HANDBOOK OF
CHILD PSYCHOLOGY

HANDBOOK OF CHILD PSYCHOLOGY

FIFTH EDITION

Volume 3:   Social, Emotional, and Personality Development

Editor-in-Chief

WILLIAM DAMON

Volume Editor

NANCY EISENBERG

John Wiley & Sons, Inc.

New York • Chichester • Weinheim • Brisbane • Singapore • Toronto

Publisher: Jeffrey W. Brown

Editor: Kelly A. Franklin

Managing Editor: Maureen B. Drexel

Composition
and Management: Publications Development Company of Texas

This text is printed on acid-free paper. ∞

This publication is designed to provide accurate and authoritative
information in regard to the subject matter covered. It is sold
with the understanding that the publisher is not engaged in
rendering professional services. If legal, accounting, medical,
psychological, or any other expert assistance is required, the
services of a competent professional person should be sought.

Library of Congress Cataloging-in-Publication Data:

Handbook of child psychology / William Damon, editor. — 5th ed.
        p.   cm.
      Includes bibliographical references and index.
      Contents: v. 1. Theoretical models of human development / Richard
   M. Lerner, volume editor — v. 2. Cognition, perception, and
   language / Deanna Kuhn and Robert Siegler, volume editors — v.
   3. Social, emotional, and personality development / Nancy Eisenberg,
   volume editor — v. 4. Child psychology in practice / Irving E.
   Sigel and K. Ann Renninger, volume editors.
      ISBN 0-471-07668-6 (v. 3 : cloth : alk. paper). — ISBN
   0-471-17893-4 (set : alk. paper)
      ISBN 0-471-34981-X (v. 3 : pbk : alk. paper).
   ISBN 0-471-33789-9 (set : alk. paper)
      1. Child psychology. I. Damon, William, 1944–   .
   BF721.H242   1997
   155.4—dc21   96-49157

Printed in the United States of America

10 9 8 7 6 5 4 3

Editorial Advisory Board

Contributors

John E. Bates, Ph.D.
Department of Psychology
Indiana University
Bloomington, Indiana

Daphne Blunt Bugental, Ph.D.
Department of Psychology
University of California, Santa Barbara
Santa Barbara, California

William Bukowski, Ph.D.
Department of Psychology
Concordia University
Montreal, Canada

Raymond Buriel, Ph.D.
Department of Psychology
Pomona College
Claremont, California

Joseph J. Campos, Ph.D.
Institute of Human Development
University of California
Berkeley, California

Avshalom Caspi, Ph.D.
Department of Psychology
University of Wisconsin
Madison, Wisconsin

John D. Coie, Ph.D.
Department of Psychology
Duke University
Durham, North Carolina

Kenneth A. Dodge
Department of Psychology
Vanderbilt University
Nashville, Tennessee

Jacqueline S. Eccles, Ph.D.
Department of Psychology
University of Michigan
Ann Arbor, Michigan

Nancy Eisenberg, Ph.D.
Department of Psychology
Arizona State University
Tempe, Arizona

Richard A. Fabes, Ph.D.
Department of Family Resources and
    Human Development
Arizona State University
Tempe, Arizona

Jacqueline J. Goodnow, Ph.D.
School of Behavioural Sciences
Macquarie University
Sydney, Australia

Harold D. Grotevant, Ph.D.
Department of Family Social Science
University of Minnesota
St. Paul, Minnesota

Susan Harter, Ph.D.
Department of Psychology
University of Denver
Denver, Colorado

Jerome Kagan, Ph.D.
Department of Psychology
Harvard University
Cambridge, Massachusetts

Carol Lynn Martin, Ph.D.
Family Resources and Human Development
Arizona State University
Tempe, Arizona

Donna Mumme, Ph.D.
Institute of Human Development
University of California
Berkeley, California

Ross D. Parke, Ph.D.
Department of Psychology
University of California
Riverside, California

Jeffrey G. Parker, Ph.D.
Department of Psychology
Pennsylvania State University
University Park, Pennsylvania

Mary K. Rothbart, Ph.D.
Department of Psychology
University of Oregon
Eugene, Oregon

Kenneth H. Rubin, Ph.D.
Center for the Study of Families, Relationships, and
    Child Development
Department of Human Development
University of Maryland
College Park, Maryland

Diane N. Ruble, Ph.D.
Department of Psychology
New York University
New York, New York

Carolyn Saarni, Ph.D.
Department of Counseling
Sonoma State University
Rohnert Park, California

Ulrich Schiefele, Ph.D.
Universität der Bundeswehr Muchen
Germany

Ross A. Thompson, Ph.D.
Department of Psychology
University of Nebraska
Lincoln, Nebraska

Elliot Turiel, Ph.D.
Graduate School of Education
University of California
Berkeley, California

Allan Wigfield, Ph.D.
Department of Human Development
College of Education
University of Maryland
College Park, Maryland

Foreword

PAUL MUSSEN

This fifth edition of the *Handbook of Child Psychology* belongs to an invaluable scholarly tradition: the presentation, at approximately 15-year intervals, of a well-planned, comprehensive, authoritative account of the current state of the field. Successive editions of the *Handbook* (or *Manual,* as it was called in the first three editions) reflect the history of the study of human development over the past half-century.

The first two editions (the second, a moderately revised version of the first) reported the accomplishments of the field in an earlier era during which there were relatively few developmental psychologists. *Description* and *measurement of changes over time* were the principal goals of research and speculation. Very little attention was paid to explanation, theory, systems, or models.

The years immediately following World War II were a watershed for science, a period marked by an immensely powerful surge in interest and activity in all sciences, including psychology. The number of scientifically trained psychologists proliferated, and fields or subdivisions within the discipline became more clearly defined. A more modern form of developmental psychology began to take shape and became a major field that was linked to other areas of psychology and allied disciplines but had its own agendas of research and theory. Continuities with earlier work were evident in new investigations and conceptualizations of standard topics—that is, topics of enduring interest—such as language, intelligence, moral behavior, the nature–nurture controversy, and social influences on development. Not surprisingly, the new investigations surpassed the earlier ones in breadth, depth, and scientific sophistication.

Most significantly, the scope of the field was immeasurably extended to include numerous new topics; innovative, more adequate methods of investigation were devised, and *explanation*—and therefore theories about mechanisms and processes—was emphasized. And, for many reasons, the new generation of developmental psychologists—many of whom were trained in other areas such as social, experimental, and clinical psychology—were generally more productive than their predecessors.

Among the myriad factors that account for the many significant advances in the field are: a basic quest for knowledge, and the self-perpetuating nature of scientific endeavors—investigations that yield interesting, sometimes unexpected, findings prompt new questions (as well as modifications of theories) and, consequently, further research. In addition, and of equal importance, developmental psychologists are generally sensitive to social issues and technological changes that may have significant impacts on children's health and development. These concerns frequently are sources of novel investigations and theories, further expanding the boundaries of the field.

Because developmental psychology had been transformed since the end of World War II, the third (1970) edition of the *Manual,* which I edited, was inevitably vastly different from the first two. In addition to up-to-date chapters on topics of continued interest, it included several chapters on theory, psycholinguistics, aggression, attachment, behavior genetics, and creativity, all of which still stand as central issues.

Like most productive scientific disciplines, developmental psychology continues to progress ceaselessly, in profound and complex ways, and at an ever-increasing rate. In 1983, the fourth edition of the *Handbook* was published. It was twice the size of the third edition, and it encompassed standard topics (usually handled in more refined and penetrating ways) and many new, fruitful areas.

Like the years following World War II, the period since 1980 has been one of unprecedented growth, change, and specialization in developmental psychology. The many theoretical and empirical developments in the discipline generated the need for this new edition. It is virtually impossible to delineate the numerous factors affecting its structure and contents, but some of the most significant influences—only a small sample, hardly an exhaustive list—can be highlighted. For example, compelling evidence of the variety and complexity of the determinants of all parameters of psychological development (and the interactions among them) cast doubt on the explanatory power of major theories that conceptualized development in terms of very few dimensions. In widely accepted current approaches and models, development is viewed as the product of multiple variables operating at multiple levels. This orientation, most explicit in several chapters of Volume 1, is also apparent in many other sections in which person–context interactions are discussed. The multivariate approach also calls attention to the limitations on generalizations from research; conclusions derived from a study with a particular population and under specified conditions may not be valid for other groups or under other circumstances. As a consequence, many chapters in this new edition include in-depth discussions of patterns of development in ethnic minorities and in diverse familial and peer group contexts. Renewed vigorous and innovative research in critical psychological parameters such as temperament, character, and emotion, reflected in several chapters, has also been significantly influenced by the multivariable approach.

As the search for the processes underlying development continues, the need to involve significant advances in other scientific disciplines accelerates. Thus, the present edition has chapters that incorporate information from the cognitive sciences, information processing, neurology, and the cultural psychology of development. Moreover, the boundaries of the field have been substantially broadened and enhanced by recent empirical work and conceptualization about psychological development throughout the life span, as reflected in several chapters.

Fortunately, in recent years, professional practitioners and policy makers have recognized the actual and potential contributions of developmental psychology to the solution of critical social and educational problems—for example, problems of parenting, childrearing in nontraditional families, effective teaching, school drop-out, and violence in television programs. Because of this recognition and the notable advances in applied research, one of the volumes of this edition is devoted exclusively to child psychology in practice.

To assist him in the extraordinarily difficult and complicated task of selecting and organizing the most prominent and exciting areas of contemporary developmental psychology, William Damon, the general editor, chose six volume editors who are recognized leaders in the field and have considerable experience in editing journals and books. Next, outstanding experts were invited to contribute critical, integrated chapters on the theoretical and substantive accomplishments of their area of expertise.

As a consequence of these authors' impeccable scholarship, intuitive and informed insights, dedication, creativity, and painstaking work, the fifth edition of the *Handbook* fully achieves its purpose: the timely presentation of an accurate and comprehensive report of the current state of developmental psychology. Readers who compare these volumes with earlier editions will be impressed with how much our understanding of human development has been enhanced in recent years, how much more solid information is available, and how much deeper and more relevant conceptualizations in the field have become. But this indispensable publication is more than an encyclopedic report, for it is enriched by thoughtful perceptions of key issues and keen insights about where matters stand and what still needs to be done. It is an invaluable aid in mapping out the future directions of this vital and dynamic field. The editors and authors have done the field of developmental psychology a great service. Everyone who is seriously interested in human development is deeply indebted to them.

Preface to The Handbook of Child Psychology, Fifth Edition

WILLIAM DAMON

THE *HANDBOOK'S* BACK PAGES—AND OURS

Developmental questions may be asked about almost any human endeavor—even about the enterprise of asking developmental questions. We may ask: How has the field of developmental study developed? In a field that has been preoccupied by continuity and change, where are the continuities and where are the changes?

Many of the chapters of this fifth edition of the *Handbook of Child Psychology* address our field's growth and progress in connection with the particular topics that they examine, and the three historical chapters (by Cairns, by Overton, and by Valsiner) present a panoramic view of our profession. As general editor of the *Handbook's* fifth edition, I wish to add a further data point: the history of the *Handbook,* which stands as an indicator of the continuities and changes within our field. The *Handbook* has long and notable credentials as a beacon, organizer, and encyclopedia of developmental study. What does its history tell us about where we have been, what we have learned, and where we are going? What does it tell us about what has changed and what has remained the same in the questions that we ask, in the methods that we use, and in the theoretical ideas that we draw on in our quest to understand human development?

It is tempting to begin with a riddle: What fifth edition has six predecessors but just three prior namesakes? Given the context of the riddle, there is not much mystery to the answer, but the reasons for it will tell us something about the *Handbook* and its history.

Leonard Carmichael was President of Tufts University when he guided Wiley's first edition of the *Handbook.* The book (one volume at that time) was called the *Manual of Child Psychology,* in keeping with Carmichael's intention of producing an "advanced scientific manual to bridge the gap between the excellent and varied elementary textbooks in this field and the scientific periodical literature. . . . "[1]

The publication date was 1946, and Carmichael complained that "this book has been a difficult and expensive one to produce, especially under wartime conditions."[2] Nevertheless, the project was worth the effort. The *Manual* quickly became the bible of graduate training and scholarly work in the field, available virtually everywhere that children's development was studied. Eight years later, now head of the Smithsonian Institution as well as editor of the book's second edition, Carmichael wrote, in the preface: "The favorable reception that the first edition received not only in America but all over the world is indicative of the growing importance of the study of the phenomena of the growth and development of the child."[3]

The second edition had a long life; not until 1970 did Wiley bring out a third edition. Carmichael was retired by then, but he still had a keen interest in the book. At his insistence, his own name became part of the title of the third edition: *Carmichael's Manual of Child Psychology.* Paul Mussen took over as editor, and once again the project flourished. Now a two-volume set, the third edition swept across the social sciences, generating widespread interest in developmental psychology and its related disciplines. Rarely had a scholarly compendium become both so dominant in its own field and so familiar in related disciplines. The set became an essential source for graduate students and advanced scholars alike. Publishers referred to *Carmichael's Manual* as the standard against which other scientific handbooks were compared. The fourth edition, published in 1983, was redesignated by John Wiley & Sons as the *Handbook of*

Child Psychology. By then, Carmichael had passed away. The set of books, now expanded to four volumes, became widely referred to in the field as "the Mussen handbook."

Words can have the power to reawaken dusty memories. When John Wiley & Sons replaced the title word *Manual* with *Handbook,* an important piece of scholarly history was inadvertently recalled. Wiley's fourth edition had a long-forgotten ancestor that was unknown to most of the new book's readers. The ancestor was called *A Handbook of Child Psychology,* and it preceded Wiley's own first edition by over 15 years. I quote here from two statements by Leonard Carmichael:

> Both as editor of the *Manual* and as the author of a special chapter, the writer is indebted . . . [for] extensive excerpts and the use of other materials previously published in the *Handbook of Child Psychology, Revised Edition.* . . .[4]

> Both the *Handbook of Child Psychology* and the *Handbook of Child Psychology, Revised Edition,* were edited by Dr. Carl Murchison. I wish to express here my profound appreciation for the pioneer work done by Dr. Murchison in producing these handbooks and other advanced books in psychology. The *Manual* owes much in spirit and content to the foresight and editorial skill of Dr. Murchison.[5]

The first quote comes from Carmichael's preface to the 1946 edition, the second from his preface to the 1954 edition. We shall never know why Carmichael waited until the 1954 edition to add the personal tribute to Carl Murchison. Perhaps a careless typist dropped the laudatory passage from a handwritten version of the 1946 preface, and its omission escaped Carmichael's notice. Perhaps eight years of further adult development increased Carmichael's generosity of spirit; or perhaps Murchison or his family complained. In any case, Carmichael from the start directly acknowledged the roots of his *Manual,* if not their author. Those roots are a revealing part of the *Handbook's* story— and of our own "back pages," as intellectual descendants of the early pioneers in the Murchison and Carmichael handbooks.

Carl Murchison was a scholar/impresario who edited *The Psychological Register;* founded and edited key psychological journals; wrote books on social psychology, politics, and the criminal mind; and compiled an assortment of handbooks, psychology texts, autobiographies of renowned psychologists, and even a book on psychic beliefs (Sir Arthur Conan Doyle and Harry Houdini were among the contributors). Murchison's first *Handbook of Child Psychology* was published by a small university press in 1931, when the field itself was still in its childhood. Murchison wrote:

> Experimental psychology has had a much older scientific and academic status [than child psychology], but at the present time it is probable that much less money is being spent for pure research in the field of experimental psychology than is being spent in the field of child psychology. In spite of this obvious fact, many experimental psychologists continue to look upon the field of child psychology as a proper field of research for women and for men whose experimental masculinity is not of the maximum. This attitude of patronage is based almost entirely upon a blissful ignorance of what is going on in the tremendously virile field of child behavior.[6]

Murchison's masculine figures of speech, of course, are from another time; they might supply good material for a social history study of gender stereotyping. That aside, Murchison was prescient in the task that he undertook and the way that he went about it. At the time this passage was written, developmental psychology was known only in Europe and in a few American labs and universities. Nevertheless, Murchison predicted the field's impending ascent: "The time is not far distant, if it is not already here, when nearly all competent psychologists will recognize that one-half of the whole field of psychology is involved in the problem of how the infant becomes an adult psychologically."[7]

For his original 1931 *Handbook,* Murchison looked to Europe and to a handful of American centers (or "field stations") for child research (Iowa, Minnesota, University of California at Berkeley, Columbia, Stanford, Yale, Clark). Murchison's Europeans included a young epistemologist named Jean Piaget, who, in an essay on "Children's Philosophies," quoted from verbal interviews of 60 Genevan children between the ages of 4 and 12 years. Piaget's chapter would provide most American readers with their introduction to his initial research program on children's conceptions of the world. Another European, Charlotte Bühler, wrote a chapter on children's social behavior. In this chapter, which still reads freshly today, Bühler described intricate play and communication patterns among toddlers—patterns that developmental psychology would not rediscover until the late 1970s. Bühler also anticipated the critiques of Piaget that would appear during the sociolinguistics heyday of the 1970s: "Piaget, in his studies on children's talk and reasoning, emphasizes that their talk is much more egocentric than social . . . that children from three to seven years accompany all their manipulations with talk which actually is not so much intercourse as monologue . . . [but] the special relationship of the child to each of the different members of the household is distinctly reflected in the respective conversations."[8] Other Europeans included Anna Freud, who wrote on "The Psychoanalysis of the Child," and Kurt Lewin, who wrote on "Environmental Forces in Child Behavior and Development."

The Americans whom Murchison chose were equally distinguished. Arnold Gesell wrote a nativistic account of his twin studies—an enterprise that remains familiar to us today—and Louis Terman wrote a comprehensive account of everything known about the "gifted child." Harold Jones described the developmental effects of birth order, Mary Cover Jones wrote about children's emotions, Florence Goodenough wrote about children's drawings, and Dorothea McCarthy wrote about language development. Vernon Jones's chapter on "children's morals" focused on the growth of *character,* a notion that was to become lost to the field during the cognitive-developmental revolution, but has lately reemerged as a primary concern in the study of moral development.

Murchison's vision of child psychology left room for an examination of cultural differences as well. He included a young anthropologist named Margaret Mead, just back from her tours of Samoa and New Guinea. In this early essay, Mead wrote that her motivation in traveling to the South Seas was to discredit the view that Piaget, Levy-Bruhl, and other nascent structuralists had put forth concerning "animism" in young children's thinking. (Interestingly, about one-third of Piaget's chapter in the same volume was dedicated to showing how it takes Genevan children years to outgrow animism.) Mead reported some data that she called "amazing": "In not one of the 32,000 drawings (by young 'primitive' children) was there a single case of personalization of animals, material phenomena, or inanimate objects."[9] Mead parlayed these data into a tough-minded critique of Western psychology's ethnocentrism, making the point that animism and other beliefs are more likely to be culturally induced than intrinsic to early cognitive development. This is hardly an unfamiliar theme in contemporary psychology. Mead also offered a research guide for developmental field workers in strange cultures, complete with methodological and practical advice, such as: translate questions into native linguistic categories; don't do controlled experiments; don't do studies that require knowing ages of subjects, which are usually unknowable; and live next door to the children whom you are studying.

Despite the imposing roster of authors that Murchison had assembled for the 1931 *Handbook of Child Psychology,* his achievement did not satisfy him for long. Barely two years later, Murchison put out a second edition, of which he wrote: "Within a period of slightly more than two years, this first revision bears scarcely any resemblance to the original *Handbook of Child Psychology.* This is due chiefly to the great expansion in the field during the past three years and partly to the improved insight of the editor."[10]

Murchison also saw fit to provide the following warning in his second edition: "There has been no attempt to simplify, condense, or to appeal to the immature mind. This volume is prepared specifically for the scholar, and its form is for his maximum convenience."[11] It is likely that sales of Murchison's first volume did not approach textbook levels. Perhaps he also received negative comments regarding its accessibility. For the record, though, despite Murchison's continued use of masculine phraseology, 10 of the 24 authors in the second edition were women.

Murchison exaggerated when he wrote that his second edition bore little resemblance to the first. Almost half of the chapters were virtually the same, with minor additions and updating. Moreover, some of the authors whose original chapters were dropped were asked to write about new topics. So, for example, Goodenough wrote about mental testing rather than about children's drawings, and Gesell wrote a more general statement of his maturational theory that went well beyond the twin studies.

But Murchison also made some abrupt changes. Anna Freud was dropped, auguring the marginalization of psychoanalysis within academic psychology. Leonard Carmichael made his first appearance, as author of a major chapter (by far, the longest in the book) on prenatal and perinatal growth. Three other physiologically oriented chapters were added as well: one on neonatal motor behavior, one on visual–manual functions during the first two years of life, and one on physiological "appetites" such as hunger, rest, and sex. Combined with the Goodenough and Gesell shifts in focus, these additions gave the 1933 *Handbook* more of a biological thrust, in keeping with Murchison's long-standing desire to display the hard-science backbone of the emerging field.

Leonard Carmichael took his 1946 *Manual* several steps further in the same direction. First, he appropriated five Murchison chapters on biological or experimental topics such as physiological growth, scientific methods, and mental testing. Second, he added three new biologically oriented chapters on animal infancy, on physical growth, and on motor and behavioral maturation (a *tour de force* by Myrtal McGraw that instantly made Gesell's chapter in the same volume obsolete). Third, he commissioned Wayne Dennis to write an adolescence chapter that focused exclusively on physiological changes associated with puberty. Fourth, Carmichael dropped Piaget and Bühler.

But five Murchison chapters on social and cultural influences in development were retained: two chapters on environmental forces on the child (by Kurt Lewin and by Harold Jones), Dorothea McCarthy's chapter on children's language, Vernon Jones's chapter on children's morality (now entitled "Character Development—An Objective Approach"), and Margaret Mead's chapter on "primitive" children (now enhanced by several spectacular photos of mothers and children from exotic cultures around the world). Carmichael stayed with three other psychologically oriented Murchison topics (emotional development, gifted children, and sex differences), but selected new authors to cover them.

Carmichael's 1954 revision—his second and final edition—was very close in structure and content to the 1946 *Manual.* Carmichael again retained the heart of Murchison's original vision, many of Murchison's original authors and chapter topics, and some of the same material that dated all the way back to the 1931 *Handbook.* Not surprisingly, the chapters that were closest to Carmichael's own interests got the most significant updating. As Murchison had tried to do, Carmichael leaned toward the biological and physiological whenever possible. He clearly favored experimental treatments of psychological processes. Yet Carmichael still kept the social, cultural, and psychological analyses by Lewin, Mead, McCarthy, Terman, Harold Jones, and Vernon Jones, and he even went so far as to add one new chapter on social development by Harold and Gladys Anderson and one new chapter on emotional development by Arthur Jersild.

The Murchison/Carmichael volumes make for fascinating reading, even today. The perennial themes of the field were there from the start: the nature–nurture debate; the generalizations of universalists opposed by the particularizations of contextualists; the alternating emphases on continuities and discontinuities during ontogenesis; and the standard categories of maturation, learning, locomotor activity, perception, cognition, language, emotion, conduct, morality, and culture—all separated for the sake of analysis, yet, as authors throughout each of the volumes acknowledged, all somehow inextricably joined in the dynamic mix of human development.

These things have not changed. Yet much in the early handbooks/manuals is now irrevocably dated. Long lists of children's dietary preferences, sleeping patterns, elimination habits, toys, and somatic types look quaint and pointless through today's lenses. The chapters on children's thought and language were done prior to the great contemporary breakthroughs in neurology and brain/behavior research, and they show it. The chapters on social and emotional development were ignorant of the processes of social influence and self-regulation that soon would be revealed through attribution research and other studies in social psychology. Terms such as *behavior genetics, social cognition, dynamic systems, information processing,* and *developmental psychopathology* were unknown. Even Mead's rendition of the "primitive child" stands as a weak straw in comparison to the wealth of cross-cultural knowledge available today.

Most tellingly, the assortments of odd facts and normative trends were tied together by very little theory throughout the Carmichael chapters. It was as if, in the exhilaration of discovery at the frontiers of a new field, all the facts looked interesting in and of themselves. That, of course, is what makes so much of the material seem odd and arbitrary. It is hard to know what to make of the lists of facts, where to place them, which ones were worth keeping track of and which ones are expendable. Not surprisingly, the bulk of the data presented in the Carmichael manuals seems not only outdated by today's standards but, worse, irrelevant.

By 1970, the importance of theory for understanding human development had become apparent. Looking back on Carmichael's last *Manual,* Paul Mussen wrote: "The 1954 edition of this *Manual* had only one theoretical chapter, and that was concerned with Lewinian theory which, so far as we can see, has not had a significant lasting impact on developmental psychology."[12] The intervening years had seen a turning away from the norm of psychological research once fondly referred to as "dust-bowl empiricism."

The Mussen 1970 handbook—or *Carmichael's Manual,* as it was still called—had an entirely new look. The two-volume set carried only one chapter from the earlier books—Carmichael's updated version of his own long chapter on the "Onset and Early Development of Behavior," which had made its appearance under a different title in Murchison's 1933 edition. Otherwise, as Mussen wrote in his preface, "It should be clear from the outset . . . that the present volumes are not, in any sense, a *revision* of the earlier editions; this is a completely new *Manual.*"[13]

And it was. In comparison to Carmichael's last edition 16 years earlier, the scope, variety, and theoretical depth of the Mussen volumes were astonishing. The field had blossomed, and the new *Manual* showcased many of the new bouquets that were being produced. The biological perspective was still strong, grounded by chapters on physical growth (by J. M. Tanner) and physiological development (by Dorothy Eichorn), and by Carmichael's revised chapter (now made more elegant by some excerpts from Greek philosophy and modern poetry). But two other cousins of biology also were represented, in an ethological chapter by Eckhard Hess, and a behavior genetics chapter by Gerald McClearn. These chapters were to define the major directions of biological research in the field for at least the next three decades.

As for theory, Mussen's *Handbook* was thoroughly permeated with it. Much of the theorizing was organized around the approaches that, in 1970, were known as the "three grand systems": (a) Piaget's cognitive-developmentalism, (b) psychoanalysis, and (c) learning theory. Piaget was given the most extensive treatment. He reappeared in the *Manual,* this time authoring a comprehensive (and some say, definitive) statement of his entire theory, which now bore little resemblance to his 1931/1933 sortings of children's intriguing verbal expressions. In addition, chapters by John Flavell, by David Berlyne, by Martin Hoffman, and by William Kessen, Marshall Haith, and Philip Salapatek, all gave major treatments to one or another aspect of Piaget's body of work. Other approaches were represented as well. Herbert and Ann Pick explicated Gibsonian theory in a chapter on sensation and perception, Jonas Langer wrote a chapter on Werner's organismic theory, David McNeill wrote a Chomskian account of language development, and Robert LeVine wrote an early version of what was soon to become "culture theory."

· With its increased emphasis on theory, the 1970 *Manual* explored in depth a matter that had been all but neglected in the *Manual's* previous versions: the mechanisms of change that could account for, to use Murchison's old phrase, "the problem of how the infant becomes an adult psychologically." In the process, old questions such as the relative importance of nature *versus* nurture were revisited, but with far more sophisticated conceptual and methodological tools.

Beyond theory building, the 1970 *Manual* addressed an array of new topics and featured new contributors: peer interaction (Willard Hartup), attachment (Eleanor Maccoby and John Masters), aggression (Seymour Feshback), indi-

vidual differences (Jerome Kagan and Nathan Kogan), and creativity (Michael Wallach). All of these areas of interest are still very much with us at century's end.

If the 1970 *Manual* reflected a blossoming of the field's plantings, the 1983 *Handbook* reflected a field whose ground cover had spread beyond any boundaries that could have been previously anticipated. New growth had sprouted in literally dozens of separate locations. A French garden, with its overarching designs and tidy compartments, had turned into an English garden, a bit unruly but often glorious in its profusion. Mussen's two-volume *Carmichael's Manual* had now become the four-volume Mussen *Handbook,* with a page-count increase that came close to tripling the 1970 edition.

The grand old theories were breaking down. Piaget was still represented by his 1970 piece, but his influence was on the wane throughout the other chapters. Learning theory and psychoanalysis were scarcely mentioned. Yet the early theorizing had left its mark, in vestiges that were apparent in new approaches, and in the evident conceptual sophistication with which authors treated their material. No return to dust-bowl empiricism could be found anywhere in the set. Instead, a variety of classical and innovative ideas were coexisting: ethology, neurobiology, information processing, attribution theory, cultural approaches, communications theory, behavioral genetics, sensory-perception models, psycholinguistics, sociolinguistics, discontinuous stage theories, and continuous memory theories all took their places, with none quite on center stage. Research topics now ranged from children's play to brain lateralization, from children's family life to the influences of school, day care, and disadvantageous risk factors. There also was coverage of the burgeoning attempts to use developmental theory as a basis for clinical and educational interventions. The interventions usually were described at the end of chapters that had discussed the research relevant to the particular intervention efforts, rather than in whole chapters dedicated specifically to issues of practice.

This brings us to the present—the *Handbook's* fifth (but really seventh) edition. I will leave it to future reviewers to provide a summation of what we have done. The volume editors have offered introductory and/or concluding renditions of their own volumes. I will add to their efforts by stating here the overall intent of our design, and by commenting on some directions that our field has taken in the years from 1931 to 1998.

We approached this edition with the same purpose that Murchison, Carmichael, and Mussen before us had shared:

"to provide," as Mussen wrote, "a comprehensive and accurate picture of the current state of knowledge—the major systematic thinking and research—in the most important research areas of the psychology of human development."[14] We assumed that the *Handbook* should be aimed "specifically for the scholar," as Murchison declared, and that it should have the character of an "advanced text," as Carmichael defined it. We expected, though, that our audience may be more interdisciplinary than the readerships of previous editions, given the greater tendency of today's scholars to cross back and forth among fields such as psychology, cognitive science, neurobiology, history, linguistics, sociology, anthropology, education, and psychiatry. We also believed that research-oriented practitioners should be included under the rubric of the "scholars" for whom this *Handbook* was intended. To that end, we devoted, for the first time, and entire volume to "child psychology in practice."

Beyond these very general intentions, we have let chapters in the *Handbook's* fifth edition take their own shape. We solicited the chapters from authors who were widely acknowledged to be among the leading experts in their areas of the field; although we know that, given an entirely open-ended selection process and budget, we would have invited a very large number of other leading researchers whom we did not have the space—and thus the privilege—to include. With only two exceptions, every author whom we invited chose to accept the challenge.

Our directive to authors was simple: Convey your area of the field as you see it. From then on, the 112 authors took center stage—with, of course, much constructive feedback from reviewers and volume editors. But no one tried to impose a perspective, a preferred method of inquiry, or domain boundaries on any of the chapters. The authors freely expressed their views on what researchers in their areas attempt to accomplish, why they do so, how they go about it, what intellectual sources they draw on, what progress they have made, and what conclusions they have reached.

The result, in my opinion, is yet more glorious profusion, but perhaps contained a bit by some broad patterns that have emerged across our garden. Powerful theoretical models and approaches—not quite unified theories, such as the three grand systems—have begun once again to organize much of the field's research and practice. There is great variety in these models and approaches, and each is drawing together significant clusters of work. Some have been only recently formulated, and some are combinations or modifications of classic theories that still have staying power.

Among the formidable models and approaches that the reader will find in this *Handbook* are the dynamic system theories, the life-span and life-course approaches, cognitive science and neural models, the behavior genetics approach, person–context interaction theories, action theories, cultural psychology, ecological models, neo-Piagetian and neo-Vygotskian models. Although some of these models and approaches have been in the making for some time, my impression is that they are just now coming into their own, in that researchers now are drawing on them more directly, taking their implied assumptions and hypotheses seriously, using them with specificity and with full control, and exploiting all of their implications for practice. A glance at the contents listings for the *Handbook's* four volumes will reveal the staggering breadth of concerns addressed through use of these models and approaches.

The other pattern that emerges is a self-conscious reflection about the notion of development. The reflection is an earnest one, yet it has a more affirmative tone than similar discussions in recent years. We have just passed through a time when the very credibility of a developmental approach was itself thrown into question. The whole idea of progress and advance, implicit in the notion of development, seemed out of step with ideological principles of diversity and equality.

Some genuine intellectual benefits accrued from that critique: the field has come to better appreciate diverse developmental pathways. But, like many critique positions, it led to excesses that created, for some in the field of developmental study, a kind of crisis of faith. For some, it became questionable even to explore issues that lie at the heart of human development. Learning, growth, achievement, individual continuity and change, common beliefs and standards—all became suspect as subjects of investigation.

Fortunately, as the contents of this *Handbook* attest, such doubts are waning. As was probably inevitable, the field's center of gravity has returned to the study of development. After all, the story of growth during infancy, childhood, and adolescence is a developmental story of multi-faceted learning, of acquisitions of skills and knowledge, of waxing powers of attention and memory, of formations and transformations of character and personality, of increases in understanding of self and others, of advances in emotional and behavioral regulation, of progress in communicating and collaborating with others, and of a host of other achievements that are chronicled in this *Handbook*. Parents and teachers in every part of the world recognize and value such developmental achievements in their children, although they do not always know how to foster them. Neither do we in all cases. But the kinds of scientific understanding that the *Handbook's* authors explicate in their chapters—scientific understanding created by themselves as well as by fellow researchers in the field of developmental study—have brought us all several giant steps toward this goal.

NOTES

1. Carmichael, L. (Ed.). (1946). *Manual of child psychology.* New York: Wiley, p. viii.

2. Carmichael, L. (Ed.). (1946). *Manual of child psychology.* New York: Wiley, p. vi.

3. Carmichael, L. (Ed.). (1954). *Manual of child psychology: Second edition.* New York: Wiley, p. v.

4. Carmichael, L. (Ed.). (1946). *Manual of child psychology.* New York: Wiley, p. vi.

5. Carmichael, L. (Ed.). (1954). *Manual of child psychology: Second edition.* New York: Wiley, p. vii.

6. Murchison, C. (Ed.). (1931). *A handbook of child psychology.* Worcester, MA: Clark University Press, p. ix.

7. Murchison, C. (Ed.). (1931). *A handbook of child psychology.* Worcester, MA: Clark University Press, p. x.

8. Buhler, C. (1931). The social participation of infants and toddlers. In C. Murchison (Ed.), *A handbook of child psychology.* Worcester, MA: Clark University Press, p. 138.

9. Mead, M. (1931). The primitive child. In C. Murchison (Ed.), *A handbook of child psychology.* Worcester, MA: Clark University Press, p. 400.

10. Murchison, C. (Ed.). (1933). *A handbook of child psychology: Second edition (Revised).* Worcester, MA: Clark University Press, p. viii.

11. Murchison, C. (Ed.). (1933). *A handbook of child psychology: Second edition (Revised).* Worcester, MA: Clark University Press, p. viii.

12. Mussen, P. (Ed.). (1970). *Carmichael's manual of child psychology.* New York: Wiley, p. x.

13. Mussen, P. (Ed.). (1970). *Carmichael's manual of child psychology.* New York: Wiley, p. x.

14. Mussen, P. (Ed.). (1983). *Handbook of child psychology.* New York: Wiley, p. vii.

Acknowledgments

The fifth edition of the *Handbook* was truly a team effort. The six volume editors have my deepest gratitude for their countless hours of devoted work. No project editor has ever had a finer group of collaborators. I also thank Kelly Franklin, of John Wiley & Sons, Inc., for her inspired editorial efforts from the time of the project's inception. Without Kelly's persistence and good sense, publication in 1998 would not have been possible.

Many people contributed invaluable advice during one or another phase of the fifth edition's production. They are far too many to mention here, even if I had managed to keep systematic records of all conversations on the project's development. The final product has benefited greatly from the insights and feedback of all those who responded.

In particular, I note two giants of the field whose wise counsel and generosity remain prominent in my mind: Paul Mussen and Eleanor Maccoby.

In slightly altered form, my preface was published in *Human Development* (March–April, 1997). I am grateful to Barbara Rogoff for her editorial help in this process, and to Anne Gregory for her help in obtaining background materials. Josef and Marsy Mittlemann's support has been vital in facilitating this and other scholarly activities at the Brown University Center for the Study of Human Development. My assistant, Pat Balsofiore, deserves our unending gratitude for her valiant work in helping to organize this vast endeavor.

William Damon

Preface to Volume 3: Social, Emotional, and Personality Development

NANCY EISENBERG

This volume has been a labor of love. When I was a graduate student, we read many of the chapters from the 1970 edition of the *Mussen Handbook of Child Psychology* in our classes. Even then, in my mind it was the "bible" of the field. Moreover, my mentor was Paul Mussen, so I frequently borrowed one of his extra copies of the *Handbook* and he gave me that copy as a gift when I graduated. When the 1983 edition of the *Handbook* was being prepared, I was fortunate as a young scholar to get to review a couple of chapters; in addition, I heard occasional grumblings from Paul Mussen about chapters that were late. At that time in my career, it was my dream that I would someday get to contribute a chapter to the *Handbook*.

Thus, I was pleased and honored (as well as a little apprehensive) when I was asked to edit a volume of this very important set of books. Editing the volume has been an exceptional learning experience. I have had the privilege to work with some of the best people in the field and to read (and re-read) a year or two before other people the very exciting work that is in this volume. I have learned much from my fellow contributors.

The contributors to this volume deserve much thanks. All of the people who were requested to contribute agreed to do so and all of the chapters were completed. This may be a record. Moreover, this set of authors spent tremendous energy and time constructing their very thoughtful and integrative chapters. Due to stringent space limitations for this edition of the *Handbook*, many of the contributors also expended considerable time cutting pages (sometimes over 100) from their original drafts. It is almost as difficult to eliminate and trim sections of a chapter that one has struggled to produce as it is to write the section in the first place!

However, the contributors were always good-natured in their responses to my repeated requests that they comply (somewhat, at least) with page restrictions. I was fortunate to work with such a talented and cooperative group of people.

I also thank the many other people who made this volume possible. First, I thank William Damon, who provided feedback on the chapters and has been the organizing and driving force of this endeavor, allowing the editors to shape their own volumes. It has been a great pleasure to work with him on this project. Numerous colleagues who critiqued the chapters in manuscript form also provided valuable insights and suggestions that enhanced the quality of the final product. Indeed, the *Handbook* is truly the result of a joint effort of many people in the discipline.

In addition, I thank my colleagues who shared their ideas with me in the course of this task. I also thank my husband, Jerry Harris, who provided support throughout and was patient with me when this task was the straw that almost broke this camel's back. I also appreciate the financial support that I received over the last three years from the National Science Foundation and the National Institutes of Mental Health, the latter of whom funded a Research Scientist Development Award and a Research Scientist Award. Finally, I thank Paul Mussen, my friend and mentor, who has provided me with intellectual and emotional support for more than two decades. It has been a privilege and joy to carry on the tradition of the *Handbook* that he established.

In this edition of the *Handbook,* there is an introductory chapter, with some of my thoughts and comments about the chapters in this volume. I hope that the readers of this volume learn as much from the chapters as I have. Enjoy.

Contents

CHAPTER 1

Introduction

NANCY EISENBERG

The goal of the authors in this volume of the *Handbook of Child Psychology* was to present state-of-the-art reviews of conceptual and empirical work on social, emotional, and personality development. This was not an easy task given the rapid advances in theory and research in the past decade or two and the reality of page limitations for the volume. Yet each author or set of authors has provided the reader with an integrative summary of the current status of an important topic within the domain of social, emotional, and personality development and, to some degree, with a vision for the future.

EMERGING THEMES

The chapters in this volume provide the reader with a perspective on the major issues and themes in the field and on the prevailing Zeitgeist in the study of social and personality development. Although any given theme or issue may not be evident in every chapter, there are certain issues that appear throughout the volume. Some issues and themes have become more salient since the last edition of the *Handbook* in 1983; these are discussed below.

Work on this chapter was supported by a National Institute of Mental Health Research Scientist Award (K05 M801321-01) and funding from the National Science Foundation (DBS-9208375) and the National Institute of Mental Health (R01 HH55052).

A Focus on Emotion

This is the first edition of the *Handbook* to include a chapter dedicated solely to the topic of emotion (rather than the more general topic of socioemotional development in infancy). The neglect of emotion in prior editions is not surprising given the history of the study of emotion in psychology in the past 50 years. Due to the influence of behaviorism and then cognitive approaches in psychology, emotion was considered a nuisance variable (and sometimes an anathema) for many years. In the past 10 to 15 years, however, emotion has become central to the study of social development, as well as to many other subdisciplines of psychology.

The current emphasis on emotion is a dramatic departure from the view of emotions in the past as intrapsychic events "which do not play a causal role in behavior and which are secondary by-products of more significant processes" (Campos, 1984, p. 148). Today emotions are viewed as motivational forces that play a role in much of our social behavior. As noted by Parke (1994), in contemporary psychology, emotions are viewed as "both products and processes of social interactions, relationships, and contexts" (p. 158).

The central role of emotion in contemporary developmental psychology is reflected in most of the chapters in this volume. This focus is, of course, most evident in the Saarni, Mumme, and Campos chapter on emotion. Saarni et al. take a functionalist perspective in which emotion is closely linked to the context and what a person is trying to do. Emotion is viewed as synonymous with the significance of a person-event transaction for the individual.

Due to the immense body of work relevant to emotion, Saarni et al. limit their coverage and focus primarily on emotion communication, the role of context in emotion, children's understanding of emotion, and how children cope with emotions and emotion-eliciting contexts. Their review of this portion of the emotion literature demonstrates that children's understanding of emotion and its expression, as well as children's communication of and coping with emotion, change considerably with age. Moreover, emotional understanding, communication, and regulation seem to have a profound influence on social interaction, although the relation between social interaction and these aspects of functioning may be reciprocal. Saarni et al.'s review reflects major domains of interest in recent work on emotion and provides a contemporary, contextually oriented perspective on emotional development.

Temperament, Personality, and Emotion

Emotion can be viewed in both situationally specific and dispositional terms. In theory and research on temperament and personality, enduring individual differences in emotional proclivities (i.e., dispositional differences) are fundamental constructs. Thus, dispositional emotion is a salient topic in the two chapters that deal with temperament and the biological bases of socioemotional functioning. The body of work pertaining or relevant to temperament is so large and inclusive at this time, and approaches to the topic vary to such a degree, that two chapters in this volume focus primarily on temperament, one authored by Mary Rothbart and John Bates and the other by Jerome Kagan.

Temperament is defined by Rothbart and Bates as constitutionally based individual differences in reactivity and self-regulation. Reactivity includes emotional responding, both in regard to specific emotions (e.g., fear) and more general constructs of emotion (e.g., negative emotionality or emotional intensity; see Larsen & Diener, 1987; Rothbart & Bates, Ch. 3, this Volume). Moreover, some aspects of temperament that are not essentially emotional involve the regulation of temperamental reactivity (e.g., inhibitory control; see Ahadi & Rothbart, 1994; Eisenberg, Fabes, & Guthrie, in press; Gray, 1987; also see Mischel, Shoda, & Peake, 1988) or are associated with particular emotions (e.g., Kagan, Ch. 4, this Volume; Rothbart, Ahadi, & Hershey, 1994). Further, there appear to be emotion-relevant

physiological correlates of some aspects of temperament (see Kagan, Ch. 4, this Volume). Thus, individual differences in dispositional emotionality and its regulation are integral to contemporary temperament theory and research.

Dispositional emotionality also plays an important role in the personality literature. Temperament-based differences in emotional reactivity are believed to feed into personality differences in childhood and adulthood. Personality has been defined as "individual differences in the tendency to behave, think, and feel in certain consistent ways" (Caspi, Ch. 6, this Volume). Personality theorists often emphasize the structure and function of personality, including not only traits, but also personal concerns (i.e., a wide array of motivational, developmental, or strategic constructs that are contextualized in time, place, or role) and life stories (McAdams, 1995).

Caspi suggests that aspects of temperament in childhood are linked to the structure of adult personality (i.e., aspects of the "big five" components of personality). For example, temperamental negative emotionality is linked to the personality construct of neuroticism and agreeableness (inversely related), whereas positive affect is associated with agreeableness and extraversion in adults. In addition, aspects of temperament believed to be involved in the regulation of emotionality and emotionally driven behavior have been linked to personality. For example, temperamental inhibition is viewed as connected to adult neuroticism and low levels of extraversion. Moreover, Ahadi and Rothbart (1994) argued that effortful control based in part on temperamental attentional regulation (an aspect of temperament) plays a role in agreeableness, as well as in proneness to anxiety in adolescence and adulthood.

Emotion and Social Behavior

In addition to playing a role in later personality, individual differences in temperamental emotionality frequently have been deemed contributors to variation among children in a range of social behaviors. For example, Thompson (Ch. 2, this Volume) concludes that temperament is related to attachment status to a modest degree. Individual differences in dispositional arousability also have been linked to aggression (see Coie & Dodge, Ch. 12, this Volume) and anger-related reactions (Eisenberg, Fabes, Nyman, Bernzweig, & Pinuelas, 1994). Further, dispositional differences in vicariously induced emotionality (e.g., empathy-related reactions such as sympathy and personal distress) have been correlated with level of prosocial behavior in specific situations and across time (see Eisenberg & Fabes, Ch. 11, this Volume). In addition, dispositional emotionality, such as irritability, fearfulness, and positive emotionality, are expected to be, and have been related, to level of adjustment, including internalizing and externalizing behavior (see Caspi, Ch. 6, this Volume; Kagan, Ch. 4, this Volume; Rothbart & Bates, Ch. 3, this Volume). Nonetheless, perhaps because researchers generally have not differentiated types of negative emotion, such as fear of novelty versus fear of strangers, prediction of specific internalizing and externalizing problems from temperamental emotionality is still difficult (see Kagan, Ch. 4, this Volume).

Dispositional emotionality also contributes to the quality of social functioning in peer interactions and relationships. However, the relation of social competence to individual differences in valence and intensity of children's emotion only recently has been a focus in empirical and conceptual work (see Eisenberg & Fabes, 1992; Hubbard & Coie, 1994; Rubin, Bukowski, & Parker, Ch. 10, this Volume). For example, it has been hypothesized that emotional reactivity affects social withdrawal (Eisenberg & Fabes, 1992) as well as information processing in social encounters, although there is relatively little research on these issues (see Crick & Dodge, 1994; Eisenberg, Fabes, Murphy, et al., 1995). Researchers have found that cheerful children appear to be relatively popular (Hubbard & Coie, 1994), whereas children prone to intense negative emotions are lower in social status (e.g., Eisenberg et al., 1993; see Rubin et al., Ch. 10, this Volume). As discussed shortly, it is likely that the regulation of emotion, as much as the emotion itself, is related to quality of social behavior in relationships.

Emotion, the Self, and Goals

Emotion is also an integral aspect of conceptions of the self. For example, self-esteem seems to be highly related to feelings of depression and hopelessness (Harter, Ch. 9, this Volume). Moreover, an understanding of emotion is viewed by Harter as affecting the child's construction of the self.

Affect also is viewed as relevant to understanding achievement-related motivation and accomplishments, which, in turn, can be expected to affect aspects of self-esteem. However, emotion is not a primary construct in most of the research and theory in this domain of investigation. Nonetheless, Eccles, Wigfield, and Schiefele (Ch. 15, this Volume) note that some achievement goals are emotional (e.g., obtaining happiness). In any case, success and failure are associated with emotional reactions, level of anxiety can affect performance, and emotion-related self-evaluations

play a role in achievement-related behavior (see Eccles et al., Ch. 15, this Volume). Consistent with an increasing awareness of emotion even in domains of study dominated by cognitive models, Eccles et al. conclude that the highest priority in the research on achievement is closer consideration of the influence of emotion on motivation.

Emotion and Morality

The role of emotion in the study of morality has varied greatly as a function of the conception of morality. In Kohlbergian work on moral reasoning, emotion plays a minor role in comparison to cognition (see Kohlberg, 1984; Rest, 1983). In contrast, emotions such as empathy-related reactions or guilt have been highlighted in some work on moral *behavior,* including theory and research on prosocial tendencies (e.g., Eisenberg & Fabes, 1990, Ch. 11, this Volume; Hoffman, 1982), guilt (Thompson, Ch. 2, this Volume; Zahn-Waxler & Kochanska, 1990), and conscience (Kochanska, 1993, 1996). For example, in work on prosocial behavior, both enduring tendencies toward experiencing moral emotions (i.e., dispositional sympathy) and situational emotional reactions (e.g., situational sympathy or guilt) are viewed as motivating altruistic action (see Eisenberg & Fabes, Ch. 1, this Volume).

Some contemporary theorists, including Wilson (1993) and Shweder (1994), assume an intuitive or biologically based emotional basis to morality (see Turiel, Ch. 13, this Volume). According to Kagan (1984), moral principles are determined by the intensity of the community's affective reactions to the specific content of the principle. Turiel (Ch. 13, this Volume) takes a somewhat more cognitive position than theorists like Hoffman, Kagan, and Shweder, concluding, "As important as are emotions, especially ones of sympathy, empathy, and respect, for moral functioning, emotions occur in and among persons who can think about them with regard to other people and in relation to complicated social agendas, goals, and arrangements. The relationships among emotions, moral judgments, reflections, and deliberations require a great deal of attention in research and in theoretical formulations."

Sex, Gender, and Emotion

As one might expect, there are sex differences in the emotions that boys and girls tend to display (Eisenberg, Martin, & Fabes, 1996; Ruble & Martin, Ch. 14, this Volume), although little is known about the degree to which boys and girls differ in internally experienced emotion (albeit adolescent girls report more depression than do boys; see

Grotevant, Ch. 16, this Volume). Nonetheless, sex differences in the degree or type of expression of anger and frustration may be a factor in the sex difference in externalizing behavior and aggression in children (see Coie & Dodge, Ch. 12, this Volume). As emotion moves center stage in the examination of many aspects of social functioning, it is likely that sex differences in the experience and expression of emotion will receive more emphasis from researchers.

Emotion in Socialization and the Socialization of Emotion

Socialization is another area in which emotion has received increased attention in recent years. As noted by Parke and Buriel (this volume), affect played a relatively minor role in socialization theories in the recent past. Until the 1980s, affect was discussed primarily in regard to the degree of warmth in the parent-child relationship. In contrast, the topic of affect and emotion permeates contemporary work on socialization.

As discussed by Bugental and Goodnow (Ch. 7, this Volume), emotion plays a central role in both biologically oriented and culturally oriented socialization theories. In biologically based theories, affect and emotion are conceived as primitive processes in need of regulation, as regulators of relationships (e.g., attachment relationships), or as consequences of socializing relationships. Often emotional processes are viewed as functional regulators of other processes central to socialization.

In recent sociocultural perspectives, the expression, experience, interpretation, and naming of emotions are derived from the culture (see Bugental & Goodnow, Ch. 7, this Volume; Kitayama & Markus, 1994; Saarni et al., Ch. 5, this Volume). Thus, socialization by the culture influences emotional reactions, as well as a range of social behaviors. As a consequence of the recent increased awareness of the cultural contributions to emotional experience and expression, a number of our current conceptions of emotional development are likely to be challenged.

Bugental and Goodnow suggest that emotion also affects a variety of cognitive processes fundamental to the socialization process, including attentional focus, memory retrieval, appraisal and response selection, and the capacity for rational or reflective processing (also see Zajonc & Marcus, 1984). Their conception of the role of emotion in socialization is more complex and encompassing than in most existing theory.

At a more concrete, empirical level, the new emphasis on emotion in the socialization process can be found in re-search on children's reactions to conflict in the family (e.g., Davies & Cummings, 1994; Eisenberg & Fabes, Ch. 11, this Volume); in a focus on the expression of emotion during family members' interactions with one another (see Grotevant, Ch. 16, this Volume); and in the emerging body of research on the socialization of children's expression and regulation of emotion and its relation to social competence (Dunn & Brown, 1994; Eisenberg & Fabes, Ch. 11, this Volume; Parke & Buriel, Ch. 8, this Volume). For example, there is some evidence that quantity or quality of expressiveness in the family is related to peer competence (e.g., Boyum & Parke, 1995; Parke & Buriel, Ch. 8, this Volume) and positive social reactions such as sympathy (e.g., Eisenberg et al., 1992; Eisenberg & Fabes, Ch. 11, this Volume). Moreover, emotion has been used as a moderator variable in examining socialization issues such as compliance and the development of internalized standards; for example, individual differences in emotionality (e.g., proneness to anxiety) have been found to affect the degree to which parental socialization practices such as reasoning are effective (Kochanska, 1993, 1996).

In summary, the topic of emotion has moved to center stage in the study of social and personality development. This surge of interest in emotion has been accompanied by, and perhaps is related causally to, elevated interest in biological inputs to development and individual differences in personality and temperament. In addition, contemporary concern with culture and context has had a powerful influence on thinking about emotional development. Moreover, because emotional experience and expression involve regulation (or the lack thereof), contemporary discussion and research on emotion regulation also has been revitalized.

A Focus on Regulation

In the past, popular approaches to the topic of regulation included emphases on parental control and discipline; children's compliance, delay of gratification, and resistance to temptation; and children's internalization of societal values regarding behaviors such as aggression and prosocial behavior (e.g., Hoffman, 1970, 1983; Maccoby & Martin, 1983; see Coie & Dodge, Ch. 12, this Volume; Eisenberg & Fabes, Ch. 11, this Volume). Although there is still considerable interest in these topics, in recent years investigators concerned with regulatory processes also have focused on mechanisms by which children regulate their emotion and emotion-driven behavior, and the relation of individual differences in regulation to social competence and adjustment.

Contemporary Work on Regulation

Contemporary work on the aforementioned topics has diverse origins in the discipline. The work of the Blocks (Block & Block, 1980) on ego control has had an important impact on this topic of study. Also important is recent work by temperament theorists who, in the past decade or so, have emphasized constructs such as attentional control (e.g., the ability to shift and focus attention), behavioral inhibition, impulsivity, and effortful control (superordinate self-regulatory systems that can assert control over the reactive and self-regulatory processes of other temperament systems; Ahadi & Rothbart, 1994; Rothbart & Ahadi, 1994). Similarly, mechanisms for adaptation discussed by coping theorists (e.g., Carver, Scheier, & Weintraub, 1989; Lazarus & Folkman, 1984) for over a decade can be viewed as modes of dealing with, or regulating, emotion and behavior in stressful contexts. In addition, some of the adult personality work on constructs such as constraint (Tellegen, 1985), persistence (Caspi, Ch. 6, this Volume), and inhibition control (Derryberry & Rothbart, 1988), as well as social psychological work on strategies for manipulating one's own mood (e.g., Erber, Wegner, & Therriault, 1996), have influenced developmentalists interested in regulatory processes.

Regulation is discussed, in one form or another, in most of the chapters in this volume. For example, Kagan examines the possible role of physiological systems and processes in regulation. Relatedly, Rothbart and Bates review parts of the growing literature pertaining to temperamental bases of regulation and the relations of temperamental regulation to social and emotional functioning. Caspi notes that constraint is a component of all contemporary systems of personality, and highlights the role of regulation in adjustment and criminality. Saarni et al. focus on social communicative mechanisms used by infants to regulate their behavior (e.g., social referencing), as well as on the development of children's ability to regulate the expression of emotion. Consistent with the conclusions of Rothbart and Bates and Caspi, Coie, and Dodge note the association of children's aggression with attentional deficits and impulsivity, particularly when combined with parent-child interactions that are coercive or disciplinary practices that are inconsistent but often punitive. Similarly, Eisenberg and Fabes report findings consistent with the view that regulatory processes are intimately involved in the vicariously induced emotions of sympathy and personal distress, as well as in the performance of prosocial behavior. Further, Eccles et al. briefly consider the issue of how motivation gets translated into regulated behavior

and note the importance of regulation in the achievement of goals and learning (Zimmerman, 1996).

Bugental and Goodnow, Parke and Buriel, Coie and Dodge, and Grotevant focus, to varying degrees, on socialization correlates of the development of regulated behavior. For example, Bugental and Goodnow discuss alternative pathways to autonomous regulation in children and argue that regulation based on fear (e.g., fear of punishment) results in very limited autonomous regulation (also see Eisenberg & Fabes, Parke & Buriel, Chs. 1 and 8, this Volume). They suggest that more productive mechanisms for inducing autonomous regulation include (a) provision of knowledge (which eventually leads to automatic action) through procedures, scripts, and behavioral routines; (b) assisted mental simulation (e.g., through reasoning); and (c) parental management and social scaffolding, by which parents orchestrate and arrange the variety and types of the child's experiences. Although the use of assisted mental simulation through reasoning was emphasized as a valuable socialization procedure over 25 years ago (e.g., Hoffman, 1970), the current focus on subtle socialization-relevant processes such as scaffolding and involvement in behavioral scripts is in striking contrast to the primary focus in the socialization literature of the past on level of parent control (Maccoby & Martin, 1983). The current focus on attachment relationships as a context for the development of emotion regulation (e.g., Bridges & Grolnick, 1995; Cassidy, 1994) is another exciting development in the area of emotional regulation (see "A Focus on Relationships" below).

The Development of Emotion-Related Regulation

Based on the literature reviewed in various chapters (e.g., the chapters of Bugental & Goodnow, Saarni et al., and Thompson), several developmental trends in emotion-related regulation are evident (also see Eisenberg, 1997; Thompson, 1994; Walden & Smith, in press). First, with increasing age in early infancy and childhood, regulation of emotion and behavior is shifted gradually from external sources in the social world (e.g., socializers) to self-initiated, internal (i.e., child-based) resources. Caregivers soothe young children, manage young children's emotion by selecting the situations they are in, and provide children with information (e.g., facial cues, narratives) to help the child interpret events. With age and cognitive development, children are better able to manage emotion themselves. Second, mentalistic strategies for emotion regulation, such as thinking about situations in a positive light, cognitive avoidance, and shifting and focusing attention, increase with age. The use of such strategies is probably facilitated by the development of children's understanding of emotion, including the factors that elicit, maintain, and modulate emotion, as well as other cognitive advances and physical changes. Third, with greater maturity, children develop greater capacity to modulate the course of their emotional arousal, for example, the intensity and duration of arousal, an ability that would be expected to have dramatic effects on behavior (e.g., aggression, venting of emotion, emotional expression). Fourth, with age, individuals likely become more adept at selecting, managing, and construing situations and relationships in a manner that minimizes the need to deal with negative emotions and stress (Carstensen, 1991). Fifth, the ability to match strategies with the nature of stressors appears to improve with development. Thus, children improve in the ability to select appropriate coping solutions for everyday problems (Berg, 1989). Moreover, children appear to become better at distinguishing between stressors that can be controlled and those that cannot, and at choosing the most effective strategies for these stressors (e.g., emotion-management strategies such as blunting or cognitive distraction in uncontrollable contexts; Altshuler, Genevro, Ruble, & Bornstein, 1995; Bull & Drotar, 1991; Hoffner, 1993).

Types of Regulation

In the literature on regulation of emotion, distinctions among various types of regulation frequently are ignored or blurred. However, it is useful to differentiate among three types of regulation when considering both development course and potential outcomes: regulation of emotion, regulation of emotion-related behavior, and regulation of the context itself. These differentiations are not always made in discussions of regulation in this volume, but they are useful for organizing the findings on regulation.

Emotion regulation can be defined as the process of initiating, sustaining, modulating, or changing the occurrence, intensity, or duration of internal feeling states and emotion-related physiological processes (see Brenner & Salovey, 1997; Thompson, 1994). Detailed discussion appears in the writings of temperament theorists who define regulation primarily in terms of modulating internal reactivity. In this work, emotion regulation frequently is operationalized as attentional processes such as shifting and focusing attention as needed (Ahadi & Rothbart, 1994; Derryberry & Rothbart, 1988; Windle & Lerner, 1986). Further, as noted previously, processes such as cognitive distraction and positive cognitive restructuring of a situation involve attentional

processes and are part of most conceptual frameworks in the coping literature. For example, Lazarus and Folkman (1984) considered emotion-focused coping—efforts to reduce emotional distress in contexts appraised as taxing or exceeding the resources of the individual—to be a major category of coping responses. As noted by Rothbart and Bates (Ch. 3, this Volume), attentional control is an aspect of temperament that predicts high-quality social functioning (also see Saarni et al., Ch. 5; Thompson, Ch. 2, this Volume, for discussion of emotion regulation).

Emotion regulation pertains to regulation of internal experience and physiological states. While emotion is aroused or experienced, it is often expressed in facial or bodily reactions, or through behaviors such as venting of emotion (yelling, crying) or aggression. Regulation of emotionally driven behavior, the second type of regulation, has not played a major role in most systems of temperament (Prior, 1992), although some temperament theorists have assessed behavioral inhibition and impulsivity (e.g., Ahadi & Rothbart, 1994; also see Gray, 1987). In addition, clinical, developmental, prevention, and personality theorists frequently have highlighted constructs such as behavioral inhibition, self-regulation, constraint, and ego control, which involve the ability to modulate the behavioral expression of impulses and feelings (Block & Block, 1980; Kochanska, 1993; Kopp, 1982; Sandler, Tein, & West, 1994; Tellegen, 1985). Literature relevant to behavioral regulation is reviewed in several chapters in this volume (e.g., Caspi; Coie & Dodge; Rothbart & Bates; Saarni et al.).

The third type of regulation—managing or regulating the stressful situation that elicited the emotional arousal—has been discussed primarily by coping theorists, who view problem-focused coping (efforts to modify the source of the problem) as an important type of coping (Lazarus & Folkman, 1984). This type of regulation generally includes planning and direct problem solving or instrumental coping and readily could be expanded to include proactive management of situations to reduce subsequent stress and negative emotion (Carstensen, 1991; Thompson, 1994; see below). As noted previously, when children are young, parents often manage situations for them, but with age children increasingly are expected to manage situations themselves as they acquire relevant cognitive and social capacities.

A related type of regulation relevant to emotion is niche picking—that is, behaviors that act to control exposure to various aspects of the environment related to emotional experience (Aspinwall & Taylor, 1997; Carstensen, 1991; Thompson, 1994). An example is when socially anxious individuals choose not to attend social events that elicit discomfort. Although niche-picking obviously is an important method of regulating emotional experience, few investigators have studied its use by children.

Appropriate regulation depends, in part, on the particular context. Effective emotion-related regulation is viewed as flexible and relevant to one's goals (Cole, Michel, & Teti, 1994; Eisenberg & Fabes, 1992). For example, appropriate expression of emotion depends on the situation and a person skilled in regulation adjusts his or her behavior accordingly. Moreover, it is important to differentiate between regulation and how it is measured. If regulation is operationalized as control or inhibition of behavior, particularly high levels are likely to be maladaptive (Block & Block, 1980). For example, some children appear to be highly inhibited temperamentally; these children are prone to fears, negative affect, avoidant behavior, and social withdrawal (Kagan, Snidman, & Arcus, 1992; see Kagan, Ch. 4, this Volume), and are more likely than other children to develop anxiety disorders in adulthood (Rosenbaum et al., 1993). Moreover, a moderate degree of behavioral control has been linked to children's resiliency, with the latter defined as resourcefulness in coping and rebounding from stress (Eisenberg et al., 1997). No doubt, the degree to which behavioral inhibition is adaptive and appropriate varies with the context.

Arousability and regulation obviously are interrelated. The individual's emotional reactivity, both at a dispositional level and in specific contexts, may influence the style that characterizes his or her coping/regulation and vice versa (Compas, 1987). However, these two constructs are distinctive and may be associated in a variety of ways. For example, some people who are relatively emotionally reactive seem to exhibit behavioral inhibition in response to a stressful stimulus (see Kagan, Ch. 4, this Volume), whereas others seem to become undercontrolled in their behavior (Block & Block, 1980; Pulkkinen, 1982; see Eisenberg & Fabes, 1992). Furthermore, the emotions associated with under- and overcontrol may differ somewhat. For instance, hostility or irritation over frustration appears to be associated particularly with underregulation, whereas overcontrolled people often are anxious or fearful about discrepancies (e.g., Bates, Bayles, Bennett, Ridge, & Brown, 1991; Rubin, Chen, & Hymel, 1993; see Kagan, Ch. 4, this Volume; Rothbart & Bates, Ch. 3, this Volume), although some undercontrolled children evidence relatively high levels of anxiety (Robins, John, Caspi, Moffitt, & Stouthamer-Loeber, 1996).

One important reason for differentiating among different types of regulation is that they may be combined in various ways that seem to be associated with different types of behavior in children (Eisenberg & Fabes, 1992). Some individuals who can be labeled highly inhibited are high in behavioral inhibition (behavioral overcontrol) but seem to be low in emotional or situational regulation. These include the highly inhibited children discussed by Kagan (Ch. 4, this Volume) who are prone to certain types of negative emotion (e.g., fear of discrepancy), are low in some markers of physiological regulation (e.g., vagal tone), and tend to withdraw rather than manage stressful situations. A second group of people are those who are underregulated—who likely are low in all three types of regulation. These individuals appear to be prone to externalizing types of problems, including criminal behavior (see Caspi, Ch. 6, this Volume; Rothbart & Bates, Ch. 3, this Volume). A third group is people who are relatively high in the ability to regulate emotions, emotionally driven behavior, and stressful situations. Such people are not *extremely* high, however, in behavioral control (i.e., behavioral inhibition). People relatively high in all three types of regulation appear to be well adjusted and socially competent (e.g., Eisenberg et al., 1993, 1996; Rothbart & Bates, Ch. 3, this Volume); Eisenberg and Fabes (1992) argued that this group is optimally regulated and likely to be resilient because they can choose from a variety of modes of regulation that which fits a given situation. Caspi (Ch. 6, this Volume) does not explicitly discuss the configuration of types of regulation contributing to each of these three heuristic categories of people, but he notes that groups of resilient, overcontrolled, and undercontrolled children similar to those described above have been differentiated in several studies (e.g., Robins et al., 1996).

Although not all individuals fit into these heuristic groupings, conceptualizing regulation in this multidimensional manner appears to have some potential for predicting adjustment and social competence (Caspi, Ch. 6, this Volume; Eisenberg & Fabes, 1992; Robins et al., 1996). Moreover, it is useful to consider the possibility that the effects of various kinds of regulation are moderated by individual differences in emotionality. For example, people who are underregulated would be expected to exhibit more reactive (i.e., emotionally driven) aggression and lower quality social skills if they also are prone to intense negative emotions (although some overcontrolled individuals occasionally lose control and engage in extremely violent actions; Baron & Richardson, 1994). This is because underregulated people would be relatively likely to have difficulty modulating their negative emotion (see Caspi et al., 1995; Derryberry & Rothbart, 1988; Eisenberg et al., 1996). Initial evidence for these predictions has been obtained (see Eisenberg, Fabes, Guthrie, et al., 1996). This is one example of the usefulness of considering moderating variables, a topic I return to later.

In summary, a recent theme in the developmental literature has been on multidimensional, emotion-related conceptions of regulation. This work is a natural accompaniment to the current emphasis on emotion and temperament, as well as the concern with adjustment, stress, and coping in the larger domain of psychology.

A Focus on Cognition

Another trend in developmental psychology in recent years has been increased interfacing of work on cognition with theory and empirical research on emotion and social behavior. Cognition plays an obvious and fundamental role in most aspects of emotional and social functioning. Saarni et al. (Ch. 5, this Volume) provide many examples of how cognitive advances in infancy and early childhood are reflected in emotion-related capabilities. For example, they note a number of competencies the child needs to undertake effective emotional communication, including (a) awareness of one's own emotional state; (b) awareness of others' emotional states; (c) skillfulness with one's subculture's emotion concepts and lexicon, including pragmatic use of subcultural emotional scripts in which emotional reactions are integrated with other social rules; (d) sympathetic responsiveness to other people's emotional distress; and (e) practical knowledge of how to use emotional expressiveness strategically in social contexts. Furthermore, the abilities to comprehend and take into account unique information about others' internal states (intentions, emotions, motivations, cognitions), to analyze elements of a social context and the consequences of various modes of action, and to devise appropriate cognitive strategies is fundamental to sensitive social interaction in relationships, management of aggressive impulses, and altruistic behavior (Coie & Dodge, Eisenberg & Fabes, Rubin et al., this Volume).

In addition, conceptions of the self are in large part cognitive constructions, although they also are imbued with emotion (Harter, Ch. 9, this Volume). In fact, Harter argues that developmental achievements in understanding others' behaviors and cognitions (e.g., how others view the self), as well as emotional processes, underlie age-related changes in self-conceptions (see Thompson, Ch. 2, this Volume).

In his chapter on moral development, Turiel (Ch. 13, this Volume) discusses a range of ways in which cognitions are integral in moral thinking. For example, cognition obviously is critical for differentiating moral from nonmoral (e.g., conventional and personal) concerns, in constructing conceptions about morality, in analyzing information about elements in a specific morally relevant situation, and in making morally relevant decisions based on situational information and values, beliefs, and goals. As is obvious from the passage from Turiel's chapter quoted earlier, he argues that cognition is at least as important (and probably more important) in moral development as is emotion.

In his discussion of early socioemotional development, Thompson (Ch. 2, this Volume) reviews some of the ways in which young children's working models of attachment figures and relationships are modified with the growth of children's understanding of psychological processes (e.g., as evident in work on the theory of mind). Individuals' working models of relationships, which have a cognitive as well as an affective component, are expected to influence relationships not only in childhood (see Rubin et al., Ch. 10, this Volume), but later in life (Main, Kaplan, & Cassidy, 1985). In addition, although Grotevant (Ch. 16, this Volume) does not focus in detail on cognitive development in adolescence, he notes the importance of self-perceptions, internal working models of relationships, and changes in reasoning ability for development during this period of life.

The role of cognition in the motivation to succeed has been a topic of considerable discussion. Eccles et al. (Ch. 15, this Volume) organize their review of theory and research on the motivation to succeed around three broad questions: Can I do this task? Do I want to do this task and why? and What do I need to do to succeed on this task? It is obvious that cognition is central to assessing and dealing with all of these questions, although, of course, emotion also plays a critical role in achievement motivation. As an example of how cognitions affect the motivation to succeed, Eccles et al. review literature concerning the ways in which children's understanding of competence-related constructs (e.g., ability, effort, task difficulty) affect motivation.

Interest in cognitive processes as explanatory mechanisms in socialization has changed markedly in recent years. In the past two decades, social learning theory accounts of socialization have become much more cognitive in orientation; in addition, cognitive constructs from the cognitive sciences and social psychology have been assimilated into developmental conceptions of socialization. In their chapter, Bugental and Goodnow (Ch. 7, this Volume) argue that socialization interactions are organized by the ways experiences are represented at a cognitive level. Cognitions often mediate or moderate socialization processes, and cognitive processes involved in socialization may be deliberate and reflective or relatively automatic. Bugental and Goodnow review numerous examples of the ways cognitive functions feed into or fuel the socialization process, including the roles of information-processing abilities, cognitive biases, appraisal processes, and cognitive scripts in socialization. For example, socialization procedures involving the provision of scripts and behavioral routines, assisted mental simulation, and parental scaffolding are likely to produce socialization outcomes in part through their effects on shaping children's cognitive schemata. Moreover, socialization is achieved partly through caregivers' influence on the development of children's conceptions of relationships, and parents' beliefs about children likely are influenced by their own working models of relationships. Like Bugental and Goodnow, Parke and Buriel (Ch. 8, this Volume) suggest that the ways parents perceive, organize, and understand their children's behaviors and beliefs are critical for appreciating how parent-child relationships are regulated and change.

Finally, cognitive perspectives such as cognitive developmental theory and schema-based models are important in contemporary work on gender issues. Among the most fundamental issues in the study of gender are the role of cognition in gender-typed behavior, the development of an understanding of gender-relevant constructs early in life, and the role of social factors in children's gender-relevant cognitions. The current focus on cognition has contributed to models of gender development in which the child's conceptions play a significant role in his or her own development (see Ruble & Martin, Ch. 14, this Volume).

In brief, cognitive processes of many sorts are being integrated into theory and research on diverse aspects of social and emotional development. This trend has resulted in richer conceptualizations of children and their social and emotional development, as well as of the socialization process.

A Focus on Contextual and Environmental Inputs to Development

Investigation of social and emotional development is becoming more differentiated and sophisticated in its conception of the social context. This change in the field is based, in part, on Bronfenbrenner's (1979, 1986) early efforts to increase the field's awareness of the various levels of the child's social ecology and the need to consider the interaction between the larger social world (e.g., the neighborhood and culture) and the family and individual. Similarly, life span psychologists have heightened our awareness of the interplay of historical, cultural, biological, and psychological influences on behavior (Baltes, Lindenberger, & Staudinger, Volume 1; Baltes, Reese, & Lipsitt, 1980; Caspi, Ch. 6, this Volume). From a life span perspective, changes in the individual's social context across the life span interact with the individual's unique history of experiences, roles, and biology to produce an individualized developmental pathway. Further, increased interest in individual differences in personality and social functioning sometimes has contributed to a focus on context as a possible explanation for these differences.

Diversity

One manifestation of current interest in the context of development is the recent emphasis in the discipline on recognizing and examining diversity. This trend is consistent with the life span emphasis on individual variation in developmental trajectories.

An emphasis on diversity can refer to a host of differences among people that are correlated with different life experiences: differences in sex and masculinity/femininity, in culture, in subcultural experiences, in socioeconomic status and associated living conditions, and in the composition and structure of families. For years, many developmentalists have acknowledged that research on differences among various groups (e.g., cultures or subcultures) is valuable in helping to delineate factors that influence diverse courses of development. However, we are finally moving beyond the point of solely identifying differences *between* groups in particular variables.

Of particular importance, developmentalists are acknowledging the value of studying differences in *processes* of development in different groups. Often in the past, the implicit assumption has been that the causes of development were similar or identical across groups but that various groups differed in degree of their exposure to various causal agents or in biological predispositions. Thus, gender, ethnicity, and other group-level variables were considered unwanted error variance and often were treated as control variables: nonpsychological and nonbehavioral variables of little interest. Investigators are finding that contributors to development, and the configuration and operation of influential factors, sometimes vary in different contexts and for different groups. Examples are provided later in the section on moderation effects.

Types and Examples of Contextual Influence

The importance of the various types of contextual influences on social and emotional development is evident in many of the chapters in this volume. Consistent with past *Handbook* chapters on socialization, Parke and Buriel (Ch. 8, this Volume) review in some detail the relations of aspects of the proximal familial context (e.g., parental socialization-related practices and cognitions) to social, personality, and emotional development. This ongoing interest in the role of the proximal family environment also is reflected in a number of other chapters, such as those focused on aggression (Coie & Dodge, Ch. 12, this Volume), prosocial development (Eisenberg & Fabes, Ch. 11, this Volume), peer relationships (Rubin et al., Ch. 10, this Volume), and adolescence (Grotevant, Ch. 16, this Volume).

However, the Parke and Buriel chapter, Bugental and Goodnow's chapter on socialization processes, and, to some degree, a number of other chapters include content pertaining to other aspects of context. These include family structure and organization (e.g., as tapped by parental employment status, marital status, and number of parents in the home) and subcultural and cultural factors. Although research on socialization in minority families and communities is still quite limited in quantity, such work has been assigned new importance in the past decade (see Parke & Buriel, Ch. 8, this Volume). Developmentalists are realizing that the values, socialization goals, and strategies in ethnic minority families may differ in important ways from those in the majority culture. Moreover, there are unique issues and challenges in regard to socialization and development in contexts where children must interact effectively in two cultures (i.e., the cultures of the minority and majority groups), cultures that often conflict in particular values and expectations. Similarly, the context of poverty—a situation in which increasing numbers of families are finding themselves—is a topic of growing interest in the developmental community (see Parke & Buriel, Ch. 8, this Volume; McLoyd, Volume 4).

Investigators with a social-cultural perspective are particularly likely to underscore the significance of the larger social context, comprised not only of ethnic and cultural groups but also of age, gender, work, religious, and national groups (see Bugental & Goodnow, Ch. 7, this Volume). From this perspective, socialization is a lifelong activity that is focused around becoming or remaining a member of one or more groups. Thus, much of socialization is learning shared practices and meanings in a particular cultural, social, and historical context. This perspective can be viewed as contributing to the theoretical background for contemporary interest in folk theories (e.g, Saarni et al., Ch. 5, this Volume), family rituals and myths (Parke & Buriel, Ch. 8, this Volume), scripts about daily patterns of living (Grotevant, Ch. 16, this Volume), and the construction of self-relevant scripts in social interactions in infancy and childhood (Harter, Ch. 9, this Volume).

Although cultural anthropology for a long time has had some influence on developmental psychology (e.g., Whiting & Whiting, 1975), interest in the role of culture in psychological development has increased in the past decade, particularly in regard to the study of emotion, the self, and moral development (e.g., Goodnow, Miller, & Kessel, 1995; Kitayama & Markus, 1994). As one example, Saarni et al. (Ch. 5, this Volume) propose that culture plays a role in the construction of the meaning of events that can elicit emotion (e.g., in emotion-relevant appraisals of events and others' behaviors and reactions) and in rendering some emotional responses more probable than others. Culture also influences how members of a society regulate and express emotion through a transactional process. Specifically, culture determines what one notices in the feedback from the body; affects communication patterns and, hence, socially induced affect; determines one's role in society and, hence, emotional experiences that are associated with roles; and influences the selection and expression of emotional responses. This view of emotion is in striking contrast to the perspective that emotional expression and feeling are strongly rooted in biology and that many or most emotion-related processes are universal.

Given the links among emotion, perceptions of the self, and relationships (Harter, Ch. 9, this Volume; Thompson, Ch. 2, this Volume), it is not surprising that contemporary theorists also expect culture to play a role in the development of the self. Harter (Ch. 9, this Volume) notes that the Western view of self may differ in important ways from that in cultures in which self-definition is deeply embedded in social relationships and obligations. This proposition is consistent with the contemporary argument that people in different cultures have strikingly different construals of the self due to cultural differences in concepts of individuality (Markus & Kitayama, 1991). In some cultures (e.g., many Asian cultures), the self is viewed as interdependent and there is emphasis on attending to others, fitting in, and harmony with others. In contrast, in many

Western cultures, independence from others rather than overt connectedness is valued. Although there may be more diversity within sociocentric groups in regard to an emphasis on individualism than sometimes is acknowledged (Turiel, Ch. 13, this Volume), it appears that there is marked variation across cultures in normative self-conceptions. This variation probably is reflected in processes underlying the development of self-perceptions early in life.

The role of culture is much more prominent in Turiel's (Ch. 13, this Volume) chapter on moral development than it was in the analogous chapter on this topic in the last edition of the *Handbook* (Rest, 1983). Although coming from a predominantly cognitive perspective, Turiel notes the dynamic interplay among various personal and social (including cultural) goals in moral development. He also acknowledges that social reasoning is flexible and takes into account different and varied aspects of the social world. In discussing contrasting perspectives on cross-cultural findings, Turiel makes the point that differences in assumptions about reality (e.g., assumptions about practices that are harmful to the dead) and in informational assumptions (e.g., in regard to the expected effects of physical punishment on children) are important to consider when interpreting cultural differences in moral and social conventional reasoning. As is evident in Turiel's chapter, there is disagreement in the field in regard to the interpretation of some cross-cultural differences in reasoning about moral and social conventional issues, with Turiel viewing moral development as being more similar across cultures than do most cultural psychologists (e.g., Shweder, Mahapatra, & Miller, 1987). However, Turiel emphasizes another aspect of context more than do most cultural psychologists; he argues that a focus on contextual variations between cultures has led to little consideration of variations in moral reasoning associated with contextual differences within cultures. Turiel and his colleagues' work (e.g., Wainryb, 1993) on diversity of perspectives within cultures stemming from factors such as gender roles and status hierarchies is an important direction for research on moral development.

The emphasis on different groups within a society as different socialization contexts is echoed in recent work on the separate cultures of girls and boys (Maccoby, 1990). Segregation by sex in childhood seems to be a universal phenomenon, although it varies to some degree with variables such as the availability of same-sex peers and opportunities to choose one's associates (Ruble & Martin, Ch. 14, this Volume). Within sex-segregated groups, girls and boys appear to develop different styles of interaction,

goals, and values. These subcultural differences likely have substantial and long-term implications for social, emotional, and personality development.

Also evident in this volume of the *Handbook* is the increased recognition in recent decades of connections between and among contexts within a society, for example, among family, school, and peer cultures (e.g., chapters by Coie & Dodge; Eccles et al.; Grotevant; Parke & Buriel; Rubin et al.). However, these connections are seldom examined in empirical study of development and in theory, or acknowledged in the real world (e.g., there often is little communication between schools and parents). Culture doubtlessly has important effects on the nature of the connections across settings within a culture; for example, the links between parents and schools may be stronger in majority culture families than for certain minority groups. However, few researchers have actually measured the role of subcultures in the forging (or inhibiting) of connections across settings within cultures.

A Focus on Biological Perspectives

There can be little doubt that there has been a resurgence of interest in individual differences, as well as in the biological and constitutional bases of individual differences. Plomin (1994) noted that 78% of the text pages in the 1983 *Handbook of Child Psychology* were devoted predominantly (more than half the pages) to normative or group difference approaches. Although no one has yet conducted a page count for this edition, it is clear that individual differences are a major focus of attention in this volume of the *Handbook*. In fact, in at least three of the chapters in this Volume, constitutionally based individual differences are the primary focus (i.e., Caspi; Kagan; Rothbart & Bates).

The current focus on constitutionally based individual differences is not unprecedented. After a period of heavy reliance on biological explanations of social behavior earlier in this century, biological perspectives appeared to go out of fashion in developmental and social psychology. Behaviorism and then social learning perspectives became more popular during the middle half of the century, whereas biologically based explanations of social behavior and personality were de-emphasized. In the past one or two decades, the pendulum has swung back once more.

Biology and Socioemotional Development

The discussion of the role of biological/constitutional factors in social, emotional, and personality development often has been heated (e.g., in response to Baumrind, 1993; Jackson, 1993; Scarr, 1992). This is not surprising because biological explanations of cognitive and social development have been used to argue for biological determinism and, consequently, can have devastating psychological, social, and policy effects. It also is true, however, that much contemporary work on the biological bases of behavior and emotion is based on complex frameworks that posit interconnected causal roles of biological/constitutional and environmental factors in human functioning. This complex view of the role of biology in development is, in general, reflected in the chapters in this volume.

For example, Bugental and Goodnow (Ch. 7, this Volume) depict development as the result of a dynamic coregulation of aspects of the individual (from neural to behavioral) and the environment (from physical to social). The emergence of structure in both people and their environments results from a process of mutual influence and regulation. They present literature consistent with the view that children are biologically prepared for socialization, and argue that biologically based differences in children (e.g., in temperament, physical attractiveness) elicit different socialization experiences from the environment. Similarly, biological factors that affect parenting are discussed, with a recognition that biologically influenced parental characteristics are played out in a social context. They further argue, using an evolutionary perspective, that humans may be designed for preferential receptivity to proximity maintenance with specific others in the presence of distress (e.g., attachments), for the use and recognition of signals denoting power or dominance, for differentiating between in-groups and out-groups in social life, and for the reciprocal obligations associated with communal life. These biological predispositions are viewed as emerging in a social context and, as was discussed previously, Bugental and Goodnow emphasize cultural factors as well as situational cognitive and emotional mediators and moderators of the socialization processes. Thus, Bugental and Goodnow view socialization in a complex process-oriented manner, influenced by the ongoing interaction of biological and environmental factors.

As is evident in Ruble and Martin's chapter (Ch. 14, this Volume) on gender development, recent interest in biological approaches, especially the influence of hormones on behavior, also is a force in the work on gender. Ruble and Martin note that the nature/nurture controversy is a central issue in gender development and is reflected in work on the development of sexual orientation, gender identity, and sex differences. Ruble and Martin emphasize that, in some cases, the effects of biological factors may be relatively easy to modify (and that the effects of environmental factors are not always easy to reverse or modify). In their view, biological and environmental factors interact in complex ways and cannot be separated in a simple manner; for example, behavior may influence hormones as well as the reverse. Ruble and Martin suggest that given the current state of theoretical development, biological approaches are more useful in terms of explaining sex differences and differences among people of the same sex than for explaining developmental changes in gender typing or situational variability.

In their chapter on aggression, Coie and Dodge (Ch. 12, this Volume) provide an example of how biological and environmental factors may jointly produce the observed sex difference in aggression. They suggest that boys' impulsivity (e.g., grabbing behavior), which probably is partly biologically mediated, may account for boys' frequent involvement in struggles over possessions as toddlers, which can then lead to later aggressive acts. However, Coie and Dodge also argue that there is little evidence for a link between genetics and physical aggression in adulthood, and that genetic differences in antisocial behavior cannot be used to explain violence in urban America because rapid secular changes in rates of violence are not consistent with genetic explanations.

Similar to Coie and Dodge (Ch. 12, this Volume), Eisenberg and Fabes (Ch. 11, this Volume) view genetic factors as contributing to both the development of prosocial and empathy-related responding in the species and to individual differences in aspects of emotionality and regulation (e.g., attentional regulation) that contribute to prosocial behavior and empathy in childhood. However, also consistent with Coie and Dodge, they do not view heredity as a major factor accounting for individual differences in prosocial behavior in childhood and adulthood, but as one that contributes to prosocial development in subtle ways (e.g., by affecting temperamental emotionality).

Biology, Temperament, and Personality

Kagan (Ch. 4, this Volume) focuses on physiological processes that play a role in temperament and social behavior. For example, he discusses cerebral asymmetry and its association with behavioral inhibition, other physiological correlates of inhibited and uninhibited behavior, and the relation of neurochemical systems in the brain to mood and action. He argues that genes make a modest contribution to individual differences in reactivity and inhibition, but that they are not omnipotent and always share power with experiential factors. As an example, Kagan notes the possibility that an infant born with a physiological tendency toward high reactivity and fearfulness, but who is in a supportive environment and experiences no major uncertainties, might undergo changes in those brain circuits that mediate emotional reactivity and, consequently, become minimally distressed.

A central focus in Kagan's chapter is on inhibited versus uninhibited behavior and its correlates. Such behavior is one aspect of temperament; Rothbart and Bates (Ch. 3, this Volume) provide a review of numerous other aspects of temperament. It is often assumed that the assertion that a behavior has a temperamental basis means that it is inherited, but current definitions of temperament are more complex. Rothbart and Bates define temperament as "constitutionally based individual differences in reactivity and self-regulation. . . . The term *constitutional* stresses the biological bases of temperament, influenced by genetic inheritance, maturation, and experience." Thus, temperament is influenced not only by inheritance, but by environmental factors that affect an individual's biological being (e.g., trauma or drugs) and by the social context.

Similarly, Caspi (Ch. 6, this Volume) defines temperament as stylistic differences among people—differences that appear early in life, show substantial stability over time, represent predictable modes of response (although they may require particular environmental elicitors), and possibly have fairly direct neurobiological correlates (adapted from Rutter, 1987; similar to Buss & Plomin, 1984). Adult personality traits are viewed as the social and cognitive elaborations of temperament. Caspi assumes that genetic factors play an important role in temperament and personality; however, based on the behavioral genetics literature, he also assumes that nonshared environmental influences (environmental factors that are not shared by twins or siblings) account for substantial variation in temperament. Further, Caspi delineates ways in which both genetic and environmental influences change with age, the different ways in which personal and environmental variables interact, and what types of environmental factors are most likely to create change (i.e., discontinuity) in personality.

Caspi reviews the pattern of findings in the behavioral genetics literature and concludes that there is relatively little evidence of shared environmental influences on personality (i.e., factors that have the same influence on children in the same family). He further notes that environmental influences often are genetically mediated in behavioral genetics studies. Such conclusions accurately reflect the behavioral genetics literature; however, interpretation of the empirical data depends on how the data are framed.

A Caveat

Work in behavioral genetics has contributed greatly to an understanding of the biological bases of behavior and is an important antidote to the view that everything is solely environmental. However, there are several limitations of the analyses used by behavioral geneticists and some of the typical conclusions found in the literature. Nothing discussed in this section is new (Baumrind, 1993; Hoffman, 1991; Lerner & von Eye, 1992; Wachs, 1993); however, given the strong emphasis on genetics in some chapters in this volume, some representation of alternative views is appropriate. Thus, some of the criticisms of the findings of behavioral geneticists and their interpretations are briefly summarized below.

First, in behavioral genetics analyses, one is forced to partition variance to genetic and shared or unshared environmental causes; proportions of the three must add up to 1. In reality, genetic and environmental factors often are inextricably intertwined and co-vary. Unfortunately, when this is the case, environmental effects tend to be labeled as genetic when, in fact, the environment plays a crucial role (McCall, 1994). In the standard statistical analyses, environment often is estimated as residual variance (depending on the analysis; Plomin, 1986; Wachs, 1993), although in some analyses, estimates of both genetic and environmental contributions are overestimated (e.g., in studies of comparisons of correlations in adoptive and nonadoptive families; Plomin, 1986). Moreover, in most behavioral genetics studies, the environment is not measured; it is assessed mainly on the basis of similarities and differences between siblings (e.g., monozygotic versus dizygotic twins or biologically related versus unrelated siblings). This may not be an adequate approach.

In addition, because the statistical techniques used in the field have, in general, been designed and used to examine only the main effects of genetic and environmental influences, the terminology and thinking based on these models often, albeit not always, have been limited to relatively simplistic conceptions of the environment and its relation to genetic factors (see Cardon & Cherny, 1994; Rowe & Waldman, 1993, for discussion of some newer techniques). In the real world, it is doubtful that genetics and environmental influences function only as main effects;

interaction effects are undoubtedly very influential. For example, Cadoret, Yates, Troughton, Woodworth, and Stewart (1995) found that for adopted children who were at genetic risk for antisocial behavior, the quality of adoptive parents' support mattered for predicting aggressive, antisocial behavior. In contrast, Cadoret et al. found little effect of support for those children who were free of the genetic risk factors.

The recent work by Turkheimer and Gottesman (1996; Turkheimer, 1997) illustrates the difficulty of measuring shared environmental effects. They conducted a series of computer simulations that indicated that some of the difficulty of identifying environmental effects in biometric models is methodological. In a dynamic system, the effects of environmental were all interactional, with little main effect. When environmental effects were examined within a single genotype, unambiguous environmental variability in phenotypic outcomes was observed; however, the shape of the relation between the environment and phenotype was nonlinear, discontinuous, and not generalizable from one genotype to another. Because the relation between environment and phenotype was inconsistent across different genotypes, when there were numerous genotypes in the simulation and they varied randomly, it was not possible to detect the effects of environment. There clearly were effects of the environment, but they were not systematic. In contrast, the effects of genotype were more systematic and easier to detect.

As noted by Wachs (1993), statistical interactions in empirical work are difficult to obtain due to several factors: (a) the use of inappropriate or imprecise measures of the environment or of individual characteristics; (b) the lack of statistical power in designs for interactions (McClelland & Judd, 1993); (c) the possibility that interactions may involve multiple environmental and organismic variables (and thus would be higher order and even more difficult to ascertain statistically); and (d) the atheoretical nature of most studies of organism-environment interaction. Wachs (1993) suggests that gene-environment interactions, like gene-environment covariance, are a unique influence on development that cannot be assigned to the genetic or environmental side. However, as noted previously, in current statistical procedures for computing hereditary and environmental contributions, variance typically is assigned to *either* hereditary or environmental factors, not both (see Plomin, DeFries, & Loehlin, 1977, for a discussion of the assignment of variance for genotype environment interactions).

Moreover, behavioral genetics analyses typically do not consider the role of environment in between-group differences or differences in mean levels of an outcome; only the relative rankings of individuals in a group are examined. Thus, if all mothers in a sample of a population were extremely stressed (e.g., due to extreme conditions during a war or extreme deprivation) and used relatively negative child-rearing techniques that resulted eventually in a high mean level of socially inappropriate behavior in the children in this population, this clear environmental effect would not be reflected in standard behavioral genetics analyses. It is a mistake to assume that being reared in different homes means encountering totally different environments; higher-order macrosystem components (e.g., economic adversity, exposure to trauma) may render homes similar in important ways that have critical consequences for development, and these effects that are not reflected in estimates of environment (Bronfenbrenner, 1986; Wachs, 1993).

An example involving physical characteristics may be useful in considering the effects of shared environment. Consider a redheaded girl with a redheaded parent in a culture in which redheads are expected to be impulsive and hotheaded. People in the society may expect the child to be hot-tempered and consequently label the girl as such even when her anger is relatively controlled. The mother may have had the same experience when she was growing up. Moreover, people may not only expect but also tolerate higher levels of uncontrolled emotion from redheaded children (e.g., when the child has a temper tantrum) than from other children because such behavior is consistent with the stereotype for redheads. Thus, others' expectations and behavior, triggered by the physical appearance of the child, may encourage the development of hot-headed behavior in the girl as well as in her parent and in other redheaded siblings. Consequently, mother and child may be more alike in the characteristic of hot-headedness than would this mother with an adopted child without red hair. Moreover, because monozygotic twins generally are concordant in redheadedness, they would be expected to exhibit greater similarity in degree of hot-headedness than would dizygotic twins (who may have different colors of hair). Thus, a physical characteristic could trigger an environmental reaction, which is primarily responsible for the similarity between redheaded monozygotic twins or between biologically related parents and children. Yet the similarity between monozygotic twins would be attributed to genetic factors rather than to the children's shared environment because redheaded monozygotic siblings are likely to be more similar to one another phenotypically than would dizygotic twins in the tendency to be hotheaded. Nonetheless, if these children were in a culture that did not have stereotypes about redheaded children, the monozygotic redheaded twins would be less likely to be hotheaded and less similar to one another in this characteristic than in the culture with the stereotype about redheads.

This scenario is further complicated by the fact that monozygotic twins are likely to spend more time together than dizygotic twins. Thus, they are more likely to be exposed to the same sampling of parenting behavior than are dizygotic twins. In addition, as noted previously, monozygotic twins, due to their similarity in physical appearance and other characteristics, may be more likely than dizygotic twins to elicit similar reactions from other socializers outside the home (e.g., peers, teachers; Baumrind, 1993; L. Hoffman, 1991; Lytton, 1977), which also may contribute to similarities in their social behavior. Although some data are consistent with the view that the assumption of equal environment holds (i.e., that monozygotic and dizygotic twins experience equal environments) for some issues (e.g., certain psychiatric disorders; Hetterma, Neale, & Kendler, 1995; Kendler, Neale, Kessler, Heath, & Eaves, 1993; Scarr & Carter-Saltzman, 1979), many of the measures used to assess similarity of environment or outcome variables are out-of-date and insensitive (Wachs, 1993; also see L. Hoffman, 1991). Thus, one simply cannot assume that the environments of monozygotic and dizygotic twins are equally similar in all ways (L. Hoffman, 1994). However, the statistics in behavior genetics studies rest on this assumption (although it also has been argued that the difference in the environments does not predict variables of importance; Plomin, DeFries, & McClearn, 1980). Moreover, in adoption studies, the assumption is that there is no genetic similarity between adopted children and parents. However, given the likelihood to selective placement of children with parents similar in some characteristics, this may not be entirely true (e.g., there may be genetically based similarities in appearance or intelligence due to matching efforts).

The notion of redheadedness having the aforementioned effect may seem unlikely, but it is clear that physical characteristics such as height and physical attractiveness do elicit specific responses from the environment (e.g., Langlois, 1986). Moreover, at a conceptual level, just because siblings react somewhat differently to the same environmental influence (e.g., maternal low education or depression)

does not mean that the environment is not shared by the siblings.* Related individuals may react differently to the same environment due to exposure to different experiences (e.g., at school or in the neighborhood).

In brief, the complex relations between biological and environmental factors and the importance of environmental factors often are masked by the way the findings in behavioral genetics studies are reported. Moreover, the use of the terms *genetic* versus *environmental* influence in behavioral genetics analyses serves to perpetuate the notion that the two types of influences are independent when they seldom are. Gene-environment covariance and interaction are unique forms of influence on development that should not be assigned exclusively to either genetic or environmental categories (Wachs, 1993). Moreover, as discussed by Horowitz (1993), genetic material is not expressed and does not influence processes in the absence of the environment. Thus, it is probably artificial to speak of a distinction between genetics and environment at all. Horowitz (1993) suggested using terms such as *organismic* and *constitutional* rather than *genetic* because they do not exclude environmental influences. In any case, our thinking about the role of genetics and environment in development, although much more sophisticated than in the past, requires further evolution.

Relatedly, as noted numerous times by authors in this volume, the psychological link between the notion of genetics and stability or invariance in behavior that is common in the field (although disclaimed by most behavioral geneticists) is out-of-date (Caspi, Ch. 6, this Volume). Plomin (1986) stated it well: "We need to pry apart the close association that the adjective *genetics* and *stable* have come to share: Longitudinally stable characteristics are not necessarily hereditary, nor are genetically influenced characters necessarily stable" (p. 4). Recent advances in the study of the role of genetics in change as well as stability of behavior are particularly relevant to developmentalists. One of the challenges for the field is to delineate the ways the environment and genetics jointly affect change in development (see Bronfenbrenner & Ceci, 1994, for an interesting perspective). A recent example is the work of Bradley et al. (1994); they found that low birthweight children raised in poverty generally have a poor prognosis for development, although those reared in environments characterized by several protective factors were relatively likely to show early signs of resiliency. Another challenge for the discipline is to identify

---

* I thank Eleanor Maccoby for her discussion of this point.

ways the environment alters constitutional (e.g., physiological) factors such as hormones that could influence development and change.

A Focus on Relationships

As noted by Rubin et al. (Ch. 10, this Volume), interest in relationships other than the parent-child relationship has grown tremendously since the 1970s, and perhaps particularly in the years since the last edition of the *Handbook*. In addition, researchers studying the family increasingly have examined not just the parent-child dyad, but also larger chunks of the family unit, associations between quality of parent-parent and parent-child relationships, and links between quality of familial interactions and quality of peer relationships (Parke & Buriel, Ch. 8, this Volume). For example, there is now evidence that marital distress and conflict are related to difficulties in friendships and child behaviors related to peer rejection (Rubin et al., Ch. 10, this Volume). Moreover, investigators have begun to study the role of social relationships outside the family (e.g., as reflected in social support) for quality of interaction within the family (see Parke & Buriel, Ch. 8, this Volume; Rubin et al., Ch. 10, this Volume) and for the provision of social opportunities for children (e.g., adult social networks as a source of potential peer contacts for children; see Parke & Buriel, Ch. 8, this Volume).

Discussion of relationships often includes references to emotion and its development. It is probable that learning about emotion and its regulation, which often occurs in the family, plays a critical role in the quality of later social relationships. Regardless of where children acquire these skills, children who understand and communicate emotion in acceptable ways are likely to have more positive relationships (see Saarni et al., Ch. 5, this Volume) than other children; in addition, the ability to regulate emotion seems to be associated with positive, other-oriented responses such as sympathy and prosocial behavior (Eisenberg & Fabes, Ch. 11, this Volume).

As noted previously, it also has been suggested that the causal link between emotion-related learning and quality of relationships can be reversed: that early attachment relationships play a role in the development of emotion regulation and reflect strategies for regulating emotion in interpersonal contexts (Bridges & Grolnick, 1995; Sroufe, Schork, Motti, Lawroski, & LaFreniere, 1984). The securely attached infant whose parent is consistently and appropriately responsive to the infant's distress signals is believed to learn that it is acceptable to express distress and to actively seek the assistance of others for comfort when upset. In contrast, avoidant infants, due in part to the parents' nonresponsiveness to their distress signals, may learn to inhibit emotional expressiveness as well as other-directed self-regulatory strategies (e.g., contact-seeking and maintaining behaviors; Braungart & Stifter, 1991; Bridges & Grolnick, 1995). Moreover, it has been argued that parental underattunement is associated with infants' inability to attend to their own affective states, label them, and incorporate them into their model of the self (see Crittenden, 1990; Harter, Ch. 9, this Volume). In contrast, parental overattunement or intrusiveness could result in a sense of incoherence about feeling states because of the emphasis on how the infant *should* feel rather than on how he or she actually feels (see Harter, Ch. 9, this Volume; Stern, 1985). Consistent with these perspectives, maternal support has been linked with the variety of coping strategies used by children to deal with stress, as well as with the use of relatively appropriate strategies (e.g., avoidant strategies in uncontrollable situations; Hardy, Power, & Jaedicke, 1993). Moreover, preschool children with secure attachments at 12 and 18 months of age have been found to be more empathic and more prosocial toward others (Kestenbaum, Farber, & Sroufe, 1989).

The internal working model developed in the context of early attachment relationships is believed to affect the quality of children's relationships because of the assumptions and expectations about relationships that are inherent in internal working models (Bretherton & Waters, 1985; Parke & Buriel, Ch. 8, this Volume; Rubin et al., Ch. 10, this Volume; Thompson, Ch. 2, this Volume). One way early attachment relationships affect other relationships is through their influence on the developing sense of self in the infant as lovable or unworthy of love (Bretherton, 1991; Harter, Ch. 9, this Volume). However, Harter (Ch. 9, this Volume) suggests that there is a need to consider how an individual's different attachments might imply different working models of relationships; this issue may have implications for the finding that self-esteem differs in different relationships (e.g., with parents, peers, teachers; Harter, Ch. 9, this Volume).

Obviously, the topic of attachment and early parent-child relationships is a central issue in the study of relationships in developmental psychology. Attachments are hypothesized to affect the development of the self, a range of cognitions relevant to quality of relationships, emotion regulation and emotions attached to various relationships, and even personality development (Eisenberg & Fabes, Ch. 11, this Volume; Harter, Ch. 9, this Volume; Nachmias,

Gunnar, Mangelsdorf, Parritz, & Buss, 1996; Rubin et al., Ch. 10, this Volume; Thompson, Ch. 2, this Volume). Thompson (Ch. 2, this Volume) reviews research pertaining to these issues and raises important questions: (a) Does attachment fully encompass early parent-infant relationships, or are there features of this relationship that are independent of the security of attachment? (b) How do features of the dyadic attachment relationship over time inhere within the child, and how rapidly does this occur? and (c) What should quality of attachment predict about a child's later functioning and why? These questions are related to issues raised by Harter (Ch. 9, this Volume) and merit additional attention in the next decade.

Peer relationships also affect the development of cognitions about the self (including those concerning self-worth and a gender-relevant self-concept) and feelings that are associated with the self and with the social world (Harter, Ch. 9, this Volume; Ruble & Martin, Ch. 14, this Volume). These feelings likely infuse children's conceptions of relationships and their valuing of other people in general. Therefore, it is not surprising that the quality of children's peer relationships has been linked to their social competencies and prosocial tendencies (Eisenberg & Fabes, Ch. 11, this Volume; Rubin et al., Ch. 10, this Volume). However, the ways in which emotions mediate associations between early quality of relationships (familial or extrafamilial) and later social outcomes have received little empirical attention, although, as mentioned previously, such associations have been discussed to some degree by attachment theorists (e.g., in theoretical work on attachment styles as modes of emotion regulation). The roles of emotion as well as cognition as mediators between quality of early relationships and later socioemotional development, and how development, characteristics of the child, and exposure to diverse relationships may moderate the process, are issues that require further study.

An Emphasis on Process (Mediation) and Moderation

As developmental psychologists have produced and accumulated more knowledge about the occurrence and frequency of variables of interest (e.g., descriptive data) as well as about relations among constructs (i.e., correlational data), they have begun to ask more complex questions than in the past. This trend is very evident in this volume of the *Handbook.* For example, in addition to routinely questioning assumptions of directionality of causality, there is evidence in a number of chapters of an increased concern with *process,* as reflected in questions

about mediation. Mediating processes are the processes underlying the relation between two variables (a predictor and a criterion). Mediators help clarify how or why a given relation occurs (Baron & Kenny, 1986).

In addition, based in part on contemporary concern with context, diversity, and individual differences, there is considerable interest in moderating variables, that is, in variables such as sex, socioeconomic class, race/ethnicity, personality, and type of situation that affect the direction or strength of the relation between an independent or predictor variable and a dependent or criterion variable (Baron & Kenny, 1986). Increasingly, psychologists have recognized that one process generally does not fit all, particularly in the study of social behavior and social development. To study moderation, investigators generally examine the interaction of the independent variable with the potential moderator (e.g., age, sex) when predicting an outcome or criterion variable or compare the equivalence of structural models for different groups.

Mediating or moderating processes are discussed directly or indirectly by all chapter authors, but are a central focus in some chapters. For example, Grotevant (Ch. 16, this Volume), in his chapter on adolescence, narrows his content focus by emphasizing studies in which mediation or moderation were examined. In addition, Rothbart and Bates (Ch. 3, this Volume) include a section in their chapter on variables that moderate the relation of temperament to other variables. Bugental and Goodnow (Ch. 7, this Volume) also explicitly emphasize moderation in the socialization process, whereas Eisenberg and Fabes (Ch. 11, this Volume) conclude that studies of moderating effects are an important deficit in the literature on prosocial development.

A few examples of how authors discuss mediation and moderation illustrate the types of issues that are the focus in contemporary work on mediation and moderation. First consider mediation. Eccles et al. (Ch. 15, this Volume) suggest that parental beliefs, practices, and resources mediate between family demographics and achievement-related outcomes. Similarly, both Grotevant (Ch. 16, this Volume) and Coie and Dodge (Ch. 12, this Volume) discuss relations between parenting and offsprings' externalizing behavior. Grotevant reviews work in which adolescents' restraint (a personality variable involving internalization of standards) mediated the relation between parenting and delinquent behavior (Feldman & Weinberger, 1994). Coie and Dodge discuss the possibility that parenting may mediate the relation between the macrolevel variable of poverty and children's aggression. Moreover, Grotevant reviews the importance of identity as a potential mediating variable (e.g., between economic hardship and psychological well-being). Consistent with Coie and Dodge, Grotevant emphasizes quality of relationships as mediators between distal environmental factors (e.g., economic resources) and adolescent adjustment, or between family structure or family cohesion and depression. For example, he cites a study by Brody et al. (1994) in which reduced financial resources led to parental depression and disruptions in caregiving, which in turn were associated with reduced self-regulation in adolescents. As noted by Grotevant, studies of this sort go far beyond the simple deficit models of poverty to demonstrate potential intervening processes. Information about such intervening processes is essential for successful intervention and prevention programs.

Bugental and Goodnow's (Ch. 7, this Volume) chapter has a strong focus on cognitive and affective mediators in the socialization process. For example, they discuss the role of automatic cognitive processing as a mediational link between parental beliefs (e.g., about control) and parenting behavior. They also suggest that temporary parental affective state can affect the parent's interpretation and cognitive processing in an ongoing parent-child interaction and, consequently, can influence the appropriateness of a parent's behavior toward a child. Goodnow and Bugental present the relations among cognition, motivation, and emotion in the context of parenting as a continuous flow process with feedback; the result is a complex and very stimulating model with numerous implications for the study of socialization.

Although mediation is emphasized in a number of the *Handbook* chapters, moderation is discussed to an even greater degree. For example, Bugental and Goodnow (Ch. 7, this Volume) consider affect and cognition as moderators of the socialization process; Kagan (this volume) mentions instances in which parental socialization and aspects of the child's temperament interact in the prediction of security of attachment or children's conscience; and Coie and Dodge (Ch. 12, this Volume) note that harsh discipline is a predictor of later aggressive behavior for white but not black children. Eccles et al. suggest that race may moderate relations between competence-related beliefs and school performance (beliefs may predict school performance for white but not black children). In addition, Eisenberg and Fabes (Ch. 11, this Volume) suggest that the interaction of individual differences in emotionality and regulation predicts children's prosocial behavior and sympathy better than the consideration of only the main effects of these predictors. Finally, Ruble and Martin, Turiel, and

others discuss ways in which sex of the child moderates the effects of social experience and various social behaviors (although authors did not always use the term *moderation*).

Grotevant (Ch. 16, this Volume) provides extensive coverage of moderation effects in his review of research on adolescents. For example, he cites Steinberg, Lamborn, Dornbusch, and Darling (1992), who proposed that parenting style (e.g., authoritative versus authoritarian parenting) moderates the influence of specific parenting practices on development in at least two ways: by transforming the nature or quality of the interaction and thus moderating the influence of the specific practices on child outcomes, and by influencing children's personality, especially children's openness to parental influence, which in turn moderates the association between parenting practices and child outcomes. Moreover, Grotevant reviews other studies in which researchers identified protective factors (e.g., adolescents' positive orientation toward school) that moderate the effect of risks on developmental outcomes.

Rothbart and Bates (Ch. 3, this Volume) explicitly evaluate whether the relation between temperament and adjustment is moderated by variables such as environmental factors (e.g., maternal control style, day care quality, parental expectations of the child's temperament), other aspects of temperament (e.g., interactions of regulation with sociability or emotionality), and sex. They believe that there are excellent theoretical reasons for expecting interaction effects in the relation of temperament with adjustment and they review some intriguing studies on the issue. However, they point out that there is not yet an adequate pattern of replicated, longitudinal results to allow them to conclude with confidence that moderation effects help explain the development of adjustment.

Given the relatively recent emphasis on moderation, it is not surprising that there is, as yet, a small and largely unreplicated body of literature on its effects. However, this is likely to change because questions of moderation are moving to the fore in many arenas of interest. The result is likely to be a more differentiated understanding of *when* relations and processes occur—an issue that is an essential complement to the more basic mediational question of *why* relations occur.

A Focus on Combining Data across Studies

A recent trend in psychology is the use of the statistical procedure of meta-analysis to combine data from many studies. With meta-analysis, investigators use quantitative procedures to "describe the typical strength of the effect or phenomenon, its variability, its statistical significance, and the nature of the moderator variables from which one can predict the relative strength of the effect or phenomenon" (Rosenthal, 1995, p. 183). As is evident in recent issues of *Psychological Bulletin,* the major journal of reviews in the discipline, meta-analysis has become a popular tool in the field.

Meta-analyses are used by some contributors to this volume; many more cite existing papers in which meta-analyses were conducted. Eisenberg and Fabes (Ch. 11, this Volume) compute meta-analyses to examine age and sex differences in prosocial behavior. Using meta-analytic techniques, they examine the effects of moderators such as type of study (e.g., experimental or correlational) on age and sex differences and examine the relation of each predictor (e.g., type of study) while controlling for the effects of other variables (e.g., type of prosocial behavior). Eisenberg and Fabes find that prosocial behavior increases with age and that the size of this age-related change is greater in experimental/structured designs than in naturalistic/correlational designs. Naturalistic/correlational designs are relatively likely to be used in studies of younger children, whereas experimental/structured designs are likely to be used with older children. After controlling for a variety of study qualities, including type of study, through the use of hierarchical regression analyses, age was still significantly related to prosocial behavior. Thus, with the use of meta-analytic techniques, Eisenberg and Fabes examine alternative hypotheses for explaining the relation of age to prosocial behavior. Procedures such as these are extremely useful for uncovering patterns of findings among many studies using a variety of methods and conducted in diverse settings.

Of course, meta-analytic procedures, like any statistical procedure, can be misused. Care must be taken in selecting studies, applying the procedures, and interpreting the results. Nonetheless, it is likely that meta-analytic procedures will be used increasingly in the future, in part because of their utility for examining moderating variables (due to the statistical power achieved by combining numerous studies).

A Focus on Application

Another trend in the developmental research has been an increased interest in application and real-world problems. This emphasis in the discipline is reflected in the fact that for the first time, one volume of the *Handbook* (Volume 4) is devoted to applied issues; thus, much of the applied work is discussed in that volume. Nonetheless, the contemporary concern with application also is reflected to some degree in this volume.

This concern can be seen in both the topics of study and the ways in which people are conducting research on certain topics. In regard to topics of study, work on aggression, regulation, coping, and social competence is burgeoning, no doubt in part because of concern in society about children's psychological health, violence, and related social issues (Coie & Dodge; Eisenberg & Fabes; Rubin et al.; Saarni et al., all this Volume). Moreover, investigators increasingly are turning their attention to the issue of development in stressful contexts such as families in poverty, one-parent families, and families of divorce (Parke & Buriel, Ch. 8, this Volume). Concern with these topics often has been spurred by heightened interest in and funding for research focused on prevention of violence, substance abuse, and psychological problems. Concern with clinical issues and prevention is not without precedent, of course; much of the early work in child development grew out of a desire to understand the origins of typical childhood problems (e.g., the longitudinal research at Berkeley).

In regard to methods of conducting research, work on topics that have been a focus of interest for a long time is increasingly being conducted outside the laboratory in real-world contexts so that findings have direct applicability to prevention, clinical, and policy issues. For example, developmentalists are becoming involved in the process of obtaining knowledge that can be used to design real-life programs that lessen the probability of negative effects from exposure to stressors (e.g., divorce, poverty) or that promote prosocial behavior or inhibit aggressive tendencies in school settings (Coie & Dodge, Ch. 12, this Volume; Eisenberg & Fabes, Ch. 11, this Volume). Moreover, developmentalists are deeply involved in evaluating programs such as day care that have implications for both families and policy (see Volume 4). It is likely that the trend for developmentalists to apply their theory and methods to real-life issues in real-world contexts will continue into the next decade and century.

SUMMARY

In general, the chapters in this volume reflect intellectual excitement and expanding possibilities due to emerging themes, constructs, and methods, and a recent permeability in the intellectual boundaries of the field. Many of the changes in the study of social and emotional development in the past decade or two can be characterized by two familiar concepts: increasing integration and differentiation. In this context, I am using the term *integration* to mean the incorporation into the study of social functioning of ideas and methods from diverse approaches and topics in developmental psychology, other subdisciplines of psychology, and even other disciplines such as sociology, genetics, and anthropology. As an example, the study of behavioral and social inhibition and deficits in social competence has been enriched by work in psychophysiology (e.g., on heart rate variability), clinical psychology and psychiatry (e.g., research on behavioral disorders and temperament), personality (e.g., research on individual differences in shyness, regulation, and coping), and social psychology (e.g., notions about the role of attributional processes in problem behaviors). Moreover, the emphasis on emotion in other areas of psychology has permeated developmental psychology. The integration of new and different methods, constructs, and theoretical perspectives has broadened not only our understanding of social and emotional development, but the entire framework upon which we design and interpret research findings.

Differentiation within the field of social development may be viewed in terms of contexts, constructs, and causal inferences. As noted previously, the burgeoning interest in context in developmental psychology is reflected in the study of many levels of influence, including diversity in culture and subculture, race and ethnicity, sex and gender, and types of families and groups. In regard to constructs, our thinking is becoming less global and more conditional, multifaceted, and complex. Similarly, proposed causal influences of various social processes are becoming more multifaceted and less simple. Researchers are increasingly acknowledging and examining the multiplicative and co-varying contributions of various types of environmental and biologically based influences on social functioning. For example, children are increasingly being viewed as producers of their environment as well as the products of socialization (e.g., Lytton, 1990), and development often is viewed as a consequence of social interactions that are shaped by contextual factors and characteristics of all participants in the interaction. Although interactional and reciprocal causal models are not new, they are becoming a part of our everyday thinking about psychological phenomena. Of course, as noted in the discussion of the analytic tools used by behavioral geneticists, implementation of complex interactive models into research designs lags behind conceptual models. However, analytic methods for exploring reciprocal, additive, and interactive causal influences, as well as analyses for examining nonlinear relations and growth curves, are becoming more common, so developmentalists are increasingly able to test complex conceptions of development empirically. The next decade will undoubtedly be an exciting time for the study of social, emotional, and personality development.

ACKNOWLEDGMENTS

I thank Richard Fabes, William Graziano, Eleanor Maccoby, Carol Martin, Adam Matheny, Paul Mussen, Nora Newcombe, and David Rowe for feedback on portions of this chapter.

REFERENCES

Ahadi, S. A., & Rothbart, M. K. (1994). Temperament, development, and the big five. In C. F. Halverson, Jr., G. A. Kohnstamm, & R. P. Martin (Eds.), *The developing structure of temperament and personality from infancy to adulthood* (pp. 189–207). Hillsdale, NJ: Erlbaum.

Altshuler, J. L., Genevro, J. L., Ruble, D. N., & Bornstein, M. H. (1995). Children's knowledge and use of coping strategies during hospitalization for elective surgery. *Journal of Applied Developmental Psychology, 16,* 53–76.

Aspinwall, L. G., & Taylor, S. E. (1997). A stitch in time: Self-regulation and proactive coping. *Psychological Bulletin, 121,* 417–436.

Baltes, P. B., Reese, H. W., & Lipsitt, L. P. (1980). Life-span developmental psychology. *Annual Review of Psychology, 31,* 65–110.

Baron, R. A., & Richardson, D. R. (1994). *Human aggression* (2nd ed.). New York: Plenum Press.

Baron, R. M., & Kenny, D. A. (1986). The moderator-mediator variable distinction in social psychological research: Conceptual, strategic, and statistical considerations. *Journal of Personality and Social Psychology, 51,* 1173–1182.

Bates, J. E., Bayles, K., Bennett, D. S., Ridge, B., & Brown, M. M. (1991). Origins of externalizing behavior problems at eight-years-of-age. In D. Pepler & K. Rubin (Eds.), *Development and treatment of childhood aggression* (pp. 93–120). Hillsdale, NJ: Erlbaum.

Baumrind, D. (1993). The average expectable environment is not good enough: A response to Scarr. *Child Development, 64,* 1299–1317.

Berg, C. A. (1989). Knowledge of strategies for dealing with everyday problems from childhood through adolescence. *Developmental Psychology, 25,*607–618.

Block, J. H., & Block, J. (1980). The role of ego-control and ego-resiliency in the organization of behavior. In W. A. Collins (Ed.), *Development of cognition, affect, and social relations: The Minnesota Symposia on Child Psychology* (Vol. 13, pp. 39–101). Hillsdale, NJ: Erlbaum.

Boyum, L. A., & Parke, R. D. (1995). Family emotional expressiveness and children's social competence. *Journal of Marriage & Family, 57,* 593–608.

Bradley, R. H., Whiteside, L., Mundfrom, D. J., Casey, P. H., Kelleher, K. J., & Pope, S. K. (1994). Early indications of resilience and their relation to experiences in the home environments of low birthweight, premature children living in poverty. *Child Development, 65,* 346–360.

Braungart, J. M., & Stifter, C. A. (1991). Regulation of negative reactivity during the strange situation: Temperament and attachment in 12-month-old infants. *Infant Behavior and Development, 14,* 349–364.

Brenner, E. M., & Salovey, P. (1997). Emotion regulation during childhood: Development, interpersonal, and individual considerations. In P. Salovey & D. Sluyter (Eds.), *Teaching in the heart of the classroom: Emotional development, emotional literacy, and emotional intelligence* (pp. 168–192). New York: Basic Books.

Bretherton, I. (1991). Pouring new wine into old bottles: The social self as internal working model. In M. R. Gunnar & L. A. Sroufe (Eds.), *Self-processes and development: The Minnesota Symposium on Child Development* (Vol. 23, pp. 1–41). Hillsdale, NJ: Erlbaum.

Bretherton, I., & Waters, E. (1985). Growing points of attachment theory and research. *Monographs of the Society for Research in Child Development, 50*(Serial No. 209).

Bridges, L. J., & Grolnick, W. S. (1995). The development of emotional self-regulation in infancy and early childhood. In N. Eisenberg (Ed.), *Review of personality and psychology* (pp. 185–211). Newbury Park, CA: Sage.

Brody, G. H., Stoneman, Z., Flor, D., McCrary, C., Hastings, L, & Conyers, O. (1994). Financial resources, parent psychological functioning, parent co-caregiving, and early adolescent competence in rural two-parent African-American families. *Child Development, 65,* 590–605.

Bronfenbrenner, U. (1979). *The ecology of human development.* Cambridge, MA: Harvard University Press.

Bronfenbrenner, U. (1986). Ecology of the family as a context for human development: Research perspectives. *Developmental Psychology, 22,* 723–742.

Bronfenbrenner, U., & Ceci, S. J. (1994). Nature–nurture reconceptualized in developmental perspective: A bioecological model. *Psychological Review, 101,* 568–586.

Bull, B. A., & Drotar, D. (1991). Coping with cancer in remission: Stressors and strategies reported by children and adolescents. *Journal of Pediatric Psychology, 16,* 767–782.

Buss, A. H., & Plomin, R. (1984). *Temperament: Early developing personality traits.* Hillsdale, NJ: Erlbaum.

Cadoret, R. J., Yates, W. R., Troughton, E., Woodworth, G., & Stewart, M. A. (1995). Genetic-environmental interaction in the genesis of aggressivity and conduct disorders. *Archives of General Psychiatry, 52,* 916–924.

Campos, J. (1984). A new perspective on emotions. *Child Abuse and Neglect, 8,* 147–156.

Cardon, L. R., & Cherny, S. S. (1994). Adoption design methodology. In J. C. DeFries, R. Plomin, & D. W. Fulker (Eds.), *Nature and nurture during middle childhood* (pp. 26–45). Oxford, England: Blackwell.

Carstensen, L. L. (1991). Selectivity theory: Social activity in life-span context. In K. W. Schaie (Ed.), *Annual review of geriatrics and gerontology* (Vol. 11). New York: Springer.

Carver, C. S., Scheier, M. F., & Weintraub, J. K. (1989). Assessing coping strategies: A theoretically based approach. *Journal of Personality and Social Psychology, 56,* 267–283.

Caspi, A., Henry, B., McGee, R. O., Moffitt, T. E., & Silva, P. A. (1995). Temperamental origins of child and adolescent behavior problems: From age 3 to age 15. *Child Development, 66,* 55–68.

Cassidy, J. (1994). Emotion regulation: Influences of attachment relationships. In N. Fox (Ed.), Emotion regulation: Behavioral and biological considerations. *Monographs of Society for Research in Child Development, 59*(Serial No. 240), 228–249.

Cole, P. M., Michel, M. K., & Teti, L. O. (1994). The development of emotion regulation and dysregulation: A clinical perspective. *Monographs of the Society for Research in Child Development, 59*(Serial No. 240), 73–100.

Compas, B. E. (1987). Coping with stress during childhood and adolescence. *Psychological Bulletin, 101,* 393–403.

Crick, N. R., & Dodge, K. A. (1994). A review and reformulation of social information-processing mechanisms in children's social adjustment. *Psychological Bulletin, 115,* 74–101.

Crittenden, P. M. (1990). Internal representational models of attachment relationships. *Infant Mental Health Journal, 11,* 259–277.

Davies, P. T., & Cummings, E. M. (1994). Marital conflict and child adjustment: An emotional security hypothesis. *Psychological Bulletin, 116,* 387–411.

Derryberry, D., & Rothbart, M. K. (1988). Arousal, affect, and attention as components of temperament. *Journal of Personality and Social Psychology, 55,* 958–966.

Dunn, J., & Brown, J. (1994). Affect expression in the family, children's understanding of emotions, and their interactions with others. *Merrill-Palmer Quarterly, 40,* 120–137.

Eisenberg, N. (1997, April). *Emotion and emotional competence in childhood.* Master lecture presented at the biennial meeting of the Society for Research in Child Development, Washington, DC.

Eisenberg, N., & Fabes, R. A. (1990). Empathy: Conceptualization, assessment, and relation to prosocial behavior. *Motivation and Emotion, 14,* 131–149.

Eisenberg, N., & Fabes, R. A. (1992). Emotion, regulation, and the development of social competence. In M. S. Clark (Ed.), *Review of personality and social psychology: Vol. 14. Emotion and social behavior* (pp. 119–150). Newbury Park, CA: Sage.

Eisenberg, N., Fabes, R. A., Bernzweig, J., Karbon, M., Poulin, R., & Hanish, L. (1993). The relations of emotionality and regulation to preschoolers' social skills and sociometric status. *Child Development, 64,* 1418–1438.

Eisenberg, N., Fabes, R. A., Carlo, G., Troyer, D., Speer, A. L., Karbon, M., & Switzer, G. (1992). The relations of maternal practices and characteristics to children's vicarious emotional responsiveness. *Child Development, 63,* 583–602.

Eisenberg, N., Fabes, R. A., & Guthrie, I. (in press). Coping with stress: The roles of regulation and development. In S. Wolchik & I. Sandler (Eds.), *Children's coping: Links between theory and intervention.* New York: Plenum Press.

Eisenberg, N., Fabes, R. A., Guthrie, I. K., Murphy, B. C., Maszk, P., Holmgren, R., & Suh, K. (1996). The relations of regulation and emotionality to problem behavior in elementary school children. *Development and Psychopathology, 8,* 141–162.

Eisenberg, N., Fabes, R. A., Murphy, B., Maszk, P., Smith, M., & Karbon, M. (1995). The role of emotionality and regulation in children's social functioning: A longitudinal study. *Child Development, 66,* 1360–1384.

Eisenberg, N., Fabes, R. A., Nyman, M., Bernzweig, J., & Pinuelas, A. (1994). The relations of emotionality and regulation to children's anger-related reactions. *Child Development, 65,* 109–128.

Eisenberg, N., Guthrie, I. K., Fabes, R. A., Reiser, M., Murphy, B. C., Holmgren, R., Maszk, P., & Losoya, S. (1997). The relations of regulation and emotionality to resiliency and competent social functioning in elementary school children. *Child Development,* 295–311.

Eisenberg, N., Martin, C. L., & Fabes, R. A. (1996). Gender development and gender differences. In D. C. Berliner & R. C. Calfee (Eds.), *The handbook of educational psychology* (pp. 358–396). New York: Macmillan.

Erber, R., Wegner, D. M., & Therriault, N. (1996). On being cool and collected: Mood regulation in anticipation of social interaction. *Journal of Personality and Social Psychology, 70,* 757–766.

Feldman, S. S., & Weinberger, D. A. (1994). Self-restraint as a mediator of family influences on boys' delinquent behavior: A longitudinal study. *Child Development, 65,* 195–211.

Goodnow, J. J., Miller, P. J., & Kessel, F. (Eds.). (1995). *Cultural practices as contexts for development: New directions in child development.* San Francisco: Jossey-Bass.

Gray, J. A. (1987). Perspectives and anxiety and impulsivity: A commentary. *Journal of Research in Personality, 21,* 493–509.

Hardy, D. F., Power, T. G., & Jaedicke, S. (1993). Examining the relation of parenting to children's coping with everyday stress. *Child Development, 64,* 1829–1841.

Hetterma, J. M., Neale, M. C., & Kendler, K. S. (1995). Physical similarity and the equal-environment assumption in twin studies of psychiatric disorders. *Behavior Genetics, 25,* 327–335.

Hoffman, L. W. (1991). The influence of the family environment on personality: Accounting for sibling differences. *Psychological Review, 110,* 187–203.

Hoffman, L. W. (1994). Commentary on Plomin. A proof and a disproof questioned. *Social Development, 3,* 60–63.

Hoffman, M. L. (1970). Moral development. In P. H. Mussen (Ed.), *Carmichael's manual of child development* (Vol. 2, pp. 261–359). New York: Wiley.

Hoffman, M. L. (1982). Development of prosocial motivation: Empathy and guilt. In N. Eisenberg (Ed.), *The development of prosocial behavior* (pp. 281–313). New York: Academic Press.

Hoffman, M. L. (1983). Affective and cognitive processes in moral internalization. In E. T. Higgins, D. N. Ruble, & W. W. Hartup (Eds.), *Social cognition and social development: A sociocultural perspective* (pp. 236–274). Cambridge, England: Cambridge University Press.

Hoffner, C. (1993). Children's strategies for coping with stress: Blunting and monitoring. *Motivation and Emotion, 17,* 91–106.

Horowitz, F. D. (1993). The need for a comprehensive new environmentalism. In R. Plomin & G. E. McClearn (Eds.), *Nature, nurture & psychology* (pp. 341–353). Washington, DC: American Psychological Association.

Hubbard, J., & Coie, J. D. (1994). Emotional determinants of social competence in children's peer relationships. *Merrill-Palmer Quarterly, 40,* 1–20.

Jackson, J. F. (1993). Human behavioral genetics, Scarr's theory, and her views on interventions: A critical review and commentary on their implications for African American children. *Child Development, 64,* 1318–1332.

Kagan, J. (1984). *The nature of the child.* New York: Basic Books.

Kagan, J., Snidman, N., & Arcus, D. M. (1992). Initial reactions to unfamiliarity. *Current Directions in Psychological Science, 1,* 171–174.

Kendler, K. S., Neale, M., Kessler, R. C., Health, A. C., & Eaves, L. J. (1993). A test of the equal-environment assumption in twin studies of psychiatric illness. *Behavior Genetics, 23,* 21–27.

Kestenbaum, R., Farber, E. A., & Sroufe, L. A. (1989). Individual differences in empathy among preschoolers: Relation to attachment history. In N. Eisenberg (Ed.), *New directions for child development: Vol. 44. Empathy and related emotional responses* (pp. 51–64). San Francisco: Jossey-Bass.

Kitayama, S., & Markus, H. R. (Eds.). (1994). *Emotion and culture: Empirical studies of mutual influence.* Washington, DC: American Psychological Association.

Kochanska, G. (1993). Toward a synthesis of parental socialization and child temperament in early development of conscience. *Child Development, 64,* 325–347.

Kochanska, G. (1996). Children's temperament, mothers' discipline, and security of attachment: Multiple pathways to emerging internalization. *Child Development, 66,* 597–615.

Kohlberg, L. (1984). *Essays on moral development: Vol. 2. The psychology of moral development.* San Francisco: Harper & Row.

Kopp, C. B. (1982). Antecedents of self-regulation: A developmental perspective. *Developmental Psychology, 18,* 199–214.

Langlois, J. H. (1986). From the eye of the beholder to behavioral reality: Development of social behaviors and social relations as a function of physical environment. In C. P. Herman, M. P. Zanna, & E. T. Higgins (Eds.), *Ontario Symposium on Personality and Social Psychology* (Vol. 3, pp. 23–51). Hillsdale, NJ: Erlbaum.

Larsen, R. J., & Diener, E. (1987). Affect intensity as an individual difference characteristic: A review. *Journal of Research in Personality, 21,* 1–39.

Lazarus, R. S., & Folkman, S. (1984). *Stress, appraisal, and coping.* New York: Springer.

Lerner, R. M., & von Eye, A. (1992). Sociobiology and human development: Arguments and evidence. *Human Development, 35,* 12–33.

Lytton, H. (1977). Do parents create, or respond to, differences in twins? *Developmental Psychology, 13,* 456–459.

Lytton, H. (1990). Child and parent effects in boys' conduct disorder: A reinterpretation. *Developmental Psychology, 26,* 683–697.

Maccoby, E. E. (1990). Gender and relationships: A developmental account. *American Psychologist, 45,* 513–520.

Maccoby, E. E., & Martin, J. A. (1983). Socialization in the context of the family: Parent-child interaction. In P. H. Mussen (Series Ed.) & E. M. Hetherington (Vol. Ed.), *Handbook of child psychology: Vol 4. Socialization, personality, and social development* (4th ed., pp. 1–101). New York: Wiley.

Main, M., Kaplan, N., & Cassidy, J. (1985). Security in infancy, childhood, and adulthood: A move to the level of representation. In I. Bretherton & E. Waters (Eds.), Growing points of attachment theory and research. *Monographs of the Society for Research in Child Development, 50*(Serial No. 209), 66–104.

Markus, H. Z., & Kitayama, S. (1991). Culture and the self: Implications for cognition, emotion, and motivation. *Psychological Review, 98,* 224–253.

McAdams, D. P. (1995). What do we know when we know a person? *Journal of Personality, 63,* 365–396.

McCall, R. B. (1994). Commentary on Plomin. Advice to the new social genetics: Lessons partly learned from the genetics of mental development. *Social Development, 3,* 54–59.

McClelland, G. H., & Judd, C. M. (1993). Statistical difficulties in detecting interactions and moderator effects. *Psychological Bulletin, 114,* 376–390.

Mischel, W., Shoda, Y., & Peake, P. K. (1988). The nature of adolescent competencies predicted by preschool delay of gratification. *Journal of Personality and Social Psychology, 54,* 687–696.

Nachmias, M., Gunnar, M., Mangelsdorf, S., Parritz, R. H., & Buss, K. (1996). Behavioral inhibition and stress reactivity: The moderating role of attachment security. *Child Development, 67,* 508–522.

Parke, R. D. (1994). Progress, paradigms, and unresolved problems: Recent advances in our understanding of children's emotions. *Merrill-Palmer Quarterly, 40,* 157–169.

Plomin, R. (1986). *Development, genetics, and psychology.* Hillsdale, NJ: Erlbaum.

Plomin, R. (1994). Nature, nurture, and social development. *Social Development, 3,* 37–53.

Plomin, R., DeFries, J. C., & Loehlin, J. C. (1977). Genotype-environment interaction and correlation in the analysis of human behavior. *Psychological Bulletin, 84,* 309–322.

Plomin, R., DeFries, J. C., & McClearn, G. E. (1980). *Behavioral genetics: A primer.* San Francisco: Freeman.

Plomin, R., & Stocker, C. (1989). Behavioral genetics and emotionality. In J. S. Reznick (Ed.), *Perspectives on behavioral inhibition* (pp. 219–240). Chicago: University of Chicago Press.

Prior, M. (1992). Childhood temperament. *Journal of Child Psychology and Psychiatry, 33,* 249–279.

Pulkkinen, L. (1982). Self-control and continuity from childhood to late adolescence. In P. B. Baltes & O. G. Brim, Jr. (Eds.), *Life-span development and behavior* (Vol. 4, pp. 63–105). New York: Academic Press.

Rest, J. R. (1983). Morality. In P. H. Mussen (Series Ed.) & J. H. Flavell & E. M. Markman (Vol. Eds.), *Handbook of child psychology: Vol. 3. Cognitive development* (4th ed., pp. 556–629). New York: Wiley.

Robins, R. W., John, O. P., Caspi, A., Moffitt, T. E., & Stouthamer-Loeber, M. (1996). Resilient, overcontrolled, and undercontrolled boys: Three replicable personality types. *Journal of Personality and Social Psychology, 70,* 157–171.

Rosenbaum, J. F., Biederman, J., Bolduc-Murphy, E. A., Faraone, S. V., Chaloff, J., Hirshfield, D. R., & Kagan, J. (1993). Converging evidence for behavioral inhibition as a risk factor for childhood-onset anxiety disorders: The MGH-Harvard collaborative project. *Harvard Review of Psychiatry, 1,* 2–16.

Rosenthal, R. (1995). Writing meta-analytic reviews. *Psychological Bulletin, 118,* 183–192.

Rothbart, M., & Ahadi, S. A. (1994). Temperament and the development of personality. *Journal of Abnormal Psychology, 103,* 55–66.

Rothbart, M. K., Ahadi, S. A., & Hershey, K. L. (1994). Temperament and social behavior in childhood. *Merrill-Palmer Quarterly, 40,* 21–39.

Rowe, D. C., & Waldman, I. D. (1993). The question "how?" reconsidered. In R. Plomin & G. E. McClearn (Eds.), *Nature, nurture and psychology* (pp. 355–373). Washington, DC: American Psychological Association.

Rubin, K. H., Chen, X., & Hymel, S. (1993). Socioemotional characteristics of withdrawn and aggressive children. *Merrill-Palmer Quarterly, 39,* 518–534.

Rutter, M. (1987). Temperament, personal, and personality disorder. *British Journal of Psychiatry, 150,* 443–458.

Sandler, I. N., Tein, J., & West, S. G. (1994). Coping, stress and the psychological symptoms of children of divorce: A cross-sectional and longitudinal study. *Child Development, 65,* 1744–1763.

Scarr, S. (1992). Developmental theories for the 1990s: Development and individual differences. *Child Development, 63,* 1–19.

Scarr, S., & Carter-Saltzman, L. (1979). Twin method: Defense of a critical assumption. *Behavior Genetics, 9,* 527–542.

Shweder, R. A. (1994). Are oral intuitions self-evident truths? *Criminal Justice Ethics, 13,* 24–31.

Shweder, R. A., Mahapatra, M., & Miller, J. G. (1987). Culture and moral development. In J. Kagan & S. Lamb (Eds.), *The emergence of morality in young children* (pp. 1–83). Chicago: University of Chicago Press.

Sroufe, L. A., Schork, E., Motti, F., Lawroski, N., & LaFreniere, P. (1984). The role of affect in social competence. In C. E. Izard, J. Kagan, & R. B. Zajonc (Eds.), *Emotion, cognition, and behavior* (pp. 289–319). Cambridge, England: Cambridge University Press.

Steinberg, L., Lamborn, S. D., Dornbusch, S., & Darling, N. (1992). Impact of parenting practices on adolescent achievement: Authoritative parenting, school involvement, and encouragement to succeed. *Child Development, 63,* 1266–1281.

Stern, D. (1985). *The interpersonal world of the infant.* New York: Basic Books.

Tellegen, A. (1985). Structures of mood and personality and their relevance to assessing anxiety, with an emphasis on self-report. In A. H. Tuma & J. D. Maser (Eds.), *Anxiety and anxiety disorders* (pp. 681–706). Hillsdale, NJ: Erlbaum.

Thompson, R. A. (1994). Emotional regulation: A theme in search of definition. *Monographs of the Society for Research in Child Development, 59*(Serial No. 240), 25–52.

Turkheimer, E. (1997). *Spinach and ice cream: Why environmental social science is so difficult.* Paper submitted for review.

Turkheimer, E., & Gottesman, I. I. (1996). Simulating the dynamics of genes and environment in development. *Development and Psychopathology, 8,* 667–677.

Wachs, T. D. (1993). The nature–nurture gap: What we have here is a failure to collaborate. In R. Plomin & G. E. McClearn (Eds.), *Nature, nurture and psychology* (pp. 375–391). Washington, DC: American Psychological Association.

Wainryb, C. (1993). The application of moral judgments to other cultures: Relativism and universality. *Child Development, 64,* 924–933.

Walden, T. A., & Smith, M. C. (in press). Emotion regulation. *Motivation and Emotion.*

Whiting, B. B., & Whiting, J. W. M. (1975). *Children of six cultures: A psychocultural analysis.* Cambridge, MA: Harvard University Press.

Wilson, J. Q. (1993). *The moral sense.* New York: Free Press.

Windle, M., & Lerner, R. M. (1986). Reassessing the dimensions of temperamental individuality across the life span: The revised dimensions of temperament survey (DOTS-R). *Journal of Adolescent Research, 1,* 213–230.

Zahn-Waxler, C., & Kochanska, G. (1990). The origins of guilt. In R. Thompson (Ed.), *The 36th annual Nebraska Symposium on Motivation: Socioemotional development* (pp. 183–258). Lincoln: University of Nebraska Press.

Zajonc, R. B., & Marcus, H. (1984). Affect and cognition: The hard interface. In C. E. Izard, J. Kagan, & R. B. Zajonc (Eds.), *Emotions, cognition, and behavior* (pp. 73–102). Cambridge, England: Cambridge University Press.

Zimmerman, B. J. (1996). Enhancing student academic and health functioning: A self-regulatory perspective. *School Psychology Quarterly, 11,* 47–66.

CHAPTER 2

Early Sociopersonality Development

ROSS A. THOMPSON

Infancy has powerful connotations to the contemporary Western mind. Infancy implies beginnings, the early formation of characteristics, skills, and dispositions that may last a lifetime. It implies vulnerability to a host of influences that may set the course of psychosocial functioning by optimizing inborn potential or blunting its expression. It implies an evolutionary legacy that is reflected not just in a maturational timetable for the developing child but also powerful incentives, in both parent and child, for behaviors that foster the child's protection and nurturance. At the center of our shared images of infancy is the mother-infant relationship where the baby discovers the self in the context of a relationship of sensitive harmony and is thus equipped with a sense of security for encountering future challenges.

We embrace this portrayal of infancy because it contains considerable truth about early development, as decades of developmental research have demonstrated. At the same time, research in many disciplines has broadened contemporary views of infancy and its place in human development. Historical and cultural studies, for example, have shown that infancy has had different connotational meanings to people of different times and societies where cultural

needs, ecological demands, and concerns about infant health shape parental expectations and investment in and responsibility for young offspring (Harkness & Super, 1995; Levine, 1988; Shorter, 1975; Super & Harkness, 1986). Divergent historical-cultural values also mean that parents seek different characteristics in offspring, whether they strive to foster animated, happy responsiveness, attentiveness and easy soothability, or benign passivity. This does not challenge the validity of contemporary views of infancy from our own culture, of course, but rather fosters an awareness of how these views reflect current societal concerns (enhancing early potential is an important value in a competitive, technological world), just as concerns about training good habits and self-control reflected the symbolic value of young children in the social-reform-minded 1920s (Beekman, 1977; Takanishi, 1978).

From cultural studies also come an appreciation of the diverse physical and social ecologies in which infants live worldwide. Mothers care for young offspring but so also do other caregivers, including fathers, sisters, aunts, grandmothers and other adult women, and older children, in contexts that range from continuous body contact (such as carrying by sling) or swaddling to extended parent-offspring separation (at child care or nighttime). Infant care may entail feeding on demand or schedule, and can occur in special settings for the child or the adult world of work and community. Early social development may be fostered by interactions that are focused on objects or people, and may involve continuous but noninteractive social contact with many partners as well as (or instead of) dyadic face-to-face play with the mother (Bornstein, 1991; Harkness & Super, 1995; Levine, 1988; Tronick, Morelli, & Ivey, 1992). These diverse cultural practices are accompanied by different ethnotheories about children and their development that guide constructions of children's needs and parents' responsibilities (Harkness & Super, 1995), and remind us that infants thrive in remarkably diverse settings beyond those with which we are most familiar. This is increasingly apparent also in the United States, where, with a growing majority of mothers of infants in the workforce, the normative use and early onset of out-of-home care means that infants encounter a range of social partners in daily life and an equally broad range of social demands, expectations, and incentives. A recognition of diverse social ecologies and an awareness of the importance of ecological connections and transitions within and between these contexts is thus essential to a contemporary view of early sociopersonality development.

At the center of this diverse ecology is the parent-child relationship. The view that a caregiver's sensitive responsiveness is an essential contribution to healthy psychosocial growth is incorporated into classic psychological theories as well as theories of natural selection, which regard the survival of offspring in terms of the parent's reproductive success. But even within an evolutionary perspective, parental solicitude is not necessarily reliable because finite parental resources of time and energy must be allocated among the many tasks related to the adult's inclusive fitness (including mate selection, promoting personal health and survival, and caring for multiple offspring), usually requiring trade-offs among these concerns. Inclusive fitness considerations may account for greater parental investment in younger than older offspring, for example, or the parent's investment in future reproductive potential over current offspring (in, for example, an impoverished environment). The contingency of parental solicitude is based on many things, including the biological relatedness of offspring, the parent's age and gender, the reproductive value of the child (e.g., health, gender, number of siblings), the caregiver's current health, environmental threats and resources, as well as the child's maturity, since the child's

growing capabilities and independence permit the reallocation of parental resources elsewhere, even before the child feels ready for it (Blurton-Jones, 1993; Clutton-Brock, 1991; Daly & Wilson, 1995; Hinde, 1986; Trivers, 1974, 1985). Because children may respond in ways to heighten parental solicitude—using persistent demands and/or deceptive practices to heighten the caregiver's responsiveness—considerable mutual monitoring of needs and investment is characteristic of parent-offspring relations (Bateson, 1994). Taken together, therefore, a natural selection perspective to early development affirms the importance of parental solicitude but underscores its contingency and indicates that potential conflict may be not only inherent in parent-offspring relations, but development enhancing.

Finally, from within developmental psychology comes a reassessment of the place of infancy within life span development. Like other beliefs about development, the current emphasis on the formative significance of infancy is based on cultural values concerning early potential, nurturance, and intervention. Developmental theorists have for so long regarded early experience as foundational for later development that the emergence of voices questioning the formative significance of infancy for later sociopersonality functioning (Fogel, 1993; Fox, 1995; Kagan, 1984; Scarr, 1992) sound jarring. Yet the central question is not whether infancy is important to later personality development but rather in what ways early experiences are influential (and in what ways not) and what are the mediating and intervening processes connecting early experiences to later development. Infancy may provide a foundation for certain later capabilities but not others: it may undergird initial social predispositions, for example, but not enduring self-representations that are contingent on more advanced cognitive skills. Similarly, early caregiving influences may have longstanding consequences if these influences are subsequently maintained, but be lost if they are not. A reassessment of the place of infancy in sociopersonality development requires examining the processes (from within and around the developing child) mediating and moderating the potentially enduring influence of early experiences. And although a contemporary respect for the resilience of young infants provides a healthy balance for traditional concerns about their vulnerability (Thompson, 1990a), the value of this reassessment is that we may also begin to perceive infancy as important in its own right, not just as a foreshadowing or foundation of later growth.

Contemporary thinking about early sociopersonality development thus embraces and articulates profound social values concerning the importance of the mother-infant relationship, the nature and functions of early care, and the significance of early experiences. But it is challenged and enlivened by current changes in the ecology of early care, as well as historical, cultural, and biological studies that provide a broadened view of infancy and early experience. This makes the contemporary study of early sociopersonality development broadly conceived but narrowly drawn because the plurality of scholarship remains focused on the mother-infant relationship, justified by the realization that (at least in most families in the United States) this is where many of the most salient, significant, and enduring early influences occur. In the context of this research, an appreciation of the cultural and ecological diversity of early care, and the complex biological incentives for that care, has been slowly emerging. Consequently, this chapter has a somewhat traditional flavor, focused as it is on familiar topics associated with early mother-infant interaction and attachment and the growth of self-understanding, self-regulation, conscience, and other early-emerging facets of personality. Consideration of these topics is informed, however, by lines of inquiry from cultural, historical, and biological research summarized above, as well as by four important new themes of contemporary reflection on these topics.

First is an interest in the developmental transition from patterns of social interaction in early infancy to the emergent representations of these interactions—and of self and others—that subsequently develop. As in other areas of developmental study, students of sociopersonality development are seeking to bridge the transition from infancy to early childhood by studying how action "moves underground" to shape representation, informed both by new discoveries about early cognitive capabilities and older theories of object relations and internalized relationships. Interestingly, the study of this transition is being advanced both by students of infancy (such as attachment researchers) extending their formulations to older children and by students of preschool cognition (such as theory of mind researchers) extending their formulations to infancy. This has resulted at times in sharply divergent portrayals of emergent early representation, but also in an important convergence of interests and questions.

Second is the growing importance of functionalist perspectives in several areas of developmental study, including attachment (Ainsworth, Blehar, Waters, & Wall, 1978), emotional development (Saarni, Mumme, & Campos, Ch. 5, this Volume), and the growth of representation

(Nelson, 1990, 1993a; Thompson, 1993). With an emphasis on the association between goals and behavioral processes, as well as the motivational and regulatory influences on behavior, functionalist accounts are well suited to the study of sociopersonality development because they embed developmental change in a social context and an agentic, developing person. These features of functionalism have methodological implications also, especially because assessments must be pertinent to the motivational context in which activity is studied and the interdependencies among behaviors. Although the history of psychological inquiry has shown that there have been important shortcomings to functional accounts, they currently provide helpful new perspectives to longstanding research questions concerning early sociopersonality growth.

Third, and perhaps most important, is a conceptual transition in models of early sociopersonality development, from socialization (emphasizing parental influences on offspring) and constructivism (emphasizing the child's active interpretation of experience) to appropriation (emphasizing the joint creation of meaning in the context of shared activity between a developing person and an older person) (Fogel, 1993; Maccoby, 1992; Rogoff, 1990). The model of appropriation, based on Vygotskian theory, underscores how social interaction provides the medium by which socioemotional skills, understanding, and perspective are jointly created as the child participates with the adult in shared activity, whether consisting of face-to-face exchanges, collaborative play, or the soothing of fear or distress. It provides a context for understanding the sensitive scaffolding of shared activities by the caregiver that, while remaining within the child's tolerances for stimulation and challenge, foster new psychosocial capabilities (Vygotsky's zone of proximal development). It also provides a perspective for understanding how the child and caregiver jointly contribute to the construction of shared meanings within the broader context of cultural values and beliefs about the goals of early development and the ecological context provided by the culture.

Finally, growing theoretical interest in the emergence and influence of close relationships is another theme that integrates and expands the three outlined above. In the view of relationship theorists (Dunn, 1993; Fogel, 1993; Hartup & Rubin, 1986; Hinde & Stevenson-Hinde, 1987; Kaye, 1982), the interactions shared by young children with close partners differ significantly from those with unfamiliar people because of the jointly constructed patterns of exchange they entail, as well as the mutual expectations, shared goals and meanings, frequency of contact, and long-standing influences that enhance the effects of close relationships on developing persons. In addition, relational partners are mutually involved in diverse activities that increase the overall impact of relationships; through encounters as varied as shared play, affectional contact, negotiating conflict, and conversations about family events, for example, siblings uniquely shape their understandings of themselves and others (Dunn, 1994). Earlier relationships may also bias a child's experience of new relationships (Sroufe & Fleeson, 1986). For these reasons, the growth and influence of close relationships remains a central concern of early sociopersonality development, albeit within a new conceptual context.

In a sense, therefore, contemporary study of early sociopersonality development includes much that is new as well as old: traditional interests in the social and emotional dimensions of early mother-infant interaction and attachment are broadened and reconceptualized in light of new themes in developmental study as well as insights from allied disciplines. This chapter is meant to capture this dynamic in the context of a research review focused especially on these new directions for the study of traditional topics. This review is admittedly selective; because research on emotional development and temperament are considered in detail in other chapters of the *Handbook* (Kagan; Rothbart & Bates; Saarni et al.), these topics are given more limited coverage than they deserve in view of their obvious relevance to early sociopersonality functioning. Similarly, issues of emergent peer relations and of the influence of day care are also largely deferred to other *Handbook* chapters. Despite these caveats, it will be clear that the questions and issues that have traditionally guided inquiry into early sociopersonality development remain provocative, informed by new theoretical views and empirical discoveries, yet also revealing a variety of new problems for future study.

RELATIONSHIPS AND THE APPROPRIATION OF MEANING

The importance of close relationships is both a traditional theme and an emergent emphasis in early sociopersonality research. Infants are influenced by close relationships before they can even conceive of relationships because they are affected by how caregivers interpret (and respond to) their facial, vocal, and gestural expressions, how adults manage infants' emotional arousal, and the ways parents structure feeding, play, and sleep routines (Thompson, 1994; Thompson & Leger, in press). Moreover, a broader network of relationships within the extended family and the community helps to define the child's conditions of care through the influence of siblings and grandparents, the support afforded parents, and the psychological well-being of the family (Cochran, Larner, Riley, Gunnarsson, & Henderson, 1990; Thompson, 1995). Early sociopersonality development is shaped, however, not just by the direct and indirect effects of influential relationships, but also by how quickly and significantly these relationships become mutually regulated contexts of shared activity that not only foster the growth of socioemotional competencies in the child but, in so doing, alter each partner's contribution to their interactive activity. In this developmental climate, parents must be responsive not only to the child's current needs and capabilities but also to the emergent skills that are fostered by the interactive activity they share, and this process of dynamic change in both child ability and parental scaffolding over time helps to guide and structure early social development. In this respect, sociopersonality growth is a co-construction in the context of shared activity.

Early Sociopersonality Growth and Shared Activity

The collaborative construction of sociopersonality growth is evident in the earliest parent-infant encounters as adults seek to interpret and respond helpfully to the child's signals. The early emergence and ubiquity of the infant cry has inspired an extensive research literature concerning the nature of the early cry as a reflection of infant state and a determinant of adult response (Boukydis, 1985; Lester, 1984; Murray, 1985). Much less attention has been devoted to developmental changes in the baby's cry and its changing impact on adult listeners, which is surprising in light of how significantly the cry evolves during the first year. In addition to morphological changes in the physical structures of cry production, neurophysiological maturation alters the cry from an involuntary, reflexive event to one that is subject to cortical regulation and inhibitory control, and concurrent psychological changes in the child (including the emergence of intentional communication, the growth of social expectations, a broadening emotional repertoire and emergent emotion self-regulatory capacities) make the cry an increasingly discriminating, instrumental signal (Thompson, Garbin, & Otten, 1996; Zeskind, 1985).

What implications does this have for parents? Leger, Thompson, Merritt, and Benz (1996) played recordings of the naturally elicited cries of 1- and 6-month-olds to adults who were either experienced or inexperienced with young children, and digitally analyzed the acoustic features of each cry pulse. They found that adults made highly reliable judgments of emotion in the cries, but the acoustic correlates of their judgments were very different for infants at each age: regardless of experience, adults "heard emotion" using much different acoustic features of the cries of 1-month-olds compared to 6-month-olds. The raspy noise of the 1-month-old cry figured prominently in their judgments of the intensity of the child's arousal, for example, but was uninfluential when the cries of older infants were heard. Their conclusion that the interpretive structure of cry perception changed in concert with the changing expressive capabilities of infants is consistent with the results of a companion study by Thompson et al. (1996), who found that experienced adults appraised the cries of 12-month-olds in a multidimensional manner, perceiving not just the intensity of arousal (as is true of cry perception with younger infants) but also more nuanced judgments of anxiety in the baby (Thompson & Leger, in press). Further research is needed to explore how the evolving interpretive structure of adult cry perception is associated with changing responsiveness that may also influence infant crying and its origins. It is also important to understand how and why caregivers increasingly perceive more complex and individualized needs and motives in the cries they hear from infants and young children.

Consider next the growth of mother-infant face-to-face interaction, an activity of considerable interest to students of infancy not because of its ubiquity or universality, but because it is a marker of broader interactive propensities that may characterize many early infant-parent relations and influence the growth of social skills and social dispositions. In middle-class homes in this country, face-to-face play typically begins to be observed at 2 to 3 months of age, after the behavioral state fluctuations of the neonatal period have subsided and longer periods of awake alertness can be observed, and it continues to about 6 or 7 months, after which more active kinds of infant-parent interaction become preeminent with the child's locomotor capabilities. Although developmental researchers have tended to evaluate the quality of face-to-face interaction in terms of the establishment and maintenance of well-coordinated activity—with adults taking the lead in doing so, partly through their sensitive scaffolding of initiatives to accord with the baby's signals (Kaye, 1979, 1982)—it is probably mistaken to portray the functional goals of face-to-face play so narrowly (M. Lamb, Morrison, & Malkin, 1987). Tronick and his colleagues (Gianino & Tronick, 1988; Tronick, 1989; Tronick & Cohn, 1989) have noted that coordinated interactions occur only about 30% or less of the time that mothers and infants engage in face-to-face interactions, and they propose that a broader variety of goals (e.g., interactive reparation and self-regulation) are also apparent and shape the social skills that young infants derive from this activity.

The salience of face-to-face play is reflected in changes in the baby's reactions during the early months of life. It is apparent, for example, that infants quickly become sensitive to the contingency inherent in the adult's responses to their behavior. This is indicated by the findings of Murray and Trevarthen (1985), who found that 2- to 3-month-olds responded animatedly when viewing live images of their mothers talking to them through closed-circuit television but later, when the same images of the mothers were replayed (and were thus noncontingent), turned away in apparent disinterest or distress (see also J. Cohn & Tronick, 1987; Symons & Moran, 1987). Young infants' generalized expectation that others will spontaneously interact and communicate with them is also revealed in studies when mothers are instructed to adopt an impassive, expressionless demeanor after a brief episode of spontaneous face-to-face play. During this "still-face" episode, 3- to 6-month-olds become more negative, and some respond with apparent social elicitations (e.g., brief smiles, momentarily increased vocalizing and reaching) that seem to reflect an expectation that the adult should behave differently (J. Cohn, Campbell, & Ross, 1991; J. Cohn & Tronick, 1983; M. Lamb et al., 1987). There is also evidence that, later in the first year, infants begin to develop discriminative social expectations for differentiated figures in their social worlds as they respond differently to mothers and fathers, based partly on the father's more vigorous, animated play style and the mother's greater involvement in quieter games and distress relief (M. Lamb, 1981a).

Another kind of expectation emerging from these early interactive experiences concerns the infant's emerging sense of agency or effectance (Watson, 1972, 1979). An awareness that their signals and actions can have predictable effects on others is fostered by the contingency inherent in the adult's responsiveness during face-to-face play, but it is also apparent in other contexts (M. Lamb, 1981b, 1981c). When infant distress is followed by parental soothing, for example, the association among the infant's arousal, a parental response, and subsequent relief is highly salient and easily learned by the baby (M. Lamb, 1981c), and there is some evidence of anticipatory soothing to the caregiver's ministrations in the early months of life (Gekoski, Rovee-Collier, & Carulli-Rabinowitz, 1983; M. Lamb & Malkin, 1986). M. Lamb and Malkin (1986) noted that during routine distress-relief encounters, for example, infants after 4 months of age began to protest if an adult arrived but did not immediately begin to soothe them.

As these studies suggest, the emergence of contingency awareness in social activity and of rudimentary expectations concerning the behavioral propensities of others transform the infant as a social partner. The growth of contingency perception means that infants can better detect the reciprocity of partners, and their interest in social interaction is further heightened by the positive affect elicited by their awareness of the efficacy of their own actions on others (Watson, 1972, 1979). Thus, whether or not a basic intersubjective capacity is innate or inherent in the infant's intermodal perception of others' actions (Meltzoff & Gopnik, 1993; Trevarthen, 1979), it is certainly consolidated in these coregulated episodes of social interaction with adults (Fogel, 1993). Equally important, these changes in the infant alter how parents perceive their young offspring as human partners with individual tendencies and developing understanding, and this deepens their attachment to the child (Robson & Moss, 1970) as well as altering their own interactive propensities.

The declining frequency of face-to-face play occurs, in part, because the infant becomes more mobile and interested in more active forms of interaction, and the emergence of self-produced locomotion introduces another network of changes in the shared activity of parent and child (Bertenthal & Campos, 1990; Campos, Kermoian, & Zumbahlen, 1992). According to Campos and his colleagues, the infant's independent locomotion has important consequences for sociopersonality growth because of its implications for agency and emotion: the child becomes more capable of goal attainment, of acting in a dangerous or disapproved manner, of wandering away from the parent, and of experiencing the varieties of emotion and feelings of self-efficacy that these activities inspire. Parents respond to these changes in ways that foster new capabilities: parents more actively monitor the child's activity, increasingly use prohibitions and sanctions, and also expect greater behavioral compliance from their locomotor offspring. As a consequence, according to these researchers, new capacities for assertiveness and attachment begin to

emerge, as well as the growth of social referencing as a means of monitoring the parent's regulatory efforts. Unfortunately, there is little research bearing on these provocative formulations, but in one study, Campos and colleagues (1992) interviewed the parents of locomotor and prelocomotor 8-month-olds and found that caregivers' perceptions of the child and reports of their own activities varied significantly based on the child's locomotor status. The parents of locomotor infants indicated that they had higher expectations of the child's compliance, used more verbal prohibitions, and engaged in greater disciplinary activity than the parents of prelocomotor infants. They also reported that their offspring showed greater sensitivity to the parents' whereabouts and their emotional signals, increased expressions of anger and frustration, and more intense affectionate behavior. These findings provide only a preliminary view of how changes in the shared activity of parents and offspring (inaugurated, in this case, by growth in the child's motoric capabilities) provoke further advances in sociopersonality functioning in the context of an altered family system, and they merit follow-up study (see also Biringen, Emde, Campos, & Appelbaum, 1995).

These advances are especially important because they occur at a time when infants are developing a dawning awareness of mental states in others, which has been regarded as an early precursor to "secondary intersubjectivity" and later theory of mind (Bretherton, McNew, & Beeghly-Smith, 1981; Stern, 1985; Tomasello, Kruger, & Ratner, 1993; Trevarthen & Hubley, 1978). In diverse behaviors that include efforts to achieve joint visual attention, imitation, and protocommunicative acts, 9- to 10-month-olds disclose a rudimentary awareness that others are intentional agents with potentially shared subjective orientations toward objects and events. As a consequence, there is a new capacity to achieve joint understanding that significantly alters the shared activity of parents and offspring.

The most widely studied manifestation of this intersubjective capacity is social referencing, in which infants respond to novel or ambiguous events based on the emotional expressions they detect in adults (Campos & Stenberg, 1981; Feinman, 1982; Klinnert, Campos, Sorce, Emde, & Svejda, 1983). Social referencing is commonly believed to arise from the child's active search for clarifying information from another's emotional reactions, reflecting the child's awareness of accessible subjective states in others when feeling uncertain. Such information gathering may, however, be derived less deliberately from the child's affective sharing in the presence of novelty or secure-base behavior when seeking reassurance (Baldwin & Moses, 1996). In either case, the importance of social referencing is twofold: it indicates that infants are fairly good consumers of emotional information from others and can enlist it in their own action tendencies, and it reflects the early emergence of socially constructed meaning through distal communication by which infants appropriate an understanding of events from more mature partners. Each are lifelong features of socialization.

The research on social referencing indicates that it has important but modest effects on infant behavior (see Feinman, Roberts, Hsieh, Sawyer, & Swanson, 1992, for a review). One reason is that whether infants visually check with adults in experimental situations involving novelty or uncertainty varies according to temperament (Hornik & Gunnar, 1988), age (Walden & Baxter, 1989; Walden & Ogan, 1988), and the infant's independent appraisal of events (Zarbatany & Lamb, 1985), and the effects of social referencing can be transient (Mumme, Fernald, & Herrera, 1996). Social referencing influences are especially apparent when infants are uncertain, but referencing can be influential even when they are not (Feinman et al., 1992). The modality of the emotional cues provided by the adult (whether mother, father, or another familiar adult) is also important; although some studies have reported changes in infant behavior based on facial expressions alone (Camras & Sachs, 1991; Klinnert, 1984; Klinnert, Emde, Butterfield, & Campos, 1986; Sorce, Emde, Campos, & Klinnert, 1985; Zarbatany & Lamb, 1985), vocal cues are also influential (Mumme et al., 1996), and referencing effects have often been based on a combination of facial, vocal, and sometimes behavioral cues (Boccia & Campos, 1989; Hirshberg & Svejda, 1990; Hornik & Gunnar, 1988; Hornik, Risenhoover, & Gunnar, 1987; Rosen, Adamson, & Bakeman, 1992; Walden & Baxter, 1989; Walden & Ogan, 1988). This is hardly surprising, since in everyday situations parents commonly provide unsolicited verbal commentary on their infants' actions, which, in light of the sensitivity of young infants to the prosody of the human voice (Fernald, 1993), can have significant regulatory and socializing influences that do not require the infant's deliberately seeking such guidance (Dunn, 1988). The reason the adult's emotional expressions have an effect on the infant is not entirely clear, since some studies have shown that the adult's signals influence the infant's general emotional demeanor (Boccia & Campos, 1989; Hirshberg & Svejda, 1990; Klinnert et al., 1986; Mumme et al., 1996; Sorce et al., 1985; Walden & Baxter, 1989), but others indicate

that referencing effects are somewhat specific to the child's reactions to particular objects or events, contrary to a generalized mood modification hypothesis (Hornik et al., 1987; Walden & Ogan, 1988). In light of the salience of a caregiver's emotional expressions to an infant in the first year (Termine & Izard, 1988), it would be unsurprising if referencing effects were not only referent-specific, but also had a broader emotional impact on the child's response to the event of shared attention.

Although there is currently considerable debate concerning the extent to which social referencing reflects the infant's deliberate information seeking rather than the use of cues that are accessed unintentionally through proximity seeking, affective sharing, and other kinds of secure-base behavior (D. Baldwin & Moses, 1996; Moore & Corkum, 1994), it is clear that referencing reveals the infant's growing capacity to appropriate meaning from shared activity with adult partners. As referencing is extended into the second and third years, moreover, it becomes integrated into the expanding repertoire of competencies by which toddlers become capable of understanding and sharing not only the emotions but also the desires and intentions of others en route to a more sophisticated psychological understanding of people. Social referencing permits toddlers, for example, to compare their own assessments of events with the cues provided by others, and thus enables a nascent comprehension of conflicting as well as shared mental states. Social referencing also becomes an important contributor to the development of self-referential emotions like pride, guilt, and shame as moral values are conveyed through the communication of the parent's affective reactions to approved and disapproved activity (Emde & Buchsbaum, 1990) and as children begin to anticipate parental reactions to their successes and failures and eventually internalize the responses they perceive (Stipek, 1995). In this respect, therefore, social referencing in toddlerhood is a contributor to self-understanding as well as understanding others' psychological states. Little is known, however, about the effects of referencing activity on the parent, although informal observations in my laboratory have revealed that adults are usually acutely aware of the child's referencing behavior and often deliberately pose salient emotional expressions to reassure, instill caution, and provide other messages. If this is confirmed, it indicates another way that changes in the child's social responding foster alterations in parent-child interaction to foster psychosocial advances that are, in many respects, at the child's "zone of proximal socioemotional development."

Taken together, by the end of the first year, infants have not only become more competently expressive and agentic, but have formulated rudimentary social expectations concerning the interactive propensities of others in general and of specific individuals in particular, as well as of themselves as effective participants in social activity. Furthermore, they have begun to grasp the shared subjectivity that helps to turn interactions into relationships and to access that subjectivity in the social encounters they share with others. This research suggests that there are two other important qualities of this developmental process. First, it occurs not just as a consequence of the socializing efforts of caregivers or the progressive unfolding of infant competencies, but rather owing to the enlistment of each in shared activity from which meaning derives: without social interaction, there are no social expectations; without an interfacing of subjective orientations, there is no shared understanding. Second, it is also apparent that emotion is central to this developmental process and, more specifically, to the connectedness that exists between infants and their partners in close relationships. It likely is true, as Hobson (1993) has argued, that the affectional connection established from shared interactions with caregivers in the first year provides a foundation for the child's emergent understanding of self and other people.

Parenting and Its Development

Parent-infant relationships are forged from the encounters of two people who each are changing over time. For the infant, these changes in behavior, cognition, and personality are salient and sometimes dramatic. For the parent, the changes are more subtle and derive from an interaction of the network of beliefs, values, and goals that arise from a lifetime with the daily experience of caring for a developing child. Recognizing that each partner is a developing individual contributes to an appreciation of the joint construction of their interactive activity and of their relational harmony.

Adults, of course, begin their encounters with a young infant biased by a personal history that shapes their goals for child rearing, expectations for developmental change, concepts of age-appropriate conduct, views about the responsibilities of parents, attitudes toward behavior control, attributions of intentionality, and beliefs about children's characteristics and needs (Goodnow & Collins, 1990; Holden, 1995; Murphey, 1992; Sigel, McGillicuddy-DeLisi, & Goodnow, 1992; Smetana, 1994). These beliefs

and attitudes are based on the confluence of many factors, including parental personality, cultural ethnotheories of development, subcultural and socioeconomic values, the belief systems of an adult's family of origin, and the conflict or concordance of each parent's attitudinal framework (Harkness & Super, 1995; Okagaki & Divecha, 1993; Vaughn, Block, & Block, 1988). Parental behavior is shaped also by the demands or support provided by the marital relationship, working environment, and broader community (Bornstein, 1995; Cochran et al., 1990; Cox, Owen, Lewis, & Henderson, 1989; Thompson, 1995). Each of these constituents of parenting can change, sometimes significantly, with the child's development, and, taken together, they constitute a remarkably dynamic network of influences (Belsky, 1984; Belsky & Isabella, 1988; M. Lamb, Chase-Lansdale, & Owen, 1979; Parke & Buriel, Ch. 8, this Volume).

The adult's representations of early childhood care, recollections of feeling loved and secure, and perceptions of the lasting impact of these experiences may also influence how parents interpret and respond to the needs of their offspring (Crowell & Treboux, 1995). The Adult Attachment Interview (AAI), developed by Main and colleagues (George, Kaplan, & Main, 1985; Main & Goldwyn, 1994), is one effort to elucidate these adult representational processes that has been conceptually influenced by attachment theory and, in particular, Bowlby's portrayal of internal "working models" (or, to Main, "states of mind") concerning self and others (see next section; a complementary approach to adult romantic relationships has also been developed by Shaver & Hazan, 1993). Based on their responses to an extensive quasi-clinical interview that assesses general and specific recollections of childhood attachment experiences and their current impact, adults are assigned to one of three AAI classifications based on the quality of discourse (especially ratings of coherence) as well as the content of recall. Adults classified as *autonomous* (Group F; typically the modal classification) report valuing attachment relationships, describe them in a balanced manner, and portray them as having been developmentally influential; their discourse is coherent, internally consistent, and nondefensive. Adults classified as *dismissing* (Group D) exhibit apparent memory lapses, tend to minimize negative experiences and deny the personal impact of attachment relationships, and their positive descriptions of their parents are often contradicted or unsupported by specific recollections—each presumed to reflect the influence of defensive processes in the recall and evaluation of attachment experiences. Finally, adults classified as *preoccupied* (Group E) seem to experience a continuing preoccupation with their parents that may be manifested in incoherent, angry, or ambivalent representations of the past and present. A secondary classification of *unresolved/disorganized* (Group U) is made when the adult's interview includes indications of past traumatic experiences in which mourning of loss seems not to have been resolved. The resemblance of these four AAI classifications to the classification system for infant Strange Situation behavior (secure, avoidant, resistant, and disorganized; see below) is not coincidental: the AAI classifications were devised through an iterative procedure specifically designed to predict the attachment classifications of adults' infant offspring in the initial Berkeley sample (Main & Goldwyn, 1988). In a sense, therefore, the AAI assesses parents' attachment-related "states of mind" that are most directly related to fostering security in offspring; alternative assessments of adult representations of early care designed to accomplish different goals would probably have resulted in different assessment or rating procedures.

In this light, it is unsurprising, but nonetheless impressive, that several studies have shown that autonomous adults are indeed more sensitively responsive to their infants than are adults in the dismissing and preoccupied groups, and their offspring are also significantly more likely to be securely attached, even when AAI classifications are derived from prenatal interviews (see Van IJzendoorn, 1995a, for a review). Although the predicted relation between parental AAI classifications and infant Strange Situation classifications is markedly weaker for preoccupied adults, the stronger relations between the remaining AAI and Strange Situation classifications requires reflection on precisely what the AAI indexes in adult respondents. As Fox (1994) and Thompson (1991) each have noted, it vastly oversimplifies the constructive quality of adult autobiographical memory to assume that either the content or the style of discourse of adults' verbal reflections in the AAI is directly tied to actual experiences of early care. Indeed, as noted later in this chapter, even young children's autobiographical recall is shaped in content and style by subsequent appropriations of parental narratives, emergent self-referent beliefs, advances in social cognition, and later experiences that alter their construals and recollections of past events. As children mature, changing family experiences are also likely to contribute to a reconstruction of the affective and representational legacy of early childhood relationships, especially when parental separation or divorce or the serious illness or death of a family member significantly alters

family functioning. In addition, representations of early family relationships are likely to be influenced by later experiences in close relationships, as well as by changes in personality, self-reflection, and implicit theories of personal growth and continuity (Ross, 1989). When consistency between early caregiving experiences and adult "states of mind" concerning attachment exists, it likely derives from the variety of intervening influences (in continuing patterns of parental care and support, enduring family practices and stories, experiences of family stress and coping, and the emerging internal constituents of self-understanding) that together maintain and reinforce early influences (Reiss, 1989).

But Van IJzendoorn (1995b) is correct that it may not matter whether the adult representations assessed by the AAI are veridical with actual early attachment experiences, are a significant reconstruction of them, or instead emerge wholly from subsequent experience and reflections. The association between adult "states of mind" concerning their early attachment history and the care they provide their offspring points to another important component of the network of parent belief systems mediating caregiving. Although it is important not to neglect the possibility that a genetically based bias shared by parent and offspring accounts for the links between adult AAI classifications and offspring attachment security (Fox, 1995), it seems more likely that one of the lessons of family experience, broadly conceived, is how to interpret, convey, and cope with strong emotion experienced in intimate relationships. The development of a secure or insecure attachment in infancy provides perhaps the first of these lessons, but others follow that may confirm or alter the lessons of infancy and eventually contribute to the representational system concerning family relationships assessed in the AAI. One of the important challenges for future research, therefore, is to better understand not only the developmental catalysts to these affective-relational beliefs, but also the relations between these beliefs and other parental attitudes, expectations, and representations that shape the care of offspring and, in particular, parental perceptions of the child's motives, dispositions, and other characteristics. Furthermore, understanding the associations between AAI classifications and adults' *contemporary* relationships with their parents (the grandparents of their offspring) is also important. Although current studies have extensively examined the discriminant validity of the AAI in relation to measures of autobiographical memory, intelligence, social desirability, social adjustment, and other features of cognitive and personality functioning, with somewhat mixed results (Bakermans-Kranenburg & Van IJzendoorn, 1993; Crowell et al., 1996; Sagi, Van IJzendoorn, Scharf, et al., 1994), further attention to convergent validity and the developmental constituents of AAI representations is warranted.

The value of further inquiry into the development of parental beliefs and attachment representations is demonstrated by the work of the Cowans on the transition to parenthood (Cowan & Cowan, 1992; Cowan, Cowan, Herning, & Miller, 1991). Their comprehensive, longitudinal study of the psychosocial functioning of a large sample of young adults and their offspring in Berkeley has shown that becoming a parent is a surprisingly dysphoric transition for most, and that coping with this transition and the quality of subsequent parenting can each be predicted by features of the couple's prenatal marital relationship and broader family networks. Moreover, parenting quality was also affected by each adult's attachment representations as assessed on the AAI and the convergence of their dual classifications (D. Cohn, Cowan, Cowan, & Pearson, 1992). As predicted, parents who were each autonomous responded more warmly when they were observed with offspring; conversely, parents who were each insecure (dismissing, preoccupied, or unresolved) were least warm. Couples in which mothers were insecure and husbands were autonomous (the reverse was infrequent in this sample) were between these groups in warmth, but, more importantly, the mothers in these dyads responded as warmly to offspring as did the mothers of jointly autonomous dyads. Similar associations were noted for measures of marital functioning (D. Cohn, Silver, Cowan, Cowan, & Pearson, 1992). The Cowans have interpreted these findings as reflecting compensatory processes within the marital dyad, with spousal support buffering the impact of one parent's insecure attachment reflections on parenting warmth.

The unanswered question from this research program is whether, over the long term, marital support of this kind might alter the insecure parent's attachment representations as that adult experiences another kind of supportive attachment relationship. This possibility is suggested by another report from this study indicating that parents who received an "earned-secure" classification (i.e., were classified autonomous despite reporting difficult, unloving early relationships with their parents) were comparable to other autonomous parents in their parenting warmth, even though they showed lingering depressive symptomatology (Pearson, Cohn, Cowan, & Cowan, 1994; see also Belsky, Pensky, & Youngblade, 1990, for similar findings). This

finding confirms how the representations derived from early experiences of care can evolve and indicates, as Main and Hesse (1990) have noted, that the security of adults' contemporary "states of mind" with respect to attachment does not depend on the actual support received from parents in early childhood, but rather on that adult's capacity subsequently to come to terms with recalled early childhood attachment experiences. It seems likely that normative life experiences in later childhood, adolescence, and adulthood provide valuable catalysts to such reflection and reassessment.

Taken together, these findings underscore not only the varied determinants of parenting but also the multifaceted origins of individual differences in parental warmth and sensitivity. They may also help to explain the changes that occur in parenting over time in response to the developing needs of offspring, evolving family circumstances, stresses and support in the marriage, work-related exigencies, the birth of additional children, the increasing age and experience of parents, other demands in adult life, as well as the immediate requirements of the context and mood (Holden, 1995; Holden & O'Dell, 1995). In a recent meta-analytic review, Holden and O'Dell (1995) found in the literature evidence for only moderate stability of parental attitudes or behavior across time (with stability depending largely on the particular construct that was measured) and little consistency in parental behavior across different situations. They proposed that parenting is primarily a process of adaptation: to the child, to the contexts in which child rearing occurs, and to the parent's own motivations and emotions. While there are apparently many contributors to consistency in parenting practices in an adult's personal history, belief systems, and personality, the confrontation of these attributes with the daily experience with a developing child (or several children in a family) makes adaptability both a desirable quality and a contributor to dynamic change in parenting. In this regard, therefore, early sociopersonality development in a young child arises out of the joint construction of meaning by two partners who are moving along concurrent, but quite different, developmental pathways.

THE GROWTH OF RELATIONSHIPS: FIRST ATTACHMENTS

Since Freud's (1940, p. 45) famous dictum that the infant-mother relationship is "unique, without parallel, established unalterably for a whole lifetime as the first and strongest love-object and as the prototype of all later love-relations," developmental theorists have in concert emphasized this relationship as a foundation for personality growth. Although psychobiological, learning, and psychoanalytic explanations have each been influential, for the past quarter-century developmental thinking about parent-infant relationships has been guided by ethological attachment theory. It is not hard to account for its potent influence. Attachment theory explores some of the most compelling questions about early sociopersonality development and its later consequences: How significant are early experiences (especially experiences in intimate relationships) for psychosocial growth? What processes guide continuity and change in personality characteristics early in life? How are childhood experiences of care linked to later social relatedness? Such questions are central to developmental theory, and the validation of the Strange Situation procedure concurrent with the growing preeminence of attachment theory enabled developmental psychologists to investigate these questions with validated and readily available empirical methods. A quarter-century of research on attachment has yielded provisional answers to central questions of developmental theory—and more questions to ponder.

Ethological Attachment Theory

Attachment may be defined as an enduring affectional tie that unites one person to another, over time and across space (Ainsworth, 1973). In his initial efforts to elucidate the impact of institutionalization and homelessness on children in the postwar period, Bowlby (1951, 1958) sought to provide a theoretical explanation for the importance of a warm and continuous relationship with a caregiver that avoided some of the problems of prevailing psychoanalytic formulations and that would improve clinical practice with the recognition of the importance of close relationships to psychological health and well-being throughout life. One of the most significant features of Bowlby's perspective is that, rather than deriving from a single conceptual view, it combined insights from several different fields: ethological theory and evolutionary biology, control systems theory, developmental psychology, as well as the psychoanalytic roots of his own training. Contemporary attachment theory is best comprehended in terms of these contributing lines of thought.

From ethology and evolutionary biology, Bowlby argued that attachment arises from one of several species-typical behavioral systems, evolved to promote infant survival, that motivate infants to seek the protective proximity of adults, especially when they are distressed, alarmed, or in danger. Such figures would become, over time, sources of protective security (or a "secure base"; Ainsworth, 1963; Ainsworth et al., 1978). Complementary behavioral systems govern exploration and fear in the infant and parenting in the adult. Thus an infant's desire to remain close to a caregiver has its own inherent, biologically adaptive motivation (rather than deriving from other, more primary motivational systems); infants are, he believed, intrinsically and normatively inclined to become attached to one or more caregivers, with complementary motivational systems fostering nurturance in adults.

Cybernetic control systems theory was borrowed to explain the flexible organization of specific attachment behaviors into an attachment behavioral system characterized by continuous goal-correctedness (in relation to the "set goal"), hierarchical organization, and the functional interrelations among specific behaviors. Bowlby believed that specific attachment behaviors are meaningful and interpretable only within the context of their broader functional organization to accomplish the behavioral system's purpose of protective proximity to a caregiver (or, more generally, a feeling of security; see Sroufe & Waters, 1977). Within this functional orientation, therefore, an infant seeking proximity to a caregiver may do so through signals (like crying or reaching), locomotion, clinging, or in other ways; the important issue is the achievement of proximity. Bowlby's control systems theory was subsequently implemented in the functionalist assessment of attachment in the Strange Situation.

In explaining the development of the attachment behavioral system, Bowlby relied heavily on the insights of contemporary developmental researchers whose portrayals of the beginnings of social responsiveness, the onset of differential social responding, and the growth of social understanding contributed to his identification of four stages in the growth of the attachment system (see also Ainsworth, 1973). These consisted of (a) an initial phase of social orientation and signaling without discrimination (from birth through 8–12 weeks); (b) a period of discriminating sociability (to about 6–8 months); (c) a stage of attachment proper, during which separation reactions, active initiative in proximity seeking, and other behavior reveal a discriminating preference for one or more specific caregivers, and (d) the formation of a goal-corrected partnership (beginning during the third or fourth year) when the child acquires greater insight into the adult's feelings and motives, and thus a more mutually regulated relationship can emerge. These formulations have diverse theoretical roots, including Piagetian portrayals of egocentrism and the growth of role taking, and ethological concepts related to the intrinsic attraction of young infants to human stimuli. Most prominent, however, is Bowlby's object-relations background, which contributed to his emphasis on early relationships, the strong emotions with which they are associated, and their long-term implications for personality and well-being, as well as his interest in the internal representations that reflect the intrapsychic experience of the developing child.

Finally, Bowlby's psychoanalytic orientation is reflected in many features of attachment theory, including formulations concerning unconscious defensive exclusion and the effects of inconsistent internal representations, the importance of transference in the therapeutic reappraisal of inadequate representations of self and others, and the role of attachment in the etiology of psychological disturbance (Bowlby, 1973, 1980, 1988). Central to many of these formulations is Bowlby's interest in the mental representations or "working models" of self and of the attachment figure that are based, he believed, on early experiences that lead to expectations of the caregiver's accessibility and responsiveness and beliefs about one's deservingness of such care. As they become consolidated over time, Bowlby argued, these representations not only permit immediate forecasts of the caregiver's behavior, but also guide future relational expectations, self-appraisal, and behaviors toward others. Thus working models become interpretive filters through which new relationships and other experiences are construed, providing implicit decision rules for relating to others that may, for better or worse, help to confirm and perpetuate intuitive expectations about oneself and others as the result of how one functions in close relationships. Bowlby believed that the risk of psychopathology was enhanced by internally incompatible working models arising from inconsistent experiences of care (such as a caregiver who acts coldly but speaks with warmth and affection) that forced the child to defensively exclude information that was inconsistent with preferred representations of self or parent, but also fostering distorted perceptions of relational experience.

In many respects, the continuing vitality as well as the future course of attachment theory draws on these diverse theoretical foundations from ethological theory and evolutionary biology, control systems theory, developmental psychology, and psychoanalysis. At the same time, as noted below, new perspectives within many of these fields—such as research on early representation and theory of mind,

cultural studies of attachment, and conceptual advances in ethology and evolutionary ecology—contribute potentially valuable new insights into the development and functioning of attachment that could hardly have been envisioned a quarter-century ago.

Although attachment theory is most commonly portrayed as a theory of individual differences in sociopersonality development (Colin, 1996; Karen, 1994), its views concerning normative developmental processes should not be neglected. Bowlby's developmental formulations concerning the growth of attachment remain heuristically important, especially in light of contemporary research on theory of mind. His regard for the centrality of emotion (whether consciously experienced or unperceived) in the appraisal processes that motivate behavior anticipates current functionalist perspectives on emotional development. This is especially apparent when the "set goal" of the attachment system is reconceptualized as the achievement of "felt security" rather than proximity per se (Sroufe & Waters, 1977). Bowlby's emphasis on close relationships as laboratories for the joint arousal and regulation of emotion (including not only fear, anxiety, and reassurance but also pride, shame, and guilt) and the diverse emotional facets of secure-base behavior (including social referencing, affective sharing, comfort seeking, and empathy) is consistent with and extends current relationship perspectives on sociopersonality growth (Sroufe, 1996). Finally, with the growth of representation and language, attachment relationships may become unique catalysts for social cognitive development as young children begin to deduce the mental, intentional, and feeling states of their attachment figures and compare them with their own, and this view was anticipated in Bowlby's fourth stage of attachment formation. In these respects, attachment theory has considerably more to offer concerning normative sociopersonality development than is commonly recognized.

Assessing Individual Differences in the Security of Attachment

Bowlby's clinical interests made individual differences in attachment the central concern, but his collaboration with Ainsworth significantly advanced his developmental theory because of Ainsworth's theoretical interests in young children's security in parental care and her Ugandan studies linking individual differences in attachment to the sensitivity of maternal care. These views were concordant with Bowlby's ethological formulations concerning the protective functions of attachment and the complementarity of infant and parental behavioral systems governing care (Ainsworth, 1963, 1967; Bretherton, 1992). In portraying individual differences in infant attachment primarily in terms of security, Ainsworth also offered a characterization that not only was congenial with the ideas of Bowlby and other contemporaries (such as Eriksonian concepts of "basic trust" in infancy), but recast the meaning of behaviors conventionally characterized as "dependent" in a more positive, psychologically constructive light.

Ainsworth devised the Strange Situation procedure to formally assess the attachment-exploration balance that had been so revealing in her Ugandan studies, recognizing the value of the attachment figure for the infant's play and exploration, but using laboratory procedures that would activate the attachment behavioral system in Baltimore infants whose circumstances of care were much different from those in Uganda. The details of the Strange Situation procedure and its assessment of attachment behavior are provided in detail elsewhere (see Ainsworth et al., 1978). In brief, the Strange Situation consists of eight episodes: an unscored, 30-second introduction to the playroom, followed by seven three-minute episodes that each entails a significant change in the social environment. After an episode of parent and baby alone (episode 2), a stranger enters and plays with the baby (episode 3), followed by the departure of the parent, leaving the infant alone with the stranger (episode 4). The parent's return (and the stranger's departure) inaugurate episode 5, which is followed by the parent's second departure (episode 6), leaving the baby alone. The stranger returns in episode 7, and the parent returns again (while the stranger departs) in episode 8. The duration of each episode (particularly the separation episodes) can be adjusted to curtail infant distress and/or provide more time for soothing. Both stranger and parent follow instructions that guide their interactions with the child while remaining responsive to the child's signals and needs.

Although the Strange Situation lasts only about 22 minutes, and occurs not at home but in an unfamiliar laboratory playroom, its validity is best appraised not in terms of its brevity or ecological realism, but rather in terms of the results of studies testing theoretical propositions concerning the antecedents, consistency, and correlates of variations in the security of attachment as it is assessed in the Strange Situation (see below). Procedural details, such as curtailing separation episodes when infants become markedly distressed and each adult's efforts to provide comfort, are enlisted not only for ethical reasons, but also to ensure that the overall distress experienced by infants in this procedure remains within manageable limits given the normative experience of American middle-class children, and thus to ensure that their behavior remains functionally organized and interpretable within the behavioral systems framework of attachment theory.

Security of Attachment in the Strange Situation

Infant behavior in the Strange Situation is assessed at various levels of detail, each consistent with the functionalist orientation of Bowlby's theory (the caregiver's behavior is typically not evaluated, even though adult behavior can vary considerably within the constraints imposed by the procedure). On one level, ratings of the infant's behavior for specific episodes provide a comparative assessment of changes in attachment-relevant activity as stress increases for the infant throughout the procedure. Detailed ratings of proximity and contact seeking, contact maintenance, resistance, avoidance, and distance interaction are each conducted on 7-point scales, with ratings of search behavior during each separation episode (see Ainsworth et al., 1978). These ratings can be used (along with measures of separation-episode distress) to statistically derive the threefold attachment classifications that more commonly index attachment security (Richters, Waters, & Vaughn, 1988; Van IJzendoorn & Kroonenberg, 1990; see also Gardner, Lamb, Thompson, & Sagi, 1986), although the classifications are most often derived inductively rather than statistically. There are other uses of these episodic interactive measures, however. Treating the Strange Situation as a mini-longitudinal study, for example, Thompson, Connell, and Bridges (1988; Connell & Thompson, 1986) noted that emotional reactions are important to the episode-by-episode organization of attachment behavior within this procedure (see also Sagi, Van IJzendoorn, & Koren-Karie, 1991).

At a second level, inclusive classifications of the security of attachment are based on the organization of the infant's behavior throughout the Strange Situation, especially during reunions with the caregiver. There are three classifications. Infants who are considered *securely-attached* (Group B) constitute about 65% of typical middle-class samples. They use the caregiver as a secure base throughout the procedure and respond positively to the adult's return, either with smiling and other distal greetings (subgroups B1 and B2) or proximity and contact seeking (subgroups B3 and B4). Infants who are *insecure-avoidant* (Group A; approximately 20% of typical samples) show avoidance of the caregiver either by failing to greet or delaying in greeting the adult during reunions, along with subtler signs of avoidance during other episodes. Infants in subgroup A2 also mingle proximity seeking with avoidant behavior, while this is much less characteristic of infants in the A1 subgroup. Infants who are *insecure-resistant* (Group C; approximately 15% of typical samples) were initially characterized by Ainsworth as "ambivalent" because they remain preoccupied with the caregiver throughout the Strange Situation, but their reunions are distinguished by resistance and other signs of anger and distress. Infants in the predominant C1 subgroup mingle proximity-seeking and contact-maintaining behaviors with resistance, while C2 subgroup infants combine resistance with marked passivity. Despite extensive instructions provided by Ainsworth and colleagues (1978), this classification system is not readily self-taught (partly because of comparative metrics incorporated within the guidelines), and novice researchers typically work collaboratively with more experienced researchers, often using a special set of training videotapes, before valid classifications are ensured.

Although these classifications seem homogeneous, each pattern of attachment organization encompasses fairly diverse behaviors. Despite the outwardly unperturbed demeanor of avoidant infants, for example, Spangler and Grossmann (1993) found that the cardiac elevations of A-group infants during the Strange Situation were comparable to those of securely attached infants. Their level of arousal is consistent with Main's (1977, 1981) portrayal of these infants as using avoidance to regulate the conflicting impulses generated by desiring contact with a rebuffing caregiver. However, other studies of their emotional and play behavior have shown that avoidant infants show few indications of emotional or behavioral self-control in comparison with B1 and B2 infants (who are comparably nondistressed), and instead seem genuinely unperturbed (Frodi & Thompson, 1985; Thompson & Lamb, 1984; see also Braungart & Stifter, 1991). The diverse meanings of avoidant behavior are also reflected in the debate concerning whether the avoidance exhibited by infants with substantial early day care experience reflects genuine insecurity (Belsky, 1988) or greater experience and ease with the challenges of the Strange Situation procedure (Clarke-Stewart, 1989; Thompson, 1988). On this issue, the research evidence is mixed (Belsky & Braungart, 1991; Fox, Sutton, & Newcombe, 1993; see M. Lamb, Ch. 2, Volume 4). In a similar manner, the two subgroups of insecure-resistant infants are behaviorally quite different within the Strange Situation for unexplained reasons, although each shows resistance during reunion episodes (Cassidy & Berlin, 1994). These considerations indicate that although classification as secure, avoidant, or resistant provides considerable insight into the organization of an infant's attachment behavior, infants within each classification behave in diverse ways, suggesting that they act securely or insecurely for much different reasons (a conclusion also supported by cultural studies of attachment reviewed below). An important, and unresearched, question concerns the meaning of these alternative patterns of behavior to parents as indicators of their competence and efficacy as caregivers, and of their child's affectional quality (Judy Ungerer, personal communication; Harwood, 1992; Harwood, Miller, & Irizarry, 1995).

A quarter-century of research using this classification procedure has revealed its substantial utility and, perhaps inevitably, some limitations. For instance, some researchers have questioned whether infants in the B4 subclassification, who show strong contact seeking but also some reunion resistance and other signs of insecurity, should properly be considered securely or insecurely attached (Sagi et al., 1985; Van IJzendoorn, Goossens, Kroonenberg, & Tavecchio, 1985). Others have proposed modifications in the classification criteria to accommodate the growing behavioral sophistication of the toddler during the second year (Schneider-Rosen, 1990).

More important is evidence that some infants do not fit satisfactorily into any of the three attachment classifications, most often because infants who would be forced into the secure classification by conventional criteria do not appear to warrant this designation because of anomalous indices of insecure behavior or because they are in caregiving circumstances (e.g., with a maltreating parent) predicted to engender insecurity. The most systematic effort to devise a new classification category to encompass these infants is the D—for disorganized or disoriented—classification developed by Main and Solomon (1986, 1990). The most important feature of this classification is that, in contrast to the A, B, and C categories, infants designated disorganized/disoriented *lack* a coherent behavioral organization within the Strange Situation for coping with heightened arousal. In other words, it is impossible to characterize them in terms of a consistent organization of attachment behavior, as is possible with the other three classifications; in this sense, infants within this classification are united only by features of disorganization and disorientation provoked by the stress of this procedure (Main and Solomon, 1990, retain an "unclassifiable" category for infants who fail to fit into existing A, B, and C classifications, but are not satisfactorily designated as D either). More specifically, indices of disorganization and disorientation include sequences or simultaneous display of contradictory behavior (e.g., calm, contented play followed immediately by angry distress); undirected, incomplete, or interrupted movements or expressions; stereotyped and anomalous postures; freezing, stilling, or slowed movements or expressions; apprehension to the parent's approach; and other behavioral markers of disorientation (see Main & Solomon, 1990, for detailed classification criteria). Like the other attachment classifications, a continuous scale used to assess these indicators of disorganization and disorientation supplements the categorical classification assignment.

The creation of this new attachment classification may help to resolve a number of dissonances between theoretical predictions and research findings that had long troubled attachment researchers. For example, several have reclassified the Strange Situation behavior of infants from high-risk families characterized by neglect or abuse in which some offspring were deemed securely attached using conventional criteria. Many of these formerly B-group infants were reclassified D using Main and Solomon's (1990) criteria (Carlson, Cicchetti, Barnett, & Braunwald, 1989; Lyons-Ruth, Connell, Grunebaum, & Botein, 1990).

Despite these promising findings, however, basic validational research remains to establish the D classification as an interpretively coherent behavioral pattern within the Strange Situation in a manner comparable to the existing A, B, and C classifications. Several researchers have found, for example, that the parents of D infants differ from others in their representations of childhood attachment experiences (Ainsworth & Eichberg, 1991; Main & Hesse, 1990), and there are some associations between disorganized attachment status and later behavioral problems (Lyons-Ruth, Alpern, & Repacholi, 1993). But it is important to systematically examine the caregiving antecedents leading to the D classification (as was done in validating the initial threefold classification system) to establish the meaning of this designation for early sociopersonality development, especially because D is distinguished from a secure attachment not by organized insecurity (as with the A and C classifications), but by disorganized and incoherent behavior. This may be a greater challenge than it first appears because D classification may reflect a more heterogeneous array of early caregiving influences and perhaps reflects several constellations of antecedents (see, for example,

Lyons-Ruth, Repacholi, McLeod, & Silva, 1991). One prospective study indicates that D classification is significantly differentiated by a history of infant abuse during the first year and by measures of maternal caregiving and risk factors, for example, but not by temperamental variables or prenatal/neonatal risk status (Carlson & Sroufe, in press). More research of this kind is needed. Once this essential validational research is accomplished and more is known about its meaning, it may then be possible to incorporate the D classification into the standard classification system.

At a third level, the Strange Situation can be used to index the general security of attachment by comparing B-group infants with a combined A- and C-group cluster. This is the procedure most commonly used by contemporary researchers. Although doing so makes it more difficult to elucidate the meanings of the varieties of insecure attachment and their unique origins and consequences—an essential task for advancing many core propositions of attachment theory—for some research purposes the difference between security and insecurity is all that is important.

The Attachment Q-Sort

This third level of assessment is also reflected in the most widely used alternative to the Strange Situation procedure: the Attachment Q-Sort (AQS) (Waters & Deane, 1985). The AQS is a systematic observational rating instrument based on Q-sort methodology: the observer is given 90 cards with short statements that are descriptive of the behavior of young children (e.g., "rarely asks mother for help"), and is asked to arrange the cards into nine piles ranging from those that are "most descriptive" of the target child to those that are "least descriptive," with a specific number of cards permitted in each pile. Within this forced-distribution format, therefore, the observer must not only sort the descriptors but also compare their relative accuracy in characterizing the target child; a thoughtful Q-sort can take an hour or more. Each card in the observer's final distribution is assigned a score based on its designated pile; these scores are then correlated with a criterion sort based on the prior ratings of a panel of attachment researchers of the hypothetically "most secure child." The correlation coefficient can be the basis for assigning children to securely attached or insecurely attached groups based on predefined cutoffs, or simply treated as a continuous security score. There are also criterion sorts for sociability (which is correlated over .80 with the criterion sort for security) and dependency (which has a small negative correlation with security) (Waters & Deane, 1985). The AQS is suitable for children ranging in age from 12 months to 5 years (Teti, Nakagawa, Das, & Wirth, 1991; Vaughn & Waters, 1990), providing considerably greater flexibility in application than the Strange Situation.

The AQS was designed to enable ratings of a broad variety of attachment-relevant behaviors in naturalistic settings, including secure-base behavior ("child keeps track of mother's location when he plays around the house"), the attachment-exploration balance ("if mother moves very far, child follows along and continues his play in the area she has moved to"), and affective responsiveness ("child quickly greets his mother with a big smile when she enters the room"). However, security scores are also influenced by other features of the child's socioemotional functioning, including the child's obedience, emotionality, and preference for novelty (Vaughn & Waters, 1990; Waters & Deane, 1985). Besides its broader behavioral content, the AQS is a much different kind of assessment than the Strange Situation; they differ in their scope and the contexts in which the child's behavior is assessed (the AQS is not limited, for example, to situations involving heightened activation of attachment behavior), the manner in which ratings are performed and their generality, and sometimes in the nature of the informant.

Research concerning the convergence of AQS security scores and attachment classifications from the Strange Situation has yielded, not surprisingly, a somewhat mixed picture. The most carefully designed initial study indicated that when well-trained observers completed the AQS after several hours of in-home observations, security scores varied significantly according to the toddler's Strange Situation classification (Vaughn & Waters, 1990); other investigators have reported the same result (Pederson, Moran, Bento, & Buckland, 1992; Seifer, Schiller, Sameroff, Resnick, & Riordan, 1996). But others have failed to find a convergence of AQS security scores and Strange Situation classifications, especially when mothers (Pederson & Moran, 1996; van Dam & Van IJzendoorn, 1988) or fathers (Youngblade, Park, & Belsky, 1993) were informants, and Sagi and his colleagues found that avoidant infants were difficult to differentiate from securely attached infants on the AQS in an Israeli kibbutzim sample (Sagi et al., 1995).

The AQS is potentially prone to the same kinds of biases that characterize any rating system, which are minimized when well-trained observers use the AQS after extensive home observations. Problems may occur, however, when parents or other caregivers are informants. One research group found, for example, that Q-sort scores for security and a social desirability measure were very highly correlated when the AQS was completed by mothers, and only when security scores were adjusted for social desirability did they converge predictably with concurrent Strange Situation classifications of infants (Belsky & Rovine, 1990). There is some evidence that maternal AQS scores are more valid and reliable when mothers are provided with considerable prior training and supervision during their ratings (Teti & McGourty, 1996; Teti et al., 1991).

Assuming that these psychometric issues can be resolved, the AQS provides a potentially valuable alternative measure of attachment security that is considerably more flexible than the Strange Situation because it can be applied to a greater range of ages and assessment contexts, permitting a broader examination of developmental changes and individual continuities in attachment. Moreover, the convergence of AQS and Strange Situation ratings contributes to the view that, despite its narrower temporal and ecological context, the Strange Situation appraises features of a young child's attachment behavior that can be observed more generally in naturalistic settings (Pederson & Moran, 1996). However, it also seems apparent that the AQS and the Strange Situation assess somewhat different aspects of attachment security, suggesting that some caution is warranted in directly comparing findings from studies using these alternative methodologies.

Other Methodologies

Recent years have witnessed the development of new procedures for evaluating the security of attachment in older children (Solomon & George, in press). It is perhaps a credit to the heuristic power of the Strange Situation that in doing so, researchers have relied largely on observations of children during extended separation-and-reunion procedures in which the child's behaviors are classified into categories that closely resemble Ainsworth's three, with the addition of an "insecure/disorganized-controlling" classification paralleling the D group (Cassidy, 1988; Main & Cassidy, 1988; Main, Kaplan, & Cassidy, 1985; see also Crittenden, 1992a). Other procedures (reviewed below in the discussion of internal representations of attachment) focus on a child's emergent "working models" of attachment through puppet, doll play, or story scenarios. These new methodologies have been used in studies of the correlates of attachment classifications at later ages, yielding predictable relations between attachment security and self-perceptions and social competence (Cassidy, 1988; Cohn, 1990; Turner, 1991; Wartner, Grossmann, Fremmer-Bombik, & Suess, 1994). More definitive conclusions, however, must await the validation of these assessments against home observations of parent-child interactions.

Creating later-age assessments of attachment security that closely resemble the Strange Situation has the advantage, of course, of fostering longitudinal comparisons of attachment using comparable assessment procedures. Using a one-hour separation-and-reunion procedure with 6-year-olds, for example, two research groups have reported that more than 80% of their samples obtained the same attachment classifications with mother in infancy and age 6 (a much higher rate, interestingly, than the reliability of the same six-year assessment over a one-month period in an independent sample: see Main & Cassidy, 1988; Wartner et al., 1994). However, the strategy of patterning later-age assessments on the Strange Situation is less useful for exploring developmental changes in the nature of attachment processes, or their behavioral manifestations, across different developmental periods. Alternative procedures might be needed to elucidate the growing range and breadth of attachment organization relevant to older children and their caregivers.

Taken together, research on the security of attachment has become broadened by the development of methodological alternatives to the Strange Situation that, while awaiting thorough validation, have the potential of enabling researchers to address larger questions about the development, consistency, and consequences of individual differences in attachment organization. In particular, the development of the AQS and preliminary evidence concerning its convergence with Strange Situation classifications provide considerable methodological flexibility in studying a range of questions that could not easily be studied using Strange Situation methodology exclusively. That these alternative methodologies have emerged from a common theoretical viewpoint, and an implicitly consensual portrayal of the nature of individual differences in security or insecurity, attests better to the heuristic power of Bowlby's theory and Ainsworth's methodology than to clear evidence that these approaches exhaust the range of possible behavioral expressions of attachment in the years beyond infancy. Indeed, these measures were designed primarily to capture the dimensions of security that have been revealed within the Strange Situation in order to study longitudinal continuity in attachment security. But

the question of what attachment is, and the nature of individual differences in attachment functioning, at later years is an empirical question to which these methodologies—and the theoretical views to follow—can usefully contribute to elucidating.

The Meaning of Attachment Classifications

Although the meaning of the behavioral patterns yielding secure and various insecure designations in the Strange Situation, AQS, and other procedures seems apparent from Bowlby's theory, a number of interpretive issues remain current in attachment theory. These issues—encompassing perspectives from natural selection, culture, and theoretical concerns within attachment theory itself—are outlined here because they are pertinent to a thoughtful assessment of research concerning the origins, stability, and correlates of attachment security reviewed subsequently.

Perspectives from Natural Selection

As Bowlby recognized, parents vary considerably in the warmth and sensitivity of their care of infants. But the reasons for this variability extend significantly beyond the important differences in parental childhood history, personality, and belief systems that his psychoanalytic orientation led him to emphasize. Besides these, other influences are highlighted by conceptualizing parent-infant attachment, as Bowlby did, within the context of natural selection. As noted earlier, current views in ethology and evolutionary ecology emphasize that parental solicitude is not necessarily reliable but rather is contingent, based on a variety of factors pertaining to an adult's inclusive fitness and its relation to caring for particular offspring. As a consequence, parent-offspring relations in many species are characterized not only by potential conflict, but also by considerable mutual monitoring of needs and investment (Bateson, 1994). Selection pressures are likely to have made offspring acutely and consciously aware of, and appropriately responsive to, variations in parental solicitude because of their relevance to the child's survival and the child's investment of personal resources toward achieving reproductive maturity, especially in an evolutionary context of high adult and infant mortality such as the one characterizing human adaptation.

Chisholm (1996) has recently argued that the three attachment classifications can be regarded as facultative (i.e., environmentally sensitive) adaptations to alternative patterns of parental investment (see also Belsky, Steinberg,

& Draper, 1991; Blurton-Jones, 1993; Hinde, 1982; Lamb, Thompson, Gardner, & Charnov, 1985; Main, 1990, for somewhat similar views). In this formulation, infants are equipped by natural selection with a variety of conditional strategies for adapting to varying patterns of parental care, so their chances of survival are enhanced by a capacity to respond appropriately to different caregiving conditions. Applying the ideas of life history theory, Chisholm argues that the securely attached pattern arises, as Bowlby believed, from sensitive and responsive parenting that reflects an ability and willingness of the adult to protect and provide for this child and that signals a relatively low level of environmental risk or danger. This attachment pattern thus permits the allocation of the infant's resources to play and exploration (consistent with Bowlby's hypothesized attachment-exploration balance) which enhances the child's potential reproductive success in various ways. By contrast, the infant's insecure-resistant behavior derives from perceptions of the parent's *inability* to invest in offspring (perhaps, in the environment of human adaptation, because of scarce food and other environmental resources, or the adult's anxiety or exhaustion), and the infant's behavioral pattern reflects a facultative adaptation for obtaining, through clingy, dependent behavior, whatever resources the parent is capable of providing. In turn, Chisholm portrays the insecure-avoidant pattern as a facultative adaptation to the parent's *unwillingness* to invest in offspring (perhaps owing to the reallocation of parental resources to other offspring or to personal survival), fostering the independence that may be necessary to obtain needed care from others (e.g., other female kin).

The determinants of these alternative patterns of parental investment are likely to be quite different in a modern, industrialized society compared to the ecological contexts characterizing most of human evolution, but the facultative adaptations that result in infants may be consistent. A study by Valenzuela (1990) with a sample of low-income, chronically underweight toddlers revealed that 93% of the children were insecurely attached, compared with a rate of 50% in a sample of low-income but adequately nourished toddlers. There is additional evidence from the comparative literature to support Chisholm's formulation. In a series of studies, Rosenblum and his colleagues explored the effects of experimentally varied foraging requirements on mother-infant dyads of bonnet macaques to examine the impact of varying conditions of environmental supply on parent-offspring attachment. In the most recent work, Andrews and Rosenblum (1988, 1991, 1993) reported that the infant offspring of mothers living in a low-foraging-demand condition, when food was easy to obtain, were more likely to comfortably depart from the mother during exploratory forays in a novel environment compared to the infant offspring of mothers living in a variable-foraging-demand condition, when access to food was unpredictable and often difficult. The diminished secure-base-like behavior of infants in the latter group was similar to that of the offspring of mothers living in a third condition, consisting of a consistently difficult foraging environment, who showed both greater independence from their mothers and also greater depressive-like behavior (Plimpton & Rosenblum, 1983; Rosenblum & Sunderland, 1982). These studies suggest that the reallocation of parental energy to subsistence in resource-poor environments—together with the direct effects of deprivation on offspring—can have a profound impact on attachment behavior.

What are the long-term implications of these early adaptations? On one hand, it is consistent with Chisholm's (1996) analysis to expect that early facultative adaptations based on perceived parental investment might change as a consequence of changing patterns of care, especially when human adaptation is concerned. As food and other environmental resources improve, for example, or as parents reallocate resources to a particular child, it would be reasonable to expect the child's attachment behavioral patterns to adapt to altered caregiving behaviors reflecting enhanced or diminished parental investment. Indeed, enduring behavioral patterns reflecting outdated conditions of parental investment would probably prove maladaptive.

On the other hand, there are eventual limits to this flexibility as organisms mature, and the behavioral patterns resulting from perceived parental investment may also affect other social ties. If a parent is unable to provide care because of environmental deprivation, for example, the children who are best adapted not only become demanding and anxiously clingy to the mother but may also compete (rather than cooperate) with peers in obtaining needed resources, or become dependent on other adults who may be better providers, and remain vigilant to signs of threat or danger in the environment (Carolyn Pope Edwards, personal communication; Hinde, 1986). Consistent with this view, the behavioral disturbances of bonnet macaques raised with their mothers under variable foraging conditions were, in adolescence, manifested in their somewhat greater agonistic encounters with peers in adolescence (Andrews & Rosenblum, 1994). Belsky and his colleagues have also argued that early attachment patterns may be related to the later timing of sexual maturity, pair bonding, and mature reproductive strategy (Belsky et al., 1991), although the evidence is mixed on this account (Moffitt, Caspi, Belsky, & Silva, 1992). It appears that the later consequences of early adaptations to perceived parental investment depend on the ecological conditions in which the child grows up, their consistency over time, other social relations, and other factors (e.g., in the culture) that influence the meaning of alternative patterns of attachment behavior.

There are several implications of this analysis for the meaning of attachment classifications. Attachment theorists now agree that there is no single species-typical pattern of sensitively responsive parental care to which infant attachment behavior is adapted, with parental insensitivity reflecting a departure from the species norm (Hinde, 1982; Hinde & Stevenson-Hinde, 1990; Main, 1990). Instead, various patterns of parental investment are species-typical, depending on environmental conditions as well as other circumstances, and natural selection has also equipped infants with alternative behavioral strategies that emerge ontogenetically in response to the infant's perceptions of parental investment. There is therefore no single biologically adaptive pattern of secure infant attachment, with insecure attachment patterns reflecting a psychologically or psychobiologically maladaptive alternative. Instead, each of the three (and possibly more) patterns of attachment most likely reflect alternative facultative adaptations to different patterns of parental investment. The immediate and longer-term consequences of these adaptations must be viewed within the context of their development; attachment patterns that are adaptive for certain rearing conditions may be maladaptive for others, and patterns that are initially adaptive may not remain so if conditions change appreciably.

Finally, this perspective highlights some of the proximate causes of secure and insecure attachment that might otherwise be neglected from a nonethological view. In particular, it emphasizes that attachment processes may be influenced by aspects of the broader social ecology of parent and child, relevant to the well-being of each, that have direct as well as indirect effects on the interactional patterns that lead to security or insecurity in the child (Belsky & Isabella, 1988). In this respect, ecological as well as interactional approaches to studying the origins of attachment security are warranted.

Perspectives from Culture

The importance of the ecological conditions that influence parental care and their effects on infant attachment is also revealed in cultural and cross-national studies of Strange Situation behavior, which were initially conceived to evaluate the extent to which the relative distribution of attachment classifications is culturally consistent, as well as the degree to which the secure pattern is modal in different societies. With the adaptational recognition that secure attachments are not necessarily more species-typical than are other attachment patterns, the question has shifted to understanding how attachment processes in alternative contexts reveal catalysts to the development of security or insecurity that may be obscured when studies occur in a single sociocultural or ecological context. Moreover, consistent with the insights from evolutionary ecology, cross-national studies of attachment have revealed that variations *within* as well as *between* nationalities are important because national groups are rarely homogeneous, and the ecological conditions of parental care can vary according to region, locality, and social class.

The relative distributions of attachment classifications in the Strange Situation revealed in the published sources listed in Table 2.1 indicate that there is considerable intranational as well as international variability in the A, B, and C patterns (few studies have used the D or A/C classifications) (see also Van IJzendoorn & Kroonenberg, 1988, 1990). Where patterns are replicated across partners or ages, they suggest that national differences are not primarily due to sampling error. However, the reasons hypothesized for this diversity are varied. In studies of Japanese and Israeli infants, for example, many infants became highly distressed during the Strange Situation (which was often abridged for this reason) and also showed heightened rates of insecure resistance. The high resistance in one Japanese sample was attributed to cultural child-rearing practices that foster mother-infant closeness and physical intimacy, which may have rendered infants unprepared for the separation episodes of the Strange Situation (Takahashi, 1986, 1990; see also Miyake, Chen, & Campos, 1985). Others, however, have attributed heightened resistance both to maternal behavior within the Strange Situation and to separation episodes that were unduly prolonged during this procedure (Grossmann & Grossmann, 1990b). This heightened rate of resistance was not observed when the same sample was tested nine months later (Takahashi, 1990) nor in an independent sample of infants from another city in Japan (Durrett, Otaki, & Richards, 1984). Procedural influences have also been hypothesized to account for the heightened rate of insecure resistance among Israeli kibbutz-reared infants, for whom the stresses of repeated encounters with a stranger during the Strange Situation (especially after two antecedent assessments of stranger

TABLE 2.1   Cross-National Comparisons of Attachment Classifications in the Strange Situation

Study	Age	N	A	B	C	D	Unclassifiable
Sweden							
Lamb et al., 1982	11–13 mos.	51					
mother			11	38	2		
father			13	36	2		
Israel							
Sagi et al., 1985	11–14 mos.						
kibbutz mother		83	7	47	28		1
kibbutz father		83	9	54	18		2
kibbutz metapelet		84	13	44	27		
city		36	1	29	6		
Sagi et al., 1994	14–22 mos.						
kibbutz communal		23	0	11	12		
(alternate classification)			0	6	7	10	
kibbutz home-reared		25	0	20	5		
(alternate classification)			0	15	2	8	
Great Britain							
Smith & Noble, 1987	15 mos.	72	16	54	2		
Japan							
Takahashi, 1986, 1990	12 mos.	60	0	41	19		
(Sapporo)	23 mos.	60	0	49	11		
Durrett et al., 1984 (Tokyo)	12 mos.	36	5	24	7		
Chile							
Valenzuela, 1990	17–21 mos.						
chronically underweight		41	13	3	12		A/C: 13
nutritionally adequate		40	9	20	9		A/C: 2
Germany							
Grossmann et al., 1981							
(Bielefeld) mother	12 mos.	49	24	16	6		3
father	13 mos.	46	25	19	1		1
(Regensburg[1])	12 or 18 mos.	54	17	30	3		4
Beller & Pohl, 1986 (Berlin)	12 mos.	40	7	31	2		
Netherlands							
Van IJzendoorn et al., 1985[2]	12–19 mos.	41	14	27	0		
	20–25 mos.	95	19	71	5		
Goossens & Van IJzendoorn, 1990	12–18 mos.						
mother		75	16	51	7		A/C:1
father		75	23	48	3		A/C:1
day care caregiver		75	21	43	6		A/C:5
United States (selected)							
Ainsworth et al., 1978	12 mos.	106	23	70	13		
Thompson et al., 1982	12.5 mos.	43	7	30	6		
(middle class)	19.5 mos.	43	6	29	8		
Egeland & Farber, 1984	12 mos.	212	46	118	48		
(low income, high risk)	18 mos.	197	44	120	33		
Carlson et al., 1989:	11–16 mos.						
maltreated		22	1	3	0		18
high-risk comparison		21	2	11	4		4
Belsky & Rovine, 1988:	12 mos.						
early & extended day care		58	13	33	12		
primarily home-reared		91	11	69	11		
Li-Repac, 1982							
(Chinese Americans)	12–18 mos.	36	9	18	9		
Lieberman et al., 1991							
(recent low-SES immigrants)	12 mos.	93	30	34	6		D + Unc. = 23
Fracasso et al., 1993							
(low-income Hispanics)	12–15 mos.	50	15	25	10		

[1] From Sagi and Lewkowicz (1987); see also Suess et al. (1992) and Wartner et al. (1994).

[2] See also Van IJzendoorn and Kroonenberg (1990).

sociability) may have proven too challenging for infants raised in a small, close-knit kibbutz community (Sagi et al., 1985; Sagi & Lewkowicz, 1987). However, resistance was also high among a comparison sample of city-dwelling infants who were recruited from day care centers. Thus, the differential impact of the Strange Situation procedure on infants from different nationalities is not entirely clear. To the extent that sample-specific variations in patterns of attachment can be reliably attributed to the differential emotional impact of the Strange Situation procedure (which was designed to be a moderately stressful assessment for middle-class infants in the United States), cross-national comparisons must be interpreted in terms of the psychological impact of procedures that may prove too stressful for infants raised under different child-rearing norms (M. Lamb et al., 1985; Levine & Miller, 1990).

More interesting explanations of the variability observed within and between national samples of Strange Situation observations focus on sociocultural and ecological influences that can account for rearing practices that foster security or insecurity. This was the approach of Klaus and Karin Grossmann and their colleagues (Grossmann & Escher-Graub, 1984; Grossmann, Grossmann, Huber, & Wartner, 1981; Grossmann, Grossmann, Spangler, Suess, & Unzner, 1985), who attributed the heightened rates of insecure-avoidance observed in their North German (Bielefeld) sample to child-rearing practices that emphasize early independence training in young children. Explanations based on child-rearing norms have also been offered to explain patterns of attachment observed in Japan (as noted above) and Israel (Sagi et al., 1985). These views provide useful directions for further studies of culture and attachment, although they often fail to account for within-cultural variability in attachment patterns, such as those observed in both Germany and Japan (see Table 2.1). Within the United States, attachment patterns vary according to socioeconomic status, which is usually attributed to the impact of stresses associated with economic impoverishment on patterns of mother-infant interaction. Other U.S. studies show variations in patterns of attachment based on ethnic or subcultural child-rearing norms (Fracasso, Busch-Rossnagel, & Fisher, 1993; Lieberman, Weston, & Paul, 1991; Li-Repac, 1982), as well as normative (Belsky & Rovine, 1988) and nonnormative (Carlson et al., 1989) variations in early child care.

These studies provide a wealth of hypotheses for future research concerning the cultural and ecological constituents of attachment security. The weakness of some of these explanations, however, is that they are based on conjectures about how cultural and ecological conditions (e.g., child-rearing norms, socioeconomic stress) influence caregivers' behaviors and/or attachment security that are seldom directly tested. It is important to know, for instance, whether theoretically predictable antecedents in mother-infant interaction comparably distinguish securely and insecurely attached infants in different cultural systems and subcultural groups (see Grossmann, 1988, and Grossmann & Grossmann 1990a, 1991, for one important effort to address this question). It is also important to identify how ecological influences that may be specific to national or subcultural groups (e.g., normative conditions of extrafamilial care) influence attachment security. To the extent that culturally normative patterns of child care are believed responsible for patterns of attachment, moreover, it is important also to examine variations in maternal behavior within the Strange Situation as well as independently of it (see Grossmann & Grossmann, 1990b).

Consequently, future cultural-ecological studies of infant-parent attachment will most profitably be based not on global distributions of attachment patterns, but on theoretically based tests of the impact of alternative caregiving conditions. In one exemplary study, Sagi and his colleagues (1994) extended the earlier findings of kibbutz-reared infants by comparing infant-mother attachment patterns in two kibbutz arrangements: a "familist" arrangement in which infants returned home for the night after spending the day in group care, and a traditional arrangement entailing communal sleeping conditions in which infants were supervised at night by professional caretakers (*metaplot*) at the end of group care and a home visit. Consistent with attachment theory, Sagi et al. (1994) predicted heightened insecurity in the traditional group because the metaplot (who rotate in and out of this role) are unable to respond promptly or develop discriminating attachments to the infants in their care. As indicated in Table 2.1, although both groups replicated earlier findings of a heightened tendency toward insecure-resistance in Israeli infants, the expectation of enhanced insecurity for infants in the traditional arrangement was confirmed.

Cultural studies of attachment can also test and refine theoretical expectations concerning the origins and correlates of attachment classifications in different nationalities. Not surprisingly, given the extent to which construals of infant needs and socialization goals are likely to vary in different national systems, efforts to replicate research findings from the United States concerning the origins of attachment security have yielded a rather mixed picture. The Grossmanns' (1991) study of attachment in Bielefeld was, for example, explicitly designed to replicate Ainsworth's findings concerning the relations between maternal sensitivity and attachment security, and while these researchers found that individual differences in maternal sensitivity at 2 and 6 months predicted later security in the Strange Situation, their findings departed from Ainsworth's results in some important ways. The variability in sensitivity distinguishing the mothers of insecurely attached infants from the mothers of secure infants was much narrower in the German sample, for example, and their predictive power ebbed throughout the first year, such that by 10 months (when mothers presumably begin to enlist child-rearing practices that encourage greater independence in offspring), variations in sensitivity no longer predicted the child's attachment security at 12 months (Grossmann et al., 1985). Fracasso and her colleagues (1993) found a comparably mixed picture in their efforts to distinguish securely from insecurely attached lower-income Hispanic infants in the South Bronx based on earlier measures of mother-infant interaction, and speculated that values of the Hispanic culture had an important mediating role (but see Leyendecker, Lamb, Fracasso, Scholmerich, & Larson, 1995, for somewhat different results). Likewise, none of a battery of measures of parental attitudes and behavior, infant behavior, and parent-child interaction obtained both prenatally and throughout the first year succeeded in discriminating infants who were securely attached from insecurely attached in Sweden (Lamb et al., 1985). To some extent, therefore, the determinants of attachment security may be specific to the cultural and ecological context.

With respect to outcomes, the importance of maintaining cultural awareness in predicting the later consequences of a secure or insecure attachment is exemplified by Oppenheim, Sagi, and Lamb (1988), who assessed 59 of the original Israeli kibbutzim infants studied by Sagi et al. (1985) at age 56–58 months on a variety of measures of socioemotional development, including social play, empathy, locus of control, ego resilience, ego control, and several personality ratings derived from adult Q-sort ratings. There were no significant differences when children who were securely or resistantly attached to mother in infancy were compared, and the same result was obtained when differences in the security of infant-father attachments were examined. When children who varied in their earlier attachments to their metaplot were compared, however, the results were largely consistent with theoretical

expectations: children who had been securely attached in the second year were, as 4-year-olds, more empathic, purposive, dominant, achievement-oriented, and independent than were those who had been insecurely attached to their communal caretakers. Although these findings may be regarded as a failure to confirm theoretical expectations concerning the consequences of a secure infant-parent attachment (since kibbutz-raised infants develop salient emotional ties to their parents, of course), they also suggest that infant-metaplot attachments provide independent developmental catalysts to later social skills, especially as they are exhibited in the child care setting where the follow-up assessments took place. In other cultural research, however, Takahashi (1990) has reported that there were no longer-term correlates of a secure or insecure attachment in the Sapporo, Japan, sample. Nor were there strong relations between attachment classifications and measures of the child's ego resiliency and ego control obtained three years later in a Netherlands sample (Van IJzendoorn, van der Veer, & van Vliet-Visser, 1987). In the German research, on the other hand, there have been a number of theoretically predicted correlates of infant attachment patterns, including predictions to measures of social skills and play at age 5 (Grossmann, 1988; Grossmann & Grossmann, 1991; Suess, Grossmann, & Sroufe, 1992).

Clearly, anticipating that the origins and correlates of secure and insecure attachments in different sociocultural and ecological contexts will be entirely consistent risks ignoring important contextual influences that may be specific to particular national and subcultural groups (Van IJzendoorn & Sagi, in press). In this sense, an infant classified as, say, insecure-resistant in one cultural setting may be much different from an infant comparably classified in a different group, and the correlates of attachment security will depend on child-rearing goals and values, cultural belief systems, and other influences on the developing child. If this is so, then a sensitive cultural analysis will also examine the construal processes by which cultural members interpret an infant's attachment behavior in light of the group's goals for socialization, needs for child rearing, and other values.

Some research of this kind has already been done. Harwood (1992; Harwood & Miller, 1991; Harwood, Miller, & Irizarry, 1995) compared lower- and middle-income Anglo mothers with lower-income Puerto Rican mothers in the values that underlie their assessments of different attachment patterns observed in the Strange Situation. While mothers in both subcultural/socioeconomic groups preferred the secure, B-type pattern, they varied in their assessments of other attachment classifications. Anglo mothers valued individual autonomy and competence and consequently commented most negatively on the clingy, dependent behavior of insecure-resistant infants. Puerto Rican mothers emphasized familial love and respect and consequently valued a child's close contact seeking (such as in the B4 classification) but responded negatively to the independence of the insecure-avoidant infants. No direct assessments of mother-infant interaction were conducted, however. In a somewhat similar line of reasoning, Jackson (1993) argues that the attachment patterns of African American infants in the United States must be appraised in light of the subcultural values and emphasis on shared caregiving that characterize many African American families.

These arguments suggest that the cultural meaning systems by which attachment patterns are construed, evaluated, accommodated, and reshaped (as children mature) are important to the development of a secure or insecure attachment (Van IJzendoorn & Sagi, in press). Adding complexity to these considerations, however, are the findings of Posada and colleagues (1995) that mothers in diverse cultures perceive the "optimally secure" child on the AQS in fairly consistent ways. Clearly, more research is needed to elucidate the relevance of culture meaning systems to infant attachment patterns and parent-infant interaction.

Broad versus Narrow Views of Attachment

Whether conceived as the prototype of later love relationships, a facultative adaptation to early patterns of parental care, or as the basis for internal representations of oneself and others, the attachment relationship assumes singular importance in portrayals of early sociopersonality development. This is why a wide variety of antecedents and correlates have been empirically studied in relation to the security of attachment. Yet there are different views within attachment theory about how pervasively attachment processes are associated with, and predict, other aspects of sociopersonality functioning. These broad versus narrow views of attachment make somewhat different claims about the factors that contribute to differences in attachment security and, in turn, what the probable consequences of these differences should be. The alternative views can be conceived best in terms of three related questions.

First, does attachment fully encompass early parent-infant relations, or are there other features of this relationship that are independent of attachment security? Bowlby (1969/1982) believed that even in infancy, attachment is only one of several aspects of the parent-child relationship and is supplemented by their complementary roles in feeding, play, instruction, and other activities that are guided by other behavioral systems. Little is known about how the development of attachment intersects with these alternative features of parent-child relationships, however, or about how they independently or jointly affect the child's later sociopersonality development. Although attachment researchers have naturally devoted much less attention to other dimensions of parent-child relationships (and some view attachment as the totality of early parent-child relations; Pederson & Moran, 1995), Bowlby's view of attachment has potentially important implications for the study of security-oriented attachment processes. For example, if the caregiver's sensitivity contributes to a secure attachment, as Bowlby believed, then sensitivity shown especially when the child is fearful, anxious, or distressed might be more influential to the development of a secure attachment than sensitivity displayed during nonstressful episodes of feeding, play, or routine care, in light of the protective functions of attachment for the child. Most broadly, this suggests that sensitivity might be differentially related to security depending on the functional contexts in which it is experienced by the baby (see Leyendecker et al., 1995; Leyendecker, Lamb, Scholmerich, & Fricke, 1995).

Second, how do features of a dyadic attachment relationship gradually inhere within a child, and how rapidly does this occur? Attachment theorists believe that attachment security begins relationally and shapes a variety of personality processes and representations of self and others. Although this formulation is useful as a broad outline, there is little consensus about what these internal constituents of attachment security are, how early they form, how long they remain dependent on continuing sensitive care, how and when they become self-perpetuating even in the context of changes in the quality of care, how they change with development, and how multiple attachments are incorporated within these internal processes. These are complex issues because there are a variety of ways that attachment security can affect emergent personality and representation, such as through the growth of individual differences in social expectations, social skills, working models of relationships, self-understanding, autobiographical memory, social cognition (such as theory of mind), and self-image. Narrower developmental portrayals tend to emphasize the rather late emergence and consolidation of these internal constituents of attachment security, their plasticity in the context of changing patterns of care, and the child's continuing reliance on the sensitivity and support of parental care for maintaining a secure attachment and its later correlates over time. Broader portrayals instead emphasize the early emergence of personality and representational facets of early attachment, their early consolidation, and their robustness in the face of later changes in the quality of care.

These alternative conceptualizations of attachment have assessment implications also. The Strange Situation and the AQS are child-centered assessments, with little accounting of concurrent parental behavior despite the theoretical importance of parental sensitivity to attachment security. Many studies of the later consequences of attachment likewise focus on child behavior independent of continuity over time in the sensitivity and supportiveness of care. Insofar as attachment researchers believe that relational support remains necessary to the maintenance of a secure attachment and its correlates, the contributions of the continuing quality of care merit greater consideration.

Third, and related to the foregoing, what should a secure or insecure attachment predict about a child's later functioning, and why? In a narrow view, the security that arises from sensitive care should foreshadow the child's later trust and confidence in the parent and, perhaps, in other close partners. In a somewhat broader view, a secure attachment should also predict the child's sociability, concern for and empathy with others—that is, a wider network of relational dispositions. In a much broader view, attachment security foreshadows cognitive competence, exploratory skill, and communication style through its effects on the child's self-confidence, initiative, and other broader personality processes. Clearly, alternative views of the correlates and consequences of a secure attachment are linked to hypotheses about how attachment influences sociopersonality growth through the generalization of social skills, the emergence of relational expectations, the growth of self-representational systems, the emergence of ego strength, facilitating exploration, and other explanations.

Although there is currently no clear consensus on these issues, greater theoretical clarity is essential for several reasons. First and foremost, the necessary search for discriminant validity in the study of the origins and consequences of attachment security is undermined if alternative theoretical views can accommodate almost any relation between attachment and other variables (Belsky & Cassidy,

1994). In this sense, it is as important to determine what a secure attachment does *not* predict, and why, as it is to understand its network of predictable consequences. Second, once clear theoretical predictions are formulated, unexpected relations between attachment and other variables can be examined more incisively. If, for example, attachment security has an apparent but unanticipated relation to later cognitive or linguistic competence, this could be due to their joint relation to a common influence (e.g., emotional sharing and discourse within the family) rather than the direct consequence of a secure attachment; these competing hypotheses permit more careful exploration of alternative developmental models. Third, and most generally, a clear and coherent set of theoretical formulations concerning the consequences of attachment is essential for theory development and, in particular, for distinguishing clear disconfirmations from inappropriate extensions of the theory (Sroufe, 1988).

In a sense, these reflections underscore the need for a more detailed theory of attachment to guide the development and interpretation of research. Although Bowlby's original and subsequent formulations provided an essential catalyst to the growth of research on infant-parent attachment, it was perhaps inevitable that a variety of implicit theories of attachment would emerge under the umbrella of Bowlby's general developmental formulations (Belsky & Cassidy, 1994). At the present, however, any effort to understand the origins and consequences of attachment security is limited by the absence of a common, consistent view of how broadly—and why—attachment is associated with sociopersonality functioning. Attempting to bootstrap such a formulation on the findings of empirical studies conceived with many different goals and agenda risks both theoretical obscurantism and holding attachment theory accountable for formulations that it should not, and perhaps cannot, embrace (Sroufe, 1988).

The Origins of Attachment Security

Early social interactions contribute to the development of infants' rudimentary expectations about other people and their own capabilities, including expectations (a) that others will spontaneously interact and communicate with them and will respond contingently to their signals, (b) that differentiated people in their social environments have distinct behavioral propensities, and (c) that they are effective in influencing others. These expectations constitute core features of social cognition early in the first year. The growth of emotional attachments to specific caregivers during the second half of the first year arises from a confluence of these differentiated expectations for others with the emotional ramifications of infant-caregiver activity, such that each caregiver becomes associated with a panoply of salient affective experiences that marks them as uniquely significant in the infant's world (Hobson, 1993).

The crucial question for attachment theorists is how these expectations contribute to the development of secure or insecure attachments. This is a more complex question not only because of the rudimentary quality of early social expectations concerning the behavioral propensities of caregivers, but also because the interactive data on which they are based are messy. Most parents are fairly adequate caregivers, and few are consistently sensitive or rejecting: their warmth and responsiveness varies depending on situational pressures and competing demands as well as personality and motivation, making the distillation of generalized expectations concerning the adult's affectionate helpfulness a challenging task. Although little is known about this process, it seems likely that the infant's perceptions of the adult's responsiveness are affected not only by the nature and regularity of the caregiver's behavior but also by the ecology of care (such as the predictability and ease of ecological demands) and characteristics of the infant. As Watson (1979) has noted, for example, contingency perception that forms the basis for an awareness of sensitive responding is affected by the base rates of both the infant's behavior and the adult's response; infants who are temperamentally fussy may, for example, have a more difficult time detecting a caregiver's sensitive responding to their cries than infants who are temperamentally more pacific (Thompson, 1986).

Sensitivity

To attachment theorists, the caregiver's sensitivity to the infant is the adult's core contribution to the development of attachment security. Sensitivity can be defined in various ways within different theoretical perspectives; within Vygotskian theory, for example, it entails the careful scaffolding of shared activity within the infant's capabilities and readiness for new challenges, while sensitivity within a learning analysis emphasizes the construction of environmental contingencies that are development enhancing. Parental sensitivity can be enlisted to accomplish various goals, whether to soothe and pacify the child, exploit teaching opportunities, or to engage the child in focused dyadic play, and the preeminence of these goals varies in different cultural and subcultural groups (Harkness & Super, 1995; Levine, 1988). Furthermore, sensitivity is likely to have different consequences for different domains of infant functioning, whether the sensitive scaffolding of play activities is used by a parent to enhance cognitive functioning, the sensitive scheduling of caregiving demands is used to foster emotional stability, or sensitive responsiveness to infant cries is used to instill confidence in the caregiver's availability when needed. Sensitivity is, in short, a broad conceptual rubric for various qualities of adult caregiving practices that can have diverse consequences for the infant's behavior.

Within attachment theory, the focus is on parental sensitivity as a catalyst to secure attachment, with sensitivity consisting of a constellation of response tendencies that includes attention to the infant's signals, accurate interpretation of their meaning, and an appropriate and prompt response (Ainsworth, Bell, & Stayton, 1974; Lamb & Easterbrooks, 1981). Although these response tendencies are conceptually dissociable, the assumption is that they usually occur in concert and contribute to the development of behavioral expectations in the infant that underlie a secure attachment (Seifer & Schiller, 1995). In this respect, sensitivity entails an empathic or sympathetic orientation to the child (Dix, 1991) or, as Bowlby (personal communication) characterized it, "respect for the child."

In general, research on the origins of attachment security supports the view that maternal sensitivity fosters a secure attachment (see Isabella, 1995; M. Lamb et al., 1985 for reviews). More specifically, mothers who respond more positively, consistently, and warmly to the infant's signals are more likely to have infants later deemed securely attached, while major deviations from this behavioral pattern are associated with insecure attachment. Indeed, a recent intervention program based on attachment theory succeeded in raising observational ratings of maternal sensitivity during the first year in a high-risk experimental group, and a higher proportion of infants from this group were subsequently deemed securely attached than from a comparison group (van den Boom, 1994). The importance of sensitive responsiveness is also seen in studies of atypical parents, such as those who are maltreating (Crittenden, 1988; Crittenden & Bonvillian, 1984; Lyons-Ruth, Connell, Zoll, & Stahl, 1987) or experience psychopathological disorders (DeMulder & Radke-Yarrow, 1991; Lyons-Ruth et al., 1990, 1991), in which marked insensitivity in maternal care is coupled with a significantly elevated proportion of insecure attachments in offspring (see review by Van IJzendoorn, Goldberg, Kroonenberg, & Frenkel, 1992).

However, it is important to note that while several studies provide fairly unequivocal support for the relation between maternal sensitivity and attachment security in typical samples (especially in contemporaneous assessments; see Pederson et al., 1990, Smith & Pederson, 1988; Teti et al., 1991; Van IJzendoorn, 1990; Wachs & Desai, 1993; see also Ainsworth et al., 1971, 1978; Isabella & Belsky, 1991; Pederson & Moran, 1995, 1996), others have not found this association (Fagot & Kavanagh, 1993; Frodi, Bridges, & Grolnick, 1985; Mangelsdorf, Gunnar, Kestenbaum, Lang, & Andreas, 1990). Most studies report somewhat inconsistent relations (across multiple assessments or measures) between antecedent measures of sensitivity and subsequent attachment, although group trends have generally (but not always) followed the predicted direction (Bates, Maslin, & Frankel, 1985; Crockenberg, 1981; Egeland & Farber, 1984; Fracasso et al., 1993; S. Goldberg, Perrotta, Minde, & Corter, 1986; Grossmann et al., 1985; Isabella, 1993; Isabella, Belsky, & von Eye, 1989; M. Lewis & Feiring, 1989a; Malatesta, Culver, Tesman, & Shepard, 1989; Miyake et al., 1985; Schneider-Rosen & Rothbaum, 1993; Scholmerich, Lamb, Leyendecker, & Fracasso, in press; Seifer et al., 1996; Stifter, Coulehan, & Fish, 1993; Van IJzendoorn, Kranenburg, Zwart-Woudstra, van Busschbach, & Lambermon, 1991). The same conclusion applies to maternal personality or behavioral attributes that are also influential in the quality of care (Belsky & Isabella, 1988; Egeland & Farber, 1984; M. Lamb, Hopps, & Elster, 1987; Levitt, Weber, & Clark, 1986; Scholmerich, Fracasso, Lamb, & Broberg, 1995; Weber, Levitt, & Clark, 1986; Zaslow, Rabinovich, Suwalsky, & Klein, 1988). Other broadly based intervention studies designed to enhance maternal sensitivity have had some success in raising parental responsiveness, but, in contrast to van den Boom's (1994) findings, this has often not changed the security of attachment in offspring (see review by Van IJzendoorn, Juffer, & Duyvesteyn, 1995). A meta-analytic review by Goldsmith and Alansky (1987) concluded that the average correlational effect size for studies associating measures of maternal sensitivity with the security of attachment was .16 (although somewhat higher with Ainsworth's original Baltimore studies included), which is a significant but modest effect; research published since this review has remained consistent with their conclusions (deWolf & Van IJzendoorn, 1997; Thompson, in press-c). In sum, the relation between maternal sensitivity and attachment security, while fairly reliable, is not highly robust.

Why? One reason may be measurement diversity: maternal sensitivity has been evaluated based on global summary ratings, discrete behavioral counts, molecular constellations of action sequences, factor-analytically-derived behavioral composites, and other strategies; ratings have been conducted at home and in laboratories; episodes for evaluating sensitivity have ranged from several multihour sessions to periods of a few minutes; and the contexts for observation have been highly structured or unstructured. In this light, it is perhaps inevitable that there is considerable variability in the association between heterogeneous assessments of sensitivity and a single index of attachment security, and any consistency in patterns of results is noteworthy. Studies in which sensitivity is appraised over long observational episodes at home will yield more valid and reliable assessments than studies entailing briefer periods in highly structured or unusual observational contexts (Leyendecker, Lamb, Scholmerich, & Fricke, 1995), although this does not account for inconsistent patterns of results *within* studies. Furthermore, even when a consistently detailed observational measure of sensitivity is used across multiple studies, the results are uneven. For example, Ainsworth's inclusive 9-point rating of maternal sensitivity was used in her original Baltimore study and also in several subsequent studies of the origins of attachment security in the Strange Situation, and have usually accounted for the strongest relations between maternal variables and the security of attachment (Egeland & Farber, 1984; S. Goldberg et al., 1986; Grossmann et al., 1985; Isabella, 1993; Pederson & Moran, 1996; see also Van IJzendoorn et al., 1991). Although mothers of secure, avoidant, and resistant infants differed significantly on this measure of sensitivity in each study, none has matched the broad range of average scores that Ainsworth observed in her Baltimore sample, and mothers of insecurely attached infants have consistently averaged above scores of 3 ("insensitive") on this measure (see Table 2.2). In other words, although mothers of insecurely attached infants are insensitive *relative* to the mothers of securely attached infants, many do not appear strikingly insensitive in an absolute sense, and the extent to which they differ from the mothers of securely attached infants varies considerably across different samples.

A second reason for the reliable, but not strong, relation between maternal sensitivity and infant security is that while sensitivity distinguishes secure from insecure infants, it does not well identify the attributes of maternal care that differentiate avoidant from resistant infants. While the sensitivity-security link is consistent with attachment theory, it leaves unexplained considerable variance in infants'

TABLE 2.2   Attachment Security and Maternal Sensitivity Ratings

Study	Sensitivity Assessment	Attachment Assessment	A	B	C
Ainsworth et al., 1971, 1978[1]	9–12 mos.	12 mos.	2.42 (N = 6)	6.48 (N = 13)	2.38 (N = 4)
Egeland & Farber, 1984[2]	6 mos.[3]	12 mos.	5.18	6.07	5.53
	6 mos.[4]	12 mos.	5.24 (N = 46)	5.76 (N = 118)	4.90 (N = 43)
Grossmann et al., 1985, personal communication[5, 1]	2 mos.	12 mos.	4.67 (N = 21)	5.86 (N = 14)	3.83 (N = 6)
	6 mos.	12 mos.	4.50 (N = 24)	5.81 (N = 16)	3.50 (N = 6)
	10 mos.	12 mos.	4.63 (N = 24)	5.12 (N = 16)	3.67 (N = 6)
Isabella, 1993, personal communication[1]	1 mo.	12 mos.	6.58 (N = 11)	6.87 (N = 14)	5.20 (N = 6)
	4 mos.	12 mos.	5.82 (N = 11)	6.67 (N = 14)	5.61 (N = 6)
	9 mos.	12 mos.	5.18 (N = 11)	6.21 (N = 12)	6.08 (N = 6)
Pederson & Moran, in press, personal communication[6, 1]	8 mos.	18 mos.	4.38	6.73	4.77
	12 mos.	18 mos.	3.28 (N = 29)	6.76 (N = 37)	4.23 (N = 13)
			B3,B4	B1,B2	A,C
Goldberg et al., 1986[7]	6 wks.	12 mos.	7.1	5.5	5.4
	3 mos.	12 mos.	6.5	5.7	5.9
	6 mos.	12 mos.	6.6	5.0	5.8
	9 mos.	12 mos.	7.0 (N = 29)	5.9 (N = 12)	6.5 (N = 14)

[1] Sensitivity assessed in various interactive contexts.
[2] Lower-income sample.
[3] Sensitivity assessed during feeding.
[4] Sensitivity assessed during play.
[5] North German (Bielefeld) sample; 3 infants unclassified.
[6] Sample included preterm and full-term infants. Correlations of 8-month sensitivity scores with maternal AQS and observer AQS scores at a 12-month home observation were .26 and .62, respectively; correlations of 12-month sensitivity scores with maternal AQS and observer AQS scores at the same 12-month observation were .41 and .89, respectively.
[7] Low birthweight preterm infants, including some twin pairs; 1 infant unclassified.

attachment organization. In response, Belsky and his colleagues have proposed, and offered empirical support for, the view that avoidant attachments arise from maternal intrusive overstimulation during the first year of life; resistant attachments develop from generally unresponsive care, with securely attached infants intermediate in the quantity of maternal stimulation and responsiveness they receive (Belsky, Rovine, & Taylor, 1984; Isabella & Belsky, 1991; Isabella et al., 1989; see also Leyendecker, Lamb, Fracasso, et al., 1995; Malatesta et al., 1989; Smith & Pederson, 1988). This formulation portrays critical maternal influences somewhat differently than do sensitivity-based views, of course, because it emphasizes the amount of stimulation as well as its quality, but it suggests that a multidimensional portrayal of

the nature of maternal care is essential in predicting attachment security.

Another explanation for the lack of robustness of the association between maternal sensitivity and infant security is that the effects of sensitivity may be contingent. Its effects may depend, as earlier noted, on the functional contexts in which it occurs; a sensitive response when the child is stressed or alarmed may foster a secure attachment more significantly than during relatively nonstressful encounters like feeding or play, as Bowlby suggested. Its effects may also be contingent on the infant's age, as Isabella (1993, 1995) has proposed and other researchers have also found, although the evidence is inconsistent (Egeland & Farber, 1984; Grossmann et al., 1985; Seifer et al., 1996).

One implication of the hypothesis that maternal sensitivity is particularly influential at specific stages of psychosocial growth, however, is that sensitivity measures should perhaps be attuned to the specific psychological challenges that infants encounter at each pertinent stage. Quick and appropriate responsiveness to infant crying may be more important earlier than later in the first year, for example, while the careful scaffolding of assistance during challenging or difficult experiences may be more influential later (see Pianta, Sroufe, & Egeland, 1989, for exemplary longitudinal research using developmentally appropriate measures of maternal sensitivity). Finally, the effects of sensitivity on attachment may be contingent on the consistency of maternal sensitivity over time. Individual differences in the sensitivity scores reported by several researchers in Table 2.2 tended to be only moderately stable over short intervals during the first year (with correlations of .30 to .50 over 8 months), which is consistent with other studies of the stability of parenting behavior (Holden & O'Dell, 1995). These findings are understandable given the significant changes that occur over this period in infant needs and capabilities, as well as parental stress and support (Crockenberg & McCluskey, 1986; Pianta et al., 1989). They suggest, however, that sensitivity may have its greatest influence on the development of attachment security when infants experience fairly reliable qualities of responsiveness over time. At present, however, none of these hypotheses can be further evaluated based on existing research.

These formulations, taken together, suggest that rather than regarding parental sensitivity as a personality attribute with generalized benefits for attachment security, it may be more useful to regard sensitivity as behavioral quality with multifaceted origins (including, as noted earlier, the influences of parent belief systems, goals for child rearing, cultural ethnotheories of development, and social stress and support) whose effects are situationally and developmentally specific. This view suggests that while sensitive care is central to a secure attachment, other developmental and ecological influences on the child may moderate its effects. Additional evidence concerning the origins of attachment adds credence to this view. The security of attachment is affected by socioeconomic status, with a greater tendency toward insecure attachment when the family faces economic, ecological, or legal stress (Egeland & Farber, 1984; Shaw & Vondra, 1993; Vaughn, Egeland, Sroufe, & Waters, 1979; Vaughn, Gove, & Egeland, 1980). In these circumstances, however, the mother's

experience of social support can enhance the likelihood of secure attachment (Crockenberg, 1981; Jacobson & Frye, 1991; Spieker & Bensley, 1994; but see Levitt et al., 1986). The quality of the marital relationship is also associated with attachment security: couples who experience poor or declining marital quality are more likely to have insecure offspring (Belsky & Isabella, 1988; Durrett et al., 1984; Goldberg & Easterbrooks, 1984; Howes & Markman, 1989). Maternal employment is complexly associated with attachment security; mothers who were employed and also reported high levels of separation anxiety were found, in one study, to exhibit greater intrusiveness during interactions with their infants, who subsequently were found to be insecurely attached (Stifter et al., 1993).

It is difficult to know, based on existing evidence, whether the impact of these features of the family ecology on attachment security are mediated primarily through their impact on the sensitivity of parental care or are instead directly influential through their effects on the baby (such as the child's witnessing angry adult encounters) or other features of child care (such as unpredictable changes in caregiving arrangements). The lessons drawn from cross-national studies of attachment as well as theoretical models of evolutionary ecology, however, suggest that the direct effects of the physicosocial ecology in which the infant lives should not be ignored (Thompson, 1993). Thus, the most powerful models predicting the security of attachment are likely to be multidimensional formulations in which the caregiver's sensitivity is viewed in the context of features of the family ecology that may moderate its effects on the development of attachment security (see, for example, the cumulative stress model of Belsky & Isabella, 1988).

The Child's Contributions

Attachment theorists recognize, of course, that security is shaped not by objective characteristics of maternal sensitivity but rather by subjective appraisals of sensitivity; it is the infant's *experience* of sensitivity, in other words, that contributes to a secure or insecure attachment (Belsky & Cassidy, 1994). This means that how sensitivity is expressed necessarily varies according to the infant's characteristics and needs (Sroufe, 1985), and how sensitivity is perceived may also vary according to the infant's attributes. From this social-cognitive perspective, a variety of infant characteristics might affect the child's perceptions of parental sensitivity and other features of responsiveness that foster feelings of security or insecurity, including temperamental features (like behavioral inhibition, distress proneness, and difficulty), experiential background (including abuse suffered by others), and psychopathology (Thompson, 1986; van den Boom, 1989). Infant characteristics may not only affect their perceptions of the sensitivity of care, but may also directly affect features of infant-parent interaction and the organization of behavioral expectations leading to a secure or insecure attachment.

The evidence concerning these formulations, however, is quite mixed. In clinical studies, a few researchers have reported markedly enhanced rates of insecure attachment (especially disorganized attachment; Goldberg, 1990) in samples of Down syndrome toddlers (Vaughn et al., 1994), high-risk premature infants (Plunkett, Meisels, Stiefel, Pasick, & Roloff, 1986), infants with congenital heart disease (S. Goldberg, Simmons, Newman, Campbell, & Fowler, 1991), and autistic children (Capps, Sigman, & Mundy, 1994). But child clinical conditions have generally not accounted for marked deviations in the relative rates of secure and insecure classifications in the Strange Situation, especially by comparison with the effects of various conditions of maternal psychopathology (Van IJzendoorn et al., 1992). To be sure, the severity of child psychopathology is an important moderator of its effects on attachment security. But when differences in attachment have been apparent in relation to child psychopathology it has not been clear whether they have been due to the impact of the child's condition on caregiver-child interaction, the differential impact of the stresses of the Strange Situation on high-risk children, and/or the validity of the Strange Situation as an index of attachment for atypical populations.

In studies of infant temperament, findings have been likewise mixed. Research directly linking parent-report measures of infant temperament with attachment classifications in the Strange Situation have generally yielded nonsignificant associations (Bates et al., 1985; Belsky & Isabella, 1988; Belsky & Rovine, 1987; Calkins & Fox, 1992; Egeland & Farber, 1984; Seifer et al., 1996; Singer, Brodzinsky, Ramsay, Steir, & Waters, 1985; Vaughn, Lefever, Seifer, & Barglow, 1989; Weber, Levitt, & Clark, 1986), although there may be a link between resistant attachment and temperamental difficulty or distress proneness (Frodi, 1983; Weber et al., 1986; see Goldsmith & Alansky, 1987). There is some evidence that parent-report temperament measures are associated with alternative groupings of attachment classifications, with infants in the C and B3/B4 groups distinguished from infants in the A and B1/B2 groups on measures of temperamental difficulty

(Belsky & Rovine, 1987; but see Mangelsdorf et al., 1990, and Seifer et al., 1996, for failures to replicate). Because infants in these two classification clusters also differ significantly on measures of separation distress in the Strange Situation (Frodi & Thompson, 1985; Thompson & Lamb, 1984), it seems likely that these temperamental variations are associated with separation reactions that are related to, but not the same as, the variations in reunion behavior that distinguish secure, resistant, and avoidant attachments (Connell & Thompson, 1986; Thompson et al., 1988). When antecedent behavioral measures of infant temperament are considered, findings are generally consistent with Ainsworth's home observational studies that insecurely attached (especially resistant) infants are fussier in mother-infant interactions and other contexts during the first year (Ainsworth et al., 1978; Belsky, Garduque, & Hrncir, 1984; Miyake et al., 1985; Seifer et al., 1996; see, however, Calkins & Fox, 1992; Mangelsdorf et al., 1990), although it is difficult to disentangle the effects of infant characteristics from the quality of maternal care.

In sorting through these diverse findings, it is important to distinguish index from construct in assessments of temperament and attachment. It seems fairly clear, for example, that parent-report temperament measures (especially indices of proneness to negative arousal) can account for meaningful variance in infants' Strange Situation behavior. But the fact that they primarily explain variations in separation distress rather than reunion behavior has led some researchers to conclude that temperament influences not whether infants develop a secure attachment, but rather *how* their security/insecurity is expressed in the Strange Situation (Belsky & Rovine, 1987). In other words, while security is believed to result from sensitive care, some infants are temperamentally prone to develop a more highly aroused style of security (B3/B4 subgroups) or insecurity (C classification), while others develop an emotionally more subdued manner of security (B1/B2 subgroups) or insecurity (A classification). However, the index of attachment is important to consider because, by contrast with the limited empirical relations between parent-report temperament measures and A/B/C classifications in the Strange Situation, researchers have rather consistently found a significant negative association between AQS security scores and parent-report temperament measures of negative emotionality (Seifer et al., 1996; Vaughn et al., 1992; Wachs & Desai, 1993). In the study by Seifer and colleagues (1996), distress-prone temperament was negatively associated with AQS security scores using both parent-report and observational temperament measures, and Vaughn and colleagues (1992) reported that the negative association between AQS security scores and parent-report temperament also increased with the child's age. It seems likely, therefore, that temperament has a meaningful albeit modest association with attachment security, especially within the broader assessment context of the AQS.

Contributing complexity to these formulations are findings concerning the concordance of infant-mother and infant-father attachments. Although initial research indicated that there was little association between attachment security to each parent—which was interpreted as further evidence against an association between temperament and attachment—a meta-analytic review by Fox, Kimmerly, and Schafer (1991) concluded that there is a modest, although significant, concordance between the attachments of infants to each parent in the Strange Situation, whether classifications were compared in terms of security/insecurity, the type of insecurity (avoidant vs. resistant), or in terms of emotionality clusters (A/B1/B2 vs. B3/B4/C). Infant temperamental quality is one explanation of interparental concordance of attachment security, although other explanations (such as the mutuality of support, caregiving goals and beliefs shared by parents, similarities in social stress, and other factors experienced in common by family members) also merit consideration.

It appears that a modest role for infant temperament in attachment security must be acknowledged. The more interesting, and important, question is *how* temperamental individuality interacts with sensitive care to shape a secure or insecure attachment; few studies offer insight on this interactive process because most focus on only the most direct association between temperament and attachment. (Indeed, most research has focused even more narrowly on the relations between attachment and temperamental difficulty or distress proneness, without exploring the multidimensional qualities of temperamental individuality and their potential effects on attachment security.) It is helpful to realize how complex the relation between infant temperament and parental care can be: a child's difficult temperament might hinder sensitive responsiveness, or instead might engage and motivate caregivers to be more responsive. Alternatively, the effects of temperament on parental responsiveness may be contingent on the availability of outside resources and support. Research findings are consistent with each of these portrayals of temperament-caregiving relations (Crockenberg, 1986). Consequently, more complex hypothesis-driven studies of the

links between temperamental individuality and specific patterns of care leading to a secure or insecure attachment are needed, such as research to elucidate the provocative conclusion of Mangelsdorf and colleagues (1990) that patterns of maternal care had different consequences for the development of security when infants who were high and low in temperamental proneness to distress were distinguished.

In the end, although research findings have failed to confirm any of the extreme positions on the relation between temperament and attachment that initially polarized discussion of this topic, they have also failed to explore thoughtful connections between temperament and attachment that are, after all, linked by their common association with the development of emotion and relationships (Goldsmith & Harman, 1994; Stevenson-Hinde, 1991). From this perspective, temperament and attachment not only share common roots, they also assume interactive roles in behavioral development. For example, toddlers who are behaviorally inhibited may especially benefit from a secure attachment relationship when coping with stressful challenges (Nachmias, Gunnar, Mangelsdorf, Parritz, & Buss, 1996). Viewed in this light, the question is not whether temperament or caregiver sensitivity has primacy in the development of attachment security, but how their joint contributions to attachment also continue to influence further growth. Such a transactional model is especially important in light of the fairly limited predictive power that temperament and sensitive care, taken alone, seem to have in predicting whether infants develop secure or insecure attachments. When such transactional processes are viewed further in the context of the broader ecology of infant care, it is likely that more powerful predictive models of attachment and later development will be confirmed.

Stability and Change in the Security of Attachment

Initially, studies of the stability of attachment in the Strange Situation emerged from concerns about the unreliability of contemporary measures of infant-parent interaction and the consequent inability of researchers to identify stable, meaningful individual differences in interactive quality (Masters & Wellman, 1974). When Waters (1978) observed 50 infants in the Strange Situation at 12 and 18 months, his findings provided an incisive demonstration that the level of behavioral analysis of Ainsworth's interactive measures and classification system could yield highly stable individual differences over a six-month period in the baby's second year. But neither this study alone (nor any other) could establish normative levels of consistency in attachment classifications. Indeed, the earliest studies of the stability of attachment security over comparable periods during the second year yielded remarkably diverse proportions of infants who obtained the same attachment classification at each age (M. Lamb et al., 1985).

As shown in Table 2.3, stability estimates have subsequently varied widely in short-term test-retest studies using the Strange Situation, making it difficult to establish a normative level of consistency in attachment classifications except with reference to characteristics of the sample and the temporal span under study. Both middle-class and lower-income samples have shown a broad range of stability estimates, and with the lowest rates of stability in middle-class samples reported in the most recent studies, it appears that attachment security cannot generally be

TABLE 2.3 Stability of Attachment Classifications in the Strange Situation

Study[1]	SES	N	Age at Time 1	Age at Time 2	Overall Stability %	B-Group Stability %	Non-B-Group Stability %
Waters, 1978	m-c	50	12 mos.	18 mos.	96	100	90
Thompson et al., 1982	m-c	43	12.5 mos.	19.5 mos.	53	67	23
Main & Weston, 1981[2]	m-c		12 mos.	20 mos.			
mothers		15			73	ni	ni
fathers		15			87	ni	ni
Owen et al., 1984[3]	m-c		12 mos.	20 mos.			
mothers		59			78	86	25
fathers		53			62	78	29
Frodi, Grolnick, & Bridges, 1985	m-c	38	12 mos.	20 mos.	66	77	25
Takahashi, 1985, 1990	m-c	48	12 mos.	23 mos.	60	ni	ni
Easterbrooks, 1989[4]	m-c	60	13 mos.	20 mos.			
mothers					58	ni	ni
fathers					56	ni	ni
Belsky et al., 1996[5]							
Pennsylvania State mothers	m-c	125	12 mos.	18 mos.	52	68	28
Pennsylvania State fathers	m-c	120	13 mos.	20 mos.	46	60	23
Pittsburgh mothers	m-c	90	12 mos.	18 mos.	46	54	31
Minneapolis study[6]	l-i		12 mos.	18 mos.			
Vaughn et al., 1979		100			62	82	38
Egeland & Sroufe, 1981							
maltreating subsample		25			48	78	31
excellent care subsample		32			81	92	50
Egeland & Farber, 1984		189			60	74	41
Lyons-Ruth et al., 1991	l-i	46	12 mos.	18 mos.			
with D classification					30	33	28
without D classification					61	59	63
Schneider-Rosen et al., 1985	l-i						
maltreated		12	12 mos.	18 mos.	42	20	57
nonmaltreated		17	12 mos.	18 mos.	76	82	67
maltreated		19	18 mos.	24 mos.	53	25	60
nonmaltreated		23	18 mos.	24 mos.	70	73	62

m-c = middle class; l-i = lower income; ni = no information

[1] Studies that did not use Ainsworth's classification system (e.g., Connell, 1976) are not included.

[2] Includes stability of "unclassified" subjects over time.

[3] Strange Situations with mothers and fathers separated by 3–6 weeks.

[4] Sample equally divided between full-term and low-birthweight preterm infants. Term status unrelated to attachment classification or its stability. Strange Situations with mothers and fathers separated by approximately 1 month.

[5] Pennsylvania State samples include exclusively firstborn sons. Pittsburgh sample recruited for a study of postpartum depression; depression was unrelated to attachment classification or its stability.

[6] Stability estimates from these studies are based on overlapping samples.

presumed to be temporally consistent. Interestingly, the addition of the D classification tends to reduce rather than increase the stability of attachment classifications, perhaps because of its heterogeneous quality (Lyons-Ruth et al., 1991; see also Belsky, Campbell, Cohn, & Moore, 1996).

The more important, and interesting, question concerns whether patterns of stability and change are lawful and predictable, or derive instead from random processes (such as measurement error). The studies listed in Table 2.3 provide some clues about the predictors of consistency and change in attachment. In general, secure attachments are far more stable over time than are insecure attachments (with the maltreated cohort from Schneider-Rosen, Braunwald, Carlson, & Cicchetti, 1985, the primary exception). This may derive, as Bowlby (1969/1982) believed, from the self-perpetuating mutual satisfactions that caregiver and infant derive from a secure attachment and the relational instability inherent in insecure attachment.

It is also apparent that the consistency of attachment classifications varies significantly by sample characteristics. On average, parent-infant attachments from middle-class samples tend to be more stable over time than are attachments in lower-income (often high-risk) samples (see, however, Belsky et al., 1996; Easterbrooks, 1989), presumably because of the greater number of unexpected stresses and changing life circumstances encountered by families in the latter conditions. In one direct test of the influence of stressful life events, Vaughn et al. (1979) found that the mothers of infants who shifted from securely attached at 12 months to insecurely attached at 18 months (N = 10) received significantly higher scores on a self-report measure of life stresses compared with the mothers of infants who maintained secure attachments at each age (N = 45). In a follow-up report that included a larger number of infants from this study, Egeland and Farber (1984) partially corroborated the influence of increasing life stress in shifts from secure to insecure attachments, but also investigated the importance of maternal personality characteristics. They found that the mothers of infants who changed from secure to insecure were (compared to the mothers of stable, securely attached infants) more aggressive and suspicious in prenatal and 3-month assessments. It is possible, therefore, that a combination of unexpected life stress and the mother's limited coping skills best account for changes in the security of attachment in this high-risk sample.

Taking their cue from the Vaughn et al. (1979) findings, Thompson, Lamb, and Estes (1982) also examined the role of changing life circumstances in their study of the stability of attachment in middle-class families. In addition to a surprisingly low rate of consistency in A, B, and C classifications, they noted that of the range of intervening events they assessed (e.g., major separations between parent and child, residential change, etc.), two overlapping events were associated with changes in attachment security: mother's return to work and the onset of regular nonmaternal care. In contrast to the Vaughn et al. (1979) findings, however, these events were associated with changes from insecurity to security as well as the reverse and reflected, they concluded, a renegotiation of familiar patterns of mother-infant interaction in the context of less severe life changes (Thompson, Lamb, & Estes, 1983). Such a view is consistent with the higher stability estimate of Main and Weston (1981) for a middle-class sample that was specifically selected to exclude such influences. Owen, Easterbrooks, Chase-Lansdale, and Goldberg (1984) did not, however, find an association between changes in attachment and shifts in maternal employment, although, interestingly, the latter was associated with changes in the security of infant-*father* attachment (which they attributed to the differential accommodation of each parent to changing maternal work patterns). Finally, Frodi et al. (1985) found no associations between the stability of attachment and intervening life events or child care patterns, but did report associations with maternal personality variables: infants who were either consistently secure or became secure from 12 to 20 months had mothers who were more sensitive and less controlling at 12 months.

It appears that it is easier to identify a broad range of short-term stability estimates in the second year than to account for their causes. Although it is commonly concluded that attachments are less stable in a context of changing family circumstances, the empirical evidence is insufficiently consistent to support this explanation taken alone. Better measures of the consistency of caregiving conditions are needed; thus far, only one research group has observed mother-infant interaction between repeated Strange Situation assessments to determine whether (and how) changes in attachment were predicated on changes in the interactive harmony of infants and caregivers. Belsky and colleagues (1996) studied consistency and change in mother-infant and father-infant attachment in a sample of 125 families, and also observed family interaction at home during a period (when infants were 15 months) that was between the two Strange Situation assessments. They found, however, that only one of twenty measures of parental sensitivity, intrusiveness, detachment, and positive or negative affect expressed at home distinguished stable from unstable infant-mother or infant-father attachments. Concurrent data concerning maternal employment changes and day care usage for this sample also did not differentiate stable from unstable attachments, partly because few families changed in these ways between the two Strange Situation assessments (Belsky, personal communication). Belsky and his colleagues suggested, however, that the increased rates of dual-career families during the past two decades might explain the differences between their stability rates and those observed by some earlier attachment researchers, since the early onset and high usage of day care by families with infants may introduce greater stresses to the attachment relationship.

This study is a model for future research on the stability of attachment, especially if measures of changing family circumstances and stress are combined with concurrent assessments of changing parent-infant interaction. As noted earlier, a complex interactive model may be needed to explain the origins of attachment security, and models of equal complexity may be needed to explain its stability, entailing a combination of family change or stress with parental personality factors and other influences (such as social support) that can heighten either resiliency or vulnerability to the impact of life stress on parent-infant attachment. In this view, therefore, the question is not whether changing life circumstances alone can explain changes in attachment, but whether these changes exceed the parent's capacities to maintain a consistent relational quality with her or his child. Although several researchers have gathered data that are pertinent to this formulation, it has not been subject to empirical test. In a study using the AQS, however, Teti, Sakin, Kucera, Corns, and Das Eiden (1996) found that attachment security in firstborn preschoolers decreased following the birth of a new sibling, and the children whose security scores dropped most dramatically had mothers with significantly higher scores on depression, anxiety, and/or hostility compared with the mothers of children who maintained high security scores. In this study, firstborns' security scores were also predicted by measures of the mothers' marital harmony and affective involvement with the firstborn. Thus the impact of the secondborn's birth on the security of mother-firstborn attachment was importantly moderated by the mother's capacities to cope successfully with the new birth, which was itself predicted not only by her personality style, but also by the support she received from her partner. Further studies of the interaction

between stressful life events, maternal coping, and changes in mother-child attachment are clearly warranted.

As this AQS study of stability and change in attachment demonstrates, the prevalent focus on short-term stability in attachment classifications in the Strange Situation (and needless debate over normative stability estimates) may become superseded by studies of longer-term consistency and change in attachment employing methodologies better suited to older children. Youngblade and her colleagues (1993), for example, have reported moderately high correlations between parent-sorted AQS security scores at 12 and 36 months, and two research groups have reported that more than 80% of the children observed in the Strange Situation as infants and in a one-hour separation-reunion procedure as 6-year-olds obtained the same attachment classification on each occasion (Main & Cassidy, 1988; Wartner et al., 1994).

Future stability studies should also examine attachments to nonparental caregivers. Howes and Hamilton (1992a) reported that attachments between preschoolers and their child care teachers were stable over 6- to 12-month intervals on observer-sorted AQS scores if their teachers remained the same. If their teachers changed, however, AQS security scores tended to be unstable until the child reached 30 months of age, after which security scores with different teachers were significantly correlated over time. What is surprising about the latter finding is not, of course, the limited stability of attachments at younger ages when teachers changed at preschool (after all, different caregivers are involved), but rather the consistency that was maintained for older children's attachment security scores even when their teachers changed. The extent to which this was due to the nature of the older child's social expectations or emergent representations of child-caregiver relationships, or to ecological factors in the preschool fostering consistency of care (especially with older children), remains to be explored further.

No investigators have yet identified the reasons accounting for stability and change in attachment in child care; in doing so, future researchers will have to explore a wider range of influences than the consistency of living circumstances and maternal personality features alone. As Bowlby (1969/1982, 1973) surmised and as subsequent attachment theorists have elaborated, children progressively construct their own representations of relationships that affect their interactions with attachment figures as well as other partners. It will be important for future investigators to examine stability and change in these mental representations of attachment as part of their ongoing research into consistency and change in attachment processes throughout life.

This is especially important as researchers will soon become capable, for the first time, of exploring in longitudinal analysis the relations between infant Strange Situation classifications (or preschool AQS scores) and adult representations of attachment many years later. As with the other research reviewed here, estimating the stability of attachment over this long period is important but is perhaps less interesting than understanding the factors contributing to consistency and change in these behavioral/representational attachment processes over time. One would expect that greater consistency in attachment would be evident when individuals (a) are securely attached early in life, (b) encounter fewer changes or disruptions in significant attachment relationships over the intervening period (such as parental separation or divorce or the death or serious illness of a parent), and (c) experience subsequent relationships that are consistent (in the security and confidence they engender) with their childhood experiences with care. But understanding the bases for longitudinal continuity from the behavioral attachments of infancy to the representational attachments of later life is additionally complicated by the need to understand how representations of childhood care themselves develop and may modify the legacy of early attachments. It is important to understand, for example, how a foundation of security in infancy may be threatened by the emotional upheaval accompanying a parent's acrimonious divorce, or how early experiences of neglect or emotional abandonment can be later comprehended with the growth of mature capacities for motivational insight and role taking. In the latter case, individuals with difficult early childhood experiences are not necessarily destined to carry insecure attachment representations throughout life if they become capable of grasping the causes, significance, and meaning of these early experiences for their present attachments. One hopes that future investigations of the continuity of attachment processes over longer spans of life incorporate assessments that provide insight into these complex developmental processes.

Attachment and Later Behavior

In a manner similar to how researchers have amassed substantial data concerning stability and change in attachment, but have neglected inquiry into its causes, they have also acquired considerable data concerning the later behaviors associated with security of attachment in infancy but little information elucidating the reasons for these associations. Virtually all attachment theorists agree that the consequences of a secure or insecure attachment arise from an interaction between the emergent internal representations and personality processes that attachment security may initially influence, and the continuing quality of parental care that fosters later sociopersonality growth. They differ, however, in the relative emphasis each places on these dual contributors to individual development, and the derivative research suggests that more thoughtfully designed studies are needed both to elucidate the influence of emerging internal representations and caregiving support over time, and their changing relative influence with the child's maturity.

An important theoretical view of the origins and consequences of attachment security is provided by Sroufe and his colleagues, who portray early personality growth within an organizational-relational perspective (Sroufe, 1979, 1990, 1996; Sroufe & Egeland, 1991; Sroufe & Fleeson, 1986, 1988). In this view, caregiver sensitivity inherently incorporates and organizes the network of dispositional (e.g., temperamental) qualities of the young infant as their attachment relationship develops, and thus the child's emergent personality is a dyadic creation. Their attachment establishes the initial organization of personality that guides later sociopersonality functioning in several ways. First, early relationships create expectations concerning relational partners and one's experience of relationships as the young child internalizes relational roles and interactions. As a consequence, according to these researchers, children choose new partners and behave with them in ways that are consistent with, and help to confirm, the expectations created from earlier attachments. Children with secure attachment histories, for example, expect the partner's positive responsiveness, and their social behavior helps to evoke such responses. Insecurely attached children instead become more dependent or hostile on the basis of having internalized a more ambivalent or unresponsive relationship, and the partner's response to their negative behavior confirms their expectations of the unreliability of others' acceptance. Second, attachments create broader internal representations of various aspects of self and others that function as interpretive filters of experience and influence motivation and emotion. From this standpoint, Sroufe argues that early attachments may underlie later differences in self-esteem, curiosity, ego resiliency, self-reliance, and other features of the emergent self-system. Finally, and most broadly, the success or failure of establishing a secure attachment relationship also influences the child's success in encountering subsequent developmental challenges, such as developing an autonomous self or establishing harmonious peer relationships. This "continuity of adaptation" (Sroufe, 1979) arises because of how the child progressively constructs more sophisticated expectations and representations of self and relationships based on the interaction of prior relational history, current relational experience, and emerging new developmental challenges. In this regard, according to Sroufe, continuing support from caregivers and others is important to maintaining and building on the foundation for personality development established initially by the primary attachment relationship.

The empirical strategy deriving from the organizational-relational perspective focuses on the developmental challenges that are salient to each period of growth to detect the continuity of personality functioning over time that may be manifested in quite different patterns of behavior. In this regard, the strongest support for this formulation derives from Sroufe's and Egeland's longitudinal follow-up study of a large, socioeconomically disadvantaged sample of families recruited initially in Minneapolis during the mid-1970s. Subsequent to a range of antecedent assessments (Egeland & Farber, 1984), infants were observed in the Strange Situation at 12 and 18 months (Vaughn et al., 1979). Subsamples were then studied in follow-up assessments of peer sociability at 20–23 months (Pastor, 1981) and in a 10- or 20-week preschool program at 47–60 months (Sroufe, 1983; Sroufe, Fox, & Pancake, 1983; see also Erickson, Sroufe, & Egeland, 1985; Kestenbaum, Farber, & Sroufe, 1989; LaFreniere & Sroufe, 1985; Sroufe & Fleeson, 1988; Sroufe, Schork, Motti, Lawroski, & LaFreniere, 1984; Troy & Sroufe, 1987) (findings from other early follow-up assessments are available in unpublished conference presentations and dissertations). In comparisons of children with consistently secure or insecure attachments from infancy, Sroufe and his colleagues found evidence for continuity in many features of later functioning. In the preschool assessments, for example, children who were initially secure were less dependent (based on several teacher ratings as well as behavioral observations) and were observed to be more empathic than were initially insecurely attached children. They were also rated by their teachers as higher on ego resiliency and self-esteem, emotional health, agency, positive affect, social competence, compliance, social skills, and empathy, and lower on negative affect; on-site observations confirmed that teachers

interacted with these children differently as well. These children were also distinguished on teacher ratings and a sociometric measure of peer popularity, as well as on several other measures. While group differences were not apparent on some measures, the continuity of predicted behavioral differences between children with secure and insecure attachments in infancy—in a context where their caregivers were not immediately present—is certainly impressive.

More recently, subsamples from this project have been studied during the early elementary school years (Renken, Egeland, Marvinney, Mangelsdorf, & Sroufe, 1989), a four-week summer camp when children were 10 (Elicker, Englund, & Sroufe, 1992; Shulman, Elicker, & Sroufe, 1994; Sroufe, Carlson, & Schulman, 1993; Urban, Carlson, Egeland, & Sroufe, 1991), with a camp reunion at age 15, and a family observation at age 13, with individual assessments at age 16, 17½, and 18 (with findings yet to be reported; see Egeland, Carlson, & Sroufe, 1993). In school, 18-month (but not 12-month) attachment classification modestly predicted teacher ratings of aggression and passive-withdrawal behavior during first through third grades (combined) for boys, although this was not true for girls. During the summer camp, children were rated by their counselors and observed by project staff throughout each day on a variety of measures of sociopersonality functioning. Children who were securely attached in infancy (N = 25) received higher ratings in social competence, emotional health/self-esteem, self-confidence, ego resiliency, and social skills, and lower ratings on dependency, and they were observed to make more friendships (especially with other children with secure attachment histories) and spent more time with friends than children who had been insecurely attached as infants (N = 22). In the most recent assessment of this sample, measures of psychopathology in adolescence were modestly, but significantly, predicted by infant attachment status (Sroufe, personal communication).

In these follow-up assessments in preschool and later years, differences between children who had earlier been identified as securely or insecurely attached were much more apparent on broad teacher- or counselor-rated personality dimensions than on discrete behavioral observations. Researchers have also had considerably more difficulty distinguishing avoidant from resistant children than in differentiating children with secure or insecure attachment histories (see, however, Sroufe, 1983; Urban et al., 1991). Moreover, it has sometimes been true that attachment at 12 or 18 months predicted later behavioral outcomes in a manner that was not replicated by the other attachment assessment, for unexplained reasons. Despite these caveats, and the absence of differences on some expected dimensions, there was clear and predicted continuity in many features of behavioral functioning that was related, according to Sroufe and his colleagues, to underlying continuity in both the quality of care that children received as well as in emergent personality processes.

A different view of continuity in behavior from early attachment is offered by Lamb and his colleagues, who have emphasized the consistency of caregiving influences that initially shape the security of attachment and later contribute to other social and personality dispositions (M. Lamb, 1987; M. Lamb et al., 1985). In this view, the same parental sensitivity and responsiveness that initially contributed to a secure attachment will, if they are maintained as the child matures, also foster greater social competence, self-esteem, resiliency, emotional health, and other markers of positive sociopersonality growth. Conversely, insensitive parenting contributes to insecure attachment and less optimal later functioning if insensitivity endures. In this sense, a secure or insecure attachment is a marker of the quality of the parent-child relationship that has continuing later influences on sociopersonality growth.

In support of this view, Lamb and his colleagues have noted that the high rates of instability in the security of attachment over as little as six months argue against the normative expectation that attachment security in infancy necessarily has long-term influences on later sociopersonality functioning. They pointed out that the strongest relations between attachment and later behavior occur in samples where caregiving influences are likely to be consistent over time, such as when children are selected for stable early attachments, or families are selected based on the absence of divorce or other disruptive intervening events, residential stability, or other factors heightening continuity in care. Moreover, several research studies indicate that the quality and consistency of parental care after infancy have a more powerful effect on later behavior than does the initial attachment relationship. For example, Easterbrooks and Goldberg (1990) found that kindergarten teachers' ratings of ego resiliency in 5- to 6-year-olds were unrelated to the security of infant-mother or infant-father attachment at 20 months. However, ego resiliency ratings were predicted by an interaction of toddler attachment and the consistency of maternal employment (as an indicator of the consistency of caregiving conditions). More optimal levels of ego resiliency were apparent in children who had

been securely attached with mothers who were stably employed, and by children with insecure early attachments whose mothers changed in employment status. Youngblade and Belsky (1992; see also Youngblade et al., 1993) found that attachment security at 12 months (with mothers) and 13 months (with fathers) poorly predicted the quality of interaction with a same-sex close friend at age 5. Measures of the harmony of mother- and father-child interaction at age 3 bore significant relations to the later peer interaction measures, however, and the poor predictive power of earlier attachment measures was explained, in part, by the very weak relation between attachment at age one and parent-child interaction measures at age 3. Absent continuity in parent-child relationships, attachment did not predict later peer interaction.

Similar findings concerning the importance of continuity of care have also appeared in the Minneapolis study. Erickson and colleagues (1985; see also Egeland, Kalkoske, Gottesman, & Erickson, 1990) noted that when infant attachment security failed to predict behavior problems at age 4½ to 5, it was often due to intervening changes in the quality of the parent-child relationship. These changes were observed especially during a series of mother-child tasks at age 42 months. At this age, children who were initially securely attached but showed later behavior problems had mothers who provided less guidance and support, and children responded less affectionately and more avoidantly to them, compared to those who were secure but without later behavior problems. Those who were initially insecurely attached but emotionally healthy at follow-up, on the other hand, had mothers who were more supportive and provided clearer structure and guidance, and children responded more affectionately and positively to them, compared to those who were initially insecure and had later behavior problems. Sroufe, Egeland, and Kreutzer (1990) also found that the predictive power of infant attachment in forecasting grade-school teacher ratings of peer competence/emotional health was significantly diminished when intervening measures of psychosocial adaptation were first entered into the predictive equation (although a lingering effect of attachment security remained apparent). When the findings of these studies are taken together, an interaction of early attachment and the quality and consistency of subsequent care seems to be more prognostic of later sociopersonality functioning than either variable taken alone.

Such a conclusion is consistent with Bowlby's (1973) view that psychosocial functioning is always a product of both developmental history and current circumstances; the positions of Lamb and Sroufe differ primarily in their relative emphasis on each and their views of the emergence and influence of the child's internal representations that mediate between personal history and current conditions. While Sroufe stresses the early growth and influence of the child's expectations of others and conceptions of self that cause the young child to approach partners with relational biases and to evoke consistent responses from them, Lamb and his colleagues emphasize the more gradual emergence of these internal constituents and the young child's continuing reliance on patterns of care that either maintain or help to alter the consequences of an initial secure or insecure attachment. Early security and the quality of subsequent care are each influential, of course, but existing research is inadequate to a further evaluation of their relative importance because research on the predictive validity of attachment in infancy has not generally been designed to examine the influence of subsequent parental care (M. Lamb et al., 1985; Waters, Kondo-Ikemura, Posada, & Richters, 1991). Because the design of follow-up studies has usually included only antecedent measures of attachment and later measures of psychosocial functioning, it is usually impossible to determine whether early attachment security is linked to later behavior because caregivers have remained sensitively supportive (or unsupportive) over time, or even whether the child's attachment has remained consistently secure or insecure. If either is true, of course, the predictive relation between attachment and later behavior may be better attributed to the continuing and contemporary influences of parental sensitivity or attachment security on behavior at follow-up. Thus, data concerning predictive relations between attachment and later behavior are often agnostic concerning its causes (Thompson, in press-b).

Properly assessing the influence of continuing patterns of care may be more difficult than expected, however, because of how each new developmental phase in early life provides challenges and opportunities for a reorganization of parent-child relations (Easterbrooks & Goldberg, 1990). Parent-child interaction changes over time as the child's emergent capabilities broaden the parent's role to include not only attachment figure but also mentor, teacher, mediator, and disciplinarian. Parents who find it easy to respond sensitively to a dependent baby may have greater difficulty with the autonomy-seeking toddler, and the quality of parental care that engenders security in a 1-year-old is different than the kind that instills confidence in a preschooler. This may be one of the reasons that conventional measures of parenting show limited stability over time (Holden & O'Dell, 1995). Consequently, accounting for intervening changes in the quality of parental care requires careful thought concerning the aspects of care that are most important to the child's later psychosocial growth, and inadequate conceptualization and measurement may misrepresent its influence. In this regard, the emphasis of Sroufe and Egeland on age-salient developmental challenges provides a good start to thinking about the facilitating qualities of parental care that are most pertinent to each developmental phase.

In considering the importance of attachment security for later behavior, it is also important to distinguish between different outcome domains. As noted earlier, although it may be reasonable to expect a secure attachment to foreshadow later parent-child relations and perhaps also the quality of other close relationships, it is theoretically less clear whether attachment should provide a foundation for sociability with unfamiliar partners, cognitive ability, or style of play (Belsky & Cassidy, 1994). Likewise, with respect to personality outcomes, expectations concerning the importance of a secure attachment for ego functioning, achievement orientation, and behavior problems rely on the nature of the theoretical formulations that associate attachment with early representations of self, predispositions toward others, and other emergent personality processes. In this regard, it might be helpful to distinguish between various kinds of developmental continuity that may be associated with a secure or insecure attachment in infancy and lead to later behavior (Thompson, in press-b).

The first kind of continuity concerns the harmony of parent-child relations: a secure attachment in infancy should provide the basis for more positive subsequent parent-child interaction. This expectation is confirmed in short-term follow-up assessments during the second year when securely attached children show greater enthusiasm and positive affect during shared tasks (Frankel & Bates, 1990; Matas, Arend, & Sroufe, 1978; see also Bates et al., 1985), and affective sharing (Waters, Wippman, & Sroufe, 1979, Study 1) and compliance during free play (Londerville & Main, 1981; see also Main, 1983; Main, Tomasini, & Tolan, 1979). Thus securely attached infants tend to maintain more harmonious relations with mothers in the second year. In each study in which concurrent maternal behavior was assessed, however, the mothers also differed in their behavior toward offspring, with mothers of securely attached children acting consistently more supportively, sensitively, and helpfully. Thus the consistency of mother-child harmony during the early years has dyadic bases. Longer-term assessments of parent-child relationships have not, however, yielded strong consistency over time. Research has not found enduring associations between attachment security in infancy and parent-child interaction at ages 2½ (in Japan: Takahashi, 1990), 3 (Youngblade & Belsky, 1992), and 5 (in the Netherlands: Van IJzendoorn et al., 1987), even though other studies have found considerable consistency between attachment assessments over longer spans of time (Main & Cassidy, 1988; Wartner et al., 1994). It appears, therefore, that short-term continuity in the harmony of parent-child relations is more reliable than longer-term consistency, perhaps because of the diminished catalysts for change in each partner's behavior over shorter periods.

Although an association between attachment security and subsequent parent-child relations is conceptually straightforward, its significance should not be underestimated, since continuing harmony heightens a young child's receptivity to various socialization influences at home, whether they concern moral internalization, emotion regulation, or cognitive achievement (Waters et al., 1991). Continuing harmony in parent-child relations suggests also that the dyad has begun to establish the kind of positive, mutually responsive relationship identified by Maccoby (1983, 1992) and MacDonald (1992) as an important contributor to positive psychosocial growth. This is thoughtfully illustrated in a study examining symbolic play and attachment (Slade, 1987; see also Belsky, Garduque, & Hrncir, 1984, for related research). As predicted, securely attached toddlers later showed longer and more complex episodes of symbolic play in the second year than did insecurely attached infants. Not surprisingly, their mothers also acted more supportively during follow-up assessments. Group differences between securely attached and insecure dyads were most apparent, however, in experimental contexts when the mother was more involved in the child's activity and could actively promote the child's play competence; in these circumstances, securely attached children showed the most advanced play. The experimenter's conclusion that "secure dyads 'work' better" (Slade, 1987) is consistent with a view of the cumulative benefits derived from a secure attachment and consistently supportive care (and also, incidentally, with a Vygotskian portrayal of the shared construction of skilled activity in the early years).

Do securely attached infants more successfully enter into other intimate relationships at later ages? A confirmation of this hypothesis would suggest that young children generalize the expectations derived from a secure or insecure attachment to other close relationships, although

other explanations (such as temperamental characteristics) also merit consideration. But the research evidence is mixed. Teti and Ablard (1989) reported that sibling pairs who were each securely attached to their parents experienced more harmonious interaction than did insecurely attached dyads (see also Volling & Belsky, 1992b), although parents assume an obvious role in maintaining this harmony. In the Minneapolis study, preschoolers with a secure attachment history were less dependent on their teachers than were insecurely attached children and were also more popular with their peers (Sroufe, 1983; Sroufe et al., 1983). Concerning peer relationships, there is further evidence that securely attached infants socialize more competently with well-acquainted peers as preschoolers (LaFreniere & Sroufe, 1985; Sroufe, 1983; Suess et al., 1992; Waters et al., 1979, Study 2). Other researchers, however, report weak or unexpected associations between attachment security and peer interactions at age 4 (Howes, Matheson, & Hamilton, 1994), interactions with close friends at age 5 (Youngblade & Belsky, 1992; Youngblade et al., 1993), self-reported loneliness at ages 5–7 (Berlin, Cassidy, & Belsky, 1995), and self-reported friendships at age 9 (Lewis & Feiring, 1989b). However, Elicker et al. (1992) and Grossmann and Grossmann (1991) have each reported greater social competence and friendships among 10-year-olds with secure attachment histories. In the only research on predictive validity using the AQS, Kerns (1994) reported that friendship pairs composed of securely attached preschoolers (assessed via maternal sorts at age 4) were, at age 5, more positive and coordinated in their interactions than pairs of insecurely attached dyads (see also Park & Waters, 1989; Kerns, 1996). In addition to offering a model of much-needed future research concerning the predictive validity of the AQS, Kerns's study also contributes to the conclusion that children with a secure attachment history seem to function more harmoniously in other close relationships, although this is more apparent in short-term rather than longer-term follow-up research.

Another kind of continuity deriving from the security of attachment concerns social skills. Thompson and Lamb (1983) proposed that in their initial encounters with unfamiliar peers and adults, securely attached infants (particularly those in the B1 and B2 subgroups) employ distal interactive skills that result in more successful interactions compared with insecurely attached infants, who are more limited by their reliance on proximal interactive modes or their avoidant behavior. Both contemporaneous and predictive studies of stranger and peer sociability in the second year have lent partial support to this view (Easterbrooks & Lamb, 1979; M. Lamb, Hwang, Frodi, & Frodi, 1982; but see Sagi, Lamb, & Gardner, 1986). Other studies also find that securely attached infants are more sociable with unfamiliar adults during the second or third year (Londerville & Main, 1981; Lutkenhaus, Grossmann, & Grossmann, 1985; Main, 1983; Main & Weston, 1981; but see Frodi, 1983), but the evidence is inconsistent concerning unfamiliar peers (e.g., Booth, Rose-Krasnor, & Rubin, 1991; Jacobson & Wille, 1986; Pastor, 1981; Takahashi, 1990), perhaps because peers are less optimal partners. Mothers were present during stranger and peer sociability assessments in these studies, of course, and each study in which concurrent maternal behavior was evaluated yielded differences indicating that the mothers of securely attached children were more supportive and child-centered with their offspring. It is thus difficult to conclude, without further research, that the security of attachment provides a repertoire of social skills that are generalized to unfamiliar partners in contexts that are independent of immediate maternal support.

A third kind of continuity from the security of attachment, and of greatest interest to attachment theorists, concerns personality functioning. Attachment theorists predict, for various reasons, that securely and insecurely attached infants will differ in emergent features of personality, and the two features that have been studied most frequently are ego resiliency and behavioral problems. Concerning ego resiliency, although Arend, Gove, and Sroufe (1979) reported that securely attached toddlers received significantly higher scores on Q-sort and behavioral measures of ego resiliency at age 5½, and Sroufe (1983) reported a similar difference for the preschool follow-up of the Minneapolis study, other researchers have not found this difference (Easterbrooks & Goldberg, 1990; Howes, Matheson, & Hamilton, 1994; Oppenheim et al., 1988; Van IJzendoorn et al., 1987; Van IJzendoorn, Sagi, & Lambermon, 1992). Concerning behavior problems, the expectation that insecurely attached infants would later exhibit greater behavioral problems has received only limited support in studies using various behavioral inventories and observations in follow-up assessments throughout the preschool years (Bates et al., 1985; Bates & Bayles, 1988; Erickson et al., 1985; Fagot & Kavanagh, 1990; M. Lewis, Feiring, McGuffog, & Jaskir, 1984), which prompted Fagot and Kavanagh (1990) to caution against drawing clinical implications from attachment classifications. Other researchers have reported that

securely attached infants are, in follow-up assessments, more curious (Arend et al., 1979), less easily frustrated (Matas et al., 1978), and more advanced in visual self-recognition (Schneider-Rosen & Cicchetti, 1984), but these have not been replicated (Frankel & Bates, 1990; Lewis et al., 1985; see also Pipp, Easterbrooks, & Harmon, 1992). In general, there are few differences between attachment groups on measures of intelligence.

Taken together, the evidence concerning the consequences of attachment security can be characterized as "modest, weak" (Belsky & Cassidy, 1994) and, like the studies of maternal sensitivity, temperament, and attachment, pointing to relations that are provocative but not robust (M. Lamb et al., 1985). A secure attachment in infancy foreshadows a more positive, mutually responsive future parent-child relationship (at least in the near term), and such infants appear capable also of forming more successful close relationships with others (again, more apparent in short-term follow-up assessments than in long-term studies). This may be due to the repertoire of social skills afforded by a secure attachment, more positive relational expectations, continuing parental support, or for other reasons. The research evidence is weakest concerning later correlates in personality functioning; with the exception of the impressive results of the Minneapolis studies, few consistent later personality outcomes of a secure or insecure attachment can be discerned. But even if later personality correlates are unclear, the correlates revealed in current research concerning parent-child relations and other close relationships are meaningful and important.

Several considerations are necessary to put these findings into proper perspective. First, the predicted outcomes of attachment security are multidetermined; many factors besides attachment contribute to individual differences in, say, behavioral problems in preschoolers, and this makes follow-up studies with single predictors like attachment status inherently low in predictive power. In many studies, in fact, outcome prediction has been boosted by the inclusion of other variables, such as measures of subsequent parent-child interaction, variables (like maternal employment) that reflect the consistency of caregiving conditions, or other psychosocial influences (like early day care experience) that may interact with attachment in predicting later behavior (Egeland & Hiester, 1995; Vaughn, Deane, & Waters, 1985). The findings of these studies confirm an obvious conclusion: regardless of the importance of a secure or insecure attachment, other influences on the child also affect later sociopersonality functioning. Second, in many instances the prediction of later psychosocial functioning has been undermined by combining avoidant and resistant classifications into an aggregate insecure group, even though differentiated outcomes might be expected for each classification. When researchers have distinguished the two insecure classifications, which are behaviorally much different in the Strange Situation, they have sometimes yielded informative results (e.g., Frodi et al., 1985). Third, as with studies of the influence of parental sensitivity on attachment, the quality of measurement is an important consideration; studies are not comparable in the duration of observations or quality of assessments that yield follow-up measures, and the inconsistent findings concerning the consequences of a secure or insecure attachment may be partially attributable to this.

Finally, it is important to consider also that insofar as it is affected by attachment security, later behavior is undoubtedly influenced by *multiple* attachments, not just the infant-mother relationship. Several studies that have examined the relative influence of infant-mother and infant-father attachments on later behavior have found that maternal attachments have generally stronger prediction, although a secure attachment to *both* parents yields the most optimal psychosocial outcomes, whereas the poorest outcomes are associated with two insecure attachments (Belsky, Garduque, & Hrncir, 1984; Easterbrooks & Goldberg, 1990; Main et al., 1985; Main & Weston, 1981; Suess et al., 1992). But the question of a hierarchy of attachment relationships may be the wrong one; because infants develop qualitatively different kinds of relationships with mothers and fathers, the bases for security and the contexts in which it is engendered with mothers and fathers may be different (Mangelsdorf, personal communication; Cox, Owen, Henderson, & Margand, 1992; Volling & Belsky, 1992a). It is more reasonable, therefore, to expect that attachment relationships with each parent might predict different aspects of later behavioral functioning, or may have different interactive influences on later behavior. This possibility remains to be studied.

Equally significant are the potential influences of extrafamilial attachments with caregivers outside the home (Howes, in press). Like parental attachments, the attachments that infants develop with extrafamilial caregivers are relationship-specific and modally secure, and are affected by the caregiver's sensitivity as well as the quality of the care setting. Further, their security is generally independent of the security of the infant-parent relationship (Goossens & Van IJzendoorn, 1990; Howes & Hamilton,

1992a, 1992b; Howes, Rodning, Galluzzo, & Myers, 1988; Sagi et al., 1985; Van IJzendoorn, Sagi, & Lambermon, 1992; see also Table 2.1). It is also apparent that the security of attachment to extrafamilial caregivers has unique psychosocial correlates that are either independent of or interact with the effects of security in infant-mother attachments (Howes et al., 1988; Oppenheim et al., 1988; see Van IJzendoorn, Sagi, & Lambermon, 1992). As noted earlier, for example, Oppenheim and colleagues (1988) found that for Israeli kibbutz-reared infants, attachments to metaplot—but not to mothers or fathers—best predicted a variety of psychosocial sequelae at age 4, and Howes et al. (1994) found that peer interaction and play were predicted by the security of attachment to child care teachers, but not to mothers (see also Howes, Hamilton, & Matheson, 1994). These findings suggest that psychosocial functioning is a complex product of various relationship influences beginning in infancy, and that nonfamilial attachments may also have a unique role in predicting later behavior.

In the end, these considerations warrant perhaps greater reflection on the central question of what behavioral consequences should be expected from infant-parent attachment security, and why (Thompson, in press-b). On one hand, the research reviewed above yields the clear conclusion that a secure attachment makes a difference for a child's future. On the other hand, the reasons for this are elusive—is it due to continuity in good parenting? social skill acquisition? social expectations? emergent working models? domain-specific effects of partner-specific attachments?—and more precise hypotheses are needed beyond the simple expectation that secure attachments should yield good future benefits. It is not hard to develop more specific predictions based on the studies reviewed above, and the design of the relevant research to test these hypotheses is equally straightforward. Among the many lessons of the research reviewed above are that consideration of the continuing quality of parental care is necessary in studies of the predictive validity of attachment security, that multiple predictors besides attachment must be enfolded into multivariate predictive models, that studies designed to explore alternative causes of developmental continuity are most desirable, and that theoretical clarity in predictive expectations is essential.

On one issue, in particular, considerably greater conceptual clarity is needed to refine predictive expectations: the nature and development of the internal representations that are believed to result from attachment security and that are believed to affect diverse aspects of later behavior.

It is possible—indeed likely—that although attachment security affects a child's emergent representations of self, others, and relationships and influences related personality processes, these representations are insufficiently mature at the time that infant attachment assessments are conducted to enable Strange Situation classifications to have significant predictive power. At later ages, however, when such representations have begun to consolidate, security of attachment may indeed have significant implications for emergent representations of self and others, as well as broader aspects of psychosocial growth. But studying these processes (using measures of attachment security suitable for later ages) depends on greater conceptual clarity of the meaning and development of such representations. Thus, we turn to this central concern of attachment theory, and of early sociopersonality development more generally, with the growth of representations of self, others, and relationships.

FROM ACTION TO REPRESENTATION

One of the signal achievements of infancy is developing and consolidating first attachments. One of the important accomplishments in the months and years that follow is a flourishing representational capacity that enables the child not only to acquire the rudiments of logical operational thought (which primarily interested Piaget), but also to conceptualize experience outside of its immediate temporal and situational context. With expanding representational ability, for example, young children can better integrate past experiences with current events and future expectations, generalize more effectively from specific incidents, characterize people (including the self) in attributional and dispositional terms, and gradually assemble a sense of personal history. Each of these achievements, and others associated with emergent understandings of emotion and morality, contributes to sociopersonality development.

To attachment theorists, these signal accomplishments are related: the security of attachment provides a foundation for the child's representations of self, the partner, and of relationships in general. Bowlby's (1969/1982, 1973, 1980) concept of internal working models, summarized earlier, describes how the behaviorally based attachment system also becomes manifested in a representational system of relationships and self. Bowlby's object-relations-based formulation is consistent, of course, with classic models of the self within psychology that emphasize the

construction of self-understanding as a consequence of important relationships (Cooley, 1902; Mead, 1934; see also Harter, Ch. 9, this Volume). The "looking glass self" is both a portrayal of the mature construction of self and a developmental account of the growth of self-understanding. Given the salience and significance of the child's attachments to caregivers—the emotional communication and understanding they share, harmony as well as conflict in goals and intentions, reassurance in the face of stress or uncertainty, and the roots of a sense of effectance, self-awareness, and self-control—it would be surprising if early relationships did not have a significant influence on the child's earliest constructions of self and assumptions about the propensities of others. In a sense, Bowlby's concept of working models provides a general formulation for conceiving how attachments have this formative influence within the broader context of sociopersonality development, and helps to foreshadow other formulations concerning the importance of "relational schemas" in interpersonal interaction (M. Baldwin, 1992). But this formulation requires greater clarity, especially in light of current research on early memory and representation, to provide useful answers to the basic question of whether, and how, attachment in infancy affects later representations of self and other, and to ensure that this formulation is not just a "catch-all, post-hoc explanation" for research findings on the outcomes of attachment security (Belsky & Cassidy, 1994; see also Hinde, 1988).

Bretherton (1990, 1991, 1993) has contributed significantly to an elaboration of Bowlby's formulations by emphasizing the gradual emergence of a young child's working models in the context of shared communication with the attachment figure that permits either open and accessible exchanges about attachment-related concerns, or instead fosters the defensive exclusion of disturbing information or feelings. To Bretherton, these communication patterns, shared over the course of parent-child interaction, contribute to the intergenerational transmission of patterns of secure or insecure relationships partly because of how adult modes of communication (and the sensitivity associated with them) bias the development of working models in offspring. In Bretherton's formulation, the preschool years are an especially significant period for the growth of working models of self and others, largely because this is when some of the constituents of such models become consolidated, such as in scripted knowledge structures that form an early basis for event representation and the growth of the child's psychological understanding of others. Based partly on this formulation, Bretherton and her colleagues (Bretherton, Ridgeway, & Cassidy, 1990) as well as other researchers (Cassidy, 1988; Main et al., 1985) have developed assessment procedures for preschoolers that use doll-play stories, drawings, responses to family photographs, and other procedures to examine attachment-related representations in age-appropriate ways.

Crittenden (1990, 1992b, 1994) has extended Bowlby's formulations somewhat differently to propose that individuals acquire multiple working models associated with different memory systems. In the order of their developmental emergence, Crittenden proposes that one kind of model based on procedural memory is associated with behavioral expectations, a second based on semantic memory consists of verbally encoded generalizations about the self and caregivers, and a third model based on episodic memory provides the basis for unconscious memories when individuals encounter disturbing and inexplicable experiences. Crittenden (like Bowlby) is particularly interested in the problems that may arise from discordant information and expectations stored in these three memory systems, such as may occur when young children's experiences of care are inconsistent with what they are told about parental solicitude. In circumstances like these, according to Crittenden, poor communication between memory systems may result from defensive processes and can contribute to splits between different features of represented experience, memory, and affect.

As Crittenden has shown, it is probably wise to regard Bowlby's working model construct not as a single representational system but rather as a variety of representations that emerge successively but interactively with development. After all, the kinds of representations that permit relatively simple behavioral predictions of a caregiver's propensities in infancy are different, in many ways, from the kinds of representations that foster later perceptions of the self as worthy or unworthy of love. Although parsing the development of working models in terms of the functioning of different memory systems is problematic in light of current work in the cognitive sciences, the effort to denote associations between the growth of working models and other features of emerging memory and representation is central to elucidating Bowlby's provocative proposal. In conceptually unpacking the working models construct, therefore, it may be helpful to distinguish among: (a) *developing event representation* by which general and specific memories of attachment-related experience are represented and retained, (b) the *growth of autobiographical memory*

in which particular events are linked by their relation to a continuing personal narrative and developing self-representation, (c) the emergence of the child's *understanding of others* by which the motives and intentions of attachment figures (and other social partners) are construed and the nature of relationships is understood, and (d) *concepts of specific attachment figures* and their characteristics. In each of these domains, the child's representational capacities develop on the basis of direct experience, maturing intellectual skills, and the guidance (e.g., shared discourse) of others, and the progressive emergence of new representational abilities provides new ways to reflect on and interpret personal experiences that incorporate and subsume earlier representations (Oppenheim & Waters, 1995). In short, representational processes encompassed within the working models construct constitute a surprisingly complex network of developing reflections, understandings, and beliefs.

Researchers have only begun to sketch the outlines of these developing representational processes; this section summarizes their conclusions as they apply to Bowlby's formulations during the early years (review sources are cited where pertinent; see also Mandler, Ch. 6, and Flavell, Ch. 17, in Volume 2, for more detailed information). As we shall see, these studies also address other aspects of sociopersonality growth in the early years, such as the emergence of the constituents of conscience, the growth of self-understanding, and the development of self-referent emotions, that are considered in more detail in the section that follows this one.

Attachment Representations in Developmental Perspective

Early Foundations

As noted earlier, the security of attachment in a 1-year-old is based, in part, on a history of sensitive or insensitive care in a context of shared activity that enables the development of basic social expectations concerning the interactive propensities of people in general, the behavioral tendencies of recognized figures in the infant's world, and the baby's personal agency or effectance, particularly in a social context. These and related social expectations have been characterized by Stern (1985, 1989a) as special kinds of generalized memory structures called RIGs (Representations of Interactions that have been Generalized). As Stern and others have noted, these rudimentary expectations are imbued with emotion that heightens their salience and biases the infant's reactions to subsequent encounters with familiar partners in specific situations. Nevertheless, the kind of contextually based responsiveness apparent in simple social expectations is not the same thing as the capacity for the independent recollection of events, in other circumstances and occasions, that is incorporated into Bowlby's working models construct, even though these expectations permit basic predictions concerning the immediate behavioral propensities of others.

There is every reason to believe that these early social expectations are retained and elaborated as the 1-year-old matures intellectually, but researchers have been hesitant to conclude that explicit memories or representations of early experiences formed in infancy are maintained in later years. There is good reason for their caution: although the mnemonic skills of 12-month-olds are surprisingly impressive, there is little evidence for the long-term retention of explicit memories created in infancy, consistent with long-standing accounts of infantile amnesia (Pillemer & White, 1989). In research using an elicited-imitation paradigm, for example, Bauer has shown that 1-year-olds can correctly reproduce simple event sequences after delays of a week or more, and that even longer retention is possible when verbal prompts and contextual cues are provided (see Bauer, 1995, for a review). But in the absence of subsequent reinstatement, verbal elaboration and encoding (e.g., in the context of parent-child discourse), rehearsal, or other mnemonic aids, there is little evidence for the long-term retention of explicit memory beyond infancy (Bauer & Wewerka, 1995).

There are, however, other nondeclarative or implicit forms of early memory that may have more lasting impact. Myers and her colleagues have reported impressive evidence for the effects of experiences in the first year on the reactions of toddlers and preschoolers to experimental stimuli one or more years later (Myers, Clifton, & Clarkson, 1987; Myers, Perris, & Speaker, 1997; Perris, Myers, & Clifton, 1990). In follow-up assessments, evidence for implicit memory of earlier events was revealed in the greater interest of experimental children in toys that control children found uninteresting, and their greater comfort or willingness to remain in experimental settings that control children found distressing or uninviting. These responses occurred even though evidence for explicit memory of their early encounters with such toys or experimental settings by experimental children was much weaker or nonexistent, especially without additional cuing. These affective responses suggest that the experiences in infancy left a lingering impact, perhaps associated with the perceptual encoding of experimental stimuli or settings. Taking a different tack, Mandler (1988, 1992) has proposed that rudimentary conceptual precursors are established late in the first year in perceptually based "image-schemas" that enable infants to represent properties of spatial relations and movement, such as elementary conceptions of containment, support, force, self-motion, and agency that permit broader inferences about animacy and inanimacy, causality, and the physical properties of objects. If this formulation of early concepts is correct, it suggests that the perceptual structures associated with certain caregiver-related experiences (e.g., contingencies associated with distress relief), charged by the heightened emotion that such encounters entail, may provide a basis for later security-relevant representations of specific caregivers.

Although these formulations suggest that certain aspects of early experiences (particularly the affective dimensions of social experience) may be retained nondeclaratively, it is important not to exaggerate the conceptual foundations that may be associated with a secure or insecure attachment at the end of the first year. As noted, there is little reason to expect that explicit memories or self-referential representations are maintained from these experiences, and there is very little research on early forms of implicit memory or their associations with later representations. These findings suggest, however, that attachment-related experiences may leave a fairly rich network of emotional associations, based on social expectations and early conceptual primitives, with attachment figures and familiar caregiving routines. Better evidence for more explicit representational processes associated with attachment-related experiences, and their progressive link to autobiographical memory and other features of understanding of self and others, appears during the second and third years of life with the developing capacity to represent and reflect on experience.

Event Representation

One of the primary functions of working models is to enable individuals to forecast the outcomes of familiar events, especially those involving attachment figures. Building on rudimentary social expectations, initial working models of familiar experiences begin to emerge during the toddler years in the form of generalized event representations, or scripts. Whereas the social expectations of the first year are contextually bound to the familiar person, actions, or situation that evokes these expectations, generalized event representations enable broader conceptualizations (or models) of common experiences to permit the child's understanding and prediction of these events outside of the immediate context. From a functionalist perspective, the growth of such early prototypical knowledge structures enables the child's comprehension and anticipation of familiar experiences such as bedtime rituals, mealtime and other regular family routines, arrivals and departures from a babysitter, and similar events (Nelson, 1978; Nelson & Gruendel, 1981). There is evidence that the rudiments of scripted knowledge structures begin to develop by the end of the second year as young children strive to achieve a more inclusive representation of the events they encounter and to integrate them into broader knowledge systems; scripts increase in scope and complexity during the years following (Hudson, 1993; Nelson, 1989).

At the same time that scripts emerge as working models of recurrent events, young children also seek to understand and represent novel experiences. Early episodic memory is often built on generalized event representations, especially when young children are reporting experiences that are distinctive variations on familiar routines (e.g., a new babysitter). Although there are impressive reports of long-term retention of episodic events by 2-year-olds (Fivush, Gray, & Fromhoff, 1987), young children's reports of specific experiences are more commonly fragmented and fallible, especially when they are retained over long periods without opportunities for verbal reinstatement, cued recall, and other mnemonic assists. Their episodic memory may also be distorted by their confusion with generalized event knowledge, such that their recollections of dinner last night become confused with the general dinner script (Nelson, 1990; Nelson & Gruendel, 1981). As children reach the end of the preschool years, however, they can increasingly distinguish the unique features of specific experiences from the features shared with routine, and this improves the quality of their memory for particular experiences (Fivush & Hamond, 1990).

How do these capacities for event representation develop? Research by Nelson and her colleagues (1989, 1993a) indicates that the content, as well as the organization and structure, of early event representation is shaped not only by the child's prelinguistic and nonverbal representations of experience, but also by the verbal structure applied to them in parent-child discourse. In the context of shared conversations, beginning as soon as children can talk about events, parents help to review, reconstruct, and consolidate the young child's memory of generalized routines

as well as of specific experiences (Fivush, 1993, 1994; Fivush & Hamond, 1990; Hudson, 1990). Furthermore, parents often help children to anticipate future events, and the verbal structure they provide may help organize the child's representation of that experience as it subsequently occurs (Nelson, 1989, 1993a). Although young children assume an increasing role in shaping the content and course of conversational exchanges with parents later in the preschool years, caregivers remain important because of the structure, memory prompts, and interpretations they provide. In short, early event representation is a joint construction of parent and child through their shared dialogue.

These researchers have also found that parents vary in their procedures for eliciting and guiding a child's representations of past events. Some parents (labeled "pragmatic" or "repetitive") use short, directive conversations centered around specific questions to cue the child's memory search, while others (labeled "elaborative") provide considerable background and contextual information for the child in a shared retelling of past events. Some studies indicate that the offspring of elaborative mothers have a more complete and sophisticated representation of their past experiences, not only because of the direct impact of parent discourse but also because of the child's appropriation of the adult's narrative approach (Fivush & Fromhoff, 1988; Hudson, 1990; Reese & Fivush, 1993; see also Nelson, 1993a). But much more research on this issue is needed.

It appears, therefore, that young children achieve considerable skill at constructing working models (or scripts) of familiar event sequences that enable them to predict the course of everyday routines, even though their recall of specific experiences remains fairly limited (Hudson, 1990, reports on one 2-year-old who became distressed when she was given her bath before—rather than after—dinner because she thought this meant that she would not be fed that evening!). Given the functions of these prototypical representations for behavioral prediction, it is hardly surprising that current studies indicate that children focus on action sequences involving people, events, and settings, with little attention to the psychological dimensions of these experiences until greater facility with mental and emotional processes in others is achieved. However, with researchers' tendency to focus on rather prosaic routines (such as restaurant visits) in their studies of scripts, little is known about children's representation of prototypical experiences that involve greater emotional and relational complexity (e.g., distress relief). Young children can easily converse about emotions (Wellman, Harris, Banerjee, & Sinclair, 1995), and the affect that is associated with such event schemas may specially mark their significance to the young child as indicators of the reliability of parental solicitude. Indeed, the content of such event schemas may be organized around the child's representations of the emotion or relational propensities entailed in these recurrent experiences, because these representations encompass the meaning that such events have for the child. But these issues also await further exploration.

These studies indicate also that the content and organization of these early representations is significantly shaped by shared conversation with adults whose style of narrative prompting may influence not just the child's immediate recall, but also their emerging mnemonic capacities. The nature and extent of these stylistic differences remain to be fully explicated, however, and the relation between individual differences in parental scaffolding of child memory and other features of their care (e.g., sensitivity, defensiveness, emotionality) remains to be explored. Indeed, as Bretherton (1993) has suggested, the quality and coherence of adults' own representations of the past may influence how they guide and organize the child's event representations, although this hypothesis has not been systematically tested.

Autobiographical Memory

Despite these advances in event representation and episodic memory, the relation between these achievements and the growth of true autobiographical memory is uncertain. Nelson (1990, 1993a, 1993b) has argued that episodic memory and autobiographical memory are not, in fact, the same. The latter requires also the integration of episodic memories for specific life events into a narrative framework of meaning to the child, which typically does not begin to be constructed until after age 3. It is after this time, Nelson argues, that events assume functional significance for reasons besides guiding current action and forecasting outcomes because they are important for self-understanding and sharing one's experiences with others. Miller (1994; Miller, Fung, & Mintz, 1996; Miller, Mintz, Hoogstra, Fung, & Potts, 1992; Miller, Potts, Fung, Hoogstra, & Mintz, 1990) has likewise argued that autobiographical narrative (or "personal storytelling") is central to self-understanding because it permits the representation of personal continuity over time and enables the evaluative framework that personal accounts inevitably entail. It is in the progressive construction of autobiographical narrative

(or a working model of the self, in Bowlby's terminology) that episodic memory becomes encoded in a manner that permits its lasting retention as part of one's personal history. Similar views have been offered by Eder (1994), Hudson (1990), Snow (1990), and Welch-Ross (1995).

According to these formulations, autobiographical memory is not created solely by the child, but rather in shared discourse with adults. This is particularly important early in the preschool years when adult narrative provides the structure and interpretive framework that establishes the significance of particular events to the child. Consider, for example, the following brief conversation between a young child and his mother about an event earlier in the morning (Dunn & Brown, 1991, p. 97):

Child: Eat my Weetabix. Eat my Weetabix. Crying.
Mother: Crying, weren't you? We had quite a battle. "One more mouthful, Michael." And what did you do? You spat it out!
Child: (Pretends to cry)

Embedded within this short exchange provoked by the child's prompt are many things: a verbal structure for event representation, a summary of the causal sequence of events leading to the child's emotional reaction, a sharing of each partner's representation of the experience, and lessons about the self in the context of moral evaluation. These are likely to be common features of early parent-child discourse; indeed, virtually any shared exchange with a caregiver about personal experiences is likely to provide young children with important and diverse lessons about the self. Such narrative sharing of events is central to the construction of autobiographical memory, according to these researchers, because it helps to reinstate and consolidate episodic memory in a manner underscoring its personal significance, partly by permitting reflection outside of the immediate situation. That autobiographical memory has a later onset than episodic memory is attributable, in this view, to the fact that prior to the fourth year, children have a very limited capacity to hold in mind the sequence of events required for narrative construction, and they are also limited in their ability to coherently share these events in verbal discourse that requires the integration of multiple perspectives about a single event. Moreover, children younger than age 3 lack the metacognitive understanding that event knowledge depends on personal experience (fostering the capacity to mnemonically "tag" events as personally significant), nor do they possess an awareness of the mental experience of remembering the personal past (Welch-Ross, 1995). The psychological self-awareness that is required for autobiographical discourse is also an important developmental prerequisite (Howe & Courage, 1993). Not surprisingly, the onset of autobiographical memory converges with the period when infantile amnesia begins to wane and during which some recall of personal experiences in adulthood is possible (Nelson, 1993a, 1993b).

Further research on the links between episodic memory and autobiographical narrative is needed (see, e.g., Bauer, 1995), but this formulation has several important implications for the initial construction of working models of the self. First, it roots this constructive process in shared dialogue in which important lessons not only about the self but also about emotion, relationships, and morality are also provided. Thus the child's earliest self-representations are likely to incorporate the parent's moral evaluations, emotional inferences, dispositional attributions to the child (e.g., perceptions of the child as rambunctious, emotionally labile, cautious or impulsive, etc.), and other features of the adult's interpretation of the situations being recounted. In this regard, these emergent self-representations may also be influenced by the mutually responsive orientation between parent and child that may (or may not) be initially established by the attachment relationship. They also incorporate cultural values; Miller and her colleagues reported that Chinese and Chinese American mothers emphasize moralistic themes and the shame inherent in misbehavior in their shared recounting of their 2-year-olds' experiences. By contrast, Anglo-American mothers de-emphasize misbehavior and attribute it benignly to the child's spunk or mischievousness in shared discourse. In each case, mothers interpret the child's experience consistently with the broader values of their culture (Miller et al., 1990, 1996). Thus the earliest co-construction of self-understanding is infused with lessons about emotion, morality, and relationships drawn from parent-child conversations.

Second, this formulation implies that at younger ages, children are more likely to internalize representations of personal experiences directly from parental narrative, whereas in later years, a greater capacity for distinguishing firsthand from secondhand memories emerges (Miller et al., 1990; Nelson, 1990). This suggests that the earliest self-representations (e.g., of the self as loved and loveable) may be more significantly influenced by the parent's memory prompts, attentional focus, and interpretations and attributions of the child's personal and emotional

predispositions than later, when the child's capacities to compare and reflect on different representations of the same experience are stronger. The child's detection of dissonance between direct experience and parental construals of that experience may thus be a rather late-developing capacity. However, this provocative formulation remains substantially untested, and further exploration of the relation between firsthand and secondhand autobiographical representation is essential in light of attachment theoretic formulations concerning the relational origins of defensive exclusion and the formation of inconsistent working models of self that may have their origins in discordant internalized information concerning the self and one's propensities. Efforts to cope with dissonant sources of personally relevant information seem particularly likely to occur in young children's representations of affective and relational experiences, especially when the child's direct experience is discordant with parental construals of the experience, or when the event arouses strong emotion in the adult.

Finally, insofar as individual differences in parental narrative style influence general and specific event representation, they are also likely to affect the growth of autobiographical memory. Parents who provide elaborative rather than pragmatic narrative structure, or who respond sympathetically rather than evaluatively to the personal accounts of offspring, or who are comfortable rather than defensive in addressing emotional themes, each may influence the construction of the child's personal history in significant ways. These parental tendencies may be neither conscious nor deliberate influences, but they are likely to significantly influence the child's emergent self-representation and, possibly, the growth of defensive processes related to self-understanding, as noted above.

In light of these formulations, it is perhaps unsurprising—although contrary to longstanding views of the nature of young children's self-understanding—that preschoolers fairly early acquire traitlike self-representations that show some stability over time (Eder, 1989, 1990) and that are similar to their mothers' conceptions of them (see Eder, 1994; Eder & Mangelsdorf, 1997, for reviews). In summarizing these findings, Eder argues that young children's earliest self-concepts are based more on how they globally feel about themselves than on specific behavioral dispositions, such that a general sense of well-being facilitates more positive attributional self-reports as well as more positive and coherent autobiographical narratives (Eder, 1994; Eder & Mangelsdorf, 1997). These generalized feelings of well-being are likely, in turn, to derive from the manner in which parents interpret and structure the child's personal accounts and their other contributions to the development of a sense of personal history.

Understanding People

Apart from (but related to) children's emergent working models of self are working models of other people, particularly attachment figures, that are built on young children's growing knowledge of the psychological as well as behavioral propensities of others, and that contribute to an understanding of relationships. A grasp of the psychological qualities of other people is a complex developmental achievement with surprisingly early origins. The burgeoning research literature on developing theory of mind indicates that 3-year-olds appreciate the agentic, goal-directed quality of human behavior, but that a fuller appreciation of motivation in terms of belief as well as desire gradually emerges during the following year or two (see Astington, 1993; Bartsch & Wellman, 1995; Flavell & Miller, Ch. 17, Volume 2; C. Lewis & Mitchell, 1994, for recent reviews). In Wellman's (1990) terms, young children proceed from an early "desire psychology" (focused especially on wants, likes, intentions, needs, and emotions) to a more sophisticated "belief-desire psychology" (encompassing also thoughts, ideas, and understanding that may or may not accord with reality) in their understanding of others.

This has important implications not only for young children's understanding of other people, but also for their understanding of relationships because it permits more refined assessments of the sharing of intentions and goals, and later of beliefs, motives, and understandings, that can affect relational quality. It also enhances young children's appreciation of the associations among various mental states in others (e.g., the links between emotions and goal achievement, and later with beliefs), the processes entailed in reconciling conflicting mental states in relationships (e.g., through compromise, apology and conciliation, persuasion, humor, turn-taking), and, thus, the interactional skills required for relational success. Later, growth in the psychological understanding of others also permits the child to balance personal goals with those of others (even when the conflict between goals is emotionally charged), to appreciate how different relationships arise with partners who have different psychological attributes, and to conceive of relationships in triadic or quadratic rather than merely dyadic contexts (Harris, 1997). Insofar as relationships (distinct from interactions) require conceptions of

another's psychological attributes (Hinde & Stevenson-Hinde, 1987), the child's capacity to conceptualize (or create a working model of) a relationship is based on at least some of these representational achievements. It is no accident, therefore, that the early preschool years are characterized by Bowlby as the fourth, "goal-corrected partnership" stage of attachment development.

To be sure, conceptions of others' minds do not emerge de novo during the third and fourth years. Early foundations of theory of mind can be seen in the emergence toward the end of the first year, as noted earlier, of behaviors like social referencing, efforts to achieve joint visual attention, and protocommunicative acts that seem to reflect a dawning awareness that others have intentional, subjective orientations that can potentially be shared or influenced. The understanding of others as intentional and agentic can be seen more clearly in the second year when children use inferences concerning the speaker's intent to derive initial word meanings (Baldwin & Moses, 1994; Tomasello, 1995) and when their earliest verbal utterances include reference to desires, perceptions, and emotions in themselves and others, together with rudimentary inferences concerning their causes (Bretherton et al., 1981; Dunn, Bretherton, & Munn, 1987; Wellman et al., 1995; see also Bretherton & Beeghly, 1982). Indeed, Bloom (1993) has argued that early language acquisition is motivated by the effort to communicate about personal (intentional, emotional) states to other people. At the same time, an expanding empathic capacity probably reflects the toddler's growing awareness of the links among external events, emotional expressions, and underlying subjectivity in others (Thompson, in press-a; Zahn-Waxler & Radke-Yarrow, 1990), and the growth of pretend play exemplifies their shared manipulation of reality and pretense (Harris & Kavanaugh, 1993). All of these emergent capacities, present in some form by the second birthday, provide early conceptual foundations for the more advanced forms of psychological understanding in the years that follow.

How do these portentous achievements in psychological understanding arise? Among the various explanations from this extensive literature—including the growth of progressively more complex theory-like conceptual systems, an expanding capacity to simulate the psychological experiences of others through role taking, and various nativist accounts (see Astington, 1993; Astington & Gopnik, 1991, for reviews)—the importance of shared social activity is becoming increasingly emphasized. Beginning during the second year, and subsequently broadening in scope and complexity with the growth of linguistic skills, young children's encounters with family members provide important contexts for learning about themselves and others, whether these interactions concern parents' reactions to the emotions of offspring, their management of conflict between siblings, toddlers' assertions of their desires, needs, and intentions to others, early conversations about the causes of others' actions and feelings, shared play or humor, or the discussion, enforcement, and internalization of moral rules (Dunn, 1988, 1994). Such encounters provide a natural laboratory for associating manifest behaviors with underlying subjective conditions, comparing personal representations of experience with those reported by others, considering (and inquiring into) the causes of psychological states, testing rudimentary conceptions of psychological causality (through assertion, denial, teasing, comforting, and persuasion), and thus constructing a facilitated comprehension of mind through discourse and interaction with others (Harris, 1996).

Consistently, therefore, with emerging evidence that individual differences in children's conceptions of mind are related to the breadth of their social networks (Perner, Ruffman, & Leekam, 1994), considerable recent research has revealed how young children's psychological understanding is facilitated by shared activity with others during the third year, which is a period of burgeoning interest in physical and psychological causality (Bartsch & Wellman, 1995; Hood & Bloom, 1979). In Dunn's research, for example, 33-month-olds who conversed most with their mothers about feelings and causal relations were more proficient in affective perspective taking and false-belief tasks seven months later (Dunn, Brown, Slomkowski, Tesla, & Youngblade, 1991) and on measures of emotional understanding at age 6 (Brown & Dunn, 1996; see also Dunn, Brown, & Beardsall, 1991). Included in such conversations are not only discussions of the child's own feelings (especially in situations entailing conflict or concerning needs), but also accounts of others' experiences that children overhear and participate in, as well as direct instruction about emotion and its consequences (see Dunn & Brown, 1991, 1993; Fivush, 1994; Miller et al., 1990; Miller & Sperry, 1987). Denham (1993) has also found that the emotional competence of 32-month-olds (when alone with strangers or an older sibling) was based on how constructively their mothers responded to their emotional expressions; in another study, preschoolers' emotional understanding was predicted by measures of mothers' emotion language and emotional responsiveness during play (Denham, Zoller, &

Couchoud, 1994; see also Denham, Cook, & Zoller, 1992; Denham, Renwick-DeBardi, & Hewes, 1994). There is also evidence in this literature for the importance of conversations with siblings and peers in young children's psychological understanding, especially in contexts of conflict, humor, and shared pretense (Brown & Dunn, 1992; Brown, Donelan-McCall, & Dunn, 1996; Slomkowski & Dunn, 1992; Tesla & Dunn, 1992; Youngblade & Dunn, 1995), and the importance of pretend role play to children's emergent understanding of others' psychological states (Harris, 1994).

Taken together, young children's working models of attachment figures, and of relationships, are considerably broadened by the progressive growth of psychological understanding during the early preschool years, and new forms of relatedness and intimacy are possible as young children become capable of understanding and sharing intentions, goals, and emotions—and later, beliefs and understandings—with others. This growing human understanding emerges from maturing conceptual capacities in the context of social experiences at home that enable children to appropriate either balanced and well-elaborated or impoverished conceptualizations of mental states in others. Equally important, young children also appropriate from these experiences the network of attributions, motivational and emotional inferences, justifications and moral evaluations, and other aspects of social understanding that arise from a caregiver's life experiences, the adult's own representations of relationships, the demands of the family ecology, and cultural values. To the extent that, as noted earlier with respect to interpreting the Adult Attachment Interview, early family experiences provide diverse lessons in how to interpret, convey, and cope with strong emotion experienced in intimate relationships, the various shared family experiences of the early preschool years are powerful contexts for such lessons. Much more research is needed, however, to elucidate how lessons about relationships as well as about emotion and morality are conveyed by early family experiences, how these lessons are appropriated through the prism of a young child's growing psychological understanding of others, and how individual differences in relational predispositions are constructed from shared encounters with parents and siblings in the home. In short, while the theory of mind literature provides useful insights into children's growing understanding of others, attachment theoretic perspectives concerning individual differences in the understanding of persons in relationships remain to be explored.

Conceiving Relationships with Attachment Figures

In light of the significant conceptual advances outlined above, it is somewhat surprising that there has not been greater attention devoted to the final phase of attachment that Bowlby (1969/1982) characterized as the "goal-corrected partnership." This is when young children become capable of more refined inferences concerning the attachment figure's emotions, thoughts, and motives, more accurate prediction of the caregiver's predispositions, goals, and intentions, and better understanding of the reasons for the parent's actions, especially concerning how they are associated with the parent's goals and not merely the child's own (Harris, 1997; Marvin, 1977; Marvin & Greenberg, 1982). In a sense, a new kind of relationship becomes possible that is not merely an extension of the security derived from infant attachment, but broadens to incorporate shared (and potentially conflicting) understandings, attitudes of mutual cooperation and respect, and the growth of new strategies for resolving conflict when it occurs. It seems that during this fourth stage of Bowlby's theory, the developmental foundation for more enduring representations and understandings of self, others, and relationships is established, warranting greater research attention than this stage has yet received.

As a consequence of these advances in psychological understanding, the child's concepts of attachment figures in general and of particular caregivers (e.g., mother, father, day care teacher) become significantly more refined. From the network of "image schemas" and rudimentary social expectations that emerged from early infancy, the preschooler becomes capable of progressively incorporating a broader array of inferences concerning the caregiver's immediate and enduring psychological dispositions, and of revising and updating these inferences with further growth in psychological understanding. To the extent to which there is continuity between these earlier conceptual "primitives" (Mandler, 1992) and later concepts of specific attachment figures, it likely consists of a prerepresentational, emotional core of feelings of well-being, uncertainty, ambivalence, or other emotions that the child associates with repeated experiences with the attachment figure over time. But even this affective core may be transformed over time owing to changes in attachment security, as well as the growth of representational capacities that enable young children to understand many features of their relationships with caregivers that were previously imponderable. These include a beginning grasp of how the caregiver's responsiveness is affected by immediate circumstances (such as distraction, stress, or the demands of a younger sibling) as well as enduring dispositions, to perceive one caregiver's warmth and sensitivity in the context of relational experience with other attachment figures, and eventually to comprehend some of the causes underlying a caregiver's dispositions and characteristics. The lesson from the literature reviewed above is that the development of working models of specific caregivers is likely to be a dynamic, multidimensional process as young children begin to comprehend the affectional reliability of different attachment figures, or the same attachment figure under different conditions, in new ways. This may result in an array of relationship models, and of understandings of self-in-relationship, within the child's expanding conceptual framework.

Conclusions

It is apparent that Bretherton's (1990, 1991, 1993) portrayal of the preschool years as a crucial period for the development and elaboration of working models of self, attachment figures, and relationships is confirmed in the research on event representation, autobiographical memory, and the emergent psychological understanding of self and others. This research indicates that these developing representational systems are shaped not just by maturing intellectual skills, but also by the collaborative construction of understanding that occurs through the young child's shared activity with parents, siblings, and other partners. Whether they are engaged in the joint recollection of recent events in the child's life, discussions of a sibling's behavior and its causes, direct instruction in moral rules or emotional management, negotiation over conflicting desires or beliefs, or shared pretend play or humor, a young child's representations of self, others, and relationships take shape through the rich array of personal and cultural meanings embedded within these encounters. In this sense, as children become conceptually capable of the kinds of broader representational capacities on which working models are based, they appropriate the meaning inherent in these diverse social experiences, and early conceptions of self and others and emergent understandings of emotion, morality, and interpersonal interaction are created and refined.

In emphasizing the importance of these achievements in the toddler and preschool years, however, it is important not to neglect the significant representational advances that occur subsequently. As children enter the school years, for example, they become capable of metarepresentation that enables them to reflect more competently on their own mental processes, including the thoughts, beliefs, emotions, and other psychological phenomena that influence their behavior and that of others (Flavell, Miller, & Miller, 1993). While a more fully achieved metarepresentational capacity awaits adolescence, new kinds of relating (and of intimacy) become possible when the child becomes more competently self-reflective and can appraise various aspects of self-in-relation-to-others more thoughtfully and insightfully. Moreover, as children and adolescents increasingly strive for inclusively coherent and internally consistent belief systems, aspects of early working models may become more subject to deliberate examination and self-initiated modification as young people reflect on their consistency with other beliefs and with current relational experience, and as they acquire more sophisticated forms of interpersonal understanding (Kobak & Cole, 1996; Selman, 1980). This is likely to be true whether they are considering their understandings of themselves, parents, relationships in general, emotional experience, or diverse other psychological phenomena.

Changing relationships within the family are one catalyst for reexamining earlier working models of self and relationships with more mature self-reflection. As children and adolescents increasingly seek autonomy from and within family relationships, strive for instrumental competence in various areas, and seek peer acceptance outside the home, parental roles as attachment figures are broadened significantly to include roles as mentors, teachers, consultants, mediators, and providers of resources but also of maturity demands. These changes in parent-offspring roles and relationships must necessarily alter earlier working models of these caregivers, as well as of the relationships they share. Furthermore, as Ainsworth (1989) has noted, other psychosocial challenges of adolescence provide further catalysts to the growth of parent-child attachment relationships and self-understanding (see also Kobak & Sceery, 1988). It is easy to see how the representations of attachment experiences that adults provide in the Adult Attachment Interview have diverse developmental catalysts.

At times, normative but significant experiences in the family can directly challenge the integrity of previously established working models of close relationships that are directly relevant to the security-oriented attachment system as it was conceived by Bowlby. Cummings and Davies (1994; Davies & Cummings, 1994) have noted, for example,

that children's experience of marital conflict has profound implications for the emotional security they feel in the home. Their "emotional security hypothesis" proposes that children can maintain secure attachments to each parent while experiencing insecurity owing to parental conflict, but intense and persistent parental arguing can also undermine the security of parent-child relations and alter the working models of attachment figures, self, and relationships that initially may have had a secure foundation from infancy. Moreover, as Cummings and Davies have noted, emotional security in preschoolers and older children is not just a function of representations of a caregiver's personal accessibility and warmth, but is also affected by the intensity of interparental conflict that they observe at home, as well as the efficacy of their own efforts to resolve and cope with parental disagreements and the extent to which children perceive themselves as the focus of conflict. The "emotional security hypothesis" not only illustrates how subsequent family experience can alter the working models provisionally established earlier in life, but also how the representations of self and others that are pertinent to emotional security at later ages have multidimensional determinants.

The account that emerges from the literature, therefore, is of a system of representations that has affective foundations in the early social expectations contributing to attachment security, but that emerges more fully and changes dynamically with the flourishing of representational ability and experiences in family interaction and discourse in preschool and subsequent years. A secure attachment in a 1-year-old does not itself provide the conceptual foundation for the working models of self and others that later emerge, but it does provide an affective core of social expectations and conceptual primitives that potentially bias the infant's subsequent attachment-related representations. Attachment experiences in infancy also inaugurate a positive, mutually responsive orientation between parent and child (or a more competitive, conflictual, or distant relationship) that, if it continues into later years, also influences how children begin to perceive themselves, their attachment figures, and other people in general. In the years that follow, the working models about which Bowlby theorized are created and refined through diverse family encounters and conversations in which the young child's striving for understanding combines with the adult's efforts to impart knowledge, socialize, reassure, and otherwise guide the child's earliest understandings of self and others. In one sense, the sensitivity that initially contributed to a secure attachment in infancy later becomes an important resource for the parent's thoughtful and supportive scaffolding of the child's understanding of human motivation, emotion, self, and relationships that emerge through these shared encounters. In another sense, however, far more than sensitivity is entailed in the co-construction of early working models, because the parent's narrative approach, emotional style, beliefs about the child and about development, sociomoral values, personal history, and cultural background also make important contributions. Moreover, experiences in later years, including witnessing marital conflict and divorce in the family, the adolescent's agonized ruminations over the self, and subsequent marriage and childbearing in young adulthood, can profoundly reshape as well as deepen these representational systems.

One of the more interesting theoretical questions emerging from this account is how early-emerging representations of self and others are related to later representations. To many attachment theorists, as noted above, there is an underlying continuity between developing representations that may change in their structure or sophistication with increasing age but retain an underlying nonpropositional, affective core. But an alternative view—specifically, that discontinuity in understandings of self, others, and relationships is likely with new representational advances—also merits consideration. Stern (1985, 1989b) has noted, for example, that the emergence of a narrative awareness of self may provoke a substantial reorganization of the toddler's earlier, preverbal understanding of self and others formed from attachment relationships and other influences in early infancy. Similar reorganizations may occur with subsequent representational advances. Brodzinsky, Schechter, and Brodzinsky (1986), for example, describe a child whose easy acceptance, as a preschooler, of the news of his adoption was later superseded by his anguished worries, as a 7-year-old, about why he had been relinquished by his biological parents, whether they might change their minds, and other concerns that are only within the conceptual capabilities of an older child. These changes resulted not from new knowledge or new experiences, but rather from how a developing understanding of relationships and of self forced a reconstruction of earlier working models (see also Brodzinsky, Singer, & Braff, 1984). It is no wonder, therefore, that Bowlby (1973, Chap. 14) portrayed working models of self and attachment figures as slowly

constructed throughout childhood and adolescence, only becoming consolidated at the end of this long period of gestation.

Such a constructivist, neo-Vygotskian perspective on working models has assessment implications. Recently, researchers who have sought to assess young children's working models of self and attachment figures have reported that children who are securely attached (either in infancy or in contemporaneous assessments) produce more coherent and elaborated responses to pictures illustrating parent-child separations or a family photograph, or respond with emotionally more positive themes to semiprojective family story stems or puppet play scenarios (see Bretherton et al., 1990; Cassidy, 1988; Main et al., 1985; Shouldice & Stevenson-Hinde, 1992; Slough & Greenberg, 1990). But, as noted by Oppenheim and Waters (1995), it is difficult to determine, using such approaches, whether variations in the coherence or elaboration of children's discourse reflect the structure of internal representations (including the influence of defensive processes), as researchers often hypothesize, or rather parental narrative style and other discourse processes as they have been appropriated by the child. The long history of research using similar kinds of semiprojective measures confirms that children's responses can also be biased by family background, social desirability, efforts to please the interviewer, and other influences that are confounded with the kind of relational history that researchers hope to assess. It is essential, therefore, that new assessments of young children's working models of self and attachment figures are based not on face validity or consistency with attachment theory alone, but on antecedent validational research that carefully explores the determinants of children's story completion or puppet play responses.

The development of carefully validated measures of early representations is especially important to evaluating some of the more provocative hypotheses of attachment theory. These include the proposal that children with different attachment histories differentially interpret interpersonal experiences (e.g., with different perceptual sets, emotional predispositions, or attributional biases), selectively attend to different social phenomena, and perceive themselves differently based on the working models created by family experience (see Belsky, Spritz, & Crnic, 1996; Laible & Thompson, 1997, for example). In addition, systematic developmental study of the emergence of these representations in the context of family experience would usefully integrate attachment theoretical propositions with the burgeoning literature on conceptual growth and family interaction during the toddler and preschool years. Furthermore, with the budding interest of social psychologists into "relational schemas" and the interpretive and dispositional characteristics they entail (M. Baldwin, 1992), attachment theorists can usefully integrate their perspectives with those of researchers in this field. Such research might provide new insights into other accomplishments of sociopersonality growth, such as the emergence of the constituents of conscience, the growth of self-understanding, and the development of self-referent emotions, to which we now turn.

BECOMING A PERSON

To some moral philosophers, "personhood" is not inherent in human existence but is instead contingent on self-awareness, moral autonomy, and other constituents of distinctly human functioning. The initial years of life witness not only the growth of relationships that shape and infuse sociopersonality growth, but also the emergence of the constituents of personhood. These developmental processes are related, and are also embedded in the broader social ecology of early sociopersonality growth (Edwards, 1995).

Self-Awareness

Although it is common to describe the second year as a period of the "emergence of the self," developmental theorists are in accord that self-awareness is a more prolonged developmental process entailing different facets of the self (Cicchetti & Beeghly, 1990; Kopp & Brownell, 1991; M. Lewis & Brooks-Gunn, 1979; Sroufe, 1990; Stern, 1985; see Harter, Ch. 9, this Volume). The earliest forms of prerepresentational self-awareness are perceptual, affective, and agentic in quality, based on the experience of self as a causal agent in social and nonsocial events and as a reactor to environmental events, particularly those that are social in nature. These experiences in the first half-year of life contribute to a nascent distinction between self and "other" (broadly conceived) and the initial organization and integration of experience around an implicit, and fairly consistent, frame of reference. This distinction later becomes consolidated with the growth of interpersonal (or intersubjective) self-awareness by the end of the first year,

accompanying the dawning awareness of others (and oneself) as subjective entities with different and potentially shareable viewpoints, revealed in efforts to achieve joint attention, protocommunicative acts, and social referencing (see, however, Moore & Corkum, 1994, for a more conservative interpretation). By the middle of the second year, another form of self-awareness emerges with the growth of visual self-recognition, such as is revealed in the well-known rouge marking test, which may reflect a capacity for objective physical self-awareness as it relates to featural characteristics (M. Lewis, 1993; M. Lewis & Brooks-Gunn, 1979). Late in the second year, toddlers exhibit emerging indications of other representational forms of self-awareness, especially in their verbal self-referential behavior, efforts to assert competence and responsibility as autonomous agents (such as by refusing assistance on tasks and insisting on "doing it myself"), and the appearance of self-referent emotions that reflect an emerging capacity for self-evaluation (Bullock & Lutkenhaus, 1990; Heckhausen, 1988; Pipp, Fischer, & Jennings, 1987; Stipek, Gralinski, & Kopp, 1990). Later still is the growth of autobiographical self-representation in which characteristics of the self are associated with past and present experiences, become part of an ongoing personal narrative, and contribute to the growth of more complex and enduring self-referential belief systems associated with self-concept and self-esteem (Miller, 1994; Povinellli, 1995; Welch-Ross, 1995).

Consistent with classic theories of the self (Cooley, 1902; Mead, 1934), developmental theorists emphasize the growth of self-awareness as a socially constituted process. Although some early features of self-awareness may derive directly from the physical effects of environmental events (such as the perception of affordances in environmental activity and contingencies in object play; see Neisser, 1991), much of the organization and continuity of early experience that fosters self-awareness derives from experiences with caregivers. This is because the manner that parents structure the infant's experience organizes self-awareness (and embeds this nascent understanding in relational experience), and also because of the affective salience and reciprocity of interaction that fosters perceptions of agency in the young infant. Later in the first year, interactive activity enhances the growth of intersubjectivity that enables further growth in self-awareness. During the second and third years, moreover, parents highlight important associations for the child between actions and their consequences and the intentions and motives that underlie their behavior, and thus help offspring to understand themselves as autonomous agents. Caregivers also assume an important role in the content and organization of narrative discourse by which children recall and internalize recollections of their personal past and begin to organize them autobiographically. As noted above, parents are likely to integrate important lessons about morality, emotion, and relationships into young children's emergent understandings of the self. Indeed, as discussed below, significant elements of self-evaluation are based on a child's appropriation of parental standards of conduct and the internalization of the adult's evaluative reactions. Young children are therefore likely to incorporate into their emergent self-understanding the varieties of attributions, inferences concerning motives and abilities, and values that characterize how parents regard them. The growth of self-awareness is thus a socially constituted process entailing significant relational influences and cultural values about the meaning of each element of the self-system. Children perceive themselves through the lens of others' regard.

The intimate connections that exist among the development of self-awareness, emotional growth, and morality—and the importance of close relationships to their development—are further illustrated in the emergence of self-referential emotions during the second and third years. By the end of the second year and increasingly in the third, the simple joy of success becomes accompanied by looking and smiling to an adult and calling attention to the feat; the simple sadness of failure becomes accompanied either by avoidance of eye contact with the adult and turning away or by reparative activity and confession; and in response to conspicuous attention toddlers increasingly respond with smiling, gaze aversion, and self-touching (Barrett, Zahn-Waxler, & Cole, 1993; Cole, Barrett, & Zahn-Waxler, 1992; Heckhausen, 1988; Lewis, 1995; Stipek, 1995; Stipek, Recchia, & McClintic, 1992; Zahn-Waxler & Robinson, 1995). Although identifying these reactions as markers of pride, shame, guilt, and embarrassment requires a "rich interpretation" of multidetermined behavioral reactions, their developmental emergence coincident with the growth of other representational dimensions of psychological self-awareness suggests the growth of a capacity for self-referent emotion at this time (M. Lewis, Sullivan, Stanger, & Weiss, 1989; but see Schneider-Rosen & Cicchetti, 1991).

The emergence of self-referent emotions shortly after the second birthday requires not only a representational capacity for self-awareness but also an appreciation of standards of conduct and the ability to apply those standards to

an assessment of one's behavior (Kagan, 1981; S. Lamb, 1991; M. Lewis, 1993). Each of these capacities is a gradual achievement in the toddler and preschool years. Stipek (1995; Stipek et al., 1992) argues cogently that early in this developmental process, parental reactions are crucial. Parents commonly articulate behavioral standards and attributions of responsibility in their interactions with offspring during the second year, owing partly to their perceptions of the child's growing capacities for compliance and achievement (Dunn, 1987, 1988; Gralinski & Kopp, 1993). In their responses to their toddlers' successes or failures, moreover, parents not only provide approval or disapproval but explicitly link their reactions to the standards measuring success or failure, whether involving moral compliance (or disobedience) or attaining competence in various skills. Furthermore, their reactions also often entail the direct induction of a self-referent evaluation, whether through the generalized "Good girl!" or "Good boy!" in circumstances warranting pride or the more specific shame inductions enlisted by the Chinese American mothers studied by Miller and colleagues (1990, 1996). Thus, it is unsurprising that early behavioral indicators of pride, shame, and guilt are profoundly social as the child anticipates parental approval or disapproval, sometimes even prior to the completion of the act (Emde, Johnson, & Easterbrooks, 1987). Parental reactions to a toddler's successes and failures are especially important because the emotional attachment between parent and child enhances the significance of the parent's reactions, and this fosters the child's adoption of the parent's standards of conduct for self-evaluation. In this regard, although it is appropriate to view self-referent emotions as building on a young child's earliest representational self-awareness, it is also true that these powerful parental messages of agency and consequence and the salient self-referent emotions with which they are associated make the earliest experiences of shame, guilt, and pride important catalysts for further growth in self-understanding, especially as they become integrated into self-referent beliefs and autobiographical memory (Barrett, 1995; Dunn, 1987). In other words, self-referent emotions may build upon representational self-awareness, but their arousal also furthers self-understanding. With the growth of more sophisticated self-representations in subsequent years, young children's experiences of pride, shame, and guilt become more independent of immediate or anticipated parental reactions by the fourth year (Stipek et al., 1992) and become increasingly apparent in the implicit comparisons entailed in competitive performance (Heckhausen, 1984).

These considerations suggest that the parent-child relationship has many facets that contribute to the socialization of self-referent emotions, including the emotional bond that makes the parent's standards and expectations of success intrinsically meaningful to offspring, the parent's emphasis on compliance or achievement, and the diverse shared experiences in which issues of moral compliance/disobedience and achievement success/failure are encountered and discussed by parent and offspring. Because of the complexity of these parenting influences, variations in young children's proneness to each of these self-referent emotions are likely to be complexly determined; it may not only be the overcritical parent whose offspring are more prone to shame or guilt, for example, but also the parent whose warmth, praise, and valuation of achievement and compliance convey high expectations for the success of offspring (Barrett, 1995; Kathleen Cain, personal communication).

Empirical evidence for these developmental pathways in self-awareness is, of course, indirect and inferential, and the bidirectional relations between increasingly complex representational forms of self-awareness and the growth of moral understanding and compliance, attributions of success and failure, and self-referent emotions particularly merit greater research attention. Current research indicates, however, that diverse facets of the parent-child relationship provide important catalysts to these developmental processes and to individual differences in the achievement and moral behavior of young children.

Managing Self

The importance of parent-child interaction to the growth of self-awareness and self-referent emotion illustrates how the parent-child relationship changes during the transition from infancy to toddlerhood. Parents must be concerned not just with establishing the child's sense of security through sensitive responsiveness but also with encouraging competence, socializing behavior in accordance with cultural expectations, and, perhaps most important, promoting self-regulation while also respecting the child's needs for autonomy and the exploration of independent desires and goals. If all goes well, a secure attachment from infancy establishes a positive, mutually responsive relationship that (together with the continuing contributions of parental sensitivity) provides a foundation for the successful negotiation, encouragement, enforcement, and adoption of behavioral standards. Even so, the need for limit setting,

maturity demands, and compliance with parental requests, together with the toddler's expanding behavioral competencies and psychological sophistication, challenge the parent-child relationship and require a broader constellation of parenting goals, strategies, and skills than were needed in infancy.

Although parents increasingly monitor and regulate the behavior of offspring with the advent of self-produced locomotion (Campos et al., 1992), these efforts commence in earnest shortly after the first birthday, owing, in part, to increased concerns with safety, preserving family possessions, consideration for others, and, later in the third year, attention to socialization goals concerning self-care, manners, and family routines (Gralinski & Kopp, 1993). Not only does the content of behavioral standards increase in scope with the child's maturity but parental strategies for eliciting compliance also change, with an early reliance on physical intervention and distraction evolving to include greater use of explanation, bargaining, indirect guidance, and other nonassertive strategies that are often more successful in enlisting the child's cooperation (Belsky, Woodworth, & Crnic, 1996; Crockenberg & Litman, 1990; Kuczynski, Kochanska, Radke-Yarrow, & Girnius-Brown, 1987). In a sense, parents "up the ante" over time by broadening the range of behavioral expectations for young offspring and using enforcement strategies that increasingly enlist the child's cooperation.

They do so, however, in a manner that is concordant with the child's growing capacities for self-management. As Kopp (1982, 1987; Kopp & Wyer, 1994) has noted, important advances occur in the growth of behavioral self-control in the preschool years. These advances occur as young children develop more sophisticated capacities for remembering, representing, and generalizing behavioral standards, begin to conceive the self as an autonomous and responsible agent, become capable of self-initiated modifications of behavior resulting from remembered standards, and (later) can engage in more continuous and self-generated monitoring of their compliance in diverse circumstances. Kopp regards the second and third years as central to the development of self-control (with the more mature and autonomous skills of self-regulation an achievement of the fourth year). During this period, for example, young children begin to exhibit spontaneous monitoring and self-correction in task activity (Bullock & Lutkenhaus, 1988), and representational self-awareness may begin to incorporate social evaluations based on children's adherence to the behavioral standards of caregivers.

It is during this period, moreover, that prototypical event representations begin to incorporate standards of conduct concerning prohibited activity, daytime routines, and rules concerning others' feelings and possessions. Consistent with this developmental outline, young children tend to show greater compliance with behavioral standards as they reach the preschool years. However, they also show a greater tendency to refuse before they comply and to negotiate, compromise, and exhibit other indicators of self-assertion. This portrayal of a greater tendency to comply and to assert autonomy both challenges and is consistent with popular portrayals of the "Terrible Twos" (Gralinski & Kopp, 1993; Kopp, 1992; Kuczynski & Kochanska, 1990; Kuczynski et al., 1987; Vaughn, Kopp, & Krakow, 1984).

Capacities for self-management develop, therefore, in a context of incrementing behavioral expectations by parents that are both responsive to and catalysts for the child's increasing self-control. Parents "up the ante" as their offspring are capable of greater compliance and, in doing so, they also foster changes in children's self-evaluative standards. However, as the constituents of self-regulation mature, parent-child interaction is also mutually shaped by the confrontation of parental efforts to noncoercively enlist the child's cooperation with the child's assertion of his or her autonomy. At the same time that parents enlist negotiation, explanation, and appeals to self-image as motivators of compliance (recognizing the intrinsic resources for self-control that have emerged in offspring), their children increasingly use such appeals as opportunities to exercise defiance as well as cooperation. Taken together, behavioral compliance becomes a developmentally calibrated joint negotiation between parents and offspring, involving the mutual accommodations of each partner to the other.

A young child's efforts to manage the self derive not just from the incentives and pressures of parental standards. They derive also from the child's striving for competence and well-being. The growth of emotion regulation illustrates how such intrinsic incentives—the maintenance of emotional stability, facilitating social interaction, fostering problem-solving competence, and similar goals—also stimulate the emergence of strategies of self-management (Kopp, 1989; Thompson, 1990b, 1994). Although infants and toddlers rely primarily on the assistance of caregivers for the regulation of emotion, there is increasing evidence of emotion self-regulation after age 2. This is apparent when young children seek the comfort of a caregiver, shift attention away from distressing events (or toward pleasurable events),

exhibit self-soothing, verbalize self-reassurance, and show other instrumental acts to alter arousing circumstances (Bridges & Grolnick, 1995; Grolnick, Bridges, & Connell, 1996; Thompson, 1990b; but see Braungart & Stifter, 1991). To be sure, even young infants exhibit behaviors (such as gaze aversion and self-stimulation) that have the consequence of modulating their arousal, but emotion self-regulation requires the deliberate enlistment of strategies of self-control to achieve desired goals, and this is a more advanced achievement. Consistent with the developmental formulations presented above, capacities for emotion self-regulation become more evident during the early preschool years.

The expected associations among emotion self-management, social competence, and healthy psychosocial well-being have made the growth of emotion self-regulation one of the more vigorous areas of theoretical inquiry in recent years (see contributors to Eisenberg & Fabes, 1992; Fox, 1994; Garber & Dodge, 1991). However, studying developing capacities for emotion self-management is a difficult research task because it requires not just the measurement of behaviors that have a purported function for emotion regulation, but also documenting their efficacy in the circumstances in which children are observed (e.g., Stifter & Braungart, 1995). This task is complicated because the goals that young children have for managing their emotions can be diverse, including not only the maintenance (or restoration) of good feelings but also creating (or restoring) good relations with peers, provoking a helpful response from others, and resisting perceived wrong or preventing its recurrence. Moreover, the behavioral strategies of emotion management by which these goals are advanced are also complex and depend on the values of social partners (e.g., how peers or adults respond to certain emotional displays), situational demands, and cultural beliefs about emotion and its public expression. Thus, individual differences in emotion regulation are not necessarily manifested in whether young children are competent peer partners or cooperate with parents (although they may), but depend on the contextual demands and incentives that children perceive and their goals for managing emotion. At times, competent emotion regulation may be best observed in the young child who loudly protests a bully's provocations when adults are nearby (but not when they are absent), or who succeeds in cajoling special favors from grandparents (but does not try the same strategies with parents). The complexity of these considerations is underscored by studies from the field of developmental psychopathology, which show that when they are faced with the potentially overwhelming emotional demands of a depressed caregiver or a maritally conflicted home, young children enlist strategies of emotion management that reflect accommodations to diverse and sometimes conflicting emotional goals; these strategies may buffer them from some stresses while leaving them vulnerable to others (Thompson & Calkins, 1996; Thompson, Flood, & Lundquist, 1995).

This functionalist analysis offers a number of unexpected directions for research on the growth of emotion regulation, including examination of children's developing understanding of their own emotional experiences, the goals underlying their efforts to manage emotion, and how these are influenced by the values of caregivers and others in the child's world (Thompson, 1994). In addition, research in this area would benefit from a focus on the dynamic features of emotion—such as the intensity, lability, persistence, latency, and range of emotional reactions—that are more often influenced by emotion self-regulatory efforts than is the discrete emotion itself (Thompson, 1990b, 1994). In other words, young children and older individuals more often seek to modify the intensity or persistence of negative emotions, or delay their onset, than to transform the valence of their arousal, partly because altering the dynamics of emotion is easier to achieve and can have satisfactory results. Consequently, research on emotion regulation should encompass these dynamic properties of emotional arousal as outcome measures. More broadly, because efforts to manage the self are forged in social contexts, greater attention to the social incentives and catalysts to the growth of behavioral and emotional self-control is warranted.

Emerging Conscience

Conscience concerns the internal regulation of behavior according to standards of conduct. According to Kochanska and Thompson (in press), the early rudiments of conscience are built on many of the constituent processes discussed above. These include the positive, mutually responsive parent-child relationship that may arise out of a secure attachment in infancy, providing the basis for the young child's receptiveness to the parent's communication and enforcement of values. They include also the early growth of event representation by which standards of conduct are embedded in prototypical knowledge structures, providing the basis for their incorporation into the

representation of diverse experiences and the prediction of behavioral outcomes when rules are obeyed and disobeyed. Rudiments of conscience are also built upon the onset and growth of social referencing by which behavioral events are imbued with emotional meaning and through which distal communication concerning disapproved or approved acts can occur (Emde & Buchsbaum, 1990). Other early constituents of conscience include the growth of representational forms of self-awareness that provide a foundation for a young child's awareness of personal agency and responsibility; the child's emergent sensitivity to standards (of wholeness, integrity, competence) and their violation (Kagan, 1981; Kochanska, Casey, & Fukumoto, 1995); and the growth of capacities for self-management and self-regulation. In contrast to traditional theories of moral development that have emphasized either the cognitive skills required for mature moral judgment or the amoral, self-interested orientation of young children to behavioral compliance, contemporary students of early conscience have focused on the variety of relational, affective, and motivational processes that contribute to distinctly nonegocentric features of initial moral development (S. Lamb, 1991).

In contrast to a traditional theoretical focus on parental discipline practices, moreover, other elements of early parent-child relationships may also contribute to conscience development (Kochanska, 1993; Kochanska & Thompson, in press). Hoffman's (1970, 1983) now classic formulation portrays the internalization of parental values in terms of the arousal generated by the discipline encounter and its consequences for the child's memory of its meaning. As he notes, parental discipline must be accompanied by some level of discomfort or anxiety to signal the importance of the parent's values and to orient and motivate the child, but the heightened distress generated by power-assertive methods may interfere with the child's processing of the parent's message and thus undermine internalization. By contrast, discipline practices that de-emphasize parental power and instead enlist rational explanations evoke more optimal levels of arousal that permit storage of the parental message in semantic memory with a justification for compliance. Although a depth of processing approach may offer a better explanation of memory and moral internalization than a focus on semantic or episodic storage—both because it better represents the effects of parental discipline procedures on memory and because it is more in concert with current work in cognitive sciences—Hoffman's formulation nevertheless provides a good foundation for examining the early growth of conscience. This is especially true when it is viewed in the context of a broader network of family influences (e.g., Dunn, Brown, & Maguire, 1995). For example, parental use of alternative control strategies, such as avoiding a discipline encounter by proactively structuring circumstances or providing anticipatory guidance, can also foster the child's cooperation (Belsky, Woodworth, & Crnic, 1996; Holden, 1983). A young child's receptiveness to parental values is influenced not only by parental reactions to misbehavior but also by the broader emotional tone of their relationship, as attachment theory predicts (Kochanska & Aksan, 1995). And interactions with siblings as well as with parents provide catalysts to early moral understanding, especially in relation to rights, possessions, and property (Dunn & Munn, 1987; Slomkowski & Dunn, 1992; Tesla & Dunn, 1992).

Moreover, parental values are also conveyed in other contexts besides discipline situations. Moral lessons are implicit as well as explicit when parents assist young children in the shared recounting of the day's events, discuss prior instances of misbehavior (such as the Weetabix vignette quoted above), or explain their response to a sibling's misconduct (Dunn, 1987, 1988; Miller et al., 1990, 1996). Moral socialization in contexts outside of the discipline encounter may have a more significant impact on internalization because in these circumstances, diminished emotional arousal and greater opportunities for reflection might enhance a young child's understanding of, memory for, and receptivity to moral lessons. Moreover, to the extent that a deeper processing of the adult's moral message is facilitated when a parent combines warmth with rational explanations during the discipline encounter, the same parental characteristics are even more likely to foster internalization of the adult's values outside of the discipline encounter. Conversely, a parent who uses threats or denigrating or demeaning speech when discussing prior misconduct will likely inhibit the child's retention of the adult's values in the same way that affectively arousing power assertion does during the discipline encounter itself. The adult's socioemotional demeanor during subsequent discussions of misconduct is important also because the content and style of the parental message may influence how children understand themselves and the impact of their misbehavior on close relationships. In short, early conscience development is fostered not only by parental discipline practices, but by many other contexts of parent-child interaction.

Kochanska (1991, 1993, 1995) has proposed that the effects of discipline practices are also moderated by a young child's temperament, finding in two studies that maternal use of nonassertive guidance and "gentle discipline" was associated with moral internalization only for toddlers who were temperamentally more fearful. Their proneness to fear and anxiety perhaps made nonpunitive discipline practices sufficiently arousing to permit effective internalization. By contrast, security of attachment was the most significant predictor of internalization for relatively fearless toddlers, which Kochanska (1995) portrays as an alternative pathway to moral internalization that builds on the positive, mutually cooperative parent-child relationship that a secure attachment can inaugurate. Moral internalization was fostered for these children not by the arousal of anxiety or distress in the discipline encounter (which was made more difficult by their temperamental fearlessness), she has argued, but rather by the young child's responsive receptivity to the parent's moral lessons.

Such experiences provide the foundation for conscience. With further growth in representational skills, young children's grasp of behavioral standards becomes more multifaceted. Rules that were initially tied to specific situations may now be generalized to novel circumstances, and a growing awareness of causal relations enables children to better understand the meaning of many behavioral standards and their applications elsewhere. Furthermore, growth in the understanding of others' emotions, desires, and thoughts permits a representational grasp of the humanistic basis for behavioral standards relevant to another's well-being. With these advances, the child becomes more genuinely morally agentic.

Although research on early conscience emphasizes, consistent with traditional developmental formulations, moral development as the internalization of parental standards, two further amendments to this approach seem warranted in view of contemporary research. First, given the growing evidence that conscience emerges not only from the prohibitive orientation of parental discipline but also from the incentives provided by a harmonious, mutually cooperative parent-child relationship, a portrayal of moral development that underscores the appropriation of norms and standards from shared activity in the family may be as well-suited to conscience development as is the traditional internalization formulation. In this complementary alternative, the growth of moral understanding arises not solely (or even primarily) from how young children respond to parental behavior in the discipline encounter, but from the varieties of interactive experiences—some focused primarily on moral compliance, but many entailing conversation, storytelling, pretend play, and other non-moralistic activities—from which parents and offspring jointly create shared understandings of behavioral standards, moral values, and compliance. By underscoring the multifaceted interactive contexts from which early conscience develops, such an approach highlights how much parents and offspring mutually create the moral environment they share in a family.

Second, and consistent with the first, the importance of an independent, humanistic basis for early conscience, based on a young child's vicarious response to others' emotions, should not be neglected (Hoffman, 1983). As 1-year-olds begin to grasp the associations among external events, emotional expressions, and underlying subjectivity in others late in the second year (Zahn-Waxler & Radke-Yarrow, 1990; Zahn-Waxler, Radke-Yarrow, Wagner, & Chapman, 1992), an understanding enhanced by subsequent linguistic access to family discourse about emotion and later growth in theory of mind, conscience development becomes rooted also in their awareness of the human consequences of wrongdoing (Thompson, 1987, in press). Although empathy is a far more motivationally complex emotional response than is often appreciated, students of conscience development are wise to attend to its potential contributions to early conscience.

BACK TO THE FUTURE

Contemporary research in early sociopersonality development is motivated by enduring questions framed within new perspectives. These enduring questions—pertaining to the formative influence of early mother-infant attachment, the bases for continuity in sociopersonality functioning from infancy to later years, and the catalysts for the development of the initial self—have provoked the interest of developmental scientists from before the dawning of psychology. Contemporary work on these questions is enlivened, however, by the insights afforded by new understandings of the nature of cognition and representation in the early years, new formulations concerning the role of emotion in sociopersonality functioning, new research insights into the nature and functioning of close relationships in the early years, and, of course, insightful, new research methodologies.

There is every reason to expect that these enduring questions will remain as central to future research on early

sociopersonality development as they have been to the past, but one might hope that when the next edition of the *Handbook* is written, some of the following advances will have occurred in theory and research.

First, it is essential that developmental scientists move beyond the rather general formulation that early relationships provide a foundation for early sociopersonality development toward greater insight into the breadth of relational processes, partners, and activities that are developmentally influential. This review has highlighted the great variety of activities shared by young children with family members that have differentiated consequences for sociopersonality functioning. They include the ways that parents interpret and respond to the socioemotional signals of offspring, the emotional cuing of social referencing, the conflict experienced by young siblings, the discussions of the day's activities by parents and offspring, and the emotional encounters among family members that provide lessons about how to interpret, convey, and cope with strong emotion in intimate relationships. Conceived within the rather narrow (but developmentally catalytic) social ecology of the family, researchers are only beginning to describe the relationship-specific influences of various family members on emergent emotion management, moral judgment, self-understanding, and other aspects of sociopersonality development; understanding continuities and changes in these relational influences over time is another formidable challenge for the future (Dunn, 1993). Conceiving the ecology of early development more broadly, however, it is also important to understand how social partners outside of the family, including child care teachers, grandparents, and peers, have direct effects on early sociopersonality functioning and also indirectly influence the child's growth through their impact on the broader family system. Most important, however, is the need for new theoretical formulations that explain how relational experience is developmentally provocative. The formulations of attachment theory have been heuristically powerful and remain influential, although (as Bowlby noted) they focus on only one dimension of parent-child relationships and thus may neglect other aspects that emerge in importance after infancy. The neo-Vygotskian approach offered in this chapter that describes sociopersonality growth in terms of the appropriation of meaning from the shared activity of the child with more mature partners, and the importance of the adult's sensitive scaffolding of manageable developmental challenges within such activity, is another potentially useful formulation, especially as it emphasizes the joint construction of understanding. But there are other potentially valuable formulations awaiting exploration.

Second, understanding the processes accounting for continuity and change in individual differences in sociopersonality functioning from infancy into later years remains a central concern, but this traditional question requires more nuanced renditions to yield more insightful answers. Attachment research has been most helpful in revealing the complicated subtexts underlying the apparently straightforward study of continuity in sociopersonality development. This literature shows that individual differences are maintained not only by emerging personality and representational processes associated with social expectations, self-understanding, and working models of relationships, but also by continuity in relational experience and support over time—and that the dynamic between these internal and extrinsic contributors to continuity changes ontogenetically. It indicates that, except in extreme circumstances, early influences are not deterministic but rather predispositional, with the strength of their effects on later behavior moderated by a variety of factors that may subsequently enhance, undermine, or alter their relation to hypothesized consequences. It reveals the critical need for a well-defined theory to identify the expected associations between early influences (such as attachment security) and specific later outcomes in light of continuity and change in intervening variables, the role of protective and risk factors in the broader social ecology, the complex relations between persons and their environments that unfold ontogenetically, and the role of the developing organism as a lifelong construer as well as recipient of early experience. The attachment literature also reveals the importance of understanding the constituents of change as well as continuity in sociopersonality growth instituted not only by significant upheavals in a child's life experiences but also by the more normative changes that occur in relational experience, self-reflection, and the life transitions that occur in childhood, adolescence, and young adulthood. All of these issues take on added importance for future study in light of the remarkably divergent patterns of continuity in attachment processes revealed in the contemporary literature, with some studies indicating minimal consistency in the security of attachment over periods as little as six months (see Table 2.3) and others finding striking consistency in individual patterns of adaptation over many years (Main & Cassidy, 1988; Wartner et al., 1994). Understanding the

bases for these variant patterns of change and continuity in sociopersonality functioning will require the construction of more elaborate developmental formulations than currently exist.

Third, the importance of integrating the developmental formulations of students of cognitive and representational development with prevailing formulations from sociopersonality theory was thoughtfully articulated more than a decade ago by Maccoby (1984), but remains a pressing concern. Depending on their interests, scientists studying children of the same age sometimes offer such strikingly different portrayals of young children's thoughts, representations, and conceptual capabilities that an integrated portrayal of early development seems impossible. To be sure, Harris (1994) has cogently argued that these alternative portrayals of early cognition and representation can urge theorists toward broader, more inclusive formulations, such as how attachment theorists' regard for the role of emotion in emergent representation should be considered carefully by students of early theory of mind. But this integrative effort can be encumbered by unshared metatheoretical assumptions about the developing person, different research methodologies, and widely different interpretations of the same empirical evidence. Yet because researchers are presumably seeking to understand common attributes of the conceptual abilities of young children, whether children are responding to an attachment story stem or a theory of mind task, the coordination of research questions and integration of research insights—possibly in the context of collaborative theoretical and empirical inquiry (see Oppenheim & Waters, 1995, for an example)—seems critical.

Finally, attention to method development is essential to progress in this field. With the move to representation and growing interest in the conceptual foundations of self-understanding, morality, and emotion regulation, students of sociopersonality development face daunting challenges in their efforts to assess the emergent understandings of very young children, and recent years have witnessed the development of potentially insightful methodological strategies for doing so. But before these strategies are enlisted into new research initiatives, careful validational work is required to identify and distinguish alternative influences on young children's responses to innovative research procedures to avoid potential misinterpretation of the meaning of their behavior. The need for foundational validational research is equally true of other domains of research reviewed in this chapter, whether concerning the development of new attachment classifications in the Strange Situation, new procedures for eliciting self-referential emotion in young children, or new strategies for revealing attachment representations in adolescents and young adults. Although validity studies are not as theoretically provocative (nor as professionally exciting) as exploring new research terrains, contemporary scholars are wise to remember how important the early years of validating the Strange Situation were to the prominence of attachment research in the decades that followed.

The vitality of this research agenda highlights the continuing importance of the traditional questions guiding the study of early sociopersonality development, especially as they are enlivened by contemporary insights into the mysteries of early sociopersonality growth.

ACKNOWLEDGMENTS

In preparing this chapter, I am grateful to a number of colleagues who have been willing to discuss these issues either in direct conversation or in the context of my "meandering ponderings" via e-mail: Patricia Bauer, Jay Belsky, Kathleen Cain, James Chisholm, Paul Harris, Russell Isabella, Grazyna Kochanska, Michael Lamb, Sarah Mangelsdorf, Douglas Teti, Judy Ungerer, and Marinus Van IJzendoorn. I am also grateful for the insightful comments of Jay Belsky, Mark Cummings, Paul Harris, Michael Lamb, Eleanor Maccoby, Alan Sroufe, and Brian Vaughn on earlier versions of this chapter. Although I have sought to identify major contributors to each of the topics reviewed here, appreciative citations to all relevant papers would have turned this review into an annotated bibliography; consequently, I offer an apology to respected colleagues whose work is not noted explicitly, but who have been influential nonetheless.

REFERENCES

Ainsworth, M. D. S. (1963). The development of infant-mother interaction among the Ganda. In B. M. Foss (Ed.), *Determinants of infant behavior* (Vol. 2, pp. 67–104). New York: Wiley.

Ainsworth, M. D. S. (1967). *Infancy in Uganda: Infant care and the growth of love.* Baltimore: Johns Hopkins University Press.

Ainsworth, M. D. S. (1973). The development of infant-mother attachment. In B. Caldwell & H. Ricciuti (Eds.), *Review of child development research* (Vol. 3, pp. 1–94). Chicago: University of Chicago Press.

Ainsworth, M. D. S. (1989). Attachments beyond infancy. *American Psychologist, 44,* 709–716.

Ainsworth, M. D. S., Bell, S. M., & Stayton, D. J. (1971). Individual differences in Strange-Situation behaviour of one-year-olds. In H. R. Schaffer (Ed.), *The origins of human social relations* (pp. 17–57). London: Academic Press.

Ainsworth, M. D. S., Bell, S. M., & Stayton, D. J. (1974). Infant-mother attachment and social development: Socialisation as a product of reciprocal responsiveness to signals. In M. P. M. Richards (Ed.), *The integration of the child into a social world* (pp. 99–135). Cambridge, England: Cambridge University Press.

Ainsworth, M. D. S., Blehar, M. C., Waters, E., & Wall, S. (1978). *Patterns of attachment.* Hillsdale, NJ: Erlbaum.

Ainsworth, M. D. S., & Eichberg, C. (1991). Effects on infant-mother attachment of mother's unresolved loss of an attachment figure, or other traumatic experience. In C. Murray Parkes, J. Stevenson-Hinde, & P. Marris (Eds.), *Attachment across the life cycle* (pp. 160–183). London: Routledge & Kegan Paul.

Ainsworth, M. D. S., & Wittig, B. A. (1969). Attachment and exploratory behavior of one-year-olds in a Strange Situation. In B. M. Foss (Ed.), *Determinants of infant behaviour* (Vol. 4, pp. 111–136). London: Methuen.

Andrews, M. W., & Rosenblum, L. A. (1988). Relationship between foraging and affiliative social referencing in primates. In J. E. Fa & C. H. Southwick (Eds.), *Ecology and behavior of food-enhanced primate groups* (pp. 247–268). New York: Liss.

Andrews, M. W., & Rosenblum, L. A. (1991). Attachment in monkey infants raised in variable- and low-demand environments. *Child Development, 62,* 686–693.

Andrews, M. W., & Rosenblum, L. A. (1993). Assessment of attachment in differentially reared infant monkeys *(Macaca radiata):* Response to separation and a novel environment. *Journal of Comparative Psychology, 107,* 84–90.

Andrews, M. W., & Rosenblum, L. A. (1994). The development of affiliative and agonistic social patterns in differentially reared monkeys. *Child Development, 65,* 1398–1404.

Arend, R., Gove, F. L., & Sroufe, L. A. (1979). Continuity of individual adaptation from infancy to kindergarten: A predictive study of ego-resiliency and curiosity in preschoolers. *Child Development, 50,* 950–959.

Astington, J. W. (1993). *The child's discovery of the mind.* Cambridge, MA: Harvard University Press.

Astington, J. W., & Gopnik, A. (1991). Theoretical explanations of children's understanding of the mind. *British Journal of Developmental Psychology, 9,* 7–31.

Bakermans-Kranenburg, M., & Van IJzendoorn, M. (1993). A psychometric study of the Adult Attachment Interview: Reliability and discriminant validity. *Developmental Psychology, 29,* 870–879.

Baldwin, D. A., & Moses, L. J. (1994). Early understanding of referential intent and attentional focus: Evidence from language and emotion. In C. Lewis & P. Mitchell (Eds.), *Children's early understanding of mind* (pp. 133–156). Hove, England: Erlbaum.

Baldwin, D. A., & Moses, L. J. (1996). The ontogeny of social information-processing. *Child Development, 67,* 1915–1939.

Baldwin, M. W. (1992). Relational schemas and the processing of social information. *Psychological Bulletin, 112,* 461–484.

Barrett, K. C. (1995). A functionalist approach to shame and guilt. In J. P. Tangney & K. W. Fischer (Eds.), *Self-conscious emotions* (pp. 25–63). New York: Guilford Press.

Barrett, K. C., Zahn-Waxler, C., & Cole, P. M. (1993). Avoiders vs. amenders: Implications for the investigation of guilt and shame during toddlerhood? *Cognition and Emotion, 7,* 481–505.

Bartsch, K., & Wellman, H. M. (1995). *Children talk about the mind.* New York: Oxford University Press.

Bates, J. E., & Bayles, K. (1988). Attachment and the development of behavior problems. In J. Belsky & T. Nezworski (Eds.), *Clinical implications of attachment* (pp. 253–299). Hillsdale, NJ: Erlbaum.

Bates, J. E., Maslin, C. A., & Frankel, K. A. (1985). Attachment security, mother-child interaction, and temperament as predictors of behavior-problem ratings at age three years. In I. Bretherton & E. Waters (Eds.), Growing points of attachment theory and research. *Monographs of the Society for Research in Child Development, 50*(1/2, Serial No. 209), 167–193.

Bateson, P. (1994). The dynamics of parent-offspring relationships in mammals. *Trends in Ecology and Evolution, 9,* 399–403.

Bauer, P. J. (1995). Recalling past events: From infancy to early childhood. In R. Vasta (Ed.), *Annals of child development* (Vol. 11, pp. 25–71). London: Jessica Kingsley.

Bauer, P. J., & Wewerka, S. S. (1995). One- to two-year-olds' recall of events: The more expressed, the more impressed. *Journal of Experimental Child Psychology, 59,*475–496.

Beekman, D. (1977). *The mechanical baby.* New York: New American Library.

Beller, E. K., & Pohl, A. (1986, April). *The Strange Situation revisited.* Paper presented at the biennial meeting of the International Conference on Infant Studies, Beverly Hills, CA.

Belsky, J. (1984). The determinants of parenting: A process model. *Child Development, 55,* 83–96.

Belsky, J. (1988). The "effects" of infant day care reconsidered. *Early Childhood Research Quarterly, 3,* 235–272.

Belsky, J., & Braungart, J. M. (1991). Are insecure-avoidant infants with extensive day-care experience less stressed by and more independent in the Strange Situation? *Child Development, 62,* 567–571.

Belsky, J., Campbell, S. B., Cohn, J. F., & Moore, G. (1996). Instability of infant-parent attachment security. *Developmental Psychology, 32,* 921–924.

Belsky, J., & Cassidy, J. (1994). Attachment: Theory and evidence. In M. Rutter & D. Hay (Eds.), *Development through life* (pp. 373–402). Oxford, England: Blackwell.

Belsky, J., Garduque, L., & Hrncir, E. (1984). Assessing performance, competence, and executive capacity in infant play: Relations to home environment and security of attachment. *Developmental Psychology, 20,* 406–417.

Belsky, J., & Isabella, R. (1988). Maternal, infant, and social-contextual determinants of attachment security. In J. Belsky & T. Nezworski (Eds.), *Clinical implications of attachment* (pp. 41–94). Hillsdale, NJ: Erlbaum.

Belsky, J., Pensky, E., & Youngblade, L. (1990). Childrearing history, marital quality and maternal affect: Intergenerational transmission in a low risk sample. *Development and Psychopathology, 1,* 291–304.

Belsky, J., & Rovine, M. (1987). Temperament and attachment security in the Strange Situation: An empirical rapprochement. *Child Development, 58,* 787–795.

Belsky, J., & Rovine, M. (1988). Nonmaternal care in the first year of life and the security of infant-parent attachment. *Child Development, 59,* 157–167.

Belsky, J., & Rovine, M. (1990). Q-sort security and first-year nonmaternal care. In W. Damon (Editor-in-Chief) & K. McCartney (Ed.), *Child care and maternal employment: A social ecology approach.* (pp. 7–22). San Francisco: Jossey-Bass.

Belsky, J., Rovine, M., & Taylor, D. G. (1984). The Pennsylvania Infant and Family Development Project: III. The origins of individual differences in infant-mother attachment: Maternal and infant contributions. *Child Development, 55,* 718–728.

Belsky, J., Spritz, B., & Crnic, K. (1996). Infant attachment security and affective-cognitive information processing at age 3. *Psychological Science, 7,* 111–114.

Belsky, J., Steinberg, L., & Draper, P. (1991). Childhood experience, interpersonal development, and reproductive strategy: An evolutionary theory of socialization. *Child Development, 62,* 647–670.

Belsky, J., Woodworth, S., & Crnic, K. (1996). Trouble in the second year: Three questions about family interaction. *Child Development, 67,* 556–578.

Berlin, L. J., Cassidy, J., & Belsky, J. (1995). Loneliness in young children and infant-mother attachment: A longitudinal study. *Merrill-Palmer Quarterly, 41,* 91–103.

Bertenthal, B., & Campos, J. J. (1990). A systems approach to the organizing effects of self-produced locomotion during infancy. In C. Rovee-Collier & L. Lipsitt (Eds.), *Advances in infancy research* (Vol. 6, pp. 1–60). Hillsdale, NJ: Erlbaum.

Biringen, Z., Emde, R. N., Campos, J. J., & Appelbaum, M. I. (1995). Affective reorganization in the infant, the mother, and the dyad: The role of upright locomotion and its timing. *Child Development, 66,* 499–514.

Bloom, L. (1993). *The transition from infancy to language: Acquiring the power of expression.* New York: Cambridge University Press.

Blurton-Jones, N. (1993). The lives of hunter-gatherer children: Effects of parental behavior and parental reproductive strategy. In M. E. Pereira & L. A. Fairbanks (Eds.), *Juvenile primates* (pp. 309–326). New York: Oxford University Press.

Boccia, M., & Campos, J. J. (1989). Maternal emotional signals, social referencing, and infants' reactions to strangers. In N. Eisenberg (Ed.), *Empathy and related emotional responses: 44* (pp. 25–49). San Francisco: Jossey-Bass.

Booth, C. L., Rose-Krasnor, L., & Rubin, K. H. (1991). Relating preschoolers' social competence and their mothers' parenting behaviors to early attachment security and high-risk status. *Journal of Social and Personal Relationships, 8,* 363–382.

Bornstein, M. H. (Ed.). (1991). *Cultural approaches to parenting.* Hillsdale, NJ: Erlbaum.

Bornstein, M. H. (1995). Parenting infants. In M. H. Bornstein (Ed.), *Handbook of parenting: Vol. 1. Children and parenting.* Hillsdale, NJ: Erlbaum.

Boukydis, C. F. Z. (1985). Perception of infant crying as an interpersonal event. In B. M. Lester & C. F. Z. Boukydis (Eds.), *Infant crying* (pp. 187–215). New York: Plenum Press.

Bowlby, J. (1951). *Maternal care and mental health.* Geneva: World Health Organization.

Bowlby, J. (1958). The nature of the child's tie to his mother. *International Journal of Psycho-Analysis, 39,* 350–373.

Bowlby, J. (1969/1982). *Attachment and loss: Vol. 1. Attachment* (2nd ed.). New York: Basic.

Bowlby, J. (1973). *Attachment and loss: Vol. 2. Separation: Anxiety and anger.* New York: Basic.

Bowlby, J. (1980). *Attachment and loss: Vol. 3. Loss: Sadness and depression.* New York: Basic.

Bowlby, J. (1988). *A secure base: Parent-child attachment and healthy human development.* New York: Basic.

Braungart, J. M., & Stifter, C. A. (1991). Regulation of negative reactivity during the Strange Situation: Temperament and attachment in 12-month-old infants. *Infant Behavior and Development, 14,* 349–364.

Bretherton, I. (1990). Open communication and internal working models: Their role in the development of attachment relationships. In R. A. Thompson (Ed.), *Socioemotional development. Nebraska Symposium on Motivation* (Vol. 36, pp. 57–113). Lincoln: University of Nebraska Press.

Bretherton, I. (1991). Pouring new wine into old bottles: The social self as internal working model. In M. R. Gunnar & L. A. Sroufe (Eds.), *Self processes and development. Minnesota Symposia on Child Psychology* (Vol. 23, pp. 1–41). Hillsdale, NJ: Erlbaum.

Bretherton, I. (1992). The origins of attachment theory: John Bowlby and Mary Ainsworth. *Developmental Psychology, 28,* 759–775.

Bretherton, I. (1993). From dialogue to internal working models: The co-construction of self in relationships. In C. A. Nelson (Ed.), *Memory and affect in development. Minnesota Symposia on Child Psychology* (Vol. 26, pp. 237–263). Hillsdale, NJ: Erlbaum.

Bretherton, I., & Beeghly, M. (1982). Talking about internal states: The acquisition of an explicit theory of mind. *Developmental Psychology, 18,* 906–921.

Bretherton, I., Fritz, J., Zahn-Waxler, C., & Ridgeway, D. (1986). Learning to talk about emotions: A functionalist perspective. *Child Development, 55,* 529–548.

Bretherton, I., McNew, S., & Beeghly-Smith, M. (1981). Early person knowledge as expressed in gestural and verbal communication: When do infants acquire a "theory of mind"? In M. Lamb & L. Sherrod (Eds.), *Infant social cognition* (pp. 333–373). Hillsdale, NJ: Erlbaum.

Bretherton, I., Ridgeway, D., & Cassidy, J. (1990). Assessing internal working models of the attachment relationship: An attachment story completion task for 3-year-olds. In M. T. Greenberg, D. Cicchetti, & E. M. Cummings (Eds.), *Attachment in the preschool years* (pp. 273–308). Chicago: University of Chicago Press.

Bridges, L. J., & Grolnick, W. S. (1995). The development of emotional self-regulation in infancy and early childhood. In N. Eisenberg (Ed.), *Review of personality and social development* (Vol. 15, pp. 185–211). Thousand Oaks, CA: Sage.

Brodzinsky, D. M., Schechter, D., & Brodzinsky, A. B. (1986). Children's knowledge of adoption: Developmental changes and implications for adjustment. In R. D. Ashmore & D. M. Brodzinsky (Eds.), *Thinking about the family: Views of parents and children* (pp. 205–232). Hillsdale, NJ: Erlbaum.

Brodzinsky, D. M., Singer, L. M., & Braff, A. M. (1984). Children's understanding of adoption. *Child Development, 55,* 869–878.

Brown, J. R., Donelan-McCall, N., & Dunn, J. (1996). Why talk about mental states? The significance of children's conversations with friends, siblings and mothers. *Child Development, 67*, 836–849.

Brown, J. R., & Dunn, J. (1991). 'You can cry, mum': The social and developmental implications of talk about internal states. *British Journal of Developmental Psychology, 9*, 237–256.

Brown, J. R., & Dunn, J. (1992). Talk with your mother or your sibling? Developmental changes in early family conversations about feelings. *Child Development, 63*, 336–349.

Brown, J. R., & Dunn, J. (1996). Continuities in emotional understanding from 3 to 6 years. *Child Development, 67*, 789–802.

Bullock, M., & Lutkenhaus, P. (1988). The development of volitional behavior in the toddler years. *Child Development, 59*, 664–674.

Bullock, M., & Lutkenhaus, P. (1990). Who am I? Self-understanding in toddlers. *Merrill-Palmer Quarterly, 36*, 217–238.

Calkins, S. D., & Fox, N. A. (1992). The relations among infant temperament, security of attachment, and behavioral inhibition at twenty-four months. *Child Development, 63*, 1456–1472.

Campos, J. J., Kermoian, R., & Zumbahlen, M. R. (1992). Socioemotional transformations in the family system following infant crawling onset. In N. Eisenberg & R. A. Fabes (Eds.), *Emotion and its regulation in early development: 55* (pp. 35–40). San Francisco: Jossey-Bass.

Campos, J. J., & Stenberg, C. R. (1981). Perception, appraisal, and emotion: The onset of social referencing. In M. E. Lamb & L. R. Sherrod (Eds.), *Infant social cognition* (pp. 273–314). Hillsdale, NJ: Erlbaum.

Camras, L. A., & Sachs, V. B. (1991). Social referencing and caretaker expressive behavior in a day care setting. *Infant Behavior and Development, 14*, 27–36.

Capps, L., Sigman, M., & Mundy, P. (1994). Attachment security in children with autism. *Development and Psychopathology, 6*, 249–261.

Carlson, E. A., & Sroufe, L. A. (in press). A prospective longitudinal study of disorganized/disoriented attachment. *Child Development*.

Carlson, V., Cicchetti, D., Barnett D., & Braunwald, K. G. (1989). Finding order in disorganization: Lessons from research on maltreated infants' attachments to their caregivers. In D. Cicchetti & V. Carlson (Eds.), *Child maltreatment* (pp. 494–528). Cambridge, England: Cambridge University Press.

Cassidy, J. (1988). Child-mother attachment and the self in six-year-olds. *Child Development, 59*, 121–134.

Cassidy, J., & Berlin, L. J. (1994). The insecure/ambivalent pattern of attachment: Theory and research. *Child Development, 65*, 971–991.

Chisholm, J. S. (1996). The evolutionary ecology of attachment organization. *Human Nature, 1*, 1–37.

Cicchetti, D., & Beeghly, M. (1990). *The self in transition: Infancy to childhood.* Chicago: University of Chicago Press.

Clarke-Stewart, K. A. (1989). Infant day care: Maligned or malignant? *American Psychologist, 44*, 266–273.

Clutton-Brock, T. J. (1991). *The evolution of parental care.* Princeton, NJ: Princeton University Press.

Cochran, M., Larner, M., Riley, D., Gunnarsson, L., & Henderson, C. R. (Eds.). (1990). *Extending families: The social networks of parents and their children.* Cambridge, England: Cambridge University Press.

Cohn, D. A. (1990). Child-mother attachment of six-year-olds and social competence at school. *Child Development, 61*, 152–162.

Cohn, D. A., Cowan, P. A., Cowan, C. P., & Pearson, J. (1992). Mothers' and fathers' working models of childhood attachment relationships, parenting styles, and child behavior. *Development and Psychopathology, 4*, 417–431.

Cohn, D. A., Silver, D. H., Cowan, C. P., Cowan, P. A., & Pearson, J. (1992). Working models of childhood attachment and couple relationships. *Journal of Family Issues, 13*, 432–449.

Cohn, J. F., Campbell, S. B., & Ross, S. (1991). Infant response in the still-face paradigm at 6 months predicts avoidant and secure attachment at 12 months. *Development and Psychopathology, 3*, 367–376.

Cohn, J. F., & Tronick, E. Z. (1983). Three-month-old infants' reaction to simulated maternal depression. *Child Development, 54*, 185–193.

Cohn, J. F., & Tronick, E. Z. (1987). Mother-infant face-to-face interaction: The sequence of dyadic states at 3, 6, and 9 months. *Developmental Psychology, 23*, 68–77.

Cole, P. M., Barrett, K. C., & Zahn-Waxler, C. (1992). Emotion displays in two-year-olds during mishaps. *Child Development, 63*, 314–324.

Colin, V. L. (1996). *Human attachment.* New York: McGraw-Hill.

Connell, D. B. (1976). *Individual differences in attachment behavior: Long-term stability and relationships to language development.* Unpublished doctoral dissertation, Syracuse University, Syracuse, NY.

Connell, J. P., & Thompson, R. A. (1986). Emotion and social interaction in the Strange Situation: Consistencies and asymmetric influences in the second year. *Child Development, 57*, 733–745.

Cooley, C. H. (1902). *Human nature and the social order.* New York: Charles Scribner's Sons.

Cowan, C. P., & Cowan, P. A. (1992). *When partners become parents.* New York: Basic Books.

Cowan, C. P., Cowan, P. A., Herning, G., & Miller, N. B. (1991). Becoming a family: Marriage, parenting, and child development. In P. A. Cowan & E. M. Hetherington (Eds.), *Family transitions: Advances in family research* (Vol. 2, pp. 79–109). Hillsdale, NJ: Erlbaum.

Cox, M. J., Owen, M. T., Henderson, V. K., & Margand, N. A. (1992). Prediction of infant-father and infant-mother attachment. *Developmental Psychology, 28,* 474–483.

Cox, M. J., Owen, M. T., Lewis, J. M., & Henderson, V. (1989). Marriage, adult adjustment, and early parenting. *Child Development, 60,* 1015–1024.

Crittenden, P. M. (1988). Relationships at risk. In J. Belsky & T. Nezworski (Eds.), *Clinical implications of attachment* (pp. 136–174). Hillsdale, NJ: Erlbaum.

Crittenden, P. M. (1990). Internal representational models of attachment relationships. *Infant Mental Health Journal, 11,* 259–277.

Crittenden, P. M. (1992a). Quality of attachment in the preschool years. *Development and Psychopathology, 4,* 209–241.

Crittenden, P. M. (1992b). Treatment of anxious attachment in infancy and early childhood. *Development and Psychopathology, 4,* 575–602.

Crittenden, P. M. (1994). Peering into the black box: An exploratory treatise on the development of self in young children. In D. Cicchetti & S. L. Toth (Eds.), *Disorders and dysfunctions of the self. Rochester Symposium on Developmental Psychopathology* (Vol. 5). Rochester, NY: University of Rochester Press.

Crittenden, P. M., & Bonvillian, J. D. (1984). The relationship between maternal risk status and maternal sensitivity. *American Journal of Orthopsychiatry, 54,* 250–262.

Crockenberg, S. (1981). Infant irritability, mother responsiveness, and social support influences on the security of infant-mother attachment. *Child Development, 52,* 857–865.

Crockenberg, S. (1986). Are temperamental differences in babies associated with predictable differences in care giving? In J. V. Lerner & R. M. Lerner (Eds.), *Temperament and social interaction during infancy and childhood: 31* (pp. 53–73). San Francisco: Jossey-Bass.

Crockenberg, S., & Litman, C. (1990). Autonomy as competence in 2-year-olds: Maternal correlates of child defiance, compliance, and self-assertion. *Developmental Psychology, 26,* 961–971.

Crockenberg, S., & McCluskey, K. (1986). Change in maternal behavior during the baby's first year of life. *Child Development, 57,* 746–753.

Crowell, J. A., & Treboux, D. (1995). A review of adult attachment measures: Implications for theory and research. *Social Development, 4,* 294–327.

Crowell, J. A., Waters, E., Treboux, D., O'Connor, E., Colon-Downs, C., Feider, O., Golby, B., & Posada, G. (1996). Discriminant validity of the Adult Attachment Interview. *Child Development, 67,* 2584–2599.

Cummings, E. M., & Davies, P. (1994). *Children and marital conflict.* New York: Guilford Press.

Daly, M., & Wilson, M. (1995). Discriminative parental solicitude and the relevance of evolutionary models to the analysis of motivational systems. In M. S. Gazzaniga (Ed.), *The cognitive neurosciences* (pp. 1269–1286). Cambridge, MA: MIT Press.

Davies, P. T., & Cummings, E. M. (1994). Marital conflict and child adjustment: An emotional security hypothesis. *Psychological Bulletin, 116,* 387–411.

DeMulder, E. K., & Radke-Yarrow, M. (1991). Attachment with affectively ill and well mothers: Concurrent behavioral correlates. *Development and Psychopathology, 3,* 227–242.

Denham, S. A. (1993). Maternal emotional responsiveness and toddlers' social-emotional competence. *Journal of Child Psychology and Psychiatry, 34,* 715–728.

Denham, S. A., Cook, M., & Zoller, D. (1992). "Baby looks *very* sad": Implications of conversations about feelings between mother and preschooler. *British Journal of Developmental Psychology, 10,* 301–315.

Denham, S. A., Renwick-DeBardi, S., & Hewes, S. (1994). Emotional communication between mothers and preschoolers: Relations with emotional competence. *Merrill-Palmer Quarterly, 40,* 488–508.

Denham, S. A., Zoller, D., & Couchoud, E. A. (1994). Socialization of preschoolers' emotion understanding. *Developmental Psychology, 30,* 928–936.

de Wolf, M. S., & Van IJzendoorn, M. H. (1997). Sensitivity and attachment: A meta-analysis on parental antecedents of infant attachment. *Child Development, 68.*

Dix, T. (1991). The affective organization of parenting: Adaptive and maladaptive processes. *Psychological Bulletin, 110,* 3–25.

Dunn, J. (1987). The beginnings of moral understanding: Development in the second year. In J. Kagan & S. Lamb (Eds.), *The emergence of morality in young children* (pp. 91–112). Chicago: University of Chicago Press.

Dunn, J. (1988). *The beginnings of social understanding.* Cambridge, MA: Harvard University Press.

Dunn, J. (1993). *Young children's close relationships.* Newbury Park, CA: Sage.

Dunn, J. (1994). Changing minds and changing relationships. In C. Lewis & P. Mitchell (Eds.), *Children's early understanding of mind* (pp. 297–310). Hove, England: Erlbaum.

Dunn, J., Bretherton, I., & Munn, P. (1987). Conversations about feeling states between mothers and their young children. *Developmental Psychology, 23,* 132–139.

Dunn, J., & Brown, J. (1991). Relationships, talk about feelings, and the development of affect regulation in early childhood. In J. Garber & K. A. Dodge (Eds.), *The development of emotion regulation and dysregulation* (pp. 89–108). Cambridge, England: Cambridge University Press.

Dunn, J., & Brown, J. (1993). Early conversations about causality: Content, pragmatics and developmental change. *British Journal of Developmental Psychology, 11,* 107–123.

Dunn, J., Brown, J., & Beardsall, L. (1991). Family talk about feeling states and children's later understanding of others' emotions. *Developmental Psychology, 27,* 448–455.

Dunn, J., Brown, J., & Maguire, M. (1995). The development of children's moral sensibility: Individual differences and emotion understanding. *Developmental Psychology, 31,* 649–659.

Dunn, J., Brown, J., Slomkowski, C., Tesla, C., & Youngblade, L. (1991). Young children's understanding of other people's feelings and beliefs: Individual differences and their antecedents. *Child Development, 62,* 1352–1366.

Dunn, J., & Munn, P. (1987). Development of justification in disputes with mother and sibling. *Developmental Psychology, 23,* 791–798.

Durrett, M. E., Otaki, M., & Richards, P. (1984). Attachment and the mother's perception of support from the father. *International Journal of Behavioral Development, 7,* 167–176.

Easterbrooks, M. A. (1989). Quality of attachment to mother and to father: Effects of perinatal risk status. *Child Development, 60,* 825–830.

Easterbrooks, M. A., & Goldberg, W. A. (1990). Security of toddler-parent attachment: Relation to children's sociopersonality functioning during kindergarten. In M. T. Greenberg, D. Cicchetti, & E. M. Cummings (Eds.), *Attachment in the preschool years* (pp. 221–244). Chicago: University of Chicago Press.

Easterbrooks, M. A., & Lamb, M. E. (1979). The relationship between quality of infant-mother attachment and infant competence in initial encounters with peers. *Child Development, 50,* 380–387.

Eder, R. A. (1989). The emergent personologist: The structure and content of 3½-, 5½-, and 7½-year-olds' concepts of themselves and other persons. *Child Development, 60,* 1218–1228.

Eder, R. A. (1990). Uncovering children's psychological selves: Individual and developmental differences. *Child Development, 61,* 849–863.

Eder, R. A. (1994). Comments on children's self-narratives. In U. Neisser & R. Fivush (Eds.), *The remembering self: Construction and accuracy in the self-narrative* (pp. 180–190). Cambridge, England: Cambridge University Press.

Eder, R. A., & Mangelsdorf, S. C. (1997). The emotional basis of early personality development: Implications for the emergent self-concept. In R. Hogan & S. Briggs (Eds.), *Handbook of personality psychology* (pp. 209–240). Orlando, FL: Academic Press.

Edwards, C. P. (1995). Parenting toddlers. In M. H. Bornstein (Ed.), *Handbook of parenting: Vol. 1. Children and parenting.* Hillsdale, NJ: Erlbaum.

Egeland, B., Carlson, E., & Sroufe, L. A. (1993). Resilience as process. *Development and Psychopathology, 5,* 517–528.

Egeland, B., & Farber, E. A. (1984). Infant-mother attachment: Factors related to its development and changes over time. *Child Development, 55,* 753–771.

Egeland, B., & Hiester, M. (1995). The long-term consequences of infant day-care and mother-infant attachment. *Child Development, 66,* 474–485.

Egeland, B., Kalkoske, M., Gottesman, N., & Erickson, M. F. (1990). Preschool behavior problems: Stability and factors accounting for change. *Journal of Child Psychology and Psychiatry, 31,* 891–909.

Egeland, B., & Sroufe, L. A. (1981). Attachment and early maltreatment. *Child Development, 52,* 44–52.

Eisenberg, N., & Fabes, R. A. (Eds.). (1992). *Emotion and its regulation in early development: 55.* San Francisco: Jossey-Bass.

Elicker, J., Englund, M., & Sroufe, L. A. (1992). Predicting peer competence and peer relationships in childhood from early parent-child relationships. In R. D. Parke & G. W. Ladd (Eds.), *Family-peer relationships: Modes of linkage* (pp. 77–106). Hillsdale, NJ: Erlbaum.

Emde, R. N., & Buchsbaum, H. K. (1990). "Didn't you hear my Mommy?": Autonomy *with* connectedness in moral self emergence. In D. Cicchetti & M. Beeghly (Eds.), *The self in transition: Infancy to childhood* (pp. 35–60). Chicago: University of Chicago Press.

Emde, R. N., Johnson, W. F., & Easterbrooks, M. A. (1987). The do's and don'ts of early moral development: Psychoanalytic tradition and current research. In J. Kagan & S. Lamb (Eds.), *The emergence of morality in young children* (pp. 245–276). Chicago: University of Chicago Press.

Erickson, M. F., Sroufe, L. A., & Egeland, B. (1985). The relationship between quality of attachment and behavior problems in preschool in a high-risk sample. In I. Bretherton & E. Waters (Eds.), Growing points of attachment theory and research. *Monographs of the Society for Research in Child Development, 50*(Serial No. 209), 147–166.

Fagot, B. I., & Kavanagh, K. (1990). The prediction of antisocial behavior from avoidant attachment classifications. *Child Development, 61,* 864–873.

Fagot, B. I., & Kavanagh, K. (1993). Parenting during the second year: Effects of children's age, sex, and attachment classification. *Child Development, 64,* 258–271.

Feinman, S. (1982). Social referencing in infancy. *Merrill-Palmer Quarterly, 28,* 445–470.

Feinman, S., Roberts, D., Hsieh, K.-F., Sawyer, D., & Swanson, D. (1992). A critical review of social referencing in infancy. In S. Feinman (Ed.), *Social referencing and the social construction of reality in infancy* (pp. 15–54). New York: Plenum Press.

Fernald, A. (1993). Approval and disapproval: Infant responsiveness to vocal affect in familiar and unfamiliar languages. *Child Development, 64,* 657–674.

Fivush, R. (1993). Emotional content of parent-child conversations about the past. In C. A. Nelson (Ed.), *Memory and affect in development. Minnesota Symposia on Child Psychology* (Vol. 26, pp. 39–77). Hillsdale, NJ: Erlbaum.

Fivush, R. (1994). Constructing narrative, emotion, and self in parent-child conversations about the past. In U. Neisser & R. Fivush (Eds.), *The remembering self: Construction and accuracy in the self-narrative* (pp. 136–157). Cambridge, England: Cambridge University Press.

Fivush, R., & Fromhoff, F. A. (1988). Style and structure in mother-child conversations about the past. *Discourse Processes, 8,* 177–204.

Fivush, R., Gray, J. T., & Fromhoff, F. A. (1987). Two-year-olds talk about the past. *Cognitive Development, 2,* 393–410.

Fivush, R., & Hamond, N. R. (1990). Autobiographical memory across the preschool years: Toward reconceptualizing childhood amnesia. In R. Fivush & J. A. Hudson (Eds.), *Knowing and remembering in young children* (pp. 223–248). Cambridge, England: Cambridge University Press.

Flavell, J. H., Miller, P. H., & Miller, S. A. (1993). *Cognitive development* (3rd ed.). Englewood Cliffs, NJ: Prentice-Hall.

Fogel, A. (1993). *Developing through relationships.* Chicago: University of Chicago Press.

Fox, N. A. (1995). Of the way we were: Adult memories about attachment experiences and their role in determining infant-parent relationships: A commentary on Van IJzendoorn. *Psychological Bulletin, 113,* 387–403.

Fox, N. A. (Ed.). (1994). The development of emotion regulation: Biological and behavioral considerations. *Monographs of the Society for Research in Child Development, 59* (Serial No. 240).

Fox, N. A., Kimmerly, N. L., & Schafer, W. D. (1991). Attachment to mother/attachment to father: A meta-analysis. *Child Development, 62,* 210–225.

Fox, N. A., Sutton, D. B., & Newcombe, N. S. (1993). *Small samples and large conclusions: A reply to Belsky & Braungart (1991).* Unpublished manuscript, University of Maryland, College Park.

Fracasso, M. P., Busch-Rossnagel, N. A., & Fisher, C. B. (1993). The relationship of maternal behavior and acculturation to the quality of attachment in Hispanic infants living in New York City. *Hispanic Journal of Behavioral Sciences, 16,* 143–154.

Frankel, K. A., & Bates, J. E. (1990). Mother-toddler problem solving: Antecedents in attachment, home behavior, and temperament. *Child Development, 61,* 810–819.

Freud, S. (1940). *An outline of psychoanalysis.* New York: Norton.

Frodi, A. (1983). Attachment behavior and sociability with strangers in premature and full-term infants. *Infant Mental Health Journal, 4,* 13–22.

Frodi, A., Bridges, L., & Grolnick, W. (1985). Correlates of mastery-related behavior: A short-term longitudinal study of infants in their second year. *Child Development, 56,* 1291–1298.

Frodi, A., Grolnick, W., & Bridges, L. (1985). Maternal correlates of stability and change in infant-mother attachment. *Infant Mental Health Journal, 6,* 60–67.

Frodi, A., & Thompson, R. A. (1985). Infants' affective responses in the Strange Situation: Effects of prematurity and of quality of attachment. *Child Development, 56,* 1280–1290.

Garber, J., & Dodge, K. A. (Eds.). (1991). *The development of emotional regulation and dysregulation.* Cambridge, England: Cambridge University Press.

Gardner, W., Lamb, M. E., Thompson, R. A., & Sagi, A. (1986). On individual differences in Strange Situation behavior: Categorical and continuous measurement systems in a cross-cultural data set. *Infant Behavior and Development, 9,* 355–375.

Gekoski, M. J., Rovee-Collier, C. K., & Carulli-Rabinowitz, V. (1983). A longitudinal analysis of inhibition of infant distress: The origins of social expectations? *Infant Behavior and Development, 6,* 339–351.

George, C., Kaplan, N., & Main, M. (1985). *Adult attachment interview.* Unpublished manuscript, University of California, Berkeley.

Gianino, A., & Tronick, E. Z. (1988). The mutual regulation model: The infant's self and interactive regulation and coping and defensive capacities In T. Field, P. McCabe, & N. Schneiderman (Eds.), *Stress and coping* (Vol. 2, pp. 47–68). Hillsdale, NJ: Erlbaum.

Goldberg, S. (1990). Attachment in infants at risk: Theory, research, and practice. *Infants and Young Children, 2,* 11–20.

Goldberg, S., Perrotta, M., Minde, K., & Corter, C. (1986). Maternal behavior and attachment in low-birth-weight twins and singletons. *Child Development, 57,* 34–46.

Goldberg, S., Simmons, R. J., Newman, J., Campbell, K., & Fowler, R. S. (1991). Congenital heart disease, parental stress, and infant-mother relationships. *Journal of Pediatrics, 119,* 661–666.

Goldberg, W. A., & Easterbrooks, M. A. (1984). Role of marital quality in toddler development. *Developmental Psychology, 20,* 504–514.

Goldsmith, H. H., & Alansky, J. A. (1987). Maternal and infant temperamental predictors of attachment: A meta-analytic review. *Journal of Consulting and Clinical Psychology, 55,* 805–816.

Goldsmith, H. H., & Harman, C. (1994). Temperament and attachment: Individuals and relationships. *Current Directions in Psychological Science, 3,* 53–57.

Goodnow, J. J., & Collins, W. A. (1990). *Development according to parents.* Hillsdale, NJ: Erlbaum.

Goossens, F. A., & Van IJzendoorn, M. H. (1990). Quality of infants' attachments to professional caregivers: Relation to infant-parent attachment and day-care characteristics. *Child Development, 61,* 832–837.

Gralinski, J. H., & Kopp, C. B. (1993). Everyday rules for behavior: Mothers' requests to young children. *Developmental Psychology, 29,* 573–584.

Grolnick, W. S., Bridges, L. J., & Connell, J. P. (1996). Emotion regulation in two-year-olds: Strategies and emotional expression in four contexts. *Child Development, 67,* 928–941.

Grossmann, K. E. (1988). Longitudinal and systemic approaches in the study of biological high- and low-risk groups. In M. Rutter (Ed.), *Studies of psychosocial risk: The power of longitudinal data* (pp. 138–157). Cambridge, England: Cambridge University Press.

Grossmann, K. E., & Escher-Graub, D. (1984, April). The status of Ainsworth's Strange Situation in North and South German attachment research. In A. Sagi (Chair), *The Strange Situation procedure: Insights from an international perspective.* Symposium conducted at the biennial meeting of the International Conference on Infant Studies, New York.

Grossmann, K. E., & Grossmann, K. (1990a). The wider concept of attachment in cross-cultural research. *Human Development, 33,* 31–47.

Grossmann, K. E., & Grossmann, K. (1990b). Preliminary observations on Japanese infants' behavior in Ainsworth's Strange Situation. Is the Ainsworth Strange Situation applicable to the study of attachment in Japanese infants? *Research and Clinical Center for Child Development Annual Report Occasional Papers No. 2, 6–17.* Hokkaido University, Sapporo, Japan.

Grossmann, K. E., & Grossmann, K. (1991). Attachment quality as an organizer of emotional and behavioral responses in a longitudinal perspective. In C. Murray Parkes, J. Stevenson-Hinde, & P. Marris (Eds.), *Attachment across the life cycle* (pp. 93–114). London: Routledge & Kegan Paul.

Grossmann, K. E., Grossmann, K., Huber, F., & Wartner, U. (1981). German children's behavior towards their mothers at 12 months and their fathers at 18 months in Ainsworth's Strange Situation. *International Journal of Behavioral Development, 4,* 157–181.

Grossmann, K., Grossmann, K. E., Spangler, G., Suess, G., & Unzner, L. (1985). Maternal sensitivity and newborns' orientation responses as related to quality of attachment in Northern Germany. In I. Bretherton & E. Waters (Eds.), Growing points of attachment theory and research. *Monographs of the Society for Research in Child Development, 50*(1/2, Serial No. 209), 233–256.

Harkness, S., & Super, C. M. (1995). Culture and parenting. In M. Bornstein (Ed.), *Handbook of parenting: Vol. 2. Biology and ecology of parenting.* Hillsdale, NJ: Erlbaum.

Harris, P. L. (1994). The child's understanding of emotion: Developmental change and the family environment. *Journal of Child Psychology and Psychiatry, 35,* 3–28.

Harris, P. L. (1996a). Between Strange Situations and false beliefs: Working models and theories of mind. In W. Koops, J. Hoeksma, & D. van den Boom (Eds.), *Early mother-child interaction and attachment: Old and new approaches* (pp. 187–199). Amsterdam, The Netherlands: Elsevier.

Harris, P. L. (1996b). Desires, beliefs, and language. In P. Carruthers & P. K. Smith (Eds.), *Theories of theories of mind* (pp. 200–220). Cambridge, England: Cambridge University Press.

Harris, P. L., & Kavanaugh, R. D. (1993). Young children's understanding of pretense. *Monographs of the Society for Research in Child Development, 58*(1, Serial No. 231).

Hartup, W. W., & Rubin, Z. (1986). *Relationships and development.* Hillsdale, NJ: Erlbaum.

Harwood, R. L. (1992). The influence of culturally derived values on Anglo and Puerto Rican mothers' perceptions of attachment behavior. *Child Development, 63,* 822–839.

Harwood, R. L., & Miller, J. G. (1991). Perceptions of attachment behavior: A comparison of Anglo and Puerto Rican mothers. *Merrill-Palmer Quarterly, 37,* 583–599.

Harwood, R. L., Miller, J. G., & Irizarry, N. L. (1995). *Culture and attachment.* New York: Guilford Press.

Heckhausen, H. (1984). Emergent achievement behavior: Some early developments. In J. Nicholls (Ed.), *Advances in motivation and achievement: Vol. 3. The development of achievement motivation* (pp. 1–32). Greenwich, CT: JAI Press.

Heckhausen, J. (1988). Becoming aware of one's competence in the second year: Developmental progression within the mother-child dyad. *International Journal of Behavioral Development, 11,* 305–326.

Hinde, R. A. (1982). Attachment: Some conceptual and biological issues. In J. Stevenson-Hinde & C. Murray Parkes (Eds.), *The place of attachment in human behavior* (pp. 60–76). New York: Basic Books.

Hinde, R. A. (1986). Some implications of evolutionary theory and comparative data for the study of human prosocial and aggressive behavior. In D. Olweus, J. Block, & M. Radke-Yarrow (Eds.), *Development of antisocial and prosocial behavior: Research, theories, and issues* (pp. 13–32). Orlando, FL: Academic Press.

Hinde, R. A. (1988). Continuities and discontinuities: Conceptual issues and methodological considerations. In M. Rutter (Ed.), *Studies of psychosocial risk: The power of longitudinal data* (pp. 367–383). Cambridge, England: Cambridge University Press.

Hinde, R. A., & Stevenson-Hinde, J. (1987). Interpersonal relationships and child development. *Developmental Review, 7,* 1–21.

Hinde, R. A., & Stevenson-Hinde, J. (1990). Attachment: Biological, cultural and individual desiderata. *Human Development, 33,* 62–72.

Hirshberg, L. M., & Svejda, M. (1990). When infants look to their parents: I. Infants' social referencing of mothers compared to fathers. *Child Development, 61,* 1175–1186.

Hobson, R. P. (1993). *Autism and the development of mind.* Hillsdale, NJ: Erlbaum.

Hoffman, M. L. (1970). Moral development. In P. H. Mussen (Ed.), *Carmichael's handbook of child psychology* (3rd ed.) (Vol. 2, pp. 261–359). New York: Wiley.

Hoffman, M. L. (1983). Affective and cognitive processes in moral internalization. In E. T. Higgins, D. Ruble, & W. Hartup (Eds.), *Social cognition and social development* (pp. 236–274). New York: Cambridge University Press.

Holden, G. W. (1983). Avoiding conflict: Mothers as tacticians in the supermarket. *Child Development, 54,* 233–240.

Holden, G. W. (1995). Parental attitudes toward childrearing. In M. H. Bornstein (Ed.), *Handbook of parenting: Vol. 3. Status and social conditions of parenting.* Hillsdale, NJ: Erlbaum.

Holden, G. W., & O'Dell, P. C. (1995). *Just how stable is parental behavior?: Meta-analysis and reformulation.* Unpublished manuscript, University of Texas at Austin.

Hood, L., & Bloom, L. (1979). What, when, and how about why: A longitudinal study of early expressions of causality. *Monographs of the Society for Research in Child Development, 44* (Serial No. 181).

Hornik, R., & Gunnar, M. R. (1988). A descriptive analysis of infant social referencing. *Child Development, 59,* 626–634.

Hornik, R., Risenhoover, N., & Gunnar, M. (1987). The effects of maternal positive, neutral, and negative affect communications on infant responses to new toys. *Child Development, 58,* 937–944.

Howe, M. L., & Courage, M. L. (1993). On resolving the enigma of infantile amnesia. *Psychological Bulletin, 113,* 305–326.

Howes, C. (in press). Attachment relationships in the context of multiple caregivers. In J. Cassidy & P. R. Shaver (Eds.), *Handbook of attachment theory and research.* New York: Guilford Press.

Howes, C., & Hamilton, C. E. (1992a). Children's relationships with child care teachers: Stability and concordance with parental attachments. *Child Development, 63,* 867–878.

Howes, C., & Hamilton, C. E. (1992b). Children's relationships with caregivers: Mothers and child care teachers. *Child Development, 63,* 859–866.

Howes, C., Hamilton, C. E., & Matheson, C. C. (1994). Children's relationships with peers: Differential associations with aspects of the teacher-child relationship. *Child Development, 65,* 253–263.

Howes, C., Matheson, C. C., & Hamilton, C. E. (1994). Maternal, teacher, and child care history correlates of children's relationships with peers. *Child Development, 65,* 264–273.

Howes, C., Rodning, C., Galluzzo, D. C., & Myers, L. (1988). Attachment and child care: Relationships with mother and caregiver. *Early Childhood Research Quarterly, 3,* 403–416.

Howes, P., & Markman, H. J. (1989). Marital quality and child functioning: A longitudinal investigation. *Child Development, 60,* 1044–1051.

Hudson, J. A. (1990). The emergence of autobiographical memory in mother-child conversation. In R. Fivush & J. A. Hudson (Eds.), *Knowing and remembering in young children* (pp. 166–196). Cambridge, England: Cambridge University Press.

Hudson, J. A. (1993). Understanding events: The development of script knowledge. In M. Bennett (Ed.), *The child as psychologist: An introduction to the development of social cognition* (pp. 142–167). New York: Harvester Wheatsheaf.

Isabella, R. A. (1993). Origins of attachment: Maternal interactive behavior across the first year. *Child Development, 64,* 605–621.

Isabella, R. A. (1995). The origins of infant-mother attachment: Maternal behavior and infant development. In R. Vasta (Ed.), *Annals of child development* (Vol. 10, pp. 57–82). London: Jessica Kingsley.

Isabella, R. A., & Belsky, J. (1991). Interactional synchrony and the origins of infant-mother attachment: A replication study. *Child Development, 62,* 373–384.

Isabella, R. A., Belsky, J., & von Eye, A. (1989). Origins of infant-mother attachment: An examination of interactional synchrony during the infant's first year. *Developmental Psychology, 25,* 12–21.

Jackson, J. F. (1993). Multiple caregiving among African Americans and infant attachment: The need for an emic approach. *Human Development, 36,* 87–102.

Jacobson, J. L., & Wille, D. E. (1986). The influence of attachment pattern on developmental changes in peer interaction from the toddler to the preschool period. *Child Development, 57,* 338–347.

Jacobson, S. W., & Frye, K. F. (1991). Effect of maternal social support on attachment: Experimental evidence. *Child Development, 62,* 572–582.

Kagan, J. (1981). *The second year: The emergence of self-awareness.* Cambridge, MA: Harvard University Press.

Kagan, J. (1984). *The nature of the child.* New York: Basic Books.

Karen, R. (1994). *Becoming attached.* New York: Warner Books.

Kaye, K. (1979). Thickening thin data: The maternal role in developing communication and language. In M. Bullowa (Ed.), *Before speech* (pp. 191–206). Cambridge, England: Cambridge University Press.

Kaye, K. (1982). *The mental and social life of babies.* Chicago: University of Chicago Press.

Kerns, K. A. (1994). A longitudinal examination of links between mother-child attachment and children's friendships in early childhood. *Journal of Social and Personal Relationships, 11,* 379–381.

Kerns, K. A. (1996). Individual differences in friendship quality: Links to child-mother attachment. In W. M. Bukowski, A. F. Newcomb, & W. W. Hartup (Eds.), *The company they keep: Friendship in childhood and adolescence.* Cambridge, England: Cambridge University Press.

Kestenbaum, R., Farber, E. A., & Sroufe, L. A. (1989). Individual differences in empathy among preschoolers: Relation to attachment history. In N. Eisenberg (Ed.), *Empathy and related emotional responses: 44* (pp. 51–64). San Francisco: Jossey-Bass.

Klinnert, M. (1984). The regulation of infant behavior by maternal facial expression. *Infant Behavior and Development, 7,* 447–465.

Klinnert, M., Campos, J. J., Sorce, J., Emde, R. N., & Svejda, M. (1983). Emotions as behavior regulators: Social referencing in infancy. In R. Plutchik & H. Kellerman (Eds.), *Emotion: Theory, research, and experience: Vol. 2. Emotions in early development* (pp. 57–86). New York: Academic Press.

Klinnert, M., Emde, R. N., Butterfield, P., & Campos, J. J. (1986). Social referencing: The infant's use of emotional signals from a friendly adult with mother present. *Developmental Psychology, 22,* 427–432.

Kobak, R. R., & Cole, H. I. (1994). Attachment and meta-monitoring: Implications for adolescent autonomy and psychopathology. In D. Cicchetti & S. L. Toth (Eds.), *Disorders and dysfunctions of the self. Rochester Symposium on Developmental Psychopathology* (Vol. 5, pp. 267–297). Rochester, NY: University of Rochester Press.

Kobak, R. R., & Sceery, A. (1988). Attachment in late adolescence: Working models, affect regulation, and representations of self and others. *Child Development, 59,* 135–146.

Kochanska, G. (1991). Socialization and temperament in the development of guilt and conscience. *Child Development, 62,* 1379–1392.

Kochanska, G. (1993). Toward a synthesis of parental socialization and child temperament in early development of conscience. *Child Development, 64,* 325–347.

Kochanska, G. (1995). Children's temperament, mothers' discipline, and security of attachment: Multiple pathways to emerging internalization. *Child Development, 66,* 597–615.

Kochanska, G., & Aksan, N. (1995). Mother-child mutually positive affect, the quality of child compliance to requests and prohibitions, and maternal control as correlates of early internalization. *Child Development, 66,* 236–254.

Kochanska, G., Casey, R., & Fukumoto, A. (1995). Toddlers' sensitivity to standard violations. *Child Development, 66,* 643–656.

Kochanska, G., & Thompson, R. A. (in press). The emergence and development of conscience in toddlerhood and early childhood. In J. E. Grusec & L. Kuczynski (Eds.), *Parenting strategies and children's internalization of values: A handbook of theoretical and research perspectives.* New York: Wiley.

Kopp, C. B. (1982). Antecedents of self-regulation: A developmental view. *Developmental Psychology, 18,* 199–214.

Kopp, C. B. (1987). The growth of self-regulation: Caregivers and children. In N. Eisenberg (Ed.), *Contemporary topics in developmental psychology* (pp. 34–55). New York: Wiley.

Kopp, C. B. (1989). Regulation of distress and negative emotions: A developmental view. *Developmental Psychology, 25,* 343–354.

Kopp, C. B. (1992). Emotional distress and control in young children. In N. Eisenberg & R. A. Fabes (Eds.), *Emotion and its regulation in early development: 55* (pp. 41–56). San Francisco: Jossey-Bass.

Kopp, C. B., & Brownell, C. A. (Eds.). (1991). The development of self: The first three years. *Developmental Review, 11,* 195–303.

Kopp, C. B., & Wyer, N. (1994). Self-regulation in normal and atypical development. In D. Cicchetti & S. L. Toth (Eds.), *Disorders and dysfunctions of the self. Rochester Symposium on Developmental Psychopathology* (Vol. 5, pp. 31–56). Rochester, NY: University of Rochester Press.

Kuczynski, L., & Kochanska, G. (1990). Development of children's noncompliance strategies from toddlerhood to age 5. *Developmental Psychology, 26,* 398–408.

Kuczynski, L., Kochanska, G., Radke-Yarrow, M., & Girnius-Brown, O. (1987). A developmental interpretation of young children's noncompliance. *Developmental Psychology, 23,* 799–806.

LaFreniere, P. J., & Sroufe, L. A. (1985). Profiles of peer competence in the preschool: Interrelations between measures, influence of social ecology, and relation to attachment history. *Developmental Psychology, 21,* 56–69.

Laible, D. J., & Thompson, R. A. (1997). *Attachment and emotional understanding in preschool children.* Unpublished manuscript, University of Nebraska.

Lamb, M. E. (1981a). Fathers and child development: An integrative overview. In M. E. Lamb (Ed.), *The role of the father in child development* (Rev. ed., pp. 1–70). New York: Wiley.

Lamb, M. E. (1981b). The development of social expectations in the first year of life. In M. E. Lamb & L. R. Sherrod (Eds.), *Infant social cognition* (pp. 155–175). Hillsdale, NJ: Erlbaum.

Lamb, M. E. (1981c). Developing trust and perceived effectance in infancy. In L. Lipsitt (Ed.), *Advances in infancy research* (Vol. 1, pp. 101–127). New York: ABLEX.

Lamb, M. E. (1987). Predictive implications of individual differences in attachment. *Journal of Consulting and Clinical Psychology, 55,* 817–824.

Lamb, M. E., Chase-Lansdale, L., & Owen, M. (1979). The changing American family and its implications for infant social development: The sample case of maternal employment. In M. Lewis & L. A. Rosenblum (Eds.), *The child and its family* (pp. 267–291). New York: Plenum Press.

Lamb, M. E., & Easterbrooks, M. A. (1981). Individual differences in parental sensitivity: Origins, components, and consequences. In M. E. Lamb & L. R. Sherrod (Eds.), *Infant social cognition* (pp. 127–153). Hillsdale, NJ: Erlbaum.

Lamb, M. E., Hopps, K., & Elster, A. B. (1987). Strange Situation behavior of infants with adolescent mothers. *Infant Behavior and Development, 10,* 39–48.

Lamb, M. E., Hwang, C. P., Frodi, A., & Frodi, M. (1982). Security of mother- and father-infant attachment and its relation to sociability with strangers in traditional and non-traditional Swedish families. *Infant Behavior and Development, 5,* 355–367.

Lamb, M. E., & Malkin, C. M. (1986). The development of social expectations in distress-relief sequences: A longitudinal study. *International Journal of Behavioral Development, 9,* 235–249.

Lamb, M. E., Morrison, D. C., & Malkin, C. M. (1987). The development of infant social expectations in face-to-face interaction: A longitudinal study. *Merrill-Palmer Quarterly, 33,* 241–254.

Lamb, M. E., Thompson, R. A., Gardner, W., & Charnov, E. L. (1985). *Infant-mother attachment: The origins and developmental significance of individual differences in Strange Situation behavior.* Hillsdale, NJ: Erlbaum.

Lamb, S. (1991). First moral sense: Aspects of and contributors to a beginning morality in the second year of life. In W. Kurtines & J. Gewirtz (Eds.), *Handbook of moral behavior and development* (pp. 171–189). Hillsdale, NJ: Erlbaum.

Leger, D. W., Thompson, R. A., Merritt, J. A., & Benz, J. J. (1996). Adult perception of emotion intensity in human infant cries: Effects of infant age and cry acoustics. *Child Development, 67,* 3238–3249.

Lester, B. M. (1984). A biosocial model of infant crying. In L. Lipsitt & C. Rovee-Collier (Eds.), *Advances in infancy research* (Vol. 3, pp. 167–212). Norwood, NJ: ABLEX.

Levine, R. A. (1988). Human parental care: Universal goals, cultural strategies, individual behavior. In R. A. Levine, P. M. Miller, & M. M. West (Eds.), *Parental behavior in diverse societies: 40* (pp. 3–12). San Francisco: Jossey-Bass.

Levine, R. A., & Miller, P. M. (1990). Commentary. *Human Development, 33,* 73–80.

Levitt, M. J., Weber, R. A., & Clark, M. C. (1986). Social network relationships as sources of maternal support and well-being. *Developmental Psychology, 22,* 310–316.

Lewis, C., & Mitchell, P. (Eds.). (1994). *Children's early understanding of mind: Origins and development.* Hove, England: Erlbaum.

Lewis, M. (1993). Self-conscious emotions: Embarrassment, pride, shame, and guilt. In M. Lewis & J. M. Haviland (Eds.), *Handbook of emotions* (pp. 563–573). New York: Guilford Press.

Lewis, M. (1995). Embarrassment: The emotion of self-exposure and evaluation. In J. P. Tangney & K. W. Fischer (Eds.), *Self-conscious emotions* (pp. 198–218). New York: Guilford Press.

Lewis, M., & Brooks-Gunn, J. (1979). *Social cognition and the acquisition of self.* New York: Plenum Press.

Lewis, M., Brooks-Gunn, J., & Jaskir, J. (1985). Individual differences in visual self-recognition as a function of mother-infant attachment relationship. *Developmental Psychology, 21,* 1181–1187.

Lewis, M., & Feiring, C. (1989a). Infant, mother, and mother-infant interaction behavior and subsequent attachment. *Child Development, 60,* 831–837.

Lewis, M., & Feiring, C. (1989b). Early predictors of childhood friendship. In T. J. Berndt & G. W. Ladd (Eds.), *Peer relationships in child development* (pp. 246–273). New York: Wiley.

Lewis, M., Feiring, C., McGuffog, C., & Jaskir, J. (1984). Predicting psychopathology in six-year-olds from early social relations. *Child Development, 55,* 123–136.

Lewis, M., Sullivan, M. W., Stanger, C., & Weiss, M. (1989). Self development and self-conscious emotions. *Child Development, 60,* 146–156.

Leyendecker, B., Lamb, M. E., Fracasso, M. P., Scholmerich, A., & Larson, C. (1995). *Playful interaction and the antecedents of attachment: A longitudinal study of Central-American and Euro-American mothers and infants.* Unpublished manuscript, National Institute of Child Health and Human Development.

Leyendecker, B., Lamb, M. E., Scholmerich, A., & Fricke, D. M. (1995). *Contexts as moderators of observed interactions: A study of Costa Rican mothers and infants from different socio-economic backgrounds.* Unpublished manuscript, National Institute of Child Health and Human Development.

Lieberman, A. F., Weston, D. R., & Pawl, J. H. (1991). Preventive intervention and outcome with anxiously attached dyads. *Child Development, 62,* 199–209.

Li-Repac, D. C. (1982). *The impact of acculturation on the child-rearing attitudes and practices of Chinese-American families: Consequences for the attachment process.* Unpublished doctoral dissertation, University of California-Berkeley.

Londerville, S., & Main, M. (1981). Security of attachment, compliance, and maternal training methods in the second year of life. *Developmental Psychology, 17,* 289–299.

Lutkenhaus, P., Grossmann, K. E., & Grossmann, K. (1985). Infant-mother attachment at twelve months and style of interaction with a stranger at the age of three years. *Child Development, 56,* 1538–1542.

Lyons-Ruth, K., Alpern, L., & Repacholi, B. (1993). Disorganized infant attachment classification and maternal psychosocial problems as predictors of hostile-aggressive behavior in the preschool classroom. *Child Development, 64,* 572–585.

Lyons-Ruth, K., Connell, D. B., Grunebaum, H. U., & Botein, S. (1990). Infants at social risk: Maternal depression and family support services as mediators of infant development and security of attachment. *Child Development, 61,* 85–98.

Lyons-Ruth, K., Connell, D. B., Zoll, D., & Stahl, J. (1987). Infants at social risk: Relations among infant maltreatment, maternal behavior, and infant attachment behavior. *Developmental Psychology, 23,* 223–232.

Lyons-Ruth, K., Repacholi, B., McLeod, S., & Silva, E. (1991). Disorganized attachment behavior in infancy: Short-term stability, maternal and infant correlates, and risk-related subtypes. *Development and Psychopathology, 3,* 377–396.

Maccoby, E. E. (1983). Let's not overattribute to the attribution process: Comments on social cognition and behavior. In E. T. Higgins, D. N. Ruble, & W. W. Hartup (Eds.), *Social cognition and social development* (pp. 356–370). Cambridge, England: Cambridge University Press.

Maccoby, E. E. (1984). Socialization and developmental change. *Child Development, 55,* 317–328.

Maccoby, E. E. (1992). The role of parents in the socialization of children: An historical overview. *Developmental Psychology, 28,* 1006–1017.

MacDonald, K. (1992). Warmth as a developmental construct: An evolutionary analysis. *Child Development, 63,* 753–773.

Mahler, M. S., Pine, F., & Bergman, A. (1975). *The psychological birth of the human infant.* New York: Basic Books.

Main, M. (1977). Analysis of a peculiar form of reunion behavior see in some day-care children: Its history and sequelae in children who are home-reared. In R. A. Webb (Ed.), *Social development in childhood: Day-care programs and research* (pp. 33–78). Baltimore: Johns Hopkins University Press.

Main, M. (1981). Avoidance in the service of attachment: A working paper. In K. Immelman, G. W. Barlow, L. Petrinovich, & M. Main (Eds.), *Behavioral development: The Bielefeld interdisciplinary project* (pp. 651–693). Cambridge, England: Cambridge University Press.

Main, M. (1983). Exploration, play, and cognitive functioning related to infant-mother attachment. *Infant Behavior and Development, 6,* 167–174.

Main, M. (1990). Cross-cultural studies of attachment organization: Recent studies, changing methodologies, and the concept of conditional strategies. *Human Development, 33,* 48–61.

Main, M., & Cassidy, J. (1988). Categories of response to reunion with the parent at age 6: Predictable from infant attachment classifications and stable over a 1-month period. *Developmental Psychology, 24,* 415–426.

Main, M., & Goldwyn, R. (1988). *Interview-based adult attachment classifications: Related to infant-mother and infant-father attachment.* Unpublished manuscript, University of California, Berkeley.

Main, M., & Goldwyn, R. (1994). *Adult attachment classification system.* Unpublished manuscript, University of California, Berkeley.

Main, M., & Hesse, E. (1990). Parents' unresolved traumatic experiences are related to infant disorganized attachment status: Is frightened and/or frightening parental behavior the linking mechanism? In M. T. Greenberg, D. Cicchetti, & E. M. Cummings (Eds.), *Attachment in the preschool years* (pp. 161–182). Chicago: University of Chicago Press.

Main, M., Kaplan, N., & Cassidy, J. (1985). Security in infancy, childhood, and adulthood: A move to the level of representation. In I. Bretherton & E. Waters (Eds.), Growing points of attachment theory and research. *Monographs of the Society for Research in Child Development, 50*(1/2, Serial No. 209), 66–104.

Main, M., & Solomon, J. (1986). Discovery of an insecure-disorganized/disoriented attachment pattern. In T. B. Brazelton & M. W. Yogman (Eds.), *Affective development in infancy* (pp. 95–124). Norwood, NJ: ABLEX.

Main, M., & Solomon, J. (1990). Procedures for identifying infants as disorganized/disoriented during the Ainsworth Strange Situation. In M. T. Greenberg, D. Cicchetti, & E. M. Cummings (Eds.), *Attachment in the preschool years* (pp. 121–160). Chicago: University of Chicago Press.

Main, M., Tomasini, L., & Tolan, W. (1979). Differences among mothers of infants judged to differ in security. *Developmental Psychology, 15,* 472–473.

Main, M., & Weston, D. R. (1981). The quality of the toddler's relationship to mother and to father: Related to conflict behavior and the readiness to establish new relationships. *Child Development, 52,* 932–940.

Malatesta, C. Z., Culver, C., Tesman, J. R., & Shepard, B. (1989). The development of emotion expression during the first two years of life. *Monographs of the Society for Research in Child Development, 54*(1/2, Serial No. 219).

Mandler, J. M. (1988). How to build a baby: On the development of an accessible representational system. *Cognitive Development, 3,* 113–136.

Mandler, J. M. (1992). How to build a baby: II. Conceptual primitives. *Psychological Review, 99,* 587–604.

Mangelsdorf, S., Gunnar, M., Kestenbaum, R., Lang, S., & Andreas, D. (1990). Infant proneness-to-distress temperament, maternal personality, and mother-infant attachment: Associations and goodness of fit. *Child Development, 61,* 820–831.

Marvin, R. S. (1977). An ethological-cognitive model for the attenuation of mother-child attachment behavior. In T. Alloway, P. Pliner, & L. Krames (Eds.), *Attachment behavior* (pp. 25–60). New York: Plenum Press.

Marvin, R. S., & Greenberg, M. T. (1982). Preschoolers' changing conceptions of their mothers: A social-cognitive study of mother-child attachment. In D. Forbes & M. T. Greenberg (Eds.), *Children's planning strategies: 18* (pp. 47–60). San Francisco: Jossey-Bass.

Masters, J. C., & Wellman, H. M. (1974). The study of human infant attachment: A procedural critique. *Psychological Bulletin, 81,* 218–237.

Matas, L., Arend, R. A., & Sroufe, L. A. (1978). Continuity of adaptation in the second year: The relationship between quality of attachment and later competence. *Child Development, 49,* 547–556.

Mead, G. H. (1934). *Mind, self, and society.* Chicago: University of Chicago Press.

Meltzoff, A. N., & Gopnik, A. (1993). The role of imitation in understanding persons and developing a theory of mind. In S. Baron-Cohen, H. Tager-Flusberg, & D. Cohen (Eds.), *Understanding other minds: Perspectives from autism* (pp. 335–366). Oxford, England: Oxford University Press.

Miller, P. J. (1994). Narrative practices: Their role in socialization and self-construction. In U. Neisser & R. Fivush (Eds.), *The remembering self: Construction and accuracy in the self-narrative* (pp. 158–179). Cambridge, England: Cambridge University Press.

Miller, P. J., Fung, H., & Mintz, J. (1996). Self-construction through narrative practices: A Chinese and American comparison of early socialization. *Ethos, 24,* 237–280.

Miller, P. J., Mintz, J., Hoogstra, L., Fung, H., & Potts, R. (1992). The narrated self: Young children's construction of self in relation to others in conversational stories of personal experience. *Merrill-Palmer Quarterly, 38,* 45–67.

Miller, P. J., Potts, R., Fung, H., Hoogstra, L., & Mintz, J. (1990). Narrative practices and the social construction of self in childhood. *American Ethnologist, 17,* 292–311.

Miller, P. J., & Sperry, L. L. (1987). The socialization of anger and aggression. *Merrill-Palmer Quarterly, 33,* 1–31.

Miyake, K., Chen, S.-J., & Campos, J. J. (1985). Infant temperament, mother's mode of interaction, and attachment in Japan: An interim report. In I. Bretherton & E. Waters (Eds.), *Growing points of attachment theory and research. Monographs of the Society for Research in Child Development, 50*(1/2, Serial No. 209), 276–297.

Moffitt, T. E., Caspi, A., Belsky, J., & Silva, P. A. (1992). Childhood experience and the onset of menarche: A test of the sociobiological model. *Child Development, 63,* 47–58.

Moore, C., & Corkum, V. (1994). Social understanding at the end of the first year of life. *Developmental Review, 14,* 349–372.

Mumme, D., Fernald, A., & Herrera, C. (1996). Infants' responses to facial and vocal emotional signals in a social referencing paradigm. *Child Development, 67,* 3219–3237.

Murphey, D. A. (1992). Constructing the child: Relations between parents' beliefs and child outcomes. *Developmental Review, 12,* 199–232.

Murray, A. D. (1985). Aversiveness is in the mind of the beholder: Perception of infant crying by adults. In B. M. Lester & C. F. Z. Boukydis (Eds.), *Infant crying* (pp. 217–239). New York: Plenum Press.

Murray, L., & Trevarthen, C. (1985). Emotional regulation of interactions between two-month-olds and their mothers. In T. M. Field & N. A. Fox (Eds.), *Social perception in infants* (pp. 177–197). Norwood, NJ: ABLEX.

Myers, N. A., Clifton, R. K., & Clarkson, M. G. (1987). When they were very young: Almost-threes remember two years ago. *Infant Behavior and Development, 10,* 123–132.

Myers, N. A., Perris, E. E., & Speaker, C. J. (1997). Fifty months of memory: A longitudinal study in early childhood. *Memory, 2,* 393–415.

Nachmias, M., Gunnar, M., Mangelsdorf, S., Parritz, R. H., & Buss, K. (1996). Behavioral inhibition and stress reactivity: The moderating role of attachment security. *Child Development, 67,* 508–522.

Neisser, U. (1991). Two perceptually given aspects of the self and their development. *Developmental Review, 11,* 197–209.

Nelson, K. (Ed.). (1978). *Event knowledge: Structure and function in development.* Hillsdale, NJ: Erlbaum.

Nelson, K. (Ed.). (1989). *Narratives from the crib.* Cambridge, MA: Harvard University Press.

Nelson, K. (1990). Remembering, forgetting, and childhood amnesia. In R. Fivush & J. A. Hudson (Eds.), *Knowing and remembering in young children* (pp. 301–316). Cambridge, England: Cambridge University Press.

Nelson, K. (1993a). Events, narratives, memory: What develops? In C. A. Nelson (Ed.), *Memory and affect in development. Minnesota Symposia on Child Psychology* (Vol. 26, pp. 1–24). Hillsdale, NJ: Erlbaum.

Nelson, K. (1993b). The psychological and social origins of autobiographical memory. *Psychological Science, 4,* 7–14.

Nelson, K., & Gruendel, J. (1981). Generalized event representations: Basic building blocks of cognitive development. In M. Lamb & A. Brown (Eds.), *Advances in developmental psychology* (pp. 131–158). Hillsdale, NJ: Erlbaum.

Okagaki, L., & Divecha, D. J. (1993). Development of parental beliefs. In T. Luster & L. Okagaki (Eds.), *Parenting: An ecological perspective* (pp. 35–67). Hillsdale, NJ: Erlbaum.

Oppenheim, D., Sagi, A., & Lamb, M. E. (1988). Infant-adult attachments on the kibbutz and their relation to socioemotional development 4 years later. *Developmental Psychology, 24,* 427–433.

Oppenheim, D., & Waters, H. A. (1995). Narrative processes and attachment representations: Issues of development and assessment. In E. Waters, B. E. Vaughn, G. Posada, & K. Kondo-Ikemura (Eds.), Caregiving, cultural, and cognitive perspectives on secure-base behavior and working models: New growing points in attachment theory and research. *Monographs of the Society for Research in Child Development, 60*(Serial No. 244), 197–215.

Owen, M. T., Easterbrooks, M. A., Chase-Lansdale, L., & Goldberg, W. A. (1984). The relation between maternal employment status and the stability of attachments to mother and to father. *Child Development, 55,* 1894–1901.

Park, K. A., & Waters, E. (1989). Security of attachment and preschool friendships. *Child Development, 60,* 1076–1081.

Pastor, D. L. (1981). The quality of mother-infant attachment and its relationship to toddlers' initial sociability with peers. *Developmental Psychology, 17,* 326–335.

Pearson, J. L., Cohn, D. A., Cowan, P. A., & Cowan, C. P. (1994). Earned- and continuous-security in adult attachment: Relation to depressive symptomatology and parenting style. *Development and Psychopathology, 6,* 359–373.

Pederson, D. R., & Moran, G. (1995). A categorical description of infant-mother relationships in the home and its relation to Q-sort measures of infant-mother interaction. In E. Waters, B. E. Vaughn, G. Posada, & K. Kondo-Ikemura (Eds.), Caregiving, cultural, and cognitive perspectives on secure-base behavior and working models: New growing points in attachment theory and research. *Monographs of the Society for Research in Child Development, 60*(Serial No. 244), 111–132.

Pederson, D. R., & Moran, G. (1996). Expressions of the attachment relationship outside of the Strange Situation. *Child Development, 67,* 915–927.

Pederson, D. R., Moran, G., Bento, S., & Buckland, G. (1992, May). *Maternal sensitivity and attachment security: Concordance of home and lab based measures.* Paper presented at the biennial meeting of the International Conference on Infant Studies, Miami, FL.

Pederson, D. R., Moran, G., Sitko, C., Campbell, K., Ghesquire, K., & Acton, H. (1990). Maternal sensitivity and the security of infant-mother attachment: A Q-sort study. *Child Development, 61,* 1974–1983.

Perner, J., Ruffman, T., & Leekam, S. R. (1994). Theory of mind is contagious: You catch it from your sibs. *Child Development, 65,* 1228–1238.

Perris, E. E., Myers, N. A., & Clifton, R. K. (1990). Long-term memory for a single infancy experience. *Child Development, 61,* 1796–1807.

Pianta, R. C., Sroufe, L. A., & Egeland, B. (1989). Continuity and discontinuity in maternal sensitivity at 6, 24, and 42 months in a high-risk sample. *Child Development, 60,* 481–487.

Pillemer, D. B., & White, S. H. (1989). Childhood events recalled by children and adults. In H. W. Reese (Ed.), *Advances in child development and behavior* (Vol. 21, pp. 297–340). San Diego: Academic Press.

Pipp, S., Easterbrooks, M. A., & Harmon, R. J. (1992). The relation between attachment and knowledge of self and mother in one- to three-year-old infants. *Child Development, 63,* 738–750.

Pipp, S., Fischer, K. W., & Jennings, S. (1987). Acquisition of self- and mother knowledge in infancy. *Developmental Psychology, 23,* 86–96.

Plimpton, E., & Rosenblum, L. (1983). The ecological context of infant maltreatment in primates. In M. Reite & N. G. Caine (Eds.), *Child abuse: The nonhuman primate data* (pp. 103–117). New York: Liss.

Plunkett, J. W., Meisels, S. J., Stiefel, G. S., Pasick, P. L., & Roloff, D. W. (1986). Patterns of attachment among preterm infants of varying biological risk. *Journal of the American Academy of Child Psychiatry, 25,* 794–800.

Posada, G., Gao, Y., Posada, R., Tascon, M., Schoelmerich, A., Sagi, A., Kondo-Ikemura, K., Haaland, W., & Wynnevaag, B. (1995). The secure-base phenomenon across cultures: Children's behavior, mothers' preferences, and experts' concepts. In E. Waters, B. E. Vaughn, G. Posada, & K. Kondo-Ikemura (Eds.), Caregiving, cultural, and cognitive perspectives on secure-base behavior and working models: New growing points in attachment theory and research. *Monographs of the Society for Research in Child Development, 60* (Serial No. 244), 27–48.

Povinelli, D. J. (1995). The unduplicated self. In P. Rochat (Ed.), *The self in early infancy* (pp. 161–192). Amsterdam, The Netherlands: North-Holland/Elsevier.

Reese, E., & Fivush, R. (1993). Parental styles of talking about the past. *Developmental Psychology, 29,* 596–606.

Reiss, D. (1989). The represented and practicing family: Contrasting visions of family continuity. In A. J. Sameroff & R. N. Emde (Eds.), *Relationship disturbances in early childhood* (pp. 191–220). New York: Basic.

Renken, B., Egeland, B., Marvinney, D., Mangelsdorf, S., & Sroufe, L. A. (1989). Early childhood antecedents of aggression and passive-withdrawal in early elementary school. *Journal of Personality, 57,* 257–281.

Richters, J. E., Waters, E., & Vaughn, B. E. (1988). Empirical classification of infant-mother relationships from interactive behavior and crying during reunion. *Child Development, 59,* 512–522.

Robson, K. S., & Moss, H. A. (1970). Patterns and determinants of maternal attachment. *Journal of Pediatrics, 77,* 976–985.

Rogoff, B. (1990). *Apprenticeship in thinking: Cognitive development in social context.* New York: Oxford University Press.

Rosen, W. D., Adamson, L. B., & Bakeman, R. (1992). An experimental investigation of infant social referencing: Mothers' messages and gender differences. *Developmental Psychology, 28,* 1172–1178.

Rosenblum, L. A., & Sunderland, G. (1982). Feeding ecology and mother-infant relations. In L. W. Hoffman, R. Gandelman, & H. R. Schiffman (Eds.), *Parenting: Its causes and consequences* (pp. 75–110). Hillsdale, NJ: Erlbaum.

Ross, M. (1989). Relation of implicit theories to the construction of personal histories. *Psychological Review, 96,* 341–357.

Sagi, A., Lamb, M. E., & Gardner, W. (1986). Relations between Strange Situation behavior and stranger sociability among infants on Israeli kibbutzim. *Infant Behavior and Development, 9,* 271–282.

Sagi, A., Lamb, M. E., Lewkowicz, K. S., Shoham, R., Dvir, R., & Estes, D. (1985). Security of infant-mother, -father, and -metapelet attachments among kibbutz-reared Israeli children. In I. Bretherton & E. Waters (Eds.), Growing points of attachment theory and research. *Monographs of the Society for Research in Child Development, 50* (Serial No. 209), 257–275.

Sagi, A., & Lewkowicz, K. S. (1987). A cross-cultural evaluation of attachment research. In L. W. C. Tavecchio & M. H. van IJzendoorn (Eds.), *Attachment in social networks* (pp. 427–459). Amsterdam, The Netherlands: Elsevier.

Sagi, A., Van IJzendoorn, M. H., Aviezer, O., Donnell, F., Koren-Karie, N., Joels, T., & Harel, Y. (1995). Attachments in a multiple-caregiver and multiple-infant environment: The case of the Israeli kibbutzim. In E. Waters, B. E. Vaughn, G. Posada, & K. Kondo-Ikemura (Eds.), Caregiving, cultural, and cognitive perspectives on secure-base behavior and working models: New growing points in attachment theory and research. *Monographs of the Society for Research in Child Development, 60*(Serial No. 244), 71–91.

Sagi, A., Van IJzendoorn, M. H., Aviezer, O., Donnell, F., & Mayseless, O. (1994). Sleeping out of home in a kibbutz communal arrangement: It makes a difference for infant-mother attachment. *Child Development, 65,* 992–1004.

Sagi, A., Van IJzendoorn, M. H., & Koren-Karie, N. (1991). Primary appraisal of the Strange Situation: A cross-cultural analysis of preseparation episodes. *Developmental Psychology, 27,* 587–596.

Sagi, A., Van IJzendoorn, M., Scharf, M., Koren-Karie, N., Joels, T., & Mayseless, O. (1994). Stability and discriminant validity of the Adult Attachment Interview: A psychometric study in young Israeli adults. *Developmental Psychology, 30,* 771–777.

Scarr, S. (1992). Developmental theories for the 1990s: Development and individual differences. *Child Development, 63,* 1–19.

Schneider-Rosen, K. (1990). The developmental reorganization of attachment relationships. In M. T. Greenberg, D. Cicchetti, & E. M. Cummings (Eds.), *Attachment in the preschool years* (pp. 185–220). Chicago: University of Chicago Press.

Schneider-Rosen, K., Braunwald, K. G., Carlson, V., & Cicchetti, D. (1985). Current perspectives in attachment theory: Illustration from the study of maltreated infants. In I. Bretherton & E. Waters (Eds.), Growing points of attachment theory and research. *Monographs of the Society for Research in Child Development, 50*(1/2, Serial No. 209), 194–210.

Schneider-Rosen, K., & Cicchetti, D. (1984). The relationship between affect and cognition in maltreated infants: Quality of attachment and the development of visual self-recognition. *Child Development, 55,* 648–658.

Schneider-Rosen, K., & Cicchetti, D. (1991). Early self-knowledge and emotional development: Visual self-recognition and affective reactions to mirror self-images in maltreated and non-maltreated toddlers. *Developmental Psychology, 27,* 471–478.

Schneider Rosen, K., & Rothbaum, F. (1993). Quality of parental caregiving and security of attachment. *Developmental Psychology, 29,* 358–367.

Scholmerich, A., Fracasso, M. P., Lamb, M. E., & Broberg, A. (1995). Interactional harmony at 7- and 10-months-of-age predicts security of attachment as measured by Q-sort ratings. *Social Development, 4,* 62–74.

Scholmerich, A., Lamb, M. E., Leyendecker, B., & Fracasso, M. P. (in press). Mother-infant teaching interactions and attachment security in Euro-American and Central-American immigrant families. *Infant Behavior and Development.*

Seifer, R., & Schiller, M. (1995). The role of parenting sensitivity, infant temperament, and dyadic interaction in attachment theory and assessment. In E. Waters, B. E. Vaughn, G. Posada, & K. Kondo-Ikemura (Eds.), Caregiving, cultural, and cognitive perspectives on secure-base behavior and working models: New growing points in attachment theory and research. *Monographs of the Society for Research in Child Development, 60*(Serial No. 244), 146–174.

Seifer, R., Schiller, M., Sameroff, A. J., Resnick, S., & Riordan, K. (1996). Attachment, maternal sensitivity, and temperament during the first year of life. *Developmental Psychology, 32,* 12–25.

Selman, R. L. (1980). *The growth of interpersonal understanding.* New York: Academic Press.

Shaver, P. R., & Hazan, C. (1993). Adult romantic attachment: Theory and evidence. In D. Perlman & W. H. Jones (Eds.), *Advances in personal relationships* (Vol. 4, pp. 29–70). London: Jessica Kingsley.

Shaw, D. S., & Vondra, J. I. (1993). Chronic family adversity and infant attachment security. *Journal of Child Psychology and Psychiatry, 34,* 1205–1215.

Shorter, E. (1975). *The making of the modern family.* New York: Basic Books.

Shouldice, A., & Stevenson-Hinde, J. (1992). Coping with security distress: The Separation Anxiety Test and attachment classification at 4.5 years. *Journal of Child Psychology and Psychiatry, 33,* 331–348.

Shulman, S., Elicker, J., & L. A. Sroufe (1994). Stages of friendship growth in preadolescence as related to attachment history. *Journal of Social and Personal Relationships, 11,* 341–361.

Sigel, I. E., McGillicuddy-DeLisi, A. V., & Goodnow, J. J. (Eds.). (1992). *Parent belief systems* (2nd ed.). Hillsdale, NJ: Erlbaum.

Singer, L. M., Brodzinsky, D. M., Ramsay, D., Steir, M., & Waters, E. (1985). Mother-infant attachment in adoptive families. *Child Development, 56,* 1543–1551.

Slade, A. (1987). Quality of attachment and early symbolic play. *Developmental Psychology, 23,* 78–85.

Slomkowski, C. L., & Dunn, J. (1992). Arguments and relationships within the family: Differences in young children's disputes with mother and sibling. *Developmental Psychology, 28,* 919–924.

Slough, N. M., & Greenberg, M. T. (1990). Five-year-olds' representations of separation from parents: Responses from the perspective of self and other. In I. Bretherton & M. W. Watson (Eds.), *Children's perspectives on the family: 48* (pp. 67–84). San Francisco: Jossey-Bass.

Smetana, J. G. (Ed.). (1994). *Beliefs about parenting: Origins and developmental implications: 66.* San Francisco: Jossey-Bass.

Smith, P. B., & Pederson, D. R. (1988). Maternal sensitivity and patterns of infant-mother attachment. *Child Development, 59,* 1097–1101.

Smith, P. K., & Noble, R. (1987). Factors affecting the development of caregiver-infant relationships. In L. W. C. Tavecchio & M. H. Van IJzendoorn (Eds.), *Attachment in social networks* (pp. 93–134). Amsterdam, The Netherlands: Elsevier.

Snow, C. E. (1990). Building memories: The ontogeny of autobiography. In D. Cicchetti & M. Beeghly (Eds.), *The self in transition: Infancy to childhood* (pp. 213–242). Chicago: University of Chicago Press.

Solomon, J., & George, C. (in press). The measurement of attachment security in infancy and childhood. In J. Cassidy & P. R. Shaver (Eds.), *Handbook of attachment theory and research.* New York: Guilford Press.

Sorce, J. F., Emde, R. N., Campos, J. J., & Klinnert, M. D. (1985). Maternal emotional signaling: Its effect on the visual cliff behavior of 1-year-olds. *Developmental Psychology, 21,* 195–200.

Spangler, G., & Grossmann, K. E. (1993). Biobehavioral organization in securely and insecurely attached infants. *Child Development, 64,* 1439–1450.

Spieker, S. J., & Bensley, L. (1994). Roles of living arrangements and grandmother social support in adolescent mothering and infant attachment. *Developmental Psychology, 30,* 102–111.

Sroufe, L. A. (1979). The coherence of individual development: Early care, attachment, and subsequent developmental issues. *American Psychologist, 34,* 834–841.

Sroufe, L. A. (1983). Infant-caregiver attachment and patterns of adaptation in preschool: The roots of maladaptation and competence. In M. Perlmutter (Ed.), *Development and policy concerning children with special needs. Minnesota Symposia on Child Psychology* (Vol. 16, pp. 41–83). Hillsdale, NJ: Erlbaum.

Sroufe, L. A. (1985). Attachment classification from the perspective of infant-caregiver relationships and infant temperament. *Child Development, 56,* 1–14.

Sroufe, L. A. (1988). The role of infant-caregiver attachment in development. In J. Belsky & T. Nezworski (Eds.), *Clinical implications of attachment* (pp. 18–38). Hillsdale, NJ: Erlbaum.

Sroufe, L. A. (1990). An organizational perspective on the self. In D. Cicchetti & M. Beeghly (Eds.), *The self in transition: Infancy to childhood* (pp. 281–307). Chicago: University of Chicago Press.

Sroufe, L. A. (1996). *Emotional development.* Cambridge, England: Cambridge University Press.

Sroufe, L. A., Carlson, E., & Schulman, S. (1993). Individuals in relationships: Development from infancy through adolescence. In D. C. Funder, R. D. Parke, C. Tomlinson-Keasey, & K. Widaman (Eds.), *Studying lives through time: Personality and development* (pp. 315–342). Washington, DC: American Psychological Association.

Sroufe, L. A., & Egeland, B. (1991). Illustrations of person-environment interaction from a longitudinal study. In T. D. Wachs & R. Plomin (Eds.), *Conceptualization and measurement of organism-environment interaction* (pp. 68–84). Washington, DC: American Psychological Association.

Sroufe, L. A., Egeland, B., & Kreutzer, T. (1990). The fate of early experience following developmental change: Longitudinal approaches to individual adaptation in childhood. *Child Development, 61,* 1363–1373.

Sroufe, L. A., & Fleeson, J. (1986). Attachment and the construction of relationships. In W. W. Hartup & Z. Rubin (Eds.), *Relationships and development* (pp. 51–71). Hillsdale, NJ: Erlbaum.

Sroufe, L. A., & Fleeson, J. (1988). The coherence of family relationships. In R. A. Hinde & J. Stevenson-Hinde (Eds.), *Relationships within families* (pp. 27–47). Oxford, England: Clarendon Press.

Sroufe, L. A., Fox, N. E., & Pancake, V. R. (1983). Attachment and dependency in developmental perspective. *Child Development, 54,* 1615–1627.

Sroufe, L. A., Schork, E., Motti, E., Lawroski, N., & LaFreniere, P. (1984). The role of affect in emerging social competence. In C. Izard, J. Kagan, & R. Zajonc (Eds.), *Emotion, cognition and behavior* (pp. 289–319). New York: Cambridge University Press.

Sroufe, L. A., & Waters, E. (1977). Attachment as an organizational construct. *Child Development, 48,* 1184–1199.

Stern, D. N. (1985). *The interpersonal world of the infant.* New York: Basic.

Stern, D. N. (1989a). The representation of relational patterns: Developmental considerations. In A. J. Sameroff & R. N. Emde (Eds.), *Relationship disturbances in early childhood* (pp. 52–69). New York: Basic.

Stern, D. N. (1989b). Crib monologues from a psychoanalytic perspective. In K. Nelson (Ed.), *Narratives from the crib* (pp. 309–319). Cambridge, MA: Harvard University Press.

Stevenson-Hinde, J. (1991). Temperament and attachment: An eclectic approach. In P. Bateson (Ed.), *The development and integration of behavior* (pp. 315–329). Cambridge, England: Cambridge University Press.

Stifter, C. A., & Braungart, J. M. (1995). The regulation of negative reactivity in infancy: Function and development. *Developmental Psychology, 31,* 448–455.

Stifter, C. A., Coulehan, C. M., & Fish, M. (1993). Linking employment to attachment: The mediating effects of maternal separation anxiety and interactive behavior. *Child Development, 64,* 1451–1460.

Stipek, D. (1995). The development of pride and shame in toddlers. In J. P. Tangney & K. W. Fischer (Eds.), *Self-conscious emotions* (pp. 237–252). New York: Guilford Press.

Stipek, D., Gralinski, J. H., & Kopp, C. B. (1990). Self-concept development in the toddler years. *Developmental Psychology, 26,* 972–977.

Stipek, D., Recchia, S., & McClintic, S. (1992). Self-evaluation in young children. *Monographs of the Society for Research in Child Development, 57*(1, Serial No. 226).

Suess, G. J., Grossmann, K. E., & Sroufe, L. A. (1992). Effects of infant attachment to mother and father on quality of adaptation in preschool: From dyadic to individual organization of self. *International Journal of Behavioral Development, 15,* 43–65.

Super, C. M., & Harkness, S. (1986). The developmental niche: A conceptualization at the interface of child and culture. *International Journal of Behavioral Development, 9,* 545–569.

Symons, D. K., & Moran, G. (1987). The behavioral dynamics of mutual responsiveness in early face-to-face mother-infant interaction. *Child Development, 58,* 1488–1495.

Takahashi, K. (1985, April). *Behavior changes in the Strange-Situation procedure among Japanese young children between the 12th and 23rd months.* Paper presented to the biennial meeting of the Society for Research in Child Development, Toronto.

Takahashi, K. (1986). Examining the Strange-Situation procedure with Japanese mothers and 12-month-old infants. *Developmental Psychology, 22,* 265–270.

Takahashi, K. (1990). Are the key assumptions of the "Strange Situation" procedure universal? A view from Japanese research. *Human Development, 33,* 23–30.

Takanishi, R. (1978). Childhood as a social issue: Historical roots of contemporary child advocacy movements. *Journal of Social Issues, 34,* 8–28.

Termine, N. T., & Izard, C. E. (1988). Infants' responses to their mothers' expressions of joy and sadness. *Developmental Psychology, 24,* 223–229.

Tesla, C., & Dunn, J. (1992). Getting along or getting your own way: The development of young children's use of argument in conflicts with mother and sibling. *Social Development, 1,* 107–121.

Teti, D. M., & Ablard, K. E. (1989). Security of attachment and infant-sibling relationships: A laboratory study. *Child Development, 60,* 1519–1528.

Teti, D. M., & McGourty, S. (1996). Using mothers vs. observers of children's secure base behavior: Theoretical and methodological considerations. *Child Development, 67,* 597–596.

Teti, D. M., Nakagawa, M., Das, R., & Wirth, O. (1991). Security of attachment between preschoolers and their mothers: Relations among social interaction, parenting stress, and mothers' sorts of the attachment Q-set. *Developmental Psychology, 27,* 440–447.

Teti, D. M., Sakin, J., Kucera, E., Corns, K. M., & Das Eiden, R. (1996). And baby makes four: Predictors of attachment security among preschool-aged firstborns during the transition to siblinghood. *Child Development, 67,* 579–596.

Thompson, R. A. (1986). Temperament, emotionality, and infant social cognition. In J. V. Lerner & R. M. Lerner (Eds.), *Temperament and social interaction during infancy and childhood: 31* (pp. 35–52). San Francisco: Jossey-Bass.

Thompson, R. A. (1987). Empathy and emotional understanding: The early development of empathy. In N. Eisenberg & J. Strayer (Eds.), *Empathy and its development* (pp. 119–145). Cambridge, England: Cambridge University Press.

Thompson, R. A. (1988). The effects of infant day care through the prism of attachment theory: A critical appraisal. *Early Childhood Research Quarterly, 3,* 273–282.

Thompson, R. A. (1990a). Vulnerability in research: A developmental perspective on research risk. *Child Development, 61,* 1–16.

Thompson, R. A. (1990b). Emotion and self-regulation. In R. A. Thompson (Ed.), *Socioemotional development. Nebraska Symposium on Motivation* (Vol. 36, pp 383–483). Lincoln: University of Nebraska Press.

Thompson, R. A. (1991). Construction and reconstruction of early attachments: Taking perspective on attachment theory and research. In D. P. Keating & H. Rosen (Eds.), *Construc-*
tivist perspectives on atypical development and developmental psychopathology (pp. 41–67). Hillsdale, NJ: Erlbaum.

Thompson, R. A. (1993). Socioemotional development: Enduring issues and new challenges. *Developmental Review, 13,* 372–402.

Thompson, R. A. (1994). Emotion regulation: A theme in search of definition. In N. A. Fox (Ed.), The development of emotion regulation: Biological and behavioral considerations. *Monographs of the Society for Research in Child Development, 59*(Serial No. 240), 25–52.

Thompson, R. A. (1995). *Preventing child maltreatment through social support: A critical analysis.* Newbury Park, CA: Sage.

Thompson, R. A. (in press-a). Reflections on early empathy. In S. Braten (Ed.), *Intersubjective communication and emotion in ontogeny: A sourcebook.* Cambridge, England: Cambridge University Press.

Thompson, R. A. (in press-b). Early attachment and later development. In J. Cassidy & P. R. Shaver (Eds.), *Handbook of attachment theory and research.* New York: Guilford Press.

Thompson, R. A. (in press-c). Sensitivity and security: New questions to ponder. *Child Development, 68.*

Thompson, R. A., & Calkins, S. (1996). The double-edged sword: Emotional regulation for children at risk. *Development and Psychopathology, 8,* 163–182.

Thompson, R. A., Connell, J. P., & Bridges, L. J. (1988). Temperament, emotion, and social interactive behavior in the Strange Situation: A component process analysis of attachment system functioning. *Child Development, 59,* 1102–1110.

Thompson, R. A., Flood, M. F., & Lundquist, L. (1995). Emotional regulation: Its relations to attachment and developmental psychopathology. In D. Cicchetti & S. L. Toth (Eds.), *Emotion, cognition, and representation. Rochester Symposium on Developmental Psychopathology* (Vol. 6, pp. 261–299). Rochester, NY: University of Rochester Press.

Thompson, R. A., Garbin, C. P., & Otten, C. (1996). *Adult perception of emotion in the cries of one-year-olds.* Unpublished manuscript, University of Nebraska-Lincoln.

Thompson, R. A., & Lamb, M. E. (1983). Security of attachment and stranger sociability in infancy. *Developmental Psychology, 19,* 184–191.

Thompson, R. A., & Lamb, M. E. (1984). Assessing qualitative dimensions of emotional responsiveness in infants: Separation reactions in the Strange Situation. *Infant Behavior and Development, 7,* 423–445.

Thompson, R. A., Lamb, M. E., & Estes, D. (1982). Stability of infant-mother attachment and its relationship to changing life circumstances in an unselected middle-class sample. *Child Development, 53,* 144–148.

Thompson, R. A., Lamb, M. E., & Estes, D. (1983). Harmonizing discordant notes: A reply to Waters. *Child Development, 54*, 521–524.

Thompson, R. A., & Leger, D. W. (in press). From squalls to calls: The cry as a developing socioemotional signal. In B. Lester, J. Newman, & F. Pedersen (Eds.), *Biological and social aspects of infant crying.* New York: Plenum Press.

Tomasello, M. (1995). Joint attention as social cognition. In C. Moore & P. J. Dunham (Eds.), *Joint attention: Its origin and role in development.* Hillsdale, NJ: Erlbaum.

Tomasello, M., Kruger, A. C., & Ratner, H. H. (1993). Cultural learning. *Behavioral and Brain Sciences, 16*, 495–511.

Trevarthen, C. (1979). Communication and cooperation in early infancy: A description of primary intersubjectivity. In M. Bullowa (Ed.), *Before speech* (pp. 321–347). Cambridge, England: Cambridge University Press.

Trevarthen, C., & Hubley, P. (1978). Secondary intersubjectivity: Confidence, confiding, and acts of meaning in the first year. In A. Lock (Ed.), *Action, gesture, and symbol: The emergence of language* (pp. 183–229). New York: Academic Press.

Trivers, R. L. (1974). Parent-offspring conflict. *American Zoologist, 14*, 249–264.

Trivers, R. L. (1985). *Social evolution.* Menlo Park, CA: Benjamin/Cummings.

Tronick, E. Z. (1989). Emotions and emotional communication in infants. *American Psychologist, 44*, 112–119.

Tronick, E. Z., & Cohn, J. F. (1989). Infant-mother face-to-face interaction: Age and gender differences in coordination and the occurrence of miscoordination. *Child Development, 60*, 85–92.

Tronick, E. Z., Morelli, G. A., & Ivey, P. K. (1992). The Efe forager infant and toddler's pattern of social relationships: Multiple and simultaneous. *Developmental Psychology, 28*, 568–577.

Troy, M., & Sroufe, L. A. (1987). Victimization among preschoolers: Role of attachment relationship history. *Journal of the American Academy of Child and Adolescent Psychiatry, 26*, 166–172.

Turner, P. J. (1991). Relations between attachment, gender, and behavior with peers in preschool. *Child Development, 62*, 1475–1488.

Urban, J., Carlson, E., Egeland, B., & Sroufe, L. A. (1991). Patterns of individual adaptation across childhood. *Development and Psychopathology, 3*, 445–460.

Valenzuela, M. (1990). Attachment in chronically underweight young children. *Child Development, 61*, 1984–1996.

van Dam, M., & Van IJzendoorn, M. H. (1988). Measuring attachment security: Concurrent and predictive validity of the parental attachment Q-set. *Journal of Genetic Psychology, 149*, 447–457.

van den Boom, D. C. (1989). Neonatal irritability and the development of attachment. In G. A. Kohnstamm, J. E. Bates, & M. K. Rothbart (Eds.), *Temperament in childhood* (pp. 299–318). New York: Wiley.

van den Boom, D. C. (1994). The influence of temperament and mothering on attachment and exploration: An experimental manipulation of sensitive responsiveness among lower-class mothers with irritable infants. *Child Development, 65*, 1457–1477.

Van IJzendoorn, M. H. (1990). Attachment in Surinam-Dutch families: A contribution to the cross-cultural study of attachment. *International Journal of Behavioral Development, 13*, 333–343.

Van IJzendoorn, M. H. (1995a). The association between adult attachment representations and infant attachment, parental responsiveness, and clinical status: A meta-analysis on the predictive validity of the Adult Attachment Interview. *Psychological Bulletin, 113*, 404–410.

Van IJzendoorn, M. H. (1995b). Of the way we are: On temperament, attachment and the transmission gap. A rejoinder to Fox. *Psychological Bulletin, 113*, 411–415.

Van IJzendoorn, M. H., Goldberg, S., Kroonenberg, P. M., & Frenkel, O. J. (1992). The relative effects of maternal and child problems on the quality of attachment: A meta-analysis of attachment in clinical samples. *Child Development, 63*, 840–858.

Van IJzendoorn, M. H., Goossens, F. A., Kroonenberg, P. M., & Tavecchio, L. W. C. (1985). Dependent attachment: B4-children in the Strange Situation. *Psychological Reports, 57*, 439–451.

Van IJzendoorn, M. H., Juffer, F., & Duyvesteyn, M. G. C. (1995). Breaking the intergenerational cycle of insecure attachment: A review of the effects of attachment-based interventions on maternal sensitivity and infant security. *Journal of Child Psychology and Psychiatry, 36*, 225–248.

Van IJzendoorn, M. H., Kranenburg, M. J., Zwart-Woudstra, H. A., van Busschbach, A. M., & Lambermon, M. W. E. (1991). Parental attachment and children's socio-emotional development: Some findings on the validity of the Adult Attachment Interview in The Netherlands. *International Journal of Behavioral Development, 14*, 375–394.

Van IJzendoorn, M. H., & Kroonenberg, P. M. (1988). Cross-cultural patterns of attachment: A meta-analysis of the Strange Situation. *Child Development, 59*, 147–156.

Van IJzendoorn, M. H., & Kroonenberg, P. M. (1990). Cross-cultural consistency of coding the Strange Situation. *Infant Behavior and Development, 13*, 469–485.

Van IJzendoorn, M. H., & Sagi, A. (in press). Cross-cultural patterns of attachment: Universal and contextual dimensions. In J. Cassidy & P. R. Shaver (Eds.), *Handbook of attachment theory and research*. New York: Guilford Press.

Van IJzendoorn, M. H., Sagi, A., & Lambermon, M. W. E. (1992). The multiple caretaker paradox: Data from Holland and Israel. In R. C. Pianta (Ed.), *Beyond the parent: The role of other adults in children's lives: 57* (pp. 5–24). San Francisco: Jossey-Bass.

Van IJzendoorn, M. H., van der Veer, R., & van Vliet-Visser, S. (1987). Attachment three years later. Relationships between quality of mother-infant attachment and emotional/cognitive development in kindergarten. In L. W. C. Tavecchio & M. H. Van IJzendoorn (Eds.), *Attachment in social networks* (pp. 185–224). Amsterdam, The Netherlands: Elsevier.

Vaughn, B. E., Block, J. H., & Block, J. (1988). Parental agreement on child rearing during early childhood and the psychological characteristics of adolescents. *Child Development, 59,* 1020–1033.

Vaughn, B. E., Deane, K. E., & Waters, E. (1985). The impact of out-of-home care on child-mother attachment quality: Another look at some enduring questions. In I. Bretherton & E. Waters (Eds.), Growing points of attachment theory and research. *Monographs of the Society for Research in Child Development, 50*(1/2, Serial No. 209), 110–135.

Vaughn, B. E., Egeland, B., Sroufe, L. A., & Waters, E. (1979). Individual differences in infant-mother attachment at twelve and eighteen months: Stability and change in families under stress. *Child Development, 50,* 971–975.

Vaughn, B. E., Goldberg, S., Atkinson, L., Marcovitch, S., MacGregor, D., & Seifer, R. (1994). Quality of toddler-mother attachment in children with Down syndrome: Limits to interpretation of Strange Situation behavior. *Child Development, 65,* 95–108.

Vaughn, B. E., Gove, F. L., & Egeland, B. (1980). The relationship between out-of-home care and the quality of infant-mother attachment in an economically disadvantaged population. *Child Development, 51,* 1203–1214.

Vaughn, B. E., Kopp, C. B., & Krakow, J. B. (1984). The emergence and consolidation of self-control from eighteen to thirty months of age: Normative trends and individual differences. *Child Development, 55,* 990–1004.

Vaughn, B. E., Lefever, G. B., Seifer, R., & Barglow, P. (1989). Attachment behavior, attachment security, and temperament during infancy. *Child Development, 60,* 728–737.

Vaughn, B. E., Stevenson-Hinde, J., Waters, E., Kotsaftis, A., Lefever, G. B., Shouldice, A., Trudel, M., & Belsky, J. (1992). Attachment security and temperament in infancy and early childhood: Some conceptual clarifications. *Developmental Psychology, 28,* 463–473.

Vaughn, B. E., & Waters, E. (1990). Attachment behavior at home and in the laboratory: Q-sort observations and Strange Situation classifications of one-year-olds. *Child Development, 61,* 1965–1990.

Volling, B. L., & Belsky, J. (1992a). Infant, father, and marital antecedents of infant-father attachment security in dual-earner and single-earner families. *International Journal of Behavioral Development, 15,* 83–100.

Volling, B. L., & Belsky, J. (1992b). The contribution of mother-child and father-child relationships to the quality of sibling interaction: A longitudinal study. *Child Development, 63,* 1209–1222.

Wachs, T. D., & Desai, S. (1993). Parent-report measures of toddler temperament and attachment: Their relation to each other and to the social microenvironment. *Infant Behavior and Development, 16,* 391–396.

Walden, T. A., & Baxter, A. (1989). The effect of context and age on social referencing. *Child Development, 60,* 1511–1518.

Walden, T. A., & Ogan, T. A. (1988). The development of social referencing. *Child Development, 59,* 1230–1240.

Wartner, U. G., Grossmann, K., Fremmer-Bombik, E., & Suess, G. (1994). Attachment patterns at age six in South Germany: Predictability from infancy and implications for preschool behavior. *Child Development, 65,* 1014–1027.

Waters, E. (1978). The reliability and stability of individual differences in infant-mother attachment. *Child Development, 49,* 483–494.

Waters, E., & Deane, K. E. (1985). Defining and assessing individual differences in attachment relationships: Q-methodology and the organization of behavior in infancy and early childhood. In I. Bretherton & E. Waters (Eds.), Growing points of attachment theory and research. *Monographs of the Society for Research in Child Development, 50*(1/2, Serial No. 209), 41–65.

Waters, E., Kondo-Ikemura, K., Posada, G., & Richters, J. E. (1991). Learning to love: Mechanisms and milestones. In M. R. Gunnar & L. A. Sroufe (Eds.), *Self processes and development. Minnesota Symposia on Child Psychology* (Vol. 23, pp. 217–255). Hillsdale, NJ: Erlbaum.

Waters, E., Wippman, J., & Sroufe, L. A. (1979). Attachment, positive affect, and competence in the peer group: Two studies in construct validation. *Child Development, 50,* 821–829.

Watson, J. S. (1972). Smiling, cooing, and "the game." *Merrill-Palmer Quarterly, 18,* 323–339.

Watson, J. S. (1979). Perception of contingency as a determinant of social responsiveness. In E. B. Thoman (Ed.), *Origins of the infant's social responsiveness* (pp. 33–64). Hillsdale, NJ: Erlbaum.

Weber, R. A., Levitt, M. J., & Clark, M. C. (1986). Individual variation in attachment security and Strange Situation behavior: The role of maternal and infant temperament. *Child Development, 57,* 56–65.

Welch-Ross, M. K. (1995). An integrative model of the development of autobiographical memory. *Developmental Review, 15,* 338–365.

Wellman, H. M. (1990). *The child's theory of mind.* Cambridge, MA: MIT Press.

Wellman, H. M. (1993). Early understanding of mind: The normal case. In S. Baron-Cohen, H. Tager-Flusberg, & D. J. Cohen (Eds.), *Understanding other minds: Perspectives from autism* (pp. 10–39). Oxford, England: Oxford University Press.

Wellman, H. M., Harris, P. L., Banerjee, M., & Sinclair, A. (1995). Early understanding of emotion: Evidence from natural language. *Cognition and Emotion, 9,* 117–149.

Youngblade, L. M., & Belsky, J. (1992). Parent-child antecedents of 5-year-olds' close friendships: A longitudinal analysis. *Developmental Psychology, 28,* 700–713.

Youngblade, L. M., & Dunn, J. (1995). Individual differences in young children's pretend play with mother and sibling: Links to relationships and understanding of other people's feelings and beliefs. *Child Development, 66,* 1472–1492.

Youngblade, L. M., Park, K. A., & Belsky, J. (1993). Measurement of young children's close friendship: A comparison of two independent assessment systems and their associations with attachment security. *International Journal of Behavioral Development, 16,* 563–587.

Zahn-Waxler, C., & Radke-Yarrow, M. (1990). The origins of empathic concern. *Motivation and Emotion, 14,* 107–130.

Zahn-Waxler, C., Radke-Yarrow, M., Wagner, E., & Chapman, M. (1992). Development of concern for others. *Developmental Psychology, 28,* 126–136.

Zahn-Waxler, C., & Robinson, J. (1995). Empathy and guilt: Early origins of feelings of responsibility. In J. P. Tangney & K. W. Fischer (Eds.), *Self-conscious emotions* (pp. 143–173). New York: Guilford Press.

Zarbatany, L., & Lamb, M. E. (1985). Social referencing as a function of information source: Mothers versus strangers. *Infant Behavior and Development, 8,* 25–33.

Zaslow, M. J., Rabinovich, B. A., Suwalsky, J. T. D., & Klein, R. P. (1988). The role of social context in the prediction of secure and insecure/avoidant infant-mother attachment. *Journal of Applied Developmental Psychology, 9,* 287–299.

Zeskind, P. S. (1985). A developmental perspective on infant crying. In B. M. Lester & C. F. Z. Boukydis (Eds.), *Infant crying* (pp. 159–185). New York: Plenum Press.

CHAPTER 3

Temperament

MARY K. ROTHBART and JOHN E. BATES

You see, a child is not born tabula rasa as one assumes. . . . Already in earliest childhood, a mother recognizes the individuality of her child; and so, if you observe carefully, you see a tremendous difference, even in very small children. Carl J. Jung (cited by Baughman, 1972, p. 180)

In this chapter, we explore historical influences and recent advances in our understanding of individual differences in temperament, differences that have been observed by parents and physicians long before their systematic study by students of human development. A *Handbook* chapter on temperament provides important recognition of our field of study, and our aim will be to present a structure for thinking about theoretical, empirical, and clinical approaches to the area. We begin with a brief history of temperament research, considering its recent history and ties to behavioral genetics and comparative psychology, its ancient roots, and its study in adulthood. In the second section, we examine the structure of temperament as it has emerged from work in child development and from major theoretical models of the neurosciences. We also note the historical search for a taxonomic structure of adult personality, relating temperament structure to the Big Three and Big Five factors of personality.

In the third section, we discuss methods and measures for the study of temperament. We consider some of the major empirical approaches to the study of temperament, their benefits and liabilities. Because the use of parent report in temperament research has recently been questioned (Kagan, 1994, Ch. 4, this Volume), we critically consider contributions of parent report to the study of temperament. In the fourth section, our major conceptual focus is on temperament and development, relating research on the stability of individual differences to developmental transformations. In the fifth section, we discuss relations between temperament and attachment. In the sixth, we consider relations between temperament and behavioral adjustment. The final section presents our conclusions and indicates future directions for the study of temperament and development. Although sections are focused on particular issues, major issues are often discussed in more than one section. For example, adjustment issues, especially those involving positive and prosocial emotions and behaviors, are considered not only in the adjustment section, but also in sections on psychobiology and the relation between attachment and temperament. Throughout the chapter, we construct a developmental model for organizing research findings. Given space limitations, our review is not comprehensive, but we hope it captures some of the major issues and approaches to the study of temperament in childhood.

HISTORY

Normative Studies

Several lines of inquiry have contributed to contemporary temperament research in child development. One is the research of the normative child psychologists in the 1920s and 1930s. These researchers observed large numbers of children to establish the normal sequences of motor and mental development. In doing so, they noted striking temperamental variability among the children they studied (Gesell, 1928, as cited in Kessen, 1965). Shirley's (1933) intensive study of a small group of infants during the first two years of life also gave an early glimpse of developmental processes in relation to individual differences in child temperament. Known for her discoveries of motor milestones in early development, Shirley did not originally intend to study temperament. Struck by individual differences in the infants' "core of personality," however, she devoted a full volume to this topic. Shirley noted that, developmentally, "both constancy and change characterize

the personality of the baby. Traits are constant enough to make it plausible that a nucleus of personality exists at birth and that this nucleus persists and grows and determines to a certain degree the relative importance of (other) traits" (1933, p. 56). Fifteen years later, Neilon (1948) followed up 15 of Shirley's 25 babies, asking judges to match Shirley's infant personality sketches to blind descriptions based on adolescent assessments. The matches were more successful than would have been expected by chance.

Gesell (1928) identified the critical importance of the child's temperament within the developmental "web of life." His views of alternative developmental pathways in relation to individual differences are illustrated in the case of C. D.: "This girl exhibited a striking degree of amenability, sociality, and good nature as early as the age of nine months. . . . She is now five years of age, and in spite of a varied experience in boarding homes and institutions she has not lost these engaging characteristics. They are part and parcel of her make-up quite as much as the lowered tempo and the lowered trend of her general development. It can be predicted with much certainty that she will retain her present emotional equipment when she is an adolescent and an adult. But more than this cannot be predicted in the field of personality. For whether she becomes a delinquent, and she is potentially one, will depend upon her subsequent training, conditioning, and supervision. She is potentially, also, a willing, helpful, productive worker. Environment retains a critical role even though heredity sets metes and bounds" (1928, cited in Kessen, 1965, p. 223).

Gesell and Shirley point to three important concepts to be further elaborated in this chapter. First, temperamental traits can be seen as inherent, constitutionally based characteristics that constitute the core of personality and influence directions for development. Second, although some stability is expected across age in temperamental traits, outcomes depend strongly on developmental processes and the social context. Finally, as in the case of C. D., a given set of temperamental characteristics provides multiple possibilities for developmental outcomes. Different trajectories and outcomes may occur for children with similar temperamental traits, and children differing in temperament may come to similar developmental outcomes via different pathways.

Behavioral Genetics and Comparative Psychology

Research in behavioral genetics and comparative psychology has made early and continuing contributions to the study of temperament. Individual differences in the expression of motivational systems have been investigated both within and across species, and selective breeding of temperament-related characteristics carried out. Major temperamental and related characteristics studied include fearfulness, activity level, impulsivity, dominance, affiliation/dependency, reactivity, and aggression (S. Diamond, 1957).

The comparative psychologist Schneirla (1959) also made important theoretical contributions. He postulated multiple approach and withdrawal systems existing across species. Approach (A) processes involved movement toward stimulation, especially stimulation of low intensity. Withdrawal (W) processes involved movement away from often higher intensity sources of stimulation. A and W processes opposed one another, so that individual variability in the strength of A and W systems would influence the likelihood of withdrawal or approach in a given situation. For many nonhuman species and neonates, "Intensity of stimulation basically determines the direction of reaction with respect to the source" (Schneirla, 1959, p. 2). With continuing development in humans, cognitive and experiential factors come to influence the operation of approach and withdrawal. Windle (1995) and Stifter (1995) have recently applied Schneirla's ideas to temperament, and later in the chapter we recognize some additional descendants of Schneirla's ideas.

Behavioral genetics study of animal populations continues today, including research on sensation seeking and related addiction proneness (e.g., Bardo, Donohew, & Harrington, 1996). One of the most exciting current approaches to the behavioral genetics of temperament in nonhumans is the Dog Genome Project, a collaborative study involving selective breeding that seeks to map the location of genes related to dogs' disease susceptibility, morphology, and behavior (e.g., Ostrander, Sprague, & Rive, 1993).

Clinical Research

A third major line of research in the early study of temperament came from biologically oriented clinicians. Bergman and Escalona (1949) identified children who were particularly reactive in one or more sensory modalities to even low intensities of stimulation. In Escalona's (1968) important book, *The Roots of Individuality,* she proposed the concept of effective experience, the idea that events in children's lives will be effectively experienced only as they are filtered through the individual child's nervous system. A given event will differ in its effects for children who differ in temperament. For example, an adult's vigorous play may

lead to pleasure in one child and distress in another. Escalona noted that objective coding of environmental events alone does not capture essential information about the child's actual reaction to them. Escalona's (1968) research samples were followed in studies of vulnerability, resiliency, and coping by Murphy and Moriarty (1976). Fries and Woolf (1953) identified and studied what they called congenital activity type; Korner (1964) studied neonatal individuality and developed an extensive assessment schedule for the newborn; and Birns (1965) and her associates developed and implemented some of the earliest laboratory assessments of temperament.

Among these clinical investigators, Thomas, Chess, Birch, Hertzig, and Korn published the first of their volumes on the extremely influential New York Longitudinal Study (NYLS) in 1963. Inspired by differences among their own children, Chess and Thomas set out to study individual differences in what they called the primary reaction patterns of infants, collecting interviews from parents of infants on different occasions. Beginning when the initial sample of 22 infants were 3 to 6 months of age, parents were extensively interviewed about their infants' behavior in specific contexts. Each infant reaction with its context was then typed on a separate sheet of paper, and Birch inductively sorted the descriptions into sets that came to represent the nine NYLS temperament dimensions (Chess & Thomas, personal communication, 1992; Thomas et al., 1963). These dimensions were activity level, approach/withdrawal, adaptability, mood, threshold, intensity, distractibility, rhythmicity, and attention span/persistence. Later, Michael Rutter suggested the term *temperament* to Thomas and Chess to describe their area of study, and this term was adopted (Chess & Thomas, personal communication, 1992).

Acceptance of Temperament Research

Reports from the NYLS arrived at an opportune time, when researchers in social development were becoming increasingly aware of the contributions of individual children to their own development. One reason was the burgeoning of infancy research, with researchers studying the "initial state" of the individual and its subsequent adaptations (Haith & Campos, 1983; Osofsky, 1979). Because the initial state varied from child to child (Korner, 1964), early differences might be seen as constituting the raw material for later development. Ideas put forward by Robert Sears and associates (e.g., Sears, Maccoby, & Levin, 1957) were also now reemerging regarding the bidirectionality of socialization effects, from child to care-giver as well as caregiver to child (Bell, 1968; Schaffer & Emerson, 1964). Finally, cognitive approaches stressed children's influences on their own development via their perceptual and cognitive mental representations. Research on temperament would now introduce the idea that individual differences in children's *emotional* processing could result in biasing of their affectively based representations of experience, with important implications for their development.

Adult Studies

Adult studies of temperament have a much longer history than developmental work, much of it under the heading of biological aspects of personality. Ideas about temperament go back to Greco-Roman physicians over 2,000 years ago and to ancient traditions in China and India (S. Diamond, 1974; Needham, 1973). Throughout these approaches, psychological characteristics were linked to the current understanding of physiology. Thus, ancient Greco-Roman physicians identified the well-known fourfold typology and linked it to the bodily humors: the sanguine individual, positive and outgoing, with a predominance of blood; the melancholic person, prone to fear and sadness, with a predominance of black bile; the choleric person, irritable and prone to aggression, with a predominance of yellow bile; and the phlegmatic person, slow to excitation, with a predominance of phlegm (S. Diamond, 1974). The fourfold typology was used throughout the Middle Ages and in the writings of Kant. By the time of Wundt (1903), however, a shift was made from positing temperamental "types" to studying dimensions of variability in temperament, a shift that has only recently been reversed in Kagan's (Ch. 4, this Volume) use of a temperament typology.

Ancient Hippocratic ideas about temperament were carried to the United States in Sheldon's work on body structure and temperament (Sheldon & Stevens, 1942), but this approach did not grow into an active movement (see discussions by Kagan, Ch. 4, this Volume; Rothbart, 1989a). Two schools of study in other countries, however, did develop into major research movements. The first was the early British factor analysis tradition (e.g., Burt, 1937), which connected the fourfold typology to behavioral dimensions of extraversion and neuroticism and led to the later psychobiological theories and laboratory work of Eysenck (1967) and Gray (1982). In the second movement, Soviet and Eastern European schools of temperament began with Pavlov's (1935/1955) observations of individual differences among dogs in conditioning experiments. This work led to an active research tradition described by Strelau (1983).

According to Pavlov, temperamental differences were linked theoretically to qualities of the central nervous system, including strength of neural activation. Strength of activation was related to the "law of strength" in classical conditioning, whereby increased intensities of the conditioned stimulus led to increased intensity of the animal's response. For some animals, however, increasing the intensity of the stimulus led to a point at which the animal failed to respond. Pavlov described these animals as having a weak nervous system. Animals with a strong nervous system maintained the law of strength even to high levels of stimulus intensity. Constructs of temperament introduced by Pavlov also included strength of inhibition, balance between activation and inhibition, and mobility, or flexibility of nervous system adjustment to changing conditions. Soviet researchers began their work by assessing these constructs in the laboratory, but encountered major problems with the lack of generality of their indexes across stimulus-and-response modalities (a phenomenon they called partiality). This led to a general shift in their focus from the laboratory to the use of questionnaire methods (Strelau, 1983).

Although British and Soviet schools took different historical directions in the study of temperament, with British researchers moving from questionnaires to the laboratory and Eastern European researchers from the laboratory to questionnaires, both schools remain actively involved in the study of temperament, and both link individual differences constructs to hypothetical nervous system function. As we note later, the British factor analytic tradition in its work on the superfactors of adult personality traits would also make contact with work on the Big Five superfactors of personality, just as the latter have made contact with research on temperament in childhood (Halverson, Kohnstamm, & Martin, 1994; Rothbart, 1989b).

CONSTRUCTS OF TEMPERAMENT

The domain of temperament can be seen as a subset of the more general area of personality. It includes individual differences in basic psychological processes constituting the affective, activational, and attentional core of personality and its development. The personality domain in turn encompasses much more than temperament, and includes skills, habits, values, and the content of social cognition. Social cognition involves the perception of the self, of others, and of the relation of the self to others and to events. These perceptions can be influenced by temperament (Derryberry & Reed, 1994b), but they involve separable processes. Allport (1961) identified temperament with emotion and gave an early definition of temperament as "the characteristic phenomena of an individual's emotional nature, including his susceptibility to emotional stimulation, his customary strength and speed of response, the quality of his prevailing mood, these phenomena being regarded as dependent upon constitutional make-up and, therefore, largely hereditary in origin" (p. 34). To Allport's emotion-based list, the NYLS added dimensions of activity level, attentional persistence, and distractibility (Thomas et al., 1963).

In this chapter, we define temperament as constitutionally based individual differences in emotional, motor, and attentional reactivity and self-regulation. Temperamental characteristics are seen to demonstrate consistency across situations, as well as relative stability over time (Bates, 1989b; Rothbart & Derryberry, 1981). The term *constitutional* stresses the biological bases of temperament, influenced by genetic inheritance, maturation, and experience. In our characterization of temperament, *reactivity* and *self-regulation* are umbrella terms for psychological processes within the temperament domain. These include more specific constructs (e.g., cardiac reactivity) as well as more general constructs (e.g., negative emotionality) and are by no means limited to general reactivity, as has been suggested by Kagan (this volume). Reactive parameters of temperament can be measured in terms of the onset, duration, and intensity of expression of affective reactions (e.g., fear, anger, positive affect), as well as variability in arousability and distress to overstimulation, activity, and attention (Rothbart & Derryberry, 1981). Self-regulatory processes, such as executive attention, serve to modulate reactivity. We believe, as does Kagan (this volume), that our current set of temperament dimensions represents only a beginning, with other important dimensions to be identified in the future.

Temperamental dispositions are the outcome of biological evolution, and are illuminated in the study of animal as well as human models (Gunnar, 1994; Strelau, 1983). An evolutionary approach developed in the important *Handbook* review by Campos, Barrett, Lamb, Goldsmith, and Stenberg (1983) linked temperament to inherited behavior patterns, including self-regulatory as well as reactive components. Because we now can also tentatively identify some of the neural structures that support emotion, arousal, and attention, an additional psychobiological level for understanding temperament is available (see Bates & Wachs, 1994).

A psychobiological analysis based on emotional and motivational structures suggests there may be less disagreement about what constitutes temperamental variables than had been previously thought. Consider the affective/motivational system of fear, including arousal, felt emotion, and motor response preparation, with responses often inhibited, and attention directed toward the fear-inducing stimulus and/or possible escape routes (Davis, Hitchcock, & Rosen, 1987). In studying this system, one can stress the motivational aspects of the individual's response (e.g., Thomas & Chess's [1977] approach/withdrawal; Kagan's [1994] behavioral inhibition), its emotional aspects (Buss & Plomin's [1975] emotionality; Goldsmith & Campos's [1982] fear), its duration and susceptibility to interventions (Rothbart's [1981] soothability), its relation to arousal (Strelau's [1983] reactivity), or multiple components of response (Rothbart & Derryberry's [1981] fear). If we take this larger view of temperament dimensions, more agreement is evident, and substantial intercorrelations among scales measuring these constructs further support this contention (Goldsmith, Rieser-Danner, & Briggs, 1991).

All of these approaches to fear refer to an evolutionarily conserved affective-motivational system that can be activated under conditions of novelty, sudden or intense stimuli, reactions to danger prepared by evolution, social interactions with unfamiliar conspecifics, and conditioned responses to punishment (Gray, 1987). All suggest that individuals vary in the threshold, intensity, and duration of their responses to these stimulus conditions. We can empirically focus on broader or more specific aspects of fear, frustration, and other reactions, including aspects that are part of other systems as well. For example, norepinephrine response is linked to fear reactions and stress reactivity, and it is also linked to cognitive arousal (Rothbart, Derryberry, & Posner, 1994). Finally, it is important to recognize that, as affective-motivational systems, temperament processes are *open* systems: the content of experience will influence their development, creating the necessity of studying links between temperament and experience.

THE STRUCTURE OF TEMPERAMENT

Recent advances in our understanding of the structure of temperament have emerged from empirical work on temperament in infancy and childhood and from psychobiological approaches identifying broad dimensions of temperamental variability. We now consider these two sources, noting that research on temperament in infants and children suggests we should revise the original list of nine NYLS dimensions to a smaller number. Much research on the structure of temperament has employed factor analysis of large sets of items within the temperament domain. Factor analysis allows researchers to see simultaneously both the relations and nonrelations among large numbers of behavior descriptors. A major limitation of the factor analytic method to keep in mind, however, is that the set of dimensions yielded by the analysis depends on the set of descriptors included in the initial data matrix.

Adult Studies

Early analysis of items assessing emotionality, activity, and intellect, performed in Great Britain, yielded factors of emotionality (later labeled neuroticism), will (consistent action resulting from effortful volition), and extraversion (e.g., Burt, 1937; Webb, 1915). These may have been the earliest versions of what are now called the Big Three superfactors of personality, represented currently by Tellegen's (1985) negative and positive emotionality and constraint and Eysenck's (1967) extraversion, neuroticism, and psychoticism. Later, in the United States, taxonomic research culled lists of trait-descriptive adjectives from the dictionary, leading to factor analytic studies that also employed personality items (Goldberg, 1993). The Big Five or Five Factor Model (FFM) personality factors were frequently extracted, and labeled extraversion, agreeableness, conscientiousness, neuroticism, and openness (Caspi, Ch. 6, this Volume; Goldberg, 1993; Halverson et al., 1994).

Infant Studies

Bates, Freeland, and Lounsbury (1979) used factor analysis to develop subscales for the Infant Characteristics Questionnaire (ICQ), designed to assess difficultness in 4- to 6-month-old infants via mother report. Initially, difficultness was defined as aspects of infant temperament that may create problems for the caregiver. The ICQ yielded four factors: (a) fussy-difficult: including overall fussing and crying, soothability, and intensity of protest of the infant (irritability), as well as an item rating the "overall degree of difficulty"; (b) unadaptable: negative reactions and slow adaptation to novelty (fear); (c) dull: low positive affect and activity which could be negatively related to approach or extraversion; and (d) unpredictable: predictability of hunger, sleep, and distress (rhythmicity). All of

Bates's factor names are worded in a "difficultness" direction. Results of this analysis foreshadowed later results in the field; individual differences in positive affect (dull) were separated from negative affect, and two kinds of negative emotions were identified: fear (unadaptability) and irritable distress (fussy-difficult). Similar factors were found with ICQ versions for 13- and 24-month-olds (Bates & Bayles, 1984).

Thomas and Chess (1977) had identified nine, not necessarily independent, dimensions of temperament in their parent interview protocols. As noted previously, the nine NYLS dimensions are activity level; rhythmicity (predictability of sleep, hunger, feeding, and elimination); approach/withdrawal (responses to novelty, conceptually resembling Kagan's behaviorally inhibited and uninhibited children); adaptability (ease of modification of response to new or altered situations); threshold; intensity (energy level of reaction); mood (negative versus positive); distractibility; and attention span/persistence. Numerous scales have been written based on the nine NYLS dimensions, including those of Carey and McDevitt and their colleagues (e.g., Carey & McDevitt, 1978; Fullard, McDevitt, & Carey, 1984; Medoff-Cooper, Carey, & McDevitt, 1993) and the Dimensions of Temperament Surveys (DOTS; Windle & Lerner, 1986).

Due to overlap among NYLS definitions, however, conceptual overlap often existed across these scales, as in the Revised Infant Temperament Scale (RITQ) developed by Carey and McDevitt (1978). For example, the RITQ mood scale includes the item "The infant is pleasant (smiles, laughs) when first arriving in unfamiliar places (friend's house, store)." This item would also fit the NYLS approach dimension, defined as the child's initial response (positive versus negative) to a new stimulus, and the NYLS mood dimension, defined in part as the amount of "pleasant, joyful, and friendly behavior" (Thomas & Chess, 1977, p. 22). Similarly, the RITQ adaptability scale includes the item "The infant adjusts within 10 min. to new surroundings (home, store, play area)." It thus overlaps conceptually with both the RITQ approach scale—which includes the item "For the first few minutes in a new place or situation (new store or home) the infant is fretful"—and the NYLS mood dimension. This content overlap suggests that some scale scores of the RITQ might be empirically highly intercorrelated, as has proven to be the case (Sanson, Prior, & Oberklaid, 1985; Sanson, Prior, Garino, Oberklaid, & Sewell, 1987). In the Australian Temperament Project (ATP) assessment of 4- to 8-month infants, the nine subscales showed substantial intercorrelations, particularly the approach, mood, and adaptability scales, with correlations ranging between .52 and .67, suggesting that some of the scales are measuring close to the same, if not the same, construct.

Concerns about lack of discriminant validity (approach, adaptability, mood) as well as low internal reliability (threshold, intensity, distractibility), led Sanson et al. (1987) to conduct an item-level factor analysis. Only two of the nine factors obtained, persistence and rhythmicity, were relatively pure representations of the original NYLS dimensions. There was no discrimination between approach and adaptability scales, and items from both scales loaded on Factor 1, which Sanson et al. (1987) labeled approach. Activity and intensity items yielded two factors, one labeled activity/reactivity, including some perceptual sensitivity items, and the other placidity, including items like "Lies quietly in bath" (from activity) and "Plays quietly with toys" (from intensity). Mood separated into items related to new situations, loading on the approach factor, and items related to caretaking procedures, loading on two additional factors: cooperation-manageability, chiefly measures of positive affect (e.g., "Happy sounds during changing"), and irritability, chiefly measures of irritable negative affect (e.g., "Cries when left alone to play"). There was evidence of a threshold factor, but it was weak and situation-specific.

Hagekull's (Bohlin, Hagekull, & Lindhagen, 1981; Hagekull, 1982) item-level factor analyses of Swedish data partly converge with those of Sanson. Items based on the NYLS yielded seven orthogonal factors for 3- to 6-month-old infants, and eight factors for 6- to 10-month-olds. Several of the factors were similar to those identified by Sanson et al. (1987): intensity/activity, similar to Sanson's activity/reactivity; regularity, similar to rhythmicity; and approach-withdrawal, similar to approach. Although Hagekull's manageability factor has a name similar to Sanson et al.'s cooperation-manageability, it is not so clearly an assessment of positive affect, and includes activity and adaptability items.

In other approaches, Buss and Plomin (1975) conceptualized temperament using the acronym that also serves as the name of their assessment instrument: EASI (emotionality, activity, sociability, impulsivity). Later, Buss and Plomin (1984) concluded that impulsivity was not established as a dimension of temperament. One concern with using the revised EAS or EASI with subjects as young as 5 months, as in the study by Rowe and Plomin (1977), is that

some of the global items in the scale do not seem appropriate for infants (e.g., "Child is off and running as soon as he wakes up in the morning," and "Child prefers quiet games such as coloring or block play to more active games"). Rowe and Plomin (1977) factor analyzed a parent-report questionnaire combining the EASI with 54 items assessing NYLS dimensions. Children ranged from age 5 months to 9 years (average = 3.6 years). The factors identified were sociability, activity, emotionality, attention span/persistence, reaction to food, and soothability.

Another search for dimensions going beyond those of the NYLS study is the rational construct-based development of the Infant Behavior Questionnaire (IBQ; Rothbart, 1981). The content of the IBQ was influenced by constructs from the NYLS, the work of Shirley (1933) and Escalona (1968), reviews of longitudinal studies of stability of personality, and S. Diamond's (1957) review of behavioral genetics and comparative studies (which also influenced Buss & Plomin, 1975). Items were originally written to represent 11 temperament constructs, but only six of these demonstrated sufficient internal reliability and lack of construct overlap with other scales. These six scales of the IBQ assessed activity level, smiling and laughter, fear, distress to limitations, duration of orienting, and soothability. The IBQ served as the basis for the Toddler Behavior Assessment Questionnaire (TBAQ; Goldsmith, 1996), the Children's Behavior Questionnaire (CBQ; Rothbart, Ahadi, & Hershey, 1994), and a self-report assessment of temperament in early adolescence (Capaldi & Rothbart, 1992). The CBQ was also influenced by an adult measure of temperament developed by Derryberry and Rothbart (1988).

In a review of the structure of temperament as indicated by results of infant studies (Rothbart & Mauro, 1990), six dimensions were identified that provide a shorter list of temperament variables for future researchers. As noted above, positive affect is differentiated from negative affect, and two kinds of negative affect are identified. The six shorter list dimensions are: (a) fearful distress, most commonly labeled withdrawal, although scales also are labeled fear and unadaptable; this scale includes adaptability (how long it takes the child to adjust to a new situation) as well as withdrawal and distress to new situations; (b) irritable distress, labeled variously irritability, fussy-difficult, distress to limitations, and anger/frustration; (c) positive affect, including the measures smiling and laughter, approach, dull, and cooperation-manageability; (d) activity level, frequently measured in infant temperament questionnaires; (e) attention span/persistence, also labeled duration of orienting or interest; and (f) rhythmicity, labeled unpredictable, rhythmicity, and regularity. The last factor tends to be small and may be influenced by the extent to which the infant is put on a schedule by the parents (Super & Harkness, 1994).

Evidence suggests that infant scales with different names are actually measuring similar constructs. Goldsmith and Rieser-Danner (1986) had both mothers and day care teachers of infants age 4–8 months fill out the RITQ (Carey & McDevitt, 1978), the ICQ (Bates et al., 1979), and the IBQ (Rothbart, 1981). The first dimension described above (distress to novelty) is assessed by all three of these instruments; IBQ fear, ICQ unadaptable, and ITQ approach-withdrawal scales. Intercorrelations across these scales were high. For mothers, they ranged from .60 to .69, with the average $r = .64$; for day care teachers, the intercorrelations ranged from .51 to .73, with the average $r = .63$ (Goldsmith & Rieser-Danner, 1986).

The second shared dimension is irritable distress, assessed by the IBQ distress to limitations, RITQ negative mood (which includes positive affect at one pole), and ICQ fussy-difficult scales. Intercorrelations among these scales for mothers ranged from .44 to .63, with an average of .54; for day care teachers, the correlations ranged from .66 to .74, with an average of .71. The third shared temperament dimension is activity level, assessed only on the RITQ and IBQ activity level scales. The correlation between these two scale scores for both mothers and day care teachers was .65. We believe that, taking overlap among scales seriously, researchers can now identify five or six variables common to rationally and factor analytically generated scales.

Childhood Studies

Factor analyses of questionnaire items based on the NYLS for older children have similarly revealed a shorter list of broad factors. Analysis of mother reports for 3- to 8-year-olds on the Thomas and Chess (1977) Childhood Temperament Questionnaire in the ATP yielded factors of inflexibility (irritability and uncooperativeness), persistence, sociability, and rhythmicity (Sanson, Smart, Prior, Oberklaid, & Pedlow, 1994); second-order factors extracted in the ATP were labeled negative emotionality, self-regulation, and sociability.

The CBQ (Rothbart, Ahadi, & Hershey, 1994), a highly differentiated parent-report measure of temperament for 3- to 8-year-olds, consistently shows three broad factors,

found also in U.S. replications and research performed in the People's Republic of China and Japan (Ahadi, Rothbart, & Ye, 1993; Kochanska, DeVet, Goldman, Murray, & Putnam, 1993). The first, called surgency, is defined primarily by the scales of approach, high-intensity pleasure (sensation seeking), activity level, and a negative contribution from shyness. The second, called negative affectivity, is defined by the scales of discomfort, fear, anger/frustration, sadness, and, loading negatively, soothability. The third factor, labeled effortful control, is defined by the scales of inhibitory control, attentional focusing, low-intensity pleasure, and perceptual sensitivity. These three factors map well upon the second-order factors identified by Sanson et al.: surgency upon sociability; negative affectivity upon negative emotionality, and self-regulation upon effortful control. The first three factors emerging from a recent factor analysis of NYLS-inspired Middle Childhood Temperament Questionnaire items (Hegvik, McDevitt, & Carey, 1982) for 8- to 12-year-olds (McClowry, Hegvik, & Teglasi, 1993) also show similarity to these factors: approach/withdrawal, negative reactivity, and task persistence. Their two smaller factors, activity and responsiveness, also parallel smaller factors in the ATP (Sanson et al., 1994).

Presley and Martin's (1994) analysis of teacher reports of 3- to 7-year-olds on the Temperament Assessment Battery for Children yielded five factors demonstrating some overlap with those described above. These include social inhibition, negative emotionality, agreeableness/adaptability, activity level, and task persistence. In their review of factor analytic studies on infant and child temperament, Martin, Wisenbaker, and Hüttunen (1994) note the robustness of the general temperament factors of negative emotionality, task persistence, adaptability, and social inhibition. They see activity level as more problematic, because it is related to both negative and positive affect in infancy.

The factors emerging also show strong conceptual similarities with the Big Three factors and three of the Big Five or FFM factors that have been extracted from analyses of self- and peer descriptions of personality in adults (Goldberg, 1993) and children (Caspi, this volume; Digman & Inouye, 1986). The negative affectivity factor from childhood measures appears to map on the broad adult dimension of neuroticism or negative emotionality. The surgency, sociability, and approach/withdrawal factors map on the broad adult dimension of extraversion or positive emotionality. The persistence, self-regulation, and effortful control factors can be seen to map upon the adult dimension of control/constraint (see Ahadi & Rothbart, 1994). More research is needed, however, to establish empirical links across these constructs. At the conceptual level, for example, personality constructs like neuroticism contain negative information about the self that may be strongly related to an individual's experiences with others; it may or may not have a strong temperamental base.

In research linking child temperament to the Big Five, Digman and Shmelyov (1996) studied teachers' ratings of 8- to 10-year-old Russian children on scales of temperament, FFM personality items, and other ratings. Temperament scores loaded substantially on four of the Big Five personality factors: (a) a temperament dimension of merry/talkative versus constrained loaded on FFM extraversion; (b) angry versus soothable loaded on FFM agreeableness; (c) impetuous versus focused loaded on FFM conscientiousness; and (d) afraid versus brave loaded on FFM emotionality. Temperament scales were not strongly convergent with the Big Five factor of intellect or openness. However, Lanthier and Bates (1995) predicted maternal and self-report openness at 17 years from measures of infant sociability, lower fears, and higher resistance to control. Lower resistance to control in infancy predicted later agreeableness, and fear and lower sociability predicted later neuroticism.

Digman and Shmelyov's (1996) results differentiated fearful distress and irritable or angry distress, as found in the infant studies and in Martin, Wisenbaker, et al.'s (1994) research on children 3- to 7-years-old. A related study by John, Caspi, Robins, Moffitt, and Stouthamer-Loeber (1994) examined mother reports for 12- to 13-year-olds on the California Child Q-set (CCQ; Block & Block, 1980). A rationally based set of FFM scales was derived from these data, with a factor analysis of the entire set. Five factors emerged, with FFM extraversion separating into two factors: sociability/expressiveness and energy/activity level. FFM Neuroticism also yielded two factors: fearful and anxious distress, and irritable distress (crying and whining).

As noted above, work to date on temperament structure in infancy and childhood suggests revisions of the original NYLS nine dimensions, including for infancy: (a) fearful distress; (b) irritable distress; (c) positive affect; (d) persistence; (e) activity level; and (f) rhythmicity. At older ages the two kinds of negative affectivity are also often differentiated. In longitudinal research, infant measures also differentially predict the two kinds of negative affect, with laboratory infant fear predicting 7-year-old fear, and

anger predicting 7-year-old anger (Rothbart, Posner, & Rosicky, 1994). There is also evidence for an approach or extraversion factor, although its Positive affect and Activity level aspects are sometimes differentiated, and in fewer studies, for agreeableness/adaptability. A conscientiousness or effortful control variable is also often found, as well as a small rhythmicity factor. The most differentiated list of constructs for older children would include (with aggregated constructs in parentheses): (a) positive affect; (b) activity level (a and b combined as approach/extraversion); (c) fearful distress; (d) irritable distress (c and d combined as general negative emotionality); (e) effortful control/task persistence; and (f) agreeableness/adaptability. In our next section, we make some tentative links between these constructs and broad dimensions of temperamental variability derived from the neurosciences.

Psychobiological Concepts and the Structure of Temperament

As noted above, behavioral temperament has historically been related to an understanding of individual physiology. Today's literature on the psychobiology of temperament is no exception. Recent advances in cognitive neuroscience have linked mental processes to brain functioning (see Posner & Raichle, 1994). Although lagging behind cognitive research, advances have also begun in the neuroscience of affect, investigating links between affective-motivational processes and brain functioning (LeDoux, 1987; Posner & Raichle, 1994). Bates and Wachs's (1994) volume documents several of these advances. Research on the behavioral genetics of temperament also indicates considerable heritability of temperamental characteristics, as noted later and by Caspi (this volume). Because genes operate via the development of physical structures, neural and neurochemical individual differences might be expected to underlie behavioral individual differences in temperament.

Some of the major theoretical constructs employed in the study of temperament have emerged from the psychobiological models of Cloninger (1987), Eysenck (1967), Gray (1982), LeDoux (1989), Panksepp (1986a), and Zuckerman (1991). The model most often applied to developmental and clinical research is Gray's theory (see Fowles, 1984; Lytton, 1990; Quay, 1993), but there is considerable agreement between the broad tendencies identified by Gray and those put forward by the other theorists. We review here constructs of approach/positive affect or extraversion, inhibition or anxiety, optimal levels of arousal and distress to overstimulation, irritability/anger, agreeableness, and attention.

Approach/Positive Affect or Extraversion

Extraverts are described as positive, reward-oriented, active and outgoing, seeking stimulation or novelty rather than avoiding it. Eysenck's (1967) model describes introverts as more arousable than extraverts, with lower optimal levels of stimulation for introverts than extraverts. Extraverts will be more likely to seek stimulation to raise their arousal to optimal levels; introverts to dampen and avoid higher levels of stimulation to maintain their levels of optimal stimulation. Gray (1975), however, accounts for introversion-extraversion in a slightly different way. He sees introversion and extraversion as arising from the relative influence of two separate systems, the approach or Behavioral Activation System (BAS) and the Behavioral Inhibition System (BIS). In Gray's model, extraverts have a relatively strong BAS in comparison with the BIS and are high in approach and active avoidance; introverts have a relatively strong BIS and are high in behavioral inhibition and anxiety. We now consider briefly some neural models of the BAS and related dimensions; the BIS is discussed later.

In Gray's model, the BAS is sensitive to cues signaling reward. It is associated with structures identified in the self-stimulation literature, including the medial forebrain bundle and lateral hypothalamus, and influences of the neurotransmitters dopamine (DA) and norepinephrine (NE). A similar model is Depue and Iacono's (1989) dopamine-related Behavioral Facilitation System (BFS). Like Gray's BAS, the BFS is involved in approach to rewarding cues, and avoidance given cues of potential relief. Depue and Iacono further suggest that when reward has been blocked or avoidance is impossible, the BFS may facilitate aggressive behavior directed toward removing an obstacle or threat. High BFS individuals will tend to experience high positive affect and anticipation of a potential reward, but will also experience frustration when a reward is blocked.

A related approach system is the *Expectancy-Foraging System* described by Panksepp (1986a). Panksepp's system also includes positive anticipation of reward-related stimuli, and is based on dopamine systems. Expectancy-Foraging System functions include motor and autonomic reactions related to locomotion, exploration, and appetitive behaviors, and emotional states such as desire, curiosity, and anticipatory eagerness. Panksepp (1986a) suggests this system also influences attention, adjusting

the sensitivities of sensory mechanisms to support behavior sequences. Gray, DePue and Iacono, and Panksepp's models all suggest that neural systems related to positive affect are closely tied to facilitated behavior, especially approach of potentially rewarding stimuli, and similar systems are discussed by Zuckerman (1991) and Cloninger (1987).

Neural structures for approach and positive emotionality have also been identified (see review by Rothbart, Derryberry, & Posner, 1994, for additional references). The limbic system contains specialized circuits for processing reward-related information: cells within the orbital frontal cortex, basolateral amygdala, and lateral hypothalamus respond when an animal is shown a reward-related visual stimulus. Damage to the basolateral amygdala can also impair the formation of associations between a stimulus and a reward. Limbic circuits that generate positive affect during intracranial self-stimulation have also been studied, although it is unclear whether they represent a general reward system or a set of more specific reward systems.

When activated by a rewarding stimulus, limbic circuits regulate endocrine, autonomic, and motor activity via neural projections to the brain stem. Behavioral approach is controlled by projections to the nucleus accumbens and pedunculopontine nucleus, two of the primary centers influencing locomotion. Limbic outputs can also facilitate approach by interacting with midbrain dopamine systems that project from the substantia nigra and ventral tegmental area. These dopamine projections influence many brain regions, particularly nuclei affecting locomotor functions. Numerous additional systems, such as central opiate and serotonin systems and gonadal hormones, also appear to interact with dopamine, contributing to approach or inhibition (Zuckerman, 1991).

In research on dopamine (DA) functioning, Netter and Rammsayer (1991) investigated effects of the DA antagonist halperidol and L-dopa to stimulate production of DA in adult subjects. Individuals high in extraversion and sensation seeking showed evidence of more highly reactive DA systems; those low on these scales showed underreactive DA systems. Depue, Luciana, Arbisi, and Collins (1994) gave adults a DA agonist, finding a positive relationship between the agonist effects and extraversion and impulsivity. In studies relating neurotransmitters and their regulating enzymes to temperament, methodological issues have been raised about whether assays of plasma, cerebrospinal fluid, or urine accurately reflect brain chemistry (Zuckerman, 1984), and there have been failures to replicate across studies. Some interesting negative relationships have been found, however, between the enzyme monoamine oxidase (MAO), which regulates the synthesis and concentration of DA and norepinephrine, and sensation seeking (see reviews by Rothbart, 1989a; Zuckerman, 1995).

In research on children, predictions from these theories about a dimension that combines approach and positive affect have been supported for infancy, where behavioral observations of smiling and laughter are related to infants' more rapid approach of objects (Rothbart, 1988). Approach reactions are also positively related to active avoidance in infancy (Rothbart, Ziaie, & O'Boyle, 1992), as predicted by Gray's theory.

Inhibition and Anxiety

In Gray's (1975) model, anxiety or the Behavioral Inhibition System (BIS) is activated in situations involving novelty, high-intensity stimulation, punishment, and evolutionarily prepared fears. Its neural substrate includes the Ascending Reticular Activating System (ARAS), orbital frontal cortex, medial septal area, and hippocampus, and the neurotransmitters norepinephrine and serotonin. The BIS is involved in passive avoidance and extinction, but not in active avoidance, which involves the BAS. In response to signals of punishment or nonreward, the ARAS activates the medial septal area, which is also monitored and modulated by the orbital frontal cortex. The medial septal area in turn leads to hippocampal theta rhythm, resulting in inhibition of reticular activity and ongoing behavior. In Gray's (1975) theory, the BIS and BAS are mutually inhibitory, competing to control the individual's motor functioning. As noted above, the BAS operates under conditions of signaled reward. When signals of punishment are added, the BIS will decrease likelihood of a response. When BIS and BAS are in conflict, the occurrence of approach will depend on the relative strength or balance between the two systems (see Fowles, 1984, for a clear explication of this model). Implications of these systems for socialization are elaborated below.

Gray (1982) found in animal studies that antianxiety drugs disinhibit behavior when passive avoidance is required. Antianxiety drugs do not affect responses chiefly affected by the BAS, suggesting an independence of the two systems. Additional evidence indicates the amygdala plays a crucial role in anxiety or fear (Davis, 1992). The central nucleus of the amygdala is interconnected with approach-related cell groups of the basolateral nucleus, but it also is key to an extended set of circuits interconnecting orbital frontal cortex, amygdala, the bed nucleus of the stria terminalis, lateral hypothalamus, central gray midbrain region, and brain stem nuclei that control specific motor and autonomic reactions. The central amygdala is well positioned for detecting potential dangers, receiving sensory information following early thalamic processing and later results of more detailed processing from association areas of the cortex (LeDoux, 1987). The central nucleus responds within 50 msec to a shock-related tone, apparently by means of a direct sensory input from the thalamus. This input is developmentally very interesting, because it may support learned fear responses in children existing prior to extensive cortical development (see Nelson, 1994; Rothbart, Derryberry, & Posner, 1994).

Fear activation is accompanied by more specific inhibition of ongoing motor programs and preparation of response systems controlling coping options such as fleeing, fighting, and hiding (see review by Rothbart, Derryberry, & Posner, 1994). Descending projections to the brain stem cell groups send serotonin and norepinephrine projections throughout the spinal cord, and may enhance the overall responsiveness of spinal motor neurons. Projections to brain stem cell groups also support autonomic and somatic components of fear, including potentiated startle, motor inhibition, facial expression, and cardiovascular and respiratory change (Davis et al., 1987). Individual variability in the structure and functioning of any of these subsystems may be related to variations in the specific behavioral expressions of fear, and multiple components of other affective motivational systems such as approach/positive affect and anger/irritable distress would also be expected.

The amygdala also appears to affect information processing within the cortex, with projections to cellular sources of the monoamine systems (noradrenergic, dopaminergic, serotonergic, and cholinergic) ascending to the cortex, projections to cortical fields via thalamic nuclei, and direct projections from amygdala to cortex. For example, the basolateral nucleus projects to frontal and cingulate regions involved in the anterior (executive) attention system (to be described later; Posner & Petersen, 1990), as well as to ventral occipital and temporal pathways involved in processing object information. Connections between amygdala and cortex, including the anterior cingulate, are consistent with the findings that anxious individuals show enhanced attention to threatening sources of information (e.g., Derryberry & Reed, 1994a). A much more detailed analysis of structures related to behavioral inhibition is found in Kagan (Ch. 4, this Volume).

In this section we have described possible neural substrates for approach/positive affect systems that are likely related to novelty, sensation, or reward seeking, and for fear linked to the inhibition of approach and sensation seeking ("harm avoidance"). One of the most important aspects of the behavioral approach and inhibition constructs for the student of social development is that they also describe individual differences in susceptibility to reward and punishment. These constructs suggest that some individuals will be more likely than others to stop a prohibited activity when there is likelihood of punishment. Similarly, potential rewards will be more motivating to some individuals than to others. In situations involving both potential rewards and punishments, such as interactions with a stranger, the balance between BAS and BIS tendencies in connection with the person's previous experience in the situation will be critical.

This theoretical model has direct applications to child socialization. If we consider a child performing an enjoyable act, such as shredding the pages of a book, the child's initial activities will be influenced by the BAS. Now the parent gives a sharp command for the child to stop. Will the child's activity be likely to be inhibited by this parental punishment? Patterson (1980) found parents of nonproblem children to be effective in stopping their children's aversive behavior on three out of four occasions when they punished. However, when parents of problem children used punishment, children were likely to continue the punished behavior (Patterson, 1980; Snyder, 1977). Although parenting skills are also involved, children's temperament is likely to make a basic contribution to this situation. Individual differences in risky behaviors and accident proneness (Matheny, 1991), mastery motivation (Harter, 1978), and affective representations of the environment (Derryberry & Reed, 1994b) are all likely to be influenced by temperamental approach and inhibition tendencies in interaction with past experience. In an excellent review, Quay (1993) has also employed Gray's constructs to analyze the development of undersocialized aggressive conduct disorder. In the next section, we describe temperament systems related to distress to overstimulation, irritability, and anger, and the controls offered by affiliative tendencies.

Optimal Levels of Stimulation and Distress to Overstimulation

We have now described individual differences in the affective-motivational systems of the BIS (anxiety/behavioral inhibition) and the BAS (positive affect/approach). How-ever, even more general temperamental processes related to arousability or reactivity have been posited to underlie approach and withdrawal. One general model incorporates the idea of optimal level of stimulation. This approach derives temperament from general arousability, and has been important in the Soviet and Eastern European schools, Eysenck's model, and in ideas more recently put forward by Bell (1974). This idea is also closely linked to the theory of Berlyne (1971), who argued that arousal potential, created by stimulus intensity, novelty, and surprise, is related to the activation of two motivational systems, one associated with pleasure and approach, elicited at lower levels, the other with distress and withdrawal, elicited at higher levels of arousal potential. The two systems oppose each other. Individual differences in the strength of each of these two systems support variability in optimal arousal, that is, the point where approach and pleasure are at their highest but withdrawal processes do not yet dominate.

As noted above, Schneirla (1959) put forward similar ideas, describing approach and withdrawal systems across species, with one influence being the intensity of the stimulus. Eysenck (1967) saw introverts as more arousable and more sensitive to stimulation at low-intensity levels than extraverts, linking this arousal to the ARAS. Introverts were then seen to experience both pleasure and discomfort at lower levels of stimulus intensity; their lower optimal level of arousal would lead them to seek lower stimulus levels. In Strelau's (1983) model, more strongly reactive individuals engage in self-regulatory activities to maintain their optimal levels of stimulation. Soviet researchers' concept of nervous system "strength" of activation or endurance under high-intensity stimulation and Strelau's reactivity construct indicate a dimension involving both sensitivity and susceptibility to distress that might be present early in life.

Developmental research on temperament is supportive of a positive relation between sensitivity and susceptibility to distress. Miller and Bates (1986) found significant positive correlations between temperature sensitivity and susceptibility to the negative emotions. In Keogh's (Keogh, Pullis, & Caldwell, 1982) Teacher Temperament Questionnaire, the third factor, labeled reactivity, included both negative affect and sensitivity items. In research with the CBQ, positive correlations between perceptual sensitivity and discomfort are regularly obtained (Goldsmith, 1996; King & Wachs, 1995; Rothbart, Posner, & Hershey, 1995). Martin, Wisenbaker, et al. (1994) have also recently reviewed three factor analytic studies, finding sensitivity items to load with items assessing negative emotionality.

Laboratory research assessing children's sensory thresholds along with their thresholds for pleasure and discomfort would be helpful in testing this theoretical relationship further.

Irritability/Anger

In Gray's (1982) model, circuits connecting the amygdala, ventromedial nucleus of the hypothalamus, central gray region of the midbrain, and somatic and motor effector nuclei of the lower brain stem process information involving unconditioned punishment and nonreward, constituting the Fight/Flight system. With detection of painful or frustrating input, these brain stem effectors produce aggressive or defensive behavior. Individual differences in the reactivity of this "Fight/Flight" system are also thought to underlie aggressive aspects of Eysenck's general psychoticism dimension, and Panksepp (1982) discusses similar neural circuitry in terms of a rage system (see review by Rothbart, Derryberry, & Posner, 1994).

Other theorists have suggested that monoaminergic systems and gonadal hormones may also contribute to aggression and hostility. As noted above, the DA system described by Depue and Iacono (1989) may facilitate irritable aggression aimed at removing a frustrating obstacle, consistent with findings that DA agonists (e.g., amphetamine) enhance aggressive behaviors. Spoont (1992) suggests that serotonergic projections from the midbrain's raphe nuclei can limit aggression by inhibiting aggression-related circuitry of the amygdala, hypothalamus, and brain stem. Animal studies have found positive relationships between testosterone and intermale aggression, but their interpretation and extension to humans is problematic (for a review, see Zuckerman, 1991). Aggressive behavior thus appears to be regulated by multiple neurochemical systems. These include behavioral inhibition and agreeableness/affiliativeness, a dimension we believe may be crucially important to social development.

Affiliativeness/Agreeableness

Because ventromedial hypothalamic lesions dramatically increase aggression, Panksepp (1986a) suggests this brain region normally inhibits aggressive behaviors controlled by the midbrain's central gray area. Hypothalamic projections allow for friendly, trusting, and helpful behaviors between members of a species by suppressing aggressive tendencies. Panksepp (1986b) indicates that these prosocial behaviors may depend in part on opiate projections from higher limbic regions (e.g., amygdala, cingulate cortex) to the ventromedial hypothalamus, with brain opiates promoting social comfort and bonding and opiate withdrawal promoting irritability and aggressiveness. Mechanisms underlying prosocial and aggressive behaviors would in this way be reciprocally related, in keeping with the bipolar agreeableness-hostility dimension found in Five Factor Models of personality. Again, however, as for extraversion-introversion, the model describes unipolar tendencies that are mutually inhibitory, rather than a single bipolar dimension of behavior.

Panksepp suggests that the general function of opioids may be to counteract stress. He notes that since pleasure is frequently experienced to stimuli associated with a return to physiological homeostasis (see also Cabanac, 1971), positive affect to opioids may be the result of associations with their antistress effects. Panksepp (1993) has also recently reviewed research suggesting links between social bonding and the hypothalamic neuropeptide oxytocin (OXY), involved in maternal behavior, feelings of social acceptance and social bonding, and reduction of separation distress. OXY is also released during sexual activity by both females and males. In Cloninger's (1987) theory, reward dependence is a dimension ranging from being emotionally dependent, warmly sympathetic, sentimental, persistent, and sensitive to social cues to being socially detached, cool, tough-minded, and independently self-willed. He sees reward dependence as related to social motivation; it is thus similar to dimensions of affiliativeness or agreeableness.

Agreeableness has been a relatively neglected individual difference variable, although Graziano's (1994) recent work is changing this situation, and MacDonald's (1992) theoretical synthesis on warmth is also an important contribution. Such a dimension would allow us to differentiate measures of sociability (outgoing social behavior that is related to an approach system) from affiliativeness, which might be expressed by individuals high or low in approach. Any temperamental predisposition to agreeableness needs to be seen as an open system, however, interacting with social experience for its outcomes. It would be of particular interest to consider both temperamental and experiential roots of agreeableness.

Neurochemical Influences

As noted above, separable neural systems related to forms of positive and negative affect process significant information through neural circuits, with these pathways appearing to some extent as parallel processing systems. These systems, however, also are regulated by more general neurochemical systems, including dopaminergic and serotonergic projections arising from the midbrain, and by circulating gonadal and corticosteroid hormones (Rothbart, Derryberry, & Posner, 1994; Zuckerman, 1995).

Neurochemical influences may provide coherence of emotional states within an individual and support more general factors of temperament. For example, serotonergic projections from the midbrain raphe nuclei appear to moderate limbic circuits related to anxiety and aggression (Spoont, 1992). Low serotonergic activity may thus increase an individual's vulnerability to both fear and frustration, contributing to the general factor of negative affectivity, including depression (Kramer, 1993). Gonadal hormones are related to both positive affect and aggressiveness (Zuckerman, 1991), possibly influencing consistent individual differences across positive and angry states. Neural structures thus can support variability at broad as well as specific levels.

Attention and Effortful Control

Brain systems have also been identified as underlying selective orienting and attentional effortful control (Posner & Raichle, 1994). Although these systems often are not considered as being involved in temperament, two of the nine behavioral dimensions identified by Thomas and Chess (1977), distractibility and attention span/persistence, specifically refer to attention. Persistence is also one of the major factors emerging from infant research. In our work on 3- to 8-year-old children, we have identified a general factor of temperament linking attentional capacities with inhibitory control (Ahadi, Rothbart, & Ye, 1993). This effortful control factor shows similarities to factors derived from NYLS items in childhood, as noted above.

Early attentional persistence or duration of orienting (Rothbart & Mauro, 1990), however, appears related to Luria's (1973) observations: "It is well known to psychologists that those features of the most elementary, involuntary attention of the type which is attracted by the most powerful or biological significant stimuli can be observed very early on, during the first few months of the child's development. They consist of turning the eyes, and then the head towards this stimulus, the cessation of all other, irrelevant forms of activity" (p. 258).

Anatomically, the posterior orienting network involves a set of cortical, midbrain, and thalamic areas (Posner & Raichle, 1994). These include portions of the parietal cortex, associated thalamic areas of the pulvinar and reticular nucli, and parts of the midbrain's superior colliculus. These areas cooperate in performing the operations needed to orient attention to a location in space. The orienting network also has close anatomical connections and interactions with an anterior executive attention network and with an arousal or vigilance network.

Infants in most instances fixate longer on novel or surprising events. After habituation to a given stimulus, it is thus possible to learn whether or not a subsequent change in the stimulus has been detected. Response to novelty is a reactive aspect of attention, and children differ both in their latency to orient and their duration of orienting to novelty (see review by Ruff & Rothbart, 1996). In the IBQ, individual differences in duration of orienting in infancy are positively related to smiling and laughter and vocal activity, suggesting that orienting may be part of an early positive reactivity that will be linked to motor approach as locomotor systems develop (Rothbart, 1988).

Later, development of the self-regulative executive attentional system allows increasing control over attention extending beyond the early reactive system (Posner, Rothbart, & Harman, 1994). This second form of attention, effortful or executive control, is related to volition and awareness of input (Posner & Rothbart, 1991, 1994). There are limits on how much we can simultaneously attend to in directed thought or action. Areas of the midfrontal lobe, including the anterior cingulate gyrus, may underlie a general executive attentional network (Vogt, Finch, & Olson, 1992). This area of the brain represents the outflow of the limbic system and is therefore closely tied to emotion. It also has close connections to adjacent motor systems. Activity of the anterior cingulate is modified by dopamine input from the underlying basal ganglia. Anterior cingulate structure consists of alternating bands of cells with close connections to the dorso-lateral frontal cortex and to the posterior parietal lobe (Goldman-Rakic, 1988), suggesting an integrative role for this area. The anterior cingulate thus might provide an important connection between widely different aspects of attention (e.g., attention to semantic content, visual location, and affective significance of an event).

The executive attention network shows evidence of development beginning in the last half of the first year of life. Infants are then gaining the ability to dissociate motor behavior from the line of sight and are able to retrieve objects by reaching away from where they are looking (A. Diamond, 1990). Changes in behavior at about 18 months suggest further development of the executive system (Rothbart, Posner, & Rosicky, 1994), and additional evidence for the development of effortful control is found between the ages of 24 to 36 months. Stroop tasks require participants to name the color of the ink (e.g., red) used to print either compatible (e.g., red) or noncompatible (blue) color words. Stroop-like conflict tasks are linked to anterior cingulate activation activity that requires the inhibition of otherwise dominant responses. Gerardi, Rothbart, Posner, and Kepler (1996) found 36-month-old children's laboratory performance on a Stroop-like task to be positively related to their mothers' reports of inhibitory control. Performance on the task was also negatively related to the children's mother-reported expressions of anger and frustration. Between 3 to 5 years, development on language-related Stroop-like tasks has also been observed (Diamond, Werker, & Lalonde, 1994).

A third attention system is related to alerting (Posner & Petersen, 1990). This system appears to involve locus coeruleus noradrenergic input to cerebral cortex (for a review see Harley, 1987). When subjects must maintain an alert state during the foreperiod of a reaction time task, or wait for an infrequent target to occur (vigilance), there is strong activity in this system (Posner & Raichle, 1994). This activity is evident in PET scans in the right lateral frontal lobe. When lesioned, this area gives rise to deficits in the ability to develop and maintain an alert state. Cells of the locus coeruleus are also particularly responsive to threatening or aversive signals in animal studies (Grant, Aston-Jones, & Redmond, 1988), indicating a potentially important role for this system in emotional states such as fear.

When one needs to be ready to detect a low probability signal, one may subjectively feel empty-headed, avoiding thoughts that might detract from detection of the signal. This "clearing of consciousness" appears to be accompanied by an increase in activation of the right frontal lobe alerting network and a reduction of neural activity in the anterior cingulate. Feelings of effort associated with inhibiting predominant responses, on the other hand, are accompanied by evidence of cingulate activation, whereas clearing the mind of distracting thoughts is accompanied by evidence of cingulate inhibition (Posner & Rothbart, 1991).

As in other aspects of attention, clearing of consciousness and maintenance of an alert state are frequently required for children's adaptive functioning. When parents or teachers ask children to prepare to switch from one activity to another or to follow instructions, individual differences among children in alerting systems may make shifting and focusing easier for some children than for others. Functioning of the alerting system has been linked to children with Attention Deficit Hyperactivity Disorder or attentional problems (Posner & Raichle, 1994). Effortful control

measures in children age 3 to 8 years are also related to measures of perceptual sensitivity (Ahadi, Rothbart, & Ye, 1993), congruent with the idea that specific arousal systems may also be involved in executive control.

Conclusions

Models from neuroscience that have been frequently employed in psychological research include those of Eysenck, Gray, Panksepp, Cloninger, Zuckerman, and Posner. The first five of these models propose quite similar general dimensions of approach, inhibition or harm avoidance, irritability (fight/flight or rage), and affiliativeness or social reward dependence, whereas Posner's model informs us of the structure of attentional systems related to orienting and effortful control. Several of these dimensions can be seen to be linked very generally to factors identified in temperament research. In addition, optimal-level models propose a link between sensitivity and affect that has found some support in the developmental literature. These general dimensions offer a beginning for future work that will more finely differentiate the temperament domain and its development. In our review, we now move to measures for the study of temperament in childhood, providing extensive evaluation of parent report measures. We then consider behavior genetics and other psychobiological approaches to the study of temperament.

MEASUREMENT APPROACHES

Several approaches have been taken to measuring temperament in children, including caregiver reports, self-reports for older children, naturalistic observations, and structured laboratory observation (see Table 3.1). Each of these kinds of measure has relative advantages, as well as disadvantages. For example, caregiver reports can tap the extensive knowledge base of caregivers who have seen the child in many different situations over a long period of time, and they are convenient—it is relatively inexpensive to develop, administer, and analyze questionnaires (Bates, 1989b, 1994; Rothbart & Goldsmith, 1985). Naturalistic observations can possess high degrees of objectivity and ecological validity. Laboratory observations allow the researcher to precisely control the context or elicitors of the child's behavior.

In addition to their respective advantages, however, each kind of technique also possesses sources of error. With caregiver report measures, for example, there is the possibility

TABLE 3.1   Potential Sources of Measurement Error in Three Child Temperament Assessment Methods

	A. Rater Characteristics Relatively Independent of Child Behavior	B. Bias in Assessment as a Function of Child Behavior or Rater-Child Interaction	C. Method Factors Relatively Independent of Both Child and Rater Characteristics
I. Parent questionnaires	1. Comprehension of instructions, questions, and rating scales 2. Knowledge of child's behavior (and general impression rater has of the child) 3. Inaccurate memory: recency effects, selective recall 4. State when completing rating task, e.g., anxiety 5. Response sets, e.g., social desirability and acquiescence 6. For ratings, knowledge of implicit reference groups 7. Accuracy in detecting and coding rare but important events 8. Kind of impression (if any) rater wants child/self to make on researcher	1. Observed child behavior occurring in response to parental behavior 2. Parents' interpretations of observed behavior a function of parental characteristics	1. Need to inquire about rarely observed situations 2. Adequacy of item selection, wording, and response options
II. Home observation measures (in vivo coding)	1. Limited capacity of coder to process all relevant behavior 2. Coding of low-intensity ambiguous behaviors 3. State of coder during observation 4. Limits of precision of coding 5. For ratings, knowledge of implicit reference groups 6. Accuracy in detecting and coding of rare, but important events	1. Caregiver-child interaction moderating behavior coded (including I.8) 2. For ratings, halo effects	1. Change in child and caregiver behavior due to presence of coder (e.g., decreased conflict) 2. Difficulties of sensitively coding the context of behavior 3. Limitations of number of instances of behavior (esp. rare ones) that can be observed 4. Lack of normative data 5. Lack of stability in observational time windows—limited sample of behavior
III. Laboratory measures (objective measures scored from videotape in episodes designed to elicit temperament-related reactions)	1. Scoring of low-intensity, ambiguous reactions 2. For ratings, knowledge of implicit reference groups 3. Limited capacity of coder to process all relevant behavior 4. State of coder during observation 5. Limits of precision of coding 6. Accuracy in detecting and coding of rare but important events	1. Effects of uncontrolled caregiver behavior or other experience prior to or during testing 2. Selection of sample, including completion of testing on the basis of child reactions (e.g., distress-prone infants not completing procedures) 3. Subtle variations in experimenter reactions to different children (e.g., more soothing behavior directed toward distress-prone infant)	1. Lack of adequate normative data 2. Limitations of number of instances of behavior that can be recorded 3. Carryover effects in repeated testing 4. Constraints on range of behavioral options 5. Novelty of laboratory setting 6. Adequate identification of episodes appropriate to evoking temperamental reactions

Adapted from Bates (1989) as adapted from Rothbart and Goldsmith (1985).

of perceptual biases in the informant. An important problem with naturalistic observation is that the expense of the procedure often prevents researchers from gaining an adequate sample of the relevant behavior. Laboratory procedures may be constrained in the particular kinds of behavior that can be elicited, and the repeated testing necessary for measuring a complex trait may be impractical or involve carryover effects. More detail on measurement issues can be found in Bates (1987, 1989b, 1994), Goldsmith and Rothbart (1991), Rothbart and Goldsmith (1985), and

Slabach, Morrow, and Wachs (1991). In this chapter, methodological issues are reviewed in association with substantive issues so that the present section can be focused on the question of the scientific acceptability of caregiver report.

Meanings of Parent Reports

Parent reports have had extensive use in clinical and developmental research, yet appropriately, researchers have also closely questioned the validity of parent reports about children's temperament. These questions have been empirically framed in varying ways, with the frame having important implications for the conclusion.

Digital versus Analog Validity

In many instances the question of the meaning of parent reports has been framed in an absolute or "digital" way, that is, as a judgment of whether parent reports are valid or not. Thomas et al. (1963) framed the question in terms of whether there was a significant correlation between parent reports and independent ratings. Finding significant correlations, they concluded that parent reports were indeed valid measures of temperament. More typically, however, on occasions when statistically significant correlations between parent ratings and independent ratings have been fairly small, the digital conclusion has been that parent reports are not valid. Any low correlation, of course, could be due to problems with independent ratings as well as parent ratings, but this is seldom concluded.

Early in the conceptual and empirical discussion of the meaning of parent reports of temperament, Kagan (1982) advocated a digital view of validity, and has continued to elaborate this view. In his recent writings, Kagan (1994, this volume) suggests parent reports are no longer worthy of use in scientific studies of temperament. We disagree. Our own position, reached more or less independently (Bates, 1994; Rothbart, 1995), is that research in the area of temperament needs several different kinds of measures. We can apply the recent statement of Vaughn et al. (1992), discussing the use of Q-sort measures of attachment security in addition to the more standard Strange Situation measure: "While researchers will require information about differences in the nature of information obtained from multiple sources, such as parents and research staff, it would be most unfortunate if pretensions to methodological rigor forced investigators to ignore sources of relevant developmental information" (p. 470).

Caregivers' Vantage versus Bias and Inaccuracy

One argument for the continued use of parent reports of temperament is that they can provide a useful perspective on children's characteristics. Temperament dimensions are by definition general patterns of responses by the child. Parents are likely to be in a good position to observe the child's behavior, especially infrequently occurring behavior that is nevertheless critical to defining a particular dimension of temperament. For example, since most families minimize noxious stimulation for their babies, it is difficult to observe such situations naturalistically. Parents, in contrast, are able to describe an infant's response to a variety of aversive stimuli. In addition, there are concerns about ecological validity as well as ethical constraints about creating such situations in the laboratory.

Kagan (1994) argues that parental experience is of dubious value because of problems with bias and inaccuracy. Bias and inaccuracy are concerns, but, as we discuss in more detail later, they are not as great a problem as Kagan suggests. Similar concerns have been extensively dealt with in personality research, and the dominant conclusion in that literature has been that traits can be reliably assessed by ratings of knowledgeable informants, including self, friends, and parents (Kenrick & Funder, 1988; Moskowitz & Schwarz, 1982). Validity is a problem for structured and naturalistic observational measures of temperament as well as parent report, and we have summarized potential sources of measurement error in three temperament assessment methods in Table 3.1.

Reliable observations of precisely defined behaviors in precisely defined situations have a high degree of objectivity. This is not tantamount to saying, however, as some writers state or imply, that these observations therefore constitute valid measures of temperament. To establish this, observational research needs to demonstrate a reliable pattern of behaviors relevant to the temperament dimension, and to demonstrate the same kinds of validity (content, construct, convergent, discriminant) that parent-report measures would be held to (Bates, 1989b; Rothbart & Goldsmith, 1985). There are some very promising laboratory assessments of temperament (e.g., Goldsmith & Rothbart, 1991; Kagan, Reznick, & Snidman, 1988; Matheny, Wilson, & Thoben, 1987), but none has become so established through rigorous and extensive validational process that it is seen as the gold standard.

Kagan (1994) also argues that the language of an individual item on a temperament questionnaire is subject to multiple interpretations. This ambiguity, however, is in fact the main reason why researchers use *scales* of items rather than individual items to measure temperament constructs. The writing of good individual items is a goal, but it is unlikely that all sources of error will thereby be eliminated. Basic psychometric theory holds that the reason a set of convergent but imperfectly correlated items tends to have better test-retest reliability, better stability over time, and better validity is that the error components of individual items tend to cancel each other out when the item scores are added to each other, yielding a closer approximation to a "true" score. This is true of aggregation across multiple observations as well as multiple items. While this is a useful principle, one need not be limited to simply adding items and hoping that error is thereby reduced. With current analytical tools, such as linear structural relations (LISREL) and structural equations (EQS), one can also explicitly model linkages between items' and scales' error components, creating latent constructs that more precisely control for measurement error. Other steps researchers can take to reduce concerns about validity are to use validity scale filters (as in the Minnesota Multiphasic Personality Inventory—MMPI) and to study the ways parents construe child behavior and the items researchers present to them (Bates, 1994).

A Components-of-Variance Approach to Validity

We prefer to frame the question of validity of parent reports of temperament in terms of components of variance, implying that validity of temperament measures should be judged on a continuum rather than as an absolute or "digital" judgment (Bates, 1980; Bates et al., 1979). Bates and his colleagues asked how much variance in parent reports could be explained by reports of independent observers. They concluded that parent reports did converge with observer indexes of temperament, and that variance in parent reports was also left unexplained by the observer indexes. Some of this variance was related to subjective factors, such as parents' tendencies to describe themselves in socially desirable terms (e.g., see reviews by Bates, 1980; Hubert, Wachs, Peters-Martin, & Gandour, 1982; Slabach, Morrow, & Wachs, 1991). In using the terms *objective* and *subjective,* we do not mean to imply an absolute categorization. Observer records of infant behavior may contain subjective components (e.g., bias due to the attractiveness of the infant), and subjective factors identified in parent reports may contain objective components (e.g., mother anxiety related to child ratings may have a temperamental basis shared genetically with the child, or mother social

desirability response set may reflect competent adaptation, see Bates, 1994).

Bates and Bayles (1984) also carried out a series of second-order analyses on data from their longitudinal study. They showed that (a) mother ratings of their children on an array of temperament and nontemperament traits showed appropriate convergent and discriminant relations on similar sets of scales from 6 months to 3 years of age, (b) fathers and mothers agreed at generally moderate levels, (c) mothers and observers (in both naturalistic and structured contexts) agreed at generally modest, but significant levels, and (d) factors such as social desirability or anxiety that could reflect subjectivity accounted for only modest portions of the variance. Measured subjective factors thus did not overshadow measured objective factors as explanations of differences in parents' perceptions of their children. In addition to the objective and subjective components of parents' perceptions, there remained error components. Matheny, Wilson, and Thoben (1987) provided independent support for this model, using a better array of laboratory measures than had been used by Bates and Bayles (1984). Their aggregated maternal report scores correlated moderately to strongly with laboratory scores of temperament: $r = .52$ at 12 months, .38 at 18 months, and .52 at 24 months. Their conclusion was that "the objective component of maternal ratings was clearly demonstrable and prominent" (Matheny et al., 1987, p. 324). They also showed that maternal personality characteristics were not only correlated with mothers' perceptions of the child, they were also correlated with their children's behavior as independently observed in laboratory situations, congruent with genetically based similarities between mother and child.

A pattern of moderate to strong validity correlations for parent report can now also be found in a number of places in the literature, and we describe some of them here. One very important requirement for ascertaining construct validity is that both measures demonstrate adequate reliability, and often it is the observational or mechanical measures, not the parent report measures, that are deficient in this regard. To produce adequate reliability, aggregation across multiple measures is often necessary (Rushton, Brainerd, & Presley, 1983). Eaton (1983) recorded activity level from actometers worn by preschoolers over repeated nursery school free play sessions. Reliability of the actometers was .13 within a single session, but rose to .75 when multiple sessions were aggregated (Eaton, 1994). Aggregated scores also correlated .75 with parent temperament ratings using the Colorado

Childhood Temperament Inventory (CCTI) activity level scale and .73 with composite staff ratings of child activity level.

Asendorpf (1990) used multiple measures on multiple occasions to assess children's behavioral inhibition to strangers (shyness) across a four-year period beginning at age 3. These measures included a parent-report measure as well as observations of children's behavior with strange adults and children. Of all the measures taken by Asendorpf, parent report consistently showed the strongest relations with other measures; for example, parent report predicted latency to talk to a stranger at 3 years with $r = .67$; the overall average r between parent report and other shyness measures across the four years ranged from .43 to .53. Laboratory measures have also been found to be positively related to the IBQ and TBAQ (see Goldsmith & Rothbart, 1991). In the future we will be particularly interested in the relations between temperament measures and tasks designed to reflect underlying brain function; we have initial indication of a positive relation between a laboratory Stroop-like model task and a CBQ measure of inhibitory control ($r = .66$) for 36-month-old children (Gerardi et al., 1996). These findings provide further validational support for parent reports of temperament.

Prenatal Perception Studies

In recent years, researchers have also studied parental perceptions of temperament before the child is born. As shown first by Mebert (1991) and later by Diener, Goldstein, and Mangelsdorf (1995), as well as other studies reviewed by these authors, mothers' and fathers' expectations of temperament are often significant predictors of postnatal ratings of temperament. Parental expectations might then be seen as reflecting general personality dispositions or questionnaire response biases of the parents. However, the picture is actually more complex.

Mebert (1991) found that both mothers' and fathers' prenatal anxiety/depression composite scores predicted, to a modest, but statistically significant degree (.19–.24), their ratings of their babies three months after birth. Parent anxiety/depression scores did not, however, correlate much with prenatal temperament expectation scores, yet parent anxiety/depression scores predicted postnatal parent anxiety/depression to a considerably greater degree than they did postnatal temperament ratings. Prenatal temperament expectations appeared to be stronger predictors of later temperament ratings than prenatal anxiety/depression scores, although the correlations were still modest. Mothers' prenatal ratings of temperament also tended to predict their postnatal counterpart temperament scales better than they did the other temperament scales.

Diener et al. (1995) report findings converging in a general way with those of Mebert (1991) and adding to the picture. One addition is the comparison of the mother-father expected temperament correlation matrix with the corresponding one after birth. Prenatally, mothers' and fathers' temperament expectations were only modestly to moderately correlated, and the correlation pattern was generally nondifferentiated; for example, mothers' expectations of unadaptability to novelty were more highly related to fathers' fussy/difficult expectations than to their unadaptability expectations. However, postnatally, the mother-father convergence was considerably stronger, and there was also a strong pattern of discriminant validity; for example, mothers' ratings of unadaptability correlated with fathers' ratings of unadaptability .67, and with fathers' ratings of difficultness only .28.

The Mebert (1991) and Diener et al. (1995) studies, along with others they review, suggest that preexisting parental personality or adjustment characteristics predict parents' postnatal perceptions of their infants, to a modest degree, and that the parents' more specific expectations for their babies' temperament predict to a slightly greater degree. Mebert (1991) and Diener et al. (1995) speculated that prenatal expectations could reflect a vague internal working model of the infant before birth, and that this model might come to influence actual temperament through the expectancy confirmation processes that social psychologists Darley and Fazio (1980) have summarized. Other interpretations are possible, however. One is that a small component of the postnatal temperament ratings may simply reflect the parents' enduring concept of the way infants are, independent of any actual infant characteristics (Hagekull, Bohlin, & Lindhagen, 1984). In addition, the fact that mother and father perceptions of the infant become so much closer in both a convergent and a discriminant sense from before to after their actual experience with the baby can be interpreted as evidence for an objective component in the ratings.

Another interpretation is that parent characteristics such as tendencies toward high levels of negative affect might be passed on to the infant genetically, as suggested by Diener et al. (1995). When challenged by the researcher to predict the future temperament of their babies, parents may also draw partly on their own temperamental characteristics and those of infants in their own families, again allowing a genetic similarity interpretation. For some predictions, parents might also draw on their perceptions of activity level of the fetus, which show convergence with ultrasound measures (Eaton & Saudino, 1992). While the prenatal expectations literature provides an interesting window on possible subjective factors in parental perceptions, specific processes involved in any linkage between prenatal and postnatal perceptions have yet to be described. In addition, the data on mothers' and fathers' perceptions suggests they are being influenced by experience with the child.

Recent Attempts to Make Parent and Observer Vantages More Similar

As indicated above, we need not assume that modest parent-observer agreement is simply a product of low validity in the parents' reports, even though some writers have argued this. Modest correlations could come in part, for example, from observers simply not seeing the behavior that parents based their reports on. Naturalistic and structured observation measures are often based on between 30 minutes and 4 hours of observation, with only a few based on as much as 6 hours total, and there is little evidence that these measures show high test-retest reliability. Two recent home observation studies attempted to address such problems.

In the first, Bornstein, Gaughran, and Segui (1991) attempted to resolve the differing experience-base problem by using structured home observations to be completed by both observers and mothers of 5-month-olds. They also compared mother ratings based on a more open time frame with observer measures from the structured observations. Bornstein et al. selected 10 behavioral items, (e.g., smile at mother, vocalize, or mouth object), and called the set of items the Infant Temperament Measure (ITM). Observers and mothers filled out parallel forms of the ITM. Mothers also filled out an ITM with a nonspecific time frame prior to the first home visit. Within a week, the home visit procedure with mother and observer ITMs was repeated, and about a week after the second visit, the mother completed another nonspecific time frame form of the ITM.

Bornstein et al. (1991) found acceptable levels of one-week test-retest reliability for both mother and observer item ratings, but on average, only modest correlations between ratings of mothers and observers in the same time frame (average $r = .24$) and negligible correlations (.10 and .12, n.s.) between the observer restricted time frame and mothers' nonspecific ratings. Bornstein et al. suggested

that mother and observer reports may each be reliable and potentially valid, but that they tap different portions of the variance in infant behavior, an appropriately cautious conclusion. A less cautious conclusion would be that the mother-observer correlations should have been higher, with the findings indicating that mothers cannot be expected to provide meaningfully objective reports, as suggested by Kagan (this volume). This latter interpretation would be difficult to accept, however: first, the ITM consisted of a very limited array of items, even for a purely observational study, and the 10 items were largely uncorrelated. A single item of behavior does not in itself define a temperament construct; measurement of a temperament characteristic requires a higher degree of aggregation of similar behaviors across similar contexts (Bates, 1989b). The ITM passed some test-retest and interobserver reliability tests, but not the content validity test.

A second problem is that on the observer form of the ITM, each item's score was the actual frequency count of the infant behavior, whereas in the mother form, the score was on a 7-point scale of grouped frequency counts, with the groupings varying from item to item. This gave some structure for mothers filling out the scale, but appears to have created scaling problems working against the original goal of having items with good distributions. For some items, the average observed frequency of the behavior (which we calculated based on Bornstein et al.'s Table 3.1) fell within the range represented by only the first scale point on the mother form. When we sorted the items into those where mother response scales had this problem and those where the distributional properties allowed more room for covariance, the average correlation for the former kind of item was .18 and for the latter kind of item .30. This might not be a statistically significant difference, but it supports the concern about the scaling. It is also interesting to note that the item with the least skew in scaling had the best average correlation across visits (.54 for mouth object).

In the second of the two studies, Seifer, Sameroff, Barrett, and Krafchuk (1994) also attempted to deal with the frame of reference problem. Seifer et al., however, used somewhat more general temperament-like items composed of triads of items at two extremes of a 5-point scale, for example, content/satisfied/comfortable versus fussy/upset/cranky, as well as a slightly greater number of items: 14 instead of 10. Factor analysis of observer ratings showed several internally consistent scales: mood, containing both positive and negative affect items; approach, including exploration versus reserve; activity, including both movement and vocal activity; intensity, including degree of engagement and reactivity; and the single item of distractibility. They called their measure the Temperament Adjective Triad Assessment (TATA), and developed parallel forms for observers and mothers. Seifer et al. also obtained considerably more observational material, collecting one 45-minute videotape each week for eight weeks, with each visit loosely structured to yield periods of infant with mother (noncaretaking), infant alone, and mother caretaking. Observational situations were analyzed separately.

Mothers completed TATA scales at the end of each observation, rating the different situations separately, just as the videotape observers did. No evidence was presented as to the factors or internal consistency in mothers' scales. Seifer et al. also used several preexisting temperament scales, such as the IBQ and the RITQ, which mothers filled out near the end of the series of eight weekly observations. Increasing weeks of aggregation produced higher levels of reliability for both observer and mother TATA scores. Observer and mother scores within situations were also correlated to a modest-to-moderate level (typically about .25 to .42), markedly better than the typical correlation between observer TATA and mother reports on the other temperament scales. Mother reports on the TATA (apparently aggregated across situations) and standard temperament scales were also correlated in expected ways, but to a lower degree than the convergence of scales of the standard instruments. Evidence of discriminant validity was not reported.

While Seifer et al. (1994) acknowledged some methodological shortcomings in their study, their preferred interpretation was that "mothers are poor reporters of their infants' behavior" (p. 1488). Although mothers' and observers' ratings converged at modest-to-moderate degrees, we would attribute less of the nonoverlapping variance to the shortcomings of mothers as reporters than did Seifer and his colleagues. Our view is that the steps taken to ensure a common frame of reference seem to have led to a slightly higher observer-parent agreement than would have been found in a more typical study, given possible measurement limits of the TATA. The Seifer et al. study took some steps toward an ideal study for establishing boundaries of the objective component of parent reports. However, there were still a number of shortcomings. First, the TATA is limited as a measure of temperament constructs. The scales have very few items. This would make it difficult for random error components of items, such as idiosyncratic

interpretations, to cancel out each other. It would also make it difficult for a scale to represent well the kinds of behavior considered to reflect a given temperament construct. In addition, the key mood scale conflates positive and negative affectivity. From a theoretical viewpoint, and based on empirical results, these are profitably assessed as separate constructs. While it is common in the literature for positive and negative affect to be conflated, for example, in questionnaires stemming from the NYLS tradition, this is less than ideal, as discussed previously.

Second, the validity of the observational system was minimally established. Reading the items, we infer that the observation situations were not optimal for all of the scales. This might have made it hard for observers to see behaviors that mothers may have seen in other situations, coloring observers' perceptions of the restricted observation periods.

Third, the aggregation strategy may have restricted possible convergence. Observer-mother agreement correlations were computed separately for the three kinds of situation, although Seifer et al. (1994) presented no evidence that the three kinds of situation really produced distinctive patterns of infant behavioral characteristics. The mother-observer correlations were each based on only about two hours of observation. High correlations may have been possible if they were based on either more total hours within situations or aggregations across situations.

Goldsmith et al. (1991) took another approach to evaluate the limits of the objective component of mother temperament ratings. They correlated mother reports with those of day care teacher reports within separate samples of preschoolers, toddlers, and infants. Using a variety of standard temperament scales, Goldsmith et al. reported strong convergence between scales from different questionnaires intended to measure the same construct and even generally acceptable divergence between scales that were expected to differ. Correlations between mother and day care teacher for two older groups were in the typical range for correlations between parents and other observers (.11–.50 for preschoolers, with the highest correlation on one of the activity-level scales, and .00–.35 for toddlers, with the highest correlation also on activity), and perhaps a little above this range for infants (.21–.60, with the highest correlation on one of the measures of approach-sociability). Day care teachers would presumably be well acquainted with the children, although Goldsmith et al. did not report the degree of acquaintance. It might therefore have been expected that the correlations would be closer to the range of parent-parent correlations (Bates, 1989b) than parent-observer correlations. However, Goldsmith et al. emphasize that "teachers and mothers observed the children in systematically different contexts" (p. 576). As evidence for potential impact of failure to control context, they cite the Hagekull et al. (1984) study.

Hagekull et al. (1984) showed that when parents were given the task of directly recording infant behavior over extended periods in specific situations, such as infants' reactions to loud sounds, their data converged strongly with independent observers' data: correlations between parent and observer direct observation data compiled in two four-hour visits ranged from .60 (for attentiveness) to .83 (for sensory sensitivity). This suggests, contrary to Seifer et al. (1994), that parents are not necessarily deficient or strongly biased in their powers of observation, especially since their training for the task was minimal. Hagekull et al. also found that open time frame, general questionnaire scales completed by the parents converged to a modest to moderately strong degree with the scales based on independent direct observation, with correlations from .21 to .63. We attribute the apparent improvements in observer-parent agreement coefficients more to the study's careful effort to observe sufficiently large numbers of key events than to conceptual or psychometric advantages in the questionnaire they used (the Baby Behavior Questionnaire). Although BBQ scales were developed through factor analysis, some of the scales in this instrument have some difficulties in interpretation, due to apparently heterogeneous content.

In summary, despite efforts by well-known research teams, the ideal large-scale study for the limits of the objective component of parent reports of temperament has not yet appeared. Studies approaching the ideal would require conceptually well-developed measures of temperament, with careful attention to both parent report and observer report forms. The design would devote extra attention to validating observer measures, testing for converging and diverging relations among indexes in the instrument as well as relations between the instrument's scales, and alternate ways of observing (e.g., summary ratings versus independently recorded molecular behavior frequencies, or naturalistic versus structured observations).

In addition, greater efforts would be made to identify and observe situations crucial in parents' perceptions of the child—for example, conditions where the child is rested or fatigued, conditions where parents are relatively responsive or relaxed versus situations where the parents are unresponsive or stressed, familiar versus unfamiliar situations, and

so on. This would probably necessitate many more hours of observation than used to date, as well as observation of rather private times in families. With ordinary naturalistic observation procedures, it would probably be difficult for many families to tolerate the necessary levels of intrusion. Other approaches, however, may yield the necessary degree of familiarity with the child's life without creating as much stress for either the family or the observer, for example, electronic activity monitors, tape recorders that switch on and off without the family's having to attend to them, or ethnographic, participant-observation methods (e.g., Henry, 1973; Rizzo, Corsaro, & Bates, 1992). The design would also pay greater attention to the contexts of temperament-relevant behavior, aggregating measures in appropriate ways to the constructs.

Although the concept of temperament implies some degree of cross-situational consistency, there is no reason to suppose that any given temperament trait should be equally well revealed in all contexts. The issue of context is crucial to all forms of temperament assessment. The question of the class of situations in which measures should be aggregated would have to be settled by further work on the situational boundaries of the specific temperament constructs.

Shall We Use Parent Reports?

We conclude that evidence to date is supportive of the use of parent-report measures of temperament. As noted by Bates (1994) and Rothbart (1995), two basic reasons to use parent-report measures are (a) that they provide a useful perspective on the personality of children, since parents can see a wide range of child behaviors, and (b) that they have established a fair degree of objective validity. In addition, parent-report measures have contributed to substantial empirical advances, such as our current understanding of the structure of temperament in relation to the Big Five or Big Three models and their parallels in psychophysiological systems (Bates, Wachs, & Emde, 1994; Rothbart, Derryberry, & Posner, 1994). A number of important results reviewed in this chapter originally emerged from research based on parent-report measures. A further reason for using parent reports is that social relationship aspects of temperament elicited from parents may in themselves be very important to understanding development.

Although observational measures are appealing, we argue that they should not at this time be the sole measure of temperament. The primary arguments for this position are that the validity of a number of such measures of temperament is not strongly established, and even if the measures were well validated, they would often be awkward and highly expensive to use. Improvements in *both* parent-report and observational measures are needed, and from the studies highlighted here, such efforts are evidently underway. It is also likely that parent reports can be made more objective, and that the subjective components can be modeled more accurately and even controlled for (see Bates, 1994). The construct validity of observational measures can be improved as well. For the present, however, temperament measures remain both under construction and under attack—and those who enter this construction zone must wear conceptual hard hats.

We now turn to a review of research that provides additional insights to guide our choice of measures, research on the neural substrates of temperament-related behavior.

PSYCHOBIOLOGICAL RESEARCH APPROACHES

Gunnar (1990) describes five assumptions guiding psychobiological research on temperament: (a) "the assumption that temperament variation is regulated by the central nervous system"; (b) "the assumption that measures of peripheral systems inform us about the physiological bases of temperament because peripheral activity is regulated centrally," allowing the use of nonintrusive measures such as heart rate or electrodermal response; (c) "the assumption that fundamental temperament and emotional processes reflect a common mammalian heritage (Panksepp, 1982)," allowing research on animal models; (d) "the assumption that the aspects of central functioning related to temperament variation are those linked to broad or general behavioral tendencies"; and (e) "Finally, as reflected in Rothbart and Derryberry's theory (1981), concepts such as reactivity or arousal and self-regulation or inhibition are central to most physiological theories of temperament" (all quotations from p. 393). We have already adopted a number of these assumptions in the course of this review; they are further illustrated in this section.

Behavioral Genetics

One reason for adopting a psychobiological approach to temperament is the body of studies indicating genetic contributions to the development of temperament and personality. Results of this work are reported extensively by Caspi (Ch. 6, this Volume), Goldsmith (1989; Goldsmith,

Losoya, Bradshaw, & Campos, 1994), Plomin (Plomin, Chipuer, & Loehlin, 1990), and for animal studies, Wimer (Wimer & Wimer, 1985). Because extensive reviews are available elsewhere, we briefly review here just three landmark papers in the area, then consider recent findings on developmental behavioral genetics that appear particularly promising for understanding temperament and social development. Heritability estimates from behavioral genetics studies calculate the proportion of phenotypic (observable) variance in a characteristic attributable to genetic variation within a population. Heritability has proven to be substantial for most broad temperament and personality traits.

In the first of these papers, using adolescent twins, Loehlin and Nichols (1976) found a number of personality traits to show moderate heritability, with environmental contributions being chiefly nonshared, that is, not linked to the adolescents' having been brought up in the same family environment. In the second paper, Henderson (1982) reviewed studies concerning extraversion (positive affect and approach) and neuroticism (proneness to anxiety, moodiness, and irritability), finding heritability estimates larger than .50 for both factors. Dizygotic (DZ) twin correlations, however, were lower than would have been expected from genetic theory (that is, approximately one-half the size of correlations for monozygotic [MZ] twins). This has often been the case in subsequent questionnaire studies of temperament (nonadditive genetic variance may also reflect assimilation-contrast effects; see Bates, 1980; Goldsmith, 1989). Adoption studies reviewed by Henderson (1982) yielded lower heritability estimates than twin studies, averaging about .30. Again, evidence for shared environment effects was not found. Average correlations for nonadoptive relatives were about .15; for adoptive relatives, about 0.

A third paper, by Tellegen, Lykken, Bouchard, and Wilcox (1988), reported studies of adult MZ and DZ twins who had been reared either together or apart. Overall correlations of traits for MZ twins reared apart were surprisingly of a magnitude usually found for identical twins raised together (average $r = .49$), with heritability estimates of about .50. Correlations for MZ twins raised apart were .61 for stress reaction (neuroticism), .48 for sense of well-being, .50 for control, .49 for low risk taking, and .46 for aggression. For the three superfactors of positive emotionality (extraversion), negative emotionality (neuroticism), and constraint (effortful and fearful control), only positive emotionality showed evidence of higher correlations for MZ and DZ twins raised together compared to twins raised apart (MZ apart $r = .34$, together $= .63$; DZ apart $r = -.07$, together $= .18$).

Goldsmith, Buss, and Lemery (in press) have recently reviewed developmental behavioral genetics research and presented their own findings. Reviewing major projects including the Louisville Twin Study (Matheny, 1987, 1989), the Colorado Twin Project (Cyphers, Phillips, Fulker, & Mrazek, 1990), the MacArthur Longitudinal Twin Study (Plomin et al., 1993), and Torgerson's Norwegian study (Torgerson & Kringlen, 1978), Goldsmith et al. reported that parent-report measures yield MZ twin correlations ranging from .50 to .80, with DZ correlations ranging from 0 to .50. For scales based on Buss and Plomin's (1984) EAS measure, DZ correlations are typically less than half MZ correlations and often near 0, creating problems for heritability estimates. Evidence for larger DZ correlations is found using observational methods (see Kagan's discussion of the genetics of behavioral inhibition, Ch. 4, this Volume), and for parent-report studies employing the IBQ (Goldsmith, 1993) and the TBAQ, but not the CBQ (Goldsmith et al., in press). Research employing these last three measures also suggests shared family influence for positive affect and approach, as did results of the MacArthur study (Plomin et al., 1993) for parent-reported positive affect (Goldsmith et al., in press). Goldsmith et al. (in press) have also found evidence for genetic and shared family influences on CBQ effortful control scales.

Goldsmith's positive affect/approach findings are congruent with Tellegen et al.'s (1988) study of MZ and DZ twins raised together and apart, suggesting possible shared family effects for positive emotionality. The shared environmental effect found by Goldsmith et al. (in press) for effortful control requires replication, but shared family experience may also prove to be important in the development of attentional control. These findings may stimulate research into conditions that promote approach, positive affect, and self-control within the social environment.

One of the major temperament longitudinal studies has been the Louisville Twin Study (Matheny, 1987). Preliminary reports on NYLS-based temperamental characteristics in parent reports collected yearly from age 1 to 9 (Matheny, 1995) indicate consistent heritable effects for activity and approach-withdrawal, contributed chiefly by low to negative correlations for DZ twins. Persistence, adaptability, and threshold scales show heritability with more substantial DZ correlations. For mood and distractibility, genetic effects were generally lacking, and for rhythmicity and intensity they were mixed. Future reports from the Louisville Twin Study can be expected to include observational data and analyses of the genetics of change in temperament scores over age, as has been carried out for the dimension of behavioral inhibition (Matheny, 1989).

Although behavioral genetics research indicates strong heritability of individual differences in temperament and personality in populations studied to date, these findings are based on the usual environmental circumstances experienced by developing children, and any heritability estimates are based on the genes and environment operating together. The results do not tell us what *might* be accomplished via environmental intervention. They also do not reveal the specific developmental processes involved in temperament and personality outcomes. To learn more about the latter questions, studies furthering our understanding of temperament and development are essential. Zuckerman (1995) addressed the question "What is inherited?" and proposed this important answer: "We do not inherit personality traits or even behavior mechanisms as such. What is inherited are chemical templates that produce and regulate proteins involved in building the structure of nervous systems and the neurotransmitters, enzymes, and hormones that regulate them. . . . How do these differences in biological traits shape our choices in life from the manifold possibilities provided by environments? . . . Only cross-disciplinary, developmental and comparative psychological research can provide the answers" (pp. 331–332).

We now recognize that experiential and environmental processes themselves build changes in brain structure and functioning (Posner & Raichle, 1994), both before and after birth (Black & Greenough, 1991). This situation is a far cry from the view that a genetic hardwiring determines our future temperament and personality, and it calls out for developmental research. We next consider two areas of developmental research taking a psychobiological perspective. Other areas that might have been reviewed here, but were not, due to space limitations, include neuroendocrine function, including cortisol reactivity (see references in this chapter to Gunnar's cortisol research, however) and neuroregulatory amines such as monoamine oxidase (for reviews see Gunnar, 1990; Rothbart, 1989a; Zuckerman, 1991).

Approach/Withdrawal and Hemispheric Asymmetry

Approach and withdrawal tendencies have been related to asymmetries in cortical functioning, and we now briefly consider models and some data in this area (for an excellent review on frontal lobe asymmetry and development, see Dawson, 1994). Kinsbourne and Bemporad (1984) proposed that neural functions coordinating attention and emotion are localized and organized along hemispheric and anterior-posterior axes of the brain. In their view, the left fronto-temporal cortex controls responses to external change, including planning and sequencing of acts. The right fronto-temporal cortex controls internal emotional arousal. Each anterior system also controls the posterior centers that provide it with information, and the two hemispheres complement rather than inhibit each other. As in the extraversion-introversion, approach-inhibition, and agreeableness-hostility interactions we have discussed above, this model describes a balance between two systems.

Fox and Davidson (1984) also proposed differences in hemispheric specialization for affect, with the left hemisphere associated with positive affect and approach (A-processes, previously described by Schneirla, 1959), and the right hemisphere with negative affect and avoidance (W-processes). They suggested that toward the end of the first year of life, development of commissural transfer permits left hemisphere inhibition of right hemisphere function, attenuating the expression of negative affect and leading to alternations between approach and withdrawal. Davidson and Fox (1982) studied 10-month infants' responses to video segments depicting positive and negative affect. Greater left hemisphere activity was found to the positive segment. In an EEG study with newborns, greater activation was found in left brain regions for a sugar stimulus, greater right activation for a water stimulus (Fox & Davidson, 1986).

Fox, Calkins, and Bell (1994) found that infants with stable right frontal EEG asymmetry between 9 and 24 months of age displayed more fearfulness and inhibition in the laboratory than other children. At 4 years, children who showed more reticence and social withdrawal were also more likely to show right frontal asymmetry. Calkins, Fox, and Marshall (1996) recently found that children selected for high motor activity and negative affect to laboratory stimulation at 4 months showed greater right frontal asymmetry at 9 months, greater mother reports of fear at 9 months, and more inhibited behavior at 14 months. However, no relation was found between behavior and frontal asymmetry at 9 and 14 months. Instead, greater activation of both right and left frontal areas was related to higher inhibition scores at 14 months. Higher motor activity associated with positive affect at 4

months also predicted higher mother-reported anger at 14 months. The authors suggest a need to differentiate between fearful and angry distress, as we have done in "The Structure of Temperament" section. They also hypothesize that high motor/high negative affect and high motor/high positive affect may be associated with later different kinds of "difficultness." For high motor/high positive affect, the "difficultness" would be associated with problems in control.

Autonomic Reactivity and Self-Regulation

By assuming general controls on peripheral reactivity, psychobiological researchers have developed models of centrally regulated systems that might be studied very early in life. Models of vagal tone have been especially exciting, because they involve both reactive and self-regulative aspects of parasympathetic tone. In this section, we consider briefly some of the research on electrodermal responding, heart rate, and vagal tone.

Electrodermal Reactivity

Several early studies reported a negative relationship between electrodermal response and extraversion (see review by Buck, 1979). Jones (1960), for example, compared the 10 highest and 10 lowest electrodermal responders age 11 to 18 in the Berkeley Adolescent Growth Study. High electrodermal responders were described by psychologists as showing emotional control, being quiet, reserved, deliberate, calm, and responsible. Low electrodermal responders were rated as more impulsive, active, and talkative, and more attention seeking, assertive, and bossy. Adult studies have also found stable individual difference in electrodermal reactivity, finding it to be negatively related to measures of extraversion (e.g., Crider & Lunn, 1971). Fowles (1982) reported that electrodermal responding, but not heart rate reactivity, was related to measures of Gray's BIS.

In more recent research, Fabes, Eisenberg, Karbon, Bernzweig, Speer, and Carlo (1994) studied kindergarten and second grade children's facial expressions of distress and skin conductance (SC) reactivity to a film about children being hurt in an accident. SC variables were used along with maternal and other variables to predict children's helping, that is, their sorting of crayons into boxes for hospitalized children. For both ages, SC reactivity, used as a marker of personal distress, was positively related to facial distress and negatively related to helping.

Results were seen to reflect an interference of personal negative affect with children's prosocial behavior. Concurrent heart rate measures were not related to other variables. In a study of older children (third and sixth graders), SC was positively related to facial expressions of distress to a film and negatively related to mothers' report of dispositional helpfulness, but for girls only (Fabes, Eisenberg, & Eisenbud, 1993). Evidence has thus been found for electrodermal response as a sign of both distress and behavioral inhibition. However, recent research by Lang and his associates (Lang, Bradley, & Cuthbert, in press) has reported that adults' SC to viewing pictures increases for *both* aversive and pleasant stimuli, so that the sympathetic response measured in SC may be more general than previously thought.

Heart Rate and Vagal Tone

Additional research has focused on heart rate and related measures, including vagal tone as a measure of parasympathetic cardiac control. In her review of heart rate (HR) research, von Bargen (1983) reported HR reactivity to stimulation to be the most stable and reliable of HR measures. As noted by Kagan (this volume), another measure, HR variability, has been linked to low behavioral inhibition in some but not all studies. Fabes, Eisenberg, Karbon, and Troyer (1994) found HR variability to be positively related to kindergarten and second grade children's instrumental coping responses to a baby's crying. Fabes et al. (1993) also found positive relationships between HR variability and measures of sympathy (dispositional sympathy for girls, concerned attention to others' distress for boys) in third and sixth grade children.

A measure designed to assess parasympathetic control of heart rate variability is respiratory sinus arrhythmia (RSA), the rhythmic fluctuation in HR occurring at the frequency of respiration (Porges, 1986). During respiration, there is an increase in HR with inspiration and a decrease with expiration. Porges statistically extracts variance associated with RSA from HR variation, and has argued that variability in RSA reflects individual differences in tonic parasympathetic vagal tone, that is, in the degree of influence of the tenth cranial nerve, the vagus, on heart rate. Fox and Davidson (1986) note that the measure of vagal tone thus derived may reflect the parasympathetic aspect of autonomic balance previously sought by Wenger (1941) and Gellhorn (1957). It may also be related to approach/withdrawal systems identified by Schneirla (1959; see Stifter, 1995). In a recent review, however, Berntson,

Cacioppo, and Quigley (1993) argue that RSA is not a direct equivalent to tonic vagal control of the heart, because it is determined by multiple peripheral and central processes. They nevertheless conclude that RSA is an important noninvasive measure that is sensitive to psychological variables.

Keeping Berntson et al.'s (1993) concerns in mind, we review some of the findings relating measures of vagal tone measure or RSA to temperamental variables. In Porges, Doussard-Roosevelt, and Maiti's (1994) model of vagal tone, young infants with high baseline levels of vagal tone also tend to be highly reactive, with emotion often expressed in irritability. They review findings that newborn infants higher in baseline RSA are more irritable and emit more distressed cries during circumcision. Baseline vagal tone is also related to the regulation or withdrawal of vagal tone. Developmentally, as self-regulation of state becomes more available, vagal tone is also related to interest and expressiveness. A relationship has been found between vagal tone and attention (for a review of these findings, see Porges, 1991), and higher vagal tone is related to sustained reductions in RSA during attention-demanding activity. Higher vagal tone is also related to greater soothability at 3 months (Huffman, Bryan, del Carmen, Petersen, & Porges, 1992). Some infants with regulatory disorders nevertheless show high RSA but do not show suppression of RSA with attention (DeGangi, DiPietro, Greenspan, & Porges, 1991).

In a longitudinal study by Stifter and Fox (1990), higher newborn vagal tone predicted mothers' ratings of their infants at 5 months as more easily frustrated and slower to approach novel situations. Concurrent relations were also found: mothers reported that infants with higher vagal tone at 5 months smiled and laughed less and were more active. Vagal tone at the newborn assessment did not, however, predict vagal tone at 5 months. There is evidence of stability of vagal tone, but only after about 9 months (Porges & Doussard-Roosevelt, in press). Gunnar, Porter, Wolf, Rigatuso, and Larson (1995) employed behavioral, cardiac, and neuroendocrine measures in a longitudinal study from the newborn period to 6 months. Infants with higher baseline vagal tone showed higher cortisol levels during and after a heelstick procedure. For a small follow-up sample, distress to limitations at 6 months as measured by the IBQ was predicted by higher vagal tone and lower percent crying during the neonatal heelstick. Higher vagal tone during recovery from the heelstick (and a trend for baseline) predicted higher IBQ smiling and laughter at 6 months.

RSA after 5 to 6 months tends to be associated with positive emotionality and approach as well as irritability. Richards and Cameron (1989) found that baseline RSA was positively correlated with parent-reported approach at 6 and 12 months, and Fox and Stifter (1989) reported more rapid approach to strangers in infants with higher RSA at 14 months. Stifter, Fox, and Porges (1989) found 5-month-olds with higher RSA to look away more often at a stranger's approach and show higher levels of interest and positive affect, although this pattern was not found at 10 months. Infants with higher baseline vagal tone may be generally more approaching and susceptible to angry irritable affect, a combination predicted by Depue and Iacono's model (1989) described above. At 9 months, Porges, Doussard-Roosevelt, Portales, and Suess (1995) found vagal tone to be positively correlated with ICQ fussy/difficultness. For a small longitudinal sample, however, even after partialling out 9-month ICQ difficulty, the 9-month vagal tone measure negatively predicted difficulty at age 3 years.

Fox and Field (1989) found a more rapid adjustment to preschool in 3-year-olds with higher vagal tone; these children also showed higher positive affect and greater adaptability. Katz and Gottman (1995) reported that children with low vagal tone at age 5 showed a stronger correlation between marital hostility at age 5 and problem behaviors at age 8 than children with high vagal tone (rs = .65 and .25), although the interaction was not significant. Katz and Gottman see their finding as congruent with a buffering effect of higher vagal tone that might operate through attentional self-regulation. Research on vagal tone further indicates the usefulness of employing multiple measures, including psychophysiological measures, parent-report and observational methods in temperament research. We expect that in the future, research in this area will employ multiple psychophysiological as well as other measures, as has been done by Gunnar et al. (1995).

Marker Tasks

Finally, a new approach linking biology and behavior involves behavioral marker tasks associated with neural functioning in specific brain areas (Posner & Raichle, 1994). For example, children's performance on Stroop-like tasks linked to neural circuits involved in attentional effortful control is related to their mothers' CBQ reports of inhibitory control and lower negative affect expression (Gerardi et al., 1996). Use of the fear-potentiated startle technique developed by Lang and his associates (Lang et al., in press) may prove to be another useful marker task,

because the underlying fear-related physiology of the potentiated startle response is now well understood. Balaban (1995) has already succeeded in measuring the potentiated startle response in 5-month-old infants.

Summary

Behavioral genetics research supports the idea that the chemical templates we inherit are reflected in our temperament and personality characteristics. Much more developmental research is needed, however, to specify how developing brain mechanisms interact with environmental events to support these outcomes. Recent investigations have linked tendencies toward approach and withdrawal to left and right hemisphere brain activity. In addition, electrodermal responding has been linked, in some studies, to the BIS and to negative emotionality. An active program currently investigates HR variability and vagal tone, with the latter taken as a measure of parasympathetic function. HR variability has been linked to prosocial responding and inversely, in some studies, to behavioral inhibition. Vagal tone has been linked to behavioral irritability, approach, positive affect, and attention, with the direction of the linkage varying depending on the age of the child. Finally, marker tasks based on specific brain-behavior relations allow noninvasive measurement of underlying processes important in the development of temperament. All of these approaches, along with the cortisol research described in other sections of the chapter and Suomi's (1986; Suomi & Novak, 1991) and others' important research on monkey models for temperament, which we have not had the space to review, are promising for tracing out the links between inherited chemical templates and structural and behavioral outcomes.

TEMPERAMENT AND DEVELOPMENT: STABILITY AND CHANGE

Early approaches to the study of temperament stressed the importance of stability of temperament over time. Thus, for Buss and Plomin (1975), to qualify as a "temperament," a dimension must demonstrate stability from its early appearance. More recent approaches to the field, however, note that temperament itself develops, so that studying changes in temperament over time as well as individual differences allows us a greater understanding of both child development and temperament (Goldsmith,

1996; Rothbart, 1989b; Rothbart & Derryberry, 1981). Repeated measures of temperamental attributes can fail to show normative stability (that is, they do not predict later from earlier measures), yet genetically related individuals show strong similarity in their change. These results have been found in behavioral genetics work on both activity level (Eaton, 1994) and behavioral inhibition (Matheny, 1989).

In this section we consider contributions of temperament to social-emotional development and the development of personality. We review research examining developmental change and instability/stability within temperament itself, in the areas of distress proneness, positive affect/approach, activity level, and attentional and effortful control. The developmental course appears to begin with individual differences in emotional and motor reactivity, influenced over time by the development of more regulatory systems, one more reactive and emotionally based (fear or behavioral inhibition), the other more self-regulative (attentional control). The first control system develops earlier than the second.

Even for dimensions showing normative stability, manifestations of temperament may change over time. The 6 year old, for example, spends much less time crying than does the 6 month old. To appropriately assess stability of temperamental characteristics, it is necessary to establish continuity in the temperament constructs studied across time. Pedlow, Sanson, Prior, and Oberklaid (1993) assessed the ATP sample at intervals from infancy to 7 to 8 years of age using multivariate analysis techniques. By using structural equation modeling, factors were identified that applied across the whole age range (approach/sociability, rhythmicity), or across several of the time intervals studied (irritability, persistence, cooperation-manageability, and inflexibility). A structural equation model correcting for attenuation of correlations due to error of measurement was then used to assess individual stability on these factors from year to year. Estimates were considerably higher than those previously reported, mostly in the range of 0.7–0.8. Even with these levels of stability, however, there was considerable room for individual change in their relative position on these characteristics, and the great majority of temperament stability correlations are in the small to moderate range.

Contributions of Temperament to Development

Temperament variables are fundamental to identifying trajectories of social-emotional and personality development. As noted above, temperament is directly implicated in learning processes. If fear of a stranger is great for one child and slight for another, avoidance of strangers may be reinforced for the first child and not for the second. If the second child not only does not experience fear, but experiences delight in the interaction with a stranger, conditioned approach to future interactions is likely. Thus positive feedback may serve to magnify initial differences. Individual differences will also promote active seeking of environments appropriate to the temperamental qualities. Scarr and McCartney (1983) have described these active genotype/environmental interactions as "niche picking." Gray's (1982) theory, however, implicates temperament in learning at an even more basic level than these examples. Extraverts, high in positive affect and approach, are seen as more susceptible to reward, and introverts, high in fear and shyness, to punishment. If we consider Gray's model seriously, it suggests that caregiver treatments will have differing developmental outcomes, given temperamental differences across children. Theories and research on moral development have also linked fearfulness to the development of internalized conscience; these will be discussed later in the chapter.

Optimal-level theories (e.g., Bell, 1974; Strelau, 1983) stress individual preferences for high or low levels of stimulation. A person easily overwhelmed by stimulation will try to keep things quiet, whereas a person who requires high levels of stimulation for pleasure will attempt to keep things exciting. Mismatches in optimal levels between a parent and child, or among siblings, are likely to require major individual adaptations. Situational demands, for example, an intense day care experience for an easily overstimulated infant or enforced quiet for a stimulus-seeking older child, may lead to problems for both the child and the caregiver.

Scarr and McCartney (1983) also describe evocative interactions, where the child's characteristics elicit reactions from others that may influence the child's development. Thus, a child's positive and outgoing disposition may serve as a protective factor in a high-risk environment (Werner, 1985). Radke-Yarrow and Sherman (1990) have noted a buffering effect that occurs when the child's characteristics meet the needs of the parent in a high-risk situation (the parent's needs may be quite idiosyncratic). These needs may be met by temperamental characteristics of the child. Acceptance by the adult then leads the child to feel there is something special or important about her or him personally. This notion is very similar to Thomas and Chess's "goodness-of-fit" argument, and will be further discussed later in the chapter.

Because temperament itself develops over time (Roth-bart, 1989b), new systems of behavioral organization (e.g., smiling and laughter, frustration) will come "on-line" over time. In addition, the development of regulative systems that serve to inhibit other actions will come to modulate characteristics previously present. In addition to the direct effects of a developing control system, children who develop a control system early versus late may have quite different experiences (Rothbart & Derryberry, 1981). For example, the child who develops fear-related behavioral inhibition late in development may have more direct interactions with potentially threatening objects or situations in the interim than the child who develops fear early. On the other hand, the child who is fearful and inhibited to the potential for danger earlier in development may spend more time watching and making sense of events in the environment than the child who is less inhibited early on.

Distress Proneness

Some evidence for longitudinal stability of distress proneness in infancy has been found, although not for preterm infants (Riese, 1987). In the Louisville Twin Study, stability of negative emotionality was found from standardized hospital and laboratory assessments during the newborn period to assessments at 9 months and 24 months (Matheny, Riese, & Wilson, 1985; Riese, 1987). Neonates were observed in the hospital from one feeding to the next, during application of a stressor, and during examiner soothing. Examiner ratings formed a cluster including irritability, resistance to soothing, activity awake, low orienting reactivity, and low reinforcement value. At 9 and 24 months, infants were observed in the laboratory, and aggregated ratings of emotional tone, attentiveness, activity, and social orientation were made at those times. Newborn irritability and resistance to soothing predicted negative emotional tone at 9 months (Matheny et al., 1985). Newborn irritability also predicted 24-month reactions of greater distress, less attentiveness to stimuli, less responsiveness to staff, and more changeability in activity level across situations (Riese, 1987).

The Louisville neonatal ratings showed *little* stability from the newborn era to either 12 or 18 months, however. Riese (1987) suggests that, during the 24-month era, increased emotionality, perhaps underlying the popular conception of the "Terrible Twos," may allow for better prediction than the more positive periods of 12 and 18 months. Her interpretation would be congruent with later developmental periods of heightened emotionality, such as adolescence, being times of a heightened potential for predictability of negative emotionality. In other studies of stability, Worobey and Lewis (1989) found that neonates who reacted strongly to PKU screening were likely to react strongly to DPT inoculations at 2 months. Larson, DiPietro, and Porges (1987) predicted 15-month fussy-difficult, unsociability, and unadaptability scores on the ICQ from newborn ratings of irritability, low alertness, and difficulty in testing as assessed in the Nebraska revision of the Neonatal Behavioral Assessment Scale (NBAS). Van den Boom (1989) also predicted later ICQ difficultness at 6 and 12 months from newborn assessments of distress proneness.

In spite of these findings, patterns of stability for distress proneness within the early months are not always found. St. James-Roberts and Plewis (1996) found parent diary records of fussing at 6 weeks predicted 10-month fussing better than did records of fussing at 3 months, and they note Fish and Crockenberg's (1981) findings of higher correlations between 1-month fussing and 9-month fussing-crying than between 3- and 9-month fussing-crying. We have also found little stability for distress from 3 months on in both parent-report and home observation measures (Rothbart, 1981, 1986). However, using a composite irritability measure derived by adapting the IBQ to younger infants, Worobey and Blajda (1989) found stability from 2 weeks to 2 months, and smaller but significant correlations between 2 months and 1 year.

There are developmental reasons to expect relative instability in distress proneness within the early months. Over the period of 1 to 3 months, infants demonstrate an inability to disengage attention from visual locations, and these changes have been related to maturation of a neural brain circuit inhibiting the superior colliculus (Johnson, Posner, & Rothbart, 1991). During this era of "obligatory looking," there is also considerable irritable crying, especially in the evening, with a peak in crying found across cultures at about 6 weeks of age in early infancy (St. James-Roberts, Bowyer, Varghese, & Sawdon, 1994). In our view, this distress may be related to infants' relative inability to regulate stimulation through the use of attention during this period. By about 4 months, obligatory looking will have greatly decreased, as will overall amounts of fussing and crying. For a short developmental window, then, changes in orienting systems may create special conditions for the elicitation of negative affect that do not exist before or later. By 4 months, greater ability to disengage orienting from a central stimulus is related to parent reports of lower negative affect and greater soothability (Johnson et al., 1991). Thus development of attention appears to first lead to distress from overstimulation that may be related to colic, and later to the capacity to avoid overstimulation through self-regulation.

There appears to be better predictiveness of later distress by measures taken at 4–6 months of age. Kagan (this volume) found distress coupled with motor reactivity to laboratory stimulation at age 4 months to predict later behavioral inhibition. This finding was replicated by Calkins and Fox (1994), who also found 4-month positive affect coupled with motor reactivity to predict later extraverted behavior. Hagekull and Bohlin's (1981) manageability factor, partly defined by low negative affect, shows moderate stability between ages 4 and 13 months, and parent-report studies have reported stability of mood from 6 months to 2 years of age (Persson-Blennow & McNeil, 1980), from 4–8 months to 1–3 years (McDevitt & Carey, 1981), and from 6–8 months to 5 years (Hüttunen & Nyman, 1982). These parent-report scales range from positive mood at one pole of the dimension to negative mood at the other, however, so either or both positive and negative emotionality may contribute to stability. Using two unipolar scales would yield more specific information about the nature of the stability.

Using more specific measures of distress, Sullivan, Lewis, and Alessandri (1992) found stability of anger in the extinction period of an arm-pulling contingency period across two-month periods (2–4 months and 6–8 months) using the Maximally Discriminative Facial Movement Coding System (MAX). Stability was also found from 4–6 months for sadness expressions. Malatesta, Culver, Tesman, and Shepard (1989) found stability of anger and sadness across 2.5–5, 5–7.5, and 7.5–22 months during mother-infant play and a reunion episode. However, whether these reactions generalize to other conditions remains at issue (Sullivan et al., 1992).

In a small longitudinal sample, we have found laboratory observations of infant fear and frustration during infancy to predict parent reports of those characteristics using the CBQ at 6–7 years. Infant fear in the laboratory was positively correlated with childhood fear, shyness, and sadness in the CBQ (Rothbart, Derryberry, & Hershey, 1995). Infant frustration also predicted both childhood frustration and approach tendencies. Over a longer period, Lanthier and Bates (1995) predicted 17-year-old maternal and self-reported neuroticism from parent reports of higher fear and lower sociability in infancy. Caspi and Silva (1995) found examiner ratings of children at age 3–4 years

predicted self-reported personality measures at age 18. Preschool children high on a cluster of examiner ratings of irritability and distractibility were found as teenagers to be low on harm avoidance (i.e., high on stimulation seeking), low on control, and high on aggression and alienation, in comparison with inhibited and with confident, well-adjusted clusters of children. The irritable-distractible preschool subgroup also scored higher than any other group on the age 18 superfactor of negative emotionality. In these predictions, children's negative reactivity was combined with a lack of attentional self-regulation to predict 18-year-old negative affect. This finding is congruent with the idea that negative affect may be regulated by attentional means (Harman, Posner, & Rothbart, in press) or, alternatively, that high distress makes attentional control difficult.

In summary, low to moderate levels of stability of distress proneness have been found during the early years, but not for all age intervals. In particular, there may be an early period of general distress proneness that does not predict later distress, but is related to an early period of obligatory attention. There is also evidence of stability between infancy and 6–7 years (Rothbart, Derryberry, & Hershey, 1995) and between early childhood and adulthood, although the latter research combines distress proneness with lack of attentional control (Caspi & Silva, 1995).

Positive Affect/Approach versus Shyness and Behavioral Inhibition

By 2–3 months, infants show a behavioral pattern that includes smiling, vocalization, and motor cycling of the limbs. This cluster of reactions was described by Kistiakovskaia in 1965 and termed the animation complex, including "smiling, quick and animated generalized movements with repeated straightening and bending of hands and feet, rapid breathing, vocal reactions, eyeblink, etc." (Kistiakovskaia, 1965, p. 39). The behavioral cluster appears to increase in duration and decrease in latency into the second and third months (Kistiakovskaia, 1965). Werner (1985) reviewed cross-cultural evidence for both an increase in smiling between 2 and 4 months, and an increase in vocalization at 3–4 months. This cluster of correlated behaviors (smiling and laughter, vocal and motor activity) is also found in parents' reports of temperament and in home observations (Rothbart, 1986). Although the pattern has been called sociability, it is displayed toward exciting and novel objects as well as to people (Bradley, 1985). Sociability therefore may be too narrow a label for this dimension, at least during early infancy.

Beyond 3–4 months, positive affect shows normative increases in expression across the first year of life, both in home observation and parent-report data (Rothbart, 1981, 1986). Stability has also been found for a composite positive emotionality variable including smiling and laughter, motor and vocal activity as assessed by parent-report and home observation across 3–9 months, and stability of a laboratory measure of smiling and laughter from 3 to 13.5 months of age (Rothbart, 1987). Smiling and laughter in infancy also predict both concurrent (Rothbart, 1988) and 6- to 7-year-old approach tendencies (Rothbart, Derryberry, & Hershey, 1995). As noted above, Pedlow et al. (1993) also found stability from infancy to 7–8 years on their dimension of approach/sociability.

Later in the first year, an important form of inhibitory control develops: some infants who were highly approaching at 5 or 6 months now come to inhibit their approach responses to unfamiliar and/or intense stimuli (Rothbart, 1988; Schaffer, 1974). In our laboratory, we found increases in infants' latency to grasp novel and intense toys from 6.5 to 10 months of age (Rothbart, 1988). Rapid approach was also positively correlated with smiling and laughter both in the laboratory and by mothers' IBQ report. Infants' approach latency to low-intensity stimuli also showed stability across 6.5 months to later ages (10 and 13.5 months), but to high intensity stimuli it did not. This finding is congruent with behavioral inhibition developing late in the first year, with inhibitory reactions particularly evident in response to high-intensity stimuli. Once inhibition of approach is established, longitudinal research suggests that individual differences in the relative strength of approach versus inhibition to novelty or challenge (recall Gray's BAS and BIS) will be a relatively enduring aspect of temperament. In familiar or low-intensity situations, however, chiefly positive activation systems may be evident. We argue that this aspect of fear (behavioral inhibition) qualifies fear as a system that modulates other response tendencies (a control system). We elaborate this argument in the discussion of Kochanska's (1993) research later in the chapter.

The resulting inhibitory state has been called response uncertainty by McCall (1979), and behavioral inhibition by Garcia-Coll, Kagan, and Reznick (1984), and has been seen as a prototype for anxiety (Suomi, 1986). Inhibited approach is elicited by perception of the novel or unfamiliar, and Gray (1982) argues that it is also influenced by the intensity of stimulation, with high levels of stimulus intensity eliciting inhibition of approach. Gray's interpretation is in keeping with definitions of behavioral inhibition that

include responses to novelty and challenge, and with predictions of later behavioral inhibition from 4-month negative reactivity. Honzik (1965) has noted that longitudinal Fels subjects' scores on spontaneity versus social interaction anxiety were stable and predictive over long periods for both males (the first three years to adulthood) and females (6–10 years to adulthood; Kagan & Moss, 1962). Bayley and Schaeffer (1963) also found their most stable and persistent category between infancy to 18 years to be active, extraverted versus inactive, introverted behavior. Tuddenham (1959) reported stability on scales indexing spontaneity versus inhibition for subjects from 14 to 33 years in the Oakland Growth Study. Finally, Honzik (1965) found that for the period between 21 months and 18 years of age, the two most stable dimensions were introversion versus extraversion and excessive reserve versus spontaneity.

These results can be added to evidence from Kagan (this volume) on stability of behavioral inhibition, and to Caspi and Silva's (1995) recent work on stability of outgoingness and inhibition. Caspi and Silva identified a group of children high on approach or confidence at age 3–4, who were outgoing and eager to undertake tasks and adjusted easily to challenging situations. At age 18, these children were relatively low on self-reported control (i.e., more impulsive) and high on social potency. Children identified in the preschool period as inhibited (fearful, with problems in sustaining attention) were, at age 18, high on harm avoidance, notably low on aggression, and low on social potency. In this study, inhibition or fearfulness served as a protective factor against the later development of aggression. This finding is also congruent with the positive correlations found between temperamental fearfulness and the development of conscience, to be described below.

Related work stemming from a theoretical framework developed by Gorenstein and Newman (1980) further suggests the relevance of constructs of activation and inhibition to socialization. Newman and his colleagues assessed the capacity of extraverted, introverted, and psychopathic individuals to use cues for punishment to withhold inappropriate approach-driven behavior. Their paradigm involved a passive avoidance procedure, also called a "go–no go" situation, where the study participants are asked to withhold responses associated with punishment. Newman, Widom, and Nathan's (1985) participants were given a series of two-digit numbers and learned by trial and error to respond to some of the numbers but not to others. Extraverts made more errors of commission to punished numbers than did introverts. In a study on 6- to 7-year-olds, Hershey (1992) found a similar result. Patterson, Kosson, and Newman

(1987) also found that individuals' tendency to slow down after a punished item was significantly related to their performance on a "go–no go" task, and found some evidence for extraverts' speeding of response to punishment.

This research suggests it is possible to separate energizing from directional influences of punishment: for introverts, goal-directed responses are often inhibited by punishment; for extraverts, goal-directed responses may be less inhibited and, under some circumstances, even activated by punishment. This analysis may also apply to younger children's functioning. Saltz, Campbell, and Skotko (1983) found, in support of Luria's (1961, 1966) observations, that increasing the loudness of a "stop" or "no go" command actually increased 3- to 4-year-old children's likelihood of performing a prohibited act. Increasing loudness decreased the likelihood of responding for children 5–6 years of age. We have noted Patterson's (1980) findings of children with aggressive problems failing to respond to parental punishment. Individual differences in approach and in passive (fearful) inhibitory control may contribute to these findings.

In summary, evidence for approach tendencies that are related to positive affect can be seen early in development. Later in infancy, approach will be modulated by development of behavioral inhibition related to fear. Once established, these tendencies toward approach versus inhibition will demonstrate significant stability over relatively long developmental periods, with important implications for social development.

Activity Level

Another major temperamental characteristic that can be measured in newborns is activity level. Activity level can also be measured prenatally using both ultrasound imaging and mother report, with relative agreement between the two indexes, and with temperamental stability found over the short periods that have been measured (Eaton & Saudino, 1992). In early research, Fries (Fries & Woolf, 1953) and Escalona (1968) identified activity level as a major dimension of individual differences among infants. Birns, Barten, and Bridger (1969) found no stability of activity level from the newborn period to ages 3–4 months, but some stability was found from 4 weeks to later assessments.

A possible explanation for instability of very early activity level is the tendency for activity to be linked to both negative and positive reactivity. When high levels of waking activity occur in the newborn they are often linked to

the expression of negative affect (e.g., Korner, Hutchinson, Koperski, Kraemer, & Schneider, 1981). Escalona (1968) observed newborns to engage in their highest motor activity during distress; positive states were associated with quiescence. Later in development, however, the infant often becomes motorically aroused while in an alert and nondistressed state, as noted by Kistiakovskaia (1965), frequently during orienting toward novel objects or when receiving caregiver stimulation (Wolff, 1965). Links between activity and newborn expression of negative affect may account for its failure to predict later activity. Indeed, when Korner et al. (1985) measured *nondistress* motor activity in the neonate, they found vigor of neonatal activity to predict high daytime activity and high approach scores on the Behavioral Style Questionnaire (BSQ) at ages 4–8 years.

Mixed findings on stability of activity level from the first year to later periods have also been reported. Stability of activity across the first year and beyond, in both parent-report and home observation measures, has been reported by Hagekull and Bohlin (1981), McDevitt and Carey (1981), Peters-Martin and Wachs (1984) and Hüttunen and Nyman (1982). However, studies using the IBQ and the TBAQ have shown instability from the first year to 18–24 months (Rothbart, Derryberry, & Hershey, 1995), and Saudino and Eaton (1993), using actometer measures in a twin study, did not find normative stability in activity level from 7 to 36 months. Nevertheless, in Saudino and Eaton's (1993) study, MZ twins were more similar than DZ twins at both ages, and MZ twins were also more concordant in their changes in activity from 7 to 36 months than were DZ twins. On the basis of their review of the literature, Buss and Plomin (1975) concluded that activity level is not stable from infancy, but that from 12 months, activity level shows moderate stability. More recently, activity level in the laboratory at 13 months has predicted activity and extraversion as well as frustration reactions at 6–7 years (Rothbart, Derryberry, & Hershey, 1995).

If we provisionally accept Buss and Plomin's (1975) conclusion that activity level does not show stability from the first year to later ages, at least two explanations are possible. One is that activity may be related to both positive and negative affectivity, with a need for the two kinds of activity to be differentiated. Thus, activity during early infancy coupled with negative affect may predict later inhibited approach; activity coupled with positive affect, later extraversion. Second, the onset of inhibition or fearfulness as a control system late in the first year of life may lower activity for a number of children in circumstances of novelty or high intensity, also creating instability. A second control over impulsive activity will also be developing late in the first year and throughout the preschool years; this is a control system related to the development of attention, to which we now turn.

Attention and Effortful Control

We noted above that attention has both reactive and self-regulative aspects, with the former developing earlier than the latter. In reactive attention, that is, visual orienting to exogenous stimulation, consistency of rates of infant looking have been found across three quite different measures in 3-month-olds: a visual discrimination paradigm, an auditory discrimination paradigm, and a measure of rate of looking toward the mother in social interaction (Coldren, Colombo, O'Brien, Martinez, & Horowitz, 1987). Byrne, Clark-Touesnard, Hondas, and Smith (1985) reported stability from 4 to 7 months in average looking time and duration of first look in visual habituation tasks.

A developmental shift in visual orienting appears to occur late in the first year of life (Ruff & Rothbart, 1996). Kagan, Kearsley, and Zelazo (1978) noted a U-shaped developmental pattern of fixation times to clay faces with scrambled and unscrambled features in both North American and Guatemalan children. From 4 to 8 months, there is a steep decline in the amount of time children spend looking at both kinds of faces. Between 13 and 36 months, however, there is an increase in looking time that is stronger for scrambled than for unscrambled faces. Kagan et al. (1978) suggest early looking patterns reflect individual differences in alertness, whereas older infants' looking represents the "richness of hypotheses surrounding representations of humans" (p. 80). They argue: "It has been our continual assumption that density of hypotheses to discrepant events is a major determinant of duration of fixation after 8 to 10 months of age. The occurrence of continuity (stability of duration of orienting) from 8 to 13 and 13 to 27 months, without comparable 8 to 27 month continuity suggests that the determinants of fixation time change between 8 and 27 months" (p. 81). No stability was found between 4 months and later measures. These changes are in keeping with findings reviewed above that signs of the anterior attention system begin to emerge toward the end of the first year, allowing increased executive control and planning, and presumably changing the meaning of individual differences in looking at objects (see also Ruff & Rothbart, 1996).

The development of effortful control, that is, the ability to inhibit a dominant response to perform a subdominant response (Gerardi et al., 1996; Rothbart, 1989b), also appears to be linked to the child's developing ability to maintain a focus of attention over an extended period. Sustained attention and the ability to delay are positively related, and both develop over the preschool years. Krakow, Kopp, and Vaughn (1981) studied sustained attention to a set of toys in 12- to 30-month-old infants. Duration increased across this period, with stability of individual differences between 12 and 18 months and between 24 and 30 months. Sustained attention was also positively related to self-control measures, independent of developmental quotient, at 24 months. Children with high sustained attention at 12 months were described by their mothers as more quiet and inactive at 24 and 36 months than children with shorter attention spans.

As in the development of behavioral inhibition, once normative changes in anterior attention have occurred, additional controls over more reactive behavior will have been added. Children may now demonstrate increased variability and flexibility in their deployment of attention from one situation to another. When the capacity for effortful control is weak in an older child, however, the child's activity may continue be driven by the intensity, novelty, or discrepancy of the stimulus, or by its associations with previous reward and punishment. Orienting may then be of long or short duration, but it will not show the flexibility of response possible when executive attentional control has been added.

Krakow and Johnson (1981), using measures of self-control under verbal instructions with younger children (age 18–30 months), found large age effects in inhibitory control. They also found moderate levels of stability of inhibitory self-control across the 12-month period. Reed, Pien, and Rothbart (1984) found strong age effects in two measures of self-control (a pinball game and Simon-says game) in a cross-sectional study of children aged 40–49 months. These studies indicate increases in self-regulation across 18 to 49 months of age. In our (Gerardi et al., 1996) research using Stroop-like tasks creating conflict between identity and location of stimuli, children 36-months-old who show greater interference in reaction time for conflicting responses were reported by their mothers as exhibiting lower levels of inhibitory control. Less accurate children were also reported as showing higher levels of anger/frustration, suggesting control over emotion as well as action.

Long-term stability in ability to delay gratification and later attentional and emotional control has been reported (Mischel, 1983). In Mischel's work, the number of seconds preschool children delayed while waiting for physically present rewards (a conflict situation) significantly predicted parent-reported attentiveness and ability to concentrate as adolescents (Shoda, Mischel, & Peake, 1990). Children less able to delay in preschool were also reported as more likely to go to pieces under stress as teenagers. In Caspi and Silva's (1995) study, preschool children characterized as "well adjusted" were described as "flexible in orientation, capable of reserve and control when it was demanded of them" (p. 492). These children showed flexibility of responsiveness, and we might expect them to have been higher in attentional and effortful control, and in Block and Block's (1980) construct of ego resiliency described later. At age 18, children identified as well adjusted by Caspi and Silva had high scores on social potency.

Attentional characteristics thus show major developments over the first years of life, with a more self-regulative (executive) system added to a more reactive (posterior) system (Rothbart, Posner, et al., 1994). As noted above, Caspi and Silva's (1995) Factor 1 (lack of control), including a combination of irritability and lack of self-regulation at age 3–4 years, was strongly related to negative emotionality at 18. Studies are now underway exploring contributions of both temperament and parent treatment to the development of self-control, as in Silverman and Ragusa's (1992) study predicting 4-year-old self-control from 24-month-old child temperament and maternal variables. Olson, Bates, and Bayles (1990) have also found relationships between parent-child interaction at 13 months and 2 years (but not at 6 months) and children's self-control at age 6. Relations were not found between 6-year-old self-control and earlier difficultness.

Two Control Systems

The developmental picture emerging describes early individual differences in motor and emotional reactivity, influenced by development of at least two temperament-related control systems, one of them part of an emotional reaction (fear), the other more completely self-regulative (attentional control), with the first system developing earlier than the second. This view is related to the theory of ego control and ego resiliency developed by Jean and Jack Block (Block & Block, 1980). The Blocks posited two control systems: one, ego control, can be seen as involving

fearful or inhibitory control over impulsive approach. The second, ego resiliency, is defined in terms of flexible adaptation to changing circumstances. This system may be related to the temperamental characteristic of attentional effortful control. Recent research by Eisenberg, Guthrie, et al. (1996) supports the predicted relationship between ego resiliency and CBQ measures of attentional control in kindergarten to third grade children. Resiliency in turn was related to social status and to teacher-reported socially appropriate behavior. A trend was also found for children's negative emotionality to be negatively related to parents' and teachers' ratings on resiliency. Positive effects of self-regulation were also significantly stronger for children who were high in negative emotionality. This is an example of a temperament X temperament interaction (for others, see the section "Temperament and Adjustment").

In the Blocks' (1980) theory, resiliency or flexibility contributes to the development of adaptation and mental health. As Block and Kremen (1996) put it, "Adaptability in the long-term requires more than the replacement of unbridled impulsivity or under-control, with categorical, pervasive, rigid impulse control. This would be over-control of impulse, restriction of the spontaneity that provides the basis for creativity and interpersonal connection. Instead and ideally, dynamic and resourceful regulation and equilibrium of impulses and inhibitions must be achieved. It is this modulation of ego-control that we more formally mean by the construct of ego-resiliency. It can be said that the human goal is to be as under-controlled as possible and as over-controlled as necessary" (1996, p. 351).

In the Blocks' (1980) ego control construct, when fear and its correlates develop in the context of a relatively constricted life, approach tendencies are strongly opposed, and rigid functioning may result. Ego resiliency, on the other hand, is strengthened by a set of life experiences that build upon capacities for both expression and control of impulses. We believe attentional effortful control may provide an important underlying control system for the development of ego resiliency, and further research along the lines of Eisenberg, Guthrie, et al. (1996) will be helpful on this topic. The Blocks' theory again stresses the importance of experience in the development of adaptation. Endogenous control systems allow cultural influence on both what is controlled and the specific self-regulatory capacities used by the child.

Fear and effortful control as passive and active systems have important implications for the expression of negative emotion and action, and both are discussed in our review of research on temperament, attachment, and adjustment. These temperamental dimensions have been put to excellent theoretical use by Kochanska (1993, 1995) in her work on the development of conscience. Kochanska posits, based on reviews of temperament research (e.g., Rothbart, 1989b), that both passive and active regulative systems, fear and effortful control, will be related to conscience development.

Another important approach taking into account both reactivity and self-regulatory control is the work of Gunnar and her colleagues (e.g., Gunnar, 1994; Gunnar et al., 1995) on cortisol reactivity. The adrenal cortex secretes steroid hormones, including the glucocorticoids, cortisol and corticosterone (Carter, 1986). These hormones increase blood glucose and work with the catecholamines to produce glucose from free fatty acids, also serving an anti-inflammatory function for injury and disease. Gunnar and her associates (1995) have investigated cortisol reactivity in relation to individual differences in temperamentally based self-regulation. Gunnar et al. found that high newborn cortisol levels predicted both higher positive affect and lower distress to limitations at age 6 months. They interpret these findings of higher stress reactivity during the newborn period predicting less distress at 6 months as "suggesting that the capacity to mount a strong stress response to pain stimuli reflects neonatal neurobehavioral organization" (p. 12).

Gunnar (1994) has also found a very interesting relationship between cortisol levels and preschool children's adjustment to a group setting. Rather than finding higher levels of cortisol for 3- to 5-year-old inhibited (and presumably stress-prone) children early in the school year, Gunnar found measures of cortisol reactivity to the school experience to be related to mother-report CBQ measures of high activity, stimulation seeking, and impulsivity, with a trend toward less shyness. Teachers also reported fewer internalizing problems, greater popularity, and independence for children with higher cortisol levels. Later in the school year, however, higher cortisol reactivity was associated with teacher reports of greater internalizing behavior and CBQ reports of sensitivity to discomfort. Gunnar suggests that temperamentally linked coping activities of children may mediate their cortisol reactions, so that more shy children will be less likely to experience stressful interactions initially because of their avoidant or inhibitory coping strategies ("niche picking"). More outgoing children will seek out stress and show its effects in early, but not later, group experience, when they are more likely to have

mastered the social challenge (Gunnar, 1994). Gunnar's work suggests the importance of studying reactive measures in the context of regulatory coping. In keeping with that suggestion, we next consider temperament in the context of dyadic social interactions in the relation between temperament and attachment.

Summary

Because temperament systems themselves develop, in this section we have presented a brief account of the early development in negative affect, fear and frustration/irritability, positive affect and approach, activity level, and attentional control. (For further information, see Saarni et al., this volume.) Some of these developmental changes lead us to expect temperamental stability within only limited time windows. Early reactive systems of emotionality and approach become overlain by the development of at least two temperamentally linked control systems. The first, behavioral inhibition of action and emotional expression, is linked to the development of fearfulness late in the first year of life. The second, effortful attentional control, develops across the preschool period and likely beyond. These two control systems are important for the internalization of societal and cultural expectations and conscience. Another likely mechanism for support of socialization is development of a social reward system, connected with children's desires to please and refrain from hurting their parents and other persons, and with a disposition toward agreeableness. Any failure of these controls may be linked to the development of behavior problems. Nevertheless, because all of these temperamental systems are open to experience, adequate socialization will be necessary for positive outcomes.

TEMPERAMENT AND ATTACHMENT

Attachment and temperament are key constructs in studies of early individual differences, and comparisons of the two constructs can shed light on our understanding of both attachment and temperament (see also Thompson, Ch. 2, this Volume). The question of relations between the two constructs has almost always been put in terms of the influence of temperament on the development of attachment, and seldom in the reverse order. Theoretical definitions may account for this bias: the attachment construct of primary interest has been attachment security. This construct is typically defined as organized thoughts, feelings, and behaviors of a child in the context of a relationship with a particular caregiver, related to feelings of safety, dependability of the caregiver, and one's own self-value (Bretherton, 1985; Sroufe, 1979). Theoretically, attachment security first develops as a function of parents' sensitive responsiveness to their infants (Ainsworth, Blehar, Waters, & Wall, 1978). Temperament, on the other hand, is typically thought of in terms of inborn tendencies that interact with environmental forces.

There are, however, theoretical reasons for thinking of temperament not only as constitutionally based and relatively stable but also as influenced by experience, both in observable patterns of behavior and in physiological response tendencies (see Bates, 1989b, for a discussion of the levels of definition of the temperament construct, from surface behavior to genetic code, and Rothbart, 1989b). The notion that temperament can develop makes it potentially interesting to think about the influence of the attachment relationship upon developing patterns of temperament (see also Goldsmith & Harmon, 1994). Nevertheless, research so far has strongly emphasized questions of how temperament may affect attachment, and this must be our emphasis, too.

Seifer and Schiller (in press) point out: "there are two important ways in which attachment and temperament might be related. The first is that temperamental variability among infants might influence interpretation of attachment assessments, and the second, that infant temperament during the first year of life may influence the nature of parent-child interactions that are important in shaping the development of attachment patterns" (ms. p. 30). For the first process, consider an infant with a temperamental predisposition to distress toward minor aversive stimuli: this infant may become highly distressed when separated from the mother in the Strange Situation, continuing to be upset in the reunion episodes, and thus more likely to be scored as insecurely attached than a less distress-prone baby with a comparably secure relationship with the mother (Thompson & Lamb, 1984). For the second process, consider a distress-prone infant whose mother is paradoxically trained by the infant to avoid the infant for relatively long periods (van den Boom, 1989): an insecure attachment may develop from this relationship pattern, which then would be diagnosed—correctly—via the Strange Situation.

Kagan (1982) and Sroufe (1985) provided an important early debate about temperament's influence on attachment measures, with Kagan arguing that temperament strongly influenced infant behavior and hence the measurement of

attachment security, and Sroufe arguing that temperament is for the most part orthogonal to attachment security. According to Sroufe, a sensitive caregiver will provide for the individual needs of an infant with any kind of temperament. Given arguments such as Sroufe's (1985), and results of our own (Bates, Maslin, & Frankel, 1985) and others' research (e.g., see meta-analysis by Goldsmith & Alansky, 1987), by the last part of the 1980s no fundamental relationship between temperament and attachment security was evident, either theoretically or empirically (Bates, 1987, 1989a). Although research often found linkages between parent reports of temperament, especially concerning tendencies to become distressed, and children's behavior in the Strange Situation, especially fussiness/resistance, it seldom found linkages between temperament measures and attachment security classification. Nevertheless, the issue has persisted.

In the years since we last wrote on this question, there have been new approaches to the temperament-attachment issue, falling within two general categories: alternative approaches to the measurement of attachment, and alternative approaches to the measurement of temperament. Historically, each approach was developing even prior to the late 1980s, but they had not yet achieved the levels of theoretical and empirical clarity evident in recent years.

The Second Wave of Attachment and Temperament Research

Q-Sort Measures Related to Temperament

The standard measure of security of attachment has been the Strange Situation. Classification is based on configuration of infant Strange Situation behavior, with categories A (avoidant) and C (resistant) regarded as insecure and B as secure. However, recently it has been increasingly recognized that since the construct of attachment security transcends the Strange Situation, there should also be alternative measures of attachment (Greenberg, Cicchetti, & Cummings, 1990). The leading alternative to the Strange Situation has been the Attachment Q-set (Vaughn & Waters, 1990; Waters & Deane, 1985). Raters sort descriptive statements into categories signifying how typical the descriptions are of the child's behavior. The attachment security of the target child is then indexed by the degree of correlation between a Q-sort for a child and the criterion Q-sort derived from attachment experts' rating a prototypical securely attached child. Q-sort and Strange Situation attachment security measures typically converge to a moderate, but not high level—they are far from equivalent. The evidence we review suggests that temperament elements are more prominent in the Q-sort measures.

Seifer, Schiller, Sameroff, Resnick, and Riordan (1996) report an unusually intensive search for relations between temperament and attachment security, using both Strange Situation and Q-sort methods, and both observer and mother temperament measures. Few temperament measures, whether from mother or observer, had significant relations with attachment security based on the Strange Situation assessment at age 12 months. There were a few borderline relations, however: insecure-resistant infants tended to be rated by mothers as more fussy-difficult on the ICQ at both 9 and 12 months, converging with prior findings that general infant negative affectivity is often associated with resistant behavior in the Strange Situation and occasionally with the C classification (Goldsmith & Alansky, 1987).

In contrast, many more temperament measures correlated significantly with attachment security Q-sorts completed by observers who made brief, weekly home visits from infant ages 4 to 12 months. Video ratings of mood in the 6- and 9-month periods, but not the 12-month period, were modestly related to observer Q-sort attachment security. In addition, each of the mother-report measures of temperament, including the RITQ and ICQ indexes of difficultness, the IBQ distress to limitations scale, and the EAS emotionality scales, was correlated with the Q-sort attachment measure, although the pattern was consistent across measures only when the temperament measures were collected at age 12 months. The highest correlations were between the IBQ distress to limitations scale (indexing anger or frustration) in all three periods and the attachment security score, with correlations ranging from .42 to .55, with lower levels of distress associated with higher levels of security. In short, Seifer et al. (1996) found both mother and observer temperament measures to be more related to observer Q-sorts than to the Strange Situation measure.

Vaughn et al. (1992) provided another answer to the temperament-attachment question. Comparing several independently collected data sets using different versions of the Attachment Q-set, different temperament measures, and children of different ages, they found that temperament, usually assessed prior to attachment assessments, converged with both mother and observer reports on the attachment Q-sorts, especially in samples where the children

were older. The temperament measures varied according to the instrument used, but all could be roughly characterized as referring to negative emotional reactivity. Children seen as higher in negative reactivity tended to be seen as lower in attachment security. Correlations ranged from nonsignificant (in two samples where the children were 6 months and 24 months, respectively) to modest (−.23 to −.35, in four samples where mother or observer Q-sorts were used with 30–36-month-olds) to moderate (−.48 in one sample using mother ratings of 3-year-olds). These correlations suggest that the Q-sort attachment security and temperamental negative reactivity constructs are related to a modest degree. While source of information is not fully confounded in these findings, it remains as at least a partial explanation for these effects.

Vaughn et al. (1992) argue that measures of temperament and attachment security cannot represent qualitatively distinct domains of behavior. Rather, both must be somewhere in the middle of a dimension primarily reflecting intrinsic characteristics of the child, at one extreme, to primarily reflecting relationship experience, at the other extreme. Particular measures of both temperament and attachment security will fall at varying points along the continuum, even though temperament measures will usually be closer to the intrinsic pole and attachment security measures closer to the relationship pole. The Q-sort index appears to fall further from the relationship extreme than does the Strange Situation index.

Teti, Nakagawa, Das, and Wirth (1991) obtained convergent findings, showing that mothers' Q-sorts on preschoolers' attachment security were correlated with their descriptions of negative, temperament-like characteristics on the Parenting Stress Index, and that both kinds of mother report measures converged with observer descriptions of mother-child interactions. The correlations differed from those reported by Vaughn et al. (1992), however, in being larger and applying to a larger array of temperament-like dimensions. Similarly, Wachs and Desai (1993) found toddlers' attachment security scores based on mother Q-sorts to be associated with maternal perceptions of more favorable toddler temperament across five of the nine RITQ scales, with the highest correlation for mood ($r = -.54$), a scale combining absence of positive and presence of negative emotional expression. Wachs and Desai also found that home observations of maternal involvement, structuring, and responsivity were related to the attachment security scores even when the relationship between temperament and attachment security was statistically controlled. They interpreted this as demonstrating that attachment security variance could not be attributed primarily to infant temperament.

Linear Combination of Attachment Behaviors

Attempts have been made to increase the operational precision of attachment security by using algorithmic combinations of coded infant behaviors. They have not yet very closely approximated the more configural Ainsworth-type classifications. One such study was performed by Izard, Haynes, Chisholm, and Baak (1991), who used an attachment security index formed by a discriminant function analysis of infant behaviors in the Strange Situation. The function correctly classified 93% of infants as either secure (B) or insecure (A + C). Izard et al. found that a mother-report temperament factor partly based on the IBQ and indexing something like the fussy-difficult factor of the ICQ, even including an attention demandingness variable (which is a key part of the Bates, 1989a, concept of difficultness), predicted the insecure attachment variable. The algorithmic-molecular measure of attachment security did not appear to filter out infant temperament to the degree of the typical configural measure.

Separation Distress and Temperament

In the past 30 years the concept of attachment has become dominated by the concept of attachment security (Ainsworth et al., 1978). Just prior to this development, however, concepts focused more often on the specific behaviors of infant and mother in a variety of situations (e.g., Maccoby & Masters, 1970). Although they are dominant, attachment security concepts do not preclude an interest in attachment behavior patterns beyond the secure and anxious patterns. Temperament studies may thus be informed by other measures of attachment, such as distress upon separation from one's caregiver. Infant separation distress differences have been observed in several studies relevant to temperament, and separation distress may have predictable antecedents and concomitants in temperament.

Belsky and Rovine (1987) found, as had others, that major attachment classifications were not related to temperament. However, they also asked whether temperament would be related to the previously observed tendency of some infants to become more distressed in the separation episodes, which in turn influences the subclassifications to which infants are assigned (e.g., Ainsworth et al., 1978; Frodi & Thompson, 1985). Infants in categories A_1 to B_2 show relatively little distress during separation; those in B_3 to C_2 become more obviously distressed. Belsky and Rovine found, in a moderately large sample, that despite the lack of relationship between standard attachment security categories and temperament measured by mother reports at 3 months on the ICQ, there was a significant modest relationship between an across-scales summary ICQ index and the A_1-B_2 versus B_3-C_2 split, with the A_1-B_2 infants lower on the index. A_1-B_2 infants also had shown greater autonomic stability and sensory orientation in Brazelton NBAS assessments than had B_3-C_2 infants. Other studies using similar general indexes of temperamental distress proneness have not replicated the Belsky and Rovine finding (Mangelsdorf, Gunnar, Kestenbaum, Lang, & Andreas, 1990; Seifer et al., 1996). However, a more specific temperament-like behavior has a more replicated linkage to attachment behavior. Early tendency to express distress during separation has been found to be related to behavior in later or more unusual separation tests. Vaughn, Lefever, Seifer, and Barglow (1989) reported indirect support for Belsky and Rovine's hypothesis, finding that infant crying during separation but not reunion episodes of the Strange Situation was related to earlier mother report of difficult temperament scores based on a composite of RITQ scales.

Gunnar, Mangelsdorf, Larson, and Hertsgaard (1989) reported another kind of confirmation of the hypothesis that temperament relates to emotional responses to the Strange Situation. Negative emotional tone (high distress/low positive affect) observed during laboratory tasks involving separation from the mother at age 9 months predicted negative emotional tone during separation episodes of the Strange Situation at 13 months, with an r of .54. Early separation distress predicted negative emotional tone in the later reunion episodes to a lesser (.24) extent, resembling the Vaughn et al. differentiation.

As an interesting contrast, Calkins and Fox (1992) found that distress in reaction to novelty at age 5 months was not associated with crying in the Strange Situation, which may imply that it is reasonable to rule out novelty fear as the interpretation of the effects found by Gunnar et al. (1989) and Vaughn et al. (1989). Kagan (this volume) has argued that distress due to separation from the caregiver involves different brain circuits from those for distress to novelty. Calkins and Fox (1992) also found that infants showing distress to arm restraint at 5 months, probably reflecting angry frustration, showed *less* crying in separation episodes at 14 months than those who had not protested arm restraint at 5 months. This resembles the finding of Seifer et al. (1996) in which the IBQ index of anger predicted observer Q-sort attachment insecurity. It may also be related to another finding Calkins and Fox (1992) reported: according to mother IBQ scores, avoidantly attached infants were the most active and securely attached infants the least active of the infants in the sample.

A third finding reported by Calkins and Fox (1992) stands as a relatively rare instance in which attachment indexes are considered as developmental antecedents (not necessarily as causes) of temperament variables: behavioral inhibition in laboratory tests in a follow-up 10 months after the attachment assessment was predicted by the standard A-B-C classifications, with A infants being least inhibited, Bs intermediate, and Cs most inhibited. This later behavioral inhibition was not associated with the A_1-B_2 versus B_3-C_2 split. There was, however, an interaction effect involving the standard attachment categories: C infants who had not cried in response to arm restraint at age 5 months (most of these same infants had been distressed at pacifier removal at 2 days and when faced with novel stimuli at 5 months) were more inhibited at 24 months than C infants who cried in response to arm restraint. These main and interaction effects relating attachment security to later behavioral inhibition may be a rare example of attachment security influencing temperament, or they may reflect inadequate measures of the antecedent temperament variables.

The studies just mentioned are far from definitive, but suggest that there may be a temperamental component in the distress behavior an infant displays in the Strange Situation, especially during separation episodes. The temperament component in the distress behavior appears to involve a tendency toward distress specific to separation from the mother; it may also involve novelty distress. In addition, it could be related to developing characteristics of affiliativeness. And, as seen in the Belsky and Rovine (1987) and other studies discussed later, it may also pertain to the integrity of the infant's sensory and internal state regulatory apparatus.

Conclusion

Recent studies defining attachment in new ways or focusing on different facets of attachment behavior have opened new vistas on possible linkages between the abstract concepts of temperament and attachment. The Q-sort studies, basing both temperament and attachment security measures on a sample of the child's behavior in everyday situations rather than on laboratory assessments, show a general tendency for mother reports of negative emotional reactivity to be associated with attachment security. This is found especially for older children, and especially, but not exclusively, when the Q-sorts are done by the mothers as opposed to observers. While common source bias may account for some of the effect, there are enough findings of validity of parent reports of both attachment security and temperament that there is likely a real overlap between behaviors marking Q-sort measures of attachment security and those marking temperament. For Q-sort and separation distress studies, however, it is important to emphasize that the overlaps are typically modest to moderate. There has also been no consistent body of evidence linking temperament as assessed by any method to attachment security in versions of the standard Strange Situation. With relatively few exceptions (e.g., Izard, Haynes, et al., 1991), studies continue to report nonrelations (e.g., see Shaw & Vondra, 1995).

Alternative Definitions of Temperament

A second approach to relating attachment and temperament involves alternative indexes of temperament. The dominant operational definitions of temperament have involved behavior patterns measured past the neonatal period, typically summing over conceptually or empirically similar behaviors in several kinds of situation. However, a number of interesting findings in the attachment area pertain to neonatal temperament measures, such as the previously mentioned ones used by Calkins and Fox (1992) and Seifer et al. (1996). First we consider measures of neonatal behavior patterns.

Neonatal Characteristics

As explained in detail in the earlier section on development of temperament, there is no reason to suppose that all temperament traits—that is, constitutionally based, relatively enduring patterns of behavior—should appear in the earliest days of life. However, as reviewed above, some neonatal behavior characteristics show at least modest degrees of stability. The neonatal characteristics with the most evidence for stability from neonatal measurement—as well as the most interesting linkages to attachment—involve irritability or proneness to distress, typically measured in the context of a standardized series of stressors, such as in the Brazelton NBAS.

One example is Belsky and Rovine's (1987) finding that infants neonatally high in autonomic stability were more often in the A_1-B_2 versus the B_3-C_2 group a year later. Bell's (1989) review suggests that neonatal behavior indexes, potentially reflecting infant characteristics largely free of environmental influences, deserve more attention as predictors of attachment security than they have so far received. Bell cites four studies (by the research groups of Crockenberg, Miyake, Egeland, and Sroufe, and the Grossmanns) showing a direct role for neonatal irritability in attachment behavior or operating via relations with maternal caregiving, which in turn may be moderated by the mother's social support. He points out the inconsistencies and methodological problems in these studies, but makes a case for the potential value of research in this area. Interestingly, a neonatal measure that Bell and his colleagues developed, reactivity in the pacifier withdrawal test (Bell, Weller, & Waldrop, 1971), predicted attachment security in one recent study: newborn infants who were more often distressed upon interruption of their sucking later cried more in the reunion episodes of a Strange Situation at age 14 months and were more likely to be categorized as insecurely attached (Calkins & Fox, 1992). The effect was not found in the separation episodes.

The research of van den Boom (1989, 1991, 1994) is a good example of the kind of research on both child characteristics and the mother-child relationship that Bell (1989) was calling for. In a preliminary study (1989, 1991), van den Boom followed 30 normal infants born to lower-SES mothers. She selected for the irritable group the 17% of infants scoring highest on an NBAS composite of peak of excitement, rapidity of buildup, and irritability. An equal number of infants who scored far below the irritability criterion formed the nonirritable group (van den Boom & Hoeksma, 1994). Since the NBAS measure was based on two administrations, at 10 and 15 days, unlike most of the research on this topic, it can be assumed that the measure was a relatively reliable marker of individual differences and not a reflection of transitory state differences. The irritable group infants were significantly more likely to be insecurely attached than the nonirritable infants when tested with their mothers in the Strange Situation at age 12 months, with irritable infants especially overrepresented in the avoidant category. Direct measures of mothers' sensitive responsiveness in the home did not predict 12-month attachment classification.

This study also demonstrated a theoretically coherent process through which the early irritability may have become translated into insecure attachment. First, among the irritable (but apparently not the nonirritable) infants, there was significant continuity from the level of neonatal irritability to the level of maternally rated difficultness on the ICQ at both 6 and 12 months of age. Second, in the irritable group, mother-infant interactions were characterized by steady low levels of responsiveness to the relatively few positive social signals the infants did give (van den Boom & Hoeksma, 1994), even though the babies' crying decreased over the first several months. The irritable group mothers, especially mothers of future A category infants, ignored infant crying for relatively long periods of time and tended to use more distal methods of soothing that are less effective than more proximal methods. Alternatively, the mothers, especially mothers of future C babies, were highly variable, sometimes responding effectively, at other times using distraction tactics that actually increased infant distress. Thus, the irritable infant may have tended to receive a kind of relatively insensitive care related to what attachment theory has specified as crucial in promoting an insecure attachment. Van den Boom (1989) interpreted this as reflecting effects of (a) infant irritable behavior suppressing maternal sensitive responsiveness and (b) the mother not using effective soothing techniques.

Van den Boom (1989, 1994) went on from her observational follow-through study to an intervention with a larger sample of all irritable infants, similarly selected. In this study, she taught 50 of the mothers, in a series of three, two-hour home visits between ages 6 and 9 months, how to be more responsive to their infants' signals. She emphasized skills in reading the infant's cues, in effective, prompt soothing, and in positively interacting with the baby when he or she was not upset. The intervention produced higher levels of observed maternal responsiveness and stimulation, as well as more infant sociability in interactions with the mother, more self-soothing, and higher levels of exploration than seen in the untreated control group. It also produced higher odds of being securely attached. Thus, van den Boom's studies not only show that highly irritable newborns may have an elevated likelihood of insecure attachments, but also that these insecure attachments can be in the avoidant (A) category rather than in the resistant (C) category, unlike the trend in several previous studies (see Bell, 1989; Goldsmith & Alansky, 1987). Moreover, van den Boom's studies show that the process by which neonatal irritability has its effect might be via mother-infant interactions characterized by relatively low levels of effective soothing and positive interaction.

Van den Boom's results, as well as earlier ones employing neonatal assessments of individual differences, raise some interesting questions. They may show a process whereby innate child characteristics interact with the qualities of caregiving to produce a major social-developmental outcome (Rothbart & Ahadi, 1994). However, the research has not yet progressed to the point where this can be concluded strongly on the basis of data. As van den Boom (1994) cautions, "So far, very few studies with irritable infants have been conducted, and those that have been done do not present concordant results" (p. 1474). If neonatal irritability is taken as the root of midinfancy irritability/difficultness, why would other studies fail to find a relationship between midinfancy distress proneness and attachment security, as shown in reviews such as Goldsmith and Alansky's (1987)? Van den Boom (1994) points out that her sample increased the chances of low levels of maternal responsiveness and of insecure attachments by being composed entirely of lower SES mothers. An alternative possibility is that some initially irritable infants may have developed their own self-regulatory strategies by the time of midinfancy.

Another implication of van den Boom's results concerns the recent issue of how attachment security may be transmitted across generations. Based on a meta-analysis, Van IJzendoorn (1995) reported that parents' own attachment cognitions predicted 22% of the variance in their children's attachment security classification. Parenting behavior differences can help explain this, but it is also possible that parental personality (based on temperament)—which may affect parenting and which may be related to child attachment (Mangelsdorf et al., 1990; Plomin & Bergeman, 1991)—is partly heritable. Fox (1995; Fox, Kimmerly, & Schafer, 1991) has argued for temperament being involved in the transmission of attachment. Van den Boom's intervention study results suggest, however, that there can be important effects of the caregiving environment upon attachment without the involvement of parent personality. Research has not yet suggested whether the converse is also true: that inherited temperament can have an effect without the mediation of parenting. Based on modern genetic theory, one would not expect such demonstrations to be easily found, but the nature of environmental support necessary for expression of temperament traits might vary from one trait to another.

Home Observation Measures of Temperament-Relevant Behaviors

As mentioned previously, there have been some notable attempts to define temperament using infant behavior observed at home. For example, Seifer et al. (1996), found observer temperament ratings neither to predict attachment security nor to support the A_1-B_2 versus B_3-C_2 hypothesis.

Another home observation study gives a somewhat different picture: Lewis and Feiring (1989) observed mother-infant interactions in one two-hour home visit at age 3 months and then assessed attachment security at 12 months using a procedure with only one separation from the mother. Infants later classified as avoidantly attached had been less sociable in three-month interactions with their mothers, that is, more object-oriented and less person-oriented than the B and C infants, consistent with the well-known tendency of A babies to focus on objects in the Strange Situation. Since B_1 and B_2 infants also show interest in objects in the Strange Situation (Ainsworth et al., 1978), one would expect that Lewis and Feiring's object- and person-orientation variables might have also distinguished the A_1-B_2 versus B_3-C_2 groups, but they did not. Lewis and Feiring pointed out that observed sociability at 3 months might reflect previous mother-infant interaction rather than inherent temperament in the infant. This could, of course, be said of any temperament measure, even one attempting to measure the wider array of situations and behaviors that would be truer to the general definition of temperament. Nevertheless, these findings at the least suggest continuity of infant-mother interaction style across nine months of development and across the home-laboratory gap. They are also congruent with the hypothesis that temperament plays a role in attachment.

Psychophysiological Measures

Psychophysiological variables are another measure of temperament-like qualities that might show linkages with attachment. Individual differences in psychophysiological responses should reflect individual differences in temperament, although we would not regard the two as synonymous. At this point research on psychophysiological characteristics in relation to attachment suggests some interesting questions regarding temperament and attachment, but no definitive conclusions. The questions most relevant to the present review concern linkages between distress responses and attachment measures. One kind of psychophysiological distress response is reactivity of the hypothalamic-pituitary-adrenocortical system, commonly measured by salivary cortisol. Gunnar et al. (1989) did not find cortisol to be related to attachment security. However, Gunnar and her associates (Nachmias, Gunnar, Mangelsdorf, & Parritz, 1996) later found that 18-month-olds who were both insecurely attached to their mothers and behaviorally inhibited to novelty showed increases in cortisol in response to novelty and a Strange Situation session. Behaviorally inhibited toddlers in a secure attachment relationship with their mothers did not show a cortisol increase, nor did uninhibited toddlers, whether securely or insecurely attached. Nachmias et al. also noted that mothers of the insecurely attached and inhibited toddlers may have contributed to the cortisol increases by insistently urging the child to approach novel stimuli, thus impeding the child's own coping efforts. Mother reports of child fearfulness on a questionnaire given prior to the experimental sessions were also predictive of cortisol responses for the insecurely attached toddlers (Gunnar, 1994). The work of Gunnar and her colleagues suggests that it is fruitful to ask not only how psychophysiological indexes of temperament might be related to attachment security, but also how attachment security might moderate the relationship between temperament and psychophysiological indexes (also see Gunnar, Larson, Hertsgaard, Harris, & Brodersen, 1992).

A second kind of psychophysiological response to stress involves sympathetic nervous system activity and negative feedback from the parasympathetic system, indexed by measures of heart rate that include heart rate period and vagal tone (Calkins & Fox, 1992). One study found relatively high heart rate variability at ages 3, 6, and 9 months to predict attachment security in the Strange Situation at 13 months, whether security was indexed by standard classifications or by a continuous function comprised of infant behavior ratings (Izard, Porges, et al., 1991). Although the heart rate variability index predicting attachment security from 3 months of age (vagal tone) filtered out sympathetic activity, the measures that predicted from 6 and 9 months of age (heart period variance) did not filter out sympathetic activity, and thus might reflect individual differences in both parasympathetic and sympathetic reactivity (Izard, Porges, et al., 1991). This result, combined with the observation that A and C babies were similar on heart rate variability, suggests a given heart rate measure might represent different kinds of process: the C babies reacted both physiologically and behaviorally to the distressing situation; the A babies were comparable to the C babies in physiological reactivity, but lower in behavioral reactivity. Izard, Porges, et al. (1991) speculate that parasympathetic responses might have been more strongly involved in the A babies' responses to the Strange Situation than in the C babies' responses. Theoretically, A babies' behavior may serve defensive functions, with strong emotions experienced but not directly expressed (e.g. Ainsworth et al., 1978; Bates & Bayles, 1988), and the Izard, Porges, et al. (1991) findings support this interpretation. Calkins and Fox (1992) did not replicate the Izard, Porges, et al. findings of prediction of attachment security with vagal tone

measures taken at ages 2 days and 5, 14, and 24 months. However, major methodological differences between the two studies make conclusions difficult. Most notably, Calkins and Fox attempted to predict attachment security with only the relatively pure index of parasympathetic reactivity, unlike Izard, Porges, et al.

In summary, based on the few relevant studies, it appears worthwhile to ask whether and how psychophysiological indexes of temperament-like responses to stressful situations relate to attachment security. Emotional and physiological responses to stressors may developmentally link the constructs of attachment and temperament in various ways. Some studies have emphasized cortisol and heart rate measures. Another candidate measure is EEG asymmetry of brain activation (Calkins & Fox, 1994). It will also be useful to ask how attachment and associated caregiving behaviors might moderate relationships between psychophysiological indexes and child temperament.

Summary

We conclude this section on temperament and attachment by noting that recent research has gone beyond the former conclusion that temperament might predict behavior in the Strange Situation but not attachment security (Bates, 1989a). Recent research has provided empirical hints that both temperament and attachment are related to the ways children regulate affect and cope with stress. Several kinds of irritability, including general neonatal irritability, distress to separation, distress to novelty, and distress to limitations, are candidate temperament variables for joining with or even interacting with the key caregiving measure of sensitive responsiveness in forecasting responses to attachment-related stressors. Object versus person orientation may also be a candidate. The question of whether temperament predicts attachment security must now be refined according to the specific kinds of temperament and attachment indexes employed: When extreme neonatal irritability is the temperament index, several results suggest that temperament may be predictive of attachment security as defined by the Strange Situation measure, and this linkage may be mediated by effects upon maternal sensitive responsiveness. When midinfancy measures are the temperament indexes, results emphasize nonlinkages to attachment security as defined by the Strange Situation. On the other hand, when attachment security is defined in terms of Q-sorts, which may reflect a more general form of attachment than the Strange Situation, a moderate degree of linkage between the two constructs has been found across a wide range of child ages. And finally, when the index of attachment is distress in the Strange Situation or other stressful situations, several findings relate early forms of distress to Strange Situation distress, indexed both by behavior and psychophysiological responses.

Seifer et al. (1996) and Gunnar (1994) point to the kinds of methodological advances needed next: several kinds of measures of temperament need to be used at multiple points in development. These measures need to be carefully related to multiple measures of the qualities of caregiver-child relations, including multiple measures of attachment. Future conceptual advances will probably hinge on clearer constructs of temperament, for example, making distinctions among separation, novelty, and limitations distress, and possibly involving converging indexes from parent-report, structured observations, and psychophysiological measures. It may be useful to measure parental as well as child temperament. In addition, in seeing the process of development from earliest infancy to the point where attachment representations are clearly visible, it may also be necessary to more carefully chart the ways in which infant and caregiver behaviors weave together interaction patterns over days and months, along the lines of van den Boom (1989, 1991). Moreover, since temperament can theoretically be altered by factors such as chronic stress or incidents of serious abuse (e.g., see Kramer, 1993), it may also be necessary to chart the ways in which aspects of the environment beyond caregiver-infant interactions, for example, family stress, relate to the emergent coping styles of the child.

TEMPERAMENT AND ADJUSTMENT

The Concept of Adjustment

We now consider the idea that temperament concepts can help explain the origins of children's individual differences in adjustment (Bates, 1989a). By using the term *adjustment* we refer to a wide range of functioning that includes psychopathology, but not merely diagnosable disorders. Variations in positive behaviors and the development of conscience are also of interest. We are more concerned with dimensions of adjustment than with supposedly qualitative categories, and use of the term adjustment indicates thinking about the child's fit to particular contexts. Children may carry qualities of functioning from one context to another, but the implications of those qualities will depend on the context and expectations within a given social relationship (Chess &

Thomas, 1984; Lerner & Lerner, 1994). In this section, we consider models for relations between temperament and adjustment, primarily focusing on children. In doing so, we discuss several relevant methodological issues. Before considering models of linkage between temperament and adjustment, however, we consider whether the two constructs have any empirical relation. If they do not, we would need to consider basic methodological and theoretical questions rather than complex models.

Does Temperament Predict Adjustment?

Although the amount of relevant evidence is not large in absolute terms, it is clear that temperament and adjustment have an empirical relation. Over the past 15 years there have been repeated demonstrations of correlations between measures of the two constructs (for previous reviews, see Bates, 1989a; Rothbart, Posner, & Hershey, 1995). These demonstrations can be sorted according to the temporal relationship between the measures of temperament and adjustment.

Concurrent Linkages

Observations of temperament-adjustment correlations when both measures are taken at approximately the same point in development are fairly common and involve a wide array of adjustment domains. A number of studies of adults demonstrate concurrent relations between basic personality dimensions, such as negative affectivity, and diagnostic categories, such as depression (Clark, Watson, & Mineka, 1994). The typical source of information in such studies is self-report. Similar information is available on relations between child and adolescent psychiatric diagnoses and parent ratings of temperament (Kashani, Ezpeleta, Dandoy, Doi, & Reid, 1991), and between parent ratings of both temperament and behavioral adjustment (Wertlieb, Weigel, Springer, & Feldstein, 1987). Observed qualities of sibling relationships are related to parent-rated temperament of the siblings (Stoneman & Brody, 1993). Parent ratings of adjustment and temperament are related in path or structural models, even when controlling for family stress and parent mental state (McClowry et al., 1994; Stevenson, Thompson, & Sonuga-Barke, 1996). Notable also is a study where negative temperament as rated by parents was related to aversive child behavior observed in family interactions, even controlling for observed problems in parenting (Fisher & Fagot, 1992). Parent ratings of the temperament of children in the preadolescent to early adolescent era are correlated with teacher ratings of classroom adjustment (Guerin, Gottfried, Oliver, & Thomas, 1994). And finally, teacher and parent reports of temperamental dimensions, as well as psychophysiological and facial expression data, all show linkages between temperament and adjustment (Eisenberg, Fabes, et al., 1996).

Although these studies have much of interest, a concurrent relation between temperament and adjustment is in itself of somewhat limited interest at this point in temperament research. One concern about the meaning of concurrent relationships between the two domains, especially when they are based on one informant's views, is that an informant may be telling about essentially the same observed behavior patterns of the child, assimilating the items of the two kinds of questionnaire to one, integrated image of the child. Indeed, Sanson, Prior, and Kyrios (1990) argued that the content of temperament and behavior problem questionnaires is similar for many of their items. They interpreted this as a form of "contamination" of the temperament scales, but one could as well talk about the contamination of behavior problem questionnaire items with temperament-like content. The basic concern, however, is that any linkage could be artifactual. Another source of artifact in single-informant studies is subjective factors in questionnaire responses (Bates & Bayles, 1984), such as the dominant mood of the mother at the time she fills out the questionnaires.

There are three, partial escapes from these concerns. The first is when the correlations between different temperament and behavior problem scales form a differentiated pattern, for example, when temperamental resistance to control or uncooperativeness is linked to aggressive or disruptive behavior problems to a greater degree than to anxiety problems, with the reverse true for temperamental fear of novelty or inhibition (Bates, 1990). This kind of pattern offers the possibility that overlap reflects meaningful continuity between the two domains, not some global, perceptual bias on the part of the informant. This is only a partial escape, because the informant could still be thinking of only one domain of behavior (current adjustment) while filling out both questionnaires. A second partial escape is when alternate sources of information about temperament and adjustment are available, for example, when temperament is measured by parent report and adjustment by naturalistic observation (e.g., as in Stoneman & Brody, 1993). This, too, is only a partial escape, because there is no assurance that the temperament measure really reflects enduring temperament rather than current child adjustment

across multiple situations. The third partial escape is to measure temperament well in advance of the age when the behavior problems or their absence may be salient. This escape, too, is only partial because there is no good theoretical reason why early behavior patterns measured as temperament might not also reflect a form of adjustment to environmental circumstances as well as more innately founded temperament. Nevertheless, although we cannot conclude that a predictive linkage shows temperament has caused the adjustment, at the very least, antecedent predictions preclude the interpretation that current adjustment is affecting the behavior patterns used to define temperament.

Antecedent Predictions

Most important for this review are studies where child temperament is assessed early in development and behavioral adjustment later. Even if one rejects the assumption that early measures are more likely to be "real" temperament, and assumes that early measures also reflect forms of adjustment, antecedent predictions still delineate the developmental process better than concurrent ones. This is of both theoretical and practical importance.

Examples of antecedent predictions of behavior problems based on parent reports and psychiatric interviews from the preschool years, throughout childhood and adolescence and into adulthood, are found in the NYLS (Chess & Thomas, 1984; Thomas, Chess, & Birch, 1968; Tubman, Lerner, Lerner, & von Eye, 1992). Other examples, sometimes extending to predictions from infancy, are found in the work of Maziade and his colleagues (Maziade, 1989), Shaw and his colleagues (Shaw, Vondra, Hommerding, Keenan, & Dunn, 1994), the Australian Temperament Project (Sanson, Smart, Prior, & Oberklaid, 1993), Earls and his colleagues (Earls & Jung, 1987), the Dunedin, New Zealand project (Caspi, Henry, McGee, Moffitt, & Silva, 1995), the work of Guerin and Gottfried (1986), Kagan and his colleagues (Biederman, Rosenbaum, Chaloff, & Kagan, 1995), Pulkkinen and her colleagues (Pulkkinen & Pitkanen, 1994), the Colorado Adoption Project (Coon, Carey, Corley, & Fulker, 1992), and the Bloomington Longitudinal Study (Bates, Bayles, Bennett, Ridge, & Brown, 1991). Most of these studies will be discussed later. A number of other studies could be listed (see reviews by Bates, 1989a; Rothbart, Posner, et al., 1995). A wide range of adjustment outcomes have been considered, from externalizing and internalizing behavior problems in preschool to psychiatric and alcohol/drug disorders in adulthood. Although the typical study's measures of both temperament and outcomes are based on parent reports, some studies have based the temperament measure on examiners' ratings of behavior in structured laboratory tasks, or based adjustment indexes on self-report or teacher report.

Predictive correlations in these studies are of modest to moderate size, with the ones between infancy measures and adjustment in late preschool and middle childhood smaller, and the ones between preschool or middle childhood and later periods larger. Although the correlations may be modest, they have been sufficiently replicated so that it is clear the effects are not chance findings. Moreover, the size of the relationship is usually not less than and is sometimes greater than predictions from other theoretically linked variables, such as qualities of parenting. Lytton (1995), for example, who performed a meta-analysis of studies predicting conduct disorder (a diagnosis of extreme externalizing problems) and criminality, found child temperament variables to be the single most powerful predictor of the outcomes, even in comparison with qualities of parenting.

Although antecedent prediction studies do not constitute proof that temperament shapes adjustment, they provide evidence that temperamental characteristics are associated with adjustment outcomes, so that we can now consider models of the role of temperament in the development of adjustment. To this point, in listing relevant studies, we have not been specific about which temperament measures predict which developmental outcomes. Many of the studies linking temperament to behavior problems have been primarily concerned with whether adversity of temperament is related to adversity of adjustment outcomes, without interest in distinctions among qualities of temperament or adjustment. However, for important theoretical and practical reasons, research questions must now be more refined (Bates, 1990). Not only are differentiated patterns of linkage more interesting, as mentioned earlier; they are also central to efforts to model developmental process.

How Does Temperament Predict Adjustment?

Temperament might be involved in the production of behavior problems or risk of disorders in a number of ways. Clark et al. (1994) listed four ways of relating mood and anxiety disorders to personality characteristics: (a) vulnerability models, in which the person is predisposed to the development of disorders, for example, in response to stressors; (b) the pathoplasty model, a variant of the vulnerability model in which personality shapes the course of a disorder,

for example, by producing an environment that maintains the disorder; (c) the scar hypothesis, in which a disorder produces enduring changes in personality, for example, increased levels of insecurity; and (d) the spectrum or continuity hypothesis, where the psychopathological condition is an extreme manifestation of the underlying personality trait. Clark et al. point out that the four models need not be mutually exclusive, and indeed, that current evidence does not allow a choice among them. Note, however, that these models might be extended to predict positive outcomes as well, for example: (a) protective models, where the person is predisposed to dealing adequately with difficult situations; (b) the positive adaptation hypothesis, in which experiences of overcoming challenge strengthen positive feelings; or (c) the spectrum or continuity hypothesis, where the positive outcome is itself the manifestation of the underlying characteristic set of characteristics, for example, a generally positive outlook on experience. Rothbart, Posner, et al. (1995) listed an even more comprehensive set of 14 possible ways in which temperament could be related to high risk conditions and psychopathology. We have reorganized this list into Table 3.2, and added to it instances of positive adaptation. The structure of Table 3.2 organizes our discussion of processes relating temperament to adjustment.

Direct Linkage

Most studies of temperament-adjustment linkages have considered direct, linear effects, where a particular temperament trait contributes to the development of an adjustment pattern. Additive effects of multiple temperament traits are also possible, for example when two or more temperament traits, such as negative affectivity and lack of impulse control, linearly increase the risk of some disorder (e.g., aggressive behavior problems, as in Bates et al., 1991). In evaluating models of direct linkage, studies considering multiple temperament traits in relation to multiple dimensions of adjustment are critical. According to modern theories of psychopathology of most relevance to temperament, individual differences in specific brain circuits are related to specific forms of motivation or functioning (Bates, 1989a; Clark et al., 1994; Fowles, 1994; Gray, 1991; MacDonald, 1988; Rothbart, Derryberry, & Posner, 1994), as discussed above. There is some, but of course not complete, agreement on what the specific systems are and how they map onto behavioral traits. In previous sections we have discussed systems controlling inhibition to novelty

TABLE 3.2 Processes That May Link Temperament and Adjustment

A. Direct, Linear Effects
  1. Temperament extreme constitutes psychopathology or positive adaptation (*e.g., extreme shyness, attention deficit disorder, high attentional control*).
  2. Temperament extreme predisposes to a closely related condition (*e.g., fearfulness → general anxiety disorder, agoraphobia/panic disorder; high attentional control → good social adjustment*).
  3. Temperament characteristics affect particular symptomatology of a disorder (*e.g., anxiety versus hopelessness in depression*).

B. Indirect, Linear Effects
  1. Temperament structures the immediate environment, which then influences development of positive adjustment or psychopathology (*e.g., high stimulation seeking → leaving home early, marrying poorly; high attentional control → planning → good school adjustment*).
  2. Temperament biases others to behave in ways that provide experiences leading to risk factors, pathology, or more positive outcome (*e.g., high positive affect → attention from caregivers in institutional situations; infant irritability → coercive cycles in parent-child interactions*).
  3. Temperament biases processing of information about self and others, predisposing to cognitively based psychopathology or positive adjustment (*e.g., negative affectivity → negatively biased social information processing → aggression; positive affectivity → positively biased social information processing → optimism about others*).

C. Temperament X Environment Interactions
  1. Temperament buffers against risk factors or stressors (*e.g., fear protecting against aggression or criminal socialization; positive affect protecting against peer or parent rejection*).
  2. Temperament heightens response to event (*e.g., negative affectivity augmenting response to stress, increasing risk of depression or likelihood of post-traumatic stress disorder; attentional orienting augmenting response to teachers' instructions*).

D. Temperament X Temperament Interactions
  1. Self-regulation of a temperament extreme qualitatively changes its expression (*e.g., high surgency with nonregulation → ADHD, whereas same trait with good regulation → high competence; high negative emotionality with low attentional control → sensitization and increasing anxiety, whereas negative emotionality plus high attentional control → no maladjustment*).
  2. One temperament trait protects against risk consequences of another temperament-based trait (*e.g., fearfulness or higher attentional control protecting against impulsivity*).

E. Miscellaneous
  1. Different temperament characteristics may predispose to similar outcomes (*e.g., shyness, impulsivity, lack of affiliativeness, and negativity may each predispose to development of social isolation*).
  2. Temperament or personality may be shaped by psychopathological disorder (*e.g., anxiety disorder → increased dependency*).

This table is an adaptation of Table 11.1 in Rothbart, Posner, and Hershey (1995). Some of the wording and examples have been changed. Note that many of the examples are theoretically plausible, but not based on empirical evidence.

and conditioned signals of punishment and nonreward, as well as unconditioned fear, positive affectivity and reward seeking, sensitivity to social rewards, and attentional control. In the present section, we use these systems as general constructs to organize the evidence on temperament and adjustment.

At this time, only a limited number of studies permit a differentiated view of temperament-adjustment linkages, and none of the studies is so free of methodological shortcomings that it can stand alone to support or reject a psychobiological systems model. However, enough convergence exists that we are confident about the broad outlines of direct linkage models.

Theoretical Expectations

Direct linkage models will become more detailed as neurobehavioral systems are better understood and as measures of adjustment are meaningfully differentiated. For now, in broad terms, one would expect early irritability, or general tendencies toward negative affect, to predict a wide variety of adaptive difficulties, including internalizing or anxiety problems as well as externalizing problems and possible deficits in positive competencies. As measures of irritability are more finely differentiated, however, more clearly defined pathways to later adjustment may be identified. For example, sensitivity to minor aversive stimuli might predispose a child to both internalizing (e.g., whining and withdrawal) and externalizing (e.g., reactive aggression) behavior problems, whereas irritability to frustration of reward or stimulation-seeking behavior (Rothbart, Posner, et al., 1995) would likely pertain more to externalizing tendencies than to internalizing ones.

Temperamental tendencies toward fearfulness, for example, as manifested in novel or potentially punishing situations, should predict internalizing-type adjustments most directly, although they may also serve to predict externalizing problems in inverse or interactive ways (discussed below). A finer differentiation of fearfulness will ultimately be important for predicting different kinds of internalizing adjustment. For example, separation distress may differ in some ways from novelty fear (see Fowles's [1994] discussion of theories placing separation fear in a panic or fight/flight brain system, and novelty fear in a behavioral inhibition system, and see our sections on Panksepp's psychobiological theory and on attachment). Positive affectivity or surgency, involving activity, stimulation seeking, assertiveness, and possibly some aspects of manageability, should be involved more closely in externalizing than in internalizing problems, except that depression has a strong component of low positive affectivity (Tellegen, 1985).

A trait of prosocial tendency, affiliation and agreeableness, perhaps involving sensitivity to social rewards (MacDonald, 1988, 1992), might prove separable from the more general extraversion or surgency (positive affectivity) systems. Low levels of prosocial interest would be expected to be associated with the development of externalizing and not internalizing problems, and perhaps with the failure to acquire positive social competencies independent of behavior problems. Finally, systems controlling attention, especially the executive system described above, would be expected to have more to do with externalizing problems than with internalizing ones. As with fear systems, however, attentional control should also play an additive or interactive role with other temperament characteristics. In addition, a well-functioning set of attentional controls is likely to be linked to more positive developmental outcomes.

Empirical Findings

In the Bloomington Longitudinal Study (BLS), infancy and toddlerhood ICQ temperamental difficultness (defined in terms of frequent and intense negative affect and attention demanding) predicted later externalizing and internalizing problems as seen in the mother-child relationship, from the preschool to the middle-childhood periods (Bates & Bayles, 1988; Bates et al., 1985; Bates et al., 1991; Lee & Bates, 1985). Early negative reactivity to novel situations (unadaptability) predicted less consistently, but when it did, it predicted internalizing problems more than externalizing problems. Early resistance to control (perhaps akin to the manageability dimension of Hagekull, 1989, and others) predicted externalizing problems more than internalizing problems. These predictions are all consistent with models where temperament extremes either constitute pathology dimensions or predispose to risk for these conditions. The linkages are modest, but they obtain from early in life, and are not eliminated by the inclusion of family and parenting characteristics in prediction, so they are not simply artifacts of family functioning. Bates (1989a) reviews other studies that provide at least partial support for the pattern obtained in the BLS, and Bates (1990) argues that the data of Sanson et al. (1990) also support this pattern.

The Dunedin Longitudinal Study (Caspi et al., 1995) provides further support, and extends measures of temperament from parent report to experimenter ratings. Ratings based on the child's behavior during testing sessions, aggregated from ages 3 and 5 years, predicted aggregated ratings of parents and teachers in late childhood (aggregating over ages 9 and 11) and early adolescence (over ages 13 and 15). Early approach (outgoing responses to strangers and new test materials—the inverse of inhibition) predicted, inversely, internalizing problems better than externalizing problems for boys. It did not predict either kind of problem for girls. Early sluggishness (a factor combining a lack of positive affect, passivity, and wariness/withdrawal from novelty) predicted later internalizing and externalizing problems for girls, but not boys, as well as the relative absence of positive competencies for both girls and boys. It is not clear how approach and sluggishness emerged separately from factor analysis describing similar dimensions, but whatever the difference between the two dimensions, they predicted outcomes differently for the two genders.

A third temperament dimension, combining lack of control, irritability and distractibility, (corresponding approximately to the resistance to control or manageability factors from parent-report questionnaires), predicted, for both genders, externalizing problems more strongly than internalizing problems or positive competencies. The discovery of differentiated patterns in studies such as the BLS and Dunedin study has occurred despite the tendency for externalizing and internalizing adjustment scores to be somewhat correlated with each other, so that the pattern is all the more remarkable. As noted in our section on development of temperament, Caspi and Silva (1995) report somewhat similar patterns of linkage between early temperament and self-reported personality patterns on Tellegen's Multidimensional Personality Questionnaire, with undercontrolled children tending as adults to be low on harm avoidance and high on social alienation, and inhibited children high on harm avoidance, low on aggression, and low on social potency.

Other studies addressing the question of differentiated linkages between temperament and adjustment include Hagekull's (1994) study. Hagekull found that parent-reported EASI sociability/shyness aggregated over mothers' and fathers' questionnaires at 28 and 36 months predicted age 48-month aggregated parent ratings of internalizing problems. Early impulsivity also predicted later externalizing but not internalizing problems, as well as lower levels of ego strength/effectance. Early activity, a variable typically placed in the extraversion or positive affect factor in the FFM of personality, predicted later externalizing and, inversely, later internalizing. Negative emotionality predicted both kinds of behavior problems as well as lowered ego strength. This pattern of findings is also consonant with the BLS and Dunedin studies.

Rothbart, Ahadi, and Hershey (1994) also provide general confirmation for the pattern. They considered concurrent relationships between parent reports of temperament on the CBQ and adjustment on a newly developed questionnaire on social behavior patterns in a group of 6- to 7-year olds. A second-order factor composite index of temperamental negative affectivity predicted the full range of social traits, including aggressiveness, guilt, help seeking, and negativity (e.g., in response to suggestion of a new activity). However, subcomponents of the general negative affect factor were associated with the social traits in a more differentiated way: fear and sadness were more related to traits such as empathy and anger, and discomfort to aggression and help seeking. A small subsample in the Rothbart, Ahadi, et al. (1994) sample had been tested in the laboratory as infants. Temperament as assessed in the laboratory five to six years earlier showed a somewhat similar pattern of linkage with the social behavior outcomes: infant laboratory activity (again, usually regarded as part of surgency or positive affectivity) predicted aggressiveness and negativity, as did early smiling (another component of surgency); infant anger/frustration predicted both higher aggressiveness and help seeking; fear predicted lower levels of aggressiveness and higher levels of empathy and guilt/shame.

Another group of four studies of multiple dimensions of temperament and adjustment can be described, all of which considered relations between parent ratings on the Middle Childhood Temperament Inventory (MCTI; Hegvik, McDevitt, & Carey, 1982) and more or less concurrent adjustment. For the sake of interpretation, we have conceptually sorted the nine NYLS-based dimensions of the MCTI into categories based on their content and published scale intercorrelations. Wertlieb et al. (1987) found parent ratings of high negative mood tended to correlate with both externalizing and internalizing disorders. Scales having to do with manageability (activity, nonadaptability, and intensity) and self-regulation (nonpersistence and nonpredictability), on the other hand, tended to have higher correlations with externalizing than with internalizing. Guerin et al. (1994) found a very similar pattern of correlations between parent temperament reports and teacher adjustment reports at age 10 years, with the exception that negative mood correlated more strongly with teacher reports of externalizing than internalizing behavior problems. Guerin et al. found similar differentials in correlations between age 10 parent temperament ratings and age 11

teacher ratings. Teglasi and MacMahon (1990) also found a similar pattern, with manageability and self-regulation temperament scales correlating more strongly with externalizing adjustment scales than with internalizing scales. In addition, their negative reaction to novelty scale was more closely associated with internalizing than externalizing scales, and mood was moderately to highly correlated with both kinds of adjustment.

McClowry et al. (1994) used factors based on the MCTI, finding negative emotional reactivity to be related to both internalizing and externalizing problems (parent rated), with low task persistence (self-regulation) correlated only with externalizing. Their approach scale did not correlate with either internalizing or externalizing. Although it is difficult to evaluate the fit of the McClowry et al. study to the other three because of its more tightly organized array of temperament variables, the studies as a group show quite similar patterns in the concurrent relations of parent perceptions of temperament and both parent and teacher perceptions of adjustment.

Biederman et al. (1990), in a longitudinal cohort of highly inhibited and highly uninhibited children, found that inhibited children accounted for the majority of diagnoses of anxiety disorder (especially phobias) in their sample, and uninhibited children the majority of the externalizing disorders (especially oppositional disorder). Despite the extreme sample, however, the two groups were not fully split: some extremely inhibited children received attention deficit diagnoses, and some extremely uninhibited children received anxiety diagnoses, such as overanxious disorder. These results are similar to the more general pattern based on parent-report studies and dimensional adjustment scores, in which there are some, if typically smaller, cross-domain correlations. Rende (1993) also provides partial confirmation for the pattern, although based on more narrow-band adjustment dimensions and only to a modest degree.

Several studies whose designs do not permit a test of the differential linkage model can be interpreted as roughly conforming to the pattern described here. For example, Eisenberg, Fabes, et al. (1996) show correlations between teacher and parent ratings of emotional and behavioral low self-regulation, lower baseline heart rate, and acting-out behavior problems. Keenan and Shaw (1994) found in a low-income sample that an ICQ composite of difficultness and resistance to control predicted laboratory measures of aggression in 18-month-old boys but not girls. Martin, Olejnik, and Gaddis (1994) found task orientation (similar to self-regulation indexes) rated by first grade teachers to predict fifth grade math and reading achievement considerably more strongly than did initial IQ, and for reading outcomes, somewhat more strongly than first grade reading achievement. Other studies confirm a relationship between temperament and adjustment, but cannot be even roughly interpreted in relation to the differentiated pattern because they present information on only a global index of adjustment, for example, Earls and Jung (1987) and Kashani et al. (1991).

In summary, findings in the literature support a direct linkage model. Specific temperament dimensions relate in a differentiated way to internalizing and externalizing adjustments, with early inhibition relating more to later internalizing and early unmanageability relating more to later externalizing, and with early negative affect relating to both outcome dimensions. Positive adjustment dimensions are not as yet clearly articulated, nor measured often enough to demonstrate differential linkages, but such measures are clearly related to temperament in understandable ways, especially in work on moral development described below (Kochanska, 1995). Evidence at this point also does not answer the question of which direct linkage models described above might apply. Given generally modest predictive relations, we would favor a vulnerability or predisposition model; a spectrum/continuity model might also apply. However, early individual differences likely become transformed via developmental processes into the more complex forms of adjustment of later years, and these processes must shape adjustment outcomes. Many child temperament researchers seem to believe, with Thomas et al. (1968), that temperament in itself does not constitute a negative versus positive adjustment, but that temperament conditions a developmental process that determines adjustment. This concept fits a vulnerability model better than a simpler continuity (or spectrum) model.

Positive Adjustment

The focus of the section just summarized has been primarily on psychopathology, or what can be called negative adjustment. Positive adjustment, however, including empathy, conscience, intelligence, self-regulation, and cooperation, is an area of at least equal importance. In our sections on Psychobiological Approaches, Temperament and Development, and Temperament and Attachment, we have presented additional evidence on such measures. Conceptually, there are two ways positive and negative adjustment can be distinguished. One is in terms of the valence of the trait/behavioral terms in the measurement scale. More interesting, however, is whether a given prosocial construct reflects

chiefly the inverse of a negative adjustment trait, for example, in the relation between cooperation and aggressive-disruptive behavior problems, or whether the construct is mostly independent of standard negative adjustment items. This question has only occasionally been addressed (e.g., Bates et al., 1991). Future research may discover how temperament antecedents of positive and negative adjustment components vary, in ways paralleling the differentiation between internalizing and externalizing (see also discussion by Rothbart [1989b] on the development of mastery motivation).

Empirical and Theoretical Limits on Continuity

As noted, predictive correlations tend to be modest to moderate in size, especially when temperament is assessed in early life. This may be partly due to measurement error. In future studies using multiple sources of both temperament and adjustment data, comparable to the state-of-the-art studies on relations between family process and adjustment (e.g., Patterson, Reid, & Dishion, 1992), measurement error can be statistically controlled in structural models to allow a more accurate estimate of relations among constructs. Limited predictive temperament-adjustment correlations may also be due to unresolved conceptual problems: one would like to think of temperament as a set of cross-situational, stable characteristics. However, as discussed in previous sections of this chapter, manifestations of temperament should be dependent on the particular eliciting situations presented to the child and the child's previous adjustments to those situations. Temperament is potentially transformed by both experience and the later-emerging temperamental tendencies, like attentional control, described above.

There is some evidence that the antecedent predictive relations between temperament and adjustment in the home are often not found between home temperament and adjustment at school (e.g., Bates et al., 1991). This could be interpreted as a sign of inadequacy of parent or teacher reports (see earlier discussion of this issue), but it could also be seen as a reflection of the discontinuities in individual differences that can occur across relationships and settings (see Hinde, 1989), as well as differences in environmental conditions or requirements. School and home differ on many qualities, including novelty, intensity of stimulation, and demand for self-control, which could easily activate different temperament traits. Especially for younger children, parents and teachers agree to only a modest degree overall on the adjustment of children, and it seems likely that a child's temperament could be expressed in rather different ways in different settings. Dumas and LaFreniere (1993), for example, observed that preschool children selected by their teachers as being anxious and withdrawn at school exhibited large amounts of resistance and open negativity in interactions with their mothers in a laboratory task. The mothers themselves were also highly negative. It is likely that little of the latter behavior was seen by the teachers, and that mothers of such children would describe their children more in terms of anger and defiance (usually considered part of the externalizing dimension) than would the teachers.

Considering stability, some might argue that limitations in temperament stability might be due to a failure to recognize qualitatively different types of individuals, rather than to inherent measurement limitations or to developmental change. Kagan et al. (1988) found that children at the extremes of the behavioral inhibition distribution show more stability across time than those from the middle of the distribution, and interpreted this as evidence for the existence of qualitatively different types as opposed to a continuum. This kind of finding has been replicated. For example, Sanson, Pedlow, Cann, Prior, and Oberklaid (1996), found greater longitudinal stability at the extreme quartiles of shyness (approach) than for the middle quartiles. They failed, however, to find evidence, as have Kagan and colleagues (Kagan, this volume), for a nonlinear pattern of correlations between shyness and other variables, such as early infancy colic and irritability or later teacher ratings. Instead, they found linear patterns of association across the quartiles of the shyness distribution. Sanson et al. also found similarly greater stability in the extreme quartiles of other dimensions of temperament.

We interpret the greater stability at the extremes of a distribution as more often reflecting statistical laws than nature's taxonomic categories. As observed in plots of our own and others' data, and as mentioned by MacDonald (1988), there is often more distance on trait scores between individuals at the tails of a distribution than in the middle of the distribution. Assuming regression to the mean or a shift for some other reason across multiple occasions of measurement, then in the middle of the distribution, a smaller movement will have more potential to shift the individual into a different quartile or change the individual's place in the bivariate distribution in ways that would reduce the correlation. In the tails of the distribution, a change would have to be larger in scale points, in many cases, for there to be a change of quartile or a shift in the bivariate distribution. The correlation coefficient is also sensitive to the range of scores, and a correlation involving only the middle of the distribution will tend to have the problem of restricted range, whereas a correlation limited to the individuals in the extreme tails (Kagan et al., 1988) will have a fuller range.

Another reason for changes in rank ordering on temperament traits or in linkage between temperament and adjustment is developmental change, and there may be lawful predictors of who will change and who will not. Asendorpf (1994) found that the adaptive behavior of shy children who are highly intelligent improves more over development than that of children who are less intelligent. Engfer (1993) found in a small sample that children who changed in shyness from their third to their seventh year also had preexisting differences. The group who changed from low to high shyness had been seen by observers to be less soothable and more moody at 8 months than the consistently low shyness group, and by their mothers as being less adaptable and having more sleep problems at 18 months. In contrast, the group who changed from high to low shyness, compared with the continued shy group, had been observed to be less moody at 8 months and seen by their mothers as less difficult (crying and restlessness) at 18 months. Their mothers also expressed less depressive and less punitive attitudes at 4 and 18 months, and were observed to be more sensitive in caregiving at 8 months.

We conclude for now that improvements in measurement will ultimately prove to be a better resolution of the stability limitation than postulating qualitative temperaments in children. These improvements include conceptually meaningful aggregation, the discovery of laws of change over development, as in the work of Asendorpf (1994), and discovery of the laws of discontinuity across settings and relationships. Discontinuities may be found via the careful description of the functional properties of situations for different children (Wachs, 1992), or in properties of children that foster cross-situational stability versus instability. We are not saying that idiographic or clustering analyses will not be productive (e.g., see Bates, 1989a); we are saying that dimensional constructs of temperament and adjustment appear to be a useful basis for both idiographic and nomothetic analyses.

Another answer to the limited size of correlations between early temperament and later adjustment indexes is to postulate that there must be other factors involved in development. This is not a radical proposal. Studies considering other factors, typically family stress and parenting practices, find they contribute in a linear fashion, over and beyond the temperament measures in explaining outcome variance (e.g., Bates et al., 1991; Earls & Jung, 1987; McClowry et al., 1994; Sanson et al., 1991; review by Sanson & Rothbart, 1995; Shaw et al., 1994; Stevenson et al., 1996). Positive parenting and the relative absence of harsh discipline and family stressors typically predict better adjustment. Some of these studies also find that multiple temperament indexes add to prediction, as do early measures of internalizing or externalizing adjustment, depending on the adjustment outcome dimension (e.g., Bates et al., 1991). School, peer group, and neighborhood characteristics might also add independently to the prediction of outcomes, although only a few researchers have considered these factors, and none we know of in relation to temperament.

Gender might also add to a predictive model. Sex differences in psychopathology are frequently found. However, a more interesting question, taken up later, is whether temperament and other antecedents of adjustment differ for girls and boys. Although reports of sex differences in temperament in early development are rare, gender differences in adjustment are pervasive, so a different process may link temperament and adjustment for girls and boys. For the present, however, we are considering additive rather than interactive models. Given that variables such as gender and parenting add to temperament predictions, the next question is how. They may constitute separate processes, each contributing in a small way to the outcome. On the other hand, they may be part of a more complex process. This brings us to the next model of temperament-adjustment linkage, that of indirect linkage.

Indirect Linkage

Temperament qualities could have a linear impact on adjustment outcomes, but through indirect processes, rather than direct ones. Two of the processes we list in Table 3.2 under the "Indirect, Linear Effects" heading involve mediation of temperament by experiences or events that would usually be considered as part of the environment (although not always; see Plomin & Bergeman, 1991). In the first, the child's temperament predisposes him or her to seek out experiences, for example, risk-taking activities that produce stressors, such as peer rejection, school failure, financial stressors, legal problems, and physical injury, that then lead to psychopathology, such as depression. There are clinical and research examples of such a process (e.g., in depression secondary to antisocial behavior in boys, Patterson et al.,

1992). In the second scenario, the child's temperament sets the stage for the quality of parenting, which then produces the adjustment (as in previously discussed interpretations of van den Boom's studies). Essentially, this involves child effects upon the socialization process, which in turn shapes the child's adjustment.

Some researchers believe that adverse temperament qualities must be mediated by parenting in the development of adjustment (e.g., Reid & Patterson, 1989). While this mediational model makes good sense—and we share the conviction that there are likely to be some indirect linkages—it has not as yet been well supported empirically. We are aware of three studies that failed in their attempts to fit their data to such a model: Stevenson et al. (in press), Fisher and Fagot (1992), and McClowry et al. (1994). Instead, they found direct effects models to fit their data better. Wills, Cleary, Filer, Mariani, and Spera (in press) provide an important exception. Building on Tarter's (1988) important review on the role of temperament in drug abuse, Wills et al. collected questionnaire data from sixth grade students. Higher activity level and negative emotionality predicted more drug use, and higher task orientation and positive emotionality predicted less drug use. These correlations were explained in a mediational model by the youths' descriptions of other aspects of their adjustment and social relations. For example, the correlations of negative emotionality and activity level with drug use were mediated by externalizing adjustment. In turn, the relations of externalizing adjustment and drug use were mediated by negative life events and having friends who used drugs. Buffering effects of positive emotionality were mediated by an index of positive coping and by reductions in the likelihood of the externalizing + deviant peers path found with negative emotionality. Wills et al. also found evidence for temperament X temperament moderator effects, to be described below.

The Wills et al. study is impressive in fitting theoretically based models to empirical data, but because it is not longitudinal and the temperament, environment, and adjustment measures were all from a single informant, it does not conclusively demonstrate developmental pathways. At this early point in the research, given the many methodological issues that have not been addressed, such as the family process and temperament measures used, and the need for longitudinal follow-through, we would prefer not to draw a conclusion from the four cross-sectional studies we have found, other than to point to these questions as very important for future research.

The third indirect process model we list in Table 3.2 involves the mediation of social information processing, which is not usually considered in this area but which also makes good sense theoretically. As argued by Rothbart, Posner, et al. (1995), emotional states are a function of emotional processing networks and the executive attentional system, which influences selection of information for conscious processing. These processes are likely to pertain to social relations. "Affective states associated with an attentional focus either on threatening stimuli or on the self may make access to information about others less accessible" (p. 319).

Dodge (1986) makes a similar argument, and research supports the mediational role of social information processing. For example, children who have received harsh treatment or abuse in early childhood are at elevated risk for aggressiveness in kindergarten and first grade (indexed by teacher and peer reports and direct observation). This risk is also mediated by a variety of social information processing characteristics assessed in responses to hypothetical vignettes. These responses, such as not attending to enough of the relevant cues, attributing hostile intent to a protagonist in an ambiguous situation, not generating enough viable alternative responses, and placing a high value on aggressive solutions, also tend to co-vary, imperfectly, with the early abuse (Dodge, Bates, & Pettit, 1990; Weiss, Dodge, Bates, & Pettit, 1992). In positive terms, this study suggests that a child who has experienced abusive discipline, yet somehow managed to avoid developing maladaptive social information processing characteristics, is not elevated in aggressiveness.

We are aware of no evidence that early temperament predisposes a child to social information processing differences, but think it plausible that they might. For example, we would hypothesize, as have Derryberry and Reed (1994a, 1994b), that at high levels of negative emotionality, some children would more readily attend to information of a negative sort, both concerning others and self. Children with low levels of attentional control or high distractibility might also be prone to gathering too little information before interpreting a social situation and choosing an action. This might lead to various forms of friction, especially with peers. On the other hand, a positive affectivity bias in the typical social situation might produce information processing in which the emotional impact of stressors is deflected. In our society, this could contribute to popularity, in that we tend to like people who overlook minor irritations and "look on the bright side." In situations where recognizing and facing adversity would be more adaptive, however, the bias toward the positive might be problematic.

At least some social information tendencies can be construed as a rational response to the actual social world of the child. For example, aggressive, rejected children really do receive more hostility from others (Olson, 1992; Trachtenberg & Viken, 1994). Empirical demonstrations of the developmental processes we have hypothesized will probably require the development of valid social information processing measures for very young children, below the age at which social information processing biases might result from temperament-induced adjustment problems.

Moderated Linkage

Another highly plausible process by which temperament and adjustment may be linked is through an interaction effect. Thomas et al. (1968) shaped thinking in this area very early when they emphasized the goodness-of-fit model for explaining the development of behavior problems. Behavior problems result from the interaction of the child's temperament profile and parental response to challenges posed by the child's temperament. Thus, a distress-prone and demanding temperament in the child may produce maladjustment only when parents respond with forceful confrontation or surrender. Most researchers agree this is a very likely model of how much development proceeds. As discussed by Bates (1989a), however, there are challenges to empirically demonstrating such effects, and in 1989 the literature had provided only a few replicated interaction effects involving temperament.

The chief exceptions described by Bates (1989a) concerned the tendency of more active (possibly more extraverted) infants to develop better cognitively under conditions of deprivation than more passive infants (e.g., Escalona, 1968), and of more difficult infants to develop less well cognitively in noisy homes than do easy infants (e.g., Wachs, 1987). Since the time of that review, a number of recent attempts have been made to detect interaction effects. We list recent findings, categorized according to the kind of factor a given temperament variable moderates or is moderated by.

Temperament X Environment Interactions

One kind of temperament X environment interaction process might involve predispositions toward negative affect and strong responses to stressors. If the same temperament is present in terms of underlying physiology, but one child is exposed to only moderate stressors while the other is exposed repeatedly to major stressors, the two children's potentials for fearfulness or stress responsiveness would differ. In one plausible scenario, given enough trauma, the brain may develop so that fearful or depressed responses might subsequently result from very minor or even nonstressful events, as a result of the formation of brain circuits that constitute a physical underpinning for sensitization or kindling (Kramer, 1993).

In a number of instances in the literature, studies are described as supporting an interactional or moderator model when they have not actually controlled for main effects. We have not located recent studies in the child temperament literature supporting a stress X temperament interaction process, although a number of studies have included parenting and family stress variables. The most relevant study (Wertlieb et al., 1987) considered interactions between family stressors and temperament in predicting adjustment and even reported finding a number of significant interaction effects. However, the analyses did not evaluate interaction effects after hierarchically removing variance associated with the main effects, so the addition of interaction effects forced out a number of the main effects. The final equations including the temperament X stress interaction effects did not explain appreciably more variance than the models with only linear, main effects terms. Apparently for this reason, Wertlieb et al. did not choose to explain the temperament X stress interaction effects. One would generally prefer the more parsimonious, main effects model to a complex, interaction effects model.

One of the most exciting current areas of research on temperament concerns the development of conscience, with both main and interaction effects predicted by theory. In direct, main effects, Kochanska (1991, 1993, 1995; Kochanska & Aksan, 1995; Kochanska et al., 1993) has used temperamental constructs of behavioral inhibition (fear), effortful control, and more recently positive affect to account for the development of conscience in young children. Recent studies besides Kochanska's have also found more fearful or inhibited children to score higher on measures of conscience (Asendorpf & Nunner-Winkler, 1992; Rothbart, Ahadi, & Hershey, 1994). Quay (1993) and Fowles (1994) have both indicated that deficiencies in a fearful control system may be linked to the development of disinhibitory psychopathologies, although in our view, the attentional control system involving effortful control will also need to be considered in these models (Rothbart & Ahadi, 1994).

An interaction effect involving child temperamental fearfulness and maternal control styles has also been found and replicated by Kochanska (1991, 1995). Highly fearful children's internalization was predicted by mothers' use of gentle, non-power-oriented discipline, interpreted as keeping levels of anxious arousal low. Nonfearful children's internalized control, on the other hand, was associated with security of attachment (indexed by mother Q-sort), interpreted as building a positive, goal-oriented partnership. Research has not yet appeared testing whether children's temperamental approach or positive affectivity interacts with parental control style in the development of conscience in a way comparable to the fear X parent treatment interaction.

In addition, Kochanska et al. (1993) has found a main effect for mother-reported high effortful control and low impulsivity as related to both active moral regulation and vigilance aspects of conscience. Girls with this pattern of characteristics also showed more affective discomfort to wrongdoing. Henry, Caspi, Moffitt, and Silva (in press) have reported an interesting temperament X environment interaction effect related to the Kochanska et al. main effect. The Henry et al. temperament variable lack of control (lack of control, irritability, and distractibility in the laboratory aggregated across sessions of testing at 3 and 5 years) had a direct, main effect on violent versus nonviolent criminal convictions among their Dunedin project subjects by age 18, and a trend main effect as to whether the adolescent had been convicted or not. However, it also interacted with whether the child had been in a single-parent family at age 13. Although the single-parent variable might have implied a number of aspects of both quality of rearing and heritable personality characteristics, it likely also signified deficiencies in the social regulation of the child. A child who was both low in temperamental control and had experienced a single-parent home was significantly more likely to have been convicted of a crime.

Hagekull and Bohlin (1995) found that Toddler Behavior Questionnaire (TBQ) manageability, aggregated over mother and father reports from ages 10, 15, and 20 months, predicted an aggregate (mother + father + day care teacher) measure of aggressiveness at age 4 years. After removing main effects, there was also a significant interaction effect involving day care quality rating and child manageability. Easy children in higher quality care were less aggressive than easy children in lower quality care, whereas difficult children's aggressiveness was not related to quality of care.

With a similar kind of analysis, but in a random-assignment treatment study, Orth and Martin (1994) found that after removing main effects for the temperament variable task orientation (significant) and the instructional method variable (computer versus teacher, not significant), there was a significant interaction of these two variables in predicting frequency of observed off-task behavior. For children at high levels of task orientation, off-task behavior was not affected by instructional method, but for children at low levels of task orientation, computer instruction led to lower rates of off-task behavior than teacher instruction.

The temperamental characteristics two siblings bring to their shared relationship have been related to the nature of their interactions. Stoneman and Brody (1993) studied combinations of sibling characteristics associated with measures of the functioning of same-gender sibling relationships. Among their findings, the highest levels of negativity/conflict were observed when siblings were both high in activity (parent report on the Dimensions of Temperament Survey-Revised [DOTS-R]) and the older one was rated as more active than the younger; the lowest levels were observed when both were low in activity. Observed conflict was also high when older siblings were high in activity and younger siblings were low in adaptability. Because temperament was assessed at the same time as the interactions, however, parents' reports of temperament may have been influenced by the sibling interactions they had themselves observed.

In other recent temperament X environment interaction studies, Lerner and Lerner (1994) summarized longitudinal work on the implications of the fit between adolescents' temperament and the kind of temperament their parents expected them to show. Among their findings, early in the sixth grade year, the degree of fit was no more related to the youth's adjustment than the youth's temperament scores alone, but over the course of the year, the fit index came to have more relationships with adjustment indexes than the temperament scores by themselves.

In summary, a number of very interesting and interpretable temperament X environment interaction effects are present in the literature, but at this point, only a few have been replicated. Direct, linear effects models have more empirical support, despite theoretically based expectations that interactive and dynamic models will eventually prove to explain development more powerfully. Models combining direct, mediator, and moderator effects may also eventually prove useful, as in the theoretical model Manassis and Bradley (1994) have developed to account for the development of anxiety disorders.

Temperament X Temperament Interactions

Another theoretically expected interaction effect involves the interactive combination of two or more different temperament traits. This is particularly likely when control systems interact with more reactive systems in the course of development. As seen in Table 3.2, we can envision a number of ways in which temperament X temperament interactions might relate to the development of adjustment differences. At this point, however, there is little evidence for such effects. It is possible that simple additive models might suffice, for example, as in predicting externalizing behavior problems by a linear combination of difficultness and resistance to control (Bates et al., 1991). However, there are indications that some interactive effects will be discovered. Eisenberg, Fabes, et al. (1996) found that negative emotionality predicted increasingly greater problem behavior (probably of an externalizing sort) as levels of self-regulation (summing attentional and ego control measures) declined. This effect applied to both teacher and parent definitions of the constructs, and was found after removing the main effects first in multiple regression models.

Another interesting example involves the possible role of anxiety as an inhibitor of aggressive tendencies. Bates, Pettit, and Dodge (1995) asked whether initial internalizing tendencies of the child, as rated by kindergarten teachers, would moderate the continuity of aggressiveness, defined by teacher and peer ratings on multiple measures. We expected that the child who is more susceptible to anxious emotions would be more likely to respond to the kind of punishments children receive for aggression in school. Although aggressiveness was highly stable from kindergarten to first grade over the whole sample (structural equation path coefficient = .93), the degree of stability was significantly lower among the third of children highest in internalizing (.76) than among the medium- (.98) and low-internalizing groups (1.00). On average, the high-internalizing group showed a slight decrease in aggressiveness. Interpreting this as a temperament X temperament interaction requires acceptance of the teacher rating of anxiety as an index of temperament. This makes sense to us, in the same way that it makes sense to consider the Caspi et al. (1995) early childhood examiners' ratings as temperament. We are currently considering the predictiveness of mothers' retrospective ratings of temperament collected months prior to the teacher anxiety ratings.

Recent findings of Rubin, Coplan, Fox, and Calkins (1995) can also be interpreted as showing a temperament X temperament interaction effect. They created extreme groups of preschoolers on the basis of two dimensions: emotion regulation, defined by mother reports of emotionality and unsoothability on the CCTI, and observed sociability in ad hoc play groups. Children who were both unsociable and poor emotion regulators were observed to be more anxious and aimless during play, and were rated by their mothers as higher on Child Behavior Checklist (CBCL) internalizing than children who were unsociable and good emotion regulators. The children showing high sociability and poor regulation were not observed to be more disruptive in laboratory play and work tasks, as had been expected, but their mothers rated them as higher in externalizing. While these findings might reflect one temperament variable moderating another, they might also reflect additive influences; the data were not analyzed and presented in a way that would allow a clear conclusion about the appropriate model.

The Wills et al. (in press) study described in the section on indirect linkage models also briefly summarized a number of temperament X temperament interaction effects. These were established both through testing cross-product interaction terms in equations after removing main effects, and by comparing nested structural equation models (as in Bates et al., 1995). In one example, high task orientation ameliorated effects of negative emotionality on drug use outcomes, for example, in reducing the relation between having drug-using peers and using drugs oneself. Again, while this is a theoretically appealing finding, temperament, mediator factors, and outcome variables were all concurrently rated by the same informant.

In summary, although we are very interested in the possibility that developmental effects of one temperament dimension might depend on the level of another, and offer three theoretically meaningful examples, results on temperament X temperament interactions are presented somewhat tentatively. We note, however, that by viewing fearful inhibition and effortful control as control systems, situations can be identified in which each control system would be expected to moderate other more reactive systems. Fear control would be expected to operate under conditions of novelty or challenge, effortful control under verbal instructions from the caregiver or experimenter or other task-related conditions.

Temperament X Gender Interactions

In contrast to the paucity of studies of temperament X temperament interactions, a number of temperament X gender interaction effects have been reported in the literature. We

mentioned a few such effects in a previous part of this section. This kind of effect suggests that developmental implications of a given temperament variable may be different for boys than for girls. This could come about because a temperamental characteristic or an adjustment outcome variable has different implications for the two sexes. It could also result from the measure's having different meanings for the two sexes, or from developmental processes linking temperament and adjustment differently for the two sexes. Hinde (1989) suggests that measures of temperament are limited. They leave out potentially important qualifiers. He describes a contrast in which highly shy preschool-age boys directed significantly more hostile actions toward their mothers and nonsignificantly more toward their peers than less shy boys, while shy girls were nonsignificantly less hostile toward their mothers and significantly less hostile toward their peers. Shyness might thus mean something quite different for the two sexes, possibly resulting from a different blend of basic characteristics, or, as Hinde and others (e.g., Eisenberg et al., 1995; Gjerde, 1995) have tended to interpret it, from social processes such as greater acceptance of shyness in girls and less acceptance of shyness in boys.

Another classic example in the literature is Kagan and Moss's (1962) finding that the stability across childhood for aggressiveness was higher in boys than in girls, and stability for dependency was greater in girls than in boys. This is again plausibly interpreted in terms of environmental selection for gender-stereotyped individual differences, although differential processes might occur in other ways as well. For example, considering the Hinde (1989) pattern, sex differences in aggressive tendencies might conflict with high fearfulness in different ways. In some boys with aggressive tendencies, fearfulness might produce considerable inner conflict, leading to occasional irritable outbursts, whereas girls would be less likely to experience this conflict. Or perhaps boys and girls, because of sex differences in dominance/aggression, might respond slightly differently on average to socialization agents' attempts to control their behavior. This may be seen in a recent study by McFadyen-Ketchum, Bates, Dodge, and Pettit (1996). Aggressive girls who received high levels of aversive control and low levels of affection from their mothers tended to show decreases in their aggressiveness at school. Aggressive boys who received similar parenting tended to show increases in school aggressiveness.

Nevertheless, after reviewing 13 recent studies considering possible moderator effects of gender in relation to the predictions from temperament to adjustment (as well as considering others reviewed by Sanson & Rothbart, 1995), we are unable to present an organized picture of how sex moderates the relations of temperament and adjustment. We considered 11 studies that interpreted at least one gender interaction effect: Caspi et al. (1995), Earls and Jung (1987), Eisenberg et al. (1996), Fagot and O'Brien (1994), Gjerda (1995), Hinde (1989), Pulkkinen and Pitkanen (1994), Rende (1993), Rothbart, Ahadi, et al. (1994), Shaw and Vondra (1995), Stevenson et al. (1996). We also considered two that looked for but did not find such effects: Bates et al. (1991) and Caspi and Silva (1995). Many of the studies finding sex X temperament interactions tended to find other ways in which the two genders showed similar processes. Some of the effects involve greater linkage for girls, and about an equal number involve greater linkage for boys. The direction of differences does not obviously relate to age of the children or to the internalizing versus externalizing nature of the temperament or adjustment variables. There thus remains the possibility that the findings might be reflections of methodological artifacts, such as idiosyncrasies in particular samples, rather than theoretically meaningful processes.

Summary

Direct, linear relations between temperament and adjustment are frequently reported, with theoretically meaningful patterns of differentiation in which particular temperament variables predict particular adjustment dimensions. Models of indirect, mediational, and moderator roles for temperament, however, are less well established. There are excellent theoretical reasons for expecting interaction effects in the relations of temperament to adjustment, and some intriguing new findings support this approach. These include Kochanska's (1995) finding that conscience development of inhibited children is stronger when the mothers use gentle discipline, whereas for uninhibited children it is stronger when there is a positive partnership with the mother, or the finding of anxiety moderating the growth of aggressiveness (Bates et al., 1995). However, there is not yet an adequate pattern of replicated, longitudinal results, testing interaction effects against linear, additive models, to allow us to strongly conclude that interaction effects help explain development.

Several other topics could be discussed in relation to the topic of temperament and adjustment, such as the ways in which temperament itself might be changed as a result of the development of adjustment difficulties or improvements

(Clark et al., 1994; Kramer, 1993); temperament in medical conditions such as premature birth (e.g., Garcia-Coll, Halpern, Vohr, Seifer, & Oh, 1992), hospitalization (e.g., see special section of the *Journal of Pediatric Nursing,* Melvin & McClowry, 1995), or childhood accidents (e.g., Matheny, 1991; Pulkkinen, 1995), and the use of temperament in solving adjustment problems (e.g., Bates et al., 1994). However, for the sake of space, we must leave these topics for another chapter. Additional important research that we have not reviewed here includes research on temperament and parent-child interaction (e.g., Casey & Fuller, 1994; review by Sanson & Rothbart, 1995), temperament and schooling (Axia, Prior, & Carelli, 1992; reviews by Martin, 1989, and Keogh, 1989), and temperament and culture (Kohnstamm, Mervielde, Besevegis, & Halverson, 1995; Super & Harkness, 1994).

CHAPTER CONCLUSIONS AND FUTURE DIRECTIONS

Several conclusions with implications for future research have emerged from our review. The first concerns developments in our understanding of the dimensional structure of temperament. The second concerns progress in the measurement of temperament. The third concerns the developmental course and plasticity of temperamental systems.

Dimensions

Over the past two decades, there has been considerable progress in identifying the broad outlines and more specific dimensions of temperament in childhood. The general framework for temperament now constitutes a revision of the NYLS dimensions, and includes broad dimensions of positive affect and approach, negative affectivity, effortful control, and possibly social orientation. These dimensions share similarities with four of the Big Five factors of personality and with all of the Big Three broad factors of personality, but they are by no means identical. Establishing the nature of linkages between early temperament characteristics and later personality will result from thoughtful future longitudinal research, one of the major continuing tasks for our area.

Within the broad domain of negative affectivity, there is strong evidence for subdimensions of fearful and irritable distress, with some suggestion that separation distress and sadness may be further differentiated from these two kinds of distress proneness. A major task for the field will be to continue to identify the more narrow dimensions of variability existing within the broad temperamental dimensions, as well as identifying constructs that do not fit within the current structure. In addition, specifying the relationship between distress to overstimulation (i.e., distress to high-intensity or rate of stimulation) and more specific forms of distress proneness such as fearfulness, irritability, separation distress, and sadness, will also be required. Current findings that distress and motor activity in response to high-intensity stimulation at age 4 months predict later behavioral inhibition or fearfulness are a good start, but we also need to know whether there are predictions to the other differentiated forms of distress, such as irritability and separation distress.

The positive relation between perceptual sensitivity and distress to overstimulation or discomfort as identified in parent-report research also requires replication in the laboratory. This finding would support Soviet theory on strength of nervous system as well as other optimal-level theories. Optimal-level theories further suggest that perceptual sensitivity will be related to the emergence of positive affect at lower levels of stimulus intensity, another project worthy of study.

The subdimensions of positive affect and approach also require further exploration: psychobiological models described above suggest the existence of a kind of general incentive motivation. However, research on parent-reported temperament has reliably identified a "food factor," in which items relating to positive or negative reactions to food do not co-vary with other aspects of positive or negative affectivity, but only with each other (see review by Rothbart, 1989b). Food incentives may thus be separable from the general incentive dimension. Social orientation or warmth may well be another separable system or systems, perhaps constituting a broad dimension related to both FFM agreeableness and separation distress. Again, important questions remain to be studied.

Investigating possible subdimensions within effortful control will also be valuable. Attentional focusing and shifting capacities are closely related in adult studies, and they are further related to inhibitory control. In younger children, however, the two attentional capacities are not as closely linked, although the ability to focus attention when requested appears to be closely related to the development of executive control. Norman and Shallice (1986) have identified the following as hallmarks of executive control: (a) planning ahead; (b) response to novel or dangerous events; (c) error correction; (d) difficult or effortful processing; and (e) conflict, as in the Stroop effect. Several of these functions have been linked to brain structures involved in anterior control, but more research will be needed to determine the degree to which they co-vary in development, and are differentiable from fear control.

Measures

Good measures of temperament are crucial to our theoretical understanding. Advances in defining the dimensional structure of temperament and understanding the neural and developmental substrates of temperament rely on advances in measurement. As an additional goal of research, we advocate continued development of sound measures, using parent report, naturalistic observation, and structured or laboratory observation measures in converging and complementary ways. We have advocated an analog approach to questions of validation, rather than a digital, yes-no approach to ascertaining the value of methods and measures. Aside from the important future work of comparing results of alternative methods, another major focus in research should be identification of *non*relationships among constructs, that is, tests for discriminant as well as convergent validity. It is partly on the basis of differential, discriminating patterns of correlations between parent reports of temperament and other measures, for example, that we are able to argue for the validity of parent reports. We have also suggested that the use of marker tasks, that is, tasks whose performance is linked to particular brain functions, can now be linked to behavioral temperament and its development, and expect further growth in this approach.

Development

As the dimensions of temperament are further delineated and measures improved, a major goal will continue to be their study in a developmental context. Future research is needed to examine whether particular developmental periods are linked to the development and plasticity of temperament systems. For example, van den Boom (1994) identified a period when the development of secure attachment may be facilitated. We do not know, however, the degree to which the timing of her intervention or specific aspects of her intervention were important. There may also be times when positive affect or effortful control systems are sensitive to environmental conditions. Schore (1994) has suggested that positive affect systems are particularly sensitive to effects of experience toward the end of the first year of life. Are there developmental periods when irritable and frustrative distress might be most easily directed toward or away from tendencies to aggressive action? These are basic developmental questions, with profound implications for our understanding of the nature of temperament and the development of personality.

Establishing closer links with our understanding of the developing neurophysiological substrate of temperament is a related task for our area. In this work, findings from each level of study will illuminate the other. Thus, behavioral research on the developing structure of temperament helps to specify the variables and operations necessary to link the psychology of temperament to its neurophysiology. Reviewers who relate parallel research carried out within these two domains will help in this work. The use of both physiological assays and behavioral measures in research designs, as well as the use of marker tasks, will lead to further advances.

Finally, we have identified possible developmental trajectories in the development of social and personality traits from early temperamental characteristics, most strongly in Kochanska's (1995) work on multiple routes to conscience. The task of identifying routes to other significant outcomes requires progress in all of the tasks described above, and it is of critical importance to our enterprise. The study of developmental trajectories requires establishing stronger links between our work and more environmentally oriented areas of our field, such as social learning and social cognition research. As we have indicated, temperament constructs do not conflict with these areas of research: the temperament dimensions we have described are open to experience, with some systems likely more open than others. In addition, the functioning of control systems will be highly dependent on what the culture indicates should be controlled. Moreover, developmentally, individual children may make quite different adaptations to differing social contexts (Cairns, 1979). Prospects for effective longitudinal research will be much improved by an integration of the study of individual differences, cross-cultural psychology, social learning, and social cognition, within a developmental framework.

Developmental research in our area may also eventually answer questions like the following: To what degree is temperament plastic and susceptible to change? To what degree does experience alter only the *expression* of temperamental characteristics? If distress and maladaptive social cognitions can result from a painful life history, how much of early temperament may have been overlain by these negative experiences? Could the original core of temperament be uncovered by imaginative assays, by intervention, by further social experience, or even by further changes in social or physical development? We know someone who through the aging process lost many of her memories, including information that had troubled her over many years and led to major conflicts within herself and with others. What remains after her memory loss is a positive and expressive person, loved by all who meet her. Was this the child she once was? If so, could other less serious interventions have uncovered it? Better yet, could developmental research inform both child rearing and children's prospects in society so that her accumulating pain might never have occurred? We have made much progress in our field in the past decades, but a number of questions remain. Many of these questions are hopeful about a future for ourselves, our parents, and our children.

ACKNOWLEDGMENTS

We wish to express our sincere gratitude to several individuals, including the critical reviewers of our chapter, who contributed so much to its construction. Megan Gunnar, Myron Rothbart, Nancy Eisenberg, Jose Antonio Carranza, Claire Kopp, and Thomas Wills all contributed helpful comments and criticisms on the entire chapter. Jack Digman reviewed the early sections, and Colleen Vande Voorde took on the extremely difficult task of putting together the manuscript. John Reid and the Oregon Social Learning Center provided important support for John E. Bates during the writing of the chapter, and Paula Bates' support was very much appreciated. We truly could not have completed the chapter without the help of these people. Mary Rothbart's work was partially sustained by grants from NIMH, Human Frontiers and the Keck Foundation; this support is gratefully acknowledged.

REFERENCES

Ahadi, S. A., & Rothbart, M. K. (1994). Temperament, development and the Big Five. In C. F. Halverson, G. A. Kohnstamm, & R. P. Martin (Eds.), *The developing structure of temperament and personality from infancy to adulthood* (pp. 189–207). Hillsdale, NJ: Erlbaum.

Ahadi, S. A., Rothbart, M. K., & Ye, R. M. (1993). Child temperament in the U.S. and China: Similarities and differences. *European Journal of Personality, 7,* 359–378.

Ainsworth, M. D. S., Blehar, M. C., Waters, E., & Wall, S. (1978). *Patterns of attachment: A psychological study of the Strange Situation.* Hillsdale, NJ: Erlbaum.

Allport, G. W. (1961). *Pattern and growth in personality.* New York: Rinehart & Winston.

Asendorpf, J. B. (1990). Development of inhibition during childhood: Evidence for situational specificity and a two-factor model. *Developmental Psychology, 26,* 721–730.

Asendorpf, J. B. (1994). The malleability of behavioral inhibition: A study of individual developmental functions. *Developmental Psychology, 30,* 912–919.

Asendorpf, J. B., & Nunner-Winkler, G. (1992). Children's moral motive strength and temperamental inhibition reduce their egoistic behavior in real moral conflicts. *Child Development, 63,* 1223–1235.

Axia, G., Prior, M., & Carelli, M. G. (1992). Cultural influences on temperament: A comparison of Italian, Italo-Australian, and Anglo-Australian toddlers. *Australian Psychologist, 27,* 52–56.

Balaban, M. T. (1995). Affective influences on startle in five-month-old infants: Reactions to facial expressions of emotion. *Child Development, 66,* 28-36.

Bardo, M. T., Donohew, R. L., & Harrington, N. G. (1996). Psychobiology of novelty-seeking and drug-seeking behavior. *Behavioral Brain Research, 77,* 23–43.

Bates, J. E. (1980). The concept of difficult temperament. *Merrill-Palmer Quarterly, 26,* 299–319.

Bates, J. E. (1987). Temperament in infancy. In J. D. Osofsky (Ed.), *Handbook of infant development* (2nd ed., pp. 1101–1149). New York: Wiley.

Bates, J. E. (1989a). Applications of temperament concepts. In G. A. Kohnstamm, J. E. Bates, & M. K. Rothbart (Eds.), *Temperament in childhood* (pp. 321–355). Chichester, England: Wiley.

Bates, J. E. (1989b). Concepts and measures of temperament. In G. A. Kohnstamm, J. E. Bates, & M. K. Rothbart (Eds.), *Temperament in childhood* (pp. 3–26). Chichester, England: Wiley.

Bates, J. E. (1990). Conceptual and empirical linkages between temperament and behavior problems: A commentary on the Sanson, Prior, and Kyrios study. *Merrill-Palmer Quarterly, 36*(2), 193–199.

Bates, J. E. (1994). Parents as scientific observers of their children's development. In S. L. Friedman & H. C. Haywood (Eds.), *Developmental follow-up: Concepts, domains and methods* (pp. 197–216). New York: Academic Press.

Bates, J. E., & Bayles, K. (1984). Objective and subjective components in mothers' perceptions of their children from age 6 months to 3 years. *Merrill-Palmer Quarterly, 30,* 111–130.

Bates, J. E., & Bayles, K. (1988). The role of attachment in the development of behavior problems. In J. Belsky & T. Nezworski (Eds.), *Clinical implications of attachment* (pp. 253–299). Hillsdale, NJ: Erlbaum.

Bates, J. E., Bayles, K., Bennett, D. S., Ridge, B., & Brown, M. M. (1991). Origins of externalizing behavior problems at eight years of age. In D. Pepler & K. Rubin (Eds.), *Development and treatment of childhood aggression* (pp. 93–120). Hillsdale, NJ: Erlbaum.

Bates, J. E., Freeland, C. A. B., & Lounsbury, M. L. (1979). Measurement of infant difficultness. *Child Development, 50,* 794–803.

Bates, J. E., Maslin, C. A., & Frankel, K. A. (1985). Attachment security, mother-child interaction, and temperament as predictors of behavior problem ratings at age three years. In I. Bretherton & E. Waters (Eds.), Growing points in attachment theory and research. *Society for Research in Child Development Monographs,* (1/2, Serial No. 209), 167–193.

Bates, J. E., Pettit, G. S., & Dodge, K. A. (1995). Family and child factors in stability and change in children's aggressiveness in elementary school. In J. McCord (Ed.), *Coercion and punishment in long-term perspectives.* New York: Cambridge University Press.

Bates, J. E., & Wachs, T. D. (Eds.). (1994). *Temperament: Individual differences at the interface of biology and behavior.* Washington, DC: American Psychological Association.

Bates, J. E., Wachs, T. D., & Emde, R. N. (1994). Toward practical uses for biological concepts of temperament. In J. E. Bates & T. D. Wachs (Eds.), *Temperament: Individual differences at the interface of biology and behavior.* Washington, DC: American Psychological Association.

Baughman, E. E. (1972). *Personality: The psychological study of the individual.* Englewood Cliffs, NJ: Prentice-Hall.

Bayley, N., & Schaeffer, E. S. (1963). Consistency of maternal and child behavior in the Berkeley Growth Study. *American Psychologist, 18*(7).

Bell, R. Q. (1968). A reinterpretation of the direction of effects in studies of socialization. *Psychological Review, 75,* 81–95.

Bell, R. Q. (1974). Contributions of human infants to caregiving and social interaction. In M. Lewis & L. A. Rosenblum (Eds.), *The effect of the infant on its caregiver* (pp. 1–19). New York: Wiley.

Bell, R. Q. (1988–1989). *Neonatal behavior predictors of security of attachment* (Annual Report, 12). Sapporo, Japan: Hokkaido University, Research and Clinical Center for Child Development.

Bell, R. Q., Weller, G. M., & Waldrop, M. (1971). Newborn and preschooler: Organization of behavior and relations between periods. *Monographs of the Society for Research in Child Development, 36*(1/2, Serial No. 142).

Belsky, J., & Rovine, M. (1987). Temperament and attachment security in the Strange Situation: An empirical rapprochement. *Child Development, 58,* 787–795.

Bergman, P., & Escalona, S. K. (1949). Unusual sensitivities in very young children. *Psychoanalytic Study of the Child, 3,* 333–352.

Berlyne, D. E. (1971). *Aesthetics and psychobiology.* New York: Appleton-Century-Crofts.

Berntson, G. G., Cacioppo, J. T., & Quigley, K. S. (1993). Respiratory sinus arrhythmia: Autonomic origins, physiological mechanisms, and psychophysiological implications. *Psychophysiology, 30,* 183–196.

Biederman, J., Rosenbaum, J. F., Chaloff, J., & Kagan, J. (1995). Behavioral inhibition as a risk factor for anxiety disorders. In J. L. March (Ed.), *Anxiety disorders in children and adolescents* (pp. 61–81). New York: Guilford Press.

Biederman, J., Rosenbaum, J. F., Hirshfeld, D. R., Faraone, S. V., Bolduc, E. A., Gersten, M., Meminger, S. R., Kagan, J., Snidman, N., & Reznick, S. (1990). Psychiatric correlates of behavioral inhibition in young children of parents with and without psychiatric disorders. *Archives of General Psychiatry, 47,* 21–26.

Birns, B. (1965). Individual differences in human neonates' responses to stimulation. *Child Development, 36,* 249–256.

Birns, B., Barten, S., & Bridger, W. (1969). Individual differences in temperamental characteristics of infants. *Transactions of the New York Academy of Sciences, 31,* 1071–1082.

Black, J. E., & Greenough, W. T. (1991). Developmental approaches to the memory processes. In J. L. Martinez, Jr. & R. P. Kesner (Eds.), *Learning and memory: A biological view* (2nd ed., pp. 61–91). San Diego, CA: Academic Press.

Block, J., & Kremen, A. (1996). IQ and ego-resiliency: Their conceptual and empirical connections and separateness. *Journal of Personality and Social Psychology, 70,* 349–361.

Block, J. H., & Block, J. (1980). The role of ego-control and ego-resiliency in the organization of behavior. In W. A. Collins (Ed.), *Minnesota Symposium on Child Psychology* (Vol. 13, pp. 39–101). Hillsdale, NJ: Erlbaum.

Bohlin, G., Hagekull, B., & Lindhagen, K. (1981). Dimensions of infant behavior. *Infant Behavior and Development, 4,* 83–96.

Bornstein, M. H., Gaughran, J. M., & Segui, I. (1991). Multimethod assessment of infant temperament: Mother questionnaire and mother and observer reports evaluated and compared at five months using the Infant Temperament Measure. *International Journal of Behavioral Development, 14,* 131–151.

Bradley, B. S. (1985). Failure to distinguish between people and things in early infancy. *British Journal of Developmental Psychology, 3,* 281–291.

Bretherton, I. (1985). Attachment theory: Retrospect and prospect. In I. Bretherton & E. Waters (Eds.), Growing points of attachment theory and research. *Monographs of the Society for Research in Child Development, 50*(1/2, Serial No. 209), 3–35.

Buck, R. W. (1979). Individual differences in nonverbal sending accuracy and electrodermal responding: The externalizing-internalizing dimension. In R. Rosenthal (Ed.), *Skill in nonverbal communication: Individual differences.* Cambridge, MA: Oelgeschlager, Gunn & Hain.

Burt, C. (1937). The analysis of temperament. *British Journal of Medical Psychology, 17,* 158–188.

Buss, A. H., & Plomin, R. (1975). *A temperament theory of personality development.* New York: Wiley.

Buss, A. H., & Plomin, R. (1984). *Temperament: Early developing personality traits.* Hillsdale, NJ: Erlbaum.

Byrne, J. M., Clark-Touesnard, M. E., Hondas, B. J., & Smith, I. M. (1985, April). *Stability of individual differences in infant visual attention.* Poster presented at the meetings of the Society for Research in Child Development, Toronto.

Cabanac, M. (1971). Physiological role of pleasure. *Science, 173,* 1103–1107.

Cairns, R. B. (1979). *Social development: The origins and plasticity of interchanges.* San Francisco: Freeman.

Calkins, S. D., & Fox, N. A. (1992). The relations among infant temperament, security of attachment, and behavioral inhibition at twenty-four months. *Child Development, 63,* 1456–1472.

Calkins, S. D., & Fox, N. A. (1994). Individual differences in the biological aspects of temperament. In J. E. Bates & T. D. Wachs (Eds.), *Temperament: Individual differences at the interface of biology and behavior* (pp. 199–217). Washington, DC: American Psychological Association.

Calkins, S. D., Fox, N. A., & Marshall, T. R. (1996). Behavioral and physiological antecedents of inhibition in infancy. *Child Development, 67,* 523–540.

Campos, J. J., Barrett, K. C., Lamb, M. E., Goldsmith, H. H., & Stenberg, C. (1983). Socioemotional development. In P. H. Mussen (Series Ed.) & M. M. Haith & J. J. Campos (Vol. Eds.), *Handbook of child psychology: Vol. 2. Infancy and developmental biology* (4th ed., pp. 783–916). New York: Wiley.

Capaldi, D. M., & Rothbart, M. K. (1992). Development and validation of an early adolescent temperament measure. *Journal of Early Adolescence, 12,* 153–173.

Carey, W. B., & McDevitt, S. C. (1978). Revision of the infant temperament questionnaire. *Pediatrics, 61,* 735–739.

Carter, C. S. (1986). The reproductive and adrenal systems. In M. G. H. Coles, E. Donchin, & S. W. Porges (Eds.), *Psychophysiology* (pp. 172–182). New York: Guilford Press.

Casey, R. J., & Fuller, L. L. (1994). Maternal regulation of children's emotions. *Journal of Nonverbal Behavior, 18,* 57–89.

Caspi, A., Henry, B., McGee, R. O., Moffitt, T. E., & Silva, P. A. (1995). Temperamental origins of child and adolescent behavior problems: From age three to age fifteen. *Child Development, 66,* 55–68.

Caspi, A., & Silva, P. A. (1995). Temperamental qualities at age three predict personality traits in young adulthood: Longitudinal evidence from a birth cohort. *Child Development, 66,* 486–498.

Chess, S., & Thomas, A. (1984). *Origins and evolution of behavior disorders.* New York: Brunner/Mazel.

Clark, L. A., Watson, D., & Mineka, S. (1994). Temperament, personality, and the mood and anxiety disorders. *Journal of Abnormal Psychology, 103,* 103–116.

Cloninger, C. R. (1987). A systematic method for clinical description and classification of personality variants. *Archives of General Psychiatry, 44,* 573–588.

Coldren, J. T., Colombo, J., O'Brien, M., Martinez, R., & Horowitz, F. D. (1987, April). *The relationship of infant visual attention across social interaction and information processing tasks.* Paper presented at the meetings of the Society for Research in Child Development, Baltimore.

Coon, H., Carey, G., Corley, R., & Fulker, D. W. (1992). Identifying children in the Colorado Adoption Project at risk for conduct disorder. *Journal of the American Academy of Child and Adolescent Psychiatry, 31,* 503–511.

Crider, A., & Lunn, R. (1971). Electrodermal lability as a personality dimension. *Journal of Experimental Research in Personality, 5,* 145–150.

Cyphers, L. A., Phillips, K., Fulker, D. W., & Mrazek, D. A. (1990). Twin temperament during the transition from infancy to early childhood. *Journal of the American Academy of Child and Adolescent Psychiatry, 29,* 393–397.

Darley, J., & Fazio, R. (1980). Expectancy confirmation processes arising in the social interaction sequence. *American Psychologist, 35,* 867–881.

Davidson, R. J., & Fox, N. A. (1982). Asymmetrical brain activity discriminates between positive versus negative affective stimuli in human infants. *Science, 218,* 1235–1237.

Davis, M. (1992). The role of the amygdala in fear and anxiety. *Annual Review of Neuroscience, 15,* 353–375.

Davis, M., Hitchcock, J. M., & Rosen, J. B. (1987). Anxiety and the amygdala: Pharmacological and anatomical analysis of the fear-potentiated startle paradigm. In G. Bower (Ed.), *The psychology of learning and motivation* (Vol. 21, pp. 263–305). San Diego, CA: Academic Press.

Dawson, G. (1994). Development of emotional expression and emotion regulation in infancy. In G. Dawson & K. Fischer (Eds.), *Human behavior and the developing brain* (pp. 346–379). New York: Guilford Press.

DeGangi, G. A., DiPietro, J. A., Greenspan, S. I., & Porges, S. W. (1991). Psychophysiological characteristics of the regulatory disordered infant. *Infant Behavior and Development, 14,* 37–50.

Depue, R. A., & Iacono, W. G. (1989). Neurobehavioral aspects of affective disorders. *Annual Review of Psychology, 40,* 457–492.

Depue, R. A., Luciana, M., Arbisi, P., & Collins, P. (1994). Dopamine and the structure of personality: Relation of agonist-induced dopamine activity to positive emotionality. *Journal of Personality and Social Psychology, 67,* 485–498.

Derryberry, D., & Reed, M. (1994a). Temperament and attention: Orienting toward and away from positive and negative signals. *Journal of Personality and Social Psychology, 66,* 1128–1139.

Derryberry, D., & Reed, M. (1994b). Temperament and the self-organization of personality. *Development and Psychopathology, 6,* 653–676.

Derryberry, D., & Rothbart, M. K. (1988). Arousal, affect and attention as components of temperament. *Journal of Personality and Social Psychology, 55,* 958–966.

Diamond, A. (1990). Developmental time course in human infants and infant monkeys, and the neural basis of inhibiting control of reaching. In A. Diamond (Ed.), *The development and neural basis of higher cognitive functions* (pp. 637–669). New York: New York Academy of Sciences.

Diamond, A., Werker, J. F., & Lalonde, C. (1994). Toward understanding commonalities in the development of object search, detour navigation, categorization, and speech perception. In G. Dawson & K. W. Fischer (Eds.), *Human behavior and the developing brain* (pp. 380–426). New York: Guilford Press.

Diamond, S. (1957). *Personality and temperament.* New York: Harper.

Diamond, S. (1974). *The roots of psychology.* New York: Basic Books.

Diener, M. L., Goldstein, L. H., & Mangelsdorf, S. C. (1995). The role of prenatal expectations in parents' reports of infant temperament. *Merrill-Palmer Quarterly, 41,* 172–190.

Digman, J. M., & Inouye, J. (1986). Further specification of the five robust factors of personality. *Journal of Personality and Social Psychology, 50,* 116–123.

Digman, J. M., & Shmelyov, A. G. (1996). The structure of temperament and personality in Russian children. *Journal of Personality and Social Psychology, 71,* 341–351.

Dodge, K. A. (1986). A social-information-processing model of social competence in children. In M. Perlmutter (Ed.), *Minnesota symposia on child psychology* (18th ed., pp. 77–125). Hillsdale, NJ: Erlbaum.

Dodge, K. A., Bates, J. E., & Pettit, G. S. (1990). Mechanisms in the cycle of violence. *Science, 250,* 1678–1683.

Dumas, J. E., & LaFreniere, P. J. (1993). Mother-child relationships as sources of support or stress: A comparison of competent, average, aggressive, and anxious dyads. *Child Development, 64,* 1732–1754.

Earls, F., & Jung, K. G. (1987). Temperament and home environment characteristics as causal factors in the early development of childhood psychopathology. *Journal of the American Academy of Child and Adolescent Psychiatry, 26,* 491–498.

Eaton, W. O. (1983). Measuring activity level with actometers: Reliability, validity, and arm length. *Child Development, 54,* 720–726.

Eaton, W. O. (1994). Temperament, development, and the Five-Factor Model: Lessons from activity level. In C. F. Halverson, Jr., G. A. Kohnstamm, & R. P. Martin (Eds.), *The developing structure of temperament and personality from infancy to adulthood* (pp. 173–187). Hillsdale, NJ: Erlbaum.

Eaton, W. O., & Saudino, K. J. (1992). Prenatal activity level as a temperament dimension? Individual differences and developmental functions in fetal movement. *Infant Behavior and Development, 15,* 57–70.

Eisenberg, N., Fabes, R. A., Guthrie, I. K., Murphy, B. C., Maszk, P., Holgren, R., & Suh, K. (1996). The relations of regulation and emotionality to problem behavior in elementary school children. *Development and Psychopathology, 8,* 141–162.

Eisenberg, N., Fabes, R. A., Murphy, M., Maszk, P., Smith, M., & Karbon, M. (1995). The role of emotionality and regulation in children's social functioning: A longitudinal study. *Child Development, 66,* 1239–1261.

Eisenberg, N., Guthrie, I. K., Fabes, R. A., Reiser, M., Murphy, B. C., Holgren, R., Maszk, P., & Losoya, S. (1996). *The relations of regulation and emotionality to resiliency and competent social functioning in elementary school children.* Manuscript submitted for publication.

Engfer, A. (1993). Antecedents and consequences of shyness in boys and girls: A 6-year longitudinal study. In K. H. Rubin & J. B. Asendorpf (Eds.), *Social withdrawal, inhibition, and shyness in childhood* (pp. 49–79). Hillsdale, NJ: Erlbaum.

Escalona, S. K. (1968). *The roots of individuality: Normal patterns of development in infancy.* Chicago: Aldine.

Eysenck, H. J. (1967). *The biological basis of personality.* Springfield, IL: Thomas.

Fabes, R. A., Eisenberg, N., & Eisenbud, L. (1993). Behavioral and physiological correlates of children's reactions to others in distress. *Developmental Psychology, 29,* 655–663.

Fabes, R. A., Eisenberg, N., Karbon, M., Bernzweig, J., Speer, A. L., & Carlo, G. (1994). Socialization of children's vicarious emotional responding and prosocial behavior: Relations with mothers' perceptions of children's emotional reactivity. *Developmental Psychology, 30,* 44–55.

Fabes, R. A., Eisenberg, N., Karbon, M., & Troyer, D. (1994). The relations of children's emotion regulation to their vicarious emotional responses and comforting behaviors. *Child Development, 65,* 1678–1693.

Fagot, B. I., & O'Brien, M. (1994). Activity level in young children: Cross-age stability, situational influences, correlates with temperament, and the perception of problem behaviors. *Merrill-Palmer Quarterly, 40,* 378–398.

Fish, M., & Crockenberg, S. (1981). Correlates and antecedents of nine-month infant behavior and mother infant interaction. *Infant Behavior & Development, 4,* 69–81.

Fisher, P. A., & Fagot, B. I. (1992, April). *Temperament, parental discipline, and child psychopathology: A social-interactional model.* Paper presented at the annual convention of the Western Psychological Association, Portland, OR.

Fowles, D. C. (1982). Heart rate as an index of anxiety: Failure of a hypothesis. In J. T. Cacioppo & R. E. Petty (Eds.), *Perspectives in cardiovascular psychophysiology* (pp. 93–126). New York: Guilford Press.

Fowles, D. C. (1984). Biological variables in psychopathology. In H. E. Adams & P. B. Suthern (Eds.), *Comprehensive handbook of psychopathology* (pp. 77–110). New York: Plenum Press.

Fowles, D. C. (1994). A motivational theory of psychopathology. In W. Spaulding (Ed.), *Nebraska Symposium on Motivation: Integrated views of motivation and emotion* (Vol. 41, pp. 181–238). Lincoln: University of Nebraska Press.

Fox, N. A. (1995). Of the way we were: Adult memories about attachment experiences and their role in determining infant-parent relationships: A commentary on Van IJzendoorn. *Psychological Bulletin, 117,* 404–410.

Fox, N. A., Calkins, S. D., & Bell, M. A. (1994). Neural plasticity and development in the first two years of life: Evidence from cognitive and socioemotional domains of research. *Development and Psychopathology, 6,* 677–696.

Fox, N. A., & Davidson, R. J. (1984). Hemispheric substrates of affect: A developmental model. In N. A. Fox & R. J. Davidson (Eds.), *The psychology of affective development* (pp. 353–382). Hillsdale, NJ: Erlbaum.

Fox, N. A., & Davidson, R. J. (1986). Taste-elicited changes in facial signs of emotion and the asymmetry of brain electrical activity in human newborns. *Neuropsychologica, 24,* 417–422.

Fox, N. A., & Field, T. (1989). Individual differences in preschool entry behavior. *Journal of Applied Developmental Psychology, 10,* 527–540.

Fox, N. A., Kimmerly, N. L., & Schafer, W. D. (1991). Attachment to mother/attachment to father: A meta-analysis. *Child Development, 62,* 210–225.

Fox, N. A., & Stifter, C. A. (1989). Biological and behavioral differences in infant reactivity and regulation. In G. Kohnstamm,

J. Bates, & M. K. Rothbart (Eds.), *Temperament in childhood* (pp. 169–183). Chichester, England: Wiley.

Fries, M. E., & Woolf, P. (1953). Some hypotheses on the role of congenital activity type in personality development. In R. Eissler (Ed.), *The psychoanalytic study of the child* (Vol. 8). New York: International Universities Press.

Frodi, A., & Thompson, R. (1985). Infants' affective responses in the Strange Situation: Effects of prematurity and quality of attachment. *Child Development, 56,* 1280–1291.

Fullard, W., McDevitt, S. C., & Carey, W. B. (1984). Assessing temperament in one- to three-year-old children. *Journal of Pediatric Psychology, 9,* 205–217.

Garcia Coll, C. T., Halpern, L. F., Vohr, B. R., Seifer, R., & Oh, W. (1992). Stability and correlates of change of early temperament in preterm and full-term infants. *Infant Behavior and Development, 15,* 137–153.

Garcia Coll, C. T., Kagan, J., & Reznick, J. S. (1984). Behavioral inhibition in young children. *Child Development, 55,* 1005–1019.

Gellhorn, E. (1957). *Autonomic imbalance and the hypothalamus.* Minneapolis: University of Minnesota Press.

Gerardi, G., Rothbart, M. K., Posner, M. I., & Kepler, S. (1996, April). *The development of attentional control: Performance on a spatial Stroop-like task at 24, 30, and 36–38-months-of-age.* Poster presented at the annual meeting of the International Society for Infant Studies, Providence, RI.

Gesell, A. (1928). *Infancy and human growth.* New York: Macmillan.

Gjerde, P. F. (1995). Alternative pathways to chronic depressive symptoms in young adults: Gender differences in developmental trajectories. *Child Development, 66,* 1277–1300.

Goldberg, L. R. (1993). The structure of phenotypic personality traits. *American Psychologist, 48,* 26–34.

Goldman-Rakic, P. S. (1988). Topography of cognition: Parallel distributed networks in primate association cortex. *Annual Review of Neuroscience, 11,* 137–156.

Goldsmith, H. H. (1989). Behavior-genetic approaches to temperament. In G. A. Kohnstamm, J. E. Bates, & M. K. Rothbart (Eds.), *Temperament in childhood* (pp. 111–132). Chichester, England: Wiley.

Goldsmith, H. H. (1993). Temperament: Variability in developing emotion systems. In M. Lewis & J. M. Haviland (Eds.), *Handbook of emotion* (pp. 353–364). New York: Guilford Press.

Goldsmith, H. H. (1996). Studying temperament via construction of the Toddler Behavior Assessment Questionnaire. *Child Development, 67,* 218–235.

Goldsmith, H. H., & Alansky, J. A. (1987). Maternal and infant temperamental predictors of attachment: A meta-analytic review. *Journal of Consulting and Clinical Psychology, 55,* 805–816.

Goldsmith, H. H., Buss, K. A., & Lemery, K. S. (in press). Toddler and childhood temperament: Expanded content, stronger genetic evidence, new evidence for the importance of environment. *Developmental Psychology.*

Goldsmith, H. H., & Campos, O. (1982). Toward a theory of infant temperament. In R. Emde & R. Harmon (Eds.), *Attachment and affiliative systems* (pp. 161–193). New York: Plenum Press.

Goldsmith, H. H., & Harman, C. (1994). Temperament and attachment: Individuals and relationships. *Current Directions in Psychological Science, 3,* 53–57.

Goldsmith, H. H., Losoya, S. H., Bradshaw, D. L., & Campos, J. J. (1994). Genetics of personality: A twin study of the Five-Factor Model and parental-offspring analyses. In C. Halverson, R. Martin, & G. Kohnstamm (Eds.), *The developing structure of temperament and personality from infancy to adulthood* (pp. 241–265). Hillsdale, NJ: Erlbaum.

Goldsmith H. H., & Rieser-Danner, L. A. (1986). Variation among temperament theories and validation studies of temperament assessment. In G. A. Kohnstamm (Ed.), *Temperament discussed: Temperament and development in infancy and childhood* (pp. 1–9). Lisse, The Netherlands: Swets & Zeitlinger.

Goldsmith, H. H., Rieser-Danner, L. A., & Briggs, S. (1991). Evaluating convergent and discriminant validity of temperament questionnaires for preschoolers, toddlers, and infants. *Developmental Psychology, 27,* 566–579.

Goldsmith, H. H., & Rothbart, M. K. (1991). Contemporary instruments for assessing early temperament by questionnaire and in the laboratory. In J. Strelau & A. Angleitner (Eds.), *Explorations in temperament: International perspectives on theory and measurement* (pp. 249–272). New York: Plenum Press.

Gorenstein, E. E., & Newman, J. P. (1980). Disinhibitory psychopathology: A new perspective and a model for research. *Psychological Review, 87,* 301–315.

Grant, S. J., Aston-Jones, G., & Redmond, D. E. (1988). Responses of primate locus coeruleus neurons to simple and complex sensory stimuli. *Brain Research Bulletin, 21,* 401–410.

Gray, J. A. (1975). *Elements of a two-process theory of learning.* New York: Academic Press.

Gray, J. A. (1982). *The neuropsychology of anxiety.* Oxford, England: Oxford University Press.

Gray, J. A. (1987). Perspectives on anxiety and impulsivity: A commentary. *Journal of Research in Personality, 21,* 493–509.

Gray, J. A. (1991). The neuropsychology of temperament. In J. Strelau & A. Angleitner (Eds.), *Explorations in tempera-*

ment: International perspectives on theory and measurement (pp. 105–128). New York: Plenum Press.

Graziano, W. G. (1994). The development of agreeableness as a dimension of personality. In C. F. Halverson, Jr., G. A. Kohnstamm, & R. P. Martin (Eds.), *The developing structure of temperament and personality from infancy to adulthood* (pp. 339–354). Hillsdale, NJ: Erlbaum.

Greenberg, M. T., Cicchetti, D., & Cummings, E. M. (Eds.). (1990). *Attachment in the preschool years: Theory, research, and intervention.* Chicago: University of Chicago Press.

Guerin, D. W., & Gottfried, A. W. (1986, April). *Infant temperament as a predictor of preschool behavior problems.* Presented at the International Conference on Infant Studies, Los Angeles.

Guerin, D. W., Gottfried, A. W., Oliver, P. H., & Thomas, C. W. (1994). Temperament and school functioning during early adolescence. *Journal of Early Adolescence, 14,* 200–225.

Gunnar, M. R. (1990). The psychobiology of infant temperament. In J. Colombo & J. Fagan (Eds.), *Individual differences in infancy: Reliability, stability and prediction* (pp. 387–410). Hillsdale, NJ: Erlbaum.

Gunnar, M. R. (1994). Psychoendocrine studies of temperament and stress in early childhood: Expanding current models. In J. E. Bates & T. D. Wachs (Eds.), *Temperament: Individual differences at the interface of biology and behavior* (pp. 175–198). Washington, DC: American Psychological Association.

Gunnar, M. R., Larson, M., Hertsgaard, L., Harris, M., & Brodersen, L. (1992). The stressfulness of separation among 9-month-old infants: Effects of social context variables and infant temperament. *Child Development, 63,* 290–303.

Gunnar, M. R., Mangelsdorf, S., Larson, M., & Hertsgaard, L. (1989). Attachment, temperament, and adrenocortical activity in infancy: A study of psychoendocrine regulation. *Developmental Psychology, 25,* 355–363.

Gunnar, M. R., Porter, F. L., Wolf, C. M., Rigatuso, J., & Larson, M. C. (1995). Neonatal stress reactivity: Predictions to later emotional temperament. *Child Development, 66,* 1–13.

Hagekull, B. (1982). Measurement of behavioral differences in infancy. *Acta University Uppsala: Abstracts of Uppsala dissertations from the Faculty of Social Sciences, 26.* Stockholm: Almquist & Wiksell International.

Hagekull, B. (1989). Longitudinal stability of temperament within a behavioral style framework. In G. A. Kohnstamm, J. E. Bates, & M. K. Rothbart (Eds.), *Temperament in childhood* (pp. 283–297). Chichester, England: Wiley.

Hagekull, B. (1994). Infant temperament and early childhood functioning: Possible relations to the Five-Factor Model. In C. J. Halverson, Jr., G. A. Kohnstamm, & R. P. Martin (Eds.), *The developing structure of temperament and personality* (pp. 227–240). Hillsdale, NJ: Erlbaum.

Hagekull, B., & Bohlin, G. (1981). Individual stability in dimensions of infant behavior. *Infant Behavior and Development, 4,* 97–108.

Hagekull, B., & Bohlin, G. (1995). Day care quality, family and child characteristics, and socioemotional development. *Early Childhood Research Quarterly, 10,* 505–526.

Hagekull, B., Bohlin, G., & Lindhagen, K. (1984). Validity of parental reports. *Infant Behavior and Development, 7,* 77–92.

Haith, M. M., & Campos, J. J. (Vol. Eds.) & P. H. Mussen (Series Ed.). (1983). *Handbook of child psychology: Vol. 2. Infancy and developmental psychobiology* (4th ed.). New York: Wiley.

Halverson, C. F., Jr., Kohnstamm, G. A., & Martin, R. P. (Eds.). (1994). *The developing structure of temperament and personality from infancy to adulthood.* Hillsdale, NJ: Erlbaum.

Harley, C. W. (1987). A role for norepinephrine in arousal, emotion and learning? Limbic modulation for norepinephrine and the Kety hypothesis. *Progress in Neuro-Pharmacology and Biological Psychiatry, 11,* 419–458.

Harman, C., Posner, M. I., & Rothbart, M. K. (in press). Distress and attention interaction in early infancy. *Motivation and Emotion.*

Harter, S. (1978). Effectance motivation reconsidered: Toward a developmental model. *Human Development, 21,* 34–64.

Hegvik, R. L., McDevitt, S. C., & Carey, W. B. (1982). The Middle Childhood Temperament Questionnaire. *Journal of Developmental and Behavioral Pediatrics, 3,* 197–200.

Henderson, N. D. (1982). Human behavior genetics. *Annual Review of Psychology, 33,* 403–440.

Henry, B., Caspi, A., Moffitt, T. E., & Silva, P. A. (in press). Temperamental and familial predictors of violent and nonviolent criminal convictions: From age three to age eighteen. *Developmental Psychology.*

Henry, J. (1973). *Pathways to madness.* New York: Vintage Books.

Hershey, K. (1992). *Concurrent and longitudinal relationships of temperament to children's laboratory performance and behavior problems.* Unpublished doctoral dissertation, University of Oregon, Eugene.

Hinde, R. A. (1989). Temperament as an intervening variable. In G. A. Kohnstamm, J. E. Bates, & M. K. Rothbart (Eds.), *Temperament in childhood* (pp. 27–33). Chichester, England: Wiley.

Honzik, M. P. (1965). Prediction of behavior from birth to maturity. *Merrill-Palmer Quarterly, 11,* 77–88.

Hubert, N. C., Wachs, T. D., Peters-Martin, P., & Gandour, M. J. (1982). The study of early temperament: Measurement and conceptual issues. *Child Development, 53,* 571–600.

Huffman, L. C., Bryan, Y. E., del Carmen, R., Petersen, F. A., & Porges, S. W. (1992). *Autonomic correlates of reactivity and self-regulation at twelve-weeks-of-age.* Unpublished manuscript, National Institute of Mental Health, Rockville, MD.

Hüttunen, M. O., & Nyman, G. (1982). On the continuity, change and clinical value of infant temperament in a prospective epidemiological study. In R. Porter & G. M. Collins (Eds.), *Temperamental differences in infants and young children* (pp. 240–247). Ciba Foundation Symposium 89. London: Pitman.

Izard, C. E., Haynes, O. M., Chisholm, G., & Baak, K. (1991). Emotional determinants of infant-mother attachment. *Child Development, 62,* 906–917.

Izard, C. E., Porges, S. W., Simons, R. F., Haynes, O. M., Hyde, C., Parisi, M., & Cohen, B. (1991). Infant cardiac activity: Developmental changes and relations with attachment. *Developmental Psychology, 27,* 432–439.

John, O. P., Caspi, A., Robins, R. W., Moffitt, T. E., & Stouthamer-Loeber, M. (1994). The "Little Five": Exploring the nomological network of the Five-Factor Model of personality in adolescent boys. *Child Development, 65,* 160–178.

Johnson, M. H., Posner, M. I., & Rothbart, M. K. (1991). Components of visual orienting in early infancy: Contingency learning, anticipatory looking and disengaging. *Journal of Cognitive Neuroscience, 3,* 335–344.

Jones, H. E. (1960). The longitudinal method in the study of personality. In I. Iscoe & H. W. Stevenson (Eds.), *Personality development in children* (pp. 3–27). Chicago: University of Chicago Press.

Kagan, J. (1982). The construct of difficult temperament: A reply to Thomas, Chess and Korn. *Merrill-Palmer Quarterly, 28,* 21–24.

Kagan, J. (1994). *Galen's prophecy: Temperament in human nature.* New York: Basic Books.

Kagan, J., Kearsley, R. B., & Zelazo, P. R. (1978). *Infancy: Its place in human development.* Cambridge, MA: Harvard University Press.

Kagan, J., & Moss, H. A. (1962). *Birth to maturity.* New York: Wiley.

Kagan, J., Reznick, J. S., & Snidman, N. (1988). Biological bases of childhood shyness. *Science, 240,* 167–171.

Kashani, J. H., Ezpeleta, L., Dandoy, A. C., Doi, S., & Reid, J. C. (1991). Psychiatric disorders in children and adolescents: The contribution of the child's temperament and the parents' psychopathology and attitudes. *Canadian Journal of Psychiatry, 36,* 569–573.

Katz, L. F., & Gottman, J. M. (1995). Vagal tone protects children from marital conflict. *Development and Psychopathology, 7,* 83–92.

Keenan, K., & Shaw, D. S. (1994). The development of aggression in toddlers: A study of low-income families. *Journal of Abnormal Child Psychology, 22,* 53–77.

Kenrick, D. T., & Funder, D. C. (1988). Profiting from controversy: Lessons from the person-situation debate. *American Psychologist, 43,* 23–34.

Keogh, B. (1989). Applying temperament research to school. In G. A. Kohnstamm, J. E. Bates, & M. K. Rothbart (Eds.), *Temperament in childhood* (pp. 437–450). Chichester, England: Wiley.

Keogh, B., Pullis, M. E., & Caldwell, J. (1982). A short form of the Teacher Temperament Questionnaire. *Journal of Educational Measurement, 19,* 323–329.

Kessen, W. (1965). *The child.* New York: Wiley.

King, B. R., & Wachs, T. D. (1995, March). *Multimethod measurement of stimulus sensitivity in infants, preschoolers, and parents.* Poster presented at the biennial meeting of the Society for Research in Child Development, Indianapolis, IN.

Kinsbourne, M., & Bemporad, B. (1984). Lateralization of emotion: A model and the evidence. In N. A. Fox & R. J. Davidson (Eds.), *The psychology of affective development* (pp. 259–292). Hillsdale, NJ: Erlbaum.

Kistiakovskaia, M. I. (1965). Stimuli evoking positive emotions in infants in the first months of life. *Soviet Psychology and Psychiatry, 3,* 39–48.

Kochanska, G. (1991). Socialization and temperament in the development of guilt and conscience. *Child Development, 62,* 1379–1392.

Kochanska, G. (1993). Toward a synthesis of parental socialization and child temperament in early development of conscience. *Child Development, 64,* 325–347.

Kochanska, G. (1995). Children's temperament, mothers' discipline, and security of attachment: Multiple pathways to emerging internalization. *Child Development, 66,* 597–615.

Kochanska, G., & Aksan, N. (1995). Mother-child mutually positive affect, the quality of child compliance to requests and prohibitions, and maternal control as correlates of early internalization. *Child Development, 66,* 236–254.

Kochanska, G., DeVet, K., Goldman, M., Murray, K., & Putnam, S. P. (1993). *Conscience development and temperament in young children.* Unpublished manuscript.

Kohnstamm, G. A., Mervielde, I., Besevegis, E., & Halverson, C. F., Jr. (1995). Tracing the Big Five in parents' free descriptions of their children. *European Journal of Personality, 9,* 283–304.

Korner, A. F. (1964). Some hypotheses regarding the significance of individual differences at birth for later development. *The Psychoanalytic Study of the Child, 19,* 58–72.

Korner, A. F., Hutchinson, C. A., Koperski, J., Kraemer, H. C., & Schneider, P. A. (1981). Stability of individual differences of neonatal motor and crying patterns. *Child Development, 52,* 83–90.

Korner, A. F., Zeanah, C. H., Linden, J., Kraemer, H. C., Berkowitz, R. I., & Agras, W. S. (1985). Relation between neonatal and later activity and temperament. *Child Development, 56,* 38–42.

Krakow, J. B., & Johnson, K. L. (1981, April). *The emergence and consolidation of self-control processes from 18 to 30 months-of-age.* Paper presented at the meetings of the Society for Research in Child Development, Boston.

Krakow, J. B., Kopp, C. B., & Vaughn, B. E. (1981, April). *Sustained attention during the second year: Age trends, individual differences, and implications for development.* Paper presented at the meetings of the Society for Research in Child Development, Boston.

Kramer, P. D. (1993). *Listening to prozac.* New York: Viking.

Lang, P. J., Bradley, M. M., & Cuthbert, B. N. (in press). Motivated attention: Affect, activation, and action. In P. J. Lang, R. F. Simmons, & M. Balaban (Eds.), *Attention and orienting.* Hillsdale, NJ: Erlbaum.

Lanthier, R. P., & Bates, J. E. (1995, May). *Infancy era predictors of the Big Five personality dimensions in adolescence.* Paper presented at the 1995 meetings of the Midwestern Psychological Association, Chicago.

Larson, S. K., DiPietro, J. A., & Porges, S. M. (1987, April). *Neonatal and NBAS performance are related to development across at 15 months.* Paper presented at meetings of Society for Research in Child Development, Baltimore.

LeDoux, J. E. (1987). Emotion. In F. Plum (Ed.), *Handbook of physiology. Section 1: The nervous system: Vol. 5. Higher functions of the brain, Part 1.* Bethesda, MD: American Physiological Society.

LeDoux, J. E. (1989). Cognitive-emotional interactions in the brain. *Cognition and Emotion, 3,* 267–289.

Lee, C. L., & Bates, J. E. (1985). Mother-child interaction at age two years and perceived difficult temperament. *Child Development, 56,* 1314–1325.

Lerner, J. V., & Lerner, R. M. (1994). Explorations of the goodness-of-fit model in early adolescence. In W. B. Carey & S. C. McDevitt (Eds.), *Prevention and early intervention: Individual differences as risk factors for the mental health of children. A festschrift for Stella Chess and Alexander Thomas* (pp. 161–169). New York: Brunner/Mazel.

Lewis, M., & Feiring, C. (1989). Infant, mother, and mother-infant interaction behavior and subsequent attachment. *Child Development, 60,* 831–837.

Loehlin, J. C., & Nichols, R. C. (1976). *Heredity, environment, and personality: A study of 850 twins.* Austin: University of Texas Press.

Luria, A. R. (1961). *The role of speech in the regulation of normal and abnormal behavior.* New York: Liveright.

Luria, A. R. (1966). *Higher cortical functions in man.* New York: Basic Books.

Luria, A. R. (1973). *The working brain: An introduction to neuropsychology.* New York: Basic Books.

Lytton, H. (1990). Child and parent effects in boys' conduct disorder: A reinterpretation. *Developmental Psychology, 26,* 683–697.

Lytton, H. (1995, March). *Child and family factors as predictors of conduct disorder and criminality.* Paper presented at biennial meetings of the Society for Research in Child Development, Indianapolis, IN.

Maccoby, E. E., & Masters, J. C. (1970). Attachment and dependency. In P. H. Mussen (Ed.), *Manual of child psychology* (3rd ed.) (Vol. 2, pp. 73–157). New York: Wiley.

MacDonald, K. (1988). *Social and personality development: An evolutionary synthesis.* New York: Plenum Press.

MacDonald, K. (1992). Warmth as a developmental construct: An evolutionary analysis. *Child Development, 63,* 753–773.

Malatesta, C. A., Culver, C., Tesman, J. R., & Shepard, B. (1989). The development of emotion expression during the first two years of life. *Monographs of the Society for Research in Child Development, 54*(1/2, Serial No. 219).

Manassis, K., & Bradley, S. J. (1994). The development of childhood anxiety disorders: Toward an integrated model. *Journal of Applied Developmental Psychology, 15,* 345–366.

Mangelsdorf, S., Gunnar, M., Kestenbaum, R., Lang, S., & Andreas, D. (1990). Infant proneness-to-distress temperament, maternal personality, and mother-infant attachment: Associations and goodness of fit. *Child Development, 61,* 820–831.

Martin, R. P. (1989). Activity level, distractibility and persistence: Critical characteristics in early schooling. In G. A. Kohnstamm, J. E. Bates, & M. K. Rothbart (Eds.), *Temperament in childhood* (pp. 451–461). Chichester, England: Wiley.

Martin, R. P., Olejnik, S., & Gaddis, L. (1994). Is temperament an important contributor to schooling outcomes in elementary school? Modeling effects of temperament and scholastic ability on academic achievement. In W. B. Carey & S. C. McDevitt (Eds.), *Prevention and early intervention: Individual differences as risk factors for the mental health of children. A festschrift for Stella Chess and Alexander Thomas* (pp. 59–68). New York: Brunner/Mazel.

Martin, R. P., Wisenbaker, J., & Hüttunen, M. (1994). The factor structure of instruments based on the Chess-Thomas model of temperament: Implications for the Big Five Model. In C. F. Halverson, G. A. Kohnstamm, & R. P. Martin (Eds.), *The developing structure of temperament and personality from infancy to adulthood.* Hillsdale, NJ: Erlbaum.

Matheny, A. P., Jr. (1987). Developmental research of twins' temperament. *Acta Geneticae Medicae et Gemellologiae, 36,* 135–143.

Matheny, A. P., Jr. (1989). Children's behavioral inhibition over age and across situations: Genetic similarity for a trait during change. Long-term stability and change in personality [Special issue]. *Journal of Personality, 57,* 215–235.

Matheny, A. P., Jr. (1991). Children's unintentional injuries and gender: Differentiation by environmental and psychosocial aspects. *Children's Environment Quarterly, 8,* 51–61.

Matheny, A. P., Jr. (1995, June–July). *Temperament stability and genetic influences for questionnaires from infancy to 9 years.* Paper presented at the meeting of the International Society for the Study of Behavioral Development, Amsterdam, The Netherlands.

Matheny, A. P., Jr., Riese, M. L., & Wilson, R. S. (1985). Rudiments of infant temperament: Newborn to nine months. *Developmental Psychology, 21,* 486–494.

Matheny, A. P., Jr., Wilson, R. S., & Thoben, A. S. (1987). Home and mother: Relations with infant temperament. *Developmental Psychology, 23,* 323–331.

Maziade, M. (1989). Should adverse temperament matter to the clinician? In G. A. Kohnstamm, J. E. Bates, & M. K. Rothbart (Eds.), *Temperament in childhood* (pp. 421–435). Chichester, England: Wiley.

McCall, R. B. (1979). Qualitative transitions in behavioral development in the first two years of life. In M. H. Bornstein & W. Kessen (Eds.), *Psychological development from infancy: Image to intention* (pp. 183–224). Hillsdale, NJ: Erlbaum.

McClowry, S. G., Giangrande, S. K., Tommasini, N. R., Clinton, W., Foreman, N. S., Lynch, K., & Ferketich, S. L. (1994). The effects of child temperament, maternal characteristics, and family circumstances on the maladjustment of school-age children. *Research in Nursing & Health, 17,* 25–35.

McClowry, S. G., Hegvik, R., & Teglasi, H. (1993). An examination of the construct validity of the Middle Childhood Temperament Questionnaire. *Merrill-Palmer Quarterly, 39,* 279–293.

McDevitt, S. C., & Carey, W. F. (1981). Stability of ratings vs. perceptions of temperament from early infancy to 1–3 years. *American Journal of Orthopsychiatry, 51,* 342–345.

McFadyen-Ketchum, S. A., Bates, J. E., Dodge, K. A., & Pettit, G. S. (1996). Patterns of change in early childhood aggressive-disruptive behavior: Gender differences in predictions from early coercive and affectionate mother-child interactions. *Child Development, 67,* 2417–2433.

Mebert, C. J. (1991). Dimensions of subjectivity in parents' ratings of infant temperament. *Child Development, 62,* 352–361.

Medoff-Cooper, B., Carey, W. B., & McDevitt, S. C. (1993). The Early Infancy Temperament Questionnaire. *Journal of Developmental and Behavioral Pediatrics, 14,* 230–235.

Melvin, N., & McClowry, S. (1995). Clinical applications of children's temperament. *Journal of Pediatric Nursing, 10,* 139–140.

Miller, E. M., & Bates, J. E. (1986, April). *Relationships between mother perceptions and observed episodes of infant distress: Components of perceived difficult temperament.* Paper presented at the meetings of the International Conference on Infant Studies, Los Angeles.

Mischel, W. (1983). Delay of gratification as process and as person variable in development. In D. Magnusson & V. P. Allen (Eds.), *Human development: An interactional perspective* (pp. 149–165). New York: Academic Press.

Moskowitz, D. S., & Schwarz, J. C. (1982). Validity comparison of behavior counts and ratings by knowledgeable informants. *Journal of Personality and Social Psychology, 42,* 518–528.

Murphy, L. B., & Moriarty, A. E. (1976). *Vulnerability, coping, and growth: From infancy to adolescence.* New Haven, CT: Yale University Press.

Nachmias, M., Gunnar, M., Mangelsdorf, S., & Parritz, R. H. (1996). Behavioral inhibition and stress reactivity: The moderating role of attachment security. *Child Development, 67,* 508–522.

Needham, J. (1973). *Chinese science.* Cambridge, MA: MIT Press.

Neilon, P. (1948). Shirley's babies after 15 years. *Journal of Genetic Psychology, 73,* 175–186.

Nelson, C. A. (1994). Neural bases of infant temperament. In J. E. Bates & T. D. Wachs (Eds.), *Temperament: Individual differences at the interface of biology and behavior* (pp. 47–82). Washington, DC: American Psychological Association.

Netter, P., & Rammsayer, T. (1991). Reactivity to dopaminergic drugs and aggression related personality traits. *Personality and Individual Differences, 12,* 1009–1017.

Newman, J. P., Widom, C. S., & Nathan, S. (1985). Passive avoidance in syndromes of disinhibition: Psychopathy and extraversion. *Journal of Personality and Social Psychology, 48,* 1316–1327.

Norman, D. A., & Shallice, T. (1986). Attention to action: Willed and automatic control of behavior. In R. J. Davidson, G. E. Schwartz, & D. Shapiro (Eds.), *Consciousness and self-regulation* (pp. 1–18). New York: Plenum Press.

Olson, S. L. (1992). Development of conduct problems and peer rejection in preschool children: A social systems analysis. *Journal of Abnormal Child Psychology, 20,* 327–350.

Olson, S. L., Bates, J. E., & Bayles, K. (1990). Early antecedents of childhood impulsivity: The role of parent-child interaction, cognitive competence, and temperament. *Journal of Abnormal Child Psychology, 18,* 317–334.

Orth, L. C., & Martin, R. P. (1994). Interactive effects of student temperament and instruction method on classroom behavior and achievement. *Journal of School Psychology, 32,* 149–166.

Osofsky, J. D. (1979). *Handbook of infant development.* New York: Wiley.

Ostrander, E. A., Sprague, G. F., Jr., & Rive, J. (1993). Identification and characterization of dinucleotide repeat (CA) on marker for genetic mapping in dogs. *Genomes, 16,* 207–213.

Panksepp, J. (1982). Toward a general psychobiological theory of emotions. *Behavioral and Brain Sciences, 5,* 407–467.

Panksepp, J. (1986a). The anatomy of emotions. In R. Plutchik & H. Kellerman (Eds.), *Emotion: Theory, research and experience: Vol. 3. Biological foundations of emotions* (pp. 91–124). San Diego, CA: Academic Press.

Panksepp, J. (1986b). The neurochemistry of behavior. *Annual Review of Psychology, 37,* 77–107.

Panksepp, J. (1993). Neurochemical control of moods and emotions: Amino acids to neuropeptides. In M. Lewis & J. M. Haviland (Eds.), *Handbook of emotions* (pp. 87–107). New York: Guilford Press.

Patterson, C. M., Kosson, D. S., & Newman, J. P. (1987). Reaction to punishment, reflectivity and passive avoidance learning in extraverts. *Journal of Personality and Social Psychology, 52,* 565–575.

Patterson, G. R. (1980). Mothers: The unacknowledged victims. *Monographs of the Society for Research in Child Development, 45*(5, Serial No. 186).

Patterson, G. R., Reid, J. B., & Dishion, T. J. (1992). *Antisocial boys.* Eugene, OR: Castalia Press.

Pavlov, I. P. (1955). General types of animal and human higher nervous activity. *Selected works.* Moscow: Foreign Language Publishing House. (Original work published 1935)

Pedlow, R., Sanson, A. V., Prior, M., & Oberklaid, F. (1993). The stability of temperament from infancy to eight years. *Developmental Psychology, 29,* 998–1007.

Persson-Blennow, I., & McNeil, T. F. (1980). Questionnaires for measurement of temperament in one- and two-year-old children: Development and standardization. *Journal of Child Psychology and Psychiatry, 21,* 37–46.

Peters-Martin, P., & Wachs, T. (1984). A longitudinal study of temperament and its correlates in the first 12 months. *Infant Behavior and Development, 7,* 285–298.

Plomin, R., & Bergeman, C. S. (1991). The nature of nurture: Genetic influences on "environmental" measures. *Behavioral and Brain Sciences, 14,* 373–427.

Plomin, R., Chipuer, H. M., & Loehlin, J. C. (1990). Behavioral genetics and personality. In L. A. Pervin (Ed.), *Handbook of personality theory and research* (pp. 225–243). New York: Guilford Press.

Plomin, R., Emde, R. N., Braungart, J. M., Campos, J., Corley, R., Fulker, D. W., Kagan, J., Reznick, J. S., Robinson, J., Zahn-Waxler, C., & DeFries, J. C. (1993). Genetic change and continuity from fourteen to twenty months: The MacArthur Longitudinal Twin Study. *Child Development, 64,* 1354–1376.

Porges, S. W. (1986.) Respiratory sinus arrhythmia: Physiological basis, quantitative methods, and clinical implications. In P. Grossman, K. Janssen, & D. Vaitl (Eds.), *Cardiorespiratory and cardiosomatic psychophysiology* (pp. 101–115). New York: Plenum Press.

Porges, S. W. (1991). Autonomic regulation and attention. In B. A. Campbell, H. Hayne, & R. Richardson (Eds.), *Attention and information processing in infants and adults* (pp. 201–223). Hillsdale, NJ: Erlbaum.

Porges, S. W., & Doussard-Roosevelt, J. A. (in press). The psychophysiology of temperament. In J. D. Noshpitz (Ed.), *Handbook of child and adolescent psychiatry.* New York: Wiley.

Porges, S. W., Doussard-Roosevelt, J. A., & Maiti, A. K. (1994). Vagal tone and the physiological regulation of emotion. In N. A. Fox (Ed.), Emotion regulation: Behavioral and biological considerations. *Monograph of the Society for Research in Child Development, 59*(2/3, Serial No. 240), 167–186.

Porges, S. W., Doussard-Roosevelt, J. A., Portales, A. L., & Suess, P. E. (1995). Cardiac vagal tone: Stability and relation to difficultness in infants and 3-year-olds. *Developmental Psychobiology, 27,* 289–300.

Posner, M. I., & Petersen, S. E. (1990). The attention system of the human brain. *Annual Review of Neuroscience, 13,* 25–42.

Posner, M. I., & Raichle, M. E. (1994). *Images of mind.* New York: Scientific American Library.

Posner, M. I., & Rothbart, M. K. (1991). Attentional mechanisms and conscious experience. In M. Rugg & A. D. Milner (Eds.), *The neuropsychology of consciousness* (pp. 91–112). London: Academic Press.

Posner, M. I., & Rothbart, M. K. (1994). Constructing neuronal theories of mind. In C. Koch & J. Davis (Eds.), *High level neuronal theories of the brain* (pp. 183–199). Cambridge, MA: MIT Press.

Posner, M. I., Rothbart, M. K., & Harman, C. (1994). Cognitive science contributions to culture and emotion. In S. Kitayama & H. R. Markus (Eds.), *Culture and emotion* (pp. 197–216). Washington, DC: American Psychological Association.

Presley, R., & Martin, R. P. (1994). Toward a structure of preschool temperament: Factor structure of the Temperament Assessment Battery for Children. *Journal of Personality, 62,* 415–448.

Pulkkinen, K., & Pitkanen, T. (1994). A prospective study of the precursors to problem drinking in young adulthood. *Journal of Studies on Alcohol, 55,* 578–587.

Pulkkinen, L. (1995). Behavioral precursors to accidents and resulting physical impairment. *Child Development, 66,* 1660–1679.

Quay, H. C. (1993). The psychobiology of undersocialized aggressive conduct disorder: A theoretical perspective. Toward a developmental perspective on conduct disorder. *Development and Psychopathology, 5,* 165–180.

Radke-Yarrow, M., & Sherman, T. (1990). Hard growing: Children who survive. In J. E. Rolf, A. S. Masten, D. Cicchetti, K. H. Neuchterlein, & S. Weintraub (Eds.), *Risk and protective factors in the development of psychopathology* (pp. 97–119). New York: Cambridge University Press.

Reed, M. A., Pien, D. P., & Rothbart, M. K. (1984). Inhibitory self-control in preschool children. *Merrill-Palmer Quarterly, 30,* 131–147.

Reid, J. B., & Patterson, G. R. (1989). The development of antisocial behaviour patterns in childhood and adolescence. *European Journal of Personality, 3,* 107–119.

Rende, R. D. (1993). Longitudinal relations between temperament traits and behavioral syndromes in middle childhood. *Journal of the American Academy of Child and Adolescent Psychiatry, 32,* 287–290.

Richards, J. E., & Cameron, D. (1989). Infant heart rate variability and behavioral developmental status. *Infant Behavior and Development, 12,* 45–58.

Riese, M. L. (1987). Temperamental stability between the neonatal period and 24 months. *Developmental Psychology, 23,* 216–222.

Rizzo, T. A., Corsaro, W. A., & Bates J. E. (1992). Ethnographic methods and interpretive analysis: Expanding the methodological options of psychologists. *Developmental Review, 12,* 101–123.

Rothbart, M. K. (1981). Measurement of temperament in infancy. *Child Development, 52,* 569–578.

Rothbart, M. K. (1986). Longitudinal observation of infant temperament. *Developmental Psychology, 22,* 356–365.

Rothbart, M. K. (1987). A psychobiological approach to the study of temperament. In G. Kohnstam (Ed.), *Temperament discussed* (pp. 63–72). Amsterdam, The Netherlands: Swets & Zeitlinger.

Rothbart, M. K. (1988). Temperament and the development of inhibited approach. *Child Development, 59,* 1241–1250.

Rothbart, M. K. (1989a). Biological processes of temperament. In G. Kohnstamm, J. Bates, & M. K. Rothbart (Eds.), *Temperament in childhood* (pp. 77–110). Chichester, England: Wiley.

Rothbart, M. K. (1989b). Temperament and development. In G. Kohnstamm, J. Bates, & M. K. Rothbart (Eds.), *Temperament in childhood* (pp. 187–248). Chichester, England: Wiley.

Rothbart, M. K. (1995). Concept and method in contemporary temperament research. Review of J. Kagan, *Galen's prophecy. Psychological Inquiry, 6,* 334–348.

Rothbart, M. K., & Ahadi, S. A. (1994). Temperament and the development of personality. *Journal of Abnormal Psychology, 103,* 55–66.

Rothbart, M. K., Ahadi, S. A., & Hershey, K. L. (1994). Temperament and social behavior in childhood. *Merrill-Palmer Quarterly, 40,* 21–39.

Rothbart, M. K., & Derryberry, D. (1981). Development of individual differences in temperament. In M. E. Lamb & A. L. Brown (Eds.), *Advances in developmental psychology* (Vol. 1, pp. 37–86). Hillsdale, NJ: Erlbaum.

Rothbart, M. K., Derryberry, D., & Hershey, K. (1995). *Stability of temperament in childhood: Laboratory infant assessment to parent report at seven years.* Unpublished manuscript.

Rothbart, M. K., Derryberry, D., & Posner, M. I. (1994). A psychobiological approach to the development of temperament. In J. E. Bates & T. D. Wachs (Eds.), *Temperament: Individual differences at the interface of biology and behavior* (pp. 83–116). Washington, DC: American Psychological Association.

Rothbart, M. K., & Goldsmith, H. H. (1985). Three approaches to the study of infant temperament. *Developmental Review, 5,* 237–260.

Rothbart, M. K., & Mauro, J. A. (1990). Questionnaire approaches to the study of infant temperament. In J. W. Fagen & J. Colombo (Eds.), *Individual differences in infancy: Reliability, stability and prediction* (pp. 411–429). Hillsdale, NJ: Erlbaum.

Rothbart, M. K., Posner, M. I., & Hershey, K. L. (1995). Temperament, attention, and developmental psychopathology. In D. Cicchetti & D. J. Cohen (Eds.), *Manual of developmental psychopathology* (Vol. 1, pp. 315–340). New York: Wiley.

Rothbart, M. K., Posner, M. I., & Rosicky, J. (1994). Orienting in normal and pathological development. *Development and Psychopathology, 6,* 635–652.

Rothbart, M. K., Ziaie, H., & O'Boyle, C. G. (1992). Self-regulation and emotion in infancy. In N. Eisenberg & R. A. Fabes (Eds.), *Emotion and its regulation in early development. New Directions for Child Development, 55,* 7–24.

Rowe, D. C., & Plomin, R. (1977). Temperament in early childhood. *Journal of Personality Assessment, 41,* 150–156.

Rubin, K. H., Coplan, R. J., Fox, N. A., & Calkins, S. D. (1995). Emotionality, emotion regulation, and preschoolers' social adaptation. *Development and Psychopathology, 7,* 49–62.

Ruff, H. A., & Rothbart, M. K. (1996). *Attention in early development: Themes and variations.* New York: Oxford University Press.

Rushton, J. P., Brainerd, C. J., & Presley, N. (1983). Behavioral development and construct validity: The principle of aggregation. *Psychological Bulletin, 94,* 18–38.

St. James-Roberts, I., Bowyer, J., Varghese, S., & Sawdon, J. (1994). Infant crying patterns in Manali and London. *Child: Care, Health & Development, 20,* 323–337.

St. James-Roberts, I., & Plewis, I. (1996). Individual differences, daily fluctuations, and developmental changes in amounts of infant waking, fussing, crying, feeding, and sleeping. *Child Development, 67,* 2527–2540.

Saltz, E., Campbell, S., & Skotko, D. (1983). Verbal control of behavior: The effects of shouting. *Developmental Psychology, 19,* 461–464.

Sanson, A. V., Pedlow, R., Cann, W., Prior, M., & Oberklaid, F. (1996). Shyness ratings: Stability and correlates in early childhood. *International Journal of Behavioural Development, 19,* 705–724.

Sanson, A. V., Prior, M., Garino, E., Oberklaid, F., & Sewell, J. (1987). The structure of infant temperament: Factor analysis of the Revised Infant Temperament Questionnaire. *Infant Behavior and Development, 10,* 97–104.

Sanson, A. V., Prior, M., & Kyrios, M. (1990). Contamination of measures in temperament research. *Merrill-Palmer Quarterly, 36,* 179–192.

Sanson, A. V., Prior, M., & Oberklaid, F. (1985). Normative data on temperament in Australian infants. *Australian Journal of Psychology, 37,* 185–195.

Sanson, A. V., Prior, M., & Oberklaid, F. (1991, April). *Structure and stability of temperament in the Australian Temperament Project.* Paper presented at the meetings of the Society for Research in Child Development, Seattle, WA.

Sanson, A. V., & Rothbart, M. K. (1995). Child temperament and parenting. In M. Bornstein (Ed.), *Parenting* (Vol. 4, pp. 299–321). Hillsdale, NJ: Erlbaum.

Sanson, A. V., Smart, D., Prior, M., & Oberklaid, F. (1993). Precursors of hyperactivity and aggression. *Journal of the American Academy of Child and Adolescent Psychiatry, 32,* 1207–1216.

Sanson, A. V., Smart, D. F., Prior, Oberklaid, F., & Pedlow, R. (1994). The structure of temperament from three to seven years: Age, sex and sociodemographic influences. *Merrill-Palmer Quarterly, 40,* 233–252.

Saudino, K. J., & Eaton, W. O. (1993). *Genetic influences on activity level: II. An analysis of continuity and change from infancy to early childhood.* Manuscript submitted for publication.

Scarr, S., & McCartney, K. (1983). How people make their own environments: A theory of genotype-environment effects. *Child Development, 54,* 424–435.

Schaffer, H. R. (1974). Cognitive components of the infant's response to strangeness. In M. Lewis & L. A. Rosenblum (Eds.), *The origins of fear* (pp. 11–24). New York: Wiley.

Schaffer, H. R., & Emerson, P. E. (1964). Patterns of response to physical contact in early human development. *Journal of Child Psychology and Psychiatry, 5,* 1–13.

Schneirla, T. C. (1959). An evolutionary and developmental theory of biphasic processes underlying approach and withdrawal. In M. R. Jones (Ed.), *Nebraska Symposium on Motivation* (Vol. 7, pp. 297–339). Lincoln: University of Nebraska Press.

Schore, A. N. (1994). *Affect regulation and the origin of the self: The neurobiology of emotional development.* Hillsdale, NJ: Erlbaum.

Sears, R. R., Maccoby, E. E., & Levin, H. (1957). *Patterns of child rearing.* Evanston, IL: Row, Peterson.

Seifer, R., Sameroff, A. J., Barrett, L. C., & Krafchuk, E. (1994). Infant temperament measured by multiple observations and mother report. *Child Development, 65,* 1478–1490.

Seifer, R., & Schiller, M. (in press). The role of parenting sensitivity, infant temperament, and dyadic interaction in attachment theory and assessment. *Monographs of the Society for Research in Child Development.*

Seifer, R., Schiller, M., Sameroff, A. J., Resnick, S., & Riordan, K. (1996). Attachment, maternal sensitivity, and temperament during the first year of life. *Developmental Psychology, 32,* 3–11.

Shaw, D. S., & Vondra, J. I. (1995). Infant attachment security and maternal predictors of early behavior problems: A longitudinal study of low-income families. *Journal of Abnormal Child Psychology, 23,* 335–357.

Shaw, D. S., Vondra, J. I., Hommerding, K. D., Keenan, K., & Dunn, M. (1994). Chronic family adversity and early child behavior problems: A longitudinal study of low income families. *Journal of Child Psychology and Psychiatry, 35,* 1109–1122.

Sheldon, W. H., & Stevens, S. S. (1942). *The varieties of human temperament.* New York: Harper & Row.

Shirley, M. M. (1933). *The first two years: A study of 25 babies.* Minneapolis: University of Minnesota Press.

Shoda, Y., Mischel, W., & Peake, P. K. (1990). Predicting adolescent cognitive and self-regulatory competencies from preschool delay of gratification: Identifying diagnostic conditions. *Developmental Psychology, 26,* 978–986.

Silverman, I. W., & Ragusa, D. M. (1992). A short-term longitudinal study of the early development of self-regulation. *Journal of Abnormal Child Psychology, 20,* 415–435.

Slabach, E. H., Morrow, J., & Wachs, T. D. (1991). Questionnaire measurement of infant and child temperament: Current status and future directions. In J. Strelau & A. Angleitner (Eds.), *Explorations in temperament: International perspectives on theory and measurement* (pp. 205–234). New York: Plenum Press.

Snyder, J. A. (1977). A reinforcement analysis of interaction in problem and nonproblem children. *Journal of Abnormal Psychology, 86,* 528–535.

Spoont, M. R. (1992). Modulatory role of serotonin in neural information processing: Implications for human psychopathology. *Psychological Bulletin, 112,* 330–350.

Sroufe, L. A. (1979). The coherence of individual development. *American Psychologist, 34,* 834–841.

Sroufe, L. A. (1985). Attachment classification from the perspective of infant-caregiver relationships and infant temperament. *Child Development, 56,* 1–14.

Stevenson, J., Thompson, M., & Sonuga-Barke, E. (1996). The mental health of preschool children and their mothers in a mixed urban/rural population: III. Latent variable models. *British Journal of Psychiatry, 168,* 26–32.

Stifter, C. A. (1995). Approach/withdrawal processes in infancy: The relationship between parasympathetic tone and infant temperament. In K. E. Hood, G. Greenberg, & E. Tobach (Eds.), *Behavioral development: Concepts of approach/withdrawal and integrative levels* (pp. 371–395). New York: Garland.

Stifter, C. A., & Fox, N. A. (1990). Infant reactivity: Physiological correlates of newborn and five month temperament. *Developmental Psychology, 26,* 582–588.

Stifter, C. A., Fox, N. A., & Porges, S. W. (1989). Facial expressivity and vagal tone in 5- and 10-month-old infants. *Infant Behavior and Development, 12,* 127–137.

Stoneman, Z., & Brody, G. H. (1993). Sibling temperaments, conflict, warmth, and role asymmetry. *Child Development, 64,* 1786–1800.

Strelau, J. (1983). *Temperament personality activity.* New York: Academic Press.

Sullivan, M. W., Lewis, M., & Alessandri, S. M. (1992). Cross-age stability in emotional expressions during learning and extinction. *Developmental Psychology, 28,* 58–63.

Suomi, S. J. (1986). Anxiety-like disorders in young nonhuman primates. In R. Gittelman (Ed.), *Anxiety disorders of childhood* (pp. 1–23). New York: Guilford Press.

Suomi, S. J., & Novak, M. A. (1991). The role of individual differences in promoting psychological well-being in rhesus monkeys. In M. A. Novak & A. J. Petto (Eds.), *Through the looking glass: Issues of psychological well-being in captive nonhuman primates* (pp. 50–56). Washington, DC: American Psychological Association.

Super, C. M., & Harkness, S. (1994). The cultural regulation of temperament-environment interactions. In M. K. Lohmander (Series Ed.), *Researching early childhood* (Vol. 2, pp. 19–53). Gothenburg, Sweden: Goteborg University Press.

Tarter, R. E. (1988). Are there inherited behavioral traits that predispose to substance abuse? *Journal of Consulting and Clinical Psychology, 56,* 189–196.

Teglasi, H., & MacMahon, B. V. (1990). Temperament and common problem behaviors of children. *Journal of Applied Developmental Psychology, 11,* 331–349.

Tellegen, A. (1985). Structures of mood and personality and their relevance to assessing anxiety, with an emphasis on self-report. In A. H. Tuma & J. D. Maser (Eds.), *Anxiety and the anxiety disorders* (pp. 681–706). Hillsdale, NJ: Erlbaum.

Tellegen, A., Lykken, D. T., Bouchard, T. J., & Wilcox, K. J. (1988). Personality similarity in twins reared apart and together. *Journal of Personality and Social Psychology, 54,* 1031–1039.

Teti, D. M., Nakagawa, M., Das, R., & Wirth, O. (1991). Security of attachment between preschoolers and their mothers: Relations among social interaction, parenting stress, and mothers' sorts of the attachment Q-set. *Developmental Psychology, 27,* 440–447.

Thomas, A., & Chess, S. (1977). *Temperament and development.* New York: Brunner/Mazel.

Thomas, A., Chess, S., & Birch, H. G. (1968). *Temperament and behavior disorders in children.* New York: New York University Press.

Thomas, A., Chess, S., Birch, H. G., Hertzig, M. E., & Korn, S. (1963). *Behavioral individuality in early childhood.* New York: New York University Press.

Thompson, R. A., & Lamb, M. E. (1984). Assessing qualitative dimensions of emotional responsiveness in infants: Separation reactions in the Strange Situation. *Infant Behavior and Development, 7,* 423–445.

Torgerson, A. M., & Kringlen, E. (1978). Genetic aspects of temperamental differences in infants. *Journal of the American Academy of Child Psychiatry, 17,* 433–444.

Trachtenberg, S., & Viken, R. J. (1994). Aggressive boys in the classroom: Biased attributions or shared perceptions? *Child Development, 65,* 829–835.

Tubman, J. G., Lerner, R. M., Lerner, J. V., & von Eye, A. (1992). Temperament and adjustment in young adulthood: A 15-year longitudinal analysis. *American Journal of Orthopsychiatry, 62,* 564–574.

Tuddenham, R. D. (1959). The constancy of personality ratings over two decades. *Genetic Psychology Monograph, 60,* 3–29.

van den Boom, D. C. (1989). Neonatal irritability and the development of attachment. In G. A. Kohnstamm, J. E. Bates, & M. K. Rothbart (Eds.), *Temperament in childhood* (pp. 299–318). Chichester, England: Wiley.

van den Boom, D. C. (1991). The influence of infant irritability on the development of the mother-infant relationship in the first six months of life. In J. K. Nugent, B. M. Lester, & T. B. Brazelton (Eds.), *The cultural context of infancy* (Vol. 2, pp. 63–89). Norwood, NJ: ABLEX.

van den Boom, D. C. (1994). The influence of temperament and mothering on attachment and exploration: An experimental manipulation of sensitive responsiveness among lower-class mothers with irritable infants. *Child Development, 65,* 1457–1477.

van den Boom, D. C., & Hoeksma, J. B. (1994). The effect of infant irritability on mother-infant interaction: A growth-curve analysis. *Developmental Psychology, 30,* 581–590.

Van IJzendoorn, M. H. (1995). Adult attachment representations, parental responsiveness, and infant attachment: A meta-analysis on the predictive validity of the adult attachment interview. *Psychological Bulletin, 117,* 387–403.

Vaughn, B. E., Lefever, G. B., Seifer, R., & Barglow, P. (1989). Attachment behavior, attachment security, and temperament during infancy. *Child Development, 60,* 728–737.

Vaughn, B. E., Stevenson-Hinde, J., Waters, E., Kotsaftis, A., Lefever, G. B., Shouldice, A., Trudel, M., & Belsky, J. (1992). Attachment security and temperament in infancy and early childhood: Some conceptual clarifications. *Developmental Psychology, 28,* 463–473.

Vaughn, B. E., & Waters, E. (1990). Attachment behavior at home and in the laboratory: Q-sort observations and Strange Situation classifications of one-year-olds. *Child Development, 61,* 1965–1973.

Vogt, B. A., Finch, D. M., & Olson, C. R. (1992). Overview: Functional heterogeneity in cingulate cortex: The anterior executive and posterior evaluative regions. *Cerebral Cortex, 2,* 435–443.

von Bargen, D. M. (1983). Infant heart rate: A review of research and methodology. *Merrill-Palmer Quarterly, 29,* 115–149.

Wachs, T. D. (1987). Specificity of environmental action as manifest in environmental correlates of infants' mastery motivation. *Developmental Psychology, 23,* 782–790.

Wachs, T. D. (1992). *The nature of nurture.* Newbury Park, CA: Sage.

Wachs, T. D., & Desai, S. (1993). Parent-report measures of toddler temperament and attachment: Their relation to each other and to the social microenvironment. *Infant Behavior and Development, 16,* 391–396.

Waters, E., & Deane, K. E. (1985). Defining and assessing individual differences in infant attachment relationships: Q-methodology and the organization of behavior. In I. Bretherton & E. Waters (Eds.), Growing points of attachment theory and research. *Monographs of the Society for Research in Child Development, 50*(Serial No. 209), 41–65.

Webb, E. (1915). Character and intelligence. *British Journal of Psychology, 1,* 3.

Weiss, B., Dodge, K., Bates, J. E., & Pettit, G. S. (1992). Some consequences of early harsh discipline: Child aggression and a maladaptive social information processing style. *Child Development, 63,* 1321–1335.

Wenger, M. A. (1941). The measurement of individual differences in autonomic balance. *Psychosomatic Medicine, 3,* 427–434.

Werner, E. E. (1985). Resilient offspring of alcoholics: A longitudinal study from birth to age 18. *Journal of Studies on Alcohol, 47,* 34–40.

Wertlieb, D., Weigel, C., Springer, T., & Feldstein, M. (1987). Temperament as a moderator of children's stressful experiences. *American Journal of Orthopsychiatry, 57,* 234–245.

Wills, T. A., Cleary, S. D., Filer, M., Mariani, J., & Spera, K. (in press). Temperament dimensions and early-onset substance use. *Journal of Abnormal Psychology.*

Wimer, R. E., & Wimer, C. C. (1985). Animal behavior genetics: A search for the biological foundations of behavior. *Annual Review of Psychology, 36,* 171–218.

Windle, M. (1995). The approach/withdrawal concept: Associations with salient constructs in contemporary theories of temperament and personality development. In K. E. Hood, G. Greenberg, & E. Tobach (Eds.), *Behavioral development: Concepts of approach/withdrawal and integrative levels* (pp. 329–370). New York: Garland.

Windle, M., & Lerner, R. M. (1986). Reassessing the dimensions of temperamental individuality across the life-span: The Revised Dimensions of Temperament Survey (DOTS-R). *Journal of Adolescent Research, 1,* 213–230.

Wolff, P. H. (1965). The development of attention in young infants. *Annals of the New York Academy of Sciences, 118,* 8–30.

Worobey, J., & Blajda, V. M. (1989). Temperament ratings at 2 weeks, 2 months, and 1 year: Differential stability of activity and emotionality. *Developmental Psychology, 25,* 257–263.

Worobey, J., & Lewis, M. (1989). Individual differences in the reactivity of young infants. *Developmental Psychology, 25,* 663–667.

Wundt, W. (1903). *Grundzuge der physiologischen pyschologie* (5th ed., Vol. 3). Leipzig: W. Engelmann.

Zuckerman, M. (1984). Sensation seeking: A comparative approach to a human trait. *Behavioral and Brain Sciences, 7,* 413–471.

Zuckerman, M. (1991). *Psychobiology of personality.* Cambridge, England: Cambridge University Press.

Zuckerman, M. (1995). Good and bad humors: Biochemical bases of personality and its disorders. *Psychological Science, 6,* 325–332.

CHAPTER 4

Biology and the Child

JEROME KAGAN

An unreserved acceptance of the idea that biological processes contribute to psychological phenomena has waxed and waned over time. Although attributing a feeling of fatigue to a bacterial infection is currently noncontroversial, the suggestion that a chronically dysphoric mood could be due, in part, to an inherited physiology has encountered more resistance during this century. One historical source of the skepticism was the decision by Greek philosophers two millennia ago to separate soul and body rather than to follow the classic Chinese philosophers and assume that mental and bodily events are joined in as seamless a unity as color, shape, and motion in the conscious perception of a cloud at sunset.

The basis for denying biology a significant role in mood and behavior during the half-century after World War I was the understandable desire, especially among Americans, to minimize biological variation among varied immigrant or

Preparation of this chapter was supported, in part, by the William T. Grant Foundation, grant number MH47077 from the National Institute of Mental Health, and by the Network on Psychopathology and Development of the John D. and Catherine T. MacArthur Foundation.

ethnic groups. This ideology was in the service of defending the optimistic hope that proper family experience and education could create a community of citizens that possessed roughly equivalent ability, motivation, civility, and capacity for happiness (May, 1959).

Second, a broad conceptual moat must be jumped when the vocabularies of biology and psychology occur in the same sentence. No one has difficulty understanding "The boy ran away because he felt afraid" because everyone's experience validates the association between a feeling of fear and the act of fleeing. But many find it more difficult to understand "The boy ran away because of a limbic discharge" because they have not consciously experienced that brain event and, further, that sentence occurs rarely in social discourse. Hence, both the sense and referential meanings of the second sentence are less clear and a causal association between flight and a limbic discharge seems less valid. Ease of assimilation is always easier when the statement contains ideas to which a listener is accustomed. Fifteenth-century Europeans would have experienced far less difficulty than modern ones in understanding, and accepting as true, the declaration: "The woman died because she was bewitched."

A third obstacle to combining biological and psychological terms, which is related to the issue of different vocabularies, is inherent in all emergent phenomena; the tides offer an example. Most people who have had the relevant education believe that the changing height of the oceans during each day is due to changes in the gravitational relation between the moon and the earth, even though there is a bit of mystery surrounding the idea that the gravitational attraction between moon and earth affects the waterline at the beach. No feeling of mystery—or certainly much less—is engendered when the linked phenomena are at the same level of description, as in "The child cried after she fell," because our phenomenology supplies the mediating feeling of pain or surprise that we know produces a cry. The contemporary public is ready to believe the recent, and surprising, declaration that a bacterium (Heliobacter pylori) can cause ulcers because it is easy to imagine how swarms of bacteria could devour the stomach's delicate mucosal lining. An earlier generation was considerably more resistant to the psychosomatic hypothesis that conflict over dependency could produce ulcers because it was harder to imagine how an unconscious psychological state could be responsible for this materialistic condition.

When the mind must leap from gravitational force to tides or from psychological states to ulcers, and the intermediate events are not completely clear, people must rely on faith in authority to accept both statements as true. When knowledge of the mediating event is incomplete, as it is for most propositions that relate brain physiology to psychology, considerable faith is required. The resulting feeling of disquiet mars the aesthetic feeling that is a distinguishing feature of a completely satisfying explanation.

THE INFLUENCES OF BIOLOGY

Biological processes affect psychological growth in two obvious but very different ways. On the one hand, the lawful maturation of the nervous system is accompanied by universal changes in emotion, cognition, and behavior. This influence can be observed during the first 20 weeks of prenatal development. For example, every one of 11 fetuses showed their first startle and hiccup before they displayed their first yawn or swallowing movement. Further, the variability in the time of appearance of 15 different reflexes was relatively small—typically less than two weeks (DeVries, Visser, & Prechtl, 1982).

Among the first facts that students of development learn are the ages when motor and cognitive milestones appear in the first two years of human development. Few developmental scholars would challenge the assertion that children can not utter their first words until the frontal and temporal lobes and their projections to other parts of the brain have reached a certain level of growth. Had Piaget (1950) anticipated the discoveries of Mishkin (1978), Squire and Zola-Morgan (1988), Goldman-Rakic (1994), and Diamond (1990), among others, he might not have insisted that the prior manipulation of objects was necessary for an 8-month-old to retrieve a small toy hidden under a cloth. Piaget might have acknowledged that the behavioral performance that signifies attainment of the first stage of the object concept is not possible until connections among sensory and motor areas, entorhinal cortex, and hippocampus have become firm. It is likely, although still to be demonstrated, that the ability to conserve mass or volume at 7 years and to reason correctly about hypothetical statements at adolescence also depend on the maturation of selected parts of the brain (see Thatcher, 1994).

The remarkable degree of concordance in the age of appearance of object permanence, fear of strangers, separation fear, symbolic play, comprehension of language, and the appreciation of right and wrong among children living in diverse parts of the world reflects the powerful influence of maturation on psychological development. This story is being told in several chapters of the second volume of this *Handbook* and a chapter on temperament by Rothbart and Bates (Ch. 3, this Volume).

Temperament

Some of the stable psychological variation found among children in all cultures represents a second domain in which biology influences growth. This idea, which is the sense meaning of the concept *temperament,* comprises the primary focus of this chapter. However, the biological processes and psychological experiences that mediate the maturation of a particular class of behavior are usually different from those that are responsible for the variation in that behavior. Fear of unfamiliar adults in infancy provides a nice example of this claim. It is believed that the display of distress to and avoidance of strangers appears in most children by 7 to 9 months as a result of maturation of circuits from limbic sites to the frontal lobe (Diamond, 1990; Kagan, 1994). The variation in the intensity and chronicity of fearful behavior to strangers is believed to be due to differences in the neural chemistry of the amygdala and experiences with strangers and not to completion of the circuits that link the limbic structures with the frontal lobe (Kagan, 1994).

Although inquiry into human temperaments is becoming more popular, there is no consensus on basic terms, measurement procedures, or robust generalizations. Hence, it is not possible in one chapter to summarize, in an integrative style, all that has been published. The interested reader is referred to several recently edited books that present the diverse views on this theme; they include Kohnstamm, Bates, and Rothbart (1989), Strelau and Angleitner (1991), Bates and Wachs (1994), and Plomin and McClearn (1993).

The structure of this chapter can be summarized easily. I present first a brief historical perspective on the concept of temperament and the reasons for its recent appeal. The chapter then presents a concise statement of the nodes of agreement and disagreement among investigators. The two most important controversies involve the validity of parental reports of children's behavior and whether temperamental qualities should be conceived of as continua or categories. The heart of the chapter is a summary of the most robust generalizations regarding the temperamental characteristics of irritability in infants and sociability and shyness in older children. The final sections consider, more briefly, the relevance of temperament to psychopathology, ethnicity, and the growth of morality. The chapter focuses on infancy and

early childhood and does not consider in any detail the interesting research on the temperamental characteristics of adolescents and adults.

SOME HISTORICAL FACTS

Early Influences

The Greeks and Romans believed that a balance among the four humors of yellow and black bile, blood, and phlegm created an opposition within each of two complementary universal qualities: warm versus cool and dry versus moist (Siegel, 1968). These qualities were related to the four fundamental substances in the world: fire, air, earth, and water. The Greeks assumed, without a detailed appreciation of genetics or physiology, that the balance among these qualities created an inner state responsible for the observed variation in rationality, emotionality, and behavior. Children were impulsive and irrational because they were born with an excess of the moist quality.

Galen, an extraordinarily perceptive second-century physician born in Asia Minor, elaborated these Hippocratic ideas by positing nine temperamental types derived from the four humors (Roccatagliatta, 1986). The ideal personality was exquisitely balanced on the complementary characteristics of warm-cool and dry-moist. In the remaining four less ideal types one pair of qualities dominated the complementary pair; for example, warm and moist dominated cool and dry. These four were the temperamental categories Galen called melancholic, sanguine, choleric, and phlegmatic. Each was the result of an excess of one of the bodily humors that produced, in turn, the imbalance in qualities. The melancholic was cool and dry because of an excess of black bile; the sanguine was warm and moist because of an excess of blood; the choleric was warm and dry because of an excess of yellow bile; and the phlegmatic was cool and moist because of an excess of phlegm.

Although the concentrations of the four humors and the relative dominance of the derived qualities were inherent in each person's physiology, they were, nonetheless, susceptible to the influence of external events, especially climate and diet. The body, naturally, became warmer and more moist in the spring; hence, people became more sanguine. When the body became cooler and drier in the fall, a melancholic mood became more prevalent. Because humans lived in different climates and ate different foods, they differed in these temperamental qualities.

Although the Chinese view of human nature articulated two millennia earlier shared some features with Galen's ideas, it differed from it in several important ways (Yosida, 1973). First, the critical balance was among sources of energy rather than the bodily humors. The energy of the universe—called ch'i—is regulated by a complementary relation between the active initiating force of yang and the more passive, completing force of yin. The two forces must be in balance for optimal physiological and psychological functioning. Like the Greeks, the Chinese linked the emotion of sadness with autumn, joy with early summer, and fear with winter. But the Greeks would have been surprised that the Chinese linked anger with spring—April and May are the months of Galen's sanguine temperament. However, the more important fact is that the Chinese were not interested in temperamental types. Because the energy of ch'i is always changing, a person's moods and behavioral style cannot be too permanent. The notion of a person inheriting a stable emotional bias was inconsistent with the Chinese premise of continual transformation. A person might be sad temporarily, but not because he or she was a melancholic type.

Galen's inferences, which remained popular in Europe until the end of the nineteenth century, were not seriously different from contemporary speculations that the brains of schizophrenics might possess an excess of dopamine while those of depressives may have insufficient norepinephrine. Kant (1785/1959) accepted Galen's four types with only minor changes but distinguished between affect and action because he recognized the imperfect relation between invisible, internal processes and overt behavior. Kant believed that humans possessed a will that could control the behavioral consequences of strong desires.

This contrast was captured in the nineteenth century in the comparison between temperament and character. The former referred to inherited emotional biases, the latter to the expression of these biases in actions that were a function of both life experiences and inborn temperament. The pragmatist, for example, was a character type who could possess either a sanguine or a melancholic temperament.

Two centuries later, Roback (1931) modernized Kant's views by suggesting that individuals inherited, to different degrees, dispositions for certain desires and emotions. But, unlike animals, humans could control behaviors that violated their ethical standards; this is Roback's version of Freud's belief that ego tames id. The sanguine type must inhibit, occasionally, the tendency to act impulsively

because of strong feelings; the melancholic must suppress the urge to become anxious and withdrawn. Thus, a temperamentally sanguine person who has made too many ill-advised decisions can become overly cautious; a melancholic who has learned to inhibit fear may appear to others to be spontaneously sociable. The idea that the character type does not always provide a reliable insight into temperament is the essence of Jung's distinction between each person's hidden anima and public persona.

Nineteenth-century essays on temperament focused on the biology of the brain and searched for visible signs of that biology on the surface of the body. Franz Gall (1835) incurred the enmity of a segment of his community by suggesting that variation in human intentions and emotions, derived from differences in brain tissue, could actually be detected with measurements of the skull. Gall's crass materialism angered many colleagues who did not believe that a person's character was determined by brain tissue and, therefore, was not controllable by each agent's will. A second reason for the hostility toward Gall is that many nineteenth-century scholars did not believe that the anatomy of the brain had any implications for human behavior because psychology was not part of natural science.

Spurzheim (1834) consolidated Gall's ideas by retaining the essential premise of a location for each primary human characteristic and, reflecting nineteenth-century prejudice, assigning more space in the cranial cavity to emotional than to intellectual processes. Love was in the cerebellum, aggression in the temporal lobe, and timidity in the upper lateral and posterior part of the head near the parietal area. The vigorous positivism in Spurzheim's arguments was motivated by the need to expunge metaphysical and religious ideas from scientific explanations of human nature; it was time to place human behavior in its proper place as a part of natural law.

Thus, by the end of the nineteenth century most scholars had accepted the fact that psychiatry rested on biology. Listen to Adolph Meyer in 1897: "We cannot conceive a disorder of the mind without a disorder of function of those cell mechanisms which embody that part of the mind" (p. 44).

The first transformation of these ideas was an expansion of the number of revealing physical features and, more important, an appreciation that these features were only indirect signs of the real, but still unknown, causes. In a book that enjoyed eight editions, Joseph Simms (1887) awarded the face more diagnostic power than Paul Ekman or Carroll

Izard would have dared. Even American schoolteachers were indoctrinated with these ideas: Jessica Fowler (1897) wrote a manual to help teachers diagnose their young pupils' psychological qualities. A "veneration for elders" was predictable from excessively drooping eyes.

Cesare Lombroso (1911) and Ernst Kretschmer (1925), in classic treatises, suggested an association between body type, on the one hand, and crime or mental disease, on the other. Lombroso acknowledged that crime had social and climatic correlates, but claimed that adults who fell at one of the extremes of a normal body type were more often represented among criminals, and dark-haired men were more likely to be criminals than those who were blonde. Kretschmer invented new names—asthenic, pyknic, and athletic—for the three classical body physiques and awarded differential vulnerability to major mental illness to the first two body types. Schizophrenics were more often tall, thin, narrow-faced asthenics; manic depressives were more often chubby, broad-faced, pyknic types.

These speculations formed the basis for Sheldon's (1940) famous book on personality and physique. Sheldon measured a large number of morphological dimensions from the photographs of 4,000 college men and collapsed the resulting 76 categories into three basic body types, each rated on a 7-point scale and each having a corresponding set of psychological qualities. The tall, thin ectomorph was an introvert; the chubby endomorph was an extrovert; and the broad, athletically built mesomorph was energetically assertive.

Sheldon's work began as the eugenics movement in America had reached a crest and was published the year that the Nazis were threatening Europe. The idea that inherited physical qualities, associated with different ethnic groups, were associated with human behavior was too close to Hitler's version of Aryan types, and this research, as well as a growing eugenics movement, stopped suddenly. Promotion of the formerly popular idea that the obvious physical differences among Scandinavians, Italians, Jews, and Blacks were linked to intelligence and morality had become a sign of both irrationality and amoral prejudice. The abrupt end to public discussion of these hypotheses is not surprising; tucked away in Sheldon's book is the provocative suggestion that Negroes are more often aggressive mesomorphs, whereas Jews are more often intellectual ectomorphs. Ernest Hooton's (1939) book, which suggested that some bodily constitutions were naturally inferior and linked to criminal behavior, had a defensive tone because he was aware of how unpopular this view had become to many Americans. Temperamental ideas, which had enjoyed the support of professors, presidents, and corporation heads during the first decade of this century, were forced underground for almost 50 years.

Freud's Influence

Freud (1933/1965) was a critical figure in this story because he made important changes in the remnants of Galen's views. First, he substituted one bodily substance, the energy of the libido, for the four humors. The idea of psychological energy, the sense meaning of libido, was not a completely novel notion. Nineteenth-century physicians had elaborated the ancient belief that amount of energy was an inherited personal quality. This "vis nervosa" was less abundant in those unfortunate persons who developed fears, depression, and neurasthenia.

Pavlov (1928) also exploited this idea to explain why some dogs became conditioned easily while others resisted the laboratory procedures and were difficult to condition. Pavlov thought that the former group of animals had a stronger nervous system, permitting them to be more resilient to the intense stimulation and unfamiliarity of the laboratory conditioning procedures. Pavlov intended that description to be flattering, because functional and adaptive evaluations, which were absent in Galen, colored temperamental concepts after Darwin's seminal work. Galen had written as if each psychological type sought an adaptation to fit his or her bodily humor. Pavlov inserted the evaluative ethic of adaptation and implied that some temperaments functioned better than others. The sanguine was the best type; the melancholic, who had a weaker brain, was the least desirable.

The idea that individuals vary in psychological energy and, therefore, in strength of brain activity may seem odd to modern readers. However, norepinephrine, the primary neurotransmitter of the sympathetic nervous system, maintains body temperature by producing bodily energy (Paxinos, 1990). Current psychiatric theory holds that depressives have low levels of central norepinephrine. The mechanism of one of the therapeutic drugs acts to increase the concentration of norepinephrine in the synaptic cleft. Moreover, infants differ in the vigor of motor activity and loudness of vocalizations. Some 4-month-olds thrash their limbs and squeal with delight; others lie passive and quiet. A high energy level leaps to mind as the best description of these infants. In the classic monograph on hysteria, Breuer and Freud (1956) wrote, "Differences which make up a man's natural temperament are based on profound differences in his nervous system—on the degree to which the functionally quiescent cerebral elements liberate energy" (p. 198).

The creative element in Freud's thinking was to award the free-floating energy of libido an origin and a target in sexuality, while accepting the popular view that heredity influenced the total amount of libido possessed.

Although Freud's early writings awarded influence both to temperamental differences in amount of libido and excitability of the nervous system, as well as childhood experiences, the latter ascended in importance in his later writings and, accordingly, the temperamental contribution faded.

The current popularity of the premise that childhood experiences are part of the causal web in adult anxiety and depression prevents a proper appreciation of the revolutionary character of Freud's ideas. Although the ancients were open to the suggestion that psychological variation within the normal range could be influenced by childhood experience—even Plato accepted that argument—the serious mental afflictions of depression, mania, and schizophrenia were regarded as solely physiological in origin. Although the ancients believed that some environmental factors were potent, including air, diet, exercise, rest, and excretion and retention of fluid, none of these causes was social in nature.

By softening the division between serious mental disorder and normal variation in worry and sadness, Freud persuaded many that both a terror of leaving home and worry about one's debts could be derivatives of the same conflict. The assumption of an experiential basis for fears and anxieties that was appropriate for all—everyone felt guilt over sexual and hostile motives—implied that every person could develop a phobia. Freud (1909) let his readers believe that "little Hans" was no different temperamentally from any other child; his extreme fear of horses was the result of very unusual experiences in his family. It is of interest that contemporary reports on children's phobias have returned to the notions prevalent decades before Freud. Clinical cases in psychiatric journals are now described as if they were physiological diseases to be treated with drugs; there is little or no discussion of conflict, trauma, or early family experience.

Psychoanalytic theory slowly turned minds away from a category of person who was especially vulnerable to acquiring a phobia to the idea of environmental encounters that produce fear. The adjective *fearful* now became a

continuous dimension on which any person could be placed. Because all individuals experienced conflict, anyone could become phobic. The idea of a vulnerable temperamental type was replaced with the notion of unusually stressful experiences.

A metaphor that captures this contrast is a bridge that collapses under a load. The traditional assumption was that all bridges must carry loads of varying weight; hence, a bridge that collapsed under a load that was in the normal range must have been structurally weak. This is the temperamental premise. Freud, and especially his followers, argued that, most of the time, the collapse was caused by an unusually heavy load. The psychological loads included childhood seduction, harsh socialization of hostility and sexuality, loss of a love object, and fear of the anger of an authoritarian parent. Even though there are many more children who are socialized harshly by autocratic parents or rejected by indifferent ones than there are hysterical patients, this theoretical stance won admirers quickly because of political factors.

Many Americans were threatened when, after the First World War, a number of prominent scientists joined by influential journalists suggested that some immigrants were less fit genetically than indigenous Americans (May, 1959). An opposing group of politically more liberal scientists and journalists quieted this provocative claim by suggesting that Pavlov's discoveries of conditioning meant that all children were essentially similar at birth and conditioned experiences supplied the only shaping hand. McDougall's (1908) acerbic critique of this position in his text *Social Psychology* was drowned out by the rising voice of Watsonian behaviorism.

RENASCENCE OF TEMPERAMENTAL IDEAS

Animal Research

The independent products of science and history have led to a return of temperamental concepts. The discovery that closely related strains of animals raised under identical laboratory conditions behaved differently to the same intrusions provided one set of persuasive facts. As an example, over 30 years ago, John Paul Scott and John Fuller (1965) observed over 250 puppies from five different breeds—basenji, beagle, cocker spaniel, Shetland sheepdog, and fox terrier—at the secluded Jackson laboratories in Bar Harbor, Maine. In one assessment of an animal's timidity, a handler took a puppy from its cage to a common room, placed the puppy one or two feet away, stood still, and observed the animal's behavior. The handler then slowly turned and walked toward the puppy, squatted down, held out his hand, stroked the puppy, and finally picked it up. The puppies who ran to the corner of the room, crouched, and issued a high-pitched yelp early in the sequence were classified as timid. The five breeds of dogs differed dramatically in degree of timidity, for the basenjis, terriers, and shelties were more timid than the beagles and cocker spaniels. But the rearing environment was important: all the dogs were less timid if they had been raised at home rather than in the laboratory. Twenty years later Goddard and Beilharz (1985) discovered that Labradors, Australian kelpies, boxers, and German shepherds differed in the avoidance of unfamiliar objects: the German shepherds were the most timid; the Labradors were the least fearful.

House cats, too, differ in timidity. The small proportion of cats who consistently withdraw to novelty and fail to attack rats have a lower threshold of excitability in specific areas of the amygdala than the majority of cats who do not withdraw and generally attack rats (Adamec, 1991). Similar stories can be told for a great many species. Mice, rats, wolves, cows, monkeys, birds, and even paradise fish differ, within species or among closely related strains, in the tendency to approach or to avoid novelty. A review of this variation by a team of evolutionary biologists concluded, "There can be little doubt that the shy-bold continuum is an important source of behavioral variation in many species that deserves the attention of behavioral ecologists" (Wilson, Clark, Coleman, & Dearstyne, 1994, p. 7).

It is not surprising that fearful behavior can be bred in animals, but it is surprising that it requires such a small number of generations. Some quail chicks become chronically immobile when placed on their back in a cradle and restricted by a human hand; remaining immobile is one measure of fear in birds. If chicks who display the fearful trait are bred with other fearful animals, it takes only eight generations to produce a relatively uniform line of birds that shows immobility for as long as two minutes. It is equally easy to establish a pedigree of birds that will show very brief periods of immobility, indicating minimal fear. It is also possible to select quail for pedigrees who secrete high or low levels of corticosterone. The strain with high levels are more fearful of novelty than those with low levels of this steroid (Jones, Satterlee, & Ryder, 1994).

Because species differ in neural circuitry and biochemistry, they also can differ in the ease with which each acquires certain conditioned responses. The intraspecific variation in vulnerability to becoming immobile to novelty, which can be due to heredity, is one form of biological preparedness.

One or Many Fear States

One obstacle to progress in understanding temperamental vulnerabilities to varied states of fear is the assumption, held by many, that there is only one basic fear state with variations in intensity. Thus, an infant monkey's distress calls to separation from the mother, a quail chick's immobility to restriction of movement, an increase in heart rate or blood pressure to a conditioned stimulus that had been paired with shock, and flight from a novel object are all regarded as indexes of the same basic fear state. The theoretical discussions of fear that are based on these observations often treat as unimportant the variation in species, incentive event, and specific response quantified. Many theorists assume that the same basic, central emotional state is generated in each of the above instances; this assumption is likely to be incorrect.

Panksepp (1990) has argued that a central nervous system circuit involving the amygdala, anterior lateral hypothalamus, and central gray, which is activated by a discrepant (or novel) event, a conditioned stimulus for pain, or biologically significant stimuli that might signify danger defines a fundamental fear state in animals and humans. This primary fear state typically produces freezing, flight, or a defensively aggressive response depending upon the imminence of the danger, the presence of a predator, and, of course, the possibility of flight (see also Panksepp, Sacks, Crepeau, & Abbott, 1991). It is important to add that this state need not be accompanied by a conscious feeling of fear and, that conscious states of worry in humans need not involve this circuit. Further, although acquiring an avoidant or distress reaction to threat or to novelty may require the amygdala, once the habit has become autonomous it can occur without the involvement of the amygdala. One trio of scientists has suggested that although the "amygdala is clearly involved in fear conditioning . . . the fear memory trace may . . . reside elsewhere" (Lavond, Kim, & Thompson, 1993, p. 326).

Although the evidence in support of Panksepp's claim is persuasive, for this pattern can be seen in both mammals and nonmammalian vertebrates, the fear circuit and its associated behaviors should be distinguished from the circuit associated with distress vocalizations by an infant mammal separated from a parent. First, the behavioral profile of the separated infant is different from the one that defines the fear state described above. Separation, unlike novelty or a conditioned stimulus that signals pain, produces neither freezing, defensive aggression, nor flight, but generates distress vocalizations. A kitten faced with an unfamiliar event often shows an arching of the back that is mediated by the central gray. A kitten separated from its mother displays a very different profile of behaviors. Thus, it is probably an error to use the distress that accompanies separation, often studied in young primates, as an ideal model for fear. This is not to say that the state created by separation is not interesting, stressful, or of theoretical importance. But this state is probably not the best probe for understanding fear to threat, a conditioned cue, or to novelty. It is of interest that posttraumatic stress disorder usually follows the experience of events that are very dangerous, such as earthquakes, or engender fear with guilt, such as witnessing atrocities, but not the loss of a loved one (Pynoos et al., 1987).

Perhaps that is why there is a low correlation between the occurrence of distress to separation in the laboratory and cries of fear to discrepant events in 1-year-old children and why a temperamental vulnerability favoring a fear reaction to discrepancy and a child's attachment classification are only modestly related (Kagan, 1994). One obvious implication of these facts is that the generalizations based on separation from caretakers, in monkeys or children, should not be applied unthinkingly to observations of fear reactions to novelty, threat, or conditioned cues.

However, Panksepp's idea of a basic fear circuit may be too ambitious; it may be wise to distinguish between fear reactions to unfamiliar events or to biologically significant stimuli that often signal danger, on the one hand, and reactions to neutral stimuli that have become conditioned cues for a fear state because of an association with pain, on the other. Freezing to a light or to a tone that had been paired with electric shock involves a circuit that shares neural sites with, but may not be identical to, the one that causes withdrawal from a looming stimulus. The former requires the central nucleus of the amygdala; the latter need not. Similarly, the rise in heart rate to a bitter liquid does not require the amygdala; the rise in heart rate to a light that is a conditioned stimulus for shock does require that structure (Finger, 1987). It may be useful, therefore, to distinguish among states of fear to: (a) unfamiliarity; (b) conditioned stimuli for pain or harm; (c) innate releasers that could signal danger or distress; and (d) reactions to

separation. The response profile, brain circuitry, and incentive conditions are not identical for these four states. Obviously, these four states are different from the state defined by anticipation of unpleasant events, a state that can be observed in older children and adults; this state is properly called anxiety, not fear. Finally, it is likely that the neurobiology that characterizes the universal appearance of any of these states is not the same as that which explains individual variation in that state.

It is reasonable to argue, given the evidence, that the meaning of the word *fear* is different when: (a) self-report of a feeling state; (b) change in behavior; or (c) increased activity in a neural circuit is the referent. If this hypothesis is correct, we will need different theoretical constructs in our discussions of fear depending upon which referent is emphasized. Even if the amygdala were involved in all of the above phenomena, that fact would be an insufficient basis for assuming the states were identical, for complex events that share a single feature can be different. Although all mammals have internal fertilization, there is still extraordinary diversity among them in many other systems—no one would confuse a mouse with a monkey.

There is also the possibility that the structure of the brain events that contribute to the psychological state of fear is different from the structure of the behavioral and/or phenomenological events that are the referents for the psychological term. That is, the two sets of phenomena might be incommensurable, as are the number of malarial parasites in a patient's blood stream and the report of the quality and the intensity of the patient's feelings of malaise. Consider as an analogy the structure of statements about hunger and feeding behavior in animals and the structure of statements describing the physiological changes that are correlated with feeding behavior. The former include latency to eat, amount of food eaten, and ease of learning an instrumental response to gain food as a function of hours of food deprivation. The latter statements refer to glucose and lipid levels in the blood, neural activity in the hypothalamus, and excitability of the receptors for fullness in the stomach. The relations between the behavioral and the biological events are complex, and there is no way, at the moment, to convert the behavioral statements to physiological ones. That conclusion means that one set of statements is not reducible to the other.

It is possible, therefore, that the meaning of the statement "The child is fearful because it ran to the mother when it saw a stranger enter the room" is not identical to, or reducible to, a detailed set of measurements of the child's brain activity as the stranger entered. The psychological and physiological data are related, but one cannot replace one sentence with the other.

Strain Differences in Fear Behavior

Nonetheless, the expectation that strain differences in behavioral reactions to novelty, threat, or danger should be associated with differences in physiology is affirmed. White rats from the Sprague Dawley strain who are very emotional in a novel environment have significantly higher concentrations of brain norepinephrine than minimally emotional rats from the same strain (Olson & Morgan, 1982). The Maudsley Reactive strain of rats, bred over generations, are fearful to unfamiliarity. The amount of defecation shown when the animal is exposed to a brightly lit open field, which is aversive for a rat, is used as the index of fear. A nonreactive strain has been bred to be minimally fearful. The differences between the reactive and nonreactive strains emerge early, by 30 days, and are not due to postnatal experiences. The reactive, compared with the nonreactive, animals have lower levels of catecholamines in body tissue and lower levels of norepinephrine in the blood, but compensate by having an increased density of beta adrenergic receptors on the heart. As a result, they display both higher heart rates and higher blood pressure (Blizard, Liang, & Emmel, 1980).

Similar strain differences exist in primate groups. South American squirrel monkeys of two different strains, reproductively isolated by only a thousand miles of jungle, vary in their morphology, physiology, and behavior (Snowdon, Coe, & Hodun, 1985). About 20 percent of rhesus monkeys are extremely fearful and timid in unfamiliar environments, have a tense muscle tone as infants, and show physiological reactivity in bodily targets that are linked to fearfulness (Suomi, 1987). There are even sanguine, melancholic, and choleric monkeys. When the behaviors of three closely related species of macaques were compared with respect to their tendency to approach or to withdraw from an unfamiliar human, bonnets were most likely to approach, whereas crabeaters, the smallest of the three species, were the most fearful. The largest animals—rhesus—were the most aggressive (Clarke, Mason, & Moberg, 1988). When these three species were observed under different conditions of novelty and restraint, the aggressive rhesus were least disturbed and showed the smallest increases in heart rate. The fearful crabeaters were the most disturbed and showed the largest increases in both heart

rate and glucocorticoids. The bonnets, who are passive and avoidant, showed modest increases in both heart rate and glucocorticoids. However, when crabeater, rhesus, and pigtail monkey infants were reared in isolation for six months, the rhesus displayed the most disturbed social behavior, whereas crabeater monkeys showed almost normal social behavior (Sackett, Ruppenthall, Farenbuch, Holm, & Greenough, 1981). Thus, the influence of temperament on development varies with the nature of the imposed stressor.

Temperamental factors are even linked to immune function in monkeys. One group of crabeater males was assigned to a stable group of four or five other monkeys for the 26 months of the experiment. A second, stressed group of animals also lived with four or five other monkeys, but the composition of the group changed each month. These frequent changes generated uncertainty in the crabeater monkey. The scientists also observed the animals twice a week for about a half hour to determine which were social and affiliative—they groomed and stayed close to other monkeys—and which were social isolates. After the two years of either stressful or minimally stressful social experience, the integrity of each animal's immune system was measured by drawing blood from each monkey for three weeks and evaluating the ability of the T lymphocytes to respond appropriately to an antigen. Lower levels of cell proliferation to the antigen index are assumed to reflect a compromised immune system. Only the animals who lived under stress and, in addition, were temperamentally prone to be social isolates showed a severely compromised immune system. The affiliative animals who had experienced the same level of stress showed a healthier immune response. This finding illustrates the principle that a disease state requires both a stress as well as a vulnerable organism (Cohen, Kaplan, Cunnick, Manuck, & Rabin, 1992).

The fact that very small variations in the genetic composition of closely related animals are associated with distinct profiles of behavior and physiology requires accommodation. If an animal's temperament influences its reaction to total isolation and its immune competence, it is likely that similar factors are operative in human psychological functions as well. Thus, diverse, independent forces combined to place temperamental ideas in a more favored position and to render them as attractive candidates in interpretations of human behavior.

However, the current receptivity to temperamental ideas cannot be understood without acknowledging the past 50 years of theory and research in neuroscience, psychology, and psychiatry. Try to imagine the history of the Civil War without a discussion of the moral attitudes of eighteenth-century New England toward slavery. The period from 1910 to 1970 was characterized by the conviction that, excepting the small number of brain-damaged children, most were fundamentally similar, and the development of different skills and personalities was due, in the main, to experience, especially conditioned habits. This popular and dominant premise was shaken by several historical events.

First, the conceptual gap between the principles of classical and operant conditioning and the novel forms observed in children's speech and behavior became difficult to repress. The resulting dissonance led, over time, to a broad dissatisfaction with the traditional view, but still no replacement for it. At the same time, Piaget's (1950) ideas of stages of psychological development became popular. Although Piaget insisted on the importance of the child's actions in the world, his arguments imposed some constraint on the effectiveness of experience. No 2-month-old could possess an object concept no matter what his or her experiences. Although Piaget did not favor the biological determinism implied by the concept of maturation, his writings created a renewed enthusiasm for maturational processes. Chomsky's ascerbic critique of Skinner's explanation of language acquisition abetted the maturational argument. Thus, the community became receptive to the influences of biology and nineteenth-century ideas about temperament. When the dissemination of PET and MRI promised an eager audience the objective quantification of the brain's resting biology, the dam of enthusiasm burst. Only two decades ago, the probability was high that a paper on behavioral genetics submitted to *Child Development* or *Developmental Psychology* would be rejected. Today similar technical reports are accepted by referees because of a change in the community's premises. The essential data have not changed very much; what has changed is the credibility of the assumption about the significance of biological processes.

There is, however, a danger in this excessive enthusiasm for genetics. A nativistic view of the infant, which is gaining popularity, resembles the preformationist assumption that a tiny child was hidden in each sperm. Infants are being awarded cognitive talents that psychologists would have satirized 25 years ago. The permissive attitude toward these claims could not have occurred without the prior perceived failures of behaviorism and psychoanalytic theory, just as the popularity of Picasso and other modernists required the prior idealism of Courbet and Monet. Picasso's *Nude in a Red Chair* would not have been regarded as a great work of art had not Western artists for the three prior centuries painted serenely beautiful, unclothed women.

A quarter-century ago, psychologists who were loyal to stimulus response learning theory invented possible explanations of almost every stable behavior. Readers will recall, for example, that Skinner (1981) suggested that operant conditioning principles could explain the child's acquisition of speech. Contemporary neuroscientists are demonstrating equally creative imaginations by proposing neurophysiological bases for many diverse and complex behaviors. I do not criticize this inventive energy, but note that, as with the earlier behavioristic accounts, most of these explanations will turn out to be either much too simple or incorrect (Hu & Fox, 1988).

Thomas and Chess

A second important reason for the return of temperamental ideas was the bold, influential work of Thomas and Chess (1977). Although Solomon Diamond (1957) anticipated the current interest in temperament at about the same time that Alexander Thomas and Stella Chess published their first papers, historical forces awarded primacy to the two psychiatrists because their categories were more closely related to parental experiences with infants and to later childhood pathology. It is useful to recall their strategy of discovery. Thomas and Chess (1977) conducted, at regular intervals, lengthy interviews with well-educated parents of infants and inferred nine temperamental dimensions together with three more abstract categories from those interviews. The nine temperamental dimensions were: (1) activity level; (2) rhythmicity or regularity of bodily functions like hunger, sleep, and elimination; (3) initial reaction to unfamiliarity, especially approach or withdrawal; (4) ease of adaptation to new situations; (5) responsiveness to subtle stimulus events; (6) amount of energy; (7) dominant mood, primarily whether happy or irritable; (8) distractibility; and (9) attention span and persistence.

The three temperamental categories represented a profile on two or more of the nine dimensions. The most frequent category, about 40 percent of the sample, was the easy child, who was regular in bodily activity and approached unfamiliar objects with a happy, engaging mood. The second, comprising about 15 percent of the sample, was slow to warm up and, like the children Kagan, Reznick, and Snidman (1988) called inhibited, they react to unfamiliarity with withdrawal and occasionally mild distress. The third category, comprising about 10 percent of the sample, was called difficult and was characterized by minimal regularity, frequent irritability, withdrawal from unfamiliarity, and poor adaptation. This category of child was most likely to develop psychiatric symptoms—two-thirds had developed such symptoms by age 10. These three categories comprised about two-thirds of the Chess and Thomas sample; the remaining third were difficult to classify.

Continuous evaluation of the children through the fifth year revealed minimal preservation of most of the dimensions. The largest correlations, about 0.3, reflected stability across the preschool years. But there was not much predictability from early infancy to age 4. As a result, Thomas and Chess concluded that the nine temperamental dimensions, as phenotypes, were not very stable. They revisited these subjects when they were between 18 and 22 years of age, using clinical interviews and questionnaires to evaluate degree of adjustment. Although there was no relation between the possession of an easy or a difficult temperament in the first two years and later adult adjustment, the children who had been classed as difficult in the third and fourth years were judged to be less able to cope with life stresses than those children who had an easy temperament. However, Chess and Thomas (1990) noted, wisely, that the outcomes of a difficult temperament depended on the goodness-of-fit—that is, the match—between the child's temperament and the family's ideals for the child. Both must be assessed if one is to predict future pathology (see Carey & McDevitt, 1978, for the stability of a difficult temperament from infancy to childhood).

Sources of Evidence

Thomas and Chess (1977) acknowledged that their nine dimensions and three categories were influenced by the nature of their evidence; namely, interviews with parents. Although this strategy is a reasonable choice as an initial probe into a complex area, it is also vulnerable to a special bias. When parents describe their infants, they typically mention qualities that are perceptually salient and contribute to the ease or difficulty of caring for the child. If car owners without extensive mechanical knowledge were interviewed about automobiles, they would probably mention fuel efficiency, ease of handling, frequency of repairs, and comfort of the ride and would be less likely to name either the structural bases for those qualities or the characteristics that are a target of public concern, like carbon monoxide emission or rigidity of the front bumpers to impact. It is not obvious that the latter characteristics are less important than the former.

Natural scientists have three choices when they begin to chart a new field: they can rely on formal theory (as physicists often do), new empirical observations (as biologists often do), or on the intuitions of the investigator or informants (more often chosen by social scientists). Each strategy is useful in the first phase of study, but history reveals that substantial progress usually follows when investigators abandon initial intuitions and generate new sources of data.

Thomas and Chess, as well as those who followed them, are not to be faulted for the categories they invented. The absence of a deep understanding of the physiological patterns that form the foundation for the many temperamental types leaves most investigators little choice but to focus on the most obvious behavioral profiles in young children; hence, activity, irritability, avoidance of novelty or danger, and smiling and laughter are among the most frequently studied temperamental characteristics. Ptolemy and Copernicus also chose the obvious when they studied the moon and the near planets. Astronomers now know that the moon and Mars are not particularly important objects in the sky; they tell us little about the origins of the solar system, have little effect on our weather, and are of little consequence for current theory in astrophysics. But five centuries ago both objects and their cycles represented interesting, lawful phenomena that could be observed and described. Scientists who chart a new domain must necessarily rely on ideas and procedures that seem most reasonable to them and to their colleagues at the time.

CONTEMPORARY CONCEPTUAL PROBLEMS

Most psychologists regard the word *temperament* as referring to the variety of stable moods and separate behavioral profiles observed in infants, children, and adults that are partially controlled by the person's biology. The initial biological bias could be the result of heredity or, in some cases, a special prenatal environment. Experimental evidence from monkeys reveals that stress during pregnancy can alter the physiology of the developing embryo and lead to postnatal changes in behavior and physiology (DiPietro, 1995; Schneider, 1992; Schneider & Coe, 1993). However, the referential meaning of temperament is not a particular set of genes, but the psychological profile that emerges when environments act upon infants who have inherited a particular physiology. The concepts *schizophrenic* and *genius,* too, refer to actualized psychological profiles and not to the genes responsible for the physiologies that contribute to those categories. The fact that biology makes a modest contribution to a stable distinctive mood or behavior does not mean that the physiology completely explains the psychological display.

Temperament as Emergent

The dramatic successes of the neurosciences have persuaded some that the anatomy and physiology that are necessary for (or make a contribution to) a behavior or emotion explain the psychological phenomenon as fully as the equation $E = mc^2$ explains the potential energy contained in a gram of plutonium. Knowledge of the biological contribution enhances our understanding of the psychological event, but it does not explain it. Necessary, but not sufficient, is what we tell students when we note why there is no snowfall on every bitterly cold day or why there is a poor relation between the degree of injury to a visceral organ and the person's perception of pain (Cervero, 1994). Rose (1995) noted, "The phenomena of human existence and experience are always simultaneously biological and social, and an adequate explanation must involve both" (p. 380).

A patient with malaria feels fatigued, feverish, and uncomfortable. The knowledge that the body contains toxins produced by malarial parasites aids understanding of the consciously felt malaise. However, a full description of the physiology of the parasite and the chemistry of its toxins, in biological language, cannot be substituted for a description of the quality and intensity of the feelings of malaise nor their changes over time.

Nonetheless, knowledge of underlying physiology enriches our conception of the psychological events. When one learns that boys and girls differ in one pair of chromosomes, one's representation of the idea of "psychological sex differences" is changed, even though the statement that girls have two X chromosomes and boys one X and one Y does not, and cannot, explain completely why depression is more common in women and homicide more frequent in men.

Each of the many temperamental profiles that has been discovered and will be discovered in the future is a concept. The more knowledge that accumulates around the concept, the more complete the cognitive appreciation of the concept and the events to which it refers. However, the biological features that enrich a temperamental concept, and are necessary for the emergent psychological profile,

cannot replace it. A small number of neurobiologists believe that one day the idea of consciousness will be reduced to a particular set of neural activities, implying that consciousness is no more than a network of circuits. The reason for rejecting that premise is the same as the rationale for rejecting the idea that a chemical description of the toxins produced by the malarial parasites is equivalent to a description of the patient's malaise. A tornado has a shape, speed, direction of motion, and color, and these features are not derivable from lengthy descriptions of groups of air molecules within the tornado. Similarly, the transparent quality of a pane of glass is not explained by a description of the chemical structure of silica. Genes select or stabilize a form, but unless we know the exact conditions under which the organism is developing it is not possible to predict or understand the final form (Goodwin, 1994). "We inherit dispositions, not destinies . . . lives are not simple consequences of genetic consignments. Genetic determinism is improbable for simple acts of the fruit fly, implausible for complex human behavior" (Rose, 1995, p. 648).

The remarkable advances in neuroscience have tempted some to hope that many psychological concepts, like fear, will eventually be replaced with a specification of a neural circuit. Such optimism is not warranted. A temporally delimited pattern of brain activation, produced by an incentive, does not necessarily reflect a person's conscious feelings. Nor can the circuit represent the sequences of thoughts, preparation for action, and autonomic reactions that will occur subsequently. All of these events are referents for the psychological state.

The psychological term *fear* is not just a momentary brain state, even though the brain state accompanies the psychological event and, therefore, cannot be ignored. The neurophysiological phenomena should be given their own conceptual label. Three different sources of evidence are often used to infer a fear state: (a) a behavioral profile; (b) a pattern of physiological reactions; and (c) self-report. At the moment, the correlations among these three profiles are not high enough to treat them as redundant. There are two complementary but different frames for descriptions of human psychological states. One originates in phenomenology, the other in physiology. The concepts, their interrelations, and their time courses are sufficiently different in the two frames that it is wise to distinguish clearly between the words that are presumed to refer to the same state.

This position is neither a defense of traditional mind-brain duality nor an attack on biological reduction. It merely states that all psychological phenomena, including temperament, are emergent with respect to underlying biological events. A particular PET scan showing high metabolic activity in areas of the visual cortex does not explain completely why a person perceives a small, red sphere moving slowly to the right rather than a large, gray background moving slowly to the left. Each perception, behavior, emotion, and thought represents more than the brain circuits that are necessary for its actualization, a position Sperry (1977) maintained during the final years of his productive career. Thus, the description of a temperamental category is not equivalent to a description of the biological features that comprise part of its foundation. A wave is more than the moving particles of water that comprise it (Einstein & Infeld, 1938).

The Complexity of Brain-Behavior Relations

The influence of a biological profile on behavior is now recognized to be complex. Earlier, and much simpler, assumptions were based on facts like the relation between a trisomy on chromosome 21 and the mental retardation of Down syndrome. This fact, and related discoveries, seduced many scientists into minimizing the indeterminacy, complexity, and counterintuitive quality of the intermediate processes between genes and a psychological profile (Hu & Fox, 1988). Consider the counterintuitive nature of the following, recently discovered fact. The activity of the sweat glands in the skin of an adult is sympathetic in origin but is mediated by cholinergic neurons. The puzzle is that the embryo's sweat gland is noradrenergic and it requires sympathetic innervation to induce a molecule that, in turn, changes the neurotransmitter from noradrenergic to cholinergic (Habecker & Landis, 1994). Very few biologists sitting quietly in their study would have imagined this enigmatic evolutionary mechanism.

Behavioral data are equally complex and it will be necessary to view variation in behaviors like aggression, affiliation, sociability, fear, and depression historically, too, for each phenotype can hide a special history. Consider two rats, one unfamiliar and one familiar with mice. If the septum of the former is lesioned, the animal is likely to attack a mouse placed in its visual field. If the rat had been familiarized with mice, however, the attack is less likely to occur following the septal surgery. Similarly, stimulation of the periaqueductal gray of a rat who formerly would not attack mice is likely to produce an attack. But if the same level of stimulation is applied to an experienced rat who has attacked mice in the past, the animal is likely to interrupt its attack when stimulation begins (Karli, 1956, 1981, 1991).

Equivalent outcomes do not always reflect the same prior conditions, even though physicists have found that assumption useful. The concept of equivalence in physics holds that if the same mathematical description applies to an event that was produced by different conditions, the phenomena are to be considered equivalent theoretically. A classic example is the concave surface of the water in a bucket that is rotating on a table. However, if one imagines the universe rotating and the bucket remaining still, the surface of the water will appear concave. Because the mathematics that describes the concave surface is the same for a rotating bucket or a rotating universe, the two events are considered equivalent. The increased reliance on complex machines that purport to measure brain states has led some scientists to a tacit acceptance of a notion of equivalence; that is, a given PET or MRI profile reflects a particular physiological state, regardless of the conditions or the context of assessment. This assumption is probably incorrect. The unconditioned nictitating membrane reflex to a puff of air involves different brain states than the conditioned form of the reflex, even though the reflex appears identical under the two conditions (the cerebellar nuclei are required for the conditioned reflex but not for the unconditioned one; Thompson et al., 1987).

One reason why there will never be a determinant relation between an underlying biology and a complex psychological profile in humans is that the historical and cultural contexts typically influence the details of the profile. The journals of the writer John Cheever (1993), who died in the second half of this century, and the biography of William James's sister Alice James (Strouse, 1980), who died 100 years earlier, imply that both writers inherited a very similar, if not identical, diathesis that favored a chronically dysphoric, melancholic mood. But Cheever, whose premises about human nature were formed when Freudian theories were ascendant, assumed that his angst was due to childhood experiences, and he tried to overcome the conflicts that he imagined his family had created with the help of drugs and psychotherapy. By contrast, Alice James believed, with a majority of her contemporaries, that she had inherited her dour mood. Hence, she concluded, after trying baths and galvanic stimulation, that because she could not change her heredity she wished to die. The historical era of these creative writers exerted a profound influence on the coping strategies each selected and, by inference, on the quality of their emotional lives.

The old view that the relation between brain and behavior was unidirectional is being replaced with a more dynamic perspective that accepts the fact that psychological states can influence not only brain physiology but also, temporarily, the degree of activity of particular genes and their products. Glucocorticoids and other chemicals produced by psychological states can turn on or off genes that control the density of receptors on neurons and, as a consequence, alter the reactivity of the central nervous system. Each afternoon as the light fades, a gene turns on and initiates a sequence of protein synthesis (Takahashi & Hoffman, 1995). Hence, a child who inherited a physiology that biased him or her to be fearful (or impulsive) might, through experience, gain control of that behavior. The new behavioral profile could change both the child's psychological state as well as the genome that contributed to his or her initial behavior. An extremely inhibited 2-year-old boy in our longitudinal sample was not very fearful as an adolescent, and the reactive sympathetic nervous system he displayed as a toddler was much less apparent when he was 13 years old (Kagan, 1994). Further, the neural structures that are necessary for the acquisition of a conditioned avoidance or a freezing response may not be necessary for long-term maintenance of the behavior. For example, the central nucleus of the amygdala is required for an animal to learn to avoid a place associated with pain. But once the association has been established over many trials, the avoidant behavior can occur without involvement of the amygdala (Parent, West, & McGaugh, 1994). Thus, the physiology that is the basis for learning an act need not be isomorphic with the physiology of its maintenance.

Specificity

A principle of specificity is as important as a belief in dynamic reciprocity in probing the relation of brain to behavior. The area of the cortex that is essential for the retrieval of words that represent actions may be different from the area that is important in the retrieval of nouns (Damasio, 1994). The areas of the brain that cause a rat to avoid an electric probe that delivered shock are not the same as those that cause the rat to bury wood chips following the same experience of shock: the amygdala is necessary for display of the former, the septum for the latter (Treit, Pesold, & Rotzinger, 1993a, 1993b). In a similar vein, the circuit that mediates defensive aggression to a noxious stimulus does not require the amygdala; the freezing response to an intruder does require the amygdala but not the hypothalamus. Further, the rise in heart rate to the intruder

is likely to involve the lateral hypothalamus (Fanselow, 1994). Thus, response profiles that scientists have regarded as indicative of fear are based on different physiologies. These robust facts imply that it will be necessary to replace abstract descriptive terms like fear with phrases that name both the incentive and the context: full sentences must replace predicates. We shall revisit this idea later.

It is a truism that the history of every science is marked by new theoretical conceptions. It is less well recognized that changes in the evidential bases for a concept, which are the product of new methods, are equally characteristic of the history of scientific disciplines. The microscope, for example, changed the meaning of life to include forms that could not be seen. The radio telescope, which permitted the measurement of microwave radiation, led to the idea of dark matter and a new conception of the mass of the cosmos.

Psychology continues to be concerned with a small number of fundamental ideas that include consciousness, emotion, memory, thought, and pathology. Prior to the invention of machines that could measure brain activity, it was understood that the definitions of each of these concepts rested either on a person's phenomenological statements or observations of behavior. But after scientists were given access first to the EEG and later to PET and MRI, the primary referents for the psychological terms changed. It is possible that, in time, the psychological information will come to be regarded as less objective, less accurate, or both. That trend is dangerous because psychological data are inherent in the meanings of words like *consciousness* and *emotion.*

Consciousness is a phenomenological state, not a pattern of electrical activity. A contributing cause or setting condition should never be confused with its emergent products. A child's perception of a gull swooping down on the sea is not synonymous with the description of the circuits that make that perception possible. No one would confuse the tides with the gravitational attraction between earth and moon, nor a burning tree with the lightning that struck it, nor obesity with levels of lipids and carbohydrates, nor a protein with the DNA and RNA that were responsible for its manufacture. Yet some scientists are committing the error of confusing ideas like perception, habit, fear, consciousness, and depression with specific neurochemistries and brain circuits. To state, correctly, that a sudden freezing reaction to a spider requires a circuit that includes the thalamus, amygdala, and central gray is not equivalent to saying that the conscious feeling of fear is nothing more than, or identical with, the discharge of that circuit. This philosophical error is chasing psychological investigations of emotion and cognition to the periphery in a legitimate excitement over the powerful advances in our understanding of the brain conditions that form the bases for a psychological state.

However, it is unlikely that the concepts that originated in psychological studies of behavior, like memory, consciousness, or fear, will map neatly on to the concepts of the neurophysiologists. Stated differently, the structure of psychological processes is different from the structure of brain processes, just as the structure of the brain is different from the molecular structure of the genes that influence its formation. It will be necessary, as we noted earlier, to invent new concepts to name the neural circuits that are activated when certain psychological states occur, rather than simply adopt the older, popular, psychological terms. For example, LeDoux, Iwata, Cichetti, and Reis (1988) have described with elegance the brain structures in a rat that are necessary for acquiring a conditioned freezing response or an increase in blood pressure to a light that had been associated with electric shock; they call these core brain structures a fear circuit. But the circuit that mediates freezing need not involve projections from the amygdala to the sympathetic chain, although the circuit that produces a rise in blood pressure does. It will be helpful if each of these circuits were given a special name that distinguished it from others and from the meaning of "fear" when used by an agoraphobic patient who tells her therapist she is afraid to leave her home.

CANDIDATE PHYSIOLOGIES

A temperamental category implies the possession of a distinct physiology; hence, we must consider what relations have been established between behavioral and psychological profiles. This chapter cannot present a detailed description of the many anatomical, physiological, and neurochemical candidates that might influence behavior and mood. However, some consideration of the most likely mechanisms may be helpful. Although it is not possible to list the biological foundations of each of the temperaments, one can speculate on potential profiles in light of what has been discovered by neuroscientists.

Gray's Ideas

Although many investigators speculate on the physiology that mediates a set of functional relations, Gray (1991) has been bolder in suggesting that variation in three basic emotional systems might account for the important human temperaments. The first, the behavioral inhibition system involving septohippocampal circuits, is activated by conditioned stimuli associated with punishment, events that are linked to omission or termination of reward, and novelty. These latter events typically produce a cessation of ongoing behavior. Presumably individual variation in the excitability of the inhibitory circuits explains why some children remain immobile longer than others when an unexpected event occurs.

The flight-fight system, which involves the amygdala, hypothalamus, and central gray, is activated by aversive events, like pain, and leads to escape. If escape is not possible, aggression is likely to occur.

The third, behavioral approach system involves the basal ganglia and accompanying dopaminergic tracts and related parts of the thalamus, as well as neocortical areas that are linked to the basal ganglia. This system, activated by events that had been associated with reward or the termination of punishment, usually elicits approach behavior (Gray, 1991).

Neurochemical Systems

A far less integrative, more conservative approach is to focus on important neurochemical systems in the brain and their relation to mood and action. For example, brain norepinephrine increases the signal-to-noise ratio in sensory areas of the brain. Hence, infants born with high levels of brain norepinephrine might show unusual sensitivities to sensory events. Some parents do report that their infants are extremely sensitive to sounds, lights, textures, or subtle tastes. Further, some conduct disorder children have low levels of DBH, an enzyme necessary in the synthesis of norepinephrine. Norepinephrine is important for the functioning of the sympathetic nervous system, especially the cardiovascular system. As a result, conduct disorder children typically have lower heart rates than control children from the same social backgrounds (Farrington, 1987).

Dopamine is an essential transmitter in mesolimbic as well as striatal areas serving motor behavior and in the frontal cortex. Because the frontal area mediates the psychological phenomena of planning, inhibition of impulsivity, and delay, it is possible that children with low levels of dopamine will be unusually impulsive in uncertain situations. The rationale for administering Ritalin to children with attention deficit disorder or hyperactivity is that it increases the level of dopamine in frontal areas.

Endorphins and other endogenous opioids probably play a role in temperament, for one of their functions is to mute activity in the nuclei of the medulla that send projections to the sympathetic nervous system and relay them back to the limbic system (Weiner, 1992). Thus, a child with high levels of these opioids might show blunted sympathetic reactions to challenge. By contrast, children with low levels might show exaggerated sympathetic reactions to the same challenge. These two types of children exist, but it is not certain that this variation in sympathetic reactivity is indeed mediated by variation in medullary opioids.

Serotonin also modulates central nervous system activity; hence, children with low serotonin levels might be susceptible to unusual mood states of excitation, anger, or depression. Some scientists have reported that violent criminals have low cerebrospinal fluid concentrations of serotonin. Drugs that block reuptake of serotonin appear to help a proportion of depressed patients (Jacobs, 1994). GABA (γ-aminobutyric acid), too, mediates inhibitory effects in all parts of the brain, and the therapeutic effects of benzodiazepenes are due, in part, to the influence of these drugs on GABA receptors. Finally, glucocorticoids—cortisol in humans—exert powerful effects on physiology and behavior, and there are temperamental differences among primates in the reactivity of the hypothalamic pituitary adrenal cortex axis to potential threats. Sapolsky (1992), who reviewed this literature, suggested that lack of control and/or a lack of predictability leads to increases in ACTH and, subsequently, increased production of cortisol by the adrenal cortex.

We could continue this discussion and list at least 100 substances affecting brain function and speculate on their relevance to human temperaments. The examples presented above were intended to illustrate the potential relations between neurochemistry and a particular temperamental quality.

Despite what has been learned about the physiology and chemistry of the brain, unfortunately, and for reasons that are not difficult to discern, a relatively small number of generalizations that unite brain physiology and behavior have been discovered. First, the physiology that is most relevant to a temperamental category probably involves a balance among several neurotransmitters or modulators and circuits. The most fundamental principle of brain function is that neurons and circuits are under both excitatory and inhibitory influences. Glutamate is excitatory, GABA is inhibitory. The septum and the bed nucleus of the stria terminalis inhibit the flight/fight reaction to threat mediated by the amygdala and the ventromedial hypothalamus.

Every behavior, therefore, will be a consequent of the operation of multiple, complementary forces. Most investigators cannot assess directly the brain's physiology or anatomy in an intact human either because the relevant methods do not exist or because it is unethical to place a child in a functional MRI or PET apparatus when there is no clinical reason for doing so. One can be hopeful that future methodological advances will permit investigators to discover that children differ genetically in both the concentration of these neurochemicals as well as the density of relevant receptors and, therefore, in cognitive, behavioral, and emotional consequences.

Use of Animal Data

Although we have noted some initial associations between neurochemistry and behavior, it is still too early to be completely confident about any conclusion that links a particular mood or behavior to a single chemical profile. The study of animals, especially primates, will hasten the time of a deeper understanding (Suomi, 1987). Adamec (1991) has been comparing the neurophysiology of a small proportion of house cats who are fearful to novelty with the much larger group of cats who are not timid. The former group shows greater excitability in the basal amygdala than does the latter. This difference in amygdalar excitability could be due to variation in CRH (corticotropin-releasing hormone), GABA, norepinephrine, opioids, or a host of other chemicals that affect the excitability of nuclei in this limbic structure. One day we will learn what profile is mediating the behavioral differences between the two groups of cats.

The behavioral profiles of animals within or among strains within a species—dogs, cats, birds, or monkeys—are analogous to the different tortoise shells Darwin saw on the Galapagos. Darwin reasoned correctly that these differences in shape and coloration were inherited, although he did not know about genes. We, too, believe that some of the stable behavioral and affective differences among animal strains, as well as among children, are due to inherited differences in neurochemistry and physiology. But, at the moment, no one knows exactly what those central physiologies might be.

Hence, investigators have to look to where the light is brightest. Psychologists examine EEG patterns and activity in the peripheral nervous system, usually variables like heart rate, vagal tone, blood pressure, pupillary dilation, salivary cortisol, and neurotransmitter metabolites in the blood or urine. Most of these measurements are removed from the more central processes of primary interest. It is likely that the genes that control the behavioral aspects of a given temperament and those that control the correlated physiological characteristics, for example, high vagal tone, are different. Hence, a child can inherit each set of genes independently. As a result, there will be only a small group of children who inherit the genes for both the behavioral and the physiological features. Most physiological measurements are susceptible to temporary affective states. Movement or laughter, for example, can produce a higher, more variable heart rate; an active, energetic child often produces high levels of salivary cortisol. Thus, it is not surprising that no single physiological variable has been a sensitive correlate of any temperamental category. Although inhibited children are more likely than uninhibited ones to show a modest heart rate acceleration to selected challenges, fewer than 50 percent of inhibited children show that reaction, and they do not do so to all challenges. Thus, an increase in heart rate to a challenge cannot be used alone to select this temperamental group.

Other Physiological Systems

Gunnar (1994), who has explored the sensitivity of salivary cortisol to detect different types of children, has also concluded that biological variables are ambiguous as to their meaning. Salivary cortisol levels are too subject to varied temporary states to be relied on alone as a sensitive sign of a stable temperamental type. Bold, outgoing preschool children are much more active than shy, timid ones early in the school year and have occasional days with very high cortisol levels. But several months later, when the originally less active, shy children have become acclimated to the school setting and venture forth to socialize with others, they begin to show occasional days with very high salivary cortisol levels. Thus, the variation in cortisol spikes is closely related to the child's temporary psychological state and level of activity. Our laboratory found no significant relation between early morning salivary cortisol levels in 87 infants 5 and 7 months old and reactivity, smiling, or fear (Kagan, 1994). A particular cortisol level has no universal meaning across a large sample of infants and young children.

Cerebral asymmetry of alpha band frequencies in the EEG as well as asymmetry in the temperature of the face and hands have proven to be modest correlates of some temperaments. For example, a large body of clinical literature implies that lesions of the anterior left hemisphere, often due to stroke, are followed by an increase in dysphoria,

while lesions of the right anterior area are followed by an indifferent mood or occasionally bouts of laughter. These and other facts suggest that the right hemisphere participates more fully in states of fear, depression, and anxiety while the left is more active in states of joy and relaxation (Davidson, 1994; Fox & Davidson, 1987). Finman, Davidson, Coton, Straus, and Kagan (1989) observed and then carefully selected groups of extremely shy-timid or social-bold children in the third year of life and obtained resting EEG measurements. The former group of shy children showed greater EEG activation—desynchronization of 6 to 12 Hz—in the right than in the left frontal area, whereas the sociable children showed greater activation on the left side. Fox, Calkins, and Bell (1994) have found a similar relation in younger children. Although most children and adults are cooler on the left side of the forehead than on the right side—mean difference of about .10°C using a thermography scanner—inhibited children are more likely than uninhibited ones to be cooler on the right side (Kagan, 1994). Because the sympathetic nervous system is more reactive on the right compared with the left side of the body, the cooler temperature on the right implies greater sympathetic activity in inhibited children.

No single peripheral physiological measure is likely to be an especially valid index of a temperamental type because each is subject to local influences that are unrelated to central brain mechanisms that are the primary features of the temperament. However, an aggregate of different measures might do better. When the standard scores for eight peripheral physiological variables that are related to limbic excitability were averaged, the correlation between this aggregate index and behavioral inhibition was much higher than was the relation between any single physiological variable and the index of inhibited behavior (Kagan, Reznick, & Snidman, 1988).

The relation between a physiological index and a temperamental quality often varies with sex of the child. Most uninhibited boys have lower and more variable heart rates than inhibited boys, but there is no comparable difference between inhibited and uninhibited girls. This fact suggests that uninhibited boys may have unusually effective opioid activity in the medullary centers that monitor heart rate.

It is also common for relations between behavior and peripheral physiology to be nonlinear. For example, the distribution of the average standard scores for heart period and heart period standard deviation (during an initial sitting baseline) was divided into quintiles for a group of over 200 14-month-old girls. A low standard score represented a high and stable heart rate (low vagal tone); a high score represented a low and variable heart rate (high vagal tone). The child's frequency of smiling to an adult examiner during a subsequent hour of testing was the same for quintiles 2 through 5, but significantly lower for the children in quintile 1, those with the highest and most stable heart rates. The same function in a group of over 200 boys revealed that those in quintile 4 (percentiles 61 to 80) smiled the most; frequencies of smiling in the other four groups were similar. Thus, the relation of heart rate to smiling across all children was decidedly nonlinear. The girls with very low resting vagal tone smiled the least; the boys with moderately high vagal tone smiled the most. These conclusions are related, but they are not equivalent.

An Interim Summary

There are several nodes of agreement among most investigators of temperament. The first is that the major structures of the limbic system—hippocampus, cingulate, septum, hypothalamus, and amygdala—and their projections to motor and autonomic targets are important participants in the variation that defines the major constructs. Second, the variation in the excitability of these brain structures is likely to be influenced by many genes rather than by a single allele. Third, the peripheral biological measurements that are often used to help to define the temperamental categories—for example, cortisol, blood pressure, heart rate, vagal tone, EEG—have only very modest associations with the behavioral components of the category (Bates & Wachs, 1994; Gunnar, 1990; Kagan, 1994). Schwartz (1995) failed to find a robust relation between any one of a large number of peripheral physiological variables and temperament in a group of adolescents who had been classified as inhibited or uninhibited in the second year of life.

This trio of agreements is set against four nodes of controversy. One node contrasts those scientists who prefer to impose an a priori theoretical order with those who are not made exceptionally uneasy by a host of tiny facts when an area of inquiry is young. The former scholars, who outnumber the latter at the present time, have tried to invent a relatively abstract theoretical structure for temperament. The smaller group, which is more Baconian and expects specificity, permits observational data to guide the invention of temperamental concepts. A leading ethologist who reviewed the literature on animal learning about 10 years ago concluded that animals consist of "specialized, dedicated, but well integrated subroutines, . . . that have been customized as appropriate for each context and each species." It is an error, Gould (1986) added, to "search for a general theory from which all learned behavior . . . is to be explained" (p. 189).

A second controversy involves the source of evidence. At present, answers to questionnaires provide most of the information; however, some argue that the correlations between questionnaire data and direct observations of children are so low that the same construct should not be used for the two sources of evidence. A third point of disagreement engages the issue of whether a temperamental quality should be conceived of as a continuum or as a qualitative category. We shall deal with these issues in this chapter.

A final, more subtle issue involves the idea of essences. Some investigators conceive of a temperamental type as an essence with a fixed behavioral and physiological profile—the way many diseases are classified. One popular strategy treats the initial temperamental profile in the first year as an original, enduring structure that is preserved, despite transformations, for life.

A less popular view holds that the child begins life with a particular temperamental profile. Each profile undergoes change as a result of experience with parents, initially, and then with teachers and peers. As each of these sets of experiences is encountered and accommodated to, important changes occur in the child. Thus, the name psychologists give to a 10-year-old who began life with an irritable temperament should describe the 10-year-old and not the irritable infant. Because many changes occur in the first dozen years, the names of the temperamental categories in infancy will differ from those used to describe the adolescent. This branching conception is similar to the biologists' view of evolution. Beagles have a biological classification as dogs even though, in the deep past, their evolutionary origin was the gray wolf. However, biologists do not regard the beagle's features as a simple, linear derivative of the traits of the gray wolf; rather, they describe the beagle's characteristics and differentiate them from those of the pit bull, whose ancestor was also the gray wolf.

There is no essential dog: some are aggressive, some are not; some are spotted, some not; some bark, some do not. What all dogs share are an evolutionary history and a select set of anatomical structures, physiologies, and behaviors. One day scientists will discover the set of critical features that define each of the many temperamental types. At present, the study of human temperaments is still at an early, phenotypic stage of inquiry. Investigators must rely on a set of external characteristics—analogous to size, color of fur, and quality of bark in dogs—that are under the control of different sets of genes.

SOURCES OF EVIDENCE: PARENT REPORT

The most frequent source of information on temperamental qualities in young children comes from parental questionnaires. Most investigators who use this form of measurement assume that the descriptions provided by the parents correspond closely to direct behavioral observations. Because the parents have more extensive contact with their child, many of which cannot be created in the laboratory, the questionnaire seems to be the method of choice. However, this decision is only wise if the parental descriptions are highly correlated with direct observations. Unfortunately, as we shall see, the correspondence is modest at best; hence, conclusions that are based on questionnaire data have a special meaning and a restricted validity. That conclusion does not mean that questionnaires should not be used, but rather that they should be combined with direct observations of the child.

There are two meanings of words intended to describe relations among events. The *sense meaning* is the thought that the word or statement expresses. The *referential meaning* is contained in the events to which the word or statement points. The morning star and the evening star have different senses but the same referent; high intelligence and genius have similar senses but different referents.

Every theoretical construct combines sense and referential meanings; hence, if the referent changes it is possible that the theoretical meaning changes also. For example, the theoretical meaning of anxiety is not the same for the following referents: (a) scores on a self-report questionnaire of anxiety; (b) a panic attack; (c) impaired recall memory following stress; and (d) an increase in heart rate (or skin conductance) to a challenge.

Older adults with lesions in the right hemisphere did not differ from controls in their ratings of the intensity of the unpleasantness of a set of slides. However, their skin conductance response to these slides was significantly lower than that of controls, hence, their subjective reports of anxiety did not match the biological evidence (Meadows & Kaplan, 1994). Thus, the validity of theoretical statements about anxiety will depend on the data used to index that state. The meaning of all theoretical statements lies with the source of the observations, which, like a puppeteer's hands shape the limp, cloth puppets into meaningful forms.

Some generalizations about human behavior, emotion, cognition, and behavior have a unique meaning because they rest on a class of data that cannot be used by scientists studying animals, namely, a person's statements about his or her emotions, beliefs, moods, and preferences. Phenomenological evidence awards special meaning to the conceptual terms for which it is the primary referent, just as the error scores of rats learning mazes award special meaning to statements about animal intelligence.

Although phenomenological data can make some contribution to an understanding of individual differences in emotions, beliefs, and personality, they should not be the only source of evidence. Few neuroscientists believe that PET scans can tell us all we need to know about the brain; few behavioral geneticists claim that heritability coefficients will tell us all we need to know about the location of genes for physiological characters. Few domains of natural science rely on only one source of data; yet, some students of human temperament have come to rely almost completely on phenomenological evidence. There are many problems with this strategy.

Sentences demand logical consistency, have a structure that is different from that of the psychic events they intend to describe, and pass through a filter that evaluates their social desirability. Further, some languages do not have words that are able to describe with accuracy certain psychological states. Finally, contrast effects and subcultural differences in the meanings that persons infer from questionnaires and interviews affect a person's replies. I now elaborate these criticisms.

A person's verbal products, whether answers to interview questions or check marks on questionnaires, have special features that are not characteristic of the phenomena the sentences are intended to describe. Over 35 years ago Charles Osgood and his colleagues (Osgood, Suci, & Tannenbaum, 1957) demonstrated that people speaking many different languages use the evaluative contrast of good versus bad as a first dividing principle in categorizing people, objects, and events. Most parents impose a construction on their child's behavior that represents their conception of the ideal child. The parent who wants an outgoing child and is threatened by a quiet one may deny the child's shyness and exaggerate his or her sociability. This evaluative frame parents impose on the description of their children colors their answers to all questions.

Second, individuals are sensitive to the logical consistency in a series of related sentences. If a mother says (or checks on a form) that her child is happy, there will be resistance to acknowledging that her child occasionally feels sad, tense, or anxious. There is no such demand for consistency in a person's behavior, physiology, or conscious feelings.

Problems with Parent Report

Each parent's symbolic-verbal summary of his or her child competes with a nonverbal representation composed of all the prior perceptual and affective experiences with the child. The verbal categories invite a consistency to which the perceptual schemata are indifferent. This deep-seated mental disposition represents a serious flaw in parental reports. That is why Bates (1994) has suggested that parental descriptions of children are influenced in a serious way by the parents' ideal for their child, even though Bates feels that such descriptions should not be ignored because of the parents' extensive experience with the child in varied contexts. Verbal descriptions of children pass through a psychological filter that removes inconsistency and exaggerates small differences to create a clearer, more consistent, and more desirable concept of the child. An infant who both smiles frequently to playful bouts but also cries to frustration presents an inconsistent profile with respect to the complementary notions of a happy or unhappy infant. As a result, many parents exaggerate one of these profiles and mute the other to avoid the inconsistency. Hence, they are likely to tell the interviewer that their baby is usually happy or usually irritable but not both (Goldsmith & Campos, 1990). It is relevant that, in one longitudinal study that used questionnaires, the *lie* scale was more stable over time than the scale that measured extroversion (Carmichael & McGue, 1994).

Third, the words in English sentences refer to discrete categories of events making it difficult to describe blends. There is no English word that describes the feeling generated when one hopes for good news about a hospitalized loved one but fears the worst, or the feeling that combines the satisfaction felt when a misfortune befalls an enemy with the feeling of guilt over the revenge. Many more examples can be given. The main point is that languages are not rich enough to describe all of the important private experiences that are within human competence. Hence, individuals must choose the best word or sentence available, even though it may be inadequate.

Fourth, every sentence assumes, often tacitly, a comparison context. When a parent reads on a questionnaire the sentence "Does your child like to go to parties?", she unconsciously compares that preference with others. If one parent compares "going to parties" with an activity that is disliked, and a second parent compares it with one that is also preferred, the former is more likely to endorse the item than the latter, even though both children like parties.

A young mother who has not had extensive experience with infants has a less accurate base for judging her first child than one who has three children. The former is prone to describe her infant as more irritable and more demanding than the latter. But if the first child of the latter parent were extremely irritable and the second only a little less irritable but still more irritable than most children, the mother is likely to rate the second child as less irritable than observations would reveal because the mother contrasts the second with the first child. This phenomenon is seen clearly in mothers of fraternal twins who usually rate the two siblings as much less similar than observers because the mother exaggerates the differences between them (Saudino & Kagan, in press).

In a large study of same-sex monozygotic and dizygotic twins, the stability of behavioral observations of shyness and fearfulness from 14 to 36 months was significantly smaller than the stability of parental ratings of the same qualities (0.3 vs. 0.6). Moreover, the heritability of the behaviorally based indexes of inhibition to unfamiliarity decreased with age, while the heritability of the parental descriptions of a similar quality increased with age. For example, the heritability of observations of inhibition from 14 to 36 months decreased from .51 at 14 months to .24 at 36 months. However, the heritability of parental descriptions of similar behaviors increased from .21 at 14 months to .37 at 36 months (Saudino & Kagan, in press). At some ages, the heritability of parental ratings of avoidant behavior in the child was close to 1.0—a value so high it is likely that the parents' ratings were a serious distortion of the children's actual behavior. One group of authors who are expert in behavioral genetics and questionnaires concluded, "Twin studies employing maternal ratings probably overestimate heritability" (Saudino, McGuire, Reiss, Hetherington, & Plomin, 1993, p. 31; see Rose, 1995 for a similar judgment).

Similarly, stability of parental ratings of children's activity level and tendency to approach novelty, across the long interval 2 to 12 years of age, was 0.4. No comparable study that relied on behavioral observations has reported such high stability coefficients over a 10-year interval (Guerin & Gottfried, 1994). A similar result was reported for activity level in children over the period 15 months to 4.5 years. The stability was much higher for parental ratings (0.6) than it was for direct observations ($r = 0.3$) (Fagot & O'Brien, 1994; see Plomin & Foch, 1980).

Fifth, individuals differ in their understanding of the meanings of words. For example, in an unpublished study of adolescents in our laboratory, some youth responded to a question about two characters they had watched in a film as if the word *anxious* meant "eager to perform well"; other adolescents who saw the same film responded as if the word anxious meant *fearful*. Similarly, the two parents of 9-month-olds did not agree in their rating of fearfulness, smiling, or sociability in their child because fathers interpreted high activity levels in the young child to reflect a positive emotional mood, whereas mothers regarded the same behavior as reflecting anger (Goldsmith & Campos, 1990).

Some mothers regard the word *shy* as referring to the child's sensitivity, others interpret it as caution, and still others treat it as referring to timidity. Thus, if a questionnaire asks, "Is your child afraid of other children?", the first two mothers will answer negatively, whereas the third will answer in the affirmative, even though the children behave similarly with peers. The answer to the apparently simple question "Is your child afraid of strangers?" is valid only if the investigator can be certain that all respondents share a similar understanding of the question and, more important, if the phrase "afraid of strangers" refers to a set of observable events that most people would agree reflected that feeling. (See Fiske, 1986, for a similar argument regarding personality questionnaires.)

The ambiguity regarding the meaning of a parent's answers to questionnaires is seen clearly in the study of identical and fraternal male twins who were asked to fill out a popular personality questionnaire. An affirmative reply to the following two questions was heritable, implying genetic influence.

1. It is hard for me to find anything to talk about when I meet a new person.
2. It is hard for me to start a conversation with strangers.

But an affirmative reply to the following two questions showed minimal heritability.

1. I feel nervous if I have to meet a lot of people.
2. I doubt whether I would make a good leader.

The two pairs of questions seem to refer to the same psychological traits, namely, a feeling of uncertainty or anxiety with others. Yet, the use of slightly different language in the second pair of questions yielded an entirely different conclusion regarding the genetic contribution to introversion (Horn, Plomin, & Rosenman, 1976). Richard Shweder (1993) has written forcefully on the difficulty of translating Hindi words for emotions into English.

Less extreme, but nonetheless real differences exist among parents within our society who have grown up in different class groups or among informants from different cultures. Thai and American school-age children, 5 to 11 years, were observed in their respective school settings by trained observers and, in addition, the teachers in each culture rated the children for problem behaviors. The teachers in Thailand reported more problem behaviors in their children than the American teachers did for American children. However, the direct observations in each culture revealed exactly the opposite pattern: the American children displayed more problem behaviors than the children in Thailand. The authors concluded, "The most valuable general lesson of this study may be that much can be learned by directly observing children's behavior rather than relying solely on the reports of informed but untrained informants" (Weisz, Chaiyasit, Weiss, Eastman, & Jackson, 1995, pp. 412–413).

Most concepts rest on more than one feature. Because the concepts that describe behaviors, acute emotions, and chronic moods have a great many features, respondents will vary in the feature they select as primary when they answer a question about their child's behavior. The question "Is your child fretful?" requires the respondent to think of a context that represents the best example of that characteristic. If one mother regards the feeding situation as quintessential and another treats separation from the mother at the day care center as the best representative, the two parents may give different replies, for there need not be a high correlation in fretfulness across the two different contexts.

When the question asks about an emotion, like cheerfulness or fear, the opportunity to emphasize different features is enhanced. If the scientist and parent have different features of the concept in mind, each will impose a different meaning on the question. Wittgenstein (1953) suggested in *Philosophical Investigations* that every sentence, written or spoken, assumes a comparison context. A linguistic description of a forest is less autonomous than my perception of a row of trees. When a mother answers a query about her child's fear of strangers, she is unconsciously comparing the idea of fear with other related concepts that can refer, for example, to anger, sensitivity, or developmental maturity. We cannot expect uniformity among parents in the final outcome of those comparisons and, as a result, similar parental replies can have different meanings.

The practice of asking parents about the past behavior or emotions of their child (as with asking adults about their own behavior or feelings) assumes that all parents impose the same symbolic meanings contained in the psychologist's questions. This assumption is probably flawed. It is unlikely that a particular mother, watching her child retreat from an unfamiliar adult, consciously concludes that her child is afraid of strangers. She may perceive the retreat but could (a) generate no categorization, (b) regard the child as tired, (c) categorize the stranger as ominous, or (d) categorize the child as behaving adaptively with strangers. This example, and many others like it, are stored in the parent's long-term memory until the day the psychologist asks, "Is your child afraid of strangers?" Contrary to the premise of those who use parental questionnaires, the consequences of that question in the consciousness of the parent are difficult to predict because the psychologist does not know what categories the parent used to store and to retrieve the relevant past observations of his or her child, nor the parent's state at the moment he or she was being questioned. It is not unreasonable to argue that at the moment the question is comprehended the act of measurement (that is, posing the question) changes the consciousness of the parent about his or her child (analogous to the quantum phenomenon where the act of measuring electrons passing through two slits changes the outcome observed from an interference pattern to two discrete foci on a screen). Put plainly, because a large number of parents do not categorize all of their child's behavior in the same way or with the concepts used by the psychologist, a particular answer—Yes, my child is afraid—cannot be treated as having equivalent meaning across a large, diverse sample of parents.

Limits of Questionnaires

The most popular sources of evidence for child and adult temperament are questionnaires constructed to assess a small number of temperamental qualities. The behavioral referents for these concepts are assumed to generalize across a broad swath of diverse situations. The questionnaires for infants and children ask about characteristics that parents are interested in and can observe easily, like irritability, smiling, activity, shyness with strangers, and fear. The questions are constraining and force a subject to select an alternative that may not fit the person's intentions exactly. If the construction of the sentence were changed, the answer might be different. For example, a questionnaire may ask, "How often does your child smile to adults?—Rate on a 5-point scale." A discerning mother might have noticed that her 1-year-old rarely smiles to men but often smiles to women. But the question does not permit that response; as a result, the parent may compute an average and rate her child as moderately affective.

Most questionnaires do not ask about qualities that are subtle, or of less interest to parents, but nonetheless might be theoretically important; for example, how long a child takes to eat, preferred use of the right or left hand, or the fullness of each smile. Obviously, investigators cannot ask parents about qualities that are not observable, like asymmetry of cerebral activation or sympathetic reactivity. Because scientists can ask parents to rate only psychological qualities that they understand using words that are part of a consensual, folk vocabulary, most psychologists must restrict their temperamental categories to a small number of easily understood ideas; for example, activity level, smiling, fear of strangers, crying to limitations, soothability, and duration of attention to events. But some scientists synthesize a temperamental construct from disparate sources of information, some of which are not available to the parent. For example, there is a small group of infants who, in addition to being minimally irritable, smile frequently and have a low heart rate, low muscle tension, and greater activation of the EEG in the left frontal area. The psychologist might invent a novel temperamental name for this combination of qualities, but he or she cannot ask a mother to rate her child on this abstract quality for she does not have access to the child's heart rate, muscle tension, or EEG readings.

Put plainly, because the parental reports describe only the child's observed behaviors, they cannot differentiate between fearful dispositions that are derivative of a temperamental bias and those that were acquired without any biological contribution. If a person trips coming down the stairs, we cannot know if the accident was due to a defect in the person's vestibular apparatus or the result of a misperception of the visual cues. Additional information is necessary to make that distinction. The same is true of temperamental categories.

Relevant Evidence

Parental personality, level of education, and social class influence parents' answers to questionnaires in systematic ways. Mothers who never attended college describe their infants as less adaptive and less sociable than do college-educated parents (Spiker, Klebanov, & Brooks-Gunn, 1992). Mothers experiencing stress, for whatever reason, have a lower frustration tolerance and, therefore, are prone to exaggerate their infant's irritability. Depressed mothers with their first child described their 6-week-old infants as more irritable than did experienced mothers or mothers free of depression (Green, 1991).

Mothers who described their children on the Carey Temperament Questionnaire as difficult were more anxious, suspicious, and impulsive than mothers who described their children as easy (Vaughn, Bradley, Joffe, Seifer, & Barglow, 1987; see also Matheny, Wilson, & Thoben, 1987; Mebert, 1991 for similar results). One set of authors commented on the problems associated with asking parents to describe emotional problems in their children: "What is clear from the present results is that current methods have limitations that must be recognized in order to forestall both poor decision making with respect to individual children in a clinical setting and misleading interpretations in research studies" (Spiker, Kraemer, Constantine, & Bryant, 1992, p. 1493).

In sum, even though parents have the opportunity to observe their children in a variety of natural situations and laboratory contexts can be artificial, there are many unique influences on parental descriptions of young children that are absent when behavior in standardized contexts is recorded on film and coded by disinterested observers. That is why the agreement between parents and observers for particular problems is low; the correlations between the two are rarely above 0.4, and usually much lower. One mother who described her child as outgoing and sociable to an interviewer in our laboratory wrote a letter to our staff a few days after she had watched her daughter interact with two unfamiliar girls in a laboratory playroom. "This was a real eye opener for me. I always thought my child was outgoing and social. I now realize that after watching her that she is actually uncomfortable with new people."

In one investigation, 50 firstborn infants were observed at home weekly from 4 to 6 months of age. The parents and the observers were consistent over time in their independent evaluations of the baby's dominant mood, approach to unfamiliarity, activity, and intensity of response. But the correlations between the parents' ratings and the observers' evaluations of the same qualities were low (about 0.2). The authors wrote, "The most important implication of our findings is . . . a cautionary message about the large

published literature based on parent report of their infant's behavioral style . . . mothers are a poor source of information about their infants' behavioral style" (Seifer, Sameroff, Barrett, & Krafchuk, 1994, pp. 1488, 1489).

In a similar study, observers visited the homes of 5-month-old infants on two occasions and noted the frequency of smiling, vocalizing, fretting, crying, banging, and kicking. The observers also asked the mothers to make ratings of these same behaviors in their infants. Once again, the two sources of data were in poor accord; the correlations averaged only about 0.2 (Bornstein, Gaughran, & Segui, 1991). An investigation relevant to work to be described later compared the laboratory behavior of 135 1-year-olds to four events that often elicit fear—for example, a toy spider or masks—with the mothers' ratings of their children's fearfulness to these events. The mothers were remarkably inaccurate in predicting how their child would behave to these unfamiliar events (Rosicky, 1993).

Agreement between parents and observers remains poor even when the children are older and can describe their fears; parents and 10-year-olds do not agree when interviewed separately about the children's moods or problems. Neither do mothers and teachers agree on the presence of behavior problems in preschool children. One team of investigators noted, "Our results question the assumption that these checklists measure stable traits or characteristics of young children" (Spiker et al., 1992, p. 1490). An exhaustive review of the degree of agreement among parents, teachers, and peers with respect to the occurrence of children's behavioral and emotional problems, in over 269 samples, revealed poor concordance among different informants as to whether a child was excessively fearful, aggressive, or impulsive. The average correlation between two different informants was less than 0.3 (Achenbach, 1985). After a review of the relevant literature, one psychologist wrote, "Good agreement between parents and child is almost never the rule" (Klein, 1991, p. 195).

Summary

We are not the first to criticize the validity of parental reports. Over 60 years ago, a team of child psychologists noted the poor relation between what actually happened during the first year of an infant's life and the mother's descriptions of those events when the children were 21 months old (Pyles, Stolz, & MacFarlane, 1935; see also Yarrow, Campbell, & Burton, 1970). Gordon Allport, in his 1937 text *Personality,* acknowledged two serious limitations of self-reports: they may be falsified by the subject and are less valid if subjects are deficient in intelligence or insight.

Gottlob Frege (1979) argued persuasively that language does not always capture a thought accurately. Each parent has an ensemble of perceptions, feelings, and ideas about the child, and there is no word or phrase that captures the complex combination of sense meaning and direct experience. Consider the inadequacy of language to describe the bond of love in a marriage of 30 years or a winter sunset over the Golden Gate Bridge.

It may be that the verbal categories parents use to describe their children's behavior, compared with the categories derived from frame-by-frame analyses of films of the children's behavior, are incommensurable. One cannot substitute one set of concepts for the other because the concepts used to describe the film analyses do not exist in the vocabulary of the parental informants. For example, the language used by Ekman (1992) and Izard (1991) to describe brief changes in facial muscles that accompany certain emotions award special meanings to words like *anger* or *fear* that are different from those understood by parents.

If talking to parents about children's behavior and moods were such an accurate source of information, the field of personality would be one of the most advanced domains in the social sciences, rather than one in disarray. Wise people have been observing children and constructing theories of their nature for a very long time. I interpret our limited progress to mean that verbal statements describing the behaviors of others, by parents or friends, has some, but limited, value because the statements are partly constructions. Bates (1983) noted, "Empirical and theoretical considerations call into question the assumption that parent reports of a difficult temperament are essentially measures of characteristics residing within the child" (p. 95). Hubert, Wachs, Peters-Martin, and Gandour (1982) state a similar message without equivocation: "No single psychometrically sound and adequately validated measure of early temperament is currently available" (p. 578).

Thus, the review of empirical research that follows will not, with some exceptions, cover the very large number of reports that have relied on parental questionnaires as the only source of evidence. The preceding discussion was detailed because it was intended as a defense of that decision. However, that conclusion does not mean that direct observations of children are free of reliability and validity problems. A single 30-minute observation of a child in one laboratory context does not guarantee a valid picture of the child's consistent behavior in more natural contexts. It is necessary to sample behavior in several situations. Further,

it is unethical to present the extreme incentives for anger or fear in a laboratory that can occur in the child's home or school. Thus, parents, but not the laboratory investigator, may have knowledge of how the child reacts to these salient provocations. A third problem with behavioral observations is the occasional lack of reliability between coders who are quantifying film records of a laboratory battery or, more seriously, making ratings of behavioral traits. Thus, generalizations about children's characteristics based on behavioral observations in a laboratory also have serious limitations, and scientists should try, when possible, to observe in the natural situations of home or of school. But, because the correlations between parental judgments and behavioral observations are low, the meanings of temperamental constructs based on direct observations are different from those based on parental report. If, as I believe, future discoveries are likely to come from direct observations, hopefully combined with parental reports, rather than from parental reports alone, it will be useful to emphasize that information and not to treat as similar the results that have been based on these two different sources of evidence.

History casts aside popular methods in all sciences. Archaeologists now use carbon dating, not informed intuition, to establish the age of a fossil. Evolutionary biologists use blood proteins together with physical similarities to assign an animal to a genus or a species. The progress from Mendel to the cloning of genes rests, in large measure, on the discovery of new methods (Kay, 1993). Very few research psychologists use the Rorschach ink blots as an index of anxiety or conflict, although less than 40 years ago that test was very popular among psychologists who studied personality. Thus, the recognition that parental reports, when used alone, are not a sufficiently valid index of a child's characteristics should be treated as progress: the cup is half full.

CONTINUOUS TRAITS OR TEMPERAMENTAL CATEGORIES

A second issue requiring explicit attention before summarizing the evidence on children's temperaments is the choice between continuous behavioral dimensions and qualitative categories. Thomas and Chess (1977) regarded the three major types of children—easy, difficult, and slow to warm up—as categories, but treated the variation within each of the nine dimensions as continuous. They wrote about the approach-withdrawal dimension as if all infants could be placed on a continuum with respect to the tendency to withdraw or to approach unfamiliar events. By failing to say otherwise, they seemed to reject the possibility that infants who usually approach unfamiliar people might be qualitatively, not just quantitatively, different from those who usually avoid strangers. It is likely, however, that extremely shy children are qualitatively different from those who are moderately shy. One reason is that extreme shyness, which is characteristic of a very small proportion of children, is linked with other characteristics that seem unrelated to shy behavior, including eye color, asymmetry of EEG activation, and sympathetic reactivity. Support for this claim is presented in later sections of this chapter.

One subtle reason why psychologists have preferred continua over categories is a derivative of the contagion of ideas that exists among disciplines. Before relativity theory, physicists assumed that object and energy were qualitatively different things. A burning log was distinct from the heat or energy the log emitted. Einstein suggested, however, that there was only the field and, therefore, only energy: "The difference between matter and field is a quantitative rather than a qualitative one" (Einstein & Infeld, 1938, p. 242). Surely, if a log and the heat it can emit can be placed on an abstract continuum of energy, psychologists could defend the notion that no individual is qualitatively different from anyone else on any psychological dimension.

A more obvious, and perhaps less controversial, reason is the training in statistics given to young psychologists. By the Second World War the use of inferential statistics became the mark of the sophisticated social scientist. The correlation coefficient, t-test, and analysis of variance should be computed on continuous variables. Hence, psychologists found it useful to assume that there were no qualitative types of people; all humans could be treated as substantially similar in their sensations, perceptions, memories, and emotions. Statistical analyses were performed on continuous scores produced by different experimental conditions, not by different kinds of people.

The domination of research in both personality and development by analyses that rely on analysis of variance and regression has frustrated a small group of investigators who have had the intuition that some subjects are qualitatively different from the majority in their sample. However, when the group of subjects is small in number, the usual inferential statistics often do not reach the popular .05 level required for referee approval. Further, there is no consensus on an algorithm that permits an investigator to conclude that some subjects belong to a distinct group.

Consider, as an example, an investigator who did not know about Down syndrome studying the relation of maternal age to children's intelligence in a sample of 600 families. The correlation between the two variables would reveal no statistically significant relation. However, examination of a scatter plot might reveal that two children with very low IQ scores had the two oldest mothers in the sample. Reflection on that fact might tempt the investigator to consider the possibility that these two children were qualitatively different from the other 598 and, perhaps, that these two families provided a clue to a relation between age of mother and intelligence of the child for a very small proportion of the population. There is an initial enthusiasm for a return to the consideration of individual cases and small subgroups with extreme scores. Research from our laboratory provides a persuasive illustration.

A Case Study

One child, from a sample of over 500 who have been followed longitudinally, showed a unique developmental profile. While being administered a standard battery of visual, auditory, and olfactory events at 8 weeks of age, this boy frowned spontaneously six times, either during or between the stimulus presentations. Spontaneous frowns are rare among all infants and especially during the quiet interval between stimulus presentations when nothing is in the infant's perceptual field. This boy continued to frown frequently to a similar laboratory battery when he was 4 months old, retaining a sad facial expression for periods as long as 30 seconds—a rare response. He emitted a sharp scream to the presentation of a moving mobile; no other 4-month-old in the sample behaved that way. When this boy was seen at 9 months, he fretted to every stimulus presentation and remained wary throughout the 60-minute battery.

This child's profile continued to be idiosyncratic at 14 months. He maintained a sad facial expression throughout the 90-minute battery, had several uncontrolled tantrums, refused the administration of most episodes by screaming, vocalized in short explosive bursts, and often showed a pained facial expression without an accompanying cry or fret—a silent expression of angst. His mother acknowledged to the examiner that he had become more aggressive lately, noting, "He walks up and bites you."

At 3.5 years of age, however, he was calmer and displayed no unusual behavior during a 90-minute session. But several weeks later, when he was observed in a play situation with an unfamiliar boy of the same age, he showed a single act of impulsive aggression that is statistically rare.

As the session started, he remained close to his mother while staring at the other boy. After five minutes, he left his mother, went to the center of the playroom, and began to punch a large inflated toy. Two minutes later, he seized the toy that the other boy was holding and retreated with it to his mother. About five minutes later—that is, 15 minutes into the session—when the other boy was inside a plastic tunnel, he picked up a wooden pole and began to strike the tunnel with force in the place where the boy was sitting. The force of the blow made the other boy cry. This unprovoked act of aggression to an unfamiliar child is a very rare event in this laboratory context, especially with both mothers present in the room (Kagan, 1994).

This boy showed unique reactions on every assessment: frequent frowning at 2 months, a scream to a mobile at 4 months, extreme fearfulness at 9 months, silent expressions of distress at 14 months, unusual resistance at 21 months, and at 3.5 years a single act of unprovoked aggression. Although the aggressive act is rare statistically, it was the only deviant act in that session. Most psychologists observing this child for the first time at 3.5 years of age would probably dismiss the aggression as reflecting greater than normal frustration on that particular day. The mother was not concerned with her son's development and did not request any additional information. However, in the light of the history described, I suspect that the impulsive act of aggression reflects a deep psychological quality and that this boy is a member of a rare temperamental category.

Meehl's Ideas

Meehl (1973, 1995) has written persuasively on the utility of considering certain behavioral profiles as qualitative taxa; schizotypy is one example. The determination of whether a sample contains qualitative types is often difficult. Factor analysis cannot reveal this fact and a bimodal distribution of scores is no guarantee either. But Meehl (1973) has described a data analytic technique which holds some promise. Briefly, the method rests on the assumption that the association between two indicators of a personality type will be largest when the population consists of two qualitative types, and will be smallest if the sample contains only one type. Consider, as an example, a sample of 500 children consisting of 125 who were born with severely impaired hearing due to hereditary forces; the remaining 375 children did not inherit this disability. The comprehension vocabulary of all the children is measured and divided into six levels from low to high competence.

The correlations between two predictors of vocabulary size—frequency of otitis infections and educational level of the parents—are computed for each of the six vocabulary levels. Because most poorly educated families are economically disadvantaged, their children are often less healthy. Both poor health and low educational attainment of parents contribute to a child's lower vocabulary score. If the sample contains only the 375 children who do not have the inherited hearing loss, the magnitude of the correlation between otitis and family educational level should be similar for each of the six levels of vocabulary ability. But if the sample also contained the 125 children with serious hearing impairment, the correlation between otitis and family education level would be much lower for those children whose very low vocabulary scores were the result of an inherited hearing impairment and much higher for the larger group without the impairment.

If a sample consists of only one qualitative type, the covariance plot should be a straight line because, it is presumed, otitis infections and low education level have the same degree of association for all ranges of vocabulary. When the correlation between the two predictors deviates from a flat line, across the range of a third variable, that fact is a clue to the possibility of qualitatively different types in the sample (Meehl, 1973, 1992).

Meehl's technique is not the only way to test for the presence of qualitative groups. Other techniques exist, including latent class analysis. The main suggestion is that investigators should be receptive to the possibility of qualitatively distinct subgroups within a sample, even when the distributions of all variables are normal. Lars Bergman (personal communication) notes that children who scored very high or very low on five different cognitive abilities were more likely to maintain their respective competences than those with less extreme scores. The author has often found, in longitudinal research, that the history of a child whose score on a contemporary variable was three standard deviations from the mean was very different from the history of the children whose scores were only two standard deviations from the mean.

Nonlinear Relations

A central tension in empirical studies of individual differences derives from a controversy over whether people differ quantitatively on the same set of dimensions—therefore, each individual is described best as a set of values on factor scores—or whether some individuals belong to qualitative groups. A strong bias for simplicity favors continuous functions over categories. The theoretical power and popular success of relativity theory in physics supports this bias. Einstein suggested that, in the frame of an observer, objects shorten as their velocity approaches the speed of light. To universalize this law in the service of parsimony, he suggested that this shortening occurs even when I swing my tennis racket, although the velocity is so small that the shortening of the object is not detectable in the frame of an observer with any current instrument. Einstein wanted one function. But he ignored the fact that water does not begin to form very tiny ice crystals as it cools from 30° to 28° centigrade. The function is nonlinear.

Nonlinear functions are common in the life sciences and, at the transition points, novel qualities emerge which are categories. For example, the behavior of a single ant, or a small number, appears random and without coherence, but, "When the density of a colony reaches a critical value . . . chaos begins to turn into order and rhythmic patterns emerge over the colony as a whole" (Goodwin, 1994, p. 189). That is, a large colony of ants has distinct qualities that cannot be predicted from or explained by an additive model that sums the behavior of a large number of ants considered one at a time.

Nonlinear functions are common in many domains of psychology; for example, the magnitude of potentiated startle in a rat has an inverted-U function with intensity of shock during training (Davis, 1984). Thus, current statistical procedures like regression can distort relations in nature (see Hinde, Tamplin, & Barrett, 1993, for a similar position). These analytic procedures assume that the forces producing the values for the variables under study are the same at all ranges; the force varies only in magnitude. This persistent preference for continua, although tacit, has been inimical to progress in psychology. A biologist phrased the case well for qualitative categories: "The study of biological form begins to take us in the direction of a science of qualities that is not an alternative to, but complements and extends, the science of quantities" (Goodwin, 1994, p. 198).

CURRENT VIEWS OF THE INFANT

The current theoretical views on temperament vary, of course, with the age of the child and the sources of evidence; hence, it is necessary that the organization of this discussion accommodate to those features. Further, it is necessary to impose a conservative and somewhat critical attitude toward some of the evidence. Infants and children differ on a large number of characteristics. It is unlikely that most of this variation is primarily temperamental in origin, even though an investigator who has implemented a cross-sectional study may claim otherwise. Thus, I shall restrict the discussion to the small number of characteristics for which most of the evidence implies a temperamental contribution to avoid the error of a half-century earlier when psychologists assumed that all of the variation among children was due to social experience.

Aesthetic considerations play a tacit role in the selection of scientific strategies. Western standards of beauty in science celebrate two different forms of discovery. In the natural sciences, especially biology and chemistry, gaining experimental control of a phenomenon through analytic techniques that often rely on machines generates an aesthetic feeling. A second strategy is to construct elegant formal theory that explains a host of diverse phenomena. Einstein's theory of relativity is a classic example. Because no student of temperament can gain experimental control of a child's behavior, most psychologists working in this domain drift toward the invention of theoretical ideas that might provide a satisfying, logical structure for the phenomena of interest.

When a domain of inquiry is young, it is natural to ask ontological questions. The Greeks asked, "What is matter?"; twentieth-century physicists have answered that question with a set of mathematical functions that predict and, therefore, presumably explain the events that follow the bombardment of a hydrogen atom with high energy. Enlightenment naturalists asked, "What is a species?"; biologists have answered with a set of relations among the evolutionary histories, anatomical and physiological features, and profiles of interbreeding among different animals. In most natural sciences, except psychology, a set of functions has replaced the earlier abstract Platonic conceptions of an object or event. That is, a set of empirical relations became the answer to the earlier ontological query.

Replacement of Platonic definitions with robust functions is moving at a slower pace in developmental psychology. Many journal reports still begin with an ontological definition of some concept, like attachment, memory, or temperament. Thomas and Chess (1977), for example, defined temperament as the style of a person's behavior; Goldsmith and Campos (1990) regard temperament as a set of processes that can modulate an emotional profile. These a priori declarations, which set up boundaries to limit the scope of the empirical work, are useful early in the investigation of a domain. But they should be abandoned when new evidence erodes their usefulness.

Consider, as an example, the variation in infant irritability, which all observers recognize as a moderately stable characteristic over the first year. A psychologist can declare that irritability is a temperamental trait. But after the second birthday, most highly irritable infants are less fretful but become timid and subdued. Thus, either a new term is needed to describe this type of 2-year-old or the investigator can move up the ladder of abstraction and declare that "ease of arousal" is the temperamental quality that unites the irritable infant with the subdued, shy 2-year-old. One problem with this solution is that other infants display "ease of arousal" in the form of babbling rather than crying, and these children develop behavioral profiles that are different from those who are irritable. Robust facts undermine most initial ontological statements. (One reason investigators like parent-report questionnaires to measure temperament is that the questions are written to prevent such undermining; for example, the questions about fear retain that concept for both infants and children.)

I do not suggest that psychologists abandon all ontological questions. It will be profitable, however, to be receptive to data and to move toward concepts that are defined by a set of related functions. For example, 20 percent of healthy 4-month-old infants become very active and fretful to auditory, visual, and olfactory stimuli; two-thirds of these easily aroused infants become fearful in the second year. This longitudinal relation begins to define a temperamental type that future investigators will refine. We can emphasize the 4-month behavior and call these infants easily aroused, or we can focus on the timid behavior at age 2 years and call these children fearful. That choice is less important than the realization that the primary meaning of either term is a set of developmental functions. New temperamental concepts will be revealed as investigators explore children's growth in detail. Psychologists should reflect before they declare the existence of a temperament and should not limit, by fiat, the number of temperamental types, no matter how attractive those choices.

Rothbart's Dimensions

Mary Rothbart's (1988, 1989) bold, synthetic ideas dominate most discussions of infant temperament. Rothbart posits two primary dimensions on which infants vary— ease of arousal and self-regulation—and both are controlled continually by the social environment. "Temperament [is defined as] constitutionally based individual differences in reactivity and self-regulation, with constitutional referring to the person's relatively enduring biological makeup inferred over time by heredity, maturation, and experience. Reactivity refers to the arousability of motor activity, affect, autonomic and endocrine responses. . . . Self-regulation refers to processes that can modulate (facilitate or inhibit) reactivity and those processes include attention, approach, withdrawal, attack, behavioral inhibition, and self-soothing" (Rothbart, 1989, p. 59).

Reactivity

Reactivity can reflect happy or distressed states. The referents for the former category are vocalization, smiling, and nondistressed motor activity; the referents for the latter are thrashing, fretting, and crying. A low-intensity stimulus usually produces vocalization and smiling; a moderately intense stimulus leads to both vocalization and fretting; and an intense stimulus more often provokes distress. Rothbart (1989) suggests that either valence can be expressed through somatic, cognitive, or neuroendocrine responses and can be experienced consciously as a feeling of pleasure or distress. Unlike most theorists, Rothbart regards conscious feeling tone as an important component of infant temperament.

The valence of the reactivity—whether a pleasant or unpleasant affect—will, of course, influence the specific self-regulatory reactions displayed. Thumb sucking or clutching a part of the body are two obvious self-regulatory reactions, as is moving toward or away from a novel incentive.

The idea of ease of arousal has obvious face validity. Fetuses and newborns differ in their reactivity to stimulation, and the variation is related to a modest degree to early postnatal behavior (Madison, Madison, & Adubato, 1986; Strauss & Rourke, 1978). In addition, maternal reports of fetal movements are moderately stable from gestational weeks 28 to 35 (Eaton & Saudino, 1992). But Rothbart writes occasionally as if the specific source of the arousing stimulation, whether visual, tactile, olfactory, or auditory, was relatively unimportant in classifying an infant as high or low in ease of arousal. She writes as if 4-month-old infants who cry to a recording of a woman speaking are similar in arousability to those who cry to a moving mobile because both types of infants were aroused, in a negative way, by an external stimulus. However, 4-month-old infants who cry in fear to a recording of a woman's voice, without the visual support of a face, are different behaviorally in the second and third years from 4-month-olds who cry to a moving mobile but not to the taped voice (Kagan, 1994). Similarly, Goldsmith and Campos (1990) found no correlation between an infant's tendency to cry when placed on the visual cliff and the tendency to cry to the appearance of a stranger.

The nature of the response is also important in judging the infant's arousal. Infants cry, fret, smile, move, or vocalize to auditory stimuli; they do or do not struggle to restraint of their arms. An infant's preferred reaction to a particular incentive is due, partly, to temperamental and maturational factors that are not yet understood. For example, in a longitudinal sample of 23 infants observed at 7, 10, 13, and 16 weeks, an index of motor arousal to varied stimuli based on limb movement increased with age, while the frequency of tongue protrusions, vocalization, and crying decreased with age. Further, only the individual variation in tongue protrusions was stable from 7 to 16 weeks (Rezendes, 1993).

Consider a second example. About 25 percent of a large sample of 4-month-old infants cried more than 6 seconds to a battery of stimuli. However, half of these infants (N = 58) also smiled on two or more occasions, while an equally large group (N = 56) never smiled. The former infants were significantly more talkative than the latter when they were 4.5 years old and showed a larger magnitude of vasoconstriction of the fingertips on the right ring finger to a film clip suggestive of fear (Kagan, unpublished).

Thus, a potential problem with the concept of "ease of arousal" is its high level of abstractness; that is, its indifference to the nature of the incentive that produced the positive or negative arousal. More important, the brain circuits that mediate the reactions of smiling and babbling are likely to be very different from those that mediate thrashing and crying (Gainotti, Caltagirone, & Zoccolotti, 1993). Hence, as Rothbart (1989) has noted, the variation in positive arousal is not highly correlated with the variation in negative arousal.

Self-Regulation

The idea of self-regulation shares some of the problems that burden ease of arousal, for Rothbart does not devote a great deal of discussion to the consequences of different forms of self-regulation. A 1-year-old infant who shows a wary face to a stranger and then retreats to the mother may be different temperamentally from one who also displays a wary face but does not retreat and, subsequently, vocalizes

to the intruder. Even though both infants may appear to be regulating the uncertainty generated by the unfamiliar adult, the former infant becomes more fearful in the second year than the latter.

Most infants do something when they are aroused by events; therefore, most self-regulate to varying degrees. It is important to attend simultaneously both to the specific source of the arousal and the specific self-regulatory behaviors that follow. It is likely that different temperamental types lie hidden within these abstract categories.

Although self-regulation seems to be an apt way to describe some of the behaviors of infants, it may be less appropriate for older children because the incentive is not an intense stimulus (and a subsequent level of arousal) but a specific emotion. When an adult dressed as a clown enters a room where a 2-year-old child has been playing quietly, most children freeze immediately and stare at the intruder. This stereotyped reaction does not occur because the clown is an intense stimulus but because it is a discrepant event, and children usually react to such discrepancies with a cessation of activity. But it is not obvious that the freezing, even if it is accompanied by a retreat to the mother, is a self-regulating reaction. It may not reduce the child's level of arousal or anxiety. Indeed, staring at an unfamiliar intruder while clutching the parent may increase the child's level of uncertainty and physiological arousal.

The idea of self-regulation is related to two older ideas: one originates in the learning theories of the 1950s, the other in Freud's writings at the turn of the century. Dollard and Miller (1950) suggested, during the 1950s, that a reinforcement was any event that reduced stimulation or internal arousal. This hypothesis appears to be derived from Freud's suggestion that humans seek quiescence: a reduction in vis nervosa. This hypothesis assumes, as a deep premise, that organisms naturally seek a low—or optimal—level of internal arousal. This idea remains popular despite the fact that children prefer to run rather than to sit and to explore rather than to play quietly in their bedroom. Freud made the bold move of changing the internal state from the amount of vis nervosa to the intensity of anxiety. That shift made the idea of nervous energy more attractive to most readers, for no one likes to feel anxious. Freud added that cognitive, affective, and behavioral reactions to an anxiety state were directed at reducing the intensity of this unpleasant state. Because anxiety is an obvious enemy, the responses to it could reasonably be called defenses. It is this idea, which remains popular among both psychiatrists and psychologists, that makes the concept of self-regulation appealing.

Specifying Conditions

I believe it may be helpful if future investigators describe the class of incentive events that generate the arousal and the accompanying behavioral reactions, always keeping in mind the child's developmental stage. Psychologists should not code crying, but rather crying to voices, restraint, novelty, or pain. They should not code smiling, but smiling to a face, a mobile, a completed goal-related action, tickling, or the violation of a norm. Two eminent students of animal behavior have noted: "careful attention to specific patterns of behavior . . . is prerequisite to an understanding of the relation between biological and behavioral systems . . . an adequate description of behavior must include reference to the stimuli and situations that normally produce that behavior and to its normal consequences in the environment" (Blanchard & Blanchard, 1988, p. 63).

The suggestion that ease of arousal and self-regulation be parsed in accord with the incentive and the nature of the infant's response does not replace Rothbart's creative ideas; rather, it allows psychologists to see her fruitful hypotheses from a different perspective. It is also in accord with Whitehead's (1928) admonition that we should not reason about predicates that are severed from their noun and object partners. The action verb *kiss* has very different meanings in the following three sentences: (a) The woman kissed her lover; (b) The baby kissed his grandmother; and (c) The winning jockey kissed his horse.

Biologists, more often than psychologists, share a consensus on particular objects and targets when they use a theoretical predicate. *Bleach* describes what rods in the retina do to light. *Phagocytosis* refers to what natural killer cells do to bacteria. *Digest* is what the intestinal villi do to proteins, fats, and carbohydrates. Social scientists are looser in their use of predicates. The predicate *learn* is often applied to diverse organisms, from worms to chimps, on the assumption that the process of learning is the same in all animals. The indifference to agents and targets is due, in part, to the fact that psychologists are primarily interested in process and not in the agents in whom those processes occur. I suspect this assumption serves a deep democratic desire to believe that all humans are alike.

Because psychology is one of the least mature sciences, its practitioners are tempted to take as a model the highly respected discipline of physics. The Newtonian declaration that force equals mass times acceleration holds for all objects—cars, stones, and snowflakes—in all earthly situations. Einstein even declared that the laws of the theory of general relativity applied in all parts of the cosmos. If psychologists were friendlier to biology than to physics, however, they would realize that specificity, not generality, is the more usual and more useful rule in the life sciences.

Strelau's Ideas

Strelau (1991, 1993) bases his conceptions of temperament on variations in the physiology of the central nervous system that were posited originally by Pavlov and more recently by Teplov (1985). Strelau suggests that an irritable infant has a weak nervous system; a minimally irritable infant has a strong one. Strelau posits three properties of the central nervous system: strength, balance, mobility. Strength is the ability to withstand excitation. Balance is the relation between excitation and inhibition. Mobility is the tendency to award priority to excitation or inhibition in a particular situation. Mobility, therefore, represents a flexibility in a reactive style.

The conceptual problems with Strelau's views are obvious. First, the characteristics of strength, balance, and mobility are assigned to the entire brain, even though modern neuroscientists suggest that the brain does not act as a whole. Second, Strelau does not try to relate these three abstract qualities to what is known about the effects of neurochemistry on the brain. Norepinephrine, CRH, glutamate, GABA, serotonin, acetylcholine, and opioids have different influences on different parts of the brain. A brain can become excitable because of excess norepinephrine or too little GABA, excessive glutamate or too little glycine. If the ideas of strength and balance have utility, they must accommodate to what is known about brain chemistry. Finally, there are hemispheric differences in level of activation: some children are more active on the right side and some more active on the left. The future will have to judge the wisdom and utility of Strelau's ideas.

Finally, it is relevant to note that many temperamental constructs have an evaluative dimension, as Osgood et al. (1957) would have predicted. Readers will recall that these scientists discovered that adults from many different cultures used the evaluative contrast good versus bad as an initial dividing principle in categorizing events and objects. Low self-regulation and a weak nervous system are bad qualities to possess. It is common for investigators probing new areas to invent constructs with an implicit evaluative dimension; survival of the fittest is one popular example from biology. But as disciplines mature, scholars replace these constructs with ideas that are more value-neutral, like genome and environmental niche. I suggest that current evaluative concepts in temperament research will also be replaced with more value-neutral concepts, such as high or low vagal tone, asymmetry of activation in the frontal lobes, and motor activity.

Infant Temperamental Qualities

We now consider the major infant qualities that have been nominated by many as temperamental. The progress in this field of inquiry over the past decade is obvious if one compares our current ideas with the state of knowledge when Bates (1987) reviewed the literature on infant temperament.

Because every behavior that can be observed shows variability over a large sample, one can claim that every response reflects a temperament. Therefore, it is important to be restrictive to some degree. By requiring evidence of stability over time and the likelihood of a biological basis, one can limit the temperamental concepts to a reasonable number.

The proper level of abstraction for a temperamental construct is difficult to resolve. At one end, there is the abstract concept of reactivity; at the other is a quality like "cries to bodily restraint during the first two months of life," where response, incentive, and age are specified. I am not certain of the most fruitful level, given current knowledge. However, if the history of biology is a useful model for psychology, it seems certain that we will make more rapid progress by staying close to the concrete phenomena and avoiding overly abstract qualities that are indifferent to the form of the behavior or the context in which the behavior occurs. The vis nervosa of 100 years ago turned out to be useless when scientists discovered a diverse set of chemicals that moderated brain activity in different ways. However, much of the existing literature uses relatively abstract categories; therefore, this chapter must accommodate to that preference.

Irritability

Examination of the extensive literature on temperamental qualities in infants and children reveals that studies of the stable variation in irritability dominate all other qualities in infants; studies of a shy-timid compared with a sociable-bold profile dominate the investigations of toddlers and children. These two facts imply that scientists who quantified other behavioral qualities did not find stable or coherent results and, therefore, did not publish these data. It is hard to believe that most developmental psychologists (over the past 40 years) restricted their observations to this small

set of characteristics. It is more likely that irritability in infancy and a timid or a sociable style in childhood are popular targets because they are obvious, relatively easy to code, of concern to American parents, and moderately stable over time.

A reasonable, relatively conservative conclusion implied by the corpus of evidence is that extremely irritable infants retain, to a modest degree, that disposition or a related derivative through part or all of the first year. Crying and fretting are stable over the first four months, and newborn irritability predicts infrequent smiling and vocalization to adults at 4 months of age (Birns, Barten, & Bridger, 1969). However, spontaneous irritability should not be confused with ease of being soothed with a pacifier. Riese (1995) reports that newborns who took a long time to be soothed by a pacifier were rated by their mothers at 9 months as more active and less likely to avoid unfamiliarity. Further, newborns whose cries were of high pitch and of shorter duration—more unpleasant to the ear—were rated by their mothers at 3 months as more irritable and difficult (Huffman et al., 1994). Extreme distress to a heel stick during the newborn period predicted degree of distress to an inoculation two months later (correlation of 0.4; Worobey & Lewis, 1989) and was related to maternal descriptions of the 6-month-old as minimally distressed by limitations but not to maternal descriptions of soothability or frequency of smiling at 6 months (Gunnar, Porter, Wolf, Rigatuso, & Larson, 1995). Facial expressions, coded in the Ekman-Izard scheme as either anger or sadness, to an inoculation were moderately stable from 2 to 19 months ($r = 0.5$; Izard, Hembree, & Huebner, 1987).

As noted, some, but not all, irritable infants develop a reserved, timid, and fearful style in the preschool years. For example, newborn twins who were unusually irritable, hard to soothe, and minimally attentive to stimulation were less sociable and more labile when they were between 9 and 24 months old (Matheny et al., 1987). Similarly, newborns who became extremely irritable to a chilled metal disk placed against their thigh, compared with those who were far less irritable, had a more serious emotional demeanor ($r = .36$) and were less sociable ($r = .38$) later (Riese, 1987). However, infant crying does not always display stability or predict later behavior (see Fish, Stifter, & Belsky, 1991, for one example).

This evidence implies that an extreme irritability to external stimulation in the opening weeks predicts a less sociable, more dour child 6 to 24 months later. It should also be noted that 4-month-old infants who show frequent irritability together with vigorous limb activity to varied classes of stimulation (these infants would be classified by Rothbart as easily aroused) were extremely fearful to unfamiliar events in the second and third years. These infants were more fearful than those who showed only irritability or only vigorous motor arousal. However, if the irritability is caused by a precocious fear reaction to unfamiliarity, then the small group of 4-month-old girls who displayed this reaction were cognitively precocious in their play at 1 year (Kagan, 1971). Thus, as noted earlier, it is necessary to specify the cause of the infant's distress.

In most of the investigations cited, the crying was either spontaneous or a reaction to visual, auditory, or painful stimuli in an infant under 4 months. In a few studies, however, the crying was produced by restraint, typically holding the infant's hands or arms. Infants who cry to this latter incentive are not similar in temperament to those who cry to visual or auditory stimulation. Infants who cry to restraint have high vagal tone; infants who cry to visual or auditory stimulation have much lower vagal tone (Fox, 1989).

The real, but modest, stability of irritability could be due to the fact that the incentive for crying changes with age. Irritability in a 2-month-old is due, in large measure, to a low threshold of responsivity to the discomfort of cold, hunger, loud noises, and bright lights. Irritability in a 9-month-old is influenced in a more important way by threshold of reaction to unfamiliarity (Hebb, 1946). Irritability in a 1-year-old is influenced, in addition, by a vulnerability to separation distress and prior conditioning experiences in which certain events have become acquired cues for distress. These are very different bases for fretting and crying in the first year. By 3 years of age, the reasons for crying are more varied and include frustrations and prior reinforcements for crying. Thus, psychologists should not be surprised that the correlation between irritability at 1 month and crying at 3 years is relatively low. If investigators had studied the preservation of a defensive reaction to loud noises and bright lights from 1 month to 3 years, the stability coefficients might be higher. Each of the small number of responses that children emit when they are distressed—crying, withdrawal, thrashing, freezing—serves different incentive conditions and involves slightly different brain circuits. The belief that if two theoretical concepts share a primary feature they reflect the same construct is retarding progress. No biologist would treat insomnia and malaria as similar conditions simply because both shared a state of "feeling fatigued."

As might be expected, extremely irritable and nonirritable infants elicit different reactions from their mothers. A group of 89 lower-class infants were observed within the first two weeks of life on the Brazelton Neonatal Behavioral Assessment Scale. One group of 15 infants were extremely irritable and another group of 15 were minimally irritable; these groups represented the top and bottom 17 percent of the sample. These infants and their mothers were observed at home monthly over the first six months. The mothers of the highly irritable, compared with the minimally irritable, infants had less physical contact with their children but soothed them more frequently during the first few months. The mothers of nonirritable infants were more constant in their soothing overtures over time. However, the two groups of mothers became increasingly similar in their responsiveness to their infants as time passed. Thus, at 6 months, the two groups of infants were observed to have experienced similar maternal behaviors, and there were few differences between the two groups in either infant or maternal behavior (Van den Boom & Hoeksma, 1994).

The consistency of the predictive association between early irritability—under 4 months—and some behavior in later childhood, although modest, implies that some infants possess a low threshold for becoming irritable to varied sources of stimulation. The next task is to determine the physiological bases for this characteristic. One possibility is an inherently low threshold in the circuit that involves the amygdala, anterior cingulate, and central gray. This circuit mediates distress cries in animals; hence, it is reasonable to suggest that the excitability of this circuit is influenced by heritable differences in the neurochemistry of these parts of the central nervous system.

All sensory modalities synapse on the amygdala (the lateral, medial, or cortical areas). It is possible that infants who inherit a low threshold of excitability to stimulation in these areas and their projections are most likely to cry to stimulation. If this physiological quality is stable, such infants should become dour and avoidant to unfamiliarity because these amygdalar nuclei and their projections to the hypothalamus, central gray, and cingulate can mediate the dysphoric reactions seen in older children.

Smiling

Crying during the opening months is more salient and more frequent than smiling and, in addition, has an analogue in the distress calls of primates. Smiling has no obvious analogue in most animals. Perhaps that is why few investigators have probed the consequences of individual differences in infant smiling, even though variation in this response appears to be heritable (Freedman & Keller, 1963; Reppucci,

1968). Frequent smiling to adults does not appear until about 3 months of age and may be impaired by damage to posterior sites in the right hemisphere (Reilly, Stiles, Larsen, & Trauner, 1995). Differences in this response appear to be stable from 3 months to the end of the first year. In one study variation in smiles to moderately discrepant events at 4 months predicted smiling following success on a cognitive test at 27 months of age, and smiling was more stable over time than either attentiveness, crying, or vocalization (Kagan, 1971).

Infants who smile and do not cry to visual or auditory stimulation become more sociable and relatively fearless in the second year (Kagan, 1994), show greater activation of the left frontal area when desynchronization of alpha frequencies in the EEG is the index of activation (Fox et al., 1994), and, if girls, are a bit heavier than infant girls who smile infrequently (Kagan, 1971).

Frequent smiling to nonsocial stimuli in young infants may reflect a special temperamental quality. We have observed a large sample of 4-month-olds who were exposed to visual, auditory, and olfactory stimuli and over half of them never smiled. However, 10 percent of the group smiled three or more times during the 45-minute battery. Although three smiles may seem to be small in an absolute sense, it represented the 90th percentile of the distribution. When these smiling infants were matched with infants of the same sex and level of motor arousal and irritability who did not smile at all, the former group had significantly lower sitting diastolic blood pressure when they were 21 months old. This result suggests that frequent smiling at 4 months is associated with low sympathetic tone in the arterial tree, an idea supported by the fact that 2-week-olds who showed high levels of heart rate variability to stimulation were frequent smilers at 4 months (Fish & Fish, 1995). High smiling may be facilitated by less intense feedback from sympathetic targets, a state that could create a lower state of arousal in the limbic system.

Activity

Activity, which is a popular temperamental category, has a special meaning after children have attained motor coordination that is different from limb movement during infancy (see Rothbart & Bates, Ch. 3, this Volume, for additional discussion). The changes in frequency and vigor of limb activity during the first year of life are so dramatic it is not surprising that observational studies do not find much preservation of variation in activity level (Dunn & Kendrick, 1981; Feiring & Lewis, 1980; Matheny, 1983). One of the best studies assessed activity in 112 healthy,

middle-class newborns using a pressure transducer mattress that distinguished activity during crying from activity during nondistress periods. Fifty of the 112 infants were assessed again when they were between 4 and 8 years of age. Activity in the older children was monitored for 24 hours using an ambulatory microcomputer along with a parental questionnaire. There was only a modest correlation between the vigor of activity during the newborn period and the proportion of vigorous activity during the day in the older children ($r = .29$). There was no correlation between day and night activity in the older children and no relation between newborn activity and the parental ratings of activity in the older children (Korner et al., 1985). The authors noted that the independence of day and night activity in children implies that the concept of general activity is not useful.

A similar study assessed activity in monozygotic (MZ) and dizygotic (DZ) twins at 7 months and 3 years using actometers. There was minimal preservation of activity but modest heritability (Saudino & Eaton, in press). By contrast, the stability and heritability of physical features like weight and the ponderal index were substantial. The absence of substantial stability of activity level in the home in a large sample of twins observed at 14, 20, and 24 months supports the conclusions described above. The stability of activity from 14 to 24 months was only .23; although statistically significant, it is quite modest, as was the heritability of activity ($h^2 = .20$; Saudino, Plomin, Campos, & DeFries, 1993). (See Saudino & Eaton, 1991, for a similar result with a smaller sample of twins, and Goldsmith & Gottesman, 1981.) Matheny (1983) also reported very modest stability of activity in a laboratory situation from 6 to 24 months but more robust heritability coefficients for MZ and DZ twins.

It seems reasonable, given the evidence summarized, to conclude that a general activity construct that does not stipulate the age of the child, the context of assessment, or time of day is not very stable and, therefore, may not be a useful concept in that abstract form.

Attentional Processes

The increasing influence of cognitive neuroscience has penetrated the study of temperament and led investigators to examine variation in the distribution of attention. Rothbart, Derryberry, and Posner (1994) present a clear summary of three aspects of attention that might turn out to be temperamental (see also Rothbart & Bates, Ch. 3, this Volume).

The posterior attention network is especially involved in directing an infant's attention to sensory stimuli. Infants differ in the rapidity and consistency with which they orient to a moving object or a sound in the periphery. It is believed that the posterior attentional network involves portions of the parietal cortex, thalamus, and parts of the superior colliculus. The activity in these sites is modulated by noradrenergic axons from the locus ceruleus.

The anterior attentional network involves parts of the prefrontal cortex, anterior cingulate cortex, and the supplementary motor area. This network participates more in effortful control of behavior and the inhibition of activity to distracting or irrelevant stimuli, as well as in the effortful search for specific targets. It is believed that dopaminergic inputs from the ventral tegmental area and the basal ganglia modulate this network.

Finally, Posner and Petersen (1990) posit a vigilance system that mediates maintenance of an alert state over a duration of time. Preliminary evidence implicates the role of the right lateral midfrontal cortex as important, which, like the posterior system, is influenced by noradrenergic axons from the locus ceruleus.

Observations of children at 1, 2, and 3.5 years of age revealed stability of inattentiveness from 2 to 3.5 years of age (Ruff, Lawson, Parinello, & Weissberg, 1990). A longitudinal study of variation in attentiveness, indexed by duration of fixation time to human faces or forms, revealed no stability from 4 months to 13 or 27 months, and only modest stability from 13 to 27 months ($r = 0.2$), although parental education predicted attentiveness for girls but not boys in the second year (Kagan, 1971). Further, variation in attentiveness was not related to the child's IQ or reading ability when the child was 10 years old (Kagan, Lapidus, & Moore, 1978). Because the psychological bases for attentiveness changed from long periods of attention to discrepancy at 4 months to the activation of cognitive structures in the second year, investigators should not expect much preservation of long fixation times.

Task orientation, observed in twin pairs from 3 to 24 months, showed reasonable heritability (Matheny, 1980). Finally, distractability in a laboratory playroom—flitting from one toy to another—in a sample of 3.5-year-old children showed modest predictability to teacher ratings of hyperactivity at 6 and 8 years of age (Carlson, Jacobvitz, & Sroufe, 1995; Riese, 1988).

In sum, activity, smiling, laughter, irritability to stimulation, distress to limitations, fear to novelty, attention, and ease of being soothed have some of the features of temperamental qualities, and these characteristics are included in the parental questionnaires created by Goldsmith and Rothbart (1991). In addition, a set of useful,

standard procedures for 1- to 2-year-olds that rely on behavioral observations in the laboratory (Lab Tab) purport to measure fear to novelty, anger proneness, pleasure, interest, and activity level (Goldsmith & Rothbart, 1991).

TEMPERAMENTS IN OLDER CHILDREN

The most popular a priori temperamental qualities that apply to children age 2 and older resemble those that dominate the study of infants, even though new characteristics emerge after the first birthday. Bates (1989) presents a summary of these qualities. The concept of *negative emotionality* refers to the display of distress, fear, and anger and is similar in sense meaning to one of the three major temperaments proposed by Buss and Plomin (1984) for adults. A second factor is *difficultness,* a derivative of the Thomas and Chess category that refers to irritability, a vulnerability to stress, and a demanding posture with adults. Bates (1980) acknowledges that this quality is, in part, a construction on the part of the parent. A third, *adaptability to novelty,* describes a child's tendency to approach unfamiliar events and situations. *Reactivity,* a fourth category, is close in meaning to Rothbart's (1989) definition of this characteristic, and *activity* is regarded as an important temperamental factor. *Attention regulation,* which refers to the tendency to shift attention when distracted by external stimulation, resembles Rothbart's (1989) infant quality of soothability. Finally, Bates (1989) suggests that *sociability and positive reactivity* comprise an important temperament. All seven of these characteristics may turn out to be stable and coherent. At the present time there is extensive evidence on adaptability to novelty and sociability, and we summarize that corpus of evidence.

Shy versus Sociable Children

A shy, subdued, timid profile, compared with a sociable, extroverted, bold one, in the presence of unfamiliar people, situations, and objects is as frequent a target of study in preschool and school-age children as irritability is in infants—and for the same reasons. The defining behaviors are frequent and easy to code, and intuition suggests that these two profiles are related to adjustment in contemporary society.

Longitudinal data from the Berkeley Guidance Study reveals that boys who were very shy in late childhood, as described by their mothers, were different from others when they were over 40 years old. The former group married, became parents, and established a career later than their less shy peers. Very shy girls, on the other hand, married at normative times, but unlike their less shy peers, did not develop a career and terminated a job when they married or had a child. These shy girls conformed to a traditional sex-role norm for that era in American history (Caspi, Elder, & Bem, 1988).

Longitudinal observations on a large group of New Zealand children affirm the preservation of a shy profile. Over 1,000 3-year-olds were rated on a variety of characteristics following a one-hour interaction in a laboratory setting. About 15 percent were rated as shy and subdued, and 30 percent as sociable and spontaneous. When these same subjects were 18 years old, they filled out a personality questionnaire. The adolescents who had been shy at 3 years of age described themselves as cautious, minimally aggressive, and likely to avoid dangerous situations (Caspi & Silva, 1995). Further, unpublished data on a Finnish longitudinal sample, followed from age 8 to age 26 years, found that an avoidant, anxious profile at age 8 (based on teacher ratings) predicted an introverted personality in adult men ($r = .34$) and a conflicted personality in adult women ($r = .47$; Lea Pulkkinen, personal communication). It is of interest that about 15 percent of this sample of Finnish 8-year-olds were rated as anxious/avoidant, a value that matches the prevalence for both American and Canadian samples.

There is an intriguing relation between season of conception and observer ratings of shyness in both American and New Zealand samples. The preschool children in a large American longitudinal cohort, the National Longitudinal Sample of Youth (NLSY), were rated on shyness by trained home visitors on two different occasions. The 15 percent of the sample who were rated as very shy on both occasions, separated by two years, were most likely to be conceived during the period from late July to late September. Thus, the brain would be completing its basic organization during the period September to November when the amount of daylight is decreasing most rapidly. The New Zealand children who were rated as shy were most likely to be conceived in January and February. Because New Zealand is in the Southern Hemisphere, daylight begins to decrease during these two months. Thus, both groups of fetuses who became shy children spent the first four months of their pregnancy at a time of decreasing daylight (Gortmaker & Kagan, in press). The decrease in daylight is accompanied by increases in level of melatonin but decreases

in serotonin in the pregnant mother. It is possible that these biochemical changes affect the brains of those embryos who are genetically disposed to develop shyness and increases the probability of that behavioral outcome. Nature can act in surprising ways.

We noted earlier that the evidence implies a modest predictive relation between variation in infant irritability and a shy or a sociable profile in the older child. However, as with irritability, a shy posture with children or adults can have different antecedents and, therefore, different meanings. A 4-year-old in a social setting can play alone because (a) uncertainty is generated over the unfamiliarity of the setting, (b) the child feels concern over being evaluated by others, (c) the child prefers to play alone, or (d) the child has experienced traumatic, fear-arousing encounters with other children and has developed a conditioned avoidance to peers. An investigator who codes only "time playing apart from other children" could have etiologically heterogeneous groups with similar scores. On the other hand, if the investigator codes several variables—time playing alone, time staring at peers, talking, smiling, and reaction to overtures from others—it will be easier to parse the isolated children into separate groups, only some of whom possess a temperamental bias to be shy. Every single class of behavior is ambiguous as to its antecedent conditions.

The research of Rubin and his colleagues, which relies on behavioral observations, is exemplary. Rubin (1993) makes a distinction between the child who plays alone but who shows signs of anxiety and the equally solitary child who is actively engaged in activities but who does not show signs of uncertainty. Both types are stable over time, but the former more often stares at peers and resembles the behaviorally inhibited child (Coplan, Rubin, Fox, Calkins, & Stewart, 1994).

Asendorpf (1991) also finds shy behavior to be stable over time, although more intelligent children show a greater decrease in shyness over time compared with their less intelligent peers (Asendorpf, 1994). Shy, reticent behavior with strangers was stable in a group of 99 German children observed in varied settings from the preschool years through the third grade ($r = 0.6$; Asendorpf, 1990). Asendorpf agrees with Rubin that a child can be shy because of the unfamiliarity of the situation, a concern over evaluation of task competence by another, or anxiety over peer rejection (Asendorpf, 1989, 1991, 1993; see also Stevenson-Hinde & Shouldice, in press, for a similar result).

A similar conclusion emerged from a study of 212 Swedish children followed over a six-year interval. Psychologists rated the children's behavior in the first and second years and annually until 6 years of age. (In addition, mothers rated their infants four times during the first year, twice during the second year, and annually until they were 6 years old.) The children who were exceptionally shy or sociable (15 percent at each end of the distribution) preserved their style from the second year of life to age 6. The stability was greater for girls than for boys and smaller in magnitude when the whole sample was treated as if sociability were a continuum (Kerr, Lambert, Stattin, & Klackenberg-Larsson, 1994).

A second group of Swedish investigators followed 144 firstborn children from 16 months through the fourth year of life, a two-year interval. Some children were attending day care and some were raised only at home. Shy behavior with an unfamiliar adult, based on observations at home, was stable from 28 to 40 months ($r = 0.4$) but not from 16 to 40 months, and there was no effect of day care attendance on shyness (Broberg, Lamb, & Hwang, 1990). "The increased contact with strange adults that followed from enrollment in out of home care did not affect children's inhibition at 28 and 40 months of age, which suggests that inhibition in the first year of life is best viewed as a fairly stable dimension that is not systematically affected by ordinary life changes like those implicit in the initiation of out of home care" (p. 1161). The fact that the children attending day care were not more sociable than those at home with their mothers surprised the authors and will surprise some developmental psychologists.

Inhibited versus Uninhibited Children

My colleagues, Nancy Snidman, Doreen Arcus, Steven Reznick, and I, regard shyness with strangers, whether peers or adults, as only one feature of a broader temperamental category called inhibition to the unfamiliar (Arcus, 1991; Kagan, 1994). Inhibited children react to many different types of unfamiliarity with an initial avoidance, distress, or subdued affect when they reach the maturational stage when discrepancies elicit uncertainty, usually 7 to 9 months in humans. The comparable ages in other species are 2 to 3 months in monkeys, 30 to 35 days in cats, and 5 to 7 days in ducklings (Kagan, 1994). The source of the unfamiliarity can be people, situations, or events. An inhibited child might, with experience, learn to control an initial avoidance of strangers and, therefore, not appear to others

to be shy. But this child might retain an avoidant style to unfamiliar nonsocial challenges or to unfamiliar places. Thus, the concept of an inhibited temperament assumes that a child can display an avoidant style in any one of a number of contexts. Membership in this temperamental category is not defined by one specific class of behavior, like shyness with an unfamiliar peer. Thus, only a proportion of shy children should be classified as inhibited.

The complementary category, called uninhibited, is characterized by a sociable, affectively spontaneous reaction to unfamiliar people, situations, and events. As with the inhibited child, the category refers to an envelope of profiles whose particular form changes with development.

Further, the behavior and the emotion displayed in a specific situation should not be regarded as conceptually separate from the biology that mediates the psychological phenomena. The idea of an inhibited (or uninhibited) child combines both phenomena. The independence of an entity, such as a child, from its functions was a major node of disagreement between Whitehead and Russell. Russell believed that the two ideas were independent, whereas Whitehead insisted that they were a unity. In the statement "Lions stalk gazelles" Russell would have argued that the predicate *stalk* was applicable to a variety of animals and could be treated as an independent function. Whitehead would have claimed that lions stalk in a particular way that is different from that of hyenas; therefore, the original idea should not be parsed into a class of agents and a class of actions that can be combined in any way. I side with Whitehead, as do all who believe that the motives, emotional mood, and posture of an agent who "gives an order to another" are different when the agent is a 3-year-old with a peer, a burglar, an army officer, or a parent of an adolescent. The behavior of inhibited children in unfamiliar social situations is not exactly like the profile of those who acquired their shy, timid demeanor through experience alone. The former group displays fewer spontaneous smiles and much greater muscle tension. Thus, it is not wise to treat the predicate *is shy* as an independent quality that is separable from the child's age, life history, and physiology and the specific context of observation.

The behavior of the inhibited child who is faced with novelty tempts one to use the word *fearful* to describe the emotional state and to assume, further, that this state is similar to, or perhaps identical with, the state created by (a) classical conditioning of a person, object, or place as a predictor of pain; (b) a biologically potent stimulus, for example, a looming object; or (c) worry over a future event.

As noted earlier, this assumption is likely to be as incorrect as the older view among cognitive scientists who regarded memory as a unitary process (Vanderwolf & Cain, 1994).

The Significance of Unfamiliarity

The states created by discrepancy, classical conditioning, evolutionarily significant stimuli, and anticipation of the future do not involve the same neural circuits. This claim rests, in part, on evidence from animal studies (Treit et al., 1993a, 1993b) and the fact that the most probable profile of responses is different for the four incentive conditions listed above. An unfamiliar event, for example, a person with a mask, typically produces cessation of activity in a 2-year-old child, a response mediated by a circuit involving the amygdala and the ventral periaqueductal gray. However, acquiring a classically conditioned rise in heart rate does not require the central gray but the amygdala and the lateral hypothalamus, together with projections to the sympathetic chain. But a startle reaction, with or without a distress call, to a sudden, looming object or a loud sound need not involve the amygdala. Classically conditioned avoidance of specific tastes, but not odors, can be acquired in rats while they are anesthetized, suggesting that the conditioned avoidance of taste stimuli may be biologically different from learned avoidance to other stimulus modalities (Rattoni, Forthman, Sanchez, Perez, & Garcia, 1988).

Unfortunately, scientists do not yet know the circuits that mediate the conscious report of anxiety or worry over a future threat or challenge. We do know that children and adults can report feeling anxious without any accompanying peripheral physiological changes. In light of this evidence, it seems reasonable to reject the idea of a unitary fear state and to assume, until data prove otherwise, that discrepancy, classical conditioning, biologically significant events, anticipation of future unpleasantness, as well as separation from a target of attachment are different physiological and psychological states, albeit members of a related family of emotions. It is reassuring that physiologists also reject the idea of a unitary state of physiological stress: hemorrhage, hypotension, and hypoglycemia produce different profiles of secratog release (Sapolsky, 1992).

The inhibited child is vulnerable to a state of fear or uncertainty to discrepancy; that statement does not mean that this child will acquire a conditioned fear reaction more easily, will be more fearful of bugs, or will worry more intensely about evaluation. By contrast, uninhibited children possess a physiology that renders them less vulnerable, but

not totally invulnerable, to becoming fearful to unfamiliar events. This degree of specificity in the use of the term *fear* will be helpful as we describe the characteristics of these two groups of children.

Rothbart (1988) detected an interesting reaction in infants that may be a correlate of later inhibition. Infants 6, 10, and 13 months old were presented with a static or moving toy and the latency to reach for the object was coded. The latencies were shorter when the toy was static, and that latency to reach was stable from 6 to 13 months ($r = .62$). Further, infants who had cried to unfamiliar events on other assessments had the longest latencies and smiled less often than those who reached for the toy quickly. This association matches a result reported by Kagan (1994).

Infant Predictors of Inhibited and Uninhibited Behavior

Observations of 4-month-old infants exposed to visual, auditory, and olfactory stimulation point to the possible physiological bases for the inhibited and uninhibited profiles that emerge by the first birthday. The early infant behaviors that are predictive of the two later categories can be understood if we assume that some infants are born with a low threshold of excitability in the amygdala and its projections to the ventral striatum, hypothalamus, cingulate, central gray, and medulla. Infants with low thresholds of excitability in the basolateral and central areas of the amygdala and their projections show high levels of vigorous motor activity, a great deal of muscle tension, and frequent irritability to a standardized 40-minute laboratory battery composed of visual, auditory, and olfactory stimulation. The 4-month-old infants who did show frequent and vigorous limb activity together with frequent distress to stimulation—about 20 percent of an unselected healthy Caucasian sample—are called high reactive. The complementary group who show low levels of motor arousal and minimal irritability to the same battery, and comprise about 40 percent of the sample, are assumed to have higher limbic thresholds to stimulation. These infants are called low reactive.

My colleagues and I have observed one cohort of over 450 infants at 4 months of age, with over 250 children studied again at both 14 and 21 months. The laboratory batteries at 14 and 21 months consisted of a variety of procedures designed to elicit uncertainty, including intrusion into the child's personal space (placing electrodes on the body or a blood pressure cuff on the arm), exposure to unfamiliar objects (robots, toy animals, papier-mâché puppets), and encounters with unfamiliar people who behaved in an atypical way or wore a novel costume. A child who cried to any one of these events or did not approach any of the unfamiliar objects when requested to do so was coded as fearful for that episode. High-reactive infants were signficantly more fearful at 14 and 21 months than were low-reactive infants. About one-third of the high-reactive infants were highly fearful at both 14 and 21 months, although only 3 percent showed minimal fear at the these two ages. By contrast, one-third of the low-reactive infants were minimally fearful at the same two ages and only 4 percent showed high fear. It is of interest that the remaining children showed intermediate levels of fearfulness.

Support for the claim that these two groups of infants, defined by a combination of motor arousal and crying to stimulation, represent qualitative categories and should not be placed on a continuum of arousal comes from the fact that when the duration of crying to the 4-month battery was either zero (the infant did not cry at all) or longer than 8 seconds, the correlation between degree of motor activity at 4 months and fearfulness at 14 months was close to zero for each of the two cry groups ($r = .13$ for the subjects who did not cry at all, and $r = .10$ for those who cried more than 8 seconds). Conversely, when the infants were divided into groups with motor scores that were low (< 40) or high (> 50), the correlation between duration of crying at 4 months and fear at 14 months was also low ($r = .25$ for those with low motor behavior; $r = .08$ for those with high motor scores). Thus, once an infant had passed the criteria for motor arousal and crying that defined high reactivity, additional motor activity or crying (within that category) had minimal consequences for how fearful the child would become later. The variation in motor behavior and crying to visual and auditory stimulation at 2 months, observed in a separate longitudinal cohort, was less predictive of fear in the second year, in part because variation in motor activity and irritability was much less striking.

Childhood Derivatives of High and Low Reactivity

When the high- and low-reactive infants were evaluated at 4.5 years of age, the former group was much more subdued; they talked and smiled less frequently during a one-hour interview with an unfamiliar female examiner. By contrast, the low-reactive children were spontaneous; they asked questions, commented on the procedures, and smiled and laughed more often. The differences between the two groups in smiling were more dramatic than the differences in talking. The three low-reactive boys who smiled the most (more than 50 times) had been the most relaxed infants when they were 4 months old (Kagan, 1997).

A small proportion of high reactives were unusual, for they talked and smiled frequently during the examination at 4 years. Although their environmental histories probably influenced this profile, it is of interest that during the original assessment at 4 months these children smiled more often than the majority of high-reactive infants who were very subdued at 4.5 years. In addition, they showed a lower and more varied heart rate when they were 14 months old. These data imply that this small group of high reactives possesses a special temperamental quality.

The fact that spontaneous conversation with a stranger is a sensitive sign of uncertainty after 3 or 4 years of age is supported by a sample of children classified as inhibited or uninhibited at 21 or 31 months and observed again at 5, 7, and 13 years of age. Infrequent talking to an unfamiliar examiner was the best correlate of the original classification of an inhibited temperament at all three ages. It is possible that the small number of children with elective mutism represent extremely inhibited children (Black, 1992).

Restraint on spontaneous conversation in an unfamiliar social situation seems to function in humans as freezing to novelty does in animals. Both responses are mediated by the fibers of the central gray that are innervated by projections from the amygdala. But restraint on spontaneous speech is not a sensitive measure of uncertainty to the unfamiliar until after the third birthday. There was no significant relation between spontaneous vocalization in the first and second year and spontaneous speech with an adult at 4 years of age. Although both variables involve making sounds, the responses are different in meaning. Absence of vocalization in the first year reflects low affective arousal; restraint on speech at 4 years reflects anticipatory anxiety. One-year-old children are not old enough to be concerned with the examiner's evaluation of them or to anticipate the laboratory procedures that might be administered. Many years ago, I suggested that there are heterotypic phenomena in development; that is, variation in an early quality predicts variation in a phenotypically different characteristic later in development (Kagan, 1971). The relation between high reactivity at 4 months and restraint on spontaneous speech and smiling at 4.5 years is an example of that principle.

The high- and low-reactive children also differed at 4.5 years in their social behavior with two other unfamiliar children of the same age and sex when trios of children were observed in a laboratory playroom for a half hour. Almost 66 percent of the low-reactive but fewer than 10 percent of the high-reactive children were outgoing and sociable with the unfamiliar children. By contrast, 40 percent of the high reactives were avoidant and quiet compared with only 10 percent of the low reactives. Although there was significant preservation of inhibited or uninhibited temperamental styles from 4 months to 4.5 years, these data also imply that environmental factors are working on each child's phenotype. However, a minority of children maintained an obvious inhibited or uninhibited profile at 14 months, 21 months, and 4.5 years. Five percent of low reactives and 13 percent of the high reactives maintained a consistently uninhibited or inhibited behavioral style across age and contexts; only one low-reactive infant became consistently inhibited and no high-reactive infant became consistently uninhibited.

The 4-year-old children who had been high reactive were also more intimidated by the examiner. In one of the episodes, the female examiner asked the older child to perform some actions that would be prohibited by most parents. For example, she opened a photo album containing pictures of herself, took out a large color photograph, and, as she handed it to the child, said, "This is my favorite picture; tear up my favorite picture." More low than high reactives either asked her why they should perform that act or, in the case of five subjects, refused to do so. Moreover, their resistance was not accompanied by any obvious signs of anxiety; they simply appeared to be less afraid of disobeying the requests of an authority figure when that request required them to violate a norm they had acquired. Almost all the high reactives were reluctant to disobey and, after a 5- to 10-second delay, tore a small corner from the photograph.

Parents of many high-reactive inhibited preschool children reported that their children are extremely sensitive to criticism. They cry, have a tantrum, or become very subdued when they are chastised. On the face of it, this response does not follow from the hypothesis that high-reactive inhibited children react to unfamiliarity with fear. Parental criticism is not an unfamiliar event in the same sense that a person dressed in a clown costume fits that definition. This developmental relation can be understood, however, if we assume that the mind/brain of a child older than 3 or 4 years is continually generating a representation of the present and immediate future, perhaps the next 30 to 60 seconds. If an event, like a chastisement, is not expected, that is, it is not in the representation

of the immediate future, it resembles a discrepant event. If the amygdala and its circuits are excited by discrepancy, there can be an extreme reaction—crying, withdrawal, or a tantrum.

It is possible that adolescents and adults who were inhibited children are more easily threatened by encounters with beliefs, opinions, or philosophical premises that are not in accord with those that have become firm beliefs. This prediction is in accord with evidence from adolescents suggesting an association between introversion and conservative attitudes. Thus, at a speculative level, it is possible that high-reactive inhibited children are more reactive to all events that are not contained in the ongoing representations of the present and immediate future.

Sympathetic Physiology

If inhibited and uninhibited children differ in their thresholds of excitability in the amygdala and its projections, high-reactive inhibited children should show evidence of greater sympathetic reactivity than low-reactive uninhibited children. Five- and 7-year-old inhibited, compared with uninhibited, children did show greater pupillary dilation, greater cardiac acceleration, and larger changes in blood pressure to appropriate stressors (Kagan, 1994). Further, more high- than low-reactive infants had higher fetal heart rates (over 140 bpm) a few weeks before birth and higher 2-week sleeping heart rates while being held erect but not when held supine. Spectral analysis of the infants' sleeping heart rates, which separate vagal from sympathetic influences, revealed that the high- compared with the low-reactive infants had greater power in the low-frequency band (between .02 and .10 Hz) when held erect, suggesting greater sympathetic reactivity (Snidman, Kagan, Riordan, & Shannon, 1995). This fact finds support in a longitudinal study of 31 pregnant mothers and their fetuses. The fetuses with high heart rates had less frequent positive affect at 6 months of age (DiPietro, 1995).

Longitudinal study of 23 infants at 7, 10, 13, and 16 weeks revealed a high correlation ($r = .72$) between motor arousal to stimulation and low-frequency power during sleep at 10 weeks, just before vagal influence is enhanced. Further, individual variation in the amount of low-frequency power during sleep was stable from 7 to 16 weeks, although level of motor arousal was not. These facts lend strong support to the hypothesis that infants who are easily aroused to display motor activity to stimulation are born with a more reactive sympathetic influence on the cardiovascular system (Rezendes, 1993).

Finally, it should be noted that a variable heart rate, reflecting less sympathetic activity in infants, seems to be linked to a tendency to approach objects (Richards & Cameron, 1989) and people (Fox, 1989) and to make more frequent facial expressions of joy (Stifter, Fox, & Porges, 1989).

An important issue in the interpretation of variation in peripheral physiological targets is whether the variation reflects relatively enduring temperamental qualities or simply a temporary state; it is likely that it reflects both. Children who are prone to be uncertain for temperamental reasons can show high and stable heart rates under resting conditions. But children who have been socialized to worry about evaluation by an adult in an unfamiliar context can resemble the first group in the heart rate profile.

Consider the following illustration. The mean resting heart rate of a group of 92 4-year-olds was obtained as the battery began. About 25 percent showed a high and stable heart rate (low vagal tone) and another 25 percent showed a low and variable heart rate (high vagal tone). The remaining children fell at neither extreme. Although more low-reactive boys had a low and variable heart rate, other children—boys and girls—who showed the low and variable profile had been significantly less fearful at 14 and 21 months than those with an initially high and stable heart rate. This fact suggests that children who are predisposed to be uncertain to an initial encounter with an unfamiliar examiner, because of either temperament or socialization, are in a psychological state that increases their sympathetic reactivity (or, perhaps, inhibits vagal activity). State and trait are often difficult to separate.

One of the many causes of variation in sympathetic reactivity is the nucleus tractus solitarius (NTS) in the medulla. This structure receives afferent information from heart, gut, respiratory organs, and taste receptors and sends them to the brain as well as sending projections downward to both branches of the autonomic nervous system. The excitability of the NTS is influenced by a large number of chemicals, including catecholamines, glutamate, GABA, and neuropeptides. The concentrations of these chemicals and the density of their specific receptors are likely to be under genetic control. Hence, the excitability of the NTS should vary with the child's genotype. It is well known that some individuals can detect subtle changes in heart rate, and this sensitivity to afferent information from the body probably influences conscious feelings and mood (Andersen & Kunze, 1994).

Although sex differences in heart rate are small for unselected volunteer samples of children, low-reactive boys in the second year have significantly lower heart rates than most children, lower than both high-reactive boys and low-reactive girls. A similar difference was noted for diastolic blood pressure to orthostatic stress. It appears that high vagal tone is associated with low reactivity in boys, but less so in girls. Because we believe that causes of low reactivity are similar in the two sexes, the sex difference in heart rate is difficult to understand. It is possible that girls inherit, independent of their 4-month reactivity, a more reactive sympathetic nervous system than boys.

Cerebral Asymmetry

When confronted with a stressful incentive, like temporary maternal absence, young children show greater EEG activation on the right, compared with the left, frontal area, where desynchronization of alpha frequencies is the index of activation (Dawson, Panagiotides, Klinger, & Hill, 1992). Thus, it is of interest that inhibited, compared with uninhibited, children show greater activation on the right frontal area under resting conditions (Davidson, 1994a, 1994b). Further, high-reactive infants show greater activation of the right frontal area during the first and second years; low-reactive infants show greater activation of the left frontal area (Fox et al., 1994). Because neural activity in the amygdala is transmitted to the frontal lobe, via the nucleus basalis, it is possible that greater desynchronization of alpha frequencies on the right frontal lobe can reflect greater activity in the right amygdala (Kapp, Supple, & Whalen, 1994; Lloyd & Kling, 1991). It appears that the greater right-sided cerebral activation that is associated with fear is more characteristic of high-reactive infants and inhibited children than of low-reactive infants and uninhibited children. It is of interest that infant chimpanzees with a right-hand bias in hand-to-mouth behavior exhibited lower arousal at 2 days of age than did infants without a clear right-hand bias (Hopkins & Bard, 1993).

Asymmetry of forehead temperature, as measured by infrared telethermography scanner, reveals a similar relation. Skin temperature is controlled by the degree of sympathetically mediated vasoconstriction in the arterioles of the forehead and the anastomoses of the fingertips. Because the sympathetic nervous system does not cross and is more reactive on the right side of the body, children with a more active right hemisphere should show greater constriction of vessels on the right side and, therefore, a cooler skin temperature on that side (Gainotti et al., 1993). Those with greater left-hemisphere activation, which is more common among children and adults, should show greater constriction on the left side (see Gur et al., 1995, for evidence of greater metabolic activity in the left cerebrum). Two-year-old girls—actually 21 months old—who had a cooler temperature on the right side of the forehead were more inhibited than those with a cooler left side (Kagan, 1994). Two-year-old boys and girls who had a cooler left compared with right side of the forehead smiled more frequently and had a lower heart rate during the laboratory battery (Kagan, Arcus, Snidman, & Rimm, 1995).

The fingertips have anastomoses and, therefore, show larger temperature changes and asymmetry than the forehead. Measurement of temperature asymmetry on the fingertips of the same children when they were 4.5 years of age revealed different profiles in high and low reactives in response to film clips suggestive of fear, sadness, and joy. Most children of both groups showed a large difference in temperature between the index finger on the left and right hands (a mean difference of 0.3°C), favoring a cooler left index finger. By contrast, more children had a cooler right compared with left ring finger (mean asymmetry of 0.4°C). However, high reactives who had been fearful at 21 months had a significantly larger asymmetry (favoring a cooler right over left ring finger) than did low reactives who were not fearful. Thus, at 21 months and 4.5 years the temperature asymmetry on the forehead and fingertips matched the asymmetry of EEG activation in inhibited and uninhibited children. Both results implied greater right-sided activation for the inhibited group.

A profile that combined low reactivity and a low heart rate at 4 months with low fear scores, frequent smiling, and a cooler left forehead in the second year was characteristic of a very small group of boys who were exuberant, sociable, and full of vitality. The existence of this small group, less than 10 percent of the large sample, is in accord with Magnusson's (1988) suggestion that investigators should search for categories of people, each defined by a distinct profile of characteristics. The fact that fewer than 10 percent of this sample of over 400 children displayed this combination challenges current practices in research, for most laboratory studies of children or adults contain fewer than 50 unselected volunteers.

Facial Skeleton

The two temperamental groups also differ in facial skeleton in ways that would not have been surprising to some nineteenth-century observers and that imply the categorical nature of these two temperaments. Infants classified as high reactive at 4 months had narrower faces (the ratio of the width of the face at the bizygomatic—high cheekbone—to the length of the face) when they were 14 months

old compared to children classified as low reactive (Arcus & Kagan, 1995). There was also a relation to contemporaneous behavior. Children with the narrowest faces at 14 months were more fearful at both 14 and 21 months than those who had very broad faces. Every one of 11 children who were high reactive at 4 months and also inhibited at 4.5 years had a facial ratio at 14 months less than .57. Every one of the 9 children who were low reactive at 4 months and uninhibited at 4.5 years had facial ratios equal to or greater than .57.

The fact that facial skeleton is a significant correlate of the two temperamental groups implies the influence of a set of genes that affects features as diverse as the growth of facial bone, ease of arousal in infancy, smiling, and fear of unfamiliar events. It is of interest that inbred mouse strains like A/JAX that are susceptible to inhibition of palatal shelf growth following pharmacological doses of glucocorticoids during gestation are more fearful in an open field than strains like C57 BL/6 that are less susceptible to the influence of this steroid on the growth of facial bone (Thompson, 1953; Walker & Fraser, 1957). This fact implies that the genes that influence the growth of facial bone in response to glucocorticoids are correlated with those that monitor fear of novelty.

Heritability

Inhibited and uninhibited profiles appear to be heritable. Identical twins are more similar in the display of shy, timid behavior during childhood than are fraternal twins (Emde et al., 1992; Matheny, 1983, 1990), matching similar conclusions based on data from adults (Davis, Luce, & Kraus, 1994). The staff at the Institute of Behavioral Genetics at the University of Colorado is conducting a longitudinal study of a large number of same-sex twin pairs first observed at 14 and 21 months who are being followed through late childhood. The heritability coefficients for inhibited and uninhibited behavior, based on direct observations in the laboratory and at home, were between 0.5 and 0.6 (Saudino & Kagan, in press). Further, the parents of inhibited and uninhibited children differ in expected ways; the parents of the inhibited children are less extroverted (based on a personality questionnaire) than the parents of uninhibited children (Rickman & Davidson, 1994).

In addition, studies of adoptive children support the role of genes. An examiner rated two groups of infants, 1 and 2 years old, during the administration of the Bayley Test. Heritability estimates were about 42 percent for an extroverted style (Braungart, Plomin, DeFries, & Fulker, 1992). Adopted siblings who were genetically unrelated but living in the same home were not more similar in this quality; the correlation was close to zero.

Variation in the stress of delivery or late prenatal experience can dilute the influence of the inherited physiology, at least temporarily. For example, an observational study of monozygotic and dizygotic twin pairs in the first week of life found no evidence of heritability for the qualities of irritability, resistance to soothing, and activity, suggesting that conditions surrounding birth are an important influence on the newborn's temperament (Riese, 1990).

Influence of Experience

Although genes make a modest contribution to infant reactivity and the inhibited and uninhibited profiles, they are not omnipotent and always share power with experience. Over one-third of high-reactive infants were not exceptionally fearful in the second year; a small number were fearless. Home observations on 50 high- and 50 low-reactive firstborn infants indicated that a mother's actions with the infant affected the probability that a high-reactive child would become inhibited. A nurturing parent who consistently protected her high-reactive infant from all minor stresses made it more, rather than less, difficult for that child to control an initial urge to retreat from strangers and unfamiliar events. Equally accepting mothers who set firm limits for their children, making mundane age-appropriate demands for cleanliness or conformity, helped their high-reactive infants overcome their fearfulness (Arcus, 1991).

The role of experience is illustrated by the variability within each temperamental category. We examined the variability in behavior with the examiner at 4.5 years within two very different groups: high-reactive girls who also showed high fear at 14 months (N = 16) and low-reactive girls who showed low fear at 14 months (N = 28). Although the former, as expected, had significantly fewer spontaneous comments and smiles compared with the latter, the variation within each group was large. For example, although one-third of the high-reactive, fearful girls had fewer than 10 spontaneous comments, one-third had more than 50 comments. One-third displayed fewer than 5 smiles, but one-third had more than 30 smiles. Within the low-reactive, low-fear girls, one-third had fewer than 27 comments and fewer than 21 smiles, but one-third had more than 70 comments and more than 35 smiles. It is fair to suggest that this broad range of outcomes at 4.5 years within these different classes of children is due, in part, to differential experience. The envelope of developmental trajectories for each temperamental group is not fixed in a rigid way.

The old view that genes are static and their effects fixed is being replaced with a dynamic picture in which some genes are so labile the change in light in the late afternoon activates them to manufacture specific proteins (Takahashi & Hoffman, 1995). These new discoveries imply that a child's experiences might be able to mute or enhance an initial temperamental disposition. Specifically, an infant born with a physiology that contributed to high reactivity and fearfulness, but who experienced subsequently a supportive environment without major uncertainties, might undergo physiological changes in those brain circuits that mediate emotional reactivity and become minimally distressed. The initial genetic endowment is not deterministic and the phenotype is subject to modification by experience.

It is likely that infants inherit a bias for at least three independent qualities. One quality is very close to Rothbart's (1989) concept of ease of arousal. The utility of this concept, as indexed by motor activity to stimulation rather than vocalization or smiling, is seen in an analysis of the relation of motor activity scores at 4 months to later behavior. The distribution of motor activity scores was divided into six groups: Group 1, the lowest 10th percentile; scores equal to or less than 10; Group 2, percentiles 11–15; scores between 11 and 24; Group 3, percentiles 16–50; scores between 25 and 45; Group 4, percentiles 51–75; scores between 46 and 69; Group 5, percentiles 76–90; scores between 70 and 99; Group 6, highest 10th percentile, equal to or greater than 100. Although the frequency of crying and fretting at 4 months increased with increasing motor activity, vocalization and smiling were unrelated to level of motor activity, suggesting that these latter two responses reflect a different form of arousal. Indeed, as noted earlier, 4-month-old infants who cried and smiled to stimulation were more talkative at 4.5 years than infants who cried but did not smile.

Summary

The data summarized affirm the utility of Rothbart's (1989) concept of ease of arousal, but add the important caveat that one must specify the behavioral reactions that define arousal. It makes a difference whether the infant vocalizes, smiles, cries, or thrashes to a moving mobile. The low-reactive girl who spoke and smiled the most at 4.5 years had very low motor arousal but very frequent vocalizations and smiles when she was 4 months old. By contrast, the low-reactive girl who never spoke or smiled at 4.5 years had an average motor activity score but very infrequent vocalization and smiling. One must also specify the age of the infant; the above conclusions apply when motor activity is measured at 4 months, not at 2, 14, or 24 months of age. Finally, one must specify the incentive for the arousal. The high-reactive infants usually cried as an accompaniment to the motor arousal generated by the visual, auditory, and olfactory stimulation. However, about 10 percent of the infants cried in fear to the discrepancy of hearing a taped female voice speak sentences without any visual support from a face, but did not cry as an accompaniment to high levels of motor arousal to a mobile. These latter infants, who were not likely to be classified as high reactive, were psychologically different from the high reactives in the second year.

A second quality is the affective state that follows arousal. This idea refers to the temperamental bias to behave in a particular way when one is aroused. Smiling compared with distress reflects a very different state that can follow an increase in arousal. High-reactive infants are easily aroused and, in addition, usually move into a state of distress following the increased arousal. Low-reactive children do not become easily aroused. On those occasions when they do, about 20 percent move into a state one might call happy or joyful. If these children are boys, they often have low and highly variable heart rates. The remaining low-reactive infants are more difficult to arouse and typically display minimal spontaneous affect—they may be Galen's phlegmatics.

A third temperamental quality, which is more speculative, refers to variation in physiological reactivity to external events. This quality may reflect differences in receptivity to salient events and may be only modestly correlated with the tendency to react to stimulation with clear motor arousal or distress. The process model that is characteristic of traditional conditioning theory and inherent in neural network schemes assumes that an input event has an identical, or a very similar, effect on the brain circuits of all individuals. Neither position acknowledges the possibility that each individual has a psychobiological layer that is more or less permeable to a particular event. The permeability, like a guard of a castle, controls, to some degree, the penetration of affectively charged information. Many years ago, Lacey (1967) suggested that if an adult had a high level of sympathetic feedback from the cardiovascular system, receptors for blood pressure in the carotid sinus would be activated and send neural impulses to the brain that would make that individual less sensitive to incoming information. Psychologists who do not rely on biological data have argued that individuals differ with regard to their openness to certain information.

An example of this phenomenon is seen in the magnitude of the cooling of the fingertips to the emotional film clips that were described earlier. More low- than high-reactive girls displayed many spontaneous comments and smiles with the unfamiliar examiner when they were 4.5 years old; these girls seemed to be more spontaneous and emotionally open than others. No high-reactive girl approached that degree of affective spontaneity. It is of interest, therefore, that low-reactive girls showed significantly greater vasoconstriction and, therefore, cooling of the ring finger than high-reactive girls to film clips that were suggestive of fear, sadness, and joy. Among the low-reactive boys, who were less emotionally expressive than girls, this effect was present, but muted.

This result hints at the possible complexity of the psychological layers that lie between an external event and a physiological reaction to that event. One might say that the children who showed greater cooling of the ring finger to the emotional films were emotionally more open to these events, or less tightly defended. Remarkably, emotionally detached, incarcerated male prisoners did not show potentiated startle to slides of unpleasant scenes, while the less-detached prisoners did show the expected potentiation (Patrick, 1994). An unpublished study from my laboratory suggests that working-class adolescent males, who were very emotionally detached during the test session, showed less Stroop interference to emotionally charged words than working-class females or middle-class adolescents of both sexes.

It is likely that investigators in the future will discover other temperamental factors that make a person more or less receptive to specific external events. These factors may not be as potent as the events that psychologists call evolutionarily significant, but the consequences are similar. We accept the fact that individuals differ in how hungry they feel after eight hours without food or how ill they feel after a cholera shot. It is becoming clear that individuals also differ in their receptivity to particular information. This receptivity affects the likelihood that the information will provoke psychological as well as physiological reactions. Temperamental factors are likely to be part of the package of processes that affect this receptivity.

Evidence for Categories

The earlier discussion of categories and continua described Meehl's (1973) strategy to determine if two or more qualitative groups of subjects are present in a particular sample. Now that the reader has a basis for understanding the predictive relation between high or low reactivity and fear in the second year, Meehl's suggestion can be applied to this corpus.

We divided the fear scores at 14 months into six roughly equal groups defined by fear scores of 0, 1, 2, 3, 4, and 5 or more fears. We then computed the average motor and cry scores, as well as the correlation between the motor and cry scores within each of the six fear groups. The motor score was similar for fear groups 1 to 4, but increased discontinuously for group 5; the cry scores increased discontinuously for group 4. This result is not surprising, for we have noted that high-reactive infants who are highly fearful have both high motor and high cry scores. The new fact is that the correlation between the motor and cry scores was highest for fear group 4 (3 or more fears) ($r = .32$, $p < .01$), while the correlations between the motor and cry scores were low for groups 1 to 3, and close to zero for groups 5 and 6. This pattern, which is in accord with Meehl's ideas, implies the presence of qualitatively different groups in the sample. High and low reactivity are two distinct temperamental categories. Once an infant attains a value for motor activity and crying that places him or her into the high-reactive group, more crying or motor arousal has minimal consequences for later fear behavior.

It is likely, moreover, that there are small, distinct subgroups within the larger low- and high-reactive groups. The total sample contained 99 low-reactive male infants—21 percent of the sample. Of this group, 31 became minimally fearful (0 or 1 fear) at both 14 and 21 months. Of this group of 31 boys, 20 smiled frequently at both 14 and 21 months. Of these 20, 8 had a low initial baseline heart rate at 4 months (< 136 bpm). Of this group of 8, 4 had facial measures at 14 months and 2 of these 4 children had broad faces (ratios > .55). Thus, we ended up with 2 boys—less than 1 percent of the original sample of children—with adequate data at 4, 14, and 21 months. One was a first- and one was a second-born child. These two boys, who combined low reactivity, low fear, frequent smiling, low 4-month baseline heart rate, and a broad face, represent a relatively rare group of children who were the most exuberant and least fearful of the 462 children.

A comparable analysis was performed on the high-reactive infant girls. Because a high baseline heart rate did not distinguish high- from low-reactive girls, the heart rate variable was not used in the analysis. There were a total of 52 high-reactive girls—11 percent of the original cohort. Of these 52, 18 (35 percent) had high fear scores (4 or more fears) at 14 and 21 months. Seven of these 18 girls (38

percent) showed infrequent smiling at both 14 and 21 months (a rating of 1 at both ages). Only 3 of these 7 girls had facial measurements; the other 4 high-reactive girls refused the procedure. However, all 3 girls had narrow faces (ratio equal to or less than .52). Hence, we estimate that about 1 percent of the original group of 462 children possessed a combination of high reactivity, high fear, infrequent smiling, and a narrow face.

The concept of emergenesis proposed by Lykken, McGue, Tellegen, and Bouchard (1992) may be helpful in understanding these small subgroups. These scientists would argue that biological sex, low reactivity at 4 months, low sympathetic tone within the cardiovascular system, ease of smiling, and the boney structure of the face are inherited independently in large populations. That is, the genes that influence each of these five features are in different locations, even though there may be a correlation among some of them. Thus, the probability of any one child inheriting the genes that contribute to all five features is relatively low: less than 1 percent of the children studied.

This fact is one reason why children with extreme scores—outliers—can be qualitatively different from those with less extreme scores. One low-reactive girl had a mean standard score for spontaneous comments and smiles at 4.5 years that placed her 3.4 standard deviations from the standardized mean; she had the highest values for these variables. The next two highest standard scores were 2.9 and 2.5 standard deviations from the mean. Nonetheless, the girl with the highest scores had markedly lower motor arousal and markedly higher vocalization at 4 months compared with the two children who had the next highest values. Indeed, the 4-month scores for the latter two children were very similar to the means for the entire sample. Thus, this girl with the highest values appeared to be qualitatively different from all other children in the sample. Perhaps statistical consultants who advise investigators to eliminate extreme outliers are offering useful advice. However, the detection of such extremes requires large samples. Meehl (1995) recommends samples of 300 or more subjects.

TEMPERAMENT AND ATTACHMENT

There is a lively controversy surrounding the contribution of inhibited or uninhibited temperaments to a child's reactions in the Ainsworth Strange Situation and, therefore, to the classifications of secure or insecure attachment

(Connell & Thompson, 1986). The Strange Situation is an unfamiliar setting; therefore, inhibited children should react with greater fear, when either left alone or with a stranger. As a result, a proportion of these children should be difficult to soothe when the mother returns. These children will be classified as type C: resistant and insecurely attached.

Infants who were classified type C at 14 months were behaviorally inhibited at 2 years, suggesting that the temperamental bias to be inhibited is contributing to their behavior in the Strange Situation (Calkins & Fox, 1992). Ten percent of Dutch infants assessed in the Strange Situation with their professional caregiver, mother, or father showed an insecure attachment to all three adults, implying a temperamental contribution to their laboratory behavior (Goosens & Van IJzendoorn, 1990). One group of authors, reflecting on these facts, wrote, "Temperament does play a role in Strange Situation behavior through its effects on the quality and intensity of the infant's separation distress. Infants who are high on fearfulness are likely to react more negatively to the separation episodes" (Thompson, Connell, & Bridges, 1988, p. 1109).

Investigators who have used maternal questionnaires to index temperament have concluded that it makes a minimal contribution to the attachment classifications. Although very few scientists have used behavioral observations to assess whether a child is inhibited, a review of a number of investigations concluded that, for most samples, children described by their mothers as irritable and distressed were later classified as insecurely attached. The authors suggested that although temperament was not the only influence on the attachment classification, nonetheless, "the empirical overlap between these behavioral domains is greater than might have been anticipated" (Vaughn et al., 1992, p. 469).

A meta-analysis of data from seven different samples (N = 498) revealed that the infant's behavior in the laboratory prior to the mother's leaving the child predicted better than chance the child's subsequent behavior and, therefore, the attachment classification. Infants that would be classified as type C showed more crying and resistance to their mother during episode 2, which occurred prior to any separation (Sagi, Van IJzendoorn, & Koren-Karie, 1991).

Further support for this view is found in an independent study of 9- and 13-month-old infants. A temperamental quality called *proneness to distress* together with the mother's personality were the best predictors of an insecure attachment. Specifically, infants who were prone to distress and had mothers with high scores on a personality trait called *constraint*—these women were rigid, had traditional views, and avoided risks—were more likely to be insecurely attached. Distressed infants reared by a mother who was low on constraint were more often securely attached. Among low-distress infants, however, there was no relation between the maternal personality and security of child attachment. Variation in maternal behavior seems to be more important for infants who are vulnerable to distress than it is for those who are minimally fretful and irritable (Mangelsdorf, Gunnar, Kestenbaum, Lang, & Andras, 1990). Thus, as Van den Boom (1994) has argued, both temperament and family experience act together to influence a child's behavior in the Strange Situation.

PSYCHOPATHOLOGY AND TEMPERAMENT

The most significant role of temperament is to modulate experience. The evidence is overwhelmingly persuasive of the fact that children and adults differ in their psychological and physiological reactions to an unexpected event, even when the event is unusually stressful, such as an earthquake, divorce, kidnapping, or witnessing a mass shooting (North, Smith, & Spitznagel, 1994). Even though the differences between adults who had an easy or difficult temperament at age 3 years were small, Chess and Thomas (1984) suggested that easy children seemed to be better-adjusted adults; Werner (1993) reports a similar result. Early temperament and experience interact in rhesus monkeys, too. High-reactive rhesus infants who are reared with peers become more fearful juveniles than high-reactive infants reared with their mothers. Moreover, high-reactive infant rhesus who experienced the stress of confinement sustained many more injuries than did low-reactive infants exposed to the same stress (Stephen Suomi, personal communication).

Only a proportion of children show psychological or biological signs of stress to threatening events. It is less clear, however, if the modulatory processes associated with temperament act directly by (a) blunting the limbic system's initial reaction to the stressor, (b) shortening the duration of the stressful reaction, or (c) acting indirectly through inhibitory processes to mute a consciously experienced stress reaction that is no less intense physiologically than it is in the majority of children. Of course, all three mechanisms are possible and each has relevance for the development of psychopathology.

Three Issues

Study of the relation of temperament to internalizing psychopathological symptoms in children and adolescents engages several issues. The first asks whether the various diagnostic categories for anxiety represent different manifestations of the same temperamental vulnerability, or whether the etiologies are distinctly different for simple phobias, social phobias, separation anxiety disorder, PTSD, and anorexia. The evidence is ambiguous, but, at the moment, most professionals favor the assumption of diagnostically separate categories.

It is possible, however, that a small group of children are born with a temperamental vulnerability to a variety of fear/anxiety states and that life experiences determine which particular symptom will be actualized. A vulnerable child who had a car accident might develop a phobia of automobiles; one who witnessed a rape might develop PTSD; an only child living in a rural area with no playmates might become a social phobic.

A second issue is the basis for arriving at a diagnosis, a theme considered earlier in the chapter. It is almost uniform practice to rely only on verbal reports of symptoms as the primary bases for the diagnosis. This fact means that if children fail to report particular feelings or thoughts, for whatever reason, or parents distort or misinterpret their child's behavior, the diagnoses will be inaccurate. Indeed, the reliability of school-age children's reports of symptoms over a two- or three-week interval was very low, and the reliability of parental reports of signs of conduct disorder was modest ($r = .48$; Schwab-Stone, Fallon, Briggs, & Crowther, 1994). Unfortunately, it is rare for clinicians or scientists to add laboratory evidence, psychological or biological, to the verbal reports when they make their diagnosis.

A final issue is the relation of the psychological symptoms to biological measures, such as cortisol level, heart rate, or blood pressure. There is no consensus on the nature of this relation. Phobic or PTSD children do not always show higher values on biological measures that are supposed to reflect a state of fear or stress. Indeed, some young infants do not show a rise in cortisol to the pain of an inoculation (Ramsay & Lewis, 1994).

Nodes of Agreement

There are, however, a few nodes of agreement. First, there is consensus that some children inherit a special physiological vulnerability to some fear or anxiety states; the evidence for a temperamental vulnerability to anger or depression is less clear. About 20 to 30 percent of first-degree relatives of children with an anxiety disorder had a similar symptom, compared with only 10 percent of controls (Weissman, 1984).

Epidemiological studies in varied Western countries agree that between 1 and 5 percent of children have simple or social phobias. The range for the looser diagnostic concept of anxiety disorder is larger—5 to 26 percent—suggesting that the clinical judgment of whether the symptom is disabling enough to be called a disorder is unreliable (Klein & Last, 1989). Finally, fear to unfamiliarity or challenge is stable from early childhood to adolescence, even though the magnitude of the stability coefficient is modest. The data from my laboratory suggest that no more than one-third of children under 5 years of age who are inhibited will be diagnosed as having an anxiety disorder 10 years later. This means that most children grow toward health. This brief summary represents what is known. Although this knowledge represents a major advance compared with the information available 100 years ago, it is, in an absolute sense, only a modest beginning.

A major conclusion is that acknowledgment of temperamental qualities will help to explain why only a minority of children react to a particular stressor with a relevant symptom, whether the stressor is an earthquake, kidnapping, divorce, or abuse. It is an established fact that only a proportion of children, usually 20 to 40 percent, react to a traumatic event with some fearful symptom. Of 40 schoolchildren who were kidnapped and terrorized for about two days, only 10 developed PTSD (Terr, 1979). In the winter of 1984, a sniper in a Los Angeles building across the street from an elementary school fired at a group of children on the playground. One child was killed and 13 were injured and a siege of several hours followed. About one month later, a group of psychologists and psychiatrists talked with the children to determine which ones were suffering from a stress disorder. Thirty-eight percent were judged to be anxious but an equal proportion, 39 percent, were not. Those who were judged anxious had a timid, avoidant personality style prior to the traumatic event (Pynoos et al., 1987).

The stress associated with entering school for the first time was only associated with an increase in respiratory illness in children who had shown both sympathetic reactivity prior to the beginning of the school year (measured by an increase in heart rate and arterial blood pressure to challenge) and, in addition, had been exposed to stressful experiences at home. Children of the same age and social class who showed low sympathetic reactivity showed no increased rate of respiratory illness, even though they may have lived in a highly stressful home environment (Boyce & Jemerin, 1990). This finding matches the study described earlier with rhesus monkeys and comparable work on adults.

One team of investigators took advantage of the fact that an earthquake occurred in Northern California (the Loma Prieta earthquake of 1989) in the middle of a study of 20 young children who were entering kindergarten. Six children showed an increase in respiratory illness after the earthquake; five showed a decline. Variation in the change in the helper-suppressor cell ratios and pokeweed mitogen response predicted which children showed the increase in respiratory illness. The children who showed an up-regulation of the two immune parameters following school entry had a significant increase in respiratory illness after the earthquake. This fact suggests that the children who perceived kindergarten entrance as stressful (indexed by the change in immune reaction) became most vulnerable to respiratory infections following the earthquake (Boyce et al., 1993).

Contributions to Pathology

It is likely that an inhibited temperament makes a modest contribution to the development of the varied syndromes called anxiety disorders. Inhibited behavior is more stable in girls than in boys, and anxiety, phobias, and panic attacks are more frequent among women than men. However, most inhibited children will not develop one of these psychiatric classifications. We estimated earlier that about 15 percent of children are both high reactive at 4 months and inhibited at 2 years. However, the best estimate of the prevalence of anxiety disorder in older children, based on a standard interview, is about 5 percent (Klein & Last, 1989). Thus, about two-thirds of high-reactive, inhibited children will not develop a profile serious enough to be characterized by a psychiatrist as anxiety disorder. Prediction of a shy, restrained, introverted adult personality from early inhibition is a much more likely outcome.

It is also likely that young children with a temperamental bias that leads them to show lack of restraint are at risk for conduct disorder or adolescent delinquency (Caspi, Henry, McGee, Moffitt, & Silva, 1995). Preschool children (from a very large sample) who were rated by teachers as showing serious lack of control were most likely to become asocial adults, even though the magnitude of the correlation was quite low (less than 5 percent of the variance). Lack of control is not a common characteristic of low-reactive, uninhibited children, but represents a different temperamental quality (see Bates, Bayles, Bennett, Ridge, & Brown, 1991, for a similar conclusion).

Although schizophrenia is much rarer than fearfulness or conduct disorder and, for that reason, should be treated in a special way, preliminary evidence suggests that some children who are at risk for later schizophrenia show qualities that require a special biology. For example, extreme disorganization in motor behavior and visual motor coordination in infancy are more characteristic of infants who will become schizophrenic (Fish, Marcus, Hans, Auerbach, & Perdue, 1992). Analysis of the home movies of young girls who later developed schizophrenia, and of their siblings who did not, revealed that the occurrence of facial expressions of joy—smiling and laughter—were infrequent in the former group. Unfortunately, this relation did not occur among the boys (Walker, Grimes, Davis, & Smith, 1993). As noted earlier, a very small number of infants display atypical profiles that can be signs of an unusual temperamental bias. These children might follow unique developmental paths.

There was a period, beginning in the late 1960s, when a small group of psychiatrists and psychologists, led by Thomas Szasz (1961), assumed that most psychiatric symptoms were cultural habits, like length of hair or the hemline of a dress. This view has far fewer adherents today as clinicians return to the ancient view that some psychopathology reflects an abnormal physiological profile. This perspective invites a comparison of psychopathology with physical diseases whose pathophysiology is known. The infectious diseases of malaria and influenza are characterized by a specific underlying pathological condition which is the basis for bodily states that are followed by conscious detection of symptoms.

Consider, as a comparison, the state of affairs in psychopathology. First, the diagnostic categories usually refer to the final stage in which the undesirable symptoms are detected consciously, by the patient or his or her relatives. If the analogy to physical illness is valid, it is likely that the symptoms are due to different pathological processes.

There is also considerable disagreement over the environmental experiences that contribute to a pathological profile. In this case, the extreme positivism of modern social science may be retarding progress. The ambiguity that surrounds valid measurement of the psychological states and personal constructions that are the central causes of psychopathology frustrates investigators. As a result, scientists are attracted to more easily measured variables such as divorce, job loss, or death of a parent. The inability to measure the patient's private construction of his or her environment leads investigators to focus on a small number of easily measured events that are regarded, a priori, as pathognomonic. These include loss of a parent, abuse, divorce, and temporary parental unemployment. However, some individuals cope well with these events; others do not. Working with many others in a large office building is not the primary cause of influenza, even though this condition can increase the probability of becoming infected.

Finally, we have to appreciate that some diagnostic profiles may have protective functions, as sickle cell anemia protects against malaria in tropical climates. A child who bullies others and steals from stores has a social problem, but these behaviors in an adolescent of illegal immigrants living in poverty in a large city may protect against a chronic depression due to deep feelings of helplessness and victimization.

ETHNICITY AND TEMPERAMENT

Differences in temperament among varied ethnic groups remain a delicate issue because of the racial and ethnic strife around the world. Many psychologists, understandably, shy away from studies that might reveal genetically based differences in mood or behavior among populations that have been reproductively isolated for a long time. A team of scientists compared the frequencies of over 100 different alleles for physiological markers in the world's geographically separate human populations by averaging the difference in frequencies to create an index of genetic distance between any pair of populations (Cavalli-Sforza, Menozzi, & Piazza, 1994). As expected, the index of genetic distance was largest when Asians, Africans, and European Caucasians were compared with each other. But even within the Caucasoid Europeans, people from Scandinavia, England, and Northern Europe were genetically different from populations living in Spain, Italy, and the Balkans. In general, the greater the geographical and linguistic distance between any two populations, and, therefore, the greater the reproductive isolation, the greater the genetic distance. It is not unreasonable to assume, therefore, that some of the alleles involved in this analysis also have implications for emotions and behavior.

Asian-Caucasian Comparisons

The most consistent set of evidence on early infant temperaments compares Asian with Caucasian infants. Over 20 years ago, Freedman and Freedman (1969) reported that newborn Asian American infants, compared with European Americans, were calmer, less labile, less likely to remove a cloth placed on their face, and more easily consoled when distressed. Nine years later, Kagan, Kearsley, and Zelazo (1978) found that Chinese American infants living in Boston were less active, less vocal, less likely to smile to stimulation, and more inhibited during the first year compared with European American infants from Boston.

Caudill and Weinstein (1969) observed Japanese infants to be less easily aroused than European American infants and Lewis, Ramsay, and Kawakami (1993) found Japanese infants to be less reactive than American infants (during well-baby examinations) and less likely to cry to inoculation. Five-month-old European American infants showed distress following arm restraint more quickly than did Japanese infants, implying a higher threshold of distress to this incentive in Asian infants (Camras, Oster, Campos, Miyake, & Bradshaw, 1992).

These differences in ease of arousal during the first year have some parallels in older children. Mothers of 6- to 7-year-old children living in Shanghai described them as less active, less impulsive, more controlled, and more shy than did mothers of children living in the Pacific Northwest (Ahadi, Rothbart, & Ye, 1993). Further, the parents of school-age Thai children, compared with those of European American children, were more concerned over low energy, low motivation, somatic problems, and forgetfulness, whereas the parents of European American children reported more concern with disobedience, aggression, and hyperactivity (Weisz, Suwanlert, et al., 1987, 1988). These differences have been regarded as reflecting primarily cultural variation in socialization practices. However, one could regard this evidence as reflecting, in part, differences in children's temperaments.

Kagan and colleagues (1994) administered the battery of visual, auditory, and olfactory stimulations described earlier to 4-month-old infants living in Boston, Dublin, and Beijing. The Caucasian infants from Dublin and Boston were more easily aroused and distressed than were the Chinese infants from Beijing. The Chinese infants were markedly lower on Rothbart's dimension of ease of arousal (Kagan et al., 1994).

It is important to note that Asian American adult psychiatric patients require a lower dose of psychotropic drugs than European American patients (Lin, Poland, & Lesser, 1986), implying that Asian populations may be at a lower level of limbic arousal. There are, as noted above, genetic differences between Asians and Europeans. The proportion of Rh-negative individuals is less than 1 percent in China but greater than 15 percent in Europe (Cavalli-Sforza, 1991). There is, in addition, greater genetic diversity in many loci determining blood groups and proteins among Caucasians than among Asians. Europeans and Asians have been reproductively isolated for over 30,000 years—over 1000 generations. It requires only 15 to 20 generations of selective breeding to produce obviously different behavioral profiles in many animal species (Mills & Faure, 1991). Perhaps scientists should consider the ethnic composition of their samples when the psychological variables they quantify bear some relation to reactivity and ease of arousal.

TEMPERAMENT AND MORAL AFFECTS

Variation in the intensity of moral emotions might be influenced by temperament. The experience of anxiety, shame, and guilt as an accompaniment to the contemplation or commission of an act that violates personal or community standards is an important source of restraint on those actions. It is likely, as Kant believed, that individuals vary in the intensity of their shame and guilt, although the biology that accounts for this variation may be different from the physiology that represents the foundation for the appearance of the moral emotions in all children. Even though parental practices and attitudes are most influential, temperamental factors might play some role. The intensity of the experienced moral affects are due to visceral efferents that originate in limbic sites and excite peripheral organs, as well as the quality of afferent traffic back from the periphery to the medulla, amygdala, and eventually, frontal cortex.

Damasio (1994) has described the case of an adult male who lost, through surgery, the ventromedial surface of his prefrontal cortex. This neural tissue receives afferent information from the amygdala, which, in turn, receives it from the heart, lung, gut, and muscles via the NTS in the medulla. Without this neuronal surface the individual cannot have the subtle anticipatory feeling of anxiety over risking money on an investment or changing jobs. This patient,

who had been an intelligent and successful man prior to the surgery, began to make impulsive decisions after the surgery despite no change in his measured intelligence.

Consider a hypothetical but common situation. A 5-year-old wants a toy that another is enjoying and thinks about seizing it. One of the factors that will influence the probability of a seizure by the envious child is a feeling of anxiety over the possible consequences of the aggressive act. Although socialization in the home will influence the intensity of that feeling, it is reasonable to suggest that children with equivalent socialization experiences will differ in the intensity of the anxiety state because of temperamental factors. This variation is related to the activation of the sympathetic nervous system and the receipt of information from limbic targets by the frontal cortex. For example, low-reactive 1- and 2-year-old infants show much less fear to an examiner's criticism compared with high reactives. Kochanska (1991b, 1993) has shown that shy, timid children raised by mothers who used reasoning in their socialization had a very strict conscience (using a projective measure of conscience). Neither the form of maternal socialization nor the child's shyness, considered alone, predicted variation in the conscience measure.

It is important to emphasize, first, that almost all children are capable of moral emotions. Further, although some children inherit a temperament that favors an exaggerated guilt reaction, such children need not show any pathology later in life. Nor is it likely that most children with a temperament favoring a less intense affective response will become juvenile delinquents. Most parents of these latter children will impose heavier socialization demands upon them. Nonetheless, if the environment is permissive of aggression, stealing, and lying, the child with a temperamental bias for a sluggish anxiety/fear reaction is probably at greater risk for asocial behavior than other children growing up in the same social context (Kochanska, 1995).

Low-reactive boys who have high vagal tone represent a special temperamental group. If these boys grow up in typical American middle-class homes with loving parents who socialize school achievement and the control of aggression, they are likely to become group leaders. The same children raised by indifferent parents in large cities may become delinquents. Antisocial adolescents who showed minimal autonomic reactivity to simple stimulation—a lower heart rate and less frequent skin conductance responses—were more likely to continue a criminal career than equally antisocial adolescents who did not become adult criminals (Raine, Venables, & Williams, 1990, 1994; see also Katz & Gottman, 1994).

It is possible that the small group of criminals who commit violent crimes (probably fewer than 5 percent of all delinquents and criminals) possess a special temperament. In a longitudinal study of a large New Zealand cohort the violent young adults were rated at ages 3 and 5 as very low on control of behavior (Henry, Caspi, & Silva, personal communication). A minority of very impulsive, minimally fearful 5-year-old boys became adolescent delinquents; only 28 percent of high-delinquent boys had been rated by their teachers eight years earlier as highly asocial (Tremblay, Pihl, Vitaro, & Dubkin, 1994). Thus, most groups of asocial adolescents probably contain only a small proportion who were born with a temperament that placed them at risk for this profile.

Constructs for Interactions

Psychologists may eventually replace the separate constructs that now describe a child and his or her relevant environments (parents, sibling, school settings) with a single construct that represents a particular temperamental type growing up in a particular set of contexts. To illustrate, instead of writing about high-reactive infants and protective, permissive families, psychologists will invent a new construct that describes the envelope of possible behavioral profiles for this category of child growing in this environment. This strategy need not replace the separate ideas of high-reactive infants and permissive family settings. This suggestion is not as strange as it may seem. Human biologists treat a genetic vulnerability to lung cancer and chronic cigarette smoking as separate conditions, but a carcinoma of the lung in a long-time smoker represents a combination of both ideas.

Put plainly, infants begin life with different biologically based qualities and varied environments. As the environments shape children into different phenotypes, it may be useful to invent new constructs to describe these emerging phenotypes, rather than to continue to state that there is an interaction between an early temperament type and a specific rearing environment.

This suggestion is a special instance of the more general rule that the construct chosen depends on the investigator's purpose. Light can be described as a wave or a particle, or as a source of heat or illumination. It will be helpful on some occasions to describe a psychological profile with a construct that combines its current features, temperamental origins, and environmental history.

SUMMARY

The inclusion of biological ideas and evidence in studies of behavior is surely a welcome development. The history of science is rich with examples of the accelerated progress that occurs when two or more previously isolated domains probe common problems with a shared vocabulary and methods. The fields of biophysics, molecular biology, and radio astronomy are obvious examples. The union, by providing new information for the new partners, refines popular terms and eliminates ideas that have outlived their usefulness. This first phase of the collaboration between biology and psychology already has revealed some new ideas, for example, the idea of only one fear state is not theoretically useful.

It is also becoming increasingly clear, as Galen anticipated, that children, like animals, inherit different biologies that, in turn, affect the manner in which environmental events influence their psychological growth. Developmental scientists should assume, from the beginning, that different temperamental types of children will not react in the same way to a given experience and invent constructs that capture that fact in an accurate way.

We have assumed for most of this century that particular environments—acute trauma or chronic conditions—have main effects and that the actions of caretakers, siblings, and peers comprise the most formative influence on behavior. We ignored the extraordinary variation in temperamental vulnerability to those experiences. There are very few incentives that provoke the same response in all children.

Temperamental factors influence the variation in physiological reactivity following an experience. High-reactive infants may inherit a neurochemistry that renders the amygdala and its multiple projections excitable. Recall that emotionally detached criminals showed less potentiation of the startle reflex than those who were emotionally spontaneous. I suspect that temperament and history act together to create a psychological barrier between an emotionally charged external event and the arousal of the limbic system, rendering the event less potent. Fifty years ago these phenomena would have been called a defense. Although all individuals can learn such defenses to protect them from distress to threatening experiences, a small proportion of children may inherit a temperament that makes it easier for them to establish these defenses. A child's experiential history determines the meaning of an event; a combination of temperament and history determines both the ease with which the meaning of an event gains access to limbic structures as well as the excitability of those structures.

The return of temperamental concepts will, inevitably, attract interest to affective phenomena and, in so doing, alert psychologists to those events that have their primary effect on emotions, rather than on behaviors, especially the emotion families named guilt, shame, fear, anxiety, sadness, excitement, and joy. Individual variation in the frequency and intensity of those affect states is influenced by temperament and the constructions that children create from their encounters. It is not unreasonable to be optimistic about the coming decades in developmental psychology if we search for the integrated profiles that emerge from biological predispositions and life histories, and not insist on reducing these profiles either to genes or to experiences. Then we will attain a synthesis as fruitful as the one that followed the recognition that both genetic change and natural selection made evolution possible.

Since Plato's *Parmenides* we know that truth does not allow itself to be grasped, that if there is an ultimate reality it retreats the closer we come to it, finally vanishing into insignificance . . . the descent is subtle and endless. This path leads us to the discovery of contingency and so it is that chance will be our constant companion. But we are looking for a different path, an ascent that will bring things together rather than disperse them, a path on which we will part with chance, just as Dante parts from Virgil at the entrance to paradise. Then beauty will be our guide. (Ekland, 1991, p. 175)

ACKNOWLEDGMENTS

I am indebted to my colleagues, Nancy Snidman, Doreen Arcus, and J. Steven Reznick, for their wisdom in our collaboration and for their constructive comments on this chapter. I also thank John Bates and Mary Rothbart for their reviews of this chapter.

REFERENCES

Achenbach, T. M. (1985). *Assessment and taxonomy of child and adolescent psychopathology.* Newbury Park, CA: Sage.

Adamec, R. E. (1991). Anxious personality in the cat. In B. J. Carroll & J. E. Barrett (Eds.), *Psychopathology and the brain* (pp. 153–168). New York: Raven Press.

Ahadi, S. A., Rothbart, M. K., & Ye, R. (1993). Children's temperament in the United States and China. *European Journal of Psychiatry, 7,* 359–377.

Allport, G. W. (1937). *Personality.* New York: Henry Holt.

Andersen, M. C., & Kunze, D. C. (1994). Nucleus tractus solitarius—gateway to neural circulatory control. In J. F. Hoffman & P. D. E. Weer (Eds.), *Annual review of physiology* (Vol. 56, pp. 93–116). Palo Alto, CA: Annual Reviews.

Arcus, D. M. (1991). *Experiential modification of temperamental bias in inhibited and uninhibited children.* Unpublished doctoral dissertation, Harvard University, Boston.

Arcus, D. M., & Kagan, J. (1995). Temperament and craniofacial skeleton in children. *Child Development, 66,* 1529–1540.

Asendorpf, J. B. (1989). Shyness as a final common pathway for two different kinds of inhibition. *Journal of Personality and Social Psychology, 57,* 481–492.

Asendorpf, J. B. (1990). Development of inhibition during childhood. *Developmental Psychology, 26,* 721–730.

Asendorpf, J. B. (1991). Development of inhibited children's coping with unfamiliarity. *Child Development 62,* 1460–1474.

Asendorpf, J. B. (1993). Abnormal shyness in children. *Journal of Child Psychiatry, 34,* 1069–1081.

Asendorpf, J. B. (1994). The malleability of behavioral inhibition. *Developmental Psychology, 30,* 912–919.

Bates, J. E. (1980). The concept of difficult temperament. *Merrill-Palmer Quarterly, 26,* 299–319.

Bates, J. E. (1983). Issues in the assessment of difficult temperament. *Merrill-Palmer Quarterly, 29,* 89–97.

Bates, J. E. (1987). Temperament in infancy. In J. D. Osofsky (Ed.), *Handbook of infant development* (2nd ed., pp. 1101–1149). New York: Wiley.

Bates, J. E. (1989). Concepts and measures of temperament. In G. A. Kohnstamm, J. E. Bates, & M. K. Rothbart (Eds.), *Temperament in childhood* (pp. 3–26). New York: Wiley.

Bates, J. E. (1994). Parents as scientific observers of their children's development. In S. L. Friedman & H. C. Haywood (Eds.), *Developmental follow-up: Concepts, domains, and methods* (pp. 197–216). New York: Academic.

Bates, J. E., Bayles, K., Bennett, D. S., Ridge, B., & Brown, M. M. (1991). Origins of externalizing behavior problems at eight years of age. In E. J. Pepler & K. H. Rubin (Eds.), *The development and treatment of childhood aggression* (pp. 93–120). Hillsdale, NJ: Erlbaum.

Bates. J. E., & Wachs, T. D. (1994). *Temperament.* Washington, DC: American Psychological Association.

Birns, B., Barten, S., & Bridger, W. (1969). Individual differences in temperamental characteristics of infants. *Transactions of the New York Academy of Sciences, 31,* 1071–1082.

Black, B. (1992). Elective mutism as a variant of social phobia. *Journal of the American Academy of Child and Adolescent Psychiatry, 31,* 1090–1094.

Blanchard, D. C., & Blanchard, R. J. (1988). Ethoexperimental approaches to the biology of emotion. In M. R. Rosenzweig & L. W. Porter (Eds.), *Annual review of psychology* (Vol. 39, pp. 43–68). Palo Alto, CA: Annual Reviews.

Blizard, D. A., Liang, B., & Emmel, D. K. (1980). Blood pressure, heart rate, and plasma catecholamines under resting conditions in rat strains selectively bred for differences in response to stress. *Behavioral and Neural Biology, 29,* 487–492.

Bornstein, M. H., Gaughran, J. M., & Segui, D. (1991). Multivariate assessment of infant temperament. *International Journal of Behavioral Development, 14,* 131–151.

Boyce, W. T., Chesterman, E. A., Martin, N., Folkman, S., Cohen, F., & Wara, D. (1993). Immunologic changes occurring at kindergarten entry predict respiratory illnesses after the Loma Prieta earthquake. *Developmental and Behavioral Pediatrics, 14,* 296–303.

Boyce, W. T., & Jemerin, J. M. (1990). Psychobiological differences in childhood stress response. *Journal of Developmental and Behavioral Pediatrics, 11,* 86–94.

Braungart, J. M., Plomin, R., DeFries, J. C., & Fulker, D. W. (1992). Genetic influences on test–retest infant temperament as assessed by Bayley's infant behavior record. *Developmental Psychology, 28,* 40–47.

Breuer, J., & Freud, S. (1956). *Studies in hysteria* [Standard edition]. London: Hogarth. (Original work published 1893–1898)

Broberg, A., Lamb, M. E., & Hwang, P. (1990). Inhibition: Its stability and correlates in 16–40-month-old children. *Child Development, 61,* 1153–1163.

Buss, A. H., & Plomin, R. (1984). *Temperament.* Hillsdale, NJ: Erlbaum.

Calkins, S., & Fox, N. A. (1992). The relations among infant temperament, security of attachment, and behavioral inhibition at 24 months. *Child Development, 63,* 1456–1472.

Camras, L. A., Oster, H., Campos, J. J., Miyake, K., & Bradshaw, D. (1992). Japanese and American infants' response to arm restraint. *Developmental Psychology, 28,* 578–583.

Carey, W. B., & McDevitt, S. C. (1978). Stability and change in individual temperament diagnoses from infancy to early childhood. *American Academy of Child Psychiatry, 17,* 331–337.

Carlson, E. A., Jacobvitz, D., & Sroufe, L. A. (1995). A developmental investigation of inattentiveness and hyperactivity. *Child Development, 66,* 37–54.

Carmichael, C. M., & McGue, M. (1994). A longitudinal study of personality change and stability. *Journal of Personality, 62,* 1–20.

Caspi, A., Elder, G. H., & Bem, D. J. (1988). Moving away from the world. *Developmental Psychology, 24,* 824–831.

Caspi, A., Henry, B., McGee, R. O., Moffitt, T. E., & Silva, P. A. (1995). Temperamental origins of child and adolescent behavior problems. *Child Development, 66,* 55–68.

Caspi, A., & Silva, P. A. (1995). Temperamental qualities at age 3 predict personality traits in young adulthood. *Child Development, 66,* 486–498.

Caudill, W., & Weinstein, H. (1969). Maternal care and infant behavior in Japan and America. *Psychiatry, 32,* 12–43.

Cavalli-Sforza, L. L. (1991). Genes, people, and languages. *Scientific American, 265,* 104–111.

Cavalli-Sforza, L. L., Menozzi, P., & Piazza, A. (1994). *The history and geography of human genes.* Princeton, NJ: Princeton University Press.

Cervero, F. (1994). Sensory innervation of the viscera. *Physiological Reviews, 74,* 95–138.

Cheever, J. (1993). *The journals of John Cheever.* New York: Ballantine Books.

Chess, S., & Thomas, A. (1984). Genesis and evolution of behavior disorders. *American Journal of Psychiatry, 141,* 1–9.

Chess, S., & Thomas, A. (1990). The New York Longitudinal Study: The young adult periods. *Canadian Journal of Psychiatry, 35,* 557–561.

Clarke, A. S., Mason, W. A., & Moberg, G. P. (1988). Differential behavioral and adrenocortical responses to stress among three macaques species. *American Journal of Primatology, 14,* 37–52.

Cohen, S., Kaplan, J. R., Cunnick, J. E., Manuck, S. B., & Rabin, B. S. (1992). Chronic social stress, affiliation, and cellular immune response in nonhuman primates. *Psychological Science, 3,* 301–304.

Connell, J. T., & Thompson, R. (1986). Emotion and social interaction in the Strange Situation. *Child Development, 57,* 733–745.

Coplan, R. J., Rubin, K. H., Fox, N. A., Calkins, S. D., & Stewart, S. L. (1994). Being alone, playing alone, and acting alone. *Child Development, 65,* 129–137.

Damasio, A. (1994). *Descartes' error.* New York: Putnam Press.

Davidson, R. J. (1994a). Asymmetric brain function, affective style, and psychopathology. *Development and Psychopathology, 6,* 741–758.

Davidson, R. J. (1994b). Temperament, affective style, and frontal lobe asymmetry. In G. P. Dawson & K. P. Fischer (Eds.), *Human behavior in the developing brain* (pp. 518–536). New York: Guilford Press.

Davis, M. (1984). The mammalian startle response. In R. C. Eaton (Ed.), *The neural mechanisms of startle behavior* (pp. 287–351). New York: Plenum Press.

Davis, M. H., Luce, C., & Kraus, S. J. (1994). The heritability of characteristics associated with dispositional empathy. *Journal of Personality, 62,* 369–391.

Dawson, G., Panagiotides, H., Klinger, L. G., & Hill, D. (1992). The role of frontal lobe functioning in the development of infant self-regulatory behavior. *Brain and Cognition, 20,* 152–175.

DeVries, J. I. P., Visser, G. H. A., & Prechtl, H. F. R. (1982). The emergence of fetal behavior. *Early Human Development, 7,* 301–322.

Diamond, A. (1990). Developmental time course in human infants and infant monkeys and the neural bases of inhibitory control and reaching. In A. Diamond (Ed.), *The development and neural bases of higher cognitive functions* (pp. 637–676). New York: New York Academy of Sciences.

Diamond, S. (1957). *Personality and temperament.* New York: Harper.

DiPietro, J. (1995, March). *Fetal origins of neurobehavioral function and individual differences.* Presented at the meeting of the Society for Research in Child Development, Indianapolis, IN.

Dollard, J., & Miller, N. E. (1950). *Personality and psychotherapy.* New York: McGraw-Hill.

Dunn, J., & Kendrick, C. (1981). Studying temperament and parent-child interaction. *Annual Progress in Child Psychiatry and Child Development,* 415–430.

Eaton, W. O., & Saudino, K. J. (1992). Prenatal activity level at the temperamental dimension. *Infant Behavior and Development, 15,* 57–70.

Einstein, E., & Infeld, L. (1938). *The evolution of physics.* New York: Simon & Schuster.

Ekland, I. (1991). *The broken dice.* Chicago: University of Chicago Press.

Ekman, P. (1992). Facial expressions of emotion. *Psychological Science, 3,* 34–38.

Emde, R. N., Plomin, R., Robinson, J., Corley, R., DeFries, J., Fulker, D. W., Reznick, J. S., Campos, J., Kagan, J., & Zahn-Waxler, C. (1992). Temperament, emotion, and cognition at 14 months: The MacArthur Longitudinal Twin Study. *Child Development, 63,* 1437–1455.

Fagot, B. I., & O'Brien, M. (1994). Activity level in young children. *Merrill-Palmer Quarterly, 40,* 378–390.

Fanselow, M. S. (1994). Neural organization of the defensive behavior system responsible for fear. *Psychonomic Bulletin and Review, 1,* 429–438.

Farrington, D. P. (1987). Implications of biological findings for criminological research. In S. A. Mednick, T. E. Moffitt, & S. A. Stack (Eds.), *The causes of crime* (pp. 42–64). New York: Cambridge University Press.

Feiring, C., & Lewis, M. (1980). Sex differences and stability in vigor, activity, and persistence in the first three years of life. *Journal of Genetic Psychology, 136,* 65–75.

Finger, T. E. (1987). Gustatory nuclei and pathways in the central nervous system. In T. E. Finger & W. L. Silver (Eds.), *Neurobiology of taste and smell* (pp. 331–353). New York: Wiley.

Finman, R., Davidson, R. J., Coton, M. B., Straus, A., & Kagan, J. (1989). Psychophysiological correlates of inhibitions to the unfamiliar in children [Abstract]. *Psychophysiology, 26,* 524.

Fish, B., Marcus, J., Hans, S. C., Auerbach, J. G., & Perdue, S. (1992). Infants at risk for schizophrenia. *Archives of General Psychiatry, 49,* 221–235.

Fish, M., Stifter, C. A., & Belsky, J. (1991). Conditions of continuity and discontinuity in infant negative emotionality. *Child Development, 62,* 1525–1537.

Fish, S. E., & Fish, M. (1995, April). *Variability in neonatal heart rate during orientation tasks and its relation to later social and coping behavior.* Presented at the meeting of the Society for Research in Child Development, Indianapolis, IN.

Fiske, D. W. (1986). Specificity of method and knowledge in social science. In D. W. Fiske & R. A. Schweder (Eds.), *Metatheory in social science* (pp. 61–82). Chicago: University of Chicago Press.

Fowler, J. A. (1897). *A manual of mental science for teachers and students.* New York: Fowler & Walls.

Fox, N. A. (1989). Psychophysiological correlates of emotional reactivity during the first year of life. *Developmental Psychology, 25,* 364–372.

Fox, N. A., Calkins, S. D., & Bell, M. A. (1994). Neural plasticity and development in the first two years of life. *Developmental Psychopathology, 6,* 677–696.

Fox, N. A., & Davidson, R. J. (1987). Electroencephalographic asymmetry in response to the approach of a stranger and maternal separation in 10-month-old infants. *Developmental Psychology, 23,* 233–240.

Freedman, D. G., & Freedman, N. (1969). Behavioral differences between Chinese-American and American newborns. *Nature, 224,* 12–27.

Freedman, D. G., & Keller, B. (1963). Inheritance of behavior in infants. *Science, 140,* 196.

Frege, G. (1979). *Posthumous writings.* Chicago: University of Chicago Press.

Freud, S. (1950). *Analysis of a phobia in a five-year-old boy.* In A. Strachey & J. Strachey (Trans.), *Collected papers of Sigmund Freud* (Vol. 3, pp. 149–295). London: Hogarth Press. (Original work published 1909)

Freud, S. (1965). *New introductory lectures on psychoanalysis.* New York: Norton. (Original work published 1933)

Gainotti, G., Caltagirone, L., & Zoccolotti, P. (1993). Left-right and cortical/subcortical dichotomies in neuropsychological study of human emotions. In F. N. Watts (Ed.), *Neuropsychological perspectives on emotion* (pp. 71–93). Hillsdale, NJ: Erlbaum.

Gall, F. J. (1835). *On the organ of the moral qualities and intellectual faculties and the plurality of the cerebral organs* (W. Lewis, Trans.). Boston: Marsh, Copen, & Lyon.

Goddard, M. E., & Beilharz, R. G. (1985). A multivariate analysis of the genetics of fearlessness in potential guide dogs. *Behavioral Genetics, 15,* 69–89.

Goldman-Rakic, P. S. (1994). Specification of higher cortical functions. In S. H. Broman & J. Grafman (Eds.), *Atypical cognitive deficits in developmental disorders* (pp. 3–17). Hillsdale, NJ: Erlbaum.

Goldsmith, H. H., & Campos, J. J. (1990). The structure of temperamental fear and pleasure in infants. *Child Development, 61,* 1944–1964.

Goldsmith, H. H., & Gottesman, I. I. (1981). Origins of variations in behavioral style. *Child Development, 52,* 91–103.

Goldsmith, H. H., & Rothbart, M. K. (1991). Contemporary instruments for assessing early temperament by questionnaire and in the laboratory. In J. Strelau & A. Angleitner (Eds.), *Explorations in temperament* (pp. 249–272). New York: Plenum Press.

Goodwin, B. (1994). *How the leopard changed its spots.* New York: Scribners.

Goosens, F. A., & Van IJzendoorn, M. H. (1990). Quality of infants' attachment to professional caregivers. *Child Development, 61,* 832–837.

Gortmaker, S., & Kagan, J. (in press). Shyness and season of birth. *Developmental Psychobiology.*

Gould, J. L. (1986). The biology of learning. In M. R. Rosenzweig & L. W. Porter (Eds.), *Annual review of psychology* (Vol. 37, pp. 163–192). Palo Alto, CA: Annual Reviews.

Gray, J. A. (1991). The neuropsychology of temperament. In J. Strelau & A. P. Angleitner (Eds.), *Explorations in temperament* (pp. 105–128). New York: Plenum Press.

Green, J. M. (1991). Mothers' perception of their 6-week-old babies. *Irish Journal of Psychology, 12,* 133–144.

Guerin, D. W., & Gottfried, A. W. (1994). Developmental stability and change in parent reports of temperament. *Merrill-Palmer Quarterly, 40,* 334–350.

Gunnar, M. R. (1990). The psychobiology of infant temperament. In J. Colombo & J. Fagen (Eds.), *Individual differences in infancy* (pp. 387–409). Hillsdale, NJ: Erlbaum.

Gunnar, M. R. (1994). Psychoendocrine studies of temperament and stress in early childhood. In J. Bates & T. Wachs (Eds.), *Temperament: Individual differences at the interface of biology and behavior.* Washington, DC: American Psychological Association.

Gunnar, M. R., Porter, F. L., Wolf, C. M., Rigatuso, J., & Larson, M. C. (1995). Neonatal stress reactivity. *Child Development, 66,* 1–13.

Gur, R. C., Mozley, L. H., Mozley, P. D., Resnick, S. M., Karp, J. S., Alavi, A., Arnold, S. E., & Gur, R. E. (1995). Sex differences in regional cerebral glucose metabolism during a resting state. *Science, 267,* 52–53.

Habecker, B. A., & Landis, S. C. (1994). Noradrenergic regulation of cholinergic differentiation. *Science, 264,* 1602–1604.

Hebb, D. O. (1946). On the nature of fear. *Psychological Review, 53,* 259–276.

Hinde, R. A., Tamplin, A., & Barrett, J. (1993). Social isolation in four-year-olds. *British Journal of Developmental Psychology, 11,* 211–236.

Hooton, E. A. (1939). *Crime and the man.* Cambridge, MA: Harvard University Press.

Hopkins, W. D., & Bard, K. A. (1993). Hemispheric specialization in infant chimpanzees (Pan troglodytes): Evidence for a relation with gender and arousal. *Developmental Psychobiology, 26,* 219–235.

Horn, J. M., Plomin, R., & Rosenman, R. (1976). Heritability of personality traits in adult male twins. *Behavioral Genetics, 6,* 17–30.

Hu, M. W., & Fox, S. W. (1988). *Evolutionary processes and metaphors.* New York: Wiley.

Hubert, N. C., Wachs, T. D., Peters-Martin, P., & Gandour, M. J. (1982). The study of early temperament. *Child Development, 53,* 571–600.

Huffman, L. C., Bryan, Y. E., Pedersen, F. A., Lester, B. M., Newman, J. D., & del Carmen, R. (1994). Infant cry acoustics and maternal ratings of temperament. *Infant Behavior and Development, 17,* 45–53.

Izard, C. E. (1991). *The psychology of emotions.* New York: Plenum Press.

Izard, C. E., Hembree, E. A., & Huebner, R. R. (1987). Infants' emotion expressions to acute pain. *Developmental Psychology, 23,* 105–113.

Jacobs, B. L. (1994). Serotonin motor activity and depression related disorders. *American Scientist, 82,* 456–463.

Jones, R. B., Satterlee, D. G., & Ryder, F. H. (1994). Fear of humans in Japanese quail selected for low or high adrenocortical response. *Physiology and Behavior, 56,* 379–383.

Kagan, J. (1971). *Change and continuity in infancy.* New York: Wiley.

Kagan, J. (1994). *Galen's prophecy.* New York: Basic Books.

Kagan, J. (1997). Temperament and the reactions to unfamiliarity. *Child Development, 68,* 139–143.

Kagan, J., Arcus, D., Snidman, N., & Rimm, S. E. (1995). Asymmetry of forehead temperature and cardiac activity. *Neuropsychology, 9,* 1–5.

Kagan, J., Arcus, D., Snidman, N., Yufeng, W., Hendler, J., & Greene, S. (1994). Reactivity in infants: A cross-national comparison. *Developmental Psychology, 30,* 342–345.

Kagan, J., Kearsley, R., & Zelazo, P. (1978). *Infancy.* Cambridge, MA: Harvard University Press.

Kagan, J., Lapidus, D. R., & Moore, M. (1978). Infant antecedents of cognitive functioning. *Child Development, 49,* 1005–1023.

Kagan, J., Reznick, J. S., & Snidman, N. (1988). Biological bases of childhood shyness. *Science, 240,* 167–171.

Kant, I. (1959). *Foundations of the metaphysics of morals* (L. Beck, Trans.). Indianapolis, IN: Bobbs-Merrill. (Original work published 1785)

Kapp, B. S., Supple, W. F., & Whalen, R. (1994). Effects of electrical stimulation of the amygdaloid central nucleus on neocortical arousal in the rabbit. *Behavioral Neuroscience, 108,* 81–93.

Karli, P. (1956). The Norway rat's killing response to the white mouse. *Behavior, 10,* 81–103.

Karli, P. (1981). Conceptual and methodological problems associated with the study of brain mechanisms underlying aggressive behavior. In P. F. Brain & D. Benton (Eds.), *Biology of aggression* (pp. 323–361). Alphenaandenrign, Holland: Sijthoff Noordhoff.

Karli, P. (1991). *Animal and human aggression.* Oxford, England: Oxford University Press.

Katz, L. F., & Gottman, J. M. (1994). Vagal tone buffers children from the effects of marital hostility. *Psychophysiology, 31,* S80.

Kay, L. E. (1993). *The molecular vision of life.* Oxford, England: Oxford University Press.

Kerr, M., Lambert, W. W., Stattin, H., & Klackenberg-Larsson, I. (1994). Stability of inhibition in the Swedish longitudinal sample. *Child Development, 65,* 138–146.

Klein, R. G. (1991). Parent-child agreement in clinical assessment of anxiety and other psychopathology. *Journal of Anxiety Disorders, 5,* 182–198.

Klein, R. G., & Last, C. G. (1989). *Anxiety disorders in children.* Newbury Park, CA: Sage.

Kochanska, G. (1991a). Patterns of inhibition to the unfamiliar in children of normal and affectively ill mothers. *Child Development, 62,* 250–263.

Kochanska, G. (1991b). Socialization and temperament in the development of guilt and conscience. *Child Development, 62,* 1379–1392.

Kochanska, G. (1993). Toward a synthesis of parental socialization and child temperament in early development of conscience. *Child Development, 64,* 325–347.

Kochanska, G. (1995). Children's temperament, mothers' discipline, and security of attachment. *Child Development, 66,* 597–615.

Kohnstamm, G. A., Bates, J. E., & Rothbart, M. K. (1989). *Temperament in childhood.* New York: Wiley.

Korner, A. F., Zeanah, C. H., Linden, J., Berkowitz, R. I., Kraemer, H. C., & Agras, W. S. (1985). The relation between neonatal and later activity and temperament. *Child Development, 56,* 38–42.

Kretschmer, E. (1925). *Physique and character* (2nd ed., W. J. H. Sprott, Trans.). New York: Harcourt Brace.

Lacey, J. I. (1967). Somatic response patterning in stress. In M. H. Appley & R. Trumbull (Eds.), *Psychological stress* (pp. 14–44). New York: Appleton-Century-Crofts.

Lavond, D. G., Kim, J. J., & Thompson, R. F. (1993). Mammalian brain substrates of aversive classical conditioning. In L. W. Porter & M. R. Rosenzweig (Eds.), *Annual review of psychology* (Vol. 44, pp. 317–342). Palo Alto, CA: Annual Reviews.

LeDoux, J. E., Iwata, J., Cichetti, P., & Reis, E. J. (1988). Different projections of the central amygdaloid nucleus mediate autonomic and behavioral correlates of conditioned fear. *Journal of Neuroscience, 8,* 2517–2529.

Lewis, M., Ramsay, D. S., & Kawakami, K. (1993). Differences between Japanese infants and Caucasian-American infants in behavioral and cortisol response to inoculation. *Child Development, 64,* 1722–1731.

Lin, K. M., Poland, R. E., & Lesser, I. N. (1986). Ethnicity and psychopharmacology. *Culture, Medicine, and Psychiatry, 10,* 151–165.

Lloyd, R. L., & Kling, A. S. (1991). Delta activity from amygdala in squirrel monkeys (Saimiri sciureus): Influence of social and environmental contexts. *Behavioral Neuroscience, 105,* 223–229.

Lombroso, C. (1911). *Crime and its causes.* Boston: Little, Brown.

Lykken, D. T., McGue, M., Tellegen, A., & Bouchard, P. J. (1992). Emergenesis. *American Psychologist, 47,* 1565–1577.

Madison, L. S., Madison, J. K., & Adubato, S. A. (1986). Infant behavior and development in relation to fetal movement and habituation. *Child Development, 57,* 1475–1482.

Magnusson, D. (1988). *Individual development from an interactional perspective.* Hillsdale, NJ: Erlbaum.

Mangelsdorf, S., Gunnar, M., Kestenbaum, R., Lang, S., & Andreas, D. (1990). Infant proneness to distress temperament, maternal personality, and mother-infant attachment. *Child Development, 61,* 820–831.

Matheny, A. (1980). Bayley's infant behavior record: Behavioral components and twin analyses. *Child Development, 51,* 1157–1167.

Matheny, A. (1983). A longitudinal twin study of stability of components from Bayley's infant behavior record. *Child Development, 54,* 356–360.

Matheny, A. (1990). Developmental behavior genetics. In M. E. Hahn, J. K. Hewitt, N. D. Henderson, & R. H. Benno (Eds.), *Developmental behavior genetics: Neural, biometrical, and evolutionary approaches* (pp. 25–38). New York: Oxford University Press.

Matheny, A., Wilson, R. S., & Thoben, A. S. (1987). Home and mother: Relations with infant temperament. *Developmental Psychology, 23,* 323–331.

May, H. (1959). *The end of American innocence.* New York: Knopf.

McDougall, W. (1908). *Introduction to social psychology.* London: Methuen.

Meadows, M. E., & Kaplan, R. F. (1994). Dissociation of autonomic and subjective responses to emotional slides in right hemisphere damaged patients. *Neuropsychologia, 32,* 847–856.

Mebert, C. J. (1991). Dimensions of subjectivity in parents' ratings of infant temperament. *Child Development, 62,* 352–361.

Meehl, P. E. (1973). Maxcov-Hitmax: A taxonomy search for loose genetic syndromes. In P. E. Meehl (Ed.), *Psychodiagnosis: Selected papers* (pp. 200–224). Minneapolis: University of Minnesota Press.

Meehl, P. E. (1995). Bootstrap taxometrics. *American Psychologist, 50,* 266–275.

Meyer, A. (1994). A short sketch of the problems of psychiatry. *American Journal of Psychiatry, 151,* 43–47. (Original work published 1897)

Mills, A. D., & Faure, J. M. (1991). Diversion selection for duration of chronic immobility and social reinstatement behavior in Japanese quail (Coturnix Japonica chicks). *Journal of Comparative Psychology, 105,* 25–38.

Mishkin, M. (1978). Memory in monkeys severely impaired by combined, but not by separate removal of amygdala and hippocampus. *Nature, 273,* 297–298.

North, C. S., Smith, E. M., & Spitznagel, E. L. (1994). Posttraumatic stress disorder and survivors of a mass shooting. *American Journal of Psychiatry, 151,* 82–88.

Olson, E. B., & Morgan, W. P. (1982). Rat brain monoamine levels related to behavioral assessment. *Life Sciences, 300,* 2095–2100.

Osgood, C. E., Suci, G. J., & Tannenbaum, P. H. (1957). *The measurement of meaning.* Urbana: University of Illinois Press.

Panksepp, J. (1990). The psychoneurology of fear. In G. D. Burrows, M. Roth, & R. Noyes (Eds.), *The neurobiology of anxiety: Vol. 3. Handbook of anxiety* (pp. 3–58). New York: Elsevier.

Panksepp, J., Sacks, D. S., Crepeau, L. J., & Abbott, B. B. (1991). The psycho and neurobiology of fear systems in the brain. In M. R. Denny (Ed.), *Fear, avoidance, and phobias* (pp. 7–59). Hillsdale, NJ: Erlbaum.

Parent, M. B., West, M., & McGaugh, J. L. (1994). Memory of rats with amygdala regions induced 30 days after footshock-motivated escape training reflects degree of original training. *Behavioral Neuroscience, 108,* 1080–1087.

Patrick, C. J. (1994). Emotion and psychopathy. *Psychophysiology, 31,* 319–330.

Pavlov, I. P. (1928). *Lectures on conditioned reflexes* (Vol. 1, W. H. Gantt, Trans.). New York: International.

Paxinos, G. (1990). *The human nervous system.* New York: Academic Press.

Piaget, J. (1950). *The psychology of intelligence.* London: Routledge & Kegan Paul.

Plomin, R., & Foch, T. T. (1980). A twin study of objectively assessed personality in childhood. *Journal of Personality and Social Psychology, 39,* 680–688.

Plomin, R., & McClearn, G. E. (Eds.). (1993). *Nature, nurture, and psychology.* Washington, DC: American Psychological Association.

Posner, M. I., & Petersen, S. E. (1990). The attention system of the human brain. *Annual Review of Neuroscience, 13,* 25–42.

Pyles, M. K., Stolz, H. R., & MacFarlane, J. W. (1935). The accuracy of mothers' reports on birth and developmental data. *Child Development, 6,* 165–176.

Pynoos, R. S., Frederick, C., Nader, K., Arroyo, W., Steinberg, A., Eth, S., Nunez, F., & Fairbanks, L. (1987). Life threat and post traumatic stress disorder in school-age children. *Archives of General Psychiatry, 44,* 1057–1063.

Raine, A., Venables, P. H., & Williams, M. (1990). Autonomic orienting responses in fifteen-year-old male subjects and criminal behavior at age 24. *American Journal of Psychiatry, 147,* 933–937.

Raine, A., Venables, P. H., & Williams, M. (1994). Autonomic nervous system factors that protect against crime. *Psychophysiology, 31,* S59.

Ramsay, D. S., & Lewis, M. (1994). Developmental changes in infant cortisol and behavioral response to inoculation. *Child Development, 65,* 1491–1502.

Rattoni, F. B., Forthman, D. L., Sanchez, M. A., Perez, J. L., & Garcia, J. (1988). Odor and taste aversions conditioned in anesthetized rats. *Behavioral Neuroscience, 102,* 726–732.

Reilly, J. S., Stiles, J., Larsen, J., & Trauner, D. (1995). Affective facial expression in infants with focal brain damage. *Neuropsychologia, 33,* 83–99.

Reppucci, C. (1968). *Hereditary influences upon distribution of attention in infancy.* Unpublished doctoral dissertation, Harvard University, Boston.

Rezendes, M. O. (1993). *Behavioral and autonomic transitions in early infancy.* Unpublished doctoral dissertation, Harvard University, Boston.

Richards, J. E., & Cameron, D. (1989). Infant heart rate variability and behavioral developmental status. *Infant Behavior and Development, 12,* 45–58.

Rickman, M. D., & Davidson, R. J. (1994). Personality and behavior in parents of temperamentally inhibited and uninhibited children. *Developmental Psychology, 30,* 346–354.

Riese, M. L. (1987). Temperament stability between the neonatal period and 24 months. *Developmental Psychology, 23,* 216–222.

Riese, M. L. (1988). Temperament in full-term and pre-term infants. *Journal of Developmental and Behavioral Pediatrics, 9,* 6–11.

Riese, M. L. (1990). Neonatal temperament in monozygotic and dizygotic twin pairs. *Child Development, 61,* 1230–1237.

Riese, M. L. (1995). Mothers' ratings of infant temperament. *Journal of Genetic Psychology, 156,* 23–32.

Roback, A. (1931). *Psychology of character* (2nd ed.). New York: Harcourt Brace.

Roccatagliatta, J. (1986). *A history of ancient psychiatry.* New York: Greenwood Press.

Rose, R. J. (1995). Genes and human behavior. In J. T. Spence, J. M. Darley, & D. P. Foss (Eds.), *Annual review of psychology* (pp. 625–654). Palo Alto, CA: Annual Reviews.

Rose, S. (1995). The rise of neurogenetic determinism. *Nature, 373,* 380–382.

Rosicky, J. (1993, March). *The assessment of temperamental fearfulness in infancy.* Presented at the Society for Research in Child Development, New Orleans.

Rothbart, M. K. (1988). Temperament and the development of inhibited approach. *Child Development, 59,* 1241–1250.

Rothbart, M. K. (1989). Temperament in childhood. In G. A. Kohnstamm, J. E. Bates, & M. K. Rothbart (Eds.), *Temperament in childhood* (pp. 59–73). New York: Wiley.

Rothbart, M. K., Derryberry, D., & Posner, M. I. (1994). A psychobiological approach to the development of temperament. In J. E. Bates & T. D. Wachs (Eds.), *Temperament* (pp. 83–116). Washington, DC: American Psychological Association.

Rubin, K. H. (1993). The Waterloo longitudinal project. In K. H. Rubin & J. B. Asendorpf (Eds.), *Social withdrawal, inhibition, and shyness in childhood* (pp. 291–314). Hillsdale, NJ: Erlbaum.

Ruff, H. A., Lawson, K. R., Parinello, B., & Weissberg, R. (1990). Long-term stability of individual differences in sustained attention in the early years. *Child Development, 61,* 60–75.

Sackett, G. P., Ruppenthall, G. C., Fahrenbuch, C. H., Holm, R. A., & Greenough, W. T. (1981). Social isolation rearing effects in monkeys vary with genotype. *Developmental Psychology, 17,* 313–318.

Sagi, A., Van IJzendoorn, M. H., & Koren-Karie, N. (1991). Primary appraisal of the Strange Situation. *Developmental Psychology, 27,* 587–596.

Sapolsky, R. M. (1992). *Stress, the aging brain, and the mechanisms of neuron death* (p. 181). Cambridge, MA: MIT Press.

Saudino, K. J., & Eaton, W. O. (1991). Infant temperament and genetics. *Child Development, 62,* 1167–1174.

Saudino, K. J., & Eaton, W. O. (1995). Continuity and change in objectively assessed temperament. *British Journal of Developmental Psychology, 13,* 81–95.

Saudino, K. J., & Kagan, J. (in press). The stability and genetics of behavioral inhibition. In R. N. Emde (Ed.), *The MALTS longitudinal study.* Unpublished manuscript.

Saudino, K. J., McGuire, S., Reiss, D., Hetherington, E. M., & Plomin, R. (1993). *Clarifying the confusion.* Unpublished paper. Center for Developmental and Health Genetics, Pennsylvania State University.

Saudino, K. J., Plomin, R., Campos, J. J., & DeFries, J. C. (1993). *Tester-rated temperament at, 14-, 20-, and 24-months.* Unpublished manuscript. Center for Developmental and Health Genetics, Pennsylvania State University.

Schneider, M. L. (1992). Prenatal stress exposure alters postnatal behavioral expression under conditions of novelty challenge in rhesus monkey infants. *Developmental Psychobiology, 25,* 529–540.

Schneider, M. L., & Coe, C. L. (1993). Repeated social stress during pregnancy impairs neuromotor development of the primate infant. *Journal of Developmental and Behavioral Pediatrics, 14,* 81–87.

Schwab-Stone, M., Fallon, T., Briggs, M., & Crowther, B. (1994). Reliability of diagnostic reporting for children aged 6 to 11 years. *American Journal of Psychiatry, 151,* 1048–1054.

Schwartz, C. (1995). *Physiological characteristics of inhibited and uninhibited adolescents.* Unpublished manuscript, Boston.

Scott, J. P., & Fuller, S. (1965). *Genetics and the social behavior of the dog.* Chicago: University of Chicago Press.

Seifer, R., Sameroff, A. J., Barrett, L. C., & Krafchuk, E. (1994). Infant temperament measured by multiple observations and mother report. *Child Development, 65,* 1478–1490.

Sheldon, W. H. (1940). *The varieties of human physique.* New York: Harper.

Shweder, R. (1993). The cultural psychology of the emotions. In M. Lewis & J. Haviland (Eds.), *Handbook of emotions* (pp. 417–434). New York: Guilford Press.

Siegel, R. E. (1968). *Galen's system of physiology and medicine.* Basel: Karger.

Simms, J. (1887). *Physiognomy illustrated* (8th ed.). New York: Murray Hill.

Skinner, B. F. (1981). Selection by consequences. *Science, 213,* 501–504.

Snidman, N., Kagan, J., Riordan, L., & Shannon, D. (1995). Cardiac function and behavioral reactivity in infancy. *Psychophysiology, 32,* 199–207.

Snowdon, C. T., Coe, C. L., & Hodun, A. (1985). Population recognition of infant isolation peeps in the squirrel monkey. *Animal Behavior, 33,* 1145–1156.

Snyder, M. (1985). To carve nature and its joints. *Psychological Review, 92,* 317–349.

Sperry, R. W. (1977). Bridging science and values. *American Psychologist, 32,* 237–245.

Spiker, D., Klebanov, P. K., & Brooks-Gunn, J. (1992, May). *Environmental and biological correlates of infant temperament.* Presented at the meeting of the International Society for Infant Studies, Miami, FL.

Spiker, D., Kraemer, H. C., Constantine, N. A., & Bryant, D. (1992). Reliability and validity of behavior problem checklist as measures of stable traits in low birth weight premature preschoolers. *Child Development, 63,* 1481–1496.

Spurzheim, J. G. (1834). *Phrenology.* Boston: Marsh, Copen, & Lyon.

Squire, L. R., & Zola-Morgan, S. (1988). Memory: Brain system and behavior. *Trends in Neurosciences, 11,* 170–175.

Stevenson-Hinde, J., & Shouldice, A. (1996). Fearfulness: Developmental consistency. In A. Sameroff & M. Haith (Eds.), *The five to seven year shift: Age of reason and responsibility* (pp. 237–252). Chicago: University of Chicago Press.

Stifter, C. A., Fox, N. A., & Porges, S. W. (1989). Facial expressivity and vagal tone in 5- and 10-month-old infants. *Infant Behavior and Development, 12,* 127–137.

Strauss, M. E., & Rourke, D. C. (1978). A multivariate analysis of the neonatal behavioral assessment scale in several samples. In A. J. Sameroff (Ed.), Organization and stability of newborn behavior. *Monographs of the Society for Research in Child Development, 43*(Nos. 5/6), 81–91.

Strelau, J. (1991). Renaissance in research on temperament. In J. Strelau & A. P. Angleitner (Eds.), *Explorations in temperament* (pp. 337–349). New York: Plenum Press.

Strelau, J. (1993). The location of the regulative theory of temperament among other temperament theories. In J. Hettema &

I. J. Dearey (Eds.), *Foundations of personality* (pp. 113–132). Amsterdam, The Netherlands: Kluwer.

Strelau, J., & Angleitner, A. (1991). *Explorations in temperament.* New York: Plenum Press.

Strouse, J. (1980). *Alice James.* Boston: Houghton Mifflin.

Suomi, S. J. (1987). Genetic and maternal contributions to individual differences in rhesus monkey biobehavioral development. In N. A. Krasnegor, E. M. Blass, M. A. Hofer, & W. P. Smotherman (Eds.), *Perinatal development* (pp. 397–420). New York: Academic Press.

Szasz, T. (1961). *The myth of mental illness.* New York: Harper.

Takahashi, J. S., & Hoffman, M. (1995). Molecular biological clocks. *American Scientist, 83,* 158–165.

Teplov, B. M. (1985). *Complete works.* Moscow: Pedagogica.

Terr, L. C. (1979). Children of Chowchilla. *Psychoanalytic Study of the Child, 34,* 547–623.

Thatcher, R. W. (1994). Cyclic cortical reorganization: Origins of human cognitive development. In G. Dawson & K. W. Fischer (Eds.), *Human behavior and the developing brain* (pp. 232–268). New York: Guilford Press.

Thomas, A., & Chess, S. (1977). *Temperament and development.* New York: Brunner/Mazel.

Thompson, R. A., Connell, J. P., & Bridges, L. J. (1988). Temperament, emotion, and social interactive behavior in the Strange Situation. *Child Development, 59,* 1102–1110.

Thompson, R. F., Donegan, N. H., Clark, G. A., Levond, D. G., Lincoln, J. S., Madden, J., Maulas, M. A., Monk, M. D., & McCormick, D. A. (1987). Neural substrates of discrete defensive conditioned reflexes, conditioned fear states, and their interaction in the rabbit. In I. Gormezano, W. F. Prokasy, & R. F. Thompson (Eds.), *Classical conditioning* (3rd ed., pp. 371–399). Hillsdale, NJ: Erlbaum.

Thompson, W. R. (1953). The inheritance of behavior. *Canadian Journal of Psychology, 7,* 145–155.

Treit, D., Pesold, C., & Rotzinger, S. (1993a). Dissociating the anti-fear effects of septal and amygdaloid lesions using two pharmacologically validated models of rat anxiety. *Behavioral Neuroscience, 107,* 770–785.

Treit, D., Pesold, C., & Rotzinger, S. (1993b). Noninteractive effects of diazepam and amygdaloid lesions in two animal models of anxiety. *Behavioral Neuroscience, 107,* 1099–1105.

Tremblay, R. E., Pihl, R. O., Vitaro, F., & Dubkin, P. L. (1994). Predicting early onset of male antisocial behavior from preschool behavior. *Archives of General Psychiatry, 51,* 732–735.

Van den Boom, D. C. (1994). The influence of temperament and mothering on attachment and exploration. *Child Development, 65,* 1457–1477.

Van den Boom, D. C., & Hoeksma, J. B. (1994). The effect of infant irritability on mother-infant interaction. *Developmental Psychology, 30,* 581–590.

Vanderwolf, C. H., & Cain, D. P. (1994). The behavioral neurobiology of learning and memory. *Brain Research Reviews, 19,* 264–297.

Vaughn, B. E., Bradley, C. F., Joffe, L. S., Seifer, R., & Barglow, R. (1987). Maternal characteristics measured prenatally are predictive of ratings of temperamental difficulty on the Carey Infant Temperament Questionnaire. *Developmental Psychology, 23,* 152–161.

Vaughn, B. E., Stevenson-Hinde, J., Waters, E., Kotsaftis, A., Lefaver, G. B., Shouldice, A., Trudel, M., & Belsky, J. (1992). Attachment security and temperament in infancy in early childhood. *Developmental Psychology, 28,* 463–473.

Walker, B. E., & Fraser, F. C. (1957). The embryology of cortisone induced cleft palate. *Journal of Embryology and Experimental Morphology, 5,* 201–209.

Walker, E., Grimes, K. E., Davis, D., & Smith, A. J. (1993). Childhood precursors of schizophrenia. *American Journal of Psychiatry, 150,* 1654–1660.

Weiner, H. (1992). *Perturbing the organism.* Chicago: University of Chicago Press.

Weissman, M. M. (1984). Depression and anxiety disorder in parents and children. *Archives of General Psychiatry, 4,* 847–849.

Weisz, J. R., Chaiyasit, W., Weiss, B., Eastman, K. L., & Jackson, E. W. (1995). A multi-method study of problem behavior among Thai and American children in school. *Child Development, 66,* 402–415.

Weisz, J. R., Suwanlert, S., Chaiyasit, W., Weiss, B., Achenbach, T., & Walter, B. R. (1987). Epidemiology of behavioral and emotional problems among Thai and American children. *Journal of the American Academy of Child and Adolescent Psychiatry, 26,* 890–898.

Weisz, J. R., Suwanlert, S., Chaiyasit, W., Weiss, B., Walter, B. R., & Anderson, W. W. (1988). Thai and American perspectives on over and under control of child behavior problems. *Journal of Consulting and Clinical Psychology, 56,* 601–609.

Werner, E. E. (1993). Risk resilience and recovery. *Development and Psychopathology, 5,* 503–515.

Whitehead, A. N. (1928). *Science and the modern world.* New York: Macmillan.

Wilson, D. S., Clark, A. B., Coleman, K., & Dearstyne, T. (1994). Shyness and boldness in human and other animals. *Trends in Ecology and Evolution, 9,* 442–446.

Wittgenstein, L. (1953). *Philosophical investigations.* New York: Macmillin.

Worobey, J., & Lewis, M. (1989). Individual differences in the reactivity of young infants. *Developmental Psychology, 25,* 663–667.

Yarrow, M. R., Campbell, J. D., & Burton, R. V. (1970). Recollections of childhood. *Monograph of the Society for Research in Child Development, 35*(5).

Yosida, M. (1973). The Chinese concept of nature. In S. Nakayama & N. Sivin (Eds.), *Chinese science* (pp. 71–90). Cambridge, MA: MIT Press.

CHAPTER 5

Emotional Development:
Action, Communication, and Understanding

CAROLYN SAARNI, DONNA L. MUMME, and JOSEPH J. CAMPOS

Extraordinary changes have been taking place in the study of emotion in the past 25 years. When the chapter dealing with socioemotional development was published in the previous edition of this *Handbook,* the study of emotion and emotional development was just emerging from 40 or more

Preparation of this chapter was conducted with the partial support of grant number HD-25066 from the National Institutes of Health, grant number MH-47543 from the National Institute of Mental Health, and a research grant from the John D. and Catherine T. MacArthur Foundation.

years of neglect. There were two principal reasons for the neglect (Campos, Barrett, Lamb, Goldsmith, & Stenberg, 1983). One was the widespread conviction that emotions were epiphenomenal, and the second was that emotions could not be measured with specificity. The 1983 chapter described the emergence of a functionalist approach to emotions, and showed how, contrary to prior thought, emotions profoundly affected cognitive, perceptual, social, and self-regulatory processes. It also described the close link between emotion and temperamental dispositions, attachment, and parent-child interactions, and documented major advances in measurement of emotion in face, voice, and action.

The remarkable surge of investigation on emotion has continued unabated in the past 15 years, and the results of such investigations are dramatically changing our conceptualization of both the nature of emotions and their function in development. Three major themes in recent research stand out: the close link between emotion and action, the social functions of emotion, and the closing of the gap in knowledge about development between infancy and adolescence.

The present chapter reflects these three emphases. We describe a recently revived way of conceptualizing emotion, one that traces its roots to the long-ignored work of John Dewey (1894, 1895). Second, we stress children's understanding of emotion and how children cope with their emotions and the environmental transactions that evoked them. Third, we are concerned with emotional development in preschool and middle childhood, when the significance of emotion is especially broad in scope. The chapter also contains a number of subordinate themes. For instance, we review some of the intriguing research that has been done with infants and toddlers on how they develop systems of emotional communication, in the process showing how the emotional expressions of others regulate the behavior of infants and children and result in empathic behavior, emotion regulation, and coping. In addition, we discuss why action has become so important in contemporary approaches to emotion and how cultural approaches to emotion are beginning to draw our attention to the importance of emotion communication in development.

A CONCEPTUAL FRAMEWORK FOR FEELING AND EMOTION

A Working Definition of Emotion

Emotions seem to be most closely linked to what a person is trying to do. One's perception and interpretation of events is never independent of the action that one can perform on it (Adolph, Eppler, & Gibson, 1993; Dewey, 1894, 1895). Indeed, an event can be defined as an opportunity for action. However, not all events generate emotion, only those in which one has a stake in the outcome. Hence, we propose as a working definition of emotion one that emphasizes action, the preparation for action, and the significance or relevance to concerns of person-environment transactions. This framework includes communication as a central aspect of action. *Emotion is thus the person's attempt or readiness to establish, maintain, or change the relation between the person and the environment on matters of significance to that person.* The definition may initially appear to be odd because of the absence of any reference to the traditional elements found in the most prevalent definitions of emotion. There is no allusion to feeling, vegetative states, facial indices of internal states, or other intrapersonal criteria. Instead, emotion is synonymous with the significance of a person-event transaction. Because the definition emphasizes what the person is trying to do, and because it comes from a conception of emotion that stresses the consequences of emotional states, this working definition of emotion is often called a functionalist one (Barrett & Campos, 1987; Campos, Mumme, Kermoian, & Campos, 1994; Frijda, 1986, 1987; Lazarus, 1991).

There are at least four ways by which events become significant. The first is a particularly powerful and pervasive one, namely, goal relevance and its corollaries. Lazarus (1991) specifically links the first step in the generation of emotion to this factor; however, goal relevance per se ensures the generation of only some kind of affect. To account for whether the affect has a positive or negative hedonic tone and a behavioral valence of approach or withdrawal, Lazarus posits the congruence or incongruence of an event to one's goals: goal congruent transactions produce positive hedonic tone, and goal incongruent transactions bring about negative tone. To explain how a specific emotion such as fear, anger, or shame comes about, he proposes the factor of ego involvement (this determines the specific nature of the emotion elicited). So, regardless of the specific goal one is working toward, a person who overcomes obstacles to goal attainment is likely to experience happiness or relief. A person who relinquishes a goal experiences sadness, regardless of whether that goal involves physical, social, or psychological loss. A person who encounters obstacles to goal attainment will show frustration or anger. The specific nature of the goal can also affect the experience of a given emotion. Thus, avoidance of threat is linked to fear, desire to atone is related to guilt, and the wish to escape the scrutiny of others following a transgression is linked to shame. Table 5.1 lists the factors that Barrett and Campos (1987) proposed for the generation and manifestation of a variety of emotional states. Some of these emotions are called primordial emotions, to denote their likely presence in the neonate and their rudimentary

TABLE 5.1 Characteristics of Some Emotion Families

Emotion Family	Goal	Appreciation re Self	Appreciation re Other	Action Tendency	Adaptive Functions	Facial Expression[b]	Physiological Reaction	Vocalic Pattern[f]
Disgust	Avoiding contamination or illness	This stimulus may contaminate me, or cause illness	[a]	Active rejection	Avoid contamination and illness; learn about substances/events/attributes to avoid; alert others re contamination	Brows lowered, nose wrinkled, with widened nasal root; raised cheeks and upper lip	Low heart rate and skin temperature; increased skin resistance[c]	Nasal, slightly tense, "very narrow," but fairly full and powerful voice
Fear	Maintaining integrity of the self (physical or psychological integrity)	This stimulus threatens my integrity	[a]	Flight; active withdrawal	Avoid danger (physical and psychological); learn about events/attributes that are dangerous; alert others re danger	Brows raised and often pulled slightly together; eyes very wide and tense, rigidly fixated on stimulus	High, stable heart rate; low skin temperature; "gasping" respiration[c]	"Narrow," extremely tense, very weak, thin, high voice
Anger	Any end state that the organism currently is invested in achieving	There is an obstacle to my obtaining my goal	[a]	Active forward movement, especially to eliminate obstacles	Attain difficult goals; learn to overcome obstacles and achieve goals; communicate power/dominance	Brows lowered and pulled together; mouth open and square or lips pressed tightly together	High heart rate and skin temperature; facial flushing[c]	"Narrow," medium to very tense, medium to extremely full voice
Sadness	Any end state that the organism currently is invested in achieving	My goal is unattainable	[a]	Disengagement; passive withdrawal	Conserve energy; learn which goals are realizable; encourage nurturance by others	Inner corners of brows moved upward; corners of mouth pulled downward, often with middle of chin pulled upward	Low heart rate;[d] low skin temperature and skin resistance	"Narrow," thin, lax, slow, or halting voice
Shame	Maintaining others' respect and affection; preserving self-esteem	I am bad (self-esteem is perceived to be impaired)	Someone/everyone notices how bad I am	Active or passive withdrawal; avoiding others; hiding of self	Behave appropriately; learn/maintain social standards; communicate submission to others and to others' standards	—	Low heart rate; blushing[e]	"Narrow," moderately lax, thin voice
Guilt	Meeting one's own internalized standards	I have done something contrary to my standards	Someone has been injured by my act	Outward movement; inclination to make reparation, to inform others, and to punish oneself	Behave prosocially; learn/maintain moral and prosocial behavior; communicate contrition/good intentions	—	High heart rate and skin conductance; irregular respiration[e]	"Narrow," tense, moderately full voice
Pride	Maintaining the respect of oneself and others	I am good (I have respect for myself)	Someone/everyone thinks (or will think) I am good	Outward/upward movement; inclination to show/inform others about one's accomplishments	Behave appropriately; learn/maintain social standards; communicate ability to meet standards	—	High heart rate[e]	"Wide," medium tense, full voice

[a] No "appreciation re other" is central to primordial or concurrent-goal emotions; however, particular family members might involve such an appreciation.
[b] These facial movements are adapted from Izard (1979).
[c] These are adapted from Ekman, Levenson, and Friesen (1983).
[d] Ekman et al. (1983) found increased heart rate with sadness; however, decreased heart rate is consistent with our theoretical position on sadness. We think it possible that most subjects in Ekman et al.'s study experienced an agitated grief state rather than a sad "giving-up" state.
[e] These are hypothesized physiological reactions.
[f] These vocalic patterns are adapted from Scherer (1986).

239

appraisal demands; others are called concurrent-goal emotions, to specify their close link to flexible goals and strivings; still others are called social emotions, to indicate their origin in social rules backed by emotion communication from significant others. For all of these emotions, goal relevance is typically the most fundamental principle of emotion generation

Not all emotions are generated by the relation of events to goals. A second way emotion can be generated is through the social signals of others, which have powerful capacities to render a person-environment transaction significant (Klinnert, Campos, Sorce, Emde, & Svejda, 1983; McIntosh, Druckman, & Zajonc, 1994). They do so because social signals can generate a contagious emotional response and tendency for action in the perceiver (Hatfield, Cacioppo, & Rapson, 1994). Social signals can also give meaning to a transaction associated with the signal (such as when an infant "catches" the mother's fear of dogs and begins to avoid them; e.g., Bowlby, 1972). Finally, social signals play a central, though underinvestigated, role in generating emotions such as pride, shame, and guilt through the enduring effects they can have as accompaniments to the approval and disapproval of others.

A third source of significance comes about through hedonic processes—specifically, when hedonic stimulation is experienced and becomes the object of one's strivings (Frijda, 1986). Hedonic stimulation refers to the sights, sounds, tastes, smells, and tactile stimulations that intrinsically produce irreducible sensations of pleasure or pain. With pleasurable hedonic experience, we are more likely to want to repeat such experience, and thus approach behavior is established; painful experience elicits the converse. Pleasure and pain are thus affectogenic in the following way. If one experiences pleasant stimulation and wants to repeat the experience, the emotion of desire is generated; similarly, if one experiences pain and wants not to repeat the experience, the emotion of aversion is created. Desire and aversion, with further development, can become the core of much more complex emotional transactions, including envy, jealousy, and rage.

The fourth way that events become significant comes from memory of transactions from the past. Although all emotion theories stress the role of memory in generating affect, we would like to emphasize the importance of past experience for the selection of strategies for responding emotionally. Such a link is best represented in the research on working models in attachment (Bretherton, 1985). For example, as Cassidy (1994) has pointed out, avoidantly attached infants typically have a history of interactions in which their attachment figure has ignored the infant's social signals, such as bids for comfort. When these bids are consistently rejected by the caregiver, the child is predisposed toward muted affect during reunions with the caregiver: the past history of ignoring social bids makes the risk of present rejection too great. By contrast, infants who are classified as ambivalently attached have a history of interaction with a figure who has responded inconsistently to their social signals. When such children are reunited with the attachment figure following separation, they show exaggerated, rather than muted, emotional reactions. Such exaggeration serves the function, in part, of ensuring the parent's responsiveness and avoiding the parent's insensitivity. Thus, past experiences determine not only the precise nature of the emotion a child undergoes (as in the case of desire and aversion discussed above), but also the manner in which the child responds to, or copes with, contemporary interactions with significant others.

Feeling and Emotion

What is the role in the emotion process of what we call "feeling," the irreducible quality of consciousness that accompanies evaluations? The layperson's conception places feeling at the core of emotion: events elicit feeling, and feeling organizes "expressions" of feeling and autonomic and instrumental behavioral reactions designed both to manifest outwardly and to deal with the feeling. However, many theorists (e.g., Lewis & Michalson, 1983; Sroufe, 1979) have proposed that feeling is absent in the young infant and comes about only after the infant has acquired the capacity to distinguish self from other, an accomplishment that begins to be shown by 9 months of age.

The functionalist approach to emotion gives feeling a major role as a facet of emotion, but not as its core. Feelings are not prior in time to other processes in emotion generation, as orthodox conceptualizations require. We propose that the origins of feeling come from four sources (Campos et al., 1994). One of these is the conscious accompaniment to the process of *appraisal,* that is, the determination of how an event impinges on one's goals (Lazarus, 1991). The appreciation of the meaning of an event shows that it *matters* to the individual, and feeling is the registration of this significance. In short, feeling accompanies the registration of events: it does not precede it.

The second source of feeling is the consciousness of the activation of goal-oriented central motor commands (efference). Efference, unlike return sensory flow to the brain (afference), has rarely been linked to consciousness in psychological theories, yet efference plays a role in the perception of self-motion as well as in one's sense of volition, that is, of "willing" a body movement to take place (Teuber, 1960). This notion of the importance of efference in generating feeling is consistent with the reasoning of Ekman, Levenson, and Friesen (1983), who discussed the importance of motoric commands to create facial patterns for bringing emotion about. It is also consistent with recent theorizing by Damasio (1994), who stated that "the brain learns to connect the fainter image of an 'emotional' body state, without having to reenact it in the body proper" (p. 155). The link between efference and emotion again renders feeling contemporary with emotion generation, not antecedent to it.

The third way feeling can be generated is through the perception of sensations coming from both smooth and striated muscles, and possibly from the effects of hormones. Our language is full of references to such internal states, such as when we talk of feeling a "cold" fear, being "flushed" in anger, having "butterflies in the stomach," and so forth. In addition, many cultures literally embody emotion by referring to somatic states that occur when one is in distress or is euphoric (Shweder, 1993). The role of feedback seems undeniable in creating aspects of feeling (Laird, 1984), but feeling is again not primary: it follows response generation.

The fourth way that feeling can be generated is through the direct perception of emotional expressions in the face, voice, and gesture of another (Hatfield et al., 1994). This is the phenomenon referred to as *socially induced affect* (McIntosh et al., 1994), which is defined as the generation of a like or complementary feeling state in the self as a result of the perception of social displays in another. This phenomenon is quite context-specific. We do not understand the circumstances in which expressions by another most directly generate a similar feeling in the perceiver, those which generate an emotional state that is similar in valence but different in quality, those in which an opposite emotional state is elicited, and those in which no feelings are generated at all. Research on the ontogeny and consequences of affect contagion and socially induced affect is sorely lacking, despite exciting work with socially deprived infant monkeys suggesting that no social experience is necessary for social signals to affect behavior in affectively appropriate ways (Kenney, Mason, & Hill, 1979; Sackett, 1966). To return to our consideration of feeling,

note again that socially induced affect renders feeling simultaneous with the detection of social signals, not prior to it. Such considerations are what have led us to propose that feeling is a facet of the emotion process, but not its core. In addition, because infants can show facial and instrumental behavior patterns of specific emotions very early in life (e.g., Gaensbauer, 1982; Stenberg & Campos, 1990), appraisal, efference, and afference are available to the young infant, and so may affect emotion contagion (Haviland & Lelwicka, 1987). We thus find no reason to deny infants younger than 9 months of age the experience of feeling.

Action Tendencies and the Flexible Manifestation of Emotion

In the course of studying blind infants, Fraiberg (1971) discovered that many parents of such children showed profound disappointment when they encountered low levels of facial responsiveness and eye contact in their children. The parents seemed to withdraw from their children and to lack the incentive to provide them with physical and social stimulation after noting their children's apparent unresponsiveness. Fraiberg discovered, however, that although blind infants were indeed relatively unresponsive *facially* during social encounters, they seemed extraordinarily articulate in expressing their emotions and social responses through the actions of their *fingers*. When this responsiveness was pointed out to the parents, they dramatically increased their levels of interaction with the infants; the infants, in turn, were able to maintain their digitally mediated level of social responsiveness.

Fraiberg's observations document an important principle about emotions: many different responses can be in the service of any given emotion. To expect, as some theories do (e.g., Ekman et al., 1983; Izard, 1977, 1991; Tomkins, 1962, 1963), a close correspondence between a given response or response pattern (e.g., a facial expression) and a given emotional state is likely to lead to errors of inference. The opposite is also true: the same response can be recruited to "express" many different emotions. Some years ago, Kagan (1971) put it well; he said that the smile serves many masters. Consider, for example, that the action of smiling can be in the service of joy, scorn, nurturance, embarrassment, stereotyped social greeting, and other emotions. Similarly, the action of doing nothing can be in the service of sadness (as in depressive withdrawal), fear (as in keeping still to avoid detection), or anger (as in passive aggressiveness). It is clear that emotions are best considered as syndromes, that is, alternative patterns of behavior, any of which, under the right circumstances, can specify the emotion (Lazarus & Averill, 1972). It is not possible to identify a priori an operational definition of a given emotion that can be applied in all circumstances: a discrete emotion thus lacks a gold standard—an ostensive definition. Neither the face, voice, gesture, specific instrumental behavior, or autonomic signatures are likely to have more than a probabilistic relation to an emotional state; even then, context must be taken into account to interpret the meaning of a response.

At present, the concept of *affect families* (Barrett & Campos, 1987; Dewey, 1934; Kagan, 1994) is used to convey the notion that each experience of a given emotion such as anger or fear is likely to differ in important ways from other emotional experiences of anger or fear. Each instance of an emotion differs from another in social signaling, type of behavior shown in context, and pattern of appraisal, yet, so long as the adaptational intent is the same for two different experiences, it can be said that the different instances bear a family resemblance to each other. It is through such adaptational intents that emotions can be classified and their differential consequences understood (Shaver, Schwartz, Kirson, & O'Connor, 1987), not by similarity in morphology.

Measuring Emotion via Action Tendencies

The absence of an ostensive criterion for a given emotional state creates serious problems of inference. One attempt to resolve this dilemma has been proposed by Frijda (1986) in his concept of *action tendencies*. Avoidance of threat, for instance, is the action tendency for fear; avoidance of social contact of the scrutinizing other is that for shame; devotion of effort to remove an obstacle is the action tendency for anger, and so on. Table 5.2 lists Frijda's proposed action tendencies and the specific emotions that they denote, a list that he considers incomplete but representative.

For Frijda, the concept of action tendency in no way refers to a response that can be measured by electromyography or by operational definition of a given response. Rather, action tendency refers to any of a number of flexibly organized phenomena that *serve the function* of, for example, avoiding threat or overcoming an obstacle. In this sense, action tendency is similar to the ethologist's conception of a behavioral system, a conception that replaced notions of fixed action patterns with appreciation of the multiplicity of ways by which an animal can attain an end (Bischof, 1975). The behavioral system for the ethologist, like the concept of a specific emotion, is defined in terms of the function those behaviors serve. How does one mea-

TABLE 5.2   Relational Action Tendencies, Activation Modes, and Inhibitions[a]

Action Tendency	End State	Function	Emotion
Approach	Access	Producing situation permitting consummatory activity	Desire
Avoidance	Own inaccessibility	Protection	Fear
Being-with	Contact, interaction	Permitting consummatory activity	Enjoyment, confidence
Attending (opening)	Identification	Orientation	Interest
Rejecting (closing)	Removal of object	Protection	Disgust
Nonattending	No information or contact	Selection	Indifference
Agonistic	Removal of obstruction	Regaining control	Anger
Interrupting	Reorientation	Reorientation	Shock
Dominating	Retained control	Generalized control	Arrogance
Submitting	Deflected pressure	Secondary control	Humility
Deactivation	—	(Recuperation?)	Sorrow
Bound activation	Action tendency's end state	Aim achievement	Effort
Excitement	—	Readiness	Excitement
Free activation	—	Generalized readiness	Joy
Inactivity	—	Recuperation	Contentment
Inhibition	Absence of response	Caution	Anxiety
Surrender	Activation decrease?	Activation decrease or social cohesion?	(Laughter, weeping)

[a] Adapted from Frijda (1986).

sure function? The functionalist's answer is: by inference from the organization of behavior, by suppositions about what the person is trying to accomplish, and by noting whether progress toward the inferred goal is proceeding smoothly or with difficulty. The identification of the operation of a discrete emotion, then, is intimately tied to the context within which the person is found and the types of behavior pattern the person shows in that setting.

Although the task of measuring emotion is much more difficult than initially thought, when emotion was restored to its place in scientific study a few years ago, there is a major precedent for measuring the organization of behavior, a precedent that is both intellectually persuasive and highly influential (Sroufe & Waters, 1977). In attachment theory, Bowlby (1969) posited that attachment could be measured by proximity seeking in times of fear or distress. Although proximity seeking can be operationalized by measuring the physical distance of the child from the attachment figure (Coates, Anderson, & Hartup, 1972; Cohen & Campos, 1974), such an approach reveals little in the way of stability of individual differences in attachment, nor is it an index that retains its manifestation as the child grows older and shows attachment patterns in a variety of different ways. Attachment theorists (e.g., Ainsworth, Blehar, Waters, & Wall, 1978) have solved this problem of measuring proximity seeking by noting first of all whether the child's behavior *in context* (of reunion with the caregiver after a distressing period of absence) manifests evidence for security or insecurity. There are many alternative ways in which attachment security can be manifested: smiling at the caregiver, making pick-up bids, showing a toy. These alternative behavioral strategies are taken as partial evidence for what Sroufe (1979; Sroufe & Waters, 1977) calls "the organization of behavior." The organization stems from the similar ends that morphologically quite different behaviors serve. Second, the crucial factors of avoidance and ambivalence in attachment are similarly inferred by judgments based on the many alternative ways that a child can give the parent the "cold shoulder treatment" specifying avoidance, or the "angry yet relieved" expression of ambivalence.

This approach to measurement of the action tendencies related to attachment needs to be generalized to the study of other emotional states. It should not be thought that such flexibility of behavior organized around an emotion is limited to the older school-age child and adult. Fraiberg's (1971) observations of blind infants' social responsiveness described above demonstrate this. So do the reactions of 8- to 9-month-old infants tested on the visual cliff, a highly

reliable fear elicitor (Scarr & Salapatek, 1970). At that age, infants can manifest fear by avoiding descending onto the glass-covered "deep" side of the cliff, or they can approach the mother, but in a manner indicative of fear. The infants do this by detouring around the deep side, hitching along the side walls of the cliff table until they reach the mother (Campos, Hiatt, Ramsay, Henderson, & Svejda, 1978). Behavioral flexibility is the rule, not the exception, in the manifestation of emotion. Restriction of such flexibility in the interests of measuring one or more responses chosen a priori by the investigator puts at risk the internal validity of a given study as well as its external or ecological validity.

Dynamic Systems Approaches to Emotion

The notion that emotion must be studied in a fashion that does justice to behavioral complexity, context, and temporal flow has led some researchers to investigate the applicability of dynamic systems approaches to the emergence of behavior patterns related to emotion (e.g., Camras, 1991; Fogel et al., 1992; Fogel & Thelen, 1987; Messinger, Fogel, & Dickson, 1997). Dynamic systems theory is an attempt to describe the organization of behavior without postulating a central organizer (such as maturation, a facial action program, localized centers in the brain). The impetus for this theory is to treat the unitary, functional, interdependent pattern of behavior in a fashion comparable to phenomena in the physical world, such as crystal growth, that spontaneously organize in the right environment without reference to any central organizer. Dynamic systems theory generates interest in a number of aspects of behavior, two of which are stability and new levels of organization. Stability is of interest because motor coordinative structures can be quite robust to environmental or motoric perturbances (e.g., saying "ba" is possible despite the obstacle of a mouthful of food). New levels of organization (called a phase shift) are of interest because they can reveal how such change takes place as the result of a change in one or more of the component elements of the phenomenon being studied. (The element driving the change is called a control parameter, and such a parameter can be found in the person, in the environment, or in their interrelation.)

Fogel et al. (1992) have proposed three principles derived from dynamic systems theory but more specifically related to emotion. The first proposition is that *emotion is a self-organizing system constituted by the interaction of many components related to individuals in their social and physical context.* For example, Fogel and his collaborators (e.g., Messinger et al., 1997) have begun to study the type of smile that is called the "felt" or Duchenne smile, be- · cause it is presumably an authentic expression—one that differs from non-Duchenne smiles, which result from the activation of display rules (Ekman, Davidson, & Friesen, 1990). (The felt/Duchenne smile involves the orbicularis oculi muscles around the eyes that result in a crow's feet appearance, as well as the upturning of the lips resulting from contraction of the zygomaticus muscle; the non-Duchenne smile involves the zygomaticus, but not the orbicularis oculi.) To clarify the nature of the smile, they have simultaneously focused on the O-shaped smile.

Consistent with the principles of dynamic systems theory, the study by Messinger et al. was longitudinal, it was conducted in naturalistic settings, the investigators devoted special attention to the temporal flow of events, and they tried to specify the coordination of components. They found that the Duchenne or felt smile was not categorically different from the O-shaped smile, being instead a manifestation resulting from the greater motoric arousal produced by the contexts within which the Duchenne smile was observed. The O-shaped smile was evident just before the Duchenne smile broke out and as the Duchenne smile was waning. What appeared to be a categorical difference between smiles was thus found to be one of intensity.

Recently, Camras (1991, 1992) conducted a longitudinal videotaped study of her daughter. This study led Camras to challenge orthodox measurements of anger faces and sad faces by using predetermined criteria and by divorcing the measurement of such facial expressions from the context within which they appeared to be observed. More specifically, Camras found that the anger face typically was observed as the child began to cry, and the sad face as the child's crying waned. Anger and sad faces were thus brief temporal manifestations on the way to or away from a full-blown distress cry. Camras proposed that such anger and sad faces have a different meaning when observed briefly in the infant than when observed at older ages, the difference being that at older ages the facial movements can occur with greater duration and in the absence of subsequent crying. Both the Fogel et al. (1992) study and the Camras (1991, 1992; Michel, Camras, & Sullivan, 1992) work demonstrate the dynamic systems principle of studying how components of behavior (in both cases, facial patterns) are organized in different contexts.

The second principle that Fogel et al. (1992) propose is that *emotions are related to the continuously evolving sequences of action.* In the same study described above, Messinger et al. (1997) described the origins and functions of the O-shaped smile. They reported that such smiles resulted from an adaptation the infant made when the mother prepared to place the infant in a feeding position or was preparing to interact with the child. The O-shape thus represents an adjustment by the child to the ongoing flow of interaction with the mother.

The third principle proposed by Fogel et al. (1992) is that *emotional development consists of the construction of categorical information out of gradient information, and the changing relationship between information and action.* The emergence of fear of heights typically after locomotor experience exemplifies the principle of how a change in gradient (i.e., continuous) information and in the relation between information and action results in a categorical change in emotional reaction to the same setting. Bertenthal and Campos (1990) proposed that such wariness of heights can occur when two powerful sources of gradient information about self-movement that ordinarily are highly correlated are unexpectedly decoupled, with the decoupling leading to a negative emotional state. One source of information about self-movement is the vestibular system, which registers the angular acceleration of a person's head. The second is visual proprioception: the flow of visual texture, especially that in the periphery of the visual field.

Ordinarily, when a baby is moving around voluntarily on a floor, the ground provides the texture for peripheral optic flow and the infant's head and body movements provide vestibular information; the two sources of information are thus coupled. However, when the infant locomotes to a drop-off, such as on the deep side of the visual cliff, the flow of visual texture slows down considerably because at the drop-off point the nearest texture starts to be much farther away than the ground had been. At the same time, vestibular information continues as before because head and body movements continue. At the drop-off, then, visual and vestibular stimulation are no longer coupled, and there is a discrepancy in information about motion of the self. That discrepancy is sufficient to produce vertigo, queasiness, or a related unpleasant state that motivates attempts to restore visual-vestibular coupling by avoiding the drop-off. In short, a quantitative shift in the rate of optic flow to the periphery creates the context for the infant experiencing a qualitatively different emotion than was being experienced prior to reaching the drop-off.

Bertenthal and Campos's (1990) explanation of the elicitation of wariness of heights leads to an explanation of why infants typically do not show wariness of heights until *after* they have acquired some locomotor experience (Campos, Bertenthal, & Kermoian, 1992). They propose that (a) prelocomotor infants are *not* very sensitive to aspects of visual proprioception (hence, they would experience no visual-vestibular decoupling and no wariness); (b) because of the way they typically hold their head and eyes straight ahead when beginning to locomote, crawling infants become sensitive to peripheral optic flow (a prediction recently confirmed by C. Higgins, Campos, & Kermoian, 1996); (c) with continued locomotor experience, visual proprioception and vestibular information about self-movement become correlated; so that (d) when there is visual-vestibular decoupling, a discrepant event occurs that leads to the vertigo or queasiness mentioned above. This explanation has recently received tentative support from a study by Campos, Kermoian, Witherington, Chen, and Dong (in press), who reported a high correlation between an infant's sensitivity to peripheral optic flow and avoidance of heights.

Note here the orchestration of elements from both the environment and the infant (i.e., the self-organization) in the generation of wariness of heights, as well as the absence of a central organizer such as maturation of fear. These elements include, from the environment, gravitational information, optic flow of texture, and a drop-off that affords the information for visual-vestibular decoupling. From the infant, the elements include the organization of crawling (which serves in this case as a control parameter), the orientation of head and eyes, the comparison of multiple sources of information specifying the same state of affairs, and reactions of vertigo, wariness, and avoidance. The person-environment transaction contributes the elements of coordination of the visual and vestibular system, the encounter with the drop-off, and the possibility of actions such as avoidance or detour behavior. In sum, as Fogel et al. (1992) note, aspects of emotional development can fit under the principle of emotion's being related to ongoing sequences of action. Research is needed to conduct similar analyses of the organization of emotional behavior.

Change in Person-Environment Relations and Emotional Development

Earlier, we proposed that any factor that changes the relation of the person to the environment will generate affect, so long as the changed person-environment relations are significant ones for the person. The development of actions related to the environment, including reaching, crawling, and walking, thus should be related to important changes in emotionality (Emde, Gaensbauer, & Harmon, 1976). For similar reasons, non-action-related, socially driven person-environment changes such as entry into school, marriage, birth of a child, divorce, and retirement should and do produce major emotional reorganizations. However, action may be a more readily observed source of changes in emotionality in early life than social changes.

Psychoanalytic theorists, such as Mahler (Mahler, Pine, & Bergman, 1975) and Spitz (1965), were the first to suggest that major affective changes are linked to the acquisition of walking. Indeed, Biringen, Emde, Campos, and Appelbaum (1995) have reported important changes in both the mother and the infant following the acquisition of upright locomotion: the mother changes in her sensitivity to affective signals from the infant, and the newly locomoting infant becomes more willful. However, the emotional reorganizations—the increased differentiation and increased intensity of emotional reactions—that take place following crawling onset have been the most systematically studied in relation to action processes. We have already seen how experience locomoting is crucial for development of aspects of the self as well as for wariness of heights, but the influence of motoric experience extends well beyond these two instances.

Emotional Communication

When crawling begins, emotional communication targeted at the infant increases substantially and can generate considerable socially induced affect (Zumbahlen & Crawley, 1996). Such affect induction comes about because the act of infant self-movement often elicits strong positive affect in caregivers, who greet the onset of locomotion with a combination of happiness and pride (Bertenthal, Campos, & Barrett, 1984). Once parents become accustomed to the child's new locomotor skills, the targeting of positive affect shifts. It now becomes directed toward encouraging the child to explore, to engage in new activities and problems, and to scrutinize events in the world. The outcome for the child is an expansion of horizons, the encounter of new and interesting environmental events, and an increase in mirrored emotional positivity and elicited curiosity and interest.

The communication of emotion, however, also has a negative side that becomes especially prominent with the emergence of new attributions of responsibility by the parent to the now mobile child. Mothers typically do not express much anger or fear to their infants prior to 8 months of age (Zumbahlen & Crawley, 1996) because prelocomotor infants are not typically considered responsible for their actions, nor are they often in situations of danger or prohibition. However, locomotion changes mothers' attributions, resulting in a sharp increase in their targeting of both anger and fear expressions toward their children as they recognize the dangers to them inherent in some objects, such as houseplants, vases, and electrical appliances (Campos, Kermoian, & Zumbahlen, 1992). If the child tests the authenticity of the maternal signals by attempting to explore a forbidden object once more, the parent's initially mild signal can become sharper and more foreboding in tone. For the child, such heightened signals can lead to apprehension and frustration (Campos et al., 1992).

Increased Prevalence of Discrete Emotions

Changes in emotion in response to the same event should also become much more frequent and complex once the child becomes mobile. This follows because the relation of events to goals changes with locomotion and results in the generation of the affects of joy, anger/frustration, and fear. For instance, as the motor responses necessary for forward propulsion become organized, the infant attains the necessary conditions for the expression of intense joy. What Buhler (1930) called "function pleasure" becomes manifest. Moreover, as the child's self-produced locomotor movements become better organized and controlled, new goals emerge because a large variety of environmental objects can be sought out successfully and a number of events can become the subject of exploration (Bertenthal et al., 1984; Gustafson, 1984). With the successful attainment of each of these goals, the infant should experience considerable joy and task engagement. This is precisely what appears to take place (Zumbahlen & Crawley, 1996).

Goal setting also creates problems. Infants can be frustrated and thus show anger, even from earliest infancy (Stenberg & Campos, 1990). Yet, for reasons similar to those in our discussion of the development of joy, with the acquisition of crawling there should be a sharp rise in the prevalence of anger-provoking encounters. As the child attempts to attain what he or she wants, it is inevitable that siblings, parents, furniture, and other structures (e.g., high places) will sometimes prevent infants from reaching their objectives. The onset of self-produced locomotion thus results in increases in anger and frustration. Anger is thus the negative side of self-initiative made possible by locomotion (Campos et al., 1992; Johnson, Emde, Pannabecker, Stenberg, & Davies, 1982).

Changes in Emotion Regulation

Finally, we address the implications of the development of self-produced locomotion for understanding developmental changes in fear and coping. According to contemporary theories of emotion (e.g., Barrett & Campos, 1987;

Lazarus, 1991), fear comes about when the child realizes that his or her actions are not adequate to cope with a threat. In short, fear comes about in part when an event is uncontrollable (Gunnar, 1980). One of the consequences of voluntary locomotion is that events that were once uncontrollable are now under the direct control of the infant. For instance, when a stranger approaches, the infant can move away from the stranger toward either the haven of the mother's lap or some other safe location. Such an example illustrates how situations that were once the source of fear are transformed through the acquisition of independent locomotion into controllable situations that are no longer feared by the child. In short, locomotion becomes a coping strategy for the child.

There is some empirical evidence that supports this prediction. In his monograph on the development of negative reactions to strangers, Bronson (1972) cited how infants showed fear of strangers at 9 months of age when they were seated in a high chair, but did not show such fear when they were freely moving about on the floor: the infant's newly developed ability to crawl permitted a coping response and a short-circuiting of fear. Subsequently, the infant's success in controlling interactions with a stranger, such as by moving away, was found to be directly related to the amount of distress shown by the infant to that stranger (Parritz, Mangelsdorf, & Gunnar, 1992).

Furthermore, the child's locomotion increases the need for vigilance to ensure the child's safety. Changes in social interaction were also reported. Following locomotor experience, infants' wariness of separation increased, as well as the manner in which they showed affection toward their fathers, siblings, and pets. Locomotor infants also bid for more play with both mother and father (Campos et al., 1992).

In sum, the onset of locomotion marks a time of major social and emotional changes in the child, the mother, and the family as a function of the child's becoming mobile. More generally, we propose that other times of change in person-environment relations will similarly be associated with increased differentiation and prevalence of emotion.

CULTURE, EMOTION, AND EMOTIONAL DEVELOPMENT

Attempts to understand how culture affects emotion and emotional development have changed considerably in the past 15 years. In the 1970s and 1980s, researchers were mostly concerned with universals in emotion expression. The search for universals generated impressive evidence on the similarity of recognition of facial expressions by preliterate peoples (Ekman, 1973; Ekman, Sorenson, & Friesen, 1969) and judges in both Western and non-Western countries (Izard, 1972). In turn, this evidence led to the widespread use of facial expressions as the preferred indices of emotional states, and motivated the "emotion revolution" of the 1970s and 1980s. The apparent universality of *recognition* of facial expression also led to studies on the *elicitation* of facial expression patterns of anger and fear in infants of different cultures (Camras, Oster, Campos, Miyake, & Bradshaw, 1992), as well as the development of methods of facial expression measurement based on anatomical criteria and judgments of emotion by coders (Izard & Dougherty, 1982; Oster & Rosenstein, in press). Although many criticisms have been leveled at research on universality of recognition (Fridlund, 1994; Russell, 1994, 1995), on the whole they have not proven entirely convincing (Ekman, 1995; Izard, 1995). As a result, the search for universals continues in cross-cultural studies of patterns of appraisal (Mesquita & Frijda, 1992), speculations about child-rearing functions (Trevarthen, 1988), and attributional biases (Morris & Peng, 1994).

Recently, the study of culture and emotions has broadened considerably beyond the issue of universality to the role of culture in the generation, manifestation, and regulation of emotion (D'Andrade, 1984; Kitayama & Markus, 1994; Lazarus, 1991). Because a complete review of culture and emotion is beyond the scope of this chapter, we will limit ourselves to an illustration of how emotion communication accompanies and helps to inculcate cultural values, affects pre- and perinatal emotionality, determines the types of event to which an infant or child is exposed, and creates the "emotional climate" within which a person is immersed.

What Is Culture and Does Culture Influence Infants?

The concept of culture is rarely defined. For our purposes, culture refers to a set of traditional, explicit and implicit beliefs, values, actions, and material environments that are transmitted by language, symbol, and behavior within an enduring and interacting group of people. Because of the centrality of symbols, language, and values for culture, most studies of culture and emotion deal with adults, and especially the language of adults (Wierzbicka, 1992). Infants and children with minimal language skills are generally

assumed to be beyond the pale of symbolic influence (Winn, Tronick, & Morelli, 1989). However, symbols, language, and values can have profound direct and indirect effects on the preverbal child. The direct effects result from diet, housing, and the material and physical implements of the culture that are used in child rearing. The indirect effects are largely mediated by two factors: the physical/social context within which the infant is raised, and the exposure of the child to the characteristic behavior patterns and nonverbal communication strategies of members of that culture (Gordon, 1989). So subtle yet powerful are these direct and indirect effects that the infant's acculturation can be said to begin at birth and maybe even before (Tronick & Morelli, 1991).

Illustrations of the Impact of Cultural Practices on Early Development

Parental Practices

Although the demands for provision of protection for infants and for meeting their needs must be universal, the way those needs are defined and met varies enormously. One way culture influences the infant is through the mother's selection of interventions for regulating social signaling, including the baby's crying and struggling. For this reason, swaddling methods have received a great deal of attention from anthropologists. They have discussed how, in Middle Eastern societies, swaddling facilitates sleep and transport (Whiting, 1981), soothes the child and permits the mother to work nearby in kibbutzim (Bloch, 1966), maximizes proximity between mother and child and facilitates responsiveness to the child's social signals in the Navaho nation (Chisholm, 1983, 1989), and brings about desirable habituation and autonomic regulation in response to stimuli in noisy environments (Landers, 1989). In the United States, by contrast, swaddling has been unpopular largely because it restricts freedom of movement (Lipton, Steinschneider, & Richmond, 1965) and possibly produces undesired yet distinctive effects on the formation of characteristic emotional dispositions (Mead, 1954), some of which, such as passivity, are not valued in the United States (Chisholm, 1989).

Another cultural variation in parenting practice evident even in the neonatal period is that of co-sleeping. Co-sleeping has been proposed as a socialization mechanism that fosters attachment throughout life by creating a powerful motivation to remain close to the parent (Abbott,

1992). Although sleeping in separate beds and separate rooms is the norm in the United States, data collected in eastern Kentucky exemplifies the widespread regional variation that can occur in co-sleeping (Abbott, 1992). Co-sleeping occurred across all social classes in eastern Kentucky, but was less common among the college-educated. Interview data suggested that co-sleeping did, in fact, facilitate greater interdependence in the family and fostered close emotional ties early in life. Findings such as these contradict widespread beliefs that the effects of co-sleeping are uniformly negative (see discussion in Morelli, Rogoff, Oppenheim, & Goldsmith, 1992).

Physical activity and infant positioning are other examples of parenting practices related to emotional development and show considerable variation across cultures. Compared to U.S. infants, Gusii infants are exposed to more light tossing and vigorous handling. Provision of such vigorous stimulation has been proposed to explain how Gusii infants overcome fear by 3 to 4 months of age (Keefer, Dixon, Tronick, & Brazelton, 1991).

A traumatic influence with potentially long-lasting consequences for the newborn is circumcision, a painful procedure often conducted without anesthesia or analgesia. It may well form the nucleus of disturbing and enduring memories for pain. Moreover, cultural variations exist in the circumcision procedure; what was at one time a religious ceremony conducted in an intimate family gathering has become routine medical practice involving medical personnel with the family excluded. The emotional climate provided to the infant during the circumcision ritual in the home (the bris) is vastly different from that provided on a plastic restraint board in a hospital nursery and also may well influence the infant's memories for pain. In addition, in religious ceremonies, the circumcised newborn is often given small amounts of wine in which sugar cubes are dissolved to drink. Such oral stimulation may help soothe the infant's pain reactions, in the same manner that Blass and Ciaramitaro (1994) have reported that sucrose does for other painful procedures.

The Significance of Exposure to Events

Culture determines the types of events to which the child is exposed. Emotional reactions are determined not only by transactions taking place in the present, but by the history of prior encounters with similar events in the past. It is as if an "adaptation level" of experience is built up, and depending on the departure of an event from that adaptation level, the child will show intense, moderate, or weak emotional reactions.

This principle of adaptation level is well exemplified in the literature on culture and attachment patterns. In the attachment literature, there is evidence that infants from northern Germany show a preponderance of apparent avoidant patterns of attachment (K. E. Grossmann, Grossmann, Huber, & Wartner, 1991). By contrast, in Japan, there is a preponderance of apparently ambivalent and hard-to-soothe infants (Miyake, Chen, & Campos, 1985). In the kibbutzim in Israel, still another pattern of behavior is shown: infants are extremely upset by the entry of strangers in the attachment-testing situation. What accounts for such different patterns of behavior (Sagi et al., 1985)? Why do children in three different areas of the world react to the same events in such dramatically different ways?

One interpretation is that the value system of a culture affects what events infants are exposed to and thus become emotionally responsive to. In northern Germany, for example, infants are frequently left alone, for instance, outside stores or supermarkets or in the home while the mother steps out briefly. The pattern of exposure or the adaptation level to being alone renders maternal separations in attachment testing not a very great departure from that to which the infant is accustomed. As a result, infants show little or no upset at a brief maternal separation and have little reason to give a strong response to the mother upon reunion. Hence, 49% of infants tested in the Ainsworth Strange Situation in Germany show the A pattern of not directing much attention to the reentry of the mother.

In Japan, there is a very different value system, one in which the mother desires very close proximity to her child. In Japan, baby-sitting is rare, and when it occurs, it is usually done by the grandparents. Accordingly, Japanese infants have very few experiences with separation from the mother; when the mother leaves the infant alone or with a stranger in the attachment test, the separation is extremely discrepant from the infant's past experience. As a result, the infant shows considerable upset, and it is thus no surprise that the infant is hard to console after experiencing intense distress on separation. The difficulty in consoling the child results in classifying the child as a C infant.

In the kibbutzim in Israel, security measures and the history of unexpected terrorist attacks makes for a strong form of xenophobia. Strangers are looked upon with distrust, and they are typically not allowed to approach infants. Because infants are very sensitive to the emotional communication of significant others by 12 months of age, they have become sensitized to be wary of strangers themselves. As a result, when a stranger enters the room and initiates contact or approach to the child, the infant is set to become intensely fearful. Interestingly, in urban Israel, where the xenophobia is usually much less evident, infants do not show such intense negative reactions to strangers.

The adaptation level of the kind of reaction that significant others typically give to the infants determines the intensity level of their negative responses. Much xenophobia in caregivers results in high levels of stranger distress; less xenophobia results in considerably lower levels. In sum, the value system of each culture (expectations of independence in northern Germany, desire for extreme proximity in Japan, and the need to protect the community in Israeli kibbutzim) leads to different levels of experience, against which new experiences are compared. The culture thus determines both exposure and the context for differential emotional reactions.

Other examples of how exposure and values interact to influence emotional-expressive behavior can be found in patterns of eye contact. Direct eye contact is usually encouraged in Western culture, where the eyes are "a window into the soul." However, in certain African societies, eye contact is generally discouraged. Certain tribes believe that eye contact allows another person to inflict harm on the infant; as a result, infants are often kept in dark corners of the living hut and held in a manner that minimizes the chance of eye contact. The end result for the infant is a cool, subdued demeanor (LeVine et al., 1994).

Still another instance of culture determining what an infant is exposed to stems from the work on multiple mothering with the Efe in central Africa (e.g., Tronick, Morelli, & Ivey, 1992). Because maternal mortality is extremely high among the Efe, the culture attempts to compensate for the negative consequences of maternal loss by fostering multiple caregiving. Infants are thus often passed from one person to another, and the infant becomes accustomed to being handled by more than one caregiver. As a result, the loss of the mother becomes much less traumatic for Efe infants than for infants elsewhere.

Culture and Emotional Climate

Emotional climate refers to the characteristic patterning and intensity of verbal and nonverbal emotional communication that is within earshot and eyeshot of an audience. Cultures often differ in their emotional climates. In some cultures, loudness and extremes of gesticulation are encouraged or tolerated; in others, quiet and peaceful expression is the expectation. Emotional climate may influence the emotional reaction of infants, children, and adults quite profoundly (Briggs, 1970).

Consider that vocal expression of affect is very pervasive and quite closely linked to the communication of discrete emotion (Scherer, 1986). It is now well known that the fetus can hear sounds in the womb from the seventh gestational month onward. As a result of the transmission of sounds through the amniotic fluid (De Casper & Fifer, 1980; De Casper, Lecanuet, Busnel, & Granier-Deferre, 1994; Fifer & Moon, 1995), the unborn infant can acquire considerable experience about patterns and intensities of emotional communication. Just as the newborn can identify his or her mother's speech within 3 days of birth, it is possible that the newborn can come into the world with built-in expectations of the society's typical emotional climate.

In Japan, the infant's emotional climate is one of soft vocalizations, few verbalizations, and much gentle stroking of the infant (Miyake, Campos, Kagan, & Bradshaw, 1986). This pattern of softness and low frequency and volume of speech has been attributed to the rice paper walls of the traditional Japanese household, together with the Japanese value for harmony and tranquillity in the home. To attain these cultural goals of harmony, mothers are charged with the responsibility of keeping the volume of communication low and the infant's crying to a minimum. Thus, Japanese mothers communicate with their infants much more by touch and less by vocalization than do U.S. mothers.

Emotional climate is thus a crucial means by which culture affects emotion. More generally, it is known that within cultures differing emotional climates have important effects on children. Thus, parental quarreling and fighting can result in infants and children of that family becoming maladjusted and insecure (Davies & Cummings, 1994).

The emphasis in this chapter should be clear: Emotions are relational and functional, they are embedded in social communicative relations, they are flexibly responsive to context, and they link our actions with our goals. Consistent with the preceding material on culture and emotional development and with a functionalist approach, in the remaining sections of the chapter we take a systems approach to emotional communication as *multichannel* (or multibehavioral), which includes facial expression, vocal quality, gesture, touch, eye contact, interpersonal distance, and so forth (Scheflen, 1974). With increased exposure and experience, young children's emotional-expressive behavior begins to resemble the normative emotional communicative patterns as prescribed by the culture in which they live. Social referencing, which will be reviewed in the next section, is a key interactive process for facilitating this learning of emotional meaningfulness.

In addition, a systems approach to communication is very useful for understanding the kinds of emotional-social phenomena that develop in the preschool and elementary school years and which will be discussed in later sections of the chapter. These phenomena include self-presentation strategies, empathy-mediated prosocial behavior, emotion management, and coping strategies, among others. Systems communication theorists (e.g., Watzlawick, Beavin, & Jackson, 1967) emphasize further that what may be most important about communication is its involvement in the *regulation* of relationships, and their notion of *metacommunication* describes this regulatory function: a message, conveyed by nonverbal behavior, communicates how the content of what is said should be understood. In short, communication about communication is intended to influence us, and such communications are typically emotion-laden. We turn next to a discussion of the early development of emotional communication, emphasizing social referencing, not only because it is a particularly well-investigated emotional communication process, but also because it illustrates this metacommunicative function of relationship regulation.

EARLY DEVELOPMENT OF EMOTIONAL COMMUNICATION

Before parents use language to communicate with their infants, they communicate and share experiences through emotional exchanges. For example, what does the infant teetering at the top of the staircase understand when his mother, looking very tense and wide-eyed, gasps, "Johnny, don't move!"? We would not expect young infants to understand the semantic meaning of their mother's communication, but we would expect them to pick up on some aspects of the emotional meaning of the communication. Does the infant respond to the sharp, high pitch in the voice or to the tensely configured face? Does the infant understand that this vocal and facial pattern signals fear? Does the infant

understand that fear connotes danger? Does the infant understand that his mother is reacting to his risky behavior and not some other concurrent event? Does the infant understand the intent of his mother's emotional display? In examining these questions, we will consider what competencies the child needs to have to be an effective user of another's emotional signals. The competencies of a sophisticated user of emotional communication include (a) sensitivity to the hedonic tone of the communication, (b) the ability to discriminate one emotional signal from another, (c) an appreciation of the discrete meanings of different emotional displays, (d) an appreciation of the referential nature of emotional signals, and (e) an awareness that emotional reactions are subjective. Although these competencies are necessary for a full understanding of an emotional communication, the infant may show appropriate responding to many forms of emotional communication before becoming fully competent in each component. In the sections below, we will elaborate these components that contribute to children's developing understanding of emotional communication.

Emotion Contagion

Stern (1985) suggests that emotion is the primary medium and the primary subject of communication in early infancy. How is it that emotion allows adults to communicate with young, preverbal infants? According to many researchers, infants can access the meaning of an emotional communication directly, via *emotional contagion* (e.g., Hatfield et al., 1994; Hoffman, 1984; Izard & Malatesta, 1987; Klinnert et al., 1983). Emotional contagion occurs when the facial, vocal, and gestural cues of one person generate a similar or complementary state in the perceiver. Of interest here is how emotional contagion enables the infant to become sensitive to the hedonic tone or message carried by an emotional signal. If infants are able to experience an emotion that is similar to the emotion being expressed by another, they may be able to discover the meaning of the other's signal at an early age.

Following Hoffman's (1984) original model of empathic development, Hatfield and her colleagues (1994) describe the variety of mechanisms through which emotional contagion can occur: conscious cognitive processes, unconditioned and conditioned responses, and motor mimicry and feedback. In the example above, Johnny may "catch" fear from his mother. His mother's shrill gasp may serve as an unconditioned stimulus and may cause Johnny's heartbeat to quicken and his hands to feel cold. He may experience these unconditioned responses as a negative state, perhaps as wariness or fear, and he may begin to cry. Or Johnny may mimic his mother's wide-eyed facial display or the sharp inhalation of breath and, via facial, vocal, and respiratory feedback, he may experience fear. Thus, the fear his mother displays in her face and in her voice may have a direct impact on the infant's emotional state. In this way, the meaning of the fear signal "Watch out" can be conveyed to the preverbal infant, without the infant's having to engage in any complex cognitive processes like perspective taking.

Although there has not been a great deal of experimental research on emotional contagion, the extant evidence suggests that infants do pick up on the positive or negative tone of an emotional signal. Two early studies (Sagi & Hoffman, 1976; Simner, 1971) provide evidence that certain emotional signals can elicit corresponding emotional states in infants, even in newborn infants. Specifically, Simner (1971) reported that 2-day-old infants were more likely to cry in response to the cry of another newborn than in response to a synthetic cry. The synthetic cry was a computer-simulated cry of similar intensity to the natural cry, so it was not merely the loudness or the rapid onset of the natural cry that elicited crying. Sagi and Hoffman (1976) replicated this finding with infants who were only 30 hours old. They suggested that this reflexive crying may represent an innate or rapidly learned form of empathic distress. Finally, a study by Martin and Clark (1982) replicated and extended these previous findings by demonstrating that neonates were more likely to cry in response to a tape recording of another neonate's cry than in response to a tape recording of their own cry, an older infant's cry, or a chimp's cry. Interestingly, this pattern of results suggests not only that neonates show an empathic distress response but also that they are able to discriminate fairly similar auditory stimuli. Their responses were peer- and species-specific. The findings from these three studies suggest that newborn infants appear to show rudimentary signs of emotion contagion and that even in the first hours of life infants show sensitivity to the negative tone of the human cry.

More recently, Haviland and Lelwica (1987) have reported evidence for an "induced-affect" effect in somewhat older infants. They investigated 10-week-old infant responsiveness to happy, sad, and angry facial and vocal expressions. The primary dependent measure in this study was infant facial expression, which was coded using the Maximally Discriminative Facial Movement Coding System (MAX). The MAX contains separate ratings for the

brow, eye, and mouth regions, and Haviland and Lelwica also coded "mouthing" as a potentially important behavioral response. They found that, by 10 weeks of age, infants responded differentially to their mothers' affective expressions. Infants showed more joy in response to mothers' expressions of happiness, more mouthing in response to sadness, and less interest and more instances of no mouth movement in response to anger. Haviland and Lelwica argue that these changes in infants' facial expressions show that infants were not simply matching their mothers' expressions, but rather were matching their mothers' *affective* states. When mothers frowned and sounded sad, infants did not show increased frowning; instead they showed more mouthing, which Haviland and Lelwica suggest may be an alternative indicator of the infants' experience of sadness or distress. The mothers' expressions seemed to have elicited an emotional experience in the infants. This is a remarkable finding, especially because Haviland and Lelwica report differential responding to the two negative expressions. As will be discussed below, the majority of evidence on infants' responsiveness to emotional signals shows that they respond differentially to positive versus negative emotions and not that they respond differentially to discrete emotions. Further research using paradigms like this, which are appropriate for both very young and older infants, will be important in the mapping out of infants' early sensitivity to emotional displays.

A recent study by Fernald (1993) suggests that the voice alone can also elicit positive or negative reactions in young infants. Fernald used an auditory preference procedure to assess 5-month-old infants' responsiveness to positive and negative vocal affect, in both familiar and unfamiliar languages. Infants' looking time to the stimuli is the key dependent variable in the standard preference procedure; if an infant shows a preference for one kind of stimuli over another (i.e., if the infant looks at one stimulus more than the other), we can infer that the infant discriminated the different stimuli. In this study, Fernald measured infants' facial expressions in addition to their looking time. Fernald found that while 5-month-olds did not look consistently longer to positive than to negative vocalizations, they did show differential and appropriate emotional responses to the vocalizations. Infants showed more positive attention and smiling when they heard approvals than when they heard prohibitions, even in unfamiliar languages. Assuming that 5-month-old infants' facial displays correspond reasonably well to their internal emotional experience, Fernald's stimuli appeared to elicit an emotional state in the infant that matched the tone of the vocalization. This series of studies demonstrates that even very young infants pick up on the hedonic tone of the messages.

A final piece of evidence suggesting that infants may have the capacity to experience emotional contagion very early comes from work on neonatal imitation (e.g., Meltzoff & Moore, 1983, 1989). In a number of studies, Meltzoff and his colleagues and others (e.g., Field, Woodson, Greenberg, & Cohen, 1982) have demonstrated that infants, in their first days and even first hours of life, imitate certain facial displays (e.g., tongue protrusions, pursed lips) and head movements. Particularly relevant to emotional communication are data from Field and her colleagues (Field et al., 1982, 1983). Field et al. report that newborn infants show more widened lips in response to modeled happy faces, more protruded lower lips to sad faces, and more wide-open mouths to surprise faces. Although there is some skepticism about these findings (Klinnert et al., 1983), which still require replication and further study, they do provide interesting food for thought. Hatfield, Cacioppo, and Rapson (1992) suggest that primitive emotional contagion is "the tendency to automatically mimic and synchronize facial expressions, vocalizations, postures, and movements with those of another person and, consequently, to converge emotionally" (pp. 153–154). Hatfield et al. (1994) argue that subjective emotional experience can be influenced by facial, vocal, and postural feedback.[1] For example, the facial feedback hypothesis predicts that an infant who imitates his mother's sad face will in turn experience a degree of sadness. Thus, if mimicry and feedback are one mechanism for emotional contagion and if newborn infants do readily imitate facial displays, then this may be one route to an early sensitivity to the hedonic tone of another's emotional signal.

Infant Perception of Facial and Vocal Emotional Displays

The majority of the research on infants' responsiveness to emotional expressions has involved testing whether infants can discriminate one emotional expression, typically

---

[1] The facial feedback hypothesis in particular has a long history in the study of emotion. See Hatfield et al. (1994) for an interesting discussion of the history of facial feedback hypotheses from the time of James and Darwin to their own current work and that of researchers like Ekman, Izard, and Zajonc.

a facial display, from another. These studies use either habituation or paired comparison procedures, in which infants are presented with live models, pictures, or films of two different expressions. Fixation time is the primary dependent measure. If the infant dishabituates when shown a new emotional expression or looks longer at one face than at another, then the infant has detected some difference between the two stimuli. For example, Nelson and Horowitz (1983) presented 2-month-old infants with happy and neutral faces in a holographic stereogram. Infants were first habituated to one facial expression and then were shown the other. Infants dishabituated to the novel face, suggesting that they were able to discriminate the change in facial expression or pose in a moving display. In a study by Schwartz, Izard, and Ansul (1985), 5-month-old infants saw photographs of females expressing fear, anger, and sadness. In this paired-comparison paradigm, infants first became familiarized to one expression, and then a novel expression was presented alongside the familiar expression. Longer looking to the novel expression was used as evidence of discrimination. Schwartz et al. found that 5-month-old infants could discriminate between fear and sadness. The 5-month-olds could also discriminate anger from fear and sadness, but only when anger was the familiarized stimulus.

Many studies similar to the two above have been conducted with infants and a few with newborns (e.g., Field et al., 1982). The general findings suggest that very young infants are able to detect differences in two faces with different expressive contents. By around 7 months of age infants are able to categorize facial expressions across different instances, such as different models or varying levels of intensity (Nelson, 1987). These studies, however, cannot tell us whether infants are actually deriving meaning from the emotional information contained in the facial expressions, and there is reason to believe that they are not. First, in very young infants, as studied by Field et al. (1982) and Nelson and Horowitz (1983), the visual system alone is probably not sufficiently developed to appreciate facial expressions as *expressions*. One-month-old infants tend to fixate only the outer contours of the face, and such limits in scanning might cause very young infants to miss key features of certain emotional displays (for a review, see Banks & Salapatek, 1983). Not until around 2 to 3 months of age do infants begin to scan both internal and external contours consistently and not until around 6 months is infant vision developed enough to discriminate most expression contrasts (Banks & Salapatek, 1983; Klinnert et al.,

1983; Nelson, 1987). However, despite these visual system limitations, research on newborn facial imitation (e.g., Meltzoff & Moore, 1983) and newborns' preference for face-like stimuli (Johnson, Dziurawiec, Ellis, & Morton, 1991) suggests that young infants may show particular sensitivity to moving faces. A second piece of evidence suggesting that young infants are not recognizing facial displays as emotional expressions comes from a study by R. Caron, Caron, and Meyers (1982). This study showed that infants ranging in age from 4 to 9 months could not discriminate toothy smiling faces from toothy angry faces. In a similar study, Oster and Ewey (1980; as cited in Oster, 1981) found that although 4-month-old infants could discriminate sad faces from toothy smiling faces, they could not discriminate sad faces from nontoothy smiling faces. These researchers concluded that the infants' discrimination of facial expression seemed to depend on the presence of specific salient features of the expressions (e.g., bared teeth) and not on the meaning of the expressions.

Of course, infants may be able to recognize emotional expressions, but the procedures used in facial expression research may not be sensitive enough to reveal infants' abilities. Facial expressions alone may be too impoverished as stimuli for young infants to succeed at emotion detection, especially since infant vision is immature at birth. Infant hearing, however, is relatively more mature at birth, and research on infants' ability to discriminate different vocal expressions of emotion might reveal greater sensitivity. In a recent discussion of the role of face and voice in infant discrimination of emotional expression, Caron (1988; as cited in Walker-Andrews & Lennon, 1991) suggested that acoustic information is probably more critical than optical information. Unfortunately, there have been only a few developmental studies on vocal affect to test this position.

A series of studies by Caron and his colleagues (A. Caron, Caron, & MacLean, 1988) showed that while 7-month-olds could discriminate between happy and angry dynamic vocal and facial expressions, the infants failed if the face alone was used. Caron et al. concluded that with similarly animated expressions like angry and happy, infants seem to rely more on the voice than the face to make discriminations. Walker-Andrews and Gronlick (1983) conducted a study in which only vocal affect varied. Five-month-old infants were habituated to, for example, a happy voice and a happy face and then heard a sad voice (the face did not change). Infants consistently looked longer at the familiar face when they heard the novel vocal expression. However, in another study, using similar procedures, Walker-Andrews and Lennon (1991) found that 5-month-olds failed to dishabituate to the novel vocal expression if they were shown a checkerboard pattern, but succeeded when shown a face, regardless of whether the facial affect matched the vocal affect. Walker-Andrews and Lennon argue that voice alone may not provide enough information for very young infants, just as face alone does not. In addition, Walker-Andrews and Lennon offer the same caution others have expressed concerning facial discrimination studies: changes in looking time may not result from an understanding of the meaning of different vocal affective expressions, but rather from a discrimination of certain acoustic variables, such as amplitude or pitch.

Studies of infant discrimination and categorization of facial and vocal emotional displays have provided fairly consistent and convincing evidence showing that infants are able to detect features of emotional displays that are critical for distinguishing one emotion from another. The ability to detect differences in various facial and vocal expressions is no doubt an important ability for human social-emotional development and perhaps even for linguistic development. Feinman (1982) suggests that the "presence of this capacity is one indication of infant readiness to be influenced by others' interpretations" (p. 451).

The face and the voice, although clearly critical in many emotional communications, are not the only modalities used for expressing emotion. Body posture and gesture are also important nonverbal sources of information (Rosenthal, Hall, DiMatteo, Rogers, & Archer, 1979). Intuition suggests, at least in western cultures, that a slumped posture conveys sadness, tensed fists convey anger, clapping conveys joy, and a puffed-up chest conveys pride. Unfortunately, there is little empirical research testing these intuitions. Some research examining adults' ability to decode bodily expressions of emotion suggests that body posture and gesture may better communicate the intensity of the emotion as opposed to the specific type of emotion, and that emotional cues expressed by the body may be more difficult to decode and more variable across cultures than those expressed on the face (e.g., Ekman, 1965; Rosenthal et al., 1979; Sogon & Masutani, 1989). We know of no published research that focuses exclusively on infants' ability to discriminate different emotionally relevant body postures, movements, or gestures. Studies of dyadic synchrony and dysynchrony (e.g., Cohn & Tronick, 1987; Field, 1995; Stern, 1985; Trevarthen, 1984) have revealed that infants are acutely sensitive to the coherence, rhythm, and tempo of social interactions. No doubt muscle tone and the speed and rhythmicity of body movements provide clues to the affective tone of the interaction, but we do not know how infants perceive or decode these cues.

The only gestural signals that have received a good deal of attention in the infancy literature are those signals that convey reference, namely, direction of eye gaze and pointing. These gestures do not signal a specific kind of emotion, rather they provide a clue as to what the signaler's emotional display is about. For example, if the mother is looking and pointing at a clump of dirt and saying to the infant, "Yuck! Nasty, don't eat!," the mother's gaze and point signal to the infant that her affect is directed toward the dirt. She is disgusted about the dirt (or about the prospect of the infant eating the dirt). As will be discussed in more detail below, it appears that around the end of the first year, infants begin to use the point and gaze gestures as cues to reference in emotional communications (Baldwin & Moses, 1994; Mumme & Fernald, 1995). Long before infants are able to engage in this relatively sophisticated following of referential gestures, it seems likely that, via emotional contagion, infants may pick up on more global emotional states that are reflected by the body. As very young infants are held close to their parent's body, the parent's rate of respiration, muscle tension, and posture may at least convey a positive or negative state to the infant. This area of research clearly warrants further study.

Social Signaling and Behavior Regulation

The discrimination studies described above have contributed a great deal to our knowledge of what infants *perceive*. In the next sections we will explore what infants *conceive* about emotional communication. When do infants begin to use emotional displays as social signals? In other words, when do infants begin to use others' emotional displays as cues to their internal states and intentions and as guides for action? As mentioned at the start of this section on emotional communication, the appropriate use of emotional signals depends on an appreciation of the discrete meaning of different emotional displays and on an appreciation of the referential nature of emotional signals. We will turn to these issues of affect specificity and referent specificity in the upcoming sections. *Affect specificity* is the awareness that certain social signals have discrete emotional meanings and specific behavioral consequences. If an infant has an appreciation of affect specificity, we would expect the infant to avoid an object if mother has

expressed fear of it, perhaps comfort mother if she has expressed sadness about the object, and perhaps approach the object and share it with mother if she has acted happy about it. At the same time, we would not expect the infant to behave in any consistent manner if mother simply made an odd or nonemotional face or noise (e.g., if she burped) when the object appeared. Affect specificity assumes that infants respond to what is emotional in the signal. *Referent specificity* is the ability to link a communicative signal, like a directed emotional signal, with its intended referent. Referent specificity involves the understanding that emotional signals are often about or in reference to specific events in the environment. Suppose an infant observes mother display fear as a mouse scurries across the room. The infant who has a grasp of referent specificity would avoid the area where the mouse was spotted and would not avoid a nearby sock or the pet chihuahua.

Research on infant social referencing provides the richest data set for examining infants' developing understanding of affect specificity and referent specificity. In its most general sense, social referencing is the process of looking to someone else for information about how to respond to, think about, or feel about some event in the environment (Campos & Stenberg, 1981; Feinman, 1982). One major goal of infant social referencing studies has been to provide insight into when infants begin to appreciate the meaning of emotional expressions and begin to respond appropriately to them. Social referencing research, with its roots in a functionalist perspective, has focused on developing naturalistic and ecologically valid approaches for testing infants' understanding of emotional communication (Campos, Barrett, Lamb, Goldsmith, & Stenberg, 1983; Klinnert et al., 1983). The infant social referencing paradigm was designed to elicit adjustive responses to emotional signals as opposed to discriminatory responses. Rather than present infants with isolated facial displays devoid of context, social referencing researchers presented expressions within a behaviorally meaningful context. The contexts were constructed to be ambiguous and to elicit a set of behaviors that could vary in predictable ways with different emotional expressions.

The typical social referencing study involves placing 9- to 18-month-old infants in a situation of uncertainty, such as at the edge of an apparent drop-off or in proximity of a noisy and unusual toy. In such situations infants are expected to look to their caregivers and, depending on whether the caregivers display a positive or negative emotional expression, approach or avoid the ambiguous event (Klinnert et al., 1983). Thus, social referencing studies set out to show not only that infants are able to discriminate different facial expressions of emotion, but also that they seek out emotional information and are able to use it to determine how to feel about and react to new situations. In the following sections we will first describe the three major paradigms used to investigate infant social referencing and the basic findings from this research. We will then focus, in particular, on how these studies address the issues of affect specificity and referent specificity.

Three Social Referencing Procedures

The *visual cliff procedure* has been used in only one published study, although it has produced the most compelling results of any infant social referencing study (Sorce, Emde, Campos, & Klinnert, 1985). In this procedure, the visual cliff is modified so that it appears to be a large step deep (about 30 cm). An experimenter places the infant on the shallow side of the cliff, and the mother stands at the deep side in front of the infant. A toy is placed on the glass on the deep side to increase the ambiguity of the situation and to attract the infant. The mother coaxes the child to the edge of the cliff and when the infant looks up at her, she poses a facial expression of emotion (happy, interest, fear, anger, and sad faces were tested). The dependent measures are infant referencing, crossing the drop-off, and hedonic tone. In this study, when 12-month-old infants approached the edge of the cliff, referenced the mother, and saw a fear face, none of the 17 infants crossed. Similarly, in response to angry faces, very few infants (2) crossed. In contrast, 14 of the 19 infants in the happy face condition and 11 of the 15 infants in the interest condition crossed the cliff after referencing their mothers. Finally, infants showed mixed responses to their mothers' sad facial displays; 6 of the 18 infants in the sad face condition crossed the cliff, the other 12 infants did not. Infants in the sad condition also referenced their mothers more often than infants in the happy, fear, and anger conditions. These findings support the proposition that infant behavior can be influenced differentially and appropriately by changes in maternal facial expressions.

The *stranger procedure* presents infants with a more common, everyday experience: the approach of an unfamiliar adult (Boccia & Campos, 1989; Feinman & Lewis, 1983; Feiring, Lewis, & Starr, 1984). Typically, a stranger enters the room and the mother greets and interacts with the stranger either positively, negatively, or not at all. The stranger then approaches the child in stages and either

picks the child up or makes a toy offer, depending on the study. The variables of interest are infant referencing the parent, smiles and toy offers to the stranger, and crying. The results from these studies have been fairly consistent, although not as clear-cut as the visual cliff findings. For example, Feinman and Lewis (1983) found that 10-month-old infants smiled more often at the stranger when their mothers spoke directly to the infant in a positive tone than in a neutral tone. However, infants did not respond consistently when their mothers spoke directly to the stranger. Thus, infants appeared to be less responsive to their mothers' emotional communications when infants were observers of the exchange rather than participants in it. Findings from a study by Boccia and Campos (1989), however, suggest that infants are responsive even when their mothers are simply responding to the stranger and not directing the emotional communication to the infant. The infants in their study behaved more positively toward the stranger when their mothers greeted the stranger with a smile and a cheery "hello" than when their mothers looked and sounded worried when the stranger entered.

The large majority of social referencing studies have used the *novel toy procedure* (e.g., Camras & Sachs, 1991; Gunnar & Stone, 1984; Hirshberg & Svejda, 1990; Hornik, Risenhoover, & Gunnar, 1987; Klinnert, 1984; Mumme, Fernald, & Herrera, 1996; Rosen, Adamson, & Bakeman, 1992; Walden & Baxter, 1989; Walden & Ogan, 1988; Zarbatany & Lamb, 1985). In nearly all of the studies, a noise-making toy creates the uncertain situation. The toy enters the room where the child and adult are sitting, and the adult responds to the toy with a facial and oftentimes vocal expression of emotion. Across the published toy studies, happy, fearful, disgusted, and neutral expressions have been used. The dependent measures have most often included infant referencing, approach or avoidance of the toy, approach to the adult, and infant affect. The findings from these various novel toy studies suggest that around 12 months of age infants regulate their toy-directed behaviors in accordance with others' emotional signals, when the face and voice are used together and, probably, when the voice alone is used, but probably not when the face alone is used.

When mothers have used only their facial expressions to convey an emotion toward a novel toy, infants have not regulated their behavior in the consistent and dramatic way that one might have expected, given the visual cliff findings. For example, in her original study, Klinnert (1984) had mothers of 12- and 18-month-old infants pose happy, fearful, and neutral expressions over the course of three trials. Infants tended to approach the toy more often and more quickly when their mothers displayed a happy face than when their mothers displayed a fear face and at an intermediate level when their mothers displayed a neutral face. However, these differences were not significant. Similarly, two subsequent studies also failed to find the predicted patterns in response to the facial displays of a friendly experimenter (Zarbatany & Lamb, 1985) and of the infant's mother (Mumme et al., 1996).

In contrast to these weak findings, novel toy studies in which mothers displayed both facial and vocal emotion have more consistently found the predicted signaling effects. Three studies using both facial and vocal signals found that 12-month-old infants showed less toy proximity in response to negative facial and vocal signals than in response to positive facial and vocal signals (Hirshberg & Svejda, 1990; Hornik et al., 1987; Rosen et al., 1992). Infants around 10 to 13 months of age have also shown appropriate responding on other measures of behavior toward the stimulus toy, such as reaching and touching (Walden & Ogan, 1988). Interestingly, in two studies in which mothers delivered only vocal signals (i.e., mothers did not display matching facial expressions), infants also responded consistent with predictions (Mumme et al., 1996; Svejda, 1981). For example, Mumme et al. (1996) found that 12-month-old infants responded to fearful vocal signals with decreased approach to the toy and increased negative affect. In this same study, Mumme et al. found that infants did not respond as predicted when mothers used only facial expressions. Thus, findings from novel toy studies are mixed and appear to depend greatly on which modalities are used in the emotional communication.

We have focused thus far only on how others' emotional signals affect infants' behavior toward the ambiguous event itself. Of course, there is another meaningful way infants can regulate their behavior, especially in the novel toy paradigm. It would be equally appropriate for infants to observe their mothers' negative reaction and then move toward their mothers for protection. Mothers' emotional displays clearly may serve to regulate attachment behavior as often as they serve to influence infants' appraisals of novel toys (Gunnar & Stone, 1984, p. 1236). The majority of novel toy studies have assessed infants' tendency to approach mothers, but the results are somewhat mixed. Klinnert (1984) found significant increases in proximity to mother when she was displaying a fearful face, but only if fear was presented in the third trial. In some studies, infants have shown significantly more approach to mothers in

the fear condition (e.g., Hirshberg & Svejda, 1990), while in others they did not (e.g., Hornik et al., 1987; Mumme et al., 1996; Walden & Ogan, 1988). In sum, the current findings suggest that emotional signals, at least when they include vocally expressed emotion, appear to have a moderately consistent influence on behavior directed toward the novel toy and a somewhat mixed influence on behavior directed toward the caregiver.

Affect Specificity: Do Infants Understand the Affective Content of Emotional Communication?

Although infants may find information that is instrumental as well as emotional in nature when they look to their caregivers or other significant people (Feinman, 1982; Rogoff, Mistry, Goncu, & Mosier, 1993; Walden, 1991), in this chapter we focus on infants' use of emotional information. To use emotional information provided by others, infants must at the very least be able to recognize facial and/or vocal emotion. As previously described, paired comparison and habituation studies have shown that infants can discriminate between different facial and vocal emotional signals. By using situations specifically designed to elicit adjustive responses to emotional signals, social referencing research has begun to tell us more about what meaning infants actually find in others' emotional displays.

The findings from social referencing research are often taken as evidence that the infant has correctly read or understood the meaning of the parent's emotional signal. However, before we accept this rich interpretation of infant behavior, we must consider carefully whether the infant has indeed regulated his or her behavior in accordance with the parent's *emotional* response. We must make sure that the infant was not responding to some other feature of the situation. It is possible that the observed behavioral regulatory effects in social referencing studies are not mediated by *affect specificity,* the traditional interpretation, but rather by some other means. This concern is analogous to the concern that prompted A. Caron et al.'s (1988) study testing whether infants could discriminate toothy smiling faces from toothy angry faces. Just as they wanted to know whether infants were discriminating emotional expressions based on the meaning of the emotional expression rather than on a specific feature of the expression (e.g., bared teeth), social referencing researchers need to determine whether the emotional meaning of the parent's signals is guiding infant behavior rather than some other feature of the signals or the situation.

The affective stimuli used in social referencing studies usually consist of positive (happy, interested) or negative (fearful, angry, disgusted) expressions. Surprisingly, no existing study has used "nonaffective" stimuli as a control. While happy expressions are familiar to infants, the exaggerated negative expressions typically used in social referencing studies are a novel experience for nearly all infants. If an infant feels uncertain about a strange situation, looks up to the caregiver for information or security, and observes, for example, a bizarre, sustained fear face that most infants have probably never seen before, the infant may become even more uncertain. According to this *uncertainty hypothesis,* it may be increasing uncertainty, especially about the *caregiver's behavior,* that causes the infant to behave differently. Inhibition of crossing behavior, as found in the fear face condition of the visual cliff study, may have been in reaction to the mother's odd facial expression or to her unresponsiveness as a social partner rather than to a "warning" signaled by the expression of fear (i.e., affect specificity). In some of our own research (Mumme, 1993), there is anecdotal evidence to suggest that some infants did take the fear face as a bizarre or funny face. For example, when one infant first referenced her mother, she smiled at the fear face, as though she thought it was part of a game. When her mother's face remained frozen and very ungamelike, however, the child sobered up. In more than this one instance, we observed infants look directly at their mothers' fearful expression and grin.

Apparently, the communication of fear may be a novel experience for mothers as well as their infants. Rosen et al. (1992) reported that in the unconstrained trials of their study, during which mothers had no strict guidelines for how to make the emotional expressions, very few of the fear messages (10.5%) were clearly fearful; nearly all the happy messages were clearly happy (91.4%). Similarly, Hornik et al. (1987) decided to have mothers deliver disgusted expressions rather than fearful expressions, because they had difficulty training mothers to express fear. Thus, the novelty of the expression in addition to its emotional content might influence the social referencing situation in a number of ways. No existing study of infant social referencing has adequately addressed the confound between negative facial expressions and novelty.

Social referencing research has also not yet tested whether specific features of the parent's emotional signal elicit the changes in infant behavior. For example, in at least two studies in which vocal emotional signals have been used (Hirshberg & Svejda, 1990; Mumme et al., 1996),

mothers in the fear condition have been instructed to begin the vocalization by drawing a breath of air sharply and to use a sharp tone with clipped phrases and rising pitch (Hirshberg & Svejda, 1990, p. 1177). Although a gasp is a natural component of a fear response, it is quite possible that this sharp initial gasp startled infants in these studies and directly induced a state of wariness in the infant. The "adjustive" responses observed in these studies—behavioral inhibition and increases in negative affect—would have been observed, whether or not the infants really understood the meaning of their mothers' emotional signals (i.e., that the vocalization signified fear or a warning of danger).

Even if the confound with novelty is eliminated and even if infants are responding to some uniquely emotional features of the signals, further research is needed to show that infants are responding appropriately to a specific emotion. Except for the visual cliff study, most studies have compared infants' responses to only one type of positive signal and one type of negative signal. Although we know that children eventually come to understand that sad expressions differ in meaning from angry expressions, which differ from fearful and disgusted expressions, we know very little about how and when this understanding comes about. This understanding is clearly critical in later social development, as understanding the meaning of others' negative signals undoubtedly plays an important role in the social construction of young children's values and opinions.

Referent Specificity: Do Infants Understand the Referential Nature of Emotional Communication?

In its most general form, social referencing involves a two-person conversation about a third event (Klinnert et al., 1983). Thus, for an infant to engage in social referencing proper, the infant must at the very least appreciate that the conversation is about some event external to the dyad. Until recently (e.g., Baldwin & Moses, 1994; Mumme & Fernald, 1995; Repacholi, 1996), only a few studies had attempted to test directly infants' understanding of the referential nature of emotional communication (e.g., Hornik et al., 1987; Walden & Ogan, 1988). Hornik et al. (1987) compared infants' responses to stimulus toys toward which mothers had targeted affective information and infants' responses to free-play toys that were scattered about the room. They found that infants were less likely to play with the stimulus toy when their mothers acted disgusted about the toy than when they acted positive about it. More important, they also found that infants' play with the free-play toys did not vary with emotion condition. The researchers interpreted this as evidence that the 12-month-old infants in their study linked the emotional signal with its referent.

Although their research design is a good first test for referent-specific responding, there are other plausible explanations for infants' behavior that do not require an understanding of reference and that were not ruled out by this procedure. First, because the free-play toys were present in the room throughout the study, they were probably not as salient as the noisy stimulus toy that appeared later. Thus, the infant's attention may have been drawn to the ambiguous toy not because it was the toy that mother was looking at, but because it was novel (Baldwin & Moses, 1996; Mumme & Fernald, 1995). Second, because the free-play toys were age appropriate and probably more familiar, or at least nonthreatening, and because they were available the entire time and were played with more overall, they may have come to function as comfort objects. Accordingly, it is not obvious why an infant in the negative emotion condition would stop playing with or, perhaps more accurately, stop holding onto a familiar toy that the infant has been enjoying up to that point. In fact, one might have predicted that infants would play more with the free-play toys in the negative condition as a distraction from the novel toy or from their mothers' odd behavior. Pilot testing in our own research (Mumme, 1993) indicated that for some children free-play toys do become comfort objects and a means of coping with negative arousal.

Using a slightly different novel toy paradigm, Walden and Ogan (1988) attempted to test for referent specificity by giving the child a chance to choose between stimulus toys at the end of the session, when the mother was no longer directing any affect toward the toys. During the stimulus presentation period, mothers directed joyful signals toward one toy in one trial and fearful signals toward a different toy in another trial, and infants were allowed to explore the toys. During the free-choice period, infants were allowed to play with whichever toy they wanted. Walden and Ogan found that older children freely chose to play with the negatively appraised toy more often, as they had in the earlier stimulus trials. Younger children chose to play with the positively appraised toy more often, as they had in the earlier stimulus trials. Walden and Ogan interpreted these findings as evidence that the younger children had associated the emotional signal with the specific toy. However, this does not explain the behavior of the older children. A more parsimonious explanation of the behavior of both age groups is that children were likely to play more in free play with the toy that they had played with more

during the stimulus presentation period. The children's familiarity or prior (harmless) contact with the toy seems as plausible an explanation for their behavior as referent specificity. In addition, because the toys were presented sequentially rather than simultaneously, the infant did not necessarily have to understand that mother was attending to the novel toy. The novel toy was the only salient object in the room during the delivery of the emotional signal and, for this reason, may have become associated with it.

To support the claim that infants respond to emotional signals with referent specificity, a study must demonstrate that infants uniquely associate the emotional signal with the object toward which the signal is directed. In addition, and of equal importance, the study must demonstrate that infants do not generalize their response to other similar objects in the environment. Thus, a study of referent specificity must also include a test for generalization. This means that the experimental situation has to include at least two equally salient, simultaneously occurring, ambiguous events, either of which could be a potential target of parental affect. This two-object presentation strategy was used in three recent studies (Baldwin & Moses, 1994; Mumme & Fernald, 1995; Repacholi & Gopnik, 1997).

Using a modified novel toy procedure, Baldwin and Moses (1994) tested whether 12- and 18-month-old infants appreciate the importance of the experimenter's attentional focus for interpreting her emotional displays. Initial findings from their laboratory suggest that infants at both ages were influenced not only by the quality of the experimenter's emotional display but also by the attentional cues. Infants reacted more positively to the target toy when the experimenter displayed pleasure than when she displayed disgust, and they did so even when initially the experimenter's focus of attention was on one toy and the infant's was on the other. However, infants also showed some inappropriate generalization to the distractor toy. Baldwin and Moses point out two limitations of procedure that may have made the task more difficult for infants and, thus, generalization more likely. First, the emotional and attentional cues may not have been strong enough, which may have reduced infants' ability to read the signals accurately. Second, the experimenter herself gave the infant the two toys at the start of the play period; this may have confused the infant about the specificity or seriousness of her emotional displays.

In another recent study, Mumme and Fernald (1995) developed a completely new procedure, which used televised stimuli, to investigate whether 12-month-old infants appreciate that a directed emotional signal refers to a specific object. In this study, infants watched video displays of an actress directing neutral, happy, or fearful facial and vocal signals at one or two novel objects. After watching the video presentation, infants were given a chance to play with the two objects. Mumme and Fernald found that infants tended to prefer the target object over the distractor in response to both neutral and happy signals. However, when the speaker reacted fearfully toward the target object, infants avoided the target, but they did not avoid the distractor. These results suggest that 1-year-old infants appear to appreciate that a directed emotional signal specifies a particular referent.

The recent studies by Baldwin and Moses (1994) and Mumme and Fernald (1995) suggest that 12-month-old infants are able to pick up on some aspect of the directionality of another's emotional signal and to regulate their responses appropriately with respect to the object that was singled out. That 12-month-old infants show an understanding of the referential nature of emotional signals is perhaps not surprising, given that infants at this age are able to follow referential gestures, such as the point (e.g., Butterworth & Grover, 1988; Corkum & Moore, 1995). Such findings have also been taken as evidence that "emotional expression affects infant behavior via an interpretive process specific to the ambiguous event rather than through a general modification of the infant's mood" (Camras & Sachs, 1991, pp. 27–28).

However, a demonstration of referent-specific responding does not rule out the possibility that infants' moods were also modified. As Klinnert, Campos, and others (e.g., Haviland & Lelwica, 1987; Stern, 1985; Termine & Izard, 1988) have argued, feeling states are also crucial to emotion and behavior regulation. They are elicited by emotional expressions of others and "are indispensable mediators of behavior regulation" (Klinnert et al., 1983, p. 80). In the study described above, Mumme and Fernald (1995) found that, in addition to their avoidance of the target object, infants in the fear condition showed an increase in their expressions of negative affect. Other studies have similarly reported changes in infant affect in response to their mothers' emotional signals (e.g., Hornik et al., 1987; Mumme et al., 1996). Changes in infant affect do not undermine referential understanding, but they do suggest that infant mood is being modified. They also show that emotional signals are not limited to influencing the infant in a purely cognitive manner. The referent-specific appraisal process of social referencing serves as only one occasion for the operation of the more fundamental processes of emotional communication (Campos et al., 1983). Clearly, in infancy, as well as

in adulthood, emotional messages can have an effect on one's emotional state and also be used as information about a specific object or person.

Infants' Awareness of the Subjectivity of Emotional Communication

A sophisticated user of emotional communication understands that others' emotional appraisals of particular events and situations are subjective in nature. For example, not everyone appraises the approach of an energetic dog in the same way. For some, the thought of the dog jumping up on them may elicit fear, whereas for others it may elicit delight. Similarly, not everyone feels the same way about liver and onions: some people love it, others are disgusted by even the smell of it. Although emotional signals need not (and may even rarely) represent the signaler's true internal *feeling* state, at some point, we do come to appreciate that emotional signals reflect others' internal states, which includes their opinions, appraisals, goals, and motivations as well as their feelings. When do infants begin to interpret emotional communications in this way?

In their observational studies of the development of empathy and sympathy, Zahn-Waxler and her colleagues have found that between 1 and 2 years of age children develop empathic concern for others in distress. In the latter part of the second year, children begin to translate this concern into prosocial actions (e.g., Zahn-Waxler & Radke-Yarrow, 1990; Zahn-Waxler, Radke-Yarrow, & King, 1979). That the children in these studies recognized that someone was in distress and that they attempted to alleviate the distress suggest that the children had some awareness of the correspondence between the person's emotional display and her emotional state of distress. In a sense, this is the flip side of the referent-specificity issue described above. In the case of empathy, the observer needs to realize that the other person's emotional signal refers to an internal state rather than to an external event. The empathic child does not comfort the broken toy that another child is crying about; instead, the empathic child comforts his or her sad friend.

In a recent dissertation, Repacholi (1996; Repacholi & Gopnik, 1997) found that at about the same age (18–19 months) infants are beginning to appreciate that disgust is also subjective. In one condition, the experimenter acted delighted with the taste of broccoli but disgusted with the taste of crackers. In the other condition, she showed the reverse preferences. When asked to share with the experimenter, the infants, who clearly had a personal preference for the crackers, responded appropriately: those infants who saw that the experimenter preferred broccoli were more likely to give her the broccoli; those who saw that she preferred crackers were more likely to give her the crackers. Just four months earlier, infants did not succeed at this task: the 14-month-old infants did not seem to understand that the experimenter's disgust with one food meant that she would prefer to eat the other.

Studies such as these suggest that toward the end of their second year, children are beginning to become aware of the fact that others' emotional reactions may differ from one's own. In this section on early emotional understanding, we have shown that even very young infants are sensitive to the quality and discriminable features of emotional signals, that infants gradually recognize that emotional displays convey specific affective information, and that these displays may refer to external events as well as to internal states. From infancy to toddlerhood there seems to be a movement away from simply reacting to others' emotional displays and toward being able to use others' emotional signals as guides for action and as cues to others' internal states, preferences, and opinions (Dunn, 1988; Harris, 1989). Eventually, children are able to anticipate and bring about emotions in others. As will be discussed in more detail in the next sections, this understanding emerges gradually during childhood and depends on other cognitive and social developments, including the development of language and a sense of self.

EMOTIONAL COMMUNICATION IN CHILDHOOD

As children enter early and middle childhood, their ever-growing cognitive capabilities, language skills, and physical coordination and the expanding social realm open up many diverse opportunities for emotional communication with others. We can examine emotional communication during childhood from the standpoint of what competencies the child needs to have to undertake effective emotional communication. Briefly, these competencies include (a) awareness of one's own emotional state; (b) awareness of others' emotional states; (c) skillfulness with one's subculture's emotion concepts and lexicon, including pragmatic use of one's subculture's emotional scripts, in which emotions are integrated with other social roles (e.g., gender roles are laden with emotion-relevant communications); (d) sympathetic responsiveness to others' emotional distress;

and (e) a practical knowledge of how to use emotional expressiveness strategically in social situations (e.g., dissembling one's emotional experience to avoid getting into trouble). In the sections below, we will elaborate on each of these components that contribute to the efficacy of emotional communication.

Awareness of Emotional Experience

For conscious awareness of one's emotional response to occur, a self-reflective capacity must have developed: children must be able to apprehend that it is they who are feeling something. Very young infants (perhaps under 6 months) would *have* emotional states but may not experience a conscious *awareness* of the emotional state (i.e., that *they* are the ones experiencing emotion). Lewis and Brooks (1978) stipulate that the infant must develop first a subjective self (self as agent) and then a self as object to have the capacity to know that one is experiencing an emotion. We can begin to infer that preverbal infants have some degree of *pragmatic* awareness of their emotional experience when they show reliable intentional behaviors to sustain or invite events (many of which are social transactions) that produce pleasurable emotional states. The phenomenon of social referencing discussed earlier also provides us with observational data that suggest that infants utilize their feeling states. More specifically, infants use their feeling states functionally as cues for adaptive action, including communicative action, such as instrumental behavior to get attention or help from caregivers.

By the time children are 2 to 3 years of age, awareness of emotional state is usually empirically examined from the standpoint of how children use emotion labels or descriptive phrases to refer to their subjective feelings. A number of studies have shown that young children spontaneously talk about their own feeling states as well as about others' emotions (e.g., Bretherton, Fritz, Zahn-Waxler, & Ridgeway, 1986; Brown & Dunn, 1991; Dunn, Bretherton, & Munn, 1987; Wellman, Harris, Banerjee, & Sinclair, 1995). The conversations between these young children and their family members also imply that they have expectancies for how they *will* feel as well as memories of how they *did* feel. In short, young children's conceptualizations about their own subjective emotional experience encompass the past, present, and future.

Children embed their awareness of their emotional state within contexts, that is, the circumstances in which their feelings arise. Harris (1994) makes an important distinction in children's understanding of *intentional targets* of emotions versus *causes* of emotions. He contends that children primarily anchor their emotions in appraisal of the object, person, or event at which the emotion is directed—for example, mad *at you,* scared *of spiders,* happy *about going to the amusement park*—as opposed to the causal or precipitating event, for example, a squabble between siblings that leads to anger, finding a big spider in one's bed, and being told that the family is going to Fun World. Wellman et al. (1995) have confirmed this finding for 2-, 3-, and 4-year-old children; however, they also found that this sort of construal did not hold for how physical pain was viewed by children. Children understood pain in terms of the eliciting or causal event rather than pain being directed at an intentional target (e.g., one would feel pain upon being pricked by a pin, but one would typically not feel pain *about* pins). The significance of this idea of intentional targets of emotions as a contextual anchor for children's understanding of their subjective emotional experience lies in how functionalist theories of emotion focus on the adaptive transactional encounter between person and environment. Functionalist views emphasize the goal-oriented nature of emotion, which is borne out by children's construal of emotions as directed at something. As will be elaborated later in this chapter, children also tend to view their experience of negative emotions as tacitly tied to how to cope with aversive emotions and distressing circumstances.

To sum up, we render our emotional experience meaningful in terms of how we *became* aware of our feelings, often based on our action and the emotion-eliciting context, and it is this meaningful construction that allows for emotional communication to others. The fact that the sequence is "meaningful" is based on children's learning their subculture's folk theories regarding what emotions are and what to do when one feels them (i.e., the embedded transactional nature of emotions; see Lutz, 1983; Saarni, 1987a). For example, consider a 4-year-old who comes home after nursery school and announces to his father, "Today I had six mads." A likely response from Dad would be, "You had what?" The boy's statement is not culturally meaningful, because Western models of emotion assume that emotions are mass nouns and not count nouns (D'Andrade, 1987). Dad might then correct his son by saying, "Oh, you mean you felt mad six times today." Dad might go on to query his son as to what he was mad about or whom he was mad at. These everyday sorts of emotion-related communicative exchanges further convey to young children that their feelings are part of a whole scenario of events, behaviors, and other people. In short, emotional experience is contextualized. Deconstructing this contextualization might be analytically interesting, but it would no longer be descriptive of how people make sense of their subjective emotional experience for the sake of communicating it meaningfully to others.

Wishes and Beliefs in Understanding Emotions

Research by Wellman and associates (Wellman & Wooley, 1990; Wellman et al., 1995) found that children as young as 2 to 3 years old could understand that emotion was connected with what one wanted or did not want. Liking, not liking, wanting, and not wanting are pivotal goal-related factors in young children's appraisals that they are readily able to communicate to others (see also Stein & Trabasso, 1989). At slightly older ages (4 to 5 years old), children begin more reliably to show in their understanding of emotional experience that beliefs and expectations are also important in predicting what one will feel. The considerable literature on the development of mind is rich with examples of preschoolers competently predicting that someone will be surprised, upset, saddened, angered, and so forth if an expectation of how an event "should" turn out does not take place (e.g., Harris, Johnson, Hutton, Andrews, & Cooke, 1991; Wellman & Banerjee, 1991; see also Wellman & Gelman, Ch. 12, Volume 2). By middle childhood, children readily comprehend that it is their mental state (appraisal) that is central to what they feel about a given target and that others with different views may experience different feelings about the same target (e.g., Harris, 1989).

Awareness of Emotional Intensity and Duration of Emotion

Few studies have directly examined children's awareness of emotional intensity or their evaluation of how long emotions last. However, Harris and his colleagues (Harris, Guz, Lipian, & Man-Shu, 1985) have examined the dissipation of emotion in children 6 to 11 years of age. Using stories featuring both positive and negative emotion-eliciting situations, all of the children believed that immediately after the incident, emotion would be very intense and then gradually would diminish in intensity. They made the same attribution about their own emotional experience. The children also believed that if one did not think about the emotion-eliciting situation (especially a negative one), one would more readily feel *less* emotional. Harris et al. interpreted children's beliefs about the waning of emotional intensity over time as associated with decreased thinking about the precipitating event and as indicative of children's capacity to reflect upon their own subjective experience. This capacity to be aware of oneself is also relevant to the development of self-conscious emotions, namely, pride, shame, guilt, hubris, envy, and embarrassment, and we turn next to a discussion of these feelings and their function in children's experience.

Self-Conscious Emotions

Lewis's work (1992a, 1992b, 1993, 1995) on the development of pride, hubris, shame, embarrassment, and guilt constitutes a cognitive appraisal view of how such emotions come about (see also Mascolo & Fischer, 1995). These emotions require that an objective self has developed; that is, children can refer to themselves and have conscious awareness of themselves as distinct from others (see also Duval & Wicklund, 1972; James, 1890). The cognitive appraisals involved include (a) recognition that there are standards to be met, (b) evaluation of the self's performance relative to these standards, and (c) attribution of responsibility to the self upon success or failure in meeting the standard. At around the time children acquire objective self-awareness (15–24 months, as measured by self-referential behavior; e.g., Lewis & Brooks-Gunn, 1979), they also become aware of parental standards for behavior, of the rules that they are expected to follow, and of desirable goals for comportment. Children learn about these standards through their family's disciplinary practices, and over the next few years their increasing cognitive sophistication also allows them to gauge the degree to which they have met the standards. Obviously, the sorts of standards young children learn are rather simple and concrete, for example, "You should say please if you want something" and "How terrible of you to bite your little sister!" As children mature, they acquire more subtle beliefs about the standards and rules that they believe they should follow and the goals that they think are worthy of striving for. Meeting these standards presumably yields positive emotional experience, both from the experience of mastery and in receiving social approval (e.g., Harter, 1978; Hunt, 1965; Reissland, 1994; Stipek, 1995).

Children also develop an appraisal of self-agency or responsibility: Have they failed or succeeded at reaching the goal, or at living up to the standard, or performing according to the rule? Although Lewis does not directly address issues of controllability here, Weiner's (e.g., 1985) work certainly informs us of how perception of controllability is directly implied in whether people feel responsible for

events or not. Dweck and Leggett (1988) have also contended that if individuals view themselves or their world as modifiable and thus controllable, they will have a different appraisal of such a context (and themselves in it), leading to different emotional sequelae, than those who view themselves and their environments as fixed and static.

Young children may believe they do "cause" things to happen, that is, that they are in control of events when in fact they are not, due to their cognitive egocentrism that blurs desire and reality. On a simple level, a 2-year-old may believe and act as though, "if I want a cookie, then I should have a cookie." But if that same young child believes that, "if I want Mommy to love me, then I have to be a good girl for her," she may then egocentrically conclude she must have been a "bad girl" when her mother simply expresses negative feelings that are unrelated to her child's behavior. Research by Zahn-Waxler and her associates (Zahn-Waxler, Cole, & Barrett, 1991; Zahn-Waxler & Kochanska, 1990; Zahn-Waxler, Radke-Yarrow, & King, 1979) suggests that young children (especially girls) growing up with depressed mothers may be particularly at risk for developing excessive "accountability" for their mothers' feelings and mood state. Such children were very careful in their interaction with others, as though others were quite fragile, and their behavior included higher levels of appeasement, apologizing, and suppression of negative emotion than comparable children of nondepressed mothers. Thus, these 2- to 3-year-old children appeared to believe unrealistically that they had control over events and over their mothers' emotional responses and/or were responsible for them.

The last cognitive appraisal that has to develop before self-conscious emotions are experienced is a focus on oneself from an evaluative standpoint, such that either the whole self or a particular aspect of the self is considered the focus of the success or failure at living up to the standard or rule or at reaching a goal. Lewis (1992a) contends that the more the whole self is globally assumed to be responsible for success or failure, the more either hubris (arrogance) or shame will be felt, respectively. When specific aspects of the self are seen as leading to success or failure, then pride or guilt will be felt, respectively. The emotional responses of pride and guilt are specific self-attributions, as in "My effort paid off" (pride) or "It was my mistake and I'll deal with this fiasco" (guilt). The prideful feelings of accomplishment and pleasure allow the individual to undertake still further challenges; the guilt felt upon one's failure at a particular event or in a particular situation allows for interpersonal repair and future improvement.

There is also a critical interpersonal context that must be taken into account in distinguishing shame and guilt, namely, whether we are observed or alone. We do not need social *exposure* to feel guilt (although it might help), but it is a significant feature in our feeling ashamed.

Differences between shame and guilt have also been argued as due to differences in felt controllability of oneself or one's action. To illustrate, if one thought one's action could be controlled (e.g., by making greater effort, by being more considerate of another's point of view), then one would feel guilty when one's action led to failure or harm to another. Shame would be felt if the breach in propriety were experienced as not under one's control (e.g., walking out of a public restroom with one's dress unknowingly hitched up in the back). Yet, we may still experience shame after a controllable breach in standards if the global self (as opposed to an action) is indicted. A common example is the shame children or youth may feel about masturbation, even when it is not socially exposed and is controllable. Such children experiencing shame have typically condemned themselves as "bad," "wicked," "unclean," and so forth. Ferguson and Stegge (1995) reviewed the attribution literature on the development of guilt and shame, and they argue that not until middle childhood do children more reliably use a causal analysis of events in reporting their emotions.

Research undertaken with children that has investigated their self-conscious emotions is steadily increasing. Tangney and Fischer's (1995) volume on self-conscious emotions contains a number of chapters that address developmental issues. Noteworthy research also includes Stipek, Recchia, and McClintic's (1992) investigation of preschoolers' self-evaluations and subsequent emotions following task success or failure; Lewis, Alessandri, and Sullivan's (1992) work, also with preschoolers, on tasks that differed in difficulty of accomplishment; Lewis, Stanger, and Sullivan's (1989) work on young children's self-conscious emotions; Ferguson, Stegge, and Damhuis's (1991) investigation of children's understanding of guilt and shame; and Griffin's (1995) study on audience judgments of the self as related to children's understanding of shame. Recently, Reimer (1996) has sought to integrate research on young children's self-conscious emotions with clinical work on adolescents and adults to examine the development of shame in later childhood and adolescence. The development and functioning of self-conscious emotions clearly need more attention at all age levels. It would appear that the development of self-conscious emotions is

especially relevant to clinical practice, whether it be the treatment of depression that occurs with a greater frequency among female adolescents or the development of effective interventions to facilitate a child's coping with the emotional aftermath of sexual abuse (see Tangney, Burggraf, & Wagner, 1995, for a review of shame, guilt, and psychopathology).

Children's Views of Emotion in Themselves versus in Others

There have been a few studies that have compared how children make sense of emotions in themselves versus in others. These suggest that there may be some degree of a positivity bias in children's assumptions of how they think they personally would feel (e.g., Harter, 1990). The expectation that one's own feelings would be more positive in tone than what others experience has parallels that appear in the literature on self-esteem (e.g., Harter, 1990; Taylor & Brown, 1988). As an illustration, Glasberg and Aboud (1982) found that 5-year-olds were much less likely than 7-year-olds to describe themselves as sad. Thus, there may be a developmental transition here that speaks to how children can both conceptualize their own emotional experience as well as anticipate their ability to cope with distressing feelings (i.e., young children may not want to think about themselves in emotionally aversive situations, as they fear they might begin to feel that way and subsequently anticipate feeling overwhelmed; see also Harter & Buddin, 1987). This positivity bias also has parallels with research on adults' self-esteem: we bias our appraisals of ourselves in that we attribute higher self-esteem and control to ourselves than our behavior in a given situation probably deserves (reviewed in Sigmon & Snyder, 1993). Children may attribute more positive feelings to themselves in how they believe they would feel in a given situation, when, if they were actually in the emotion-evoking situation, their experience might not be as positive as they had anticipated. The big qualification to these studies, two of which are described below, is that they use interview strategies, asking children to verbalize their anticipation of how they would feel if in the same situation as a story protagonist, or to describe how they believe they emotionally responded in the past in a situation similar to that of a story protagonist. In other words, these studies may be eliciting children's knowledge of our culture's folk theory of emotion rather than their own spontaneously occurring emotional experience. The assumption here, of course, is that one is socialized according to the general tenets of one's cultural folk theory of emotion and that, as a consequence, one's spontaneous emotional behavior will presumably have some congruence with the cultural consensus of the predicted emotional experience for a given situation. In fact, children as young as 4 years of age have been found to understand many connections between situational causes and emotions in a fashion similar to adults (e.g., Barden, Zelko, Duncan, & Masters, 1980), but obviously there are many subtleties that still elude them at this young age.

One study that compared children's expectations for how they would feel in contrast to what other children would feel was undertaken by Karniol and Koren (1987). They presented to 6-year-olds a series of brief scenarios and asked the children what they would feel if this happened to them and how the boy or girl in the scenario would feel. They were also asked to justify their responses. Karniol and Koren's data suggest (at least in this age group) that children make different inferences about their own anticipated emotional experience than they do about others'. Specifically, the feelings children predicted for others were more negative than those predicted for themselves. They also spontaneously gave more coping suggestions for how to transform the negative situations into more positive contexts when they were asked to infer how they would personally feel. Last, when evaluating their own emotional response as opposed to others', the children were more focused on the consequences to themselves of the story situation. What is interesting here theoretically is that children do not appear to be simply "reading off" some sort of prototypical script for how one is likely to feel in a situation. If they did, then there would be little difference between what children thought they themselves would feel versus what others would feel. Karniol and Koren argue that children use unique information available about the self as a way to flesh out their inferences for how they would feel in a situation. For predicting hypothetical reactions, they probably do use more common social stereotypic scripts, but for themselves, some element of anticipated coping with the emotion-eliciting event is built into their inferred reaction.

The second study was undertaken with school-age children (Saarni, 1987, 1989). Adults' and school-age children's expectations were compared relative to what parental reactions would be to children's emotional-expressive behavior in situations that varied according to whether expressing one's genuine emotion would contribute to hurting someone's feelings, or whether the genuine emotional display would make the child more vulnerable and distressed. The children were interviewed about story protagonists in several such situations and at the end of each story were asked what they personally would do in the situation. Even though the children often described the story protagonists as concealing or somehow dissembling their genuine feelings to avoid making themselves even more vulnerable (e.g., "If she shows that she's scared of shots, then when she gets it, it'll hurt more"), for themselves they anticipated that they would indeed express their genuine feelings, either because they anticipated parental support for doing so or because they felt their feelings would be quite intense and therefore could not be dissembled. On the other hand, if they did believe that expressing their real feelings would hurt the feelings of someone else, they anticipated that both their own as well as the story protagonists' emotional-expressive behavior would be monitored to avoid that predicament (e.g., "Well, even if you don't like what your grandpa got you for your birthday, you should try to smile and say thank you").

Saarni's and Karniol and Koren's data may be similar, in that the children appear to scan the situations for how they would cope if they were in that situation; then they respond with anticipated emotional reactions that already have embedded in them their expectations as to how they think they will be able to cope with the demands of the situation. Thus, if children's real feelings give them a sense of fragility or vulnerability, but their parents are nearby to comfort and support them, then expressing genuine feelings is acceptable, and effective coping lies in being with those who provide an "emotional safety net." Interestingly, other data collected with different methods and in another region of the country (the Midwest) found a gender difference in children's expectations about whether they would reveal their negative feelings to their parents. Fuchs and Thelen (1988) found that boys were less likely than girls to communicate sadness (a vulnerability-inducing emotion) to their parents, but if they were to do so, they would be more likely to reveal their sadness to their mothers. Such boys apparently would minimize or otherwise modify the expression of their vulnerable emotions, such as sadness, with their fathers. Adopting an emotional front or dissembling the expression of one's feelings then becomes the more adaptive coping response for such school-age boys if they do not anticipate a supportive interpersonal context for the display of genuine emotions.

Awareness of Multiple Emotions

Awareness of experiencing multiple emotions or conflicting emotions (as in ambivalence) is a development that may appear as early as 5 to 6 years of age (Stein & Trabasso, 1989) or not until late childhood (Donaldson & Westerman, 1986; Harter & Whitesell, 1989), depending on the criteria and methods of eliciting such understanding from children. Stein and Trabasso examined 5- and 6-year-olds and determined that at this age children could readily describe people who made them feel good *and* bad or whom they liked *and* did not like. However, Stein and Trabasso cautioned that this did not mean that children *simultaneously* felt conflicting feelings; rather, they first focused on one situation to which they attached values and attributions, responded emotionally to its impact on them (e.g., "I don't like her, because she took my Halloween candy"), and then focused on another situation with its accompanying values and attributions and responded emotionally to its impact (e.g., "But I like her when she plays with me"). Thus, ambivalence for Stein and Trabasso was viewed as a *sequential* process with different appraisals attached to the different or polarized emotional responses; they suggested that this process was the same for adults, just much more rapid.

Studies conducted by Harter and Whitesell (1989) and Donaldson and Westerman (1986) are similarly concerned with children's cognitive construction of their own emotional experience, particularly when multiple emotions are involved. Harter and Whitesell focused on the cognitive developmental prerequisites for understanding the simultaneity of multiple emotions embedded in a situation or relationship and used Fischer's (1980) skill theory as their organizational framework (see also Harter, 1986). Not until children had access to "representational mappings" (Harter's level 3, mean age 10 years) were they able to integrate opposite valence emotions (happy and sad) about different targets that co-occur in a *situation* (e.g., "I'm glad I get to live with my dad, but I'm sad about not being able to live with Mom too"). In level 4, children (now probably preadolescents) could integrate simultaneously opposite valence emotions about the same *target* (e.g., "I love my dad, even though I'm mad at him right now"). Harter and Whitesell acknowledged that what may occur as we cognitively integrate contrasting emotions about the same target is a rapid oscillation between the multiple emotion-eliciting aspects of a relationship or situation.

Harter and Buddin (1987) also pointed out that it is not known whether children might experience simultaneously two (or even more) emotions but can only cognitively construct an explanation about the experience that focuses on one emotion. They also noted that in some situations children may experience only one overwhelming emotion, for example, fear, but as they seek to cope with the scary situation or have to communicate about it to someone else, they begin to cognitively construct a more complex system of appraisals about the emotion-eliciting situation or relationship.

Donaldson and Westerman (1986) used methodology that allowed them to probe whether children recognized that contradictory feelings toward the same target could influence or interact with one another. They found that not until age 10 to 11 years did children understand such an interaction of contradictory feelings. A common occurrence is when children of divorced parents admit to not always wanting to see the noncustodial parent because they reexperience the pain of loss and anger at their parents for breaking up the family, but they experience as well their love for the absent parent. They may end up coping with the emotional conflict by withdrawing from it and may be quite aware of doing so (from an 11-year-old: "Well, I'd just get upset seeing him, so it was easier just not to, but then I feel guilty sometimes that I don't want to visit him.").

Last, a study by Wintre, Polivy, and Murray (1990) examined understanding of concurrent emotions for a given situation in four age groups, ranging from 8 to 20 years old. They sought to distinguish between understanding that an event could elicit a variety of feelings, though not all at the same time, and understanding that an event might elicit simultaneous, co-occurring emotions or feelings. Their methodological approach used hypothetical emotion-eliciting events, but the children did not need to nominate emotions themselves; rather, they could choose from among a selection provided by the experimenter. Thus, verbal production was minimized. Their results suggested that children as young as 8 could predict that as many as three emotions could be elicited simultaneously for some situations. The pattern for 8-year-olds was not markedly different from that of the young adults, and Wintre et al. concluded that their data supported Russell and Ridgeway's (1983) finding that children use a taxonomy of emotion concepts similar to that used by adults.

The Ability to Discern and Understand Others' Emotional Experiences

The ability to understand what others are feeling develops in conjunction with awareness of one's own feelings, with one's ability to empathize, and with the ability to conceptualize causes of emotions and their behavioral consequences. In addition, the more we learn about how and why people act as they do, the more we can *infer* what is going on for them emotionally, even if it is not especially obvious or may even be counterintuitive.

Facial Expressions and Emotion-Eliciting Situations

In their review, Lewis and Michalson (1985) emphasized that the meanings attributed to facial expressions and eliciting situations are variable, for already by age 2 family "rules" or customs may be in place that influence what sort of facial expression is likely to occur in a particular situation. Adolescents, for example, may match a sad facial expression almost as often as an angry facial expression to a situation in which damage is intentionally done to one's achievement. Thus, adolescents recognize that one's expression may be a *social* response and not necessarily limited to one's emotional response. Some people may have learned that a sad expression upon having one's achievement damaged may elicit repair or compensation from the perpetrator; others may have learned that by expressing anger, they can prevent the perpetrator from doing such damage again in the future. Both are legitimate instrumental expressive responses intended to influence the social exchange. Indeed, as Lewis and Michalson concluded, facial expressions can have a dual function: they can be *signs,* in which case they bear a one-to-one correspondence to internal emotional states, or they can function as *symbols,* in which case they point to something else, for example, placating someone, deterring someone, or presenting oneself in a more favorable light. The dissociation of facial expression from internal emotional experience will be taken up in detail later in this chapter.

A review by Gross and Ballif (1991) of research on children's understanding of emotions in others based on facial expression cues and situational elicitors of emotion concluded, not surprisingly, that as children matured, they became more accurate in their inferences about what others were feeling. The easiest emotions to figure out were positive ones: smiling faces and situations depicting pleasure and getting what one wants were readily comprehended as associated with happiness. Negative facial expressions depicting sadness, fear, or anger were more difficult for children to decode, but if paired with a detailed emotion-eliciting situational context, children were much more likely to infer the negative emotion in question. By age 4, children can also nominate the sorts of situations that "go with" a simple set of emotions (Barden et al., 1980).

As children mature, they combine both facial and situational cues as they attempt to discern and understand the emotional experience of others (e.g., Hoffner & Badzinski, 1989). Wiggers and van Lieshout (1985) suggested that when there was a contradiction between a facial expression and the emotion-eliciting situation, school-age children were more likely to opt for whichever cue was more clearly presented. An example used by Wiggers and van Lieshout is a scenario depicting a boy with a weak smile about to get a fearsome injection. The situation, in this case, is more definitively portrayed than the boy's facial expression, and as a result, children conclude that the boy is anxious or afraid, despite the attempt at a smile. Children also recognize that others might feel a mixture of feelings about a situation. As an illustration, Camras (personal communication cited in Lewis & Michalson, 1985) interviewed 5- and 6-year-old children using several different stories, for example, "My friend came home from school one day and his mother told him that the family dog had just had puppies. My friend didn't even know his dog was going to have puppies." The children were then asked to infer the story protagonist's feelings. Happiness and surprise were equally selected, but some children thought disgust might occur as well.

Strayer (1986) has documented that by age 5 to 6 years, children are able to provide reasonable determinants for emotions experienced both by the self and by others. She elicited this information by asking the children open-ended questions about their experience (e.g., "Tell me what would make you feel happy"). She next examined several thematic shifts in situational determinants of emotion, such as impersonal versus interpersonal attributions, achievement themes, the role of fantasy, and degree of agency or control. Older children (7–8 years) made more use of interpersonal and achievement themes relative to the younger children (5–6 years), and there were no significant differences in explanations given for whether the emotion was experienced by oneself or by somebody else.

The preceding conclusions were largely based on research that was done by having children appraise hypothetical vignettes, photos, and the like. Fabes, Eisenberg, Nyman, and Michealieu (1991) investigated 3- to 6-year-old children's understanding of others' emotions in naturalistic settings. They found that happy reactions were more often correctly identified (according to adult standards) than negative reactions, thus replicating the general outcome of interview-based research. Fabes et al. also examined children's understanding of the causes of emotions and found that children could more readily identify causes for negative emotions. They interpreted this result as based on the greater intensity of negative emotional states and concurred with Stein and Trabasso's (1989) conclusion that children more readily evaluate the causes for goal failure (i.e., any undesired outcome). A developmental difference found by Fabes et al. was that their youngest children tended to attribute causes to wants and needs, whereas the older children in kindergarten more often made use of others' personality traits in their construal of what gave rise to the emotional response. This use of personalized information in understanding others' emotional experience is further examined in the next section.

Taking into Account Unique Information about the Other

The most relevant studies for more fully describing this feature of understanding others' emotional experience were conducted by Gnepp and Gould (1985) and Gnepp and Chilamkurti (1988) and theoretically elaborated by Gnepp (1989a). Gnepp and Gould examined whether children (ages 5–10) could use information about a story character's past experience (e.g., being rejected by one's best friend) to predict how the character would feel in a new situation (e.g., subsequently meeting the best friend on the playground). Not unexpectedly, the youngest children were more likely to use the current situational information to infer what the character was feeling (e.g., she would be happy at seeing her best friend), and older children were more likely to infer the character's emotional state by taking into account the prior experience (e.g., she would feel sad upon seeing her best friend). An interaction also occurred between the hedonic tone (positive/negative) of the emotion and the use of personal information: if the story character experienced a negative *emotion* at Time 1 but encountered a commonly assumed positive *situation* at Time 2, then children were more likely to use prior personal history information when inferring how the character would feel at Time 2. Gnepp (1989b) suggests that children must first recognize what a person's perspective was at Time 1 and then must apply that inferred perspective from Time 1 to Time 2 to come up with the atypical emotional response.

In an analogous investigation, Gnepp and Chilamkurti (1988) presented stories to elementary school children and adults in which characters' personality traits were systematically described as either desirable or undesirable. The story characters then had some experience befall them, and the children were to infer the emotional reaction of the character to this new experience. Older children and adults were more likely to take into account the prior trait information in inferring the emotional response of the character in the new situation. The younger children (6-year-olds) were less consistent in doing so, but a number were able to take personality trait information into account when inferring how someone might emotionally respond to an emotion-eliciting event, even when the emotional reaction might be atypical for the eliciting event.

These two investigations show us that by school entry, children are on their way to superimposing multiple frames of reference onto one another across time intervals to predict or infer other people's emotional responses. In Gnepp's research, a distinction was not made between emotional state and emotional-expressive behavior; the assumption was that children would infer emotional state. Whether children could also infer what sort of expressive behavior would be displayed, and whether it would be congruent with an atypical internal emotional state or with the consensually defined typical emotion response to the situation, was not part of the focus of these studies.

Attribution of Causality and Inference of Emotion in Others

Weiner and Graham (1984; Graham & Weiner, 1986; Weiner, 1985; also reviewed in Thompson, 1989) are concerned with how we infer others' emotions, and, for that matter, reflect upon our own, by examining what we believe to be the causes of these emotional experiences. In particular, Weiner and Graham focus on several attributions that they argue shape the kinds of inferences we make. The first is the dimension of *stability,* the extent to which an event will recur. When we attribute causes of emotional experience to something within the individual, we are using an *internal locus,* according to Weiner and Graham. When our causal attribution is about the environment (e.g., the cultural context), then the locus is *external.* Another feature that contributes very importantly to our perception of emotional causes is the perceived *controllability* of the eliciting event, of ourselves, and of the emotional experience itself.

When we combine these three aspects of attributions about causes of emotion, namely, stability (ranging from random/rare to high recurrence), locus (internal or external), and controllability (ranging from none to a lot), we gain considerable insight into how people *expect* themselves to feel in future situations as well as how they *explain* why they felt as they did in a situation. For example,

Yirmiya and Weiner (1986) found that by about age 7 children attributed an angry reaction to those who were intentionally harmed by others. Younger children could discriminate controllable acts from accidental ones, but they did not necessarily use such thinking in their attribution of causes for feeling angry as opposed to feeling sad (e.g., Graham, 1988).

From a developmental standpoint, Thompson (1989) has argued that the attribution dimensions suggested by Weiner and Graham need to be viewed in a broad way, for children may demonstrate use of these dimensions in their causal search for understanding one emotional experience, for example, anger, but fail to use them in understanding their own or another's feelings in another situation, for example, one involving ambivalent feelings. Thompson also emphasized the need to consider individual differences in the use of such attributions; that is, what may be viewed as controllable by one subculture may not be so viewed by another.

Taking a different view of how children use attributions in understanding emotions, Levine (1995) examined 5- and 6-year-old children's beliefs about causes for angry and sad reactions in hypothetical situations. She found that when children inferred angry responses, they more often focused on the aversiveness of the outcome and believed that the protagonist's goal should be reinstated. For inferred sadness, the children more often mentioned the loss felt by the protagonist and the impossibility of goal reinstatement. It was the child's attribution that determined the inferred emotion rather than the actual event depicted in the stories. Thus, the same episode involving a child who cannot go outside to play because of an injury was variously construed as anger provoking (e.g., "He's mad because he has to stay inside and he doesn't want to") or as sadness inducing (e.g., "He's sad because he wants to play outside but he can't"). Thus, Levine's work suggests that while children may learn to pair situations with particular emotions, what may be more pivotal to their beliefs about what sort of emotion will be felt are their expectations regarding goal outcome.

Social Competence and Discerning Others' Feelings

Several investigators have gathered data that suggest that children with emotional problems or who have been abused show deficits in their understanding of links between facial expression and emotion, in their producing facial expressions, and in their discriminating emotion expressions (Camras, Grow, & Ribordy, 1983; Feldman, White, & Lobato, 1982; Walker, 1981). Do children who are exceptionally socially competent show an enhancement of understanding emotion and expression linkages? Custrini and Feldman (1989) reported that among girls, but not among boys, degree of social competence greatly influenced their overall accuracy score in encoding and decoding others' emotions. Girls who were below average in social competence scored well below boys, regardless of the boys' social competence level, and the highest-scoring children were girls who were above average in social competence. Other research undertaken by Walden and Field (1988) suggested that preschoolers who obtained high sociometric peer preferences as play partners were also those who tended to be better at discriminating among emotional facial displays and who tended to demonstrate high spontaneous expressivity (but they did not excel in posed expressions). Another study undertaken by Edwards, Manstead, and McDonald (1984) with somewhat older children demonstrated a similar relationship: children's sociometric rating was positively related to their ability to recognize facial expressions of emotion.

Further support for a link between social effectiveness and emotion knowledge can be found in research undertaken by Denham, McKinley, Couchoud, and Holt (1990) and in a study on family-peer connections by Cassidy, Parke, Buttkovsky, and Braungart (1992). In the Denham et al. study, preschoolers were observed for nine months and their sociometric ratings were also established (which were modified and subsequently referred to as their *likability* among their peers). Observations of naturally occurring emotion episodes in the preschool were collected, as were measures of children's understanding of emotion. Among the latter was a task that required the children to select a situationally appropriate facial expression from a felt board and place it on a puppet's otherwise neutral face, so that the affixed expression properly matched the situation that had been enacted by the puppet. Their results showed that children who demonstrated greater knowledge of emotion in the puppet task (especially in understanding anger and fear) were perceived by their peers as more likable. Their results also indicated that prosocial behavior was positively related to likability, but emotion knowledge in the puppet task was unrelated to prosocial behavior.

In the Cassidy et al. (1992) study of kindergarten children, emotion understanding was measured by interviewing the children about identification of emotional facial expressions, how particular emotions were situationally elicited, and what the social consequences were to such emotions. They found that children who demonstrated more complex emotion understanding were more accepted by their peers. The investigators also looked at parental expressiveness and determined that mothers' expressiveness in the home was also positively related to their children's peer acceptance. The authors suggested that the children may have learned from their parents' expressiveness appropriate ways to negotiate relations with their peers.

Problematic Outcomes and Understanding Others' Feelings

Discerning and understanding others' feelings does not necessarily always contribute to one's skill at emotional communication. Paradoxically, in certain circumstances, some children would be better off tuning out others' emotional behavior. Children who are exposed to and involved in their parents' depressed feelings represent one group who are at risk for an aversive emotion-socialization experience, and another group consists of those children exposed to marital conflict accompanied by overt anger. Obviously, it is unrealistic to assume that children can tune out their parents' negative emotions, but outcomes do not bode well for children if such experiences are frequent, intense, and started early in life. Investigations of how children of chronically depressed parents (for the most part, mothers) develop emotionally have been reviewed by Downey and Coyne (1990) and Zahn-Waxler and Kochanska (1990). Research on children who witness interadult anger has been reviewed by Cummings and Davies (1994).

Zahn-Waxler and her associates (Zahn-Waxler, Cummings, Iannotti, & Radke-Yarrow, 1984; Zahn-Waxler & Robinson, 1995; Zahn-Waxler, Cole, & Barrett, 1991) noticed in their work with children of chronically depressed mothers that such young children appeared to be overinvolved and overresponsible in their interaction with their distressed mothers. Some of these children attributed the cause of their mothers' distress to themselves and developed a seemingly precocious repertoire of strategies for "repairing" their mothers' unhappiness. Zahn-Waxler and her colleagues saw in this behavior a contradictory blend of impotence and omnipotence, which contributed to the children's becoming vulnerable to inappropriate guilt when they failed to make their mothers happy. The seeds of depression were perhaps also planted in such failure: helplessness was frequently experienced by such children, for they could not reliably succeed in pleasing their mothers.

Zahn-Waxler and her colleagues (1984) found that when young children were involved with emotionally troubled parents, the children were constantly having to cope with both their parents' distress and the demands that

such negative emotional experiences placed on them. At the same time, these children were having to maintain and "nourish" their attachment to their parents (as opposed to the parents more appropriately nurturing the attachment to the children). These excessive emotional demands appeared to contribute to an intergenerational transmission of maladaptive emotion socialization. Not surprisingly, depressed parents tend to have children who later also show depressive tendencies.

In the research on children exposed to adults' anger and conflict, children as young as 4 years readily recognize such interactions as angry ones and respond to them with verbalized negative feelings of their own (Cummings, Vogel, Cummings, & El-Sheikh, 1989). With children younger than 4, verbal report cannot be reliably used, but general distress and emotional arousal have been observed in children ages 10 to 20 months when they were exposed to angry parents (Cummings, Zahn-Waxler, & Radke-Yarrow, 1981). Across a series of investigations on school-age children, Cummings and his colleagues found a pattern that suggested that boys in the age range of 6 to 9 years were more likely to respond to interadult anger and conflict with their own anger and aggression; girls were more likely to experience distress and anxiety. Children perceived angry conflict between adults accompanied by physical aggression as the most reprehensible. Cummings and his colleagues (Cummings, Ballard, & El-Sheikh, 1991) also investigated age changes in responses of older children and adolescents to witnessed interadult anger. They found that the 9- to 11-year-olds had the strongest negative reaction to the staged interadult anger, and the oldest adolescents (17–19 years old) had the least. Interestingly, the gender difference found was reversed from that noted above with younger children: adolescent girls reported more anger than boys, who, in turn, reported more sadness. Cummings et al. speculate that this reversal of sex differences among adolescents may be a function of the boys feeling sympathetic distress for the couple engaged in the mock conflict, whereas the girls may have felt aggravated at this couple having this ridiculous and petty conflict. What is unclear is the extent to which adolescents felt self-involved as they responded to this staged argument.

What does stand out in these studies is that the youngest children were the most ardently involved in having an aversive reaction. Thus, we may infer that the younger the child, the greater the stress when exposed to angry, hostile conflicts between adults. Given that this research was undertaken with mock conflicts between adults whom the children and youth did not know, one can only surmise how much more involving and upsetting it is for children exposed to their parents' anger and conflict. Indeed, clinically oriented research on such families shows that such youngsters are at risk for developing behavior problems, for becoming victims and victimizers themselves, and thus for perpetuating the cycle of abuse (e.g., Egeland, Jacobvitz, & Sroufe, 1988; Grych & Fincham, 1990).

The Ability to Use Concepts, Lexicon, and Scripts Relevant to Emotion and Expression

The ability to represent our emotional experience through words, imagery, and symbolism of varied sorts allows us to undertake two major accomplishments. The first is that we can communicate our emotional experiences to others across time and space, whether this takes the form of talking on the telephone about how we felt about what happened yesterday or painting a picture of a maelstrom to represent our inner turmoil. The second accomplishment is more strictly intrapsychic; by having access to representations of our emotional experiences, we can further elaborate them, integrate them across contexts, and compare them with others' representations about emotional experiences. Some of the developments in awareness of our own multiple feelings or in understanding others' atypical emotions described earlier in this chapter could not be undertaken if we did not have access to a language or representational system for symbolically encoding and communicating our emotional experiences. Being able to comprehend emotion *scripts* also entails representations that become elaborated with development (Abelson, 1981). Scripts may be thought of as paradigms or prototypical scenarios that entail a sequence of causal links; they can also be coordinated with scripts for other sorts of social behavior. Thus, some emotions, for example, anger, may have scripts that differ according to gender, status, age group, subculture, and so forth.

Assuming an intact nervous system and an environment that is not overwhelmingly trauma-filled, children do show some commonalities in our culture in learning how to represent emotion. However, individual differences and cultural influence are again strong forces in the development of language-based emotion concepts, which is not surprising, since one of the critical functions of an emotion lexicon is to be able to communicate with others, which obviously entails their reciprocal communication about emotion (see illustrative research by Denham, Cook, & Zoller, 1992; Dunn & Brown, 1994).

Development of Emotion Language and Lexicon

Bretherton, Fritz, Zahn-Waxler, and Ridgeway (1986) reviewed the relevant literature on children's acquisition of emotion words, and what follows is substantially drawn from their material. They note that many toddlers can use emotion words toward the end of the second year, but as Smiley and Huttenlocher (1989) caution, what may be included as an emotion word, for example, crying, may simply be a behavioral action noted by the young child and conceivably is not used by the child to denote internal emotional state. By 3 years of age children can much more readily label the emotions of others in addition to their own feelings; they can refer to emotional experiences in the past and anticipate them in the future. Increasingly, they can also verbally address the consequences of emotional states as well as the situational causes of emotions; for example, "Grandma mad. I wrote on wall."

Children can also apply emotion terms to pretend play by age 2.5 years, and, indeed, listening to children talk as they enact fantasies with their figurative toys (e.g., dolls, action figures, stuffed animals, etc.) is an excellent way to observe a young child's competence with emotion language, for they construct both the causes of the figure's emotional response and the consequences of the emotion, including how the figure copes. Denham and Auerbach (1995) analyzed the emotional content of mothers and preschoolers' dialogues while looking at picture books together (whose contents were emotion-laden). They found that such an interaction was rich with adult-child exchanges that included affect labeling and causes and consequences of emotional experience. In addition, both mothers and children used their emotion-descriptive language in ways that suggested social influence of the other; for example, mothers who limited themselves to simple comments about the emotion-laden material in the picture books had children who asked more questions to engage their mothers more. However, those mothers who made use of verbal explanation to a very great degree appeared to stimulate their children further to use more complex and elaborated emotion-descriptive language. These children tended to respond with more guiding and socializing language about the characters' emotional experience (e.g., "We don't hit cats with baseball bats," from the coding appendix).

Researchers have also studied parents' reports of their children's understanding and use of emotion-descriptive words. Using parents' ratings on checklists of words indicating emotion states (e.g., happy), emotion traits (e.g., good), and physical states (e.g., sleepy, clean), Ridgeway, Waters, and Kuczaj (1985) tabulated at six-month intervals (starting at 18 months and extending to 6 years of age) the percentages of children comprehending the emotion word and also using it. The most frequently understood words at 18 months were *sleepy, hungry, good, happy, clean, tired,* and *sad* (50–83% comprehension). The toddlers' use of these words in their own verbal production was much lower; 50% used the word *good,* whereas only 7% used the word *sad.* By age 6, children comprehended such words as *nervous* (83%), *embarrassed* (77%), *jealous* (60%), and *miserable* (53%). Their corresponding production of these words was half to two-thirds of the percentages for comprehension.

Going beyond the description of frequency and range of feeling-state words, Dunn, Bretherton, and Munn (1987) investigated naturally occurring conversations in the home between young children and their mothers and siblings. They were particularly interested in determining what sorts of functions conversations about feelings had in the social exchange within the home and how children communicated causes of feelings in their exchanges with others. They followed the young children from age 18 months to 24 months and found that conversations about causes of feelings increased significantly in the six months they tracked the children. They also found that the vast majority of feeling-state conversations were with the mother as opposed to the older sibling, although feeling-state conversations involving all three occurred more often than between just the two children. What this finding suggests is that access to an adult who is interested in their feelings may be pivotal to children's having opportunities both to talk about emotions and have their understanding of emotions elaborated. Mothers tended to use conversations about feelings as a functional way to guide or explain something to their children, whereas the children were more likely to use feeling-descriptive words simply to comment on their own reaction or observation of another. Thus, they were learning to communicate their own self-awareness of feeling states to their mothers, who in turn were likely to communicate *meaningfulness* to their children by using guiding, persuading, clarifying, or otherwise interpretive feeling-related language.

Dunn et al.'s (1987) research suggests that mothers anchored for their young children *how* to make sense of what they were experiencing in themselves and occasionally what others experienced. Interestingly, Dunn et al. found a considerable decrease in mothers' responses to the children's use of distress-related feeling words as they matured

from 18 to 24 months. This may be an example of mothers trying to de-emphasize their children's attention to distress. Alternatively, by 24 months these children may be going through the "Terrible Twos" stage with their attendant bids for autonomy at all costs; they end up experiencing more distress because their mothers set limits (e.g., "No, you cannot put your toys in the toilet!") and therefore thwart them, causing a greater frequency of distress episodes which the mothers prudently ignore.

Dunn, Brown, and Beardsall (1991) continued their research on naturally occurring conversations about feelings in the home, but this time extended their longitudinal study of children from when they were 3 years old to age 6. They again focused on children and mothers' exchanges around causes and consequences of feelings and additionally tracked how disputes and conflicts in the home provided occasions for emotional growth in terms of how children were exposed to and had to use emotion-descriptive language to negotiate the conflict. They found a tremendous range in variability among the children in frequency of "feeling talk": from 0 to 27 occasions per hour of observation. The mothers also showed a similar variability, ranging from 0 to 22 occasions of feeling talk per hour of observation. Unfortunately, Dunn et al. did not provide information as to whether the mother-child dyads were matched in their rates of feeling talk. Given the findings of their earlier study, where mothers were pivotal in providing opportunities for children to verbally communicate about their feelings, we can only speculate that if a mother did not talk much about feelings and related inner states, very likely her child did not either.

Relative to disputes, Dunn et al. found that an average of 22% of feeling talk concerned conflicts between child and mother, or with the sibling, or among all three; the range was again considerable, varying from 0 to 75% across households. When disputes were being negotiated, 67% of the conversations included reference to causes of feelings, whereas conversations that did not focus on conflicts referred to causes of feelings only 45% of the time.

Dunn et al. (1991) also examined the relation between their various measures of feeling talk (taken at age 3) and a measure of social sensitivity at age 6. They assessed social sensitivity by using Rothenberg's (1970) audiotapes of a man and a woman in scenarios that depicted happiness, anger, anxiety, and sadness. The children were asked to describe the emotional transitions that occurred from the beginning to the end of the tapes, and the adequacy of their commentary provided the rating for social sensitivity. The significant correlations between the Rothenberg measure and the feeling talk variables assessed at age 3 were impressive: they ranged from a high of .47 with diversity of feeling themes present in mother-child conversations (e.g., themes as diverse as pain, disgust, distress, pleasure, etc.) to a low of .34 for incidence of disputes. In between were conversations about causes of feelings and total number of feeling talk conversations between mothers and children. Although these correlations might not seem terribly large, when one takes into account that these measures span three years, to obtain that sort of continuity in children's understanding of and sensitivity to emotional cues at age 6 with their earlier conversations about feelings with their mother at age 3 is really quite impressive.

The special role played by conflict should also be reassuring to parents. As taxing as disputes with one's preschooler may be, they play an important role in children's learning to understand their own and others' feelings and to acquire the emotional lexicon to make themselves understood by others. As Dunn and Brown (1991) point out, when children are feeling bad, they are motivated to express, verbally and otherwise, their feelings to get their needs attended to. For them to attain that goal, they need to learn to communicate their feelings in ways that regulate not only their own behavior but that of others as well. Learning to express affection to a parent is also a highly effective way to elicit positive attention, and Dunn and Brown are emphatic in their contention that children desire pleasurable interaction, not just attention to their distress or pain.

Another study by Dunn and Brown (1994) shed further light on the effects of family emotional expression on children's acquisition of emotion-descriptive language. Again they found that occasions of negative feeling on the part of the child were when most emotion-related discourse occurred between mother and child. What this study also documented that was quite intriguing was that if families were characterized as high in frequency of anger and distress expression, the children were *less* likely to be engaged in discourse about feelings. But if the families were low in frequency of negative emotional expression, when a negative emotional event did occur for the child, there was a greater likelihood of an emotion-related conversation to ensue between child and parent. This research suggests that children's acquisition of emotion-descriptive language is anchored in relationship contexts: if everyone is angry or distressed a lot of the time, an episode of distress on the part of a child may be viewed as trivial. What may be metacommunicated in such families is that a child's feelings are not very important. We can surmise how differences in the families' emotional milieus provide varying preparatory stages for their children's later emotional experiences in the world beyond the home (see, e.g., Davies & Cummings's review on marital conflict and child adjustment, 1994).

Structural Analysis of Emotion-Descriptive Language

Moving on to older children, Russell and Ridgeway (1983) examined emotion-descriptive adjectives used by children in elementary school. They found that these words could be statistically analyzed with principal-components analyses and multidimensional scaling. The result was that two bipolar dimensions were found that provided an organizational structure for the many emotion-related terms used by schoolchildren. These two dimensions were degree of pleasure or hedonic tone and degree of arousal.

This dimensional analysis of emotion concepts is of interest, for it suggests something about the way emotion is categorized and perhaps even organized as subjective experience. A number of cross-cultural comparisons have been made on emotion concepts used by adults in other languages (reviewed by Russell, 1991), and the pleasure/displeasure dimension has been reliably found in all the cultures studied. The arousal dimension has sometimes been mixed with degree of dominance/submissiveness. Perhaps in these cultures, as probably in our own, dominance is associated with high energy or arousal vis-à-vis others, whereas submissiveness is associated with low energy. Russell suggests that hedonic tone is relevant in all cultures in terms of how feeling states are differentiated, but the English word *emotion* is not necessarily present in all languages, although an equivalent term is more the rule than the exception (exceptions appear to be the language of Tahitians, Bimin-Kuskusmin of Papua New Guinea, Gidjingali aborigines of Australia, Ifalukians of Micronesia, Chewong of Malaysia, and Samoans; cited in Russell, 1991). In these few cultures where no term similar to emotion exists, feelings may be referred to as arising within certain body parts or organs; for example, the Chewong view the liver as the source of what might be called thoughts and feelings. The significance of the virtually universal presence of the pleasure/aversion dimension in emotion-descriptive concepts may indicate that what experiencing pleasure/aversion does for us is a basic function: it is embedded in our approach/avoidance actions vis-à-vis the contexts we live in (see Frijda, 1986, 1987, for further discussion of action tendencies).

Emotion Script Learning

Acquisition of emotion-descriptive concepts continues throughout childhood and into adolescence, but little research has examined these older age groups. Further development of emotion language in the school-age child and adolescent may be found in their greater ability to add variety, subtlety, nuance, and complexity to their use of emotion-descriptive words with others. What may also develop is that children's *scripts* for understanding emotional experience are reciprocally influenced by their growing access to increasing complexity of emotion concepts. Russell (1991) defines emotion scripts as "a knowledge structure for a type of event whereby the event is thought of as a sequence of subevents" (p. 442). An example based on a child experiencing anger should clarify this definition. Note that the numbers indicate the sequence of subevents contained within a script for anger; the words in parentheses indicate the general subevent meaning:

1. Eleven-year-old Kate felt betrayed (offense) when Ellen blabbed all over the class the secret she had told her, namely, that her parents were getting divorced (Ellen's act was intentional and harmful to an innocent person).

2. Kate glared at Ellen across the classroom (expression of negative emotion directed at the offender).

3. Kate felt herself getting hot and tense; she broke the tip of her pencil pressing down so hard on the paper (physical changes accompanying the negative emotion).

4. Kate imagined what she could do to Ellen to get back at her (retribution).

5. During the next recess Kate sneaked back into the classroom and poured liquid rubber cement on Ellen's chair seat (reciprocal harm done to the offender).

Russell notes that even within the same culture scripts for the same emotions may differ from person to person, for emotion scripts are linked to other *belief networks*. This is a significant point, for when a script for anger, as an example, is linked to a network of concepts about, for example, gender role, then the anger script may well have additional emphases or omissions if one's machismo or one's femininity is implicated in the anger episode. What is important to

consider here is that scripts for different emotions may merge (or one emotion may cycle into another) under certain circumstances, particularly if individuals appraise a situation as salient for certain beliefs they hold about themselves (see also Lewis, 1992a, for a discussion of links between gender and shame scripts).

Emotion scripts may merge with gender-role socialization, as suggested by some of the gender differences found for how anger and sadness are talked about in families. For example, gender differences in learning to talk about feelings were found by Dunn, Bretherton, and Munn (1987) in their study of young British children and their mothers. Little girls received more comments and inquiries about feelings from their mothers and from their older siblings than did little boys; however, the boys and girls themselves were similar in their initiation of conversations about feelings. In a similar vein, Fivush (1991) undertook an exploratory study with mothers of 3-year-old boys and girls and found that mothers tended to talk in a more elaborate fashion about sadness with their daughters and about anger with their sons. She found that mothers tended to embed their discussions of feelings in social frameworks more with their daughters than with their sons. Relative to script notions, she also found that when anger was involved, mothers emphasized relationship repair with their daughters and were more accepting of retaliation by their angry sons.

Last, cultural influence and the acquisition of an emotional lexicon are inseparable, for societies use language to regulate emotion within social interaction. Many societies emphasize some emotional responses over others by attaching special importance to certain emotion-descriptive words. In U.S. culture, the word *love* is such an emotionally loaded word. Much anthropological research has been done that examines emotion-descriptive language. The reader is referred to Russell's (1991) excellent review that examines cultural similarities and differences in how emotions are categorized in different languages and cultures and to his recent edited volume on this topic (Russell, Fernandez-Dols, Manstead, & Wellenkamp, 1996). Another useful perspective is that of ethnotheories (or folk theories) of emotion; Lutz's work (1988; Lutz & White, 1986) is a source for learning further about emotion lexicons viewed from an ethnotheory perspective. Illustrative of this perspective are Ochs's (1986) review of Samoan children's acquisition of emotion-descriptive language and A. Eisenberg's (1986) ethnographic study of the emotional and social functions of verbal banter (teasing) in recently immigrated Mexican children.

Empathy and the Communication of Sympathy

Conceptual Issues

Empathy, *feeling with* others, and sympathy, *feeling for* others, are emotional responses that connect us with others. Beginning in early infancy, it is clear that very young babies respond to others' emotional-expressive behavior (see preceding discussion on social referencing). Thus, this early attentiveness to emotional-expressive cues paves the way for later vicariously induced emotion, for one cannot be "induced" to experience another's emotional state unless one notices it and considers it salient. Sympathy differs from empathy in that it can be experienced when responding to purely symbolic information, such as reading about someone's distress or hearing about someone's unfortunate circumstances. Empathy tends to be defined as a more immediate emotional response that is experienced by the observer upon witnessing someone's emotional state, and experiencing empathy may give rise to sympathy and its accompanying feelings of concern for the other's plight (e.g., N. Eisenberg & Fabes, 1990).

However, some individuals experience empathy in a way that yields a decidedly aversive emotional reaction. N. Eisenberg and Fabes (1990) refer to this reaction as personal distress. Such a reaction to another's negative emotional state more often leads to an avoidance of the upset person, for personally distressed individuals focus on themselves as they struggle to reduce their own negative emotional reaction. In contrast, a sympathetic response to someone's upsetness more typically leads to concern and prosocial overtures. An extensive literature has developed in recent years on empathy, sympathy, and personal distress in children (comprehensive reviews include N. Eisenberg & Fabes, 1990, 1992; N. Eisenberg & Miller, 1987), and some of the major findings will be discussed below.

The consensus appears to be that empathy and sympathy require the cognitive acquisition of a self distinguished from others and to some degree the ability to figure out the emotional state of the other, for example, to recognize that the other person is *feeling something* (N. Eisenberg & Strayer, 1987). This view of empathy would exclude emotional contagion effects, but the conditioned or reflexively shared emotional responding that we see in emotion contagion may be thought of as a precursor to empathy or as

quasi-empathy (Thompson, 1987, 1990). However, having the capacity for self-other differentiation and perspective taking vis-à-vis another's emotional state sounds emotionally detached, and empathic responding is in fact quite emotionally engaged.

Strayer (1987) is emphatic about the emotional involvement that is central to experiencing empathy: "An intelligent psychopath may have good role taking skills, but may use them only to manipulate others for personal gain. Again, the affective aspect of empathy is critical" (p. 225). In a subsequent analysis of empathy in children, Strayer (1989) makes an important developmental distinction between an empathic response that essentially is derived from the young child's focus on the emotion-eliciting *events* that are impacting on another (e.g., watching child A hit child B and becoming distressed about witnessing the event of hitting), as opposed to an empathic response that stems from *participation* in the emotional reaction of the impacted individual (e.g., showing distress upon seeing a crying child but without having seen the precipitating event). The former, event-focused empathy relies on a rather concrete cognitive awareness of what sort of situations "cause" emotions; the latter, participatory empathy requires cognitive awareness of and attributions about the internal states of others. Thus, Strayer does include cognitive developmental complexity in her assessment of empathy, because representations, whether of emotion-eliciting events or of emotion-experiencing people, determine the quality of the empathic response. Furthermore, what can elicit an empathic response in children or adults will depend heavily on what sorts of representations they are capable of.

A significant contributor to experiencing personal distress rather than the more functional sympathetic response is the disposition to experience emotional overarousal and more intense levels of vicariously induced negative emotion (N. Eisenberg, Fabes, et al., 1988; N. Eisenberg, Schaller, et al., 1988). These researchers found that heart rate acceleration was associated with a personal distress response, whereas sympathy co-occurred with heart rate deceleration. In the latter study, children's heart rate and facial expressions were better predictors of their subsequent helpful overtures than their self-report. Self-report of feeling empathic concern for others may be unreliable because of children's tendency to present their responses in socially desirable ways (see also N. Eisenberg & Lennon, 1983, for a critique of empathy self-report measures in the context of sex differences, and Lennon &

Eisenberg, 1987, for a critique of a variety of types of self-report measures yielding inconsistent age differences). We will return to further discussion of personal distress responses when we take up individual differences in empathy and sympathy.

Considerable research has also been done on children's prosocial behavior and its relation to empathy and/or perspective taking (see N. Eisenberg & Fabes, Ch. 11, this Volume; Kurtines & Gewirtz, 1991), and it will not be further reviewed here. We concur with the position taken by Zahn-Waxler (1991), who believes that the origins of prosocial and altruistic behavior are to be found in the dynamic emotional exchanges of the attachment relationship between parent and infant. She notes that the social exchange and cooperative turn-taking that has been observed between caregiver and infant "create a world of shared meaning, empathic understanding and appropriate linking of one's own emotions with those of others that then generalize beyond the parent-child dyad" (p. 156). In sum, the emotional attunement between parent and baby is essentially the crucible in which empathy and concern for others' well-being are forged.

Children's Attempts to Influence Another's Emotional State

Related to sympathetically intervening on someone's behalf is seeking to change how someone is feeling; this commonly takes the form of trying to cheer someone up, to calm someone down, or to reassure someone who is scared. Empathy or sympathy may be involved when one attempts to influence another's emotional experience, but not necessarily; being able to understand what the other is feeling is critical, as is an awareness of any relevant personal information about the target person. Obviously there are also other occasions that are clearly not prosocially intended in which we attempt to influence another's feelings, for example, when we appease an irrational bully, tease someone to anger or to tears, or try to distract someone from his or her distress so that we do not have to feel bad anymore (the personal distress reaction described earlier). A few studies have been undertaken that examined children's attempts to influence others' feelings (e.g., Covell & Abramovitch, 1987; McCoy & Masters, 1985), but the investigators did not provide observational data on just how children went about this emotion-influencing process. However, a study with elementary school children did shed light on what children do when they attempt to influence someone's feelings (Saarni, 1992).

In this study, elementary school children met individually on two separate occasions with a "market researcher" confederate. The first time, she was visibly in a happy emotional state and engaged the children warmly; on the second occasion, she was in a sad, depressed state. Prior to the second meeting the children were asked to help cheer up the sad market researcher, and all agreed to do so. Results indicated that among the youngest children were those who did appear to display personal distress upon witnessing the sad researcher's demeanor. The oldest children (11–12 years), although showing the most positive behavior toward the sad researcher, also revealed the most tension-filled expressive behavior, for example, biting their lips, touching themselves, and so on. However, their conversational fluency, combined with their positive expressive behavior, suggested that these oldest children were more self-contained and less influenced by the sad researcher's emotional-expressive behavior. Their strategy for influencing the sad researcher's emotional state seemed to be one of trying to direct the interaction toward a more amicable exchange, but they showed some degree of accompanying tension or uncertainty about whether they were effective.

Individual Differences in Empathy and Sympathy

Gender Differences. When gender differences have been found (reviewed in N. Eisenberg & Fabes, Ch. 11, this Volume; Eisenberg & Lennon, 1983; Lennon & Eisenberg, 1987; Zahn-Waxler, Cole, & Barrett, 1991), they have tended to occur in conjunction with other contributing influences (such as the nature of the method used to measure empathy) or contexts (such as when demand characteristics were obviously oriented toward eliciting sympathetic responsiveness or if the context involved close relationships). One cannot simplistically and globally conclude that one gender is more empathic than the other. However, one's *subsequent* action relative to feeling empathy or sympathy may well reflect gender-role influence; for example, men have been found to help strangers more readily than women, but women undertake the majority of nurturing and caring for others in close relationships (reviewed in Zahn-Waxler, Cole, & Barrett, 1991; see also Golombok & Fivush, 1994, for further discussion of gender differences and empathy). Zahn-Waxler et al. note that girls are socialized to be attuned more to their relations with others and to feel responsible for others' well-being. When feeling responsible for others is conjoined with discomfort, guilt and empathy may merge together, particularly if family socialization patterns have led children to acquire an overgeneralized sense of responsibility for others' well-being (Zahn-Waxler & Robinson, 1995). They argue that young girls are more likely to develop this pattern and consequently may become more "vulnerable to establishing beliefs about their over-responsibility, unworthiness, and blameworthiness for the problems of others" (Zahn-Waxler & Robinson, 1995, p. 165). Such self-attributions are evident in depression, and by early adolescence girls exceed boys in incidence of depression. It appears that a healthy dose of self-interest may inoculate young girls against such feelings, and Zahn-Waxler et al. (1991) point out in their review that a masculine gender-role orientation (regardless of one's sex) appears to protect one against depression, as it is associated with assertive self-interest.

Temperament and Personality Differences. Eisenberg, Fabes, Carlo, and Karbon (1992) reviewed studies that suggested some patterns about what sorts of children are most likely spontaneously to behave in a sympathetic and prosocial manner. They note that preschoolers who are socially expressive (although not always in a positive fashion), assertive, demonstrate sympathy, and are capable of reasoning about others' needs are those children who are most likely *spontaneously* to help, share, and comfort others in distress. Interestingly, compliant children who shared or helped when directly asked were more likely to react with personal distress when confronted with another's distress. These children also tended to be rejected by their peers when they did comply (especially if they were boys); they were generally less socially responsive, and their level of moral reasoning was not related to their degree of prosocial or altruistic behavior.

N. Eisenberg and Fabes (1992) proposed that personal distress reactions to vicariously induced emotion are related to individuals' negative emotionality, including arousability and intensity. According to these authors, being able to regulate one's emotional arousal requires neurophysiological regulation, attentional control processes, cognitive appraisal of emotion-eliciting events, construal of internal subjective emotion cues, and coping with situational demands. Children high in regulatory capacity were hypothesized to be more likely to modulate their emotional arousal when experiencing vicariously induced emotion such that they could focus their attention on the target rather than on themselves—as would be the case if their arousal became excessive and potentially aversive. This sort of optimally modulated level of arousal was assumed to be associated

with sympathy reactions rather than personal distress responses.

Recently, N. Eisenberg, Fabes, Murphy, et al. (1996) investigated this pattern of emotion regulation and sympathy in children ages 5 to 8 years who had been participants in a short-term longitudinal study for about two years. They collected data on the children's attentional control, impulsivity/inhibition, general self-control, emotional intensity (based on mother and teacher reports), as well as vagal tone and heart rate, respiration, and skin conductance during a distressing film. Teacher reports were also collected on a variety of instruments that evaluated children's social skills, popularity with peers, and prosocial behavior. Children's social competence was further assessed with parent reports and several child measures, including sociometric ratings and puppet enactments of peer interaction strategies. Their complex results included determining that emotionally unregulated children were low in sympathy, regardless of their emotional intensity, whereas for children who were moderately or highly regulated, sympathy increased in conjunction with their general emotional intensity. Individual differences in attentional control two years earlier also predicted sympathetic responses. In general, their results confirmed the relation between negative emotionality and personal distress reactions, but these differed by gender. The relation held for boys, whose sympathy was especially related to their social competence, but for girls the picture was inconsistent, possibly due to the gender-role linkage between femininity and sympathy.

Socialization Influence. N. Eisenberg, Fabes, Carlo, and Karbon (1992) also described a couple of socialization studies that suggested that sympathetic mothers produce sympathetic daughters, and sympathetic fathers produce sympathetic sons (N. Eisenberg, Fabes, Schaller, Miller, et al., 1991; Fabes, Eisenberg, & Miller, 1990). Modeling would seem to be a key socializing agent here. Adult women who report empathy after watching distressing films also describe their families of origin in ways that indicate that positive emotions and sympathetic and vulnerable feelings were freely expressed. Along similar lines, in the N. Eisenberg, Fabes, Schaller, Carlo, and Miller (1991) investigation, parents' attitudes were assessed using the Parental Attitude toward Children's Expressiveness Scale (PACES; Saarni, 1990), which was modified for use with preschoolers. Parents who reported restrictive attitudes toward their children's emotional displays had children who seemed more inclined to experience personal distress rather than sympathetic concern when describing their reaction to another's distress. This effect was more noticeable when the parents espoused controlling beliefs about their children's emotional displays, even when the emotional displays simply expressed the child's own vulnerable feelings (e.g., sadness, anxiety), as opposed to showing one's genuine feelings without regard for whether they could hurt someone else's feelings (e.g., showing annoyance toward a well-intentioned gift giver). Parents who restricted their children's emotional displays in circumstances where others' feelings might be hurt—but not when their children expressed vulnerable feelings—appeared to have more sympathy-oriented children. The most impacted children appeared to be boys of mothers who endorsed controlling attitudes about their sons' display of emotions in situations where only self-related vulnerable feelings were involved; these boys were the most likely to show personal distress reactions.

Several studies have also examined relations between children's empathy or sympathy and parental empathy, discipline style, and altruistic behavior. Strayer and Roberts (1989) found that for 6-year-old children prosocial behavior in their families was positively related to their display of empathy, although the parents' empathy was not related to their children's empathy. Research undertaken by P. Miller, Eisenberg, Fabes, Shell, and Gular (1989) with 4- and 5-year-olds and their mothers yielded very interesting results about how maternal emotional intensity during hypothetical disciplinary encounters with their children might be a significant moderator of their children's responsiveness to vicarious emotion. They also found that high-intensity parental emotion when combined with negative-control disciplinary style was related to lower levels of children's sympathetic responsiveness. In a later study, N. Eisenberg, Fabes, Carlo, Troyer, et al. (1992) found that mothers' sympathy and encouragement of prosocial behavior were related to their daughters' sympathetic responses, whereas mothers' verbal reports of their feelings during a distressing film were related to their sons' sympathy. For both sons and daughters (age 5–8), the expression of dominant negative feelings in the family was associated with children more likely experiencing personal distress during an evocative film.

A couple of longitudinal studies that examined empathy and family influence are worth mentioning here. N. Eisenberg and McNalley (1993) examined relations between

mothers' child-rearing practices over an eight-year period and their adolescents' (age 15–16) perspective taking and vicariously induced emotion. They found that mothers who expressed positive emotions and minimal negative affect with their children were more likely to have sympathetic daughters and sons who scored lowed in personal distress. Warm maternal communication was also associated with increased perspective taking in youth of both sexes. However, mothers' own sympathy was not significantly related to their adolescents' sympathy.

The last study to be mentioned here was undertaken by Koestner, Franz, and Weinberger (1990) with adults who had been participants in a longitudinal study since their preschool years. Empathic concern at age 31 was most strongly related to the following variables assessed when the adults were 5 years old: fathers' involvement in child care, mothers' tolerance of their children's dependency, inhibition of children's aggression, and satisfaction with the role of mother (fathers were not asked about their satisfaction with their parental role, but their high involvement with their children would seem to show that they were satisfied). The authors' conclusion is worth quoting: "children are most likely to grow up to be empathically concerned adults when both of their parents enjoyed being involved with them and when their affiliative and aggressive needs were differentially responded to, with the former being permitted and encouraged and the latter inhibited" (p. 714). The authors note with concern that the high incidence of divorce and the all-too-common subsequent diminished contact between fathers and their children could result in reduced empathy and associated prosocial behavior in children affected by early divorce.

Child Abuse and Empathy. Several studies have been conducted that examined physically abused children's reactions to distress in others (e.g., Hoffman-Plotkin & Twentyman, 1984; Main & George, 1985; Trickett & Kuczynski, 1986). Physically abused children show a multitude of problems, but most obvious is their more intense and frequent aggressiveness compared to nonabused children. To illustrate, Main and George (1985) observed young preschoolers' responses to other children's distress in day care settings. The target children were all from poor homes, with many of the households dependent on welfare and with only one parent in the home. Half of these children had been reported as having been maltreated; the other half did not have any incidence of maltreatment. The abused children (who were quite young: 1 to 3 years of age) showed no comforting gestures toward the child involved in the mishap; even worse, they sometimes moved in on the distressed child in a threatening and hostile fashion and attacked the crying child. At other times they began to fuss as well and even showed apprehension or anxiety toward the distressed child. Quite different responses were shown by the nonabused children (who were also 1 to 3 years old): they looked at the distressed child, offered tentative touches or pats, and about one-third demonstrated active prosocial behavior toward the unhappy child. For this very young age group, this proportion of prosocial behavior was about the same as that obtained with middle-class children; thus, the stress of poverty did not in itself affect young children's developing sense of empathy and concern for others.

Empathy and its derivative, sympathy, are critical to emotional communication; indeed, responsiveness to others' emotions is critical to human evolution (e.g., MacLean, 1985). The development of empathy such that it becomes linked with altruistic, prosocial behavior obviously promotes the well-being of those who need support or help, but it also facilitates the well-being of individuals who respond sympathetically. The preceding research suggests that such individuals enjoy more favorable relations with their peers, may themselves be more effective parents, and are able to regulate their emotional arousal such that they can effectively intervene to assist another.

The Ability to Differentiate Internal Emotional Experience from External Expression

Based on their collective social-emotional experiences over time, infants gradually learn to synchronize their emotional states and expressive behavior relative to an eliciting situation, but by no means do they necessarily begin life with an automatic "readout" of clearly discernible expressions that map onto reliably defined situational elicitors of emotion. Camras (1992) presented persuasive arguments and data for infants' acquisition of emotion *systems* of responses, including expressive behavior, which are heavily influenced by context. Her descriptions of her own daughter's early emotional-expressive development suggest that in seemingly neutral or even positive situations, a very young infant may express a number of facial expressions denoting a variety of interpretive meanings (e.g., adult observers might judge them as indicative of anger, pain, sadness, disgust, or

interest). In short, the coordination of skeletal muscle patterning, situational "appraisal" (if we may call it that in the first weeks of life), and functional adaptation begins in a rather loose fashion and progresses toward socially defined *scripts* for what sorts of emotions are elicited by what sorts of situations and accompanied by what sorts of expressive behavior.

By the preschool years, if not earlier, young children also learn how to introduce disparities between their internal emotional state and their external expressive behavior. Such discrepancies indicate that young children have begun to differentiate their inner emotional experience from what they express in their behavior—especially to others. Perhaps the earliest form of this differentiation between internal state and external expression is the *exaggeration* of emotional-expressive behavior to gain someone's attention (a trivial injury becomes the occasion to howl loudly and solicit comfort and attention). Blurton-Jones (1967) reported that children ages 3 to 4 in a free-play situation were more likely to cry after injuring themselves if they noticed a caregiver looking at them; they were less likely to cry if they thought they were unattended. *Minimization* may be the next form of differentiation to appear; it consists of dampening the intensity of emotional-expressive behavior, despite feeling otherwise. *Neutralization* describes the adoption of a "poker face," but it is probably relatively difficult to carry off; indeed, Ekman and Friesen (1975) suggest that *substitution* of another expression that differs from what one genuinely feels is probably a more successful strategy (e.g., smiling despite feeling anxious).

Whether one is trying to protect one's vulnerability, enhance some advantage to oneself, or promote the well-being of another for whom one cares about, being able to monitor one's emotional-expressive behavior strategically is adaptive, and children learn to do so with increasing finesse as they mature (Saarni, 1989). In the following discussion of specific research, this discrepancy between internal subjective feeling and external emotional expression is referred to as *emotional dissemblance*. The term *emotion management* is used to refer to children's regulating their experience of emotion by monitoring their expressive behavior. This last topic is also a significant link to the next section on children's coping with aversive emotions in social contexts.

Types of Emotional Dissemblance

Emotional dissemblance can be divided into two broad categories: the first is more rule driven—that is, there is a fair degree of consensus and predictability in North American middle-class culture about "when, where, and with whom" emotional-expressive behavior is to be managed—and the second is more situation-dependent and tends to occur due to immediate need or expedience (such as avoiding getting into trouble). This second category contains essentially deceptive or situational-strategic expressive maneuvers, which will be addressed later.

The first category includes cultural and personal display rules, which are essentially predictable social customs for how one expresses one's feelings appropriately (Ekman & Friesen, 1975). All cultures have display rules, but obviously they vary considerably in content and application. In contrast to personal display rules, cultural display rules have the added advantage of being generally agreed to by most members of a culture or subculture, and thus they permit smooth, predictable social exchange. As an illustration of cultural display rules, Saarni (1984) conducted a study in which elementary school children were observed trying to monitor their expressive behavior to meet the cultural display rule "Look agreeable when someone gives you a gift, even if you don't like it." The children met individually with an ostensible market researcher, did a small task, and then received candy and money. This first session provided baseline data for what their expressive behavior was upon receiving a desirable gift. A couple of days later they returned to do another task and this time were presented with a grab bag of wrapped gifts. They received a dull and inappropriate baby toy for their effort. The videotapes of their unwrapping the baby toy and having to interact with the market researcher provided the following results: 6-year-old boys were uniformly negative in their expressive behavior; the youngest girls and both boys and girls of 8 and 9 years frequently demonstrated what was categorized as transitional behavior, defined as behavior that was not exactly negative, but the children did not appear to be adopting positive expressive behavior either. The transitional category also contained what might be called socially anxious behaviors such as glancing back and forth between the baby toy and the experimenter, touching one's face here and there, and biting one's lips. These children were aware that they could not just run out of the room (as some of the youngest boys attempted to do), but they also did not have a firm grasp on how to implement the cultural display rule "Look agreeable when you get a gift, even if you don't like it." Thus, they were tense and sought out social guidance, such as when they glanced back and forth between the gift and the experimenter. By contrast, the oldest children

(10–11 years), especially the girls, were most likely to express positive behavior toward the market researcher, despite receiving a dumb baby toy.

Cole (1986) replicated this study with several methodological changes and extended the sample down to age 4 years. She found that across this age span children made an attempt to inhibit negative expressive displays when receiving an undesirable gift (which they had previously rated as indeed undesirable). She also found that a separate sample of 3- to 4-year-old girls smiled when in the presence of the examiner, regardless of the nature of the gift they received, but when the examiner was absent and they received an undesired gift, they did not inhibit their disappointment. This pattern of results was also obtained by Josephs (1994) with German preschool girls. This suggests that it is the *social* context that might be highly important here for understanding what sort of expressive display is revealed rather than an internal emotional state (for theoretical exploration of such effects, see Cappella, 1981; Fridlund, 1991; Zivin, 1985, 1986b).

Cole, Jenkins, and Shott (1989) also examined facial expression control among elementary school-age, congenitally blind children. They found that these children also produced smiles when receiving a disappointing gift from an examiner, despite not being able to observe others' reciprocal expressive behavior. They were more likely than the comparison sighted sample to verbalize the need to deflect attention away from the disappointment by using conversational strategies (e.g., changing the subject).

Garner (1995) also used the disappointing gift paradigm with preschoolers and examined the frequency of positive displays upon receiving the undesirable gift in conjunction with (a) maternal ratings of the child's temperamental dimension of emotional intensity, (b) ratings of the family's expressiveness, and (c) the child's emotion knowledge. She found that higher incidence of positive displays, despite getting a disappointing gift, was associated with lower emotional intensity ratings and report of less sadness in the family and with higher levels of emotion understanding by the child and more report of positive emotion in the family. Girls also produced more positive behavior than boys. Thus, individual differences in adoption of this particular cultural display rule may be due to the combined influence of social-cognitive knowledge, temperament, parental modeling of emotional-expressive behavior, and gender-related socialization.

Personal display rules are often more idiosyncratic, and their function differs from cultural display rules as well.

Whereas the latter is for the sake of predictable and conventional social exchanges, personal display rules function to help one feel as though one is coping more adequately with an emotionally taxing situation. They are strategies that are often understood as coping efforts by others who may know the individual well or who share a similar cultural background. There is virtually no systematic research on children's use of personal display rules in management of their emotional-expressive behavior; however, research on children's coping efforts reviewed in the next section is related.

Direct Deception in Emotional-Expressive Behavior

In addition to cultural and personal display rules, there is also ordinary deceptive emotional-expressive behavior. The key difference here is a relative lack of social consensus or predictability: one deliberately puts on a dissimulated facial expression, tone of voice, and so forth in a *particular and immediate situation* to mislead another about one's emotional experience so as to gain some advantage or to avoid some distinct disadvantage. A fairly large literature has begun to emerge on children's deception in recent years, and although the majority of it examines verbal lies, some studies have also observed children's emotional-expressive behavior while they are lying (e.g., Chandler, Fritz, & Hala, 1989; Feldman, Jenkins, & Popoola, 1979; Josephs, 1993, 1994; Lewis, 1993; Lewis, Stanger, & Sullivan, 1989). As an illustration, a series of studies by Josephs (1994) showed that 4- and 5-year olds were quite capable of deceiving others by adopting misleading expressive behavior, but she found that they did not necessarily articulate this understanding. In other words, these young children demonstrated a tacit or pragmatic understanding of what to do behaviorally, but their verbalized knowledge did not reveal that they "knew what they knew" (or how they behaved).

In one of her studies, Josephs (1993) also determined that the children were capable of concealing a *positive* emotion, which had heretofore not been empirically or systematically examined. The children were seen individually by two research assistants. One assistant left the room, and Josephs arranged for the child to pretend along with the other research assistant that a glass of fruit juice was sweetened juice, when in fact it was quite sour, to trick the first assistant upon her return. While this assistant was out of the room, the children were generally quite gleeful in their *Schadenfreude* (malicious pleasure) in anticipation of the reaction of the assistant upon drinking sour juice. Thus,

they had to conceal their positive emotional-expressive behavior for the ruse to succeed. Josephs found that the children showed many tension-related behaviors (e.g., hands over their mouths, rather obvious attempts to conceal smiles, and incipient giggles) and considerable glancing back and forth between assistants when the deceived assistant returned. However, some smiling did occur, and prolonged eye contact with the deceived assistant seemed to be a common strategy the children used to try to maintain a neutral expression.

Components of Emotional Dissemblance

As summarized by Shennum and Bugental (1982), in North America children gradually acquire *knowledge* about when, where, with whom, and how to express behaviorally their feelings. They also need to have the *ability to control* the skeletal muscles involved in emotional-expressive behavior. They need to have the *motivation* to enact display rules in the appropriate situations. Last, they need to have reached a certain complexity of *cognitive representation*. We will address each of these components in turn.

Knowledge. In an early study, Saarni (1979a) interviewed elementary school children about when and why they would conceal their own feelings of hurt/pain and fear. The majority of their reasons referred to wanting to avoid embarrassment or derision from others for revealing vulnerable feelings. Getting attention, making someone feel sorry for oneself, and getting help were also among the reasons mentioned for dissembling one's emotional-expressive behavior. Significant age differences appeared only when children were questioned about when it would be appropriate to express one's genuine feelings; older children were more likely to cite many more such occasions than younger children, suggesting that the older children (10–11 years) perceived the expression of emotion, whether genuine or dissembled, as a regulated act. The older children were more likely to make reference to the degree of affiliation with an interactant, status differences, and controllability of both emotion and circumstances as contextual qualities that affected the genuine or dissembled display of emotion. However, across all ages, the most common reason cited for when genuine feelings would be expressed was if they were experienced as very intense (and thus less controllable).

More recent research has elaborated on these contextual influences in children's understanding of emotional-expressive behavioral management. Gross and Harris

(1988) determined that 6-year-olds (and even some 4-year-olds) could recognize that others could be misled by adoption of dissembled facial expressions. Underwood, Coie, and Herbsman (1992) found that elementary school children reported that they would be more likely to mask angry expressive behavior with their teachers than with their peers, thus recognizing the salience of authority and possible risk if anger were to be directly expressed. Doubleday, Kovaric, and Dorr (1990) investigated children's understanding of social norms regarding control of expressive behavior; they found that as children matured, their endorsement of such norms increased. These investigators also confirmed that children acquire expression norms as well, consistent with the earlier results of Saarni (1979a) that older children view both dissembled and genuine expressions of emotion as regulated acts.

Meerum Terwogt and Olthof (1989) also reviewed this topic and concluded that older children (age 10) evaluate their emotion from a wider social perspective and can anticipate the impact on others that their expressive display would likely have. Finally, Underwood (1996) found that age differences in reporting dissemblance of emotion varied according to the emotion felt, with older children reporting greater likelihood of masking disappointment and blunting of very positive affect and younger children (age 8) more likely to mask anger. Across emotion, girls expected more negative reactions from peers to "mismanaged" emotional-expressive behavior than boys did, and children generally expected less positive peer response to "extremely honest" emotional displays (see also Saarni, 1988).

Ability to Implement Emotional Dissemblance. Control of skeletal muscles, especially in the face, is critical to being able to modify one's emotional-expressive behavior and thus dissemble the outward expression of one's feelings. Children begin to be able to do this modification voluntarily at a young age (2–3 years), and it is readily apparent in their pretend play; for example, they mimic postures, expressions, vocal qualities, and the like of assorted fantasy characters. However, when it comes to deliberately adopting emotional expressions, posing of facial expressions proves to be difficult, especially negatively toned expressions (e.g., Lewis, Sullivan, & Vasen, 1987; Odom & Lemond, 1972). The difficulty in posing fear, disgust, sadness, and the like may be due to the fairly consistent socialization pressure in our culture to inhibit negative displays of emotion. As Lewis et al. point out, when asked

to produce a scared face, the young children in their sample produced *scary* faces instead.

Motivation. In a study with elementary school children, Saarni (1979b) investigated children's knowledge of how to manage emotional-expressive behavior and their expectations about what motivated story characters to undertake such management strategies. When the children were asked to explain why the character's feelings had not been genuinely expressed, four broad categories of motivation were apparent in their responses:

1. *Avoidance of negative outcomes or enhancement of positive outcomes.* This common motive is well illustrated in a recent study by Davis (1995). She had children play a game in which a desirable prize and an undesirable one were placed in separate, open boxes; the toys inside were visible only to the child. The children were told to deceive the experimenter by pretending to like both prizes, and if they succeeded in "tricking" the experimenter to believe they really liked both, they would be able to keep both prizes. If they did not succeed, then the experimenter took both prizes. Thus, for the children to get the attractive prize, they had to persuasively manage their expressive behavior so as to look positive for both attractive and unattractive prizes. The results showed that the girls were more successful than the boys at suppressing negative expressive behaviors toward the unattractive prize. The girls also revealed a greater number of social monitoring behaviors (e.g., rapid glancing at the experimenter) as well as tension behaviors (e.g., touching one's face), and they appeared to monitor the social exchange more closely than did the boys, which may have facilitated their expression management. Davis concludes that girls do have more ability in managing the expression of their negative feelings, and she suggests that individual differences (e.g., temperament) may interact with gender-role socialization to yield the pattern she observed.

2. *Protection of one's self-esteem.* Illustrative research is discussed by Meerum Terwogt and Olthof (1989), who found that boys were reluctant to express fear because they worried they would be viewed as cowards by their peers. As noted earlier, Fuchs and Thelen (1988) also reported that boys were loathe to reveal their sadness to their fathers but might consider doing so to their mothers. Maintenance of self-image appeared to be the chief motive for these boys, and emotion management was

sought by adoption of a stoic "emotional front." Interestingly, Diener, Sandvik, and Larsen (1985) reported that across the life span, women consistently scored higher than men on self-reported affect intensity. The expressive blunting of vulnerable emotions such as fear and sadness by boys may contribute to this reduced affective intensity.

3. *Maintenance or enhancement of relationships,* that is, concern for others' well-being. As an illustration of this motive for emotional dissemblance, von Salisch (1991) probed how children actually regulated a relationship by monitoring what they expressed. She developed a computer game that was rigged: the computer was cast as the opponent and a pair of children were to play as a team. If the airplane crashed on the screen, it meant the children had lost; in fact, its demise was random but appeared to the children to have been caused by one of them. The participating children were 11 years old, and von Salisch was able to have the pairs consist of either best friends or casual acquaintances. In her analyses of the actual conflict episodes, the most frequent expressive behavior was smiling, followed by signs of tension, then contempt, and finally anger (only 3% of the expressions). In many cases the children also verbalized reproaches about the crash, but then accompanied the reproach by smiling. Between close friends the incidence of smiling was greater than between acquaintances, and between girls in close friend pairs, genuine smiles were especially notable in their reciprocity, even through these girls more frequently verbalized their negative feelings about their friend's game-playing skill (or ostensible lack thereof). The boys in close friendship pairs tended to verbalize less, but they showed more signs of tension than any other group. In essence, these preadolescent boys and girls used their smiles to reassure their friend that the *relationship* was still on firm ground, despite their reproaching their friend for "incompetence" in making them lose the game against the computer. Clearly, expressive behavior has among its functions more than simply the display of emotion; it is also a *social* message. What von Salisch's research shows us is that children are adept at using this social function of emotional-expressive behavior to manage their relationships, and they do so in a discriminating fashion.

4. *Norms and conventions.* These are the cultural display rules that provide us with consensually agreed-upon scripts for how to manage our emotions. Two responses

of 9- to 10-year-old children illustrate their notions of what are norms for emotional dissemblance: "You shouldn't yell at a grown-up" and "You should apologize, even though you don't feel like it." It is probably noteworthy that cultural display rules often have "shoulds" associated with them. At least two factors might account for why children do not consistently perform cultural display rule scripts, despite knowing them: first, the social stakes may not be sufficiently high for them to feel motivated to do so; second, their distressed, hurt, or angry feelings may be experienced as too intense to allow for emotional dissemblance. As mentioned earlier (Saarni, 1979a), intensity of feeling was cited by school-age children as the chief reason for when feelings would be genuinely expressed. The research by Garner (1995) described earlier also indicated that emotional intensity as a temperament factor may influence the likelihood of adopting emotional dissemblance in certain situations.

These four categories for why we may be motivated to dissemble the expression of our feelings are not necessarily exhaustive, but they all have one significant feature in common: they are concerned with interpersonal consequences, and it is the varying nature of these social consequences that yields the differences among motives. Even the self-esteem motive for dissemblance does not occur in a social vacuum, for the self is embedded in a history of social relationships.

Cognitive Representation. As was already suggested by Josephs's (1993) research, a pragmatic or implicit knowledge of emotional dissemblance is likely to precede an articulated and verbalized understanding of expressive dissimulation. Within the theory of mind literature, a large body of research has emerged concerned with children's understanding of real versus apparent phenomena, and this distinction has been applied to inner emotional state as "real" and external expressive behavior as "apparent." By school entry, children generally understand that how one looks on one's face is not necessarily how one feels on the inside (e.g., Harris & Gross, 1988). Thus, relatively young children understand that the appearance of one's facial expression can be misleading about the actual emotional state experienced. By age 6 many children can provide justifications for how appearances can conceal reality, in this case, the genuine emotion felt by an individual. Harris and Gross (1988) examined young children's rationales for why story characters would conceal their emotions by adopting misleading facial expressions. A significant number of the 6-year-olds interviewed gave very complex justifications that included describing the intent to conceal their feelings and to mislead another to believe something other than what was really being emotionally experienced (e.g., "She didn't want her sister to know that she was sad about not going to the party"). Children younger than 6 can readily adopt pretend facial expressions, but they are not likely to be able to articulate the embedded relationships involved in deliberate emotional dissemblance.

These embedded relationships refer to how one wants another to perceive an apparent self, not the real self. In other words, by age 6 children readily grasp that emotional dissemblance has as its basic function the creation of a false impression on others. Because the construct *false impression* seems to have a rather negative connotation, a more useful way to look at this development is to view children as acquiring effective *self-presentations,* which are not false or phony aspects of the self, but rather reveal the degree to which children embrace social interaction with flexibility and resourcefulness as they adapt the range of behaviors available to them in their expressive repertoire to the exigencies of the interpersonal transaction facing them. DePaulo (1991) has provided us with a definitive review of what is known about the development of self-presentation, emphasizing nonverbal behavior. She makes the important point that as children grow older, more of their peers and adult networks hold them accountable for being able to regulate and manage their emotional-expressive behavior. Thus, there is a continual reinforcement of motivation to manage how one presents oneself to others.

Cultural Differences in Emotional Dissemblance

Mesquita and Frijda's (1992) review of cultural variation in emotions suggests that on the most general level most researchers agree that virtually universal is the phenomenon of "response inhibition, or the existence of some measure of emotion and expression control" (p. 198). However, they also state that one of the most significant sources of variation in cultural experience of emotion lies in regulatory processes, whether these are the sort that prohibit certain emotions from being experienced and/or expressed or the sort that prescribe what one should feel and express emotionally under certain circumstances. Thus, on the more specific and descriptive level, cultures vary widely in terms of what one is expected to feel, and when, where, and with whom one may express assorted feelings. In short, folk theories of emotion are as variable as cultures are. To give some

specificity to how these folk theories reveal themselves in children's responses to researchers investigating understanding of misleading expressions and display rules, several studies will be described that were carried out with Japanese, African American, and Indian and English children.

Japanese Children.   Gardner, Harris, Ohmoto, and Hamazaki (1988) evaluated Japanese children's (ages 4–6) understanding of whether facial expressions could be adopted to mislead another about one's real feelings. The instruction was made explicit to the children that what a story protagonist would express would not be congruent with what she felt internally. Similar to results of an earlier study with British children, the 4-year-olds lagged behind the 6-year-olds in understanding that this distinction could be made. Gardner et al. interpreted their findings from the viewpoint common in the appearance-reality literature, which is that young children have a cognitive barrier, as it were, to comprehending simultaneous and mutual incompatibilities or contradictions that co-occur or are contained within the same object or event. It should be pointed out that this study required the children to *verbalize* their understanding; a tacit or pragmatic behavioral enactment of misleading expressions was not investigated (cf., Josephs, 1993).

African American Children.   Underwood, Coie, and Herbsman (1992) examined children's expectations of when to mask expressions of anger in response to videotaped hypothetical vignettes that featured a child interacting with either a teacher or another child. The children were all urban African American children in a low-income neighborhood; they ranged in age from 8 to 13. Children were asked to put themselves in the protagonist's shoes and respond with what they would do. They generally suggested genuine expressions of anger toward peers but were more likely to inhibit the expression of their anger toward teachers. This audience difference makes sense strategically, since teachers have authority over children, and the display of anger toward a peer is not the sort of expression of emotion that renders one vulnerable or "weak." If anything, displaying anger may well facilitate making the impression on one's peers that one is strong or invincible.

An interesting gender effect was also found, namely, that the preadolescent girls were less likely than the boys of the same age to expect themselves to mask anger toward teachers. Underwood et al. speculate that in this American subculture it may be resourceful for boys to present themselves as emotionally "contained" (e.g., stoic, unruffled) and for girls to present themselves as assertive. Underwood et al. also found that children who nominated masking anger also tended to do so if sadness was felt as well; in other words, negative emotions in general were proposed as being likely targets of masking strategies. Last, the investigators thought they would see more usage of display rule reasoning in this sample due to the children's being older than those in other studies, but, in fact, many children preferred genuine displays of anger. Four conditions may be involved here: the nature of the emotion felt (anger); the fact that displaying the anger was not sampled as occurring in close relationships (where it could hurt the feelings of people one cares about); that the intensity of the emotion was not perceived as controllable (and therefore not "maskable"); and there may well be a bias for children to prefer genuine displays of emotion for themselves but to attribute dissembled displays to others (e.g., Karniol & Koren, 1987; Saarni, 1991).

Indian and English Children.   Joshi and MacLean (1994) compared 4- and 6-year old children in Bombay and England on their understanding that expressive behavior need not be congruent with subjectively felt emotion. They systematically varied child-child stories and child-adult stories, since children are more likely to endorse genuine displays of emotion with peers (e.g., see the study by Underwood et al., 1992, mentioned above). More than three times as many 4-year-old Indian girls than English girls endorsed the idea that children would inhibit or use misleading facial expressions to conceal a negative emotion when interacting with an adult. Indian and English boys did not differ. The authors emphasize a socialization interpretation of their findings, describing the sort of intense pressures applied to young Indian girls to adopt deferential and highly regulated decorum in the presence of adults. They also highlight the fact that this early acquisition of understanding that negative emotions are to be concealed from adults, especially by Indian girls, is brought about not by greater concern for the feelings of others but by fear of punishment for acting improperly.

In summary, the ability to maneuver one's emotional-expressive behavior according to interpersonal contexts and how one feels gives one a rich repertoire of communicative behavior. The intermingling of emotional experience and social interaction is also evident in children's acquisition of emotional dissemblance and emotion management

strategies. There are highly adaptive and functional reasons for humans to be able to dissociate their emotional-expressive behavior from their internally felt, subjective emotional experience. One is being able to have reasonably satisfactory relationships with others; another is to be able to get others to provide support and validation for oneself; still another is to exert one's influence on others, as in impression management, persuasive communication, and the like. A reason that children are particularly likely to endorse is that it helps one to avoid getting into trouble, and finally, the omnipresent self-appraisal system has its antennae out to try to create experiences that strengthen or protect the self rather than undermine it. Coping effectively with interpersonal conflict and other situational stressors has much to do with both how we regulate our subjective experience of emotion as well as what we communicate expressively to others. We turn next to this topic.

COPING WITH AVERSIVE EMOTIONS AND DISTRESSING CIRCUMSTANCES

Regulatory Processes

Before we move into the specifics of children's coping skills, we need to define emotion regulation, for being able to modulate one's degree of emotional arousal facilitates one's coping with an environmental stressor or conflict. As will be shown in the discussion of several research studies, both high intensity of feeling and high frequency of negative feelings (i.e., a low threshold for experiencing aversive emotions) appear to be aspects of emotion regulation that interfere with efficacy of coping, especially in the social arena. There appears to be a convergence on a definition of emotion regulation that takes into account (a) temperamental reactivity (Rothbart & Bates, Ch. 3, this Volume; Thompson, 1994); (b) those processes that involve deployment of attention; (c) the components of emotion (physiological, expressive, and subjective experience); and (d) approach/avoidance tendencies, whereby the latter is understood to include individual differences in inhibition (e.g., Thompson, 1990). Brenner and Salovey's (1997) definition of emotion regulation combines these elements: it is the relative capacity to manage one's emotional reactivity (including intensity and duration of arousal) such that alterations in one's physiological-biochemical system, behavioral-expressive system, and experiential-cognitive system are effected. We also add the emphasis of the relational and functionalist perspective, used in this chapter, such that emotional regulatory processes should be understood as occurring within contexts construed as personally meaningful to the individual. Last, optimal emotion regulation also contributes to a sense of well-being or emotional equilibrium, a sense of self-efficacy, and a sense of connectedness to others (see Skinner & Wellborn, 1994, for an elaboration) insofar as effective emotion regulation facilitates constructive problem-solving strategies and appropriate appraisal of context (including its social aspects). Thompson (1990, 1991, 1994) has written comprehensively about emotion and self-regulation, and the reader is referred to his excellent essays for further detail.

Development of Emotion Regulation and Coping

Thompson (1991) has reviewed the maturing emotion regulatory capacities of the infant's nervous system and concluded that during the first year, excitatory and inhibitory processes are stabilized such that infants gradually develop a greater ability to inhibit or minimize the intensity and duration of emotional reactions; at the same time, they also acquire a greater diversity of emotional responses. Examples of early regulation of emotional arousal are young infants' soothing themselves through sucking or withdrawal from excessive stimulation, but equally critical is that caregivers assist infants in learning how to regulate their arousal though attending to their infants' distress and providing comfort (see also J. Campos, Campos, & Barrett, 1989; Casey & Fuller, 1994). Thompson has also argued that parents' emotion regulatory interventions may, over time, contribute significantly to their children's style of emotion regulation. His illustration is that of parents who wait until their child's upset has escalated to high levels before they intervene. The effect is that they reinforce their child's rapid rise time of distress and high intensity of responding, which in turn makes it harder for the parents to soothe their infant due to its high level of emotional arousal.

An extensive literature on emotion regulation has emerged since the last *Handbook of Child Psychology* was published, for example, the reviews by Thompson already cited, Brenner and Salovey (1997), Fox's edited *Monograph* (1994); the special section of *Developmental Psychology* (Dodge, 1989); McCoy and Masters (1990); Meerum Terwogt and Olthof (1989), and others. Many investigators also use the terms *coping* and *emotion regulation* interchangeably, and Brenner and Salovey (1997) explicitly state that "coping is synonymous with emotion regulation; both are processes in which the child uses available strategies to manage stressful encounters." In examining developmental trends in emotion regulation, it makes sense to combine the research findings of coping studies with those of emotion regulation investigations: effective coping is inseparable from effective emotion regulation and vice versa.

Coping research has typically focused on *strategies* used to manage stress-provoking experience. In examining what changes about these coping strategies as children mature, we find that although use of situation-oriented problem solving is accessible throughout childhood, it becomes more targeted to the specific problem at hand, and children's repertoire of problem-solving strategies broadens with age (e.g., Altshuler & Ruble, 1989; Band & Weisz, 1988; Compas, Malcarne, & Fondacaro, 1988). With age, their ability to consider a stressor from a number of different angles increases, and thus older children can more readily consider different problem solutions relative to these different perspectives (Aldwin, 1994). They learn to recruit social support more effectively as well as more subtly, for example, through effective self-presentation strategies that garner social approval. They expand their capacity to tolerate aversive emotion to the degree that appraisal processes can be redirected and thus reduce distress. If appraisal indicates that control over the situational stressor or conflict is minimal or extremely risky, then effective emotional regulation may also involve distraction, cognitively reframing the meaning of the difficult situation, and use of cognitive blunting or sensitizing (Miller & Green, 1985). Denial and dissociation appear to be less adaptive coping strategies, in that emotions are split off from their eliciting context for short-term gain but at long-term expense (see Fischer & Ayoub, 1994, for further discussion of affective splitting).

Finally, perceived control over the stressful situation is relevant to how coping efforts are undertaken (S. Miller & Green, 1985; Skinner, 1991; Skinner & Wellborn, 1994). Cortez and Bugental (1995) found that children primed for self-control in a fear-inducing situation showed enhanced information processing. In an earlier study, Graham, Doubleday, and Guarino (1984) determined that children associated perceived self-control with anger and guilt reactions, in that they saw the causes of these emotions as controllable. As children mature, they become better able to distinguish uncontrollable stressors from controllable ones (Aldwin, 1994); for the uncontrollable situations, older children are more likely to nominate "blunting" coping strategies, which include reframing, distraction, and avoidance through anticipatory planfulness (Hoffner, 1993; Miller & Green, 1985). Younger children's avoidance is more often of the "escape" sort, such as hiding under the bed to avoid an unpleasant event (Aldwin, 1994).

A large literature has developed examining the different coping strategies mentioned above, and for further elaboration, the reader is referred to Aldwin's (1994) volume on stress, coping, and development; Compas, Phares, and Ledoux's (1989) review of coping interventions for children and adolescents; Cramer's (1991) volume on defense processes; Miller and Green's (1985) chapter on coping with stress and frustration; Skinner and Wellborn's (1994) discussion of coping during childhood and adolescence from a motivational perspective; and Sorensen's (1993) text on children's stress and coping using their diaries and artwork.

Brenner and Salovey (1997) propose a framework for the analysis of coping and emotion regulation that includes several key dimensions: (a) the controllability of the stressor, as described above; (b) the degree to which the individual invokes solitary strategies as opposed to socially interactive ones; and (c) the use of internal/intrapsychic strategies as opposed to situational-focused strategies. We elaborate on the dimensions of solitary-social strategies and intrapsychic-situational strategies below as they manifest themselves in children at different developmental stages.

The solitary/social dimension in regulatory strategies is readily illustrated by our use of physical exercise to dissipate tension, frustration, and other dysphoric states. Children soothe themselves with physical activities such as thumb sucking; they also make good use of solitary fantasy play as a regulatory strategy (e.g., Slade & Wolf, 1994). On the other hand, throughout our lives we seek social support (e.g., help, comfort) as a way to cope with stressors and regulate our emotional experience. However, the younger the child, the more likely reliance will be on social support (e.g., see reviews by Cole & Kaslow, 1988; Maccoby, 1983; Rossman, 1992). Young children rely on adults to provide safe environments such that their ability to cope is not overwhelmed (e.g., Thompson, 1991), and caregivers provide direct teaching of coping strategies as well as modeling how to cope (e.g., P. Miller, Kliewer, Hepworth, & Sandler, 1994). Rossman (1992) found that young elementary school-age children (6–7 years) were more likely to cite parents as sources of support, whereas older children were more likely to turn to their peers.

The internal/external dimension becomes more salient in older children's coping and emotion regulation due to their facility to introspect and use metacognition in their understanding of themselves. Meerum Terwogt and Olthof (1989) have reviewed a number of studies that suggested that the cognitive developmental gains of middle childhood facilitated self-reflection, thus permitting children to use more cognitive strategies to render emotional experience less aversive (by using distraction, thinking optimistically, and being able to shift perspectives to allow for more positive appraisals). On the other hand, Harris and Lipian (1989) found what they called "cognitive slippage" in school-age children when dealing with immediate and acute stress, in this case, hospitalization. Compared with unstressed children, the hospitalized children seemed to regress to less mature ways of thinking and understanding cognitive and emotional processes. Compas, Phares, and Ledoux's (1989) review also noted older children's greater ease in using internally focused strategies. Band and Weisz (1988) obtained nominations from 6- to 12-year-olds about what they did to feel better: addressing the problematic situation was used by the children most often when they had control over the circumstances, but noteworthy was the significant increase with age in the use of intrapsychic strategies (e.g., reframing) when control was limited.

A methodological concern is that virtually all of these studies used children's and youths' verbal self-report, which may confound the increased ability to use internally focused strategies with the greater verbal skills that also accompany maturation. It is probable that young children (preschoolers) can also access intrapsychic strategies although they cannot verbalize for us that they are doing so. For example, dissociation is an intrapsychic coping strategy, and it is used by young children as a way of distracting themselves from an intensely stressful situation. It is probably useful when children feel powerless and overwhelmed (e.g., van der Kolk & Fisler, 1994).

Individual Differences in Coping Efficacy

In the subsequent sections concerned with individual differences, we will also address some of the methodological issues facing researchers investigating emotion regulation and coping in children. We have already noted the effect verbal self-report may have on the development of coping strategies such that we may be underestimating younger children's use of intrapsychic regulatory strategies. Other significant methodological influences include source of report (e.g., parents versus teachers), context (e.g., school versus home, mildly stressful encounters versus highly stressful ones that elicit different intensities of emotion, as in the Harris and Lipian [1989] study cited above), and, when the situation is selected by the investigator, the degree of control the individual has in that situation (e.g., relatively low control with aversive medical procedures versus relatively high control with getting one's homework done).

The Influence of Temperament

The notion of temperament is multifaceted and fraught with many definitional and measurement problems (e.g., J. Campos, Campos, & Barrett, 1989; Derryberry & Rothbart, 1988; Goldsmith & Campos, 1982; Rothbart & Bates, Ch. 3, this Volume; Strelau, 1987), but it is a useful construct for thinking about the influences on how children develop different styles of coping. Temperament may be viewed as a collection of dispositions that characterize the individual's style in responding to environmental change (or the lack thereof). These dispositions include reactivity, arousability, and temporal dimensions such as latency of response. Some theorists also include as temperamental traits sociability, approach/avoidance tendencies, and degree of attentional control. Most theorists working with temperament regard these dispositions as applicable to both emotional and nonemotional behavior, and many contend that temperamental dispositions have a biophysiological contribution that is influenced by one's genetic makeup (Strelau, 1987).

When we look at temperament as applied to how a person responds *emotionally* to evocative stimulation, then we can examine the intensity of emotional response (both negative and positive valence), the threshold of arousal of emotional response, the duration (and other temporal aspects) of the emotional response, and even the proclivity for what sort of hedonic tone of emotional response is generated (i.e., negative versus positive reactions to change). The construct *emotionality* has typically been used to refer to temperament's influence on emotional experience; "high" emotionality is often assumed to refer to high intensity of emotional reaction, frequently combined with a negative hedonic tone (but see Strelau's [1987] review of six different definitions of emotionality, some of which do not associate a negative hedonic tone with high levels of emotional intensity of response).

Using temperament in this fairly global fashion as having to do with how we dispositionally tend to modulate our emotional reactions, we can examine how individual differences in temperament may influence coping efficacy. This approach was taken by Eisenberg and her colleagues in several different research projects on preschoolers' coping efficacy relative to their social functioning (e.g., N. Eisenberg & Fabes, 1994; N. Eisenberg, Fabes, Miller, et al., 1990; N. Eisenberg, Fabes, Minore, et al., 1994; N. Eisenberg, Fabes, Murphy, Maszk, Smith, & Karbon, 1995). We will describe three additional studies from Eisenberg's lab in some detail.

In one investigation, Eisenberg, Fabes, Bernzweig, et al. (1993) looked at 4- to 6-year-old children whose emotional intensity level was rated by both their mothers and their teachers and then examined the children's social competence (teacher ratings) and sociometric ratings (peer popularity). They also evaluated the children's coping strategies by having the teachers and mothers rate the children's likelihood of using assorted coping strategies (similar to those previously described) in hypothetical situations. Among their very complex results was that greater social competence of boys (but not girls) could be predicted by their displaying constructive coping strategies (e.g., problem solving) and not displaying excessive negative emotion. For girls, social competence could be predicted from their use of avoidant coping strategies rather than by their engaging in acting out or conflict-escalating behaviors. For both boys and girls, high emotional intensity was associated with lower levels of constructive coping and with lower levels of attentional control (shifting and distractable attention vs. focused attention, as assessed by teachers). In short, those 4- to 6-year-olds who frequently showed high-intensity negative emotions were more likely to be distractable and to demonstrate less constructive coping. They were also regarded by their teachers as less socially mature and by their peers as less attractive as playmates.

In a second study with the same 4- to 6-year-olds, Eisenberg, Fabes, Nyman, Bernzweig, and Pinuelas (1994) investigated relations among temperament (more specifically, emotionality, operationally defined as intensity of reaction and negative tone of emotion), children's ability to control their attention, coping skills, and their management of anger with their peers. The pattern of their findings was complex, with some results occurring only for teacher-rated behaviors but not for mother-rated behaviors. The sex of the child was again a variable that affected some of the patterning of results. Overall, children whose temperament was characterized by low levels of emotionality displayed anger reactions that were socially desirable; that is, the children used nonhostile verbal strategies to try to deal with the anger provocation. This pattern was stronger for boys than girls, and boys who used socially desirable anger responses were also rated as higher in attentional control. Girls who tended to escape the situation when angered were viewed by teachers as socially skilled; that is, the girls' avoidance of anger was apparently seen as not contributing to an escalation of conflict, a desirable outcome from teachers' standpoint. Although the authors were not studying gender-role socialization, it is noteworthy that teachers' approval of sex-typed behaviors (e.g., the girls' avoidance of conflict), even at this relatively young age, may be influencing children's subsequent style of coping with such gender-role-laden emotions as anger.

The last study to be described here is a longitudinal investigation of emotionality and regulation in children's social functioning (N. Eisenberg, Fabes, Murphy, et al., 1996). The children had been assessed when they were preschoolers and again when they were 6 to 8 years of age. Emotionality was again defined by measures of emotional intensity and tendency to experience negative affect (parent and teacher reports). Regulation was defined by measures of attentional control (focusing, shifting) and impulsivity/inhibition; these were also completed by both teachers and parents, as were instruments assessing children's coping styles. The children's vagal tone was also measured as a nonverbal index of regulatory capacity (vagal tone is likely to be suppressed during sustained attention or episodes of "mental effort"; see Porges, 1991). The children's social functioning was evaluated by means of teacher ratings of the children's social skills, popularity, prosocial behavior, and levels of aggression, insecurity, and disruptive behavior. Parent reports were also collected on their children's social functioning by having them rate their children's problem behaviors in social interaction.

These complex data sets were aggregated in various ways, and the results revealed how significant methodological issues are: parental and teacher reports were often uncorrelated; social functioning at school was often unrelated to social functioning at home; and boys and girls had opposite patterns of vagal tone relative to desirable social functioning. Emotional intensity was associated with constructive coping and socially desirable behavior at school (with negative emotionality controlled), whereas negative emotionality, as distinguished from emotional intensity per se, was associated with behavioral problems. However, this pattern was evident only for boys. High attentional control combined with constructive coping as assessed when the

children were preschoolers predicted prosocial behavior in elementary school (teacher ratings only). This difference in context, school versus home, may be due to children's acting differently in the two settings, the different demands for behavioral control in the two settings, and teachers and parents possibly attending to different features of emotionality, coping, attentional control, and social behavior. Last, this study illustrates the importance of taking gender into account. The social meanings attributed to children's behavior by adults are laden with gender-related beliefs, and the children themselves have already been exposed to considerable gender-role socialization. Psychologically oriented ratings reflect this influence and make it difficult to ascertain just what the relations are among temperament, coping, and social functioning.

Although the construct of temperament allows us to consider what children might "inherently" bring with them as they seek to cope with stressful circumstances, it is unlikely that temperament solely affects how constructive one's coping style is. Bear in mind that the social environment has also been modulating and *giving meaning* to the young child's emotional behavior all along, which includes such temperamental dimensions as intensity, hedonic tone, temporal factors, and the like. Cultures that value expressive restraint might ascribe rather different meanings to, for example, intensity of emotional response, than cultures that do not have such an orientation. The point to be made here is that in the long run, adequacy of coping will be best determined by whether individuals experience themselves as efficacious in the sociocultural context in which they find themselves.

Family Influences on Children's Coping

Another possible influence on children's coping strategies is their early attachment experience with significant caregivers. There is relatively little longitudinal research in this area, although provocative retrospective accounts are available that suggest links between quality of attachment in early life with subsequent emotion regulatory "style" (e.g., Kobak & Sceery, 1988; Main, Kaplan, & Cassidy, 1985). Cassidy (1994) has recently theorized how attachment history and emotion regulation may be linked and the reader is referred to her work for further detail; we will provide only a brief summary of her thinking here. She argues that negative emotions such as anger and fear for the securely attached infant come to be associated with maternal sympathetic assistance and that these negative feelings are associated neither with any sort of invalidation of the young child nor with denial of the negative feelings. What this does for emotional regulation is that the young child comes to be able to tolerate aversive emotion temporarily, such that he or she can begin to make sense of the frustrating or conflictful situation that faces him or her and figure out an adaptive coping response.

The anxiously attached infant, on the other hand, has often experienced its caregiver's rejection when it sought comfort for its distress. Such an infant learns that some emotions are not acceptable and maybe not even safe. It develops a wariness and avoidance of its caregiver and begins to regulate its emotions by minimizing their expression when in the presence of the caregiver. Cassidy (1994) cites some studies that indicated that insecurely attached infants interacted responsively with their mothers when *not* distressed or needing care. But when experiencing emotional distress, they ended up suppressing their negative emotional display *so as to maintain* caregiver involvement. In other words, the infant's emotional regulation strategy seems to be "Mom will stay with me if I don't raise any fuss." The cost to the infant, however, is constant emotional vigilance and suppression of normal distress. In short, development of adaptive problem-solving and support-seeking coping strategies may be short-circuited for insecure infants. This is again an area that needs research attention; a recent review on marital conflict and children's emotional security by Davies and Cummings (1994) provides many suggestions for further investigation.

Family Conflict and Dysfunction.   Given the relatively few studies that have tracked quality of attachment to children's subsequent coping competence, the ways that families contribute to individual children's coping competence are far from well understood. There is a larger body of research that has examined the effects of marital conflict and anger on children's functioning, the latter having some links with how well children cope with the aversive feelings that they themselves experience. Cummings and Davies (1994) have reviewed this area, and, not surprisingly, the general conclusion they reach is that many children do not fare well when faced with frequent and intense marital conflict, an outcome echoed in other investigators' work (e.g., Emery, 1988; Grych & Fincham, 1990). If verbal and physical aggression is common between spouses, the boys in particular appear to develop aggressive, externalizing behavior problems. Daughters also demonstrate behavior problems, but more of the girls also show acute distress, which may account for why Vuchinich, Emery,

and Cassidy (1988) found that girls were more likely to intervene in parental conflicts. Angry exchanges between parents are felt by children as very stressful, even when the children play no role in the dispute, and the immediate coping strategies that children bring to bear on such a family crisis probably pivot on the children's perception of controllability of the dispute.

Children growing up with depressed or psychiatrically disturbed parents have also been studied for how such a family environment influences children's emotional and social functioning. Obviously, parental dysfunction co-occurs with higher frequency with other stressful events for children such as divorce, chronic unemployment, and spousal conflict. Goodman, Brogan, Lynch, and Fielding (1993) investigated the socio-emotional functioning of children (5–10 years) who had a depressed mother; the children were subdivided further into three groups: some also had a disturbed father in the home, some were in mother-custody homes, and some had a well father in the home. They also had a comparison sample of children whose mothers and fathers were neither depressed nor psychiatrically disturbed.

Their results indicated that it was the combination of a depressed mother *and* a disturbed father that was associated with the greatest number of problems among *older* children. Apparently, as the children matured, living in an emotionally strained household with two psychiatrically ill parents began to take its toll. Younger children did not yet demonstrate such negative effects. Also reconfirmed in their study were the problematic effects that divorce has on children when living with a depressed parent, particularly on self-regulation variables (e.g., Emery, 1988). Such children tended to be rated as undercontrolled, for example, more often aggressive and impulsive. Children who had a well father and a depressed mother who were still married and living together did not differ from the children of well parents except for being rated by their teachers as somewhat less popular among their peers.

Parenting Style.   Looking at more ordinary families, Hardy, Power, and Jaedicke (1993) examined several parenting variables (supportiveness, structure, and control) and children's coping with "daily hassles." Given the homogeneous middle-class sample, they found that only maternal supportiveness and structure were related to children's coping. Specifically, very supportive mothers in moderately low-structured homes had children who generated more coping strategies across situations; mothers who provided more structure had children who used fewer aggressive coping strategies. Supportive mothers also had children who reported more avoidant coping strategies when the children perceived the stressor as uncontrollable. Hardy et al. concluded that children's coping is multifaceted and that for this age group (9–10 years) distinctive coping styles or patterns were not discernible. However, it is noteworthy that parental supportiveness was found to be significantly related to the breadth of repertoire of coping strategies.

Sex Differences

Some researchers have found sex differences in children's coping strategies, usually in interaction with some other variable, and others have not found significant sex differences. For example, Altshuler and Ruble (1989) found no sex differences across the ages from 5 to 12 in children's nomination of coping strategies for situations involving uncontrollable stress (getting an injection and having a cavity filled). Compas et al. (1988) found that sixth grade girls generated more coping strategies than same-aged boys for dealing with academic and interpersonal problem situations; by the eighth grade the boys had caught up and even slightly exceeded the girls in generating a greater number of coping strategies, but the difference was not significant.

Similar to other research on the *understanding* of emotional and cognitive phenomena, sex does not appear to be a major contributor to differences in children's cognitive construal of how coping or emotional processes work (e.g., Saarni, 1995). However, sex differences frequently appear when adults make ratings of children's coping (see the N. Eisenberg et al. studies described above) and when children's and youths' actual coping behaviors are observed (e.g., Bull & Drotar's [1991] study on children and youth with cancer). In this latter study, girls were more likely to use emotion-focused strategies as a way to cope with pain. Girls' greater use of internalizing processes when emotionally stressed (e.g., worrying, anxiety, self-blame, withdrawal) suggests coping strategies of a distancing or emotionally focused sort (see Rossman, 1992; Zahn-Waxler, Cole, & Barrett, 1991), whereas distressed boys may be more likely to use physical exercise when they feel bad, or they may more often endorse anger expression as a coping strategy (Rossman, 1992).

In their review, Golombok and Fivush (1994) conclude that differential gender-role socialization accounts for much of the gender-linked variation in emotional experience and behaviors, including vulnerability to emotional distress. Brody and Hall (1993), in their review of gender and emotion, similarly conclude that gender-role socialization contributes to gender differences on emotion-related processes, but they also contend that females' superior language skills in early childhood may be a factor that facilitates parents' talking about feelings more with their daughters, with the result that girls attend more and give greater significance to emotional experience. The result for coping competence may well favor girls when they are in uncontrollable circumstances; they may be more able to use emotion-focused strategies at a younger age than boys. Altshuler and Ruble's (1989) research did not confirm this, but their contexts for eliciting *verbal* reports of coping strategies were aversive medical procedures, a rather limited sampling of contexts.

Interestingly, Compas et al.'s (1988) research did reveal that girls more often suggested emotion-focused coping strategies for academic failure than did boys, who more frequently suggested problem-solving coping strategies for academic failure; yet both boys and girls viewed academic failure as relatively more controllable than interpersonally stressful circumstances. If these young adolescent girls are reporting emotion-focused coping strategies for something they also view as comparatively under their control, then one might infer an element of denial, avoidance, or helplessness in such emotion-focused coping strategies. Coping adaptiveness is likely to be compromised when something problematic is under one's control but one acts as though it is not.

Social Maturity Differences

Most of us would conclude that it is not very socially acceptable to beat up someone as a way to solve a dispute, nor is it socially effective to stay in bed all day and weep helplessly about not getting an invitation to a party. Avoidance seems inherently reinforcing: one escapes from something onerous. What incentive is there for acquiring constructive coping strategies other than one's desire to be a decent sort of person? One important incentive is that one's peers will generally like one more if one uses constructive coping strategies, and most children do want to be liked by their peers. As mentioned earlier, N. Eisenberg, Fabes, Bernzweig, et al. (1993) and N. Eisenberg, Fabes, Nyman, et al. (1994) found that children in the age range of 4 to 6 were rated as more socially competent by teachers and also by their peers as more attractive playmates when they used constructive coping strategies (problem solving as opposed to aggression). An earlier study by Richard and Dodge

(1982) with older children (second through fifth grades), who were also all boys, obtained parallel results. In their study of the boys' verbal reports to hypothetical stories, those boys who had been identified by peers and teachers as either aggressive or isolated children were found to generate fewer coping solutions to interpersonal conflicts as compared to boys nominated as cooperative and well liked. All of the boys generated effective coping solutions on the first round, so to speak, but subsequent suggested coping strategies for the aggressive and isolated boys tended to be either aggressive in tone or ineffective. There was no statistical difference between the aggressive and the isolated boys, which seems surprising, since the latter were selected for their shyness and tendency to be alone. There were also no age differences. Thus, the authors' results extend the N. Eisenberg et al. research in further confirming that children who are well liked tend to have broader coping repertoires that include a greater number of effective problem-solving strategies.

Kliewer (1991) obtained rather different results in her study of elementary school-age children. She found that children rated by teachers as socially competent were most likely to endorse using active avoidance of problem situations as a coping strategy. It may be that when teachers rate social competence, they are looking for children who do not give them a lot of trouble in the classroom. Thus, children who do not contribute to any escalation of conflict will tend to be viewed as socially desirable and therefore as competent. Similar to N. Eisenberg et al.'s research, children who were highly emotionally expressive were also rated as using avoidant strategies less often. It appears as though children who are emotionally "in your face" come off as problematic to teachers, or they may be somewhat impulsive in temperament and tend not to weigh solutions to problems as readily as more reflective children might. Similar findings were also reported by Rubin, Coplan, Fox, and Calkins (1995), who determined that preschoolers who were very socially interactive and at the same time were poor emotion regulators were rated by their parents as having externalizing problems, especially disruptiveness.

In a small but intensive study of thirty-eight 5- and 6-year-old children's coping styles and adjustment, Carson, Swanson, Cooney, Gillum, and Cunningham (1992) found that a passive-aggressive style of coping was most often associated with impaired social development. Similarly, impulsive acting out, dependency, externalizing, and internalizing behaviors and ratings were associated with adjustment difficulties. In evaluating the children's exposure

to stressful events in their lives, the authors found some relation between major stress exposure and social adjustment, but what seemed to be more directly linked to the children's social competence was the family's flexibility, support, and confidence in approaching major upheavals. These family variables may have influenced the children's emergent coping repertoire such that more adaptive coping strategies were developed and applied to other sorts of stressors experienced by the children and subsequently assessed in this investigation.

Depressed Children and Coping

Chronically sad children probably have good reason to be sad: an accumulation of losses, disappointments, humiliations, stressors, and conflicted family relationships have taken their toll on their capacity to persist in enduring the onslaught of negative events in their lives. Hopelessness is a key feature of their depression, and while a minority of depressed children and youths are suicidal, those who do attempt suicide do report considerable hopelessness (Asarnow, Carlson, & Guthrie, 1987). Research on depressed children is extensive, and much of that work indicates that depressed children very likely have other concurrent difficulties or disorders (e.g., anxiety disorder, adjustment disorder, conduct disorder, Attention Deficit Hyperactivity Disorder; Asarnow et al., 1987). Thus, it comes as no surprise that depressed children have a variety of difficulties in coping with stressors and with aversive emotions. Relevant to how depressed children cope when confronted by challenging circumstances, we shall briefly describe the research program undertaken by Garber and her associates (Garber, Braafladt, & Zeman, 1991).

In a small-sample study, Garber et al. asked children between the ages of 8 and 17 to nominate what they would do to change an aversive feeling. (Age and sex patterns were not reported, if there were any.) The psychiatric clinic–referred depressed children were more likely to suggest avoidance or negative coping strategies to alter the bad feeling. The nondepressed children, who were seen at a medical clinic, more often reported using problem-focused and active distraction strategies. The depressed children did not differ from the nondepressed in suggesting ways to maintain or prolong positive emotional states; rather, it was when feeling negative emotions that the depressed children appeared to get "locked into" a negative expectancy mode that biased them toward using coping strategies that were more likely to be self-defeating choices. These sorts of ineffective coping behaviors were more likely to have the consequence that the depressed children would find themselves isolated or in trouble with others. Garber et al. also noted that very few children nominated seeking social support for when they were feeling bad, nor did they often report using cognitive reframing strategies, that is, transforming the meaning of the difficult situation mentally, using counterarguments to refute irrational beliefs, and the like.

In summary, as children mature, their growing cognitive sophistication, exposure to varied social models, and breadth of emotional-social experience contribute to their being able to generate more coping solutions to problematic situations. The older they are when faced with severe trauma, the more able they are to see the situation from various perspectives (including those held by other people who may be part of the problematic situation) and figure out a way to resolve it. With maturity, they become more accurate in their appraisals of how much control they really have over the situation and of what risks might accompany taking control of a very difficult situation (e.g., intervening in a fight). Effective coping in Western cultures involves acknowledgment of one's feelings, awareness of oneself as having some degree of agency, and a functional appraisal of the problematic situation and one's role in it. By late childhood or early adolescence, Western children who have enjoyed secure attachment within their supportive families and escaped severe trauma should generally be capable of this sort of emotionally competent coping.

CONCLUSION

Our conclusion will take the form of raising a number of questions and issues for future research and theory development as based on the main sections covered in this chapter: (a) generation of emotion in human development, (b) social referencing, (c) understanding emotion in oneself and in others, (d) the language of emotion, (e) vicarious emotional responsiveness, (f) display of emotion, whether dissembled or genuine, and (g) coping and emotion regulation.

Generation of Emotion

In our opening discussion of culture and emotional development, we raised the issue of adaptation level as a feature of exposure to emotion-eliciting events that can differ across cultures and thus influence the generation of

emotional response. This topic is rich with possibilities for descriptive research as well as more controlled studies. Similarly, the topic of cultural differences in emotional climates as related to differential probabilities of emotion generation in children is worthy of further investigation. As an example, consider how students who come to school from a noncompetitive subcultural emotional climate may exhibit different emotional responses when faced with having to demonstrate academic achievement within a competitive context (instead of being galvanized, they might withdraw).

Another question about the generation of emotion is with regard to self-conscious emotions. The role of the self has been emphasized theoretically and empirically in this chapter, but what other contextual variables might play a significant role in generating shame, pride, guilt, and so forth? An interesting possibility is whether the nature of the emotion-laden signal from someone else (e.g., a scornful tone of voice, a look of contempt) could initiate a shamed response without the shamed individual's ever having felt that a breach of standards occurred or that any action that the individual undertook was his or her fault. Would such emotion-laden signals be more likely to have this shame-generating effect on others if the relationship was significant between them (e.g., such as between a parent and a child)?

The larger question of the conditions under which socially induced affect is likely to occur deserves more attention. We have some studies on contagion, many studies on social referencing, and some recent thought-provoking studies examining naturally occurring dyadic exchanges that suggest a rich dovetailing of emotional responses (e.g., von Salisch, 1991) that appear dependent on the nature of the relationship between the interactants (e.g., close friendship rather than more distant acquaintanceship). From a functionalist/relational standpoint, how does socially induced emotion affect relationships? Some of the research on the effects of troubled marriages on children's peer relationships appears relevant to how to investigate emotion-laden relationship transactions witnessed by children that subsequently influence their extrafamilial social interaction (e.g., Kahen, Katz, & Gottman, 1994).

Social Referencing

Nature of the Social Signal

We do not really know how sensitive infants are at different ages to such cues as their caregivers' respiration, differences in body posture, variation in movement, and so forth. When we examine societies that employ different caregiving routines than Western cultures, such as the use of body slings, we might well find that cues generated by mothers, other than vocal, facial, and gestural behavior, play an important role in infants' early emotional regulation. In these different cultural contexts, infants themselves can also signal their mothers more readily because of mothers' proximity. In addition, an infant carried on the mother's body may not only access more maternal cues to ascertain the emotional meaning of an otherwise ambiguous situation, but the infant's proximity to the mother provides the mother with more immediate and near continuous, albeit subtle, information about her baby's emotional state. These sorts of potentially powerful contextual influences on mother-infant emotion communication are neglected in the artifice of controlled laboratory-based studies on social referencing.

Sensitivity to Context

How does one tell what the emotional display is targeted toward? Young infants may not be that sensitive to emotional-expressive differences between sad and angry displays, but to what extent are they able to figure out when an angry display means to avoid the signaler (because it is Mom who is angry at the baby) as opposed to avoiding the situation (Mom is angrily talking on the phone)? Becoming able to distinguish those cues that differentiate when one is the target of maternal displeasure as opposed to the situation that one is in (or is witnessing) is a critical topic that relates to the *functions* emotion communication has in developing the foundation of emotion meaningfulness. Research reviewed in this chapter suggests that there are lingering sources of confusion for young children about affective processes when their experience includes chronic family conflict and/or abuse (e.g., Cummings & Davies, 1994; Hoffman-Plotkin & Twentyman, 1984; Main & George, 1985). There are profound qualitative contextual differences between witnessing one's parents fight and witnessing one's parent argue with a neighbor, but we are not able to say specifically what the determinants are that contribute to young children's discernment of these differences and thereby regulate themselves accordingly. Their "action tendencies" clearly differ in these two conflict situations by school entry, but data for distinctions such as these are difficult to obtain in infancy and early childhood without creating laboratory contexts utterly divorced from infants' ordinary and meaningful worlds.

Understanding Emotion in Oneself and in Others

Some of the exciting questions for research under this topic also have relevance for clinical application. Specifically, the links between self-conscious emotions and the developmental course of affective disturbance require further study (e.g., shame/depression and shame/rage cycles). Another question regards the role of the self: Is the self-positivity bias found in some of the research reviewed related to self-protective factors, or is it actually reflective of the difference between what children "know" of their cultural folk theory about emotions and what they know about their own considerably richer experience? Media exposure may play a role here as well.

There are also methodological questions to consider. How are our data on children's understanding of their own and others' emotions influenced by (a) verbal self-report versus others' ratings of children, (b) naturalistic versus contrived laboratory observations, (c) interpersonal context effects (e.g., peers vs. adults), and (d) the ever-present issues presented by individual differences? How do these methodological differences affect our theory development about emotion? As an example, Levine's (1995) use of strategic questions and careful interviewing techniques allowed her to determine that children's beliefs about what sort of emotion would be felt in assorted situations were more dependent on their expectations about *goal outcome* than on their learning some stereotyped association that X emotion is paired with Y situation. In short, children apparently use a functional theory of emotion, with goal outcomes being the link with what is expected emotionally.

Language of Emotion

Emotion-Laden Dialogues

Between 1 and 3 years of age, toddlers do a remarkable job of attending to others' emotional-expressive behavior, to their emotion-descriptive conversations and verbal attributions, and to the social consequences of emotional experience. For example, getting a time-out for the first time for an inopportune tantrum at age 2½ can be a compelling learning experience for an otherwise "indulged" youngster, as is hearing a vivid story about one's mother fighting with someone (e.g., Miller & Sperry, 1987). But do we really know what the gradient is that infants move along as they change from "reacting" to others' emotional-expressive signals to engaging in the impressive negotiations of 18-month-olds? As an illustration of children's negotiation skills,

Dunn (1988) cited a delightful dialogue between a toddler and her mother after the child pulled her mother's hair; she was reproached and told not to, but the child insisted "Yes," while smiling. Mother then said, "It's not kind to pull hair, is it?", to which the child responded with "Nice!" Dunn appropriately inferred that these young children appeared to want "to upset their mothers—and to enjoy the consequences of their actions" (p. 17). Dunn noted that during the second year children increased the frequency with which they looked at their parent or caregiver, all the while smiling or laughing as they obviously pursued a forbidden activity. Being able to invite positive overtures by smiling even as one deliberately provokes disciplinary intervention is skillful negotiation indeed. In any case, such exchanges as these suggest considerable and rapid change in the social organization of emotion communication in just a few months. Both experimental and naturalistic studies are needed to describe these significant changes in detail, for they will illuminate our understanding of emotion processes as well as social-communicative development.

Script Linkages

How emotion scripts and other social scripts interact with one another in human development presents a wide-open terrain of interesting research possibilities. We have speculated about the links between gender role and emotion scripts, but other emotion script linkages occur with occupational roles, family roles, roles of those with power and those without power, and so forth. Family systems thinkers, sociologists, and social psychologists have examined the transactions among these belief systems, but developmental psychologists have not systematically examined how these social roles interface with one another and with emotion scripts in the contexts experienced by the developing child. Our hunch is that as children's and youths' social roles expand, they elaborate their beliefs about how emotion works by deepening the contextualization of emotional experience. Social cognitive research on this topic would broaden our understanding of how emotion is integrated by children and youths into the values (or stigma) of the roles they assume.

Vicarious Emotional Responsiveness

It is intuitively appealing to view the infant-parent attachment relationship as the basis for children's developing empathic and sympathetic responsiveness to others in distress (e.g., Zahn-Waxler, 1991). But research by N. Eisenberg and her colleagues (Eisenberg, Fabes, Minore, et al.,

1994) suggests that this may be moderated by a disposition to experience over-arousal, and thus personal distress is elicited in an otherwise sympathy-eliciting situation. Research that examines early and enduring family dynamics in conjunction with variables such as temperament and gender-role socialization would help us to understand better the development of sympathy and its concomitant prosocial action.

Another vexing question has to do with what variables come into play such that children and youths who demonstrate emotional responsiveness with their in-group members will turn around and experience little emotional responsiveness to those outside their group. Obvious examples include the violent confrontations between gangs, but how does one explain young children ganging up on another child who is simply vulnerable? What processes and incentives for dehumanization occur such that empathy is short-circuited? Possible sociobiological explanations and the function played by the presence of a group need to be accompanied by detailed contextual analyses for us to better understand this failure of empathy.

Display of Emotion

Several research issues will be described here. First, there is little systematic research on children's use of personal display rules for coping with aversive circumstances by managing their expressive displays in a strategic fashion. Second, if children adopt a dissembled emotional-expressive display and it results in efficacious outcomes for them (e.g., their status is enhanced as a result of their confident self-presentation, despite their having felt quite nervous), how is their subjective emotional experience thereby changed? Will the change endure when they face similar encounters? Anecdotal report suggests that parents urge their children to take risks with their emotional vulnerability, especially with their peers but also in the performance and achievement domain, and to try to conceal their anxiety so that they can succeed in whatever the endeavor is. But how does this affect children the next time they face similar challenges to their self-esteem?

Related questions concern how intensity of felt emotion might be influenced by habitual suppression of particular emotions. As an example, if boys tend to be socialized to mask feelings of vulnerability and are reinforced for adopting stoic "emotional fronts," what happens over time to their sensitivity toward feeling these vulnerable emotions or being able to acknowledge them? Similarly, how does membership in a particular group (e.g., a gang) contribute to chronic masking of "group-dystonic" emotions, thereby dampening one's conscious awareness of these feelings (e.g., fear, sympathy toward those outside one's group)?

Finally, the influence of individual differences in displays of emotional-expressive behavior is very great, and many descriptive studies could be undertaken to flesh out our knowledge of these differences and how they influence emotional-social communication. Differences in self-presentation strategies or impression management are also underresearched from a developmental standpoint. Cultural influence is assumed, but how exactly does it manifest itself? Especially intriguing for culturally diverse societies is the question of how members of subcultures apply display rules when with people from other subcultures. Studying bicultural individuals might be most revealing as to how one cultivates "expressive display style-switching."

Coping and Emotion Regulation

Given that most of the research on "mental" or internally focused coping strategies relies on verbal self-report from school-age children, we may be underestimating younger children's use of intrapsychic ways of regulating their emotion in aversive circumstances. We have some clinical resources available that suggest the sorts of defenses young children employ (e.g., denial, dissociation), but might there be other strategies, perhaps something like a "proto-reframing" that young children access as a way of redefining the situation for themselves? How would we empirically investigate this without subjecting young children to unwarranted stress? The collision of ethics and research on children's coping is a familiar one.

Contextual influence is very great in investigations of coping and emotion regulation: *Who* is the source of the data (e.g., parents vs. teachers), *where* are the data collected (e.g., home vs. school), *what* is the intensity of the emotion felt by children that is the focus of coping and/or regulation, and *how* much control over the circumstances do children believe they have (accurately or inaccurately)? To complicate things further, the influence of such social categories as gender affect all of the above contextual influences. We do not know the influence of other important social categories such as ethnic identity and immigration status on coping and emotion regulation; these latter two social categories may also interact with the likelihood of economic distress in children's families, which, in turn, may influence the degree of perceived control poor children believe themselves to have.

More research is needed (especially longitudinal studies) on the influence of family dynamics on children's coping competence. Particularly needed are studies that track dysfunctional families receiving supportive interventions and then assess the coping skills of the children affected by these interventions. If parents learn to become more effective parents, do their children's coping skills eventually expand in variety, become more targeted to the problem at hand, and provide a greater sense of well-being to the children? This is one of the central questions facing social programs that focus on family maintenance or family preservation (e.g., Behrman, 1993), especially where the programs strive to reduce intergenerational transmission of dysfunctional parenting and emotional disturbance.

The questions for future research suggested here are simply a sample of those to be considered. Given our functionalist perspective, our proposed research questions emphasize context, goals, and the embeddedness of emotion in interpersonal transactions. Obvious omissions include psychophysiological questions about emotional development, which are many, but beyond the scope of this chapter. The field of emotional development has expanded tremendously in the years since the last *Handbook of Child Psychology* chapter on emotional development was published. We anticipate not only continued interest in basic research in emotional development but also an increasing dual focus on applied or clinical outcomes and theories of emotional development.

ACKNOWLEDGMENTS

We gratefully acknowledge the assistance in the preparation of this chapter of Dr. Rosemary Campos, Dr. Chen Hong Tu, and Amy Brotman. Part of the chapter was written while the third author was a Fellow at the Center for Advanced Study in the Behavioral Sciences. He is grateful for the support of grants from the John D. and Catherine T. MacArthur Foundation (grant number 8900078) and the National Science Foundation (grant number SBR-9022192).

REFERENCES

Abbott, S. (1992). Holding on and pushing away: Comparative perspectives on an eastern Kentucky child-rearing practice. *Ethos, 20,* 33–65.

Abelson, R. P. (1981). Psychological status of the script concept. *American Psychologist, 36,* 715–729.

Adolph, K. E., Eppler, M. A., & Gibson, E. J. (1993). Development of perception of affordances. In C. Rovee-Collier & L. Lipsitt (Eds.), *Advances in infancy research* (Vol. 8, pp. 50–97). Norwood, NJ: ABLEX.

Ainsworth, M., Blehar, M., Waters, E., & Wall, S. (1978). *Patterns of attachment.* Hillsdale, NJ: Erlbaum.

Aldwin, C. (1994). *Stress, coping, and development.* New York: Guilford Press.

Altshuler, J., & Ruble, D. (1989). Developmental changes in children's awareness of strategies for coping with uncontrollable stress. *Child Development, 60,* 1337–1349.

Asarnow, J., Carlson, G., & Guthrie, D. (1987). Coping strategies, self-perceptions, hopelessness, and perceived family environments in depressed and suicidal children. *Journal of Consulting and Clinical Psychology, 55,* 361–366.

Baldwin, D. A., & Moses, L. J. (1994). Early understanding of referential intent and attentional focus: Evidence from language and emotion. In C. Lewis & P. Mitchell (Eds.), *Children's early understanding of mind* (pp. 133–156). Hillsdale, NJ: Erlbaum.

Baldwin, D. A., & Moses, L. J. (1996). The ontogeny of social information gathering. *Child Development, 67,* 1915–1939.

Band, E., & Weisz, J. (1988). How to feel better when it feels bad: Children's perspectives on coping with everyday stress. *Developmental Psychology, 24,* 247–253.

Banks, M., & Salapatek, P. (1983). Infant visual perception. In P. Mussen (Series Ed.) & M. Haith & J. Campos (Vol. Eds.), *Handbook of child psychology: Vol. 2. Infancy and developmental psychobiology* (4th ed., pp. 435–571). New York: Wiley.

Barden, R. C., Zelko, F., Duncan, S. W., & Masters, J. C. (1980). Children's consensual knowledge about the experiential determinants of emotion. *Journal of Personality and Social Psychology, 39,* 968–976.

Barrett, K., & Campos, J. (1987). Perspectives on emotional development: II. A functionalist approach to emotions. In J. Osofsky (Ed.), *Handbook of infant development* (2nd ed., pp. 555–578). New York: Wiley.

Behrman, R. (Ed.). (1993). *Home visiting: The future of children, 3.* Los Altos, CA: David and Lucille Packard Foundation.

Bertenthal, B., & Campos, J. (1990). A systems approach to the organizing effects of self-produced locomotion during infancy. In C. Rovee-Collier & L. Lipsitt (Eds.), *Advances in infancy research* (pp. 2–60). Hillsdale, NJ: Erlbaum.

Bertenthal, B., Campos, J., & Barrett, K. (1984). Self-produced locomotion: An organizer of emotional, cognitive, and social development in infancy. In R. Emde & R. Harmon (Eds.), *Continuities and discontinuities in development* (pp. 175–210). New York: Plenum Press.

Biringen, Z., Emde, R., Campos, J., & Appelbaum, M. (1995). Affective reorganization in the infant, the mother, and the dyad. *Child Development, 66,* 499–514.

Bischof, N. (1975). A systems approach toward the functional connections of attachment and fear. *Child Development, 46,* 801–817.

Blass, E., & Ciaramitaro, V. (1994). A new look at some old mechanisms in human newborns. *Monographs of the Society for Research in Child Development, 59*(Serial No. 239).

Bloch, A. (1966). The Kurdistani cradle story. *Clinical Pediatrics, 5,* 641–645.

Blurton-Jones, N. (1967). An ethological study of some aspects of social behaviour of children in nursery school. In D. Morris (Ed.), *Primate ethology.* London: Weidenfeld and Nicolson.

Boccia, M., & Campos, J. J. (1989). Maternal emotional signals, social referencing, and infants' reactions to strangers. In N. Eisenberg (Ed.), *New directions for child development* (Vol. 44, pp. 25–49). San Francisco: Jossey-Bass.

Bowlby, J. (1969). *Attachment and loss: Vol. 1. Attachment.* New York: Basic Books.

Bowlby, J. (1972). *Attachment and loss: Vol. 2. Separation.* New York: Basic Books.

Brenner, E., & Salovey, P. (1997). Emotion regulation during childhood: Developmental, interpersonal, and individual considerations. In P. Salovey & D. Sluyter (Eds.), *Emotional literacy and emotional development* (pp. 168–192). New York: Basic Books.

Bretherton, I. (1985). Attachment theory: Retrospect and prospect. In I. Bretherton & E. Waters (Eds.), Growing points in attachment theory and research. *Monographs of the Society for Research in Child Development, 50*(1/2, Serial No. 209).

Bretherton, I., Fritz, J., Zahn-Waxler, C., & Ridgeway, D. (1986). Learning to talk about emotions: A functionalist perspective. *Child Development, 57,* 529–548.

Briggs, J. (1970). *Never in anger.* Cambridge, MA: Harvard University Press.

Brody, L., & Hall, J. (1993). Gender and emotion. In M. Lewis & J. Haviland (Eds.), *Handbook of emotions* (pp. 447–460). New York: Guilford Press.

Bronson, G. (1972). Infants' reactions to unfamiliar persons and novel objects. *Monographs of the Society for Research in Child Development, 37*(Serial No. 148).

Brown, J. R., & Dunn, J. (1991). "You can cry, mum": The social and developmental implications of talk about internal states. *British Journal of Developmental Psychology, 9,* 237–256.

Buhler, C. (1930). *The first year of life.* New York: John Day.

Bull, B., & Drotar, D. (1991). Coping with cancer in remission: Stressors and strategies reported by children and adolescents. *Journal of Pediatric Psychology, 16,* 767–782.

Butterworth, G., & Grover, L. (1988). The origins of referential communication in human infancy. In L. Weiskrantz (Ed.), *Thought without language* (pp. 5–24). Oxford, England: Clarendon Press.

Campos, J. (1994, Spring). The new functionalism in emotion. *SRCD Newsletter.*

Campos, J., Barrett, K. C., Lamb, M. E., Goldsmith, H. H., & Stenberg, C. (1983). Socioemotional development. In P. H. Mussen (Series Ed.) & M. Haith & J. Campos (Vol. Eds.), *Handbook of child development: Vol. 2. Infancy and developmental psychobiology* (4th ed., pp. 435–571). New York: Wiley.

Campos, J., Bertenthal, B., & Kermoian, R. (1992). Early experience and emotional development: The emergence of wariness of heights. *Psychological Science, 3,* 61–64.

Campos, J., Campos, R., & Barrett, K. (1989). Emergent themes in the study of emotional development and emotion regulation. *Developmental Psychology, 25,* 394–402.

Campos, J., Hiatt, S., Ramsay, D., Henderson, C., & Svejda, M. (1978). The emergence of fear on the visual cliff. In M. Lewis & L. Rosenblum (Eds.), *The origins of affect.* New York: Wiley.

Campos, J., Kermoian, R., & Witherington, D. (1996). An epigenetic perspective on emotional development. In R. Kavanaugh, B. Zimmerberg, & S. Fein (Eds.), *Emotion: Interdisciplinary perspectives* (pp. 119–138). Hillsdale, NJ: Erlbaum.

Campos, J., Kermoian, R., Witherington, D., Chen, H., & Dong, Q. (in press). Activity, attention, and developmental transitions in infancy. In P. Lang & M. Balaban (Eds.), *Attention and orienting: Sensory and motivational processes.* Hillsdale, NJ: Erlbaum.

Campos, J., Kermoian, R., & Zumbahlen, M. (1992). Socioemotional transformations in the family following infant crawling onset. In N. Eisenberg & R. Fabes (Eds.), *New directions in child development: Emotion and its regulation in early development* (Vol. 5, pp. 25–40). San Francisco: Jossey-Bass.

Campos, J., Mumme, D., Kermoian, R., & Campos, R. (1994). A functionalist perspective on the nature of emotion. In N. Fox (Ed.), The development of emotion regulation: Biological and behavioral considerations. *Monographs of the Society for Research in Child Development, 59*(2/3, Serial No. 240).

Campos, J., & Stenberg, C. R. (1981). Perception, appraisal and emotion: The onset of social referencing. In M. E. Lamb & L. R. Sherrod (Eds.), *Infant social cognition: Empirical and theoretical considerations* (pp. 274–313). Hillsdale, NJ: Erlbaum.

Camras, L. A. (1991). Conceptualizing early infant affect: View II and reply. In K. Strongman (Ed.), *International review of studies on emotion* (Vol. 1, pp. 16–28, 33–36). New York: Wiley.

Camras, L. A. (1992). Expressive development and basic emotions. *Cognition and Emotion, 6,* 267–283.

Camras, L. A., Grow, G., & Ribordy, S. C. (1983). Recognition of emotional expressions by abused children. *Journal of Clinical and Child Psychology, 12,* 325–328.

Camras, L. A., Oster, H., Campos, J., Miyake, K., & Bradshaw, D. (1992). Japanese and American infants' responses to arm restraint. *Developmental Psychology, 28,* 578–583.

Camras, L. A., & Sachs, V. B. (1991). Social referencing and caretaker expressive behavior in a day care setting. *Infant Behavior and Development, 14,* 27–36.

Cappella, J. (1981). Mutual influence in expressive behavior: Adult-adult and infant-adult dyadic interaction. *Psychological Bulletin, 89,* 101–132.

Caron, A. J., Caron, R. F., & MacLean, D. J. (1988). Infant discrimination of naturalistic emotional expressions: The role of face and voice. *Child Development, 59,* 604–616.

Caron, R. F., Caron, A. J., & Myers, R. S. (1982). Abstraction of invariant face expressions in infancy. *Child Development, 53,* 1008–1015.

Carson, D., Swanson, D., Cooney, M., Gillum, B., & Cunningham, D. (1992). Stress and coping as predictors of young children's development and adjustment. *Child Study Journal, 22,* 273–302.

Casey, R., & Fuller, L. (1994). Maternal regulation of children's emotions. *Journal of Nonverbal Behavior, 18,* 57–89.

Cassidy J. (1994). Emotion regulation: Influences of attachment relationships. In N. Fox (Ed.), The development of emotion regulation: Biological and behavioral considerations. *Monographs of the Society for Research in Child Development, 59*(2/3, Serial No. 240), 228–249.

Cassidy, J., Parke, R., Butkovsky, L., & Braungart, J. (1992). Family-peer connections: The roles of emotional expressiveness within the family and children's understanding of emotions. *Child Development, 63,* 603–618.

Chandler, M., Fritz, A., & Hala, S. (1989). Small-scale deceit: Deception as a marker of two-, three-, and four-year-olds' early theories of mind. *Child Development, 60,* 1263–1277.

Chisholm, J. S. (1983). *Navajo infancy.* New York: Aldine.

Chisholm, J. S. (1989). Biology, culture and the development of temperament: A Navajo example. In J. K. Nugent, B. M. Lester, & T. B. Brazelton (Eds.), *The cultural context of infancy: Vol. 1. Biology, culture, and infant development* (pp. 341–364). Norwood, NJ: ABLEX.

Coates, B., Anderson, E., & Hartup, W. (1972). Interrelations in the attachment behavior of human infants. *Developmental Psychology, 6* 218–237.

Cohen, L., & Campos, J. (1974). Father, mother and stranger as elicitors of attachment behaviors in infancy. *Developmental Psychology, 10,* 146–154.

Cohn, J. F., & Tronick, E. Z. (1987). Mother-infant face-to-face interaction: The sequence of dyadic states at 3, 6, and 9 months. *Developmental Psychology, 23,* 68–77.

Cole, P. (1986). Children's spontaneous control of facial expression. *Child Development, 57,* 1309–1321.

Cole, P., Jenkins, P., & Shott, C. (1989). Spontaneous expressive control in blind and sighted children. *Child Development, 60,* 683–688.

Cole, P., & Kaslow, N. (1988). Interactional and cognitive strategies for affect regulation: Developmental perspective on childhood depression. In L. Alloy (Ed.), *Cognitive processes in depression* (pp. 310–343). New York: Guilford Press.

Compas, B., Malcarne, V., & Fondacaro, K. (1988). Coping with stressful events in older children and young adolescents. *Journal of Consulting and Clinical Psychology, 56,* 405–411.

Compas, B., Phares, V., & Ledoux, N. (1989). Stress and coping preventive interventions for children and adolescents. In L. Bond & B. Compas (Eds.), *Primary prevention and promotion in the schools* (pp. 319–340). London: Sage.

Corkum, V., & Moore, C. (1995). Development of joint visual attention infants. In C. Moore & P. Dunham (Eds.), *Joint attention: Its origins and role in development*. Hillsdale, NJ: Erlbaum.

Cortez, V., & Bugental, D. (1995). Priming of perceived control in young children as a buffer against fear-inducing events. *Child Development, 66,* 687–696.

Covell, K., & Abramovitch, R. (1987). Understanding emotion in the family: Children's and parents' attributions of happiness, sadness, and anger. *Child Development, 58,* 985–991.

Cramer, P. (1991). *The development of defense mechanisms.* New York: Springer-Verlag.

Cummings, E. M., Ballard, M., & El-Sheikh, M. (1991). Responses of children and adolescents to interadult anger as a function of gender, age, and mode of expression. *Merrill-Palmer Quarterly, 37,* 543–560.

Cummings, E. M., & Davies, P. (1994). *Children and marital conflict.* New York: Guilford Press.

Cummings, E. M., Vogel, D., Cummings, J. S., & El-Sheikh, M. (1989). Children's responses to different forms of expression of anger between adults. *Child Development, 60,* 1392–1404.

Cummings, E. M., Zahn-Waxler, C., & Radke-Yarrow, M. (1981). Young children's responses to expressions of anger and affection by others in the family. *Child Development, 52,* 1274–1282.

Custrini, R., & Feldman, R. S. (1989). Children's social competence and nonverbal encoding and decoding of emotion. *Journal of Child Clinical Psychology, 18,* 336–342.

Damasio, A. (1994). *Descartes' error: Emotion, reason, and the human brain.* New York: Grosset & Dunlap.

D'Andrade, R. (1984). Cultural meaning systems. In R. Shweder & R. LeVine (Eds.), *Culture theory: Essays on mind, self, and emotion* (pp. 88–119). New York: Cambridge University Press.

D'Andrade, R. (1987). A folk model of the mind. In D. Holland & N. Quinn (Eds.), *Cultural models in language and thought* (pp. 112–148). New York: Cambridge University Press.

Davies, P., & Cummings, M. (1994). Marital conflict and child adjustment: An emotional security hypothesis. *Psychological Bulletin, 116,* 387–411.

Davis, T. (1995). Gender differences in masking negative emotions: Ability or motivation? *Developmental Psychology, 31,* 660–667.

Dawson, G., Hessl, D., & Frey, K. (1994). Social influences on early developing biological and behavioral systems related to risk for affective disorder. *Development and Psychopathology, 5,* 759–779.

DeCasper, W., & Fifer, W. (1980). Of human bonding: Newborns prefer their mothers' voices. *Science, 208,* 1174–1176.

DeCasper, W., Lecanuet, J.-P., Busnel, M.-C., & Granier-Deferre, C., & Maugeais, K. (1994). Fetal reactions to recurrent maternal speech. *Infant Behavior and Development, 17,* 159–164.

Denham, S., & Auerbach, S. (1995). *Mother-child dialogue about emotions and preschoolers' emotional competence.* Paper presented at the biennial meeting of the Society for Research in Child Development, Indianapolis, IN.

Denham, S., Cook, M., & Zoller, D. (1992). "Baby looks very sad": Implications of conversations about feelings between mother and preschooler. *British Journal of Developmental Psychology, 10,* 301–315.

Denham, S., McKinley, M., Couchoud, E., & Holt, R. (1990). Emotional and behavioral predictors of preschool peer ratings. *Child Development, 61,* 1145–1152.

DePaulo, B. (1991). Nonverbal behavior and self-presentation: A developmental perspective. In R. S. Feldman & B. Rime (Eds.), *Fundamentals of nonverbal behavior* (pp. 351–397). New York: Cambridge University Press.

Derryberry, D., & Rothbart, M. (1988). Arousal, affect, and attention as components of temperament. *Journal of Personality and Social Psychology, 55,* 958–966.

Dewey, J. (1894). The theory of emotion: I. Emotional attitudes. *Psychological Review, 1,* 553–569.

Dewey, J. (1895), The theory of emotion: II. The significance of emotions. *Psychological Review, 2,* 13–32.

Dewey, J. (1934). *Art as experience.* New York: Minton, Balch.

Diener, E., Sandvik, E., & Larsen, R. (1985). Age and sex effects for affect intensity. *Developmental Psychology, 21,* 542–546.

Dodge, K. (1989). Coordinating responses to aversive stimuli: Introduction to a special section on the development of emotion regulation. *Developmental Psychology, 25,* 339–342.

Donaldson, S. K., & Westerman, M. A. (1986). Development of children's understanding of ambivalence and causal theories of emotion. *Developmental Psychology, 22,* 655–662.

Doubleday, C., Kovaric, P., & Dorr, A. (1990). *Children's knowledge of display rules for emotional expression and control.* Paper presented at the annual meeting of the American Psychological Association, Washington, DC.

Downey, G., & Coyne, J. C. (1990). Children of depressed parents: An integrative review. *Psychological Bulletin, 108,* 50–76.

Dunn, J. (1988). *The beginnings of social understanding.* Cambridge, MA: Harvard University Press.

Dunn, J., Bretherton, I., & Munn, P. (1987). Conversations about feeling states between mothers and their young children. *Developmental Psychology, 23,* 132–139.

Dunn, J., & Brown, J. (1991). Relationships, talk about feelings, and the development of affect regulation in early childhood. In J. Garber & K. Dodge (Eds.), *The development of emotion regulation and dysregulation* (pp. 89–108). Cambridge, England: Cambridge University Press.

Dunn, J., & Brown, J. (1994). Affect expression in the family, children's understanding of emotions, and their interactions with others. *Merrill-Palmer Quarterly, 40,* 120–137.

Dunn, J., Brown, J., & Beardsall, L. (1991). Family talk about feeling states and children's later understanding of others' emotions. *Developmental Psychology, 27,* 448–455.

Duval, S., & Wicklund, R. (1972). *A theory of objective self-awareness.* New York: Academic Press.

Dweck, C., & Leggett, E. (1988). A social-cognitive approach to motivation and personality. *Psychological Review, 95,* 256–273.

Edwards, R., Manstead, A., & MacDonald, C. J. (1984). The relationship between children's sociometric status and ability to recognize facial expressions of emotion. *European Journal of Social Psychology, 14,* 235–238.

Egeland, B., Jacobvitz, D., & Sroufe, A. (1988). Breaking the cycle of abuse. *Child Development, 59,* 1080–1088.

Eisenberg, A. R. (1986). Teasing: Verbal play in two Mexicano homes. In B. B. Schieffelin & E. Ochs (Eds.), *Language socialization across cultures* (pp. 182–198). Cambridge, England: Cambridge University Press.

Eisenberg, N., & Fabes, R. (1990). Empathy: Conceptualization, assessment, and relation to prosocial behavior. *Motivation and Emotion, 14,* 131–149.

Eisenberg, N., & Fabes, R. (1992). Emotion, regulation, and the development of social competence. In M. S. Clark (Ed.), *Emotion and social behavior: Vol. 14. Review of personality and social psychology* (pp. 119–150). Newbury Park, CA: Sage.

Eisenberg, N., & Fabes, R. (1995). The relation of young children's vicarious emotional responding to social competence, regulation, and emotionality. *Cognition and Emotion, 9,* 203–228.

Eisenberg, N., Fabes, R., Bernzweig, J., Karbon, M., Poulin, R., & Hanish, L. (1993). The relations of emotionality and regulation to preschoolers' social skills and sociometric status. *Child Development, 64,* 1418–1438.

Eisenberg, N., Fabes, R., Bustamante, D., Mathy, R., Miller, P., & Lindholm, E. (1988). Differentiation of vicariously induced emotional reactions in children. *Developmental Psychology, 24,* 237–246.

Eisenberg, N., Fabes, R., Carlo, G., & Karbon, M. (1992). Emotional responsivity to others: Behavioral correlates and socialization antecedents. In N. Eisenberg & R. Fabes (Eds.), *New directions in child development: Emotion and its regulation in early development* (Vol. 5, pp. 57–73). San Francisco: Jossey-Bass.

Eisenberg, N., Fabes, R., Carlo, G., Troyer, D., Speer, A., Karbon, M., & Switzer, G. (1992). The relations of maternal practices and characteristics to children's vicarious emotional responsiveness. *Child Development, 63,* 583–602.

Eisenberg, N., Fabes, R., Miller, P., Shell, C., Shea, R., & May-Plumlee, T. (1990). Preschoolers' vicarious emotional responding and their situational and dispositional prosocial behavior. *Merrill-Palmer Quarterly, 36,* 507–529.

Eisenberg, N., Fabes, R., Minore, D., Mathy, R., Hanish, L., & Brown, T. (1994). Children's enacted interpersonal strategies: Their relations to social behavior and negative emotionality. *Merrill-Palmer Quarterly, 40,* 212–232.

Eisenberg, N., Fabes, R., Murphy, B., Karbon, M., Smith, M., & Maszk, P. (1996). The relations of children's dispositional empathy-related responding to their emotionality, regulation, and social functioning. *Developmental Psychology, 32,* 195–209.

Eisenberg, N., Fabes, R., Murphy, B., Maszk, P., Smith, M., & Karbon, M. (1995). The role of emotionality and regulation in children's social functioning: A longitudinal study. *Child Development, 66,* 1360–1384.

Eisenberg, N., Fabes, R., Nyman, M., Bernzweig, J., & Pinuelas, A. (1994). The relations of emotionality and regulation to children's anger-related reactions. *Child Development, 65,* 109–128.

Eisenberg, N., Fabes, R., Schaller, M., Carlo, G., & Miller, P. A. (1991). The relations of parental characteristics and practices to children's vicarious emotional responding. *Child Development, 62,* 1393–1408.

Eisenberg, N., Fabes, R., Schaller, M., Miller, P. A., Carlo, G., Poulin, R., Shea, C., & Shell, R. (1991). Personality and socialization correlates of vicarious emotional responding. *Journal of Personality and Social Psychology, 61,* 459–470.

Eisenberg, N., & Lennon, R. (1983). Sex differences in empathy and related capacities. *Psychological Bulletin, 94,* 100–131.

Eisenberg, N., & McNally, S. (1993). Socialization and mothers' and adolescents' empathy-related characteristics. *Journal of Research on Adolescence, 3,* 171–191.

Eisenberg, N., & Miller, P. (1987). The relation of empathy to prosocial and related behaviors. *Psychological Bulletin, 101,* 91–119.

Eisenberg, N., Schaller, M., Fabes, R., Bustamante, D., Mathy, R., Shell, R., & Rhodes, K. (1988). Differentiation of personal distress and sympathy in children and adults. *Developmental Psychology, 24,* 766–775.

Eisenberg, N., & Strayer, J., (Eds.). (1987). *Empathy and its development.* Cambridge, England: Cambridge University Press.

Ekman, P. (1965). Communication through nonverbal behavior: A source of information about an interpersonal relationship. In S. S. Tomkins & C. Izard (Eds.), *Affect, cognition, and personality.* New York: Springer.

Ekman, P. (1973). *Darwin and facial expression.* New York: Academic Press.

Ekman, P. (1995). Strong evidence for universals in facial expressions: A reply to Russell's mistaken critique. *Psychological Bulletin, 115,* 268–287.

Ekman, P., Davidson, R., & Friesen, W. (1990). The Duchenne smile: Emotional expression and brain physiology II. *Journal of Personality and Social Psychology, 58,* 342–353.

Ekman, P., & Friesen, W. V. (1975). *Unmasking the face.* Englewood Cliffs, NJ: Prentice-Hall.

Ekman, P., Levenson, R. W., & Friesen. W. V. (1983). Autonomic nervous activity distinguishes between emotions. *Science, 221,* 1208–1210.

Ekman, P., Sorensen, E., & Friesen, W. (1969). Pan-cultural elements in the facial expression of emotion. *Science, 164,* 86–88.

Emde, R., Gaensbauer, T., & Harmon, R. (1976). *Emotional expression in infancy: A biobehavioral study. Psychological issues* (Vol. 10, No. 37). New York: International Universities Press.

Emery, R. E. (1988). *Marriage, divorce, and children's adjustment.* London: Sage.

Fabes, R., Eisenberg, N., & Miller, P. (1990). Maternal correlates of children's vicarious emotional responsiveness. *Developmental Psychology, 26,* 639–648.

Fabes, R., Eisenberg, N., Nyman, M., & Michealieu, Q. (1991). Young children's appraisals of others' spontaneous emotional reactions. *Developmental Psychology 27,* 858–866.

Feinman, S. (1982). Social referencing in infancy. *Merrill-Palmer Quarterly, 28,* 445–470.

Feinman, S., & Lewis, M. (1983). Social referencing at ten months: A second-order effect on infants' responses to strangers. *Child Development, 54,* 878–887.

Feiring, C., Lewis, M., & Starr, M. D. (1984). Indirect effects and infants' reaction to strangers. *Developmental Psychology, 20,* 485–491.

Feldman, R. S., Jenkins, L., & Popoola, O. (1979). Detecting of deception in adults and children via facial expressions. *Child Development, 50,* 350–355.

Feldman, R. S., White, J. B., & Lobato, D. (1982). Social skills and nonverbal behavior. In R. S. Feldman (Ed.), *Development of nonverbal behavior in children* (pp. 259–277). New York: Springer-Verlag.

Ferguson, T., & Stegge, H. (1995). Emotional states and traits in children. In J. Tangney & K. Fischer (Eds.), *Self-conscious emotions: The psychology of shame, guilt, embarrassment and pride* (pp. 174–197). New York: Guilford Press.

Ferguson, T., Stegge, H., & Damhuis, I. (1991). Children's understanding of guilt and shame. *Child Development, 62,* 827–839.

Fernald, A. (1984). The perceptual and affective salience of mothers' speech to infants. In L. Feagans, C. Garvey, R. Golinkoff, M. T. Greenberg, & J. Bohannon (Eds.), *The origins and growth of communication* (pp. 5–29). Norwood, NJ: ABLEX.

Fernald, A. (1992). Human maternal vocalizations to infants as biologically relevant signals: An evolutionary perspective. In J. H. Barkow, L. Cosmides, & J. Tooby (Eds.), *The adapted mind: Evolutionary psychology and the generation of culture* (pp. 391–428). Oxford, England: Oxford University Press.

Fernald, A. (1993). Approval and disapproval: Infant responsiveness to vocal affect in familiar and unfamiliar languages. *Child Development, 64,* 657–674.

Fernald, A., & Kuhl, P. (1987). Acoustic determinants of infant preference for motherese speech. *Infant Behavior and Development, 10,* 279–293.

Field, T. (1995). The effects of mother's physical and emotional unavailability on emotion regulation. *Monographs of the Society for Research in Child Development, 59,* 208–227.

Field, T. M., Woodson, R., Cohen, D., Greenberg, R., Garcia, R., & Collins, K. (1983). Discrimination and imitation of facial expressions by term and preterm neonates. *Infant Behavior and Development, 6,* 485–489.

Field, T. M., Woodson, R., Greenberg, R., & Cohen, D. (1982). Discrimination and imitation of facial expressions by neonates. *Science, 218,* 179–181.

Fifer, W., & Moon, C. (1995). The effects of fetal experience with sound. In J.-P. Lecanuet, W. Fifer, N. Krasnegor, & W. Smotherman (Eds.), *Fetal development: A psychobiological perspective* (pp. 351–366). Hillsdale, NJ: Erlbaum.

Fischer, K. (1980). A theory of cognitive development: The control and construction of hierarchies of skills. *Psychological Review, 87,* 477–531.

Fischer, K., & Ayoub, C. (1994). Affective splitting and dissociation in normal and maltreated children: Developmental pathways for self in relationships. In D. Cicchetti & S. Toth (Eds.), *Rochester Symposium on Development and Psychopathology: Vol. 5. Disorders and dysfunctions of the self* (pp. 149–222). Rochester, NY: University of Rochester Press.

Fivush, R. (1991). Gender and emotion in mother-child conversations about the past. *Journal of Narrative and Life History, 1,* 325–341.

Fogel, A., Nwokah, E., Dedo, J., Messinger, D., Dickson, L., Matusov, E., & Holt, S. (1992). Social process theory of emotion: A dynamic systems approach. *Social Development, 1,* 122–142.

Fogel, A., & Thelen, E. (1987). Development of early expressive and communicative action: Reinterpreting the evidence from a dynamic systems perspective. *Developmental Psychology, 23,* 747–761.

Fox, N. A. (1994). Dynamic cerebral processes underlying emotion regulation. In N. Fox (Ed.), The development of emotion regulation: Biological and behavioral considerations. *Monographs of the Society for Research in Child Development, 59*(2/3, Serial No. 240), 152–166.

Fraiberg, S. (1971). *Insights from the blind.* New York: Basic Books.

Fridlund, A. (1991). Evolution and facial action in reflex, social motive, and paralanguage. *Biological Psychology, 32,* 3–100.

Fridlund, A. (1994). *Human facial expressions: An evolutionary view.* New York: Academic Press.

Frijda, N. (1986). *The emotions.* Cambridge, England: Cambridge University Press.

Frijda, N. (1987). Emotion, cognitive structure, and action tendency. *Cognition and Emotion, 1,* 115–143.

Fuchs, D., & Thelen, M. (1988). Children's expected interpersonal consequences of communicating their affective states and reported likelihood of expression. *Child Development, 59,* 1314–1322.

Gaensbauer, T. (1982). The differentiation of discrete affects: A case report. *Psychoanalytic Study of the Child, 37,* 29–66.

Gaensbauer, T., & Hiatt, S. (1980). Anaclitic depression in a three-and-one-half-month-old child. *American Journal of Psychiatry, 137,* 841–842.

Garber, J., Braafladt, N., & Zeman, J. (1991). The regulation of sad affect: An information-processing perspective. In J. Garber & K. Dodge (Eds.), *The development of emotion regulation and dysregulation* (pp. 208–240). New York: Cambridge University Press.

Gardner, D., Harris, P. L., Ohmoto, M., & Hamazaki, T. (1988). Japanese children's understanding of the distinction between real and apparent emotion. *International Journal of Behavioral Development, 11*(2), 203–218.

Garner, P. (1995). *Antecedents of preschoolers' emotional control in the disappointment paradigm.* Paper presented at the biennial meeting of the Society for Research in Child Development, Indianapolis, IN.

Glasberg, R., & Aboud, F. (1982). Keeping one's distance from sadness: Children's self-report of emotional experience. *Developmental Psychology, 18,* 287–293.

Gnepp, J. (1989a). Children's use of personal information to understand other people's feelings. In C. Saarni & P. Harris (Eds.), *Children's understanding of emotion* (pp. 151–180). Cambridge, England: Cambridge University Press.

Gnepp, J. (1989b). Personalized inferences of emotions and appraisals: Component processes and correlates. *Developmental Psychology, 25,* 277–288.

Gnepp, J., & Chilamkurti, C. (1988). Children's use of personality attributions to predict other people's emotional and behavioral reactions. *Child Development, 59,* 743–754.

Gnepp, J., & Gould, M. E. (1985). The development of personalized inferences: Understanding other people's emotional reactions in light of their prior experiences. *Child Development, 56,* 1455–1464.

Goldbeck, T., Tolkmitt, F., & Scherer, K. R. (1988). Experimental studies on vocal affect communication. In K. R. Scherer (Ed.), *Facets of emotion: Recent research* (pp. 119–137). Hillsdale, NJ: Erlbaum.

Goldsmith, H., & Campos, J. (1982). Toward a theory of infant temperament. In R. Emde & R. Harmon (Eds.), *The development of attachment and affiliative systems: Psychobiological aspects* (pp. 161–193). New York: Plenum Press.

Golombok, S., & Fivush, R. (1994). *Gender development.* New York: Cambridge University Press.

Goodman, S., Brogan, D., Lynch, M., & Fielding, B. (1993). Social and emotional competence in children of depressed mothers. *Child Development, 64,* 516–531.

Gordon, S. (1989). The socialization of children's emotions: Emotional culture, competence, and exposure. In C. Saarni & P. Harris (Eds.), *Children's understanding of emotions* (pp. 319–349). New York: Cambridge University Press.

Graham, S. (1988). Children's developing understanding of the motivational role of affect: An attributional analysis. *Cognitive Development, 3,* 71–88.

Graham, S., Doubleday, C., & Guarino, P. (1984). The development of relations between perceived controllability and the emotions of pity, anger, and guilt. *Child Development, 55,* 561–565.

Graham, S., & Weiner, B. (1986). From attributional theory of emotion to developmental psychology: A round-trip ticket? Developmental perspectives on social-cognitive theories [Special issue]. *Social Cognition, 4*(2), 152–179.

Griffin, S. (1995). A cognitive-developmental analysis of pride, shame, and embarrassment in middle childhood. In J. Tangney & K. Fischer (Eds.), *Self-conscious emotions: The psychology of shame, guilt, embarrassment and pride* (pp. 219–236). New York: Guilford Press.

Gross, A. L., & Ballif, B. (1991). Children's understanding of emotion from facial expressions and situations: A review. *Developmental Review, 11,* 368–398.

Gross, D., & Harris, P. L. (1988). False beliefs about emotion: Children's understanding of misleading emotional displays. *International Journal of Behavioral Development, 11,* 475–488.

Grossmann, K. E., Grossmann, K., Huber, F., & Wartner, U. (1981). German children's behavior toward their mothers at 12 months and their fathers at 18 months in Ainsworth's Strange Situation. *International Journal of Behavioral Development, 4,* 157–181.

Grych, J., & Fincham, F. (1990). Marital conflict and children's adjustment: A cognitive-contextual framework. *Psychological Bulletin, 108,* 267–290.

Gunnar, M. R. (1980). Control, warning signals, and distress in infancy. *Developmental Psychology, 16,* 281–289.

Gunnar, M. R., & Stone, C. (1984). The effects of positive maternal affect on infant responses to pleasant, ambiguous, and fear-provoking toys. *Child Development, 55,* 1231–1236.

Gustafson, G. (1984). Effects of the ability to locomote on infants' social and exploratory behaviors: An experimental study. *Developmental Psychology, 20,* 307–405.

Hardy, D., Power, T., & Jaedicke, S. (1993). Examining the relation of parenting to children's coping with everyday stress. *Child Development, 64,* 1829–1841.

Harris, P. L. (1989). *Children and emotion: The development of psychological understanding.* Oxford, England: Basil Blackwell.

Harris, P. L. (1994). The child's understanding of emotion: The developmental process and the family environment. *Journal of Child Psychology and Psychiatry, 35,* 3–28.

Harris, P. L., & Gross, D. (1988). Children's understanding of real and apparent emotion. In J. W. Astington, P. L. Harris, & D. R. Olson (Eds.), *Developing theories of mind* (pp. 295–314). Cambridge, England: Cambridge University Press.

Harris, P. L., Guz, G. R., Lipian, M. S., & Man-Shu, Z. (1985). Insight into the time-course of emotion among western and Chinese children. *Child Development, 56,* 972–988.

Harris, P. L., Johnson, C., Hutton, D., Andrews, G., & Cooke, T. (1989). Young children's theory of mind and emotion. *Cognition and Emotion, 3*(4), 379–400.

Harris, P. L., & Lipian, M. S. (1989). Understanding emotion and experiencing emotion. In C. Saarni & P. Harris (Eds.), *Children's understanding of emotion* (pp. 241–258). Cambridge, England: Cambridge University Press.

Harter, S. (1978). Effectance motivation reconsidered: Toward a developmental model. *Human Development, 21,* 34–64.

Harter, S. (1986). Cognitive-developmental processes in the integration of concepts about emotions and self. *Social Cognition, 4,* 119–151.

Harter, S. (1990). Developmental differences in the nature of self-representations: Implications for the understanding, assessment, and treatment of maladaptive behavior. *Cognitive Therapy and Research, 14,* 113–142.

Harter, S., & Buddin, B. J. (1987). Children's understanding of the simultaneity of two emotions: A five-stage developmental acquisition sequence. *Developmental Psychology, 23,* 388–399.

Harter, S., & Whitesell, N. R. (1989). Developmental changes in children's understanding of single, multiple, and blended emotion concepts. In C. Saarni & P. Harris (Eds.), *Children's understanding of emotion* (pp. 81–116). Cambridge, England: Cambridge University Press.

Hatfield, E., Cacioppo, J. T., & Rapson, R. L. (1992). Primitive emotional contagion. In M. S. Clark (Ed.), *Emotion and social behavior: Review of personality and social psychology* (Vol. 14, pp. 151–177). Newbury Park, CA: Sage.

Hatfield, E., Cacioppo, J. T., & Rapson, R. L. (1994). *Emotional contagion.* Cambridge, England: Cambridge University Press.

Haviland, J. M., & Lelwica, M. (1987). The induced affect response: 10-week-old infants' responses to three emotional expressions. *Developmental Psychology, 23,* 97–104.

Hazan, C., & Shaver, P. (1994). Attachment as an organizational framework for research on close relationships. *Psychological Inquiry, 5,* 1–22.

Held, R., & Hein, A. (1963). Movement-produced stimulation in the development of visually guided behavior. *Journal of Comparative and Physiological Psychology, 81,* 394–398.

Hiatt, S., Campos, J., & Emde, R. (1979). Facial patterning and infant emotional expression: Happiness, surprise, and fear. *Child Development, 50,* 1020–1035.

Higgins, C., Campos, J., & Kermoian. R. (in press). The origins of visual proprioception. *Developmental Psychology.*

Hirshberg, L. M., & Svejda, M. (1990). When infants look to their parents: I. Infants' social referencing of mothers compared to fathers. *Child Development, 61,* 1175–1186.

Hoffman, M. (1977). *Empathy: Its development and prosocial implications. Nebraska Symposium on Motivation.* Lincoln: University of Nebraska Press.

Hoffman, M. (1984). Interaction of affect and cognition in empathy. In C. Izard, J. Kagan, & R. Zajonc (Eds.), *Emotions, cognition, and behavior* (pp. 103–131). New York: Cambridge University Press.

Hoffman-Plotkin, D., & Twentyman, C. (1984). A multimodal assessment of behavioral and cognitive deficits in abused and neglected preschoolers. *Child Development, 55,* 795–802.

Hoffner, C. (1993). Children's strategies for coping with stress: Blunting and monitoring. *Motivation and Emotion, 17,* 91–106.

Hoffner, C., & Badzinski, D. (1989). Children's integration of facial and situational cues to emotion. *Child Development, 60,* 411–422.

Hornik, R., Risenhoover, N., & Gunnar, M. (1987). The effects of maternal positive, neutral, and negative affective communications on infant responses to new toys. *Child Development, 58,* 937–944.

Hunt, J. McV. (1965). Intrinsic motivation and its role in psychological development. In D. Levine (Ed.), *Nebraska Symposium on Motivation* (pp. 189–282). Lincoln: University of Nebraska Press.

Izard, C. (1972). *The face of emotion.* New York: Appleton-Century-Crofts.

Izard, C. (1977). *Human emotions.* New York: Plenum Press.

Izard, C. (1991). *The psychology of emotions.* New York: Plenum Press.

Izard, C. (1995). Innate and universal facial expressions: Evidence from developmental and cross-cultural research. *Psychological Bulletin, 115,* 288–299.

Izard, C. E., & Dougherty, L. (1982). Two complementary systems for measuring facial expressions in infants and children. In C. E. Izard (Ed.), *Measuring emotions in infants and children.* New York: Cambridge University Press.

Izard, C. E., & Malatesta, C. Z. (1987). Perspectives on emotional development: I. Differential emotions theory of early emotional development. In J. Osofsky (Ed.), *Handbook of infant development* (pp. 494–554). New York: Wiley.

James, W. (1890). *The principles of psychology.* New York: Holt.

Johnson, M. H., Dziurawiec, S., Ellis, H., & Morton, J. (1991). Newborns' preferential tracking of face-like stimuli and its subsequent decline. *Cognition, 40,* 1–19.

Johnson, W., Emde, R., Pannabecker, B., Stenberg, C., & Davies, M. (1982). Maternal perception of infant emotion from birth through 18 months. *Infant Behavior and Development, 5,* 312–322.

Josephs, I. (1993). *The regulation of emotional expression in preschool children.* New York: Waxmann Verlag.

Josephs, I. (1994). Display rule behavior and understanding in preschool children. *Journal of Nonverbal Behavior, 18,* 301–326.

Joshi, M. S., & MacLean, M. (1994). Indian and English children's understanding of the distinction between real and apparent emotion. *Child Development, 65,* 1372–1384.

Kagan, J. (1971). *Change and continuity in infancy.* New York: Wiley.

Kagan, J. (1994). On the nature of emotion. In N. Fox (Ed.), The development of emotion regulation: Biological and behavioral considerations. *Monographs of the Society for Research in Child Development, 59*(2/3, Serial No. 240), 7–24.

Kahen, V., Katz, L. F., & Gottman, J. (1994). Linkages between parent-child interaction and conversations of friends. *Social Development, 3,* 238–254.

Karniol, R., & Koren, L. (1987). How would you feel? Children's inferences regarding their own and others' affective reactions. *Cognitive Development, 2,* 271–278.

Keefer, C., Dixon, S., Tronick, E., & Brazelton, T. (1991). Cultural mediation between newborn behavior and later development: Implications for methodology in cross-cultural research. In J. Nugent, B. Lester, & T. Brazelton (Eds.), *The cultural context of infancy: Vol. 2. Multicultural and interdisciplinary approaches to parent-infant relations* (pp. 39–61). Norwood, NJ: ABLEX.

Kenney, M., Mason, W., & Hill, S. (1979). Effects of age, objects, and visual experience on affective responses of rhesus monkeys to strangers. *Developmental Psychology, 15,* 176–184.

Kitayama, S., & Markus, H. (1994). Introduction to cultural psychology and emotion research. In S. Kitayama & H. Markus (Eds.), *Emotion and culture* (pp. 1–19). Washington, DC: American Psychological Association.

Kliewer, W. (1991). Coping in middle childhood: Relations to competence, Type A behavior, monitoring, blunting, and locus of control. *Developmental Psychology, 27,* 689–697.

Klinnert, M. D. (1984). The regulation of infant behavior by maternal facial expression. *Infant Behavior and Development, 7,* 447–465.

Klinnert, M. D., Campos, J. J., Sorce, J. F., Emde, R. N., & Svejda, M. (1983). Emotions as behavior regulators: Social referencing in infancy. In R. Plutchik & H. Kellerman (Eds.), *Emotion: Theory, research and experience* (pp. 57–86). New York: Academic Press.

Kobak, R., & Sceery, A. (1988). Attachment in late adolescence: Working models, affect regulation, and representations of self and others. *Child Development, 59,* 135–146.

Koestner, R., Franz, C., & Weinberger, J. (1990). The family origins of empathic concern: A 26-year longitudinal study. *Journal of Personality and Social Psychology, 58,* 709–717.

Kurtines, W., & Gewirtz, J. (Eds.). (1991). *Handbook of moral behavior and development: Vol. 1. Theory: Vol. 2. Research: Vol. 3. Application.* Hillsdale, NJ: Erlbaum.

Ladd, D. R., Silverman, K., Tolkmitt, F., Bergmann, G., & Scherer, K. R. (1985). Evidence for the independent function of intonation contour type, voice quality, and FO range in signalling speaker affect. *Journal of the Acoustical Society of America, 78,* 435–444.

Laird, J. (1984). The real role of facial response in the experience of emotions: A reply to Tourangeau and Ellsworth and others. *Journal of Personality and Social Psychology, 47,* 909–917.

Landers, C. (1989). A psychobiological study of infant development in South India. In J. K. Nugent, B. Lester, & T. B. Brazelton (Eds.), *The cultural context of infancy: Vol. 1. Biology, culture, and infant development* (pp. 169–207). Norwood, NJ: ABLEX.

Lazarus, R. (1991). *Emotion and adaptation.* New York: Oxford University Press.

Lazarus, R., & Averill, J. (1972). Emotion and cognition with special reference to anxiety. In C. Spielberger (Ed.), *Anxiety: Current directions in theory and research* (pp. 242–283). New York: Academic Press.

Lennon, R., & Eisenberg, N. (1987). Gender and age differences in empathy and sympathy. In N. Eisenberg & J. Strayer (Eds.), *Empathy and its development* (pp. 195–217). New York: Cambridge University Press.

Levine, L. (1995). Young children's understanding of the causes of anger and stress. *Child Development, 66,* 697–709.

LeVine, R., Dixon, S., LeVine, S., Richman, A., Leiderman, P. H., Keefer, C. H., & Brazelton, T. B. (1994). *Child care and culture: Lessons from Africa.* New York: Cambridge University Press.

Lewis, M. (1992a). *Shame: The exposed self.* New York: Free Press.

Lewis, M. (1992b). The role of the self in social behavior. In F. Kessel, P. M. Cole, & D. Johnson (Eds.), *Self and consciousness: Multiple perspectives.* (pp. 19–44). Hillsdale, NJ: Erlbaum.

Lewis, M. (1993). Self-conscious emotions: Embarrassment, pride, shame, and guilt. In M. Lewis & J. Haviland (Eds.), *The handbook of emotions* (pp. 563–573). New York: Guilford Press.

Lewis, M. (1995). Embarrassment: The emotion of self-exposure and evaluation. In J. Tangney & K. Fischer (Eds.), *Self-conscious emotions: The psychology of shame, guilt, embarrassment and pride* (pp. 198–218). New York: Guilford Press.

Lewis, M., Alessandri, S., & Sullivan, M. W. (1992). Differences in shame and pride as a function of children's gender and task difficulty. *Child Development, 63,* 630–638.

Lewis, M., & Brooks, J. (1978). Self-knowledge and emotional development. In M. Lewis & L. Rosenblum (Eds.), *The development of affect* (pp. 205–226). New York: Plenum Press.

Lewis, M., & Brooks-Gunn, J. (1979). *Social cognition and the acquisition of self.* New York: Plenum Press.

Lewis, M., & Michalson, L. (1983). *Children's emotions and moods: Developmental theory and measurement.* New York: Plenum Press.

Lewis, M., & Michalson, L. (1985). Faces as signs and symbols. In G. Zivin (Ed.), *The development of expressive behavior* (pp. 153–178). New York: Academic Press.

Lewis, M., Stanger, C., & Sullivan, M. W. (1989). Deception in 3-year-olds. *Developmental Psychology, 25,* 439–443.

Lewis, M., Sullivan, M., Stanger, C., & Weiss, M. (1989). Self-development and self-conscious emotions. *Child Development, 60,* 146–156.

Lewis, M., Sullivan, M., & Vasen, A. (1987). Making faces: Age and emotion differences in the posing of emotional expressions. *Developmental Psychology, 23,* 690–697.

Lipton, E. L., Steinschneider, A., & Richmond, J. B. (1965). Swaddling, a child care practice: Historical, cultural and experimental observations. *Pediatrics, 34,* 521–567.

Lutz, C. (1983). Parental goals, ethnopsychology, and the development of emotional meaning. *Ethos, 11,* 246–262.

Lutz, C. (1988). Ethnographic perspectives on the emotion lexicon. In V. Hamilton, G. H. Bower, & N. Frijda (Eds.), *Cognitive perspectives on emotion and motivation* (pp. 399–419). Norwell, MA: Kluwer Academic Press.

Lutz, C., & White, G. M. (1986). The anthropology of emotions. *Annual Review of Anthropology, 15,* 405–436.

Maccoby, E. (1983). Social-emotional development and response to stressors. In N. Garmezy & M. Rutter (Eds.), *Stress, coping and development in children* (pp. 217–234). New York: McGraw-Hill.

MacLean, P. (1985). Brain evolution relating to family, play, and the separation call. *Archives of General Psychiatry, 42,* 405–417.

Mahler, M., Pine, F., & Bergman, A. (1975). *The psychological birth of the human infant.* New York: Basic Books.

Main, M., & George, C. (1985). Responses of abused and disadvantaged toddlers to distress in agemates: A study in the day care setting. *Developmental Psychology, 21,* 407–412.

Main, M., Kaplan, N., & Cassidy, J. (1985). Security in infancy, childhood, and adulthood: A move to the level of representation. In I. Bretherton & E. Waters (Eds.), Growing points of attachment theory and research. *Monographs of the Society for Research in Child Development, 50*(1/2, Serial No. 209), 66–104.

Manstead, A. S., Wagner, H. L., & MacDonald, C. J. (1984). Face, body, and speech as channels of communication in the detection of deception. *Basic & Applied Social Psychology, 5*(4), 317–332.

Martin, G. B., & Clark, R. D. (1982). Distress crying in neonates: Species and peer specificity. *Developmental Psychology, 18,* 3–9.

Mascolo, M., & Fischer, K. (1995). Developmental transformations in appraisals for pride, shame, and guilt. In J. Tangney & K. Fischer (Eds.), *Self-conscious emotions: The psychology of shame, guilt, embarrassment and pride* (pp. 64–113). New York: Guilford Press.

McCoy, C., & Masters, J. (1985). The development of children's strategies for the social control of emotion. *Child Development, 56,* 1214–1222.

McCoy, C., & Masters, J. (1990). Children's strategies for the control of emotion in themselves and others. In B. S. Moore & A. Eisen (Eds.), *Affect and social behavior* (pp. 231–268). New York: Cambridge University Press.

McIntosh, D. N., Druckman, D., & Zajonc, R. B. (1994). Socially induced affect. In D. Druckman & R. A. Bjork (Eds.), *Learning, remembering, believing: Enhancing human performance* (pp. 251–276, 364–371). Washington, DC: National Academy Press.

Mead, M. (1954). The swaddling hypothesis: Its reception. *American Anthropologist, 56,* 395–409.

Meerum Terwogt, M., & Olthof, T. (1989). Awareness and self-regulation of emotion in young children. In J. Raarni & P. Harris (Eds.), *Children's understanding of emotion* (pp. 209–240). Cambridge, England: Cambridge University Press.

Meltzoff, A. N., & Moore, M. K. (1983). Newborn infants imitate adult facial gestures. *Child Development, 54,* 702–709.

Meltzoff, A. N., & Moore, M. K. (1989). Imitation in newborn infants: Exploring the range of gestures imitated and the underlying mechanisms. *Developmental Psychology, 25,* 954–962.

Mesquita, B., & Frijda, N. (1992). Cultural variations in emotion: A review. *Psychological Bulletin, 112,* 179–204.

Messinger, D., Fogel, A., & Dickson, L. (1997). In J. Russell & J.-M. Fernandez-Dols (Eds.), *New directions in the study of facial expression.* New York: Cambridge University Press.

Michel, G. F., Camras, L. A., & Sullivan, J. (1992). Infant interest expressions as coordinative motor structures. *Infant Behavior and Development, 15,* 347–358.

Miller, P., Eisenberg, N., Fabes, R., Shell, R., & Gular, S. (1989). Mothers' emotional arousal as a moderator in the socialization of children's empathy. In N. Eisenberg (Ed.), *New directions for child development: 44. Empathy and related emotional responses* (pp. 65–83). San Francisco: Jossey-Bass.

Miller, P., Kliewer, W., Hepworth, J., & Sandler, I. (1994). Maternal socialization of children's postdivorce coping: Development of a measurement model. *Journal of Applied Developmental Psychology, 15,* 457–487.

Miller, P., & Sperry, L. (1987). The socialization of anger and aggression. *Merrill-Palmer Quarterly, 33,* 1–31.

Miller, S. M., & Green, M. L. (1985). Coping with stress and frustration: Origins, nature, and development. In M. Lewis &

C. Saarni (Eds.), *The socialization of emotions* (pp. 263–314). New York: Plenum Press.

Miyake, K., Campos, J., Kagan, J., & Bradshaw, D. (1986). Issues in socioemotional development in Japan. In H. Azuma, K. Hakuta, & H. Stevenson (Eds.), *Kodomo: Child development and education in Japan* (pp. 238–261). San Francisco: Freeman.

Miyake, K., Chen, S., & Campos, J. (1985). Infant temperament, mother's mode of interaction, and attachment in Japan. In I. Bretherton & E. Waters (Eds.), Growing points in attachment theory and research. *Monographs of the Society for Research in Child Development, 50*(1/2, Serial No. 209), 276–297.

Morelli, G., Rogoff, B., Oppenheim, D., & Goldsmith, D. (1992). Cultural variation in infants' sleeping arrangements: Questions of independence. *Developmental Psychology, 28,* 604–613.

Morris, M., & Peng, K. (1994). Culture and cause: American and Chinese attributions for social and physical events. *Journal of Personality and Social Psychology, 67,* 949–971.

Mumme, D. L. (1993). *Rethinking social referencing: The influence of facial and vocal affect on infant behavior.* Unpublished doctoral dissertation, Stanford University, Stanford, CA.

Mumme, D. L., & Fernald, A. (1995). *Infants' use of gaze in interpreting emotional signals.* Unpublished manuscript.

Mumme, D. L., Fernald, A., & Herrera, C. (1996). Infants' responses to facial and vocal emotional signals in a social referencing paradigm. *Child Development, 67,* 3219–3237.

Nelson, C. A. (1987). The recognition of facial expression in the first two years of life: Mechanisms of development. *Child Development, 58,* 889–909.

Nelson, C. A., & Horowitz, F. D. (1983). The perception of facial expressions and stimulus motion by 2- and 5-month-old infants using holographic stimuli. *Child Development, 56,* 868–877.

Ochs, E. (1986). From feelings to grammar: A Samoan case study. In B. B. Schieffelin & E. Ochs (Eds.), *Language socialization across cultures* (pp. 251–272). Cambridge, England: Cambridge University Press.

Odom, R., & Lemond, C. (1972). Developmental differences in the perception and production of facial expressions. *Child Development, 43,* 359–369.

Oster, H. (1981). "Recognition" of emotional expression in infancy. In M. E. Lamb & L. R. Sherrod (Eds.), *Infant social cognition: Empirical and theoretical considerations* (pp. 274–313). Hillsdale, NJ: Erlbaum.

Oster, H., & Rosenstein, D. (in press). *Baby FACS: Analyzing facial movement in infants.* Palo Alto, CA: Consulting Psychologists Press.

Parritz, R., Mangelsdorf, S., & Gunnar, M. (1992). Control, social referencing, and the infant's appraisal of threat. In S. Feinman (Ed.), *Social referencing and the social construction of reality in infancy* (pp. 209–228). New York: Plenum Press.

Porges, S. (1991). Vagal tone: An autonomic mediator of affect. In J. Garber & K. Dodge (Eds.), *The development of emotion regulation and dysregulation* (pp. 111–128). New York: Cambridge University Press.

Reimer, M. (1996). "Sinking into the ground": The development and consequences of shame in adolescence. *Developmental Review, 16,* 321–363.

Reissland, N. (1994). The socialization of pride in young children. *International Journal of Behavioral Development, 17,* 541–552.

Repacholi, B. M. (1996). *Components of children's early emotion understanding: Evidence from 14- and 18-month-olds.* Unpublished doctoral dissertation, University of California, Berkeley.

Repacholi, B. M., & Gopnik, A. (1997). Early reasoning about desires: Evidence from 14- and 18-month-olds. *Developmental Psychology, 33,* 12–21.

Richard, B. A., & Dodge, K. (1982). Social maladjustment and problem solving in school-aged children. *Journal of Consulting and Clinical Psychology, 50,* 226–233.

Ridgeway, D., Waters, E., & Kuczaj, S. A. (1985). Acquisition of emotion-descriptive language: Receptive and productive vocabulary norms for ages 18 month to 6 years. *Developmental Psychology, 21,* 901–908.

Rogoff, B., Mistry, J., Goncu, A., & Mosier, C. (1993). Guided participation in cultural activity by toddlers and caregivers. *Monographs of the Society for Research in Child Development, 58.*

Rosen, W. D., Adamson, L. B., & Bakeman, R. (1992). An experimental investigation of infant social referencing: Mothers' messages and gender differences. *Developmental Psychology, 28,* 1172–1178.

Rosenthal, R., Hall, J., DiMatteo, M., Rogers, P., & Archer, D. (1979). *Sensitivity to nonverbal communication: The PONS test.* Baltimore: Johns Hopkins University Press.

Rossman, B. R. (1992). School-age children's perceptions of coping with distress: Strategies for emotion regulation and the moderation of adjustment. *Journal of Child Psychology and Psychiatry, 33,* 1373–1397.

Rubin, K., Coplan, R., Fox, N., & Calkins, S. (1995). Emotionality, emotion regulation, and preschoolers' social adaptation. *Development and Psychopathology 7,* 49–62.

Russell, J. A. (1991). Culture and the categorization of emotion. *Psychological Bulletin, 110,* 426–450.

Russell, J. A. (1994). Is there universal recognition of emotion from facial expression? A review of the cross-cultural studies. *Psychological Bulletin, 115,* 102–141.

Russell, J. A. (1995). Facial expression of emotion: What lies beyond minimal universality? *Psychological Bulletin, 118,* 379–391.

Russell, J. A., Fernandez-Dols, J. M., Manstead, A., & Wellenkamp, J. (Eds.). (1996). *Everyday conceptions of emotion: An introduction to the psychology, anthropology and linguistics of emotion.* Hingham, MA: Kluwer.

Russell, J. A., & Ridgeway, D. (1983). Dimensions underlying children's emotion concepts. *Developmental Psychology, 19,* 795–804.

Saarni, C. (1979a). *When not to show what you feel: Children's understanding of the relations between emotional experience and expressive behavior.* Paper presented at the meeting of the Society for Research in Child Development, San Francisco.

Saarni, C. (1979b). Children's understanding of display rules for expressive behavior. *Developmental Psychology, 15,* 424–429.

Saarni, C. (1984). An observational study of children's attempts to monitor their expressive behavior. *Child Development, 55,* 1504–1513.

Saarni, C. (1987a). Cultural rules of emotional experience: A commentary on Miller and Sperry's study. *Merrill-Palmer Quarterly, 33,* 535–540.

Saarni, C. (1987b). *Children's beliefs about parental expectations for emotional-expressive behavior management.* Paper presented at the biennial meeting of the Society for Research in Child Development, Baltimore.

Saarni, C. (1988). Children's understanding of the interpersonal consequences of dissemblance of nonverbal emotional-expressive behavior. *Journal of Nonverbal Behavior, 12,* 275–294.

Saarni, C. (1989). Children's beliefs about emotion. In M. Luszez & T. Nettelbeck (Eds.), *Psychological development: Perspectives across the life-span* (pp. 69–78). Amsterdam, The Netherlands: Elsevier.

Saarni, C. (1990). *Psychometric properties of the Parental Attitude toward Children's Expressiveness Scale (PACES).* Unpublished manuscript, Sonoma State University. (ERIC Document Reproduction Service No. ED 317-301)

Saarni, C. (1991). *Social context and management of emotional-expressive behavior: Children's expectancies for when to dissemble what they feel.* Paper presented at the biennial meeting of the Society for Research in Child Development, Seattle, WA.

Saarni, C. (1992). Children's emotional-expressive behaviors as regulators of others' happy and sad states. *New Directions for Child Development, 55,* 91–106.

Saarni, C. (1995). *Children's coping strategies for aversive emotions*. Paper presented at the biennial meeting of the Society for Research in Child Development, Indianapolis, IN.

Sackett, G. (1966). Monkeys reared in isolation with pictures as visual input. *Science, 154,* 175–176.

Sagi, A., & Hoffman, M. L. (1976). Empathic distress in the newborn. *Developmental Psychology, 12,* 175–176.

Sagi, A., Lamb, M., Lewkowicz, K., Shoham, R., Dvir, R., & Estes, D. (1985). Security of infant-mother, -father, and -metapelet attachments among kibbutz reared Israeli children. In I. Bretherton & E. Waters (Eds.), Growing points in attachment theory and research. *Monographs of the Society for Research in Child Development, 50*(1/2, Serial No. 209).

Scarr, S., & Salapatek, P. (1970). Patterns of fear development during infancy. *Merrill-Palmer Quarterly, 16,* 53–90.

Scheflen, A. (1974). *How behavior means.* Garden City, NY: Anchor Press.

Scherer, K. R. (1986). Vocal affect expression: A review and model for further research. *Psychological Bulletin, 98,* 143–165.

Schwartz, G. M., Izard, C. E., & Ansul, S. E. (1985). The 5-month-old's ability to discriminate facial expressions of emotion. *Infant Behavior and Development, 8,* 65–67.

Shaver, P., Schwartz, J., Kirson, D., & O'Connor, C. (1987). Emotion knowledge: Further exploration of a prototype approach. *Journal of Personality and Social Psychology, 52,* 1061–1086.

Shennum, W. A., & Bugental, D. B. (1982). The development of control over affective expression in nonverbal behavior. In R. S. Feldman (Ed.), *Development of nonverbal behavior in children* (pp. 101–118). New York: Springer-Verlag.

Shweder, R. A. (1993). The cultural psychology of the emotions. In M. Lewis & J. M. Haviland (Eds.), *Handbook of emotions* (pp. 417–434). New York: Guilford Press.

Sigmon, S., & Snyder, C. R. (1993). Looking at oneself in a rose-colored mirror: The role of excuses in the negotiation of a personal reality. In M. Lewis & C. Saarni (Eds.), *Lying and deception in everyday life* (pp. 148–165). New York: Guilford Press.

Simner, M. L. (1971). Newborn's response to the cry of another infant. *Developmental Psychology, 5,* 136–150.

Skinner, E. (1991). Development and perceived control: A dynamic model of action in context. In M. R. Gunnar & L. A. Sroufe (Eds.), *Minnesota Symposium on Child Psychology: Vol. 23. Self processes in development* (pp. 167–216). Hillsdale, NJ: Erlbaum.

Skinner, E., & Wellborn, J. (1994). Coping during childhood and adolescence: A motivational perspective. In R. Lerner (Ed.), *Life-span development and behavior* (pp. 91–133). Hillsdale, NJ: Erlbaum.

Slade, A., & Wolf, D. (Eds.). (1994). *Children at play: Clinical and developmental approaches to meaning representation.* New York: Oxford University Press.

Smiley, P., & Huttenlocher, J. (1989). Young children's acquisition of emotion concepts. In C. Saarni & P. Harris (Eds.), *Children's understanding of emotion* (pp. 27–49). Cambridge, England: Cambridge University Press.

Sogon, S., & Masutani, M. (1989). Identification of emotion from body movements: A cross-cultural study of Americans and Japanese. *Psychological Reports, 65,* 35–46.

Sorce, J. F., Emde, R. N., Campos, J., & Klinnert, M. D. (1985). Maternal emotional signaling: Its effect on the visual cliff behavior of 1-year-olds. *Developmental Psychology, 21,* 195–200.

Sorensen, E. S. (1993). *Children's stress and coping.* New York: Guilford Press.

Spitz, R. (1965). *The first year of life.* New York: International Universities Press.

Sroufe, L. A. (1979). Socioemotional development. In J. Osofsky (Ed.), *Handbook of infant development* (pp. 462–516). New York: Wiley.

Sroufe, L. A., & Waters, E. (1977). Attachment as an organizational construct. *Child Development, 48,* 1184–1199.

Stein, N., & Trabasso, T. (1989). Children's understanding of changing emotional states. In C. Saarni & P. Harris (Eds.), *Children's understanding of emotion* (pp. 50–80). Cambridge, England: Cambridge University Press.

Stenberg, C., & Campos, J. (1990). The development of anger expressions in infancy. In N. Stein, B. Leventhal, & T. Trabasso (Eds.), *Psychological and biological approaches to emotion* (pp. 247–282). Hillsdale, NJ: Erlbaum.

Stern, D. N. (1985). *The interpersonal world of the infant.* New York: Basic Books.

Stern, D. N., Spieker, S., & MacKain, K. (1982). Intonation contours as signals in maternal speech to prelinguistic infants. *Developmental Psychology, 18,* 727–735.

Stipek, D. (1995). The development of pride and shame in toddlers. In J. Tangney & K. Fischer (Eds.), *Self-conscious emotions: The psychology of shame, guilt, embarrassment and pride* (pp. 237–252). New York: Guilford Press.

Stipek, D., Recchia, S., & McClintic, S. (1992). Self-evaluation in young children. *Monographs of the Society for Research in Child Development, 57*(Serial No. 226).

Strayer, J. (1986). Children's attributions regarding the situational determinants of emotion in self and others. *Developmental Psychology, 17,* 649–654.

Strayer, J. (1987). Affective and cognitive perspectives on empathy. In N. Eisenberg & J. Strayer (Eds.), *Empathy and its development* (pp. 218–244). New York: Cambridge University Press.

Strayer, J. (1989). What children know and feel in response to witnessing. In C. Saarni & P. Harris (Eds.), *Children's understanding of emotion* (pp. 259–292). Cambridge, England: Cambridge University Press.

Strayer, J., & Roberts, W. (1989). Children's empathy and role-taking: Child and parental factors and relations to prosocial behavior. *Journal of Applied Developmental Psychology, 10,* 227–239.

Strelau, J. (1987). Emotion as a key concept in temperament research. *Journal of Research in Personality, 31,* 510–528.

Svejda, M. J. (1981). *The development of infant sensitivity to affective messages in the mother's voice.* Unpublished doctoral dissertation, University of Denver, Denver, CO.

Tangney, J., Burggraf, S., & Wagner, P. (1995). In J. Tangney & K. Fischer (Eds.), *Self-conscious emotions: The psychology of shame, guilt, embarrassment and pride* (pp. 343–367). New York: Guilford Press.

Tangney, J., & Fischer, K. (Eds.). (1995). *Self-conscious emotions: The psychology of shame, guilt, embarrassment, and pride.* New York: Guilford Press.

Taylor, S. E., & Brown, J. D. (1988). Illusion and well-being: A social psychological perspective on mental health. *Psychological Bulletin, 103,* 193–210.

Termine, N. T., & Izard, C. E. (1988). Infants' responses to their mothers' expressions of joy and sadness. *Developmental Psychology, 24,* 223–229.

Teuber, H. L. (1960). Perception. In J. Field, H. Magoun, & V. E. Hall (Eds.), *Handbook of physiology: Sec. 1. Neurophysiology* (Vol. 3). Washington, DC: American Physiological Society.

Thompson, R. A. (1987). Empathy and emotional understanding: The early development of empathy. In N. Eisenberg & J. Strayer (Eds.), *Empathy and its development* (pp. 119–145). Cambridge, England: Cambridge University Press.

Thompson, R. A. (1989). Causal attributions and children's emotional understanding. In C. Saarni & P. Harris (Eds.), *Children's understanding of emotion* (pp. 117–150). Cambridge, England: Cambridge University Press.

Thompson, R. A. (1990). Emotion and self-regulation. In R. A. Thompson (Ed.), *Socioemotional development. Nebraska Symposium on Motivation* (Vol. 36, pp. 367–467). Lincoln: University of Nebraska Press.

Thompson, R. A. (1991). Emotional regulation and emotional development. *Educational Psychology Review, 3,* 269–307.

Thompson, R. A. (1994). Emotion regulation: A theme in search of definition. In N. Fox (Ed.), Emotion regulation: Behavioral and biological considerations. *Society for Research in Child Development Monographs, 59*(Serial No. 240), 25–52.

Tomkins, S. (1962). *Affect, imagery, and consciousness: Vol. 1. The positive affects.* New York: Springer-Verlag.

Tomkins, S. (1963). *Affect, imagery, and consciousness: Vol. 2. The negative affects.* New York: Springer-Verlag.

Trevarthen, C. (1984). Emotions in infancy: Regulators of contact and relationships with persons. In K. Scherer & P. Ekman (Eds.), *Approaches to emotions.* Hillsdale, NJ: Erlbaum.

Trevarthen, C. (1988). Universal cooperative motives: How infants begin to know the language and culture of their parents. In G. Jahoda & I. Lewis (Eds.), *Acquiring culture: Cross-cultural studies in child development* (pp. 37–90). London: Croom Helm.

Trickett, P., & Kuczynski, L. (1986). Children's misbehaviors and parental discipline strategies in abusive and nonabusive families. *Developmental Psychology, 22,* 115–123.

Tronick, E., & Morelli, G. (1991). Foreword. In J. Nugent, B. Lester, & T. Brazelton (Eds.), *The cultural context of infancy: Vol. 2. Multicultural and interdisciplinary approaches to parent-infant relations* (pp. ix-xiii). Norwood, NJ: ABLEX.

Tronick, E., Morelli, G., & Ivey, P. (1992). The Efe forager infant and toddler's pattern of social relationships: Multiple and simultaneous. *Developmental Psychology, 28,* 568–577.

Underwood, M. K. (1996). *Peer social status and children's choices about the expression and control of positive and negative emotions.* Unpublished manuscript, Department of Psychology, Reed College, Oregon.

Underwood, M. K., Coie, J., & Herbsman, C. (1992). Display rules for anger and aggression in school-age children. *Child Development, 63,* 366–380.

van der Kolk, R., & Fisler, R. (1994). Childhood abuse and neglect and loss of self-regulation. *Bulletin of the Menninger Clinic, 58,* 145–168.

von Salisch, M. (1991). *Kinderfreundschaften.* Gottingen, Germany: Hogrefe.

Vuchinich, S., Emery, R., & Cassidy, J. (1988). Family members as third parties in dyadic family conflict: Strategies, alliances and outcomes. *Child Development, 59,* 1293–1302.

Walden, T. A. (1991). Infant social referencing. In J. Garber & K. Dodge (Eds.), *The development of emotion regulation and dysregulation* (pp. 69–88). Cambridge, England: Cambridge University Press.

Walden, T. A., & Baxter, A. (1989). The effect of context and age on social referencing. *Child Development, 60,* 1511–1518.

Walden, T. A., & Field, I. (1988). *Preschool children's social competence and production and discrimination of affective expressions.* Unpublished manuscript, Vanderbilt University, Nashville, TN.

Walden, T. A., & Ogan, T. A. (1988). The development of social referencing. *Child Development, 59,* 1230–1240.

Walker, E. (1981). Emotion recognition in disturbed and normal children: A research note. *Journal of Child Psychology and Psychiatry, 22,* 263–268.

Walker-Andrews, A. S., & Gronlick, W. (1983). Discrimination of vocal expressions by young infants. *Infant Behavior and Development, 6,* 491–498.

Walker-Andrews, A. S., & Lennon, E. (1991). Infants' discrimination of vocal expressions: Contributions of auditory and visual information. *Infant Behavior and Development, 14,* 131–142.

Watzlawick, P., Beavin, J., & Jackson, D. (1967). *Pragmatics of human communication: A study of interactional patterns, pathologies, and paradoxes.* New York: Norton.

Weiner, B. (1985). An attributional theory of achievement motivation and emotion. *Psychological Review, 92,* 548–573.

Weiner, B., & Graham, S. (1984). An attributional approach to emotional development. In C. Izard, J. Kagan, & R. Zajonc (Eds.), *Emotions, cognition, and behavior* (pp. 167–191). New York: Cambridge University Press.

Wellman, H., & Banerjee, M. (1991). Mind and emotion: Children's understanding of the emotional consequences of beliefs and desires. *British Journal of Developmental Psychology, 9,* 191–214.

Wellman, H., Harris, P. L., Banerjee, M., & Sinclair, A. (1995). Early understanding of emotion: Evidence from natural language. *Cognition and Emotion, 9,* 117–149.

Wellman, H., & Wooley, J. (1990). From simple desires to ordinary beliefs: The early development of everyday psychology. *Cognition, 35,* 245–275.

Werker, J. F., & McLeod, P. J. (1989). Infant preference for both male and female infant-directed talk: A developmental study of attentional and affective responsiveness. *Canadian Journal of Psychology, 43,* 230–246.

Whiting, J. (1981). Environmental constraint on infant care practices. In R. H. Munroe, R. L. Munroe, & B. Whiting (Eds.), *Handbook of cross-cultural human development.* New York: Garland STPM Press.

Wierzbicka, A. (1992). Talking about emotions: Semantics, culture, and cognition. *Cognition and Emotion, 6,* 285–319.

Wiggers, M., & van Lieshout, C. (1985). Development of recognition of emotions: Children's reliance on situational and facial expressive cues. *Developmental Psychology, 21,* 338–349.

Winn, S., Tronick, E. Z., & Morelli, G. A. (1989). The infant and the group: A look at Efe caretaking practices in Zaire. In J. K. Nugent, B. M. Lester, & T. B. Brazelton (Eds.), *The cultural context of infancy: Vol. 1. Biology, culture, and infant development* (pp. 87–109). Norwood, NJ: ABLEX.

Wintre, M., Polivy, J., & Murray, M. (1990). Self-predictions of emotional response patterns: Age, sex, and situational determinants. *Child Development, 61,* 1124–1133.

Yirmiya, N., & Weiner, B., (1986). Perceptions of controllability and anticipated anger. *Cognitive Development, 1,* 273–280.

Zahn-Waxler, C. (1991). The case for empathy: A developmental review. *Psychological Inquiry, 2,* 155–158.

Zahn-Waxler, C., Cole, P. M., & Barrett, K. C. (1991). Guilt and empathy: Sex differences and implications for the development of depression. In J. Garber & K. Dodge (Eds.), *The development of emotion regulation and dysregulation* (pp. 243–272). New York: Cambridge University Press.

Zahn-Waxler, C., Cummings, E. M., Iannotti, R., & Radke-Yarrow, M. (1984). Young offspring of depressed parents: A population at risk for affective problems. In D. Cicchetti & K. Schneider-Rosen (Eds.), Childhood depression. *New Directions for Child Development, 26,* 81–105.

Zahn-Waxler, C., & Kochanska, G. (1990). The origins of guilt. In R. A. Thompson (Ed.), *Socioemotional development. Nebraska Symposium on Motivation* (Vol. 36, pp. 183–258). Lincoln: University of Nebraska Press.

Zahn-Waxler, C., & Radke-Yarrow, M. (1990). The origins of empathic concern. *Motivation and Emotion, 14,* 107–130.

Zahn-Waxler, C., Radke-Yarrow, M., & King, R. (1979). Child rearing and children's prosocial initiations toward victims of distress. *Child Development, 50,* 319–330.

Zahn-Waxler, C., & Robinson, J. (1995). Empathy and guilt: Early origins of feelings of responsibility. In J. Tangney & K. Fischer (Eds.), *Self-conscious emotions* (pp. 143–173). New York: Guilford Press.

Zarbatany, L., & Lamb, M. E. (1985). Social referencing as a function of information source: Mothers versus strangers. *Infant Behavior and Development, 8,* 25–33.

Zivin, G. (1985). Separating the issues in the study of expressive development: A framing chapter. In G. Zivin (Ed.), *The development of expressive behavior* (pp. 3–22). New York: Academic Press.

Zivin, G. (1986a). Clarifying the framework of expressive behavior: A reply to Hinde and to Izard and Haynes. *Merrill-Palmer Quarterly, 32,* 321–325.

Zivin, G. (1986b). Processes of expressive behavior development. *Merrill-Palmer Quarterly, 32,* 103–140.

Zumbahlen, M., & Crawley, A. (1996). *Infants' early referential behavior in prohibition contexts: The emergence of social referencing?* Paper presented at the meetings of the International Conference on Infant Studies, Providence, RI.

CHAPTER 6

Personality Development across the Life Course

AVSHALOM CASPI

There are many ways to think about and to study personality. I favor focusing on individual differences in personality because differences between individuals are the most remarkable feature of human nature.

Individual differences are the stuff of natural selection. In both genetic and cultural evolution, selection pressures operate on differences between persons. In genetic evolution, mutation introduces variability in genes—stretches of chemical information—whose phenotypic expressions are subject to selection pressures. In cultural evolution, social innovation introduces variability in "memes" (rhymes with *genes*)—ideas, fashions, customs, and other "stretches of social information"—and these, too, are subject to selection pressures: they thrive or die because of their adaptation to environmental conditions (Dawkins, 1976, p. 206). Individual differences are the stuff of life.

Not surprisingly, individual differences are ubiquitous: they pervade all aspects of life. Some individuals are tall, others short; some shy, others outgoing; some process new information quickly, others slowly. In fact, individual differences within a group are generally greater than differences between groups, and regardless of the group in which they are observed individual differences have real-world consequences. Individual differences thus demand scientific scrutiny: How do they arise? How do they shape social experience?

And because, as I will show, individual differences in personality *do* shape social experience, individual differences are fundamental to applied practice and policy considerations. Teachers, police officers, and CEOs—all practitioners who draw on basic research in psychology—wish to know the reasons for and the consequences of variation in the population. Why do some children have difficulty concentrating? Do individual differences in aggression make a difference in later life? What qualities

Preparation of this chapter was supported by grants from the National Institute of Mental Health (MH49414) and the William T. Grant Foundation, and by the Vilas Foundation of the University of Wisconsin.

311

predict job success? The triumviral task of describing, predicting, and explaining individual differences is one of the most important contributions that psychology can make to society.

A DEVELOPMENTAL APPROACH TO THE STUDY OF PERSONALITY DIFFERENCES

A developmental approach to the study of individual differences in personality seeks to answer three questions. First, what are the origins of personality differences? Efforts to answer this question examine how biological and environmental forces give shape to emergent personality differences in the course of human development (Grusec & Lytton, 1988). Second, how is continuity achieved? Efforts to answer this question treat the continuity of personality not as a given, but as a phenomenon requiring both confirmation and explanation (Caspi & Bem, 1990). Third, how do people change? Efforts to answer this question specify the conditions that modify behavior patterns and life trajectories (Laub & Sampson, 1993).

Distinct questions about the origins, continuity, and change of personality differences demand distinct answers. Indeed, some of the most striking confusions about personality development result from mistaking answers to one question as answers to another. Such confusion is striking in discussions about genetic influences on behavior. Behavior-genetic analyses are concerned primarily with the origins of individual differences. Because evidence from behavior-genetic studies points to the considerable heritability of many personality characteristics, it is frequently concluded that genetic effects also explain how continuity is achieved. This is not necessarily so; genetic sources of influence on individual differences do not preclude the possibility that continuities in these differences are mediated environmentally (Rutter, 1991). Similar confusion characterizes the analysis of continuity and change. Longitudinal evidence points to the significant continuity of personality across the life course. Less is known about how such continuity is achieved and about whether the processes that promote change are simply the opposite of processes that promote continuity (Rutter, 1988). In fact, continuity and change may demand separate theoretical treatments because unique processes promote each of them.

The goal of this chapter is to summarize what I think we know about the origins, continuity, and change of individual differences in personality. The answers are sometimes obvious, sometimes surprising, and sometimes unsatisfactory.

The chapter is divided into four sections. The first section offers a personality primer and sketches the conceptual and methodological concerns of modern personality research. The second section summarizes research evidence about the genetic and environmental origins of personality differences, and explores how early-emerging temperamental differences become elaborated into personality differences. The third section looks at personality from a longitudinal perspective and examines processes that promote continuity across the life course. The fourth section examines the multiple meanings of the term *change* and seeks to answer whether people can and do change.

PERSONALITY PSYCHOLOGY: A SKETCH OF RECENT ADVANCES

If individual differences are the sine qua non of personality psychology, which differences should we focus on? Individuals differ from one another in appearance, social background, the statuses they occupy, and the roles they play. This chapter focuses on individual differences in personality traits. Personality traits refer to individual differences in the tendency to behave, think, and feel in certain consistent ways. Trait models are often caricatured as static, nondevelopmental conceptions of personality. This misapprehension arises because temperamental and personality traits are thought to represent stable and enduring psychological differences between persons; ergo, they are static. Few personality researchers subscribe to this conclusion. Rather, contemporary personality research has sought to formulate the ways in which personality differences, in transaction with environmental circumstances, organize behavior in dynamic ways over time. Personality traits are thus organizational constructs; they influence how individuals organize their behavior to meet environmental demands and new developmental challenges. As Allport (1937) noted, personality traits are "modi vivendi, ultimately deriving their significance from the role they play in advancing adaptation within, and mastery of, the personal environment" (p. 342).

In preparing this chapter, I used Allport's (1937) text as a guide. This choice is occasioned by the realization that, by and large, Allport had it right (Funder, 1991). Allport claimed the concept of personality traits was tenable and railed against "fictionism," the alternative view that personality traits are social constructions in the eyes of beholders: "Scarcely anyone has ever thought of questioning the existence of traits as the fundamental dispositions of personality. In common speech everyone presupposes traits when he characterizes himself or his acquaintances. . . . Normally the psychologist too talks in these terms. But as soon as he enters his laboratory or class-room he is likely to leave common sense behind him. . . . Rightly he thinks of common sense as a faulty guide. Yet in the matter of human traits common sense is remarkably well-seasoned with experience, and scarcely deserves the complete rebuff it receives" (p. 286).

Allport was also prescient. He anticipated numerous challenges to the study of personality that have arisen over the past 50 years, and in many instances he presaged the research conclusions. In fact, traits have been revived as basic concepts in the study of personality (Wiggins & Pincus, 1992), and this revival has begun to influence developmental research (Halverson, Kohnstamm, & Martin, 1994; Hartup & van Lieshout, 1995). Because there are still misconceptions about personality traits, I open this chapter with a personality psychology primer whose purpose is to summarize recent advances in theory and research.

The Reality of Personality Traits

The most daring challenge to the study of personality has been the possibility that there is no such thing. Kenrick and Funder (1988) reviewed data concerning seven pessimistic claims about the existence of personality traits. The kernels of these claims, or "trait-dismissive hypotheses" (Tellegen, 1991), were contained in Mischel's (1968) critique of trait models of personality. Over the past 25 years, many studies tested these trait-dismissive hypotheses, and the accumulated data, far from dismissing traits, have contributed to the renaissance of the trait as an essential psychological construct. Here are the trait-dismissive claims, and Kenrick and Funder's (1988) summary of their empirical status.

The first claim is that personality is "in the eye of the beholder." According to this claim, human observers routinely make inferential errors about the mainsprings of human behavior, and the perception of traitlike behavioral uniformity in the behavior of other people is idiosyncratic if not illusory. The difficulty with this claim is that observers agree to a substantial degree in their perception of other people.

The second claim is that demonstrations of agreement are the result of semantic generalization. According to this claim, observers use an implicit theory of personality to judge the behavior of other persons and make their ratings of others on the basis of similarity of meaning, that is, on the basis of what words go with other words. The difficulty with this claim is that observers don't just agree about what words go with other words; they also agree about the people to whom the specific words apply.

The third claim is that agreement reflects consensus about high base-rate characteristics in the population. According to this claim, observers agree in their personality judgments of other people because they know people in general but not any one person in particular; it is thus easy to agree that someone, in fact anyone, "wishes to be liked." The difficulty with this claim is that high base rates can only account for agreement when observers fail to make distinctions between the persons they rate. High base rates cannot account for agreement when observers differentiate among the persons they rate.

The fourth claim is that observers may well differentiate among the persons they judge, but they do so on the basis of erroneous stereotypes. According to this claim, observers agree in their ratings of specific persons because they share and use stereotypes (e.g., about appearance) to evaluate these persons. The difficulty with this claim is that the use of stereotypes cannot account for evidence that observers increasingly agree with each other the more they have gotten to know the persons they rate, nor for evidence that these ratings are correlated with behavioral measures.

The fifth claim is that observers agree with each other because they talk among themselves and with the person being rated. According to this claim, observers agree in their ratings of specific persons because the persons rated have acquired or created a unique reputation for themselves. The difficulty with this claim is that strangers who have not had a chance to "negotiate" their agreement with each other or with the person being rated agree in their judgments of that person.

The sixth claim is that observers agree in their evaluations of other persons simply because they have observed those persons in the same or in related situations. According to this claim, agreement about other persons' personalities is a by-product of watching them in the same situation. The difficulty with this claim is that different observers who get to know the same target person in different situations agree about their personalities.

Kenrick and Funder (1988; Funder, 1995) marshaled evidence to counter the six aforementioned claims. This evidence supports Allport's (1937) contention that "there must be something really there, something objective in the nature of the individual himself that compels observers, in spite of their own prejudices, to view him in essentially the same way" (p. 288). But there is a seventh claim: Personality traits are unimportant.

The Importance of Personality Traits

Mischel (1968) used the term *personality coefficient* to describe those correlations, usually of the .3 magnitude, typically found between scores on personality tests and nontest behaviors. This descriptive summary paved the way for others to claim that personality traits are simply unimportant. This claim has generated the following questions and answers.

Is the "Situation Coefficient" Bigger?

If effect sizes associated with personality variables are small, do situation factors play a stronger role in determining behavior? Here arises a communication problem traceable to the historic bifurcation of psychology (Cronbach, 1975). Psychologists who study individual differences typically report effect sizes, whereas experimental psychologists typically report only significance tests. In fact, when effect sizes are calculated for experimental manipulations (e.g., for classic demonstrations of situational influences on bystander intervention or obedience to authority), the resulting "situation coefficient" is remarkably similar to the personality coefficient, ranging from .36 to .42 (Funder & Ozer, 1983). Of course, these classic experiments are remarkable not for their statistical strength of association but because their results violated expectations about human behavior. That, however, hardly makes the personality evidence less credible scientifically.

Is .3 Low?

To demonstrate the meaning of correlations, Rosenthal and Rubin (1982) developed a procedure to convert effect size estimates into a contingency table display. The results are striking. Consider a correlational analysis showing that a new intervention program can explain 9% of the total variation in outcome among children at risk for behavior problems. It is unlikely that most social scientists would herald it a successful program. In fact, however, such a correlation (.3) suggests that whereas fully 65% of the children in the control group would develop behavior problems, only 35% of the children enrolled in the intervention program would develop behavior problems. The correlation coefficient of .3 is thus associated with a reduction of 30% in the outcome of interest! More generally, Ozer (1985) suggests that theoretical grounds should inform the choice between r or

r^2 as the coefficient of determination. If one is interested in predicting variance in one variable from a second variable, the correlation squared is appropriate. If one is interested in the percent of variance common to two variables (that is, in whether a latent trait underlies both variables), the correlation is appropriate.

Can We Improve on .3?

According to Epstein (1983), many studies find low correlations between trait measures and behavior measures, as well as little cross-situational consistency in behavior, because they examine single behavioral acts that are low in reliability and generality. More accurate estimates of personality-behavior relations emerge when investigators create aggregated scores by combining several behavioral measures of the same trait (Rushton, Brainerd, & Pressley, 1983). This is not just a psychometric truism; it is also a substantive claim about the strong practical significance of personality traits. For example, it does not matter much if on occasion a student is late for class (a single behavioral act that is low in reliability and generality), but the student who is habitually late and often neglects to submit work on time is likely to incur the wrath of teachers and to lose out in formal education.

Sampling decisions also affect estimates of personality-behavior relations. Sample selection biases jeopardize both external and internal validity (Berk, 1983). If particular cases are systematically underrepresented in a sample the regression lines between personality and behavior will yield biased and inconsistent estimates of population regression lines. Unfortunately, the majority of psychological studies rely on samples of convenience (e.g., school samples, clinic samples), which systematically exclude particular cases (e.g., school dropouts, individuals who do not seek treatment). The exclusion of these cases may truncate the range of scores on psychological variables of interest to personality researchers and thereby reduce observed effect sizes. (The problem may be more serious because propositions about psychological processes, not just effect sizes, that are derived from studies of select samples may not generalize to other samples; see Sears, 1986.)

Is Specific Behavior Determined by Only One Trait?

Debates about the personality coefficient are based on the implicit assumption that every behavior is the product of a single trait. This is implausible, for behavior is more likely determined by multiple traits. This multiple-trait perspective has important implications for effect size estimates.

To explain this point, Ahadi and Diener (1989) conducted a Monte Carlo simulation. They used a simulation study because, in the real world, it is impossible to fully know all the determinants of a specific behavior. Their simulation study showed that small to moderate correlations are the rule, even in the case of completely determined behavior. For example, when a specific behavior was totally determined by three traits, working additively, the upper-bound trait-behavior correlation was about .5. Even this upper-bound estimate may be too generous, for it is based on two extreme assumptions: only three psychological traits completely determine a specific behavior and these three traits can combine only additively, not multiplicatively. In sum, it may be unreasonable (and under most conditions, statistically inconceivable) to expect enormous effect sizes.

Do Traits Have Any Practical Relevance?

Personality traits have been shown to shape developmental outcomes in multiple domains and in different age groups. Research in criminology shows that personalty differences are related to delinquency in different countries, different age cohorts, across gender, and across race (Caspi et al., 1994). Research in organizational psychology shows that personality differences are related to measures of job performance and may offer incremental validity over cognitive measures (Barrick & Mount, 1991). Research in health psychology shows that personality differences are related to risk- and health-promoting behaviors (Friedman et al., 1995), and knowledge of these psychological differences can be used to design health campaigns and educational programs (Jaccard & Wilson, 1991). These empirical findings are not simply the result of shared item content on measures of personality and measures of behavior. Studies that avoid the problem of predictor-criterion item overlap and that use different and multiple data sources suggest that personality traits are alive and well (Deary & Matthews, 1993).

The unproductive bifurcation of personality and clinical psychology is also drawing to an end. Although there remain methodological issues to resolve in relating normal and abnormal psychology, research shows that different forms of psychopathology are related to variations in normal personality traits (e.g., Krueger et al., 1996a). The possibility that traits and disorders reflect phenotypic expressions of the same underlying process holds the promise for advances in etiology (Nigg & Goldsmith, 1994). It is also possible for personality psychology to contribute to differential treatment planning, especially in terms of choosing feedback procedures and intervention strategies (e.g., Horowitz, Rosenberg, Baer, Ureno, & Villasenor, 1988). In all, when research is carefully done—that is, when reliable and valid measures of personality are selected, when multiple and independent outcomes are secured, when sampling biases are avoided, and when the problem of predictor-criterion item overlap is eliminated—the data point to the reality and consequential nature of personality differences.

The Developing Structure of Personality: Current Conceptions and Controversies

A perusal of psychology journals gives the impression that there exist thousands of personality traits. Given so many personality concepts and corresponding measures, the scientific description of personality would appear to be futile. Indeed, one of the most fundamental problems in the study of individual differences has been to develop a taxonomy of personality traits. The purpose of such a taxonomy is to "facilitate the accumulation and communication of empirical findings" about the many different personality concepts and measures studied by behavioral scientists (John, 1990, p. 66).

A (Brief) Summary of Research on Personality Structure across the Life Span

Progress in developing a taxonomy of personality traits has been facilitated by the recognition that personality is organized hierarchically (Eysenck, 1947; Hampson, John, & Goldberg, 1986). At the highest level are those broad traits (e.g., extraversion) representing the most general dimensions of individual differences in personality. At successively lower levels are more specific traits (e.g., sociability, activity) that are, in turn, composed of more specific responses (e.g., talkative, enthusiastic, energetic). In this hierarchical scheme, higher-order constructs can be shown to account for the observed covariation among lower-order constructs (Digman, 1990). Not surprisingly, the search for the structure of personality yields somewhat different results depending at which level personality factors are derived, how factors are extracted, and how they are rotated. The result is an uneasy tension between multidimensional trait models and general factor models (Watson, Clark, & Harkness, 1994).

Multidimensional trait models focus on specific traits (e.g., sociability, activity, dominance, achievement, altruism) and have been developed on the basis of both theoretical concerns and pragmatic considerations. For example, the Personality Research Form assesses traits derived from Murray's system of "needs" (Jackson, 1984). The Sixteen Personality Factor Questionnaire, the product of factor analytic research, assesses source traits thought to constitute an individual's personality (Cattell, Eber, & Tatsuoka, 1970). The California Psychological Inventory assesses traits that are thought to reflect universal, folk concepts of personality (Gough, 1986). General factor models emphasize the importance of a smaller number of superfactors rather than a larger number of more specific traits. In fact, most multidimensional models appear to represent specific traits that can be accounted for by more general superfactors (McCrae, 1989). Among the best established and validated general factor models are Eysenck's (Eysenck & Eysenck, 1985) three-factor system, Tellegen's (1985; Tellegen & Waller, in press) model of personality structure, and the five-factor model (John, 1990).

Eysenck initially proposed two general superfactors of personality, neuroticism and Extraversion, later supplemented with a third factor, psychoticism, which more accurately reflects disinhibition (Zuckerman, 1991). Tellegen proposed a similar three-factor model including Negative Emotionality, Positive Emotionality, and Constraint. Other researchers suggest that most personality traits fall within five, rather than three, broad content domains. Researchers who favor a five-factor model have been guided by the lexical hypothesis, which posits that most socially relevant and salient personality characteristics have become encoded in everyday language. Words arise in language because they are needed. Accordingly, the personality terms contained in the natural language may provide an extensive, yet finite, set of attributes that people who share that language have found important and useful in their interactions with each other. Historically, Allport (1937, p. 304) provided the basis for later taxonomic work by listing the personality terms found in an unabridged dictionary. Cattell (1945) used this list as a starting point for his multidimensional model of personality structure, but other researchers who continued the lexical research tradition found that five factors represent sufficiently well the structure of these adjectives. Goldberg (1993) dubbed these factors "the Big Five."

Each of the so-called Big Five factors summarizes a domain of individual differences that is extremely broad and includes a large number of distinct, more specific personality characteristics. To illustrate the meaning of the factors, Table 6.1 lists four trait adjectives (John, 1990) and

four California Adult Q-Sort (CAQ) items (McCrae, Costa, & Busch, 1986) that define the positive pole of each dimension. These five factors have been found repeatedly in studies of adults, using different instruments, different data sources, and different languages (Digman, 1990; Goldberg, 1993; John, 1990).

The five-factor model overlaps to a considerable extent with the three-factor models of Eysenck and Tellegen (Church, 1994; Watson et al., 1994). Neuroticism or Negative Emotionality is common to all systems; it describes the extent to which the person experiences the world as distressing or threatening. Extraversion or Positive Emotionality is also common to all systems; it describes the extent to which the person actively engages the world or avoids intense social experiences. Conscientiousness or Constraint describes the extent and strength of impulse control: whether the person is able to delay gratification in the service of more distant goals or is unable to modulate impulsive expression. Agreeableness describes a person's interpersonal nature on a continuum from warmth and compassion to antagonism. Agreeable persons are empathic, altruistic, helpful, and trusting, whereas antagonistic persons are abrasive, ruthless, manipulative, and cynical. (Eysenck's psychoticism factor may represent a combination of low Conscientiousness and low Agreeableness; Costa and McCrae, 1995.) Openness to Experience describes the depth, complexity, and quality of a person's mental and experiential life.

Are these traits merely psycholexical artifacts? According to Buss (1991), they are much more. From his "personality as an adaptive landscape" view, these five traits represent the most salient and important dimensions of an individual's social survival needs. We judge others—and are judged by others—according to those psychological dimensions that provide information to the group about adaptational potential, and the Big Five summarize those personality traits that are most relevant to adaptation to the social landscape.

Whereas the study of personality structure in adulthood has influenced research on adult development and aging (McCrae & Costa, 1990), the study of personality structure in childhood has been all but neglected. The trait domains most frequently studied by developmentalists (e.g., shyness, sociability, altruism, withdrawal, impulsivity) have not been related to each other in a coherent taxonomic framework. Indeed, most investigations of personality development focus their study on the origins and developmental course of a single personality dimension. Revelle (1993) noted that the result is a research discipline filled

Table 6.1 Examples of Trait Adjectives, California Adult Q-Sort Items, and California Child Q-Sort Items Defining the Big Five Factors

| Big Five Factor | Factor Definers | | |
	Adjectives[a]	Adult Q-Sort Items[b]	Child Q-Sort Items[c]
Extraversion	Active	Skilled in play, humor	Emotionally expressive
	Assertive	Facially, gesturally expressive	A talkative child
	Enthusiastic	Behaves assertively	Makes social contact easily
	Outgoing	Gregarious	Not inhibited or constricted
Agreeableness	Generous	Sympathetic, considerate	Warm and responsive
	Kind	Arouses liking	Helpful and cooperative
	Sympathetic	Warm, compassionate	Develops genuine and close relationships
	Trusting	Basically trustful	Tends to give, lend, and share
Conscientiousness	Organized	Dependable, responsible	Persistent in activities, does not give up easily
	Planful	Able to delay gratification	Attentive and able to concentrate
	Reliable	Not self-indulgent	Planful; thinks ahead
	Responsible	Behaves ethically	Reflective; thinks and deliberates before speaking or acting
Neuroticism	Anxious	Thin-skinned	Fearful and anxious
	Self-pitying	Basically anxious	Tends to go to pieces under stress; becomes rattled and disorganized
	Tense	Concerned with adequacy	Not self-reliant, not confident
	Worrying	Fluctuating moods	Appears to feel unworthy; thinks of self as "bad"
Openness/Intellect	Artistic	Wide range of interests	Curious and exploring
	Curious	Introspective	Appears to have high intellectual capacity (whether or not expressed in achievement)
	Imaginative	Values intellectual matters	Creative in perception, thought, work, or play
	Wide interests	Aesthetically reactive	Has an active fantasy life

[a] Adjective checklist items defining the factor in a study of 280 men and women who were rated by 10 psychologists during an assessment weekend at the Institute of Personality Assessment and Research, Berkeley (John, 1990).

[b] Abbreviated California Adult Q-sort items defining the factor in a study of 403 men and women who Q-sorted themselves as part of their participation in the Baltimore Longitudinal Study of Aging (McCrae, Costa, & Busch, 1986).

[c] Abbreviated California Child Q-sort items defining the factor in two independent studies: (a) a study of 720 Dutch boys and girls who were Q-sorted by parents and teachers (van Lieshout & Haselager, 1993, 1994) and (b) a study of 350 African American and Caucasian boys aged 12–13 enrolled in the Pittsburgh Youth Study who were Q-sorted by their mothers (John et al., 1994).

with many studies of convergent validity and few studies of discriminant validity. Halverson et al. (1994) made a strong case that research on life span personality development will remain unintegrated unless child psychologists begin to study the structure of personality.

Some research suggests that the five-factor model may provide a reasonable representation of personality structure in late childhood and adolescence (Digman, 1989; Graziano & Ward, 1992). Using teacher ratings of subjects ranging in age from 7 to 13, Digman replicated five factors that he interpreted as childhood equivalents of the Big Five. However, the personality descriptors used in this research were selected from prior research on the Big Five in adulthood. Several other studies used free-response techniques and found that the Big Five dimensions account for a significant portion of parents' and teachers' descriptions of children's behavior (Havill, Allen, Halverson, & Kohnstamm, 1994; Mervielde, 1994) as well as for children's descriptions of other persons (Donahue, 1994).

Two large-scale studies used the California Child Q-Sort (CCQ) to study personality structure in childhood and adolescence. These studies did not use an item pool selected from adult research on the Big Five. Rather, the CCQ was used in these studies because this personality measure does not favor or represent any one theoretical viewpoint; it reflects a general language for describing a broad range of variations in personality and provides a comprehensive description of children and adolescents.

One study used a Dutch translation of the CCQ to explore the structure of personality in a sample ranging in age from 3 to 16 (van Lieshout & Haselager, 1993, 1994). Q-sort descriptions were provided by parents and teachers for over 700 boys and girls. Factor analyses, performed for different age groups, revealed that the first five principal components corresponded to the Big Five personality factors. A second study used the CCQ to explore the structure of personality in an ethnically diverse sample of boys aged 12 to 13 (John, Caspi, Robins, Moffitt, & Stouthamer-

Loeber, 1994). Q-sort descriptions were provided by mothers for over 300 African American and Caucasian boys, and the results also pointed to five factors corresponding to the five-factor model. To illustrate the convergence of findings across the two independent studies, as well as their resemblance to findings from studies of personality structure in adulthood, Table 6.1 lists four CCQ items that define the positive pole of each Big Five dimension. It appears that the Big Five personality dimensions can be measured in childhood and in adolescence, in boys and in girls, and in youngsters of different racial-ethnic groups. In addition, both the Dutch and the American analyses suggest that, at least in childhood and early adolescence, the Big Five may be supplemented by two additional factors, activity and irritability. Analyses showed that these factors exist at the same level of breadth as the other five dimensions and are independent of the Big Five.

In summary, research suggests that the five-factor model provides a generalizable and comprehensive representation of personality trait structure in adulthood. Inspired by these robust findings, studies with children and adolescents are confirming the replicability of the five-factor model in younger age groups. Moreover, analyses of the construct validity of these traits suggest that they are related to theoretically and socially important developmental outcomes such as juvenile delinquency, externalizing and internalizing behavior disorders, and school performance (John et al., 1994). In later sections, I consider how these findings may spur research on the development and emergence of personality. For now, I answer a more practical question.

What Advantages Do Structural Models of Personality Offer Developmental Research?

Students of personality development face a bewildering array of measures and scales from which to choose. Moreover, measures with the same name often measure concepts that are not the same, and measures with different names often measure constructs that overlap considerably in their content. As long as "each assessor has his own pet units and uses a pet battery of diagnostic devices" (Allport, 1958, p. 258), isolated empirical findings are unlikely to be integrated.

John (1990) suggested that an empirically based taxonomy of personality traits is more likely than any one researcher or any one theory to integrate the diverse systems of personality description. Rather than replacing all other systems, a personality taxonomy serves three research functions (Briggs, 1989):

- It improves communication among researchers who are using different variables to study closely related phenomena; connecting multiple and different measures of personality to an established and validated personality structure helps to organize and integrate diffuse research findings.

- It provides researchers with a structure to use when they develop new measures of personality; locating new measures in relation to what is already known eliminates redundancy and elucidates psychological constructs.

- It enables researchers to connect personality measures to more elaborate nomological networks and thereby to interpret research and generate new hypotheses about the origins of individual differences in personality.

To illustrate how a taxonomy may help to integrate research findings about child development, consider evidence from the Minnesota Mother-Child Project, an important longitudinal study that has used the CCQ to explore outcomes among children at risk for developmental difficulties. A report from this project showed that incompetent maternal care during the first few years of life predicted individual differences on a measure of "passive withdrawal" among boys during the elementary school years (Renken, Egeland, Marvinney, Mangelsdorf, & Sroufe, 1989). Unfortunately, there is little other published information about this trait. One way to connect passive withdrawal to a more elaborate nomological network is to examine its relation to the five-factor model. To do this, I used data from the Pittsburgh Youth Study, where we collected CCQ descriptions of several hundred boys. In this sample, I scored Renken et al.'s (1989) CCQ measure of passive withdrawal and correlated it with measures of the Big Five (John et al., 1994). The results show that passive withdrawal is negatively correlated with Extraversion ($r = -.69$) and somewhat positively correlated with Agreeableness ($r = .37$); the five-factor model thus provides an integrative framework in which a new measure can be classified.

These correlations do not mean that passive withdrawal is not a meaningful personality dimension. Rather, they suggest that passive withdrawal may be part of a more elaborate nomological network. Thus, even in the absence of other research about passive withdrawal it is possible to generate further predictions about the origins of individual differences in this trait by linking it to higher-order super-factors about which more information is known. Rather than work in isolation from research in personality psychology and its strong psychometric tradition, it is possible for students of child development to integrate new findings and develop new measures in conjunction with established and validated models.

To illustrate how a taxonomy may help to integrate research findings about adult development, consider evidence about personality and health. Researchers who have studied the association between the Type A behavior complex and coronary heart disease now believe that hostility may be the lethal personality component (Dembroski, Mac-Dougall, Costa, & Grandits, 1989). Unfortunately, efforts to replicate this association have been hampered by the absence of information about the construct validity of measures of hostility. Some measures of hostility appear to reflect subjective feelings of anger and irritation, whereas other measures of hostility reflect overt interpersonal expressions such as verbal outbursts (Smith, Sanders, & Alexander, 1990).

One way to clarify what measures of hostility measure is to examine their relation to the five-factor model. Smith and Williams (1992) note that hostility is a facet or component of both Neuroticism and Agreeableness (vs. antagonism), and this may explain the inconsistent association observed between different measures of hostility and coronary disease. Measures of hostility that reflect feelings of anger and irritation are facets of Neuroticism, and Neuroticism does not predict actual health outcomes; rather, it predicts health complaints (Watson & Pennebaker, 1989). In contrast, measures of hostility that reflect overt interpersonal expressions are facets of Agreeableness (vs. antagonism); antagonism may thus be the salient personality risk factor for coronary heart disease. By using a taxonomic model, students of adult development can make conceptual and measurement refinements in understanding the course of illness across the life span and begin to study neuroendocrinological and other physiological mechanisms that link specific personality traits and health.

By illustrating the research functions of a taxonomic system, I do not mean to advocate studying personality variation only at the highest level of abstraction, that is, in terms of broad and general superfactors. The Big Five are too broad to capture all the interesting variations in human personality, and distinctions at the level of more specific traits are necessary. As John and Robins (1993) note, the advantage of broad categories, such as those described by the five-factor model, is their substantial bandwidth; the disadvantage of broad categories is their low fidelity. For example, in both childhood and adulthood, shyness and sociability appear to be correlated at the empirical level, but at the same time they appear to be distinct at the construct level (Asendorpf & Meier, 1993; Cheek & Buss, 1981; Eisenberg, Fabes, & Murphy, 1995). A broad general factor such as Extraversion may thus overlook important etiological differences between specific traits. There is much to learn from studying variation at different levels of the personality trait hierarchy, but this does not obviate the need to understand how different levels are related hierarchically to each other.

This section emphasized the usefulness of the five-factor model. Of course, it is but one of several models that has proven useful in organizing and integrating findings about personality differences in fields as diverse as behavioral genetics (Loehlin, 1992), gerontology (Costa & McCrae, 1992), and organizational psychology (Barrick & Mount, 1991). Shortcomings of this model have been discussed (e.g., Block, 1995; Eysenck, 1991; McAdams, 1992), but none of these diminishes the usefulness of structural models per se.

A personality taxonomy is simply an evolving classification system whose purpose is to integrate and guide research. Indeed, there are historical parallels between the use of structural models in personality psychology and the use of a standardized model for describing and diagnosing mental illness in psychiatry. Prior to the advent of the *Diagnostic and Statistical Manual of Mental Disorders III* (*DSM-III;* American Psychiatric Association, 1980), clinicians and researchers did not have available explicit criteria to define the boundaries of diagnostic categories. Clinical diagnoses were difficult to compare, and cross-sample replications were hard to conduct. The development of *DSM-III* provided a common language with which clinicians and researchers could communicate about the disorders they were treating or investigating; *DSM-III* was a big improvement over *DSM-II*. *DSM-III* had its share of problems, and subsequent modifications to this system (*DSM-III-R, DSM-IV*) testify to the need for a flexible and evolving system that can accommodate new empirical information (Cantwell & Rutter, 1994). We can similarly hope that the use of a generally accepted trait taxonomy will help to impose structure on unintegrated research findings, reduce the likelihood that old traits will be reinvented under new labels, and advance the study of personality development across the life span.

Traits and Types, Dimensions and Categories

Thus far I used the term personality structure to refer to the pattern of covariation of traits across individuals. Personality structure can also refer to the organization of traits within the individual (Allport, 1958). Whereas most research on personality development focuses on the relative standing of persons on single variables, the more appropriate unit of analysis may be the person, not the variable. Person-centered research focuses on the configuration of multiple variables within the person; on how different variables are organized within the person and how this organization defines different types of persons. Such a model of the person as a system of interacting components is absent from most studies of personality, although investigators have called for approaches in which the person, not the variable, is the focus of analysis (e.g., Bem, 1983; Bergman & Magnusson, 1991). The focus of typological research is to discover the basic categories of human nature and in so doing to "carve nature at its joints" (Gangestad & Snyder, 1985).

However, just as the study of personality traits has been hampered by the absence of a structural model, the study of personality types has been held back by the absence of empirically derived personality typologies. It is unknown what, if any, personality types exist in the normal (nonpathological) population, and this determination cannot be made by establishing arbitrary cut-points along a distribution of scores (Meehl, 1992, p. 117). The designation of a "type" on the basis of extreme scores in a distribution alone is a dangerous enterprise. In the absence of a compelling theoretical cut-point, and without the use of statistical techniques that can detect whether a trait is dimensional or taxonic (dichotomous), the use of extreme scores is likely to generate findings that are sample-specific. Typological models of personality need to be held to the same empirical standards as dimensional models of personality: replicability, generalizability, and construct validity.

The most prominent empirical work on personality types is Block's (1971) study of Lives Through Time. Block employed the Q-sort technique of personality description to analyze continuity and change from early adolescence to adulthood in the Berkeley Guidance and Oakland Growth studies. Block had clinically trained judges complete independent Q-sorts of the study participants. In the Q-sort technique, a sorter describes an individual's personality by sorting a set of cards containing personality attributes into piles ranging from attributes that are least characteristic to those that are most characteristic of the individual. This produces a person-centered description because the sorter explicitly compares each attribute with other attributes within the same individual. The resemblance between two individuals is indexed by the correlation between their respective Q-sorts, which reflects the degree to which the attributes specified by the Q-sort are ordered the same way within the two individuals. The method of inverse factor analysis can then be used to identify clusters of individuals with similar Q-sort profiles.

Block (1971) identified five personality types among males. Three of these types represented groups of individuals with stable personalities across adolescence and adulthood: ego-resilients were well-adjusted and interpersonally effective; vulnerable overcontrollers were rigidly overcontrolled and maladapted; and unsettled undercontrollers were impulsive and antisocial. The remaining two types represented groups of individuals who showed patterns of personality change from early adolescence to adulthood: belated adjusters were maladjusted during adolescence but functioning effectively in adulthood, whereas anomic extraverts showed the opposite trend.

It is important to determine whether this particular cleavage of "nature at its joints" represents a generalizable personality typology. For example, the types may be specific to these samples, which included individuals who were almost exclusively White, above-average in intelligence, and who grew up several generations ago. Moreover, these same types were not apparent among females. Evidence for a generalizable typology requires that the types replicate across a broad range of populations.

Subsequent studies adopting a person-centered approach have now found three replicable personality types that converge with those identified by Block (1971). This convergence is noteworthy as the studies differ in numerous ways, including age, gender, ethnicity, the historical period and geographic location in which the study participants grew up, the source of personality information used to derive the types, and even the way the types were derived. Table 6.2 summarizes these facets of generalizability.

Extending Block's earlier work to a different sample, Klohnen and Block (personal communication, 1995) performed a typological analysis of young adults using Q-sort descriptions provided by interviewers on the basis of extensive individual assessments. They found three replicable personality types among males and females. The largest

Table 6.2   Generalizability of Three Empirically Derived Personality Types across Eight Studies

	Block (1971)	Klohnen & Block (1995)	Robins et al. (1996)	van Lieshout et al. (1995)	Hart et al. (1997)	York & John (1992)	Caspi & Silva (1995)	Pulkkinen (1996)
Personality Types								
1	Ego-resilients	Resilients	Resilients	Resilients	Resilients	Individuated	Well-adjusted	Resilients Individuated
2	Vulnerable overcontrollers	Overcontrollers	Overcontrollers	Overcontrollers	Overcontrollers	Traditional	Inhibited	Introverts/ Anxious
3	Unsettled undercontrollers	Undercontrollers	Undercontrollers	Undercontrollers	Undercontrollers	Conflicted	Undercontrolled	Conflicted/ Undercontrolled
Facets of Generalizability								
Subjects	84 boys/men	106 men & women	300 boys	79 boys & girls	168 boys & girls	103 women	1,024 boys & girls	138 men & 137 women
Age	Both 13 & 35 yrs	23 yrs	12–13 yrs	7, 10, & 12 yrs	7 yrs	43 yrs	3 yrs	26 yrs
Birth cohort	1920s	1960s	Late 1970s	Early 1970s	1970s	1937–39	1972–73	1960s
Geographical region	San Francisco Bay Area	San Francisco Bay Area	Pittsburgh	The Netherlands	Iceland	San Francisco Bay Area	New Zealand	Finland
Data source	Clinical judgments	Interviewer assessments	Caregiver reports	Teacher reports	Interviewer assessments	Clinical judgments	Examiner observations	Self-reports
Instrument used	Adolescent & Adult Q-sort	Adult Q-sort	Child Q-sort	Child Q-sort	Child Q-sort	Adult Q-sort	Behavior ratings	Scale scores from multiple questionnaires
Type derivation	Q-factors across time	Q-factors	Replicated Q-factors	Cluster analysis	Q-factors	Replicated Q-factors	Replicated clusters	Cluster analysis

group was made up of resilients who were well-functioning cognitively, emotionally, and interpersonally; male and female overcontrollers were without many interpersonal skills, shy, and inward looking; undercontrollers were hostile, disagreeable, and showed little concern for others. In a representative sample of Pittsburgh public school boys, Robins, John, Caspi, Moffitt, and Stouthamer-Loeber (1996) performed a typological analysis using Q-sort descriptions provided by primary caregivers and found three personality types that generalized across Black and White youth and that converged with Block's. In a sample of 7-, 10-, and 12-year-old Dutch boys and girls, van Lieshout, Haselager, Risken-Walraven, and van Aken (1995) performed a typological analysis using Q-sort descriptions provided by teachers. They found three personality types that generalized across age and sex and that converged with the groupings and the external correlates reported by Robins et al. (1996). A typological analysis using Q-sort descriptions of 7-year-old Icelandic children also found three personality types (Hart, Hofman, Edelstein, & Keller, 1997). When the authors conducted a longitudinal follow-up of these three types of children in adolescence, they found external correlates that replicated those reported by Robins et al. (1996). Another comparison can be made with the research of York and John (1992), who identified four replicable personality types in middle-aged women. Three of their types correspond to those identified here. The first (and again most prevalent type), labeled individuated, was substantially more resilient; the second (traditional) was overcontrolled; and the third type (conflicted) shared features with undercontrollers, specifically the undercontrolled expression of antagonism and hostility.

The four studies just reviewed all relied on Q-sort descriptions. But other data sources reveal similar findings. Caspi and Silva (1995) used cluster analysis to identify five replicable types in a New Zealand birth cohort, based on behavior ratings by examiners when the children were 3 years old. Three of these types match the types in Table 6.2. The well-adjusted type was the most prevalent and resembled the resilient type; the second type, given the label inhibited, parallels the overcontrolling type and was described as restrained, shy, fearful, and easily upset; the third, undercontrolled type, included children described as impulsive, restless, and distractible. Pulkkinen (1996) used extensive personality self-report data to identify personality types among young Finnish adults. The three male types (labeled resilients, introverts, and conflicted) identified in her study clearly match the other types in Table 6.2. Although the female types were less clearly defined, they, too, correspond with the three types in Table 6.2: a large group of adjusted individuals which included two subgroups of women (labeled feminines and individuated), differing from each other principally in their adherence to or separation from conventional female roles—and two smaller groups characterized by their anxious and undercontrolled behavior, respectively.

In summary, three replicable personality types seem to emerge in different studies. The convergence across studies is not perfect, and more typological research needs to be done before anything close to a comprehensive, generalizable personality typology can be said to exist. Special attention should be given to the generalizability of the types across sex, both in terms of the structure of the types and their developmental correlates. Despite its ancient history as a concept, the empirical study of personality types is still in its infancy. Nonetheless, the findings in Table 6.2 show sufficient convergence across studies to suggest that the three replicable personality types constitute a minimally necessary set. That is, if broadly defined personality types are studied in a large, heterogeneous sample, one should find one well-adjusted type, one maladjusted overcontrolling type, and one maladjusted undercontrolling type. At this point, these three types are good candidates to become an integral part of any generalizable personality typology. This does not mean that there are only three personality types, just as the five-factor model does not imply that there are only five personality dimensions. It simply means that at the broadest level of generalization, psychological theories must account for the development of these types. As a starting point for further typological research, the costs and benefits of having relatively few types must be weighed against those of having a larger number of types. A large number of types provides a differentiated system that respects the diversity of personalities in the population, but at the risk of including small and possibly unreplicated groupings of individuals. Thus, any refined typological model will need to provide evidence for its expected incremental validity.

Typological conceptions of temperament and personality are enjoying a renaissance in developmental psychology

(Kagan, 1994). Still, it is not known whether the dimensional or the categorical approach provides a more accurate reflection of personality organization (Livesley, Schroeder, Jackson, & Jang, 1994), and it is not yet known whether the empirical types identified in the person-centered research reviewed above reflect "true" types (i.e., discrete natural classes). This debate, however, should not obscure the possibility that trait dimensions and person typologies are complementary rather than competing systems (John & Robins, 1994). According to this perspective, the typological approach identifies categories of individuals based on their particular configuration of traits, and thus provides a bridge between purely variable-centered research (which emphasizes the traits on which all individuals differ) and purely person-centered research (which emphasizes the unique patterning of traits within an individual).

The Ontological Status of Personality Traits

Irrespective of one's preference for traits or types, dimensions or categories, variable- or person-centered approaches, each investigator must wrestle with the ontological status of traits (or types), because their substantive interpretation necessarily informs the nature of subsequent empirical inquiries.

It is possible to distinguish between three conceptions of traits or types: descriptive, dispositional, and explanatory (Zuroff, 1986). According to the first, descriptive-summary conception, traits are summary variables that describe observable consistencies in a person's past behavior. As demonstrated by criterion-oriented studies, a descriptive-summary conception serves useful predictive purposes. However, because this conception bypasses the explanatory work of psychology, it is unlikely, by itself, to yield theoretical insights about personality development: "It contributes no more to the science of psychology than rules for boiling an egg contribute to the science of chemistry" (Loevinger, 1957, p. 641).

According to a second, dispositional conception, traits represent a tendency to behave in certain kinds of ways if in certain kinds of situations. Personality differences are here treated as if-then conditional propositions (Mischel, 1990). "Dominant" individuals dominate when there are subjects for domination, but not when they are alone. Likewise, "intelligent" persons solve problems given the presence of problems; one is not constantly "acting smart." Dispositions differ from descriptive summaries in that they indicate nothing about the occurrence of behavior in the absence of eliciting stimuli (Wakefield, 1989; Zuroff, 1986).

According to a third, realist conception, traits are explanatory concepts. Whereas the descriptive and dispositional conceptions of traits outlined above regard behavioral attributes as "samples of response classes," a realist conception treats them as indicators or "signs of internal [psychological] structures" (Wiggins, 1973, pp. 368, 370). Whereas the dispositional, if-then conception of traits is agnostic with regard to explanation, a realist conception attempts to postulate underlying processes that lead traits to cause certain intentional states (Tellegen, 1991). "Personality is and does something. . . . It is what lies behind specific acts and within the individual. The systems that constitute personality are in every sense determining tendencies, and when aroused by suitable stimuli provoke those adjustive and expressive acts by which personality comes to be known" (Allport, 1937, pp. 48–49).

According to the realist conception, traits are not observable entities but hypothetical constructs, and like all such constructs their usefulness needs to be demonstrated and refuted through the procedures of construct validation. The process of "construct validation is nothing more or less than hypothesis testing" in which a construct becomes known by virtue of the interlocking system of laws in which it occurs (Hogan & Nicholson, 1988, p. 622), and the task of empirical research is to keep tightening the nomological net (Meehl, 1986). In this sense, researchers need to embed traits in process theories that lead to new and testable hypotheses about social, psychological, and biological phenomena throughout the life course (Zuroff, 1986). Trait explanations are not an end; rather, they are "placeholders" in an evolving search for fuller explanations of action and motivated behavior (Fletcher, 1993; Wakefield, 1989). Central to this evolving search are the three research goals introduced at the beginning of this chapter: to identify the origins of personality differences, to examine how they are maintained, and to explore how they may change across the life course. For the remainder of this chapter, I turn to these three topics.

THE ORIGINS OF INDIVIDUAL DIFFERENCES IN PERSONALITY

A fundamental assumption guiding the study of personality development is that early-emerging temperamental differences shape the course of development, its problematic presentations and healthful outcomes (Rutter, 1987). Individual differences in temperament refer to stylistic differences between people, to "differences that appear early in life, show substantial stability over time, represent predictable modes of response, and possibly have fairly direct neurobiological correlates" (Rutter, 1987, p. 447). Adult personality traits, to use Rutter's (1987) distinction, represent the social and cognitive elaborations of this endowment. In this section I ask: What are the origins of these individual differences, and how are temperamental differences elaborated into personality traits?

Genetic and Environmental Influences

If genotypic differences influence behavioral variation, genetic similarity should create personality similarities. Of course, environmental similarity may also create personality similarities. To estimate the relative roles that genes and environments play in personality development, behavioral geneticists employ two basic research designs: twin studies and adoption studies.

Twin studies compare monozygotic (MZ) twins, who are genetically identical, to dizygotic (DZ) twins, who have no more genes in common than other first-degree relatives (50% on average). This design assumes that, if the trait-relevant variation in the environments of MZ and DZ twins is the same, genetic influences are revealed if MZ twins are more similar than DZ twins. In addition, by comparing MZ and DZ twins who have been reared together to MZ and DZ twins who have been reared apart, it is possible to estimate the effects of environmental similarity on twin resemblance above and beyond the effects associated with genetic similarity.

Adoption studies compare pairs of genetically unrelated siblings growing up in the same family. In addition, adoption studies enable researchers to compare parent-child resemblance among parents and children who are genetically related and among parents and children who are unrelated. This design assumes that, if there is no selective placement with regard to trait-relevant environmental variation (e.g., no matching of biological and adoptive parents by the adoption agency), genetic influences will be revealed if correlations in adoptive families are negligible relative to correlations observed in biological families.

Twin and adoption studies are "natural experiments" that yield correlations between family members who share genes and environments to differing degrees. In addition to distinguishing between genetic and environmental variation for a given trait, behavioral geneticists have noted that environmental variance can be divided into two components (Rowe & Plomin, 1981). Shared environmental factors are those that have the same influence on children in the same family; these factors make members of a family similar to one another. For example, growing up in a poor family or in a divorced home may create similarities between siblings. Nonshared environmental factors are those that have a different influence on children in the same family; these factors make members of a family different from one another. For example, attending different schools or parental favoritism may create differences between siblings. The advent of model-fitting techniques has made it possible to examine the fit of alternative gene-environment models to twin and adoption data. Model fitting involves fitting different simultaneous equations to observed familial correlations and estimating the genetic and environmental values of the parameters associated with the best-fitting model (Loehlin, 1992).

Genetic and Environmental Influences on Temperamental Differences in Childhood

It is surprisingly difficult to summarize this evidence because different studies have used different measures of temperament and the relations between these different measures are not well established (Goldsmith, Rieser-Danner, & Briggs, 1991). A reliable summary may be furnished by combining evidence from three studies that used the same temperament measures (Bayley's Infant Behavior Record; IBR) on two occasions during the second year of life. Examiners in the Louisville Twin Study, the Colorado

Adoption Project, and the MacArthur Longitudinal Study of Twins rated children in these studies on three dimensions of temperament: affect-extraversion refers to the extent to which the child is positive and outgoing; activity refers to the child's activity level and energy expenditure; task-orientation refers to the child's persistence, attention, and goal-directed activity (Braungart, Plomin, DeFries, & Fulker, 1992; Emde et al., 1992; Matheny, 1980; Plomin et al., 1993).

The results from these studies are summarized in Figure 6.1, which shows correlations for the three IBR temperament dimensions for MZ twins, DZ twins, biological siblings, and adoptive siblings. In general, the rank order of the correlations is consistent with a genetic hypothesis: MZ twins who are genetically identical are most similar; adoptive siblings who are genetically unrelated are least similar; DZ twins and biological siblings, both of whom share about 50% of their genes, fall between MZ twins and adoptive siblings in their phenotypic similarity. Models fit to these data point to significant genetic influences on temperament, with somewhat clearer effects toward the end of the second year. Shared environmental influences on temperament are minimal. However, nonshared environmental influences account for substantial variation in these temperamental traits (Braungart et al., 1992; Plomin et al., 1993).

Whereas behavior-genetic studies of temperament in early childhood tend to rely on observational ratings, such studies in later childhood and adolescence have tended

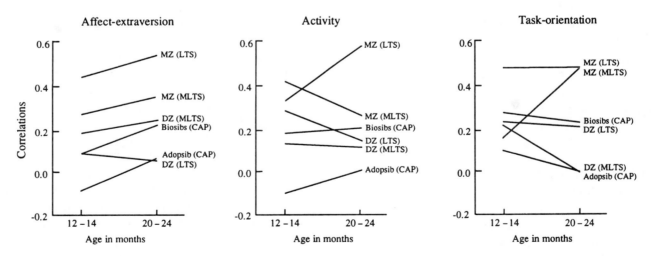

Figure 6.1 Correlations of MZ twins, DZ twins, biological siblings, and adoptive siblings on three dimensions of temperament during the second year of life. MZ = Monozygotic twins; DZ = Dizygotic twins; Biosibs = Biological siblings; Adopsibs = Adoptive siblings. LTS = Louisville Twin Study; MLTS = MacArthur Longitudinal Twin Study; CAP = Colorado Adoption Project.

to rely on parental reports. The temperamental dimensions of emotionality, activity, and sociability have been rated by parents in several independent twin studies (Buss & Plomin, 1984; Matheny & Dolan, 1980; Plomin et al., 1993; Saudino, McGuire, Reiss, Hetherington, & Plomin, 1995). Table 6.3 summarizes these findings about temperament during the first two decades of life. It shows that MZ twins are much more similar to each other than DZ twins, suggesting a substantial genetic influence on childhood temperament. However, these findings are limited by their reliance on parents as the sole source of data for assessing twin similarity, a problem discussed in a later section.

Genetic and Environmental Influences on Personality Differences in Adolescence and Adulthood

Loehlin (1992) fit different gene-environment models to a meta-analysis of twin and adoption studies of personality. He accomplished this in two steps. First, he organized according to the Big Five scheme the many different personality measures that have been administered in twin and family studies. Second, he fit different gene-environment models to data about the Big Five traits. Figure 6.2 summarizes the results of this meta-analysis.

Figure 6.2 shows that genetic effects are important for all traits and account for 22% to 46% of the total variation in each of the Big Five factors. Model-fitting efforts also point to a second factor that may indicate either (a) a special MZ environmental effect or (b) nonadditive genetic effects. Special MZ environmental effects refer to the possibility that MZ twins resemble each other more than other first-degree relatives because their environments are different from those of other first-degree relatives. Nonadditive genetic effects refer to the possibility that MZ twins resemble each other more than other first-degree relatives

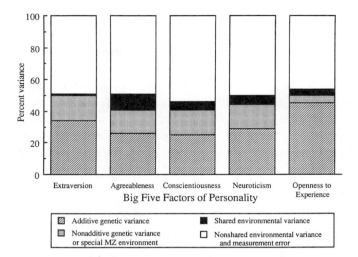

Figure 6.2 Genetic and environmental influences on the Big Five factors of personality. From *Genes and Environment in Personality Development,* by J. C. Loehlin, 1992, Sage Publications.

because they share the entire configuration of their genes. As Figure 6.2 shows, to the extent that nonadditive genetic effects are important, it may be that altogether between 40% to 50% of the variation in personality traits is heritable. I consider the meaning of this factor in greater detail in the next section.

The results in Figure 6.2 also highlight important environmental influences on personality traits. As with studies of temperament, the results show that the contribution of the shared family environment is small and accounts for 10% or less of the total variation in each of the Big Five factors. The largest factor—accounting for approximately 50% of variation in personality traits—refers to nonshared environmental variation, as well as gene-environment interactions and errors of measurement. In the following sections, I examine the implications and limitations of findings about genetic, shared-environmental, and nonshared-environmental influences.

Genetic Influences

Genetic influences on childhood temperament and on adolescent and adult personality are substantial. In the personality domain, these estimates are especially clear-cut for traits related to Extraversion and Neuroticism. These trait domains have been measured extensively in behavior-genetic studies. The estimates for the remaining three traits (Agreeableness, Conscientiousness, Openness to Experience) are less consistent across different studies because

Table 6.3 Correlation of MZ and DZ Twins on Parental Ratings of Temperament during the First Two Decades of Life

Average age (in years) of twins	Temperament Dimension					
	Emotionality		Activity		Sociability	
	MZ	DZ	MZ	DZ	MZ	DZ
1.5[a]	.43	−.03	.55	−.24	.44	.07
5.0[b]	.63	.12	.62	−.13	.53	−.03
8.5[c]	.45	.11	.56	.06	.66	.19
10–18[d]	.56	.27	.73	.19	.52	.05

[a] Data for 1.5-year-olds are from Plomin et al., 1993; Table 2.
[b] Data for 5.0-year-olds are from Buss & Plomin, 1984; Table 9.2.
[c] Data for 8.5-year-olds are from Matheny & Dolan, 1980; Table 3.
[d] Data for 10–18-year-olds are from Saudino et al., 1995; Table 2.

these trait domains have been measured less extensively (Loehlin, 1992).

As more twin and adoption studies of personality have accumulated, two peculiar findings have emerged. The first is that in some twin studies, MZ correlations are more than twice the size of DZ correlations (see the correlations in Table 6.3). This is peculiar because, in terms of additive genetic variance, MZ twins are only twice as similar to each other as DZ twins; the ratio of MZ correlations to DZ correlations should not exceed 2. This finding is made all the more peculiar by a second finding: twin studies tend to yield higher heritability estimates than adoption studies (e.g., Loehlin, Willerman, & Horn, 1987).

There are at least two explanations for these findings, a genetic and an environmental explanation. The genetic explanation suggests that the effect of genes is not merely additive, but nonadditive as well. Most behavior-genetic models assume that genetic influences on personality are additive; that is, genes add up according to gene dosage and relatives should thus resemble each other in proportion to their genetic relatedness. But it is conceivable that genetic influences on personality are also nonadditive; genes may interact with one another in different ways that geneticists call dominance and epistasis (Plomin, DeFries, & McClearn, 1990). If genetic interactions are important, they will contribute to the greater similarity of MZ twins compared to other kin because genetic configurations are identical in MZ twins; MZ twins are identical for both additive and nonadditive genetic effects. Lykken, McGue, Tellegen, and Bouchard (1992) suggest that nonadditive genetic effects are important in personality development. They discuss the process of *emergenesis,* by which they mean that some personality traits may be "an emergent property of a configuration of genes or perhaps a configuration of more basic traits that are themselves partly genetic in origin" (p. 1569).

The environmental explanation suggests that different environmental processes may characterize the homes of MZ and DZ twins. One possibility is that environmental factors increase MZ similarity relative to DZ similarity ("assimilation" effects); another possibility is that environmental factors decrease DZ similarity relative to MZ similarity ("contrast" effects). Both environmental processes may account for MZ:DZ ratios greater than 2 and for higher estimates of heritability in twin studies relative to adoption studies. For example, whereas twin studies show substantial genetic influences on parent ratings of childhood emotionality, activity, and sociability (see Table 6.3),

at least one adoption study revealed no evidence of genetic influences on these dimensions (Plomin, Coon, Carey, DeFries, & Fulker, 1991). It is possible that parental ratings inflate MZ twin similarity and deflate DZ and adoptive sibling similarity. Parents may contrast their DZ twins, nontwin siblings, and adoptive siblings but not their MZ twins. Differential contrasts may create differences between nonidentical first-degree relatives. Such contrast effects may even account for the negative correlations between DZ twins in Table 6.3. Of course, it is possible that these contrast effects emerge primarily in parents' ratings of their children's temperament and do not generalize to other data sources, thus underscoring the need to gather data from multiple sources in future behavior-genetic studies of personality development.

The available evidence from twin and adoption studies does not firmly establish whether nonadditive genetic effects or special environmental processes provide better fits to the data. Moreover, this problem is difficult to sort out because the substantive accounts of the data are confounded with the source of measurement. Indeed, it may be that both explanations are correct; nonadditive genetic variance may be important for some personality traits, and both assimilation and contrast effects may play a role in producing some similarities between first-degree relatives (Bergeman et al., 1993; Saudino et al., 1995).

In general, there is little evidence pointing to differential heritability; genetic influences appear to account for a similar percent of the variation in most personality traits. As shown in Figure 6.2, Openness to Experience may be an exception; Loehlin's (1992) estimates point to a very large effect of additive genes on Openness. This should be regarded cautiously because there is less research about Openness relative to the remaining Big Five traits. However, if this finding withstands the rigors of replication, it may be that the relatively greater heritability of Openness reflects its significant correlation with IQ (e.g., John et al., 1994). Intelligence traits yield higher heritabilities than personality traits (Bouchard, 1993), and to the extent that Openness is suffused with IQ variation it may yield higher heritabilities than other personality traits.

It should be noted that almost the entire corpus of behavior-genetic research on personality in adolescence and adulthood is based on self-reports. Although self-reports tend to agree with other data sources (e.g., peer reports), they are limited by self-knowledge and self-presentational biases. More generally, relying on a single data source confounds method variance and trait variance. A strategy to separate method variance from trait variance is to gather, in the context of a behavior-genetic study, personality data from multiple sources. Heath, Neale, Kessler, Eaves, and Kendler (1992) collected personality data from twins using both self-reports and twin reports about each twin. They found similar genetic influences on personality traits whether these were assessed with self-reports or with ratings by the respondent's cotwin. It is hoped that future behavior-genetic studies will more routinely include multiple sources of personality data.

Shared Environmental Influences

Shared environmental influences on temperament and personality are very small. Plomin (1986, pp. 69–70) described three ways of estimating shared environmental influence: (a) in twin studies, from the remainder of variance after genetic variance, variance due to nonshared environment, and error are taken out; (b) in studies of identical twins raised together and apart, by assessing whether those pairs who are raised together are more similar than those pairs who are raised apart; and (c) in adoption studies, from the correlation between genetically unrelated children who are raised in the same family. When the results from these various efforts are tallied, it appears that shared environmental experiences do not create similarities among family members on most personality traits, values, and social attitudes (Plomin & Daniels, 1987).

There are at least two exceptions to this sweeping conclusion; one concerns attitudes toward love and the other concerns juvenile delinquency. Waller and Shaver (1994) showed that individual differences in "romantic love styles," measured via self-reports of attitudes toward love and romantic relationships, were influenced by shared environmental factors. The results indicated that resemblances between adult twins in their love styles were due to their exposure to the same childhood environment irrespective of genetic relatedness. The authors speculate that, unlike other personality traits, "love styles are inherently relational . . . and may be learned during early familial or shared extrafamilial interactions and subsequently played out in romantic relationships" (Waller & Shaver, 1994, pp. 272–273).

Rowe (1983; Rowe, Rodgers, & Meseck-Bushey, 1992) found that the best-fitting model to twin data of juvenile delinquency was a model including both genetic and shared environmental influences. Shared environmental effects typically refer to factors such as social class or child-rearing practices that are shared by members of a twin pair

and should thus serve to make members of the pair similar to each other. Rowe, however, speculated that with regard to delinquency the shared-environment effect may not necessarily reflect criminogenic home environments as provided by parents. Rather, the shared-environment effect may be the result of mutual influence within twin pairs. Twin pairs may commit crimes together, and siblings may model delinquent behavior for one another. Genetic factors and mutual environmental influence may combine to produce delinquent behavior among members of the same family.

"Love styles" and delinquency may not be personality traits per se, but I mention these two findings because they show that behavior-genetic studies have been used to identify shared-environment effects on social behavior; biometric models do not stack the deck against shared environmental influences. Aside from these studies, there is little other replicable evidence that shared environmental influences create similarities among family members (see Figure 6.2). This research evidence has not gone unchallenged. In fact, it has proven more controversial than evidence about the heritability of personality (Hoffman, 1991). Below, I summarize and evaluate four reactions to this evidence.

The first reaction has been disbelief: The behavior genetic findings must be wrong because research has documented associations between measures of the family environment and measures of children's personality. However, most of the research that shows significant correlations among family climate, parental discipline, and caregiver beliefs with children's personalities does not test whether the environment-behavior correlations are mediated genetically. As Wachs (1983) noted, "correlations between parental behaviors and child development are commonly viewed as due solely to the contributions of the environment; rarely do we find consideration of the possibility that these correlations may reflect the contribution of shared genes that influence both the parents' behavior and the child's development" (p. 397).

To consider this possibility, Plomin, Loehlin, and DeFries (1985) studied correlations between measures of the environment and measures of children's personality in nonadoptive and in adoptive homes. Here is the rationale for their study: In nonadoptive homes, parents and children share both their environment and their genes, whereas in adoptive homes, parents and children share only their environment. Thus, in nonadoptive homes the correlation between environmental measures and children's personality can be mediated environmentally and genetically; in adoptive homes, this correlation can be mediated only by environmental processes. If the correlations between environmental measures and children's personality were the same in both types of homes, there would be little reason to doubt the role of shared environmental influences. However, if these correlations were stronger in nonadoptive homes than in adoptive homes, there would be reason to surmise that environmental influences are genetically mediated.

The results showed that correlations between measures of the environment and children's personalities were stronger in nonadoptive than in adoptive homes, suggesting that shared genetic variance between parents and children creates an environment that has a significant influence on children. In the absence of shared genetic variance between parents and children, environmental influences were minimal. Because socialization theories do not posit genetic relatedness as a prerequisite for environmental influences on personality development, Scarr and Grajec (1982, p. 374) noted that the presence of genotype-environment correlations in biologically related families renders many "socialization" findings uninterpretable.

The second reaction to evidence that shared environmental influences are small is part of a more general critique: Most behavior-genetics studies only "estimate" the influence of the environment; they do not measure environmental factors (Hoffman, 1991; Wachs, 1983). It is important to design behavior-genetic studies that directly measure whether specific environmental factors make children in the same family similar to one another. For example, as part of a twin study of psychiatric disorders, Kendler, Neale, Kessler, Heath, and Eaves (1992) reported that childhood parental loss (through divorce or death) is associated with increased adult risk for depression and anxiety among siblings; parental loss thus appears to be a specific shared environmental factor that makes children who grow up in the same family similar to each other. This study illustrates the important etiological contributions that can be made by behavior-genetic studies that measure specific shared environmental influences.

Still, the interpretation of even this shared environmental effect is not straightforward. Brody and Crowley (1995) questioned whether parental loss, brought on by divorce or even death, is a purely environmental influence. They noted that both divorce and premature death have been linked to heritable personality traits such as neuroticism (e.g., Allgulander, 1994; McGue & Lykken, 1992). Thus, parental

loss in childhood, whether due to divorce or to premature death, may be associated with heritable characteristics (e.g., neuroticism) that are linked, in turn, with depression and anxiety disorders in adulthood. Brody and Crowley (1995) noted that their "speculations are not meant to suggest that an environmental interpretation of the effect of parental loss in childhood on adult psychopathology is wrong—rather, these speculations are offered in order to establish the difficulty of forming unambiguous inferences about environmental influences" (p. 70) even when using a genetically controlled design. Be that as it may, behavior-genetic research designs that measure the environment are better suited to identify specific experiences that influence personality development than are research designs that do not use genetic controls.

A third reaction to evidence that shared environmental influences are small has been to raise the possibility that shared environmental influences may be nonlinear. In her analysis of the "average expectable environment," Scarr (1992, 1993) suggested that shared family experiences within a normal range of environments may have little influence on personality development. However, grossly substandard or dysfunctional environments may influence personality development. According to Scarr, shared family experiences may have little influence on personality development because wide variations within the average expectable environment represent "functionally equivalent opportunities" for developmental experiences (Scarr, 1992). Most shared family environments offer individuals sufficient latitude to construct experiences that are correlated with their genes. However, outside the average expectable environment, beyond its conditional boundaries, shared family experiences may be very influential. Whether variations between the average expectable environment and a dysfunctional environment are more influential than variations within the average expectable environment—that is, whether shared environmental influences are nonlinear—remains an unanswered empirical question. Moreover, a test of nonlinear influences requires behavior-genetic studies that allow for the possibility that nonlinear environmental effects derive from genetic influences (Willerman, 1979a). Such severe environments, however, are not well represented in most behavior-genetic studies.

Some see political danger in the concept of the average expectable environment (Baumrind, 1993). This concept also needs scientific specification. How is it possible to determine in what kind of average expectable environment the human child evolved? If it is not a timeless, eternal invariant, how does the concept of the average expectable environment incorporate cultural evolution and social-historical change, which, arguably, have been more rapid than genetic evolution? Scarr (1993) argued that a useful theory of environmental influences on personality development will need to distinguish between evolutionary imperatives and cultural variants. That is, such a theory will need to specify species-normal environmental features that lead to "species-typical development" and to distinguish these features from cultural and subcultural features that influence culturally defined "normal development" (Tooby & Cosmides, 1990).

A fourth reaction to evidence that shared environmental influences are small is provided by life span researchers who distinguish between two types of shared family influences: the shared rearing environment of childhood and the shared marital environment of adulthood. They argue that generalizations about the absence of shared family experiences should be confined to claims about development in childhood and adolescence, in one's family of origin, whereas shared family experiences in adulthood, in one's family of destination, may be more influential.

To understand this distinction, it is necessary to reexamine the definitions of shared environment and nonshared environment. Jinks and Fulker (1970) originally described this partition of the environment as between- and within-families, although the methods they described were appropriate for understanding environmental sources of variance in twins and siblings. Rowe and Plomin (1981) and all subsequent investigators have in practice also adopted this perspective: shared variation is variation between siblings of different families; nonshared variation is variation among siblings within the same family. Transforming the between- and within-family distinction to a between- and within-sibling pair (whether adopted, biological, or twin) contrast is appropriate when studying development in the years from infancy through late adolescence. But what about when studying development in adulthood?

If the categorization as shared or nonshared of a specific environmental influence within a household is to remain constant across generations, then the reference family must remain constant. In the study of adults, the reference family must then be the family of destination, and the shared environment refers to the common environment of spouses and their children. For at least some (although not all) purposes, between- and within-family effects should be understood in terms of variation between and within spouse pairs. A shared (between-family) environmental effect (e.g., family income) could fail to increase the similarity of children in the same family while greatly increasing the similarity of their parents on a wide range of phenotypic characteristics.

To explore this distinction, Caspi, Herbener, and Ozer (1992) analyzed data about personality values and attitudes in married couples across 20 years. Their results suggested that shared experiences in the marital environment serve to maintain similarities between couples over time; in the absence of shared environmental influences, couples would become increasingly different from one another, like strangers in their own home. The authors argued that across time, married couples actively construct a "shared environment" that helps them to maintain their similarity to one another.

These findings do not challenge or undermine the conclusion of Plomin and Daniels (1987) and others who find that the impact of the shared rearing environment is negligible. Behavior genetic studies have focused on environments shared by siblings in their families of origin, whereas Caspi et al. (1992) focused on environments shared by spouses in their families of destination. The use of shared and nonshared environment to refer to resemblance between spouses rather than siblings may be a bit confusing. It also accurately reflects the complexity of individual life span development as it unfolds during different stages of family development and generational succession (Hill & Mattessich, 1979). Thus, while shared environmental experiences in one's family of origin may contribute little to development in childhood and adolescence, shared environmental influences in one's family of destination may contribute a great deal to continued development in adulthood.

Nonshared Environmental Influences

Behavior-genetic findings are mistakenly interpreted to show that environmental experiences are unimportant. In fact, almost every behavior-genetics study highlights the role of environmental influences; as shown in Figure 6.2, nonshared environmental influences account for most of the variation in personality differences. These nonshared influences reflect experiences unique to each child—experiences not shared with siblings—that tend to make children in the same family different from each other (Plomin & Daniels, 1987).

It will be recalled, however, that the component of variance implicating nonshared environmental factors also includes variance associated with measurement error and with gene-environment interactions. In theory, it is possible that measurement error and gene-environment interactions exaggerate the importance of nonshared environmental variation. But in practice these factors do not appear to invalidate the conclusion that nonshared environmental influences create personality differences. Measurement errors probably inflate estimates of nonshared environmental variation, but the routine use of reliable measures in contemporary research obviates this problem to some degree; there is "true score" variation in the nonshared component of Figure 6.2. Gene-environment interactions probably do not inflate estimates of nonshared environmental variation. Such interactions, if significant, would suggest that the effect of the genotype depends on the environment. Possible gene-environment interaction effects have been implicated in some studies of crime and aggression (Cadoret, Yates, Troughton, Woodworth, & Stewart, 1995; Mednick, Moffitt, Gabrielli, & Hutchings, 1986) and schizophrenia (Cannon et al., 1993), but there have been fewer explorations of this question using personality data. What evidence does exist suggests that gene-environment interactions are few in number, small in magnitude, inconsistent, and difficult to interpret (Bergeman, Plomin, McClearn, Pedersen, & Friberg, 1988; Plomin, DeFries, & Fulker, 1988).

What are the most important nonshared environmental influences on personality development? To identify these specific nonshared environmental influences it is necessary to (a) rethink traditional sampling strategies in socialization research and (b) design new ways to measure environmental influences.

First, studies of personality development will need to include more than one child from each family to identify specific environmental experiences that make children in the same family different from each other. Developmental psychologists have traditionally sampled one child per family because shared environmental experiences were assumed to account for significant variation in personality differences. Behavior-genetic evidence indicates that this assumption may be wrong, suggesting that studies of personality development that include at least two siblings from the same household are more likely to yield information about specific environmental influences on personality development. The study of multiple children in the same family raises new sampling and statistical problems. Rovine (1994) provides a review of methodological issues in estimating associations between nonshared environmental factors and personality differences between siblings.

Second, studies of personality development will need to devise and incorporate new methods of measuring nonshared environmental influences. Behavior-genetic studies have estimated a large component of variance in personality differences that implicates nonshared environmental factors. These factors now need to be measured and related to personality differences (Dunn & Plomin, 1990).

In terms of the family environment, it is possible that many of the relevant parental child-rearing tactics have already been identified in previous studies but that these influence personality development in relative rather than absolute terms. Relative differences in socialization experiences between children within a family may have more influence on personality development than absolute differences between children in different families. For example, parental love may matter a lot if one is loved less than one's sibling but may matter little if one is raised in a more loving home than average (Rutter & Rutter, 1993).

Several questionnaire and observational studies have shown that relative differences in how siblings are treated are correlated with personality differences between siblings. Daniels (1986) developed the Sibling Inventory of Differential Experience to assess differences between the experiences of siblings in the same family and found that the sibling who received more maternal affection was more likely to be sociable. In a study of sibling differences in behavior problems, Dunn, Stocker, and Plomin (1990) found that the sibling who received more maternal affection was less likely to exhibit internalizing symptomatology. Of course, family environment constructs such as maternal affection have been featured in research on personality development for many decades. The construct is not novel; what is novel is the suggestion that the influence of maternal affection on personality development may be understood better as a nonshared environmental experience, that is, by focusing on differences in maternal affection within the family rather than by focusing on family-by-family differences in maternal affection.

In addition to differences within the family, differential peer experiences, differential experiences with teachers, and, more broadly, differential neighborhood experiences represent potentially potent sources of nonshared environmental variation. These extrafamilial influences may assume greater influence in the lives of today's children than in those of previous generations. There is suggestive evidence that the association between familial socioeconomic status and some developmental outcomes has declined over the twentieth century. White (1982) speculated that "the increased availability to people of all SES levels of such things as television, movies, community groups and organizations" has reduced the long-term influence of the shared rearing environment on some developmental outcomes and shifted the bulk of environmental influence to extrafamilial factors (p. 468).

Thus far, studies of nonshared extrafamilial influences have focused primarily on the peer group (Baker & Daniels, 1990; Daniels, 1986). Harris (1995) and Rowe (1994) have elaborated some of the group processes—rather than dyadic influences—that may shape children's personality and behavior. Beyond the peer group, it may be important to consider the influence of neighborhoods on children's development. In highly mobile societies, it is likely that even siblings who differ in age by only a few years may grow up in different neighborhoods (Featherman, Spenner, & Tsunematsu, 1988). A focus on neighborhood characteristics is a decidedly sociological contribution to the study of life course development. Sociologists have not focused on personality differences per se, although they have identified ecological conditions associated with the development of problem behavior (e.g., Brewster, 1994; Sampson & Groves, 1989). Differential neighborhood experiences may be important nonshared environmental factors that influence the development of personality differences among children from the same family. Just as the study of multiple children in the same family imposes new research demands, so will the study of individuals nested within different communities complicate methodological requirements (Farrington, Sampson, & Wikstrom, 1993).

Once specific nonshared environmental influences are identified, researchers will need to wrestle with the problem of directionality: Are nonshared environmental experiences causes of personality differences, or are personality differences causes of nonshared experiences? Cross-sectional studies that examine differential experiences between siblings cannot answer this question. For example, it is possible that differences in siblings' internalizing symptoms may contribute to their receiving different treatment from their mothers rather than differential treatment producing these sibling differences (e.g., Stoneman & Brody, 1993). Longitudinal studies that control for initial differences between siblings may help to untangle this problem of directionality between differential experiences and personality differences (McGuire, Dunn, & Plomin, 1995).

A related possibility is that correlations between specific nonshared environmental factors and specific developmental outcomes may be genetically mediated. Indeed, many of the correlations between differences in sibling experiences and differences in their personalities are difficult to interpret because differential sibling experiences are imbued with genetic variation. For example, some of the dimensions assessed by the Sibling Inventory of Differential Experience are heritable (Baker & Daniels, 1990), suggesting that correlations between measures of differential experience and individual differences in personality may be mediated genetically. The genetic mediation of nonshared environmental influences is not so mysterious: it means siblings interpret and shape experiences in ways that are correlated with their personality characteristics. Sibling differences may be due less to objective differences in their treatment within their family than to differences in the way siblings "evoke responses from others, actively select or ignore opportunities, and construct their own experiences" (Scarr, 1992, p. 14).

A more convincing search for specific nonshared environmental factors that are free of genetic mediation may be carried out with MZ twins. Because differences between MZ twins are due entirely to nonshared environmental factors, studies that relate differential environmental experiences to personality differences between MZ twins may be used to identify specific nonshared environmental influences. This approach has been used with limited success in studies of psychopathology comparing discordant MZ twins (Gottesman, 1991), but I am not aware of any such studies of normal personality variation.

Another approach involves measuring specific nonshared environmental factors in different kinship types that vary in their genetic resemblance. Rodgers, Rowe, and Li (1994) used data from over 7,000 5- to 11-year-old children to identify four kinship pair types: twin, full-sibling, half-sibling, and cousin pairs. Using a regression technique that controls for both genetic and shared environmental influences, Rodgers et al. (1994) identified several nonshared differences in parental treatment that were free of genetic mediation and that predicted pair differences in problem behavior. For example, the twin, full sibling, half-sibling, or cousin who experienced a poorer home environment quality relative to his or her pair member had more behavior problems. This study shows that it is possible to specify nonshared, within-family environmental differences that are free of genetic influence.

Because the study of within-family environmental differences is relatively recent, it is not yet possible to enumerate those specific nonshared influences that contribute to long-term personality differences. Studies of personality development that include multiple children from the same household and that control for genetic influences are bound to yield new insights about these factors (Hetherington, Reiss, & Plomin, 1994).

Age Changes in Genetic and Environmental Influences on Personality

Behavior-genetic studies have been conducted with twins across the life span, from infancy to senescence. This wide age range has enabled researchers to examine age differences in the effects of genes and environments on personality. Does heritability change with age? Do environmental influences change over the life span?

To address these questions, McCartney, Harris, and Bernieri (1990) conducted a developmental meta-analysis of twin studies of personality. For each study, they obtained information about the average age of the twins and about the MZ and DZ intraclass correlations. By calculating, across studies, the association between the twins' age and the twins' similarity, they estimated whether twins become more or less alike over time. The results showed that the correlation between age and twin similarity was negative, suggesting that as twins grow up they become increasingly different.

Of special interest is the finding that MZ and DZ twins diverged across time to the same degree. This suggests that the "growing apart" of twins over the life span may be attributed to the increasing importance of nonshared environmental influences that contribute to differences between twins and the concomitant, decreasing importance of shared rearing effects on twin resemblance as twins age. Moreoever, it is unlikely that the increasing influence of nonshared environmental influences is mediated genetically because the negative correlation between age and twin resemblance was the same for both MZ and DZ twins. This interpretation is consistent with the findings that adult MZ twins in less frequent contact are less similar to each other than twins who see each other frequently (Rose, Koskenvuo, Kaprio, Sarna, & Langinvainio, 1988). It appears that experiential differences contribute to personality differences between twins as they grow older.

The evidence adduced by McCartney et al. (1990) is based on a comparison of multiple cross-sectional studies of children and of adults. Because such comparisons may confound age and cohort effects, longitudinal behavior-genetic studies are needed to determine whether there are age changes in genetic and environmental influences on personality. In fact, two recent longitudinal studies showed

that genetic and environmental influences are moderated by age. A study of twins who completed the Multidimensional Personality Questionnaire at age 20 and again at age 30 showed declines in heritability for measures of Negative Emotionality and Positive Emotionality, but not for Constraint (McGue, Bacon, & Lykken, 1993). This pattern was replicated in a larger, cross-sequential analysis of twins from age 18 to 59. Viken, Rose, Kaprio, and Koskenvuo (1994) found that the heritability of Neuroticism and Extraversion decreased during young adulthood and began to stabilize thereafter. Moreover, the decreases in heritability—at least for Positive Emotionality/Extraversion—were associated with increases in the influence of nonshared environmental influences.

The possibility that nonshared environmental influences may increase with age is consistent with the hypothesis that beyond the first two decades of life, personality development may be increasingly influenced by nonnormative life events that are unique to each individual (Baltes, Reese, & Lipsitt, 1980). It is not clear, however, whether the increasing influence of nonnormative events reflects the greater frequency of such events in adulthood or the cumulative influence of nonnormative events over the life span.

In general, it appears that shared rearing influences on personality are small and fade in importance with age. Genetic influences are substantial. As shown by the data reported earlier in Figure 6.1, these influences seem to increase from infancy to childhood and, as suggested by McCartney et al. (1990), genetic influences may decline a bit after young adulthood. Nonshared environmental influences are substantial and continue to increase throughout adulthood. At this point, it is only possible to provide this impressionistic account because the vast majority of the extant studies use different cross-sectional samples and different measures.

Implications and Directions for Future Research

Modern behavioral genetics has been responsive to methodological and substantive criticism. Numerous studies have directly tested the equal environments assumption. Newer studies are relying less on self-reports and are increasingly using multimethod, multi-occasion assessments of psychological variables. Measures of the environment are increasingly incorporated into behavioral genetic studies, enabling researchers to focus on developmental processes. Finally, theoretical advances have served to clarify the meaning of heritability and the concept of reaction range. However, there is still much to learn. Little is known about the psychological and environmental experiences of twins and adoptees and how the experiences of twins differ from those of singletons. There is little research about twin-twin relationships and about relationships between adoptive versus biological siblings. In addition, little is known about biological and neurodevelopmental differences between MZ and DZ twins and how these may influence psychological and behavioral outcomes (see Bouchard & Propping, 1993).

Although methodological innovations and replications in behavior-genetics research are exciting, the descriptive work is far from complete. As noted earlier, there are some inconsistencies between studies, and it is not clear whether these should be ascribed one of a number of different substantive interpretations or attributed to sampling and measurement differences. Moreover, most behavior-genetic studies continue to recruit relatively selective samples that potentially underrepresent the extent of variation—behavioral and environmental—in the population. Inconsistencies may be resolved as more descriptive work accumulates, and even more robust findings may alert researchers to the most heritable dimensions of personality. This "signpost function" of behavior-genetics research is important for molecular genetics research, whose starting point is, after all, the phenotype (Goldsmith, 1994). Advances in molecular genetics—particularly a shift from the search for single-gene disorders to methods involving the search for multiple genes—may generate a better understanding of the origins of individual differences (Plomin, Owen, & McGuffin, 1994).

With regard to personality research, behavior-genetic findings serve two important functions. Behavior-genetic studies are important for life span research because they help to specify and more clearly define behavioral phenotypes, just as they may help to identify new diseases (Rutter, 1991). For example, evidence that genetic influences on adult criminality are substantial whereas genetic influences on juvenile delinquency are less so suggests that these two constructs—seemingly the "same"—may be somewhat distinct, and that different etiological factors may be implicated in antisocial behavior at different ages (DiLalla & Gottesman, 1989). Behavior-genetic studies may thus be used to help elucidate developmental and situational distinctions between behaviors at different points in the life span and help to validate or refute phenotypic distinctions in developmental research. Similarly, behavior-genetic research can shed light on the etiology of age-related disorders such as depression. Epidemiological studies show that depressive disorders increase during adolescence and young adulthood, but it is not clear whether this increase is related to increasing psychosocial stressors or to the turning on of genetic influences. Behavior-genetic studies can clarify these competing accounts by studying similarities and differences in genetic and environmental influences on childhood-onset versus adult-onset cases of depression (Rutter, Silberg, & Simonoff, 1993). Such work is critical for measurement in longitudinal-developmental research because it enables researchers to establish whether or not they are measuring similar or distinct phenotypes at different ages. In this way, behavior-genetics research may help to improve psychiatric nosologies and personality taxonomies.

Behavior-genetic findings are also important for research on personality development because they suggest that family transmission effects are genetic as well as social. Dual inheritance complicates the interpretation of research findings because genetic variation can work in surprising ways and may generate correlations between variables that are not directly or obviously related to genotypes, correlations for which psychologists inadvertently construct ill-informed theories (Scarr, 1985).

Consider the finding that girls who grow up in father-absent homes are likely to mature physically at an earlier age than girls who grow up with both biological parents present (e.g., Moffitt, Caspi, Belsky, & Silva, 1992). What is the interpretation of this correlation between "family stress" and early physical maturation? It is possible to link these results to cognate research about the effects of environmental stress on the socioendocrinology of mammalian reproduction and to proffer sociobiological speculations that family stress causes early maturation (e.g., Belsky, Steinberg, & Draper, 1991). But a more parsimonious explanation may be contained in a genetic inheritance model: the timing of physical maturation is heritable. Consider this scenario suggested by Surbey (1990). Early maturers spend time with older peers, date earlier, and engage in sexual intercourse at a younger age than later maturing girls. Not surprisingly, they marry earlier and first give birth at a younger age. This observation, coupled with the fact that early marriages are more likely to dissolve, suggests that early-maturing women are likely to raise their own children in father-absent homes; that is, early maturation may indirectly "cause" later family stress. But, whether fathers leave or not, early-maturing mothers will tend to have early-maturing daughters. In sum, genetic inheritance and genotype-environment correlations may account for the observed association between family stress and early physical maturation, and possibly for the intergenerational transmission of early parenthood as well. When interpreting research findings, it is imperative to examine whether genetic variation may have produced social covariation.

I provide this research illustration because, in this case, the genetic inheritance model strikes most social scientists as prudent and parsimonious. But in other cases, this type of interpretation provokes disbelief. Consider the association between the intellectual environment of the home and children's IQ. Much has been written about covariation between the home environment and children's cognitive development, but this research often ignores genetic variation. Longstreth et al. (1981) showed that the association between the intellectual environment of the home and child IQ is, in part, a function of maternal IQ. It appears that maternal IQ, which research has shown to be heritable (Bouchard & McGue, 1981), predicts both features of the socialization environment and child IQ. Here, then, is another case in which genetic variation (in IQ) may produce social covariation (i.e., correlations between features of the socialization environment and child outcomes). Or consider the association between parental divorce and children's conduct problems. Much has been written about covariation between family discord and children's externalizing problems, but this research often ignores genetic variation. Lahey et al. (1988) showed that the association between parental divorce and child conduct problems is, in part, a function of parental antisocial personality disorder. Parental antisocial personality disorder, which research has shown to be heritable (Nigg & Goldsmith, 1994), may predict both parental divorce and child conduct disorder. Here, too, is a case in which genetic variation may produce social covariation.

The possibility that genetic variation produces social covariation alerts researchers to the need to incorporate genetic inheritance models in developmental theories. The bar has been lifted for standards of proof for socialization theories of personality development. Behavior-genetic studies have also suggested that shared environmental factors may not be the most important influences on personality development. This knowledge contradicts conventional wisdom about how environmental experiences influence personality development and challenges traditional approaches to the study of socialization. As Scarr (1988) has noted, individual differences in personality arise from genetic differences and from environmental differences

within families, not from environmental differences between families. Environmental influences do not operate on a family-by-family basis; rather they operate on an individual-by-individual basis (Braungart et al., 1992).

From Temperament to Personality

Many theorists surmise that the origins of personality can be identified in temperamental characteristics, in early-appearing individual differences that index a person's characteristic style of approach and response to the environment (Goldsmith et al., 1987). In fact, Buss and Plomin (1984) refer to temperamental characteristics as "early emerging personality traits."

But this conjecture is difficult to substantiate empirically because it requires costly longitudinal studies, from birth to adulthood. Such studies are rare. As I show in a later section, "Personality Continuity across the Life Course," there is evidence about long-term continuities of personality characteristics from late childhood to adulthood (e.g., Farrington, 1983; Huesmann, Eron, Lefkowitz, & Walder, 1984; Magnusson, 1988; Moskowitz & Schwartzman, 1989; Pulkkinen, 1986; Robins, 1966). There is also evidence about personality continuities across lengthy periods of adult life (e.g., Conley, 1985; McCrae & Costa, 1990). However, evidence about continuities from temperamental variables in early childhood—from the first three to five years of life—to individual differences in adolescence and adulthood is sparse. My aim in this section is to evaluate research evidence about the temperamental origins of individual differences in later behavior problems and personality. My review is limited to studies that span periods of developmental reorganization, from early childhood across to late childhood and through to young adulthood. I do not review cross-sectional or short-term longitudinal studies that assess temperament, behavior problems, and personality within specific developmental periods. I incorporate studies of individual differences in behavior problems into my review because these may provide important evidence about temperamental influences on psychological dimensions in the normal range. Indeed, measurement and empirical distinctions between "normal" and "abnormal" personality variation are rather murky.

Temperament and Later Behavior Problems

Several longitudinal studies have linked early temperamental styles to later behavior problems (see Rothbart & Bates, this volume). Chess and Thomas (1987) found that the "easy/difficult" temperament constellation, when measured at ages 3, 4, and 5, was significantly related to later "adjustment" problems within the home, at school, and during early adulthood. Block (1993; Block, Block, & Keyes, 1988) showed that from age 3 to early adulthood, individuals maintain their relative position on two dimensions of personality functioning: ego resiliency and ego control. Early-emerging differences on these dimensions of personality are also implicated in later behavior problems. For example, undercontrolled children at age 3 were likely to report more drug use as adolescents. Corroborating results were reported by Tremblay, Pihl, Vitaro, and Dobkin (1994). Boys rated by their preschool teachers as high on impulsivity were significantly more likely to self-report involvement in antisocial behavior during late childhood and early adolescence. Caspi, Henry, McGee, Moffitt, and Silva (1995) showed that observers' ratings of children's temperament at ages 3 and 5 correlated in theoretically coherent ways with independent parent and teacher reports of behavior problems from late childhood through midadolescence. Impulsive, irritable, and distractible boys and girls had more behavior problems, especially externalizing symptoms of conduct disorder, hyperactivity, and inattention; sociable, confident, and self-reliant boys exhibited fewer internalizing problems; shy, fearful, and passive children, especially girls, were more anxious and inattentive in adolescence.

Shorter-term longitudinal studies have also linked childhood temperament to later behavior problems (e.g., Hirshfeld et al., 1992; Sanson, Smart, Prior, & Oberklaid, 1993). Bates (Bates, Bayles, Bennett, Ridge, & Brown, 1991; Bates, Maslin, & Frankel, 1985) reported that management problems in infancy were associated with later externalizing problems; negative reactions to novelty predicted later internalizing problems; and negative emotionality predicted both externalizing and internalizing outcomes. Corroborating results are provided by Rende (1993), who reported that mothers' ratings of their children's emotionality were positively related to mothers' later ratings of their children's internalizing and externalizing problems. In addition, mothers' early ratings of their children's sociability were negatively related to later reports of internalizing problems.

It is difficult to summarize the various studies cited above because they used different temperament scales and different outcome measures. The correlations between different temperament scales are often unknown. The relations between different measures of behavior problems are equally indeterminate; classification and case-identification procedures differ across studies, and it is unclear—within specific areas of disorder, such as anxiety problems or conduct problems—whether the studies have actually assessed the same type of disorder.

Moreover, each of the studies is not without some limitation. First, some have focused on small, homogeneous samples or single-sex samples, whereas other studies have focused on children referred for treatment or on those identified on the basis of extreme temperament scores. The generalizability of results may be compromised by the selective nature of the samples.

Second, many studies relied on reports of temperament and behavior problems from the same rater at different ages, most often on reports provided over time by mothers. Using these reports to estimate behavioral continuity is problematic because observed continuities may reflect continuities in children's characteristics as well as, to some unknown extent, continuities in maternal characteristics (Bates, 1994).

Third, it is not clear in many studies if measures of temperament and measures of behavior problems represent distinct constructs or if these measures are simply different degrees of the same phenomenon. At the extreme ends of the distribution, measures of temperamental differences may actually assess early, subclinical manifestations of later behavior disorders (Rutter, 1987). Indeed, there is conceptual similarity between some temperament dimensions (e.g., distractibility) and behavior problems (e.g., attention deficit disorder). Item overlap between questionnaire measures of temperament and behavior problems may also blur the distinction between the two constructs (Sanson, Prior, & Kyrios, 1990). Although it is possible to distinguish conceptually between temperament and behavior problems (Bates, 1990; Rutter, 1987), it is not clear that conceptual distinctions have been matched at the measurement level.

A fourth problem concerns whether correlations between temperament variables and behavior problems represent associations throughout the range of normal variation or represent associations at the extremes of population distributions. Studies of this topic are needed to determine whether there are continuities or discontinuities between normality and disorder and for understanding the links between normal and abnormal development. A promising step in this direction may be provided by applying behavior-genetic methods to temperament and psychopathology data to test whether the genetic contribution to extreme scores in a distribution differs from the etiology of the rest of the scores in a distribution (Plomin, 1991).

Fifth, some studies focus on broad or undifferentiated measures of childhood behavior. Global measures, such as "difficult" temperament or a count of behavioral difficulties, provide useful predictive information, but they may obscure differences in the developmental importance of distinct behavioral characteristics. McDevitt (1986) has cautioned that "as the generality of a concept increases, its sensitivity and ability to provide useful information clinically or theoretically decreases. It is one thing to know that a child is temperamentally [or behaviorally] difficult but without knowing which dimensions are problematic it would be impossible to offer meaningful assistance" (p. 36).

In combination, the available evidence highlights the important role of early temperament in the development of later behavior problems. But the evidence is not without interpretive problems. What would constitute better evidence? The ideal study would examine links between childhood temperament and later behavior problems (a) in a representative general population sample, (b) with independent information about children provided by multiple sources (e.g., observers, teachers, parents) and multiple methods (e.g., behavioral observations, ratings), (c) using measures that eliminate predictor-criterion overlap in the measurement of temperament and behavior problems, (d) that test whether observed correlations between the two constructs represent associations throughout the distribution or are the product of extremes in the distribution, (e) with the aim of clarifying whether temperamental characteristics in early childhood have predictive specificity for later psychopathology. Ideally, an exploration of the links between temperamental characteristics and later behavior problems should begin in infancy and continue through adolescence, because the prevalence of clinical disorders and behavior problems, both internalizing and externalizing, tends to increase during and following puberty (Newman et al., 1996).

Until then, two general conclusions are warranted (Bates, Wachs, & Emde, 1994). Temperamental measures of "difficultness" appear to predict both internalizing and externalizing behavior problems. Difficultness includes negative emotional expression, impulsivity, restlessness, and distractibility. Temperamental measures of inhibition or "unadaptability" are more clearly related to internalizing than externalizing problems, although at least two studies report that these temperamental qualities are also

related to attention problems (Caspi et al., 1995; Hirshfeld et al., 1992).

Temperament and Later Personality

About this topic, where speculation has been robust, the data remain fragmentary (e.g., Rothbart & Ahadi, 1994). Surprisingly, there has been virtually no contact between child psychologists who study temperament and personality psychologists who are concerned with personality differences. However, there are indications of important studies on the horizon.

Future research linking temperament to the development of personality may be facilitated by two parallel achievements: the development of a consensual system for describing the structure of individual differences in temperament and the development of such a system for personality differences. In a previous section, I described one such system in the domain of personality: the five-factor model offers an integrative framework for studying personality differences. In the domain of temperament, conceptual reviews, as well as factor analytic studies, have arrived at five to seven basic "consensus" dimensions of infant and childhood temperament that might show continuity with later behavior (e.g., Martin, Wisenbaker, & Hüttunen, 1994). Five of these dimensions are shown in Figure 6.3. Two other dimensions are represented in a more limited fashion in existing temperament inventories and appear to apply to infancy. One is regularity, which mainly refers to the predictability of biological functions; the other is soothability, which has two facets: susceptibility to external soothing techniques and self-calming ability.

Wachs (1994) noted that advances in the measurement of individual differences in temperament and personality

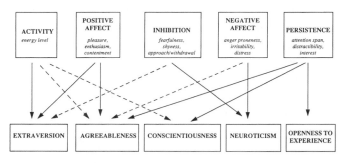

Figure 6.3 Hypothesized links between childhood temperament and adult personality structure. Solid lines represent hypothesized positive correlations; dashed lines represent hypothesized negative correlations.

should provide the beginning and endpoint for future developmental research on the connection between early temperament and later personality. Others have suggested that the five-factor model may provide "a target framework for attempting to identify how infant and child temperamental dimensions may interact with each other and the environment to create variation in (adult) personality" (Ahadi & Rothbart, 1994, p. 174). For the most part, this research has yet to be conducted. The following is a summary of hypothesized connections based on suggestive evidence (see Figure 6.3).

Activity Level. Activity level, consisting of rapid tempo and motor vigor, may be most closely linked to the trait domain of Extraversion/Positive Emotionality, which includes such surgent characteristics as active, dominant, outgoing, and energetic (John, 1990). Cross-sectional studies of different age groups provide suggestive evidence about this link. In factor analytic studies of children, activity level emerges as a distinct individual-difference dimension (Martin et al., 1994). It remains a distinct dimension at least through early adolescence (John et al., 1994). However, factor analytic studies of adults show that measures of activity are subsumed by a higher-order factor: Extraversion (e.g., Zuckerman, Kuhlman, & Camac, 1988). Eaton (1994) suggested that, with age, activity level changes from a primary to a secondary dimension of individual differences. There may be two reasons for this developmental shift. First, it is possible that childhood activity level reflects but an age-specific manifestation of a more enduring personality characteristic. For example, dominance may be reflected in physical vigor in childhood and in social presence and leadership skills in adulthood. Second, it is possible that the physically dominated, activity temperament factor in childhood is a less salient feature of adult behavior, or it may remain an important part of everyday behavior (e.g., exercise) that is simply not reflected in adult personality inventories.

Several studies have also shown that activity level may be associated with increased risk for externalizing behavior problems (e.g., Moss, Blackson, Martin, & Tarter, 1992). Other studies have linked externalizing behavior problems in adolescence and adulthood to lower scores on personality measures of Constraint/Conscientiousness and Agreeableness (Krueger et al., 1996a), suggesting a link between childhood activity level and low behavioral Constraint/Conscientiousness and low Agreeableness. A 20-year longitudinal study confirms these predictions (Franz,

1996). Observer-based measures of activity level at ages 3 and 4 were significantly linked to outgoing behavior, self-control problems, and interpersonal conflicts at age 23. These longitudinal findings, somewhat stronger for males than females, were also partially replicated using actometer measures of activity level in early childhood.

Positive Affect. The temperament dimension of positive affect encompasses reward-seeking activities that are expressed in pleasure, enthusiasm, and contentment (Bates et al., 1994). This dimension may be most closely linked to the adult factors of Extraversion and Agreeableness. Suggestive evidence for this link is provided by studies that have tried to predict infant temperament from parental personality. For example, Goldsmith, Losoya, Bradshaw, and Campos (1994) showed that temperamental measures of positive affect in infancy (e.g., smiling and laughter) are associated with parental personality measures of Positive Emotionality. By themselves, parent-offspring correlations do not speak to the question of developmental continuity in the lives of offspring, although behavior-genetic studies may shed some light on developmental continuity by demonstrating that the associations between parent personality and child temperament are mediated genetically. Such studies, however, are no substitute for necessary longitudinal demonstrations.

Inhibition. Temperamentally inhibited children are cautious in approaching new objects and situations, and physiological studies reveal differences between inhibited and uninhibited children in sympathetic reactivity (Kagan, Reznick, & Snidman, 1988). As noted earlier, behavioral inhibition has been linked to internalizing problems, suggesting it may be linked (negatively) to the trait domain of Extraversion, which captures a constellation of characteristics such as social withdrawal, shyness, and social discomfort. The fearlike component of behavioral inhibition—as revealed both behaviorally and physiologically—may also be linked to that constellation of characteristics of Neuroticism that describes an individual who is easily rattled, brittle under stress, and anxious in unpredictable situations.

Negative Affect. Measures of this construct—including irritability, fussing, anger, and lack of control—have received the most research attention. In terms of adult personality expression, individual differences in negative affect are most likely to be linked to neuroticism and agreeableness, to the extent that the latter dimension may be associated with the inhibition of negative affect (Graziano, 1994). Suggestive evidence for these links is provided by research, summarized earlier, showing that measures of negative affect in early childhood predict both internalizing and externalizing behavior problems.

Persistence.   Persistence, which refers to individual differences in children's attentional capacities—attention span, distractibility, task orientation, and interest—may be most closely linked to Constraint/Conscientiousness. Low behavioral Constraint captures multiple elements of persistence and impulse control in task and achievement settings, and suggestive research points to links between task persistence and school-related behaviors (Martin, 1989). However, direct tests of the link between temperament measures of persistence and personality measures of Constraint are, for the most part, still outstanding. To the extent that individual differences in persistence reflect the flexible use of attentional and social mechanisms (i.e., self-regulation), this temperamental quality may also be linked to the personality dimension of Agreeableness (Eisenberg & Fabes, 1992), a prediction that has received support in cross-sectional and short-term longitudinal studies (e.g., Eisenberg, Fabes, Murphy, Maszk, et al. 1995).

Individual differences in persistence may also be related to Openness to Experience, whose defining characteristics are imagination, fantasy, curiosity, and an eagerness to learn and experience new things. One study, using an experimental paradigm to tax children's persistence (e.g., the ability to delay gratification), showed that children who score high on Openness are better able to resist immediate gratification (Krueger et al., 1996b), possibly because they can avoid focusing on the immediate reward and can pass the time in the private realm of imagination and fantasy (Mischel, Ebbesen, & Zeiss, 1973). Tests of the link between temperamental measures of persistence and Openness will need to verify that this connection is independent of measured intelligence, for performance on intelligence tests has been shown to be correlated with measures of persistence as well as with Openness in different developmental periods (John et al., 1994; Martin, 1989). More generally, little is known about how cognitive skills may moderate the links between childhood temperament and later personality development.

The isomorphism between the structure of temperament and the structure of personality is striking, but it may be more apparent than real (Hartup & van Lieshout, 1995). A similar number of factors with similar labels at different ages does not constitute a developmental model. A meaningful developmental model will be advanced by the following research programs: (a) longitudinal studies that document empirical relations between temperament and personality measures using independent data sources, (b) studies of social learning processes that document how nonshared environmental influences (e.g., unique reinforcement histories) interact with temperamental differences to shape personality variation, and (c) experimental studies that establish whether the same processes are correlated with psychological differences at different ages, such as studies showing similar correlations in childhood and in adulthood between selective activation of left prefrontal cortex and measures of positive affect and selective activation of right prefrontal cortex and measures of negative affect (Davidson, 1992). All three research programs should allow for the likelihood that a one-to-one correspondence does not characterize the relation between temperament dimensions and personality dimensions. Because environmental influences may deflect developmental trajectories, variations on one trait dimension may have multiple sources of temperamental variation, and variations on different traits may evolve from a common temperamental source.

It is also possible that a purely dimensional approach may yield a confusing developmental portrait because orthogonal dimensions of temperament conceal distinct types of children who are characterized by unique temperamental configurations. Person-centered research may offer a more promising approach to uncover developmental continuities (Block, 1993). Using this approach in a longitudinal study from age 3 to age 18, Caspi and Silva (1995) reported evidence consistent with some of the predictions outlined above. At age 3, "undercontrolled" children were described by examiners as irritable, impulsive, and impersistent; they had difficulty sitting still, were rough and uncontrolled in their behavior, and labile in their emotional responses. At age 18, these children scored high on traits indexing Negative Emotionality and low on traits indexing Constraint. They described themselves as danger seeking, impulsive, prone to respond with strong negative emotions to everyday events, and enmeshed in adversarial relationships. At age 3, "inhibited" children were described by examiners as shy and fearful. At age 18, these children were characterized by an overcontrolled, restrained personality and a nonassertive interpersonal style. They preferred safe activities over dangerous ones, were cautious rather than impulsive, and were lacking in social potency; they were submissive, not fond of leadership roles, and had little desire to influence others.

How Early Can We Tell?

The strength of associations between temperamental characteristics in early childhood and later behavior problems and personality differences is weak to moderate. However, the fact that it is possible to chart connections from the first few years of life—as early as age 3—to adolescence and young adulthood is a significant achievement, for this was a contested point less than two decades ago (Kagan, 1980).

The second year of life may be the crucial dividing line for predicting later personality differences because of the intercorrelated cognitive-emotional changes that take place during this period. During the second year of life, perceptual and cognitive changes enable children to master object permanence, defer imitation, and engage in symbolic play (Kagan, 1981). Self-conscious emotions such as embarrassment and shame also begin to appear at this time (Astington, 1993). These capacities may be necessary for children to form mental representations of their social world and to develop beliefs and expectations that are then affirmed by an expanding and reactive social environment (Kagan, 1984). It is possible that continuity or predictability may not emerge until infants experience these major developmental reorganizations during the second year of life.

There are other reasons to doubt the feasibility of prediction prior to the second year of life. It is possible that much of the observed variation in infant behavior is due to transient conditions, such as temporary allergies. As these conditions disappear with growth, so may their associated behavioral tendencies (Kagan, 1984). It is also possible that predictability may not emerge until a later age because early psychological differences are especially likely to be modified by the child's subsequent experiences with the environment (Chess & Thomas, 1987). Temperamental dimensions in infancy are the entire "personality" of the newborn, but whether they show continuity may depend on the degree of "fit" between the child's temperamental characteristics and the socialization context (Wachs, 1994).

But before giving up on predicting later personality from infant temperament, consider the parallel case of predicting IQ. For many years, psychologists argued that intellectual performance scores obtained in the earliest years of life correlated poorly with IQ scores at later ages, implying that infancy and toddlerhood may be especially plastic developmental periods for intellectual status. But new evidence is challenging this claim. This evidence emerges from studies that are using new measures of "infant intelligence." Whereas earlier studies relied on infant tests that measured sensory and motor behavior, more recent studies rely on infant tests that measure habituation to stimuli and recognition memory, which are conceptually closer to the construct of intelligence. Habituation refers to differences in the amount of time that infants attend to unfamiliar stimuli placed in their view. Theoretically, more intelligent infants need less time to thoroughly explore a stimulus, and they sooner turn attention away. Recognition memory refers to the extent to which infants look at a new stimulus more than they look at a stimulus they have been shown before. Theoretically, more intelligent infants are likely to remember the repeated stimulus and will glance at it only briefly. Studies have shown that assessments of habituation and recognition memory in the first year of life predict later IQ quite well; the median correlation is .45 (McCall & Carriger, 1993).

What implications do these findings have for the prediction of personality? According to Asendorpf (1992a), these findings highlight the distinction between the stability of individual differences and the continuity of psychological constructs. Correlations across time may be low either because the rank order of individuals has changed over time or because the construct *intelligence* is indexed by different behaviors at different ages. Thus, it may be that, relative to previous measures of infant intelligence, habituation and recognition paradigms tap an information-processing mechanism that is more similar to those skills tapped by later IQ tests. With regard to the prediction of personality differences, it may be that behavioral indicators in early childhood and those in later adolescence and adulthood have unequal validity coefficients; that is, they do not adequately reflect the behavioral expression of the same personality construct. Further advances in prediction will be made only if we are able to operationalize the same trait construct at different ages.

From Temperament to Personality: The Process of Elaboration

The process of developmental elaboration refers to the mechanisms by which those temperamental attributes that are part of each individual's genetic heritage accumulate response strength through their repeated reinforcement and become elaborated into cognitive structures strongly primed for accessibility. Of course, it will never be possible to fully account for this process. This is not a heretical proposition, but a sober appraisal of the human condition. Meehl (1978, p. 811) argued that much of personality development resembles a "random walk," a series of stochastic events that collectively and cumulatively contribute to differences between individuals. Bandura (1982) similarly argued that some life paths are determined by chance encounters that have their own causes. However, these observations do not require relinquishing the quantitative, nomothetic treatment of personality development. It may not be possible to predict the stochastic events and chance encounters that shape one's life course, but it is possible to study how early dispositional differences influence the way these events are "experienced" (Scarr, 1988).

If temperament is the core around which subsequent personality dimensions develop, it is important to understand how phenotypes emerge out of person-environment transactions. This elaboration may involve at least six processes, which are listed below in the order of their hypothesized developmental emergence. For example, learning processes and environmental elicitation are hypothesized to influence the course of subsequent personality development already in the first few months of life; environmental construal and social comparison processes can influence personality development only following the emergence of necessary cognitive functions in early and middle childhood; and environmental selection and manipulation require the emergence of self-regulatory functions in later childhood and adolescence.

Learning Processes. The fact that some responses are learned only after extensive training, if at all, suggests that there are basic individual differences in the learning process (Bolles, 1970). Temperamental differences may influence several learning mechanisms that are involved in the elaboration process, including discrimination learning, extinction, reinforcement, and punishment (Bandura, 1961). For example, Eysenck (1977), in his autonomic conditioning theory of adult antisocial personality disorder, hypothesized that stimulus generalization should be enhanced through parents' verbal labeling of misbehaviors as "naughty," "bad," or "wicked." But children with verbal-skill deficits might not profit from the labeling of a class of behaviors as punishment-attracting; they may have to learn by trial and error. Verbally impaired children thus experience more frequent punishment events than verbally adept children, but with proportionately less result in curbing

their problem behaviors. Kochanska (1991, 1995) found that the influence of maternal discipline on the development of conscience was moderated by temperamental differences. Maternal rearing styles that deemphasized power assertion were linked to children's moral orientation, but only if the children were anxious; among nonfearful children, a responsive mother-child relationship was linked to children's moral orientation. Temperamental differences thus appear to shape the learning process.

Environmental Elicitation. Temperamental differences also elicit different reactions from the environment (Bell & Chapman, 1986). Individual differences in temperament influence how adults react to children over the course of development, beginning already in the first few months of life (e.g., van den Boom & Hoeksma, 1994). Research about this process is especially well developed in regard to "difficult" temperament; much less is known about other temperamental differences. However, research has shown that individual differences in temperament and personality traits are reliably expressed in unique verbal and nonverbal behaviors, and that other persons in the immediate environment react to these behaviors and use this information to make inferences and attributions (Borkenau & Liebler, 1995; Gifford, 1994). It is possible that these observable "markers" of temperament traits lead primary caretakers and other adults to attribute psychological qualities to children that are subsequently internalized as part of children's emerging self-concept. Research on developmental changes in children's understanding of personality—and the relation of this changing understanding to internalization—suggests that this process may start to take hold during middle childhood. For example, adults' verbal messages (reinforcements, attributions) to children about their personal characteristics and behavior appear to influence children's subsequent behavior only once children develop an understanding of personality consistency, at around 7 to 8 years of age (Eisenberg, Cialdini, McCreath, & Shell, 1987; Grusec & Redler, 1980).

Environmental Construal. With the emergence of belief systems and expectations, temperamental differences may also begin to influence how environmental experiences are construed, thus shaping each person's "effective experience" of the environment (Hartup & van Lieshout, 1995). For example, temperamental differences in impulse control may influence children's reaction to demands for effortful attention and concentration in educational settings (e.g.,

Mischel, Shoda, & Peake, 1988), turning school into a frustrating experience for some and an engaging experience for others. Research about the construal process stems from the cognitive tradition in personality psychology that emphasizes each person's subjective experience and unique perception of the world (Mischel, 1990). This research focuses on what people "do" mentally (Cantor, 1990), demonstrating that social information processing—including attention, encoding, retrieval, and interpretation—is a selective process shaped by individual differences in temperament and personality (Fiske & Taylor, 1991). Research on temperament and information processing is especially well developed in regard to introversion-extraversion and anxiety; much less is known about other temperamental differences (Derryberry & Reed, 1994a; Larsen, 1992; Revelle, 1993).

Social and Temporal Comparisons. With increased cognitive sophistication (e.g., role-taking skills), two social psychological processes are hypothesized to influence self-evaluations: children learn about themselves by comparing and contrasting themselves to others (social comparisons) as well as to themselves over time (temporal comparisons). Suls and Mullen (1982) proposed that the salience of these comparison processes changes across the life course. Age-related changes in social cognition, as well as changing social roles, suggest that temporal comparisons are especially salient in childhood and old age, whereas social comparisons are salient in adolescence and in much of adulthood. Most of the research on comparison processes has focused on achievement-related behaviors; less is known about how these processes are related to the course of personality development, although this area of research is potentially fertile because social comparisons in sibling relationships represent a potent source of nonshared environmental influence on personality (Tesser, 1980). Moreover, little is known about how temperamental differences influence comparison processes (Derryberry & Reed, 1994b). It is possible that attentional biases shape the type of comparison information to which different children attend, and that this contributes to individual differences in self-evaluation. Temperamental differences may also influence responsivity to different types of comparison information and thereby influence emotional reactions (e.g., fear, sadness, or shame) to social and temporal comparisons.

Environmental Selection. As self-regulatory competencies increase with age, individuals begin to make choices and display preferences that may reinforce and sustain their characteristics. Indeed, the most striking differences among individuals are to be found not by studying their responses to the same situation but by studying how they construct new situations (Wachtel, 1973). Although the mechanisms that produce such person-situation correlations are not entirely understood, it is apparent that different persons, by virtue of their behaviors and characteristics, construct social contexts and generate life situations that are congruent with their personalities (Hammen, 1991). A person's selection and creation of environments is thus one of the most individualizing and pervasive expressions of his or her personality, and research has shown that individuals' dispositions can lead them to select situations that, in turn, reinforce and sustain those same dispositions (e.g., Buss, 1987; Emmons, Diener, & Larsen, 1986; Magnus, Diener, Fujita, & Payot, 1993; Snyder & Ickes, 1985).

Environmental Manipulation. Once the self-concept is firmly established, individuals also begin to alter, modify, and manipulate the environments in which they find themselves (Buss, 1987). For example, observational studies reveal individual differences in the strategies children use to influence and change the behavior of others (Raush, 1965). Experimental studies likewise show that people alter social situations so that they receive feedback from their environment that confirms their personality characteristics. They do this by adopting behavioral strategies that confirm their self-conceptions and by resisting feedback that clashes with their self-conceptions (Swann, 1987). Each of us projects signs, uses symbols, and engages in behaviors that are consistent with our personality characteristics and that serve to "bring social reality into harmony with our personality" (Swann, 1983, p. 33).

I have described six processes through which endogenous-biological and experiential-learning sources of influence may serve to elaborate an initial disposition over time so that it increasingly organizes emotion, thought, and action. Research is now needed on each of these processes in relation to different temperamental traits. The emergence of a consensual system for describing individual differences in temperament may facilitate such a research program and enable students of personality development to shift their concern from studies of structure (e.g., describing the structure of individual differences) to studies of developmental processes (e.g., the elaboration of a temperamental trait over time).

The processes outlined above are hypothesized to promote the elaboration of temperamental differences into personality traits, and they highlight the increasingly important role, with age, of the emerging self-concept and social relations. In the next section I turn to longitudinal studies of personality traits, where I consider, in greater detail, the transactional processes that promote stable individual differences across the life course.

PERSONALITY CONTINUITY ACROSS THE LIFE COURSE

What types of continuity are observed? What are the factors that affect continuity? What are the mechanisms that promote the continuity of personality across the life course? My purpose in this section is to discuss the conceptual and methodological issues involved in answering such questions, not to provide an exhaustive review of longitudinal studies or their findings. Young, Savola, and Phelps (1991) have compiled an overview of longitudinal studies. Moss and Susman (1980) summarize classic longitudinal studies of personality development. I begin by considering two interpretive issues in longitudinal research on personality development. First, I evaluate the use of retrospective longitudinal methods. Second, I explore the implications of historical change for the interpretation of longitudinal research.

Prospective and Retrospective Studies of Personality Development

Prospective versus Retrospective Data Gathering

Many psychological theories subscribe to the view that what is past is prologue. Prospective-longitudinal studies, in which information is obtained from the same persons assessed repeatedly over time, offer the most promising method for linking events and behaviors across the life course and for identifying the antecedents of particular conditions. In the absence of these studies, researchers often turn to retrospective studies for convenience and ask people to report about the past (Robins, 1988).

Because of a variety of cognitive and motivational factors, people may be inefficient and inaccurate processors of information about their past (Bradburn, Rips, & Shevell, 1987). Although numerous cautionary notes have been issued about the use of retrospective data, studies of personality

development continue to use the retrospective method to gather reports of socialization experiences as well as recollections of earlier temperament and personality characteristics. This is unfortunate because retrospective reports are plagued by two problems (Halverson, 1988).

The first is that there is little agreement between what people say about the past and what is known about the past from concurrent data sources (i.e., from data collected in the past; e.g., Henry, Moffitt, Caspi, Langley, & Silva, 1994; Yarrow, Campbell, & Burton, 1970). The second is that memory is a reconstructive process and people may distort the past. This problem poses special difficulties when evaluating intervention programs and when studying continuity and change. Ross (1989) found that people's recollections of their earlier attributes and personal histories are guided by their own "implicit theories" about stability and change. People formulate recollections of past events and earlier attributes in biased and self-serving ways.

Although the psychological past is difficult to retrieve reliably or accurately, memories of the past—real or imagined—are of functional significance: they give shape and meaning to current behaviors and conditions (Cohler, 1982). However, the use of retrospective reports as valid and veridical accounts of the past is unwarranted; it serves to generate findings that may be misleading in research, clinical, and legal settings (Loftus, 1993). At the very least, Brewin, Andrews, and Gotlib (1993) recommend that, if using retrospective reports, researchers should adopt more structured methods that may enhance recall and should seek to complement retrospective self-reports with corroborating data from other independent sources.

Follow-Up versus Follow-Back Data Analysis

The distinction between prospective and retrospective data gathering is often confused with the distinction between follow-up and follow-back data analysis. Data gathered prospectively can be analyzed using one of two different strategies (Rutter & Garmezy, 1983). In the follow-back strategy, researchers examine the childhood characteristics of adults with a known outcome (e.g., antisocial personality disorder). In the follow-up strategy, researchers examine which childhood characteristics predict the outcome of interest.

The difference between the two data analytic strategies is the difference between reference points. In follow-back designs, researchers move back in time from the outcome of interest; in follow-up designs, researchers move forward in time to the outcome of interest. Follow-back and follow-up data analysis designs thus provide different types of information about longitudinal relations. Sometimes this evidence does not converge. For example, it is possible for the majority of adults with antisocial personality disorder to have had rejecting parents without a majority of rejected children becoming adults with an antisocial personality disorder. Whereas follow-back designs provide suggestive evidence about connections between child and adult behavior, only follow-up designs "provide data interpretable in terms of predictive risk" (Parker & Asher, 1987, p. 361). Inferences about developmental continuities are strongest when both types of data analytic designs are applied to data collected prospectively (e.g., Henry, Caspi, Moffitt, & Silva, 1996).

Historical Change and Personality Development

A limitation of most longitudinal studies is their historical specificity. This is because simple longitudinal studies assess members of a single birth cohort. Accordingly, it is unknown to what extent knowledge about personality development is historically specific. This is, of course, a problem in the social sciences generally, but it typically remains unacknowledged; both data and theory are presented as if they were transhistorically valid. Those who deal with longitudinal data have been somewhat more sensitive to the issue.

Social scientists have articulated three responses to this question. The *metatheoretical response* has been articulated by social psychologists who question whether psychology is science or history (e.g., Gergen, 1982). According to this view, all theory and "findings" are historically conditioned and socially constructed. However, social constructionism as a philosophical perspective negates the possibility of basing applied social practices on scientific findings (Smith, 1994).

The *methodological response* has been led by developmental psychologists who have observed that simple longitudinal designs confound three types of effects: age, cohort (year of birth), and period (time of measurement; Baltes, Cornelius, & Nesselroade, 1979). Age effects reflect the influence of maturation or aging, as illustrated by a decline for most individuals on speeded ability tests. Cohort and period effects are historical in nature. Historical influence takes the form of a cohort effect when social change differentiates the life patterns of successive birth cohorts. For example, members of relatively small population birth cohorts may encounter more favorable employment opportunities

because of less competition for jobs than members of relatively large population birth cohorts (Glenn, 1980). Historical influences take the form of period effects when specific influences, such as wars, exert a relatively uniform effect across successive birth cohorts. For example, marriage and divorce rates increased with mobilization and demobilization in the Second World War. Age, cohort, and period effects are confounded in simple longitudinal studies because chronological age is defined by birth year (cohort) and year of measurement (period).

Schaie (1965) proposed a general developmental model that addressed the task of estimating the three effects (age, cohort, and period) in relation to psychological functioning. This model has clarified ambiguities emerging from cross-sectional and single-cohort longitudinal designs, but for other purposes the model is more limited. Some have argued that the methodological requirements of the model are uneconomical and unnecessary (McCall, 1977). Others have noted that the model does not solve the conceptual problem of linking historical influences to human development (Elder, Caspi, & Burton, 1988).

Consider a study by Nesselroade and Baltes (1974). To test whether secular changes influenced personality development, they administered personality tests to four adolescent cohorts born in 1954, 1955, and 1957 on three occasions, in 1970, 1971, and 1972. The results showed a period effect whereby from 1970 to 1971–1972 all adolescents, independent of their age, showed a decline in impulse control. The authors made some effort to explain these findings, but the design is inappropriate for linking historical circumstances to behavior; it uses little more than speculation to explain historical variations. Baltes et al. (1979) noted that the promise of cohort analysis will remain unfulfilled until specific historical changes can be linked to specific changes in psychological functioning. The treatment of historical influences as cohort or period effects in itself provides no clues about such linkages. In that sense, a cohort difference is like an age difference or a social class difference; it remains an empty finding until it can be translated into psychological processes or events.

The *social-historical response* has been led by life course sociologists who have sought to sketch the flow of influence from macrohistorical developments to the world of the individual and to relate social changes to personality development (Elder, Modell, & Parke, 1993). Elder's (1974, 1979) examination of two birth cohorts who lived through the Great Depression and World War II exemplifies this approach. With pre-Depression birth dates that differed by only eight years, these cohorts experienced dramatically different historical times. Members of the Oakland cohort (born 1920–1921) were young children during the prosperous 1920s and entered adolescence during the hard times of the Great Depression. In contrast, members of the Berkeley cohort (born 1928–1929) encountered family hardships during the vulnerable years of early childhood, and the developmental tasks of adolescence were accompanied by the disruptions of war mobilization. Although economic deprivation produced similar changes in the family environments of children in both cohorts, the differential developmental effects of these changes on the two cohorts were still evident at midlife.

In considering historical influences, it is important to draw two distinctions. First, one must distinguish between historical influences on mean levels of variables and historical influences on the correlational structure among variables. Secular changes tend to influence the average level of particular psychological characteristics in the population, but secular changes seldom alter the correlations between variables, either within or across developmental periods (McCall, 1977; Nesselroade & Baltes, 1984). Second, it is important to distinguish between biological and social adaptation and to recognize that different variables may be more or less susceptible to historical influence. Baltes (1987) suggested that cohort differences are most pronounced in relation to those aspects of development that are not stabilized in the process of genetic and cultural evolution. For example, there are few observable historical effects on cognitive development among children in developed countries, but there are marked historical effects on values, attitudes, and beliefs (Stewart & Healy, 1989). However, it is not clear how these latter historical changes have influenced children's socialization experiences. For example, evidence points to historical changes in the traits that parents desire and value most in their children (Alwin, 1988), but the mean levels of these personality traits do not appear to have changed over this same period (McCrae & Costa, 1988).

Although there is little compelling evidence for historical changes in personality traits, some evidence suggests that mental health problems are on the rise (Achenbach & Howell, 1993; Lewinsohn, Rohde, Seeley, & Fischer, 1993). However, the interpretation of these trends is not straightforward. One possibility is that there have been mean level increases in those personality traits (e.g., neuroticism) that predispose toward mental health problems. A second possibility is that the change is not in levels of personality traits

per se but rather in person-environment interactions. For example, secular changes in depression may be the result of new and increased environmental stressors that have led to the expression of depression among vulnerable individuals (Brody & Crowley, 1995). It is difficult to draw conclusions about the effects of historical changes on personality development on the basis of changing mean levels and prevalence rates alone.

Historically Specific Findings and Transhistorical Generalizations: An Epistemological Dilemma

The historian Zuckerman (1993) argued that the coupling of developmental psychology and history represents a "dangerous liaison" because it is unclear whether psychologists are willing to abandon their quest for lawlike predictions. Indeed, analyses like Elder's (1979) raise the larger epistemological issue of how we can move from historically specific findings to a more general understanding of life course processes. Sometimes it is easy to extract the general finding behind relatively superficial historical differences. For example, a study of men born in the 1920s found that low ego control in adolescence predicted midlife drinking problems (Jones, 1981). A more recent study of children born in the late 1960s found that low ego control at ages 3 and 4 predicted marijuana use at age 14 (Block et al., 1988). Clearly, the historical change in the drug of choice is trivial; the general finding is obvious.

Sometimes the general finding is more obscure. For example, intellectual competence in a sample of women born in the 1920s was positively correlated with the number of children they had during the postwar baby boom (Livson & Day, 1977), but in both earlier and later samples of women, the correlation between tested intelligence and fertility was negative. Livson and Day noted that their historically specific findings were useful "only if they are interpreted not as direct if-then relationships, but as providing an understanding of the intrapsychic and interpersonal characteristics that mediate one's child-bearing response to a social context prevailing during the period in which fertility decisions are made" (p. 321).

Sometimes psychological processes may remain general even when the psychological content is historically specific. In 1985, Schuman and Scott (1989) asked a large probability sample of Americans to mention which national or world events that had occurred over the past 50 years were especially important. The results showed that regardless of when they were born, most adults identified events that occurred when they were in their late teens or early

20s. Adults who were 70 and older in 1985 identified the Great Depression (50 years earlier) as the most important event; adults who were in their late 30s and 40s in 1985 identified JFK's assassination (20 years earlier) as the most important event; and adults who were 18 to 23 in 1985 identified terrorism, the preoccupation of the early 1980s, as the most important event. These data suggest that the content of collective memories is variable across birth cohorts; the intersection of personal biography and national history leaves a unique impression on each cohort's memory. But beyond the changing content of collective memories, a more general process of personality development appears to be at work: the data highlight the salience of adolescence and young adulthood in political socialization and hint about a sensitive period for the formation of political opinions and for learning about society.

The tension between historical specificity and transhistorical generality is analogous to the tension between idiographic and nomothetic approaches to personality, and the choice of strategy is largely a matter of the investigator's metatheoretical taste. The data themselves place no constraints on the specificity or universality of the inferences drawn or the theories constructed therefrom. As Geertz (1973, chap. 2) observed, "It is not whether phenomena are empirically common that is critical in science . . . but whether they can be made to reveal the enduring natural processes that underlie them . . . [T]he road to the general, to the revelatory simplicities of science, lies through a concern with the particular, the circumstantial, the concrete." Research on personality development that is conducted without a sense of history, without recognition that phenotypic expressions represent a point of articulation between biological, social, and historical processes, may thus miss the point. Ironically, psychologists may have to be historically specific to grasp the more general essence of phenomena examined in the study of personality development.

Types of Continuity Observed in Longitudinal Research

The assertion that an individual's personality has changed or remained the same over time is ambiguous. The boy who has daily temper tantrums when he is 2 but weekly tantrums when he is 9 has increased his level of emotional control; he has changed in absolute terms. But if he ranks first in temper tantrums among his peers at both ages, he has not changed in relative terms. Further ambiguity arises if the form of the behavior changes. If this boy emerges into

adulthood as a man who is irritable and moody, we may grant that the phenotype has changed but claim that the underlying genotype has not. A third ambiguity arises when a claim of continuity rests on observations not of an individual but of a sample of individuals. The continuity of an attribute at the group level may be masking large but mutually canceling changes at the individual level. There are, in short, several meanings denoted by the term *continuity*. The purpose of this section is to disentangle those meanings.

Differential Continuity

Differential continuity refers to the consistency of individual differences within a sample of individuals over time, to the retention of an individual's relative placement in a group. This most common definition of continuity is typically indexed by a correlation coefficient.

Evidence about differential continuity has been marshaled using different self-report personality inventories (e.g., Carmichael & McGue, 1994; Costa, McCrae, & Arenberg, 1980; Finn, 1986; Helson & Moane, 1987; McCrae & Costa, 1990; McGue et al., 1993 Siegler, George, & Okun, 1979; Stevens & Truss, 1985). Personality ratings by clinicians, acquaintances, and spouses reveal temporal continuities as well (e.g., Block, 1971; Conley, 1985; Costa & McCrae, 1988). These studies offer three major conclusions about differential continuity (Clarke & Clarke, 1984; Conley, 1984a; Olweus, 1979; Schuerger, Zarrella, & Hotz, 1989). First, differential continuity tends to increase as the age of study participants increases. Second, differential continuity tends to decrease as the time interval between observations increases. Third, aging changes by themselves have little effect on the ordering of individual differences in adulthood.

These conclusions hold for most psychological variables, but there is some evidence that different types of variables may exhibit different degrees of differential continuity. Measures of intellectual performance show the strongest continuities; personality variables such as the Big Five are next; and political attitudes and measures of self-opinions (e.g., self-esteem, life satisfaction) are last, showing correlations between .2 and .4 over 5- to 10-year intervals (Conley, 1984a). What accounts for this hierarchy of consistency?

It is unlikely that these differences are simply a function of the differential reliability of the three kinds of variables because this hierarchy obtains even when the measures are corrected for unreliability. However, a related methodological consideration is that ability tests demand maximal performance, whereas personality and attitude questionnaires assess representative, typical performance. The former may yield evidence of greater continuity. Willerman, Turner, and Peterson (1976) showed that, for the purpose of predicting behavior, personality tests modeled on an ability format tend to outperform traditional personality tests that sample typical performance. It is also possible that consistencies in social behavior require environmental supports, whereas cognitive activities may be supported more by internal feedback systems (Cairns, 1979). This interpretation may account for the relatively lower continuities observed among attitudes, which may be especially susceptible to changes in sociocultural context (Alwin, 1994). Finally, it is noteworthy that this hierarchy of continuity roughly parallels the size of the heritability coefficients for the three kinds of variables, suggesting that genetic and gene-environment correlations may be contributing to continuity. Consistent with this hypothesis, Tesser (1993) showed that, even within the domain of attitudes, those with higher heritabilities are more resistant to change than attitudes with lower heritability.

Some investigators have suggested that the differential continuity of personality may be influenced by social norms (e.g., Block, Gjerde, & Block, 1991; Caspi, Bem, & Elder, 1989; Kerr, Lambert, Stattin, & Klackenberg-Larsson, 1994). For example, Kagan and Moss (1962) found a number of continuities from childhood to adulthood that were related to the sex of the individual and the gender-appropriateness of the behaviors being assessed. Passivity and dependency showed continuity for females but not for males; aggression showed continuity for males but not for females. These findings suggest that individuals who do not conform to the culture's norms are likely to be pressured to change. But caution is needed in evaluating evidence about sex differences in continuity. First, many studies that examine sex differences in the correlational structure among variables fail to test whether these differences are statistically significant (Cohen, Cohen, & Brook, 1995). Second, longitudinal researchers who test for sex differences, but do not find them, typically report findings pooled across males and females, thus obscuring the absence of sex differences in most studies.

The interpretation of differential continuity must also take into account extraneous sources of influence. For example, correlation coefficients depend on the amount of variability in the measures. Thus, because of restricted range, homogeneous samples may show less continuity than unselected populations. Similarly, systematic attrition may alter the composition of longitudinal samples in ways that affect variability. If more extreme individuals are unavailable for follow-up relative to less extreme individuals, the homogeneity of the sample will increase, and the apparent temporal continuity of personality will be artifactually attenuated.

Changes in variability—and hence changes in estimates of differential continuity—can also arise for substantive reasons. The use of the correlation coefficient as an index of temporal continuity implicitly assumes that variability remains constant across the period of development under study. But, as Wohlwill (1980) notes, "Many dimensions conform to [a] model of individuation emerging at some point during development and increasing over a period of time, only to converge toward a terminal level at which differences are either eliminated . . . or greatly attenuated in amount . . . [Differential continuity] must be considered in relation to the overall pattern of differentiation over the course of development characterizing a particular variable" (p. 408). In the realm of personality development, Haan (1981) suggested that increased heterogeneity may reflect individuated ways of meeting new, age-specific situational challenges, whereas increased homogeneity may indicate that individuals accommodate to common experiences with similar solutions.

Absolute Continuity

Absolute continuity refers to constancy in the quantity or amount of an attribute over time. Conceptually, it connotes the continuity of an attribute within a single individual, but it is typically assessed empirically by examining group means (e.g., Conley, 1985; Schaie & Parham, 1976; Siegler et al., 1979).

Costa and McCrae (1988) reported that there is little consistent evidence for age changes in mean levels of personality traits during adulthood. Working with the five-factor model of personality traits, they gathered data on two occasions, six years apart, from 983 participants who ranged in age between 21 and 96. They conducted three different types of analyses: cross-sectional analyses in which individuals of different ages were compared to each other; longitudinal analyses in which the same individuals were retested over time; and cross- and time-sequential analyses in which individuals of the same birth cohort (cross-sequential) or of the same age (time-sequential) were compared at different times of measurement. Costa and McCrae also gathered spouse reports for a subset of their sample to try to replicate the cross-sectional and longitudinal analyses with different data sources.

The results of these analyses are summarized in Table 6.4, where a zero indicates no age effect, a minus sign indicates a decline with age, a plus sign indicates an increase with age, and the strength of the age effect is indicated by the number of signs. The results in Table 6.4 suggest that there are few consistent age-related personality changes in adulthood. In fact, the lack of convergence among the cross-sectional, longitudinal, and sequential approaches—and the failure to replicate evidence of change using different data sources—led McCrae and Costa (1990) to conclude that sampling differences, practice effects, time of measurement artifacts, and selective mortality may well render spurious many aging effects.

Personality changes have been noted when study participants are first tested as adolescents and young adults (e.g., Carmichael & McGue, 1994; Haan, Millsap, & Hartka, 1986; Helson & Moane, 1987; McGue et al., 1993; Mortimer, Finch, & Kumka, 1982; Stein, Newcomb, & Bentler, 1986; Stevens & Truss, 1985). In general, the evidence points to normative age-related decreases on personality traits related to Neuroticism or Negative Emotionality and to increases on personality traits related to Conscientiousness or Constraint. From late adolescence through early adulthood, most people become less emotionally labile, more responsible, and more cautious. Some personality changes have also been noted when people are tested very late in life, but it is not clear whether these are normative aging effects or the influence of poor health (Mendelsohn et al., 1995).

Most research focusing on age-related mean level changes has not been guided by theoretical concerns, although several theories have been formulated on the basis of clinical work (Neugarten, 1977). For example, Guttman (1975) suggested that the advent of parenthood establishes gender-role distinctions in young adulthood. To succeed as caregivers, women need to suppress elements of aggression; to succeed as economic providers, men need to suppress elements of affiliation. After the demands of parenthood are over, earlier suppressed elements of personality can be expressed again. Studies by Helson (Helson & Moane, 1987; Wink & Helson, 1992) are consistent, in part, with this crossover account. The results showed that, during their late 20s, women increased in femininity and self-discipline but, in their later years, they decreased in femininity and increased in confidence, dominance, and coping skills. In contrast, men increased in affiliation during the postparental period. It is not clear, however, whether these personality changes were attributable to parenthood per se or to secular changes in the lives of the study participants, who were born in the 1930s. In a longitudinal analysis of changes predicted by Erikson's stage theory of psychosocial development, Whitbourne, Zuschlag, Elliot, and Waterman (1992) used a quantitative measure that indicates the extent to which psychosocial crises are successfully resolved. They found evidence of increased psychosocial resolution of Eriksonian crises with age. This pattern of mean level changes is consistent with Erikson's writings, although it does not test the strong version of his theory that psychosocial development proceeds according to an epigenetic principle.

Despite the absence of consistent evidence for developmental changes in personality traits after young adulthood, absolute changes have been observed when individuals cross important life course transitions. For example, a

Table 6.4 Age Effects on the Big Five Personality Traits: Results from Cross-Sectional, Longitudinal, and Cross-Sequential Analyses

Big Five Traits	Cross-Sectional		Longitudinal		Cross-Sequential
	Self-Report	Spouse Rating	Self-Report	Spouse Rating	Self-Report
Neuroticism	– –	– – –	–	+	0
Extraversion	– – –	– – –	0	0	+
Openness	– – –	– –	0	0	+
Agreeableness	+	0	– – –	NA	– – –
Conscientiousness	0	+ + +	–	NA	–

Note: Minus signs indicate a negative association of the variable with age; plus signs indicate a positive association. Effects accounting for less than 2% of the variance are marked with one sign; those accounting for 2% to 5% are marked with two signs; and those accounting for more than 5% are marked with three signs. Zeros indicate nonsignificant effects. Longitudinal analyses of Agreeableness and Conscientiousness were conducted only for self-reports.

Source: P. T. Costa Jr., & R. R. McCrae (1988). Personality in adulthood: A six-year longitudinal study of self-reports and spouse ratings on the NEO Personality Inventory. *Journal of Personality and Social Psychology, 54,* 853–863.

study of primiparous couples from the third semester of pregnancy to six months postpartum found mean level shifts not just in role behaviors, but also in sex-typed personality and identity measures (Feldman & Aschenbrenner, 1983). It is important, however, to underscore the difference between absolute continuity and differential continuity. A sample of individuals may show change in mean levels of the trait over time but still preserve their rank ordering across occasions. Physical height is an obvious example. Another example is provided by the study of primiparous couples cited above. Despite the absolute changes the study participants showed in their sex-typed personality characteristics across the transition from expectancy to parenthood, the differential continuity displayed by the same attributes was quite high.

Although the distinction between absolute and differential indices is not difficult to grasp, it has often led to misinterpretations. For example, the observation that the correlation for estimates of intelligence between adopted children and their biological mothers is usually higher than that between these children and their adoptive mothers often leads to the inference that the environment has little effect on IQ. In fact, the mean IQ scores of early-adopted children suggest that they can benefit from enriched family environments (Turkheimer, 1991).

It is also important to note that the assessment of absolute continuity requires that the same attribute be measured on successive occasions. Absolute continuity has no meaning if the "same" attribute actually refers to different phenotypic expressions of a personality variable. Thus, absolute continuity cannot be assessed over long-time intervals where identical behaviors cannot be assessed. For example, it is not possible to assert than an individual who is irritable and moody as an adult is more or less ill-tempered in absolute terms than he or she was as a child who had weekly temper tantrums.

So far, in discussing absolute continuity, I have focused on objective indices of personality. But there is also research that examines subjective continuity and change (Ryff, 1984). For example, Woodruff and Birren (1972) retested a sample of middle-aged adults 25 years after they had originally completed a personality test. In addition to describing their current selves, they were asked to complete the same test as they thought they had answered it in adolescence. Although there were, in fact, very few age changes over the 25-year span, study participants perceived many such changes. The differences between actual and perceived discontinuities suggest that the flow of psychological time (subjective

age) may be relatively independent of calendar time and may exert an effect on behavior that is also independent of chronological age (Rossi, 1980).

Structural Continuity

Structural continuity refers to the persistence of correlational patterns among a set of variables across time. Typically, such continuity is assessed by examining the similarity of covariation patterns among item and factor relations across repeated measurements. The technical work involved in testing whether a factor structure is invariant across age and in determining whether variables have equivalent measurement properties at different ages can be accomplished with structural equation models (Bollen, 1989).

Structural change may indicate a developmental transformation. For example, factor analyses of mental test items in infancy and early childhood suggest that there are qualitative changes in the nature of intelligence (McCall, Eichorn, & Hogarty, 1977). Some developmental psychologists believe that structural invariance should always be established before investigating other kinds of stability (Baltes, Reese, & Nesselroade, 1977). This strategy has been adopted by several groups of researchers investigating the development of individual differences in temperament and personality. Pedlow, Sanson, Prior, and Oberklaid (1993) studied the structure of temperament during the first decade of life. From infancy to age 8, temperament was measured on six occasions using maternal reports. Structural equation modeling was used to examine whether the temperament factors that emerged on these multiple measurement occasions showed measurement equivalence. The results pointed to substantial measurement equivalence for several temperament dimensions (e.g., approach, persistence), although this evidence is restricted to maternal perceptions of their children over time. Future research on structural stability and change should include multiple sources of data (e.g., parent reports, teacher reports, and observer ratings) to disentangle rater effects from developmental changes.

In adulthood, researchers working with trait models of personality have based their research on factor analytically derived measures of personality whose structure has been shown to be invariant (Costa & McCrae, 1992). Although there do not appear to be qualitative structural shifts beyond adolescence in the personality variables examined in most studies, there may be qualitative shifts in other psychosocial domains, such as in "theories of oneself" (Brim,

1976). Research employing spontaneously generated descriptions of the self points to qualitative changes in adolescents' self-conceptions (Damon & Hart, 1986). As in the example of the differentiation of abilities cited earlier, it is possible that the self-concept of young children, which is relatively undifferentiated, may evolve to become more complex later in childhood both because of cognitive changes and because the person acquires a larger set of roles and corresponding identities (see Harter, Ch. 9, this Volume).

Ipsative Continuity

Absolute, differential, and structural continuities are indexed by statistics that characterize a sample of individuals. However, continuity at the group level may not mirror continuity at the individual level. For this reason, some researchers examine ipsative continuity, which explicitly refers to continuity at the individual level. Ipsative continuity denotes continuity in the configuration of variables within an individual across time. Ipsative continuity could also be called morphogenic (Allport, 1962) or person-centered continuity. The latter term derives from Block's (1971) distinction between a variable-centered approach to personality, which is concerned with the relative standing of persons across variables, and a person-centered approach, which is concerned with the salience and configuration of variables within the person. An ipsative approach to the study of development seeks to discover continuities in personality functioning across development by identifying each person's salient attributes and their intraindividual organization.

Very little longitudinal research has been conducted from an ipsative point of view. An exception is Block's *Lives Through Time* (1971), in which he employed the Q-sort technique of personality description to analyze continuity and change. Continuity and change were indexed by computing correlations across the set of attributes—Q-correlations—between an individual's Q-sort profiles from different measurement occasions; the higher the correlation, the more the configuration of attributes within the individual remained stable across time. Block's analysis showed that aggregate indices of continuity mask large individual differences in personality continuity. For example, the average Q-correlations between early and late adolescence exceeded .70, and those between late adolescence and adulthood exceeded .50, but the intraindividual Q-correlations ranged from moderately negative to the maximum imposed by measurement error. Other studies of

personality continuity and change between childhood and adolescence report average Q-correlations ranging from .43 to .71, with considerable variability in the distribution of these scores; intraindividual Q-correlations ranged from −.44 to .92, indicating that from childhood to adolescence people vary widely in how much continuity or change they exhibited (Asendorpf & van Aken, 1991; Ozer & Gjerde, 1989). Furthermore, Asendorpf and van Aken (1991) found meaningful individual differences in intraindividual continuity: in two samples, the most resilient children showed the most continuity of personality patterns across time. The authors speculated that, relative to more brittle children, ego-resilient children are better equipped to shape their environments in ways that are correlated with their dispositions; they can thus stabilize their personality by adapting their changing environments to their unique characteristics. These findings confirm Block's (1971) report that those persons whose personalities remained stable from adolescence to adulthood (nonchangers) were quite different from those whose personalities changed (changers). In particular, nonchangers of both sexes were more intellectually, emotionally, and socially successful as adolescents than the changers, and a measure of adjustment also showed them to be better adjusted.

The advantage of these Q-sort indices of continuity is that they reference the continuity of each individual within the sample. Unlike assessments of continuity in traditional variable-centered research, these indices do not require reference to other sample members to derive their meaning. The disadvantage of these indices is that they do not yield information about the continuity of individuals along any single attribute (Buss, 1985). Continuity is thus regarded as a general quality of personality only with respect to a set of complex characteristics (Cronbach & Gleser, 1953). This definition is problematic: we can assume that people show personality continuity only if the original measurement covered a large proportion of the significant dimensions of personality. To overcome these limitations, Asendorpf (1992b) proposed a technique for deriving measures of each individual's continuity with respect to specific personality dimensions.

Coherence

The kinds of continuity discussed so far refer to homotypic continuity—continuity of similar behaviors or phenotypic attributes over time. The concept of coherence enlarges the definition of continuity to include heterotypic continuity—continuity of an inferred genotypic attribute presumed to underlie diverse phenotypic behaviors. Moss and Susman (1980) suggested that specific behaviors in childhood may not predict phenotypically similar behaviors later in adulthood, but may still be associated with behaviors that are conceptually consistent with the earlier behaviors (Livson & Peskin, 1980). Kagan (1969) noted that heterotypic continuities are most likely to be found from the earlier years of life, when children go through numerous rapid changes. In contrast, homotypic continuities are more likely to be found after puberty, when psychological organization nears completion.

Examples of heterotypic continuities were reported by Ryder (1967), who reexamined the data from Kagan and Moss's (1962) longitudinal study, *Birth to Maturity*. Childhood task persistence was related to adult achievement orientation. Similarly, childhood aggression, sociability, physical adventurousness, and nonconformity were related to adult sexual behavior. Another example of coherence is provided in a 22-year follow-up study of men and women who had been rated as aggressive by their peers in late childhood (Huesmann et al., 1984). As adults, the men were likely to commit serious criminal acts, abuse their spouses, and drive while intoxicated, whereas the women were likely to punish their offspring severely. Other examples of personality coherence include the finding that the developmental antecedents of adult Type A behavior may be found in phenotypically dissimilar temperamental attributes in childhood (MacEvoy et al., 1988; Steinberg, 1985).

It is important to emphasize that coherence and heterotypic continuity refer to conceptual rather than literal continuity among behaviors. Accordingly, the investigator who claims to have discovered coherence must have a theory—no matter how rudimentary or implicit—that specifies the "genotype" or provides the basis on which the diverse behaviors and attributes can be said to belong to the same equivalence class. In what sense is adult sexual behavior a "derivative" of childhood physical adventurousness? In what way is driving while intoxicated the "same thing" as pushing and shoving other children?

As these examples illustrate, the "theories" behind claims of coherence often amount to appeals to the reader's intuition. Often they are post hoc interpretations of empirical relations discovered in large correlation matrices (Moss & Susman, 1980). With the notable exception of the psychoanalytic theory of psychosexual stages and their adult sequelae, most personality theories do not specify links between personality variables at different developmental periods, a topic to which I now turn.

To study the coherence of personality development it is necessary to trace personality variables through social changes while tracking their continuities. For this strategy to yield meaningful insights, it is necessary to include both temporal and contextual dimensions in the measurement of personality differences. Indeed, the artificial separation of temporal and contextual dimensions in the prediction of behavior obscures development and adaptation; people do not move across time without also moving across situations (Conley, 1984b). According to Ozer (1986), "the notion of coherence refers to a pattern of findings where a construct, measured by several different methods, retains its psychological meaning as revealed in relationships to a variety of other measures" (p. 52) across time and in different contexts.

Below I review three conceptual approaches to the problem of studying personality coherence across the life course. Each of these social-developmental approaches provides a framework for understanding coherence by focusing on the distinctive ways individuals organize their behavior to meet new environmental demands and developmental challenges.

An Organizational-Adaptational Perspective. Sroufe and his colleagues (1979; 1989; Sroufe, Carlson, & Shulman, 1993) have used Anna Freud's (1980) concept of *developmental lines* as a heuristic device for the study of personality coherence. By outlining the tasks and milestones that can be expected in the course of development, from infancy through adolescence, they have designed assessment procedures that capture the organization of behavior in different developmental periods. Longitudinal data show that continuity across development can be discerned in children's adaptational profiles with respect to the challenges they face at each developmental phase. This general approach enables Sroufe and his colleagues to confer conceptual coherency on their findings that individuals who are securely attached as infants later explore their environments as toddlers (Matas, Arend, & Sroufe, 1978), are less dependent on their teachers in the preschool years (Sroufe, Fox, & Pancake, 1983), attain higher sociometric status and display greater competence in peer relations in late childhood (Urban, Carlson, Egeland, & Sroufe, 1991), and appear to establish appropriate cross-sex relationships in adolescence (Sroufe, Bennett, et al., 1993).

Invariant behavior patterns do not emerge in these findings. Instead, we see a predictable and meaningful way of relating to the environment in different social settings at different ages. The continuities of personality are thus expressed not through the constancy of behavior across time and in diverse circumstances, but through the consistency over time in the ways persons characteristically modify their changing contexts as a function of their behavior.

A Sociological Perspective.   Beyond childhood, the search for coherence becomes more complicated, and it may be that a purely psychological approach is insufficient for the analysis of personality continuity and change as the individual increasingly negotiates social roles defined by the culture. Indeed, some researchers have found it useful to adopt a sociocultural perspective and to conceive of the life course as a sequence of culturally defined, age-graded roles that the individual enacts over time (Caspi, 1987; Helson, Mitchell, & Moane, 1984).

Helson introduced the concept of a *social clock project* as a framework for studying life span development. The concept of a social clock focuses attention on the age-related life schedules of individuals in particular cultures and cohorts, and organizes the study of lives in terms of patterned movements into, along, and out of multiple role-paths such as education, work, marriage, and parenthood. In this fashion, the life course can be charted as a sequence of social roles that are enacted over time, and personality coherence can be explored by investigating consistencies in the ways different persons select and perform different social-cultural roles.

In her 30-year longitudinal study of female college seniors, who were first studied in 1958–1960, Helson examined the personality antecedents and consequences of adherence to a Feminine Social Clock (FSC) and a Masculine Occupational Clock (MOC). For example, women who adhered to the FSC were earlier in life characterized by a desire to do well and by a need for structure; women in this birth cohort who adhered to a MOC were earlier in life more rebellious and less sensitive to social norms. Helson et al. (1984, p. 1079) were thus able to identify "culturally salient need-press configurations through time" and to show predictable and meaningful relations between personality and behavior in different social settings at different ages.

An Evolutionary Psychology Perspective.   Bouchard (1995) correctly argued that a purely sociocultural perspective on the life course "ignores the fact that life-histories themselves are complex evolved adaptations" (p. 91). An evolutionary perspective complements the sociocultural perspective by exploring how personality variation is related to those adaptively important problems with which human beings have had to repeatedly contend. Evolutionary psychology thus focuses attention on the coherence of behavioral strategies that people use in, for example, mate selection, mate retention, reproduction, parental care, kin investment, status attainment, and coalition building (see Buss, 1991). It focuses research on the genetically influenced strategies and tactics that individuals use for survival and reproduction.

An evolutionary perspective on the life course offers a fusion of concerns in evolutionary theory, behavior genetics, and demography (Stearns, 1992). For example, using the evolutionary perspective, Draper and Belsky (1990) and Gangestad and Simpson (1990) have offered intriguing hypotheses about personality characteristics and reproductive strategies that facilitate adaptations in different environments at different ages. Although these and other specific models have not yet been tested in the context of longitudinal studies, they show the promise of evolutionary psychology for organizing longitudinal-developmental data on personality coherence.

The STORI Is in the Data

It is now recognized that prediction and explanation in longitudinal research are best achieved by gathering data from multiple sources using multiple methods (Bank & Patterson, 1992). Building on distinctions proposed by Cattell (1957) and Block (1977), it is possible to identify five different sources of personality data: **S**-data are Self-observations, ratings, and descriptions, including responses to personality inventories and interviews; **T**-data are derived from performance Tests and objective laboratory measurements; **O**-data are Observational assessments that capture moment-to-moment behavioral variations, often using video technology; **R**-data come from life Records and include family, educational, occupational, and marital histories, as well as records from agencies such as schools, hospitals, and the police; **I**-data are Informant ratings of the individual by peers, parents, teachers, and other observers. Multiple data sources enable researchers to tell the STORI of personality development (Moffitt, 1991).

In general, S- and I-data display strong continuities across time, correlate well with each other, and predict real-life records (R-data). T- and O-data tend to show lower continuities across time, although they can predict well in longitudinal studies if they are carefully conceived and operationalized. When crossing between the fields of developmental psychology and personality psychology, one can discern tension in the preference for different data sources. It is unfortunate that these tensions have turned into prejudice, for different data sources are differentially suited for answering different questions (Cairns & Green, 1979; Moskowitz, 1986). For example, S- and I-ratings may predict long-term outcomes in part because they tend to eliminate the situational sources of variance found in T- and O-data. When making ratings, informants implicitly sum over situations while taking context into account in a way that behavior sampling ignores. Such ratings, of course, may be culturally conditioned. But in some instances this may be precisely why they are more predictive of future outcomes than are more "objective" assessments. Future outcomes are themselves frequently the product of culturally conditioned reactions of others to the individual. But S- and I-ratings are not the method of choice if one is interested in examining the functional relations between an individual's behaviors and other ongoing events in the situation. Despite their lower differential stability, O-assessments that preserve the precise actions of individuals are better suited for analyzing how social behavior patterns are maintained and changed over time (Cairns & Green, 1979). Different data sources provide different but crucial information about continuity and change in personality development.

More generally, multimethod data collection in longitudinal research is prescribed for the following reasons: (a) different data sources often provide complementary information; (b) comparisons across data sources can yield substantive information about the phenomena of interest; (c) confirmatory factor analytic methods can be used to build and test competing theoretical models of constructs with multiple indicators from multiple sources; (d) when multiple sources are used to measure a construct, the "true score" variance may be more readily separated from metric sources of error variance; (e) when data are missing from one source, alternative data may still be available from other sources.

Mechanisms of Continuity

There is now an extensive database of research documenting and describing continuities in personality development across the life span. Efforts to go beyond description to the more difficult task of explanation, however, are far less developed. Nevertheless, recent attempts to integrate environmental, genetic, and transactional processes of personality development appear promising.

Environmental Influences

One continuity-promoting mechanism is so mundane that it is often overlooked: behavior patterns may show continuity across the life course because the environment remains stable. To the extent that parental demands, peer influences, and teacher expectancies remain stable over time, we could expect such environmental stability to promote behavioral continuities (e.g., Bloom, 1964; Cairns & Hood, 1983; see Thompson, Ch. 2, this Volume).

Several longitudinal studies have shown that there is a good deal of continuity in the "psychological press" of children's socialization environments. For example, Hanson (1975) found that environmental variables known to be related to IQ (e.g., parental involvement with the child, freedom to engage in verbal expression, direct teaching of language behavior) showed significant continuities from early to late childhood. Another study of children who were assessed at age 4 and again at age 13 found that the stability of an environmental-risk score ($r = .77$) was not less than the stability of IQ scores ($r = .72$; Sameroff, Seifer, Baldwin, & Baldwin, 1993). Significant continuities have also been found in parent reports of child-rearing practices from childhood to adolescence (McNally, Eisenberg, & Harris, 1991; Roberts, Block, & Block, 1984). Thus, maternal control, expression of affect, and achievement emphasis have been shown to be highly consistent over an eight-year period from childhood through adolescence. Observational studies also reveal significant continuities across time. Maternal sensitivity shows significant continuity from infancy to early childhood (Pianta, Sroufe, & Egeland, 1989), and parenting practices that are correlated with children's aggressive acts are stable across childhood and adolescence (Patterson & Bank, 1989).

These longitudinal "environmental correlations" are about the same magnitude as longitudinal "personality correlations." If the environments of most children are as stable as these data suggest, then the continuities observed in personality measures may simply reflect the cumulative and continuing continuities of those environments. What is needed is a formal test evaluating the possibility that environmental continuities account for observed personality continuities. Whether one would then consider personality continuity to be an "artifact" of environmental continuity or "real" personality continuity may depend on one's theoretical predilections.

It is also unclear from the available studies whether environmental continuity is the product or the cause of stable individual differences. For example, it is possible that features of the environment may reflect the stable and enduring features of individuals who make up the environment. It is even possible that features of the environment may reflect heritable characteristics of individuals.

Plomin and Bergeman (1991) showed that the measures commonly used to assess socialization environments may be confounded with genetic variation. Using data from twin and adoption studies, they decomposed the variance in measures of the environment into genetic and environmental components of variance. Of course, environments per se

> have no DNA and can show no genetic influence. However, measures of the environment . . . may be perfused with characteristics of individuals. To the extent that this is the case, measures of the environment can show genetic influence. Consider an environmental construct such as parental responsiveness. We might think of this construct as existing "out there" independent of individuals. However, when we measure the construct, we are in fact measuring parental behavior, and this measure can be analyzed as a phenotype in quantitative genetic analyses in order to investigate the extent to which inter-individual genetic differences and environmental differences contribute to phenotypic variance for this measure. If the measure is really "out there" independent of individuals, it will show no genetic influence. (p. 374)

Plomin and Bergeman's (1991) empirical review showed that a variety of measures typically used to study socialization environments are subject to substantial genetic influence. To appreciate the implications of their findings, it is useful to first group environmental measures into a taxonomy. I rely on the taxonomic system introduced by Moos (1973), in which he identified six methods of measuring the environment.

According to Moos (1973), environments can be measured in terms of their functional properties. At this level of analysis, environments are characterized by the reinforcement consequences that persons are apt to experience for particular behaviors. This level is represented by "objective" measures of parental behavior toward children (e.g., observations of maternal affection, attention, and responsiveness). According to Plomin and Bergeman (1991), these measures of the environment are subject to substantial genetic influence.

Environments can also be measured in terms of their psychosocial climate. How much emphasis is placed on doing well in school? How much encouragement does the child receive? Such characteristics determine the atmosphere of a social setting and are represented by various "subjective" or perceived climate scales (e.g., the Moos Family Environment Scales of Cohesion, Conflict, Achievement; measures of social support). According to Plomin and Bergeman (1991), these measures also show substantial genetic influence.

A third level of environmental measurement focuses on characteristics of milieu inhabitants. This may include, in addition to easily ascertainable demographic characteristics, the salient interests, abilities, attitudes, and personality traits of persons in the environment. Consider peer relationships. The peer group is an important environment; children's peers define norms for tolerable conduct and play an important role in the consolidation of behavior patterns. Research has shown that individuals select peers who are similar to themselves, and they do so with regard to heritable attributes. For example, twin studies have shown that more genetically similar siblings select more similar peer groups with respect to achievement orientation, delinquency, and popularity (Baker & Daniels, 1990). Thus, according to Plomin and Bergeman (1991), the characteristics of milieu inhabitants appear to show substantial genetic influence.

According to Moos (1973), there are three additional methods by which environments can be measured. Organizational structure refers to structural characteristics of settings (e.g., schools) such as population density, teacher-student ratio, and teacher continuity. Behavioral settings are characterized by the spatial and social properties that regulate activities among group members. Finally, ecological dimensions refer to various geographic and manufactured features of environments. These three measures of the environment are most likely immune to genetic influence.

In sum, measures of the environment that are most frequently used by psychologists and sociologists in their studies of human development are saturated with genetic variation. What appear to be stable and enduring features of the environment may be a reflection of stable, enduring, and partially heritable individual differences. How can partially heritable individual differences contribute to measures of the socialization environment? With regard to measures of the family environment, there are at least two possibilities: a "child-based explanation" and a "parent-based explanation." Both explanations draw on concepts of genotype-environment correlation (Plomin, DeFries, & Loehlin, 1977), and both explanations can be tested in multivariate genetic analyses (Plomin, 1994).

The child-based explanation suggests that features of the family environment are products of parents' responding to gene-based characteristics of their children and of children's seeking out particular experiences from their parents. The parent-based explanation suggests that features of the family environment are determined, in part, by individual differences in parents' personalities. Thus, active genotype-environment correlations may account for associations between parental personality traits (e.g., sociability) and parenting styles (e.g., warmth). Remarkably, this latter topic has been all but neglected in developmental psychology. Whereas hundreds of studies have correlated parenting styles with measures of children's personality, only a handful of studies have considered the possibility that parents' personalities may shape their parenting styles. This is a curious omission because parental personality forms a critical part of children's developmental context (Goldsmith et al., 1994). In an important longitudinal demonstration, Belsky, Crnic, and Woodworth (1995) showed that measures of parental personality traits predict observational assessments of their parenting behavior.

Studies that have examined the possible genetic mediation of the family environment by children's temperamental characteristics or by parents' personality characteristics suggest that genetic effects on temperamental and personality traits may account, in part, for genetic effects on measures of the environment, as assessed, for example, by the Home Observation for Measurement of the Environment (HOME) or by the Family Environment Scales (Plomin, 1994). According to Plomin (1994), it appears that "when an environmental measure and a behavioral measure are both moderately heritable, as is typically the case, the phenotypic correlation between them is mediated in part by genetic factors" (p. 149). So far, however, multivariate genetic analyses have been done with only a few samples and require replication. Moreover, the results suggest that traditional temperament and personality measures—whether of the child or the parent—account for a small fraction of the genetic variation in measures of the environment. The results are thus tentative, but the new hypotheses and the availability of new methods promise important findings over the next decade.

Genetic Influences

Behavior-genetic methods can be used to answer three distinct questions about personality development: Are there genetic influences on individual differences in personality at a given age? Are there changes in the magnitude of genetic effects across age? Are personality change and continuity influenced by genetic factors? In previous sections, I reviewed evidence about the first two questions. In this section, I review evidence about the third, distinct question: distinct because it is possible for heritable characteristics to show change and for nonheritable characteristics to show continuity.

The quantitative methods that behavioral geneticists use to estimate genetic and environmental components of phenotypic variance at a given point in time can be extended to estimate genetic contributions to continuity and change across time (Plomin & Nesselroade, 1990). Genetic factors can contribute both to personality change between measurement occasions and to personality continuity across measurement occasions. Genetic influences on personality change may be explored in twin studies by analyzing within-person change scores; that is, by fitting behavior-genetic models to the change scores of MZ and DZ twins. Genetic influences on change would be implied by the finding that MZ twins are more likely than DZ twins to change in concert. Genetic influences on personality continuity may be explored in twin studies by analyzing cross-twin correlations, that is, by fitting behavior-genetic models to the correlation between Twin A's score at t_1 and Twin B's score at t_2.

Both of these analytic approaches have been used to analyze longitudinal behavior-genetic studies. Unfortunately, there are only a few such studies, and these are difficult to compare because of wide differences in the age of study participants and in the measures used.

Age-to-Age Change. Some of the earliest studies of genetic influences on change were performed with children in the Louisville Twin Study. Even though assessments of temperament across 6, 12, 18, 24, and 30 months of age showed low to modest stabilities, within-pair analyses revealed that MZ twins were more likely to change in concert than were DZ twins (Matheny, 1980, 1983, 1989). An earlier study of adaptability showed only modest correlations between two laboratory settings and large mean level changes in behavior across age, and yet MZ twin pairs remained more similar to one another across both settings and ages than did DZ twin pairs (Matheny & Dolan, 1975). These results suggest that changes in childhood temperament may be under some genetic influence, a finding that has been partially replicated in the MacArthur Longitudinal Twin Study (Plomin et al., 1993).

Turning to adolescence and adulthood, the picture looks very different. One of the earliest studies of genetic influence on change examined twins who completed personality inventories at age 16 and again at age 28 (Dworkin, Burke, Maher, & Gottesman, 1976, 1977). The results showed that changes in trait levels from adolescence to adulthood were influenced by genetic similarity. However, subsequent and larger studies yield mixed evidence about this point. At least two short-term longitudinal studies, as well as one adoption study, did not find evidence for genetic influences on age-to-age personality changes (Eaves & Eysenck, 1976; Loehlin, Horn, & Willerman, 1990; Pogue-Geile & Rose, 1985). It appears that there may be genetic contributions to temperament and personality change in childhood but only slight, if any, genetic contributions to personality change in adulthood. In fact, most of the personality change observed in late adolescence and adulthood appears to be due to unique individual experiences, that is, to nonshared environmental influences.

Age-to-Age Continuity.   Even fewer studies have explored genetic contributions to temporal continuity by analyzing cross-twin correlations. A notable exception is the MacArthur Longitudinal Twin Study, where the heritability of cross-twin correlations has been studied from 14 to 20 months of age (Plomin et al., 1993). In this analysis, the heritability of the cross-twin correlations provides an estimate of the genetic contribution to phenotypic stability. Analyses of both observational measures and parental reports of infant temperament suggest that, between 14 and 20 months of age, a significant portion of the phenotypic stability of temperament may be accounted for by genetic factors.

Turning to adulthood, at least one longitudinal study has examined the genetic and environmental etiology of age-to-age continuity. McGue et al. (1993) administered the Multidimensional Personality Questionnaire to a sample of twins on two occasions 10 years apart. The results showed that the MZ cross-twin correlations were consistently and significantly larger than the DZ cross-twin correlations. The authors estimate that approximately 80% of phenotypic stability may be associated with genetic factors.

Although the results of these studies suggest that genetic factors can influence the continuity of personality, they do not address the mechanisms by which they do so. One possibility is to examine physiological mechanisms. This is illustrated by Kagan's research on shyness or "inhibition to the unfamiliar." Individual differences in behavioral inhibition are heritable and stable, and, at least in

early childhood, their phenotypic stability appears to be influenced by genetic factors (Plomin et al., 1993). Kagan, Reznick, and Snidman (1988) have suggested that inherited variations in threshold of arousal in selected limbic sites may be contributing to longitudinal consistencies in this behavioral style (see Kagan, Ch. 4, this Volume). Another possibility is that genetic factors exert their influence on phenotypic stability through gene-environment correlations; thus, personality continuity across the life course may be the result of transactional processes that are, in part, genetically influenced.

Person-Environment Transactions across the Life Course

There are many kinds of transactions, but three play particularly important roles both in promoting the continuity of personality across the life course and in controlling the trajectory of the life course itself (cf. Buss, 1987; Plomin, DeFries, & Loehlin, 1977; Scarr & McCartney, 1983). Reactive transactions occur when different individuals exposed to the same environment experience it, interpret it, and react to it differently. Evocative transactions occur when an individual's personality evokes distinctive responses from others. Proactive transactions occur when individuals select or create environments of their own. (I deliberately use the term *person-environment transaction* rather than *interaction* or *correlation* because the first term is methodologically neutral, whereas the latter terms have specific statistical and data analytic connotations; see Rutter, 1983; Wachs & Plomin, 1991.)

Reactive Person-Environment Transactions.   Different individuals exposed to the same environment experience it, interpret it, and react to it differently. Each individual extracts a subjective psychological environment from the objective surroundings, and it is that subjective environment that shapes both personality and subsequent social interaction.

This is the basic tenet of the phenomenological approach historically favored by social psychology and embodied in the famous dictum that if people "define situations as real, they are real in their consequences" (Thomas & Thomas, 1928). It is also the assumption connecting several prominent theories of personality development: Epstein's (1991) writings on the development of self-theories of reality; Tomkins's (1979) description of scripts about the self and interpersonal interactions; and Bowlby's (1973) analysis of working models—mental representations of the self and others—that develop in the context of interactional experiences.

All three theories assert that people continually revise their "self-theories," "scripts," and "working models" as a function of experience. But if these function as filters for social information, the question is also raised about how much revision actually occurs (Gurin & Brim, 1984). The answer is provided by social psychologists whose research on the cognitive features of internal organizational structures suggests that self-schemata—psychological constructs of the self—screen and select from experience to maintain structural equilibrium (Greenwald, 1980; Westen, 1991). Accordingly, once a schema becomes well-organized it makes individuals selectively responsive to information that is congruent with their expectations and self-views (Markus, 1977). A host of cognitive processes (e.g., primacy effects, anchoring bias, confirmatory bias) may promote consistency and impair people's ability to change (e.g., Cantor & Kihlstrom, 1987; Nisbett & Ross, 1980; Snyder, 1984). In these several ways, persistent ways of perceiving, thinking, and behaving may be preserved by features of the cognitive system. Indeed, because of these features the course of personality is likely to be quite conservative and resistant to change.

The role of cognitive factors in promoting the continuity of individual differences in personality and psychopathology has been detailed by Dodge (1986; Crick & Dodge, 1994; see Coie & Dodge, this volume), whose social-information-processing model of children's social adjustment includes five steps. The first step is to encode information about the event, searching the situation for informative cues; the second step is to interpret the cues and arrive at some decision about their meaning and significance; the third step is to search for possible responses to the situation; the fourth step is to consider the consequences of each potential response and to select a response from the generated alternatives; and the fifth step is to carry out the selected response. Research has identified individual differences in processing social information at all of these steps and in different combinations of steps. These differences are seen in comparisons of aggressive and depressed children (Quiggle, Garber, Panak, & Dodge, 1992). Aggressive children search the situation for fewer cues before they make an attributional decision, are prone to make hostile attributions, are more likely to generate aggressive responses, and appear to believe that aggression will yield tangible rewards to solving problems. In contrast, depressed children are more likely to attend to negative cues,

are prone to make internal, stable, and global attributions for negative events, and believe that assertive responses will be ineffective.

A basic assumption of this and other social-information-processing models is that early temperamental characteristics in combination with early social experiences can set up anticipatory attitudes that lead the individual to project particular interpretations onto new social relationships and situations. This is accomplished through a variety of informational processes in which the person interprets new events in a manner that is consistent with his or her experientially established understanding of self and others. Individuals are thus hypothesized to elicit and selectively attend to information that confirms rather than disconfirms their self-conceptions (Darley & Fazio, 1980; Snyder, 1984; Swann, 1983, 1987). This promotes the stability of the self-concept, which, in turn, promotes the continuity of behavioral patterns that are congruent with that self-concept (Snyder & Ickes, 1985). Social-information-processing models thus recognize both a cognitive and a motivational component in latent mental structures such as "self-theories," "scripts," "working models" and schemata (Crick & Dodge, 1994). In a sense, social information processing is dynamic, for it activates idiosyncratic representations of particular situations and thus "carries" our responses to the interpersonal world (Markus & Cross, 1990, p. 594).

Moreover, individual differences in social information processing may reflect unconscious mental processes; that is, individual differences may play a more important role in automatic rather than in controlled processing of social information (e.g., Rabiner, Lenhart, & Lochman, 1990). Indeed, psychoanalytic concepts (e.g., transference) are implicit in cognitive perspectives on personality development (Erdelyi, 1985). For example, methodologically sophisticated N = 1 studies and experimental studies using the tools of research in social cognition have shown how recurring emotional states organize experience and how individuals transfer affective responses developed in the context of previous relationships to new relationships (e.g., Andersen & Baum, 1994; Horowitz et al., 1994). The integration of cognitive and psychodynamic perspectives may shed light on the enduring puzzle of personality continuity.

To summarize, following Block (1982), dispositional differences may be maintained across the life course because individuals repeatedly utilize "existing adaptive structures or schemes to integrate or make sense of new experiential elements" (p. 283). In his revisionist account of the (psycho)dynamics of assimilation and accommodation, Block (1982) argued that Piagetian theory is suited to understanding personality functioning in longitudinal perspective. Viewed sequentially, as distinct adaptive strategies, the Piagetian dynamics of assimilation and accommodation suggest that, when individuals encounter disequilibrating experiences, they seek to equilibrate first via assimilation. When assimilative efforts cannot help impose structure on a changing world, people accommodate.

Block (1982) suggested that the Piagetian scenario suits the physical world but that its application to the social world is problematic because the social world is reactive. People thus find that assimilative efforts inadvertently create an assimilable world. Consider the aggressive child. The evidence reviewed earlier showed that aggressive children are likely to make hostile attributions about new social encounters; aggressive children attempt to "make sense of new experiential elements" by utilizing and invoking characteristic schemata. In a nonreactive world, these attributions might be sorted out and new schemata might be integrated until more adaptive person-environment transactions are achieved. But in a reactive world, biased interpretations may create corresponding facts. If hostile attributions have fueled hostile exchanges in the past, aggressive children are correct in their present interpretation of the new situation (Trachtenberg & Viken, 1994). Indeed, as I discuss next, persistent ways of perceiving, thinking, and behaving are not preserved simply by psychic forces, nor are they entirely attributable to features of the cognitive system; they are also maintained by the consequences of everyday action (Wachtel, 1977).

Evocative Person-Environment Transactions.   Individuals evoke distinctive reactions from others on the basis of their unique personality characteristics. The person acts; the environment reacts; and the person reacts back in mutually interlocking evocative transactions. Such transactions continue throughout the life course and promote the continuity of personality.

Already very early in life children evoke consistent responses from their social environment (Chess & Thomas, 1987). Numerous studies have shown that children's behavior can affect disciplinary strategies and subsequent interactions with adults and peers (Bell & Chapman, 1986). For example, as part of a longitudinal study, Buss, Block, and Block (1980; Buss, 1981) used an actometer to measure activity level in 3- and 4-year-old children. Observations of family interactions when the children were 5 revealed that

parents of highly active children were impatient and hostile with their children and frequently got into power struggles with them. When the children were 7, they were described by their teachers as aggressive, manipulative, noncompliant, and more likely to push limits and stretch the rules. These findings suggest that early-developing temperamental features influence socialization processes in multiple settings.

It is also through evocative transactions that phenomenological interpretations of situations—the products of reactive interaction—are transformed into situations that are "real in their consequences." As discussed earlier, expectations can lead an individual to project particular interpretations onto new situations and relationships, and thence to behave in ways that corroborate those expectations (Wachtel, 1977).

The process through which evocative person-environment transactions can sustain individual differences in antisocial behavior has been explored by Patterson (1982), who has identified the reinforcement arrangements that typify the coercive family process. It appears that children's coercive behaviors lead adult family members to counter with punitive and angry responses, often escalating to an ever-widening gulf of irritation until the parents of such children eventually withdraw from aversive interactions with their children. One outcome of such negative reinforcement is that children who coerce others into providing short-term payoffs in the immediate situation may thereby learn an interactional style that continues to "work" in similar ways in later social encounters and with different interaction partners. The immediate reinforcement not only short-circuits the learning of more controlled interactional styles that might have greater adaptability in the long run, it also increases the likelihood that coercive behaviors will recur whenever similar interactional conditions arise again. Moreover, the long-term costs associated with short-term rewards are severe. Early coercive family interactions portend deteriorated family management practices when antisocial children reach adolescence. At this point, parents of antisocial children are less likely to supervise and monitor their pubescent boys; their inept disciplinary strategies, in turn, predict persistent and progressively more serious delinquency among their offspring.

The social learning interpretation of coercive family systems is that "family members and antisocial children alternate in the roles of aggressors and victims, each inadvertently reinforcing the coercive behavior of the other" (Patterson & Bank, 1989, p. 190). But there is an additional interpretation: parents and children possess similar aggressive traits as determined by their shared genes. Rowe (1987) observed that shared heredity may render the social learning interpretation incomplete and suggested that social-interactional analyses of biological and adoptive parent-child dyads are needed to estimate the contribution of social learning mechanisms to behavioral continuity independent of shared heredity.

Although such social-interactional studies have not been conducted, experimental research shows that children evoke predictable responses from adults independent of shared heredity. In an experimental study of unrelated mothers and children, Anderson, Lytton, and Romney (1986) observed conduct-disordered and nonproblem boys interacting with mothers in unrelated pairs. The conduct-disordered boys evoked more negative reactions from both types of mothers than did nonproblem boys, but the two types of mothers did not differ from each other in their negative reactions. It appears that adults respond to the behaviors of children rather than create differences between the children. It may be that early temperamental differences contribute to the development of later personality differences by evoking responses from the interpersonal environment that reinforce the child's initial tendencies (Lytton, 1990). Of course, Lytton (1990) is not simply substituting one "main effects" model (parental influence) with another such model (child influence). A transactional model recognizes that partners react back and forth in mutually interlocking evocative transactions; parents and children contribute to the continuity of dispositional characteristics by evoking congruent responses from each other. The application of new statistical techniques for analyzing family interaction data may help to decompose how different individuals and relationships in the family conspire to maintain behavioral continuity (Cook, Kenny, & Goldstein, 1991).

It is also likely that the behavioral process just described is mediated by belief systems and expectancies. Parents respond not only to children's actual behaviors, but also on the basis of expectations they have formed about their children's behavior. For example, when Anderson et al. (1986) observed related as well as unrelated mother-child pairs, they found that mothers of problem-behavior boys were more negative when interacting with their own children than when interacting with other children who were characterized by similar behavior problems. Parental expectations may thus serve to maintain personality differences between children by eliciting behaviors that confirm the adults' expectations (e.g., Bugental & Shennum, 1984).

Such findings raise a larger question about the role that self-fulfilling prophecies play in generating personality continuity. Do adult expectations create persistent differences between children or do adult expectations serve to maintain preexisting differences between children? Although some research purports to show that social expectations may often create social reality, this research has been critically reevaluated. Jussim and Eccles (1995) noted that much of the experimental research on self-fulfilling prophecies is problematic because such experiments lead subjects to develop false expectations about the people with whom they interact. Such experiments only allow inferences about the influence of false beliefs on behavior and cannot disentangle the influence of erroneous expectations from accurate expectations. According to Jussim and Eccles (1995), research purporting to demonstrate a self-fulfilling prophecy must show that the influence of expectations on behavior is not the product of accuracy: "Accurate beliefs cannot create self-fulfilling prophecies because, by definition, self-fulfilling prophecy refers to initially false beliefs becoming true" (p. 76).

Jussim and Eccles (1995) have examined whether naturally occurring expectations influence behavior through a self-fulfilling prophecy or whether expectations influence behavior because expectations are, in fact, accurate beliefs. The results suggest that adults' expectations predict children's behavior because these expectations are quite accurate. It does not appear that social expectations create personality continuity; rather, these expectations appear to maintain preexisting differences between individuals.

Individuals also manifest their personalities in expressive behavior, and research has shown that specific personality traits are associated with specific expressions of emotion. Facial expressions of emotion are especially important in evocative person-environment transactional processes for they convey information to others about what the individual is feeling and about how the individual is likely to act (Ekman, 1993). Keltner (Keltner, Bonano, Caspi, Krueger, & Stouthamer-Loeber, 1996; Keltner, Moffitt, & Stouthamer-Loeber, 1995) has shown that personality differences among adolescents are manifest in facial behavior. For example, boys scoring high on Neuroticism were significantly more likely to express negative emotions (e.g., anger, contempt, fear); boys scoring high on Extraversion were significantly more likely to express positive emotions (e.g., enjoyment); and boys scoring high on Openness to Experience were significantly more likely to express amusement.

The finding that personality traits are registered in facial expressions suggests that personality-related expressions of emotion may influence the course of social development. For example, extraverts, who show more positive emotions, may elicit congruent emotions in others that, in turn, enhance the expression and stability of the extraverted personality (Thorne, 1987). Similarly, neurotic individuals, who show negative emotions, are likely to create social contexts in which others either avoid them or mirror and reciprocate their negative emotions (Hammen, 1991). The "social processes that revolve around the mutual expression of emotion are one subtle yet powerful way in which personality shapes the social environment" (Keltner et al., 1996).

Proactive Person-Environment Transactions. As children grow older, they can move beyond the environments imposed by their parents and begin to select and construct environments of their own. The most consequential environments for personality development are interpersonal environments, and the personality-sustaining effects of proactive transactions are most apparent in friendship formation, in mate selection, and in the world of work. Social selections may maintain and elaborate initial personality differences between people, and proactive transactions may account for the age-related increase in the magnitude of stability coefficients across the life span.

Friends tend to resemble each other in physical characteristics, values, attitudes, and behaviors (e.g., Cairns, Cairns, Neckerman, Gest, & Gariepy, 1988; Dishion, Patterson, Stoolmiller, & Skinner, 1991; Kandel, 1978). Whereas popular wisdom holds that members of peer groups are similar because peers influence their friends to behave in similar ways, empirical studies suggest that members of peer groups are similar because individuals selectively choose to affiliate with similar others (e.g., Ennett & Bauman, 1994). Billy and Udry (1985) examined the contribution of three mechanisms to similarities between friends: selection, in which individuals acquire friends on the basis of behavioral similarity; influence, in which peers influence their friends to behave like them; and deselection, in which individuals deselect friends whose behavior is different from their own. In general, social selection is the most important factor contributing to peer similarities in attitudes and behaviors. Children, adolescents, and adults do not congregate randomly; they choose activities that are compatible with their own dispositions and select companions who are similar to themselves. The similarity-attraction function appears to

be continuous across the life span (Byrne & Griffitt, 1966), reflecting two processes: attraction to the similar and repulsion from the dissimilar (Rosenbaum, 1986).

Cairns and Cairns (1994) suggest that affiliations with similar others may serve as guides for norm formation and the consolidation of behavior patterns over time. Continuities in social networks may thus contribute to behavioral continuity because the demands of the social environment remain relatively stable over time. Moreover, consistency in how members of the social network relate to the individual may contribute to behavioral continuity because it affects how individuals view and define themselves.

These mutually supportive dynamics of social selection and social influence are illustrated by research on the psychosocial implications of pubertal timing (Magnusson, 1988). Adolescents of the same age vary greatly in their level of pubertal development, and differences in the timing of puberty have implications for behavioral development; for example, early-maturing girls are more likely to engage in delinquency. This association between early maturation and juvenile delinquency appears to be mediated by the social composition of girls' social networks. Early-maturing girls gravitate toward chronologically older peers who resemble them somatically; older peers, in turn, function as norm transmitters, sanctioning and even encouraging norm-breaking behaviors among early-maturing girls. Thus, the social network, whose composition is in part determined by social selection, serves as a convoy throughout development, providing support for new social behaviors.

Research on marriage similarly indicates that people tend to choose partners who are similar to themselves. Positive assortative mating has been documented—in descending order of magnitude—for physical characteristics, cognitive abilities, values and attitudes, and personality traits (Epstein & Guttman, 1984). Because of its genetic, social, and psychological consequences, assortative mating has consequences for personality development.

Assortative mating has genetic consequences (Willerman, 1979b). For example, assortative mating for a trait with a genetic component will produce a population distribution for that trait that differs from the distribution that would obtain under conditions of random mating. In particular, assortative mating decreases variability within families, increases variability between families, and increases the standard deviation of trait scores by increasing the frequency of extreme scorers, high and low. (Significant assortative mating may also mask nonadditive genetic effects in twin studies. Assortative mating adds to the similarity of DZ twins but not to the similarity of MZ twins who are genetically identical. This effectively reduces the differences between MZ and DZ correlations and may mask nonadditive genetic effects.)

Assortative mating also has social consequences. Even if there is no genetic component to the traits for which there is assortative mating, couples will, on average, differ more from other couples than they would under conditions of random mating. Moreover, to the extent that parent-child resemblance is related to environmental factors associated with these traits, entire families will differ from each other (Willerman, 1979b). In fact, increases in assortative mating may increase social inequality within and between generations (Mare, 1991).

Assortative mating may also have implications for the course of personality development in adulthood. In particular, similarities between spouses might create an environment that reinforces initial tendencies (Buss, 1984). This proactive transactional process is documented in a longitudinal study of Bennington College students. The political liberalism acquired by the women while at Bennington in the 1930s was sustained over the subsequent 50 years of their lives, in part because they selected liberal friends and husbands who continued to support their politically liberal attitudes (Alwin, Cohen, & Newcomb, 1991). In a 10-year longitudinal study of couples, Caspi and Herbener (1990) found that persons who married a partner similar to themselves were subsequently more likely to show personality continuity over time. It may be that through assortative mating individuals set in motion processes of social interchange that help to sustain their dispositions, for in selecting marriage partners, individuals also select the environments they will inhabit and the reinforcements to which they will be subject for many years (Buss, 1987).

So far I discussed the tendency to form friendships with similar others and the tendency to marry similar others as if these were different tendencies. In fact, they reflect a common inclination to affiliate with similar others. In a unique longitudinal design, Kandel, Davies, and Baydar (1990) examined continuities in the tendency to form dyadic relations with similar others. Using a sample of triads (i.e., longitudinal sample members matched with a best friend in adolescence and with a partner in adulthood), they examined the correlation between two latent variables, the first defining friendship similarity in adolescence, the second defining marital similarity in adulthood. The results revealed significant continuity from adolescence to adulthood—across different types of relationships—in the tendency of individuals to affiliate with others who are similar to them.

Work conditions may also play an important role in promoting personality continuity across adulthood (Mortimer, Lorence, & Kumka, 1986). An example of the personality-sustaining effects of proactive transactions comes from Kohn and Schooler's (1983) longitudinal studies of personality and work. The original purpose of this research was to investigate the source of social class differences in parents' values for their children. This research showed that certain features of the work environment (e.g., the amount of autonomy in the workplace, the degree of routinization on the job) were associated with personal values of self-direction or conformity. For example, workers who have greater freedom on the job and are involved in more complex and challenging work are more likely to value self-direction in their offspring; workers who experience more routine work are more likely to value conformity in their offspring.

But these findings did not tackle the nature of the causal relations between occupational conditions and psychological functioning. In longitudinal analyses, Kohn and Schooler (1983) have shown that the relations are reciprocal. Workers who value self-direction and are intellectually flexible tend to select substantively complex work; in turn, substantively complex jobs continue to nurture the intellectual flexibility of workers and contribute to the development of autonomy values in adulthood.

These findings demonstrate the mutually supportive dynamics of two processes in life course development: social selection, according to which individuals are likely to selectively enter specific life contexts, and social causation, according to which select life contexts are likely to shape subsequent behavior. The critical difference between these two processes lies in their locus of causation, yet both perspectives must be incorporated in life course analyses. To understand continuity across the life course it is necessary to locate individuals in their particular environments, to ask how they got there and how those environments continue to nourish initial differences (Dohrenwend et al., 1992).

Life Course Consequences of Person-Environment Transactions.   Reactive, evocative, and proactive transactions enable an individual's personality both to shape itself and to promote its own continuity through the life course. These same processes also enable an individual's personality to influence the life course itself. In particular, person-environment transactions can produce two kinds of consequences in the life course: cumulative consequences and contemporary consequences.

Consider the boy who has temper tantrums. His ill temper may provoke school authorities to expel him (evocative transaction), or may cause him to experience school so negatively (reactive transaction) that he chooses to quit (proactive transaction). In either case, leaving school may limit his future opportunities, channeling him into frustrating, low-level jobs. These jobs may then lead to an erratic worklife characterized by frequent job changes and bouts of unemployment, possibly disrupting his marriage. In this scenario, occupational and marital outcomes are cumulative consequences of his childhood personality. Once set in motion by childhood temper tantrums, the chain of events takes over and culminates in the adult outcomes.

It is also possible that contemporary consequences will arise if this boy carries his ill temper with him into adulthood. He is likely to explode when frustrations arise on the job or when conflicts arise in his marriage. This can lead to an erratic work life and unstable marriage. In this scenario, the same occupational and marital outcomes are contemporary consequences of his current personality, rather than consequences of earlier events such as quitting school.

Caspi et al. (1989) examined these two hypothetical scenarios using data from the longitudinal Berkeley Guidance Study. They identified men who had a history of childhood temper tantrums at ages 8 to 10 and then traced the continuities and consequences of this personality style across the subsequent 30 years of the study participants' lives. The path analysis displayed in Figure 6.4 reveals evidence, albeit indirect, for both cumulative and contemporary consequences.

Cumulative consequences are implied by the effect of childhood ill-temperedness on occupational status at midlife. Ill-temperedness predicts lower educational attainment, which, in turn, predicts occupational status. But there is no direct effect of ill-temperedness on occupational status. In other words, boys with a history of tantrums arrive at lower occupational status at midlife because they truncated their formal education. (The subsequent path between occupational status and erratic work life cannot be interpreted unequivocally because they are contemporaneous variables.)

Contemporary consequences are implied by the direct link between ill-temperedness and erratic work life. Men with a childhood history of ill-temperedness continue to be ill-tempered in adulthood, where it gets them into trouble in

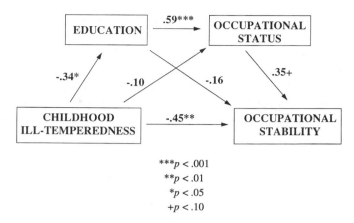

Figure 6.4 Midlife occupational outcomes as a function of childhood ill-temperedness. From "Continuities and Consequences of Interactional Styles across the Life Course," by A. Caspi, D. J. Bem, & G. H. Elder, Jr., 1989, *Journal of Personality, 57,* 375–406. Copyright © 1989 by Duke University Press. Reprinted with permission.

the world of work. (A history of childhood ill-temperedness also affects the domestic sphere; almost 50% of the men with histories of tantrums had divorced by age 40, compared with only 22% of the other men.) As noted earlier, reactive, evocative, and proactive transactions not only shape personality and mediate its continuity over time; these processes also enable the personality to influence the trajectory of the life course itself.

CHANGE IN THE LIFE COURSE

The field of personality development is replete with contested claims, including those about continuity and change. I have already presented evidence about personality continuity. Much of this evidence also pointed to change. For example, behavior-genetic studies showed that as MZ twins grow up, they grow apart (McCartney et al., 1990); studies of personality traits showed that only a portion of the variance in personality measures is predictable across time (McCrae & Costa, 1990); and person-centered studies pointed to the reorganization of personality attributes for at least some persons (Block, 1971). To be sure, the study of continuity and change is also replete with subjective judgments. Do correlations of .5 over a 10-year period highlight connectedness in development, or do they underscore the malleability of personality? Do seemingly inconsistent behaviors reflect personality transformations or the changing but lawful expressions of personality dispositions? My objective in this section is to review conceptual and methodological issues in the study of personality change across the life course. I suggest that whether personality variables show continuity or change depends on which aspects of personality an investigator chooses to focus, on how change is defined, and on how change is assessed.

Change and the Measurement of Personality

Whether personality variables show continuity or change depends, in part, on the unit of analysis that is used to measure personality differences. McAdams (1994) suggested that whether personality changes depends on whether psychologists measure *dispositional traits, personal concerns,* or *life narratives.* Dispositional traits, as reviewed in the previous section, show significant continuity across development. Under the heading of personal concerns, McAdams refers to constructs such as personal projects (Little, Lecci, & Watkinson, 1992), personal strivings (Emmons, 1986), and life tasks (Cantor, 1990), which are personality units that index the particular concerns and motivations of persons at a particular point in time. These variables are expected to show developmental changes that correspond to biosocial changes and changes in age-graded roles, but the necessary longitudinal research—cutting across developmental periods—has yet to be carried out (Nurmi, 1993). Under the heading of life narratives, McAdams refers to the "internalized and evolving story" that each person forges by reconstructing the past, evaluating the present, and anticipating the future. In theory, such narratives are continually reconstructed across the life span, but such variables have not been explored in longitudinal research.

Like McAdams, Helson and Stewart (1994) distinguished among *personality traits, personal styles* (e.g., values), and *personal formations* (e.g., identities). They argue that measures representing these three domains yield different evidence about continuity and change. Thus, stable traits can coexist with changing values, ambitions, responsibilities, and commitments.

Costa and McCrae (1994) distinguished between *basic tendencies* and *characteristic adaptations.* Basic tendencies refer to "the abstract underlying potentials of the individual, including personality traits," whereas characteristic adaptations refer to "attitudes, roles, relationships and goals" that are thought to be the developmental product of

transactions between basic tendencies and environmental demands. Costa and McCrae argued that basic tendencies may remain stable across the life course despite change in characteristic adaptations.

According to Clausen (1993), change in characteristic adaptations may come about as a result of three different environmental sources of influence. First, change may be brought about by *sociocultural transformations* during a person's lifetime. In the process of moving across the age-graded life course, persons are exposed to a different slice of historical experience and adjust their behavior to prevailing norms, deprivations, and opportunities. It is not clear, however, whether such historical changes are also linked to changes in basic tendencies. Second, change may be brought about when persons encounter *new responsibilities and demands* as they assume new roles and relationships. For example, cohabitation, marriage, and employment place new role demands on persons, although it is not clear whether the assumption of new roles and relationships has lasting effects on basic tendencies (Cowan & Cowan, 1992). Third, change may be brought about by *traumatic circumstances,* such as the death of a family member or unemployment. However, it is not clear whether such acute stressors produce transitory changes or give rise to new and persisting traits. It may be that persisting personality change is a function of the extent to which acute stressors generate persisting environmental changes (Rutter, 1986).

The influence of these various types of environmental change on characteristic adaptations may also be contingent on the personality dispositions that persons bring to the change situation itself. Studies of social change, role change, and traumatic life change have shown that characteristic adaptations are shaped both by the requirements of the new situation and by the psychological resources persons bring to the newly changed situation. For example, as individuals assume new roles they inevitably acquire new skills and develop new goals, but how they enact these roles—whether in an impulsive or planful manner, with warmth or aloofness—may depend on stable, basic tendencies. Basic tendencies appear to influence characteristic adaptations to new circumstances (Elder & Caspi, 1990).

The distinction between basic tendencies and characteristic adaptations is also relevant to discussions of planned, psychotherapeutic change. According to Kazdin (1992), what evidence does exist for the effectiveness of therapy suggests that it influences characteristic adaptations—skills, goals, concerns—but does not change personality traits. Whether change in characteristic adaptations endures may depend on changing and maintaining those environmental circumstances that support new adaptations. Unfortunately, few therapy-outcome studies measure multiple units of personality, and the distinction between the relative malleability of characteristic adaptations and basic tendencies remains to be evaluated empirically in therapy-outcome studies (Brody, 1994).

Pervin (1994) offered a somewhat different distinction, suggesting that affective, cognitive, and behavioral components of personality functioning are differentially stable or resistant to change: affects may be more stable than cognitions, and cognitions more stable than behaviors. Although some psychotherapy researchers (Prochaska, DiClemente, & Norcross, 1992) suggest that the modification of a target behavior (behavioral change) may precede or induce change at other levels (e.g., cognitive changes), there is little evidence to support such claims of relative or sequential malleability. Moreover, psychopharmaceutical interventions raise doubts about such sequential hypotheses and about the extent to which the behavioral components of a trait are separable from their correlated cognitions or psychobiological mechanisms (Andreasen, 1984).

The Multiple Meanings of Change

In an earlier section of this chapter I discussed the multiple meanings of the term continuity. The term *change* is also ambiguous, as is its measurement. I review three meanings of change: change as measurement error, change as the absence of continuity, and change as a turning point in the life course.

Change as Measurement Error

Implicit in many analyses of change in behavioral development is the assumption that the effects of measurement errors on observed developmental sequences are generally benign and that observed changes over time faithfully reflect the processes of continuity and change in behavior. This is a questionable assumption; it is more likely that the presence of measurement errors in longitudinal-developmental sequences produces inflated estimates of change in these sequences as a result of some component of the apparent change reflecting the effects of measurement error rather than true change. For these reasons, it is important to develop analytic methods for distinguishing between true change and change due to measurement error. Moreover, it is likely that simple corrections for

measurement unreliability may not be sufficient in some longitudinal analyses. If unreliability changes over time it may be necessary to develop models that allow both (in)stability and (un)reliability to vary with age in longitudinal designs (Alwin, 1994).

Studies that focus on correlates of change need to be particularly sensitive to distinctions between true change and change that can be accounted for by measurement error. Two recent longitudinal studies, one of personality and the other of intelligence, suggest that it is difficult to identify individuals who exhibit true change. In the personality domain, McCrae (1993) suggested that changes in personality-trait scores in adulthood may largely reflect errors of measurement. He used several techniques to try to identify individuals who showed systematic change and discovered that such groups could not be reliably distinguished. In the cognitive domain, Moffitt, Caspi, Harkness, and Silva (1993) suggested that changes in intellectual performance (IQ) from middle childhood through adolescence are mostly unreliable. Although their study focused on intellectual rather than personality traits, it highlights two more general problems in the study of change. First, their study underscores the need to identify individuals who exhibit "reliable" levels of change as opposed to those whose change does not exceed what is expected given measurement error. Second, their study shows that reliable intraindividual patterns of change often reflect a rebounding, "level-maintaining" or "level-seeking," phenomenon, raising larger, conceptual questions about why change is not incremental or sustained.

Scarr and McCartney's (1983) developmental theory of person → environment effects may help to account for this level-maintaining or level-seeking process of change. According to this theory, children evoke responses and select experiences that are matched with their traits. Thus, perturbations in performance (as a result of a bad cold or a single semester with an extraordinary teacher) can be swamped, in the long run, by evocative and active processes that generate conditions that support, foster, and recreate trait-matched levels of performance. The Scarr-McCartney (1983) theory is especially compelling because it can accommodate the Moffitt et al. (1993) finding that children "rebound" from increased and improved intellectual performance just as often as they "rebound" from poorer performance. It is reasonable that some children should spontaneously recover from a temporary setback in IQ test performance. But why should the IQ test performance of children fall after it has improved? The theory of genotype-environment effects suggests that children's test performance can improve as long as environmental intervention is aggressive. However, if left to their own devices, children may evoke responses and seek environments that are less intellectually demanding and more comfortably matched with their abilities. More generally, the Scarr-McCartney model may be applied to account for the transient course of reliable natural history change in trait levels, as well as for patterns of relapse commonly observed in psychotherapy-outcome studies and in educational interventions (e.g., Entwisle & Alexander, 1992).

The problem of measurement error in the study of change is familiar to researchers who favor variable-centered approaches to the study of development. Numerous statistical techniques are available for dealing with measurement error in longitudinal models with continuously distributed variables (Bollen, 1989). However, many psychologists use categorical variables to classify children into groups. For example, longitudinal studies in developmental psychopathology typically study children who have been classified into a particular group on the basis of psychiatric diagnostic information. Such studies seek to establish the extent of change or "remission" in behavior disorders and to determine the correlates of change. Similarly, researchers who favor person-centered approaches over variable-centered approaches often wish to determine the extent of change among types of children. For example, what environmental circumstances are associated with inhibited children becoming sociable? What events are associated with children securely attached to their mothers becoming insecurely attached? To address these questions, developmental researchers use categorical measures.

Such categorical data are not immune to measurement error. In fact, measurement error may bedevil the interpretation of change in categorical data more so than the interpretation of change in dimensional data. It may do so not for statistical reasons, but for conceptual reasons: to report that a child no longer meets diagnostic criteria for an anxiety disorder implies a more profound psychological change than to report that a child has shifted in his location on a continuous distribution of anxiety scores in a sample.

Statistical techniques are available for examining the influence of errors of measurement in longitudinal studies of dichotomously scored outcome variables, but these techniques are less familiar to psychologists. Fergusson and Horwood (Fergusson, Horwood, Caspi, Moffitt, & Silva, 1996; Fergusson, Horwood, & Lynskey, 1995) have adapted such models (e.g., latent Markov models) to study stability and change in various childhood disorders. For example, a study of disruptive behavior from age 7 to 13 revealed that children with disruptive behavior problems showed a large apparent remission of these problems with the passage of time, but much of this remission was illusory and arose from errors of measurement in the classification of disruptive behaviors. It is important for researchers who favor person-centered approaches to incorporate such models into their developmental studies.

The aforementioned studies have implications for clinical practice and treatment studies, as well as for developmental research. Unless due regard is taken of errors of measurement in longitudinal data, much of what is interpreted as change in behavior over time may turn out to be little more than the presence of random errors and noise in test measures.

Change as the Absence of Continuity

The term change can denote some kind of systematic change or the absence of continuity. Conceptually, both continuity and systematic change are positive phenomena in their own right; both can be sought as figures against a background of randomness. But just as the claim of personality coherence requires a theory that specifies the basis on which the diverse phenotypic behaviors can be said to cohere, so a claim of systematic change requires a theory that specifies in what way the observed absence of continuity is "systematic." And just as it is more difficult to sustain a claim of coherence than to demonstrate one of the empirically simpler forms of continuity, so it is more difficult to sustain a claim of systematic change than to demonstrate a simple absence of continuity. Not surprisingly, then, when the term change appears in the literature, it most frequently denotes merely the absence of continuity.

The absence of continuity may reflect lack of predictability, or it may reflect one of at least three methodological problems. The first problem, discussed earlier, is posed by unreliable measures that may mask meaningful behavioral continuities across time. The second problem is posed by developmental specificity. Because personality dispositions may change their behavioral manifestations over time, cross-time correlations may fail to yield meaningful continuities if the assessed behaviors are phenotypically similar but conceptually unrelated. The third problem is posed by the ambiguous meaning of age or time in longitudinal-developmental research. As discussed below, this ambiguity arises from the multiple meanings of age and from changes in the situations that are sampled at different ages.

Although developmental research is fundamentally concerned with understanding behavioral change as a function of age, theory seldom guides the choice of assessment intervals in longitudinal studies of personality development. More often, the vagaries of funding dictate these decisions. However, age has multiple meanings—biological, cognitive, social, historical—which must be specified to make sense of longitudinal data (Rutter, 1989). For example, individual differences in biological age vary widely among adolescents of the same chronological age and may influence the magnitude of correlations between childhood and adolescent measures of personality functioning (Magnusson, 1988). To illustrate, Figure 6.5 shows developmental curves for four different individuals. Although the growth curves are similar, individual differences in the onset of growth may alter the nature of correlational findings across some developmental periods (from t_1 to t_2) relative to other developmental periods (from t_1 to t_3). Low stability coefficients cannot be taken as evidence of low temporal continuity without regard to the nature of developmental functions and the multiple meanings of age (Magnusson & Allen, 1983).

The absence of continuity over time may also reflect changes in the situations that are sampled at different ages.

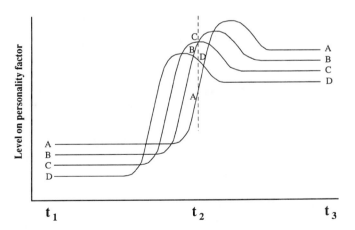

Figure 6.5 Developmental curves for four individuals (A, B, C, and D) showing levels on a personality factor across time. From "Implications and Applications of an Interactional Perspective for Human Development," by D. Magnusson & V. L. Allen, 1983, in *Human Development: An Interactional Perspective,* pp. 370–389. Copyright © 1983 by Academic Press, Inc. Reprinted with permission.

It is difficult to evaluate the absence of continuity without evaluating the situations in which behavior is assessed. For example, in studies of individual differences in nonhuman primates, Suomi (1983) reported that measures of temperamental differences in anxiety showed significant longitudinal correlations when monkeys were assessed in new and relatively stressful situations, whereas measures taken in more familiar situations failed to correlate significantly over time. Thus, longitudinal assessments that are carried out in different situations appear to yield different conclusions about the role of individual differences in the course of social development. It may not be the time interval that matters but the similarity of environmental demands on different measurement occasions that determines the extent of observed continuity. Indeed, some researchers have proposed that behavioral continuities are most likely to emerge in the life course whenever individuals experience social discontinuities that are characterized by novelty, ambiguity, and uncertainty (Caspi & Moffitt, 1993). As suggested by research on "strong" versus "weak" situations and their effect on personality assessment, dispositional factors may be more pronounced in unstructured settings in which individuals must rely on their own traits to guide their behavior than in settings in which pre- and proscribed role expectations make the situation more predictable (Snyder & Ickes, 1985).

Related to this point is the notion of *sleeper effects,* defined as "a lag between a cause and open manifestation of the effect" (Kagan & Moss, 1962, p. 277). Although there is little replicable evidence about sleeper effects in personality development (Moss & Susman, 1980), claims about the absence of continuity should be evaluated with regard to the possibility that early individual differences may resurface on some occasions during development. For example, Jacobs and Nadel (1985) proposed a model of phobias according to which, under stress, "residues of early experience are reinstated and incorporated into adult memory where they directly control behavior" (p. 512). In a sense, the introduction of a novel stimulus can induce spontaneous recovery of "forgotten" associations as well as the disinhibition of previously extinguished behavior. Some primate studies report developmental findings that are consistent with this model. Rhesus monkeys reared in isolation in early life show many bizarre emotional behaviors. Although some of these behavior problems can be corrected through rehabilitation, the deleterious effects of isolation may reemerge in later life when rehabilitated monkeys are placed in a challenging situation where they again display bizarre emotional behaviors reminiscent of their infantile reactions to isolation (Kraemer, 1992).

Not all change is measurement artifact or simply the absence of continuity. Real people show real change over time, and the trajectories of real lives can be altered both by chance events and by planned interventions. However, these real changes are more likely to be discovered and explained after researchers account for error-caused changes and for changes that are little more than the absence of continuity.

Change as a Turning Point in the Life Course

A life course perspective is uniquely suited to investigate processes of continuity and change because it draws attention to the role of individual differences and environmental circumstances in guiding life patterns. Two central concepts inform the analysis of life course dynamics: trajectories and transitions (see Elder, Ch. 16, Volume 1). A trajectory is a pathway over the life span, such as a work life, a marital history, the course of a mental illness, or a criminal career. Trajectories are thus long-term patterns of behavior that are marked by a sequence of relatively discrete transitions. Transitions are specific life events, such as a first job, a divorce, a psychotic episode, a hospitalization, or an arrest. Transitions are thus embedded in trajectories and evolve over shorter time spans; they are "changes in state that are more or less abrupt" (Elder, 1985, p. 32). Sampson and Laub (1993) note that "the long-term view embodied by the life-course focus on trajectories implies a strong connection between experiences in childhood and experiences in adulthood [whereas] the simultaneous, shorter-term view embodied by the life-course focus on transitions also implies that some life events can modify and redirect life paths" (p. 8). Thus, the life-course perspective is concerned with understanding both continuity and change in life patterns.

A major concept in the life course perspective is the dynamic process whereby the interlocking nature of trajectories and transitions generates *turning points* in development (Elder, 1985). That is, despite the connection between childhood and adult experiences, turning points can modify life trajectories—they can "redirect paths." For some individuals, turning points are radical "turnarounds." In most instances, however, turning points are part of a more gradual and unfolding process (Pickles & Rutter, 1991). Change is not discrete but appears to be an incremental process.

Three longitudinal-prospective studies have contributed information about turning points in the life course. All three studies suggest that specific life events and social ties in early adulthood can counteract, at least to some extent, the trajectories of child development. These life events include military service, marriage, and work, and studies of these turning points offer clues about how change may occur in the life course.

Military Service as a Turning Point. The first study, a follow-up investigation of children who grew up in the Great Depression, illustrates how new social roles may induce change in life opportunities. How did the large number of children growing up in families on public aid withstand and rise above their misfortune? Elder (1986, 1987) found that part of the answer centers on military experience as a turning point. Men who grew up in deprived circumstances could break the cycle of disadvantage by entering the service, especially if they did so at a relatively young age.

According to Elder, three features of military life may have promoted behavioral change. The first feature is the "knifing-off" of past experience: the military separated recruits from their past and made their prior identities irrelevant. The second feature of military life is the "time-out" or "psychosocial moratorium" offered by military service: the military gave youths a chance to take a break from the conventional expectations and pressures of the age-graded life course and to consider where they were going. It also delayed marriage and family formation and thus reduced the social and psychological burden on this already vulnerable group of men. The third feature of military life is "the broadened range of perspective, social knowledge, and basic skills" instilled by the military: the military offered youths a source of self-esteem and new skills that they could apply upon reentry into civilian life. Of course, these are not the only features of the transition to military life, but together they define a developmental pathway that may have offered a promising route to life change. Indeed, men who entered the military at a relatively young age became more self-confident, ambitious, and successful. Sampson and Laub (1996) have extended these findings to a different sample, showing that, even after controlling for preservice selection differences, entering military service at a young age as well as overseas duty provided an opportunity for men to redirect their lives.

Marriage to a Supportive Spouse as a Turning Point. A second study of change in the life course focused on marital support in early adult life as a protective factor that modifies the continuity of deviant behavior. This "study" is, in fact, a series of longitudinal replications using both high-risk and general population samples (Pickles & Rutter, 1991; Quinton & Rutter, 1988; Quinton, Pickles, Maughan, & Rutter, 1993; Rutter, Quinton, & Hill, 1990).

Consistent with evidence about the continuity of personality development, Quinton and Rutter found that youth with conduct disorders went on to experience diverse troublesome outcomes in adulthood. But there was also considerable heterogeneity in outcomes, leading the authors to attempt to "account for major discontinuities, as well as continuities in development." In this connection, "marital support from a nondeviant spouse stood out as a factor associated with a powerful protective effect" (Rutter et al., 1990, p. 152). In their dual concern with continuity and change, Quinton and Rutter offered a useful metaphor: chain links. Continuity from childhood adversity to adult difficulties involves multiple links in a chain with each link dependent on the presence of other links. However, there are also many opportunities for change, for each link in the chain can be unfastened. Much like Elder's study of military experience, Quinton and Rutter's study suggests that events during the transition to adulthood may modify life course trajectories; in particular, a nondeviant partner may help to promote discontinuity.

Social Bonds as a Turning Point.   In a third study along similar lines, Sampson and Laub (1993) theorized that social ties to adult institutions (e.g., family, community, and work) may modify the persistence of antisocial behavior from childhood through adulthood. Their research focused on the transition to adulthood and, in turn, the new role demands from full-time employment, military service, and marriage. Like Quinton and Rutter, Sampson and Laub emphasize the quality or strength of social ties more than the occurrence or timing of life events. For example, "marriage per se may not increase social control, but close emotional ties increase the social bond between individuals and, all else equal, should lead to a reduction in criminal behavior" (Sampson & Laub, 1990; p. 611). Similarly, "employment alone may not increase social control. It is employment coupled with job stability, job commitment, and ties to work that should increase social control and, all else equal, lead to a reduction in criminal behavior" (p. 611).

To test these hypotheses, Sampson and Laub (1993) analyzed the natural histories of two groups of boys who differed in childhood antisocial behavior; one was a group of 500 delinquents and the other a group of 500 controls matched on age, IQ, SES, and ethnicity. The results showed continuities from childhood to adulthood. But there was also considerable heterogeneity in adult outcomes that could be accounted for by the quality and strength of social ties in the transition to adulthood. Consistent with their theory of adult development and informal social control, Sampson and Laub found that job stability and marital attachment in young adulthood were significantly related to changes in the life course; for example, the stronger the adult ties to work and family, the less crime and deviance among both delinquents and controls. Hence, much like Quinton and Rutter, the Sampson and Laub study suggests that social ties embedded in the transition to adulthood (e.g., marital attachment, job stability) may help to explain emergent discontinuities in development.

The studies summarized above provide convergent clues about change in the life course, although even these studies do not directly address the question of whether the observed changes reflect changes in characteristic adaptations or changes in basic tendencies. Moreover, although the evidence reviewed above suggests that change does in fact occur, it also raises a puzzle: Why do some individuals change and others do not? To learn more about turning points in the life course, it is important to account for differential developmental change among individuals.

Laub and Sampson (1993) advanced three hypotheses about differential change. The first is that change involves chance. This hypothesis follows from Bandura's (1982) observation that chance encounters generate opportunities for change: "Although the separate chains of events in a chance encounter have their own causal determinants, their intersection occurs fortuitously rather than through deliberate plan" (p. 749). The second hypothesis is that change comes about as a result of both individual and structural characteristics. Laub and Sampson (1993) note that macrosocial opportunity structures—whether, for example, in the labor market or in the marriage market—can affect who has the opportunity to change. Unfortunately, linkages between individual and structural levels of analysis are rare in empirical research. Theories are available on the micro and macro levels, but there is little theoretical guidance for connecting the two. The third hypothesis is that there are predictable individual differences in who responds to change-potentiating life events. According to Laub and Sampson (1993), the same events and opportunities do not have the same meaning for every person; rather, the change process may be explained by the "confluence of objective and subjective contingencies."

Quinton and Rutter provide an example of one such "subjective contingency" in their studies of continuity and change in conduct disorders (Pickles & Rutter, 1991; Quinton et al., 1993). They showed that a "planning disposition" helped to structure differential developmental trajectories among girls with a history of conduct disorder; that is, planning appeared to be the critical mediating link in the chain of discontinuity. Planful girls were less likely to affiliate with deviant peers and more likely to choose nondeviant partners, thus enhancing their prospect for salutary outcomes in adulthood. Such competence may be a significant predictor of discontinuity in other maladaptive behaviors as well. Asendorpf (1994) reports that across childhood, socially competent children are more likely to overcome their inhibition than less competent children. According to Clausen (1993), planful competence may be especially important during middle and late adolescence, when the ability to make choices is critical.

In sum, change is clearly possible. Researchers are gaining a better appreciation of the circumstances under which systematic change may take place, and they are learning that the situational requisites that define turning points in the life course are more specialized than previously thought. Advances have been made in clarifying the standards of proof for change and in spelling out the methodological requirements for longitudinal studies that focus on turning points in the life course. Pickles and Rutter (1991) provide an excellent introduction on how to translate conceptual models into statistical models in the study of change.

Can Personality Change versus Does Personality Change: Lessons from Treatment Research about How to Measure Change

The question of whether or not people do change is often confused with the question of whether or not people can change. These two questions reflect a larger tension between two different research traditions that McCall (1977) labeled *can* versus *does* research. *Can* research asks: Can factor X produce change in Y under certain conditions? *Does* research asks: Under typical conditions, does factor X produce change in Y? The distinction between these research traditions has important implications for research on personality development because their yield is not always the same. For example, attribution research on coping suggests that people are motivated to provide explanations for stressful events, and that these internal cognitive processes mediate the adjustment process. But field studies have challenged the core assumption of the attribution-adjustment hypothesis, suggesting that most persons are typically unconcerned with attributional issues (Downey, Silver, & Wortman, 1990). Likewise, experimental socialization studies suggest that adult attributions can strengthen children's behavior (e.g., altruism), but it is not clear if in practice adults make such attributions (Grusec & Lytton, 1988). Inferences about the processes of personality development—as they *do* rather than as they *can* unfold—are often compromised by the absence of transcontextual validity from lab to life (Weisz, 1978).

The *can* versus *does* distinction can be used to contrast treatment studies that are designed to change personality and longitudinal studies that provide a naturalistic description of personality change. A review of psychotherapy treatment studies is beyond the scope of this chapter, but it should be noted that it is not even clear whether results from controlled therapy-outcome studies generalize to conventional clinical therapy (Weisz, Weiss, & Donenberg, 1992). "Research therapy" is usually performed on recruited participants with homogeneous symptom presentation using treatment techniques that focus on the homogeneous symptom cluster. The therapists are trained before implementing the treatment program and treatment integrity is assured by supervising and monitoring the therapists. In contrast, conventional "clinic therapy" is usually performed on referred participants with heterogeneous symptom presentation using treatment techniques directed at a wide range of problems. Moreover, treatment integrity of clinic therapy is often difficult to sustain. According to Weisz et al. (1992), the relatively standardized conditions of "research therapy" enhance the effectiveness of psychotherapy; although standardization is a scientific virtue, it does not reflect conventional conditions and thus raises concerns about whether "positive lab findings can be generalized to the clinics where most therapy occurs" (p. 1578).

Whatever the benefits of psychotherapy, psychotherapy research offers at least four important lessons about how to measure change in longitudinal studies of personality. I summarize these lessons in the hope they will be incorporated more routinely in longitudinal-developmental research programs that attempt to study change, both in basic tendencies and characteristic adaptations. (For a treatment of statistical issues, see Collins & Horn, 1991.)

Statistical versus Clinical Significance of Personality Change

Studies of personality development may profit from examining definitional debates in clinical psychology, where outcome-evaluation studies have long struggled with the ambiguous meanings of change. In outcome-evaluation studies, treatment effects are typically reported as significant if there are significant group mean-level differences in repeated-measurement designs. However, statistically significant differences may be the result of many small changes among many people or of a few large changes among a few people. Moreover, statistical significance bears no necessary relation to clinical significance (i.e., whether the change altered the life of the individual).

Whether or not psychotherapeutic change is clinically significant depends on therapeutic goals. Accordingly, there are many different definitions of clinical significance (Jacobson & Truax, 1991; Kazdin, 1990). Symptom reduction, measured by the extent to which presenting symptoms are reduced over the course of treatment, is perhaps the most common definition of change. Change may also be defined by increases in positive functioning, which may be demonstrated by bringing behavior into normative, nonclinical levels of functioning. Social validation provides an additional criterion for clinically significant change; change that is recognized by significant others may constitute especially meaningful change. Research on change is further complicated by the finding that different indices of change are not highly correlated. For example, an evaluation of treatments for antisocial children revealed that decreases in behavioral problems were only weakly correlated with increases in prosocial behaviors (Kazdin, Bass, Siegel, & Thomas, 1989). Apparently, symptom reduction does not imply improved positive functioning. The interpretation of change is thus restricted to its definition in any particular study.

Multimethod and Multisource Approaches to Measuring Personality Change

To assess personality change it is important to rely on multiple measures gathered from multiple sources using multiple methods. "Heteromethod" assessments reduce the likelihood that estimates of change will be contaminated by method variance (Brody, 1990). Studies of change that use personality data from multiple sources (e.g., parent, teacher, peer, and self-ratings) are more powerful because they can be used to separate correlated method variance from true change scores (Patterson, 1993). Multisource longitudinal assessments are also important because they can be used to distinguish change in self-perception from behavioral change as it registers on significant others.

Specificity versus Generality of Personality Change

To assess the extent of change, it is important to evaluate the specificity or generality of observed change. Brody (1990) noted that most interventions attempt to reduce symptomatic expressions of a particular disorder. As a result, most therapy-outcome studies measure symptoms, not dispositions, and cannot resolve the question of whether the symptom or the disposition has changed. He suggested that confidence in the view that the disposition has changed would be bolstered by demonstrations that a change in specific symptom expression has generalized to other related symptoms.

The distinction between symptom change and dispositional change is important in light of cross-sectional and longitudinal evidence that most psychiatric conditions are comorbid; that is, certain disorders (e.g., anxiety disorders and depression, antisocial personality and substance dependence) are likely to co-occur within individuals. Brody and Crowley (1995) suggest that convincing evidence of personality change needs to include evidence of symptom reductions across co-occuring disorders that are related to the disposition in question. How such change would be manifest may depend on the mechanisms that underlie comorbidity (Caron & Rutter, 1991). For example, if two disorders share a common set of temperamental or personality risk factors, dispositional change may be demonstrated by symptom changes in both disorders. If two disorders overlap because one disorder constitutes a risk factor for the other disorder, dispositional change may be demonstrated by evidence that changes in symptom levels of one disorder are associated over time with the reduced probability of developing the other disorder.

Modeling Trajectories of Personality Change

To demonstrate change it is important to implement long-term follow-ups. Many psychotherapy-outcome studies are limited to evidence of change at the conclusion of therapy and do not demonstrate enduring effects over time. The possibility of relapse—and the conditions that give rise to it—must be evaluated (Brody, 1990). More generally, it is now recognized that two measurement occasions are not sufficient to describe longitudinal change. The use of two measurement occasions, whether in naturalistic or in treatment studies, assumes that the form of change is constant across time and that there are no individual differences in the form of change. As such, two-wave longitudinal studies cannot answer questions about intraindividual change nor about individual differences in intraindividual change (Gottman & Rushe, 1993). The study of change requires data from multiple follow-up occasions. With such data it is possible to model change—and to study the correlates of change—using hierarchical linear models. At the within-subjects level of analysis, these models estimate each individual's "growth" curve or change trajectory; at the between-subjects level, these models test for differences in the within-subject parameters. Within-subject parameters can be used to describe quantitative change on a wide range of variables, such as vocabulary level, attitudes, and personality traits. The between-subject differences can include variables such as social background, treatment conditions, and individual-difference variables that are hypothesized to influence trajectories of change (e.g., Raudenbush & Chan, 1993).

CONCLUSION

Evidence about the origins, continuity, and change of personality differences depends on well-designed longitudinal research. Only longitudinal studies can chart growth, identify developmental sequences, establish the temporal ordering of variables across time, trace behavioral connections across development, and reveal the implications of early behavior for later adjustment. In the social sciences, explanatory efforts can only follow those descriptive studies that establish social facts. But poorly designed studies may generate pseudofacts and thereby induce "pseudoproblems, which cannot be solved because matters are not what they purport to be" (Merton, 1959, p. xv).

The reader will have noted that, in my survey of personality development, I have more successfully identified methodological limitations than I have unearthed definitive findings. My concluding comments are thus devoted to sketching the requirements for improved longitudinal studies of personality development. In this section, I summarize four points that have been reiterated in different sections of this chapter: Longitudinal designs can be improved (a) by integrating epidemiological concepts and methods into studies of personality development, (b) by using genetic controls to study developmental processes,

(c) by relying on theoretically informed data collection schedules to focus on homotypic and heterotypic continuities across periods of maturational and social change in the life course, and (d) by gathering data from multiple sources using multiple methods.

Studies of personality development must be improved with regard to sampling, which continues to be psychology's Achilles' heel. The majority of longitudinal studies of personality development rely on samples of convenience, primarily from schools and clinics, and pay little attention to the implications of selective sampling (both inadequate specification and inadequate representation) and nonrandom attrition, although these problems have been shown to be serious (Weinberger, Tublin, Ford, & Feldman, 1990). Longitudinal-epidemiological designs can uniquely address questions about etiology, continuity, and change in personality development. Although epidemiological studies tend to focus on the abnormal, such studies also provide critical information about normal developmental processes (Costello & Angold, 1995). Rutter (1982) reviewed the advantages of longitudinal-epidemiological studies for developmental research. Their most important advantages follow from a concern with the study of populations. First, population-based studies are less biased than referred (e.g., clinic-based) and institutional (e.g., school-based) samples typically used in research on personality development. Clinic samples are atypical and school samples exclude entire segments of the population (e.g., truants, dropouts, children with disabilities). The use of biased samples may alter the distribution of variables and may also influence associations between variables, either concealing significant findings or producing illusory findings (Berk, 1983; Cohen & Cohen, 1984). Second, population-based studies provide information about norms and base rates of psychological phenomena. Such information is critical for drawing valid clinical and research inferences and for deriving predictions about individuals from information about groups. Third, population-based studies yield crucial information about the influence of missing data on developmental findings. Missing data in longitudinal research—either because study members could not be located or because they refused to participate—are seldom random, and population-based studies, especially birth registers, provide more precise estimates of the effects of systematic attrition on inferences from longitudinal research.

Human behavioral genetic findings suggest that inferences about environmental influences on personality differences are ambiguous unless the effects of heritability are taken into account. This fact underscores the need for genetic controls in research on personality development. Many behavior-genetic studies can be faulted for relying on unrepresentative samples (e.g., many twin samples tend to involve middle-class volunteers). However, ordinary sibling studies may provide many of the same advantages for controlling for genetic influence as twin and adoption studies. The combination of sibling studies, supplemented with adoption and twin studies, may make it possible to address key developmental questions about the origins of personality differences that cannot be addressed by between-family studies with no genetic controls (Rowe, 1987, 1989). For example, what are the most important shared and non-shared environmental influences on personality development? How do such influences change with age? Are these "environmental" influences mediated genetically? What accounts for differences between siblings who are raised in the same family and exposed to many of the "same" experiences? In addition, longitudinal behavior-genetic designs make it possible to examine sources of continuity and change in personality development and to study the mechanisms underlying person-environment transactions over time.

A perennial problem that plagues longitudinal research is the problem of developmental follow-up: When and how frequently should assessment intervals be scheduled? This question is further complicated by the fact that personality dispositions change their behavioral manifestations over time. How is it possible to anticipate the changing expression of a disposition across time and in diverse circumstances? Longitudinal studies may get a handle on this problem by organizing data collection around well-defined developmental tasks, whether these tasks are defined by evolutionary imperatives, sociological realities, or maturational changes. The organization of data collection around such developmental tasks offers "natural experiments" that may provide leverage for testing hypotheses about the mechanisms involved in generating both continuity and change (Caspi & Moffitt, 1993). In particular, longitudinal studies that trace their samples across periods of environmental-maturational changes offer an opportunity to test competing hypotheses about how individuals select and shape their environments (social selection) and how environments influence individuals (social causation). Longitudinal behavior-genetic data would be of special use during periods of environmental-maturational change in the life course, enabling researchers to test these dynamic processes of selection and causation using appropriate genetic controls.

Finally, although psychologists typically invest more resources developing sophisticated instruments with which to measure their constructs than in drawing appropriate samples, longitudinal studies continue to be limited by the use of single data sources (e.g., parent reports) and single methods of measurement (e.g., rating scales). All measurement instruments are fallible. Each data method and data source is associated with systematic (and random) error, and can only partially and imperfectly tap latent constructs of interest. Multiple methods and sources can be used to unconfound method variation from trait variation. Estimates of latent constructs derived from multiple methods and sources are required for demonstrating both continuity and change in personality development.

ACKNOWLEDGMENTS

I am grateful to John Bates, Nancy Eisenberg, and Robert Plomin for their comments on earlier drafts of this chapter, and to Oliver John, Robert Krueger, and Terrie Moffitt for their many contributions to my thinking about the topics reviewed here. This chapter reviews materials available to me through December 1995.

REFERENCES

Achenbach, T. M., & Howell, C. T. (1993). Are American children's problems getting worse? A 13-year comparison. *Journal of the American Academy of Child and Adolescent Psychiatry, 32,* 1145–1154.

Ahadi, S., & Diener, E. (1989). Multiple determinants and effects sizes. *Journal of Personality and Social Psychology, 56,* 398–406.

Ahadi, S., & Rothbart, M. K. (1994). Temperament, development, and the Big Five. In C. F. Halverson, Jr., G. A. Kohnstamm, & R. P. Martin (Eds.), *The developing structure of temperament and personality from infancy to adulthood* (pp. 189–207). Hillsdale, NJ: Erlbaum.

Allgulander, C. (1994). Suicide and mortality patterns in anxiety neurosis and depressive neurosis. *Archives of General Psychiatry, 51,* 708–712.

Allport, G. W. (1937). *Personality: A psychological interpretation.* New York: Holt.

Allport, G. W. (1958). What units shall we employ? In G. Lindzey (Ed.), *Assessment of human motives* (pp. 238–260). New York: Rinehart.

Allport, G. W. (1962). The general and the unique in psychological science. *Journal of Personality, 30,* 405–422.

Alwin, D. F. (1988). From obedience to autonomy: Changes in traits desired in children, 1924–1978. *Public Opinion Quarterly, 52,* 33–52.

Alwin, D. F. (1994). Aging, personality, and social change: The stability of individual differences over the adult life span. In D. L. Featherman, R. M. Lerner, & M. Perlmutter (Eds.), *Life-span development and behavior* (Vol. 12, pp. 135–185). Hillsdale, NJ: Erlbaum.

Alwin, D. F., Cohen, R. L., & Newcomb, T. M. (1991). *Political attitudes over the life span: The Bennington women after fifty years.* Madison: University of Wisconsin Press.

American Psychiatric Association. (1980). *Diagnostic and statistical manual of mental disorders.* Washington, DC: Author.

American Psychiatric Association. (1987). *Diagnostic and statistical manual of mental disorders.* Washington, DC: Author.

American Psychiatric Association. (1994). *Diagnostic and statistical manual of mental disorders.* Washington, DC: Author.

Andersen, S. M., & Baum, A. (1994). Transference in interpersonal relations: Inferences and affect based on significant-other representations. *Journal of Personality, 62,* 459–497.

Anderson, K. E., Lytton, H., & Romney, D. M. (1986). Mothers' interactions with normal and conduct-disordered boys: Who affects whom? *Developmental Psychology, 22,* 604–609.

Andreasen, N. C. (1984). *The broken brain: The biological revolution in psychiatry.* New York: Harper & Row.

Asendorpf, J. B. (1992a). A Brunswikean approach to trait continuity: Application to shyness. *Journal of Personality, 60,* 53–77.

Asendorpf, J. B. (1992b). Beyond stability: Predicting interindividual differences in intraindividual change. *European Journal of Personality, 6,* 103–117.

Asendorpf, J. B. (1994). The malleability of behavioral inhibition: A study of individual developmental functions. *Developmental Psychology, 30,* 912–919.

Asendorpf, J. B., & Meier, G. H. (1993). Personality effects on children's speech in everyday life: Sociability-mediated exposure and shyness-mediated reactivity to social situations. *Journal of Personality and Social Psychology, 64,* 1072–1083.

Asendorpf, J. B., & van Aken, M. A. G. (1991). Correlates of the temporal consistency of personality patterns in childhood. *Journal of Personality, 59,* 689–703.

Astington, J. W. (1993). *The child's discovery of the mind.* Cambridge, MA: Harvard University Press.

Baker, L. A., & Daniels, D. (1990). Nonshared environmental influences and personality differences in adult twins. *Journal of Personality and Social Psychology, 58,* 103–110.

Baltes, P. B. (1987). Theoretical propositions of life-span developmental psychology: On the dynamics between growth and decline. *Developmental Psychology, 23,* 611–626.

Baltes, P. B., Cornelius, S. W., & Nesselroade, J. R. (1979). Cohort effects in developmental psychology. In J. R. Nessel-

roade & P. B. Baltes (Eds.), *Longitudinal research in the study of behavior and development* (pp. 1–39). New York: Academic Press.

Baltes, P. B., Reese, H. W., & Lipsitt, L. P. (1980). Life-span developmental psychology. *Annual Review of Psychology, 31,* 65–110.

Baltes, P. B., Reese, H. W., & Nesselroade, J. R. (1977). *Life-span developmental psychology: Introduction to research methods.* Monterey, CA: Brooks/Cole.

Bandura, A. (1961). Psychotherapy as a learning process. *Psychological Bulletin, 58,* 143–159.

Bandura, A. (1982). The psychology of chance encounters and life paths. *American Psychologist, 37,* 747–755.

Bank, L., & Patterson, G. R. (1992). The use of structural equation modeling in combining data from different types of assessment. In J. C. Rosen & P. McReynolds (Eds.), *Advances in psychological assessment* (Vol. 8, pp. 41–74). New York: Plenum Press.

Barrick, M. R., & Mount, M. K. (1991). The big five personality dimensions and job performance: A meta analysis. *Personnel Psychology, 44,* 1–26.

Bates, J. E. (1990). Conceptual and empirical linkages between temperament and behavior problems: A commentary on the Sanson, Prior, & Kyrios study. *Merrill-Palmer Quarterly, 36,* 193–199.

Bates, J. E. (1994). Parents as observers of their children's development. In S. Friedman & H. C. Haywood (Eds.), *Developmental follow-up: Concepts, domains, and methods.* San Diego, CA: Academic Press.

Bates, J. E., Bayles, K., Bennett, D., Ridge, B., & Brown, M. (1991). Origins of externalizing behavior problems at eight years of age. In D. Pepler & K. Rubin (Eds.), *The development and treatment of childhood aggression.* Hillsdale, NJ: Erlbaum.

Bates, J. E., Maslin, C., & Frankel, K. (1985). Attachment security, mother-child interaction, and temperament as predictors of behavior-problem ratings at age three years. In I. Bretherton & E. Waters (Eds.), *Monographs of the Society for Research in Child Development, 50*(Serial No. 209).

Bates, J. E., Wachs, T. D., & Emde, R. N. (1994). Toward practical uses for biological concepts of temperament. In J. E. Bates & T. D. Wachs (Eds.), *Temperament: Individual differences at the interface of biology and behavior* (pp. 275–306). Washington, DC: American Psychological Association.

Baumrind, D. (1993). The average expectable environment is not good enough: A response to Scarr. *Child Development, 64,* 1299–1317.

Bell, R. Q., & Chapman, M. (1986). Child effects in studies using experimental or brief longitudinal approaches to socialization. *Developmental Psychology, 22,* 595–603.

Belsky, J., Crnic, K., & Woodworth, S. (1995). Personality and parenting: Exploring the mediating role of transient mood and daily hassles. *Journal of Personality, 63,* 905–929.

Belsky, J., Steinberg, L., & Draper, P. (1991). Childhood experience, interpersonal development and reproductive strategy: An evolutionary theory of socialization. *Child Development, 62,* 647–670.

Bem, D. J. (1983). Constructing a theory of the triple typology: Some (second) thoughts on nomothetic and idiographic approaches to personality. *Journal of Personality, 51,* 566–577.

Bergeman, C. S., Chipuer, H. M., Plomin, R., Pedersen, N. L., McClearn, G. E., Nesselroade, J. R., Costa, P. T., Jr., & McCrae, R. R. (1993). Genetic and environmental effects on openness to experience, agreeableness, and conscientiousness: An adoption/twin study. *Journal of Personality, 61,* 159–179.

Bergeman, C. S., Plomin, R., McClearn, G. E., Pedersen, N., & Friberg, L. (1988). Genotype-environment interaction in personality development: Identical twins reared apart. *Psychology and Aging, 3,* 399–406.

Bergman, L. R., & Magnusson, D. (1991). Stability and change in patterns of extrinsic adjustment problems. In D. Magnusson, L. R. Bergman, G. Rudinger, & B. Torestad (Eds.), *Problems and methods in longitudinal research* (pp. 323–346). Cambridge, MA: Cambridge University Press.

Berk, R. A. (1983). An introduction to sample selection bias in sociological data. *American Sociological Review, 48,* 386–398.

Billy, J. O. G., & Udry, R. (1985). Patterns of adolescent friendship and effects on sexual behavior. *Social Psychology Quarterly, 48,* 27–41.

Block, J. (1971). *Lives through time.* Berkeley, CA: Bancroft Books.

Block, J. (1977). Advancing the psychology of personality: Paradigmatic shift or improving the quality of research. In D. Magnusson & N. S. Endler (Eds.), *Personality at the crossroads: Current issues in interactional psychology* (pp. 37–63). Hillsdale, NJ: Erlbaum.

Block, J. (1982). Assimilation, accommodation, and the dynamics of personality development. *Child Development, 53,* 281–295.

Block, J. (1993). Studying personality the long way. In D. Funder, R. D. Parke, C. Tomlinson-Keasey, & K. Widaman (Eds.), *Studying lives through time: Personality and development* (pp. 9–41). Washington, DC: American Psychological Association.

Block, J. (1995). A contrarian view of the Five-Factor approach to personality description. *Psychological Bulletin, 117,* 187–215.

Block, J., Block, J. H., & Keyes, S. (1988). Longitudinally foretelling drug usage in adolescence: Early childhood personality and environmental precursors. *Child Development, 59,* 336–355.

Block, J., Gjerde, P. F., & Block, J. H. (1991). Personality antecedents of depressive tendencies in 18-year-olds: A prospective study. *Journal of Personality and Social Psychology, 60,* 726–738.

Bloom, B. S. (1964). *Stability and change in human characteristics.* New York: Wiley.

Bollen, K. A. (1989). *Structural equations with latent variables.* New York: Wiley.

Bolles, R. C. (1970). Species-specific defense reactions and avoidance learning. *Psychological Review, 77,* 32–48.

Borkenau, P., & Liebler, A. (1995). Observable attributes as manifestations and cues of personality and intelligence. *Journal of Personality, 63,* 1–25.

Bouchard, T. J., Jr. (1993). Genetic and environmental influences on adult personality: Evaluating the evidence. In J. Hettema & I. J. Deary (Eds.), *Foundations of personality* (pp. 15–44). Boston: Kluwer.

Bouchard, T. J., Jr. (1995). Longitudinal studies of personality and intelligence: A behavior genetic and evolutionary psychology perspective. In D. Saklofske & M. Zeidner (Eds.), *International handbook of personality and intelligence* (pp. 81–106). New York: Plenum Press.

Bouchard, T. J., Jr., & McGue, M. (1981). Familial studies of intelligence: A review. *Science, 212,* 1055–1059.

Bouchard, T. J., Jr., & Propping, P. (Eds.). (1993). *Twins as a tool of behavioral genetics.* Chichester, England: Wiley.

Bowlby, J. (1973). *Attachment and loss: Vol. 2. Separation.* New York: Basic Books.

Bradburn, N. M., Rips, L. J., & Shevell, S. K. (1987). Answering autobiographical questions: The impact of memory and inference on surveys. *Science, 236,* 157–161.

Braungart, J. M., Plomin, R., DeFries, J. C., & Fulker, D. W. (1992). Genetic influence on tester-rated infant temperament as assessed by Bayley's Infant Behavior Record: Nonadoptive and adoptive siblings and twins. *Developmental Psychology, 28,* 40–47.

Brewin, C. R., Andrews, B., & Gotlib, I. H. (1993). Psychopathology and early experience: A reappraisal of retrospective reports. *Psychological Bulletin, 113,* 82–98.

Brewster, K. L. (1994). Race differences in sexual activity among adolescent women: The role of neighborhood characteristics. *American Sociological Review, 59,* 408–424.

Briggs, S. R. (1989). The optimal level of measurement for personality constructs. In D. M. Buss & N. Cantor (Eds.), *Personality psychology: Recent trends and emerging directions* (pp. 246–260). New York: Springer-Verlag.

Brim, O. G., Jr. (1976). Life span development of the theory of oneself: Implications for child development. In H. W. Reese (Ed.), *Advances in child development and behavior* (pp. 242–253). New York: Academic Press.

Brody, N. (1990). Behavior therapy versus placebo: Comment on Bowers and Clum's meta-analysis. *Psychological Bulletin, 107,* 106–109.

Brody, N. (1994). .5 + or − .5: Continuity and change in personal dispositions. In T. F. Heatherton & J. L. Weinberger (Eds.), *Can personality change?* (pp. 59–81). Washington, DC: American Psychological Association.

Brody, N., & Crowley, M. J. (1995). Environmental (and genetic) influences on personality and intelligence. In D. Saklofske & M. Zeidner (Eds.), *International handbook of personality and intelligence* (pp. 59–80). New York: Plenum Press.

Bugental, D. B., & Shennum, W. A. (1984). Difficult children as elicitors and targets of adult communication patterns: An attributional-behavioral transactional analysis. *Monographs of the Society for Research in Child Development, 49*(Serial No. 205).

Buss, A. H., & Plomin, R. (1984). *Temperament: Early developing personality traits.* Hillsdale, NJ: Erlbaum.

Buss, D. M. (1981). Predicting parent-child interactions from children's activity level. *Developmental Psychology, 17,* 59–65.

Buss, D. M. (1984). Toward a psychology of person-environment correspondence: The role of spouse selection. *Journal of Personality and Social Psychology, 47,* 361–377.

Buss, D. M. (1985). The temporal stability of acts, trends, and patterns. In C. D. Spielberg & J. N. Butcher (Eds.), *Advances in personality assessment* (pp. 165–196). Hillsdale NJ: Erlbaum.

Buss, D. M. (1987). Selection, evocation, and manipulation. *Journal of Personality and Social Psychology, 53,* 1214–1221.

Buss, D. M. (1991). Evolutionary personality psychology. *Annual Review of Psychology, 42,* 459–491.

Buss, D. M., Block, J. H., & Block, J. (1980). Preschool activity level: Personality correlates and developmental implications. *Child Development, 51,* 401–408.

Byrne, D., & Griffitt, W. (1966). A developmental investigation of the law of attraction. *Journal of Personality and Social Psychology, 4,* 699–702.

Cadoret, R. J., Yates, W. R., Troughton, E., Woodworth, G., & Stewart, M. (1995). Genetic-environmental interaction in the genesis of aggressivity and conduct disorders. *Archives of General Psychiatry, 52,* 916–924.

Cairns, R. B. (1979). *Social development.* San Francisco: Freeman.

Cairns, R. B., & Cairns, B. D. (1994). *Lifelines and risks: Pathways of youth in our time.* New York: Cambridge University Press.

Cairns, R. B., Cairns, B. D., Neckerman, H. J., Gest, S. D., & Gariepy, J. L. (1988). Social networks and aggressive behavior: Peer support or peer rejection. *Developmental Psychology, 24,* 815–823.

Cairns, R. B., & Green, J. A. (1979). How to assess personality and social patterns: Observations or ratings? In R. B. Cairns (Ed.), *The analysis of social interactions.* Hillsdale, NJ: Erlbaum.

Cairns, R. B., & Hood, K. E. (1983). Continuity in social development: A comparative perspective on individual difference prediction. In P. B. Baltes & O. G. Brim, Jr. (Eds.), *Life-span development and behavior* (Vol. 5, pp. 301–358). New York: Academic Press.

Cannon, T. D., Mednick, S. A., Parnas, J., Schulsinger, F., Praestholm, J., & Vestergaard, A. (1993). Developmental brain abnormalities in the offspring of schizophrenic mothers. *Archives of General Psychiatry, 50,* 551–564.

Cantor, N. (1990). From thought to behavior: "Having" and "doing" in the study of personality and cognition. *American Psychologist, 45,* 735–750.

Cantor, N., & Kihlstrom, J. (1987). *Personality and social intelligence.* Englewood Cliffs, NJ: Prentice-Hall.

Cantwell, D. P., & Rutter, M. (1994). Classification: Conceptual issues and substantive findings. In M. Rutter, E. Taylor, & L. Hersov (Eds.), *Child and adolescent psychiatry* (3rd ed., pp. 3–22). Oxford, England: Blackwell.

Carmichael, C. M., & McGue, M. (1994). A longitudinal family study of personality change and stability. *Journal of Personality, 62,* 1–20.

Caron, C., & Rutter, M. (1991). Comorbidity in child psychopathology: Concepts, issues and research strategies. *Journal of Child Psychology and Psychiatry, 32,* 1063–1080.

Caspi, A. (1987). Personality in the life course. *Journal of Personality and Social Psychology, 53,* 1203–1213.

Caspi, A., & Bem, D. J. (1990). Personality continuity and change across the life course. In L. Pervin (Ed.), *Handbook of personality: Theory and research* (pp. 549–575). New York: Guilford Press.

Caspi, A., Bem, D. J., & Elder, G. H., Jr. (1989). Continuities and consequences of interactional styles across the life course. *Journal of Personality, 57,* 375–406.

Caspi, A., Henry, B., McGee, R. O., Moffitt, T. E., & Silva, P. A. (1995). Temperamental origins of child and adolescent behavior problems: From age 3 to age 15. *Child Development, 66,* 55–68.

Caspi, A., & Herbener, E. S. (1990). Continuity and change: Assortative marriage and the consistency of personality in adulthood. *Journal of Personality and Social Psychology, 58,* 250–258.

Caspi, A., Herbener, E. S., & Ozer, D. J. (1992). Shared experiences and the similarity of personalities: A longitudinal study of married couples. *Journal of Personality and Social Psychology, 62,* 281–291.

Caspi, A., & Moffitt, T. E. (1993). When do individual differences matter? A paradoxical theory of personality coherence. *Psychological Inquiry, 4,* 247–271.

Caspi, A., Moffitt, T. E., Silva, P. A., Stouthamer-Loeber, M., Krueger, R. F., & Schmutte, P. S. (1994). Are some people crime-prone? Replications of the personality-crime relationship across countries, genders, races, and methods. *Criminology, 32,* 163–195.

Caspi, A., & Silva, P. A. (1995). Tempermental qualities at age 3 predict personality traits in young adulthood: Longitudinal evidence from a birth cohort. *Child Development, 66,* 486–498.

Cattell, R. B. (1945). The principal trait clusters for describing personality. *Psychological Bulletin, 42,* 129–161.

Cattell, R. B. (1957). *Personality and motivation structure and measurement.* Yonkers-on-Hudson, New York: World Book.

Cattell, R. B., Eber, A. A., & Tatsuoka, A. (1970). *Handbook for the Sixteen Personality Factor Questionnaire (16PF) in clinical, educational, industrial, and research psychology, for use with all forms of the test.* Champaign, IL: Institute for Personality and Ability Testing.

Cheek, J. M., & Buss, A. H. (1981). Shyness and sociability. *Journal of Personality and Social Psychology, 41,* 330–339.

Chess, S., & Thomas, A. (1987). *Origins and evolution of behavior disorders: From infancy to early adult life.* Cambridge, MA: Harvard University Press.

Church, T. A. (1994). Relating the Tellegen and Five Factor models of personality structure. *Journal of Personality and Social Psychology, 67,* 898–909.

Clarke, A. D. B., & Clarke, A. M. (1984). Consistency and change in the growth of human characteristics. *Journal of Child Psychology and Psychiatry, 25,* 191–210.

Clausen, J. A. (1993). *American lives.* New York: Free Press.

Cohen, P., & Cohen, J. (1984). The clinician's illusion. *Archives of General Psychiatry, 41,* 1178–1182.

Cohen, P., Cohen, J., & Brook, J. S. (1995). Bringing in the sheaves, or just gleaning? A warning regarding the investigation of sex differences in association. *International Journal of Methods in Psychiatric Research, 5,* 140–144.

Cohler, B. J. (1982). Personal narrative and life course. In P. B. Baltes & O. G. Brim, Jr. (Eds.), *Life-span development and behavior* (4th ed., pp. 205–241). New York: Academic Press.

Collins, L. M., & Horn, J. L. (1991). *Best methods for the analysis of change.* Washington, DC: American Psychological Association.

Conley, J. J. (1984a). The hierarchy of consistency: A review and model of longitudinal findings on adult individual differences in intelligence, personality, and self-opinion. *Personality and Individual Differences, 5,* 11–25.

Conley, J. J. (1984b). Relation of temporal stability and cross-situational consistency in personality: Comment on the Mischel-Epstein debate. *Psychological Review, 91,* 491–496.

Conley, J. J. (1985). Longitudinal stability of personality traits: A multitrait-multimethod-multioccasion analysis. *Journal of Personality and Social Psychology, 49,* 1266–1282.

Cook, W. L., Kenny, D. A., & Goldstein, M. J. (1991). Parental affective style risk and the family system: A social relations model analysis. *Journal of Abnormal Psychology, 100,* 492–501.

Costa, P. T., Jr., & McCrae, R. R. (1988). Personality in adulthood: A six-year longitudinal study of self-reports and spouse ratings on the NEO personality inventory. *Journal of Personality and Social Psychology, 54,* 853–863.

Costa, P. T., Jr., & McCrae, R. R. (1992). Trait psychology comes of age. In T. B. Sonderegger (Ed.), *Nebraska Symposium on Motivation: Psychology and aging* (Vol. 39, pp. 169–204). Lincoln: University of Nebraska Press.

Costa, P. T., Jr., & McCrae, R. R. (1994). Set like plaster: Evidence for the stability of adult personality. In T. F. Heatherton & J. L. Weinberger (Eds.), *Can personality change?* (pp. 21–40). Washington, DC: American Psychological Association.

Costa, P. T., Jr., & McCrae, R. R. (1995). Primary traits of Eysenck's P-E-N system: Three- and five-factor solutions. *Journal of Personality and Social Psychology, 69,* 308–317.

Costa, P. T., McCrae, R. R., & Arenberg, D. (1980). Enduring dispositions in adult males. *Journal of Personality and Social Psychology, 38,* 793–800.

Costello, E. J., & Angold, A. (1995). Developmental epidemiology. In D. Cicchetti & D. J. Cohen (Eds.), *Developmental psychopathology* (Vol. 1, pp. 23–56). New York: Wiley.

Cowan, P., & Cowan, C. (1992). *When partners become parents.* New York: Basic Books.

Crick, N. R., & Dodge, K. A. (1994). A review and reformulation of social information-processing mechanisms in children's social adjustment. *Psychological Bulletin, 115,* 74–101.

Cronbach, L. J. (1975). Beyond the two disciplines of scientific psychology. *American Psychologist, 30,* 116–127.

Cronbach, L. J., & Gleser, G. C. (1953). Assessing the similarity between profiles. *Psychological Bulletin, 50,* 456–473.

Damon, W., & Hart, D. (1986). Stability and change in children's self-understanding. *Social Cognition, 4,* 102–118.

Daniels, D. (1986). Differential experiences of siblings in the same family as predictors of adolescent sibling personality differences. *Journal of Personality and Social Psychology, 51,* 339–346.

Darley, J., & Fazio, R. H. (1980). Expectancy confirmation processes arising in the social interaction sequence. *American Psychologist, 35,* 867–881.

Davidson, R. J. (1992). Emotion and affective style: Hemispheric substrates. *Psychological Science, 3,* 39–43.

Dawkins, R. (1976). *The selfish gene.* New York: Oxford University Press.

Deary, I. J., & Matthews, G. (1993). Personality traits are alive and well. *The Psychologist,* 299–311.

Dembroski, T. M., MacDougall, J. M., Costa, P. T., Jr., & Grandits, G. A. (1989). Components of hostility as predictors of sudden death and myocardial infarction in the Multiple Risk Factor Intervention Trial. *Psychosomatic Medicine, 51,* 514–522.

Derryberry, D., & Reed, M. A. (1994a). Temperament and attention: Orienting toward and away from positive and negative signals. *Journal of Personality and Social Psychology, 66,* 1128–1139.

Derryberry, D., & Reed, M. A. (1994b). Temperament and the self-organization of personality. *Development and Psychopathology, 6,* 653–676.

Digman, J. M. (1989). Five robust trait dimensions: Development, stability, and utility. *Journal of Personality, 57,* 195–214.

Digman, J. M. (1990). Personality structure: Emergence of the five-factor model. *Annual Review of Psychology, 41,* 417–440.

DiLalla, L. F., & Gottesman, I. I. (1989). Heterogeneity of causes for delinquency and criminality: Lifespan perspectives. *Development and Psychopathology, 1,* 339–349.

Dishion, T. J., Patterson, G. R., Stoolmiller, M., & Skinner, M. L. (1991). Family, school, and behavioral antecedents to early adolescent involvement with antisocial peers. *Developmental Psychology, 27,* 172–180.

Dodge, K. A. (1986). A social-information-processing model of social competence in children. In M. Perlmutter (Ed.), *Minnesota Symposia on Child Psychology* (18th ed., pp. 77–125). Hillsdale, NJ: Erlbaum.

Dohrenwend, B. P., Levav, I., Shrout, P. E., Schwartz, S., Naveh, G., Link, B. G., Skodol, A. E., & Stueve, A. (1992). Socioeconomic status and psychiatric disorders: The causation-selection issue. *Science, 255,* 946–952.

Donahue, E. M. (1994). Do children use the Big Five, too? Content and structural form in personality description. *Journal of Personality, 62,* 45–66.

Downey, G., Silver, R. C., & Wortman, C. B. (1990). Reconsidering the attribution-adjustment relation following a major negative event: Coping with the loss of a child. *Journal of Personality and Social Psychology, 59,* 925–940.

Draper, P., & Belsky, J. (1990). Personality development in evolutionary perspective. *Journal of Personality, 58,* 141–161.

Dunn, J., & Plomin, R. (1990). *Separate lives: Why siblings are so different.* New York: Basic Books.

Dunn, J., Stocker, C., & Plomin, R. (1990). Nonshared experiences within the family: Correlates of behavioral problems in middle childhood. *Development and Psychopathology, 2,* 113–126.

Dworkin, R. H., Burke, B. W., Maher, B. A., & Gottesman, I. I. (1976). A longitudinal study of the genetics of personality. *Journal of Personality and Social Psychology, 34,* 510–518.

Dworkin, R. H., Burke, B. W., Maher, B. A., & Gottesman, I. I. (1977). Genetic influences on the organization and development of personality. *Developmental Psychology, 13,* 164–165.

Eaton, W. O. (1994). Temperament, development, and the five-factor model: Lessons from activity level. In C. F. Halverson, Jr., G. A. Kohnstamm, & R. P. Martin (Eds.), *The developing structure of temperament and personality from infancy to adulthood* (pp. 173–187). Hillsdale, NJ: Erlbaum.

Eaves, L., & Eysenck, H. (1976). Genetic and environmental components of inconsistency and unrepeatability in twins' responses to a neuroticism questionnaire. *Behavior Genetics, 6,* 145–160.

Eisenberg, N., Cialdini, R. B., McCreath, H., & Shell, R. (1987). Consistency-based compliance: When and why do children become vulnerable. *Journal of Personality and Social Psychology, 52,* 1174–1181.

Eisenberg, N., & Fabes, R. A. (1992). Emotion, regulation, and the development of social competence. In M. S. Clark (Ed.), *Review of personality and social psychology* (Vol. 14, pp. 119–150). Newbury Park, CA: Sage.

Eisenberg, N., Fabes, R. A., & Murphy, B. C. (1995). Relations of shyness and low sociability to regulation and emotionality. *Journal of Personality and Social Psychology, 68,* 505–517.

Eisenberg, N., Fabes, R. A., Murphy, B., Maszk, P., Smith, M., & Karbon, M. (1995). The role of emotionality and regulation in children's social functioning: A longitudinal study. *Child Development, 66,* 1360–1384.

Ekman, P. (1993). Facial expression and emotion. *American Psychologist, 48,* 384–392.

Elder, G. H., Jr. (1974). *Children of the Great Depression.* Chicago: University of Chicago Press.

Elder, G. H., Jr. (1979). Historical change in life patterns and personality. In P. B. Baltes & O. G. Brim, Jr. (Eds.), *Lifespan development and behavior* (Vol. 2, pp. 117–159). New York: Academic Press.

Elder, G. H., Jr. (1985). Perspectives on the life course. In G. H. Elder, Jr. (Ed.), *Life course dynamics: Trajectories and transitions, 1968–1980* (pp. 23–49). Ithaca, NY: Cornell University Press.

Elder, G. H., Jr. (1986). Military times and turning points in men's lives. *Developmental Psychology, 22,* 233–245.

Elder, G. H., Jr. (1987). War mobilization and the life course. *Sociological Forum, 2,* 449–472.

Elder, G. H., Jr., & Caspi, A. (1990). Studying lives in a changing society: Sociological and personological explorations. In A. Rabin, R. Zucker, R. Emmons, & S. Frank (Eds.), *Studying persons and lives* (pp. 201–247). New York: Springer.

Elder, G. H., Jr., Caspi, A., & Burton, L. M. (1988). Adolescent transitions in developmental perspective: Sociological and historical insights. In M. Gunnar & W. A. Collins (Eds.), *Minnesota Symposium on Child Psychology* (Vol. 21, pp. 151–179). Hillsdale, NJ: Erlbaum.

Elder, G. H., Jr., Modell, J., & Parke, R. D. (Eds.). (1993). *Children in time and place: Developmental and historical insights.* New York: Cambridge University Press.

Emde, R. N., Plomin, R., Robinson, J., Corley, R., DeFries, J., Fulker, D. W., Reznick, J. S., Campos, J., Kagan, J., & Zahn-Waxler, C. (1992). Temperament, emotion, and cognition at fourteen months: The MacArthur Longitudinal Twin Study. *Child Development, 63,* 1437–1455.

Emmons, R. A. (1986). Personal strivings: An approach to personality and subjective well-being. *Journal of Personality and Social Psychology, 51,* 1058–1068.

Emmons, R. A., Diener, E., & Larsen, R. J. (1986). Choice and avoidance of everyday situations and affect congruence: Two models of reciprocal interactionism. *Journal of Personality and Social Psychology, 51,* 815–826.

Ennett, S. T., & Bauman, K. E. (1994). The contribution of influence and selection to adolescent peer group homogeneity: The case of adolescent cigarette smoking. *Journal of Personality and Social Psychology, 67,* 653–663.

Entwisle, D., & Alexander, K. (1992). Summer setback: Race, poverty, school composition, and mathematics achievement in the first two years of school. *American Sociological Review, 57,* 72–84.

Epstein, E., & Guttman, R. (1984). Mate selection in man: Evidence, theory and outcome. *Social Biology, 31,* 243–278.

Epstein, S. (1983). Aggregation and beyond: Some basic issues on the prediction of behavior. *Journal of Personality, 51,* 360–392.

Epstein, S. (1991). Cognitive-experiential self-theory: Implications for developmental psychology. In M. Gunnar & L. A. Sroufe (Eds.), *Minnesota Symposia on Child Psychology* (Vol. 23, pp. 79–123). Hillsdale, NJ: Erlbaum.

Erdelyi, M. H. (1985). *Psychoanalysis: Freud's cognitive psychology.* New York: Freeman.

Eysenck, H. J. (1947). *Dimensions of personality.* London: Routledge & Kegan Paul.

Eysenck, H. J. (1977). *Crime and personality.* London: Routledge & Kegan Paul.

Eysenck, H. J. (1991). Dimensions of personality: 16, 5 or 3? Criteria for a taxonomic paradigm. *Personality and Individual Differences, 12,* 773–790.

Eysenck, H. J., & Eysenck, M. (1985). *Personality and individual differences: A natural science approach.* New York: Plenum Press.

Farrington, D. P. (1983). Offending from 10 to 25 years of age. In K. Van Dusen & S. A. Mednick (Eds.), *Prospective studies of crime and delinquency* (pp. 17–38). Boston: Kluwer-Nijhoff.

Farrington, D. P., Sampson, R. J., & Wikstrom, P.-O. (Eds.). (1993). *Integrating individual and ecological aspects of crime.* Stockholm: National Council for Crime Prevention.

Featherman, D. L, Spenner, K. I., & Tsunematsu, N. (1988). Class and the socialization of children: Constancy, change, or irrelevance? In E. M. Hetherington, R. M. Lerner, & M. Perlmutter (Eds.), *Child development in life span perspective* (pp. 69–90). Hillsdale, NJ: Erlbaum.

Feldman, S. S., & Aschenbrenner, B. G. (1983). Impact of parenthood on various aspects of masculinity and femininity: A short-term longitudinal study. *Developmental Psychology, 19,* 278–289.

Fergusson, D. M., Horwood, L. J., Caspi, A., Moffitt, T. E., & Silva, P. A. (1996). The (artefactual) remission of reading disability: Psychometric lessons in the study of stability and change in behavioral development. *Developmental Psychology, 32,* 132–140.

Fergusson, D. M., Horwood, L. J., & Lynskey, M. T. (1995). The stability of disruptive childhood behaviors. *Journal of Abnormal Child Psychology, 23,* 379–396.

Finn, S. E. (1986). Stability of personality self-ratings over 30 years: Evidence for an age-cohort interaction. *Journal of Personality and Social Psychology, 50,* 813–818.

Fiske, S. T., & Taylor, S. (1991). *Social cognition.* New York: McGraw-Hill.

Fletcher, G. J. O. (1993). The scientific credibility of common-sense psychology. In K. H. Craik, R. Hogan, & R. N. Wolfe (Eds.), *Fifty years of personality psychology* (pp. 251–268). New York: Plenum Press.

Franz, C. E. (1996). *The implications of preschool tempo and motoric activity level for personality two decades later.* Manuscript submitted for publication.

Freud, A. (1980). *Normality and pathology in childhood.* London: Hogarth Press and the Institute of Psycho-Analysis.

Friedman, H. S., Tucker, J. S., Schwartz, J. E., Tomlinson-Keasey, C., Martin, L. R., Wingard, D. L., & Criqui, M. H.

(1995). Psychosocial and behavioral predictors of longevity. *American Psychologist, 50,* 69–78.

Funder, D. C. (1991). Global traits: A neo-Allportian approach to personality. *Psychological Science, 2,* 31–39.

Funder, D. C. (1995). On the accuracy of personality judgment: A realistic approach. *Psychological Review, 102,* 652–670.

Funder, D. C., & Ozer, D. (1983). Behavior as a function of the situation. *Journal of Personality and Social Psychology, 44,* 107–112.

Gangestad, S. W., & Simpson, J. A. (1990). Toward an evolutionary history of female sociosexual variation. *Journal of Personality, 58,* 69–96.

Gangestad, S. W., & Snyder, M. (1985). "To carve nature at its joints": On the existence of discrete classes in personality. *Psychological Review, 92,* 317–349.

Geertz, C. (1973). *The interpretation of cultures.* New York: Basic Books.

Gergen, K. J. (1982). *Toward transformation in social knowledge.* New York: Springer.

Gifford, R. (1994). A lens-mapping framework for understanding the encoding and decoding of interpersonal dispositions in nonverbal behavior. *Journal of Personality and Social Psychology, 66,* 398–412.

Glenn, N. D. (1980). Values, attitudes, and beliefs. In O. G. Brim, Jr. & J. Kagan (Eds.), *Constancy and change in human development* (pp. 596–640). Cambridge, MA: Harvard University Press.

Goldberg, L. R. (1993). The structure of phenotypic personality traits. *American Psychologist, 48,* 26–34.

Goldsmith, H. H., Buss, A. H., Plomin, R., Rothbart, M. K., Thomas, A., Chess, S., Hinde, R. A., & McCall, R. B. (1987). Roundtable: What is a temperament? Four approaches. *Child Development, 58,* 505–529.

Goldsmith, H. H. (1994, Winter). The behavior-genetic approach to development and experience: Contexts and constraints. *SRCD Newsletter,* 1–10.

Goldsmith, H. H., Losoya, S. H., Bradshaw, D. L., & Campos, J. J. (1994). Genetics of personality: A twin study of the five-factor model and parent-offspring analyses. In C. F. Halverson, Jr., G. A. Kohnstamm, & R. P. Martin (Eds.), *The developing structure of temperament and personality from infancy to adulthood* (pp. 241–265). Hillsdale, NJ: Erlbaum.

Goldsmith, H. H., Rieser-Danner, L. A., & Briggs, S. (1991). Evaluating convergent and discriminant validity of temperament questionnaires for preschoolers, toddlers, and infants. *Developmental Psychology, 27,* 566–579.

Gottesman, I. I. (1991). *Schizophrenia genesis: The origins of madness.* New York: Freeman.

Gottman, J. M., & Rushe, R. H. (1993). The analysis of change: Issues, fallacies, and new ideas. *Journal of Consulting and Clinical Psychology, 61,* 907–910.

Gough, H. G. (1986). *California Psychological Inventory.* Palo Alto, CA: Consulting Psychologists Press.

Graziano, W. G. (1994). The development of agreeableness as a dimension of personality. In C. F. Halverson, Jr., G. A. Kohnstamm, & R. P. Martin (Eds.), *The developing structure of temperament and personality from infancy to adulthood* (pp. 339–354). Hillsdale, NJ: Erlbaum.

Graziano, W. G., & Ward, D. (1992). Probing the Big Five in adolescence: Personality and adjustment during a developmental transition. *Journal of Personality, 60,* 425–439.

Greenwald, A. G. (1980). The totalitarian ego: Fabrication and revision of personal history. *American Psychologist, 35,* 603–618.

Grusec, J. E., & Lytton, H. (1988). *Social development.* New York: Springer.

Grusec, J. E., & Redler, E. (1980). Attribution, reinforcement, and altruism: A developmental analysis. *Developmental Psychology, 16,* 525–534.

Gurin, P., & Brim, O. G., Jr. (1984). Change in self in adulthood: The example of sense of control. In P. B. Baltes & O. G. Brim, Jr. (Eds.), *Life-span development and behavior* (Vol. 6, pp. 282–334). New York: Academic Press.

Guttman, D. L. (1975). Parenthood: Key to the comparative psychology of the life cycle. In N. Datan & L. Ginsberg (Eds.), *Life-span developmental psychology: Normative life crises* (pp. 167–184). New York: Academic Press.

Haan, N. (1981). Common dimensions of personality development. In D. Eichorn, J. A. Clausen, H. Haan, M. P. Honzik, & P. H. Mussen (Eds.), *Present and past in middle life* (pp. 151–177). New York: Academic Press.

Haan, N., Millsap, R., & Hartka, E. (1986). As time goes by: Change and stability in personality over fifty years. *Psychology and Aging, 1,* 220–232.

Halverson, C. F., Jr. (1988). Remembering your parents: Reflections on the retrospective method. *Journal of Personality, 56,* 435–443.

Halverson, C. F., Jr., Kohnstamm, G. A., & Martin, R. P. (Eds.). (1994). *The developing structure of temperament and personality from infancy to adulthood.* Hillsdale, NJ: Erlbaum.

Hammen, C. (1991). Generation of stress in the course of unipolar depression. *Journal of Abnormal Psychology, 100,* 555–561.

Hampson, S. E., John, O. P., & Goldberg, L. R. (1986). Category breadth and hierarchical structure in personality: Studies of asymmetries in judgments of trait implications. *Journal of Personality and Social Psychology, 51,* 37–54.

Hanson, R. A. (1975). Consistency and stability of home environmental measures related to IQ. *Child Development, 46,* 470–480.

Harris, J. R. (1995). Where is the child's environment? A group socialization theory of development. *Psychological Review, 102,* 458–489.

Hart, D., Hofman, V., Edelstein, W., & Keller, M. (1997). The relation of childhood personality types to adolescents behavior and development: A longitudinal study of Icelandic children. *Developmental Psychology, 33,* 195–205.

Hartup, W. W., & van Lieshout, C. F. M. (1995). Personality development in social context. *Annual Review of Psychology, 46,* 655–687.

Havill, V. L., Allen, K., Halverson, C. F., & Kohnstamm, G. A. (1994). Parents' use of Big Five categories in their natural language descriptions of children. In C. F. Halverson, Jr., G. A. Kohnstamm, & R. P. Martin (Eds.), *The developing structure of temperament and personality from infancy to adulthood* (pp. 371–386). Hillsdale, NJ: Erlbaum.

Heath, A. C., Neale, M. C., Kessler, R. C., Eaves, L. J., & Kendler, K. S. (1992). Evidence for genetic influences on personality from self-reports and informant ratings. *Journal of Personality and Social Psychology, 63,* 85–96.

Helson, R., Mitchell, V., & Moane, G. (1984). Personality and patterns of adherence and nonadherence to the social clock. *Journal of Personality and Social Psychology, 46,* 1079–1096.

Helson, R., & Moane, G. (1987). Personality change in women from college to midlife. *Journal of Personality and Social Psychology, 53,* 176–186.

Helson, R., & Stewart, A. (1994). Personality change in adulthood. In T. F. Heatherton & J. L. Weinberger (Eds.), *Can personality change?* (pp. 201–225). Washington, DC: American Psychological Association.

Henry, B., Caspi, A., Moffitt, T. E., & Silva, P. A. (1996). Temperamental and familial predictors of violent and non-violent criminal convictions: From age 3 to age 18. *Developmental Psychology, 32,* 614–623.

Henry, B., Moffitt, T. E., Caspi, A., Langley, J., & Silva, P. A. (1994). On the "remembrance of things past": A longitudinal evaluation of the retrospective method. *Psychological Assessment, 6,* 92–101.

Hetherington, E. M., Reiss, D., & Plomin, R. (Eds.). (1994). *Separate social worlds of siblings: The impact of nonshared environment on development.* Hillsdale, NJ: Erlbaum.

Hill, R., & Mattessich, P. (1979). Family development theory and life-span development. In P. B. Baltes & O. G. Brim, Jr. (Eds.), *Life-span development and behavior* (pp. 161–204). San Diego, CA: Academic Press.

Hirshfeld, D. R., Rosenbaum, J. F., Beiderman, J., Bolduc, E. A., Faraone, S. V., Snidman, N., Reznick, J. S., & Kagan, J. (1992). Stable behavioral inhibition and its association with anxiety disorder. *Journal of the American Academy of Child and Adolescent Psychiatry, 31,* 103–111.

Hoffman, L. W. (1991). The influence of the family environment on personality: Accounting for sibling differences. *Psychological Bulletin, 110,* 187–203.

Hogan, R., & Nicholson, R. A. (1988). The meaning of personality test scores. *American Psychologist, 43,* 621–626.

Horowitz, L. M., Rosenberg, S. E., Baer, B. A., Ureno, G., & Villasenor, V. S. (1988). Inventory of Interpersonal Problems: Psychometric problems and clinical applications. *Journal of Consulting and Clinical Psychology, 56,* 885–892.

Horowitz, M. J., Milbrath, C., Jordan, D. S., Stinson, C. H., Ewert, M., Redington, D. J., Fridhandler, B., Reidbord, S. P., & Hartley, D. (1994). Expressive and defensive behavior during discourse on unresolved topics: A single case study of pathological grief. *Journal of Personality, 62,* 527–563.

Huesmann L. R., Eron, L. D., Lefkowitz, M. M., & Walder, L. O. (1984). Stability of aggression over time and generations. *Developmental Psychology, 20,* 1120–1134.

Jaccard, J., & Wilson, T. (1991). Personality factors influencing risk behaviors. In J. N. Wasserheit, S. O. Aral, & K. K. Holmes (Eds.), *Research issues in human behavior and sexually transmitted diseases in the AIDS era.* Washington, DC: American Society for Microbiology.

Jackson, D. N. (1984). *Personality Research Form.* Port Huron, MI: Research Psychologists Press.

Jacobs, W. J., & Nadel, L. (1985). Stress-induced recovery of fears and phobias. *Psychological Review, 92,* 512–531.

Jacobson, N. S., & Truax, P. (1991). Clinical significance: A statistical approach to defining meaningful change in psychotherapy research. *Journal of Consulting and Clinical Psychology, 59,* 12–19.

Jinks, J., & Fulker, D. W. (1970). Comparison of the biometrical, MAVA, and classical approaches to the analysis of human behavior. *Psychological Bulletin, 73,* 311–349.

John, O. P. (1990). The "Big Five" factor taxonomy: Dimensions of personality in the natural language and in questionnaires. In L. Pervin (Ed.), *Handbook of personality: Theory and research* (pp. 66–100). New York: Guilford Press.

John, O. P., Caspi, A., Robins, R. W., Moffitt, T. E., & Stouthamer-Loeber, M. (1994). The "Little Five": Exploring the five-factor model of personality in adolescent boys. *Child Development, 65,* 160–178.

John, O. P., & Robins, R. W. (1993). Gordon Allport: Father and critic of the Five-Factor Model. In K. H. Craik, R. T. Hogan, & R. N. Wolfe (Eds.), *Fifty years of personality research* (pp. 215–236). New York: Plenum Press.

John, O. P., & Robins, R. W. (1994). Traits and types, dynamics and development: No doors should be closed in the study of personality. *Psychological Inquiry, 5,* 137–142.

Jones, M. C. (1981). Midlife drinking patterns: Correlates and antecedents. In D. Eichorn, J. A. Clausen, N. Haan, M. P. Honzik, & P. H. Mussen (Eds.), *Past and present in middle life* (pp. 223–242). New York: Academic Press.

Jussim, L., & Eccles, J. (1995). Naturally occurring interpersonal expectancies. In N. Eisenberg (Ed.), *Review of personality and social psychology* (Vol. 15, pp. 74–108). Thousand Oaks, CA: Sage.

Kagan, J. (1969). The three faces of continuity in human development. In D. A. Goslin (Ed.), *Handbook of socialization theory and research* (pp. 983–1002). Chicago: Rand McNally.

Kagan, J. (1980). Perspectives on continuity. In O. G. Brim, Jr. & J. Kagan (Eds.), *Constancy and change in human development* (pp. 26–74). Cambridge, MA: Harvard University Press.

Kagan, J. (1981). *The second year.* Cambridge, MA: Harvard University Press.

Kagan, J. (1984). *The nature of the child.* New York: Basic Books.

Kagan, J. (1994). *Galen's prophecy: Temperament in human nature.* New York: Basic Books.

Kagan, J., & Moss, H. A. (1962). *Birth to maturity.* New York: Wiley.

Kagan, J., Reznick, J. S., & Snidman, N. (1988). Biological bases of childhood shyness. *Science, 240,* 167–171.

Kandel, D. B. (1978). Similarity in real-life adolescent friendship pairs. *Journal of Personality and Social Psychology, 36,* 306–312.

Kandel, D. B., Davies, M., & Baydar, N. (1990). The creation of interpersonal contexts: Homophily in dyadic relationships in adolescence and young adulthood. In L. N. Robins & M. R. Rutter (Eds.), *Straight and devious pathways from childhood to adulthood* (pp. 221–241). New York: Cambridge University Press.

Kazdin, A. E. (1990). Psychotherapy for children and adolescents. *Annual Review of Psychology, 41,* 21–54.

Kazdin, A. E. (1992, August). *Can personality change?* Lecture presented at the American Psychological Association Science Weekend Symposium, Washington, DC.

Kazdin, A. E., Bass, D., Siegel, T., & Thomas, C. (1989). Cognitive-behavioral therapy and relationship therapy in the treatment of children referred for antisocial behavior. *Journal of Consulting and Clinical Psychology, 57,* 522–535.

Keltner, D., Bonano, G., Caspi, A., Krueger, R., & Stouthamer-Loeber, M. (1996). *Personality and facial expressions of emotion.* Unpublished manuscript, University of California, Berkeley.

Keltner, D., Moffitt, T. E., & Stouthamer-Loeber, M. (1995). Facial expressions of emotion and psychopathology in adolescent males. *Journal of Abnormal Psychology, 104,* 644–652.

Kendler, K. S., Neale, M. C., Kessler, R. C., Heath, A. C., & Eaves, L. J. (1992). Childhood parental loss and adult psychopathology in women: A twin perspective. *Archives of General Psychiatry, 49,* 109–116.

Kenrick, D. T., & Funder, D. C. (1988). Profiting from controversy: Lessons from the person-situation debate. *American Psychologist, 43,* 23–34.

Kerr, M., Lambert, W. W., Stattin, H., & Klackenberg-Larsson, I. (1994). Stability of inhibition in a Swedish longitudinal sample. *Child Development, 65,* 138–146.

Kochanska, G. (1991). Socialization and temperament in the development of guilt and conscience. *Child Development, 62,* 1379–1392.

Kochanska, G. (1995). Children's temperament, mothers' discipline, and security of attachment: Multiple pathways to emerging internalization. *Child Development, 66,* 597–615.

Kohn, M. L., & Schooler, C. (1983). *Work and personality: An inquiry into social stratification.* Norwood, NJ: ABLEX.

Kraemer, G. W. (1992). A psychobiological theory of attachment. *Behavioral and Brain Sciences, 15,* 493–541.

Krueger, R., Caspi, A., Moffitt, T. E., Silva, P., & McGee, R. (1996a). Personality traits are differentially linked to psychopathology: A multi-trait/multi-diagnosis study of an adolescent birth cohort. *Journal of Abnormal Psychology, 105,* 299–312.

Krueger, R., Caspi, A., Moffitt, T. E., White, J., & Stouthamer-Loeber, M. (1996b). Delay of gratification, personality, and psychopathology: Is low self-control specific to externalizing problems? *Journal of Personality, 64,* 107–129.

Lahey, B. B., Hartdagen, S. E., Frick, P. J., McBurnett, K., Connor, R., & Wynd, G. W. (1988). Conduct disorder: Parsing the confounded relation to parental divorce and antisocial personality. *Journal of Abnormal Psychology, 97,* 334–337.

Larsen, R. J. (1992). Neuroticism and selective encoding and recall of symptoms: Evidence from a combined concurrent-retrospective study. *Journal of Personality and Social Psychology, 62,* 480–488.

Laub, J. H., & Sampson, R. J. (1993). Turning points in the life course: Why change matters to the study of crime. *Criminology, 31,* 301–325.

Lewinsohn, P. M., Rohde, P., Seeley, J. R., & Fischer, S. A. (1993). Age-cohort changes in the lifetime occurrence of depression and other mental disorders. *Journal of Abnormal Psychology, 102,* 110–120.

Little, B. R., Lecci, L., & Watkinson, B. (1992). Personality and personal projects. *Journal of Personality, 60,* 501–525.

Livesley, W. J., Schroeder, M. L., Jackson, D. N., & Jang, K. L. (1994). Categorical distinctions in the study of personality disorder: Implications for classification. *Journal of Abnormal Psychology, 103,* 6–17.

Livson, N., & Day, D. (1977). Adolescent personality antecedents of completed family size. *Journal of Youth and Adolescence, 6,* 311–324.

Livson, N., & Peskin, H. (1980). Perspectives on adolescence form longitudinal research. In J. Adelson (Ed.), *Handbook of adolescent psychology* (pp. 47–98). New York: Wiley.

Loehlin, J. C. (1992). *Genes and environment in personality development.* Newbury Park, CA: Sage.

Loehlin, J. C., Horn, J. M., & Willerman, L. (1990). Heredity, environment, and personality change: Evidence from the Texas Adoption Project. *Journal of Personality, 58,* 221–243.

Loehlin, J. C., Willerman, L., & Horn, J. (1987). Personality resemblance in adoptive families: A 10-year follow-up. *Journal of Personality and Social Psychology, 53,* 961–969.

Loevinger, J. (1957). Objective tests as instruments of psychological theory [Monograph]. *Psychological Reports, 3*(Suppl. 9), 635–694 .

Loftus, E. F. (1993). The reality of repressed memories. *American Psychologist, 48,* 518–537.

Longstreth, L. E., Davis, B., Carter, L., Flint, D., Owen, J., Rickert, M., & Taylor, E. (1981). Separation of home intellectual environment and maternal IQ as determinants of child IQ. *Developmental Psychology, 17,* 532–541.

Lykken, D. T., McGue, M., Tellegen, A., & Bouchard, T. J., Jr. (1992). Emergenesis: Genetic traits that may not run in families. *American Psychologist, 47,* 1565–1577.

Lytton, H. (1990). Child and parent effects in boys' conduct disorder: A reinterpretation. *Developmental Psychology, 26,* 683–697.

MacEvoy, B., Lambert, W. W., Karlberg, P., Karlberg, J., Klackenberg-Larsson, I., & Klackenberg, G. (1988). Early affective antecedents of adult Type A behavior. *Journal of Personality and Social Psychology, 54,* 108–116.

Magnus, K., Diener, E., Fujita, F., & Payot, W. (1993). Extraversion and neuroticism as predictors of objective life events: A longitudinal analysis. *Journal of Personality and Social Psychology, 65,* 1046–1053.

Magnusson, D. (1988). *Individual development from an interactional perspective.* Hillsdale, NJ: Erlbaum.

Magnusson, D., & Allen, V. (1983). An interactional perspective on human development. In D. Magnusson & V. Allen (Eds.), *Human development: An interactional perspective.* New York: Academic Press.

Mare, R. D. (1991). Five decades of educational assortative mating. *American Sociological Review, 56,* 15–32.

Markus, H. (1977). Self-schemata and processing information about the self. *Journal of Personality and Social Psychology, 35,* 63–78.

Markus, H., & Cross, S. (1990). The interpersonal self. In L. Pervin (Ed.), *Handbook of personality: Theory and research* (pp. 576–608). New York: Guilford Press.

Martin, R. B. (1989). Activity level, distractibility, and persistence: Critical characteristics in early schooling. In G. A. Kohnstamm, J. E. Bates, & M. K. Rothbart (Eds.), *Temperament in childhood* (pp. 451–461). Chichester, England: Wiley.

Martin, R. P., Wisenbaker, J., & Hüttunen, M. (1994). Review of factor analytic studies of temperament measures based on the Thomas-Chess structural model: Implications for the Big Five. In C. F. Halverson, Jr., G. A. Kohnstamm, & R. P. Martin (Eds.), *The developing structure of temperament and personality from infancy to adulthood* (pp. 157–172). Hillsdale, NJ: Erlbaum.

Matas, L., Arend, R., & Sroufe, L. A. (1978). Continuity of adaptation in the second year: The relationship between quality of attachment and later competence. *Child Development, 49,* 547–556.

Matheny, A. P., Jr. (1980). Bayley's Infant Behavior Record: Behavioral components and twin analyses. *Child Development, 51,* 1157–1167.

Matheny, A. P., Jr. (1983). A longitudinal study of stability of components from Bayley's Infant Behavior Record. *Child Development, 54,* 356–360.

Matheny, A. P., Jr. (1989). Children's behavioral inhibition over age and across situations: Genetic similarity for a trait during change. *Journal of Personality, 57,* 215–235.

Matheny, A. P., Jr., & Dolan, A. B. (1975). Persons, situation, and time: A genetic view of behavioral change in children. *Journal of Personality and Social Psychology, 32,* 1106–1110.

Matheny, A. P., Jr., & Dolan, A. B. (1980). A twin study of personality and temperament during middle childhood. *Journal of Research in Personality, 14,* 224–234.

McAdams, D. P. (1992). The five-factor model in personality: A critical appraisal. *Journal of Personality, 60,* 329–361.

McAdams, D. P. (1994). Can personality change? Levels of stability and growth in personality across the life span. In T. F. Heatherton & J. L. Weinberger (Eds.), *Can personality change?* (pp. 299–313). Washington, DC: American Psychological Association.

McCall, R. B. (1977). Challenges to a science of developmental psychology. *Child Development, 48,* 333–344.

McCall, R. B., & Carriger, M. S. (1993). A meta-analysis of infant habituation and recognition memory performance as predictors of later IQ. *Child Development, 64,* 57–79.

McCall, R. B., Eichorn, D. H., & Hogarty, P. S. (1977). Developmental changes in mental performance. *Monographs of the Society for Research in Child Development, 38*(Serial No. 171).

McCartney, K., Harris, M. J., & Bernieri, F. (1990). Growing up and growing apart: A developmental meta-analysis of twin studies. *Psychological Bulletin, 107,* 226–237.

McCrae, R. R. (1989). Why I advocate the Five-Factor Model: Joint factor analyses of the NEO-PI with other instruments. In D. M. Buss & N. Cantor (Eds.), *Personality psychology: Recent trends and emerging directions* (pp. 237–245). New York: Springer-Verlag.

McCrae, R. R. (1993). Moderated analyses of longitudinal personality stability. *Journal of Personality and Social Psychology, 65,* 577–585.

McCrae, R. R., & Costa, P. T., Jr. (1988). Recalled parent-child relations and adult personality. *Journal of Personality, 56,* 417–434.

McCrae, R. R., & Costa, P. T., Jr. (1990). *Personality in adulthood.* New York: Guilford Press.

McCrae, R. R., Costa, P. T., Jr., & Busch, C. M. (1986). Evaluating comprehensiveness in personality systems: The California Q-Set and the five-factor model. *Journal of Personality, 54,* 430–446.

McDevitt, S. C. (1986). Continuity and discontinuity of temperament in infancy and early childhood: A psychometric perspective. In R. Plomin & J. Dunn (Eds.), *The study of temperament: Changes, continuities and challenges* (pp. 27–39). Hillsdale, NJ: Erlbaum.

McGue, M., Bacon, S., & Lykken, D. T. (1993). Personality stability and change in early adulthood: A behavioral genetic analysis. *Developmental Psychology, 29,* 96–109.

McGue, M., & Lykken, D. T. (1992). Genetic influence on risk of divorce. *Psychological Science, 3,* 368–373.

McGuire, S., Dunn, J., & Plomin R. (1995). Maternal differential treatment of siblings and children's behavioral problems: A longitudinal study. *Development and Psychopathology, 7,* 515–528.

McNally, S., Eisenberg, N., & Harris, J. D. (1991). Consistency and change in maternal child-rearing practices and values: A longitudinal study. *Child Development, 62,* 190–198.

Mednick, S. A., Moffitt, T. E., Gabrielli, W. F., & Hutchings, B. (1986). Genetic factors in criminal behavior. In J. Block, D. Olwues, & M. R. Yarrow (Eds.), *The development of antisocial and prosocial behavior.* New York: Academic Press.

Meehl, P. E. (1978). Theoretical risks and tabular asterisks: Sir Karl, Sir Ronald, and the slow progress of soft psychology. *Journal of Consulting and Clinical Psychology, 46,* 806–834.

Meehl, P. E. (1986). What social scientists don't understand. In D. W. Fiske & R. A. Shweder (Eds.), *Metatheory in social science* (pp. 315–338). Chicago: University of Chicago Press.

Meehl, P. E. (1992). Factors and taxa, traits and types, differences of degree and differences in kind. *Journal of Personality, 60,* 117–172.

Mendelsohn, G. A., Dakof, G. A., & Skaff, M. (1995). Personality change in Parkinson's disease patients: Chronic disease and aging. *Journal of Personality, 63,* 233–257.

Merton, R. K. (1959). Notes on problem-finding in sociology. In R. K. Merton, L. Bloom, & L. S. Cottrell, Jr. (Eds.), *Sociology today: Problems and prospects* (pp. ix-xxxiv). New York: Basic Books.

Mervielde, I. (1994). A five-factor model classification of teachers' constructs on individual differences among children age 4 to 12. In C. F. Halverson, Jr., G. A. Kohnstamm, & R. P. Martin (Eds.), *The developing structure of temperament and personality from infancy to adulthood* (pp. 387–397). Hillsdale, NJ: Erlbaum.

Mischel, W. (1968). *Personality and assessment.* New York: Wiley.

Mischel, W. (1990). Personality dispositions revisited and revised. In L. Pervin (Ed.), *Handbook of personality: Theory and research* (pp. 111–134). New York: Guilford Press.

Mischel, W., Ebbesen, E. B., & Zeiss, A. R. (1973). Selective attention to the self: Situational and dispositional determinants. *Journal of Personality and Social Psychology, 27,* 129–142.

Mischel, W., Shoda, Y., & Peake, P. K. (1988). The nature of adolescent competencies predicted by preschool delay of gratification. *Journal of Personality and Social Psychology, 54,* 687–696.

Moffitt, T. E. (1991). *An approach to organizing the task of selecting measures for longitudinal research* (Tech. Rep.). Madison: University of Wisconsin.

Moffitt, T. E., Caspi, A., Belsky, J., & Silva, P. A. (1992). Childhood experience and the onset of menarche. *Child Development, 63,* 47–58.

Moffitt, T. E., Caspi, A., Harkness, A. R., & Silva, P. A. (1993). The natural history of change in intellectual performance: Who changes? How much? Is it meaningful? *Journal of Child Psychology and Psychiatry, 34,* 455–506.

Moos, R. (1973). Conceptualizations of human environments. *American Psychologist, 28,* 652–665.

Mortimer, J. T., Finch, M. D., & Kumka, D. (1982). Persistence and change in development: The multi-dimensional self concept. In P. B. Baltes & O. G. Brim, Jr. (Eds.), *Life-span development and behavior* (Vol. 4, pp. 264–310). New York: Academic Press.

Mortimer, J. T., Lorence, J., & Kumka, D. (1986). *Work, family, and personality: Transition to adulthood.* Norwood, NJ: ABLEX.

Moskowitz, D. S. (1986). Comparison of self-reports, reports by knowledgeable informants, and behavioral observations data. *Journal of Personality, 54,* 294–317.

Moskowitz, D. S., & Schwartzman, A. E. (1989). Painting group portraits: Assessing life outcomes for aggressive and withdrawn children. *Journal of Personality, 57,* 723–746.

Moss, H. A., & Susman, E. J. (1980). Longitudinal study of personality development. In O. G. Brim, Jr. & J. Kagan (Eds.), *Constancy and change in human development* (pp. 530–595). Cambridge, MA: Harvard University Press.

Moss, H. B., Blackson, T. C., Martin, C. S., & Tarter, R. E. (1992). Heightened motor activity level in male offspring of substance abusing fathers. *Biological Psychiatry, 32,* 1135–1147.

Nesselroade, J. R., & Baltes, P. B. (1974). Adolescent personality development and historical change: 1970–1972. *Monographs of the Society for Research in Child Development, 39*(Serial No. 154).

Nesselroade, J. R., & Baltes, P. B. (1984). Sequential strategies and the role of cohort effects in behavioral development: Adolescent personality (1970–1972) as a sample case. In S. A. Mednick, M. Harway, & K. M. Finello (Eds.), *Handbook of longitudinal research* (Vol. 1, pp. 55–87). New York: Praeger.

Neugarten, B. L. (1977). Personality and aging. In J. E. Birren & K. W. Schaie (Eds.), *Handbook of the psychology of aging* (pp. 626–649). New York: Van Nostrand-Reinhold.

Newman, D. L., Moffitt, T. E., Caspi, A., Magdol, L., Silva, P. A., & Stanton, W. (1996). Psychiatric disorder in a birth cohort of young adults: Prevalence, comorbidity, clinical significance, and new case incidence from age 11 to 21. *Journal of Consulting and Clinical Psychology, 64,* 552–562.

Nigg, J. T., & Goldsmith, H. H. (1994). Genetics of personality disorders: Perspectives from personality and psychopathology research. *Psychological Bulletin, 115,* 346–380.

Nisbett, R., & Ross, L. (1980). *Human inference: Strategies and shortcomings of social judgment.* Englewood Cliffs, NJ: Prentice-Hall.

Nurmi, J. E. (1993). Adolescent development in an age-graded context: The role of personal beliefs, goals, and strategies in the tackling of developmental tasks and standards. *International Journal of Behavioral Development, 16,* 169–189.

Olweus, D. (1979). Stability of aggressive reaction patterns in males: A review. *Psychological Bulletin, 86,* 852–875.

Ozer, D. J. (1985). Correlation and the coefficient of determination. *Psychological Bulletin, 97,* 307–315.

Ozer, D. J. (1986). *Consistency in personality: A methodological framework.* New York: Springer.

Ozer, D. J., & Gjerde, P. F. (1989). Patterns of personality consistency and change from childhood through adolescence. *Journal of Personality, 57,* 483–507.

Parker, J. G., & Asher, S. R. (1987). Peer relations and later personal adjustment: Are low-accepted children at risk? *Psychological Bulletin, 102,* 357–389.

Patterson, G. R. (1982). *Coercive family process.* Eugene, OR: Castalia Press.

Patterson, G. R. (1993). Orderly change in a stable world: The antisocial trait as chimera. *Journal of Consulting and Clinical Psychology, 61,* 911–919.

Patterson, G. R., & Bank, L. (1989). Some amplifying mechanisms for pathologic processes in families. In M. R. Gunnar & E. Thelen (Eds.), *Systems and development: The Minnesota Symposia on Child Psychology* (Vol. 22, p. 167–209). Hillsdale, NJ: Erlbaum.

Pedlow, R., Sanson, A., Prior, M., & Oberklaid, F. (1993). Stability of maternally reported temperament from infancy to 8 years. *Developmental Psychology, 29,* 998–1007.

Pervin, L. A. (1994). Personality stability, personality change, and the question of process. In T. F. Heatherton & J. L. Weinberger (Eds.), *Can personality change?* (pp. 315–330). Washington, DC: American Psychological Association.

Pianta, R. C., Sroufe, L. A., & Egeland, B. (1989). Continuity and discontinuity in maternal sensitivity at 6, 24, and 42 months in a high-risk sample. *Child Development, 60,* 481–487.

Pickles, A., & Rutter, M. (1991). Statistical and conceptual models of "turning points" in developmental processes. In D. Magnusson, L. R. Bergman, G. Rudinger, & B. Torestad (Eds.), *Problems and methods in longitudinal research: Stability and change* (pp. 133–165). Cambridge, England: Cambridge University Press.

Plomin, R. (1986). *Development, genetics, and psychology.* Hillsdale, NJ: Erlbaum.

Plomin, R. (1991). Genetic risk and psychosocial disorders: Links between the normal and abnormal. In M. Rutter & P. Casaer (Eds.), *Biological risk for factors for psychosocial disorders* (pp. 101–138). Cambridge, England: Cambridge University Press.

Plomin, R. (1994). *Genetics and experience: The interplay between nature and nurture.* Thousand Oaks, CA: Sage .

Plomin, R., & Bergeman, C. S. (1991). The nature of nurture: Genetic influence on "environmental" measures. *Behavioral and Brain Sciences, 14,* 373–386.

Plomin, R., Coon, H., Carey, G., DeFries, J. C., & Fulker, D. W. (1991). Parent-offspring and sibling adoption analyses of parental ratings of temperament in infancy and childhood. *Journal of Personality, 59,* 705–732.

Plomin, R., & Daniels, D. (1987). Why are children in the same family so different from one another? *Behavioral and Brain Sciences, 10,* 1–16.

Plomin, R., DeFries, J. C., & Fulker, D. W. (1988). *Nature and nurture during infancy and early childhood.* New York: Cambridge University Press.

Plomin, R., DeFries, J. C., & Loehlin, J. C. (1977). Genotype-environment interaction and correlation in the analysis of human behavior. *Psychological Bulletin, 84,* 309–322.

Plomin, R., DeFries, J. C., & McClearn, G. E. (1990). *Behavioral genetics: A primer.* New York: Freeman.

Plomin, R., Kagan, J., Emde, R. N., Reznick, J. S., Braungart, J. M., Robinson, J., Campos, J., Zahn-Waxler, C., Corley, R., Fulker, D. W., & DeFries, J. C. (1993). Genetic change and continuity from fourteen to twenty months: The MacArthur Longitudinal Twin Study. *Child Development, 64,* 1354–1376.

Plomin, R., Loehlin, J. C., & DeFries, J. C. (1985). Genetic and environmental components of "environmental" influences. *Developmental Psychology, 21,* 391–402.

Plomin, R., & Nesselroade, J. R. (1990). Behavioral genetics and personality change. *Journal of Personality, 58,* 191–220.

Plomin, R., Owen, M. J., & McGuffin, P. (1994). The genetic basis of complex human behaviors. *Science, 264,* 1733–1739.

Pogue-Geile, M., & Rose, R. J. (1985). Developmental genetic studies of adult personality. *Developmental Psychology, 21,* 547–557.

Prochaska, J. O., DiClemente, C. C., & Norcross, J. C. (1992). In search of how people change: Applications to addictive behaviors. *American Psychologist, 47,* 1102–1114.

Pulkkinen, L. (1986). The role of impulse control in the development of antisocial and prosocial behavior. In D. Olweus, J. Block, & M. Radke-Yarrow (Eds.), *Development of antisocial and prosocial behavior: Research, theories, and issues* (pp. 149–175). New York: Academic Press.

Pulkkinen, L. (1996). Female and male personality styles: A typological and developmental analysis. *Journal of Personality and Social Psychology, 70,* 1288–1306.

Quiggle, N. L., Garber, J., Panak, W. F., & Dodge, K. A. (1992). Social information processing in aggressive and depressed children. *Child Development, 63,* 1305–1320.

Quinton, D., Pickles, A., Maughan, B., & Rutter, M. (1993). Partners, peers, and pathways: Assortative pairing and continuities in conduct disorder. *Development and Psychopathology, 5,* 763–783.

Quinton, D., & Rutter, M. (1988). *Parenting breakdown: The making and breaking of intergenerational links.* Aldershot, England: Avebury.

Rabiner, D. L, Lenhart, L., & Lochman, J. E. (1990). Automatic versus reflective social problem solving in relation to children's sociometric status. *Developmental Psychology, 26,* 1010–1016.

Raudenbush, S. W., & Chan, W.-S. (1993). Application of a hierarchical linear model to the study of adolescent deviance in an overlapping cohort design. *Journal of Consulting and Clinical Psychology, 61,* 941–951.

Raush, H. L. (1965). Interaction sequences. *Journal of Personality and Social Psychology, 2,* 487–499.

Rende, R. D. (1993). Longitudinal relations between temperament traits and behavioral syndromes in middle childhood. *Journal of the American Academy of Child and Adolescent Psychiatry, 32,* 287–290.

Renken, B., Egeland, B., Marvinney, D., Mangelsdorf, S., & Sroufe, L. A. (1989). Early childhood antecedents of aggression and passive-withdrawal in early elementary school. *Journal of Personality, 57,* 257–281.

Revelle, W. (1993). Individual differences in personality and motivation: "Non-cognitive" determinants of cognitive performance. In A. Baddeley & L. Weiskrantz (Eds.), *Attention: Selection, awareness, and control* (pp. 346–373). Oxford, England: Oxford University Press.

Roberts, G. C., Block, J. H., & Block, J. (1984). Continuity and change in parents' child-rearing practices. *Child Development, 55,* 586–597.

Robins, L. N. (1966). *Deviant children grown up.* Baltimore: Williams & Wilkins.

Robins, L. N. (1988). Data gathering and data analysis for prospective and retrospective longitudinal studies. In M. Rutter (Ed.), *Studies of psychosocial risk* (pp. 315–324). Cambridge, England: Cambridge University Press.

Robins, R. W., John, O. P., Caspi, A., Moffitt, T. E., & Stouthamer-Loeber, M. (1996). Resilient, overcontrolled, and undercontrolled boys: Three replicable personality types. *Journal of Personality and Social Psychology, 70,* 157–171.

Rodgers, J. L., Rowe, D. C., & Li, C. (1994). Beyond nature versus nurture: DF analysis of nonshared influences on problem behaviors. *Developmental Psychology, 30,* 374–384.

Rose, R. J., Koskenvuo, M., Kaprio, J., Sarna, S., & Langinvainio, H. (1988). Shared genes, shared experiences, and similarity of personality: Data from 14,288 adult Finnish co-twins. *Journal of Personality and Social Psychology, 54,* 161–171.

Rosenbaum, M. E. (1986). The repulsion hypothesis: On the non-development of relationships. *Journal of Personality and Social Psychology, 51,* 1156–1166.

Rosenthal, R., & Rubin, D. (1982). A simple, general purpose display of magnitude of experimental effect. *Journal of Educational Psychology, 74,* 166–169.

Ross, M. (1989). Relation of implicit theories to the construction of personal histories. *Psychological Review, 96,* 341–357.

Rossi, A. (1980). Aging and parenthood in the middle years. In P. B. Baltes & O. G. Brim, Jr. (Eds.), *Life-span development and behavior* (Vol. 3, pp. 138–205). New York: Academic Press.

Rothbart, M. K., & Ahadi, S. A. (1994). Temperament and the development of personality. *Journal of Abnormal Psychology, 103,* 55–66.

Rovine, M. J. (1994). Estimating nonshared environment using sibling discrepancy scores. In E. M. Hetherington, D. Reiss, & R. Plomin (Eds.), *Separate social worlds of siblings: The impact of nonshared environment on development* (pp. 33–61). Hillsdale, NJ: Erlbaum.

Rowe, D. C. (1983). Biometrical genetic models of self-reported delinquent behavior: A twin study. *Behavior Genetics, 13,* 489–573.

Rowe, D. C. (1987). Resolving the person-situation debate: Invitation to an interdisciplinary dialogue. *American Psychologist, 42,* 218–227.

Rowe, D. C. (1989). Personality theory and behavioral genetics: Contributions and issues. In D. M. Buss & N. Cantor (Eds.), *Personality psychology: Recent trends and emerging directions* (pp. 294–307). New York: Springer.

Rowe, D. C. (1994). *The limits of family influence: Genes, experience, and behavior.* New York: Guilford Press.

Rowe, D. C., & Plomin, R. (1981). The importance of non-shared (E$_1$) environmental influences in behavioral development. *Developmental Psychology, 17,* 517–530.

Rowe, D. C., Rodgers, J. L., & Meseck-Bushey, S. (1992). Sibling delinquency and the family environment: Shared and unshared influences. *Child Development, 63,* 59–67.

Rushton, J. P., Brainerd, C. J., & Pressley, M. (1983). Behavioral development and construct validity: The principle of aggregation. *Psychological Bulletin, 94,* 18–38.

Rutter, M. (1982). Epidemiological-longitudinal approaches to the study of development. In W. A. Collins (Ed.), *Minnesota Symposia on Child Psychology* (Vol. 15, pp. 105–144). Hillsdale, NJ: Erlbaum.

Rutter, M. (1983). Statistical and personal interactions: Facets and perspectives. In D. Magnusson & V. L. Allen (Eds.), *Human development: An interactional perspective* (pp. 295–319). New York: Academic Press.

Rutter, M. (1986). Meyerian psychobiology, personality development, and the role of life experiences. *American Journal of Psychiatry, 143,* 1077–1087.

Rutter, M. (1987). Temperament, personality, and personality disorder. *British Journal of Psychiatry, 150,* 443–458.

Rutter, M. (1988). Longitudinal data in the study of causal processes: Some uses and some pitfalls. In M. Rutter (Ed.), *Studies of psychosocial risk: The power of longitudinal data* (pp. 1–28). Cambridge, England: Cambridge University Press.

Rutter, M. (1989). Age as an ambiguous variable in developmental research: Some epidemiological considerations from developmental psychopathology. *International Journal of Behavioral Development, 12,* 1–34.

Rutter, M. (1991). Nature, nurture, and psychopathology: A new look at an old topic. *Development and Psychopathology, 3,* 125–136.

Rutter, M., & Garmezy, N. (1983). Developmental psychopathology. In E. M. Hetherington (Ed.), *Handbook of child psychology: Vol. 4. Socialization, personality, and social development* (4th ed., pp. 775–911). New York: Wiley.

Rutter, M., Quinton, D., & Hill, J. (1990). Adult outcome of institution-reared children: Males and females compared. In L. N. Robins & M. Rutter (Eds.), *Straight and devious pathways from childhood to adulthood* (pp. 135–157). New York: Cambridge University Press.

Rutter, M., & Rutter, M. (1993). *Developing minds.* New York: Basic Books.

Rutter, M., Silberg, & Simonoff, E. (1993). Whither behavioral genetics? A developmental psychopathological perspective. In R. Plomin & G. E. McClearn (Eds.), *Nature, nurture, and psychology* (pp. 433–456). Washington, DC: American Psychological Association.

Ryder, R. G. (1967). Birth to maturity revisited: A canonical reanalysis. *Journal of Personality and Social Psychology, 7,* 168–172.

Ryff, C. D. (1984). Personality development from the inside: The subjective experience of change in adulthood and aging. In P. B. Baltes & O. G. Brim, Jr. (Eds.), *Life-span development and behavior* (Vol. 6, pp. 244–278). Orlando, FL: Academic Press.

Sameroff, A. J., Seifer, R., Baldwin, A., & Baldwin, C. (1993). Stability of intelligence from preschool to adolescence: The influence of social and family risk factors. *Child Development, 64,* 80–97.

Sampson, R. J., & Groves, W. B. (1989). Community structure and crime: Testing social disorganization theory. *American Journal of Sociology, 94,* 774–802.

Sampson, R. J., & Laub, J. H. (1990). Crime and deviance over the life course: The salience of adult social bonds. *American Sociological Review, 55,* 609–627.

Sampson, R. J., & Laub, J. H. (1993). *Crime in the making: Pathways and turning points through life.* Cambridge, MA: Harvard University Press.

Sampson, R. J., & Laub, J. H. (1996). Socioeconomic achievement in the life course of disadvantaged men: Military service as a turning point, circa 1940–1965. *American Sociological Review, 61,* 347–367.

Sanson, A., Prior, M., & Kyrios, M. (1990). Contamination of measures in temperament research. *Merrill-Palmer Quarterly, 36,* 179–192.

Sanson, A., Smart, D., Prior, M., & Oberklaid, F. (1993). Precursors of hyperactivity and aggression. *Journal of the American Academy of Child and Adolescent Psychiatry, 32,* 1207–1216.

Saudino, K. J., McGuire, S., Reiss, D., Hetherington, E. M., & Plomin, R. (1995). Parent ratings of EAS temperaments in twins, full siblings, half siblings, and step siblings. *Journal of Personality and Social Psychology, 68,* 723–733.

Scarr, S. (1985). Constructing psychology: Making facts and fables for our times. *American Psychologist, 40,* 499–512.

Scarr, S. (1988). How genotypes and environments combine: Development and individual differences. In N. Bolger, A. Caspi, G. Downey, & M. Moorehouse (Eds.), *Persons in context: Developmental processes* (pp. 217–244). Cambridge, England: Cambridge University Press.

Scarr, S. (1992). Developmental theories for the 1990s: Development and individual differences. *Child Development, 63,* 1–19.

Scarr, S. (1993). Biological and cultural diversity: The legacy of Darwin for development. *Child Development, 64,* 1333–1353.

Scarr, S., & Grajec, S. (1982). Similarities and differences among siblings. In M. E. Lamb & B. Sutton-Smith (Eds.), *Sibling relationships.* Hillsdale, NJ: Erlbaum.

Scarr, S., & McCartney, K. (1983). How people make their own environments: A theory of genotype to environment effects. *Child Development, 54,* 424–435.

Schaie, K. W. (1965). A general model for the study of developmental problems. *Psychological Bulletin, 64,* 92–107.

Schaie, K. W., & Parham, I. A. (1976). Stability of adult personality traits: Fact or fable? *Journal of Personality and Social Psychology, 34,* 146–158.

Schuerger, J. M., Zarrella, K. L., & Hotz, A. S. (1989). Factors that influence the temporal stability of personality by questionnaire. *Journal of Personality and Social Psychology, 56,* 777–783.

Schuman, H., & Scott, J. (1989). Generations and collective memories. *American Sociological Review, 54,* 359–381.

Sears, R. O. (1986). College sophomores in the laboratory: Influences of a narrow data base on social psychology's view of human nature. *Journal of Personality and Social Psychology, 51,* 515–530.

Siegler, I. C., George, L. K., & Okun, M. A. (1979). Cross-sequential analysis of adult personality. *Developmental Psychology, 15,* 350–351.

Smith, M. B. (1994). Selfhood at risk: Postmodern perils and the perils of postmodernism. *American Psychologist, 49,* 405–411.

Smith, T. W., Sanders, J. D., & Alexander, J. F. (1990). What does the Cook and Medley Hostility Scale measure? Affect, behavior, and attributions in the marital context. *Journal of Personality and Social Psychology, 58,* 699–708.

Smith, T. W., & Williams, P. G. (1992). Personality and health: Advantages and limitations of the five-factor model. *Journal of Personality, 60,* 395–423.

Snyder, M. (1984). When beliefs create reality. In L. Berkowitz (Ed.), *Advances in experimental social psychology* (pp. 248–305). Orlando, FL: Academic Press.

Snyder, M., & Ickes, W. (1985). Personality and social behavior. In E. Aronson & G. Lindzey (Eds.), *Handbook of social psychology* (Vol. 2, pp. 248–305). New York: Random House.

Sroufe, L. A. (1979). The coherence of individual development. *American Psychologist, 34,* 834–841.

Sroufe, L. A. (1989). Pathways to adaptation and maladaptation: Psychopathology as developmental deviation. In D. Cicchetti (Ed.), *The emergence of a discipline: Rochester Symposium on Development Psychopathology.* Hillsdale, NJ: Erlbaum.

Sroufe, L. A., Bennett, C., Englund, M., Urban, S., & Shulman, S. (1993). The significance of gender boundaries in preadolescence: Contemporary correlates and antecedents of boundary violation and maintenance. *Child Development, 64,* 455–466.

Sroufe, L. A., Carlson, E., & Shulman, S. (1993). Individuals in relationships: Development from infancy through adolescence. In D. C. Funder, R. D. Parke, C. Tomlinson-Keasey, & K. Widaman (Eds.), *Studying lives through time* (pp. 315–342). Washington, DC: American Psychological Association.

Sroufe, L. A., Fox, N., & Pancake, V. (1983). Attachment and dependency in developmental perspective. *Child Development, 54,* 1615–1627.

Stearns, S. C. (1992). *The evolution of life histories.* New York: Oxford University Press.

Stein, J. A., Newcomb, M. D., & Bentler, P. M. (1986). Stability and change in personality: A longitudinal study from early adolescence to young adulthood. *Journal of Research in Personality, 20,* 276–291.

Steinberg, L. (1985). Early temperamental antecedents of adult Type A behaviors. *Developmental Psychology, 21,* 1171–1180.

Stevens, D. P., & Truss, C. V. (1985). Stability and change in adult personality over 12 and 20 years. *Developmental Psychology, 21,* 568–584.

Stewart, A., & Healy, J. M., Jr. (1989). Linking individual development and social changes. *American Psychologist, 44,* 30–42.

Stoneman, Z., & Brody, G. H. (1993). Sibling temperaments, conflict, warmth, and role asymmetry. *Child Development, 64,* 1786–1800.

Suls, J., & Mullen, B. (1982). From the cradle to the grave: Comparison and self-evaluation across the life-span. In J. Suls (Ed.), *Psychological perspectives on the self* (Vol. 1, pp. 97–125). Hillsdale, NJ: Erlbaum.

Suomi, S. J. (1983). Social development in rhesus monkeys: Consideration of individual differences. In A. Oliverio & M. Zapella (Eds.), *The behavior of human infants* (pp. 71–92). New York: Plenum Press.

Surbey, M. K. (1990). Family composition, stress, and human menarche. In T. E. Ziegler & F. B. Bercovitch (Eds.),

Socioendocrinology of primate reproduction (pp. 11–32). New York: Wiley-Liss.

Swann, W. B., Jr. (1983). Self-verification: Bringing social reality into harmony with the self. In J. Suls & A. G. Greenwald (Eds.), *Psychological perspectives on the self* (Vol. 2, pp. 33–66). Hillsdale, NJ: Erlbaum.

Swann, W. B., Jr. (1987). Identity negotiation: Where two roads meet. *Journal of Personality and Social Psychology, 53,* 1038–1051.

Tellegen, A. (1985). Structure of mood and personality and their relevance to assessing anxiety, with an emphasis on self-report. In A. H. Tuma & J. D. Maser (Eds.), *Anxiety and the anxiety disorders* (pp. 681–706). Hillsdale, NJ: Erlbaum.

Tellegen, A. (1991). Personality traits: Issues of definition, evidence, and assessment. In W. M. Grove & D. Cicchetti (Eds.), *Thinking clearly about psychology: Vol. 2. Personality and psychopathology* (pp. 10–35). Minneapolis: University of Minnesota.

Tellegen, A., & Waller, N. G. (in press). Exploring personality through test construction: Development of the Multidimensional Personality Questionnaire. In S. R. Briggs & J. M. Cheek (Eds.), *Personality measures: Development and evaluation.* Greenwich, CT: JAI Press.

Tesser, A. (1980). Self-esteem maintenance in family dynamics. *Journal of Personality and Social Psychology, 39,* 77–91.

Tesser, A. (1993). The importance of heritability in psychological research: The case of attitudes. *Psychological Review, 100,* 129–142.

Thomas, W. I., & Thomas, D. (1928). *The child in America.* New York: Knopf.

Thorne, A. (1987). The press of personality: A study of conversations between introverts and extraverts. *Journal of Personality and Social Psychology, 53,* 718–726.

Tomkins, S. S. (1979). Script theory: Differential magnification of affects. In H. E. Howe, Jr. & R. A. Dienstbier (Eds.), *Nebraska Symposium on Motivation* (Vol. 26, pp. 201–236). Lincoln: University of Nebraska Press.

Tooby, J., & Cosmides, L. (1990). On the universality of human nature and the uniqueness of the individual: The role of genetics and adaptation. *Journal of Personality, 58,* 17–67.

Trachtenberg, S., & Viken, R. J. (1994). Aggressive boys in the classroom: Biased attributions or shared perceptions? *Child Development, 65,* 829–835.

Tremblay, R. E., Pihl, R. O., Vitaro, F., & Dobkin, P. L. (1994). Predicting early onset of male antisocial behavior from preschool behavior. *Archives of General Psychiatry, 51,* 732–739.

Turkheimer, E. (1991). Individual and group differences in adoption studies of IQ. *Psychological Bulletin, 110,* 392–405.

Urban, J., Carlson, E., Egeland, B., & Sroufe, L. A. (1991). Patterns of individual adaptation across childhood. *Development and Psychopathology, 3,* 445–460.

van den Boom, D. C., & Hoeksma, J. B. (1994). The effect of infant irritability on mother-infant interaction: A growth-curve analysis. *Developmental Psychology, 30,* 581–590.

van Lieshout, C. F. M., & Haselager, G. J. T. (1993). *The Big Five personality factors in the Nijmegen California Child Q-set (NCCQ).* Nijmegen, The Netherlands: University of Nijmegen.

van Lieshout, C. F. M., & Haselager, G. J. T. (1994). The Big Five personality factors in Q-sort descriptions of children and adolescents. In C. F. Halverson, Jr., G. A. Kohnstamm, & R. P. Martin (Eds.), *The developing structure of temperament and personality from infancy to adulthood* (pp. 293–318). Hillsdale NJ: Erlbaum.

van Lieshout, C. F. M., Haselager, G. J. T., Risken-Walraven, J. M., & van Aken, M. A. G. (1995). *Personality development in middle childhood.* Paper presented at the meeting of the Society for Research in Child Development, Indianapolis, IN.

Viken, R. J., Rose, R. J., Kaprio, J., & Koskenvuo, M. (1994). A developmental genetic analysis of adult personality: Extraversion and neuroticism from 18 to 59 years of age. *Journal of Personality and Social Psychology, 66,* 722–730.

Wachs, T. D. (1983). The use and abuse of environment in behavior-genetic research. *Child Development, 54,* 396–407.

Wachs, T. D. (1994). Fit, context, and the transition between temperament and personality. In C. F. Halverson, Jr., G. A. Kohnstamm, & R. P. Martin (Eds.), *The developing structure of temperament and personality from infancy to adulthood* (pp. 209–220). Hillsdale, NJ: Erlbaum.

Wachs, T. D., & Plomin, R. (Eds.). (1991). *Conceptualization and measurement of organism-environment interaction.* Washington, DC: American Psychological Association.

Wachtel, P. L. (1973). Psychodynamics, behavior therapy, and the implacable experimenter: An inquiry into the consistency of personality. *Journal of Abnormal Psychology, 82,* 324–334.

Wachtel, P. L. (1977). *Psychoanalysis and behavior therapy.* New York: Basic Books.

Wakefield, J. C. (1989). Levels of explanation in personality theory. In D. M. Buss & N. Cantor (Eds.), *Personality psychology: Recent trends and emerging directions* (pp. 333–346). New York: Springer.

Waller, N. G., & Shaver, P. R. (1994). The importance of nongenetic influences on romantic love styles: A twin-family study. *Psychological Science, 5,* 268–274.

Watson, D., Clark, L. A., & Harkness, A. R. (1994). Structures of personality and their relevance to psychopathology. *Journal of Abnormal Psychology, 103,* 18–31.

Watson, D., & Pennebaker, J. W. (1989). Health complaints, stress, and distress: Exploring the central role of negative affectivity. *Psychological Review, 96,* 234–254.

Weinberger, D. A., Tublin, S. K., Ford, M. E., & Feldman, S. S. (1990). Preadolescents' social-emotional adjustment and selective attrition in family research. *Child Development, 61,* 1374–1386.

Weisz, J. R. (1978). Transcontextual validity in developmental research. *Child Development, 49,* 1–12.

Weisz, J. R., Weiss, B., & Donenberg, G. R. (1992). The lab versus the clinic: Effects of child and adolescent psychotherapy. *American Psychologist, 47,* 1578–1585.

Westen, D. (1991). Social cognition and object relations. *Psychological Bulletin, 109,* 429–455.

Whitbourne, S. K., Zuschlag, M. K., Elliot, L. B., & Waterman, A. S. (1992). Psychosocial development in adulthood: A 22-year sequential study. *Journal of Personality and Social Psychology, 63,* 260–271.

White, K. R. (1982). The relation between socioeconomic status and academic achievement. *Psychological Bulletin, 91,* 461–481.

Wiggins, J. S. (1973). *Personality and prediction: Principles of personality assessment.* Reading, MA: Addison-Wesley.

Wiggins, J. S., & Pincus, A. L. (1992). Personality: Structure and assessment. *Annual Review of Psychology, 43,* 473–504.

Willerman, L. (1979a). Effects of families on intellectual development. *American Psychologist, 34,* 923–929.

Willerman, L. (1979b). *The psychology of individual and group differences.* San Francisco: Freeman.

Willerman, L., Turner, R. G., & Peterson, M. (1976). A comparison of the predictive validity of typical and maximal personality measures. *Journal of Research in Personality, 10,* 482–492.

Wink, P., & Helson, R. (1992). Personality change in women and their partners. *Journal of Personality and Social Psychology, 65,* 597–605.

Wohlwill, J. F. (1980). Cognitive development in childhood. In O. G. Brim, Jr. & J. Kagan (Eds.), *Constancy and change in human development* (pp. 359–444). Cambridge, MA: Harvard University Press.

Woodruff, D. S., & Birren, J. E. (1972). Age changes and cohort differences in personality. *Developmental Psychology, 6,* 252–259.

Yarrow, M. R., Campbell, J. D., & Burton, R. V. (1970). Recollections on childhood: A study of the retrospective method. *Monographs of the Society for Research in Child Development, 35*(Serial No. 138).

York, K., & John, O. P. (1992). The four faces of Eve: A typological analysis of women's personality at midlife. *Journal of Personality and Social Psychology, 63,* 494–508.

Young, C. H., Savola, K. L., & Phelps, E. (1991). *Inventory of longitudinal studies in the social sciences.* Newbury Park, CA: Sage.

Zuckerman, M. (1991). *Psychobiology of personality.* Cambridge, England: Cambridge University Press.

Zuckerman, M., Kuhlman, D. M., & Camac, C. (1988). What lies beyond E and N? Factor analyses of scales believed to measure basic dimensions of personality. *Journal of Personality and Social Psychology, 54,* 96–107.

Zuckerman, Mi. (1993). History and developmental psychology, a dangerous liaison: A historian's perspective. In G. H. Elder, Jr., J. Modell, & R. D. Parke (Eds.), *Children in time and place: Developmental and historical insights* (pp. 230–240). New York: Cambridge University Press.

Zuroff, D. C. (1986). Was Gordon Allport a trait theorist? *Journal of Personality and Social Psychology, 51,* 993–1000.

CHAPTER 7

Socialization Processes

DAPHNE BLUNT BUGENTAL and JACQUELINE J. GOODNOW

In the course of experience with others, people develop competencies in living and working together. They come to share—or at least to anticipate—each others' ways of acting, thinking, and feeling. *Socialization* is the term used to describe the process by which these accomplishments occur. In its most general sense, socialization may be defined as the continuous collaboration of "elders" and "novices," of "old hands" and "newcomers" in the acquisition and honing of skills important for meeting the demands of group life.

The study of socialization has experienced a new burst of energy after languishing somewhat from a high point in the 1960s and 1970s (Bronfenbrenner, 1994, p. xi). In part, the new burst comes from opening up the content matter of socialization. Socialization has come to be perceived as having to do with every aspect of life rather than concentrated on

the development of correct or moral behaviors. In part, the new burst comes also from the recognition that the processes of socialization do not take the form of any simple internalization of the standards of others. Instead, children—if we take them for the moment as prototypical novices—have come to be seen as actively contributing to events and as doing so in ways that change as the children themselves change: physically, cognitively, and socially.

Moreover, the socialization process has come to be seen as one in which many people have an investment. For children, the stakeholders include the young themselves, along with parents, friends, siblings, teachers, storekeepers, police, neighbors, policymakers, and so on. Sometimes the interests of these stakeholders fit neatly together, in which case change takes the form of increasingly smooth synchronization. At other times, people differ in their goals or in the routes they wish to follow toward a shared goal. The child (or any novice) may want to be counted as a full-fledged member of the group. Others, for a variety of reasons, may want to direct that progression along a particular course. Teachers and school administrators may hope to produce students who are academically accomplished. Policymakers may wish to have schools and family environments that yield a productive workforce. In these cases, some processes of negotiation, compromise, or mutual attempts at control will inevitably be involved.

Above all, the new burst of interest has come from a change in conceptual positions. That change has not taken the form of any single new grand theory. Instead, it has taken the form of several new ways of conceptualizing human processes in general, including socialization processes. Neuroscience provides one such emergent framework. Changing perspectives within the cognitive sciences offer other windows. Expanded interest in the effects of social and cultural contexts provides another set of insights.

The main body of this chapter takes three of these perspectives and applies them to the topic of socialization. We have labeled the three *biological, cognitive,* and *social-cultural.* The detailed nature of each emerges as we proceed. Briefly, however, a biological perspective starts from the view that humans are "prepared" for the socialization process. They come equipped with certain perceptual sensitivities and response tendencies that set them up for the specialized processes involved in socializing relationships. A cognitive perspective considers the ways in which people think about socializing events: the ways they attend to them, interpret them, categorize them, remember them, process them, transform their meaning, and tag them in terms of their emotional/motivational significance. A social-cultural perspective reminds us that socialization is influenced by the nature of the larger groups to which parents and children belong: by features, for example, such as the requirements for membership in various groups, the degree of consensus or diversity that exists, or the extent of pressure toward adopting particular social identities.

We see the understanding of socialization as best pursued by taking these particular perspectives or vantage points and seeing where they lead. To bring them together, however, we have asked what each has to say about some cross-cutting themes and questions. First, we ask about the various ways in which the subject matter of socialization is conceptualized within biological, cognitive, and social-cultural perspectives: What are the outcomes of interest? What are the relevant processes? Second, we ask about the

various assumptions made regarding causal effects: Who is influencing whom? What are the multiple sources of influence on the course of socialization, and how do they fit together? Finally, we ask whether socialization should be viewed as a single process or a set of processes and what each perspective has to say about methods of research. This same set of themes and questions, pursued in the course of considering each perspective, provides as well the framework for the first section of the chapter, where we briefly look backwards to review the shape of changes in the study of socialization, and for the last, where we consider the ways in which the various perspectives may be integrated.

Our orientation is not without bias. To start with, there is a bias toward material that is from psychology or is easily related to psychological research and theory. We use developmental psychology as our central launching base, adding to it the insights that may be afforded by other fields within psychology (social psychology, cognitive psychology, social psychophysiology, behavior genetics) and outside of psychology (sociology, anthropology, biology, psychiatry). In the interest of breadth, the research we cite is representative—not exhaustive. We hope this serves as an advance apology to our colleagues for the selective lens we have used in reviewing this literature.

In addition, there is an age bias in the material presented. The studies we have drawn from deal predominantly with children and adolescents. We recognize that socialization is a lifelong phenomenon and that the nature of the processes involved may vary from one age period to another. The bulk of the literature, however, like the title of this *Handbook,* concentrates on the earlier parts of the life span (childhood and adolescence). Processes that occur during these ages may be thought of as socialization prototypes. They may also be thought of as time periods when socialization is most needed and is most likely to have lasting effects.

BACKGROUND AND CROSS-CUTTING THEMES

Cutting across studies of socialization are several recurring themes. We use these themes to bring out the lines along which historical change has shaped current research, and then pursue them further in developing the three selected perspectives. These themes have to do with (a) expanding the content covered within studies of socialization, (b) adding cognition and affect to a concentration on actions, (c) specifying directions and sources of influence, and (d) asking whether any single account of socialization will fit all occasions, and if not, how occasions differ from one another.

The Subject Matter of Socialization: Moving beyond Conflict and Control

"A prudent and kind mother of my acquaintance was . . . forced to whip her little daughter . . . eight times successively in the same morning, before she could master her stubbornness and obtain compliance in a very easy and indifferent manner. If she had left off sooner, and stopped at the seventh whipping, she had spoiled the child for ever . . . but wisely persisting till she had bent her mind and suppled her will, the only end of correction and chastisement, she established her authority thoroughly and had ever after a very ready compliance and obedience in all things" (Locke, as cited by Cleverly, 1971, p. 56).

From Locke's perspective, socialization is about obedience and compliance. Across all situations, only one process is pointed to: the "suppling" of the child's will through punishment that inhibits a natural tendency to be "stubborn." The only variables considered are the actions of the two parties. If the parent acts in an insistent and sustained way, the child will act in a conforming fashion. Only the parent's actions really matter. All influence flows from the parent to the child, with the child contributing only an original tendency toward sin and defiance. The ideal methods are those that promote the child's taking over the task of controlling his or her own actions in desired ways—without external pressure or supervision.

Locke's focus on control has been echoed in subsequent conceptual formulations. A position similar to his was taken and then modified within the early formulations of learning theory, psychoanalytic theory, and sociological/anthropological theory.

Learning Theory

The emphasis on impulse control and compliance as goals of socialization continued into recent times through the formulations of general learning theory. Socialization continued to be conceptualized as a way of dealing with the basic nature of children, framed mainly in terms of "drives," including a natural pursuit of pleasure, a spontaneous orientation toward own concerns rather than the concerns of others, an initial lack of tolerance for frustration, with aggression as its sequel. If not effectively channeled, these tendencies ran counter to the interests of others—and ultimately the

interests of the child. Consistent with this emphasis, attention was directed to ways of most effectively shaping the child's behavior and fostering impulse control.

One break in this pattern came in the form of increasing interest in the ways children come to display moral values: avoiding behaviors that place a burden on others, contributing to the support of self and others, keeping and maintaining close relationships, ultimately serving as responsible parents (Maccoby, 1992), and generally acting in a variety of prosocial ways. This shift in focus matched to a fair degree a break in conceptual approaches to learning. General learning theory, with its emphasis on the direct experience of rewards and sanctions, had difficulty accounting for the socialization of altruism (producing benefit for others in the absence of benefit to oneself). Bandura's (1969) social learning theory, with its emphasis on learning based on opportunities to observe the actions and fates of others, could more easily account for such behaviors. Attention turned then to the ways in which parental modeling of concern for others fostered prosocial responses among children (e.g., Eisenberg, Fabes, Schaller, Carlo, & Miller, 1991; Fabes, Eisenberg, & Miller, 1990; Grusec, 1991).

Psychoanalytic Theory

Early psychoanalytic views of socialization again placed children and parents/society in an oppositional role. The basic nature of the child was described by Freud (1965) as primitive and hedonistic in nature, with aggressive and sexual impulses acting as prime forces. Parents and society in turn were seen as forces that served to "civilize" the brutish child. As in approaches from learning theory, parental management mattered. The main dimension, however, had to do with the degree of gratification offered to the child (too much, too little, or a judicious mixture) in the course of experiences such as breast-feeding or toilet training. Early experiences were regarded as particularly critical, with their effects carried forward primarily by the way they influenced personality structure, for example, by the way they influenced the nature of defense mechanisms or the strength of the superego.

In time, classical psychoanalytic theory displayed several changes. In the work of Erikson (1959), for example, the concept of early critical points was broadened to cover the life span; greater emphasis was placed on the possibility of being able, at later points, to work through the problems left unresolved at earlier ages; and the framing in terms of opposition and conflict gave way to a framing in terms of challenges. The sharpest break from the notion of a conflictual relationship between parents and children, however, came with Bowlby's (1969) emphasis on the adaptive quality of these relationships. Bowlby drew from ethology and evolutionary biology to make the argument that over evolutionary time, relationships between caregivers and their offspring had taken shapes that ensured the survival and adaptive skills of the young. The first steps toward that goal took the form of actions, on both sides, that ensured proximity and, in many species, affectional ties between parents and their young. Retained from the psychoanalytic perspective, however, was a strong concern with the ways in which the impact of early experiences was carried forward. That concern is at the core of proposals that the attachment patterns developed in early life are carried forward in the form of working models that are brought to later close relationships or to one's own performance as a parent (e.g., Bowlby, 1980; Bretherton, 1980).

Sociological and Anthropological Theory

Once again, the early view of socialization was that individuals were intrinsically at odds with the requirements of society. That sense of opposition, however, gave rise to a dilemma: How can societies function if individuals are basically asocial and devoted to the pursuit of self-interest? Part of the answer was seen as lying in the general power of socialization. In Small's (1905) description, "we may use the terms 'socialization' and 'civilization' interchangeably" (p. 363). A further part of the answer was seen as lying in the more specific process of internalization. Less regulation from others is needed if people take over their own regulation, adopting as their own the standards of others, building their own conscience in the light of what they have experienced in the course of interactions with others. A great deal of anthropology's interest in Freudian theory, for example, stemmed from interest in the concept of internalization and in the hypothesis that this process was influenced by specified and observable child-rearing practices (e.g., Whiting & Child, 1953).

Over time, however, as internalization came to be questioned as an adequate account of socialization, the picture of individuals as intrinsically asocial softened, and the range of content areas that socialization came to cover broadened (Wentworth, 1980). Increasingly, sociologists came to regard socialization as referring to the ways novices or newcomers—as children or as adults—came to participate in the social structure, with particular emphasis on the ways they came to participate in those parts of the social structure that had to do with work, production, and the distribution of power or resources (e.g., Kohn, 1977; Levine & Moreland, 1991; Willis, 1977). Anthropologists, in turn, moved more toward regarding socialization as concerned with the ways new members of a culture came to acquire the various parts of a cultural pattern, parts that might range from forms of initiation to ways of naming, talking, child rearing, housing, producing food, or exchanging gifts.

New Directions (Summary of Changes)

An emerging shift in ways of viewing socialization involves a broadening of relevant content. Increasing concerns with ways to foster socially positive actions added one such extension. As a further extension, socialization is increasingly seen as part of every aspect of social life, starting with the early establishment of proximity and affectional ties to a caregiver. This extension is reflected in the current coupling of the term socialization to a wide range of content areas: from language (e.g., Schieffelin & Ochs, 1986), to emotion (e.g., Capatides & Bloom, 1993; Kitayama & Markus, 1994), cognition (e.g., Goodnow, 1990; Wertsch, 1991b), the management of health and safety (e.g., Peterson & Brown, 1994; Tinsley, 1992), the negotiation of disagreement and differences in power (e.g., Kuczynski & Kochanska, 1990), and the construction of a sense of self (e.g., Markus & Kitayama, 1991).

The Emerging Role of Cognition and Affect: Moving beyond Actions

Historically, the central concern within the socialization literature has been with actions, and with the assumed causal connection between the actions of parents and the actions of children. Many studies of socialization did stop with demonstrating correlations between the methods parents used at one point and the actions that children displayed. Baumrind's (1967, 1971) division of parental styles into authoritarian, authoritative, and permissive continues as the classic example of this approach. Studies of this type are well represented in the 1983 *Handbook* chapter on socialization by Maccoby and Martin.

There are, however, some major limitations to analyses that stop with overt actions. Referring to research conducted within Baumrind's typology, Darling and Steinberg (1993) noted: "despite consistent evidence that authoritative parents produce competent children, we still do not really know how or why. Both the attribution and social learning perspectives offer interesting hypotheses about the mechanism through which such an association might come about, but the empirical evidence necessary to allow us to judge which hypotheses are correct is lacking. . . . If we are to move beyond a 'family address' model of parenting and understand the processes through which parenting style influences children, models of parenting style must account for the crucial mediating processes" (pp. 491–492). Consistent with this call, increasing interest in the search for mediating processes has appeared within a number of conceptual frameworks.

Social Learning Theory

Within Bandura's conceptualizing of social learning, we saw emerging concern with the *cognitive* organization of experience, that is, the ways in which observational information is organized for later use. Bandura (1977) suggested that the individual stores information concerning the observed and the possible outcomes of actions even without directly practicing those actions or experiencing the observed outcomes. Moving beyond the simpler notion of "imitation," it was pointed out that observational learning occurs even in the absence of reinforcement. The socialization process could now be interpreted in terms of the child's cognitive representation of the environment and self. In conceptualizing the ways children gain autonomous control over their own behavior, Bandura introduced notions of self-regulation and self-efficacy. At the heart of these notions was the idea that individuals develop domain-specific beliefs about their own efficacy as a function of their history of performance within that domain, their observations of the performance of others within that domain, the verbal persuasions of others with respect to their efficacy in that domain, and their current state of emotional arousal (with excessive levels of arousal having negative consequences for performance and success expectancies). Optimal socialization was described in terms of the opportunities created for children to see that their actions on the environment are efficacious.

Within social learning theory accounts, the emphasis was not entirely cognitive. Attention was also given to the particular ways affect influences the learning process. To take one proposal, the emotions of participants within the socialization process may influence their receptivity to the learning process. For example, children have been found to be more likely to comply with maternal requests after they have been placed in a positive mood (Lay, Waters, & Park, 1989). In similar fashion, evidence emerged that parental affect was an important mediator within the socialization process. For example, parents showed declines in effectiveness as "managers" in response to chronic or temporary stressors that led them to be more irritable or depressed (Conger, Patterson, & Ge, 1995; Patterson, 1996).

Concerns with affect from the perspective of social learning theory have also focused on children's affective processes as *end products* of socialization. Beyond managing the circumstances that influence children's emotional responses, parents may also model patterns of emotional response and emotion regulation (Eisenberg & Fabes, 1991; Eisenberg, Miller, Schaller, Fabes, et al., 1988; Halberstadt, 1986; Malatesta-Magai, 1991). Affect and affect regulation appeared to represent a socialization end product in which observational learning was particularly effective. For example, parents' advocated or modeled patterns of regulatory control over emotions influence the ways children come to experience and express emotions (Dunn & Brown, 1991; Eisenberg, Fabes, Carlo, & Karbon, 1992; Roberts & Strayer, 1987). As suggested by Thompson (1994), "Parents have fairly clearly defined expectations for the emotional behavior of their offspring that change with situational demands and the child's developing capabilities for the self-management of emotion, and they use a broadened range of direct and indirect influence strategies to socialize the child's emotional behavior" (p. 42).

Social Cognition Theory

Drawing primarily from cognitive and social cognitive theory, increasing consideration has been given to the role of information processing in socialization. In particular, attention has been given to the role of *parental* beliefs and appraisal processes as sources of influence on their interactions with children. Parke (1978) pointed out that—up to that point—most contingency analyses of mother-infant interaction credited the mother with the same degree of cognitive complexity as the infant. This concern led Parke to emphasize the "thinking parent." The striking differences observed in socialization processes may reflect variations in parental cognitions, for example, their differing subjective "timetables" for development (e.g., Goodnow, Cashmore, Cotton, & Knight, 1984; Hess, Kashiwagi, Azuma, Price, & Dickson, 1980; Ninio & Bruner, 1978), their stable, affectively tagged biases in interpreting child actions (e.g., Bugental, 1992; Strassberg, 1995), or their momentary changes in interpretations of child actions as a function of changing emotional states (e.g., Dix, 1992). In similar fashion, children's response to their social experiences are increasingly being understood in terms of the joint influences of cognition and affect (e.g., Crick &

Dodge, 1994). We give detailed consideration to these issues within our discussion of cognitive approaches to socialization.

Biologically Based Theories

Approaches to socialization that have biological origins have regularly given consideration to the emotional components of such processes, either as primitive processes in need of regulation, as regulators of relationships, or as consequences of socializing relationships. For Freud (1965), an optimal socializing environment involved the channeling of the child's primitive unconscious emotions into societally acceptable channels. For Bowlby (1973), an optimal socializing environment prevented the experience of separation or neglect, thus limiting the child's negative emotional reactions to such stressful experiences. Additionally, Bowlby (1980) introduced a cognitive component to early relationships by describing the infant as building a "working model" of relationships on the basis of early experiences with parents.

Moving away from the earlier view of emotion as disruptive, we have seen a recent shift toward conceptualizations that focused on the functional nature of emotion (Campos, Campos, & Barrett, 1989), including the adaptive role of emotion within socialization processes. Functionalist views of emotion (influenced by bioevolutionary models of emotion) also focused on the role of emotional regulatory processes (Thompson, 1991). Emotional processes came to be understood not only as in need of regulation to maintain their adaptive quality but also as functional regulators of other processes.

Social-Cultural Theories

Psychologists were far from alone in their concern with how to add cognition and affect to analyses of socialization actions. Affect as an outcome of socialization has long been a concern among anthropologists interested in psychoanalytic accounts of the way childhood experiences lead to adult personality structure, mediated by internalization (e.g., Whiting & Child, 1953). Cognition entered the picture in two primary ways. The first was by way of a concern with parents' ideas as contributing to parents' actions. That concern ranges from Fischer and Fischer's (1963) early description of New England parents as believing in the need to "divine" and then "maximize the potential" of each individual child rather than regarding all young children as basically alike and as having common needs, to LeVine's (1974; LeVine et al., 1994) interest in

parents' goals for themselves and their children. The second was by way of interest in a particular quality of ideas, cutting across content. This quality was the extent to which ideas were shared by members of a group. Interest in this quality of ideas is not unknown in developmental psychology (e.g., Deal, Halverson, & Wampler, 1989; Resnick, Levine, & Teasley, 1991). It is more widespread, however, within certain subareas of social psychology (notably, social representations theory; e.g., Duveen & Lloyd, 1990; Moscovici, 1981) and anthropology (notably, within analyses of cultural models; e.g., D'Andrade & Strauss, 1992; Holland & Quinn, 1987). In the section on socialcultural perspectives, we shall have occasion to consider proposals with regard to culturally shared ideas. In essence, however, interest in the concept of culturally shared ideas has often been accompanied by an interest in (a) the way ideas are "socially distributed" (in effect, the issue of who shares what ideas), (b) the need people experience to move toward ideas that enable them to communicate easily with others or to establish common ground with them, (c) the ways a body of shared ideas forms a set from which individuals can draw in the course of selecting or constructing their own viewpoints, and (d) the ways degrees of consensus can give rise to the sense that a particular viewpoint is "natural" or an option open to question and choice. As we shall see in the section on socialcultural perspectives, one of the recent moves involves the reinclusion of affect to what had become for a while a markedly cognitive picture.

New Directions (Summary of Changes)

In short, we have seen an "unpacking" of the global action-oriented stylistic variables that have been used in the past to explore the constituent processes. We are increasingly concerned with emotion and cognition—as well as behaviors. At the same time, we are moving in some new directions in our conceptualization of the ways emotion and cognition enter into socialization processes. For example, we are increasingly concerned with the ways these processes are interwoven and the ways such interweavings change over time.

Directions and Sources of Influence in Socialization Transactions

The original emphasis within studies of socialization was on single-source, one-way effects. Parents shape children, society shapes individuals. The reaction to this emphasis took two directions. One took the form of arguing for a more active role for the person seen as being molded. Where, it was asked, is the child's contribution? Where is the individual as an active agent within society? The second direction took the form of asking how multiple sectors of any social context are interrelated. Once we begin to see parents as far from being the sole influence on children, and we add siblings, grandparents, friends, teachers, the media, and the community to the list, we come face-to-face with the questions: How are these multiple sectors related to one another? Do they speak with one voice to the child, or do they send competing messages? Does experience with one sector facilitate events in another sector? Does a good experience in one sector act as a buffer against the effects of poor experiences in another? Does variety create difficulty for the child or increase the options available?

The first of these two directions (searching for each individual's active contribution and influence on the other) was more likely to be taken by researchers interested in the analysis of face-to-face interactions. The second (putting together multiple sources of influence) was more likely to be taken by researchers starting from an interest in the nature and the impact of the social context. The two directions overlap. For the moment, however, we shall treat the two as separate.

Double Influences: Two-Way Effects

In general, the progression has been from a deterministic view in which influence flows from parents to children, to proposals for reversing the direction of effects (e.g., children are seen as shapers of parents or as the primary producers of their environments), to interest in the nature of interlocking or mutual influence.

The first phase prompted a large body of research directed toward documenting the nature of parental effects and locating the dimensions (e.g., warmth/hostility, restrictiveness/permissiveness) that might differentiate one method from another. Maccoby and Martin's (1983) review in an earlier *Handbook* amply documents this line of research. The second phase is represented by strong versions of a "child effects" (Bell, 1968) position, with children seen as producing their own environments, either by triggering particular responses in their parents or by actively selecting some environments rather than others (e.g., Scarr & McCartney, 1983). The third phase is the one to which we direct attention. Within it, children no longer play a determinist role. Instead, they are considered "active contributors" (Engfer, Walper, & Rutter, in press), and the

question arises as to how children's contributions mesh with those of their parents or of other parties.

Within this third phase, there is a large set of proposals. We shall divide them in terms of whether the overall emphasis is on a relatively easy dovetailing or on varying degrees of tension or conflict, and in terms of their general conceptual base. As before, we note how similar directions of change emerged, in somewhat different forms, within several conceptual positions.

Attachment Theory. Dovetailing models predominated here, in particular with respect to the form of mutual responsiveness between mothers and infants. For Ainsworth and her colleagues (Ainsworth, Blehar, Waters, & Wall, 1978), for example, socialization was "a byproduct of reciprocal responsiveness to signals." Even physiological systems may be seen as displaying dovetailing. Hofer (1987), for example, proposed a linkage of the physiological homeostasis systems of mother and infant, with the internal states of each open to regulation by the partner. McKenna's (1990) description of mother and infant as performing a "dreaming tango" provides another example. He has demonstrated that when mothers and infants sleep together, the breathing patterns of both develop a joint rhythm, a rhythm that helps the infant get back into a regular pattern after momentary blocks.

At the same time, attachment systems have also been conceptualized as involving tension. Well-functioning mother-infant systems have been described as involving "interactive errors" that require a coordinated state of repair (Tronick, 1989). Security of attachment is in turn associated not with the extremes of maternal sensitivity, but with maternal sensitivity that is in the mid-range. Those infants who are more experienced in managing mismatches are, in turn, better able to develop self-regulatory skills and maintain engagement within stressful interactions (Gianino & Tronick, 1988; Tronick, 1989).

Learning Theory. Here both dovetailing and tension models emerged. The former are best illustrated by studies based on Vygotskian theory. Within these studies, the novice provides signals as to what he or she is ready for, and the expert phases in help or withdraws assistance, as needed. This kind of mutuality has appeared under several labels, with "scaffolding" (Wood, Bruner, & Ross, 1976) and "guided participation" (Rogoff, 1990) being the most common. Most of the studies have been concerned with cognitive development. The same patterning has, however, also been noted as occurring within the provision of assistance for entering social groups, with demonstrated benefits for the child's later social skills (e.g., Finnie & Russell, 1988).

What is the nature of models that see two-way effects as involving some greater degree of tension or conflict? Overall, we may place these along a continuum of varying degrees of tension. The gentlest model is one that represents parents as faced with a discrepancy between their perceptions of and hopes for their children and the perceptions and hopes maintained by the children themselves. Over time, parents resolve this discrepancy by adjusting their perceptions (e.g., Collins & Luebker, 1995). A stronger degree of tension is illustrated by Bell's (1977) "control-system" model focused on "mutual adjustment and accommodation" (p. 65). Within this model, each party is seen as aiming at keeping each other's behavior within an upper and lower limit. Each works, for example, toward raising the level of arousal or involvement when it is felt to be too low, or dampening it when it is felt to be too high. Control, then, is not intended to be absolute. The goal is behavior within a range, leaving some options on each side.

A notch higher on the tension scale is the kind of model suggested by Kuczynski and his colleagues (e.g., Kuczynski, 1997; Kuczynski & Kochanska, 1990; Kuczynski, Kochanska, Radke-Yarrow, & Girnius-Brown, 1987). They see tension as more endemic, perhaps because they are considering actions between parents and preschoolers on occasions that involve parents issuing directives to their children. Most studies of directives, especially at this age level, are framed in terms of the achievement of compliance. In an important change of frame, Kuczynski and his colleagues argued that these occasions were about negotiation rather than compliance. Mothers might in fact be described as using these occasions to carry out a major task within socialization: encouraging children to develop acceptable forms of negotiation (reasonable ways to say "no," or to ask, "Can I do it after dinner?"), or accommodation (e.g., "I'll see what I can do"), and to abandon or to use with discretion the technique of direct defiance.

As an example of the end-point of the scale, we choose Patterson's (1982) account of "escape conditioning" in families with aggressive boys: the mother makes an aversive intrusion, the child counterattacks, the mother backs off, the child terminates the counterattack. The child's "win" increases the likelihood that he or she will counterattack successfully on the next occasion. In such systems, the skirmishing is constant, and the tension unresolved by the development of any mutually acceptable ways of negotiating. It may be lowered by one party coming to give up, but it is not *resolved.*

Anthropological and Sociological Theory. As in psychological theory, there has been a shift away from simple determinism, in this case, from a view of society as shaping individuals. One move has taken the form of pointing out that society's constraints are far from uniform. Pressures are exerted more in some areas than in others, leaving the latter open to greater freedom in action and interpretation (e.g., D'Andrade, 1984). In addition, constraints are often more severe for some people than for others. Access to knowledge in many content areas, for example, is often restricted to a chosen few, with others advised that this knowledge is inappropriate, irrelevant, taboo, or beyond their capacity (e.g., Bourdieu, 1979; Foucault, 1980).

A further move away from simple determinism has taken the form of arguing that society and individuals are always interdependent. This type of proposal is expressed in a variety of ways. Contexts and individuals are said, for instance, to shape each other, to create, sustain, or construct each other, to be inseparable variables (e.g., Cole, 1985; Cole, Barrett, & Zahn-Waxler, 1992; Giddens, 1979; Kulick, 1992; Mehan, 1979; Packer, 1993; Shweder, 1990; Valsiner, 1989).

From this array, we single out at this point two proposals that utilize a particular term (coconstruction) and that have prompted studies that may readily be seen as developmental in nature. (Both have been strongly influenced by Vygotskian theory, but that is not their only base.)

As Winegar (1988) points out, the term coconstruction has been used in two main senses. In one, the emphasis falls on society as providing content that is interpreted by people with changing capacities and backgrounds. Society, for instance, provides invariances, patterns, and texts of various kinds. Meaning, however, is given by the perceivers or readers. That kind of proposal gives rise to a general conceptual position with regard to the nature of meaning (e.g., Wozniak, 1993). It also prompts studies asking about the extent to which, within families, fathers and mothers take the same position (a way of describing the patterns that children encounter), and these levels of agreement are correlated with the accuracy of a child's perception of the views that parents hold (e.g., Alessandri & Wozniak, 1989; Wozniak, 1993).

In the second meaning of the term, the emphasis is on everyday social transactions as providing a basis for establishing, negotiating, and redefining meanings and procedures. A specific example is provided by a study of the way arrangements for snack time at a preschool evolved over the first two months of school, shifting to accommodate the several goals and interests of both teachers and children (Winegar, 1988). These interactions, Winegar points out, are not simply occasions for children to learn teachers' scripts. Instead, teachers and children "jointly *construct* the organization and social meaning of the activity. In this sense, social procedures, conventions, and events are *inter*individual constructions of social organization" (p. 8, emphasis in original).

Multiple Sources, Multiple Intersections

As a way of framing the various lines of discussion about double directions of effects, we divided proposals in terms of the extent to which they emphasized a relative ease of fit or varying degrees of tension. In all cases, we assumed that between any two parties or any two segments of society, there are always two-way effects. The issue was one of describing the forms that these might take.

For proposals that concern multiple sources of influence, we again adopt a simplifying device. We divide proposals into three types that have been prominent in anthropological and sociological theory or in psychological approaches that have been strongly influenced by those disciplines. All three lay out multiple components within some kind of "space." They differ, however, in the way the components are fitted together.

Chain-style models have the longest history. In the simplest form, parents may be described as agents of society. Society, parents, and children are represented on a simple line. Problematic within this view, however, is the assumption that there are identical interests between "parents" and "society." At the very least, this assumption does not fit with any feeling on the part of parents that they need to protect children from the "outside world."

In a more complex version of chain-style models, parents are no longer seen as simple agents. Instead, they may act as funnels or conduits through which the larger society impinges on the lives of children. Conditions such as climate or the nature of food production, for instance, influence parents' child-rearing practices, and these in turn influence what children learn and come to be like (e.g., Whiting & Whiting, 1975). That influence may come about not simply because of what parents do directly but also because parents assign children to settings that then alter the opportunities open to children; for example, they may alter the opportunities for interaction with a range of other-aged children (Whiting, 1974). Over time, models of this

kind have become more complex and less stringlike. In one model, for example, economic stress affects parents' moods, and those moods alter both their interactions with their children and their interactions with each other (essentially providing two channels into an effect on the way children are treated; e.g., Elder & Caspi, 1988). By and large, however, these models contained relatively little allowance for children's being directly affected by circumstances outside the family. ("Resourceful children," however, are a feature of a later "hard times" analysis by Elder and his colleagues; Elder, Nguyen, & Caspi, 1985.)

Geographical models also have a substantial history. They are probably most familiar to psychologists in the form of Bronfenbrenner's (1979) early ecological model, with the term ecology used to describe children, parents, community, and so on, as forming a set of nested sectors. The descriptive adjective *geographical* is taken from Goodnow (1995) as a way of highlighting the metaphor contained within "ecological" or "habitat" models of development as a journey—a journey in which the individual moves from one sector to another, along paths that may need to be hacked out or may be made easier by the presence of well-worn paths and helpful guides. Within models of this kind, the particular role of parents may then be to act as guides, managers, mentors, or interpreters. Proposals of this kind cut across models based on Bronfenbrenner's approach and models stemming from expansions of learning theory (e.g., Parke & Bhavnagri, 1989; Patterson, 1996). Outside psychology they are to be found in discussion of "cultural capital" (e.g., Bourdieu & Passeron, 1977). Parents, the argument runs, may provide their children not only with economic capital but also with capital in the form of knowledge about the ways the system works. The children of parents with substantial schooling, for instance, inherit considerable knowledge of the ways the school system works, and that knowledge provides them with a decided advantage.

System-style models have less to say about chains or routes and more to say about dynamics. They have been particularly prominent within analyses that seek a way of describing both the interconnections among members of a family and the interconnections among the various parts of a social context. To reduce some complex proposals to a simple form, these models propose that various parts of any unit form a whole such that change in any one part flows on to change in others, either dampening or heightening the conditions already existing there and, in time, giving rise to a new but never permanent stabilization (e.g., Hinde & Stevenson-Hinde, 1987; Rutter, in press; Sameroff & Chandler, 1975). As a concrete example, we may take Sameroff and Chandler's proposal that risk factors at birth do not in themselves give rise to later difficulties. They create, however, a condition of vulnerability to later stresses, and the combination of risk factors at birth with a socially disadvantaged family increases considerably the likelihood that later difficulties will occur. Now there is no simple chain; instead, there may be aspects of spread, spillover, magnification, or buffering.

To varying degrees, these various models have given rise to some of the same questions. In all of them, for example, concern has arisen about how to make sure that individuals, children or adults, appear as actively influencing the settings they encounter. In all of them, the question has also arisen: What are the features of various components that make a difference to the nature of these active contributions or the way components are fitted together?

We single out two particular proposals. In one of these, the feature highlighted has been the extent to which a setting facilitates or makes difficult the achievement of an individual's goals. How far, Dix (1991) has asked, does a particular environment make it easy or difficult for parents to achieve their goals for children? How far, to make the issue more one of interpretation, do parents see the world as friendly or hostile and describe it in these terms to their children (e.g., Reiss, Oliveri, & Curd, 1983)?

In the second proposal, the feature highlighted is the extent to which the world encountered is diverse or all of a piece. One might ask what kind of a world it is that children are being introduced into, that parents are monitoring or tracking. One might also ask whether new contexts serve to facilitate or constrain the meeting of parents' and children's interests. The "outside world" may then be described in terms of the ways it facilitates or impedes the achievement of parental goals for a child (Dix, 1991), or the achievements, by parents or children, of a positive view of oneself (Tajfel, 1981). The "outside world" may also be described in terms of the opportunities it offers them. When parents assign their children to workplaces or schools, they may be moving them into a world where there is little opportunity to interact with other children or into a world (the school world, for instance) in which most of the opportunities are restricted to interactions with same-age children, with little exposure to children who are older or younger than they (B. Whiting, 1974). To take one last description, the "outside world" may be one that is marked by heterogeneity or homogeneity with regard to its ideologies or to the kinds of interpersonal relationships that are expected to be developed. Parents and peers, for example,

may not give the same message, a difference once thought to be an automatic source of difficulty but increasingly seen as offering the possibility of benefit and mutual facilitation (e.g., Corsaro & Eder, 1990; Hartup, 1983; Youniss & Damon, 1992).

Under what circumstances, we now need to ask, is the presence of a variety of messages or positions an occasion for confusion and conflict, or an opportunity for discovering alternatives and making a creative choice? As we shall see later, that last description (heterogeneity/homogeneity with the possibility of contested positions or competing "voices"; Wertsch, 1991a) is a type of approach often considered within social-cultural perspectives. For the moment, we shall simply signpost it as a point to which we return.

New Directions (Summary of Changes)

Concerns with directionality and sources of influence within socialization have moved in two directions. First, we have seen an increasing focus on the interlocking nature of mutual-influence processes. Second, the analysis of multiple, intersecting influences has moved toward finding not only ways of laying out a number of pieces within some kind of space but also ways of sketching out some of the dynamics within the influences that these pieces exert on one another, dynamics that are essential to locate if we are to build a picture of how socialization proceeds when both distal and proximal influences are involved and when a number of people, often with varying interests, have a stake in what happens.

Is Socialization a Single Process or a Set of Processes?

Within the history of socialization theory, we have seen competing views in representing the continuity of relevant processes. One view suggests that socialization proceeds by way of a single process that cuts across all situations. The same principles of social learning or drive theory, the same critical features of parental practices, the same steps toward cultural transmission, the same forms of preparatory training for later roles, might then be easily applied across the board. Another view suggests that socialization involves a set of processes that are qualitatively distinct. For some, such differences are stage-like and represent a progression across the course of development. The processes that predominate at one stage are replaced by other processes as the child moves in a directional course toward adulthood. For others, such differences are modular and operate in the service of different socialization tasks. In pursuing this theme, we are addressing an issue that has been a continuing point of controversy in the socialization literature. Questions have repeatedly been raised concerning the extent to which socialization processes follow the same "rules" at different points in development and in different types of relationships.

Questioning of Single-Process Theories

Learning Theory. Researchers coming from a general learning theory perspective—over time—have increasingly noted the limits of basic processes originally believed to influence all aspects of learning. A first breach in that wall came with evidence of predispositions to attend to particular stimuli and to respond in particular ways: predispositions that seemed to reflect "prelearning" (Seligman, 1970), and that resisted attempts to override them. In principle, if reinforcement processes explain all learning, then they should apply equally to all learning situations. In practice, however, it turned out to be extremely difficult to establish and maintain responses that are incompatible with species-specific responses (e.g., Breland & Breland, 1966). Such findings might have been discounted as involving highly specific stimuli and responses of infrahumans. This point of view became less defensible, however, when the argument was made that large sectors of human behavior are marked by some particular predispositions. The area of language is one such area; the area of attachment is another; the area of emotion is a third. These areas have occupied largely separate literatures, with the work of Chomsky (1988) standing out in the first, that of Bowlby (1973) in the second, and that of Hoffman (1981) on empathy and sympathetic distress in the third. Common, however, was the view that learning and socialization proceed in quite different ways when some particular predispositions to learning are present.

Similar limitations were found in applying general learning theory to the processes of socialization. As noted by Patterson (1996), researchers operating within a learning theory tradition were frustrated by the fact that there was no linear relationship between rate of reinforcement and rate of response, that the conditions that influenced generalizability were difficult to specify, and that some types of performance did not seem to be responsive to the same organizational rules as others. Surprisingly, even contingent positive reinforcement did not prove to be equally effective in all domains. For example, mothers who show an extremely high contingency of *positive* responses (i.e., who are "overattuned") are more likely to have children who demonstrate high levels of *negative* affect (Malatesta, Culver, Tesman, & Shepard, 1989). Reinforcement was also found to be more relevant for some domains than others. For example, prosocial responses (unlike some other response systems) were *not* likely to be strengthened by the provision of positive reinforcement (e.g., Grusec, 1991). But, at the same time, it was just as obvious that certain types of training (e.g., methods used by Patterson and his colleagues; Patterson, Dishion, & Chamberlain, 1993) were very effective (and replicable) in altering other types of behavior (e.g., antisocial behavior), in particular with younger children. These conflicting findings supported the emerging view that the principles of learning theory do not apply in a equipotential fashion to all domains of learning.

Attachment Theory. Questions concerning the continuity of socializing processes arose early on from within attachment theory. Early relationships between parents and infants appeared to be governed by a different set of rules than those that operated at later ages. The processes suggested by learning theorists as organizers of socialization did not appear to operate in any simple fashion within attachment relationships. For example, *prompt* attention to the infant's severe distress cries but *delayed* response to mild distress cries appear to decrease the duration of crying activity at later ages (Bell & Ainsworth, 1972; Hubbard & Van IJzendoorn, 1991), suggesting the presence of different operating principles. Additionally, attachment relationships have been found to be strengthened only by the provision of particular kinds of positive outcomes or "benefits" (e.g., predictable availability of comfort) and are not strengthened by other benefits. Most notably, Harlow's (e.g., Harlow & Harlow, 1965) groundbreaking work with monkeys documented the irrelevance of food as a basis for attachment. In the same way, shared play activities appear to represent a benefit that is not salient to this domain (Bretherton, 1985; Higley et al., 1992). Again, it appears that different types of socializing relationships may be organized according to different principles.

Moral Development. Questions have been raised about the different types of "rules" that are involved in different stages or processes of moral thought. Is there a single general capacity for the understanding of rules, or are some kinds of rules understood differently than others? It has been suggested by some that basic moral rules (e.g., rules that involve avoiding harm to others, establishing the rights of others) appear to involve a different "social domain" than do conventional rules, rules concerning "socially appropriate" forms of communication or behavior (Laupa & Turiel, 1995; Turiel, 1983). Although the justifications offered for moral and conventional judgments change across the course of development, children as young as 3 years of age can distinguish between moral and conventional rules (e.g., Nucci & Turiel, 1978). Children understand moral rules as universal and immutable; that is, they believe that such rules are not open to regulation or control by authority figures or consensus decisions. Conventional rule systems, on the other hand, are seen as properly falling within the regulatory domain of those in power (e.g., parents); additionally, they are believed to be subject to negotiation and change on the basis of shared agreement. Moral rules, then, are less open to the influences of socialization than are conventional rules. They are also less likely to give rise to occasions of conflict and negotiation between parents and children. In contrast, conflict and negotiation are likely to occur when an issue falls into the conventional domain (Smetana, 1988) or into the domain labeled "personal decision making" (a domain covering issues such as the choice of one's friends or clothing; Nucci & Weber, 1995; Smetana, 1995; Smetana & Asquith, 1994).

Contextual Variations in Socialization. Another challenge to the notion of single-process explanations of socialization came from developmentalists who have focused their attention on peer relationships (and peer socialization). Beginning with the work of Piaget (1948), peer influence processes have regularly been identified as involving a distinctive type of socialization. Youniss, McLellan, and Strouse (1995) suggested that "Peer relationships are marked by use of symmetrical reciprocity and guided by the overarching principle of cooperation by equals" (p. 102), an organizational principle that differs from the unilateral authority or power asymmetry that is more characteristic of adult-child relationships. Harris (1995) recently proposed that socialization is context-specific and that the central tasks of socialization are accomplished within the peer groups of childhood and adolescence, not through dyadic relationships.

Domain Specificity of Socialization: A Proposition

Across biological, cognitive, and social-cultural perspectives, we explore the possibility that socialization within different types of relationships involves distinctive sensitivities

and regulatory processes. In doing so, we are borrowing the notion of domain specificity from cognitive psychology. A basic debate in the area of cognitive psychology has concerned the extent to which the architecture of the brain is best thought of as an equipotential processing system or a system that consists of special-purpose processing modules (e.g., Fodor, 1983; Hirschfeld & Gelman, 1994). Cognitive domains have been conceptualized as representing bodies of knowledge that act as guides to partitioning the world and that facilitate the solving of recurring problems faced by organisms within that world (Hirschfeld & Gelman, 1994). Although the focus of this debate has been on perceptual and cognitive processes, the same basic issues may apply to social and emotional processes. We consider the possibility here that socializing processes operate according to different "rules," reflecting the different tasks or problems associated with different categories of relationships.

In examining the evidence for socialization patterns as involving distinctive social domains, we suggest the following criteria:

1. Interactions within different domains are organized around distinctive socialization "tasks."
2. The perceptual sensitivities and social cues that operate within different socialization domains are distinctive to those domains.
3. The regulatory processes that serve to organize different socialization domains are distinctive to those domains.
4. The relationship patterns that characterize different domains operate as natural categories in the organization of social thought.

Within the socialization literature, four commonly identified types of relationships are attachment relationships, reciprocity-based relationships, hierarchical relationships, and relationships based on social identity. At most points in the life course, human relationships may be parsed into these domains. Relationships between the same individuals operate according to different "rules" based upon the changing nature of their relationship and the changing nature of the immediate context. Thus, the interaction between a given parent and child may be governed by attachment principles when the child is highly dependent (common in infancy and recurring at later times of stress). The struggles between the parent and the same child as a toddler (or early adolescent) may more typically involve power-based principles. During collaborative activity (work or play) involving the parent and the child, interactions are more likely to involve principles of reciprocity. At other times, the dyadic relationship may be based upon their shared identity as a family or as community members, in which case, interactions are organized around the principles of social identity. The proposed social domains are represented diagrammatically in Figure 7.1.

Attachment relationships represent overlapping systems in which each individual ultimately stands to gain by maintaining proximity with the other person, in particular under conditions of threat or danger. In the prototypical attachment relationship (parent and infant), the relationship is asymmetrical; that is, the focus is on maintenance of the child's safety—an outcome that provides direct survival advantages for the young (but ultimate reproductive advantages for both). The relationship is regulated by perceptual processes (parent and infant readily identify each other), emotional processes (parent and infant experience distress during separation), communication processes (infants employ a signalling system to call parents under conditions of distress), and proximity tracking processes (visual tracking or search processes by parent or infant). Finally, the re-establishment of proximity after separation serves to reduce distress responses for both.

Identity relationships involve symmetrical, overlapping systems in which each individual stands to gain by their shared identity with others who are similar in socially-important ways (Tajfel, 1982). Social identity is jointly established by similarity to some and differences from others. Relationships based upon shared social identity have been conceptualized as serving the goals of common defense, and (for humans) the establishment/protection of

social self-esteem. Identity-based relationships provide benefits for similarity and group loyalty, and costs for dissimilarity or defection. The physical or symbolic presence of group members serves to reduce distress in response to threat, and the possibility of exclusion from that group induces anxiety (Caporael & Brewer, 1991). Identity-based socialization focuses on the acquisition of shared norms and routines that facilitate the smooth, coordinated flow of group-level activities as well as the acquisition of skills and knowledge that are valued within that group. Although identity-based socialization begins in families (e.g., Dunn & Brown, 1991), peer groups (e.g., cliques, gangs) serve as prototypes of identity-based socializing relationships.

Hierarchical relationships involve the management of competing interests between individuals with unequal control or resources. Regulating mechanisms are directed to negotiating the division of power or resources based upon each individual's current position within a hierarchical system. For example, dominance and submission cues are used to signal the power-based capabilities and intentions of interactants. Although hierarchical relationships may be of many different types, the relationship between parents and young children represents a prototypic exemplar (Bugental, 1993). Power assertion involves efforts to induce the compliance or deference of others, or to reduce the resistance of others by means of control over future outcomes (reward and punishment). Direct parental power assertion is employed in the service of facilitating children's (short-term) compliance and the attempted establishment of adult authority. Socialization processes are more likely to be characterized by power-based interaction when expected or established hierarchical relationships are challenged or contested (e.g., when toddlers show resistance to parental constraints; when adolescents contest the authority of parents).

Reciprocal relationships involve the maximization of benefits to the self through the negotiation of reciprocal exchange with functional equals. Such relationships are based upon implicit social contracts between parties who have equivalent levels of resources and needs. Reciprocal relations can be broadly defined to include not only short-term tit-for-tat exchange of resources but also mutuality of expressed positive affect (Foot, Chapman, & Smith, 1977; Pataki, Shapiro, & Clark, 1994). They have also been conceptualized as involving mutual expectations that support would be available if needed within enduring relationships (Tooby & Cosmides, 1996). The relationship between friends represents the prototypical example of

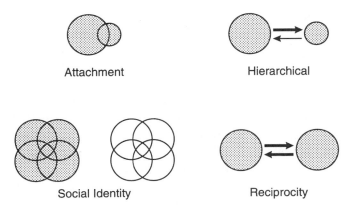

Figure 7.1 Proposed socialization domains.

Attachment   Hierarchical

Social Identity   Reciprocity

reciprocity-based relationships (e.g., Corsaro & Eder, 1990; de Cooke, 1992). However, in many contexts (e.g., during play) the relationship between parents and children may also be framed in terms of reciprocity. Even very young children respond positively and appropriately to a parental style that is based on reciprocity (Parpal & Maccoby, 1985), and indeed reciprocity (of positive affect) is a central regulating feature of adaptive interactions between caregivers and infants.

New Directions (Summary of Changes)

In the face of evidence that socialization shows systematic variations across settings, a notion of domain-specific socialization has been suggested. The proposal, although integrating evidence drawn from many different perspectives, is speculative. Therefore, we shall consider evidence related to this notion from the three perspectives: biological, cognitive, and social-cultural. We first consider the ways humans are selectively and distinctively prepared for socialization in terms of biological processes. We then move on to consider the extent to which different types of socializing relationships are represented cognitively as natural categories. Finally, we consider evidence for the social/cultural construction of different socialization domains.

BIOLOGICAL PERSPECTIVES ON SOCIALIZATION

As our first step in presenting the processes involved in socialization, we consider the ways we may be thought of as biologically prepared for socialization. Historically, theories that have focused on biological influences on development and those that have focused on environmental influences represented opposing views. As noted earlier, we have more recently come to recognize the integrated, unified nature of such processes (e.g., Kagan, 1989). Indeed, we have increasingly focused on the ways we are biologically designed to "create" culture. When we focus attention on our shared biological heritage, our attention is directed to the ways we are preferentially "designed" to facilitate the accomplishment of certain social "tasks," tasks that (within our history as humans) have been essential for adaptive functioning, for example, care of the young, establishing communication processes with conspecifics, acquiring culturally shared skills and knowledge. We may be thought of as *selectively* prepared for acquisition of

social knowledge and adaptation to the demands of social living.

Our primary focus is on human processes. Although humans share with infrahumans many processes that help to prepare the young for group life, they appear to be unique in their capacity to "teach," that is, to *deliberately* transmit knowledge to others (Boyd & Richerson, 1995; Tomasello, Savage-Rumbaugh, & Kruger, 1993). The *receptive* capacity of the young for acquiring skills of group life is also more advanced in humans; that is, humans have a unique capacity for symbolizing, forethought, and self-reflection that allows the acquisition of knowledge in ways that extend beyond the constraints of immediate situations and time periods (Tomasello, in press). Although some of these receptive capacities are shared with other higher primates (e.g., social imitation), they are much more developed in humans (e.g., Nagell, Olguin, & Tomasello, 1993).

In considering the biological influences on socialization, we first consider the possible role of our *shared evolutionary history,* that is, the ways humans may have evolved to manage the care and training of dependent children. We then move on to review evidence for *individual variations* in the ways parents and children are biologically prepared for socialization; here we consider the role of genetic, prenatal, neurohormonal, and other biological influences. Finally, we consider the evidence for biologically influenced variations in socialization processes across *different social domains.*

Biological Preparation for Socialization as a Coevolutionary Process

The successful accomplishment of socialization tasks may be framed in terms of either distal or proximal adaptation. Concerns with distal adaptations stem from an evolutionary perspective. That is, when thinking in terms of distal adaptations, we are concerned with the extent to which certain types of socialization processes yielded reproductive advantages across *vast time periods* within our early history as humans. We suggest that humans have evolved in ways that (a) facilitate the general capability for shared engagement with the environment, and (b) foster the accomplishment of specialized socialization tasks. Such adaptations continue into present times due to the very short evolutionary history associated with modern society (Tooby & Cosmides, 1990). Alternately, we may think in terms of proximal adaptiveness, that is, the extent to which socialization processes yield advantages in the present time and within particular contextual milieus. Obviously, there may be inconsistencies between the two. Adaptations that once served us well (e.g., gender specialization in care of the young) are often maladaptive in contemporary society.

In considering the issue of biological preparation for socialization, we are presenting a view that is discrepant from tabula rasa notions of socialization: that the child is completely shapable as a function of experience. Instead, socialization is conceptualized as involving shared sensitivities and reciprocal response patterns that act to selectively channel and direct the course of interpersonal interaction. As suggested by Wozniak (1993):

> As 20 years of infancy research have persuasively documented, babies appear to be born into the world with a cognitive system preadapted to mutuality of expectation, to intersubjectivity, and to interaction. If so, this suggests that the typical (and, indeed, Piagetian) assumption that babies are born into the world preadapted for acting on objects and become socialized by learning how to interact with that special category of strangely variable and unpredictable objects called people, must be abandoned. Instead, we must start from the radically different premise that babies are born into the world with a cognitive system preadapted to the mutuality of expectations that defines intersubjectivity and that what they must learn is that actions on objects are a special case, a case in which you don't have to concern yourself with what the objects think you happen to be doing. (p. 82)

First of all, we may think in terms of the *general* ways in which children are biologically prepared for socialization processes. Young children may be thought of as prepared for human interaction in general and for socialization in particular, a concept described as reflecting "social fittedness" (Emde, Biringen, Clyman, & Oppenheim, 1991). The brain opioid system has been shown to have an important role in the emergence and regulation of social affect in the developing animal. For example, opioids (and opioid antagonists) have been found to influence infant separation distress, maternal retrieval of the young, and juvenile play (Panksepp, Nelson, & Bekkedal, 1997). Infants are prepared to manifest "easily understood" social signals and to be responsive to the social features of their environment. Early indications of such preparation appear through presocial abilities available at birth that have significance for social engagement, for example, primitive capacities for imitation (Meltzoff & Moore, 1992), "empathic distress" (Sagi & Hoffman, 1976), and social signaling of emotional states (Izard, 1993). Infants show early preferences for

face-like stimuli (e.g., Sherrod, 1981), for human voices (DeCasper & Spence, 1991), and for human types of movement (e.g., Bertenthal, Proffitt, Spetner, & Thomas, 1985). The social signals produced by infants (e.g., smiles, cries) serve to *motivate* those in their environment. For example, the infant cry not only serves an alerting mechanism, it also compels action (Murray, 1979). The "demand" property of infant cries is suggested by differences shown between hearing and nonhearing parents in their response to cries; that is, hearing parents respond much more quickly than do nonhearing parents to the witnessed cry of infants (Murray, 1979).

The signals produced by the young and the perceptual sensitivities of the young are well-designed for coregulation processes. In explaining these processes, Krebs and Dawkins (1984) have suggested a coevolutionary process that involves both a "manipulator" role for social signals (they serve to motivate the actions of others) and a "mindreader" role (signals are used to predict the actions of others). Such signals are highly sensitive to the social context. For example, infant smiles (as with other emotional signals) are more likely to occur in the presence of an audience (Jones & Raag, 1989). Both in humans and infrahumans, strong evidence has emerged for the importance of audiences as a source of influence on communicative acts (e.g., Fridlund, 1991). Additionally, infants show a specialized sensitivity to human faces. Even at birth, infants are more likely to visually track face-like patterns than scrambled faces (Morton & Johnson, 1991). Neuroanatomical support for specific sensitivities to faces and eye movements of others has emerged from the work of Perrett and his colleagues (e.g., Perrett et al., 1990).

Among humans, there appears to be a generalized preparation for adults to be responsive to the characteristics of the young and a generalized tendency of infants to respond to the communication characteristics of speech directed to them. Such sensitivities may represent coevolutionary processes that foster the possibility of shared child care and multiple attachment processes. For example, it has been well established that the "babyish" facial qualities associated with immaturity (e.g., big eyes, large forehead, small nose) are reliable elicitors of specialized reactions (e.g., Hess & Polt, 1960). Children with a more babyish quality to their faces are likely to be subject to lowered cognitive expectations than are other children (Zebrowitz, Kendall-Tackett, & Fafel, 1991). Additionally, Eisenberg, Roth, Bryniarski, and Murray (1984) found that *small* girls are perceived as more dependent. Such responses have been characterized in terms of biologically prepared "affordances"; that is, humans show a predisposition to respond with approach behavior to the visual cues associated with immaturity. The pervasiveness of this effect is demonstrated by the fact that babyish facial qualities of *adults* elicit differential reactions from others; for example, they are judged to have more "childlike" traits (Zebrowitz & Montepare, 1992).

Particular attention has been given within the empirical literature to infant-directed speech (IDS), that is, to the specialized ways adults communicate to infants. Such patterns appear to be automatic, unlearned, and nonconscious in nature (Fernald, 1993; Papousek & Papousek, 1991). From an evolutionary perspective, IDS represents a species-typical parental strategy ("intuitive parenting") that contributes to infant survival (Papousek & Papousek, 1991). Consistent with this view, there is a high level of communality across cultures in the extent to which parents produce higher pitch and a wide pitch range (along with longer pauses and shorter utterances) in their interactions with infants (Fernald, Taeschner, Dunn, Papousek, et al., 1989), properties that in turn suit the capabilities and preferences of young infants. For example, infants show enhanced auditory sensitivity to higher-level frequencies (500–2,000 Hz region; Sinnott, Pisoni, & Aslin, 1983), and even at birth they show a preference for IDS (Cooper & Aslin, 1990). The universal nature of IDS provides support for the biologically prepared nature of such processes. The distinctive advantages of IDS for interactions with infants is revealed by the negative reactions to this form of speech when it is directed to other audiences; for example, "baby talk" directed to competent (older) adults serves to *disrupt* rather than enhance the listener's effectiveness (Caporael & Culbertson, 1986).

Controversy Concerning Evolutionary Approaches

Given the apparent utility of an evolutionary perspective, why has it been so controversial? One limitation rests in its post hoc nature. However, perhaps the test of usefulness lies in the extent to which an approach generates new questions or insights in accounting for phenomena that otherwise seem strange or irrational. We have also seen an encouraging movement toward the application of experimental methods in testing questions generated from the vantage point of evolutionary psychology, for example, the assessment of the extent to which certain processes are unusually accessible, mandatory, and automatic in response to certain social cues (e.g., Cosmides & Tooby, 1992). Additionally, our increased understanding of the biological

"hardware" of social interaction (e.g., specific areas of the brain involved in social perception) provides more tangible evidence of the ways we have evolved to solve problems of group life and to adaptively make use of the prolonged period of dependence of the young.

A second argument made against evolutionary approaches is that they are unnecessary. From this point of view, the adaptive processes that occur within the life course in the service of meeting proximal goals provide a sufficient explanation of socialization processes. A counterargument can be made that many commonly observed socialization processes often do *not* serve contemporary goals. So, for example, the derogation of outgroup members that becomes focal in middle childhood is not only harmful to individual victims, it may also divide groups in arbitrary and damaging ways. One need only think of the "colors" used to identify rival gangs—and the ritual acts of violence that are used to instantiate membership into a gang—to recognize the extent to which some processes that served distal goals are regularly maladaptive in contemporary social contexts. Evolutionary approaches (e.g., Tooby & Cosmides, 1990) that are mindful of the distinctions between adaptations in ancestral and current environments (focusing on the former) have clear advantages over earlier approaches that blurred the distinctions between proximal and distal adaptiveness (implying that what was adaptive in the past continued to be adaptive in the present).

Third, negative reactions to biological positions (as a whole) have often been based on the assumption that biological theories necessarily imply a view of human functioning as rigidly designed and lacking flexibility in the ways those designs may be implemented. Contemporary evolutionary psychology gives full attention to the ways different circumstances trigger different behavioral accommodations (Nisbett, 1990). It would indeed be a badly designed system that locked us into particular response patterns that limited our ways of coping with variations in environmental demands. The evidence we present here (reviewed later in this section) suggests that the range of adaptations that are available for accommodation to changing environments (e.g., ways of maintaining proximity within attachment relationships) is indeed extremely wide.

Biological Variations in Preparation for Socialization

Adults and children may also be thought of as varying in the extent to which they are biologically prepared for socialization. In particular, attention has been directed to biologically influenced variables that influence the extent to which and the ways in which partners to the socialization process react to interpersonal interaction.

Biologically Influenced Variations in Parents

Potential biological and genetic contributions to parenting are easily overlooked (DiLalla & Gottesman, 1991). Historically, little systematic attention has been directed to differences between adults in the extent to which they are biologically "prepared" to *provide* socialization. At the same time, socialization deficits have regularly been observed among parents who show certain types of temperament or affective patterns that are subject to genetic influence.

Particular attention has been directed to parental depression as a predisposing factor that influences the course of socialization. Recent research by Campbell, Cohn, and Meyers (1995) provided evidence concerning the significance of *chronic* depression (a pattern subject to genetic influence; e.g., Kendler et al., 1994) as a source of influence on maternal response to infants. Of those women who met diagnostic criteria for depression, those who were chronically depressed (six months or longer) were less positive to their infants during all types of interactions assessed (feeding, face-to-face, and toy play). Additionally, infants themselves were less positive during face-to-face interactions with chronically depressed mothers. Supporting the importance of chronic depression, Teti, Gelfand, Messinger, and Isabella (1995) found that preschool children who lacked coherent attachment strategies (having instead avoidant, ambivalent, or disorganized strategies) were more likely to have chronically depressed mothers than were children who demonstrated coherent (secure) strategies.

We have also seen emerging interest in genetically influenced differences between parents as risk factors for *coercive* family processes (DiLalla & Gottesman, 1991). Attention has been given to the potential utility of considering genetic influences on antisocial patterns (e.g., Brunner, Nelan, Breakefield, Ropers, & Van Oost, 1993; Gottesman & Goldsmith, 1994); antisocial behaviors in adults may act as risk factors for antisocial responses of children, either directly through genetic transmission or indirectly through the kinds of socializing environments they provide. There is also mounting evidence that physically abusive parents show an unusual level of reactivity to stress (a pattern that is subject to genetic influence; e.g., Rothbart & Ahadi, 1994). Wolfe (1985), in reviewing the literature on physical abuse, pointed out that a shared feature of abusive parents is a tendency to be hyperreactive to many

sources of stress (not simply caregiving stress); their responses to stress include not only heightened levels of hostility but also greater frequency of depressive symptoms or illness. This elevated level of reactivity has also been shown to be reflected in autonomic reactions that abusive parents manifest in response to relevant social cues. That is, abusive parents show elevations in defensive arousal when presented with social stimuli that have relevance for caretaking (e.g., videotapes or audiotapes of children or caregiving sequences; Frodi & Lamb, 1980; Wolfe, Fairbanks, Kelly, & Bradlyn, 1983). Of particular interest was the observation that such parents do not respond selectively to affective distinctions in social cues provided by children; for example, they show heart rate increases both in response to infant cries and infant smiles.

Biological Variations in Children: Significance for Socialization

Effect of Biological Variations in Children on Socializing Environments. The role of genetics as a perceived source of influence on the developing child has changed in recent years. We have seen many inroads on the view of genetics as producing simple main effects on child development. We are now more likely to think of the ways genetic variations come to influence both the modification and the selection of socializing environments across the life course (Belsky, 1993; Plomin & Neiderhiser, 1992). Plomin and his colleagues have demonstrated that family environmental influences on child behaviors and disorders are largely nonshared (Plomin, 1994); that is, children experience primarily individual environments within the home. These environmental variations in turn are influenced by genetic variations in the children themselves. Specifically, more than a quarter of the variance in a variety of home environment measures can be accounted for by genetic variations in children (Plomin, Reiss, Hetherington, & Howe, 1994). These very stable findings suggest that genetic differences between children serve as important sources of influence on socializing environments. As suggested by Plomin, these findings challenge the historical view of children (from behaviorism) as passive recipients of environmental effects.

The perceived role of genetic influences is not, however, without controversy. Scarr (1992) advanced a strong "child effects" position by proposing that children, as a function of their genetic endowment, *create their own experiences* from the environments they encounter. She argued that socialization practices have little influence on children's development once their environments reach some minimum "average expectable" or "good enough" level. Although critics took issue with a number of the points made by Scarr (Baumrind, 1993; Jackson, 1993), one criticism that is relevant to our discussion here concerns the relative contributions of children and parents to socialization outcomes.

There can be little question that children do indeed influence their own environments in important ways, but such impact is not uniform across parents. Parental variables also act as *moderators* of the extent to which and the ways in which children "create" their own socializing environments (e.g., Beckwith & Cohen, 1989; Crockenberg, 1981; Goldberg, Lojkasek, Gartner, & Corter, 1989). For example, low birthweight infants are at risk for a variety of adverse outcomes; however, as pointed out by Baumrind (1993), those negative outcomes are attenuated when such children are reared in optimal, responsive environments. Under ordinary circumstances, risk factors (e.g., low birthweight, nonoptimal socializing environments) are likely to be correlated. But at the same time, it is important to recognize the possible effects of altered environments. As suggested by Bronfenbrenner and Ceci (1994), the interactions between organism and environment have indeed been found to serve as powerful predictors of the child's later outcomes. Ultimately, the differences between Scarr and her critics rest less on a dispute as to whether children influence their environments as on the expected malleability of child responses as a function of *possible* socializing environments.

Child Temperament.   Concerns with "child effects" on socialization have focused heavily on child temperament variables, many of which have been found to be genetically influenced (Emde et al., 1992; Gottesman & Goldsmith, 1994). Research that has focused on temperament has suggested the possibility that children differ in their *receptivity to socialization processes* and in the extent of their receptivity to socialization at different points in development (Cairns, Gariepy, & Hood, 1990). Dienstbier (1984) was an early voice pointing out that children who experience little distress following misdeeds may be more likely to receive harsh responses from parents. More recently, Kochanska (1993) has suggested that children are more receptive to socialization and the development of conscience to the extent that they are *emotionally reactive to punishment* (i.e., they experience anxiety in response to actual or potential misdeeds), and to the extent that they engage in effective self-regulation.

Even in infancy, autonomic reactivity of children (in response to stressors) acts as a predictor of response to socialization (Kagan & Snidman, 1991; Rothbart & Derryberry, 1981). For example, newborns who showed high reactivity to heel stick procedures (e.g., more crying, short heart periods, high cortisol, and low vagal tone) showed lower scores on distress to limitations (a temperament measure) at 6 months of age (Gunnar, Porter, Wolf, Rigatuso, & Larson, 1995); this particular response pattern has been interpreted as reflecting anger. This relationship is consistent with the emerging view of strong reactivity to aversive stimuli as predictive of *adaptive* neurobehavioral organization in the newborn. Thus, infants who show high levels of reactivity in the first 2 months of life have been found to show lower levels of reactivity to the same stimuli at 6 months (possibly suggesting increasing regulation). Additionally, Gunnar et al. observed a rapid return of cardiac responses to baseline among those infants who showed other indications of "health," suggesting the importance of self-righting responses.

There has also been a continuing interest in children's self-regulatory ability (i.e., children's ability to inhibit or suppress undesired actions and perform desired actions). By age 2, children typically show a variety of negative emotions in response to actual or potential misdeeds (Hoffman, 1983), and within the third year, they attempt to take reparative actions in response to misdeeds (Cole, Barrett, & Zahn-Waxler, 1992). Children who are deficient in manifesting such responses are likely to be less receptive to socialization efforts of parents and to have a poorly developed conscience. In the same way, socialization efforts are less likely to succeed with children who have low self-regulatory skills. Children who fail to show usual gains in self-regulatory ability that emerge during the second year of life (Kopp, 1982) are less able to meet the socialization goals of parents—even if they show usual levels of emotional reactivity. At the other extreme, children who respond to socialization conflict with increases in stress (as reflected, for example, in increasing levels of cortisol production) have been found to show increasing levels of internalizing and anxiety disorders in the future (Granger, Weisz, McCracken, Ikeda, & Douglas, 1996).

Kochanska (1994) has directed empirical attention to variations in children's temperament and their receptivity to *particular* parental approaches to socialization. For example, she demonstrated that gentle maternal discipline in which there was a de-emphasis on power was a useful strategy with fearful, anxious children but not with nonfearful, nonanxious children. The most successful route to conscience development of "fearless" children, on the other hand, appears to be rooted in the quality of their early relationship with parents; that is, a warm, responsive relationship with parents acts to compensate for deficits associated with child fearlessness. Thus, it appears that variations in child temperament influence the means by which they may be most effectively socialized. In short, the effects of different socializing experiences are not absolute; instead, they reflect the "fit" between the socializing environment and the characteristics of the child.

Although the focus of genetic research has been on variations associated with childhood problems, it has also been recognized that some genetically influenced variations may also serve as protective factors against more negative socialization experiences. For example, temperamentally easy children are "protected" from the hostility that characterizes parents with certain types of mental disorders (Rutter, 1978).

Age-Related Changes in Children. Morton and Johnson (1991) have suggested that the infant enters the world with a sensitivity to faces; with maturing cortical development and experience, they learn to identify and respond selectively to faces of members of their own species. In addition, emerging control of the visual system lies at the heart of early preparation of the infant for social interaction. For example, infants can regulate their interaction with others by initiating eye contact or terminating it. Baron-Cohen (1994) has suggested that infants are biologically enabled to develop the capacity for joint attention. Specifically, he proposed that this capacity develops through an eye direction detection mechanism. That is, infants are not only attracted to the eyes of others in the service of establishing mutual engagement with each other, they also have the capacity to use the eye movements of others as a source of information about other events. By tracking the eye movements of others, children are able to "envision" their intended actions. Ultimately, this process allows a concept of mind, i.e., a concept that others have beliefs that may differ from one's own, and which act as the basis for their actions (Leslie, 1994; Premack & Woodruff, 1978). In the absence of this capacity (e.g., as is true for autistic children; Baron-Cohen, 1991), children's ability to negotiate within their social environment is severely impaired).

With the development of relevant perceptual and neural systems, capacities for shared involvement with the social world become even more apparent. Trevarthen (1988) has referred to such sensitivities as involving an innate capacity for intersubjectivity. In support of such notions, Adamson and Bakeman (1991) have documented the universally-observed progression in which infants shape their early social environments first through social alertness, then through interpersonal engagement, and finally through joint object involvement. Fogel (1994) suggested that "Development is the result of a dynamic co-regulation among the various components of the individual (from neural to behavioral) and the environment (from physical to social) such that neither individuals nor environments are defined fully in advance: Rather, the emergence of structure in both individuals and environments is the result of the process of their mutual regulation" (p. 7).

Attention has also been given to the normal hormonal changes that occur during pubescence—and the ways in which such changes may indirectly influence socialization. For example, higher levels of estradiol and androstenedione (two of the hormones involved in growth and sexual development during puberty) have been found to predict higher levels of aggression in girls—as reflected in their expressions of anger and defiance in interaction with parents (Inoff-Germain et al., 1988). Similar patterns have been found in pubescent boys. For example, higher levels of androstenedione in boys are related to greater acting-out behavior (Susman et al., 1987). Consistent with these findings, both boys and girls (between the ages of 9 and 14) who manifest early timing of puberty also have been found to show differences in social-emotional response patterns; specifically, such children are more likely to manifest psychopathology—combined with increased time in association with peers (Susman, Nottelmann, Cutler, & Chrousos, 1985). It should be pointed out that the observed effects of hormones on social behaviors were unaffected by statistical controls for age and pubertal stage; as a result, hormonal influences can be seen as independent sources of influences beyond those associated with *visible* changes associated with increased sexual maturity.

Other Biological Influences. Child variations that are significant for socialization also include biologically influenced factors beyond those that reflect temperament or maturation. Variations may be associated with a wide range of pathological prenatal, perinatal, or postnatal conditions and experiences. For example, children who have unusual or aversive communicative characteristics or stimulus properties are at risk for more negative socialization experiences. This grouping includes such features as abnormal cries (e.g., Frodi, 1981; Zeskind & Shingler, 1991), high irritability or fuss/cry behavior (e.g., Bates, 1987; Belsky, Rovine, & Taylor, 1984), or communication disorders (e.g., DeLissovoy, 1979; Sigel, Stinson, & Flaugher, 1993). Particular attention has been given to parental reactions to "at risk" infants (e.g., preterm) with unusual cry properties. Children with these vocal characteristics not only elicit negative reactions from adults, they also elicit different autonomic responses. For example, Bryan and Newman (1988) found that the predominant response of women (mothers and nonmothers) to the cries of high-risk infants was heart rate acceleration (consistent with mobilization for action), whereas the predominant response to cries of low-risk infants was heart rate deceleration (consistent with attentional orienting).

Children may also manifest stimulus features that foster positive socializing environments or that buffer against negative environments. For example, there is an extensive literature showing the more positive reactions of adults (including parents) to physically attractive than to unattractive children and infants (e.g., Langlois, Ritter, Casey, & Sawin, 1995). Additionally, physically attractive girls are not subject to the explosive reactive style that is common among fathers experiencing stress (Elder et al., 1985), showing the potential buffering effects of the child's appearance.

A new area of research is emerging in which we are discovering that the child's physical development is influenced by extreme experiences in socializing environments. For example, increasing attention has been given to the effects of unusually stressful early experiences on the developmental course of sexual maturation. Belsky, Steinberg, and Draper (1991) have proposed an evolutionary account of *divergent* developmental pathways in response to environmental stress. Following up on evidence for a relationship between childhood stress (e.g., father absence), early menarche (Moffitt, Caspi, & Belsky, 1990), and precocial sexual activity (e.g., Draper & Harpending, 1982), they suggested that this pattern might be thought of as making sense as a biological adaptation. They went on to propose that this association may be mediated at both psychological and physiological levels. Belsky et al. (1991) state, "Fundamentally, evolution has primed humans to learn particular lessons during the first 5–7 years of life that will shape their subsequent pair-bonding and child-rearing behavior" (p. 648). In optimal environments, humans show a prolonged period of dependence and delayed sexual maturation and focus their efforts on establishing enduring pair bonds (a "quality" pattern of mating and rearing that is consistent with expectations of relationship security). But in nonoptimal environments, children acquire information concerning the tenuous predictability of interpersonal support, an experience that leads to an acceleration of sexual maturation and short-term pair bonds (a "quantity" pattern of mating and rearing that may be optimal in risky environments). Belsky et al. also proposed that the relationship between early stress and timing of puberty is mediated by neuroendocrine responses; that is, stress has a direct effect on somatic development.

Maccoby (1991), in criticizing this position, offered a number of counterarguments. For example, she suggested that a quantity reproductive strategy would act against the reproductive interests of young women who cannot count on secure relationships. Additionally, she cited animal evidence suggesting the *higher* involvement of males in the feeding and protection of the young in environments or in time periods in which resources are scarce.

At the same time, support for the effects of early childhood stress on the functioning of the neurohormonal system has been increasing. Evidence is appearing for a relationship between stressors such as sexual abuse and children's neurohormonal response. An analogy has been drawn between the neurohormonal responses of children to stress and the neurohormonal responses found for adults experiencing posttraumatic stress disorder (DeBellis, Lefter, Trickett, & Putnam, 1994; Perry, 1994).

Biological Evidence for Variations across Socialization Domains

Finally, we explore the evidence that socialization processes may be parsed into different social domains on the basis of biological influences. In taking a biological perspective, we consider the ways we may be preferentially and distinctively designed for receptivity to proximity maintenance with specific others in the presence of distress, for use and recognition of signals for power or dominance, for identifying the lines that divide "us" and "them" in group life, and for the reciprocal obligations that are involved within communal life.

Interactions within different types of social arrangements have evolved to solve very different kinds of problems. Regulatory systems that evolved to handle different aspects of social life emerged at different points in our phylogenetic history. For example, dominance signals and power hierarchies appeared among social vertebrates in response to competition for scarce resources, but reciprocal exchange processes only emerged among mammals and became highly developed among primates. Identity processes are apparent even among social insects, but attachment processes only appeared among mammals or birds in which there was a period of dependence of the young.

Although notions of domain specificity or modularity need not imply an evolutionary base, it is reasonable to explore the possibility that the often observed differences in socialization in different contexts (e.g., attachment-based relationships, compliance-oriented socialization, negotiated relationship between peers, etc.) may have evolved as a function of the distal advantages they served. A. Fiske (1992) proposed a domain-specific view of social relationships in which he suggested a developmental progression in the emergence of different types of relationships. Although his focus was on the cognitive organization of such relationship categories (and we discuss his cognitive formulations later in the chapter), he also proposed that such categories have an evolutionary base. From a neuroscience perspective, Panksepp (Panksepp et al., 1997) has proposed that the mammalian brain, although revealing some shared neurochemical influences on social behavior, also includes special-purpose sociomotivational systems that involve distinct brain circuits. From an evolutionary standpoint, MacDonald (1992) proposed a discrete systems theory of socialization. In discussing different socialization systems, he focused on the distinctiveness of attachment relationships and "affectional relationships." He suggested that the former are regulated by fear (in the absence of the attachment object), whereas the latter are regulated by positive feelings of warmth and affection. Attachment systems are ubiquitous among mammals but affectional ties are relatively rare. Additionally, even when affectional ties are present, the processes involved are independent of those shown within attachment relationships. MacDonald also suggested that attachment relationships have a general utility in that they provide security in the face of threat, whereas affectional ties form the basis for *high-quality* investment in the young over a prolonged period of dependency (MacDonald focuses on the significance of such ties for paternal investment). Both of these processes have traditionally been viewed as components of *secure* attachment among humans (Ainsworth, Bell, & Stayton, 1971), but it is important to keep in mind that they are potentially separable components of early relationships. We focus here on security/safety when discussing attachment, and

on affection/positive responsiveness when discussing the reciprocity domain.

The socialization domains proposed earlier are more extensive than those proposed by MacDonald and are more specifically developmental than those proposed by A. Fiske. In support of the proposed model, we next consider the evidence for biologically influenced sensitivities and responses that are selectively associated with the proposed domains.

Attachment Domain. Within developmental psychology, attachment—possibly more than any other type of relationship—has been seen as involving distinctive perceptual sensitivities and regulatory processes. Even at birth, the human infant is simultaneously prepared to (a) be responsive to social cues that facilitate the establishment of the identity of others, and (b) produce signals that allow others to identify him or her as unique individuals. For example, neonates, as a function of their prenatal sensitivity to voices, respond differentially (and preferentially) to the voice of their own mother (DeCasper & Spence, 1991). The cry of the infant, in turn, is so unique that it allows for easy parental identification of individual children (Gustafson, Green, & Cleland, 1994). In reciprocal fashion, mothers are highly responsive to the distress vocalizations of their own offspring, as well as to ongoing and recently-occurring sources of environmental threat or danger to the infant (Fairbanks, 1996).

Within the psychobiology literature, there is evidence that distress responses associated with the attachment domain are mediated by the brain opioid system (Panksepp, Normansell, Herman, Bishop, & Crepeau, 1988). In support of this notion, pharmacological research (with infrahuman primates) has demonstrated that the introduction of the opioid antagonist naloxone leads to an increase in the rate of distress vocalizations of separated infants, whereas the introduction of the opioid agonist morphine leads to decreased vocalizations (Wiener, Coe, & Levine, 1988). Additionally, there is evidence that separation-induced changes in pituitary-adrenal hormones are modulated by opioid agonists and antagonists (Kalin, Shelton, & Barksdale, 1988). Reciprocally, maternal retrieval of the young (in rats and dogs) and maternal distress in response to separation from the young are reduced by the introduction of morphine.

Among human infants, separation responses are associated with increases in activation of the hypothalamic-pituitary-adrenocortical (HPA) axis. For example, infants

(9–11 months) separated from their mothers for 30 minutes show increases in salivary cortisol levels, a distress response reflecting activation of the HPA axis (Larson, Gunnar, & Hertsgaard, 1991). Additionally, the children in the separation condition who showed the highest levels of behavioral distress also showed the highest levels of cortisol. Using animal models, Hofer (1987) has suggested that mothers regulate the behavioral and physiological responses of attached infants through specific thermal, olfactory, and tactile cues. There is also an emerging literature suggesting that the physical proximity of a parent during the infant's sleep states serves an adaptive regulatory function. McKenna and his colleagues (McKenna, 1990; McKenna & Mosko, 1990) demonstrated that parental breathing patterns during co-sleeping act to regulate the breathing patterns of young infants. This coregulatory process leads to shorter sleeping bouts and easier arousal of infants, which may in turn correct for breathing control errors associated with sudden infant death syndrome.

Across species, there is enormous variation in the differential sensitivity of males versus females to the stimulus cues provided by the young. Among humans, we see a mixed picture. Although mothers and fathers share their involvement with children, the mother's role is typically more focused on caretaking, and the father's role is more focused on play (Parke, 1995), a pattern that appears even when fathers assume a role as primary caregiver (Lamb et al., 1982). Although fathers and mothers appear to be equally proficient in "reading" infant distress signals (Parke, 1995), there are some indications that mothers are more responsive to infant signals (Power, 1985). Additionally, males show a different pattern of autonomic response to infant cries (heart rate deceleration) than do females (heart rate acceleration; Power, Hildebrandt, & Fitzgerald, 1982). The response of males is more consistent with an orienting response (consistent with alertness for possible sources of danger), and the response of females is more consistent with mobilization for action (consistent with proximity seeking; Lin, 1997).

Social Identity Domain. Increasing attention is being given to socialization that involves influence processes between group members with a shared social identity (Harris, 1995). The earliest capabilities that are needed for the activation of the social identity domain involve social categorization processes. One of the most basic categories is the establishment of others as familiar or unfamiliar, a process suggested by Meltzoff and Moore (1992) to be assisted by precocial imitation processes. At birth, infants show a capacity for social imitation (e.g., imitating the exaggerated facial expressions of others). Meltzoff and Moore (1994) have gone on to demonstrate that infants also show imitative *memory,* that is, imitating a response pattern previously seen for a particular person. They suggest that such processes are part of an *identification* process; that is, the identity of another person (as a familiar or unfamiliar other) is established by repeating a facial action previously shown by that individual. This process does not seem to be part of the turn-taking system involved in reciprocal interactions, in that imitation does not form part of a continuous sequence of action (e.g., imitations are made of static facial patterns as well as changing patterns).

The perceptual capability for response to grouping variables appears to emerge in infancy. Premack and Premack (1994, 1995) propose that awareness of the properties of groups emerges as a "primitive" during late infancy. As young as 10 months of age (Sugarman, 1983), the infant has a tendency to bring physically similar objects together. The Premacks note that infants expect physically similar objects to form groups and physically dissimilar objects not to form groups. But if infants are shown that physically dissimilar objects do indeed cohere and move with each other, they are subsequently interpreted as a group. The Premacks also argue that infants expect group members to be reciprocal and to act alike: repeated actions of one group member are expected for other group members. Knowledge of the properties of outgroups is also expected to be a part of this primitive knowledge structure (prerogatives extended to members and withdrawn from nonmembers). Thus, the awareness of intragroup and intergroup properties may be present as a basic perceptual capacity.

Children are able (a) to identify perceptual differences between social categories (gender, age, etc.) in early infancy (Fagan & Singer, 1979; Leinbach & Fagot, 1993), (b) to make ingroup/outgroup comparisons as young as 3 (Yee & Brown, 1992), and (c) to show ingroup bias as young as 5 (Yee & Brown, 1992). However, ingroup/outgroup distinctions are not fully instantiated until middle childhood. It is not until this age that ingroup preference is also associated with active segregation and outgroup derogation processes. By middle childhood, we see pronounced voluntary self-segregation by gender. Gender segregation (and outgroup derogation based upon gender) is universally observed and is strikingly resistant to change efforts (Sroufe, Bennett, Englund, Urban, & Shulman, 1993).

Children do not segregate themselves in this way because of adult efforts; instead, they can *only* be integrated by very active adult intervention (Thorne & Luria, 1986).

The Premacks (1995) suggest that males are more sensitive than girls to group-based distinctions. Certainly, we know that, across cultures, boys are more likely to show a preference for group relationships than are girls (Thorne & Luria, 1986). Although the preponderance of observations of such distinctions have been concerned with middle childhood, male preferences for group relationships emerge among children as young as 3 and 4 years of age (Benenson, 1993).

Hierarchical Domain. In general, social animals show a high sensitivity to the physical or social power of conspecifics. It appears that we may be biologically prepared for making very fast decisions with respect to the relative power of others. It has been suggested that the quickest decisions that are made in forming snap judgments of others involve assessments of their social extroversion or power (Fisek & Ofshe, 1970; Levesque & Kenny, 1993). Young primates have been found to be sensitive to cues to social power even before they are sensitive to physical cues with strong biological significance, for example, cues to the presence of a predator (e.g., Cheney & Seyfarth, 1985).

There is evidence for the coevolution of matched social cues and sensitivities both in infants and socializers with respect to the hierarchical domain. Fernald and her colleagues (e.g., Fernald et al., 1989) have demonstrated that, across cultures, caregivers share common vocal properties in communicating messages of power or control to infants—not through *what* they say but *how* they say it (prohibition messages such as a sharply voiced "No!"). That is, initial preparation for parental control involves the association of particular acoustical properties (e.g., short, loud, staccato speech) with verbal prohibitions. These sounds, in turn, reliably elicit inhibitory responses from infants (Fernald et al.), even when produced in languages that are unfamiliar to the child. Equivalent processes have been found across cultural groupings (German, Italian, and Japanese), supporting the notion of a universally adaptive signaling system.

No account of socialization within the hierarchical domain would be complete without some consideration of gender differences. Dominance or power struggles are more characteristic of male than female interactions, beginning in early childhood (Maccoby, 1990). Although any notion of biological contributions to gender differences is subject to controversy, the evidence with respect to biological influences on intermale aggression struggles is (arguably) substantial (Maccoby, 1980). Higher androgen levels in early adolescent children (boys or girls) have been found to predict aggressiveness (Susman et al., 1987); however, the presence of androgens has greater significance for male aggression because of the higher concentration levels involved. Although increased levels of testosterone can be a *consequence* of successful aggression (winners showing increasing levels and losers showing decreasing levels; e.g., Gladhue, Boechler, & McCaul, 1989; Mazur & Lamb, 1980), chronic testosterone also acts as a predictor of aggression among young males (e.g., Archer, 1990). To some extent, then, the relatively high focus on dominance and power management among fathers and sons (e.g., Power & Shanks, 1989; Snow, Jacklin, & Maccoby, 1983) may be influenced by biological factors.

Reciprocity Domain. Reciprocal relationships focus on the exchange of matched outcomes. In early infancy, children show abilities that are consistent with the establishment of reciprocal engagement with others of the same species. At the earliest stages (simple turn-taking), this involves a simple quid pro quo exchange of matched actions or affect: in infancy, for example, the reciprocal processes involved in the exchange of smiles. Affectional or playful exchanges may be thought of as beginning with the establishment of interpersonal engagement—usually through reciprocal gaze—followed by a turn-taking exchange of positive events such as vocalizations, touches, sounds, or laughter. It has been suggested that social reciprocity is deeply rooted in primate phylogeny (e.g., Silk, 1992), and serves to organize group life for unrelated as well as related community members.

In arguing for reciprocity processes as distinct from proximity-maintenance processes, we should point out that interactions between infants and caregivers set the stage for many types of relationships, not just proximity-seeking relationships (a point made by Bretherton, 1980). As suggested by Belsky and Cassidy (in press), "It would . . . be a mistake to label as an attachment behavior the child's approach to mother in order to engage in peekaboo. . . . In addition to serving as attachment figure, the mother may serve also as playmate, teacher, or disciplinarian" (p. 8). Here we focus on the distinction between the parent as a secure source of safety (security aspect of attachment domain) as opposed to a positively responsive interaction partner (reciprocity domain). Interaction within the reciprocity domain is less likely to have the preferential quality of the basic attachment domain. Children show a wide range of choices in selecting a partner for play or "conversation" but show a high degree of selectivity in choosing an individual to provide safety (Tracy, Lamb, & Ainsworth, 1976). It appears that mutual responsiveness in the service of proximity maintenance is functionally separable from mutual responsiveness in the service of other goals (e.g., exchange of positive affect, play, cooperation).

Reciprocal exchange processes may be thought of in terms of implicit social contracts. The provision of benefits to others in an implicit contractual or reciprocal arrangement appears to extend beyond relationships with kin (e.g., Hoffman, 1981). Therefore, it is important to understand how such interactions are regulated in a manner that provides mutual benefits among unrelated individuals. In a series of empirical investigations, Cosmides and Tooby (1992) tested the hypothesis that the human mind is designed to keep track of the reciprocal provision of benefits within social interactions. They argued that humans are extremely sensitive to violations of social contracts. In other words, a mechanism is present for detecting those who "cheat" on reciprocal obligations. The mind may be thought of as "prepared" to acquire social exchange information in the same way that it is "prepared" to acquire language. In testing this hypothesis, Cosmides and Tooby tested the improved ability of individuals to solve logical problems (Wason task) when these are framed as social exchange contracts. In confirmation of their predictions, they demonstrated that research participants easily solve problems framed as social exchange processes but have difficulty with identical problems constructed in an identical fashion logically but lacking the exchange implications. Tooby and Cosmides (1996) have suggested mechanisms whereby reciprocity processes become extended into long-term friendships; they suggest that there is a reciprocal process of mutual "investment" between individuals who provide cues that they have the capability and willingness to provide uniquely beneficial help to each other if needed in the future.

There is evidence that even young children engage in reciprocal interactions that are consistent with a notion of social contracts. For example, toddlers (aged 2.5–3 years) have been found to demonstrate reciprocal exchange; initially toy-deprived children with whom another child shared toys were subsequently more willing to share toys with that child (Levitt, Weber, Clark, & McDonnell, 1985). The more limited exchanges of early childhood are replaced with more stable friendships based upon durable patterns of reciprocity in middle childhood, and deepened to include more intimacy during adolescence (Newcomb & Bagwell, 1995).

Flexibility in the Instantiation of Socialization Domains. Although biological influences on processes within socialization domains provide initial sensitivities and regulatory processes, they also allow for flexibility in means of implementation. As one illustration, we may think in terms of the flexibility shown by children in their ability to cope with different attachment environments. Indeed, Main (1990) has suggested that infants have evolved with the capacity to respond flexibly to variations in their caregiving environments. She proposed that infants employ "conditional behavioral strategies" that enhance the chances of securing and maintaining proximity with caregivers. Such strategies appear to be "automatic" and do not require conscious effort. Cassidy (1994), operating from this framework, proposed that children employ different but adaptive emotion-regulation strategies as ways of maintaining a relationship with caregivers. Thus, the child who has experienced a *rejecting* mother may minimize his or her own expression of negative affect to prevent future rejection. Alternatively, a child who has experienced an *overinvolved* mother may similarly reduce contact by a strategy of emotional withdrawal. On the other hand, a child who has experienced an *unavailable* mother may show relatively high levels of negative affect to increase the chances of getting her attention (see Thompson, Ch. 2, this Volume).

There is also a wide range of options in the ways proximity may be maintained within attachment relationships. In the United States, high levels of visual engagement are maintained between mothers and infants. But in other cultural settings (e.g., the Gusii of Kenya), there are social "rules" that act against protacted gaze (LeVine, 1990; LeVine & LeVine, 1988; Tronick, 1989). At the same time, it is often common in such groups for mothers to hold their infants more than do Western mothers. Even among infants reared in Western cultures, infants respond to maternal touch as compensatory for absence of facial engagement (e.g., Stack & Muir, 1992). Bornstein et al. (1992) observed that maximum differences in mother-infant behavior across cultures (New York, Paris, and Tokyo) occurred in maternal responses to infant looking and in the extent to which mothers spoke to or stimulated their infants. In similar fashion, continuous care and contact between the child and *one* primary caregiver—often advocated as a model for secure attachment (Bowlby, 1980)—represents a historical and cultural anomaly in caregiving arrangements (Lamb & Sternberg, 1992; Tronick, Morelli, & Ivey, 1992). The highly responsive, face-to-face (and exclusive) mother-child interaction advocated in Western culture may indeed be quite uncommon in other cultures, including cultures in which children grow up "to be healthy, sane, and successful" (Blurton-Jones, 1993, p. 310).

At a more general level, human socialization processes allow for a great deal of flexibility as a function of our capability for imagining alternative realities in planning future actions. As a metaphor, one may think in terms of the design of complex versus simple human-machine systems. Simple systems are often designed to respond in fixed ways to prespecified inputs; such systems are highly efficient for the management of routine operations or for the management of events that would excessively tax a human operator. More complex systems include these automated components, but they also include an "override" feature in which an operator may flexibly introduce a wide range of responses. Sperber (1994), arguing for the domain-specific nature of the mind, has suggested that flexibility in the cognitive-perceptual functioning of humans occurs as a function of the *interconnected* nature of cognitive domains. The same process may be true for social domains. In humans, the capability to envision alternative perspectives or future options across interconnected *social* domains provides the flexibility to consider a wide variety of response possibilities.

Methodological Issues within a Biological Approach

As socialization researchers increasingly explore the contributions of biological variables, new methodologies have appeared within the literature. We now see regular references to psychophysiological measures, hormonal assays, and more. Unsurprisingly, we also see increases in the use of a team approach in conducting this type of research (e.g., combining the theoretical interests of developmentalists with the technical expertise of neuroscientists). Whether questions address such issues as the physiological consequences of stressful caregiving experiences, genetic differences in children that lead to a heightened level of autonomic reactivity to stress, or hormonal changes in puberty that have consequences for socializing relationships, the methods employed involve a high level of technology and specific expertise. Additionally, the relevant fields

of developmental psychophysiology, developmental neuroscience, and developmental behavioral genetics have been relatively isolated as specialty areas rather than mainstream concerns within the field as a whole. As knowledge and training are expanded on these topics, biological approaches will not only become more available to researchers, they may also be more comprehensible to and better accepted by developmentalists.

One of the better-developed methodological approaches (with origins in biological theory) involves the analysis of (nonverbal) communication between parents and children. In particular, a great deal of attention has been given to the communication signals shown in interactions between parents and infants. Well-developed observational systems for coding infant facial expressions (e.g., the maximally discriminative facial movement coding system [MAX], Izard, Huebner, Risser, & Dougherty, 1980; and Baby Facial Action Coding System [FACS], Oster, Hegley, & Nagel, 1992) have become easily accessible to researchers interested in coding early expressive behavior as a source of influence on socialization and as a consequence of differential patterns of parenting. Additionally, the methods used for coding infant vocal signals (or parental voice properties) have been facilitated by increasingly accessible signal-processing technology. Using acoustical analysis, researchers have explored a number of important questions with respect to infant cries, for example, regularities in parental social responses to normal infant cries (Gustafson & Deconti, 1990); differential parental responses to normal versus abnormal cry patterns (e.g., Lester et al., 1992); and differences between parents in their affective and psychophysiological responses to abnormal cry patterns (e.g., Crowe & Zeskind, 1992). Strengthening the inferences that may be drawn from this literature, experimental methods have also been introduced (experimental variations in the temporal properties of cries) to verify the nature of cry features that elicit more negative perceiver-response patterns (Zeskind, Klein, & Marshall, 1992).

Developmentalists interested in evolutionary theory have increasingly extended an earlier focus on possible origins of currently observed processes to include the direct assessment of natural social competencies and preferences. Such approaches have focused on early competencies and preferences that originally appear without experience and that often show a high degree of universality in their manifestation. The extensive cross-cultural work of Fernald and her colleagues (described earlier) on the manifestations of infant-directed speech spoken in the child's native language versus three unfamiliar languages (e.g., Fernald & Morikawa, 1993) is a good case in point. This approach affords the generalizability that follows from the use of cross-cultural research with the inferential capabilities that follow from the use of experimental methodology. When combined with detailed acoustical analysis of the spontaneous vocal productions of mothers across cultures (yielding shared features in the communication of meanings), a strong test is made of coevolutionary explanations of early communication patterns.

Utility of Biological Perspectives

In reviewing the literature on biological perspectives on socialization, we have suggested that socialization involves generalized preparation for social life, combined with specialized preparation for socialization within distinctive social domains. We have also pointed out variations in preparation of socialization as a function of genetic factors or experiential factors that have a physiological impact. The utility of biological approaches comes from the window they provide on basic "design" features in the ways we are set up for socialization. They suggest the distinctive regulatory processes that govern socialization within different domains, thus accounting for the limitations consistently found in providing any general-purpose explanation for socialization processes. Just as our knowledge about perception is facilitated by an understanding of our differential sensitivities to physical stimuli and by an understanding of the regulatory processes that maintain effective visual engagement with the physical environment, our knowledge about socialization is facilitated by an understanding of the differential sensitivities to social stimuli and by an understanding of the regulatory processes that serve to maintain effective engagement with the social world.

An awareness of biological influences on social processes allows us insight into why some socialization processes are more easily implemented than others. As an analogy, think of the relative ease with which children learn spoken language (for which we appear to be biologically prepared) and the relative difficulty with which children learn written language (for which we do not appear to be biologically prepared). In similar fashion, children are highly responsive to certain types of socialization (e.g., learning group "rules," learning to manage reciprocal relationships) and relatively resistant to other socialization efforts (e.g., nighttime separation from parents in infancy, gender integration in middle childhood). As relevant knowledge becomes available from social neuroscience and psychoneuroendocrinology, new insights will be available with respect to the ways are prepared for social processes in general and socialization processes in particular.

The integrated nature of biological approaches with the perspectives that follow is suggested by a comment from Bandura (1989): "Genetic factors and neural systems affect behavioral potentialities and place constraints on capabilities. Both experiential and physiological factors interact, often in intricate ways, to determine behavior. Even in behavioral patterns that are formed almost entirely through experience, rudimentary elements are present as part of the natural endowment. . . . [A]ction patterns regarded as instinctual, because they draw heavily on inborn elements, require appropriate experience to be developed. Sensory systems and brain structures are alterable by environmental influences. . . . [D]ichotomous thinking, which separates activities neatly into innate and acquired categories, is seriously inaccurate" (p. 52).

COGNITIVE PERSPECTIVES ON SOCIALIZATION

In the previous section, we focused on the ways we may be biologically prepared or "designed" for socialization, and on the ways these predispositions help account for both similarities and variations in the way that socialization interactions unfold across the life course. Socialization interactions are organized also by the way experiences are represented at a cognitive level: representations that provide one source of malleability for biologically based predispositions and that in themselves are a further source of similarity and variation in socialization interactions and their effects.

As suggested earlier, increasing attention has been given to the role of cognition as an organizer of socialization processes. Instead of directing exclusive attention to ultimate "input" variables (parental practices) and "output" variables (child internalization and compliance), we now ask about the mediating and moderating processes (cognitive and affective) that operate within such systems. At first glance, this might seem like a return to an earlier period in which we asked parents to tell us about their views of caregiving and about their caregiving practices—an approach that yielded little reliable information about what parents actually *did* (S. Miller, 1988). However, as we reintroduce a concern with cognitions, we offer reformulations that borrow contemporary concepts from social cognition—framed within a developmental perspective.

In this section, we begin by considering the changing ways cognitive processes are included in our understanding of socialization. To what extent do relevant cognitions act as deliberate, reflective processes that guide socialization decisions or as fast-acting processes that play out their effects in a relatively automatic fashion? What is the nature of the relationship between cognition and affect within socializing relationships? How do cognitions facilitate transitions to autonomous self-regulation? We then move on to consider variability in the content of socializing cognitions, that is, the differences in the ways socializing processes are represented cognitively. We consider the origins of such differences in the unique history of individuals, in culturally diverse beliefs about socialization, and in universally shared ways of thinking about different socialization domains.

Cognitions: How Do They Operate within Socializing Interactions?

Controlled versus Automatic Cognitive Processes

When parents are asked, in interviews or on questionnaires, to give their views about parenting or development, the opportunity usually exists for some relatively slow, reflective appraisal of events. During actual interactions, however, that kind of opportunity is not likely to occur. During actual interactions, parents respond at the same time they are engaged in other tasks. The fast response given to a child's attention bids while a parent is simultaneously caring for another child, watching TV, fixing a meal, and so on, cannot easily be compared to a slow, considered response to questions about caregiving practices or beliefs about children.

To cover both types of situations, we would do well to borrow from the cognitive literature, where a distinction has been made between "controlled" processes (effortful, controllable, slow, and making substantial use of attentional resources) and "automatic" processes (effortless, uncontrollable, fast, and making low use of attentional resources; Anderson, 1983; Johnson & Hasher, 1987; Shiffrin & Schneider, 1977). Epstein (1994) has used the terms *rational* versus *experiential* to capture this distinction. A parent responding to an *ongoing* caregiving interaction is very likely to rely on ways of thinking that can be accessed quickly and effortlessly. These ways of thinking are sometimes close to the surface because of the priming effects of a recent event. They are also often highly accessible because they have been overlearned; such overlearned structures have been described as chronically accessible

schemas (Bargh, 1994), social representations (Moscovici, 1981), social scripts (Read, 1987), and narratives (Bruner, 1992). They act to influence what we attend to in the social environment (e.g., Erdelyi, 1974), what kinds of emotions or motives we experience in response to particular types of social events (Bargh & Gollwitzer, 1994; Fiske & Pavelchak, 1986), and what types of thoughts and response tendencies come to mind. When confronted with an attention-demanding event, these overlearned knowledge structures can be easily accessed to provide an explanation or guide to action, a "front-end" step that is consistent with Lazarus's (1991) notion of primary appraisal.

The notion of relationship schemas as easily accessed is consistent with the fast preappraisal processes suggested by others as operating within relationships (e.g., Fletcher & Fincham, 1991). Bugental and her colleagues (Bugental, Lyon, Krantz, & Cortez, 1997), employing a construct of "caregiving schemas," have demonstrated that parents make schema-consistent judgments in a fast, effortless manner; that is, they make schema-consistent judgments just as quickly when they are concurrently engaged in a cognitively demanding task as when they are not. In the same way, children may respond to parents at an automatic level. For example, Patterson (1995) suggested that children's antisocial response patterns within coercive caregiving exchanges may reflect "automatic" or "schematic" routines that are played out without reflective thought. Supporting this notion, Bargh, Chen, and Burrows (1996) have observed that social knowledge and structures, when primed, automatically trigger construct-consistent behavioral routines.

Inclusion of a role for automatic processes does *not* preclude a role for slower, more reflective processes within socializing interactions. Within the stress and coping literature (Lazarus, 1991), it has been suggested that fast primary appraisal processes are followed by slower appraisals of the implications of significant events and the possible ways of coping with them. Epstein (1994) described such processes as "rational," noting that personal constructions in the rational system have often been referred to as "beliefs," whereas those in the experiential system have been referred to as "schemata." The majority of research on parental cognitions has indeed focused on beliefs, and it is only recently that we see an emergent interest in schemata.

Within approaches that focus on parents and children as rational processors, individuals are seen as responding to socializing events with a search for meaning, combined with response selection or goal setting. The search may include explanatory analyses, for example, "Why did Johnny just ignore me?", as well as coping appraisals, for example, "Can I control this situation?" and "Is anybody watching?" Such processes have been clearly demonstrated in the work of Holden (1988). In this program of research, Holden has called attention to the fact that parents respond to moment-by-moment cues in making their behavioral decisions; that is, immediate cues present in the caregiving environment may at times act as a greater source of influence than long-standing parental beliefs. Parents also respond to the probable success of different strategies with different children at different times and in different circumstances. So, for example, they are more likely to physically punish a child at home than in a public setting. They are also more likely to select physical punishment as a response strategy with younger children, a decision that may be thought of as reflecting an appraisal of situational realities (e.g., Wauchope & Straus, 1989).

Continuous-Flow Influences among Cognition, Attention, and Affect

A traditional view of information processing brought a linear model to our understanding of socializing interactions. The processing of information was conceptualized as an ordered series of steps that included encoding and representation processes, response-search and decision processes, and response-enactment processes (Dodge, 1986). Such approaches were limited on two bases: first, they were constrained by their assumption of linearity in information processing; second, they were constrained by the absence of a specific role for emotions. Such constraints were, however, consistent with prevailing beliefs about the inappropriateness of including a role for emotion within information-processing systems. For example, Siegler in 1983 observed, "The information-processing approach will not prove very helpful in studying social, emotional, and personality development. . . . People's feelings of love, hate, anger, fear and joy are perhaps the ways in which they differ most from computers. No doubt, all of these emotions involve the manipulation of symbols, but considerably more also is involved. It is difficult to capture this 'considerably more' within the information-processing framework" (p. 201).

Although this outlook might have proved accurate if we had retained an exclusive focus on cognitive parameters, researchers concerned with socialization (and other social interactions) have increasingly explored the ways emotions play a part other than as a nuisance variable or source of interference with cognition. Conceptualized within this framework, emotions involve "processes of establishing, maintaining, or disrupting the relation between the organism and the environment on matters of significance to the person" (Campos et al., 1989, p. 394). Changes in the perceived role of emotion brought with them changes in the conceptualizations of information-processing systems. Increasing attention has been directed to the role of emotion as a regulatory factor within information-processing. As noted by Hoffman (1986), "Affect may initiate, accelerate or terminate information-processing; it may determine which sector of the environment is processed and which processing modes operate; it may organize recall and influence category accessibility; it may contribute to the formation of emotionally charged schemata and categories; it may provide inputs for social cognition; and it may influence decision-making" (p. 260).

Consistent with these general changes, Crick and Dodge (1994) amended Dodge's earlier model to reflect a continuous process in the processing of information within relationships. Just as interpersonal processes have increasingly been conceptualized as involving corrections, adjustments, and accommodations as the interaction proceeds, intrapersonal events have come to be represented as involving continuously correcting processes. That is, emotional states influence what is perceived and how it is processed, and the interpretations made of ongoing events subsequently influence emotional reactions and perceptual biases. Affect and cognition are appropriately conceptualized as interwoven processes. For example, cognitions may be thought of as knowledge structures that are affectively tagged on the basis of associations involved in their initial creation (Fiske & Pavelchak, 1986). From this standpoint, parental beliefs or ways of thinking about their own relationships with children (and child beliefs or ways of thinking about their own relationships with parents) are integrally tied to associated affective processes. So, for example, in a challenging caregiving encounter, participants may not only bring to mind their overlearned ways of interpreting such events, they also may simultaneously experience the emotion that is associated with that interpretation. We now turn to consideration of the various ways affect is both influenced and acts as a source of influence within socializing interactions.

Affect and Attentional Focus. As an early step in socializing interactions, participants may be thought of as deploying attention to ongoing events. Indeed, ongoing events that have strong affective implications (e.g., a child's distress cry) may trigger attention automatically (e.g., Christianson, 1992). Such affect-eliciting events serve to disrupt other ongoing processes due to the demands they place on attentional resources (e.g., Ellis & Ashbrook, 1989). As a result, the individual is likely to show a narrowing of attention (Easterbrook, 1959) along with disruptions in cognitive processing on complex tasks (Tversky & Kahneman, 1973). For example, the parent's narrowed attention to the needs of an injured child may limit the ability to look up the phone number of a doctor. Reciprocally, this process is also important for the child's ability to process information during socializing encounters. For example, parental disciplinary tactics that generate excess levels of affect in the child may limit the child's understanding of the message (Hoffman, 1983). Thus, a child who is being yelled at will focus his or her attention on the frightening parent and may direct little attention to the semantic content of the parent's spoken words. The event will subsequently be recalled as an isolated memory and is unlikely to be integrated into semantic memory (Hoffman, 1983). Additionally, the child who is being yelled at may engage in emotion-regulation strategies (e.g., looking down, "tuning out") that further constrain attention. In research by Bugental and her colleagues (Bugental, Blue, Cortez, Fleck, & Rodriguez, 1992), children viewing a videotape of a potentially stressful interaction between an adult and child manifested increases in autonomic arousal in response to fear cues, a response that was associated with subsequent memory deficits in recalling witnessed events.

Affect and Cognitive Biases. From another standpoint, affect may serve to selectively guide the individual's memory retrieval. For example, mood states may act to increase the accessibility of mood-consistent thoughts (Baumgardner & Arkin, 1988). Affect not only serves to influence the selective retrieval of affect-consistent cognitions through associative networks (Bower, 1981), it may also act to increase perceptual vigilance for events that are affect consistent. That is, stimulus events that match one's current affective state are perceived more efficiently than are other stimuli (Niedenthal & Setterlund, 1994).

On a long-term basis, *chronic* affective states have indeed been found to have a continuing effect on parental processing patterns. Thus, parents who are characteristically depressed, anxious, or angry are more likely to perceive children as acting in deliberately negative ways (Brody & Forehand, 1988; Dix, Reinhold, & Zambarano, 1990). Affective responses not only influence the individual's assessment of eliciting events, they also spill over to influence the evaluation of irrelevant events (Mayer,

Gaschke, Braverman, & Evans, 1992). Thus, parents who are depressed may not only make negative judgments about events in their own personal lives, they may also make negatively biased judgments about unrelated actions of their children. For example, they may easily interpret a child's behavior as a personal rejection. As another example, Dodge, Bates, and Pettit (1990) have shown that children of harsh or abusive parents manifest negative biases in their processing of relevant social cues.

Temporary affective states of parents may also influence the kinds of interpretations that easily come to mind. Dix (1991) has been extensively concerned with the organizing effects of parental affect on adaptive and maladaptive parenting processes. He has suggested that within well-functioning family systems, positive emotions predominate and act to facilitate mutual responsiveness and coordinated activity; negative emotions, in turn, provide adaptive corrections. However, within maladaptive systems, negative emotions predominate and lead to "parenting that is hypersensitive, avoidant, punitive, overly controlling, and focused on self rather than child-concerns" (Dix, 1991, p. 20). Dix et al. (1990) observed that mothers in angry moods show biased interpretations of the causes of child behavior depicted in videotaped vignettes. In comparison with mothers in a neutral mood state, angry mothers were particularly likely to show negative attributional biases in response to child misbehaviors. Rubin and Mills (1992) found that parental choice of directive or coercive responses to undesired child behavior was clearly associated with negative affect (e.g., anger, disappointment) in reaction to those behaviors. Mash and Johnston (1990) have also suggested that depressed mood may exert a direct effect on parental interpretations of child behaviors. In support of this expectation, Krech and Johnston (1992) demonstrated a positive relationship between depressed mood and mothers' negative perceptions of child behaviors.

Affect and Appraisal/Response Selection. Ultimately, affect or arousal serves to influence the attentional resources that are available for more reflective appraisal processes and evaluative judgments (Clore, Schwarz, & Conway, 1994). Elevated levels of affect or defensive arousal act to interrupt or constrain "rational" or reflective appraisal processes (Vasta, 1982; Zillmann, Bryant, Cantor, & Day, 1975). Thus, an overwrought parent may deliver a swat or yell in response to an apparent child misbehavior before it is indeed possible to fully understand what has happened. Zillmann et al. described this process as accounting for the bypassing of careful interpretive processes under conditions of high autonomic arousal. Correspondingly, parents (or children) in a state of high autonomic arousal are more likely than less aroused individuals to make use of low-level inference processes; for example, they are more likely to engage in correspondent inference (inferring children's motives on the basis of their behavior, even when there is evidence that their behavior is situationally constrained). As a result, parental responses are selected on the basis of very limited cognitive appraisal. Vasta suggested that abusive parents (who are often autonomically more reactive than other parents) are more prone to preemptive processing. In similar fashion, Dodge and his colleagues (Crick & Dodge, 1994; Dodge & Somberg, 1987) have shown that socially maladjusted children are also more prone to preemptive processing.

Feedback from Appraisal to Affect. Just as affective and motivational processes may come to influence appraisal processes, appraisal processes may act back to influence affect (as part of a continuous-flow process). Weiner and his colleagues (Himelstein, Graham, & Weiner, 1991; Weiner, 1986) have focused on the affective consequences of attributional activity, including the explanations that parents give for the behavior of their children. From this view, affect occurs in response to the attributional analysis of events rather than to the events per se. So, for example, parents might experience pride after making the attribution that their child had won a contest as a function of hard work. Alternatively, they experience disappointment or anger if the child won the contest by cheating. A similar account is offered by theories that focus on the relationship between cognitive appraisal and emotion. Appraisal theories (e.g., Ellsworth & Smith, 1988; Lazarus, 1991; Smith & Lazarus, 1993) focus on emotional responses to the assessment of the implications of events. Thus, parents with low perceived control in the caregiving relationship might easily respond to caregiving events as sources of threat and appraise their coping potential as low—processes that subsequently lead to an anxious style of parenting.

Cognitions and Communication

Ultimately, we are concerned with the interpersonal interactions of socialization participants. We are interested in the nature of their dialogue, their affective signals, and the behaviors they produce. Thus, it is important to assess the influence of cognitions on communication processes.

For example, parents with low perceived control within the caregiving relationship—in particular, during interactions with children who pose a challenge to their competence—reveal distinctive communication patterns: they are more likely to produce highly controlling verbalizations (e.g., Janssens, 1994) and low levels of positive affect (e.g., Bugental, Blue, & Lewis, 1990). Such responses are consistent with their implicit views of their own (limited) capabilities and children's (malevolent) intentions.

Increasingly, however, we are concerned not only with the words or nonverbal responses used in socializing interactions but also with the nature and signal clarity of messages (e.g., Grusec & Goodnow, 1994; Kochanska, 1994). For example, communication inconsistencies and ambiguities have been observed within many types of poorly functioning families, including those in which family members are particularly prone to anger, aggression, or depression (e.g., Weinberger, 1994; Zahn-Waxler, Iannotti, Cummings, & Denham, 1990). The uncertainties that are engendered by erratic, inconsistent parental communication strategies may have general negative consequences for children's social compliance as well as their ability to experience trust within interpersonal relationships (Rotenberg, Simourd, & Moore, 1989; Shifflett-Simpson & Cummings, 1996; Wahler & Dumas, 1986). Such messages may also lead to social disengagement in children as they withdraw from the uncertainties generated (Gianino & Tronick, 1988). It has even been suggested that children may misbehave to reduce indiscriminate responses from parents by triggering a predictable coercive bout (Wahler, Williams, & Cerezo, 1990).

In any analysis of children's responses to parental communication patterns, however, it is critical to consider differential response patterns that reflect the child's *level of development*. For example, younger children have greater difficulty understanding unclear parental messages (e.g., affectively inconsistent messages) than do older children. Across middle childhood, children acquire an increased understanding of the use of deception and cultural "display rules" in the production of complex messages (e.g., Saarni, 1984), a change that reflects increased understanding of discrepancies between what others feel and what they display (e.g., Saarni, 1988).

Cognitions and Autonomous Regulatory Activity

A mainstay of the socialization literature has been a concern with the extent to which children ultimately come to act in ways that have been encouraged by socializing adults—in the absence of the continued influence of those adults. In this case, attention has focused on the child's capacity to regulate his or her actions without the assistance or supervisory presence of others. This type of regulation has sometimes been taken as a sign of *internalization*. This term, however, may have multiple meanings (e.g., Lawrence & Valsiner, 1993). To avoid the unidirectional implication of this term, we shall stay with the term *autonomous regulatory activity*. In doing so, we are not implying that such actions are free of social influence. Our use of the term refers to regulatory activity of the child that occurs without the *explicit* influence of others. Even self-generated actions may be influenced by "implicit audiences," that is, response patterns reflect the implicit sharing of an experience with others who are not actually present (Fridlund, 1991).

Alternative Pathways to Autonomous Regulation. Autonomous regulatory activity may be initially acquired and subsequently maintained by different means:

1. *Fear.* The most automatic type of autonomous regulation involves an association between particular stimulus cues and particular affective responses. For example, a child who has been punished in response to some event may respond with immediate fear to similar cues in the future. To the extent such punishment was severe and/or the child highly reactive, preemptory processing may occur. That is, the child shows an emotional response to stimulus cues that leads to a bypassing of further thought and the implementation of emotion-regulation processes, for example, avoidance. In other words, parental injunctions are implemented on the basis of perceptual and affective rather than controlled cognitive responses. Within the framework of Craik and Lockhart's (1972) depth-of-processing theory, children showing fear-based regulation only process to the level of recognizing the stimulus (matching it with some previous event) but fail to then go on to relate the stimulus to other cognitive structures stored in memory. As noted earlier, when children focus on the parent as a *source* of fear-inducing messages, they are less likely to integrate the parent's message into a full understanding of the disciplinary event. As a result, fear-based processes comprise a very limited type of autonomous regulation, but one that continues as a function of strong associations between perceptual cues and fear responses. Traditional social learning

positions categorized this type of self-regulation as conditioned avoidance responses (Parke, 1974).

2. *Procedures, scripts, and behavioral routines.* From a variety of sources (parents, other children, the media), children acquire a knowledge of the ways most people act, think, and feel in given situations. Once overlearned, these procedures and routines may come to operate in automatic fashion. Grooming routines (e.g., washing one's face, brushing one's teeth) may come to be played out without reflective consideration; at the same time, one has a sense of unease if they are not followed. Rules, once acquired, may come to be unquestioned. We will return to this issue in the section on social-cultural perspectives.

For the moment, however, we draw attention to the question: What kinds of behaviors are most subject to this type of autonomous regulation? The most probable candidates appear to share two features. First, they fall within the area that has been labeled as involving conventional morality (Turiel, 1983). For example, they have to do with ways to eat or dress, with rules of politeness or of contributions to the household. These are by and large areas where appeals to inductive reasoning (e.g., appeals based on the need to avoid harm to others) have little or no force. Custom then, rather than enlightenment, is expected to supply the basis for behavioral maintenance. Second, such behaviors fall into areas that parents identify as the "child's responsibility," behaviors that should ultimately occur without reminders, assistance, or extrinsic rewards.

3. *Assisted mental simulation.* Autonomous regulation may involve processes that represent cognitive coconstructions of parents and children. Parents who use rational appeals or reasoning are essentially assisting the child in running a mental "simulation" of the potential outcomes of different courses of action (including the affective outcomes of those experiences). To the extent this process is successfully shared, the child stores an event-outcome association (containing both cognitive and affective components) in memory. The participation of the parent is that of a director of the child's search and appraisal processes rather than as a direct advocate of desired responses or as a purveyor of consequences for particular courses of action. As a result, the acquired content and strategic knowledge may be thought of as involving "information-based" self-regulation. For example, as part of disciplinary encounters, parents may

guide children's thoughts to consider the impact their misbehavior has had on someone else, along with their own feelings of guilt or empathic distress in response to the imagined suffering of another. What is acquired is a regulatory strategy along with information stored in the process of the simulation.

This third type of self-regulation follows from socialization tactics described by Hoffman (1983) as involving "induction" (parental use of reasoning or explanations) and by Sigel (1993) as involving "distancing" strategies that psychologically separate the child from the immediate, ongoing present (e.g., reconstructing past events, considering alternatives, anticipating or predicting future events). Using Tulving's (1972) distinction between episodic and semantic memory, Hoffman suggested that induction tactics lead the child to store and organize relevant information within semantic memory rather than episodic memory. Episodic memory is employed for the storage of specific, perceptually indexed temporal events, whereas semantic memory is employed for the storage of organized knowledge structures, that is, underlying meanings. Highly affect-inducing events (such as the use of a fear-inducing tactic by a parent) are stored in episodic memory, whereas less affectively intense events (such as a parental induction) are more likely to become integrated into semantic memory. In the latter case, then, the child will remember the message but not the parent as the source of that message; additionally (as noted by Hoffman), the child will also integrate this information with similar information taken from other incidents (which, in turn, results in the acquisition of a more general concept).

4. *Parental management/social scaffolding.* Vygotskian thinking has highlighted the ways socializers may optimally provide support: offering it when the child or the novice cannot succeed alone, phasing it out as the person being assisted is increasingly able to act without help. Most of the research in this area has dealt with the development of cognitive skills. The concepts, however, may well be applied to the development of social skills (Maccoby, 1992) and profitably considered together with the role of parents as "managers" or "arrangers" of children's experiences (e.g., Bradley & Caldwell, 1995; Parke & Buriel, Ch. 8, this Volume). Parents may arrange situations that provide the opportunity for children to learn some action-outcome sequence on their own. For example, they may facilitate their children's entry into play groups or sporting activities that foster experiences with

reciprocity and fair play (e.g., Finnie & Russell, 1988). A parent may also provide opportunities to help others, to take care of others, or to take routine responsibility for household jobs that benefit others—opportunities that are likely to promote nurturance, altruism, and social responsibility (e.g., Eisenberg, Cialdini, McCreath, & Shell, 1987; Grusec, Goodnow, & Cohen, in press; Whiting & Whiting, 1975). Moving out to the broader society, there have also been concerns with community circumstances that *prevent* parents from being able to manage their children's environment, for example, chronic violence and poverty (Osofsky, 1995).

Development of and Receptiveness to Autonomous Regulation. A cognitive view of socialization implies no necessary developmental progression in types of autonomous regulation. Based upon their experiences in different content areas, children may reveal the effects of different types of socializing influences. Thus, a given child may not steal on the basis of fear, may show courtesy to others on the basis of a politeness rule, may make a donation to a needy child in response to a mental simulation, and may reciprocate the kindness of a teammate on the basis of direct experience with cooperative group activities.

At the same time, children's increasing levels of cognitive development and increased exposure to nonfamilial influences can be expected to make them more receptive to different types of autonomous regulation at different points in their development. *Parental management of the child's environment* represents a socialization strategy that is available at all ages, but is likely to be less effective at older ages. During infancy (and even before the birth of a child) parents serve as the primary designers of children's environmental opportunities. At later ages, peers, educational institutions, and popular culture (e.g., media) serve as additional and increasing sources of influence that are only partially controlled by parents. In similar fashion, the use of *fear* as a source of influence on autonomous self-regulation (conditioned avoidance) serves as a mechanism that is available at all ages but that is most likely to have enduring effects if introduced at younger ages. As suggested by Crick and Dodge (1994), "early experiences lay down neural paths (especially in the first several years of life, when synaptic pathways can be created at a more rapid rate than in later life). These paths are traversed repeatedly in subsequent social interactions so that they become well worn and automatic. After multiple trials over many years, the paths become characterized by enhanced efficiency and complexity but also, paradoxically, by rigidity and resistance to change" (p. 81).

There appears to be a particularly important "window of opportunity" for children's acquisition of *procedures and behavioral routines* when they first move out to explore their environment. Toddlers show a high degree of receptivity to the acquisition of rules, a skill that follows the emergence of representational thought as a mechanism that allows them to keep rules "in mind" (Emde et al., 1991). Children's receptivity to *assisted mental simulations* increases as they acquire a more sophisticated understanding of others and of social causality. Both Hoffman (1983) and Emde et al. (1991) suggest that this type of "internalization" begins at about 3 years of age. As children acquire the capacity to understand that others may have beliefs that differ from their own—and that others act on their beliefs even when those beliefs are false (e.g., Hala, Chandler, & Fritz, 1991)—they have a greatly expanded capacity to understand the alternative outcomes that may follow from both their own actions and the actions of others. This capacity increases, of course, during middle childhood as children acquire an enhanced capacity to consider present events and future possibilities in the light of past events and changing contexts (e.g., Gnepp & Gould, 1985; Ruble, Newman, Rholes, & Altshuler, 1988).

Uniformities and Variations in Cognitions about Socializing Relationships

Over the past 15 years there has been an explosion of research concerned with parents' ways of thinking about children and parenting (for overviews, see Goodnow, 1988a; Goodnow & Collins, 1990; Grusec, Hastings, & Mammone, 1994; S. Miller, 1988; Murphey, 1992; Sigel, McGillicuddy-DeLisi, & Goodnow, 1992), along with a more limited concern with children's ways of thinking about socialization. Researchers have focused on (a) the validity of cognitions; (b) variations in cognitions as a function of personal history; (c) variations in cognitions as a function of social-cultural history; (d) variations in cognitions as a function of phase of development; and (e) variations in cognitions as a function of context.

Validity of Cognitions

A continuing concern with cognitions about socialization has been with their validity, that is, the extent to which parental ideas or thoughts correspond in some way to "reality." One concern has been with the correspondence between parental cognitions and interpersonal outcomes. If we know a parent holds some belief, we ask: What parental practices do they use or affect do they reveal? How do their children respond? What is the evidence for successful (or problematic) socialization? Alternatively, concern has been directed to the "truth value" of parental cognitions. For example, how well do the beliefs that parents hold about children correspond to reality?

Predictive Validity.   Historically, the greatest concern has been with the predictive validity of parental cognitions, as reflected in parental behavior, child behavior, or caregiving outcomes. It has been shown repeatedly that such relationships are equivocal at best (Hess, Holloway, Dickson, & Price, 1984; Holden & Edwards, 1989; McGillicuddy-DeLisi, 1985). In accounting for our failure to confirm such relationships, a number of explanations have been proposed. First, research concerned with belief-behavior relationships in the socialization literature has been plagued with methodological problems. Holden and Edwards (1989) have detailed the myriad limitations that have characterized the assessment of parental beliefs, for example, ill-defined classes of responses (beliefs, values, attitudes, behavioral intentions, self-perceptions), questionable reliability and validity of measures, and lack of coherent structure of measures.

As a second explanation, it has been suggested that we are asking the wrong questions. Sigel (1992), in reviewing the long history of the Educational Testing Service (ETS) in exploring the relationship between parental beliefs and behaviors, concluded that parental beliefs may be conceptualized in quite diverse ways. For example, as social scientists, we define the nature of beliefs that are of interest to us in exploring theoretical questions, but our notions of important beliefs may bear little correspondence to the implicit theories that parents hold about parenting (S. Miller, 1988). Thus, it may be that we are looking at the "wrong" beliefs.

Alternatively, it may be that we have focused on overly simplistic effects. Bugental and Shennum (1984) suggested that social cognitions act in a *moderator* role within socializing interactions; that is, cognitions influence what one attends to, how events are appraised, and how one feels in different settings—but they do not act as direct determiners of behavior or outcomes.

Concurrent Validity.   Another approach has focused on the concurrent validity of beliefs, in terms of the relationship between *parents'* naïve beliefs about children and other sources of evidence about children (e.g., Azar, Robinson, Hekimian, & Twentyman, 1984; S. Miller, 1988). Parents have been asked what they believe about children's abilities (at different ages), what they believe about children's motives or intentions, and what they believe about the causal influences on children's actions. Research focused on such issues has revealed that parental beliefs about child behaviors—despite their variability—are fairly well-rooted in reality (S. Miller, 1988). For example, Dix and his colleagues (Dix et al., 1990; Dix, Ruble, Grusec, & Nixon, 1986: Dix, Ruble, & Zambarano, 1989) have shown that greater control is attributed to children as they become older and more competent. Additionally, children are held more responsible for behaviors that are easy to control than for behaviors that are hard to control (Dix & Lochman, 1990).

Attention has also been given to the *convergence between children's beliefs about parents and other evidence concerning parental responses.* One line of research has focused on the differences in children's views of mothers versus fathers. As with parents' views of children, children's views of parents show a reasonable degree of congruence with the ways parents act. For example, both the United States and in Asian countries, mothers are thought to be high on warmth/kindness and fathers are thought to be high on control/strictness (Berndt, Cheung, Lau, Hau, & Lew, 1993; Block, 1984), a perception that loosely corresponds with objectively observed differences (e.g., Collins & Russell, 1991; Huston, 1983; Lamb, Frodi, Hwang, Frodi, & Steinberg, 1982).

Variations in Cognitions as a Function of Personal History

As noted by Goodnow (1985), developmentalists entered this field with an expectation that parents acquired their beliefs on the basis of their personal experiences with children. Although beliefs about individual children may be influenced by their direct experiences as socializers (e.g., Holden, 1988), it is becoming apparent that ideas about parenting are also shaped in advance of becoming a parent (e.g., S. Miller, 1988; Moss & Jones, 1977; Ninio, 1988) and may indeed be in place at very young ages (e.g., Melson, Fogel, & Toda, 1986). For example, parental beliefs about appropriate socializing practices may mirror those they have experienced; thus, Holden and Zambarano (1992) found a significant relationship between children's personal history of spanking (high frequency) and their

subsequent advocacy of spanking. In short, children learn the "acceptability" of parenting practices from their parents. Additionally, parents may acquire biased ways of interpreting their social experiences as a function of their own history as children.

Attachment Styles. During the past few years, extensive attention has been given to the ways children come to represent relationships on the basis of their earliest attachment relationships (Main, Kaplan, & Cassidy, 1985; Thompson, Ch. 2, this Volume; Van IJzendoorn, 1992). From their early experiences with parents, children develop "working models" of relationships that include a representation of both self and parent (Bowlby, 1980). These representations or knowledge structures act as organizers of the child's understanding of the ways the social world functions (Bretherton, 1990), along with their views of themselves in relationship to others (Bowlby, 1980). Those children who come to believe that others are available to them and interact with them in positive, responsive ways are more likely to feel secure within those relationships and to develop a secure working model of relationships. Working models (whether secure or insecure) may be thought of as "attachment styles" that come to influence close relationships with others throughout the course of development and on into adulthood (Hazan & Shaver, 1987). Sroufe and Fleeson (1986) have argued that the inclusion of others as well as self within working models prepares the child for complementary roles associated with the parent as well as for the original role of the self; thus, the role of the parent may subsequently be played out when children reach adulthood and become parents. Consistent with this notion, adult attachment categories (as revealed in the Adult Attachment Interview [AAI]) have been found to predict the attachment categories of their own children (Benoit & Parker, 1994; Van IJzendoorn, 1995). Attachment styles not only influence an individual's expectations of others, they also influence social information processing. For example, secure individuals are quicker to identify words with implications for positive interpersonal outcomes, whereas insecure individuals are quicker to identify words with implications for negative outcomes (Baldwin, Fehr, Keedian, Seidel, & Thompson, 1993).

Social Self-Efficacy and Social Attributions. One approach to variations in cognitions has focused on parents' perceptions of their own ability to influence children, a notion that is consistent either with Bandura's (1977;

Grusec, 1992) notions of self-efficacy or with attributional constructs that focus on perceived controllability of socialization outcomes. Such constructs are typically understood as having their origins in the individuals own history—either with their own children or in their past relationships with their own parents. The central focus within this approach has been to determine differences among parents in their perceived competence within caregiving relationships. Just as self-efficacy perceptions guide responses in other domains, parents' beliefs about their ability to perform well in the socialization domain influence their practices, and may ultimately come to act in a self-confirming fashion. In support of this view, Teti and Gelfand (1991) found that parents who were low in self-efficacy (in the domain of infant care) were also low in socialization competence and high in depression. From a different framework, researchers have also demonstrated that expected control over socialization serves to influence *actual* outcomes (e.g., Affleck & Tennen, 1991). There has been relatively little attention directed to the role of children's individual attributions or self-efficacy as a factor in socializing relationships (see Loeb, 1975; MacKinnon-Lewis, Lamb, Dechman, Rabiner, & Curtner, 1994 for exceptions).

Relationship Schemas. Another approach has focused on cognitions about the joint influence of parents and children on the socialization relationship. Within the close relationships literature, there has been an increasing interest in *relationship schemas,* that is, the ways we represent others in our self-schemas (e.g., Markus & Kitayama, 1991), the ways we represent significant others (Andersen & Glasman, 1996), and the ways we directly represent our interpersonal, dyadic relationships (Aron, Aron, Tudor, & Nelson, 1991; Baldwin, 1992). Consistent with these changes, we have seen an increase in research on dyadic aspects of parental cognitions. One focus of interest has been on the relative power or control that parents attribute to themselves versus their children (e.g., Bugental et al., 1993; Bugental & Shennum, 1984; Stratton & Swaffer, 1988). Those parents who attribute high control to children and low control to self (in particular, for negative caregiving outcomes) have been found to be at elevated risk for caregiving conflict, for example, physical abuse (Bugental, Blue, & Cruzcosa, 1989; Stratton & Swaffer, 1988). Maltreating parents more easily interpret child resistance or unresponsiveness as both intentional and personally directed at them (e.g., Dietrich, Berkowitz, Kadushin, & McGloin, 1990). Individuals who perceive themselves as "power disadvantaged" are hypervigilant to the possibility of interpersonal threat and are more likely than others to select coercive tactics in efforts to regain control (Kipnis, 1976; Raven & Kruglanski, 1970).

There is also evidence that low perceived interpersonal control is associated with avoidance as a regulatory strategy in response to distress. Grusec et al. (1994) demonstrated that parents with low perceived control (as measured by the Parent Attribution Test) are more likely to reveal an avoidant attachment history; that is, they showed a dismissive response pattern during the AAI. Thus, relationship schemas appear to be influenced by the parent's own early history.

From a different perspective, there has been an emergent effort to understand control beliefs within entire families using the Social Relations Model (Cook, 1993). From this standpoint, the behavior of each family member toward all others is influenced by the individual, the other person, and the relationship between the two. Cook developed the Interpersonal Sense of Control Scale (ISOC) to assess dimensions commonly identified in the locus of control construct, that is, internality, powerful others, and fate/chance. In confirmation of his expectations, the individual family member's interpersonal sense of control was found to depend on the characteristics of the other person; for example, family member A had a stronger sense of control (higher "effectance") with respect to member B if B reported high acquiescence to A.

Variations in Cognitions as a Function of Phase of Development

Grusec and Goodnow (1994) have offered a general frame for integrating the limited evidence available on variations in cognitions about socialization as a function of phase of development. They have distinguished three phases in children's processing and proposed that each is influenced by different conditions. The first has to do with the child's perception of the parent's intention. This perception may be accurate or inaccurate. The conditions seen as especially relevant range from the clarity of the parent's statements to the child's degree of interest in accuracy, interpretive skill, interpretive biases, and emotional state. The second phase has to do with the child's acceptance or rejection of the perceived message. Here the conditions seen as likely to have particular relevance range from aspects of appraisal processes (e.g., the child's judgments of the parent's position as fair or as appropriate to the occasion) to the warmth of the relationship between parent and child. The third phase has to do with the child's sense of an accepted message as self-generated, a phase seen as influenced especially by the child's perception of pressure from others. This third phase is adopted from Hoffman (1983); the first two are an expansion of proposals by Cashmore and Goodnow (1985) and Goodnow (1992). The three phases are used by Grusec and Goodnow (1994) as a frame for pulling together proposals about children's processing from a variety of sources, ranging from research by Dodge and his colleagues (e.g., Dodge, Coie, Pettit, & Price, 1990) on bias in children's interpretations of ambiguous situations to research by Nucci (1984) on children's judgments of fair or appropriate behavior.

Variations in Cognitions as a Function of Social-Cultural History

Beliefs about socialization may also be based upon "ready-made" cultural interpretations of children and socializing events (Goodnow, 1985), with these supplying a pool or a "landscape" (Lightfoot & Valsiner, 1992) of possibilities. Added to this general proposal has been the argument that any selection from the pool always displays transformation on its way to becoming adopted as one's own position (Lawrence & Valsiner, 1993; Lightfoot & Valsiner, 1992; Valsiner, 1989). That argument prompts the question: Which ideas are likely to display the most and the least degrees of transformation? Murphey (1992), for instance, has suggested that general or abstract beliefs about children or parenting are more likely to remain unchanged than are specific ideas about ways to interact with particular children on particular occasions.

We may ask: What conditions influence the nature of the selection from the pool or the landscape? The range of alternatives may be narrow or large (a condition we return to in the section on social-cultural perspectives). In addition, selection may be influenced by a variety of parental factors: their exposure to various views of parenting, their need to justify actions taken, their sense of need for advice from experts, their perceptions of the qualities that children may need in the future (Goodnow & Collins, 1990). Ideas about gender provide one example. All societies contain ideas about the extent to which children need to be "toughened up" to cope with a world that will not always be gentle. The extent to which toughening is seen as needed for both boys and girls, however, appears to vary with the parent's perception of the qualities children need to cope with life within or outside the family. In societies where women as adults have considerable influence in their own

right, for instance, there is less emphasis on obedience rather than independence for girls (Low, 1989), a condition that seems likely to apply also within cultures. In families marked by low income and high degrees of stress, both girls and boys may be encouraged to be tough (Miller & Sperry, 1988).

As a second example, we take the extent to which parents' ideas are "traditional," "modern," or "paradoxical" (Palacios, 1990). Traditional in these discussions refers to beliefs that children are hard to influence, in large part because their characteristics are seen as innately shaped. Modern refers to the more optimistic perception of children as malleable. In several countries, traditional views of this kind have been found to be prevalent among parents with fewer years of schooling or in occupations with low socioeconomic status (McGillicuddy-DeLisi, 1992; S. Miller, 1988; Palacios, in press; Schaefer & Edgerton, 1985). These perceptions might reflect the extent to which parents are in circumstances that allow them to have an impact on what happens to their children. A role for exposure to particular viewpoints, however, is pointed to by some of Palacios's (1990, in press) findings. In his Spanish sample, paradoxical beliefs (an inconsistent mixture of traditional and modern) were concentrated within groups that combined exposure to traditional village beliefs and to the views presented in formal schooling or by medical/educational experts. Bits of each position then came to be held, without any resolution of their inconsistency. Exposure is also pointed to by the finding that in Kenya, Mexico, and the United States, the extent of mothers' schooling predicted the extent to which they were verbally responsive with their infants (Richman, Miller, & LeVine, 1992).

Variations in Cognitions as a Function of Context

Cognitive representations of socializing relationships may also be thought of as varying across context or setting. In different settings, parents and/or children may access different scripts as guides to their response patterns. Such contextually anchored distinctions may either be tightly conceptualized as reflecting the manifestation of natural social categories (or modules), or more loosely conceptualized as reflecting commonly occurring responses to different types of socializing settings.

Relationship Cognitions as Natural Categories. Arguing for notions of modularity, A. Fiske (1992) proposed that the various groupings of human relationships are organized on the basis of natural categories and are enacted in terms of domain-specific "scripts" or "grammars." He proposed that human relationships are spontaneously categorized by perceivers into four basic types:

1. Communal sharing (CS) relationships (relationships that involve equal sharing and common identity among group members); attachment as well as group relations are included in this category.
2. Authority-ranked (AR) relationships (hierarchical groups in which some individuals have more power than others).
3. Equality-matched (EM) relationships (relationships characterized by quid pro quo provision of benefits between members).
4. Market-priced (MP) relationships (in which members act on the basis of rationally weighed subjective utilities of member resources and actions).

Fiske (1992) proposed that these relationship types can be thought of as distinctive modules, each of which involves "a distinct form of representation, used for integrating and interpreting experience and guiding action in a specific sphere" (p. 690). Supporting this notion, he observed the same basic domains of interaction in a traditional West African village as in Western cultures, but, at the same time, the ways these domains were implemented varied as a function of cultural variables.

Fiske and his colleagues (Fiske, 1993; Fiske, Haslam, & Fiske, 1991) have also provided support for this basic model by showing that processing errors (e.g., misnamings, memory errors) are likely to be consistent with specialized relationship categories or grammars. For example, processing errors in which one person is confused with another reveal a shared category of social relationships. Thus, a parent may confuse the names of children or the names of work colleagues but will not show confusion errors across these categories. In exploring the universality of such processes, the strongest evidence was provided for CS, EM, and AR relationship categories.

Influences of Settings.   Cognitions about socializing relationships have also been thought of as varying across settings in a less modular fashion. Grusec and Goodnow (1994) have pointed out the variations that occur in disciplinary practices as a function of socialization *situations,* a variable that does not imply the categorical notion of socialization "domains" but does suggest variations in socialization across settings. Consistent with Hoffman's (1970) idea that different situations "pull" different types of parental discipline, they proposed that regularities have been observed in the control strategies used by parents in response to different types of misdeeds. So, for example, violations of social conventions (e.g., violation of politeness rules) are followed by reasoning (but not power assertion); antisocial acts (e.g., stealing) are followed by reasoning and power assertion, whereas damage to physical objects is followed by punitive power assertion.

Variations in control strategies in different contexts, in turn, are represented in the thinking of both adults and children. That is, regulatory strategies are thought of in terms of their "fairness" or appropriateness for different types of events. For example, children believe it is appropriate for adults to intervene and provide punishment in response to moral transgressions (e.g., stealing). But at the same time, they feel that such interventions are inappropriate for conventional transgressions (Tisak, 1986) or failure to act in a prosocial fashion (Grusec & Pedersen, 1989). At a later age, adolescents consider that home and paid work differ in the extent to which thought needs to be given to the feelings of others, with males drawing the distinction between these two spheres more sharply than do females (Goodnow & Warton, 1991).

Socialization settings may also be parsed on the basis of relevant goals. Dix (1992), for example, has noted the differences in parents' response on the basis of their application of self-oriented goals (personal goals of parents), empathic goals (attempts to understand and facilitate immediate child goals), and socialization goals (rules and expectations imposed on child in service of long-term welfare of child).

Methodological Issues within a Cognitive Approach

Increasing Assessment of Moderating and Mediating Relationships

The field has moved beyond a reliance on simple correlational approaches (linking socialization practices and socialization outcomes) to approaches that allow an assessment of mediating and moderating processes. Increasing interest in the role of cognitions and affect within socializing transactions has fostered the development of new types of measures. Although there is a long history of observational research focused on behaviors, we now see an increased interest in response patterns that are not directly observable. As one example, increasing use is being made of psychophysiological assessment of adults and children during interactions. Donovan, Leavitt, and colleagues (Donovan & Leavitt, 1989; Donovan, Leavitt, & Walsh, 1990) demonstrated that mothers with an "illusory sense of control" were more likely than other mothers to show defensive autonomic arousal (e.g., heart rate increases) in response to uncontrollable encounters with infants. A similar pattern of findings was observed for "low-power" mothers paired with an apparently unresponsive child (Bugental et al., 1993). Additionally, methods have been introduced that allow the on-line assessment of thoughts and affective responses during the course of family interactions (e.g., Gottman & Levenson, 1985) or during simulated interactions (Davison, Navarre, & Vogel, 1995). Such approaches not only provide a window on mediating processes during the course of socialization, they also are well suited to the assessment of interaction *sequences* and have the advantage of being relatively nonreactive.

New Uses of Experimental Designs

Experimental tests of different models of socialization have been used to supplement naturalistic observations. Historically, there has been a greater reliance on experimental methods in socialization research framed within a social psychological tradition than within biological, anthropological, or sociological traditions. As cognitive approaches to socialization are more likely to borrow from social psychological theory (than are biological or social-cultural approaches), their tenets are more often tested by experimental designs. The focus of newer experimental designs has been to create situations that provide good experimental realism; that is, situations are created that generate cognitive and affective responses equivalent to those found in more natural settings.

A feature that has been increasingly incorporated into experimental designs involves the use of ambiguous settings. Patterns shown within ambiguous settings have been found to be particularly revealing of chronic patterns of information processing and interaction within socializing relationships (e.g., Bugental et al., 1990; Dix et al., 1990; Strassberg, 1995). In the absence of clear expectations regarding appropriate behavior, research participants must engage in appraisal processes that easily expose their selectively biased ways of interpreting child behaviors and socializing events.

As another approach, research strategies have been devised that place high demands or stresses on socializing participants, thus revealing patterns that might otherwise

be unobserved (equivalent to the advantages offered by the Strange Situation test in the assessment of attachment). For example, Donovan, Leavitt, and their colleagues (Donovan & Leavitt, 1989; Donovan et al., 1990) created a "learned helplessness" situation by exposing mothers to an infant's cry that they could not terminate.

Creative use has also been made of vignette approaches in which parents (as well as children) are exposed to realistically portrayed "socialization scenarios." For example, mothers of children who manifest behavior problems have been found to show negatively biased interpretations of child behaviors presented in a scenario format (e.g., MacKinnon-Lewis et al., 1994; Strassberg, 1995).

Utility of Cognitive Perspectives

Consideration of the role of cognitions allows insight into the bases of both stability and change in socializing interactions. At one level, cognitions may be understood as stable organizers of expectations, interpretations, emotional responses, and behaviors in parent-child or other socializing relationships. Such structures may have their origins in many different sources. To some extent, they may reflect "natural social categories"; that is, they may involve representations of social domains for which we are biologically prepared. At the same time, they may reflect cultural constructions that are perpetuated across generations as organizers of ways of understanding and managing children and parent-child relationships. Alternatively, they may be strongly influenced by the individual's own unique social history. Whatever the source, stable beliefs ultimately serve to organize and maintain particular kinds of socializing interactions. Although the preponderance of research has focused on the effects of parental cognitions, increasing attention has been given to the origins and functioning of such cognitions in children's early relationships, as well as to the perpetuation of socialization cognitions across generations. Rather than viewing cognitions as stable traits, however, we are now more likely to see them as organizers of reactions to triggering events. For example, parents who show negative interpretive biases will not respond with anger under all circumstances; they may simply be more easily "triggered" to anger in response to behavior that is ambiguous or might appear to be confrontational. We have suggested here that stable relationship cognitions are highly accessible during the course of "challenging" socializing interactions. Such knowledge structures may in fact be thought of as providing default interpretations.

Spontaneously activated cognitions or schemas serve as initial framers of the thoughts that first come to mind and the feelings that are triggered in response to relevant events.

At another level, cognitions also come into play in the service of flexibility or change. Here we think in terms of relatively slow, reflective, controlled, or effortful cognitive activity. Such activity is more likely to be observed when parents (or others) are not constrained by concurrent demands that limit their processing capacity. Under these favorable processing circumstances, reflective thought may incorporate information from the immediate environment; opening (default) thoughts and feelings may then be "corrected" on the basis of new information or alternative interpretations. For example, the spontaneous reaction of annoyance to a persistently crying child may be modified by the awareness that the child is tired or sick; it may be reduced by an awareness that other family members are available for assistance or exacerbated by isolation and the unavailability of help or support from others.

We have suggested the importance of an interdisciplinary approach in understanding the role of cognition as an organizer of socializing relationships. Ideas drawn from contemporary attachment theory and social cognition theory may be profitably integrated in understanding the ways cognitions serve to organize socializing relationships. Methodology drawn from communication research and psychophysiological research elucidates the complex mediating processes that occur during the course of socializing interactions. Whether concern is directed to short-term socializing episodes or long-term socialization history, complex transactional systems are best understood as moderated by overlearned cognitions or schemas and mediated by the complex on-line interwoven influences of thought, affect, arousal, and communicative behavior.

SOCIAL-CULTURAL PERSPECTIVES

What can a third set of perspectives add to what has already been said? In this section, we apply that question to issues that by now will be familiar: the overall nature of socialization; the ways influences intersect; the interconnections among actions, ideas, and feelings; the ways occasions of socialization differ from one another.

In broad terms, social-cultural perspectives underline the significance of the world outside the family, the significance of "the larger social context." The more specific

questions and proposals then stem from the ways that larger social context and its connections to individuals and families are conceptualized.

In many cases, for instance, the larger context is thought of as made up of social groups: age, gender, work, ethnic, religious, or national groups. Socialization is then perceived as being about becoming or remaining a member of one or more groups. That view of socialization underlines its being a lifelong activity. It also prompts the questions: How can we go beyond simply saying that people become members of a group? What does membership involve? How can we describe gradations of membership, or variations in position within a group, and the ways these are related to socialization?

Social contexts are also often defined in terms of the extent to which they display particular qualities. A quality often emphasized in analyses of socialization, for instance, is the extent to which there is consensus or diversity within the social world. When consensus is the case, most people in the group act, think, or feel in similar ways. Socialization can then be thought of as coming to think and act in the ways that others do: interpreting the world by the same "cultural models" (e.g., D'Andrade & Strauss, 1992), participating in the same "cultural practices" (e.g., Ortner, 1985), or "communities of practice" (e.g., Lave, 1991). When diversity applies, the presence of a variety of ways of acting, thinking, and feeling may simply offer the individual a degree of choice. The diverse ways may also, however, be actively competitive with one another or antagonistic to one another. Socialization may then involve coming to terms with the fact that some ways of acting, thinking, and feeling are arbitrarily defined as better than others (e.g., Wertsch, 1991b), or with the experience of encountering others who seek to undermine the efforts of one set of socializers, to undo or "dismantle" (Michaels, 1991) what they have achieved.

We shall have occasion to consider a number of ways of conceptualizing the larger social context, concentrating on their implications for socialization. Throughout, we draw from several disciplines: anthropology and sociology, together with some parts of social and developmental psychology. We draw also from studies of socialization in both childhood and adulthood. The emphasis falls on concepts and models. We ask, for example, what it means to say that meanings or practices are "shared," "negotiated," "privileged," "contested," or "coconstructed." The emphasis falls also on proposals that offer links to concepts already familiar in developmental psychology. Without these links, much of what appears in social-cultural analyses may seem irrelevant to developmentalists. Finally, the emphasis falls on proposals that suggest research directions that include but are by no means limited to cross-cultural comparisons. That method is often highly rewarding for the study of socialization but a great deal of research may proceed without it and still be informed by social-cultural perspectives (Goodnow, in press).

The coverage we offer is necessarily highly selective. There is currently a great deal of material emerging with regard to the significance of the social-cultural-historical contexts of development, adding to much that was written before the current wave. In this *Handbook* alone, for example, the reader interested in social-cultural perspectives may turn to the chapter by Parke and Buriel (a chapter on ethnic and ecological approaches to socialization, Ch. 8, this Volume) as well as to chapters on cognition and collaboration by Rogoff, on gender by Ruble and Martin (Ch. 14, this Volume), and on the cultural psychology of development by Shweder and a large group of colleagues. Our own concentration must be on material that is specifically relevant to socialization and that expands on themes already present within the description offered of other perspectives. Our hope, however, is that the description and demystification of some proposals with regard to socialization will contribute to a cumulative understanding of social-cultural perspectives.

What Is the General Nature of Socialization?

In essence, social-cultural perspectives argue for the need to regard socialization as (a) concerned with every aspect of development, (b) lifelong, (c) concerned with the emergence of the new as well as the reproduction of the old, and (d) concerned with membership in groups. The first feature has been noted in the introduction to this chapter. The second and third will be briefly noted, leaving the major space for the fourth.

Socialization as a Lifelong Phenomenon

This feature is nicely brought out by the argument that the elderly in institutions are "socialized into dependency" (Baltes, 1986). It is also underlined by a widespread and long-standing interest in the ways by which we come to know what is expected or tolerated within a variety of work groups (e.g., Brim & Wheeler, 1966; Chaiklin & Lave, 1993; Levine & Moreland, 1991; Merton, Reader, & Kendall, 1957). These studies are sometimes labeled studies in "occupational socialization" (e.g., Brim & Wheeler,

1966) and sometimes studies in "apprenticeship" (e.g., Geer, 1972). The unifying proposal is that socialization can occur at any point over the life span that involves the entry of a novice or a newcomer into an already established group (Levine & Moreland, 1991; Wentworth, 1980).

Socialization as Beyond Reproduction

"In earlier decades it was conventional wisdom to think of cultures as integrated, stable sets of meanings and practices unproblematically reproduced through socialized actors. Now, anthropologists are beginning to stress conflict, contradiction, ambiguity, and change in cultural understandings—the ways in which cultural understandings are 'contested' and 'negotiated' in current jargon" (Strauss, 1992, p. 1). The study of socialization then shifts away from a concentration on continuity. Instead, attention is given to the ways it allows for novelty (e.g., D'Andrade, 1992), displays a creative adaptation to shifting circumstances (e.g., B. Whiting & Edwards, 1988), contains approval of divergence from old ways (e.g., Goodnow, 1992, 1995), tolerates "acceptable ignorance" (Goodnow, 1996a), or offers explicit advice to children that they should not repeat their parents' lives (Cooper et al., 1994).

Socialization as Related to Membership in Groups

References to socialization as dealing with being or becoming a member of a group abound in anthropology and sociology. As an example, we single out Wentworth's (1980) analysis of socialization as referring to a particular set of interactions: interactions that are most marked at the time of entry into a group (they may also occur at other times) and that always, even when the cast of characters is large, involve at least one of "two social types: a novice and a member" (p. 85).

What does it mean, however, to say that people become members of a group, or that newcomers interact with established members? The implications are several.

Membership as the Acquisition of Shared Meanings and Practices.   In the course of socialization, the novice may be described as encountering and as coming to understand "cultural models": shared ways of looking at the world or interpreting events (e.g., D'Andrade & Strauss, 1992; Holland & Quinn, 1987). In some cases, these models may acquire various degrees of "directive force," guiding or initiating action (D'Andrade & Strauss, 1992). At the least, what will emerge are degrees of intersubjectivity, in the sense that each of us will know what others mean when they nod, wink, or use particular words, and each of us will know that the other understands (D'Andrade, 1987).

The adjective *cultural,* when added to *models,* refers to the same meanings or interpretations being used or understood by all or most members of a group. The same kind of referent applies to the phrase *cultural practices.* The term *practices* refers to everyday routines; the adjective *cultural* is again added when a recurring way of acting, thinking, or feeling (acting especially) is observed by many or most of a group (e.g., Bourdieu, 1977, 1990; Ortner, 1985; see also the several chapters in Goodnow, Miller, & Kessel, 1995). Whether the reference is to models or practices, however, there is no expectation that everyone in a group will be identical with every other. These are essentially "consensus models" (Romney, Weller, & Batchelder, 1986), prompting questions about the extent to which they are shared and the manner in which they are distributed among members of a group (e.g., Reid & Valsiner, 1986), and about the conditions that give rise to the occurrence—or to the assumption by individuals—of various degrees of similarity or difference among members of a group (e.g., Frijda & Mesquita, 1994; Mesquita & Frijda, 1992).

Gradations of Membership or Position in a Group. In its simplest terms, membership may refer to becoming or not becoming a member of a group, to being in or out. Socialization may then be seen as directed toward making it possible to meet the entry qualifications (parents might add socialization toward ways of coping with being excluded). There are as well, however, grades of membership or variations of position within a group. Moreland and Levine (1989), for example, describe socialization into groups as going through several phases. In the first, the individual is a prospective member. The main processes involve reconnaissance and recruitment, with investigation on both sides: Do I wish to join this group? Do we want this person as a member? In the second, the individual is a new member. This is the phase normally labeled "socialization." The main processes are now seen as processes of accommodation and assimilation, with "newcomers" and "oldtimers" working out how far each will bend to the other's definitions of what membership requires. In the third, the individual is a full member. The main processes now have to do with the maintenance of commitment on both sides, often involving a search for a specialized place for the individual in the group. If these negotiations fail, the individual may move to a fourth phase, becoming a marginal member of the group, with reduced commitment. The oldtimers may now engage in resocialization, aimed at

bringing the individual back to full rather than marginal membership. At some point, however, the individual becomes an ex-member, either because time requires it or because the resocialization efforts either are not made wholeheartedly or are unsuccessful. As Moreland and Levine (1989) point out, their model "applies primarily . . . to small, autonomous, and voluntary groups" but the breakdown by phases of membership and associated processes could well be applied also to family groups.

Gradations of membership are also at the heart of Lave and Wenger's (1991) description of learning or socialization as involving change in the form of an individual's participation in activities that involve others. In this description, people move over time from marginal or peripheral participation in the activities of a group (being a tolerated eavesdropper, a minor helper, or a small voice in a large choir are examples) to occupying a more central position. In a further kind of differentiation, with less implication of movement, one may be a member of a group but be accorded only some of the privileges of membership: one may be allowed, for example, to live in an area but not to vote, to own property, or to exercise a voice in what happens (Pateman, 1988). Socialization may then be directed toward persuading individuals who are assigned a marginal place to accept that position as their permanent place. Social positions, however, are seldom single in kind. Women, for example, may come to know that they should act in one way toward dominant males; toward women or "lesser" males, however, they may act quite differently. There is then no static or general role into which they, or any other persons, are socialized (e.g., Holloway, 1984).

Variations in the type of membership one holds, or in one's position within a group, offer first of all ways of breaking down phases and objectives within socialization. The nature of one's position may influence one's vulnerability to the opinions or pressures of others. Parents who are unfamiliar with the school system, for example, are likely to take on the views that teachers hold about the nature of intelligence, if only to be able to communicate easily with these more established members of the school group (Mugny & Carugati, 1989). Newcomers are most likely to have to depend on the way that oldtimers describe to them the world they are about to enter (Wentworth, 1980). The nature of one's position in a group is also likely to alter one's view of events and of other people. In Finland, for example, parents who are more economically advantaged are more likely than parents who are less advantaged to regard intelligence and school performance as biologically based (in a sense, as a tribute to their parents' genes; Raty, Snellman, Mantysaari-Hetekorpi, & Vornanen, in press). In the United States, parents with substantial years of schooling are less likely to see "the school" as a monolithic structure and more likely to perceive it as made up of people who are differentially approachable when their help is needed (Alexander & Entwisle, 1988).

Membership and Identity. Membership is not only about entering a group or coming to occupy a particular position or set of positions within it. Involved also is the development of a sense of identity, both social identity and personal identity. The former aspect of identity (social identity) is especially prominent in analyses based on social-cultural perspectives. Socialization is about "becoming" one of a group. To take a variety of titles, it is about "becoming a Kwoma" (J. Whiting, 1941), "becoming an elder" (J. Whiting, 1981), "becoming a policeman" (Hopper, 1977), or "becoming a male stripper" (Dressel & Petersen, 1982).

Socialization is also about the placement of individuals in a number of social categories: the categories of male and female (Maccoby, 1988), or the categories of jocks, nerds, and burn-outs, to take some from Eckert's (1991) analysis of a U.S. high school. In the course of socialization, this orientation emphasizes, people come to think of themselves in social identity terms ("I am a . . ."). They also come to know the categories that exist, the categories they are usually assigned to, the categories it is desirable or feasible to aim at, and, in Tajfel's (1981) analysis, the categories that amount to social oblivion and are at all costs to be avoided. Those categories in turn may determine the extent to which one is predisposed to go along with or to resist socialization (Tajfel, 1981). To be classed as "one of those people," for example, is hardly conducive to accepting the opinions of the people making such judgments.

There is a corollary to these aspects of identity. What is acquired may often be not only a view of the group one has now joined but also a view of other groups. What is acquired may be a sense of compatible and incompatible memberships. In the latter, return to an earlier status is impossible: "Now that you are an X, you may no longer be a Y." What is acquired also may be a downgrading of the outgroup. In some analyses, membership of even arbitrary groups (the experimental assignment, for example, to group X or group Y) brings with it a favored view of the group to which one has been assigned and a less favored view of the group to which one has not been assigned (e.g., Tajfel & Turner, 1986). In others, active steps are taken to ensure

that new members understand that nonmembers are lesser beings, with strict rules about fraternization. The fierceness with which males and females in primary school enforce gender boundaries is an example (e.g., Sroufe et al., 1993; Thorne & Luria, 1986).

Change within and between Individuals. Social-cultural perspectives do not rule out interest in the occurrence of change within the individual in the course of socialization. Added, however, is an interest in the way change within an individual alters the nature of the connection to others: alters not only the relationship between people who form a closely attached dyad or a family but also the relationships among members of any group. For a specific example, we take an account of Girl Scouts selling cookies in a part of the United States (Rogoff, Baker-Sennett, Lacasa, & Goldsmith, 1995). In the course of experience in selling, they point out, there is a change in the skills and perceptions of the individual. At the same time, change occurs in the relationship between the learner and all the other participants in the practice: the customers, the helping hands, other sellers, the Scout leader. Change also occurs in the practice itself. As individuals adapt their ways of selling to the times that they and their customers have available, and to the resources that they and their customers may use (calculators, credit cards, faxed order forms, etc.), the practice itself changes, along with that change there occurs change in the way the individual is introduced into the practice and the nature of the skills acquired. Needed now, Rogoff et al. (1995) argue, is not only the exploration of the third kind of change (they offer as an example a historical account of change in the practice of cookie selling) but also the recognition that all three types of change are inseparably interwoven and occur simultaneously rather than linearly.

In sum, social-cultural perspectives encourage one to take a broad and group-related view of the general nature of socialization. That view alters the ways we describe the goals or the outcomes of socialization. It also alters, we have suggested, the view taken of what influences the course of socialization. Expanding that suggestion forms our next step.

Sources and Directions of Influence

What does it mean to say that, within socialization interactions, people influence one another? Or that any socialization interaction is affected by people and conditions that go well beyond family dyads? Those questions, and some ways of answering them, were raised at the beginning of this chapter and have been the subject of comment in the perspectives we have so far considered. Some of that discussion has already been informed by social-cultural perspectives. What is added by a closer look?

Directions of Influence: Models Highlighting Fluid Change

In the early section on cross-cutting themes, we outlined some of the ways any two parties to a socialization interaction influence one another. To those proposals, we now add two models, both emphasizing the constantly changing nature of the ways mutual influence operates in practice.

Model 1: Negotiated Meanings. Conflicts between children provide an example. Within what have been called "interpretive approaches to socialization" (Corsaro & Miller, 1992, p. 1), conflicts between children are increasingly recognized as ways children define and redefine the nature of their friendship, working out between them the way they should treat each other if they wish to be still regarded as a friend or as a "best friend" (e.g., Goodwin, 1990; Rizzo, 1992; Selman & Schultz, 1990).

The same negotiation of meanings, it has been pointed out, occurs in more formal teaching-learning situations. Both teacher and learner move toward some agreed-upon definition of what "the task" shall be, a definition that is again likely to be fluid or understood as renegotiable within some agreed-upon time span or circumstances (e.g., Elbers, Maier, Hoekstra, & Hoogsteder, 1992; Newman, Griffin, & Cole, 1989). In related fashion, newcomers and old-timers in work groups negotiate with each other with regard to the level of commitment that the newcomer should bring to a job and the extent to which the interests of each should accommodate to the interests of the other (Levine & Moreland, 1991; Moreland & Levine, 1989). The approach, one should note, does not assume that the two parties bring equal power to the negotiation. That is unlikely to be the case in any expert-novice or adult-child interaction (Verdonik, Flapan, Schmit, & Weinstock, 1988). It does insist, however, on there being input and influence on both sides.

Those examples of negotiated meanings are between individuals. That restriction, however, need not always be the case. Meanings may also be negotiated between more macro segments of society. The meanings of terms such as "abuse," "harassment," "ethnic," or "discrimination" provide examples. In all such cases, the meaning of a term or an event is not handed down from on high and passively accepted. Instead, there are varying degrees of debate and disagreement before a meaning is settled on as adequate for the moment: adequate until the next negotiation or agreement has to be worked through.

Model 2: Change in One Party and Change in the Other Are Intrinsically Inseparable. In essence, this model argues against treating individuals and contexts as independent variables. Parents and children, or individuals and society, the argument runs, cannot exist without each other. "The family," for instance, may be said to "construct" people, in the sense of contributing to the personal identity that its members come to feel and to the social identity that others may assign to them. More strictly, one cannot be "a member of the family" unless a family exists. But "the family" in itself exists only insofar as its members define it as an entity and contribute to its being so. In similar fashion, an ethnic group may "construct" its members, in the sense of offering them, among other things, a label and/or a language by which they can identify themselves. But the nature of "the ethnic group" must change if its members decide to accept some aspects of membership and not others, or if many decide to cease defining themselves as part of it.

It is easy to say that "people and society construct one another," and the phrasing does serve several purposes. It reminds us once again that influence flows in more than one direction. It also serves to remind us that social structures are not static, any more than individuals are. Even after they have been established, social structures need to be maintained, and the conditions that affect the occurrence of a continued life may be different from those that affect the initial establishment. The question still remains: How do such concepts work out in practice?

Kulick (1992) provides a detailed example. He reports the disappearance of a local language from one generation to another, despite the assertion of parents that the local language should be maintained and despite a history of local identity—of a group's claim to distinctiveness—being based, for this and other subgroups in New Guinea, on the presence of a local language. Kulick brings out with care the way the disappearance is contributed to by several factors: a pattern of language socialization being left largely to older siblings rather than being the responsibility of parents; those older siblings being in schools that place a higher value on a new national language ("pidjin") than on the local language; and the children's observations that the local language is used more for "domestic" issues than for public or "important" affairs. As the children change, then, so also does the group. To retain any claim to distinctiveness, the group now needs to redefine itself in terms other than language.

Multiple Sources, Multiple Intersections

Within the early section on cross-cutting themes, we drew attention to the presence in the literature of three general types of proposals, all stemming from relatively familiar social-cultural perspectives. In one of these, parents, children, and a variety of external influences were seen as forming parts of a chain, simply or complexly defined. In a second, the several parts were fitted into more of a spatial map, with an emphasis placed on development as a form of traveling from one physical or social site (family, for instance) to others (schools, peer groups, neighborhoods, sports grounds, workplaces, etc.). In the third, the emphasis was on the ways the several parts of families and contexts could be regarded as forming a system, in which change in any one part or in the interconnection between any two inevitably flowed on to other parts until a new but temporary stabilization was achieved. A further look at social-cultural perspectives adds several concepts that enrich all three models.

The additions are fourfold. They have to do with (a) the place of socialization in relation to other activities, (b) contexts as marked by varying degrees of layering and contest, (c) contexts and the concept of access, and (d) contexts as they are perceived.

Socialization as Part of a Web of Other Activities. The socialization of children is the main source of examples. Parents, it has been pointed out, do far more than give active attention to the way children should be socialized. Both they and their children are engaged in a number of other activities both in the home and outside it. That aspect of social context is made particularly clear in studies of agricultural societies, where the mothers are heavily committed to raising food or to maintaining their status as valuable workers (e.g., LeVine et al., 1994). The phenomenon, however, is certainly not restricted to agricultural settings, nor are two general implications for the study of socialization. (These are implications over and beyond one already noted: the increased likelihood that involvement in other activities may tip the scales toward heuristic or automatic processing rather than deliberate or systematic thought.)

The first of these further implications is that we would do well to regard parents as approaching socialization with a number of goals in mind. The actions they take may then stem from the need to balance several goals or to trade success in one direction for success in another. The second is that we may need to modify accounts that emphasize parents as preparing children for a future world of peers, school, or paid work. Children, we are reminded, are also being guided toward patterns of sleeping, eating, moving, talking, and working that fit into the ongoing, here-and-now involvement of adults with other adults. This guidance begins in infancy and at an early age gives rise to large cultural differences in behaviors that may seem matters of physiological maturity (sleeping through the night, for example; Super, 1981).

Contexts as Involving Layering and Contest. The web of activities into which a particular task such as child rearing has to be fitted provides one way of describing interconnections. A further way consists of asking about the extent to which the several parts of the social world are aligned or in competition with one another. The social world may be "multilayered" (Watson-Gegeo, 1992, p. 50). Its several sectors contain the same message, building a cumulative pattern. To take an example from the area of gender, expectations about being "male" or "female" are conveyed by multiple routes: by everyday phrases ("women and children," to use Thorne's, 1987, example), the titles of schoolbooks (e.g., "Look, Jane, look; See Dick run"), or the arrangements of spaces ("ladies' rooms," "men's rooms").

In contrast to layering, what may exist is the presence of "contest" between ways of acting or ways of looking at the world. The concept of contest is of long standing, dating back at least to Gramsci's (1971) description of the social world as made up of "hegemonic" and "counterhegemonic" viewpoints. In essence, the notion of contest draws attention to two features of the social world. The first feature is the presence of diversity or multiplicity. Most social groups have more than one way of proceeding or of viewing the world. Within modern society, for example, there are both formal and alternative medicine, both formal and alternative education, both major studios and independent producers, both established churches and smaller sects, both majority and minority languages or voices. The same point may be extended to families, where again there may be both a majority and a minority voice.

The second feature underlined by the notion of contest is the significance of the way each viewpoint or practice is regarded by the other. Tolerance accompanied by mutual respect is one situation. Tolerated existence accompanied by scorn is another. A precarious tolerance that may disappear at an unpredictable moment is still another. In all cases, however, there is between parts of the social world some degree of emotionally toned appraisal and some degree of inequality in access to status or other resources. To adopt part of Wertsch's (1991a) description of the ways children come to speak in the classroom, some "voices" have a more "privileged" status than others. The rewarded voice in many classrooms, for example ("privileged" in the sense that the status it is accorded is not earned), is the "voice of science": citing facts, producing numbers, downplaying personal experience or personal anecdote, adopting a rational and impersonal frame for the description of any event (Wertsch, 1991a).

We single out the concept of contest and differential privilege for several reasons. The first is that it enriches the concept of diversity, a term that in itself does not capture the presence of tension, evaluation, and differential status. The second is that it offers an addition to the concept of system that has become part of psychologists' repertoire of ways to look at the larger social world. To the image of change in one part of a system as flowing on to change in other parts, we may now add the image of some parts making preemptive moves to establish their dominance over others. The third is that the notion of contest and privilege helps account for some of the socialization experiences that children and newcomers encounter. What happens in many cases is not simply that the newcomer is taught how to enter the new social world. What also happens is that there is an active "dismantling" and replacement of the newcomer's ways of speaking, telling stories, presenting an argument, asking questions, communicating by words or silences (e.g., Cazden, 1993; Heath, 1983; Wertsch, 1991a: the term *dismantling* comes from Michaels, 1991).

Most of the data on dismantling comes from studies of the experience of minority children in classrooms run by teachers who do not share their values. It is of interest, however, that adult socialization into work groups has also been noted as involving efforts aimed at "convincing newcomers that their previous identities, assumptions, and knowledge are no longer valid and, hence, must be replaced" (Levine & Moreland, 1991, p. 271). These efforts may include harsh initiations that underline the newcomers' ignorance and incompetence and may serve the function of demonstrating to the newcomers "how dependent they are on oldtimers" (p. 271). The phenomenon of dismantling is apparently widespread. Some joint consideration of the child and the adult studies would now seem useful to discover its forms and functions in various socialization situations.

Contexts Defined by Access. Parke and Buriel (Ch. 8, this Volume) point out that Mexican Americans occupy a particular position within the United States. It is not only that parental goals in this group may vary from those in other social groups. Significant also is the ease of access to information about Mexican settings and to Mexico as a place to which parents and/or children might return. That ease of parental access then alters the actions that parents may take.

To Parke and Buriel's point, we add the proposal that the "socializee's" access to other settings and other options also matters. Television provides one example. It provides access to a great deal of information that was previously "private" or "restricted" (knowledge, for instance, about sex or about the fact that people in authority may make errors and have personal frailties). As a result, change inevitably occurs in the way people in authority—physicians, politicians, parents—attempt to control or to persuade (Meyrowitz, 1985). Parents, for example, may seek to restrict children's access. They may also find themselves having to change the ways they manage children's experiences: shifting, for instance, from the role of shield or barrier to the role of interpreter, providing a position from which inevitably encountered events should be viewed.

At a more adult level, the significance of access to options is brought out by a vivid case history (Lawrence, Benedikt, & Valsiner, 1993) and by Tajfel's (1981) analysis of "social creativity." The case history describes the life of a young woman brought up in an extremely orthodox Jewish group. By way of books borrowed from the library, she discovers that there are other ways of viewing the world, a discovery that ultimately leads to a series of painful steps away from membership in the group. Tajfel's analysis starts from the argument that a significant part of our social experience consists of being assigned to social categories. We may be defined, for instance, as "female," "blue stockings," "nice women," "black," "Irish," or as "soft scientists." Such assignments, however do not always fit well with our self-esteem. To avoid a negative self-image (and in Tajfel's view of the individual, maintaining a positive self-image is a major motive), we may then make two moves. One is to define oneself out of the category: to "pass," to have oneself accepted, for instance, as "a different kind of woman," as "white," or as "close to biology or neurophysiology." The other is to attempt to change the value attached by the group to the dimension of the difference. To take one example, "Irish," with its connotation within several parts of the world of poor immigrants, may become redefined as "Celtic," with evidence attached of a long and powerful history. To take another, group efforts may be made to redefine the value of skin color or hair quality (as in the redefinition involved in "Black is Beautiful"), or the value of being female (as in the argument that women's approaches to relationships and politics would lead to a kinder and more peaceful world).

In effect, an individual may attempt a redefinition or a repositioning by way of individual action or by involvement in group action. The choice between the several actions, in Tajfel's (1981) proposal, is determined not only by qualities within the individual but also by the possibility of access to the new group and to support for any challenge. When the price of "passing" is high, or when "passing" is difficult (e.g., the screening procedures are stringent or one's features are undisguisable), then the likelihood increases of attempts to question or redefine the values that give rise to the negative image and to make common cause with others who offer more positive definitions of one's social identity.

Perceptions of the Larger World.   Socialization must clearly be influenced not only by the way that the world "is" but also by the way it is perceived. It is, for instance, both the reality and the perceptions of access that influence what one does and how one feels. To bring out that point, and to relate perceptions to specific aspects of socialization interactions, we concentrate on one particular aspect of perceptions: perceptions of the outside world as supporting or undermining one's socialization efforts.

The majority of the examples come from socialization by parents. When the outside world is expected to contain people who will be supportive and caring, for example, the parent's actions appear geared toward preparing the child to invite care or to reward offers of care. In Fijian society, for instance, care by siblings or by adults other than parents is normative. It is appropriate then that Fijian infants are faced outward when sitting on the mother's lap and are encouraged both to respond warmly to the attentions offered by other women and to learn welcoming forms of greetings (West, 1988).

What happens when the outside world is expected to be less welcoming? One possibility is that children are protected from exposure, kept in the cocoon of the family for as long as possible. Another possibility is that children will be prepared with some "advance arming" or "advance armor-plating." Watson-Gegeo (1992) provides one example: Kwara'ae children are warned not to expect too much benefit from going to school, and the past experience of others in the family is cited as evidence for caution. Blurton-Jones (1993) provides another, an analogue of urban "stranger danger": in an area where thick bush makes it easy to lose sight of home base, children are warned of the dangers of wandering, with stories provided not only of children who become lost but also of the monsters who lurk in the bush. Thornton, Chatters, Taylor, and Allen (1990) provide a third, in the form of African American parents giving their children explicit advice about racial discrimination, advice most likely to be given when the families are living in mixed neighborhoods, where presumably encounters with discrimination are more likely to occur than if a neighborhood is less integrated. Miller and her colleagues (Miller, Potts, Fung, Hoogstra, & Mintz, 1990; Miller & Sperry, 1988) provide a fourth: they describe mothers in low-income African American families telling stories about everyday incidents in which they have acted in a feisty, self-assertive fashion, coping effectively with a world that seeks to take advantage of them; it is a genre of stories that children then begin to use in describing their own experiences, constructing in the process a sense of self as well as a sense of what the social world is like.

Phenomena of this kind are certainly not restricted to interactions between parents and children. Newcomers in adult work groups, Moreland and Levine (1989) note, may also be kept within a circle of trustworthy oldtimers, away from people who might be less willing, less able, or less trustworthy when it comes to passing on the culture of the work group. For any age group, however, there are several gaps in the kind of picture we have painted. One has to do with the nature of "cocooning" or "pre-arming" strategies. The other has to do with the perceptions that give rise to particular strategies. If we take parents as an example, their strategies seem likely to stem from a pair of perceptions: perceptions of the world (e.g., as friendly or hostile, as reinforcing one's own message or as undermining it) and perceptions of the child (e.g., as vulnerable or as potentially strong if some advance armor or advance training in defensive strategies can be provided). The data available, however, are sparse, and we would benefit from studies that explore combinations of perception, in a fashion similar to the combinations considered in the section on cognitive perspectives for the relative attributions of power to oneself as an adult and to a child (e.g., Bugental & Shennum, 1984).

Actions, Thoughts, and Feelings

At several points in this chapter, we have noted that accounts of processes in socialization need to go beyond an exclusive concern with overt actions, incorporating attention to ideas and emotions. In the face of this emphasis, it may seem strange that we begin a discussion of what social-cognitive perspectives add on this score by turning to the nature of actions, placing that ahead of suggestions with regard to the places of cognition and affect.

A Special Place for Actions: The Significance of Cultural Practices

Social-cultural perspectives contain an emphasis on repeated, everyday ways of acting: ways of speaking, expressing emotion, marking differences between males and females, dividing work between parents or between parents and children. The area of gender provides an accessible example. From the start, parents and children may be thought of as "doing gender" (a phrase from West & Zimmerman, 1987). Parents, for example, give their male and female children different names, dress them differently, hold them differently, give them different activities that then become part of children's sense of what males and females do and of what they themselves, as a boy or a girl, should do. The routine nature of these activities gives rise to their being called *practices*. The adjective cultural, as we noted earlier, is added when a routine is followed by most members of a group.

Practice approaches are widespread within anthropology and sociology. Bourdieu (1977, 1990) and Lave (e.g., 1988; Lave & Wenger, 1991) are two well-known sources. Ortner (1985) provides a review of practice approaches in anthropology; Schieffelin and Ochs (1986) cover their use in studies of language socialization; Lancy (1996) draws attention to routines ranging from involvement in work to bedtime stories; A. Fiske (in press) brings out especially the general absence of explanatory talk for most of the routines to which children are introduced. The several chapters in Goodnow, Miller, and Kessel (1995) cover a number of overlaps between anthropology and developmental psychology, with the chapter by Miller and Goodnow (1995) drawing on Miller's expertise to provide a bridge to studies of narrative. Approaches of this kind clearly have an affinity with approaches emphasizing the importance of

"routines," "activities," and "activity systems" (e.g., Cole, 1988; Engestrom, 1993; Tharp & Gallimore, 1988). As Cole (1995) comments, the lines of overlap and demarcation among these conceptual approaches are as yet far from clear. Yet to be explored also is the nature of overlap with the overlearned and automatically processed procedures considered in the section on cognitive perspectives, and with the family practices that Parke and Buriel (Ch. 8, this Volume) draw attention to: family rituals displayed either on special occasions or in such everyday events as the greeting routinely offered to people returning home at the end of a day (e.g., Fiese, 1992; Sameroff & Fiese, 1992). Cutting across these proposals, however, is a common orientation toward thinking about socialization in terms of what people routinely do.

Why are practice approaches of particular interest within the study of socialization? One reason is that they offer an addition to the more conventional emphasis, in psychologists' analyses of socialization, on special moments: on occasions, for instance, when a child breaks a rule or engages in a tantrum and the parent responds with reason or discipline. These moments of conflict are undoubtedly important within socialization. They are certainly the occasions when rules or principles are most likely to be made explicit, as Dunn and her colleagues (e.g., Dunn, 1988; Dunn & Munn, 1985) have made especially clear. They are unlikely, however, to be the only route to socialization.

A second basis for interest is that practices may provide a particular link between actions and identity. Routine ways of solving problems—routine recourse to pencil and paper, for example—may come to mark for oneself and others whether one is a "practical" or a "schooled," "book-oriented" person (Nunes, 1995). Routines also may serve as a basis for negotiating a change in one's identity. Ways of dressing or of doing one's hair, for example, become ways adolescents signal to parents or peers the group they currently identify with (B. Miller, 1995).

The third and last reason for an interest in the concept of practices is that it brings to the surface two models for the ways actions and ideas are interrelated in the course of socialization. In one of these, the emphasis is on the actions in themselves, with ideas or principles occupying a decidedly secondary position. Routines are seen as developing an inertia or a momentum of their own. They may be accompanied by particular legitimations, but these may have little relationship to what is done and are not to be regarded as the necessary sources for actions (Bourdieu, 1977,

1990). The very nature of practices—their routine, shared quality—may in fact lead away from any reflection or questioning (e.g., Watson-Gegeo, 1992).

In the alternative model, the argument offered is that practices are the route by which children or novices come to know the principles they are expected to follow. Within any cultural group, for example, there are preferred arrangements for sleeping spaces (arrangements related to who shall share a bed or a room with what other members of the family). There are as well arrangements that elicit strong disapproval: arrangements that in some cultures take the form of a young child's sleeping alone, in others the form of a young child's sharing the parents' space. Behind these practices are principles related to the protection of the young child, the avoidance of incest, the avoidance of girls of a "sexual age" sleeping alone and unchaperoned, and the privacy of the married couple: principles that are given different priority in different cultures (Shweder, Jensen, & Goldstein, 1995). In related fashion, routine contributions to the work of a household are seen as providing a base for learning the meanings of responsibility and the expected nature of relationships among family members (Goodnow, 1996b; Goodnow & Warton, 1991). This second kind of position does not assume that practices and principles are aligned in one-to-one fashion. Children may in fact need to learn that practices and expressed principles need not coincide. What is emphasized, however, is that the everyday practices in which children participate provide a base for coming to know about principles in action, a route to understanding that is over and above the explicit statements or clarifications that are more likely to occur at moments of transgression and overt discussion. Emphasized also is the need to ask in future research what children and adults themselves perceive to be the connections among what is done, what is said, and what is understood to be the message behind the practice.

Steps in Processing Socialization Episodes

In the section on cognitive perspectives, we noted approaches that break socialization into several phases, using Grusec and Goodnow's (1994) analysis as one example and then bringing out the recursive nature of any series of phases. Stepwise approaches to processing have also been effectively used by several psychologists to bring out the interplay of culture, cognition, and emotion, primarily by way of asking how cultural conditions influence specific steps (e.g., Ellsworth, 1994; Frijda & Mesquita, 1994; Posner, Rothbart, & Harman, 1994). We follow the same general approach, offering—for the analysis of each step—suggestions drawn from social-cultural perspectives. To keep the possibilities within manageable limits, we restrict ourselves to two suggestions for each step. We also confine the breakdown by limiting it to four steps and by making no attempt to include the continuous "cross-talk" between people emphasized in the section on cognitive perspectives.

Step 1: An Expectation Is Expressed or Indicated. Social-cultural perspectives highlight some particular differences between one expectation and another and some of the particular ways an expectation is signaled.

Expectations emerge as differing first of all in the extent to which an expectation is marked as serious, as needing to be noticed and considered. All cultures mark some qualities as essential to develop, leaving others as options (e.g., D'Andrade, 1984; Goodnow, 1996a). Parents in various class groups, to take a proposal from Rodman (1963), differ in the extent to which they exhibit "value-stretch": a readiness to scale down an expectation when difficulty or resistance is encountered. The seriousness of the expectation is seen as signaled in a variety of ways, primarily by the affective quality of a statement, the tone of voice in which a statement is delivered and, a feature emphasized by Watson-Gegeo (1992), the use of particular forms of language or oratory that all members of the group come to recognize.

The second highlighted feature for expectations has to do with the expected contributions of each party. What matters is not simply what one individual should do but how that participation will be related to the contributions of others. This feature is suggested especially by analyses of teaching-learning situations. Implicit in these situations are social contracts between teacher and learner (e.g., Rommetveit, 1987), contracts that may vary from one social group to another but are in each case expected to be understood. Across cultures, for instance, differences occur in the extent to which children are expected to be alert for opportunities to observe what adults do (Rogoff, Mistry, Goncu, & Mosier, 1993), to aim at doing a task "by themselves" (Wertsch, Minick, & Arns, 1984), to proceed by tackling only what they can manage without help (Greenfield & Lave, 1982), and to rely on adults being ready to step in and take on part of the labor (Ochs, 1990). How such expected divisions of labor are signaled is not yet clear. Ochs's (1990) analysis of divisions of work in Samoan language exchanges, however, points to the importance of whether adults routinely guess at what a child has in mind as against ignoring an unclear statement or insisting that the child make a clearer statement, with both of these being ways to indicate that the task of making oneself understood belongs to the child.

Step 2: The Individual Notices, Interprets, and Encodes the Expectation.   We single out again two particular additions from social-cultural perspectives. The first of these has to do with the significance of what other people in the group are doing. When all or most people in a group act, think, or feel the same way about a topic, for example, the likelihood is higher that the individual will not engage in any systematic processing and will assume that others hold the same views as he or she does (e.g., Mesquita & Frijda, 1992). When there is more diversity within a group, and especially when there is some degree of contest between viewpoints, the chances are higher that some degree of reflection will occur, unless the individual has already been prepared to feel negatively toward particular sources of information and to discount the relevance to self of the options that in theory these sources present.

The second condition highlighted has to do with a particular contribution from the group. This is the availability of a set of categories into which people or events may be placed. Biological perspectives offer the possibility that we arrive in the world ready to partition the world in some ways rather than others. For instance, we appear to be alert from the start to some particular differences in relationships. In contrast, some cognitive perspectives—notably, those derived from Piagetian theory—have emphasized the extent to which individuals construct categories on the bases of their own experience. Social-cultural perspectives offer a further alternative. They underline the ways the group offers "prepackaged" categories for people or events (the term is from Shweder, 1982). Prepackaged categories are by no means static. We come to know the categories that are available and what they cover. We also come to know how to alter, bend, or transform the available categories in ways that suit our purposes but still allow some degree of communication with others. In the course of all these transformations or constructions, however, social-cultural perspectives remind us of the presence in most cases of an existing set of categories that provides a starting point or that moderates invention. Needed, as Dowd (1990) points out, is an "appreciation for the creative and transformative powers of human beings, as well as for the constraining power of social structures" (p. 139).

Step 3: The Individual Adopts a Stance toward the Perceived Expectation: Feels Positively or Negatively about It, Accepts It in Whole or in Part, Questions, Negotiates, Resists, or Rejects It.   From what social-cultural perspectives offer, we single out again two particular additions. The first has to do with the extent to which cultures promote particular evaluative stances toward various kinds of sources: old texts, classical philosophers, members of the bourgeoisie, people over 30. All these categories may be singled out as untrustworthy, irrelevant, or fit subjects for parody and scorn (Bakhtin, 1965; Wertsch, 1991a, 1991b).

The second addition has to do with analyses of resistance. Social-cultural perspectives underline the need to consider both active and passive forms of resistance and to keep in mind their links to identity. More finely, resistance to the socialization pressures of one group may promote solidarity with another. Resisting or breaking the rules set by adults may be the route into solidarity with one's peers, even in nursery school (e.g., Corsaro, 1988). Resistance to the achievement or productivity pressures brought by teachers or by supervisors in the workplace may be the way by which young males establish their identity as one of "the lads" (Willis, 1977).

Step 4: The Individual Gives Some Indication of What Is Understood and of His or Her Stance; This Indication Is Noticed and Interpreted by Others.   In effect, a new cycle starts. Psychologists' analyses of this step concentrate on parent-child interactions. They ask, for instance, about the conditions under which children disguise or make blatant a difference with their parents (e.g., Goodnow, 1995), or parents move toward reducing the divergence between their positions and the positions of their adolescent children (e.g., Collins & Luebker, 1995). Social-cultural perspectives draw attention to the need to ask: Under what conditions do members of a group, other than parents, become involved? Cultures differ in the extent to which people feel that it is appropriate for others to offer parents unsolicited comment or advice (Keller, Miranda, & Gauda, 1984), or, in any situation marked by distress or conflict, to carefully look the other way until calm has been restored (Mesquita, cited by Frijda & Mesquita, 1994).

The Place of Affect

We have proposed that social-cultural perspectives offer some specific additions and alternatives relevant to particular steps within a socialization interaction. If the additions appear to be predominantly cognitive in style, this is in large part because that is where the emphasis within social-cultural perspectives has often fallen. In line with developments in other perspectives, the emphasis on affect as a critical process is relatively recent. Part of the current burst of activity, however, is an attempt to break away from the concept of affect as a given, physiological state—with culture then entering the picture as a set of rules regulating its display. The alternative view regards the experience, the interpretation, and the naming of emotions as culturally constructed (e.g., Briggs, 1992; White, 1994). That general alternative has given rise to several lines of research on emotion and culture. The volume edited by Kitayama and Markus (1994) brings together a number of these; Jenkins (1994) offers a summary particularly concerned with anthropological research.

From these several analyses, we draw out some proposals that are specifically relevant to socialization and to the possible links between cognition and affect. The first of these is an addition to the notion of "shared meanings" or "cultural understandings." What is shared, it is pointed out, are not only semantic meanings but also affective significance (D'Andrade, 1992; Frijda & Mesquita, 1994). People come to feel similar emotions—pleasure, horror, approval, disgust—in particular situations.

The second addition takes the form of proposing that what we observe most readily when we look at how others behave is the way they feel about an event. This kind of proposal is especially clear in Frijda and Mesquita's (1994) merger of cognitive and affective processes. When all or most people respond with affect to an event, they propose, that topic is likely to become a "focal concern" for the individual, increasing the likelihood that he or she will then monitor carefully for its occurrence, feel more certain of his or her judgments, regard "alternative interpretations of the situation or alternative reactions as inconceivable" (Frijda & Mesquita, 1994, p. 69), and perceive what happens with regard to this object or event as relevant to one's own concerns. That perceived relevance to one's own concerns, in Frijda and Mesquita's analysis, is then the critical step toward arousal and the attachment of affect to the situation. In a further extension of the notion that what we notice most is the way that people feel about an event, Mesquita has proposed that cultures vary in the extent to which we are socialized into being alert for particular kinds of emotion (ignoring some, responding to others), into responding in particular ways (into rational or empathic responses, for example), and into recognizing the

cues that mean acknowledgment of the emotion and a particular kind of response will be welcome rather than felt to be intrusive (Mesquita, cited by Frijda & Mesquita, 1994). In effect, affect serves as a direct base for others coming to play an active role in the socialization we so often treat as a two-party interaction.

Differentiating among Occasions for Socialization

In the opening section on cross-cutting themes, we set out the argument that no single account of socialization is likely to apply to all occasions, and that ways need to be found to differentiate among occasions. What do social-cultural perspectives add on this score? One proposal has already been cited in the section on cognitive perspectives. This is A. Fiske's (1992) proposal that some types of relationships are universal and biologically given, a proposal accompanied by evidence that people do not make categorization errors across types. To that proposal we may now add another, from Whiting and Edwards (1988), based on the appearance in several cultural groups of a distinction that is difficult to attribute to socialization. This is to the effect that children spontaneously respond to "lap" children with nurturance and to "knee" or "yard" children (provided they are younger than oneself) with attempts at dominance. This spontaneous differentiation presents mothers on the one hand with a behavior they need only encourage and, on the other, with a behavior that may run counter to what they wish to see.

Social-cultural perspectives contain as well a number of proposals that are not couched in terms of domain specificity but that point to dimensions that may be used to differentiate among occasions of socialization. Some of the dimensions proposed (e.g., variations as a function of the importance of a goal to the parent) might stem from any perspective. More specific to social-cultural perspectives is the proposal that the way socialization proceeds varies with the position in the group of the people involved. Socialization cannot proceed in the usual ways, for example, when the child is in the position of knowing more about the larger social world than the parent does: when the child is in the position of being the "culture-broker" (this point is amply brought out by Parke and Buriel, Ch. 8, this Volume). Socialization has also been pointed to as proceeding in different ways as a function of what others in the group provide or are perceived as offering. Some approaches are feasible when there are others in the group who provide support, who validate a parent's efforts, or to whom some of the tasks of socialization can be entrusted. Quite different strategies are likely to occur when others in the group provide, instead of consensus or validation from like-minded others, a heterogeneous set of viewpoints, contest, antagonism, few possibilities for task sharing, and, if encounters with an undermining diversity are likely, a need for parents to provide the child with some protective armor. In all these circumstances, what is underlined is the nature of conditions within a group or groups, extending beyond the individual or the family.

Research Methods and Utility of Social-Cultural Perspectives

We ended the analysis of each of the earlier sets of perspectives—biological and cognitive—with a general comment on utility. For social-cultural perspectives, we combine that comment with some discussion of research methods. Traditionally, research based on social-cultural perspectives has been associated with two particular methods: comparisons across cultural groups and across subgroups within a culture. We shall concentrate on methods that are additions to this traditional pair.

That concentration does not deny the value of comparisons across cultural groups or across subgroups in a culture. As Parke and Buriel (Ch. 8, this Volume) emphasize, we need always to ask whether the accounts we construct on the basis of data gathered with one group apply to other groups. Only by sampling groups outside the Western world, for instance, can we discover that infants can become deeply attached to their mothers without the eye-to-eye contact that we see as an essential part of bonding between mother and child (LeVine, 1990), that children emerge with linguistic skills in place even though their parents do not engage in verbal prompts and verbal games with them (e.g., Ochs, 1990), and that they are not irreparably damaged by the practice of sleeping in a parent's bed or a parent's room until what many would regard as the much-too-late age of 6 or 7 years or later (e.g., Shweder et al., 1995). In addition, it is only by sampling groups other than one's own and by coming to know that they may regard "our" methods of child rearing with horror (e.g., LeVine et al., 1994), that we become aware of the extent to which socialization into any group seems to bring with it the assumption that one's own ways are normal, natural, and—if not necessary for healthy development—at least optimal. We need to step outside our own groups, then, both to test theoretical positions and to become aware of the implications of labels such as "mainstream," "minority," "ethnic," and "other."

What, then, is possible if we concentrate on analyses within a social group? Throughout the course of this section, a number of suggestions have been made. At this point, we single out a few for particular comment (for a number of others, see Goodnow, in press). One recommendation is for increased attention to everyday practices and their specific effects. At the moment, that recommendation is most strongly represented by studies of the way talk proceeds, with talk covering both everyday conversation and family stories (e.g., Fiese, Hooker, Kotary, Schwagler, & Rimmer, 1995; Goodwin, 1990; Miller, 1992; Ochs, 1990; Schieffelin, 1990). Talk illustrates par excellence the dependence of meaning on the social context, and the expectation that the novice will pick up the contextual meaning. The meaning of the phrase *How are you?*, for example, depends on how it is asked, when, by whom, and of whom. In addition, talk or discourse provides a superb vehicle for analyzing the ways people negotiate what a word shall mean (for example, the meaning of *fair* or *a friend*). In talk, as well, one can observe the way differences in power and the nature of expected relationships enter directly into the experience of a child. Family conversations, for example, bring out not only the content of what is said but the opportunity to observe who initiates, who interrupts, who interrogates, who evades interrogation and by what means (Ochs & Taylor, 1992). The larger family structure, indeed the larger social structure, is laid bare. Talk, however, is by no means the only everyday practice that offers a base for studying socialization. We might well explore practices related to eating, sleeping, forms of dress, or divisions of work, choosing among these on the basis of their particular links to specific outcomes, such as a family's sense of cohesion and identity (e.g., Fiese, 1992), a child's development of concern for others (e.g., Grusec, Goodnow, & Cohen, 1996), or a child's coming to recognize a hierarchy of moral principles (e.g., Shweder et al., 1995).

A further large recommendation takes the form of asking how other people enter into any two-party interaction. The interactions we choose as a focus may be between two people: child and parent, novice and member, student and teacher. In the background of that interaction, however, and at times entering directly into it, are other people. How do we begin to put together those "others" and our chosen pair or trio? Social-cultural perspectives suggest several possibilities. They draw attention to socialization as preparation for participation and membership in a group or in several groups, highlighting the need to ask how these future groups are perceived by the preparers and what conditions influence the particular ways preparation proceeds: ways that may range from demonstrating how to make friends to providing a child with some advance armor for the slights expected to be probable or inevitable.

Social-cultural perspectives draw attention also to the variety of ways others provide information about ways of acting, thinking, and feeling, providing an expanded view of the social referencing often noted as occurring within two-party interactions and adding to what we know about developmental changes in social comparisons. We might well ask how children use their perceptions of others—in particular, their perceptions of what "most others" are like—as a base for constructing social categories or prototypes, for working out one's position in a group, for coming to understand what is important to know or to be, and for developing a sense of the options or degrees of negotiability that may be feasible for oneself.

Others may also enter socialization interactions in more direct fashion. On the one hand, they are a source of activities and demands that may support or compete with socialization tasks. Even more directly, other people may intervene in the interaction, a possibility that prompts us to ask about the principles that regulate when various kinds of intervention are regarded as feasible or reasonable. We know at this point that there are cultural variations in when advice from others about child rearing is regarded as reasonable or as intrusive (Keller, Miranda, & Gauda, 1984). We know also that cultural groups vary in the ways they signal that involvement would be welcomed or found unacceptable (Mesquita, cited in Frijda & Mesquita, 1994). We are some distance, however, from understanding the several ways—direct or indirect—by which the presence, the viewpoints, and the involvement of others in socialization influence specific aspects of the socialization process.

In short, the specific research strategies for exploring the impact of the social group may vary. The aim in all cases, however, is to create some merger between a focus on interactions between two people and the recognition that other members of the social group are also part of that interaction.

A Final Comment on the Socio-Cultural Perspective. All told, we have aimed at bringing out several benefits to starting from a social-cultural perspective. As a minimum, we hope we have dispelled the notion that these perspectives involve studies of a particularly limited kind: studies that ask only whether a socialization practice observed in one social class or one culture is observed in others, that are limited to descriptions of unusual events in exotic "other" places, that frame socialization in the one-way

terms of "society" shaping individuals, that ignore individual variations in their preoccupation with groups, and that are remote from the usual concerns with cognition and affect with which most developmental psychologists are familiar. There is only one other preconception that we have not addressed. This is the incompatibility that may be thought to exist between biological and social-cultural perspectives. We noted in the section on biological perspectives that this incompatibility is a misconception. To make the point again, we draw attention to the frequent presence in anthropology of researchers with an interest in "evolutionary" perspectives (e.g., LeVine et al., 1994; Werner, 1988). We draw attention also to the presence in this *Handbook* of arguments to the effect that an interest in culture and an interest in physiological states can go hand in hand. Physiological states are not simply states that cultures come to terms with, they are themselves altered by cultural patterns and conditions. In effect, while each set of perspectives has its own particular utility, they do not pull in completely opposite directions.

INTEGRATION

In pulling together the common threads that we have found across socialization perspectives, we return to the crosscutting themes that we introduced at the start of the chapter. In particular, we focus on the ways these positions may be interwoven to give a reformulated picture of the "tasks" of socialization, the many faces and functions of socialization, the constituent components of socialization, and the various forms that mutual influence may take. The approaches we have offered complement rather than compete with each other in accounting for socialization for life tasks.

What Are the Changes in the Subject Matter of Socialization?

The term socialization refers both to a social end product and to the changes that occur by way of social interactions. In both senses of the word, views of socialization have undergone a shift that broadens what is considered, and calls for a closer look at activities and interactions in the course of everyday life.

From a biological perspective, the shifting view of socialization has taken the form of asking what is (or historically *was)* critical to the welfare of the child and the group, and then asking about the skills needed to achieve those tasks. Attention turns, for example, to the perceptual skills needed to identify others, the mental capacity to envision the thoughts of others, mental algorithms that "keep track" of equity within relationships, and emotional and neural responses that promote and sustain proximity between mother and infant. The bases of these skills are sought in biology. Biologically, the argument runs, we are prepared to "tune in" to the social signals that act to establish and maintain social relationships in particular ways.

Cognitive perspectives bring into play the "operating principles" that govern the organized ways we think about others within socializing relationships. The cognitive task is one of understanding, predicting, and coping with the continuous flow of interactive events within socializing relationships—in the service of joint goals. Such processes include easily retrieved information drawn from one's personal history, the group's shared history, and universally shared ways of conceptualizing different kinds of relationships. Additionally, however, cognitions also include slower appraisal processes that allow the envisioning of alternative perspectives and future options. Effective socialization involves the facilitation of such processes among novices by those with greater knowledge or experience.

Breadth again is the message from social-cultural perspectives. Socialization covers any task or content area that is part of learning a cultural pattern or that is part of learning about the positions and places that one might occupy in a social structure or in the groups that are part of that structure. The bases to such learning are typically sought in the patterns of everyday life, in the apparently mundane routine arrangement of ordinary tasks rather than in the more occasional moments of transgression followed by discipline.

Taken together, these shifts may be characterized as moving from the extraordinary to the ordinary. They reflect a shift to a concern with the capacity to engage in life with others: to communicate with them, understand them, share feelings with them, invest in the welfare of those with whom we share a social identity, work together toward consensually valued goals, and negotiate disputes when goals differ.

What Are the Relevant Processes Involved in Socialization?

In discussing changes within the socialization literature, we have pointed out the increased understanding that is offered by moving beyond concerns with actions and insular theories. Increasingly, we have seen the inclusion of affective and cognitive variables as mediators and moderators of behavior. Once again, however, the different perspectives highlight the different ways actions, emotions, and cognitions may come to be interwoven.

Emotions

From a biological perspective, emotions serve both as a self- and social-regulation process. Emotions are conceptualized from the standpoint of their regulatory role in the management of inner states. They are also conceptualized in terms of their value as social signals and social regulators; that is, emotional signals provide information regarding the intentions of others, as well as directly serving to motivate particular responses from others.

From a cognitive perspective, emotions both regulate and are regulated by cognitions. Indeed, social cognitions increasingly have been conceptualized in terms of associated affective processes (Fiske & Pavelchak, 1986). For example, affect serves to influence the amount of attention that is available for information acquisition, memory retrieval or storage, and appraisal processes. Affect also serves to *focus* those processes on salient aspects of the environment, salient representations of past events, and salient response options.

Within social-cultural perspectives, affect again is seen as an integral part of the ideas we hold and the practices we follow. In addition to this place within the experience of individuals, however, affect emerges as a critical part of our experiences with others. Interactions with others give rise to the experience and labeling of particular emotions. In addition, affect serves as a particular kind of signal to others. It is a signal of the importance of a position or event. When all or most of the group one belongs to, for example, display horror at the violations of some norm or delight at some achievement, then we come to monitor for situations that might give rise to these behaviors. As well, affect is a way we signal to others whether their involvement in our actions will be welcome or not.

Cognitions

Throughout this chapter, we have pointed to the many ways cognitions act to influence actions and feelings within socializing interactions. At this point, we draw attention to one particular feature of cognition that has appeared in all three perspectives. Its surface form varies somewhat from one perspective to another, but the same basic quality is present throughout. This quality has to do with the extent to which processing is deliberative and systematic, or relatively fast and automatic. We draw attention to this issue due to the fact that within psychology, socialization has often been thought of as a deliberate, intentional process by which cultural values are knowingly transmitted from one generation to the next. In actual fact, however, socializing influences often operate in a much more automatic fashion. Automatic processes operate as historically efficient, easily accessible shortcuts in dealing with emotionally significant events. But once they become established, they may persist without regard for their continuing usefulness.

From a biological perspective, children and caregivers are prepared to show perceptual sensitivities and information organization that occur in ways that may be thought of as automatic. The automaticity of such processes is suggested by their occurrence in the absence of learning, and their resistance to modification—even when no longer serving adaptive functions. Processes that helped to solve problems in our historical past may persist despite their lack of utility in solving present-day problems.

Automaticity in the cognitive domain appears in terms of "front-end" processes that allow participants in socializing interaction to easily access experiential information as organizers of actions. Relationship schemas or internal working models become established as overlearned representations that subsequently influence later relationships (Hazan & Shaver, 1987). Deliberative or systematic processing may be the exception, brought into play when something is puzzling or when some well-practiced heuristics do not achieve what is wanted.

Where, then, does an absence of careful thought appear within social-cultural perspectives? It appears in particular strength with reference to the importance of practices. When parents' ways of rearing children are shared by others and are part of routine daily life, little thought may be given to why one might proceed in one way rather than another. In similar fashion, children who are introduced into ways of acting, thinking, and feeling by being immersed in activities that are pursued in routine fashion, with little explanation offered as to why they are being undertaken, are likely to take for granted those ways of acting, thinking, and feeling. Habit and custom rather than reflection are likely to become the basis of what emerges.

Who Is Influencing Whom?
Double Direction of Effects

Possibly the greatest area of convergence across the perspectives explored in this chapter has occurred with respect to conceptions of directions of effects. On all sides,

we now see the emergence of new metaphors as we reformulate our thinking about the forms that double directions of influence may take (e.g., Kuczynski, 1993). The specific forms of bidirectionality that are highlighted vary from one perspective to another; from each perspective, attempts are being made to go beyond the simple statement that children and caregivers (or individuals and society) affect one another.

A biological approach focuses on the ways we are selectively prepared to jointly engage in social interactions and to act as coconstructors of culture within that frame. The emerging evidence supporting this position acts to signal the end of a tabula rasa approach to socialization—and associated interests in child compliance. In its place, we see a redefinition of interests in bidirectional effects or joint contributions to socialization to include consideration of the ways both parties are prepared for the socialization process.

From a cognitive perspective, we have pointed out the increasing variety of ways that cognitive processes (as well as interactions) may be thought of as "shared." In earlier conceptualizations of reciprocity, a turn-taking metaphor was popular, such as might be found in radio contact between individuals at distant locations. First, one individual acts and then the other responds; this response in turn acts as a signal for the first person. What is lacking within this way of thinking about reciprocal interaction is the continuous nature of interactions. One of the earliest moves away from narrow conceptualizations of reciprocal processes (turn-taking *dyads)* was to represent socialization metaphorically as systems, thus suggesting that dyads are embedded in larger social structures. We also see increasing use of terminology that conceptualizes socialization as a collaborative process, that is, the shared creation of social interactions and social knowledge (e.g., coregulation, coconstruction, attunement). Finally, we have seen a movement toward a focus on the continuous "interplay" within such interactions (e.g., Emde, 1993; Hinde, 1992). Children and their socializers are seen as participating in a shared, intersubjective world in which relationships and culture are being continuously created and revised.

Social-cultural perspectives pick up some of the same emphasis on continuous creation and revision. The bases to this continuous revision, however, are perceived in a different way. One basis stems from a less rosy picture of coregulation than developmental psychologists often propose. Interactions, it is often proposed, may take the form of mutual pressure and resistance. Shifting degrees of influence are then inevitable in the wake of shifting degrees of interest in pressing or resisting or shifting capacities to do so. The other basis stems from a double concern that is not prominent within the other two perspectives. The concern is with the need to explain both how ways of acting, thinking, and feeling persist over time, and how innovations and changes come about (in one version of this double concern, the need is to account for both the "reproduction" and the "production" of society). That double concern leads toward a distinction between the establishment of a way of proceeding and its maintenance. Establishment does not mean that a way of proceeding may be expected to stay firmly in place; on the contrary, the need for constant support or validation may be the state to assume as natural. An established way of proceeding may then exert an influence because it is already in place. Influence from other sources is inevitable, however, when the effort or the agreement of others is needed to keep it in place. On either basis, bi-directionality is taken as a given. The problem now faced is how to account for its shifting form.

Finally, we may ask whether there is some general model that might encompass all of the suggested ways of viewing mutual influence within the socialization process. One possibility consists of proposing that each party provides constraints and opportunities for the other. Historically, the socialization literature has emphasized the constraints and opportunities that adults provide for the young. Attention has also been directed to the constraints that are provided by the young. Equally important, however, are the opportunities that are provided by the young. The young provide opportunities for older members of the group in the form of mutations, variations, and innovations (Campbell, 1965). They also present their caregivers with the responsibility of looking after a highly vulnerable other who relies upon them to survive and who needs protection from dangers that they cannot cope with unaided. If that responsibility is accepted, there comes the opportunity for both a changed view of self and a changed view of the world.

Is Socialization a Single Process or a Set of Processes?

From each vantage point we have taken, we have seen evidence that argues against socialization as involving a single set of rules that applies across all situations and at all ages. At the same time, it seems equally unlikely that there is an unlimited set of routes to socialization, with a new route for each and every occasion. We have accordingly been alert to what each perspective offers as an alternative way forward, avoiding the procrustean bed of all-purpose theories as well as the potential chaos of unlimited specificity or situatedness. What has emerged is the value of thinking in terms of particular domains or "families" of situations that appear to operate according to different operating rules.

From a biological perspective, it may be suggested that coevolutionary processes have prepared adults and children for functioning within different types of situations, that is, the shared domains of social life. The socialization tasks of interest are those that are universal in nature and that have been of critical importance in our evolutionary history. The socialization categories (or domains) proposed have to do with the maintenance of proximity under conditions of potential threat, establishing one's place in power-ranked hierarchies, establishing the group one belongs to (the "us" and "them" of social life), and establishing ways of negotiating shared costs and benefits in work and play.

Social cognitive views of relationships have traditionally taken a domain-general view, in which social processes are organized by the same principles as nonsocial processes. Such views may overestimate the extent to which processes that act to regulate our nonsocial experiences are the same as those that govern our social experiences. Increasingly, however, we are coming to believe that the ways we think about the social world are distinguishable from the ways we think about the nonsocial world (Brewer, 1994). Additionally, we have seen distinctions emerge between different types of social situations, both in developmental and adult theories of social cognition. Different "rules" apply on the basis of the various characteristics of the people being thought about (e.g., their gender, their age, their identity as one of "us" or one of "them"), the nature of the perceived relationship (e.g., Clark, Helgeson, Mickelson, & Pataki, 1994; Fiske et al., 1991), or the nature of the social judgments involved (e.g., the moral vs. conventional domains proposed by Turiel, 1983).

Social-cultural perspectives offer a further set: a concern with differentiations in terms of the extent to which various ways of acting, thinking, and feeling are regarded as important, as requiring effort to establish, as open to choice or experimentation, and as involving actions that are likely to be supported, rather than undermined, by others in the group.

The particular grouping of situations (and the associated processes) may vary with different perspectives on socialization. Shared across perspectives, however, is the view that particular sensitivities, expectations, processing forms, and affective qualities are associated with particular socialization tasks.

CONCLUSION

As a final thought, it is interesting to note the increasing questions that have emerged concerning the extent to which parents have any unique effect on children's development. Maccoby and Martin ended their 1983 review with a question concerning the robustness of reported effects of socializing adults on children. Scarr (1992) again raised this question in her concern with "good enough" parenting, that is, the extent to which variations in parenting have any consequences once some minimum level of acceptability is reached. Harris (1995) suggested that, within the range of effects usually studied, parents have no effect on the ultimate psychological characteristics of their children. In her analysis, the group is the main source of socialization. In a slightly different vein, behavior geneticists noted that the environments experienced by children growing up in the same family are primarily unshared (Plomin, 1994), suggesting either that (a) socialization is dyad-specific or (b) we have underestimated the similarities in socialization across families (of those families operating in similar environments).

So what conclusion would we reach at this point in our review? First of all, it may be that there is indeed a high degree of communality in the socialization of coordinated routines with others in carrying out daily life tasks, the understanding and predictions of commonly occurring interactive events, and the solving of shared problems. At the same time, we should not throw out the need for consideration of nonshared patterns of socialization. Nonshared patterns may range from those that are biological (e.g., genetic variations that influence receptivity to socialization), to those that are experiential (e.g., settings that place stresses on socializing systems), to those that are multiply determined (e.g., biological changes that follow from extreme experiences, and that in turn act to modify future experiences). In short, variations in socialization and the circumstances of socialization have clear implications for successful adaptation to the demands of group life. It must always be recognized that there are certain kinds of environments that are "toxic" to effective socialization. Ultimately, then, we are also concerned with the social policies that impact on the contexts of socialization. The direction for the future includes consideration of the interplay of complex forces that guide the course of socialization in the world as we know it. At the same time, our study of socialization needs to include consideration of the "possible worlds" we may create.

ACKNOWLEDGMENTS

We would like to express our appreciation to Marilynn Brewer, Leda Cosmides, Joan Grusec, Frank Kessel, Bert Moore, and Ross Parke for their thoughtful suggestions on earlier drafts of the manuscript. In addition, we would like to thank Nancy Eisenberg for her valued input as Volume Editor.

REFERENCES

Adamson, L. G., & Bakeman, R. (1991). The development of shared attention during infancy. *Annals of Child Development, 8,* 1–41.

Affleck, G., & Tennen, H. (1991). Appraisal and coping predictors of mother and child outcomes after newborn intensive care. *Journal of Social and Clinical Psychology, 10,* 424–447.

Ainsworth, M. D. S., Bell, S. M., & Stayton, D. J. (1971). Individual differences in Strange Situation behavior of 1-year-olds. In H. R. Schaffer (Ed.), *The origins of human social relations* (pp. 17–57). London: Academic Press.

Ainsworth, M. D. S., Blehar, M. C., Waters, E., & Wall, S. (1978). *Patterns of attachment: A psychological study of the Strange Situation.* Hillsdale, NJ: Erlbaum.

Alessandri, S., & Wozniak, R. H. (1989). Perception of the family environment and intrafamilial agreement in belief concerning the adolescent. *Journal of Early Adolescence, 9,* 67–81.

Alexander, K. L., & Entwisle, D. R. (1988). Achievement in the first two years of school: Patterns and processes. *Monographs of the Society for Research in Child Development, 53*(2, Serial No. 218).

Andersen, S. M., & Glasman, N. S. (1996). Responding to significant others when they are not there: Effects on interpersonal inference, motivation, and affect. In R. M. Sorrentino & E. T. Higgins (Eds.), *Handbook of motivation and cognition* (Vol. 3, pp. 262–321). New York: Guilford Press.

Anderson, J. R. (1983). *The architecture of cognition.* Cambridge, MA: Harvard University Press.

Archer, J. (1990). The influence of testosterone on human aggression. *British Journal of Psychology, 82,* 1–28.

Aron, A., Aron, E. N., Tudor, M., & Nelson, G. (1991). Close relationships as including other in self. *Journal of Personality and Social Psychology, 60,* 241–253.

Azar, S. T., Robinson, D. R., Hekimian, E., & Twentyman, C. T. (1984). Unrealistic expectations and problem-solving ability in maltreating and comparison mothers. *Journal of Consulting and Clinical Psychology, 52,* 687–691.

Bakhtin, M. (1965). *Rabelais and his world.* Cambridge, MA: MIT Press.

Baldwin, M. W. (1992). Relational schemas and the processing of social information. *Psychological Bulletin, 112,* 461–484.

Baldwin, M. W., Fehr, B., Keedian, E., Seidel, M., & Thompson, D. W. (1993). An exploration of the relational schema underlying attachment styles: Self-report and lexical decision approaches. *Personality and Social Psychology Bulletin, 19,* 746–754.

Baltes, M. M. (1986). The etiology and maintenance of dependence in the elderly: Three phases of operant research. *Behavior Therapy, 19,* 301–319.

Bandura, A. (1969). Social learning of moral judgments. *Journal of Personality and Social Psychology, 11,* 275–279.

Bandura, A. (1977). Self-efficacy: Toward a unifying theory of behavior change. *Psychological Review, 84,* 191–215.

Bandura, A. (1989). Social cognitive theory. *Annals of Child Development, 6,* 1–60.

Bargh, J. A. (1994). The four horsemen of automaticity: Awareness, intention, efficiency, and control in social cognition. In R. W. Wyer, Jr. & T. K. Srull (Eds.), *Handbook of social cognition* (2nd ed., pp. 1–40). Hillsdale, NJ: Erlbaum.

Bargh, J. A., Chen, M., & Burrows, L. (1996). Automaticity of social behavior. *Journal of Personality and Social Psychology, 71,* 230–244.

Bargh, J. A., & Gollwitzer, P. M. (1994). Environmental control of goal-directed action: Automatic and strategic contingencies between situations and behavior. *Nebraska Symposium on Motivation, 41,* 71–124.

Baron-Cohen, S. (1991). The theory of mind deficit in autism: How specific is it? *British Journal of Developmental Psychology, 9,* 301–314.

Baron-Cohen, S. (1994). How to build a baby that can read minds. *Cahiers de Psychologie Cognitives, 13,* 1–40.

Bates, J. E. (1987). Temperament in infancy. In J. D. Osofsky (Ed.), *Handbook of infant development* (pp. 1101–1149). New York: Wiley.

Baumgardner, A. H., & Arkin, R. M. (1988). Affective state mediates causal attributions for success and failure. *Motivation and Emotion, 12,* 99–111.

Baumrind, D. (1967). Child care practices anteceding three patterns of preschool behavior. *Genetic Psychology Monographs, 75,* 43–88.

Baumrind, D. (1971). Current patterns of parental authority. *Developmental Psychology, 4,* 1–103.

Baumrind, D. (1993). The average expectable environment is not good enough: A response to Scarr. *Child Development, 64,* 1299–1317.

Beckwith, L., & Cohen, S. (1989). Maternal responsiveness with preterm infants and later competency. In M. H. Bornstein (Ed.), *Maternal responsiveness: Characteristics and consequences* (pp. 75–88). San Francisco: Jossey-Bass.

Bell, R. A. (1968). A reinterpretation of the direction of effects in studies of socialization. *Psychological Review, 75,* 81–95.

Bell, R. A. (1977). Socialization findings re-examined. In R. Q. Bell & L. V. Harper (Eds.), *Child effects on adults* (pp. 53–84). Hillsdale, NJ: Erlbaum.

Bell, R. A., & Ainsworth, M. D. (1972). Infant crying and maternal responsiveness. *Child Development, 43,* 1171–1190.

Belsky, J. (1993). Etiology of child maltreatment: A developmental-ecological analysis. *Psychological Bulletin, 114,* 413–434.

Belsky, J., & Cassidy, J. (in press). Attachment: Theory and evidence. In M. Rutter, D. Hay, & S. Baron-Cohen (Eds.), *Developmental principles and clinical issues in psychology and psychiatry.* Oxford, England: Blackwell.

Belsky, J., Rovine, M., & Taylor, D. G. (1984). The Pennsylvania Infant and Family Development Project: III. The origins of individual differences in infant-mother attachment: Maternal and infant contributions. *Child Development, 55,* 718–728.

Belsky, J., Steinberg, L., & Draper, P. (1991). Childhood experience, interpersonal development, and reproductive strategy: An evolutionary theory of socialization. *Child Development, 62,* 647–670.

Benenson, J. F. (1993). Greater preference among females than males for dyadic interaction in early childhood. *Child Development, 64,* 544–555.

Benoit, D., & Parker, K. C. H. (1994). Stability and transmission of attachment across three generations. *Child Development, 65,* 1444–1456.

Berndt, T. J., Cheung, P. C., Lau, S., Hau, K., & Lew, W. J. F. (1993). Perceptions parenting in Mainland China, Taiwan, and Hong Kong: Sex differences and societal differences. *Developmental Psychology, 29,* 156–164.

Bertenthal, B. I., Proffitt, H. D. R., Spetner, N. B., & Thomas, M. A. (1985). The development of infant sensitivity to biomechanical motions. *Child Development, 56,* 531–543.

Block, J. H. (1984). *Sex role identity and ego development.* San Francisco: Jossey-Bass.

Blurton-Jones, N. (1993). The lives of hunter-gatherer children: Effects of parental behavior and parental reproductive strategy. In M. E. Pereira & L. A. Fairbanks (Eds.), *Juvenile primates: Life history, development, and behavior* (pp. 309–326). New York: Oxford University Press.

Bornstein, M. H., Tamis-LeMonda, C. S., Tal, J., Ludemann, P., Toda, S., Rahn, C. W., Pecheux, M., Azuma, H., & Vardi, D. (1992). Maternal responsiveness to infants in three societies: The United States, France, and Japan. *Child Development, 63,* 808–821.

Bourdieu, P. (1977). *Outline of a theory of practice.* Cambridge, England: Cambridge University Press.

Bourdieu, P. (1979). *Distinction: A social critique of the judgment of taste.* London: Routledge & Kegan Paul.

Bourdieu, P. (1990). *A logic of practice.* Palo Alto, CA: Stanford University Press.

Bourdieu, P., & Passeron, J.-C. (1977). *Reproduction in education, society, and culture.* Beverly Hills: Sage.

Bower, G. H. (1981). Mood and memory. *American Psychologist, 36,* 129–148.

Bowlby, J. (1969). *Attachment and loss: Vol. 1. Attachment.* New York: Basic Books.

Bowlby, J. (1973). *Attachment and loss: Vol. 2. Separation.* New York: Basic Books.

Bowlby, J. (1980). *Attachment and loss: Vol. 3. Loss.* New York: Basic Books.

Boyd, R., & Richerson, P. J. (1995). Life in the fast lane: Rapid cultural change and the human evolution process. In J. P. Changeux & J. Chavaillon (Eds.), *Origins of the human brain. Symposia of the Fyssen Foundation* (pp. 155–169). Oxford, England: Oxford University Press.

Bradley, R. H., & Caldwell, B. M. (1995). The acts and conditions of the caregiving environment. *Developmental Review, 15,* 38–85.

Breland, K., & Breland, M. (1966). *Animal behavior.* New York: Macmillan.

Bretherton, I. (1980). Young children in stressful situations: The supporting role of attachment figures and unfamiliar caregivers. In G. V. Coelho & P. I. Ahmed (Eds.), *Uprooting and development* (pp. 179–210). New York: Plenum Press.

Bretherton, I. (1985). 1. Attachment theory: Retrospect and prospect. *Monograph of the Society for Research on Child Development. 50*(1/2, Serial No. 209), 3–35.

Bretherton, I. (1990). Open communication and internal working models: Their role in the development of attachment relationships. In R. A. Thompson (Ed.), *Socioemotional development: Nebraska Symposium on Motivation, 1988* (pp. 57–113). Lincoln: University of Nebraska Press.

Brewer, M. B. (1994, June). *The social origins of human nature.* Keynote address presented at the fourth annual Society for Personality and Social Psychology Preconference, Washington, DC.

Briggs, J. (1992). Mazes of meaning: How a child and a culture create each other. In W. A. Corsaro & P. J. Miller (Eds.), *Interpretive approaches to children's socialization* (pp. 25–50). San Francisco: Jossey-Bass.

Brim, O. G., & Wheeler, S. (1966). *Socialization after childhood: Two essays.* New York: Wiley.

Brody, G. H., & Forehand, R. (1988). Multiple determinants of parenting: Research findings and implications for the divorce process. In E. M. Hetherington & J. D. Arasteh (Eds.), *Impact of divorce, single parenting, and stepparenting on children* (pp. 117–133). Hillsdale, NJ: Erlbaum.

Bronfenbrenner, U. (1979). *The ecology of human development.* Cambridge, MA: Harvard University Press.

Bronfenbrenner, U. (1994). Foreword. In R. A. LeVine, S. Dixon, S. LeVine, A. Richman, P. H. Leiderman, C. H. Keefer, & T. B. Brazelton (Eds.), *Child care and culture: Lessons from Africa* (pp. xi–xviii). Cambridge, England: Cambridge University Press.

Bronfenbrenner, U., & Ceci, S. J. (1994). Nature–nurture reconceptualized in developmental perspective: A bioecological model. *Psychological Review, 101,* 568–586.

Bruner, J. (1992). The narrative and construction of reality. In H. Beilin & P. B. Pufall (Eds.), *Piaget's theory: Prospects and possibilities* (pp. 229–248). Hillsdale, NJ: Erlbaum.

Brunner, H. G., Nelan, M., Breakefield, X. O., Ropers, H. H., & Van Oost, B. A. (1993). Abnormal behavior associated with point mutation in the structural gene for monoamine oxidase A. *Science, 262,* 578–580.

Bryan, Y. E., & Newman, J. D. (1988). Influence of infant cry structure on the heart rate of the listener. In J. D. Newman (Ed.), *The physiological control of mammalian vocalization* (pp. 413–432). New York: Plenum Press.

Bugental, D. B. (1992). Affective and cognitive processes within threat-oriented family systems. In I. E. Sigel, A. McGillicuddy-DeLisi, & J. Goodnow (Eds.), *Parental belief systems: The psychological consequences for children* (pp. 219–248). New York: Erlbaum.

Bugental, D. B. (1993). Communication in abusive relationships: Cognitive constructions of interpersonal power. *American Behavioral Scientist, 36,* 288–308.

Bugental, D. B., Blue, J., Cortez, V., Fleck, K., Kopeikin, H., Lewis, J., & Lyon, J. (1993). Social cognitions as organizers of autonomic and affective responses to social challenge. *Journal of Personality and Social Psychology. 64,* 94–103.

Bugental, D. B., Blue, J. B., & Cruzcosa, M. (1989). Perceived control over caregiving outcomes: Implications for child abuse. *Developmental Psychology, 25,* 532–539.

Bugental, D. B., Blue, J. B., & Lewis, J. (1990). Caregiver cognitions as moderators of affective reactions to "difficult" children. *Developmental Psychology, 26,* 631–638.

Bugental, D. B., Lyon, J. E., Krantz, J., & Cortez, V. (1997). Who's the boss? Accessibility of dominance ideation among individuals with low perceptions of interpersonal power. *Journal of Personality and Social Psychology, 72,* 1297–1309.

Bugental, D. B., & Shennum, W. A. (1984). "Difficult" children as elicitors and targets of adult communication patterns: An attributional-behavioral transactional analysis. *Monographs of the Society for Research in Child Development, 49* (No. 1).

Cairns, R. B., Gariepy, J. L., & Hood, K. E. (1990). Development, microevolution, and social behavior. *Psychological Review, 97,* 49–65.

Campbell, D. T. (1965). Variation and selection-retention in sociocultural evolution. In H. R. Barringer, G. I. Blanksten, & R. W. Mack (Eds.), *Social change in developing areas: A reinterpretation of evolutionary theory* (pp. 19–49). Cambridge MA: Schenkman.

Campbell, S. B., Cohn, J. F., & Meyers, T. (1995). Depression in first-time mothers: Mother-infant interaction and depression chronicity. *Developmental Psychology, 31,* 349–357.

Campos, J. J., Campos, R. B., & Barrett, K. C. (1989). Emergent themes in the study of emotional development and emotion regulation. *Developmental Psychology, 25,* 394–402.

Capatides, J. B., & Bloom, L. (1993). Underlying process in the socialization of emotion. *Advances in Infancy Research, 8,* 99–135.

Caporael, L. R., & Brewer, M. B. (1991). The quest for human nature: Social and scientific issues in evolutionary psychology. *Journal of Social Issues, 47,* 1–9.

Caporael, L. R., & Culbertson, G. R. (1986). Verbal response modes of baby talk and other speech at institutions for the aged: Language, communication and the elderly [Special issue]. *Language and Communication, 6,* 99–112.

Cashmore, J. A., & Goodnow, J. G. (1985). Agreement between generations: A two-process approach. *Child Development, 56,* 493–501.

Cassidy, J. (1994). Emotion regulation: Influences of attachment relationships. *Monographs of the Society for Research in Child Development, 59* (Nos. 2/3), 228–283.

Cazden, C. (1993). Vygotsky, Hymes and Bakhtin: From word to utterance and voice. In E. Forman, N. Minick, & C. A. Stone (Eds.), *Contexts for learning* (pp. 197–212). New York: Oxford University Press.

Chaiklin, S., & Lave, J. (Eds.). (1993). *Understanding practice.* Cambridge, England: Cambridge University Press.

Cheney, D. L., & Seyfarth, R. M. (1985). Social and non-social knowledge in vervet monkeys. *Philosophical Transactions of the Royal Society of London, 308,* 187–201.

Chomsky, N. (1988). *Language and problems of knowledge.* Cambridge, MA: MIT Press.

Christianson, S. A. (1992). Emotional stress and eyewitness memory: A critical review. *Psychological Bulletin, 112,* 284–309.

Clark, M. S., Helgeson, V. S., Mickelson, K., & Pataki, S. (1994). In R. S. Wyer, Jr. (Ed.), *Handbook of social cognition* (pp. 189–238). Hillsdale, NJ; Erlbaum.

Clark, M. S., & Mills, J. (1989). Interpersonal attraction in exchange and communal relationships. *Journal of Personality and Social Psychology, 57,* 12–24.

Cleverly, J. F. (1971). *The first generation: School and society in early Australia.* Sydney, Australia: Sydney University Press.

Clore, G. L., Schwarz, N., & Conway, M. (1994). Affective causes and consequences of social information processing. In R. S. Wyer & T. K. Srull (Eds.), *Handbook of social cognition* (Vol. 2, pp. 323–417). Hillsdale, NJ: Erlbaum.

Cole, M. (1985). The zone of proximal development: Where culture and cognition create each other. In J. V. Wertsch (Ed.), *Culture, communication, and cognition: Vygotskian perspectives* (pp. 146–161). Cambridge, England: Cambridge University Press.

Cole, M. (1988). Cross-cultural research in the socio-historical tradition. *Human Development, 31,* 137–152.

Cole, M. (1995). The supra-individual envelope of development: Activity and practice, situation and context. In J. J. Goodnow, P. J. Miller, & F. Kessel (Eds.), *Cultural practices as contexts for development* (pp. 105–118). San Francisco: Jossey-Bass.

Cole, P. M., Barrett, K. C., & Zahn-Waxler, C. (1992). Emotion displays in 2-year-olds during mishaps. *Child Development, 63,* 314–324.

Collins, W. A., & Luebker, C. (1995). Parent and adolescent expectancies: Individual and relational significance. In J. F. Smetana (Ed.), *Beliefs about parenting: Origins and developmental consequences* (pp. 65–80). San Francisco: Jossey-Bass.

Collins, W. A., & Russell, G. (1991). Mother-child and father-child relationships in middle childhood and adolescence: A developmental analysis. *Developmental Review, 11,* 99–136.

Conger, R. D., Patterson, G. R., & Ge, X. (1995). It takes two to replicate: A mediational model for the impact of parents' stress on adolescent adjustment. *Child Development, 66,* 80–97.

Cook, W. L. (1993). Interdependence and the interpersonal sense of control: An analysis of family relationships. *Journal of Personality and Social Psychology, 64,* 587–601.

Cooper, C. R., Azmitia, M., Garcia, E. E., Ittel, A., Lopez, E., Rivera, L., & Marinex-Chavez, R. (1994). Aspirations of low-income Mexican-American and European-American parents for their children and adolescents. In F. Villarruel & R. M. Lerner (Eds.), *Environments for socialization and learning* (pp. 65–81). San Francisco: Jossey-Bass.

Cooper, R. P., & Aslin, R. N. (1990). Preferences for infant-directed speech in the first month after birth. *Child Development, 61,* 15–23.

Corsaro, W. A. (1988). Routines in the peer culture of American and Italian nursery school children. *Sociology of Education, 61,* 1–14.

Corsaro, W. A., & Eder, D. (1990). Children's peer culture. *Annual Review of Sociology, 16,* 197–220.

Corsaro, W. A., & Miller, P. J. (Eds.). (1992). *Interpretive approaches to socialization.* San Francisco: Jossey-Bass.

Cosmides, L., & Tooby, J. (1992). Cognitive adaptations for social exchange. In J. H. Barkow, L. Cosmides, & J. Tooby (Eds.), *The adapted mind: Evolutionary psychology and the generation of culture* (pp. 163–228). New York: Oxford University Press.

Craik, F. I., & Lockhart, R. S. (1972). Levels of processing: A framework for memory research. *Journal of Verbal Learning and Verbal Behavior, 11,* 671–684.

Crick, N. R., & Dodge, K. A. (1994). A review and reformulation of social information-processing mechanisms in children's social adjustment. *Psychological Bulletin, 115,* 74–101.

Crockenberg, S. B. (1981). Infant irritability, mother responsiveness, and social support influences on the security of infant-mother attachment. *Child Development, 52,* 857–865.

Crowe, H. P., & Zeskind, P. S. (1992). Psychophysiological and perceptual responses to infant cries varying in pitch: Comparison of adults with low and high scores on the Child Abuse Potential Inventory. *Child Abuse and Neglect, 16,* 19–29.

Crowell, J. A., O'Connor, E., Wollmers, G., Sprafkin, J., & Rao, U. (1992). Mothers' conceptualizations of parent-child relationships: Relation to mother-child interaction and child behavior problems. *Development and Psychopathology, 3,* 431–444.

D'Andrade, R. G. (1984). Cultural meaning systems. In R. A. Shweder & R. A. LeVine (Eds.), *Culture theory: Essays on mind, self, and emotion* (pp. 88–119). Cambridge, England: Cambridge University Press.

D'Andrade, R. G. (1987). A folk model of the mind. In D. Holland & N. Quinn (Eds.), *Cultural models in language and thought* (pp. 112–148). Cambridge, England: Cambridge University Press.

D'Andrade, R. G. (1992). Schemas and motivations. In R. G. D'Andrade & C. Strauss (Eds.), *Human motives and cultural models* (pp. 23–44). Cambridge, England: Cambridge University Press.

D'Andrade, R. G., & Strauss, C. (Eds.). (1992). *Human motives and cultural models.* Cambridge, England: Cambridge University Press.

Darling, N., & Steinberg, L. (1993). Parenting style as context: An integrative model. *Psychological Bulletin, 113,* 487–496.

Davison, G. C., Navarre, S. G., & Vogel, R. S. (1995). The articulated thoughts in simulated situations paradigm: A think-aloud approach to cognitive assessment. *Current Directions in Psychological Science, 4,* 29–33.

Deal, J. E., Halverson, C. F., & Wampler, K. S. (1989). Parental agreement on child-rearing orientations: Relations to parental, marital, family, and child characteristics. *Child Development, 60,* 1025–1034.

DeBellis, M. D., Lefter, L., Trickett, P. K., & Putnam, F. W. (1994). Urinary catecholamine excretion in sexually-abused girls. *Journal of the American Academy of Child and Adolescent Psychiatry, 33,* 320–377.

DeCasper, A. J., & Spence, M. J. (1991). Auditory mediated behavior during the perinatal period. In M. J. S. Weiss & P. R. Zelazo (Eds.), *Newborn attentional biological contrasts and the influence of experience* (pp. 142–176). Norwood, NJ: ABLEX.

DeCooke (1992). Children's understanding of indebtedness as a feature of reciprocal help exchanges between peers. *Developmental Psychology, 28,* 948–954.

DeLissovoy, V. (1979). Toward the definition of "abuse provoking child." *Child Abuse and Neglect, 3,* 341–350.

Dienstbier, R. A. (1984). The role of emotion in moral socialization. In C. Izard, J. Kagan, & R. B. Zajonc (Eds.), *Emotions, cognitions, and behaviors* (pp. 484–513). New York: Cambridge University Press.

Dietrich, D., Berkowitz, L., Kadushin, A., & McGloin, J. (1990). Some factors influencing child abusers' justification of their child abuse. *Child Abuse and Neglect, 14,* 337–345.

DiLalla, L. F., & Gottesman, I. I. (1991). Biological and genetic contributors to violence: Widom's untold tale. *Psychological Bulletin, 109,* 125–129.

Dix, T. (1991). The affective organization or parenting: Adaptive and maladaptive processes. *Psychological Bulletin, 110,* 3–25.

Dix, T. (1992). Parenting on behalf of the child: Empathic goals in the regulation of responsive parenting. In I. E. Sigel, A. V. McGillicuddy-DeLisi, & J. J. Goodnow (Eds.), *Parental belief systems: The psychological consequences for children* (2nd ed., pp. 319–346). Hillsdale, NJ: Erlbaum.

Dix, T. (1993). Attributing dispositions to children: An interactional analysis of attributions in socialization. *Personality and Social Psychology Bulletin, 19,* 633–643.

Dix, T., & Lochman, J. E. (1990). Social cognition and negative reactions to children: A comparison of mothers of aggressive and nonaggressive boys. *Journal of Social and Clinical Psychology, 9,* 414–438.

Dix, T., Reinhold, D. P., & Zambarano, R. J. (1990). Mothers' judgments in moments of anger. *Merrill-Palmer Quarterly, 36,* 465–486.

Dix, T., Ruble, D. N., Grusec, J. E., & Nixon, S. (1986). Social cognition in parents: Inferential and affective reactions to children of three age levels. *Child Development, 57,* 879–894.

Dix, T., Ruble, D. N., & Zambarano, R. J. (1989). Mothers' implicit theories of discipline: Child effects, parent effects, and the attribution process. *Child Development, 57,* 879–894.

Dodge, K. A. (1986). A social information processing model of social competence in children. In M. Perlmutter (Ed.), *Minnesota Symposium on Child Psychology* (Vol. 18, pp. 77–125). Hillsdale, NJ: Erlbaum.

Dodge, K. A., Bates, J. E., & Pettit, G. S. (1990). Mechanisms in the cycle of violence. *Science, 250,* 1678–1683.

Dodge, K. A., Coie, J. D., Pettit, G. S., & Price, J. M. (1990). Peer status and aggression in boys' groups: Developmental and contextual analyses. *Child Development, 61,* 1289–1309.

Dodge, K. A., & Somberg, D. R. (1987). Hostile attributional biases among aggressive boys are exacerbated under conditions of threats to the self. *Child Development, 58,* 213–224.

Donovan, W. L., & Leavitt, L. A. (1989). Maternal self-efficacy and infant attachment: Integrating physiology, perceptions, and behavior. *Child Development, 60,* 460–472.

Donovan, W. L., Leavitt, L. A., & Walsh, R. O. (1990). Maternal self-efficacy: Illusory control and its effect on susceptibility to learned helplessness. *Child Development, 61,* 1638–1647.

Dowd, J. J. (1990). Ever since Durkheim: The socialization of human development. *Human Development, 33,* 138–159.

Draper, P., & Harpending, H. (1982). Father absence and reproductive strategy: An evolutionary perspective. *Journal of Anthropological Research, 38,* 255–273.

Dressel, P. L., & Petersen, D. (1982). Becoming a male stripper: Recruitment, socialization, and ideological development. *Work and Occupations, 9,* 387–406.

Dunn, J. (1988). *The beginnings of social understanding.* Cambridge, MA: Harvard University Press.

Dunn, J., & Brown, J. (1991). Becoming American or English? Talking about the social world in England and the United States. In M. H. Bornstein (Ed.), *Cultural approaches to parenting: Crosscurrents in contemporary psychology* (pp. 155–172). Hillsdale, NJ: Erlbaum.

Dunn, J., & Munn., P. (1985). Becoming a family member: Family conflict and the development of understanding. *Child Development, 56,* 480–492.

Duveen, G., & Lloyd, B. (1990). *Social representations and the development of knowledge.* Cambridge, England: Cambridge University Press.

Easterbrook, J. A. (1959). The effect of emotion on cue utilization and the organization of behavior. *Psychological Review, 66,* 183–201.

Eckert, P. (1991). *Jocks and burnouts: Social categories and identity in the high school.* New York: Teachers College Press.

Eisenberg, N., Cialdini, R. B., McCreath, H., & Shell, R. (1987). Consistency-based compliance: When and why do children become vulnerable? *Journal of Personality and Social Psychology, 52,* 1174–1183.

Eisenberg, N., & Fabes, R. A. (1991). Prosocial behavior and empathy: A multimethod, developmental perspective. In M. Clark (Ed.), *Review of personality and social psychology* (Vol. 12, pp. 34–61). Newbury Park, CA: Sage.

Eisenberg, N., Fabes, R. A., Carlo, G., & Karbon, M. (1992). Emotional responsivity to others: Behavioral correlates and socialization antecedents. In N. Eisenberg & R. A. Fabes (Eds.), *Emotion and its regulation in early development* (pp. 57–73). San Francisco: Jossey-Bass.

Eisenberg, N., Fabes, R. A., Schaller, M., Carlo, G., & Miller, P. (1991). The relations of parental characteristics and practices to children's vicarious emotional responding. *Child Development, 62,* 1393–1408.

Eisenberg, N., Fabes, R. A., Schaller, M., Miller, P., Carlo, G., Poulin, R., Shea, C., & Shell, R. (1991). Personality and socialization correlates of vicarious emotional responding. *Journal of Personality and Social Psychology, 61,* 459–470.

Eisenberg, N., Miller, P., Schaller, M., Fabes, R. A., Bustamente, D., Mathy, R. M., Shell, R., & Rhodes, K. (1988). Differentiation of personal distress and sympathy in children and adults. *Developmental Psychology, 24,* 766–775.

Eisenberg, N., Roth, K., Bryniarski, K. A., & Murray, E. (1984). The effects of height on adults' attributions of competency and children's social and cognitive competencies. *Sex Roles, 11,* 719–734.

Elbers, E., Maier, R., Hoekstra, T., & Hoogsteder, M. (1992). Internalization and adult-child interaction. *Learning and Instruction, 2,* 101–118.

Elder, G. H., Jr., & Caspi, A. (1988). Economic stress in lives: Developmental perspective. *Journal of Social Issues, 44,* 25–45.

Elder, G. H., Jr., Nguyen, T. V., & Caspi, A. (1985). Linking family hardship to children's lives. *Child Development, 56,* 361–375.

Ellis, H. C., & Ashbrook, P. W. (1989). The "state" of mood and memory research: A selective review. Mood and memory: Theory, research and applications [Special issue]. *Journal of Social Behavior and Personality, 4,* 1–21.

Ellsworth, P. C. (1994). Sense, culture, and sensibility. In S. Kitayama & H. R. Markus (Eds.), *Emotion and culture* (pp. 23–50). Washington, DC: American Psychological Association.

Ellsworth, P. C., & Smith, C. A. (1988). From appraisal to emotion: Differences among unpleasant feelings. *Motivation and Emotion. 12*, 271–302.

Emde, R. N. (1993). Infant emotions and the caregiving environment. In R. N. Emde, J. D. Osofsky, & P. M. Butterfield (Eds.), *The IFEL pictures: A new instrument for interpreting emotions* (pp. 27–49). Madison, WI: International University Press.

Emde, R. N., Biringen, Z., Clyman, R. B., & Oppenheim, D. (1991). The moral self of infancy: Affective core and procedural knowledge. *Developmental Review, 11*, 251–270.

Emde, R. N., Plomin, R., Robinson, J., Corley, R., DeFries, J., Fulker, D. W., Reznick, J. S., Campos, J., Kagan, J., & Zahn-Waxler, C. (1992). Temperament, emotion, and cognition at fourteen months: The MacArthur Longitudinal Twin Study. *Child Development, 63*, 1437–1455.

Engfer, A., Walper, S., & Rutter, M. (in press). Individual characteristics as a force in development. In M. L. Rutter & D. F. Hay (Eds.), *Developmental principles and clinical issues in psychology and psychiatry.* Oxford, England: Blackwell.

Engstrom, Y. (1993). Developmental studies of work as a testbench of activity theory: The case of primary care medical practice. In S. Chaiklin & J. Lave (Eds.), *Understanding practice* (pp. 64–103). New York: Cambridge University Press.

Epstein, S. (1994). Integration of the cognitive and the psychodynamic unconscious. *American Psychologist, 49*, 709–724.

Erdelyi, M. H. (1974). A new look at the New Look: Perceptual defense and vigilance. *Psychological Review, 81*, 1–25.

Erel, O., & Burman, B. (1995). Interrelatedness of marital relations and parent-child relations: A meta-analytic review. *Psychological Bulletin, 118*, 108–132.

Erikson, E. H. (1959). *Identity and the life-cycle.* New York: International University Press.

Fabes, R. A., Eisenberg, N., & Miller, P. A. (1990). Maternal correlates of children's vicarious emotional responsiveness. *Developmental Psychology, 26*, 639–648.

Fagan, J. F., & Singer, L. T. (1979). The role of simple feature differences in infants' recognition of faces. *Infant Behavior and Development, 2*, 39–45.

Fairbanks, L. A. (1996). Individual differences in maternal style. *Advances in the Study of Behavior, 25*, 579–611.

Fernald, A. (1993). Approval and disapproval: Infant responsiveness to vocal affect in familiar and unfamiliar languages. *Child Development, 64*, 657–674.

Fernald, A., & Morikawa, H. (1993). Common themes and cultural variations in Japanese and American mothers' speech to infants. *Child Development, 64*, 637–656.

Fernald, A., Taeschner, T., Dunn, J., Papousek, M., Boysson-Bardies, B., & Fukui, I. (1989). A cross-language study of prosodic modifications in mothers' and fathers' speech to preverbal infants. *Journal of Child Language, 16*, 477–501.

Fiese, B. H. (1992). Dimensions of family rituals across two generations: Relation to adolescent identity. *Family Process, 31*, 151–162.

Fiese, B. H., Hooker, K. A., Kotary, L., Shwagler, J., & Rimmer, M. (1995). Family stories in the early stages of parenthood. *Journal of Marriage and the Family, 57*, 763–770.

Finnie, V., & Russell, A. (1988). Preschool children's social status and their mothers' behavior and knowledge in the supervisory role. *Developmental Psychology, 24*, 789–801.

Fischer, J. L., & Fischer, A. (1963). The New Englanders of Orchardtown, U.S.A. In B. B. Whiting (Ed.), *Six cultures: Studies of child rearing* (Vol. 5, pp. 869–1009). New York: Wiley.

Fisek, M. H., & Ofshe, R. (1970). The process of status evolution. *Sociometry, 22*, 327–346.

Fiske, A. P. (1992). The four elementary forms of sociality: Framework for a unified theory of social relations. *Psychological Review, 99*, 689–723.

Fiske, A. P. (1993). Social errors in four cultures: Evidence about the elementary forms of social relations. *Journal of Cross-Cultural Psychology, 24*, 67–94.

Fiske, A. P. (in press). Learning a culture the way informants do: Observing, imitating, and participating. *Ethos.*

Fiske, A. P., Haslam, N., & Fiske, S. T. (1991). Confusing one person with another: What errors reveal about the elementary forms of social relations. *Journal of Personality and Social Psychology, 60*, 656–674.

Fiske, S. T., & Pavelchak, M. A. (1986). Category-based versus piecemeal-based responses: Developments in schema-triggered affect. In R. M. Sorrentino & E. T. Higgins (Eds.), *Handbook of motivation and cognition: Foundations of social behavior* (pp. 167–203). New York: Guilford Press.

Fletcher, G. J. O., & Fincham, F. D. (1991). Attribution processes in close relationships. In G. J. O. Fletcher & F. D. Fincham (Eds.), *Cognition in close relationships* (pp. 7–35). Hillsdale, NJ: Erlbaum.

Fodor, J. (1983). *The modularity of mind: An essay on faculty psychology.* Cambridge, MA: MIT Press.

Fogel, A. (1994). Development and relationships: A dynamic model of communication. In J. B. Slater (Ed.), *Advances in the study of behavior* (Vol. 24, pp. 1–49). San Diego, CA: Academic Press.

Foot, H. C., Chapman, A. J., & Smith, J. R. (1977). Friendship and social responsiveness in boys and girls. *Journal of Personality and Social Psychology, 35*, 401–411.

Ford, D. M., & Lerner, R. M. (1992). *Developmental systems theory.* Newbury Park, CA: Sage.

Freud, S. (1965). *Normality and pathology in childhood.* New York: International Universities Press.

Fridlund, A. J. (1991). Sociality of solitary smiling: Potentiation by an implicit audience. *Journal of Personality and Social Psychology, 60,* 229–240.

Frijda, N. H., & Mesquita, B. (1994). The social roles and functions of emotions. In S. Kitayama & H. R. Markus (Eds.), *Emotion and culture* (pp. 51–88). Washington, DC: American Psychological Association.

Frodi, A. M. (1981). Contribution of infant characteristics to child abuse. *American Journal of Mental Deficiency, 85,* 341–349.

Frodi, A. M., & Lamb, M. E. (1980). Child abusers' responses to infant smiles and cries. *Child Development, 51,* 238–241.

Geer, B. (1972). *Learning to work.* Beverly Hills, CA: Sage.

Gianino, A., & Tronick, E. Z. (1988). The mutual regulation model: The infant's self and interactive regulation and coping and defensive capacities. In T. M. Field, P. M. McCabe, & N. Schneiderman (Eds.), *Stress and coping across development* (pp. 47–68). Hillsdale, NJ: Erlbaum.

Giddens, A. (1979). *Central problems in social theory.* London: Macmillan.

Gladhue, B. A., Boechler, M., & McCaul, K. D. (1989). Hormonal response to competition in men. *Aggressive Behavior, 15,* 409–422.

Glick, J. (1985). Culture and cognition revisited. In E. Neimark, R. DeLisis, & J. L. Newman (Eds.), *Moderators of competence* (pp. 99–116). Hillsdale, NJ: Erlbaum.

Gnepp, J., & Gould, M. E. (1985). The development of personalized inferences: Understanding other people's emotional reactions in light of their prior experiences. *Child Development, 56,* 1455–1464.

Goldberg, S., Lojkasek, M., Gartner, G., & Corter, C. (1989). Maternal responsiveness and social development in preterm infants. In M. H. Bornstein (Ed.), *Maternal responsiveness: Characteristics and consequences* (pp. 89–104). San Francisco: Jossey-Bass.

Goodnow, J. J. (1985). Change and variation in parents' ideas about childhood and parenting. In I. E. Sigel (Ed.), *Parental belief systems* (pp. 235–270). Hillsdale, NJ: Erlbaum.

Goodnow, J. J. (1988a). Parents' ideas, actions, and feelings: Models and methods from developmental and social psychology. *Child Development, 59,* 286–320.

Goodnow, J. J. (1988b). Children's household work: Its nature and functions. *Psychological Bulletin, 103,* 5–26.

Goodnow, J. J. (1990). The socialization of cognition: What's involved? In J. W. Stigler, R. A. Shweder, & G. Herdt (Eds.), *Culture and human development* (pp. 259–286). Chicago: University of Chicago Press.

Goodnow, J. J. (1992). Parents' ideas, children's ideas: The bases of congruence and divergence. In I. Sigel, A. V. McGillicuddy-DeLisi, & J. J. Goodnow (Eds.), *Parental belief systems* (pp. 293–318). Hillsdale, NJ: Erlbaum.

Goodnow, J. J. (1995). Acceptable disagreement across generations. In J. Smetana (Ed.), *Beliefs about parenting: Origins and developmental implications* (pp. 51–64). San Francisco: Jossey-Bass.

Goodnow, J. J. (1996a). Acceptable ignorance, negotiable disagreement: Alternative views of learning. In D. H. Olson & N. Torrance (Eds.), *Handbook of psychology in education: New models of teaching, learning, and schooling* (pp. 345–368). Hillsdale, NJ: Erlbaum.

Goodnow, J. J. (1996b). From household practices to parents' ideas about work and interpersonal relationships. In S. Harkness & C. Super (Eds.), *Parents' cultural belief systems* (pp. 313–344). New York: Guilford Press.

Goodnow, J. J. (in press). Parenting and the transmission and internalization of values: From social-cultural approaches to within-family analyses. In J. E. Grusec & L. Kuczynski (Eds.), *Parenting strategies and children's internalization of values: A handbook of theoretical and research approaches.* New York: Wiley.

Goodnow, J. J., Cashmore, J. A., Cotton, S., & Knight, R. (1984). Mothers' developmental timetables in two cultural groups. *International Journal of Psychology, 19,* 193–205.

Goodnow, J. J., & Collins, A. W. (1990). *Development according to parents: The nature, sources, and consequences of parents' ideas.* Hillsdale, NJ: Erlbaum.

Goodnow, J. J., Miller, P. J., & Kessel, F. (Eds.). (1995). *Cultural practices as contexts for development.* San Francisco: Jossey-Bass.

Goodnow, J. J., & Warton, P. (1991). The social basis of social cognition: Interactions about work and lessons about relationships. *Merrill-Palmer Quarterly, 37,* 27–58.

Goodwin, M. H. (1990). *He-said-she-said: Talk as social organization among black children.* Bloomington: Indiana University Press.

Gottesman, I. I., & Goldsmith. H. H. (1994). Developmental psychopathology of antisocial behavior: Inserting genes into its ontogenesis and epigenesis. In C. A. Nelson (Ed.), *Threats to optimal development: Integrating biological, psychological, and social risk factors. The Minnesota Symposia on Child Psychology* (Vol. 27, pp. 69–104). Hillsdale, NJ: Erlbaum.

Gottman, J. M., & Levenson, R. W. (1985). A valid procedure for obtaining self-report of affect in marital interactions. *Journal of Clinical and Counseling Psychology, 53,* 151–160.

Gramsci, A. (1971). *Selections from the prison notebooks of Antonio Gramsci.* London: Lawrence & Wisnart.

Granger, D. A., Weisz, J. R., McCracken, J. T., Ikeda, S. C., & Douglas, P. (1996). Reciprocal influences among adrenocortical activation, psychosocial processes, and the behavioral adjustment of clinic-referred children. *Child Development, 67,* 3250–3262.

Greenfield, P. M., & Lave, J. (1982). Cognitive aspects of informal education. In D. Wagner & H. Stevenson (Eds.), *Cultural perspectives on child development* (pp. 181–207). San Francisco: Freeman.

Grusec, J. E. (1991). Socializing concern for others in the home. *Developmental Psychology, 27,* 338–342.

Grusec, J. E. (1992). Social learning theory and developmental psychology: The legacies of Robert Sears and Albert Bandura. *Developmental Psychology, 28,* 776–786.

Grusec, J. E., & Goodnow, J. J. (1994). The impact of parental discipline methods on the child's internalization of values: A reconceptualization of current points of view. *Developmental Psychology, 30,* 4–19.

Grusec, J. E., Goodnow, J. J., & Cohen, L. (1996). Household work and the development of concern for others. *Developmental Psychology, 32,* 999–1007.

Grusec, J. E., Hastings, P., & Mammone, N. (1994). Parenting cognitions and relationship schemas. In J. Smetana (Ed.), *Beliefs about parenting: Origins and developmental implications* (pp. 5–20). San Francisco: Jossey-Bass.

Grusec, J. E., & Mammone, N. (1994). Features and sources of parents' attributions about themselves and their children. In N. Eisenberg (Ed.), *Review of personality and social psychology* (Vol. 15, pp. 49–73). Thousand Oaks, CA: Sage.

Grusec, J. E., & Pedersen, J. (1989, April). *Children's thinking about prosocial and moral behavior.* Paper presented at the biennial meeting of the Society of Research in Child Development, Kansas City, KS.

Gunnar, M. R., Porter, F. L., Wolf, C. M., Rigatuso, J., & Larson, M. C. (1995). Neonatal stress reactivity: Predictions to later emotional temperament. *Child Development, 66,* 1–13.

Gustafson, G. E., & Deconti, K. A. (1990). Infants' cries in the process of normal development. Infant cry researchers: Papers from the Third International Workshop [Special issue]. *Early Child Development and Care, 65,* 45–56.

Gustafson, G. E., Green, J. A., & Cleland, J. W. (1994). Robustness of individual identity in the cries of human infants. *Developmental Psychobiology, 27,* 1–9.

Hala, S., Chandler, M., & Fritz, A. S. (1991). Fledgling theories of mind: Deception as a marker of 3-year-olds' understanding of false belief. *Child Development, 62,* 83–97.

Halberstadt, A. G. (1986). Family socialization of emotional expression and nonverbal communication styles and skills. *Journal of Personality and Social Psychology, 51,* 827–836.

Harlow, H., & Harlow, M. (1995). The affectional system. In A. Schrier & J. R. Harris (Eds.), Where is the child's environment? A group socialization theory of development. *Psychological Review, 102,* 458–489.

Harris, J. R. (1995). Where is the child's environment? A group socialization theory of development. *Psychological Review, 102,* 458–489.

Hartup, W. W. (1983). Peer relations. In P. Mussen (Ed.), *Handbook of child psychology: Vol. 4. Socialization, personality, and social development* (pp. 103–196). New York: Wiley.

Hazan, C., & Shaver, P. (1987). Romantic love conceptualized as an attachment process. *Journal of Personality and Social Psychology, 52,* 511–524.

Heath, S. B. (1983). *Ways with words: Language, life and work in communities and classrooms.* Cambridge, England: Cambridge University Press.

Hess, E. H., & Polt, J. M. (1960). Pupil size as related to interest value of visual stimuli. *Science, 132,* 349–350.

Hess, R. D., Holloway, S. D., Dickson, W. P., & Price, G. G. (1984). Maternal variables as predictors of children's school readiness and later achievement in vocabulary and mathematics in sixth grade. *Child Development, 55,* 1902–1912.

Hess, R. D., Kashiwagi, K., Azuma, H., Price, G. G., & Dickson, R. D. (1980). Parental expectations for mastery of developmental tasks in Japan and the United States. *International Journal of Psychology, 15,* 259–271.

Higley, J. D., Hopkins, W. D., Thompson, W. W., Byrne, E. A., Hirsch, R. M., & Suomi, S. J. (1992). Peers as primary attachment sources in yearling rhesus monkeys (Macaca mulatta). *Developmental Psychology, 28,* 1163–1171.

Himelstein, S., Graham, S., & Weiner, B. (1991). An attributional analysis of maternal beliefs about the importance of child-rearing practices. *Child Development, 62,* 301–310.

Hinde, R. A. (1992). Developmental psychology in the context of older behavioral sciences. *Developmental Psychology, 28,* 1018–1029.

Hinde, R. A., & Stevenson-Hinde, J. (1987). Interpersonal relationships and child development. *Developmental Review, 7,* 1–21.

Hirschfeld, L. A., & Gelman, S. A. (1994). Toward a topography of mind: An introduction to domain specificity (pp. 3–36). In L. A. Hirschfeld & S. A. Gelman (Eds.), *Mapping the mind.* Cambridge, England: Cambridge University Press.

Hofer, M. A. (1987). Early social relationships: A psychobiologist's view. *Child Development, 58,* 633–647.

Hoffman, M. L. (1970). Moral development. In P. H. Mussen (Ed.), *Carmichael's manual of child psychology* (Vol. 2, pp. 261–359). New York: Wiley.

Hoffman, M. L. (1981). Is altruism part of human nature? *Journal of Personality and Social Psychology, 40,* 121–137.

Hoffman, M. L. (1983). Affective and cognitive processes in moral internalization. In E. T. Higgins, D. Ruble, & W. Hartup (Eds.), *Social cognition and social development: A sociocultural perspective* (pp. 236–274). Cambridge, England: Cambridge University Press.

Hoffman, M. L. (1986). Affect, cognition, and motivation. In R. M. Sorrentino & E. T. Higgins (Eds.), *Handbook of motivation and cognition: Foundations of social behavior* (pp. 244–280). New York: Guilford Press.

Holden, G. W., (1988), Adults' thinking about a child-rearing problem: Effects of experience, parental status, and gender. *Child Development, 59,* 1623–1632.

Holden, G. W., & Edwards, I. A. (1989). Parental attitudes toward child rearing: Instruments, issues, and implications. *Psychological Bulletin, 106,* 29–58.

Holden, G. W., & Zambarano, R. J. (1992). Passing the rod: Similarities between parents and their young children in orientations toward physical punishment. In I. E. Sigel, A. V. McGillicuddy-DeLisi, & J. J. Goodnow (Eds.), *Parental belief systems: The psychological consequences for children* (2nd ed., pp. 143–174). Hillsdale, NJ: Erlbaum.

Holland, D., & Quinn, N. (Eds.). (1987). *Cultural models in language and thought.* Cambridge, England: Cambridge University Press.

Holloway, S. D. (1984). Causal attributions of mothers concerning their children's academic achievement. *Dissertation Abstracts International, 44,* 3014.

Hopper, M. (1977). Becoming a policeman: Socialization of cadets in a police academy. *Urban Life, 6,* 149–170.

Hubbard, F. O. A., & Van IJzendoorn, M. H. (1991). Maternal unresponsiveness and infant crying across the first 9 months: A naturalistic longitudinal study. *Infant Behavior and Development, 14,* 299–312.

Huston, A. C. (1983). Sex-typing. In P. H. Mussen (Series Ed.) & E. M. Hetherington (Vol. Ed.), *Handbook of child psychology: Vol. 4. Socialization, personality, and social development* (pp. 387–468). New York: Wiley.

Inoff-Germain, G., Arnold, G. S., Nottelmann, E. D., Susman, E., Cutler, G. B., Jr., & Chrousos, G. P. (1988). Relations between hormone levels and observational measures of aggressive behavior of young adolescents in family interaction. *Developmental Psychology, 24,* 129–139.

Isabella, R. A., & Belsky, J. (1991). Interactional synchrony and the origins of infant-mother attachment: A replication study. *Child Development, 62,* 373–384.

Izard, C. E. (1993). Four systems of emotion activation: Cognitive and noncognitive processes. *Psychological Review, 100,* 68–90.

Izard, C. E., Haynes, O. M., Chisholm, G., & Baak, K. (1991). Emotional determinants of infant-mother attachment. *Child Development, 62,* 906–917.

Izard, C. E., Huebner, R. R., Risser, D., & Dougherty, L. (1980). The young infant's ability to produce discrete emotion expressions. *Developmental Psychology, 16,* 132–140.

Jackson, J. F. (1993). Human behavioral genetics, Scarr's theory, and her views on interventions: A critical review and commentary on their implications for African-American children. *Child Development, 64,* 1318–1332.

Janssens, J. M. A. M. (1994). Authoritarian child rearing, parental locus of control, and the child's behavioral style. *International Journal of Behavioral Development, 17,* 485–501.

Jenkins, J. J. (1994). Culture, emotion, and psychopathology. In S. Kitayama & H. R. Markus (Eds.), *Emotion and culture* (pp. 307–338). Washington, DC: American Psychological Association.

Johnson, M. K., & Hasher, L. (1987). Human learning and memory. *Annual Review of Psychology, 38,* 631–668.

Jones, S. S., & Raag, T. (1989). Smile production in older infants: The importance of a social recipient for the facial signal. *Child Development, 60,* 811–818.

Kagan, J. (1989). Temperamental contributions to social behavior. *American Psychologist, 44,* 668–674.

Kagan, J., Resnick, J. S., & Snidman, N. (1988). Biological bases of childhood shyness. *Science, 240,* 167–171.

Kagan, J., & Snidman, N. (1991). Temperamental factors in human development. *American Psychologist, 46,* 856–862.

Kalin, N. H., Shelton, S. E., & Barksdale, C. M. (1988). Opiate modulation of separation-induced distress in non-human primates. *Brain Research, 440,* 285–292.

Keller, H., Miranda, D., & Gauda, G. (1984). The naive theory of the infant and some maternal attitudes: A two-country study. *Journal of Cross-Cultural Psychology, 15,* 165–179.

Kendler, K. S., Walters, E. E., Truett, K. R., Heath, A. C., Neale, M. C., Martin, M. G., & Eaves, C. J. (1994). Sources of individual differences in depressive symptoms: Analysis of two samples of twins and their families. *American Journal of Psychiatry, 151,* 1605–1614.

Kipnis, D. (1976). *The powerholders.* Chicago: University of Chicago Press.

Kitayama, S., & Markus, H. R. (Eds.). (1994). *Emotion and culture: Empirical studies of mutual influence.* Washington, DC: American Psychological Association.

Kochanska, G. (1993). Toward a synthesis of parental socialization and children's temperament in early development of conscience. *Child Development, 64,* 325–347.

Kochanska, G. (1994). Beyond cognition: Expanding the search for the early roots of internalization and conscience. *Developmental Psychology, 30,* 20–22.

Kohn, M. L. (1977). *Class and conformity: A study of values* (2nd ed.). Chicago: University of Chicago Press.

Kopp, C. B. (1982). Antecedents of self-regulation: A developmental perspective. *Developmental Psychology, 18,* 199–214.

Kopp, C. B. (1989). Regulation of distress and negative emotions: A developmental view. *Developmental Psychology, 25,* 343–354.

Krebs, J. R., & Dawkins, R. (1984). Animal signals: Mind-reading and manipulation. In J. R. Krebs & N. B. Davies (Eds.), *Behavioral ecology: An evolutionary approach* (pp. 380–402). Oxford, England: Blackwell.

Krech, K. H., & Johnston, C. (1992). The relationship of depressed mood and life stress to maternal perceptions of child behavior. *Journal of Clinical Child Psychology, 21,* 115–122.

Kuczynski, L. (1993, May). *Evolving metaphors of bidirectionality in socialization and parent-child relations.* Paper presented at the meetings of the Canadian Psychological Association, Montreal.

Kuczynski, L. (1997, April). *Accomodation/negotiation: A model of compliance within relationships.* Paper presented at the meetings of the Society for Research in Child Development, Washington, DC.

Kuczynski, L., & Kochanska, G. (1990). Development of children's noncompliance strategies from toddlerhood to age 5. *Developmental Psychology, 26,* 398–408.

Kuczynski, L., Kochanska, G., Radke-Yarrow, M., & Girnius-Brown, O. (1987). A developmental interpretation of young children's noncompliance. *Developmental Psychology, 23,* 799–806.

Kuczynski, L., Zahn-Waxler, C., & Radke-Yarrow, M. (1987). Development and content of imitation in the second and third years of life: A socialization perspective. *Developmental Psychology, 23,* 276–282.

Kulick, D. (1992). *Language shift and cultural reproduction: Socialization, self and syncretism in a Papua New Guinea village.* New York: Cambridge University Press.

Lamb, M. E., Frodi, A. M., Hwang, C.P, Frodi, M., & Steinberg, J. (1982). Mother- and father-infant interactions involving play and holding in traditional and non-traditional Swedish families. *Developmental Psychology, 18,* 215–221.

Lamb, M. E., & Sternberg, K. J. (1992). Sociocultural perspectives on nonparental childcare. In M. E. Lamb, K. J. Sternberg, C. P. Hwang, & A. G. Broberg (Eds.), *Nonparental childcare: Cultural and historical perspectives* (pp. 1–23). Hillsdale, NJ: Erlbaum.

Lancy, D. F. (1996). *Playing on the mother-ground: Cultural routines for children's development.* New York: Guilford Press.

Langlois, J. H., Ritter, J. M., Casey, R. J., & Sawin, D. B. (1995). Infant attractiveness predicts maternal behaviors and attitudes. *Developmental Psychology, 31,* 464–472.

Larson, M. C., Gunnar, M. R., & Hertsgaard, L. (1991). The effects of morning naps, car trips, and maternal separation on adrenocortical activity in human infants. *Child Development, 62,* 362–372.

Laupa, M., & Turiel, E. (1995). Social domain theory. In W. M. Kurtines & J. L. Gewirtz (Eds.), *Moral development: An introduction* (pp. 455–474). Boston: Allyn & Bacon.

Lave, J. (1988). *Cognition in practice.* New York: Cambridge University Press.

Lave, J. (1991). Situating learning in communities of practice. In L. S. Resnick, J. M. Levine, & C. D. Teasley (Eds.), *Perspectives on socially shared cognition* (pp. 63–84). Washington, DC: American Psychological Association.

Lave, J., & Wenger, E. (1991). *Situated learning: Legitimate peripheral participation.* New York: Cambridge University Press.

Lawrence, J. A., Benedikt, R., & Valsiner, J. (1993). Homeless in the mind: A case history of personal life in and out of a close orthodox community. *Journal of Social Distress and the Homeless, 1,* 157–176.

Lawrence, J. A., & Valsiner, J. (1993). Conceptual roots of internalization: From transmission to transformation. *Human Development, 36,* 150–167.

Lay, K., Waters, E., & Park, K. A. (1989). Maternal responsiveness and child compliance: The role of mood as a mediator. *Child Development, 60,* 1405–1411.

Lazarus, R. S. (1991). *Emotion and adaptation.* New York: Oxford University Press.

Leinbach, M. D., & Fagot, B. I. (1993). Categorical habituation to male and female faces: Gender schematic processing in infancy. *Infant Behavior and Development, 16,* 317–332.

Leslie, A. M. (1994). ToMM, ToBY, and agency: Core architecture and domain specificity. In L. A. Hirschfeld & S. A. Gelman (Eds.), *Mapping the mind: Domain specificity in cognition and culture* (pp. 119–148). Cambridge, England: Cambridge University Press.

Lester, H. M., Boukydis, C. Z., Garcia-Coll, C. T., Hole, W., & Peucker, M. (1992). Infantile colic: Acoustic cry characteristics, maternal perception of cry, and temperament. *Infant Behavior and Development, 15,* 15–26.

Levesque, M. J., & Kenny, D. A. (1993). Accuracy of behavioral predictions at zero acquaintance: A social relations analysis. *Journal of Personality and Social Psychology, 65,* 1178–1187.

Levine, J. M., & Moreland, R. L. (1991). Culture and socialization in work groups. In L. B. Resnick, J. M. Levine, & S. D. Teasley (Eds.), *Perspectives on socially shared cognition* (pp. 257–182). Washington, DC: American Psychological Association.

LeVine, R. A. (1974). *Culture and personality: Contemporary readings.* Chicago: Aldine.

LeVine, R. A. (1990). Infant environments in psychoanalysis: A cross-cultural view. In R. Stigler, R. Shweder, & G. Herdt (Eds.), *Cultural psychology: Essays on comparative human development* (pp. 454–476). New York: Cambridge University Press.

LeVine, R. A., Dixon, S., LeVine, S., Richman, A., Leiderman, P. H., Keefer, C. H., & Brazelton, T. B. (1994). *Child care and culture: Lessons from Africa.* Cambridge, England: Cambridge University Press.

LeVine, R. A., & LeVine, S. E. (1988). Parental strategies among the Gusii of Kenya. In R. A. LeFien, P. M. Miller, & M. M. West (Eds.), *Parental behavior in diverse societies* (pp. 27–35). San Francisco: Jossey-Bass.

Levitt, M. J., Weber, R. A., Clark, M. C., & McDonnell, P. (1985). Reciprocity of exchange in toddler sharing behavior. *Developmental Psychology, 21,* 122–123.

Lightfoot, C., & Valsiner, J. (1992). Parental belief system under the influence: Social guidance of the construction of personal cultures. In I. E. Sigel, A. V. McGillicuddy-DeLisi, & J. J. Goodnow (Eds.), *Parental belief systems: The psychological consequences for children* (2nd ed., pp. 393–414). Hillsdale, NJ: Erlbaum.

Lin, E. K. (1997, April). *The signalling value of children's voices on adults.* Paper presented at the meetings of the Society for Research in Child Development, Washington, DC.

Loeb, R. C. (1975). Concomitants of boys' locus of control examined in parent-child interactions. *Developmental Psychology, 11,* 353–358.

Low, B. S. (1989). Cross-cultural patterns in the training of children: An evolutionary perspective. *Journal of Comparative Psychology, 103,* 311–319.

Maccoby, E. E. (1980). Sex differences in aggression: A rejoinder. *Child Development, 51,* 964–980.

Maccoby, E. E. (1988). Gender as a social category. *Developmental Psychology, 24,* 755–765.

Maccoby, E. E. (1990). Gender and relationships: A developmental account. *American Psychologist, 45,* 513–520.

Maccoby, E. E. (1991). Different reproductive strategies in males and females. *Child Development, 62,* 676–681.

Maccoby, E. E. (1992). The role of parents in the socialization of children: An historical overview. *Developmental Psychology, 28,* 1006–1017.

Maccoby, E. E., & Martin, J. (1983). Socialization in the context of the family: Parent-child interaction. In P. H. Mussen (Series Ed.) & E. M. Hetherington (Vol. Ed.), *Handbook of child psychology: Vol. 4. Socialization, personality, and social development* (pp. 1–101). New York: Wiley.

MacDonald, K. B. (1992). Warmth as a developmental construct: An evolutionary position. *Child Development, 63,* 753–773.

MacKinnon-Lewis, C., Volling, B. L., Lamb, M. E., Dechman, K., Rabiner, D., & Curtner, M. E. (1994). A cross-contextual analysis of boys' social competence: From family to school. *Developmental Psychology, 30,* 325–333.

Main, M. (1990). Cross-cultural studies of attachment organization: Recent studies, changing methodologies, and the concept of conditional strategies. *Human Development, 33,* 48–61.

Main, M., Kaplan, N., & Cassidy, J. (1985). Security in infancy, childhood and adulthood: A move to the level of representation. In I. Bretherton & E. Waters (Eds.), Growing points of attachment theory and research. *Monographs of the Society for Research in Child Development, 50*(1/2, Serial No. 209).

Malatesta, C. Z., Culver, C., Tesman, J. R., & Shepard, B. (1989). The development of emotion expression during the first two years of life. *Monographs of the Society for Research in Child Development, 54*(1/2, Serial No. 219).

Malatesta-Magai, C. (1991). Development of emotional expression during infancy: General course and patterns of individual difference. In J. Garber & K. A. Dodge (Eds.), *The development of emotional regulation and dysregulation* (pp. 49–68). Cambridge, England: Cambridge University Press.

Markus, H. M., & Kitayama, S. (1991). Culture and the self: Implications for cognition, emotion, and motivation. *Psychological Review, 98,* 234–253.

Mash, E., & Johnston, C. (1990). Determinants of parenting stress: Illustrations from families of hyperactive children and families of physically abused children. *Journal of Clinical Child Psychology, 19,* 313–328.

Mayer, J. D., Gaschke, Y. N., Braverman, D. L., & Evans, T. W. (1992). Mood-congruent judgment is a general effect. *Journal of Personality and Social Psychology, 63,* 119–132.

Mazur, A., & Lamb, T. A. (1980). Testosterone, status and mood in human males. *Hormones and Behavior, 14,* 236–246.

McGillicuddy-DeLisi, A. V. (1985). The relationship between parental beliefs and children's cognitive level. In I. E. Sigel (Ed.), *Parental belief systems* (pp. 7–24). Hillsdale, NJ: Erlbaum.

McGillicuddy-DeLisi, A. V. (1992). Parents' beliefs and children's personal-social development. In I. E. Sigel, A. V. McGillicuddy-DeLisi, & J. J. Goodnow (Eds.), *Parental belief systems: The psychological consequences for children* (2nd ed., pp. 115–142). Hillsdale, NJ: Erlbaum.

McKenna, J. J. (1990). Evolution and the sudden infant death syndrome (SIDS): I. Infant response to parental contact. *Human Nature, 1,* 145–177.

McKenna, J. J., & Mosko, C. (1990). Evolution and the sudden infant death syndrome (SIDS): III. Infant arousal and parent-infant co-sleeping. *Human Nature, 1,* 291–330.

Mehan, H. (1979). *Learning lessons.* Cambridge, MA: Harvard University Press.

Melson, G. F., Fogel, A., & Toda, S. (1986). Children's ideas about infants and their care. *Child Development, 57,* 1519–1527.

Meltzoff, A. N., & Moore, M. K. (1992). Early imitation within a functional framework: The importance of person identity, movement, and development. *Infant Behavior and Development, 15,* 479–505.

Meltzoff, A. N., & Moore, M. K. (1994). Imitation, memory, and the representation of persons. *Infant Behavior and Development, 17,* 83–99.

Merton, R. K., Reader, G. R., & Kendall, P. L. (1957). *The student physician.* Cambridge, MA: Harvard University Press.

Mesquita, B., & Frijda, N. F. (1992). Cultural variations in emotions: A review. *Psychological Bulletin, 112,* 179–204.

Meyrowitz, J. (1985). *No sense of place: The impact of electronic media on social behavior.* New York: Oxford University Press.

Michaels. S. (1991). The dismantling of narrative. In A. McCabe & C. Petersen (Eds.), *Developing narrative structure* (pp. 303–351). Hillsdale, NJ: Erlbaum.

Miller, B. D. (1995). Precepts and practices: Researching identity formation among Indian Hindu adolescents in the United States. In J. J. Goodnow, P. J. Miller, & F. Kessel (Eds.), *Cultural practices as contexts for development* (pp. 71–86). San Francisco: Jossey-Bass.

Miller, P. J. (1992). Narrative practices and the social construction of self in childhood. *American Ethologist, 17,* 292–311.

Miller, P. J., & Goodnow, J. J. (1995). Cultural practices: Towards an integration of culture and development. In J. J. Goodnow, P. J. Miller, & F. Kessel (Eds.), *Cultural practices as contexts for development* (pp. 5–16). San Francisco: Jossey-Bass.

Miller, P. J., Potts, R., Fung, H., Hoogstra, L., & Mintz, J. (1990). Narrative practices and the construction of self in childhood. *American Ethnologist, 17,* 292–311.

Miller, P. J., & Sperry, L. L. (1987). The socialization of anger and aggression. *Merrill-Palmer Quarterly, 33,* 1–31.

Miller, P. J., & Sperry, L. L. (1988). Early talk about the past: The origins of conversational stories of personal experience. *Journal of Child Language, 15,* 293–315.

Miller, S. A. (1988). Parents' beliefs about children's cognitive development. *Child Development, 59,* 259–285.

Moffitt, T., Caspi, A., & Belsky, J. (1990, March). *Family context, girls' behavior, and the onset of puberty: A test of a sociobiological model.* Paper presented at the biennial meetings of the Society for Research in Adolescence, Atlanta, GA.

Moreland, R. L., & Levine, J. M. (1989). Newcomers and old-timers in small groups. In P. B. Paulus (Ed.), *Psychology of group influence* (2nd ed., pp. 143–186). Hillsdale, NJ: Erlbaum.

Morton, J., & Johnson, M. H. (1991). CONSPEC and CONLERN: A two-process theory of infant face recognition. *Psychological Review, 98,* 164–181.

Moscovici, S. (1981). On social representations. In J. P. Forgas (Ed.), *Social cognition* (pp. 181–209). New York: Academic Press.

Moss, H. A., & Jones, S. J. (1977). Relations between maternal attitudes and maternal behaviors as a function of social class. In P. H. Leiderman, S. R., Tulkin, & A. Rosenfeld (Eds.), *Culture and infancy* (pp. 439–465). New York: Academic Press.

Mugny, G., & Carugati, F. (1989). *Social representations of intelligence.* Cambridge, England: Cambridge University Press.

Murphey, D. A. (1992). Constructing the child: Relations between parents' beliefs and child outcomes. *Developmental Review, 12,* 199–232.

Murray, A. D. (1979). Infant crying as an elicitor of parental behavior: An examination of two models. *Psychological Bulletin, 86,* 191–215.

Nagell, K., Olguin, R. S., & Tomasello, M. (1993). Processes of social learning in the tool use of chimpanzees (Pan troglodytes) and human children (Homo sapiens). *Journal of Comparative Psychology, 107,* 174–186.

Newcomb, A. F., & Bagwell, C. L. (1995). Children's friendship relations: A meta-analytic review. *Psychological Bulletin, 117,* 306–347.

Newman, D., Griffin, P., & Cole, M. (1989). *The construction zone: Working for cognitive change in school.* Cambridge, England: Cambridge University Press.

Niedenthal, P. M., & Setterlund, M. C. (1994). Emotion congruence in perception. *Personality and Social Psychology Bulletin, 20,* 401–411.

Ninio, A. (1988). The effects of cultural background, sex and parenthood on beliefs about the timetable of cognitive development in infancy. *Merrill-Palmer Quarterly, 34,* 369–388.

Ninio, A., & Bruner, J. (1978). The achievement and antecedents of labelling. *Journal of Child Language, 5,* 1–15.

Nisbett, R. E. (1990). Evolutionary psychology, biology, and cultural evolution. *Motivation and Emotion, 14,* 255–263.

Nucci, L. P. (1984). Evaluating teachers as social agents: Students' ratings of domain appropriate and domain inappropriate teacher responses to transgressions. *American Educational Research Journal, 21,* 367–378.

Nucci, L. P., & Turiel, E. (1978). Social interactions and the development of social concepts in preschool children. *Child Development, 49,* 400–407.

Nucci, L. P., & Weber, E. K. (1995). Social interactions in the home and the development of young children's conceptions of the personal. *Child Development, 66,* 1438–1452.

Nunes, T. (1995). Cultural practices and the conception of individual differences. In J. J. Goodnow, P. J. Miller, & F. Kessel

(Eds.), *Cultural practices as contexts for development* (pp. 91–104). San Francisco: Jossey-Bass.

Ochs, E. (1982). Talking to children in Western Samoa. *Language in Society, 11,* 77–104.

Ochs, E. (1990). Indexicality and socialization. In J. W. Stigler, R. A. Shweder, & G. Herdt (Eds.), *Culture and human development* (pp. 287–308). Chicago: University of Chicago Press.

Ochs, E., & Taylor, C. (1992). Family narratives as political activity. *Discourse and Society, 3,* 301–318.

Ortner, S. (1985). The psychologist in psychotherapeutic practice: Motivations, satisfactions, and stresses. *Dissertation Abstracts International, 45,* 3954.

Osofsky, J. D. (1995). The effects of exposure to violence on young children. *American Psychologist, 50,* 782–788.

Oster, H., Hegley, D., & Nagel, L. (1992). Adult judgments and fine-grained analysis of infant facial expressions: Testing the validity of a priori coding formulas. *Developmental Psychology, 28,* 1115–1131.

Packer, M. J. (1993). Away from internalization. In E. A. Forman, N. Minick, & C. A. Stone (Eds.), *Contexts for learning* (pp. 254–265). New York: Oxford University Press.

Palacios, J. (1990). Parents' ideas about the development and education of their children: Answers to some questions. *International Journal of Behavioral Development, 13,* 137–155.

Palacios. J. (in press). Parents' and adolescents' ideas on children, origins and transmission of intracultural diversity. In S. Harkness & C. M. Super (Eds.), *Parents' cultural belief systems.* New York: Guilford Press.

Panksepp, J., Nelson, E., & Bekkedal, M. (1997). Brain systems for the mediation of social separation-distress and social-reward. *Annals of the New York Academy of Sciences, 807,* 87–100.

Panksepp, J., Normansell, L., Herman, B., Bishop, P., & Crepeau, L. (1988). Neural and neurochemical control of the separation distress call. In J. D. Newman (Ed.), *The physiological control of mammalian vocalization* (pp. 263–299). New York: Plenum Press.

Papousek, H., & Papousek, M. (1991). Innate and cultural guidance of infants' integrative competencies: China, the United States, and Germany. In M. H. Bornstein (Ed.), *Intersections with attachment* (pp. 97–122). Hillsdale, NJ: Erlbaum.

Parke, R. D. (1974). Rules, roles and resistance to deviation: Recent advances in punishment, discipline and self-control. In A. D. Pick (Ed.), *Minnesota Symposium on Child Psychology* (Vol. 8, pp. 111–143). Minneapolis: University of Minnesota Press.

Parke, R. D. (1978). Parent-infant interaction: Progress, paradigms, and problems. In G. P. Sackett (Ed.), *Observing behavior* (Vol. 1, pp. 69–94). Baltimore: University Park Press.

Parke, R. D. (1995). Fathers and families. In M. Bornstein (Ed.), *Handbook of parenting* (pp. 27–63). Hillsdale, NJ: Erlbaum.

Parke, R. D., & Bhavnagri, N. P. (1989). Parents as managers of children's peer relationships. In D. Belle (Ed.), *Children's social networks and social supports* (pp. 241–259). New York: Wiley.

Parpal, M., & Maccoby, E. E. (1985). Maternal responsiveness and subsequent child compliance. *Child Development, 56,* 1326–1334.

Pataki, S. P., Shapiro, D., & Clark, M. S. (1994). Children's acquisition of appropriate norms for friendship and acquaintance: Children's friendships [Special issue]. *Journal of Social and Personal Relationships, 11,* 427–442.

Pateman, C. (1988). *The sexual contract.* Cambridge, MA: Polity Press.

Patterson, G. R. (1982). *Coercive family process.* Eugene, OR: Castalia Press.

Patterson, G. R. (1995). Coercion as a basis for early age of onset for arrest. In J. McCord (Ed.), *Coercion and punishment in long-term perspective* (pp. 81–105). New York: Cambridge University Press.

Patterson, G. R. (1996). Some characteristics of a developmental theory for early onset delinquency. In J. J. Haugaard & M. F. Lenzenweger (Eds.), *Frontiers of developmental psychopathology.* New York: Oxford University Press.

Patterson, G. R., Dishion, T. J., & Chamberlain, P. (1993). Outcomes and methodological issues relating to treatment of antisocial children. In T. R. Giles (Ed.), *Handbook of effective psychotherapy* (pp. 43–88). New York: Plenum Press.

Perrett, D., Harries, M., Mistlin, A., Hietanen, J., Benson, P., Bevan, R., Thomas, S., Oram, M., Ortega, J., & Brierley, K. (1990). Social signals analyzed at the single cell level: Someone is looking at me, something touched me, something moved! *International Journal of Comparative Psychology, 4,* 25–55.

Perry, B. D. (1994). Neurobiological sequelae of childhood trauma: PTSD in children. In M. M. Murburg (Ed.), *Catecholamine function in posttraumatic stress disorder: Emerging concepts* (No. 42., pp. 233–255). Washington, DC: American Psychiatric Press.

Peterson, L., & Brown, D. (1994). Integrating child injury and abuse-neglect research: Common histories, etiologies, and solutions. *Psychological Bulletin, 116,* 293–315.

Piaget, J. (1948). *The moral judgment of the child.* Glencoe, IL: Free Press.

Plomin, R. (1994). The Emmanuel Miller Memorial Lecture 1993: Genetic research and identification of environmental influences. *Journal of Child Psychology and Psychiatry and Allied Disciplines, 35,* 817–834.

Plomin, R., & Neiderhiser, J. M. (1992). Genetics and experience. *Current Directions in Psychological Science, 1*, 160–163.

Plomin, R., Reiss, D., Hetherington, E. M., & Howe, G. W. (1994). Nature and nurture: Genetic contributions to measures of the family environment. *Developmental Psychology, 30*, 32–43.

Posner, M. I., Rothbart, M. K., & Harman, C. (1994). Cognitive science's contribution to culture and emotion. In S. Kitayama & H. R. Markus (Eds.), *Emotion and culture* (pp. 197–218). Washington, DC: American Psychological Association.

Power, T. G. (1985). Mother- and father-infant play: A developmental analysis. *Child Development, 56*, 1514–1524.

Power, T. G., Hildebrandt, K. A., & Fitzgerald, H. E. (1982). Adults' responses to infants varying in facial expressions and perceived attractiveness. *Infant Behavior and Development, 5*, 33–44.

Power, T. G., & Shanks, J. A. (1989). Parents as socializers: Maternal and paternal views. *Journal of Youth and Adolescence, 18*, 203–220.

Premack, D., & Premack, A. J. (1994). Moral belief: Form versus content. In L. A. Hirschfeld & S. A. Gelman (Eds.), *Mapping the mind: Domain specificity in cognition and culture* (pp. 149–168). Cambridge, England: Cambridge University Press.

Premack, D., & Premack, A. J. (1995). Origins of human social competence. In M. S. Gazzaniga (Ed.), *The cognitive neurosciences* (pp. 205–218). Cambridge, MA: MIT Press.

Premack, D., & Woodruff, G. (1978). Does the chimpanzee have a "theory of mind"? *Behaviour and Brain Sciences, 4*, 515–516.

Raty, H., Snellman, L., Mantysaari-Hetekorpi, H., & Vornanen, A. (in press). Parents' views on the comprehensive school and its development. *Scandinavian Journal of Educational Research.*

Raven, B. H., & Kruglanski, A. W. (1970). Conflict and power. In P. Swingle (Ed.), *The structure of conflict* (pp. 69–110). San Diego, CA: Academic Press.

Read, S. J. (1987). Constructing causal scenarios: A knowledge structure approach in causal reasoning. *Journal of Personality and Social Psychology, 52*, 288–302.

Reid, B. V., & Valsiner, J. (1986). Consistency, praise, and love: Folk theories of American parents. *Ethos, 14*, 1–15.

Reiss, D., Oliveri, M., & Curd, K. (1983). Family paradigm and adolescent social behavior. *New Directions for Child Development, 22*, 77–92.

Resnick, L., Levine, J., & Teasley, S. D. (1991). *Perspectives on socially shared cognition.* Washington, DC: American Psychological Association.

Richman, A. L., Miller, P. M., & LeVine, R. A. (1992). Cultural and educational variations in maternal responsiveness. *Developmental Psychology, 28*, 614–621.

Rizzo, T. A. (1992). The role of conflict in children's friendship development. In W. A. Corsaro & P. J. Miller (Eds.), *Interpretive approaches to children's socialization* (pp. 93–112). San Francisco: Jossey-Bass.

Roberts, W., & Strayer, J. (1987). Parents' responses to the emotional distress of their children: Relations with children's social competence. *Developmental Psychology, 23*, 414–422.

Rodman, H. (1963). The lower-class value stretch. *Social Forces, 42*, 205–215.

Rogoff, B. (1990). The joint socialization of development by young children and adults. In M. Lewis & S. Feinman (Eds.), *Social influences and socialization in infancy: Genesis of behavior* (Vol. 6, pp. 253–280). New York: Plenum Press.

Rogoff, B., Baker-Sennett, J., Lacasa, P., & Goldsmith, D. (1995). Development through participation in sociocultural activity. In J. J. Goodnow, P. J. Miller, & F. Kessel (Eds.), *Cultural practices as contexts for development* (pp. 45–66). San Francisco: Jossey-Bass.

Rogoff, B., Mistry, J., Goncu, A., & Mosier, C. (1993). Guided participation in cultural activity by toddlers and caregivers. *Monographs of the Society of Research in Child Development, 58*(8, Serial No. 236).

Rommetveit, R. (1987). Meaning, context, and control: Convergent trends and controversial issues in current social-scientific research on human cognition and communication. *Inquiry, 30*, 77–99.

Romney, A. K., Weller, S. C., & Batchelder, W. H. (1986). Culture as consensus: A theory of culture and informant accuracy. *American Anthropologist, 88*, 313–332.

Rotenberg, K., Simourd, L., & Moore, D. (1989). Children's use of a verbal-nonverbal consistency principle to infer truth and lying. *Child Development, 60*, 309–322.

Rothbart, M. K., & Ahadi, S. A. (1994). Temperament and the development of personality: Personality and psychopathology [Special issue]. *Journal of Abnormal Psychology, 103*, 55–66.

Rothbart, M. K., & Derryberry, D. (1981). Development of individual differences in temperament. In M. E. Lamb & A. L. Brown (Eds.), *Advances in developmental psychology* (Vol. 1, pp. 37–86). Hillsdale, NJ: Erlbaum.

Rubin, K. H., & Mills, R. S. L. (1992). Parent's thoughts about children's socially adaptive and maladaptive behaviors: Stability, change, and individual differences. In I. I. Sigel, A. V. McGillicuddy-DeLisi, & J. J. Goodnow (Eds.), *Parental belief systems: The psychological consequences for children* (2nd ed., pp. 41–70). Hillsdale, NJ: Erlbaum.

Ruble, D. N., Newman, L. S., Rholes, W. S., & Altshuler, J. (1988). Children's "naive psychology": The use of behavioral and situational information for the prediction of behavior. *Cognitive Development, 3*, 89–112.

Rutter, M. (1978). Family, area and school influences in the genesis of conduct disorders. In L. Hersov, M. Berger, &

D. Shaffer (Eds.), *Aggression and antisocial behaviour in childhood and adolescence* (Vol. 1, pp. 95–113). Oxford, England: Pergamon Press.

Rutter, M. (in press). Continuities, transitions, and turning points in development. In M. Rutter & D. Hay (Eds.), *Development through life: A handbook for clinicians*. Oxford, England: Blackwell.

Saarni, C. (1984). An observational study of children's attempts to monitor their expressive behavior. *Child Development, 55,* 1504–1513.

Saarni, C. (1988). Children's understanding of the interpersonal consequences of dissemblance of nonverbal emotional-expressive behavior. *Journal of Nonverbal Behavior, 12,* 275–294.

Sagi, A., & Hoffman, M. L. (1976). Empathic distress in the newborn. *Developmental Psychology, 12,* 175–176.

Sameroff, A. J., & Chandler, M. J. (1975). Reproductive risk and the continuum of caretaking causality. In F. D. Horowitz (Ed.), *Review of child development research* (Vol. 4, pp. 187–244). Chicago: University of Chicago Press.

Sameroff, A. J., & Fiese, B. H. (1992). Family representations of development. In I. E. Sigel, A. V. McGillicuddy-DeLisi, & J. J. Goodnow (Eds.), *Parental belief systems* (2nd ed., pp. 347–369). Hillsdale, NJ: Erlbaum.

Scarr, S. (1992). Developmental theories for the 1990s: Development and individual differences. *Child Development, 63,* 1–19.

Scarr, S., & McCartney, K. (1983). How people make their own environment: A theory of genotype-environment effects. *Child Development, 54,* 424–435.

Schaefer, E. S., & Edgerton, M. (1985). Parent and child correlates of parental modernity. In I. E. Sigel (Ed.), *Parental belief systems* (pp. 287–318). Hillsdale, NJ: Erlbaum.

Schieffelin, B. B. (1990). *The give and take of everyday life: Language socialization of Kaluli children.* Cambridge, England: Cambridge University Press.

Schieffelin, B. B., & Ochs, E. (Eds.). (1986). *Language socialization across cultures.* Cambridge, England: Cambridge University Press.

Seligman, M. E. (1970). On the generality of the laws of learning. *Psychological Review, 77,* 406–418.

Selman, R. L., & Schultz, L. H. (1990). *Making a friend in youth: Developmental theory and peer therapy.* Chicago: University of Chicago Press.

Shaver, P. R., & Hazan, C. (1993). Adult romantic attachment: Theory and evidence. In D. Perlman & W. Jones (Eds.), *Advances in personal relationships* (Vol. 4, pp. 29–70). London: Jessica Kingsley.

Sherrod, L. R. (1981). Issues in cognitive-perceptual development: The special case of social stimuli. In M. Lamb &

L. Sherrod (Eds.), *Infant social cognition: Empirical and theoretical considerations* (pp. 11–36). Hillsdale, NJ: Erlbaum.

Shifflett-Simpson, K., & Cummings, E. M. (1996). Mixed message resolutions and children's responses to interadult conflict. *Child Development, 67,* 437–448.

Shiffrin, R. M., & Schneider, W. (1977). Controlled and automatic information process: II. Perceptual learning, automatic attending, and a general theory. *Psychological Review, 84,* 127–188.

Shweder, R. A. (1982). Beyond self-constructed knowledge. *Merrill-Palmer Quarterly, 28,* 41–69.

Shweder, R. A. (1990). Cultural psychology: What is it? In J. W. Stigler, R. A. Shweder, & G. Herdt (Eds.), *Cultural psychology* (pp. 1–46). Cambridge, England: Cambridge University Press.

Shweder, R. A., Jensen, L. A., & Goldstein, W. M. (1995). Who sleeps by whom revisited: A method for extracting the moral goods implicit in practice. In J. J. Goodnow, P. J. Miller, & F. Kessel (Eds.), *Cultural practices as contexts for development: New directions for child development* (pp. 21–39). San Francisco, CA: Jossey-Bass.

Siegler, T. D. (1983). Information processing approaches to development. In P. H. Mussen (Series Ed.) & W. Kessen (Vol. Ed.), *Handbook of child psychology: Vol. 1. History, theory and methods* (pp. 129–212). New York: Wiley.

Sigel, I. E. (1992). The belief-behavior connection: A resolvable dilemma. In I. E. Sigel, A. V. McGillicuddy-DeLisi, & J. J. Goodnow (Eds.), *Parental belief systems: The psychological consequences for children* (pp. 433–456). Hillsdale, NJ: Erlbaum.

Sigel, I. E. (1993). The centrality of a distancing model for the development of representational competence. In R. R. Cocking & K. A. Renninger (Eds.), *The development and meaning of psychological distance* (pp. 141–158). Hillsdale, NJ: Erlbaum.

Sigel, I. E., McGillicuddy-DeLisi, A. V., & Goodnow, J. J. (Eds.). (1992). *Parental belief systems: The psychological consequences for children.* Hillsdale, NJ: Erlbaum.

Sigel, I. E., Stinson, E. T., & Flaugher, J. (1993). Family process and school achievement: A comparison of children with and without communication handicaps. In R. E. Cole & D. Reiss (Eds.), *How do families cope with chronic illness? Family research consortium: Advances in family research* (pp. 95–120). Hillsdale, NJ: Erlbaum.

Silk, J. B. (1992). The patterning of intervention among male bonnet macaques: Reciprocity, revenge, and loyalty. *Current Anthropology, 33,* 318–324.

Sinnott, J. M., Pisoni, D. B., & Aslin, R. N. (1983). A comparison of pure tone auditory thresholds in human infants and adults. *Infant Behavior and Development, 6,* 3–17.

Small, A. W. (1905). *General sociology.* Chicago: University of Chicago Press.

Smetana, J. (1995). Parenting styles and beliefs about parental authority. In J. Smetana (Ed.), *Beliefs about parenting* (pp. 21–36). San Francisco: Jossey-Bass.

Smetana, J. (1988). Adolescents' and parents' conceptions of parental authority. *Child Development, 59,* 321–335.

Smetana, J., & Asquith, P. (1994). Adolescents' and parents' conceptions of parental authority and personal autonomy. *Child Development, 65,* 1147–1162.

Smith, C. A., & Lazarus, R. S. (1993). Appraisal components, core relational themes, and the emotions. *Cognition and Emotion, 7,* 233–269.

Snow, M. E., Jacklin, C. N., & Maccoby, E. E. (1983). Sex-of-child differences in father-child interaction at one year of age. *Child Development, 54,* 227–232.

Sperber, D. (1994). The modularity of thought and the epidemiology of representations. In L. A. Hirschfeld & S. A. Gelman (Eds.), *Mapping the mind* (pp. 39–67). Cambridge, England: Cambridge University Press.

Sroufe, L. A., Bennett, C., Englund, M., Urban, J., & Shulman, S. (1993). The significance of gender boundaries in pre-adolescence: Contemporary correlates and antecedents of boundary violation and maintenance. *Child Development, 64,* 455–466.

Sroufe, L. A., & Fleeson, J. (1986). Attachment and the construction of relationships. In W. Hartup & Z. Rubin (Eds.), *Relationships and development* (pp. 52–71). Hillsdale, NJ: Erlbaum.

Stack, D. M., & Muir, D. W. (1992). Adult tactile stimulation during face-to-face interactions modulates 5-month-olds' affect and attention. *Child Development, 63,* 1509–1525.

Strassberg, Z. (1995). Social information-processing in compliance situations by mothers of behavior-problem boys. *Child Development, 66,* 376–389.

Stratton, P., & Swaffer, R. (1988). Maternal causal beliefs for abused and handicapped children. *Journal of Reproductive and Infant Psychology, 6,* 201–216.

Strauss, C. (1992). Models and motives. In R. G. D'Andrade & C. Strauss (Eds.), *Human motives and cultural models* (pp. 1–20). Cambridge, England: Cambridge University Press.

Sugarman, D. B. (1983). The development of children's physical and social causal explanations. *Dissertation Abstracts International, 44,* 363.

Super, C. M. (1981). Behavioral development in infancy. In R. H. Munroe, R. L. Munroe, & B. B. Whiting (Eds.), *Handbook of cross-cultural human development* (pp. 181–270). New York: Garland.

Super, C. M., Harkness, S., van Tijen, N., van der Flugt, E., Fintelman, M., & Dijkstra, J. (in press). The three R's of Dutch childrearing and the socialization of infant arousal. In S. Harkness & C. M. Super (Eds.), *Parents' cultural belief systems.* New York: Guilford Press.

Susman, E. J., Inoff-Germain, G., Nottelman, E. D., Loriaux, D. L., Cutler, G. G., Jr., & Chrousos, G. P. (1987). Hormones, emotional dispositions, and aggressive attributes in young adolescents. *Child Development, 58,* 1114–1134.

Susman, E. J., Nottelmann, E. D., Inoff, G. E., Dorn, L. D., Cutler, G. B., Jr., Loriaux, D. L., & Chrousos, G. P. (1985). The relation of relative hormonal levels and physical development and social-emotional behavior in young adolescents: Time of maturation and psychosocial functioning in adolescence [Special issue]. *International Journal of Youth and Adolescence, 14,* 245–264.

Tajfel, H. (1982). Social psychology of intergroup relations. *Annual Review of Psychology, 33,* 1–39.

Tajfel, J. (1981). *Human groups and social categories: Studies in social psychology.* Cambridge, England: Cambridge University Press.

Tajfel, H., & Turner, J. C. (1986). The social identity theory of intergroup behavior. In S. Worchel & W. G. Austin (Eds.), *Psychology of intergroup relations* (pp. 33–47). Chicago: Nelson-Hall.

Teti, D. M., & Gelfand, D. M. (1991). Behavioral competence among mothers of infants in the first year: The mediational role of maternal self-efficacy. *Child Development, 62,* 918–929.

Teti, D. M., Gelfand, D. M., Messinger, D. S., & Isabella, R. (1995). Maternal depression and the quality of early attachment: An examination of infants, preschoolers, and their mothers. *Developmental Psychology, 31,* 364–376.

Tharp, R. G., & Gallimore, R. (1988). *Rousing minds to life: Teaching, learning, and schooling in social context.* Cambridge, England: Cambridge University Press.

Thompson, R. A. (1991). Emotional regulation and emotional development. *Educational Psychology Review, 3,* 269–307.

Thompson, R. A. (1994). Emotion regulation: A theme in search of definition. *Monographs of the Society for Research in Child Development, 59*(2/3), 250–283.

Thorne, B. (1987). Re-visioning women and social change: Where are the children? *Gender and Society, 1,* 85–109.

Thorne, B., & Luria, Z. (1986). Sexuality and gender in children's daily worlds. *Social Problems, 33,* 176.

Thornton, M. C., Chatters, L. M., Taylor, R. J., & Allen, W. R. (1990). Sociodemographic and environmental correlates of racial socialization by Black parents. *Child Development, 61,* 401–409.

Tinsley, B. J. (1992). Multiple influences on the acquisition and socialization of children's health attitudes and behavior: An integrated review. *Child Development, 63,* 1043–1069.

Tisak, M. (1986). Children's conceptions of parental authority. *Child Development, 57,* 166–176.

Tomasello, M. (in press). Uniquely primate, uniquely human. *Developmental Science.*

Tomasello, M., Savage-Rumbaugh, S., & Kruger, A. C. (1993). Imitative learning of actions on objects by children, chimpanzees, and enculturated chimpanzees. *Child Development, 64,* 1688–1705.

Tooby, J., & Cosmides, L. (1990). The past explains the present: Emotional adaptations and the structure of ancestral environments. *Ethology and Sociobiology, 11,* 375–424.

Tooby, J., & Cosmides, L. (1995). Mapping the evolved functional organization of mind and brain. In M. S. Gazzanga (Ed.), *The cognitive neurosciences* (pp. 1185–1197). Cambridge, MA: MIT Press.

Tooby, J., & Cosmides, L. (1996). Friendship and the banker's paradox: Other pathways to the evolution of adaptations for altruism. In J. M. Smith, W. G. Runciman, & R. I. M. Dunbar (Eds.), *Evolution of social behavior patterns in primates and man* (Vol. 88, pp. 119–143). London: British Academy.

Tracy, L. R., Lamb, M. E., & Ainsworth, M. D. S. (1976). Infant approach as related to attachment. *Child Development, 47,* 571–578.

Trevarthen, C. (1988). Universal cooperative motives: How infants begin to know the language and culture of their parents. In G. Jahoda & I. M. Lewis (Eds.), *Acquiring culture: Cross cultural studies in child development* (pp. 37–90). London: Croom Helm.

Tronick, E. Z. (1989). Emotions and emotional communication in infants. Children and their development: Knowledge base, research agenda, and social application [Special issue]. *American Psychologist, 44,* 112–119.

Tronick, E. Z., Morelli, G. A., & Ivey, P. K. (1992). The Efe forager infant and toddler's pattern of social relationships: Multiple and simultaneous. *Developmental Psychology, 28,* 568–577.

Tulving, E. (1972). Episodic and semantic memory. In E. Tulving & W. Donaldson (Eds.), *Organization of memory.* New York: Academic Press.

Turiel, E. (1983). *The development of social knowledge: Morality and convention.* New York: Cambridge University Press.

Tversky, A., & Kahneman, D. (1973). Availability: A heuristic for judging frequency and probability. *Cognitive Psychology, 5,* 207–232.

Valsiner, J. (1989). *Culture and human development.* Lexington, MA: D. C. Haith.

Valsiner, J. (in press). Culture and human development: A co-constructivist perspective. In P. van Geert & L. Mos (Ed.), *Annals of theoretical psychology* (Vol. 10). New York: Plenum Press.

Van IJzendoorn, M. H. (1992). Intergenerational transmission of parenting: A review of studies in non-clinical populations. *Developmental Review, 12,* 76–99.

Van IJzendoorn, M. H. (1995). Adult attachment representations, parental responsiveness, and infant attachment: A meta-analysis on the predictive validity of the Adult Attachment Interview. *Psychological Bulletin, 117,* 411–415.

Vasta, R. (1982). Physical child abuse: A dual-component analysis. *Developmental Review, 2,* 125–149.

Verdonik, F., Flapan, V., Schmit, C., & Weinstock, J. (1988). The role of power relationships in children's cognition: Its significance for research on cognitive development. *Quarterly Newsletter of the Laboratory of Comparative Human Cognition, 10,* 80–85.

Wahler, R. G., & Dumas, J. E. (1986). Maintenance factors in coercive mother-child interactions: The compliance and predictability hypotheses. *Journal of Applied Behavior Analysis, 19,* 13–22.

Wahler, R. G., Williams, A. J., & Cerezo, A. (1990). The compliance and predictability hypotheses: Sequential and correlational analyses of coercive mother-child interactions. *Behavioral Assessment, 12,* 391–407.

Watson-Gegeo, K. A. (1992). Thick explanation in the ethnographic study of child socialization: A longitudinal study of the problem of schooling for Kwara'ae (Solomon Islands) children. In W. A. Corsaro & P. J. Miller (Eds.), *Interpretive approaches to children's socialization* (pp. 51–66). San Francisco: Jossey-Bass.

Wauchope, B. A., & Straus, M. A. (1989). Physical punishment and physical abuse of American children: Incidence rates by age, gender, and occupational class. In M. A. Straus & R. J. Gelles (Eds.), *Physical violence in American families: Risk factors and adaptations to violence in 8,145 families* (pp. 1–15). New Brunswick, NJ: Transaction.

Weinberger, D. A. (1994, February). *Relations between parents' distress and self-restraint and adolescents' adjustments.* Paper presented at the meeting of the Society for Research on Adolescence, San Diego, CA.

Weiner, B. (1986). *An attributional theory of motivation and emotion.* New York: Springer-Verlag.

Wentworth, W. M. (1980). *Context and understanding: An inquiry into socialization theory.* New York: Elsevier.

Werner, E. E. (1988). A cross-cultural perspective on infancy. *Journal of Cross-Cultural Psychology, 19,* 96–113.

Wertsch, J. V. (1991a). *Voices of the mind.* Cambridge, England: Cambridge University Press.

Wertsch, J. V. (1991b). A sociocultural approach to socially shared cognition. In L. B. Resnick, J. M. Levine, & S. D. Teasley (Eds.), *Perspectives on socially shared cognition* (pp. 85–100). Washington, DC: American Psychological Association.

Wertsch, J. V., Minick, N., & Arns, F. J. (1984). The creation of context in joint problem-solving. In B. Rogoff & J. Lave (Eds.), *Everyday cognition: Its development in social context* (pp. 151–171). Cambridge, MA: Harvard University Press.

West, C., & Zimmerman, D. H. (1987). Doing gender. *Gender and Society, 1,* 125–151.

West, M. M. (1988). Parental values and behavior in the Outer Fiji islands. In R. A. LeVine, P. M. Miller, & M. M. West (Eds.), *Parental behavior in diverse societies* (pp. 13–26). San Francisco: Jossey-Bass.

White, G. M. (1994). Affecting culture: Emotion and morality in everyday life. In S. Kitayama & H. R. Markus (Eds.), *Emotion and culture* (pp. 219–240). Washington, DC: American Psychological Association.

Whiting, B. B. (1974). Folk wisdom and child rearing. *Merrill-Palmer Quarterly, 20,* 9–19.

Whiting, B. B., & Edwards, C. P. (1988). *Children of different worlds: The formation of social behavior.* Cambridge, MA: Harvard University Press.

Whiting, B. B., & Whiting, J. W. M. (1975). *Children of six cultures: A psychocultural analysis.* Cambridge, MA: Harvard University Press.

Whiting, J. W. M. (1941). *Becoming a Kwoma.* New Haven, CT: Yale University Press.

Whiting, J. W. M. (1981). Aging and becoming an elder: A cross-cultural comparison. In J. G. Marsh (Ed.), *Aging.* New York: Academic Press.

Whiting, J. W. M., & Child, I. L. (1953). *Child training and personality: A cross-cultural study.* New Haven, CT: Yale University Press.

Wiener, S. G., Coe, C. L., & Levine, S. (1988). Endocrine and neurochemical sequelae of primate vocalizations. In J. D. Newman (Ed.), *The physiological control of mammalian vocalization* (pp. 367–394). New York: Plenum Press.

Willis, P. (1977). *Learning to labour.* Aldershot Hampshire, England: Gower.

Winegar, L. T. (1988). Children's emerging understanding of social events: Co-construction and social process. In J. Valsiner (Ed.), *Social co-construction and environmental guidance in development* (pp. 2–27). New York: ABLEX.

Wolfe, D. A. (1985). Child-abusive parents: An empirical review and analysis. *Psychological Bulletin, 97,* 462–482.

Wolfe, D. A., Fairbanks, J. A., Kelly, J. A., & Bradlyn, A. S. (1983). Child abusive parents' physiological responses to stressful and nonstressful behavior in children. *Behavioral Assessment, 5,* 363–372.

Wood, D., Bruner, J. S., & Ross, G. (1976). The role of tutoring in problem solving. *Journal of Child Psychology and Psychiatry and Allied Disciplines, 17,* 89–100.

Wozniak, R. H. (1993). Co-constructive metatheory for psychology: Implications for an analysis of families as specific social contexts for development. In R. H. Wozniak & K. W. Fischer (Eds.), *Development in context: Acting and thinking in specific environments* (pp. 77–91). Hillsdale, NJ: Erlbaum.

Yee, M. D., & Brown, R. (1992). Self-evaluations and intergroup attitudes in children aged 3 to 9. *Child Development, 63,* 619–629.

Youniss, J., & Damon, W. (1992). Social construction in Piaget's theory. In H. Beilin & P. Pufall (Eds.), *Piaget's theory: Prospects and possibilities* (pp. 267–286). Hillsdale, NJ: Erlbaum.

Youniss, J., McLellan, J. A., & Strouse, D. (1995). "We're popular, but we're not snobs": Adolescents describe their crowds. In R. Montemayer (Ed.), *Advances in adolescent development* (Vol. 5, pp. 101–122). Newbury Park, CA: Sage.

Zahn-Waxler, C., Iannotti, R. J., Cummings, E. M., & Denham, S. (1990). Antecedents of problem behaviors in children of depressed mothers. *Development and Psychopathology, 2,* 271–291.

Zebrowitz, L. A., Kendall-Tackett, K., & Fafel, J. (1991). The influence of children's facial maturity on parental expectations and punishments. *Journal of Experimental Child Psychology, 52,* 221–238.

Zebrowitz, L. A., & Montepare, J. M. (1992). Impressions of babyfaced individuals across the life span. *Developmental Psychology, 28,* 1143–1152.

Zeskind, P. S., Klein, L., & Marshall, T. M. (1992). Adults' perceptions of experimental modifications of durations of pauses and expiratory sounds in infant crying. *Developmental Psychology, 28,* 1153–1162.

Zeskind, P. S., & Shingler, E. A. (1991). Child abusers' perceptual responses to newborn infant cries varying in pitch. *Infant Behavior and Development, 14,* 335–347.

Zillmann, D., Bryant, J. J., Cantor, J. R., & Day, K. D. (1975). Irrelevance of mitigating circumstances in retaliatory behavior at high levels of excitation. *Journal of Research in Personality, 9,* 282–293.

CHAPTER 8

Socialization in the Family: Ethnic and Ecological Perspectives

ROSS D. PARKE and RAYMOND BURIEL

Socialization is the process whereby an individual's standards, skills, motives, attitudes, and behaviors change to conform to those regarded as desirable and appropriate for his or her present and future role in any particular society. Many agents and agencies play a role in the socialization process, including family, peers, schools, and the media.

Moreover, it is recognized that these various agents function together rather than independently. Families have been recognized as an early pervasive and highly influential context for socialization. Children are dependent on families for nurturance and support from an early age, which accounts, in part, for their prominence as a socialization agent.

In this chapter, we have several goals. Our primary goal is to expand our framework for conceptualizing the family's role in socialization. This takes several forms, including treating the family as a social system in which the full range of subsystems including

Preparation of this chapter was facilitated by National Science Foundation grants BNS 8919391 and SBR 9308941, NICHD grant HD 32391, and NIMH R01 MH 54154 grant to Parke.

parent-child, marital, and sibling systems are recognized. The diversity of family forms has increased in the past several decades, and a second goal is to explore the implications of various family configurations for the socialization process. Third, cultural and ethnic variations in family traditions, beliefs, and practices are increasingly being recognized, and a further aim of this chapter is to explore how ethnic diversity informs our understanding of family socialization. Fourth, our goal is to locate family socialization in an ecological context to appreciate how family environments shape and constrain their socialization practices. We demonstrate the value of a life course perspective on socialization that recognizes the importance of both developmental changes in adult lives and the historical circumstances under which socialization unfolds. Finally, we recognize that families are increasingly diverse in terms of their organization, form, and lifestyle. Some issues are beyond the scope of the chapter, including the recent work on gay and lesbian families, as well as research on adopted children (see Brodinsky, Lang, & Smith, 1995; C. Patterson, 1995, for reviews of these issues).

THEORETICAL APPROACHES TO SOCIALIZATION WITHIN THE FAMILY: HISTORICAL AND CONTEMPORARY PERSPECTIVES

Historical Perspectives on Family Socialization Theory

To appreciate these goals, a brief overview of historical changes in socialization theory is necessary. The history of this field over the past century can be traced to two theoretical perspectives: behaviorism and psychoanalysis (Maccoby, 1992). In the 1920s, John Watson offered a learning theory approach to socialization that was based largely on conditioning as a major explanatory mechanism. This approach was clearly Euro-American in terms of its endorsement of the modifiability of behavior and its clear commitment to an environmentally based analysis. At the same time, behavioral views were not developmental and assumed that the same explanatory principles apply equally to children at all ages. This legacy continued under Skinner and his followers in the behavior modification movement who applied these principles to children's behavior (Bijou & Baer, 1961).

The other major legacy was Freudian psychoanalysis. Perhaps no other theoretical view has had so wide an influence—albeit often unrecognized and unacknowledged—than Freudian theory. Freud's stage theory of development, with its emphasis on the importance of early experience as a determinant of later social and personality development, was a major force in socialization research for nearly half a century. Although it was difficult to test as originally formulated, the theory nevertheless provided the outlines for the major socialization products such as aggression, dependency, moral development, and sex typing, as well as the major sets of formative experiences in the family, especially the centrality of the mother-child relationship.

In the late 1930s, the fusion of Hullian learning theory with psychoanalysis (N. Miller & Dollard, 1941) provided the opportunity to empirically evaluate the propositions of psychoanalytic theory by translating them into Hullian drive-reduction language. This led to several well-known studies by J. Whiting and Child (1953) and Sears, Maccoby, and Levin (1957). Whiting tested various Freudian-based propositions about the impact of child-rearing practices, such as feeding, weaning, and toilet training on later development in a variety of different cultures, while Sears evaluated these hypotheses in American-based interview studies of child-rearing practices. As Maccoby (1992) noted: "These large scale efforts to merge psychoanalytic and behavior theory and then to predict children's personality attributes from parental socialization methods, were largely unsuccessful" (p. 1009). Moreover, the field moved away from the long-standing commitment to the search for a few principles that would explain large domains of development (Parke, Ornstein, Rieser, & Zahn-Waxler, 1994). Since that time there has been a retreat from wide-scope theorizing. As Kessen (1982) observed, "At an accelerated rate, child psychologists as a society of colleagues have moved away from the general process, general-principle specification of their intellectual task. More and more, we have turned from the search for singular general laws of development" (p. 36). In the past 25 to 30 years, the degree of specialization has increased sharply; in place of grand theories, a variety of minitheories aimed at limited and specific aspects of development have emerged.

The 1960s and 1970s marked the advent of further developments in socialization theory. First, social learning theory (Bandura, 1977; Bandura & Walters, 1963) emerged as an alternative to the Hullian-Freudian legacy. (For a detailed account of this theoretical development, see Grusec, 1992.) The distinguishing feature of this approach was the emphasis on imitation or observational learning, which emphasized the central role of cognition in social learning and reduced dependence on external reinforcement for the acquisition of new behaviors. In terms of method, social learning theory relied on the experimental analogue approach in contrast to the retrospective interview approaches of Sears and his colleagues. Moreover, in a break with the Freudian tradition, social learning theorists placed much greater emphasis on the plasticity and modifiability of the organism at different points in development and downplayed the psychoanalytically based concept of early experience as a constraining condition on later development.

At the same time, the role of social contingencies in shaping parent-child interaction was receiving increased attention (Gewirtz, 1969). Studies of parent-infant interaction (e.g., Stern, 1977), as well as interactions of parents and children, especially aggressive and/or deviant children, were flourishing (Cairns, 1979; Patterson, 1980). These studies were important reminders of the bidirectional and mutually influential nature of the socialization process (R. Bell, 1968; Sears, 1951).

As approaches to socialization, these theories were limited in a variety of ways. First, they were largely nondevelopmental, and it was generally assumed that the principles applied equally to children at all ages. This is surprising in view of the increased interest in the role of cognition in social learning theory (Bandura, 1977). While there were some exceptions (Coates & Hartup, 1969), most of the work remained nondevelopmental. Second, the role of affect was given a relatively minor role. Third, genetic factors and biological constraints were given relatively short shrift in the theorizing of the 1960s and 1970s. Fourth, the agents of socialization were still narrowly defined as primarily mothers. In the late 1960s, John Bowlby's (1969) fusion of psychoanalysis and ethology into his influential theory of attachment and loss foreshadowed a variety of changes that materialized in the 1970s and beyond. Concepts of biological preparedness for social interaction combined with emphasis on the importance of early close relationships served to anticipate modern concepts of biological constraints (Schaffer, 1971) as well as revive early notions of the importance of early experience and critical periods. Finally, Bowlby's focus on the dyad as the unit of analysis led to the recognition of the importance of *relationships* for development.

In the late 1970s to the present, a variety of changes have taken place in our theoretical approaches to socialization that have not served simply to correct some of the shortcomings of these earlier analyses but to extend our frameworks into new domains as well.

Contemporary Perspectives on Family Socialization Theory

Several themes are evident in current theoretical approaches to socialization. First, the rise of systems theory (Sameroff, 1983, 1994; Thelen, 1989) has transformed the study of socialization from a parent-child focus to an emphasis on the family as a social system. To understand fully the nature of family relationships, it is necessary to recognize the interdependence among the roles and functions of all family members. It is being increasingly recognized that families are best viewed as social systems. Consequently, to understand the behavior of one member of a family, the complementary behaviors of other members also need to be recognized and assessed. For example, as men's roles in families shift, changes in women's roles in families must also be monitored.

Second, family members—mothers, fathers, and children—influence each other both directly and indirectly (Hinde & Stevenson-Hinde, 1988; Minuchin, 1985; Parke, Power, & Gottman, 1979). Examples of fathers' indirect impact include various ways fathers modify and mediate mother-child relationships. In turn, women affect their children indirectly through their husbands by modifying both the quantity and the quality of father-child interaction. Children may indirectly influence the husband-wife relationship by altering the behavior of either parent, consequently changing the interaction between spouses.

Third, different units of analysis are necessary to understand families. While the individual level—child, mother, and father—remains a useful and necessary level of analysis, recognition of relationships among family members as units of analysis is necessary. The marital, mother-child, and father-child relationships require separate analysis (Parke & O'Neil, 1997). Finally, the family as a unit that is independent of the individual or dyads within the family requires recognition (Sigel & Parke, 1987).

Fourth, under the influence of Bronfenbrenner's (1979, 1989) ecological theory, recognition is being given to the embeddedness of families within a variety of other social systems, including both formal and informal support systems as well as the cultures in which they exist (Parke & Kellam, 1994; Tinsley & Parke, 1984). These include a wide range of extrafamilial influences such as extended families, informal community ties such as friends and neighbors, work sites, and social, educational, and medical institutions (Repetti, 1994; Tinsley & Parke, 1984).

Fifth, developmental considerations are increasingly central to our socialization theories, and the importance of considering family relationships from a variety of developmental perspectives is now recognized. While developmental changes in infant and child perceptual, motor, cognitive, and socioemotional capacities continue to represent the most commonly investigated aspect of development, other aspects of development are viewed as important as well. Under the influence of life course and life span perspectives (Elder, Ch. 3, Vol. 1; Hetherington & Baltes, 1988; Parke, 1988), the importance of examining developmental changes in adults is gaining recognition because parents continue to change and develop during adult years. For example, age at the time of the onset of parenthood can have important implications for how females and males manage their maternal and paternal roles. This involves an exploration of the tasks faced by adults such as self-identity, education, and career and an examination of the relationship between these tasks and the demands of parenting.

Developmental analysis need not be restricted to the level of the individual—either child or parent. Relationships, such as the marital relationship or the mother-infant or father-infant relationship, may follow separate and partially independent developmental courses over childhood (Belsky et al., 1989; Parke, 1988). In turn, the mutual impact of different sets of relationships on each other will vary as a function of the nature of the developmental trajectory. Families change their structure (e.g., through the addition of a new child or the loss of a member through death, separation, or divorce) over time, as well as their norms, rules, and strategies. Tracking the family unit itself over development is an important and relatively neglected task.

A major shift in the 1990s is the challenge to the universality of our socialization theories. This challenge takes a variety of forms. First, as cross-cultural work in development accumulated, it became evident that generalizations from a single culture (e.g., U.S.) may, in fact, not be valid in other cultural contexts (Rogoff, 1990). Second, studies of social class differences in socialization challenged the generality of findings even within one cultural or national context (Hoff-Ginsberg & Tardif, 1995). Finally, there were reminders (e.g., Graham, 1992) that our efforts to understand cultural and racial diversity in our country were severely limited. After her review of journals between 1970 and 1989 revealed that only a small percentage of publications focused on minority samples, Graham (1992) suggested that the lack of a strong empirical base about the development of minority children and families has resulted in "sets of isolated and outdated findings often of questionable soundness" (p. 632). Currently, there is an increased awareness of the importance of both recognizing *and* studying variations in families and family socialization strategies in other cultures (B. Whiting & Edwards, 1988) as well as across ethnic groups within our own culture (Harrison, Wilson, Pine, Chan, & Buriel, 1990). It is important to examine the diversity of familial organization, goals, and strategies *across* ethnic groups, but it is equally critical to explore variations *within* different ethnic groups (Harrison et al., 1990). While there are many similarities across groups and within groups, appreciation of the variations is of central concern.

Another assumption that underlies current socialization theorizing involves the recognition of the impact of secular shifts on families. In recent years, there has been a variety of social changes in U.S. society that have had a profound impact on families. These include the declines in fertility and family size, the changes in the timing of the onset of parenthood, the increased participation of women in the workforce, the rise in rates of divorce, and the subsequent increase in the number of single-parent families (Cherlin, 1992; Parke, 1996). The ways these society-wide changes impact on interaction patterns between parents and children merit examination.

A closely related theme involves the recognition of the importance of the historical time period in which the family interaction is taking place. Historical time periods provide the social conditions for individual and family transitions: examples include the 1960s (the Vietnam War era), the 1930s (the Great Depression), and the 1980s (Farm Belt Depression; Conger & Elder, 1994). Across these historical time periods, family interaction may, in fact, be quite different due to the peculiar conditions of the particular era. These distinctions among different developmental trajectories, as well as social change and historical period effects, are important because these different forms of change do not always harmonize (Elder & Hareven, 1993; Parke & Tinsley, 1984). For example, a family event such as the birth of a child—the transition to parenthood—may have very profound effects on a man who has just begun a career in contrast to the effects on one who has advanced to a stable occupational position. Moreover, individual and family developmental trajectories are embedded within both the social conditions and the values of the historical time in which they exist (Hareven, 1977). The role of parents, as is the case with any social role, is responsive to such fluctuations.

To understand the nature of parent-child relationships within families, a multilevel and dynamic approach is required. Multiple levels of analysis are necessary to capture the individual, dyadic, and family unit aspects of operation within the family itself as well as to reflect the embeddedness of families within a variety of extrafamilial social systems. The dynamic quality reflects the multiple developmental trajectories that warrant consideration in understanding the nature of families in infancy.

The central processes that are involved in accounting for *both* the choice and regulation of socialization strategies and the effects of socialization on the developing child have undergone a major revision (see Bugental & Goodnow, Ch. 7, this Volume, for a detailed review of this issue). Briefly, the renewed interest in the biological bases of behavior has clearly altered our views of socialization. This interest takes several forms, including the role of genetics across development. This work has produced a more sophisticated understanding of the potential role genetics can play not only in the onset of certain behaviors, but in the unfolding of behavior across development. Moreover, Plomin's (1990) reformulation of genetic questions has led to studies of the effects of nonshared family environment on children's development. Finally, this work has underscored the fact that individual differences between children—some of which are genetically based—play a central role in eliciting and shaping parents' socialization strategies. It is well accepted in contemporary accounts of socialization that the child is an active contributor to his or her own socialization. A second focus is found in studies of hormones and behavior, especially during infancy and adolescence (Gunnar, 1987). Third, the increased use of psychophysiological assessments with families represents a further instance of how biological processes are changing socialization studies (Gottman & Katz, 1989). Fourth, the resurgence of interest in the use of evolutionary approaches to the study of socialization is producing new and provocative hypotheses and research directions (Belsky, Steinberg, & Draper, 1991; MacDonald, 1992). Fifth, the role of parents as socializers of children's physical health is being recognized (Tinsley, 1992; Tinsley & Lees, 1995).

Affect is increasingly viewed as a central socialization process (Gottman, Katz, & Hooven, 1996; Parke, 1994). The study of affect has assumed a variety of forms, including the development of emotion regulation (Bridges & Grolnick, 1995; Eisenberg & Fabes, 1994), the development of

emotional production and understanding, and the role of emotion in the enactment of the parenting role (Dix, 1991). Cognition is viewed as central to socialization as well. Again, the role of cognition comes in many guises, including the child's own cognitive capacities as a determinant of socialization strategies, as well as parents' cognitions, beliefs, and values concerning their parental role as constraints on their socialization practices. Equally crucial for appreciating how parent-child relationships are regulated and change is the recognition of the importance of the ways parents perceive, organize, and understand their children's behaviors and beliefs (Goodnow & Collins, 1990; Parke, 1978a). Underlying much of current socialization research is the recognition that these processes are interdependent, mutually influencing each other. Cognition and affect, for example, generally operate together in determining parenting practices (e.g., Dix, 1991).

Just as processes are viewed as interdependent, there is an increasing appreciation of the need for perspectives from a variety of disciplines to understand the family socialization process. No longer restricted to developmental psychology, the field of family socialization is increasingly multidisciplinary. History, anthropology, sociology, demography, pediatrics, psychiatry, and economics are all fields that are playing an increasing role in the study of socialization (Parke, Ornstein, et al., 1994).

FAMILY SYSTEMS APPROACH TO SOCIALIZATION

Consistent with a family systems viewpoint, recent research has focused on a variety of subsystems, including parent-child, marital, and sibling systems. In the next several sections of this chapter we will focus on each of these subsystems as contexts for socialization. Finally, we will examine recent attempts to conceptualize the family as a unit of analysis.

The Parent-Child Subsystem: A Tripartite Approach

In this section we consider the parent-child subsystem and the relation between this subsystem and children's social adaptation. While it has been common in traditional paradigms to focus on the impact of parent-child interaction, the parent-child relationship, or parental child-rearing styles, according to Parke, Ornstein, et al.'s (1994) tripartite model (see Figure 8.1), this represents only one pathway. In the

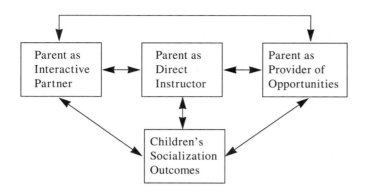

Figure 8.1 A tripartite model of parental socialization. Adapted from Parke et al., 1994.

tripartite model, the impact of parent-child interaction is not explicitly to modify or enhance children's relationships with extrafamilial social partners. In addition, this scheme posits that parents may influence their children through a second pathway, namely, in their role as direct instructor, educator, or consultant. In this role, parents may explicitly set out to educate their children concerning appropriate norms, rules, and mores of the culture. This second socialization pathway may take a variety of forms. Parents may serve as coaches, teachers, and supervisors as they provide advice, support, and directions about strategies for managing new social situations or negotiating social challenges or dilemmas. In a third role, parents function as managers of their children's social lives and serve as regulators of opportunities for social contacts and cognitive experiences. Researchers and theorists have begun to recognize the "managerial" function of parents and to appreciate the impact of variations in how this managerial function influences child development (Hartup, 1979; Parke, 1978b; Parke, Ornstein, et al., 1994). By managerial, we refer to the ways parents organize and arrange the child's home environment and set limits on the range of the home setting to which the child has access and the opportunities for social contact with playmates and socializing agents outside the family.

Parent-Child Relationships: Interaction and Child-Rearing Styles

In this section, we consider first descriptive studies of differences in the quantity of mother versus father involvement with their children as well as qualitative differences in styles of interaction. Then we will explore the implications of parent-child interactive style and level of involvement for children's socialization outcomes.

Not all forms of parental involvement are conceptually equivalent. Lamb, Pleck, and Levine (1985) have distinguished various types of parental involvement: interaction, availability, and responsibility. "Interaction refers to the parent's direct contact with his child through caregiving and shared activities. Availability is a related concept concerning the child's potential availability for interaction, by virtue of being present or accessible to the child whether or not direct interaction is occurring. Responsibility refers to the role the parent takes in ascertaining that the child is taken care of and arranging for resources to be available for the child" (p. 125).

Several further distinctions have been offered (Radin, 1993). Specifically, it is important to distinguish involvement in child care activities and involvement in play, leisure, or affiliative activities with the child. There are different determinants of these two types of parental involvement (Levy-Shiff & Israelashvili, 1988). Radin (1993) also suggests that absolute and relative involvement need to be distinguished because prior work (e.g., Pleck, 1983) suggests that these two indices are independent and may affect both children's and adults' views of role distributions in different ways.

Quantitative Assessments of Mother and Father Involvement in Intact Families. Two approaches to the issue of parental involvement merit distinction. The extent to which mothers and fathers in intact families participate in child care needs to be distinguished from the level of involvement of parents (usually father) who are not coresident with their children for a variety of reasons, including divorce or out-of-wedlock births. In this section, we will focus on the former aspect of the issue and in later sections, on adolescent parenthood, father visitation of nonresidential parenthood.

In spite of current shifts in cultural attitudes concerning the appropriateness and desirability of shared roles and equal levels of participation in routine caregiving and interaction for mothers and fathers, the shifts are more apparent than real in the majority of intact families. Fathers spend less time with their infants and children than mothers (Lamb et al., 1985), not only in the United States, but in other countries such as Great Britain, Australia, France, and Belgium (Lamb, 1987). Mothers and fathers differ in the amount of time they spend in actual interaction with their children. In a longitudinal study of middle- and working-class families in which mothers, fathers, and their infants were observed at infant's ages of 1, 3, and 9 months, mothers were found to respond to, stimulate, express positive affection toward, and provide more basic care for their infants at all time points. Fathers exceeded mothers in the extent to which they engaged in personal activities such as reading and television viewing (Belsky & Volling, 1987).

Recent studies of African American and Hispanic American families confirm the pattern found in Euro-American households. Middle-class as well as lower-class African American fathers were less involved in caregiving than mothers (Hossain & Roopnarine, 1994). Lower-income Hispanic American fathers of infants showed a similar pattern (Hossain, Field, Malphus, Valle, & Pickens, 1995). Comparisons across ethnic groups (African, Hispanic, and Euro-American) revealed few differences in level of father involvement (Hossain et al., 1995). These findings are important in light of past negative characterizations of low-income African American and Hispanic American fathers as uninvolved. Clearly, exclusively stereotyping fathers of these ethnic backgrounds is inaccurate and outdated (J. McAdoo, 1993). Much of the earlier work was based on single-parent families and failed to recognize the large differences within cultural groups.

These findings are consistent with the more general proposition that pregnancy and birth of a first child, in particular, are occasions for a shift toward a more traditional division of roles (Cowan & Cowan, 1992). Of particular interest is the fact that this pattern held regardless of whether the initial role division between husbands and wives was traditional or egalitarian (Cowan & Cowan, 1992). "Despite the current rhetoric and ideology concerning equality of roles for men and women, it seems that couples tend to adopt traditionally defined roles during times of stressful transition such as around the birth of a first child" (C. Cowan, Cowan, Coie, & Coie, 1978, p. 20).

The overall pattern of contact time between mothers and fathers with their children that is evident in infancy continues into middle childhood and adolescence (W. A. Collins & Russell, 1991). In a study of middle childhood (6- to 7-year-olds), Russell and Russell (1987) found that Australian mothers were available to children 54.7 hours/week compared to 34.6 hours/week for fathers. Mothers also spent more time alone with children (22.6 hours/week) than did fathers (2.4 hours/week). However, when both parents and child were together, mothers and fathers initiated interactions with children with equal frequency and children's initiations toward each parent were similar. Adolescents and parents show a similar pattern: 14- to 18-year-olds spent twice as much time with their mothers alone each day

(Montemeyer & Brownlee, 1987). From infancy through adolescence, mothers and fathers clearly differ in terms of their degree of involvement with their children.

Qualitative Effects: Stylistic Differences in Mother and Father Interaction. Fathers participate less than mothers in caregiving but spend a greater percentage of the time available for interaction in play activities. In Euro-American families, Kotelchuck (1976) found that fathers spent a greater percentage of their time with their infants in play than do mothers, although in absolute terms mothers spent more time than fathers in play with their children. In recent studies of African American (Hossain & Roopnarine, 1994) and Hispanic American (Hossain et al., 1995) families, fathers spent a greater percentage of their time with children in play than mothers; the quality of play across mothers and fathers differed too. With young infants, older infants, and toddlers, fathers play more physically arousing games than do mothers. In contrast, mothers play more conventional motor games or toy-mediated activities, and are more verbal and didactic (Parke, 1996).

Nor are these effects evident only in infancy. MacDonald and Parke (1984) found that fathers engaged in more physical play with their 3- and 4-year-old children than mothers, although mothers engaged in more object-mediated play than fathers. According to a survey (MacDonald & Parke, 1986), fathers' distinctive role as a physical play partner changes with age. Physical play is highest between fathers and 2-year-olds; when children are between 2 and 10 years of age there is a decreased likelihood that fathers will engage them physically.

In spite of the decline in physical play across age, fathers remain more physical in their play than mothers. In an Australian study of parents and their 6- to 7-year-old children (Russell & Russell, 1987), fathers were more involved in physical/outdoor play interactions and fixing things around the house and garden than mothers. In contrast, mothers were more actively involved in caregiving and household tasks, in schoolwork, reading, playing with toys, and helping with arts and crafts. In adolescence, the quality of maternal and paternal involvement continues to differ. Just as in earlier developmental periods, mothers and fathers may complement each other and provide models that reflect the tasks of adolescence: connectedness and separateness. Recent evidence suggests that fathers may help adolescents develop their own sense of identity and autonomy by being more "peerlike" and more playful (joking and teasing), which is likely to promote more equal and egalitarian exchanges (Larson & Richards, 1994; Shulman & Klein, 1993). "Fathers, more than mothers, conveyed the feeling that they can rely on their adolescents, thus fathers might serve as a 'facilitating environment' for adolescent attainment of differentiation from the family and consolidation of independence" (Shulman & Klein, 1993, p. 53). Nor is this developmental shift in the father role restricted to one culture. Mexican fathers are affectionate and playful with younger children, but shift to a more reserved and distant play style during adolescence (Madsen, 1973). Although the style of fathers' involvement as a play or recreational partner appears to have reasonable continuity from infancy through adolescence, the meaning and function of this interaction style shifts across development. The positive affect associated with fathers' play in infancy is not as evident in adolescence, although other goals of this age period may be facilitated by this more playful egalitarian style.

A word of caution is in order, because fathers in several other cultures do not show this physical play style. In some cultures that are very similar to U.S. culture, such as in England and Australia, there are similar parental sex differences in play style (Russell & Russell, 1987). In contrast, research in several other cultures do not find that physical play is a central part of the father-infant relationship (Lamb, 1987; Roopnarine & Carter, 1992). Neither in Sweden nor among Israeli kibbutz families were fathers more likely to play with their children or to engage in different types of play (Hwang, 1987). Similarly, Chinese, Malaysian, and Indian mothers and fathers reported that they rarely engaged in physical play with their children (Roopnarine, Lu, & Ahmeduzzaman, 1989). Observations of Aka pygmies of Central Africa suggest that mothers and fathers rarely, if ever, engage in a vigorous or physical type of play (Hewlett, 1991). Instead, both display affection and engage in plenty of close physical contact. In other cultures, such as in Italy, other women in the extended family or in the community are more likely than mothers or fathers to play physically with infants (New & Benigni, 1987).

Why do mothers and fathers play differently? Both biological and environmental factors probably play a role. Experience with infants, the amount of time spent with infants, the usual kinds of responsibilities that a parent assumes—all of these factors influence the parents' style of play. The fact that fathers spend less time with infants and children than mothers may contribute as well. Fathers may use their distinctive arousing style as a way to increase their salience in spite of more limited time. Biological factors cannot be ignored in light of the fact that male monkeys

show the same rough-and-tumble physical style of play as U.S. human fathers (Parke & Suomi, 1981). Male monkeys, moreover, tend to respond more positively to bids for rough-and-tumble play than females (Meany, Stewart, & Beatty, 1985). "Perhaps [both monkey and human] males may be more susceptible to being aroused into states of positive excitement and unpredictability than females" (Maccoby, 1988, p. 761), speculation that is consistent with gender differences in risk taking and sensation seeking (Zuckerman, 1991). In addition, human males, whether boys or men, tend to behave more boisterously and show more positive emotional expression and reactions than females (Charlesworth & Dzur, 1987). Together, these pieces of the puzzle suggest that predisposing biological differences between males and females may play a role in the play patterns of mothers and fathers. At the same time, the cross-cultural data underscore the ways cultural and environmental contexts shape play patterns of mothers and fathers and remind us of the high degree of plasticity of human social behaviors.

Parent-Child Interaction and Children's Adaptation. Two approaches to this issue of the impact of parent-child interaction on children's socialization outcomes have been utilized in recent research. Some have adopted a typological approach and examined styles or types of child-rearing practices (e.g., Baumrind, 1973). Others have adopted a social interaction approach by focusing on the nature of the interchanges between parent and child (G. Patterson, 1981; see Maccoby & Martin, 1983, for a more detailed review).

The Typological Approach. Perhaps the most influential typology has been offered by Baumrind (1973), who distinguished three types of parental child rearing. She found that *authoritative* but not *authoritarian* or overly *permissive* behavior by parents led to positive emotional, social, and cognitive development in children. *Authoritative parents* were not intrusive and did permit their children considerable freedom within reasonable limits, but were firm and willing to impose restrictions in areas in which they had greater knowledge or insight. They did not yield to their children's attempts to coerce them into acquiescing to their demands. Such discipline gave children the opportunity to explore their environment and gain interpersonal competence without the anxiety and neurotic inhibition associated with hostile, restrictive, power-assertive discipline practices, or the inexperience in conforming to the demands and needs of others associated with extreme permissiveness. In general, these parents demonstrated high warmth and moderate restrictiveness, expecting appropriately mature behavior from their children and setting reasonable limits but being responsive and attentive to their children's needs; their child-rearing behavior was associated with the development of self-esteem, adaptability, competence, internalized control, popularity with peers, and low levels of antisocial behavior.

In contrast, the *authoritarian parents* of the conflicted-irritable children were rigid, power assertive, harsh, and unresponsive to the children's needs. In such families, children have little control over their environment and receive few gratifications. They may feel trapped and angry but fearful of asserting themselves in a hostile environment. This results in the unhappy, conflicted, neurotic behavior often found in these children.

Finally, in spite of the *permissive parents'* reasonably affectionate relationship with their children, their excessively lax and inconsistent discipline and encouragement of the free expression of their children's impulses were associated with the development of uncontrolled, impulsive behavior in their children. Both authoritarian and permissive parents viewed their children as being dominated by primitive, self-centered impulses over which they have little control. However, the permissive parents thought that free expression of these impulses was healthy and desirable, whereas the authoritarian parents perceived them as something to be suppressed.

In a longitudinal study, Baumrind (1991) has followed her authoritarian, authoritative, and permissive parents and their children from the preschool period through adolescence. She found that authoritative parenting continued to be associated with positive outcomes for adolescents as with younger children, and that responsive, firm parent-child relationships were especially important in the development of competence in sons. Moreover, authoritarian child rearing had more negative long-term outcomes for boys than for girls. Sons of authoritarian parents were low in both cognitive and social competence: their academic and intellectual performance was poor, and they were unfriendly and lacking in initiative, leadership, and self-confidence in their relations with their peers.

Maccoby and Martin (1983) extended the Baumrind typology based on combinations of the warm/responsive, unresponsive/rejecting dimension and the restrictive/demanding, permissive/undemanding dimension and added a fourth type of parenting style characterized by neglect

	Accepting, Responsive, Child-Centered	Rejecting, Unresponsive, Parent-Centered
Demanding, controlling, restrictive	Authoritative-reciprocal, high in bidirectional communication	Authoritarian, power-assertive
Undemanding, low in control attempts, permissive	Indulgent	Neglecting, ignoring, indifferent, uninvolved

Figure 8.2 A two-dimensional classification of parenting patterns. Adapted from Maccoby & Martin (1983).

and lack of involvement (see Figure 8.2). These are disengaged parents who are "motivated to do whatever is necessary to minimize the costs in time and effort of interaction with the child" (Maccoby & Martin, 1983, p. 49). Such parents are motivated to keep the child at a distance and focus on their own needs rather than the needs of the child. They are parent-centered rather than child-centered. With older children, this is associated with the parents' failure to monitor the child's activity, to know where the child is, what the child is doing, and who the child's companions are. This pattern of parenting has been related to several different types of personality characteristics in parents and to social change and stressful life events. For example, parental detachment is often found in depressed mothers (Egeland & Sroufe, 1981), who have difficulty mobilizing themselves to be responsive to their children's needs and are more likely to be influenced by their own emotional state than to respond contingently to their children's behavior (Kochanska, 1991). Moreover, in times of stress such as during marital discord or divorce, because of their own anxiety and emotional neediness, some parents may relentlessly pursue self-gratification at the expense and neglect of their children's welfare (Patterson & Capaldi, 1991).

In infants such a lack of parental involvement is associated with disruptions in attachment (Thompson, Ch. 2, this Volume); in older children it is associated with impulsivity, aggression, noncompliance, moodiness, and low self-esteem (Baumrind, 1991). Adolescents and young adults from neglecting homes are more likely to have drinking problems, be truant, spend time on the streets with friends who are disliked by the parents, be precociously sexually active, and have a record of arrests (Baumrind, 1991; Pulkkinen,

1982). Lack of parental monitoring is strongly associated with the risk of delinquent behavior (Baumrind, 1991; Patterson, Reid, & Dishion, 1992). It is not just that children with disengaged parents are socially incompetent, irresponsible, immature, and alienated from their families; they also show disruptions in peer relations and in cognitive development, achievement, and school performance (Baumrind, 1991; Hetherington & Clingempeel, 1992). It is the combined impact of not having the skills to be able to gain gratification in either social or academic pursuits that frequently leads to delinquency in children with neglecting parents (Patterson et al., 1992). Clearly, parental involvement plays an important role in the development of both social and cognitive competence in children.

The Status of the Typological Approach.   This approach has been challenged on three fronts. First, questions remain concerning the processes that contribute to the relative effectiveness of these different styles. The task of identifying the components that account for the effectiveness of various styles is far from complete.

One of the major concerns about the focus on parental *style* is the limited attention to the delineation of the processes that account for the effects of different styles on children's development. Throughout the history of socialization research there has been a tension between molar and molecular levels of analysis. Over the past three decades the pendulum has swung back and forth between these levels of analysis. Currently these two strands of research coexist and are seldom united in a single study. On the molecular side, the work of G. Patterson (1981), Gottman (1994), and Tronick (1989) can be cited; on the molar side, the search for typological answers to parenting style continues (Baumrind, 1989, 1991; Steinberg, Dornbusch, & Brown, 1992). Some exceptions can be noted: Hetherington and Clingempeel (1992), for example, have used parenting style in combination with sequential analyses of children's levels of compliance to parental control. This type of analysis represents a useful bridging of the two levels.

In an attempt to resolve this issue, Darling and Steinberg (1993) have argued that parental style and parental practices need to be distinguished. Parenting style is "a constellation of attitudes toward the child that are communicated to the child and create an emotional climate in which parents' behaviors are expressed" (p. 493). In contrast to style, "parenting practices are behaviors defined by specific content and socialization goals" (p. 492). These authors cite attending school functions and spanking as examples of

parenting practices. Style is assumed to be independent of both the content of parenting behavior and the specific socialization content. Figure 8.3 displays their contextual model of parenting style. Critical to their model is the assumption that parenting style has its impact on child outcomes indirectly. First, style transforms the nature of parent-child interaction and thereby moderates the impact of specific practices. Second, they posit that style modifies the child's openness to parental influence, which in turn moderates the association between parenting practices and child outcomes.

Other schemes represent a similar distinction. Dix (1991), for example, has argued that emotion is a central contextual variable in understanding parenting behavior. Moreover, the Dix argument focuses specifically on the affective processes that are involved in parenting and provides a research agenda that links cognition and affect as central determinants of parenting behavior

A second concern focuses on the issue of direction of effects. It is unclear whether the styles described by Baumrind are, in part, in response to the child's behavior (Lewis, 1981). Placing the typology work in a transactional framework (Sameroff, 1994; Sameroff & Chandler, 1974) would, in fact, argue that children with certain temperaments and/or behavioral characteristics determine the nature of the parental style. (See Bates, 1987; Kochanska, 1993; Rothbart & Ahadi, 1994, for reviews.)

A third concern is the universality of the typological scheme. Recent studies have raised serious questions about the generalizability of these styles across either SES or ethnic/cultural groups. Two questions are involved here: first, does the rate of utilization of different styles vary across

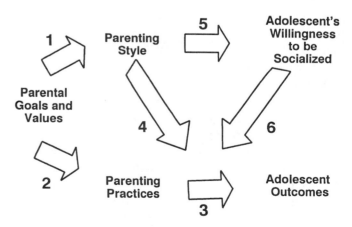

Figure 8.3 Contextual model of parenting style. From Darling & Steinberg (1993).

groups, and second, are the advantages in terms of positive social outcomes associated with a particular style (e.g., authoritative) similar across groups? The answer to both of these questions seems to be negative. In lower-SES families, parents are more likely to use an authoritarian as opposed to an authoritative style, but this style is often an adaptation to the ecological conditions such as increased danger and threat that may characterize the lives of poor families (Furstenberg, 1993; Kelley, Power, & Wimbush, 1992). Moreover, as noted below, studies find that the use of authoritarian strategies under these circumstances may be linked with more positive outcomes for children (Baldwin, Baldwin, & Cole, 1990). A second challenge to the presumed universal advantage of authoritative child-rearing styles comes from cross-ethnic studies. In Chinese families, authoritarian styles of child rearing are also more common, and some have argued that the application of those stylistic categories to Chinese parents may be "ethnocentric and misleading" (R. Chao, 1994, p. 1111), because these child-rearing types represent a U.S. perspective that emphasizes an individualistic view of childhood socialization and development. As argued in more detail in our discussion of ethnic variations in child-rearing practices, accumulating evidence underscores the nonuniversality of these stylistic distinctions and suggests the importance of developing concepts that are based on an indigenous appreciation of the culture in question. In summary, it is evident that contextual and cultural considerations need to be given more attention in typological approaches to child rearing.

The Parent-Child Interactional Approach. Research in this tradition is based on the assumption that face-to-face interaction with parents may provide the opportunity to learn, rehearse, and refine social skills that are common to successful social interaction with other social partners. The research has yielded several conclusions. First, the style of the interaction between parent and child is linked to a variety of social outcomes including aggression, achievement, and moral development (see Coie & Dodge, Ch. 13, this Volume; Eccles, Ch. 15, this Volume; Turiel, Ch. 12, this Volume). To illustrate this approach, studies of children's social competence will be considered. Recent studies have found that parents who are responsive, warm, and engaging are more likely to have children who are more socially competent (Putallaz, 1987). Moreover, recent evidence suggests that high levels of positive synchrony and low levels of nonsynchrony in patterns of mother-child interaction are related to school adjustment as

rated by teachers, peers, and observers (Harrist, Pettit, Dodge, & Bates, 1994). In contrast, parents who are hostile and controlling have children who experience more difficulty with age-mates (J. Barth & Parke, 1993; MacDonald & Parke, 1984; Pettit, Dodge, & Brown, 1988). Moreover, these findings are evident in the preschool period (Harrist et al., 1994; MacDonald, 1987; Pettit et al., 1988) as well as middle childhood (Dishion, 1990; Henggeler, Edwards, Cohen, & Summerville, 1992).

Recent evidence suggests that family interaction patterns not only relate to concurrent peer relationships, but predict peer relationships at later times. In their study of third-grade children, Henggeler et al. (1992) found that children of fathers who were responsive to their children's requests became more popular over the school year than children of less responsive fathers. Similarly, J. Barth and Parke (1993) found that parents who were better able to sustain their children in play predicted better subsequent adaptation to kindergarten.

Although there is overlap between mothers and fathers, evidence is emerging that fathers make a unique and independent contribution to their children's social development. Recent studies (Isley, O'Neil, & Parke, 1996) have shown that fathers continue to contribute to children's social behavior with peers—after accounting for mothers' contributions. Although father involvement is quantitatively less than mother involvement, fathers have an important impact on their offspring's development. Quality rather than quantity of parent-child interaction is the important predictor of cognitive and social development.

Not only are differences in interactive style associated with children's social competence, but the nature of the emotional displays during parent-child interaction are important as well. The affective quality of the interactions of popular children and their parents differs from the interactions of rejected children and their parents. Consistently higher levels of positive affect have been found in both parents and children in popular dyads than in rejected dyads (Parke, Burks, Carson, & Cassidy, 1992). While negative parental affect is associated with lower levels of peer acceptance (Isley et al., 1996), Carson and Parke (1996) found that children of fathers who are likely to respond to their children's negative affect displays with negative affect of their own are less socially skilled (less altruistic, more avoidant, and more aggressive) than their preschool classmates. The results for the reciprocity of negative affect were evident only for fathers, which suggests that men may play a particularly salient role in children's learning how to manage negative emotions in the context of social interactions. Boyum and Parke (1995) confirmed the importance of parental negative affect for children's social development, but demonstrated that father anger is a particularly salient predictor of children's social acceptance by peers. Less-accepted children were likely to receive angry affect from their fathers during home observations of family dinner. This finding underscores the importance of distinguishing among specific affective displays rather than relying on categories of negative or positive emotions.

Together, these recent findings lead to a revision in traditional thinking about the ways that mothers and fathers influence their children's development. According to the sociologist Talcott Parsons (1951; Parsons & Bales, 1955), mothers were viewed as the emotional brokers in the family and fathers' role was an instrumental one. Instead, this recent work suggests that fathers may play a much larger role in socialization of children's emotion than earlier theories suggested. And it is through the management of their own emotions and their reactions to their children's emotions that fathers may have their greatest impact on their children's social relationships with peers and friends.

In summary, both the nature of parent-child interaction and the affective quality of the relationship are important correlates of children's social development.

Beyond Description: Processes Mediating the Relations between Parent-Child Interaction and Children's Social Competence. A variety of processes have been hypothesized as mediators between parent-child interaction and peer outcomes. These include emotion encoding and decoding skills, emotional regulatory skills, cognitive representations, attributions and beliefs, and problem-solving skills (Ladd, 1992; Parke, Burks, Carson, Neville, & Boyum, 1994). It is assumed that these abilities and beliefs are acquired in the course of parent-child interchanges over the course of development and, in turn, guide the nature of children's behavior with their peers; these styles of interacting with peers may, in turn, determine children's level of acceptance by their peers. We focus on two sets of processes that seem particularly promising candidates for mediator status: affect management skills and cognitive representational processes. Figure 8.4 summarizes these two sets of mediating factors.

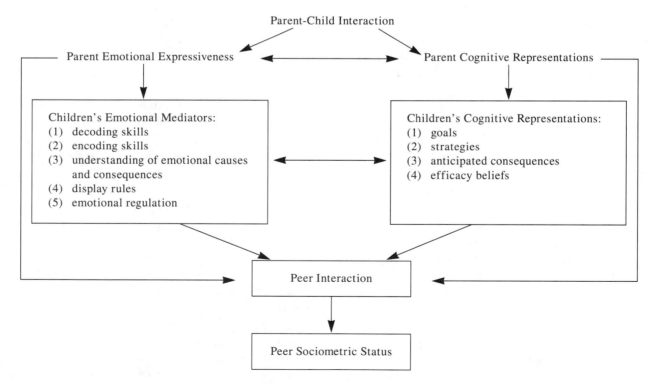

Figure 8.4   Emotional and cognitive mediating links between family and peer systems.

Affect Management Skills.   Children learn more than specific affective expressions, such as anger or sadness or joy, in the family. They learn a cluster of processes associated with the understanding and regulation of affective displays, which we term affect management skills (Parke et al., 1992). It is assumed that these skills are acquired during the course of parent-child interaction and, in turn, are available to the child for use in other relationships. Moreover, it is assumed that these skills play a mediating role between family and children's social competence.

One set of skills that is of relevance to successful peer interaction and may, in part, be acquired in the context of parent-child play, especially arousing physical play, is the ability to clearly encode emotional signals and to decode others' emotional states. Through physically playful interaction with their parents, especially fathers, children may be learning how to use emotional signals to regulate the social behavior of others. In addition, they may learn to accurately decode the social and emotional signals of other social partners. Several studies have found positive relationships between children's ability to encode emotional expressions and children's popularity with peers (see Hubbard & Coie, 1994, for a review). Successful peer interaction requires not only the ability to recognize and produce emotions, but also a social understanding of emotion-related experiences, of the meaning of emotions, of the cause of emotions, and of the responses appropriate to others' emotions. Cassidy, Parke, Butkovsky, and Braungart (1992), in a study of 5- and 6-year-old children, found that a higher level of peer acceptance was associated with greater (a) ability to identify emotions, (b) acknowledgment of experiencing emotion, (c) ability to describe appropriate causes of emotions, and (d) expectations that they and their parents would respond appropriately to the display of emotions. Similarly, Denham, McKinley, Couchoud, and Holt (1990) found that children's understanding of the type of emotion that would be elicited by different situations was positively related to peer likability. Family emotional expressiveness—an index of the extent to which family members express emotion in the course of everyday interaction—has emerged as a further link between family and peer systems, providing guidelines for the use of emotion in ongoing social interchanges. The expressiveness concept extends emotional learning beyond the acquisition of specific skills, such as encoding or decoding, to the utilization of rules about emotion in multiple contexts (Halberstadt, 1991). Several studies have found cross-generational similarities between mother's (Denham,

1993), father's (Boyum & Parke, 1995), and children's level of expressiveness. Consistent with the assumption that expressiveness is learned in the family and that children transfer their expressive style to their interactions with others outside the family, several studies (Boyum & Parke, 1995; Cassidy et al., 1992) found links between family expressiveness and peer competence. For example, Boyum and Parke (1995) found that parents who were positively emotionally expressive had children who were higher in social competence. These studies suggest that family emotional expressiveness may be one pathway by which children learn to understand and express their emotions in a socially appropriate manner.

Emotional Regulation.   Research is emerging that suggests that parental support and acceptance of children's emotions is related to children's ability to manage emotions in a constructive fashion. Several theorists recently have suggested that these emotional competence skills are, in turn, linked to social competence with peers (Denham, 1993; Eisenberg & Fabes, 1992; Parke, 1994). Parental comforting of children when they experience negative emotion has been linked with constructive anger reactions (Eisenberg & Fabes, 1994). Similarly, several studies have suggested that parental willingness to discuss emotions with their children is related to children's awareness and understanding of others' emotions (Denham, Cook, & Zoller, 1992; Dunn & Brown, 1994). Similarly, Eisenberg, Fabes, Schaller, Carlo, and Miller (1991) found that parental emphasis on direct problem solving was associated with sons' sympathy, whereas restrictiveness in regard to expressing one's own negative emotions was associated with sons' physiological and facial indicators of personal distress. This pattern of findings is consistent with recent work by Gottman, Katz, and Hooven (1996) on parents' emotion philosophy or meta-emotion. By meta-emotion these researchers refer to parents' emotions about their own and their children's emotions; metacognitive structure refers to an organized set of thoughts, a philosophy and an approach to one's own emotions and to one's children's emotions. Gottman et al. (1996), in a longitudinal analysis, found that fathers' acceptance and assistance with children's sadness and anger at 5 years of age was related to their children's social competence with peers at 8 years of age. Moreover, fathers' assistance with anger predicted academic achievement. Gender of child influenced these relationships: when fathers help daughters with sadness, the daughters are rated as more competent by their teachers;

when fathers help their daughters regulate anger, girls are rated as more socially competent by their teachers, show higher academic achievement, and their dyadic interaction with a best friend is less negative. Fathers who are more accepting of their sons' anger and assist their boys in regulating anger have sons who are less aggressive. Similarly, Roberts (1994) found that father's comforting and acceptance of their children's emotional distress is linked with more positive peer relationships.

Together, these studies suggest that various aspects of emotional development—encoding, decoding, cognitive understanding, and emotional regulation—play an important role in accounting for variations in peer competence. Our argument is that these aspects of emotion may be learned in the context of family interaction and serve as mediators between the parents and peers. At the same time, the contribution of genetics to individual differences in emotionality and emotional regulation probably also plays a role in the emergence of these emotional processes (Eisenberg & Fabes, 1994; Kochanska, 1993). Finally, the direction of effects remains unclear in these relations; probably both parent and child mutually influence each other in the development of affect management skills.

Cognitive Representational Models: Another Possible Mediator between Parents and Peers. One of the major problems facing the area of family-peer relationships is how children transfer the strategies that they acquire in the family context to their peer relationships. A variety of theories assumes that individuals process internal mental representations that guide their social behavior. Attachment theorists offer working model notions (Bowlby, 1969; Bretherton & Waters, 1985), whereas social and cognitive psychologists have provided an account involving scripts or cognitive maps that could serve as a guide for social action (Baldwin, 1992; Bugental, 1991).

Researchers within the attachment tradition have examined attachment-related representations and found support for Bowlby's argument that representations vary as a function of child-parent attachment history (see Thompson, Ch. 2, this Volume). For example, children who had been securely attached infants were more likely in their drawings to represent their family in a coherent manner, with a balance between individuality and connection, than were children who had been insecurely attached.

Research in a social interactional tradition reveals links between parent and child cognitive representations of social relationships. Burks and Parke (1996) found some evidence for similarities between children and mothers in their goals, attributions, and anticipated consequences when they responded to a series of hypothetical social dilemmas. These studies suggest that children may learn cognitive representational schemas through their family relationships, although the precise mechanisms through which these schemas are acquired is not yet specified.

Next, we turn to an examination of the evidence in support of the general hypothesis that parents of children of different sociometric status differ in terms of their cognitive models of social relationships. Several aspects of cognitive models including attributions, perceptions, values, goals, and strategies have been explored (see Grusec, Hastings, & Mammone, 1994; Mills & Rubin, 1993, for recent reviews). Pettit, Dodge, and Brown (1988) found that mothers' attributional biases concerning their children's behavior (e.g., the extent to which they view an ambiguous provocation as hostile or benign) and the endorsement of aggression as a solution to interpersonal problems were related to children's interpersonal problem-solving skill that, in turn, was related to their social competence. Other evidence suggests that parents hold different patterns of beliefs about problematic social behaviors such as aggression and withdrawal and that these patterns are associated with their children's membership in various sociometric status groups (Rubin & Mills, 1990). This work is important because it suggests that parents do, in fact, have sets of beliefs concerning children's social behavior that may, in part, govern their behavior (Goodnow & Collins, 1990; Parke, 1978b).

MacKinnon-Lewis and her colleagues (1994) found that mothers' and sons' hostile attributions were significantly related to the coerciveness of their interactions. Moreover, mothers' attributions were related to reports of their children's aggression in the classroom. Similarly, Rubin, Mills, and Rose-Krasnor (1989) found a link between mothers' beliefs and their preschoolers' social problem-solving behavior in the classroom. Mothers who placed higher values on such skills as making friends, sharing with others, and leading or influencing other children had children who were more assertive, prosocial, and competent social problem solvers. Additionally, the degree to which mothers viewed social behavior as controllable rather than as externally caused was associated with higher levels of social competence among their children. In related work, Spitzer, Estock, Cupp, Isley-Paradise, and Parke (1992) assessed perceptions of *parental influence* (e.g., how much influence parents feel they have regarding their children's social behavior) as well as perceptions of *parental efficacy* (e.g., how easy or hard they found it to help their children's social behavior). Parents, especially mothers, who were high in both perceptions of influence and efficacy had children who were higher in their levels of social acceptance as rated by peers and teachers.

Spitzer and Parke (1994) explored the links between parent and child cognitive representations of social relationships. In this study, parents and their children responded to a series of vignettes reflecting interpersonal dilemmas by indicating how they might react in each situation. They found that the cognitive representations of social behavior of *both* fathers and mothers were related to their children's representations. Moreover, mothers who were low in their use of relational and prosocial strategies had children with high levels of peer-nominated aggression, while mothers who provided specific and socially skilled advice had more popular children. Fathers' strategies that were rated high on confrontation and instrumental qualities were associated with low teacher ratings of children's prosocial behavior and high teacher ratings of physical and verbal aggression, avoidance, and being disliked. Fathers with relational goals had children who were less often nominated as aggressive by their peers and rated by teachers as more liked and less disliked.

Together, this set of studies suggests that cognitive models of relationships may be transmitted across generations, and these models, in turn, may serve as mediators between family contexts and children's relationships with others outside of the family (see Bugental & Goodnow, Ch. 7, this Volume; Parke & O'Neil, 1996, for reviews). Finally, this work underscores the fact that *both* children and parents actively construct their own dyadic relationships, but also other social relationships as well. Moreover, both are influenced in their behavior with each other by these cognitive constructions. One issue that needs more attention is how child and adult constructions change across development (Steinberg, 1996) and how the pattern of mutual influence between parent and child changes as the child develops. As Maccoby (1984, 1992) has argued, coordination and coregulation rather than simply a bidirectional pattern of influence probably increasingly characterize the parent-child relationship in middle childhood and adolescence.

Parental Instruction, Advice Giving, and Consultation

Learning about relationships through interaction with parents can be viewed as an indirect pathway because the goal is often not explicitly to influence children's social relationships with extrafamilial partners such as peers. In contrast, parents may influence children's relationships directly in their role as instructor, educator, or advisor. In this role, parents may explicitly set out to educate their children concerning appropriate ways of initiating and maintaining social relationships and learning social and moral rules.

Several recent studies have examined these issues. In a study of parental supervision, Bhavnagri and Parke (1991) found that children exhibited more cooperation and turn taking and had longer play bouts when assisted by an adult than when playing without assistance. Adult assistance enhanced the quality of play for younger (2–3.5 years) more than older (3.5–6 years) children, which suggests that parental facilitation may be more important for younger children, who are beginning to acquire social skills, than for older children. While both fathers and mothers were effective facilitators of their children's play with peers, under natural conditions, mothers are more likely to play this supervisory/facility role than fathers (Bhavnagri & Parke, 1991; Ladd & Golter, 1988).

The quality of advice that mothers provided their children prior to entry into an ongoing play dyad varied as a function of children's sociometric status (Finnie & Russell, 1988; A. Russell & Finnie, 1990). Mothers of well-accepted children were more specific and helpful in the quality of advice they provided. In contrast, mothers of poorly accepted children provided relatively ineffective kinds of verbal guidance, such as "Have fun," "Stay out of trouble." The advice in their subsequent instructions was too general to be of value to the children.

As children develop, the forms of management shift from direct involvement or supervision of the ongoing activities of children and their peers to a less public form of management, involving advice or consultation concerning appropriate ways of handling peer problems. This form of direct parental management has been termed *consultation* (Ladd, LeSieur, & Profilet, 1993) or *decontextualized discussion* (Lollis, Ross, & Tate, 1992). Interestingly, this role has received surprisingly little attention, in view of the extensive literature on coaching as a strategy to aid children with social skill deficits (Ladd, 1981).

Cohen (1989), in a study of third graders and their mothers, found that some forms of consulting were associated with positive outcomes, whereas other forms were linked with poor social relationships. When mothers were supportive but noninterfering the outcomes were positive. On the other hand, mothers who were too highly involved (e.g., interfering) had children who were socially withdrawn.

Do parents provide this kind of guidance under everyday conditions? This issue of naturally occurring advice was recently addressed in a study of preschoolers (Laird, Pettit, Mize, Brown, & Lindsey, 1994). These investigators found that about half of the mothers of the preschoolers in the study reported that they frequently engage in conversations with their children about peer relationships. Rates of conversation about peers were related to both peer and teacher ratings of social competence. Advice giving was a unique predictor of peer-rated competence even after controlling for the amount of conversation. Finally, the extent to which the child initiated the conversation was a further positive predictor of peer-rated competence. Although it is based on self-reports, this work extends prior work by demonstrating the impact of maternal advice giving in ecologically valid contexts.

These studies suggest that direct parental influence in the form of supervision and advice giving can significantly increase the interactive competence of young children and illustrates the utility of examining direct parental strategies as a way of teaching children about social relationships. In all of these studies, the direction of effects is difficult to determine and parents may be responding to their children's level of social skill. Experimental and longitudinal studies would help place these studies on a clearer interpretative footing.

Parents as Managers of Children's Opportunities

Parents influence their children's social relationships through their direct interactions with their children. But parents also function as managers of their children's social lives (Hartup, 1979; Parke, 1978b) and serve as regulators of opportunities for social contact with extrafamilial social partners. This parental role is of theoretical importance in light of the recent claims that parents' impact on children's development is limited and peer-group-level processes account for major socialization outcomes (Harris, 1995). In contrast to this view, we conceptualize the parental management of access to peers as a further pathway through which parents influence their children's development.

Mothers and fathers differ in their degree of responsibility for management of family tasks. From infancy through middle childhood, mothers are more likely to assume the managerial role than fathers. In infancy, this means setting boundaries for play (Power & Parke, 1982), taking the child to the doctor, and arranging for day care. Mothers are higher in all of these domains than fathers. In middle childhood, Russell and Russell (1987) found that mothers continue to assume more managerial responsibility (e.g.,

directing the child to have a bath, to eat a meal, and to put away toys).

Parental Monitoring. One way parents can affect their children's social relationships is through monitoring of their children's social activities. This form of management is particularly evident as children move into preadolescence and adolescence and is associated with the relative shift in importance of family and peers as sources of influence on social relationships. Moreover, direct monitoring is more common among younger children, whereas distal monitoring is more evident among adolescents. Monitoring refers to a range of activities, including the supervision of children's choice of social settings, activities, and friends. These studies indicate that parents of delinquent and antisocial children engage in less monitoring and supervision of their children's activities, especially with regard to children's use of evening time, than parents of nondelinquent children (C. Patterson & Stouthamer-Loeber, 1984). Dishion (1990) has confirmed these earlier findings. Low parental supervision and monitoring (e.g., not knowing their child's whereabouts, not setting clear rules for behavior) were positively linked with peer rejection. As will be argued below, it is unlikely that parental discipline and interaction and monitoring are independent. In support of this view, Dishion found that *both* inconsistent, negative, and punitive discipline and low monitoring were related to emergence of antisocial behavior, which, in turn, was linked with rejection by peers. Consistent with this study is the work of Steinberg (1986), who found that children in grades 6 to 9, especially girls who are on their own after school, are more susceptible to peer pressure to engage in antisocial activity (e.g., vandalism, cheating, stealing) than are their adult-supervised peers. In addition, Steinberg found that monitoring may be more important for some families than for others; specifically, children of parents who were high in their use of authoritative parenting practices (Baumrind, 1978) were less susceptible to peer pressure in the absence of monitoring. On the other hand, children of parents who were low in authoritative child rearing were more susceptible to peer pressure in nonsupervised contexts. Nor are the effects of monitoring limited to a reduction in the negative aspects of peer relations. As Krappmann (1986) found, preadolescents of parents who were well informed about their children's peer relationships and activities had closer, more stable, and less problem-ridden peer relationships. Isolation of other conditions or variables that alter the impact of monitoring would be worthwhile.

Parental Participation in Children's Organized Activities. In addition to choosing a neighborhood as a way of increasing access to children, parents influence their children's social behavior by interfacing between children and institutional settings, such as child-oriented clubs and organizations (e.g, Brownies, Cub Scouts). These mediational activities are important because they permit the child access to a wider range of social activities and opportunities to practice developing social skills that may, in turn, contribute to their social development.

There are sex-of-parent and social class differences in these activities. Mothers communicate more frequently than fathers with child care staff (Joffe, 1977) and have more frequent contact with teachers in elementary schools (Lightfoot, 1978). O'Donnell and Stueve (1983), in a study of 5- to 14-year-old children, found marked social class differences both in children's utilization of community organizations and in the level of maternal participation. Working-class children were only half as likely to participate in activities as were their middle-class peers and were more likely to use facilities on an occasional rather than a regular basis. Middle-class mothers were more likely to sign their children up for specific programs, whereas working-class mothers were less likely to involve their children in planned activities. Finally, economically advantaged mothers participated more heavily than working-class mothers.

Unfortunately, we know relatively little about how these opportunities for participation relate to children's social behavior with their peers. One exception is Bryant (1985), who found that participation in formally sponsored organizations with unstructured activities was associated with greater social perspective-taking skill among 10-year-old children, but had little effect on 7-year-olds. In light of the importance of this skill for successful peer interaction (Hartup, 1983), this finding assumes particular significance. Moreover, it suggests that activities that "allow the child to experience autonomy, control and mastery of the content of the activity are related to expressions of enhanced social-emotional functioning on the part of the child" (Bryant, 1985, p. 65). In support of this argument, Ladd and Price (1987) found that children who were exposed to a higher number of unstructured peer activities (e.g., at church, school, the swimming pool, or library) were less anxious and had fewer absences at the beginning of kindergarten.

Although we have limited understanding of how these activities differ as a function of children's age, it appears that there is an increase with age in participation in sponsored organizations with structured activities (e.g., clubs, Brownies, organized sports), with participation most prevalent among preadolescent children (Bryant, 1985; O'Donnell & Stueve, 1983). Finally, more attention to the ways fathers participate in these types of activities is needed, especially in light of their shifting roles (Parke, 1996).

Parent as Social Initiator and Arranger. Parents play an important role in the facilitation of their children's development by initiating contact between their own children and potential play partners, especially among younger children (Bhavnagri & Parke, 1991). Studies by Ladd et al. (1993) suggest that parents' role as arranger may play a facilitory part in the development of their children's friendships. Children of parents who tended to arrange peer contacts had a larger range of playmates and more frequent play companions outside of school than children of parents who were less active in initiating peer contacts. When children entered kindergarten, boys but not girls with parents who initiated peer contacts were better accepted by their peers than were boys with noninitiating parents. Moreover, parents' peer management (initiating peer contacts, purchasing toys for social applications) of younger preschool children prior to enrollment in preschool was, in turn, linked to the time that children spent in peers' homes. Finally, Krappmann (1986) found that preadolescents whose parents played an active role in stimulating and arranging peer contacts on behalf of their children had more stable and closer peer relationships than children of less active parents.

Children's own initiation activity has been linked with measures of social competence. Children who initiated a larger number of peer contacts outside of school tended to be better liked by their peers in preschool settings (Ladd et al., 1993). This finding serves as a corrective to the view that initiation activity is only a parental activity and reminds us that variations in the level of activity played by children in organizing their own social contacts is an important correlate of their social competence.

Future research should detail how parental and child initiating activities shift over the course of development. It is clear that parental initiating is important, but over time initiating decreases and the factors that govern this decrease are important issues to explore. Moreover, it is critical to understand when parental initiation activity can, in fact, be beneficial and when it is detrimental to children's emerging social competence. Younger children may learn through observation of their parents how to initiate social contacts. On the other hand, as the child grows older, social competence may, in fact, be negatively affected if insufficient independence in organizing their social contacts is not permitted. At the least, a child may regard it as inappropriate for a parent to continue to initiate on the child's behalf beyond a certain age; parental micromanagement may be viewed as interfering rather than helpful and a potential source of embarrassment for the child.

Together, these studies provide evidence of the possible facilitory role of parents in the development of social competence. However, the issue of direction of effects remains unresolved. Perhaps parents are more likely to initiate activities on behalf of socially competent children than for less competent offspring. Little is known, however, about the possible determinants of parental utilization of neighborhood social resources, including other children as playmates. In a later section, we address how neighborhood conditions may alter parental management.

Adult Social Networks as a Source of Potential Peer Contacts for Children.   In addition to the role played by parents in arranging children's access to other children, parents' own social networks, including the child members of parental social networks, provide a source of possible play partners for children. Several theorists (Cochran & Brassard, 1979; Coleman, 1988) have suggested ways these two sets of relationships may be related. First, the child is exposed to a wider or narrower band of possible social interactive partners by exposure to the members of the parents' social network. Cochran and his colleagues (Cochran, Larner, Riley, Gunnarsson, & Henderson, 1990) have provided support for the overlap between parental and child social networks. Specifically, these investigators found that 30% to 44% of 6-year-old children's social networks were also included in the mothers' networks. In other words, children often listed other children as play partners who were children of their mothers' friends. Finally, the overlap was higher in the case of relatives than nonrelatives, but both kin and nonkin adult networks provided sources of peer play partners for young children. The extent to which the child has access to the social interactions of his or her parents and members of their social network may determine how well the child acquires particular styles of social interaction. However, little direct evidence in support of this assumption is available.

Another way these two networks are linked was proposed by Coleman (1988), who argues that when both parents and their children are acquainted with other parents and their children, they form network closure. According to Coleman, when network closure exists, there are likely to be more shared values and more social control over their

offspring, which, in turn, would be related to better social outcomes. In support of this view, Darling, Steinberg, Gringlas, and Dornbusch (1995) found that social integration (as indexed by network closure) and value consensus were related to adolescent social and academic outcomes. Specifically, adolescents who reported high degrees of contact among their parents, friends, and their friends' parents as well as high levels of interaction with nonfamily adults were less deviant and higher in academic achievement than their peers who were less socially integrated. However, neighborhood effects were evident, with positive effects present only when the neighborhoods were "positive." In poor neighborhoods, integration produced negative effects. Moreover, the quality of parenting received by other children in the network influences children's own social outcomes. When the majority of parents in the network were authoritative in their child rearing, adolescents had lower levels of deviant behavior (e.g., substance abuse), especially when adolescents perceived their own parents as authoritative as well (Fletcher, Darling, Steinberg, & Dornbusch, 1995). While more detailed and precise measures of network closure are needed, this focus on the overlap of networks and its link with children's development is a promising one.

Several studies suggest that the quality of adult social networks relates to children's social behavior. In an Australian study, Homel, Burns, and Goodnow (1987) found positive relationships between the number of "dependable" friends that parents report and 11-year-old children's self-rated happiness, the number of regular playmates, and maternal ratings of children's social skills. Second, parents' affiliation with various types of formal community organizations was related to children's happiness, school adjustment, and social skills. The reliance on self-reports limits the value of these findings, but they do support the importance of parental or at least maternal social networks as a factor in potentially affecting children's social relationships. Recently, J. Lee, O'Neil, Parke, and Wang (1997) extended this work by showing a relation between parents' enjoyment of friends in their network and independent peer ratings. The more parents enjoyed their friends, the less the child was disliked and perceived as aggressive. Moreover, the more contact parents had with relatives, the less disliked children were by their peers.

Oliveri and Reiss (1987) found distinctive patterns of relations between maternal and paternal networks and the networks of adolescent children. The structural aspects (size, density) of networks were more closely related to maternal than paternal network qualities. This finding is consistent with prior work that suggests that mothers function as social arrangers and "kin keepers" more than do fathers. In contrast, the relationship aspects of adolescent social networks (positive sentiment between individuals, help received from network members) more closely resembled those aspects of fathers' social network characteristics. This is consistent with the view that fathers may, in fact, play an important role in the regulation of emotion, a central ingredient in the maintenance of close personal relationships (Parke et al., 1992). A variety of mechanisms is probably involved in accounting for these patterns, including the increased availability of social initiation and maintenance strategies. Finally, in view of the social support function of social networks, some of the above effects concerning children's outcomes may be due to an indirect effect, namely, the impact of social networks on the quality of parenting. We return to this issue later in the chapter.

Beyond the Parent-Child Dyad: The Marital Subsystem as a Contributor to Children's Socialization[1]

In the preceding section, parents were conceptualized as active influences, both direct and indirect, on the development of children's social competence and understanding of relationships. Considerable evidence emerged in support of the parent-child relationship as a primary socializing influence on children's social development in general, and on the development of specific relationship skills. However, children's experiences in families extend beyond their interactions with parents. Evidence is beginning to emerge that suggests that children's understanding of relationships also is shaped through their active participation in other family subsystems (e.g., child-sibling), as well as through exposure to the interactions of other dyadic subsystems (e.g., parent-parent) or participation in triadic relationships (e.g., child-sib-parent, child-parent-parent).

Influence of Marital Satisfaction and Discord on Child Outcomes

Considerable evidence indicates that marital functioning is related to children's short-term coping and long-term adjustment. Although the size of the associations is not always large, a range of studies links marital discord and conflict to outcomes in children that are likely to impair the quality

---

[1] The next two sections were adapted from Parke & O'Neil (1997).

of interpersonal relationships, including antisocial behavior (Emery, 1988), internalizing and externalizing behavior problems (Katz & Gottman, 1993), and changes in cognitions, emotions, and physiology in response to exposure to marital conflict (Cummings & Davies, 1994; Gottman & Katz, 1989). Although little empirical work has been directed specifically toward examination of the "carryover" of exposure to marital conflict to the quality of children's relationships with significant others such as peers and siblings, exposure to marital discord is associated with poor social competence and problematic peer relationships (Cummings & Davies, 1994; Gottman & Katz, 1989).

Mechanisms Linking Marital Discord to Children's Adjustment: Indirect and Direct Effects

Two alternative, but not mutually exclusive models, have been proposed to account for the impact of marital relations on children's developmental outcomes. Until recently, theoretical frameworks typically conceptualized marital discord as an indirect influence on children's adjustment that operated through its effect on family functioning and the quality of parenting (Fauber & Long, 1991). Factors such as affective changes in the quality of the parent-child relationship, lack of emotional availability, and adoption of less optimal parenting styles (Easterbrooks & Emde, 1988) have been implicated as potential mechanisms through which marital discord disrupts parenting processes. A second model (Cummings & Davies, 1994; Grych & Fincham, 1990) focuses on the direct effects of witnessed marital conflict on children's outcomes, rather than on the indirect or mediated effects.

Indirect Effects. A sizable body of literature supports the view that these two family subsystems (parent-child and husband-wife) are related. In a recent meta-analytic review, Erel and Burman (1995) gathered 68 studies that met a variety of criteria, including independent assessment of marital and parent-child relationships. Their review provided clear support for a positive relationship between the quality of the marital relationship and the quality of the parent-child relationship. As Erel and Burman concluded: "The composite mean weighted effect size representing the association between marital and parent-child quality was 0.46 or approximately one standard deviation in the direction of more positive parent-child relationships in families with more positive relations and more negative parent-child relationships in families with more negative marital relations" (p. 126). Even when their meta-analysis was restricted to studies of high research quality or to studies using independent raters and a between-subjects design, the effect sizes were reduced but remained significant. Their review leaves little doubt about the relationship between marriage and parent-child relationships.

Theoretically, two models have been offered to account for these effects: the spillover hypothesis and the compensatory hypothesis. According to the spillover perspective, mood or behavior in one subsystem transfers to another subsystem (e.g., from marital subsystem to parent-child subsystem; see Easterbrooks & Emde, 1988; Emery, 1988, for reviews). In contrast, the compensatory hypothesis suggests that positive parent-child relationships can be maintained even in the face of martial conflict and can serve as a buffer for children (Erel & Burman, 1995). The meta-analysis clearly supports the spillover hypothesis and offers no support for the compensatory concept. In fact, the analysis underscores the difficulty of buffering children from marital conflict and discord. Parents may try to buffer their children by limiting their opportunities to witness marital conflicts and disputes; however, as Erel and Burman suggest, "they cannot shield them from the negative impact that marital discord has on the parent-child relationships" (p. 128). Unfortunately, Erel and Burman's conclusions were largely restricted to Caucasian and intact families.

A variety of factors have been proposed as potential moderators of the relation between the marital subsystem and the parent-child subsystem, including gender of parent, gender of child, age of child, and birth order. Although Erel and Burman (1995) found little support for several potential moderators of the link between marital and parent-child subsystems (birth order, target of observation, sex of parent, and sex of parent and child), they note, "there may well be combinations of variables (e.g., sex of parent × child age or sex of child × sample type interactions) that moderate the association between marital and parent-child relations" (p. 128). In view of these concerns, the literature on potential moderators of this linkage will be briefly addressed.

A sizable body of evidence suggests that the quality of the father-child relationship is more consistently associated with the quality of the marital relationship and/or with the amount and quality of marital support than is the mother-child relationship (see Cowan & Cowan, 1992; Parke, 1996, for reviews). For example, Belsky, Gilstrap, and Rovine (1984) found that fathers' overall engagement of the infant was reliably and positively related to overall marital engagement at infant ages of 1, 3, and 9 months, whereas maternal engagement was related to the marital relationship

only when the infant was 1 month old. Similarly, Belsky and Volling (1986) found a stronger link between fathering and martial interaction than between mothering and marital interaction. Dickie (1987) found that the level of emotional and cognitive support provided by the spouse successfully discriminated high- and low-competent fathers but failed to do so in the case of mothers. This suggests that spousal support is more critical for adequate parenting on the part of fathers than mothers. In a short-term longitudinal study of the antecedents of father involvement, Feldman, Nash, and Aschenbrener (1983) measured marital relationship during the third trimester of the wives' pregnancies and again at 6 months postpartum. Marital relations predicted father involvement in caregiving, playfulness, and satisfaction with fatherhood. Moreover, fathers reacted more to changes in marital relationships than mothers. Finally, as marriages deteriorated, men became more negative and intrusive fathers, whereas mothers were less affected by shifts in marital quality (Belsky, Youngblade, Rovine, & Volling, 1991).

These findings suggest that successful paternal parenting is more dependent on a supportive marital relationship than is maternal parenting. A number of factors may aid in explaining this relation. First, there is prior evidence that the father's level of participation is, in part, determined by the extent to which the mother permits participation (Dickie & Carnahan, 1980). Second, because the paternal role is less well articulated and defined than the maternal role, spousal support may serve to help crystallize the boundaries of appropriate role behavior (Parke, 1996). Third, men have fewer opportunities to acquire and practice skills that are central to caregiving activities during socialization and therefore may benefit more than mothers from informational (i.e., cognitive) support.

Even if research eventually indicates that mother-child and father-child relationships are equally associated with marital relations, mothers and fathers may influence their children's outcomes in different ways. Katz and Kahen (1993) found that when parents used a mutually hostile pattern of conflict resolution, fathers were more likely to be intrusive and children were more likely to express anger during a parent-child interaction task. In addition, fathers' intrusiveness predicted more negative peer play and more aggressive play with a best friend. Interestingly, this study also suggests that an individual parent's style of handling conflict may be related to the quality of the *partner's* relationships with children in the family. When fathers were angry and withdrawn in a conflict resolution task, mothers were more critical and intrusive during interactions with their child. Maternal criticism and intrusiveness, in turn, were associated with unresponsiveness or "tuning out" by the child during mother-child interactions and higher levels of teacher-rated internalizing symptoms. Similarly, P. Cowan, Cowan, Schulz, and Heming (1994) examined the influence of marital quality on children's social adaptation to kindergarten, with results suggesting evidence of both direct and indirect links to children's social adjustment. Internalizing difficulties (e.g., shy/withdrawn qualities) were predicted by the influences of marital functioning on parenting quality, whereas externalizing difficulties (e.g., aggressive/antisocial qualities) were predicted directly by qualities of marital interaction.

Family systems theory suggests that not only does marital discord interfere with the mother-child and father-child relationship, it also may impair qualities of the mother-father-child triadic relationship by interfering with the effectiveness of how the mother and father work together with the child. Westerman and Schonholtz (1993) found that fathers', but not mothers', reports of marital disharmony and disaffection were significantly related to the effectiveness of joint parental support toward their child's problem-solving efforts. Joint parental support was, in turn, related to fathers' and teachers' reports of children's behavior problems. As Gottman (1994) has shown, women tend to engage and confront, while men tend to withdraw in the face of marital disharmony. Perhaps men's lack of involvement in the triadic family process may account for these findings.

Direct Effects of Marital Relationships on Children's Outcomes. Despite progress in elucidating specific parenting processes that are impaired by interparental conflict, evidence suggests that parental conflict is also associated with behavior problems independent of its influence on the parent-child relationship. Accordingly, attention has turned to elucidating specific processes by which the marital relationship itself *directly* influences children's immediate functioning and long-term adjustment. A parallel research trajectory has been movement away from a focus on global measures of marital satisfaction to a focus on specific aspects of marital interaction that are most likely to influence children's immediate cognitive, emotional, and physiological functioning. These immediate responses or "microprocesses," in turn, have been hypothesized to be critical links to children's long-term social adjustment in the face of interparental conflict (Cummings & Davies, 1994; Grych & Fincham, 1990). Recent studies

show that the form of expression of marital conflict plays a critical role in how children react. More frequent interparental conflict and more intense or violent forms of conflict have been found to be particularly disturbing to children and likely to be associated with externalizing and internalizing difficulties (Cummings & Davies, 1994). Conflict that was child-related in content was more likely than conflict involving other content to be associated with behavior problems in children, such as greater shame, responsibility, self-blame, and fear of being drawn into the conflict (Grych, Seid, & Fincham, 1991).

Resolution of conflict, even when it was not viewed by the child, reduces children's negative reactions to exposure to interadult anger and conflict. Exposure to unresolved conflict has been found to be associated with negative affect and poor coping responses in children (Cummings & Davies, 1994). In addition, the manner in which conflict is resolved may also influence children's adjustment. Katz and Gottman (1993) found that couples who exhibited a hostile style of resolving conflict had children who tended to be described by teachers as exhibiting antisocial characteristics. When husbands were angry and emotionally distant while resolving marital conflict, children were described by teachers as anxious and socially withdrawn.

Conflict is inevitable in most parental relationships and is not detrimental to family relationships and children's functioning under all circumstances. Although disagreements that are extremely intense and involve threat to the child are likely to be more disturbing to the child, when conflict is expressed constructively, is moderate in degree, is expressed in the context of a warm and supportive family environment, and shows evidence of resolution, children may learn valuable lessons regarding how to negotiate conflict and resolve disagreements (Cummings & Davies, 1994).

Less well understood are the specific emotional regulatory and cognitive processing mechanisms through which exposure to interparental conflict is "carried over" into children's understanding of close relationships and social competence with others. Two recent conceptual frameworks have emerged to examine these carryover questions. Using a cognitive-conceptual model, Grych and Fincham (1990) focus on the cognitive and affective meaning that exposure to conflict has for the child. They suggest that certain dimensions of interparental conflict (e.g., intensity and content of conflict) and contextual factors (e.g., family emotional climate, past history) are used by the child to appraise the personal relevance of interadult conflict. Three appraisals influence the child's coping responses to interparental conflict, including the level of perceived threat to the child, the child's perceived coping efficacy, and causal attributions and ascription of blame made by the child. Over time, a family environment that is characterized by high interparental conflict may play a role in the development of children's cognitive models of familial and extrafamilial relationships by exposing children to hostile and negative interpretations of interpersonal experiences and social situations (Cummings & Davies, 1994) and by undermining the child's sense of efficacy in regard to how to cope in social situations with peers and significant others. Further, children who are exposed to chronic levels of intense, unresolved conflict also may feel the threat of imminent separation, which may influence the child's responses in the face of conflict.

Some evidence exists to suggest that the quality of the marital relationship may shape the cognitive dimensions of the family climate. Spouses in discordant marriages are more likely than those in happy marriages to focus on negative aspects of interactions with their partners, to overlook positive behaviors, and to attribute their partners' behaviors to hostile intentions (Bradbury & Fincham, 1989). Children who are exposed to marital discord may develop similar attribution processes in response to interactions with significant others. Modeling of negative behavior patterns that children observe when exposed to marital conflict may be an important mechanism through which nonadaptive interaction styles are transmitted to children.

In an alternative model, Davies and Cummings (1994) downplay cognitive factors and emphasize the primacy of emotions as organizers of interpersonal experience. In an extension of the literature linking attachment security in the parent-child relationship and quality of emotional functioning, they propose that emotional security also derives from the quality of the marital relationship. They posit that the emotion-laden quality of marital conflict contributes to emotionality's playing a primary role relative to cognitive processes in determining how children react to interparent conflict. They propose that several interrelated processes account for the impact of emotional security on children's functioning: emotional security (a) affects the ability of the child to regulate his or her own emotions, (b) influences the child's motivation to intervene to regulate the parents' behavior, and (c) affects the cognitive appraisals and internal representations of family relationships that are made by children.

Evidence suggests that chronic, intense marital conflict undermines children's emotional regulatory abilities. Gottman and Katz (1989) found that maritally distressed couples employed a parenting style that was cold, unresponsive, angry, and low in limit setting and structuring. Children who were exposed to this style of parenting exhibited high levels of stress hormones and displayed more anger and noncompliance. In addition, these children tended to play at low levels with peers and displayed more negative peer interactions. Not all problematic marriages are similar. Some problematic marriages are likely to be characterized by lower levels of openly expressed anger and hostility and higher levels of active withdrawal from interaction. Children in marriages characterized by withdrawal rather than interaction accompanied by anger react differently (Katz & Gottman, 1994). These authors argue that withdrawal may be even more stressful for children than an angry but engaged marital relationship.

Although more work is clearly needed before conclusions regarding the mechanisms through which interparental conflict influences children's understanding of relationships, a number of potential mechanisms have been suggested. The challenge lies in applying these models to future investigations of the links between children's exposure to interparental interaction and their adjustment. Finally, prior work has been largely developmental or restricted largely to young children. Little is known about the impact of exposure to marital conflict on adolescents, especially the effects on their own emerging friendships and close relationships.

The Sibling Subsystem as a Contributor to Children's Socialization

Descriptions of the normative patterns that characterize sibling relationships over the course of development (Dunn, 1988) suggest that, in addition to parents, siblings may play a critical role in the socialization of children. In fact, most children are likely to spend more time in direct interaction with siblings than with parents and significant others (Dunn, 1993; Larson & Richards, 1994). Interactions with siblings provide a context for the expression of a range of positive social behaviors as well as numerous conflictual encounters and experiences with conflict resolution (Dunn, 1988). Further, this array of interactions between siblings has been found to be typified by greater emotional intensity than the behavioral exchanges that characterize other relationships (Katz, Kramer, & Gottman, 1992).

Sibling relationships have been hypothesized to contribute to children's socialization in a number of significant ways. A social learning framework analogous to the one posited to explain parental contributions to the development of children's social competence (Parke et al., 1988) predicts that through their interactions with siblings, children develop specific interaction patterns and social understanding skills that generalize to relationships with other children. In addition, relationships with siblings may provide a context in which children can practice the skills and interaction styles that have been learned from parents or others (McCoy, Brody, & Stoneman, 1994). Older siblings function as tutors, managers, or supervisors of their younger brother or sister's behavior during social interactions (Edwards & Whiting, 1993) and may function as gatekeepers who extend or limit opportunities to interact with children outside of the family (Weisner, 1987). Also paralleling the indirect influence that the observation of parent-parent interaction has on children, a second avenue of influence on children's development is their observation of parents interacting with siblings. These interactions have been hypothesized to serve as an important context in which children deal with issues of differential treatment and learn about complex social emotions such as rivalry and jealousy.

Influence of Siblings on Child Outcomes

Children's experiences with siblings provide a context in which interaction patterns and social understanding skills may generalize to relationships with other children (McCoy et al., 1994). According to Stocker and Dunn (1990), interactions with siblings provide a setting in which children "develop social understanding skills which may enable them to form particularly close relationships with a child of their choice, a close friend" (p. 227). There is a mixed body of evidence in support of links between sib-sib patterns of interaction and interaction styles between friends and peers. Some studies find little evidence of a link between sibling and peer interaction, while others find evidence of transfer of either positive or negative interactive skills from sibs to peers (see Dunn, 1988, for review). Putallaz and Sheppard (1992) have posited that children with adequate social skills exhibit cross-situational specificity by adapting to the specific demands of each social relationship—behaving in a more reciprocal, egalitarian manner with classmates and in a more asymmetric, hierarchical fashion with siblings. In contrast, among children who lack social competence, deficits in social skills such

as heightened aggressiveness and inability to initiate interaction will generalize across sibling and peer contexts.

Other recent studies continue to show only modest evidence of straightforward carryover of interaction styles between children's relationships, and when associations emerge they may be complicated by birth order effects and other processes (Dunn, 1993; Stocker & Dunn, 1990). Adding further complexity to the emerging picture of how sibling and peer relationships are linked are findings from recent studies that suggest that the sibling relationship may play a role in compensating for other problematic relationships by providing an alternative context for experiencing satisfying social relationships and protecting children from the development of adjustment difficulties. East and Rook (1992), for example, found that children who were socially isolated in their peer relationships were buffered from adjustment problems when they reported positive relationships with a favorite sibling. Similarly, Stocker (1994) reported support for the compensatory role of at least one positive relationship (either sibling, friend, or mother) as protection from the development of behavioral conduct difficulties.

Less is known about the reverse effect, namely, the impact of friendship on sibling relationships. Recently, Kramer and Gottman (1992) examined the role that positive relationships with peers play in children's adaptation to the birth of a new sibling. Children who displayed a more positive interaction style with a best friend and who were better able to manage conflict and negative affect behaved more positively toward their new sibling at 6 months and 14 months. The authors suggest that management of conflict, a skill that is particularly useful when interacting with siblings, may be more likely to be learned in interactions with peers than in direct interactions with parents.

The challenge for future work is to discover the contexts under which strong, weak, or compensatory connections might be expected between relationship systems as well as the processes through which children's experiences with siblings are translated into relationship skills that are used in other relationships. For example, greater generalization of hostile, aggressive interaction styles in both sibling and peer systems may emerge when children lack adequate relationship skills (Putallaz & Sheppard, 1992) or when children are experiencing stressful, negative family relationships (Dunn, 1993). In contrast, under other circumstances, the associations between sibling relationships and relationships outside the family may be moderated by a number of features that uniquely characterize each relationship. As Dunn (1993) has argued, friendship involves a mutual and reciprocated relationship with another individual, whereas sibling relationships do not necessarily share these qualities. In contrast to sib-sib relationships, friend and peer relationships represent a more diverse combination of backgrounds, experiences, and temperaments that may generate interaction styles that are the result of two unique individuals' approach to relationships. Further, there appear to be different role expectations for sibling and friend relationships that may differentially influence interaction styles. The challenge of future work will be to more systematically examine the moderating and mediating influences of these factors to better unravel normative patterns of associations between sibling and peer relationships.

Siblings as Managers of Children's Social Lives

Just as parents function as managers of children's social lives, siblings in many cultures perform similar management functions in relation to their younger siblings. Cross-cultural work indicates that in both African and Polynesian cultures, children, especially girls, become involved in sibling caretaking activities at an early age (Weisner, 1993). Relatively little is known, however, about the caregiving role of siblings in contemporary Euro-American families. Patterns of sibling interaction in New England families suggests that formal caregiving responsibilities may not be as common in American culture as in other cultures (B. Whiting & Edwards, 1988). However, Bryant (1989) suggests that although parents may not formally assign caretaking duties to children, children frequently voluntarily assume the roles of caretaker, tutor, and teacher of younger siblings and make unique contributions to the socialization of young children. Most work examining these roles has focused on the influence that instruction from older siblings may have on children's cognitive development (Rogoff, 1990). Relatively little is known about the role that siblings play as supervisors, managers, or advisors of children's social lives. Given the amount of time that most children spend in the company of siblings, this is an area that clearly is ripe for future investigation.

Beyond the Sibling Dyad: Children's Observations of Parental Interactions with Siblings

Not only are children active participants in relationships, they also witness the interactions of other family subsystems. Children appear to be particularly attentive to parent-sibling interactions that involve the expression of affect (e.g., disputes or games) and actively attempt to intervene in these interactions to draw attention to themselves (Dunn & Shatz, 1989). Further, as family systems theory predicts, the birth of a sibling is linked to changes in the relationship between mother (or father) and the firstborn child, with changes being moderated by the quality of the parent-child relationship and gender of the firstborn child (Dunn & Kendrick, 1982; Howe & Ross, 1990). In families with firstborn girls, if the mother-daughter relationship was particularly positive before the birth of the sibling, a more hostile relationship was likely to develop between the firstborn daughter and her sibling. In contrast, when mother and daughter had a more conflictual relationship, siblings were more likely to have a close, friendly relationship with one another one year later (Dunn & Kendrick, 1982). Just as the negative impact of marital conflict appears to be ameliorated when parents have conversations with the child regarding the conflict, evidence also suggests that parental management strategies are likely to moderate the child's reaction to a new sibling, perhaps by influencing the child's attribution processes. Dunn and Kendrick (1982) found that if mother used conversation to help the child think of his or her infant sibling in more positive ways, the child reacted in a more positive way. These findings suggest that close monitoring and sensitivity to relative differences in relationships begin to emerge early in children's significant relationships, and social comparison and cognitive-attributional processes may play an important role in how information about relationships is understood. From an early age, children appear to take an active role in the construction of their relationships.

Future Directions for Sibling Research

More fruitful investigation of the links between relationships may come with movement from a socialization framework to a relationships framework. Dunn (1993) points out that one disadvantage of a socialization approach is that it does not adequately take into account the fact that even when a child acquires social competencies through interactions in one relationship, he or she may not be motivated to apply these skills in another relationship. In contrast, a relationships perspective takes into account the fact that each relationship reflects a unique set of demands and rewards as well as different challenges to a child's sociocognitive abilities. This may lead to the generation of questions concerning the unique aspects of the child (e.g., temperament, attachment security, self-confidence), the relationship partner, the dynamic of the relationship itself, and the broader social ecology (e.g., family stress, life transitions) that may contribute to a child's being motivated or disinclined to behave in a socially competent manner. As Dunn (1993) points out, the goal is to specify "for *which* children, at *which* stages of development, *which* dimensions of particular relationships are likely to show associations with other relationships" (p. 125). A final value of the renewed focus on siblings is the contribution that this work is making to our understanding of the relative roles of genetics and environment in studies of socialization and development (Dunn, 1993; Plomin, 1994).

The Family Unit as a Contributor to Children's Socialization

Parent-child, marital, and sibling influences are clearly the most well-researched aspects of socialization. However, consideration of these units of analysis alone is insufficient, for they fail to recognize the family unit itself as a separate and identifiable level of analysis (Parke, 1988). Consistent with a systems theory perspective (Sameroff, 1994), the properties, functions, and effects of the family unit cannot necessarily be inferred from these smaller units of analysis. Families as units change across development in response to changes in the individual members, life circumstances, and scheduled and unscheduled transitions. Families develop distinct "climates" (Moos & Moos, 1981), "styles" of responding to events (Reiss, 1981), and "boundaries" (Boss, 1983), which, in turn, provide differing socialization contexts for the developing child. Reiss (1989) argues that the family regulates the child's development through a range of processes, including paradigms, myths, stories, and rituals: "According to this perspective the stability and coherence of these processes reside not within individuals, but in the *co-ordinated practices* of the entire family . . . the interaction of the group—above and beyond the memories of individuals—conserves relationships and regulates and perpetuates many aspects of ongoing family life" (p. 188). Recent evidence suggests the potential importance of these family-level processes for understanding socialization in the family.

Family Paradigms

Reiss and Oliveri (1983) have offered a useful starting point for this analysis by providing a typology of family paradigms:

> A paradigm is a set of enduring assumptions about the social world shared by all family members. Although family members may disagree about specific percepts of their social world, their more deeply seated convictions and experiences

concerning its safety, equitability and familiarity are shared. Families can be distinguishable from one another by the nature of their paradigms, and three dimensions have been useful in clarifying those differences. Families high on *configuration* believe the social world to be ordered, understandable and through diligent exploration, masterable; families low on this dimension see the world as chaotic, unknown, and dangerous. Families high on *coordination* see the world as treating each member in the same fashion and viewing the family as a single group; families low on the dimension see the world as divided and functioning differently for each member. Finally, families who delay *closure* see the world as novel, exciting, and intriguing; families with early closure see the world as familiar and reminiscent. (p. 81)

These investigators have demonstrated the utility of this level of analysis in a variety of ways (Reiss, 1981). First, the paradigm is useful in predicting the type of pathology or disturbance that an individual might develop in response to a stressful event. For example, families with low configurations and low coordination—families that may be experiencing isolation among family members and pessimism that environmental problems can be solved—may, when sufficiently stressed, be at risk for the development of delinquency in children. In contrast, low coordination may also predispose family members to alcoholism if other stresses are sufficiently great. Second, the paradigm may be of value in terms of understanding the type of coping processes in which a family may engage and the targets selected to help in terms of stress. For example, Oliveri and Reiss (1981) found that delayed closure was positively associated with the size of the preferred-kin network; families who are open have relationships with a wide range of kin. Coordination was positively related to *shared connection:* the degree to which parents and children in the same family jointly interacted in the same subgroupings within the kin network. High-configuration families showed low shared connection between the child and his or her parents. It is assumed that families who feel they can master their social world encourage their children to form their own distinct social ties with their relatives. Similarly, configuration was related positively to the size of the adolescent's network of friends and acquaintances (Reiss, 1981). Finally, coordination was positively related with the degree of interconnectedness of the kin network (i.e., the extent to which kin know each other).

These family styles would be of varying value for successful adaptation to stress, in part, depending on the type of stressor. For example, in the case of divorce, children in a high-configuration family might fare best because they would have strong ties outside the family that could provide support. Similarly, being high on coordination may be beneficial when the stressful event is shared by the family (e.g., an illness, a hurricane), because this would yield support for all family members. On the other hand, low coordination, in which each family member has developed separate social ties, may be more beneficial when the stress affects family members differently, as in the case of divorce; families who maintain similar social ties may suffer due to the necessity of choosing which member of the family to support in the crisis.

Other methods of conceptualizing the family as a unit, such as family boundaries (Boss, 1983), have been suggested. According to this concept, the definition of which members are included in the functional family system has proven useful in determining how families react to stressful changes such as the case of a POW father or an alcoholic mother. In the first case, the missing father can be treated as psychologically present but physically absent, which may prolong the family's redefinition of its boundaries excluding the missing member. Alternatively, in the case of the alcoholic mother, the individual is physically present but psychologically absent, which, in turn, produces ambiguity concerning the boundaries of the family unit.

Many questions remain concerning the utility of this level of analysis. The relative utility of various schemes for conceptualizing family units in terms of their value for understanding family reaction to stressful change remains untested. Little is known yet concerning the ontogenesis of these types of family paradigms. Do these paradigms change over time, or are they stable? Although it is clear that there is short-term test-retest reliability, longitudinal studies are necessary to determine the long-term stability or instability of these family paradigms. For example, do these paradigms shift with the developmental levels of the children in the family? Second, these paradigms may be useful not only as a way of characterizing response to stress but can be treated as dependent variables as well. In this case, the shifts along paradigm dimensions would be used as a way of characterizing the reaction to stress.

Family Myths

Myths refer to beliefs that influence family process, provide continuity across generations, and are generally not open to discussion or debate (Sameroff, 1994). Wamboldt and Reiss (1989) argue that family myths influence mate selection and marital satisfaction. Individuals can set aside destructive family myths by marrying a person with a different and perhaps healthier history of family myths. To date, there is little direct evidence of the impact of family myths on children's development.

Family Stories

Family stories have received more attention as vehicles for socialization of young children. Stories are vehicles for the transmission of family values and for teaching family roles. The study of stories as socialization vehicles has taken a variety of forms, in part, depending on the disciplinary perspective of the investigator. Culturally oriented investigators (e.g., Miller & Sperry, 1987) have established that stories occur in naturalistic contexts in exchanges between parents and children or while children are present. In home observations of African American toddlers in south Baltimore, they found that mothers told informal narratives in the presence of their children about events in which someone became angry or responded with verbal or nonverbal aggression. Through these stories children learn to distinguish between justified and unjustified anger.

Family-of-origin experiences may be transmitted across generations through stories and shared memories and, in turn, shape contemporary interactions between family members. Fiese (1990), for example, found that mothers who told stories of their own childhood that emphasized affiliative, nurturant, and playful themes engaged in more turn-taking and reciprocal interactions. Mothers who told stories of achievement and rejection were less engaged and more intrusive and directive. Not only are stories related to family interaction patterns, they are linked to children's social competence as well. Putallaz, Costanzo, and Smith (1991) found that mothers with predominantly anxious/lonely recollections of their own childhood experiences with peers took an active role in their children's social development and had the most socially competent children. In this case, mothers may be compensating for their own difficult childhoods. Finally, stories change across development. Fiese (1990) found that mothers of 8- to 12-year-old boys told stories of their childhood that represented themes of overcoming obstacles and facing adversity—a very different set of themes than that transmitted in the stories told to toddlers.

Family Rituals

Rituals have been recognized for decades as an important aspect of family life (Bossard & Ball, 1950), but only in the past decade has the socialization function of rituals become apparent (Fiese, 1994). As Sameroff (1994) notes: "Family rituals may range from highly stylized religious observances such as first communion or bar mitzvahs to less articulated daily interaction patterns such as the type of greeting made when someone returns home" (p. 209). Central to the concept of rituals is the fact that they provide meaning to family interactions. Wolin, Bennett, and Jacobs (1988) have identified three types of family rituals: family celebrations (e.g., holidays or rites of passage [weddings]), family traditions (e.g., birthday customs, family vacations), and patterned routines (e.g., dinnertime, bedtime routines, weekend activities). Methodological progress has recently been marked by development of a Family Ritual Questionnaire (Fiese & Kline, 1993).

Of importance is the fact that rituals serve a protective function. Wolin, Bennett, and Jacobs (1988) found that children who came from families that were able to preserve family rituals such as dinner and holiday routines were less likely to become alcoholics as adults. Other studies (Fiese, 1992) report that families who attach more meaning to their rituals have adolescents who are higher in self-esteem. In sum, rituals are a powerful index of family functioning and may serve as a protective factor for the child. Questions remain about the uniqueness of rituals relative to other forms of family routines or child-rearing practices. Are rituals independent vehicles of socialization or merely a reflection of more central causal influences, such as the quality of the parent-child relationship? For example, rituals may be less likely in families of alcoholics, which suggests that degree of alcoholism, either alone or in combination with the lack of rituals, may contribute to future drinking problems. Evidence is needed concerning the contribution of family-level variables independent of individual or dyadic levels of analysis. Similarly, the direction of causality in these studies remains unclear. Do harmonious families participate more in family rituals, or does the active participation in these activities contribute to increased family well-being? While the answers to these questions are unclear, it is evident that we need to expand our search of avenues along which socialization is enacted in families. Finally, the origin of family-level differences is an issue that has received little attention. In light of recent demonstrations (e.g., Plomin et al., 1994) that genetics may play a role in accounting for variations in measures of family home environments, answers are most likely to derive from designs that recognize the contributions of both genetic and environmental factors in accounting for the emergence of family-level differences.

Putting the Pieces Together: Toward a Multiple-Sources Model of Socialization within the Family

Our family systems viewpoint argues for the construction of a comprehensive model in which the contributions of parent-child, parent-parent, and sibling relationships all are recognized. Figure 8.5 outlines a comprehensive model of family socialization that includes the influence of all family members. To date, few studies have addressed how these subsystems combine to produce their impact on children's relationship learning (see Katz et al., 1992; McCoy et al., 1994, for recent exceptions). Little is known about the relative weight of parent-child relationships versus other family relationships (Parke & O'Neil, 1997). Nor do we understand how the impact of these different relationships changes as the child develops. The most crucial issue remains, namely, the specification of the pathways through which these different relationships exert their influence. It is evident from our model that multiple pathways are possible, and there is support for both direct and mediated effects. As noted earlier, marital relationships exert both direct (e.g., witnessed) and indirect effects (e.g., marital relationships influence parent-child patterns). Similarly, parent-child relationships could influence marital relationships. For example, a disciplinary encounter with a difficult-to-control child could, in turn, trigger a marital conflict due to disagreement about

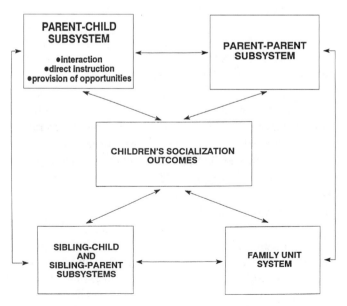

Figure 8.5 Model indicating the hypothesized relations among family subsystems and children's socialization outcomes.

the child's misbehavior or management of the child, the carryover of negative mood, or the alignment of parent and child against a third party. Less is known about the impact of parent-child relationships on marital interactions than the reverse effects.

Moreover, recent research has begun to identify individual differences across families or family typologies as well as at the level of family subsystems such as marital dyads (D. Bell & Bell, 1989; Filsinger, 1991). As a next step, can we characterize families usefully in terms of the relative importance of various subsystems? Some families may invest heavily in directly parenting their children but tend to protect their children from their marital problems. Earlier evidence suggests that exposure to marital conflict is higher for boys than girls (Emery, 1988). Similarly, some families may encourage close sib-sib relationships, while others tend to encourage sibs to form separate social spheres. In turn, this kind of social arrangement will result in different types of socialization outcomes.

Do all combinations produce equally socially competent children, or are some ingredients in this mix more important than others? Do different combinations produce different but equally well-adjusted children in terms of their social relationships? Can children in a family with a poor marriage compensate by investing "relationship energy" into another subsystem such as the sib-sib or parent-child systems? Studies of divorce (Hetherington et al., 1989) suggest that a close sib-sib relationship can help buffer children during a stressful divorce.

DETERMINANTS OF FAMILY SOCIALIZATION STRATEGIES

One of the major advances in the field has been a recognition of the importance of understanding the determinants of parenting behavior (Belsky, 1984). For a long time, developmentalists were concerned about the impact of particular styles or practices on children (Baumrind, 1967; Sears et al., 1957). There was less concern with the conditions that alter parenting behaviors themselves. Several trends have converged to stimulate this interest. First, the recognition of child effects (Bell, 1968) led to a reevaluation of the role of the child in eliciting and shaping parental behaviors. Second, renewed interest in contextual-ecological issues (Bronfenbrenner, 1979, 1989) has led to research on how contextual factors shape parenting practices. Third and closely linked is the increased focus on how cultural,

racial, and ethnic background modify parenting behavior (Harrison et al., 1990). Fourth, interest in the life course perspective (Elder, Ch. 16, Vol. 1; Parke, 1988) has led to a focus on the ways that timing of entry into parenting roles alters the enactment of parental behaviors. Fourth, recognition of the role of parental cognitions (e.g., goals, values, attributions) has fueled interest in how cognition shapes parental behavior (Goodnow & Collins, 1990; Parke, 1978b).

In this section, a variety of factors will be considered. Belsky (1984) proposed a three-domain model of the determinants of parenting, which included personal resources of the parents, characteristics of the child, and contextual sources of stress and support. Some of this work relevant to this model will be reviewed, and recent work on ethnic variations in parenting will be reviewed to expand upon this earlier theoretical scheme.

Child Characteristics

Child characteristics take two forms: universal predispositions that are shared by all children and individual differences in particular characteristics. Over the past several decades, an impressive amount of evidence has documented that infants are biologically prepared for social, cognitive, and perceptual challenges, and these prepared responses play a significant role in facilitating children's adaptation to their environment. This evolutionary approach, which was championed early by Bowlby (1958), has continued to receive support (see Bugental & Goodnow, Ch. 7, this Volume; Wozniak, 1993, for reviews). Under the influence of recent advances in behavior genetics (e.g., Plomin, 1994; Rowe, 1994), there is increasing recognition of the role of individual differences in a wide variety of behavioral characteristics in shaping parental socialization strategies. Perhaps the most well-researched determinant of parenting behavior is infant and child temperament (Bates, 1987; Kochanska, 1993). Although debates continue about the relative contributions of genetic and experimental factors to the emergence of individual differences in temperament (Bates, 1987; Rothbart & Ahadi, 1994), there is no doubt that temperament plays an important role as a determinant of parental socialization tactics. Infants with difficult temperaments elicit more arousal and distress from caregivers than less difficult infants (Bates, 1987). Children who are more difficult may elicit increasingly coercive strategies from parents (Patterson, Reid, & Dishion, 1992). On the other hand, fearful children may respond optimally to subtle parental socialization strategies (Wachs & Gandour, 1983). Other characteristics, in addition to temperament, have been examined, including activity level, social responsiveness, and compliance level. In general, the more active, less responsive, and more noncompliant children elicit more negative parenting and more negative parental arousal and affect (see Bell & Harper, 1977, for a review). The impact of these individual differences on parental socialization behavior is not independent of environmental conditions. In a classic study, Crockenberg (1981) showed that the impact of a difficult infant temperament on the parent-infant attachment relationship varied as a function of the degree of social support available to the mother, which underscores the potential modifiability of temperament-based influences.

Personal Resources

A variety of studies support the prediction that personal resources—conceptualized as knowledge, ability, and motivation to be a responsible caregiver—alter parenting behaviors (Belsky, 1984). Particularly striking are recent studies of how parental psychopathology such as depression will alter parenting behavior. A variety of studies has documented that from early infancy onward the patterns of interaction between depressed and nondepressed parents (usually mothers) and their offspring are markedly different. When interacting with their infants, depressed mothers show flat affect and provide less stimulation as well as less contingent responsivity than nondepressed mothers; in turn, their infants show less attentiveness, fewer contented expressions, more fussiness, and lower activity levels (Field, 1992). Moreover, as Field, Healy, Goldstein, and Guthertz (1990) found in a study of 3-month-old infants and their depressed and nondepressed mothers, depressed mothers and their infants matched negative behavior states more often and positive behavior states less often than did nondepressed dyads. Differences are particularly evident when depression is protracted and not merely transient (Campbell, Cohn, & Meyers, 1995). These investigators found that women whose depressions lasted through the child's sixth month were less positive with their infants during feeding, toy play, and face-to-face interaction than those whose depression was short-lived. Moreover, the babies of the mothers with sustained depression were less positive during face-to-face interaction than the other babies. This study is particularly important because all the mothers met diagnostic criteria for depression.

These differences in style of interaction may place the infant at risk for later developmental problems. Several studies have found that infants of depressed mothers are more likely to develop insecure attachment. For example, Radke-Yarrow and Zahn-Waxler (1985) found that infants of severely depressed mothers were more likely to develop insecure attachment classification. More recent investigations have found links between severe and chronic depression and disorganized attachment behavior (Campbell et al., 1995; Lyons-Ruth, Connell, Grunebaum, & Botein, 1990; this attachment category refers to infants who lack a coherent strategy for accessing their attachment figures and who show confused, conflictful, and fearful behavior in the Strange Situation; see Thompson, Ch. 2, this Volume). Nor are the effects on child-parent attachment restricted to infancy. Teti, Gelfand, Messinger, and Isabella (1995) recently found that a similar pattern of insecure attachment was evident among preschool-age children of depressed mothers. Moreover, in the preschoolers a higher proportion of the depressed group were classified as disorganized. Finally, parenting stress and objective ratings of maternal behavioral competence were both higher among the depressed mothers, a finding consistent with earlier work that suggests that shifts in parenting quality are mediating the effects of maternal depression on children's outcomes. While no follow-up studies have revealed the long-term outcomes for these children, other studies of the developmental course of children with poor attachment histories reveal that these children are at risk for later relationship difficulties in adolescence (Sroufe, Carlson, & Shulman, 1993). Just as in the case of individual differences in infants and children, recent theorists have argued that some of these individual differences across parents, such as depression and proneness to abuse or coerciveness, may, in part, be genetically based (Gottesman & Goldsmith, 1994). Studies addressing the interplay of genetically based individual differences among infants and parents and environmental factors that enhance or suppress the influence of these characteristics would be valuable.

Social Support and Family Socialization Strategies

Families exist as units with other social organizations within society and thus need to be viewed within their social context. Recognition of the role of the community and community agents as modifiers of family modes of interaction is necessary for an adequate theory of socialization.

Recognition of the embeddedness of families in a set of broader social systems such as community and culture or, in Bronfenbrenner's (1979, 1989) terms, the meso and macro systems is only a first step. The next important task is to articulate the ways these other levels of social organization affect family functioning and to explore the ways these influence processes take place. It should be noted that community influence, regardless of its form, can be either positive or negative; this view stands in contrast to the view that high degree of connectedness with community resources is, ipso facto, positive. In addition, it is assumed that influence between communities and families is bidirectional. It is assumed that the ways communities and families are related will vary across the developmental span. Moreover, the influence of support systems on families may either be direct or indirect in its effects. Finally, availability and utilization need to be separately considered; families may have friends, relatives, and neighbors available, but fail to utilize these members of their informal social network in times of stress or crises or on a day-to-day basis.

Informal Support Systems

Informal support systems refer to (a) unstructured social networks, which consist of a person's relatives, friends, neighbors, coworkers, and other acquaintances who interact with the person, and (b) structured social support systems, which include a variety of neighborhood or community-based organizations or groups usually not officially generated, controlled, or funded by local or other government officials (Cochran & Brassard, 1979). Each of these types of social support systems can help families function in a variety of ways: providing instrumental physical and financial support, providing emotional/social support, and providing informational support.

Families are particularly likely to rely on external social support systems under conditions of high stress or family crisis. The premature birth of an infant constitutes one example of this type of situation. Evidence (Parke & Tinsley, 1984) indicates that parents are more likely to use social support systems when their infants are born prematurely than when their infants are born at term. Crnic, Greenberg, Ragozin, Robinson, and Basham (1983) reported positive relationships between informal social support and parenting attitudes and behavior. Mothers with higher levels of community support were more responsive, gratified with the interactions, and affectionate, as were their infants. Recently, Goldstein, Diener, and Mangelsdorf (1995) found

that women with larger networks were found to be more sensitive in interactions with their infants than women with smaller networks. Jennings, Staff, and Conners (1991) reported similar links between size of social networks and parent-child interaction with 4-year-olds. Specifically, they found that mothers who were more satisfied with their personal networks and mothers with larger maternal networks demonstrated more optimal maternal behavior, as indexed by higher levels of praise and less intrusive control. In turn, these altered interaction patterns may lead to different patterns of infant-parent attachment, with higher social support associated with more secure attachment (Crockenberg, 1981). However, as noted earlier, infant characteristics such as temperament may modify the relationship between social support and parent-infant relationships. Especially in the case of irritable infants, utilization of social support was associated with secure attachment. This illustrates the interplay of individual characteristics (temperament) and the role of the social environment (social support networks) on later infant-parent relationships (Crockenberg, 1981).

Formal Support Systems

Although review of various types of formal support systems is beyond the scope of this chapter, several general conclusions can be drawn. First, a variety of programs has demonstrated the malleability of parenting behavior and the positive impact of formal interventions for child functioning (see Cowan, Cowan, & Powell, Ch. 1, Volume 4). Second, both preventive and interventive efforts are important strategies for increasing parent effectiveness (C. Cowan & Cowan, 1992; Olds, 1988). Third, there is an increasing trend toward two-generation interventions. As Smith and Zaslow (1995) note, these types of programs involve the integration of "two kinds of family supports, namely (a) self-sufficiency services designed to improve the parents' education level, vocational skills and employment status and (b) child development services that may include preventive health care, parenting education and high-quality child care or early childhood education. The programs also provide other services designed to meet the individual needs of the parent and family such as transportation and assistance obtaining social services" (p. 1). These types of interventions that target both adult and child are clearly consistent with a life course view of parenting that recognizes the importance of adult developmental status and needs. Fourth, formal support programs are increasingly sensitive to the variability in families in terms of structure, ethnicity, and needs, and a goal of recent intervention efforts is to match families and strategies to increase program effectiveness (Smith & Zaslow, 1995).

Ecological Determinants: Neighborhoods and Family Socialization Strategies

Neighborhoods influence child and adolescent development directly by exposure to the physical and social challenges and opportunities that neighborhoods offer and indirectly by shifts in parental socialization practices in response to the ecology of different neighborhoods.

Do neighborhoods make a difference to children's development? Several approaches have been used to address this issue. Early studies, such as Bryant (1985) examined children's perceptions of neighborhood resources during a "neighborhood walk." She found that children in neighborhoods characterized as richer in social and physical resources were higher in perspective taking and internal locus of control. Using census tract data to characterize neighborhoods has become a common strategy in more recent studies. In an Australian study, Homel and Burns (1989) found that children who lived in the most disadvantaged, inner-city neighborhoods were lower on several indices of social adjustment including sense of loneliness, feelings of rejection, worry, anger, and life dissatisfaction than children in less disadvantaged neighborhoods. Similarly in the United States, several investigators (Brooks-Gunn, Duncan, Klebanov, & Sealand, 1993a; Coulton & Pandey, 1992) found that children in high poverty areas had lower reading scores and higher rates of low birth-weight infants and juvenile delinquency. Neighborhood effects are not independent of family characteristics. Kupersmidt, Griesler, DeRosier, Patterson, and Davis (1995) examined second- through fifth-grade children's behavioral adjustment as a function of the combined influence of neighborhood characteristics (based on census tract data) and family context. Better quality neighborhoods may serve a protective function for some families (e.g., African American children from low-income single-parent families) while exacerbating the problems for other families (e.g., Euro-American, low-income children from single-parent families). However, the interplay between ethnicity, family type, and neighborhood is far from settled, since Brooks-Gunn et al. (1993b) found that low-income African American adolescents did not benefit from residing in a more affluent neighborhood. In summary, although several studies have found evidence of "neighborhood effects" across a number of development outcomes in both children and adolescents, these effects appear to be modest after taking into account "family effects." According to Furstenberg, Eccles, Elder, Cook, and Sameroff (in press), "place of residence has not told us much about the success and failure of urban youth . . . parents and their children differ far more within particular neighborhoods than they do between areas. Family variations in neighborhoods are expressed by different socialization styles, featuring particular management strategies and child outcomes (p. 13)."

In support of the Furstenberg et al. argument, a number of studies have found that neighborhoods are important contextual determinants of parental socialization strategies and underscore the particular value of considering context in understanding these strategies. Since minority families often reside in relatively dangerous and threatening neighborhoods, child-rearing practices may be adapted to suit this set of ecological conditions. While an authoritative child-rearing style may be productive of social and academic competence in children and youth residing in low-risk environments (Baumrind, 1978; Steinberg, Dornbusch, & Brown, 1992), recent research has questioned the generality of these findings. Baldwin, Baldwin, and Cole (1990) found that poor minority parents who used more authoritarian child-rearing practices had better-adjusted children than those relying on authoritative strategies. Similarly, McCarthy and Lord (1993) found that 11- to 14-year-old Black children whose parents use more controlling strategies report less depression than Black children who use less controlling strategies. For White children, there was no relationship between parental control and depression. In addition, opportunities for child decision making was more important in reducing the child's depression in less dangerous environments. Increased opportunities for decision making also had negative consequences, as reflected in higher rates of acting-out behavior for White children than Black children. Recently, O'Neil and Parke (1997) demonstrated the importance of distinguishing subjective and objective views of neighborhoods. These investigators found that when mothers and fathers perceived their neighborhoods as dangerous and low in social control, they placed more restrictions on their fourth-grade children's activities. Parental perceptions were more consistently related to parenting practices than objective ratings of neighborhood quality. Moreover, maternal regulatory strategies serve as mediators of the relation between parental perceptions of neighborhood quality and social competence. Mothers who perceived problems in their neighborhood had children who were higher in social competence, but this was mediated by shifts toward more restrictive parental management strategies.

Finally, recent work also suggests that social integration of parents within the neighborhood may be an important predictor of more adequate parenting practices (Furstenberg, 1993; Steinberg, Darling, & Fletcher, 1995; Wilson, 1995). The findings of Steinberg, Darling, and Fletcher (1995) suggest, for example, that "adolescents benefit directly from the increased exchange of resources allowed by parents' social integration" (p. 456) and that parents who are more socially integrated may also be more vigilant about children's behavior, particularly when families reside in neighborhoods for which "good parenting" is the norm. On the other hand, social integration into a neighborhood characterized by a high proportion of deviant parents can have a harmful effect on adolescent outcomes. The message of these recent studies underscores a basic tenet, namely that "the family is the primary proximal setting through which community influence on children's development is transmitted" (Steinberg et al., 1995, p. 457). Although these studies suggest that neighborhoods are an important factor in accounting for children's developmental outcomes, much remains to be learned about the different mechanisms that account for neighborhood effects and how these mechanisms shift across development.

Socioeconomic Status as a Determinant of Family Socialization Strategies

There is a long history of research concerning the links between socioeconomic status and/or social class and parenting beliefs and practices (Bronfenbrenner, 1958; Davis & Havighurst, 1946). While the debate continues concerning the best strategy for measuring SES (Entwisle & Astone, 1994; Hauser, 1994), most scholars agree that SES is multiply determined and therefore the links with parenting are likely to be multiple as well. Also, in contrast to traditional assumptions that SES is a static state, recent work (e.g., Featherman, Spenner, & Tsunematsu, 1988) has clearly shown that SES is a dynamic concept. Over the course of childhood and adolescence, families change social class, and change is greatest in the youngest ages. Over 50% of U.S. children change social class prior to entering school.

While some developmentalists (e.g., Bronfenbrenner, 1958) have argued that SES is only a proxy variable, others (e.g., Featherman et al., 1988) view it as a "variable—albeit

a multifaceted complex variable—that acts as an organizing force in the daily lives of parents and children" (Hoff-Ginsberg & Tardif, 1995, p. 170). In a recent application of the developmental niche approach (Super & Harkness, 1986), Hoff-Ginsberg and Tardif (1995) argue: "In the developmental niche model, the multiple variables that define SES act jointly, as an organizing force in the lives of families and individuals. It is also true, however, that the multiple variables that define SES may act separately, each influencing different domains of parenting. The specific relations between particular components of SES are correlated. Nonetheless, a full account of the effects of SES on parenting will describe the separate contributions to parenting of the multiple variables that define SES and will also describe how the multiple variables act in concert" (p. 171). In spite of the controversies surrounding the interpretation of this variable, there are SES differences in parental socialization practices and beliefs.

Several differences are evident. First, SES differences in parenting style have been found. Lower-SES parents are more authoritarian and more punitive than higher-SES families (Kelley, Sanchez-Hucies, & Walker, 1993). Second, interaction styles differ across SES levels. First, lower-SES mothers are more controlling, restrictive, and disapproving than higher-SES mothers (Hart & Risley, 1995). Second, there are more SES differences on language measures than on nonverbal measures with higher-SES mothers being more verbal than low-SES mothers (Hart & Risley, 1995; Hoff-Ginsberg, 1991). Specifically, "higher SES mothers not only talk more, but provide object labels, sustain conversational topics longer, respond more contingently to their children's speech, and elicit more talk from their children than lower SES mothers" (Hoff-Ginsberg & Tardif, 1995, p. 177). Of interest is the fact that some SES differences are independent of race and poverty. In China, where there are relatively small differences in income across groups who vary in terms of education, Tardif (1993) found that less-educated parents used more imperatives with their toddlers than better-educated mothers. Similarly, Hess and Shipman (1965), in their early classic studies of cognitive socialization, found clear SES differences in African American lower-class and middle-class families.

Parental cognitions—ideas, beliefs, values—clearly play a major mediating role in accounting for SES differences (Luster, Rhoader, & Haas, 1989); ecological factors, such as neighborhood conditions, clearly play a role as well. One of the challenges in this area is to determine the roles of parental ideas and beliefs and the ecological conditions under which families are operating in determining parental socialization strategies. A more detailed exploration of socioeconomic circumstances is clearly a first step. Perhaps extreme circumstances such as unsafe and dangerous living conditions will override parental beliefs and play a more determining role, whereas beliefs may play a more powerful role under less extreme conditions. Specification of the types of parenting behavior that are altered by different factors is also of interest. Perhaps differences in verbal stimulation will not vary across contexts within class, but control strategies may be more responsive to environmental circumstances.

Ethnicity as a Determinant of Family Socialization Strategies

Recent cross-cultural and intracultural theories have emphasized the importance of socialization goals, values, and beliefs as organizing principles for understanding cultural variations (Super & Harkness, 1995; B. Whiting & Edwards, 1988). In contrast to the older cultural deficit models of socialization, the more recent models emphasize how ecological demands shape socialization goals, values, and practices and are viewed as adaptive strategies to meet the demands of the ecological settings.

In the recent past, cultural deficit models were popular explanations for the socialization and child outcome differences observed between ethnic minorities and Euro-Americans. Thus, for example, if Mexican Americans did poorly in school, it was because their culture allegedly discourages achievement motivation (Demos, 1962); if they lived in poverty, it was because their culture encourages fatalism (Kuvlesky & Patella, 1971); and, if they were involved in delinquent behaviors, it was because of the violent and antisocial nature of their culture (Carroll, 1980; Heller, 1966). This cultural deficit perspective was reinforced by the popularity of two-group studies that compared samples of Euro-Americans with ethnic minorities and assumed that differences between the groups were cultural in nature. In effect, ethnicity was equated with culture as if all members of an ethnic group were equally involved with the ethnic culture. An assumption inherent in many of the conclusions of these studies was that ethnic minorities needed to assimilate or become "like Euro-Americans" to correct deficiencies in their development (Ginsberg, 1972; Ramirez & Castaneda, 1974). More recently, the focus on ethnic minority families has shifted away from majority-minority differences in developmental

outcomes toward an understanding of the adaptive strategies ethnic minorities develop in response to both majority and minority cultural influences on their development. Ecological (Bronfenbrenner, 1979) and family systems perspectives (Minuchin, 1985) have been useful in explaining how the socialization goals for children derive from their parents' experiences with adaptive strategies that have helped them meet the ecological challenges faced as ethnic minorities.

One of the major problems that confront researchers who engage in cross-cultural research or research on different ethnic groups within a culture is the issue of the equivalence of measures across groups. In recognition of the fact that most standard measures of family values and functioning are developed and standardized in White middle-class populations, significant efforts have been made to develop culturally and linguistically equivalent measures. One recent innovation is the use of focus groups consisting of members of the ethnic group of interest to generate items and issues that are culturally relevant (Gomel, Tinsley, & Clark, 1995; Vázquez-García, García-Coll, Erkut, Alarcón, & Tropp, 1995). Focus groups are also being used as an integral part of the scale-construction process; they make recommendations for wording changes and identify culturally inappropriate items. Another innovation is the use of translation and back translation to ensure that the meaning is retained in the translation process. In addition, a dual-focus approach (Vázquez-García et al., 1995) is being used, by which new concepts and items that arise in the course of the translation process are generated simultaneously in both languages. Recent work by Knight and colleagues (1994) have provided models for establishing scalar equivalence of commonly used questionnaires for assessment of family functioning. Recent theoretical and statistical advances in scaling can be usefully applied to this issue of cross-group equivalency as well. Specifically, Reise and his colleagues (Flannery, Reise, & Widaman, 1995; Reise, Widaman, & Pugh, 1993) have utilized item response theory (IRT) techniques to address the equivalence of scales across groups. The utility of this approach for establishing gender equivalence (Flannery et al., 1995) and cross-cultural equivalence (e.g., China vs. the United States; Reise et al., 1993) suggests that this strategy can be used to establish scalar equivalence across different ethnic groups within our own culture as well. The thorny methodological issues in this area are by no means resolved, but the increased awareness of these problems has spurred significant recent advances (Betancourt & Lopez, 1993).

Ethnic Minorities in U.S. Society

Ethnicity refers to an individual's membership in a group sharing a common ancestral heritage based on nationality, language, and culture (Betancourt & Lopez, 1993). Psychological attachment to the group is also a dimension of ethnicity, referred to as ethnic identity (Alba, 1990). Sometimes ethnicity includes a biological or racial component (F. Barth, 1969) that is evident in the phenotype of the group members. Culture is a multidimensional construct referring to the shared values, behaviors, and beliefs of a people that are transmitted from one generation to the next. The term *minority group* implies relative powerlessness and discrimination (Greenfield & Cocking, 1994). Ethnicity, culture, and minority group status come together in the experiences of certain groups in the United States, namely American Indians, Latinos, African Americans, and Asian Americans. The histories of these groups in the United States are different, but have common features of exploitation and subordination by the cultural majority: (a) the forceful removal of American Indians from their ancestral homelands and placement in reservations; (b) Latinos' incorporation through military conquest of the southwest and ambivalent immigration policies that at times encourage immigration (the Bacero Program) and at other times deports even U.S. citizens of Mexican descent; (c) the enslavement of Africans and segregation after emancipation; and (d) ambivalent immigration policies toward Asians and their internment during wartime.

Acculturation and Assimilation in U.S. Society. The European immigrants that came to this country at the turn of this century underwent acculturation and assimilation in their transformation into Euro-Americans. Acculturation is the process of learning the language, values, and social competencies of the larger society (Ramirez, 1984). Assimilation is a possible outcome of acculturation that involves the replacement of the ancestral culture with the culture of the host society (Ramirez, 1983). As European immigrants and their descendants acculturated and eventually replaced their immigrant culture with the mainstream culture, and were in turn accepted as "Americans" by the larger society, they achieved assimilation. For European immigrants, the process of assimilation was completed by the second generation. That is, the native-born children of immigrants replaced their parents' culture with "American" culture and were accepted as "Americans." Assimilation was motivated both by the desire to become part of the mainstream and to eliminate societal prejudice and

discrimination against ethnic immigrants (A. Portes & Rumbaut, 1990). Assimilation of these European immigrants was aided by their European phenotype, which they shared with members of the larger society, who were themselves descendants of earlier English and German immigrants. Although ethnicity persists in varying degrees among assimilated Euro-Americans, it is largely "symbolic ethnicity." Alba (1990) notes that symbolic ethnicity is a vestigial attachment to a few ethnic symbols that impose little cost on everyday life.

Ethnicity and cultural variation from the Euro-American mainstream remain enduring facts of life for peoples in the United States of non-European descent, including American Indians, Latinos, African Americans, and Asian Americans. Although peoples in these groups have been in contact with Euro-Americans for centuries, and have acculturated to varying degrees, they have not assimilated. The non-European phenotype of these four groups heightens awareness of their "ethnicity" and triggers beliefs about their behaviors. Often, these beliefs are in the form of stereotypes that disparage the lives and cultures of ethnic minorities. Ethnic minorities also have stereotypes of Euro-Americans; however, because Euro-Americans are more economically and politically empowered, their stereotypes of ethnic minorities are more influential in society. In fact, individual members of ethnic minority groups may even internalize Euro-Americans' stereotypes of ethnic minorities (Buriel & Vasquez, 1982), which then yield self-fulfilling prophecies about the behavior of ethnic minorities.

The sum of these experiences has influenced the individual and group beliefs about what it means to be a member of an ethnic minority group in the United States. Ethnic minority status has potent meaning for persons in the group because of the difficulties and conflicting developmental challenges group members have experienced in attempting to coexist with the Euro-American culture (Harrison et al., 1990).

Minority Child Socialization

As with most children, socialization of ethnic minority children usually takes place in a family setting that includes adult caregivers. These adult caregivers are usually biological parents but may also include grandparents, relatives, godparents, and other adults who are not biologically related to the children. In addition to ensuring children's physical health and survival, parents attempt to inculcate in children values and behaviors that help them adapt to their environment as it is perceived by the parents. The parents' individual history of interaction with the larger sociocultural context, including their awareness of their ethnic group's history within the larger society, affects the manner in which they socialize their children. An important dimension of socialization in many ethnic minority families is teaching children how to interact effectively in dual cultural contexts: the context of their ethnic group and the context of the larger Euro-American society (Boykin & Toms, 1985). Harrison et al. (1990) have adopted an ecological orientation to explain the diverse environmental influences that contribute to the socialization of ethnic minority children. They conceptualize the socialization of ethnic minority children in terms of the interconnectedness between the status of ethnic minority families, adaptive strategies, socialization goals, and child outcomes. Family status has to do with the socioeconomic resources available to ethnic group members such as housing, employment, health care, and education. Despite considerable within-group diversity in socioeconomic status, a growing number of ethnic minority children live in poverty. Adaptive strategies are the cultural patterns that promote the survival and well-being of group members. Some of these cultural patterns are adaptations of the original ethnic culture to life circumstances in the United States. For instance, family extendedness expresses itself in the mobilization of extended family in response to child care needs. Other cultural patterns may arise as a result of coping with the conflicting behavioral demands of being an ethnic minority in a predominately Euro-American society. Thus, biculturalism, which is the simultaneous adoption of two cultural orientations, arose originally in response to conflicting cultural demands but is now part of what constitutes the ethnic minority culture. Biculturalism, for example, characterizes the lives of many Mexican Americans and other ethnic minorities (LaFromboise, Coleman, & Gerton, 1993). In addition to family extendedness and biculturalism, other adaptive strategies discussed by Harrison et al. (1990) include role flexibilities and ancestral worldviews. Emerging out of the adaptive strategies of adults are the socialization goals that they endeavor to inculcate in children to help them meet the ecological challenges they will face as ethnic minorities in a class- and race-conscious society. Ethnic pride and interdependence are two important socialization goals that enable ethnic minority children to function competently as members of both their minority culture and the larger society (Harrison et al., 1990). Ethnic pride imparts a sense of personal self-worth in the face of

societal prejudice and discrimination (Walker, Taylor, McElroy, Phillip, & Wilson, 1995). Interdependence sustains effective intergroup relations that strengthen ethnic group solidarity (Staples & Johnson, 1993).

Ethnic Minority Families

Taken as a whole, ethnic minority families constitute the fastest growing segment of the U.S. population. According to H. McAdoo (1993), if present trends in immigration and birthrates continue until the end of the twentieth century, the Asian American population will increase by 22%, the Latino population by 21%, the African American population by 12%, and the Euro-American population by only 2%. These demographic shifts will inevitably change the way we think about families as well as our research priorities in areas of child socialization.

Two groups, Latinos and Asian Americans, warrant special attention due to their rapidly increasing numbers and immigrant backgrounds which pose special challenges to researchers. Between 1980 and 1990, the Asian American population nearly doubled in size, growing from 3.5 million to 6.5 million. As the fastest growing ethnic group in the country, it is estimated that by the year 2000, Asian Americans will number about 10 million. Also by the year 2000, Latinos will replace African Americans as the nation's largest ethnic minority group, and number about 35 million. The number of Latino and Asian American families will grow, in large measure, due to immigration, both documented and undocumented. As immigrant groups, Latinos and Asian Americans share common characteristics, including diverse subpopulations with distinct histories, non-English native languages, and a relatively young age. Both groups also include economic immigrants who seek a better quality of life in this country, and political immigrants who seek refuge from persecution in their countries of origin. Owing to their different motivations for immigrating to this country, economic and political immigrants may have different adaptation strategies that influence their socialization goals for children. For example, political immigrants may expect to return to their countries of origin when conditions there improve and consequently may resist acculturating influences more than economic immigrants (Rumbaut, 1995).

The continual influx of Latino and Asian immigrants into this country means that these two ethnic groups will be constantly characterized by within-group differences in generational status and degree of acculturation. First-generation immigrant parents generally acculturate more slowly than their children (Szapocznik & Kurtines, 1980), particularly after the onset of children's schooling. Yet, despite the more rapid acculturation of children in immigrant families, the socialization of these children is heavily influenced by the socialization goals of their parents' culture and also the adaptive strategies developed by immigrants to survive in this country. As the children of immigrants grow and start their own families, their children, the third generation, are socialized in family ecologies that are socioculturally distinct from the ecologies of their parents. The generational status of parents and children contributes to variations in the sociocultural ecologies of families that have implications for child rearing (Buriel, 1993a). The importance of generational status to diversity in family ecologies is illustrated with an example using Mexican Americans, the largest immigrant group in the United States.

Generational Differences in Family Ecologies. The first generation includes those persons born in Mexico who later immigrated to the United States. Some of these persons immigrate as single young adults or as married couples; others are brought to this country as young children by their parents. It is not uncommon for parents to immigrate with only some of their children, leaving the other children in Mexico under the care of relatives. As the parents' economic condition improves, children in Mexico are brought to the United States. Under these circumstances, children often experience multiple socializing influences in both Mexico and the United States. At the time of immigration, adults have usually completed the extent of their lifetime formal education in Mexico, seven years on average (Bean, Chapa, Berg, & Sowards, 1994), which is one year over compulsory education in Mexico. School-age immigrant children have usually begun their schooling in Mexico and then continue it in this country after immigration. Preschool immigrant children begin and complete their schooling in the United States. Family income is typically low in the first generation due to parents' lower education and limited knowledge of English. In the first six to eight years after immigration, it is not uncommon for immigrants to live with families of relatives or friends (Blank, 1993) who assist parents with child care. After eight years, the rate of immigrant families living in single-family households is about 75%, which is the same as for U.S. Mexican Americans (Blank, 1993). First-generation children are socialized in home environments influenced by immigrant Mexican culture, which includes elements of

Mexican culture as well as the adaptive strategies parents associate with the immigrant experience that parents convert into socialization goals (Buriel, 1993a; Delgado-Gaitan, 1994). Elements of Mexican cultural socialization include familism, respect for adults, and interdependence among family and ethnic group members (Delgado-Gaitan, 1994; Rueschenberg & Buriel, 1989; Sabogal et al., 1987). Socialization goals related to the immigrant experience are self-reliance (Buriel, 1993a) and biculturalism (Buriel, 1993b). Immigrant parents and their children both prefer a "Mexican" ethnic identity (Buriel & Cardoza, 1993) and use Spanish as their primary home language. The parents' and other family members' exposure to English often comes through children's participation in the U.S. schooling system. As a result, many immigrant children serve as interpreters for their parents, which means they are often given adultlike responsibility when acting as the family's representative to the outside English-speaking world. Because these children interpret both the language and culture of the larger society, they are referred to as "cultural brokers" (Buriel & DeMent, 1993; Buriel, DeMent, & Chavez, 1995). Child cultural brokers play an important role in helping immigrant families adapt and survive in a new environment. There are, however, extraordinary pressures and developmental challenges associated with the role of being a child cultural broker. For this reason, child cultural brokers will be discussed in more detail later in this chapter.

Generally speaking, the second generation represents the U.S.-born children of immigrant parents. The family environments of second-generation children are in many ways similar to those of their first-generation peers, owing to the foreign-born status of their parents. There are, however, some important differences between the two generations that are reflected in the sociocultural characteristics of the family. For example, in some cases the immigrant parents of second-generation children came to the United States as single young adults who later became partners in generationally endogamous marriages (Murguia, 1982). As a result they have lived longer in the United States. In those cases where parents came from Mexico as young children, they may have attended U.S. schools for some or all of their education. For these reasons, the family incomes of second-generation children are higher than their peers' in the preceding generation. Cultural synergisms are most apparent in the families of second-generation children. Thus, while Spanish is usually the native language of second-generation children, English becomes their dominant language after the onset of schooling. However, Spanish continues as the primary language of parents, which creates a strong motivation for the development of bilingualism. Parents encourage the learning of English but also stress the retention of Spanish, as that is the language used to demonstrate respect to adults. Retention of Spanish may therefore help preserve parental authority during the more rapid acculturation of children. Socialization of second-generation children is similar to that of the first generation, although the outcomes are attenuated by prolonged exposure to Euro-American culture (Buriel, 1993a). For example, the longer families live in the United States, the more socialization practices and child behaviors shift in an individualistic direction, particularly in the area of critical thinking (Delgado-Gaitan, 1994). In the area of ethnic identity, foreign-born parents prefer a "Mexican" identity, but their second-generation children prefer either a "Mexican American" or "Chicano" identity (Buriel & Cardoza, 1993).

The third generation refers collectively to all persons of Mexican descent whose parents were born in the United States. This includes persons in the fourth and subsequent generations whose grandparents and great-grandparents were born in this country. Due to immigration and birthrate differences between generations, third-generation children are in the minority within the Mexican American population and are expected to remain in that position for the next half century (Edmonston & Passel, 1994). The third generation is distinguished from the two previous generations by the absence of any direct parental links to Mexico involving immigration. Consequently, socialization goals derived from immigrant adaptation strategies are not a direct part of the socialization experiences of third-generation children (Buriel, 1993a). Nevertheless, since many members of the third generation continue living in ethnic neighborhoods (barrios) heavily populated by immigrants, socialization practices still retain some immigrant influences. For example, familism, or the expectation of support from family members, continues as a socialization goal into later generations (Keefe & Padilla, 1987), even after controlling for socioeconomic status (Sabogal et al., 1987). Persons in the third generation are also socialized in homes where all family members are U.S. citizens, where English is the primary language of parents and children (Lopez, 1982), where parental schooling has taken place exclusively in the United States, and where children and parents express a "Mexican American" ethnic identity (Buriel & Cardoza, 1993). Laosa (1982) theorizes that U.S. schooling alters the child-rearing practices of Mexican American parents. Mothers with less education, who are likely to be immigrants, use more modeling to instruct children, whereas mothers with more schooling, who are likely to be native-born, use more inquiry and praise to instruct children. According to Laosa (1982), this shift in maternal teaching style occurs because more highly schooled mothers increasingly take on the teaching style of the school, which emphasizes inquiry and praise. Buriel (1993a) also found that among parents of third-generation children, parental schooling was associated with a child-rearing style involving more support, control, and equality. Divorce is more common among parents of third-generation children, which has implications for child socialization (Oropesa & Landale, 1995). Teacher ratings of Mexican American children indicate more school maladjustment in boys from single-parent (mothers only) homes than in boys from two-parent homes or in girls of either family type (LeCorgne & Laosa, 1976). Father absence may be more deleterious for boys in third-generation families because it represents the loss of a disciplinarian at a time when boys are most susceptible to negative peer pressures such as gangs. Although family incomes are higher in the third generation, schooling outcomes are lower than in the previous generation. Second-generation children complete more years of schooling and have higher educational aspirations than their third-generation peers (Bean et al., 1994; Buriel, 1987, 1994). Kao and Tienda (1995) have also documented lower educational achievement in third-generation Asian Americans relative to their first- and second-generation peers.

It is apparent that generational status introduces sociocultural variations into family ecologies that have important implications for the socialization of children and their developmental outcomes. An adequate study of Latino and Asian American socialization must take into account generation and acculturation and their influence on human development. In addition, the developmental and socialization implications associated with generation and acculturation may also have relevance for other U.S. ethnic minorities not typically included in the category of immigrants. Thus, African American families moving from the ghetto into a predominately Euro-American neighborhood may describe their experiences in such terms as "the first generation of their family to live around mostly White people" or "having to adapt or acculturate to an all-White environment." The same set of experiences may also hold true for American Indian families moving off the reservation to live in a mostly non-Indian environment or for American

Indian children attending government boarding schools far from their reservation (Garcia-Coll, Meyer, & Brillon, 1995).

For Latinos and Asian Americans, acculturation across generations is not a uniform process. Within each generation there is considerable diversity in terms of individuals' involvement with both the native culture and Euro-American culture. In addition, acculturation is not a unidirectional process such that movement toward Euro-American culture is necessarily associated with a corresponding loss of the native culture. Ecological variables such as degree of societal discrimination, educational and employment opportunities, and opportunities to participate in the native culture can all contribute to variations in both the rate and direction of acculturation across generations. Changes in any of these environmental systems (Bronfenbrenner, 1986) can affect the sociocultural nature of family ecologies and impact on the cultural socialization of children.

Bicultural Adaptation

For Mexican Americans, the proximity of Mexico and the fact that the southwestern United States was once a part of Mexico create many opportunities for members of this group to participate in their native culture. For Latinos and Asian Americans, a high rate of immigration resulting in densely populated ethnic communities also creates powerful environmental influences for retention of many aspects of the native cultures. Finally, for all ethnic minorities, a non-European phenotype triggers many societal stereotypes and prejudices that limit access to the larger society and its institutions (Buriel, 1994; Harrison, Serafica, & McAdoo, 1990). The combination of all these environmental and ethnic group influences differentially operate within and between ethnic minority groups, giving rise to adaptation strategies that do not conform to the assimilationist orientation of European immigrants and their descendants. Instead, many ethnic minority group members strive for a bicultural orientation that allows for acculturation to Euro-American culture while simultaneously retaining aspects of the native culture. This bidirectional adaptation strategy permits individuals to meet the dual cultural expectations that characterize the lives of ethnic minorities as they move in and out of minority and majority cultural environments. The bicultural person learns to function optimally in more than one cultural context and to switch repertoires of behavior appropriately and adaptively as called for by the situation (Harrison et al., 1990). Although all ethnic minority groups have expressed biculturalism in some form as an

important adaptive strategy (Harrison et al., 1990), the majority of research has focused on immigrant groups, especially Mexican Americans (Keefe & Padilla, 1987; LaFromboise et al., 1993).

Using Mexican Americans as an example, Figure 8.6 illustrates a bidirectional model of cultural adaptation. This bidirectional model posits four acculturation adaptation styles for Mexican immigrants and their descendants, depending upon their involvement with both Mexican immigrant culture and Euro-American culture. The four acculturation styles are the bicultural orientation, the Mexican orientation, the marginal orientation, and the Euro-American orientation. Ramirez (1983) has defined biculturalism as the simultaneous adoption of the language, values, and social competencies of two cultures. Since culture is multidimensional in nature, involvement in either culture can vary along different dimensions and at different rates. Cultural involvement is represented on a scale of 1 to 5. Thus, persons expressing a bicultural orientation are those above 3 on both Mexican and Euro-American culture. The Mexican orientation is characterized by those individuals who are primarily involved in Mexican culture. This category usually includes many adult recent immigrants, as well as a few later-generation persons living in rural areas. Also included in this category are the elderly

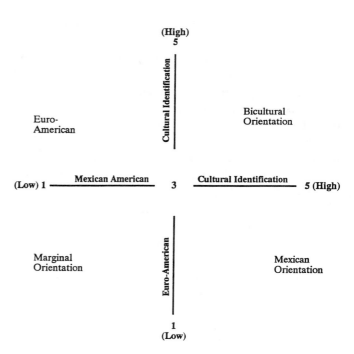

Figure 8.6   Bidirectional model of acculturation.

parents of immigrants who are brought to this country to live with the families of their adult children after the children become financially stable. For these elderly persons, a Mexican orientation seems well suited to their life experiences, which, at their stage in life, revolve mostly around family and community rather than schooling and the labor market. The marginal orientation includes a minority of individuals who have become "deculturated" (Berry, 1980; Buriel, 1984) from their ancestral culture and simultaneously alienated from the larger Euro-American society. Deculturation evolves from societal denigration of the ethnic group and the internalization of society's stereotypes of Mexican Americans (Buriel, 1984). Ogbu's (1987) description of Mexican Americans (as well as American Indians and African Americans) as "caste-like" minorities is probably accurate only for the minority of individuals who adopt a marginal orientation. For example, Vigil (1988) has described hard-core Mexican American gang members in terms characteristic of the marginal orientation. Those who are not gang members, on the other hand, are described as expressing either a traditional or bicultural orientation. Individuals in the Euro-American quadrant of the bidirectional model are those who are primarily involved and identified with Euro-American culture; that is, their preference for friends, language, and social activities are those characteristic of Euro-American culture.

To date, the majority of empirical research on acculturation and biculturalism has been done with adult and adolescent samples. A small but growing body of research in this area indicates that ethnic minorities who develop bicultural competencies have better physical and psychological health than those who do not (Buriel & Saenz, 1980; LaFromboise et al., 1993). Gutierrez and Sameroff (1990) have shown that mothers' biculturalism is positively associated with the complexity of their concepts about children's development (Sameroff & Fiel, 1985). They found that more acculturated and more bicultural mothers scored higher in their concepts of development. In addition, the mothers who were the most bicultural had the highest concept of development scores when compared to the other Mexican American mothers and a sample of highly acculturated Euro-American mothers. They concluded that bicultural mothers have insights into two cultures and realize that the child development beliefs associated with each culture are appropriate in different contexts within the same society. LaFromboise et al. (1993) connect biculturalism to self-efficacy theory (Bandura, 1977) by using the term *bicultural efficacy* to describe the belief, or confidence,

that one can live effectively, and in a satisfying manner, within two cultural groups without compromising one's sense of cultural identity.

Child Cultural Brokers

Most immigrant parents do not speak English, many live in communities where little English is spoken, and they rely on their children to translate for them. "With responsibility as interpreters of the new culture and language, immigrant children are often in a position with no one to translate or interpret for them. Traditional intergenerational authority relationships change and the child also becomes very involved in the worries and concerns of the family, such as hassles with landlords, arranging for medical care, and dealing with the legal system" (Olsen & Chen, 1988, p. 31). Because these children of immigrants represent the link between their parents' culture and Euro-American society, they are referred to here as cultural brokers.

To date, the unique situation of children as cultural brokers has not been investigated. Child cultural brokers are unique because in addition to the stress related to their own acculturation, they experience additional stressors arising from their role as mediators between their parents and U.S. society. In public, child cultural brokers act with adult authority on behalf of their parents, but at home they are expected to behave as children and show deference and respect to parents. These conflicting expectations and responsibilities represent a form of role strain (Pearlin, 1983) that may raise children's anxiety to debilitating levels and lower their general well-being.

Whether children's brokering role promotes or undermines their long-term adjustment remains to be seen. However, family background characteristics, such as socioeconomic status, parents' English proficiency, and family support, are likely to moderate the stress associated with the brokering role. In addition, individual characteristics of children, such as their level of self-esteem, biculturalism, and academic self-confidence, are likely to influence adjustment to their brokering role.

The unique situation of child cultural brokers has important implications for their socioemotional development. The experience of acting on behalf of parents in negotiations with adult agents of U.S. society may promote self-efficacy for managing social interactions. Self-efficacy research with Latinos and Asian Americans (Solberg, O'Brien, Villareal, Kennel, & Davis, 1993) has not dealt with children nor the effects of acculturation. Child cultural brokers are also likely to develop insight and sensitivity to parental roles due to the often personal nature of the situations they broker. The affective bond between parent and child is thus likely to be strengthened for children who serve as cultural brokers. Finally, child cultural brokers not only represent their parents to adults outside the family, they also transmit the messages of those outsiders to their parents. In brokering situations, children act as adults in interactions with their parents, which often gives rise to role reversals involving the transmission of information. That is, child cultural brokers must sometimes "teach" parents things about the new culture while still demonstrating deference and respect consistent with their status as children. Child cultural brokers must assume a higher-status teaching role without causing parents to lose face in public or in the family. The instructional demands inherent in brokering are thus likely to promote instructional strategies by children that achieve the transmission of information to adults without causing embarrassment to parents.

On a more global level, these children represent their parents' link to mainstream society; often they must negotiate economic, legal, and health-related transactions between their parents and societal institutions (e.g., explaining tax forms, filling out insurance claims, and applying for health care benefits; Buriel & DeMent, 1993). In effect, these children serve to teach their parents about U.S. culture and perform many duties ordinarily reserved for adults in this society.

Socialization Concerns in Ethnic Minority Families

African American Families. Today, approximately 96% of all African Americans are descendants of slaves (Reed, 1982) who exhibited extraordinary resiliency to survive in this country without benefit of any human rights. The socially disruptive effects of slavery were felt in all spheres of life, including family formation and functioning. According to M. Wilson (1992), the focus on African American family research has recently shifted from a pathological/disorganizational model to a strength/resilient model. This shift is characterized by (a) an examination of African American families within an African American sociocultural context, (b) a consideration of the role of grandmothers and other extended family members in child-rearing and child development activities, and (c) an analysis of the presence of fathers rather than their absence within the family.

Nobles, Goddard, Cavil, and George (1987) have defined the African American family as follows: "The African American family is a term used to characterize a group of people who are biologically and spiritually bonded or connected and whose members' relations to each other and the outside world are governed by a particular set of cultural beliefs, historical experiences and behavioral practices" (p. 22). Sudarkasa (1993) notes that to understand families, households, and socialization of children among African Americans, it is important to understand that these groupings evolved from African family structure in which coresidential families were the norm. Sudarkasa suggests that the type and quality of adaptations to slavery and life in America were perhaps facilitated by the West African heritage of African Americans. From her studies of West African culture, she contends that African extended-family traditions may have proved useful in preserving family ties and for the socialization of children in the face of the disruptive aspects of slavery and its aftermath. Greenfield and Cocking (1994) have also argued that more attention needs to be paid to the positive heritage that ethnic minority socialization practices owe to their culture of origin. Characteristics of African American extended-kin systems noted most frequently in the literature include: (a) a high degree of geographical propinquity; (b) a strong sense of family and familial obligation; (c) fluidity of household boundaries, with great willingness to absorb relatives, both real and fictive; (d) frequent interaction with relatives; (e) frequent extended-family get-togethers for special occasions and holidays; and (f) a system of mutual aid (Harrison et al., 1990; Hatchett & Jackson, 1993). Some might surmise that extended-kin behavior among African Americans is a response to poverty rather than an authentic cultural characteristic of the group. However, there is evidence (H. McAdoo, 1978) that higher-SES African Americans have greater activity within kin networks than their lower-SES counterparts. This suggests that higher-SES African Americans continue to derive physical and psychological benefits from these behaviors. Boykin (1983; Boykin & Toms, 1985) has also noted similarities between the West African traditions of spirituality, harmony, affect, and communalism and African American culture.

The influence of the extended family among African Americans is important because of the large number of female-headed households that require child-rearing assistance and economic support (M. Wilson, 1992). The proportion of African American households with elderly heads that have young family members is also high, about one in three families (Pearson, Hunter, Ensminger, & Kellam, 1990). When coupled with the fact that many African American grandparents live in close proximity to their married children and families, it is obvious that African American grandparents have many opportunities to influence the development of their grandchildren. Pearson et al. (1990) found that in multigenerational households, mothers were the primary caregivers, followed by grandmothers and then fathers. Grandmothers also showed more supportive behaviors in mother/grandmother families than in mother/father/grandmother families. In mother-absent families, grandmothers were more involved in control and punishment of children. Tolson and Wilson (1990) found that the presence of grandmothers in African American families increases the moral-religious emphasis in the household. Nobles et al. (1987) note that such religious emphasis helps to sustain the African American family and reinforce the sense of family and family solidarity. While some research suggests that children are better adjusted in grandmother households (Staples & Johnson, 1993), other research suggests that intergenerational conflict may offset the positive effects of grandmother presence.

Male-present households were the norm in poor African American communities in the period between 1880 and 1925 (Staples & Johnson, 1993). Until the 1980s, most African American families included two parents; today, approximately 42% of all African American children live in two-parent families (U.S. Census Bureau, 1994). Despite the statistical norm of two-parent families until recently, much of the research on African American fathers focused either on fathers' absence or their maladaptive responses to familial roles (Bowman, 1993). Now, a small but growing body of research is beginning to focus on African American husband-fathers who remain with their families. Bowman (1993) notes that researchers are beginning to document the high level of involvement among African American husband-fathers in child rearing, family decision making, and the economic provider role. J. McAdoo (1993) notes that across several studies, African American spouses share equally in the major decisions in the family. From an exchange theory perspective, cooperation in decision making has been essential because in most families both spouses have had to work to overcome the lower wages earned by the husband (J. McAdoo, 1993).

Previous research suggests that persistent economic marginality among African American fathers may lessen their perceptions of the quality of family life and contribute to their separation from their families (Farley & Allen, 1987; W. Wilson, 1987). Bowman (1993) has adopted a role strain model to investigate how African American males perceive economic marginality and how

cultural resources facilitate adaptive modes of coping. He has shown that subjective cultural strengths, which are transmitted across generations, appear to reduce harmful effects of provider role barriers among husband-fathers and to facilitate adaptive coping. In particular, religious beliefs appear to be strongly associated with effective coping. Bowman also found that in his national sample, African American husband-fathers were much more likely to have jobs (75%) than unmarried fathers (58%). Among African American fathers, joblessness appears to be a major factor distinguishing the growing numbers of unmarried fathers from traditional husband-fathers.

When African American fathers from working-class backgrounds discipline children, the discipline is more often physical than verbal and delivered in accordance to the transgression's consequences rather than the child's intent (Staples & Johnson, 1993). Although these parents may use physical discipline, they rarely couple this with withdrawal of love from children, which may eliminate some of the anxiety and resentment associated with this disciplinary method. Because African American socialization stresses obedience to adults and may involve physical discipline, parents have often been described as harsh, rigid, and strict (P. Portes, Dunham, & Williams, 1986). The disciplinary style of African American parents is sometimes referred to as being parent-centered rather than child-centered because it does not primarily take into account the desires of the child (Kelley, Power, & Wimbush, 1992). These descriptions of African American parents and their disciplinary style fail to take into account the settings in which parents must raise children and the adaptive value connected to their parent-centered approach to child rearing. Growing up in dangerous neighborhoods brings with it greater risks for involvement in antisocial behavior, which can have serious personal consequences, whether one is a victim or a perpetrator. Under these circumstances, strict obedience to parental authority is an adaptive strategy that parents may endeavor to maintain through physical discipline (Kelley et al., 1992). This disciplinary method may also serve to impress upon children the importance of following rules in society and the consequences incurred from breaking those rules when one is a member of an ethnic or racial group that is unfairly stereotyped as violent (Willis, 1992). Kelley and her colleagues (Kelley et al., 1992; Kelley, Sanchez-Hucles, & Walker, 1993) note, however, that there is considerable diversity in the disciplinary methods used by African American parents. Younger mothers and mothers raising their children alone use more physical discipline. Mothers with less education use more restrictive disciplinary practices that include insensitivity, inflexibility, and inconsistent parental behavior. Mothers who are more involved in organized religion also express more child-oriented disciplinary attitudes (Kelley et al., 1992; Kelley et al., 1993).

An important socialization goal of many ethnic minority parents is fostering a sense of ethnic pride in children (Harrison et al., 1990). Some parents believe that in order for their children to successfully confront the hostile social environment they will encounter as African Americans, it is necessary to teach them to be comfortable with their Blackness (Harrison, 1985; Peters, 1985). Bowman and Howard's (1985) study of a national sample of African American three-generational families indicated that the manner in which parents oriented their children toward racial barriers was a significant element in children's motivation, achievement, and prospects for upward mobility. Parents of successful children emphasized ethnic pride, self-development, awareness of racial barriers, and egalitarianism in their socialization practices. Using a national sample, Thornton, Chatters, Taylor, and Allen (1990) also report that two out of three African American parents indicate that they either spoke or acted in a manner intended to racially socialize children. African American parents envisioned racial socialization as involving messages regarding their experiences as minority group members, themes emphasizing individual character and goals, and information related to African American cultural heritage. In addition, Thorton et al. found that (a) older parents were more likely than younger parents to view racial socialization information as a necessary element of the socialization process; (b) that mothers were more likely than fathers to educate children about race; (c) that never-married parents, both women and men, were less likely than their married counterparts to racially socialize their children; (d) that fathers residing in the Northeast were more likely than those living in the South to racially socialize children; and (e) that mothers living in racially integrated neighborhoods were more likely to socialize their children to racial matters than were mothers living in all–African American communities.

American Indian Families. At one time in the recent past American Indians were known as the "Vanishing Americans." Since 1940, however, the American Indian population has increased at every census count. The Indian population was 345,000 in 1940, but in 1990 numbered nearly 2,000,000 American Indians and Alaska Natives

(Trimble & Medicine, 1993). American Indians are a socioculturally diverse group consisting of over 450 distinct tribal units who speak over 100 different languages (Trimble & Medicine, 1993). Typically, American Indians prefer their tribal designation over the term American Indian (Burgess, 1980). The Navajo of New Mexico and Arizona is the largest tribe, with more than 170,000 members. Other large tribes include the Cherokee, Sioux, and Chippewa, as well as the Aleuts and Eskimos.

Today, approximately 70% of American Indians live off reservations (Banks, 1991), mostly in urban areas. For example, Los Angeles, California, has the largest concentration of American Indians in the United States. Despite this, most research on American Indians focuses on those living on reservations. Due to cultural differences and discrimination, many Indians have a difficult time adjusting to life in urban areas. For this reason, many reservation Indians who migrate to urban areas tend to settle in cities and towns near reservations and to maintain contact with family on the reservation (Banks, 1991). Such living arrangements close to the reservation are more conducive to the development of biculturalism than when Indians live in large urban areas further removed from reservations. Contact with Euro-Americans and other cultural groups such as Latinos have introduced changes in traditional Indian values and behaviors. Consequently, it is necessary to consider level of acculturation in research involving American Indians. Joe (1994) notes that most studies with American Indians simply state that the sample was made up of Navajo, Sioux, or members of some other tribe, without reference to the study participants' level of acculturation.

American Indian families may be characterized as a collective cooperative social network that extends from the mother and father union to the extended family and ultimately the community and tribe (Burgess, 1980). American Indian tribes are resilient in that they have withstood attempts at extermination, removal from their traditional lands, extreme poverty, removal of their children to boarding schools, loss of self governance, and assimilationist policies aimed at destroying Indian languages, traditions, dress, religions, and occupations (Harjo, 1993). A strong extended-family system and tribal identity characterizes many urban and rural American Indian families (Harrison et al., 1990). Extended-family systems have helped American Indians cope with adversity both on and off the reservation. American Indian patterns of extended family include several households representing significant relatives that give rise to village-like characteristics even in urban areas.

In such families, grandparents retain an official and symbolic leadership role. Children seek daily contact with grandparents and grandparents monitor children's behavior and have a voice in child rearing (Lum, 1986). Despite the many social problems faced by American Indian families, such as poverty, alcoholism, accidents, and adolescent suicide, the majority are two-parent families. In 1980, 7 out of 10 American Indian families included married couples living together (Banks, 1991).

Although there are variations among tribes in their value orientations, there are nevertheless some common themes across many groups that can be characterized as traditional American Indian values. These include (a) present-time orientation—a primary concern for the present and acceptance of time as fluid and not segmented; (b) respect for elders—with age comes experience that is transmitted as knowledge that is essential for group survival and harmony in life; (c) identity with the group—self-awareness has meaning only within the context of the family and tribe so that the interests of the family and tribe are the same as one's own self-interest; (d) cooperation and partnership—among the Pueblo Indians a common saying is "Help each other so the burden won't be so heavy" (Suina & Smolikin, 1994, p. 121); the concept of partnership and sharing is stressed as the desirable way of conducting most activities; and (e) living in harmony with nature—nature, like time, is indivisible, and the person is an integral part of the flow of nature and time.

Traditional American Indian values constitute a worldview that is fundamentally different from Western assumptions about the "proper" relationships among people, the environment, and time. Trimble and Medicine (1993) argue that in its present form, psychology cannot properly describe and explain traditional-oriented American Indian affective and behavioral patterns. A traditional-oriented American Indian worldview represents an "indigenous psychology" (Kim & Berry, 1993; Ramirez, 1983) that can only be understood when examined from ecological and sociohistorical perspectives that do not assume the superiority of a Western worldview.

Within traditional-oriented Indian culture, the uses of knowledge and learning are prescribed to help individuals live fulfilling lives as fully integrated members of the family and tribe. For example, among the Navajo, knowledge is organized around three life goals. First there is knowledge that lasts throughout one's lifetime and has to do with language, kinship, religion, customs, values, beliefs, and the purpose of life (Joe, 1994). This kind of knowledge is usually taught informally and using a variety of sources. Among the Pueblo Indians, teaching and learning at this stage is thought to be the responsibility of all Pueblo members (Suina & Smolkin, 1994). The second area of knowledge involves learning an occupation or the means to making a living. This learning often requires an apprenticeship and involves a narrower range of teaching experts such as herders, weavers, and hunters. Learning is through listening, watching, and doing, with a strong emphasis placed on modeling and private practicing of the emerging skill (Suina & Smolkin, 1994). At this stage, children also learn the appropriate context for the use of their knowledge. The person learns how one's knowledge is enmeshed with the history, culture, and survival goals of the tribe. The third category of knowledge is the most restrictive because it is reserved for those interested in becoming healers and religious leaders (Joe, 1994). These are lifetime commitments involving specialized instruction that is usually in addition to learning other means of livelihood.

The influence of traditional-oriented Indian culture on child rearing varies from tribe to tribe and from family to family depending on their contact with Euro-American society. The establishment of boarding schools for American Indian children, far removed from the reservation, was a deliberate attempt to destroy traditional child-rearing practices (Harjo, 1993). Between 1890 and 1920, children were forcibly removed from their families for up to 12 years, and parents and relatives were not allowed to visit children during the school year (Harjo, 1993). From 1920 to the 1970s, boarding schools were still a usual part of the childhood and adolescent experience of most Indian children. Among the many deleterious effects of boarding schools were the deprivation of children from adult parenting models and an undermining of parental authority. Today most Indian grandparents and parents are products of government boarding schools, which impacts on the quality of their parenting. Child abuse, particularly in the form of neglect, is cited as a major reason for the removal of Indian children from their families and tribes. As recently as 1980, Indian children were placed out of homes at a rate five times higher than other children (Harjo, 1993).

According to Berlin (1987), a major concern of some tribes is the infant- and child-rearing abilities of adolescents, which are critical for the tribes' survival. Greater tribal self-determination in the areas of education (the Indian Self-Determination and Education Assistance Act of 1975), family life (the Indian Child Welfare Act of 1978), and culture (the American Indian Religious Freedom Act of 1978) have made it possible for some Indian tribes and families to recover traditional child-rearing practices. The socialization goal is to prepare children to be proud and competent members of an integrated family and tribal system, and to selectively adopt those aspects of Euro-American culture that can contribute to the well-being of the group (Berlin, 1987).

Asian American Families. The Asian American population includes people from 28 Asian countries or ethnic groups (Takanishi, 1994). It is a very diverse group in terms of languages, cultures, generations in the United States, and reasons for immigrating to the United States. The first Asian immigrants came from China in the 1840s. However, due to discriminatory immigration policies against Asians, the number of Asian Americans remained low until recent times. The growth of the Asian American population in recent years has been accompanied by shifts in ethnicity and national origin. Before 1970, Japanese Americans were the largest Asian ethnic group (41%), followed by Chinese (30%) and Filipinos (24%). By 1990, the three largest Asian groups in the United States no longer included Japanese Americans. Instead, the three largest groups are Chinese (24%), Filipino (20%), and Indo-Chinese (Vietnamese, Cambodian, Hmong, and Laotian, totaling over 14%; S. Lee & Edmonston, 1994).

Historically, Japanese, Chinese, and Filipino immigrants came to the United States primarily to improve their economic status. However, Indo-Chinese have arrived primarily as political immigrants or refugees. At the end of the Vietnam War in 1975, 130,000 refugees found asylum in the United States. Beginning in 1978, a massive flow of Indo-Chinese refugees (boat people or second wave) occurred, abruptly ending in 1992 (Rumbaut, 1995). Unlike economic immigrants, political immigrants leave their homelands involuntarily. Usually refugees suffer more psychological problems and have a more difficult time adjusting to life in the United States than economic immigrants. In addition, they tend to experience more undesirable change in the process of acculturation, a greater threat of danger, and a decreasing sense of control over their lives (Rumbaut, 1991).

Little empirical research exists on the structure and process of Asian American families. Among the studies in this area, most have sampled from Chinese and Japanese American populations. Often, examination of Asian American families is for the purpose of identifying the family characteristics that contribute to children's academic performance. Consequently, there is very little research on the

adaptive strategies and socialization goals of Asian American parents that bears on the socioemotional development of children. Discussions of Asian American families usually invoke Confucian principles to explain family structure and roles. Confucius developed a hierarchy defining one's role, duties, and moral obligations within the state. This hierarchical structure is also applied to the family and each member's role is dictated by age and gender. Typically Asian American families are seen as patriarchal, with the father maintaining authority and emotional distance from other members (Ho, 1986; Wong, 1988, 1995). Wives are subordinate to their husbands, but in their role as mothers they have considerable authority and autonomy in child rearing. Traditionally, the family exerts control over family members, who are taught to place family needs before individual needs. Children show obedience and loyalty to their parents and, especially in the case of male children, are expected to take care of elderly parents (filial piety). Confucian influences on family life are stronger in some Asian American populations (e.g., Chinese and Vietnamese) than others (e.g., Japanese) due to differences in immigration patterns and degree of Westernization of the country of origin. Length of U.S. residence and acculturation also contribute to extensive within-group differences in family structure and roles. Kibria (1993) found that large Vietnamese families varying in age and gender fared better economically than smaller nuclear families. The larger extended family enabled households to connect to a variety of social and economic resources. In Vietnamese families, the kin group is seen as more important than the individual. This perspective has its source in Confucian principles, especially ancestor worship (Kibria, 1993). Ancestor worship for Vietnamese Americans consists of devotion in caring for an altar containing pictures of deceased family members and praying at ritually prescribed times (C. Chao, 1992). This act affirms the sacredness, unity, and timelessness of the kin group. It is this belief that one's kin group is an economic safety net that creates extended families and multiple-family households.

Aspects of traditional Asian child-rearing practices appear to be continued by Asian American families (Uba, 1994). Studies tend to be focused primarily upon characteristics of parental control. Chiu (1987) compared the child-rearing attitudes of Chinese, Chinese American, and Euro-American mothers. Chinese mothers endorsed restrictive and controlling behavior more than Chinese American and Euro-American mothers, and Chinese American mothers were more restrictive and controlling in their child-rearing attitudes than Euro-American mothers. The intermediate position of Chinese American mothers suggests that their child-rearing attitudes are shifting toward Euro-American norms due to acculturation.

R. Chao (1994) has argued that the traditional view of Chinese parents as authoritarian, restrictive, and controlling is misleading because these parenting behaviors do not have cross-cultural equivalence for Euro-Americans and Chinese: these child-rearing concepts are rooted in Euro-American culture and are not relevant for describing the socialization styles and goals of Chinese parents. According to R. Chao (1994), "The 'authoritarian' concept has evolved from American culture and psychology that is rooted in both evangelical and Puritan religious influences" (p. 1116). Instead, Chinese parenting should be viewed from the concepts of *chiao shun* and *guan*. *Chiao shun* means "training" or "teaching in appropriate behaviors." Parents and teachers are responsible for training children by exposing them to examples of proper behavior and limiting their view of undesirable behaviors. However, training in the Euro-American sense is conceptualized in terms of strict discipline. This is not the case for Chinese, for whom training is accomplished in the context of a supportive and concerned parent or teacher. The word *guan* means "to govern," "to care for or to love," and parental care and involvement is seen as an aspect of *guan*. Thus, control and governance have positive connotations for the Chinese. Using a middle-class sample, R. Chao (1994) compared Euro-American and immigrant Chinese American mothers on standard measures of control and authoritarian parenting, as well as measures of *chiao shun* and *guan*. R. Chao found that Chinese American mothers scored higher on standard measures of parental control and authoritarian parenting. However, they also scored higher on measures reflecting the concepts of *chiao shun* and *guan*. Thus, although Chinese American mothers scored high on the Euro-American concepts of parental control and authoritarian parenting, their parenting style could not be described using Euro-American concepts. Instead, the style of parenting used by the Chinese American mothers is conceptualized as a type of training performed by parents who are deeply concerned and involved in the lives of their children.

The value of this approach is that it helps resolve paradoxes in the current literature. In a series of studies of ethnicity and achievement, Steinberg, Dornbusch, and Brown (1992) have found that Asian American students rated their parents as higher on authoritarian parenting than Euro-American or Hispanic groups. Although their parents scored lower on the optimal parental style of authoritativeness, Asian students had the highest achievement scores (Steinberg et al., 1992). The R. Chao (1994) study suggests that confusion between authoritarian and training child-rearing concepts among Chinese respondents may account for the paradox. In short, Chinese simply have a different set of child-rearing values and styles that are distinct from the traditional U.S. child-rearing schemes.

Future research on socialization in Asian American families should consider the influence of *chiao shun* and *guan* and their relation to parenting goals. As the Asian American population grows due to immigration, the concepts of *chiao shun* and *guan* are likely to be reinforced and exert continued influence on the parenting styles of Asian American parents. At the same time, as the Asian American population extends itself across more generations, parenting styles are likely to change due to acculturation. Future research with Asian American families must therefore take into account within-group differences in child-rearing practices due to generation and acculturation.

Latino Families. The term *Latino* is used here to describe those persons often referred to as Hispanics. *Hispanic* is a word coined by the Department of Commerce to enumerate persons in the United States whose ancestry derives from the Spanish-speaking countries and peoples of the Americas. Many people in this group prefer Latino over Hispanic because Latino is the Spanish word for describing this group, whereas Hispanic is an English word imposed on the group. The Latino population consists primarily of Mestizo peoples born of the Spanish conquest of the Americas who intermixed with populations indigenous to the geographic areas. Although the language of Mestizos is Spanish, much of their culture is a hybrid of Spanish and Native American influences. Child-rearing, in particular, is heavily influenced by Native American cultures because it was the Native American women who bore the children of the Spanish conquistadores and raised them in their extended families. As these children grew, they formed unions with other Mestizos and Native Americans and extended the predominately Native American child-rearing practices across generations through their children.

Today, Mexican Americans make up the vast majority of Latinos (64%), followed by Central and South Americans (13%), Puerto Ricans (10.6%), and Cuban Americans (4.7%; U.S. Department of Commerce, 1993). It is estimated that if current immigration trends continue, more than half of the Latino population for the next 50 years will be made up of immigrants and their children (Edmonston & Passel, 1994). This means that the Latino population will be characterized by sociocultural diversity and change as new immigrants and their children adapt to life in the United States. The direction and nature of this change will be influenced by the sociocultural ecology of the United States, which itself is being gradually transformed by the growing numbers of Latinos and Asians of immigrant families.

Ramirez and Castaneda (1974) have described the cultural values of Latinos in terms of four conceptual categories: (a) identification with family, community, and ethnic group; (b) personalization of interpersonal relationships; (c) status and roles based on age and gender; and (d) Latino Catholic ideology. The following discussion of these values is with the understanding that there are important subgroup (Cuban American, Mexican American, Puerto Rican, Central and South American) variations as well as variations due to acculturation, generation, and social class.

Identification with Family, Community, and Ethnic Group.   Latino child-rearing practices encourage the development of a self-identity embedded firmly within the context of the *familia* (family). One's individual identity is therefore part of a larger identity with the familia.

The desire to be close to the familia often results in many members of the same familia living in the same community. The familia network extends further into the community through kinships formed by intermarriage among familias and *el compadrazco,* which is the cultural practice of having special friends become godparents of children in baptisms. Adults united through el compadrazco, called *compadres* and *comadres,* have mutual obligations to each other similar to those of brothers and sisters. Vidal (1988) found that Puerto Rican godparents served as role models and social supports for their godchildren, and regarded themselves as potential surrogate parents in the event of the parents' death. Extended familia ties in the community give rise to a sense of identity with one's community.

The worldview of many Latinos includes a sense of identity with *La Raza* (the Race), which is a sense of peoplehood shared by persons of the Americas who are of Mestizo ancestry.

Personalization of Interpersonal Relationships.   Latino culture places a heavy emphasis on sensitivity to the social domain of the human experience. Individuals are socialized to be sensitive to the feelings and needs of others and to personalize interpersonal relationships *(personalismo).* This socialization goal encourages the development of cooperative social motives while discouraging individual competitive behaviors that set apart the individual from the group (Kagan, 1984). In a collectivist culture where working as a group is important, knowing how to cooperate is a valuable social skill.

The paramount importance of the social domain for Latinos is reflected in the term *bien educado,* which literally translated means "well educated." In Latino culture, however, the term is used to refer not only to someone with a good formal education but also to a person who can function successfully in any interpersonal situation without being disrespectful or rude. Okagaki and Sternberg (1993) found that Mexican immigrant parents emphasized social skills as equal to or more important than cognitive skills in defining an "intelligent" child. Children in particular are expected to be bien educados in their relations with adults. Addressing adults in Spanish with the formal "you" *(usted)* rather than the informal "you" *(tu)* is an example of being bien educado. Thus, if children lose Spanish and cannot communicate with Spanish monolingual adults, they may be unable to achieve the status of being bien educado in their community.

Status and Roles Based on Age and Gender.   Latino culture has clearly defined norms of behavior governing an individual's actions within the familia and the community. Age and gender are important determinants of status and respect. Children are expected to be obedient and respectful toward their parents, even after they are grown and have children of their own. An authoritarian parenting style has been reported among Latinos (Dornbusch, Ritter, Leiderman, Roberts, & Fraleigh, 1987; Schumm et al., 1988). Yet, as R. Chao (1994) has shown, in the context of non-Western cultures, this parenting style may be experienced as parental support and concern. Grandparents, and older persons in general, receive much respect and have considerable status owing to their knowledge of life. Consequently, children are taught to "model" themselves after adults, and as a result modeling becomes a preferred teaching style (Laosa, 1980).

Gender also influences a person's role in the familia and community. Males are expected to have more knowledge about politics and business, while females are expected to know more about child rearing, health care, and education.

Because politics and business expose males more to the outside world, they are often perceived as the dominant figures in the familia. However, decision-making studies in the United States reveal that Latino husbands and wives most often share responsibility for major family decisions (R. Cooney, Rogler, Hurrell, & Ortiz, 1982; Ybarra, 1982; Zavella, 1987). These findings challenge the stereotype of the macho Latino male. Another stereotype is that Latino gender roles prevent women from working outside the home. However, U.S. Department of Commerce (1988) statistics show 51% of Latinas in the labor force compared to 56% for non-Latinas. Among young women, the percentage of working Latinas actually exceeds that of non-Latinas.

Latino Catholic Ideology.   Religion strongly influences the lives of Latinos inasmuch as Latino Catholicism reinforces and supports cultural values. Latino Catholicism is a synthesis of Spanish European Catholicism and indigenous religious beliefs and practices. Identity with family and community is facilitated through such religious practices as weddings and el compadrazco, which help extend family networks. Identity with the ethnic group is reinforced by the common Catholic religion shared by more than 80% of La Raza. Religious symbols are often used as markers of ethnic identity. For example, the image of the Virgen of Guadalupe, the Mestizo equivalent of the Virgin Mary, is both a religious symbol and a symbol for La Raza. The cultural emphasis on respect, group harmony, and cooperation in interpersonal relations is in line with the religious themes of peace, community, and self-denial.

The Role of Family in Latino Adaptation.   The family plays an important role in the adaptation of Latinos to life in the United States. During the first 10 years following immigration, it is not uncommon for immigrants and their children to live in extended households that include relatives and other nonfamily members (Blank, 1993). However, as immigrants move out of extended households, they prefer to establish single households in the surrounding area, thus retaining some of the benefits of extended kin and friends, such as social support.

The longer immigrants live in the United States, the more their family networks expand. Family networks grow through marriage and birth and from continued immigration of family members. Thus, even as individual family members become acculturated, their local extended family becomes larger (Keefe & Padilla, 1987). Second- and third-generation Mexican Americans have larger and more integrated extended families than immigrants (Keefe & Padilla, 1987). Griffith and Villavicencio (1985) report that for Mexican Americans, education and income are the best predictors of contact and support from family members. This suggests that involvement with family is not maintained solely for socioeconomic reasons.

Involvement with family members through visits and exchange of services represents the behavioral component of familism. Another component is attitudinal in nature and has to do with feelings of loyalty, solidarity, and reciprocity among family members. Unlike behavioral familism, attitudinal familism is partially susceptible to change with acculturation. Sabogal and his colleagues (Sabogal et al., 1987) identified three dimensions of attitudinal familism: familial obligations, perceived support from family, and family as referents. They found that for Latinos, familial obligations and family as referent decreased across generations. Perceived support from family, however, remained the same despite changes in acculturation and generational status. Thus, it appears that the perception of support from family is high even among immigrants with fewer family members, and remains high as more family members are added across generations.

A small number of studies suggests that despite the disruptions of immigration, immigrant family environments are less stressful than native-born family environments. Thus, McClintock and Moore (1982) found that immigrant mothers had more harmonious interactions with their children than native-born Mexican American mothers. Other studies (Casas & Ortiz, 1985; de Anda, 1984; Golding, Burman, Timbers, Escobar, & Karno, 1985) also report more marital satisfaction and spousal support among immigrant couples compared to their native-born peers. When acculturation level is used to differentiate Mexican American families, similar results emerge. Thus, low-acculturated Mexican American parents were more likely to be low in stress and to be satisfied with family life and spouse personality during the stage of raising preadolescent children than their more acculturated counterparts (D. Olsen, Russell, & Sprenkle, 1980). Even when chronic childhood illness is present in the family, immigrant families seem to cope better than native-born families (Chavez & Buriel, 1988).

A recent study by Buriel (1993a) found that early assumption of responsibility was a dominant socialization goal of Mexican immigrant parents that persists into adolescence. Buriel (1993a) also found that there was greater similarity in socialization styles among immigrant mothers and fathers than among native-born mothers and fathers. Similar findings have been reported by Zepeda and Espinosa (1990). Consensus in socialization styles may reflect an area of domestic interdependence conditioned by the immigrant experience. That is, since immigrants lack extended kinship networks, parents may depend more on each other for the socialization of children, which encourages agreement in parents' socialization styles.

Family research with Latinos has often focused on how immigration and acculturation affect the adaptation of individual family members. However, the family can be viewed as an adapting entity with its own developmental processes. The family unit undergoes its own development, which transcends the development of its individual members. From a systems perspective (Kaye, 1985; Ramirez, 1983) the Mexican American family can be thought of as an open system with both internal and external aspects of functioning. Internal aspects include the family's patterns of relationships and interactions and also the structure of the family. External aspects include the family's interactions with outside social systems including social institutions and the larger context of U.S. society. Rueschenberg and Buriel (1989) have shown that the Mexican American family is capable of adapting to U.S. social systems while retaining many of its internal characteristics that are cultural in nature.

Perspectives on Ethnic Influences on Family Socialization

Research on ethnic minority families in the United States has not kept pace with their rapid rate of growth. Until recently, ethnic minority families were lumped together under the category of "minority," which overlooked important differences among ethnic groups as well as significant diversity within individual groups. Most often, the intent of research with ethnic minority families has been to compare them against Euro-American families to identify differences between these groups. An implicit assumption in many of these two-group studies is that ethnic minority families are not yet "like" Euro-American families, and that this developmental lag is responsible for the problems besetting ethnic minority families. Only of late have some researchers begun to eschew two-group studies in favor of single-group studies that examine sociocultural variations within ethnic minority families and their relation to child outcomes. Much of this research is guided by either an ecological or systems perspective that seeks to understand how parents adapt to the challenges they face as ethnic minorities in U.S. society and how these experiences contribute to socialization goals they hold for their children.

The value of the concepts of collectivism and individualism that have been used to distinguish Euro-American families from ethnic minority families (Greenfield & Cocking, 1994; Okagaki & Divecha, 1993) is being questioned as well (Scott-Jones, Lewis, & Shirley, 1996). As our review has indicated, both individualism and collectivism are important elements in the socialization of *both* Euro-American and ethnic minority families and to continue to draw sharp contrasts using these terms serves only to promote stereotypes that are no longer valid. Scott-Jones et al. (1996) have recently suggested the adoption of Sampson's (1985, 1988) notion of ensembled individualism, which "reflects the importance of both individual development and commitment to family as complementary, intertwined elements in the socialization goals of ethnic families" (Scott-Jones et al., 1996, p. 8). While the precise terminology that is best suited to capture the complexity of ethnic family socialization is still evolving, it is clear that *both* individual and collectivist features will continue to be recognized as important in describing ethnic families.

At present, and for the foreseeable future, the growth of ethnic minority families will be due primarily to immigration from Latin America and Asia. Research with families of these groups needs to take into account the acculturation level of parents and children and the effects this has on family processes and child outcomes. Intergenerational differences in acculturation, for example, can create role strains between parents and children that have implications for child-rearing styles, disciplinary practices, and overall parent-child relations. Together with acculturation, recognition of biculturalism as both an adaptation strategy and socialization goal should guide future research. The effects of prejudice and discrimination on ethnic minorities, in such areas as social and emotional development, ethnic identity, and achievement motivation, deserve much more attention. Language development research should also give greater attention to second-language acquisition (usually English) and bilingualism and their relation to cognitive development and school achievement. Much more attention must also be given to the role of ethnic minority fathers, grandparents, and extended family members in the socialization of children. Finally, more observational studies with ethnic minority families should be encouraged. Observational research has the potential for yielding a contextual richness about the family environments of ethnic minorities that can lead to more culturally relevant insights and theories about their socialization experiences.

THE IMPACT OF SOCIAL CHANGE ON FAMILY SOCIALIZATION

Families are not static but dynamic and are continuously confronted by challenges, changes, and opportunities. A number of societywide changes have produced a variety of shifts in the nature of family relationships. Fertility rates and family size have decreased, the percentage of women in the workforce has increased, the timing of onset of parenthood has shifted, divorce rates have risen, and the number of single-parent families has increased (Cherlin, 1992; Hernandez, 1993). These social trends provide an opportunity to explore how families adapt and change in response to these shifting circumstances and represent "natural experiments" in family coping and adaptation. Moreover, they challenge our traditional assumption that families can be studied at a single point in historical time because the historical contexts are constantly shifting. Our task is to establish how socialization processes operate similarly or differently under varying historical circumstances. In this section, three issues from this myriad of changes—the impact of timing of parenthood, the effects of recent shifts in family employment and unemployment patterns, and the impact of divorce and remarriage—are explored to illustrate the impact of social change on parent-child and family relationships. Some of these changes are scheduled or planned, such as reentry into the workforce and delaying the onset of parenthood; other changes, such as job loss and divorce, are unscheduled or nonnormative transitions. According to a life course view both scheduled and unscheduled transitions need to be examined (Hetherington & Baltes, 1988; Elder, Ch. 3, Volume 1) to fully appreciate how these different types of change alter family socialization strategies. These family transitions are adult-focused in contrast to child-focused transitions (e.g., entry to day care, junior high school) and underscore our assumption that adult developmental issues need to be directly addressed to understand how these transitions alter parental socialization beliefs and behaviors. At the same time, child developmental status will play a major role in determining how adults respond to these transitions. As we argued earlier, it is insufficient to focus on individual levels of analysis—either adult or child.

Instead, individual, dyadic, triadic, and family units each follows its own developmental trajectory, and the interplay among these separate developmental trajectories can produce a diverse set of effects on the functioning of the units themselves. In addition, the role that these units (individual, dyad, family) play in modifying the impact of family transitions will vary as a result of these interlocking developmental curves. Both the timing and nature of family transitions and reactions to these alterations will be determined by the points at which particular individuals, dyads, triads, and families fall along their respective developmental life course trajectories. Moreover, individual families can vary widely in terms of the particular configuration of life course trajectories. To illustrate:

> Consider how the developmental status of the child (individual level) may alter the husband-wife relationship (dyadic level). As Hetherington, Cox, and Cox (1985) found, the stress on the marital relationship on newly married parents is greater when the stepdaughter is an adolescent than when the girl is younger. Similarly, the developmental levels of the child and the couple relationship may interact not only in determining the degree to which change is stressful, but in determining the onset of a stressful event. For example, the probability of divorce may increase when children achieve independence and leave home. Individual and dyadic units may interact with family levels of analysis. As a couple's relationship changes over time, the associated family paradigm may, in turn, shift. A marriage that is deteriorating may lead to the family decreasing its level of coordination as the couple begins to view each member separately and not as a single group. (Parke, 1988, p. 174)

The central premise is that the particular configuration of these multiple sets of developmental trajectories needs to be considered to understand the impact of societal change on families (Parke, 1988).

Timing of Parenthood and Family Socialization

Patterns of the timing of the onset of parenting have undergone profound changes over the past several decades. An increasing number of women have babies earlier and later than in previous decades. Although the actual teen birthrate between 1960 and 1992 has declined, the number of births to young mothers (under 17 years old) has actually risen slightly (Brooks-Gunn & Chase-Lansdale, 1995). Black teens are most at risk for early parenthood, with one out of five Black children born to an unmarried teenager (Cherlin, 1992). The other trend, delayed childbearing, is even more dramatic: between 1972 and 1982, the percentage of women who waited until their 30s to have their first child doubled (R. Collins & Coltrane, 1994); in 1988, women over 30 accounted for 35% of births to women (Cherlin et al., 1991). This trend toward later parenthood was especially marked among White women; Black women, on average, have their children at earlier ages than White women (Cherlin et al., 1991).

A number of factors needs to be considered to understand the impact on parenting of childbearing at different ages. First, the *life course context,* which is broadly defined as the point at which the individual has arrived in his or her social, educational, and occupational timetable, is an important determinant. Second, the *historical context,* namely, the societal and economic conditions that prevail at the time of the onset of parenting, interacts with the first factor in determining the effects of variations in timing.

Early-Timed Parenthood

Recently, theorists have cast this issue in a risk-and-resiliency framework, which leads to a search for the factors that exaggerate the problems as well as the conditions that may protect teen parents and their offspring from adverse outcomes. There is also considerable variability in both the short- and long-term outcomes for teen parents, and the older assumptions about the inevitability of negative life course outcomes is being challenged (Furstenberg, Brooks-Gunn, & Morgan, 1987). As Hetherington (1995) recently argued, "there are multiple pathways to successful outcomes with new experiences, options and decisions encountered on the path that may sustain a developmental trajectory or deflect an individual onto a new course. It is not the inevitability of outcomes but the flexibility and diversity in the response to teenage parenthood . . . that is notable" (p. 3).

The most significant aspect of early entry into parenthood is that it is a nonnormative event and can be viewed as an accelerated role transition. As McCluskey, Killarney, and Papini (1983) note, "School age parenting may produce heightened stress when it is out of synchrony with a normative life course. Adolescents may be entering parenting at an age when they are not financially, educationally, and emotionally ready to deal with it effectively" (p. 49). In addition, adolescent childbearers are at higher medical risk due to poorer diets, malnutrition, and less intensive and consistent prenatal care (Brooks-Gunn & Chase-Lansdale,

1995). Teenage childbearing is also strongly associated with higher levels of completed fertility and closer spacing of births (Hoffreth & Hayes, 1987). In the educational sphere, early childbearing is negatively associated with educational attainment, especially for females (Brooks-Gunn & Furstenberg, 1986). African American females are more likely than Caucasians to complete high school after becoming mothers, in part due to the fact that they receive more help from family members and have lower marriage rates (Brooks-Gunn & Chase-Lansdale, 1995). Similarly, early onset of parenthood is linked with diminished income and assets as well as poverty, relative to individuals who delay childbearing (Hoffreth & Hayes, 1987); again, the effect is particularly severe for women. In turn, this has long-term occupational consequences, with early childbearers overrepresented in blue-collar jobs and underrepresented in the professions. Another issue is that early childbearing is more likely to be unplanned (Brooks-Gunn & Chase-Lansdale, 1995). Only 14% of teenage pregnancies were planned, 37% were unintended, 14% resulted in miscarriage, and 35% in abortions (Moore, Snyder, & Glei, 1995). Similarly, 92% of births to African American teenagers and 54% of births to Caucasian teenagers were out of wedlock (Brooks-Gunn & Chase-Lansdale, 1995). In 1960, 40% of teenage girls were married by age 19. In 1992, 93% of the births to African American teenagers and 61% of White teenagers were to unmarried adolescents (Snyder & Fromboluti, 1993). Other estimates differ but still suggest a higher-than-average probability that adolescents are unmarried at the time of conception and/or at the time of delivery. Marriage often occurs in the first two years after delivery; again, estimates vary but approximately one-quarter of the unmarried women tend to marry within two years (Furstenberg, Brooks-Gunn, & Chase-Lansdale, 1989). However, there is a trend over the past two decades suggesting that more recent cohorts are less likely to marry to legitimate a premarital pregnancy than older cohorts were (Cherlin, 1992; Hetherington, 1995). As Cherlin (1992) has argued, marriage and childbearing are becoming less linked and should be viewed as following separate trajectories. Moreover, this holds across a variety of ethnic and age groups (Hetherington, 1995; Moore et al., 1995).

Although teens do not generally marry, when they do, their marriages tend to be highly unstable. Separation and divorce are two to three times as likely among adolescents as among couples who are 20 years or older (Furstenberg et al., 1989). In view of the low rates of marriage and high rates of separation and divorce for adolescents, adolescent fathers, in contrast to "on-schedule" fathers, have less contact with their offspring. However, contact is not absent; in fact, studies of unmarried adolescent fathers indicate a surprising amount of paternal involvement for extended periods following the birth. Recent data based on a national representative sample of young unwed fathers indicated that 75% of young fathers who lived away from their children at birth never lived in the same household with them (Lerman & Ooms, 1993). However, many unwed fathers remain in close contact with their children, with nearly 50% visiting their youngest child at least once a week and nearly 25% almost daily; only 13% never visited, and 7% visited only yearly. These estimates were based on fathers' own reports, but other work that relies on maternal reports yield lower contact estimates. Mott (1993) found about 40% visited once a week and 33% never visited or visited only yearly.

Several studies report declines in contact as the child develops. According to one national survey, 57% of adolescent unwed fathers visited once a week when the child was 2 or under, 40% for ages 2 to 4.5 years, 27% for ages 4.5 to 7.5, and 22% for 7.5 years and older (Lerman & Ooms, 1993). Nearly 33% of the fathers of the oldest group never visited their offspring. These declines in father participation continue across childhood and adolescence. Furstenberg and Harris (1992, 1993) found that under 50% of the children lived at least some time with their biological father at some point during their first 18 years, but only 9% lived with their father during the entire period. Instead, children spent about one-third of their childhood with their fathers, and this was more likely to occur in early childhood. During the preschool period, nearly 50% of the children were either living with their father or saw him on a weekly basis. By late adolescence, 14% were living with him, and only 15% were seeing him as often as once a week; 46% had no contact, but 25% had seen him occasionally in the preceding year.

On balance, the stereotype of the uncaring and irresponsible teenage father is probably overstated and more myth than reality—at least for some young fathers. One of the major barriers to continued involvement is the difficulty of finding employment and the instability of available jobs (Bowman, 1993). Fathers who rarely or never visit are less likely to pay child support, which, in turn, adds to the mother's financial burden and may indirectly have negative effects on the children (Furstenberg & Harris, 1993). Finally, Euro-American (30%) and Hispanic (37%) fathers

are more likely to have no contact with their offspring than African American fathers (12%).

Risk, Resiliency, and Long-Term Outcomes for Mothers and Children.   What are the long-term effects of teenage motherhood on the teenager and her children? Instead of a deficit perspective, researchers are embracing risk-and-resiliency models. Two studies (Furstenberg, Brooks-Gunn, & Morgan, 1987; Horowitz, Klerman, Kuo, & Jekal, 1991) have provided insights into the long-term consequences by following teen mothers as they enter middle age. Perhaps the most surprising finding was the diversity in outcomes. Instead of all teen mothers being inevitably destined to a life of poverty and welfare dependence, many were faring quite well in their early 30s. In the Furstenberg et al. (1987) sample, for example, one-third had completed high school (of those who had dropped out earlier, during pregnancy) and nearly one-third completed some post–high school education. About three-quarters of the mothers were working and only one-quarter were on welfare. Family size was similar to that of older mothers (approximately two children). Several factors concerning educational experience—being at age-appropriate grade level at pregnancy, having parents with more than grade 10 education, attending a special school for pregnant teens, and having high aspirations at the time of birth—predicted positive outcomes for teenage mothers. Limiting childbearing and early completion of high school after childbirth and growing up in a non-welfare-dependent family were further predictions of positive outcomes in the middle years. Similar findings were reported for the Horowitz et al. (1991) study of New Haven teenagers. Two features limit the generalizability of these studies: both focused only on African American women who lived in the eastern United States (Baltimore or New Haven); the structural/sociological orientation resulted in limited attention to psychologically based individual differences (e.g., coping, self-efficacy) that could have accounted for the relative success of some teenage mothers. Nevertheless, these studies are important reminders that teenage childbearing need not lead to negative life course outcomes.

In spite of the fact that some teenage mothers may develop well, evidence is clear that the offspring of teen mothers are at high risk for long-term developmental problems. Teenage mothers interact differently than on-time mothers with their infants and children (see Brooks-Gunn & Chase-Lansdale, 1995; Brooks-Gunn & Furstenberg, 1986; Osofsky, Hann, & Peebles, 1993, for reviews). A variety of observational studies suggests that teenage mothers provide a less stimulating and less verbal environment for their infants and young children. Although they are equally warm as older mothers, they are more restrictive with their young children, have unrealistic developmental timetables, have lower educational aspirations for their children, and provide a home environment that is less conducive to learning. A promising new direction has been charted by Osofsky et al. (1993), who suggest that affect regulation and emotional availability may both be lower in adolescent mothers, which may be a further contributor to some of the negative outcomes for their offspring.

Finally, there are a variety of deleterious effects of early childbearing for the offspring. First, there is a greater risk of lower IQ, academic achievement, and retention in grade (Furstenberg et al., 1989). Nor are the effects short-lived: they tend to persist throughout the school years (Hoffreth, 1987). Social behavior is affected as well, with children of teenage parents being at greater risk of social impairment (e.g., undercontrol of anger, feelings of inferiority, fearfulness) and mild behavior disorders (e.g., aggressiveness, rebelliousness, impulsivity; Brooks-Gunn & Furstenberg, 1986). In assessing the effects of early childbearing, it is important to remember that the deleterious impact on children is due to both teenage mothers and teenage fathers. Clearly, early-timed parenthood has profound consequences for partners and their offspring. At the same time, it is important to remember that there is variation among early-timed parents as well as late-timed parents.

A major limitation of this body of literature is the near exclusive focus on African American adolescents. Since the ecology of family arrangements differs in African American and Caucasian samples (McLoyd, 1989), generalizability of conclusions across groups is difficult. Some recent work on Hispanic American teenage mothers has provided a corrective to this problem. Wassermann, Brunelli, Raul, and Alvarado (1994) have examined parenting, child-rearing attitudes, and social support in two groups of Hispanic American mothers (whose ethnic backgrounds were Dominican Republic and Puerto Rico), a group of African American adolescent mothers, and comparison samples of older mothers from each ethnic group. In spite of several similarities across the ethnic groups (e.g., teenage mothers are more depressed, did less childcare, provided less stimulating home environments than older mothers), there were interesting ethnic group differences. African American mothers had more social support than Hispanic American mothers, and Puerto

Rican mothers reported more social support than Dominican Republic American mothers. Child-rearing attitudes differed as well, with Hispanic American mothers more strict than African American mothers, and Dominican Republic American mothers stricter than their Puerto Rican counterparts. Other studies (e.g., Garcia-Coll, Meyer, & Brillon, 1995) underscore the culture-specific nature of the timing of pregnancy interactions patterns, marriage patterns, and type and amount of familial support.

A Family Systems Perspective on Teenage Parenthood. A promising trend in recent conceptualizations of this issue is the recognition that "the advent of teenage motherhood has effects on several members of the family, not just the teenage mother" (Brooks-Gunn & Chase-Lansdale, 1995, p. 39). It is common for the teenage mother to reside with her parents or other relatives.

According to recent national estimates (Hernandez, 1993), the percentage of infants in 1980 who resided with grandparents in the home were 42% for never-married mothers and 25% for ever-married mothers. Coresidence is particularly prevalent among African American families and is twice as likely than for Caucasian single mothers (Hernandez, 1993). Similarly Hispanic American rates of coresidence are higher than for Caucasian mothers (Baydar & Brooks-Gunn, 1995).

A family systems perspective (Minuchin, 1985), which stresses the interrelationships among the members of the multigenerational household, is useful for exploring this issue. Recent studies have focused on the interaction patterns of mothers, grandmothers, and infants or children. According to Chase-Lansdale, Brooks-Gunn, and Zamsky (1994), coresidence is beneficial when the mother is very young (16 and under at first birth). Coresident mothers and grandmothers both displayed more positive and less harsh parenting than those who lived separately. However, when the mother was older at the birth of the first child, coresidence was related to poorer parenting patterns for women in both generations. Similarly, Shapiro and Mangelsdorf (1994) found that among younger adolescents, support from the family of origin was positively associated with more optimal parenting, whereas for older adolescents' support from family was negatively related to optimal parenting. Brooks-Gunn and Chase-Lansdale (1995) offer a life span interpretation: "Living together may be difficult for both generations—the young mother who is balancing needs for autonomy and needs for childcare simultaneously and the grandmother who is balancing the demands of adult mid-life (work, relationships, parenting) with unanticipated child-care demands (Burton, 1990)" (1995, pp. 43–44).

What is the impact of coresidence on the developing child? Although early studies (Furstenberg, 1976; Kellam, Ensminger, & Turner, 1977) documented positive effects of coresidence for the children of teenage mothers, more recent studies have yielded a mixed picture. For both Caucasian and African American children (Brooks-Gunn, Berlin, & Aber, 1993), living in a multigenerational household was associated with poorer reading and verbal scores in preschool and early elementary school. Pope, Casey, Bradley, and Brooks-Gunn (1993) found that teenage mothers of low-birthweight infants benefited from coresidence, as indexed by higher IQ scores at age 3. Perhaps in the case of low-birthweight babies where the burden of care is higher, coresidence may be beneficial.

Historical Considerations. Is the experience of achieving parenthood during adolescence different in earlier historical periods than in the present? First, as rates of adolescent childbearing rise and the event becomes less nonnormative or deviant, the social stigma associated with the event may decrease. Second, in combination with increased recognition that adolescent fathers have a legitimate and potentially beneficial role to play, the opportunity for adolescent fathers to participate has probably expanded. Third, the increased availability of social support systems such as special schools, social welfare, intervention programs, and day care make it somewhat easier for adolescent parents to simultaneously balance educational and occupational demands with parenting demands. The experience of adolescent parenthood is likely to vary across historical periods.

Late-Timed Parenthood

A variety of contrasts exists between becoming a parent in adolescence and initiating parenthood 15 to 20 years later. In contrast to adolescent childbearing, when childbearing is delayed (i.e., age 30 or over), education is generally completed and career development is well underway for both males and females.

Mothers who delay childbearing may interact differently with their infants. Ragozin, Bashman, Crnic, Greenberg, and Robinson (1982), in a comparison of mothers between 18 and 38 years of age, found positive increases in caretaking responsibility and satisfaction with parenting and a negative linear relationship for social time away from their infants. Moreover, affect directed toward their infants

increased with maternal age. Similarly, older mothers were more successful in eliciting vocal and imitative responses from their infants—an index of their social and cognitive teaching skills. However, these mother-infant interaction effects were evident only for primiparous mothers, and as parity increased, the relationship between maternal age and parity became negative. As Ragozin et al. note, "it appears that having previously experienced parenthood, a mother becomes more interested in extra-familial roles as she grows older—more ready to 'get on with her life.' Thus, older multiparous women exhibit less positive affect and less optimal behavior toward infants. In contrast, the older primiparous woman, having more experience in non-parenting roles, is more committed to the parenting experience" (p. 633). In summary, not only career patterns are affected by timing of parenthood, but, as this study clearly illustrates, maternal roles and behavior are affected as well. Unfortunately, Ragozin et al. provide no information concerning the extrafamilial work patterns of these women.

What are the consequences of these patterns for father involvement? Men who have their children early have more energy for certain types of activities that are central to the father role, such as physical play (MacDonald & Parke, 1986). Similarly, the economic strain that occurs early is offset by avoiding financial problems in retirement due to the fact that children are grown up and independent earlier. In turn, early fathering generally means beginning grandfathering at a younger age, which in turn permits the early-timed father to be a more active grandparent (Tinsley & Parke, 1988). When men become fathers early, there are two main disadvantages: financial strain and time strain, due to the competing demands imposed by trying simultaneously to establish a career as well as a family. The late-timed father's career is more settled, permitting more flexibility and freedom in balancing the demands of work and family. Also, patterns of preparental collaboration between the parents may already be established and persist into the parenthood period. Daniels and Weingarten (1982) found that three times as many late-timed fathers, in contrast to their early-timed counterparts, had regular responsibility for some part of the daily care of a preschool child. Possibly, the increase in paternal responsibility assumed by fathers in late-timed families may account for the more optimal mother-infant interaction patterns observed by Ragozin et al. (1982). T. Cooney, Pedersen, Indelicato, and Palkovitz (1993) found in a nationally representative sample that late-timed fathers were more likely to be classified as being highly involved and experiencing positive affect associated with the paternal role than on-time fathers. Finally, men who delayed parenthood until their late 20s contributed more to indirect aspects of child care, such as cooking, feeding, cleaning, and doing laundry than men who assumed parenthood earlier (Coltrane & Ishii-Kuntz, 1991).

There are qualitative differences in styles of interaction for on-time versus late-timed fathers. In a self-report study, MacDonald and Parke (1986) found that age of parent is negatively related to the frequency of physical play. Even after controlling for the age of the child, the size of the relation is reduced but generally reveals the same pattern. However, this relation appears stronger for some categories of play than for others. Some physical activities, such as bounce, tickle, chase, and piggyback, that tend to require more physical energy on the part of the play partner, show strong negative relation with the age of the parent. The negative correlation between age of parent and physical play may be due to either the unwillingness or inability of older parents to engage in high-energy, affectively arousing activities, such as physical play, or to the fact that children may elicit less physical activity from older parents. Perhaps older fathers are less tied to stereotypic paternal behavior, adopting styles more similar to those that have been considered traditionally maternal (Parke & Neville, 1995).

Recent observational studies of father-child interaction confirm these early self-report investigations. Volling and Belsky (1991), who studied fathers interacting with their infants at 3 and 9 months, found that older fathers were more responsive, stimulating, and affectionate at both ages. In another observational study, Neville and Parke (in press) examined the play patterns of early- and late-timed fathers interacting with their preschool-age children: the early fathers (average age 25 years) relied on physical arousal to engage their children, whereas the delayed fathers (average age 36 years) relied on more cognitive mechanisms to remain engaged.

Clearly, the timing of the onset of parenthood is a powerful organizer of both maternal and paternal roles. In the future, investigators need to examine not only both maternal and paternal interaction patterns with each other and their children, but within the context of careers as well. Finally, more detailed attention to cohort issues is warranted. Presumably, the decision to delay the onset of parenthood is easier in the 1990s than in earlier decades due to increased acceptance of maternal employment, less rigid role definitions for men and women, and the greater availability of support services such as day care that would permit different career-family arrangements.

Women's and Men's Employment Patterns and Family Socialization

The relations between employment patterns of both women and men and their family roles are increasingly being recognized (Crouter, 1994; Gottfried, Gottfried, & Bathurst, 1995). In this section, a variety of issues concerning the links between the worlds of work and family are considered to illustrate the impact of recent shifts in work patterns on both men's and women's family roles. The impact of changes in the rate of maternal employment on both quantitative and qualitative aspects of mother and father participation is examined, as well as the influence of variations in family work schedules.

Since the mid-1950s, there has been a dramatic shift in the participation rate of women in the labor force. The rise has been particularly dramatic for married women with children. Between 1950 and 1990, the employment rate for married mothers of children increased dramatically to over 70% (Hernandez, 1993). How have these shifts affected the quantity and quality of the mother's and father's contribution to family tasks such as housework and child care, and what are the implications for children's development?

Maternal Employment and Socialization

Impact on Mother and Father Household Roles.   Do fathers' and mothers' rates of participation in family tasks shift toward greater equity as a function of maternal employment? Problems arise in interpreting the main data source—time-use studies—because these studies often fail to control for family size and age of children. As Hoffman (1984) noted, "Since employed-mother families include fewer children, in general, and fewer preschoolers and infants, in particular, there are fewer childcare tasks to perform" (p. 439). Therefore, the differences between families with employed and nonemployed mothers may, in fact, be underestimated. A second problem is that the differentiation of tasks performed by fathers is often very crude, and in some studies it is impossible to determine what specific aspects of the father's family work—such as primary child care, non-care-related child contact, and housework—are affected. In spite of these limitations, some trends are clear.

One recent estimate (Coltrane, 1996) suggests that "men's average contributions to inside housework have roughly doubled since about 1970, whereas women's contributions have decreased by a third . . . the late 1980s men were doing about 5 hours per week or about 20–25% of the inside chores" (p. 53). These trends are slightly higher in the case of dual-career families. These trends do not negate the fact that the majority of household tasks, including child care (Biernat & Wortman, 1991), are still performed by women (Ferree, 1991). Moreover, this increase often emerges as a result of women reducing the amount of time they devote to housework and child care rather than as a result of increases in the absolute amount of time men devote to these tasks (Pleck, 1983; Robinson, 1988). These findings are not without significance for children's development because the impact of the mother and the father on children is likely to be different in families in which the father and the mother are more equal in their household participation. "By assuming partial responsibility for home and/or child care, such a husband relieves his wife of some of her responsibilities, freeing her time for more unhurried interaction with the child. . . . The husband's participation has a beneficial impact on the mother-child relationship and so affects the child's development indirectly" (Lamb & Bronson, 1978, p. 7). When fathers persist in a traditional paternal role and refuse to participate, both mother and child may suffer.

Moreover, there is some evidence for absolute increases in fathers' contributions to family work when mothers are employed, especially in father-child contact. Pleck (1983) found that fathers with employed wives performed about one-half hour per day more family work that includes housework, child care, and parent-child contact. Although the proportion of time fathers in the Pleck study spent in child-centered activity and housework was not determined, other evidence indicates that child care time is more likely to increase than housework time (Coltrane, 1996; Hoffman, 1984). In fact, child care by fathers has shown the most dramatic increase in the past decade compared to household work (Coltrane, 1996). The level of paternal child care has shifted since the mid 1980s, and men contribute nearly one-third to this activity in dual-earner couples. In fact, in a recent survey, O'Connell (1993) found that the percentage of children whose fathers cared for them during their mothers' work hours rose to 20% in 1991, after a steady level of around 15% since 1977. These modest absolute increases assume greater importance because they directly affect the nature of the father-child relationship.

Child variables, such as age, appear to determine whether or not fathers' family involvement shifts with maternal employment. Several early studies (G. Russell, 1982; Walker & Woods, 1976) found that fathers increased their family work involvement when their children were infants or preschool-age children. Recently, Gottfried, Bathhurst, and Gottfried (1994), in a prospective analysis, found that maternal employment status when the child was 3.5 years old predicted greater father involvement with their children at 8 and 12 years of age. As Gottfried and colleagues note: "These analyses are significant in that they show that future patterns of increased involvement with children are established in the preschool years in relation to employment. For families in which mothers enter the workforce earlier, fathers appear to establish increased involvement with their children, and this pattern continued into early adolescence" (p. 145). Age of the child is not the only variable, however; other factors such as employment onset in relationship to the family's developmental cycle as well as the reason for employment need to be considered. Both the age of the parents and their point in the occupation cycle will affect paternal involvement and may interact with maternal employment.

Examination of the quantitative shifts in father behavior as a consequence of maternal employment is only one aspect of the issue; it is also necessary to examine the impact of this shift on the quality of the father-child relationship. Shifts in style of father-infant interaction may also occur as a function of maternal employment. Pederson, Anderson, and Cain (1980) assessed the impact of dual-wage-earner families on mother and father interaction patterns with their 5-month-old infants. Fathers in single-wage-earner families tended to play with their infants more than mothers did, but in the two-wage-earner families, the mothers' rate of social play was higher than the fathers' rate of play. In fact, the fathers in these dual-wage-earner families played at a lower rate than even the mothers in the single-wage-earner families. Because the observations took place in the evenings after both parents returned from their jobs, Pedersen and colleagues suggested that the mother used increased play as a way of reestablishing contact with her infant after being away from home for the day. This behavior of the mother is consistent with studies of maternal employment and infant attachment that found no relation between employment status and the quality of infant-mother attachment (Hoffman, 1989) but found evidence of insecure infant-father attachment in dual-career families, although only for sons and not daughters (Chase-Lansdale & Owen, 1987).

Finally, McHale, Crouter, and Bartko (1991), in a sample of fourth and fifth grade children, found that both work status of spouses and role arrangements in families (traditional vs. egalitarian) may, in fact, be independent contributors to father participation. To understand the effects of father participation on children, it is important to consider both work status of parents and family type (traditional vs. egalitarian). McHale et al. found that an inequitable division of parents' work and family roles related to poorer socioemotional adjustment of children. Children from traditional dual-earner families were more anxious and depressed and rated themselves lower in terms of both peer social acceptance and school competence than did children from families characterized by an equitable division in parents' work and family roles (e.g., traditional single-earner and egalitarian dual-earner families).

A caveat is in order, because not all women want to work outside the home, nor do all women want help with household and child care tasks. Although many researchers find that the personal life satisfaction of employed mothers, whether they are professional or blue-collar workers, is higher than for the nonemployed, this is not the case for all mothers. A match between their wishes and their employment status worked best. The positive link between dual roles for mothers and their personal happiness is found only for women who wanted to work outside the home (Grove & Zeiss, 1987). Similarly, mothers of infants who preferred employment but stayed at home were more depressed than either mothers whose employment status was consistent with their desires or employed mothers who indicated a preference for nonemployment (Hock & DeMeis, 1990). The quality of the job and the stability of child care arrangements can also alter the relationship between dual-career status and women's satisfaction (Baruch & Barnett, 1987; Goldberg & Easterbrooks, 1988). Not surprisingly, poor child care and an uninteresting job can make one rethink the advantages of a more traditional lifestyle. Similarly, Ross (1987) has found that fathers' assistance in household and child care tasks has a positive effect on their wives if they want help; if they do not want increased father involvement, there are negative effects, and fathers are viewed as interfering in their wives' domain (Ross, 1987). Congruence between parental preferred roles and their actual roles is a major determinant of the impact of maternal employment on children and families as well as on women themselves.

Implications of Maternal Employment for Children's Development. In addition to exploring mother and father roles as a function of maternal employment, the issue of shifts in the nature of the child's home environment has been examined to assess the impact of employment on children's development. In spite of earlier concerns about the potential deleterious effects of maternal employment on children's development, research suggests that with adequate child care it does not usually have detrimental effects on children (Gottfried & Gottfried, 1988; Hoffman, 1989).

Several domains of children's development have been examined, including gender roles, achievement, and behavior problems. Maternal employment is associated with more egalitarian views of gender roles by their children, particularly by their daughters (Hoffman, 1989). In middle-class families, maternal employment is related to higher educational and occupational goals in children (Hoffman, 1989). Maternal employment is also associated with fewer traditional feminine interests and characteristics in daughters. Daughters of working as compared to nonworking mothers often perceive the woman's role as involving freedom of choice, satisfaction, and competence, and they themselves are career- and achievement-oriented, independent, assertive, and high in self-esteem (Hoffman, 1989). Sons of working mothers, in contrast to sons of unemployed mothers, not only perceive females as more competent, but also view men as warmer and more expressive.

One of the limitations of many earlier studies in this area is the lack of long-term follow-up to assess potential delayed effects of early maternal employment on children's development. In a recent longitudinal study, Gottfried et al. (1994) found that maternal employment was not related to children's development across age (infancy to age 12), developmental domain, and gender. Moreover, prospective analyses indicated that there were no sleeper effects associated with maternal employment. The children of employed and nonemployed mothers were similar in cognitive, socioemotional, academic, motivational, and behavioral domains from infancy through adolescence. This conclusion is not surprising in light of the finding that the home environment and parenting of employed and nonemployed mothers were very similar in terms of stimulation, nurturing, parent-child interactions, and family climate. Cohort effects need to be considered in interpreting these findings. As maternal employment becomes more common, the differential effects on select areas of development (e.g., gender roles, independence) may decrease. In part, this may be due to the fact that the shift in maternal employment is part of a changing set of cultural attitudes concerning male and female roles that all children, regardless of their family employment arrangements, are exposed to.

The pattern of findings suggests that variations within employed and nonemployed mothers are more significant for child outcomes than differences between groups. In support of this shift away from a "social address" model to a process-oriented approach, Gottfried et al. (1994) found that processes such as parental involvement and the quality of the home environment (as indexed by the Home Scale) were clearly linked to children's development—regardless of maternal employment status.

There is some evidence that the child-rearing practices of working mothers may differ from those of nonemployed mothers, particularly in the area of independence training. Except in cases where mothers feel guilty about leaving their children to work, employed mothers encourage their children to become self-sufficient and independent and to assume responsibility for household tasks at an earlier age (Hoffman, 1989). This early independence training may be beneficial in leading to high achievement motivation, achievement behavior, and competence (Hoffman, 1989). However, maternal employment in some families is also associated with less supervision and monitoring of school-aged children (Crouter, MacDermid, McHale, & Perry-Jenkins, 1990). Lack of monitoring is associated with especially adverse consequences for boys: lower school performance, more behavior problems, and an increase in mother-child conflict (Crouter et al., 1990). For both boys and girls, lack of supervision is associated with earlier dating behavior, precocious sexuality, and greater peer involvement (Dornbusch et al., 1985).

In summary, the results of studies of maternal employment suggest that it does not usually have detrimental effects on children; in fact, positive consequences usually have been obtained, especially for girls. However, the effects of maternal employment can be evaluated only in relation to other factors, such as the reason why the mother is working, the mother's satisfaction with her role, the demands placed on other family members, the attitudes of the other family members toward the mother's employment, and the quality of substitute care and supervision provided for the children.

Quality of Mother and Father Work and Family Socialization

Instead of examining whether or not one or both parents are employed, researchers have begun to address the issue of the impact of the quality and nature of work on parenting of both mother and father behavior. As Crouter (1994) recently noted, there are two types of linkage. One type of research focuses on work as an "emotional climate," which, in turn, may have carryover effects to the enactment of roles in home settings; the focus is generally on short-term or transitory effects. A second type of linkage focuses on the type of skills, attitudes, and perspectives that adults acquire in their work-based socialization as adults and how these variations in job experience alter their behavior in family contexts. In contrast to the short-term perspective of the spillover of emotional climate research, this type of endeavor involves more enduring and long-lasting effects of work on family life.

Work in the first tradition has been conducted by Repetti (1989, 1994), who studied the impact of working in a high-stress job (air traffic controller) on subsequent family interaction patterns. She found that the male air traffic controllers were more withdrawn and less angry in marital interactions after high-stress shifts and tended to be behaviorally and emotionally withdrawn during interactions with their children as well. Although high workload is associated with withdrawal, negative social experiences in the workplace have a different effect. In addition, distressing social experiences at work were associated with higher expressions of anger and greater use of discipline during interaction with the child later in the day. Repetti views this as a "spillover effect" in which there is transfer of negative feelings across settings. Consistent with these findings is the work of Bolger, Delongis, Kessler, and Wethington (1989); they found that work-related stress (e.g., arguments, heavy workloads) was associated with more negative marital interactions and less household work.

Other research suggests that positive work experiences can enhance the quality of fathering. Grossman, Pollock, and Golding (1988) found that high job satisfaction was associated with higher levels of support for their 5-year-olds' autonomy and affiliation in spite of the fact that positive feelings about work were negatively related to the quantity of time spent interacting with their child. This finding underscores the importance of distinguishing quantity and quality of involvement.

One caveat: In contrast to the Repetti (1989, 1994) studies, the Grossman et al. (1988) study focused on general job satisfaction and demandingness rather than daily fluctuations in the level of positivity or negativity experienced in the work setting. Future studies need to assess these two aspects of job-related affect and involvement separately.

Research in the second tradition of family-work linkage, namely, the effects of the nature of men's occupational roles on their fathering behavior, dates back to the classic work of Kohn and Schooler (1983) and D. Miller and Swanson (1954). Men who experience a high degree of occupational autonomy value independence in their children, consider children's intentions when determining discipline, and use reasoning and withdrawal of rewards instead of physical punishment. In contrast, men who are in highly supervised jobs with little autonomy value conformity and obedience, focus on consequences rather than intentions, and use more physical forms of discipline. In short, they repeat their job-based experiences in their parenting roles.

Greenberger and O'Neil (1991) extended Kohn's original work by focusing on the implications of job characteristics not only for the parenting behavior of both mothers and fathers but, in turn, the effects of these variations in parenting for children's development. Fathers with more complex jobs (i.e., characterized by mentoring others versus taking instruction or serving others) spend more time alone with sons and more time developing their sons' skills (e.g., academic, athletic, mechanical, interpersonal), but this is not the case for daughters. In fact, they spend more time in work and work-related activities if they have daughters. In addition, these fathers tend to behave more warmly and responsively to sons and use less harsh and less lax control with sons, but report more firm but flexible control with daughters. Fathers who have jobs characterized by a high level of challenge (e.g., expected to solve problems, high level of decision making) devote more time to developing sons' skills, give higher quality explanations to their sons, and use less harsh and more firm but flexible control in their interactions with their boys. Finally, fathers with time-urgent jobs (work fast most of the day, little time for breaks) spend more time on work activities, less time interacting, and use less lax control if they have daughters. To summarize, when fathers have complex, stimulating, and challenging jobs, sons seem to benefit much more than daughters. In contrast, mothers' job characteristics are, in general, less predictive of their parenting than fathers' job attributes, but again, when there is a link, sons seem to benefit (higher quality explanations, warmth, and responsivity) more than daughters. Mothers show fewer relationships in part due to the more heavily culturally scripted nature of maternal roles. According to these researchers, different processes may account for the work-home linkages due to stimulating or challenging jobs and complexity of occupation. Greenberger and O'Neil (1991) argue that "spillover of positive mood" may account for the relationships between stimulating/challenging jobs and good fathering, whereas "complexity of work with people may

increase fathers' intellectual and emotional flexibility in dealing with their sons" (p. 13; see also Greenberger, O'Neil, & Nagel, 1994).

As these studies clearly suggest, the parents' work experiences impact on their parenting behavior. However, the process probably operates in both directions in which parents' home experience affects their job performance as well. In fact, arguments at home with a wife or with a child increased the chances of arguments with coworkers and supervisors the next day (Bolger et al., 1989). Perhaps positive home-based experiences create a positive mood and possibly enhance one's workday. These studies underscore the importance of moving beyond employment status per se to a detailed exploration of the nature of work in our future studies of family-work linkages.

Job Loss and Unemployment

Another unscheduled transition that has received attention is the impact of job loss on families (Conger & Elder, 1994; McLoyd, 1989).

Marital Relationships.   Economic stress is associated with increases in marital conflict and instability. Classic studies from the Great Depression (Liker & Elder, 1983) report that income loss in the early 1930s was positively linked to marital conflict several years later; marital tension was associated with higher rates of separation and divorce. Contemporary studies are consistent with the earlier work. Conger et al. (1990) found that the quality of behavior exchange between couples linked economic difficulties to satisfaction in the relationship. They found that several aspects of economic hardship (low income, income loss, and unstable work) were positively associated with marital hostility.

Indirect effects models have also gained support in both classic and more recent studies. In the Depression-era research, Liker and Elder (1983) found that economic stress influences marital quality, in part due to increases in men's tense, explosive, and irritable behavior. The role of women in the process in the earlier era was less clear. Recently, Conger, Ge, and Lorenz (1994) found that depression mediated the effects of economic stress on marriage for women, while irritability served this role for men. Of interest is the fact that "contemporary women were more directly influenced by economic stress than those living during the depression years because of their greater responsibility in family economic life" (Conger et al., 1994, p. 203). In addition, the state of the marital relationship prior to economic hardship can significantly impact on the parents' adjustment, with a strong marital relationship serving to buffer the impact of stressors (Elder & Caspi, 1988).

Parent-Child Relationships.   Several aspects of the parent-child relationship are altered by economic stress, including parenting style, parent discipline, parental problem solving, and levels of parent-child conflict and monitoring. Research suggests that parenting behavior is adversely affected as indexed by increased parental hostility and less consistent and effective but harsher discipline (Conger & Elder, 1994; Elder, 1974; McLoyd, 1989). Moreover, under conditions of stress, parental monitoring will be adversely affected, with less vigilance on the part of the parent (Crouter, MacDermid, McHale, & Perry-Jenkins, 1990). Although conditions of unemployment or underemployment increase fathers' availability and involvement in child care, unemployed fathers report fewer nurturing behaviors than employed fathers (Harold-Goldsmith, Radin, & Eccles, 1988). Recent research has focused on modifying and mediating variables. Several studies indicate that social support has a positive impact on parent-child relationships under conditions of stress (Conger & Elder, 1994; McLoyd, Jayaratne, Ceballo, & Borquez, 1994). Child temperament and physical attractiveness also modify parenting practices: temperamentally difficult children are treated more harshly by unemployed fathers than temperamentally easy offspring (Elder, Van Nguyen, & Caspi, 1985); similarly, physically unattractive daughters are treated more harshly, and attractive girls, in some cases, received more support and less harshness (Elder et al., 1985). The quality of the prior father-child relationship is another determinant of how stress impacts changes in the relationship. A positive relationship prior to job loss served as a protective factor in buffering the child from deterioration of the father-child relationship (Elder et al., 1985). Similarly, a positive (warm and affectionate) mother-child relationship reduced harsh treatment of the child by the father. A disinterested, aloof mother, in contrast, was linked with harsh paternal treatment of the child (Elder et al., 1985).

Impact on Children.   A variety of adverse effects on children accompany unemployment and economic stress. Several negative outcomes have been identified, including increased mental health problems, depression and loneliness, and lowered self-esteem (McLoyd, 1989). Gender differences are evident as well: girls respond to stress with internalizing problems, and boys tend to show externalizing

behaviors (Conger & Elder, 1994). Recent longitudinal studies confirm the earlier findings from cross-sectional studies. Conger, Ge, Elder, Lorenz, and Simons (1994) interviewed parents and their adolescents over a three-year period (grades 7–9). Economic pressure at Wave 1 directly impacted parent-child financial conflict at Wave 2, which in turn was related to adolescent internalizing and externalizing behavior at Wave 3. Moreover, these investigators found support for indirect pathways as well; specifically, an indirect path between parental depressed mood and marital conflict in turn alters parental hostility, which was linked to adolescent internalizing and externalizing measures. Even though there were predictable gender differences in levels of symptomatology for boys and girls (i.e., greater externalizing for boys and greater internalizing for girls), the paths were similar for both sexes. While the Depression-era data suggest that boys are more affected than girls (Elder, 1974), the contemporary findings "may reflect a secular trend toward greater expectations regarding males and females" (Conger, Ge, Elder, Lorenz, & Simons, 1994, p. 557). Similar support for an indirect pathway model comes from McLoyd et al.'s (1994) examination of the impact of unemployment among African American single mothers on parenting and adolescent socioemotional functioning.

In summary, studies of the impact of unemployment have clearly been fruitful avenues for exploring how families adapt and cope in response to stressful change and underscore the value of a family systems approach to the study of socialization.

Divorce, Custody, and Remarriage

Divorce has a profound impact on families, producing changes and stress in fathers, mothers, and children. The annual divorce rate in the United States doubled between 1960 and 1986. Today about half of all new marriages are likely to end in divorce. In Denmark, Germany, Sweden, and Switzerland, the rates have doubled; in Canada, France, and the Netherlands, the rates have tripled since the mid-1960s. In Great Britain, the rate of marital breakup increased sixfold. Although the divorce rate has stabilized or even dropped slightly in the United States in the early 1990s, it is still at its all-time high. In the United States 60% and in Great Britain nearly 75% of the divorces involve children. One-third of children will experience their parent's remarriage, and 62% of remarriages end in divorce (Sorentino, 1990). Clearly, more parents and children are undergoing multiple marital transitions and rearrangements in family relationships.

Divorce is often viewed as a single event or a crisis, but it is more useful to think of it as "a sequence of experiences involving a transition in the lives of children" (Hetherington, 1979, p. 851). Often, a period of conflict and disagreement among family members precedes the separation. As recent evidence suggests, parent conflict can have serious effects on the developing child, including increased aggression and anger and heightened sensitivity to conflict (Cummings & Davies, 1994). Even when children are not directly involved in marital disputes, witnessed discord can have a marked negative impact on them—a reminder that marriage and parenting are closely linked. Although divorce is a serious step, with consequences for all family members, continual and chronic parental conflict itself can be a negative influence on children. Boys may be especially vulnerable because boys are more likely than girls to be exposed to parental conflict: parents fight more frequently and longer in the presence of their sons than their daughters (Hetherington, Cox, & Cox, 1982). As is noted below, this increased exposure to conflict before the divorce may contribute to the difficulties that mothers and sons experience after the divorce.

After the separation, there is often a lengthy period of family disorganization and disruption and at the same time a search for new strategies for handling the new and different life situation. Eventually, a new phase occurs in which the single-parent family settles on a new but stable and organized lifestyle. A variety of factors such as the cause of the divorce, the financial status of the family, the age and gender of the children, the kind of separation settlement, and especially the custody arrangements and the kinds of social support available from relatives, friends, and neighbors can influence how quickly and how successfully families adjust to divorce.

Maternal Custody

Mothers usually have physical custody of children after the breakup of a marriage, and most of our knowledge of the impact of divorce on children focuses on mother-custody families.

Divorce may cause psychological upset, but it has practical implications as well. As Weitzman (1985) argues, women suffer much more economic hardship than men following a breakup. One estimate found that women suffered about a 30% decline in income in the year after divorce, whereas noncustodial fathers retain 90% of their predivorce income (McLanahan & Booth, 1989). Divorced women generally return to their predivorce income levels, but generally due to remarriage (Duncan & Hoffman, 1985).

Fathers' failure to pay child support contributes to the economic plight of divorced mother-custody families as well. In 1990, only about half of divorced women received child support awards, but only 30% ever received full payments (Current Populations Reports, 1991). Moreover, child support payments decrease across time (Furstenberg & Cherlin, 1991). And children suffer as a consequence, with 10% of Euro-American children and 14% of African American children slipping into poverty in the year after their parents' separation (Duncan & Hoffman, 1985). As a result of the divorce, they often have to move to smaller homes in less desirable neighborhoods, moves that involve not only loss of friends and neighbors but possibly poorer schools and more crime and threats to personal safety.

In combination with the economic, social, and emotional strains accompanying divorce, divorce can have serious consequences, at least in the short run, for both mothers and fathers as individuals. In the first year following divorce, parents felt more anxious, depressed, and angry than nondivorced parents (Hetherington et al., 1982). The effects were more severe and lasted longer for divorced mothers than for fathers—particularly mothers of boys: even after two years they were still feeling less competent, more anxious, and angrier than married mothers or mothers of girls (Hetherington et al., 1982; Hetherington & Jodl, 1994). However, many fathers continue to suffer emotionally from the loss of regular contact with their children.

Short-Term Effects on Children

Both mothers and fathers are less effective parents after divorce, especially in the first year, although there is a clear pattern of improvement over time (Hetherington, 1989). According to Hetherington's examination of the impact of divorce on young children's adjustment, divorced parents settled for less mature behavior from their children than parents from intact families would accept and expected their children to accept fewer responsibilities—a factor that may contribute to the household disorganization that often accompanies divorce.

Divorced mothers generally showed less affection toward their children of either sex than did married mothers, and especially toward their sons (Hetherington, 1989). Besides being less affectionate, the divorced mothers treated their sons more harshly and gave them more threatening commands, though they did not systematically enforce them. Fathers, on the other hand, tended to be permissive and indulgent, a pattern that probably made it more difficult for mothers to control their children. The boys in divorced families were less compliant and more aggressive than boys in intact families.

After two years, the situation was much better, with both parents and children adapting to the situation. Fathers became more restrictive with their children, and mothers became less restrictive. Even after two years, however, the boys in the divorced families were still more aggressive, more impulsive, and more disobedient toward their mothers than either girls in divorced families or children in intact families (Hetherington, 1989, 1993).

Numerous other studies provide the same general profile of the short-term effects of divorce. After divorce, parenting quality shifts as mothers are more erratic and less able to control and monitor their children's behavior. Sons and mothers have the most difficult time and engage in coercive, escalating negative exchanges. Girls suffer too and are noncompliant, angry, and dependent in the first year after divorce, but they recover sooner than their male siblings (Hetherington, Stanley-Hagan, & Anderson, 1989; Stevenson & Black, 1995).

Long-Term Effects on Children

In a follow-up at six years, Hetherington (1989) found that in families in which the mother was still single, the girls who were relatively well adjusted after two years remained in good social and emotional shape after six years, with a close relationship with their mothers. These girls did have more responsibility and more power within the family. Although the adjustment profile is reasonable for girls in the preschool and elementary school years, adjustment problems are more evident at the onset of adolescence. During the teen years, girls of divorce may show increased conflict with their mothers, increased noncompliance, antisocial behavior, emotional disturbance, loss in self-esteem, and problems in heterosexual relations and sexual behavior (Chase-Lansdale & Hetherington, 1990; Newcomber & Udry, 1987; Zaslow, 1988). Especially if the girls were early maturers, there was more alienation and disengagement from their families. While girls do well in the short run, there seems to be a long-term sleeper effect in adolescent girls and in young women as well. The risk of being a teenage mother increased three times as a result of divorce, from 11% in intact families to 33% in divorced families. In a follow-up study of girls who had experienced divorce early in their lives, Hetherington (1988) found that these young women were more likely to have married at a young age, to have been pregnant before marriage, and to have selected husbands who were more psychologically unstable

and less educated and economically secure than women in intact or widowed families. Moreover, national survey studies of nationally representative samples confirm the increased difficulties in heterosexual relationships for young women of divorce (Furstenberg & Cherlin, 1991). Adult women from divorced families were more likely than those from nondivorced families to have higher rates of divorce themselves (Hetherington, 1987).

What about the long-term adjustment of boys? In the Hetherington study (1989, 1993), boys remained problematic for their mothers and themselves. Divorced mothers continued to spend less time with their sons and feel less close to daughters or sons than mothers in nondivorced families. Moreover, the mothers continued to be ineffective in their control efforts and continued to engage in coercive interactions with their sons. Monitoring of boys was lower in divorced nonremarried households, and the boys engaged in more antisocial behavior and spent more time away from home with peers.

Finally, national survey studies suggest that divorce is related to several negative outcomes (McLanahan & Sandefur, 1994). The risk of dropping out of high school was 31% for children of divorced families or over twice as high as children in intact families (13%). This outcome has serious long-term implications and may reduce future employment and educational opportunities.

Perhaps the most dramatic evidence of the long-term effects of divorce comes from a recent study of the predictors of longevity (Freidman et al., 1995). In a follow-up investigation of a group of gifted children originally studied by Lewis Terman in the 1920s, individuals who experienced parental divorce during childhood were likely to die sooner than those whose parents stayed married. Although these individuals were more likely themselves to divorce as adults, even after taking this into account, parental divorce was still a predictor of premature death. Clearly, divorce has long-term consequences, although the mechanisms by which divorce alters longevity are still not clearly understood. Finally, there may be cohort effects because divorce was much less normative in the 1920s and 1930s than in the present era.

Individual Contributors: Age, Gender, and Temperament

Individual characteristics of children may contribute to the effects of divorce on children's subsequent adaptation. The role of age of the child at the time of divorce remains inconclusive, because age at divorce, the time elapsed since divorce, and the child's age are confounded (Hetherington,

1995). Although some national survey studies indicate that preschool-age children are most negatively affected by divorce (Zill, Morrison, & Corio, 1993), divorce is probably traumatic for children of all ages. Because children at different developmental stages have different levels of comprehension and different strategies for coping with the changes surrounding divorce, their pattern of reactions are likely to differ as well. Preschoolers tend to blame themselves for the divorce; moreover, they do not understand their parents' emotions, needs, and behavior. Because young children have only poorly formed concepts of families, they often are uncertain about new living arrangements or new patterns of contact between themselves and the departing parent. This often leads to excessive fears of being abandoned and exaggerated hopes of reconciliation (Hetherington et al., 1989).

Children who are older at the time of divorce react differently. Seven- and 8-year-old children are less likely to blame themselves, but fears of abandonment and rejection are common and their interpersonal understanding is still limited. Only by adolescence are children able to understand the divorce process, to assign responsibility for the divorce, to resolve loyalty conflicts with their parents, and to cope with the economic and social changes that often accompany divorce. However, "if the home situation is particularly painful adolescents, more than younger children, do have the option to disengage and seek gratification elsewhere such as in the neighborhood, peer group or school" (Hetherington, 1979, p. 855). One-third of older children and adolescents become disengaged from their families, and this involvement in the wider community can have either positive or negative effects. If the involvement translates into more time on school issues and closer friendships with well-behaved peers, that's all for the better. On the other hand, if weakened family ties lead to joining a gang or drinking and drug use, the results can be damaging for the adolescent (Chase-Lansdale & Hetherington, 1990).

Similarly, the impact of gender remains unresolved. As noted above, many earlier studies of preadolescent children found that boys were more negatively affected by divorce than girls. More recent studies, especially those involving adolescents, are less likely to report marked gender differences. As in the case of age, boys and girls react differently and at different ages to divorce. Personality and temperament differences are important as well. Hetherington (1989), for example, found that temperamentally difficult boys receive more negative treatment from divorced mothers, especially if the mother is depressed, under high

stress, and receives little social support. At the same time, Hetherington (1989, 1995) has found evidence for a "steeling" or "inoculation" effect, in which children are better able to deal with stress as a result of exposure to and successful coping with current stressors (Hetherington, 1995; Rutter, 1987). Girls who are temperamentally easy actually emerge with enhanced coping skills after the experience of a moderately stressful and supportive divorce. As Hetherington (1995) noted, "the psychologically poor get poorer and the psychologically rich get richer when confronting the changes and challenges of divorce" (p. 28).

Children's Maladjustment: An Outcome or a Contributor to Divorce?

Most research on divorce assesses children's functioning after the divorce, but perhaps children are already having difficulties even before the divorce. In support of this view, Jeanne Block and her colleagues found that the increased aggression in adolescent boys after divorce was evident 11 years prior to the marital breakup (Block, Block, & Gjerde, 1986). Nor is this an isolated finding. In a recent study of two large representative samples, a British sample of 14,476 children and an American sample of 2,270 children, Cherlin et al. (1991) studied children's behavior problems before and after divorce. Again, there were preexisting behavior problems as well as predivorce family conflict that accounted for the nearly half of the impact of the divorce on children's adjustment. Preexisting problems were especially important for predicting postdivorce adjustment for boys. While these studies suggest that divorce has a negative impact on children, we should be cautious about attributing all postdivorce effects to the divorce itself. As Emery and Forehand (1994) argued, "The small differences in psychological adjustment found between children from married and divorced families are at least partially an effect of either pre-divorce family distress or perhaps genetic factors that are linked with both an increased rate of divorce and more behavior problems among children" (p. 89). However, when the predivorce behavior problems are controlled, the differences between children in divorced and nondivorced families are reduced but still evident (Hetherington, 1995).

Father's Role When Mother Has Custody

Even when the mother has custody of the children, the father remains important. Hetherington (1993) found that, at first, many divorced fathers had almost as much face-to-face contact with their children as fathers in intact homes—a reminder that many fathers in nondivorced families do not spend much time with their children. However, there is generally a gradual decline in father-child contact after divorce. In the National Survey of Children, a representative sample of children and families studied since the mid-1970s, fewer than 20% of the fathers had weekly contact with their offspring and another 20% saw them less than once a month. Nearly 50% of the fathers in this study had not visited their children in the previous year. Ten years after the divorce, a mere 10% of children still had weekly contact with their fathers, and nearly 66% had no contact in the previous year (Furstenberg, Nord, Peterson, & Zill, 1983). More recent studies suggest that the situation may be improving, but only slightly. Seltzer and Bianchi (1988) found that 37% of fathers saw their children once a month or more, and only 35% never had contact with their children.

More dramatic evidence of an increase in contact comes from a recent longitudinal study of 1,100 divorcing couples in California, where 64% of children reported seeing their fathers during the preceding month after more than three years after separation (Maccoby & Mnookin, 1992). However, many of these families had legal joint custody arrangements, which may have inflated the figures. In contrast, mothers who do not have custody are more likely to maintain contact with their children (Seltzer & Bianchi, 1988). Whereas 35% of fathers have no contact with their children, the rate for noncustodial mothers is 19%, with 46% maintaining at least monthly contact with their children. Society clearly defines women as mothers even when they no longer live with their children—another indication of the clear cultural guidelines that shape the definition of motherhood.

A variety of factors may account for fathers' "retreat from parenthood" (Furstenberg & Cherlin, 1991). Most of these factors flow from the circumstances of life after divorce rather than the quality of the father-child relationship before separation. In fact, predivorce parenting is not a good barometer of how involved a father will be with his children after the divorce (Hetherington et al., 1989). Residential mobility and geographic distance decrease visitation due to the practical difficulties of maintaining contact. Remarriage may help some children and wives, but it decreases contact between biological fathers and their children. Nor does it matter who remarries; whether it is mother or father who remarries, the result is similar: fathers decrease contact with their biological children. More affluent fathers maintain ties more often than poorer

fathers, in part because they can afford to visit and have the funds to make the contact mutually enjoyable. The custodial parent's attitude is important too. Between 25 and 50% of mothers interfere with or make visitation more difficult. Just as in intact families (Parke, 1996), mothers also serve as "gatekeepers" in divided families. Nor does the legal system help very much, since most states are lax in enforcing a father's right to spend time with his child or even prevent mothers from moving out of state (McLanahan & Sandefur, 1994).

Paternal Custody

Although we tend to take for granted maternal custody in divorce cases, it is a twentieth-century phenomenon. Before this century, under English law, children (and wives) were viewed as property of the husband, and fathers were nearly always granted custody of their children. A father had to be grossly unfit before an exception was made. In our century, by contrast, until very recently fathers were typically awarded custody only if the mother was viewed as exceptionally incompetent.

The view that mothers are uniquely suited, both biologically and psychologically, to raise children has prevailed. And this attitude is generally held by the courts, who "have long paid lip service to a `best interest' doctrine when child custody is at issue, but in practice, courts have been guided by the generalization that the mother should be awarded custody except in extreme circumstances" (Santrock & Warshak, 1979, p. 113). Since the 1970s, the situation has shifted, and the inevitability of maternal custody is being challenged. Currently, approximately 11.4% of divorced fathers have custody of their children in the United States. However, many more fathers indicate that they would like physical custody than actually seek this arrangement. In a recent California study, of the 33% of fathers who indicated they desired physical custody of their children, more than half either failed to request custody or requested mother custody in their legal court documents (Maccoby & Mnookin, 1992). Apparently women have a higher interest in retaining custody than men—in spite of the legal and ideological shifts that our society has undergone over the past two decades. Several factors may account for these findings. Many men may feel less well prepared for sole custody and the responsibilities of child care than women who have been socialized more clearly into a caregiver role. Or perhaps some men view the possibility of winning a custody dispute as low, which leads them not to pursue custody. Moreover, men who receive custody tend to be older, be more established, and have higher socioeconomic status than men who are not awarded custody. Finally, men are more likely to gain custody after remarrying. Together, these findings suggest that men who gain custody are not representative of divorced fathers in general and indicate the need for caution in interpreting the findings on the effects of father custody on children (Emery, 1988).

How do fathers with custody affect their children's development? A small number of studies have compared the adjustment of children in mother and father custody homes (Emery, 1988; Stevenson & Black, 1995). The major finding is that children who live with their same-sex parent are better adjusted than those who live with their opposite-sex parent. Santrock and Warshak (1979) found that father-custody boys and mother-custody girls were found to be more socially competent and more satisfied with their living arrangements than children who lived with their opposite-sex parent. However, we need to be careful about drawing strong conclusions from this study because only 20 father-custody and 20 mother-custody families were involved and the range of outcomes that was assessed was limited.

A more ambitious evaluation of the impact of father custody on children's development was recently completed by Clarke-Stewart and Hayward (1996). A sample of 5- to 13-year-old children, 72 in father custody and 115 in mother custody, was assessed using both parental and child reports of psychological well-being. Children in father custody displayed higher self-esteem, less anxiety and depression, and fewer "difficult" behaviors than children in mother custody. Although both boys and girls did better in father than mother custody, the effects were stronger for boys. Children did best when they were in father custody—and the custodial parent was happier and more affluent—and when they spent holidays and did a broad range of activities with the noncustodial parent. Again, boys are more likely to benefit from this set of factors, whereas girls appear to be mainly affected by contact with the nonresidential parent.

Nor are these findings evident in only small-scale studies or in young children (Amato & Keith, 1991). Peterson and Zill (1986), in a study of a 1981 national sample of 1,400 children ages 12 to 16, found similar beneficial effects of living with a same-sex parent after divorce. Antisocial behavior, depression, and impulsive/hyperactive behavior were all lower for children residing with a same-sex parent following the family breakup. Others report that high school students living with the same-sex parent were less likely to drop out of school than were students living

with the opposite-sex parent—unless the custodial parent had remarried (Zimiles & Lee, 1991).

However, we need to be careful in interpreting these findings or in generalizing from these studies to all divorced fathers. In fact, one recent large-scale study (Buchanan, Maccoby, & Dornbusch, 1992, 1996) raises doubts about the benefits of father custody. In this investigation, adolescent adjustment and family processes were examined in a group of 522 adolescents (10.5 to 18 years old) living in mother, father, or dual residence arrangements 4.5 years after parental separation. Various aspects of adolescent adjustment, including depression, anxiety, deviance, grades, and school effort were assessed through telephone interviews with the adolescents. Adolescents in father residence had poorer adjustment than adolescents in mother and dual residence arrangements, although the differences between groups were small. Father-resident adolescents were more deviant than mother-resident respondents and had lower grades than dual or to a lesser degree mother-residence adolescents. Nor did Buchanan et al. find that adolescents did better when living with their same-sex parent. The superiority of the mother-residence arrangement was evident for both boys and girls, although the effects were stronger for girls. The link between residence and adjustment was primarily indirect, mediated by differences in closeness to and monitoring by the residential parent. Poorer adjustment in father residence was related to poorer monitoring by residential fathers. For children of both sexes, poorer adjustment in father residence may be due, in part, to less close relationships with the residential parent, which makes it difficult for the residential parent to effectively monitor their adolescent's activities. In the case of girls in father residence, poor adjustment may have been due to an elevated frequency of residence changes, which in turn may have contributed to the poor paternal monitoring of girls. A similar pattern of poorer paternal monitoring, using parental rather than adolescent reports was found by Maccoby and Mnookin (1992). Another study of over 400 eighth graders living in mother-only or father-only homes also failed to find *any* evidence that boys and girls benefit significantly from living with their same-sex parent (Downey & Powell, 1993).

In light of the conflicting evidence, no firm conclusions concerning the wisdom of same-sex custody and residence arrangements following separation and divorce are warranted. Moreover, more attention should be paid to the factors that enhance child adjustment, such as fostering close ties between parents and offspring, minimizing post-divorce parent-parent conflict and maintaining vigilance to their children's lives, interests, and activities—processes which may be important, regardless of the residential arrangements. Clearly, we need to be cautious about basing any judicial decisions about mother versus father custody on the evidence that is available.

Joint Custody

In view of the increasing evidence that fathers are competent caregivers and mothers are more active participants in the outside workforce, it is not surprising that the doctrine of sole custody has been reexamined. Perhaps children and ex-spouses would all benefit if joint custody was an option in cases of divorcing adults with children. "At its best, joint custody presents the possibility that each family member can 'win' in post divorce life rather than insisting that a custody decision identify 'winners' and 'losers': mothers and fathers each win a significant future role in the lives of offspring and children win as a consequence" (Thompson, 1994, p. 17).

Joint custody can take two main forms. Legal joint custody refers to an arrangement by which both mother and father retain and share responsibility for decisions concerning their children's lives but generally physically reside with one of their parents. Under a joint physical custody arrangement, the children live with both parents for certain periods of time throughout the year. While the length and timing of these periods vary, it is expected that children will have physical access to both parents on a regular basis.

To examine the impact of joint custody on children, Maccoby and Mnookin (1992) followed 1,100 families beginning with their separation, through the divorce, and for another two-and-a-half years, for a total of three-and-a-half years. Nearly 80% of the families had joint legal custody, although generally mothers receive sole physical custody in over 67% of the cases, whereas fathers receive sole physical custody less than 10% of the time. Even when joint physical custody is the legal decision, only about half the children actually live in dual-residence arrangements, while a third live with their mothers. Overall, more than two-thirds of the families opted for a mother-residence arrangement and continued with this residence plan for the three-year period. However, boys were more likely to live with their fathers or in dual residence than girls, who more often lived with their mothers. Moreover, older children were more likely to live with their fathers than their mothers, and children between 3 and 8 were most likely to be in dual-residence arrangements. Arrangements are not static; over one-quarter of the children had changed houses during the three years of the study. Moreover, nearly half of the children in mother-residence families changed—either increased or decreased—the amount of contact that they had with their fathers.

To understand the impact of differing custody arrangements on children, we first need to consider patterns of co-parenting. Only about a quarter of the families were able to cooperate. Another 25 to 30% of the parents were conflicted, and 30 to 40% were disengaged, with the parents avoiding contact with each other and practicing "parallel," uncoordinated parenting in the two residences. Over time, conflicting parenting decreased and disengagement increased. In a follow-up, four-and-a-half years after separation, adolescents (10- to 18-year-olds) were interviewed to assess their feelings about their parenting arrangements and their own adjustment (Buchanan, Maccoby, & Dornbusch, 1991). "Feeling caught" between parents was more likely to occur in high-conflict/low-cooperation families in which children are asked to carry messages between parents and to inform each parent of the other's activities. Adolescents of parents who had disengaged from one another were less likely to feel this way than adolescents whose parents were still in "conflict," but more likely to feel caught than adolescents of parents who were cooperating. Dual-residence arrangements are particularly harmful when parents continue to be in conflict. Older adolescents and girls were more likely to feel caught in the between-parent squeeze. Adolescents with higher feelings of being caught were more likely to experience depression and anxiety and engage in more deviant behavior (e.g., smoking, drugs, fighting, cheating, stealing) than adolescents who experienced more interparental cooperation.

This pattern of findings is consistent with earlier smaller studies; namely, that it is the degree of parental conflict rather than custody arrangements themselves that seems to be the best predictor of children's adjustment (Luepnitz, 1982). Joint custody is clearly not a panacea for divorced families or for divorced fathers in particular. Fathers' influence and contact with their children seem less governed by custody arrangements than by other factors such as geographic distance and relationships with their ex-spouses. In the long run, the advantage of joint custody may be its "symbolic value to parents and children" (Emery, 1988, p. 93)—a sign to fathers that they retain some rights and obligations as a parent and a message to their children that their fathers are still part of their larger family and a significant figure in their lives. At the same time, it is evident that joint custody is not a problem-free solution, especially if interparental conflict continues after divorce. Evaluations of the long-term impact of differing types of custody arrangements on children as well their parents are needed.

Stepparenting and Children's Adjustment

Another role is emerging for men as a result of the increasing number of divorces and remarriages: the role of stepfather. Some estimate that 75% of women and 80% of men will remarry after a divorce. Moreover, about 40% of U.S. children will spend some time in a stepparent family before they are 18 (Glick, 1989). In 1978, 10% of children in the United States lived with one biological parent and a stepparent, usually a stepfather; by 1990, 15% of U.S. children were living with a stepparent (Hernandez, 1993). Of particular significance for some children is that remarriage may only be another temporary life course "waystation rather than a destination" (Hetherington & Clingempeel, 1992, p. 9) because the rate of divorce in remarried families is about 10% higher than in first marriages (Furstenberg & Cherlin, 1991). Divorce is most likely to occur in remarried families in the first five years, the period in which the new stepfamily is trying to work out an acceptable organizational system.

How do stepfathers function in the parenting role? As Hetherington (1989) found, stepfathers, in contrast to biological fathers, tended to be disengaged and less likely to have an authoritative parenting style involving warm, responsive, but firm discipline and good communication. Over time things improved, at least in the case of boys. Toward girls, disengagement remained the main parenting style.

Both the age and gender of the children contribute to the degree of success or failure that the new stepfamily achieves (Hetherington, 1989; Stevenson & Black, 1995). Very young children and postadolescent children tend to accept a stepparent more easily than do adolescents. Adolescence is a particularly difficult age period for children to undergo the changes associated with remarriage. In a recent longitudinal study of remarriage, Hetherington and Clingempeel (1992) examined how well 9- to 13-year-olds cope with this type of transition. Although remarriage improves the adjustment of younger children, especially boys, the introduction of a stepfather does not alleviate the adjustment problems in adolescents. Adolescents in remarried families demonstrated a variety of problems, both externalizing disorders such as acting out and disruptive behavior and internalizing problems such as depression and withdrawal. Moreover, they were less competent socially and academically than children from nondivorced families.

At a 26-month follow-up, there was little improvement for adolescents in remarried families (Hetherington & Clingempeel, 1992).

Gender is another determinant of stepparent effectiveness. While some studies show that boys have more adjustment problems in single mother-headed households than girls, when remarriage occurs the gender picture is reversed (Emery, 1988; Stevenson & Black, 1995). Boys who often have been involved in coercive relationships with their custodial mothers may have little to lose and much to gain from the addition of a caring stepfather. Daughters, on the other hand, may feel the intrusion of stepfathers into their close relationship with their mothers as more threatening and disruptive. In preadolescent children, divorce has more adverse consequences for boys and remarriage for girls. However, these gender differences should be viewed cautiously, since large-scale national studies have generally not found clear differences in boys' and girls' adaptation to remarriage (Allison & Furstenberg, 1989; Furstenberg & Cherlin, 1991). Age seems to be important, because recent studies of remarriage when children were in adolescence have found few gender differences (Hetherington & Clingempeel, 1992).

What are the long-term effects on children of growing up in a home with a stepfather? The evidence is mixed (Stevenson & Black, 1995). Some investigators report that the presence of a stepfather has beneficial effects, especially for teaching boys the behaviors traditionally considered masculine. Others are less positive about the impact of "reconstituted" families. In a national survey of children, Zill (1978) found that children living with mothers and stepfathers were significantly more likely to be seen as "needing help" than were children in mother-father or single-parent homes. Clearly, divorce and the subsequent adjustments that children must make are difficult, and remarriage may bring new problems and require even further new adjustments. However, parents and stepparents who are sensitive to the child's needs can develop good family relationships. Finally, it is important to underscore that only about 25% of children in remarried families experience any long-term adverse effects (Emery, 1988). While not an insignificant number, it is clear that the vast majority of children in remarried families are doing quite well.

Social scientists are much better at describing the complexities of problems such as divorce, custody, and remarriage than they are at prescribing solutions for individual children and families. We can describe the impact of divorce and remarriage on children and their parents *in general,* but the best path for individual children, mothers, and fathers can be guided only in part by these findings. In the final analysis, decisions about divorce, custody, and remarriage need to be informed by the unique circumstances of individual lives and the values, priorities, and prospects of individual families (Parke, 1996).

Single versus Multiple Transitions

To date, societal changes such as shifts in the timing of parenting, work participation, and divorce have been treated relatively independently, but, in fact, these events co-occur rather than operate in any singular fashion (Parke & Tinsley, 1984). As earlier work (Simmons & Blyth, 1987) on the impact of multiple transitions—such as the onset of puberty and entry into junior high school—on children's adjustment has found, co-occurrence of several changes can have a cumulative impact on the adolescent's adaptation. Similarly, as the number of environmental risk variables increase, the level of family functioning and child outcomes decrease (Rutter, 1987; Sameroff et al., 1987). One would expect that the co-occurrence of the arrival of a new infant accompanied by job loss would have very different effects than either of these events occurring singly. Moreover, the impact of any historical change may be different as a result of its occurrence in the same period as another change or changes. For example, women's increased presence in the workplace and delay in the onset of parenthood vary, and probably each event has different meaning without the other change. This implies the research need for multivariate designs to capture the simultaneous impacts of multiple events on family socialization strategies.

REMAINING ISSUES AND FUTURE TRENDS

A number of issues remain to be examined in future research if we are to describe fully the complexities, specify the determinants and processes, and outline the consequences of family-child relationships. These include the choice of the unit of analysis, the effects of family variation, types of developmental change, the role of historical change, and methodological and contextual issues.

Unit of Analysis

Current work is clearly recognizing the importance of considering parents from a family systems perspective.

However, our conceptual analysis of dyadic and triadic units of analysis is still limited (Barrett & Hinde, 1988; Filsinger, 1991; Parke, 1988). Considerable progress has been made in describing the behavior of individual interactants (e.g., mother, father, child) within dyadic and to a lesser extent triadic settings, but less progress has been achieved in developing a language for describing interaction in dyadic and triadic terms. Even if such terms as *reciprocal* and *synchronous* hold promise, there remains little real advance in this regard. In addition, greater attention needs to be paid to the family as a unit of analysis. A number of researchers have offered different taxonomies of family types or typologies that move us to this level of analysis (Kreppner, 1989; Reiss, 1981), but to date little effort has been made to apply these notions systematically to family relationships in childhood.

Parenting and Family Variation

One of the clear advances of the past decade is recognition of the importance of individual differences in children; one of the next advances will be the recognition of individual differences among families. Recognition of individual variability across families implies the necessity of expanding sampling procedures. In spite of demands for a greater awareness of family diversity, the range of family types that are studied is still relatively narrow. Although progress has been made in describing interaction patterns of parents and children in different cultures (Bornstein, 1991; Roopnarine & Carter, 1992) and in different ethnic groups in the United States (Harrison et al., 1990), this work represents only a beginning. Particularly critical is an extension of earlier work on parent-child relationships in other ethnic groups to other subsystems such as the marital, sibling, and family systems. Evaluation of family systems notions in families with different ethnic backgrounds, organizations, and structures will provide an opportunity to test the generality of this theoretical perspective. Finally, recent work on gay and lesbian families (C. Patterson, 1995) and the effects on children of growing up in these alternative family arrangements is raising important questions about the necessity of male-female family arrangements for the rearing of children.

Types of Developmental Change

Developmental issues need to be addressed more fully to include children at a wider range of ages. In spite of

Maccoby's (1992) plea, we still are only beginning to map developmental changes in parental socialization strategies. Moreover, we need to move beyond childhood and examine more closely parental relationships with their adult children—if we are to achieve a life span view of family socialization. Although development traditionally has marked change in the individual child, it is evident from this review that this perspective is too limited and that parents, as well as children, continue to develop across time (Elder, Ch. 3, Volume 1; Parke, 1988). Parents' management of a variety of life course tasks, such as marriage, work, and personal identity, will clearly determine how they will execute parental tasks; in turn, these differences may find expression in measures of parent-child interaction. Because developmental shifts in children's perceptual, cognitive, and social development in turn may alter parental attitudes and behaviors and/or the nature of the adults' own developmentally relevant choices, such as work or career commitment, this clearly argues for the recognition of two developmental trajectories: a child developmental course and an adult developmental sequence. The description of the interplay between these two types of developmental curves is necessary to capture adequately the nature of developmental changes in a family's role in the socialization process.

Monitoring Secular Trends

There is a continuing need to monitor secular trends and to describe their impact on family relationships (Parke & Stearns, 1993). Secular change is complex and clearly does not affect all individuals equally or on all behavior patterns to the same extent. In fact, it is a serious oversimplification to assume that general societal trends can isomorphically be applied across all individual children, parents, and families. Moreover, better guidelines are necessary to illuminate which aspects of processes within families are most likely to be altered by historical events and which processes are less amenable to change. For example, the structural dynamics of early interaction (Stern, 1977) as well as some qualitative aspects of early parent-infant interactive style may be insulated from the influence of secular shifts. Are fathers biologically prepared to interact in a more physical way, and mothers in a more verbal mode? If this assumption about differences in parental play style is, in fact, true, rates of interactions would be more likely to change than style when employment opportunities for men and women become more equal. Alternatively, the restraints may be more solely environmental, and as opportunities for

adult male and female participation in child care and child rearing equalize, some maternal-paternal stylistic differences may diminish.

Methodological and Design Issues

It is likely that no single methodological strategy will suffice to explain the development of family socialization. Instead, a wide range of designs and data collection and data analysis strategies is necessary. To date, there is still a paucity of information concerning interrelations across molar and molecular levels of analysis. However, it is becoming increasingly clear that a microanalytic strategy is not always more profitable in terms of describing relationships among interactive partners; in fact, in some cases, ratings may be a more useful approach. A set of guidelines concerning the appropriate level of analysis for different questions would be helpful.

Parents' own reports continue to be underutilized in most research. Self-reports are not a substitute for observational data but can provide important information that can aid in interpretation of observed patterns (Goodnow & Collins, 1990; Parke, 1978b). Other types of self-reports than structured interviews and questionnaires need to be more frequently employed. Focus groups are commonly used in other disciplines but seldom have been used by psychologists. A focus group is a type of group interview that relies on an emergent process of interaction among group members to produce data and insights that would not be found without such interaction (Morgan, 1988). Focus groups are excellent forums in which to explore micro-level experiences of families as well as examining similarities and differences across different genders, socioeconomic classes, and ethnic groups. These provide a unique opportunity for parents and children to articulate their concerns, values, and goals in a context that is less constrained than the usual interview format. This technique is of particular value in the early stages of research with understudied populations (see Gomel, Tinsley, & Clark, 1995; Vásquez-García et al., 1995, for illustrations of the use of focus groups with African American and Hispanic American groups). Moreover, quantitative analytic strategies have recently become available for use with the type of qualitative verbal reports generated by focus groups (Richards & Richards, 1991). Recent computer programs (e.g., Nudist 3.3, Non-numerical Unstructured Data Indexing, Searching and Theory Building) allow the researcher to explore patterns in the data that aid in grounded theory construction, while simultaneously allowing for the application of a coding scheme to the transcript text and then converting the coded text into quantitative information. Gomel, Tinsley, and Clark (1995) recently successfully utilized this Nudist program in a focus group study of the impact of economic downturn on ethnic minority families. Ethnographic methodologies can play an important role in family research as well, particularly to gain a better understanding of contextual factors that affect parental functioning (Burton, 1995).

Reliance on nonexperimental strategies may be insufficient to address the important issue of direction of effects in work on the impact of parents on children and families. Experimental strategies have been underutilized in studies of families (Cummings, 1995). By experimentally modifying either the type of parental behavior or level of involvement, firmer conclusions concerning the direct causative role that parents play in modifying their children's and their spouses' development will be possible. Intervention studies (e.g., Dickie & Carnahan, 1980; Parke, Hymel, Power, & Tinsley, 1980) aimed at modifying fathering behavior provide models for this type of work; by extending these studies to include measures of child, mother, and father development, they could provide evidence of the impact of changes in parenting behavior on developmental outcomes. Moreover, these experimentally based interventions have clear policy implications by exploring the degree of plasticity of parenting behavior. Similarly, studies in which child behavior is either experimentally modified (Bell & Chapman, 1986) or children with known characteristics (e.g., hyperactivity, conduct disorder) are paired with parental surrogates (Anderson, Lytton, & Romney, 1986) are needed to capture the bidirectionality of family influence effects. By expanding the range of family members or subsystems that are measured, to include nontargeted individuals and subsystems, the impact of modifying the behavior of one family member on other parts of the family system could be evaluated. These interventions can serve as a vehicle for evaluation of alternative theoretical views of parenthood and socialization. More recognition of the utility of combined sampling strategies is needed. Recently, researchers have begun to use multistage sampling strategies, in which survey-level information on a national representative sample is secured in combination with the selection of a subsample for purposes of more intensive analyses, such as in-depth interviews or observations (Plomin, Reiss, Hetherington, & Howe, 1994). This strategy ensures greater confidence in the generalizability of the findings and gains access to process-level variables.

In terms of research design, under the influence of the behavior geneticists (Plomin, 1994; Rowe, 1994), there has been an increased focus on the value of nonshared environmental designs that allow measurement of the differential impact of families on different children within the same family. Although some have argued for the decreased use of traditional between-family designs that still form the foundation of most of our knowledge of family effects (Plomin, 1994), others (e.g., Hoffman, 1991) have argued for the continued utility of both types of designs with the goal of discovering "what environmental conditions might lead to sibling similarity and dissimilarity" (Hoffman, 1991, p. 199). More conceptual work is clearly needed to provide guidelines concerning the value of within- and between-family designs for different variables and issues.

Contextual Issues

Greater attention needs to be paid to the role of context in determining family relationships. How do parent-child interaction patterns shift between home and lab settings and across different types of interaction contexts such as play, teaching, and caregiving? Moreover, it is important to consider the social as well as the physical context. Recognition of the embeddedness of parents in family contexts is critical; in turn, conceptualizing families as embedded in a variety of extrafamilial social settings is important for understanding variation in family functioning. In this regard, it is necessary to recognize that variations in family structure and in ethnicity and social class will modify significantly the ways in which social networks are organized and utilized. For example, the role of the extended family is much more prominent in some groups, such as African American, than in other groups (Wilson, 1986). Similarly, single-parent families may be more directly embedded in community-based social networks than are two-parent families. Descriptions of these variations are necessary for an adequate understanding of the role of extrafamilial networks on parent and family functioning.

Locating Families in a Network of Socialization Influences

One of the major challenges is to determine the unique contribution of families to socialization outcomes as well as the limits of family effects (Harris, 1995; Rowe, 1994). As Maccoby and Martin (1983) argued in their review of the relations between parental functioning and characteristics of children, "in most cases the relationships that have appeared are not large, if one thinks in terms of the amount of variance accounted for" (p. 82). Their conclusion is still valid if we assume a narrow view of family influence as the direct impact of parents on their children. However, our increased recognition of the family as a *partner* with other institutions—peers, schools, media, religious institutions, and government policymakers that together influence children's development—has significantly expanded our view of the family's role in the socialization process. Further, it suggests that the family—directly and indirectly—may have a larger impact on children's outcomes than previously thought. As we have argued, families serve not just as direct influences on children but also as indirect influences in their roles as managers, modifiers, and negotiators on behalf of children in relation to these social institutions. However, our understanding of the ways families influence their children's socialization through their links with other institutions is still poorly understood. Moreover, these agents and institutions (e.g., schools, peers) play a direct as well as indirect role through the family in the socialization process.

Several issues need to be addressed. What are the unique roles that families play in socialization? Are some kinds of outcomes specifically within the family purview, such as the development of early social attachments? Are other outcomes influenced largely by other groups (e.g., tastes in music and fashion)? How do the relative roles of family and other agents shift across development? Perhaps the most interesting question concerns the ways families coordinate their socialization roles with other agents and institutions. Successful socialization requires a gradual sharing of responsibility for socialization with other groups, but we know relatively little about this process of coordination and mutual sharing across socialization agents. It is unhelpful to continue to posit linear models of decreasing family influence across development; instead, we need models that help us understand the changing nature of family influence relative to other groups and the mechanisms that maintain family values and orientation after direct influence has subsided. Recent work on the intergenerational transmission of working models of relationships (Thompson, Ch. 1, this Volume) testifies to the prolonged influence of childhood socialization on later adult parenting roles. In fact, this work anticipates one of the major themes of future research, namely, the impact of childhood socialization patterns on later adult development—not just in parenting, but in other types of adult relationships including marital, friendship, and work relationships. Closely related is the issue of how families and other institutions are linked. Recent work has focused on family-peer linkages (Parke et al., 1994), family-work ties (Crouter, 1994), and family-school relationships (Kellam, 1994), but less attention has been devoted to links between the family and religious institutions, the legal system, and social service systems. Nor are the processes that promote or constrain family involvement with other institutions well understood. Finally, the bidirectional nature of the linkage needs more attention so that we understand the dynamic and mutual influence of families on other institutions and vice versa.

CONCLUSION

Families continue to play a central role in the socialization process, but their role has undergone dramatic changes during the past several decades. To continue to develop our understanding, it is critical to monitor how changing ecologies of families of different ethnic backgrounds, in turn, are modifying the socialization strategies of families. Only by a better understanding of these changes will we be able to offer meaningful assistance and support for families. And only by achieving these goals will we be able to fulfill our aim of providing optimal conditions for promoting children's development.

ACKNOWLEDGMENTS

Thanks to Terri DeMent, Nancy Eisenberg, Halford Fairchild, Joan Grusec, Eleanor Maccoby, Lawrence Steinberg, and Barbara Tinsley for their comments on earlier versions of our chapter. Finally, thanks to Tracy Bunker for her preparation of the manuscript.

REFERENCES

Ahmeduzzaman, M., & Roopnarine, J. (1992). Sociodemographic factors, functioning style, social support, and fathers' involvement with preschools in African-American intact families. *Journal of Marriage and the Family, 54,* 699–707.

Alba, R. D. (1990). *Ethnic identity.* New Haven, CT: Yale University Press.

Allison, P. D., & Furstenberg, F. F. (1989). How marital dissolution affects children: Variations by age and sex. *Developmental Psychology, 25,* 540–549.

Amato, P. R., & Keith, B. (1991). Parental divorce and the wellbeing of children: A meta-analysis. *Psychological Bulletin, 110,* 26–46.

Anderson, K. E., Lytton, H., & Romney, D. M. (1986). Mothers' interactions with normal and conduct-disordered boys: Who affects whom? *Developmental Psychology, 22,* 604–609.

Baldwin, A., Baldwin, C., & Cole, R. E. (1990). Stress-resistant families and stress-resistant children. In J. E. Rolf, A. S. Masten, D. Cicchetti, K. N. Wechterlein, & S. Weintraub (Eds.), *Risk and protective factors in the development of psychopathology* (pp. 257–280). New York: Cambridge University Press.

Baldwin, M. J. (1992). Relational schema and the processing of information. *Psychological Review, 112,* 461–484.

Bandura, A. (1977). *Social learning theory.* Englewood Cliffs, NJ: Prentice-Hall.

Bandura, A., & Walters, R. H. (1963). *Social learning and personality development.* New York: Holt, Rinehart and Winston.

Banks, J. A. (1991). *Teaching strategies for ethnic studies* (5th ed.). Boston: Allyn & Bacon.

Barrett, J., & Hinde, R. A. (1988). Triadic interactions: Mother–first born–second born. In R. A. Hinde & J. Stevenson-Hinde (Eds.), *Towards understanding families* (pp. 181–190). Oxford, England: Oxford University Press.

Barth, F. (1969). *Ethnic groups and boundaries.* Boston: Little, Brown.

Barth, J. M., & Parke, R. D. (1993). Parent-child relationship influences on children's transition to school. *Merrill-Palmer Quarterly, 39,* 173–195.

Baruch, G. K., & Barnett, R. C. (1987). Role quality and psychological well-being. In F. Crosby (Ed.), *Spouse, parent, worker* (pp. 63–84). New Haven, CT: Yale University Press.

Bates, J. E. (1987). Temperament in infancy. In J. Osofsky (Ed.), *Handbook of Infancy* (2nd ed., pp. 1101–1149). New York: Wiley.

Baumrind, D. (1967). Child care practices anteceding 3 patterns of preschool behavior. *Genetic Psychology Monographs, 75,* 43–88.

Baumrind, D. (1973). The development of instrumental competence through socialization. In A. D. Pick (Ed.), *Minnesota Symposium on Child Psychology* (Vol 7, pp. 3–46). Minneapolis: University of Minnesota Press.

Baumrind, D. (1978). Parental disciplinary patterns and social competence in youth. *Youth and Society, 9,* 239–276.

Baumrind, D. (1989). Rearing competent children. In W. Damon (Ed.), *Child development today and tomorrow* (pp. 349–378). San Francisco: Jossey-Bass.

Baumrind, D. (1991). Parenting styles and adolescent development. In J. Brooks-Gunn, R. Lerner, & A. C. Peterson (Eds.), *The encyclopedia of adolescence* (pp. 746–758). New York: Garland.

Baydar, N., & Brooks-Gunn, J. (1995). *Profiles of America's grandmothers: Those who provide care for their grandchildren and those who do not.* Unpublished manuscript, Columbia University, New York, NY.

Bean, F. D., Chapa, J., Berg, R. R., & Sowards, K. (1994). Educational and sociodemographic incorporation among Hispanic immigrants to the United States. In B. Edmonston & J. S. Passel (Eds.), *Immigration and ethnicity: The integration of America's newest arrivals* (pp. 73–100). Washington, DC: The Urban Institute Press.

Bell, D. C., & Bell, L. G. (1989). Micro and macro measurement of family systems concepts. *Journal of Family Psychology, 3,* 137–157.

Bell, R. Q. (1968). A reinterpretation of the direction of effects in studies of socialization. *Psychological Review, 75,* 81–95.

Bell, R. Q., & Chapman, M. (1986). Child effects in studies using experimental or brief longitudinal approaches to socialization. *Developmental Psychology, 22,* 595–603.

Bell, R. Q., & Harper, L. V. (1977). *Child effects on adults.* Hillsdale, NJ: Erlbaum.

Belsky, J. (1984). The determinants of parenting: A process model. *Child Development, 55,* 83–96.

Belsky, J., Gilstrap, B., & Rovine, M. (1984). The Pennsylvania Infant and Family Development Project: I. Stability and change in mother-infant and father-infant interaction in a family setting at one, three and nine months. *Child Development, 55,* 692–705.

Belsky, J., Rovine, M., & Fish, M. (1989). The developing family system. In M. R. Gunnar & E. Thelen (Eds.), *Systems and development. The Minnesota Symposia on Child Psychology* (Vol. 22, pp. 119–166). Hillsdale, NJ: Erlbaum.

Belsky, J., Steinberg, L., & Draper, P. (1991). Childhood experience, interpersonal development, and reproductive strategy: An evolutionary theory of socialization. *Child Development, 62,* 647–670.

Belsky, J., & Volling, B. L. (1987). Mothering, fathering and marital interaction in the family triad: Exploring family systems processes. In P. Berman & F. Pedersen (Eds.), *Men's transition to parenthood: Longitudinal studies of early family experience* (pp. 43–64). Hillsdale, NJ: Erlbaum.

Belsky, J., Youngblade, L., Rovine, M., & Volling, B. (1991). Patterns of marital change and parent-child interaction. *Journal of Marriage and the Family, 53,* 487–498.

Berlin, I. N. (1987). Effects of changing Native American cultures on child development. *Journal of Community Psychology, 15,* 299–306.

Berry, J. W. (1980). Acculturation as varieties of adaptation. In A. M. Padilla (Ed.), *Acculturation: Theory, models, and some new findings* (pp. 9–25). Boulder, CO: Westview Press.

Betancourt, H., & Lopez, S. R. (1993). The study of culture, ethnicity, and race in American Psychology. *American Psychologist, 48,* 629–637.

Bhavnagri, N., & Parke, R. D. (1991). Parents as direct facilitators of children's peer relationships: Effects of age of child and sex of parent. *Journal of Personal and Social Relationships, 8,* 423–440.

Biernat, M., & Wortman, C. (1991). Sharing of home responsibilities between professionally employed women and their husbands. *Journal of Personality and Social Psychology, 60,* 844–860.

Bietel, A., & Parke, R. D. (1996). *Maternal attitudes as a determinant of father involvement.* Unpublished manuscript, University of Illinois, Champaign, IL.

Bijou, S. W., & Baer, D. M. (1961). *Child development: A systematic and empirical theory* (Vol. 1). New York: Appleton-Century-Crofts.

Blank, S. (1993). *Household formation and Mexican immigrants: An alternative strategy for meeting the goals of recent migration.* Paper presented at the 20th annual Center for Studies of the Family Conference, Brigham Young University, Provo, UT.

Block, J. H., Block, J., & Gjerde, P. F. (1986). The personality of children prior to divorce: A prospective study. *Child Development, 57,* 827–840.

Bolger, N., DeLongis, A., Kessler, R. C., & Wethington, E. (1989). The contagion of stress across multiple roles. *Journal of Marriage and the Family, 51,* 175–183.

Bornstein, M. H. (Ed.). (1991). *Cultural approaches to parenting.* Hillsdale, NJ: Erlbaum.

Boss, P. G. (1983). The marital relationship: Boundaries and ambiguities. In H. I. McCubbin & C. R. Figley (Eds.), *Stress and the family* (Vol. 1, pp. 26–40). New York: Bruner/Mazel.

Bossard, J., & Boll, E. (1950). *Ritual in family living.* Philadelphia: University of Pennsylvania Press.

Bowlby, J. (1958). The nature of the child's tie to his mother. *International Journal of Psycho-Analysis, 39,* 350–373.

Bowlby, J. (1969). *Attachment and loss* (Vol. 1). New York: Basic Books.

Bowman, P. J. (1993). The impact of economic marginality among African American husbands and fathers. In H. P. McAdoo (Ed.), *Family ethnicity* (pp. 120–137). Newbury Park, CA: Sage.

Bowman, P. J., & Howard, C. S. (1985). Race-related socialization, motivation and academic achievement: A study of Black youth in three-generation families. *Journal of the American Academy of Child Psychiatry, 24,* 134–141.

Boykin, A. W. (1983). The academic performance of Afro-American children. In J. Spence (Ed.), *Achievement and achievement motives* (pp. 321–371). San Francisco: Freeman.

Boykin, A. W., & Toms, F. D. (1985). Black child socialization: A conceptual framework. In H. P. McAdoo & J. L. McAdoo (Eds.), *Black children: Social, educational, and parental environments* (pp. 33–51). Newbury Park, CA: Sage.

Boyum, L., & Parke, R. D. (1995). Family emotional expressiveness and children's social competence. *Journal of Marriage and Family, 57,* 593–608.

Bradbury, T. N., & Fincham, F. D. (1989). Behavior and satisfaction in marriage: Prospective mediating processes. *Review of Personality and Social Psychology, 10,* 119–143.

Bretherton, I., & Waters, E. (Eds.). (1985). Growing points of attachment theory and research. *Monographs of the Society for Research in Child Development, 50*(1/2, Serial No. 209).

Bridges, L. J., & Grolnick, W. S. (1995). The development of emotional self-regulation in infancy and early childhood. In N. Eisenberg (Ed.), *Review of Personality and Social Psychology, 15,* 185–211.

Brodinsky, D. M., Lang, R., & Smith, D. W. (1995). Parenting adopted children. In M. Bornstein (Ed.), *Handbook of parenting* (Vol. 3, pp. 209–232). New York: Wiley.

Bronfenbrenner, U. (1958). Socialization and social class through time and space. In E. E. Maccoby, R. M. Newcomb, & E. Harley (Eds.), *Readings in social psychology* (pp. 400–425). New York: Holt, Rinehart and Winston.

Bronfenbrenner, U. (1979). *The ecology of human development.* Cambridge, MA: Harvard University Press.

Bronfenbrenner, U. (1986). Ecology of the family as a context for human development: Research perspectives. *Developmental Psychology, 22,* 723–742.

Bronfenbrenner, U. (1989). Ecological systems theory. In R. Vasta (Ed.), *Annals of child development* (Vol. 6, pp. 187–250). Greenwich, CT: JAI Press.

Brooks-Gunn, J., Berlin, L. J., & Aber, J. L. (1993, November). *A consideration of self-sufficiency and parenting in the context of the Teenage Parent Demonstration Program.* Paper presented at the 2nd National Head Start research conference, Washington, DC.

Brooks-Gunn, J., & Chase-Lansdale, P. L. (1995). *Adolescent parenthood.* In M. Bornstein (Ed.), *Handbook of parenting* (pp. 113–150). Hillsdale, NJ: Erlbaum.

Brooks-Gunn, J., Duncan, G. J., Pamela, K., & Sealand, N. (1993). Do neighborhoods influence child and adolescent development? *American Journal of Sociology, 99,* 353–395.

Brooks-Gunn, J., & Furstenberg, F. F. (1986). The children of adolescent mothers: Physical, academic and psychological outcomes. *Developmental Review, 6,* 224–251.

Bryant, B. (1985). The neighborhood walk: Sources of support in middle childhood. *Monographs of the Society for Research in Child Development, 50*(3, Serial No. 210).

Bryant, B. K. (1989). The child's perspective of sibling caretaking and its relevance to understanding social-emotional functioning and development. In P. G. Zukow (Ed.), *Sibling interaction across cultures: Theoretical and methodological issues* (pp. 143–164). New York: Springer-Verlag.

Buchanan, C. M., Maccoby, E. E., & Dornbusch, S. M. (1991). Caught between parents: Adolescents' experience in divorced families. *Child Development, 62,* 1008–1029.

Buchanan, C. M., Maccoby, E. E., & Dornbusch, S. M. (1992). Adolescents and their families after divorce: Three residential arrangements compared. *Journal of Research on Adolescence, 2,* 261–291.

Buchanan, C. M., Maccoby, E. E., & Dornbusch, S. M. (1996). *Adolescents after divorce.* Cambridge, MA: Harvard University Press.

Bugental, D. (1991). Affective and cognitive processes within threat-oriented family systems. In I. E. Sigel, A. V. McGillicuddy-DeLisi, & J. J. Goodnow (Eds.), *Parental belief systems: The psychological consequences for children* (2nd ed., pp. 219–248). Hillsdale, NJ: Erlbaum.

Burgess, B. J. (1980). Parenting in the Native American community. In M. D. Fantini & R. Cardenas (Eds.), *Parenting in a multicultural society* (pp. 63–73). New York: Longman.

Buriel, R. (1984). Integration with traditional Mexican American culture and sociocultural adjustment. In J. L. Martinez & R. Mendoza (Eds.), *Chicano psychology* (2nd ed., pp. 95–130). New York: Academic Press.

Buriel, R. (1987). *Academic performance of foreign- and native-born Mexican Americans: A comparison of first-, second-, and third-generation students and parents.* New Directions for Latino Public Policy Research, Working Paper No. 14. A project for the Inter-University Program for Latino Research and the Social Science Research Council, New York.

Buriel, R. (1988). *Latino value systems and their educational implications.* Psychology Department, Pomona College, Claremont, CA.

Buriel, R. (1993a). Childrearing orientations in Mexican American families: The influence of generation and sociocultural factors. *Journal of Marriage and the Family, 55,* 987–1000.

Buriel, R. (1993b). Acculturation, respect for cultural differences and biculturalism among three generations of Mexican American and Euro-American school children. *Journal of Genetic Psychology, 154,* 531–543.

Buriel, R. (1994). Immigration and education of Mexican Americans. In A. Hurtado & E. E. Garcia (Eds.), *The educational achievement of Latinos: Barriers and successes* (pp. 197–226). Santa Cruz, CA: Regents of the University of California.

Buriel, R., & Cardoza, D. (1993). Mexican American ethnic labeling: An intrafamilial and intergenerational analysis. In M. Bernal & G. Knight (Eds.), *Ethnic identity* (pp. 197–210). Albany: State University of New York Press.

Buriel, R., & Chavez, J. M. (1988). Mother-child interactions involving a child with epilepsy: A comparison of immigrant and native-born Mexican Americans. *Journal of Pediatric Psychology, 13,* 349–361.

Buriel, R., & DeMent, T. (1993). *Children as cultural brokers: Recollections of college students.* Psychology Department, Pomona College, Claremont, CA.

Buriel, R., DeMent, T., & Chavez, D. (1995). *Children and stress: Interpreting for immigrant parents.* Psychology Department, Pomona College, Claremont, CA.

Buriel, R., & Saenz, E. (1980). Psychocultural characteristics of college-bound and noncollege-bound Chicanas. *Journal of Social Psychology, 110,* 245–251.

Buriel, R., & Vasquez, R. (1982). Stereotypes of Mexican descent persons: Attitudes of three generations of Mexican Americans and Anglo American adolescents. *Journal of Cross-Cultural Psychology, 13,* 59–70.

Burks, V. S., & Parke, R. D. (1996). Parent and child representations of social relationships: Linkages between families and peers. *Merrill-Palmer Quarterly, 42,* 358–378.

Burton, L. M. (1990). Teenage childbearing as an alternative life-course strategy in multigeneration black families. *Human Nature, 1,* 123–143.

Burton, L. M. (1995). Intergenerational patterns of providing care in African-American families with teenage childbearers: Emergent patterns in an ethnographic study. In V. L. Bengston, K. W. Shaie, & L. M. Burton (Eds.), *Adult intergenerational relations: Effects of societal change* (pp. 79–125). New York: Springer.

Cairns, R. B. (1979). *Social development: The origins and plasticity of interchanges.* San Francisco: Freeman.

Campbell, S. B., Cohn, J. F., & Meyers, T. (1995). Depression in first-time mothers: Mother-infant interaction and depression chronicity. *Developmental Psychology, 31,* 349–357.

Carroll, J. C. (1980). A cultural-consistency theory of family violence in Mexican-American and Jewish ethnic groups. In M. A. Straus & G. T. Hotaling (Eds.), *The social causes of husband-wife violence.* Minneapolis: University of Minnesota Press.

Carson, J., & Parke, R. D. (1996). Reciprocal negative affect in parent-child interactions and children's peer competency. *Child Development, 67,* 2217–2226.

Casas, J. M., & Ortiz, S. (1985). Exploring the applicability of the dyadic adjustment scale for assessing level of marital adjustment with Mexican Americans. *Journal of Marriage and the Family, 47,* 1023–1027.

Cassidy, J., Parke, R. D., Butkovsky, L., & Braungart, J. M. (1992). Family-peer connections: The role of emotional expressiveness within the family and children's understanding of emotions. *Child Development, 63,* 603–618.

Chan, S. (1991). *Asian Americans: An interpretive history.* Boston: Twayne.

Chao, C. M. (1992). The inner heart: Therapy with Southeast Asian families. In L. A. Vargas & J. D. Koss-Chioino (Eds.), *Working with culture: Psychotherapeutic intervention with ethnic minority children and adolescents* (pp. 157–181). San Francisco: Jossey-Bass.

Chao, R. K. (1994). Beyond parental control and authoritarian parenting style: Understanding Chinese parenting through the cultural notion of training. *Child Development, 65,* 1111–1119.

Charlesworth, W. R., & Dzur, C. (1987). Gender comparison of preschoolers' behavior and resource utilization in group problem solving. *Child Development, 58,* 191–200.

Chase-Lansdale, P. L., Brooks-Gunn, J., & Zamsky, E. S. (1994). Young African-American multigenerational families in poverty: Quality of mothering and grandmothering. *Child Development, 65*(2), 373–393.

Chase-Lansdale, P. L., & Hetherington, E. M. (1990). The impact of divorce on life-span development: Short and long-term effects. In D. Featherman & R. M. Lerner (Eds.), *Life span development and behavior* (Vol. 10, pp. 105–150). Orlando, FL: Academic Press.

Chase-Lansdale, P. L., Mott, F. L., Brooks-Gunn, J., & Phillips, D. A. (1991). Children of the NLSY: A unique research opportunity. *Developmental Psychology, 27,* 918–931.

Chase-Lansdale, P. L., & Owen, M. T. (1987). Maternal employment in a family context: Effects on infant-mother and infant-father attachments. *Child Development, 58,* 1505–1512.

Chavez, D., & Buriel, R. (1988). Mother-child interactions involving a child with epilepsy: A comparison of immigrant and native-born Mexican Americans. *Journal of Pediatric Psychiatry, 13,* 349–361.

Chavez, L. (1990). Co-residence and resistance: Strategies for survival among undocumented Mexicans and Central Americans in the United States. *Urban Anthropology, 19,* 31–61.

Cherlin, A. J. (1992). *Marriage, divorce and remarriage.* Cambridge, MA: Harvard University Press.

Cherlin, A. J., Furstenberg, F. F., Jr., Chase-Lansdale, P. L., Kiernana, K. E., Robins, P. K., Morrison, D. R., & Teitler, J. O. (1991). Longitudinal studies of effects of divorce on children in Great Britain and the United States. *Science, 252,* 1386–1389.

Chiu, L. H. (1987). Child-rearing attitudes of Chinese, Chinese-American, and Anglo-American mothers. *International Journal of Psychology, 22,* 409–419.

Clarke-Stewart, K. A., & Hayward, C. (1996). Advantages of father custody and contact for the psychological well-being of school age children. *Journal of Applied Developmental Psychology, 17,* 239–270.

Coates, B., & Hartup, W. W. (1969). Age and verbalization in observational learning. *Developmental Psychology, 1,* 556–562.

Cochran, M., & Brassard, J. A. (1979). Child development and personal social networks. *Child Development, 50,* 601–616.

Cochran, M., Larner, M., Riley, D., Gunnarsson, L., & Henderson, C., Jr. (1990). *Extending families: The social networks of parents and their children.* Cambridge, England: Cambridge University Press.

Cohen, J. S. (1989). *Maternal involvement in children's peer relationships during middle childhood.* Unpublished doctoral dissertation, University of Waterloo, Waterloo, Ontario, Canada.

Coleman, J. (1988). Social capital in the creation of human capital. *American Journal of Sociology, 94,* 95–120.

Collins, R., & Coltrane, S. (1994). *Sociology of marriage and the family* (4th ed.). Chicago: Nelson-Hall.

Collins, W. A., & Russell, G. (1991). Mother-child and father-child relationships in middle childhood and adolescence: A developmental analysis. *Developmental Review, 11,* 99–136.

Coltrane, S. (1996). *Family man.* New York: Oxford University Press.

Coltrane, S., & Ishii-Kuntz, M. (1992). Men's household work: A life course perspective. *Journal of Marriage and the Family, 54,* 43–57.

Conger, R. D., & Elder, G. H. (Eds.). (1994). *Families in troubled times: Adapting to change in rural America.* New York: Aldine.

Conger, R. D., Elder, G. H., Lorenz, F. O., Conger, K. J., Simons, R. L., Whitbeck, L. B., Huck, S., & Melby, J. N. (1990). Linking economic hardship to marital quality and instability. *Journal of Marriage and the Family, 52,* 643–656.

Conger, R. D., Ge, X., Elder, G. H., Lorenz, F. O., & Simons, R. L. (1994). Economic stress, coercive family process and developmental problems of adolescents. *Child Development, 65,* 541–561.

Conger, R. D., Ge, X., & Lorenz, F. O. (1994). Economic stress and marital relations. In R. D. Conger & G. H. Elder (Eds.), *Families in troubled times* (pp. 187–203). New York: Aldine.

Cooney, R. S., Rogler, L. H., Hurrell, R., & Ortiz, V. (1982). Decision making in intergenerational Puerto Rican families. *Journal of Marriage and the Family, 44,* 621–631.

Cooney, T. M., Pedersen, F. A., Indelicato, S., & Palkovitz, R. (1993). Timing of fatherhood: Is "on-time" optimal? *Journal of Marriage and the Family, 55,* 205–215.

Coulton, C. L., & Pandey, S. (1992). Geographic concentration of poverty and risk to children in urban neighborhoods. *American Behavioral Scientist, 35,* 238–257.

Cowan, C. P., & Cowan, P. (1992). *When partners become parents.* New York: Basic Books.

Cowan, C. P., Cowan, P. A., Coie, L., & Coie, J. D. (1978). Becoming a family: The impact of a first child's birth on the couple's relationship. In W. B. Miller & L. F. Newman (Eds.), *The first child and family formation* (pp. 293–324). Chapel Hill, NC: Carolina Population Center.

Cowan, P. A., Cowan, C. P., Schulz, M. C., & Heming, G. (1994). Prebirth to preschool family factors in children's adaptation to kindergarten. In R. D. Parke & S. Kellam (Eds.), *Exploring family relationships with other social contexts* (pp. 75–114). Hillsdale, NJ: Erlbaum.

Crnic, K. A., Greenberg, M. T., Ragozin, A. S., Robinson, N. M., & Basham, R. B. (1983). Effects of stress and social support on mothers and premature and full-term infants. *Child Development, 54,* 209–217.

Crockenberg, S. B. (1981). Infant irritability, mother responsiveness, and social support influences on the security of infant-mother attachment. *Child Development, 52,* 857–865.

Crouter, A. C. (1994). Processes linking families and work: Implications for behavior and development in both settings. In R. D. Parke & S. Kellam (Eds.), *Exploring family relationships with other contexts* (pp. 9–28). Hillsdale, NJ: Erlbaum.

Crouter, A. C., MacDermid, S., McHale, S. M., & Perry-Jenkins, M. (1990). Parental monitoring and perceptions of children's school performance and conduct in dual- and single-earner families. *Developmental Psychology, 26,* 649–657.

Cummings, E. M. (1995). Usefulness of experiments for the study of the family. *Journal of Family Psychology, 9,* 175–185.

Cummings, E. M., & Davies, P. T. (1994). *Child and marital conflict: The impact of family dispute and resolution.* New York: Guilford Press.

Current Populations Reports. (1991). U.S. Bureau of the Census, N 181, p. 23. Washington, DC: U.S. Government Printing Office.

Daniels, P., & Weingarten, K. (1982). *Sooner or later: The timing of parenthood in adult lives.* New York: Norton.

Darling, N., & Steinberg, L. (1993). Parenting style as context: An integrative model. *Psychological Bulletin, 113,* 489–496.

Darling, N., Steinberg, L., Gringlas, & Dornbusch, S. (1995). *Community influences on adolescent achievement and deviance: A test of the functional community hypothesis.* Unpublished manuscript, Temple University, Philadelphia, PA.

Davies, P. T., & Cummings, E. M. (1994). Marital conflict and child adjustment: An emotional security hypothesis. *Psychological Bulletin, 116,* 387–411.

Davis, A., & Havighurst, R. J. (1946). Social class and color differences in child-rearing. *American Sociological Review, 11,* 698–710.

de Anda, D. (1984). Informal support networks of Hispanic mothers: A comparison across age groups. *Journal of Social Service Research, 7,* 89–105.

Delgado-Gaitan, C. (1994). Socializing young children in Mexican-American families: An intergenerational perspective. In P. M. Greenfield & R. R. Cocking (Eds.), *Cross-cultural roots of minority child development* (pp. 55–86). Hillsdale, NJ: Erlbaum.

Demos, G. D. (1962). Attitudes of Mexican-American groups toward education. *Journal of Social Psychology, 57,* 249–256.

Denham, S. A. (1993). Maternal emotional responsiveness to toddlers' social-emotional functioning. *Journal of Child Psychology and Psychiatry, 34,* 715–728.

Denham, S. A., Cook, M., & Zoller, D. (1992). "Baby looks very sad": Implications of conversations about feelings between mother and preschooler. *British Journal of Developmental Psychology, 10,* 301–315.

Denham, S. A., McKinley, M., Couchoud, E. A., & Holt, R. (1990). Emotional and behavioral predictors of preschool peer ratings. *Child Development, 61,* 1145–1152.

Dickie, J. (1987). Interrelationships within the mother-father-infant triad. In P. Berman & F. Pederson (Eds.), *Men's transition to parenthood* (pp. 113–143). Hillsdale, NJ: Erlbaum.

Dickie, J., & Carnahan, S. (1980). Training in social competence: The effect on mothers, fathers and infants. *Child Development, 51,* 1248–1251.

Dishion, T. J. (1990). The family ecology of boys' peer relations in middle childhood. *Child Development, 61,* 874–892.

Dix, T. (1991). The affective organization of parenting: Adaptive and maladaptive processes. *Psychological Bulletin, 110,* 3–25.

Dornbusch, S. M., Carlsmith, J., Bushwall, S., Ritter, P., Leiderman, H., Hastorf, A., & Gross, R. (1985). Single parents, extended households and the control of adolescents. *Child Development, 56,* 326–341.

Dornbusch, S. M., Ritter, P. L., Leiderman, P. H., Roberts, D. F., & Fraleigh, M. J. (1987). The relation of parenting style to adolescent school performance. *Child Development, 58,* 1244–1257.

Downey, D. B., & Powell, B. (1993). Do children in single parent households fare better with same-sex parents? *Journal of Marriage and the Family, 55,* 55–72.

Duncan, G. J., & Hoffman, S. D. (1985). Economic consequences of marital instability. In M. David & J. Smeeding (Eds.), *Horizontal equity, uncertainty and economic well-being* (pp. 427–470). Chicago: University of Chicago Press.

Dunn, J. (1988). *The beginnings of social understanding.* Cambridge, MA: Harvard University Press.

Dunn, J. (1993). *Young children's close relationships.* Newbury Park, CA: Sage.

Dunn, J., & Brown, J. (1994). Affect expression in the family, children's understanding of emotions and their interactions with others. *Merrill-Palmer Quarterly, 40,* 120–137.

Dunn, J., & Kendrick, C. (1982). *Siblings: Love, envy and understanding.* New York: Academic Press.

Dunn, J., & Shatz, M. (1989). Becoming a conversationalist despite (or because of) having an elder sibling. *Child Development, 60,* 399–410.

Durrett, M. E., O'Bryant, S., & Pennebaker, J. W. (1975). Child-rearing reports of White, Black, and Mexican-American families. *Developmental Psychology, 11,* 871.

East, P. L., & Rook, K. S. (1992). Compensatory patterns of support among children's peer relationships: A test using school friends, nonschool friends, and siblings. *Developmental Psychology, 28,* 163–172.

Easterbrooks, M. A., & Emde, R. N. (1988). Marital and parent-child relationships: The role of affect in the family system. In R. Hinde & J. Stevenson-Hinde (Eds.), *Relationships within families* (pp. 83–103). Oxford, England: Clarendon Press.

Edmonston, B., & Passel, J. S. (1994). The future immigrant population of the United States. In B. Edmonston & J. S. Passel (Eds.), *Immigration and ethnicity* (pp. 317–353). Washington, DC: The Urban Institute Press.

Edwards, C. P., & Whiting, B. B. (1993). "Mother, Older Sibling and Me": The overlapping roles of caregivers and companions in the social world of two- and three-year-olds in Ngeca, Kenya. In K. MacDonald (Ed.), *Parent-child play: Descriptions and implications* (pp. 305–329). Albany: State University of New York Press.

Egeland, B., & Sroufe, L. A. (1981). Attachment and early maltreatment. *Child Development, 52,* 44–52.

Eisenberg, N., & Fabes, R. A. (1992). Young children's coping with interpersonal anger. *Child Development, 63,* 116–128.

Eisenberg, N., & Fabes, R. A. (1994). Emotion regulation and the development of social competence. In M. Clark (Ed.), *Review of personality and social psychology* (pp. 119–150). Newbury Park, CA: Sage.

Eisenberg, N., Fabes, R. A., Schaller, M., & Miller, P. (1991). Personality and socialization correlates of vicarious emotional responding. *Journal of Personality and Social Psychology, 61,* 459–470.

Elder, G. H. (1974). *Children of the Great Depression.* Chicago: University of Chicago Press.

Elder, G. H., & Caspi, A. (1988). Human development and social change: An emerging perspective on the life course. In N. Bolger, A. Caspi, G. Downey, & M. Moorehouse (Eds.), *Persons in context: Developmental processes* (pp. 77–113). Cambridge, England: Cambridge University Press.

Elder, G. H., & Hareven, T. K. (1993). Rising above life's disadvantage: From the Great Depression to war. In G. H. Elder, J. Modell, & R. D. Parke (Eds.), *Children in time and place* (pp. 47–72). New York: Cambridge University Press.

Elder, G. H., Van Nguyen, T., & Caspi, A. (1985). Linking family hardship to children's lives. *Child Development, 56,* 361–375.

Emery, R. E. (Ed). (1988). *Marriage, divorce and children's adjustment.* Newbury Park, CA: Sage.

Emery, R. E., & Forehand, R. (1994). Parental divorce and children's well-being: A focus on resilience. In R. J. Haggerty, L. R. Sherrod, N. Garmezy, & M. Rutter (Eds.), *Stress, risk and resilience in children and adolescents: Processes, mechanisms, and interventions* (pp. 64–99). New York: Cambridge University Press.

Entwisle, D. R., & Astone, N. M. (1994). Some practical guidelines for measuring youths' race/ethnicity and socioeconomic status. *Child Development, 65,* 1521–1540.

Erel, O., & Burman, B. (1995). Interrelatedness of marital relations and parent-child relations: A meta-analytic review. *Psychological Bulletin, 118,* 108–132.

Escovar. P. L., & Lazarus, P. J. (1982). Cross-cultural child-rearing practices: Implications for school psychology. *School Psychology International, 3,* 143–148.

Farley, R., & Allen, W. R. (1987). *The color line and the quality of American life.* New York: Russell-Sage Foundation.

Fauber, R. L., & Long, N. (1991). Children in context: The role of the family in child psychotherapy. *Journal of Consulting and Clinical Psychology, 59,* 813–820.

Featherman, D. L., Spenner, K. I., & Tsunematsu, N. (1988). Class and the socialization of children: Constancy, change, or irrelevance? In E. M. Hetherington, R. M. Lerner, & M. Perlmutter (Eds.), *Child development in life-span perspective* (pp. 67–90). Hillsdale, NJ: Erlbaum.

Feldman, S. S., Nash, S. C., & Aschenbrenner, B. G. (1983). Antecedents of fathering. *Child Development, 54,* 1628–1636.

Ferree, M. M. (1991). The gender division of labor in two-earner marriages: Dimensions of variability and change. *Journal of Family Issues, 12,* 158–180.

Field, T. (1992). Infants of depressed mothers. *Development and Psychopathology, 4,* 49–66.

Field, T., Healy, B., Goldstein, S., & Guthertz, M. (1990). Behavior state matching and synchrony in mother-infant interactions of non-depressed dyads. *Developmental Psychology, 26,* 7–14.

Fiese, B. H. (1990, April). *Family stories: Mothers' stories of their childhood and relation to mother-toddler interaction in a free-play setting.* Paper presented at the International Conference on Infant Studies, Montreal, Canada.

Fiese, B. H. (1992). Dimensions of family rituals across two generations: Relation to adolescent identity. *Family Process, 31,* 151–162.

Fiese, B. H. (1995). Family rituals. In D. Levinson (Ed.), *Encyclopedia of marriage and the family* (pp. 275–278). New York: Macmillan.

Fiese, B. H., & Kline, C. A. (1993). Development of the Family Ritual Questionnaire (FRQ): Initial reliability and validation studies. *Journal of Family Psychology, 6,* 290–299.

Filsinger, E. E. (1991). Empirical typology, cluster analysis and family-level measurement. In T. W. Draper & A. C. Marcos (Eds.), *Family variables* (pp. 90–104). Newbury Park, CA: Sage.

Finnie, V., & Russell, A. (1988). Preschool children's social status and their mothers' behavior and knowledge in the supervisory role. *Developmental Psychology, 24,* 789–801.

Flannery, W. P., Reise, S. P., & Widaman, K. F. (1995). An item response theory analysis of the general and academic scales of the Self-Description Questionnaire II. *Journal of Research in Personality, 29,* 168–188.

Fletcher, A. C., Darling, N. E., Steinberg, L., & Dornbusch, S. M. (1995). The company they keep: Relation of adolescent's adjustment and behavior to their friends' perception of authoritative parenting in the social network. *Developmental Psychology, 31,* 300–310.

Freidman, H. S., Tucker, J. S., Schwartz, J. E., Tomlinson-Keasey, C., Martin, L. R., Wingard, D. L., & Criqui, M. H. (1995). Psychosocial and behavioral predictors of longevity. *American Psychologist, 50,* 69–78.

Furstenberg, F. F., Jr. (1976). *Unplanned parenthood: The social consequences of teenage childbearing.* New York: Free Press.

Furstenberg, F. F., Jr. (1993). How families manage risk and opportunity in dangerous neighborhoods. In W. J. Wilson (Ed.), *Sociology and the public agenda* (pp. 231–258). Newbury Park, CA: Sage.

Furstenberg, F. F., Jr., Brooks-Gunn, J., & Chase-Lansdale, L. (1989). Teenaged pregnancy and child bearing. *American Psychologist, 44,* 313–320.

Furstenberg, F. F., Jr., Brooks-Gunn, J., & Morgan, P. (1987). *Adolescent mothers in later life.* New York: Cambridge University Press.

Furstenberg, F. F., Jr., & Cherlin, A. J. (Eds.). (1991). *Divided families.* Cambridge, MA: Harvard University Press.

Furstenberg, F. F., Jr., Eccles, J., Elder, G. H., Cook, T. D., & Sameroff, A. (in press). *Urban families and adolescent success.* Chicago: University of Chicago Press.

Furstenberg, F. F., Jr., & Harris, K. M. (1992). The disappearing American father? Divorce and the waning significance of biological parenthood. In S. J. South & S. E. Tolnay (Eds.), *The changing American family* (pp. 197–223). Boulder, CO: Westview Press.

Furstenberg, F. F., Jr., & Harris, K. M. (1993). When and why fathers matter: Impacts of father involvement on children of adolescent mothers. In R. I. Lerman & T. J. Ooms (Eds.), *Young unwed fathers* (pp. 117–138). Philadelphia: Temple University Press.

Furstenberg, F. F., Jr., Nord, C. W., Peterson, J. L., & Zill, N. (1983). The life course of children and divorce: Marital disruption and parental conflict. *American Sociological Review, 48,* 656–668.

Garcia-Coll, C. T., Meyer, E. C., & Brillon, L. (1995). Ethnic and minority parenting. In M. H. Bornstein (Ed.), *Handbook of parenting* (pp. 189–209). Hillsdale, NJ: Erlbaum.

Gentemann, K. M., & Whitehead, R. L. (1983). The cultural broker concept in bicultural education. *Journal of Negro Education, 52,* 118–129.

Gewirtz, J. (1969). Mechanisms of social learning: Some roles of stimulation and behavior in early human development. In D. Goslin (Ed.), *Handbook of socialization theory and research* (pp. 57–212). New York: Rand McNally.

Ginsberg, H. (1972). *The myth of the deprived child.* Englewood Cliffs, NJ: Prentice-Hall.

Glick, P. C. (1989). The family life cycle and social change. *Family Relations, 38,* 123–129.

Goldberg, W. A., & Easterbrooks, M. A. (1988). Maternal employment when children are toddlers and kindergartners. In A. E. Gottfried & A. M. Gottfried (Eds.), *Maternal employment and children's development: Longitudinal research* (pp. 121–154). New York: Plenum Press.

Golding, J. M., Burnam, M. A., Timbers, D. M., Escobar, J. I., & Karno, M. (1985). *Acculturation and distress: Social psychological mediators.* Paper presented at the annual meeting of the American Psychological Association, Los Angeles, CA.

Goldstein, L. H., Diener, M. L., & Mangelsdorf, S. C. (1995). Maternal characteristics and social support across the transition to motherhood: Associations with maternal behavior. *Journal of Family Psychology, 10,* 60–71.

Gomel, J. N., Tinsley, B. J., & Clark, K. M. (1995, March). *Family stress and coping during times of economic hardship: A multi-ethnic perspective.* Paper presented in the symposium The Effects of Economic Downturn and Joblessness on Children and Families at the biennial meeting of the Society for Research in Child Development, Indianapolis, IN.

Goodnow, J. J., & Collins, W. A. (1990). *Development according to parents: The nature, sources and consequences of parents' ideas.* Hillsdale, NJ: Erlbaum.

Gordon, M. M. (1964). *Assimilation in American life.* New York: Oxford University Press.

Gottesman, I. I., & Goldsmith, H. H. (1994). Developmental psychopathology of antisocial behavior: Inserting genes into its ontogenesis and epigenesis. In C. A. Nelson (Ed.), *Threats to optimal development. The Minnesota Symposia on Child Psychology* (Vol. 27, pp. 69–104). Hillsdale, NJ: Erlbaum.

Gottfried, A. E., Bathurst, K., & Gottfried, A. W. (1994). Role of maternal and dual-earner employment status in children's development: A longitudinal study from infancy through early adolescence. In A. E. Gottfried & A. W. Gottfried (Eds.), *Redefining families: Implications for children's development* (pp. 55–97). New York: Plenum Press.

Gottfried, A. E., & Gottfried, A. W. (Eds.). (1988). *Maternal employment and children's development: Longitudinal research.* New York: Plenum Press.

Gottfried, A. E., Gottfried, A. W., & Bathurst, K. (1995). Maternal and dual-earner employment status and parenting. In M. Bornstein (Ed.), *Handbook of parenting* (pp. 139–159). Hillsdale, NJ: Erlbaum.

Gottman, J. M. (1994). *What predicts divorce?* Hillsdale, NJ: Erlbaum.

Gottman, J. M., & Katz, L. F. (1989). Effects of marital discord on young children's peer interaction and health. *Developmental Psychology, 25,* 373–381.

Gottman, J. M., Katz, L. F., & Hooven, C. (1996). *Meta-emotion: How families communicate emotionally.* Mahwah, NJ: Erlbaum.

Graham, S. (1992). Most of the subjects were white and middle class. *American Psychologist, 47,* 629–639.

Greenberger, E., & O'Neil, R. (1991, April). *Characteristics of fathers' and mothers' jobs: Implications for parenting and children's social development.* Paper presented at the biennial meeting of the Society for Research in Child Development, Seattle, WA.

Greenberger, E., O'Neil, R., & Nagel, S. K. (1994). Linking workplace and homeplace: Relations between the nature of adults' work and their parenting behaviors. *Developmental Psychology, 30,* 990–1002.

Greenfield, P. M., & Cocking, R. R. (1994). *Cross-cultural roots of minority child development.* Hillsdale, NJ: Erlbaum.

Griffith, J., & Villavicencio, S. (1985). Relationships among acculturation, sociodemographic characteristics, and social supports in Mexican American adults. *Hispanic Journal of Behavioral Sciences, 7,* 75–92.

Grossman, F. K., Pollack, W. S., & Golding, E. (1988). Fathers and children: Predicting the quality and quantity of fathering. *Developmental Psychology, 24,* 82–91.

Grove, W. R., & Zeiss, C. (1987). Multiple roles and happiness. In F. Crosby (Ed.), *Spouse, parent, worker* (pp. 125–137). New Haven, CT: Yale University Press.

Grusec, J. E. (1992). Social learning theory and developmental psychology: The legacies of Robert R. Sears & Albert Bandura. *Developmental Psychology, 28,* 776–786.

Grusec, J. E., Hastings, P., & Mammone, N. (1994). Parenting cognitions and relationship schemas. In J. G. Smetana (Ed.), *Beliefs about parenting: Origins and developmental implications.* San Francisco: Jossey-Bass.

Grych, J. H., & Fincham, F. D. (1990). Marital conflict and children's adjustment: A cognitive-contextual framework. *Psychological Bulletin, 101,* 267–290.

Grych, J. H., Seid, M., & Fincham F. D. (1991, April). *Children's cognitive and affective responses to different forms of interparental conflict.* Paper presented at the biennial meetings of the Society for Research in Child Development, Seattle, WA.

Gunnar, M. (1987). Psychological studies of stress and coping: An introduction. *Child Development, 58,* 1403–1407.

Gutierrez, J., & Sameroff, A. (1990). Determinants of complexity in Mexican-American and Anglo-American mothers' conceptions of child development. *Child Development, 61,* 384–394.

Halberstadt, A. G. (1991). Socialization of expressiveness: Family influences in particular and a model in general. In R. S. Feldman & R. Rime (Eds.), *Fundamentals in nonverbal behavior* (pp. 106–160). New York: Cambridge University Press.

Hareven, T. K. (1977). Family time and historical time. *Daedalus, 106,* 57–70.

Harjo, S. S. (1993). The American Indian experience. In H. P. McAdoo (Ed.), *Family ethnicity* (pp. 199–207). Newbury Park, CA: Sage.

Harold-Goldsmith, R., Radin, N., & Eccles, J. S. (1988). Objective and subjective reality: The effects of job loss and financial stress on fathering behaviors. *Family Perspective, 22,* 309–325.

Harris, J. R. (1995). Where is the child's environment? A group socialization theory of development. *Psychological Review, 102,* 458–489.

Harrison, A. O. (1985). The black family's socializing environment. In H. McAdoo & J. McAdoo (Eds.), *Black children* (pp. 174–193). Beverly Hills, CA: Sage.

Harrison, A. O., Serafica, F., & McAdoo, H. (1984). Ethnic families of color. In R. D. Parke (Ed.), *The family: Review of child development research* (Vol. 7, pp. 329–371). Chicago: University of Chicago Press.

Harrison, A. O., Wilson, M. N., Pine, C. J., Chan, S. Q., & Buriel, R. (1990). Family ecologies of ethnic minority children. *Child Development, 61,* 347–362.

Harrist, A. W., Pettit, G. S., Dodge, K. A., & Bates, J. E. (1994). Dyadic synchrony in mother-child interaction-relation with children's subsequent kindergarten adjustment. *Family Relations, 43,* 417–424.

Hart, B., & Risley, T. R. (1995). *Meaningful differences in the everyday experience of young American children.* Baltimore: Brookes.

Hartup, W. W. (1979). The social worlds of childhood. *American Psychologist, 34,* 944–950.

Hartup, W. W. (1983). Peer relations. In P. Mussen & E. M. Hetherington (Eds.), *Handbook of child psychology* (4th ed.) (Vol. 4, pp. 103–196). New York: Wiley.

Hatchett, S. J., & Jackson, J. S. (1993). African American extended kin systems: An assessment. In H. P. McAdoo (Ed.), *Family ethnicity.* Newbury Park, CA: Sage.

Hauser, R. M. (1994). Measuring socioeconomic status in studies of child development. *Child Development, 65,* 1541–1545.

Heller, C. (1966). *Mexican-American youth: Forgotten youth at the crossroads.* New York: Random House.

Henggeler, S. W., Edwards, J. J., Cohen. R., & Summervile, M. B. (1992). Predicting changes in children's popularity: The role of family relations. *Journal of Applied Developmental Psychology, 12,* 205–218.

Hernandez, D. J. (Ed). (1993). *America's children.* New York: Russell-Sage Foundation.

Hess, R. D., & Shipman, V. C. (1965). Early experience and the socialization of cognitive modes in children. *Child Development, 36,* 869–886.

Hetherington, E. M. (1979). Divorce: A child's perspective. *American Psychologist, 34,* 851–856.

Hetherington, E. M. (1987). *Long-term impact of divorce on children's marital stability.* Unpublished manuscript, University of Virginia, Charlottesville.

Hetherington, E. M. (1988). *The impact of the experience of divorce during childhood on women's adult adjustment.* Unpublished manuscript, University of Virginia, Charlottesville.

Hetherington, E. M. (1989). Coping with family transitions: Winners, losers and survivors. *Child Development, 60,* 1–14.

Hetherington, E. M. (1993). A review of the Virginia Longitudinal Study of Divorce and Remarriage: A focus on early adolescence. *Journal of Family Psychology, 7,* 39–56.

Hetherington, E. M. (1995, March). *The changing American family: Teenaged childbearing and divorce.* Paper presented at the biennial meeting of the Society for Research in Child Development, Indianapolis, IN.

Hetherington, E. M., & Baltes, P. B. (1988). Child psychology and life-span development. In E. M. Hetherington, R. M. Lerner, & M. Perlmutter (Eds.), *Child development in life span perspective* (pp. 1–20). Hillsdale, NJ: Erlbaum.

Hetherington, E. M., & Clingempeel, G. (Eds.). (1992). Coping with marital transitions. *Monographs of the Society for Research in Child Development, 57*(Serial No. 227).

Hetherington, E. M., Cox, M., & Cox, R. (1979). Play and social interaction in children following divorce. *Journal of Social Issues, 35,* 26–49.

Hetherington, E. M., Cox, M., & Cox, R. (1982). Effects of divorce on parents and children. In M. E. Lamb (Ed.), *Nontraditional families: Parenting and child development* (pp. 233–288). Hillsdale, NJ: Erlbaum.

Hetherington, E. M., Cox, M., & Cox, R. (1985). Long-term effects of divorce and remarriage on the adjustment of children. *Journal of the American Academy of Child Psychiatry, 24,* 518–530.

Hetherington, E. M., & Jodl, K. M. (1994). Stepfamilies as settings for child development. In A. Booth & J. Dunn (Eds.), *Stepfamilies: Who benefits? Who does not?* (pp. 55–79). Hillsdale, NJ: Erlbaum.

Hetherington, E. M., Stanley-Hagan, M., & Anderson, E. R. (1989). Marital transitions: A child's perspective. *American Psychologist, 44,* 303–312.

Hewlett, B. S. (1991). *Intimate fathers: The nature of context of Aka Pygmy paternal infant care.* Ann Arbor: University of Michigan Press.

Hinde, R. A., & Stevenson-Hinde, J. (Eds.). (1988). *Relationships within families: Mutual influences.* Oxford, England: Clarendon Press.

Ho, D. Y. F. (1986). Chinese patterns of socialization: A critical review. In M. H. Bond (Ed.), *The psychology of the Chinese people* (pp. 1–37). Hong Kong: Oxford University Press.

Hock, E., & DeMeis, D. (1990). Depression in mothers of infants: The role of maternal employment. *Developmental Psychology, 26,* 285–291.

Hoff-Ginsberg, E. (1991). Mother-child conversation in different social classes and communicative settings. *Child Development, 62,* 782–796.

Hoff-Ginsberg, E., & Tardif, T. (1995). Socioeconomic status and parenting. In M. Bornstein (Ed.), *Handbook of parenting* (pp. 161–188). Hillsdale, NJ: Erlbaum.

Hoffman, L. W. (1984). Work, family and the socialization of the child. In R. D. Parke, R. Emde, H. McAdoo, & G. P. Sackett (Eds.), *Review of child development research: The family* (Vol. 7, pp. 223–281). Chicago: University of Chicago Press.

Hoffman, L. W. (1989). Effects of maternal employment in the two-parent family. *American Psychologist, 44*(2), 283–292.

Hoffman, L. W. (1991). The influence of the family environment on personality: Accounting for sibling differences. *Psychological Bulletin, 110,* 187–203.

Hoffreth, S. L. (1987). Social and economic consequences of teenage parenthood. In S. L. Hoffreth & C. D. Hayes (Eds.), *Risking the future: Adolescent sexuality, pregnancy and childbearing* (Vol. 2, pp. 207–263). Washington, DC: National Academy of Sciences Press.

Hoffreth, S. L., & Hayes, C. D. (Eds.). (1987). *Risking the future: Adolescent sexuality, pregnancy and childbearing* (Vol. 2). Washington, DC: National Academy of Sciences Press.

Hogan, D. P., Hao, L. X., & Parish, W. L. (1990). Race, kin networks and assistance to mother-headed families. *Social Forces, 68,* 797–812.

Homel, R., & Burns, A. (1989). Environmental quality and the wellbeing of children. *Social Indicators Research, 21,* 133–158.

Homel, R., Burns, A., & Goodnow, J. (1987). Parental social networks and child development. *Journal of Social and Personal Relationships, 4,* 159–177.

Horwitz, S. M., Klerman, L. V., Kuo, H. S., & Jekel, J. F. (1991). School-age mothers: Predictors of long-term educational and economic outcomes. *Pediatrics, 87,* 862–867.

Hossain, Z., Field, T., Malphus, J., Valle, C., & Pickens, J. (1995). *Fathers' caregiving in low-income African-American and Hispanic American families.* Unpublished manuscript, University of Miami, Medical School.

Hossain, Z., & Roopnarine, J. L. (1993). Division of household labor and child care in dual-earner African-American families. *Sex Roles, 29*(9/10), 571–583.

Hossain, Z., & Roopnarine, J. L. (1994). African-American fathers' involvement with infants: Relationship to their functioning style, support, education and income. *Infant Behavior and Development, 17,* 175–184.

Howe, N., & Ross, H. S. (1990). Socialization perspective taking and the sibling relationship. *Developmental Psychology, 26,* 160–165.

Hubbard, J. A., & Coie, J. D. (1994). Emotional correlates of social competence in children's peer relationships. *Merrill-Palmer Quarterly, 40,* 1–20.

Hwang, P. (1987). The changing role of Swedish fathers. In M. E. Lamb (Ed.), *The father's role: Cross-cultural perspectives* (pp. 197–226). Hillsdale, NJ: Erlbaum.

Isley, S., O'Neil, R., & Parke, R. D. (1996). The relation of parental affect and control behavior to children's classroom acceptance: A concurrent and predictive analysis. *Early Education and Development, 7,* 7–23.

Jennings, K. D., Staff, V., & Conners, R. E. (1991). Social networks and mothers' interactions with their preschool children. *Child Development, 62,* 966–978.

Joe, J. R. (1994). Revaluing Native-American concepts of development and education. In P. M. Greenfield & R. R. Cocking (Eds.), *Cross-cultural roots of minority child development* (pp. 107–113). Hillsdale, NJ: Erlbaum.

Joffe, C. E. (1977). *Friendly intruders.* Berkeley: University of California Press.

Kagan, S. (1984). Interpreting Chicano cooperativeness: Methodological and theoretical considerations. In J. L. Martinez, Sr.

& R. H. Mendoza (Eds.), *Chicano psychology* (2nd ed., pp. 289–333). New York: Academic Press.

Kao, G., & Tienda, M. (1995). Optimism and achievement: The educational performance of immigrant youth. *Social Science Quarterly, 76,* 1–19.

Katz, L. F., & Gottman, J. M. (1993). Patterns of marital conflict predict children's internalizing and externalizing behaviors. *Developmental Psychology, 29,* 940–950.

Katz, L. F., & Gottman, J. M. (1994). Patterns of marital interaction and children's emotional development. In R. D. Parke & S. G. Kellam (Eds.), *Exploring family relationships with other social contexts* (pp. 49–74). Hillsdale, NJ: Erlbaum.

Katz, L. F., & Kahen, V. (1993). *Marital interaction patterns and children's externalizing and internalizing behaviors: The search for mechanisms.* Paper presented at the biennial meetings of Society for Research in Child Development, New Orleans, LA.

Katz, L. F., Kramer, L., & Gottman, J. M. (1992). Conflict and emotions in marital, sibling, and peer relationships. In C. U. Shantz & W. W. Hartup (Eds.), *Conflict in child and adolescent development* (pp. 122–149). Cambridge, England: Cambridge University Press.

Kaye, K. (1985). Toward a developmental psychology of the family. In L. L'Abate (Ed.), *The handbook of the family psychology and therapy* (Vol. 1, pp. 38–72). Homewood, IL: Dorsey Press.

Keefe, S. E., & Padilla, A. M. (1987). *Chicano ethnicity.* Albuquerque: University of New Mexico Press.

Kellam, S. G. (1994). The social adaptation of children in classrooms: A measure of family childrearing affectiveness. In R. D. Parke & S. G. Kellam (Eds.), *Exploring family relationships with other social contexts* (pp. 147–168). Hillsdale, NJ: Erlbaum.

Kellam, S. G., Ensminger, M., & Turner, R. J. (1977). Family structure and the mental health of children. *Archives of General Psychiatry, 34,* 1012–1022.

Kelley, M. L., Power, T. G., & Wimbush, D. D. (1992). Determinants of disciplinary practices in low-income Black mothers. *Child Development, 63,* 573–582.

Kelley, M. L., Sanchez-Hucies, J., & Walker, R. (1993). Correlates of disciplinary practices in working- to middle-class African-American mothers. *Merrill-Palmer Quarterly, 39,* 252–264.

Kessen, W. (1982). The child and other cultural inventions. In F. S. Kessel & A. W. Siegel (Eds.), *The child and other cultural inventions* (pp. 26–39). New York: Praeger.

Kibria, N. (1993). *Family tightrope: The changing lives of Vietnamese Americans.* Princeton, NJ: Princeton University Press.

Kim, U., & Berry, J. W. (1993). *Indigenous psychologies.* Newbury Park, CA: Sage.

Knight, G., Virdin, L. M., & Roosa, M. (1994). Socialization and family correlates of mental health outcomes among Hispanic and Anglo American children: Consideration of cross-ethnic scale equivalence. *Child Development, 65,* 212–224.

Kochanska, G. (1991). Patterns of inhibition to the unfamiliar in children of well and affectively ill mothers. *Child Development, 61,* 85–98.

Kochanska, G. (1993). Toward a synthesis of parental socialization and child temperament in early development of conscience. *Child Development, 64,* 325–347.

Kohn, M. L., & Schooler, C. (1983). *Work and personality: An inquiry into the impact of social stratification.* Norwood, NJ: ABLEX.

Kotelchuck, M. (1976). The infant's relationship to the father: Experimental evidence. In M. E. Lamb (Ed.), *The role of the father in child development* (pp. 329–344). New York: Wiley.

Kramer, L., & Gottman, J. M. (1992). Becoming a sibling—with a little help from my friends. *Developmental Psychology, 28,* 685–699.

Krappmann, L. (1986). *Family relationships and peer relationships in middle childhood: An explanatory study of the association between children's integration into the social network of peers and family development.* Paper presented at the Family Systems and Life-Span Development Conference, Max Planck Institute, Berlin, FRG.

Kreppner, K. (1989). Linking infant development in context research to the investigation of life-span family development. In K. Kreppner & R. M. Lerner (Eds.), *Family systems and life-span development* (pp. 33–64). Hillsdale, NJ: Erlbaum.

Kupersmidt, J. B., Griesler, P. C., De Rosier, M. E., Patterson, C. J., & Davis, P. W. (1995). Childhood aggression and peer relations in the context of family and neighborhood factors. *Child Development, 66,* 360–375.

Kuvlesky, W. P., & Patella, V. M. (1971). Degree of ethnicity and aspirations for upward mobility among Mexican American youth. *Journal of Vocational Behavior, 1,* 231–244.

Ladd, G. W. (1981). Effectiveness of a social learning method for enhancing children's social interaction and peer acceptance. *Child Development, 52,* 171–178.

Ladd, G. W. (1992). Themes and theories: Perspective on processes in family-peer relationships. In R. Parke & G. Ladd (Eds.), *Family-peer relationships: Modes of linkage* (pp. 3–34). Hillsdale, NJ: Erlbaum.

Ladd, G. W., & Golter, B. S. (1988). Parents' management of preschoolers' peer relations: Is it related to children's social competence? *Developmental Psychology, 24,* 109–117.

Ladd, G. W., LeSieur, K., & Profilet, S. M. (1993). Direct parental influences on young children's peer relations. In S. Duck (Ed.), *Learning about relationships* (Vol. 2, pp. 152–183). London: Sage.

Ladd, G. W., & Price, J. M. (1987). Predicting children's social and school adjustment following the transition from preschool to kindergarten. *Child Development, 58,* 1168–1189.

LaFromboise, T., Coleman, H. L. K., & Gerton, J. (1993). Psychological impact of biculturalism: Evidence and theory. *Psychological Bulletin, 114,* 395–412.

Laird, R. D., Pettit, G. S., Mize, J., Brown, E. G., & Lindsey, E. (1994). Mother-child conversations about peers: Contributions to competence. *Family Relations, 43,* 425–432.

Lamb, M. E. (1987). *The father's role: Cross-cultural perspectives.* Hillsdale, NJ: Erlbaum.

Lamb, M. E., & Bronson, S. K. (1978, November). *The role of the father in child development: Past presumptions, present realities, and the future potential.* Paper presented at Conference of Fatherhood and the Male Single Parent, Omaha, NE.

Lamb, M. E., Pleck, J. H., & Levine, J. A. (1985). The role of the father in child development: The effects of increased paternal involvement. In B. Lahey & E. E. Kazdin (Eds.), *Advances in clinical child psychology* (Vol. 8, pp. 229–266). New York: Plenum Press.

Laosa, L. M. (1980). Maternal teaching strategies in Chicano and Anglo-American families: The influence of culture and education on maternal behaviors. *Child Development, 51,* 759–765.

Laosa, L. M. (1982). School, occupation, culture, and family: The impact of parental schooling on the parent-child relationship. *Journal of Educational Psychology, 74,* 791–827.

Larson, R., & Richards, M. H. (1994). *Divergent realities: The emotional lives of mothers, fathers and adolescents.* New York: Basic Books.

Leadbeater, B. J., & Linares, O. (1992). Depressive symptoms in Black and Puerto Rican adolescent mothers in the first three years postpartum. *Development and Psychopathology, 4,* 451–468.

LeCorgne, L. L., & Laosa, L. M. (1976). Father absence in low-income Mexican-American families: Children's social adjustment and conceptual differentiation of sex-role attributes. *Developmental Psychology, 12,* 471.

Lee, J., O'Neil, R., Parke, R. D., & Wang, S. (1997). *Parental and child networks as correlates of children's social competence.* Unpublished manuscript, University of California, Riverside.

Lee, S. M., & Edmonston, B. (1994). The socioeconomic status and integration of Asian immigrants. In B. Edmonston & J. S. Passel (Eds.), *Immigration and ethnicity* (pp. 101–138). Washington, DC: The Urban Institute Press.

Lerman, R. L., & Ooms, T. J. (1993). *Young unwed fathers.* Philadelphia: Temple University Press.

Levy-Shiff, R., & Israelashvili, R. (1988). Antecedents of fathering: Some further exploration. *Developmental Psychology, 24,* 434–440.

Lewis, C. C. (1981). The effects of parental firm control: A reinterpretation of findings. *Psychological Bulletin, 90,* 547–563.

Lightfoot, S. L. (1978). *Worlds apart: Relationships between families and schools.* New York: Basic Books.

Liker, J. K., & Elder, G. H. (1983). Economic hardship and marital relations in the 1930s. *American Sociological Review, 48,* 343–359.

Lollis, S. P., Ross, H. S., & Tate, E. (1992). Parents' regulation of children's peer interactions: Direct influences. In R. Parke & G. Ladd (Eds.), *Family-peer relationships: Modes of linkage* (pp. 255–281). Hillsdale, NJ: Erlbaum.

Lopez, D. E. (1982). *Language maintenance and shift in the United States today: The basic patterns and their social implications: Vol. 1. Overview and summary.* Los Alamitos, CA: National Center for Bilingual Research.

Luepnitz, D. A. (Ed.). (1982). *Child custody: A study of families after divorce.* Lexington, MA: Lexington Books.

Lum, D. (1986). *Social work practice and people of color: A process-stage approach.* Monterey, CA: Brooks/Cole.

Luster, T., Rhoader, K., & Haas, B. (1989). The relation between parental values and parenting behavior: A test of the Kohn hypothesis. *Journal of Marriage and the Family, 51,* 139–147.

Lyons-Ruth, K., Connell, D. B., Grunebaum, H. U., & Botein, S. (1990). Infants at social risk: Maternal depression and family support as mediators of infant development and security of attachment. *Child Development, 61,* 85–98.

Maccoby, E. E. (1984). Socialization and developmental change. *Child Development, 55,* 317–328.

Maccoby, E. E. (1988). Gender as a social category. *Developmental Psychology, 24,* 755–765.

Maccoby, E. E. (1992). The role of parents in the socialization of children: An historical overview. *Developmental Psychology, 28,* 1006–1017.

Maccoby, E. E., & Martin, J. A. (1983). Socialization in the context of the family: Parent-child interaction. In P. H. Mussen (Series Ed.) & E. M. Hetherington (Vol. Ed.), *Handbook of child psychology: Vol. 4. Socialization, personality, and social development* (4th ed., pp. 1–101). New York: Wiley.

Maccoby, E. E., & Mnookin, R. (Eds.). (1992). *Dividing the child.* Cambridge, MA: Harvard University Press.

MacDonald, K. B. (1987). Parent-child physical play with rejected, neglected and popular boys. *Developmental Psychology, 23,* 705–711.

MacDonald, K. B. (1992). Warmth as a developmental construct: An evolutionary position. *Child Development, 63,* 753–773.

MacDonald, K. B., & Parke, R. D. (1984). Bridging the gap: Parent-child play interaction and peer interactive competence. *Child Development, 55,* 1265–1277.

MacDonald, K. B., & Parke, R. D. (1986). Parent-child physical play: The effects of sex and age of children and parents. *Sex Roles, 7–8,* 367–379.

MacKinnon-Lewis, C., Volling, B. L., Lamb, M. E., Dechman, K., Rabiner, D., & Curtner, M. E. (1994). A cross-contextual analysis of boys' social competence: From family to school. *Developmental Psychology, 30,* 325–333.

Madsen, W. (1973). *The Mexican-American of South Texas.* New York: Holt, Rinehart and Winston.

McAdoo, H. P. (1978). Factors related to stability in upwardly mobile black families. *Journal of Marriage and the Family, 40,* 761–776.

McAdoo, H. P. (1993). Ethnic families: Strengths that are found in diversity. In H. P. McAdoo (Ed.), *Ethnic families: Strength in diversity* (pp. 3–14). Newbury Park, CA: Sage.

McAdoo, J. L. (1993). The roles of African-American fathers: An ecological perspective. *Families in Society: The Journal of Contemporary Human Services, 74,* 28–34.

McCarthy, K. A., & Lord, S. E. (1993, March). *Contextual factors related to family management strategies in high risk environments.* Poster presented at the biennial meeting of the Society for Research in Child Development, New Orleans, LA.

McClintock, E., & Moore, J. W. (1982). *Interactional styles of immigrant and later generation Mexican American mother-child pairs.* Paper presented at the second Symposium on Chicano Psychology, University of California, Riverside.

McCluskey, K. A., Killarney, J., & Papini, D. R. (1983). Adolescent pregnancy and parenthood: Implications for development. In E. C. Callahan & K. A. McCluskey (Eds.), *Life-span developmental psychology: Non-normative life events.* New York: Academic Press.

McCoy, J. K., Brody, G. H., & Stoneman, Z. (1994). A longitudinal analysis of sibling relationships as mediators of the link between family processes and youths' best friendships. *Family Relations, 43,* 400–408.

McHale, S. M., Crouter, A. C., & Bartko, W. T. (1991). Traditional and egalitarian patterns of parental involvement: Antecedents, consequences and temporal rhythms. In R. Lerner & D. Featherman (Eds.), *Advances in life-span development* (Vol. 9). Hillsdale, NJ: Erlbaum.

McLanahan, S., & Booth, K. (1989). Mother-only families: Problems, prospects and politics. *Journal of Marriage and the Family, 51,* 557–580.

McLanahan, S., & Sandefur, G. (1994). *Growing up with a single parent.* Cambridge, MA: Harvard University Press.

McLoyd, V. C. (1989). Socialization and development in a changing economy: The effects of paternal job and income loss on children. *American Psychologist, 44,* 293–302.

McLoyd, V. C., Jayaratne, R. E., Ceballo, R., & Borquez, J. (1994). Unemployment and work interruption among African-American single mothers: Effects on parenting and adolescent socioemotional functioning. *Child Development, 65,* 562–589.

Meany, M. J., Stewart, J., & Beatty, W. W. (1985). Sex differences in social play: The socialization of sex roles. In J. S. Rosenblatt, C. Bear, C. W. Bushnell, & P. Slater (Eds.), *Advances in the study of behavior* (Vol. 15, pp. 1–58). New York: Academic Press.

Miller, D. R., & Swanson, G. E. (1954). *The changing American parent.* New York: Wiley.

Miller, N., & Dollard, J. (1941). *Social learning and imitation.* New Haven, CT: Yale University Press.

Miller, P., & Sperry, L. L. (1987). The socialization of anger and aggression. *Merrill-Palmer Quarterly, 33,* 1–31.

Mills, R. S. L., & Rubin, K. H. (1993). Parental ideas as influences on children's social competence. In S. Duch (Ed.), *Learning about relationships* (pp. 98–117). Newbury Park, CA: Sage.

Minuchin, P. (1985). Families and individual development: Provocations from the field of family therapy. Family Development [Special issue]. *Child Development, 56,* 289–302.

Montemayor, R., & Brownlee, J. (1987). Fathers, mothers and adolescents: Gender-based differences in parental roles during adolescence. *Journal of Youth and Adolescence, 16,* 281–291.

Moore, K. A., Snyder, N. O., & Glei, D. (1995). *Facts at a glance.* Washington, DC: Child Trends.

Moos, R. H., Insel, P. M., & Humphrey, B. (1974). *Manual for the Family Environment Scale.* Palo Alto, CA: Consulting Psychologists Press.

Moos, R. H., & Moos, B. S. (1981). *Family Environment Scale manual.* Palo Alto, CA: Consulting Psychologists Press.

Morgan, D. L. (1988). *Focus groups as qualitative research.* Newbury Park, CA: Sage.

Mott, F. (1993). *Absent fathers and child development: Emotional and cognitive effects at ages five to nine.* Unpublished report, Ohio State University, Columbus.

Murguia, E. (1982). *Chicano intermarriages: A theoretical and empirical study.* San Antonio, TX: Trinity University Press.

Neville, B., & Parke, R. D. (in press). Waiting for paternity: Interpersonal and contextual implications of the timing of fatherhood. *Sex Roles.*

New, R., & Benigni, L. (1987). Italian fathers and infants: Cultural constraints on paternal behavior. In M. E. Lamb (Ed.), *The father's role: Cross-cultural perspectives* (pp. 139–168). Hillsdale, NJ: Erlbaum.

Newcomber, S., & Udry, J. R. (1987). Parental marital status effects on adolescent sexual behavior. *Journal of Marriage and the Family, 49,* 235–240.

Nobles, W. W., Goddard, L. L., Cavil, W. E., & George, P. Y. (1987). *African-American families: Issues, insight, and directions.* Oakland, CA: Black Family Institute.

O'Connell, M. (1993). *Where's papa? Father's role in child care* (Population Trends and Public Policy). Washington, DC: Population Reference Bureau.

O'Donnell, L., & Stueve, A. (1983). Mothers as social agents: Structuring the community activities of school aged children. In H. Lopata & J. H. Pleck (Eds.), *Research in the interweave of social roles: Jobs and families: Vol. 3. Families and jobs.* Greenwich, CT: JAI Press.

Ogbu, J. V. (1987). Variability in minority responses to schooling: Nonimmigrants vs. immigrants. In G. Spindler & L. Sprindler (Eds.), *Interpretive ethnography of education: At home and abroad* (pp. 255–280). Hillsdale, NJ: Erlbaum.

Okagaki, L., & Divecha, D. J. (1993). Development of parental beliefs. In T. Luster & L. Okagaki (Eds.), *Parenting: An ecological perspective* (pp. 35–67). Hillsdale, NJ: Erlbaum.

Okagaki, L., & Sternberg, R. J. (1993). Parental beliefs and children's school performance. *Child Development, 64,* 36–56.

Olds, D. L. (1988). The prenatal/early infancy project. In R. Price, E. Cowen, R. Lorion, & J. Ramos-McKay (Eds.), *14 ounces of Prevention* (pp. 9–23). Washington, DC: American Psychological Association.

Oliveri, M. E., & Reiss, D. (1981). A theory-based empirical classification of family problem-solving behavior. *Family Process, 20,* 409–418.

Oliveri, M. E., & Reiss, D. (1987). Social networks of family members: Distinctive roles of mothers and fathers. *Sex Roles, 17,* 719–736.

Olsen, D. H., Russell, C. S., & Sprenkle, D. H. (1980). Circumplex model of marital and family systems: II. Empirical studies and clinical interventions. In J. P. Vincent (Ed.), *Advances in family interventions, assessment, and theory* (Vol. 1, pp. 128–176). Greenwich, CT: JAI Press.

Olsen, L., & Chen, M. T. (1988). *Crossing the schoolhouse border: Immigrant students and the California public schools.* San Francisco: California Tomorrow Policy Research Report.

O'Neil, R., & Parke, R. D. (1997, March). *Objective and subjective features of children's neighborhoods: Relations to parental regulatory strategies and children's social competence.* Paper presented at the biennial meeting of the Society for Research in Child Development, Washington, DC.

Oropesa, R. S., & Landale, N. S. (1995). *Immigrant legacies: The socioeconomic circumstances of children by ethnicity and generation in the United States* (Working Paper 95-01R). Population Research Institute, Pennsylvania State University, University Park, PA.

Osofsky, J. D., Hann, D. M., & Peebles, C. (1993). Adolescent parenthood: Risks and opportunities for parents and infants. In C. Zeanah (Ed.), *Handbook of infant mental health* (pp. 106–119). New York: Guilford Press.

Paine, R. (1971). *Patrons and brokers in the East Arctic.* Toronto: University of Toronto Press.

Parke, R. D. (1978a). Parent-infant interaction: Progress, paradigms, and problems. In G. P. Sackett (Ed.), *Observing behavior: Vol. 1. Theory and applications in mental retardation* (pp. 69–95). Baltimore: University Park Press.

Parke, R. D. (1978b). Children's home environments: Social and cognitive effects. In I. Altman & J. F. Wohlwill (Eds.), *Children and the environment* (pp. 33–81). New York: Plenum Press.

Parke, R. D. (1988). Families in life-span perspective: A multilevel developmental approach. In E. M. Hetherington, R. M. Lerner, & M. Perlmutter (Eds.), *Child development in life span perspective* (pp. 159–190). Hillsdale, NJ: Erlbaum.

Parke, R. D. (1994). Progress, paradigms and unresolved problems: A commentary on recent advances in our understanding of children's emotions. *Merrill-Palmer Quarterly, 40,* 157–169.

Parke, R. D. (1996). *Fatherhood.* Cambridge, MA: Harvard University Press.

Parke, R. D., Burks, V., Carson, J., Neville, B., & Boyum, L. (1994). Family-peer relationships: A tripartite model. In R. D. Parke & S. Kellam (Eds.), *Advances in family research: Vol. 4. Family relationships with other social systems* (pp. 115–145). Hillsdale, NJ: Erlbaum.

Parke, R. D., Cassidy, J., Burks, V. M., Carson, J. L., & Boyum, L. (1992). Familial contribution to peer competence among young children: The role of interactive and affective processes. In R. D. Parke & G. W. Ladd (Eds.), *Family-peer relationships: Modes of linkage* (pp. 107–134). Hillsdale, NJ: Erlbaum.

Parke, R. D., Hymel, S., Power, T. G., & Tinsley, B. R. (1980). Fathers and risk: A hospital-based model intervention. In D. B. Sawin, R. C. Hawkins, L. O. Walker, & J. H. Penticuff (Eds.), *Psychosocial risks in infant-environment transactions* (pp. 174–189). New York: Bruner/Mazel.

Parke, R. D., & Kellam, S. (Eds.). (1994). *Advances in family research: Vol. 4. Family relationships with other social systems.* Hillsdale, NJ: Erlbaum.

Parke, R. D., MacDonald, K. B., Beitel, A., & Bhavnagri, N. (1988). The role of the family in the development of peer relationships. In R. D. Peters & R. J. McMahon (Eds.), *Social*

learning and systems approaches to marriage and the family (pp. 17–44). New York: Brunner/Mazel.

Parke, R. D., & Neville, B. (1995). Late-timed fatherhood: Determinants and consequences for children and families. In J. L. Shapiro, M. J. Diamond, & M. Greenberg (Eds.), *Becoming a father* (pp. 104–116). New York: Springer.

Parke, R. D., & O'Neil, R. (1997). The influence of significant others on learning about relationships. In S. Duck (Ed.), *The handbook of personal relationships* (2nd ed., pp. 29–59). New York: Wiley.

Parke, R. D., Ornstein, P. A., Rieser, J. J., & Zahn-Waxler, C. (1994). The past as prologue: An overview of a century of developmental psychology. In R. D. Parke, P. A. Ornstein, J. J. Rieser, & C. Zahn-Waxler (Eds.), *A century of developmental psychology* (pp. 1–75). Washington, DC: American Psychological Association.

Parke, R. D., Power, T. G., & Gottman, J. M. (1979). Conceptualization and quantifying influence patterns in the family triad. In M. E. Lamb, S. J. Suomi, & G. R. Stephenson (Eds.), *Social interaction analysis: Methodological issues* (pp. 231–253). Madison: University of Wisconsin Press.

Parke, R. D., & Stearns, P. N. (1993). Fathers and child rearing. In G. H. Elder, J. Modell, & R. D. Parke (Eds.), *Children in time and place* (pp. 147–170). New York: Cambridge University Press.

Parke, R. D., & Suomi, S. (1981). Adult male-infant relationships: Human and nonhuman primate evidence. In K. Immelman, G. Barlow, M. Main, & L. Petrinovitch (Eds.), *Behavioral development: The Bielefeld Interdisciplinary Project* (pp. 700–725). New York: Cambridge University Press.

Parke, R. D., & Tinsley, B. R. (1984). Fatherhood: Historical and contemporary perspectives. In K. McCluskey & H. Reese (Eds.), *Life span development: Historical and generational effects* (pp. 203–248). New York: Academic Press.

Parsons, T. (1951). *The social system.* Glencoe, IL: Free Press.

Parsons, T., & Bales, R. F. (1955). *Family, socialization and interaction process.* Glencoe, IL: Free Press.

Patterson, C. J. (1995). Families of the lesbian baby boom: Parents' division of labor and children's adjustment. *Developmental Psychology, 31,* 115–123.

Patterson, G. R. (1980). Mothers: The unacknowledged victims. *Monographs of the Society for Research in Child Development, 45,* 64.

Patterson, G. R. (1981). *Coercive family process.* Eugene, OR: Castalia Press.

Patterson, G. R., & Capaldi, D. M. (1991). Antisocial parents: Unskilled and vulnerable. In P. A. Cowan & E. M. Hetherington (Eds.), *Family transitions* (pp. 195–218). Hillsdale, NJ: Erlbaum.

Patterson, G. R., Reid, J. B., & Dishion, T. J. (1992). *Antisocial boys.* Eugene, OR: Castalia Press.

Patterson, G. R., & Stouthamer-Loeber, M. (1984). The correlation of family management practices and delinquency. *Child Development, 55,* 1299–1306.

Pearlin, L. I. (1983). Role strain and personal stress. In H. G. Kaplan (Ed.), *Psychosocial stress: Trends in theory and research* (pp. 3–32). New York: Academic Press.

Pearson, J. L., Hunter, A. G., Ensminger, M. E., & Kellam, S. G. (1990). Black grandmothers in multigenerational households: Diversity in family structure and parenting involvement in the Woodlawn community. *Child Development, 61,* 434–442.

Pedersen, F. A., Anderson, B. J., & Cain, R. L. (1980). Parent-infant and husband-wife interactions observed at age five months. In F. A. Pedersen (Ed.), *The father-infant relationship* (pp. 71–86). New York: Praeger.

Peters, M. (1985). Racial socialization of young black children. In H. McAdoo & J. McAdoo (Eds.), *Black children* (pp. 159–173). Beverly Hills, CA: Sage.

Peterson, J. L., & Zill, N. (1986). Marital disruption, parent-child relationships, and behavior problems in children. *Journal of Marriage and the Family, 48,* 295–307.

Pettit, G. S., Dodge, K. A., & Brown, M. M. (1988). Early family experience, social problem solving patterns, and children's social competence. *Child Development, 59,* 107–120.

Phinney, J. S., Chavira, V., & Tate, J. D. (1993). The effects of ethnic threat on ethnic self concept and own-group ratings. *Journal of Social Psychology, 133*, 469–478.

Pleck, J. H. (1983). Husbands' paid work and family roles: Current research issues. In H. H. Lopata & J. H. Pleck (Eds.), *Research on the interview of social roles: Vol. 3. Families and jobs* (pp. 231–333). Greenwich, CT: JAI Press.

Plomin, R. (1990). *Nature and nurture: An introduction to behavioral genetics.* Belmont, CA: Brooks/Cole.

Plomin, R. (1994). Genetic research and identification of environmental influences. *Journal of Child Psychology and Psychiatry, 35,* 817–834.

Plomin, R., Reiss, D., Hetherington, E. M., & Howe, G. W. (1994). Nature and nurture: Genetic contributions to measures of the family environment. *Developmental Psychology, 30,* 32–43.

Pope, S., Casey, P., Bradley, R., & Brooks-Gunn, J. (1993). The effect of intergenerational factors on the development of low birth weight infants born to adolescent mothers. *Journal of the American Medical Association, 269,* 1396–1400.

Portes, A., & Rumbaut, R. G. (1990). *Immigrant America.* Berkeley: University of California Press.

Portes, P. R., Dunham, R. M., & Williams, S. (1986). Assessing childrearing style in ecological settings: Its relation to culture, social class, early age intervention, and scholastic achievement. *Adolescence, 21,* 723–735.

Power, T. G., & Parke, R. D. (1982). Play as a context for early learning: Lab and home analyses. In I. E. Sigel & L. M. Laosa (Eds.), *The family as a learning environment* (pp. 147–178). New York: Plenum Press.

Pulkkinen, L. (1982). Self-control and continuity from childhood to late adolescence. In P. B. Baltes & O. G. Brim, Jr. (Eds.), *Life-span development and behavior* (Vol. 4, pp. 63–105). New York: Academic Press.

Putallaz, M. (1987). Maternal behavior and sociometric status. *Child Development, 58,* 324–340.

Putallaz, M., Costanzo, P. R., & Smith, R. B. (1991). Maternal recollections of childhood peer relationships: Implications for their children's social competence. *Journal of Social and Personal Relationships, 8,* 403–422.

Putallaz, M., & Sheppard, B. H. (1992). Conflict management and social competence. In C. U. Shantz & W. W. Hartup (Eds.), *Conflict in child and adolescent development* (pp. 330–355). Cambridge, England: Cambridge University Press.

Radin, N. (1993). Primary caregiving fathers in intact families. In A. Gottfried & A. Gottfried (Eds.), *Redefining families* (pp. 11–54). New York: Plenum Press.

Radke-Yarrow, M., & Zahn-Waxler, C. (1984). Roots, motives and patterns in children's prosocial behavior. In E. Staub, D. Bar-Tal, J. Karylowski, & J. Reykowski (Eds.), *Origins and maintenance of prosocial behaviors* (pp. 155–176). New York: Plenum Press.

Ragozin, A. S., Bashan, R. B., Crnic, K. A., Greenberg, M. T., & Robinson, N. M. (1982). Effects of maternal age on parenting role. *Developmental Psychology, 18,* 627–634.

Ramirez, M., III. (1983). *Psychology of the Americas.* New York: Pergamon Press.

Ramirez, M., III, & Castaneda, A. (1974). *Cultural democracy, bicognitive development and education.* New York: Academic Press.

Reed, J. (1982). Black Americans in the 1980s. *Population Bulletin, 37,* 1–37.

Reise, S. P., Widaman, K. F., & Pugh, R. M. (1993). Confirmatory factor analysis and item response theory: Two approaches for exploring measurement invariance. *Psychological Bulletin, 114,* 552–566.

Reiss, D. (1981). *The family's construction of reality.* Cambridge, MA: Harvard University Press.

Reiss, D. (1989). The represented and practicing family: Contrasting visions of family continuity. In A. J. Sameroff & R. N. Emde (Eds.), *Relationship disturbances in early childhood* (pp. 191–220). New York: Basic Books.

Reiss, D., & Oliveri, M. E. (1983). The family's construction of social reality and its ties to its kin network: An exploration of causal direction. *Journal of Marriage and the Family, 45,* 81–91.

Repetti, R. L. (1989). Effects of daily workload on subsequent behavior during marital interaction: The roles of social withdrawal and spouse support. *Journal of Personality and Social Psychology, 57*(4), 651–659.

Repetti, R. L. (1994). Short-term and long-term processes linking perceived job stressors to father-child interactions. *Social Development, 3,* 1–15.

Richards, L., & Richards, P. (1991). The transformation of qualitative method: Computational paradigm and research processes. In N. Fielding & R. M. Lee (Eds.), *Using computers in qualitative research* (pp. 38–53). London: Sage.

Roberts, W. (1994, June). *The socialization of emotional expression: Relation with competence in preschool.* Paper presented at the meetings of the Canadian Psychological Association, Penticton, British Columbia.

Robinson, J. (1988). Who's doing the housework? *American Demographics, 10,* 24–28.

Rogoff, B. (1990). *Apprenticeship in thinking: Cognitive development in social context.* New York: Oxford University Press.

Rohner, R. P., & Pettengill, S. M. (1985). Perceived parental acceptance-rejection and parental control among Korean adolescents. *Child Development, 56,* 524–528.

Roopnarine, J. L., & Carter, D. B. (Eds.). (1992). *Parent-child socialization in diverse cultures.* Norwood, NJ: ABLEX.

Roopnarine, J. L., Lu, M., & Ahmdezzaman, M. (1989). Parental reports of early patterns of caregiving play and discipline in India and Malaysia. *Early Child Development and Care, 50,* 109–120.

Rosier, K. B., & Corsaro, W. A. (1993). Competent parents, complex lives: Managing parenthood in poverty. *Journal of Contemporary Ethnography, 22,* 171–204.

Ross, C. (1987). The division of labor at home. *Social Forces, 65,* 816–833.

Rothbart, M. K., & Ahadi, S. A. (1994). Temperament and the development of personality. *Journal of Abnormal Psychology, 103,* 55–66.

Rowe, D. (1994). *The limits of family effects.* New York: Guilford Press.

Rubin, K. H., & Mills, R. S. L. (1990). Maternal beliefs about adaptive and maladaptive social behaviors in normal, aggressive and withdrawn preschoolers. *Journal of Abnormal Child Psychology, 18,* 419–435.

Rubin, K. H., Mills, R. S. L., & Rose-Krasnor, L. (1989). Maternal beliefs and children's competence. In B. Schneider, G. Attili, J. Nadel, & R. Weissberg (Eds.), *Social competence in developmental perspective* (pp. 313–331). Amsterdam, The Netherlands: Kluwer Academic.

Rueschenberg, E., & Buriel, R. (1989). Mexican American family functioning and acculturation: A family systems perspective. *Hispanic Journal of Behavioral Sciences, 11,* 232–244.

Rumbaut, R. G. (1991). The agony of exile: A study of the migration and adaptation of Southeast Asian refugee adults and children. In F. L. Ahearn, Jr. & J. A. Garrison (Eds.), *Refugee children: Theory, research, and practice* (pp. 53–91). Baltimore: Johns Hopkins University Press.

Rumbaut, R. G. (1995a). The crucible within: Ethnic identity, self-esteem, and segmented assimilation among children of immigrants. *International Migration Review, 28,* 748–794.

Rumbaut, R. G. (1995b). Vietnamese, Laotian, and Cambodian Americans. In P. G. Min (Ed.), *Asian Americans: Contemporary trends and issues* (pp. 232–270). Thousand Oaks, CA: Sage.

Russell, A., & Finnie, V. (1990). Preschool children's social status and maternal instructions to assist group entry. *Developmental Psychology, 26*(4), 603–611.

Russell, G. (1982). Shared-caregiving families: An Australian study. In M. E. Lamb (Ed.), *Nontraditional families* (pp. 139–172). Hillsdale, NJ: Erlbaum.

Russell, G., & Russell, A. (1987). Mother-child and father-child relationships in middle childhood. *Child Development, 58,* 1573–1585.

Rutter, M. (1971). Parent-child separation: Psychological effects on children. *Journal of Child Psychology and Psychiatry, 12,* 233–260.

Rutter, M. (1987). Psychosocial resilience and protective mechanisms. *American Journal of Orthopsychiatry, 57,* 316–331.

Sabogal, F., Marin, G., Otero-Sabogal, R., VanOss-Marin, B., & Perez, E. J. (1987). Hispanic familism and acculturation: What changes and what doesn't. *Hispanic Journal of Behavioral Sciences, 9,* 397–412.

Sameroff, A. J. (1983). Developmental systems: Contexts and evolution. In P. H. Mussen (Series Ed.) & W. Kessen (Vol. Ed), *Handbook of child psychology: Vol. 1. History, theory and methods* (pp. 237–294). New York: Wiley.

Sameroff, A. J. (1994). Developmental systems and family functioning. In R. D. Parke & S. G. Kellam (Eds.), *Exploring family relationships with other social contexts* (pp. 199–214). Hillsdale, NJ: Erlbaum.

Sameroff, A. J., & Chandler, M. J. (1974). Reproductive risk and the continuum of caretaking casualty. In F. D. Horowitz (Ed), *Review of child development research* (Vol. 4, pp. 187–244). Chicago: University of Chicago Press.

Sameroff, A. J., & Feil, L. A. (1985). Parental conceptions of development. In I. E. Sigel (Ed.), *Parental belief systems: The psychological consequences for children* (pp. 83–105). Hillsdale, NJ: Erlbaum.

Sameroff, A. J., Seifer, R., Zax, M., & Barocas, R. (1987). Early indicators of developmental risk: Rochester longitudinal study. *Schizophrenia Bulletin, 13,* 383–394.

Sampson, E. E. (1985). The decentralization of identity: Toward a revised concept of personal and social order. *American Psychologist, 40,* 1203–1211.

Sampson, E. E. (1988). The debate of individualism: Indigenous psychologies of the individual and their role in personal and societal functioning. *American Psychologist, 43,* 15–22.

Santrock, J. W., & Warshak, R. (1979). Father custody and social development in boys and girls. *Journal of Social Issues, 35,* 112–125.

Schaffer, H. R. (1971). *The growth of sociability.* Harmondsworth, England: Penguin Books.

Schank, R. C., & Abelson, R. P. (1977). *Scripts, plans, goals and understanding.* Hillsdale, NJ: Erlbaum.

Schumm, W. R., McCollum, E. E., Bughaighis, M. A., Jurich, A. P., Bollman, S. R., & Reitz, J. (1988). Differences between Anglo and Mexican American family members on satisfaction with family life. *Hispanic Journal of Behavioral Sciences, 10,* 39–53.

Scott-Jones, D., Lewis, L. T., & Shirley, K. (1996). *Successful pathways through middle childhood: The role of ethnic families of color.* Paper presented at the meeting of the MacArthur Foundation Joint Task Force on Family Processes, Philadelphia, PA.

Sears, R. R. (1951). A theoretical framework for personality and social behavior. *American Psychologist, 6,* 476–483.

Sears, R. R., Maccoby, E. E., & Levin, H. (1957). *Patterns of child-rearing.* Evanston, IL: Row-Peterson.

Seltzer, J. A. (1991). Relationships between fathers and children who live apart: The father's role after separation. *Journal of Marriage and the Family, 52,* 79–101.

Seltzer, J. A., & Bianchi, S. M. (1988). Children's contact with absent parents. *Journal of Marriage and the Family, 50,* 663–678.

Shapiro, J. R., & Mangelsdorf, S. C. (1994). The determinants of parenting competence in adolescent mothers. *Journal of Youth and Adolescence, 23,* 621–641.

Shulman, S., & Klein, M. M. (1993). Distinctive role of the father in adolescent separation-individuation. In S. Shulman & W. A. Collins (Eds.), *Father-adolescent relationships* (pp. 41–58). San Francisco: Jossey-Bass.

Sigel, I., & Parke, R. D. (1987). Conceptual models of family interaction. *Journal of Applied Developmental Psychology, 8,* 123–137.

Simmons, R. G., & Blyth, D. A. (1987). *Moving into adolescence: The impact of pubertal change and school context.* New York: Aldine.

Simons, R. L., Lorenz, R. O., Conger, R. D., & Wu, C.-I. (1992). Support from spouse as a mediator and moderator of the disruptive influence of economic strain on parenting. *Child Development, 63,* 1282–1301.

Smith, S., & Zaslow, M. (1995). Rationale and policy context for two-generation interventions. In S. Smith (Ed.), *Two-generation programs for families in poverty: A new intervention strategy* (pp. 1–35). Norwood, NJ: ABLEX.

Snyder, T. D., & Fromboluti, C. S. (1993). *Youth indicators 1993.* Washington, DC: National Center for Education Statistics.

Solberg, V. S., O'Brien, K., Villareal, P., Kennel, R., & Davis, B. (1993). Self-efficacy and Hispanic college students: Validation of the College Self-Efficacy Instrument. *Hispanic Journal of Behavioral Sciences, 15,* 80–95.

Sorrentino, J. (1990). The changing family in international perspective. *Monthly Labor Review, 113,* 41–46.

Spitzer, S., Estock, S., Cupp, R., Isley-Paradise, S., & Parke, R. D. (1992). *Parental influence and efficacy beliefs and children's social acceptance.* Unpublished manuscript, University of California, Riverside.

Spitzer, S., & Parke, R. D. (1994). *Family cognitive representations of social behavior and children's social competence.* Paper presented at the meeting of the American Psychological Society, Washington, DC.

Sroufe, A. L., Carlson, E., & Shulman, S. (1993). The development of individual relationships: From infancy through adolescence. In D. Funder, R. D. Parke, C. Tomlinson-Keasey, & K. Widaman (Eds.), *Studying lives through time: Approaches to personality and development* (pp. 315–342). Washington, DC: American Psychological Association.

Staples, R., & Johnson, L. B. (1993). *Black families at the crossroads.* San Francisco: Jossey-Bass.

Steinberg, L. (1986). Latchkey children and susceptibility to peer pressure: An ecological analysis. *Developmental Psychology, 22,* 433–439.

Steinberg, L. (1996, January). *The assessment of parent-child relations in the study of developmental psychopathology: A conceptual framework and methodological proposal.* Paper presented at the meeting of the MacArthur Foundation Joint Task Force on Family Processes, Philadelphia, PA.

Steinberg, L., Darling, N. E., & Fletcher, A. C. (1995). Authoritative parenting and adolescent development: An ecological journey. In P. Moen, G. H. Elder, & K. Luscher (Eds.), *Examining lives in context* (pp. 423–466). Washington, DC: American Psychological Association.

Steinberg, L., Dornbusch, S., & Brown, B. (1992). Ethnic differences in adolescent achievement: An ecological perspective. *American Psychologist, 47,* 723–729.

Stern, D. N. (1977). *The first relationship.* Cambridge, MA: Harvard University Press.

Stevenson, M. R., & Black, K. N. (1995). *How divorce affects offspring: A research approach.* Dubuque, IA: Brown & Benchmark.

Stocker, C. (1994). Children's perceptions of relationships with siblings, friends, and mothers: Compensatory processes and links with adjustment. *Journal of Child Psychology and Psychiatry, 35,* 1447–1459.

Stocker, C., & Dunn, J. (1990). Sibling relationships in childhood: Links with friendships and peer relationships. *British Journal of Developmental Psychology, 8,* 227–244.

Sudarkasa, N. (1988). Interpreting the African heritage in Afro-American family organization. In H. P. McAdoo (Ed.), *Black families* (pp. 37–53). Newbury Park, CA: Sage.

Sudarkasa, N. (1993). Female-headed African American households: Some neglected dimensions. In H. P. McAdoo (Ed.), *Family ethnicity* (pp. 81–89). Newbury Park, CA: Sage.

Suina, J. H., & Smolkin, L. B. (1994). From natural culture to school culture to dominant society culture: Supporting transitions for Pueblo Indian students. In P. M. Greenfield & R. R. Cocking (Eds.), *Cross-cultural roots of minority child development* (pp. 115–130). Hillsdale, NJ: Erlbaum.

Super, C. M., & Harkness, S. (1986). The developmental niche: A conceptualization at the interface of child and culture. *International Journal of Behavioral Development, 9,* 545–569.

Super, C. M., & Harkness, S. (1995). Culture and parenting. In M. Bornstein (Ed.), *Handbook of parenting* (Vol. 2, pp. 211–234). Hillsdale, NJ: Erlbaum.

Szapocznik, J., & Kurtines, W. (1980). Acculturation, biculturalism, and adjustment among Cuban Americans. In A. M. Padilla (Ed.), *Acculturation: Theory, models and some new findings* (pp. 139–161). Boulder, CO: Westview Press.

Takanishi, R. (1994). Continuities and discontinuities in the cognitive socialization of Asian-originated children: The case of Japanese Americans. In P. M. Greenfield & R. R. Cocking (Eds.), *Cross-cultural roots of minority child development* (pp. 351–362). Hillsdale, NJ: Erlbaum.

Tardif, T. (1993). *Adult-to-child speech and language acquisition in Mandarin Chinese.* Unpublished manuscript, Yale University Press, New Haven, CT.

Teti, D. M., Gelfand, D. M., Messinger, D. S., & Isabella, R. (1995). Maternal depression and the quality of early attachment: An examination of infants, preschoolers and their mothers. *Developmental Psychology, 31,* 395–405.

Thelen, E. (1989). Self-organization in developmental processes: Can systems approaches work? In M. R. Gunnar & E. Thelen (Eds.), *Systems and development. The Minnesota Symposia on Child Psychology* (Vol. 22, pp. 77–117). Hillsdale, NJ: Erlbaum.

Thompson, R. A. (1994). Fatherhood and divorce. In L. S. Quinn (Ed.), *The future of children: Children and divorce.* Palo Alto, CA: Packard Foundation.

Thornton, M. C., Chatters, L. M., Taylor, R. J., & Allen, W. R. (1990). Sociodemographic and environmental correlates of racial socialization by Black parents. *Child Development, 61,* 401–409.

Tinsley, B. J. (1992). Multiple influences on the acquisition and socialization of children's health attitudes and behavior: An integrative review. *Child Development, 63,* 1043–1069.

Tinsley, B. J. & Lees, N. B. (1995). Health promotion for parents. In M. Bornstein (Ed.), *Handbook of parenting* (Vol. 4, pp. 187–204). Mahwah, NJ: Erlbaum.

Tinsley, B. J., & Parke, R. D. (1984). The person-environment relationship: Lessons from families with preterm infants. In D. Magnusson & V. Allen (Eds.), *Human development: An interactional perspective* (pp. 93–110). New York: Academic Press.

Tinsley, B. J., & Parke, R. D. (1988). The contemporary role of grandfathers in young families. In P. Bronstein & C. P. Cowan (Eds.), *Fatherhood today: Men's changing role in the family* (pp. 236–250). New York: Wiley.

Tolson, T. F. J., & Wilson, M. N. (1990). The impact of two and three generational Black family structure on perceived family climate. *Child Development, 61,* 416–428.

Trimble, J. E., & Medicine, B. (1993). Diversification of American Indians: Forming an indigenous perspective. In U. Kim & J. W. Berry (Eds.), *Indigenous psychologies* (pp. 133–151). Newbury Park, CA: Sage.

Tronick, E. (1989). Emotions and emotional communication in infants. *American Psychologist, 44,* 112–119.

Uba, L. (1994). *Asian Americans: Personality patterns, identity and mental health.* New York: Guilford Press.

Unger, D. G., & Wandersman, A. (1985). The importance of neighbors: The social, cognitive, and affective components of neighboring. *American Journal of Community Psychology, 13,* 139–169.

Unger, D. G., & Wandersman, L. P. (1996). Social support and adolescent mothers: Action research contributions to theory and application. *Journal of Social Issues, 41,* 29–45.

U.S. Census Bureau. (1994). *The diverse living arrangements of children: Summer 1991.* Washington, DC: U.S. Government Printing Office.

U.S. Department of Commerce. (1988). *The Hispanic population in the United States: March 1988* (Current Population Reports, Series P-20, No. 431). Washington, DC: U.S. Government Printing Office.

U.S. Department of Commerce. (1993). *The Hispanic population in the United States: March 1993* (Current Population Reports, Series P20-475). Washington, DC: U.S. Government Printing Office.

Valdivieso, R., & Davis, C. (1988). *U.S. Hispanics: Challenging issues for the 1990s* (Population Reference Bureau, Number 17). Washington, DC: U.S. Government Printing Office.

Vázquez-García, H. A., García-Coll, C., Erkut, S., Alarcón, O., & Tropp, L. (1995). *An instrument for the assessment of family values and functioning of Latino parents*. Poster presented at the biennial meeting of the Society for Research in Child Development, Indianapolis, IN.

Vidal, C. (1988). Godparenting among Hispanic Americans. *Child Welfare, 67,* 453–459.

Vigil, J. D. (1988). *Barrio gangs*. Austin: University of Texas Press.

Volling, B. L., & Belsky, J. (1991). Multiple determinants of father involvement during infancy in dual-earner and single-earner families. *Journal of Marriage and the Family, 53,* 461–474.

Wachs, T. D., & Gandour, M. J. (1983). Temperament, environment and six months cognitive-intellectual development. *International Journal of Behavioral Development, 6,* 135–152.

Walker, K., Taylor, E., McElroy, A., Phillip, D., & Wilson, M. N. (1995). Familial and ecological correlates of self-esteem in African American children. In M. N. Wilson (Ed.), *New directions for child development: 68. African American family life: Its structure and ecological aspects* (pp. 23–34). San Francisco: Jossey-Bass.

Walker, K., & Woods, M. (1976). *Time use: A measure of household production of family goods and services*. Washington, DC: American Home Economics Association.

Wallerstein, J. S., & Kelly, J. B. (1980a). California's children of divorce. *Psychology Today, 13,* 71–72.

Wallerstein, J. S., & Kelly, J. B. (Eds.). (1980b). *Surviving the break-up: How children actually cope with divorce*. New York: Basic Books.

Wamboldt, F. S., & Reiss, D. (1989). Defining a family heritage and a new relationship identity: Two central tasks in the making of a marriage. *Family Process, 28,* 317–335.

Wasserman, G. A., Brunelli, S. A., Rauh, V. A., & Alvarado, L. E. (1994). The cultural context of adolescent childrearing in three groups of urban minority mothers. In G. Lamberty & C. Garcia Coll (Eds.), *Puerto Rican women and children: Issues in health, growth and development* (pp. 137–160). New York: Plenum Press.

Weisner, T. (1987). Socialization for parenthood in sibling caretaking societies. In J. B. Lancaster, J. Altmann, A. S. Rossi, & L. R. Sherrod (Eds.), *Parenting across the life span: Biosocial dimensions* (pp. 237–270). Hawthorne, NY: Aldine.

Weisner, T. S. (1993). Overview: Sibling similarity and difference in different cultures. In C. W. Nuckolls (Ed.), *Siblings in South Asia: Brothers and sisters in cultural context* (pp. 1–17). New York: Guilford Press.

Weitzman, L. J. (1985). *The divorce revolution: The unexpected social and economic consequences for women and children in America*. New York: Free Press.

Westerman, M. A., & Schonholtz, J. (1993). Marital adjustment, joint parental support in a triadic problem-solving task, and child behavior problems. *Journal of Clinical Child Psychology, 22,* 97–106.

Whiting, B. B., & Edwards, C. P. (1988). *Children of different worlds: The formation of social behavior*. Cambridge, MA: Harvard University Press.

Whiting, J. W. M., & Child, I. L. (1953). *Child training and personality: A cross-cultural study*. New Haven, CT: Yale University Press.

Willis, W. (1992). Families with African American roots. In E. W. Lynch & M. J. Hanson (Eds.), *Developing cross-cultural competence: A guide for working with young children and their families* (pp. 121–150). Baltimore: Brookes.

Wilson, M. N. (1986). The Black extended family: An analytical consideration. *Developmental Psychology, 22,* 246–258.

Wilson, M. N. (1992). Perceived parental activity of mothers, fathers, and grandmothers in three generational Black families. In A. K. Hoard Burlew, W. C. Banks, H. P. McAdoo, & D. A. Azibo (Eds.), *African American psychology* (pp. 87–104). Newbury Park, CA: Sage.

Wilson, W. J. (1987). *The truly disadvantaged: The inner city, the underclass, and public policy*. Chicago: University of Chicago Press.

Wilson, W. J. (1995). Jobless ghettos and the social outcomes of youngsters. In P. Moen, G. H. Elder, & K. Luscher (Eds.), *Examining lives in context* (pp. 527–543). Washington, DC: American Psychological Association.

Wolin, S. J., Bennett, L. A., & Jacobs, J. S. (1988). Assessing family rituals. In E. Imber-Black, J. Roberts, & R. Whiting (Eds.), *Rituals and family therapy* (pp. 230–256). New York: Norton.

Wong, M. G. (1988). The Chinese American family. In C. H. Mindel, R. W. Habenstein, & R. Wright, Jr. (Eds.), *Ethnic families in America: Patterns and variations* (3rd ed., pp. 230–257). New York: Elsevier.

Wong, M. G. (1995). Chinese Americans. In P. G. Min (Ed.), *Asian Americans: Contemporary trends and issues* (pp. 58–94). Thousand Oaks, CA: Sage.

Wozniak, R. H. (1993). Co-constructive metatheory for psychology: Implications for an analysis of families as specific social contexts for development. In R. H. Wozniak & K. W. Fischer (Eds.), *Development in context: Acting and thinking in specific environments* (pp. 77–91). Hillsdale, NJ: Erlbaum.

Ybarra, L. (1982). When wives work: The impact on the Chicano family. *Journal of Marriage and the Family, 44,* 169–177.

Zavella, P. (1987). *Women's work and Chicano families: Cannery workers of the Santa Clara Valley.* Ithaca, NY: Cornell University Press.

Zazlow, M. T. (1988). Sex differences in children's response to parental divorce: Research methodology and post-divorce forms. *American Journal of Orthopsychiatry, 58,* 355–378.

Zepeda, M., & Espinosa, M. (1990, April). *The impact of acculturation on the parenting beliefs of Mexican-Americans.* Poster presented at the 7th International Conference on Infant Studies, Montreal, Canada.

Zill, N. (1978). *Divorce, marital happiness, and mental health of children: Findings from the Foundation for Child Development national survey of children.* Paper prepared for the National Institute of Mental Health Workshop on Divorce and Children, Bethesda, MD.

Zill, N., Morrison, D. R., & Corio, M. J. (1993). Long-term effects of parental divorce on parent-child relationships, adjustment and achievement in young adulthood. *Journal of Family Psychology, 7,* 91–103.

Zimiles, H., & Lee, V. E. (1991). Adolescent family structure and educational progress. *Developmental Psychology, 27,* 314–320.

Zuckerman, M. (1991). Sensation-seeking: The balance between risk and reward. In L. P. Lipsitt & L. Mitnick (Eds.), *Self-regulatory behavior and risk taking: Causes and consequences* (pp. 143–152). Norwood, NJ: ABLEX.

CHAPTER 9

The Development of Self-Representations

SUSAN HARTER

Attention to self processes has burgeoned since the 1983 *Handbook of Child Psychology*. The field has witnessed a return to classic issues that plagued historical scholars of the self. In addition, shifts in emphasis, including new themes and characterizations of the self, have emerged. In this chapter, the theoretical formulations of selected historical scholars of the self whose influence is still very much in evidence are first reviewed, followed by those historical developments since the turn of the century. A major contemporary thrust has been the emphasis on the *functions* of the self, which is summarized. Then attention turns to the development of self-representations in infancy, in an attempt to provide an integrated account of the major ontogenetic changes. The normative development of self-representations in childhood and adolescence are then addressed, applying contemporary stage models.

The focus then shifts to individual differences in self-evaluations. Theory and findings on *discrepancies* between

one's perceived and ideal self-concepts are reviewed, followed by evidence for James's (1890, 1892) model in which the discrepancy between perceived successes and aspirations for success influences global self-esteem. James also set the stage for multidimensional and hierarchical models of the self, which are reviewed. This discussion serves as a springboard to a consideration of multiple selves versus the unified self, with implications at adolescence for behaviors that are viewed as unauthentic. Attention then shifts to theory and research on the social sources of self-evaluation, building upon the tradition of symbolic interactionists and emphasizing the role of socializing agents. The topics described above speak to the antecedents of self-representations. However, other considerations include the stability of such representations over time and situation as well as their *accuracy*. Attention then turns to selected correlates of self-esteem, followed by implications for intervention. Issues involving autonomy and connectedness are also considered. The liabilities of self-development are then summarized, followed by concluding comments.

Historical Roots of Contemporary Issues Involving Self-Development

The history of interest in the self can be traced back to Greek philosophy, as revealed in the injunction to "know thyself." However, contemporary scholars of the self-concept typically pay major intellectual homage to James (1890, 1892) and to such symbolic interactionists as Cooley (1902), Mead (1925, 1934), and Baldwin (1895, 1906), scholars in whom there has been a recent resurgence of interest. The reader interested in the history of the self prior to the turn of the century is referred to excellent treatments by Baumeister (1987), Broughton (1987), and Logan (1987). The historical contributions of James and the symbolic interactionists will be presented as a general conceptual backdrop, followed by a consideration of more contemporary issues.

The Legacy of William James

The contributions of James (1890, 1892) were legion. Of paramount importance was his distinction between two fundamental aspects of the self, the "I" and the "Me," the self as subject and the self as object. For James, the I was the knower, in contrast to the Me, which represented an empirical aggregate of things objectively known about the self. It is the Me that came to be labeled the self-concept and that has received major attention. For James, however, it was essential to posit an I-self, the active agent responsible for constructing the Me-self. The I-self also demonstrated more specific types of awareness, for example, a concern with one's personal continuity through time and the distinctness of oneself as a person. The I-self/Me-self dichotomy has remained viable (Damon & Hart, 1988; Harter, 1983) and has led to recent elaborations, particularly by infancy researchers.

For James (1890), the Me-self could be subdivided into "constituents," namely, the *material self,* the *social self,* and the *spiritual self.* The material self subsumed the bodily self as well as one's possessions. The social self consisted of those characteristics recognized by others. Given the potential diversity of others' opinions, James concluded that "a man has as many social selves as there are individuals who recognize him and carry an image of him in their mind" (p. 190). The spiritual self was considered to be an inner core comprised of one's thoughts,

dispositions, moral judgments, and so on that were more enduring aspects of the self. James also sought to impose a hierarchical structure onto these self constituents. At the bottom of the hierarchy is the material self. The social self occupies the next position, given his assumption that we should care more about human ties and honor among others than about our bodies or wealth. The spiritual self, which James regarded as "supremely precious," occupies the highest tier. Thus, James paved the way for future models in which the self is viewed as multidimensional and hierarchical.

In differentiating various aspects of the self, including the multiplicity of social selves, James (1890) noted that these multiple selves may not all speak with the same voice. For example, James observed that "Many a youth who is demure enough before his parents and teachers, swears and swaggers like a pirate among his tough young friends" (p. 169). James further noted that this multiplicity can be harmonious, for example, when one is tender to his children but also stern to the soldiers under his command. Alternatively, there may be a "discordant splitting" if one's different selves are experienced as contradictory. The "conflict of the different Me's" could also be observed in the incompatibility of potential adult roles. James himself fantasized about his own desires to be handsome, athletic, rich, witty, a bon vivant, lady-killer, philosopher, philanthropist, statesman, warrior, and African explorer, as well as a tone-poet and a saint! He knowingly concluded that, because all of these roles could not possibly coexist, it was necessary to selectively choose, suppressing the alternatives. Thus, "the seeker of his truest, strongest, deepest self must review the list carefully, and pick out the one on which to stake his salvation" (p. 174).

The repudiation of particular attributes or roles was not, for James (1890), necessarily damaging to the individual's overall sense of worth, the "average tone of self-feeling which each one of us carries about" (p. 171). Thus, his own deficiency at Greek led to no sense of humiliation because he had no *pretensions* to be proficient at Greek. The role of pretensions became paramount in James's formulation of the causes of self-esteem. Self-esteem could not simply be reduced to the aggregate of perceived successes, but rather represented a ratio of successes to one's *pretensions.* If one's perceived successes were equal to or greater than one's pretensions or aspirations for success, high self-esteem would result. Conversely, if pretensions exceeded successes, that is, if one were unsuccessful in domains in which one had aspirations, one would experience low self-esteem. Critical to this formulation is the assumption that lack of success in an area in which one does *not* have pretensions (e.g., Greek for James) will not erode one's self-esteem, since it can be discounted. Thus, both the presence and absence of pretensions figured heavily in James's theorizing. He argued that abandoning certain pretensions can be as much a relief as striving to meet goals: "How pleasant is the day when we give up striving to be young" (1890, p. 201).

In James, therefore, we find many themes that anticipate contemporary issues about the self. These include the distinction between I and Me selves, a multidimensional, hierarchical view of the Me-self, the potential conflict between different Me-selves, and a formulation concerning the causes of self-esteem.

The Contribution of the Symbolic Interactionists

In contrast to James, the symbolic interactionists placed primary emphasis on how social interactions with others profoundly shaped the self. Thus, for Cooley (1902), Mead (1925, 1934), and Baldwin (1895, 1906), the self is viewed as a *social construction,* crafted through linguistic exchanges (symbolic interactions) with others. Cooley's looking-glass-self formulation was perhaps the most metaphorical, in that significant others constituted a social mirror into which the individual gazes to detect others' opinions toward the self. These opinions, in turn, are incorporated into one's sense of self. Cooley contended that what becomes the self is what we imagine that others think of us, including our appearance, motives, deeds, and character. One then comes to own these reflected appraisals. Such a "self-idea" was comprised of three components: (a) the imagination of our appearance to the other person, (b) the imagination of that person's judgment of that appearance, and (c) an associated self-affect.

These components gradually become removed from their initial social sources through an implied internalization process. Cooley (1902) wrote that the adult is "not immediately dependent upon what others think; he has worked over his reflected self in his mind until it is a steadfast portion of his thought, an idea and conviction apart, in some measure, from its external origin. This sentiment requires time for its development and flourishes in mature age rather than in the open and growing period of youth" (p. 199). Thus, Cooley's views on the internalization of others' opinions about the self paved the way for a more developmental perspective on how the attitudes of others are incorporated into the self. Moreover, the more mature

sense of self is not buffeted about by potentially transient or disparate views of significant others. As Cooley observed, the person with "balanced self-respect has stable ways of thinking about the image of self that cannot be upset by passing phases of praise or blame" (p. 201).

In Mead (1925, 1934), we find an elaboration of the themes identified by Cooley, with an even greater insistence on the role of social interaction. For Mead (1925), "We appear as selves in our conduct insofar as we ourselves take the attitude that others take toward us. We take the role of what may be called the 'generalized' other" (p. 270). Mead (1925) also spoke to the origins of these attitudes in childhood. He postulated a two-stage developmental process through which the child adopted the attitudes of others toward the self, labeling these stages the "play" and the "game." The "play" involved the imitation of adult roles, which Mead documented in his description of the young child "continually acting as a parent, a teacher, a preacher, a grocery man, a policeman, a pirate, or an Indian" (p. 270). In the subsequent stage of *games,* there are prescribed procedures and rules. "The child must not only take the role of the other, as he does in the play, but he must assume the various roles of all the participants in the game and govern his actions accordingly. If he plays first base, it is as the one to whom the ball will be thrown from the field or from the catcher. Their organized reaction becomes what I have called the 'generalized other' that accompanies and controls his conduct. And it is this generalized other in his experience which provides him with a self" (p. 271). Thus, the individual comes to adopt the generalized perspective of a group of significant others who share a particular societal perspective on the self.

It was Baldwin (1895, 1906) who provided the most detailed formulation on the social origins of the self in childhood. For Baldwin, the knowledge of both self and other was intimately related, beginning in infancy. He described the "bipolar self," with the self as one pole and the other person, the "alter," as the opposite pole. Baldwin described the developmental emergence of infants' awareness that other people have experiences like their own, leading to an equation of self and other. *Imitative* processes became paramount to self-development, in that toddlers adopt caregivers' behaviors as models for their own behavior. Thus, children come to be part of someone else through imitation and the internalization of the actions, thoughts, and attitudes of others, absorbing "copies" from their social interactions with others. Young children not only imitate and internalize the standards of others but project their sense of self onto others. Thus, children expect other family members to adhere to these standards as well. More so than other symbolic interactionists, Baldwin highlighted the reciprocity between the development of a sense of self and of the sense of others.

In Cooley, Mead, and Baldwin we can identify several themes that have found their way into contemporary treatments of the self. Paramount is the role of the opinions of others in shaping the self-concept, through social interaction. Cooley hinted at a developmental internalization process whereby the reflected appraisals of specific others become incorporated in the form of relatively *enduring* attitudes about the self, a process that has implications for the stability of the self-concept. For Mead, a more generalized sense of self was internalized. In Baldwin we observe the significance of social imitative processes in fashioning a sense of self and other, founded upon the infant's realization that others have subjective experiences like the self. As such, Baldwin anticipated later contentions concerning the infant's rudimentary "theory of mind." Finally, Cooley's observation that self-judgments are accompanied by self-*feelings* highlighted the role of affective processes in self-concept development.

Self Psychology in the 20th Century

During the early period of introspection, inquiry into topics concerning the self and psyche flourished. However, with the emergence of radical behaviorism, such constructs were excised from the scientific vocabularies of many theorists for whom the writings of James and the symbolic interactionists gathered dust on the shelf. Historically, it is of interest to ask why the self was for so long an unwelcome guest at the behaviorists' table. Why was it that constructs such as self, including self-esteem, ego strength, sense of omnipotence, narcissistic injury, feelings of unconscious rejection, and so on, did little to whet the behaviorist's appetite? Several related reasons appear responsible.

The very origins of the behaviorist movement rested on the identification of *observables*. Thus, hypothetical constructs were both conceptually and methodologically unpalatable. Cognitions in general, and self-representations in particular, were deemed unmeasurable because they could not be operationalized as observable behaviors. Moreover, self-report measures designed to tap self-constructs were not included on the methodological menu because people were assumed to be very inaccurate judges of their own behavior. Those more accepting of introspective methodologies found the existing measures of self-concept ungratifying, in large

part because their content was overly vague and general. Finally, self-constructs were not satisfying to the behaviorist's palate because their *functions* were not clearly specified. The very cornerstone of behavioral approaches rested upon a functional analysis of behavior. In contrast, approaches to the self did little more than implicate self-representations as *correlates* of behavior, affording them little explanatory power as causes or mediators of behavior.

Several shifts in emphasis, beginning in the second half of the century, have allowed self-constructs to become more palatable. Hypothetical constructs, in general, gained favor as parsimonious predictors of behavior, often far more economical in theoretical models than a multitude of discrete observables. In addition, we witnessed a cognitive revolution within the fields of both child and adult psychology (Bruner, 1990). For developmentalists, Piagetian models came to the forefront. For experimental and social psychologists, numerous cognitive models found favor. With the emergence of this revolution, self theorists jumped on the bandwagon, resurrecting the self as a *cognitive* construction, as a constellation of mental representations that constitute a theory of self (e.g., Brim, 1976; Case, 1985; Epstein, 1973, 1981; Fischer, 1980; Greenwald, 1980; Kelly, 1955; Markus, 1977, 1980; Sarbin, 1962). Finally, self-representations gained legitimacy as behaviorally oriented therapists were forced to acknowledge that the spontaneous self-evaluative statements of their clients seemed powerfully implicated in their pathology.

A more *sociocultural* perspective on the history of the self has been offered by Gergen (1991), who identifies three major periods: romanticism, modernism, and postmodernism. Romantic visions of the self flourished during the late eighteenth and the nineteenth centuries, during which the vocabulary about the self emphasized such commodities as love, passion, loyalty, intrinsic worth, morality, creative inspiration, and will. Thus, one's psychological interior, namely, those characteristics that constituted the depths of one's soul, was accentuated. The period of modernism was ushered in by the scientific and technological advances of the twentieth century. Emerging values of reason, objective evidence, and rational utility were incompatible with, and therefore replaced, the romanticist perspective. The machine became the metaphor for the self. Individuals were characterized in computer terminology, for example, as networks of associations, perceptual mechanisms, and cognitive structures, all of which highlighted *rationality* as the essence of humanity. From a developmental perspective, proper molding by one's family and wider societal forces would result in the well-designed person whose behavior would be self-directing, authentic, trustworthy, and consistent. As Gergen (1991) has observed, "modernist man is genuine rather than phony, principled, rather than craven, stable, rather than wavering" (p. 44).

Modernism, for Gergen (1991), has more recently given rise to our current period of *postmodernism,* which he partially traces to further advances in technology (see also Overton, 1994). In developing his portrait of the "saturated" self, Gergen observes that easy access to air travel, electronic and express mail, fax machines, cellular phones, beepers, and answering machines have all dramatically accelerated our social connectedness. As a result, contemporary life has become a dizzying swirl of social relations where the "social caravan in which we travel through life remains always full" (p. 62). For Gergen, these changes have profound implications for the self. The demands of different relationships lead to a cacophony of multiple selves whose voices do not necessarily harmonize. Moreover, the need to craft different selves to conform to the particular relationship at hand leads to doubt about one's true identity, in that the sense of an obdurate, core self is compromised as one plays out one's role as "social chameleon." The erosion of one's belief in an essential and immutable self is a topic to which we shall return in considering the issues of authenticity that emerge during adolescence and continue into adulthood.

Contemporary Perspectives on the Functions of the Self

Far from considering the self as an epiphenomenon, contemporary theorists emphasize a variety of functions that the self performs. Attachment theorists (e.g., Bretherton, 1991; Cassidy, 1990; Cicchetti, 1990; Sroufe, 1990) have observed how working models of the self have *organizational* significance, providing infants and young children with a set of expectations that allow them to more efficiently guide their behavior in future situations. The development of self-relevant scripts also provides the toddler with predictive structure; moreover, the emergence of autobiographical memories, scaffolded by the narrative coconstruction of the self, serves to define the self and cement social bonds (e.g., Crittenden, 1994; Fivush, 1987; Hudson, 1990a, 1990b; Nelson, 1993; Snow, 1990). For those focusing on childhood and adolescence, self-structures serve to shape goals (e.g., Dweck, 1991; Ruble & Frey, 1991) and to provide self-guides that aid in appropriate social behaviors and

self-regulation (e.g., Higgins, 1991). Social psychologists who address adult self processes have also articulated a number of similar functions. Markus and colleagues (e.g., Markus & Kityama, 1991; Markus & Nurius, 1986; Markus & Wurf, 1987; Oyserman & Markus, 1993) have focused on how the self organizes, interprets, and gives meaning to experience, regulates affect, and motivates action by providing incentives, standards, plans, and scripts (see also Carver & Scheier, 1990; Greenwald, 1980). Moreover, the construction of future, possible selves (Markus & Wurf, 1987) further organizes behavior and energizes the individual to pursue selected goals. Discrepancies between one's real and ideal self-concepts can also motivate individuals to achieve their ideals in the service of self-improvement (Banaji & Prentice, 1994; Bandura, 1990; Oosterwegel & Oppenheimer, 1993; Rogers, 1951).

Epstein and colleagues (e.g., Epstein, 1991; Epstein & Morling, 1995) have identified four basic needs that require the construction of the I-self. The individual needs to (a) maintain a favorable sense of Me-self, (b) maximize pleasure and minimize pain, (c) develop and maintain a coherent picture of the world, and (d) maintain relatedness with others. The first self-enhancement function has also been addressed by others (e.g., Beach & Tesser, 1995; Steele, 1988; Tesser, 1988; Tesser & Cornell, 1991). Other social psychologists have emphasized more specific motives. For example, Greenberg, Pyszczynski, and Solomon (1995) concur that the pursuit of positive self-esteem is a superordinate goal toward which humans aspire. However, they also argue that self-esteem serves as an anxiety buffer against what they see as adults' terror over their eventual death. Leary and Downs (1995) have identified a different social function, namely, to avoid social exclusion. They argue that behaviors that maintain self-esteem tend to decrease the likelihood that one will be ignored, avoided, or rejected by other people. Clearly, across different theorists addressing different stages of development, the functions of various self-representations have surfaced as important considerations.

THE DEVELOPMENT OF SELF-REPRESENTATIONS DURING INFANCY

The "New Look" in Infancy Research and Theory

Within the field of infancy, several general shifts have characterized recent work in self-development, some of which are evident in the field at large. There has been a renewed homage to William James, observed in the prolif-eration of terminology to capture more specific features of the distinction between the I-self and the Me-self during infancy. Tributes to the formulations of symbolic interac-tionists such as Cooley, Mead, and Baldwin are also very much in evidence as theorists and researchers place in-creasing emphasis on the role of social interaction and on links between knowledge of the self and knowledge of the other. Moreover, theorists have increasingly emphasized the *function* that early infant-caregiver interactions play in fashioning the self as well as the organizing function that the infant self, in turn, plays in one's present and future be-havior. In addition, there has been a shift from a focus on autonomy as an end point of self-development in infancy to a focus on the dual goals of *autonomy* and *connectedness.* More attention has also been devoted to the role of *affect* in formulations about the infant self. Moreover, there has been increasing emphasis on the *integration* of cognitive, social, and affective processes and their impact on the de-velopment of the self. Analyses of *memory* processes and the role of *narrative* in the coconstruction of the self have also proliferated.

A number of features of the "new look" are unique to the period of infancy. For example, most theorists now take exception to the classic psychoanalytic view that during the early months the infant is not differentiated from the mother. Similarly, infant behavior shortly after birth is no longer characterized as random or disorganized; rather, the focus is on the initial presence and rapid development of organized action patterns. Moreover, infants are credited with numerous capabilities not heretofore observed in their repertoire (e.g., amodal and cross-modal linkages, and imi-tation). Finally, the importance of mirror behavior in pro-moting self-development has been muted, as emphasis on the role of the caregiver as a *social* mirror has swelled.

More Recent Distinctions between the I-Self and the Me-Self

There has been a proliferation of contrasts between I and Me selves. Lewis and Brooks-Gunn (1979) initially distin-guished the *existential self* from the *categorical self.* The task for the I-self is to realize that it is existential in that it *exists* as separate from others. Self as *object* is referred to as the categorical self because toddlers must develop cate-gories (e.g., age and gender) by which to define themselves. More recently, Lewis (1991, 1994) has adopted new termi-nology. He now refers to the I-self as the "machinery of the self" that represents basic biological and perceptual

processes operative prior to 15 to 18 months and continu-ing beyond. Lewis describes the Me-self as the "idea of me," namely, cognitive representations of the self that do not emerge until the second half of the second year. The machinery of the self-system is also referred to as "subjec-tive self-awareness" because when attention is directed away from the self to external objects, people, and events, one is the *subject* of consciousness. In contrast, the "idea of me" can also be described as "objective self-awareness," which involves focusing on the self as the *object* of con-sciousness. For Lewis, many of the earliest self processes do not require the "idea of me" or objective self-awareness.

Pipp (1990, 1993) makes a similar distinction, contrast-ing *sensorimotor* working models that appear prior to 15 to 18 months with *representational* working models that appear after this developmental transition. Sensorimotor working models are composed of temporally based interaction se-quences with caregivers. As such, they bear a strong re-semblance to "generalized event structures" (Fivush, 1987; Nelson, 1986; Stern, 1985). Pipp describes feeding routines as one example of such sensorimotor scripts, in that the in-fant learns that first one is put in the high chair, then given a bib, then fed, and so on. Representational working models, in contrast, require linguistically expressed knowledge of the self, analogous to Lewis's "idea of me."

Other distinctions overlap with these characterizations. For example, Rochat (in press) describes the I-self as the *situated self,* making reference to the fact it refers to the self as agent in relation to the other and the environment, contrasting it with the *identified self,* namely, the empirical Me-self. A similar distinction has been drawn by Case (1991) in his characterizations of the *implicit self* (the I-self) and the *explicit self* (the Me-self). In emphasizing the I-self's relationship to the environment, Neisser (1991) makes reference to the *ecological self.* Such a self involves the perception of acting on the environment, sharing fea-tures with the I-self as agent. For Neisser, an *interpersonal self* next evolves in the context of the reciprocity of gestures and vocalizations with caregivers, allowing an awareness of behaviors that invite continued mutuality. Such a self does not yet require "an idea of me." Neisser reserves the term *extended* or *remembered self* for what seems more analogous to the representational Me-self in that it is based upon memories and narrative conventions. It is apparent that the distinctions between infant I-self and Me-self features are flourishing. Moreover, across these various theorists and researchers (see also Butterworth, 1990; Har-ter, 1983; Watson, 1990) there is considerable agreement on the point that I-self features precede the emergence of Me-self features. In the next section we will examine the origins and development of these infant selves.

Current Conceptualizations of the Ontogeny of Infant Self-Development: An Integration

It is instructive to observe how the material on infancy was organized in my 1983 *Handbook* review of the infant literature on the self. Each of a number of stage models (e.g., cognitive developmental models, Mahler's model, Ainsworth's model, etc.) was analyzed *separately* and presented in parallel. It was urged that eventually we need to integrate these frameworks to provide a comprehensive model of the development of infant self-understanding. Some 15 years later, such an integration appears possible, particularly given newer frameworks and findings.

A major contention of most current conceptualizations of infant self-development is that newborns are biologically predisposed to engage in interactions with caregivers from birth. This assumption has historical roots in the theorizing of Bowlby (1969, 1979, 1980) and has become increasingly popular among contemporary theorists (Bretherton, 1987, 1991; Case, 1991; Emde, 1988; Neisser, 1991; Pipp, 1990; Rochat, in press; Sander, 1975; Sroufe, 1990; Stern, 1985). As Case observes, in paying homage to Baldwin, Cooley, and Mead, the first sense of self is formed in the crucible of children's intimate relations and is profoundly influenced by these interactive experiences. Similarly, Sander argues that there is an organization of self that exists at the outset and that resides in the dyadic system of infant and caregiver. For this reason, it is critical that one characterizes how the self arises from an organized caregiving matrix (Sroufe, 1990).

The Newborn Period (0 to 4 Months)

For contemporary theorists, the central task during the first few months is the experience and formation of *organization* (see Cicchetti, 1991; Rochat, in press; Sroufe, 1990; Stern, 1985). However, they argue that the infant does not experience total nonorganization, and thus take issue with James's characterization of the world of the newborn as one of buzzing confusion, random behaviors, and disorganization. Theorists (see Butterworth, 1990; Gibson, 1993; Neisser, 1991; Rochat, 1993; Stern, 1985) also find the traditional view that the newborn is in a state of *undifferentiation* vis-à-vis the caregiver to be untenable, given recent findings. Such a view was most forcefully argued by

Mahler (1965, 1967, 1968), although those within the cognitive-developmental tradition also questioned the newborn's ability to differentiate self from other (Bertenthal & Fischer, 1978; Lewis & Brooks-Gunn, 1979).

The newborn must form links between isolated experiences and extract invariances about the self as well as the caregiver. In so doing, there is an emergence of the organization and integration of the perceptual and sensorimotor systems. These early acquisitions are attained during what Sander (1975) labels the stage of "initial regulation." The infant's state and caregiver intervention are coordinated, leading to the establishment of a predictable, comfortable pattern of sleeping, feeding, elimination, quieting, and arousal. For Sroufe (1990), such dyadic *physiological* regulation is the prototype for later *psychological* regulation, characterized by coordinated sequences of *behavioral* interactions. As Ainsworth (1973, 1974) initially observed, newborns engage in behaviors representing signals to caregivers that promote proximity and contact in the service of meeting their needs; however, during this stage of *preattachment,* psychological bonds between infant and caregiver have yet to be established.

Aiding infants in creating an emerging organization are several capacities present at the beginning of life. There is increasing evidence that infants possess crossmodal perception, demonstrating the ability to transfer perceptual experiences from one sensory modality to another (Meltzoff & Moore, 1983, 1985, 1989). Meltzoff (1990) has proposed that the infant possesses a *supramodal* representational system, allowing the visual, motor, and possibly auditory systems to "speak the same language" from birth. Stern (1985) and, more recently, Meltzoff review considerable evidence for links between these systems that should greatly facilitate the infant's extraction of self-invariance and other-invariance from the stream of experience.

In discussing the identification of invariants, Stern (1985) adopts a constructivist perspective, describing these acquisitions and the development of sensorimotor schemes as cognitive constructions (see also Case, 1991). He leaves open the possibility that certain relationships may be the direct result of perception. More recently, certain theorists such as Neisser (1991) and Rochat (in press) have taken issue with the cognitive constructivist position in the extreme. Rather, they adopt a Gibsonian perspective (J. J. Gibson, 1979; E. J. Gibson, 1993), in which knowledge begins with perception, arguing that infant behavior is inextricably tied to the environment's affordances for action. Neisser's *ecological self* and Rochat's *situated self* also make reference to the infant's relationship with the environment.

The young infant's capacity for *imitation* also contributes to the emerging sense of self because behaviors modeled by significant others are adopted by the self (Baldwin, 1906; Kagan, 1981; Mead, 1934; Meltzoff, 1990; Stern, 1985). As Meltzoff's (1990) review of his and others' work indicates, some primitive capacity to copy the actions of adults appears to be present from birth. Moreover, young infants can imitate *novel* acts that are not in their behavioral repertoire. Meltzoff conjectures that the infant's imitation of caregivers' behavior may contribute to the subsequent grasp of others' minds and emotions. The fact that young infants can imitate others' physical expressions suggests that they can detect similarities, at least at the *behavioral* level, between the self and others. Meltzoff interprets the phenomenological experience of the infant: "If the other is producing the same behavior I produce when I am experiencing a particular emotional state, then perhaps the other is experiencing the same emotion" (p. 161).

Another important feature of early experiences leading to the emerging sense of self and other is *affect* (see Emde, Biringen, Clyman, & Oppenheim, 1991; Stern, 1985). For Stern, the infant primarily experiences "vitality affects," namely, rushes of pleasure or displeasure, rather than discrete, categorical affects (e.g., joy, anger, sadness). If such affective reactions are yoked to particular sensorimotor experiences, they will contribute to the emerging process of organization. Moreover, infants experience a "vitality affective mother" who may soothe the infant with her voice and with gentle strokes simultaneously. The capacity for cross-modal matching enhances the infant's ability to experience and bring organization to such an emergent other. As Case (1991) has observed, the baby's representation of its world in the first few months involves the construction "of small islands of sensory-affective coherence, in what is otherwise a rather vast and uncharted spatio-temporal sea" (p. 215).

The Period of 4 to 10 Months

During this period, the infant becomes increasingly differentiated from caregivers, which in turn permits new levels of relatedness, including the development of an interpersonal self. Mahler (1968) initially observed behaviors such as the infant's reaction to separation (e.g., distress, gazes toward the door where mother left) that suggest that the

infant can differentiate self from mother. Ainsworth (1973, 1974) has reported similar observations; however, she focused more on how the infant's proximity-seeking behavior and ability to be comforted by the mother when distressed signals *attachment in the making.* Thus, for Mahler, this period represents the beginning of the separation/individuation process, whereas for Ainsworth it signals the potential for developing an emotional bond of connectedness.

Another acquisition of this period is the development of a sense of *agency,* a rudimentary form of James's I-self. Cognitive-developmentalists, employing visual-recognition paradigms, observe that infants become aware of the cause-and-effect relationship between their own body movements and the moving visual image in the mirror, inferring the emergence of a sense of oneself as an active agent in space (Bertenthal & Fischer, 1978; Lewis & Brooks-Gunn, 1979). More recent work indicates that infants acquire an earlier sense of agency for the self than for mother, since infants have more experience with their own bodies than with their mothers' (Pipp, 1993; Pipp, Easterbrooks, & Harmon, 1992). Stern (1985) has described self-agency, namely, a sense of volition over self-generated acts (e.g., I can make the mobile move), as one of several I-self functions to emerge during this period. Another is self-coherence, the sense of being a physical whole with boundaries and a locus of integrated action, giving agency a place of residence.

Bandura (1990) has traced the early roots of *self-efficacy* to this period, noting that infants acquire a sense of personal agency when they realize that they can control certain environmental events, particularly when sensitive caregivers aid in this process (see also Schaffer & Blatt, 1990). Case (1991) observes that infants are particularly likely to display exuberance when they demonstrate their control over inanimate objects, such as making a mobile move, suggesting their sense of self as agent. These affectively charged responses are not feelings *about* the self, but they imply a clear *sense* of the Jamesian I-self. The pleasure that infants derive from mastery has also been a theme in the writings of other theorists and investigators (Connell & Wellborn, 1991; Deci & Ryan, 1995; Stipek, Recchia, & McClintic, 1992; White, 1959).

Most of the developmental acquisitions of this period occur in the context of intense social interaction with caregivers. Games, for example, walking fingers ("I'm going to get you"), peekaboo, and so on, offer repetitive acts that also contain slight variations. Such experiences are ideally suited to teach infants to identify invariants about the self and others. As contemporary theorists (e.g., Bretherton, 1987; Case, 1991; Cicchetti & Beeghly, 1990; Emde, 1988; Emde et al., 1991; Neisser, 1993; Pipp, 1990; Sander, 1975; Sroufe, 1990; Stern, 1985) emphasize, these acquisitions require interactions with a "self-regulating other." Sander has described how, during this stage of "reciprocal exchange," sensitive caregivers craft and coordinate an organized system of behavioral sequences around the infant. Such reciprocal exchanges occur around feeding, dressing, and simple games. Infants cannot *create* such organization independently, but they are capable of participating in sensorimotor routines. As Sroufe (1990) has observed, the reciprocity is in part illusory, given the high level of scaffolding by the caregiver who makes adjustments to accommodate the infant's behavior. Such sequences are not yet authored by the infant. For Sander, it is not until approximately 7 months that the infant actively chooses or *initiates* activities to promote reciprocal exchanges with the caregiver.

Numerous theorists have pointed to the role of affect in these exchanges. Stern (1985) has observed that the infant comes to experience patterned inner qualities of affects that arise across related but somewhat different events. For example, joy will be signaled by mother's making a funny face, grandmother's tickling, and father's throwing the infant in the air. Emde and colleagues (Emde, 1988; Emde et al., 1991) have posited an affective core to early self-development wherein the regularity with which one experiences one's emotions provides a background for a sense of both the continuity and the coherence of the self. However, affect will only serve these functions if there is a sensitive, self-regulating other who is scaffolding reciprocal interactions. Sander (1975) has also observed how repetition of highly organized sequences of interactions commonly culminate in mutual delight, arguing that such shared affect becomes a part of infants' overall representation of their experience. Case (1991) concurs, noting that during this period an increasingly differentiated set of affects emerges (e.g., joy, anger, and sadness) and that these are lawfully related to the interactions in which babies and their mothers engage.

Stern (1985) has proposed a preverbal mechanism through which infants average and store these routines: representations of interactions that have been generalized (RIGs). RIGs constitute an extended form of "episodic" memory (Tulving, 1972). For example, in the first game of peekaboo, the infant lays down a memory of that specific episode. After repeated peekaboo experiences, each similar but with slight variations, the infant will form a generalized representation: a peekaboo RIG. For others (e.g., Crittenden, 1994; Emde et al., 1991; Neisser, 1991; Pipp, 1993), these generalizations represent procedural knowledge. Such generalized event structures constitute the building blocks for constructing *working models* of self and mother. Others have argued that the first such representations are actually working models *of the relationship* (Bretherton, 1991; Cassidy, 1990; Pipp, 1990; Sroufe, 1990).

The Period of 10 to 15 Months

According to earlier formulations, this period represented further differentiation of the self from caregivers, as well as an increasing sense of oneself as an agent. From a cognitive-developmental perspective, such self-other differentiation involves an appreciation that the self is an active, independent agent separate from others who are also independent agents. For Mahler (1968), further differentiation is observed in the infant's greater tolerance for separation, as the infant practices new skills and explores the environment. When a need does arise, the infant seeks to reestablish contact with the mother in what Mahler referred to as a "refueling" process. Ainsworth's (1973, 1974) observations converge. From her attachment perspective, good caregivers provide a "secure base" from which infants can move out to explore their world. Thus, the attachment and exploration systems are interlocked, in that the need to remain connected prevents infants from straying too far or for too long.

More contemporary theories place emphasis on the forms of *shared* experiences and interpersonal connection. For example, during this period, infants come to realize that their subjective experiences, their attention, intentions, and affective states can be shared with another (see Stern, 1985; Trevarthen, 1988). According to these theorists, this achievement represents a rudimentary form of a "theory of mind" in that infants apparently discover that they have a mind and that other people have minds as well, and that the subject matter of minds can be shared or interfaced. Evidence for the sharing of subjective experience can be observed in a number of arenas. Displays of *joint attention,* for example, the gesture of pointing and the act of following another's line of vision, are among the first overt acts that permit inferences about the sharing of perspectives. Infants not only visually follow the direction of a caregiver's pointing, but after observing the target, they look back to obtain feedback to confirm that they have indeed arrived at the intended target.

The sharing of *intentions* represents another such arena, in that the infant utilizes protolinguistic forms of requesting. For example, if the mother is holding a cookie, the infant will reach out, palm upward, making grasping movements and imperative intonations. Case (1991) has also described *infants'* efforts to share with their mothers aspects of their transactions with toys. Sroufe (1990) has observed that there is a qualitative shift in the caregiver-infant system during this period, with clear evidence for a social *relationship,* whereas previously it was primarily organized interaction. The sharing of *affective states* can also be observed. A primary example involves displays of social referencing (see Campos & Stenberg, 1980). In situations of uncertainty, infants look to their mothers to detect and utilize maternal affect as a guide to their own behavioral and affective reactions.

Another form of mutuality can be observed in *parental imitation* of their infants' behavior. Meltzoff (1990) describes how parents function as *social mirrors* in this regard. His research reveals that infants show a preference for adults who imitate their actions with toys (compared to adults who engage in infantlike toy behavior that is not imitative). The inference is that infants can recognize the self-other equivalence involved when an adult imitates them. Maternal vocal imitation of the infant in the form of "motherese" represents another form of social mirroring (Cooper & Aslin, 1990; Fernald & Kuhl, 1987). Meltzoff contends that adult imitation of infants performs an important function for self-development. Parental imitation represents a natural avenue for infants to discover what their acts look like. Their observations of parent behavior enhance and solidify their sense of the self as a causal agent.

These forms of mutuality converge with Emde's (1988) concept of the *we-self* (or "we-go") that emerges during this period. Through reciprocal interactions with the caregiver, leading to shared meaning, a sense of "we" emerges, in addition to a sense of the I-self. The internalization of this executive we-self serves to empower infants, to give them an added sense of control, and to aid in self-regulation, particularly in situations where the mother is not present. This process has features in common with the formation of internal working models as described by attachment theorists. As noted earlier, contemporary attachment researchers (Bretherton, 1991; Cassidy, 1990; Main, Kaplan, & Cassidy, 1985; Pipp, 1990; Sroufe, 1990; Sroufe & Fleeson, 1986) emphasize that a working model of the *relationship* is first developed. Out of this initial working model emerge working models of both the caregiver and the self.

Bretherton (1991) has recently suggested a refinement of Bowlby's (1979, 1980) concept of working models, viewing them as schema *hierarchies* derived from actual transactions with the caregiver (see also Crittenden, 1994). With regard to the working model of the *relationship,* at the lowest level of such hierarchies are interactional schemata that are very close to experience (a preverbal event representation that is analogous to "When I hurt, my mommy always comes to comfort me"). At the next level are more general schemata ("My mommy is usually there for me when I need her") that subsume the lower-level schemata of need-fulfilling events with mother. At the top of the hierarchy would be "My mother is a loving person" and "I am loved." It is only at the next stage that these hierarchies become more differentiated, such that a working model of *self* would emerge, with "I am a lovable person" at the top of that hierarchy, given a positive child-rearing history.

One challenge to contemporary attachment theorists is how to think about the fact that the young child can develop different attachment styles with different caregivers, which in turn implies different working models (Bretherton, 1991; Cassidy, 1990). These investigators have raised the question of whether and how such representations (which may be quite incompatible, e.g., lovable versus worthless) become integrated into an overarching model of the self. There are those who favor the notion of a single self, in the form of a hierarchically organized model (e.g., Crittenden, 1994), whereas others find this view untenable and argue for a model of multiple selves (Kagan, 1991). We will revisit this issue in treatments of the adolescent and adult self.

The Period of 15 to 18 Months

This period is noteworthy for the emergence of the *Me-self,* the sense of the self as an *object* of one's knowledge. For example, visual-recognition studies reveal that infants can, for the first time, recognize their own facial features in a mirror (Bertenthal & Fischer, 1978; Lewis & Brooks-Gunn, 1979). From this observation it is inferred that infants have developed a perceptual model for what they look like, an internal representation that can be compared to their external mirror image (see also Case, 1991). Interestingly, recent research (Pipp, 1993) has revealed that infants develop featural recognition for caregivers before they can recognize themselves. The fact that the eyes are directed outward should bias infants to acquire visual knowledge of their mothers' face before they form a schema for their own face.

The more psychodynamic models emphasize facets of the infant-caregiver *social* interaction. During what Sander (1975) has labeled a period of *self-assertion,* the infant begins to determine goals and activities independent of the mother and at times in opposition to the mother's wishes. For Mahler, this period represents a "rapprochement crisis" because the infant's attempts to coerce the environment, including the mother, are often frustrated, and ambivalence is often intense. Thus, infants' awareness that they are not omnipotent and cannot control the caregivers' need-fulfilling behaviors leads to anger and aggressive behaviors toward caregivers (see also Kohut, 1977). Both Mahler and Ainsworth have observed that separation distress is also very common during this period. Here one can also appreciate the contribution of those visual-recognition studies documenting the fact that not only does the infant develop an appreciation for the *self* as an independent agent but also for the separate agency of *others.* The inability to control mother, coupled with separation distress, requires an awareness that self and other are each independent agents who may not necessarily always share the same agenda.

The Period of 18 to 30 Months

Infants are developing not only representations of the self but, as noted above, schemata for caregivers. For Mahler (1967, 1968), the image of mother has very functional properties. She has asserted that the earliest images are not sufficiently stable to be comforting during the mother's absence. However, during what she labels a period of "consolidation," beginning at approximately 24 months, the infant is better able to tolerate separation from the mother. She has inferred from these observations that not only is the mother clearly perceived as a separate person in the outside world, but that she has a more stable and comforting existence in the child's internal representational world. While Mahler marked this as a goal of the separation/individuation process, Ainsworth (1973, 1974) emphasized the goals of attachment in what she labels the *goal-corrected partnership* of this period. Thus, the toddler develops a greater understanding of those factors that influence the mother's behavior and can more skillfully induce her to accommodate her plans to the child's own desires or to reach some compromise. Sander (1975) has also suggested that the toddler develops a new level of *self*-understanding that he terms "self constancy." In less sanguine interactions with a caregiver, toddlers learn that they can take a stance contrary to that of the parent, but that their "good self" will still be recognized such that the facilitative pattern of

interaction can be restored. Thus, such a pattern fosters self-schemata in which the representation of self as active initiator and organizer is conserved.

The development of *language* represents a potent acquisition in the development of the self (Stern, 1985). Language allows for the verbal expression and representation of the Me-self, the categorical self that Lewis (1991, 1994) has more recently relabeled the "idea of me." As the language literature and visual-recognition studies have revealed, during this stage the infant comes to label the self and other with appropriate personal pronouns (see Bates, 1990) as well as by name. Language makes possible what Neisser (1991, 1993) refers to as the "extended or remembered self." Verbal and representational skills also permit the shift from an "explicit" self that is sensorimotor in nature to an "implicit" self that Case (1991) terms the "referential me-self." As others have noted (Hart & Karmel, in press; Lewis, 1991, 1994; Sander, 1975; Sroufe, 1990; Stern, 1985), with the emergence of linguistic and symbolic representational capabilities, toddlers move to a new level of awareness of the self as an object.

The emergence of language also provides toddlers with the symbolic ability to represent parental rules and standards and their ability to meet them (Kagan, 1981; Lewis, 1991, 1994). For Emde (1988; Emde et al., 1991) these acquisitions form the earliest manifestations of moral behavior and elevate the we-self to a new level. The internalization of rules and prohibitions represents a more sophisticated form of social referencing in that toddlers now check with caregivers about the *appropriateness* of their behavior. Unlike Mahler, who placed more emphasis on the battle of wills that might ensue, Emde has focused on how the internalization of rules and prohibitions actually *empowers* toddlers, allowing them to regulate their own behavior and to resist temptation in situations where the caregiver is not present. Kagan (1981) has addressed the toddler's adoption of another type of caregiver's standards concerning competence and achievement. He reports that toddlers express distress when they cannot succeed on tasks that have been modeled by adults, from which he infers that they have a rudimentary form of self-awareness signaling that they have not measured up to the standards.

Self in Memory and the Role of Narrative in the Coconstruction of the Self

With the emergence of language comes the ability to construct a narrative of one's "life story" and therefore to develop a more enduring portrait of the self. Our understanding of the processes of memory and the construction of narratives has increased dramatically since the last *Handbook*. Developmentalists (see Crittenden, 1994; Fivush, 1987; Fivush & Hudson, 1990; Nelson, 1986, 1993) now distinguish between a number of types of memories, elaborating on Tulving's (1972, 1983) initial distinction between semantic and episodic memory. *Semantic memory* refers to verbally encoded, context-free or generalized information, which, when applied to the self, would represent summary trait knowledge (e.g., I am a good girl). *Episodic memory* refers to the memory of an experience that happened once, at a specific time and place. Episodic memories are initially relegated to a holding pattern. If the episodes are reinstated frequently, they are transformed into generic event memory or *scripts,* namely, schemata derived from experience that sketch the general outline of a familiar event without providing details about the specific time and place. Finally, *autobiographical memory* is another special form of episodic memory that codifies experiences of the self. These memories are very personal and have long-lasting significance for the individual, becoming the basis for one's own life story. As Nelson (1993) has pointed out, an initial function of autobiographical memories is that they allow one, through language, to share these recollections with significant others, which serves to cement social bonds. Autobiographical memory (see also Hudson, 1990a, 1990b; Snow, 1990) is also referred to as *personal narrative memory* (Eisenberg, 1983; Nelson, 1986).

Very young children can construct episodic memories for particular events as well as generic event memory or scripts (e.g., of bedtime rituals). However, there are no autobiographical memories before the age of 2, and the average age is 3.5 (Pillemer & White, 1989). This infantile amnesia can only be overcome by learning from adults how to formulate their own memories as *narratives*. Thus, parents recount stories about a child's past experiences that are told to the child. With increasing age and language facility, children take on a more active role as parent and child *coconstruct* the memory of a shared experience (Eisenberg, 1983; Hudson, 1990a, 1990b; Nelson, 1986, 1993; Rogoff, 1990; Snow, 1990). However, for the young child such narratives are still highly scaffolded by parents who model aspects of experience that they feel are important to codify and remember (Fivush, Gray, & Fromhoff, 1987; Nelson, 1989). Through these experiences, an autobiographic account of the *self* is created. Moreover, findings demonstrate individual differences in maternal styles of narrative construction (Bretherton, 1993; Nelson, 1993).

For example, Tessler (1991) distinguished between an *elaborative* style (where mothers present an embellished narrative) and a *pragmatic* style (focusing more on useful information). Elaborative mothers were more effective in establishing and eliciting memories with their young children.

For most developmental memory researchers, *language* is the critical acquisition allowing one to establish a personal narrative and to overcome infantile amnesia (Fivush & Hamond, 1990; Hudson, 1990a, 1990b; Nelson, 1990; Pillemer & White, 1989). The mastery of language in general, and of personal pronouns in particular, enables young children to think and talk about the I-self and to expand their categorical knowledge of the Me-self (Bates, 1990; Miller, Potts, Fung, Hoogstra, & Mintz, 1990). Moreover, representations of the self in language are further facilitated by acquisition of the *past tense,* which occurs toward the latter half of the third year.

Howe and Courage (1993) have argued, however, that the emergence of language is not sufficient to explain the demise of infantile amnesia and the emergence of an ability to create autobiographical memory. They note that *self-knowledge* is also required. That is, an appreciation for the self as an independent entity with actions, attributes, affects, and thoughts that are distinct from those of others is required for the development of autobiographical memory. Without the clear recognition of an independent I-self and Me-self, there can be no referent around which personally experienced events can be organized. Thus, for Howe and Courage, the emergence of self-knowledge is the cornerstone in the development of autobiographical memory that further shapes and solidifies a sense of self.

Linguistic interactions with parents also impact the developing child's representation of self in *semantic* memory (Bowlby, 1979; Nelson, 1989, 1993; Snow, 1990). As Bowlby first noted, early semantic memory is conferred by one's caregivers. Parents convey considerable descriptive and evaluative information about the child (e.g., "You're a big boy," "You are so smart"), as well as about rules and standards and the extent to which the child has met them. Consistent with Cooley's (1902) model of the looking-glass self, children incorporate these labels and evaluations into their self-definition in the form of general *trait* knowledge (represented in semantic memory). Thus, the linguistic construction of the self is a highly interpersonal process, with caregivers making a major contribution to its representation in both autobiographical and semantic memory.

Language as a Double-Edged Sword

Language clearly promotes heightened levels of relatedness and allows for the creation of a personal narrative. Stern (1985), however, has also alerted us to the liabilities of language, arguing that language can drive a wedge between two simultaneous forms of interpersonal experience, as it is lived and as it is verbally represented. The capacity for objectifying the self through verbal representations allows one to transcend, and therefore potentially distort, one's immediate experience and to create a fantasied construction of the self. There is also the potential for incorporating the biases of caregivers' perspectives on the self, since initially they dictate the content of narratives incorporated in autobiographical memory (Bowlby, 1980; Bretherton, 1987; Crittenden, 1994; Pipp, 1990). Children may receive subtle signals that certain episodes should not be retold or are best "forgotten" (Dunn, Brown, & Beardsall, 1991). Bretherton describes another process, "defensive exclusion," in which negative information about the self or other is not incorporated because it is too psychologically threatening (see also Cassidy & Kobak, 1988). Wolf (1990) further describes several mechanisms such as deceit and fantasy whereby the young child, as author of the self, can select, edit, or change the "facts" in the service of personal goals, hopes, or wishes (see also Dunn, 1988).

Such distortions may well contribute to the formation of a self that is perceived as *unauthentic* if one accepts the falsified version of experience. Winnicott (1958) has observed that intrusive or overinvolved mothers lead infants, in their desire to comply with maternal demands and expectations, to present a false outer self that does not represent their own inner experiences. Moreover, such parents may reject the infant's "felt self," approving only of the falsely presented self (Crittenden, 1994). As Stern (1985) notes, the display of false-self behavior, selected because it meets the needs and wishes of someone else, incurs the risk of alienating oneself from those inner experiences that represent one's true self (see also Main & Solomon, 1990). Thus, linguistic abilities allow one not only to share one's experiences with others but to withhold them as well.

Individual Differences in the Representation of the Self

Traditional psychodynamic theorists such as Sullivan (1953) and Winnicott (1958) placed heavy emphasis on how the quality of mother-infant interactions influenced self-development. Winnicott described a pattern of "good enough" mothering that would promote healthy self-development. The "good enough" mother responds promptly and appropriately to the infant's demands, thereby engendering feelings of "omnipotence" or power, which certain theorists consider to be a critical precursor of positive feelings about the self (Erikson, 1950; Kohut, 1977). She also responds positively to the infant's mastery attempts. During periods when the infant's needs are met, the "good enough" mother retreats, supporting the capacity for the infant to be alone, which Winnicott considered essential to the development of a stable sense of self. Small failures in parental responsiveness eventually lead to the infant's disappointment in the parent and lessen feelings of omnipotence. However, according to both Winnicott and Kohut, these experiences play a vital role in self-other differentiation, allowing the child both to separate from the parent and to become more reality-oriented (see also Mahler, 1968).

From an attachment theory perspective, a working model of *self* can only be considered within the context of the caregiver-infant relationship from which it emerged. Thus, as Bowlby (1969) contended, children who experience parents as emotionally available, loving, and supportive of their mastery efforts will construct a working model of the self as lovable and competent. In contrast, a child who experiences attachment figures as rejecting or emotionally unavailable and nonsupportive will construct a working model of the self as unlovable, incompetent, and generally unworthy. Thus, individual differences in the *content* of a child's working model of self will be influenced by parental responsiveness. The importance of these working models is that they are assumed to generalize, and to characterize relationships with those beyond caregivers.

Sroufe (1990) has further distinguished between securely attached infants and two insecurely attached groups, those that are ambivalently attached and those described as avoidant. Secure children who have experienced responsive caregiving should develop a working model of the self as effective. Ambivalently attached infants, whose caregivers were inconsistently available, should construct a working model of the self as ineffective, weak, and uncertain. Those with a history of avoidant attachment, where caregivers were not available, should develop working models in which the self is unworthy and lacks competence. Sroufe presents longitudinal data supporting these hypotheses within the contexts of preschools and summer camps. Those with insecure attachment histories manifested lower levels of *behaviorally manifested* and *teacher- or counselor-rated* self-esteem than did those with secure attachment histories. Differences in self-*confidence* were also observed on problem-solving tasks, particularly between the securely and the anxiously attached groups. Both groups of insecurely attached individuals report forms of social withdrawal from peers (see also Rubin, Stewart, & Coplan, 1995).

It should be noted that the *self-presentation* by avoidants on verbal self-report measures is often quite positive. In fact, Cassidy (1988) has reported that, as young children, many describe themselves as "perfect," in contrast to ambivalently attached children whose descriptions were typically negative. Securely attached children generally described themselves in positive terms but also admitted to being less than perfect. Similar patterns have been found for ratings and descriptions of adults (Cassidy & Kobak, 1988). Avoidants appear to idealize the self as well as the parent. These findings have been interpreted as revealing defensively high self-esteem, in an attempt to consciously or unconsciously mask feelings of unworthiness.

Interactions with caregivers also affect the structure and *organization* of the working model (Bretherton, 1991). Insensitive caregivers who ignore the child's signals will produce insecurely attached children whose working models are less coherently organized from the outset and less likely to become well integrated. Parental *underattunement* leads to impoverished working models because it undermines the infants' ability to attend to their affective states, label them, and incorporate them into their self-portrait (Crittenden, 1990, 1994). The child may also *defensively* exclude painful experiences at the hands of insensitive caregivers. At the other extreme, Stern (1985) has observed that parental *overattunement* (or intrusiveness) represents a form of emotional theft because the parent accentuates how the infant *should* feel rather than how the infant actually *does* feel. Thus, actual feeling states are not shared but become isolated, contributing to fragmentation or lack of coherence (see also Crittenden, 1990).

Crittenden (1990, 1994) has further distinguished between securely attached and both types of insecurely attached individuals. Her findings reveal that those with a history of *secure* attachment can access and integrate the various memory systems, can view themselves from several perspectives, and can accept both their desirable and

undesirable features. They can also reason more openly with parents about the motives for their misbehavior. These features allow them to evaluate the self more realistically and aid in the construction of a self-narrative (see also Cassidy, 1990). Those with an *avoidant* attachment history, individuals labeled "defended," have less access to their various memory systems, given that some features of the true self are held out of awareness, whereas others have been defensively "corrected" (Crittenden, 1988). Those with an *ambivalent* attachment history, labeled "coercive," also have more fragmented and distorted working models. Their tendency to blame others for their misbehavior robs them of the opportunity to integrate behavioral aspects of the self into their working models. Moreover, the inconsistent parenting they have experienced prevents them from developing an organized or coherent set of internal representations.

Concluding Comments on Self-Development during Infancy

Efforts in the field of infancy have increased dramatically in the past 15 years, providing us with a much more detailed picture of self-development during the early years of life. Moreover, an integration of perspectives allows for a much more comprehensive understanding of how the cognitive, social, and affective combine to enhance our understanding of the emerging I- and Me-selves. Perhaps the most notable advances can be observed in the critical role assigned to caregivers. Whereas in earlier work caregiving styles were related to *individual differences* in child self-related behaviors, recent conceptualizations and supportive evidence point to the major role that caregiver-infant interactions play in influencing the *normative* progression of self-development through the levels described. Far from representing an endogenously driven unfolding of self structures, the emergence of both I- and Me-self functions is dependent on organizing experiences at the hands of sensitive caregivers. However, there is an imbalance in this literature in that theory and inference on the links between caregiver behaviors and infant self-development far outweigh empirical research evidence. Moreover, the developmental progression identified is primarily descriptive. Future efforts need to document these relationships directly and identify more precisely those mechanisms and transition rules that underlie the developmental shifts proposed.

SELF-REPRESENTATIONS IN CHILDHOOD AND ADOLESCENCE

The Limitations of Earlier Findings and Frameworks

Earlier work, reviewed in my *Handbook* chapter (Harter, 1983), was largely *descriptive* and focused primarily on the *content* of self-representations, namely, how the Me-self evolves over development. Investigators sought to document developmental differences in self-representations through the coding of spontaneously generated descriptions of the self (Bannister & Agnew, 1977; Guardo & Bohan, 1971; McGuire, 1981; Montemayor & Eisen, 1977; Mullener & Laird, 1971; M. Rosenberg, 1979). These efforts identified broad, discontinuous, qualitative shifts in how the self was described. However, there was little analysis of the structural organization of self-descriptions. Given that many theorists (e.g., Epstein, 1973, 1981; Greenwald, 1980; Kelly, 1955; Markus, 1980) had forcefully argued that the self is a *cognitive construction,* an analysis of how cognitive-developmental shifts might be implicated in reported age differences seemed warranted. Thus, in the earlier *Handbook* chapter, it was suggested that the broad, three-stage progression reflected in the findings could be interpreted within a Piagetian framework (Piaget, 1960). Thus, the young child's rendering of the self in terms of concrete, observable characteristics such as physical attributes, material possessions, behaviors, and preferences that were not coherently organized was consistent with the cognitive abilities and limitations of the preoperational period. The earlier studies reported that in middle to later childhood the self was described in terms of traitlike constructs (e.g., smart, honest, shy), which required the type of hierarchic organizational skills that emerged during concrete operations. Thus, the trait label "smart" could subsume the behavioral manifestations of scholastic competence in several school subjects (e.g., doing well at reading, spelling, and math). During adolescence, findings documented the emergence of more abstract self-definitions based on psychological processes such as inner thoughts, emotions, attitudes, and motives. Such a self-portrait was consistent with formal operational advances such as the ability to construct higher-order abstractions and the capacity for introspection.

However, within the general field of cognitive development, there have since been numerous critiques of Piagetian theory (see Case, 1985, 1992; Feldman, 1994; Fischer, 1980; Fischer & Canfield, 1986; Flavell, 1985; Flavell, Miller, & Miller, 1993; Pascual-Leone, 1988; Siegler, 1991), critiques that also have specific implications for our understanding of self-development. As Case (1992) observes, Piagetian theory painted a picture of cognitive development that was "too monolithic, universal, and endogenous" (p. 10). For example, findings documenting the tremendous unevenness or *décalage* in development across domains argued against some single, underlying set of integrated cognitive structures (see also Costanzo, 1991; Graziano & Waschull, 1995). Moreover, the theory is primarily descriptive, with insufficient attention to specific underlying processes and transition rules. The broad shifts that Piaget identified have also been viewed as too discontinuous. In addition, there was little emphasis on individual differences in the rate of cognitive development, as well as on the potential for different pathways of development. Finally, issues involving contextual factors that might affect cognitive development were virtually ignored (e.g., specific child-rearing, instructional, and broader cultural influences).

The theorists cited above have, therefore, adopted various neo-Piagetian frameworks that have been infused with concepts and methodologies from information-processing perspectives. Several common principles across these newer frameworks represent contemporary solutions to those problems identified in Piaget's theory. For example, a greater number of structural levels has been identified, with more emphasis on the continuity of development. Higher structures are considered to build upon and incorporate lower structures that become more intercoordinated. Décalage is accepted as the rule, rather than the exception; therefore, it is expected that the particular level of development at which one is functioning will vary across different domains of knowledge. The particular processes and transition rules that govern such development have become more precise. For example, certain neo-Piagetians focus on memory functions and their development (e.g., Case, 1985, 1992; Pascual-Leone, 1988). Other mechanisms include practice and the automatization of skills (e.g., Case, 1985; Siegler, 1991). Siegler, from an information-processing perspective, also identifies encoding and strategy construction. Encoding involves the identification of the most important features of objects and events that form the basis for internal representations. Strategy construction refers to processes through which concepts are combined to form categories or higher-order generalizations. Such processes may also be influenced by contextual factors. For example, the child's culture as well as more proximal family values and educational instruction will play an important role in dictating what features of events and objects, including the self, are most salient (see also Bem, 1985; Rogoff, 1990; Vygotsky, 1978). Moreover, such contextual factors will partially determine how particular structures are coordinated (see also Costanzo, 1991). The inclusion of experiential variables also contributes to an understanding of individual differences in the rate and manner in which structures are integrated. Although experience, instruction, and practice influence the progression through cognitive levels, most neo-Piagetians acknowledge that there are constraints on the upper limit that one may achieve at any given age. For example, brain development in general, and working memory capacity in particular, represent such constraints.

Many of these contemporary principles have direct relevance for the development of the self, particularly given the well-accepted perspective that the self is a cognitive construction. Such principles provide a framework for considering how particular cognitive-developmental changes in the I-self, as agent, knower, and constructor, influence

the differences we observe in the Me-self, the self as known or constructed. From a neo-Piagetian perspective, the self is viewed as one particular domain of knowledge where the level of development may differ from that in other domains. Normative developmental changes in self-representations will be presented against this backdrop. Three influences will be highlighted: how cognitive development affects the (a) structure, content, valence, and accuracy of the self-concept; how it (b) mediates the impact of the reactions of socializing agents to the self; and (c) how the social context, in turn, impacts these cognitive-developmental acquisitions. Major developmental shifts are summarized in Table 9.1.

Developmental Differences in Self-Representations during Childhood and Adolescence

Toddlerhood to Early Childhood

Theory and evidence (see Case, 1992; Fischer, Hand, Watson, Van Parys, & Tucker, 1984; Griffin, 1992; Harter, in press-a; Higgins, 1991; Watson, 1990) indicates that the young child can construct very concrete cognitive representations of observable features of the self (e.g., "I know

Table 9.1   Normative Developmental Changes in Self-Representations during Childhood and Adolescence

Age Period	Structure/Organization	Salient Content	Valence/Accuracy
Toddlerhood to Early Childhood	Isolated representations; lack of coherence, coordination; all-or-none thinking.	Concrete, observable characteristics; taxonomic attributes in the form of abilities, activities, possessions.	Unrealistically positive; inability to distinguish real from ideal selves.
Early to Middle Childhood	Rudimentary links between representations; links typically opposites; all-or-none thinking.	Elaboration of taxonomic temporal comparisons with own past performance.	Typically positive; inaccuracies persist.
Middle to Late Childhood	Higher-order generalization that subsumes several behaviors; ability to integrate opposing attributes.	Trait labels that focus on abilities and interpersonal characteristics; comparative assessments with peers.	Both positive and negative evaluations; greater accuracy.
Early Adolescence	Intercoordination of trait labels into simple abstractions; abstractions compartmentalized; all-or-none thinking; don't detect, integrate, opposing abstractions.	Social skills/attributes that influence interactions with others or one's social appeal.	Positive attributes at one point in time; negative attributes at another; leads to inaccurate overgeneralizations.
Middle Adolescence	Initial links between single abstractions, often opposing attributes; cognitive conflict caused by seemingly contradictory characteristics.	Differentiation of attributes associated with different roles and relational contexts.	Simultaneous recognition of positive and negative attributes; instability, leading to confusion and inaccuracies.
Late Adolescence	Higher-order abstractions that meaningfully integrate single abstractions and resolve inconsistencies, conflict.	Normalization of different role-related attributes; attributes reflecting personal beliefs, values, and moral standards.	More balanced, stable view of both positive and negative attributes; greater accuracy.

my ABCs, I can count, I can run fast, I live in a big house"). Damon and Hart (1988) label these "categorical identifications," in that the young child understands the self only as separate, taxonomic attributes that may be physical (e.g., "I have blue eyes"), active (e.g., "I play ball"), social (e.g., "I have two sisters"), or psychological (e.g., "I am happy"). Case (1992) has referred to this level as "inter-relational," in that young children can forge rudimentary links in the form of discrete event-sequence structures that are defined in terms of physical dimensions, behavioral events, or activity. However, they cannot coordinate two such structures (see also Griffin, 1992), in part because of working memory constraints that prevent the young child from holding several features in mind simultaneously.

Fischer's (1980) formulation is very similar. He has labeled these initial structures "single representations." Such structures are highly differentiated from one another because the cognitive limitations at this stage render the child incapable of integrating single representations into a coherent self-portrait. One manifestation of this self structure is the inability to acknowledge that one can possess opposing attributes, for example, *good* and *bad* or *nice* and *mean* (Fischer et al., 1984). Children also deny that they can experience two *emotions*, both same-valence (e.g., mad and sad) as well as opposite-valence emotions (e.g., happy and sad), at the same time (Harris, 1983; Harter & Buddin, 1987).

Moreover, self-evaluations during this period are likely to be unrealistically positive, since young children have difficulty distinguishing between their desired and their actual competence, a confusion initially observed by both Freud (1952) and Piaget (1932). For contemporary cognitive-developmentalists, this problem stems from another cognitive limitation of this period: the inability to bring social comparison information to bear meaningfully on their competencies (Frey & Ruble, 1990). The ability to use social comparison toward the goals of self-evaluation requires that the child be able to relate one concept (one's own performance) to another (someone else's performance), a skill that is not sufficiently developed in the young child.

Higgins (1991), building upon the models of Case (1985), Fischer (1980), and Selman (1980), has focused more on the interaction between the child's cognitive abilities and the role of socializing agents. He has provided evidence that at Case's stage of interrelational development, very young children can place themselves in the same *category* as the parent who shares their gender, which forms an initial basis for *identification* with that parent. For example, the young boy can evaluate his overt behavior with regard to the question: "Am I doing what Daddy is doing?" Attempts to match that behavior (as well as cultural ideals concerning gender-appropriate behavior), will determine which attributes become incorporated into the young child's self-definition. Thus, one observes the influence of the socializing environment upon the self.

Higgins (1991) has noted that at the interrelational stage, young children can also form structures allowing them to detect the fact that their behavior evokes a reaction in caregivers, which in turn causes psychological reactions in the self. These experiences shape the self to the extent that the child chooses to engage in behaviors designed to please the parents. Stipek et al. (1992), in a laboratory study, provided empirical evidence for this observation, demonstrating that slightly before the age of 2, children begin to anticipate adult reactions, seeking positive responses to their successes and attempting to avoid negative responses to failure. They also found that children at this age show rudimentary appreciation for adult standards, by turning away from adults and hunching their shoulders as a reaction to failure (see also Kagan, 1984, who has reported similar distress reactions). Although young children are beginning to recognize that their behavior has an impact on others, their I-self cannot yet evaluate their Me-self, consistent with the first stage of Selman's (1980) developmental model of self-awareness.

Early to Middle Childhood

At the next level, children show some abilities to intercoordinate concepts that were previously compartmentalized (Case, 1985; Fischer, 1980). For example, they can form a category or representational *set* that relates a number of their competencies (good at running, jumping, climbing) to one another. Of particular interest are the structures that Fischer labels "representational mappings," a level that was missing in earlier developmental models. Mappings represent links that are unidirectional or nonreversible. Thus, representations are linked or mapped onto one another. One very common type of mapping involves a link in the form of *opposites*. For example, in the domain of physical concepts, children can oppose up and down, taller and shorter, thinner and wider, although they cannot yet demonstrate the reversible operation required for conservation. Educational instruction as well as television programming (e.g., *Sesame Street*) serve to facilitate the detection and utilization of such opposites.

With regard to descriptions of self and other, the ability to oppose attributes perceived as "good" and "bad" (e.g., nice versus mean, smart versus dumb) is especially salient (Fischer, Shaver, & Carnochan, 1990; Harter, 1986a; Ruble & Dweck, 1995). Given that "good" is defined as the opposite of "bad," and that the young child continues to identify self-attributes as positive, such a cognitive construction precludes the young child from acknowledging negative characteristics (although *others* may be perceived as bad). At this particular level, the child overdifferentiates good and bad. The very structure of such mappings, therefore, results in the unidimensional or all-or-none thinking that typically leads to self-descriptions that remain laden with virtuosity. (In child-rearing situations involving harsh discipline for misbehavior, or for a subset of children with very negative socialization histories involving abuse, maltreatment, or neglect, children may at times conclude that they are *all bad*. However, the underlying structure is the same, namely, a mapping in the form of opposites that results in all-or-none, unidimensional thinking.) In Case's theory and its application to the self (Griffin, 1992), similar structures are posited. In fact, this stage is labeled "unidimensional" thinking. Evidence reveals that although children at this level can develop representational sets or categories for self-attributes and self-emotions, they cannot as yet integrate attributes or affects of opposing valence, for example, smart versus dumb (Harter, 1986a), nice versus mean (Fischer et al., 1984), and happy versus sad (Harter & Buddin, 1987).

Nor do these self-descriptors appear to meet those criteria that would distinguish them as true "trait" labels. That is, they do not possess the structure of higher-order generalizations that integrate lower-order behavioral features of the self (Case, 1985; Fischer et al., 1984; Harter, 1988a; Siegler, 1991), a structure that emerges in middle to late childhood. Moreover, Ruble and Dweck (1995) suggest that while descriptors such as smart and dumb, nice and mean, and so on may sound like trait labels, their use at this age may not represent a true understanding of inner dispositional qualities. They indicate that the evidence is inconclusive and that further research is necessary to clarify the nature of such attributes in the young child's vocabulary.

Higgins (1991) has moved beyond a consideration of the structural features of self-descriptors at this age level, examining how an increasing cognitive appreciation for the perspective of *others* influences self-development. The relational structures of this level allow children to realize that socializing agents have a particular *viewpoint* (not merely a reaction) toward them and their behavior. As Selman (1980) has observed, the improved perspective-taking skills at this age permit children to realize that others are actively *evaluating* the self (although they have not yet internalized these evaluations sufficiently to evaluate the self independently). Nevertheless, as Higgins argues, the viewpoints of others begin to function as "self-guides," as children come to further identify with what they perceive socializing agents expect of the self. These self-guides function to aid children in the regulation of their behavior. The findings of Stipek et al. (1992) provide direct evidence that these processes begin to be observed shortly after the age of 3.

One can recognize, in these observations, mechanisms similar to those identified by Bandura (1991) in his theory of the development of self-regulation. Early in development, children's behavior is more externally controlled by reinforcement, punishment, direct instruction, and modeling. Gradually, children come to anticipate the reactions of others and to internalize the rules of behavior set forth by significant others. As these rules become more internalized or personal standards, children's behavior comes more under the control of evaluative self-reactions (self-approval, self-sanctions), aiding in self-regulation and the selection of those behaviors that promote positive self-evaluation. The contribution of cognitive-developmental theory is to more clearly identify those cognitive structures making such developmental acquisitions possible. Moreover, the structures underlying such a shift represent precisely those processes required for the emergence of the *looking-glass self,* based upon the incorporation of the opinions of significant others. However, they undergo further development at subsequent levels.

With regard to the interaction between cognitive-developmental level and the socializing environment, there are also some advances in the ability to utilize social comparison information, although there are also limitations. Frey and Ruble (1985, 1990) as well as Suls and Sanders (1982) have provided evidence that children first focus on *temporal* comparisons (how I am performing now, compared to when I was younger) and age norms, rather than comparisons with agemates. Such temporal comparisons are particularly gratifying given the rapid skill development at this age level, and therefore such comparisons contribute to the positive self-evaluations that typically persist at this age level. Evidence (see Ruble & Frey, 1991) now reveals that younger children do engage in certain forms of social comparison, however, it is directed toward different goals than for older children. For example, young children use such information to determine if they have received their fair share of rewards rather than for purposes of self-evaluation. Moreover, findings reveal that young children show an interest in others' performance to obtain information about the task demands that can facilitate their understanding of mastery goals and improve their learning (Frey & Ruble, 1985). However, they do not yet utilize such information to assess their competence, in large part due to the cognitive limitations of this period.

Middle to Late Childhood

The major advance of this age period is the ability to coordinate self-representations that were previously differentiated or considered to be opposites. In Case's (1985, 1992) theory, this level is labeled "bidimensional" thought. Identifying similar structures, Fischer labels this stage "representational systems." Siegler's (1991) strategy construction processes at this level also include higher-order generalizations of features previously compartmentalized. These frameworks lead to the expectation, supported by the studies cited earlier, that the child is capable of forming higher-order concepts, namely trait labels, based upon the integration of more specific behavioral features of the self. Thus, the higher-order generalization that one is smart integrates observations of success in both English and social studies. Similarly, the child could construct a hierarchy for the construct "dumb," coordinating perceptions of lack of ability in math and in science. In the domain of social relationships, the self can be viewed as both rowdy (with close friends and with kids on the bus) as well as shy (around someone they don't know and with someone who is more competent). Thus, concepts previously viewed as opposing can now be integrated, leading to both positive and *negative* self-evaluations.

Such bidimensional thought is applied to emotion concepts as well, as a growing number of empirical studies indicates (Carroll & Steward, 1984; Donaldson & Westerman, 1986; Fischer et al., 1990; Gnepp, McKee, & Domanic, 1987; Harris, 1983; Harris, Olthof, & Meerum-Terwogt, 1981; Harter, 1986a; Harter & Buddin, 1987; Reissland, 1985). Thus, one can develop a representational system by integrating happy (when one is playing sports) with sad (when my efforts on the team are not successful). With the emerging ability to integrate positive and negative concepts about the self, the child is much less likely to engage in the type of all-or-none thinking observed in the previous stages, where typically only one's positive attributes were touted.

As a result, self-descriptions begin to represent a more balanced presentation of one's abilities in conjunction with one's limitations, perceptions that are likely to be more veridical with others' views of the self.

For Case (1991), the emergence of these structures will partially depend upon experiences in which two lower-order features, for example, perceptions of smartness and dumbness, are activated simultaneously or in rapid sequence. Thus, events that make each of these attributes salient will foster such bidimensional structures. Moreover, Case emphasizes the general role of *practice*. Repeated exposure to such events (e.g., "On my report card I got an A in English but only a C+ in Math") should reinforce this type of intercoordination. One can imagine scenarios in which there would be little environmental support for such integration. For example, children who are severely abused typically develop negative self-perceptions that lead them not only to feel unworthy and unlovable, but to experience a profound sense of inner badness, as if they were inherently "rotten to the core," as revealed in clinical observations (Briere, 1992; Harter, in press-b; Herman, 1992; Terr, 1990; Westen, 1993) as well as research (Fischer & Aboud, 1993). In abusing environments, family members typically offer and continue to reinforce negative evaluations of the child that are then incorporated into the self-portrait. As a result, there may be little scaffolding for the kind of self structure that would allow the child to develop as well as integrate both positive and negative self-evaluations. Moreover, negative self-evaluations that become *automatized* (Siegler, 1991) may be even more resistant to change.

Further evidence for the effects of experience on level of self-development comes from clinical cases in which children in this age period continue to engage in all-or-none thinking in the domain of their symptomatology (e.g., dyslexia, conduct disorder), concluding that they are all dumb or all bad (Harter, 1977). However, in other domains (e.g., conservation), they may be quite capable of integrating the necessary components. At a more normative level, differential socialization can affect the self structures of girls versus boys. Laboratory studies reveal that parents provide more negative feedback for girls than for boys, despite no gender differences in actual performance (Lewis, Allesandri, & Sullivan, 1992). Similar observations are reported in classrooms, where girls receive more negative and less positive feedback from teachers (Dweck & Leggett, 1988; Eccles & Blumefeld, 1985). This differential treatment contributes to the more negative self-evaluations of girls and may well interfere with a more balanced sense of self in which positive as well as negative attributes are emphasized.

The more balanced view of self, in which both positive and negative attributes of the self are acknowledged, is also fostered by social comparison. A number of studies conducted in the 1970s and early 1980s (reviewed in Frey & Ruble, 1990; Ruble & Frey, 1991) have presented evidence that it is not until middle childhood that one utilizes comparisons with others as a barometer of the skills and attributes of the self. As Damon and Hart's (1988) model and supportive evidence also indicates, in middle childhood comparative assessments with peers in the service of self-evaluation become particularly salient. From a cognitive-developmental perspective, the ability to use social comparison information toward the goal of *self-evaluation* requires that children compare their own performance to that of another, a skill that is not sufficiently developed at younger ages. In addition to the contribution of advances in cognitive development (see also Moretti & Higgins, 1990), age stratification in school stimulates greater attention to individual differences between agemates (Mack, 1983). More recent findings reveal that the primary motive for children in this age period to utilize social comparison is for personal competence assessment. Moreover, with increasing age, children shift from more conspicuous forms of social comparison to more subtle avenues as they become more aware of the negative social consequences of overt forms, for example, being accused of boasting about their superior performance (Pomerantz, Ruble, Frey, & Greulich, 1995).

The ability to utilize social comparison information for the purpose of self-evaluation is founded on cognitive-developmental advances and supported by the socializing environment. In addition to providing a basis for self-evaluation, it also aids in self-other differentiation, an ongoing developmental task. However, it also ushers in potential liabilities, as others have cogently observed (Maccoby, 1980; Moretti & Higgins, 1990), contributing to individual differences in self-evaluation. With the emergence of the ability to rank-order the performance of other students in the class, all but the most competent children will fall short. Jacobs (1983) has noted that this is a major liability for children with learning disabilities. Other research supports this observation in that mainstreamed learning-disabled students were found to have more negative perceptions of their scholastic competence than those in self-contained classrooms restricted only to learning-disabled students (Renick & Harter, 1989). Thus, the very ability and penchant to compare the self with others makes one's self-concept vulnerable in those domains that are valued (e.g., scholastic competence, athletic prowess, and peer popularity). Moreover, to the extent that negative self-evaluations are now organized as relatively stable dispositional *traits* (rather than mere behaviors), they may be more resistant to disconfirmation.

The advances of this period also have implications for those looking-glass-self processes that require the ability to incorporate the opinions of significant others. For Higgins (1991), the newfound cognitive ability to form dispositional traits leads children to construct a more general evaluation of themselves as a *person*. This observation is consistent with our own empirical work demonstrating that the concept of global self-worth, namely, how much one likes oneself as a person, does not emerge until middle childhood (Harter, 1990a). Higgins has further observed that children can now focus on the "type of person" that others desire or expect them to be. Further cognitive acquisitions at this age allow the child to incorporate these expectations into self-guides that become even more internalized. Thus, as Selman (1980) also notes, the child incorporates both the standards and opinions of significant others, allowing the I-self to directly evaluate the Me-self.

Early Adolescence

During this period, the young adolescent becomes capable of thinking abstractly (Case, 1985; Fischer, 1980; Flavell, 1985; Harter, 1983; Higgins, 1991). The ability to construct abstractions can be applied to inanimate features of one's world as well as to self and others. This cognitive advance represents further intercoordination, in that now trait labels are integrated in abstractions. For example, one may construct an abstraction of the self as intelligent by combining such traits as smart and creative. One also may create an abstraction that the self is an "airhead" given situations where one feels dumb and uncreative. Similarly, one may construct abstractions that one is an extrovert (integrating the traits of rowdy and talkative) as well as that one is an introvert in certain situations (when one is shy and quiet). With regard to emotion concepts, one can be depressed (combining sad and mad) as well as cheerful (combining happy and excited). With regard to the *content* of these abstractions, Damon and Hart (1988) report that in the self-portraits of young adolescents, interpersonal attributes and social skills that influence interactions with others or one's social appeal are typically quite salient.

From a traditional Piagetian perspective, the formal operational skills that emerge during this age period should not only usher in abstract thinking but should equip the adolescent with the tools to construct a formal, hypothetico-deductive theory (Piaget, 1960). Such a theory, whether about physical phenomena in the universe or psychological attributes of the self, should meet certain criteria, for example, internal consistency, and should represent an integrated nomological network of postulates (Epstein, 1973). However, a neo-Piagetian analysis, supported by evidence, indicates that the newfound abstract representations are compartmentalized; that is, they are quite distinct from one another (Case, 1985; Fischer, 1980; Harter, 1990b; Higgins, 1991). For Fischer, they are overdifferentiated from one another because the young adolescent lacks "cognitive control" over such abstractions and therefore can only think about them as isolated self-attributes. However, this inability to integrate seemingly contradictory characteristics of the self (intelligent versus airhead, extrovert versus introvert, depressed versus cheerful) has the psychological advantage of sparing the adolescent conflict over opposing attributes in one's self-theory (Harter & Monsour, 1992). As Higgins observes, the increased differentiation functions as a cognitive buffer, reducing the possibility that negative attributes in one sphere may spread or generalize to another sphere (see also Linville, 1987; Simmons & Blyth, 1987).

Middle Adolescence

During this period, further cognitive links are forged (Case, 1985; Fischer, 1980), and the teenager can now begin to relate one abstraction to another (e.g., one can simultaneously recognize that one is both intelligent and an airhead, both an extrovert and an introvert, both cheerful and depressed). Within Fischerian theory, these abstract "mappings" bear features in common with the earlier representational mappings, in that such links often take the form of opposites. However, the mapping structure is an immature form of relating two abstract concepts to one another because one cannot yet integrate such self-representations in a manner that would resolve the apparent contradiction. Thus, at the level of abstract mappings, the adolescent still does not possess the cognitive tools necessary to construct an integrated theory of self in which the postulates, namely, personal attributes, are internally consistent. Moreover, an awareness of the opposites within one's self-portrait causes considerable intrapsychic conflict, confusion, and distress (Fischer et al., 1990; Harter & Monsour, 1992; Higgins, 1991), given the inability to coordinate these seeming contradictions. Mappings also lead to instability in the self-portrait, another form of lack of cognitive control. As a result, adolescents at this stage

may frequently demonstrate all-or-none thinking (Harter, 1990b), vacillating from one extreme to the other (e.g., they may view themselves as brilliant at one point in time and a total airhead at another).

A major contextual factor contributing to the contradictions experienced at this age level involves socialization pressure to develop different selves in different roles or relationships (Erikson, 1968; Grotevant & Cooper, 1986; Hill & Holmbeck, 1986; M. Rosenberg, 1986). Such pressures provide a backdrop for the emergence of the "conflict of the different Me's" (James, 1890). Several studies have provided evidence that the self-descriptions of adolescents vary across different roles, for example, self with parents, close friends, romantic partners, and classmates (Gecas, 1972; Griffin, Chassin, & Young, 1981; Hart, 1988; Harter & Monsour, 1992; M. Rosenberg, 1986). Conflicts between opposing attributes in these different relational contexts have been found to be particularly problematic for adolescents at this age, in comparison to attributes within a role (Harter & Bresnick, 1996). Higgins (1991) describes this new vulnerability in terms of conflicting *self-guides* across different roles, as adolescents attempt to meet the incompatible expectations of parents versus peers. Such discrepancies have been found to produce confusion, uncertainty, and indecision with regard to self-regulation and self-evaluation, consistent with the findings reported above.

The vulnerability of this period is exacerbated by the ability to think about one's thinking and to reflect on internal events, which brings about a dramatic increase in introspection (see Broughton, 1978; Erikson, 1968; Harter, 1990b; M. Rosenberg, 1979). In their search for a coherent self, adolescents in this age period are often morbidly preoccupied with how they appear in the eyes of others (see also Elkind, 1967; Lapsley & Rice, 1988). Such self-consciousness includes the search for "who I am," as the adolescent seeks to establish self-boundaries and more clearly sort out the multiple Me's that provide for a very crowded self-landscape. The creation of a coherent self-portrait also shifts to a larger canvas during this and the subsequent period, where broad brush strokes must come to define the social, occupational, religious, and political *identities* that one will assume (see Grotevant, Ch. 16, this Volume).

Late Adolescence

The cognitive advances during this period involve the construction of higher-order abstractions that represent the meaningful intercoordination of single abstractions. As such, they should provide the older adolescent with new cognitive solutions for developing a more integrated theory of self. Neo-Piagetians (see Case, 1985; Fischer, 1980) observe that developmental acquisitions at these higher levels typically require greater scaffolding by the social environment, in the form of support instruction, and so on, for individuals to function at their optimal level. If these new skills are fostered, they should aid the adolescent in integrating opposing attributes in a manner that does not produce conflict or distress. For example, one could integrate one's extroversion and introversion by constructing the higher-order abstraction that one is "flexible" across different social situations that pull for one or the other stance. One may integrate one's tendencies to be both intelligent and an airhead under the higher-order abstraction of "inconsistent." Cheerful and depressed could similarly be coordinated under the rubric of "moody." Such higher-order abstractions provide self-labels that bring meaning and therefore legitimacy to what formerly appeared to be troublesome contradictions within the self.

Findings (Harter & Bresnick, 1996; Harter & Monsour, 1992) indicate that not only do older adolescents utilize these strategies, but they also seek to normalize inconsistency by asserting that it would be strange and undesirable to display the same attributes across different relational contexts. Higgins (1991) has described the reduction in conflict as a function of further levels of internalization. Thus, adolescents come to construct their *own* standards that represent an integration of a complex array of alternative self-guides that become less tied to their social origins. These findings are consistent with those of Damon and Hart (1988), who have reported that in late adolescence, the self is described in terms of an organized system of beliefs and values that include dimensions of personal choice and moral standards.

FACTORS INFLUENCING INDIVIDUAL DIFFERENCES IN SELF-EVALUATIONS

Discrepancies between Real and Ideal Self-Concepts

In addition to constructing perceptions of one's actual attributes, individuals create representations for what they *want* to, or feel they *should,* be like, namely, an *ideal* self. The contrast between real and ideal self-images parallels James's distinction between perceptions of one's actual success and one's aspirations. The real/ideal terminology

found its way into the clinical literature through the efforts of Rogers and his colleagues (Rogers & Dymond, 1954). In Rogers's view, the magnitude of the disparity between real and ideal selves among adults was a primary index of maladjustment. More recently, developmentalists have become interested in the real/ideal disparity construct.

One developmental issue concerns the age at which children are able to develop a sense of the ideal self that can then be compared to perceptions of the real self. According to Higgins and colleagues (Higgins, 1991; Moretti & Higgins, 1990), the ability to construct ideal self-representations, which he terms "self-guides," emerges in middle childhood during the stage of "late dimensional development." As described in an earlier section, prior to this age level, children develop representations for what *others* want them to do. The advance in middle childhood is that children *internalize* these expectations in the form of self-guides that can now be compared to their perceptions of the real self. As Higgins has noted, a discrepancy between these two representations ushers in potential vulnerabilities, particularly since the child can now conceptualize the self in terms of dispositional traits that are viewed as relatively stable.

Developmentalists have also been interested in whether there are age-related changes in the *magnitude* as well as the meaning of real/ideal disparities. In a seminal series of studies, Zigler and his colleagues (reviewed in Glick & Zigler, 1985) challenged Rogers's assumptions that self-image disparity is necessarily indicative of maladjustment, suggesting an alternative developmental framework. Their findings revealed that in children and adolescents, the discrepancy between one's real and ideal self-images increases with development, as assessed by age as well as a broad array of measures of cognitive maturity. They argued that individuals at higher developmental levels should employ a greater number of categories and should make finer distinctions within each category than an individual at a lower developmental level. Their reasoning was that this increasing cognitive differentiation should increase the probability of a greater disparity between any two complex judgments, including those regarding real and ideal self-images. An alternative hypothesis for developmental increases in the discrepancy between real and ideal self-images comes from the work of Leahy and colleagues (Leahy & Shirk, 1985), who view developmental increases in *role-taking ability* as critical. From a symbolic interactionist position, taking the role of others toward the self may lead one to construct more realistic (less positive) views of the self and/or to internalize increasingly higher standards of behavior. These two shifts would lead to greater disparity between one's self-evaluations and one's standards. Their findings indicate that higher self-image disparity and a more positive ideal image were associated with greater role taking.

There has been considerable advancement in theorists' thinking about real/ideal self-image discrepancies. Noteworthy are the greater number of distinctions that have been made between different facets of the real and ideal self. M. Rosenberg (1979) observes that the distinction between one's idealized self-image (a pleasant fantasy) and one's "committed" self-image (what is taken seriously) is frequently overlooked. Thus, academics may have a fantasized image of winning a Nobel prize, whereas their committed image is to obtain tenure. Rosenberg suggests that in earlier work, where respondents were asked what they would "ideally" like to be, we do not know if they responded in terms of a more fantasized ideal or the self that one is earnestly committed to become.

Further distinctions have been put forth by Higgins (1987, 1991). He distinguishes among (a) the *actual self,* the representation of the attributes that either you or a significant other believes you actually possess; (b) the *ideal self,* the representation of the attributes that you or another would *like* you, ideally, to possess; and (c) the *ought self,* a representation of the attributes that you or another believes you should or *ought* to possess (given expectations about your duties, obligations, or responsibilities). In addition to specifying the particular cognitive structures necessary to construct such discrepancies, Higgins has reported that different types of discrepancies will produce different forms of psychological distress. Thus, discrepancies between one's actual and one's ideal self produce *dejection-related* emotions (e.g., sadness, discouragement, depression). In contrast, discrepancies between one's actual self and the self one ought to become produce *agitation-related* emotions such as feeling worried, threatened, or on edge.

Higgins (1991) has also predicted that the *magnitude* of these discrepancies is critical; if it is relatively large, it will represent an index of maladjustment. Zigler and colleagues (Rosales & Zigler, 1989), in an attempt to reconcile their developmental position with the maladjustment position of Rogers and Higgins, observe that there may be a point beyond which the discrepancy becomes debilitating. They also note that one needs to consider not just the discrepancy per se but also the absolute level of real and ideal ratings, since the same discrepancy associated with a negative

sense of one's real self may produce more distress than if it was associated with a more positive evaluation. However, this contention has yet to be empirically investigated.

Certain theorists have also emphasized the *positive* function of discrepancies in motivating behavior. Rosales and Zigler (1989) have argued that some degree of real-ideal differentiation is necessary as a source of motivation. Bandura (1990) has also described how people actually produce discrepancies by creating challenging standards that mobilize them toward a goal; goal attainment then reduces the discrepancy, leading the person to set even higher standards. In these more recent efforts, one observes that the field has moved away from views that emphasize either implications for maladjustment *or* the developmental underpinnings of self-discrepancies and their function, toward a more thoughtful consideration of both.

Closely related to the contrast between real and ideal selves is the distinction between real and *possible* selves (Markus & Nurius, 1986). Here, we can appreciate James's (1890) characterization of "immediate and actual" selves as well as "remote and potential" selves. Possible selves represent both the hoped for as well as dreaded selves, and function as incentives that clarify those selves that are to be approached as well as avoided. Markus and her colleagues (see Markus & Wurf, 1987) contend that possible selves have a very important *motivational* function. From their perspective, it is most desirable to have a balance between positive expected selves and negative feared selves so that positive possible selves (e.g., obtaining a well-paying job, wanting to be loved by family, hoping to be recognized and admired by others) can give direction to desired future states, whereas negative possible selves (e.g., being unemployed, feeling lonely, being socially ignored) can clarify what is to be avoided (cf., Ogilvie and Clark's, 1992, concept of "undesired" selves). Markus and colleagues report findings supporting these motivational functions in adolescents and adults.

To return to a consideration of developmental issues, Oosterwegel and Oppenheimer (1993) have recently examined a number of discrepancies across the ages of 6 to 18, building upon the models of Markus and of Higgins. In keeping with Markus's orientation, they note that possible self-concepts function as standards for the real self-concept. In addition to distinguishing between real and possible selves, they address how subjects evaluate themselves, how they *think* others (e.g., parents and peers) evaluate them (as Higgins urges), as well as how others *actually do* evaluate them. These investigators do not replicate Zigler's findings showing an increase in the disparity between children's evaluation of their real and possible selves. As explanations, they cite differences in methodology and the possibility that Zigler's procedures may have pulled for the more "fantasy" ideal, whereas theirs may have induced a consideration of more committed possible selves (M. Rosenberg, 1979).

However, Oosterwegel and Oppenheimer (1993) have found that the distance between real and possible selves increases from age 6 to age 12 for children's perceptions of their parents' perspective (i.e., their perceptions of what their parents think of them relative to what they think parents *want* them to be like). Thus, increasingly, children feel that they are disappointing their parents, discrepancies that have negative emotional consequences. They report the opposite effect for discrepancies "within the person." That is, subjects profit from discrepancies between what they think they are like and what they think parents think they are like, and between their ideal for themselves and what they think is their parents' ideal for them. They also observe that children's ideals come closer to their parents' ideals with age (up to age 12). They interpret these findings as demonstrating that with age, children become better able to take the perspective of parents and adjust their own ideas accordingly, consistent with Leahy and Shirk's (1985) analysis.

Future work needs to focus on contextual factors that may influence the magnitude and function of real ideal discrepancies. For example, Plummer and Graziano (1987) examined the impact of grade retention on the discrepancy between real and ideal self-images as well as on self-esteem. Paradoxically, their findings indicated that the retained children reported lower ideal selves, resulting in lower discrepancies, and higher self-esteem compared to children who were not retained. Future research should not only consider contextual variables but a broader range of outcomes to identify how discrepancies promote as well as hinder adjustment.

The Jamesian Discrepancy Model

There is clear convergence between the self-image disparity work and James's model emphasizing the need to consider perceptions of success in relation to pretensions or aspirations. For James, this relationship represented the primary antecedent of global self-esteem. Thus, individuals who perceive the self positively in domains where they aspire to excel will have high self-esteem. Those who fall short of their ideals will experience low self-esteem. From a Jamesian perspective, inadequacy in domains deemed unimportant to the self will not adversely affect self-esteem; for example, if athletic prowess is not an aspiration for an unathletic individual, self-esteem will not be negatively affected. Thus, high self-esteem individuals are able to *discount* the importance of domains in which they are not competent, whereas low self-esteem individuals appear unable to devalue success in domains of inadequacy.

There is a growing body of literature revealing that individuals do differentially value some domains more highly than others. For example, Kelly (1955) observed that the self-theory contained *core* constructs more critical to the evaluation and maintenance of one's identity than peripheral constructs. More recently, Markus and Wurf (1987) have argued that self-descriptions differ in their importance. Their findings indicate that some attributes possess high personal relevance and function as central characteristics, whereas other attributes are less personally relevant and more peripheral. Other findings (Harter & Monsour, 1992) indicate that adolescents can construct a self-portrait in which they differentiate the most central or important self-descriptors from those that are less and least important.

With regard to testing the Jamesian hypothesis more specifically, M. Rosenberg (1979) has provided some of the earliest evidence with children that the importance of a domain will influence the degree to which success and failure affect overall self-evaluation. Focusing on the centrality of one characteristic, likability, he found that among those who cared about being likable, the relationship between perceived likability and global self-esteem was much stronger than for those to whom this quality mattered little. With adult subjects, Tesser and his colleagues (Tesser, 1980; Tesser & Campbell, 1983) have also demonstrated that if a dimension is highly relevant to one's self-definition, performance judged to be inferior will threaten one's sense of self-esteem. In our work we have directly examined the Jamesian hypothesis across an age span of 8 to 55. With regard to operationalization, participants evaluate their adequacy or competency across age-relevant domains and also rate the *importance* of each domain. We have employed importance ratings rather than ideal-self judgments because the construct of importance is closer to Rosenberg's concept of the "committed ideal" and avoids the potential confound with a fantasized ideal. In numerous studies across the life span (see Harter, 1985a, 1986b, 1990a, 1993, in press-d), competence in domains deemed important is more highly correlated with global self-esteem (*r* of .70) than competence in domains judged unimportant (*r* of .30).

Marsh (1986, 1993), who has also explored the role of importance, has been less successful in predicting global self-esteem from weighted scores that take into account importance. However, he does agree that common sense and a variety of theoretical hypotheses lead to the expectation that the effect of a specific component of self-concept on self-esteem *should* vary as a function of the individual importance of each component. It is worth noting that merely correlating domain-specific self-evaluations with self-esteem (ignoring the importance of domains) will yield correlations that approach in magnitude those that include only self-perceptions for those domains judged important, because the domains that investigators typically select are those that have high salience or importance to most individuals, as Marsh also argues. However, the more appropriate test of the value of the Jamesian hypothesis lies in a comparison of the correlations with self-esteem of domains rated important or central with those rated *unimportant*. As noted above, the magnitude of the differences between these two correlations (.70 versus .30) is quite convincing.

A Jamesian perspective can be applied to findings revealing that the self-esteem of European American and African American youth does not typically differ (see Crain, 1996; Hare & Castenell, 1985; Iheanacho, 1988; S. Rosenberg, 1988). To the extent that African American values differ, the two racial groups may well base their self-esteem upon different domains that are judged important. For example, there is a stronger correlation between school grades and self-esteem among European Americans than African Americans (Cross, 1985). Assuming that people value those areas in which they are competent and try to excel in those areas that they value, African American adolescents come to value those nonschool activities in which they feel efficacious and devalue their negative academic experiences (Hare & Castenell, 1985). For example, athletic prowess, musical talent, acting ability, sexuality, and certain antisocial behaviors may become more highly valued and therefore represent compensatory pathways to maintaining self-esteem.

However, several studies suggest that when African American students attend racially integrated schools, they may have more difficulty defending their own value system, which in turn leads to lowered self-esteem (see Powell, 1985; S. Rosenberg, 1988). These studies reveal that those African American students in segregated or racially isolated schools report higher self-concepts than those in desegregated schools. There are also related regional differences, in that those African American students in racially segregated schools in the South have higher self-esteem than those in the North (Powell, 1985). These findings have been interpreted in terms of the shared values of school administrators and parents as well as the greater cultural and psychological cohesion provided by community and family within the segregated school setting (see also Spencer & Markstrom-Adams, 1990).

According to the Jamesian perspective, domain-specific evaluations are the *antecedents* of global self-esteem. Recently, the directionality of these links has been questioned. Brown (1993a, 1993b) has argued that self-esteem is an affectively based, fluid construct that generalizes to specific domains. Thus, if one's self-esteem is high, it imbues the self with many positive qualities. He reports findings that are consistent with such a claim but not conclusive. My own research group has also been concerned with the directionality of the link between domain-specific self-evaluations and self-esteem, focusing on the domain of perceived physical appearance. This domain was selected because the correlations between appearance and self-esteem range from .65 to .82 across samples, clearly demonstrating a strong link. Rather than take a stance on which directionality best captures this relationship, we have examined adolescents' *perception* of the directionality of this link (Harter, 1993). Approximately 60% of adolescents report that self-perceptions of appearance impact their self-esteem; the remaining 40% report that self-esteem affects their views of how they look. We find that the former orientation is particularly pernicious for females. Those adolescent girls who indicate that their appearance determines their worth as a person also report more negative evaluations of their looks, lower self-esteem, and more depressed affect.

Global versus Differentiated Models of Self

In distinguishing between material, social, and spiritual selves, James set the stage for a *multidimensional* model of the self. However, James also ushered in the concept of *global self-esteem,* postulating that there was a certain average tone of self-feeling that individuals possess. Cooley (1902) voiced a similar sentiment in identifying an overall sense of self-respect. Although the global and dimensional perspectives are not necessarily antithetical, child researchers initially embraced the concept of overall self-esteem. Coopersmith (1967) viewed self-esteem as global in nature, arguing that children do not make differentiations among the domains of their life. Unfortunately, inadequacies in his methodology led to this erroneous conclusion (see Harter, 1983). In contrast, although Piers and Harris (1964) began with the assumption that self-esteem was relatively unidimensional, their empirical work documented that children do make different evaluative judgments across domains, leading them to conclude that the self-concept is multifaceted.

Within recent years, there has been a dramatic shift away from global, unidimensional models of self. The prevailing models, supported by extensive data, clearly reveal that a multidimensional model of self far more adequately describes the phenomenology of self-evaluations (see Bracken, 1996; Harter, 1982, 1985b, 1990a, 1993, in press-d; Hattie, 1992; Marsh, 1986, 1987, 1993; Marsh & Hattie, 1996; Mullener & Laird, 1971; Oosterwegel & Oppenheimer, 1993; Shavelson & Marsh, 1986). These investigators have demonstrated the multidimensional nature of self-evaluations through factor analytic studies of self-concept measures. Such studies demonstrate that given individuals judge themselves differently across domains, providing a *profile* of self-evaluations. Moreover, these investigators have provided considerable evidence for the convergent and divergent validity of these measures, bolstering the appropriateness of a domain-specific approach (see also Graziano & Ward, 1992, who have linked domain-specific self-perceptions to teachers' ratings of the Big Five personality dimensions).

The number of domains that can be differentiated increases with development across the periods of early childhood, middle and late childhood, adolescence, and adulthood (see Harter, 1990a, for a listing of the specific domains at each developmental period). For example, the Self-Perception Profile for Children (Harter, 1985b) taps five specific domains: scholastic competence, athletic competence, peer likability, physical appearance, and behavioral conduct, in addition to global self-worth. The Self-Perception Profile for Adolescents (Harter, 1988b) adds three new domains: close friendship, romantic appeal, and job competence. Additional domains are included on the Self-Perception Profile for College Students (Neemann & Harter, 1987) and the Self-Perception Profile for Adults (Messer & Harter, 1989). Another popular series of multidimensional instruments has been developed by Marsh and Hattie (1996). Their Self-Description Questionnaires tap domains appropriate for children, adolescents, and young

adults, in addition to assessing general self-concept. The Multidimensional Self-Concept Scale developed by Bracken (1995) is the most recent such measure. For a comprehensive review of these and other self-concept measures, see Keith and Bracken (1996). The Harter and Marsh scales have also been reviewed by Wylie (1989).

Although there has been a shift to a multidimensional focus, these investigators have retained global self-esteem or self-worth in their models and measures (see also M. Rosenberg, 1979). Findings reveal that beginning in middle childhood, individuals can make global judgments of their worth as a person as well as provide specific self-evaluations across a variety of domains. Younger children, however, do not possess a conscious, verbalizable concept of their overall self-esteem, nor are self-evaluations in domains as clearly differentiated (Harter & Pike, 1984). However, younger children do exude a sense of their self-esteem, and these behavioral manifestations (e.g., displays of confidence) can be reliably rated by observers (Haltiwanger, 1989; Harter, 1990a).

The Shift to Hierarchical Models

An appreciation for both global and domain-specific self-evaluations naturally led theorists to speculate on the links between the two types of self-judgments. This, in turn, produced a number of *hierarchical* models in which global self-esteem or self-concept is placed at the apex and particular domains and subdomains are nested underneath. The original models were more conceptually than empirically derived. For example, Epstein (1973) suggested that the postulates one has about the self are hierarchically arranged, with self-esteem as the superordinate construct. Epstein's second-order postulates include general competence, moral self-approval, power, and love worthiness (see also Coopersmith, 1967). Lower-order postulates, for example, those organized under competence, include assessments of general mental and physical ability. The lowest-order postulates represent further subcategories. Epstein contends that as one moves from lower-order to higher-order postulates, they become increasingly important to the maintenance of the individual's self-theory.

A somewhat different hierarchical model can be found in the theorizing of Shavelson, Hubner, and Stanton (1976), who initially identified two broad classes, academic and nonacademic self-concepts, nested under general self-concept at the apex. The nonacademic self-concept is subdivided into social, emotional, and physical domains; physical self-concept is further differentiated into physical ability and physical appearance.

The academic self-concept is subdivided into particular school subjects: English, history, math, and science. Self-perceptions at lower levels were hypothesized to have a causal impact on those at the next levels; for example, perceptions of math competence "cause" perceptions of overall academic achievement, which in turn impact general self-concept (Byrne, 1995). Marsh and colleagues have conducted extensive research on this model, employing hierarchical confirmatory factor analytic and multitrait, multimethod statistical procedures applied to data from the Self-Description Questionnaires (see Hattie, 1992; Marsh, 1993; Marsh, Byrne, & Shavelson, 1992; Marsh & Hattie, 1996). More recent refinements have further subdivided the academic domain (Marsh, 1993). Song and Hattie (1984) have also modified the original Shavelson et al. model, imposing a somewhat different constellation of domains. An even more complex hierarchical model has been developed by L'Ecuyer (1992).

There has been some, though not unequivocal, empirical support for these models. It should also be noted that in refinements of these hierarchical frameworks, there appears to be the assumption that the more domains, the better the model. However, the *value* of these more molecular approaches has not been sufficiently justified, either theoretically or empirically. For example, it is not clear how the proliferation of domains aids in our understanding of self processes, including potential correlates and outcomes. Nor has much attention focused on developmental, individual, and cultural differences in such hierarchies.

Another assumption underlying many of these hierarchical models is that people organize or structure the vast amount of information they have about themselves into categories that they relate to one another (Marsh et al., 1992). However, one has to ask whether the *statistical* structure extracted does, in fact, mirror the psychological structure as it is phenomenologically experienced by individuals. The statistical procedures employed do *not* directly tap the manner in which *people themselves* organize self-constructs. Thus, the hierarchical models reflected in statistical solutions may confirm theories in the minds of psychologists but not necessarily the actual self-theories in the minds of individuals (Harter, 1986b; see Hattie, 1992, for an excellent discussion and critique of hierarchical models). Procedures that directly tap the manner in which people organize their own self-constructs are required.

Linville (1987), for example, has reported that there are clear individual differences in the complexity of the self-structure when subjects themselves are asked to sort self-traits. Complexity refers to both the number of levels in the hierarchy and the number of categories or degree of differentiation. Other sorting procedures also reveal categorization principles that differ from those proposed in the hierarchical models. For example, in asking adolescent subjects to sort self-attributes in central, intermediate, and peripheral categories, Harter and Monsour (1992) found that the *valence* of the attributes was more salient than the particular content domain (academic self, social self, etc.). The vast majority of central attributes were positive in valence, whereas negative attributes were relegated to the periphery of one's self-portrait. Findings by Showers (1995) also point to interesting individual differences in how subjects organize self-attributes that are positive and negative in valence. Certain individuals employ what she terms "evaluative compartmentalization" in which positive attributes that cut across roles or domains form one category, whereas negative attributes across those same roles form a separate category. In contrast, others employ "evaluative integration" in which attributes are categorized by role (me with friends versus me with my boss). Within each separate role there are both positive and negative attributes.

Indeed, there has been a growing literature describing a proliferating number of alternative models of the cognitive organization of self (see reviews in Greenwald & Pratkanis, 1984; Higgins & Bargh, 1987; Kihlstrom, 1993; Kihlstrom & Cantor, 1984; Klein & Kihlstrom, 1986; Srull & Wyer, 1993). As these reviews indicate, certain researchers have developed the notion of self as a hierarchical category structure building upon the initial formulation of Rosch (1975) and Cantor and Mischel (1979). Others have viewed the self as a dynamic system of schemata, a memory structure in which certain attributes are more closely linked to the self than others (Markus, 1977; Markus & Sentis, 1982; Markus & Wurf, 1987). Others claim that self-knowledge is organized around "prototypes" that also serve to structure one's perceptions of other people (e.g., Kuiper, 1981; S. Rosenberg, 1988). Still others view the self as a multidimensional space, demonstrating that multidimensional scaling techniques reveal individual differences in how self-attributes are organized (e.g., Breckler & Greenwald, 1982). Most recently, controversy has surrounded a variety of models that speak to whether general trait knowledge is represented in memory independently of specific trait-relevant behavioral knowledge (see Srull & Wyer, 1993). A review of these issues and models is beyond the scope of this chapter. However, it is clear that while hierarchical models of the self-concept have enjoyed some popularity, increasingly there are alternative theories that are based on the direct examination of how individuals process information about self-relevant and irrelevant attributes in laboratory studies.

Multiple Selves versus the Unified Self

One index of the multiplicity of the self can be observed in the fact that, beginning in middle childhood, individuals, on self-report inventories, evaluate themselves differently across a variety of domains. Another index can be observed in the proliferation of different role-related selves during adolescence. Historically, James set the stage for the consideration of the multiple selves that may be manifest in different interpersonal roles or relationships, including their potential contradictions. However, theorists in the first half of the century did not embrace James's contentions. As Gergen (1968) has noted, there was historical resistance to such a stance in the form of a "consistency ethic." Thus, many scholars placed major emphasis on the importance of maintaining an integrated, unified self (Allport, 1961; Horney, 1950; Jung, 1928; Lecky, 1945; Maslow, 1954; Rogers, 1951). Epstein (1973, 1981) formalized these observations under the rubric of the unity principle, emphasizing that one of the most basic needs of the individual is to preserve the unity and coherence of the conceptual system that defines the self.

The pendulum would appear to have swung back to an emphasis on multiplicity, with increasing zeal for models depicting how the self varies across situations. In contrast to the emphasis on unity, several social psychologists (Gergen, 1968, 1982; Mischel, 1973; Vallacher, 1980) began to argue that the most fruitful theory of self must take into account the multiple roles that people adopt. That is, people are compelled to adjust their behavior in accord with the specific situational and relational context, such that consistency across contexts may be inappropriate if not potentially damaging. In the extreme, high self-monitors (Snyder, 1987) frequently and flexibly alter their self-presentation in the service of creating a positive impression, enacting behaviors they feel are socially appropriate, and preserving critical relationships.

Gergen (1991) has more recently elevated the argument to new heights in his sociocultural treatise on the "saturated" or "populated" self. Gergen observes that individuals have been forced to contend with a swirling sea of multiple social relationships, which requires the construction of numerous, disparate selves and the suspension of any demands for personal coherence. Lifton (1993) similarly describes the emergence of a "protean self" (named after Proteus, the Greek sea god who possessed many forms) that has emerged from confusion due to uncontrollable historical forces, rapid societal and economic changes, and social uncertainties. For both Gergen and Lifton, these contemporary selves represent flexibility and resiliency, although for Gergen, they also make one vulnerable to an erosion of the belief in a core, essential self.

Other social psychologists have turned their attention to the more empirical investigation of multiple self-representations in adults (e.g., Ashmore & Ogilvie, 1992; Higgins, Van Hook, & Doorfman, 1988; Kihlstrom, 1993; Markus & Cross, 1990; S. Rosenberg, 1988; Stryker, 1987). Each of these investigators agrees that the self is multifaceted rather than a monolithic, unitary cognitive structure. However, there is less unanimity on the nature of the structure of such selves and on the extent to which multiple representations are integrated. For some, the notion of a hierarchy is preserved (e.g., Kihlstrom). For others (e.g., Ashmore & Ogilvie), multiple selves form a somewhat loose "confederation." For others, certain (but not all) subsets of self-attributes are interconnected (Higgins et al., 1988). Alternatively, theorists such as Kagan (1991) assert that the multiply represented qualities of self do not become integrated into an abstract, unitary self. This latter position is consistent with the application of recent distributed process models (see Costanzo, 1991; Graziano & Waschull, 1995), in which cognitive modules in the form of initially discrete self-schemata may not necessarily become coordinated.

One solution for preserving some sense of a unified self can be found in those theorists who have emphasized the role of autobiographical *narratives* in the construction of the adult self (Freeman, 1992; Gergen & Gergen, 1988; McAdams, in press; Oyserman & Markus, 1993). In developing a self-narrative, the individual creates a sense of continuity over time as well coherent connections among self-relevant life events. In constructing such a life story, the I-self is assigned an important agentic role as author, temporally sequencing the Me-selves into a coherent self-narrative that provides meaning and direction. An emphasis on narrative also highlights the interpersonal nature of the self, in that narratives are both socially derived and sustained (see also Ashmore & Ogilvie's, 1992, concept of "self-with-other" representations).

From a developmental perspective, there is considerable evidence for differentiation during adolescence, where there is a proliferation of selves that vary as a function of social context. As documented in an earlier section, these include self with father, mother, close friend, romantic partner, and peers, as well as the self in the role of student, on the job, and as athlete. Moreover, theory and findings point to the conflict, confusion, and distress caused by perceived contradictions in attributes across these roles, particularly during mid-adolescence. Another potential liability involves the emergence of confusion over which of one's multiple selves is the "true" self.

True- versus False-Self Behavior during Adolescence

A number of theorists and researchers have documented the fact that during adolescence, issues involving the authenticity of one's behaviors become very salient. Broughton (1981) describes the preoccupation with real and false or phony selves that emerges during adolescence. Selman (1980) discusses a similar theme, noting that the adolescent comes to distinguish between the true self, which consists of one's inner thoughts and feelings, and one's outer self, namely, manifest feelings or behaviors. M. Rosenberg (1979) observes that with the shift toward introspection, formerly unquestioned assumptions about the self "become problematic self-hypotheses and the search for the truth about the self is on" (p. 255).

In our own work (Harter & Monsour, 1992), we became alerted to the emergence of concerns over false-self behavior within the context of an examination of the proliferation of multiple selves during adolescence. In describing their contradictory role-related attributes, many adolescents spontaneously agonized about "which was the real me." In subsequent studies, we asked adolescents to define true and false selves. Adolescents' descriptions of their true selves include: "stating my true opinion," "expressing my true feelings," "saying what I really think and feel," and "acting the way *I* want to behave and not how someone else wants me to be." False selves are described as the opposite, namely, "being phony," "not saying what you think," "putting on an act," "expressing things you don't really believe or feel," and "changing yourself to be something that someone *else* wants you to be."

In asking adolescents directly about the extent to which they engage in true- versus false-self behavior, there is considerable variability in the levels they report. Theoretical analyses described in the section on infancy (e.g., by Bleiberg, 1984; Deci & Ryan, 1995; Stern, 1985; Winnicott, 1965) pointed to antecedents of behaviors in which children would act in ways that did not match their inner emotions, thoughts, and desires. Common across these analyses are caregivers who do not validate the child's true

self but instead force the child to comply with externally imposed standards of behavior, both of which conspire to lead to the suppression of one's authentic self. In our own research, we have documented a model of these processes among adolescents.

Core to this model was the inclusion of the construct "conditionality of support," which we defined as the extent to which the adolescent feels that support is only forthcoming if one meets high, and seemingly unrealistic, standards or expectations of parents or peers. Conditionality was contrasted to unconditional positive regárd (Rogers, 1951; Rogers & Dymond, 1954), which Rogers considered essential to high self-esteem. Previous findings (Harter, Marold, & Whitesell, 1992) have indicated that conditionality is actually not perceived as supportive and, as a result, undermines self-esteem. The best-fitting model documents that *conditionality* as well as *level* of support lead to *hopelessness* about obtaining support, which in turn predicted level of true/false-self behavior. Thus, the highest levels of false-self behavior are reported by those adolescents who are receiving relatively low levels of support that they perceived to be conditional, leading them to feel hopeless about pleasing others, which in turn causes them to suppress their true self as a potential means of garnering the desired support (see also Harter, in press-d).

Interestingly, adolescents not only acknowledge that they engage in behavior that they consider "false," but they can report on their motives for doing so (Harter, Marold, Whitesell, & Cobbs, in press). Three classes of reasons stand out: (a) because others (and therefore they) devalue their true self (motives consistent with those cited in the clinical literature); (b) because they want to make a good impression on others and/or gain their approval (motives that have features in common with self-monitoring and impression management); and (c) because they want to experiment with being different, trying on other roles (more developmentally normative motives of role experimentation). Moreover, there are powerful correlates of these motive choices. Those citing the motives involving devaluation of the self report the worst outcomes in terms of engaging in the highest levels of false-self behavior, not knowing who their true self really is, and having lower self-esteem coupled with depressed affect. Those reporting the more normative developmental motives of role experimentation report the most positive outcomes, with those reporting the social motives of approval seeking and impression management (the majority of subjects) falling in between.

It should be noted that the starting point for this research was the acknowledgment by adolescents that they were engaging in behavior that they themselves perceived as false. However, as the social monitoring literature with adults (see Snyder, 1987) and with children (see Graziano & Waschull, 1995) indicates, individuals who monitor and alter their behavior across relational contexts typically do so to present themselves in a manner that will be appropriate to the context, will not hurt others' feelings, and is accommodating, to foster or preserve the relationship. Individual differences among children reveal that parents differentially socialize children toward such goals. From this perspective, the situation-specific behaviors of those monitoring their actions and their expression of emotions represent flexibility and not necessarily false-self behavior (see also Paulhus, 1985, who reports that self-deception and impression management are independent factors). Our own interest, however, is in those individuals for whom self-presentation is *acknowledged* to be false-self behavior, including the consequences of these perceptions.

Adolescents' descriptions of false-self behavior in our studies also reveal that a primary manifestation is the suppression of one's thoughts, opinions, and feelings. These observations converge with what Gilligan and her colleagues (Gilligan, 1982; Gilligan, Lyons, & Hanmer, 1989) label "loss of voice." For Gilligan, loss of voice becomes problematic for females, beginning in adolescence, when they begin to identify with the cultural role of the "good woman" (nice, polite, and quiet, if not shy). Observations of their own mothers as well as the realization that women's opinions are not highly valued in this society contribute to the suppression of self, as does the perception that to speak one's opinion might threaten relationships with significant others.

Gilligan finds some support for her contention in interview studies with adolescent girls (she has not studied boys). However, in our own research employing questionnaire procedures (Harter, in press-c; Harter, Waters, & Whitesell, in press; Harter, Waters, Whitesell, & Kastelic, in press), we find no gender differences at either the middle or high school levels. Rather, there are dramatic individual differences that are predicted by an additive combination of level of perceived support for voice as well as gender *orientation*. The higher the level of support for voice, the more adolescents are able to voice their opinions. Masculine and androgynous adolescents of both sexes report higher levels of voice than do those with a feminine orientation. Interestingly, among females, femininity is a

particular liability in public contexts (e.g., school and group social situations) where the cultural role of the "good woman" is most likely to be provoked. Feminine girls do not report lack of voice with parents and close friends.

Critical to this issue are findings indicating that 75% of adolescents report that lack of voice represents false-self behavior and that it *bothers* them not to be able to speak their mind. The study of voice is of further concern because our findings reveal that suppression of one's true self takes its toll on the well-being of both sexes. Results indicate that among both adolescents and adults, those who do not receive validation for the expression of their true or authentic self engage in false-self behavior, which in turn is associated with low self-esteem, hopelessness, and depressed affect (Harter, Marold, Whitesell, & Cobbs, 1996; Harter, Waters, Pettitt, Whitesell, Kofkin, & Jordan, in press). These findings converge with observations from those at the Stone Center, which also note the lack of zest and depressive symptomatology that accompany the suppression of one's authentic self (Jordan, 1991; Jordan, Kaplan, Miller, Stiver, & Surrey, 1991). Kolligian (1990) also reports findings that perceived fraudulence in adults is accompanied by pressures to excel, evaluation anxiety, self-criticism, and depressive tendencies. These findings emphasize a constellation of negative outcomes for those individuals who report engaging in false-self behavior. However, as Gergen (1991) contends in describing the "saturated" self, we are all potentially at risk for becoming alienated from our true selves, given contemporary societal demands that we adopt the role of social chameleon.

Social Sources of Self-Evaluation: The Role of Socializing Agents

The preceding discussion has focused primarily on cognitive *process* variables and their impact on *structural* features of the developing self. However, to understand the *content* and *valence* of self-representations, we need to revisit the contentions of such symbolic interactionists as Cooley (1902) and Mead (1925, 1934), who focused on the incorporation of the appraisals of significant others. Although many contemporary scholars pay homage to these earlier formulations, there have been noticeable refinements. There has been increasing attention to the role of developmental factors, as the earlier analysis of how internalization processes emerge at different age levels revealed (see Connell & Wellborn, 1991; Higgins, 1991; Selman, 1980). Attention has also focused on the issue of *whose* opinions are internalized. Furthermore, the accuracy of one's perceptions of the opinions of others has been questioned, as has the directionality of the link between the opinions of others and self-evaluations.

The Impact of Significant Others

As emphasized in the section on infancy, the role of caregivers is critical to the development of many self processes. Particularly relevant to the *content* of self-representations are the observations of attachment theorists who have noted how toddlers begin to develop a rudimentary working model of the self in reaction to the responsiveness of caregivers (Bowlby, 1969; Bretherton, 1991; Sroufe, 1990). Thus, young children who experience parents as sensitive to their needs and supportive of their mastery efforts will construct a model of the self as lovable and competent. In contrast, the young child who experiences the parent as rejecting or neglectful will form a model of the self as unworthy. At this developmental level, however, the toddler, in all likelihood, is not consciously aware of these influences.

From a symbolic interactionist perspective, rudimentary skills necessary for the development of a looking-glass self begin to emerge at about 2 years of age. Stipek et al. (1992) report that toward the goal of anticipating positive parental responses and avoiding negative reactions, 2-year-olds begin to develop an appreciation for parental standards. In addition, they show some initial ability to evaluate whether or not they have met these standards. Thereafter, children gradually begin to internalize these standards, allowing them to engage in self-evaluation independent of adults' reactions. Further contributing to looking-glass-self processes is the increasing ability throughout childhood to appreciate parents' evaluative perspectives toward the self. Through increasing perspective-taking skills, children come to recognize not only that parents have standards that they expect to be met, but that parents form an evaluative opinion about the child (Higgins, 1991; Leahy & Shirk, 1985; Oosterwegel & Oppenheimer, 1993; Selman, 1980). Oosterwegel and Oppenheimer report that as children move into adolescence, their own self-evaluations increasingly parallel the evaluations of their parents.

There is a growing body of empirical evidence revealing that parental approval is particularly critical in determining the self-esteem of children, supporting the looking-glass-self formulation. Coopersmith (1967) was among the first to describe how the socialization practices of parents impacted children's self-esteem. Parents of children with high self-esteem (a) were more likely to be accepting, approving, affectionate, and involved; (b) enforced rules consistently and encouraged children to uphold high standards of behavior; (c) preferred noncoercive disciplinary practices, discussing the reasons why the child's behavior was inappropriate; and (d) were democratic in considering the child's opinion around certain family decisions. More recent studies have built upon Baumrind's (1989) typology of parenting styles, linking them to child and adolescent self-evaluations. For example, Lamborn, Mounts, Steinberg, and Dornbusch (1991) report that adolescents of authoritative parents report significantly higher self-concepts in the domains of social and academic competence than do those with authoritarian or neglectful parents.

Additional evidence reveals that parental support, particularly in the form of approval and acceptance, is associated with high self-esteem and the sense that one is lovable (see reviews by Feiring & Taska, 1996; Harter, in press-d). Richards, Gitelson, Petersen, and Hurtig (1991) present evidence refining this general relationship, demonstrating that support from mothers has a greater impact on male adolescents, whereas paternal support is more highly related to females' self-esteem. While types of support other than approval may contribute to self-esteem, findings from our laboratory indicate that approval or acceptance is most highly predictive, instrumental support is least predictive, and emotional support falls in between (Robinson, in press). From a looking-glass-self perspective, others' approval of the self should be most readily incorporated as approval of oneself as a person, namely self-esteem. While emotional and instrumental support from significant others should be a welcome sign of caring, it could also serve as a sign of one's weaknesses rather than one's strengths, undermining one's sense of efficacy. Building upon Nadler and Fisher's (1986) model, Shell and Eisenberg (1992) provide an interesting developmental analysis of the conditions under which aid from others should and should not pose a threat to one's self-esteem. For example, among older children who have developed trait conceptualizations of self-attributes (e.g., smart versus dumb), help from others could be interpreted as feedback that they are "dumb," leading to negative self-evaluations and a sense of helplessness.

More comprehensive models linking family factors to child and adolescent self-esteem have recently begun to emerge. These models are moving away from an emphasis on structural features (e.g., birth order, number of siblings, family intactness) to a consideration of more psychological process variables that influence children's self-representations. For example, Hattie (1992) presents a model in which such structural features, including social status, are included; however, family psychological characteristics, such as expectations and encouragement of the child, rewards and punishments, and family activities and interests, play a major role. Feiring and Taska (1996) present a heuristic model that identifies family factors impacting the child's self-representations, building upon attachment theory. For example, they suggest that during childhood, positive interactions between caregiver and child (e.g., affectionate contact upon reunion) coupled with a warm and reliable relationship will foster positive self-representations within the family context (e.g., I am loved, valued, accepted) as well as more global self-evaluations that transcend family relationships (e.g., I am worthwhile, secure, and autonomous). They review isolated findings consistent with pieces of the model, but observe that there is relatively little research that comprehensively addresses many of the issues in their model.

In their review, Feiring and Taska (1996) observe that within the family systems literature, attention has recently turned to the impact of siblings upon developing self-representations. Age-related status is one influence, in that an older sibling may come to view the self as nurturant or dominant, whereas the younger sibling will identify more with the role of being nurtured or dominated. Social comparison with siblings represents another avenue through which the self-concept is impacted, depending upon how one measures up to the siblings with whom one is compared. De-identification is another pathway to self-definition as children attempt to be *different* from siblings, in part to avoid intense competition.

The field is also beginning to examine how *dysfunctional* families influence the developing child's sense of self. For example, research (reviewed by Feiring & Taska, 1996) reveals that children and adolescents from alcoholic families report lower self-esteem. Considerable evidence also reveals that children from *abusive* families suffer a constellation of assaults to the self system (see reviews by Harter, in press-c; Putnam, 1993; Westen, 1993). There are disruptions in both I-self functions (e.g., impaired sense of agency, disturbances in the sense of self-coherence as well as of self-continuity over time) and Me-self manifestations

(e.g., large discrepancies between real and ideal selves, low self-esteem, excessive self-blame, and the suppression of one's authentic self).

From a developmental perspective, parental approval has been found to be more predictive of self-esteem than is approval from *peers* (outside the family) among *younger* children (Nikkari & Harter, 1993; Pekrun, 1990; M. Rosenberg, 1979). M. Rosenberg has observed that younger children's conclusions about what they are like rest heavily on the perceived judgments of external authority, particularly parental authority. Knowledge of the self is regarded as absolute and resides in those with superior wisdom, a conclusion consistent with Piaget's (1932) observations of children's understanding of rules and sources of moral judgment. Thus, during childhood, parents are considered to be more *credible* sources of information on the self (see also Oosterwegel & Oppenheimer, 1993). According to Rosenberg, respect for parental knowledge declines with development and peer evaluations rise in importance (see also Pekrun, 1990).

Evidence only partially confirms these claims. For example, although the correlation between peer approval and self-esteem has been found to increase with development, the correlation between parental approval and self-esteem does not decline, at least through adolescence (Harter, 1990a). This pattern is consistent with the recent conclusions of Oosterwegel and Oppenheimer (1993), who emphasize the importance of parents' opinions of the self well into adolescence. Others also report that while peers become more important as one moves into adolescence, parents continue to remain central; their role may be transformed, but it is not diminished (see Buhrmester & Furman, 1987; Lamborn & Steinberg, 1993; Ryan & Lynch, 1989). Correlations between parent approval and self-esteem have been observed to decline, however, when adolescents make the transition to college (Harter & Johnson, 1993).

With regard to the role of the appraisals of peer groups on self-esteem, different types of peers have differential influence. At every developmental level we have investigated—middle to late childhood, adolescence, the college years, and early to middle age adulthood (Harter, 1990a)—we have consistently found that approval from peers in the more public domain (e.g., classmates, peers in organizations, work settings, etc.) is far more predictive of self-esteem than is approval from one's close friends. We interpret this finding to suggest that support from others in the more public domain may better represent acceptance from the "generalized other," approval that may be perceived as more "objective" or from more credible sources, than the support from one's close friends. This is not to negate the importance of close friend support, which would appear to be critical as a source of acceptance, feedback, and clarification of values. Such close friend support would seem to function as a secure psychological base from which one can reemerge to meet the challenges of the generalized other, whose acceptance appears critical to maintaining high self-esteem.

For some adolescents, the opinions of selected subgroups rather than of mainstream classmates become critical to one's self-definition. For example, failure to meet the standards of the dominant group may produce negative self-attitudes, which in turn cause such adolescents to seek the company of teenage groups or gangs where prevalent societal standards are ignored and delinquent behaviors are admired (Kaplan, 1980). Through these identifications, one's level of self-esteem can be elevated. For example, evidence reveals that boys who suffered the biggest reduction in self-esteem when they entered high school were able to restore their self-esteem by engaging in delinquent behavior (Bynner, O'Malley, & Bachman, 1981).

A looking-glass-self perspective can also be applied to the relationship between self-esteem and ethnicity. The majority of comparisons have been made between European American and African American youth. Overall, particularly when SES is controlled, the pattern of findings reveals little in the way of systematic differences in self-esteem (see Crain, 1996). Interestingly, among African American youth, the relationship between the attitudes of significant others toward the self (especially family members as well as African American friends and teachers) has been found to be somewhat stronger than among European American youth (S. Rosenberg, 1988). It has been suggested that not only is the African American community a source of positive self-concept in African American children but that under certain conditions the African American family can filter out racist, destructive messages from the White community, supplanting such messages with more positive feedback that will enhance self-esteem (Barnes, 1980). More recent treatments of ethnicity suggest the need for much more complex models that take into account a variety of risk factors, stressors, contextual variables, social support, and relatedness to others in predicting self-perceptions, including their impact on positive and negative outcomes (see Connell, Spencer, & Aber, 1994; Spencer, 1995). This is clearly the direction in which the

field needs to move to thoughtfully address the complexity of the issues involving ethnicity and the self.

Accuracy of the Perceptions of Others' Appraisals

As others have observed, the reflected appraisal process consists of three elements: (a) self-appraisals, (b) the *actual* appraisals of significant others, and (c) the individual's *perceptions* of the appraisals of others, referred to as *reflected* appraisals (Felson, 1993; Kenny, 1988; Kinch, 1963). An increasing body of research reveals that there is a stronger relationship between reflected appraisals and self-appraisals than between the actual appraisals of significant others and self-appraisals (Berndt, in press; Felson, 1993; John & Robbins, 1994; M. Rosenberg, 1979; Shrauger & Schoeneman, 1979). Thus, although Mead (1934) initially claimed that "We are more or less unconsciously seeing ourselves as others see us" (p. 68), M. Rosenberg (1979) qualifies Mead's principle, suggesting that "We are more or less unconsciously seeing ourselves as we think others who are important to us and whose opinion we trust see us" (p. 97). For example, Ooosterwegel and Oppenheimer's (1993) developmental data reveal that as children move into adolescence, they come to perceive their parents' opinions of them to be more negative than the judgments of parents actually are. A number of mechanisms to account for the discrepancy between the actual appraisals of others and one's perceptions of these appraisals have been suggested (Berndt, in press; Juhasz, 1992; Kenny, 1988; Shrauger & Schoeneman, 1979). In addition to the importance of the individual making an evaluative judgment, the salience of the dimension on which one is being evaluated will have an effect, as will biases toward either self-enhancement or modesty. Distortions may also reflect the need to make feedback congruent with one's own self-perceptions.

Communication of Approval

Symbolic interactionists, particularly Mead, placed heavy emphasis upon the direct communication of others' evaluations in the form of language, evaluations that were then incorporated into a sense of self. Certain theorists (e.g., Ashmore & Ogilvie, 1992) suggest that such a model is too passive and mechanical, arguing that in our interactions with others we not only encode their verbalizations but also affective, verbal, motoric, and behavioral information about the other as well as the self. Felson (1993) as well as Shrauger and Schoeneman (1979) also report findings demonstrating that the opinions of others may be gleaned through channels other than direct communication. Negative evaluations, less likely to be communicated directly, may be inferred from the absence of positive feedback. Third parties may also serve as a source of information about others' appraisals. In addition, observing how people whose opinions matter evaluate *others* provides indirect information as to how such people evaluate the self. Shared standards and social comparison processes represent another route through which the opinions of others can be inferred. That is, shared *standards* may be communicated directly by others; individuals then engage in social comparison to determine whether their performance measures up to these standards. If they feel it does not, they conclude that those others whose standards they share must think poorly of them. Conversely, if they meet these standards, they infer that others must be evaluating them positively.

Directionality of the Link between Actual and Reflected Appraisals

A number of investigators have questioned the assumption that the inferred appraisals of others necessarily *precede* self-evaluations (Felson, 1993; Juhasz, 1992; Leahy & Shirk, 1985). The alternative is also plausible, namely, that self-evaluations may be driving one's perceptions of the other's opinions. Felson has reported evidence that children who like themselves assume that parents' and peers' reactions to them are favorable, leading to an alternative interpretation that he terms the "false consensus effect." Both effects, the internalization of others' opinions as well as the assumption that if one likes the self, others in turn will manifest their approval, are likely to be operative. Such reciprocity was acknowledged by Felson and Zielinski (1989), who inferred that "Support increases self-esteem, which increases support (or perceived support), which in turn increases self-esteem" (p. 219).

Another fruitful approach involves an examination of which perspective is dominant from the individual's own point of view (Harter, Stocker, & Robinson, 1996). Do adolescents consciously endorse a looking-glass-self metatheory, or the opposite directionality? Findings reveal that approximately half of the participants did acknowledge that they need to have other people evaluate them positively in order to like themselves as a person (our definition of self-esteem). The other half endorsed the competing metatheory that if one likes oneself as a person, then others will necessarily like or support the self. Moreover, the findings revealed liabilities for those

endorsing the first, looking-glass-self orientation. Such individuals reported a greater preoccupation with others' opinions, lower support, more fluctuating support, and lower and more fluctuating self-esteem, compared to those who felt that their self-esteem would impact the opinions of others. The first group was also judged by teachers to be more socially distracted from schoolwork.

Developmentally, a looking-glass-self model represents the mechanism through which opinions of others come to impact the self initially. However, the healthiest developmental course would appear to be one in which the standards and opinions of others are eventually internalized, such that truly *self*-evaluations become the standards that guide behavior (see Higgins, 1991). Damon and Hart (1988) come to a similar conclusion, observing that adolescents who do not move to the stage of internalized standards but continue to rely on external social standards and feedback will be at risk because they will not have developed an internalized, relatively stable sense of self that will form the basis for subsequent identity development.

The Stability of Self-Representations

The section on multiple selves described how individuals vary their behavior depending upon the relational context. In this section, the focus will be on stability and/or change in the *valence* of one's self-representations, namely, how favorably one evaluates the self. That is, do such evaluations change with *development* as well as with *situation* at any one point in development? With regard to developmental change, the evidence reveals that self-evaluative judgments become less positive as children move into middle childhood (Frey & Ruble, 1985, 1990; Harter, 1982; Harter & Pike, 1984; Stipek, 1981). Investigators attribute such a decline to the greater reliance on social comparison information and external feedback, leading to more realistic judgments about one's capabilities (see also Crain, 1996; Marsh, 1989). A growing number of studies suggests that there is another decline at early adolescence (ages 11–13), after which self-esteem and domain-specific self-evaluations gradually become more positive over the course of adolescence (Dusek & Flaherty, 1981; Engel, 1959; Marsh, Parker, & Barnes, 1985; Marsh, Smith, Marsh, & Owens, 1988; O'Malley & Bachman, 1983; Piers & Harris, 1964; M. Rosenberg, 1986; Savin-Williams & Demo, 1984; Simmons, Rosenberg, & Rosenberg, 1973).

Many of the changes reported coincide with the educational transition to junior high school. Eccles and colleagues

(Eccles & Midgley, 1989; Eccles, Midgley, & Adler, 1984) and Simmons and colleagues (Blyth, Simmons, & Carlton-Ford, 1983; Nottelmann, 1987; Simmons & Blyth, 1987; Simmons, Blyth, Van Cleave, & Bush, 1979; Simmons, Rosenberg, & Rosenberg, 1973; Wigfield, Eccles, MacIver, Reuman, & Midgley, 1991) have postulated that differences in the school environments of elementary and junior high schools are in part responsible. Junior high school brings more emphasis on social comparison and competition, stricter grading standards, more teacher control, less personal attention from teachers, and disruptions in social networks, all of which leads to a mismatch between the structure of the school environment and the needs of young adolescents. The numerous physical, cognitive, social, and emotional changes further jeopardize the adolescent's sense of continuity, which may in turn threaten self-esteem (Leahy & Shirk, 1985). A number of studies (e.g., Blyth et al., 1983; Nottelmann, 1987; Rosenberg & Simmons, 1972; Simmons et al., 1979; Simmons & Rosenberg, 1975; Wigfield et al., 1991) also report lower self-esteem for girls than for boys (see also Block & Robins, 1993, who find that the gender gap widens from ages 14 to 23).

The magnitude of the self-esteem decline is also related to the timing of school shifts and to pubertal change (Brooks-Gunn & Peterson, 1983; Simmons & Blyth, 1987). Those making the shift from sixth to seventh grade show greater losses of self-esteem than those who make the school transition a year later, from seventh to eighth grade. Moreover, students making the earlier change, particularly girls, do not recover these losses in self-esteem during the high school years. Early-maturing girls fare the worst: they are the most dissatisfied with their bodies, in part because they tend to be somewhat heavier and do not fit the cultural stereotype of female attractiveness. This in turn has a negative effect on their self-esteem. Furthermore, according to the developmental readiness hypothesis (Simmons & Blyth, 1987), early-maturing girls are not yet emotionally prepared to deal with the social expectations that surround dating and with the greater independence that early maturity often demands (see Lipka, Hurford, & Litten, 1992, for a general discussion of the effects of being "off-time" in one's level of maturational development).

Several interpretations have been offered for the gradual gains in self-esteem that follow from eighth grade through high school (McCarthy & Hoge, 1982). Gains in personal autonomy may provide more opportunity to select performance domains in which one is competent, consistent with

a Jamesian analysis. Increasing freedom may allow more opportunities to select support groups that will provide esteem-enhancing approval, consistent with the looking-glass-self formulation. Increased role-taking ability may also lead teenagers to behave in more socially acceptable ways that garner the acceptance of others. A study by Hart, Fegley, and Brengelman (1993) provides some confirming evidence. In describing their past and present selves, adolescents asserted that with time they have become more capable, mature, personable, and attractive, describing how they shed undesirable cognitive, emotional, and personality characteristics.

An analysis of changes in *mean* level of self-esteem, however, may mask individual differences in response to educational transitions (see also Block & Robins, 1993). Findings (Harter, 1986b; Johnson & Harter, 1995) on both the transition to junior high school and to college have identified three groups: those whose self-esteem increases, those whose self-esteem decreases, and those whose level of self-esteem remains the same. These investigators contend that self-esteem should only be altered if theoretically derived *antecedents* of self-esteem change, leading to an examination of instability or stability as a function of the determinants of self-esteem identified by James (competence in domains of importance) and Cooley (approval from significant others). Results indicate that those whose self-esteem increased across educational transitions displayed greater competence in domains of importance and reported more social approval in the new school environment. Students whose self-esteem decreased reported both a decline in competence for valued domains and reported less social support after the transition. Students showing no changes in self-esteem reported minimal changes in both competence and social support. Demo and Savin-Williams (1992) have also adopted a more idiographic approach, demonstrating that while nearly half of their sample demonstrated self-esteem stability, the remaining subjects manifested varying degrees of instability.

The extent to which self-representations vary as a function of *situation* is a second context in which the issue of the stability and malleability of the self-concept has been raised. James scooped contemporary theorists and researchers on this issue, arguing that whereas the barometer of our self-esteem rises and falls from one day to another, there is nevertheless a certain average tone of self-feeling, independent of the reasons we may have for momentary self-satisfaction or discontent. There is considerable evidence that the self-concept is relatively stable.

For example, Swann (1985, 1987) provides evidence demonstrating individuals' elaborate and ingenious strategies for self-verification; people go to great lengths to seek information that confirms their self-concept and are highly resistant to information that threatens their view of self (see also Epstein, 1991; Greenwald, 1980; Markus, 1977; M. Rosenberg, 1979). Epstein observes that "people have a vested interest in maintaining the stability of their personal theories of reality, for they are the only systems they have for making sense of their world and guiding their behavior" (p. 97).

On the other hand, considerable evidence reveals that situational factors can lead to short-term changes in self-evaluation (Baumgardner, Kaufman, & Levy, 1989; Gergen, 1967, 1982; Heatherton & Polivy, 1991; Jones, Rhodewalt, Berglas, & Skelton, 1981; Markus & Kunda, 1986; M. Rosenberg, 1986; Savin-Williams & Demo, 1983; Tesser, 1988). Gergen's position is perhaps the most extreme; he has argued that people are capable of marked shifts in their public presentation that are not necessarily accompanied by self-alienation. In an effort to reconcile these positions, Markus and Kunda have invoked the construct of the "working self-concept." According to their view, the individual possesses a stable universe of core self-conceptions. The working self-concept is a subset of these self-conceptions, a temporary structure, elicited by those situational factors that occur at any given point in time. Thus, the self-concept is also malleable to the extent that the content of the working self-concept changes. Their empirical findings strongly support such a position (see also Greenwald & Pratkanis, 1984).

There is a growing consensus that, as James originally suggested, individuals possess both a *baseline* self-concept and a *barometric* self-concept (see reviews by Demo & Savin-Williams, 1992; M. Rosenberg, 1986). Thus, people have a core sense of self that is relatively consistent over time; however, there are also situational variations around this core self-portrait. Others have come to a similar conclusion, postulating that individuals display both trait and state self-esteem (Heatherton & Polivy, 1991; Leary & Downs, 1995). Within the context of hierarchical models of the self, theorists have argued that higher-order schemata are far more resistant to modification than lower-order, situation-specific constructs (Epstein, 1991; Hattie, 1992). Epstein notes that such higher-order schemata have typically been acquired early in development and are often derived from emotionally significant experiences to which the individual may have little conscious access, making the beliefs difficult to alter.

With regard to the barometric self, adolescence is a time when fluctuations appear to be the most flagrant (Blos, 1962; Demo & Savin-Williams, 1992; Harter, 1990b; Leahy & Shirk, 1985; M. Rosenberg, 1986). Those of a cognitive-developmental persuasion (e.g., Fischer, 1980; Harter, 1990b; Harter & Monsour, 1992; Higgins, 1991) have attributed these fluctuations to limitations in the ability to cognitively control seemingly contradictory self-attributes (shy versus outgoing), particularly during middle adolescence. Psychoanalytic thinkers (e.g., Blos, 1962; Kohut, 1977) attribute fluctuations to the intense heightened narcissism and self-preoccupation of adolescents whose self-esteem swings from grandiosity to battered self-devaluation. M. Rosenberg (1986) focuses more on how socialization factors influence the volatility of the self during adolescence. Thus, he observes that the adolescent is preoccupied with what others think of the self but has difficulty divining others' impressions, leading to ambiguity about the self. Moreover, different significant others may have different impressions of the self, creating contradictory feedback.

Self-esteem may also vary as a function of the *relational context*. In a recent study, adolescents were asked to describe their feelings of self-worth in four contexts: with parents, teachers, male classmates, and female classmates (Harter, Waters, & Whitesell, 1996). A very clean four-factor solution revealed that self-esteem differs across these contexts. In fact, some participants report the entire range (e.g., one adolescent girl reported the lowest possible self-esteem score with parents and the highest possible score with female classmates). There are clear individual differences, however, revealed in the discrepancy between one's lowest and highest relational self-esteem scores. There are those with negligible discrepancies, reflecting considerable stability, those with moderate discrepancies, and those with very large discrepancies, indicating considerable variation in self-esteem across relational constructs.

Such a focus on *individual differences* is the third major context in which issues of stability and change in self-evaluations have been examined. Kernis and colleagues (Greenier, Kernis, & Waschull, 1995; Kernis, 1993; Kernis, Cornell, Sun, Berry, & Harlow, 1993) have been the major proponents of such an approach. According to these investigators, those prone to short-term fluctuations in self-esteem demonstrate enhanced sensitivity to evaluative events, ego involvement (versus task involvement), preoccupation with self-evaluation, and overreliance on social sources of self-esteem (see also Deci & Ryan, 1987; M. Rosenberg, 1986). Findings indicating greater fluctuations in self-esteem for those who consciously endorse a looking-glass-self orientation (approval determines my self-esteem) are consistent with this individual difference approach (Harter et al., 1996). It was speculated that the developmental precursors may have involved parenting characterized by inconsistent approval and/or conditional support. Greenier et al. (1995) also conjectured that inconsistent as well as controlling feedback will undermine the development of a stable sense of worth (see also Deci & Ryan, 1987, 1995).

Consistent with their individual difference approach, Kernis and colleagues distinguish between individuals with stable and unstable self-esteem at two *levels* of self-esteem, high and low. They have been particularly interested in illuminating the differential reactions to success and failure feedback of those both high and low in self-esteem, whose self-esteem is *unstable*. For those with high self-esteem, instability is associated with strategies in which one continually seeks favorable feedback and defensively reacts to negative feedback (e.g., by questioning its legitimacy) to defend one's fragile sense of high self-esteem. Another manifestation of defensiveness is a heightened tendency to become angry or hostile. For those with low self-esteem, instability is associated with attempts to avoid continuous negative feedback that might lead to global conclusions about one's inadequacy or worthlessness. Thus, for Kernis and colleagues, it is not sufficient to consider only level of self-esteem, given that different styles also are related to the stability of self-esteem.

Dweck and colleagues (Dweck, 1991; Dweck & Elliott, 1983; Dweck & Leggett, 1988) have approached the issue of individual differences from another perspective, examining differences in the *theories* older children hold about stability or change in traits over situation or time. Specifically, they have examined the implicit theories that children develop about self-attributes that concern *intelligence*, attributional patterns that have implications for behavior. They identify two types of self-theories, which they label "entity" and "incremental" conceptualizations of one's intelligence. Children who are entity theorists consider their intellectual ability to be fixed and therefore uncontrollable. Such children focus on performance outcomes and are oriented toward gaining approval and avoiding negative feedback. If they receive negative evaluations, their confidence is eroded and they develop behavior patterns of helplessness in the face of challenge or failure. In contrast, children who are incremental theorists believe that their intelligence is malleable. As a result, they are oriented toward learning goals that will allow them to increase their competence. Such children are very mastery-oriented in

the face of challenge as well as failure. More recently, Dweck and colleagues have extended their analysis to traits in the social realm, with similar implications. This work is particularly important in its demonstration of the *function* of particular self-theories in influencing behavior.

The Accuracy of Self-Evaluations

There is a growing body of developmental literature revealing that young children are relatively inaccurate judges of their abilities, but that accuracy increases with age (Harter, 1985a; Harter & Pike, 1984; Leahy & Shirk, 1985; Phillips & Zimmerman, 1990; Stipek, 1981, 1984). The clearest picture emerges when one compares teachers' evaluations with self-ratings of competence. Among young children the correlations are modest to negligible. Findings also indicate that even when young children are exposed to repeated failures, they do not lower their expectations for success; rather, they persist in holding high and unrealistic beliefs about their abilities (Parsons & Ruble, 1977). As argued elsewhere (Harter, 1988a), young children's inaccurate and inflated self-evaluations should be understood as "normative distortions" and the result of their failure to differentiate the *wish* to be competent from the reality. Stipek (1984) provides experimental evidence that young children's unrealistically high performance expectations are intruded upon by personal desires.

With increasing development, children's estimates of their ability become more realistic, due to several different processes. The emergence of the cognitive ability to engage in social comparison leads to lower and more realistic self-evaluations (e.g., Frey & Ruble, 1985, 1990; Ruble & Frey, 1991). Cognitive-developmental advances also allow one to make the distinction between real and ideal self-concepts (e.g., Glick & Zigler, 1985; Higgins, 1991; Oosterwegel & Oppenheimer, 1993). Moreover, the development of perspective-taking abilities provides children with a more accurate rendering of others' views of their abilities and attributes (Leahy & Shirk, 1985; Oosterwegel & Oppenheimer, 1993; Selman, 1980) that are incorporated into the looking-glass self. Concomitantly, children manifest an increasing capacity for self-reflection (Leahy & Shirk, 1985). Finally, during childhood there is an increasing differentiation between concepts of effort and ability and their relationship to one another (Nicholls, 1990). The realization that extreme effort implies less ability contributes to more realistic appraisals of one's competencies.

There is some evidence that the progression toward more realistic self-evaluations is not completely linear. Findings

(Harter, 1982) have indicated that the correlation between perceived scholastic competence and teachers' ratings of students' competence gradually increased from third through sixth grade. However, the correlation plummeted with the transition to junior high school in seventh grade, after which it recovered substantially in eighth and ninth grades. The new school environment brings different academic expectations and shifting standards of social comparisons in the face of a new social reference group. Initially, these changes may lead to ambiguity that results in unrealistic self-evaluations, requiring that students construct new criteria by which to judge their competence (Harter, Whitesell, & Kowalski, 1992). As a more general consideration, most developmental transitions present new tasks to be mastered, which may cause doubt and anxiety about one's abilities as well as challenge existing self-representations, leading to potential alterations and inaccuracies in one's self-perceptions (see also Mack, 1983).

There are also *individual differences* in the degree to which self-evaluations are veridical with more objective indices (Harter, 1985a; Leahy & Shirk, 1985; Phillips & Zimmerman, 1990). In our own work, we have identified three groups of middle school children: those who seriously *overrate* their competence relative to the teacher's judgment, those who seriously *underrate* their competence, and those whose ratings are *congruent* with the teacher's. Interestingly, in a preference for challenge task (Harter, 1985a), both underraters and the overraters selected easier tasks than did the accurate raters (groups were matched on actual ability). It would appear that the underraters operate in accord with their beliefs of low incompetence, whereas overraters prefer less challenge to avoid failure and thereby protect their inflated sense of competence.

Phillips and Zimmerman (1990) have been particularly interested in high-achieving students who seriously underestimate their scholastic competence. They also find that underraters are guided more by their inaccurate self-perceptions than by their actual capabilities. Those who manifest this "illusion of incompetence" reported unrealistically low expectations for success, displayed evaluation anxiety, and were reluctant to perform challenging achievement tasks. Moreover, they believed that significant adults judged their abilities unfavorably, suggesting that they had incorporated these perceived evaluations into their self-concepts. Gender differences revealed that, beginning in the ninth grade, girls were overrepresented among underraters and perceived their mothers to expect less of them and to hold them to less stringent achievement standards than did boys.

With regard to the overestimation of one's abilities, a critical consideration involves the *magnitude* of the discrepancy between perceived and actual competence. Large discrepancies, such as those that defined the overraters and underraters in the studies described above, signal liabilities; for example, they prohibit preference for challenging activities that might promote further learning. However, veridical self-evaluations can be self-limiting. For example, it has been demonstrated that depressed individuals are more likely to report realistic self-appraisals; in contrast, nondepressed persons are likely to view themselves as more capable than they really are (e.g., Alloy & Abramson, 1979; Asarnow & Bates, 1988; Lewinsohn, Mischel, Chaplain, & Barton, 1980).

Some degree of overestimation, if not excessive, represents one of many self-enhancing biases that most (nondepressed) people exhibit (Banaji & Prentice, 1994; Baumeister, Tice, & Hutton, 1989). Thus, high self-esteem individuals construe events and process information so as to promote positive self-perceptions, which in turn serves to preserve feelings of self-worth (see Blaine & Crocker, 1993; Brown, 1993a, 1993b; Dunning, 1993; Greenwald, 1980; Greenwald & Pratkanis, 1984; Pelham & Swann, 1989; Steele, 1988; Taylor & Brown, 1988). In his "self-ffirmation theory," Steele has addressed the strategies through which individuals modify their beliefs about the self in the service of this goal (see also Taylor, 1983; Tesser & Cornell, 1991). While the overestimation strategy represents some distortion, such self-enhancement may improve task performance (Bandura, 1989; Brown, 1993b; Taylor & Brown, 1988). Taylor and Brown conclude that the self-enhancing strategies associated with high self-esteem are functional, as evidenced by the fact that self-esteem is consistently linked to other indices of psychological adjustment. Although most of these efforts have focused on adult subjects, data with children reveal that high self-esteem students see themselves as slightly more competent than do their teachers, in both their most competent and least competent domains (Harter, 1986b). Low self-esteem children show little tendency to inflate their judgments of competence; in fact, for their lowest competence domain they view themselves as less capable than do their teachers.

Other self-enhancement strategies displayed by high self-esteem individuals include downward comparisons in which the self is considered superior to others (Baumeister, 1991a; Brown, 1986, 1993a, 1993b; Markus, Cross, & Wurf, 1990; Wood, 1989). Dunning (1993) reviews those studies that demonstrate this "above average effect" in numerous domains, a strategy that Markus and Kityama (1991) feel is particularly prevalent in Western cultures. In their self-evaluation maintenance theory, Tesser and colleagues (Beach & Tesser, 1995; Tesser, 1988) identify another strategy for self-enhancement, namely, basking in the glory of the accomplishments of a close other (e.g., a spouse) with whom one identifies. Such a process will only serve the intended goal if success in the given domain of comparison is not vitally important to the individual's self-definition. However, these processes have not been examined in children, as a function of age, to determine at what point in their development such processes might emerge.

The functional value of self-enhancement strategies and self-serving biases has been touted by many social psychologists. However, others adopt a less sanguine perspective. Baumeister (1991b, 1993) observes the risks that accompany a preoccupation with self-presentation, high self-monitoring, and the maintenance of a highly positive self-image involving egoistic illusions. He cites the potential for disconfirmation from others, vulnerability to attack, the pressure of living up to the inflated self-image, and overconfidence that may create interpersonal difficulties. Others (Blaine & Crocker, 1993; Brown, 1993a, 1993b; De La Ronde & Swann, 1993) have pointed to similar liabilities. Brown observes that an overemphasis on positive outcomes can undermine the stability of the self-concept. Recall Kernis's (1993) findings that those with high but unstable self-esteem are also prone to hostility. De La Ronde and Swann observe that such overestimation can rob the individual of opportunities to gain an understanding of what one is truly like.

Deci and Ryan (1995) also cite the dangers of developing a false self if self-esteem is based primarily on impression management and is contingent upon living up to the externally imposed evaluation criteria of others. Such "contingent self-esteem" is contrasted to "true self-esteem" derived from more autonomous actions that involve self-determination based upon internal standards, leading to a genuine sense of efficacy. Deci and Ryan argue that the latter orientation leads to a more stable and integrated sense of self that can be shared with others in a more mutual, authentic relationship. Exploring the more practical implications of this issue, Damon (1995) and Seligman (1993) have recently questioned what they consider to be an overemphasis by educators and clinicians on promoting high self-esteem among our youth or among depressed individuals, particularly when these efforts lead to an inflated sense of esteem. They see such efforts as misguided and possibly detrimental, arguing that they divert educators from teaching skills, deprive students of the thrill of actual accomplishment, and distract clinicians from identifying the more specific causes of psychological problems such as depression.

Selected Correlates of Self-Esteem

Perceived Physical Appearance

In shifting to multidimensional, hierarchical models of the self, many investigators have been interested in whether some domains are more predictive of global self-esteem than others. In our own work (Harter, 1990a), we have found that perceived physical appearance repeatedly heads the list as the domain most highly correlated (rs between .65 and .82) with self-esteem, from early childhood through adulthood, with no gender differences in the magnitude of these correlations. Other investigators examining this link in children and adolescents have obtained similar relationships (Lenerz, Kuchner, East, Lerner, & Lerner, 1987; Lerner & Brackney, 1978; Lerner & Karabenick, 1974; Lerner, Orlos, & Knapp, 1976; Marsh, 1987; Padin, Lerner, & Spiro, 1981; Pomerantz, 1979; Simmons & Rosenberg, 1975). Moreover, the correlation is just as high in special populations such as the intellectually gifted and the learning disabled, where one might anticipate that perceived scholastic competence would bear a stronger relationship to self-esteem, given its presumed salience (Harter, 1993).

Numerous findings in the adult literature reveal that perceived physical appearance and self-esteem are inextricably linked (Adams, 1982; Berscheid, Walster, & Bohrnstedt, 1973; Davies & Furnham, 1986; Feingold, 1992; Franzoi & Shields, 1984; Hatfield & Sprecher, 1986; Jackson, 1992; Korabik & Pitt, 1980; Lerner, Karabenick, & Stuart, 1973; Longo & Ashmore, 1995; Mathes & Kahn, 1975; McCaulay, Mintz, & Glenn, 1988; Messer & Harter, 1989; Mintz & Betz, 1988; Neemann & Harter, 1987; Rosen & Ross, 1968; Ryckman, Robbins, Thornton, & Cantrell, 1982; Silberstein, Striegel-Moore, Timko, & Rodin, 1988). Moreover, self-evaluations are found to be more highly related to perceived attractiveness than to actual physical attractiveness (see Feingold, 1992).

The literature also documents the fact that females are typically more dissatisfied with their appearance than are males (Adams, 1982; Birtchnell, Dolan, & Lacey, 1987; Cohn et al., 1987; Davies & Furnham, 1986; Fallon & Rozin, 1985; McCaulay et al., 1988; Mintz & Betz, 1988; Silberstein et al., 1988; Stager & Burke, 1982). This dissatisfaction begins in middle childhood (Maloney, McGuire,

& Daniels, 1988; Mellin, 1988; Salmons, Lewis, Rogers, Gatherer, & Booth, 1988; Stein, in press). In our own work (Harter, 1993), we find that in early childhood, girls and boys are equally satisfied with their looks. Boys continue to evaluate their appearance positively as they move through the school years. However, beginning in fourth grade, there is a systematic decline for girls such that by the end of high school girls' evaluations of their appearance are dramatically lower than are boys'. Other investigators have reported similar findings, particularly among adolescents (Allgood-Merten, Lewinsohn, & Hops, 1990; Nolen-Hoeksema, 1987; Simmons & Blyth, 1987).

Girls' self-esteem also declines with age, leading to gender differences; however, the drop is not as precipitous as it is for perceived appearance. Self-esteem has been found to be particularly low for those females who acknowledge that they are basing their self-esteem on their appearance (Harter, 1993). Culturally, messages about the importance of appearance begin at an early age. Studies reveal that adults begin to react to physical appearance when one is an infant and toddler (Langlois, 1981; Maccoby & Martin, 1983). Those who are attractive by societal standards are responded to with more positive attention than those judged to be less attractive. Thus, from an early age, the physical self is highly salient in provoking evaluative psychological reactions that are incorporated into the child's emerging sense of worth. Moreover, findings reveal that young children are well aware of the cultural criteria for attractiveness (Cavior & Lombardi, 1973).

Many point to the emphasis that society and the media place on appearance at every age (see Adams, 1982; Andersen, 1992; Elkind, 1979; Hatfield & Sprecher, 1986; Kilbourne, 1994; Nemeroff, Stein, Diehl, & Smilack, 1994; Silverstein, Perdue, Peterson, & Kelly, 1986). Movies, television, magazines, rock videos, and advertising all tout the importance of physical attractiveness, glamorizing the popular role models whom females and males should emulate. However, the standards are particularly punishing and very narrow for women. Ubiquitous standards regarding desirable bodily characteristics such as thinness have become increasingly unrealistic for women within the past two decades (see Garner, Garfinkel, Schwartz, & Thompson, 1980; Heatherton & Baumeister, 1991; Jackson, 1992; Wiseman, Gray, Mosimann, & Ahrens, 1992), making it difficult to live up to these ideals.

Another major liability can be observed in the eating-disordered behavior of females, for whom the incidence is much higher than for men (e.g., Greenfeld, Quinlan, Hard-

ing, Glass, & Bliss, 1987; Raciti & Norcross, 1987; Rand & Kuldau, 1992; Streigel-Moore, Silberstein, & Rodin, 1986). In addition to considerable body dissatisfaction and body distortion, studies report that eating-disordered females report much lower self-esteem than normal comparison groups (Baumeister, 1991b; Crowther & Chernyk, 1986; Gross & Rosen, 1988; Heatherton & Baumeister, 1991; Mintz & Betz, 1988; Mizes, 1988; Williamson et al., 1995). Baumeister and colleagues (Baumeister, 1990, 1991a) have developed the thesis that symptoms such as binge eating represent an attempt to escape from unflattering images of oneself. Such an escape narrows one's attention and deconstructs normal cognitive functioning, which in turn disengages normal inhibitions about overeating. There is considerable evidence that eating-disordered women experience depression in addition to low self-esteem (Bennett, Borgen, & Spoth, 1987; Crowther & Chernyk, 1986; Gross & Rosen, 1988; Heatherton & Baumeister, 1991; Kaye, Gwirtsman, George, Weiss, & Jimerson, 1986; Mizes, 1988; Vanderheyden, Fekken, & Boland, 1988). Such a finding is not surprising given the inextricable link between low self-esteem and depression, a topic to which we next turn.

Depression

There is clear historical precedent for including negative self-evaluations as one of a constellation of symptoms experienced in depression, beginning with Freud's (1968) observations of the low self-esteem displayed by adults suffering from depressive disorders. Those within the psychoanalytic tradition have continued to afford low self-esteem a central role in depression (Bibring, 1953; Blatt, 1974; Malmquist, 1983). More recently, a number of theorists who have addressed the manifestations of depression in children and adolescents, as well as adults, have focused heavily on cognitive components involving the self. For example, attention has been drawn to the role of *self-deprecatory ideation, low self-esteem,* and *hopelessness* in depression (Abramson, Metalsky, & Alloy, 1989; Battle, 1987; Baumeister, 1990; Beck, 1975; Greenberg, Pyszczynski, & Solomon, 1995; Hammen & Goodman-Brown, 1990; King, Naylor, Segal, Evans, & Shain, 1993; Kovacs & Beck, 1978, 1986), to *attributional style* (Abramson, Seligman, & Teasdale, 1986; Blaine & Crocker, 1993; Nolen-Hoeksema, Girus, & Seligman, 1986; Seligman, 1975; Seligman & Peterson, 1986), *self-complexity* (Linville, 1987), *pessimism* (Carver & Scheier, 1991), and *self-discrepancies* (Bandura, 1990; Baumeister, 1990; Carver & Scheier, 1991; Harter, 1990a, 1993; Higgins, 1987;

Kaslow, Rehm, & Siegel, 1984; McCauley, Mitchell, Burke, & Moss, 1988).

In several models, there is a causal pathway from self-discrepancies (failure to live up to standards) to low self-esteem and depressed affect (e.g., Baumeister, 1990; Harter, 1990a). In Baumeister's model, failure to meet one's standards, coupled with intense self-awareness, leads to global dissatisfaction with the self and depressive affect. In an effort to escape from these painful negative self-evaluations, individuals narrow their attentional focus and cognitively "deconstruct," that is, dismantle logical thought processes. Such deconstruction in turn removes the typical inhibitions against suicidal behaviors, putting individuals at risk for terminating their lives.

In our own model (Harter, Marold, & Whitesell, 1992), failure to live up to one's standards is captured by the Jamesian discrepancy between perceived competence and the importance of success. In addition, we have included approval from peers and parents, in keeping with Cooley's (1902) looking-glass-self model. In earlier versions of the model, self-esteem was postulated to have a causal impact on depression. However, self-esteem and depressed affect are so highly related (rs from .72 to .80), as is general hopelessness, that it is impossible to statistically model their directionality. Thus, they have been combined into a depression composite. Empirical evidence reveals that the competence in domains of importance and approval from significant others strongly impact the depression composite, which in turn is highly predictive of suicidal ideation. Issues of directionality continue to intrigue and plague theorists and researchers. We have determined, through interview procedures probing into the phenomenological experience of the directionality of self-esteem and depressed affect, that about half of adolescents report that low self-esteem precedes or causes depressed affect, whereas the remaining half report that they first experience depressed affect that then ushers in feelings of low self-esteem (Harter & Jackson, 1993; Harter & Marold, 1993). Moreover, there are systematic correlates of each directionality orientation.

Higgins's (1991) model also identifies failure to meet standards set for the self, although he does not posit global self-esteem as an intervening variable. He provides evidence that discrepancies between one's ideal self, in the form of what one would *like* to be (in contrast to what one thinks one "ought" to be), and the perception of one's real self produce dejection-related emotions such as depression. Of interest are findings by Ogilvie and Clark (1992),

who report that while such real/ideal discrepancies do predict depressive affect, discrepancies between real and *undesired* selves are even more predictive. These authors argue that undesired selves are more securely established markers for assessing present-day well-being than ideal selves because they are more likely to have actually been experienced.

A number of investigators report that girls are more at risk than boys for negative self-evaluative patterns that may serve as precursors to depressive reactions, particularly beginning in adolescence (see Dweck & Leggett, 1988; Nolen-Hoeksema, 1987, 1990; Nolen-Hoeksema & Girgus, 1994; Petersen, Sarigiani, & Kennedy, 1991; Ruble, Greulich, Pomerantz, & Gochberg, 1993). These authors review evidence pointing to a number of socialization factors. Because many girls are socialized to be concerned with pleasing others, failure to meet externally imposed standards may lead to more evaluation anxiety. Girls also experience more socialization pressure to conform to adult standards and values, making the experience of failure more likely. In addition, standards imposed by others undermine mastery motivation, which in turn limits opportunities for learning and success (see also Deci & Ryan, 1995). Moreover, girls are more likely to be monitored, and their activities outside the home are more likely to be restricted, further precluding mastery opportunities that are more available to boys, who are allowed more independence. The authors cited above also provide evidence that cultural stereotypes of dependency, passivity, and helplessness for females (in contrast to competence, confidence, control, and power for males), further exacerbate this pattern.

Nolen-Hoeksema and Girgus (1994) suggest that these risk factors in childhood predispose females to depression in the face of the greater challenges they face, compared to boys, during adolescence. It is at this point in development that the incidence of depressive reactions for females begins to exceed that for males (see also Brooks-Gunn & Petersen, 1991; Nolen-Hoeksema, 1990; Rutter, 1986; Weissman & Klerman, 1977). In addition to those factors identified above, they note that females are more likely to base their self-esteem on the approval of others, which puts them at risk for depression. Such reliance limits the control over a sense of personal well-being, a factor that places the individual at increased risk for depression (e.g., Abramson et al., 1989). Findings reviewed by Nolen-Hoeksema and Girgus reveal that females are more likely than males to endorse more helpless, self-defeating attributions. These authors also report that females are more likely to engage in rumination that is also predictive of depressive symptoms. In addition, adolescent girls react more negatively than do boys to increases in body fat and weight gain, and such body dissatisfaction also contributes to depressive reactions (Brooks-Gunn, 1988; Rierdan, Koff, & Stubbs, 1988, 1989). Other stressors facing some adolescent girls are sexual abuse, rape, and unwanted advances (see also reviews by Harter, in press-b; Putnam, 1993; Westen, 1993, which describe the deleterious effects of abuse on both I-self and Me-self processes). Nolen-Hoeksema and Girgus conclude that the greater number of risk factors for girls interacts with these biological and social challenges at adolescence, leading to the emergence of substantial gender differences in depression.

Implications for Intervention

One arena for interventions with children and adolescents has been the school system, where educational programs have been designed to maintain or enhance academic self-concept and global self-esteem. The goals of these different educational programs reflect two competing orientations toward change. As Caslyn and Kenny (1977) have noted, "self-enhancement" theorists believe that efforts should focus on enhancing self-concept and self-esteem directly, for example, by giving students affectively based exercises that encourage them to feel good about themselves in general. In contrast, "skill" theorists argue that attitudes about the self are consequences of successful achievement, and thus pedagogical efforts should be directed toward enhancing specific academic skills. In recent years, the pendulum has clearly shifted toward the skill-learning orientation in which interventions are directed toward specific domains.

Elsewhere (Harter, 1988a), I have suggested the usefulness of distinguishing between the *goal* of a program (e.g., enhanced self-esteem) and the *target* of our interventions, arguing that while self-esteem enhancement may be a goal, one's intervention strategies should be directed toward its *determinants*. For example, our own model identifies two general antecedents: competence in domains of importance (from James) and approval from significant others (from Cooley). Within this framework, interventions to enhance self-esteem should strive to reduce the competence/importance discrepancy and either find routes to increase approval from significant others or provide compensatory support figures from whom the child or adolescent can

garner more positive regard. Based on the lack of the success of the more general, affectively based programs in the 1960s and 1970s, it appears that efforts to enhance the child's self-worth *directly* will have little impact, particularly given certain developmental factors that will preclude the effectiveness of such a strategy (see Harter, 1988a, in press-d).

Others have offered similar arguments. Greenberg et al. (1995) hypothesize that by encouraging the acquisition of skills and creative achievement, such activities may, as a by-product, result in more stable, high self-esteem. In his meta-analysis of a variety of program interventions, Hattie (1992) concludes that cognitively based programs are consistently and significantly more effective than affectively based programs (see also Strein, 1988). Hattie suggests that the cognitively oriented interventions target smaller, more definable goals that are also more amenable to measurement. Marsh (Craven, Marsh, & Debus, 1991; Marsh & Hattie, 1996; Marsh & Peart, 1988) shares this perspective, noting that interventions directed at impacting particular domains, and that are assessed at the domain-specific level, will be the most successful. For example, in his own work, he finds that academic interventions have substantial effects on the academic components of the self-concept but little effect on nonacademic components and vice versa. Bracken (1995) has also argued that the lack of success of certain intervention programs is due to the fact that global self-concept is insufficiently sensitive to specific treatments. Thus, he recommends interventions that directly address the various self-concept components. Given the hierarchical nature of both the Marsh and Bracken models, one would infer that global self-concept at the apex would be enhanced as well, although not to the same degree.

Other theorists such as Damon (1995) and Seligman (1993) have also argued against the direct global self-enhancement position. Each suggests that efforts to enhance self-esteem to promote school achievements have been misguided. However, they adopt a more radical stance on the issue of the importance of global self-esteem. It is Damon's contention that self-esteem has been overrated as a commodity, and that the effusive praise that parents or teachers heap on children to make them feel good is often viewed with suspicion by children and interferes with the goal of building specific skills in the service of genuine achievement. Seligman further argues that low self-esteem is merely an epiphenomenon, a reflection that "one's commerce with the world is going badly," with little explanatory power in and of itself.

At one level, self-esteem would appear to have little explanatory power because as a mediator, it has been causally implicated in so many different child and adolescent problem behaviors, including depression and suicide, eating disorders, antisocial behaviors and delinquency (most recently gang membership), and teen pregnancy (see Mecca, Smelser, & Vasconcellos, 1989, who review evidence on the links between self-esteem and these problem behaviors). Knowing that a child or adolescent has low self-esteem, therefore, will not allow us to predict which *particular* outcome will ensue. However, in our zeal for parsimonious explanatory models, we must not ignore the fact that the *phenomenological* self-theory as experienced by children, adolescents, and adults is not necessarily parsimonious. Self-representations and self-evaluative judgments appear as very salient constructs in one's working model of self and as such wield powerful influences on affect and behavior. Thus, the challenge is to develop models that identify the specific antecedents of different outcomes but preserve the role of self-representations as phenomenological mediators.

In the spirit of more specific interventions, Hattie (1992) also suggests that providing the child with realistic expectancies that are somewhat higher than the individual's actual level of accomplishment may lead to achievements that in turn will enhance the domain-relevant sense of efficacy and self-concept (cf., Bandura, 1990). Thus, both the agentic sense of the I-self as well as the self-evaluative component of the Me-self can be affected. Others have targeted those *attributional* variables that affect one's sense of self and that are implicated in depression. For example, external attributions in which others are seen as responsible for one's successes or blamed for one's failures will impede self-concept change (Gold, 1994; Tice, 1994), as will internal attributions for negative events that are global and stable because they are associated with depressed affect and low self-esteem (Seligman & Peterson, 1986). Thus, strategies in which there is a cognitive/verbal reframing of one's attributions, shifting to global, stable, internal attributions for one's successes, have been suggested as another form of intervention (see Pope, McHale, & Craighead, 1988; Seligman, 1993). These suggestions are consistent with the findings of Grusec and colleagues (e.g., Grusec & Redler, 1980), who observed that children who attribute their prosocial behavior to a trait were found to engage in more prosocial behavior than those who attributed the same behavior to external factors (see also Eisenberg, Cialdini, McCreath, & Shell, 1987, who link

children's views on the value of consistency to prosocial behaviors).

As discussed in the previous section, perceptions of one's attractiveness are inextricably tied to self-esteem as well as depression. Interventions in this domain are admittedly challenging. Pope et al. (1988) offer a number of suggestions. Consistent with the attributional literature, they feel it is important to shift the individual's attribution away from stable and global attributions about unattractiveness ("I'm ugly, and will always be ugly"; "I'm ugly and therefore worthless"). Although they suggest that some counseling around dress and hygiene may be appropriate, they do not recommend cosmetic overhauls that pander to the ideals of attractiveness touted in the media. Rather, they suggest that interventionists communicate the fact that such ideals are virtually unattainable, and therefore individuals should alter the standards for what they should look like. From a Jamesian perspective, reducing the discrepancy between one's ideal body image and one's perceptions of one's looks should serve to bolster self-esteem. Pope et al. also recommend cognitive restructuring such that individuals shift their focus from concerns about appearance to other domains (academic, athletic, interpersonal, or moral) where they are, or can be, more successful. Another reframing intervention is inherent in our own findings on the perceived directionality of link between appearance and self-esteem (Harter, 1993). Those who feel that their appearance is a determinant of their self-esteem are particularly at risk for low self-esteem and depression. Thus, efforts should attempt to shift such individuals to the perception that qualities leading to the approval of their *inner* self as a worthwhile person will lead to their acceptance of their *outer* self, namely, how they think they look.

A number of other types of interventions have been recommended along the spectrum from educational programs to more formal therapies (see the chapter contributions in Brinthaupt & Lipka, 1994). For example, on the educational front, Beane (1994) describes the "ecological" approach, in which one attempts to alter features of the broader school environment such that it provides a more self-enhancing atmosphere (e.g., shifting from an emphasis on external control to self-direction). More specific therapeutic approaches have been based on cognitive therapy (e.g., Beck, 1976; Seligman, 1993), rational therapy (Ellis, 1958; Zastrow, 1994), and psychoanalytic interventions (e.g., Wexler, 1991) based upon the formulation of Kohut (1977).

A major problem with many intervention efforts is their failure to employ an adequate program evaluation strategy. Elsewhere, I have enumerated suggestions to bolster assessment efforts (Harter, 1990c, in press-d), a few of which are summarized here: (a) select instruments that specifically tap the constructs that are the targets of the intervention and that have sound psychometric properties (see also Hattie, 1992); (b) attempt to specify a *pattern* of predictions, indicating what outcomes should be affected and what outcomes should *not* be affected, including sensitive measures of each (see also Marsh & Hattie, 1996); (c) include measures of the actual *processes* thought to be responsible for self-concept change; (d) rather than expect overall mean gains, identify subgroups who may and may not profit from the intervention, attempting to identify the factors leading to these different outcomes. There may exist marvelous intervention programs whose efficacy has not been demonstrated due to the failure to include appropriate assessment and data analytic strategies.

Autonomy and Connectedness

Much of the content of this chapter has presented a very Western view of the self. Constructs such as self-concept, self-esteem, self-verification, self-enhancement, self-affirmation, and so on, all make reference to goals that involve the maintenance of positive self-evaluations for the *individual*. As many have observed (e.g., Guisinger & Blatt, 1993; Jordan, 1991; Kim & Berry, 1933; Markus & Kityama, 1991; Sampson, 1988), the Western view of self emphasizes separateness, autonomy, independence, individualism, and distinctness. In contrast, most non-Western societies have adopted a more sociocentric ideal in which self-definition is deeply embedded in the matrix of social relationships and obligations.

Shweder and colleagues (Shweder, 1991; Shweder & Bourne, 1982; Shweder & Miller, 1991) have made the distinction between *egocentric* and *sociocentric* cultures, giving the United States and India as respective examples of each. The Western self emerges in a context that values the privacy, autonomy, and freedom of the individual and where personhood is more abstract. In contrast, in societies such as India, the person is regulated by strict rules of interdependence that are context-specific and particularistic. These cultural differences are associated with differences in the nature of self-descriptions (Shweder & Miller, 1991). In India, such descriptions focus on behavioral acts that are context-dependent, namely, situated in time and place (e.g., "I bring cakes to my family on festival days"). Americans, however, emphasize situation-free personality traits and dispositional factors (e.g., "I am friendly").

Triandis (1989a, 1989b) builds upon a similar distinction between *individualistic* and *collectivist* cultures (introduced by Hsu, 1983) and discusses implications for the salience of private versus public selves. In individualistic cultures, the individual is the basic unit of society, personal goals are valued over group goals, and there is an emphasis on privacy and autonomy. In collectivist societies, such as Japan and China, priority is given to the goals of the ingroup whose belief systems one shares; within this ingroup, obedience and harmony are demanded. Triandis observes that in individualistic cultures, the private self is more salient than the public self; however, there is greater overlap between these two selves given the values of frankness and honesty. In collectivist cultures, the public self is more likely to be on display, and there is a greater disparity between public and private selves because the individual presents socially desirable attributes that may be very different from one's "true" self behind the mask (Doi, 1986; see also Hart & Edelstein, 1992, who have provided similar cross-cultural analyses).

In focusing more specifically on how the self is construed in such cultures, Markus and Kityama (1991) have distinguished between *independent* and *interdependent* conceptions of self. The former, which characterizes the Western self, locates crucial representations *within* the individual, where salient identities are quite distinct from those of others. In an interdependent self system (e.g., among the Japanese), individuals are not defined by their uniqueness but by their social connectedness to others (see also Cousins, 1989). Markus and Kityama's analysis extends to the cognitive, emotional, and motivational consequences of the culturally dependent construal of self. For example, they observe that unlike English, the Japanese language contains emotion concepts that refer specifically to relational issues (Doi, 1973).

The distinction between individuality and connectedness has also been applied to differences in the self system of men and women. Within the gender literature, a number of women theorists have challenged the individualistic conceptualizations of development and adaptation, models that were put forth *by* men and were primarily applicable *to* men (Chodorow, 1978; Gilligan, 1982; Miller, 1986). As Miller observes, the notion of the "self" that we inherited does not appear to characterize women's experience. For Gilligan, issues involving interpersonal connection and the ethics of caregiving were conspicuously absent in the traditional male-dominated psychological models. These and other writers have pointed to gender differences in self-definition. Men's sense of worth is closely linked to autonomy and the sense of personal accomplishment, whereas women emphasize connectedness and sensitivity to others (Eagly, 1987; Josephs, Markus, & Tafarodi, 1992; Miller, 1986; Oyserman & Markus, 1993). Gilligan and colleagues (Gilligan, Lyons, & Hanmer, 1989) and Rubin (1985) further describe the liabilities of the different orientations adopted by women and men. Given the importance to women of connectedness, they are threatened by separation and have difficulty with individuation. In contrast, men are less likely to form close relationships and are threatened by intimacy and connectedness.

Chodorow (1978) has offered a developmental perspective on the origins of such gender differences. She has argued that the greater individuality of males stems from the fact that the young boy is driven to create boundaries between himself and his mother upon discovering that he is of a different sex and therefore must relinquish his earlier identification with the mother. In addition, a growing literature points to differences in the socialization of girls and boys, noting that girls are socialized to be cooperative, friendly, empathic, and obedient, whereas boys are socialized to be assertive, creative, confident, and independent (see Basow, 1992; Beale, 1994).

Certain researchers have directly identified the links between particular gender-related characteristics and self-esteem. For example, Block and Robins (1993) report that the ability to relate to others in an interpersonally positive manner promotes self-esteem in females, whereas lack of emotion, independence, and personal uninvolvement are more highly related to self-esteem in males. In their longitudinal study (ages 14–23) they find that males and females come to be more similar to one another over time (see also Pratt, Pancer, Hunsberger, & Manchester, 1990); however, the long-recognized basic interpersonal asymmetry is still observed. Block and Robins observe that females are still socialized to "get along," whereas males are socialized to "get ahead." In this same sample, Thorne and Michaelieu (1994) examined the memories of males and females with both low and high self-esteem at age 23. High self-esteem males recounted experiences in which they had successfully asserted themselves, whereas high self-esteem women recalled memories of wanting to help female friends. Low self-esteem men's memories focused on failures to avoid conflict or to establish intimate relationships with girlfriends, whereas low self-esteem women were concerned with failures to obtain approval or validation from friends.

Despite such findings, it would appear that the constructs of autonomy and connectedness have been dichotomized too sharply and have been too readily generalized to characterize the styles of men and women, respectively. Views of development that have focused solely on growth toward self-focused autonomy or the primacy of other-focused connection have each contributed to distortions about what constitutes healthy development. Thus, it is refreshing to observe the recent emphasis on healthy adaptation as an *integration* of autonomy and connectedness. A number of theorists and investigators of various periods of the life span are now arguing that a continuing developmental task involves individuation that is best achieved in a context of connectedness and ongoing transformations in relationships with significant others.

As observed in the section on infancy, there has been increasing dissatisfaction with formulations (e.g., Mahler's and those of earlier cognitive-developmentalists) that touted autonomy as the major developmental accomplishment of the first two years of life. In contrast, attachment theorists have emphasized how separation is facilitated by secure attachments. Stern (1985) places considerable emphasis on how the subjective self emerges from the context of intersubjective relatedness in which shared attention and intentions as well as affective attunement are key processes. Emde's (1988) concept of the we-self further underscores how reciprocal interactions between infant and caregiver lead to the development of shared meaning, serve to empower the infant, and aid in self-regulation.

A number of scholars who have focused on adolescence have also argued that concepts such as autonomy and connectedness should not be polarized. For example, Cooper, Grotevant, and colleagues (Cooper, Grotevant, & Condon, 1983; Grotevant & Cooper, 1986) emphasize that while one task of adolescence is to individuate from parents, another goal is to remain psychologically connected to the family in the process (see also Hill & Holmbeck, 1986). Deci and Ryan (1995) also observe that too often autonomy and relatedness are viewed as competing orientations. They argue that individuation during adolescence is facilitated not by detachment from parents but rather by continued emotional attachment. These themes have also been addressed in the work of Collins (1990) and of Allen, Hauser, Bell, and O'Connor (1994).

Blatt and colleagues (Blatt, 1990; Guisinger & Blatt, 1993) make a similar argument that can be applied to adulthood. They contend that both individuality and relatedness to others develop throughout the life span as a dialectical process. They review analyses that point to how our overemphasis on individualistic values has led to a number of liabilities, including alienation from others, narcissism, violence, and the devaluation of women. Blatt (1995) has also argued that an exaggeration of either relatedness or isolation of the self distinguishes different types of psychopathology: a distorted preoccupation with issues of interpersonal relatedness leads to what Blatt terms "anaclitic" disorders, whereas a preoccupation with issues involving isolation of the self leads to "introjective" disorders. Moreover, Blatt observes correspondences between these two orientations and the two types of insecure attachment, preoccupied and avoidant, respectively.

A similar perspective has been advanced by members of the Stone Center at Wellesley College (Jordan, 1991; Jordan et al., 1991; Miller, 1986). Their concept of "self-in-relation" makes reference to their conviction that the deepest sense of oneself is continuously formed in connection with others and is inextricably tied to growth within the relationship. Mutual empathy is a cornerstone. As Jordan (1991) observes, "In true empathic exchange, each is both object and subject, mutually engaged in affecting and being affected, knowing and being known" (p. 141). From this point of view, relatedness with others brings clarity and reality to the self.

Empirical efforts have built recently upon this tradition (Harter, Waters, Pettitt, et al., in press). We have introduced a trichotomy of adult relationship styles in which self-focused autonomy and other-focused connection are viewed as extremes. The third style, mutuality, represents an adaptive blend of autonomy and connectedness. Examining partner combinations, it was demonstrated that other-focused women with self-focused male partners fared the worst with regard to perceived validation by the partner and the ability to be their authentic self. Partners of both genders who display the style of mutuality reported the highest levels of validation and authentic-self behavior. Self-focused men paired with other-focused women, a stereotypic pattern described in the literature, fell in between. Thus, both extreme styles were associated with attributes that are self-limiting and which have, as correlates, lower self-esteem and a greater tendency toward depressed affect.

THE LIABILITIES OF SELF-DEVELOPMENT

At the outset of the chapter, it was observed that most contemporary self theorists have highlighted numerous positive functions that the self performs. However, as others have also noted, there are costs to development (Leahy, 1985), and new cognitive advances usher in potential vulnerabilities for the self system (Higgins, 1991). These liabilities are apparent at every level of development. For example, in infancy, the ability to differentiate the self from other dramatically reduces one's sense of omnipotence and control over others, leading to frustration, anxiety, and anger. With the development of language, making possible the construction of an autobiographical self, falsified self-representations that do not represent one's authentic experience can be constructed. The emergence of the cognitive ability to construct representational mappings leads to all-or-none thinking, such that in the face of failure or censure, young children may conclude that they are "all bad."

In middle childhood, the emerging ability to make social comparisons allows for the possibility that many who fall short of others will develop perceptions of incompetence and inadequacy. The capacity to construct ideal selves also makes possible discrepancies between the real and the ideal self that can threaten the self-system. The development of the concept of traits as relatively stable attributes of the self further exacerbates the tendency toward global negative judgments in the face of perceived failure. The increasing capacity for role taking will promote the awareness and subsequent internalization of the evaluations of significant others. However, if these evaluations are negative, this looking-glass-self process will contribute to lowered self-esteem. The related ability to criticize the self will also put one in jeopardy if self-judgments are unfavorable. Emerging cognitive abilities also scaffold the construction of a hierarchy of self-evaluations in which self-schemata at the apex (e.g., global self-esteem) are more resistant to change. If such schemata are negative, other liabilities such as depressive reactions may ensue.

During adolescence, the emergence of introspection, self-consciousness, and self-reflection may also pose threats to the self system. Moreover, with the advent of abstract mappings in middle adolescence, the individual may revert to all-or-none thinking as well as experience conflict between proliferating multiple selves. This multiplicity, in turn, provokes concern and confusion over which is the real self. Furthermore, if the true self is not accepted by significant others, false-self behavior will ensue, behavior that is associated with lower self-esteem and depressed affect.

These processes continue into adulthood, during which time self-evaluations for many become more stable. Unfavorable self-evaluations, resistant to change, will be associated with other negative outcomes such as depression. For those with unstable high self-esteem, other liabilities include preoccupation with the self and hostility, which may interfere with productivity and interpersonal relations with others. Excessive overestimation of one's capabilities also predisposes individuals to the risks of egoistic illusions that may negatively impact one's relationship with others. Finally, the adoption of either an overly autonomous or an overly connected self style with intimate partners may well lead to a sense of alienation or disconnection from both self and others. In the face of all of these potential liabilities, one can well appreciate why the self apparatus has also been provided with numerous processes to protect and enhance the self. Such functions may well be necessary given that development, by its very nature, poses challenges for individuals as they try to navigate a successful journey through the life span.

CONCLUSIONS

As we move toward the twenty-first century, the self is alive and well on many fronts. New life has been breathed into James's distinction between the I-self and the Me-self. Moreover, there has been increasing emphasis on how those changing cognitive processes that define the I-self as knower influence the nature of the Me-self, the self theory that is constructed at each developmental period. There has also been a resurgence of interest in the formulations of those symbolic interactionist and social self theorists, namely, Cooley, Mead, and Baldwin, who placed heavy emphasis on how interactive processes with caregivers shaped the developing self. Thus, concepts such as the looking-glass self (Cooley), the generalized other (Mead), and the bipolar self (Baldwin) have been granted new lifeblood. The developing individual has also been afforded a more *active* role in the construction of the self. For example, the original looking-glass-self models emphasized the relatively passive and unidirectional incorporation of the opinions of significant others. More recently, investigators have turned their attention to the individual's more active contribution to such a process. In addition to a more complex analysis of the antecedents of self-representations, there has been more focus on the *consequences* of self-evaluative judgments. Many of these efforts extend to pathological implications, for example, the role of negative evaluations observed in depressive and eating disorders, as well as to suggestions for intervention.

Although there are liabilities to self-development, the more positive *functions* of self processes have also been increasingly highlighted. Conceptualizations in which the self is postulated to organize experience, give direction to behavior, and provide psychological protection have proliferated. Moreover, the *structure* of the self has received increasing attention. Cognitive-developmentalists have suggested how developing cognitive structures impact the organization as well as the content of self-representations. Information-processing models have articulated self structures and processes with increasing specificity, particularly for the period of adulthood. Domain-specific models, in which self-concepts are viewed as more differentiated, have become increasingly popular. There has also been more emphasis on the creation of *multiple selves* appropriate to different relational contexts.

Affect has taken center stage in many conceptualizations of the self. Progress can also be observed in the greater emphasis on the *integration* of cognitive, social, and affective processes in self-development. Greater attention to *process* variables has expanded our understanding of the mechanisms and motivations underlying such phenomena as self-evaluation, self-presentation, self-enhancement, and self-monitoring. Moreover, across the life span, there has been a welcome shift away from formulations that tout autonomy as the desired, teleological end point of self-development and toward models emphasizing the dual goals of autonomy with connectedness.

Despite these advances, there is considerable future work to be accomplished. Many of the developmental analyses are still largely theoretical and descriptive, and they lack specificity as well as a solid, empirical foundation, particularly with regard to underlying mechanisms and transition rules. Although investigators of adult self processes have achieved a greater level of specificity, we know little about how such processes emerge developmentally. Across all developmental levels, much more attention should be given to contextual variables that impact self-representations. Finally, we need to be clear about why we should *care* about the self. That is, we need to document how self-representations have critical consequences in the everyday lives of children, adolescents, and adults, lest our efforts be misguided. These are the exciting challenges that face us in the future.

REFERENCES

Abramson, L. Y., Metalsky, G. I., & Alloy, L. B. (1989). Hopelessness and depression: A theory-based subtype of depression. *Psychological Review, 96,* 358–372.

Abramson, L. Y., Seligman, M. E. P., & Teasdale, J. D. (1986). Learned helplessness in humans: Critique and reformulation. In J. C. Coyne (Ed.), *Essential papers on depression* (pp. 106–138). New York: New York University Press.

Adams, G. R. (1982). Physical attractiveness. In A. G. Miller (Ed.), *In the eye of the beholder: Contemporary issues in stereotyping* (pp. 54–79). New York: Praeger.

Ainsworth, M. (1973). The development of infant-mother attachment. In B. Caldwell & H. Ricciuto (Eds.), *Review of child development research* (Vol. 3, pp. 1–94). Chicago: University of Chicago Press.

Ainsworth, M. (1974). Infant-mother attachment and social development: Socialization as a product of reciprocal responsiveness to signals. In M. Richards (Ed.), *The integration of the child into the social world* (pp. 99–135). Cambridge, MA: Cambridge University Press.

Allen, J. P., Hauser, S. T., Bell, K. L., & O'Connor, T. G. (1994). Longitudinal assessment of autonomy and relatedness in adolescent-family interactions as predictors of adolescent ego development and self-esteem. *Child Development, 64,* 179–194.

Allgood-Merten, B., Lewinsohn, P. M., & Hops, R. (1990). Sex differences and adolescent depression. *Journal of Abnormal Psychology, 99,* 55–63.

Alloy, L., & Abramson, L. (1979). Judgment of contingency in depressed and nondepressed students: Sadder but wiser? *Journal of Experimental Psychology, 108,* 441–485.

Allport, G. W. (1961). *Pattern and growth in personality.* New York: Holt, Rinehart and Winston.

Andersen, A. E. (1992). Diet vs. shape content of popular male and female magazines: A dose-response relationship to the incidence of eating disorders? *International Journal of Eating Disorders, 11(3),* 283–287.

Asarnow, J. R., & Bates, S. (1988). Depression in child psychiatric inpatients: Cognitive and attributional patterns. *Journal of Abnormal Child Psychology, 16,* 601–615.

Ashmore, R. D., & Ogilvie, D. M. (1992). He's such a nice boy . . . when he's with Grandma: Gender and evaluation in

self-with-other representations. In T. M. Brinthaupt & R. P. Lipka (Eds.), *The self: Definitional and methodological issues* (pp. 236–290). Albany: State University of New York Press.

Baldwin, J. M. (1895). *Mental development of the child and the race: Methods and processes.* New York: Macmillan.

Baldwin, J. M. (1906). *Mental development in the child and the race* (3rd ed.). New York: Kelley.

Banaji, M. R., & Prentice, D. A. (1994). The self in social contexts. In L. W. Porter & M. R. Rosenzweig (Eds.), *Annual review of psychology* (Vol. 45, pp. 297–325). New Haven, CT: Yale University Press.

Bandura, A. (1989). Self-regulation of motivation and action through internal standards and goal systems. In L. Pervin (Ed.), *Goal concepts in personality and social psychology* (pp. 19–86). Hillsdale, NJ: Erlbaum.

Bandura, A. (1990). Conclusion: Reflections on nonability determinants of competence. In R. J. Sternberg & J. Kolligian, Jr. (Eds.), *Competence considered* (pp. 316–352). New Haven, CT: Yale University Press.

Bandura, A. (1991). Self-regulation of motivation through anticipatory and self-regulatory mechanisms. In R. A. Dienstbier (Ed.), *Perspectives on motivation: Nebraska Symposium on Motivation* (Vol. 38, pp. 79–94). Lincoln: University of Nebraska Press.

Bannister, D., & Agnew, J. (1977). The child's construing of self. In J. Cole (Ed.), *Nebraska Symposium on Motivation* (pp. 99–125). Lincoln: University of Nebraska Press.

Barnes, E. J. (1980). The Black community as a source of positive self-concept for Black children: A theoretical perspective. In R. Jones (Ed.), *Black psychology* (pp. 123–147). New York: Harper & Row.

Basow, S. A. (1992). *Gender stereotypes and roles* (3rd ed.). Pacific Grove, CA: Brooks/Cole.

Bates, E. (1990). Language about me and you: Pronominal reference and the emerging concept of self. In D. Cicchetti & M. Beeghly (Eds.), *The self in transition: Infancy to childhood* (pp. 1–15). Chicago: University of Chicago Press.

Battle, J. (1987). Relationship between self-esteem and depression among children. *Psychological Reports, 60,* 1187–1190.

Baumeister, R. F. (1987). How the self became a problem: A psychological review of historical research. *Journal of Personality and Social Psychology, 52,* 163–176.

Baumeister, R. F. (1990). Suicide as escape from self. *Psychological Review, 97,* 90–113.

Baumeister, R. F. (1991a). *Escaping the self.* New York: Basic Books.

Baumeister, R. F. (1991b). *Meaning of life.* New York: Guilford Press.

Baumeister, R. F. (1993). Understanding the inner nature of low self-esteem: Uncertain, fragile, protective, and conflicted. In

R. F. Baumeister (Ed.), *Self-esteem: The puzzle of low self-regard* (pp. 201–218). New York: Plenum Press.

Baumeister, R. F., Tice, D. M., & Hutton, D. G. (1989). Self-presentational motivations and personality differences in self-esteem. *Journal of Personality, 57,* 547–579.

Baumgardner, A. H., Kaufman, C. M., & Levy, P. E. (1989). Regulating affect interpersonally: When low self-esteem leads to greater enhancement. *Journal of Personality and Social Psychology, 56,* 907–921.

Baumrind, D. (1989). Rearing competent children. In W. Damon (Ed.), *Child development today and tomorrow* (pp. 349–378). San Francisco: Jossey-Bass.

Beach, S. R. H., & Tesser, A. (1995). Self-esteem and the extended self-evaluation maintenance model: The self in social context. In M. H. Kernis (Ed.), *Efficacy, agency, and self-esteem* (pp. 145–168). New York: Plenum Press.

Beal, C. R. (1994). *Boys and girls: The development of gender roles.* New York: McGraw-Hill.

Beane, J. A. (1994). Cluttered terrain: The schools' interest in the self. In T. M. Brinthaupt & R. P. Lipka (Eds.), *Changing the self* (pp. 69–88). Albany: State University of New York Press.

Beck, A. T. (1975). *Depression: Causes and treatments.* Philadelphia: University of Pennsylvania Press.

Beck, A. T. (1976). *Cognitive therapy and the emotional disorders.* New York: New American Library.

Bem, S. (1985). Androgyny and gender schema theory. In T. B. Sonderegger (Ed.), *Nebraska Symposium on Motivation* (Vol. 32, pp. 179–236). Lincoln: University of Nebraska Press.

Bennett, N. A. M., Borgen, F. H., & Spoth, R. L. (1987). Bulimic symptoms in high school females: Prevalence and relationship with multiple measures of psychological health. *Journal of Community Psychology, 19*(1), 13–28.

Berndt, T. J. (in press). The social self-concept. In B. A. Bracken (Ed.), *Handbook of self-concept.* New York: Wiley.

Berscheid, E., Walster, E., & Bohrnstedt, G. (1973, November). Body image: The happy American body: A survey report. *Psychology Today,* 119–131.

Bertenthal, B. I., & Fischer, K. W. (1978). Development of self-recognition in the infant. *Developmental Psychology, 14,* 44–50.

Bibring, E. (1953). The mechanism of depression. In P. Greenacre (Ed.), *Affective disorders: Psychoanalytic contribution to their study* (pp. 61–92). New York: International Universities Press.

Birtchnell, S. A., Dolan, B. M., & Lacey, J. H. (1987). Body image distortion in non-eating disordered women. *International Journal of Eating Disorders, 6*(3), 385–391.

Blaine, B., & Crocker, J. (1993). Self-esteem and self-serving biases in reactions to positive and negative events: An integrative review. In R. F. Baumeister (Ed.), *Self-esteem: The puzzle of low self-regard* (pp. 55–81). New York: Plenum Press.

Blatt, S. J. (1974). Levels of object representation in anaclitic and introjective depression. *Psychoanalytic Study of the Child, 29,* 107–157.

Blatt, S. J. (1990). Interpersonal relatedness and self-definition: Two personality configurations and their implications for psychopathology and psychotherapy. In J. L. Singer (Ed.), *Repression and dissociation: Implications for personality theory, psychopathology and health* (pp. 299–335). Chicago: University of Chicago Press.

Blatt, S. J. (1995). Representational structures in psychopathology. In D. Cicchetti & S. Toth (Eds.), *Rochester Symposium on Developmental Psychopathology: Emotion, cognition, and representation* (Vol. 6, pp. 1–35). Rochester, NY: University of Rochester Press.

Bleiberg, E. (1984). Narcissistic disorders in children. *Bulletin of the Menninger Clinic, 48,* 501–517.

Block, J., & Robins, R. W. (1993). A longitudinal study of consistency and change in self-esteem from early adolescence to early adulthood. *Child Development, 64,* 909–923.

Blos, P. (1962). *On adolescence.* New York: Free Press.

Blyth, D. A., Simmons, R. G., & Carlton-Ford, S. (1983). The adjustment of early adolescents to school transitions. *Journal of Early Adolescence, 3,* 105–120.

Bowlby, J. (1979). *The making and breaking of affectional bonds.* London: Tavistock.

Bowlby, J. (1980). *Attachment and loss: Vol. 3. Loss, sadness, and depression.* New York: Basic Books.

Bowlby, J. (1982). *Attachment and loss: Vol. 1. Attachment.* New York: Basic Books. (Original work published 1969)

Bracken, B. (1996). Clinical applications of a context-dependent multi-dimensional model of self-concept. In B. Bracken (Ed.), *Handbook of self-concept* (pp. 463–505). New York: Wiley.

Breckler, S. J., & Greenwald, A. G. (1982). *Charting coordinates for the self-concept in multidimensional trait space.* Paper presented at the symposium, Functioning and Measurement of Self-Esteem, American Psychological Association, Washington, DC.

Bretherton, I. (1987). New perspectives on attachment relations: Security, communication, and internal working models. In J. D. Osofsky (Ed.), *Handbook of infant development* (2nd ed., pp. 1061–1100). New York: Wiley.

Bretherton, I. (1991). Pouring new wine into old bottles: The social self as internal working model. In M. R. Gunnar & L. A. Sroufe (Eds.), *Self processes and development: The Minnesota*

Symposia on Child Development (Vol. 23, pp. 1–42). Hillsdale, NJ: Erlbaum.

Bretherton, I. (1993). For dialogue to internal working models: The co-construction of self in relationships. In R. Nelson (Ed.), *Memory and effect development: The Minnesota Symposia on Child Development* (Vol. 26, pp. 71–97). Hillsdale, NJ: Erlbaum.

Briere, J. (1992). *Child abuse trauma: Theory and treatment of the lasting effects.* Newbury Park, CA: Sage.

Brim, O. B. (1976). Life span development of the theory of oneself: Implications for child development. In H. W. Reese (Ed.), *Advances in child development and behavior* (Vol. 11, pp. 82–103). New York: Academic Press.

Brinthaupt, T. M., & Lipka, R. P. (Eds.). (1994). *Changing the self: Philosophies, techniques, and experiences.* Albany: State University of New York Press.

Brooks-Gunn, J. (1988). Antecedents and consequences of variations in girls' maturational timing. *Journal of Adolescent Health Care, 9,* 365–373.

Brooks-Gunn, J., & Petersen, A. C. (1983). *Girls at puberty: Biological and psychological perspectives.* New York: Plenum Press.

Brooks-Gunn, J., & Petersen, A. C. (1991). Studying the emergence of depression and depressive symptoms during adolescence. *Journal of Youth and Adolescence, 20,* 115–119.

Broughton, J. M. (1978). The development of the concepts of self, mind, reality, and knowledge. In W. Damon (Ed.), *Social cognition* (pp. 75–100). San Francisco: Jossey-Bass.

Broughton, J. M. (1981). The divided self in adolescence. *Human Development, 24,* 13–32.

Broughton, J. M. (1987). The psychology, history, and ideology of the self. In K. S. Larsen (Ed.), *Dialectics and ideology in psychology* (pp. 1–29). Norwood, NJ: ABLEX.

Brown, J. D. (1986). Evaluations of self and others: Self-enhancement biases in social judgments. *Social Cognition, 4,* 353–376.

Brown, J. D. (1993a). Motivational conflict and the self: The double-bind of low self-esteem. In R. F. Baumeister (Ed.), *Self-esteem: The puzzle of low self-regard* (pp. 117–127). New York: Plenum Press.

Brown, J. D. (1993b). Self-esteem and self-evaluation: Feeling is believing. In J. Suls (Ed.), *Psychological perspectives on the self* (Vol. 4, pp. 27–58). Hillsdale, NJ: Erlbaum.

Bruner, J. (1990). *Acts of meaning.* Cambridge, MA: Harvard University Press.

Buhrmester, D., & Furman, W. (1987). The development of companionship and intimacy. *Child Development, 58,* 1101–1113.

Butterworth, G. (1990). Self-perception in infancy. In D. Cicchetti & M. Beeghley (Eds.), *The self in transition: Infancy to childhood* (pp. 119–137). Chicago: University of Chicago Press.

Bynner, J. M., O'Malley, P. M., & Bachman, J. C. (1981). Self-esteem and delinquency revisited. *Journal of Youth and Adolescence, 10,* 407–441.

Byrne, B. M. (1995). Academic self-concept: Its structure, measurement, and relation with academic achievement. In B. A. Bracken (Ed.), *Handbook of self-concept* (pp. 287–316). New York: Wiley.

Campos, J., & Stenberg, C. (1980). Perception, appraisal, and emotion: The onset of social referencing. In M. Lamb & L. Sherrod (Eds.), *Infant social cognition* (pp. 273–314). Hillsdale, NJ: Erlbaum.

Cantor, N., & Mischel, W. (1979). Prototypes in person perception. In L. Berkowitz (Ed.), *Advances in experimental social psychology* (Vol. 12, pp. 3–52). New York: Academic Press.

Carroll, J. J., & Steward, M. S. (1984). The role of cognitive development in children's understandings of their own feelings. *Child Development, 55,* 1486–1492.

Carver, C. S., & Scheier, M. F. (1990). Origins and functions of positive and negative affect: A control-process. *Psychological Review, 97,* 19–35.

Carver, C. S., & Scheier, M. F. (1991). Self-regulation and the self. In J. Strauss & G. R. Goethals (Eds.), *The self: Interdisciplinary approaches* (pp. 168–207). New York: Springer-Verlag.

Case, R. (1985). *Intellectual development: Birth to adulthood.* New York: Academic Press.

Case, R. (1991). Stages in the development of the young child's first sense of self. *Developmental Review, 11,* 210–230.

Case, R. (1992). *The mind's staircase.* Hillsdale, NJ: Erlbaum.

Caslyn, R. J., & Kenny, D. A. (1977). Self-concept of ability and perceived evaluation of others: Cause or effect of academic achievement? *Journal of Educational Psychology, 69,* 136–145.

Cassidy, J. (1988). Child-mother attachment and the self at age six. *Child Development, 57,* 331–337.

Cassidy, J. (1990). Theoretical and methodological considerations in the study of attachment and the self in young children. In M. T. Greenberg, D. Cicchetti, & E. M. Cummings (Eds.), *Attachment in the preschool years: Theory, research, and intervention* (pp. 87–120). Chicago: University of Chicago Press.

Cassidy, J., & Kobak, R. R. (1988). Avoidance and its relationship to other defensive processes. In J. Belsky & T. Nezworski (Eds.), *Clinical implications of attachment* (pp. 300–326). Hillsdale, NJ: Erlbaum.

Cavior, N., & Lombardi, D. A. (1973). Developmental aspects of judgment of physical attractiveness in children. *Developmental Psychology, 8*(1), 67–71.

Chodorow, N. (1978). *The reproduction of mothering.* Berkeley: University of California Press.

Cicchetti, D. (1990). The organization and coherence of socio-emotional, cognitive, and representational development: Illustrations through a developmental psychopathology perspective on Down syndrome and child maltreatment. In R. Thompson (Ed.), *Nebraska Symposium on Motivation: Socioemotional development* (Vol. 36, pp. 266–375). Lincoln: University of Nebraska Press.

Cicchetti, D. (1991). Fractures in the crystal: Developmental psychopathology and the emergence of self. *Developmental Review, 11,* 271–287.

Cicchetti, D., & Beeghly, M. (1990). Perspectives on the study of the self in transition. In D. Cicchetti & M. Beeghly (Eds.), *The self in transition: Infancy to childhood* (pp. 1–15). Chicago: University of Chicago Press.

Cohn, L. D., Adler, N. E., Irwin, C. E., Jr., Millstein, S. G., Kegeles, S. M., & Stone, G. (1987). Body-figure preferences in male and female adolescents. *Journal of Abnormal Psychology, 96*(3), 276–279.

Collins, W. A. (1990). Parent-child relationships in the transition to adolescence: Continuity and change in interaction, affect, and cognition. In R. Montemayor, G. R. Adams, & T. P. Gullota (Eds.), *From childhood to adolescence: A transitional period?* (Vol. 2, pp. 85–106). Newbury Park, CA: Sage.

Connell, J. P., Spencer, M. B., & Aber, J. L. (1994). Educational risk and resilience in African-American youth: Context, self, action, and outcomes in school. *Child Development, 65,* 493–506.

Connell, J. P., & Wellborn, J. G. (1991). Competence, autonomy, and relatedness: A motivational analysis of self-system processes. In M. R. Gunnar & L. A. Sroufe (Eds.), *Self processes and development: The Minnesota Symposium on Child Development* (Vol. 23, pp. 43–78). Hillsdale, NJ: Erlbaum.

Cooley, C. H. (1902). *Human nature and the social order.* New York: Charles Schribner's Sons.

Cooper, C. R., Grotevant, H. D., & Condon, S. M. (1983). Individuality and connectedness both foster adolescent identity formation and role taking skills. In H. D. Grotevant & C. R. Cooper (Eds.), *Adolescent development in the family: New directions for child development* (pp. 43–59). San Francisco: Jossey-Bass.

Cooper, R. P., & Aslin, R. N. (1990). Preference for infant-directed speech in the first month after birth. *Child Development, 61,* 1584–1595.

Coopersmith, S. (1967). *The antecedents of self-esteem.* San Francisco: Freeman.

Costanzo, P. R. (1991). Morals, mothers, and memories: The social context of developing social cognition. In R. Cohen &

R. Siegel (Eds.), *Context and development* (pp. 91–132). Hillsdale, NJ: Erlbaum.

Cousins, S. D. (1989). Culture and self-perception in Japan and the United States. *Journal of Personality and Social Psychology, 56,* 124–131.

Crain, R. M. (1996). The influences of age, race, and gender on child and adolescent multidimensional self-concept. In B. A. Bracken (Ed.), *Handbook of self-concept* (pp. 395–420). New York: Wiley.

Craven, R. G., Marsh, H. W., & Debus, R. (1991). Effects of internally focused feedback and attributional feedback on the enhancement of academic self-concept. *Journal of Educational Psychology, 83,* 17–26.

Crittenden, P. M. (1988). Relationships at risk. In J. Belsky & T. Nezworski (Eds.), *Clinical implications of attachment* (pp. 136–174). Hillsdale, NJ: Erlbaum.

Crittenden, P. M. (1990). Internal representational models of attachment relationships. *Infant Mental Health Journal, 11,* 259–277.

Crittenden, P. M. (1994). Peering into the black box: An exploratory treatise on the development of self in young children. In D. Cicchetti & S. L. Toth (Eds.), *Rochester Symposium on Developmental Psychopathology: Disorders and dysfunctions of the self* (Vol. 5, pp. 79–148). Rochester, NY: University of Rochester Press.

Crittenden, P. M., & DiLalla, D. (1988). Compulsive compliance: The development of an inhibitory coping strategy in infancy. *Journal of Abnormal Child Psychology, 16,* 585–599.

Cross, W. E. (1985). Black identity: Rediscovering the distinction between personal identity and reference group orientation. In M. B. Spencer, G. C. Brookings, & W. R. Allen (Eds.), *Beginnings: The social and affective development of Black children* (pp. 155–171). Hillsdale, NJ: Erlbaum.

Crowther, J. H., & Chernyk, B. (1986). Bulimia and binge eating in adolescent females: A comparison. *Addictive Behaviors, 11,* 415–424.

Damon, W. (1995). *Greater expectations: Overcoming the culture of indulgence in America's homes and schools.* New York: Free Press.

Damon, W., & Hart, D. (1988). *Self-understanding in childhood and adolescence.* New York: Cambridge University Press.

Davies, E., & Furnham, A. (1986). Body satisfaction in adolescent girls. *British Journal of Medical Psychology, 59,* 279–287.

Deci, E. L., & Ryan, R. M. (1987). The support of autonomy and the control of behavior. *Journal of Personality and Social Psychology, 53,* 1024–1037.

Deci, E. L., & Ryan, R. M. (1995). Human autonomy: The basis for true self-esteem. In M. H. Kernis (Ed.), *Efficacy, agency, and self-esteem* (pp. 31–46). New York: Plenum Press.

De La Ronde, C., & Swann, W. B., Jr. (1993). Caught in the crossfire: Positivity and self-verification strivings among people with low self-esteem. In R. F. Baumeister (Ed.), *Self-esteem: The puzzle of low self-regard* (pp. 147–161). New York: Plenum Press.

Demo, D. H., & Savin-Williams, R. C. (1992). Self-concept stability and change during adolescence. In R. P. Lipka & T. M. Brinthaupt (Eds.), *Self-perspectives across the life span* (pp. 116–150). Albany: State University of New York Press.

Doi, T. (1973). *Anatomy of dependence* (J. Bester, Trans.). Tokyo: Kodansha.

Doi, T. (1986). *The anatomy of conformity: The individual versus society.* Tokyo: Kodansha.

Donaldson, S. K., & Westerman, M. A. (1986). Development of children's understanding of ambivalence and causal theories of emotion. *Developmental Psychology, 22,* 622–655.

Dunn, J. (1988). *The beginnings of social understanding.* Cambridge, MA: Harvard University Press.

Dunn, J., Brown, J., & Beardsall, L. (1991). Family talk about feeling states and children's later understanding of others' emotions. *Developmental Psychology, 27,* 445–448.

Dunning, D. (1993). Words to live by: The self and definitions of social concepts and categories. In J. Suls (Ed.), *Psychological perspectives on the self* (pp. 99–126). Hillsdale, NJ: Erlbaum.

Dusek, J. B., & Flaherty, J. (1981). The development of the self during the adolescent years. *Monograph of the Society for Research in Child Development, 46*(Whole No. 191), 1–61.

Dweck, C. S. (1991). Self-theories and goals: Their role in motivation, personality and development. In R. Dienstbier (Ed.), *Nebraska Symposium on Motivation* (pp. 199–235). Lincoln: University of Nebraska Press.

Dweck, C. S., & Elliott, E. S. (1983). Achievement motivation. In P. H. Mussen (Series Ed.) & E. M. Hetherington (Vol. Ed.), *Handbook of child psychology: Vol. 4. Social and personality development* (pp. 643–691). New York: Wiley.

Dweck, C. S., & Leggett, E. L. (1988). A social-cognitive approach to motivation and personality. *Psychological Review, 95,* 256–273.

Eagly, A. (1987). *Sex differences in social behavior: A social role interpretation.* Hillsdale, NJ: Erlbaum.

Eccles, J. S., & Blumefeld, P. (1985). Classroom experiences and student gender: Are there differences and do they matter? In L. C. Wilkinson & C. B. Marrett (Eds.), *Gender influences in the classroom* (pp. 79–113). New York: Academic Press.

Eccles, J. S., & Midgley, C. (1989). Stage/environment fit: Developmentally appropriate classrooms for early adolescents. In R. Ames & C. Ames (Eds.), *Research on motivation in education* (Vol. 3, pp. 139–181). San Diego, CA: Academic Press.

Eccles, J. S., Midgley, C., & Adler, T. (1984). Grade-related changes in the school environment: Effects on achievement motivation. In J. G. Nicholls (Ed.), *The development of achievement motivation* (pp. 283–331). Greenwhich, CT: JAI Press.

Edelmann, R. J. (1987). *The psychology of embarrassment.* Chichester, England: Wiley.

Eisenberg, N. (1983). *Early descriptions of past experiences: Scripts as structure.* Princeton, NJ: Educational Testing Service.

Eisenberg, N., Cialdini, R. B., McCreath, J., & Shell, R. (1987). Consistency based compliance: When and why do consistency procedures have immediate effects? *Journal of Behavioral Development, 12,* 351–368.

Eisenberg, N., Fabes, R. A., Miller, P. A., Fultz, J., Shell, R., Mathy, R. M., & Reno, R. R. (1989). Relation of sympathy and personal distress to prosocial behavior: A multi-method study. *Journal of Personality and Social Psychology, 58,* 55–66.

Elkind, D. (1967). Egocentrism in adolescence. *Child Development, 38,* 1025–1034.

Elkind, D. (1979). Growing up faster. *Psychology Today, 12,* 38–45.

Ellis, A. (1958). Rational psychotherapy. *Journal of General Psychology, 58,* 35–49.

Emde, R. N. (1988). Development terminable and interminable: Innate and motivational factors from infancy. *International Journal of Psychoanalysis, 69,* 23–25.

Emde, R. N., Biringen, A., Clyman, R. B., & Oppenheim, D. (1991). The moral self of infancy: Affective core and procedural knowledge. *Developmental Review, 11,* 251–270.

Engel, M. (1959). The stability of the self-concept in adolescence. *Journal of Abnormal and Social Psychology, 58,* 211–217.

Epstein, S. (1973). The self-concept revisited or a theory of a theory. *American Psychologist, 28,* 405–416.

Epstein, S. (1981). The unity principle versus the reality and pleasure principles, or the tale of the scorpion and the frog. In M. D. Lynch, A. A. Norem-Hebeisen, & K. Gergen (Eds.), *Self-concept: Advances in theory and research* (pp. 82–110). Cambridge, MA: Ballinger.

Epstein, S. (1991). Cognitive-experiential self theory: Implications for developmental psychology. In M. R. Gunnar & L. A. Sroufe (Eds.), *Self processes and development: The Minnesota Symposium on Child Development* (Vol. 23, pp. 111–137). Hillsdale, NJ: Erlbaum.

Epstein, S., & Morling, B. (1995). Is the self motivated to do more than enhance and/or verify itself? In M. H. Kernis (Ed.), *Efficacy, agency, and self-esteem* (pp. 9–26). New York: Plenum Press.

Erikson, E. H. (1950). *Childhood and society.* New York: Norton.

Erikson, E. H. (1968). *Identity, youth, and crisis.* New York: Norton.

Fallon, A. E., & Rozin, P. (1985). Sex differences in perceptions of desirable body shape. *Journal of Abnormal Psychology, 94,* 102–105.

Feingold, A. (1992). Good-looking people are not what we think. *Psychological Bulletin, 111,* 304–341.

Feiring, C., & Taska, L. S. (1996). Family self-concept: Ideas on its meaning. In B. Bracken (Ed.), *Handbook of self-concept* (pp. 317–373). New York: Wiley.

Feldman, D. H. (1994). *Beyond universals in cognitive development* (2nd ed.). Norwood, NJ: ABLEX.

Felson, R. B. (1993). The (somewhat) social self: How others affect self-appraisals. In J. Suls (Ed.), *Psychological perspectives on the self* (Vol. 4, pp. 1–26). Hillsdale, NJ: Erlbaum.

Felson, R. B., & Zielinski, M. (1989). Children's self-esteem and parental support. *Journal of Marriage and the Family, 51,* 727–735.

Fernald, A., & Kuhl, P. K. (1987). Acoustic determinants of infant preference for motherese speech. *Infant Behavior and Development, 10,* 279–293.

Fischer, K. W. (1980). A theory of cognitive development: The control and construction of hierarchies of skills. *Psychological Review, 87,* 477–531.

Fischer, K. W., & Aboud, C. (1993). Affective splitting and dissociation in normal and maltreated children: Developmental pathways for self in relationships. In D. Cicchetti & V. Carlson (Eds.), *Child maltreatment: Theory and research on the causes and consequences of child abuse and neglect.* New York: Cambridge University Press.

Fischer, K. W., & Canfield, R. (1986). The ambiguity of stage and structure in behavior: Person and environment in the development of psychological structure. In I. Levin (Ed.), *Stage and structure: Reopening the debate* (pp. 246–267). New York: Plenum Press.

Fischer, K. W., Hand, H. H., Watson, M. W., Van Parys, M., & Tucker, J. (1984). Putting the child into socialization: The development of social categories in preschool children. In L. Katz (Ed.), *Current topics in early childhood education* (Vol. 5, pp. 27–72). Norwood, NJ: ABLEX.

Fischer, K. W., Shaver, P., & Carnochan, P. (1990). How emotions develop and how they organize development. *Cognition and Emotion, 4,* 81–127.

Fivush, R. (1987). Scripts and categories: Interrelationships in development. In U. Neisser (Ed.), *Concepts and conceptual development: Ecological and intellectual factors in categorization* (pp. 107–139). Cambridge, England: University of Cambridge Press.

Fivush, R., Gray, J. T., & Fromhoff, F. A. (1987). Two-year-olds talk about the past. *Cognitive Development, 2,* 393–409.

Fivush, R., & Hamond, N. R. (1990). Autobiographical memory across the preschool years: Toward reconceptualizing childhood amnesia. In R. Fivush & J. A. Hudson (Eds.), *Knowing and remembering in young children* (pp. 223–248). New York: Cambridge University Press.

Fivush, R., & Hudson, J. A. (Eds.). (1990). *Knowing and remembering in young children.* New York: Cambridge University Press.

Flavell, J. H. (1985). *Cognitive development* (2nd ed.). Englewood Cliffs, NJ: Prentice-Hall.

Flavell, J. H., Miller, P. H., & Miller, S. A. (1993). *Cognitive development* (3rd ed.). Englewood Cliffs, NJ: Prentice-Hall.

Franzoi, S. L., & Shields, S. A. (1984). The body esteem scale: Multidimensional structure and sex differences in a college population. *Journal of Personality Assessment, 48*(2), 173–178.

Freeman, M. (1992). Self as narrative: The place of life history in studying the life span. In T. M. Brinthaupt & R. P. Lipka (Eds.), *The self: Definitional and methodological issues* (pp. 15–43). Albany: State University of New York Press.

Freud, S. (1952). *A general introduction to psychoanalysis.* New York: Washington Square Press.

Freud, S. (1968). Mourning and melancholia. In J. Strachey (Ed.), *The standard edition of the complete works of Sigmund Freud* (Vol. 14, pp. 201–221). London: Hogarth Press. (Original work published 1917)

Frey, K. S., & Ruble, D. N. (1985). What children say when the teacher is not around: Conflicting goals in social comparison and performance assessment in the classroom. *Journal of Personality and Social Psychology, 48,* 550–562.

Frey, K. S., & Ruble, D. N. (1990). Strategies for comparative evaluation: Maintaining a sense of competence across the life span. In R. J. Sternberg & J. Kolligian, Jr. (Eds.), *Competence considered* (Vol. 7, pp. 167–189). New Haven, CT: Yale University Press.

Garner, D. M., Garfinkel, P. E., Schwartz, D., & Thompson, M. (1980). Cultural expectations of thinness in women. *Psychological Reports, 47,* 483–491.

Gecas, V. (1972). Parental behavior and contextual variations in adolescent self-esteem. *Sociometry, 36,* 332–345.

Gergen, K. J. (1967). To be or not to be the single self. In S. M. Journal (Ed.), *To be or not to be: Existential perspectives on the self* (pp. 62–91). Gainesville: University of Florida Press.

Gergen, K. J. (1968). Personal consistency and the presentation of self. In C. Gordon & J. Gergen (Eds.), *The self in social interaction* (pp. 299–308). New York: Wiley.

Gergen, K. J. (1982). From self to science: What is there to know? In J. Suls (Ed.), *Psychological perspectives on the self* (Vol. 1, pp. 129–149). Hillsdale, NJ: Erlbaum.

Gergen, K. J. (1991). *The saturated self.* New York: Basic Books.

Gergen, K. J., & Gergen, M. M. (1988). Narrative and the self as relationship. In L. Berkowitz (Ed.), *Advances in experimental social psychology* (Vol. 21, pp. 17–56). New York: Academic Press.

Gibson, E. J. (1993). Ontogenesis of the perceived self. In U. Neisser (Ed.), *The perceived self: Ecological and interpersonal sources of self-knowledge* (pp. 25–42). New York: Cambridge University Press.

Gibson, J. J. (1979). *The ecological approach to visual perception.* Boston: Houghton-Mifflin.

Gilligan, C. (1982). *In a different voice: Psychological theory and women's development.* Cambridge, MA: Harvard University Press.

Gilligan, C., Lyons, N., & Hanmer, T. J. (1989). *Making connections.* Cambridge, MA: Harvard University Press.

Glick, M., & Zigler, E. (1985). Self-image: A cognitive-developmental approach. In R. Leahy (Ed.), *The development of the self* (pp. 1–48). New York: Academic Press.

Gnepp, J., McKee, E., & Domanic, J. A. (1987). Children's use of situational information to infer emotion: Understanding emotionally equivocal situations. *Developmental Psychology, 23,* 114–123.

Gold, M. (1994). Changing the delinquent self. In T. M. Brinthaupt & R. P. Lipka (Eds.), *Changing the self* (pp. 89–108). Albany: State University of New York Press.

Graziano, W. G., & Ward, D. (1992). Probing the Big Five in adolescence: Personality and adjustment during a developmental transition. *Journal of Personality, 60,* 425–439.

Graziano, W. G., & Waschull, S. B. (1995). Social development and self-monitoring. In N. Eisenberg (Ed.), *Social development: Review of personality and social psychology* (Vol. 15, pp. 233–260). London: Sage.

Greenberg, J., Pyszczynski, T., & Solomon, S. (1995). Toward a dual-motive depth psychology of self and social behavior. In M. H. Kernis (Ed.), *Efficacy, agency, and self-esteem* (pp. 73–101). New York: Plenum Press.

Greenfeld, D., Quinlan, D. M., Harding, P., Glass, E., & Bliss, A. (1987). Eating behavior in an adolescent population. *International Journal of Eating Disorders, 6,* 99–111.

Greenier, K. D., Kernis, M. H., & Waschull, S. B. (1995). Not all high (or low) self-esteem people are the same: Theory and research on stability of self-esteem. In M. H. Kernis (Ed.), *Efficacy, agency, and self-esteem* (pp. 51–68). New York: Plenum Press.

Greenwald, A. G. (1980). The totalitarian ego: Fabrication and revision of personal history. *American Psychologist, 7,* 603–618.

Greenwald, A. G., & Pratkanis, A. R. (1984). The self. In R. S. Wyer & T. K. Srull (Eds.), *Handbook of social cognition* (Vol. 3, pp. 129–178). Hillsdale, NJ: Erlbaum.

Griffin, N., Chassin, L., & Young, R. D. (1981). Measurement of global self-concept versus multiple role-specific self-concepts in adolescents. *Adolescence, 16,* 49–56.

Griffin, S. (1992). Structural analysis of the development of their inner world: A neo-structural analysis of the development of intrapersonal intelligence. In R. Case (Ed.), *The mind's staircase* (pp. 123–146). Hillsdale, NJ: Erlbaum.

Gross, J., & Rosen, J. C. (1988). Bulimia in adolescents: Prevalence and psychosocial correlates. *International Journal of Eating Disorders, 7*(1), 51–61.

Grotevant, H. D., & Cooper, C. R. (1986). Individuation in family relationships. *Human Development, 29,* 83–100.

Grusec, J. E., & Redler, E. (1980). Attribution, reinforcement, and altruism: A developmental analysis. *Developmental Psychology, 16,* 525–535.

Guardo, C. J., & Bohan, J. B. (1971). Development of a sense of self-identity in children. *Child Development, 42,* 1909–1921.

Guisinger, S., & Blatt, S. J. (1993). Individuality and relatedness: Evolution of a fundamental dialectic. *American Psychologist, 49,* 104–111.

Haltiwanger, J. (1989, April). *Behavioral referents of presented self-esteem in young children.* Paper presented at the meeting of the Society for Research in Child Development, Kansas City, MO.

Hammen, C., & Goodman-Brown, T. (1990). Self-schemas and vulnerability to specific life stress in children at risk for depression. *Cognitive Therapy and Research, 14,* 215–227.

Hare, B. R., & Castenell, L. A., Jr. (1985). No place to run, no place to hide: Comparative status and future prospects of Black boys. In M. B. Spencer, G. K. Brookings, & W. R. Allen (Eds.), *Beginnings: The social and affective development of Black children* (pp. 21–42). Hillsdale, NJ: Erlbaum.

Harris, P. L. (1983). What children know about the situations that provoke emotion. In M. Lewis & C. Saarni (Eds.), *The socialization of affect* (pp. 117–130). New York: Plenum Press.

Harris, P. L., Olthof, T., & Meerum-Terwogt, M. (1981). Children's knowledge of emotion. *Journal of Child Psychology and Psychiatry, 45,* 247–261.

Hart, D. (1988). The adolescent self-concept in social context. In D. K. Lapsley & F. C. Power (Eds.), *Self, ego, and identity* (pp. 71–90). New York: Springer-Verlag.

Hart, D., & Edelstein, W. (1992). Self-understanding development in cross-cultural perspective. In T. M. Brinthaupt &

R. P. Lipka (Eds.), *The self: Definitional and methodological issues* (pp. 291–322). Albany: State University of New York Press.

Hart, D., & Fegley, S. (1994). Social imitation and the emergence of a mental model of self. In S. T. Parker, R. W. Mitchell, & M. L. Boccia (Eds.), *Self-awareness in animals and humans* (pp. 149–165). New York: Cambridge University Press.

Hart, D., Fegley, S., & Brengelman, D. (1993). Perceptions of past, present and future selves among children and adolescents. *British Journal of Developmental Psychology, 11,* 265–282.

Hart, D., & Karmel, M. P. (in press). Self-awareness and self-knowledge in humans, apes, and monkeys. In A. Russon, K. Bard, & S. Parker (Eds.), *Reaching into thought.* New York: Cambridge University Press.

Harter, S. (1977). A cognitive-developmental approach to children's expression of conflicting feelings and a technique to facilitate such expression in play therapy. *Journal of Consulting and Clinical Psychology, 45,* 417–432.

Harter, S. (1982). The perceived competence scale for children. *Child Development, 53,* 87–97.

Harter, S. (1983). Developmental perspectives on the self-system. In P. H. Mussen (Series Ed.) & E. M. Hetherington (Vol. Ed.), *Handbook of child psychology: Vol. 4. Social and personality development* (4th ed., pp. 275–385). New York: Wiley.

Harter, S. (1985a). Competence as a dimension of self-evaluation: Toward a comprehensive model of self-worth. In R. Leahy (Ed.), *The development of the self* (pp. 55–122). New York: Academic Press.

Harter, S. (1985b). *The self-perception profile for children.* Unpublished manual, University of Denver, Denver, CO.

Harter, S. (1986a). Cognitive-developmental processes in the integration of concepts about emotions and the self. *Social Cognition, 4*(2), 119–151.

Harter, S. (1986b). Processes underlying the construction, maintenance, and enhancement of the self-concept in children. In J. Suls & A. G. Greenwald (Eds.), *Psychological perspectives on the self* (Vol. 3, pp. 137–181). Hillsdale, NJ: Erlbaum.

Harter, S. (1988a). Developmental and dynamic changes in the nature of the self-concept: Implications for child psychotherapy. In S. Shirk (Ed.), *Cognitive development and child psychotherapy* (pp. 119–160). New York: Plenum Press.

Harter, S. (1988b). *The self-perception profile for adolescents.* Unpublished manual, University of Denver, Denver, CO.

Harter, S. (1990a). Causes, correlates and the functional role of global self-worth: A life-span perspective. In J. Kolligian & R. Sternberg (Eds.), *Perceptions of competence and incompetence across the life-span* (pp. 67–98). New Haven, CT: Yale University Press.

Harter, S. (1990b). Adolescent self and identity development. In S. S. Feldman & G. R. Elliot (Eds.), *At the threshold: The developing adolescent* (pp. 352–387). Cambridge, MA: Harvard University Press.

Harter, S. (1990c). Issues in the assessment of the self-concept of children and adolescents. In A. La Greca (Ed.), *Childhood assessment: Through the eyes of a child* (pp. 292–325). New York: Allyn & Bacon.

Harter, S. (1993). Causes and consequences of low self-esteem in children and adolescents. In R. F. Baumeister (Ed.), *Self-esteem: The puzzle of low self-regard* (pp. 87–116). New York: Plenum Press.

Harter, S. (in press-a). Developmental changes in self-understanding across the 5 to 7 year shift. In A. Sameroff & M. Haith (Eds.), *Reason and responsibility: The passage through childhood.* Chicago: University of Chicago Press.

Harter, S. (in press-b). The effects of child abuse on the self-system. In B. B. Rossman & M. S. Rosenberg (Eds.), *Multiple victimization of children: Conceptual, developmental, research, and treatment issues.* New York: Haworth Press.

Harter, S. (in press-c). *The personal self in social context: Barriers to authenticity.* Rutgers Symposium on Self and Identity.

Harter, S. (in press-d). *Developmental approaches to self processes.* New York: Guilford Press.

Harter, S., & Bresnick, S. (1996). *Developmental and gender differences in role-related opposing attributes within the adolescent self-portrait.* Unpublished manuscript, University of Denver, Denver, CO.

Harter, S., & Buddin, B. J. (1987). Children's understanding of the simultaneity of two emotions: A five-stage developmental acquisition sequence. *Developmental Psychology, 23*(3), 388–399.

Harter, S., & Jackson, B. K. (1993). Young adolescents' perceptions of the link between low self-worth and depressed affect. *Journal of Early Adolescence, 33,* 383–407.

Harter, S., & Johnson, C. (1993). *Changes in self-esteem during the transition to college.* Unpublished manuscript, University of Denver, Denver, CO.

Harter, S., & Marold, D. B. (1993). The directionality of the link between self-esteem and affect: Beyond causal modeling. In D. Cicchetti & S. L. Toth (Eds.), *Rochester Symposium on Developmental Psychopathology: Disorders and dysfunctions of the self* (Vol. 5, pp. 333–370). Rochester, NY: University of Rochester Press.

Harter, S., Marold, D. B., & Whitesell, N. R. (1992). A model of psycho-social risk factors leading to suicidal ideation in young adolescents. *Development and Psychopathology, 4,* 167–188.

Harter, S., Marold, D. B., Whitesell, N. R., & Cobbs, G. (1996). A model of the effects of parent and peer support on adolescent false self behavior. *Child Development, 67,* 360–374.

Harter, S., & Monsour, A. (1992). Developmental analysis of conflict caused by opposing attributes in the adolescent self-portrait. *Developmental Psychology, 28*(2), 251–260.

Harter, S., & Pike, R. (1984). The pictorial scale of perceived competence and social acceptance for young children. *Child Development, 55,* 1969–1982.

Harter, S., Stocker, C., & Robinson, N. (1996). The perceived directionality of the link between approval and self-worth: The liabilities of a looking glass self orientation among young adolescents. *Journal of Adolescence, 6,* 285–308.

Harter, S., Waters, P. L., Pettitt, L., Whitesell, N., Kofkin, J., & Jordan, J. (in press). Autonomy and connectedness as dimensions of relationship styles in adult men and women. *Journal of Personal and Social Relations.*

Harter, S., Waters, P., & Whitesell, N. R. (in press). False self behavior and lack of voice among adolescent males and females. *Developmental Psychology.*

Harter, S., Waters, P., Whitesell, N. R., & Kastelic, D. (in press). Lack of voice as a manifestation of false self behavior among adolescents: The school setting as a stage upon which the drama of authenticity is enacted. *Educational Psychologist.*

Harter, S., Whitesell, N., & Kowalski, P. (1992). Individual differences in the effects of educational transitions on young adolescents' perceptions of competence and motivational orientation. *American Educational Research Journal, 29,* 777–808.

Hatfield, E., & Sprecher, S. (1986). *Mirror, mirror . . . The importance of appearance in everyday life.* New York: State University of New York Press.

Hattie, J. (1992). *Self-concept.* Hillsdale, NJ: Erlbaum.

Heatherton, T. F., & Ambady, N. (1993). Self-esteem, self-prediction, and living up to commitments. In R. F. Baumeister (Ed.), *Self-esteem: The puzzle of low self-regard* (pp. 131–142). New York: Plenum Press.

Heatherton, T. F., & Baumeister, R. F. (1991). Binge eating as escape from self-awareness. *Psychological Bulletin, 110,* 86–108.

Heatherton, T. F., & Polivy, J. (1991). Development and validation of a scale for measuring state self-esteem. *Journal of Personality and Social Psychology, 60,* 895–910.

Herman, J. (1992). *Trauma and recovery.* New York: Basic Books.

Hermans, H. J. M., Kempen, H. J. G., & van Loon, R. J. P. (1992). The dialogical self. *American Psychologist, 47,* 23–33.

Higgins, E. T. (1987). Self-discrepancy: A theory relating self and affect. *Psychological Review, 94,* 319–340.

Higgins, E. T. (1991). Development of self-regulatory and self-evaluative processes: Costs, benefits, and tradeoffs. In M. R. Gunnar & L. A. Sroufe (Eds.), *Self processes and development: The Minnesota Symposia on Child Development* (Vol. 23, pp. 125–166). Hillsdale, NJ: Erlbaum.

Higgins, E. T., & Bargh, J. A. (1987). Social cognition and social perception. *Annual Review of Psychology, 38,* 369–425.

Higgins, E. T., Van Hook, E., & Dorfman, D. (1988). So self-attributes form a cognitive structure? *Social Cognition, 6,* 177–207.

Hill, J. P., & Holmbeck, G. N. (1986). Attachment and autonomy during adolescence. In G. J. Whitehurst (Ed.), *Annals of child development* (Vol. 3, pp. 145–189). Greenwich, CT: JAI Press.

Hill, J. P., & Lynch, M. E. (1983). The intensification of gender-related role expectations during early adolescence. In J. Brooks-Gunn & A. C. Petersen (Eds.), *Girls at puberty* (pp. 201–228). New York: Plenum Press.

Horney, K. (1950). *Neurosis and human growth.* New York: Norton.

Howe, M. L., & Courage, M. L. (1993). On resolving the enigma of infantile amnesia. *Psychological Bulletin, 113,* 305–326.

Hsu, F. L. K. (1983). *Rugged individualism reconsidered.* Knoxville: University of Tennessee Press.

Hudson, J. A. (1990a). Constructive processes in children's autobiographical memory. *Developmental Psychology, 26,* 180–187.

Hudson, J. A. (1990b). The emergence of autobiographical memory in mother-child conversation. In R. Fivush & J. A. Hudson (Eds.), *Knowing and remembering in young children* (pp. 166–196). New York: Cambridge University Press.

Iheanacho, S. O. (1988). Minority self-concept: A research review. *Journal of Instructional Psychology, 15,* 3–11.

Jackson, L. A. (1992). *Physical appearance and gender: Sociobiological and sociocultural perspectives.* New York: State University of New York Press.

Jacobs, D. H. (1983). Learning problems, self-esteem, and delinquency. In J. E. Mack & S. L. Ablon (Eds.), *The development and sustenance of self-esteem in childhood* (pp. 209–222). New York: International Universities Press.

James, W. (1890). *Principles of psychology.* Chicago: Encyclopedia Britannica.

James, W. (1892). *Psychology: The briefer course.* New York: Henry Holt.

John, O. P., & Robbins, R. W. (1994). Accuracy and bias in self-perception: Individual differences in self-enhancement and the role of narcissism. *Journal of Personality and Social Psychology, 66,* 206–219.

Johnson, C., & Harter, S. (1995). *The effect of the transition to college on students' self-esteem.* Unpublished manuscript, University of Denver, Denver, CO.

Jones, E. E., Rhodewalt, E., Berglas, S., & Skelton, J. A. (1981). Effect of strategic self presentation in subsequent self-esteem. *Journal of Personality and Social Psychology, 41,* 407–421.

Jordan, J. V. (1991). The relational self: A new perspective for understanding women's development. In J. Strauss & G. Goethals (Eds.), *The self: Interdisciplinary approaches* (pp. 136–149). New York: Springer-Verlag.

Jordan, J. V., Kaplan, A. G., Miller, J. B., Stiver, J. L., & Surrey, L. P. (Eds.). (1991). *Women's growth in connection.* New York: Guilford Press.

Josephs, R. A., Markus, H., & Tafarodi, R. W. (1992). Gender differences in the source of self-esteem. *Journal of Personality and Social Psychology, 63,* 391–402.

Juhasz, A. M. (1992). Significant others in self-esteem development: Methods and problems in measurement. In T. M. Brinthaupt & R. P. Lipka (Eds.), *The self: Definitional and methodological issues* (pp. 204–235). Albany: State University of New York Press.

Jung, C. G. (1928). *Two essays on analytical psychology.* New York: Dodd, Mead.

Kagan, J. (1981). *The second year: The emergence of self-awareness.* Cambridge, MA: Harvard University Press.

Kagan, J. (1984). *The nature of the child.* New York: Basic Books.

Kagan, J. (1991). The theoretical utility of constructs for self. *Devlopmental Review, 11,* 244–250.

Kaplan, H. (1980). *Deviant behavior in defense of self.* New York: Academic Press.

Kaslow, N. J., Rehm, L. P., & Siegel, A. W. (1984). Social-cognitive and cognitive correlates of depression in children. *Journal of Abnormal Child Psychology, 12,* 605–620.

Kaye, W. H., Gwirtsman, H. E., George, D. T., Weiss, S. R., & Jimerson, D. C. (1986). Relationship of mood alterations to bingeing behaviour in bulimia. *British Journal of Psychiatry, 149,* 479–485.

Keith, L. K., & Bracken, B. A. (1996). Self-concept instrumentation: An historical and evaluative review. In B. A. Bracken (Ed.), *Handbook of self-concept* (pp. 91–170). New York: Wiley.

Kelly, G. A. (1955). *The psychology of personal constructs.* New York: Norton.

Kenny, D. (1988). Interpersonal perception: A social relations analysis. *Journal of Social and Personal Relationships, 5,* 247–261.

Kernis, M. H. (1993). The roles of stability and level of self-esteem in psychological functioning. In R. F. Baumeister (Ed.), *Self-esteem: The puzzle of low self-regard* (pp. 167–180). New York: Plenum Press.

Kernis, M. H., Cornell, D. P., Sun, C., Berry, A., & Harlow, T. (1993). There's more to self-esteem than whether it is high or low: The importance of stability of self-esteem. *Journal of Personality and Social Psychology, 65*(6), 1190–1204.

Kihlstrom, J. F. (1993). What does the self look like? In T. K. Srull & R. S. Wyer, Jr. (Eds.), *The mental representation of trait and autobiographical knowledge about the self: Advances in social cognition* (Vol. 5, pp. 79–90). Hillsdale, NJ: Erlbaum.

Kihlstrom, J. F., & Cantor, N. (1984). Mental representations of the self. In L. Berkowitz (Ed.), *Advances in experimental social psychology* (Vol. 17, pp. 2–40). New York: Academic Press.

Kilbourne, J. (1994). Still killing us softly: Advertising and the obsession with thinness. In P. Fallon, M. Katzman, & S. Wooley (Eds.), *Feminist perspectives on eating disorders* (pp. 395–418). New York: Guilford Press.

Kim, U., & Berry, J. W. (1993). *Indigenous psychologies: Research and experience in cultural context.* Newbury Park, CA: Sage.

Kinch, J. W. (1963). A formalized theory of the self-image. *American Journal of Sociology, 74,* 251–258.

King, C. A., Naylor, M. W., Segal, H. G., Evans, T., & Shain, B. N. (1993). Global self-worth, specific self-perceptions of competence, and depression in adolescents. *Journal of the American Academy of Child and Adolescent Psychiatry, 32,* 745–752.

Klein, S. B., & Kihlstrom, J. F. (1986). Elaboration, organization, and the self-reference effect in memory. *Journal of Experimental Psychology: General, 115,* 26–38.

Kohut, H. (1977). *The restoration of the self.* New York: International Universities Press.

Kolligian, J., Jr. (1990). Perceived fraudulence as a dimension of perceived incompetence. In R. J. Sternberg & J. Kolligian, Jr. (Eds.), *Competence considered* (pp. 261–285). New Haven, CT: Yale University Press.

Korabik, K., & Pitt, E. J. (1980). Self concept, objective appearance and profile self perception. *Journal of Applied Social Psychology, 10*(6), 482–489.

Kovacs, M., & Beck, A. T. (1978). Maladaptive cognitive structures in depression. *American Journal of Psychiatry, 135,* 525–533.

Kovacs, M., & Beck, A. T. (1986). Maladaptive cognitive structures in depression. In J. C. Coyne (Ed.), *Essential papers on depression* (pp. 212–239). New York: New York University Press.

Kuiper, N. A. (1981). Convergent evidence for the self as a proto-type: The "inverted-URT effect" for self and other judgments. *Personality and Social Psychology Bulletin, 7,* 438–443.

Lamborn, S. D., Mounts, N. S., Steinberg, L., & Dornbusch, S. M. (1991). Patterns of competence and adjustment among adolescents from authoritative, authoritarian, indulgent, and neglectful families. *Child Development, 62,* 1049–1065.

Lamborn, S. D., & Steinberg, L. (1993). Emotional autonomy redux: Revisiting Ryan and Lynch. *Child Development, 64,* 483–499.

Langlois, J. H. (1981). Beauty and the beast: The role of physical attractiveness in the development of peer relations and social behavior. In S. S. Brehm, S. M. Kassin, & F. X. Gibbons (Eds.), *Developmental social psychology: Theory and research* (pp. 47–63). New York: Oxford University Press.

Lapsley, D. K., & Rice, K. (1988). The "New Look" at the imaginary audience and personal fable: Toward a general model of adolescent ego development. In D. K. Lapsley & F. C. Power (Eds.), *Self, ego, and identity: Integrative approaches* (pp. 109–129). New York: Springer-Verlag.

Leahy, R. L. (1985). The costs of development: Clinical implications. In R. L. Leahy (Ed.), *The development of the self* (pp. 267–294). New York: Academic Press.

Leahy, R. L., & Shirk, S. R. (1985). Social cognition and the development of the self. In R. L. Leahy (Ed.), *The development of the self* (pp. 123–150). New York: Academic Press.

Leary, M. R., & Downs, D. L. (1995). Interpersonal functions of the self-esteem motive: The self-esteem system as a sociometer. In M. H. Kernis (Ed.), *Efficacy, agency, and self-esteem* (pp. 123–140). New York: Plenum Press.

Lecky, P. (1945). *Self-consistency: A theory of personality.* New York: Island Press.

L'Ecuyer, R. (1992). An experiential-developmental framework and methodology to study the transformations of the self-concept from infancy to old age. In T. M. Brinthaupt & R. P. Lipka (Eds.), *The self: Definitional and methodological issues* (pp. 96–136). Albany: State University of New York Press.

Lenerz, K., Kucher, J. D., East, P. L., Lerner, J. V., & Lerner, R. M. (1987). Early adolescents' physical organismic characteristics and psychosocial functioning: Findings from the Pennsylvania Early Adolescent Transition Study. In R. M. Lerner & T. T. Foch (Eds.), *Biological-psychosocial interactions in early adolescence* (pp. 212–239). Hillsdale, NJ: Erlbaum.

Lerner, R. M., & Brackney, B. E. (1978). The importance of inner and outer body parts attitudes in the self-concept of late adolescents. *Sex Roles, 4,* 225–238.

Lerner, R. M., & Karabenick, S. A. (1974). Physical attractiveness, body attitudes, and self-concept in late adolescents. *Journal of Youth and Adolescence, 3,* 307–316.

Lerner, R. M., Karabenick, S. A., & Stuart, J. L. (1973). Relations among physical attractiveness, body attitudes, and self-concept in male and female college students. *Journal of Psychology, 85,* 119–129.

Lerner, R. M., Orlos, J. B., & Knapp, J. R. (1976). Physical attractiveness, physical effectiveness, and self-concept in late adolescents. *Adolescence, 11,* 313–326.

Lewinsohn, P. M., Mischel, W., Chaplain, W., & Barton, R. (1980). Social competence and depression: The role of illusory self-perceptions. *Journal of Abnormal Psychology, 89,* 203–212.

Lewis, M. (1991). Ways of knowing: Objective self-awareness or consciousness. *Developmental Review, 11,* 231–243.

Lewis, M. (1994). Myself and me. In S. T. Parker, R. W. Mitchell, & M. L. Boccia (Eds.), *Self-awareness in animals and humans: Developmental perspectives* (pp. 20–34). New York: Cambridge University Press.

Lewis, M., Allesandri, S. M., & Sullivan, M. W. (1992). Differences in shame and pride as a function of children's gender and task difficulty. *Child Development, 63,* 630–638.

Lewis, M., & Brooks-Gunn, J. (1979). *Social cognition and the acquisition of self.* New York: Plenum Press.

Lifton, R. J. (1993). *The protean self.* New York: Basic Books.

Linville, P. W. (1987). Self-complexity as a cognitive buffer against stress-related illness and depression. *Journal of Personality and Social Psychology, 52,* 663–676.

Lipka, R. P., Hurford, D. P., & Litten, M. J. (1992). Self in school: Age and school experience effects. In R. P. Lipka & T. M. Brinthaupt (Eds.), *Self-perspectives across the life span* (Vol. 3, pp. 93–115). Albany: State University of New York Press.

Logan, R. D. (1987). Historical change in prevailing sense of self. In K. Yardley & T. Honess (Eds.), *Self and identity: Psychological perspectives* (pp. 222–241). Chicester, England: Wiley.

Longo, L. C., & Ashmore, R. D. (1995). The looks-personality relationship: Self-orientations as shared precursors of subject physical attractiveness and self-ascribed traits. *Journal of Applied Social Psychology, 25,* 371–398.

Maccoby, E. (1980). *Social development.* New York: Wiley.

Maccoby, E., & Martin, J. (1983). Socialization in the context of the family: Parent-child interaction. In P. H. Mussen (Series Ed.) & E. M. Heatherington (Vol. Ed.), *Handbook of child psychology: Vol. 4. Socialization, personality and social development* (pp. 1–102). New York: Wiley.

Mack, J. E. (1983). Self-esteem and its development: An overview. In J. E. Mack & S. L. Ablong (Eds.), *The development and sustaining of self-esteem* (pp. 1–44). New York: International Universities Press.

Mahler, M. S. (1965). On the significance of the normal separation-individuation phase: With reference to research in symbiotic child psychosis. In M. Schur (Ed.), *Drives, affects, behavior* (Vol. 2, pp. 161–169). New York: International Universities Press.

Mahler, M. S. (1967). On human symbiosis and the vicissitudes of individuation. *Journal of the American Psychoanalytic Association, 15,* 740–763.

Mahler, M. S. (1968). *On human symbiosis and the vicissitudes of individuation: Vol. 1. Infantile psychosis.* New York: International Universities Press.

Main, M., Kaplan, N., & Cassidy, J. (1985). Security in infancy, childhood, and adulthood: A move to the level of representation. In I. Bretherton & E. Waters (Eds.), Growing points in attachment theory and research. *Monographs of the Society for Research in Child Development, 50*(1/2, Serial No. 209), 66–104.

Main, M., & Solomon, J. (1990). Procedures for identifying infants as disorganized/disoriented during the Ainsworth Strange Situation. In M. Greenberg, D. Cicchetti, & M. Cummings (Eds.), *Attachment during the preschool years: Theory, research, and intervention* (pp. 121–160). Chicago: University of Chicago Press.

Malmquist, C. P. (1983). The functioning of self-esteem in childhood depression. In J. E. Mack & S. L. Ablong (Eds.), *The development and sustenance of self-esteem in childhood* (pp. 189–208). New York: International Universities Press.

Maloney, M. J., McGuire, J. B., & Daniels, S. R. (1988). Reliability testing of a children's version of the Eating Attitude Test. *Journal of the American Academy of Child and Adolescent Psychiatry, 27,* 541–543.

Markus, H. (1977). Self-schemata and processing information about the self. *Journal of Personality and Social Psychology, 35,* 63–78.

Markus, H. (1980). The self in thought and memory. In D. M. Wegner & R. R. Vallacher (Eds.), *The self in social psychology* (pp. 42–69). New York: Oxford University Press.

Markus, H., & Cross, S. (1990). The interpersonal self. In L. A. Pervin (Ed.), *Handbook of personality: Theory and research* (pp. 576–608). New York: Guilford Press.

Markus, H., Cross, S., & Wurf, E. (1990). The role of the self-system in competence. In R. J. Sternberg & J. Kolligian, Jr. (Eds.), *Competence considered* (pp. 205–226). New Haven, CT: Yale University Press.

Markus, H., & Kityama, S. (1991). Culture and the self: Implications for cognition, emotion, and motivation. *Psychological Review, 98,* 224–253.

Markus, H., & Kunda, Z. (1986). Stability and malleability of the self-concept. *Journal of Personality and Social Psychology, 51,* 858–866.

Markus, H., & Nurius, P. (1986). Possible selves. *American Psychologist, 41,* 954–969.

Markus, H., & Sentis, K. (1982). The self in social information processing. In J. Suls (Ed.), *Social psychological perspectives on the self* (Vol. 1, pp. 41–70). Hillsdale, NJ: Erlbaum.

Markus, H., & Wurf, E. (1987). The dynamic self-concept: A social psychological perspective. In M. R. Rosenweig & L. W. Porter (Eds.), *Annual Review of Psychology, 38,* 299–337.

Marsh, H. W. (1986). Global self-esteem: Its relation to specific facets of self-concept and their importance. *Journal of Personality and Social Psychology, 51,* 1224–1236.

Marsh, H. W. (1987). The hierarchical structure of self-concept and the application of hierarchical confirmatory factor analysis. *Journal of Educational Measurement, 24,* 17–19.

Marsh, H. W. (1989). Age and sex effects in multiple dimensions of self-concept: Preadolescence to early adulthood. *Journal of Educational Psychology, 81,* 417–430.

Marsh, H. W. (1990). The structure of academic self-concept: The Marsh/Shavelson model. *Journal of Educational Psychology, 82,* 623–636.

Marsh, H. W. (1993). Academic self-concept: Theory, measurement, and research. In J. Suls (Ed.), *Psychological perspectives on the self* (Vol. 4, no. 3, pp. 59–98). Hillsdale, NJ: Erlbaum.

Marsh, H. W., Byrne, B. M., & Shavelson, R. J. (1992). A multidimensional, hierarchical self-concept. In T. M. Brinthaupt & R. P. Lipka (Eds.), *The self: Definitional and methodological issues* (pp. 44–95). Albany: State University of New York Press.

Marsh, H. W., & Hattie, J. (1996). Theoretical perspectives on the structure of self-concept. In B. A. Bracken (Ed.), *Handbook of self-concept* (pp. 38–90). New York: Wiley.

Marsh, H. W., Parker, J., & Barnes, J. (1985). Multidimensional adolescent self-concepts: Their relationship to age, sex, and academic measures. *American Educational Research Journal, 22,* 422–444.

Marsh, H. W., & Peart, N. (1988). Competitive and cooperative physical fitness training programs for girls: Effects on physical fitness and on multidimensional self-concepts. *Journal of Sport and Exercise Psychology, 10,* 390–407.

Marsh, H. W., Smith, I. D., Marsh, M. R., & Owens, L. (1988). The transition from single-sex to coeducational high schools: Effects on multiple dimensions of self-concept and on academic achievement. *American Educational Research Journal, 25,* 237–269.

Maslow, A. H. (1954). *Motivation and personality.* New York: Harper & Row.

Mathes, E. W., & Kahn, A. (1975). Physical attractiveness, happiness, neuroticism, and self-esteem. *Journal of Psychology, 90,* 27–30.

McAdams, D. (in press). The unity of identity. In R. D. Ashmore & L. Jussim (Eds.), *The Rutgers Symposium on Self and Social Identity.*

McCarthy, J., & Hoge, D. (1982). Analysis of age effects in longitudinal studies of adolescent self-esteem. *Developmental Psychology, 18,* 372–379.

McCaulay, M., Mintz, L., & Glenn, A. A. (1988). Body image, self-esteem, and depression proneness: Closing the gender gap. *Sex Roles, 18*(7/8), 381–391.

McCauley, E., Mitchell, J. R., Burke, P., & Moss, S. (1988). Cognitive attributes of depression in children and adolescents. *Journal of Consulting and Clinical Psychology, 56,* 903–908.

McGuire, W. (1981). The spontaneous self-concept as affected by personal distinctiveness. In A. A. Norem-Hebeisen & M. Lynch (Eds.), *Self-concept* (pp. 211–239). Cambridge, MA: Ballinger.

Mead, G. H. (1925). The genesis of the self and social control. *International Journal of Ethics, 35,* 251–273.

Mead, G. H. (1934). *Mind, self, and society from the standpoint of a social behaviorist.* Chicago: University of Chicago Press.

Mecca, A. M., Smelser, N. J., & Vasconcellos, J. (Eds.). (1989). *The social importance of self-esteem.* Berkeley: University of California Press.

Mellin, L. M. (1988). Responding to disordered eating in children and adolescents. *Nutrition News, 51,* 5–7.

Meltzoff, A. N. (1990). Foundations for developing a concept of self: The role of imitation in relating self to other and the value of social mirroring, social modeling, and self practice in infancy. In D. Cicchetti & M. Beeghly (Eds.), *The self in transition: Infancy to childhood* (pp. 139–164). Chicago: University of Chicago Press.

Meltzoff, A. N., & Moore, M. K. (1983). Newborn infants imitate adult facial gestures. *Child Development, 54,* 702–709.

Meltzoff, A. N., & Moore, M. K. (1985). Cognitive foundations and social functions of imitation and intermodal representation in infancy. In J. Mehler & R. Fox (Eds.), *Neonate cognition: Beyond the blooming, buzzing confusion* (pp. 139–156). Hillsdale, NJ: Erlbaum.

Meltzoff, A. N., & Moore, M. K. (1989). Imitation in newborn infants: Exploring the range of gestures imitated and the underlying mechanisms. *Developmental Psychology, 25,* 954–962.

Messer, B., & Harter, S. (1989). *The self-perception profile for adults.* Unpublished manual, University of Denver, Denver, CO.

Miller, J. B. (1986). *Toward a new psychology of women* (2nd ed.). Boston: Beacon Press.

Miller, P. J., Potts, R., Fung, H., Hoogstra, L., & Mintz, J. (1990). Narrative practices and the social construction of self in childhood. *American Ethnologist, 17,* 292–311.

Mintz, L. B., & Betz, N. E. (1988). Prevalence and correlates of eating disordered behaviors among undergraduate women. *Journal of Counseling Psychology, 35*(4), 463–471.

Mischel, W. (1973). Toward a cognitive social learning reconceptualization of personality. *Psychological Review, 80,* 252–283.

Mizes, J. S. (1988). Personality characteristics of bulimic and non-eating-disordered female controls: A cognitive behavioral perspective. *International Journal of Eating Disorders, 7*(4), 541–550.

Montemayor, R., & Eisen, M. (1977). The development of self-conceptions from childhood to adolescence. *Developmental Psychology, 13,* 314–319.

Moretti, M. M., & Higgins, E. T. (1990). The development of self-esteem vulnerabilities: Social and cognitive factors in developmental psychopathology. In R. J. Sternberg & J. Kolligian, Jr. (Eds.), *Competence considered* (pp. 286–314). New Haven, CT: Yale University Press.

Mullener, N., & Laird, J. D. (1971). Some developmental changes in the organization of self-evaluations. *Developmental Psychology, 5,* 233–236.

Nadler, A., & Fischer, J. D. (1986). The role of threat to self-esteem and perceived control in recipient reaction to help: Theory development and empirical validation. In L. Berkowitz (Ed.), *Advances in experiental social psychology* (Vol. 19, pp. 81–122). San Diego, CA: Academic Press.

Neemann, J., & Harter, S. (1987). *The self-perception profile for college students.* Unpublished manual, University of Denver, Denver, CO.

Neisser, U. (1991). Two perceptually given aspects of the self and their development. *Developmental Review, 11,* 197–209.

Neisser, U. (1993). The self perceived. In U. Neisser (Ed.), *The perceived self: Ecological and interpersonal sources of self-knowledge* (pp. 3–24). New York: Cambridge University Press.

Nelson, K. (1986). *Event knowledge: Structure and function in development.* Hillsdale, NJ: Erlbaum.

Nelson, K. (Ed.). (1989). *Narratives from the crib.* Cambridge, MA: Harvard University Press.

Nelson, K. (1990). Remembering, forgetting, and childhood amnesia. In R. Fivush & J. A. Hudson (Eds.), *Knowing and remembering in young children* (pp. 301–316). New York: Cambridge University Press.

Nelson, K. (1993). Events, narratives, memory: What develops? In C. A. Nelson (Ed.), *Memory and affect. Minnesota Symposia on Child Psychology* (Vol. 26, pp. 1–24). Hillsdale, NJ: Erlbaum.

Nemeroff, C. J., Stein, R. I., Diehl, N. S., & Smilack, K. M. (1994). From the Cleavers to the Clintons: Role choices and body orientation as reflected in magazine article content. *International Journal of Eating Disorders, 16*(2), 167–176.

Nicholls, J. G. (1990). What is ability and why are we mindful of it? A developmental perspective. In R. J. Sternberg & J. Kolligian, Jr. (Eds.), *Competence considered* (pp. 11–40). New Haven, CT: Yale University Press.

Nikkari, D., & Harter, S. (1993). *The antecedents of behaviorally-presented self-esteem in young children.* Unpublished manuscript, University of Denver, Denver, CO.

Nolen-Hoeksema, S. (1987). Sex differences in unipolar depression: Evidence and theory. *Psychological Bulletin, 101,* 259–282.

Nolen-Hoeksema, S. (1990). *Sex differences in depression.* Stanford, CA: Stanford University Press.

Nolen-Hoeksema, S., & Girgus, J. S. (1994). The emergence of gender differences in depression during adolescence. *Psychological Bulletin, 115,* 424–443.

Nolen-Hoeksema, S., Girgus, J. S., & Seligman, M. E. P. (1986). Learned helplessness in children: A longitudinal study of depression, achievement, and explanatory style. *Journal of Personality and Social Psychology, 51,* 435–442.

Nottelmann, E. D. (1987). Competence and self-esteem during the transition from childhood to adolescence. *Developmental Psychology, 23,* 441–450.

Ogilvie, D. M., & Clark, M. D. (1992). The best and worst of it: Age and sex differences in self-discrepancy research. In R. P. Lipka & T. M. Brinthaupt (Eds.), *Self-perspectives across the life span* (pp. 186–222). Albany: State University of New York Press.

O'Malley, P., & Bachman, J. (1983). Self-esteem: Change and stability between ages 13 and 23. *Developmental Psychology, 19,* 257–268.

Oosterwegel, A., & Oppenheimer, L. (1993). *The self-system: Developmental changes between and within self-concepts.* Hillsdale, NJ: Erlbaum.

Overton, W. (1994). The arrow of time and the cycle of time: Concepts of change, cognition, and embodiment. *Psychological Inquiry, 5,* 215–237.

Oyserman, D., & Markus, H. R. (1993). The sociocultural self. In J. Suls (Ed.), *Psychological perspectives on the self* (Vol. 7, pp. 187–220). Hillsdale, NJ: Erlbaum.

Padin, M. A., Lerner, R. M., & Spiro, A. (1981). Stability of body attitudes and self-esteem in late adolescents. *Adolescence, 62,* 371–384.

Parsons, J., & Ruble, D. (1977). Developmental changes in attributions of descriptive concepts to persons. *Journal of Personality and Social Psychology, 48,* 1075–1079.

Pascual-Leone, J. (1988). Organismic processes for neo-Piagetian theories: A dialectical causal account of congitive development. In A. Demetrious (Ed.), *The neoPiagetian theories of cognitive development: Toward an integration* (pp. 25–65). Amsterdam, The Netherlands: North-Holland/Elsevier.

Paulhus, D. L. (1985). Self-deception and impression management in test responses. In A. Angleitner & J. S. Wiggins (Eds.), *Personality assessment via questionnaires* (pp. 251–278). New York: Spinger-Verlag.

Pekrun, R. (1990). Social support, achievement evaluations, and self-concepts in adolescence. In L. Oppenheimer (Ed.), *The self-concept: European perspectives on its development, aspects, and applications* (pp. 107–119). Berlin: Springer.

Pelham, B. W. (1993). On the highly positive thoughts of the highly depressed. In R. F. Baumeister (Ed.), *Self-esteem: The puzzle of low self-regard* (pp. 183–196). New York: Plenum Press.

Pelham, B. W., & Swann, W. B., Jr. (1989). From self-conceptions to self-worth: On the sources and structure of global self-esteem. *Journal of Personality and Social Psychology, 57,* 672–680.

Petersen, A. C., Sarigiani, P. A., & Kennedy, R. (1991). Adolescent depression: Why more girls? *Journal of Youth and Adolescence, 20,* 247–271.

Phillips, D. A., & Zimmerman, M. (1990). The developmental course of perceived competence and incompetence among competent children. In R. J. Sternberg & J. Kolligian, Jr. (Eds.), *Competence considered* (pp. 41–66). New Haven, CT: Yale University Press.

Piaget, J. (1932). *The moral judgment of the child.* New York: Harcourt, Brace, & World.

Piaget, J. (1960). *The psychology of intelligence.* Patterson, NJ: Littlefield, Adams.

Piers, E. V., & Harris, D. B. (1964). Age and other correlates of self-concept in children. *Journal of Educational Psychology, 55,* 91–95.

Pillemer, D. B., & White, S. H. (1989). Childhood events recalled by children and adults. In H. W. Reese (Ed.), *Advances in child development and behavior* (Vol. 21, pp. 297–340). San Diego, CA: Academic Press.

Pipp, S. (1990). Sensorimotor and representational internal working models of self, other, and relationship: Mechanisms of connection and separation. In D. Cicchetti & M. Beeghly (Eds.), *The self in transition: Infancy to childhood* (pp. 243–264). Chicago: University of Chicago Press.

Pipp, S. (1993). Infants' knowledge of self, other, and relationship. In U. Neisser (Ed.), *The perceived self: Ecological and interpersonal sources of self-knowledge* (pp. 41–62). Cambridge, MA: Cambridge University Press.

Pipp, S., Easterbrooks, M. A. M., & Harmon, R. J. (1992). The relation between attachment and knowledge of self and mother in one- to three-year-old infants. *Child Development, 63,* 738–750.

Plummer, D. L., & Graziano, W. G. (1987). Impact of grade retention on the social development of elementary school children. *Developmental Psychology, 23,* 267–275.

Pomerantz, E. V., Ruble, D. N., Frey, K. S., & Greulich, F. (1995). Meeting goals and confronting conflict: Children's changing perceptions of social comparison. *Child Development, 66,* 723–738.

Pomerantz, S. C. (1979). Sex differences in the relative importance of self esteem, physical self-satisfaction, and identity in predicting adolescent satisfaction. *Journal of Youth and Adolescence, 8*(1), 51–61.

Pope, A. W., McHale, S. M., & Craighead, W. E. (1988). *Self-esteem enhancement with children and adolescents.* Boston: Allyn & Bacon.

Powell, G. J. (1985). Self-concepts among Afro-American students in racially isolated minority schools: Some regional differences. *Journal of the American Academy of Child Psychiatry, 24,* 142–149.

Pratt, M. W., Pancer, M., Hunsberger, B., & Manchester, J. (1990). Reasoning about the self and relationships in maturity: An integrative complexity analysis of individual differences. *Journal of Personality and Social Psychology, 59*(3), 575–581.

Putnam, F. W. (1993). Dissociation and disturbances of the self. In D. Cicchetti & S. Toth (Eds.), *Disorders and dysfunctions of the self: Rochester Symposium on Developmental Psychopathology* (Vol. 5, pp. 251–266). Rochester, NY: University of Rochester Press.

Raciti, M. C., & Norcross, J. C. (1987). The EAT and EDI: Screening, interrelationships and psychometrics. *International Journal of Eating Disorders, 6*(4), 579–586.

Rand, C. S., & Kuldau, J. M. (1992). Epidemiology of bulimia and symptoms in a general population: Sex, age, race, and sociometric status. *International Journal of Eating Disorders, 11*(1), 37–44.

Reissland, N. (1985). The development of concepts of simultaneity in children's understanding of emotions. *Journal of Child Psychology and Psychiatry, 26,* 811–824.

Renick, M. J., & Harter, S. (1989). Impact of social comparisons on the developing self-perceptions of learning disabled students. *Journal of Educational Psychology, 81*(4), 631–638.

Richards, M. H., Gitelson, I. B., Petersen, A. C., & Hurtig, A. L. (1991). Adolescent personality in girls and boys: The role of mothers and fathers. *Psychology of Women Quarterly, 15,* 65–81.

Rierdan, J., Koff, E., & Stubbs, M. L. (1988). Gender, depression, and body image in early adolescents. *Journal of Early Adolescence, 8,* 109–117.

Rierdan, J., Koff, E., & Stubbs, M. L. (1989). A longitudinal analysis of body image as a predictor of the onset and persistence of adolescent girls' depression. *Journal of Early Adolescence, 9,* 454–466.

Robinson, N. S. (in press). Evaluating the nature of perceived support and its relation to perceived self-worth in adolescents. *Journal of Research on Adolescence.*

Rochat, P. (1993). Hand-mouth coordination in the newborn: Morphology, determinants, and early development of a basic act. In M. Savelsbergh (Ed.), *The development of coordination in infancy. Advances in psychology series* (pp. 265–288). Amsterdam, The Netherlands: Elsevier.

Rochat, P. (in press). Early objectification of the self. In P. Rochat (Ed.), *The self in infancy: Theory and research.* Amsterdam, The Netherlands: North-Holland/Elsevier.

Rogers, C. R. (1951). *Client-centered therapy.* Boston: Houghton Mifflin.

Rogers, C. R., & Dymond, R. (1954). *Psychotherapy and personality change.* Chicago: University of Chicago Press.

Rogoff, B. (1990). *Apprenticeship in thinking.* New York: Oxford University Press.

Rosales, I., & Zigler, E. F. (1989). Role taking and self-image disparity: A further test of cognitive-developmental thought. *Psychological Reports, 64,* 41–42.

Rosch, E. R. (1975). Cognitive representations of semantic categories. *Journal of Experimental Psychology: General, 104,* 192–233.

Rosen, G. M., & Ross, A. O. (1968). Relationship of body image to self-concept. *Journal of Consulting and Clinical Psychology, 32*(1), 100.

Rosenberg, M. (1979). *Conceiving the self.* New York: Basic Books.

Rosenberg, M. (1986). Self-concept from middle childhood through adolescence. In J. Suls & A. G. Greenwald (Eds.), *Psychological perspective on the self* (Vol. 3, pp. 107–135). Hillsdale, NJ: Erlbaum.

Rosenberg, M., & Simmons, R. G. (1972). *Black and White self-esteem: The urban school child.* Washington, DC: American Sociological Association.

Rosenberg, S. (1988). Self and others: Studies in social personality and autobiography. In L. Berkowitz (Ed.), *Advances in experimental social psychology* (Vol. 21, pp. 56–96). New York: Academic Press.

Rubin, L. (1985). *Just friends: The role of friendship in our lives.* New York: Harper.

Ruble, D. N., & Dweck, C. (1995). Self-conceptions, person conception, and their development. In N. Eisenberg (Ed.), *Review of personality and social psychology: Development and social psychology: The interface* (Vol. 15, pp. 109–139). Thousand Oaks, CA: Sage.

Ruble, D. N., & Frey, K. S. (1991). Changing patterns of comparative behavior as skills are acquired: A functional model of self-evaluation. In J. Suls & T. A. Wills (Eds.), *Social comparison: Contemporary theory and research* (pp. 70–112). Hillsdale, NJ: Erlbaum.

Ruble, D. N., Greulich, F., Pomerantz, E. M., & Gochberg, B. (1993). The role of gender-related processes in the development of sex differences in self-evaluation and depression. *Journal of Affective Disorders, 29,* 97–128.

Rutter, M. (1986). The developmental psychopathology of depression: Issues and perspectives. In M. Rutter, C. E. Izard, & P. B. Read (Eds.), *Depression in young people* (pp. 3–32). New York: Guilford Press.

Ryan, R., & Lynch, J. (1989). Emotional autonomy versus detachment: Revisiting the vicissitudes of adolescence and young adulthood. *Child Development, 60,* 340–356.

Ryckman, R. M., Robbins, M. A., Thornton, B., & Cantrell, P. (1982). Development and validation of a physical self-efficacy scale. *Journal of Personality and Social Psychology, 42,* 891–900.

Salmons, P. H., Lewis, V. J., Rogers, P., Gatherer, A. J. H., & Booth, D. A. (1988). Body shape dissatisfaction in schoolchildren. *British Journal of Psychiatry, 153*(Suppl. 2), 27–31.

Sampson, E. E. (1988). The debate on individualism: Indigenous psychologies and their role in personal and societal functioning. *American Psychologist, 43,* 15–22.

Sander, L. (1975). Infant and caretaking environment: Investigation and conceptualization of adaptive behavior in a series of increasing complexity. In E. J. Anthony (Ed.), *Explorations in child psychiatry* (pp. 129–166). New York: Plenum Press.

Sarbin, T. R. (1962). A preface to a psychological analysis of the self. *Psychological Review, 59,* 11–22.

Savin-Williams, R. C., & Demo, D. H. (1983). Situational and transitional determinants of adolescent self-feelings. *Journal of Personality and Social Psychology, 44,* 820–833.

Savin-Williams, R. C., & Demo, D. H. (1984). Developmental change and stability in adolescent self-concept. *Developmental Psychology, 20,* 1100–1110.

Schaffer, C. E., & Blatt, S. J. (1990). Interpersonal relationships and the experience of perceived efficacy. In R. J. Sternberg & J. Kolligian, Jr. (Eds.), *Competence considered* (pp. 229–245). New Haven, CT: Yale University Press.

Seligman, M. E. P. (1975). *Helplessness: On depression, development, and death.* San Francisco: Freeman.

Seligman, M. E. P. (1993). *What you can change and what you can't.* New York: Fawcett Columbine.

Seligman, M. E. P., & Peterson, C. (1986). A learned helplessness perspective on childhood depression: Theory and research. In M. Rutter, C. E. Izard, & P. B. Read (Eds.), *Depression in young people: Developmental and clinical perspectives* (pp. 223–249). New York: Guilford Press.

Selman, R. (1980). *The growth of interpersonal understanding.* New York: Academic Press.

Shavelson, R. J., Hubner, J. J., & Stanton, G. C. (1976). Validation of construct interpretations. *Review of Educational Research, 46,* 407–441.

Shavelson, R. J., & Marsh, H. W. (1986). On the structure of self-concept. In R. Schwarzer (Ed.), *Anxiety and cognition.* Hillsdale, NJ: Erlbaum.

Shell, R. M., & Eisenberg, N. (1992). A developmental model of recipients' reaction to aid. *Psychological Bulletin, 111,* 413–433.

Showers, C. (1995). The evaluative organization of self-knowledge: Origins, process, and implications for self-esteem. In M. H. Kernis (Ed.), *Efficacy, agency, and self-esteem* (pp. 101–122). New York: Plenum Press.

Shrauger, J. S., & Schoeneman, T. J. (1979). Symbolic interactionist view of self-concept: Through the looking glass darkly. *Psychological Bulletin, 86,* 549–573.

Shweder, R. A. (1991). *Thinking through cultures.* Cambridge, MA: Harvard University Press.

Shweder, R. A., & Bourne, E. (1982). Does the concept of person vary cross-culturally? In R. Shweder & R. LeVine (Eds.), *Culture theory: Essays on mind, self, and emotion* (pp. 158–199). New York: Cambridge University Press.

Shweder, R. A., & Miller, G. (1991). The social construction of the person. In R. Shweder (Ed.), *Thinking through cultures* (pp. 156–185). Cambridge, MA: Harvard University Press.

Siegler, R. S. (1991). *Children's thinking* (2nd ed.). Englewood Cliffs, NJ: Prentice-Hall.

Silberstein, L. R., Striegel-Moore, R. H., Timko, C., & Rodin, J. (1988). Behavioral and psychological implications of body dissatisfaction: Do men and women differ? *Sex Roles, 19*(3/4), 219–232.

Silverstein, B., Perdue, L., Peterson, B., & Kelly, E. (1986). The role of the mass media in promoting a thin standard of bodily attractiveness for women. *Sex Roles, 14*(9/10), 519–532.

Simmons, R. G., & Blyth, D. A. (1987). *Moving into adolescence: The impact of pubertal change and school context.* New York: Aldine de Gruyter.

Simmons, R. G., Blyth, D. A., Van Cleave, E. F., & Bush, D. (1979). Entry into early adolescence: The impact of school structure, puberty, and early dating on self-esteem. *American Sociological Review, 44,* 948–967.

Simmons, R. G., & Rosenberg, F. (1975). Sex, sex roles, and self-image. *Journal of Youth and Adolescence, 4,* 229–258.

Simmons, R. G., Rosenberg, F., & Rosenberg, M. (1973). Disturbances in the self-images at adolescence. *American Sociological Review, 38*, 553–568.

Snow, K. (1990). Building memories: The ontogeny of autobiography. In D. Cicchetti & M. Beeghly (Eds.), *The self in transition: Infancy to childhood* (pp. 213–242). Chicago: University of Chicago Press.

Snyder, M. (1987). *Public appearances, private realities: The psychology of self-monitoring.* New York: Freeman.

Song, I. S., & Hattie, J. A. (1984). Home environment, self-concept, and academic achievement: A causal modeling approach. *Journal of Educational Psychology, 76*, 1269–1281.

Spencer, M. B. (1995). Old issues and new theorizing about African-American youth: A phenomenological variant of ecological systems theory. In R. L. Taylor (Ed.), *Perspectives on their status in the United States* (pp. 37–70). Westport, CT: Praeger.

Spencer, M. B., & Markstrom-Adams, C. (1990). Identity processes among racial and ethnic minority children in America. *Child Development, 61*, 290–310.

Sroufe, L. A. (1990). An organizational perspective on the self. In D. Cicchetti & M. Beeghly (Eds.), *The self in transition: Infancy to childhood* (pp. 281–308). Chicago: University of Chicago Press.

Sroufe, L. A., & Fleeson, J. (1986). Attachment and the construction of relationships. In W. Hartup & Z. Rubin (Eds.), *Relationships and development* (pp. 51–71). New York: Cambridge University Press.

Sroufe, L. A., Fox, N., & Pancake, V. (1983). Attachment and dependency in developmental perspective. *Child Development, 54*, 1615–1627.

Srull, T. K., & Wyer, R. S., Jr. (Eds.). (1993). *Advances in social cognitive: Vol. 5. The mental representation of trait and autobiographical knowledge about the self.* Hillsdale, NJ: Erlbaum.

Stager, S. F., & Burke, P. J. (1982). A reexamination of body build stereotypes. *Journal of Research in Personality, 16*(4), 435–446.

Steele, C. M. (1988). The psychology of self-affirmation: Sustaining the integrity of the self. In L. Berkowitz (Ed.), *Advances in experimental social psychology* (Vol. 21, pp. 261–302). San Diego: Academic Press.

Stein, R. (in press). Physical self-concept. In B. A. Bracken (Ed.), *Handbook of self-concept.* New York: Wiley.

Stern, D. (1985). *The interpersonal world of the infant.* New York: Basic Books.

Stipek, D. J. (1981). Children's perceptions of their own and their classmates' ability. *Journal of Educational Psychology, 73*, 404–410.

Stipek, D. J. (1984). Young children's performance expectations: Logical analysis or wishful thinking? In J. Nicholls (Ed.), *Advances in motivation achievement* (Vol. 3, pp. 33–56). Greenwich, CT: JAI Press.

Stipek, D. J., Recchia, S., & McClintic, S. (1992). Self-evaluation in young children. *Monographs of the Society for Research in Child Development, 57*(1/84, Serial No. 226).

Streigel-Moore, R. H., Silberstein, L. R., & Rodin, J. (1986). Toward an understanding of risk factors for bulimia. *American Psychologist, 41*(3), 246–263.

Strein, W. (1988). Classroom-based elementary school affective education programs: A critical review. *Psychology in the Schools, 25*, 288–296.

Stryker, S. (1987). Identity theory: Developments and extensions. In K. Yardley & T. Honess (Eds.), *Self and identity* (pp. 212–232). New York: Wiley.

Sullivan, H. (1953). *The interpersonal theory of psychiatry.* New York: Norton.

Suls, J., & Sanders, G. (1982). Self-evaluation via social comparison: A developmental analysis. In L. Wheeler (Ed.), *Review of personality and social psychology* (Vol. 3, pp. 67–89). Beverly Hills, CA: Sage.

Swann, W. B., Jr. (1985). Self-verification: Bringing social reality into harmony with the self. In J. Suls & A. G. Greenwald (Eds.), *Social psychological perspectives on the self* (Vol. 2, pp. 33–66). Hillsdale, NJ: Erlbaum.

Swann, W. B., Jr. (1987). Identity negotiation: Where two roads meet. *Journal of Personality and Social Psychology, 53*, 1038–1051.

Taylor, S. E. (1983). Adjustment to threatening events: A theory of cognitive adaptation. *American Psychologist, 38*, 1161–1173.

Taylor, S. E., & Brown, J. D. (1988). Illusion and well-being: A social psychological perspective on mental health. *Psychological Bulletin, 103*, 193–210.

Terr, L. (1990). *Too scared to cry.* New York: Basic Books.

Tesser, A. (1980). Self-esteem maintenance in family dynamics. *Journal of Personality and Social Psychology, 39*, 77–91.

Tesser, A. (1988). Toward a self-evaluation maintenance model of social behavior. In L. Berkowitz (Ed.), *Advances in experimental social psychology* (Vol. 21, pp. 181–227). New York: Academic Press.

Tesser, A., & Campbell, J. (1983). Self-definition and self-evaluation maintenancy. In J. Suls & A. G. Greenwald (Eds.), *Psychological perspectives on the self* (Vol. 2, pp. 34–53). Hillsdale, NJ: Erlbaum.

Tesser, A., & Cornell, D. (1991). On the confluence of self processes. *Journal of Experimental Social Psychology, 27*, 501–526.

Tessler, M. (1991). *Making memories together: The influence of mother-child joint encoding on the development of autobiographical memory style.* Unpublished doctoral dissertation, City University of New York Graduate Center.

Thorne, A., & Michaelieu, Q. (1994, August). *Situating adolescent gender and self-esteem with personal memories.* Paper presented at the annual meeting of the American Psychological Association, Los Angeles, CA.

Tice, D. M. (1994). Pathways to internalization: When does overt behavior change the self-concept? In T. M. Brinthaupt & R. P. Lipka (Eds.), *Changing the self* (pp. 229–250). Albany: State University of New York Press.

Trevarthen, C. (1988). Universal co-operative motives: How infants begin to know the language and culture of their parents. In G. Jahoda & I. M. Lewis (Eds.), *Acquiring culture: Cross-cultural studies in child development* (pp. 116–135). New York: Croom Helm.

Triandis, H. C. (1989a). Cross-cultural studies of individualism and collectivism. In R. A. Diestbier & J. J. Berman (Eds.), *Nebraska Symposium on Motivation: Cross-cultural perspectives* (Vol. 370, pp. 232–259). Lincoln: Nebraska University Press.

Triandis, H. C. (1989b). The self and social behavior in differing cultural contexts. *Psychological Review, 96,* 506–520.

Tulving, E. (1972). Episodic and semantic memory. In E. Tulving & W. Donaldson (Eds.), *Organization of memory* (pp. 382–403). New York: Academic Press.

Tulving, E. (1983). *Elements of episodic memory.* New York: Oxford University Press.

Vallacher, R. R. (1980). An introduction to self-theory. In D. M. Wegner & R. R. Vallacher (Eds.), *The self in social psychology* (pp. 3–30). New York: Oxford University Press.

Vanderheyden, D. A., Fekken, G. C., & Boland, F. J. (1988). Critical variables associated with bingeing and bulimia in a university population: A factor analytic study. *International Journal of Eating Disorders, 7*(3), 321–329.

Vygotsky, L. S. (1978). *Mind in society: The development of higher psychological processes.* Cambridge, MA: Harvard University Press.

Watson, M. (1990). Aspects of self development as reflected in children's role playing. In D. Cicchetti & M. Beeghly (Eds.), *The self in transition: Infancy to childhood* (pp. 281–307). Chicago: University of Chicago Press.

Weissman, M. M., & Klerman, G. L. (1977). Sex differences in the epidemiology of depression. *Archives of General Psychiatry, 34,* 98–111.

Westen, D. (1993). The impact of sexual abuse on self structure. In D. Cicchetti & S. Toth (Eds.), *Disorders and dysfunctions of the self: Rochester Symposium on Developmental Psychopathology* (Vol. 5, pp. 223–250). Rochester, NY: University of Rochester Press.

Wexler, D. B. (1991). *The adolescent self: Strategies for self-management, self-soothing, and self-esteem.* New York: Norton.

White, R. (1959). Motivation reconsidered: The concept of competence. *Psychological Review, 66,* 297–333.

Wigfield, A., Eccles, J. S., MacIver, D., Reuman, D. A., & Midgley, C. (1991). Transitions during early adolescence: Changes in children's domain-specific self-perceptions and general self-esteem across the transition to junior high school. *Developmental Psychology, 27*(4), 552–565.

Williamson, D. A., Netemeyer, R. G., Jackman, L. P., Anderson, D. A., Funsch, C. L., & Rabalais, J. Y. (1995). Structural equation modeling of risk factors for the development of the eating disorder symptoms in female athletes. *International Journal of Eating Disorders, 17*(4), 387–393.

Winnicott, D. W. (1958). *From peadiatrics to psychoanalysis.* London: Hogarth Press.

Winnicott, D. W. (1965). *The maturational processes and the facilitating environment.* New York: International Universities Press.

Wiseman, C. V., Gray, J. J., Mosimann, J. E., & Ahrens, A. H. (1992). Cultural expectations of thinness in women: An update. *International Journal of Eating Disorders, 11*(1), 85–89.

Wolf, D. P. (1990). Being of several minds: Voices and version of the self in early childhood. In D. Cicchetti & M. Beeghly (Eds.), *The self in transition: Infancy to childhood* (pp. 183–212). Chicago: University of Chicago Press.

Wood, J. V. (1989). Theory and research concerning social comparisons of personal attributes. *Psychological Bulletin, 106,* 231–248.

Wylie, R. C. (1989). *Measures of self-concept.* Lincoln: University of Nebraska Press.

Zastrow, C. (1994). Conceptualizing and changing the self from a rational therapy perspective. In T. M. Brinthaupt & R. P. Lipka (Eds.), *Changing the self* (pp. 175–120). Albany: State University of New York Press.

CHAPTER 10

Peer Interactions, Relationships, and Groups

KENNETH H. RUBIN, WILLIAM BUKOWSKI, and JEFFREY G. PARKER

Preparation of this chapter was aided, in part, by a Senior Research Fellowship to the first author from the Ontario Mental Health Foundation while he was affiliated with the University of Waterloo, by a grant to the second author from the W. T. Grant Foundation Faculty Scholars Program, and by a faculty fellowship to the third author from the University of Michigan.

Experiences with peers constitute an important developmental context for children. Within these contexts, children acquire a wide range of skills, attitudes, and experiences that influence their adaptation across the life span. Accordingly, peers are powerful socialization "agents" contributing beyond the influence of family, school, and neighborhood to children's social, emotional, and cognitive well-being and adjustment.

These opening remarks are substantiated in sections that follow. We begin, however, by commenting briefly on identifiable developments in the study of children's peers since the publication of the last *Handbook of Child Psychology*. In 1983, Willard W. Hartup noted the "astonishing" acceleration of research interest that had taken place since his earlier review of the field for the 1970 *Manual of Child Psychology*. He indicated that this interest was particularly noteworthy because the topic had all but been ignored by researchers in the 1950s and 1960s. Indeed, the literature had become so voluminous that Hartup was forced, by practical constraints, to restrict his 1983 chapter primarily to research published in the previous decade.

Our task of reviewing the literature on peer interaction, relationships, and groups is ever more daunting. We have inherited, from Hartup, the responsibility of examining a body of theory and research for which the growth trajectory continues upward. To provide the reader with an appreciation of what has transpired since Hartup's review in 1983, we invite consideration of the following. Since the publication of Hartup's chapter, an encyclopaedic collection of relevant research monographs and texts have appeared, including *Peer Relationships and Social Skills in Childhood: Issues in Assessment and Training* (Schneider, Rubin, & Ledingham, 1985); *Conversations of Friends: Speculations on Affective Development* (Gottman & Parker, 1986); *Process and Outcome in Peer Relationships* (Mueller & Cooper, 1986); *Peer Interaction of Young Children* (Howes, 1988); *Peer Relationships in Child Development* (Berndt & Ladd, 1989); *Social Competence in Developmental Perspective* (Schneider, Attili, Nadel, & Weissberg, 1989); *Children's Social Networks and Social Supports* (Belle, 1989); *Peer Rejection in Childhood* (Asher & Coie, 1990); *Family-Peer Relationships: Modes of Linkage* (Parke & Ladd, 1992); *Close Friendships in Adolescence* (Laursen, 1993a); *Friendship and Peer Relations in Children* (Erwin, 1993); and *The Company They Keep: Friendship during Childhood and Adolescence* (Bukowski, Newcomb, & Hartup, 1996).

The rapid expansion of interest in this topic is also chronicled in the emergence and growth of the field's unofficial professional organization and conference. In 1983, a small group of about 30 researchers met in Detroit, just prior to the biennial meeting of the Society for Research in Child Development (SRCD). The roster of participants was compiled informally and included most of the active researchers studying children's peer relationships. The participants described their current research, and there was lively discussion of specific studies and broader methodological and conceptual issues in the field. By the second meeting, prior to the 1985 SRCD meetings in Toronto, the group had grown to 80 "members," thereby forcing participation in simultaneously running discussion groups focused on issues such as correlates and consequences of peer rejection, intervention, assessment and methodological issues, and so on. The SRCD Preconference on Peer Relations, as the meeting became known, has continued to convene and, by 1995, its directory listed 202 researchers.

Clearly, research concerned with children's peers has witnessed enormous recent growth in both breadth and depth. To cover this field adequately, we have partitioned this chapter into several segments. In the first section, we pay brief homage to those researchers who established, historically, areas of investigation that are still active today. Next, we suggest that the peer system consists of multiple levels of analysis, namely, individual characteristics, social interactions, dyadic relationships, and group membership and composition. Our thesis is that interactions, relationships, and groups reflect social participation at different interwoven orders of complexity. Our goal in introducing these levels of analysis is to establish a framework for further discussion of the development and significance of children's peer experiences. Moreover, discussion of the interactions, relationships, and group levels of social complexity allows subsequent commentary on conceptual and assessment issues that pertain to individual differences in children's behavioral tendencies and peer relationships.

There has yet to emerge an all-encompassing theory of peer interactions and relationships. However, there exist many "grand" theories in which are expressed views about the significance of peer interactions and relationships for normal growth and development. Thus, in the third section, we discuss theories relevant to the understanding of the peer system.

Next we describe normative patterns of development from infancy through late childhood and early adolescence. In the fifth section, we introduce the individual level of analysis by discussing the contributions of social competence to children's peer experiences. In so doing, we acknowledge characteristics that children bring with them to their interactions with peers or their involvements in relationships and groups.

Researchers who study children's peer experiences have long maintained a healthy interest in measurement and measurement issues. In the sixth section, we distinguish among individuals, interactions, relationships, and groups in our discussion of measurement issues.

In the final sections of the chapter we review the voluminous literature that has emerged concerning the origins and consequences of individual differences in children's experiences with peers. We pay particular attention to the proximal and distal correlates of variables associated with individual differences in popularity and friendship. We consider also the developmental prognosis for children whose peer interaction patterns and relationships are deviant from the norm.

Our chapter concludes with the presentation of two developmental models in which are described pathways to difficulties with peers, as well as a discussion of some of the directions that future research might take.

PEER INTERACTIONS AND RELATIONSHIPS: A HISTORICAL OVERVIEW

The study of children's peer interactions and relationships has had a long and rich history. Charlotte Buhler (1931), in the first *Handbook* chapter on "The Social Behavior of the Child," gave credit to Will S. Monroe (1899) for having conducted the first empirical study of children's peer relationships. Using questionnaires, Monroe asked 2,000 school-age children about the qualities they valued in their chums, their preferred toys and games, and the organization of children's clubs and "gangs." Monroe's report was not developmental; systematic comparisons across age were not made. And to the extent that this study was not followed up in a programmatic fashion by others, the report appears to have been an isolated one.

Of the 253 papers cited by Buhler in her original *Handbook* chapter, 156 were published in German and only 85 in English. Among the early German studies reviewed by Buhler (1931) were developmental examinations of social interaction in infants and toddlers (Buhler); studies of antisocial and other "disliked tendencies" in children and adolescents (e.g., Hetzer); investigations of the evolution of different leadership roles played by children in their peer groups (Winkler-Hermaden), and observational studies of the development of friendship networks in 6- and 10-year-old boys (Reininger). Thus, prior to the Second World

War, German laboratories were producing research of high quality on topics not unknown to contemporaneous peer relationships researchers—topics including peer group acceptance, friendship, leadership, and peer group structure. Often the correlates or concomitants of these relationship variables were examined—variables such as family constellation, institutionalization, and poverty. These are clearly topics we continue to grapple with in contemporary research.

Early North American Research

North American–based research concerning children's peer interactions and relationships began to blossom in the 1920s, when the first Child Welfare Research Stations came into existence. These interdisciplinary research centers produced new observational and statistical procedures to examine developmental and individual differences in children's social behaviors, interactions, and peer relationships. For example, monograph 1 in the Child Development Series published by the University of Toronto's St. George's School for Child Study was titled "Method in Social Studies of Young Children" (Bott, 1933). Among the topics that attracted research interest at the time were the development of social participation (Parten, 1932); assertiveness (Dawe, 1934); sympathetic and altruistic behaviors (Murphy, 1937); conflict and aggression (Maudry & Nekula, 1939); leadership, dominance, and "ascendant behavior" (Hanfmann, 1935); friendship (Challman, 1932); group dynamics (Lewin, Lippit, & White, 1938); peer group structure and composition (Moreno, 1934); and the correlates of individual differences in social skills and competence (Koch, 1935).

By the beginning of the Second World War, however, the study of children's social behaviors, interactions, and peer relationships began to lose its luster. Nevertheless, it was during this period that sociometric techniques were initially developed (Bronfenbrenner, 1944). As we demonstrate later, the development of sociometric methods for children provided researchers with a framework for studying one aspect of the peer system, that of *popularity*. And, using these new procedures, investigators examined correlates of sociometric popularity (e.g., Bonney, 1944). As the United States and Canada entered the war, however, those who had studied children turned their attention to performing warfare-related tasks, and the number of personnel working at child welfare research stations was depleted considerably (see Renshaw, 1981, for a review of the peer relationships research conducted prior to 1940).

Post–World War II

Following the Second World War, some research attention was redirected toward the study of children's development in the peer context. For example, Baldwin (1949) examined the relations between observed peer interaction styles and parenting behaviors and attitudes. But, by and large, the end of the war and the arrival of the Cold War fostered limited research concern about children and their extrafamilial social relationships. Instead, attention was directed to children's academic and intellectual prowess. With the launching of the *Sputnik* satellite by the USSR in 1957, the pressures to train children to become academically achievement oriented and skilled at earlier ages and at faster rates than ever before moved developmental researchers away from the earlier focus on children's social worlds.

Although children's peer interactions and relationships were relatively neglected, *parent*-child interactions and relationships remained critical areas of inquiry. Parents were viewed as the primary socializers of children's achievement motives and behaviors (e.g., Rosen & D'Andrade, 1959). Thus, although developmental psychologists continued to study children's social interactions and relationships, the primary focus was on the parent-child unit.

In the 1960s, the rediscovery of Piaget's developmental theory provided an impetus for a structurally oriented research climate that captured the interest of psychologists throughout the Western world. A brief glance at the journal *Child Development* during the 1960s and 1970s attests to the domination of the Piagetian zeitgeist. This focus on cognition, coupled with continued interest in achievement motivation and behavior, created an environment that was not particularly attuned to the significance of peer interaction and relationships. North American preoccupation with attempts to "disprove" Piaget by (a) altering the traditional Genevan research paradigms or (b) attempting to *train* concrete operations dominated journal space. These empirical challenges were designed to demonstrate that cognitive operations could be taught, or that they could be demonstrated, at earlier ages than those proposed initially by Piaget and his colleagues. This research mandate to demonstrate earlier and faster learning of cognitive operations fit well within the achievement orientation of the times.

Ironically, whilst *not* believing Piaget about the trainability of cognitive operations and the ages at which such operations could be developed, researchers in the 1960s and early 1970s nonetheless appeared to accept the premise that young children were primarily egocentric and neither willing nor able to understand the thoughts, feelings, and spatial perspectives of their peers. Egocentrism also stood in the way of making mature moral judgments and decisions (Kohlberg, 1963). Given these assumptions, the mind-set seemed to be that studying children's peer relationships would not be productive, at least until the mid-elementary school ages when concrete operations emerged and egocentric thought vanished.

The aforementioned research and educational climate was subsequently united with a significant sociopolitical event. In the 1960s, President Lyndon Johnson proclaimed a War on Poverty in the United States. This effort led to the development of early education prevention and intervention programs for which the primary foci were cognitive and language development and the development of an achievement orientation in young children. As a consequence, nursery schools in which the primary emphasis was the socialization of relationships and social skills were replaced by early education centers designed to prepare "at-risk" children for elementary school. Additionally, cognitively oriented preschool programs (e.g., Montessori), became increasingly favored by the achievement-oriented middle classes of the 1960s and 1970s.

Despite the emphasis on early cognitive and language development, the preschool and day care movements of the 1960s and 1970s may have been partly responsible for the reemergence of peer relationships research. In particular, the enormous growth in the numbers of early education and care centers in North America was dictated, not only by the need to prevent educational failure among the socioeconomically impoverished, but also by the need for out-of-home care for dual-income middle-class households. Given that North American children were entering organized peer-group settings at earlier ages than ever before and were remaining with peers in age-segregated schools for more years than their cohorts of previous generations, it would have been shortsighted and irresponsible for developmental researchers to ignore the importance of children's peer relationships and social skills.

Current thinking about the significance of peer interactions and relationships for normal development is certainly neither novel nor discontinuous with earlier writings. Piaget (1932) himself implicated peer *interaction,* discourse, and negotiation as crucial elements likely to provoke higher levels of operational thinking. Mead (1934) and Sullivan (1953) also wrote persuasively about the importance of friendship and peer *relationships* for adaptive development. Thus, by the end of the 1960s, the time appeared ripe for child developmentalists to be reminded of their early roots during early decades of the twentieth century. This reminder was issued by Hartup in his 1970 *Manual of Child Psychology* chapter. Hartup's message concerning the significance of children's peer interactions and relationships fell fast on the heels of a seminal review by John Campbell (1964). These chapters, and Hartup's (1983) revision, have clearly proved provocative. The extent to which provocation has elicited research production becomes evident in the sections that follow.

INTERACTIONS, RELATIONSHIPS, AND GROUPS: ORDERS OF COMPLEXITY IN CHILDREN'S PEER EXPERIENCES

Children's experiences with peers can be best understood by referring to several levels of social complexity: within individuals, within interactions, within relationships, and within groups (Hinde, 1987). Moreover, events and processes at each level are constrained and influenced by events and processes at other levels. *Individuals* bring to social exchanges more or less stable social orientations, temperaments that dispose them to be more or less aroused physiologically to social stimuli, and a repertoire of social skills for social perception and social problem solving. Over the short term, their *interactions* with other children vary in form and function in response to fluctuations in the parameters of the social situation, such as the partner's characteristics, overtures, and responses. Further, most interactions are embedded in longer-term *relationships,* and thus are influenced by past and anticipated future interactions. Relationships may take many forms and have properties that are not relevant to interactions. At the same time, the nature of a relationship is defined partly by the characteristics of its members, its constituent interactions, and, over the long term, the kinds of relationships individuals form depend on their history of interactions in earlier relationships. Finally, individual relationships, in turn, are embedded within *groups,* or networks of relationships with more or less clearly defined boundaries (e.g., cliques, teams, school classes). As the highest level of social complexity, groups are defined by their constituent relationships and, in this sense, by the types and diversity of interactions that are characteristic of the participants in those relationships. But groups are more than mere aggregates of relationships;

through emergent properties such as norms or shared cultural conventions, groups help define the type and range of relationships and interactions that are likely or permissible. Further, groups have properties and processes, such as hierarchical organization and cohesiveness, that are not relevant to descriptions of children's experiences at lower levels of social complexity.

To further complicate matters, at any level of social organization the understanding of participants will necessarily differ from that of outsiders (Furman, 1984). Humorous anecdotes shared among friends, for example, can strike outsiders as unnecessarily cruel (e.g., gossip). Children with many friends can still feel lonely, and seemingly innocuous acts can have great significance to members of a friendship, who understand them differently than do outsiders. Given that neither "insiders" nor "outsiders" can claim any specific hegemony on the truth, researchers must be prepared to cross and recross perspectives as the problem dictates.

The enormous complexity of the multiple, interrelated levels of social organization that underpin peer experiences can make the prospect of understanding these experiences and their influence on children seem truly dim. Historically, distinctions among the various levels and perspectives of children's peer experiences often have been blurred. For example, investigators have confused phenomena from different levels (e.g., failing to distinguish between group acceptance and friendship) or perspectives (e.g., accepting one child's declaration as evidence of friendship without verifying the reciprocity of this sentiment), and have also sometimes been too facile in making inferences about experiences at one level from measurements at another (e.g., assuming that children who are aggressive in interaction cannot be well liked or have friends). Nevertheless, over the past 15 years, recognition and articulation of the multiple levels of analysis and perspectives that comprise the peer system have greatly increased. Especially significant in this regard has been the contribution of Robert Hinde (e.g., 1976, 1979, 1987, 1995; see also Bateson, 1991), who has articulated the features and dialectical relations among successive levels of social complexity.

Borrowing heavily from Hinde, in this section we discuss the nature of three successive levels of complexity in children's experiences with peers: *interactions, relationships,* and *groups.* Our goal is to set the framework for subsequent discussion of the development and significance of children's peer experiences. The interaction, relationship, and group levels of social complexity are also important to the conceptualization and assessment of individual differences in children's behavioral tendencies, because individuals can be compared with respect to their functioning at these levels; therefore, the present section serves as an orienting framework for our later discussion of measurement issues. As we indicated, a hierarchy of social complexity also properly should include processes at work at the individual (versus interactional, relationship, or group) level of description (Hinde, 1987). These processes would include children's social-emotional/temperamental dispositions and social knowledge and skills repertoires. Within the literature on children's peer experiences, the individual level has been the focus of much interest. However, rather than introduce this well-developed literature here, we embed its discussion into sections on children's interactions and relationships.

Interactions

The simplest order of complexity of peer experience involves interactions. *Interaction* is the braiding of the behaviors of two individuals into a social exchange of some duration. Behaviors that simply (and only) complement one another (like riding on either end of a teeter-totter) would ordinarily not be considered true interaction unless it were amply clear that they were jointly undertaken. Instead, the term *interaction* is reserved for dyadic behavior in which the participants' actions are interdependent such that each actor's behavior is both a response to and stimulus for the other participant's behavior. At its core, an interaction comprises "such incidents as Individual A shows behavior X to Individual B, or A shows X to B and B responds with Y" (Hinde, 1979, p. 15). Conversational turn-taking is a quintessential illustration of this: thus, Child A requests information from Child B ("What's your name?"); Child B responds ("My name is Lara, what's yours?"); Child A replies ("Camilla"); and so on.

Of course, such a simple exchange as that of Camilla and Lara belies the richness and enormous complexity of the ways that children of most ages communicate with and influence one another. Thus, besides introducing themselves, children in conversation may argue, gossip, comfort, and support one another, self-disclose, and joke, among other things. And, during interaction, children compete, fight, withdraw, respond to provocation, and engage in a host of other behaviors that includes everything from ritualized sexual contact to rough-and-tumble play to highly structured

sociodramatic fantasy. Indeed, if one begins to consider the diversity of children's exchanges with one another, one may despair of ever being able to describe, let alone understand, children's interactional experiences. In practice, researchers have been less interested in cataloguing the myriad interactional experiences than in understanding the origins and consequences of three broad childhood behavioral tendencies: (a) moving toward others, (b) moving against others, and (c) moving away from others. As a consequence, our current understanding of children's experiences at the interactional level is disproportionately organized around the constructs of sociability and helpfulness, aggression, and withdrawal. As much of this literature is oriented toward individual differences among children along these dimensions of interaction, we review this research in later sections. Indeed, we suggest temperamental factors that may set individuals apart from one another vis-à-vis the tendencies to socialize with, aggress against, and withdraw from others during opportunities for peer interaction. Developmental trends in these behaviors are described in the subsequent section.

Although many social exchanges have their own inherent logic (as in the question-answer sequence of Camilla and Lara), it is also the case that the forms and trajectories of episodes of interaction are shaped by the relationships in which they are embedded. For example, friends are more committed to resolving conflict with each other than nonfriends and are more likely than nonfriends to continue to interact following a disagreement (Hartup & Laursen, 1995; Laursen, 1993b). Beyond this, children engaged in interaction vary their behavior as a function of their short-term and long-term personal goals, their understanding of their partner's thoughts and feelings in the situation, the depth of their repertoire of alternative responses, and various "ecological" features of the context of the interactions, such as the presence of bystanders, the physical setting, their own and their partner's relative standing in the group, and the operative local customs or "scripts" for responding. It is precisely the demonstration of such range and flexibility in responding to the challenges of interpersonal interaction, *when considered at the individual level of analysis,* that many writers think of as social competence (e.g., Rubin & Rose-Krasnor, 1992).

Relationships

Relationships introduce a second and higher-order level of complexity to children's experiences with peers.

Relationships involve a succession of interactions between two individuals known to each other. Importantly, because the individuals are known to each other, the nature and course of each interaction are influenced by the history of past interactions between the individuals as well as by their expectations for interactions in the future. It has been suggested that the degree of closeness of a relationship is determined by such qualities as the frequency and strength of influence, the diversity of influence across different behaviors, and the length of time the relationship has endured. In a close relationship, influence is frequent, diverse, strong, and enduring. Alternatively, relationships can be defined with reference to the predominant *emotions* that participants typically experience within them (e.g., affection, love, attachment, enmity). Hinde (1979, 1995) further suggests that an essential element of a relationship is *commitment*, or the extent to which the partners accept their relationship as "continuing indefinitely or direct their behaviors towards ensuring its continuance or towards optimizing its properties" (Hinde, 1979, p. 29). Finally, it is important to note that, although as social scientists we may speak of abstract categories of relationships (sibling, best friend, enemy, etc.), children view each instance of these relationships in a particularized way; to children, relationships of even the same general category are not interchangeable.

As a form of social organization, dyadic relationships share features with larger social organizations, such as a family, a class, or a team. In a particularly insightful analysis, McCall (1988) noted that dyads, like larger organizational structures, undergo role differentiation, specialization, and division of labor: "Members' lines of action differ one from the other yet remain interdependent in certain ways" (p. 473). Moreover, participants in a relationship are aware that their relationship, though it may be very much their own local creation, is supported by an objectified, institutionalized social form: "When persons say they are friends, usually they can point to cultural images, rules of conduct, and customary modes of behavior to confirm their claims" (Suttles, 1970, p. 98). In addition, parties to a relationship have a sense of shared membership and belonging: "A sense of shared fate tends to arise as members discover that the surrounding world treats them not so much as separate individuals but rather as a couple, or unit" (McCall, 1988, p. 471). Finally, the creation of a shared culture is a vital part of dyadic relationships. This shared culture includes normative expectations regarding appropriate activities, patterns of communication and revelation, relations to external persons and organizations, and so on. It also includes private terms, or neologisms, for shared concerns or common activities, and rituals, or "dyadic traditions," arising from the routinization of recurrent dyadic activities (such as meeting at the same place after school or flipping a special coin to resolve a dispute).

These are all features that relationships have in common with other, larger social organizations. However, McCall (1988) indicates that there are certain attitudinal features of the participants in a dyadic relationship that are distinct to this level of social organization and vital to understanding its functioning and impact on interactions and individuals. For example, unlike most social organizations, dyadic relationships do not vary in membership size. Having only two members, the dyad is peculiarly vulnerable, for the loss of a single member ends its existence. Because members appreciate this vulnerability, issues of commitment, attachment, and investment loom larger in dyadic relationships than in other forms of social organization. Indeed, an understanding of the surface behavior of members of relationships can be elusive unless note is taken of the deeper meaning of behavior vis-à-vis the relationship's mortality. This same sense of mortality is likely to contribute to a special sense of uniqueness ("There has never been a friendship quite like ours") and to what McCall calls a "sense of consecration," or a feeling that each member must take responsibility for what happens within the relationship.

In the literature on children's peer experiences, one form of dyadic relationship has received attention above all others: *friendship*. The issue of what constitutes friendship is a venerable philosophical debate beyond the scope of this chapter. However, some points from this debate warrant noting here because of their operational significance.

First, almost every psychologist who studies friendship regards it as a *reciprocal* relationship that must be affirmed or recognized by both parties. Reciprocity is the factor that distinguishes between friendship and the nonreciprocal attraction of only one partner to another. From an assessment perspective, methods that do not verify that the perception of friendship is shared between partners prove difficult because children are sometimes motivated by self-presentational goals to designate as friends other children who do not view them as friends in return (Berndt, 1984). Thus, in the absence of assessing reciprocity, methods of identifying friends may confuse desired relationships with actual ones.

A second point of consensus is that *reciprocity of affection* represents the essential, though not necessarily exclusive, tie that binds friends to one another (Hays, 1988). The interdependence of the two partners derives primarily from socioemotional rather than instrumental motives. It is customary, of course, for children to seek one another out for instrumental reasons. Similarity of talents or interests may bring together children who might not otherwise interact. For example, work and sports teams, musical groups, and even delinquent gangs comprise members who are not necessarily friends. Similarities or complementarities of talents and interests may lead to friendship and can help sustain them; however, they do not constitute the basis of the friendship itself. The basis is reciprocal affection.

Third, friendships are voluntary, not obligatory or prescribed. It is the case that in some cultures and in some circumstances, children may be assigned their "friends," sometimes even at birth. Although these relationships may take on some of the features and serve some of the same interpersonal ends as voluntary relationships, most scholars would agree that their involuntary nature argues against confusing them with friendship.

A final point is that relationships must be understood according to their place within the network of other relationships. It has been suggested, for example, that children's friendships are influenced by the relationships they have at home with parents and siblings (Hinde, 1987). That is, it has been posited that children's conceptualizations and feelings about their primary relationships are internalized and lead (a) to expectations about what relationships outside of the family might and should be like, and (b) to particular interpersonal behaviors and interactions with peers that reflect their internalized models of relationships (Bowlby, 1973; Sroufe & Fleeson, 1986). Whereas parent-child relationships may influence the early development and maintenance of children's peer relationships, it would make sense to expect that the relations between relationship systems become increasingly reciprocal and mutual with increasing child age. That is, the quality of the child's peer relationships is likely to influence the quality of the parent-child relationship and perhaps even the relationship between the child's parents.

Groups

A *group* is a collection of interacting individuals who have some degree of reciprocal influence over one another. Groups often form spontaneously, out of common interests or circumstances, but they are also established formally, the most ubiquitous example being the school class.

Hinde (1979) suggests that a group is the structure that emerges from the features and patterning of the relationships and interactions present within a population of children. Accordingly, groups possess properties that arise from the manner in which the relationships are patterned but that are not present in the individual relationships themselves. Examples of such properties include *cohesiveness*, or the degree of unity and inclusiveness exhibited by the children or manifested by the density of the interpersonal relationships; *hierarchy*, or the extent of intransitivity in the ordering of the individual relationships along interesting dimensions (e.g., if Fred dominates Richard and Richard dominates Peter, does Fred dominate Peter?); and *heterogeneity*, or consistency across members in the ascribed or achieved personal characteristics (e.g., sex, race, age, intelligence, attitudes toward school). Finally, every group has *norms*, or distinctive patterns of behaviors and attitudes that characterize group members and differentiate them from members of other groups.

Many of our most important means for describing groups speak to these emergent properties. Thus, researchers may address the degree to which the relationships and interactions in a group are segregated along sex or racial lines; they may compare the rates of social isolation among groups that differ in composition; or they may investigate the extent to which a group's hierarchies of affiliation, dominance, and influence are linear and interrelated. In addition, group norms can be used as a basis for distinguishing separate "crowds" within the networks of relationships among children in high school (e.g., B. Brown, 1989). The emergent properties of groups also shape the experiences of individuals in the groups. Thus, crowd *labels* constrain, in important ways, adolescents' freedom to explore new identities; *status hierarchies* influence the formation of new friendships; *segregation* influences the diversity of children's experiences with others; and *cohesiveness* influences children's sense of belonging. As such, the group can influence the individual.

Many of the classic studies of children concerned the peer group per se, including that of Lewin, Lippitt, and White (1938) concerning group climate, and Sherif, Harvey, White, Hood, and Sherif's (1961) examination of intragroup loyalty and intergroup conflict. In addition, theorists who have stressed the importance of children's peer experiences (e.g., Cairns, Xie, & Leung, in press) have generally conceptualized the group as an important developmental context that shapes and supports the behaviors of its constituent members.

In spite of the importance of the group, little attention has been paid to the assessment of group phenomena. This is surprising because researchers often cite experiences with peers with reference to the "peer group." Recently, Cairns et al. (in press) have argued that this neglect can be attributed to the complex conceptual and methodological issues related to the study of group structure and organization.

Finally, it is worth noting that the construct that has dominated the peer literature during the past 15 years, namely that of *popularity,* is both an individual- and a group-oriented phenomenon. Measures of popularity refer to the group's view of an individual vis-à-vis the dimensions of liking and disliking (Bukowski & Hoza, 1989). In this regard, popularity is a group construct and the processes of rejection and acceptance are group processes. Yet, despite this reality, most peer researchers treat popularity as characteristic of the individual (Newcomb, Bukowski, & Pattee, 1993). This confusion exemplifies the significance of recognizing the inextricable links between different levels of analysis. As Bronfenbrenner (1944) wrote over 50 years ago, the study of the peer system requires the "envisagement of the individual and the group as developing organic units" (p. 75).

Summary

To understand children's experiences with peers, researchers have focused on children's interactions with other children and on their involvements in peer relationships and groups. Analyses within each level—interactions, relationships, groups—are, of course, scientifically legitimate and raise interesting questions. However, researchers have not always demonstrated a clear understanding of the important ways in which processes at one level are influenced by those at the others. As such, they have sometimes overlooked ways in which conclusions drawn at single levels of analysis can be limited. For example, the observation of two children at play can reveal the rates at which they display different behaviors and the patterning of these behaviors with respect to one another. It can be misleading, however, to attribute these characteristics of interaction solely to individual differences in social competence or temperament; one must also consider relational interdependencies, that is, unique adjustments made by Persons A and B to one another that define their particular relationship. And events transpiring within a given relationship also reflect realities outside the relationship; for

example, tensions produced by individuals' loyalties to other friends in the peer group may affect the quality of social interaction between two specific children.

Finally, our emphasis on multiple levels of analysis provides us with a basic conceptual model of social competence. Researchers have often treated measures of peer experiences (e.g., sociometric status) as indices of social competence. Our view is that social competence within the peer system refers to a child's capacity to engage effectively and successfully at each level of analysis. By this we mean that a competent child will be able to (a) become engaged in a peer-group structure and participate in group-oriented activities, (b) become involved in satisfying relationships constructed upon balanced and reciprocal interactions, and (c) satisfy individual goals and needs and develop accurate and productive means of understanding experiences with peers on both the group and dyadic levels.

THEORIES RELEVANT TO THE STUDY OF CHILDREN'S PEER INTERACTIONS, RELATIONSHIPS, AND GROUPS

Personality Theorists

Psychoanalytic Perspectives

Psychoanalytic or neopsychoanalytic theorists have generally viewed neither childhood peer interaction nor children's peer relationships as playing a significant role in development. Instead, these authors view much of the child's development as resulting from parental behavior and the quality of the parent-child relationship. If peer interaction or relationships are considered by these psychoanalytic writers, they are viewed as extensions of parent-child relationships, as arenas for the playing out of biologically based psychosexual and aggressive drives, or as markers of adaptive or maladaptive psychosexual development. For example, Anna Freud (1949) regarded the peer milieu as a relatively safe, extrafamilial context within which adolescents could work out their aggressive and sexual drives. She also regarded the emergence of qualitatively positive peer relationships as an index of healthy development.

Perhaps the only psychoanalytically oriented theorist to ascribe developmental significance to children's peer relationships is Peter Blos. For Blos (1967), the major event of adolescence is the process of *individuation* by which adolescents restructure their childhood relationships with their parents and strive to achieve qualitatively different relationships with peers. Individuation involves renegotiating dependency relationships with parents; such renegotiation is precipitated, in part, by adolescent sexual drives. It also involves the introduction of new themes into relationships with peers. Responding to erotic drives, the adolescent turns toward the peer group as a means of finding sexual outlets and venues of emotional closeness; previously, such closeness was available only from parents.

As a function of restructuring their relationships with parents, adolescents come to experience turmoil and anxiety accompanied by feelings of despair, worthlessness, discouragement, and vulnerability. According to Blos (1967), adolescents' capacities to cope with these feelings and experiences rest with their ability to establish qualitatively distinct forms of supportive relationships with peers. In the process of separating from parents, and prior to achieving a state of personal autonomy, adolescents turn to peers for "stimulation, belongingness, loyalty, devotion, empathy, and resonance" (p. 177).

One potential pitfall of the individuation process for adolescents is that some teenagers become overly dependent on peers, conforming to the norms and standards of the group too readily as part of their search for security outside the family. Blos (1967) argued that, in such cases, dependence on peers is problematic because it precludes the promotion of independence and autonomy. But more generally, it is argued that the peer group is a major determinant of an adolescent's ability to achieve a sense of autonomy and independence from the family.

Sullivan's Theory of Personality Development

In his developmental model of interpersonal relationships, Harry Stack Sullivan (1953) characterized children's peer relationships during the early childhood and the early school-age years as organized largely around play and common activities. During the juvenile period (from approximately age 7 to 9 years), however, children become increasingly concerned about their place within the peer group as a whole and a sense of "belonging" to the group becomes increasingly important.

As children enter early adolescence, the central feature of the peer group shifts from the group to the dyad. Sullivan (1953) proposed that during early adolescence, children begin to develop "chumships," or close, intimate, mutual relationships with same-sex peers. As a relationship between "coequals," chumships were distinct from the

hierarchical relationships that children experienced with their parents. Accordingly, Sullivan argued that this close relationship was a child's first true interpersonal experience based on reciprocity and exchange between equals.

As for the *functions* of peer relationships, Sullivan (1953) argued that the peer system is essential for the development of a sense of well-being. He proposed that the experience of being isolated from the group, during the juvenile period, would lead a child to have concerns about his or her own competencies and acceptability as a desirable peer. Consequently, Sullivan suggested that children who are unable to establish a position within the peer group would develop feelings of inferiority that could contribute to a sense of psychological ill-being. One posited outcome of the lack of supportive chumships was the development of loneliness, or "the exceedingly unpleasant and driving experience connected with the inadequate discharge of the need for human intimacy" (p. 290).

Consistent with the developmental perspective described above, Sullivan (1953) argued that the early adolescent shift from group to dyad allowed participation in deep, enduring chumships. It was within chumships that children had their first opportunities to experience a sense of self-validation. This validation would emanate, in large part, from their recognition of the positive regard and care in which their chums held them. Sullivan went so far as to argue that the positive experiences of having a "chum" in adolescence would be so powerful as to enable adolescents to overcome trauma that may have resulted from prior family experiences.

The Symbolic Interactionist Perspective

Following the lead of William James (1890), who posited that humans have "an innate propensity to get ourselves noticed, and noticed favorably, by our kind" (p. 293), writers such as Cooley (1902) and Mead (1934) argued that people define themselves according to how they believe they are perceived by others. To Mead (1934), for example, the ability to self-reflect, to consider the self in relation to others, and to understand the perspectives of others was largely a function of participation in organized, rule-governed activities with peers. He suggested that exchanges among peers, whether experienced in the arenas of cooperation or competition, conflict or friendly discussion, allowed the child to gain an understanding of the self as both a subject and an object. Understanding that the self could be an object of others' perspectives gradually evolved into the conceptualization of a "generalized other" or an organized and coordinated perspective of the "social" group. In turn, recognition of the "generalized other" led to the emergence of an organized sense of self.

Thus, according to symbolic interactionist theory, exchanges between the individual and the peer group are essential to the formation of a "self-concept" and a concept of the "other," two constructs thought to be mutually interdependent.

Cognitive Developmental Perspectives

The Piagetian Perspective

Piaget (1932) suggested that children's relationships with peers could be distinguished, in both form and function, from their relationships with adults. The latter relationships were construed as being complementary, asymmetrical, and falling along a vertical plane of dominance and power assertion. As such, children's interactions with adults about cognitions, ideas, and beliefs were thought to be marked by more emotional wariness and less openness and spontaneity than their interactions with age-mates. By contrast, peer exchanges allowed children to actively explore their ideas rather than risk their devaluation and criticism by adult authority figures. It was also proposed that children come to accept adult's notions, thoughts, beliefs, and rules, not necessarily because they understand them, but rather because obedience is viewed as required. Along the same lines, adults were less likely to follow the dictates of children. Peer relationships, on the other hand, were portrayed as being balanced, egalitarian, and as falling along a more or less horizontal plane of dominance and power assertion. Thus, it was in the peer context that children could experience opportunities to examine conflicting ideas and explanations, to negotiate and discuss multiple perspectives, to decide to compromise with or to reject the notions held by peers. These peer interactive experiences were believed to result in positive and adaptive developmental outcomes for children, such as the ability to understand others' thoughts, emotions, and intentions.

Empirical support for these contentions is drawn from neo-Piagetian research demonstrating that when children work together to solve given problems, they are more likely to advance their knowledge base through discussion than if they work independently and alone (e.g., Doise & Mugny, 1984). Developmental change occurs because differences of opinion provoke cognitive disequilibria that are sufficiently

discomforting so as to elicit attempts at resolution. Each interactant must construct, or reconstruct, a coordinated perspective of the original set of ideas to reinstate a sense of cognitive equilibrium.

From this perspective, it is cognitive, *intrapersonal* conflict that evokes a search for homeostasis and resultant developmental change. This intrapersonal conflict may be instigated by disagreements about ideas, thoughts, beliefs; it is unlikely, however, that mean-spirited *interpersonal* conflict and hostility brings with it cognitive advancement. In other words, recent views on the role of conflict center on the notion that disagreements between peers about things personal, interpersonal, and impersonal are best resolved through the cooperative exchange of explanations, questions, and reasoned dialogue (e.g., Rogoff, 1990). If the exchange of conflicting ideas is marked by hostility, dysregulated or disabling emotions are not likely to promote cognitive growth and development.

Contemporary perspectives on the role of peer exchange for cognitive growth can be seen in the work of co-constructivist thinkers such as Azmitia (1988; Azmitia & Montgomery, 1993) and Hartup (in press). These writers introduce the notion that the quality of the relationship between the peers who are interacting with each other may contribute to cognitive and social-cognitive growth and development. For example, *friends* can challenge each other with relative impunity. Given that friends are more sensitive to each other's needs and more supportive of each others' thoughts and well-being than nonfriends, it may be that children are more likely to talk openly and challenge each others' thoughts and deeds in the company of friends than nonfriends. If this is the case, one would expect exchanges between friends to be more promoting of cognitive and social-cognitive growth than nonfriend peer exchanges. Data supportive of this view are found in Azmitia and Montgomery (1993) and Nelson and Aboud (1985) and are reviewed in relevant sections below.

Vygotsky's Perspective

According to Vygotsky (1978), cognitive growth and development are a function, in large part, of interpersonal exchange. Vygotsky invoked the principle of the "zone of proximal development" (ZPD) to explain the significance of social interaction. The ZPD represented the distance between what the child could do independently and what he or she could do with the collaboration or assistance of others. Vygotsky indicated that typically, assistance was provided by the child's parents. But more recently, researchers such as Tudge (1992) and Rogoff (1990) have argued that the child's peers can play the role of coconstructivist. Thus, pairing with a more competent, "expert" peer may assist the child's movement through the ZPD (Gauvain & Rogoff, 1989; Messer, Joiner, Loveridge, Light, & Littleton, 1993).

One difference between the Piagetian and Vysgotskian perspectives of the links among peer interaction, peer relationships, and growth and development lies in Piaget's belief that it was peer *conflict* that evoked change, whereas Vygotsky contended that it was *cooperation* and the pooling of ideas that promoted change. In fact, contemporary accounts suggest that conflicting ideas and differences in opinion actually elicit cooperation between partners (Wertsch, 1984). If partners are positively disposed to one another, it behooves them to discuss their differences, to negotiate, to compromise—in short, to cooperate to move forward, not only cognitively, but also emotionally in their relationship. Thus, recent studies of the role that *conflict* plays in cognitive and social-cognitive growth include, in the phenomenon's definition, components of disagreement as well as explanation, questions, agreements, and compromise (e.g., Damon & Killen, 1982; Dimant & Bearison, 1991; Roy & Howe, 1990). A rapprochement between the Piagetian and Vygotskian positions would suggest that intrapersonal, cognitive conflict triggers the child's attempts to regain some semblance of cognitive homeostasis. If such intrapersonal cognitive conflict is associated with conflictual, negative-spirited interpersonal exchange, cognitive growth is less likely to result than anger, fear, or some other disabling emotion. Alternatively, if cognitive conflict is associated with "reasoned dialogue" (Damon & Killen, 1982), cooperative coconstruction may occur, resulting in a new, more cognitively mature perspective.

In summary, recent research based on the constructivist theories of Piaget and Vygotsky reveals that:

1. Children can and do make cognitive advances when they *cooperatively* exchange and discuss conflicting perspectives on various issues (Nelson & Aboud, 1985).
2. Children working together can solve problems that neither partner is capable of solving alone (Doise & Mugny, 1984).
3. Discussing problems with a peer who has superior knowledge is more likely to evoke intrapersonal conflict and cognitive advancement than discussions with a less

competent peer (Gauvain & Rogoff, 1989; Messer et al., 1993; Tudge, 1992; Tudge & Winterhoff, 1993).
4. Transactive exchanges during which children openly criticize each others' ideas and clarify and elaborate their own ideas are more often observed in the company of friends than of nonfriends (e.g., Azmitia & Montgomery, 1993) or of parents (Kruger & Tomasello, 1986; Nelson & Aboud, 1985).

Peer Relationships, Peer Interaction, and Moral Development

Moral development involves changes in children's reasoning, affect, and behavior in regard to principles and constructs such as benevolence, justice, and reciprocity. Clearly, peers experience, on a regular basis, interactions involving the distribution of resources, object disputes, and the need for helping and caring behaviors. Yet, the extent to which peers play a role in moral development varies from theory to theory.

Kohlberg's Theory

Kohlberg's (Kohlberg & Deissner, 1991) theory of moral development centers on explaining the development of universal principles of justice. Moral development, to Kohlberg, is reflected primarily by changes in the individual's thinking about conflicts involving competing rights and responsibilities. Kohlberg emphasized the importance of developing cognitive capacities to integrate various perspectives when arriving at moral decisions.

In describing influences on moral development, Kohlberg focused primarily on the parent-child relationship; peer relationships were given little consideration as particular contexts within which principles of morality could develop. Nevertheless, the evocative processes in parent-child interaction that were described by Kohlberg as responsible for developmental change in moral thinking can also be observed in friendship relations.

According to Kohlberg (Kohlberg & Deissner, 1991), two processes are involved in moral development. The first process forms the basic conditions for moral development that are involved in any sociomoral interaction regardless of the special nature of the relationship. This includes exposure to internal cognitive moral conflict, exposure to disagreements between persons, and role-taking opportunities. The second process, identified by Kohlberg as "moral attachment," involves the processes of basic imitation and perceived likeness to persons with whom the child has formed a close relationship. Through these secondary processes, children develop a sense of a "shared self" with others, which sensitizes them to social reinforcement contingencies and creates a feeling of obligation or responsibility to others' welfare, their expectations, and to the maintenance of the relationship itself.

Clearly, one can see a role for peer relationships, and the quality thereof, in moral development. However, the emphasis on the development of cognitive structures in Kohlberg's model may diminish the attention devoted to the potential importance and power that affective bonds with peers and friends may exert on morality.

Piaget's Theory

Piaget (1932) proposed that children develop two different types of moral values as a result of qualitatively different forms of interaction with parents and peers. To make sense of a world in which there is an imbalance of power between adult and child, the child must learn respect for authority and social tradition. Piaget called this "unilateral respect" (p. 44), a phenomenon that led to unreflective obedience to parental constraints and demands. However, peers provide the child with an opportunity to develop "mutual respect" that, in turn, contributes to a transformation in understanding of the origins of morality. According to Piaget, it is through cooperation, conflict, and negotiation with others *of an equal status* that moral behavior ceases to be attributed to external causes (e.g., adult control). And, when the perspectives of peers vary from their own, children find discussion, debate, and negotiation more facile in the company of equals than in the company of adults. Thus, it is through interactions and relationships with one's peers that the child "will not only discover the boundaries that separate his self from the other person, but will learn to understand the other person and be understood by him" (p. 90).

For Piaget then, moral reasoning occurs as a function of coconstruction between equals. The kind of cooperation and mutual sensitivity that Piaget describes as fundamental to the process of moral reasoning has been observed to occur between peers (Damon & Killen, 1982), and especially between friends (e.g., Newcomb & Brady, 1982). By suggesting that interaction and mutual respect lead to processes of collaboration and cooperation, Piaget implied a unique role for friendship in moral reasoning.

Sullivan and Moral Development

The trust, intimacy, commitment, and affection that characterize friendship make it a unique setting for moral development. According to Sullivan (1953), it was within the bounds of friendship that a young adolescent develops a sense of "what should I do to contribute to the happiness or to support the prestige and feeling of worth-whileness of my chum" (p. 245). Clearly, Sullivan saw the affective ties of friendship as a precondition for the acquisition of particular moral sensitivities.

Learning and Social Learning Theories, Peer Interaction, and Peer Relationships

The traditional learning theory perspective has been that children are behavior control and behavior change agents for each other. Peers punish or ignore nonnormative social behavior and reward or reinforce positively those behaviors considered culturally appropriate and competent. Thus, to the extent that children behave in a socially appropriate manner, they develop positive relationships with their peers; to the extent that children behave in a socially incompetent or nonnormative manner, peer rejection may result.

Perhaps the most relevant and influential social learning theory was that formulated originally by Bandura and Walters (1963). In their monograph, *Social Learning and Personality Development,* Bandura and Walters noted that children can learn novel social behaviors by observing others. Moreover, children can use observational information about the consequences of specific social behaviors to guide their own exhibition or inhibition of these behaviors.

This modeling perspective provides a powerful argument for how the social behaviors of children are quickly and effectively organized, reorganized, and redirected. Observational learning promotes adaptation to new circumstances and new relationships (Cairns, 1979). As Cairns noted, however, once learned, social behaviors are subject to maintenance and change; thus, it is argued that the demonstration of socially learned behaviors will be maintained or inhibited by its actual or expected consequences. Further, the social contexts within which reinforcement and punishment occur (or are expected to occur) matter. The source of the reinforcement or punishment, how, when, and where the consequences are administered, and whether or not the child believes that he or she can actually produce the desired behavior all affect the production, reproduction, or inhibition of the given behavior. For example, Bandura (1989) has speculated that children set standards of achievement for themselves and that they are likely to self-administer reinforcement when the standards are met, and punishment when they are not. Self-reinforcement is applied when children see themselves as having exceeded the norms for their relevant comparison group of peers; self-punishment is consequent to having failed to meet perceived group norms.

Also, children's beliefs, cognitions, and ideas about the administrators of reward/punishment can influence the strength of the given behaviors. Is the administrator a competent or incompetent peer; an aggressive or nonaggressive age-mate; a younger or older child? Moreover, the age of the child who is processing this social information must assuredly be of some significance. To the extent that researchers have generally ignored these issues, social learning theory still has some way to go in advancing an understanding of the establishment, maintenance, and dissolution/inhibition of children's peer-directed behaviors.

Human Ethology

Ethology "is the subdiscipline of biology concerned with the biological bases of behavior, including its evolution, causation, function, and development" (Cairns, 1979, p. 358). Although there is no particular ethological theory pertaining specifically to the evolutionary significance of peer interaction or peer relationships, the *methods* used by animal behaviorists have often been adopted by those who study children's social behaviors, peer relationships, and the structural dynamics of the peer group (e.g., Strayer, 1989). To the extent that Bowlby's (1973) ethologically oriented theory of parent-infant attachment relationships has come to influence the study of peer relationships (see below), some consideration of human ethological theory is warranted.

The kinds of questions asked by ethologists were outlined many years ago by Tinbergen (1951). He suggested that when an organism produces a given behavior, the scientist must ask: (a) Why did the individual demonstrate the particular behavior at the specific time he or she did? (b) How did the individual come to produce such a behavior at such times? and (c) What is the functional significance or survival value of the produced behavior? These questions focus concern on features of motivation, learning and development, and evolutionary adaptation, respectively (Blurton-Jones, 1972).

A central tenet of ethological theory is that social behavior, relationships, and organizational structures are limited by biological constraints related to their adaptive, evolutionary function (Hinde & Stevenson-Hinde, 1976).

Thus, *aggression,* for example, is viewed as a means by which members of the species survive; protect themselves, their significant others, and their progeny; and ensure reproductive success (Lorenz, 1966). *Altruism* is also seen as a basic facet of human nature, ensuring survival of the species. Likewise, the *attachment relationship,* formed during infancy between parent and child, not only guarantees the protection of the young from discomfort and threatening predators, but also provides the child with an internalized "working model" (Bowlby, 1973) of what human relationships could, should, or might be like. In this latter case, the quality of the primary relationship engenders a set of internalized relationship expectations that affect the initiation and maintenance of extrafamilial (e.g., peer) relationships.

Given the assumption that behavior is best understood when observed in natural settings, ethological theory has influenced contemporary methodologies. Thus, investigators have devoted considerable effort to distinguish *observationally* among different forms and functions of what, on the surface, appear to be the same basic behavioral phenomena. For example, one can distinguish among physical, verbal, and relational aggression (the *forms*) and between hostile and instrumental aggression (the putative *functions;* see Coie & Dodge, this volume). Such distinctions are drawn on the basis of examining the gestures and facial expressions of the interacting individuals, as well as the ecological (venues) and interpersonal (quality of relationships) contexts within which social interactions occur.

Relatedly, ethological theory and the questions derived from it evoke analyses of the psychological meanings of different forms of the same behavior. For example, do instrumental and hostile aggression have different developmental origins and different proximal and distal causes? Similarly does the frequent expression of behavioral solitude when engaging in constructive activity have different developmental origins and different proximal and distal causes than the frequent expression of behavioral solitude when observing others (Coplan, Rubin, Fox, Calkins, & Stewart, 1994)? Likewise, does a given behavior have the same psychological meaning when produced by a 2-, 4-, and 10-year-old? Clearly, these are questions pertinent to the study of peer *interaction.* And, given the normalcy/abnormalcy of social behaviors in different contexts and at different ages, it is also clear how questions derived from ethological theory are relevant to the study of children's peer *relationships.*

PEER INTERACTIONS, RELATIONSHIPS, AND GROUPS: A DEVELOPMENTAL PERSPECTIVE

As in other spheres, with development, children's peer experiences show patterns of increasing diversity, complexity, and integration. In some cases, the impetus for these developments rests within children (i.e., changes in interpersonal understanding or interpersonal concerns), whereas others derive from situational or contextual phenomena (Higgins & Parsons, 1983). Organizational features of the environment, for example, help to define the timetable for many developments in peer relationships. In any case, whatever their origins, it is possible to trace over age many developmental mileposts in the *interactional* (changes in the frequency or forms of specific behaviors), *relational* (changes in qualities of friendships or patterns of involvement in friendships), and *group* (changes in configurations of and involvement in cliques and crowds) levels of children's involvement with other children.

Infancy and the Toddler Years

Interaction

Early researchers of children's peer experiences were impressed by what they regarded as the significant social shortcomings in infants. Buhler (1935), for example, reported that prior to the first six months of life, babies were oblivious to each other's presence. And it was argued that throughout much of the first year, infants were interested in each other as objects, but not as social partners with whom the development of a relationship was possible (e.g., Maudry & Nekula, 1939). Such a view appears less often in contemporary readings, but it has not disappeared completely; for example, it has been noted that the peer interactions of infants are diffuse and fragmented. These interactions are seen as illustrating the inability of babies to comprehend the social and cognitive needs, capacities, or zones of proximal development of their age-mates (Hay, 1985).

Infants do have obvious social limitations. Yet, careful observation of infants reveals remarkable strides taken during the first year of life. For example, by 2 months of age, infants are aroused by the presence of peers and engage in mutual gaze (Eckerman, 1979). By 6 to 9 months, they direct looks, vocalizations, and smiles at one another; often such initiations are returned in kind, thereby demonstrating

the existence of social interest (Hay, Pederson, & Nash, 1982; Vandell, Wilson, & Buchanan, 1980).

During the final quarter of the first year, infants increasingly watch each other. Their smiles, finger points, vocalizations, and playful activities are often met with appropriate, contingent responses and imitations by their infant play partners. These very first imitative acts are often focused on objects, and according to Mueller and Silverman (1989), represent the first evidence of shared meanings between peers and may lay the foundation for the later development of cooperative peer activity.

Thus, several important social skills and behaviors emerge during the first year of life. These include (a) the seemingly intentional direction of smiles, frowns, and gestures to their play partners (Hay et al., 1982); (b) the careful observation of peers, representing a clear sign of social interest (Eckerman, 1979); and (c) the response, often in kind, to their play partner's behaviors (Mueller & Brenner, 1977).

During the second year of life, toddlers demonstrate monumental gains in their social repertoires. With the emergence of locomotion and the ability to use words to communicate, social interchanges become increasingly complex. Interactive bouts become lengthier (Bronson, 1981; Eckerman & Stein, 1990; Ross & Conant, 1992), and toddler play becomes organized around particular themes or "games."

According to Ross (1982), the typical toddler game involves extended and patterned interchanges characterized by the mutual exchange of gaze, the direction of social actions to one another, the production of appropriate responses to these social actions, and the demonstration of turn-taking behaviors. Often, these toddler games are marked by reciprocal imitative acts. Reciprocity of imitation suggests not only that a given child is socially interested in the playmate to the point at which he or she is willing to copy that playmate's behavior, but also that he or she is also aware of the partner's interest in him or her (i.e., an awareness of being imitated). Mutual imitation, which increases rapidly during the second year, appears to lay the basis for later emerging cooperative interchanges involving pretense (Howes, 1992).

In summary, social skills in toddlerhood comprise (a) the ability to coordinate behavior with that of the play partner (e.g., Baudonierre, Garcia-Werebe, Michel, & Liegois, 1989); (b) imitation of the peer's activity and an awareness of being imitated (Eckerman, 1993); (c) turn-taking that involves *observe peer–respond to peer–observe and wait–respond to peer* interchange sequences (Goldman & Ross, 1978; Howes, 1988; Ross, Lollis, & Elliot, 1982); (d) the demonstration of helping and sharing behaviors (e.g., Rheingold, Hay, & West, 1976); and (e) the ability to respond appropriately to the peer partner's characteristics (Brownell, 1990; Howes, 1988).

These developments promote more effective social commerce between toddlers and contribute a generally positive affective quality to their interaction. However, toddler social interaction is also marked by conflict (e.g., Hay & Ross, 1982). Indeed, it appears as if many of those toddlers who frequently initiate conflicts with peers are the most socially outgoing and initiating (E. Brown & Brownell, 1990). It is also the case that (a) toddlers who lose conflicts are more likely than the initial victor to initiate the immediately subsequent conflict (Hay & Ross, 1982); and (b) toddlers are highly attentive to, and are more likely to imitate and initiate interactions with, highly sociable agemates (E. Brown & Brownell, 1990; Howes, 1983, 1988). Taken together, these data suggest that during the second year of life, toddlers not only display social skills of modest complexity, but also demonstrate preferences for peers who carry with them a variety of attractive characteristics. Such interpersonal preferences may indicate that toddlers are readily capable of establishing *relationships* with agemates, a possibility we consider next.

Relationships

It has been demonstrated that toddlers are more likely to initiate play, direct positive affect to, and engage in complex interactions with familiar than unfamiliar playmates (Howes, 1988). But can familiarity be equated with the existence of a relationship?

According to Ross and Lollis (1989), toddlers do develop positive relationships as they become increasingly familiar with one another. Indeed, these toddler relationships allow the observer to predict the sorts of interchanges that will transpire between dyadic partners (Ross, Conant, Cheyne, & Alevisos, 1992). It is the predictability of the quality of interchange that marks a dyad as constituting a friendship.

Ross and colleagues (Ross et al., 1992) have carried out an elegant series of studies to demonstrate that toddlers not only can and do develop relationships, but also that their relationships can be characterized in several different ways. Ross and colleagues begin by noting that a relationship may be inferred when "Neither the characteristic behavior of Child One, nor the behavior that others typically direct to Child Two, nor the independent, additive influences of both factors taken together are sufficient to predict the behavior of Child One to Child Two. In that sense, relationships cannot be derived from the individual characteristics of the participants; the relationship itself influences the interaction between them" (p. 1).

To this end, Ross and colleagues (Ross et al., 1992) have demonstrated that toddlers develop *reciprocal* relationships, not only in terms of the mutual exchange of positive overtures, but also in terms of agonistic interactions. Positive interactions are directed specifically to those who have directed positive initiations to the child beforehand; conflict is initiated specifically with those who have initiated conflictual interactions with the child beforehand.

To the extent that reciprocal interchanges of positive overtures may characterize particular dyads, it may be said that toddlers do have friendships. Although the terms of reference and the operationalizing principles vary from those of Ross and colleagues, other researchers have proposed that toddlers have "friends." For example, Howes (1983, 1988) defined toddler friendship as encompassing the response to a peer's overture at least *once,* the production of at least *one* complementary or reciprocal dyadic exchange, and the demonstration of positive affect during at least *one* such exchange. Vandell and Mueller (1980) identified toddler friends as those who initiated positive social interaction more often with each other than with other potential partners. In short, during the toddler period, friendships, as defined above, do exist. It is doubtful, however, that they carry the same strength of psychological meaning as the friendships of older children. Nevertheless, these early relationships may lay the groundwork for the establishment and maintenance of friendships throughout the childhood years.

Groups

Insofar as the group represents the highest level of social complexity, it is hardly surprising that this level has not yet proved to be an important level of description when describing very young toddler's experiences with peers. To be sure, even young toddlers spend much time in small groups, such as with day care mates. But there is not much empirical evidence that this level of social organization is salient to, or influential on, these young children. Nevertheless, some authors (e.g., Legault & Strayer, 1990) have observed dominance hierarchies even within small groups of young toddlers, as well as subsets of children who invest greater attention and interaction to one another than to nonmembers. Interestingly, some members of these groups appear more central to their functioning than others, perhaps illustrating the very earliest examples of individual differences in popularity and influence.

Early Childhood

Interaction

From 24 months to 5 years, the frequency of peer interaction increases and becomes more complex. One classic description of the changes over this period was offered by Mildred Parten (e.g., 1932). Parten described six social participation categories that purportedly unfolded as stages as children matured. In order of presumed maturity, these categories included unoccupied behavior; solitary play; onlooker behavior (the child observes others but does not participate in the activity); parallel play (the child plays beside but not with other children); associative play (the child plays and shares with others); and cooperative play (the child engages others in interaction that is well coordinated and defined by a division of labor). From her data, Parten concluded that between the ages of 2 and 5 years, children engage in increasing frequencies of associative and cooperative play and in decreasing frequencies of idle, solitary, and onlooker behavior.

In spite of the very limited database on which she based her developmental conclusions (a sample of only 40 children attending the University of Minnesota laboratory preschool), Parten's (1932) social participation taxonomy and her reported findings dominated the literature concerning children's interactive behavior for almost 50 years. Indeed, it became commonplace to characterize the typical 3-year-old preschooler as a solitary or parallel player and referring to the typical 5-year-old as spending much of his or her time in associative or cooperative play.

A more critical reading of Parten's study and subsequent attempts at replication (e.g., Barnes, 1971; Rubin, Watson, & Jambor, 1978) suggests a more complex set of conclusions. To begin with, children at all ages engage in unoccupied, onlooking, solitary, parallel, and group activities (Howes & Matheson, 1992). Even at 5 years, children spend *less* of their free-play time in classroom settings interacting with others than being alone or near others (Barnes, 1971; Rubin et al., 1978). Indeed, the frequency of parallel play appears to remain constant from 3 to 5 years (Barnes, 1971; Rubin et al., 1978). Yet, despite its modest placement in Parten's hierarchy of social participation, parallel play appears to serve as an important bridge

to more truly interactive exchanges. More precise, sequential observations of preschool interaction reveal that parallel play often serves as an entrée into more complex, cooperative activity (Bakeman & Brownlee, 1980). Put another way, competent entry into ongoing peer activity appears to involve the ability to observe what the play participants are doing (onlooking activity), to approach and play beside potential play partners (parallel play), and, finally, to engage the players in conversation about the ongoing activity. As such, a simple consideration of the frequency of particular forms of social participation masks the functional significance of the behavior. Watching and playing near but not with others is not necessarily immature. Rather, these behaviors may be sequenced in a competent manner to gain entry into an ongoing play activity.

Further attesting to the limits of Parten's original social participation categories is the fact that the categories of solitary, parallel, and group behavior comprise a variety of play forms that differ in cognitive complexity (see Rubin, Fein, & Vandenberg, 1983, for a review). Thus, whether alone, near, or with others, children may produce simple sensorimotor behaviors (*functional play,* e.g., aimlessly bouncing a ball), construct structures from blocks or draw with crayons (constructive play), or engage in some form of pretense (*dramatic* or pretend play). These cognitive forms of play (Rubin et al., 1983), when examined within their social context, reveal interesting developmental trends. For example, solitary sensorimotor behaviors become increasingly rare over the preschool years, whereas the relative frequency of solitary construction or exploration remains the same (Rubin et al., 1978). Furthermore, the only types of social interactive activity to increase over the preschool years are sociodramatic play and games with rules. That is, age differences are apparent only for particular forms of social participation. Thus, in contrast to Parten's characterization, it does not appear to be a simple matter of solitary play disappearing over time, being replaced by social interactive activity. Rather, it is the form that solitary or parallel or social activity takes that is of developmental significance (Rubin et al., 1978).

Perhaps the most complex form of group interactive activity during the preschool years is *sociodramatic play.* The ability to engage easily in this form of social activity represents mastery of one of the essential tasks of early childhood: the will and skill to share and coordinate decontextualized and substitutive activities (e.g., Garvey, 1990). Researchers have reported that by the third year of life, children are able to share symbolic meanings through social pretense (e.g., Howes, 1984, 1988; Howes & Matheson, 1992; Howes, Unger, & Siedner, 1989). This is a remarkable accomplishment, as it involves the capacity to take on complementary roles, none of which matches real-world situations, and to agree on the adoption of these imaginary roles within a rule-governed context.

The ability to share meaning during pretense has recently been referred to as "intersubjectivity" (Goncu, 1993; see also Mueller & Brenner, 1977). Goncu has reported that quantitative differences are present in the extent to which the social interchanges of 3- versus 4.5-year-olds comprise indices of shared meaning or intersubjectivity. For example, the social interactions of older preschoolers involve longer sequences or turns. With increasing age, play partners become better able to agree with each other about the roles, rules, and themes of their pretense. They are also better able to maintain their play interactions by adding new dimensions to their expressed ideas. These developments reflect the preschooler's capacity to take the perspective of the play partner or, even more important, reflect the increasing sophistication of preschoolers' naive "theory of mind" (DiLalla & Watson, 1988).

Clearly, the demonstration of elaborate forms of social pretense during the preschool years is impressive. But is the experience of sociodramatic play developmentally significant? According to Howes (1992), sociodramatic play serves three essential developmental functions. First, it creates a context for mastering the communication of meaning. Second, it provides opportunities for children to learn to control and compromise; these opportunities arise during discussions and negotiations concerning pretend roles and scripts and the rules guiding the pretend episodes. Third, social pretense allows for a "safe" context within which children can explore and discuss issues of intimacy and trust. Researchers have demonstrated that engaging in sociodramatic play is associated with social perspective-taking skills and the display of skilled interpersonal behavior (e.g., Garvey, 1990).

In summary, as pretend play becomes more interactive, it serves increasingly sophisticated psychological functions. At first, social pretense provides opportunities for developing communication skills (Garvey, 1974). Subsequently, it allows children opportunities to negotiate roles, rules, and play themes and to practice a variety of roles within particular play scripts (Goncu, 1993). Thus, the addition of understanding pretense and sharing this understanding with

others (Goncu, 1993) represents a significant milestone in the social lives of young children.

In addition to developmental differences in the extent to which children interact with one another or engage in cooperative endeavors requiring shared meanings, several other significant advances are made during the preschool period. For one, positive social behaviors become more commonplace with increasing age. Researchers have demonstrated that 4-year-olds direct approval and affection to their peers more often than 3-year-olds (see Eisenberg & Fabes, this volume). On the other hand, the frequency of aggression also increases with age. However, the proportion of aggressive to friendly interactions actually decreases with age (see Coie & Dodge, Ch. 12, this Volume).

Finally, older preschool-age children direct more speech to their peers than do their younger counterparts (Levin & Rubin, 1983). It is important to note, however, that the successful outcome of a verbally directed request is predicted by its technical quality. Preschoolers whose language is comprehensible, who assure that they have obtained listener attention, and who are within arm's length of their social targets are more likely to meet their social goals than those whose verbal directives are less skillfully evinced (Mueller, 1972).

It has also been reported that during the preschool period, children alter their speech to suit the needs of their listeners. For example, Shatz and Gelman (1973) found that the utterances directed to 2-year-old listeners were shorter and less grammatically complex than those directed to age-mates or adults. Similar adjustments to the characteristics of their social targets have been reported in studies of interpersonal problem-solving overtures (Krasnor & Rubin, 1983; Rubin & Krasnor, 1983). These authors reported that preschool children altered their requestive strategies given target characteristics such as age and gender.

Taken together, the data reviewed above certainly raise questions concerning Piaget's (1959) assumption that the speech of preschoolers is characterized primarily by its socially egocentric quality. Indeed, approximately 60% of preschoolers' utterances are socially directed, comprehensible, and result in appropriate responses (Levin & Rubin, 1983; Mueller, 1972). Furthermore, it has been shown that young children recognize when their verbal repertoires are limited and, in such circumstances, will resort to the use of gestures to communicate meaning (e.g., Evans & Rubin, 1979). These studies of gestural communication actually shed light on a seemingly forgotten or ignored aspect of

Piaget's original writings and research concerning egocentric thought and speech. Piaget recognized the significance of gestural communication and wrote that in the explanations of young children, "gestures play as important a part as words" (p. 77). In fact, it may well be that Piaget's "take" on communicative competence was poorly understood, or at best, misjudged for many years. In Piaget's own research, he indicated that only 35 to 40% of young children's utterances were "egocentric." This leads to the obvious conclusion that in at least 60% of the cases, young children demonstrated communicative competence. If one were to add to *verbal* expression the appropriate and comprehensible use of gestures, preschoolers would clearly be regarded as communicatively skilled.

Although preschoolers do demonstrate communicative skill, growth does occur during this period. For example, Garvey (1984) reported that older preschoolers (4.5- to 5-year-olds) were more likely than younger preschoolers (3.5- to 4.5-year-olds) to use indirect (declarative, interrogative, inferred) than direct (imperative) requests. Given that the indirect request form is the more sophisticated (and skilled) means by which to communicate one's personal wishes to a peer, it can be concluded that during early childhood, pragmatic skills are developed and do improve.

Relationships

During early childhood, children express preferences for some peers over others as playmates. It appears that one important influence on this process is that preschoolers are attracted to peers who are similar to them in some noticeable regard. For example, similarities in age and sex draw young children together. Furthermore, preschoolers appear to be attracted to peers whose behavioral tendencies are similar to their own, a phenomenon known as *behavioral homophyly* (Rubin, Lynch, Coplan, Rose-Krasnor, & Booth, 1994).

Once preschoolers form friendships, their behavior with these individuals is distinct from their behavior with other children who are familiar but not friends. For example, positive social exchanges and mutuality occur more among friends than nonfriends (e.g., Baudonniere, 1987; Baudonniere et al., 1989). Children as young as 3.5 years direct more social overtures, engage in more social interaction, and play in more complex ways with their friends as compared to nonfriends (e.g., Doyle, 1982; Gottman, 1983; Hinde, Titmus, Easton, & Tamplin, 1985). As well, preschool-age friends tend to cooperate and exhibit more positive social behaviors with each other than with nonfriends (e.g., Charlesworth & LaFreniere, 1983; Masters & Furman, 1981).

It is not only the positive aspects of behavior that differentiate preschool friendships from nonfriendships; compared to nonfriends, preschool friends also demonstrate more quarreling and more active (assaults and threats) and reactive (refusals and resistance) hostility (Hinde et al., 1985). Hartup and his colleagues (Hartup & Laursen, 1991; Hartup, Laursen, Stewart, & Eastenson, 1988) have demonstrated that preschool children engage in more conflicts overall with their friends than with neutral associates. Of course, these differences are best understood by recognizing that friends spend much more time actually interacting with each other than do nonfriends. Hartup and his colleagues also report qualitative differences in how preschool friends and nonfriends resolve conflicts and in what the outcomes of these conflicts are likely to be. Friends, as compared with nonfriends, make more use of negotiation and disengagement, relative to standing firm, in their resolution of conflicts. In terms of conflict outcomes, friends are more likely to have equal resolutions, relative to win or lose occurrences. Also, following conflict resolution, friends are more likely than neutral associates to stay in physical proximity and continue to engage in interaction.

In summary, preschoolers behave differently in the company of friends than of nonfriends. When they interact with friends, preschoolers engage in more prosocial behaviors as well as more conflicts than when with nonfriends. These conflicts are most likely to be resolved through negotiation, and the outcomes are usually equitable. These differences suggest that preschoolers view friendship as a unique context, separate and qualitatively different from their experiences with nonfriends.

Groups

Drawing from ethological theory, a number of researchers have examined the social structures of preschool playgroups. Most research concerning group structure and hierarchies has focused on the importance of dominance (toughness and assertiveness) in determining ranks within the group. According to Markovits and Strayer (1982), social dominance essentially involves asymmetrical relationships. They distinguish between "dyadic dominance," which refers to the balance of social power between two individuals in a social group, and "group dominance structures," which refer to the organizational system that summarizes the coordination of all such dyadic relationships. These group dominance structures are more commonly referred to as "dominance hierarchies." Essentially, dominance hierarchies are stable orderings of individuals that serve to predict who will prevail under conditions of conflict between group members.

Many researchers have found that the social dominance hierarchy is an important organizational feature of the preschool peer group (e.g., Strayer and Strayer, 1976; Vaughn & Waters, 1981). And, in keeping with a central tenet of the ethological perspective, researchers have argued that dominance hierarchies develop naturally in groups to serve adaptive functions. In the case of preschool-age children, dominance hierarchies appear to reduce overt aggression among members of the group (LaFreniere & Charlesworth 1983; Strayer, 1984). The observations of exchanges between children in which physical attacks, threats, and object conflicts occur reveal a consistent pattern of winners and losers. And the child who loses in an object struggle rarely initiates conflict with children who have been "victorious" over those to whom the child has lost (Strayer & Strayer, 1976).

It is interesting to note, however, that although dominance relationships are observable in the interactive behaviors of preschoolers, the children themselves have difficulty articulating their existence. Thus, researchers have found that, when asked, preschoolers cannot agree on who is the toughest or strongest in their classrooms, and often nominate themselves (Strayer, Chapeskie, & Strayer, 1978).

In summary, even in early childhood, one can identify children who are more or less skilled in manipulating their peers or in meeting their interpersonal goals. Of course, dominance hierarchies reflect primarily differences in children's success in struggles over objects. However, achieving the acquisition of desired objects is only one of many interpersonal goals that preschool children may have. Consequently, it remains unknown whether preschool children who have risen to the top of the preschool dominance hierarchy are those who develop and maintain positive relationships with their peers, not only in preschool, but thereafter as well.

Middle Childhood and Preadolescence

The school-age years represent a dramatic shift in social context for most children in Western cultures (Higgins &

Parsons, 1983). One simple barometer of change is that the proportion of social interaction that involves peers increases; approximately 10% of the social interaction for 2-year-olds involves peers, whereas the comparable figure for children in middle childhood is more than 30% (the rest being with siblings, parents, and adults). Other changes include the size of the peer group (which becomes considerably larger than it had been during the preschool period) and how peer interaction is supervised (peer interactions become less closely supervised by parents and other adults). Thus, in the years leading up to adolescence, children are brought into contact with a more diverse set of peers, albeit generally with those who are similar to them in age.

The settings of peer interaction also change in middle childhood and early adolescence. Preschool children's peer contacts are centered in the home and in day care centers, whereas school-age children come into contact with peers in a wide range of settings. The settings for peer interaction in middle childhood have not been well described. Zarbatany, Hartmann, and Rankin (1990) have reported that the most frequent contexts for peer interaction among middle-class young adolescents include, in order of their frequency, conversing, "hanging out," being together at school, talking on the telephone, traveling to and from school, watching TV and listening to records, and noncontact sports. Boys and girls differed on only one of these activities: more peer interaction took place during phone conversations for girls than for boys. In order of their perceived *importance,* this sample of early adolescents ranked noncontact sports, watching TV and listening to records, conversing, talking on the telephone, physical games, parties, and "hanging out" as the most important contexts for peer interaction. Each of these activities was as important for boys as for girls, with the exception of noncontact sports. An important aspect of this research is that these contexts were associated with very different types of peer interaction. Noncompetitive activities facilitated socializing and the development of relationships, whereas competitive activities provided opportunities for identifying unique aspects of the self. According to Zarbatany et al. (1990), the full range of activities is necessary for early adolescents to derive broad benefits from peer experiences.

Interaction

There appear to be few changes in the amount of negative behaviors shown by individual children across the school-age period. However, the form of aggressive behaviors changes. Verbal aggression (insults, derogation, threats) gradually replaces direct physical aggression. Further, relative to preschoolers, the aggressive behavior of 6- to 12-year-olds is less instrumental (directed toward possessing objects or occupying specific territory) and more specifically hostile toward others (Coie & Dodge, this volume). With regard to positive social behavior, Eisenberg and Fabes (this volume) report the levels of generosity, helpfulness, or cooperation that children direct to their peers increase somewhat during the primary school years, but that changes are not observed in adolescence.

One striking difference between peer interaction in older and younger children is the decline of pretend play across middle childhood. By the time children reach early adolescence, this form of interaction is almost absent from children's interactions with age-mates (Baumeister & Senders, 1989). There is a similar decline in the frequency of rough-and-tumble play during middle childhood, although this decrease is not as sharp or as complete as that of pretense. Replacing these forms of interaction are games with or without formal rules, and activities structured by adults. In these latter activities, children's interactions with peers are highly coordinated, involving both positive and negative forms of behavior.

Children's concerns about acceptance in the peer group rise sharply during middle childhood, and these concerns appear related to an increase in the salience and frequency of gossip (Eder, 1985; Parker & Gottman, 1989). At this age, gossip reaffirms children's membership in important same-sex social groups and reveals, to its constituent members, the core attitudes, beliefs, and behaviors comprising the basis for inclusion in or exclusion from these groups. Teasley and Parker (1995) recently examined the topics of gossip, and how gossip is influenced by parameters of the interpersonal context during middle childhood. These authors reported that much gossip among children at this age is negative, involving the defamation of third parties. However, gossip takes other important forms. For example, a great deal of children's gossip involves discussion of the important interpersonal connections among children; that is, children discuss and debate whether other children are friends, enemies, dating, and so on. Generally these discussions are not strongly pejorative; instead, children appear concerned with consolidating their separate "social maps" of the structure of the larger group. Much of children's gossip involves discussion of others' admirable traits. The gossip of boys and girls is more similar than different. However, there is some evidence that boys who are not close friends use gossip to find common ground between them, whereas girls who are not close friends avoid gossip more than close friends. Also, compared to boys, girls engage in more discussion of real or imagined romantic relationships among their peers.

Another form of interaction emerging during middle childhood is bullying and victimization (Olweus, 1993a). Bullying refers to acts of verbal and physical aggression on the part of a bully that are directed toward particular peers (i.e., victims). Bullying accounts for a substantial portion of the aggression that occurs in the peer group (Olweus, 1993a). The dimension that distinguishes bullying from other forms of aggressive behavior is its specificity. That is, bullies direct their behavior toward only certain peers, comprising approximately 10% of the school population (Olweus, 1984, 1993a; Perry, Kusel, & Perry, 1988). Research on bullying suggests that bullies are characterized by strong tendencies toward aggressive behavior, relatively weak control over their aggressive impulses, and a tolerance for aggressive behavior. Further, Perry, Perry, and Kennedy (1992) note that bullies are most likely to use force unemotionally and outside of an ongoing flow of conflict or interaction. Also, bullies generally do not experience much resistance to their aggressive acts. Finally, there is evidence that children who are disproportionately the victims of bullying behavior tend to be anxious, insecure, and isolated from the remainder of the peer group (Olweus, 1993b). Victimized children appear also to lack self confidence, self-esteem, and prosocial skills (Perry et al., 1992). Some authors have concluded that victims of bullying are unlikely to be aggressive themselves (e.g, Olweus, 1993b); others report that children victimized through bullying actually show high levels of aggression (e.g., Perry et al., 1992).

Relationships

The period of middle childhood and early adolescence brings marked changes in children's understanding of friendship. To chart these changes, researchers have asked children questions such as "What is a best friend?" (Youniss, 1980) and "What do you expect from a best friend?" (Bigelow, 1977). Researchers have shown that young children's conceptions of a friend are anchored in the here-and-now and not easily separated from social activity itself. Early school-age children have friendship concepts that transcend any specific activity, and thus have continuity over time. But during the early school years, children can still be very instrumental and concrete in what they view as a friendship or appropriate friendship behavior. For example, Bigelow (1977) suggested that children's friendship conceptions at the start of middle childhood (7–8 years) go through a *reward-cost stage:* friends are individuals who are rewarding to be with, whereas nonfriends are individuals who are difficult or uninteresting to be with. A friend is someone who is convenient (i.e., who lives nearby), has interesting toys or possessions, and shares the child's expectations about play activities. This conception evolves across the period of middle childhood and early adolescence. By about 10 to 11 years, children go through a *normative stage,* in which shared values and rules become important and friends are expected to stick up for and be loyal to one another. Later, at 11 to 13 years, children's concept of a friend enters an *empathetic stage,* at which friends are seen as sharing similar interests, as required to make active attempts to understand each other, and as willing to engage in self-disclosure.

According to Selman (1980; Selman & Schultz, 1990), the engine that drives these developmental changes in children's friendship conceptions is perspective-taking ability. Young children do not yet realize that other people feel or think about things differently from themselves. By middle childhood, analyses of children's discussions of friendship and friendship issues indicate a maturing appreciation that feelings and intentions, not just manifest actions, keep friends together or drive them apart. Children also begin to appreciate that others' thoughts and feelings concerning social events may differ from their own. Nevertheless, these social-cognitive advances are insufficient to move children beyond a unilateral concern with their own, not their partner's, subjective experiences in the relationship. This explains their preoccupation with only their own side of rewards-costs of the interaction equation. This unilateral perspective subsides eventually, however, and children begin to express an understanding that both parties in a relationship must coordinate and adjust their needs and actions to one another in mutually satisfying ways. But their understanding of friendship does not include an expectation that friendships can weather specific arguments or negative events. As late childhood/early adolescence begins (around 11 or 12 years), however, most children realize that friendship implies an affective bond having continuity over time, distance, and events.

Youniss (1980) has argued that children's friendship expectations develop in conjunction with the child's understanding of reciprocity. Young children, who believe that their own contribution toward a friendship is the most

important, are more likely to understand friendship in terms of momentary interactions and how they themselves are affected. By adolescence, friendship is perceived as an ongoing relationship, and friends are people on whom one can count for understanding and intimate social support.

To many researchers, children's ideas about relationships in general, and about friendship in particular, develop in a hierarchical, stage-like manner. Thus, it is assumed that the understanding of relationships is progressive, unidirectional and nonreversible, hierarchical, and qualitatively different from one stage to the next. Evidence in support of this stage-like model of friendship conceptions emanates largely from the work of Selman (1980). He has demonstrated that a child's ideas of friendship can generally be coded at or around a single stage or level. Furthermore, longitudinal research indicates that the development of friendship conceptions is generally progressive and invariant; over a two-year longitudinal period, Selman found that 83% of his sample demonstrated progressive change. The remaining 17% of the sample maintained their original levels of conceptual development.

Berndt (1981), however, has argued that children's conceptions of friendship relationships do not change in a stage-like manner but rather represent the cumulative assimilation of basically unrelated themes or dimensions, such as commonalities in play interests and self-disclosure. According to Berndt (1996), children do not abandon initial notions about play and mutual association when they eventually recognize the importance of intimacy and loyalty. This notion deserves further research given that current empirical evidence does not preclude the possibility that understanding friendship develops cumulatively rather than hierarchically.

Although the underlying mechanisms by which the understanding of friendships develops remain relatively unknown, certain generalizations are plausible. Essentially, children's conceptions about friendship reflect their own transitions from the world of the concrete to the abstract. What children may require and desire in a friendship develops as a function of their growing understanding of their social worlds. Beginning in early childhood, this world is cognitively differentiated, and becomes more so with time (Berndt & Perry, 1986). Eventually, children begin to realize that a friendship can serve as both a resource and a context that differs from the conditions that exist with nonfriends.

In other studies in which elementary school-age children have been asked to describe their friendships, children draw sharper distinctions between the supportiveness of friends and nonfriends with increasing age (Berndt & Perry, 1986, 1990). Moreover, children's descriptions of their friendships indicate that loyalty, self-disclosure, and trust increase with age, although these trends are more likely to be observed in girls than in boys (Berndt, 1986; Berndt & Perry, 1986; Buhrmester, 1996; Furman & Buhrmester, 1985; Sharabany, Gershoni, & Hofman, 1981). Older children of both sexes also possess more intimate knowledge of their friends (Diaz & Berndt, 1982), describe their friends in a more differentiated and integrated manner (Peevers & Secord, 1973), and see their friendships as more exclusive and individualized (Sharabany et al., 1981; Smollar & Youniss, 1982).

Changes in the understanding of friendship are accompanied by changes in the patterns and nature of involvement in friendships across middle childhood. Children's friendship choices are more stable and more likely to be reciprocated in middle childhood than at earlier ages, although it is not clear that either the reciprocity or stability of friendship increases across the period of middle childhood itself (Berndt & Hoyle, 1985; Epstein, 1986). In addition, the number of children's reported "close friends" increases with age up to about 11 years after which it begins to decline (see Epstein, 1986). Moreover, as is commonly observed, children's liking for and friendship involvement with opposite-sex peers drops off precipitously after 7 years of age (Epstein, 1986; Hayden-Thompson, Rubin, & Hymel, 1987; Leaper, 1994a).

With respect to the *features* of children's friendships in middle childhood and early adolescence, Newcomb and Bagwell (1995) report that children are more likely to behave in positive ways with friends than with nonfriends and to ascribe positive characteristics to their interactions with friends. This pattern of findings is observed across a broad range of studies using a variety of methods, including direct observations (e.g., Newcomb & Brady, 1982), interviews (Berndt, 1985; Berndt, Hawkins, & Hoyle, 1986), and hypothetical dilemmas (Rotenberg & Slitz, 1988). More importantly, Newcomb and Bagwell's meta-analysis showed that the expression of affect varied considerably for pairs of friends and nonfriends during middle childhood and early adolescence. In their interactions with friends, relative to interaction with nonfriends, children show more affective reciprocity and emotional intensity and enhanced levels of emotional understanding. In this regard, friendship is not only a socially positive relational context, but it also provides opportunities for the expression and regulation of affect (Parker & Gottman, 1989). And consistent with the aforementioned views of Sullivan (1953), it has been found that these friend-nonfriend differences are stronger during early adolescence than during either middle childhood or the preschool years.

One of the few dimensions of interaction in which there are no differences between friends and nonfriends is that of *conflict*. Research has shown repeatedly that after early childhood, pairs of friends engage in about the same amount of conflict as pairs of nonfriends (Hartup, 1992; Laursen, Hartup, & Koplas, 1996). There is, however, a major difference in the conflict resolution strategies that friends and nonfriends adopt. The Newcomb and Bagwell (1995) meta-analysis, for example, showed that friends were more concerned about achieving an equitable resolution to conflicts. More specifically, Laursen et al. (1996) and Hartup (1996) report that friends are more likely than nonfriends to resolve conflicts in a way that will preserve or promote the continuity of their relationship. In this respect, experience within friendship is linked to the development of social competence in the sense that within the friendship relation, children and adolescents show a concern for a balance between individual and communal goals.

Before leaving our discussion of relationships in middle childhood and early adolescence, note must be made of one form of social relationship at this age that thus far has not received much empirical inquiry: the *bully-victim dyad*. It has been observed that bullies and victims form asymmetrical pairs in which the victim serves as the recipient of a bully's aggressive acts. The emergence of these dyads has been explained as the result of an aggressive child's search for a peer who will not retaliate against the aggressor's actions (G. Patterson, Littman, & Bricker, 1967). Once a victim has been found, the aggressor tends to direct his or her aggressive behaviors toward the victimized peer. Surprisingly, there is evidence that victimized children do not necessarily dislike the bullies who victimize them. Dodge, Price, Coie, and Christopoulos (1990) reported that when asked to indicate which of their peers they disliked, victimized children were not more likely to nominate the bullies who victimized them than they were to nominate other children.

Groups

A new form of social involvement that emerges in middle childhood is participation in stable, polydyadic social groups, or cliques (Crockett, Losoff, & Peterson, 1984; Eder, 1985). Cliques are voluntary, friendship-based groups and stand in contrast to the activity or work groups to which children can be assigned by circumstance or by adults. Cliques generally range in size from three to nine children and almost always comprise same-sex, same-race members (Epstein, 1986; Kindermann, McCollom, & Gibson, 1995). The prevalence of cliques has generally not been investigated among children younger than 10 or 11 years of age. By 11 years of age, however, children report that most of their peer interaction takes place in the context of the clique, and nearly all children report being a member of one (Crockett et al., 1984).

Apart from cliques, the other primary organizational feature of children's groups in middle childhood and early adolescence is the popularity hierarchy. As these hierarchies are discussed in great length later, we note here only that children's appreciation of their own and other children's popularity greatly increases at this age. Indeed, children can express great consternation and concern over their acceptance by peers and their real or imagined status (or lack thereof) in the popularity hierarchy (Gavin & Furman, 1989; Parker & Gottman, 1989). Parker, Rubin, Price, and DeRosier (1995) note that such concern may be partly explained by developmental changes in social comparison processes that accompany entry into middle childhood (Ruble, 1983). Whereas the younger child is likely to evaluate his or her behavioral performance against a set of absolute standards, in middle childhood evaluations are more likely to be based on comparisons with others. On the other hand, children's social insecurities are almost certainly also fueled by the sometimes capricious manner with which in-group and out-group status can shift at this age. For example, Kanner, Feldman, Weinberg, and Ford (1987) found that close to one in three 11-year-olds reported the experience of losing a friend or being picked last by peers for an activity, and almost two out of three children reported being teased by peers within the previous month.

Adolescence

Interaction

The trend toward spending increasingly substantial amounts of time with peers continues in adolescence. For example, Csikszentmihalyi and Larson (1984) asked adolescents to keep records of their activities, moods, and companions at random intervals across a one-week period. During a typical week, even discounting time spent in classroom instruction, high school students spend almost one-third (29%) of their waking hours with peers, an amount more than double that spent with parents and other adults (13%). Moreover, adolescent peer interaction takes place with less adult guidance and control than peer interaction in middle childhood, and is more likely to involve individuals of the opposite sex (B. Brown, 1990).

Relationships

Adolescence also heralds a significant advance in how children conceptualize friendship (Selman & Schultz, 1990). Preadolescents understand a great deal about the reciprocal operations and obligations of friendship, about the continuity of friendships, and about the psychological grounds that evoke behavior. But preadolescents tend to view friendships in overly exclusive terms; they regard relationships with third parties as inimical to the basic nature of friendship commitment. The significant change at adolescence, however, is that individuals begin to accept the other's need to establish relationships with others and to grow through such experiences. In particular, adolescents recognize an obligation to grant friends a certain degree of autonomy and independence. Thus, their discussions of friendship and friendship issues show fewer elements of possessiveness and jealousy and more concern with how the relationship helps the partners enhance their respective self-identities.

During adolescence, youngsters report that they have fewer friends on average than younger children (Epstein, 1986). Nonetheless, same-sex friends account for an increasingly larger proportion of adolescents' perceived primary social network, and friends equal or surpass parents as sources of support and advice to adolescents in many significance domains (e.g., Adler & Furman, 1988; Buhrmester, 1996; Furman & Buhrmester, 1985, 1992). Also, the friendships of adolescents are relatively stable (Berndt, Hawkins, & Hoyle, 1986; Berndt & Hoyle, 1985).

One hallmark of friendship in adolescence is its emphasis on intimacy and self-disclosure (Buhrmester, 1996). Studies consistently indicate that adolescents report greater levels of intimacy in their friendships than do younger children (Buhrmester & Furman, 1986; Youniss & Smollar, 1985). Furthermore, observations of adolescent friends indicate that intimate self-disclosure is a highly salient feature of friendship interaction (Parker & Gottman, 1989). Parker and Gottman (1989; see also Gottman & Parker, 1986) speculate that salience of self-disclosure in friendship during adolescence plays a role in aiding the understanding of themselves and their own and others' significant relationships. Although self-disclosure is sometimes apparent in the interactions of younger friends, in adolescent friendships, unlike at earlier ages, self-disclosure prompts lengthy and sometimes emotionally laden, psychological discussions about the nature of the problem and possible avenues to its resolution (Parker & Gottman, 1989).

Groups

As in middle childhood, cliques are readily observed in adolescence, and membership in cliques is related to adolescents' psychological well-being and ability to cope with stress (Hansell, 1981). Nevertheless, Shrum and Cheek (1987) reported a sharp decline from 11 to 18 years of age in the proportion of students who were clique members, and a corresponding increase with age in the proportion of children who had ties to many cliques and children whose primary ties were to other children who existed at the margins of one or more cliques. These authors concluded that there is a general loosening of clique ties across adolescence, a process they label "degrouping." This interpretation meshes well with recent data suggesting that both the importance of belonging to a group and the extent of intergroup antagonism decline steadily across the high school years (B. Brown, Eicher, & Petrie, 1986; Gavin & Furman, 1989). It is consistent also with the observations of ethnographers, who report a dissipation of clique boundaries and a sense of cohesiveness among senior high school class members (Larkin, 1979).

A structural change in group composition that accompanies adolescent development is the integration of the sexes. According to Dunphy (1963), initially isolated, single-sex cliques in early adolescence eventually build closer ties to opposite-sex cliques. These ties eventually draw these groups together into a loose association of cliques, thereby permitting new social activities. Toward the end of adolescence, these loose associations dissolve into isolated, tighter units that are heterosexually composed and defined by dyadic dating relationships. B. Brown (1989) noted recently, however, that Dunphy's ethnographic description has never been formally replicated. Further, Dunphy's research was carried out in Australia over 40 years ago; thus, the original descriptions may not prove representative of group and clique structure among contemporary youth. In addition to the possibility of cohort or generational differences in adolescent group or clique structure, there is the likelihood that differences could be found among contemporary youth who reside, for example in rural versus urban areas,

in large versus small communities, or in schools or neighborhoods varying in socioeconomic strata.

Whereas cliques represent small groups of individuals linked by friendship selections, the concept of peer subcultures, or "crowds" (B. Brown, 1990), is a more encompassing organizational framework for segmenting adolescent peer social life. A crowd is a reputation-based collective of similarly stereotyped individuals who may or may not spend much time together (B. Brown, 1990). Crowds are defined by the primary attitudes or activities their members share. Thus, crowd affiliation is assigned through the consensus of the peer group and is not selected by the adolescents themselves. B. Brown lists the following as common crowd labels among American high school students: jocks, brains, eggheads, loners, burnouts, druggies, populars, nerds, and greasers (see also Castlebury & Arnold, 1988; Eckert, 1989). Crowds place important restrictions on children's social contacts and relationships with peers (B. Brown, 1989; Eckert, 1989; Eder, 1985); for example, cliques are generally formed within (versus across) crowds. Crowd labels may also constrain adolescents' abilities to change their lifestyles or explore new identities by "channeling" them into relationships and dating patterns with those sharing the same crowd nomenclature or classification (Eckert, 1989; Eder, 1985).

Crowd membership is an especially salient feature of adolescent social life, and children's perceptions of crowds change in important ways with age. For example, between the ages of 13 and 16 years, adolescents alter the ways they identify and describe the crowds in their school (O'Brien & Bierman, 1987). Whereas young adolescents focus on the specific behavioral proclivities of group members, older adolescents center on members' dispositional characteristics and values. This observation reflects broader changes that characterize developmental shifts in person perception between the childhood and adolescent years (Barenboim, 1981; see also Flavell & Miller, Vol. 2). Importantly, this change in person perception appears to augment the influence that peer groups have on individuals—influences affecting the adolescent's appearance, engagement in illicit acts, attitudes, and values (O'Brien & Bierman, 1987).

But it is also the case that the prototypicality and exhaustivity of crowd labels wax and wane with development. B. Brown and Clasen (1986) found that, when students were asked to name the major crowds in their school, the proportion of responses that fell into typical crowd categories rose from 80% in sixth grade (approximately 12 years) to 95% in ninth grade (age 15 years), then fell steadily through twelfth grade (age 18 years). The average number of crowds named increased with age, from just under eight at 12 years to over ten by 18 years. Adolescence also brings with it the recognition of various crowd types ("druggies," "brains," "punkers," "grungers") that are rarely mentioned by younger children. And the percentage of students who are able to correctly identify their peer-rated crowd membership increases with age (B. Brown, Clasen, & Neiss, 1987).

Summary

In this section, we have outlined developmental differences that mark the changing nature of social interactions and peer relationships from infancy to adolescence. We hope this review will prove sufficient to provide a normative basis for the discussion that follows concerning the development of individual differences in children's social behaviors and peer relationships. Further discussion of developmental differences and changes in the expression of social behavior and the understanding of social phenomena can be found in current *Handbook* chapters, especially those authored by Coie and Dodge (Ch. 12, this Volume), Eisenberg and Fabes (Ch. 11, this Volume), and Flavell and Miller (Ch. 17, Volume 2).

The nature of children's peer experiences changes with age because of a complex mix of developments with regard to four factors: intrapersonal (i.e., changes in interpersonal understanding and concerns), interpersonal (changes in the frequency or forms of specific behaviors), dyadic (changes in qualities of friendships or patterns of involvement in friendships), and group (changes in configurations of and involvement in cliques and crowds). Furthermore, these different factors are not orthogonal; rather, they interlock in complex ways. For example, children's cognitions about interpersonal behaviors, friendships, and the crowds and cliques in their school change with age. The qualitative and developing nature of children's friendships assuredly has some effect on children's expectations of friends; also, changing friendship expectations likely lead children to change friends or to take existing friendships in new directions.

SOCIAL SKILLS AND SOCIAL COMPETENCE

Thus far, we have used a developmental perspective to examine the characteristic social behaviors that children typically display during interactions with acquaintances and friends. Some of these social behaviors represent developmental milestones of a sort. For example, imitation of peers in infancy and toddlerhood and the "shared meanings" connoted by the demonstration of social pretense among preschoolers represent seemingly skilled forms of social exchange.

But what is it that defines *social skill?* And is social skill equivalent to *social competence?* These are important issues to consider if one is to address questions concerning children's peer interactions and relationships. After all, it seems reasonable to suggest that social skills and the demonstration of social competence are essential for the initiation and maintenance of positive social relationships; alternatively, it is just as reasonable to suggest that socially unskilled behaviors and peer judgments of social incompetence will contribute to difficulty in initiating and maintaining positive peer relationships.

Social Skills

Just as cognitive skills are behaviors that permit children to perform well on cognitive tasks, researchers have generally been comfortable with defining social skills as discrete behaviors that lead children to solve social tasks or achieve social success. As such, it is probably impossible to compile a complete list of discrete social skills, as the tasks of social life and the avenues to social success can be expected to change with time, context, and culture. Nevertheless, the requirements of social life are general enough that a reasonable and representative list of social skills might include: (a) to understand the thoughts, emotions, and intentions of others; (b) to abstract information about the social partner and the milieu in which the potential interaction is to take place; (c) to generate various means by which to strike up a conversation or interaction, to maintain one, to end one on a positive note, and so on; (d) to understand the consequences of one's social actions for the self as well as for the "target"; (e) to make mature moral judgments that serve to guide social action; (f) to behave positively and altruistically; (g) to appropriately express positive emotions and inhibit negative ones; (h) to inhibit negative behaviors that might result from negative thoughts and feelings about the social partner; (i) to communicate verbally and nonverbally in ways that will result in the partner's social comprehension; and (j) to attend to other's communicative attempts and be willing to comply with the requests of the social partner (see Schneider et al., 1989, for relevant reviews).

In short, social skills comprise thoughts, emotions and the regulation thereof, and observable behaviors. Clearly, however, the examples cited above will not be seen in the repertoires of all children. Individual as well as developmental differences exist. For example, in *infancy,* social skills include the direction of smiles, frowns, and gestures to play partners; the careful observation of peers, representing a clear sign of social interest; and the response, often in kind, to the play partner's behaviors. During the *second and third years* of life, social skills comprise the ability to coordinate behavior with that of the play partner; imitation of the peer's activity and an awareness of being imitated; turn-taking that involves observe peer–respond to peer–observe and wait–respond to peer interchange sequences; the demonstration of helping and sharing behaviors; and the ability to respond appropriately to the peer partner's characteristics. Further, during the *preschool years,* socially skilled behaviors are marked by the abilities to share meanings through social pretense and rough-and-tumble play; to use speech forms that indicate an understanding of the listener's characteristics; and to spontaneously direct prosocial behaviors to peers. In sections that follow, we discuss the significance of individual differences in social skills. Much of this work, however, is not directed to the study of infants and toddlers; this represents an area for future research endeavors.

Social Competence

Insofar as social competence is concerned, it has been suggested repeatedly that there are as many definitions as there are researchers currently gathering data on the topic (e.g., Putallaz & Gottman, 1981). We offer a sampling of definitions, in the chronological order in which they appeared in print: "an organism's capacity to interact effectively with its environment" (White, 1959, p. 297); "the effectiveness or adequacy with which an individual is capable of responding to various problematic situations which confront him" (Goldfried & D'Zurilla, 1969, p. 161); "an individual's everyday effectiveness in dealing with his environment" (Zigler, 1973, p. 44); "a judgment by another that an individual has behaved effectively" (McFall, 1982, p. 1); "attainment of relevant social goals in specified social contexts, using appropriate means and resulting in positive developmental outcomes" (Ford, 1982, p. 324); the ability "to make use of environmental and personal resources to achieve a good developmental outcome" (Waters & Sroufe, 1983, p. 81); and "the ability

to engage effectively in complex interpersonal interaction and to use and understand people effectively" (Oppenheimer, 1989, p. 45).

Several common properties are shared in these definitions. First, in defining social competence, most of the authors make reference to *effectiveness.* Second, competence appears to imply that one is able to guide the behaviors and contingent responses of others to meet one's own needs or goals. It is necessary, however, to distinguish between the effective manipulation of others in the Machiavellian sense and influencing others using conventionally accepted means in accord with one's local knowledge about the norms and standards of the present social milieu. Thus, McFall's (1982) notion that social competence refers to a "judgment call" based on the display of skilled behavior is an important one. Furthermore, Ford's (1982) suggestion that competence involves the use of "appropriate means" is significant.

Drawing from the definitions noted above, as well as from others found in the work of Dodge (1986), Gresham (1981), Strayer (1989) and many others, Rubin and Rose-Krasnor (1992) have defined social competence as *the ability to achieve personal goals in social interaction while simultaneously maintaining positive relationships with others over time and across situations.* A significant feature of this definition is its implicit recognition of the importance of balancing personal desires against social consequences. This emphasis reflects the essential duality of self and other, placing the individual within a social and personal context. The conceptualization of self and other as interdependent is an important feature of several personality theories (Sullivan, 1953), in gender-role theory (Leaper, 1994b), and in philosophy (Harré, 1984). Accordingly, this definition is valuable because it points to the complex goals that persons confront as individuals and as members of groups. It is in this regard that individuals, as well as social scientists, have struggled with the tension between agentic and communal orientations.

The definition of social competence just offered allows distinctions to be made between acceptable and unacceptable social successes and between adaptive social cognitions and unadaptive social "outcomes." As the reader will note in the chapter by Coie and Dodge (this volume), aggressive children often get their way when attempting to exact goods and services from their peers. Nevertheless, the means by which success is attained is not likely to be judged as competent by peers and adults in the aggressive child's social milieu. It is the case that socially unsuccessful children often demonstrate the underlying social cognitive knowledge of how to interact appropriately and successfully with their peers; unfortunately, because they are unable to regulate their feelings of social wariness and anxiety, they experience interpersonal failure despite their social-cognitive acumen (e.g., Rubin, Coplan, Fox, & Calkins, 1995; Stewart & Rubin, 1995).

Several models currently exist of the processes involved in the child's demonstrating those social behaviors that result ultimately in judgments of competence. These models are worthy of chapters in their own right, and a review of them is beyond the scope of this chapter. Thus, we refer interested readers to the work of Dodge and colleagues (Crick & Dodge, 1994; Dodge, Pettit, McClaskey, & Brown, 1986) and Rubin and Krasnor (1986; Rubin & Rose-Krasnor, 1992).

SOCIAL BEHAVIORS, INTERACTIONS, RELATIONSHIPS, AND GROUPS: ASSESSMENT ISSUES

The perspective we have adopted for this chapter assumes that children's experiences with peers occur at several orders of social complexity, from interactions to relationships to groups. Implied in such a formulation is that these levels of analysis provide separate windows on the adjustment of individual children with peers. That is, to the extent that individual differences exist in children's adaptation or success with peers, such differences will be reflected in their (a) social interactions, (b) abilities to develop and sustain friendships, and (c) acceptance in peer groups. Because, as we have argued, each level of complexity has emergent properties not relevant to lower or higher levels, each affords researchers a unique perspective on children's adjustment with peers. At the same time, important connections exist across levels; thus, we would also expect consistencies in adjustment, such as links between social behavior and group acceptance or social behavior and quality of friendship. We examine these issues in this section.

Children's Behaviors and Interactions with Peers

The assessment of children's behaviors with peers represents a tradition of differential child psychology. Although parents, clinicians, and archival data have all served as sources of information about the valence and nature of children's peer interactions, the most common sources are the reports of other children or teachers or structured observations (Coie, Dodge, & Kupersmidt, 1990; Newcomb et al., 1993).

Observations of Behavior

There has been a long tradition of observing children in either naturalistic or laboratory-based play groups and then coding their behavior to reflect particular constructs. For example, *observational procedures* have been used to index the frequency with which individuals engage in particular behavioral styles (e.g., aggression, sociodramatic play, reticence/social wariness, sharing), adopt particular roles vis-à-vis their partners (e.g., dominant versus submissive roles), or demonstrate social competence (e.g., are successful at entering playgroups). Several well-known coding systems have been developed for these purposes, and discussions of these techniques can be found elsewhere (e.g., Ladd & Price, 1993). These coding schemes have been used profitably to reliably distinguish between children along a variety of behavioral dimensions. For example, Rubin, Coplan, et al. (1995) have illustrated how time sampling can be used to identify extremely withdrawn and extremely aggressive children. Their observational taxonomy considers both the specific behavioral activity (e.g., categories of play, aggression, rough-and-tumble activities, unoccupied and onlooker behaviors, and conversations with peers) and the social context of the activity (i.e., whether it occurs during solitary, parallel, or group activities). The procedure allows the measurement of the relative frequencies of social interactive behaviors, different dimensions of solitude, and aggression and rough-and-tumble play.

Although observational methods offer many advantages over the assessments discussed next, they also have specific limitations. First, observations are time-, energy-, and money-consuming. Whereas peer and teacher assessments can be conducted in minutes or hours, observations can require weeks or months of data collection. Second, as children get older, it becomes increasingly difficult to observe them during free play (although recent advances in remote audiovisual recording allow observations of children's conversations and interactions from afar; Asher & Gabriel, 1993; Pepler & Craig, 1995). Third, observations may be reactive: children who are aware that they are being observed may behave in atypical manners, perhaps suppressing negative behaviors or increasing the production of prosocial behaviors.

Peer Assessments

In lieu of direct observations, researchers have often relied on children for information about who it is in the peer group that behaves competently or incompetently or has qualitatively good or poor relationships. Hymel and Rubin (1985) note the following advantages of peer informants. First, as "insiders," peers can identify characteristics of children and of relationships that are considered relevant from the perspectives of those who ultimately determine a child's social status and integration within the peer group. Second, the judgments of peers are based on many extended and varied experiences with those being evaluated. For example, peers may be able to consider low-frequency but psychologically significant events (e.g., a punch in the nose or taking someone's valued possession) that lead to the establishment and maintenance of particular social reputations. These latter events may be unknown to nonpeer "outsiders." Third, peer assessments of children's behaviors and relationships represent the perspectives of many observers with whom the target child has had a variety of personal relationships. The chance that error will be introduced by some idiosyncratic aspect of any single reporter's experience with the child is therefore correspondingly reduced.

In peer assessment techniques, children are given a set of target behaviors or personality descriptions and asked the extent to which each applies to a particular child (e.g., "is a good leader," "gets into fights," "likes to play alone"). Moreover, in practice, researchers are usually interested in the reputations of all children in a group, and therefore, all children are asked for their impressions of every other group member. As such, a behavioral profile becomes available for each child. Two of the most commonly used assessment instruments, the Revised Class Play (RCP; Masten, Morison, & Pellegrini, 1985) and the Pupil Evaluation Inventory (PEI; Pekarik, Prinz, Liebert, Weintraub, & Neale, 1976), produce factor scores for the dimensions of sociability and likableness, aggression, and withdrawal.

Recent advances in the use of peer assessments have provided a more refined articulation of the dimensions underlying children's social behavior. Consistent with Coie et al.'s (1990) argument that the use of global measures, such as a single index of aggression, may not adequately capture the particular features of children's behavior with peers, investigators have reconsidered the value of relying on three broad indices of social behavior. Accordingly, the range of dimensions has been expanded and the unidimensional structure of each factor has been reconstrued. For example, Crick and Grotpeter (1995) have developed a set of items to measure *relational aggression,* or the tendency to hurt others by manipulating their friendships (e.g., spreading rumors, forming exclusive coalitions). In regard to social withdrawal, Rubin and Mills (1988) proposed two more specific constructs, one form of isolation emanating from the actions of the group (i.e., isolation due to ostracism) and the other reflecting the child's own preference for being alone or anxiety with social interaction.

Peer behavioral assessment assumes that children's impressions of one another are established over time. Indeed, it has long been assumed that a major advantage of this technique is that it permits researchers to identify children who engage in behaviors that are salient to other children but too infrequent or too subtle for researchers to observe with any reliability. But a disadvantage of peer assessments is that once behavioral reputations consolidate, they can be resistant to change (Hymel, Wagner, & Butler, 1990). Thus, even though a child's behavior may have changed, his or her reputation for this behavior persists with peers. As such, the data reaching the researcher may not fully reflect the current state of "reality." In addition, reputations are probably unduly influenced by infrequent but salient events (e.g., embarrassing social gaffes, poignant aggressive outbursts). Although characteristic of the child, the child's reputation for this behavior may overstate the frequency with which it appears in his or her social interchanges. Finally, and relatedly, there is evidence that children's recall of their peers' abilities and behavior is affected by their own behavioral reputation, level of peer status, age, and liking for the target; situational factors; and the target's sex, age, and sociometric status (e.g., Hymel, 1986; Younger & Boyko, 1987).

Teacher Assessments

Teachers can provide useful and rich data concerning low-frequency social exchanges that may contribute toward the quality of a child's peer relationships. One advantage of teacher assessments over peer assessments is that the collection of data is more efficient and less time-consuming. A second advantage is that, because they themselves are not members of the peer group, teachers may be more objective in their assessments of social behavior. On the other hand, teachers may bring with them an "adultomorphic" perspective that carries with it value judgments about social behaviors that might differ from those of children. Furthermore, teachers may carry with them biases that influence the ways they react to their pupils; such teacher reactions may strongly influence children's peer preferences and judgments (White & Kistner, 1992).

Teacher *referrals* are one source of data on children with behavioral difficulties (e.g., Gresham, 1981). Many objections might be leveled against this approach, however. In the first place, teachers refer children for academic behaviors (e.g., learning disabilities, motivational problems) that may have only minor implications for social difficulties with peers (but see Coie & Krebiehl, 1984). Second, even when problematic behavior toward peers is the basis for referral, it is not clear that such referrals will take place when the behavior is not also disruptive of classroom routines and academic progress. Thus, as Strain and Kerr (1981) have noted, the referral rates for aggressive and acting-out problems exceed those for internalizing (fearful, anxious, socially withdrawn) behavior. Further, teachers' decisions to refer children may in some cases be as heavily influenced by the sex of the child as the nature of the child's behavioral difficulties (La Greca, 1981).

By far the most common form of data comprise *teacher ratings*. A partial list of the most prevalent of these standardized or semistandardized measures includes Achenbach and Edelbrock's (1986) Child Behavior Checklist (CBCL), the Preschool Behavior Questionnaire (PBQ, Behar & Stringfield, 1974), and the Connors' Rating Scale (CRS; Connors, 1969).

Agreement among Sources

Achenbach, McConaughy, and Howell (1987) reported that the correlations between reports of children's behavioral problems average about .60 between similar informants seeing children under generally similar conditions (e.g., pairs of teachers; pairs of parents); .28 between different types of informants seeing the child under different conditions (e.g., parents versus teachers); and .22 between children's self-reports and reports by others, including parents, teachers, and mental health workers. Age, sex, and the specific topography of the behavior under consideration have all been shown to be important factors influencing agreement. For example, agreement between teachers and peers concerning social withdrawal appears to increase with age from early to late childhood (Hymel, Rubin, Rowden, & LeMare, 1990; Ledingham, Younger, Schwartzman, & Bergeron, 1982), primarily because social withdrawal takes on increased salience to peers (but not teachers) with increasing age. As another example, Lancelotta and Vaughn (1989) report better agreement between teachers and peers concerning boys' aggression than girls' aggression, and

that teachers and peers agree more readily on some types of aggression (e.g., unprovoked physical aggression) than others (e.g., provoked physical aggression, verbal disparagement). Thus, it would appear as if no single source can substitute for all the others. The goal is not to determine which assessment procedure yields the singular truth about the child, but to use what each one reveals about the child's functioning in particular areas or contexts.

Children's Relationships with Friends

Considering the complexity and the abstractness of friendship, it is not surprising that measuring differences in individual children's friendship experiences presents several challenges.

Participation in Friendship

Perhaps the most basic question regarding individual differences in friendship is whether or not a child is engaged in a friendship relation. Participation in a friendship is typically operationalized according to whether a child's identification of a peer as a friend is reciprocated. In early childhood, it is common to ask parents or teachers to identify whether a child is a friend of another child (Gottman, 1983; Howes, 1988). Typically, researchers do not give these informants specific criteria by which the presence of a friendship should be determined. Instead, it is often simply assumed that these informants share the researcher's definition of friendship, which may or may not always be the case.

With older children, researchers rely primarily on reciprocal sociometric nomination procedures to assess children's involvement in friendships (Bukowski & Hoza, 1989; Price & Ladd, 1986). Typically, children are presented with a roster or a set of pictures of their same-sex classmates (or some other functionally similar group) and asked to circle or otherwise indicate which members are their best or close friends. The pattern of choices is then examined to identify children who nominate one another. Less often, investigators have used reciprocated high ratings as an index of friendship, either alone or in conjunction with friendship nominations (Berndt & Hoyle, 1985; Berndt & Hoyle, 1985; Bukowski, Hoza, & Newcomb, 1994). Both procedures are consistent with the definition of friendship that we presented earlier; namely, that friendship requires reciprocity, that it refers to a free choice on the part of the two children involved, and that it is predicated upon affectional concerns rather than instrumental issues. In spite of the apparent simplicity of this operationalization, many problems can limit the validity of these measures. One problem is whether one has adequately assessed the entire domain of a child's peer relationships. Although the peer group at school is typically a child's most salient peer group, it is almost always the case that children have friends outside of school, in their neighborhood or in connection with sports or recreational activities. In this regard, the sole use of school-based data underestimates the extent of children's friendship relations. This problem is further exacerbated if assessments allow only for the nomination of classmates: friendships with children in other classrooms at school are overlooked.

A second problem occurs when children are permitted only a limited number of friendship nominations (e.g., three choices). This practice may arbitrarily restrict the number friendships a child may have. Furthermore, when the number of choices is specified, children who have one or two classroom friends may feel compelled to add to their list the names of children who are not actually their best friends (Hallinan, 1981). This creates the possibility for overestimating the actual number of friendships these children have.

Friendship Quality

In addition to determining whether a child is engaged in a friendship relation, investigators have shown an increasing concern with the characteristics or qualities of children's relationships with their best friends. Given that children's understanding of friendship changes with age, it is not surprising that there are age differences in the properties of children's friendships. And considering the wide variations in individual characteristics that children bring with them to their friendships, it is reasonable to expect that not all friendships will be alike. Such differences are likely to be related to children's subsequent adjustment, and thus investigators have sought to develop procedures for reliably and validly assessing them. The most common approach involves assessing the features of children's friendships through children's own reports (e.g., Adler & Furman, 1988; Berndt & Perry, 1986; Buhrmester, 1990; Bukowski, Hoza, & Boivin, 1994; Furman & Buhrmester, 1985; Parker & Asher, 1993b). Furman (1996) has recently noted that assessments of this type are usually conducted with questionnaires or interview procedures, and are predicated on the belief that a child's impression of a relationship is the best index of this relationship for the child. Drawing from theoretical accounts of friendship (e.g., Sullivan, 1953), the dimensions typically assessed relate to (a) the

functions of friendship (e.g., provision of companionship, level of intimate disclosure, degree of helpfulness and advice), (b) *conflict and disagreements,* and (c) the *affective properties* of the friendship (e.g., the affective bonds between friends).

Observational techniques have also sometimes been used to study friends' behavior with one another (Berndt, 1987; Doyle, 1982; Gottman & Parker, 1986; Hartup, 1989, 1992; Parker & Herrera, in press), although far less frequently than self-reports (Price & Ladd, 1986). Part of the reluctance of researchers to use observational approaches may stem from the formidable task of isolating the contributions of individual members to the observed patterns of dyadic interaction (Furman, 1984; Hinde & Stevenson-Hinde, 1986). This is a very real concern, but recently some promising observational methods for describing interdyad variation have appeared (e.g., Gottman & Katz, 1989; Howes, 1988; Kramer & Gottman, 1992; Park & Waters, 1989; Youngblade, Park, & Belsky, 1993). Thus far, observational procedures have been used with children up to the age of 7 or 8 years, but their applicability to older children is clear and in some cases extensions along these lines have begun.

Children's Adjustment in the Group

Much of the dramatic increase in interest in children's peer relationships during the past 15 years can be traced to advances in *sociometry.* New techniques for measuring popularity, especially a procedure developed by Coie, Dodge, and Coppotelli (1982), gave researchers an important means by which to represent the extent to which a child is liked and disliked by peers. These procedures were attractive because they were simple and powerful. They were simple in the sense that they could be used easily; they were powerful in the sense that they produced concise, apparently comprehensive, and conceptually appealing representations of the peer group.

Advances in sociometric technology were not completely new; instead, they are best viewed as extensions and refinements of previous work. As such, these advances constitute an important renaissance of fundamental issues in the literature on sociometry.

Sociometry: A Brief Historical Overview

Sociometry has its roots in the work of the American psychiatrist Jacob Moreno (1934). Moreno believed that interpersonal relationships and experiences should be understood via consideration of two fundamental aspects of interpersonal experience: attractions and repulsions. Moreno defined *attractions* as the positive forces that bring persons together, and *repulsions* as the negative forces that would keep persons apart. Moreno did not see these forces as antithetical, but instead as two sides of a triangular model for which the third side was the dimension of *indifference*. In the absence of feelings of attraction to (or repulsion from) another person, an individual could feel either repulsed (or attracted) or indifferent.

To assess these views, Moreno asked individuals to indicate (a) whether they like to associate with (i.e., attraction), (b) do not like to associate with (i.e., repulsion), or (c) are indifferent to each member of a given social group. These procedures were subsequently adopted, in the 1940s, by researchers interested in understanding children's social experiences and relationships (e.g., Hunt & Solomon, 1942). Methodological advances in sociometry were made, in turn, by Bronfenbrenner (1943, 1944), Thompson and Powell (1951), and Dunnington (1957), such that by the late 1950s, researchers had developed an index of a child's "status" in the peer group. Three sociometric classifications included a *low-status* group comprising children who were high in rejection and low in acceptance; a *high-status* group comprising children above a probabilistic criterion on acceptance and below a probabilistic criterion on rejection; and an *average* group consisting of all remaining children. Unfortunately, no index was provided for children to whom peers were *indifferent*.

Almost 30 years later, Peery (1979) described a system of sociometric classification based on the two derivative dimensions described originally by Dunnington in 1957 (*status* and *notice*). Peery renamed these dimensions *social preference* and *social impact*. Social preference refers to a child's general likability within the peer group and is defined as the difference between the number of times a child is chosen as liked and the number of times he or she is chosen as disliked. Social impact refers to the child's overall visibility in the group and is defined as the sum of positive and negative nominations. With this taxonomic model, children could be assigned to one of four groups: *popular* (above the mean in impact and preference), *rejected* (above the mean in impact and below it in preference), *amiable* (below the mean in impact and above it in preference), or *isolated* (below the mean on both impact and preference). With this new classification scheme, researchers had at their disposal, for the first time, a clearly articulated model of sociometric classification that distinguished among rejected, neglected, and popular children.

Following Peery (1979), several new sociometric classification taxonomies were developed. The most frequently used classification systems appear to be those developed by Coie et al. (1982) and Newcomb and Bukowski (1983). These schemes are rooted in the conceptual framework Peery developed, but have two main advantages. First, children must receive very high or very low numbers of nominations to fall into the extreme groups. Second, each of these systems provides for a more differentiated set of groups. These groups have been labeled (a) *popular*—children who receive many positive nominations and few negative nominations (high impact, high preference); (b) *rejected*—children who receive few positive nominations and many negative nominations (high impact, low preference); (c) *neglected*—children who receive few positive and negative nominations (low impact); (d) *average*—children who receive an average number of positive and negative nominations (midrange on both variables); and (e) *controversial*—children who receive many positive and many negative nominations (high impact, midrange on preference).

Rating Scale Approaches

Rating scales have been used in sociometric research for at least five decades (e.g., Thompson & Powell, 1951). The rating scale technique requires children to rate each of his or her classmates on a Likert-type scale, according to some specified criterion ("How much do you like this person?" or "How much do you like to play/work with this person?"). In this regard, rating scales assess children's views toward their peers according to a continuum from highly liked (or accepted) to highly disliked (or rejected). The average rating that a child receives from all peer group members constitutes an index of popularity.

An advantage of the rating scale measure is that it provides a sensitive evaluation system. Sociometric procedures that include both acceptance and rejection *nominations* essentially produce a three-category system in which each child identifies each of the other children in the nominating pool as being (a) highly liked, (b) highly disliked, or (c) neither of these. Rating scales provide more sensitive data than nominations because they allow for more differentiation among peers, especially those who would fall into the "neither" category. A second noteworthy advantage of the rating scale procedure is that it eliminates the need to request that children identify those peers they *dislike;* requesting negative nominations may constitute an ethical dilemma for some children.

Recently, Asher and Dodge (1986) have used rating scale data to produce three scores: (a) a sum indicating the number of times a child received the *lowest* rating on the scale; (b) a sum indicating the number of times the child received the *highest* rating on the scale; and (c) an average of the received ratings. Whereas Asher and Dodge used the first score as an index of rejection or disliking, the sum of highest scores appears to be a measure of acceptance, and the average score received appears to be a measure of preference.

Short-Term Stability of Children's Acceptance/Rejection by the Peer Group

An index of reliability and practical utility is derived from evidence that given sociometric procedures produce stable results across short time intervals. Hunt and Solomon (1942) reported that the stability of sociometric acceptance was approximately .85 across one-week intervals in a sample of school-age boys attending a summer camp. Stability increased as the boys spent more time together. More recently, Asher and Dodge (1986) found that over a six-month school interval, the Time 1–Time 2 correlations were (a) .55 and .55 for measures of acceptance assessed with peer nominations and peer ratings, respectively; (b) .65 for rejection ratings; and (c) .68 and .69 for preference when measured by nominations and ratings, respectively. Similar stability data have been reported for varying short terms, and for varying age groups, by Coie and Dodge (1983) and Bukowski and Newcomb (1984), and more recently by Chen, Rubin, and Li (1995).

Short-term stability has also been assessed with regard to the sociometric classifications we described earlier. In general, the data reveal that the popular, rejected, and average classifications are more stable than all others, whereas neglected and controversial status are consistently reported to be highly unstable (e.g., Asher & Dodge, 1986; Newcomb & Bukowski, 1984).

Long-Term Stability of Children's Acceptance/Rejection by the Peer Group

Studies of the long-term stability of popularity are more frequent than studies of short-term stability; however, there is less convergence among their findings. In the 1940s, Bonney (1944) reported correlations between assessments of acceptance made at one-year intervals to be .84 from grade 2 to grade 3, and roughly .76 from grade 3 to grade 4. The correlations observed in other studies have been lower. For example, Rubin and Daniels-Beirness

(1983) reported that the one-year stability of sociometric ratings from kindergarten to grade 1 (age 5–6 years) was .48. Hymel et al. (1990) found that the correlation of peer acceptance ratings from grade 2 (age 8 years) to grade 5 (age 11 years) was .56.

Roff, Sells, and Golden (1972) assessed the stability of acceptance, rejection, and preference in a large sample of children followed from grade 3 to grade 6. Acceptance and preference were observed to be more stable than rejection, and the stability of all three variables decreased as the size of the intervening period increased. For example, from grade 3 to grade 4, the correlations for acceptance, preference, and rejection were .52, .53, and .38, whereas across the interval from grade 3 to grade 6 the corresponding correlations were .42, .45, and .34. Roff et al.'s findings have been replicated in some studies (e.g., Bukowski & Newcomb, 1984), but not in others (e.g., Coie & Dodge, 1983). Perhaps the only unequivocal conclusion that one can draw from this literature is that sociometric variables are moderately stable, and that impact tends to be less stable than the other variables.

Several researchers have measured the long-term consistency of sociometric classification (e.g., Coie & Dodge, 1983; Newcomb & Bukowski, 1984). In general, the category of peer rejection is the most stable. The stability of neglect and controversial status rarely exceeds 30%.

Problems with Sociometric Classification

Although it is clear that the procedures developed in the 1980s have provided researchers with reliable, valid, and practical means of measuring individual differences in popularity, it is also the case that there are problems with the assessments that these techniques provide. One problem concerns the use of cutoff scores to form extreme groups. As Dunnington (1957) and Thompson and Powell (1951) noted long ago, the cutoffs used to designate groups were designed to make statistical sense rather than to reflect an underlying psychological meaning. A second problem is that the variables on which sociometric classifications are based (i.e., the underlying dimensions of preference and impact) are *continuous*. The sensitivity of these continuous measures is lost when it is parsed to serve the needs of a procrustean classification procedure.

A third problem is that sociometric groups differ along several dimensions. For example, *rejected* and *popular* children differ along the dimensions of acceptance and rejection; thus, if one were to observe differences between the outcomes experienced by these two groups of children, it would be difficult to know which of these two dimensions would account for the differences.

Finally, we have already mentioned that, at times, researchers and practitioners have found the use of sociometric negative nominations discomforting. Do such assessments represent an ethical dilemma for the nominators, the nominees, and the researcher? It has been suggested that the administration of negative nomination measures (often completed in group settings) may implicitly sanction negative judgments about peers, lead children to view disliked peers even more negatively or interact with them in even less positive ways, and serve to increase the salience of their marginal status within the group (Bell-Dolan, Foster, & Sikora, 1989). While such concerns may indeed be valid, at least two studies—one conducted with preschool children (Hayvren & Hymel, 1984) and the other with fifth grade children (Bell-Dolan et al., 1989)—have demonstrated that sociometric testing does not necessarily have negative implications for the children involved. Still, minimizing the potential risks involved in the administration of negative nomination measures would appear imperative (see Bell-Dolan, Foster, & Christopher, 1992; Vasa, Maag, Torrey, & Kramer, 1994, for further discussion).

Summary

During the 1980s there was intense interest in distinguishing groups on the basis of sociometric status. Surprisingly, however, the interest in sociometry was primarily practical and functional; little attention was given to either the conceptual roots of the concept of popularity, or to the complex issues related to the study of individuals within groups. Whereas the use of sociometric groups has waned, concern with these other topics is likely to increase in the next phase of peer acceptance research.

Assessments of the Peer Group

Typically, groups have been studied for three reasons. First, investigators have sought to determine whether and how a child is embedded into a group structure. These group structures are not formal groups organized by adults, but instead are formed naturally and spontaneously by the children themselves. To determine whether a child is a member of such a group, investigators (e.g., Cairns, Cairns, & Neckerman, 1989; Kindermann, 1995) typically ask children to identify who, in a large group (e.g., all the children in a

school grade), they associate with. By so doing, one can develop a representation of how many children each child is linked to and whether there are particular patterns of links between sets of children. A group is defined as a set of children who are highly interrelated. Once it has been determined that a child is part of a group, one can assess how strong the child's links to the group are. Is the child linked to many other children in the group, to just a few, or perhaps to only one other child? The goal of this assessment is to provide an index of the child's position within the social network. The criteria that are used to determine a child's group membership have been discussed by Cairns, Xie, and Leung (in press).

Second, following the determination that a child is a member of a group, one can assess the group's structural properties. These properties typically consist of (a) group size, (b) the position of the group within the broader community of peer groups, and (c) the patterns of association within the group. *Size* refers simply to the number of children within the group. The *position of the group* within the broader peer group refers to how many links the group has to other collectives in the general community of peers. And *group structure* refers to how many links there are among group members. In a *dense* group, most members would be linked to others; in a *loosely organized* group, some members would have no links to others at all.

Finally, a third goal is to assess the psychological characteristics of children's groups. Examples of this approach can be seen in the above described work of B. Brown (1989) and Kindermann et al. (1995). In their research, group profiles are schematized, representing the interest and characteristics that its members share. Kindermann and colleagues, for example, have shown that groups vary considerably in their emphasis on academic performance.

PROXIMAL CORRELATES OF CHILDREN'S PEER RELATIONSHIPS

The understanding of the origins and correlates of individual differences in children's experiences with peers comprises the largest corpus of peer relationships research in the past 15 years. Much of this research has focused on the processes and variables that either provide the basis for or are correlated with children's popularity in the peer group; a much smaller proportion of the research extant is focused on the correlates and antecedents of individual differences at the level of the dyad (e.g., friendship). Of course, many researchers have examined factors associated with variability at the level of the individual (e.g., behavioral tendencies to be aggressive, altruistic, or withdrawn). Since this research is covered in other *Handbook* chapters, it will not be reviewed herein.

The literature on individual differences in popularity and friendship can be divided into two domains. First, the largest concentration of investigations center on the *individual* characteristics associated with acceptance or rejection in the peer group. Most of this work focuses on either the display of particular forms of social behavior or the ways that children think about their social environments. In the present discussion, we examine the *proximal* correlates of popularity. A second body of research is concerned with the associations between sociometric status and the child's family relationship experiences and the social and personal environments in which the child functions. This literature deals with the *distal* correlates of popularity. Although researchers appear to have their own preferences with regard to whether they examine proximal or distal correlates of group acceptance, it is necessary to remind the reader that these factors are truly interdependent; indeed, the study of the links between proximal and distal factors has become the central theme of much contemporary research. Nevertheless, as investigators began to identify the roots of popularity, their primary concern was to identify conceptually meaningful variables that might be associated with the child's status among peers.

Proximal Correlates—Popularity

In the early 1980s, researchers set out to develop a behavioral explanation of peer acceptance and rejection (Putallaz & Gottman, 1981). The vast majority of the studies were correlational, predicated on the assumption that behaviors and cognitions are likely to be antecedents, rather than consequences, of experiences with peers. Direct evidence supporting this assumption has been sparse, but that which exists generally confirms this perspective. Thorough reviews of the literature on the correlates of popularity are already available (e.g., Coie et al., 1990; Newcomb et al., 1993; Parker et al., 1995). Therefore, we provide only a summary and commentary on this literature. Our discussion is divided into three sections. First, we examine literature related to associations between behavioral processes and sociometric status; then we discuss the

social-cognitive correlates of status. We conclude our discussion with an evaluation of the behavioral and social-cognitive models that have been proposed to explain variations in children's experiences with peers.

Behavioral Correlates of Popularity

The relevant research reviewed below is organized around the sociometric classifications of *popular, rejected, neglected, controversial,* and *average*. When particularly relevant, rating scale data are reviewed as well.

Research on the associations between the behavioral profiles and sociometric status classifications of children has drawn upon the methods of (a) behavioral observation, (b) peer assessment, and (c) teacher ratings described in the preceding section. Typically, investigators have searched for behavioral differences between children from the different sociometric groups. This attempt to link behavior and sociometric status is not new. Indeed, until relatively recently, it was not uncommon to find some authors who equated sociometric membership with distinctive behavioral profiles. For example, some authors would assume that popular children were invariably helpful and even-tempered, rejected children were invariably aggressive, and neglected children were invariably socially withdrawn. This expectation, though attractive in its simplicity, has not held up well to empirical scrutiny. Instead, as we show below, simple one-to-one relations between specific behaviors and specific sociometric classifications have rarely been found.

Popular Children. Researchers have shown that popular children are skilled at initiating and maintaining qualitatively positive relationships. When entering new peer situations, popular children are more likely than members of other sociometric status groups to consider the frame of reference common to the ongoing playgroup and to establish themselves as sharing in this frame of reference (Putallaz, 1983; Putallaz & Gottman, 1981). Popular children are also less likely to draw unwarranted attention to themselves when entering ongoing playgroups. That is, they do not talk exclusively or overbearingly about themselves and their own social goals or desires, and they are not disruptive of the group's activity (Dodge, McClaskey, & Feldman, 1985; Dodge, Schlundt, Schocken, & Delugach, 1983). In addition, when entering the ongoing play of both familiar and unfamiliar children, popular children speak clearly, respond contingently to their prospective playmates, and otherwise demonstrate communicative competence that allows the maintenance of connected, coherent interaction (Black & Hazen, 1990).

Popular children are also viewed as cooperative, friendly, sociable, and sensitive by peers, teachers, and observers (e.g., Coie et al., 1982; Dodge, Coie, & Brakke, 1982; Newcomb & Bukowski, 1983, 1984). Specifically, popular children are more likely to be helpful, to interact actively with other children, to show leadership skills, and to engage in constructive play.

One important finding is that popular children do not differ from average children on all aspects of aggression. In a meta-analysis of research on popularity, Newcomb et al. (1993) distinguished between assertive/agonistic behaviors and behaviors that reflected disruptiveness. Popular children did not differ from others on the former category of behavior, whereas they did on the latter. Popular children, it appears, can engage in some forms of assertive behavior, but they rarely engage in behaviors that are likely to interfere with the actions and goals of others.

Rejected Children.   The most commonly cited behavioral correlate of peer rejection is aggression. This finding emerges regardless of whether aggression is indexed by peer evaluations (e.g., Carlson, Lahey, & Neeper, 1984; Cillessen, Van IJzendoorn, van Lieshout, & Hartup, 1992; French, 1988; Rubin, Chen, & Hymel, 1993), teacher ratings (Coie & Kupersmidt, 1983; Dodge, 1983; French & Waas, 1985), or observations (Coie & Kupersmidt, 1983). The association between rejection and aggression appears to be rather broad; Newcomb et al. (1993) revealed that rejected children, relative to average, popular, and neglected children, showed elevated levels on three forms of aggression: disruptiveness, physical aggression, and negative behavior (e.g., verbal threats).

The data we have described above are generally based on correlational research. A small number of studies, however, provide evidence of a causal link between aggression and rejection. Two of these are the groundbreaking playgroup studies of Dodge (1983) and Coie and Kupersmidt (1983). In these cleverly designed investigations, the interactions among *unfamiliar* peers in small groups were observed in a laboratory context over several days. Each child's behavior was observationally coded; in addition, each child was assessed in a sociometric interview at the end of each play session. Gradually, some of the children became popular and others became rejected. The behavior that most clearly predicted peer rejection was aggression.

This same conclusion was reached by Bukowski and Newcomb (1984), who studied the emergence of popularity in a group of early adolescent boys and girls who had recently entered the same middle school. Using a longitudinal design, they found that the direct path between aggression at the initial assessment (in the autumn of the year) and rejection at subsequent assessments was significant even after all indirect links between these measures had been accounted for. Similar findings emanate from a longitudinal study reported recently by Kupersmidt, Burchinal, and Patterson (1995).

It is clear, however, that aggression is not the only factor linked to rejection. Detailed analyses indicate that aggressive children comprise only between 40 and 50% of the rejected group (Bierman, 1986; Bierman, Smoot, & Aumiller, 1993; Cillessen et al., 1992; French, 1988). Also, the data indicate that aggression may not lead to rejection if it is balanced by a set of positive qualities that facilitate links with other children. Indeed, Cairns, Cairns, Neckerman, Gest, and Gariépy (1988) have shown that aggressive children who are competent at developing a social support network are unlikely to be rejected. Moreover, several researchers have shown that there is a high level of heterogeneity among the behavioral tendencies of rejected children. For example, Newcomb and Bukowski (1984), using a profile analysis, showed that whereas some rejected early adolescents were aggressive, others were very immature (i.e., other children saw them as "acting like a baby"). Paralleling these findings, researchers have reported consistently that children who are highly socially withdrawn, timid, and wary comprise between 10 and 20% of the rejected group (e.g., Cillessen et al., 1992; French, 1988, 1990; Parkhurst & Asher, 1992; Volling, MacKinnon-Lewis, Rabiner, & Baradaran, 1993). Another perspective on this latter statistic is that when extremely withdrawn children are identified, approximately 25% of them fall into the sociometrically rejected group (e.g., Rubin et al., 1993).

Furthermore, it appears as if the association between social withdrawal and peer dislike or rejection follows a distinct developmental course. Withdrawn preschoolers and kindergartners do not appear to be rejected by their peers (Rubin, 1982b). This may be the case largely because the phenomenon of social withdrawal is not particularly salient to young children (Younger, Gentile, &

Burgess, 1993). However, in middle and especially late childhood, social withdrawal becomes salient to the peer group and is judged as a marker of social deviance. It is during this period that extremely withdrawn children become more actively disliked by peers than their more sociable age-mates (Hymel & Rubin, 1985; Rubin, Hymel, & Mills, 1989). To this end, it is now common practice to identify not one, but at least two types of sociometrically rejected children: rejected-withdrawn (or submissive) and rejected-aggressive children (e.g., Boivin, Thomassin, & Alain, 1989; Cillessen et al., 1992; French, 1988, 1990; Hymel, Bowker, & Woody, 1993; Parkhurst & Asher, 1992; Perry, Kusel, & Perry, 1988).

Neglected Children. Neglected children have been shown to interact with their peers less frequently than average children, and to be less sociable and less aggressive, disruptive, and negative than other children, including those in the average group (Coie & Dodge, 1988; Coie & Kupersmidt, 1983; Dodge, Coie, & Brakke, 1982). Coie and Dodge (1988) also note that neglected children are not only low in aggression, but they appear to actively avoid aggressive encounters. It should be pointed out, however, that although these differences may be large enough to reach statistical significance, their absolute size is actually rather modest.

One issue that has been debated in the literature is whether sociometrically neglected children are more socially withdrawn than other children (Rubin, LeMare, & Lollis, 1990). Although, as indicated, neglected children do appear to interact with peers less frequently than do other children, no consistent evidence has emerged that suggests that neglected children display social anxiety, extreme social wariness, or high social withdrawal. Although Dodge et al. (1982), Coie and Kupersmidt (1983), and Coie and Dodge (1988) have reported that sociometrically neglected children are more withdrawn than average children, other researchers have not found such differences (e.g., Cantrell & Prinz, 1985; Coie et al., 1982; Rubin et al., 1993). Indeed, as we have indicated, there is a tendency for highly socially withdrawn children to be sociometrically rejected rather than neglected.

In short, few, if any, discrete behaviors have been found to be distinctive of sociometrically neglected children (Newcomb, et al., 1993). Although future research may yet uncover such differences, it should be recalled that sociometric neglected status is relatively unstable, even over short periods. In that light, the fact that there are few strong associations between neglected status and specific behaviors is unsurprising.

Controversial Children. Consistent with its size and its relative instability, little attention has been paid to the controversial group. Sociometrically, this group is unique in that controversial children are high on both acceptance and rejection. Accordingly, controversial children appear to have many of the characteristics of both popular *and* rejected children. In perhaps the only study in which the authors appeared specifically interested in the controversial group, Coie and Dodge (1988) reported that controversial boys, like rejected boys, were aggressive and disruptive, socially withdrawn, prone to anger and rule violations, and highly active. On the other hand, they reported that controversial boys were like popular boys in that they show high levels of helpfulness, cooperation, leadership, and, in some instances, social sensitivity.

Summary. Scores of studies have been conducted to identify the behavioral correlates of popularity. General conclusions can be drawn as to the features that distinguish popular, rejected, neglected, controversial, and average children from one other. These differences generally fall along a positive/negative continuum. Rejected children show high levels of negative behaviors and low levels of positive behaviors, whereas the opposite pattern is characteristic of popular children. Average children show moderate amounts of positive and negative behaviors, neglected children demonstrate low levels of each form of social behavior, and controversial children show high levels of both positive and negative behaviors.

These studies have been successful in the sense that they converge on the general conclusions offered above; however, they have been unsuccessful in producing a behavioral theory of peer acceptance and rejection. To this end, investigators have attempted to understand the association between behavior and peer status by turning to the aforementioned models of social competence. In our earlier discussion, we argued that social competence refers to a child's ability to be successfully engaged at all levels of complexity, that is, in interactions, in relationships, and in groups. The factors linked to rejection (i.e., aggression, disruptiveness, hostility) appear to be those that would make interactions and belonging to a group difficult, especially insofar as these factors make it difficult for others to pursue their own goals. On the other hand, the factors that are characteristic of the children in the popular group (e.g., helpfulness, moderate levels of self-assertion, sensitivity) appear to be those that facilitate interaction with others, being valued by the peer group, and allowing the pursuit of individual goals.

Variations in the Behavioral Correlates of Popularity: Sex, Group, and Cultural Differences

Groups have norms, or standards, regarding the "goodness" of particular acts. The acceptability of a behavior, and of the child who displays that behavior, is determined by whether or not the behavior conforms to the group's norms. If a behavior is universally valued, then it should correlate with popularity; if the normalcy of a behavior varies across groups, then the extent to which the behavior is linked to popularity should vary across these groups also. It is this logic that has provided the basis for much of the research on group variations in the correlates of popularity.

Sex Differences

Given the widespread concern with sex differences in the literature on child development, it seems surprising to discover how very little work exists on the topic of peer acceptance. Typically, researchers have failed to examine whether general findings are equally valid for boys and girls. For that matter, much of the early work focused solely on boys (e.g., Coie & Kupersmidt, 1983; Dodge, 1983), despite published calls for the examination of sex differences in the causes, proximal and distal correlates, and prospective outcomes of peer acceptance and rejection (e.g., Rubin, 1983). Further, sex differences have been neglected despite the long-standing view that the relationships formed and maintained by females are qualitatively distinct from those of males (Fine, 1987; Hinde, 1987; Leaper, 1994a; Maccoby, 1986) and the evidence that some aspects of social behavior may be differentially normative for boys and for girls (e.g., Hughes, 1991; Humphreys & Smith, 1987).

Not only is research sparse, but that which does exist has failed to produce a consistent set of findings. For example, when sex differences are not considered, the strongest correlate of unpopularity and rejection is aggression. Following the line of thinking that deviant behavior is associated with rejection, and assuming that aggression is more common among boys than girls (Coie & Dodge, this volume), one might expect that it would be a stronger correlate

of peer rejection or unpopularity for girls than boys. Contradicting this hypothesis, Coie et al. (1982) reported that peer nominations for the item "starts fights" were more strongly associated with popularity for boys than girls. Similarly, LaGreca (1981) reported that teacher ratings of aggression were predictive of measures of peer acceptance for boys but not for girls. Other researchers, however, have either failed to find sex differences in the link between aggression and rejection or unpopularity (e.g., Crick & Grotpeter, 1995), have reported that aggression is more strongly associated with rejection or unpopularity for girls than boys (Bukowski, Gauze, Hoza, & Newcomb, 1993), or have noted developmental differences in the association between aggression and lack of peer acceptance. With regard to the latter, Rubin and Cohen (1986) found that at 7 years of age, aggression was associated with unpopularity for girls but not boys; at 8 years of age, aggression was equally related to unpopularity for the two sexes. One particularly noteworthy aspect of the Bukowski et al. study was the finding that aggression was a stronger correlate of both same- and other-sex popularity for girls compared with boys. This pattern shows that it is not that boys and girls have different norms for aggressive behavior but that boys and girls, in general, see aggression as being less acceptable for girls than for boys. In a way, these data reflect adult norms for children as well; for example, Mills and Rubin (1990) found that both fathers and mothers were less accepting of their daughters' than their sons' aggression.

As for social withdrawal, the data appear even more inconsistent than that for aggression. LaGreca (1981) reported that socially withdrawn girls were less popular among peers than withdrawn boys. French (1990) found that, in contrast to boys, withdrawal rather than aggression differentiated deviant rejected girls from other girls. No differences have been reported by other investigators (e.g., Bukowski et al., 1993; Coie & Dodge, 1983; Rubin & Cohen, 1986). Regarding popularity, again relevant data are few and far between. Rubin and Cohen (1986) found that both sexes reported that children who were regarded by their peers as sensitive, socially competent, and as leaders were popular.

Moving away from the more common correlates of peer acceptance, it is noteworthy that sex differences *do* exist when behavior that is typical for a sex is considered. Put another way, the correlates described above centered on aggression and withdrawal, two behaviors thought to be deviant from the norm for *both* boys and girls. However, in an observational study of 8- and 10-year-olds, Moller, Hymel, and Rubin (1992) distinguished styles of play that were preferred by females from styles of play that were preferred by males. The children were also administered a sociometric rating. The authors found that the relation between the same- or opposite-sex-preferred play scores and popularity were nonsignificant for females in either age group. For males, however, the frequent demonstration of female-preferred play was significantly, and negatively, associated with acceptance, not only by boys, but also by girls. This relation held only for the 10-year-old males who frequently produced female-stereotyped play.

These latter data are in keeping with a study by Berndt and Heller (1986). Using scenarios in which they described a child who had chosen activities either consistent or inconsistent with gender stereotypes, the participants were asked to make judgments of the actor's popularity among peers. The authors found that 9- and 12-year-old children demonstrated a greater negative reaction to sex-inconsistent behavior than did 5-year-olds. Furthermore, they found this intolerance was greater for boys than for girls in that it was more appropriate for girls to behave in a sex-inconsistent manner. The two studies just described are reminiscent of one published earlier by Fagot (1985), who found that boys who deviate from same-sex play norms suffer more peer ridicule than their more sex-role-stereotyped age-mates. Again, this researcher found that in comparison to males, females who engaged in opposite-sex activities underwent less peer alienation.

Taken together, the research on the correlates of popularity for boys versus girls reveals one consistent finding. Males who display female-stereotyped behavior are disliked by both same- and opposite-sex peers; females who display male-stereotyped behavior are generally accepted by both same- and opposite-sex peers. These relations appear to gain strength with increasing age. Nevertheless, it is important to note that the relevant data for examining sex differences in the correlates of peer acceptance and rejection are sparse. This gap in the literature is striking, and it severely compromises our current understanding of the peer system (see Ruble & Martin, this volume, for further discussion).

Variations across Groups

The argument that a child's popularity will be associated with particular peer-group norms has been the central focus of two investigations. Wright, Giammarino, and Parad (1986) examined the differences in the correlates of popularity in groups at a summer camp for boys with behavioral and emotional problems. For highly aggressive groups of children, the correlation between peer preference and aggression was very low. In nonaggressive groups, this association between preference and aggression was of moderate strength. The opposite pattern was seen in these same groups when social withdrawal was considered. Withdrawal was strongly and negatively correlated to preference in the high-aggression groups and uncorrelated to preference in the low-aggression groups. Wright et al. replicated these findings in another sample, as did Boivin, Dodge, and Coie (1995). Three of the five behaviors they examined (reactive aggression, proactive aggression, and solitary play) were more negatively linked to a measure of social preference when high levels of this behavior were nonnormative, and unrelated to preference when high levels on this behavior were normative. The association between rough-and-tumble play and preference did not vary as a function of its normativeness, whereas the association between positive interactions and social preference was strong and positive when positive interaction was normative and unrelated to preference when positive behaviors were nonnormative.

These studies show clearly that the association between a particular form of behavior and popularity depends on whether the behavior is normative for a group. Considering the importance of group norms as moderators of the associations between behaviors and popularity, researchers should be cautious about drawing very broad conclusions about the correlates of popularity. Indeed, researchers would do well to assess the *person/group interaction* as a major determinant of peer acceptance and rejection.

Variations across Cultures

The latter conclusion is particularly relevant for an understanding of the correlates of popularity across cultures. Somewhat surprisingly, cross-cultural research on the correlates of popularity has been aimed at broadly replicating findings from North American samples. Little attention has been devoted to examining specific hypotheses derived from an understanding of norms that may be specific to particular cultures. Generally, investigators have taken measures originally developed for use within a Western cultural context, and have employed them within other cultural milieus. The general conclusion from this research has been that aggression and helpfulness are associated with popularity in a wide range of cultures (e.g., Khatri, 1995; Schneider, Tomada, Labovitz, Tassi, & Innocenti, 1995).

On the other hand, culture-specific findings have been observed for the construct of withdrawal. Whereas Western cultures typically value independence and self-assertion, children in China are encouraged to be dependent, cautious, self-restrained, and behaviorally inhibited (Ho, 1986). Such behaviors are generally considered indices of accomplishment, mastery, and maturity (King & Bond, 1985). Similarly, shy, reticent, and quiet children are described as "good" and well behaved. In accord with these standards, researchers have revealed that among Chinese children, sensitive, cautious, and inhibited behavior is positively associated with competent and positive social behavior and with peer acceptance (Chen et al., 1995; Chen, Rubin, & Sun, 1992). These findings support the notion that the link between behavior and popularity will vary as a function of cultural norms. Thus, researchers would do well not to generalize findings drawn from children of one cultural group to children from another.

Summary

We have highlighted the notion that acceptance by the peer group (typically defined by classroom composition) is driven by conformity to or deviation from *behavioral* norms. Such a view is admittedly simple conceptually, and does not take into account the possibility that correlates of popularity may vary according to whether one is acquiring or maintaining one's status within a group. Coie (1990) focused on exactly this theme by arguing that it is too facile and developmentally unproductive to continue to examine how, and whether, individual behavioral characteristics are linked to sociometric status either contemporaneously or predictively. Instead, Coie has proposed that there is a need to determine how the fit between a child and the other members of the group will influence the emergence, maintenance, and consequences of a child's liking and disliking experiences with peers. This proposal is likely to serve as an important research agenda for the next generation of studies on popularity.

Social-Cognitive Correlates of Popularity

A wide range of social-cognitive variables have been studied in relation to children's acceptance by peers, including perspective taking (Rubin, 1972), causal attributions (Dodge & Frame, 1982), problem-solving processes (Pettit, Dodge, & Brown, 1988; Rubin & Krasnor, 1986), cue-detection skills (Dodge, Murphy, & Buchsbaum, 1984), the selection of interpersonal goals (Dodge, Asher, & Parkhurst, 1989), and

children's reasoning about others' motives and dispositions (Juvonen, 1991). In this section, we review research in which social cognition has been associated with sociometric status.

We begin first with a brief description of social information processing models that are relevant to the study of children's skilled and unskilled social behaviors. In one model, Rubin and Krasnor (1986) speculated that, when children face an interpersonal dilemma (e.g., making new friends or acquiring an object from someone else), their thinking follows a particular sequence. First, children select a social goal or a representation of the desired end state of the problem-solving process. Second, they examine the task environment; this involves reading and interpreting relevant social cues. For example, social status, familiarity, and age of the participants in the task environment are likely to influence the child's goal and strategy selection (Krasnor & Rubin, 1983). Third, they access and select strategies; this process involves generating possible plans of action for achieving the perceived social goal and choosing the most appropriate one for the specific situation. Fourth, they implement the chosen strategy. Finally, it is proposed that children evaluate the outcome of the strategy; this involves assessing the situation to determine the relative success of the chosen course of action in achieving the social goal. If the initial strategy is unsuccessful, the child may repeat it, or may select and enact a new strategy, or may abandon the situation entirely.

Dodge's (1986) influential model also consists of five stages: (1) the encoding of social cues; (2) the interpretation of encoded cues; (3) the accessing and generation of potential responses; (4) the evaluation and selection of responses; and (5) the enactment of the chosen response. The processes that occur in steps 1 and 2 lead to an interpretation of a situation based on the information that is available to them; for example, a child may develop an impression of the motives of a peer with whom they are interacting. In steps 3 and 4, children consider alternative choices, evaluating the likely outcomes of each option, and then choose one that is then enacted in step 5.

The models proposed by Rubin and Krasnor (1986) and Dodge (1986) posit a sequential organization between steps, although each of them allows for feedback between steps. Each one also recognizes that children bring with them to each situation a set of biological predispositions as well as a database of past experiences. Moreover, each one assumes that a child's database will be continually updated following experiences.

Recently, Crick and Dodge (1994) offered a reformulation of the original Dodge model, including three important improvements. First, they added a new component to the model, the *clarification of goals*. Second, they moved away from a serial processing model and instead proposed that the subcomponents of their model would occur in parallel. Instead of conceptualizing the components of their model as fitting a hierarchy, they argued that each component draws upon and contributes to a shared database that informs subsequent interpretations and decisions. Third, they incorporated a role for peer evaluations and responses, pointing in particular to the effects of peer experience on subsequent social-cognitive processes.

Children who have difficulties in their peer relationships demonstrate characteristic deficits or qualitative differences in performance at various stages of these social information processing models. First, rejected children can be distinguished from their nonrejected counterparts on the basis of their spontaneous *motives* for social engagement. Popular children, for example, are more inclined to indicate that the reason for interacting with others is to establish new, or enhance ongoing, relationships. Rejected children, on the other hand, are more likely to be motivated by goals that would reasonably be expected to undermine their social relationships, such as "getting even with" or "defeating" their peers (Crick & Dodge, 1989; Rabiner & Gordon, 1992; Slaby & Guerra, 1988).

Second, when considering the motives or intentions of others, rejected children, especially rejected-aggressive children, are more disposed than their popular counterparts to assume that negative events are the product of malicious, malevolent intent on the part of others (Crick & Dodge, 1994; Dodge & Frame, 1982; Quiggle, Garber, Panak, & Dodge, 1992; Sancilio, Plumert, & Hartup, 1989). This bias is evident when children are asked to make attributions for others' behaviors in situations where something negative has happened but the motives of the instigator are unclear. In these ambiguous situations, rejected-aggressive children appear unwilling to give a provocateur the benefit of the doubt, for example, by assuming that the behavior occurred by accident.

There is also evidence that peers process information about rejected children in biased ways. Thus, children are more likely to assume that a negative act was deliberate and intentional when it was committed by a rejected-aggressive classmate than when committed by a popular classmate (Dodge et al., 1986). It would appear then that the social-cognitive environment surrounding the behavior of rejected-aggressive children is permeated by mistrust: both the child and his or her peers regard one another's actions with suspicion.

Given such mutual suspicion, it is not surprising that researchers have found that the interpersonal problem-solving strategy repertoires of rejected-aggressive children are also less adequate than those of other, nonrejected children. When asked how they would go about solving social problems (e.g., obtaining a desired object, trying to make friends with another child, soliciting help from a peer) or reacting to provocations by peers (e.g., reacting to having been hit in the back with a ball by peers for whom the intent of the action is ambiguous), rejected children generate fewer strategies than their more popular age-mates (Asarnow & Callan, 1985; Pettit et al., 1988). Furthermore, they are likely to suggest more agonistic and fewer prosocial solutions or resolutions to social dilemmas (Asarnow & Callan, 1985; Quiggle et al., 1992; Rubin & Daniels-Beirness, 1983). Thus, the social-cognitive response repertoires of rejected, especially rejected-aggressive, children are more restricted than those of other children, and the strategies they do suggest are less kind and more agonistic than those suggested by nonrejected children.

In addition, rejected-aggressive children feel more efficacious in using hostile, hurtful strategies to meet their social goals (Crick & Dodge, 1989). And finally, research conducted before the distinction between different sociometric classifications suggests that unpopular children are more inclined to interpret social outcomes in a less positive light than their more popular age-mates. Hymel (1986) found, for example, that unpopular children were more likely to expect social failure; furthermore, their analyses of the consequences of social interchanges were often self-defeating in nature. Several researchers have reported that rejected or unpopular children perceive their social successes as unstable and externally caused, whereas their social failures are viewed as stable and internally caused (e.g., Hymel & Franke, 1985).

It is important to note, at this point, that the social-cognitive concomitants of peer rejection vary for children who have been characterized as aggressive on the one hand, or socially wary, submissive, and withdrawn on the other. Indeed, multiple scenarios may be necessary to explain the relations between social-cognitive processes and peer acceptance-rejection. For example, aggressive children, ostensibly already rejected by peers, misinterpret the social motives of others, are themselves motivated by negative concerns, and thus choose from a restricted range of

interpersonal problem-solving strategies and choose agonistic strategies. The process leading to the enactment of
aggression and the behavioral display itself will probably
reinforce an already negative peer profile.

The scenario for rejected-submissive or withdrawn children may be different. Researchers have found that socially
withdrawn 4- and 5-year-olds suggest during interviews
that they would use more adult-dependent and nonassertive
social strategies to solve their interpersonal dilemmas
(Rubin, 1982a). Yet, despite their actual production of
unassertive strategies, withdrawn children are more often
rebuffed by their peers than are nonwithdrawn children
(Rubin & Borwick, 1984). This finding suggests that withdrawn children, although not sociometrically rejected in
the early years, do experience qualitatively poor peer relationships as evidenced by the experience of behavioral
rebuff (Rubin, 1985).

By the middle school years, non-aggressive-rejected
children, unlike like their rejected-aggressive counterparts,
do *not* have difficulties interpreting social cues and generating competent solutions to hypothetical interpersonal
dilemmas (Rabiner, Lenhart, & Lochman, 1990; Rubin,
1985). Their problem is in the production, or enactment,
phase of the processing sequence (Rubin & Borwick, 1984;
Stewart & Rubin, 1995). Researchers have speculated that
social dilemmas evoke emotionally anxious-fearful reactions in withdrawn children; their inability to regulate and
overcome their wariness is proposed to result in an unassertive, submissive social problem-solving style. Interestingly, however, there has been little research in which the
relations between emotion and affect regulation and social
information processing have been studied (Crick & Dodge,
1994).

Attribution theory provides a conceptual framework for
understanding the link between social-cognitive processes
and experiences with peers. Using an attributional approach, Goetz and Dweck (1980) explored the association
between children's interpretations of an experience with
peers (i.e., being rejected from joining a pen pal club) and
their subsequent behavior. They found that children who attributed failure to be accepted into a pen pal club to *personal internal causes,* were debilitated in later attempts to
gain entry into the club.

These data suggest that if children interpret social experiences negatively, inappropriately, and inaccurately, they
may prove to be their own worst enemies. Such negative biases are likely to contribute to their already problematic
social relationships. In the case of rejected-aggressive

children, demonstrated deficits in social-cognitive processing suggest that these children may have difficulty understanding the consequences of their behaviors for others,
and in understanding that their social failures can be attributed to internal, stable causes (see Coie & Dodge, Ch. 12,
this Volume, for a complete review). In short, they may not
claim responsibility for their production of agonistic social
behaviors ("They made me do it!") or for their negative social reputations. Indeed, given their social-cognitive inadequacies, rejected-aggressive children may not realize that
their interactive styles are perceived negatively by peers.

Alternatively, the socially withdrawn child may be able
to think through interpersonal dilemmas in an adequate,
competent manner. Nevertheless, when confronted by the
"real-life" social world, withdrawn children may be less
able to meet their social goals than are their nonwithdrawn
peers. The experience of peer noncompliance noted above
is likely to have an unfortunate outcome for the sensitive,
wary, withdrawn child. It is this type of sensitive-rejected
child who would attribute social failures to internal, stable
characteristics, and who would respond to peer rebuff by
expressing loneliness, dissatisfaction with his or her social
relationships, and negative self-appraisals of social skills.

Self System Correlates of Popularity

Earlier, we suggested that peer rejection does not represent
a homogeneous classification of children. The distinction
among subtypes of rejected children is especially significant insofar as the relevant literature on the self system is
concerned.

To begin with, children, on average, view themselves in
a positive light. Moreover, researchers have consistently
reported that popular or accepted children are more likely
to feel and think positively about themselves and their social competencies, and to perceive social situations as relatively comforting and easy to deal with (Harter, 1982;
Kurdek & Krile, 1982; Ladd & Price, 1986; Wheeler &
Ladd, 1982). Unpopular or rejected children report being
more socially dissatisfied and anxious in the peer milieu
than their accepted, nonrejected age-mates (Hymel &
Franke, 1985; LaGreca, Dandes, Wick, Shaw, & Stone,
1988).

More recently, researchers have found that it is only
rejected-withdrawn children (also variously described as
submissive, sensitive, wary) who believe they have poor social skills and relationships (Boivin & Begin, 1989; Boivin
et al., 1989; Hymel, Bowker, & Woody, 1993). *Rejected-*

aggressive children do not report thinking poorly about their social competencies or their relationships with peers (C. Patterson, Kupersmidt, & Griesler, 1990). These findings are in keeping with the results of recent studies concerning withdrawn and aggressive children; it is only the former group that reports having difficulty with their social skills and peer relationships (Hymel et al., 1990; Hymel et al., 1993; Rubin, Chen, & Hymel, 1993).

Given rejected-withdrawn children's negative perceptions of their social competencies and relationships, and given their negative experiences in the peer group, it is not surprising that these children report more loneliness and social detachment than popular children or children who are rejected but aggressive (e.g., Boivin et al., 1989). These relations have been reported throughout childhood and early adolescence (Asher & Wheeler, 1985; Cassidy & Asher, 1992; Crick & Ladd, 1993; Parkhurst & Asher, 1992). Neglected sociometric status has not been found to be associated with risk for loneliness (Asher & Wheeler, 1985; Asher & Williams, 1987).

In summary, although rejected children tend to report that they are less competent, less efficacious, and less satisfied with reference to their social skills and peer relationships, this conclusion appears true only for rejected children who are withdrawn, timid, or submissive. Sociometrically neglected children have not been found to report more loneliness or dissatisfaction with their social circumstances than sociometrically average children.

Proximal Correlates of Friendship

Peer researchers have not devoted nearly as much attention to the correlates of friendship as they have to the correlates of popularity. Studies in this area also lack the methodological consistency seen in the sociometric research. Studies of the correlates of friendship typically involve either a comparison of children with and without friends, or an assessment of why a child will become a friend of one peer but not another (Parker & Asher, 1993b).

With regard to the first issue, studies of preschoolers (e.g., Howes, Matheson, & Wu, 1992) indicate that friendless children are less likely than other children to initiate and maintain play with peers. This lack of social skill is seen also in older children (Eason, 1985). Among older children, there is evidence also that those with friends, relative to those who are friendless, are more prominent in the group, more stimulating, and more popular than others (Clark & Drewry, 1985). Studies that have controlled for

the differences in popularity between friended and friendless children have pointed to a more specific set of features that linked to friendship. McGuire and Weisz (1982), for example, revealed that when popularity is controlled, friended and friendless children differ in altruism and emotional perspective taking (see Eisenberg & Fabes, Ch. 11, this Volume).

Theory and research on the processes of interpersonal attraction are also relevant to the study of friendship. By considering the processes that underlie attraction and friendship formation, one can begin to understand the factors that distinguish friended and friendless children. What is it that attracts children to one another? Psychologists have suggested that attraction among children is guided by concordances or similarities in age, sex, and ethnicity/race (Hartup, 1989). Beyond such physical or *surface* information (e.g., age, sex, race, physical attractiveness), relatively little is known about the relations in early and middle childhood between other forms of similarity and preferential personal attraction (Hartup, 1989). What *is* known derives generally from databases comprising older children and adolescents. For example, Hymel and Woody (1991) found that middle school-aged children reported liking those who were similar to them in terms of politeness and sense of humor. Gest, Graham-Berman, and Hartup (1991) noted that self-reported similarity in sociability and sensitivity distinguished friend from nonfriend dyads. In adolescence, similar attitudes, aspirations, and intellect appear to aid in the maintenance of friendship bonds (e.g., Smollar & Youniss, 1982). Based on this perspective, it appears that children who are different from the other boys and girls in the group are those who are less likely to have a friend.

Another important factor that draws children together is *behavioral homophyly*. In a recent study of initially unfamiliar quartets of 7-year-olds, Rubin, Lynch, et al. (1994) reported that children who offer a clear and discriminating preference for one previously *unfamiliar* peer over another demonstrate behaviors concordant with the preferred peer. This concordance was especially marked with regard to the cognitive maturity of their play. Importantly, behavioral concordance was exhibited when the discriminating child was *not playing* with his or her preferred playmate; as such, the authors concluded that children who display similar behaviors when they are *not* playing together are more likely to be attracted to each other than children whose play styles differ.

These findings imply that the more distinct a child is from the group, the more difficulty he or she may have forming friendships. Thus again, group norms and characteristics seem important in the determination of a child's peer relationships. In one group, a child may have many opportunities for friendship if his or her characteristics are like those of others in the group; in another group within which the child is more distinctive, it is less likely that he or she will have a friend.

Research on *friendship formation* also indicates the type of children who will have trouble forming friendships. For example, in a longitudinal study of children aged 3 to 9 years, Gottman (1983) found that those who were in the process of becoming friends were more likely to communicate clearly, have more positive exchanges, and resolve conflicts more effectively than children who would not become friends. As the relationship progressed, communication clarity and self-disclosure become increasingly important. Thus, it would appear that friendships form when partners are able to establish some sense of commonality and community. This is accomplished through clear channels of mutual communication, thus allowing full understanding and the avoidance or resolution of conflicts.

Once friendships are established, cooperation and reciprocity become key elements of successful relationships (Hartup, 1989). Thus, the child's ability to engage in joint communication and cooperative activities with a peer as well as to successfully resolve conflicts with that peer appear to be important behavioral skills for friendships.

DISTAL PREDICTORS OF CHILDREN'S SOCIAL SKILLS AND PEER RELATIONSHIPS

The quality of children's extrafamilial social lives is likely a product of factors internal and external to the child. Drawing from Hinde (1976, 1979, 1987), for example, it seems reasonable to suggest that characteristics of the *individual,* such as biological or dispositional factors (e.g., temperament) may influence the quality of children's peer relationships. It is equally plausible that the *interactions* and *relationships* children experience with their parents are important. Of course, parenting behaviors are influenced by parental beliefs about child rearing and child behavior. But parental behavior and beliefs are, themselves, influenced by parental personality, mental health status, and the parent's own childhood experiences (Belsky, 1984). Thus, these latter variables may also have implications for children's interactions and relationships with peers. Finally, contextual factors, such as poverty, parental

illness, and marital conflict, are likely to play a role in promoting or jeopardizing children's social competence and later adjustment with peers. These *ecological factors* may be more or less directly influential on the development of peer difficulties.

In the following section, we present a brief review of some of the distal factors that may influence children's social interactions and peer relationships. We begin with a short discussion of the role of *individual* or dispositional temperament and biological factors. Following this, we examine the association between the parent-child and child-peer *relationship* systems. We focus primarily on research conducted within the framework of attachment theory. Following our discussion of attachment theory, we examine the relevant literature on parenting beliefs and behaviors. Finally, we briefly review some of the family contextual factors that appear to influence children's peer relationships and social skills.

Temperament, Social Behaviors, and Peer Relationships

Temperament has been defined as "characteristic individual differences in the intensive and temporal parameters of expression of emotionality and arousal" (Campos, Campos, & Barrett, 1989, p. 399). Researchers who study temperament in children report that individuals differ not only in the ease with which positive and negative emotions may be aroused (emotionality; Buss & Plomin, 1984), but also in the ease with which emotions, once aroused, can be regulated (Derryberry & Rothbart, 1984).

Surprisingly perhaps, studies of emotional reactivity and regulation in childhood are relatively limited (Thompson, Ch. 2, this Volume). Yet, one can construe dispositional dimensions as reflections of reactivity and regulation. Take, for example, the constructs of difficult temperament, activity level, and inhibition/sociability. Difficult temperament refers to the frequent and intense expression of negative affect (Thomas & Chess, 1977). Fussiness and irritability would be characteristic of a "difficult" infant or toddler. In reactivity/regulation terminology, the "difficult" child is one whose negative emotions are easily aroused and difficult to soothe or regulate. The highly active baby/toddler is one who is easily excited and motorically facile. Again, these children are easily aroused, that is, highly reactive. Inhibited infants/toddlers are timid, vigilant, and fearful when faced with novel social stimuli; like the other groups of children, their emotions are easily aroused and difficult to regulate. Finally, children who are outgoing and open in response to social novelty are described as sociable (Kagan, 1989).

Each of these temperamental characteristics is relatively stable, and each is related to particular constellations of social behaviors that we described above as characteristic of either popular or rejected children. For example, infants and toddlers who have been identified as having difficult and/or active temperaments are more likely to behave in aggressive, impulsive ways in early childhood (e.g., aggression; Bates, Bayles, Bennett, Ridge, & Brown, 1991). And, as we noted earlier, undercontrolled, impulsive, and aggressive behavior is associated contemporaneously and predictively with peer relationships characterized by rejection (e.g., Bates et al., 1991). Similarly, behavioral inhibition, an individual trait identified in infancy and toddlerhood, predicts the display of socially withdrawn behavior in early and middle childhood (Calkins & Fox, 1992; Kagan, 1989). As mentioned earlier, social withdrawal in middle childhood is also a strong correlate of peer rejection.

Related to the above, it has been suggested that dispositional characteristics related to emotion regulation may lay the basis for the emergence of children's social behaviors and relationships. For example, Rubin, Coplan, Fox, and Calkins (1995) have argued that the social consequences of emotion dysregulation vary in accord with the child's behavioral tendency to approach and interact with peers during free play. They found that sociable children whose approach behaviors lacked regulatory control were disruptive and aggressive; those who were sociable but able to regulate their emotions were socially competent. Unsociable children who were good emotion regulators appeared to suffer no ill effects of their lack of social behavior; when playing alone, they were productive engagers in constructive and exploratory activity. They were neither anxious among peers nor rated by parents as having socioemotional difficulties. Unsociable children who were poor emotion regulators were more behaviorally anxious and wary, more reticent than constructive when playing alone, and rated by parents as having more internalizing problems than their other age-mates. Thus, emotionally dysregulated preschoolers may behave in ways that will solicit peer rejection and inhibit the development of qualitatively adaptive friendships. Further, this is the case for emotionally dysregulated sociable as well as unsociable children.

The results of Rubin et al.'s (1995) study are clearly in keeping with findings from Eisenberg and colleagues' extensive research program on young children's emotional arousal and regulation. In this work, Eisenberg and colleagues (e.g., Eisenberg et al., 1993; Eisenberg, Fabes, Nyman, Bernzweig, & Pinuealas, 1994; Fabes & Eisenberg, 1992) have found that the extent to which provocation by peers results in anger as well as the lack of regulatory control (e.g., retaliation) is negatively associated with teacher ratings of preschoolers' peer acceptance and social competence. Alternatively, preschoolers who are able to cope with anger-provoking situations by seeking support or by shifting their attention to nonprovocative stimuli (constructive coping) are viewed by their teachers as more popular and socially competent. Interestingly, these results are stronger for boys than girls.

Relatedly, in a two-year follow-up study of these preschoolers, Eisenberg, Fabes, Murphy, Maszk, Smith, and Karbon (1995) reported that aggression in elementary school children could be predicted by displays of negative emotionality (responding to provocation with anger) and the relative lack of emotion regulation (responding to provocation by retaliating and not with constructive coping) during preschool. Again these findings were particularly strong for boys, but not for girls.

Finally, in a study of 5- to 10-year-olds, Stocker and Dunn (1990) found that sociability and emotionality were associated with the quality of children's *friendships* as well as their general acceptance in the peer group. Children reported to be more sociable were rated as having more positive relationships with friends and judged to be more popular with peers than children who were less sociable. And children reported to be highly emotional had less successful relationships with friends and peers than children who were low in emotionality. Unfortunately, unlike the recent Rubin, Coplan, et al. (1995) study described above, the authors did not examine the interactive relations between sociability and emotionality insofar as they might predict qualitative dimensions of friendship. This would appear to be a reasonable topic of future study.

In summary, researchers suggest that individual, dispositionally based characteristics may set the stage for the development of particular types of parent-child relationships and for the development of social behavioral profiles that ultimately predict the quality of children's peer relationships. Although this argument is being examined in a number of current research programs, it is nevertheless the case that individual differences in emotional arousability, the intensity of emotional expression, and the regulation of negative affect as they relate to and perhaps predict children's interactions and relationships in the peer group remain very much understudied.

Parent-Child Attachment Relationships, Social Behaviors, and Peer Relationships

According to Hartup (1985), parents serve at least three functions in the child's development of social competence and qualitatively positive peer relationships. First, parent-child *interaction* is a context within which many competencies necessary for social interaction develop. Second, the parent-child *relationship* constitutes a safety net permitting the child the freedom to examine features of the social universe, thereby enhancing the development of social skills. Third, it is within the parent-child relationship that the child begins to develop expectations and assumptions about interactions and relationships with other people.

The Parent-Child Attachment Relationship

A basic premise of attachment theory is that "The young child seeks and explores new relationships within the framework of expectations for self and others that emerges from the primary relationship" (Sroufe & Fleeson, 1986, p. 52) In most cases, it is the mother-infant relationship that is the most significant. Thus, it is suggested that the early mother-infant relationship lays the groundwork for children's understanding of and participation in subsequent familial and extrafamilial relationships. And, since the quality of attachment relationships with the mother may vary, subsequent social success and relationships with peers is expected to vary as well.

The putative, proximal causes of the development of a secure attachment relationship, at least insofar as the parent is concerned, are the expressions of responsivity, warmth, and sensitivity (e.g., Belsky & Cassidy, 1995). The sensitive and responsive parent is able and willing to recognize the infant's or toddler's emotional signals, to consider the child's perspective, and to respond promptly and appropriately according to the child's needs. In turn, it is posited that the child develops a working belief system that incorporates the parent as someone who can be relied upon for protection, nurturance, comfort, and security; a sense of trust in relationships results from the secure infant/toddler-parent bond. Furthermore, the child forms a belief that the self is competent and worthy of positive response from others. Thus, attachment theory predicts at least three influences on children's internal working models that bear on

their developing interactive skills and social relationships with peers (Elicker, Englund, & Sroufe, 1992). First, a secure attachment relationship with the primary caregiver promotes *positive social expectations:* children are disposed to engage other children and expect peer interaction to be rewarding. Second, their experience with a responsive and empathic caregiver builds the rudiments of a social understanding of *reciprocity.* Finally, responsive and supportive parental care lays the foundation for the development of *a sense of self-worth and self-efficacy.* This internal outlook is thought to be important to promoting curiosity, enthusiasm, and positive affect, characteristics that other children find attractive.

The process by which a secure attachment relationship is thought to result in the development of social competence and positive relationships with peers may be described briefly as follows. The "internal working model" of the securely attached young child allows him or her to feel secure, confident, and self-assured when introduced to novel settings; this sense of felt security fosters the child's active exploration of the social environment (Sroufe, 1983). In turn, exploration of the social milieu leads to peer interaction and play (Rubin et al., 1983). And, as we noted earlier, peer interaction and play allow children to experience the interpersonal exchange of ideas, perspectives, roles, and actions. From such social interchanges, children develop skills that lead to the development of positive peer relationships.

Alternatively, the development of an insecure attachment relationship is posited to result in the child's developing an internal working model that interpersonal relationships are rejecting or neglectful (Bretherton & Waters, 1985). According to Bowlby (1973), a baby whose parent has been inaccessible and unresponsive is frequently angry because the parent's unresponsiveness is painful and frustrating. At the same time, because of uncertainty about the parent's responsiveness, the infant is apprehensive and readily upset by stressful situations. To protect against these intolerable emotions, the infant purportedly develops ego defense strategies that involve excluding from conscious processing any information that, when processed in the past, aroused anger and anxiety (Bowlby, 1969). In situations that could arouse these emotions, the infant blocks the conscious awareness and the processing of thoughts, feelings, and desires associated with his or her need of the parent. This blockage deactivates the behavioral system mediating attachment behavior and inhibits the behavioral expression of attachment-related thoughts and emotions (Thompson, Ch. 2, this Volume).

Attachment theorists have suggested also that the expectations and assumptions that infants hold about others, and the means by which they cope with these cognitions, are internalized and carried forward into subsequent relationships (Bowlby, 1973). Thus, it has been proposed that, in their subsequent peer relationships, insecure "avoidant" infants are guided by previously reinforced expectations of parental rejection; hence, they are believed to perceive peers as potentially hostile and tend to strike out proactively and aggressively (Troy & Sroufe, 1987). Insecure "ambivalent" infants, on the other hand, are thought to be guided by a fear of rejection; consequently, in their extrafamilial peer relationships they are posited to attempt to avoid rejection through passive, adult-dependent behavior and withdrawal from the prospects of peer interaction (Renken, Egeland, Marvinney, Sroufe, & Mangelsdorf, 1989).

The Parent-Child Attachment Relationship and Children's Social Behaviors: Empirical Support

Recent research supports many of these premises. With regard to social behaviors, securely attached infants are more likely than their insecure counterparts to demonstrate socially competent behaviors among peers during the toddler (e.g., Pastor, 1981), preschool (e.g., Booth, Rose-Krasnor, & Rubin, 1991; Erickson, Sroufe, & Egeland, 1985), and elementary school periods (e.g., Elicker et al., 1992; Renken et al., 1989). Insecure-avoidant babies later exhibit more hostility, anger, and aggressive behavior in preschool settings than their secure counterparts (e.g., LaFreniere & Sroufe, 1985; Troy & Sroufe, 1987). Insecure-ambivalent infants are more whiney, easily frustrated, and socially inhibited at 2 years than their secure age-mates (e.g., Fox & Calkins, 1993). At 4 years of age, children classified at 1 year as ambivalent infants have been described as lacking in confidence and assertiveness (Erickson et al., 1985), and at 7 years as passively withdrawn (Renken et al., 1989).

It is also the case that secure and insecure attachments, as assessed in early and mid-childhood are associated contemporaneously with and predictive of adaptive and maladaptive social behaviors, respectively. For example, children who experience a secure relationship with their mothers have been found to be more sociable and competent than their insecure counterparts, whereas insecure

children exhibit more aggression and withdrawal (Cohn, 1990; Rose-Krasnor, Rubin, Booth, & Coplan, 1996). Furthermore, insecurity of attachment, as assessed in early and mid-childhood, *predicts* the subsequent display of both aggression and withdrawal (Booth, Rose-Krasnor, McKinnon, & Rubin, 1994).

The Parent-Child Attachment Relationship and Children's Peer Relationships: Empirical Support

Recent evidence suggests also that infants with secure attachment histories are later more popular in the peer group during the preschool (LaFreniere & Sroufe, 1985) and elementary school years (Elicker et al., 1992) than their insecurely attached counterparts. Furthermore, there appears to be a contemporaneous association between the security of parent-child attachment and peer popularity as assessed in middle childhood (Cohn, 1990).

Researchers have also found significant associations between the quality of children's attachment relationships and the subsequent quality of their best friendships. Thus, Youngblade and Belsky (1992) have reported that securely attached infants were less likely than insecure infants to have negative and asynchronous friendships at 5 years of age. Their data replicated and extended the findings of Park and Waters (1989), who observed dyads of 4-year-old best friends. In dyads where both members were securely attached, the interaction was more harmonious, less controlling, more responsive, and more positive when infant-mother attachment histories were more positive and harmonious than in dyads in which one member was insecurely attached.

Summary

There is growing evidence that the quality of parent-child attachment relationships predicts socially skilled behaviors, peer acceptance, and qualitatively good friendships. The reader is cautioned, however, that any firm conclusions on these matters are premature at this time. It is the case that several researchers have been unable to demonstrate contemporaneous or predictive links between attachment status and children's social behaviors and relationships (e.g., Bates, Maslin, & Frankel, 1985). Thus, according to Belsky and Cassidy (1995), additional research is required to determine whether antecedent or contemporaneous attachment security plays a causal role or, instead, simply correlates with indices of developmental psychopathology via yet-to-be studied, third-variable mechanisms.

Parenting Beliefs and Children's Social Behaviors and Peer Relationships

As noted above, sensitive, responsive parenting is associated with the development of secure parent-infant attachment relationships, whereas insensitive, unresponsive, and intrusive parenting styles are associated with insecure parent-infant attachment relationships. Also, as noted above, security of attachment is concurrently and predictively associated with the demonstration of competent social behavior; in turn, social competence predicts peer popularity and close friendship relations. Given these associations, it should not be surprising that parenting behavior is associated with the development and production of socially competent behavior, as well as with acceptance in the peer milieu. We begin our discussion of the relations between parenting and children's peer relationships with a brief overview of the relevant literature on parental beliefs (see also Bugental & Goodnow, Ch. 7, this Volume).

Parental Beliefs

Parents' ideas, beliefs, and perceptions about the development and maintenance of children's social behaviors and relationships predict, and presumably partially explain, the development of socially adaptive and maladaptive interactive behaviors and peer relationships in childhood. This is true because parents' child-rearing practices represent a behavioral expression of their ideas about how children become socially competent, how family contexts should be structured to shape children's behaviors, and how and when children should be taught to initiate and maintain relationships with others (Laosa & Sigel, 1982).

Parents' Beliefs about Adaptive Child Behaviors and Relationships

Presumably, the more parents think it is important for their children to be socially competent, the more likely they will promote social skills in their children. In general, parents view their children optimistically and forecast healthy developmental outcomes for them. Parents of socially competent children believe that, in early childhood, parents should play an active role in the socialization of social skills via teaching and providing peer interaction opportunities. They believe also that when their children display maladaptive behaviors, it is due to transitory and situationally caused circumstances (Goodnow, Knight, & Cashmore, 1985). Parents whose preschoolers display socially incompetent behaviors (such as social reticence, hostility,

aggression), on the other hand, are less likely to endorse strong beliefs in the development of social skills (Rubin, Mills, & Rose-Krasnor, 1989). Furthermore, they are more likely to attribute the development of social competence to internal factors ("Children are born that way"), to believe that incompetent behavior is difficult to alter, and to believe that interpersonal skills are best taught through direct instructional means (Rubin et al., 1989).

One conclusion that may derive from these findings is that parental involvement in the promotion of social competence is mediated by strong beliefs in the importance of social skills. When a socially competent child demonstrates poor social performance, parents who place a relatively high value on social competence are likely to become the most involved and responsive. Over time, such involvement may be positively reinforced by the child's acquisition of social skills. At the same time, parents are likely to value the social skills displayed by their children, and these children will be perceived as interpersonally competent and capable of autonomous learning. Hence, parental beliefs and child characteristics will influence each other in a reciprocal manner (Mills & Rubin, 1993; see Miller, 1995, for a relevant review).

The Child as Parental Belief Evocateur

In keeping with the perspective that the parent-child relationship reflects the contributions of both partners, it is important to understand that parental beliefs may be evoked by child characteristics and behavior. For example, the "problematic" child who demonstrates maladaptive social behaviors and who does not get along with his or her peers is likely to evoke different parental emotions and cognitions than the "normal" child (Bugental, 1992). When this latter group of children behave in maladaptive or socially inappropriate manners, they may activate parental feelings of concern, puzzlement, and, in the case of aggression, anger. These affects are regulated by the parent's attempts to understand, rationalize, or justify the child's behavior and by the parent's knowledge of the child's social skills history and the known quality of the child's social relationships at home, at school, and in the neighborhood. Thus, in the case of nonproblematic children, the evocative stimulus produces adaptive, solution-focused parental ideation that results in the parent's choice of a reasoned, sensitive, and responsive approach to dealing with the problem behavior (Bugental, 1992). In turn, the child views the parent as supportive and learns to better understand how to behave and feel in similar situations as they occur in the future. As such, a reciprocal connection is developed between the ways and means of adult and child social information processing.

But how does the socially incompetent child's presentation of socially maladaptive behavior affect the parent? In the case of aggressive children, any hostile behavior, whether directed at peers, siblings, or parents, evokes strong parental feelings of anger and frustration (Rubin & Mills, 1990). These feelings, when left unregulated, predict the use of power-assertive and restrictive disciplinary techniques (Hart, DeWolf, Wozniak, & Burts, 1992; Pettit et al., 1988). This type of low warmth–high control parental response, mediated by affect and beliefs/cognitions about the intentionality of the child behavior, the historical precedence of child aggression, and the best means to control child aggression, is likely to evoke negative affect and cognitions in the child. The result of this interplay between parent and child beliefs, affects, and behavior may be the reinforcement and extension of family cycles of hostility (Dishion, Duncan, Eddy, Fagot, & Fetrow, 1994).

Parental reactions to social wariness and fearfulness are less well understood. Researchers have found that when children produce a high frequency of socially wary, withdrawn behaviors their parents (a) recognize this as a problem; (b) express feelings of concern, sympathy, guilt, embarrassment, and, with increasing child age, a growing sense of frustration; and (c) are more inclined to attribute their children's social reticence to dispositional traits (Mills & Rubin, 1993). Perhaps in an attempt to regulate their own expressed guilt and embarrassment emanating from their children's ineffectual behaviors, mothers of socially withdrawn preschoolers indicate that they would react to their children's displays of social withdrawal by providing them with protection and direct instruction. To release the child from social discomfort, the parents of socially wary children have indicated that they would solve the child's social dilemmas by asking other children for information desired by the child, obtaining objects desired by the child, or requesting that peers allow the child to join them in play (Mills & Rubin, 1993). Relatedly, socially withdrawn preschoolers are more likely than their nonwithdrawn age-mates to believe that it is appropriate to ask an adult to help them solve their interpersonal dilemmas (Rubin, 1982b).

In summary, it is suggested that parental beliefs influence parental behavior; in turn, parental behavior influences the development, maintenance, and inhibition of children's social behaviors, which, as we noted earlier, influence the quality of their peer relationships. Consistent with this view, parents of aggressive and withdrawn children have been found to differ from those of average children in the ways they think about socializing social skills and in the ways they report reacting to their children's maladaptive behaviors. We turn now to the relevant research on parental behaviors.

Parenting Behaviors and Children's Social Skills and Peer Relationships

Parents may influence the development of social behaviors, interaction patterns, and ultimately, the quality of their children's peer relationships by (a) providing opportunities for their children to have contact with peers; (b) monitoring their children's peer encounters (when necessary); (c) coaching their children to deal competently with interpersonal peer-related tasks; and (d) disciplining unacceptable, maladaptive peer-directed behaviors (e.g., Pettit & Mize, 1993).

Parental Coaching and Monitoring

Recent research suggests that parents vary widely in the extent of their efforts to provide opportunities for peer interaction for their children and to coach their children in specific social skills. Moreover, the available evidence suggests that parents' efforts in these areas have implications for their children's success with peers (Ladd, Profilet, & Hart, 1992; Pettit & Mize, 1993). Ladd and Golter (1988), for example, found that parents who actively arranged peer contacts and who indirectly supervised these contacts had preschoolers who were better liked by their peers. In addition, children whose parents relied on indirect rather than direct monitoring of their children's peer contacts were less hostile toward peers. In a follow-up, short-term longitudinal study, Ladd and Hart (1992) found that mothers' over- as well as underinvolvement in arranging and monitoring peer contacts could be detrimental to children's social success, at least among boys. Boys whose mothers were moderately involved in initiating their child's peer contacts displayed significant gains in peer status over time compared to boys with over- and underinvolved mothers. Girls made significant gains in peer status only when their own efforts to initiate contact with other children were large in comparison to those of their mothers (i.e., when their mothers were underinvolved).

Like Ladd and colleagues, Bhavnagri and Parke (1991) found that mothers often arranged for and supervised play sessions with peers for their children. These authors also found that mothers were far more likely than fathers to arrange and supervise children's contacts with other children, a disparity that was also noted by Ladd and Golter (1988).

Parents also regularly supervise and coach their children's peer activities. Finnie and Russell (1988), for example, found that during play with an unfamiliar age-mate, mothers of unpopular children were more likely to avoid supervising their children and to supervise their children less skillfully than mothers of more popular children. Mothers of more popular children were more active and effective in supervising their children's peer-related behaviors than mothers of less well-accepted children. Mothers of more popular children suggested that they would encourage their children to employ positive and assertive strategies for handling hypothetical interpersonal problems involving peers; mothers of less popular children suggested that they would coach their children to be more avoidant in response to hypothetical problems involving peers. In a follow-up study, Russell and Finnie (1990) examined mothers' instructions to their child immediately prior to the child's opportunity to play with an unfamiliar child. Mothers of popular children were more likely than mothers of low-status (rejected and neglected) children to make group-oriented statements during both the anticipatory instruction period as well as during the play session itself. Mothers of low-status children were more disruptive of their children's play.

In summary, recent research on parental monitoring and coaching indicates that when parents are involved in effective ways in coaching their children through difficulties with peers, facilitating their children's play with peers, and providing their children with opportunities to play with peers, their children are more popular among their age-mates. However, all of the research in this area is correlational. It is entirely possible that the observed differences between the mothers of socially popular and unpopular children are a consequence, rather than the cause, of their children's success with peers. Thus, it would be timely to examine whether very young children identified as being relatively unpopular with peers could "shake" their early reputations if their parents were "trained" in parental monitoring and coaching skills.

Parenting Behaviors

It seems quite clear that children whose peer relationships suffer experience less than optimal parenting. Parents (usually mothers) of unpopular and/or peer-rejected children have been reported to use inept, harsh, and authoritarian disciplinary and socialization practices more frequently than those of their more popular counterparts (e.g., Bierman & Smoot, 1991; Dishion, 1990). These data seem to hold true for parents of preschoolers through elementary schoolers. Alternatively, parents of popular children use more feelings-oriented reasoning and induction, warm control (authoritative), and more positivity during communication than their unpopular counterparts (e.g., Finnie & Russell, 1988; Hart et al., 1992; Hart, Ladd, & Burleson, 1990; MacDonald & Parke, 1984; Putallaz, 1987; Roopnarine & Adams, 1987).

In regard to the actual process that links parenting to the child's peer relationships, it is possible to consider that parenting styles may promote particular child behaviors that mark a child for acceptance or rejection. To this end, researchers have demonstrated that mothers of socially competent children are more child-centered, more feelings-oriented, warmer, and more likely to use positive verbalizations, reasoning, and explanations than mothers of less competent children (e.g., Denham & Grout, 1992; Finnie & Russell, 1988; Hinde & Tamplin, 1983; Pettit & Mize, 1993).

With regard to socially incompetent behaviors, researchers have shown consistently that aggressive children have parents who model and inadvertently reinforce aggressive and impulsive behavior, and who are cold and rejecting, physically punitive, and inconsistent in their disciplinary behaviors. In addition to parental rejection and the use of high power-assertive and inconsistent disciplinary strategies, parental permissiveness, indulgence, and lack of supervision have often been found to correlate with children's aggressive behavior (see Rubin, Stewart, & Chen, 1995, for a recent extensive review of related literature). It may not be difficult to understand these associations given that parental tolerance and neglect of the child's aggressive behavior may actually have the implication of legitimization and encouragement of aggression. Importantly, these findings appear to have cross-cultural universality (e.g., Chen & Rubin, 1994; Whiting & Edwards, 1988).

Compared to the literature on the parenting behaviors associated with undercontrolled, aggressive children, little is known about social wariness and withdrawal. Research concerning the parenting behaviors and styles associated with social withdrawal focuses clearly on two potential socialization contributors: overcontrol and overprotection.

Parents who use high power-assertive strategies and who place many constraints on their children tend to rear shy, reserved, and dependent children. Thus, the issuance of parental commands combined with constraints on exploration and independence may hinder the development of competence in the social milieu. Restrictive control may also deprive the child of opportunities to interact with peers. As such, it should not be surprising that children who are socially withdrawn are on the receiving end of parental overcontrol and overprotection (e.g., East, 1991; Hart et al., 1992; LaFreniere & Dumas, 1992). These findings concerning parental overcontrol and restriction stem from very few studies, most of which center on children of preschool age. Furthermore, the contexts within which parents of socially withdrawn children display overcontrol and overprotection have not been well specified. Thus, unlike the literature on the parents of aggressive children, the socialization correlates and causes of social withdrawal are not well known. This dearth of data represents an open research agenda for future investigation.

Parenting Behaviors: Summary

In summary, there is some support for the contention that parental behavior is associated, not only with the development of children's social competence, but also with their peer relationships. The assumption has been that parenting leads to social competence/incompetence, which in turn leads to peer acceptance/rejection. This causal model has been tested recently in two studies.

Dishion (1990) examined the relations among grade school boys' sociometric status, academic skills, antisocial behavior, and several elements of parental discipline practices and family circumstances. Results indicated that, compared with other boys, sociometrically rejected boys had parents who were significantly more likely to engage in inept and negative disciplinary practices. Disadvantaged family circumstances (e.g., poverty, low SES) and stressful events were also linked to poor adjustment with peers, but further analysis of this relation suggested that the link was indirect, that is, mediated primarily by parenting practices. Causal modeling further suggested that the relation between inept parenting and peer rejection was itself mediated by boys' antisocial behavior and academic difficulties. That is, lower levels of parental skill were associated with higher levels of antisocial behavior and lower levels of academic performance; antisocial behavior and poor academic performance, in turn, were associated with higher levels of peer rejection.

These findings have been replicated and extended in a similar study conducted in the People's Republic of China (Chen & Rubin, 1994). Not only was the pathway from parental authoritarian, punitive disciplinary practices to child aggression to peer rejection replicated, but the authors revealed that parental warmth and authoritative control predicted social competence, which in turn predicted peer acceptance. These latter results suggest that the pathways to peer acceptance and rejection may be generalized across cultures.

Finally, when one considers extremes of parenting behavior, it has recently been shown that physical abuse predicts the abilities of children to understand the emotions of others, which in turn predicts isolation by peers (Rogosch, Cicchetti, & Aber, 1995; see also Cicchetti, Lynch, Shonk, & Manly, 1992, for a thorough discussion of the associations between child maltreatment and peer relationships).

Many methodological and other issues remain. However, the existing research supports the general conclusion that socially successful children have mothers (and, where examined, fathers) who are more feelings-oriented, more positive, more skillful, more likely to use inductive reasoning, and less negative and coercive in their interaction with their children than their socially unsuccessful counterparts. The limits that the correlational nature of this work place on our interpretation should be recognized, however. Although it is likely that parents' behaviors have an influence on their children's behavior and success with peers, it must be acknowledged that parents' behavior may be elicited by their children's characteristics (Lytton, 1990). Relatedly, it should be noted that, with few exceptions, research in this area focuses on the *concurrent* relations between parental practices and children's social adjustment with peers, and not these relations over time. Thus, although we take this work as generally supportive of a link between early parental behaviors and children's later social success, this link has not been explicitly demonstrated.

The Ecology of Parenting

An examination of the "determinants of parenting" is well beyond the scope of this chapter. Instead, we refer the interested reader to Belsky (1984) and Dix (1991. Nevertheless, it is appropriate to briefly note several factors that are particularly relevant to the study of children's social behaviors and peer relationships.

First, *parental psychopathology* is associated with parenting styles known to be related to children's maladaptive social behaviors and peer relationships. For example, maternal depression is associated with a lack of parental involvement, responsivity, spontaneity, and emotional support that may result from feelings of hopelessness and helplessness (Downey & Coyne, 1990). Given these findings, it should not be surprising that parental depression is associated with social inhibition, wariness, and withdrawal in early childhood (Kochanska, 1991; Rubin, Both, Zahn-Waxler, Cummings, & Wilkinson, 1991). When depressed parents attempt to gain some element of control in their lives, they resort to overcontrolling, authoritarian patterns of child rearing (e.g., Gelfand & Teti, 1990). This mix of parental uninvolvement and overcontrol is likely responsible for reports that parental depression is associated with both social withdrawal and aggression in childhood. How it is that some children of depressed parents develop social behavioral patterns of social withdrawal and wariness whereas others become aggressive is unknown.

Second, *marital distress and conflict* has been linked to poor social outcomes in children, including friendship difficulties and child behaviors related to peer rejection (e.g., Gottman & Katz, 1989). Marital distress, conflict, and dissatisfaction predict negative attitudes about child rearing as well as insensitive, unresponsive parenting behaviors Gottman & Katz, 1989; Jouriles et al., 1991). As noted above, these parenting styles are associated with the development of social behaviors in children that are known to predict peer rejection. Also, spousal conflict and hostility can affect children directly by providing them with models of coercive interpersonal behavior (Emery, 1992).

Third, *parents' recollections and reconstructions of their own childhood peer experiences* appear to shape their concern over their children's peer experiences and their strategies for assisting their children through problems they encounter in peer relationships. Putallaz and colleagues (e.g., Putallaz, Costanzo, & Klein, 1993) have found that mothers who recall their own childhood peer relationships positively report being more nurturing as parents and judge their children as more socially competent than mothers who regard their childhood peer interactions negatively. Negative recollections of childhood peer relationships were not necessarily connected to poor child outcomes, however. Specifically, one group of mothers who regarded their early peer relationships negatively were distinctive in their tendency to recall anxious/lonely peer experiences. These mothers described themselves as nurturant and made more efforts than other mothers to positively influence their children's peer experiences (e.g., by enrolling them in social activities). Although

these mothers did not view their children as particularly socially competent, their children were rated as the most socially competent by peers, teachers, and objective observers.

Finally, *poverty and parental unemployment* produces sufficient stress in the family so as to interfere with the ability of a parent to be sensitive and responsive to the needs of a child (e.g.,. Booth et al., 1991; McLoyd, 1989). Economic stress, brought on by the lack of financial resources, makes scarce the availability of necessary goods. It also creates feelings of frustration, anger, and helplessness that can be translated into less than optimal child-rearing styles. Stressful economic situations predict parental negativism and inconsistency (Lempers, Clark-Lempers, & Simons, 1989; Weiss, Dodge, Bates, & Pettit, 1992). Given these findings, it should not be surprising that behavioral maladaptation as well as peer rejection are associated with chronic stress and economic disadvantage (C. Patterson, Vaden, & Kupersmidt, 1991). However, as Dishion's (1990) findings indicate, links between these factors and children's adjustment with peers are likely to be complex and not necessarily direct

Summary

It is now quite apparent that children's social behaviors and the quality of their peer relationships are a product, in part, of the quality of their relationships with their parents, the parenting behaviors they experience, and the ecological factors that impinge on the family unit. Children who experience harsh or neglectful parenting, who develop insecure relationships with their parents, and who live in ecologically stressful environments may be considered "at risk" for developing maladaptive social and emotional behavioral styles and peer rejection. It is important to note, however, that among the factors affecting children's social behavioral and relationship development, one must not neglect the child's dispositional, temperamental characteristics. There is every reason to believe that infant temperament may set the stage for the development of particular types of parent-child relationships and for the development of social behavioral profiles that ultimately predict the quality of children's peer relationships.

It must be acknowledged that the associations between each of the factors discussed above and the quality of children's social behaviors and relationships have not been examined in any single study. And although one may posit relations between (a) temperament and attachment, (b) attachment and parent and child behaviors, (c) parent and child behaviors and the quality of children's relationships, and (d) the overarching relation between family and cultural ecology, the *full* range of associations suggested herein have not been examined in any one research program.

CHILDHOOD PEER EXPERIENCES AND LATER ADJUSTMENT

Our goal, in this section, is to provide a summary of research in which the primary focus has been to identify aspects of childhood peer relationship experiences that predict subsequent adaptation and maladaptation. The predictors we examine fall at the levels of dyadic (friendship) and group (peer acceptance) *relationships.* Although we fully recognize that social behaviors (e.g., aggression), dispositions (e.g., temperament), and interactions (e.g., interactive conflict evoked by differences of opinion) may predict adaptive and malevolent "outcomes," relevant discussions are presented elsewhere in this volume.

Methodological Issues

The associations between the quality of peer relationships in childhood and subsequent difficulties have generally been examined in one of two ways (Parker et al., 1995). First, using *retrospective, case-control,* or *follow-back* designs, researchers have asked whether maladjusted and adjusted adolescents or adults differed as children in terms of their adjustment with peers. Second, with the *prospective, cohort,* or *follow-up* design, researchers have asked whether popular and unpopular children differ in terms of their incidence of later psychological and educational adaptation. These designs have been differentially informative insofar as the relation between peer relationships and later adjustment is concerned.

Retrospective Studies

Retrospective, or follow-back, studies usually begin with the identification, in adolescence or adulthood, of a particular target group (e.g., school dropouts, psychiatrically referred patients, persons with a criminal record). Typically, the focal group is matched with a sample of nonsymptomatic participants. Data concerning the quality of children's peer relationships and social skills are accessed from school or professional records. These archival data are then examined to discover symptomatic versus nonsymptomatic between-group differences.

By and large, retrospective studies have had, as their focus, the examination of the childhood peer experiences of adolescents and adults known to have psychiatric and/or psychological dysfunctions. For example, Kohn and Clausen (1955) found that 18% of the adult schizophrenics they interviewed reported that as children, they had played alone nearly all of the time, whereas the comparative rate for a matched group of nondisordered control study participants was only 2%.

One difficulty with accepting such findings is that retrospective interviews may invite conscious or unconscious distortion of childhood histories from respondents who have been identified as psychologically disturbed adults (Garmezy, 1974). Furthermore, retrospection requires an enormous recall capacity; asking someone to remember events that occurred many years previously simply represents a generous invitation to response bias. To avoid these limitations, researchers interested in the etiology of maladaptation have referred to child guidance clinic records for insights about the individual's peer relationships history (e.g., Ricks & Berry, 1970; Roff, 1963). One obvious advantage of this procedure over the retrospective interview is that the peer relationships data were collected, more or less systematically, by teachers and social workers *while the subject was still a child.* This procedure avoids the potential for inaccuracies from memory limitations and selective recall.

Case-control follow-back studies suggest strongly that psychologically maladjusted adults are far more likely to have had poor peer experiences than their normal counterparts (e.g., Ricks & Berry, 1970; Roff, 1961, 1963). But, like retrospective investigations, these case-control reports have serious methodological shortcomings (Garmezy, 1974; Parker & Asher, 1987). Perhaps the most serious limitation is the question of whether the findings can be generalized to those disordered adults who do *not* have a history of having been seen in a child clinic. Children treated or assessed at such venues have adjustment difficulties to begin with and thus represent a very select subset of children.

There are some early follow-back studies, however, in which the researchers relied neither on retrospective interviews nor child clinic records. These investigations provide some of the strongest cases for accepting, as developmentally significant, children's peer relationships histories. Cowen, Pedersen, Bagigian, Izzo, and Trost (1973), for example, asked third-grade children to select classmates who they thought would be most appropriate for certain roles in a hypothetical class play. Children who received many nominations for items reflecting maladaptive behavior (mostly items centered on aggression and withdrawal) were assumed to have poor peer relationships. Eleven to 13 years later, there was established a countywide psychiatric registry that made it possible to identify those third-grade children who had subsequently received public or private psychiatric care. Adults whose names appeared in the psychiatric registry were matched and compared with former classmates whose names were absent from the registry. Cowen et al. (1973) found that adults under psychiatric care received significantly more nominations for undesirable roles, a greater proportion of undesirable to total role nominations, and more overall nominations (desirable and undesirable). Thus, during childhood, the registry adults were viewed in a negative light by their peers. Of particular significance was the finding that the aforementioned peer nominations were the *only* indices to discriminate reliably between registry and nonregistry adults, a result that has proven to be a highly evocative marker of the significance of childhood peer relationships for present-day researchers.

In summary, the evidence from follow-back studies consistently supports the view that psychological and educational maladjustment in adolescence and adulthood is associated with histories of problematic childhood peer relationships. These findings are reported regardless of whether the investigators used retrospective interviews, examined child guidance clinic records, or focused on school records. Indeed, these follow-back studies suggest that, under some circumstances, indices of childhood peer adjustment distinguish disordered from nondisordered adults when many other intellectual and demographic variables do not (e.g., Cowen et al., 1973).

Prospective Studies

Prospective, or follow-up studies, in which peer measures from one time are used to predict adjustment measures at a later time provide a distinct advantage over retrospective data sets. For one, the peer relationships measures are temporally antecedent to the adjustment measures; for another, reliance on subjective memory or on school record information that was not gathered with the intention of having it reviewed in later years is avoided. In the review that follows, we examine the evidence for a predictive association between the quality of children's peer relationships and ensuing academic and psychological well- or ill-being.

Peer Relationships and Academic Adjustment

For the most part, the best and most consistent predictive outcomes of the lack of peer acceptance or childhood peer rejection are school related. For many years, it has been known that being disliked in childhood predicts academic difficulties, truancy, and high school dropout rates (e.g., Barclay, 1966; Ullman, 1957). The school and classroom must assuredly lose its luster when many of a child's peers demonstrate and target their negative feelings toward the child. This is likely to be the case, not only for the child who was doing poorly in school to begin with, but also for the intellectually competent child. Withdrawing via truancy or by dropping out may serve as the escape route for children who are consistently rejected by peers.

Wentzel and Asher (1995) have reported contemporaneous differences among average, neglected, rejected-aggressive, rejected-submissive, and controversial young adolescents on measures of school adjustment. Popular children were viewed as helpful, good students. Neglected children were also viewed by their peers as being good, highly academically motivated students, and were seen by teachers as independent and self-assured. Rejected children were perceived by teachers and peers as being weak students and lacking in self-assurance. Among the rejected children, rejected-aggressive students were observed to have the most problems. These children, relative to average children and rejected-submissive children, showed little interest in school, were perceived by teachers as dependent, and were seen by peers and teachers as inconsiderate, noncompliant, and prone to causing trouble in school. Clearly, many of the problems that lead to rejection, such as the display of disruptive and aggressive behavior, make it difficult for a child to adjust to the climate of most classrooms.

Longitudinal research supports the latter scenario. Ollendick, Weist, Borden, and Greene (1992) reported that children who were actively disliked by their peers were anywhere from two to seven times more likely to fail a subsequent grade than better accepted children. Similarly, Coie, Lochman, Terry, and Hyman (1992), in a three-year longitudinal study, found that higher levels of social rejection predicted later grade retention and poorer adjustment to the transition to middle school. Likewise, based on a four-year longitudinal study, DeRosier, Kupersmidt, and Patterson (1994) reported that the experience of peer rejection in any one of the first three years of their study placed children at significantly greater risk for absenteeism in the fourth year, even after statistically controlling for initial levels of absenteeism.

Given these longitudinal connections between peer rejection and later poor school performance and truancy, it is not surprising to learn that children who have troubled relations with their peers are more likely to drop out of school than are other children. For example, Parker and Asher (1987) reported that, on the whole, unaccepted children, particularly girls, drop out of school at a rate two to eight times greater than that of accepted children; approximately 25% of low-accepted elementary school children drop out, compared to about 8% of other children. More recently, Ollendick and colleagues (1992) found, in a five-year longitudinal study, that 17.5% of rejected children had dropped out of school before the end of ninth grade, compared to 3.1% of neglected children and 5.4% of popular or average children. The particularly low dropout rate for the neglected group is consistent with Wentzel and Asher's (1995) observations regarding neglected children's superior adjustment to school relative to other boys and girls.

The data presented thus far make it clear that peer rejection in childhood is associated with subsequently assessed academic difficulties. It is important to note, however, that not all recent studies paint such a negative portrait. For example, in a longitudinal study with a representative sample of 475 12-year-olds, Cairns et al. (1989) found little reason to conclude that peer rejection by itself carries risk of later dropping out. Instead, the most powerful precursors of later dropping out were aggression and academic difficulties, especially when the latter were simultaneously present. Indeed, many school dropouts appeared to have very satisfactory social lives. Cairns et al. caution against viewing dropping out as a purely individual phenomenon. Potential school dropouts in their study appeared to gravitate to peers who shared their negative dispositions toward school.

These latter findings are important because they suggest that peer-group norms may influence academic performance. Relatedly, in a study of elementary schoolers, Kindermann (1993) identified the subgroups that constituted the larger peer groups in the children's classrooms. Each group was assessed according to its overall level of academic motivational orientation. He found that children typically associated with peers who had a motivational orientation similar to their own. Moreover, using a longitudinal design, he found that children's motivational orientations toward school were in accord with the initial orientation of the peer group in which they were constituents. These findings reflect the impact that peer-group orientations and norms may have on children's academic behaviors and attitudes.

Supporting Kindermann's (1993) data is a recent report by Hymel, Comfort, Schonert-Reichl, and McDougall (in press), who noted that adolescents who drop out of school are more likely than other students to have associated with peers who do not regard school as useful and important. These authors argued that the two variables from the peer system that appear to be associated with school drop out are peer rejection and close association with peers who place little emphasis on academic achievement and active school participation.

Finally, in a series of recent studies of young children, Ladd and colleagues (Ladd, 1990, 1991; Ladd, Kochenderfer, & Coleman, 1996) have demonstrated the potential influence of close dyadic relationships on academic performance. In a study of the transition to kindergarten, Ladd (1990) obtained repeated measures of friendship, sociometric status, and school adjustment during the transition to kindergarten. Although children's personal attributes (mental age and prior school experience) predicted early school performance, measures of social adjustment with peers were much better by comparison. Children with many friends at the time of school entry developed more favorable attitudes toward school in the early months than children with fewer friends. Those who maintained their friendships also liked school better as the year went by. Making new friends in the classroom also predicted gains in school performance. By comparison, measures of school performance at the start of the transition to kindergarten did not generally forecast gains in social adjustment. And children who were rejected by peers were less likely than other children to have positive attitudes toward school, and they were less likely to show a positive school performance. These findings show clearly that even during the early childhood years, friendships with peers are strongly linked to children's academic success. Because Ladd used a longitudinal design in which initial assessments of academic orientation and peer relationships were accounted for, his findings suggest a causal link between friendship and academic outcome.

In a subsequent study, Ladd et al. (1996) examined the association between children's perceptions of best friendship quality in kindergarten and indices of scholastic adjustment (school-related affect, perceptions, involvement, and performance) in grade school (transition from kindergarten to grade school). Their main finding replicated, at the dyadic level, one of the findings observed by Kindermann (1993) at the group level. Specifically, Ladd et al. reported that children who viewed their friendships as a source of validation or aid, tend to feel happier at school, see their classmates as supportive, and develop positive attitudes toward school. They reported also that conflict with one's best friend was positively associated with school adjustment difficulties, although this association was stronger for boys than for girls.

In summary, it appears reasonable to conclude that children's peer relationships play a central role in promoting or maintaining academic adaptation. It is clear also that this role occurs at several levels of peer-group analysis. Peer rejection may serve the purpose of making school an unwelcome venue for children and adolescents, and the lack of friends may fail to provide the necessary support for children and adolescents to fare well in school. Alternatively, a child's peer group may actually serve to develop and reinforce poor school-related goals and behaviors. Thus, the role of the peer culture appears too significant to be dismissed in practical efforts designed to encourage promising school aspirations and performance; indeed, this is an area that requires further empirical and practical substantiation in the future.

Peer Relationships and Psychological Adjustment

Ample evidence exists that difficulties with peers place a child at risk for developing subsequent problems of a psychological nature. For example, in one of the earliest follow-up studies that included measures of peer acceptance, Janes and her colleagues (e.g., Janes, Hesselbrock, Myers, & Penniman, 1979) interviewed 187 adult men and women who had been referred to a child guidance clinic more than a decade earlier. At the time of their clinic referral, the participants' elementary school teachers had completed a lengthy behavioral checklist that assessed classroom academic performance and attitudes, relationships with other children, shyness and withdrawal, neurotic behaviors, and leadership. Janes et al. found that teachers' simple notation that the child "failed to get along with other children" related to several adult variables. Boys whose teachers checked this item were twice as likely as boys whose teachers did not to report later having been fired because of something they had done, having been in

trouble with the law, or having been arrested. They were also somewhat more likely to enter the military or to report that they had been hospitalized for psychiatric disorder. (Girls were not examined in this analysis.) No other teacher item, including indications of aggressiveness or shyness, predicted later problematic adult outcomes.

As we noted earlier, however, studies of child *clinic* samples do not constitute an adequate test of the predictive/causal relation between the quality of childhood peer experiences and ensuing psychological adaptation. This methodological weakness has been remedied in subsequent longitudinal studies. For example, Roff et al. (1972) collected peer-status information from approximately 38,000 8- to 11-year-old children. They found that children with very low social preference scores were 1.5 to 2 times more likely than more accepted children to become delinquent prior to age 14.

Because the Roff et al. (1972) study predated current concern for sociometric status classification, the risk attached to rejection was not cleanly separated from the risk attached to neglected peer status. Several recent studies have addressed this issue. Kupersmidt and Coie (1990) reported the findings of a longitudinal study in which they followed-forward a group of fifth-grade children for seven years. Children identified as sociometrically rejected were twice as likely to be delinquent (35%) in adolescence than was the case for the sample base rate (17%). As one might expect from earlier discussion, sociometrically neglected children did not appear to suffer any negative outcome from their earlier peer status.

In a second study, Ollendick et al. (1992) followed sociometrically rejected, neglected, popular, controversial, and average-status 9-year-old children for five years, documenting the incidence of subsequent delinquent, behavioral, and psychological disturbance. At the follow-up, rejected children were perceived by their peers as less likable and more aggressive than popular and average children. Rejected children were also perceived by their teachers as having more conduct problems, aggression, motor excess, and attentional problems than their popular and average counterparts. Moreover, rejected children reported higher levels of conduct disturbance and substance abuse, and committed more delinquent offenses than the popular and average children.

Controversial children were similar to rejected children on most measures. For example, children in the two groups committed similar numbers of delinquent offenses. Neglected children, on the other hand, did not differ from average children on any measure and differed from popular children only on the locus of control and peer evaluation measures.

Similar findings concerning the predictive outcomes of rejected status have been reported more recently by Bierman and Wargo (1995) and Coie, Terry, Lenox, Lochman, and Hyman (1995). In both of these longitudinal studies, peer rejection in combination with the early display of aggressive behavior predicted externalizing problems. Interestingly, these findings held true whether the outcomes were assessed after only two years (Bierman & Wargo, 1995) or after four years (Coie et al., 1995).

The studies reported above focus mainly on psychological difficulties of *undercontrol* (e.g., delinquency, aggression). Although a contemporaneous link between peer rejection and problems of an *overcontrolled,* internalizing nature has been established (e.g., Cassidy & Asher, 1992), especially among rejected-withdrawn or wary children (e.g., Boivin, Hymel, & Bukowski, 1995; Parkhurst & Asher, 1992; Renshaw & Brown, 1993), researchers have not demonstrated a similar relation longitudinally. Instead, investigators have demonstrated that social withdrawal/reticence/wariness in childhood predicts subsequent difficulties of psychological overcontrol. For example, Rubin and colleagues followed-forward a group of children from kindergarten (age 5 years) to the ninth grade (age 15 years). They reported that passive withdrawal, in kindergarten and grade 2, predicted self-reported feelings of depression, loneliness, and negative self-worth, and teacher ratings of anxiety in the fifth grade (age 11 years) (Hymel, Rubin, et al., 1990; Rubin & Mills, 1988). In turn, social withdrawal in the fifth grade predicted self-reports of loneliness, depression, negative self-evaluations of social competence, feelings of not belonging to a peer group that could be counted on for social support, and parental assessments of internalizing problems in the ninth grade (Rubin, Chen, McDougall, Bowker, & McKinnon, 1995).

These latter findings have been supported in other recent reports. For example, Renshaw and Brown (1993) found that passive withdrawal at ages 9 to 12 years predicted loneliness assessed one year later. Morison and Masten (1991) indicated that children perceived by peers as withdrawn and isolated in middle childhood were more likely to think negatively of their social competencies and relationships in adolescence. And finally, Hoza, Molina, Bukowski, and Sippola (1995) reported that passive withdrawal in middle childhood predicted internalizing problems two years hence.

Findings concerning the longitudinal, predictive association between a social characteristic (e.g., aggression) and subsequent outcome raise an important question about the earlier reviewed studies in which childhood peer rejection and ensuing externalizing problems were described. That is, can the predictive relation between early peer rejection and later externalizing problems be attributed primarily to the *behaviors* that likely "caused" rejection to begin with? Few researchers have addressed this issue. Nevertheless, Kupersmidt and Coie (1990), as well as others (e.g., Bierman, 1993), have reported a conditional, predictive relation among aggressive behavior, rejection, and psychological adjustment, wherein a rejected child's risk for externalizing difficulties is enhanced for some negative outcomes when that child is characteristically aggressive. In this regard, examining social withdrawal/wariness and its concomitants (e.g., negative self-appraisals of social skills and social relationships) may enhance the prediction of later internalizing problems.

Finally, it is presently unknown whether risk for later maladjustment varies according to the chronicity of peer ostracism. Given the less than perfect stability of rejected status, it would seem reasonable to ask whether psychological risk status is equivalent for children with chronic versus episodic and transient rejection by peers. To address this question, DeRosier, Kupersmidt, and Patterson (1994) followed 640 7- to 9-year-old children for four years. They found that children who were more chronically rejected over the first three years of the study were at greatest risk for behavior problems in the fourth year, even after controlling for initial level of adjustment. Similarly, Burks, Dodge, and Price (1995) have found that chronic rejection in middle childhood predicts the subsequent development of internalizing difficulties (depression, loneliness) six years later. Their results held only for boys who had been rejected for two consecutive years; chronicity of rejection did not predict internalizing problems for girls. The authors speculated that girls' rejection by the larger peer group may be less severe than the lack of close, intimate relationships with a friend.

This notion that friendship may buffer rejected children from negative outcomes has been examined in a number of recent studies. Interestingly, however, the findings in these studies have been somewhat counterintuitive. For example, Hoza et al. (1995) and Kupersmidt, Burchinal, and Patterson (1995) reported that having a best friend actually *augmented* negative outcomes for children who were earlier identified as rejected and aggressive. One explanation for these findings emanates from research by Cairns et al. (1988), and more recently by Tremblay, Mâsse, Vitaro, and Dobkin (1995). These investigators found that the friendship networks of rejected-aggressive children comprise other aggressive children; as such, the existence of a friendship network supportive of maladjusted behavior may actually exacerbate the prospects of a negative developmental outcome for rejected children.

Summary

Studies of the predictive relations between children's peer relationships and their subsequent academic and psychological adjustment generally support the notion that peer rejection represents a risk factor for normal development. Furthermore, the data extant reveal that the types of friends a child may have, or the groups in which he or she participates, may influence individual adaptation. Taken together, these findings suggest that knowledge of a child's peer rejection or lack of friendships in childhood should raise a warning flag for teachers, parents, and professionals.

Despite these conclusions, however, it is important to note that most of the longitudinal studies reviewed above do not allow for a causal interpretation of data. As Kupersmidt, Coie, and Dodge (1990) have pointed out, an interpretation of causality is warranted only when other potential pathways between the initial peer measures and the subsequent adjustment variables have been accounted for. For example, the initial level of adjustment must be controlled or accounted for if an unequivocal conclusion about causal relations is to be reached.

A further issue that needs to be considered, prior to making judgments about causal relations, is that of multicollinearity. We have noted that there is neither conceptual nor empirical independence among measures of peer experiences taken from different levels of social complexity. For example, measures of aggression and group acceptance are intercorrelated. One repercussion of such associations is that if one wants to conclude that a given measure from the peer domain predicts some outcome, it is necessary to control for the other measures with which the predictor may be confounded.

Considering how a set of measures will function together to affect outcome will also satisfy substantive objectives as well as methodological concerns. Inherent in theoretical positions regarding the peer system is the notion that experience within one domain of the peer system may compensate for, or enhance, experience within another domain. For example, if it is true that friends influence one another, then the experience of having a friend will vary according to what the friend is like. Or, as we have shown, the experience of being rejected by peers appears to be different for children who are aggressive and those who are nonaggressive. The implication of these concerns regarding the associations among measures from different domains of the peer system is that using a single-factor model to understand the link between peer experiences and outcome is likely to result in both an empirical and conceptual dead end.

CONCEPTUALIZING DEVELOPMENTAL PATHWAYS TO ADAPTIVE AND MALADAPTIVE PEER INTERACTIONS AND RELATIONSHIPS

In this chapter, we have reviewed literature concerning developmental norms in children's peer interactions, relationships, and groups; the developmental significance of peer interaction, discussion, and shared differences of opinion; the importance of friendship; the significance of social skills and social competence; the assessment of children's peer experiences; the proximal and distal predictors of peer acceptance; and the outcomes of qualitative differences in peer relationships histories. Additionally, we have reviewed the research on sex and cultural differences in children's peer interactions, relationships, and groups, although these two subareas appear to require further investigation.

In reviewing the relevant research, we admit to not having interconnected the individual, interactional, and relationships pieces into a larger, theoretical or conceptual statement of substance. Although we will allow the reader to pass judgment on the degree of substance, we conclude by offering descriptions of developmental pathways that may prove heuristically helpful to those motivated to develop programmatic research in the topics reviewed herein. Thus, the following descriptions represent attempts to "put it all together." We should note that the following pathways models are largely derived from previous work we have published (e.g., Parker et al., 1995; Rubin, Hymel, Mills, & Rose-Krasnor, 1991); readers are referred to these earlier versions.

Transactional Models of Development

According to Sameroff (1987), development is a dynamic, multidirectional process influenced by child characteristics, family and environmental characteristics, and the interactions and interdependencies thereof. Proponents of transactional models of development view the child as an active organizer, and changer, of his or her environment. In turn, these changes function to produce transformations in the child. In the models below, we describe how children might come to develop competent or incompetent social interactional styles and adaptive or maladaptive peer relationships.

A Pathway to Peer Acceptance

We begin with two assumptions. First, acceptance by peers is largely a function of the child's social skills; in normal circumstances, all else is secondary. Second, the development of social skills and subsequent peer acceptance derives from the interaction of intra-individual, inter-individual, and macrosystemic forces. More specifically, the road to peer acceptance and the positive outcomes that may follow is probably the joint product of the child's dispositional and biologically based characteristics, his or her parents' socialization practices, the quality of relationships within and outside of the family, and the forces of culture, stress, and social support impinging on the child and the family.

Adopting a developmental and sequential approach, we posit that the combination of (a) an even-tempered, easy disposition, (b) the experience of sensitive and responsive parenting, and (c) the general lack of major stresses or crises during infancy and early childhood conspire to predict the development of secure parent-child attachment relationships. Drawing from the early research on continuities of infant attachment, we hypothesize that these secure primary relationships influence the development of social and emotional adjustment (see Bretherton & Waters, 1985).

Thankfully, most infants and toddlers have relatively easygoing dispositions (Thomas & Chess, 1977) and develop *secure* relationships with their parents (Ainsworth, Blehar, Waters, & Wall, 1978). These relationships appear to be caused and maintained, in part, by having parents who are in tune with the child's behaviors (e.g., Isabella & Belsky, 1991). Such sensitive and responsive parents may, from time to time, be angered and put off by their child's behavior; however, given such circumstances, they are accepting of the child and do not remain angry, hostile, or resentful. It is worth noting that parental responsivity and sensitivity is probably easier to deliver when one's infant is relatively easygoing and when the family unit is relatively stress-free.

Within the context of a secure relationship, then, a conceptual link to the development of social competence can be suggested. This link draws its underpinnings from the notion that a primary attachment relationship results in the child's development of a belief system that incorporates the parent as available and responsive to his or her needs. The internal working model provides the child with the felt security and confidence to explore the peer milieu and to engage in healthy bouts of peer interaction. Also, as we noted earlier in the chapter, it is during peer interaction that children experience the interpersonal exchange of ideas, perspectives, roles, and actions. From social negotiation, discussion, and conflict with peers, children learn to understand others' thoughts, emotions, motives, and intentions. In turn, armed with these new social understandings, children are able to think about the consequences of their social behaviors, not only for themselves but also for others. As we indicated above, the development of these social-cognitive abilities is thought to result in the production of socially competent behaviors.

Once socially competent behavior is demonstrated by the child and recognized by the parent, the secure parent-child relationship may be nurtured and maintained by the child's display of socially appropriate behavior in extrafamilial settings and by parents who are emotionally available, sharply attuned to social situations and to the thoughts and emotions of the child, able to anticipate the child's behaviors and the consequences of the child's actions, and able to predict the outcomes of their own actions for the child. For example, the confident, secure child's competent play with peers will probably be reinforced by parents who believe that such activity is both desirable and necessary for normal development. As indicated earlier, parents of socially competent children provide opportunities for them to play with peers, and they tend to carefully monitor their children's social activities. Furthermore, the sensitive, competent parent uses distancing strategies (Sigel, 1982) that focus the child on alternative means to tackle given problems ("What are all the things you can do in order to . . . ?"). Such a parent also queries the child about potential consequences of the child's suggested strategies, and helps the child deal flexibly with his or her social failures.

This competent, secure relationship system serves both parent and child well, and, barring any undue circumstances, an outcome of social competence can be predicted. As we have reviewed above, a significant outcome of social competence, however defined, is the establishment and maintenance of peer acceptance. Peer acceptance enables the child to continue to interact with age-mates and school-mates in positive ways. Furthermore, the demonstration of competence is likely to gain the child close friendship relations—supportive relationships that provide the child with confidence and security in the extrafamilial milieu.

A Pathway to Aggression and Rejection

Not all children are socially competent, accepted by their peers, and fortunate to have close friendships. In previous writings, we have described two possible developmental pathways to peer rejection and social isolation (see Rubin et al., 1991). One pathway begins with an infant who is perceived by his or her parents as having a *difficult* temperament. We do not suggest that all such infants are at risk; however, infants who are viewed by parents as irritable and overactive and who are born into less than desirable situations may be recipients of less than optimal care (Thompson, Ch. 2, this Volume). Consistent with these speculations are findings that temperamentally irritable infants often have mothers who are more aggressive, less nurturant, more anxious, and less responsive than mothers of nondifficult babies (e.g., Egeland & Farber, 1984). Family living conditions, however, may be critical mediating factors; for example, Crockenberg (1981) reported that mothers of temperamentally difficult babies who have social and financial support are less negative in their interactions with their infants than other high-risk mothers. For some families, then, the interaction between infant dispositional characteristics and ecological setting conditions may promote parenting practices that result in the establishment of insecure, perhaps hostile, early parent-child relationships.

As described in other chapters in this volume (e.g., Parke & Buriel), existing data suggest that there is a group of insecure babies who have already established hostile relationships with their primary caregivers by 12 or 18 months. And as we noted earlier, researchers have found that when these insecure avoidant infants reach preschool age, they often direct their hostility, anger, and aggression against peers (Troy & Sroufe, 1987).

Once expressed in a relatively consistent manner, aggression, from very early in childhood, is a highly salient determinant of peer rejection (Coie & Kupersmidt, 1983). Thus, it follows logically (and, indeed, empirically) that children who are rejected by their peers because of their proactive hostility may soon become precluded from the very activities that supposedly aid in the development of social skills: peer interaction, negotiation, and discussion.

Furthermore, the aggressive child is unlikely to trust his or her peers, and aggressive children believe that negative social experiences are usually caused intentionally by others. This mistrust and misattribution to others of hostile intention suggests that the aggressive child's peer relationships can be characterized as hostile and insecure.

Furthermore, given the salience of aggression on school grounds, it is not surprising that teachers often request meetings with the parents of aggressive perpetrators. These school-based appraisals must assuredly be discomforting to parents, especially to those parents who have not enjoyed a secure and pleasant relationship with their child or to those experiencing a good deal of stress. One may posit at least two possible outcomes from these teacher-parent meetings: (a) Parents may attribute their child's maladaptive behavior to dispositional or biological factors, thereby alleviating themselves of the responsibility of having to deal with aggressive displays. This type of attributional bias may lead to parental feelings of helplessness in the face of child aggression and thus, predict a permissive or laissez-faire response to aggressive behavior. (b) Parents may attribute their child's behaviors to external causes and utilize overly harsh, power-assertive techniques in response to their child's maladaptive behavior. Both the neglect of aggression and the harsh treatment of it, especially in an environment lacking warmth, are likely to create even more problems for the child, the parents, and for their relationships (Forgatch, 1991).

In summary, we propose that socially incompetent, aggressive behaviors may be the product of difficult temperament, of insecure parent-child relationships, of authoritarian *or* laissez-faire parenting, of family stress, and, most likely, of the joint interactions among "all of the above." One result of aggression and hostility is likely to be rejection by most peers and potential supportive associations with children of like "character."

A Pathway to Social Wariness, Withdrawal, and Rejection

The second pathway to peer rejection begins with newborns who may be biologically predisposed to have a low threshold for arousal when confronted with social (or nonsocial) stimulation and novelty. Recent research concerning temperamental inhibition has shown that under conditions of novelty or uncertainty, some babies demonstrate physical and physiological changes that suggest that they are hyperarousable (e.g., Kagan, 1989), a characteristic that may make them extremely difficult for their parents to soothe and comfort (Kagan, Reznick, Clarke,

Snidman, & Garcia-Coll, 1984). Consequently, under some circumstances, parents may react to easily aroused and wary babies with insensitivity, nonresponsivity, and/or neglect. Each of these parental variables also predicts the development of insecure parent-infant attachment relationships. And for those dispositionally wary infants who develop insecure attachment relationships with their parents, one might posit a developmental prognosis of social withdrawal.

Support for these conjectures derives from several recent sources. First, there is some evidence of an association between temperament and attachment. Fox and Calkins (1993) for example, have demonstrated that infants who are highly reactive to mildly stressful, novel social events are more likely to be classified as anxious-resistant infants than are their less reactive counterparts. Thus, they argue that behavioral and physiological assessments of *infant reactivity,* especially to situations involving mild stress or the introduction of novelty, predict attachment status of an anxious-resistant quality in infancy.

As we noted earlier, the social behaviors of toddlers and preschoolers who have an insecure anxious-resistant attachment history are thought to be guided largely by fear of rejection. Conceptually, psychologists have predicted that when these insecurely attached children are placed in group settings with peers, they attempt to avoid rejection through the demonstration of passive, adult-dependent behavior and withdrawal from social interaction. Empirically, several researchers have provided support for these conjectures. For example, it has been reported that infants who experience an anxious-resistant attachment relationship are more whiney, easily frustrated, and socially inhibited at 2 years of age than their secure counterparts (Fox & Calkins, 1993; Matas, Arend, & Sroufe, 1978). Anxious-resistant infants also tend to be less skilled in peer interaction and to be rated by their teachers as more dependent, helpless, tense, and fearful (Pastor, 1981). At 4 years, anxious-resistant babies have been described as lacking in confidence and assertiveness (Erickson et al., 1985) and, at 7 years, as passively withdrawn (Renken et al., 1989). Thus, both conceptually and empirically, there is reason to believe that a relation exists between dispositionally based reactivity to novel stimulation, the quality of the parent-infant attachment relationship, and subsequent socially inhibited and withdrawn behavior.

As we noted earlier, children who refrain from interacting with peers may preclude themselves from (a) establishing normal social relationships, (b) the experience of normal social interactive play behaviors, and (c) the development of those social and cognitive skills that are supposedly encouraged by peer relationships and social play. Thus, one can predict a developmental sequence in which an inhibited, fearful, insecure child withdraws from the social world of peers, fails to develop those skills derived from peer interaction and, because of this, becomes increasingly anxious and isolated from the peer group.

Furthermore, it is now well established that with increasing age, social reticence or withdrawal becomes increasingly salient to the peer group (Younger & Boyko, 1987). It is also known that perceived deviation from age-normative social behavior is associated with the establishment of negative peer reputations. Thus, by the mid to late years of childhood, social withdrawal and anxiety are as strongly correlated with peer rejection and unpopularity as is aggression (e.g., French, 1988).

Unlike their aggressive counterparts, however, anxiously withdrawn children rarely get into trouble by acting out at home or school. Yet, given their reticence to explore their environments, these children may demonstrate difficulties in asserting themselves or resolving interpersonal problems. Sensing the child's difficulties and perceived helplessness, some parents may try to provide instrumental aid directly by manipulating their child's social behaviors in a power-assertive, highly controlling, authoritarian manner (e.g., telling the child how to act or what to do). Others may respond by overprotecting and infantilizing their children; these parents may choose what appears to them to be the simplest and most humane course of action by taking over the solution of their child's social dilemmas (e.g., intervening during object disputes, inviting potential playmates to the home). The choice of parenting styles is likely determined by the stresses facing the parent. Thus, the overstressed, overhassled parent may choose a quick-fix approach that reflects impatience and anger; an authoritarian, overcontrolling choice of action. The overprotective parent may actually be an oversensitive and extremely responsive parent who cannot bear to see his or her child in difficulty. Whatever the inspirations for parenting styles of overcontrol, overinvolvement, and overprotection, it is nevertheless the case that these socialization strategies have long been linked conceptually to social withdrawal in childhood; these associations, however, have rarely been investigated.

At any rate, parental overdirectiveness and overprotection are likely to maintain rather than to ameliorate the postulated problems associated with social inhibition. Either parenting style likely will not help the child deal firsthand with his or her social interchanges and dilemmas;

they probably do little to aid in the development of a belief system of social self-efficacy, and they likely perpetuate feelings of insecurity within and outside of the family. Thus, just as socially incompetent, externalizing forms of behavior are posited to be maintained by unproductive parent-child interchanges and continued maladaptive relationships, so too are internalizing forms of behavior.

In summary, in this developmental model, we posit that an inhibited temperament, when responded to with insensitivity, overprotection, and/or overcontrol, will predict the establishment of an insecure attachment relationship (see also Mangelsdorf, Gunnar, Kestenbaum, Lang, & Andreas, 1990; Rubin, Hastings, Stewart, Henderson, & Chen, in press). Felt insecurity may lead to an impoverished exploratory style that precludes the opportunity to experience those forms of peer exchanges hypothesized to promote the development of social competence. The relatively slow development of social competence, when combined with wariness and felt insecurity, may lead to peer rejection, and for this particular group of children, the development of negative self-appraisals of competence, which in turn exacerbate withdrawal from peers.

A Caveat

We recognize fully that many, if not most, infants with either a fearful, wary, inhibited temperament, or a difficult, irritable/angry disposition do *not* develop insecure attachment relationships and do *not* behave in either a socially withdrawn or aggressive fashion during the preschool and elementary school years. Indeed, in most studies of the predictive relations between infant difficult temperament and the subsequent development of attachment relationships, no clear predictive picture emerges (e.g., Bates et al., 1985). Thus, it may be posited that skilled parenting, under conditions of limited stress and optimal support, can buffer the effects of potentially "negative" biology. Basically, this is the classic argument of *goodness of fit* between parental characteristics and infant dispositional characteristics offered originally by Thomas and Chess (1977).

Likewise, we contend that a wary or difficult temperament is *not* necessary for the development of social behavioral deviations from the norm. We hold that both parental overcontrol and undercontrol, and a lack of parental warmth and sensitivity, especially when accompanied by familial stress and a lack of social support, can interact to deflect the temperamentally easygoing infant to pathways of social behavioral and relationships difficulties. Needless to say,

these latter statements represent testable hypotheses reaching out for empirical substantiation.

Summary

Transactional models such as the ones offered above represent formidable research challenges. Children's social behaviors, social-cognitions, and family and peer relationships are not expected to remain constant over time, and patterns of change over time must be used to predict subsequent changes and organism states. Progress in studying transactional models of development has been aided largely by the evolution of particular statistical procedures (e.g., structural equation modeling, growth curve analyses, survival analyses) for examining bidirectional and reciprocal influences in multivariate longitudinal data sets; nevertheless, the number of investigations incorporating these techniques has been very limited. Future growth in our understanding of the relations between children's individual, dispositional characteristics, social interaction styles, and the quality of their social relationships will require the acceptance of transactional models of development and, for better or worse, the comprehension of heretofore rarely used statistical procedures.

CONCLUSIONS

In this chapter, we have examined the literature on children's peer interactions, relationships, and groups. One of our goals was to provide the reader with an up-to-date perspective of the relevant theory and research. In so doing, we discovered an enormous amount of valuable material. Yet, our search of the literature also revealed some obvious omissions in the study of children's peer-related experiences. Thus, in this last section of the chapter, we attempt to set an agenda for future research on children's peer interactions, relationships, and groups.

Individual Differences in Toddlers' Peer Experiences

There is developing an extensive literature concerning extrafamilial social relationships in very young children. Much of this work is normative and centers on the emergent social repertoires of infants and toddlers. For example, in our review we indicated that by the end of the second year of life, toddlers are able to engage in complementary and reciprocal interactive behaviors with peers. Unlike the research we described concerning the social skills and peer relationships of older children, however, little attention has been addressed to individual differences in social competence and peer relationships in the toddler period. This vacuum may be a product of thinking that social skills are range restricted or that qualitative differences in peer relationships are impossible to sort out at this period of childhood. Yet, if dispositional and socialization factors vary in infancy, it seems likely that individual differences may be present in the second and third years of life—differences that may predict and/or lead to adaptation or maladaptation to the developmental milestone of preschool or kindergarten entry. Given the normative information available concerning the emergent social skills of toddlers, the question of early individual differences now appears timely.

The Role of the Family

Interest in the parent-child attachment relationship has played a catalytic role in bringing researchers who study the family together with researchers who study children's peer groups. Drawing upon Bowlby's construct of internal working models, researchers using an attachment framework have only just begun to examine whether early parent-child relationships affect later social behavioral development and the quality of children's extrafamilial relationships.

The alliance of attachment research with research on children's peer relationships will undoubtedly yield rich dividends. But it is important to provide a cautionary note regarding some potential omissions of significance. For example, research on the parenting antecedents of children's peer relationships skills is almost solely focused on the "contributions" of mothers. Future research must clearly address how fathers may influence children's peer interactions and relationships (Parke & Buriel, Ch. 8, this Volume). Generally speaking, fathers have not received much attention within the attachment literature, and controversy surrounds the validity of father-child attachment classifications (Dunn, 1993). As Parker et al. (1995) noted, "It would be unfortunate if the very salutary influence of attachment research on the study of children's peer relationships has the unintended consequence of further directing attention away from fathers" (p. 143). The same general point can be made about the need for further research on sibling influences, another area that has received scant attention in the literature on children's peer relationships (Dunn, 1993).

Finally, the quality of the interactions and relationships between parents, or between parents and siblings, has not been well examined insofar as it affects children's extrafamilial peer interactions and relationships. Assuredly, exposure to family conflict and violence (and alternatively, family supportiveness and well-being) must carry some weight in determining children's out-of-home interactions and relationships. And whether children's out-of-home relationships can serve as protectors against the potentially malevolent consequences of exposure to and personal experience of family violence is a question of some concern for future research (Cicchetti et al., 1992).

Friendships, Peer Relationships, and Social Adaptation

Experiencing difficulties with peers is a consistent risk factor for later adjustment. Although this association is robust, it remains the case that only a subset of children with poor peer relationships—perhaps about one-third (Parker et al., 1995)—actually experience later maladjustment beyond adolescence. Thus, it would appear that most children with poor peer relationships do not suffer deleterious outcomes. Comparisons among rejected children who do and do not ultimately develop later disorders may offer clues to family, genetic, demographic, behavioral, and other factors that either increase risk of or protect children from later maladaptation; this represents yet another agenda for future research.

One potential buffer against negative outcome might be the relationship the child has with a close friend. Yet, this field is in its infancy insofar as having available standard procedures for identifying and qualifying children's friendships. Typically, the identification of friendships relies on sociometric techniques developed and refined principally in the context of efforts to gauge children's peer acceptance or group standing. As a result, a great deal is known about how the assessment of peer acceptance and the assignment of children to sociometric status groups is affected by variations in the instructions given to children, the testing context, and the mathematical algorithms employed to assign children to groups (Newcomb et al., 1993). Notably lacking, however, is much understanding of how these and other parameters of sociometric assessment affect the identification of friendships. Some researchers (e.g., Parker & Asher, 1993a, 1993b) have argued that operational decisions such as how sociometric nomination items are worded, the number of nominations children are permitted, whether children nominate other children rather than rate them on a continuum, and how sociometric data are aggregated affect the interpretation of friendship variables. In particular, these authors have worried that some decisions conflate the association between friendship involvement and acceptance by the peer group. Others (e.g., Bukowski, Hoza, & Newcomb, 1994) have countered that most of these operational factors are nuances that do not have large practical significance. The current literature provides little guidance on assessment issues and controversies of this type.

An additional matter is that the distinction between friendship and group acceptance may be important for understanding the adolescent and adult outcomes of peer relationships difficulties. Because most of the risk literature predates concern for the distinction between friendship and group acceptance, researchers have not provided significant insights about this matter. Perhaps, as Gottman (1983) warned, "the correlation between peer sociometric data and later functioning can be accounted for, to some extent, by the problems encountered by [the subset of] children who go through childhood without any friends" (p. 2). Obviously, future research must address Gottman's provocative challenge. It may well be that the long-term implications of difficulties in the domains of friendship and group acceptance will prove to be different.

While sociometric assessments of friendships and peer acceptance are appropriate and valid, it must be remembered that, by themselves, they do not provide insights into the day-to-day experiences of children with significant difficulties in peer relationships. Few data exist, for example, on the frequency with which peer-rejected children are excluded from playground games, experience teasing and taunts, or are otherwise victimized by other children. The high levels of loneliness and social dissatisfaction reported by rejected children suggest that their day-to-day commerce with peers is generally negative. As we have reviewed, however, there is substantial variability among rejected children in their reports of loneliness and other signs of subjective distress. This variability may partly account for the heterogeneity that rejected children show in their long-term adjustment and positive responses to remedial interventions (Asher, Parkhurst, Hymel, & Williams, 1990). An important direction for future research, then, should be greater systematic effort to obtain observational data on rejected children's experiences with peers, especially outside the classroom. In other words, we recommend that researchers step up their efforts to understand the experiences that contribute to making rejection by peers and friendlessness stressful for children.

Not only is there a general lack of observational data related to processes of acceptance and rejection, there is also a dearth of observational data concerning processes of friendship. For example, we know a great deal more about support as a *property* of children's friendships than we do about the *process* of support in these relationships. Very little is understood, for example, about how children respond when their friends raise emotional issues, how self-disclosure unfolds in the course of the conversations among friends of different ages or sexes, or how advice is offered or received in friendships. Further efforts are needed to stimulate work in this area.

Gender and Peer Experiences

Over the years, there has emerged a literature on sex differences in social behavior and relationships. Yet, not much is known about the possibility that the peer culture can play different functions for boys and girls. For example, it is the case that virtually nothing is known about the causes and consequences of peer acceptance and rejection for boys and girls. Given that for much of childhood, children interact primarily with same-sex peers, and given that boys and girls characteristically display rather different social behaviors (Ruble & Martin, Ch. 14, this Volume), it would not be surprising to discover that there might be sex differences in the forms and functions of children's peer groups. And if the forms and functions of *friendship* groups differ between the sexes, it would also seem important to determine whether friendships serve to differentially (or similarly) protect boys and girls from family and/or peer abuse and rejection. Indeed, it may even be that the friendships children form mirror the relationships they develop within their families. As such, the close friendships of boys and girls may actually promote or exacerbate dysfunctional behavior. The mechanisms by which this possibility may occur, and whether they are different for boys and girls, are fruit for future investigation.

Culture and Peer Experiences

What we know about the development and correlates, causes, and outcomes of children's social behaviors and relationships is constrained by the cultures in which we study these phenomena. By far the vast majority of the published literature on children's peer experiences is derived from studies conducted in North America and Western Europe. Simply put, we know very little about the development and significance of particular social interactive behaviors and peer acceptance, rejection, and friendship in non-Western cultures; even less is known about how cultures may vary, one from another, in these areas. It has already been established that the psychological "meanings" of some social behaviors differ from culture to culture (e.g., Chen et al., 1992; Chen, Rubim, & Z. Li, 1995). Further work, in this regard, is called for. Additionally, whether the forms and functions of children's peer and friend relationships vary across cultures would seem especially important to consider.

Within cultures, there appear to be subcultures of peer groups that are ill-understood at the present time (Hartup, 1996). Take, for example, the growing numbers of street children in large urban communities throughout the world (e.g. Rabinovitch, 1994; Verma & Kumar, 1996). Virtually nothing is known about the structures of and supportive facilities within these groups. One may assume that not all children growing up "on the streets" will become dysfunctional adults. The question remains, therefore, whether some elements of street culture are supportive and protective for some children. Clearly, this is a "real-world" problem that requires the immediate attention of researchers.

The Significance of Intervention

As noted earlier, many authors have assumed that where poor peer adjustment is found to predict later problematic outcomes, the poor peer adjustment is in some way *responsible*, at least in part, for the later negative outcome. We have indicated that this assumption may have merit, given that poor peer adjustment constitutes a stressor for children and deprives children of important socialization opportunities. There now exists an extensive literature addressing how to improve children's social skills (Asher, 1985; Asher, Parker, & Walker, 1996; Bond & Compas, 1989). It is this intervention literature that provides an opportunity to test some of the causal pathways implicated in the link between poor peer relationships and later adjustment. Specifically, through intervention, researchers can learn whether improvements in adjustment with peers also reduce children's relative risk for subsequent adjustment disturbances. This strategy has not be sufficiently exploited to date.

Relatedly, we indicated that children's friendships serve a variety of functions, including the provision of emotional and social support. We also noted that children's ideas about friendship become increasingly abstract with age.

Furthermore, children's friendships are posited to play an increasingly important role with age. Yet little is known about the potential adaptive effects of friendship, or about *when* it is in childhood that friendship can serve as an accelerator, promoter, or inhibitor of adaptation or as a buffer against the ill effects of parental or peer neglect or rejection. This issue of the functional significance of friendship may prove very helpful in the planning of intervention programs for children who have poorly developed social skills and peer relationships.

Our review is now complete. Yet, as we look back at the concluding section just written, we realize how very many interesting and important questions remain unanswered. This should not be surprising given that the modern history of peer research began only a quarter of a century ago with Willard Hartup's 1970 chapter in this *Handbook*. But growth begets growth, and it is encouraging to realize that there will be no shortage of topics for us to study as we enter the next millennium.

ACKNOWLEDGMENTS

The authors extend their sincere appreciation to Shelley Hymel for her astute and helpful editorial review of the original draft of this manuscript.

REFERENCES

Achenbach, T. M., & Edelbrock, C. S. (1986). *Child behavior checklist and youth self-report.* Burlington, VT: Author.

Achenbach, T. M., McConaughy, S. H., & Howell, C. T. (1987). Child/adolescent behavioral and emotional problems: Implications of cross-informant correlations for situational specificity. *Psychological Bulletin, 101,* 213–232.

Adler, T., & Furman, W. (1988). A model for children's relationships and relationship dysfunctions. In S. W. Duck (Ed.), *Handbook of personal relationships: Theory, research, and interventions* (pp. 211–228). London: Wiley.

Ainsworth, M. D. S., Blehar, M. C., Waters, E., & Wall, S. (1978). *Patterns of attachment.* Hillsdale, NJ: Erlbaum.

Asarnow, J. R., & Callan, J. W. (1985). Boys with peer adjustment problems: Social cognitive processes. *Journal of Consulting and Clinical Psychology, 53,* 80–87.

Asher, S. R. (1985). An evolving paradigm in social skills training research with children. In B. H. Schneider, K. Rubin, & J. E. Ledingham (Eds.), *Children's peer relations: Issues in assessment and intervention* (pp. 157–174). New York: Springer-Verlag.

Asher, S. R., & Coie, J. D. (Eds.). (1990). *Peer rejection in childhood.* New York: Cambridge University Press.

Asher, S. R., & Dodge, K. A. (1986). Identifying children who are rejected by their peers. *Developmental Psychology, 22,* 444–449.

Asher, S. R., & Gabriel, S. W. (1993). Using a wireless transmission system to observe conversation and social interaction on the playground. In C. H. Hart (Ed.), *Children on playgrounds* (pp. 184–209). Albany: State University of New York Press.

Asher, S. R., Parker, J. G., & Walker, D. L. (1996). Distinguishing friendship from acceptance: Implications for intervention and assessment. In W. M. Bukowski, A. F. Newcomb, & W. W. Hartup (Eds.), *The company they keep: Friendship during childhood and adolescence* (pp. 366–405). New York: Cambridge University Press.

Asher, S. R., Parkhurst, J. T., Hymel, S., & Williams, G. A. (1990). Peer rejection and loneliness in childhood. In S. R. Asher & J. D. Coie (Eds.), *Peer rejection in childhood.* New York: Cambridge University Press.

Asher, S. R., & Wheeler, V. A. (1985). Children's loneliness: A comparison of rejected and neglected peer status. *Journal of Consulting and Clinical Psychology, 53,* 500–505.

Asher, S. R., & Williams, G. A. (1987, April). New approaches to identifying rejected children of school. In G. W. Ladd (Chair), *Identification and treatment of socially rejected children in school settings.* Symposium conducted at the annual meeting of the American Educational Research Association, Washington, DC.

Azmitia, M. (1988). Peer interaction and problem solving: When are two heads better than one? *Child Development, 59,* 87–96.

Azmitia, M., & Montgomery, R. (1993). Friendship, transactive dialogues, and the development of scientific reasoning. *Social Development, 2,* 202–221.

Bakeman, R., & Brownlee, J. R. (1980). The strategic use of parallel play: A sequential analysis. *Child Development, 51,* 873–878.

Baldwin, A. L. (1949). The effect of home environment on nursery school behavior. *Child Development, 20,* 49–62.

Bandura, A. (1989). Social cognitive theory. In R. Vasta (Ed.), *Annals of child development: Six theories of child development: Revised formulations and current issues* (Vol. 6, pp. 1–60). Greenwich, CT: JAI Press.

Bandura, A., & Walters, R. H. (1963). *Social learning and personality development.* New York: Holt, Rinehart and Winston.

Barclay, J. R., (1966). Sociometric choices and teacher ratings as predictors of school dropout. *Journal of Consulting and Clinical Psychology, 53,* 500–505.

Barenboim, C. (1981). The development of person perception in childhood and adolescence: From behavioral comparisons to psychological constructs to psychological comparisons. *Child Development, 52,* 129–144.

Barnes, K. E. (1971). Preschool play norms: A replication. *Developmental Psychology, 5,* 99–103.

Bates, J. E., Bayles, K., Bennett, D. S., Ridge, B., & Brown, M. M. (1991). Origins of externalizing behavior problems at eight years of age. In D. J. Pepler & K. H. Rubin (Eds.), *The development and treatment of childhood aggression* (pp. 93–120). Hillsdale, NJ: Erlbaum.

Bates, J. E., Maslin, C. A., & Frankel, K. A. (1985). Attachment security, mother-infant interaction and temperament as predictors of behavior problem ratings at age three years. In I. Bretherton & E. Waters (Eds.), Growing points of attachment theory and research. *Monographs of the Society for Research in Child Development,* (Serial No. 209, 167–193).

Bateson, P. (Ed.). (1991). *The development and integration of behaviour: Essays in honour of Robert Hinde.* Cambridge, England: Cambridge University Press.

Baudonniere, P. (1987). Dyadic interaction between 4-year-old children: Strangers, acquaintances, and friends: The influence of familiarity. *International Journal of Psychology, 22,* 347–362.

Baudonniere, P., Garcia-Werebe, M., Michel, J., & Liegois, J. (1989). Development of communicative competencies in early childhood: A model and results. In B. H. Schnieder, G. Attili, J. Nadel, & R. P. Weissberg (Eds.), *Social competence in developmental perspective* (pp. 175–193). Boston: Kluwer Academic.

Baumeister, R. F., & Senders, P. S. (1989). Identity development and the role of structure of children's games. *Journal of Genetic Psychology, 150,* 19–37.

Behar, L., & Stringfield, S. (1974). A behavioral rating scale for the preschool child. *Developmental Psychology, 10,* 601–610.

Bell-Dolan, D., Foster, S., & Christopher, J. M. (1992). Children's reactions to participating in a peer relations study: Child, parent, and teacher reports. *Child Study Journal, 22,* 137–156.

Bell-Dolan, D., Foster, S., & Sikora, D. (1989). Effects of sociometric testing on children's behavior and loneliness in school. *Developmental Psychology, 25,* 306–311.

Belle, D. (1989). *Children's social networks and social supports.* New York: Wiley.

Belsky, J. (1984). The determinants of parenting: A process model. *Child Development, 55,* 83–96.

Belsky, J., & Cassidy, J. (1995). Attachment: Theory and evidence. In M. Rutter, D. Hay, & S. Baron-Cohen (Eds.), *Developmental principles and clinical issues in psychology and psychiatry.* Oxford, England: Blackwell.

Berndt, T. J. (1981). Relations between social cognition, non-social cognition, and social behavior: The case of friendship. In J. H. Flavell & L. Ross (Eds.), *Social cognitive development* (pp. 176–199). Cambridge, England: Cambridge University Press.

Berndt, T. J. (1984). Sociometric, social-cognitive, and behavioral measures for the study of friendship and popularity. In T. Field, J. L. Roopnarine, & M. Segal (Eds.), *Friendship in normal and handicapped children* (pp. 31–52). Norwood, NJ: ABLEX.

Berndt, T. J. (1985). Prosocial behavior between friends in middle childhood and early adolescence. *Journal of Adolescence, 5,* 307–313.

Berndt, T. J. (1986). Children's comments about their friendships. In M. Perlmutter (Ed.), *Minnesota Symposia on Child Psychology: Vol. 18. Cognitive perspectives on children's social and behavioral development* (pp. 189–212). Hillsdale, NJ: Erlbaum.

Berndt, T. J. (1987). The distinctive features of conversations between friends: Theories, research, and implications for socio-moral development. In W. M. Kurtines & J. L. Gewitz (Eds.), *Moral development through social interaction* (pp. 281–300). New York: Wiley.

Berndt, T. J. (1996). Friendship quality affects adolescents' self-esteem and social behavior. In W. M. Bukowski, A. F. Newcomb, & W. W. Hartup (Eds.), *The company they keep: Friendship during childhood and adolescence* (pp. 346–365). New York: Cambridge University Press.

Berndt, T. J., Hawkins, J. A., & Hoyle, S. G. (1986). Changes in friendship during a school year: Effects on children's and adolescents' impressions of friendship and sharing with friends. *Child Development, 57,* 1284–1297.

Berndt, T. J., & Heller, K. A. (1986). Gender stereotypes and social inferences: A developmental study. *Journal of Personality and Social Psychology, 50,* 889–898.

Berndt, T. J., & Hoyle, S. G. (1985). Stability and change in childhood and adolescent friendships. *Developmental Psychology, 21,* 1007–1015.

Berndt, T. J., & Ladd, G. W. (1989). *Peer relationships in child development.* New York: Wiley.

Berndt, T. J., & Perry, T. B. (1986). Children's perceptions of friendships as supportive relationships. *Developmental Psychology, 22,* 640–648.

Berndt, T. J., & Perry, T. B. (1990). Distinctive features and effects of early adolescent friendships. In R. Montmeyer, G. R. Adams, & T. P. Gullotta (Eds.), *From childhood to adolescence: A transitional period?* (pp. 269–287). Newbury Park, CA: Sage.

Bhavnagri, N., & Parke, R. D. (1991). Parents as direct facilitators of children's peer relationships: Effects of age of child and sex of parent. *Journal of Social and Personal Relationships, 8,* 423–440.

Bierman, K. L. (1986). The relation between social aggression and peer rejection in middle childhood. In R. J. Prinz (Ed.), *Advances in behavioral assessment of children and families* (Vol. 2, pp. 151–178). Greenwich, CT: JAI Press.

Bierman, K. L. (1993, March). *Social adjustment problems of aggressive-rejected, aggressive, and rejected boys: A longitudinal analysis.* Paper presented at the biennial meeting of the Society for Research in Child Development, New Orleans, LA.

Bierman, K. L., & Smoot, D. L. (1991). Linking family characteristics with poor peer relations: The mediating role of conduct problems. *Journal of Abnormal Child Psychology, 19,* 341–356.

Bierman, K. L., Smoot, D. L., & Aumiller, K. (1993). Characteristics of aggressive-rejected, aggressive (nonrejected), and rejected (nonaggressive) boys. *Child Development, 64,* 139–151.

Bierman, K. L., & Wargo, J. B. (1995). Predicting the longitudinal course associated with aggressive-rejected, aggressive (nonrejected), and rejected (nonaggressive) status. *Development and Psychopathology, 7,* 669–682.

Bigelow, B. J. (1977). Children's friendship expectations: A cognitive developmental study. *Child Development, 48,* 246–253.

Black, B., & Hazen, N. (1990). Social status and patterns of communication in acquainted and unacquainted preschool children. *Developmental Psychology, 26,* 379–387.

Blos, P. (1967). *The second individuation process of adolescence: Psychoanalytic study of the child* (Vol. 22). New York: International Universities Press.

Blurton-Jones, N. (1972). Characteristics of ethological studies of human behavior. In N. Blurton-Jones (Ed.), *Ethological studies of child behavior* (pp. 3–36). Cambridge, England: Cambridge University Press.

Boivin, M., & Begin, G. (1989). Peer status and self-perception among early elementary school children: The case of rejected children. *Child Development, 60,* 591–596.

Boivin, M., Dodge, K. A., & Coie, J. D. (1995). Individual-group behavioral similarity and peer status in experimental play groups of boys: The social misfit revisited. *Journal of Personality and Social Psychology, 69,* 269–279.

Boivin, M., Hymel, S., & Bukowski, W. M. (1995). The roles of social withdrawal, peer rejection, and victimization by peers in predicting loneliness and depressed mood in childhood. *Development and Psychopathology, 7,* 765–785.

Boivin, M., Thomassin, L., & Alain, M. (1989). Peer rejection and self-perceptions among early elementary school children: Aggressive rejectees versus withdrawn rejectees. In B. H. Schneider, G. Attili, J. Nadel, & R. P. Weissberg (Eds.), *Social competence in developmental perspective* (pp. 392–393). Boston: Kluwer Academic.

Bond, L. A., & Compas, B. E. (Eds.). (1989). *Primary prevention and promotion in the schools.* Newbury Park, CA: Sage.

Bonney, M. E. (1944). Relationship between social success, family size, socioeconomic background, and intelligence among school children grades three to five. *Sociometry, 7,* 26–39.

Booth, C. L., Rose-Krasnor, L., McKinnon, J., & Rubin, K. H. (1994). Predicting social adjustment in middle childhood: The role of preschool attachment security and maternal style. *Social Development, 3,* 189–204.

Booth, C. L., Rose-Krasnor, L., & Rubin, K. H. (1991). Relating preschoolers' social competence and their mothers' parenting behaviors to early attachment security and high-risk status. *Journal of Social and Personal Relationships, 8,* 363–382.

Bott, H. (1933). *Method in social studies of young children* (Child Developmental Series 1, No. 1). University of Toronto Studies.

Bowlby, J. (1969). *Attachment and loss: Vol. 1. Attachment.* New York: Basic Books.

Bowlby, J. (1973). *Attachment and loss: Vol. 2. Separation, anxiety and anger.* New York: Basic Books.

Bretherton, I., & Waters, E. (Eds.). (1985). Growing points in attachment theory and research. *Monographs of the Society for Research in Child Development, 50*(Serial No. 209).

Bronfenbrenner, U. (1943). A constant frame of reference for sociometric research: Pt. 1. Theory and technique. *Sociometry, 6,* 363–397.

Bronfenbrenner, U. (1944). A constant frame of reference for sociometric research: Pt. 2. Experiment and inference. *Sociometry, 7,* 40–75.

Bronson, W. C. (1981). Toddlers' behaviors with agemates: Issues of interaction, cognition, and affect. *Monographs of Infancy, 1,* 127.

Brown, B. B. (1989). The role of peer groups in adolescents' adjustment to secondary school. In T. J. Berndt & G. W. Ladd (Eds.), *Peer relationships in child development* (pp. 188–216). New York: Wiley.

Brown, B. B. (1990). Peer groups and peer cultures. In S. S. Feldman & G. R. Elliott (Eds.), *At the threshold* (pp. 171–196). Cambridge, MA: Harvard University Press.

Brown, B. B., & Clasen, D. R. (1986). *Developmental changes in adolescents' conceptions of peer groups.* Paper presented at the biennial meetings of the Society for Research in Adolescence, Madison, WI.

Brown, B. B., Clasen, D. R., & Neiss, J. D. (1987, April). *Smoke through the looking glass: Adolescents' perceptions of peer group status.* Paper presented at the biennial meeting of the Society for Research in Child Development, Baltimore, MD.

Brown, B. B., Eicher, S. A., & Petrie, S. (1986). The importance of peer group ("crowd") affiliation in adolescence. *Journal of Adolescence, 9,* 73–96.

Brown, E., & Brownell, C. (1990). *Individual differences in toddlers' interaction styles.* Paper presented at the International Conference on Infant Studies, Montreal, Canada.

Brownell, C. (1990). Peer social skills in toddlers: Competencies and constraints illustrated by same-age and mixed-age interaction. *Child Development, 61,* 838–848.

Bugental, D. B. (1992). Affective and cognitive processes within threat-oriented family systems. In I. E. Sigel, A. V. McGillicuddy-DeLisi, & J. J. Goodnow (Eds.), *Parental belief systems: The psychological consequences for children* (pp. 219–248). Hillsdale, NJ: Erlbaum.

Buhler, C. (1929). Spontaneous reactions of children in the first two years. *Proceedings and Papers of the Ninth International Congress of Psychology,* 99–100.

Buhler, C. (1931). The social behavior of the child. In C. Murchison (Ed.), *A handbook of child psychology* (pp. 393–431). New York: Russell & Russell.

Buhler, C. (1935). *From birth to maturity: An outline of the psychological development of the child.* London: Routledge & Kegan Paul.

Buhrmester, D. (1990). Intimacy of friendship, interpersonal competence, and adjustment during preadolescence and adolescence. *Child Development, 61,* 1101–1111.

Buhrmester, D. (1996). Need fulfillment, interpersonal competence, and the developmental contexts of friendship. In W. M. Bukowski, A. F. Newcomb, & W. W. Hartup (Eds.), *The company they keep: Friendship during childhood and adolescence* (pp. 158–185). New York: Cambridge University Press.

Buhrmester, D., & Furman, W. (1986). The changing functions of friends in childhood. A neo-Sullivanian perspective. In V. J. Derlega & B. A. Winstead (Eds.), *Friendship and social interaction* (pp. 41–62). New York: Springer-Verlag.

Bukowski, W. M., Gauze, C., Hoza, B., & Newcomb, A. F. (1993). Differences and consistency in relations with same-sex and other-sex peers during early adolescence. *Developmental Psychology, 29,* 255–263.

Bukowski, W. M., & Hoza, B. (1989). Popularity and friendship: Issues in theory, measurement, and outcome. In T. J. Berndt & G. W. Ladd (Eds.), *Peer relations in child development* (pp. 15–45). New York: Wiley.

Bukowski, W. M., Hoza, B., & Boivin, M. (1994). Measuring friendship quality during pre- and early adolescence: The development and psychometric properties of the friendship qualities scale. *Journal of Social and Personal Relationships, 11,* 471–484.

Bukowski, W. M., Hoza, B., & Newcomb, A. F. (1994). Using rating scale and nomination techniques to measure friendships and popularity. *Journal of Social and Personal Relationships, 11,* 485–488.

Bukowski, W. M., & Newcomb, A. F. (1984). The stability and determinants of sociometric status and friendship choice: A longitudinal perspective. *Developmental Psychology, 20,* 265–274.

Bukowski, W. M., Newcomb, A. F., & Hartup, W. W. (Eds.). (1996). *The company they keep: Friendship during childhood and adolescence.* New York: Cambridge University Press.

Burks, V. S., Dodge, K. A., & Price, J. M. (1995). Models of internalizing outcomes of early rejection. *Development and Psychopathology, 7,* 683–696.

Buss, A. H., & Plomin, R. (1984). *Temperament: Early developing personality traits.* Hillsdale, NJ: Erlbaum.

Cairns, R. B. (1979). *Social development: The origins and plasticity of interchanges.* San Francisco: Freeman.

Cairns, R. B., Cairns, B. D., & Neckerman, H. J. (1989). Early school dropout: Configurations and determinants. *Child Development, 60,* 1437–1452.

Cairns, R. B., Cairns, B. D., Neckerman, H., Gest, S., & Gariépy, J.-L. (1988). Social networks and aggressive behavior: Peer support or peer rejection? *Developmental Psychology, 24,* 815–823.

Cairns, R. B., Xie, H., & Leung, M. C. (in press). The popularity of friendship and the neglect of social networks: Toward a new balance. In W. M. Bukowski & A. H. N. Cillessen (Eds.), *Sociometry then and now: Recent developments in the study of children's peer groups.* San Francisco: Jossey-Bass.

Calkins, S., & Fox, N. A. (1992). The relations among temperament, security of attachment and behavioral inhibition at 24 months. *Child Development, 63,* 1456–1472.

Campbell, J. D. (1964). Peer relations in childhood. In M. Hoffman & L. W. Hoffman (Eds.), *Review of child development research* (pp. 289–322). New York: Russell-Sage Foundation.

Campos, J. J., Campos, R. G., & Barrett, K. C. (1989). Emergent themes in the study of emotional development and emotion regulation. *Developmental Psychology, 25,* 394–402.

Cantrell, S., & Prinz, R. J. (1985). Multiple perspectives of rejected, neglected, and accepted children: Relationship between sociometric status and behavioral characteristics. *Journal of Consulting and Clinical Psychology, 53,* 884–889.

Carlson, C. L., Lahey, B. B., & Neeper, R. (1984). Peer assessment of social behavior of accepted, rejected, and neglected children. *Journal of Abnormal Child Psychology, 12,* 189–198.

Cassidy, J., & Asher, S. R. (1992). Loneliness and peer relations in young children. *Child Development, 63,* 350–365.

Castlebury, S., & Arnold, J. (1988). Early adolescent perceptions of informal groups in a middle school. *Journal of Early Adolescence, 8,* 97–107.

Challman, R. C. (1932). Factors influencing friendships among preschool children. *Child Development, 3,* 146–158.

Charlesworth, W. R., & LaFreniere, P. (1983). Dominance, friendship, and resource utilization in preschool children's groups. *Ethology and Sociobiology, 4,* 175–186.

Chen, X., & Rubin, K. H. (1994). Family conditions, parental acceptance, and social competence and aggression in Chinese children. *Social Development, 3,* 269–290.

Chen, X., Rubin, K. H., & Li, B. (1995a). Social and school adjustment of shy and aggressive children in China. *Development and Psychopathology, 7,* 337–349.

Chen, X., Rubin, K. H., & Li, Z. (1995b). Social functioning and adjustment in Chinese children: A longitudinal study. *Developmental Psychology, 31,* 531–539.

Chen, X., Rubin, K. H., & Sun, Y. (1992). Social reputation and peer relationships in Chinese and Canadian children: A cross-cultural study. *Child Development, 63,* 1336–1343.

Cicchetti, D., Lynch, M., Shonk, S., & Manly, J. T. (1992). An organizational perspective on peer relations in maltreated children. In R. D. Parke & G. W. Ladd (Eds.), *Family-peer relationships: Modes of linkage* (pp. 345–383). Hillsdale, NJ: Erlbaum.

Cillessen, A. H., Van IJzendoorn, H. W., van Lieshout, C. F., & Hartup, W. W. (1992). Heterogeneity among peer-rejected boys: Subtypes and stabilities. *Child Development, 63,* 893–905.

Clark, M. L., & Drewry, D. L. (1985). Similarity and reciprocity in the friendships of elementary school children. *Child Study Journal, 15,* 251–264.

Cohn, D. A. (1990). Child-mother attachment of six-year-olds and social competence at school. *Child Development, 61,* 152–162.

Coie, J. D. (1990). Towards a theory of peer rejection. In S. R. Asher & J. D. Coie (Eds.), *Peer rejection in childhood* (pp. 365–401). Cambridge, MA: Cambridge University Press.

Coie, J. D., & Dodge, K. A. (1983). Continuities and changes in children's social status: A five-year longitudinal study. *Merrill-Palmer Quarterly, 29,* 261–281.

Coie, J. D., & Dodge, K. A. (1988). Multiple sources of data on social behavior and social status. *Child Development, 59,* 815–829.

Coie, J. D., Dodge, K. A., & Coppotelli, H. (1982). Dimensions and types of social status: A cross-age perspective. *Developmental Psychology, 18,* 557–570.

Coie, J. D., Dodge, K., & Kupersmidt, J. B. (1990). Peer group behavior and social status. In S. R. Asher & J. D. Coie (Eds.), *Peer rejection in childhood* (pp. 17–59). New York: Cambridge University Press.

Coie, J. D., & Krehbiehl, G. (1984). Effects of academic tutoring on the social status of low-achieving, socially rejected children. *Child Development, 55,* 1465–1478.

Coie, J. D., & Kupersmidt, J. (1983). A behavioral analysis of emerging social status in boys' groups. *Child Development, 54,* 1400–1416.

Coie, J. D., Lochman, J. E., Terry, R., & Hyman, C. (1992). Predicting early adolescent disorder from childhood aggression and peer rejection. *Journal of Consulting and Clinical Psychology, 60,* 783–792.

Coie, J. D., Terry, R., Lenox, K., Lochman, J., & Hyman, C. (1995). Childhood peer rejection and aggression as predictors of stable patterns of adolescent disorder. *Development and Psychopathology, 7,* 697–714.

Connors, C. (1969). A teacher rating scale for use in drug studies with children. *American Journal of Psychiatry, 126,* 152–156.

Cooley, C. H. (1902). *Human nature and the social order.* New York: Scribner.

Coplan, R. J., Rubin, K. H., Fox, N. A., Calkins, S., & Stewart, S. L. (1994). Being alone, playing alone, and acting alone: Distinguishing between reticence and passive- and active-solitude in young children. *Child Development, 65,* 129–138.

Cowen, E. L., Pedersen, A., Babigian, H., Izzo, L. D., & Trost, M. A. (1973). Long-term follow-up of early detected vulnerable children. *Journal of Consulting and Clinical Psychology, 41,* 438–446.

Crick, N. R., & Dodge, K. A. (1989). Children's perception of peer entry and conflict situations: Social strategies, goals, and outcome expectation. In B. Schneider, J. Nadel, G. Attili, & R. Weissberg (Eds.), *Social competence in development perspective* (pp. 396–399). Boston: Kluwer Academic.

Crick, N. R., & Dodge, K. A. (1994). A review and reformulation of social information-processing mechanisms in children's social adjustment. *Psychological Bulletin, 115,* 74–101.

Crick, N. R., & Grotpeter, J. K. (1995). Relational aggression, gender, and social-psychological adjustment. *Child Development, 66,* 710–722.

Crick, N. R., & Ladd, G. W. (1993). Children's perceptions of their peer experiences: Attributions, loneliness, social anxiety, and social avoidance. *Development Psychology, 29,* 244–254.

Crockenberg, S. B. (1981). Infant irritability, mother responsiveness, and social support influences on the security of mother-infant attachment. *Child Development, 52,* 857–865.

Crockett, L., Losoff, M., & Peterson, A. C. (1984). Perceptions of the peer group and friendship in early adolescence. *Journal of Early Adolescence, 4,* 155–181.

Csikszentmihalyi, M., & Larson, R. (1984). *Being adolescent.* New York: Basic Books.

Cummings, E. M. (1987). Coping with background anger in early childhood. *Child Development, 58,* 976–984.

Damon, W., & Killen, M. (1982). Peer interaction and the process of change in children's moral reasoning. *Merrill-Palmer Quarterly, 28,* 347–378.

Dawe, H. C. (1934). Analysis of two hundred quarrels of preschool children. *Child Development, 5,* 135–157.

Denham, S. A., & Grout, L. (1992). Mothers' emotional expressiveness and coping: Relations with preschoolers' social-emotional competence. *Genetic, Social, and General Monographs, 118,* 73–101.

DeRosier, M., Kupersmidt, J., & Patterson, C. (1994). Children's academic and behavioral adjustment as a function of the chronicity and proximity of peer rejection. *Child Development, 65,* 1799–1813.

Derryberry, D., & Rothbart, M. K. (1984). Emotion, attention, and temperament. In C. E. Izard, J. Kagan, & R. B. Zajonc (Eds.), *Emotions, cognitions, and behavior.* Cambridge, England: Cambridge University Press.

Diaz, R. M., & Berndt, T. J. (1982). Children's knowledge of a best friend: Fact or fancy? *Developmental Psychology, 18,* 787–794.

DiLalla, L. F., & Watson, M. W. (1988). Differentiation of fantasy and reality: Preschoolers' reactions to disruptions in their play. *Developmental Psychology, 24,* 286–291.

Dimant, R. J., & Bearison, D. J. (1991). Development of formal reasoning during successive peer interactions. *Developmental Psychology, 27,* 277–284.

Dishion, T. J. (1990). The family ecology of boys' peer relations in middle childhood. *Child Development, 61,* 874–892.

Dishion, T. J., Duncan, T. E., Eddy, J. M., Fagot, B. I., & Fetrow, R. (1994). The world of parents and peers: Coercive exchanges and children's social adaptation. *Social Development, 3,* 255–268.

Dix, T. (1991). The affective organization of parenting: Adaptive and maladaptive processes. *Psychological Bulletin, 110,* 3–25.

Dodge, K. A. (1983). Behavioral antecedents of peer social status. *Child Development, 54,* 1386–1399.

Dodge, K. A. (1986). A social information processing model of social competence in children. In M. Perlmutter (Ed.), *Minnesota Symposium on Child Psychology* (Vol. 18, pp. 77–125). Hillsdale, NJ: Erlbaum.

Dodge, K. A., Asher, S. R., & Parkhurst, J. T. (1989). Social life as a goal coordination task. In C. Ames & R. Ames (Eds.), *Research on motivation in education* (Vol. 3, pp. 107–135). San Diego, CA: Academic Press.

Dodge, K. A., Coie, J. D., & Brakke, N. P. (1982). Behavior patterns of socially rejected and neglected preadolescents: The role of social approach and aggression. *Journal of Abnormal Child Psychology, 10,* 389–410.

Dodge, K. A., & Frame, C. M. (1982). Social cognitive biases and deficits in aggressive boys. *Child Development, 53,* 620–635.

Dodge, K. A., McClaskey, C. L., & Feldman, E. (1985). A situational approach to the assessment of social competence in children. *Journal of Consulting and Clinical Psychology, 53,* 344–353.

Dodge, K. A., Murphy, R. R., & Buchsbaum,K. (1984). The assessment of intention-cue detection skills in children: Implications for developmental psychopathology. *Child Development, 55,* 163–173.

Dodge, K. A., Pettit, G. S., McClaskey, C. L., & Brown, M. M. (1986). Social competence in children. *Monographs of the Society for Research in Child Development, 51*(2), 1–80.

Dodge, K. A., Price, J. M., Coie, J. D., & Christopoulos, C. (1990). On the development of aggressive dyadic relationships in boys' peer groups. *Human Development, 33,* 200–270.

Dodge, K. A., Schlundt, D. G., Schocken, I., & Delugach, J. D. (1983). Social competence and children's social status: The role of peer group entry strategies. *Merrill-Palmer Quarterly, 29,* 309–336.

Doise, W., & Mugny, G. (1984). *The social development of the intellect.* Oxford, England: Pergamon Press.

Downey, G., & Coyne, J. C. (1990). Children of depressed parents: An integrative review. *Psychological Bulletin, 108,* 50–76.

Doyle, A. (1982). Friends, acquaintances, and strangers: The influence of familiarity and ethnolinguistic background on social interaction. In K. H. Rubin & H. S. Ross (Eds.), *Peer relations and social skills in childhood* (pp. 229–252). New York: Springer-Verlag.

Dunn, J. (1993). *Young children's close relationships: Beyond attachment.* Newbury Park, CA: Sage.

Dunnington, M. J. (1957). Investigation of areas of disagreement in sociometric measurement of preschool children. *Child Development, 28,* 93–102.

Dunphy, D. C. (1963). The social structure of urban adolescent peer groups. *Sociometry, 26,* 230–246.

Eason, L. J. (1985). *An investigation of children's friendships: The relation between cognitive and social development and demonstration of prosocial behaviors.* Unpublished doctoral dissertation, University of Georgia.

East, P. L. (1991). The parent-child relationships of withdrawn, aggressive, and sociable children: Child and parent perspectives. *Merrill-Palmer Quarterly, 37,* 425–444.

Eckerman, C. O. (1979). The human infant in social interaction. In R. Cairns (Ed.), *The analysis of social interactions: Methods, issues, and illustrations* (pp. 163–178). Hillsdale, NJ: Erlbaum.

Eckerman, C. O. (1993). Imitation and toddlers' achievement of co-ordinated action with others. In J. Nadel & L. Camaioni (Eds.), *New perspectives in early communicative development* (pp. 116–156). New York: Routledge & Kegan Paul.

Eckerman, C. O., & Stein, M. R. (1982). The toddler's emerging interactive skills. In K. H. Rubin & H. S. Ross (Eds.), *Peer re-*

lationships and social skills in childhood (pp. 47–71). New York: Springer-Verlag.

Eckerman, C. O., & Stein, M. R. (1990). How imitation begets imitation and toddler's generation of games. *Developmental Psychology, 26,* 370–378.

Eckert, P. (1989). *Jocks and burnouts: Social categories and identity in the high school.* New York: Teachers' College Press.

Eder, D. (1985). The cycle of popularity: Interpersonal relations among female adolescents. *Sociology of Education, 58,* 154–165.

Egeland, B., & Farber, E. A. (1984). Infant-toddler attachment: Factors related to its development and changes over time. *Child Development, 55,* 753–771.

Eisenberg, N., Fabes, R. A., Bernzweig, J., Karbon, M., Poulin, R., & Hanish, L. (1993). The relations of emotionality and regulation to preschoolers' social skills and sociometric status. *Child Development, 64,* 1418–1438.

Eisenberg, N., Fabes, R. A., Murphy, B., Maszk, P., Smith, M., & Karbon, M. (1995). The role of emotionality and regulation in children's social functioning: A longitudinal study. *Child Development, 66,* 1418–1438.

Eisenberg, N., Fabes, R. A., Nyman, M., Bernzweig, J., & Pinuelas, A. (1994). The relations of emotionality and regulation to children's anger-related reactions. *Child Development, 65,* 109–128.

Elicker, J., Englund, M., & Sroufe, L. A. (1992). Predicting peer competence and peer relationships in childhood from early parent-child relationships. In R. Parke & G. Ladd (Eds.), *Family-peer relationships: Modes of linkage* (pp. 77–106). Hillsdale, NJ: Erlbaum.

Emery, R. E. (1992). Family conflicts and their developmental implications: A conceptual analysis of meanings for the structure of relationships. In C. U. Shantz & W. W. Hartup (Eds.), *Conflict in child and adolescent development* (pp. 270–298). New York: Cambridge University Press.

Epstein, J. L. (1986). Friendship selection: Developmental and environmental influences. In E. Mueller & C. Cooper (Eds.), *Process and outcome in peer relationships.* New York: Academic Press.

Erickson, M. F., Sroufe, L. A., & Egeland, B. (1985). The relationship between quality of attachment and behaviour problems in preschool in a high-risk sample. In I. Bretherton & E. Waters (Eds.), Growing points of attachment theory and research. *Monographs of the Society for Research in Child Development, 50*(1/2, Serial No. 209), 147–166.

Erwin, P. (1993). *Friendship and peer relations in children.* New York: Wiley.

Evans, M., & Rubin, K. H. (1979). Hand gestures as a communicative mode in school-aged children. *Journal of Genetic Psychology, 135,* 189–196.

Fabes, R. A., & Eisenberg, N. (1992). Young children's coping with interpersonal anger. *Child Development, 63,* 116–128.

Fagot, B. I. (1985). Beyond the reinforcement principle: Another step toward understanding sex roles. *Developmental Psychology, 21,* 1097–1104.

Fine, G. A. (1987). *With the boys: Little league baseball and preadolescent culture.* Chicago: University of Chicago Press.

Finnie, V., & Russell, A. (1988). Preschool children's social status and their mothers' behavior and knowledge in the supervisory role. *Developmental Psychology, 24,* 789–801.

Ford, M. E. (1982). Social cognition and social competence in adolescence. *Developmental Psychology, 18,* 323–340.

Forgatch, M. S. (1991). The clinical science vortex: A developing theory of anti-social behavior. In D. J. Pepler & K. H. Rubin (Eds.), *The development and treatment of childhood aggression* (pp. 291–316). Hillsdale, NJ: Erlbaum.

Fox, N. A., & Calkins, S. D. (1993). Pathways to aggression and social withdrawal: Interactions among temperament, attachment, and regulation. In K. H. Rubin & J. Asendorpf (Eds.), *Social withdrawal, inhibition, and shyness in childhood* (pp. 81–100). Hillsdale, NJ: Erlbaum.

French, D. C. (1988). Heterogeneity of peer rejected boys: Aggressive and nonaggressive subtypes. *Child Development, 59,* 976–985.

French, D. C. (1990). Heterogeneity of peer rejected girls. *Child Development, 61,* 2028–2031.

French, D. C., & Waas, G. A. (1985). Behavior problems of peer-neglected and peer-rejected elementary-age children: Parent and teacher perspectives. *Child Development, 56,* 246–252.

Freud, A. (1949). *Psychoanalytic study of the child* (Vol. 4). New York: International Universities Press.

Furman, W. (1984). Issues in the assessment of social skills of normal and handicapped children. In T. Field, M. Siegal, & J. Roopnarine (Eds.), *Friendships of normal and handicapped children.* New York: ABLEX.

Furman, W. (1996). The measurement of friendship perceptions: Conceptual and methodological issues. In W. M. Bukowski, A. F. Newcomb, & W. W. Hartup (Eds.), *The company they keep: Friendships in childhood and adolescence* (pp. 41–65). Cambridge, England: Cambridge University Press.

Furman, W., & Buhrmester, D. (1985). Children's perceptions of the personal relationships in their social networks. *Developmental Psychology, 21,* 1016–1024.

Furman, W., & Buhrmester, D. (1992). Age and sex differences in perceptions of networks and personal relationships. *Child Development, 63,* 103–115.

Garmezy, N. (1974). Children at risk: The search for antecedents of schizophrenia: Part 1. Conceptual models and research methods. *Schizophrenia Bulletin, 1,* 14–89.

Garvey, C. (1974). Some properties of social play. *Merrill-Palmer Quarterly, 20,* 163–180.

Garvey, C. (1984). *Children's talk.* Cambridge, MA: Harvard University Press.

Garvey, C. (1990). *Play.* Cambridge, MA: Harvard University Press.

Gauvin, M., & Rogoff, B. (1989). Collaborative problem solving and children's planning skills. *Developmental Psychology, 29,* 139–151.

Gavin, L. A., & Furman, W. (1989). Age differences in adolescents' perceptions of their peer groups. *Developmental Psychology, 25,* 827–834.

Gelfand, D. M., & Teti, D. M. (1990). The effects of maternal depression on children. *Clinical Psychological Review, 10,* 329–353.

Gest, S. D., Graham, S. A., & Hartup, W. W. (1991, July). *Social network affiliations and social representations of second and third grade children.* Paper presented at the biennial meeting of the International Society for the Study of Behavioral Development, Minneapolis, MN.

Goetz, T. E., & Dweck, C. S. (1980). Learned helplessness in social situations. *Child Development, 39,* 246–255.

Goldfried, M. R., & D'Zurilla, T. J. (1969). A behavior-analytic model for assessing competence. In C. D. Spielberger (Ed.), *Current issues in clinical and community psychology* (pp. 151–198). New York: Academic Press.

Goldman, B. D., & Ross, H. S. (1978). Social skills in action: An analysis of early peer games. In J. Glick & K. A. Clarke-Stewart (Eds.), *Studies in social and cognitive development: Vol. 1. The development of social understanding.* New York: Gardner Press.

Goncu, A. (1993). Development of intersubjectivity in the dyadic play of preschoolers. *Early Childhood Research Quarterly, 8,* 99–116.

Goodnow, J. J., Knight, R., & Cashmore, J. (1985). Adult social cognition: Implications of parents' ideas for approaches to development. In M. Perlmutter (Ed.), *Cognitive perspectives and behavioral development: Vol. 18. The Minnesota Symposia on Child Psychology* (pp. 287–329). Hillsdale, NJ: Erlbaum.

Gottman, J. M. (1983). How children become friends. *Monographs of the Society for Research in Child Development, 48*(3, Serial No. 201).

Gottman, J. M., & Katz, L. F. (1989). Effects of marital discord on young children's peer interactions and health. *Developmental Psychology, 25,* 373–381.

Gottman, J. M., & Parker, J. G. (Eds.). (1986). *Conversation of friends: Speculations on affective development.* New York: Cambridge University Press.

Gresham, F. (1981). Validity of social skills measures for assessing social competence in low-status children: A multivariate investigation. *Developmental Psychology, 17,* 390–398.

Hallinan, M. T. (1981). Recent advances in sociometry. In S. R. Asher & J. M. Gottman (Eds.), *The development of children's friendships* (pp. 91–115). New York: Cambridge University Press.

Hanfmann, E. P. (1935). Social structure of a group of kindergarten children. *American Journal of Orthopsychiatry, 5,* 407–410.

Hansell, S. (1981). Ego development and peer friendship networks. *Sociology of Education, 54,* 51–63.

Harré, R. (1984). *Personal being.* Cambridge, MA: Harvard University Press.

Hart, C. H., DeWolf, D., Wozniak, P., & Burts, D. C. (1992). Maternal and paternal disciplinary styles: Relations with preschoolers' playground behavioral orientations and peer status. *Child Development, 63,* 879–892.

Hart, C. H., Ladd, G. W., & Burleson, B. R. (1990). Children's expectations of the outcomes of social strategies: Relations with sociometric status and maternal disciplinary styles. *Child Development, 61,* 127–137.

Harter, S. (1982). The perceived competence scale for children. *Child Development, 53,* 89–97.

Hartup, W. W. (1970). Peer interaction and social organization. In P. H. Mussen (Ed.), *Carmichael's manual of child psychology* (Vol. 2, pp. 361–456). New York: Wiley.

Hartup, W. W. (1983). Peer relations. In P. H. Mussen (Series Ed.) & E. M. Hetherington (Vol. Ed.), *Handbook of child psychology: Vol. 4. Socialization, personality, and social development* (pp. 103–196). New York: Wiley.

Hartup, W. W. (1985). Relationships and their significance in cognitive development. In R. A. Hinde, A. Perret-Clermont, & J. Stevenson-Hinde (Eds.), *Social relationships and cognitive development* (pp. 66–82). Oxford, England: Clarendon Press.

Hartup, W. W. (1989). Behavioral manifestations of children's friendships. In T. J. Berndt & G. W. Ladd (Eds.), *Peer relationships in child development* (pp. 46–70). New York: Wiley.

Hartup, W. W. (1992). Conflict and friendship relations. In C. U. Shantz & W. W. Hartup (Eds.), *Conflict in child and adolescent development* (pp. 185–215). Cambridge, England: Cambridge University Press.

Hartup, W. W. (1996). The company they keep: Friendships and their developmental significance. *Child Development, 67,* 1–13.

Hartup, W. W. (in press). Cooperation, close relationships, and cognitive development. In W. M. Bukowski, A. F. Newcomb, & W. W. Hartup (Eds.), *The company they keep: Friendships in childhood and adolescence.* Cambridge, England: Cambridge University Press.

Hartup, W. W., & Laursen, B. (1991). Relationships as developmental contexts. In R. Cohen & A. W. Siegel (Eds.), *Context and development* (pp. 253–279). Hillsdale, NJ: Erlbaum.

Hartup, W. W., & Laursen, B. (1995). Conflict and context in peer relations. In C. H. Hart (Ed.), *Children on playgrounds.* Albany: State University of New York Press.

Hartup, W. W., Laursen, B., Stewart, M. A., & Eastenson, A. (1988). Conflicts and the friendship relations of young children. *Child Development, 59,* 1590–1600.

Hay, D. F. (1985). Learning to form relationships in infancy: Parallel attainments with parents and peers. *Developmental Review, 5,* 122–161.

Hay, D. F., Pedersen, J., & Nash, A. (1982). Dyadic interaction in the first year of life. In K. H. Rubin & H. S. Ross (Eds.), *Peer relationships and social skills in childhood* (pp. 11–40). New York: Springer-Verlag.

Hay, D. F., & Ross, H. (1982). The social nature of early conflict. *Child Development, 53,* 105–113.

Hayden-Thompson, L., Rubin, K. H., & Hymel, S. (1987). Sex preferences in sociometric choices. *Developmental Psychology, 23,* 559–562.

Hays, R. B. (1988). Friendship. In S. W. Duck (Ed.), *Handbook of personal relationships: Theory, research, and interventions* (pp. 391–408). London: Wiley.

Hayvren, M., & Hymel, S. (1984). Ethical issues in sociometric testing: The impact of sociometric measures in interaction behavior. *Developmental Psychology, 20,* 844–849.

Higgins, E. T., & Parsons, J. E. (1983). Social cognition and the social life of the child: Stages as subcultures. In E. T. Higgins, D. N. Ruble, & W. W. Hartup (Eds.), *Social cognition and social development* (pp. 15–62). Cambridge, England: Cambridge University Press.

Hinde, R. A. (1976). On describing relationships. *Journal of Child Psychology and Psychiatry, 17,* 1–19.

Hinde, R. A. (1979). *Towards understanding relationships.* London: Academic Press.

Hinde, R. A. (1987). *Individuals, relationships and culture.* Cambridge, England: Cambridge University Press.

Hinde, R. A. (1995). A suggested structure for a science of relationships. *Personal Relationships, 2,* 1–15.

Hinde, R. R., & Stevenson-Hinde, J. (1976). Toward understanding relationships: Dynamic stability. In P. Bateson & R. Hinde (Eds.), *Growing points in ethology* (pp. 451–479). Cambridge, England: Cambridge University Press.

Hinde, R. A., & Stevenson-Hinde, J. (1986). Relating childhood relationships to individual characteristics. In W. W. Hartup

& Z. Rubin (Eds.), *Relationships and development* (pp. 27–50). Hillsdale, NJ: Erlbaum.

Hinde, R. A., & Tamplin, A. (1983). Relations between mother-child interaction and behavior in preschool. *British Journal of Developmental Psychology, 1,* 231–257.

Hinde, R. A., Titmus, G., Easton, D., & Tamplin, A. (1985). Incidence of "friendship" and behavior with strong associates versus non-associates in preschoolers. *Child Development, 56,* 234–245.

Ho, D. Y. F. (1986). Chinese patterns of socialization: A critical review. In M. H. Bond (Ed.), *The psychology of Chinese people* (pp. 1–37). New York: Oxford University Press.

Howes, C. (1983). Patterns of friendship. *Child Development, 54,* 1041–1053.

Howes, C. (1984). Sharing fantasy: Social pretend play in toddlers. *Child Development, 56,* 1253–1258.

Howes, C. (1988). Peer interaction of young children. *Monographs of the Society for Research in Child Development, 53*(No. 217).

Howes, C. (1992). *The collaborative construction of pretend.* Albany: State University of New York Press.

Howes, C., & Matheson, C. C. (1992). Sequences in the development of competent play with peers: Social and social-pretend play. *Developmental Psychology, 28,* 961–974.

Howes, C., Matheson, C. C., & Wu, F. (1992). Friendships and social pretend play. In C. Howes, O. Unger, & C. C. Matheson (Eds.), *The collaborative construction of pretend.* Albany: State University of New York Press.

Howes, C., Unger, O., & Siedner, L. B. (1989). Social pretend play in toddlers: Parallels with social pretend play and solitary pretend. *Child Development, 60,* 77–84.

Hoza, B., Molina, B., Bukowski, W. M., & Sippola, L. K. (1995). Aggression, withdrawal and measures of popularity and friendship as predictors of internalizing and externalizing problems during early adolescence. *Development and Psychopathology, 7,* 787–802.

Hughes, F. P. (1991). *Children, play, and development.* Boston: Allyn & Bacon.

Humphreys, A. P., & Smith, P. K. (1987). Rough-and-tumble, friendship, and dominance in school children: Evidence for continuity and change with age. *Child Development, 58,* 201–212.

Hunt, J., & Solomon, R. (1942). The stability and some group correlates of group status in a summer camp group of young boys. *American Journal of Psychology, 55,* 33–45.

Hymel, S. (1986). Interpretations of peer behavior: Affective bias in childhood and adolescence. *Child Development, 57,* 431–445.

Hymel, S., Bowker, A., & Woody, E. (1993). Aggressive versus withdrawn unpopular children: Variations in peer and self-perceptions in multiple domains. *Child Development, 64,* 879–896.

Hymel, S., Comfort, C., Schonert-Reichl, M., & McDougall, P. (in press). Academic failure and school dropout: The influence of peers. In K. Wentzel & J. Juvonen (Eds.), *Social motivation: Understanding children's school adjustment.* Cambridge, England: Cambridge University Press.

Hymel, S., & Franke, S. (1985). Children's peer relations: Assessing self-perceptions. In B. H. Schneider, K. H. Rubin, & J. E. Ledingham (Eds.), *Children's peer relationships: Issues in assessment and intervention* (pp. 75–92). New York: Springer-Verlag.

Hymel, S., & Rubin, K. H. (1985). Children with peer relationship and social skills problems: Conceptual, methodological, and developmental issues. In G. J. Whitehurst (Ed.), *Annals of child development* (Vol. 2, pp. 254–297). Greenwich, CT: JAI Press.

Hymel, S., Rubin, K. H., Rowden, L., & LeMare, L. (1990). Children's peer relationships: Longitudinal predictions of internalizing and externalizing problems from middle to late childhood. *Child Development, 61,* 2004–2021.

Hymel, S., Wagner, E., & Butler, L. (1990). Reputational bias: View from the peer group. In S. R. Asher & J. Coie (Eds.), *Peer rejection in childhood* (pp. 156–186). Cambridge, England: Cambridge University Press.

Hymel, S., & Woody, E. (1991, April). *Friends versus non-friends: Perceptions of similarity across self, teacher, and peers.* Paper presented at the biennial meeting of the Society for Research in Child Development, Seattle, WA.

Isabella, R. A., & Belsky, J. (1991). Interaction synchrony and the origins of infant-mother attachment: A replication study. *Child Development, 62,* 373–384.

James, W. (1890). *The principles of psychology.* New York: Henry Holt.

Janes, C. L., Hesselbrock, V. M., Myers, D. G., & Penniman, J. H. (1979). Problem boys in young adulthood: Teachers' ratings and twelve-year follow-up. *Journal of Youth and Adolescence, 8,* 453–472.

Janes, C. L., Hesselbrock, V. M., & Schechtman, J. (1980). Clinic children with poor peer relations: Who refers them and why? *Child Psychiatry and Human Development, 11,* 113–125.

Jouriles, E. N., Murphy, C. M., Farris, A. M., Smith, D. A., Richters, J., & Waters, E. (1991). Marital adjustment, parental disagreements about child rearing and behavior problems in boys: Increasing the specificity of the marital assessment. *Child Development, 62,* 1424–2433.

Juvonen, J. (1991). Deviance, perceived responsibility, and peer reactions. *Developmental Psychology, 27,* 672–681.

Kagan, J. (1989). Temperamental contributions to social behavior. *American Psychology, 44,* 668–674.

Kagan, J., Reznick, S. J., Clarke, C., Snidman, N., & Garcia-Coll, C. (1984). Behavioral inhibition to the unfamiliar. *Child Development, 55,* 2212–2225.

Kanner, A. D., Feldman, S. S., Weinburg, D. A., & Ford, M. E. (1987). Uplifts, hassles, and adaptational outcomes in early adolescents. *Journal of Early Adolescence, 7,* 371–394.

Khatri, P. (1995, March). *Behavioral and academic correlates of sociometric status among rural Indian children.* Paper presented at the biennial meeting of the Society for Research in Child Development, Indianapolis, IN.

Kindermann, T. A. (1993). Natural peer groups as contexts for individual development: The case of children's motivation in school. *Developmental Psychology, 29,* 970–977.

Kindermann, T. A. (1995). Distinguishing "buddies" from "bystanders": The study of children's development within natural peer contexts. In T. A. Kindermann & J. Valsiner (Eds.), *Development of person-context relations.* Hillsdale, NJ: Erlbaum.

Kindermann, T. A., McCollom, T. L., & Gibson, E., Jr. (1995). Peer networks and students' classroom engagement during childhood and adolescence. In K. Wentzel & J. Juvonen (Eds.), *Social motivation: Understanding children's school adjustment.* New York: Cambridge University Press.

King, A. Y. C., & Bond, M. H. (1985). The confucian paradigm of man: A sociological view. In W. S. Teng & D. Y. H. Wu (Eds.), *Chinese culture and mental health* (pp. 29–45). New York: Academic Press.

Koch, H. (1935). Popularity among preschool children: Some related factors and techniques for its measurement. *Child Development, 4,* 164–175.

Kochanska, G. (1991). Patterns of inhibition to the unfamiliar in children of normal and affectively ill mothers. *Child Development, 62,* 250–263.

Kohlberg, L. (1963). Moral development and identification. In H. W. Stevenson (Ed.), *Child psychology* (62nd Yearbook of the National Society for the Study of Education). Chicago: University of Chicago Press.

Kohlberg, L. (1969). Stage and sequence: The cognitive-developmental approach to socialization. In D. A. Goslin (Ed.), *Handbook of socialization theory and research.* Chicago: Rand McNally.

Kohlberg, L., & Diessner, R. (1991). A cognitive developmental approach to moral attachment. In J. L. Gewirtz & W. M. Kurtines (Eds.), *Intersections with attachment.* Hillsdale, NJ: Erlbaum.

Kohn, M., & Clausen, J. (1955). Social isolation and schizophrenia. *American Sociological Review, 20,* 265–273.

Kramer, L., & Gottman, J. M. (1992). Becoming a sibling: "With a little help from my friends." *Developmental Psychology, 28,* 685–699.

Krasnor, L., & Rubin, K. H. (1983). Preschool social problem solving: Attempts and outcomes in naturalistic interaction. *Child Development, 54,* 1545–1558.

Kruger, A. C., & Tomasello, M. (1986). Transactive discussions with peers and adults. *Developmental Psychology, 22,* 681–685.

Kupersmidt, J. B., Burchinal, M., & Patterson, C. J. (1995). Developmental patterns of childhood peer relations as predictors of externalizing behavior problems. *Development and Psychopathology, 7,* 649–668.

Kupersmidt, J. B., & Coie, J. D. (1990). Preadolescent peer status, aggression, and school adjustment as predictors of externalizing problems in adolescence. *Child Development, 61,* 1350–1362.

Kupersmidt, J. B., Coie, J. D., & Dodge, K. A. (1990). The role of poor peer relationships in the development of disorder. In S. R. Asher & J. D. Coie (Eds.), *Peer rejection in childhood* (pp. 274–308). Cambridge, England: Cambridge University Press.

Kurdek, L. A., & Krile, D. (1982). A developmental analysis of the relation between peer acceptance and both interpersonal understanding and perceived social self-competence. *Child Development, 53,* 1485–1491.

Ladd, G. W. (1990). Having friends, keeping friends, making friends, and being liked by peers in the classroom: Predictors of children's early school adjustment? *Child Development, 61,* 312–331.

Ladd, G. W. (1991). Family-peer relations during childhood: Pathways to competence and pathology? *Journal of Social and Personal Relationships, 8,* 307–314.

Ladd, G. W., & Golter, B. S. (1988). Parents' initiation and monitoring of children's peer contacts: Predictive of children's peer relations in nonschool and school settings? *Developmental Psychology, 24,* 109–117.

Ladd, G. W., & Hart, C. H. (1992). Creating informal play opportunities: Are parents' and preschoolers' initiations related to children's competence with peers? *Developmental Psychology, 28,* 1179–1187.

Ladd, G. W., Kochenderfer, B. J., & Coleman, C. C. (1996). Friendship quality as a predictor of young children's early school adjustment. *Child Development, 67,* 1103–1118.

Ladd, G. W., & Price, J. M. (1986). Promoting children's cognitive and social competence: The relation between parents' perceptions of task difficulty and children's perceived and actual competence. *Child Development, 57,* 446–460.

Ladd, G. W., & Price, J. M. (1993). Play styles of peer-accepted and peer-rejected children on the playground. In C. H. Hart (Ed.), *Children on playgrounds: Research perspectives and applications* (pp. 130–161). New York: State University of New York Press.

Ladd, G. W., Profilet, S., & Hart, C. H. (1992). Parent's management of children's peer relations: Facilitating and supervising children's activities in the peer culture. In R. D. Parke & G. W. Ladd (Eds.), *Family-peer relationships: Modes of linkage* (pp. 215–254). Hillsdale, NJ: Erlbaum.

LaFreniere, P. J., & Charlesworth, W. R. (1983). Dominance, attention, and affiliation in a preschool group: A nine-month longitudinal study. *Ethology and Sociobiology, 4*(2), 55–67.

LaFreniere, P. J., & Dumas, J. E. (1992). A transactional analysis of early childhood anxiety and social withdrawal. *Development and Psychopathology, 4,* 385–402.

LaFreniere, P. J., & Sroufe, L. A. (1985). Profiles of peer competence in the preschool: Interrelations between measures, influence of social ecology, and relations to attachment history. *Developmental Psychology, 21,* 56–69.

LaGreca, A. (1981). Peer acceptance: The correspondence between children's sociometric scores and teacher's ratings of peer interventions. *Journal of Abnormal Child Psychology, 9,* 167–178.

LaGreca, A. M., Dandes, S. K., Wick, P., Shaw, K., & Stone, W. L. (1988). Development of the Social Anxiety Scale for Children: Reliability and concurrent validity. *Journal of Clinical Child Psychology, 17,* 84–91.

Lancelotta, G. X., & Vaughn, S. (1989). Relation between types of aggression and sociometric status: Peer and teachers perceptions. *Journal of Educational Psychology, 81.*

Laosa, M., & Sigel, I. E. (1982). *Families as learning environments for children.* New York: Plenum Press.

Larkin, R. W. (1979). *Suburban youth in cultural crisis.* New York: Oxford University Press.

Laursen, B. (Ed.). (1993a). *Close friendships in adolescence.* San Francisco: Jossey-Bass.

Laursen, B. (1993b). Conflict management among close peers. In B. Laursen (Ed.), *Close friendships in adolescence* (pp. 39–54). San Francisco: Jossey-Bass.

Laursen, B., Hartup, W. W., & Koplas, A. L. (1996). Towards understanding peer conflict. *Merrill-Palmer Quarterly, 42,* 76–102.

Leaper, C. (1991). Influence and involvement in children's discourse: Age, gender, and partner effects. *Child Development, 62,* 797–811.

Leaper, C. (1994a). Exploring the consequences of gender segregation on social relationships. In C. Leaper (Ed.), *Childhood gender segregation: Causes and consequences* (pp. 67–86). San Francisco: Jossey-Bass.

Leaper, C. (Ed.) (1994b). *Childhood gender segregation: Causes and consequences.* San Francisco: Jossey-Bass.

Ledingham, J., Younger, A., Schwartzman, A., & Bergeron, G. (1982). Agreement among teacher, peer and self-ratings of children's aggression, withdrawal and likeability. *Journal of Abnormal Child Psychology, 10,* 363–372.

Legault, F., & Strayer, F. F. (1990). The emergence of sex-segregation in preschool peer groups. In F. F. Strayer (Ed.), *Social interaction and behavioral development during early childhood.* Montreal, Quebec: La maison d'ethologie de Montreal.

Lempers, J. D., Clark-Lempers, D., & Simons, R. L. (1989). Economic hardship, parenting and distress in adolescence. *Child Development, 60,* 25–39.

Lever, J. (1976). Sex differences in games children play. *Social Problems, 23,* 478–487.

Levin, E., & Rubin, K. H. (1983). Getting others to do what you wanted them to do: The development of children's requestive strategies. In K. Nelson (Ed.), *Child language* (Vol. 4). Hillsdale, NJ: Erlbaum.

Lewin, K., Lippit, R., & White, R. K. (1938). Patterns of aggressive behavior in experimentally created "social climates." *Journal of Social Psychology, 10,* 271–299.

Lorenz, K. (1966). *On aggression.* London: Methuen.

Lytton, H. (1990). Child and parent effects on boys' conduct disorder: A reinterpretation. *Developmental Psychology, 26,* 683–697.

Maccoby, E. E. (1986). Social groupings in childhood: Their relationship to prosocial and antisocial behavior in boys and girls. In D. Olweus, J. Block, & M. Radke-Yarrow (Eds.), *Development of antisocial and social behavior* (pp. 263–284). New York: Academic Press.

Maccoby, E. E. (1990). Gender and relationships. *American Psychologist, 45,* 513–520.

MacDonald, K., & Parke, R. D. (1984). Bridging the gap: Parent-child play interactions and peer interactive competence. *Child Development, 55,* 1265–1277.

Mangelsdorf, S., Gunnar, M., Kestenbaum, R., Lang, S., & Andreas, D. (1990). Infant proneness-to-distress temperament, maternal personality and mother-infant attachment: Associations and goodness of fit. *Child Development, 61,* 820–831.

Markovits, H., & Strayer, F. F. (1982). Toward an applied social ethology: A case study of social skills among blind children. In K. H. Rubin & H. S. Ross (Eds.), *Peer relationships and social skills in childhood* (pp. 301–322). New York: Springer-Verlag.

Masten, A. S., Morison, P., & Pellegrini, D. S. (1985). A revised class play method of peer assessment. *Developmental Psychology, 3,* 523–533.

Masters, J. C., & Furman, W. (1981). Popularity, individual friendship selection, and specific peer interaction among children. *Developmental Psychology, 17,* 344–350.

Matas, L., Arend, R. A., & Sroufe, L. A. (1978). The continuity of adaptation in the second year: Relationship between quality of attachment and later competence. *Child Development, 49,* 547–556.

Maudry, M., & Nekula, M. (1939). Social relations between children of the same age during the first two years of life. *Journal of Genetic Psychology, 54,* 193–215.

McCall, G. J. (1988). The organizational life cycle of relationships. In S. W. Duck (Ed.), *Handbook of personal relationships* (pp. 467–484). New York: Wiley.

McFall, R. M. (1982). A review and reformulation of the concept of social skills. *Behavioral Assessment, 4,* 1–33.

McGuire, K. D., & Weisz, J. R. (1982). Social cognition and behavior correlates of preadolescent chumship. *Child Development, 53,* 1478–1484.

McLoyd, V. C. (1989). Socialization and development in a changing economy: The effects of paternal job and income loss on children. Children and their development: Knowledge base, research agenda, and social policy application [Special issue]. *American Psychologist, 44,* 293–302.

Mead, G. H. (1934). *Mind, self, and society.* Chicago: University of Chicago Press.

Messer, D. J., Joiner, R., Loveridge, N., Light, P., & Litteton, K. (1993). Influences on the effectiveness of peer interaction: Children's level of cognitive development and the relative ability of partners. *Social Development, 2,* 279–294.

Miller, S. A. (1995). Parents' attributions for their children's behavior. *Child Development, 66,* 1557–1584.

Mills, R. S. L., & Rubin, K. H. (1990). Parental beliefs about problematic social behaviors in early childhood. *Child Development, 61,* 138–151.

Mills, R. S. L., & Rubin, K. H. (1993). Socialization factors in the development of social withdrawal. In K. H. Rubin & J. Asendorpf (Eds.), *Social withdrawal, inhibition and shyness in childhood* (pp. 117–150). Hillsdale: Erlbaum.

Moller, L., Hymel, S., & Rubin, K. H. (1992). Sex typing in play and popularity in middle childhood. *Sex Roles, 26,* 331–353.

Monroe, W. S. (1899). Play interests of children. *American Educational Review, 4,* 358–365.

Moreno, J. L. (1934). *Who shall survive? A new approach to the problem of human interrelations.* Washington, DC: Nervous and Mental Disease.

Morison, P., & Masten, A. S. (1991). Peer reputation in middle childhood as a predictor of adaptation in adolescence: A seven year follow-up. *Child Development, 62,* 991–1007.

Mueller, E. (1972). The maintenance of verbal exchanges between young children. *Child Development, 43,* 930–938.

Mueller, E., & Brenner, J. (1977). The origins of social skills and interaction among playgroup toddlers. *Child Development, 48,* 854–861.

Mueller, E., & Cooper, C. (Eds.). (1986). *Process and outcome in peer relationships.* New York: Academic Press.

Mueller, E., & Silverman, N. (1989). Peer relations in maltreated children. In D. Cicchetti & V. Carlson (Eds.), *Child maltreatment: Theory and research on the causes and consequences of child abuse and neglect* (pp. 529–578). New York: Cambridge University Press.

Murphy, L. B. (1937). *Social behavior and child psychology: An exploratory study of some roots of sympathy.* New York: Columbia University Press.

Nelson, J., & Aboud, F. E. (1985). The resolution of social conflict between friends. *Child Development, 56,* 1009–1017.

Newcomb, A. F., & Bagwell, C. (1995). Children's friendship relations: A meta-analytic review. *Psychological Bulletin, 117,* 306–347.

Newcomb, A. F., & Brady, J. E. (1982). Mutuality in boys' friendship relations. *Child Development, 53,* 392–395.

Newcomb, A. F., & Bukowski, W. M. (1983). Social impact and social preference as determinants of children's peer group status. *Developmental Psychology, 19,* 856–867.

Newcomb, A. F., & Bukowski, W. M. (1984). A longitudinal study of the utility of social preference and social impact sociometric classification schemes. *Child Development, 55,* 1434–1447.

Newcomb, A. F., Bukowski W. M., & Pattee, L. (1993). Children's peer relations: A meta-analyic review of popular, rejected, neglected, controversial, and average sociometric status. *Psychological Bulletin, 113,* 99–128.

O'Brien, S. F., & Bierman, K. L. (1987). Conceptions and perceived influence of peer groups: Interviews with preadolescents and adolescents. *Child Development, 59,* 1360–1365.

Ollendick, T. H., Weist, M. D., Borden, M. G., & Greene, R. W. (1992). Sociometric status and academic, behavioral, and psychological adjustment: A five-year longitudinal study. *Journal of Consulting and Clinical Psychology, 60,* 80–87.

Olweus, D. (1984). Stability in aggressive and withdrawn, inhibited behavior patterns. In R. M. Kaplan, V. J. Konecni, & R. W. Novaco (Eds.), *Aggression in children and youth* (pp. 104–136). The Hague: Nijhoff.

Olweus, D. (1993a). *Bullying at school: What we know and what we can do.* Oxford, England: Blackwell.

Olweus, D. (1993b). Victimization by peers: Antecedents and long-term outcomes. In K. H. Rubin & J. B. Asendorpf (Eds.), *Social withdrawal, inhibition and shyness in childhood* (pp. 315–341). Hillsdale, NJ: Erlbaum.

Oppenheimer, L. (1989). The nature of social action: Social competence versus social conformism. In B. Schneider, G. Attili, J. Nadel, & R. Weissberg (Eds.), *Social competence in developmental perspective* (pp. 40–70). Dordrecht, The Netherlands: Kluwer.

Park, K. A., & Waters, E. (1989). Security of attachment and preschool friendships. *Child Development, 60,* 1076–1081.

Parke, R. D., & Ladd, G. W. (1992). *Family-peer relationships: Modes of linkage.* Hillsdale, NJ: Erlbaum.

Parker, J. G., & Asher, S. R. (1987). Peer relations and later personal adjustment: Are low-accepted children at risk? *Psychological Bulletin, 102,* 357–389.

Parker, J. G., & Asher, S. R. (1993a). Beyond group acceptance: Friendship and friendship quality as distinct dimensions of children's peer adjustment. In D. Perlman & W. H. Jones (Eds.), *Advances in personal relationships* (Vol. 4, pp. 261–294). London: Kingsley.

Parker, J. G., & Asher, S. R. (1993b). Friendship and friendship quality in middle childhood: Links with peer group acceptance and feelings of loneliness and social dissatisfaction. *Developmental Psychology, 29,* 611–621.

Parker, J. G., & Gottman, J. M. (1989). Social and emotional development in a relational context: Friendship interaction from early childhood to adolescence. In T. J. Berndt & G. W. Ladd (Eds.), *Peer relations in child development* (pp. 95–131). New York: Wiley.

Parker, J. G., & Herrera, C. (in press). Interpersonal processes in friendships: A comparison of maltreated and nonmaltreated children's experiences. *Developmental Psychology.*

Parker, J. G., Rubin, K. H., Price, J., & DeRosier, M. E. (1995). Peer relationships, child development, and adjustment: A developmental psychopathology perspective. In D. Cicchetti & D. Cohen (Eds.), *Developmental psychopathology: Vol. 2. Risk, disorder, and adaptation* (pp. 96–161). New York: Wiley.

Parkhurst, J. T., & Asher, S. R. (1992). Peer rejection in middle school: Subgroup differences in behavior, loneliness, and interpersonal concerns. *Developmental Psychology, 28,* 231–241.

Parten, M. B. (1932). Social participation among preschool children. *Journal of Abnormal and Social Psychology, 27,* 243–269.

Pastor, D. L. (1981). The quality of mother-infant attachment and its relationship to toddlers' initial sociability with peers. *Developmental Psychology, 17,* 326–335.

Patterson, C. J., Kupersmidt, J. B., & Griesler, P. C. (1990). Children's perceptions of self and of relations with others as a function of sociometric status. *Child Development, 61,* 1335–1349.

Patterson, C. J., Vaden, N. A., & Kupersmidt, J. B. (1991). Family background, recent life events, and peer rejection during childhood. *Journal of Social and Personal Relationships, 8,* 347–361.

Patterson, G. R., Littman, R., & Bricker, W. (1967). Assertive behavior in children: A step toward a theory of aggression. *Monographs of the Society for Research in Child Development, 32*(Serial No. 113).

Peery, J. C. (1979). Popular, amiable, isolated, rejected: A reconceptualization of sociometric status in preschool children. *Child Development, 50,* 1231–1234.

Peevers, B. H., & Secord, P. F. (1973). Developmental changes in attribution of descriptive concepts to persons. *Journal of Personality and Social Psychology, 27,* 120–128.

Pekarik, E. G., Prinz, R. J., Liebert, D. E., Weintraub, S., & Neale, J. M. (1976). The Pupil Evaluation Inventory: A sociometric technique for assessing children's social behavior. *Journal of Abnormal Child Psychology, 4,* 83–97.

Pepler, D. J., & Craig, W. (1995). A peek behind the fence: Naturalistic observations of aggressive behavior with remote audiovisual recording. *Developmental Psychology, 31,* 548–553.

Perry, D. G., Kusel, S. J., & Perry, L. C. (1988). Victims of peer aggression. *Developmental Psychology, 24,* 807–814.

Perry, D. G., Perry, L., & Kennedy, E. (1992). Conflict and the development of antisocial behavior. In C. Shantz & W. W. Hartup (Eds.), *Conflict in child and adolescent development.* New York: Cambridge University Press.

Pettit, G. S., Dodge, K. A., & Brown, M. M. (1988). Early family experience, social problem solving patterns, and children's social competence. *Child Development, 59,* 107–120.

Pettit, G. S., & Mize, J. (1993). Substance and style: Understanding the ways in which parents teach children about social relationships. In S. Duck (Ed.), *Learning about relationships* (pp. 118–151). Newbury Park, CA: Sage.

Piaget, J. (1932). *The moral judgment of the child.* Glencoe, IL: Free Press.

Piaget, J. (1959). *The language and thought of the child.* New York: Harcourt, Brace, & World.

Price, J. M., & Ladd, G. W. (1986). Assessment of children's friendships: Implications for social competence and social adjustment. In R. J. Prinz (Ed.), *Advances in behavioral assessment of children and families* (Vol. 2, pp. 121–150). Greenwich, CT: JAI Press.

Putallaz, M. (1983). Predicting children's sociometric status from their behavior. *Child Development, 54,* 1417–1426.

Putallaz, M. (1987). Maternal behavior and children's sociometric status. *Child Development, 58,* 324–340.

Putallaz, M., Constanzo, P. R., & Klein, T. P. (1993). Parental ideas as influences on children's social competence. In S. Duck (Ed.), *Learning about relationships* (pp. 63–97). Newbury Park, CA: Sage.

Putallaz, M., & Gottman, J. M. (1981). Social skills and group acceptance. In S. R. Asher & J. M. Gottman (Eds.), *The development of children's friendships* (pp. 116–149). New York: Cambridge University Press.

Quiggle, N., Garber, J., Panak, W., & Dodge, K. A. (1992). Social-information processing in aggressive and depressed children. *Child Development, 63,* 1305–1320.

Rabiner, D. L., & Gordon, L. (1992). The coordination of conflicting social goals: Differences between rejected and nonrejected boys. *Child Development, 63,* 1344–1350.

Rabiner, D. L., Lenhart, L., & Lochman, J. E. (1990). Automatic versus reflective social problem solving in relation to children's sociometric status. *Developmental Psychology, 26,* 1010–1016.

Rabinovich, E. P. (1994). Sedentary homeless children in Sao Paulo, Brazil: Their houses, their families, their lives. In W. Koops, B. Hopkins, & P. Engelen (Eds.), *Abstracts of the thirteenth biennial meeting of ISSBD* (p. 433). Amsterdam, The Netherlands: Logon.

Renken, B., Egeland, B., Marvinney, D., Sroufe, L. A., & Mangelsdorf, S. (1989). Early childhood antecedents of aggression and passive-withdrawal in early elementary school. *Journal of Personality, 57,* 257–281.

Renshaw, P. E. (1981). The roots of peer interaction research: A historical analysis of the 1930's. In S. R. Asher & J. M. Gottman (Eds.), *The development of children's friendships* (pp. 1–28). New York: Cambridge University Press.

Renshaw, P. E., & Brown, P. J. (1993). Loneliness in middle childhood: Concurrent and longitudinal predictors. *Child Development, 64,* 1271–1284.

Rheingold, H. L., Hay, D., & West, M. J. (1976). Sharing in the second year of life. *Child Development, 47,* 1148–1158.

Ricks, D., & Berry, J. C. (1970). Family and symptom patterns that precede schizophrenia. In M. Roff & D. Ricks (Eds.), *Life history research in psycho-pathology* (Vol. 1, pp. 31–39). Minneapolis: University of Minnesota Press.

Roff, M. (1961). Childhood social interactions and young adult bad conduct. *Journal of Abnormal Social Psychology, 63,* 333–337.

Roff, M. (1963). Childhood social interactions and young adult psychosis. *Journal of Clinical Psychology, 19,* 152–157.

Roff, M., Sells, B. B., & Golden, M. M. (1972). *Social adjustment and personality development.* Minneapolis: University of Minnesota Press.

Rogoff, B. (1990). *Apprenticeship in thinking: Cognitive development in social context.* Oxford, England: Oxford University Press.

Rogosch, F., Cicchetti, D., & Aber, J. L. (1995). The role of child maltreatment in early deviations in cognitive and affective processing abilities and later peer relationship problems. *Development and Psychopathology, 7,* 591–609.

Roopnarine, J. L., & Adams, G. R. (1987). The interactional teaching patterns of mothers and fathers with their popular, moderately popular, or unpopular children. *Journal of Abnormal Child Psychology, 15,* 125–136.

Rose-Krasnor, L., Rubin, K. H., Booth, C. L., & Coplan, R. J. (1996). Maternal directiveness and child attachment security as predictors of social competence in preschoolers. *International Journal of Behavioral Development, 19,* 309–325.

Rosen, B. C., & D'Andrade, R. (1959). The psychosocial origins of achievement motivation. *Sociometry, 22,* 185–218.

Ross, H. S. (1982). The establishment of social games amongst toddlers. *Developmental Psychology, 18,* 509–518.

Ross, H. S., & Conant, C. L., (1992). The social structure of early conflict: Interactions, relationships, and alliances. In C. U. Shantz & W. W. Hartup (Eds.), *Conflict in child and adolescent development.* Cambridge, England: Cambridge University Press.

Ross, H. S., Conant, C., Cheyne, J. A., & Alevizos, E. (1992). Relationships and alliances in the social interactions of kibbutz toddlers. *Social Development, 1,* 1–17.

Ross, H. S., & Lollis, S. P. (1989). A social relations analysis of toddler-peer relationships. *Child Development, 60,* 1082–1091.

Ross, H. S., Lollis, S. P., & Elliott, C. (1982). Toddler-peer communication. In K. H. Rubin & H. S. Ross (Eds.), *Peer relationships and social skills in childhood* (pp. 73–98). New York: Springer-Verlag.

Rotenberg, K., & Slitz, D. (1988). Children's restrictive disclosure to friends. *Merrill-Palmer Quarterly, 34,* 203–215.

Roy, A. W., & Howe, C. (1990). Effects of cognitive conflict, socio-cognitive conflict and imitation on children's socio-legal thinking. *European Journal of Social Psychology, 20,* 241–252.

Rubin, K. H. (1972). Relationship between egocentric communication and popularity among peers. *Developmental Psychology, 7,* 364.

Rubin, K. H. (1982a). Non-social play in preschoolers: Necessary evil? *Child Development, 53,* 651–657.

Rubin, K. H. (1982b). Social and social-cognitive developmental characteristics of young isolate, normal and sociable children. In K. H. Rubin & H. S. Ross (Eds.), *Peer relationships and social skills in childhood* (pp. 353–374). New York: Springer-Verlag.

Rubin, K. H. (1983). Recent perspectives on sociometric status in childhood: Some introductory remarks. *Child Development, 54,* 1383–1385.

Rubin, K. H. (1985). Socially withdrawn children: An "at risk" population? In B. Schneider, K. H. Rubin, & J. Ledingham (Eds.), *Children's peer relations: Issues in assessment and intervention* (pp. 125–139). New York: Springer-Verlag.

Rubin, K. H., & Borwick, D. (1984). The communication skills of children who vary with regard to sociability. In H. Sypher & J. Applegates (Eds.), *Social cognition and communication.* Hillsdale, NJ: Erlbaum.

Rubin, K. H., Both, L., Zahn-Waxler, C., Cummings, M., & Wilkinson, M. (1991). The dyadic play behaviors of children of well and depressed mothers. *Development and Psychopathology, 3,* 243–251.

Rubin, K. H., Chen, X., & Hymel, S. (1993). Socioemotional characteristics of withdrawn and aggressive children. *Merrill-Palmer Quarterly, 39,* 518–534.

Rubin, K. H., Chen, X., McDougall, P., Bowker, A., & McKinnon, J. (1995). The Waterloo Longitudinal Project: Predicting internalizing and externalizing problems in adolescence. *Development and Psychopathology, 7,* 751–764.

Rubin, K. H., & Cohen, J. S. (1986). Predicting peer ratings of aggression and withdrawal in the middle childhood years. In R. J. Prinz (Ed.), *Advances in behavioral assessment of children and families* (Vol. 2, pp. 179–206). Greenwich, CT: JAI Press.

Rubin, K. H., Coplan, R. J., Fox, N. A., & Calkins, S. (1995). Emotionality, emotion regulation, and preschoolers' social adaptation. *Development and Psychopathology, 7,* 49–62.

Rubin, K. H., & Daniels-Beirness, T. (1983). Concurrent and predictive correlates of sociometric status in kindergarten and grade one children. *Merrill-Palmer Quarterly, 29,* 337–351.

Rubin, K. H., Fein, G., & Vandenberg, B. (1983). Play. In P. H. Mussen (Series Ed.) & E. M. Hetherington (Vol. Ed.), *Handbook of child psychology: Vol. 4: Socialization, personality and social development* (pp. 693–774). New York: Wiley.

Rubin, K. H., Hastings, P. D., Stewart, S. L., Henderson, H. A., & Chen, X. (in press). The consistency and concomitants of inhibition: Some of the children, all of the time. *Child Development.*

Rubin, K. H., Hymel, S., & Mills, R. S. L. (1989). Sociability and social withdrawal in childhood: Stability and outcomes. *Journal of Personality, 57,* 237–255.

Rubin, K. H., Hymel, S., Mills, R. S. L., & Rose-Krasnor, L. (1991). Conceptualizing different developmental pathways to and from social isolation in childhood. In D. Cicchetti & S. L. Toth (Eds.), *Rochester Symposium on Developmental Psychopathology: Vol. 2: Internalizing and externalizing expressions of dysfunction* (pp. 91–122). Hillsdale, NJ: Erlbaum.

Rubin, K. H., & Krasnor, L. R. (1983). Age and gender differences in the development of a representative social problem solving skill. *Journal of Applied Developmental Psychology, 4,* 463–475.

Rubin, K. H., & Krasnor, L. R. (1986). Social-cognitive and social behavioral perspectives on problem solving. In M. Perlmutter (Ed.), *Cognitive perspectives on children's social and behavioral development. The Minnesota Symposia on Child Psychology* (Vol. 18, pp. 1–68). Hillsdale, NJ: Erlbaum.

Rubin, K. H., LeMare, L. J., & Lollis, S. (1990). Social withdrawal in childhood: Developmental pathways to peer rejection. In S. R. Asher & J. D. Coie (Eds.), *Peer rejection in childhood* (pp. 217–249). New York: Cambridge University Press.

Rubin, K. H., Lynch, D., Coplan, R., Rose-Krasnor, L., & Booth, C. L. (1994). "Birds of a feather . . . ": Behavioral concordances and preferential personal attraction in children. *Child Development, 65,* 1778–1785.

Rubin, K. H., & Mills, R. S. L. (1988). The many faces of social isolation in childhood. *Journal of Consulting and Clinical Psychology, 6,* 916–924.

Rubin, K. H., & Mills, R. S. L. (1990). Maternal beliefs about adaptive and maladaptive social behaviors in normal, aggressive, and withdrawn preschoolers. *Journal of Abnormal Child Psychology, 18,* 419–435.

Rubin, K. H., Mills, R. S. L., & Rose-Krasnor, L. (1989). Maternal beliefs and children's social competence. In B. Schneider, G. Attili, J. Nadel, & R. Weissberg (Eds.), *Social competence in developmental perspective* (pp. 313–331). Boston: Kluwer Academic.

Rubin, K. H., & Rose-Krasnor, L. (1992). Interpersonal problem solving. In V. B. Van Hassett & M. Hersen (Eds.), *Handbook of social development* (pp. 283–323). New York: Plenum Press.

Rubin, K. H., Stewart, S., & Chen, X. (1995). Parents of aggressive and withdrawn children. In M. Bornstein (Ed.), *Handbook of parenting* (Vol. 1, pp. 255–284). Hillsdale, NJ: Erlbaum.

Rubin, K. H., Watson, K., & Jambor, T. (1978). Free play behaviors in preschool and kindergarten children. *Child Development, 49,* 534–536.

Ruble, D. (1983). The development of social comparison processes and their role in achievement-related self-socialization. In E. T. Higgins, D. Ruble, & W. W. Hartup (Eds.), *Social cognition and social behavior: Developmental perspectives* (pp. 134–157). New York: Cambridge University Press.

Russell, A., & Finnie, V. (1990). Preschool social status and maternal instructions to assist group entry. *Developmental Psychology, 26,* 603–611.

Sameroff, A. J. (1987). The social context of development. In N. Eisenberg (Ed.), *Contemporary topics in developmental psychology* (pp. 273–291). New York: Wiley.

Sancilio, F. M., Plumert, J. M., & Hartup, W. W. (1989). Friendship and aggressiveness as determinants of conflict outcomes in middle childhood. *Developmental Psychology, 25,* 812–819.

Schneider, B. H., Attili, G., Nadel, J., & Weissberg, R. P. (1989). *Social competence in developmental perspective.* Boston: Kluwer Academic.

Schneider, B. H., Rubin, K. H., & Ledingham, J. E. (Eds.). (1985). *Children's peer relations: Issues in assessment and intervention.* New York: Springer-Verlag.

Schneider, B. H., Tomada, G., Labovitz, G., Tassi, F., & Innocenti, F. (1995, March). *Aggression, competition, and social competence in two cultures: A closer look.* Paper presented at the biennial meeting of the Society for Research in Child Development, New Orleans, LA.

Selman, R. L. (1980). *The growth of interpersonal understanding: Developmental and clinical analyses.* New York: Academic Press.

Selman, R. L., & Schultz, L. H. (1990). *Making a friend in youth: Developmental theory and pair therapy.* Chicago: University of Chicago Press.

Sharabany, R., Gershoni, R., & Hofman, J. (1981). Girlfriend, boyfriend: Age and sex differences in intimate friendship. *Developmental Psychology, 17,* 800–808.

Shatz, M., & Gelman, R. (1973). The development of communication skills: Modifications in the speech of young children as a function of the listener. *Monographs of the Society for Research in Child Development, 38*(No. 38).

Sherif, M., Harvey, O. J., White, B. J., Hood, W. R., & Sherif, C. (1961). *Inter-group conflict and cooperation: The Robbers Cave experiment.* Norman: University of Oklahoma Press.

Shrum, W., & Cheek, N. H. (1987). Social structure during the school years: Onset of the degrouping process. *American Sociological Review, 52,* 218–223.

Sigel, I. E. (1982). The relationship between parental distancing strategies and the child's cognitive behavior. In L. M. Laosa & I. E. Sigel (Eds.), *Families as learning environments for children* (pp. 47–86). New York: Plenum Press.

Slaby, R. G., & Guerra, N. B. (1988). Cognitive mediators of aggression in adolescent offenders: 1. Assessment. *Developmental Psychology, 24,* 580–588.

Smollar, J., & Youniss, J. (1982). Social development through friendship. In K. H. Rubin & H. S. Ross (Eds.), *Peer relationships and social skills in childhood* (pp. 277–298). New York: Springer-Verlag.

Sroufe, L. A. (1983). Infant-caregiver attachment and patterns of adaptation in preschool: The roots of maladaptation. In M. Perlmutter (Ed.), *Minnesota Symposia on Child Psychology* (Vol. 16, pp. 41–83). Hillsdale, NJ: Erlbaum.

Sroufe, L. A., & Fleeson, J. (1986). Attachment and the construction of relationships. In W. Hartup & Z. Rubin (Eds.), *The nature and development of relationships.* Hillsdale, NJ: Erlbaum.

Stewart, S. L., & Rubin, K. H. (1995). The social problem solving skills of anxious-withdrawn children. *Development and Psychopathology, 7,* 323–336.

Stocker, C., & Dunn, J. (1990). Sibling relationships in childhood: Links with friendships and peer relationships. *British Journal of Developmental Psychology, 8,* 227–244.

Strain, P., & Kerr, M. (1981). Modifying children's social withdrawal: Issues in assessment and clinical intervention. In

M. Herson, R. Eisler, & P. Miller (Eds.), *Progress in behavior modification* (Vol. 2, pp. 203–248). New York: Academic Press.

Strayer, F. F. (1984). Biological approaches to the study of the family. In R. D. Parke, R. Emde, H. Macadoo, & G. P. Sackett (Eds.), *Review of child development research: Vol. 7. The family.* Chicago: University of Chicago Press.

Strayer, F. F. (1989). Co-adaptation within the early peer group: A psychobiological study of social competence. In B. H. Schneider, G. Attili, J. Nadel, & R. Weissberg (Eds.), *Social competence in developmental perspective* (pp. 145–174). Boston: Kluwer Academic.

Strayer, F. F., Chapeskie, T. R., & Strayer, J. (1978). The perception of preschool dominance relations. *Aggressive Behavior, 4,* 183–192.

Strayer, F. F., & Strayer, J. (1976). An ethological analysis of social agonism and dominance relations among preschool children. *Child Development, 47,* 980–989.

Sullivan, H. S. (1953). *The interpersonal theory of psychiatry.* New York: Norton.

Suttles, G. D. (1970). Friendship as a social institution. In G. J. McCall, M. McCall, N. K. Denzin, G. D. Suttles, & S. Kurth (Eds.), *Social relationships* (pp. 95–135). Chicago: Aldine.

Teasley, S. D., & Parker, J. G. (1995, March). *The effects of gender, friendship, and popularity on the targets and topics of preadolescents' gossip.* Paper presented at the biennial meeting of the Society for Research in Child Development, Indianapolis, IN.

Thomas, A., & Chess, S. (1977). *Temperament and development.* New York: Brunner/Mazel.

Thompson, G., & Powell, M. (1951). An investigation of the rating-scale approach to the measurement of social status. *Educational and Psychological Measurement, 11,* 440–455.

Tinbergen, N. (1951). *The study of instinct.* London: Oxford University Press.

Tremblay, R. E., Mâsse, L. C., Vitaro, F., & Dobkin, P. L. (1995). The impact of friends' deviant behavior on early onset of delinquency: Longitudinal data from 6 to 13 years of age. *Development and Psychopathology, 7,* 649–668.

Troy, M., & Sroufe, L. A. (1987). Victimization among preschoolers: Role of attachment relationship history. *Journal of the American Academy of Child and Adolescent Psychiatry, 26,* 166–172.

Tudge, J. (1992). Processes and consequences of peer collaborations: A Vygotskian analysis. *Child Development, 63,* 1364–1379.

Tudge, J., & Winterhoff, P. (1993). Can young children benefit from collaborative problem solving? Tracing the effects of partner competence and feedback. *Social Development, 2,* 242–259.

Ullman, C. A. (1957). Teachers, peers, and tests as predictors of adjustment. *Journal of Educational Psychology, 48,* 257–267.

Vandell, D. L., & Mueller, E. (1980). Peer play and friendships during the first two years. In H. Foot, A. Chapman, & J. Smith (Eds.), *Friendship and social relations in children* (pp. 181–208). New York: Wiley.

Vandell, D. L., Wilson, K. S., & Buchanan, N. R. (1980). Peer interaction in the first year of life: An examination of its structure, content, and sensitivity to toys. *Child Development, 51,* 481–488.

Vasa, S. F., Maag, J. W., Torrey, G. K., & Kramer, J. J. (1994). Teachers' use and perceptions of sociometric techniques. *Journal of Psychoeducational Assessment, 12,* 135–141.

Vaughn, B., & Waters, E. (1981). Attention structure, sociometric status, and dominance: Interrelations, behavioral correlates and relationships to social competence. *Developmental Psychology, 17,* 275–288.

Verma, S., & Kumar, S. (1996, March). *Voices from the streets: Family life experiences of street children in Chandigarh.* Poster presented at the sixth biennial meeting of the Society for Research on Adolescence, Boston, MA.

Volling, B. L., MacKinnon-Lewis, C., Rabiner, D., & Baradaran, L. P. (1993). Children's social competence and sociometric status: Further exploration of aggression, social withdrawal, and peer rejection. *Development and Psychopathology, 5,* 459–483.

Vygotsky, L. S. (1978). *Mind in society: The development of higher psychological processes.* Cambridge, MA: Harvard University Press.

Waters, E., & Sroufe, L. A. (1983). Social competence as a developmental construct. *Developmental Review, 3,* 79–97.

Weiss, B., Dodge, K. A., Bates, J. E., & Pettit, G. S. (1992). Some consequences of early harsh discipline: Child aggression and maladaptive social information processing study. *Child Development, 63,* 1312–1335.

Wentzel, K. R., & Asher, S. R. (1995). The academic lives of neglected, rejected, popular, and controversial children. *Child Development, 66,* 754–763.

Wertsch, J. V. (1984). The zone of proximal development: Some conceptual issues. In B. Rogoff & J. V. Wertsch (Eds.), *Children's learning in the "zone of proximal development."* San Francisco: Jossey-Bass.

Wheeler, V. A., & Ladd, G. W. (1982). Assessment of children's self-efficacy for social interactions with peers. *Developmental Psychology, 18,* 795–805.

White, K. J., & Kistner, J. (1992). The influence of teacher feedback on young children's peer preferences and perceptions. *Developmental Psychology, 28,* 933–940.

White, S. (1959). Motivation reconsidered: The concept of competence. *Psychological Review, 66,* 297–333.

Whiting, B. B., & Edwards, C. P. (1988). *Children of different worlds: The formation of social behavior.* Cambridge, MA: Harvard University Press.

Wright, J. C., Giammarino, M., & Parad, H. W. (1986). Social status in small groups: Individual-group similarity and the social "misfit." *Journal of Personality and Social Psychology, 50,* 523–536.

Youngblade, L. M., & Belsky, J. (1992). Parent-child antecedents of five-year-olds' close friendships: A longitudinal analysis. *Developmental Psychology, 1,* 107–121.

Youngblade, L. M., Park, K. A., & Belsky, J. (1993). Measurement of young children's close friendship: A comparison of two independent assessment systems and their associations with attachment security. *International Journal of Behavioral Development, 16,* 563–587.

Younger, A. J., & Boyko, K. A. (1987). Aggression and withdrawal as social schemas underlying children's peer perceptions. *Child Development, 58,* 1094–1100.

Younger, A. J., Gentile, C., & Burgess, K. (1993). Children's perceptions of withdrawal: Changes across age. In K. H. Rubin & J. Asendorpf (Eds.), *Social withdrawal, inhibition, and shyness in childhood* (pp. 215–236). Hillsdale, NJ: Erlbaum.

Youniss, J. (1980). *Parents and peers in social development: A Sullivan-Piaget perspective.* Chicago: University of Chicago Press.

Youniss, J., & Smollar, J. (1985). *Adolescent relations with mothers, fathers, and friends.* Chicago: University of Chicago Press.

Zarbatany, L., Hartmann, D. P., & Rankin, D. B. (1990). The psychological functions of preadolescent peer activities. *Child Development, 61,* 1067–1980.

Zigler, E. (1973). Project Head Start: Success or failure? *Learning, 1,* 43–47.

CHAPTER 11

Prosocial Development

NANCY EISENBERG and RICHARD A. FABES

Writing of this chapter was supported by a grant from the National Science Foundation (DBS-9208375) to both authors and a Research Scientist Development Award from the National Institute of Mental Health (K02 MH00903) to Nancy Eisenberg.

Prosocial behavior—voluntary behavior intended to benefit another—is of obvious importance to the quality of social interactions between individuals and among groups. However, scientists did not devote much attention to prosocial development prior to 1970, perhaps because of the greater salience of the consequences of aggression, criminality, and immorality for society. In the 1970s, however, there was a sudden and notable increase in work on prosocial behavior in social and developmental psychology, with about 2% of the articles in the two premier developmental psychology journals concerning this topic (Bar-Tal, 1984). Interest in prosocial behavior continued in the 1980s and beyond. However, the number of studies primarily on prosocial behavior has dropped somewhat in the past few years, whereas studies in which prosocial has been examined in the larger context of social competence may have increased. Thus, the study of prosocial development is in its adolescence; much work has been conducted since 1970, but both relevant theory and the conceptual integration of existing empirical findings are in need of further development. In addition, there are relatively few theories pertaining to prosocial behavior in comparison to many other areas of study (e.g., achievement, aggression).

The purpose of this chapter is severalfold. First, although there is considerable empirical work on prosocial development, the field is at a stage where it is still possible to bring together, integrate, and interpret a large portion of the empirical work scattered across many literatures. We have tried to accomplish this task, although, due to space constraints, we built upon some previously published reviews and omitted some topics. In our review, we generally emphasize topics of central importance to prosocial development and issues that have emerged in the past decade. Further, we have confined our coverage to a somewhat narrow definition of prosocial responding (e.g., literature on cooperation or the allocation of rewards generally is not emphasized).

Other goals are to pinpoint some of the gaps and weaknesses in the work on prosocial behavior and to stimulate integration of this work with research and theory on other aspects of development. In our view, developments in work on emotion, regulatory abilities, social competence, interactions in familial systems (e.g., conflict in families), and other contemporary topics are highly relevant and can be used to broaden our understanding of prosocial responding.

As stated previously, we define prosocial behavior as voluntary behavior intended to benefit another. Prosocial behaviors may be performed for a host of reasons, including egoistic, other-oriented, and practical concerns. Of particular importance for an understanding of morality, however, is the subgroup of prosocial behaviors labeled *altruism*. One common definition of altruism is intrinsically motivated, voluntary behavior intended to benefit another: acts motivated by internal motives such as concern for others or by internalized values, goals, and self-rewards rather than by the expectation of concrete or social rewards or the avoidance of punishment (Eisenberg & Mussen, 1989). Because of the emphasis on internalized motives and values, altruism is particularly relevant to an understanding of the development of morality. However, because it usually is impossible to differentiate between altruistically motivated actions and those motivated by less noble concerns, it is necessary to focus on the broader domain of prosocial behaviors.

In our view, emotion plays an important role in the development of prosocial values, motives, and behaviors. Particularly relevant are *empathy*-related emotions. Definitions of empathy vary; we define it as an affective response that stems from the apprehension or comprehension of another's emotional state or condition, and that is identical or very similar to what the other person is feeling or would be expected to feel.

It is important to differentiate empathy from related vicarious emotional responses, particularly sympathy and personal distress. *Sympathy* is an affective response that frequently stems from empathy (but can derive directly from perspective taking or other cognitive processing), and consists of feelings of sorrow or concern for the distressed or needy other (rather than the same emotion as the other person). *Personal distress* also frequently stems from exposure to another's state or condition; however, it is a self-focused, aversive emotional reaction to the vicarious experiencing of another's emotion (e.g., discomfort, anxiety; see Batson, 1991; Eisenberg, Shea, Carlo, & Knight, 1991).

As is discussed later, empathy and sympathy have been strongly implicated in prosocial development and action. Thus, these vicarious emotional reactions are examined to some degree throughout the chapter. However, our focus on empathy-related emotions is confined to their relevance for prosocial behavior and their relations to variables considered to be antecedents or correlates of children's prosocial behavior.

In the initial sections of this chapter, we briefly discuss philosophical perspectives on prosocial development, as well as several grand psychological theories that have influenced the field. Then the empirical literature related to prosocial responding in children is reviewed. In the final sections of the chapter, a model for integrating the various factors believed to relate to prosocial responding is presented briefly, and gaps in the field and future directions are discussed.

PHILOSOPHICAL ROOTS OF PROSOCIAL BEHAVIOR

Philosophical concepts of prosocial behavior and sympathy often have roots in religious doctrine. As an example, the commandment "Thou shalt love they neighbor as thyself" is a basic tenet in Judaism and Christianity. Similarly, the parable of the Good Samaritan who pitied and helped an injured man (Luke 10:29–37) often is cited as an example for Christians. In Buddhism, the *via positiva* outlines the virtues necessary to reach *Nirvana* (ultimate happiness), including *dana* (giving), *metta* (kindness), *mudita* (sympathetic joy), and *karuna* (compassion). Indeed, the importance of compassion and altruism is fundamental tenets in Buddhism (Dalai Lama, personal communication, October 1995). Similar principles are evident in many religions.

Given the influence of religion in philosophy, it is not surprising that the sources of prosocial and moral behaviors have been discussed by philosophers for centuries. Of particular relevance, philosophers have debated whether any human action is truly unselfish and, relatedly, whether it is unreasonable to behave in a manner contrary to one's own self-interest (the doctrine of ethical egoism). According to Thomas Hobbes (1651/1962), a vocal advocate of egoism and self-love, selfishness might produce helping, but the motivation for such prosocial action would primarily be to relieve the helper's own distress. He also believed that the only motivation for cooperative action lay in the fear of some outside agent.

Later philosophers began to refute the doctrine of ethical egoism. For example, Rousseau (1773/1962) believed that human nature was basically good and that humans have an innate sensitivity toward others. In his view, if individuals were able to develop this natural state of nobility and sensitivity, a strong sense of moral obligation to others and concern for the common good would emerge. He believed society corrupts this innate moral nature.

Kant (1785/1956) also refuted the doctrine of ethical egoism and argued that if an action is one's duty, that is reason enough to do it, independent of one's own interests.

According to Kant, prosocial and moral behavior and values involve will and self-control and stem from universal, impartial principles that are totally detached from emotion.

Similarly, Nagel (1970) differentiated between "pure" rational altruism and behavior motivated by sympathy, love, or other emotions. In his view, the involvement of affect in the helping process tainted its purity. In contrast, David Hume (1748/1975) argued that moral emotions such as sympathy, benevolence, and concern for humanity are fundamental incentives of human action and that prosocial behaviors often are based on these incentives. Susceptibility to sympathy and empathy was viewed as an innate human propensity. Similarly, sympathy and related affective responses were core elements of A. Smith's (1759/1982) moral and social system. Smith believed that sympathy was an innate endowment, instigated by the perception of others' conditions and the desire to see them happy for purely altruistic reasons. However, for Smith, sympathy was not solely a primitive awareness of others' suffering; it was a complex capacity influenced by awareness of aspects of the situation or the person involved.

Lawrence Blum (1980) has been particularly vocal in refuting some of Kant's ideas about the role of emotion in morality. He pointed out that rational processes do not always produce moral action and that the sense of duty (viewed by Kant as rational) is no more immune to the distorting and weakening effects of personal feelings than is sympathy for another. Blum further suggested that because emotions such as sympathy and empathy promote perspective taking and understanding of others, they sometimes produce rationality and may induce more and higher-quality prosocial behavior than does rationality.

In summary, philosophers have viewed people as primarily egoistic, primarily noble and generous, or somewhere in between. Philosophical debate about the nature and existence of altruism is alive and well in contemporary psychology, particularly in social psychology (e.g., Batson, 1991). However, given the difficulty in discriminating motives for children's prosocial behavior, philosophical concerns are not highly salient in developmental work and are reflected primarily in work on empathy and sympathy and in work on moral judgment influenced by cognitive developmental theory (discussed subsequently). Indeed, much of the influence of philosophy on theory and research concerning prosocial behavior has been through its influence on the grand theories in developmental psychology.

PSYCHOLOGICAL THEORIES

Recent work on prosocial behavior has been influenced by a number of mini-theories, such as Hoffman's theoretical contributions to understanding empathy (1982) and socialization (1970b, 1983), and Grusec's (e.g., 1983; Grusec & Goodnow, 1994) and Staub's (1979, 1992) thinking about socialization. Some of these conceptual frameworks are referred to briefly later in this chapter. In addition to such mini-theories, the grand theories that have had considerable influence on developmental psychology have affected thinking about prosocial development, particularly in the past. Thus, pertinent ideas in psychoanalytic, learning, social learning, and cognitive developmental theory are reviewed briefly.

Psychoanalytic Theory

In Freud's psychoanalytic theory, children are born with innate, irrational sexual and aggressive impulses directed toward self-gratification (the id). They develop a conscience or superego at about age 4 to 6 years as a means of resolving the conflict between their own hostile and sexual impulses and their fears of parental hostility or the loss of parental love. The superego is the outcome of the process of identification by which children "internalize" their parents and "introject" their values. Once children develop a superego, they may behave prosocially due to guilt inflicted by the conscience for not doing so or based on the internalization of values consistent with prosocial behavior (e.g., S. Freud, 1933/1968).

In many versions of psychoanalytic theory, guilt, self-destructive tendencies, and sexual strivings underlie altruism (Fenichel, 1945; Glover, 1968). Prosocial actions often are defense mechanisms used to by the ego (the rational part of personality) to deal with the superego. As examples, a person may act prosocially to conceal and keep in check avaricious tendencies, a defense called reaction formation, or a person may subordinate his or her interests to those of others as a means of resolving internal conflict (A. Freud, 1946).

However, Freud and other psychoanalysts sometimes have acknowledged more positive roots of altruism. For example, S. Freud (1930) asserted that, "Individual development seems to us a product of the interplay of two trends, the striving for happiness, generally called 'egoistic,' and the impulse towards merging with others in the community, which we call 'altruistic'" (p. 134).

Other psychoanalytic theorists, such as Ekstein (1978), have built on Freud's emphasis on the importance of the early mother-child relationship: "Those first preverbal cues between mother and infant, this first struggle between waiting and satisfying one's self, are the external organizers of later empathic understanding and of sympathy and altruism. Good mothering, analysts maintain, makes for good empathy. Empathy is the forerunner of the capacity for imitation, for identification and for internalization" (p. 169).

Perhaps the greatest contribution of psychoanalytic work to theory on prosocial responding is the construct of identification. Social learning theorists in the 1960s and 1970s adapted this construct to refer to children's internalization of parents' norms, values, and standards as a consequence of a positive parent-child relationship (e.g., Hoffman, 1970b; Rutherford & Mussen, 1968). This theoretical perspective had a significant impact on the early work on the socialization of altruism.

Behaviorism and Social Learning Theory

Early behaviorists posited that children learn primarily through mechanisms such as conditioning and contingencies. Behaviors that are reinforced continue; those that are punished drop from the child's repertoire. This perspective is reflected in some of the relatively early work on the role of reinforcement and punishment in promoting prosocial behavior (e.g., Gelfand, Hartmann, Cromer, Smith, & Page, 1975; Hartmann et al., 1976) and in work concerning the development of empathy through conditioning (Aronfreed, 1970).

In modifications of behaviorism, social learning theorists allow internal cognitive processes to play a greater role. For example, contingencies need not actually occur; people learn through observation and verbal behavior the likely consequences of a behavior. Imitation is viewed as a critical process in the socialization of moral behavior and standards (Bandura, 1986).

In current cognitive social learning theory, the interplay of cognition and environmental influences in moral development is complex. According to Bandura (1986, 1991; also see Hoffman, 1983), moral rules or standards of behavior are fashioned from information from a variety of social sources, including tuition, others' evaluative social reactions, and models. Based on experience, people learn what factors are morally relevant and how much value to attach to each. For example, socializers provide information about behavioral alternatives, expectations, and possible contingencies for different courses of action, model moral behaviors, reinforce and punish children for various actions, and influence the development of self-evaluative reactions (e.g., guilt). Moreover, thought, behavior, and environmental events all interact and influence one another, and the individual's attentional and regulatory processes play a role in the learning of moral behavior.

Cognitive Developmental Theory

The cognitive developmental perspective on morality, as represented by the work of Piaget (1932/1965) and Kohlberg (e.g., 1969, 1984), concerns primarily the development of moral reasoning and other social cognitive processes rather than moral behavior. Kohlberg described moral development as an invariant, hierarchical sequence of stages of moral reasoning, which progress as a function of sociocognitive development (e.g., perspective taking; Turiel, Ch. 13, this Volume). Each stage is viewed as distinct or qualitatively different in structure from previous stages and is believed to displace and reintegrate or reorganize structures at lower stages. These moral judgment stages were "described in cognitive structural terms even in regard to 'affective' aspects of moral judgment, like guilt, empathy, etc." (Kohlberg, 1969, p. 390). Thus, Kohlberg emphasized the contributions of cognition, particularly perspective taking, to morality and minimized (but did not fully neglect) the contributions of emotion and socialization. Moreover, because of Piaget's and Kohlberg's assumption that young children have limited perspective-taking abilities, for years investigators influenced by cognitive developmental work assumed that other-oriented prosocial behavior was not likely to emerge until the early school years.

The cognitive developmental perspective is discussed at length by Turiel (Ch. 13, this Volume). Its primary relevance for this chapter is that Kohlberg's theory influenced Eisenberg's (e.g., Eisenberg, 1986) work on prosocial moral reasoning. However, although Eisenberg views sociocognitive development as playing an important role in the development of prosocial moral reasoning, she does not view all her stages of reasoning as universal or as involving hierarchical integration of lower stages. Rather, environmental and emotional factors are believed to play a considerable role in the development and use of prosocial moral reasoning. Thus, Eisenberg's conception of moral reasoning differs considerably from the traditional cognitive developmental perspective.

Now that the religious, philosophical, and theoretic roots of work on prosocial responding have been reviewed briefly, we turn to the review of the empirical literature. We first examine the potential origins of prosocial behavior (biological, cultural, and socialization), followed by consideration of the sociocognitive, empathy-related, dispositional, and situational correlates of prosocial behavior. In the final sections, age and sex differences in prosocial behavior are considered.

BIOLOGICAL DETERMINANTS OF PROSOCIAL BEHAVIOR

Based on evolutionary theory and sociobiology, there has been considerable discussion of the biological bases of altruism in animals and humans. Much of the existing work on the biological origins of prosocial behavior concerns the validity of evolutionary explanations for prosocial behavior. Because evolutionary theories are not directly relevant to a developmental focus on prosocial behavior, we do not discuss them in this chapter (Eisenberg, Fabes, & Miller, 1990; Trivers, 1971; E. Wilson, 1978). Rather, research relevant to the heritability of prosocial tendencies and possible biological mediators of these tendencies is reviewed.

Is There an Innate Bias toward Prosocial Tendencies?

Some theorists have argued that humans are biologically predisposed to experience empathy and positive other-oriented emotions and, thus, are biologically predisposed to enact altruistic behavior. For example, Hoffman (1981) cited (a) evolutionary arguments that altruism and empathy are widespread among humans, (b) research concerning a possible neural basis for empathy in the limbic system, and (c) the fact that 1- and 2-day-old infants cry in response to another infant's cry (e.g., Martin & Clark, 1982) as evidence of the innate basis of empathy and altruism. The presence of helping and sharing among many animals (E. Wilson, 1978) also supports the notion of a biological basis for altruism. In addition, the Dalai Lama (personal communication, October 1995), the leader of a large branch of the Buddhist religion, has argued that the near-universal tendency for infants to develop attachments involving love and caring is evidence that there is a strong biological predisposition toward altruism.

It appears that humans are biologically equipped to experience empathy and to develop prosocial behaviors; otherwise, prosocial behaviors probably would not be so common among people, even young children. Perhaps more interesting issues concern the role of biology in individual differences in empathy and altruism and the neural-physiological processes that may play a role in prosocial development.

Heritability of Prosocial Tendencies

Twin studies have been used to examine the genetic contribution to individual differences in prosocial responding. In these studies, if the correlation between scores on prosocial responding is higher for identical twins than for fraternal twins, the difference is attributed to genetic effects to the degree that common environmental sources are assumed to be roughly equal for the two types of twins.

In twin studies involving self-report data from adults, researchers found that approximately 50% of the variance in twins' altruism, empathy, and nurturance was accounted for by genetic factors. Most of the remaining 50% of the variance was accounted for by idiosyncratic differences in the environments of the twins (and not by common shared environment; Matthews, Batson, Horn, & Rosenman, 1981; Rushton, Fulker, Neal, Nias, & Eysenck, 1986; also see Davis, Luce, & Kraus, 1994). It is important to note, however, that the participants in these studies were adults. Given that common shared variance is likely to decrease with age (Scarr & McCartney, 1983), it may not be surprising that common environments had so little effect in this study.

More recently, Zahn-Waxler, Emde, and colleagues (Plomin et al., 1993; Zahn-Waxler, Robinson, & Emde, 1992) examined twin children's reactions to simulations of distress in others (in both home and laboratory settings). Estimates of heritability indicated a significant genetic component for empathic concern, prosocial acts, and maternal reports of prosocial acts at 14 months of age, albeit the variance accounted for was much less than 50% for all but maternal reports. At 20 months, empathic concern (sympathy) during simulations and maternal reports of prosocial acts (but not prosocial acts themselves) continued to evidence significant genetic contributions. Unresponsiveness and active indifference also showed genetic

influence at both time periods; however, there was no evident of heritability for self-distress at either 14 or 20 months (Zahn-Waxler, Robinson, & Emde, 1992). Moreover, Plomin et al. (1993) found no evidence for genetic influence on change in a composite index of empathy from 14 to 20 months of age, although genetic factors partially accounted for stability over time in empathy.

Neurophysiological Underpinnings of Prosocial Responding

Behavioral genetics research has merely documented the presence and size of genetic contributions to prosocial behavior; it does not identify the conditions or processes of organism-environment interaction through which genotypes are transformed into phenotypes. Research and theory on the neurological processes may provide a mechanism for mediation between genetics and overt behavior. For example, Panksepp (1986) suggested that brain opioids influence the degree to which social contact is reinforcing and that fluctuations in brain opioids and the underlying emotive systems affect altruistic behavior. Panksepp also hypothesized that during social interactions (which are affected by brain opioids), animals may become better attuned to the emotions of their conspecifics and thereby become better able to alleviate others' distress when it occurs.

Panksepp (1986) asserted that all mammalian helping behavior arises from the "nurturant dictates of brain systems that mediate social bonding and maternal care" (p. 44). This view is consistent with that of MacLean (1985), who argued that the basis for altruism lies in maternal behavior, affiliation, and play, which are mediated in part by the limbic system of the brain. MacLean further suggested that it is the development of the prefrontal neocortex, which occurred relatively recently in evolution and is most distinctive in humans, that provides the basis for concern for others and a sense of responsibility and conscience (also see Brothers, 1989).

Research and theory related to temperament may provide additional mechanisms for explicating links between constitutional factors and prosocial behavior. If certain traits with a constitutional basis relate to prosocial behavior, then research on the neural bases for these traits may help us understand the neural mechanisms that are linked to the development of prosocial behavior. For example, temperamentally based regulatory processes may play a role in sympathetic responding and prosocial behavior. Although work in regard to the physiological underpinnings of temperament is preliminary, it is likely to yield information pertaining to the biological bases of prosocial responding in the future.

In summary, it is likely that biological factors play some role in individual differences in empathy and prosocial behavior. However, much of the relevant research on biological mechanisms comes from work with nonhumans, and existing behavioral genetics work is limited in quantity and scope. Further, pertinent theory is very speculative, and issues regarding cause and effect are still unresolved. For example, increased opioid production may affect play and gregarious behaviors, but it is also likely that play and gregarious behaviors affect opioid production. Finally, as is reviewed shortly, there is impressive evidence that the environment plays a critical role in prosocial development. The key to understanding human prosocial behavior lies in determining how biological influences, prior environmental influences on the child, and the current context jointly affect prosocial behavior and development (with the influence of biology being probablistic rather than deterministic; Wachs, 1994).

CULTURAL FACTORS

Research on the cultural bases of prosocial responding provides insights into the role of the environment, in contrast to strictly biological factors, in prosocial development. However, despite current interest in cultural influences on emotion and behavior, there has been surprisingly little research concerning cultural influences on prosocial development. Nonetheless, it is clear from the anthropological literature and psychological studies in non-Western cultures that societies vary greatly in the degree to which prosocial and cooperative behaviors are normative (e.g., Mead, 1935). In studies of individual cultures, some writers have described societies in which prosocial and communal values and behaviors are (or were in the past) highly valued and common, such as the Aitutaki (a Polynesian island people; Graves & Graves, 1983) and the Papago tribe in Arizona (Rohner, 1975; see Eisenberg, 1992, for a review). In contrast, other social and behavioral scientists have described cultures in which prosocial behaviors were rare and cruelty or hostility was the norm, such as the Ik of Uganda (Turnbull, 1972) and the Alorese (on an island east of Java; Rohner, 1975; also see Goody, 1991). Moreover, societal experiments such as the communally oriented kibbutz in Israel support the view

that subcultural variations can have a substantial impact on prosocial values and behavior (Aviezer, Van IJzendoorn, Sagi, & Schuengel, 1994).

Research in which prosocial behaviors and values have been contrasted across cultures is consistent with single-culture studies in highlighting the importance of culture in prosocial development. Relevant investigations include laboratory studies, naturalistic observational research, and studies of moral reasoning and values in various cultures.

Laboratory Studies

Much of the work on cross-cultural and subcultural variation in prosocial behavior is embedded in the research on cooperation, competition, and allocation behavior. In many studies, cooperation involved overt self-gain; thus, this work is not reviewed. However, it is noteworthy that researchers consistently have found that children from traditional rural and semi-agricultural communities and relatively traditional subcultures (e.g., Mexican American children) are more cooperative than children from urban or Westernized cultures (see Eisenberg & Mussen, 1989).

In other studies, children were asked to make a series of choices concerning the distribution of chips (or other objects) to the self and a peer when giving the peer more chips did not change the child's own yield. In general, Mexican American children give more to the peer than do AngloAmerican children (Kagan & Knight, 1979, 1981; Knight, Nelson, Kagan, & Gumbiner, 1982), and the difference increases in magnitude from age 5 to 6 years to age 8 to 9 years (Knight & Kagan, 1977b). Sometimes, however, there have been no significant differences between groups in the selection of options in which the peer received more chips than the child (e.g., Kagan & Knight, 1981; Knight & Kagan, 1982; Knight, Nelson, et al., 1982; also see Graziano, Musser, Rosen, & Shaffer, 1982). The tendency to choose more for the peer than for the self is stronger in second- than third-generation Mexican American children (Knight & Kagan, 1977a), suggesting effects of acculturation.

In another variation on this task, some of the choices allow the child to give more to the peer at a cost to the self. Mexican American or Mexican children still tend to give more chips overall to a peer than do Anglo American children, although the two groups of children sometimes have differed in regard to specific choices involving cost to the self (Kagan & Madsen, 1972b; Knight, Kagan, & Buriel, 1981) and sometimes have not (e.g., Avellar & Kagan,

1976; Kagan, 1977). Mexican American children with a stronger ethnic identity have been found to display more concern with others' outcomes on this type of task, although few children maximized others' outcomes at a cost to the self (Knight, Cota, & Bernal, 1993). On a similar task, Cook Island Polynesian children were more generous than were New Zealand city and rural children (Graves & Graves, 1983).

Findings for other types of prosocial tasks have not produced consistent evidence of cultural effects. For example, rural Mexican children and Anglo American city children were equally likely to help a peer in a noncompetitive context (Kagan & Madsen, 1972a), and Mexican American and Anglo American children did not differ in anonymous sharing of candy with an unspecified classmate (Hansen & Bryant, 1980). Israeli kibbutz fifth-grade boys, but not girls, shared more than did city children (Nadler, Romek, & Shapira-Friedman, 1979), although 5-year-old kibbutz and city children did not differ in prosocial behavior (Bizman, Yinon, Mivtzari, & Shavit, 1978; also see Bar-Tal, Raviv, & Shavit, 1981). Differences in kibbutz and non-kibbutz people may increase with age; researchers have found that kibbutz adults are more helpful than people raised in small agricultural communities without a communal philosophy and than city dwellers in Israel (Yinon, Sharon, Azgad, & Barshir, 1981).

Observational Research

Systematic observation of prosocial behavior in different cultures is rare. In the classic study by Whiting and Whiting (1973, 1975), prosocial behavior was operationalized as a composite index of offering helping (including food, toys, and helpful information), offering support, and making helpful suggestions. Cultures in which children scored relatively high on prosocial behavior (Kenya, Mexico, Philippines) tended to differ from the other three cultures (Okinawa, India, and the United States) on several dimensions. In prosocial cultures, people tended to live together in extended families, the female role was important (with women making major contributions to the economic status of the family), work was less specialized, and the government was less centralized. Further, children's prosocial behavior was associated with early assignment of chores and taking on responsibility for the family's economic welfare and the welfare of family members (also see Whiting & Edwards, 1988). Consistent with the data on chores, Graves and Graves (1983), in an observational study of Polynesian

children from Aitutaki, found that children, particularly girls, from urban settings performed fewer chores and were less prosocial than were children raised in traditional extended families.

More recently, Stevenson (1991) found that the incidence of sharing, comforting, and helping in Taiwanese, Japanese, and U.S. kindergarten classes was lowest in the United States (albeit relatively high in all groups). Stevenson and others have argued that Chinese and Japanese societies generally put great emphasis on socializing children to be responsible and prosocial toward others in the group (e.g., the family, the group in the classroom, and the society; also see Hieshima & Schneider, 1994). For example, privileges and social acknowledgment in the classroom are dependent on group rather than individual accomplishments. However, parental valuing of prosocial behavior appears to have declined from the 1950s and 1960s to the 1980s in the People's Republic of China (Lee & Zhan, 1991). Moreover, as was observed by Stevenson (1991), a strong emphasis on subordinating the self to the group interest can be used to justify aggression toward outsiders and ethnocentrism.

Although children in some non-Western cultures may be more prosocial than children in industrialized Western societies, there are few data on processes that may mediate cultural differences in prosocial behavior. Some researchers have hypothesized that tender, responsive parenting is an important factor in cultural differences in prosocial dispositions (e.g., Mead, 1935; Rohner, 1975), but there is little direct evidence for this idea (Knight, Kagan, & Buriel, 1982). Moreover, Goody (1991) argued that although some small-scale face-to-face societies (e.g., the African Mbuti) foster prosocial behavior within a secure, benevolent setting involving warm parent-child and peer relationships, other cultures view the outside world as dangerous and use fear to foster dependence among members of the group.

Moral Reasoning, Values, and Beliefs about Social Responsibility

Cultural norms regarding the importance of harmony among people and social responsibility clearly differ across cultures and subcultures (e.g., Stevenson, 1991). For example, Joan Miller and her colleagues (J. Miller, Bersoff, & Harwood, 1990) have found that Hindu Indian culture forwards a broader and more stringent duty-based view of social responsibility than does American culture. Hindu

Indians, school-aged and adult, tend to focus more than Americans on nonresponsiveness to others' needs in discussing moral conflicts and view interpersonal responsibilities as at least as important as justice-related obligations (J. Miller & Bersoff, 1992). In contrast, Americans tend to view interpersonal responsiveness and caring as less obligatory and more of a personal choice, particularly if the other's need is moderate or minor, or if friends or strangers (rather than parents and children) are potential recipients (J. Miller et al., 1990). J. Miller and Bersoff (1992) argued that a personal morality of interpersonal responsiveness and caring (such as that in the United States) is linked to a strong cultural emphasis on individual rights.

A body of work relevant to an understanding of cross-cultural variation in cognition about prosocial behavior is the research on prosocial moral reasoning (also see Ma, 1985). Among industrial Western cultures, relatively few cross-cultural differences in reasoning have been noted, although minor differences have been found. For example, school-age children in Germany and Israel have been found to emphasize direct reciprocity more than children from the United States (Eisenberg, Boehnke, Schuhler, & Silbereisen, 1985; Fuchs, Eisenberg, Hertz-Lazarowitz, & Sharabany, 1986), and Israeli kibbutz children tend to verbalize high levels of concern with the humanness of recipients and internalized values and norms (Fuchs et al., 1986; also see Eisenberg, Hertz-Lazarowitz, & Fuchs, 1990). Moreover, Carlo, Koller, Eisenberg, Pacheco, and Loguercio (1996) found that Brazilian urban adolescents used less internalized (i.e., higher level) prosocial moral reasoning than did adolescents from the United States, although their reasoning was similar otherwise. The similarities in reasoning in Western cultures are much greater than the differences, and even Japanese children's prosocial moral reasoning resembles that of children from urbanized Western cultures (Munekata & Ninomiya, 1985). Moreover, the reasons that German, Polish, Italian, and American adolescents attribute to themselves for helping or not helping are somewhat similar, although some differences have been found (Boehnke, Silbereisen, Eisenberg, Reykowski, & Palmonari, 1989; also see Silbereisen, Lamsfuss, Boehnke, & Eisenberg, 1991).

In contrast, the prosocial moral reasoning of children and adults from non-Western, nonindustrial cultures may differ considerably from that of people from Western cultures. Tietjen (1986) found that although younger Maisen children from Papua New Guinea differed little in their prosocial moral reasoning from children in Western cultures, Maisen adults' moral reasoning was less sophisticated than that of Western adults. Maisen adults' reasoning, however, was probably appropriate for a small, traditional society in which others' physical and psychological needs, costs for prosocial behavior, and pragmatic concerns are paramount to everyday life. Of particular interest, Maisen children's reasoning became more hedonistic as they entered school and hedonism peaked in third grade, perhaps due to exposure to Western values, whereas Western children's hedonistic reasoning initially is quite high and decreases with age in elementary school (Eisenberg, 1986).

One difficulty in making cross-cultural comparisons is that cultures differ considerably in valuing of different types of prosocial actions. For example, Hindu Indians view prosocial behavior performed because of reciprocity considerations as more moral than do American adults (J. Miller & Bersoff, 1994). Further, Middle Eastern third graders in Israel seem to value requested acts of consideration more, and spontaneous acts less, than do Israeli Jewish children of Western heritage (Jacobsen, 1983). Thus, Westerners may value prosocial acts that appear to be based on endogenous motivation more than do people from traditional cultures, whereas people from traditional cultures value prosocial actions that reflect responsiveness to others' stated needs and reciprocal obligations.

Summary

There appear to be differences across cultures in the degree to which children display prosocial behavior in the classroom and everyday life, although most of this prosocial behavior is directed toward known individuals and much of it may not be costly. Further, prosocial moral reasoning and prosocial values can vary greatly among cultures that differ in degree of modernity and in religious and cultural values. In some cultures, helpfulness and social responsibilities are emphasized more than individual rights, gain, and achievement, and this difference in values is reflected in thinking about prosocial behavior.

It is not as clear whether there are cross-cultural differences in prosocial actions directed toward those who are not part of the child's group, especially if assisting has a cost. Further, it is not known if aspects of socialization in the family besides assignment of chores play a role in the observed cross-cultural variation. There is a strong need for work in which factors that mediate and moderate cross-cultural differences in prosocial behavior are examined.

SOCIALIZATION WITHIN AND OUTSIDE THE FAMILY

Familial structure, socialization within the family, and socialization by peers and in the schools are factors that may augment or counteract cultural influences. These potential influences are now examined. However, it is necessary to note briefly limitations of the existing research, including an overreliance on parental reports of the child's prosocial proclivities and of socialization measures, the use of very brief observations to measure behavior (which may not be generalizable), and a dearth of data from non-Western cultures and minority populations. Further, most of the work is correlational so that causal relations cannot be ascertained. The prevailing view of socialization is that the parent-child relationship is bidirectional in influence and complex (Bugental & Goodnow, this volume), and this relationship (and its outcomes) is embedded in the larger family, neighborhood, and culture. However, this complexity generally is not reflected in the existing empirical research on the socialization of prosocial behavior.

Demographic Features of Families and Family Members

Intuitively, one might expect children's prosocial behavior to be related to the socioeconomic status (SES) of their families. Poorer children might be expected to horde scarce resources or, due to increased demand for participation in caregiving chores, to be relatively helpful and likely to comfort others in distress (Whiting & Whiting, 1975).

In fact, findings in regard to the relation of SES to prosocial behavior are inconsistent. Researchers have found results favoring higher-SES children (e.g., middle-class; Doland & Adelberg, 1967; Payne, 1980; Ramsey, 1988; Raviv & Bar-Tal, 1981), lower-SES children (Eisenberg, Fabes, Carlo et al., 1993; Gupta, 1982; Knight, 1982; Rehberg & Richman, 1989; Ugurel-Semin, 1952), and neither (Barrett, Radke-Yarrow, & Klein, 1982; Dreman & Greenbaum, 1973; Hertz-Lazarowitz, Fuchs, Sharabany, & Eisenberg, 1989). As suggested by Call, Mortimer, and Shanahan (1995), one possibility is that higher SES is associated with some types of prosocial behavior outside of the home, whereas lower SES is associated with helpfulness in the home setting.

Family structure might play a role in social status differences in prosocial behavior. Rehberg and Richman (1989) found that preschool boys from father-absent homes comforted (but did not help) a peer more than did girls and boys from two-parent homes (also see Richman, Berry, Bittle, & Himan, 1988). Children's comforting behavior was positively related with parental dependency on the child, and such dependency (including the need for help with chores) was particularly high for boys in mother-headed homes. However, other researchers have not found effects of father absence on measures of prosocial responding (Call et al., 1995; Hoffman, 1971; Rigby, 1993, Santrock, 1975a). Further, Keith, Nelson, Schlabach, and Thompson (1990) found that 10- to 14-year-olds from two-parent families in which one parent was not employed participated in more volunteer activities than did adolescents from single-parent families.

Parental presence versus absence may have effects on children's prosocial development. Musun-Miller (1991) found that siblings were more helpful in the presence of their mothers than in mother's absence. In a single-parent family, the parent often may not be at home, and this may lessen opportunities for the socialization of certain types of sibling- or peer-related prosocial behaviors or for involvement in volunteer activities out of the home. Children from single-parent families also might be more likely to work, and work does not appear to foster adolescents' concern for others (Steinberg, Greenberger, Garduque, Ruggiero, & Vaux, 1982).

Findings for family size also are inconsistent. Some investigators have found that family size and prosocial behavior or sympathy are unrelated (Cauley & Tyler, 1989; Dreman & Greenbaum, 1973; Gelfand et al., 1975; Handlon & Gross, 1959; Harris, 1967; Hull & Reuter, 1977; Loban, 1953). Others have found that children in a large family are more generous (Ugurel-Semin, 1952) but less likely to help in emergency situations (Staub, 1971a, 1971c) or comfort a peer (Rehberg & Richman, 1989). Staub speculated that children from small families are more self-assured and, consequently, are more likely to take initiative and intervene spontaneously to help someone else. In contrast, perhaps children in larger families, due to the need to engage in chores, are particularly likely to learn everyday helping and sharing behaviors. Consistent with this reasoning, Weissbrod (1976) found that large family size was related to slower helping in an emergency but higher levels of generosity.

Findings concerning ordinal position are limited. Firstborn children, particularly girls, have been found to be more willing to give commodities to peers (Knight, 1982; Sharma, 1988a) and to intervene in an emergency (Staub, 1971c). Moreover, older siblings, in comparison to younger siblings, more often behave prosocially in sibling interactions (Brody, Stoneman, MacKinnon, & MacKinnon, 1985; Bryant & Crockenberg, 1980; Dunn & Munn, 1986; Eisenberg, Fabes, Karbon, Murphy, Carlo, & Wosinski, 1996; Furman & Buhrmester, 1985; Stoneman, Brody, & MacKinnon, 1986; Whiting & Whiting, 1975). However, other investigators have found no relation between birth order and various measures of prosocial responding (Gelfand et al., 1975; Harris, 1967; Honig, Douthit, Lee, & Dingler, 1992; Hull & Reuter, 1977; Musun-Miller, 1991; Rheingold, Hay, & West, 1976) or sympathy (Loban, 1953; Wise & Cramer, 1988), or have found younger siblings to be more prosocial than firstborns (Raviv & Bar-Tal, 1981). In general, it appears that older children are somewhat more prosocial, especially in regard to actual (rather than reported) prosocial behavior and in interactions with younger children. However, it is possible that only children are not particularly prosocial (Chong-de, 1988).

Parental Disciplinary Practices

Many investigators have examined the relations of specific disciplinary practices to children's prosocial behavior.

Inductions

A disciplinary practice of particular salience in the study of prosocial behavior is parental inductions (i.e., techniques in which the adult gives explanations or reasons for requiring the child to change his or her behavior; Hoffman, 1970b). Hoffman (1970b, 1983) argued that inductions are likely to promote moral development because they induce an optimal level of arousal for learning (i.e., they elicit the child's attention, but are unlikely to disrupt learning). Further, inductions are not likely to be viewed as arbitrary by the child and thereby induce resistance; rather, they focus children's attention on consequences for others of their behavior, thereby capitalizing on children's capacity to empathize and experience guilt. Hoffman further suggested that over time, inductive messages are experienced as internalized because the child plays an active role in processing the information (which is encoded and integrated with information contained in other inductions), and the focus is on the child's action and its consequences rather than on the parent as the disciplinary agent. Thus, over time, children are likely to remember the causal link between their actions and consequences for others rather than the external pressure or the specific disciplinary context.

In research on inductions, investigators generally have tried to assess the degree to which parents use reasoning as a general mode of discipline, not simply to promote prosocial behavior (as for experimental studies on preaching). Inductions can be of several sorts: they can appeal to justice, including fairness of the consequences of the child's behavior for another; appeal to legitimate authorities (Henry, 1980); or provide matter-of-fact, nonmoralistic information (Henry, 1980; Hoffman, 1970a). In addition, inductions may be focused on the consequences of the child's behavior for either the parent or for the other person involved in the situation (often called peer-oriented). Hoffman (1970b) argued that peer-oriented inductions are likely to be most effective because they may induce sympathy. Although type of induction seldom has been differentiated in research studies, there is some evidence of peer-oriented inductions' efficacy (Thompson & Hoffman, 1980).

The degree to which parental inductions have been linked to prosocial behavior varies considerably across studies and across measures of prosocial responding. Results of studies in which the type of reasoning was not specified are particularly varied. Some researchers have obtained at least some evidence—often for one sex or grade group and not another—of a positive relation between parental use of inductive discipline and prosocial responding (Bar-Tal, Nadler, & Blechman, 1980; Dlugokinski & Firestone, 1974; Feshbach, 1978; Mussen, Rutherford, Harris, & Keasey, 1970; Oliner & Oliner, 1988). Others, often studying small samples (Mullis, Smith, & Vollmers, 1983; Trommsdorff, 1991), have not (Janssens & Gerris, 1992).

When researchers have differentiated among types of induction, results also have been somewhat mixed, with findings often varying by sex, age, or socioeconomic group, or measure of prosocial responding. However, usually investigators have found at least some support for a relation between prosocial behavior or sympathy and inductions focused on peers' or others' feelings or state (Hoffman & Saltzstein, 1967; Stanhope, Bell, & Parker-Cohen, 1987; also see Iannotti, Cummings, Pierrehumbert, Milano, & Zahn-Waxler 1992). For example, P. Miller, Eisenberg, Fabes, Shell, and Gular (1989) found that inductions regarding peers were positively related to children's sad reactions to viewing others in distress and, when delivered by mothers with affective intensity, to low levels of facial distress (an index of personal distress rather than sympathy).

Consistent with P. Miller et al.'s (1989) findings, Zahn-Waxler, Radke-Yarrow, and King (1979) found that maternal use of affectively charged explanations, particularly those including moralizing, was related to toddlers' prosocial behavior in the second and third year of life. Explanations delivered without affect were not effective, perhaps because the toddlers were unlikely to attend or to think that their mothers were serious. However, parental inductions delivered in situations involving relatively high degrees of anger, particularly inductions that are guilt-inducing, seem to be associated with low levels of preschoolers' parent-directed prosocial behavior (Denham, Renwick-DeBardi, & Hewes, 1994).

Different types of inductions may be associated with different moral orientations. Hoffman (1970b) found that children oriented toward conventional principles without regard to extenuating circumstances (i.e., who were rigid) had fathers who reported using inductions about harm to the parent. Children who were more humanistic (i.e., who stressed human needs as the underlying reason for compliance with rules and considered extenuating circumstances) reported that their mothers used more matter-of-fact inductions that pointed out the pragmatic requirements of the situation. There were no differences between the groups in receipt of inductions regarding peers, and both groups of children were exposed to inductions more than were children oriented toward external punishment as a reason for behavior.

Using a different conceptual framework, Karylowski (1982) compared Polish high school girls high in prosocial behavior motivated by concern about another's well-being (exocentric) with girls high in prosocial behavior motivated by its anticipated effects on one's own feelings of moral satisfaction and pride (endocentric). The former group was exposed to fewer inductions pointing out inconsistencies with regard to the requirements of the child's social role and more other-oriented inductions. Relatedly, Hoffman (1975a) found that parents who reported victim-oriented discipline (which often includes other-oriented inductions) tended to have same-sex children who were prosocial. Victim-oriented discipline seems to enhance the level of children's interpersonal understanding (e.g., perspective taking), which is associated with higher guilt, including concern about harm to another (de Veer & Janssens, 1994).

The configuration of parenting practices appears to influence the effectiveness of inductions. Inductions are more effective at promoting prosocial behavior if they are verbalized by parents who typically do not use power-assertive (punitive) techniques (Hoffman, 1963; also see Dlugokinski & Firestone, 1974) or are part of a pattern of democratic parenting (Dekovic & Janssens, 1992). In a study in which inductions were not correlated with prosocial behavior, maternal and paternal use of induction, combined with parental demands for mature behavior and

low power assertion, was linked to children's self-reported empathy, which in turn was associated with teachers' reports of the children's prosocial behavior (Janssens & Gerris, 1992).

In summary, the empirical findings on the relation of inductions to children's prosocial behavior vary considerably across studies. This is not surprising given that researchers often have not differentiated among various types of inductions and the measures of both induction and prosocial behavior differ across studies. Nonetheless, it appears that inductions that are victim- or peer-oriented are linked to some degree with children's prosocial behavior. Research on fathers is rare, so it is difficult to draw any firm conclusions about the role of paternal inductions. Further, the degree and valence of the association between inductive discipline and children's prosocial behavior likely varies as a function of the larger configuration of the parent's disciplinary practices, the child's socialization history, and the degree of affect associated with the delivery of inductions.

In addition, some of the inconsistency in findings may stem from failure to focus on critical dimensions of parental messages. Grusec and Goodnow (1994) argued that internalization of parental messages likely depends on children's accurate perception of the message (including its content, the rules implied in the message, and the parent's intentions and investment in the message) and children's acceptance of the message. According to Grusec and Goodnow, accurate perception of the message is influenced by the clarity, redundancy, and consistency of the message, as well as fit of the message to the child's developmental level. Acceptance is deemed as more likely if the message is perceived as appropriate by the child, is motivating (e.g., if empathy or insecurity is aroused), and fosters the perception that the value inherent in the message is self-generated. Grusec and Goodnow also hypothesized that parental responsivity or past willingness to comply with the child's wishes promotes the child's willingness to comply with the parents' wishes. Thus, it may be productive to examine clarity of parents' messages and variables related to children's acceptance of the message as moderators of the relation between parental inductions and children's prosocial behavior.

Power-Assertive, Punitive Techniques of Discipline

Researchers generally have found that socializers' use of power-assertive techniques of discipline such as physical punishment or deprivation of privileges is either unrelated (Feshbach, 1978; Janssens & Gerris, 1992; Mussen et al., 1970; Olejnik & McKinney, 1973; Zahn-Waxler et al.,

1979; also see Kochanska, Padavich, & Koenig, 1996) or negatively related (Bar-Tal, Nadler, & Blechman, 1980; Dlugokinski & Firestone, 1974; also see Janssens & Gerris, 1992) to children's prosocial development. Likewise, a punitive, authoritarian parenting style has been unrelated (Iannotti et al., 1992) or negatively related (Dekovic & Janssens, 1992) to children's prosocial behavior. Moreover, physical abuse of children has been linked to low levels of children's empathy and prosocial behavior (George & Main, 1979; Howes & Eldredge, 1985; Main & George, 1985; Straker & Jacobson, 1981; see P. Miller & Eisenberg, 1988), as well as inappropriate behavior (e.g., aggression) toward distressed peers (Howes & Eldredge, 1985; Klimes-Dougan & Kistner, 1990; Main & George, 1985). Indeed, researchers seldom have obtained positive relations between power assertion and children's prosocial behavior (see, however, Hoffman & Saltzstein, 1967; Knight, Kagan, & Buriel, 1982). The frequent use of power-assertive techniques by socializers who also are hostile and distant appears to be particularly inimicable to moral (including prosocial) development and may hinder the effectiveness of other socialization techniques that usually promote prosocial development (Dekovic & Janssens, 1992; Hoffman, 1963; also see Janssens & Gerris, 1992).

Indeed, power assertion has been associated with an external moral orientation (Hoffman, 1970a). As argued by Hoffman (1970a), children often attribute prosocial behavior induced by power-assertive techniques to external motives such as fear of detection or punishment (Dix & Grusec, 1983; Smith, Gelfand, Hartmann, & Partlow, 1979).

Nonetheless, as noted by Hoffman (1983) and Baumrind (1971), there is a difference between the occasional use of power-assertive techniques in the context of a positive parent-child relationship and the use of punishment as the preferred, predominant mode of discipline. When power-assertive techniques are used in a measured and rational manner by parents who generally are supportive and use non-power-assertive disciplinary techniques, there may be no negative effects on children's social behavior (Baumrind, 1971). Rescuers of Jews in Nazi Europe reported that the punishment they received from their parents was not a routine response and was linked to specific behaviors rather than used gratuitously (Oliner & Oliner, 1988). Further, consistent with the view that the use of reasoning can moderate the effects of punishment (if punishment is not the preferred mode of discipline), P. Miller et al. (1989) found that maternal report of using physical techniques (including physical punishment) was positively associated with preschoolers' empathic sadness when viewing others in distress, but only for children whose mothers also used relatively high levels of inductive discipline (cf. Hoffman, 1963).[1]

Of course, punishment can induce immediate compliance with a socializer's expectations for prosocial behavior if the socializer monitors the child's behavior (Morris, Marshall, & Miller, 1973) or is in view (DePalma, 1974), particularly if the contingency between lack of prosocial behavior and punishment is specified (Hartmann et al., 1976). However, these effects often extinguish when punishment is removed (Hartmann et al., 1976). Nevertheless, social disapproval, unlike material punishment (e.g., fines for not helping), has been associated with children's attributing their own donating to internal motives (Smith et al., 1979). Thus, it is possible that social disapproval (verbal punishment) can be used to enhance internally motivated prosocial behavior. However, most middle-class mothers in Western cultures such as the United States infrequently use punishment (especially physical punishment) to induce helping or in response to children's failure to help (Grusec, 1982; Zahn-Waxler et al., 1979).

Appropriate versus Inappropriate Parental Control

Perhaps the critical issue is whether the degree of power and control asserted by the parent is excessive and arbitrary versus reasonable. Parental demands and expectations for socially responsible and moral behavior have been associated with socially responsible and prosocial behavior (e.g., Baumrind, 1971, 1988; Dekovic & Janssens, 1992; Janssens & Gerris, 1992). Other research indicates a link between appropriate parental control (rather than leniency) and children's empathy (Bryant, 1987) and women's (but not men's) sympathy in adulthood (Koestner, Franz, & Weinberger, 1990). Finally, Greenberger and Goldberg (1989) found that parental demands for prosocial behavior in their 3- and 4-year-olds were associated with parental demands for self-control and independence, as well as fathers' firm responsive control. In middle-class families, parental demands for prosocial behavior may be part of a child-rearing pattern in which mature behavior is expected. In contrast, parental valuing of mere compliance, which often may lead to arbitrary overcontrol, has been linked to low levels of prosocial behavior with mothers and peers (Eisenberg, Wolchik, Goldberg, & Engel, 1992).

---

[1] Here and throughout the chapter, the term *cf.*, which means "compare with," signifies "contrast with" and is used to indicate that contrary findings were obtained in a study.

Parental Warmth and Quality of the Parent-Child Relationship

Intuitively, it would seem that warm, supportive socializers would rear prosocial children. However, support for this assumption is mixed. In a number of studies, a positive relation between an index of maternal warmth/support and prosocial or sympathetic responding has been obtained, at least for some measures (Bar-Tal, Nadler, & Blechman, 1980; Bryant & Crockenberg, 1980; Eberly, Montemayor, & Flannery, 1993; Frankel, Lindahl, & Harmon, 1992; Janssens & Gerris, 1992; Rigby, 1993; Robinson, Zahn-Waxler, & Emde, 1994; Zahn-Waxler et al., 1979; also see Eisenberg, Fabes, Schaller, Carlo, & Miller, 1991), particularly for boys (Feshbach, 1978; Hoffman, 1975a; Hoffman & Saltzstein, 1967; Rutherford & Mussen, 1968). In contrast, a number of investigators have obtained no evidence of a relation between parental warmth (or rejection) and children's prosocial behavior or sympathy (Iannotti et al., 1992; Koestner et al., 1990; Turner & Harris, 1984).

Support for the role of parental nurturance or warmth also can be gleaned from several other bodies of data. For example, researchers have found that mothers with sensitive comforting skills have children who have the ability to provide sensitive comforting (Burleson & Kunkel, 1995). Similarly, sympathetic parents tend to have same-sex children in elementary school who are helpful (Eisenberg, Fabes, Carlo, & Karbon, 1992; Fabes, Eisenberg, & Miller, 1990) or prone to sympathy rather than egoistic personal distress (Eisenberg, Fabes, Carlo, Troyer, et al., 1992; Eisenberg, Fabes, Schaller, Carlo, & Miller, 1991; Eisenberg & McNally, 1993; Fabes et al., 1990). Links between parental empathy (rather than sympathy) and children's empathy have been mixed, with some researchers obtaining positive relations (Barnett, Howard, King, & Dino, 1980; Trommsdorff, 1991) and others obtaining no or inconsistent correlations (Barnett, King, Howard, & Dino, 1980; Kalliopuska, 1984; Strayer & Roberts, 1989).

There also is some evidence, albeit limited, that children with secure attachments at a young age are more sympathetic at 3.5 years of age (Waters, Hay, & Richters, 1986) and display more prosocial behavior and/or concern for others at approximately age 5 (Iannotti et al., 1992; Kestenbaum, Farber, & Sroufe, 1989), although they do not offer more toys to others at 20 to 23 months of age (Pastor, 1981). Waters et al. (1986) suggested that children with secure attachments differentially attend to their parent, are positively oriented to the parent, are familiar with and reproduce parents' actions, and are responsive to parental control and wish to avoid parental censure. These tendencies would be expected to enhance the effectiveness of parents' attempts to socialize prosocial behavior. Staub (1992) argued that the quality of early attachments is important to the development of a sense of connection to others and positive valuing of other people, two characteristics with conceptual links to intrinsically based caring for other people (also see Oliner & Oliner, 1988). However, in families in which the child or parent has significant psychological problems, the link between attachment and prosocial behavior likely varies in a complex manner with the type of prosocial behavior and the target of the behavior (Radke-Yarrow, Zahn-Waxler, Richardson, Susman, & Martinez, 1994).

It is likely that the degree of association between prosocial responding and parental warmth is moderated by other socialization practices. Dekovic and Janssens (1992) found that democratic parenting, involving both parental warmth and support, combined with inductions, demandingness, and the provision of suggestions, information, and positive comments, was associated with Dutch children's prosocial behavior as reported by teachers and peers (also see Baumrind, 1971, 1988; Forliti & Benson, 1986). Similarly, Robinson et al. (1994) found that mothers who were relatively negative *and* controlling had children who tended to decrease rather than increase in empathy from 14 to 20 months of age (for those toddlers moderate or high in empathy at 14 months). Moreover, as is discussed in the section on modeling, socializers who are nurturant and model prosocial behavior seem to promote costly prosocial behavior in children (e.g., Yarrow & Scott, 1972; Yarrow, Scott, & Waxler, 1973). Nurturance may serve as a background or contextual variable that enhances the child's receptivity to parental influence, including parental inductions, preachings, and moral standards (Hoffman, 1970b). Thus, whereas parental warmth combined with a high degree of parental permissiveness probably does not foster prosocial behavior involving self-denial, nurturance combined with directive child-rearing practices (setting of standards and induction, for example) seems to promote the development of prosocial behavior (Oliner & Oliner, 1988).

Parental Emphasis on Prosocial Values

Because parents who hold prosocial values would be expected to teach and model prosocial behavior, it is reasonable to expect a relation between parental prosocial values and children's prosocial behavior. Empirical findings provide mixed support for this association. Eisenberg, Wolchik, et al. (1992) found a positive correlation between fathers', but not mothers', reports of their own prosocial values and children's observed prosocial behavior when they were preschoolers, but not when they were toddlers. However, Hoffman (1975a), using a similar measure of parental report of values, found positive relations between peer nominations of fifth graders' prosocial behavior (including prosocial behavior, guilt, and rule following) and both maternal (for girls) and paternal (for both sexes) altruistic values.

In other studies, researchers have examined parents' reports of emphasizing prosocial values or have derived measures of this construct from observations. Some investigators has found no evidence of a relation between measures of parental emphasis on prosocial responding and children's prosocial behavior or empathy (Turner & Harris, 1984), whereas others have obtained mixed (Bryant & Crockenberg, 1980) or positive relations (Olejnik & McKinney, 1973; Trommsdorff, 1991).

Perhaps the most compelling evidence for the importance of parental prosocial values comes from studies of people who have exhibited unusual tendencies toward altruism. Rescuers in Nazi Europe often recalled learning values of caring from parents and the other most influential person in their lives (Oliner & Oliner, 1988; also see Hart & Fegley, 1995). Rescuers reported that their parents felt that ethical values were to be extended to all human beings. Interestingly, rescuers did not differ from nonrescuers in reported exposure to values that are not particularly prosocial such as honesty and equity. In another study of rescuers in Nazi Europe, rescuers reported a strong identification with parents who taught morals (London, 1970). However, it should be noted that real-life moral exemplars often solidify their values or even develop new moral values in adulthood in the process of interacting with other adults who discuss value issues and jointly engage in moral activities with the individual (Colby & Damon, 1992). Thus, it is likely that the socialization of other-oriented values, even if it begins in one's family of origin, is a continuing dynamic process.

Modeling

Because of the importance of modeling in social learning theory (e.g., Bandura, 1986), numerous researchers have examined whether children's prosocial behavior varies as a function of exposure to prosocial versus selfish models. Much of the relevant research has been conducted in laboratory studies using strangers or brief acquaintances as models and donating as the index of prosocial behavior. Thus, the generalizability of much of the laboratory research to real-life settings involving familiar models and to other types of prosocial actions has been questioned. However, the experimental laboratory literature is supplemented by a smaller body of work, often correlational in design, in which real-life situations and familiar models have been used. Given that, in general, there is consistency across the experimental and correlational research, it is possible to have confidence in the larger pattern of findings.

Laboratory Studies

In the prototypic laboratory study of modeling of prosocial behavior, children earn prizes, tokens, or money by winning a game, view or do not view a model, and then are provided an opportunity to donate to needy children or children who did not get to play the game. In general, children who view a generous or helpful model are more generous or helpful than those exposed to a control condition (often a model who had no opportunity to donate; Elliott & Vasta, 1970; Gray & Pirot, 1983; Grusec, 1972; Harris, 1970, 1971; Israel & Raskin, 1979; Kipper & Yinon, 1978; Liebert & Fernandez, 1970; Liebert & Poulos, 1971; Owens & Ascione, 1991; Rice & Grusec, 1975; Rushton & Littlefield, 1979; Rushton & Teachman, 1978; Sims, 1978; Staub, 1971a; White & Burnam, 1975; Yarrow et al., 1973; cf. White, 1972).

Children also tend to donate more when they view a generous model than a selfish model (e.g., Bryan & Walbek, 1970a, 1970b; Dressel & Midlarsky, 1978; Gupta & Bhargava, 1977; Harris, 1971; Lipscomb, Larrieu, McAllister, & Bregman, 1982; Lipscomb, McAllister, & Bregman, 1985; Midlarsky, Bryan, & Brickman, 1973; Presbie & Coiteux, 1971; Rushton, 1975; Rushton & Owen, 1975). Further, multiple models may be more effective than one model (Liebert & Fernandez, 1970) or inconsistent models (Wilson, Piazza, & Nagle, 1990) for inducing precise imitation of donating, and very generous models induce more modeling than moderately generous models (Rushton & Littlefield, 1979; Sharma, 1988b).

In some of the studies in which mixed or no effects of modeling were obtained, sample sizes were quite small (Rogers-Warren & Baer, 1976; Rogers-Warren, Warren, & Baer, 1977); children were engaged in an assigned task that would be disrupted if they assisted (Sukemune, Dohno, &

Matsuzaki, 1981); or donations were not anonymous, so children who viewed a selfish model or no model may have donated merely because they felt the adult experimenter expected donations (Bryan, Redfield, & Mader, 1971; Lipscomb, Bregman, & McAllister, 1983; Parish, 1977; Sharma, 1988b). In yet other studies that will be discussed shortly, only models with certain characteristics (e.g., high nurturance) were effective (Gray & Pirot, 1983; Yarrow et al., 1973).

In most laboratory studies of modeling, prosocial behavior is modeled only once; thus, it is impressive that some investigators have obtained evidence of generalization to new behaviors or settings (Harris, 1971; Midlarsky & Bryan, 1967; Rushton, 1975; Yarrow et al., 1973), although others have found only partial (Elliott & Vasta, 1970) or no evidence of generalization (Gray & Pirot, 1983; Harris, 1970; Rushton & Littlefield, 1979; Rushton & Teachman, 1978). Further, a number of investigators have found effects of modeling days to months later (Israel & Raskin, 1979; Rice & Grusec, 1975; Rushton, 1975; Rushton & Littlefield, 1979; Wilson et al., 1990; cf. Rushton & Owen, 1975). However, stability of effects sometimes was found for modeling only when combined with other procedures such as rehearsal (White, 1972), positive reinforcement (Rushton & Teachman, 1978), or the provision of internal self-attributions (Grusec, Kuczynski, Rushton, & Simutis, 1978).

According to social learning theory, one reason people may imitate models is because they view them receiving rewards for prosocial behavior. Some researchers have found that children imitate reinforced models more than models who have not been reinforced (Franco, 1978; Israely & Guttmann, 1983; Presbie & Coiteux, 1971), particularly if the reinforcement is praise rather than a concrete reward (Elliott & Vasta, 1970) and the model does not also engage in self-praise (Presbie & Coiteux, 1971). However, not all investigators have found that praise enhances imitation of models (Ascione & Sanok, 1982; Gupta & Bhargava, 1977; Harris, 1970). Further, it appears that children are more generous after exposure to a model who appears to derive happiness from engaging in prosocial behavior, that is, who accompanies his or her prosocial acts with statements such as "I feel wonderful" (Bryan, 1971; Midlarsky & Bryan, 1972; Rushton, 1975; Rushton & Owen, 1975). Such statements may be viewed as expressions of vicarious internal reinforcement, and children may be more likely to assist if they think that they will obtain similar internal reinforcements for helping or sharing.

As might be expected, some models are imitated more than others. Models who control valued resources (Grusec, 1971) appear to be relatively powerful models, as are models perceived as competent (Eisenberg-Berg & Geisheker, 1979). Nurturance of a model also has an effect on children's imitation of prosocial behavior, although findings depend upon the experimental context. When the prosocial behavior tested is low cost to the children and is something they probably want to do (e.g., help when they hear someone in distress), those briefly exposed to warm models imitate prosocial behavior more than children exposed to a nonnurturant model (Weissbrod, 1976; also see Staub, 1971a). In contrast, when prosocial behavior involves self-denial (e.g., donations), short-term exposure to a warm model seems to have little effect (Grusec & Skubiski, 1970; Midlarsky & Bryan, 1967; Rosenhan & White, 1967) or may even reduce donating behavior (Grusec, 1971; Weissbrod, 1976, 1980). Thus, short-term noncontingent warmth seems to disinhibit children to do as they please, including assisting distressed others and keeping valued commodities for themselves. However, in real life, adult-child interactions are never entirely noncontingent. In fact, there is evidence that preschool children model the prosocial behaviors and nurturance of adults with whom they have had an extended nurturant relation (Yarrow & Scott, 1972; Yarrow et al., 1973; also see Morishita, 1985).

Modeling by Real-Life Socializers

The limited literature pertaining to children's modeling of parents' prosocial behavior is scattered, correlational, and often can be interpreted in more than one way. Nonetheless, in general the research is consistent with the view that children model parents' prosocial behavior.

In the first two years of life, children do not seem consistently to model maternal sharing or helping of a distressed person (Hay & Murray, 1982; Zahn-Waxler et al., 1979). However, mothers' modeling of helping behaviors such as participation in household chores seems to enhance the likelihood of 1- and 2-year-olds helping their mothers (Rheingold, 1982). For very young children, modeling of the action itself (as well as eliciting the child's attention) likely fosters the child's learning of the desired behavior and focuses the child's attention on the helping action.

Moreover, the data on real-life altruists suggest an effect of parental modeling. Rosenhan (1970) studied a group of Caucasian young adults who participated in the civil rights movement in the United States in the late 1950s and the 1960s. Their activities entailed both considerable costs and physical danger. Activists who were highly involved and committed to the cause reported that their parents were both nurturant and actively involved in working for altruistic and humanitarian causes. In contrast, individuals who were less involved and committed reported that their parents preached prosocial values but often did not practice altruism. Similarly, Clary and Miller (1986) found that volunteers at a crisis counseling agency who maintained their commitment (rather than quitting) were somewhat more likely to report ($p < .10$) that their parents were nurturant and altruistic. Moreover, Hart and Fegley (1995) found that African American and Latin American adolescents' care exemplars were more likely than other youth to incorporate aspects of parentally related representations (e.g., what their mothers were like or expected of them) in their self-representation. Finally, in two different studies, rescuers of Jews in Nazi Europe described their parents as having acted in accordance with strong moral convictions (London, 1970; Oliner & Oliner, 1988).

Of course, the data from studies of adult altruists are not only correlational in design but involve retrospective data. Even if people's recall of parental practices were unbiased and accurate, it is possible that their own altruism stemmed from family factors other than modeling (such as discipline), exposure to cultural or community values, or a variety of other factors. Nonetheless, research findings on parents of prosocial offspring converge with the experimental laboratory findings in implicating modeling in the development of prosocial tendencies.

Nondisciplinary Verbalizations

Adults' verbalizations relevant to prosocial behavior have been examined in nondisciplinary contexts (situations in which the parent is not responding to the child's misbehavior), as well as in disciplinary situations. Three types of verbalizations have been examined: (a) statements merely about what the other person, usually a model, intends to do; (b) preachings that contain content about desired behavior; and (c) instructions or prompts.

Statement of Intentions

In a number of laboratory studies, models merely state if they plan to donate or not but do not actually have an opportunity to share. Statements of the intent to share sometimes foster generosity, even four months later (Rice & Grusec, 1975). However, statements of intention may have less effect than does viewing the actual performance of donating

(Grusec, 1972; Rice & Grusec, 1975), and sometimes only have an effect in specific circumstances (Grusec & Skubiski, 1970; Rice & Grusec, 1975). Adults' statements of prosocial intentions may be similar to symbolic modeling.

Preachings

In studies of the effects of preachings or exhortations, the preacher states what should be done, but does not explicitly tell the child to do it. Often the preacher also gives reasons why one should assist or why one should not. The preacher may verbalize to himself or herself, as if thinking through the issue (Eisenberg-Berg & Geisheker, 1979), or direct the preaching to the child (e.g., Bryan & Walbek, 1970a, 1970b; Rushton, 1975).

In many studies on preachings, an adult or peer confederate in a laboratory study wins some commodity that he or she can donate to a charity. The preacher exhorts while playing the game, and may or may not have an opportunity to actually donate. Preachings often are normative in content, with the preacher stating what should be done and stating either prosocial or selfish norms (e.g., "It's a nice thing [not such a nice thing] to give to the crippled children"; Bryan & Walbek, 1970a). In a neutral control group, the preacher typically would make normatively neutral statements such as "This game is fun."

Most researchers have found no effects, or inconsistent effects, of normative preachings on children's donating behavior (e.g., Bryan, Redfield, & Mader, 1971; Bryan & Walbek, 1970a, 1970b; Rushton & Owen, 1975; cf. Zarbatany, Hartmann, & Gelfand, 1985). In one study of elementary school children, normative preachings were associated with enhanced sharing on a two-month follow-up measure, albeit not on the immediate postpreaching test of donation. However, the effect that was obtained generally was an undermining effect of selfish preachings (which interacted with the effect of the model; Rushton, 1975). Nonetheless, normative preachings seem to foster generosity if the preaching is very strong in its emphasis on the importance of helping (Anderson & Perlman, 1973) or if the preacher promoting donating is an adult likely to have direct power over the children (Eisenberg-Berg & Geisheker, 1979).

In addition, empathy-inducing preachings that emphasize the emotional consequences of assisting for the recipients of aid have been found to elicit more private donations than selfish preachings (Dressel & Midlarsky, 1978), neutral control preachings (Dlugokinski & Firestone, 1974; Eisenberg-Berg & Geisheker, 1979; Perry, Bussey, &

Freiberg, 1981; C. Smith, 1983; C. Smith, Leinbach, Stewart, & Blackwell, 1983), punitive, threatening preachings (Perry et al., 1981), or preachings in which the adult merely asked the child to share or emphasized that the child would still have some candy left if he or she shared (Burleson & Fennelly, 1981). Empathy-inducing preachings also have been found to enhance elementary school children's effort and success when helping a peer (Ladd, Lange, & Stremmel, 1983), have been related to prosocial behavior a week later, and generalize to new prosocial behaviors (Smith, 1983).

Not all researchers have found effects of empathy-inducing preachings (e.g., Lipscomb et al., 1983; Rosser, 1982). It is quite possible that the wording in some studies may have led the children to believe that the adult or the beneficiary would be angry at them for not helping, which might evoke reactance rather than empathy (McGrath & Power, 1990), or compliance rather than internalization. Preachings may work best if children feel that they have a choice of whether to assist and if the preachings highlight the positive outcomes of helping for another. McGrath, Wilson, and Frassetto (1995) found that adults' appeals enhanced donating if they referred to the peer-beneficiary in the appeal *and* if children did not feel forced to give. In addition, children were more generous if exposed to a message stating that the focus of the appeal (adult or child) would be happy if they donated rather than sad if they did not. Similarly, Grusec, Saas-Kortsaak, and Simutis (1978) obtained evidence of the generalizability and stability of the effect of exposure to preachings emphasizing the positive emotional consequences of assisting for the beneficiary.

In two studies, an adult's preachings undermined helping an adult to pick up paper clips that had spilled (Grusec, Saas-Kortsaak, & Simutis, 1978; Staub, 1971c). Perhaps exposure to preachings highlights the power differential between adults and children so that children feel inhibited in helping adults with simple tasks. Further, the results of one study suggest that empathic preachings are effective only for children who have been exposed to inductive discipline at home (rather than relatively high degrees of power assertion; Dlugokinski & Firestone, 1974).

In summary, preachings that are other-oriented in content and focus on the positive effects of prosocial action on others' emotional states appear to be relatively effective for fostering prosocial behavior. However, the generalizability of the findings on preachings is limited by the fact that most of the research has been conducted with middle to late elementary school-aged, middle-class children in a laboratory setting in which the preacher was a stranger or adult acquaintance. Nonetheless, it is impressive that exposure to brief preachings on one occasion from adults with whom children have little relationship can influence their behavior, particularly prosocial behaviors performed in another setting or at a later date (Grusec, Saas-Kortsaak, & Simutis, 1978). Findings such as these complement the research on socializers' inductive disciplinary practices and provide further support for the conclusion that practices that induce children to consider the effects of their behavior for others can promote prosocial behavior.

Prompts and Directives

It is not surprising that children who are instructed or prompted to help or share tend to do so (Gelfand et al., 1975; Hay & Murray, 1982; Israel & Raskin, 1979; C. Smith et al., 1983). However, the degree to which they follow instructions varies with the nature of the instructions, albeit in a complex manner. Some researchers have found that directive instructions (instructions that tell the child to share) result in greater prosocial behavior (e.g., donating) than permissive instructions (instructions that tell the child that he or she might want to share, but don't have to), even if the child's prosocial actions are anonymous (e.g., Brown & Israel, 1980; Israel & Brown, 1979; Israel & Raskin, 1979; Weissbrod, 1980; White & Burnam, 1975). In fact, the effects of directive instructions have been found to persist over 11 days (Israel & Brown, 1979), and even four weeks (Israel & Raskin, 1979). However, directive instructions often are not effective for all ages or both sexes (Israel & Raskin, 1979; Kawashima, 1980; White & Burnam, 1975). Further, there is evidence that constraining directives are less effective with older than younger children (White & Burnam, 1975), particularly over time (Israel & Raskin, 1979; cf. Israel & Brown, 1979), and that permissive instructions foster older children's donating if combined with modeling (White & Burnam, 1975).

Direct requests for prosocial behavior may be particularly important for younger children because of their limited abilities to understand others' emotions and situational cues (Denham, Mason, & Couchoud, 1995). However, if instructions are highly constraining, they may induce reactance. Further, after the early years, children are unlikely to attribute behavior perceived as forced to internal motivation (Lepper, 1983) and, consequently, may not enact prosocial behavior when they can subsequently freely choose to assist in an unsupervised setting (McGrath & Power, 1990).

Related to prompting or directing a child to be prosocial is assigning a child responsibility for handling situations involving prosocial action. When children were identified as the ones with personal responsibility for a situation in which an opportunity of helping in an emergency or donating then arose (Staub, 1970a), children tended to help or share more, particularly if they had training relevant to helping (Peterson, 1983a, 1983b) or were not in a large group of children (Maruyama, Fraser, & Miller, 1982). Encouraging children to engage in work that benefits members of the family fosters a concern for the welfare of others (Grusec, Goodnow, & Cohen, 1996). Adults' verbalizations that encourage children to feel responsible and in control may encourage self-initiated responsible behavior.

Reinforcement for Prosocial Behavior

As is predicted by learning theory, concrete (Fischer, 1963) and social (Bryan, Redfield, & Mader, 1971; Doland & Adelberg, 1967; Eisenberg, Fabes, Carlo, & Karbon, 1992; Eisenberg, Fabes, Carlo, Speer, et al., 1993; Gelfand et al., 1975; Grusec & Redler, 1980; Rushton & Teachman, 1978) reinforcements have been found to increase children's prosocial behavior, at least in the immediate context. Further, parental reports of reinforcing children's sympathetic and prosocial behavior have been associated with girls' (but not boys') concerned or sad reactions to others in distress (Eisenberg, Fabes, Carlo, Troyer, et al., 1992). However, social reinforcement such as praise for the prosocial behavior sometimes does not have an effect even in the immediate context (Fischer, 1963; Mills & Grusec, 1989; also see Kagan & Knight, 1984).

Although concrete rewards may induce prosocial behavior in the given context, the long-term effect of concrete rewards may be negative. Consistent with Lepper's (1983) notion that the provision of concrete rewards undermines intrinsic motivation (and also may induce children to attribute their prosocial actions to external motivation), Szynal-Brown and Morgan (1983) found that third-grade children ᐧwho were promised tangible rewards if the younger children they tutored did well were less likely to engage in teaching activities during a subsequent free-choice period than were tutors who were not promised rewards for teaching. Those children promised rewards that were not contingent on the pupil's learning were in between the aforementioned two groups in regard to teaching, but

did not differ significantly from either. Further, Fabes, Fultz, Eisenberg, May-Plumlee, and Christopher (1989) found that the use of material rewards for elementary school children's helping behavior undermined their subsequent anonymous prosocial behavior during a free-choice situation, particularly for children whose mothers valued the use of rewards. Moreover, mothers who felt relatively positive about using rewards reported that their children were less prosocial than did mothers who were less enthusiastic about the use of rewards. These findings suggest that concrete rewards may undermine prosocial behavior for children who are frequently exposed to rewards. Rewards may be salient for these children and, consequently, they may be particularly likely to attribute their initial prosocial behavior to the external reward (rather than to an internal motive).

The effects of social reinforcement may vary as a function of type of praise and age of the child. Praise that attributes the children's positive behavior to their dispositional kindness or internal motives (e.g., because they enjoy helping others) seems to be more effective than praise involving simply labeling of the act as positive (Grusec & Redler, 1980; Mills & Grusec, 1989; the provision of dispositional attributions is a special type of praise and is discussed further shortly). Although Grusec and Redler (1980) found that social reinforcement for prosocial actions (without an internal attribution) increased elementary school children's prosocial behavior in the immediate context, it was not associated with the generalization of prosocial behavior to a new situation for 5- or 8-year-olds. In contrast, 10-year-olds exposed to social reinforcement were more likely than children who were not reinforced to engage anonymously in a different prosocial behavior. Grusec and Redler hypothesized that older children may interpret reinforcement for a specific action as having implications for a variety of situations, whereas younger children do not view praise for a given act as having broader relevance. Other researchers, however, have not found that the effects of reinforcement generalize to new prosocial behaviors (e.g., Rushton & Teachman, 1978). Unfortunately, in most situations in which reinforced behaviors have generalized to new settings or have been durable over time, reinforcement was combined with modeling or other techniques (e.g., Barton & Ascione, 1979; Barton, Olszewski, & Madsen, 1979; Rogers-Warren & Baer, 1976; Rushton & Teachman, 1978).

Eisenberg, Wolchik, et al. (1992) found that parents' social reinforcement of toddlers' prosocial behaviors (toward the parent) at 1 to 2 years of age was positively correlated with the child's prosocial behavior in the play session, but not with the other parent. Moreover, reinforcement of the toddlers' prosocial behaviors requested by the parent was *negatively* correlated with children's compliant prosocial behavior with a peer at 3 to 4 years of age. Similarly, Grusec (1991) found that 4-year-olds who most frequently received no response for their prosocial actions from parents were marginally *more* prosocial than children who received acknowledgments or social approval. Perhaps young children who are low in prosocial behavior sometimes elicit high levels of praise from parents who are trying to modify their behavior.

Provision of Attributions or Dispositional Praise

Elementary school children are likely to act in a prosocial manner on a subsequent occasion if they initially are induced to behave prosocially and are provided with internal attributions (i.e., dispositional praise) for their actions (e.g., "I guess you're the kind of person who likes to help others whenever you can. Yes, you are a very nice and helpful person"; Grusec & Redler, 1980). Children provided with such praise are more helpful or generous even weeks later than are children who are provided with no attribution (Grusec, Kuczynski, et al., 1978; Grusec & Redler, 1980; Holte, Jamruszka, Gustafson, Beaman, & Camp, 1984; cf. Eisenberg, Cialdini, McCreath, & Shell, 1987) or with an attribution attributing prosocial behavior to the fact that the adult experimenter expected such behavior (Grusec, Kuczynski, et al., 1978).

The provision of internal attributions is believed to foster a prosocial self-image, which then results in enhanced prosocial behavior (Grusec & Redler, 1980). Although Mills and Grusec (1989) obtained only weak, inconsistent support for this supposition, other research provides indirect support for the mediating role of the child's self-concept in the association between dispositional attributions and enhanced prosocial behavior in children. For example, prosocial attributions are not effective in situations in which children are likely to feel that their initial prosocial behavior (the one to which the attribution was attached) was due to external pressure (e.g., direct instructions to assist; Grusec, Kuczynski, et al., 1978). In such situations, one would expect no alteration in children's self-concept because they are likely to attribute their prosocial action to external pressure. Furthermore, consistent with a self-concept explanation, the provision of internal attributions was found to be more effective for children who did not have an accurate perception of their own prosocial dispositions or who did not perceive themselves as prosocial than for children who accurately perceived themselves to be prosocial (and were unlikely to change their self-perception; Holte et al., 1984).

If changes in children's self-concepts mediate the effects of dispositional attributions, the provision of internal attributions would not be expected to be effective until children have some understanding of personality traits and their stability. Consistent with this view, Grusec and Redler (1980) found that the provision of internal attributions was effective in enhancing prosocial behavior of mid- and later-elementary school children both immediately and long term (e.g., a week or more later). In contrast, the effects of the character attributions were very limited for kindergartners. Further, Eisenberg, Cialdini, McCreath, and Shell (1989) found that elementary school children who were induced to engage in prosocial behavior *and* provided with internal attributions were more helpful if they demonstrated the ability to label traits accurately. Thus, although definitive research has not been conducted (the ability to understand traits was only inferred from the age of the child in the Grusec and Redler studies), an understanding of traits may be essential if internal attributions are to foster children's prosocial behavior. Moreover, an understanding of the implications of dispositional praise may not only affect children's self-perceptions, but also arouse positive affect (Mills & Grusec, 1989). Such positive affect could serve to cue thoughts and memories compatible with prosocial behavior (e.g., about positive outcomes of prosocial behavior) or may simply reinforce prosocial behavior.

Learning by Doing (and the Foot-in-the-Door Effect)

Children's participation in prosocial activities seems to foster prosocial behavior at a later time, although boys sometimes may exhibit some reactance in the short term (Staub, 1979, 1992). This pattern of findings has been obtained both using experimental procedures (Eisenberg, Cialdini, et al., 1987; Staub, 1979) and in research linking prosocial proclivities to participation in household chores (perhaps particularly those that benefit others; Rehberg & Richman, 1989; Richman et al., 1988; Whiting & Whiting, 1973; cf. Gelfand et al., 1975). In addition, adolescents' and young adults' participation in voluntary community service (which can be considered as practice) sometimes has been linked to greater feelings of commitment to helping others (Yates & Youniss, 1996) and the attitude that society has the obligation to meet the needs of others (albeit there was no increase in reported personal responsibility; Hamilton & Fenzel, 1988; Rutter & Newmann, 1989). Rehearsal or practice in laboratory studies also seems to promote prosocial tendencies in that context, although researchers frequently have combined rehearsal with modeling or other procedures, so the effects of rehearsal cannot be isolated (Barton, 1981; Barton & Ascione, 1979; Barton et al., 1979; Barton & Osborne, 1978; Rosenhan & White, 1967; White, 1972; cf. White & Burnam, 1975).

The effects of practice appear to be moderated by the age and characteristics of the child. Eisenberg, Cialdini, et al. (1987) found that inducing children to donate through noncoercive suggestion in one context was associated with enhanced helping a couple of days later, but only for children in mid-elementary school or older. The effects of practice were stronger for children who valued consistent behavior than for those who did not. Partially consistent with the latter finding, Eisenberg, Cialdini, et al. found that for girls (but not boys), an initial helping experience was related to children's enacted behavior in hypothetical sharing situations, but only for girls who valued consistent behavior.

The findings on the effects of practice are similar to those obtained by social psychologists studying compliance (i.e., the foot-in-the-door effect) in adulthood. Although the processes underlying the findings for adults are unclear (Dillard, 1991), a common explanation is that engaging in the initial prosocial behavior changes the actor's self-perception in regard to prosocial behavior and/or the actor's attitude about helpfulness. A self-concept explanation is consistent with Eisenberg, Cialdini, et al.'s (1989) finding that the effects of an initial helping experience were primarily for children with an elementary understanding of trait labels (because an understanding of traits is necessary for a stable self-concept) and with Eisenberg, Cialdini, et al.'s (1987) finding that practice had an effect only for children old enough to understand consistency in personality. However, there is little direct evidence that a more sophisticated understanding of the stability of personality is necessary for the foot-in-the-door effect.

Moreover, processes unrelated to self-concept likely contribute to the finding that initial helping experiences foster subsequent prosocial action. Staub (1992) argued that one must engage in prosocial behavior to develop an interest in it and to acquire the motivation to enact similar behavior in future contexts. It also is possible that engaging in prosocial behavior provides empathic rewards, increases children's feelings of competence to help, and results in social approval.

Emotion Socialization and Prosocial Tendencies

A relatively recent development in the prosocial literature has been the focus on links between the socialization of emotion and children's prosocial behavior and empathy-related reactions, particularly the latter. The results of this research are consistent with the view that parental practices that help children to cope with their own negative emotion in a constructive fashion foster sympathy and prosocial behavior rather than personal distress reactions. This presumably is because children who cannot adequately cope with their emotions tend to become overaroused and, consequently, experience a self-focused, aversive response (i.e., personal distress) when confronted with another's distress (Eisenberg, Fabes, Murphy, et al., 1994).

For example, Eisenberg, Fabes, Schaller, Carlo, and Miller (1991) found that mothers who emphasized to their sons the need to control their own negative emotions (e.g., sadness and anxiety) had sons who exhibited facial and physiological (skin conductance and heart rate) markers of distress when they viewed a sympathy-inducing film, but reported low distress in reaction to the film. Thus, these boys seemed prone to experience distress when confronted with others' distress, but seemed not to want others to know what they were feeling.

In contrast, same-sex parents' restrictiveness in regard to emotional displays that could be *hurtful to others* (e.g., gaping at a disfigured person) has been linked to elementary school children's reports of dispositional and situational sympathy (Eisenberg, Fabes, Schaller, Carlo, & Miller, 1991). Parents who discourage their children from expressing emotions hurtful to others may be educating their children about the effects of emotional displays on others. However, maternal restrictiveness in regard to the display of hurtful emotions was associated with distress in kindergarten girls. It appeared that mothers who were restrictive in this regard with kindergarten girls were less supportive in general. Thus, for younger children, such maternal restrictiveness may have reflected age-inappropriate restrictiveness or low levels of support (Eisenberg, Fabes, Carlo, Troyer, et al., 1992).

A method of coping that often is successful in dealing with emotional arousal is directly acting upon the problem, that is, trying to change factors in the environment that have caused the stress or distress (Lazarus & Folkman, 1984). Initial findings indicate that boys whose parents encourage them to deal instrumentally with situations causing their own sadness or anxiety are likely to experience sympathy rather than personal distress in empathy-inducing contexts

(Eisenberg, Fabes, Schaller, Carlo, & Miller, 1991). Further, parents' encouragement of direct problem solving as a way to cope with emotion has been associated with the amount of girls' (but not boys') comforting of a crying infant (Eisenberg, Fabes, Carlo, et al., 1993).

Mothers' discussion of their own and their children's emotions also seems to relate to children's vicarious emotional responding. In a study in which mothers viewed an empathy-inducing film with their children in a nondisciplinary context, mothers' verbal linking of the events in the film with children's own experiences was associated with children's heightened vicarious emotional responding of all kinds (sadness, distress, and sympathy). Further, mothers' references to their own sympathy and sadness and their statements about perspective taking or the film protagonist's feelings or situation were associated with boys' reports of sympathy and sadness (Eisenberg, Fabes, Carlo, Troyer, et al., 1992). In addition, mothers' reports of trying to find out why their children feel bad, helping their children talk about their negative emotions, and listening to their children when they were anxious or upset have been associated with girls' comforting of an infant (Eisenberg, Fabes, Carlo, et al., 1993).

The aforementioned findings are consistent with other research in which parental willingness to discuss emotion has been linked to empathy (e.g., M. Barnett, Howard, King, & Dino, 1980), although there are some discrepancies in the pattern of findings (M. Barnett, King, Howard, & Dino, 1980; Eisenberg, Fabes, Schaller, Carlo, & Miller, 1991). For example, Trommsdorff (1995) found that German and Japanese mothers who focused on their children's emotions in stressful situations by verbalizing or matching their emotions had 5-year-old daughters who were prone to experience distress rather than sympathy when exposed to another's sadness. Perhaps mothers tend to attend to the emotions of daughters who are easily distressed. Alternatively, Trommsdorff suggested that girls who experience too strong a degree of empathy from their caretaker may experience more distress in empathy-inducing contexts because of less developed self-other differentiation. Another possibility is that some mothers may overarouse their children by focusing too much on distress, with the consequence that the children do not learn to regulate their distress.

It is likely that the manner in which mothers talk about emotional events partially accounts for the nature of the relation between maternal verbalizations and children's empathy-related and prosocial responding. Denham and Grout (1992) found that preschoolers' prosocial behavior at school was positively related to mothers' tendencies to explain their own sadness. Fabes, Eisenberg, Karbon, Bernzweig, et al. (1994) examined how mothers told their kindergarten and second-grade children empathy-evoking stories (e.g., about a child whose pet died). For kindergartners, maternal displays of positive rather than negative emotion while telling the story were correlated with children's sympathy, low personal distress, and helpfulness on a behavioral task. Interestingly, mothers displayed more of this positive expressiveness with younger children and if they viewed their children as reactive to others' distresses. Thus, it appeared as if mothers were reacting to characteristics of their children (i.e., age and emotional vulnerability) and were attempting to buffer younger and vulnerable children from emotional overarousal. Further, this buffering was positively associated with young children's helpful behavior. In contrast, second graders' helpfulness as well as sympathy and low personal distress (assessed with physiological and facial measures) were correlated with a maternal style that combined warmth with directing the child's attention to the stories. For older children, buffering of negative emotion may not be necessary, whereas it may be important to direct the child's attention to others in a way that does not induce reactance.

In summary, although the data are scant, it appears that parental practices that help children to regulate their negative emotion rather than become overaroused are likely to foster sympathy and prosocial behavior rather than personal distress. However, there may be a fine line between parental practices that help children to regulate and to understand their own emotion and practices that overly focus children's attention on negative emotion. Moreover, the effects of parental emotion-related practices might be expected to vary with the child's emotional reactivity. More work is needed to delineate the ways parental behaviors are associated with children's behavioral and emotional reactions to others' negative emotions and moderators of this relation.

Expression of Emotion and Conflict in the Home

Frequency and valence of emotion expressed in the home appear to be linked to children's prosocial behavior, albeit in a complex manner. In regard to positive emotion, relations, when obtained, generally are positive (Denham & Grout, 1992; Eisenberg, Fabes, Schaller, Miller, et al., 1991; Garner, Jones, & Miner, 1994), a finding that is consistent with the modest association between prosocial behavior and parental support, warmth, and sympathy. However, researchers sometimes have found no relations between familial or maternal positive emotion and children's sympathy (Eisenberg, Fabes, Carlo, Troyer, et al., 1992) or prosocial behavior (Denham & Grout, 1993).

At first glance, findings regarding negative emotion in the home are quite inconsistent and puzzling. On the one hand, conflict in the family is associated with prosocial behavior toward family members (Cummings, Zahn-Waxler, & Radke-Yarrow, 1981). Even very young children exposed to parental conflict sometimes try to comfort or help their parents, and this tendency increases with age in the early years (Cummings, Zahn-Waxler, & Radke-Yarrow, 1984). Further, siblings (but not peers) exposed to conflict between their mother and another adult seemed to try to buffer the stress for one another by either acting prosocially toward one another (for boys) or increasing their rates of positive affect (for girls; Cummings & Smith, 1993). Moreover, young children are more likely to respond with prosocial behavior toward a parent, as well as with anger, distress, and support seeking, if familial conflict is frequent (Cummings et al., 1981) or is physical in nature (Cummings, Pellegrini, Notarius, & Cummings, 1989). Similarly, Cummings, Hennessy, Rabideau, and Cicchetti (1994) found that physically abused boys (approximately age 5) were more likely than nonabused boys to respond to anger between their mother and another adult with coping (including comforting the mother); however, they also were relatively likely to exhibit aggression and anger.

In the studies by Cummings and his colleagues, children were exposed to enacted conflicts or mothers reported on actual conflicts in the home. Other investigators have examined the relation of reported prevalence of hostile, negative emotion in the home environment or maternal simulations of anger situations. Garner, Jones, and Miner (1994) did not find a significant relation between mothers' reports of dominant negative affect or their own anger directed toward children and children's caregiving to a sibling. In contrast, Denham and her colleagues found that preschoolers' prosocial real-life reactions to their peers' emotional displays were negatively related to mothers' reports in a diary of frequency of their own anger at home (Denham & Grout, 1992) and intense maternal simulations of anger (when enacting events in a photograph; Denham et al., 1994), and were positively related to mothers' reports of rational expressions of anger (Denham & Grout, 1992). Similarly, high levels of familial or maternal dominant

negative emotion (e.g., anger) have been linked to low levels of sympathetic concern and high levels of personal distress (Crockenberg, 1985; Eisenberg, Fabes, Carlo, Troyer, et al., 1992). However, prosocial behavior also was positively related to mothers' reports of *experiencing* externalizing emotions (anger, scorn, disgust) on a questionnaire (Denham & Grout, 1993). Of course, the expression and experience of emotions may differ considerably.

Thus, Cummings and his colleagues have found that exposure to conflict, including ongoing conflict in the home, is related to increased prosocial reactions toward children's mothers and siblings (but not peers; E. Cummings & Smith, 1993), whereas, in general, reports and displays of maternal anger and externalizing emotion have been linked to low levels of peer-directed prosocial behavior and sympathy and high levels of personal distress. This apparently discrepant pattern of findings can be interpreted in a meaningful way if one views exposure to adult conflict as undermining children's emotional security, inducing distress, and evoking coping responses from the child calculated to minimize the stress in his or her social environment (Davies & Cummings, 1994). Given that children frequently cannot readily escape from conflict in the home, they often may attempt to alleviate their distress by intervening and comforting family members. However, children exposed to high-intensity or ongoing anger may tend to become overaroused by others' negative emotions and experience self-focused personal distress in reaction to others' negative emotion (Eisenberg et al., 1994). If this is the case, children would be expected to try to escape from dealing with others' distress if possible. In brief, it appears that exposure to high levels of anger and conflict may induce attempts by children to minimize self-related negative emotional (and physical) consequences of conflict but does not foster the capacity for sympathy or other-oriented (rather than self-oriented) prosocial behavior.

Negative emotions need not always be harsh and dominant; often, emotions such as sadness, fear, and loss are expressed in the home. In studies of children from typical families, maternal report of such submissive negative emotion (Halberstadt, 1986) has been negatively related to children's caregiving toward a younger sibling (Garner, Jones, & Miner, 1994), but positively related to girls' (but not boys') sympathy (Eisenberg, Fabes, Carlo, Troyer, et al., 1992). Further, preschoolers' prosocial reactions to peers' emotions have been related to low- rather than high-intensity enacted sadness by mothers (Denham et al., 1994) and low maternal tension/fear in a parent-child interaction

(Denham & Grout, 1993). In contrast, children's peer-oriented prosocial actions have not been significantly related to frequency of mothers' reported expressions of sadness or tension at home in front of their children (Denham & Grout, 1992) or mothers' reports of experiencing internalizing negative emotions (Denham & Grout, 1993). Thus, the findings in regard to the relation between children's exposure to parents' softer negative emotions and their prosocial behavior are inconsistent.

Perhaps what is important is whether such emotion is dealt with constructively in the home and if children learn ways to manage emotions such as sadness so that they are likely to experience sympathy rather than personal distress when exposed to others' negative emotion. Denham and Grout (1992) found that mothers' reported expressions of tension/fear and sadness at home were positively related to children's peer-oriented prosocial behavior if mothers expressed their tension in a positive manner or explained their sadness. Further, as discussed previously, parental emotion-related socialization efforts have been linked to children's empathy-related responding (see section on emotion socialization). Moderate exposure to others' sadness, tension, and fear, combined with parental behaviors that foster constructive coping with negative emotion, may be optimal for enhancing other-oriented prosocial behavior.

Summary of Research on Discipline and Socializers' Practices, Beliefs, and Characteristics

It would appear that some constellation of parental practices, beliefs, and characteristics, as well as the emotional atmosphere of the home, are related to children's prosocial development. The findings generally are consistent with Staub's (1992) assertion that the development of prosocial behavior is enhanced by a sense connection to others (e.g., through attachment and a benign social environment), exposure to parental warmth (which fosters a positive identity and sense of self as well as attachment), adult guidance, and children's participation in prosocial activities. However, numerous factors believed by Staub to contribute to prosocial development and to derive from socialization—such as emotional independence, a sense of responsibility for others, the capacity for independence, broad experience, and moral courage—seldom have been examined in studies with children.

Moreover, although it usually is assumed that environmental factors account for the findings on the socialization of emotion, genetically mediated factors likely partially account for the pattern of findings (Caspi, Ch. 6, this Volume). For example, it is possible that prosocial, sympathetic parents have prosocial children not only because of socialization, but also because of shared genetic predispositions. Recall that Plomin et al. (1993) found that genetic factors accounted for much of the consistency in twins' empathy from age 14 to 20 months. The role of genetic factors in associations between parent practices or characteristics and children's prosocial behavior is an important but neglected issue.

However, Plomin et al. (1993) also found that nonshared (unique) environmental experience accounted for some consistency and for the substantial degree of change in empathy over the aforementioned period. Part of this variance likely is due to unique features of each twin's interactions with his or her parents. Moreover, genetic explanations cannot readily account for findings in experimental socialization studies in which parents were not involved (e.g., many of the studies on modeling, preaching, and learning by doing).

Further, most researchers who have studied socialization correlates of prosocial responding have taken a top-down perspective; the role of the child's characteristics in the socialization process has been virtually ignored. Yet it is highly likely that children's personality and temperament influence and interact with parental characteristics and beliefs in determining the quality of the parent-child relationship and parental socialization efforts. Consistent with this view, adults use more reasoning about the consequences of acts and less bargaining with material rewards to induce prosocial behavior for children who are responsive and attentive than for children who are not (Keller & Bell, 1979). The role of the child in the socialization of prosocial behavior is a key topic for further attention.

Other Familial and Extrafamilial Influences

Of course, people and institutions other than parents in children's environments are potential socializers of children's prosocial actions. Unfortunately, research on the role of nonparental influences is in the rudimentary stages, and researchers studying the various environmental influences seldom have considered multiple familial models (including multiple family members) or the influence of various types of potential socializers (e.g., peers and the school context). (For discussion of the effects of television, see Eisenberg & Mussen, 1989; Hearold, 1986; Huston & Wright, Ch. 15, Volume 4.)

Siblings

Because siblings are familiar and uninhibited with one another, they would be expected to play a considerable role in the development of children's social understanding and interpersonal skills (Dunn & Munn, 1986). In fact, even 1- to 2-year-old children exhibit prosocial behavior toward their siblings (Dunn & Kendrick, 1982). Preschool-age children enact relatively high rates of comforting behavior to distressed younger siblings (Howe & Ross, 1990; Stewart & Marvin, 1984) but show relatively low rates of responsiveness to unfamiliar younger children (Berman & Goodman, 1984). Because older siblings often act as caregivers to younger siblings, the sibling relationship provides children with opportunities to learn about others' needs and caring effectively for others.

As discussed previously, the child's ordinal position in the sibling dyad likely affects opportunities and expectations for prosocial behavior. Older children are more likely to enact prosocial behaviors directed toward younger siblings and younger siblings accept reciprocal roles by displaying high rates of compliance and modeling (Brody, Stoneman, MacKinnon, & MacKinnon, 1985; Dunn & Munn, 1986; Lamb, 1978b; Stoneman, Brody, MacKinnon, 1986). Moreover, there is some evidence that older sisters are particularly likely to engage in prosocial interactions with their siblings (Blakemore, 1990; Brody et al., 1985; Stoneman et al., 1986; Whiting & Whiting, 1973, 1975; cf. Brody, Stoneman, & Mackinnon, 1986). Due to gender roles, older girls may be expected to help, comfort, and teach younger siblings (Kaneko & Hamazaki, 1987). Indeed, by early adulthood, people are less defensive about accepting aid from a sister, particularly an older sister, than from a brother (especially a younger brother; Searcy & Eisenberg, 1992).

Siblings' prosocial behavior may be related in complex ways. Although Bryant and Crockenberg (1980) found that older and younger siblings' prosocial behaviors did not correlate, older and younger siblings' helping, sharing, and comforting were correlated with the other sibling's willingness to accept help. Moreover, although Dunn and Munn (1986) found little relation between older and younger siblings' prosocial behavior, younger siblings' cooperation and prosocial behavior were positively related to older siblings' giving and cooperation six months later. Further, siblings who expressed negative affect in a high percentage of their interactions were relatively unlikely to behave prosocially with one another. However, Stillwell and Dunn (1985), with a small sample, found only weak evidence of an association between quality of sibling interaction and children's sharing with a sibling.

Because sibling relationships are embedded in the family, it is not surprising that mothers' behaviors are linked to prosocial behavior between siblings. For example, when mothers discussed their newborn's feelings and needs with an older sibling, the older child was more nurturant toward the infant. Further, friendly interest in the infant persisted and predicted prosocial behavior toward the younger sibling three years later (Dunn & Kendrick, 1982). In another study, nurturant maternal responsiveness to young daughters' needs was correlated with younger siblings' comforting of and sharing with their older sibling. In contrast, mothers' unavailability was associated with older daughters' prosocial behavior toward their younger siblings (Bryant & Crockenberg, 1980). The latter finding is similar to Brody, Stoneman, and MacKinnon's (1986) finding that maternal valuing of a separate life from children was associated with older siblings' helping and managing their younger siblings. Perhaps older siblings, especially daughters, are expected to take a nurturant helping role when mother is unavailable relatively often.

Because sibling caregiving provides children with opportunities to learn about others' perspectives and emotions, children with sibling caregiving experience may develop relatively mature perspective-taking skills and therefore respond relatively appropriately and effectively in caregiving situations (see section on perspective taking). Stewart and Marvin (1984) found a positive relation between perspective taking and sibling caregiving; however, Howe and Ross (1990) did not (although perspective taking was related to friendly behavior between siblings). In addition, Garner, Jones, and Palmer (1994) found that emotional role-taking skills, but not cognitive perspective taking, predicted sibling caregiving behavior. Perspective taking about emotions may be a more relevant skill for sibling caregiving than is the case for cognitive perspective taking, although the latter has been emphasized in most studies of perspective taking and sibling interactions. Of course, even if correlated, sibling caregiving may not directly enhance perspective taking. For example, the correlation may be due to the fact that high-perspective-taking siblings are likely to be asked by parents to take care of younger siblings (Stewart & Marvin, 1984).

In summary, sibling interactions may be an important context for learning caregiving behaviors (particularly for older siblings) and the development of perspective taking. However, little is known about the ways the larger familial context moderates the development of prosocial responding in the sibling relationship.

Peer Influences on Prosocial Development

Developmental theorists frequently have tied the acquisition of morality to processes inherent in social interaction with peers (Piaget, 1932/1965; Sullivan, 1953; Youniss, 1980). For example, they have argued that because peer interactions involve association with equals and, frequently, cooperation, reciprocity, and mutuality, peer interaction may provide an optimal atmosphere for the acquisition of concepts and behaviors reflecting justice, kindness, and concern for another's welfare (Youniss, 1980). Consistent with this view, Tesson, Lewko, and Bigelow (1987) found that prosocial themes pertaining to issues such as reciprocity, sincerity and trust, helping and solving problems, and sensitivity to others' feelings were prominent in 6- to 13-year-old children's reports of the social rules they used in peer relationships.

Moreover, researchers have found that the quality of children's prosocial behavior directed toward peers and adults differs somewhat, particularly at younger ages. When asked to give examples of kindness directed toward peers, 6- to 14-year-olds tended to cite giving-sharing, playing, physical assistance, understanding, and teaching. In contrast, they cited primarily being good or polite, doing chores, and obeying in regard to adults (Youniss, 1980). Further, preschoolers provide more authority- and punishment-related reasons for complying with adults' than peers' requests, and more other-oriented or relational (friendship, liking) motives for complying with peers' requests (Eisenberg, Lundy, Shell, & Roth, 1985). With age, children appear to be slightly more likely to define kindness toward adults in a manner similar to peer-directed kindness, that is, as involving acts demonstrating concern rather than compliance (Youniss, 1980). Thus, peer interactions may provide a context that is conducive to the development of prosocial behavior motivated by other-oriented concerns rather than compliance, particularly in regard to prosocial actions directed toward individuals outside the family.

Other research also is consistent with the notion that peer interactions are important for the development of empathy, sympathy, and an other-orientation. According to maternal reports, infants and toddlers cry more in response to cries of peers than of adults (Zahn-Waxler, Iannotti, & Chapman, 1982). Children observed adults cry relatively infrequently, and when they did they generally did not cry. When children cried in response to adults' distress, it usually was in reaction to angry interactions such as fights

between parents. Moreover, prosocial behavior (when it occurred) was enacted more often in response to a child's than an adult's distress, and most of the children's prosocial actions to adults were directed toward their own parents. These findings further support the assertion that interactions with peers may be particularly important for the development of sympathy and prosocial responding, particularly directed to people besides parents (see Zahn-Waxler, Radke-Yarrow, Wagner, & Chapman, 1982).

Peers also may affect prosocial development because of their roles as models. Prosocial peer models sometimes have been found to be effective in eliciting selfishness (Ascione & Sanok, 1982) and prosocial behavior in the laboratory (Bryan & Walbek, 1970a, for boys but not girls; Elliot & Vasta, 1970; Owens & Ascione, 1991; cf. Ascione & Sanok, 1982; Barton, 1981). Familiarity and liking of peer models may be important factors in influencing children's prosocial behavior: peers have greater identification with fellow peers and may experience more freedom to try out new behaviors with peers than they do with adults (Damon, 1977). However, findings in this regard are sparse and are not readily interpretable (Owens & Ascione, 1991). In one study, children with a history of receiving social reinforcement from peers were more likely to model the donating behavior of a peer from whom they had received frequent rewards than the behavior of a nonrewarding peer. In contrast, children with a history of infrequent peer reinforcement imitated the prosocial behavior of a nonrewarding rather than rewarding peer (Hartup & Coates, 1967). Thus, characteristics of the child and the peer model likely influence whether children imitate peers' prosocial actions. (The role of friendship status on prosocial behavior is reviewed shortly.)

Researchers also have found that peer reinforcement affects children's self-regulated and moral behavior (e.g., Furman & Masters, 1980). Peers respond relatively frequently in a reinforcing manner (i.e., continue with conversation or play, give approval, thank, or smile) to peers' prosocial actions (Eisenberg, Cameron, Tryon, & Dodez, 1981; cf. Peterson, Ridley-Johnson, & Carter, 1984), but few investigators have examined whether such reinforcement has an effect on children's prosocial behavior. Eisenberg et al. (1981) found that preschool girls who engaged in relatively high levels of spontaneous prosocial behavior were those who received marginally more positive reinforcement for their prosocial actions from peers (also see Lennon & Eisenberg, 1987a). However, a similar association was not found for boys, and preschoolers (especially boys) who were high in compliant (requested) prosocial actions received low levels of positive reinforcement for their compliant prosocial actions. Sociable children were particularly likely to receive positive peer reactions when they enacted compliant prosocial actions, and children who responded positively to other children's spontaneous prosocial behaviors were likely to receive positive peer reactions for their own spontaneous and compliant prosocial behavior. Thus, children who were more assertive, sociable, and positive may have elicited the most peer reinforcement when they engaged in prosocial behavior. A cyclical process may occur in which socially competent children elicit more positive peer reactions for prosocial behavior, which in turn increases their prosocial behavior (with the reverse process occurring for children low in social skills).

In brief, peer interactions seem to provide optimal, or at least unique, opportunities for prosocial behavior, and peer responses in such contexts may influence the type and degree of potential prosocial responses (Zahn-Waxler et al., 1982). However, the role of peer interaction in older children's and adolescents' prosocial behavior seldom has been examined, and little is known about the degree to which the effects of peers are moderated by other variables (e.g., the nature of interactions with other socializers and characteristics of the child, the peer group, or the context).

The Role of School Programs on Children's Prosocial Behavior

Children likely receive considerable moral education and training in schools. However, little is known about the effects of school experiences on children's prosocial behavior.

One avenue for examining the potential impact of the school context on children's prosocial behavior is to assess the natural occurrence of prosocial behavior in the classroom. Hertz-Lazarowitz (1983; Hertz-Lazarowitz et al., 1989) found that naturally occurring prosocial behaviors in school classrooms (grades 1–12) were relatively rare (only 1.5–6.5% of total behaviors). Researchers usually have noted low frequencies of prosocial behavior in the preschool class, although estimates vary considerably with the operationalization of prosocial behavior (e.g., Caplan & Hay, 1989; Denham & Burger, 1991; Eisenberg, Cameron, Tryon, & Dodez, 1981; Eisenberg-Berg & Hand, 1979; Strayer, Wareing, & Rushton, 1979). Further, in studies of preschoolers, teachers rarely reinforced (Eisenberg et al., 1981) or encouraged (Caplan & Hay, 1989) children's prosocial behavior. These findings suggest that the typical classroom environment may not be conducive to eliciting frequent prosocial interaction among children. Salient and unambiguous expectations regarding prosocial behavior

may be necessary to elicit more spontaneous prosocial actions in the classroom.

Moreover, structuring classes to provide children with opportunities to help others may promote prosocial behavior. Bizman et al. (1978) found that Israeli kindergartners enrolled in classes that contained younger peers were more altruistic than those enrolled in classes that were homogeneous in regard to age. Further, elementary school Israeli students in active classrooms in which cooperation and individualized learning were emphasized helped peers more than students in traditional classrooms (Hertz-Lazarowitz et al., 1989).

One way to assess the effects of preschool and day care on children's prosocial development is to examine differences in children who attend school and those who do not. Clarke-Stewart (1981) suggested that attendance in group child care has a temporarily accelerating effect on social development and found that prosocial behavior was higher for children with nonparental care; however, evidence in support of this contention is equivocal. Schenk and Grusec (1987) found that home-care children were more likely than day care children to behave prosocially in situations involving an adult stranger, whereas the two groups were similar on helping unknown children. Other researchers have produced results that indicate that out-of-home care per se does not have any reliable or consistent effects on children's emerging social and prosocial development (Austin et al., 1991).

Although differences between home versus group care children may be limited, quality of the caregiving situation likely moderates the degree and type of influence preschools have on children's prosocial behavior and attitudes. Quality of the day care or preschool environment has been associated with children's self-regulation (Howes & Olenick, 1986), empathy and social competence (Vandell, Henderson, & Wilson, 1988), considerateness (Phillips, McCartney, & Scarr, 1987), and positive peer-related behaviors (including prosocial behaviors; Broberg, Hwang, Lamb, & Ketterlinus, 1989). Moreover, warm, supportive interactions with teachers have been associated with preschool children's modeling of teachers' prosocial actions (Yarrow et al., 1973) and positive interactions among students in the elementary school classroom (Serow & Solomon, 1979). In addition, Howes, Matheson, and Hamilton (1994) found that children classified as securely attached to their current and first preschool teachers were rated as more considerate and empathic with unfamiliar peers than were children classified as having an insecure (especially ambivalent) relationship with their teachers.

Contemporaneous teacher-child relationships better differentiated peer outcomes for children than did contemporary maternal attachment relations or child care history. Thus, degree and type of influence exerted by school experiences, as well as durability of effects on prosocial responding, probably vary as a function of quality of care received and the child's relationship with the teacher (as well as quality of care received from parents at home).

Based on the previously described literature concerning the socialization of prosocial attitudes and behavior, some investigators have attempted to design school-based programs aimed at fostering prosocial responding. For example, Solomon and colleagues (Solomon, Watson, Delucchi, Schaps, & Battistich, 1988; Watson, Solomon, Battistich, Schaps, & Solomon, 1989) developed a program, the Child Development Project (CDP), in which teachers were trained to maintain positive personal relationships with their students and to utilize a child-centered approach to classroom management emphasizing inductive discipline and student participation in rule setting. Other aspects of the program were designed to promote social understanding, highlight prosocial values, and provide helping activities; however, these program components were viewed as playing a more limited, supportive role in the program (Battistich, Watson, Solomon, Schaps, & Solomon, 1991).

Across five consecutive years of implementation (kindergarten through fourth grade), students in the program classrooms, compared to control classes, generally scored higher on ratings of prosocial behavior. These patterns held when both teachers' general competence and students' participation in cooperative activities were controlled, suggesting that program effects on children's prosocial behavior were not due simply to differences in teacher-initiated cooperative interactions or to more efficiently organized and managed classrooms (Solomon et al., 1988).

Interestingly, children enrolled in the program evidenced the highest ratings for prosocial and harmonious behavior and control children the lowest in kindergarten. Thus, it appears that the impact of this program was greatest when first introduced. The degree to which program effects generalized beyond the immediate classroom environment was unclear (Battistich et al., 1991). However, the teachers in the program had only one year of experience in implementing the program and the effects may have been more sustained given additional time for teachers to develop their techniques and fully integrate the program into the ongoing routine of the classroom.

In another longitudinal test of the effects of the CDP, the program was used with a cohort of students who began in kindergarten and continued through eighth grade (Solomon, Battistich, & Watson, 1993). Of particular interest, measures of prosocial reasoning and conflict resolution were obtained each year. Comparison students reasoned higher than CDP children at kindergarten, but CDP students reasoned at higher levels from first grade on, although the within-year difference was significant only in second grade. In general, CDP students also evidenced higher conflict resolution scores (indicating consideration of others' needs and a reliance on the use of compromise and sharing) than comparison students. Program effects appeared to be greater when combined across years (effects were not consistently significant within years). However, the CDP was implemented in schools with mostly advantaged White children. The extent to which the CDP would be effective with more diverse samples of children is unclear.

Other school-based programs have been designed to promote empathy. Although some seem to have been minimally effective (e.g., Kalliopuska & Tiitinen, 1991), Feshbach and Feshbach (1982) found that empathy training significantly increased incidents of prosocial behaviors in school-age children. Moreover, the use of cooperative educational techniques in classroom activities has been found to promote acceptance of others (Johnson & Johnson, 1975) as well as cooperation and prosocial behavior (Hertz-Lazarowitz & Sharan, 1984; Hertz-Lazarowitz, Sharan, & Steinberg, 1980; Matusov, Bell, & Rogoff, 1993).

Some researchers have developed school-based programs that include a formal curriculum component. For example, Ascione (1992) studied the effects of a humane education program when used with first, second, fourth, and fifth graders for nearly 40 hours over the school year. There was relatively little immediate evidence of an effect for younger children, although there was an effect on humane attitudes a year later (Ascione & Weber, 1993). Humane attitudes were enhanced for the fourth graders in the immediate posttest and for fourth and fifth graders a year later. Human-directed empathy increased for both fourth and fifth graders on both the initial and one-year posttest.

In summary, although prosocial behavior often may not be fostered in the classroom, quality early schooling and supportive relationships between children and their teachers have been associated with the development of prosocial behavior. Moreover, school-based programs designed to enhance prosocial values, behaviors, and attitudes in children can be effective in fostering children's prosocial attitudes and behaviors toward both humans and animals. However, most programs have involved relatively weak and short interventions that may not be adequate for some groups of children. Further, evaluation of the programs sometimes has been hampered by the fact that control groups have been exposed to similar content or experiences as the experimental group, albeit to a lesser degree (e.g., Ascione, 1992). Variation in instruction among teachers within a treatment group also may be problematic. These issues are critical if one hopes to argue that such programs are cost-effective and impactful, especially in contexts where resources and time are limited.

COGNITIVE AND SOCIOCOGNITIVE CORRELATES OF PROSOCIAL DEVELOPMENT

Numerous theorists have hypothesized that cognitive and sociocognitive skills, particularly perspective taking and moral reasoning, foster prosocial responding (Batson, 1991; Eisenberg, 1986; Hoffman, 1982; Staub, 1979). Moreover, it is likely that certain types of prosocial experiences provide experiences that enhance children's sociocognitive skills. The relevant literature on cognitive/sociocognitive capabilities and prosocial development is now reviewed, with an emphasis on updating earlier reviews. (See Eisenberg, 1986, for a review of children's understanding of, and attributions about, others' kindness.)

Intelligence, Cognitive Capacities, and Academic Achievement

Because cognitive abilities may underlie the ability to discern others' need or distress or the capacity to devise ways to respond to others' need, it would be logical to expect a modest relation between measures of intelligence and prosocial responding, particularly prosocial behavior involving higher-level moral reasoning or the sophisticated cognitive skills. Some investigators have obtained moderate positive correlations (e.g., often .30 to .40) between measures of intelligence and self-report (Ma & Leung, 1991; Weidman & Strayhorn, 1992) and other measures of prosocial behavior (Abroms & Gollin, 1980; Krebs & Sturrup, 1982; Mussen et al., 1970; Zahn-Waxler et al., 1982; also see Lourenco, 1993). In addition, there is weak, albeit somewhat inconsistent, support for a positive relation

between scores on achievement tests and children's empathy (Feshbach, 1978; Feshbach & Feshbach, 1987) and sympathy (Wise & Cramer, 1988). However, other researchers have found no significant relations between tests of intelligence (or scholastic ability) and children's prosocial behavior (Grant, Weiner, & Rushton, 1976; Jennings, Fitch, & Suwalsky, 1987; Rubin & Schneider, 1973; Rushton & Wiener, 1975; Turner & Harris, 1984; also see Harris, 1967) or have obtained mixed or inconsistent relations with prosocial behavior (Friedrich & Stein, 1973; Payne, 1980; Severy & Davis, 1971; Strayer & Roberts, 1989) or sympathy (Loban, 1953; Wise & Cramer, 1988). This pattern of findings is consistent with the view that intelligence is associated with certain types of prosocial responding, or prosocial behavior in some contexts.

As previously noted, intelligence may be linked to the quality of both children's motivation for assisting and the helping act itself. For example, Bar-Tal, Korenfeld, and Raviv (1985) found that intelligent fifth graders engaged in higher quality (more internally motivated), but not higher quantity, prosocial behavior than their less intelligent peers. Few investigators have examined the quality of the actual helping behavior of children varying in intelligence. We now examine some cognitive and sociocognitive abilities that may mediate the modest association between intelligence and prosocial responding.

Perspective Taking

It is commonly assumed that perspective-taking skills increase the likelihood of individuals identifying, understanding, and sympathizing with others' distress or need (e.g., Batson, 1991; Eisenberg, Shea, Carlo, & Knight, 1991; Feshbach, 1978; Hoffman, 1982). For example, Hoffman (1982) proposed that improvement in young children's perspective-taking ability is critical to children's abilities to differentiate between their own and others' distresses and to accurately understand the nature of others' emotional reactions. These skills are believed to foster empathy and sympathy and, consequently, prosocial behavior. Burleson (1985) further suggested that people skilled at perspective taking are able not only to discern and pursue the goal of improving another's condition, but also to pursue and achieve goals associated with sensitive comforting (e.g., the goals of protecting the other's self-concept).

Information about others' internal states can be obtained by means of imagining oneself in another's position or through other processes such as accessing stored mental associations and social scripts or deduction (Karniol, 1995). Children also may have "theories" about others' internal states that they use to infer how others feel (Eisenberg, Murphy, & Shepard, 1997). For convenience, and because it generally is difficult to identify the processes underlying performance on perspective taking tasks, the term perspective-taking is used to refer to the ability to engage in any of these processes when they result in knowledge about others' internal states.

At least three kinds of perspective taking have been discussed: (a) perceptual—the ability to take another's perspective visually; (b) affective—the ability (or tendency) to understand another's emotional state; and (c) cognitive or conceptual—the ability (or tendency) to understand another's cognitions. In a review of the existing literature in the early 1980s including mostly studies of children, Underwood and Moore (1982) found that all three types of perspective taking were positively related to prosocial behavior. Moreover, a number of studies not included in the Underwood and Moore review contain evidence of an association between perspective taking and prosocial behavior (including comforting skills), although findings sometimes have been significant for only some of the examined associations (Adams, 1983; Ahammer & Murray, 1979; Bender & Carlson, 1982; Bengtsson & Johnson, 1992; Burleson, 1984; Burleson & Kunkel, 1995; Dekovic & Gerris, 1994; Denham, 1986; Denham & Couchoud, 1991; Denham et al., 1994; Eisenberg, Carlo, Murphy, & Van Court, 1995; Estrada, 1995; Garner, Jones, & Miner, 1994; Garner, Jones, & Palmer, 1994; Hudson, Forman, & Brion-Meisels, 1982; Jennings et al., 1987; Krebs & Sturrup, 1982; Marsh, Serafica, & Barenboim, 1981; McGuire & Weisz, 1982; Stewart & Marvin, 1984; J. Strayer & Roberts, 1989; Tabor & Shaffer, 1981; also see Cutrona & Feshbach, 1979; Staub, 1971c). In contrast, no such association has been found in some studies not reviewed by Underwood and Moore (e.g., Abroms & Gollin, 1980; Astington & Jenkins, 1995; Bar-Tal, Korenfeld, & Raviv, 1985; Jones, 1985; Lalonde & Chandler, 1995; Peterson, 1983a; J. Strayer, 1980; Zahn-Waxler et al., 1982). Nonetheless, to our knowledge, in only three studies has perspective taking been significantly negatively related to children's prosocial behavior (Barrett & Yarrow, 1977, for low-assertive boys only; Lemare & Krebs, 1983; Iannotti, 1985, who obtained positive, negative, and nonsignificant correlations).

Positive findings were obtained in many studies despite the fact that most researchers used single measures of perspective-taking abilities or prosocial behavior rather than more reliable indexes created by aggregation across measures. The association does not seem to be due merely to increases in both perspective taking and prosocial behavior with age; often, the age range of the study participants was narrow or findings were maintained when age was controlled (e.g., Burleson, 1984; Burleson & Kunkel, 1995; Garner, Jones, & Palmer, 1994; see Underwood & Moore, 1982).

It is unrealistic to expect measures of perspective taking to relate to prosocial behavior in all circumstances (Eisenberg, 1986). In fact, the relation seems to be stronger when there is a match between the type of perspective-taking skills assessed and the type of level of understanding likely to promote prosocial behavior in the given context (Carlo, Knight, Eisenberg, & Rotenberg, 1991; also see Hudson et al., 1982). Moreover, in some circumstances, perspective-taking skills may be unimportant because prosocial actions are enacted in a relatively automatic fashion due to either their low cost (Langer, Blank, & Chanowitz, 1978) or the compelling, crisis-like nature of the situation. In many other contexts, prosocial behavior may be motivated by any number of factors other than knowledge of another's internal state, such as social approval or internalized values (although perspective taking may enhance prosocial behavior in situations involving the potential for social evaluation; Froming, Allen, & Jensen, 1985).

Further, some people may perspective-take but lack the motivation, skills, or social assertiveness required to take action. In support of the importance of moderating variables, perspective taking has been linked to prosocial behavior for children who are socially assertive (Barrett & Yarrow, 1977; Denham & Couchoud, 1991) or person-oriented (i.e., participate in group activities; Ujiie, 1981–1982), but not for children lacking in these qualities. Similarly, the effects of perspective taking on prosocial behavior sometimes appear to be mediated or moderated by children's empathic/sympathetic responding (Barnett & Thompson, 1985; Roberts & Strayer, 1996; also see Wiggers & Willems, 1983). In one study, children who donated money to help a child who had been burned were those who not only evidenced relatively sophisticated perspective-taking skills, but also were sympathetic and understood units and value of money (Knight, Johnson, Carlo, & Eisenberg, 1994).

In summary, it appears that children with higher perspective-taking skills are somewhat more prosocial, particularly if their perspective-taking abilities are those relevant to the prosocial task and if they have the relevant social skills (e.g., assertiveness) and emotional motivation (e.g., sympathy) to act on the knowledge obtained by perspective taking. Perspective-taking skills may be involved in discerning others' needs, providing sensitive help, and evoking the affective motivation for prosocial action (i.e., sympathy, empathy, or guilt). Moreover, it is likely that children with mature perspective-taking abilities are provided with more opportunities to be prosocial; for example, older siblings with better perspective-taking skills are more frequently asked by their mothers to provide caregiving to younger siblings (Stewart & Marvin, 1984). In future work, the mediators and moderators of associations between perspective taking and prosocial behavior merit particular attention.

Person Attributions and Expressed Motives

As discussed previously, there are relatively clear developmental trends in the motives that children report or reflect in their prosocial behavior (via the situations in which they choose to assist another). Of course, it is recognized that children sometimes may report socially desirable motives or may have little access to their motives (see Eisenberg, 1986, for a discussion of these issues). Nonetheless, investigators have explored the relation between expressed motives and actual prosocial behavior. Although some researchers have not obtained much evidence of a link between expressed motives and prosocial behavior (Eisenberg, Cameron, Pasternack, & Tryon, 1988; Eisenberg, Pasternack, Cameron, & Tryon, 1984; see Eisenberg, 1986), most investigators have found some support for an association between level of expressed motives and quantity (e.g., Bar-Tal, Korenfeld, & Raviv, 1985; Bar-Tal, Raviv, & Leiser, 1980; Dreman & Greenbaum, 1973) or quality (i.e., maturity; Bar-Tal et al., 1985; Raviv, Bar-Tal, & Lewis-Levin, 1980; Wright, 1942; also see Dreman, 1976) of prosocial behavior. In addition, C. Smith et al. (1979) found that children who rated their own donating as relatively intrinsically (rather than extrinsically) motivated donated more than did other children. Although Bar-Tal and Nissim (1984) obtained no relation between expressed motives and helping, they obtained motives only from adolescents who helped and not from nonhelpers.

Thus, in general, there appears to be a modest relation between children's expression of motives for prosocial behavior and the quantity and quality of their prosocial actions. As discussed by Eisenberg (1986), it is unclear whether children's motives influence their prosocial responding or if children formulate motives post hoc to the execution of behavior based on self-observation. In support of the former explanation, C. Smith et al. (1979) found that individual differences in expressed internality of motives were associated with donating, whereas environmental contingencies (e.g., rewards and punishments) that might influence post hoc evaluations were not. In any case, it is likely that people have greater access to their cognitive processes when a task is not so overlearned that it can be performed in a mindless manner. Therefore, it is probable that expressed motives are more accurate for prosocial acts that are not performed automatically—that is, when the potential benefactor must consider whether or not to assist. However, at this time, data to test this idea are not available (see, however, Eisenberg & Shell, 1986).

Moral Reasoning

In general, investigators have hypothesized that there should be some link between children's moral reasoning and their behavior. For example, Krebs and Van Hesteren (1994) argued as follows: "Advanced stages give rise to higher quantities of altruism than less advanced stages because they give rise to greater social sensitivity, stronger feelings of responsibility, and so on. . . . Inasmuch as higher stages of development include lower stages, they enable people to engage in the forms of altruism that stem from their most advanced stages plus the forms of altruism that stem from all the earlier stages they have acquired. . . . We propose that advanced stage-structures give rise to forms of altruism that are (a) purer (i.e., more exclusively devoted to enhancing the welfare of others, as opposed to the self) and (b) deeper (i.e., that benefit others in less superficial and less transient ways) than less advanced structures" (p. 136).

The fact that prosocial actions can be motivated by a range of considerations, including altruistic, pragmatic, and even self-oriented concerns, obviously attenuates the degree to which one might expect associations between general level of moral reasoning and observed prosocial actions. However, prosocial behavior motivated by a particular type of concern (e.g., empathy) is likely to be correlated with use of types or levels of reasoning reflecting that concern, although not necessarily with overall level of reasoning.

In early reviews of the literature on the association between moral reasoning and prosocial behavior, Blasi (1980) and Underwood and Moore (1982) concluded that there was support for the hypothesized positive association. However, they reviewed numerous studies with adult participants, studies involving distributions of rewards, and research on self-attributions. In published studies with only child participants, prosocial behavior has been either positively related to aspects of Piaget's scheme of moral judgment (e.g., intentionality, distributive justice; Emler & Rushton, 1974) or nonsignificantly related (Bar-Tal et al., 1985; Bar-Tal & Nissim, 1984; Grant et al., 1976). Kohlbergian prohibition- and justice-oriented moral reasoning (or modified versions thereof) also has been positively related to children's prosocial behavior in some studies (Harris, Mussen, & Rutherford, 1976; Rubin & Schneider, 1973; cf. Hoffman, 1975b; Santrock, 1975b).

It is logical to expect a greater correspondence between moral reasoning and prosocial behavior if the moral reasoning dilemma concerns reasoning about prosocial behavior rather than another type of behavior. In fact, Levin and Bekerman-Greenberg (1980) found that the strength of the positive relation between reasoning about sharing and actual prosocial behavior was somewhat greater if the dilemma and sharing task were similar in content. When researchers have assessed children's moral reasoning about dilemmas involving helping or sharing behavior, generally moral reasoning has been associated with at least some measures of prosocial behavior (e.g., Eisenberg, Carlo, et al., 1995; Eisenberg, Shell, et al., 1987; Larrieu & Mussen, 1986; also see Borg, Hultman, & Waern, 1978, and Eisenberg, 1986, for a review). In addition, children reasoning at developmentally mature levels are less likely than children reasoning at lower levels to say they would discriminate between people close to them and others when deciding whether to help (Eisenberg, 1983; also see Ma, 1992). However, predicted findings have not been obtained in all studies (Schenk & Grusec, 1987; Simmons & Zumpf, 1986).

Moreover, in most studies, not all measures of prosocial moral judgment have been related to all measures of prosocial behavior. Hedonistic reasoning and needs-oriented reasoning (i.e., rudimentary other-oriented reasoning) tend to be negatively and positively related, respectively, to prosocial behavior (e.g., Carlo, Koller, Eisenberg, Pacheco, & Loguercio, 1996; Eisenberg, Boehnke, et al., 1985; Eisenberg, Carlo, et al., 1995; Eisenberg et al., 1984; Eisenberg & Shell, 1986; Eisenberg-Berg & Hand, 1979; Eisenberg, Shell, et al., 1987; Eisenberg, Miller, Shell, McNalley, & Shea, 1991). In addition, sometimes a mode of reasoning

that is relatively sophisticated for the age-group (Miller, Eisenberg, Fabes, Shell, & Gular, 1996; Schenk & Grusec, 1987) or an overall level of reasoning index (Eisenberg, Carlo, et al., 1995; Eisenberg, Miller, et al., 1991; Eisenberg-Berg, 1979b; Levin & Bekerman-Greenberg, 1980) has been significantly associated with prosocial behavior. Thus, types of reasoning that clearly reflect a self- versus other-orientation and are developmentally mature for the age-group are likely to predict prosocial responding.

The nature of the enacted prosocial behavior also seems to be a critical variable. In observational studies, prosocial moral reasoning most often has been significantly related to preschoolers' spontaneous sharing behaviors rather than helping behaviors (which, in these studies, generally entailed little cost) or prosocial behaviors performed in compliance with a peer's request (Eisenberg et al., 1984; Eisenberg-Berg & Hand, 1979). Spontaneous prosocial behaviors are more likely than requested prosocial behaviors to be performed for internal, altruistic reasons; preschoolers who are relatively high in responding to peers' requests appear to be those who are nonassertive and, consequently, are targets of peers' requests (Eisenberg et al., 1981; Eisenberg, Fabes, Miller, Shell, et al., 1990; Eisenberg et al., 1984).

Moreover, in laboratory studies involving elementary or high school students, prosocial moral reasoning more frequently has been associated with prosocial actions that incur a cost (e.g., donating or volunteering time after school) than with behaviors low in cost (e.g., helping pick up dropped paper clips; Eisenberg, Boehnke, et al., 1985; Eisenberg & Shell, 1986; Eisenberg, Shell, et al., 1987; Eisenberg-Berg, 1979b; also see Miller, Eisenberg, Fabes, & Shell, 1996). Eisenberg and Shell (1986) hypothesized that low-cost behaviors are performed rather automatically, without much cognitive reflection, moral or otherwise. In contrast, moral reasoning is more likely to be associated with children's prosocial behavior in situations involving a cost because consideration of the cost is likely to evoke cognitive conflict and morally relevant decision making.

It is probable that the relation between moral judgment and prosocial behavior also is moderated by other variables, particularly for lower-level modes of reasoning (at higher levels, moral principles may be sufficient motivation to help). One likely moderator is sympathetic responding. Consistent with this view, Miller et al. (1996) found that preschoolers who reported sympathy for hospitalized children and who were relatively high in use of needs-oriented reasoning were especially likely to help hospitalized children at a cost to themselves. Affective motivation such as sympathy (and perhaps guilt) often may be necessary to spur the individual to action.

The relation between moral judgment and prosocial behavior may be partially mediated by differential social skills of high and low moral reasoning children. Bear and Rys (1994) found that second- and third-grade boys (but not girls) who were high in hedonistic reasoning and low in needs-oriented reasoning were deficient in social competence, high in acting-out behaviors, and relatively unpopular with peers. Perhaps children who tend to be self- rather than other-oriented, due to their own self-related priorities and to reduced opportunities to interact in positive ways with peers, are less likely than other children to develop the social skills needed to comprehend and intervene in prosocial contexts. Casting children's moral reasoning in the larger context of the development of competent social functioning may provide new insight into why children low in prosocial moral judgment often are unlikely to perform spontaneous or costly prosocial actions.

EMPATHY-RELATED EMOTIONAL RESPONDING

As discussed previously, psychologists (e.g., Batson, 1991; Eisenberg, 1986; Feshbach, 1978; Hoffman, 1982; Staub, 1979) and philosophers (Blum, 1980; Hume, 1748/1975), have proposed that prosocial behavior, particularly altruism, often is motivated by empathy or sympathy. Links between empathy or sympathy and prosocial behavior have been presumed to exist both within specific contexts (e.g., Batson, 1991; Eisenberg & Fabes, 1990) and at the dispositional level (i.e., people with a dispositional tendency toward empathy/sympathy are expected to be altruistic in general; Eisenberg & Miller, 1987; Staub, 1979).

Although many psychologists have assumed that empathy plays a role in prosocial behavior, in a meta-analytic review, Underwood and Moore (1982) found that empathy was *not* significantly related to prosocial behavior. Many of the studies they reviewed were conducted with children, and most involved a particular type of measure: the picture/story measure of empathy. With this type of measure, children are presented with a series of short vignettes, often illustrated, about children in emotionally evocative contexts (e.g., when a child loses his or her dog). After each vignette, the child is asked "How do you feel?" or a similar question. If children say they felt an emotion similar to that which the

story protagonist would be expected to feel, they typically are viewed as empathizing.

More recently, the validity of this sort of measure has been seriously questioned (Eisenberg & Lennon, 1983; Eisenberg-Berg & Lennon, 1980; Lennon, Eisenberg, & Carroll, 1983). In fact, the degree of association between measures of empathy-related responding and prosocial behavior appears to vary as a function of the measure of empathy. In a more recent meta-analytic review of the literature, Eisenberg and Miller (1987) found no significant relation between prosocial behavior and picture/story measures (or children's self-reported reactions to enactments or to videotapes of others in distress or need). In contrast, there were significant positive associations for non-self-report measures of empathy-related responding and self-report measures for older adolescents and adults. Thus, it seemed that there was a problem with the types of self-report measures used in most studies of children's empathy. Although questionnaire and facial measures of empathy generally were associated with children's prosocial behavior, at the time of the Eisenberg and Miller review there were few published studies including facial measures or the use of questionnaires with preschool or early elementary school children (see Eisenberg & Miller, 1987, for references before 1987; also see Bengtsson & Johnson, 1992; J. Strayer & Roberts, 1989).

In recent years, it has become clear that it is essential to differentiate among various empathy-related emotional reactions. Batson (1991) hypothesized that sympathy (as defined at the beginning of this chapter) is intimately linked with other-oriented motivations and, consequently, with other-oriented, altruistic helping behavior. In contrast, personal distress is viewed as involving the egoistic motivation of alleviating one's own distress; therefore, it is expected to be linked with prosocial behavior only when the easiest way to reduce one's own distress is to eliminate the other's distress (e.g., when one cannot escape contact with the empathy-inducing person).

Consistent with his theorizing, Batson and his colleagues, in laboratory studies with adults, have found that sympathy is more likely to be associated with helping than is personal distress when it is easy for people to escape contact with the person needing assistance (see Batson, 1991; also see Carlo, Eisenberg, Troyer, Switzer, & Speer, 1991; Eisenberg, Fabes, Miller, Schaller, et al., 1989). In a series of studies, Eisenberg, Fabes, and their colleagues and students have obtained similar findings with children. First they demonstrated that children and adults exhibit different heart rate (HR), skin conductance, facial, and (to some degree) self-reported reactions in situations likely to induce vicarious sympathy and distress (or personal distress). For example, children and adults exhibited HR deceleration when confronted with a sympathy-inducing stimulus and HR acceleration and higher skin conductance when viewing a distressing film or talking about distressing events (Eisenberg, Fabes, et al., 1988, 1991; Eisenberg, Fabes, Carlo, et al., 1992; Eisenberg, Schaller, et al., 1988). Then Eisenberg, Fabes, and colleagues examined the relation of these markers of sympathy and personal distress to prosocial responding. In their studies, children's prosocial behavior was as anonymous as possible and children did not have to deal in any way with the needy other(s) if they did not want to do so. Across a variety of studies in which children were shown empathy-inducing videotapes, Eisenberg, Fabes, and colleagues found that children who exhibited facial or physiological (i.e., heart rate or skin conductance) markers of sympathy tended to be relatively prosocial when given an opportunity to assist someone in the film and people similar to those in the film (e.g., hospitalized children). In contrast, those who exhibited evidence of personal distress, particularly boys, tended to be less prosocial (Eisenberg, Fabes, Carlo, et al., 1993; Eisenberg, Fabes, Miller, Shell, et al., 1990; Eisenberg, Fabes, Miller, et al., 1989; Fabes, Eisenberg, Karbon, Bernzweig, et al., 1994; Fabes, Eisenberg, Karbon, Troyer, & Switzer, 1994; Fabes, Eisenberg, & Miller, 1990; Miller et al., 1996). Self-report measures tended to be less consistently related to children's prosocial behaviors (Eisenberg & Fabes, 1990, 1991). Fabes, Eisenberg, and Eisenbud (1993) also found that skin conductance (a marker of personal distress) predicted girls' (but not boys') low *dispositional* (rather than situational) helpfulness (i.e., ratings of trait helpfulness rather than prosocial behavior in the same context). Moreover, facial reactions of sympathy (Eisenberg, Fabes, Miller, Shell, et al., 1990; Eisenberg, McCreath, & Ahn, 1988) or global empathy (Lennon, Eisenberg, & Carroll, 1986) have been linked to prosocial behavior in another context.

Of course, not all markers of sympathy or personal distress in Eisenberg, Fabes, and their colleagues' research predicted prosocial behavior in all studies (or sometimes for both sexes; e.g., Eisenberg, Fabes, Karbon, et al., 1996; Miller et al., 1996). Nonetheless, the overall pattern of findings is rather consistent. Further, research in other laboratories has provided some support for Eisenberg and Fabes's findings. For example, Zahn-Waxler and her colleagues found that sympathetic concern and prosocial actions seemed to co-occur in the behavior of children aged

14 and 20 months (Zahn-Waxler, Robinson, & Emde, 1992) and 4 to 5 years (Zahn-Waxler, Cole, Welsh, & Fox, 1995), although self-distress in reaction to another's emotion (Zahn-Waxler, Robinson, & Emde, 1992) and arousal (Zahn-Waxler et al., 1995) were unrelated to prosocial behavior in toddlers. In addition, Zahn-Waxler et al. (1995) found (a) children's HR deceleration during exposure to sadness (at the peak interval) was associated with three of four measures of prosocial responding, and (b) behavioral/facial measures of concerned attention were positively related to prosocial behavior directed toward the target of concern. Further, Trommsdorff (1995) obtained positive correlations between German and Japanese 5-year-old girls' sympathetic reactions to an adult's sadness and the girls' prosocial behavior. Distress reactions were negatively related to German girls' prosocial behavior but were unrelated to Japanese girls' prosocial behavior. In one study in which the expected relation was not obtained, facial expressions of distress and concern were combined into one index (Roberts & Strayer, 1996). Moreover, HR markers of reactions to empathy-inducing films seem to predict prosocial behavior within but not across contexts (e.g., Eisenberg, Fabes, Miller, Shell, et al., 1990).

Preschoolers' personal distress reactions also have been positively related to children's tendency to engage in compliant, requested prosocial behaviors in other contexts (Eisenberg, Fabes, Miller, Shell, et al., 1990; Eisenberg, McCreath, & Ahn, 1988). Compliant prosocial behavior has been correlated with low assertiveness, low levels of positive peer reinforcement, and low levels of positive response to peers' prosocial actions, as well as lower levels of social interaction than has spontaneous prosocial behavior. Children high in compliant prosocial responding, especially boys, seem to be nonassertive and perhaps are viewed as easy targets by their peers (Eisenberg et al., 1981; Eisenberg, McCreath, & Ahn, 1988; Larrieu, 1984). Eisenberg and Fabes (1992) hypothesized that young children who exhibit high levels of compliant behavior with peers are relatively low in social competence and emotion regulation and engage in requested prosocial behaviors as a means of curtailing unpleasant social interactions and the resultant negative emotion.

In Eisenberg and Miller's (1987) review, there were relatively few studies of the relation between children's prosocial behavior and children's self-reported empathy-related responding as assessed with questionnaires. Recent studies support the view that questionnaire measures tapping either empathy (Eisenberg, Miller, et al., 1991; Eisenberg, Shell, et al., 1987; also see Barnett, Howard, et al.,

1981) or sympathy (Eisenberg, Carlo, et al., 1995; Eisenberg, Miller, et al., 1991; Estrada, 1995; Knight et al., 1994) tend to be positively related to some measures of children's prosocial behavior in Asian cultures (e.g., in Japan; Ando, 1987; Asakawa, Iwawaki, Mondori, & Minami, 1987) as well as in Western societies. Relations between empathy or sympathy and prosocial behavior seem to be most consistent for self-reported or relatively costly prosocial behavior (Eisenberg, Miller, et al., 1991; Eisenberg, Miller, et al., 1987). Moreover, self-reported empathy often has been related to some measures of prosocial behavior and not others (e.g., Larrieu & Mussen, 1986; J. Strayer & Roberts, 1989; also see Roberts & Strayer, 1996). However, empathy questionnaires often contain items that may reflect personal distress or sympathy in addition to empathy. Children's self-reported personal distress on questionnaires tends not to be related to children's prosocial behavior (Eisenberg, Carlo, et al., 1995; Eisenberg, Miller, et al., 1991), although a weak negative relation was obtained in one study with adolescents (Estrada, 1995). It is likely that questionnaire measures of personal distress, which have been adapted from work with adults, are not ideal for children.

Further, modified versions of the picture/story procedure have been more consistently correlated with prosocial behavior than in the past. For example, Miller et al. (1996) used a self-report measure in which preschoolers pointed at labeled visual depictions of emotional expressions to indicate their reactions to an empathy-inducing videotape and then rated the intensity of their empathic arousal. They found that children's reports of sadness and low levels of happiness were related to helping children like those in the videotape; reported sympathy was correlated with helping an injured adult in another context. J. Strayer (1993) developed a measure of empathy that combines degree of affective sharing experienced (i.e., degree of match between own and stimulus person's emotion) with the child's cognitive attribution for his or her own emotion. The measure contains seven levels of cognitive mediation varying in level of interpersonal understanding and perspective taking. High scores on this measure have been linked to a variety of measures of prosocial behavior, particularly for boys (Roberts & Strayer, 1996), as well as with greater expressed willingness to help and report of relatively high numbers of helping strategies when children were asked how they would respond to situations depicted in videotapes (J. Strayer & Schroeder, 1989).

In brief, recent research findings are consistent with the conclusion that sympathy and sometimes empathy (depending on their operationalization) are positively related to prosocial behavior, whereas personal distress, particularly as assessed with nonverbal measures, is negatively related to prosocial behavior. As might be expected, there is more evidence of associations within contexts than across contexts, although children with a sympathetic disposition appear to be somewhat more prosocial in general than are other children. In addition, there is evidence that the effects of sympathy are moderated by dispositional perspective taking (Knight et al., 1994) and moral reasoning (Miller et al., 1996). Thus, it is important to identify dispositional and situational factors that influence when and whether empathy-related situational reactions and dispositional characteristics are related to prosocial behavior.

PERSONALITY CORRELATES OF PROSOCIAL BEHAVIOR

There are a number of aspects of children's personalities or dispositions besides those already discussed that might be expected to relate to children's prosocial responding. Some of the most frequently examined are reviewed in this section.

Although differences in personality may reflect both constitutional and environmental factors, some personality characteristics, such as the tendency to experience negative emotions, seem to have a genetic basis (e.g., Plomin et al., 1993). Thus, some of the research on personality correlates—particularly those aspects of personality viewed as part of temperament—is relevant to an understanding of the constitutional bases of prosocial behavior and empathy. Moreover, information on the personality correlates of prosocial behavior may provide clues to the environmental origins of prosocial behavior when there is evidence of a link between a given aspect of personality and socialization.

The assertion that there are personality correlates of prosocial behavior implies a more basic assumption: that there is some consistency in children's prosocial responding. The issue of consistency—that is, of the existence of an altruistic (or moral) personality—has been an issue of debate for many years and continues to be a topic of considerable interest in the social psychological literature (Batson, 1991; Carlo, Eisenberg, et al., 1991; Eisenberg, Miller, et al., 1989). This issue is reviewed in moderate detail in other sources (Eisenberg & Mussen, 1989; Graziano & Eisenberg, 1997); thus, this literature is merely summarized briefly.

Consistency of Prosocial Behavior

Although findings differ considerably across measures of prosocial behavior and studies, there is evidence of modest consistency across situations and time. Evidence of consistency is weakest in studies of infants and preschoolers (e.g., Dunn & Munn, 1986; Eisenberg, Cameron, Pasternack, & Tryon, 1988; Eisenberg, McCreath, & Ahn, 1988; Eisenberg et al., 1984; Iannotti, 1985; Richman et al., 1988; J. Strayer & Roberts, 1989), although often some evidence of consistency has been obtained (Denham, 1986; Denham & Couchoud, 1991; Denham et al., 1994; Radke-Yarrow & Zahn-Waxler, 1984; Rheingold et al., 1976; Rutherford & Mussen, 1968; Stanhope et al., 1987; F. Strayer et al., 1979; Yarrow et al., 1976; Zahn-Waxler, Robinson, & Emde, 1992). Findings in the elementary school years are somewhat more consistent than those during the earlier years. Although nonsignificant correlations among prosocial indexes have been obtained in some studies (e.g., Krebs & Sturrup, 1982; Weissbrod, 1976), positive relations among measures of prosocial responding, across situations, raters, or time, often have been obtained (e.g., Bar-Tal & Raviv, 1979; Berndt, 1981a; Dekovic & Janssens, 1992; Dlugokinski & Firestone, 1974; Eisenberg, Shell, et al., 1987; Elliott & Vasta, 1970; Rubin & Schneider, 1973; Rushton & Littlefield, 1979; Rushton & Teachman, 1978; Rushton & Wiener, 1975; Tremblay, Vitaro, Gagnon, Piche, & Royer, 1992, Vitaro, Gagnon, & Tremblay, 1990, 1991). In the preschool and school years, correlations among measures may be particularly likely to occur between acts directed toward the same target (e.g., peer versus teacher; Payne, 1980; F. Strayer et al., 1979) and when aggregate measures of prosocial behavior are used (e.g., F. Strayer et al., 1979).

Evidence of consistency is strongest in studies of adolescents' prosocial and empathic tendencies (Davis & Franzoi, 1991; Eisenberg, Carlo, et al., 1995; Eisenberg, Miller, et al., 1991). For example, Savin-Williams, Small, and Zeldin (1981; Small, Zeldin, & Savin-Williams, 1983; Zeldin, Savin-Williams, & Small, 1984; Zeldin, Small, & Savin-Williams, 1982) found impressive consistency between peer ratings and observations of prosocial behavior in a natural setting, and across observations in different situations.

In summary, it appears that there is some consistency across measures and time in children's prosocial behavior, particularly for older children. Given the wide range of measures of prosocial behavior and the diversity of motives likely to be associated with this range of behaviors, it is impressive that investigators frequently have found significant relations across situations or time. Correlations would be expected to be considerably stronger if researchers could control for the motives underlying prosocial behavior (e.g., assess only altruistically motivated prosocial behavior; see Yarrow et al., 1976) and for cognitive and personality (e.g., assertiveness) prerequisites for various measures of prosocial behavior. A complex conceptualization of prosocial tendencies, one that acknowledges the fact that prosocial behaviors are motivated by numerous factors and facilitated or limited by person variable, would be beneficial in guiding future work regarding consistency in prosocial responding.

Personality Correlates

Aspects of temperament or personality are associated with individual differences in both the inclination to assist others and in the tendency to enact prosocial behaviors when motivationally inclined to do so. Given the correlational nature of associations between personality variables and prosocial behavior, causal relations are difficult to prove. Nonetheless, the literature on personality correlates provides some clues regarding why certain people are more prosocial in general, and why some people but not others assist in certain contexts.

Sociability and Shyness

Sociability and shyness, which likely have a temperamental basis (Kagan, Ch. 4 and Rothbart & Bates, Ch. 3, this Volume), appear to influence if and when children assist. In preschool and beyond, children prone to participate in activities at school (Jennings et al., 1987; Ujiie, 1981–1982), who tend to approach novel people and things (Stanhope et al., 1987), and who are sociable rather than shy or socially anxious are somewhat more likely to help than are other children (Howes & Farver, 1987; S. Miller, 1979; Silva, 1992; cf. Farver & Branstetter, 1994; O'Connor & Cuevas, 1982; Rutherford & Mussen, 1968). Further, high school students' social anxiety has been positively correlated with dispositional personal distress but not sympathy (Davis & Franzoi, 1991).

Sociability is particularly likely to be associated with the performance of prosocial behaviors that are spontaneously emitted (rather than in response to a request for assistance; Eisenberg et al., 1981; Eisenberg et al., 1984; Eisenberg-Berg & Hand, 1979) and directed toward an unfamiliar person in an unfamiliar setting (rather a familiar person at home; Stanhope et al., 1987). Further, extroversion (which includes an element of sociability) was related to elementary school children's helping in an emergency when another peer was present (but not when the child was alone) and to helping by approaching the other person; introverts tended to help in ways that did not involve approaching the injured person (Suda & Fouts, 1980). Thus, sociable children seem to be more prosocial than their peers when assisting another involves social initiation or results in social interaction. Moreover, according to preliminary evidence, shyness may be more likely to inhibit prosocial behavior involving contact with another if a child is relatively young (e.g., in middle rather than late elementary school; Eisenberg, Fabes, Karbon, et al., 1996).

Social Competence and Socially Appropriate Behavior

Given that prosocial behavior is socially appropriate in many contexts, it is not surprising that children's prosocial behavior often is correlated with indexes of socially appropriate behavior. Specifically, although not all researchers have obtained significant results (Marcus & Jenny, 1977; Stockdale, Hegland, & Chiaromonte, 1989), prosocial children tend to be viewed by adults as socially skilled and constructive copers (Eisenberg, Fabes, Karbon, Murphy, Wosinski, et al., 1996; Lenrow, 1965; Peterson et al., 1984). They are high in social problem-solving skills (Marsh et al., 1981), positive social interaction with peers (Farver & Branstetter, 1994; Howes & Farver, 1987; Ramsey, 1987; see Weidman & Strayhorn, 1992), developmentally advanced play (Howes & Matheson, 1992; also see Karpova & Murzinova, 1988), and cooperation (e.g., Dunn & Munn, 1986; Jennings et al., 1987; S. Miller, 1979), and are low in aggression (Barrett, 1979; Day, Bream, & Pal, 1992; Eisenberg, Carlo, et al., 1995; Ma & Leung, 1991; Ladd & Profilet, 1996; S. Miller, 1979; Rutherford & Mussen, 1968; also see Silva, 1992; Weidman & Strayhorn, 1992). There also is some evidence that psychoticism (Saklofske & Eysenck, 1983), Machiavellianism (Barnett & Thompson, 1985), competitiveness (Barnett, Matthews, & Howard, 1979), and aggression, acting-out behaviors, and delinquency (e.g., Cohen & Strayer, 1996; see P. Miller & Eisenberg, 1988) are associated with low empathy, whereas social competence is linked to sympathy (Eisenberg & Fabes, 1995) and empathy (Adams, 1983; see Eisenberg & Miller, 1987).

The relation between aggressiveness and prosocial behavior may be complex in the early years. In one study (Yarrow et al., 1976), there was a positive correlation between prosocial and aggressive behavior for young boys (but not girls) below the mean in exhibited aggression, whereas there was a negative relation between prosocial behavior and aggression for boys above the mean in aggression. A similar pattern of relations was not found for a sample of only elementary school children (Barrett, 1979; also see Cairns & Cairns, 1994). For those young children who are relatively nonaggressive overall, aggression often may be indicative of assertiveness rather than hostility, and aggressive actions often may reflect assertiveness rather than hostility or intent to harm another (Eisenberg & Mussen, 1989).

Consistent with the link between socially appropriate behavior and prosocial behavior, preschoolers' prosocial and sympathetic responding has been linked to having a close friend (Farver & Branstetter, 1994; Mannarino, 1976; McGuire & Weisz, 1982) and status with peers (Coie, Dodge, & Kupersmidt, 1990; Das & Berndt, 1992; Dekovic & Gerris, 1994; Dekovic & Janssens, 1992; Hampson, 1984; Loban, 1953; Ramsey, 1988; Raviv, Bar-Tal, Ayalon, & Raviv, 1980; Tremblay et al., 1992; also see Ladd & Oden, 1979; cf. Eisenberg, Cameron, et al., 1988; L. Harris, 1967; McGuire & Weisz, 1982). For example, stability of children's status as rejected by peers in early elementary school is predicted by children's low levels of prosocial behavior (Vitaro et al., 1990), and children's skill at comforting predicts whether children are rejected, neglected, or accepted by peers (Burleson et al., 1986; cf. Burleson & Waltman, 1987). In addition, mature prosocial moral reasoning has been positively correlated with sociometric status as well as teachers' reports of social competence and low levels of acting-out behavior (Bear & Rys, 1994). Thus, children who are prosocial tend to have positive relationships and interactions with peers.

Degree of social competence or popularity also may affect the types of prosocial behaviors children prefer to perform. For example, Hampson (1984) found that popular prosocial adolescents tended to engage in peer-related prosocial behavior, whereas less popular helpers preferred non-peer-related tasks. Peer acceptance may affect children's comfort level when helping peers; alternatively, people who prefer to help in ways that do not involve social contact with peers may be less popular due to avoidance of peer-oriented prosocial behavior.

Assertiveness and Dominance

Assertiveness and dominance also have been associated with frequency and type of children's prosocial behaviors. Assertive children (e.g., those who issue commands or defend their possessions) are relatively high in sympathy versus personal distress reactions (Eisenberg, Fabes, Miller, Shell, et al., 1990) and prosocial behavior (Barrett, 1979; Barrett & Yarrow, 1977; Denham & Couchoud, 1991; Larrieu & Mussen, 1986; cf. Eisenberg-Berg, Hand, & Haake, 1981), particularly spontaneously emitted (unrequested) instances of helping and sharing (Eisenberg et al., 1984; cf. Eisenberg et al., 1981). A certain level of assertiveness may be necessary for many children to spontaneously approach others needing assistance (Midlarsky & Hannah, 1985). However, children who are not simply assertive but seek to dominate others may be low in prosocial behavior (Krebs & Sturrup, 1982). In contrast, nonassertive, nondominant children tend to be prosocial in response to a request (Eisenberg et al., 1981; Eisenberg & Giallanza, 1984; Eisenberg et al., 1984; Larrieu, 1984), apparently because they frequently are asked for help or sharing (probably due to their compliance; Eisenberg, McCreath, & Ahn, 1988; Eisenberg et al., 1981).

Self-Esteem and Related Constructs

It appears that there is a positive relation between children's self-esteem and their prosocial tendencies, but more so for older than younger children. In studies of preschoolers and elementary school children, investigators often have found no evidence of a relation between self-reports of self-esteem or self-concept and measures of prosocial behavior (Cauley & Tyler, 1989; DeVoe & Sherman, 1978; Kagan & Knight, 1979, for altruism/group enhancement; Rehberg & Richman, 1989). However, in studies of children in fourth grade to high school, investigators usually have found that prosocial children have a positive self-concept (Jarymowicz, 1977; Larrieu & Mussen, 1987; S. Miller, 1979; Mussen et al., 1970; Rigby & Slee, 1993; also see Tyler & Varma, 1988) and are high in self-efficacy (Sugiyama, Matsui, Satoh, Yoshimi, & Takeuchi, 1992), whereas children high in need for approval sometimes may not help due to fear of disapproval (Staub & Sherk, 1970). Perhaps young children's self-reports of their self-concepts do not adequately tap relevant dimensions of their self-conceptions. However, it is possible that young children's self-concepts often are uncorrelated with their prosocial behavior because their self-concepts are not based on enduring characteristics of the self relevant to prosocial responding (Harter, Ch. 9, this Volume).

It also is probable that the relation between self-concept or self-esteem and prosocial behavior varies as a function of the psychological significance or quality of the prosocial act. For example, children who are anxious or emotionally unstable may enact prosocial behaviors to ingratiate or due to fear of disapproval or overreactivity to social distress. In fact, there is some evidence that boys who are particularly high in prosocial behavior performed or promised in a public context are anxious, inhibited, and emotionally unstable (Bond & Phillips, 1971; O'Connor, Dollinger, Kennedy, & Pelletier-Smetko, 1979).

The association between older children's self-conceptions and prosocial behavior probably is bidirectional in regard to causality. Children who feel good about themselves may be able to focus on others' needs because their own needs are being met; further, they may feel that they have the competencies needed to assist others. In addition, it has been argued that involvement in activities that help others may foster the development of self-efficacy (Yates & Youniss, 1996). It is reasonable to assume that the performance of socially competent behavior, including prosocial behavior, and children's self-concepts are intricately related during development.

Values and Goals

An important component of the self is one's values. Colby and Damon (1992) noted two morally relevant characteristics that were dramatically evident in adult moral exemplars: (a) exemplars' certainty or exceptional clarity about what they believed was right and about their own personal responsibility to act in ways consistent with those beliefs, and (b) the unity of self and moral goals, that is, the central place of exemplars' moral goals in their conceptions of their own identity and the integration of moral and personal goals. Consistent with Colby and Damon's findings, Hart and Fegley (1995) found that adolescents who demonstrated exceptional commitments to care for others were particularly likely to describe themselves in terms of moral personality traits and goals and to articulate theories of self in which personal beliefs and philosophies were important. Further, values, ascription of personal responsibility to oneself for assisting others, and prosocial personal norms frequently are cited as motivators of altruism in the literature on adult altruists (e.g., Schwartz & Howard, 1984; Staub, 1978).

In research with normal (i.e., nonclinical) children, there also is evidence that prosocial behavior is correlated with measures of moral functioning, including other-oriented values (Dlugokinski & Firestone, 1974; Larrieu & Mussen, 1986), social responsibility (O'Connor & Cuevas, 1982; Savin-Williams et al., 1981), integrative goals (i.e., concern with the maintenance and promotion of other individuals or social groups; Estrada, 1995), and guilt (Chapman, Zahn-Waxler, Cooperman, & Iannotti, 1987; see Zahn-Waxler, Radke-Yarrow, & King, 1983; cf. Hoffman, 1975b; Santrock, 1975b). Further, adolescents sometimes cite moral values and responsibility for others as reasons for enacting prosocial behaviors (Carlo, Eisenberg, & Knight, 1992; Eisenberg, Carlo, et al., 1995). Thus, it appears that older children and adolescents who have internalized moral (including altruistic) values and who view morality as central to their self-concept are particularly likely to be altruistic.

Regulation and Emotionality

Prosocial children tend to be well regulated and low in impulsivity (Block & Block, 1973, detailed in Eisenberg & Mussen, 1989; Bond & Phillips, 1971, for boys only; Braband & Lerner, 1975; Eisenberg, Fabes, Karbon, et al., 1996; Long & Lerner, 1974; Rai, Bhargva, & Rai, 1989; Silva, 1992; cf. Rutherford & Mussen, 1968; Weissbrod, 1976). Similarly, sympathy (but not empathy; Saklofske & Eysenck, 1983) has been linked to regulation in children (Eisenberg & Fabes, 1995; Eisenberg, Fabes, Murphy, et al., 1996), whereas personal distress sometimes has been associated with low regulation among adults (Eisenberg, Fabes, Murphy, et al., 1994; Eisenberg & Okun, 1996; cf. Eisenberg & Fabes, 1995) and infants (Ungerer et al., 1990). Physiological emotional regulation, as assessed by heart rate variance or vagal tone, also has been associated with children's comforting (Eisenberg, Fabes, Karbon, et al., 1996) and dispositional sympathy (Fabes et al., 1993), although findings for girls have been positive for maternal report of girls' sympathy (Fabes et al., 1993) but negative for girls' self-reported sympathy/empathy (Eisenberg, Fabes, Murphy, et al., 1996). In addition, resilient children, who may be viewed as optimally regulated, tend to be prosocial and empathic (J. Strayer & Roberts, 1989).

Children who are emotionally positive—a characteristic that often is viewed as an outcome of emotional regulation (e.g., Eisenberg & Fabes, 1992)—also tend to be prosocial (Denham, 1986; Denham & Burger, 1991; Eisenberg et al., 1981; Rutherford & Mussen, 1968; cf. Farver & Branstetter, 1994) and empathic/sympathetic (Eisenberg, Fabes, Murphy, et al., 1996; Robinson et al., 1994; J. Strayer, 1980; also see Eisenberg et al., 1994). In contrast, the data pertaining to the relation between negative emotionality and prosocial responding are more complex. *Prosocial behavior* generally has been negatively related to children's negative emotionality, including anger, fear, anxiety, or

sadness (Denham, 1986; Denham & Burger, 1991; Eisenberg, Fabes, Karbon, Murphy, Wosinski, et al., 1996; Ma & Leung, 1991, for girls; S. Miller, 1979, for girls; O'Connor & Cuevas, 1982; Tremblay et al., 1992; cf. Farver & Branstetter, 1994; Denham et al., 1991). However, the relation of negative emotionality to *sympathy/empathy* has been negative (Eisenberg, Fabes, Murphy, Karbon, et al., 1996; Roberts & Strayer, 1996, for anger; also see Zahn-Waxler et al., 1982), nonsignificant (Eisenberg & Fabes, 1995), or positive. In particular, children's empathy (or empathy and sympathy; Robinson et al., 1994) has been positively associated with a composite of young toddlers' emotionality (including sadness, guilt, and fear; Robinson et al., 1994), toddlers' crying (Howes & Farver, 1987), children's negative emotionality as assessed by Eysenck's neuroticism scale (Saklofske & Eysenck, 1983), parents' ratings of children's sadness (Rothbart, Ahadi, & Hershey, 1994), and teachers' reports of whining and pouting (for boys: S. Miller, 1979). Further, intensity (rather than frequency) of negative emotions when they are experienced has been associated with low levels of sympathetic concern among younger children (Eisenberg & Fabes, 1995), but with high sympathy and personal distress in adults (Eisenberg et al., 1994; Eisenberg & Okun, 1996).

Thus, in general, prosocial behavior and sympathy or empathy have been linked to dispositional positive emotionality. Further, prosocial behavior has been consistently associated with low negative emotionality, as has children's, but not infants' or adults', sympathy. In contrast, relations for empathy have been quite inconsistent. The inconsistencies in findings may be due to both type and intensity of the negative emotion experienced; moreover, findings may vary depending on whether the data are self-report (as for studies with adults) or other-report (as in much of the work with children). Relations between negative emotionality and sympathy/empathy or prosocial behavior seem to be negative particularly for externalizing types of emotions (e.g., anger) and when adults are reporting on children's negative emotional intensity. Especially in the classroom setting, children's anger and frustration seem to be salient to teachers (Eisenberg, Fabes, Bernzweig, et al., 1993); thus, teacher-report measures of negative emotional intensity frequently may tap intensity of externalizing emotions. In contrast, in relevant studies in which adults reported on their own negative emotionality, they usually reported on internalizing negative emotions (e.g., sadness or anxiety) as much as (and usually more than) externalizing negative emotions.

In addition, intensity of negative emotion may be related to whether people experience sympathy or personal distress, which, in turn, predicts prosocial behavior. Eisenberg et al. (1994) proposed that situational emotional over-arousal due to empathy is associated with personal distress, whereas moderate empathic responding is associated with sympathy (also see Hoffman, 1982). If people can maintain their vicarious emotional reactions within a tolerable range, they are likely to experience how needy or distressed others feel, but are relatively unlikely to become overwhelmed by their emotion and, consequently, self-focused. In contrast, people who are overaroused by vicarious negative emotion are expected to experience the emotion as aversive and experience a distressed, self-focused reaction (i.e., sometimes labeled personal distress; Batson, 1991). Consistent with this view, general negative emotional arousal has been found to result in a self-focus (Wood, Saltzberg, & Goldsamt, 1990), and empathically induced distress reactions are associated with higher skin conductance reactivity than is sympathy (Eisenberg, Fabes, Schaller, Carlo, & Miller, 1991; Eisenberg, Fabes, Schaller, Miller, et al., 1991).

Based on this line of reasoning, Eisenberg and Fabes (1992) proposed that *individual* differences in the dispositional tendency to experience sympathy versus personal distress vary as a function of dispositional differences in both typical level of emotional intensity (Larsen & Diener, 1987) and individuals' ability to regulate their emotional reactions. People high in constructive modes of regulation such as behavioral and emotional regulation skills (e.g., who have control over the expression of emotion and their ability to focus and shift attention; Derryberry & Rothbart, 1988) were hypothesized to be relatively high in sympathy regardless of emotional intensity. Well-regulated people would be expected to modulate their negative vicarious emotion and maintain an optimal level of emotional arousal—one that has emotional force and enhances attention, but is not so aversive and physiologically arousing that it engenders a self-focus. In contrast, people low in the ability to regulate their emotion, especially if they are emotionally intense, were hypothesized to be low in dispositional sympathy. Further, measures of susceptibility to display anger and frustration probably reflect low regulation and high emotional reactivity and, consequently, would be expected to relate to personal distress and low prosocial behavior.

Some support has been obtained for Eisenberg and Fabes's (1992) ideas. As noted previously, regulation has been linked to high sympathy and low personal distress.

Further, low and moderate levels of negative emotional intensity, but not high levels, have been associated with situational concern (Eisenberg & Fabes, 1995), and children who experience more negative emotion than that of the empathy-eliciting stimulus person (i.e., become overaroused) are relatively low in empathy/sympathy (J. Strayer, 1993). In addition, there is limited evidence that unregulated children are low in sympathy regardless of their level of emotional intensity, whereas, for moderately and highly regulated children, level of sympathy increases with level of emotional intensity (Eisenberg, Fabes, Murphy, et al., 1996; also see Eisenberg, Fabes, Karbon, et al., 1996). Also consistent with Eisenberg and Fabes's ideas, Lenrow (1965) found that preschoolers high in overt distress *and* active coping (which can be viewed as regulation; Eisenberg, Fabes, Bernzweig, et al., 1993) were relatively helpful, and Rothbart et al. (1994) found a negative relation between anger and empathy only when regulation (and surgency) was controlled in the analysis.

Thus, there is initial support for the notion that a predisposition to experience negative emotions such as sadness, fear, and anxiety is associated with sympathy primarily for individuals who are well regulated (especially in regard to the regulation of emotion). Positive relations between negative emotionality and sympathy/empathy in the literature also may be due to sympathetic people being relatively likely to express or report their emotions (Roberts & Strayer, 1996). People who are well regulated are unlikely to be overwhelmed by their negative emotion and probably are viewed by others as relatively low in negative emotionality; thus, it is not surprising that children's prosocial behavior usually has been associated with *adults'* reports of low levels of children's negative emotionality. In future work on empathy-related reactions, it will be useful to differentiate among various types of negative emotions (e.g., externalizing and internalizing emotions), between expressed (i.e., observable) and experienced emotion, and between individuals' general emotional intensity and intensity of solely negative emotionality.

SITUATIONAL INFLUENCES

As would be expected for nearly any social behavior, a variety of situational factors appears to influence children's prosocial responding. Evidence on the situational correlates of prosocial behavior demonstrates the scope and diversity of environmental factors on children's prosocial behavior. Due to space constraints, we briefly provide a few examples and then discuss one situational factor—identity of the recipient—in somewhat more detail.

Costs and Benefits, Mood State, and Situationally Relevant Skills

It is no surprise that children's prosocial behavior varies as a function of situational costs and benefits (e.g., Barnett, Thompson, & Schroff, 1987; Mosbacher, Gruen, & Rychlak, 1985; Zinser & Lydiatt, 1976; Zinser, Perry, Bailey, & Lydiatt, 1976; Zinser, Perry, & Edgar, 1975). It is likely that costs undermine younger children's prosocial behavior more than that of older children, whereas older children are more likely to recognize the possible gains (physical, psychological, or moral) for assisting others (Lourenco, 1990, 1993; L. Perry, Perry, & Weiss, 1986).

Relatedly, toddlers (Levitt, Weber, Clark, & McDonnell, 1985), school-age children (e.g., Dreman, 1976; Fishbein & Kaminski, 1985; Furby, 1978; M. Harris, 1970, 1971; Staub & Sherk, 1970) and adolescents (Berkowitz, 1968; Berkowitz & Friedman, 1967; Cox, 1974) frequently assist an individual more if that person previously helped or shared with them. Moreover, the ability of a recipient to reciprocate in the future seems to be an important determinant of elementary school children's tendencies to help or share (Dreman & Greenbaum, 1973; Furby, 1978; Peterson, 1980). Although relevant data are sparse, the effect of prior receipt of aid on children's prosocial behavior appears to diminish with age from kindergarten to third grade (Peterson, Hartmann, & Gelfand, 1977). In contrast, the influence of future reciprocation may increase during the school years (Peterson, 1980; also see Eisenberg, Carlo, et al., 1995; Eisenberg, Miller, et al., 1991). Reciprocity concerns may be particularly salient to middle-class boys in Western cultures, especially those with fathers engaged in entrepreneurial rather than bureaucratic occupations (Berkowitz, 1968; Berkowitz & Friedman, 1967; Dreman & Greenbaum, 1973). However, there appear to be national and cross-cultural differences in the degree to which children are influenced by reciprocity concerns (Berkowitz, 1968; Gupta, 1982; Krishnan, 1989).

Children are particularly likely to assist people who clearly will benefit from assistance, for example, people who are distressed (Garner, Jones, & Palmer, 1994) or in need (e.g., Fouts, 1972; Kennedy & Thurman, 1982; Midlarsky & Hannah, 1985; Tabor & Shaffer, 1981; Zinser & Lydiatt, 1976; Zinser et al., 1975; cf. Katz, Katz, & Cohen, 1976). Further, this tendency seems to increase with age (Ladd et al., 1983). Children over age 6 (Weiner & Graham, 1989) also are somewhat more likely to pity (Graham, Doubleday, & Guarino, 1984) and help recipients who did not have control over the cause of their need (e.g., Barnett, 1975; D. Miller & Smith, 1977).

Children's temporary mood also affects their helping or sharing. Children generally help more when in a positive mood (Carlson, Charlin, & Miller, 1988; Cialdini, Kenrick, & Baumann, 1982). In contrast, often children become less helpful or generous after experiencing failure or contemplating sad events in their lives, especially if their prosocial behavior is anonymous (e.g., Barden, Garber, Duncan, & Masters, 1981; Cialdini & Kenrick, 1976; Moore, Underwood, & Rosenhan, 1973; Underwood, Froming, & Moore, 1977). However, children sometimes help more when saddened, and this tendency may increase with age, perhaps because helping acquires secondary reinforcement value during the socialization process due to its pairing with positive events such as social reinforcement (Cialdini & Kenrick, 1976; see Cialdini et al., 1982). Currently, the relation of negative mood state to children's prosocial behavior is unclear and controversial (Carlson & Miller, 1987; Cialdini & Fultz, 1990; see Eisenberg, 1991; Eisenberg & Mussen, 1989, for reviews).

Children, particularly those in early and mid-elementary school, frequently report that they do not help others because they believe themselves to be incompetent to do so in the particular context (Barnett et al., 1987; Midlarsky & Hannah, 1985; also see Caplan & Hay, 1989). Peterson (1983a) found that children who had been shown how to assist in a particular situation were more likely to help than were other children without the relevant prior knowledge (also see Peterson, 1983b). In other situations, children and adolescents have the skills to assist but feel that someone else (e.g., an adult) is responsible (Caplan & Hay, 1989), or they are not sure that it is appropriate for them to intervene (Midlarsky & Hannah, 1985; Staub, 1970b). Thus, children are more likely to help in an emergency when they have been assigned responsibility in the given context (Peterson, 1983a; Staub, 1970a) or have been given permission to enter the room where the emergency occurred (Staub, 1971b).

Identity and Characteristics of the Recipient

The degree to which children are prosocial frequently depends on the identity and characteristics of the potential recipient (Eisenberg & Pasternack, 1983). Children prefer to help people who are relatively important in their lives. Infants and young children direct more social and prosocial behavior to parents than siblings (Lamb, 1978a, 1978b) and unknown adults (Rheingold et al., 1976). School-aged children assist siblings more than unknown peers (Ma & Leung, 1992). By adolescence, help is as likely (Zeldin et al., 1984) or more likely (Zeldin et al., 1982, 1984) to be directed toward known peers as toward known, nonfamilial adults (e.g., counselors). The central role of peers in adolescents' lives may account for the latter findings.

Status of a recipient also affects children's prosocial behavior. Popular children tend to receive more help and support from close friends (Parker & Asher, 1993) and peers (Raviv, Bar-Tal, Ayalon, & Raviv, 1980) than do other children. Popular preschool children also receive more help than they give (Marcus & Jenny, 1977). In addition, children and adults report that they are more likely to assist people they like (Ma, 1985) or who are likable (Furby, 1978; also see Barnett et al., 1987).

Given that children tend to help others who they like, it is not surprising that children often share or help friends or liked peers more than less liked peers (Buhrmester, Goldfarb, & Cantrell, 1992; Ma & Leung, 1992; Staub & Sherk, 1970), acquaintances (Birch & Billman, 1986; Buhrmester et al., 1992; Farver & Branstetter, 1994; Howes & Farver, 1987; Jones, 1985; Kanfer, Stifter, & Morris, 1981; also see Knight & Chao, 1991; Knight, Bohlmeyer, Schneider, & Harris, 1993; Werebe & Baudonniere, 1988), and unknown peers (Kanfer et al., 1981). Indeed, children, especially older children and girls (e.g., Parker & Asher, 1993; Sharabany, Gershoni, & Hofman, 1981), generally conceptualize friendships as involving prosocial interchanges (e.g., emotional support, helping, sharing; Berndt & Das, 1987; Bigelow & La Gaipa, 1975; Bigelow, Tesson, & Lewko, 1992; Youniss, 1980; Zarbatany, Ghesquiere, & Mohr, 1992) and report that friends are more supportive than acquaintances (Berndt & Perry, 1986; also see Frankel, 1990). Even children as young as 4 or 5 years or in elementary school report more sympathy toward the plight of a friend or liked peer than toward an acquaintance (Costin & Jones, 1992) or disliked peer (Bengtsson & Johnson, 1987). Prosocial behavior among friends appears to be motivated by not only liking and concern (Costin & Jones, 1992), but also loyalty, consideration of reciprocity obligations, and the fact that friends more often ask for sharing or help (Birch & Billman, 1986).

Although liking of a recipient often seems to enhance children's prosocial behavior, the research on friendships suggests that liking is not the only factor that affects whether children assist others. Sometimes children are equally prosocial to friends and other peers or even help or share less with friends (Berndt, 1981b; Fincham, 1978; Staub & Noerenberg, 1981; also see Gershman & Hayes, 1983; Sharabany & Hertz-Lazarowitz, 1981). A lack of preferential treatment for friends may be stronger in elementary school children than among older children (Berndt, 1985; Berndt, Hawkins, & Hoyle, 1986; cf. Eisenberg, 1983). In studies in which children had to choose between friends and strangers, children apparently assisted people they did not know well to eliminate inequities between a stranger and a friend, because they said their friends would understand, or to gain an unknown person's approval or friendship (Berndt, 1981a; Staub & Noerenberg, 1981; Wright, 1942).

The context influences whether children share more with friends than with other peers. Buhrmester et al. (1992) found that although children tended to share more with friends than with acquaintances or disliked peers, fourth graders shared more in public with disliked peers, whereas eighth graders shared more with friends. Buhrmester et al. suggested that children in mid-elementary school are discovering ingratiation tactics and may overuse them until, with age, they gain the understanding that overt ingratiation often is viewed negatively. Moreover, children, particularly school-age boys (Berndt, 1981b; Staub & Noerenberg, 1981), are less likely to favor a friend in situations involving potential competition. Berndt (1982) suggested that elementary school children are concerned about performing equally or better than their friends, and that boys are particularly likely to compete because their attitudes toward competition are more positive than are those of girls. Consistent with Berndt's arguments, children anticipating or having experienced a competitive encounter generally respond less charitably toward a needy person not involved in the competition (Barnett, Matthews, & Corbin, 1979). This pattern appears to hold particularly for older elementary school boys (Barnett & Bryan, 1974; McGuire & Thomas, 1975). However, children's preference for sharing rather than competing with friends may increase between middle childhood and early adolescence. Indeed, Berndt et al. (1986) found that close friends shared less in fourth grade but more in eighth grade than did children who were no longer close friends (also see Berndt, 1985).

AN INTEGRATIVE MODEL OF PROSOCIAL BEHAVIOR

As should now be evident, we view prosocial behavior as the outcome of multiple individual and situational factors.

A simplified model of the major variables viewed as contributing to the performance of prosocial behavior (and steps in the process itself) is depicted in Figure 11.1 (see Eisenberg, 1986, for extended discussion of this model). This heuristic model can be used to integrate many of the topics discussed earlier in this chapter.

Briefly, in our model, biological factors are viewed as having an effect on both the child's individual characteristics (e.g., sociocognitive development, empathy, sociability) and parental interactions with the child (i.e., socialization experiences). The child's individual characteristics and socialization experiences affect one another and, together with objective characteristics of the situation, influence how the child interprets events involving another's need or distress in a specific context. For example, individual differences in perspective taking and in decoding skills, which likely are influenced by socialization experiences as well as heritability (e.g., genetic effects on intelligence), may affect whether a child notices another's distress, as might the clarity of the distressed other's nonverbal and verbal cues of emotion (a situational factor). In addition, the child's temporary state, for example, his or her mood, often may determine his or her attention to or interpretation of a situation. Level of arousal seems to alter

the ways people interpret others' verbal statements and facial expressions (Clark, Milberg, & Erber, 1984).

How the child interprets the situation logically leads to and affects the child's identification of prosocial actions and the child's recognition of his or her ability to engage in these actions. If a child believes he or she is capable of assisting, the child must then decide whether he or she intends to assist. The child's emotional reactions (e.g., sympathy or personal distress), his or her evaluation of the costs and benefits in the situation, and the child's attributions about the cause of the other's need or distress (e.g., whether the needy person is responsible for his or her situation) are examples of motivationally relevant situational evaluations and emotional reactions that can play a role in this decision. In addition, the decision of whether to engage in prosocial action is affected by antecedent person variables such as individual differences in concern about social approval, values, personal goals, and self-identity in regard to the trait of altruism (see Figure 11.1).

In the given context, the various relevant moral and nonmoral factors—be they perceived costs and benefits, values, sympathetic emotion, or other factors—influence the individual's relative hierarchy of goals in the particular situation. Often goals, needs, or values conflict in a situation

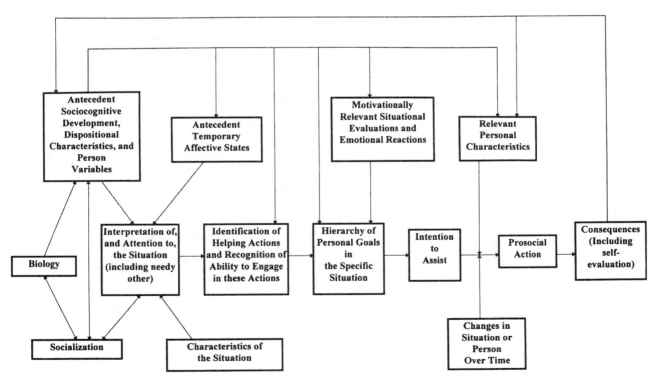

Figure 11.1   Heuristic model of prosocial behavior. Adapted from Eisenberg, 1986.

and must be prioritized. This ordering of personal goals undoubtedly varies across individuals and across situations for a given person (see Figure 11.1). For example, in a situation in which important people are present, social approval needs may be salient (particularly for people who value such approval). On the other hand, in another situation in which there are material costs for assisting, valuing of the object to be shared or donated will be particularly relevant for some people (but not for others who do not value the commodity). Moreover, if the situation evokes an emotional reaction such as sympathy or personal distress, then other- or self-related goals linked to those emotional reactions will be salient.

The values, goals, and needs that underlie personal goals and their relative importance (in general and in specific contexts) change with age (e.g., Bar-Tal et al., 1980). In our view, an individual's values, goals, and needs, as expressed in one's prosocial moral reasoning, provide some insight into the child's typical hierarchy of goals, needs, and values (i.e., one's general hierarchy rather than one's hierarchy in a specific context), although, as noted previously, different factors will be particularly salient in different situations (Eisenberg, 1986). Because other-oriented values based in part on perspective taking, sympathetic reactions, or the capacity for abstract principles increase with age (Eisenberg, 1986), one would expect prosocial moral goals to rank higher in the hierarchies of older than younger children.

Thus, the hierarchy of an individual's goals (or priorities) in the particular situation is viewed as determining whether the child *intends* to assist. However, even if the child intends to perform a prosocial behavior, he or she may not be able to do so due to the lack of relevant personal competencies (physical, psychological, or material) such as the social initiative needed to intervene or appropriate helping skills. In addition, the situation may change, as might the potential benefactor's situation, prior to the actual helping opportunity. For example, the potential benefactor may receive help from someone else before the child can assist.

Finally, there are consequences of engaging in prosocial behavior (or choosing not to do so). For example, children who help may develop new helping competencies or sociocognitive skills in the process that can be applied in future situations. In addition, the act of assisting another may affect the degree to which an individual develops a prosocial self-concept (e.g., Eisenberg, Cialdini, et al., 1987). These consequences are reflected in the future in terms of the child's ongoing dispositional/person variables (see Figure

11.1), as well as in the range of the child's prosocial-relevant personal competencies. Thus, there is a cycle by which children's prosocial behavior (or the lack thereof) has consequences for future prosocial responding.

THE DEVELOPMENT OF PROSOCIAL BEHAVIOR

Despite the volume of research on prosocial behavior in the past 25 years, there has been little consensus on whether or not there are age-related changes in the development of prosocial tendencies (e.g., Hay, 1994; Moore & Eisenberg, 1984; Radke-Yarrow, Zahn-Waxler, & Chapman, 1983). Thus, the literature on age changes in prosocial responding is examined in some detail.

Theory

For many years the study of morality was dominated by cognitive perspectives in which morality was assumed to develop only after the child was capable of sociocognitive processes such as moral reasoning and an understanding of intentionality (e.g., Piaget, 1932/1965; see Rest, 1983). Thus, it was not until the 1970s that investigators started to study prosocial behavior in young children with very limited sociocognitive development. The theoretical work of Hoffman (1982) was a stimulus for much of the early thinking about the early emergence of empathy and prosocial behavior.

Hoffman (1982) proposed four levels of feelings that result from the coalescence of vicarious affect and the cognitive sense of the other and that are linked to prosocial behavior. In the first stage, infants experience empathic distress through one or more of the simpler modes of empathy (e.g., based on reactive crying, conditioning, mimicry) before they acquire a sense of others as separate physical entities. Thus, in the first year of life, infants are unable to differentiate their own distress from that of another and experience global distress—a diffuse and generalized state encompassing both the distressed person as well as themselves. At this stage, infants are likely to seek comfort for themselves when exposed to others' distress.

At the next level—egocentric empathy—children are capable of distinguishing self from others, but cannot fully differentiate between their own and the other person's internal states. Thus, they are apt to respond to others' distresses in ways that they themselves find comforting (e.g., seek their own mother to comfort another child, even if the other child's mother is available). Such helping is not purely egocentric because their attempts to help reflect appropriate empathic affect.

With the onset of perspective-taking abilities at 2 to 3 years of age, young children increasingly become aware that other people's feelings are independent of, and sometimes differ from, their own. Children become capable of empathizing with a wider range of emotions and can be aroused empathically by information pertinent to someone's feelings even when that person is not physically present. Moreover, prosocial actions reflect an awareness of others' unique needs and situations. However, until they are in late childhood or early adolescence, children's empathic responses are restricted to another's immediate, transitory, and situation-specific distress. With greater cognitive maturity (including sophisticated perspective-taking skills and the ability to think abstractly) and the awareness of their own and other people's continuing existence, children can empathize with the general condition of others (including deprivation, oppression, and incompetence). Thus, the adolescent is able to comprehend and respond to the plight of an entire group or class of people, such as the impoverished, politically oppressed, or mentally retarded.

Empirical Studies of the Development of Prosocial Behavior

Although there are relatively few studies of prosocial behavior in young children, there is support for some of Hoffman's (1982) assertions. For example, there is evidence that, as discussed by Hoffman, newborn infants display reactive crying to another infant's cry, but not to a synthetically produced cry (Simner, 1971). However, reactive crying is not found in all infants nor in all situations (Hay, Nash, & Pederson, 1981; Martin & Clark, 1982), and it is unclear whether such crying reflects primitive empathy, conditioned responses, or emotional contagion (Thompson, 1987).

True empathy seems to emerge at 12 to 18 months of age. Hay et al. (1981) reported that 6-month-old infants rarely became distressed by the crying of a peer. Zahn-Waxler and Radke-Yarrow (1982; Zahn-Waxler, Radke-Yarrow, Wagner, & Chapman, 1992), however, found that 38- to 61-week-olds tended to respond to others' distresses that they did not cause with orienting and sometimes distress cries or even positive affect. Distress cries and positive emotion decreased with age in the first years of life,

and by 12 and 18 months of age, infants sometimes reacted to others' emotional distress with prosocial interventions. Toddlers 86 to 109 weeks of age responded with prosocial behavior to about one-third of the distress events they witnessed (also see Kaneko & Hamazaki, 1987). Consistent with Hoffman's theory, toddlers approximately 1.5 to 2 years of age who recognize themselves in the mirror are relatively likely to experience empathy and exhibit prosocial behavior (Bischof-Kohler, 1991; Johnson, 1982; Zahn-Waxler, Radke-Yarrow, Wagner, & Chapman, 1992). It should be noted, however, that many infant researchers believe that infants do differentiate between self and other during the first year of life (Harter, Ch. 9, this Volume), so it is likely that it is the differentiation of one's own and others' internal states that is most relevant. Consistent with the notion that rudimentary perspective-taking skills shape the quality of young children's responses to others' distress, in the second year of life and at age 4 to 5 years, children's tendencies to try to test hypotheses about why another is distressed have been linked to children's prosocial behavior (Zahn-Waxler et al., 1995; Zahn-Waxler, Robinson, & Emde, 1992).

Young children clearly are capable of responding empathically to others' distress, but they also sometimes respond to others' distress with ignoring, avoidance, or aggressive behaviors, and toddlers' responsiveness to peers' cries is relatively infrequent. Howes and Farver (1987) and Phinney, Feshbach, and Farver (1986) found in only about 20% of peer crying incidents did a child respond in any way, although many of these responses were prosocial; 70% of incidents were totally ignored, and only 40% of the children were ever observed to respond prosocially. Individual differences in children, situations, and experiential factors appear to influence a particular child's response (Farver & Branstetter, 1994).

There is evidence that prosocial actions that are not likely to be motivated by empathy (i.e, are not in response to distress cues) occur by 12 months of age. For example, 12-month-olds frequently release an object into the hand or lap of the mother (West & Rheingold, 1978). However, such giving may reflect attempts to engage the mother rather than the desire to benefit the mother. Regardless, sharing and helping behavior is even more evident during the second year of life (Hay, 1979; Zahn-Waxler & Radke-Yarrow, 1982). Rheingold, Hay, and West (1976) found that all 24 18-month-olds in their study shared a variety of objects with their mothers, fathers, and unfamiliar persons, often without prompting. Children in the second year of life also help their mothers care for their baby siblings (Dunn,

Kendrick, & MacNamee, 1981) and spontaneously assist with household chores (Rheingold, 1982).

Although it is clear that even young children evidence prosocial behavior, the developmental patterns associated with the acquisition of prosocial behavior remain relatively unclear. Hay (1994) suggested that prosocial behavior is exhibited at relatively low rates from age 3 to 6 years and actually drops in frequency after the second year of life. However, one of the two published studies that Hay (1994) cited as support for an age-related decline did not include a measure of prosocial behavior. Hay herself concluded in another paper that "no clear evidence was found in this study for an overall decline in sharing with increasing age" (Hay, Caplan, Castle, & Stimson, 1991, p. 992). This issue is examined in more detail shortly.

Viewed more generally, the extant literature appears to support the conclusion that as children get older there is increasing evidence of altruistic concern and related prosocial action (Bar-Tal, Raviv, & Leiser, 1980), particularly in studies of donation behavior (Radke-Yarrow et al., 1983). This linear trend may not hold, however, for children of all ages or for all measures. For example, Radke-Yarrow et al. (1983) concluded the following: (a) age trends in regard to children's comforting, caregiving, and sympathy after age 2 are inconsistent; (b) helping is either positively related or unrelated to age; and (c) sharing increases with age, but primarily when sharing is with hypothetical others (i.e., people with whom the child has not interacted). Moreover, Zarbatany, Hartmann, and Gelfand (1985) found that elementary school children's generosity increased with age only when adult experimenters were present and were relatively obtrusive. Thus, it appears that age differences in children's prosocial behavior vary according to type of prosocial behavior and characteristics of the situation.

To reexamine the issue of age-related changes in prosocial behavior, Fabes and Eisenberg (1996) conducted a meta-analysis of age differences in children's prosocial behavior. In their meta-analysis, they collected and coded 179 studies yielding 478 effect sizes. Their criteria for including studies in the prosocial analyses were as follows: (a) the participants were not sampled from a clinical population (handicapped children, delinquents; there were relatively few clinical populations and our focus was on normative development); (b) participants were children and/or adolescents not over the age of 21; (c) the article was published; (d) the data reported were for individual children rather than data at the dyadic, triadic, or class levels; and (e) the index of prosocial behavior was for real rather than pretend or play prosocial behavior. Studies of cooperation versus competition also were excluded. For each study, they coded several factors: (a) sample size for older and younger children; (b) type of index (instrumental helping, sharing/donating, kindness/considerateness, comforting, aggregated index of prosocial behavior); (c) method (observation, self-report, other-report [peers, parents, teachers]); (d) design (correlational/naturalistic, structured/experimental); (e) target of prosocial response (children, adults, unknown/unspecified); (f) mean age of sample; (g) mean age of oldest and youngest children in sample; and (h) year of publication.

Fabes and Eisenberg (1996) took two approaches to their analysis of age differences in prosocial behavior. First, they examined effect sizes as a function of the specific age group comparison. Because some of the studies utilized correlational analyses to examine the relation of the age to prosocial behavior ($n = 55$), specific comparisons between age-related groups could not be calculated. Thus, for the analysis of prosocial behavior as it relates to specific age comparisons, they primarily relied on those studies in which specific age groups were contrasted ($n = 125$; see Table 11.1). Second, Fabes and Eisenberg were interested in the predictors of the magnitude of effect sizes in age differences in prosocial behavior. In this analysis, they used all available studies and computed least square weighted regression analyses.

To examine specific age-related changes, children were categorized into one of the following age groups (based on the mean age of the children in a particular age group): (a) infants (less than 3 years of age); (b) preschool (3–6 years of age); (c) childhood (7–12 years of age); and (d) adolescents (13–17 years of age). The final sample of effect sizes in the meta-analysis of age differences in prosocial behavior included 265 effects from the 125 studies (excluding nonindependent effect sizes and 12 outliers; see Table 11.1).[2]

As can be seen in Table 11.1, the data from the Fabes and Eisenberg meta-analysis indicated that the overall mean unweighted effect sizes obtained were positive for both the full and partial data sets, indicating a difference favoring older children. They then examined effect sizes broken down for each age group, as well as each categorical coding classification broken down by age group (reproduction of these data is

---

[2] A complete list of the studies, codings, effect sizes, and procedures is available from the authors.

Table 11.1 Descriptive Summary of Age Differences in Prosocial Behavior

Variable	Value
Effect Sizes Used in Age Group Analyses (n = 265)[a]	
M unweighted effect size	0.38
95% confidence interval (lower/upper)	0.33/0.43
Median unweighted effect size	0.40
Mean Age in Years of Older/Younger Group by Age Group Comparison for Age Group Analyses	
Infant/Infant	2.00 / 1.40
Preschool/Infant	4.58 / 2.13
Preschool/Preschool	5.59 / 3.90
Childhood/Preschool	9.03 / 5.43
Childhood/Childhood	10.40 / 7.59
Adolescent/Preschool	12.50 / 5.67
Adolescent/Childhood	13.36 / 9.04
Adolescent/Adolescent	15.71 / 12.98

Note. Data taken from Fabes and Eisenberg (1996). Effect sizes are unbiased estimates and are positive for differences favoring older children.
[a] Only those effect sizes calculated from comparisons of children of specific ages, with only one effect size per age-group comparison per study (excluding studies that included young adults and excluding the outliers).

presented in Table 11.2). Each effect size was weighted by the reciprocal of its variance (d+; see Hedges & Olkin, 1985).

The effect sizes summarized for each of the age group comparisons were positive (indicating that the older age group evidenced greater prosocial behavior). Further, all age group comparison effect sizes were significant except for those in the preschool/infant and adolescent/adolescent (within adolescent) age groups. The largest effect size was found in the comparison of adolescents to preschoolers, with moderate effect sizes found for comparisons of infant/infant, childhood/preschool, and childhood/childhood groupings, and small effect sizes found for preschool/infant, adolescent/childhood, and adolescent/adolescent (i.e., adolescent groups of different ages) age group comparisons (see Table 11.2).

Importantly, Fabes and Eisenberg (1996) found that age differences in prosocial behavior sometimes varied as a function of study qualities; this was not surprising given that the homogeneity statistic (Q) was significant for the total sample and for a number of subgroup comparisons. Variation in the magnitude of age differences in prosocial behavior as a function of the type of prosocial behavior was not significant for the three youngest age group comparisons. Across the remaining age group comparisons, the

Table 11.2 Categorical Models for Age Differences in Prosocial Behavior Effect Sizes

Variables and Class	Number of Effects	Weighted Effect Size (d +)	95% Confidence Interval for d+ (lower/upper)
Overall	265	0.26****	0.23/0.29
Age Group Comparison			
Infant/Infant	10	0.26*	0.06/0.45
Preschool/Infant	11	0.15[a]	−0.01/0.30
Preschool/Preschool	30	0.24[b]****	0.13/0.35
Childhood/Preschool	75	0.33[c]*****	0.28/0.39
Childhood/Childhood	85	0.30[d,h,i]****	0.26/0.35
Adolescent/Preschool	6	0.68[a,b,e,f,h]****	0.48/0.87
Adolescent/Childhood	37	0.13[e,g,i]****	0.06/0.19
Adolescent/Adolescent	11	0.06[c,d,f]	−0.03/0.16

Type of Prosocial Behavior (by age group)

Variables and Class	Number of Effects	Weighted Effect Size (d +)	95% Confidence Interval for d+ (lower/upper)
Infant/Infant			
Instrumental help	4	0.34*	0.03/0.64
Comforting	0		
Sharing/donating	3	0.06	−0.27/0.40
Aggregated index	3	0.38*	0.01/0.75
Preschool/Infant			
Instrumental help	2	0.21	−0.35/0.51
Comforting	1	0.00	−0.60/0.60
Sharing/donating	2	0.27	−0.07/0.61
Aggregated index	6	0.09	−0.12/0.31
Preschool/Preschool			
Instrumental help	3	0.08	−0.35/0.51
Comforting	2	0.53*	0.05/1.01
Sharing/donating	10	0.26**	0.07/0.45
Aggregated index	15	0.22***	0.07/0.36
Childhood/Preschool			
Instrumental help	16	0.64[a,b,c]****	0.50/0.79
Comforting	9	0.28[a]***	0.09/0.47
Sharing/donating	41	0.36[b,d]****	0.28/0.43
Aggregated index	9	0.16[c,d]***	0.06/0.26
Childhood/Childhood			
Instrumental help	17	0.40[a]****	0.29/0.52
Comforting	6	0.18*	0.07/0.30
Sharing/donating	59	0.34[b]****	0.28/0.40
Aggregated index	3	0.09[a,b]	−0.07/0.24
Adolescent/Preschool			
Instrumental help	1	1.39****	0.42/2.37
Comforting	2	0.54***	0.16/0.91
Sharing/donating	3	0.69****	0.46/0.92
Aggregated index	0		
Adolescent/Childhood			
Instrumental help	22	0.02[a]	−0.06/0.11
Comforting	2	0.33	−0.06/0.72
Sharing/donating	7	0.65[a,b]****	0.45/0.85
Aggregated index	6	0.13[b]	−0.02/0.27
Adolescent/Adolescent			
Instrumental help	9	−0.01	−0.14/0.12
Comforting	0		
Sharing/donating	2	0.14*	0.01/0.27
Aggregated index	0		

(Continued)

Table 11.2   (Continued)

Variables and Class	Number of Effects	Weighted Effect Size ($d+$)	95% Confidence Interval for $d+$ (lower/upper)
Method (by age group)			
Infant/Infant			
Observation	8	0.21*	0.01/0.43
Self-report	0		
Other-report	2	0.47*	0.01/0.92
Preschool/Infant	All codings were from observational studies.		
Preschool/Preschool			
Observation	28	0.23****	0.12/0.35
Self-report	2	0.28	−0.09/0.65
Other-report	0		
Childhood/Preschool			
Observation	64	0.41[a]****	0.34/0.47
Self-report	5	0.45[b]****	0.25/0.65
Other-report	6	0.08[a,b]	−0.03/0.19
Childhood/Childhood			
Observation	71	0.34[a]****	0.29/0.40
Self-report	12	0.25****	0.16/0.35
Other-report	2	0.06[a]	−0.10/0.23
Adolescent/Preschool			
Observation	5	0.71****	0.50/0.92
Self-report	1	0.49****	−0.01/0.99
Other-report	0		
Adolescent/Childhood			
Observation	26	0.18[a]****	0.10/0.27
Self-report	6	−0.06[a,b]	−0.19/0.07
Other-report	6	0.26[b]**	0.06/0.46
Adolescent/Adolescent			
Observation	7	0.08	−0.08/0.24
Self-report	4	0.06	−0.06/0.16
Other-report	0		
Design (by age group)			
Infant/Infant			
Naturalistic/ correlational	6	0.16	−0.09/0.41
Experimental/ structured	4	0.41**	0.11/0.71
Preschool/Infant	All effect sizes were from naturalistic/correlational studies.		
Preschool/Preschool			
Naturalistic/ correlational	20	0.19***	0.06/0.32
Experimental/ structured	10	0.35****	0.15/0.55
Childhood/Preschool			
Naturalistic/ correlational	13	0.12[a]*	0.02/0.22
Experimental/ structured	62	0.42[a]****	0.35/0.48
Childhood/Childhood			
Naturalistic/ correlational	9	0.13[a]**	0.04/0.22
Experimental/ structured	76	0.36[a]****	0.30/0.41

Table 11.2   (Continued)

Variables and Class	Number of Effects	Weighted Effect Size ($d+$)	95% Confidence Interval for $d+$ (lower/upper)
Adolescent/Preschool	All effect sizes were from structured/experimental studies.		
Adolescent/Childhood			
Naturalistic/ correlational	9	0.00[a]	−0.11/0.11
Experimental/ structured	28	0.20[a]****	0.12/0.28
Adolescent/Adolescent			
Naturalistic/ correlational	8	−0.07[a]	−0.21/0.07
Experimental/ structured	3	0.17[a]**	0.04/0.29
Target (by age group)			
Infant/Infant			
Child	2	−0.02	−0.37/0.60
Adult	7	0.33**	0.07/0.64
Unknown/unspecified	1	0.68**	0.13/1.23
Preschool/Infant			
Child	9	0.19*	0.02/0.37
Adult	1	−0.03	−0.44/0.39
Unknown/unspecified	1	0.00	−0.59/0.59
Preschool/Preschool			
Child	28	0.23****	0.12/0.35
Adult	0		
Unknown/unspecified	2	0.28	−0.08/0.65
Childhood/Preschool			
Child	61	0.39[a,b]****	0.33/0.46
Adult	2	1.16[a,c]****	0.76/1.56
Unknown/unspecified	12	0.12[b,c]*	0.01/0.22
Childhood/Childhood			
Child	76	0.33[a]****	0.28/0.38
Adult	3	0.67[b]****	0.34/1.00
Unknown/unspecified	6	0.13[a,b]*	0.02/0.25
Adolescent/Preschool			
Child	5	0.69****	0.48/0.89
Adult	0		
Unknown/unspecified	1	0.60****	0.03/1.17
Adolescent/Childhood			
Child	26	0.12***	0.04/0.20
Adult	2	0.31	−0.06/0.68
Unknown/unspecified	9	0.12***	0.01/0.24
Adolescent/Adolescent			
Child	5	0.18[a]***	0.06/0.29
Adult	6	−0.14[a]	−0.31/0.07
Unknown/unspecified	0		

Note. Data taken from Fabes and Eisenberg (1996). Effect sizes are positive for differences favoring older children. Age classifications: Infants = less than 3 years of age; Preschool = 3–6 years of age; Childhood = 7–12 years of age; Adolescent = 13–17 years of age. Analyses computed with outliers included produced similar results.

[a–i] Within each coding category for each age comparison grouping, effect sizes with similar alphabetic superscripts are significantly different (post hoc contrasts), *ps* at least < .05. *p < .05; **p < .01; ***p < .005; ****p < .001.

magnitudes of age differences were relatively constant in size when the type of prosocial behavior was an aggregated index, sharing, or comforting. In contrast, the magnitude of effect sizes in instrumental helping varied more across these age group comparisons. The magnitudes of effect sizes were relatively high when the type of prosocial behavior was instrumental help for childhood/preschool and childhood/childhood comparisons and relatively low for the adolescent/childhood and adolescent/adolescent comparisons (see Table 11.2).

The magnitudes of the effect sizes differed significantly by the method of collection (e.g., observation, self-report, other-report) only for childhood/preschool, childhood/childhood, and adolescent/childhood comparison groups. Specifically, for both the childhood/preschool and childhood/childhood age comparison groups, effect sizes for age differences were higher when measured by observation or self-report than when measured by reports obtained from others (e.g., parents, peers, and/or teachers). For the adolescent/childhood comparisons, effect sizes were significantly smaller when measured by self-report methods than by observational or other-report methods (see Table 11.2).

A very consistent pattern of findings was obtained when the effect sizes were broken down by the type of design. For all age comparison groups in which effect sizes could be calculated, effect sizes were greater in experimental/structured designs than in naturalistic/correlational designs (although these were not significant for infant/infant and preschool/preschool comparisons). Finally, the magnitude of the effect size differed significantly by the target of the prosocial behavior, but this was true only for childhood/preschool, childhood/childhood, and adolescent/adolescent comparison groups. In the first two age comparison groups, effect sizes were largest when the target was an adult and lowest when the target was unknown/unspecified (with child targets in between). In contrast, for the adolescent/adolescent comparison, the effect size was greater when the target was a child in comparison to an adult.

There also were age-related differences in study characteristics. For example, instrumental help was relatively unlikely to be used as a measure of prosocial behavior for children under 7 years of age. Moreover, naturalistic/correlational designs were relatively likely to be used with younger children, whereas experimental/structured designs were likely to be used with older children. Additionally, adults were likely to be used as targets of children's prosocial behavior at the youngest and oldest age group comparisons, whereas children were likely to be targets for groups not at the extremes (see Table 11.2). Thus, age-related differences in prosocial behavior may be a function of differences in study characteristics that vary with the age of the sample.

To explore this possibility, Fabes and Eisenberg (1996) examined the prediction of age differences in prosocial behavior while controlling for study qualities (using all 265 studies). Study characteristics included method, design, target, type of prosocial behavior, data type (cross-sectional age group comparisons versus correlational), mean age of sample, age of youngest and oldest children in sample, sample size, and year of publication. After controlling for other study qualities (through the use of hierarchical regression analyses), mean age of sample, age of youngest children in sample, sample size, and year of publication were significantly, inversely related to effect sizes. Age differences in prosocial behavior were found to be smaller as the mean age of the sample and the youngest children in the sample increased, as the sample size increased, and in studies published later. In contrast, effect sizes were larger as the age of the oldest children in the sample increased.

Although sharing and aggregated indexes significantly predicted age differences in prosocial behavior prior to controlling for study characteristics, effect sizes were not predicted by type of prosocial measure (instrumental help, sharing/donating, aggregated, comforting) after partialing out other study qualities. However, after controlling for study qualities, effect sizes were found to be significantly predicted by self- or other-reports (i.e., they were larger when measured by self- or other-reports). When study characteristics were *not* controlled, the finding for self-reports was not significant and age differences were smaller when other-reports were used (in comparison to self-reports and observations).

The findings of Fabes and Eisenberg's (1996) meta-analysis suggest that age differences in prosocial behavior are complex: they differed in magnitude as a function of the specific age comparison made, the way in which prosocial behavior was studied, and the type of age-related analysis reported. However, combining across all studies and study qualities, they found a significant, positive effect size for age differences in prosocial behavior. Thus, these data support the conclusion that as children get older, prosocial behaviors generally are more likely to occur. This pattern was found for all specific cross-age group comparisons, although there was considerable variation in the magnitude of effect sizes across different age group comparisons (see Table 11.2). We now turn to a discussion of the possible developmental processes that may contribute to these differences.

Processes Potentially Related to Changes with Age in Prosocial Responding

For some theorists, the primary source of the increase in prosocial and altruistic behavior across age is sociocognitive development (e.g., Burleson, 1984), including attentional processes (attending to the needs of others), evaluative processes (evaluating behaviors and situations in terms of moral standards), and planning processes (Krebs & Van Hesteren, 1994). In our view, these processes encompass more than purely sociocognitive development, and other aspects of responding (e.g., moral emotions, regulatory capacities) may partially account for age-related changes in prosocial behavior.

As noted by Krebs and Van Hesteren (1994) and Hoffman (1982), attention to the needs of others transforms egoistic affect to other-oriented affect, rendering it more altruistic. Throughout infancy and childhood, children develop an increasingly refined understanding of others' emotional states and cognition processes, and are better able to decode other people's emotional cues (K. Barnett, Darcie, Holland, & Kobasigawa, 1982; see Eisenberg, Murphy, & Shepard, 1997). As is discussed previously, such perspective-taking and related sociocognitive skills are associated with prosocial responding. Moreover, with age, children are more likely to have the social experience necessary to perceive need in social contexts in which overt cues of distress are ambiguous or subtle (Pearl, 1985).

Children's abilities to evaluate situational factors and behavioral options also become more complex and probably more accurate with age (Black, Weinstein, & Tanur, 1980). Younger children appear to weigh costs to the self more than do older children when deciding whether or not to assist others (Eisenberg, 1986) and are less attuned to the benefits of prosocial behavior (Lourenco, 1990, 1993; Perry et al., 1986). These age-related differences in the analysis of costs and benefits likely contribute to age-related differences in prosocial behavior.

Moreover, numerous researchers have suggested that the quality of children's motivation for assisting others changes with age (e.g., Eisenberg, 1986; Krebs & Van Hesteren, 1994). Bar-Tal, Raviv, and Leiser (1980) proposed that children's helping behavior develops through six stages that differ in quality of motivation. The first three stages

involve helping behaviors that are compliant and in which the child anticipates the gain of material rewards (or the avoidance of punishment). The next two stages involve compliance with social demands and/or concern with social approval and generalized reciprocity. The final stage represents true altruism without self-focused concern in which helping is an end in itself.

Bar-Tal and colleagues have found some support for their hypothesized developmental changes in children's motives for helping: older children tend to assist more often than do younger children in contexts in which the effects of compliance and rewards or costs are minimized (Bar-Tal et al., 1980; Raviv, Bar-Tal, & Lewis-Levin, 1980; see Bar-Tal, 1982; Eisenberg, 1986). Although Bar-Tal and colleagues sought to delineate a developmental sequence in prosocial motivation, the data concerning this issue are inconclusive (i.e., it is not clear whether all of their proposed stages actually emerge in the specified order; see Eisenberg, 1986). Moreover, children's reported motives for their prosocial behavior change in ways that generally are consistent with Bar-Tal's stages. Although even preschoolers sometimes give simple other-oriented and pragmatic reasons for their peer-directed prosocial actions (Eisenberg, Lundy, Shell, & Roth, 1985; Eisenberg et al., 1984; Eisenberg-Berg & Neal, 1979), researchers generally have found a decrease with age in self-oriented, hedonistic reasons for helping and an increase in other-oriented, internalized, and altruistic motives and reasons for prosocial behavior (e.g., Bar-Tal & Nissim, 1984; Bar-Tal et al., 1980; Ugurel-Semin, 1952; see Bar-Tal, 1982; Eisenberg, 1986). Findings vary with contextual variables (e.g., if an adult is present; see Eisenberg, 1986) and are not always consistent (Boehnke et al., 1989; Hertz-Lazarowitz, 1983); nonetheless, overall the evidence of developmental change in children's motives for assisting others is relatively compelling (Eisenberg, 1986).

Like Bar-Tal, Krebs, and Van Hesteren (1994) proposed age-related forms of altruism, ranging from egocentric and exchange stages (egocentric accommodation and instrumental cooperation, stages 1 and 2, respectively), to concern with others' evaluation and behaving in a socially acceptable manner (stage 3), to altruism motivated by the desire to fulfill an internalized sense of social responsibility (e.g., conscientious altruism, stage 4). The higher-level adult stages are motivated by the desire to uphold self-chosen, internalized utilitarian values (e.g., maximizing benefits to all; autonomous altruism, stage 5), the goal of fostering maximally balanced and integrated social relations (e.g., upholding the rights of all people, including the self; integrated altruism, stage 6), and the goal of universal love stemming from a cosmic feeling of oneness with the universe and a selfless ethic of responsible universal love, service, and sacrifice that is extended to others without regard for merit (universal self-sacrificial love, stage 7). Of course, children or adolescents would not be expected to obtain the higher-level stages. Although Krebs and his colleagues have not explicitly tested the validity of their stages, they based them upon data collected by other investigators concerned with the development of moral reasoning, prosocial behavior, and empathy.

Age-related changes in children's evaluative processes and prosocial-relevant goals are reflected in children's prosocial moral reasoning (i.e., reasoning about moral dilemmas in which one person's needs or wants conflict with those of others in a context in which the role of authorities, laws, rules, punishment, and formal obligations is minimal). In research on prosocial moral reasoning, typically individuals are presented with hypothetical moral conflicts (e.g., about helping an injured child rather than going to a social event), and their reasoning about the conflicts is elicited.

Based on both cross-sectional and longitudinal research, Eisenberg and her colleagues (1986; Eisenberg, Miller, et al., 1991) have identified an age-related sequence of children's prosocial reasoning. Preschool and early elementary school children tend to use primarily hedonistic reasoning or needs-oriented (primitive empathic) prosocial reasoning. Hedonistic reasoning decreases sharply in elementary school and increases slightly in adolescence; needs-oriented reasoning increases until mid-childhood and then levels off in use. In elementary school, children's reasoning begins to reflect concern with others' approval and enhancing interpersonal relationships, as well as the desire to behave in stereotypically "good" ways. However, such reasoning (particularly approval reasoning) appears to decline somewhat in high school.

Beginning in late elementary school or thereafter, children begin to express reasoning reflecting abstract principles, internalized affective reactions (e.g., guilt or positive affect about the consequences of one's behavior for others or living up to internalized principles and values), and self-reflective sympathy and perspective taking. Thus, although children and adolescents alike sometimes verbalize immature modes of reasoning, with age children's moral reasoning becomes more abstract, somewhat less self-oriented, and increasingly based on values, moral principles, and moral emotions (Carlo, Eisenberg, & Knight, 1992; Carlo, Koller, Eisenberg, Pacheco, & Loguercio, 1996; Eisenberg,

1986; Eisenberg, Carlo, et al., 1995; Eisenberg, Miller, et al., 1991; Eisenberg-Berg, 1979a). As discussed previously, these age-related changes are linked to prosocial behavior; thus, the processes reflected in children's moral reasoning likely play some role in the age-related increase in quantity and quality of prosocial behavior. However, these processes may include age-related changes in goals and values as well as in sociocognitive skills required for high-level moral reasoning (Eisenberg, 1986).

Sociocognitive processes may underlie the development of children's prosocial behaviors, but engaging in these processes does not ensure that prosocial actions will be enacted. As discussed previously, Eisenberg and Fabes (1992) suggested that individuals who are optimally regulated (i.e., use moderate amounts of inhibitory control and are relatively high in flexible and constructive coping and attentional regulation) are relatively likely to engage in spontaneous prosocial behavior. Because some regulatory capacities likely increase with age (Block & Block, 1980; Mischel, Shoda, & Rodriguez, 1989), one would expect older children, relative to younger ones, to be more likely to respond sympathetically and with prosocial behavior in emotionally evocative situations.

Developmental changes in both children's emotion regulation and in their sociocognitive skills (e.g., Hoffman, 1982) would be expected to contribute to developmental changes in prosocial behavior in part by influencing children's tendencies to respond empathically or sympathetically (Eisenberg, Fabes, Murphy, et al., 1994). Lennon and Eisenberg (1987b), in a review of the literature, found that age differences in empathy varied with the specific index of empathy used. In general, self-report of empathy was positively associated with age in preschool and elementary school years. However, findings were inconsistent with older children and adolescents. Facial/gestural indexes appeared to be either inversely related or unrelated to age in the early school years, perhaps due to increases with age in children's ability to mask their emotions. To examine this issue further, Fabes and Eisenberg (1996) conducted a separate meta-analysis of age differences in empathy in studies published since 1983 and found an overall unweighted effect size of .24 (favoring older children). Moreover, Fabes and Eisenberg found that effect sizes in empathy varied significantly by method; they were significant and larger for observational and self-report indexes than for nonverbal (facial/physiological) or other-report measures (for which the effects sizes were not significant). These findings are consistent with the view that age-related changes in vicarious emotional responding may contribute to changes with age in prosocial responding.

Developmental changes in children's experience-based competencies also affect their ability to engage in prosocial behavior. Peterson (1983a, 1983b) found that when children were specially trained on relevant tasks, age-related increases in helping evaporated. The data in our meta-analysis also suggest that experience-based developmental competencies may contribute to age-related differences in prosocial behavior. For example, age differences in prosocial behavior were relatively pronounced when the index of prosocial behavior was instrumental helping. Older children may provide more direct, instrumental assistance because they possess greater physical and social competence than do younger children.

In summary, developmental changes in prosocial behavior are complex and are influenced by a variety of methodological factors. Moreover, the precise developmental mechanisms involved in producing these changes are not yet fully explicated and likely involve cognitive, social, motivational/emotional, and physical processes and capabilities. The next wave of research should include studies devoted to identifying when and how age-related changes in sociocognitive, emotional, and regulatory capabilities jointly affect prosocial responding.

SEX DIFFERENCES IN CHILDREN'S PROSOCIAL BEHAVIOR

Based on stereotypic gender roles, females generally are expected and believed to be more responsive, empathic, and prosocial than are males, whereas males are expected to be relatively independent and achievement oriented (Broverman, Vogel, Broverman, Clarkson, & Rosenkrantz, 1972; Parsons & Bales, 1955; Spence, Helmreich, & Stapp, 1974). Further, cross-cultural work has verified that gender differences in prosocial responding are not limited to only a few cultures and may develop with age. For example, Whiting and Edwards (1973) found that helpfulness and support giving generally were greater for girls than boys across six different cultures, although these differences were significant for older but not younger children.

Despite the prevailing view that females are more prosocial than males, the empirical evidence is equivocal (see Moore & Eisenberg, 1984; Radke-Yarrow et al., 1983, for reviews). In fact, Eagly and Crowley (1986) conducted a meta-analysis of sex differences in older adolescents' and adults' helping behavior and found that *men* helped more than women, particularly in situations involving instrumental and chivalrous assistance. Importantly, sex differences in helping were inconsistent across studies and were successfully predicted by various attributes of the studies. Until recently, however, a similar meta-analysis has not been conducted with studies of children.

Fabes and Eisenberg (1996) examined sex differences as well as age differences in children's prosocial responding. In this meta-analysis, they used the same procedures and criteria as those used in their meta-analysis of age differences. The resulting sample consisted of 259 studies yielding a total of 450 effect sizes (M age = 7.93 years). However, only one effect size was used per sample (i.e., when different variables were used for a single sample, one was selected randomly). Thus, the final number of effect sizes for the meta-analysis was 272. For the sample of effect sizes, the mean unweighted effect size was modest (.18) and positive (indicating a difference favoring females; see Table 11.3).[3]

As before, Fabes and Eisenberg (1996) broke down sex differences in prosocial behavior by each categorical coding classification (see Table 11.4). Although it is clear that the overall sex difference presented in Table 11.4 differed from zero (the value indicating exactly no sex difference), the effect sizes in this sample were found not to be consistent across studies (the Q statistic often was significant).

For type of prosocial behavior studied, the sex difference was significantly greater for aggregated indexes or indexes reflecting kindness/considerateness than for indexes reflecting instrumental help, comforting, or sharing. Moreover, sex differences were significantly greater when prosocial responding was measured with self-reports or reports from others than with observational methods. The magnitude of the sex difference also was greater in correlational/naturalistic studies than in structured/experimental studies. Finally, sex differences in prosocial behavior were significantly greater when the target was an adult or was unspecified than when the target was another child (see Table 11.4).

Once again, Fabes and Eisenberg (1996) examined the prediction of effect sizes in sex differences as a function of study qualities by conducting hierarchical regression analyses. When controlling for other variables, the sex

---

[3] A complete list of the studies, codings, effect sizes, and procedures is available from the authors.

Table 11.3 Descriptive Summary of Sex Differences in Prosocial Behavior

Variable	Value
Effect Sizes Used in Analyses ($n = 272$)[a]	
M unweighted effect size	0.18
95% confidence interval (lower/upper)	0.14/0.21
Median unweighted effect size	0.00

Note. Data taken from Fabes and Eisenberg (1996). Positive effect sizes indicate larger difference favoring girls.

[a] Independent effect sizes excluding outliers.

difference in prosocial behavior was greater for larger samples and when the age span of study participants was relatively small. Year of publication and age of study participants did not predict sex differences once other study characteristics were controlled (although older age and recent publication date were associated with a larger sex difference prior to controlling for study characteristics).

Table 11.4 Categorical Models for Sex Differences in Prosocial Behavior Effect Sizes

Variables and Class	Number of Effect Sizes	Weighted Effect Size ($d +$)	95% Confidence Interval for $d+$ (lower/upper)
Overall	272	0.20****	0.18/0.22
Type of Prosocial Behavior			
Instrumental help	62	0.14[a,b]****	0.09/0.20
Being kind/considerate	9	0.42[a,d,e]****	0.29/0.54
Comforting	20	0.17[e,f]****	0.09/0.25
Sharing/donating	117	0.13[c,d]****	0.10/0.17
Aggregated index	64	0.31[b,c,f]****	0.27/0.35
Method			
Observation	196	0.13[a,b]****	0.10/0.16
Self-report	36	0.28[a]****	0.22/0.32
Other-report	40	0.33[b]****	0.27/0.39
Design			
Correlational/ naturalistic	120	0.26[a]****	0.23/0.29
Structured/ experimental	152	0.14[a]****	0.11/0.17
Target of Prosocial Behavior			
Child	190	0.15[a,b]****	0.12/0.18
Adult	23	0.28[a]****	0.19/0.38
Unknown/unspecified	59	0.28[b]****	0.24/0.32

Note. Data taken from Fabes and Eisenberg (1996). Effect sizes are positive for differences favoring females. Analyses computed with outliers included produced similar results. ****All effect sizes were significantly different from zero, all $ps < .001$.

[a]–[e]Within each category, mean effect sizes with similar alphabetic superscripts are significantly different (posthoc ps at least $< .05$, see text).

When the effects of other study qualities were controlled, the category of instrumental help was significantly less predictive of sex differences in prosocial behavior than were other types of prosocial indexes. Indexes of being kind, sharing, and the aggregated index of prosocial behavior did not differ each other once study characteristics were controlled, and there was no effect of design (correlational/naturalistic versus structured/experimental) when other study qualities were controlled (although more effects were obtained for naturalistic/correlational designs prior to controlling for study characteristics). Sex differences continued to be greater when measured by self- or other-reports relative to observation of behavior. Finally, when the targets of the prosocial behavior were adults, effect sizes for the sex difference were still greater.

The results of Fabes and Eisenberg's (1996) meta-analysis of sex differences in prosocial behavior support Eagly and Crowley's (1986) conclusion that sex differences in adults' prosocial behavior are inconsistent across studies and vary as a function of the qualities of the studies. In contrast to Eagly and Crowley's findings, Fabes and Eisenberg's data indicate that *girls* tend to be more prosocial than boys. However, it is also the case that the results of Fabes and Eisenberg's meta-analysis indicated that there was a significant amount of variance left unexplained. We now briefly examine the extant literature with an eye toward understanding what factors may account for the unexplained variance.

In the Fabes and Eisenberg (1996) meta-analysis, sex differences in prosocial behavior varied with the type of prosocial behavior. Sex differences (favoring girls) were larger for indexes of kindness/considerateness and for the aggregated indexes than for help or sharing in the initial post hoc contrasts. However, when study characteristics were controlled, the sex difference was significantly smaller for instrumental helping than for other measures and only marginally greater for kindness/consideration. Aggregated measures, which were strong predictors in the univariate analyses, did not differ from other measures of prosocial behavior when study characteristics were controlled. The finding that the sex difference was weakest for instrumental helping is particularly interesting because many of the studies in the adult literature in which men helped more assessed instrumental helping (Eagly & Crowley, 1986).

Because the kindness/consideration and the aggregated indexes often were measured with self- or other-reports, whereas helping and sharing have tended to be measured with observational procedures, the relatively large sex differences in the former global indexes may be partially a function of methodology. Fabes and Eisenberg found that sex differences were greater for self-report and other-report data than for observational data and that kindness/consideration and aggregated indexes did not differ significantly from other types of prosocial behavior in the degree of sex difference once study characteristics (including whether self-report, other-report, or observational measures were used) were controlled. Berman (1980) noted that sex differences in children's responsiveness to young children were greatest when responsiveness was indexed by self-reports. Berman found little sex difference for studies with physiological indexes and mixed results in studies with behavioral indexes. Similarly, Eisenberg and Lennon (1983) found that sex differences in empathy favoring females were large for self-report measures, whereas no sex differences were evident when the measure of empathy was either physiological or unobtrusive observation of nonverbal reactions to another's emotional state.

Sex differences in self- and other-reported prosocial behavior may reflect people's conceptions of what boys and girls are *supposed* to be like rather than how they actually behave. Parents emphasize prosocial behaviors and politeness more with their daughters than their sons (Power & Parke, 1986; Power & Shanks, 1989). Moreover, peers, parents, and teachers tend to perceive girls as more prosocial than behavioral or self-reported data indicate is actually the case (Bernzweig, Eisenberg, & Fabes, 1993; Bond & Phillips, 1971; Shigetomi, Hartmann, & Gelfand, 1981). Parents even attribute girls' actions to inborn factors significantly more often than boys' actions, whereas boys' prosocial actions are more likely to be viewed as due to environmental factors (Gretarsson & Gelfand, 1988). These findings are consistent with the view that girls' reputations for prosocial behavior are greater than the actual sex difference. Nonetheless, it should be noted that there was a small sex difference favoring girls even in observational studies.

Sex differences in the literature may also be due, in part, to biases in measures of prosocial behavior. Zarbatany, Hartmann, Gelfand, and Vinciguerra (1985) argued that measures used to evaluate children's prosocial tendencies include a disproportionate number of sex-biased items favoring girls (items pertaining to feminine activities). They found that masculine items (e.g., helping get a cat out of a tree) elicited endorsements for boys, and feminine-related and neutral items elicited endorsements for girls. These data support the notion that the sex differences in prosocial behavior are due in part to the items included on measures of prosocial behavior. Consistent with the masculine role and findings for adults (Eagly & Crowley, 1986), boys often may help as much or more than girls in situations in which there is some risk or need for certain types of instrumental activities.

The conditions under which prosocial action is measured also may influence the degree to which sex differences in prosocial behavior are found. In their univariate meta-analyses (i.e., when study characteristics were not controlled), Fabes and Eisenberg (1996) found that sex differences favoring girls tended to be larger when measured in naturalistic/correlational contexts than in structured/experimental contexts. Again, this may have to do with the fact that self- or other-reports are likely to be used in correlational designs. The multivariate analysis failed to reveal a significant effect of design once the other study qualities were controlled.

Fabes and Eisenberg (1996) found that, with increasing age, sex differences in prosocial behavior tended to get larger, although this effect was eliminated once other study qualities were controlled. Because type of study was associated with age, with older children involved in more naturalistic/correlational studies, it is likely that controlling for design eliminated the association between sex and prosocial behavior.

Findings in regard to sex differences in empathy and sympathy, like those for prosocial behavior, vary with the method used to assess empathy-related responding. As mentioned previously, Eisenberg and Lennon (1983; Lennon & Eisenberg, 1987a), in a meta-analytic review, found large differences favoring females for self-report measures of empathy, especially questionnaire indexes. No gender differences were found when the measure of empathy was either physiological or unobtrusive observations of nonverbal behavior. In more recent work in which sympathy and personal distress were differentiated, investigators have obtained similar findings, although they occasionally have found weak sex differences in facial reactions (generally favoring females; Eisenberg, Fabes, Schaller, & Miller, 1989; Eisenberg, Martin, & Fabes, 1996). Eisenberg and Lennon (1983) suggested that the general pattern of results was due to differences among measures in the degree to which both the intent of the measure was obvious and people could control their responses. Sex differences were greatest when demand characteristics were high (i.e., it was clear what was being assessed) and individuals had conscious control over their responses (i.e., self-report indexes were used);

sex differences were virtually nonexistent when demand characteristics were subtle *and* study participants were unlikely to exercise much conscious control over their responding (i.e., physiological indexes). Thus, when sex-related stereotypes are activated and people can easily control their responses, they may try to project a socially desirable image to others or to themselves.

Fabes and Eisenberg (1996) also conducted a follow-up meta-analysis of empathy data published since Eisenberg and Lennon's (1983) first review and found an overall unweighted effect size (favoring girls) of .34. Relatively large effect sizes were found in self-report studies (significantly larger than in the studies involving other methods) and in studies where the targets of the empathic response were unspecified/unknown individuals. Moreover, sex differences were larger with samples of older children. When sex differences were examined by method, significant sex differences favoring girls were obtained with self-report indexes (weighted effect size of .60) and observational measures (in which a combination of behavioral and facial reactions usually were used, .29). No sex differences were obtained for nonverbal facial and physiological measures. Further, the sex difference in self-reported empathy/sympathy increased with mean age of the sample (beta = .24). Sex differences in reported empathy may increase as children become more aware of, and perhaps are more likely to internalize in their self-image, sex-role stereotypes and expectations.

Whereas there are no sex differences in prosocial moral reasoning in young children, in later elementary school and beyond, girls use more of some relatively sophisticated types of prosocial moral reasoning than do boys, whereas boys sometimes verbalize more of less mature types of reasoning (Carlo et al., 1992; Eisenberg, Carlo, et al., 1995; Eisenberg, Miller, et al., 1991; Eisenberg, Shell, et al., 1987). Moreover, in adolescence, femininity is positively related to internalized prosocial moral reasoning (but also related to hedonistic reasoning for males; Carlo et al., 1996). At this time, it is unclear the degree to which these sex differences, which generally are relatively weak, are due to real differences in moral reasoning or to differences in the ways adolescent males and females view themselves and desire to be viewed by others. However, the previously discussed finding that children's moral reasoning frequently is related to their prosocial behavior is consistent with the view that children's prosocial moral reasoning does not reflect merely children's desire to reason in a socially acceptable manner.

Although boys and girls may not differ greatly in some measures of prosocial behavior and empathy, people may tend to view girls as more prosocial because they are lower in overt aggression (Coie & Dodge, Ch. 12, this Volume). If one defines prosocial behavior broadly as including unwillingness to harm others, it may be realistic to view girls as more prosocial. Moreover, it is quite possible that the patterns of girls' and boys' prosocial behaviors differ. For example, girls and women may be more likely to embed prosocial actions in personal relationships, whereas boys and men may be more likely to engage in impersonal, instrumental acts of prosocial behavior (e.g., Eagly & Crowley, 1986). Thus, the psychological significance of males' and females' prosocial actions may differ somewhat.

In summary, although girls appear to be more prosocial than boys in their behavior, the issue of sex differences in prosocial responding and their origins is far from resolved. At this time it is difficult to determine the degree to which any sex difference reflects a difference in moral orientation versus other factors (e.g., self-presentation). It also is unclear whether the sex difference changes with age: although age was related to effect size in the univariate analysis, there was no effect of age when study characteristics were controlled. In the future, there is a need to assess better the developmental trajectory of any sex differences and to investigate the origins of sex differences in prosocial behavior.

CHALLENGES AND FUTURE DIRECTIONS

At the beginning of this chapter, we suggested that the study of prosocial behavior is in its adolescence. As is evident in our review, there is considerable research on antecedents and correlates of children's prosocial responding. This work has provided a rudimentary understanding of the range of factors that may foster prosocial action, although in many cases it is premature to confidently assume causation. At this time, the field would benefit from new emphases, both in terms of methods and in regard to conceptual frameworks and empirical foci.

Methodological Issues

An important next step in studying prosocial behavior is to focus on both the mediators and moderators of the bivariate relations obtained in much of the empirical literature. A focus on mediation (the notion that A → B → C) would enhance our understanding of the processes related to prosocial development and behavior. For example, little is known about factors that mediate (i.e., B in the mediational process) the relation between particular socialization influences (e.g., inductions) and children's prosocial behavior or empathy-related responding. As hypothesized by Hoffman (1983), do inductions actually affect perspective taking and empathy, which then foster prosocial action? Do some parental emotion-related practices enhance children's ability to regulate emotion, which then promotes sympathy? Examination of mediational processes requires that investigators refine their conceptual explanations and go beyond looking at global associations to focus more on process-oriented explanations.

In contrast, a focus on moderation forces investigators to think about the ways various predictors of prosocial responding interact in their potential influence (moderation usually is examined by assessing the interaction between two predictors; Baron & Kenny, 1986). We live in a multivariate world, and behavior is no doubt determined by numerous factors. For example, as discussed previously, Knight et al. (1994) found that children who donated to needy children were those who were not only high in perspective taking, but also were high in sympathy and understood money (the commodity to be donated). In many instances, a combination of personal characteristics or parenting practices may have more potent effects than any single variable. Moreover, moderational designs could be used to examine questions related to the ways child characteristics (e.g., degree of emotional intensity) and parental practices (e.g., ways in responding to children's empathy-related emotion) jointly predict children's prosocial responding. As one example, parental encouragement that children experience empathic emotion may be related to sympathy (and prosocial behavior) for children who are low or moderate in emotional reactivity but may increase the probability of emotional overarousal and personal distress in highly emotional children. In fact, in work on conscience and compliance, Kochanska (1995) found that temperamental characteristics of the child moderate relations between maternal socialization and measures of conscience. In addition, it is important to go beyond simple moderational models to examine the ways in which configurations of numerous variables (e.g., child-rearing practices) predict prosocial outcomes.

As noted previously, most of the research on prosocial responding is correlational. To better examine issues of causality, longitudinal designs and structural equation modeling can be used to test causal hypotheses (although structural modeling can only assess if a causal sequence is consistent with the data and does not prove causality). Further, experimental research designs could be used more frequently to complement correlational data. Because experimental designs usually (but need not) require the use of relatively artificial laboratory situations, recently researchers have been shying away from experiments. Yet laboratory experiments can be valuable in testing ideas about causality drawn from naturalistic, correlational research. We do not intend to minimize the real need for ecologically valid research; however, a multimethod approach in terms of the design of studies is necessary because different methods can be used to address somewhat different questions, including questions about causality. In addition, the convergence of findings across methods increases one's confidence in the veracity of the findings.

Another limitation of much of the research on prosocial responding is the heavy reliance on self-report data in tapping predictors of prosocial behavior, empathy-related responding, and, to a limited degree, prosocial behavior itself. Again, a multimethod approach is needed, one that includes measures as diverse as observations, self- and other-report data, behavioral assessments, and physiological and facial indexes. All measures have clear limitations, but different measures have different limitations. Thus, a multimethod approach can be expected to provide a richer and more accurate understanding of prosocial development.

Conceptual and Content-Related Directions

In regard to both conceptual and content issues, the study of prosocial behavior would benefit from greater integration with work on related issues. Prosocial behavior can be regarded in a manner similar to most interpersonal behaviors—in terms of its social appropriateness and social and personal outcomes both in specific situations and in the long term. In many but not all settings, prosocial behavior is a socially appropriate behavior; indeed, prosocial behaviors frequently are included in measures of social competence. Thus, conceptual work on social competence and the development of interpersonal competence in attachment and peer relationships is relevant to an understanding of prosocial development. Moreover, research on moral emotions such as guilt, moral cognitions, and the development of an egoistic or antisocial orientation could be used to a greater degree than in the past to inform our understanding of prosocial behavior, particularly altruism. In brief, work on prosocial behavior has been too isolated from work on related topics, and greater integration across content domains would have broad benefits. We tried to make some inroads in this direction in this chapter, although our attempts were limited by the need to cover much material in a limited space.

Of particular value and interest from our perspective is contemporary work on emotionality and regulation, including the work on temperament and the biological bases of emotion and regulatory capacities, the socialization of emotion and of coping with emotion, and the development of coping and regulatory capacities. In many, albeit not all, situations, morally relevant emotions such as empathy, sympathy, personal distress, guilt, and pride play a role in prosocial behavior. As discussed previously, individual differences in children's emotionality (particularly their emotional reactivity) and in their ability to regulate emotion arousal appear to be related to whether children experience sympathy or egoistic, personal distress in helping contexts. Thus, an understanding of emotion and its regulation is critical to the study of prosocial responding. Further, enactment of prosocial behaviors often involves not only emotional regulation, but also behavioral regulation, particularly if prosocial action requires self-denial. Thus, developmental change and individual differences in children's abilities to inhibit their behavior, delay gratification, and activate behavior when desirable are issues of considerable importance to understanding prosocial development.

Although temperamental factors likely contribute to individual differences in emotionality, regulation, and morally relevant emotions, socialization (including at a cultural level) and other environmental factors doubtlessly affect children's abilities and tendencies to regulate their emotion and behavior. Environmental factors associated with optimal regulation and moderate levels of emotionality likely foster prosocial responding, including sympathy. Thus, the growing bodies of literature on the socialization of emotion and coping, as well as cultural influences on emotion and its regulation, also are highly relevant to a comprehensive perspective on prosocial development.

It is important to note that not only has the field of prosocial behavior been relatively intellectually isolated from relevant literature on other topics, but investigators studying other issues often have not attended sufficiently to findings in the domain of prosocial development. Much of what has been learned about prosocial behavior and empathy-related reactions is relevant to the study of aggression, psychopathology (particularly externalizing behavior), guilt, socialization mechanisms, peer relationships, and the development of socially competent behavior. The broader field of developmental psychology, as well as psychology in general, would benefit if the boundaries between content areas, as well as across disciplines, were more permeable.

ACKNOWLEDGMENTS

The authors wish to thank Pat Maszk, Sherri Souza, Leslee Adler, and Sarah Coburn for their help in obtaining materials for our review. Appreciation also is expressed to Carolyn Zahn-Waxler, Bill Damon, and Bill Graziano for their comments on earlier drafts of this manuscript.

REFERENCES

Abroms, K. I., & Gollin, J. B. (1980). Developmental study of gifted preschool children and measures of psychosocial giftedness. *Exceptional Children, 46,* 334–341.

Adams, G. R. (1983). Social competence during adolescence: Social sensitivity, locus of control, empathy, and peer popularity. *Journal of Youth and Adolescence, 12,* 203–211.

Ahammer, I. M., & Murray, J. P. (1979). Kindness in the kindergarten: The relative influence of role playing and prosocial television in facilitating altruism. *International Journal of Behavioral Development, 2,* 133–157.

Anderson, J. A., & Perlman, D. (1973). Effects of an adult's preaching and responsibility for hypocritical behavior on children's altruism. *Proceedings of the 81st Annual Convention, American Psychological Association,* 291–292.

Ando, K. (1987, July). *The development of empathy in prosocial behavior.* Paper presented at the meeting of the International Society for the Study of Behavioral Development, Tokyo.

Aronfreed, J. (1970). The socialization of altruistic and sympathetic behavior: Some theoretical and experimental analyses. In J. Macaulay & L. Berkowitz (Eds.), *Altruism and helping behavior* (pp. 103–126). New York: Academic Press.

Asakawa, K., Iwawaki, S., Mondori, Y., & Minami, H. (1987, July). *Altruism in school and empathy: A developmental study of Japanese pupils.* Paper presented at the meeting of the International Society for the Study of Behavioral Development, Tokyo.

Ascione, F. R. (1992). Enhancing children's attitudes about the humane treatment of animals: Generalization to human-directed empathy. *Antrozoos, 5,* 176–191.

Ascione, F. R., & Sanok, R. L. (1982). The role of peer and adult models in facilitating and inhibiting children's prosocial behavior. *Genetic Psychology Monographs, 106,* 239–259.

Ascione, F. R., & Weber, C. V. (1993, March). *Children's attitudes about the humane treatment of animals and empathy: One-year follow up of a school-based intervention.* Paper presented at the biennial meeting of the Society for Research in Child Development, New Orleans, LA.

Astington, J. W., & Jenkins, J. M. (1995). Theory of mind development and social understanding. *Cognition and Emotion, 9,* 151–165.

Austin, A. M. B., Braeger, T., Schvaneveldt, J. D., Lindauer, S. L. K., Summers, M., Robinson, C., & Armga, C. (1991). A comparison of helping, sharing, comforting, honesty, and civic awareness for children in home care, day care, and preschool. *Child and Youth Care Forum, 20,* 183–194.

Avellar, J., & Kagan, S. (1976). Development of competitive behaviors in Anglo-American and Mexican-American children. *Psychological Reports, 39,* 191–198.

Aviezer, O., Van IJzendoorn, M. H., Sagi, A., & Schuengel, C. (1994). "Children of the dream" revisited: 70 years of collective early child care in Israeli Kibbutizim. *Psychological Bulletin, 116,* 99–116.

Bandura, A. (1986). *Social foundations of thought and action: A social cognitive theory.* Englewood Cliffs, NJ: Prentice-Hall.

Bandura, A. (1991). Social cognitive theory of moral thought and action. In W. M. Kurtines & J. L. Gewirtz (Eds.), *Handbook of moral behavior and development* (Vol. 1, pp. 45–103). Hillsdale, NJ: Erlbaum.

Barden, R. C., Garber, J., Duncan, S. W., & Masters, J. C. (1981). Cumulative effects of induced affective states in children: Accentuation, inoculation, and remediation. *Journal of Personality and Social Psychology, 40,* 750–760.

Barnett, K., Darcie, G., Holland, C. J., & Kobasigawa, A. (1982). Children's cognitions about helping. *Developmental Psychology, 18,* 267–277.

Barnett, M. A. (1975). Effects of competition and relative deservedness of the other's fate on children's generosity. *Developmental Psychology, 11,* 665–666.

Barnett, M. A., & Bryan, J. H. (1974). Effects of competition with outcome feedback on children's helping behavior. *Developmental Psychology, 10,* 838–842.

Barnett, M. A., Howard, J. A., King, L. M., & Dino, G. A. (1980). Antecedents of empathy: Retrospective accounts of early socialization. *Personality and Social Psychology Bulletin, 6,* 361–365.

Barnett, M. A., Howard, J. A., King, L. M., & Dino, G. A. (1981). Helping behavior and the transfer of empathy. *Journal of Social Psychology, 115,* 125–132.

Barnett, M. A., King, L. M., Howard, J. A., & Dino, G. A. (1980). Empathy in young children: Relation to parents' empathy, affection, and emphasis on the feelings of others. *Developmental Psychology, 16,* 243–244.

Barnett, M. A., Matthews, K. A., & Corbin, C. B. (1979). The effect of competitive and cooperative instructional sets on children's generosity. *Personality and Social Psychology Bulletin, 5,* 91–94.

Barnett, M. A., Matthews, K. A., & Howard, J. A. (1979). Relationship between competitiveness and empathy in 6- and 7-year-olds. *Developmental Psychology, 15,* 221–222.

Barnett, M. A., & Thompson, S. (1985). The role of perspective taking and empathy in children's Machiavellianism, prosocial behavior and motive for helping. *Journal of Genetic Psychology, 146,* 295–305.

Barnett, M. A., Thompson, S., & Schroff, J. (1987). Reasons for not helping. *Journal of Genetic Psychology, 148,* 489–498.

Baron, R. M., & Kenny, D. A. (1986). The moderator-mediator variable distinction in social psychological research: Conceptual, strategic, and statistical considerations. *Journal of Personality and Social Psychology, 51,* 1173–1182.

Barrett, D. E. (1979). Relations between aggressive and prosocial behaviors in children. *Journal of Genetic Psychology, 134,* 317–318.

Barrett, D. E., Radke-Yarrow, M., & Klein, R. E. (1982). Chronic malnutrition and child behavior: Effects of early caloric supplementation on social and emotional functioning at school age. *Developmental Psychology, 18,* 541–556.

Barrett, D. E., & Yarrow, M. R. (1977). Prosocial behavior, social inferential ability, and assertiveness in young children. *Child Development, 48,* 475–481.

Bar-Tal, D. (1982). Sequential development of helping behavior: A cognitive-learning approach. *Developmental Review, 2,* 101–124.

Bar-Tal, D. (1984). American study of helping behavior: What? Why? and Where? In E. Staub, D. Bar-Tal, J. Karylowski, & J. Reykowski (Eds.), *Development and maintenance of prosocial behavior* (pp. 5–27). New York: Plenum Press.

Bar-Tal, D., Korenfeld, D., & Raviv, A. (1985). Relationships between the development of helping behavior and the development of cognition, social perspective, and moral judgment. *Genetic, Social, and General Psychology Monographs, 11,* 23–40.

Bar-Tal, D., Nadler, A., & Blechman, N. (1980). The relationship between Israeli children's helping behavior and their perception on parents' socialization practices. *Journal of Social Psychology, 111,* 159–167.

Bar-Tal, D., & Nissim, R. (1984). Helping behavior and moral judgment among adolescents. *British Journal of Developmental Psychology, 2,* 329–336.

Bar-Tal, D., & Raviv, A. (1979). Consistency in helping-behavior measures. *Child Development, 50,* 1235–1238.

Bar-Tal, D., Raviv, A., & Leiser, T. (1980). The development of altruistic behavior: Empirical evidence. *Developmental Psychology, 16,* 516–524.

Bar-Tal, D., Raviv, A., & Shavit, N. (1981). Motives for helping behavior: Kibbutz and city children in kindergarten and school. *Developmental Psychology, 17,* 766–772.

Barton, E. J. (1981). Developing sharing: An analysis of modeling and other behavioral techniques. *Behavior Modification, 5,* 386–398.

Barton, E. J., & Ascione, F. R. (1979). Sharing in preschool children: Facilitation, stimulus generalization, response generalization, and maintenance. *Journal of Applied Behavior Analysis, 12,* 417–430.

Barton, E. J., Olszewski, M. J., & Madsen, J. J. (1979). The effects of adult presence on the prosocial behavior of preschool children. *Child Behavior Therapy 1,* 271–286.

Barton, E. J., & Osborne, J. G. (1978). The development of classroom sharing by a teacher using positive practice. *Behavior Modification, 2,* 231–250.

Batson, C. D. (1991). *The altruism question: Toward a social-psychological answer.* Hillsdale, NJ: Erlbaum.

Battistich, V., Watson, M., Solomon, D., Schaps, E., & Solomon, J. (1991). The Child Development Project: A comprehensive program for the development of prosocial character. In W. M. Kurtines & J. L. Gewirtz (Eds.), *Handbook of moral behavior and development: Vol. 3. Application* (pp. 1–34). New York: Erlbaum.

Baumrind, D. (1971). Current patterns of parental authority. *Developmental Psychology Monographs, 4,* 1–103.

Baumrind, D. (1988). *Familial antecedents of social competence in middle childhood.* Unpublished manuscript.

Bear, G. G., & Rys, G. S. (1994). Moral reasoning, classroom behavior, and sociometric status among elementary school children. *Developmental Psychology, 30,* 633–638.

Bender, N. N., & Carlson, J. S. (1982). Prosocial behavior and perspective-taking of mentally retarded and nonretarded children. *American Journal of Mental Deficiency, 86,* 361–366.

Benedict, R. (1934). *Patterns of culture* (6th ed.). Boston: Houghton Mifflin.

Bengtsson, H., & Johnson, L. (1987). Cognitions related to empathy in 5- to 11-year-old children. *Child Development, 58,* 1001–1012.

Bengtsson, H., & Johnson, L. (1992). Perspective taking, empathy, and prosocial behavior in late childhood. *Child Study Journal, 22,* 11–22.

Berkowitz, L. (1968). Responsibility, reciprocity, and social distance in help giving: An experimental investigation of English social class differences. *Journal of Experimental Social Psychology, 4,* 46–63.

Berkowitz, L., & Friedman, P. (1967). Some social class differences in helping behavior. *Journal of Personality and Social Psychology, 5,* 217–225.

Berman, P. W. (1980). Are women more responsive than men to the young? A review of developmental and situational variables. *Psychological Bulletin, 88,* 668–695.

Berman, P. W., & Goodman, V. (1984). Age and sex differences in children's responses to babies: Effects of adults' caretaking requests and instructions. *Child Development, 55,* 1071–1077.

Berndt, T. J. (1981a). Age changes and changes over time in prosocial intentions and behavior between friends. *Developmental Psychology, 17,* 408–416.

Berndt, T. J. (1981b). Effects of friendship on prosocial intentions and behavior. *Child Development, 52,* 636–643.

Berndt, T. J. (1982). The features and effects of friendship in early adolescence. *Child Development, 53,* 1447–1460.

Berndt, T. J. (1985). Prosocial behavior between friends in middle childhood and early adolescence. *Journal of Early Adolescence, 5,* 307–317.

Berndt, T. J., & Das, R. (1987). Effects of popularity and friendship on perceptions of the personality and social behavior of peers. *Journal of Early Adolescence, 7,* 429–439.

Berndt, T. J., Hawkins, J. A., & Hoyle, S. G. (1986). Changes in friendship during a school year: Effects on children's and adolescents' impressions of friendship and sharing with friends. *Child Development, 57,* 1284–1297.

Berndt, T. J., & Perry, T. B. (1986). Children's perceptions of friendships as supportive relationships. *Developmental Psychology, 22,* 640–648.

Bernzweig, J., Eisenberg, N., & Fabes, R. A. (1993). Children's coping in self- and other-relevant contexts. *Journal of Experimental Child Psychology, 55,* 208–226.

Bigelow, B. J., & La Gaipa, J. J. (1975). Children's written descriptions of friendships: A multidimensional analysis. *Developmental Psychology, 11,* 857–858.

Bigelow, B. J., Tesson, G., & Lewko, J. H. (1992). The social rules that children use: Close friends, other friends, and "other kids" compared to parents, teachers, and siblings. *International Journal of Behavioral Development, 15,* 315–335.

Birch, L. L., & Billman, J. (1986). Preschool children's food sharing with friends and acquaintances. *Child Development, 57,* 387–395.

Bischof-Kohler, D. (1991). The development of empathy in infants. In M. E. Lamb & H. Keller (Eds.), *Infant development: Perspectives from German-speaking countries* (pp. 245–273). Hillsdale, NJ: Erlbaum.

Bizman, A., Yinon, Y., Mivtzari, E., & Shavit, R. (1978). Effects of the age structure of the kindergarten on altruistic behavior. *Journal of School Psychology, 16,* 154–160.

Black, C. R., Weinstein, E. A., & Tanur, J. M. (1980). Development of expectations of altruism versus self-interest. *Journal of Social Psychology, 111,* 105–112.

Blakemore, J. E. O. (1990). Children's nurturant interactions with their infant siblings: An exploration of gender differences and maternal socialization. *Sex Roles, 22,* 43–57.

Blasi, A. (1980). Bridging moral cognition and moral action: A critical review of the literature. *Psychological Bulletin, 88,* 1–45.

Block, J., & Block, J. H. (1973, January). *Ego development and the provenance of thought: A longitudinal study of ego and cognitive development in young children.* Progress report for the National Institute of Mental Health. (Grant No. MH16080).

Block, J. H., & Block, J. (1980). The role of ego-control and ego-resiliency in the organization of behavior. In W. A. Collins (Ed.), *Development of cognition, affect, and social relations. The Minnesota Symposia on Child Psychology* (Vol. 13, pp. 39–101). Hillsdale, NJ: Erlbaum.

Blum, L. A. (1980). *Friendship, altruism and morality.* London: Routledge & Kegan Paul.

Boehnke, K., Silbereisen, R. K., Eisenberg, N., Reykowski, J., & Palmonari, A. (1989). The development of prosocial motivation: A cross-national study. *Journal of Cross-Cultural Psychology, 20,* 219–243.

Bond, N. D., & Phillips, B. N. (1971). Personality traits associated with altruistic behavior of children. *Journal of School Psychology, 9,* 24–34.

Borg, A., Hultman, E., & Waern, Y. (1978). Conflict resolution and social understanding in six to twelve year old boys. *Scandinavian Journal of Psychology, 19,* 53–62.

Braband, J., & Lerner, M. J. (1975). "A little time and effort" ... Who deserves what from whom. *Personality and Social Psychology Bulletin, 1,* 177–179.

Broberg, A., Hwang, C., Lamb, M., & Ketterlinus, R. D. (1989). Child care effects on socioemotional and intellectual competence in Swedish preschoolers. In J. S. Lande, S. Scarr, & N. Gunzenhauser (Eds.), *Caring for children: Challenge to America* (pp. 49–76). Hillsdale, NJ: Erlbaum.

Brody, G. H., Stoneman, Z., & MacKinnon, C. E. (1986). Contributions of maternal child-rearing practices and play contexts to sibling interactions. *Journal of Applied Developmental Psychology, 7,* 225–236.

Brody, G. H., Stoneman, Z., MacKinnon, C. E., & MacKinnon, R. (1985). Role relationships and behavior between preschool-aged and school-aged sibling pairs. *Developmental Psychology, 21,* 124–129.

Brothers, L. (1989). A biological perspective on empathy. *American Journal of Psychiatry, 146,* 10–19.

Broverman, I. K., Vogel, S. R., Broverman, D. M., Clarkson, F. E., & Rosenkrantz, P. S. (1972). Sex-role stereotypes: A current appraisal. *Journal of Social Issues, 28,* 59–78.

Brown, M. S., & Israel, A. C. (1980, September). *Effects of instructions, self-instructions and discipline on children's donating.* Paper presented at the meeting of the American Psychological Association, Montreal.

Bryan, J. H. (1971). Model affect and children's imitative altruism. *Child Development, 42,* 2061–2065.

Bryan, J. H., Redfield, J., & Mader, S. (1971). Words and deeds about altruism and the subsequent reinforcement power of the model. *Child Development, 42,* 1501–1508.

Bryan, J. H., & Walbek, N. H. (1970a). The impact of words and deeds concerning altruism upon children. *Child Development, 41,* 747–757.

Bryan, J. H., & Walbek, N. H. (1970b). Preaching and practicing generosity: Children's actions and reactions. *Child Development, 41,* 329–353.

Bryant, B. K. (1987). Mental health, temperament, family, and friends: Perspectives on children's empathy and social perspective taking. In N. Eisenberg & J. Strayer (Eds.), *Empathy and its development* (pp. 245–270). Cambridge, England: Cambridge University Press.

Bryant, B. K., & Crockenberg, S. B. (1980). Correlates and dimensions of prosocial behavior: A study of female siblings with their mothers. *Child Development, 51,* 529–544.

Buhrmester, D., Goldfarb, J., & Cantrell, D. (1992). Self-presentation when sharing with friends and nonfriends. *Journal of Early Adolescence, 12,* 61–79.

Burleson, B. R. (1984). Age, social-cognitive development, and the use of comforting strategies. *Communication Monographs, 51,* 140–153.

Burleson, B. R. (1985). The production of comforting messages: Social-cognitive foundations. *Journal of Language and Social Psychology, 4,* 253–273.

Burleson, B. R., Applegate, J. L., Burke, J. A., Clark, R. A., Delia, J. G., & Kline, S. L. (1986). Communicative correlates of peer acceptance in childhood. *Communication Education, 35,* 349–361.

Burleson, B. R., & Fennelly, D. A. (1981). The effects of persuasive appeal form and cognitive complexity on children's sharing behavior. *Child Study Journal, 11,* 75–90.

Burleson, B. R., & Kunkel, A. W. (1995, March). *Socialization of emotional support skills in childhood: The influence of parents and peers.* Poster presented at the biennial meeting of the Society for Research in Child Development, Indianapolis, IN.

Burleson, B. B., & Waltman, P. A. (1987). Popular, rejected, and supportive preadolescents: Social-cognitive and communicative characteristics. In M. L. McLaughlin (Ed.), *Communication yearbook* (Vol. 10, pp. 533–552). Newbury Park, CA: Sage.

Cairns, R. B., & Cairns, B. D. (1994). *Lifelines and risks: Pathways of youth in our time.* Cambridge, England: Cambridge University Press.

Call, K. T., Mortimer, J. T., & Shanahan, M. J. (1995). Helpfulness and the development of competence in adolescence. *Child Development, 66,* 129–138.

Caplan, M. Z., & Hay, D. F. (1989). Preschoolers' responses to peers' distress and beliefs about bystander intervention. *Journal of Child Psychology and Psychiatry, 30,* 231–242.

Carlo, G., Eisenberg, N., & Knight, G. P. (1992). An objective measure of adolescents' prosocial moral reasoning. *Journal of Research on Adolescence, 2,* 331–349.

Carlo, G., Eisenberg, N., Troyer, D., Switzer, G., & Speer, A. L. (1991). The altruistic personality: In what contexts is it apparent? *Journal of Personality and Social Psychology, 61,* 450–458.

Carlo, G., Knight, G. P., Eisenberg, N., & Rotenberg, K. (1991). Cognitive processes and prosocial behavior among children: The role of affective attributions and reconciliations. *Developmental Psychology, 27,* 456–461.

Carlo, G., Koller, S., Eisenberg, N., Pacheco, P., & Loguercio, A. (in press). Prosocial cognitions, emotions, and behaviors: A cross-cultural study of adolescents from Brazil and the United States. *Developmental Psychology.*

Carlson, M., Charlin, V., & Miller, N. (1988). Positive mood and helping behavior: A test of six hypotheses. *Psychological Bulletin, 55,* 211–229.

Carlson, M., & Miller, N. (1987). Explanation of the relation between negative mood and helping. *Psychological Bulletin, 102,* 91–108.

Cauley, K., & Tyler, B. (1989). The relationship of self-concept to prosocial behavior in children. *Early Childhood Research Quarterly, 4,* 51–60.

Chapman, M., Zahn-Waxler, C., Cooperman, G., & Iannotti, R. (1987). Empathy and responsibility in the motivation of children's helping. *Developmental Psychology, 23,* 140–145.

Chong-De, L. (1988). Moral development in a changing world: A Chinese perspective. *School Psychology International, 9,* 13–19.

Cialdini, R. B., & Fultz, J. (1990). Interpreting the negative mood/helping literature via mega-analysis: A contrary view. *Psychological Bulletin, 107,* 110–114.

Cialdini, R. B., & Kenrick, D. T. (1976). Altruism as hedonism: A social development perspective on the relationship of negative mood state and helping. *Journal of Personality and Social Psychology, 34,* 907–914.

Cialdini, R. B., Kenrick, D. T., & Baumann, D. J. (1982). Effects of mood on prosocial behavior in children and adults. In N. Eisenberg (Ed.), *The development of prosocial behavior* (pp. 339–359). New York: Academic Press.

Clark, M. S., Milberg, S., & Erber, R. (1984). Effects of arousal on judgments of others' emotions. *Journal of Personality and Social Psychology, 46,* 551–560.

Clarke-Stewart, K. A. (1981). Observation and experiment: Complementary strategies for studying day care and social development. In S. Kilmer (Ed.), *Advances in early education and day care* (Vol. 2, pp. 227–250). Greenwich, CT: JAI Press.

Clary, E. G., & Miller, J. (1986). Socialization and situational influences on sustained altruism. *Child Development, 57,* 1358–1369.

Cohen, D., & Strayer, J. (1996). Empathy in conduct disordered and comparison youth. *Developmental Psychology, 32,* 988–998.

Coie, J. D., Dodge, K. A., & Kupersmidt, J. B. (1990). Peer group behavior and social status. In S. R. Asher & J. D. Coie (Eds.), *Peer rejection in childhood* (pp. 17–59). Cambridge, England: Cambridge University Press.

Colby, A., & Damon, W. (1992). *Some do care: Contemporary lives of moral commitment.* Toronto: Free Press.

Costin, S. E., & Jones, D. C. (1992). Friendship as a facilitator of emotional responsiveness and prosocial interventions among young children. *Developmental Psychology, 28,* 941–947.

Cox, N. (1974). Prior help, ego development, and helping behavior. *Child Development, 75,* 594–603.

Crockenberg, S. (1985). Toddlers' reactions to maternal anger. *Merrill-Palmer Quarterly, 31,* 361–373.

Cummings, E. M., Hennessy, K. D., Rabideau, G. J., & Cicchetti, D. (1994). Responses of physically abused boys to interadult anger involving their mothers. *Developmental Psychopathology, 6,* 31–41.

Cummings, E. M., & Smith, D. (1993). The impact of anger between adults on siblings' emotions and social behavior. *Journal of Child Psychology and Psychiatry, 34,* 1425-1433.

Cummings, E. M., Zahn-Waxler, C., & Radke-Yarrow, M. (1981). Young children's responses to expressions of anger and affection by others in the family. *Child Development, 52,* 1274–1282.

Cummings, E. M., Zahn-Waxler, C., & Radke-Yarrow, M. (1984). Developmental changes in children's reactions to anger in the home. *Journal of Child Psychology and Psychiatry, 25,* 63–74.

Cummings, J. S., Pellegrini, D. S., Notarius, C. I., & Cummings, E. M. (1989). Children's responses to angry adult behavior as a function of marital distress and history of interparent hostility. *Child Development, 60,* 1035–1043.

Cutrona, C. E., & Feshbach, S. (1979). Cognitive and behavioral correlates of children's differential use of social information. *Child Development, 50,* 1036–1042.

Damon, W. (1977). *The social world of the child.* San Francisco: Jossey-Bass.

Das, R., & Berndt, T. J. (1992). Relations of preschoolers' social acceptance to peer ratings and self-perceptions. *Early Education and Development, 3,* 221–231.

Davies, P. T., & Cummings, E. M. (1994). Marital conflict and child adjustment: An emotional security hypothesis. *Psychological Bulletin, 116,* 387–411.

Davis, M. H., & Franzoi, S. (1991). Stability and change in adolescent self-consciousness and empathy. *Journal of Research in Personality, 25,* 70–87.

Davis, M. H., Luce, C., & Kraus, S. J. (1994). The heritability of characteristics associated with dispositional empathy. *Journal of Personality, 62,* 369–391.

Day, D. M., Bream, L. A., & Pal, A. (1992). Proactive and reactive aggression: An analysis of subtypes based on teacher perceptions. *Journal of Clinical Child Psychology, 21,* 210–217.

Dekovic, M., & Gerris, J. R. M. (1994). Developmental analysis of social cognitive and behavioral differences between popular and rejected children. *Journal of Applied Developmental Psychology, 15,* 367–386.

Dekovic, M., & Janssens, J. M. A. M. (1992). Parents' child-rearing style and children's sociometric status. *Developmental Psychology, 28,* 925–932.

Denham, S. A. (1986). Social cognition, prosocial behavior, and emotion in preschoolers: Contextual validation. *Child Development, 57,* 194–201.

Denham, S. A., & Burger, C. (1991). Observational validation of ratings of preschoolers' social competence and behavior problems. *Child Study Journal, 21,* 185–291.

Denham, S. A., & Couchoud, E. A. (1991). Social-emotional predictors of preschoolers' responses to adult negative emotion. *Journal of Child Psychology and Psychiatry, 32,* 595–608.

Denham, S. A., & Grout, L. (1992). Mothers' emotional expressiveness and coping: Relations with preschoolers' social-emotional competence. *Genetic, Social, and General Psychology Monographs, 118,* 75–101.

Denham, S. A., & Grout, L. (1993). Socialization of emotion: Pathway to preschoolers' emotional and social competence. *Journal of Nonverbal Behavior, 17,* 205–227.

Denham, S. A., Mason, T., & Couchoud, E. A. (1995). Scaffolding young children's prosocial responsiveness: Preschoolers' responses to adult sadness, anger, and pain. *International Journal of Behavioral Development, 18,* 489–504.

Denham, S. A., Renwick-DeBardi, S., & Hewes, S. (1994). Emotional communication between mothers and preschoolers: Relations with emotional competence. *Merrill-Palmer Quarterly, 40,* 488–508.

DePalma, D. J. (1974). Effects of social class, moral orientation and severity of punishment of boys' moral responses to transgression and generosity. *Developmental Psychology, 10,* 890–900.

Derryberry, D., & Rothbart, M. K. (1988). Arousal, affect, and attention as components of temperament. *Journal of Personality and Social Psychology, 55,* 958–966.

de Veer, A. J. E., & Janssens, J. M. A. M. (1994). Victim-orientated discipline, interpersonal understanding, and guilt. *Journal of Moral Education, 23,* 165–182.

DeVoe, M. W., & Sherman, T. M. (1978). A microtechnology for teaching prosocial behavior to children. *Child Study Journal, 8,* 83–91.

Dillard, J. P. (1991). The current status of research on sequential-request compliance techniques. *Personality and Social Psychology Bulletin, 17,* 283–288.

Dix, T., & Grusec, J. E. (1983). Parental influence techniques: An attributional analysis. *Child Development, 54,* 645–652.

Dlugokinski, E. L, & Firestone, I. J. (1974). Other centeredness and susceptibility to charitable appeals: Effects of perceived discipline. *Developmental Psychology, 10,* 21–28.

Doland, D. J., & Adelberg, K. (1967). The learning of sharing behavior. *Child Development, 38,* 695–700.

Dreman, S. B. (1976). Sharing behavior in Israeli school children: Cognitive and social learning factors. *Child Development, 47,* 186–194.

Dreman, S. B., & Greenbaum, C. W. (1973). Altruism or reciprocity: Sharing behavior in Israeli kindergarten children. *Child Development, 44,* 61–68.

Dressel, S., & Midlarsky, E. (1978). The effects of model's exhortations, demands, and practices on children's donation behavior. *Journal of Genetic Psychology, 132,* 211–223.

Dunn, J., Kendrick, C., & MacNamee, R. (1981). The reaction of first-born children to the birth of a sibling: Mothers' reports. *Journal of Child Psychology and Psychiatry, 22,* 1–18.

Dunn, J., & Kendrick, D. (1982). *Siblings: Love, envy, and understanding.* Cambridge, MA: Harvard University Press.

Dunn, J., & Munn, P. (1986). Siblings and the development of prosocial behavior. *International Journal of Behavioral Development, 9,* 265–284.

Eagly, A. H., & Crowley, M. (1986). Gender and helping behavior: A meta-analytic review of the social psychological literature. *Psychological Bulletin, 100,* 283–308.

Eberly, M. B., Montemayor, R., & Flannery, D. J. (1993). Variation in adolescent helpfulness toward parents in a family context. *Journal of Early Adolescence, 13,* 228–244.

Eisenberg, N. (1983). Children's differentiations among potential recipients of aid. *Child Development, 54,* 594–602.

Eisenberg, N. (1986). *Altruistic emotion, cognition, and behavior.* Hillsdale, NJ: Erlbaum.

Eisenberg, N. (1991). Meta-analytic contributions to the literature on prosocial behavior. *Personality and Social Psychology Bulletin, 17,* 273–282.

Eisenberg, N. (1992). *The caring child*. Cambridge, MA: Harvard University Press.

Eisenberg, N., Boehnke, K., Schuhler, P., & Silbereisen, R. K. (1985). The development of prosocial behavior and cognitions in German children. *Journal of Cross-Cultural Psychology, 16,* 69–82.

Eisenberg, N., Cameron, E., Pasternack, J., & Tryon, K. (1988). Behavioral and sociocognitive correlates of ratings of prosocial behavior and sociometric status. *Journal of Genetic Psychology, 149,* 5–15.

Eisenberg, N., Cameron, E., Tryon, K., & Dodez, R. (1981). Socialization of prosocial behavior in the preschool classroom. *Developmental Psychology, 17,* 773–782.

Eisenberg, N., Carlo, G., Murphy, B., & Van Court, P. (1995). Prosocial development in late adolescence: A longitudinal study. *Child Development, 66,* 1179–1197.

Eisenberg, N., Cialdini, R., McCreath, H., & Shell, R. (1987). Consistency-based compliance: When and why do children become vulnerable? *Journal of Personality and Social Psychology, 52,* 1174–1181.

Eisenberg, N., Cialdini, R. B., McCreath, H., & Shell, R. (1989). Consistency-based compliance in children: When and why do consistency procedures have immediate effects? *Journal of Behavioral Development, 12,* 351–367.

Eisenberg, N., & Fabes, R. A. (1990). Empathy: Conceptualization, assessment, and relation to prosocial behavior. *Motivation and Emotion, 14,* 131–149.

Eisenberg, N., & Fabes, R. A. (1991). Prosocial behavior and empathy: A multimethod, developmental perspective. In P. Clark (Ed.), *Review of personality and social psychology* (Vol. 12, pp. 34–61). Newbury Park, CA: Sage.

Eisenberg, N., & Fabes, R. A. (1992). Emotion, regulation, and the development of social competence. In M. S. Clark (Ed.), *Review of personality and social psychology: Vol. 14. Emotion and social behavior* (pp. 119–150). Newbury Park, CA: Sage.

Eisenberg, N., & Fabes, R. A. (1995). The relation of young children's vicarious emotional responding to social competence, regulation, and emotionality. *Cognition and Emotion, 9,* 203–228.

Eisenberg, N., Fabes, R. A., Bernzweig, J., Karbon, M., Poulin, R., & Hanish, L. (1993). The relations of emotionality and regulation to preschoolers' social skills and sociometric status. *Child Development, 64,* 1418–1438.

Eisenberg, N., Fabes, R. A., Bustamante, D., Mathy, R. M., Miller, P. A., & Lindholm, E. (1988). Differentiation of vicariously induced emotional reactions in children. *Developmental Psychology, 24,* 237–246.

Eisenberg, N., Fabes, R. A., Carlo, G., & Karbon, M. (1992). Emotional responsivity to others: Behavioral correlates and socialization antecedents. In N. Eisenberg & R. A. Fabes (Eds.), *New directions in child development* (No. 55, pp. 57–73). San Francisco: Jossey-Bass.

Eisenberg, N., Fabes, R. A., Carlo, G., Speer, A. L., Switzer, G., Karbon, M., & Troyer, D. (1993). The relations of empathy-related emotions and maternal practices to children's comforting behavior. *Journal of Experimental Child Psychology, 55,* 131–150.

Eisenberg, N., Fabes, R. A., Carlo, G., Troyer, D., Speer, A. L., Karbon, M., & Switzer, G. (1992). The relations of maternal practices and characteristics to children's vicarious emotional responsiveness. *Child Development, 63,* 583–602.

Eisenberg, N., Fabes, R. A., Karbon, M., Murphy, B. C., Carlo, G., & Wosinski, M. (1996). Relations of school children's comforting behavior to empathy-related reactions and shyness. *Social Development, 5,* 330–351.

Eisenberg, N., Fabes, R. A., Karbon, M., Murphy, B. C., Wosinski, M., Polazzi, L., Carlo, G., & Juhnke, C. (1996). The relations of children's dispositional prosocial behavior to emotionality, regulation, and social functioning. *Child Development, 67,* 974–992.

Eisenberg, N., Fabes, R. A., & Miller, P. A. (1990). The evolutionary and neurological roots of prosocial behavior. In L. Ellis & H. Hoffman (Eds.), *Crime in biological, social, and moral contexts* (pp. 247–260). New York: Praeger.

Eisenberg, N., Fabes, R. A., Miller, P. A., Fultz, J., Mathy, R. M., Shell, R., & Reno, R. R. (1989). The relations of sympathy and personal distress to prosocial behavior: A multimethod study. *Journal of Personality and Social Psychology, 57,* 55–66.

Eisenberg, N., Fabes, R. A., Miller, P. A., Shell, C., Shea, R., & May-Plumlee, T. (1990). Preschoolers' vicarious emotional responding and their situational and dispositional prosocial behavior. *Merrill-Palmer Quarterly, 36,* 507–529.

Eisenberg, N., Fabes, R. A., Murphy, B., Karbon, M., Maszk, P., Smith, M., O'Boyle, C., & Suh, K. (1994). The relations of emotionality and regulation to dispositional and situational empathy-related responding. *Journal of Personality and Social Psychology, 66,* 776–797.

Eisenberg, N., Fabes, R. A., Murphy, B. C., Karbon, M., Smith, M., & Maszk, P. (1996). The relations of children's dispositional empathy-related responding to their emotionality, regulation, and social functioning. *Developmental Psychology, 32,* 195–209.

Eisenberg, N., Fabes, R. A., Schaller, M., Carlo, G., & Miller, P. A. (1991). The relations of parental characteristics and practices to children's vicarious emotional responding. *Child Development, 62,* 1393–1408.

Eisenberg, N., Fabes, R. A., Schaller, M., & Miller, P. A. (1989). Intercorrelations and developmental changes in indices of empathy. In N. Eisenberg (Ed.), *New directions in child development* (No. 44, pp. 86–126). San Francisco: Jossey-Bass.

Eisenberg, N., Fabes, R. A., Schaller, M., Miller, P. A., Carlo, G., Poulin, R., Shea, C., & Shell, R. (1991). Personality and socialization correlates of vicarious emotional responding. *Journal of Personality and Social Psychology, 61,* 459–470.

Eisenberg, N., Fabes, R. A., & Shea, C. (1989). Gender differences in empathy and prosocial moral reasoning: Empirical investigations. In M. M. Brabeck (Ed.), *Who cares? Theory, research, and educational implications of the ethic of care* (pp. 127–143). New York: Praeger.

Eisenberg, N., & Giallanza, S. (1984). The relation of mode of prosocial behavior and other proprietary behaviors to toy dominance. *Child Study Journal, 14,* 115–121.

Eisenberg, N., Hertz-Lazarowitz, R., & Fuchs, I. (1990). Prosocial moral judgment in Israeli kibbutz and city children: A longitudinal study. *Merrill-Palmer Quarterly, 36,* 273–285.

Eisenberg, N., & Lennon, R. (1983). Gender differences in empathy and related capacities. *Psychological Bulletin, 94,* 100–131.

Eisenberg, N., Lundy, N., Shell, R., & Roth, K. (1985). Children's justifications for their adult and peer-direct compliant (prosocial and nonprosocial) behaviors. *Developmental Psychology, 21,* 325–331.

Eisenberg, N., Martin, C. L., & Fabes, R. A. (1996). Gender development and gender effects. In D. C. Berliner & R. C. Calfee (Eds.), *The handbook of educational psychology* (pp. 358–396). New York: Macmillan.

Eisenberg, N., McCreath, H., & Ahn, R. (1988). Vicarious emotional responsiveness and prosocial behavior: Their interrelations in young children. *Personality and Social Psychology Bulletin, 14,* 298–311.

Eisenberg, N., & McNally, S. (1993). Socialization and mothers' and adolescents' empathy-related characteristics. *Journal of Research on Adolescence, 3,* 171–191.

Eisenberg, N., & Miller, P. (1987). The relation of empathy to prosocial and related behaviors. *Psychological Bulletin, 101,* 91–119.

Eisenberg, N., Miller, P. A., Schaller, M., Fabes, R. A., Fultz, J., Shell, R., & Shea, C. (1989). The role of sympathy and altruistic personality traits in helping: A re-examination. *Journal of Personality, 57,* 41–67.

Eisenberg, N., Miller, P. A., Shell, R., McNalley, S., & Shea, C. (1991). Prosocial development in adolescence: A longitudinal study. *Developmental Psychology, 27,* 849–857.

Eisenberg, N., Murphy, B., & Shepard, S. (1997). The development of empathic accuracy. In W. Ickes (Ed.), *Empathic accuracy* (pp. 73–116). New York: Guilford Press.

Eisenberg, N., & Mussen, P. (1989). *The roots of prosocial behavior in children.* Cambridge, England: Cambridge University Press.

Eisenberg, N., & Okun, M. (1996). The relations of dispositional regulation and emotionality to elders' empathy-related responding and affect while volunteering. *Journal of Personality, 64,* 157–183.

Eisenberg, N., & Pasternack, J. (1983). Inequalities in children's prosocial behaviors: Whom do children assist? In R. L. Leahy (Ed.), *Child's construction of inequality* (pp. 179–205). New York: Academic Press.

Eisenberg, N., Pasternack, J. F., Cameron, E., & Tryon, K. (1984). The relation of quality and mode of prosocial behavior to moral cognitions and social style. *Child Development, 155,* 1479–1485.

Eisenberg, N., Schaller, M., Fabes, R. A., Bustamante, D., Mathy, R., Shell, R., & Rhodes, K. (1988). The differentiation of personal distress and sympathy in children and adults. *Developmental Psychology, 24,* 766–775.

Eisenberg, N., Shea, C. L., Carlo, G., & Knight, G. (1991). Empathy-related responding and cognition: A "chicken and the egg" dilemma. In W. Kurtines & J. Gewirtz (Eds.), *Handbook of moral behavior and development: Vol. 2. Research* (pp. 63–88). Hillsdale, NJ: Erlbaum.

Eisenberg, N., & Shell, R. (1986). The relation of prosocial moral judgment and behavior in children: The mediating role of cost. *Personality and Social Psychology Bulletin, 12,* 426–433.

Eisenberg, N., Shell, R., Pasternack, J., Lennon, R., Beller, R., & Mathy, R. M. (1987). Prosocial development in middle childhood: A longitudinal study. *Developmental Psychology, 24,* 712–718.

Eisenberg, N., Wolchik, S., Goldberg, L., & Engel, I. (1992). Parental values, reinforcement, and young children's prosocial behavior: A longitudinal study. *Journal of Genetic Psychology, 153,* 19–36.

Eisenberg-Berg, N. (1979a). Development of children's prosocial moral judgment. *Developmental Psychology, 15,* 128–137.

Eisenberg-Berg, N. (1979b). The relationship of prosocial moral reasoning to altruism, political liberalism, and intelligence. *Developmental Psychology, 15,* 87–89.

Eisenberg-Berg, N., & Geisheker, E. (1979). Content of preachings and power of the model/preacher: The effect on children's generosity. *Developmental Psychology, 15,* 168–175.

Eisenberg-Berg, N., & Hand, M. (1979). The relationship of preschooler's reasoning about prosocial moral conflicts to prosocial behavior. *Child Development, 50,* 356–363.

Eisenberg-Berg, N., Hand, M., & Haake, R. (1981). The relationship of preschoolers' habitual use of space to social, prosocial, and antisocial behavior. *Journal of Genetic Psychology, 138,* 111–121.

Eisenberg-Berg, N., & Lennon, R. (1980). Altruism and the assessment of empathy in the preschool years. *Child Development, 51,* 552–557.

Eisenberg-Berg, N., & Neal, C. (1979). Children's moral reasoning about their own spontaneous prosocial behavior. *Developmental Psychology, 15,* 228–229.

Eisenberg-Berg, N., & Neal, C. (1981). Children's moral reasoning about self and others: Effects of identify of the story character and cost of helping. *Personality and Social Psychology Bulletin, 7,* 17–23.

Ekstein, R. (1978). Psychoanalysis, sympathy, and altruism. In L. G. Wispe (Ed.), *Altruism, sympathy, and helping: Psychological and sociological principles* (pp. 165–175). New York: Academic Press.

Elliott, R., & Vasta, R. (1970). The modeling of sharing: Effects associated with vicarious reinforcement, symbolization, age, and generalization. *Journal of Experimental Child Psychology, 10,* 8–15.

Emler, N. P., & Rushton, J. P. (1974). Cognitive-developmental factors in children's generosity. *British Journal of Social and Clinical Psychology, 13,* 277–281.

Estrada, P. (1995). Adolescents' self-reports of prosocial responses to friends and acquaintances: The role of sympathy-related cognitive, affective, and motivational processes. *Journal of Research on Adolescence, 5,* 173–200.

Fabes, R. A., & Eisenberg, N. (1996). *An examination of age and sex differences in prosocial behavior and empathy.* Unpublished data, Arizona State University.

Fabes, R. A., Eisenberg, N., & Eisenbud, L. (1993). Behavioral and physiological correlates of children's reactions to others' distress. *Developmental Psychology, 29,* 655–663.

Fabes, R. A., Eisenberg, N., Karbon, M., Bernzweig, J., Speer, A. L., & Carlo, G. (1994). Socialization of children's vicarious emotional responding and prosocial behavior: Relations with mothers' perceptions of children's emotional reactivity. *Developmental Psychology, 30,* 44–55.

Fabes, R. A., Eisenberg, N., Karbon, M., Troyer, D, & Switzer, G. (1994). The relations of children's emotion regulation to their vicarious emotional responses and comforting behavior. *Child Development, 65,* 1678–1693.

Fabes, R. A., Eisenberg, N., & Miller, P. (1990). Maternal correlates of children's vicarious emotional responsiveness. *Developmental Psychology, 26,* 639–648.

Fabes, R. A., Fultz, J., Eisenberg, N., May-Plumlee, T., & Christopher, F. S. (1989). The effects of reward on children's prosocial motivation: A socialization study. *Developmental Psychology, 25,* 509–515.

Farver, J. A. M., & Branstetter, W. H. (1994). Preschoolers' prosocial responses to their peers' distress. *Developmental Psychology, 30,* 334–341.

Fenichel, O. (1945). *The psychoanalytic theory of neurosis.* New York: Norton.

Feshbach, N. D. (1978). Studies of empathic behavior in children. In B. A. Maher (Ed.), *Progress in experimental personality research* (Vol. 8, pp. 1–47). New York: Academic Press.

Feshbach, N. D., & Feshbach, S. (1982). Empathy training and the regulation of aggression: Potentialities and limitations. *Academic Psychology Bulletin, 4,* 399–413.

Feshbach, N. D., & Feshbach, S. (1987). Affective processes and academic achievement. *Child Development, 58,* 1335–1347.

Fincham, F. (1978). Recipient characteristics and sharing behavior in the learning disabled. *Journal of Genetic Psychology, 133,* 143–144.

Fischer, W. F. (1963). Sharing in preschool children as function of amount and type of reinforcement. *Genetic Psychology Monographs, 68,* 215–245.

Fishbein, H. D., & Kaminski, N. K. (1985). Children's reciprocal altruism in a competitive game. *British Journal of Developmental Psychology, 3,* 393–398.

Forliti, J. E., & Benson, P. L. (1986). Young adolescents: A national study. *Religious Education, 81,* 199–224.

Fouts, G. T. (1972). Charity in children: The influence of "charity" stimuli and an audience. *Journal of Experimental Child Psychology, 13,* 303–309.

Franco, A. C. S. P. (1978). Altruism in children as a function of deservedness of reward, story telling and vicarious reinforcement. *Philippine Journal of Psychology, 11,* 3–14.

Frankel, K. A. (1990). Girls' perceptions of peer relationship support and stress. *Journal of Early Adolescence, 10,* 69–88.

Frankel, K. A., Lindahl, K., & Harmon, R. J. (1992). Preschoolers' response to maternal sadness: Relationships with maternal depression and emotional availability. *Infant Mental Health Journal, 13,* 132–146.

Freud, A. (1946). A form of altruism. In A. Freud (Ed.), *The ego and the mechanisms of defense* (pp. 122–136). New York: International Universities Press.

Freud, S. (1930). *Civilization and its discontents* (J. Riviere, Trans.). London: Hogarth Press.

Freud, S. (1968). *New introductory lectures on psychoanalysis.* London: Hogarth. (Original work published 1933)

Friedrich, L. K., & Stein, A. H. (1973). Aggressive and prosocial television programs and the natural behavior of preschool children. *Monographs of the Society for Research in Child Development, 38*(4, Serial No. 151), 1–64.

Froming, W. J., Allen, L., & Jensen, R. (1985). Altruism, role-taking, and self-awareness: The acquisition of norms governing altruistic behavior. *Child Development, 56,* 1223–1228.

Fuchs, I., Eisenberg, N., Hertz-Lazarowitz, R., & Sharabany, R. (1986). Israeli city and American children's moral reasoning about prosocial moral conflicts. *Merrill-Palmer Quarterly, 32,* 37–50.

Furby, L. (1978). Sharing: Decisions and moral judgments about letting others use one's possessions. *Psychological Reports, 43,* 595–609.

Furman, W., & Buhrmester, D. (1985). Children's perceptions of the personal relationships in their social networks. *Developmental Psychology, 21,* 1016–1024.

Furman, W., & Masters, J. C. (1980). Peer interactions, sociometric status, and resistance to deviation in young children. *Developmental Psychology, 16,* 229–236.

Garner, P. W., Jones, D. C., & Miner, J. L. (1994). Social competence among low-income preschoolers: Emotion socialization practices and social cognitive correlates. *Child Development, 65,* 622–637.

Garner, P. W., Jones, D. C., & Palmer, D. J. (1994). Social cognitive correlates of preschool children's sibling caregiving behavior. *Developmental Psychology, 30,* 905–911.

Gelfand, D. M., Hartmann, D. P., Cromer, C. C., Smith, C. L., & Page, B. C. (1975). The effects of instructional prompts and praise on children's donation rates. *Child Development, 46,* 980–983.

George, C., & Main, M. (1979). Social interactions of young abused children: Approach, avoidance, and aggression. *Child Development, 50,* 306–318.

Gershman, E. S., & Hayes, D. S. (1983). Differential stability of reciprocal friendships and unilateral relationships among preschool children. *Merrill-Palmer Quarterly, 29,* 169–177.

Glover, E. (1968). *The birth of the ego.* London: Allen & Unwin.

Goody, E. (1991). The learning of prosocial behaviour in small-scale egalitarian societies: An anthropological view. In R. A. Hinde & J. Groebel (Eds.), *Cooperation and prosocial behaviour* (pp. 106–128). Cambridge, England: Cambridge University Press.

Graham, S., Doubleday, C., & Guarino, P. A. (1984). The development of relations between perceived controllability and the emotions of pity, anger, and guilt. *Child Development, 55,* 561–565.

Grant, J. E., Weiner, A., & Rushton, J. P. (1976). Moral judgment and generosity in children. *Psychological Reports, 39,* 451–454.

Graves, N. B., & Graves, T. D. (1983). The cultural context of prosocial development: An ecological model. In D. L. Bridgeman (Ed.), *The nature of prosocial development* (pp. 243–264). New York: Academic Press.

Gray, R., & Pirot, M. (1983). The effects of prosocial modeling on young children's nurturing of a "sick" child. *Psychology and Human Development, 1,* 41–46.

Graziano, W. G., & Eisenberg, N. (1997). Agreeableness: A dimension of personality. In R. Hogan, J. Johnson, & F. Briggs (Eds.), *Handbook of personality psychology* (pp. 795–824). San Diego, CA: Academic Press.

Graziano, W. G., Musser, L. M., Rosen, S., & Shaffer, D. R. (1982). The development of fair-play standards in same-race and mixed-race situations. *Child Development, 53,* 938–947.

Greenberger, E., & Goldberg, W. A. (1989). Work, parenting, and the socialization of children. *Developmental Psychology, 25,* 22–35.

Gretarsson, S. J., & Gelfand, D. M. (1988). Mothers' attributions regarding their children's social behavior and personality characteristics. *Developmental Psychology, 24,* 264–269.

Grusec, J. E. (1971). Power and the internalization of self-denial. *Child Development, 42,* 93–105.

Grusec, J. E. (1972). Demand characteristics of the modeling experiment: Altruism as a function of age and aggression. *Journal of Personality and Social Psychology, 22,* 139–148.

Grusec, J. E. (1982). The socialization of altruism. In N. Eisenberg (Ed.), *The development of prosocial behavior* (pp. 65–90). New York: Academic Press.

Grusec, J. E. (1983). The internalization of altruistic dispositions: A cognitive analysis. In E. T. Higgins, D. N. Ruble, & W. W. Hartup (Eds.), *Social cognition and social development: A sociocultural perspective* (pp. 275–293). Cambridge, England: Cambridge University Press.

Grusec, J. E. (1991). Socializing concern for others in the home. *Developmental Psychology, 27,* 338–342.

Grusec, J. E., & Goodnow, J. J. (1994). Impact of parental discipline methods on the child's internalization of values: A reconceptualization of current points of view. *Developmental Psychology, 30,* 4–19.

Grusec, J. E., Goodnow, J. J., & Cohen, L. (1996). Household work and the development of concern for others. *Developmental Psychology, 32,* 999–1007.

Grusec, J. E., Kuczynski, L., Rushton, J. P., & Simutis, Z. M. (1978). Modeling, direct instruction, and attributions: Effects on altruism. *Developmental Psychology, 14,* 51–57.

Grusec, J. E., & Redler, E. (1980). Attribution, reinforcement, and altruism: A developmental analysis. *Developmental Psychology, 16,* 525–534.

Grusec, J. E., Saas-Kortsaak, P., & Simutis, Z. M. (1978). The role of example and moral exhortation in the training of altruism. *Child Development, 49,* 920–923.

Grusec, J. E, & Skubiski, L. (1970). Model nurturance, demand characteristics of the modeling experiment, and altruism. *Journal of Personality and Social Psychology, 14,* 352–359.

Gupta, P. (1982). Altruism or reciprocity: Sharing behaviour in Hindu kindergarten children. *Psychological Studies, 27,* 68–73.

Gupta, P., & Bhargava, P. (1977). Sharing behaviour in children as a function of model generosity and vicarious reinforcement. *Psychologia, 20,* 221–225.

Halberstadt, A. G. (1986). Family socialization of emotional expression and nonverbal communication styles and skills. *Journal of Personality and Social Psychology, 51,* 827–836.

Hamilton, S. F., & Fenzel, L. M. (1988). The impact of volunteer experience on adolescent social development: Evidence of program effects. *Journal of Adolescent Research, 3,* 65–80.

Hampson, R. B. (1984). Adolescent prosocial behavior: Peer group and situational factors associated with helping. *Journal of Personality and Social Psychology, 46,* 153–162.

Handlon, B. J., & Gross, P. (1959). The development of sharing behavior. *Journal of Abnormal and Social Psychology, 59,* 425–428.

Hansen, B. K., & Bryant, B. K. (1980). Peer influence on sharing behavior of Mexican-American and Anglo-American boys. *Journal of Social Psychology, 110,* 135–136.

Harris, L. A. (1967). A study of altruism. *Elementary School Journal, 68,* 135–141.

Harris, M. B. (1970). Reciprocity and generosity: Some determinants of children. *Child Development, 41,* 313–328.

Harris, M. B. (1971). Models, norms, and sharing. *Psychological Reports, 29,* 147–153.

Harris, S., Mussen, P., & Rutherford, E. (1976). Some cognitive, behavioral, and personality correlates of maturity of moral judgment. *Journal of Genetic Psychology, 128,* 123–135.

Hart, D., & Fegley, S. (1995). Altruism and caring in adolescence: Relations to self-understanding and social judgment. *Child Development, 66,* 1346–1359.

Hartmann, D. P., Gelfand, D. M., Smith, C. L., Paul, S. C., Cromer, C. C., Page, B. C., & LeBenta, D. V. (1976). Factors affecting the acquisition and elimination of children's donation behavior. *Journal of Experimental Child Psychology, 21,* 328–338.

Hartup, W. W., & Coates, B. (1967). Imitation of a peer as a function of reinforcement from the peer group and rewardingness of the model. *Child Development, 38,* 1003–1016.

Hay, D. F. (1979). Cooperative interactions and sharing between very young children and their parents. *Developmental Psychology, 15,* 647–653.

Hay, D. F. (1994). Prosocial development. *Journal of Child Psychology and Psychiatry, 35,* 29–71.

Hay, D. F., Caplan, M. Z., Castle, M. Z., & Stimson, C. A. (1991). Does sharing become "rational" in the second year of life? *Developmental Psychology, 27,* 987–993.

Hay, D. F., & Murray, P. (1982). Giving and requesting: Social facilitation of infants' offers to adults. *Infant Behavior and Development, 5,* 301–310.

Hay, F. D., Nash, A., & Pedersen, J. (1981). Responses of six-month-olds to the distress of their peers. *Child Development, 52,* 1071–1075.

Hearold, S. (1986). A synthesis of 1043 effects of television on social behavior. In G. Comstock (Ed.), *Public communication and behavior* (Vol. 1, pp. 65–133). New York: Academic Press.

Hedges, L. V., & Olkin, I. (1985). *Statistical methods for meta-analysis.* New York: Academic Press.

Henry, R. M. (1980). A theoretical and empirical analysis of "reasoning" in the socialization of young children. *Human Development, 23,* 105–125.

Hertz-Lazarowitz, R. (1983). Prosocial behavior in the classroom. *Academic Psychology Bulletin, 5,* 319–338.

Hertz-Lazarowitz, R., Fuchs, I., Sharabany, R., & Eisenberg, N. (1989). Students' interactive and non-interactive behaviors in the classroom: A comparison between two types of classrooms in the city and the kibbutz in Israel. *Contemporary Educational Psychology, 14,* 22–32.

Hertz-Lazarowitz, R., & Sharan, S. (1984). Enhancing prosocial behavior through cooperative learning in the classroom. In E. Staub, D. Bar-Tal, J. Karylowski, & J. Reykowski (Eds.), *Development and maintenance of prosocial behavior: International perspectives on positive morality* (pp. 423–443). New York: Plenum Press.

Hertz-Lazarowitz, R., Sharan, S., & Steinberg, R. (1980). Classroom learning style and cooperative behavior of elementary school children. *Journal of Educational Psychology, 72,* 97–104.

Hieshima, J. A., & Schneider, B. (1994). Intergenerational effects on the cultural and cognitive socialization of third- and fourth-generation Japanese Americans. *Journal of Applied Developmental Psychology, 15,* 319–327.

Hobbes, T. (1962). *Leviathan* (M. Oakeshotte, Ed.). New York: Dutton. (Original work published 1651)

Hoffman, M. L. (1963). Parent discipline and the child's consideration for others. *Child Development, 34,* 573–588.

Hoffman, M. L. (1970a). Conscience, personality, and socialization techniques. *Human Development, 13,* 90–126.

Hoffman, M. L. (1970b). Moral development. In P. H. Mussen (Ed.), *Carmichael's manual of child development* (Vol. 2, pp. 261–359). New York: Wiley.

Hoffman, M. L. (1971). Father absence and conscience development. *Developmental Psychology, 4,* 400–406.

Hoffman, M. L. (1975a). Altruistic behavior and the parent-child relationship. *Journal of Personality and Social Psychology, 31,* 937–943.

Hoffman, M. L. (1975b). Sex differences in moral internalization and values. *Journal of Personality and Social Psychology, 32,* 720–729.

Hoffman, M. L. (1981). Is altruism part of human nature? *Journal of Personality and Social Psychology, 40,* 121–137.

Hoffman, M. L. (1982). Development of prosocial motivation: Empathy and guilt. In N. Eisenberg (Ed.), *The development of prosocial behavior* (pp. 281–313). New York: Academic Press.

Hoffman, M. L. (1983). Affective and cognitive processes in moral internalization. In E. T. Higgins, D. N. Ruble, & W. W. Hartup (Eds.), *Social cognition and social development: A sociocultural perspective* (pp. 236–274). Cambridge, England: Cambridge University Press.

Hoffman, M. L., & Saltzstein, H. D. (1967). Parent discipline and the child's moral development. *Journal of Personality and Social Psychology, 5,* 45–57.

Holte, C. S., Jamruszka, V., Gustafson, J., Beaman, A. L, & Camp, G. C. (1984). Influence of children's positive self-perceptions on donating behavior in naturalistic settings. *Journal of School Psychology, 22,* 145–153.

Honig, A. S., Douthit, D., Lee, J., & Dingler, C. (1992). Prosocial and aggressive behaviours of preschoolers at play in secular and church-based day care. *Early Child Development and Care, 83,* 93–101.

Howe, N., & Ross, H. S. (1990). Socialization, perspective-taking, and the sibling relationship. *Developmental Psychology, 26,* 160–165.

Howes, C., & Eldredge, R. (1985). Responses of abused, neglected, and non-maltreated children to the behaviors of their peers. *Journal of Applied Developmental Psychology, 6,* 261–270.

Howes, C., & Farver, J. (1987). Toddlers' responses to the distress of their peers. *Journal of Applied Developmental Psychology, 8,* 441–452.

Howes, C., & Matheson, C. C. (1992). Sequences in the development of competent play with peers: Social and social pretend play. *Developmental Psychology, 28,* 961–974.

Howes, C., Matheson, C. C., & Hamilton, C. E. (1994). Maternal, teacher, and child care history correlates of children's relationships with peers. *Child Development, 65,* 264–273.

Howes, C., & Olenick, M. (1986). Family and child care influences on toddlers' compliance. *Child Development, 57,* 202–216.

Hudson, L. M., Forman, E. A., & Brion-Meisels, S. (1982). Role taking as a predictor of prosocial behavior in cross-age tutors. *Child Development, 53,* 1320–1329.

Hull, D., & Reuter, J. (1977). The development of charitable behavior in elementary school children. *Journal of Genetic Psychology, 131,* 147–153.

Hume, D. (1975). *Enquiry into human understanding* (P. Nidditch, Ed.). Oxford, England: Clarendon Press. (Originally published 1748)

Iannotti, R. J. (1985). Naturalistic and structured assessments of prosocial behavior in preschool children: The influence of empathy and perspective taking. *Developmental Psychology, 21,* 46–55.

Iannotti, R. J., Cummings, E. M., Pierrehumbert, B., Milano, M. J., & Zahn-Waxler, C. (1992). Parental influences on prosocial behavior and empathy in early childhood. In J. M. A. M. Janssens & J. R. M. Gerris (Eds.), *Child rearing: Influence on prosocial and moral development* (pp. 77–100). Amsterdam, The Netherlands: Swets & Zeitlinger.

Israel, A. C., & Brown, M. S. (1979). Effects of directiveness of instructions and surveillance on the production and persistence of children's donations. *Journal of Experimental Child Psychology, 27,* 250–261.

Israel, A. C., & Raskin, P. A. (1979). Directiveness of instructions and modeling: Effects on production and persistence on children's donations. *Journal of Genetic Psychology, 135,* 269–277.

Israely, Y., & Guttmann, J. (1983). Children's sharing behavior as a function of exposure to puppet-show and story models. *Journal of Genetic Psychology, 142,* 311–312.

Jacobsen, C. (1983). What it means to be considerate: Differences in normative expectations and their implications. *Israel Social Science Research, 1,* 24–33.

Janssens, J. M. A. M., & Gerris, J. R. M. (1992). Child rearing, empathy and prosocial development. In J. M. A. M. Janssens & J. R. M. Gerris (Eds.), *Child rearing: Influence on prosocial and moral development* (pp. 57–75). Amsterdam, The Netherlands: Swets & Zeitlinger.

Jarymowicz, M. (1977). Modification of self-worth and increment of prosocial sensitivity. *Polish Psychological Bulletin, 8,* 45–53.

Jennings, K. D., Fitch, D., & Suwalsky, J. T. D. (1987). Social cognition and social interaction in three-year-olds: Is social cognition truly social? *Child Study Journal, 17,* 1–14.

Johnson, D. B. (1982). Altruistic behavior and the development of the self in infants. *Merrill-Palmer Quarterly, 28,* 379–388.

Johnson, D. W., & Johnson, R. T. (1975). *Learning together and alone: Cooperation, competition, and individualization.* Englewood Cliffs, NJ: Prentice-Hall.

Jones, D. C. (1985). Persuasive appeals and responses to appeals among friends and acquaintances. *Child Development, 56,* 757–763.

Kagan, S. (1977). Social motives and behaviors of Mexican-American and Anglo-American children. In J. L. Martinez (Ed.), *Chicano psychology* (pp. 45–86). New York: Academic Press.

Kagan, S., & Knight, G. P. (1979). Cooperation-competition and self-esteem: A case of cultural relativism. *Journal of Cross-Cultural Psychology, 10,* 457–467.

Kagan, S., & Knight, G. P. (1981). Social motives among Anglo-American and Mexican-American children: Experimental and projective measures. *Journal of Research in Personality, 15,* 93–106.

Kagan, S., & Knight, G. P. (1984). Maternal reinforcement style and cooperation-competition among Anglo American and Mexican American children. *Journal of Genetic Psychology, 145,* 37–46.

Kagan, S., & Madsen, M. C. (1972a). Experimental analyses of cooperation and competition of Anglo-American and Mexican children. *Developmental Psychology, 6,* 49–59.

Kagan, S., & Madsen, M. C. (1972b). Rivalry in Anglo-American and Mexican children of two ages. *Journal of Personality and Social Psychology, 24,* 214–220.

Kalliopuska, M. (1984). Relation between children's and parents' empathy. *Psychological Reports, 54,* 295–299.

Kalliopuska, M., & Tiitinen, U. (1991). Influence of two developmental programs on the empathy and prosociability of preschool children. *Perceptual and Motor Skills, 72,* 323–328.

Kaneko, R., & Hamazaki, T. (1987). Prosocial behavior manifestations of young children in an orphanage. *Psychologia, 30,* 235–242.

Kanfer, F. H., Stifter, E., & Morris, S. J. (1981). Self-control and altruism: Delay of gratification for another. *Child Development, 52,* 674–682.

Kant, E. (1956). *Groundwork of the metaphysics of moral law.* London: Hutchinson. (Original work published 1785)

Karniol, R. (1995). Developmental and individual differences in predicting others' thoughts and feelings: Applying the transformation rule model. In N. Eisenberg (Ed.), *Review of personality and social psychology: Vol. 15. Social development* (pp. 27–48). Thousand Oaks, CA: Sage.

Karpova, S. N., & Murzinova, N. I. (1988). The importance of play and schoolwork in the assimilation of moral norms by 6–7-year-olds. *Vestnik Moskowskogo Universiteta, Ser. 14, Psikhologiya, 2,* 43–48.

Karylowski, J. (1982). Doing good to feel good vs. doing good to make others feel good: Some child-rearing antecedents. *School Psychology International, 3,* 149–156.

Katz, P. A., Katz, I., & Cohen, S. (1976). White children's attitudes toward blacks and the physically handicapped: A developmental study. *Journal of Educational Psychology, 82,* 20–24.

Kawashima, K. (1980). Effects of presence of another and learning styles on donating behavior in children. *Japanese Journal of Psychology, 50,* 345–348.

Keith, J. G., Nelson, C. S., Schlabach, J. H., & Thompson, C. J. (1990). The relationship between parental employment and three measures of early adolescent responsibility: Family-related, personal, and social. *Journal of Early Adolescence, 10,* 399–415.

Keller, B. B., & Bell, R. Q. (1979). Child effects on adult's method of eliciting altruistic behavior. *Child Development, 50,* 1004–1009.

Kennedy, A. B., & Thurman, S. K. (1982). Inclinations of non-handicapped children to help their handicapped peers. *Journal of Special Education, 16,* 319–327.

Kestenbaum, R., Farber, E. A., & Sroufe, L. A. (1989). Individual differences in empathy among preschoolers: Relation to attachment history. *New Directions in Child Development, 44,* 51–64.

Kipper, D. A., & Yinon, Y. (1978). The effect of modeling with expressed conflict on children's generosity. *Journal of Social Psychology, 106,* 277–278.

Klimes-Dougan, B., & Kistner, J. (1990). Physically abused preschoolers' responses to peers' distress. *Developmental Psychology, 26,* 599–602.

Knight, G. P. (1982). Cooperative-competitive social orientation: Interactions of birth order with sex and economic class. *Child Development, 53,* 664–667.

Knight, G. P., Bohlmeyer, E. M., Schneider, H., & Harris, J. D. (1993). Age differences in temporal monitoring and equal sharing in a fixed-duration sharing task. *British Journal of Developmental Psychology, 11,* 143–158.

Knight, G. P., & Chao, C. (1991). Cooperative, competitive, and individualistic social values among 8- to 12-year-old siblings, friends, and acquaintances. *Personality and Social Psychology Bulletin, 17,* 201–211.

Knight, G. P., Cota, M. K., & Bernal, M. E. (1993). The socialization of cooperative, competitive, and individualistic preferences among Mexican American children: The mediating role of ethnic identity. *Hispanic Journal of Behavioral Sciences, 15,* 291–309.

Knight, G. P., Johnson, L. G., Carlo, G., & Eisenberg, N. (1994). A multiplicative model of the dispositional antecedents of a prosocial behavior: Predicting more of the people more of the time. *Journal of Personality and Social Psychology, 66,* 178–183.

Knight, G. P., & Kagan, S. (1977a). Acculturation of prosocial and competitive behaviors among second- and third-generation Mexican-American children. *Journal of Cross-Cultural Psychology, 8,* 273–284.

Knight, G. P., & Kagan, S. (1977b). Development of prosocial and competitive behaviors in Anglo-American and Mexican-American children. *Child Development, 48,* 1385–1394.

Knight, G. P., & Kagan, S. (1982). Siblings, birth order and cooperative-competitive social behavior: A comparison of Anglo-American and Mexican-American children. *Journal of Cross-Cultural Psychology, 13,* 239–249.

Knight, G. P., Kagan, S., & Buriel, R. (1981). Confounding effects of individualism in children's cooperation-competition social motive measures. *Motivation and Emotion, 5,* 167–178.

Knight, G. P., Kagan, S., & Buriel, R. (1982). Perceived parental practices and prosocial development. *Journal of Genetic Psychology, 141,* 57–65.

Knight, G. P., Nelson, W., Kagan, S., & Gumbiner, J. (1982). Cooperative-competitive social orientation and school achievement among Anglo-American and Mexican-American children. *Contemporary Educational Psychology, 7,* 97–106.

Kochanska, G. (1995). Children's temperament, mothers' discipline, and security of attachment: Multiple pathways to emerging internalization. *Child Development, 66,* 597–615.

Kochanska, G., Padavich, D. L., & Koenig, A. L. (1996). Children's narratives about hypothetical moral dilemmas and objective measures for their conscience: Mutual relations and socialization antecedents. *Child Development, 67,* 1420–1436.

Koestner, R., Franz, C., & Weinberger, J. (1990). The family origins of empathic concern: A 26-year longitudinal study. *Journal of Personality and Social Psychology, 58,* 709–717.

Kohlberg, L. (1969). Stage and sequence: The cognitive-developmental approach to socialization. In D. A. Goslin (Ed.), *Handbook of socialization theory and research* (pp. 325–480). New York: Rand McNally.

Kohlberg, L. (1984). *Essays on moral development: Vol. 2. The psychology of moral development.* San Francisco: Harper & Row.

Krebs, D. L., & Sturrup, B. (1982). Role-taking ability and altruistic behavior in elementary school children. *Journal of Moral Education, 11,* 94–100.

Krebs, D. L., & Van Hesteren, F. (1994). The development of altruism: Toward an integrative model. *Developmental Review, 14,* 103–158.

Krishnan, L. (1988). Recipient need and anticipation of reciprocity in prosocial exchange. *Journal of Social Psychology, 128,* 223–231.

Ladd, G. W., Lange, G., & Stremmel, A. (1983). Personal and situational influences on children's helping behavior: Factors that mediate helping. *Child Development, 54,* 488–501.

Ladd, G. W., & Oden, S. (1979). The relationship between peer acceptance and children's ideas about helpfulness. *Child Development, 50,* 402–408.

Ladd, G. W., & Profilet, S. M. (1996). The Child Behavior Scale: A teacher-report measure of young children's aggressive, withdrawn, and prosocial behaviors. *Developmental Psychology, 32,* 1008–1024.

Lalonde, C. E., & Chandler, M. J. (1995). False belief understanding goes to school: On the social-emotional consequences of coming early or late to a first theory of mind. *Cognition and Emotion, 9,* 167–185.

Lamb, M. E. (1978a). Interactions between eighteen-month-olds and their preschool-aged siblings. *Child Development, 49,* 51–59.

Lamb, M. E. (1978b). The development of sibling relationships in infancy: A short-term longitudinal study. *Child Development, 49,* 1189–1196.

Langer, E. J., Blank, A., & Chanowitz, B. (1978). The mindlessness of ostensibly thoughtful action. *Journal of Personality and Social Psychology, 36,* 635–642.

Larrieu, J. A. (1984, March). *Prosocial values, assertiveness, and sex: Predictors of children's naturalistic helping.* Paper presented at the biennial meeting of the Southwestern Society for the Research in Human Development, Denver, CO.

Larrieu, J. A., & Mussen, P. (1986). Some personality and motivational correlates of children's prosocial behavior. *Journal of Genetic Psychology, 147,* 529–542.

Larsen, R. J., & Diener, E. (1987). Affect intensity as an individual difference characteristic: A review. *Journal of Research in Personality, 21,* 1–39.

Lazarus, R. S., & Folkman, S. (1984). *Stress, appraisal, and coping.* New York: Springer.

Lee, L. C., & Zhan, G. Q. (1991). Political socialization and parental values in the People's Republic of China. *International Journal of Behavioral Development, 14,* 337–373.

Lemare, L., & Krebs, D. (1983). Perspective-taking and styles of (pro)social behavior in elementary school children. *Academic Psychology Bulletin, 5,* 289–298.

Lennon, R., & Eisenberg, N. (1987a). Gender and age differences in empathy and sympathy. In N. Eisenberg & J. Strayer (Eds.), *Empathy and its development* (pp. 195–217). New York: Cambridge University Press.

Lennon, R., & Eisenberg, N. (1987b). Emotional displays associated with preschoolers' prosocial behavior. *Child Development, 58,* 992–1000.

Lennon, R., Eisenberg, N., & Carroll, J. (1983). The assessment of empathy in early childhood. *Journal of Applied Developmental Psychology, 4,* 295–302.

Lennon, R., Eisenberg, N., & Carroll, J. (1986). The relation between empathy and prosocial behavior in the preschool years. *Journal of Applied Developmental Psychology, 3,* 219–224.

Lenrow, R. B. (1965). Studies of sympathy. In S. S. Tompkins & C. E. Izard (Eds.), *Affect, cognition, and personality* (pp. 264–294). New York: Springer.

Lepper, M. R. (1983). Social-control processes and the internalization of social values: An attributional perspective. In E. T. Higgins, D. N. Ruble, & W. W. Hartup (Eds.), *Social cognition and social development: A sociocultural perspective* (pp. 294–330). Cambridge, England: Cambridge University Press.

Levin, I., & Bekerman-Greenberg, R. (1980). Moral judgment and moral reasoning in sharing: A developmental analysis. *Genetic Psychological Monographs, 101,* 215–230.

Levitt, M. J., Weber, R. A., Clark, M. C., & McDonnell, P. (1985). Reciprocity of exchange in toddler sharing behavior. *Developmental Psychology, 21,* 122–123.

Liebert, R. M., & Fernandez, L. E. (1970). Effects of single and multiple modeling cues on establishing norms for sharing. *Proceedings of the 78th Annual Convention, American Psychological Association,* 437–438.

Liebert, R. M., & Poulos, R. W. (1971). Eliciting the "norm of giving": Effects of modeling and presence of witness on children's sharing behavior. *Proceedings of the 79th Annual Convention, American Psychological Association,* 345–446.

Lipscomb, T. J., Bregman, N. J., & McAllister, H. A. (1983). The effect of words and actions on American children's prosocial behavior. *Journal of Psychology, 114,* 193–198.

Lipscomb, T. J., Larrieu, J. A., McAllister, H. A., & Bregman, N. J. (1982). Modeling and children's generosity: A developmental perspective. *Merrill-Palmer Quarterly, 28,* 275–282.

Lipscomb, T. J., McAllister, H. A., & Bregman, N. J. (1985). A developmental inquiry into the effects of multiple models on children's generosity. *Merrill-Palmer Quarterly, 31,* 335–344.

Loban, W. (1953). A study of social sensitivity (sympathy) among adolescents. *Journal of Educational Psychology, 44,* 102–112.

London, P. (1970). The rescuers: Motivational hypotheses about Christians who saved Jews from the Nazis. In J. Macaulay & L. Berkowitz (Eds.), *Altruism and helping behavior* (pp. 241–250). New York: Academic Press.

Long, G. T., & Lerner, M. J. (1974). Deserving the "personal contract" and altruistic behavioral by children. *Journal of Personality and Social Psychology, 29,* 551–556.

Lourenco, O. M. (1990). From cost-perception to gain-construction: Toward a Piagetian explanation of the development of altruism in children. *International Journal of Behavioral Development, 1990,* 119–132.

Lourenco, O. M. (1993). Toward a Piagetian explanation of the development of prosocial behaviour in children: The force of negational thinking. *British Journal of Developmental Psychology, 11,* 91–106.

Ma, H. K. (1985). Cross-cultural study of the hierarchical structure of human relationships. *Psychological Reports, 57,* 1079–1083.

Ma, H. K. (1992). The relation of altruistic orientation to human relationships and moral judgment in Chinese people. *International Journal of Psychology, 27,* 377–400.

Ma, H. K., & Leung, M. C. (1991). Altruistic orientation in children: Construction and validation of the Child Altruism Inventory. *International Journal of Psychology, 26,* 745–759.

Ma, H. K., & Leung, M. C. (1992). Effects of age, sex, and social relationships on the altruistic behavior of Chinese children. *Journal of Genetic Psychology, 153,* 293–303.

MacLean, P. D. (1982, May). *Evolutionary brain roots of family, play, and the isolation call.* Paper presented at the annual meeting of the America Psychiatric Association, Toronto.

MacLean, P. D. (1985). Brain evolution relating to family, play and the separation call. *Archives of General Psychiatry, 42,* 405–417.

Main, M., & George, C. (1985). Responses of abused and disadvantaged toddlers to distress in agemates: A study in the day care setting. *Developmental Psychology, 21,* 407–412.

Mannarino, A. P. (1976). Friendship patterns and altruistic behavior in preadolescent males. *Developmental Psychology, 12,* 555–556.

Marcus, R. F., & Jenny, B. (1977). A naturalistic study of reciprocity in the helping behavior of young children. *The Alberta Journal of Educational Research, 23,* 195–206.

Marsh, D. T., Serafica, F. C., & Barenboim, C. (1981). Interrelationships among perspective taking, interpersonal problem solving and interpersonal functioning. *Journal of Genetic Psychology, 138,* 37–48.

Martin, G. B., & Clark, R. D. (1982). Distress crying in neonates: Species and peer specificity. *Developmental Psychology, 18,* 3–9.

Maruyama, G., Fraser, S. C., & Miller, N. (1982). Personal responsibility and altruism in children. *Journal of Personality and Social Psychology, 42,* 658–664.

Matthews, K. A., Batson, C. D., Horn, J., & Rosenman, R. H. (1981). Principles in his nature which interest him in the fortune of others: The heritability of empathic concern for others. *Journal of Personality, 49,* 237–247.

Matusov, E., Bell, N., & Rogoff, B. (1993, March). *Collaboration and assistance in problem solving by children differing in cooperative schooling backgrounds.* Paper presented at the biennial meeting of the Society for Research in Child Development, New Orleans, LA.

McGrath, M. P., & Power, T. G. (1990). The effects of reasoning and choice on children's prosocial behaviour. *International Journal of Behavioural Development, 13,* 345–353.

McGrath, M. P., Wilson, S. R., & Frassetto, S. J. (1995). Why some forms of inductive reasoning are better than others: Effects of cognitive focus, choice, and affect on children's prosocial behavior. *Merrill-Palmer Quarterly, 41,* 347–360.

McGuire, J. M., & Thomas, M. H. (1975). Effects of sex, competence, and competition on sharing behavior in children. *Journal of Personality and Social Psychology, 32,* 490–494.

McGuire, K. D., & Weisz, J. R. (1982). Social cognition and behavior correlates of preadolescent chumship. *Child Development, 53,* 1478–1484.

Mead, M. (1935). *Sex and temperament in three primitive societies.* New York: Morrow.

Midlarsky, E., & Bryan, J. H. (1967). Training charity in children. *Journal of Personality and Social Psychology, 5,* 408–415.

Midlarsky, E., & Bryan, J. H. (1972). Affect expressions and children's imitative altruism. *Journal of Experimental Research on Personality, 6,* 195–203.

Midlarsky, E., Bryan, J. H., & Brickman, P. (1973). Aversive approval: Interactive effects of modeling and reinforcement on altruistic behavior. *Child Development, 44,* 321–328.

Midlarsky, E., & Hannah, M. E. (1985). Competence, reticence, and helping by children and adolescents. *Developmental Psychology, 21,* 534–541.

Miller, D. T., & Smith, J. (1977). The effect of own deservingness and deservingness of others on children's helping behavior. *Child Development, 48,* 617–620.

Miller, J. G., & Bersoff, D. M. (1992). Culture and moral judgment: How are conflicts between justice and interpersonal responsibilities resolved? *Journal of Personality and Social Psychology, 62,* 541–554.

Miller, J. G., & Bersoff, D. M. (1994). Cultural influences on the moral status of reciprocity and the discounting of endogenous motivation. *Personality and Social Psychology Bulletin, 20,* 592–602.

Miller, J. G., Bersoff, D. M., & Harwood, R. L. (1990). Perceptions of social responsibilities in India and in the United States: Moral imperatives or personal decisions? *Journal of Personality and Social Psychology, 58,* 33–47.

Miller, P., & Eisenberg, N. (1988). The relation of empathy to aggression and externalizing/antisocial behavior. *Psychological Bulletin, 103,* 324–344.

Miller, P. A., Eisenberg, N., Fabes, R. A., & Shell, R. (1996). Relations of moral reasoning and vicarious emotion to young children's prosocial behavior toward peers and adults. *Developmental Psychology, 32,* 210–219.

Miller, P. A., Eisenberg, N., Fabes, R. A., Shell, R., & Gular, S. (1989). Socialization of empathic and sympathetic responding. In N. Eisenberg (Ed.), *The development of empathy and related vicarious responses. New directions in child development* (pp. 65–83). San Francisco: Jossey-Bass.

Miller, S. M. (1979). Interrelationships among dependency, empathy, and sharing. *Motivation and Emotion, 3,* 183–199.

Mills, R. S. L., & Grusec, J. (1989). Cognitive, affective, and behavioral consequences of praising altruism. *Merrill-Palmer Quarterly, 35,* 299–326.

Mischel, W., Shoda, Y., & Rodriguez, M. L. (1989). Delay of gratification in children. *Science, 244,* 933–938.

Moore, B. S., & Eisenberg, N. (1984). The development of altruism. *Annals of Child Development, 1,* 107–174.

Moore, B. S., Underwood, B., & Rosenhan, D. L. (1973). Affect and altruism. *Developmental Psychology, 8,* 99–104.

Morishita, M. (1985). The influence of the perceived teacher model attitude of acceptance-rejection on children's aggressive or altruistic behavior through modeling. *Japanese Journal of Psychology, 56,* 138–145.

Morris, W. N., Marshall, H. M., & Miller, R. S. (1973). The effect of vicarious punishment on prosocial behavior in children. *Journal of Experimental Child Psychology, 15,* 222–236.

Mosbacher, B. J., Gruen, G. E., & Rychlak, J. F. (1985). Incentive value: The overlooked dimension in childhood sharing. *Journal of Genetic Psychology, 146,* 197–204.

Mullis, R. L., Smith, D. W., & Vollmers, K. E. (1983). Prosocial behaviors in young children and parental guidance. *Child Study Journal, 13,* 13–21.

Munekata, H., & Ninomiya, K. (1985). Development of prosocial moral judgments. *Japanese Journal of Educational Psychology, 33,* 157–164.

Mussen, P., Rutherford, E., Harris, S., & Keasey, C. (1970). Honesty and altruism among preadolescents. *Developmental Psychology, 3,* 169–194.

Musun-Miller, L. (1991). Effects of maternal presence on sibling behavior. *Journal of Applied Developmental Psychology, 12,* 145–147.

Nadler, A., Romek, E., & Shapira-Friedman, A. (1979). Giving in the kibbutz: Pro-social behavior of city and kibbutz children as affected by social responsibility and social pressure. *Journal of Cross-Cultural Psychology, 10,* 57–72.

Nagel, T. (1970). *The possibility of altruism.* Oxford, England: Clarendon Press.

O'Connor, M., & Cuevas, J. (1982). The relationship of children's prosocial behavior to social responsibility, prosocial reasoning, and personality. *Journal of Genetic Psychology, 140,* 33–45.

O'Connor, M., Dollinger, S., Kennedy, S., & Pelletier-Smetko, P. (1979). Prosocial behavior and psychopathology in emotionally disturbed boys. *American Journal of Orthopsychiatry, 49,* 301–310.

Olejnik, A. B., & McKinney, J. P. (1973). Parental value orientation and generosity in children. *Developmental Psychology, 8,* 311.

Oliner, S. P., & Oliner, P. M. (1988). *The altruistic personality: Rescuers of Jews in Nazi Europe.* New York: Free Press.

Owens, C. R., & Ascione, F. R. (1991). Effects of the model's age, perceived similarity, and familiarity on children's donating. *Journal of Genetic Psychology, 152,* 341–357.

Panksepp, J. (1982). Toward a general psychobiological theory of emotion. *Brain and Behavioral Sciences, 5,* 407–468.

Panksepp, J. (1986). The psychobiology of prosocial behaviors: Separation distress, play, and altruism. In C. Zahn-Waxler, E. M. Cummings, & R. Iannotti (Eds.), *Altruism and aggression: Biological and social origins* (pp. 19–57). Cambridge, England: Cambridge University Press.

Parish, T. S. (1977). The enhancement of altruistic behaviors in children through the implementation of language conditioning procedures. *Behavioral Modification, 1,* 395–404.

Parker, J. G., & Asher, S. R. (1993). Friendship and friendship quality in middle childhood: Links with peer group acceptance and feelings of loneliness and social dissatisfaction. *Developmental Psychology, 29,* 611–621.

Parsons, T., & Bales, R. F. (1955). *Family, socialization, and interaction processes.* New York: Free Press.

Pastor, D. L. (1981). The quality of mother-infant attachment and its relationship to toddlers' initial sociability with peers. *Developmental Psychology, 17,* 326–335.

Payne, F. D. (1980). Children's prosocial conduct in structural situations and as viewed by others: Consistency, convergence, and relationships with person variables. *Child Development, 51,* 1252–1259.

Pearl, R. (1985). Children's understanding of others' need for help: Effects of problem explicitness and type. *Child Development, 56,* 735–745.

Perry, D. G., Bussey, K., & Freiberg, K. (1981). Impact of adults' appeals for sharing on the development of altruistic dispositions in children. *Journal of Experimental Child Psychology, 32,* 127–138.

Perry, L. C., Perry, D. G., & Weiss, R. J. (1986). Age differences in children's beliefs about whether altruism makes the actor feel good. *Social Cognition, 4,* 263–269.

Peterson, L. (1980). Developmental changes in verbal and behavioral sensitivity to cues of social norms of altruism. *Child Development, 51,* 830–838.

Peterson, L. (1983a). Influence of age, task competence, and responsibility focus on children's altruism. *Developmental Psychology, 19,* 141–148.

Peterson, L. (1983b). Role of donor competence, donor age, and peer presence on helping in an emergency. *Developmental Psychology, 19,* 873–880.

Peterson, L., Hartmann, D. P., & Gelfand, D. M. (1977). Developmental changes in the effects of dependency and reciprocity cues on children's moral judgments and donation rates. *Child Development, 48,* 1331–1339.

Peterson, L., Ridley-Johnson, R., & Carter, C. (1984). The supersuit: An example of structured naturalistic observation of children's altruism. *Journal of General Psychology, 110,* 235–241.

Phillips, D., McCartney, K., & Scarr, S. (1987). Child-care quality and children's social development. *Developmental Psychology, 23,* 537–543.

Phinney, J., Feshbach, N., & Farver, J. (1986). Preschool children's responses to peer crying. *Early Childhood Research Quarterly, 1,* 207–219.

Piaget, J. (1965). *The moral judgment of the child.* New York: Free Press. (Original work published 1932)

Plomin, R., Emde, R. N., Braungart, J. M., Campos, J., Kagan, J., Reznick, J. S., Robinson, J., Zahn-Waxler, C., & DeFries, J. C. (1993). Genetic change and continuity from fourteen to twenty months: The MacArthur Longitudinal Twin Study. *Child Development, 64,* 1354–1376.

Power, T. G., & Parke, R. D. (1986). Patterns of early socialization: Mother- and father-infant interaction in the home. *International Journal of Behavioral Development, 6,* 331–341.

Power, T. G., & Shanks, J. A. (1989). Parents as socializers: Maternal and paternal views. *Journal of Youth and Adolescence, 18,* 203–220.

Presbie, R. J., & Coiteux, P. F. (1971). Learning to be generous or stingy: Imitation of sharing behavior as a function of model generosity and vicarious reinforcement. *Child Development, 42,* 1033–1038.

Radke-Yarrow, M., & Zahn-Waxler, C. (1984). Roots, motives, and patterns in children's prosocial behavior. In E. Staub, D. Bar-Tal, J. Karylowski, & J. Reykowski (Eds.), *Development and maintenance of prosocial behavior: International perspectives on positive behavior* (pp. 81–99). New York: Plenum Press.

Radke-Yarrow, M., Zahn-Waxler, C., & Chapman, M. (1983). Children's prosocial dispositions and behavior. In P. H. Mussen (Ed.), *Carmichael's manual of child psychology* (Vol. 4, pp. 469–546). New York: Wiley.

Radke-Yarrow, M., Zahn-Waxler, C., Richardson, D. T., Susman, A., & Martinez, P. (1994). Caring behavior in children of clinically depressed and well mothers. *Child Development, 65,* 1405–1414.

Rai, S. N., Bhargva, M., & Rai, B. K. (1989). Effects of age and impulsiveness on altruism. *Indian Journal of Current Psychological Research, 4,* 121–128.

Ramsey, P. G. (1987). Possession episodes in young children's social interactions. *Journal of Genetic Psychology, 148,* 315–325.

Ramsey, P. G. (1988). Social skills and peer status: A comparison of two socioeconomic groups. *Merrill-Palmer Quarterly, 34,* 185–202.

Raviv, A., & Bar-Tal, D. (1981). Demographic correlates of adolescents' helping behavior. *Journal of Youth and Adolescence, 10,* 45–53.

Raviv, A., Bar-Tal, D., Ayalon, H., & Raviv, A. (1980). Perception of giving and receiving help by group members. *Representative Research in Social Psychology, 11,* 140–151.

Raviv, A., Bar-Tal, D., & Lewis-Levin, T. (1980). Motivations for donation behavior by boys of three different ages. *Child Development, 51,* 610–613.

Rehberg, H. R., & Richman, C. L. (1989). Prosocial behaviour in preschool children: A look at the interaction of race, gender, and family composition. *International Journal of Behavioral Development, 12,* 385–401.

Rest, J. R. (1983). Morality. In P. H. Mussen (Series Ed.) & J. Flavell & E. Markman (Vol. Eds.), *Handbook of child psychology* (Vol. 3, pp. 556–629). New York: Wiley.

Rheingold, H. L. (1982). Little children's participation in the work of adults, a nascent prosocial behavior. *Child Development, 53,* 114–125.

Rheingold, H. L., Hay, D. F., & West, M. J. (1976). Sharing in the second year of life. *Child Development, 47,* 1148–1158.

Rice, M. E., & Grusec, J. E. (1975). Saying and doing: Effects on observer performance. *Journal of Personality and Social Psychology, 32,* 584–593.

Richman, C. L., Berry, C., Bittle, M., & Himan, M. (1988). Factors related to helping behavior in preschool-age children. *Journal of Applied Developmental Psychology, 9,* 151–165.

Rigby, K. (1993). School children's perceptions of their families and parents as a function of peer relations. *Journal of Genetic Psychology, 154,* 501–513.

Rigby, K., & Slee, P. T. (1993). Dimensions of interpersonal relation among Australian children and implications for psychological well-being. *Journal of Social Psychology, 133,* 33–42.

Roberts, W., & Strayer, J. (1996). Empathy, emotional expressiveness, and prosocial behavior. *Child Development, 67,* 449–470.

Robinson, J. L., Zahn-Waxler, C., & Emde, R. N. (1994). Patterns of development in early empathic behavior: Environmental and child constitutional influences. *Social Development, 3,* 125–145.

Rogers-Warren, A., & Baer, D. M. (1976). Correspondence between saying and doing: Teaching children to share and praise. *Journal of Applied Behavioral Analysis, 9,* 335–354.

Rogers-Warren, A., Warren, S. F., & Baer, D. M. (1977). A component analysis: Modeling, self-reporting, and reinforcement of self-reporting in the development of sharing. *Behavior Modification, 1,* 307–322.

Rohner, R. P. (1975). *They love me, they love me not.* New Haven, CT: HRAF Press.

Rosenhan, D. L. (1970). The natural socialization of altruistic autonomy. In J. Macaulay & L. Berkowitz (Eds.), *Altruism and helping behavior* (pp. 251–268). New York: Academic Press.

Rosenhan, D. L., & White, G. M. (1967). Observation and rehearsal as determinants of prosocial behavior. *Journal of Personality and Social Psychology, 5,* 424–431.

Rosser, R. A. (1982). Information use by preschool children in altruistic decision-making: An exploratory investigation of donating behavior. *Journal of Genetic Psychology, 141,* 19–27.

Rothbart, M. K., Ahadi, S. A., & Hershey, K. L. (1994). Temperament and social behavior in childhood. *Merrill-Palmer Quarterly, 40,* 21–39.

Rousseau, J. J. (1962). *Emile.* New York: Columbia University Press. (Original work published 1773)

Rubin, K. H., & Schneider, F. W. (1973). The relationship between moral judgment, egocentrism, and altruistic behavior. *Child Development, 44,* 661–665.

Ruble, T. L. (1983). Sex stereotypes: Issues of change in the 1970s. *Sex Roles, 9,* 397–402.

Rushton, J. P. (1975). Generosity in children: Immediate and long-term effects of modeling, preaching, and moral judgment. *Journal of Personality and Social Psychology, 31,* 459–466.

Rushton, J. P., Fulker, D. W., Neal, M. C., Nias, D. K. B., & Eysenck, H. J. (1986). Altruism and aggression: The heritability of individual differences. *Journal of Personality and Social Psychology, 50,* 1192–1198.

Rushton, J. P., & Littlefield, C. (1979). The effects of age, amount of modeling, and a success experience on seven- to eleven-year-old children's generosity. *Journal of Moral Education, 9,* 55–56.

Rushton, J. P., & Owen, D. (1975). Immediate and delayed effects of TV modelling and preaching on children's generosity. *British Journal of Social and Clinical Psychology, 14,* 309–310.

Rushton, J. P., & Teachman, G. (1978). The effects of positive reinforcement, attributions, and punishment on model induced altruism in children. *Personality and Social Psychology Bulletin, 4,* 322–325.

Rushton, J. P., & Wheelwright, M. (1980). Validation of donating to charity as a measure of children's altruism. *Psychological Reports, 47,* 803–806.

Rushton, J. P., & Wiener, J. (1975). Altruism and cognitive development in children. *British Journal of Social and Clinical Psychology, 14,* 341–349.

Rutherford, E., & Mussen, P. (1968). Generosity in nursery school boys. *Child Development, 39,* 755–765.

Rutter, R. A., & Newmann, F. M. (1989). The potential of community service to enhance civic responsibility. *Social Education, 53,* 371–374.

Saklofske, D. H., & Eysenck, S. B. G. (1983). Impulsiveness and venturesomeness in Canadian children. *Psychological Reports, 52,* 147–152.

Santrock, J. W. (1975a). Father absence, perceived maternal behavior, and moral development in boys. *Child Development, 46,* 753–757.

Santrock, J. W. (1975b). Moral structure: The interrelations of moral behavior, moral judgment, and moral affect. *Journal of Genetic Psychology, 127,* 201–213.

Savin-Williams, R. C., Small, S. A., & Zeldin, R. S. (1981). Dominance and altruism among adolescent males: A comparison of ethological and psychological methods. *Ethology and Sociobiology, 2,* 167–176.

Scarr, S., & McCartney, K. (1983). How people make their own environments: A theory of genotype—environment effects. *Child Development, 54,* 424–435.

Schenk, V. M., & Grusec, J. E. (1987). A comparison of prosocial behavior of children with and without day care experience. *Merrill-Palmer Quarterly, 33,* 231–240.

Schwartz, S. H., & Howard, J. A. (1984). Internalized values as motivators of altruism. In E. Staub, D. Bar-Tal, J. Karylowski, & J. Reykowski (Eds.), *International perspectives on positive development* (pp. 229–255). New York: Plenum Press.

Searcy, E., & Eisenberg, N. (1992). Defensiveness in response to aid from a sibling. *Journal of Personality and Social Psychology, 62,* 422–433.

Serow, R. C., & Solomon, D. (1979). Classroom climates and students' intergroup behavior. *Journal of Educational Psychology, 71,* 669–676.

Severy, L. J., & Davis, K. E. (1971). Helping behavior among normal and retarded children. *Child Development, 42,* 1017–1031.

Sharabany, R., Gershoni, R., & Hofman, J. E. (1981). Girlfriend, boyfriend: Age and sex differences in intimate friendship. *Developmental Psychology, 17,* 800–808.

Sharabany, R., & Hertz-Lazarowitz, R. (1981). Do friends share and communicate more than non-friends? *International Journal of Behavioral Development, 4,* 45–59.

Sharma, V. (1988a). Effect of birthorder, age and sex on helping behaviour of children. *Indian Journal of Psychometry and Education, 19,* 91–96.

Sharma, V. (1988b). Effect of model's amount of donation and justification on imitative altruism. *Psycho-Lingua, 18,* 39–46.

Shigetomi, C. C., Hartmann, D. P., & Gelfand, D. M. (1981). Sex differences in children's altruistic behavior and reputations for helpfulness. *Developmental Psychology, 17,* 434–437.

Silbereisen, R. K., Lamsfuss, S., Boehnke, K., & Eisenberg, N. (1991). Developmental patterns and correlates of prosocial motives. In L. Montada & H. W. Bierhoff (Eds.), *Altruism in social systems* (pp. 82–104). Goettingen, West Germany: Hofrefe.

Silva, F. (1992). Assessing the child and adolescent personality: A decade of research. *Personality and Individual Differences, 13,* 1163–1181.

Simmons, C. H., & Zumpf, C. (1986). The gifted child: Perceived competence, prosocial moral reasoning, and charitable donations. *Journal of Genetic Psychology, 147,* 97–105.

Simner, M. L. (1971). Newborn's response to the cry of another infant. *Developmental Psychology, 5,* 136–150.

Sims, S. A. (1978). Sharing by children: Effects of behavioral example, induction, and resources. *Journal of Psychology, 100,* 57–65.

Small, S. A., Zeldin, R. S., & Savin-Williams, R. C. (1983). In search of personality traits: A multimethod analysis of naturally occurring prosocial and dominance behavior. *Journal of Personality, 51,* 1–16.

Smith, A. (1982). *A theory of moral sentiments.* Indianapolis: Liberty Classics. (Original work published 1759)

Smith, C. L. (1983). Exhortations, rehearsal, and children's prosocial behavior. *Academic Psychology Bulletin, 5,* 261–271.

Smith, C. L., Gelfand, D. M., Hartmann, D. P., & Partlow, M. E. Y. (1979). Children's causal attributions regarding help giving. *Child Development, 50,* 203–210.

Smith, C. L., Leinbach, M. D., Stewart, B. J., & Blackwell, J. M. (1983). Affective perspective-taking, exhortations, and children's prosocial behavior. In D. L. Bridgeman (Ed.), *The nature of prosocial development* (pp. 113–137). New York: Academic Press.

Solomon, D., Battistich, & Watson, M. (1993, March). *A longitudinal investigation of the effects of a school intervention program on children's social development.* Paper presented at the biennial meeting of the Society for Research in Child Development, New Orleans, LA.

Solomon, D., Watson, M. S., Delucchi, K. L., Schaps, E., & Battistich, V. (1988). Enhancing children's prosocial behavior in the classroom. *American Educational Research Journal, 25,* 527–554.

Spence, J. T., Helmreich, R. L., & Stapp, J. (1974). The Personal Attributes Questionnaire: A measure of sex-role stereotypes and masculinity-femininity. *JSAS: Catalog of Selected Documents in Psychology, 4,* 43(Ms. No. 617).

Stanhope, L., Bell, R. Q., & Parker-Cohen, N. Y. (1987). Temperament and helping behavior in preschool children. *Developmental Psychology, 23,* 347–353.

Staub, E. (1970a). A child in distress: The effects of focusing responsibility on children on their attempts to help. *Developmental Psychology, 2,* 152–153.

Staub, E. (1970b). A child in distress: The influence of age and number of witnesses on children's attempts to help. *Journal of Personality and Social Psychology, 14,* 130–140.

Staub, E. (1971a). A child in distress: The influence of nurturance and modeling on children's attempts to help. *Developmental Psychology, 5,* 124–132.

Staub, E. (1971b). Helping a person in distress: The influence of implicit and explicit rules of conduct on children and adults. *Journal of Personality and Social Psychology, 17,* 137–145.

Staub, E. (1971c). The use of role playing and induction in children's learning of helping and sharing behavior. *Child Development, 42,* 805–817.

Staub, E. (1978). *Positive social behavior and morality: Vol. 1. Social and personal influences.* New York: Academic Press.

Staub, E. (1979). *Positive social behavior and morality: Vol. 2. Socialization and development.* New York: Academic Press.

Staub, E. (1992). The origins of caring, helping, and nonaggression: Parental socialization, the family system, schools, and cultural influence. In P. M. Oliner, L. Baron, L. A. Blum, D. L. Krebs, & M. Z. Smolenska (Eds.), *Embracing the other: Philosophical, psychological, and historical perspectives on altruism* (pp. 390–412). New York: New York University Press.

Staub, E., & Noerenberg, H. (1981). Property rights, deservingness, reciprocity, friendship: The transactional character of children's sharing behavior. *Journal of Personality and Social Psychology, 40,* 271–289.

Staub, E., & Sherk, L. (1970). Need for approval, children's sharing behavior, and reciprocity in sharing. *Child Development, 41,* 243–252.

Steinberg, L. D., Greenberger, E., Garduque, L., Ruggiero, M., & Vaux, A. (1982). Effects of working on adolescent development. *Developmental Psychology, 18,* 385–395.

Stevenson, H. W. (1991). The development of prosocial behavior in large-scale collective societies: China and Japan. In R. A. Hinde & J. Groebel (Eds.), *Cooperation and prosocial behaviour* (pp. 89–105). Cambridge, England: Cambridge University Press.

Stewart, R. B., & Marvin, R. S. (1984). Sibling relations: The role of conceptual perspective-taking in the ontogeny of sibling caregiving. *Child Development, 55,* 1322–1332.

Stillwell, R., & Dunn, J. (1985). Continuities in sibling relationships: Patterns of aggression and friendliness. *Journal of Child Psychology and Psychiatry, 26,* 627–637.

Stockdale, D. F., Hegland, S. M., & Chiaromonte, T. (1989). Helping behaviors: An observational study of preschool children. *Early Childhood Research Quarterly, 4,* 533–543.

Stoneman, Z., Brody, G. H., & MacKinnon, C. E. (1986). Same-sex and cross-sex siblings: Activity choices, roles, behavior, and gender stereotypes. *Sex Roles, 15,* 495–511.

Straker, G., & Jacobson, R. S. (1981). Aggression, emotional maladjustment, and empathy in the abused child. *Developmental Psychology, 17,* 762–765.

Strayer, F. F., Wareing, S., & Rushton, J. P. (1979). Social constraints on naturally occurring preschool altruism. *Ethology and Sociobiology, 1,* 3–11.

Strayer, J. (1980). A naturalistic study of empathic behaviors and their relation to affective states and perspective-taking skills in preschool children. *Child Development, 51,* 815–822.

Strayer, J. (1993). Children's concordant emotions and cognitions in response to observed emotions. *Child Development, 64,* 188–201.

Strayer, J., & Roberts, W. (1989). Children's empathy and role taking: Child and parental factors, and relations to prosocial behavior. *Journal of Applied Developmental Psychology, 10,* 227–239.

Strayer, J., & Schroeder, M. (1989). Children's helping strategies: Influences of emotion, empathy, and age. *New Directions in Child Development, 44,* 85–103.

Suda, W., & Fouts, G. (1980). Effects of peer presence on helping in introverted and extroverted children. *Child Development, 51,* 1272–1275.

Sugiyama, K., Matsui, H., Satoh, C., Yoshimi, Y., & Takeuchi, M. (1992). Effects of self-efficacy and outcome expectation on observational learning of altruistic behavior. *Japanese Journal of Psychology, 63,* 295–302.

Sukemune, S., Dohno, K., & Matsuzaki, M. (1981). Model and motivational cost effects on helping behavior through modeling in preschool children. *Basic Factors and Learning Modes in Observational Learning by Children,* 41–47.

Sullivan, H. S. (1953). *The interpersonal theory of psychology.* New York: Norton.

Szynal-Brown, C., & Morgan, R. R. (1983). The effects of reward on tutor's behaviors in a cross-age tutoring context. *Journal of Experimental Child Psychology, 36,* 196–208.

Tabor, C., & Shaffer, D. R. (1981). Effects of age of benefactor, attractiveness of the recipient, and the recipient's need for assistance on prosocial behavior in children's dyads. *Social Behavior and Personality, 9,* 163–169.

Tesson, G., Lewko, J. H., & Bigelow, B. J. (1987). The social rules that children use in their interpersonal relations. *Contributions of Human Development, 18,* 36–57.

Thompson, R. A. (1987). Empathy and emotional understanding: The early development of empathy. In N. Eisenberg & J. Strayer (Eds.), *Empathy and its development* (pp. 119–145). New York: Cambridge University Press.

Thompson, R. A., & Hoffman, M. L. (1980). Empathy and the development of guilt in children. *Developmental Psychology, 16,* 155–156.

Tietjen, A. (1986). Prosocial reasoning among children and adults in a Papua New Guinea society. *Developmental Psychology, 22,* 861–868.

Tremblay, R. E., Vitaro, F., Gagnon, C., Piche, C., & Royer, N. (1992). A prosocial scale for the preschool behaviour questionnaire: Concurrent and predictive correlates. *International Journal of Behavioral Development, 15,* 227–245.

Trivers, R. L. (1971). The evolution of reciprocal altruism. *Quarterly Review of Biology, 46,* 35–57.

Trommsdorff, G. (1991). Child-rearing and children's empathy. *Perceptual Motor Skills, 72,* 387–390.

Trommsdorff, G. (1995). Person-context relations as developmental conditions for empathy and prosocial action: A cross-cultural analysis. In T. A. Kindermann & J. Valsiner (Eds.), *Development of person-context relations* (pp. 189–208). Hillsdale, NJ: Erlbaum.

Turnbull, C. M. (1972). *The mountain people.* New York: Simon & Schuster.

Turner, P. H., & Harris, M. B. (1984). Parental attitudes and preschool children's social competence. *Journal of Genetic Psychology, 144,* 105–113.

Tyler, F. B., & Varma, M. (1988). Help-seeking and helping behavior in children as a function of psychosocial competence. *Journal of Applied Developmental Psychology, 9,* 219–231.

Ugurel-Semin, R. (1952). Moral behavior and moral judgment of children. *Journal of Abnormal and Social Psychology, 47,* 463–474.

Ujiie, T. (1981–1982). Altruistic behavior, social cognition and person orientation in preschool children. In K. Miyake (Ed.), *Research and Clinical Center for Child Development: Annual report* (pp. 63–69). Sappora, Japan: Faculty of Education, Hokkaido University.

Underwood, B., Froming, W. J., & Moore, B. S. (1977). Mood attention and altruism: A search for mediating variables. *Developmental Psychology, 13,* 541–542.

Underwood, B., & Moore, B. (1982). Perspective-taking and altruism. *Psychological Bulletin, 91,* 143–173.

Ungerer, J. A., Dolby, R., Waters, B., Barnett, B., Kelk, N., & Lewin, V. (1990). The early development of empathy: Self-regulation and individual differences in the first year. *Motivation and Emotion, 14,* 93–106.

Vandell, D. L., Henderson, V. K., & Wilson, K. S. (1988). A longitudinal study of children with day-care experiences of varying quality. *Child Development, 59,* 1286–1292.

Vitaro, F., Gagnon, C., & Tremblay, R. E. (1990). Predicting stable peer rejection from kindergarten to grade one. *Journal of Clinical Child Psychology, 1990,* 257–264.

Vitaro, F., Gagnon, C., & Tremblay, R. E. (1991). Teachers' and mothers' assessment of children's behaviors from kindergarten to grade two: Stability and change within and across informants. *Journal of Psychopathology and Behavioral Assessment, 13,* 325–343.

Wachs, T. D. (1994). Genetics, nurture, and social development: An alternative viewpoint. *Social Development, 3,* 66–70.

Waters, E., Hay, D., & Richters, J. (1986). Infant-parent attachment and the origins of prosocial and antisocial behavior. In D. Olweus, J. Block, & M. Radke-Yarrow (Eds.), *Development of antisocial and prosocial behavior: Research, theories, and issues* (pp. 97–125). Orlando, FL: Academic Press.

Watson, M., Solomon, D., Battistich, V., Schaps, E., & Solomon, J. (1989). The Child Development Project: Combining traditional and developmental approaches to values education. In L. Nucci (Ed.), *Moral development and character education: A dialogue* (pp. 51–92). Berkeley, CA: McCutchan.

Weidman, C. S., & Strayhorn, J. M. (1992). Relations between children's prosocial behaviors and choices in story dilemmas. *Journal of Psychoeducational Assessment, 10,* 330–341.

Weiner, B., & Graham, S. (1989). Understanding the motivational role of affect: Life-span research from an attributional perspective. *Cognition and Emotion, 3,* 401–419.

Weissbrod, C. S. (1976). Noncontingent warmth induction, cognitive style, and children's imitative donation and rescue effort behaviors. *Journal of Personality and Social Psychology, 34,* 274–281.

Weissbrod, C. S. (1980). The impact of warmth and instruction on donation. *Child Development, 51,* 279–281.

Werebe, M. J. G., & Baudonniere, P. M. (1988). Friendship among preschool children. *International Journal of Behavioral Development, 11,* 291–304.

West, M. J., & Rheingold, H. L. (1978). Infant stimulation of maternal instruction. *Infant Behavior and Development, 1,* 205–215.

White, G. M. (1972). Immediate and deferred effects of model observation and guided and unguided rehearsal on donating and stealing. *Journal of Personality and Social Psychology, 21,* 139–148.

White, G. M., & Burnam, M. A. (1975). Socially cued altruism: Effects of modeling, instructions, and age on public and private donations. *Child Development, 46,* 559–563.

Whiting, B. B., & Edwards, C. P. (1973). A cross-cultural analysis of sex differences in the behavior of children aged three through 11. *Journal of Social Psychology, 91,* 171–188.

Whiting, B. B., & Edwards, C. P. (1988). *Children of different worlds.* Cambridge, MA: Harvard University Press.

Whiting, B. B., & Whiting, J. W. M. (1975). *Children of six cultures: A psychocultural analysis.* Cambridge, MA: Harvard University Press.

Whiting, J. W. M., & Whiting, B. B. (1973). Altruistic and egoistic behavior in six cultures. In L. Nader & T. Maretzki

(Eds.), *Cultural illness and health* (pp. 56–66). Washington, DC: American Anthropological Association.

Wiggers, M., & Willems, H. (1983). Female preschoolers' verbal and nonverbal empathic responses to emotional situations and facial expressions. *International Journal of Behavioral Development, 6*, 427–440.

Wilson, C. C., Piazza, C. C., & Nagle, R. J. (1990). Investigation of the effect of consistent and inconsistent behavioral example upon children's donation behaviors. *Journal of Genetic Psychology, 151*, 361–376.

Wilson, E. O. (1978). *On human nature.* Cambridge, MA: Harvard University Press.

Wise, P. S., & Cramer, S. H. (1988). Correlates of empathy and cognitive style in early adolescence. *Psychological Reports, 63*, 179–192.

Wood, J. V., Saltzberg, J. A., & Goldsamt, L. A. (1990). Does affect induce self-focused attention? *Journal of Personality and Social Psychology, 58*, 899–908.

Wright, B. A. (1942). Altruism in children and the perceived conduct of others. *Journal of Abnormal and Social Psychology, 37*, 218–233.

Yarrow, M. R., & Scott, P. M. (1972). Imitation of nurturant and nonnurturant models. *Journal of Personality and Social Psychology, 23*, 259–270.

Yarrow, M. R., Scott, P. M., & Waxler, C. Z. (1973). Learning concern for others. *Developmental Psychology, 8*, 240–260.

Yarrow, M. R., Waxler, C. Z., Barrett, D., Darby, J., King, R., Pickett, M., & Smith, J. (1976). Dimensions and correlates of prosocial behavior in young children. *Child Development, 47*, 118–125.

Yates, M., & Youniss, J. (1996). A developmental perspective on community service in adolescence. *Social Development, 5*, 85–111.

Yinon, Y., Sharon, I., Azgad, Z., & Barshir, I. (1981). Helping behavior of urbanites, Moshavniks, and Kibbutzniks. *Journal of Social Psychology, 113*, 143–144.

Youniss, J. (1980). *Parents and peers in social development: A Sullivan-Piaget perspective.* Chicago: University of Chicago Press.

Zahn-Waxler, C., Cole, P. M., Welsh, J. D., & Fox, N. A. (1995). Psychophysiological correlates of empathy and prosocial behaviors in preschool children with problem behaviors. *Development and Psychopathology, 7*, 27–48.

Zahn-Waxler, C., Iannotti, R., & Chapman, M. (1982). Peers and prosocial development. In K. H. Rubin & H. S. Ross (Eds.), *Peer relationships and social skills in childhood* (pp. 133–162). New York: Springer-Verlag.

Zahn-Waxler, C., & Radke-Yarrow, M. (1982). The development of altruism: Alternative research strategies. In N. Eisenberg-Berg (Ed.), *The development of prosocial behavior* (pp. 109–137). New York: Academic Press.

Zahn-Waxler, C., Radke-Yarrow, M., & King, R. A. (1979). Child rearing and children's prosocial initiations toward victims of distress. *Child Development, 50*, 319–330.

Zahn-Waxler, C., Radke-Yarrow, M., & King, R. (1983). Early altruism and guilt. *Academic Psychology Bulletin, 5*, 247–259.

Zahn-Waxler, C., Radke-Yarrow, M., Wagner, E., & Chapman, M. (1992). Development of concern for others. *Developmental Psychology, 28*, 126–136.

Zahn-Waxler, C., Robinson, J., & Emde, R. N. (1992). The development of empathy in twins. *Developmental Psychology, 28*, 1038–1047.

Zarbatany, L., Ghesquiere, K., & Mohr, K. (1992). A context perspective on early adolescents' friendship expectations. *Journal of Early Adolescence, 12*, 111–126.

Zarbatany, L., Hartmann, D. P., & Gelfand, D. M. (1985). Why does children's generosity increase with age: Susceptibility to experimenter influence or altruism? *Child Development, 56*, 746–756.

Zarbatany, L., Hartmann, D. P., Gelfand, D. M., & Vinciguerra, P. (1985). Gender differences in altruistic reputation. *Developmental Psychology, 21*, 97–101.

Zeldin, R. A., Savin-Williams, R. C., & Small, S. A. (1984). Dimensions of prosocial behavior in adolescent males. *Journal of Social Psychology, 123*, 159–168.

Zeldin, R. S., Small, S. A., & Savin-Williams, R. C. (1982). Prosocial interactions in two mixed-sex adolescent groups. *Child Development, 53*, 1492–1498.

Zinser, O., & Lydiatt, E. W. (1976). Mode of recipient definition, affluence of the recipient, and sharing behavior in preschool children. *Journal of Genetic Psychology, 129*, 261–266.

Zinser, O., Perry, J. S., Bailey, R. C., & Lydiatt, E. W. (1976). Racial recipients, value of donations, and sharing behavior in children. *Journal of Genetic Psychology, 129*, 29–35.

Zinser, O., Perry, J. S., & Edgar, R. M. (1975). Affluence of the recipient, value of donations, and sharing behavior in preschool children. *Journal of Psychology, 89*, 301–305.

CHAPTER 12

Aggression and Antisocial Behavior

JOHN D. COIE and KENNETH A. DODGE

Since the publication of the preceding edition of this *Handbook,* American society has witnessed profound growth in the rate of serious violence and antisocial behavior among its youth, particularly among disadvantaged adolescents (Blumstein, in press). Between 1982 and 1992, the per capita murder rate among youths under age 18 rose 60% (Uniform Crime Reports, 1992). This trend follows a 40-year pattern, in which violent crime has risen 600% since 1953 (Skogan, 1989). In the eyes of the American public, crime and violence now rank as the most important problems facing this country (Berke, 1994), and homicide is now the leading cause of death among urban males aged 15 to 24 (Centers for Disease Control, 1991; Huesmann & Miller, 1994). The problem is acutely American: Teenagers in the United States are at least four times more likely to be murdered than are teenagers in 21 other industrialized countries (Goldstein, 1992).

These rapid changes in American society have been paralleled by changes in the research on the development of

The authors acknowledge the support of Research Scientist Awards K05 MH00797 and K05 MH01027.

aggressive and antisocial behavior. Research in the past 20 years has increasingly focused on the development of chronically antisocial individuals (e.g., Why does this person become more violent than most people?) in contrast to research on specieswide patterns in aggressive behavior (e.g., Why is the human species aggressive?). This shift has been exemplified in numerous longitudinal studies of individual differences in aggressive behavioral development across the life span. Important breakthroughs have been made in the genetic, biological, socialization, environmental, and contextual factors relating to aggression and other antisocial behavior. These advances have shaped much of this chapter.

OVERVIEW

Four questions guide the organization of this chapter:

1. What is the developmental course of aggression and antisocial behavior in human beings?
2. What factors lead humans to aggress against each other?
3. What stability and change occur in the life course of individual differences in antisocial behavior?
4. Why do some individuals become more antisocial than others?

The first two questions address the issues of specieswide human aggression. The last two questions address the developmental course and determinants of individual differences in aggression.

Much has been learned about specieswide, age-related changes in aggressive and antisocial behavior. Cairns (1979) has pointed out that, in terms of frequency of aggressive acts, preschoolers are the most aggressive humans, and there is a log-linear decrease in frequency with advancing age. Adolescence brings a temporary increase in aggression and antisocial activity, especially in delinquent acts and serious violence (Moffitt, 1993a). Aggression and antisocial behavior in adulthood take on different forms from that of childhood, with domestic violence perhaps being the most common type of adult aggression. Finally, antisocial behaviors, in general, appear to wane after age 40. This material is covered in the section Aggressive and Antisocial Development in the Human Species.

We also know a great deal about the proximal determinants of these acts of aggression. An individual's perception of goal blocking and threat by another person is highly associated with retaliatory aggression. Likewise, the contexts in which aggressive acts will be rewarded with instrumental gain are aggression inducing. The section Specieswide Antecedents of Aggressive Acts focuses on these determinants.

Our knowledge of specieswide determinants of aggressive behavior has spawned hypotheses and empirical studies of individual differences in aggression. In general, the shift from a study of specieswide patterns of aggression to a study of the predictors of stable individual differences in aggression has led to dramatic increases in knowledge over the past decade. Aggressive behavior patterns become increasingly stable during the early school years, and early aggressive behavior is predictive of adolescent and adulthood antisocial behavior. Evidence supporting these conclusions is reviewed in the section Stability of Individual Differences in Aggression and Antisocial Behavior.

The determinants of these stable individual differences have received perhaps the greatest attention in the past decade. Family and twin studies suggest some heritability of antisocial behaviors, through temperament, hyperreactivity, or attention deficits. Biological factors such as hormones, neurotransmitters, exposure to environmental toxins, and resting heart rate have been implicated as correlates of individual differences in aggression. Ecological factors, including poverty, neighborhood violence, subcultural modeling of aggression, family stressors, and racial discrimination, certainly play a prominent role in aggressive development. Particular attention has been placed on early socialization in the family. The quality of the parent-child relationship, as it interacts with contextual stressors, seems to be predictive of early aggression. Particular discipline patterns, such as coercion, inconsistent and harsh punishment, and physical abuse are associated with later heightened aggressive behavior. The importance of reciprocal effects between child characteristics and parent-child interactions has also been realized. Individual differences in these early ecological and family experiences have been found to be predictive of later cognitive and emotional processes in children, including academic readiness, moral development, hypervigilance to hostile cues, hostile attributional biases, aggressive social problem solving, and beliefs in the efficacy of aggressive behavior. These mental processes, in turn, are known to be predictive of later aggressive behavior.

As the child enters school, cognitive processes mediate the effects of these experiences on aggressive behavior. Peer relations also play an important role. Rejection by peers in the early school years is predictive of, and perhaps incrementally contributes to, later aggressive behavior. In early adolescence, the aggressive child's peer interactions may become influenced increasingly by deviant peer groups, often as a result of social alienation from mainstream socializing institutions. The pattern of poor-quality relationships with family and mainstream peer groups and institutions continues into adulthood, when the most serious cases of aggressive behavior problems take the form of antisocial personality disorder. Research speaking to each of these issues is reviewed, in sequence, in the section Determinants of Individual Differences in Antisocial Behavior.

Brief sections covering definitions and historical background precede the substantive review of research relating to each of these four major questions. First, definitions of antisocial behavior and aggression are discussed, along with the relation between these two terms and other concepts from law and psychiatry. We also include a brief section on the importance of examining gender, ethnic group, and cultural effects on rates of antisocial behavior and on the correlates of antisocial behavior. Following this section is a necessarily abbreviated treatment of the major theoretical perspectives on human aggression that have influenced the research of the past few decades.

In reading the sections on the developmental course of aggression and antisocial behavior and the development of individual differences, it is important to keep in mind the distinction between specieswide patterns of change in the form and frequency of this behavior and the factors underlying the emergence of stable patterns of individual activity. It is also true that some of the same factors that lead virtually all humans to aggress in certain circumstances will contribute to individual propensities for antisocial activity. Although there is some repetition between these sections, the latter section is organized to describe as closely as possible the temporal sequence in which these different factors have their greatest influence. The latter goal is inherently self-defeating because most factors continue to have influence across the life course, often interacting with each other. Research on each factor often has been dominated by a focus on certain developmental periods, and this fact has guided some of the decisions on sequencing.

DEFINING AGGRESSION AND ANTISOCIAL BEHAVIOR

Although definitional issues are important in reviews such as this one, the difficulties of making precise definitions with clear boundary designations always emerge. This is the case for defining antisocial behavior and aggression. Previous editions of the *Handbook* have restricted the discussion

of antisocial behavior to aggression, perhaps because that form of antisocial behavior has most often been studied by psychologists and animal ethologists. Over the past 10 years, research in this area has increasingly emphasized individual differences in aggression and this shift has led to the recognition that aggressive behaviors often occur in a context of other antisocial behaviors, including noncompliance with adults, delinquency, substance abuse, cheating, early and risky sexual activity, and vandalism (Elliott & Morse, 1989; Jessor, Donovan, & Costa, 1991). These behaviors do not fit a narrow definition of aggression, but they have been studied with aggression, as part of a more general syndrome of antisocial behavior pattern. The comorbidity of aggression with other antisocial behaviors suggests that an understanding of the etiology and developmental course of aggression might be enhanced by including it in the broader class of antisocial behaviors (Menard & Elliott, 1994). Substance use and abuse, as well as participation in drug sales activities, have particular significance in any discussion of contemporary antisocial behavior. The increased rates of violence and homicide in the United States, especially for teenage males, parallel the rise in illegal substance use in our society. Nonetheless, an explicit treatment of developmental issues relating to substance use and trafficking is not included in this chapter because of space limitations. The most recent survey and interview measures of antisocial activity include items dealing with substance use and sales. Thus, results of longitudinal findings of delinquency encompass this category of antisocial activity.

Although definitions of aggression and antisocial activity usually have considerable overlap, there are important differences among them. The definition of aggression embraced by Parke and Slaby, "behavior that is aimed at harming or injuring another person or persons" (1983, p. 50), is similar to the broader definition that Loeber offered for antisocial behaviors, namely those "that inflict physical or mental harm or property loss or damage on others, and which may or may not constitute the breaking of criminal laws" (1985, p. 6). This definition includes aggression but is not restricted to it. Sometimes aggression is defined broadly enough to include property loss or damage, as in the case of instrumental aggression; however, the feature of instrumental aggression that makes it aggressive, in our view, is the use or threat of force to obtain possession. An important difference in the two definitions is the inclusion of intent in the Parke and Slaby definition, a distinction that we endorse for reasons that will be discussed later.

Loeber's definition of antisocial behavior makes reference to violations of criminal code. For children and adolescents, legal violations constitute delinquency, although some delinquent acts such as truancy and running away from home do not fit with what is usually meant by antisocial activity. Conversely, fighting and threats of harm occur frequently among school-age children, yet this behavior is rarely considered as a possible cause for arrest even though the same acts by adults would be construed as assault. A further ambiguity to this definitional issue is the relation of the psychiatric term, conduct disorder, to the antisocial category. Conduct disorder is diagnosed by the frequency of problem behaviors exhibited by a child or adolescent across a given time period (three or more across a 6-month period). The term is applied to individuals rather than acts and is considered to reflect a diagnostic syndrome. Oppositional defiant disorder, disobedience or disrespect for adults often accompanied by irritability, is a psychiatric syndrome that is distinct from conduct disorder and is most often applied to preschool children, but it is thought to be predictive of conduct disorder (for a detailed treatment of conduct and oppositional defiant disorders, see Hinshaw & Anderson, 1996). Antisocial behavior, therefore, can be thought of as inclusive of activities that define delinquency or conduct disorder and is often described as disruptive behavior because of its impact on social order.

Because antisocial or disruptive behavior is a heterogeneous set of behaviors, there have been a number of attempts to establish dimensions of antisocial behavior by factor analytic or multidimensional scaling techniques. Frick et al. (1993) conducted a meta-analysis of factor analytic studies of oppositional defiant disorder and conduct disorder behaviors. They extracted two dimensions of antisocial behavior from studies describing more than 23,000 youth. As Figure 12.1 demonstrates, one dimension runs from overt to covert behaviors, a distinction that Loeber and Schmaling (1985b) found to be quite robust, and the other dimension consists of more destructive to less destructive behaviors. The resulting quadrants constitute the categories of aggression, oppositional, status violations and property violations.

Because of the extensive research on aggressive behavior, it is worth taking time to consider the complexities of defining aggression. The definition arrived at by Parke and Slaby (1983) relied heavily on an earlier discussion of the topic by Hartup and deWit (1974), who concluded that various definitions have relied on one or more of four aspects of the phenomenon: (a) topographical qualities of a

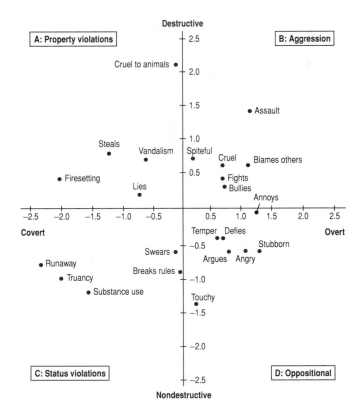

Figure 12.1 Two dimensions of child antisocial behavior emerging from a meta-analysis of parent and teacher ratings (Frick et al., 1993).

behavior, (b) antecedents of a behavior, (c) effects of a behavior, and (d) the social judgment about a behavior made by an observer.

Definition Based on Topography

Ethologists have had some success in using directly observable features of a behavior without regard to its antecedents, consequences, or context to define an act of aggression. Terms such as "beating movement" (Blurton Jones, 1967) and "high-magnitude behavior" (Walters, 1964) have helped define agonistic acts in lower species. The obvious advantage to this approach is that by distinguishing the act from its determinants one can scientifically study the determinants of aggression in a nontautological manner. Topographically based definitions of human aggression have been unsuccessful (Parke & Slaby, 1983). In humans, "The range of their aggressions is much greater, the conditions of elicitation are less restricted, and the effects of experience are more pervasive than in the various nonhuman species" (Hartup & deWit, 1974, p. 597). In addition, the social judgment of an act as aggressive is subjective and highly dependent on its context, antecedents, consequences, and the values of the judge. Students of human aggression have been forced to live with the confound between determinant and act in studying aggression.

Definition Based on Antecedent Conditions

A major definitional approach has been to rely on the antecedent conditions preceding an act of aggression to declare a behavior as aggressive. Dollard, Doob, Miller, Mowrer, and Sears (1939) offered the definition of aggression as "behavior for which the goal response is the injury of the person toward whom it is directed." The antecedent condition, the intent to harm, is placed squarely at the core of the construct of aggression. Although this definition has guided an enormous body of research, it has two major problems. First, intentionality is not a directly observable feature of a behavior; it must be inferred. The reliability and validity of this judgment is often a problem. The attribution of intent necessary to define an act as aggressive often presumes freedom of choice and personal culpability, features that give the science of aggression a problem. As Averill (1982) noted, angry aggression might be considered as a "passion," driven by internal emotions that "force" action on an individual. Does this interpretation imply that aggression in the heat of passion is not intentional at all, but rather is a forced outcome of circumstances? Behavioral scientists have problems with inferring intentionality to the subject of their inquiry but also difficulty in restraining themselves from such inferences. Second, a focus on antecedents of aggression ignores that subclass of aggression that is outcome focused (e.g., acquisition of a peer's toy or a store's money).

Even though defining an act as aggressive based on antecedents is problematic, an antecedent-oriented approach could be used to subclassify types of aggressive acts based on their antecedents for the purpose of further inquiry. Mating, hunger, protection of young, and self-defense are antecedent conditions that may define useful distinctions in subclasses of aggression.

Definition Based on Outcomes

The effects approach defines aggression as "behavior that results in injury of another individual" (Parke & Slaby, 1983, p. 549). This approach avoids the pitfalls of the inference-of-intent approach previously described (Buss, 1961), but it leads to three new problems. First, injury can result

unintentionally from the behavior of others. The slip of a dentist drill might produce injury, but such behavior would not normally be labeled as aggressive. Second, this approach excludes behaviors that appear obviously aggressive but do not lead to injury, such as the gunfire of a sniper that happens to miss its target. Likewise, quantifying degrees of aggressiveness based on degrees of injury could be misleading, as in the case of a gunshot victim who survives or dies as a function of the skill level of an emergency room surgeon. Finally, a focus on outcomes leads to a theory of aggression that is more instrumental than emotional, thus deemphasizing a major part of the phenomenon. The approach of Buss (1961) and Bandura (1983) seems to be limited by this emphasis.

The Social Judgment Approach to Defining Aggression

Walters and Parke (1964) have suggested that aggression is a culturally determined label applied to a behavior following the social judgment of an observer. Intention and other antecedent conditions, as well as injury and other outcomes, may be part of a cultural definition. According to this approach, judges weight antecedents, mitigating factors, degree of injury, the situational context, the status of the aggressor and the victim, and other factors in labeling an act as aggressive. These judges use community standards in applying this label, much like courts and jurors use standards to judge guilt and culpability of criminal actions (Dodge, 1991). From this viewpoint, definitions of aggression vary across cultures, and the basis of a culture's definition becomes a scientifically observable phenomenon worthy of inquiry in itself (Averill, 1982). Parke and Slaby (1983) embraced this perspective in their review of the field but offered a tentative definition of aggression that included both antecedent and outcome perspectives: "aggression is defined in a minimal way as behavior that is aimed at harming or injuring another person or persons" (p. 550).

A Multifactor Framework

Brain (1994) suggests that four conditions define aggression as a heterogeneous category rather than an entity. First of all, aggressive acts must have the potential for harm or damage, even though not all acts that have the potential for harm could be considered aggressive. Second, aggression must be intentional, even though this judgment may not always be reliable and will vary from aggressor to victim to impartial judge. Third, aggression, to most biologists, involves arousal, although here, too, the judgment may be difficult. Finally, the act must be aversive to the victim. Rather than provide precise boundaries to the concept, Brain's criteria provide a multifactor framework for recognizing the broad category of events to be covered. This framework, taken together with Parke and Slaby's minimalist definition, serves as the basic conception of aggression for this chapter.

Defining Subtypes of Aggression

As is the case with antisocial behavior, more generally, aggression can be subdivided according to different antecedents and different intentions or goals. Moyer (1976) described differences in the form and function of aggression that are related to hunger, crowding, self-defense, and other antecedent conditions. Other antecedent distinctions might include provocation, interpersonal loss, social rejection, and authority directives (Dodge, McClaskey, & Feldman, 1985). Still other subclassifications have been made among the various outcomes or goals of aggression. Coie, Dodge, Terry, and Wright (1991) distinguished two subtypes of outcome-oriented aggression, bullying and instrumental aggression. Bullying is behavior directed toward interpersonal dominance of another person, whereas instrumental aggression is coercive behavior directed toward a noninterpersonal goal such as object possession.

These two different approaches to defining aggression, one based on antecedents and the other on outcomes, suggest a theoretically based subclassification. Aggression that appears to be a response to antecedent conditions such as goal blocking and provocation, and responses that are primarily interpersonal and hostile in nature can be considered *reactive;* in contrast, aggression that occurs in anticipation of self-serving outcomes can be called *proactive* (Dodge & Coie, 1987). Likewise, it may be possible to characterize persons as primarily reactively aggressive and others as primarily proactively aggressive. Similar subclassifications have referred to hostile versus instrumental aggression (Hartup, 1974) and affective versus instrumental aggression (Lorenz, 1966). For some individuals, aggressive behavior is predominantly reactive, whereas for others it is proactive; however, in the Dodge and Coie (1987) study of boys in elementary school, most aggressive boys displayed both forms.

The perspective of this chapter is that human aggressive behavior, because of its many adaptive features, has evolved to be part of a broader social communication system (Tedeschi & Felson, 1994). Aggression must be interpreted as a social event. It has meaningful subtypes and multiple topographies, antecedents, and functions. To understand processes in specific aggressive events may require subclassification and behavioral analysis. To understand the broader adaptive (and maladaptive) functions of aggression may require integration with other antisocial patterns.

ISSUES OF GENDER, ETHNICITY, AND CULTURAL SPECIFICITY

For too long, the scientific study of human aggression has largely been the study of Western white male aggressive behavior. Scientists have now become aware of the important gender, ethnic, and cultural differences in the measurement and study of aggression.

The definition of aggression may vary according to gender, ethnicity, or culture. The social judgment approach to defining aggression (Walters & Parke, 1964) stipulates that whether or not a behavior is classified as aggressive depends, in part, on features of the judge, aggressor, and victim. Because of its contrast with or assimilation to group base rates in aggression, a particular act might be classified as aggressive or not, depending on the circumstances. Thus, the same act that is displayed by a boy and labeled as aggressive might be interpreted by coders and peers as nonaggressive if displayed by a girl (Fagot & Hagan, 1985). Estimates of base rate differences across gender and ethnic groups may vary to the extent that these differences in judgment occur.

A second issue is that the valid measurement of aggressive behavior may vary across groups. Elliott and Ageton (1980) suggested that many self-report measures of delinquent behavior are deficient because they include only a limited set of behavioral items, they use ambiguous or truncated response sets, and the scoring of item responses into scales is conducted in a misleading manner. These problems have contributed to inaccurate estimations of social class differences in delinquency. For example, middle-class youth more commonly admit to borrowing the family car without permission. If this is coded as auto theft, then middle-class rates will be inflated compared with lower-class rates. Thus, measures used to study aggressive behaviors may yield less valid results in some groups compared with other groups.

A related issue is that behaviors constituting the class called aggression may vary across groups. Crick and Grotpeter (1995) have argued that one reason for the apparent gender discrepancy in base rates of aggression is that aggression has been inappropriately defined as being limited to direct acts of physical or verbal assault. If the definition is expanded to include relationally destructive behavior, such as exclusionary behavior and destruction of another's reputation, then base rates for girls begin to approach those for boys.

These points have obvious implications for interpreting age differences in aggressive behaviors. If the measure of aggression is frequency of direct destructive acts, including biting and hitting, 4-year-olds may be the most aggressive humans on earth; on the other hand, if homicide is the criterion measure, then 18-year-olds are the most aggressive humans.

A final issue concerns the possibility that the antecedents and correlates of aggressive behaviors might vary across groups. It has been speculated that different developmental models might be needed to explain aggression in boys versus girls and in majority versus minority children. Rowe, Vazsonyi, and Flannery (1994) have argued that covariance matrices among antecedent and outcome variables in a wide range of domains are largely invariant across ethnic groups, and that different models of development are unnecessary. In contrast, Ogbu (1993) and others have suggested that the cultural circumstances of being in a minority group necessitate different socialization strategies and, in turn, lead to different developmental pathways to aggressive behavior. Consistent with this thesis are findings by Deater-Deckard, Dodge, Bates, and Pettit (in press) that physically harsh discipline is an early predictor of later child aggressive behavior in white children but not in African American children. Whether these findings constitute different developmental models across ethnic groups (vs. different validity of measurements, or contextual qualifiers on a general model) is unclear. However, the importance of examining developmental models separately in various gender, ethnic, and cultural groups has become recognized and is likely to characterize research over the next decade.

HISTORICAL PERSPECTIVES ON THEORY AND EMPIRICAL INQUIRY

In the modern era, scholarly inquiry in aggressive behavior has been dominated by broad theories, and the major excitement has occurred through sweeping theoretical debates (see Parke & Slaby, 1983, for a detailed summary of

theories). These debates have addressed the very nature of the human species. Beginning with the Greek philosophers such as the Stoics and Seneca (Averill, 1982), one argument has been that aggression is instinctive to humans by biological imperative (see arguments from Hobbes, 1651/1969, through James, 1890, and Freud, 1930), and the role of culture is to rein in this instinct. In contrast, Rousseau (see Jimack, 1911) and Locke (1690/1913) viewed the newborn as a *tabula rasa*. Aggression reflects societal influences that can either enslave or inspire the species. Perhaps in response to the horrors of a world war, Freud (1930) suggested that humans are born with both a death instinct and a life-giving erotic instinct, and he framed the major modern question: Is aggressive behavior in humans biologically inevitable?

Following the Hobbesian tradition, the frustration-aggression hypothesis of Dollard et al. (1939) posited a drive theory that aggressive behavior is an inevitable, specieswide response to perceived goal blocking. They suggested that frustration necessarily results in aggression and that all aggressive behavior is instigated by frustration. This hypothesis led to the first major systematic empirical studies of aggression, and the empirical findings disputed the premise. Revisionists of this perspective (e.g., Berkowitz, 1962, 1989) have noted that frustration does not always lead to aggression (Davitz, 1952), but maintain the hypothesis that frustration creates a drivelike readiness to aggress, namely the arousal of anger.

The ethological approach of Lorenz (1966) similarly suggested the inevitability of aggressive behavior, but emphasized instead the instinctual system that relied on internal energy that is generated even in the absence of external stimuli. This aggressive energy, according to Lorenz, builds up over time and must be released periodically. The adaptive species-preserving functions of intraspecific aggression are to balance the distribution of the species across a limited ecology, to allow for the natural selection of the fittest of the species through combat, and to promote the selection of the most able family defenders against extraspecific threat. Thus, aggressive behavior has evolved as a necessary, species-preserving, component of human adaptation.

The Lockeian perspective has been framed by Bandura (1973), who argued that aggressive behavior develops through social learning processes. Most empirical inquiry in human aggression over the past two decades has been inspired by this perspective. Learning processes that have been identified include imitation of aggressive models, direct operant reinforcement for aggressive acts, and vicarious reinforcement through observational learning. Bandura acknowledges the biological constraints on human learning but argues that these constraints are much less restrictive than in other species.

Social learning theorists have described the way aggressive behavior patterns are acquired. Complementary to this learning theory perspective has been an emerging social information-processing perspective, which describes the mental process through which aggressive behaviors are generated and displayed in social interactions (see Dodge, 1986; Huesmann, 1988; Rubin & Krasnor, 1986). The origins of this description are cognitive-developmental theory (Flavell, 1977) and problem-solving theory (Newell & Simon, 1972). According to this perspective, in response to a social stimulus such as teasing, human beings proceed through a series of information-processing steps, leading to behavioral responses that might include aggression. These steps include encoding and representation of stimulus information, mentally accessing and evaluating behavioral responses, and enacting selected responses. Representation of an encoded stimulus as threatening, coupled with the accessing of an aggressive response that is evaluated favorably, is likely to lead to aggressive behavior (Dodge, 1980).

Biological theories have been posed and supported as well. Aggressive genetic relatives (DiLalla & Gottesman, 1989), difficult temperament (Plomin, 1983), neuropsychological deficits (Moffitt, 1993b), low IQ (West, 1982), psychophysiological indicators such as low resting heart rate and low skin conductance (Fowles, 1988; Raine, 1993), the sex hormone testosterone (Olweus, Mattison, Schalling, & Low, 1988), and neurotransmitters such as low CSF 5-HIAA (Asberg, Traskman, & Thoren, 1976) have all been implicated as markers of aggression-prone individuals. However, most of these theories have been attempts to explain individual differences in patterns of aggressive behavior rather than specieswide explanations of the occurrence of aggression or within-individual accounts of changes in aggressive responding. As a group, these theories have not been specific enough to account for specific aggressive events.

The modern debates among these instinctive, psychosocial, and biological theories have been enormously useful because they have inspired a diversity of rich, empirical knowledge. The debates themselves, however, have not been resolvable, perhaps because the theories are too broad. Scholars in the field understand that aggressive behavior is extraordinarily complex, that different theoretical perspectives can best explain different aspects of aggressive development, and that a comprehensive understanding will require an integrated, theoretical model with multiple features. In the past, the developmental aspects of aggressive behavior largely have been ignored in theory. Age differences in the form and function of aggression have not been discussed adequately, and life-course models of individual differences in aggressive development have been formulated only recently.

The values of the emerging field of developmental psychopathology (Garber, 1984; Sroufe & Rutter, 1984), however, have changed the study of aggressive development remarkably in the past decade. Microbehavioral analyses of aggressive events have been supplemented by epidemiological studies of the life course of aggression. Models of reciprocal influence, transactional development, and biological-psychosocial interaction have been formulated. An immediate result has been a greater understanding of the development of chronic aggression, acquired through longitudinal studies of population-based samples. This basic knowledge has led to major prevention efforts that are currently underway and will add further to the understanding of aggressive development.

AGGRESSIVE AND ANTISOCIAL DEVELOPMENT IN THE HUMAN SPECIES

Aggressive behavior is a universal characteristic of the human species. Charting specieswide patterns of growth and change in aggressive behavior across the life span is complicated, however, because different growth curves apply to different measures of aggression in different contexts with different subgroups. Even though infancy and toddlerhood can be considered the period of highest frequency in aggression, the most dangerously aggressive period is late adolescence and early adulthood. The goal of this section and of the following one is to detail these specieswide patterns of growth and change and the factors associated with them.

Different measures of aggressive behavior provide discrepant pictures of aggressive development. Direct observations of rates of conflict indicate linear decreases from the age of 12 months to 30 months (Holmberg, 1977; Maudry & Nekula, 1939). In contrast, some types of physical aggression (e.g., stamping and hitting) increase across this period and only later decline (Goodenough, 1931). Still a different pattern is evidenced in verbal acts of aggression, which sharply increase from 24 months to 48 months, coincident with language development (Jersild & Markey, 1935), but then stabilize. Physical fighting is a common form of male aggression in the prepubescent years. Finally, criminal homicides present a different developmental function altogether, with peaks at ages 18 to 20 years (Fingerhut & Kleinman, 1990).

Some of these discrepancies occur because the construct of antisocial behavior itself changes across development. Grabbing objects, tattling on others, and homicide are all valid measures, but developmental norms and base rates render their validity different at different ages. Farrington (1993) suggests that different measures at different ages (e.g., fighting at age 8, vandalism at age 12, and homicide at age 18) may be indicators of the same underlying antisocial construct or may indicate developmental sequences across different but correlated constructs. Cairns (1979) has described the concept of continuity across development as involving numerous aspects, including intraindividual continuity (absolute stability), interindividual continuity (relative stability in rank), organizational continuity (the fact that the biological organism is fundamentally the same from birth to death), factor structure continuity (whether covariance matrices in variables are identical across ages), process continuity (whether rates of change or factors in change vary across age), and societal or generational continuity (whether the construct is conceptualized similarly across time by societies). Aggressive behavior is such a complex developmental construct partly because even though its intraindividual, factor structure, and process continuities are weak, its interindividual continuity is strong.

The Emergence of Anger in Infancy

The fundamental human emotion of anger is crucial to survival because of its self-regulatory and social communication functions (Stenberg & Campos, 1990). It prepares the body physiologically and psychologically to initiate self-protective and instrumental activity (Frijda, 1986; Izard, 1977), and it has been conjectured to be an important reason for the adaptation and survival of the species (Lorenz, 1966). When not controlled properly, anger is a source of much human misery.

If anger is functional and innate (Ekman, 1972; Tomkins, 1963), when does it emerge, and what are its earliest elicitors? Surprisingly, the answers to these fundamental ontogenetic questions are still being debated. Averill (1982) suggested that anger is expressed only after considerable

socialization. In contrast, the behaviorist John B. Watson claimed that physical restraint invariantly elicits a "rage" response (i.e., crying, screaming, and face flushing) even among neonates (Watson & Morgan, 1917); however, later studies revealed that observers could not reliably detect this response or distinguish it from pain or discomfort (M. Sherman, 1927).

Stenberg and Campos (1990) suggested that research on infant anger has been hampered by the lack of a uniform metric for anger expression that can be distinguished from other negative emotions, such as pain and discomfort. Poor reliability of scoring may be due to vague operational definitions of anger. They proposed the use of Ekman and Friesen's (1975) two patterns of facial expression of anger that have been found to have cross-cultural uniformity. In both patterns, the eyebrows lower and draw together, the eyelids narrow and squint, and the cheeks elevate; in one pattern, the mouth is open and square, and in the other, the lips are pressed together tightly. They also distinguished these responses from equally discrete pain responses. Using these definitions, Stenberg, Campos, and Emde (1983) found that pulling a biscuit out of an infant's mouth will reliably produce an anger facial expression by seven months of age. In addition, the expression is not randomly emitted but rather is targeted, often at the mother, even when a stranger has withdrawn the biscuit.

Stenberg and Campos (1990) used a forearm restraint procedure to elicit responses in 1-, 4-, and 7-month old infants. They grasped the infant's forearms, pulled them together, and held them approximately 6 inches in front of the infant's torso for up to 3 minutes. Even though 1-month-olds did display undifferentiated negative facial expressions, not one of the 16 infants of this age tested displayed a discrete anger template, that differentiated the anger expression from all other negative expressions. In contrast, 5 of the 16 infants at 4 months and 6 of the 16 infants at 7 months displayed the discrete anger template. Thus, even though the capacity for negative emotional expression is present by 1 month of age, it is over the course of the first 4 months of life that a distinct anger response becomes coordinated.

At what age does anger expression come to have a social communication function? Stenberg and Campos (1990) found that, following restraint, 1-month-olds turned their heads randomly, but 4-month-olds turned their heads toward the frustrator or the frustrator's hands. Immediately following the onset of the first display of anger, 7-month-olds, but not 4-month-olds, turned their heads not toward the frustrator but toward their mothers. Thus, Stenberg and Campos (1990) concluded, "By at least 4 months anger facial displays may function as discrete social signals. These signals are at first directed proximally to the immediate source of frustration, but by 7 months they become expressed directly to social objects such as the mother" (pp. 270–271). Of course, the failure to observe a discrete anger expression in 1-month-olds does not rule out its existence at this age, because other stimuli might have elicited the anger response or other observational codes might be necessary to detect a different form of anger at an early age. Still, the empirical findings by Stenberg and Campos (1990) that angry facial displays are present early in life and are directed toward the source of frustration are precisely as Darwin (1872) had suggested they would be. These findings are also consistent with a functionalist view of anger as social communication (Campos, Campos, & Barrett, 1989).

Aggression and Conflict in the Second Year of Life

Trivers (1974) suggested that conflict, anger, and aggression necessarily increase in frequency and intensity across early development, especially in mammalian species that undergo a prolonged period of symbiosis between mother and infant. Following a period of total dependence by the infant, the mother is motivated to help the infant achieve independence for survival, but the infant is ambivalent and may be motivated to sustain the mother's attention. The infant's growing size and weight or the birth of a younger sibling may accelerate the mother's interest in pushing the infant/toddler toward independence, as well as the toddler's interest in keeping the mother's attention (Dunn, 1988). Thus, mother-infant conflict will be inevitable, especially in the second year of life as the individuation process intensifies (Mahler, 1968). Individual differences in anger expression may also emerge during this period, related to difficult temperament (Bates, 1980; Thomas, Chess, & Birch, 1968), or insecure attachment (Sroufe, 1985). Indeed, systematic observations reveal increased oppositional behavior, including temper tantrums and aggression, in the second year (Wenar, 1972).

Mothers trained to observe their toddlers in naturalistic settings report that anger occurs during an average of 7% of all one-minute time intervals, with cross-individual ranges from 0% to 33% (Radke-Yarrow & Kochanska, 1990). Even as early as 24 months of age, the consistency of anger responses across time is at least moderately high

($r = .56$), suggesting that individual differences in anger expression emerge early in life.

The earliest documented observations of peer-directed aggression have been found at the end of the first year of life. This period coincides with emerging interest in one's own possessions, in control over one's own activities, and in peer communication. Six-month-olds appear not to be bothered by peers who grab their objects or invade their space (Hay, Nash, & Pedersen, 1983). By 12 months of age, however infants respond to peer provocations with protest and aggressive retaliation (Caplan, Vespo, Pedersen, & Hay, 1991). Up to half of all peer exchanges among children 12 to 18 months old can be characterized as involving conflict (Holmberg, 1977; Maudry & Nekula, 1939), although most conflicts do not involve aggressive behavior (Shantz & Shantz, 1985). Hay and Ross (1982) found that 87% of 21-month-old children participated in at least one conflict during four 15-minute laboratory peer group observation sessions. The conflicts generally were of short duration (mean length = 23 seconds), even when there was no adult intervention. Most conflicts concerned object possession struggles. Interestingly, verbal communication of resistance was more effective than motor-behavioral resistance in preventing a peer from taking one's toy. Differences in responding during conflict between 12-month-olds and 24-month-olds were not so much in frequency of aggressive retaliation but, rather, in the emergent use of speech in conflict and in the emergence (but still infrequent use) of prosocial attempts to resolve conflicts peacefully (Loeber & Hay, 1993).

Aggression in the Preschool Years

Physical aggression decreases and verbal aggression increases normatively between 2 and 4 years of age (Cairns, 1979; Jersild & Markey, 1935). Goodenough (1931) used parent diaries to find that stamping and hitting increased until age 2 and then declined sharply, being replaced by verbally aggressive statements. Jenkins, Bax, and Hart (1980) found that parental concerns about behavior problems and management peak at age 3, in contrast with earlier peaks for toileting, eating, and sleeping problems. Other epidemiological studies have revealed high rates (up to 13%) of tantrum, peer fighting, and frustration tolerance problems in 3-year-olds, with declines thereafter (Crowther, Bond, & Rolf, 1981; Earls, 1980; Richman, Stevenson, & Graham, 1982). As Campbell (1990) noted, "It seems unlikely that such a large proportion of young children is showing clinically significant symptoms. Rather, these studies suggest that many of the behaviors that can be problematic for parents are extremely common in the general population" (p. 59).

The most frequent elicitors of aggression in infancy are physical discomfort and the need for attention, but these become replaced by "habit training" in the third year and by peer conflicts and conflicts over material possessions (Fabes & Eisenberg, 1992a) in the fourth and fifth years. Dawe (1934) found that quarrels over possessions were the most frequent elicitors of aggression during this age period. Abramovitch, Corter, and Lando (1979) found that siblings become a predominant source of agonistic behavior for preschoolers, with 45% of all interactions between younger and older siblings involving conflict. Most of the time, it is the older sibling who initiates the conflict, through threats, object grabbing, or insults. The younger sibling may learn aggressive behaviors through imitation of older siblings during these exchanges (Dunn & Kendrick, 1982), just as preschoolers acquire aggressive behaviors in the classroom through exposure to aggressive peer encounters (Patterson, Littman, & Bricker, 1967).

Numerous factors may account for the gradual decline in aggression across the late preschool period. The development of language is an obvious factor that may help children inhibit aggressive motor behaviors through symbolic communication of needs (Kagan, 1981). Preschool children referred to speech clinics for delays in language development often demonstrate a range of aggressive behavior problems (Cantwell, Baker, & Mattison, 1979), and children referred to psychiatric clinics often display unsuspected language problems (Cohen, Davine, & Meloche-Kelly, 1989). Epidemiological surveys have shown a correlation between language delays and aggressive behavior problems in normative samples (Richman et al., 1982). Whereas language development may help a child inhibit aggression, language delays may contribute to peer relationship problems that, in turn, result in aggressive conflicts (Campbell, 1990). But language also provides children with yet another means of aggressing (through insults, threats, and name-calling), so the decline in overall aggression must be ascribed to additional factors.

Mischel (1974) suggests that the emerging ability to delay gratification may account for this decline. Through interpersonal exchanges, children acquire cognitive strategies for delaying gratification (e.g., distraction, mentally representing delayed rewards) that may help them avoid impulsive grabbing of others' possessions and hitting. During the preschool years, peers provide feedback to aggressors that results in the decline of aggression. The development of dominance hierarchies (Strayer & Trudel, 1984) and of genuine peer understanding also contribute to this decline (Zahn-Waxler, Radke-Yarrow, & King, 1979). The ability to delay gratification, in turn, may be aided by the corresponding development of broader representational abilities (Gelman & Baillargeon, 1983), including perspective taking (Selman, 1980), empathy (Zahn-Waxler et al., 1979), and memory strategies (Brown, Bransford, Ferrara, & Campione, 1983). Kopp (1982) has articulated a broader theory of emergent emotional self-regulation during this period, with children progressing from externally controlled regulation to internally mediated cognitive controls. Block and Block (1980) have framed related arguments in terms of developing ego control during these years. It is likely that these cognitive changes are paralleled by increases in neural sophistication that also may account for some of the decline of impulsive aggression.

The Emergence of Sex Differences

Relatively few sex differences in the rate of aggressive behaviors have been found in infancy and toddlerhood (Hay & Ross, 1982; Loeber & Hay, 1993), but by the time that children interact in naturally occurring preschool groups, the differences become striking (Loeber & Hay, 1993; Maccoby & Jacklin, 1980). Boys engage in more conflict and more forceful aggressive acts (Smith & Green, 1974), both physically and verbally (Maccoby & Jacklin, 1980), as well as in both hostile and instrumental ways (Hartup, 1974). This emergent sex difference appears to hold across socioeconomic groups (Baumrind, 1971; Maccoby & Jacklin, 1980), as well as across cultures (Whiting & Whiting, 1975), including Britain (Smith & Green, 1974), America, Switzerland, and Ethiopia (Omark, Omark, & Edelman, 1975), and the developing countries of Kenya, India, Philippines, Mexico, and Okinawa (Whiting & Edwards, 1973). This sex difference also widens across later development, as girls outgrow their tendency toward oppositional behavior at an earlier age than do boys (Richman et al., 1982). By adolescence, the sex difference in juvenile court appearances is at least fourfold (Snyder et al., 1987). The sex difference in self-reported delinquent acts as assessed in the National Youth Survey is threefold (Elliott, Ageton, Huizinga, Knowles, & Canter, 1983), with the sex difference in self-reported serious violent offending being sixfold at age 18 (Elliott, Huizinga, & Morse, 1987). The sex difference in homicide is even greater (Uniform Crime Reports, 1992).

Even though it is highly likely that biological differences set in motion the early development of sex differences in aggression, this effect is equally likely to be indirect and mediated by social experiences (which also may have biological correlates). For example, even though sex differences in aggression are not yet apparent in the first year, these differences are foreshadowed by early peer interaction styles. In laboratory settings, 6-month-old boys are more likely to grab toys held by same-age peers than are 6-month-old girls (Hay et al., 1983). At this young age, peers do not object to this intrusion, and conflict does not usually result. At later ages, however, when peers learn to recognize social rules of possession and begin to protest when an object has been taken from them, conflict is likely to unfold and aggression is likely to occur. The impulsive grabbing behavior of boys may account for their frequent involvement in toddlerhood object-possession struggles, which, in turn, lead to aggressive acts. Thus, a biologically mediated gender effect on impulsivity may account for early sex differences in involvement in conflict and aggression. Another gender difference is that girls use more verbal objection and negotiation during conflicts than boys do, which may prevent the escalation of conflicts into aggression (Eisenberg, Fabes, Nyman, Bernzweig, & Pinuelas, 1994). In addition, the aggressive acts by young girls are displayed in a manner that is more likely to lead to ignoring by peers than are those by boys, which are more often met with resistance (Fagot & Hagan, 1985). Ignoring an aggressive act often leads to its termination, whereas resistance continues the struggle (Fagot & Hagan, 1985).

Other early sex differences may have similar indirect effects on the development of aggressive behaviors. Male newborns show less sensitivity to pain than do female newborns (Lipsett & Levy, 1959), suggesting that boys may be more likely than girls to continue with proactively assertive/aggressive behaviors even following peer rebuke. At 21 months of age, girls deliberate more during conflicts, taking longer to respond, than do boys (Hay & Ross, 1982). This slower, less impulsive, pace may prevent the escalation from conflict to aggression. Likewise, during social exchanges, young girls are more likely than boys to withdraw from competition for objects (Charlesworth & Dzur, 1987; Charlesworth & LaFreniere, 1982), thus preventing the escalation to aggression. Boys attend to high-action stimuli, such as in television,

more than girls do (Anderson, Choi, & Lorch, 1987), and thus, may be differentially affected by the viewing of televised violence (Huesmann & Eron, 1986).

Initial sex differences in behavioral style and aggression become more pronounced through the sex-group segregation that develops naturally and with societal support during the preschool period (Maccoby, 1986). In contrast to girls' play groups, boys' groups generally are larger, more public, rougher, and more concerned with competition and dominance rank. Maccoby (1986) argued that these features of same-sex group life potentiate enduring sex differences in aggressive behavior.

Adults' cultural stereotypes and sex-differentiated behavior toward boys and girls may provide yet another pathway in the emergence of sex differences. Rubin, Provenzano, and Luria (1974) found that parents, especially fathers, evaluate their newborn sons as stronger, hardier, and more well-coordinated than daughters, whereas they viewed newborn girls as more delicate, weaker, and more awkward. Whether or not these differences are objectively true, the sex-stereotypic conceptions of their children that parents form may well guide socialization practices, leading to self-fulfilling prophecies in behavioral outcomes. Likewise, both men and women who watched a video of a toddler named Chris tended to rate Chris as stronger, more assertive, and more aggressive when told that Chris was a boy than when told Chris was a girl (Gurwitz & Dodge, 1975). Condry and Condry (1976) obtained a similar effect with videotaped infant stimuli. Adults rated an infant's reaction to a jack-in-the-box as "anger" when they thought the infant was male and "fear" when they though the infant was female. Whatever their origins, sex differences in the frequency, form, and function of aggressive behaviors tend to persist throughout the life span, from toddlerhood forward.

Aggression in the Elementary School Years

Most children display aggression less frequently during the elementary school years, but a select few become highly troublesome to peers, parents, and teachers (Loeber & Hay, 1993). By the end of elementary school, playground researchers usually abandon the study of physical aggression through direct observation methods because of insufficient instances of readily observable aggressive behaviors (especially when children know they are being observed; an exception is Pepler & Craig's, 1995, hidden playground video camera technique), giving way instead to the more common use of peer nomination and contrived play group methods to study aggressive children (Coie, Dodge, & Kupersmidt, 1990).

With the gradual decline in the rate of aggression comes a shift in its form and function. Aggressive behaviors become increasingly person-oriented and hostile across this period, in contrast with the relatively nonsocial, instrumental nature of aggression in the preschool period; and major eliciting of aggression come to include perceived threats and derogations to one's ego and esteem (Hartup, 1974). The emergent recognition that another may be acting with intentional and hostile motives instigates increased retaliatory, angry responding (Dodge, 1980). During the early elementary school years, children learn that some actions are unintended whereas others are under the actor's volitional control, with the result that the attribution that another has acted with hostile intent has an inflammatory effect (Shantz & Voydanoff, 1973).

An important distinction made during this age period is between reactive and proactive aggression. Animal behaviorists have long distinguished between hostile-affective (reactive) aggression, characterized by intensive patterned autonomic arousal, anger, and defensive postures that lead to frenzied attacks in response to perceived threat, and instrumental (proactive) aggression, characterized by little autonomic activation but highly patterned appetitive behavior oriented toward a reward (Lorenz, 1966; Reis, 1974). Price and Dodge (1989) and Coie et al. (1991) have distinguished these behaviors in direct observations of children aged 5 to 9. Atkins and Stoff (1993) have developed a laboratory analogue task to elicit these behaviors. During a competitive game, 8- to 12-year-old children are given the opportunity to respond to an obstructive peer with either a goal-blocking response (instrumental aggression) or a loud noise (hostile aggression). Hostile aggressive responding was found to be uniquely correlated with poor impulse control on other measures (Atkins, Stoff, Osborne, & Brown, 1993). Finally, teacher ratings have also validly distinguished reactive and proactive aggression (Dodge & Coie, 1987).

During the early school years, covert forms of antisocial behavior such as lying, cheating, and stealing emerge in greater frequency, along with overt forms carried over from the preschool years (Loeber & Schmaling, 1985a, 1985b). Sex differences in both direct and indirect aggressive behaviors are maintained across the elementary school years (Maccoby & Jacklin, 1980), despite Feshbach's (1970) speculation that girls would rival boys in the display of indirect aggression. Although Feshbach (1970) was incorrect about a broad category of indirect aggression, the distinction between physical and psychological aggression is a meaningful one. Reconceptualizations of the topography of aggressive behavior have emphasized a type of relational aggression that is peculiar to girls at this age (Crick & Grotpeter, 1995). Relational aggression includes attempts to exclude peers from group participation, besmirch another's reputation, and gossip about another's negative attributes. Girls display this pattern more than boys (who more likely display overt aggression), with reasonable stability across time, and significant correlations with other peer and social-cognitive problems (Crick, 1995).

It is during the elementary school years that many children, boys especially, are referred to mental health clinics for conduct problems. Lahey and Loeber (1994) have outlined a developmental trajectory for aggressive conduct problems, beginning with oppositional defiant disorder (ODD), which is characterized by temper tantrums and defiant, irritable, blameful, argumentative, and annoying behavior. These behaviors are not uncommon at 4 to 5 years of age (Achenbach & Edelbrock, 1983) but become less common and clinically problematic by age 8 (Loeber, Lahey, & Thomas, 1991). Children diagnosed with these problems at age 12 have been found by retrospective report typically to have displayed the problems since elementary school onset (Lahey, Loeber, Quay, Frick, & Grimm, 1992). These findings suggest that oppositional behaviors are normative in preschool, but the usual developmental course is to shed these problems by age 8. Clinically referred children in elementary school typically do not present with these problems as new symptoms; rather, these children have been unable to outgrow these problems that have carried over from earlier times (Loeber, Tremblay, Gagnon, & Charlebois, 1989).

Some ODD children begin to diversify their deviant repertoire in the elementary school years (usually about ages 8–11) to include setting fires, lying, fighting, weapon use, and vandalism (Lahey et al., 1992). This pattern is called conduct disorder (CD), and its prevalence in the United States is about 9% of males and 2% of females (American Psychiatric Association, 1994). Canadian survey data on 3,300 children indicate a prevalence of 7% of males and 3% of females (Offord, Boyle, & Racine, 1989). Between 11 and 13 years, a subset of children who could be diagnosed as CD begin to diversify their deviant behaviors even further to include violent criminal behavior such as mugging, breaking and entering, and forced sex.

Aggression in the Adolescent Years

Loeber (1982) concluded that most longitudinal studies show decrements in ratings of aggressive behavior as children enter adolescence. Despite this species-typical decrease in the perceived frequency of aggressive acts, however, adolescence is when serious acts of violence increase, as recent crime statistics demonstrate in the United States. In some peer cultures, physical aggression becomes more socially acceptable in adolescence (Coie, Terry, Zakriski, & Lochman, 1995; Ferguson & Rule, 1980), although it is generally confined to male-male conflicts (Cairns, Cairns, Neckerman, Ferguson, & Gariepy, 1989). In the United States, the escalation of violence is paralleled by the availability of firearms. In Cairns' sample, 85% of adolescent males had direct access, with 49% owning guns (Sadowski, Cairns, & Earp, 1989). Even in a culture where firearms are not readily available, Farrington (1989b) found that 96% of his sample of 400 inner-city London males admitted committing at least one common criminal offense during adolescence and young adulthood.

Data from the National Youth Survey (NYS) of 1,725 youths first surveyed in 1976 provide a detailed picture of the onset, prevalence, and course of violent offending in the United States (Elliott, 1994; Elliott et al., 1983). Violent offending almost always begins in the adolescent years. Self-reports of serious violent offenses (SVOs, defined as aggravated assault, robbery, or rape, necessarily involving some injury or a weapon) rise sharply from the age of 12 to 20. The onset hazard rate (first-time offending) for SVOs is almost zero (< 0.5%) through age 11 but doubles between ages 13 and 14 and rises sharply to 5.1% at age 16. The onset rate then halves between ages 16 and 18 and declines to less than 1% after age 20. Thus, over half of the persons who become involved in serious violent offending, prior to age 27, commit their first violent offense between the ages of 14 and 17, and almost all offenders commit their first offense before age 21. Not only is the rise in first-time offending dramatic, the overall prevalence rates for offending in adolescence are startlingly high. As depicted in Figure 12.2, at the peak age of 17, 19% of males and 12% of females reported committing at least one SVO.

Official arrest records reported by the FBI (Uniform Crime Reports, 1992) indicate three to four times lower prevalence rates of SVOs and a similar but lagged (delayed) curvilinear developmental function (Fingerhut & Kleinman, 1990). At age 17, about 15% of all boys in the United States are arrested (Snyder et al., 1987). The relations

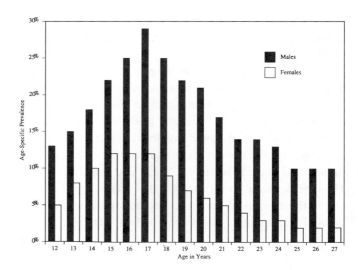

Figure 12.2 Age-specific prevalence of self-reported serious violent offending for males and females. Data are extracted from Elliott's (1994) report of respondents in the National Youth Survey.

among self-report, arrest, and incarceration data have been summarized by Huizinga and Elliott (1987) as follows. Of those adolescents who commit offenses, only 15% to 33% are in fact arrested (Farrington, 1989b). Of those arrested, about 64% are referred to juvenile or adult court, and of those referred to court, only about 2% to 10% are incarcerated. Thus, very few offenders are ever incarcerated. Because those arrested probably are a very biased group of all offenders, due to gender, socioeconomic, and racial discrimination, arrest records and self-reports provide different pictures of violence (Huizinga & Dunford, 1985). Based solely on arrest records, Weiner (1989) concluded that most first-time SVOs occur between ages 18 and 24. However, as noted by Elliott (1994), "If we assume the accuracy of both (self-report and official record) measures, it appears that most first arrests for a violent offense in a serious violent career take place several years after the initiation into this type of behavior and extend into ages where the hazard rate for initiation is close to 0" (p. 10).

Gender differences are striking: Violent crime arrest prevalence differentials may be as high as 8 to 1 (Hamparian, Schuster, Dinitz, & Conrad, 1978), although this difference may be slightly decreasing across time, as the secular rate of robbery and assault is increasing more rapidly for girls than boys (Kruttschnitt, 1994). Gender differences occur in self-reports of antisocial activity but are less pronounced than for arrest records, due partly to gender biases in arrest patterns but also, perhaps, to more serious offending in boys than girls (even controlling for rates of offending). The NYS data indicate that 42% of males report committing a serious violent offense at some time in their youthful lives, in contrast with 16% for females (Elliott, 1994). However, girls who become involved in SVOs do so at an earlier age than boys. The peak age for onset for girls is 14, in contrast to 16 for boys (Elliott, 1994).

Race differences in aggression in the social context of America are almost negligible in the elementary school years (Achenbach, 1991), but are more pronounced in adolescence. Arrest record data indicate that even though African American youth make up 15% of the juvenile population, they account for 52% of those arrested for juvenile violent crimes (Dryfoos, 1990). The lifetime chances that an urban African American male will be arrested for an FBI "index" offense (murder, forcible rape, aggravated assault, robbery, burglary, larceny, auto theft) is 50%, in contrast to 14% for urban White males (Blumstein & Cohen, 1987). The problem is so great that more African American male adolescents are incarcerated or on probation for a crime than are gainfully employed (Edelman, 1992). Self-reports indicate a much narrower race difference in actual behavior, however. The black-to-white ratio in prevalence of SVOs is about 5 to 4, a statistically significant but substantially small effect (Elliott, 1994). When socioeconomic class confounds are controlled, this ratio is reduced to about 7 to 6. Elliott (1994) has reported that the higher prevalence rate of self-reported SVOs among African Americans can be almost entirely accounted for by the particularly high risk of onset between the ages of 13 and 16 for African American male adolescents. This age period obviously is a risky one for this group in terms of self-reported SVOs, but an even more tragic time in terms of arrest rates, and rates of victimization.

These data suggest common developmental patterns in serious violence that begin with minor aggressive acts and delinquent behaviors in middle childhood and progress to frequent and serious offending by age 17. The initiation of substance use and sexual activity adds incrementally to the risk for increased aggressive behavior during this period (Jessor et al., 1991). Elliott (1994) concludes that minor forms of delinquent behavior and alcohol use typically precede more serious forms of violence. Aggravated assault precedes robbery in 85% of cases, and robbery precedes rape in 72% of cases. Thus, the developmental path for a

small portion of the population involves progressively serious and violent behaviors, although most offenders usually desist from crime in early adulthood.

Aggression in Adulthood

Most self-report studies indicate that between ages 18 and 25 the overall rate of aggressive behavior begins to decline. Virtually no new cases of antisocial behavior begin in adulthood (Robins, 1966). In the Cambridge study, Farrington (1993) found that self-reported prevalence of all criminal behaviors, including violence, decreased markedly in early adulthood. For example, self-reports of burglary decreased from 11% at age 18 to 5% at age 21 and 2% at both ages 25 and 32. In the National Youth Survey, Elliott, Huizinga, and Menard (1989) found that self-reported offending peaked at age 17 and declined linearly in subsequent years (see Figure 12.2). Official arrest record data indicate a similar decline in violent offending in adulthood, although the decline as measured by arrests begins later and is less sharp than that by self-reports (Blumstein, Farrington, & Moitra, 1985).

The majority of the decline in offending in early adulthood can be attributed to the termination of crime by that majority of persons who had been low-frequency offenders in the first place. High-frequency offenders, called "career criminals," apparently continue their high rates of offending, when they are not in prison, until about age 40 and only then begin their decline (Blumstein & Cohen, 1987). These career offenders, often diagnosed with antisocial personality disorder (American Psychiatric Association, 1994), almost always begin their careers in early life and continue their antisocial behavior through young adulthood. Nearly half of those children initiating a serious violent offense prior to age 11 continue their violent careers into their 20s, in contrast to just one fourth of those initiating their violent career between ages 11 and 12. The ratios are even lower for persistence among those initiating violence later in adolescence (Elliott, 1994). By age 40, approximately, termination from criminal offending in this select group occurs at a rate of about 15% per year.

There is a significant exception to the general pattern of decline in serious violence in early adulthood. Among African American males, there is no decline in violence from age 22 to 30. Nearly twice as many African Americans continue their violent careers as do whites; thus, the violent careers of African Americans last longer than they do for whites (Elliott, 1994), in sharp contrast to the finding of few race differences in the propensity for initial violence. It seems that the underclass, especially poor African American males, are unable to escape the "system" of incarceration, labeling, unemployment, and negative identity once the course of violence begins. As Elliott (1994), concluded, "Once involved in a lifestyle that includes serious forms of violence, theft, and substance use, persons from disadvantaged families and neighborhoods find it very difficult to escape. They have fewer opportunities for conventional adult roles, and they are more deeply embedded in and dependent upon the gangs and the illicit economy that flourish in their neighborhoods. . . . Poverty is related less to the onset of violence than to the continuity of violence, once initiated" (p. 19).

It is important to note that there is no race disparity in continuing violence among persons employed between ages 18 and 20; nor is there a race disparity among those persons who are married or living with a partner. The evidence suggests that those persons who can establish stable work and family life careers, regardless of ethnicity, tend to end their involvement in criminal violence (Rutter, 1989). As Elliott (1994) pointed out, these findings have enormous implications for the focus of intervention, which might be directed toward job training and economic opportunity.

An important caveat to these findings is that almost all of these studies fail to include child abuse and spousal battery as instances of violence. Thus, it might be misleading to conclude that adulthood brings about less violence. Straus and Gelles (1990) reported that 16% of American couples report physically assaulting each other, and 11% report physically abusing their children, in the past 12 months; however, systematic epidemiological research that would adequately describe the life course and origins of child and spouse abuse does not yet exist. Huesmann, Eron, Lefkowitz, and Walder (1984) have reported some continuity between peer-directed aggression at age 8 and spousal and child abuse at age 30, suggesting that this behavior may have similar antecedents to other forms of violence.

SPECIESWIDE ANTECEDENTS OF AGGRESSIVE ACTS

This section is devoted to understanding the major developmental antecedents of aggressive behaviors in the human species. Origins of stable individual differences are discussed in later sections.

Ecological Conditions

Disparities in violent crime rates across geographic regions implicate the crowded inner city as one setting for high rates of violence (Hammond & Yung, 1991). In a classic work, Shaw and McKay (1942) argued that the three community structural variables of poverty, ethnic heterogeneity, and high residential mobility are associated with high violent crime rates that persist across time, even after the entire population in a community changes. Empirical research over the past half-century largely supports this contention (Sampson & Laub, 1993). However, numerous examples of contrary findings suggest that these community factors are not *always* associated with aggression. What must be understood are the processes and mechanisms operating in poor, urban, ethnically diverse, and residentially mobile settings that account for heightened crime and violence.

To understand these processes, many scholars point to the pernicious effects of poverty on the family unit (McLoyd, 1990; Wilson, 1987). Controlling for other community variables, poverty within the family increases the probability not only of adult crime but also of peer-directed aggressive behavior by children (Guerra, Huesmann, Tolan, Van Acker, & Eron, 1995; Patterson, Kupersmidt, & Vaden, 1990) and adolescents (Spencer, Dobbs, & Phillips, 1988). McLoyd (1990) has suggested that poverty increases parents' psychological distress and impairs their social support systems, which, in turn, will diminish parents' effectiveness and increase their coerciveness toward their children. She has demonstrated the powerful effects of poverty on single African American mothers. These effects, in turn, may lead to child aggression. Consistent with this formulation, Guerra, Huesmann, Tolan, et al. (1995) found that, among urban Chicagoans, poverty was correlated with stressful life events and a lack of parental involvement in religious support systems; these two factors, in turn, accounted for the effect of poverty on peer-nominated aggression. Sampson and Laub (1994) reanalyzed the Glueck and Glueck (1950) longitudinal data set involving 1,000 Depression-era white families and found that the structural variable of family poverty influenced family processes of harsh discipline, low supervision, and poor parent-child attachment, which, in turn, influenced juvenile delinquency. Family process accounted for two thirds of the effect of poverty on delinquency. Likewise, Dodge, Pettit, and Bates (1994) found that harsh physical discipline by parents accounted for about half of the effect of low socioeconomic status on children's aggressive behavior.

Other early environmental conditions appear to have similar effects on children's aggression, and these effects also may be mediated through disruptions in parenting. These conditions include parental divorce (Kolvin, Miller, Scott, Gatzanis, & Fleeting, 1990), parental conflict (McCord, 1991c), being born to a teenage (Morash & Rucker, 1989) or single (Blum, Boyle, & Offord, 1988) parent, being raised in a large family (Rutter, Tizard, & Whitmore, 1970), and being parented by convicted felons (Farrington, 1992; McCord, 1977; Robins, 1978). These factors likely share a common pathway through effects on parenting quality, although they may have more direct effects or may be linked to child aggression through common genes.

By school age, ecological conditions in the neighborhood and school environment have effects on aggression that operate more directly, or at least independently of parenting. Kellam (1990) described pronounced and persistent differences in rates of aggressive behavior across schools, and even across classrooms within schools. These effects seem to hold even after controlling for socioeconomic status and other demographic factors, suggesting a broad environmental effect that might be attributable to local norms, contingencies, and attitudes. Furthermore, Werthamer-Larsson, Kellam, and Wheeler (1991) found that characteristics of classrooms, such as academic achievement environments, influence the overall rate of aggressive behaviors.

Among adolescents and young adults, aggressogenic environmental setting conditions include school detachment and dropout (Thornberry, Lizotte, Krohn, Farnworth, & Jang, 1991), unsupervised interaction with deviant peers (Elliott, Huizinga, & Ageton, 1985; Farrington, 1989a), the onset of unemployment (Farrington, Gallagher, Morley, St. Ledger, & West, 1986), membership in a gang (Thornberry, 1987), involvement in a drug market (Blumstein, in press), being arrested and stigmatized as a criminal for a past offense (Blumstein et al., 1985), and abnormally high temperature (through season of the year or more transient conditions such as a non-air-conditioned subway, E. Anderson, 1990). As noted earlier, however, these effects are rarely universal, they often interact with other factors, and they reciprocally influence each other in cumulative ways. For example, randomized experiments reveal that arrest for domestic violence reduces repeat violence among the

employed but actually increases repeat violence among the unemployed (L. Sherman, 1992). L. Sherman (1993) argues that arresting an unemployed person in this context only serves to increase defiant recidivism among those who are already disaffected and are particularly threatened and vulnerable.

Because of the apparent situational specificity of environmental effects, rather than simply cataloging a long list of environmental factors in aggression, it may be more important to understand common processes that account for such effects. According to Berkowitz's (1989, 1990, 1994) cognitive-neoassociationistic perspective, an environmental variable will lead to aggression to the extent that it induces negative affect, thoughts, and memories. Theories of interpersonal relations (e.g., Heider, 1958; Jones & Davis, 1965; Kelley, 1979) suggest that attribution processes mediate environmental effects. Wilson and Herrnstein's (1985) rational theory of crime emphasizes the individual's analysis of the environment in terms of expected benefits versus expected costs. Together, these theories suggest that an environmental variable will influence human aggressive behavior if it affects one or more of three mental processes: (a) the perception of threat and experience of irritation or fear; (b) the accessibility of aggressive responses in one's memorial repertoire; and (c) the evaluation that aggression will lead to desirable positive consequences.

Factors That Enhance the Attribution of Threat

One of the most consistent findings from laboratory studies is that provocation leads to retaliatory aggression, even in young children (Ferguson & Rule, 1988; Shantz & Voydanoff, 1973). Frustration and goal blocking have long been known to induce anger under both experimental and natural conditions (Berkowitz, 1989). Studies over the past two decades have indicated, however, that the *perception* of provocation is far more important than the provocation itself in instigating aggression (Dodge, Murphy, & Buchsbaum, 1984; Nasby, Hayden, & DePaulo, 1979). If a child who is pushed from behind in line at school or who receives an excessively severe punishment from a teacher interprets such an environmental threat as malevolently intended and foreseeable, that child is likely to retaliate aggressively (Ferguson & Rule, 1988). Even kindergarten children, however, can refrain from aggressing when they make a nonmalevolent interpretation of a negative event (Shantz & Voydanoff, 1973). Environmental factors that facilitate a hostile attribution include information about the provocateur as acting consistently negatively over time and distinctively negatively toward the perceiver, as well as information that others consensually interpret the provocateur's actions similarly (Kelley, 1973). Inferences of hostile intent are more likely when the provocateur continues to harm the perceiver despite feedback or threats of punishment, exerts special effort to cause the harm, or seems happy when causing the harm (Rule & Ferguson, 1986). Children also learn when to attribute hostile intent and make moral judgments of a provocateur through socialization (Rule & Ferguson, 1986). Berkowitz (1993) suggested that environmental conditions leading to pervasive negative affect (such as high temperatures, unpleasant living conditions, and foul odors) will also increase the likelihood of anger responses to current threats, even when the unpleasant environmental condition is unrelated to the current threat. He argues that the conscious ascription of blame to the provocateur is not as essential as the experience of displeasure when the stimulus is presented.

It is only a short inferential leap to suggest that attributions of hostile intent and experiences of anger in response to current provocative stimuli are more likely if a child is growing up under circumstances of pervasive violence, harm, and deprivation: when provocateurs regularly assault the child; when assaults regularly occur toward the child's family, peers, and ethnic group; and when peer groups and family also interpret provocateurs as being hostile. These conditions characterize many environments of poverty and ethnic heterogeneity, and some subcultures (e.g., gangs). In such environments, hypervigilance to hostile cues and attributions of threat may occasionally be adaptive, and retaliatory aggression may be common.

Factors That Increase the Accessibility of Aggressive Responses

A second mechanism leading to aggressive responding is the accessing of aggressive responses from memory during interpersonal exchanges. Biological factors that define the species both afford certain aggressive behaviors and limit the range and rate of learning of aggressive strategies (Bandura, 1991). Ecological and environmental factors operate through two steps: (a) exposure to aggressive behavioral stimuli that place aggressive responses in one's repertoire; and (b) factors that increase the accessibility of aggressive responses that are already in one's repertoire.

Observational Learning

Bandura's classic studies (1973; Bandura, Ross, & Ross, 1963) indicate that "children can acquire entire repertoires of novel aggressive behavior from observing aggressive models and can retain such response patterns over extended periods" (Bandura, 1983, p. 6). Imitation is an evolved characteristic that is present even among neonates (Meltzoff & Moore, 1977). Aggressive models can be observed in a child's family members, community subculture, or mass media. Social learning theory (Bandura, 1977, 1983) articulates four processes by which modeling can activate aggressive behavior: (a) directive functions, through which an aggressive response enters a child's repertoire because of the positive consequences for aggressing that are vicariously taught; (b) disinhibitory functions, in which modeled aggression reduces fear of negative consequences; (c) emotional arousal, in which the aggressive model facilitates aggression by arousing observers; and (d) stimulus-enhancing effects, in which the objects used in aggression receive heightened attention and provide instruction for the aggressive use of these objects.

Aggressive models teach more than just specific behaviors. They teach general constructs and strategies for acting; when observers synthesize modeled behaviors into patterns that follow regularized sequences, those patterns form *scripts* that are laid down in memory (Collins, 1982; Huesmann, 1988). Information about the category of aggression, its elicitors, and its consequences constitutes aggressive *schemas* (Shank & Abelson, 1977); schemas guide attention and interpretation to future stimuli and can therefore enrich scripts for action. Through observation and experience, children develop an understanding of aggression that includes expectations for what produces aggression, how aggression is performed, elements of an aggression category (including emotions and actions), and the likely consequences of this behavior (Rule & Ferguson, 1986). Once having acquired an aggression script, when a child encounters difficult situations, that script governs expectations and prescribes behavioral strategies. Strongly developed scripts, acquired through observational learning, can lead to aggressive responding.

Huesmann (1988) suggested that aggression scripts are developed through active attention to aggressive models. Aggressive behaviors can be acquired through repeated exposure to multiple stimulating aggressive acts in diverse contexts displayed by models who are both heroes and identification figures for the observer, followed by opportunities to practice aggressing with impunity so that complex scripts for aggressing become part of a child's memorial repertoire for extraction in future situations. Living with a violent family or in a neighborhood in which the heroes are violent, interacting with antisocial peers who present repeated chances to act aggressively, and watching television violence all represent opportunities to learn aggressive scripts.

Priming of Aggressive Constructs

The extraction of aggressive scripts and specific aggressive responses from memory can occur either through active problem solving (Rubin & Krasnor, 1986) or nonconscious priming. Berkowitz (1993) suggests that certain stimuli induce an associative network of internal responses that he calls "the anger/aggression syndrome," which include physiological reactions, motor tendencies, feelings, thoughts, and memories. Higgins and King (1981) and Wyer and Srull (1989) have suggested that these responses are activated through an association in memory between a stimulus and one aspect of the response, which then spreads the activation to the entire syndrome through secondary associations. Priming effects are short-lived but powerful and automatic (Bargh, Chaiken, Raymond, & Hymes, in press). Wann and Branscombe (1990), for example, found that experimentally giving students the names of aggressive persons and sports increased the likelihood that the students would subsequently attribute hostile intent to an ambiguous target person. Herr (1986) found that a similar priming stimulus could lead students to behave in a hostile manner toward a partner in an unrelated task.

Many factors influence the probability that a particular stimulus will prime aggressive responses. Aggressive script responses that are laid down in memory with great frequency, drama, and recency are likely to be at the top of the "storage bin" and primed (Wyer & Srull, 1989); scripts that have multiple complex associations in memory are likely to be easily and chronically accessible (Bargh & Thein, 1985) because many stimuli can instigate associations to the script. Thus, growing up in an environment in which violence is normative will increase the accessibility of aggressive constructs in future situations. Certain persons who are nonreflective about their own behavior or are in impaired pathological states (Bargh, 1989) are "ripe" for priming effects. Stressful environments may render children vulnerable to aggressive priming. Finally, situational cues that are self-relevant (Strauman & Higgins, 1987) and not overly engrossing, but are aggression-related (such as easy access to weapons, Goldstein, 1994) or semantically related to one's ideographic aggressive schema (Carver, Ganellan, Froming, & Chambers, 1983) are likely to have priming effects.

Lack of Alternatives to Aggression

The likelihood that aggressive behavior is accessed from memory is only partly a function of its salience and priming potential; it is also a function of the salience and accessibility of alternatives to aggression. Thus, environments that fail to offer children competent and effective nonaggressive solutions to interpersonal dilemmas present risks for aggressive behavior by default (Rubin & Krasnor, 1986).

Factors That Enhance the Belief That Aggression Will Be Successful

Social learning theory stipulates that environments induce aggression not only by making aggressive responses accessible (through modeling) but also by promoting the belief that aggression is normative, morally appropriate, and will lead to desired positive consequences (through reinforcement, Bandura, 1991). According to Bandura (1983), "[In] societies that provide extensive training in aggression, attach prestige to it, and make its use functional, people spend a great deal of time threatening, fighting, maiming, and killing each other" (p. 11).

Direct and Vicarious Reinforcement

The most direct path to aggressive beliefs is one's own experience. Patterson et al. (1967) found that children who were victimized by peers and who occasionally succeeded in stopping those attacks through counteraggression became more likely to fight in the future; in contrast, those children who avoided peers and thus avoided victimization did not become aggressive over time. This analysis suggests that aggression "works" in children's peer culture: Environments that allow children to be exposed to aggression, to try out aggression, and to experience its positive instrumental consequences are likely to have children who develop aggressively. Of course, it is conceivable that environments might expose children to multiple trials of aggression that "fail," but few examples come to mind; the successful environments are ones that lack aggressive models and devalue aggressive conduct altogether (Mead, 1935).

Bandura (1991) suggests that reinforcement can take the form of tangible rewards, social and status rewards, reduction of aversive treatment, and expressions of injury by the victim. Just as powerful as direct reinforcement, according to Bandura (1991), is the observation of other persons being reinforced for aggressing. In this case, the person learns through vicarious means that aggression leads to desired consequences.

Rational Decision Making

Wilson and Herrnstein (1985) proposed that criminal behavior (and aggression more broadly) involves a rational decision in which the participant considers the expectation of benefits and their probabilities (e.g., peer approval, instrumental gain) versus the expectation of costs and their probabilities (e.g., legal punishment, parental disapproval). Crick and Dodge (1994) proposed that children may consider instrumental, interpersonal, intrapersonal, and moral outcomes in their evaluations. They may evaluate a possible behavior in terms of these outcomes, assign weights (estimates of value) to these categories, and perform mental arithmetic to decide on a behavioral response. Thus, environments that afford a positive cost/benefit ratio will show high rates of aggression. Clarke and Cornish (1983) conducted a rational decision analysis of youthful burglary and found that important deciding factors included whether a house was occupied, whether it had a burglar alarm or dog, and whether it reflected affluence. Not surprisingly, Becker (1974) concludes that offenders typically estimate the risk of being caught as very low (whether valid or not); thus, a rational analysis can still lead to risky (and ill-informed) behavior by some individuals.

As young children develop the ability to represent mentally the anticipated consequences of their behavior (usually, between ages 5 and 10; Werner, 1961), they become more skilled at deciding when to aggress. The rate of their aggression might not necessarily decrease, but their behavior will become more reasoned.

Normative Beliefs

Huesmann and Guerra (Guerra, Huesmann, & Hanish, 1995) have proposed that consensual social norms influence children's aggressive behavior. Children learn these norms through perception, identification with reference groups, and personal evaluation. Huesmann and Guerra assessed children's normative beliefs about the consequences of aggressing and found that the male culture more strongly endorses the use of aggression than does the female culture, and that normative endorsement increases across age during the school years. Thornberry (1987) has found that being a part of a gang can often overwhelm an adolescent with norms for expected aggression.

Moral Disengagement

Through socialization, most children learn self-restraints including anticipatory self-censuring and evaluations that aggression will be punished. These adaptive self-reactive patterns have been described in field studies by Bandura and Walters (1959) and in laboratory studies by Perry and Bussey (1977) as major mechanisms in the control of aggression. Bandura (1991) argues that otherwise moral children perform aggressive acts through processes that disengage the usual self-reactions from such conduct. Several processes can contribute to moral disengagement. Cognitive restructuring can involve justifying aggressive action on the grounds that it will lead to a higher moral end (e.g., self-respect). This restructuring involves the minimization of one's own moral violations by comparing them with more reprehensible acts. This minimizing is particularly easy when a child is growing up amidst truly flagrant inhumanities (e.g., child abuse, homicide, rape, discrimination). Euphemistic labeling (e.g., "trains," "get-back," "just teaching him a lesson," McCall, 1994) further minimizes the perceived seriousness of the act.

A second set of dissociative processes involves distorting the relation between actions and their effects. When aggressing with a group, individuals can diffuse their own responsibility for their actions or deflect responsibility elsewhere (e.g., to authority, as in Milgram's, 1974, obedience experiments, or to society more broadly for allowing the entire group to behave aggressively). A third set of disengagement processes operates on the perceptions of the victims. Dehumanization through labels ("cracker," "nigger") can lead to self-exoneration for inhumane acts. Modern urban life tends to foster such dehumanization processes as a result of high social mobility, anonymity, and the castelike categorization of persons into ingroup and outgroup members. Finally, aggressive actions commonly are justified by attributing blame for the action to the victim. Because most aggressive acts occur within a sequence of escalating interpersonal exchanges, aggressors often find it easy to select from the chain of events an act by the victim that "merits" aggressive retaliation. Studies by Bandura and Caprara (1995) demonstrate that measures of moral disengagement by children based on these concepts are linked to their rates of aggressive behavior and emotional irascibility.

Moral disengagement can occur quickly within a social exchange, but more frequently it evolves gradually through cultural influence and reinforcement for partial disengagement. Children learn across time whether disengagement is allowed, and they learn to disengage more quickly and with less apparent justification in environments that provide little opposition.

A Case of Pervasive Environmental Influence: The Effects of Television Violence

Perhaps no greater cultural influence on children's aggressive development can be found than the effects of viewing violence on television. Laboratory studies over the past quarter-century demonstrate that viewing televised aggressive models leads immediately to increased aggressive behavior, whether assessed by aggression toward "Bobo" dolls (Bandura et al., 1963) or toward peers (Björkqvist, 1985; Josephson, 1987). Laboratory effects also include increased aggressive cognition and higher systolic blood pressure (Bushman & Geen, 1990). Field studies repeatedly demonstrate significant, albeit modest, correlations between viewing of television violence and current aggressiveness, even when numerous confounding factors (such as parental supervision and socioeconomic status) are controlled (Comstock & Paik, 1991; Huesmann & Eron, 1986). The effect is fairly linear: The more a child watches TV violence, the more aggressive that child becomes.

Longitudinal studies indicate that the effects of repeated viewing of violence are even greater over long periods of time. Eron, Huesmann, Lefkowitz, and Walder (1972) began studying the entire third-grade population of Columbia County, New York—875 children—in 1960 and found that boys' television violence preferences at age 8, as assessed by their mothers, predicted aggressiveness at age 18 ($r = .31$). This finding held even when age 8 aggression and age 18 television violence viewing were controlled statistically. Continued follow-ups to age 30 showed that age 8 TV violence predicted self-reported aggression and seriousness of criminal arrests, even when social class, intelligence, parenting, age 8 aggression, and age 30 TV violence viewing all were controlled statistically (Huesmann, 1986). Huesmann and Eron (1986) attempted to replicate these findings in a cross-national longitudinal study of

1,683 6- to 8-year-old children in Australia, Finland, Israel (urban and kibbutz), Poland, and the United States. In all cultures except Australia and the Israeli kibbutz, the findings indicated that early TV violence viewing, controlling for earlier aggressiveness, incremented the prediction of aggressiveness three years later. Huesmann and Bachrach (1988) suggested that the absence of effects in the Israeli kibbutz culture was due to the low levels of TV violence available and a cultural norm that disparaged televised violence. Unlike the earlier study, this more recent study demonstrated that the effects of TV violence extended to girls as well as to boys.

Meta-analytic reviews of the most rigorous studies in the field (Comstock & Paik, 1991; Wood, Wong, & Chachere, 1991) indicate that the effects of TV violence are robust and account for about 10% of the variance in child aggression, which approximately equals the magnitude of effect of cigarette smoking on lung cancer. This finding appears to be one of the most rigorously tested and robust effects in all of developmental psychology.

Qualifications on the Effects of TV Violence

Several factors have been found to moderate the effects of viewing television violence on aggression. First, the effects hold more strongly for children than for adults (Huesmann & Miller, 1994), perhaps because the effects act more strongly on the individual's development of a repertoire than on the accessing of responses already in one's repertoire. Also, children's attention to the sensational aspects of TV violence is relatively great, and their comprehension of subtle moralities is limited, thereby increasing the impact (Collins, 1982). Second, the effect is larger when the lag in measurement between TV viewing and child aggression is greater, suggesting that effects cumulate across time (Huesmann, 1986).

Next, the effects of viewing television violence are greater if the child believes that the violence on television is real (Huesmann, Lagerspetz, & Eron, 1984), perhaps because perceived reality increases salience and the encoding of scripts (Huesmann, 1986). Likewise, the effects are greater if the child viewer identifies with the violent TV character, that is, believes that the character is like the self (Huesmann, Lagerspetz, & Eron, 1984). The family context in which TV violence is viewed is another qualifier, in that children who watch violence without parental supervision and in home contexts in which harsh discipline is utilized are subject to greater influence by TV violence (Singer & Singer, 1981).

The importance of these qualifiers is indicated by an experiment by Huesmann and colleagues (Huesmann, Eron, Klein, Brice, & Fischer, 1983). They randomly assigned 169 third graders who watched a great deal of violent TV to either an intervention designed to help children become immune to the effects of TV violence or to a placebo control group. The intervention consisted of attempts to get children to understand that violence on television is not real, that special effects created the impressions of violence, and that in real life most people use nonaggressive means to solve the problems depicted on television. In addition, the children were induced to create a film to show other children "who had been fooled by TV" as a way of getting these children to adopt nonviolent attitudes and to see TV violence as problematic. The intervention succeeded in changing children's attitudes, relative to the control group, and the intervention group subsequently received lower peer-nominated aggression scores than the control group.

The context in which violence is shown is also an important qualifier. Violence that is displayed by heroes, without negative consequences for the hero being clearly shown and with the violence being legitimized, will have stronger negative effects (Bandura, 1983). However, instances of TV violence that result in punishment can lead to increased aggression if they are shown repeatedly, apparently because of desensitization (Huesmann & Miller, 1994). Other qualifiers on the effects of TV violence, such as the child's initial level of aggression and differential effects for boys versus girls, have received less conclusive support (Huesmann & Miller, 1994; Rule & Ferguson, 1986).

How Does TV Violence Have Its Effect?

Huesmann (1986) has argued that a cumulative learning process is responsible for the effects of television violence on long-term outcomes, and that several different social learning effects are responsible. These effects are the result of televised violence, not television per se (Bandura, 1983). The first effect is that children learn new ways of aggressing by watching aggressive models, and more importantly, the strategies that they observe take on primary places in their memorial repertoires. Viewing hundreds of thousands of violent acts over a childhood period is likely to make these strategies highly accessible.

Second, TV violence weakens the child's restraints over aggression (Bandura, 1983). The excitement of violent acts is often intrinsically stimulating and reinforcing merely by observation. The consequences of violence depicted for the aggressor are rarely negative, at least immediately. Violent acts are displayed by heroes and are rationalized in the context of the story as "good triumphing over evil." The effect is to teach the child that aggression is an appropriate tool for people who think they are in the right. Third, children's beliefs about the consequences of violence are shaped by the observed consequences. Children who watch a great deal of TV violence are relatively likely to believe that aggression is justified, that victims deserve their fate, and that aggression is an appropriate strategy for heroes (Rule & Ferguson, 1986).

Fourth, TV violence desensitizes the observer, who habituates to its negative effects. Repeated viewing of violence results in less emotional responding over time (Cline, Croft, & Courrier, 1973), decreased skin potential and vasoconstriction (Björkqvist & Didrikkson, 1985), and greater tolerance for aggression (Rule & Ferguson, 1986). These effects stand in paradox to other findings that viewing TV violence arouses observers and increases emotional sensitivity; however, these latter effects may be obtained only by less frequent viewers (Rule & Ferguson, 1986). The long-term effect is to lessen emotional responsivity. An immediate effect, however, is to prime aggressive scripts from memory, thereby increasing their readiness for enactment as well as enriching the scripts themselves (Berkowitz, 1989; Huesmann, 1986). Huesmann (1986) points out that even though the long-term influence of TV violence is known to be greater for young children than for adults, the immediate cue-retrieval and priming functions hold for all humans and may even be greater for young adults who have richer scripts to be accessed.

Another effect of TV violence is to alter the observer's sense of reality. Frequent viewers of TV violence, compared with less frequent viewers, believe that real-world violence is more common, that the world is less safe, that group stereotypes are more valid, and that their chances of being victimized are greater (Gerbner & Gross, 1976). Finally, viewing TV violence leads children to fantasize about their own potential aggressive actions, especially if they identify with the aggressive character observed. Repeated fantasizing about aggressing is correlated, in turn, with actual aggressive behavior (Huesmann & Eron, 1986).

It appears that repeated viewing of television violence in the elementary school years leads to increased aggression later in life through processes of strategy acquisition, modification of perceived consequences for aggressing, decreased emotional responsivity, and the shaping of violent images of the world. In turn, viewing of TV violence in young adulthood serves to cue aggressive scripts from memory and to prime aggressive action.

Bidirectional Influences

Huesmann and Miller (1994) point out that initially aggressive children are the ones most likely to want to watch TV violence in the first place. This fact has led Freedman (1984) to argue that the effects of violence viewing are small, mostly artifactual, and explained by correlated third variables. However, the bulk of evidence (Huesmann, Eron, Berkowitz, & Chafee, 1991) suggests otherwise. The relation between TV violence viewing and aggression is clearly reciprocal and transactional over time. Seemingly small effects can have huge impact, especially for broad social factors (Abelson, 1981; Rosenthal, 1986). TV violence is but one component in aggressive development, although a powerful one.

THE STABILITY OF INDIVIDUAL DIFFERENCES IN AGGRESSION AND ANTISOCIAL BEHAVIOR

Over the past decade, scholars have increasingly turned their attention to the problem of individual differences in antisocial behavior. Evidence for the stability of individual differences in aggression and antisocial behavior has been the stimulus for a surgence of research on the factors contributing to that stability. The fact that some individuals consistently exhibit antisocial behaviors more than others calls for developmentally organized explanations. These continuities exist despite age-based differences in frequency and seriousness and despite society's efforts to constrain antisocial behavior. Does this stability persist for some people but not others? Are there predictable sequences of antisocial activity that characterize the consistently antisocial life course? These are some of the questions that are addressed in this section.

Stability of Aggression

In his well-known review of evidence for the stability of aggression, Olweus (1979) concluded that among males, individual differences in aggression rivaled the construct of intelligence for traitlike stability. This review of 16 longitudinal studies covering periods from 6 months to 21 years yielded stability correlations that decreased only moderately with the length of time interval covered. The regression line calculated on the basis of these 16 studies yielded stability coefficients ranging from .76 for a 1-year interval to .60 for a 10-year interval. The source of information on aggression employed in most of the 16 studies involved ratings of behavior by teachers or peers, although a few short-term stability estimates were based on direct observations. Olweus compared stability coefficients from these observational measures with those based on ratings and found similar levels of stability for each method, suggesting that the high stability in aggression is not merely an artifact of measurement source.

Stability estimates from studies more recent than those reviewed by Olweus reflect somewhat lower figures, but these figures are consistent with the idea that aggression is remarkably stable across time. Cairns, Cairns, Neckerman, Gest, and Gariepy (1988) found that teachers' ratings across an 8-year period resulted in a stability coefficient of .38, and Coie and Dodge (1983) reported that peer-based ratings across a 5-year period correlated at .49. Pulkkinen (1981) obtained a stability coefficient of .37 based on peer ratings of a Finnish sample followed from age 8 to age 14. Moskowitz, Schwartzman, and Ledingham (1985) also employed peer ratings in their 3-year follow-up of first, fourth, and seventh graders. Stability correlations ranged from .45 to .69 with older cohorts having higher stability. Each of these studies included both boys and girls and followed them across at least one significant school transition in which the peer group changed substantially, thus ruling out the likelihood that these results could be attributed primarily to group bias and stereotyping effects.

The most extensive longitudinal study of individual aggressiveness covered a span of 22 years, from age 8 to age 30 (Huesmann, Eron, et al., 1984). Peer ratings were used for the original assessments, as were those at age 18, at which point the male stability correlation was .38. At age 30, self-ratings of physical aggression on 193 males correlated significantly ($r = .25$) with the age 8 peer ratings. (Childhood aggression ratings had similar correlations to adult criminal offending.) Aggression ratings by wives ($n = 88$) also were significantly correlated ($r = .27$) with the age 8 peer ratings. These same correlations were not significant for the female sample, although self-ratings of punishment toward their children and MMPI scores were significantly correlated with age 8 aggression ratings, as was the case for males.

For the most part, when separate stability analyses have been conducted for males and females, equivalent levels of stability generally have been found. Olweus (1981) reviewed six studies in which the average estimate was .50 for males and .44 for females. Comparable stability for males and females was reported by Cairns and Cairns (1994), Pulkkinen (1981), and Moskowitz et al. (1985). Thus, even though males consistently display more physical and serious forms of aggression, whereas females tend to use more indirect forms of aggression (Lagerspetz & Björkqvist, 1994), the consensus now seems to be that aggression is a characteristic that is stable for both males and females.

Stability of Antisocial Behavior

Because specific forms of antisocial behavior change across contexts and age, researchers have searched for continuity at the broader level of the antisocial construct. Studies of early child behavior problems show convincing evidence of continuity between disobedience and defiance of adults, aggression toward peers, impulsivity and hyperactivity at age 3 or so, and similar or more serious behavior problems in later childhood. Richman, Stevenson, and Graham (1982) reported that 62% of the 3-year-olds exhibiting discipline and impulsivity problems at that age continued to show these problems, as well as peer problems, at age 8. Campbell (1987) found moderate stability of behavior problems from age 3 to age 6; furthermore, 67% of those who showed significant problems at age 6 met the *DSM-III* criteria for conduct problems at age 9 (Campbell & Ewing, 1990). A growing literature on early childhood behavior problems suggests a high degree of continuity of problems from preschool into the school years (e.g., Fischer, Rolf, Hasazi, & Cummings, 1984; McGee, Silva, & Williams, 1984). Among boys, Keenan, Shaw, Giovanelli, Greenstein, and Delliquadri (1995) have traced a developmental sequence of noncompliance at 18 months to aggression at 2 years to more generalized externalizing problems at 5 years.

Loeber and his colleagues have proposed a developmental pathway for chronic offenders that begins with hyperactivity and oppositional behavior in the preschool years, followed by aggressive behavior in the early school years, and then to more varied forms of delinquency in preadolescence and adolescence (Loeber, 1988b). Findings from the Pittsburgh Youth Study indicate that the aggressive/versatile pathway is the most common developmental sequence for serious and chronic adolescent offenders. Those children who are both overtly aggressive and engage in covert acts of delinquency typify the highest risk group (Loeber & Schmaling, 1985b). Prospective and retrospective data describing the age of onset for various antisocial acts provide some support for this framework (Loeber, Wung, Keenan, Giroux, Stouthamer-Loeber, Van Kammen, & Maughan 1993). In contrast to the idea that disruptive behavior is a heterogeneous category with development that follows a single pathway of increasing severity (Jessor et al., 1991; Jessor & Jessor, 1977), Loeber and his colleagues have identified three pathways for which stepwise sequences of increasing severity in antisocial behavior seem to hold. Authority conflict moves from initial stubbornness to defiance to authority avoidance (truancy, running away). Covert behaviors escalate from lying and shoplifting to property damage (fire setting) and then to such delinquent acts as stealing cars, selling drugs, and breaking and entering. The overt pathway begins with bullying or annoying others and progresses to physical fighting and then to violent acts (e.g., attacking someone, forced sex). Of those boys who entered any step of these sequences, the majority fit the hypothesized pathways, with most boys entering the overt and covert paths at the first step. Boys who escalated along the overt pathway also tended to escalate along the covert pathway, although the converse was not true. Finally, boys whose antisocial activity followed the overt pathway and at least one other pathway were the ones most apt to have court records for violent offending, although combinations involving covert offending were associated with more general self-reported delinquency (Loeber et al., 1993). The involvement of individuals in more than one pathway may be the key to more serious offending in later life.

These findings not only support the hypothesis that early antisocial behavior predicts later antisocial behavior, but also provide a more specific illustration of two more general points made by Robins (1966, 1978) about the relation between childhood conduct problems and adult antisocial behavior. Robins concluded that it was rare to find an antisocial adult who had not shown a pattern of conduct problems as a child and, second, that less than half of the children who displayed conduct problems would go on to become antisocial adults. One reason for the latter conclusion is that many behavior problems, such as oppositional behavior among toddlers or minor forms of delinquency in adolescence, are almost normative and describe a large portion of these age groups.

In general for males, the earlier the age of onset of conduct problems, the greater the likelihood of continuing antisocial behavior in later life (Farrington, Loeber, & Van Kammen, 1990). This point is supported by a large number of longitudinal studies that link aggression and conduct problems in middle childhood (ages 8–10) to delinquency and antisocial behavior in adolescence and adulthood (Coie, Terry, Lenox, Lochman, & Hyman, 1995; Eron, Huesmann, Dubow, Romanoff, & Yarmel, 1987; Haapasalo

& Tremblay, 1994; Patterson, 1993; Pulkkinen, 1982; Roff & Wirt, 1984; Stattin & Magnusson, 1989; Thornberry, Wolfgang, & Figlio, 1987; Viemero, 1992; West & Farrington, 1973). Reviewing seven longitudinal studies of males, Stouthamer-Loeber and Loeber (1989) concluded that the mean relative improvement over chance in predicting delinquency from childhood aggression averaged about 33%. Patterson, Crosby, and Vuchinich (1992), using structured multiple regression analyses, found that a childhood antisocial trait, together with social disadvantage (i.e., family stress), could account for 30% of the variance in predicting age of first arrest. Furthermore, Patterson and Yoerger (1993) estimate a correlation of .74 between the age of first arrest and a pattern of chronic offending in their Oregon Youth Study sample of 200 males. Finally, in a study of a large New Zealand birth cohort, White, Moffitt, Earls, Robins, and Silva (1990) were able to classify 66% of the sample who became delinquent by age 15, on the basis of preschool behavior. Having preschool behavior problems was the strongest predictor of subsequent delinquency and worked equally well for girls and boys, a conclusion also reached by Stouthamer-Loeber and Loeber.

These impressive findings on the continuity of antisocial behavior also can be interpreted as indicating that most children discontinue their antisocial behavior as they grow older (Robins, 1978), even though a substantial number continue in this deviant pathway. This seeming paradox of continuity and desistance has been resolved by several theorists as evidence of different life course patterns of antisocial activity. One pattern is the early-starting pathway (Moffitt, 1993a; Patterson, Capaldi, & Bank, 1991).

In the Patterson et al. (1991) early-starter model, early family interactions are seen as having the central role in promoting antisocial development. Parents inadvertently reinforce antisocial behaviors and fail to punish them. The consistency of these discipline failures and the deficits in social skills that result for the child leave early starting antisocial youth with few resources for adapting to conventional social life. As these children's behaviors become increasingly coercive, parental control diminishes still further and the children avoid the demands of school and begin to explore an increasing variety of antisocial acts (Patterson, 1995). Moffitt (1993a) assigned primary causality to neuropsychological deficits that are associated with attention problems and hyperactivity in childhood. The impulsivity and irritability of these children make it difficult for their parents to manage them, particularly because many of the parents share their child's temperament. The problematic parent-child interactions that evolve are part of what Caspi and Bem (1990) refer to as cumulative continuity, the sustaining of children's antisocial behavior by the reactions of parents to their children's difficult behaviors. Cumulative consequences have a self-perpetuating impact above and beyond that produced by the stability of traits such as impulsivity. Like Patterson, Moffitt believes that these "life-course-persistent" antisocial children have little opportunity to acquire prosocial abilities and wind up being ensnared by the consequences of their antisocial behavior.

A second pattern of antisocial behavior is displayed by a late-starter group (Patterson et al., 1991). Moffitt (1993a) refers to this group as the adolescence-limited type because her assumption is that this group accounts for the discontinuity between juvenile delinquency and adult criminality. The delinquency of this group begins in adolescence in response to the gap between emerging biological maturity and adult constraints on adolescents' autonomy. In her longitudinal analyses of the New Zealand sample, Moffitt (1990) found that 32% of previously nondelinquent boys had become delinquent between ages 11 and 15. Unlike the life-course-persistent group to whom Moffitt ascribes a certain element of psychopathology, the delinquency of the adolescence-limited group is viewed as an exaggeration of age-normative trends in response to the social circumstances of adolescence.

Comorbidity Issues

An epidemiological study of Ontario youth from age 4 to 16 provides some support for Moffitt's contention about psychopathology and the two paths to adolescent delinquency. Offord, Boyle, and Racine (1991) found high comorbidity between diagnoses of conduct disorder and other diagnoses in the 4- to 11-year-old sample. Almost 60% had a diagnosis of hyperactivity. However, comorbidity was much less frequent among the 12- to 16-year-old group, particularly for the males. Comorbidity for hyperactivity was approximately half as common in the older group. Females showed greater comorbidity between emotional disorders and conduct disorders than males (Offord et al., 1991), whereas Rutter et al. (1970) found similar rates of comorbidity for males and females in their Isle of Wight study. These patterns are what Moffitt would predict at adolescence with the influx of newly delinquent youth whose violations are not connected to more pervasive disorder. In a longitudinal study of urban African American adolescents (Coie, Terry, Lenox, et al., 1995), those youth who were aggressive and rejected by peers as 8-year-olds (fitting the life-course-persistent profile) had consistently high rates of antisocial activity and psychological problems such as depression and anxiety throughout the adolescent period.

Biederman, Newcorn, and Sprich (1991) also found strong comorbidity for conduct disorder and attention deficit/hyperactivity disorder, which is not surprising because childhood hyperactivity is itself highly predictive of adolescent and adult antisocial behavior (Farrington et al., 1990; Magnusson, 1987). The constellation of variables such as hyperactivity, inattention, and impulsivity is at least partially independent of the conduct disorder category, having different family history correlates and heritability estimates (Hinshaw, 1994), and hyperactivity adds to the predictability of adolescent and adult offending obtained by childhood aggression. Nonetheless, in predicting persistence of antisocial behavior from other childhood factors, impulsivity and hyperactivity are significant factors representing a consistent lifestyle of problems in self-control (Pulkkinen, 1986, 1988). Children who are comorbid for attention deficits/hyperactivity have the earliest onset of conduct disorder and exhibit greater physical aggression and persistence of antisocial behavior (Hinshaw, Lahey, & Hart, 1993).

The substantial comorbidity of conduct disorder and anxiety or depression found in epidemiological studies of adolescents and adults (Zoccolillo, 1992) raises the question of direction of influence between serious antisocial behavior and emotional problems. Kovacs, Paulauskas, Gatsonis, and Richards (1988) found that 16% of depressed children also had conduct disorder at the point of first diagnosis that usually seemed to be a consequence of the depression. Similarly, Puig-Antich (1982) found that conduct disorder symptoms occurred at the same time or later than depressive symptoms. In the Kovacs et al. study, however, which was longitudinal, conduct problems did not usually disappear when depression went into remission. Loeber, Stouthamer-Loeber, Van Kammen, and Farrington (1991) also found depression to be predictive of the onset of antisocial activity in the preadolescent cohort of the Pittsburgh Youth Study. In a 4-year longitudinal study of anxiety and conduct disorder, Lahey and McBurnett (reported in Hinshaw et al., 1993) found that boys with comorbid conduct disorders and anxiety were less aggressive during the 9- to 10-year-old period than boys with only conduct disorder, but were more aggressive during the following 2 years. These results suggest a

delayed impact of emotional problems on antisocial behavior, although more complex developmental processes may be involved.

DETERMINANTS OF INDIVIDUAL DIFFERENCES IN ANTISOCIAL BEHAVIOR

The preceding section provided substantial evidence for the stability of aggressive and antisocial behavior across the life course. The same data also demonstrated that there is considerable individual variation in antisocial activity across time and settings. In this section we examine a series of factors that seem to be influential in determining initial involvement in the antisocial path, as well as factors that influence persistence in or desistance from this pathway. The section is organized from a life-course perspective, taking into account as much as possible the particular relevance of certain factors to different developmental segments of the life course. In noting the evidence for discontinuity, as well as continuity, in crime across the life course, Sampson and Laub (1992) have argued that both discontinuity and continuity can be explained by sociological influences. Sampson and Laub argue that factors in adult development and changes in informal social control help to explain changes in adult criminal offending. This same point can be extended to factors in child and adolescent development. Caspi (1987) contends that antisocial children continue to behave antisocially in adolescence and adulthood not only as a matter of trait stability but also because of the impact that their antisocial behavior has on a succession of environmental factors. The converse, then, can also be argued, namely that discontinuity may be explained by environmental factors that support prosocial development. An examination of factors whose presence or absence relates to persistence or desistance of antisocial behavior will be a major consideration in this section.

Heritability

Perhaps no aspect of the study of human aggression has been more divisive and controversial than the question of heritability. It is an obvious but trivial assertion that all violent behavior (indeed, all behavior) begins with an individual's genetic endowment. Genes account for species-specific patterns of human aggressive behavior as well as differences between humans and other species. However, most behavior-genetic theories and studies are concerned with understanding individual differences within the human species. Humans share over 99% of their genes with each other by virtue of being human beings (Britten, 1986), so genetic theories of individual differences postulate that variations in the remaining 1% of genes account for vast differences in aggressive behavior across humans. Still, the evidence from some of these studies is indeed consistent with this hypothesis (see Carey, 1994; Gottesman & Goldsmith, 1994; and Raine, 1993, for excellent reviews).

Methodological Issues

Even though the concern of behavior-genetic studies is with explaining an individual's development, these studies yield estimates of the genetic contribution at the population, not individual, level. That is, it is never possible to use behavior-genetic information that a particular trait is heritable to conclude that the behavior of a particular individual or group is due to genetic, versus environmental, causes.

Likewise, the estimate of the magnitude of the genetic contribution to aggressive behavior is fully a function of the range in genetic and environmental characteristics of a population. That is, because the magnitude estimates are apportioned reciprocally between genetic and environmental influences; a population for which environmental influences are relatively small (perhaps due to little cross-person variation in these factors) will necessarily demonstrate relatively strong genetic influence and vice versa. For example, in a population where almost all children are raised in similar secure and nonharsh circumstance, the estimated environmental influence will be small and the genetic influence will be estimated to be large. Carey (1994) notes that this description characterizes pre-1960 Sweden and Denmark, where most behavior-genetic data on aggression have been collected, and it especially characterizes the adoptive families of many studies because public policies often require adoptive parents to pass screening on criminal history and discipline practice. "One could argue that (the) relative cultural and socioeconomic homogeneity (of Scandinavian samples) would provide a ripe medium for maximizing genetic effects" (Carey, 1994, p. 45). Thus, the estimate of the magnitude of genetic, versus environmental, loading for aggression in any particular study will vary greatly according to fluctuations in the genetic and environmental parameters of the population and should not be generalized to any other population.

The most common methods for examining behavior-genetic effects have been twin studies and adoption studies (Carey, 1994; Raine, 1993). In the former, the similarity in behavior of identical twins (monozygotic, MZ; sharing 100% of genes) is contrasted with the similarity of fraternal twins (dyzogotic, DZ; sharing about 99.5% of genes or half of the nonspecies-specific genes) (Raine, 1993). Assuming identical environmental treatment for both types of twins (a controversial assumption), one can conclude that higher concordance in behavior for MZ than DZ twins implies heritability. Adoption studies overcome the assumption of identical treatment. In these studies, offspring who have been reared apart from their biological parents are matched in behavior scores to their biological, as well as adoptive, parents. Concordance between biological parent-offspring pairs is assumed to be evidence for heritability.

Unlike Mendelian characteristics such as eye color, aggressive behavior is not inherited directly. Rather, one might inherit a *liability* for aggressive behavior, which is a hypothetical latent factor of probabilistic risk (Carey, 1994). Furthermore, most theorists now eschew the notion of an aggressive gene. "Notions such as 'genes for crime' are nonsense" (Gottesman & Goldsmith, 1994, p. 72). Genes code for proteins and enzymes, which can influence physiological processes that, in turn, can instigate environmental processes that affect behavior, including aggressive behavior (Raine, 1993). Thus, it is hypothesized that what may be inherited are biological genotypes that influence physiological phenotypes such as steroid hormones and their receptors, neurotransmitter levels, and central nervous system reactivity (Gottesman & Goldsmith, 1994). In turn, these physiological characteristics may predispose one toward behavioral characteristics and cognitive styles such as impulse control, the need for stimulation, activity level, anxiety processes, and frustration tolerance levels. Depending on environmental context, these behavioral and cognitive characteristics might lead to aggressive behavior or to a more socially acceptable outcome such as politics or corporate leadership. Thus, the most likely genetic pathways for aggression involve gene-environment interactions (Raine, 1993).

Heritable characteristics related to aggression are most likely transmitted through polygenetic paths, rather than Mendelian single-gene effects. The fact that multiple and different genes may be implicated in aggressive behavior (a principle called genetic heterogeneity, Gottesman & Goldsmith, 1994) and the same genes may lead to both aggressive and nonaggressive behaviors (a principle called pleiotropy) renders the genetic analysis of behavior "a daunting task" (Gottesman & Goldsmith, 1994, p. 72).

Chromosomal Disorders

The hypothesis that chromosomal disorders are responsible for aggressive behavior has received a great deal of attention, especially regarding the XYY syndrome. According to Carey's (1994) review, this hypothesis has proven not to account for a large proportion of aggressive behavior problems, because these disorders are rare and the effects are rather small (for a possible exception, see Brunner, Nelen, Breakfield, Ropers, & Van Oost, 1993, who identified a single pedigree with X-linked transmission of a syndrome of mental retardation and aggressive behavioral disturbance).

Behavior-Genetic Studies

Even with these caveats, evidence has mounted that genetic factors are a necessary part of any comprehensive theory of individual differences in aggressive development. The role played by genes varies, however, across development and across measures of aggressive behavior. For example, the MZ and DZ twin similarity in laboratory-assessed emotionality (e.g., irritability, reactivity, negative affectivity) in the Louisville Twin Study was nearly identical at the neonatal stage of development (Riese, 1990), indicating no heritable contribution, but MZ twin similarity became significantly greater than DZ twin similarity by nine months of age and continued to be greater over time (Matheny, 1989), indicating moderate heritability of negative emotional behavior. These findings run counter to the mistaken assumption that genetic influences are greatest at birth. Dynamic analyses reveal different genetic influence patterns across life. For example, Goldsmith and McArdle's structural modeling analyses (cited in Gottesman & Goldsmith, 1994) indicate that genetic influences in reactivity increase from age 4 to 7, whereas genetic influences in persistence are captured fully by age 4. Both in toddlerhood (Goldsmith, 1993) and childhood (Goldsmith, Jaco, & Elliott, 1986), parent-reported indices of temperament among MZ and DZ twins reveal "moderate" heritability (Gottesman & Goldsmith, 1994).

Twin studies of childhood externalizing problems using parents' reports on Achenbach's Child Behavior Checklist (CBCL) reveal higher intraclass correlations for MZ than DZ twins among 3- to 7-year-olds (Aggression Scale rs of .78 versus .31, Ghodsian-Carpey & Baker, 1987) and among older ($M = 11$ years) children (CBCL Delinquent Scale rs of .72 vs. .55 and Aggression Scale rs of .75 vs. .45, Edelbrock, Rende, Plomin, & Thompson, 1992). Similar results have been found in the Netherlands, with moderate genetic effects on the CBCL Aggression Scale among 3-year-old twins (Van Den Oord, Verhulst, & Boomsma, 1992) as well as older adoptees (Van Den Oord, Boomsma, & Verhulst, 1992). There is no known twin proband study of psychiatrically diagnosed conduct disorder (Gottesman & Goldsmith, 1994), but Eaves et al. (1993) have reported greater MZ than DZ concordance for latent classes of conduct disorder symptoms.

In contrast, both twin and adoption studies reveal relatively little evidence for the heritability of adjudicated juvenile delinquency (see reviews by Carey, 1994; Raine, 1993; Rutter, Boltin, et al., 1990). Interestingly, Rowe (1985) reported a heritability estimate of .34 for *self-reported* delinquent behavior among 265 twin pairs. Raine (1993) concluded that "antisocial behavior is not heritable when legally defined in adolescence, but is heritable when adolescent antisociality is measured by self-report measures or when childhood behavior is assessed by mothers" (p. 75).

Vulnerability to adult nonviolent crime appears more clearly to be heritable. Raine's (1993) review of 10 twin studies covering samples from diverse countries (e.g., United States, Japan, Denmark, England, Germany) indicates substantial heritability, with MZ twins about twice as likely to be concordant as DZ twins. Christiansen (1977), found a heritability estimate of .54 in a sample of over 3,000 Danish twin pairs. Fourteen of the 15 known adoption studies reveal heritability as well, although with much lower estimates (Raine, 1993). Cadoret (1978) used multiple regression analyses to find that only 3% of the variance in crime is due to genetic factors. Major possible reasons for the discrepancy between twin and adoption studies in estimated magnitude of genetic influence include likely imitation of behavior between twins (Carey, 1992) and the tendency in twin studies to report how much of the *explained* variance is due to genetic (vs. environmental) factors, in contrast to the tendency in adoption studies to report how much of the *total* variance is due to genetic factors (Raine, 1993).

Unlike the supportive evidence for heritability of nonviolent crime, all three known adoption studies of violent crime have found nonsignificant heritability estimates (Bohman, Cloninger, Sigvardsson, & von Knoring, 1982; Mednick, Gabrielli, & Hutchings, 1984; Sigvardsson, Cloninger, Bohman, & von Knoring, 1982). These findings run counter to the mistaken hypothesis that more serious and violent offending would be genetically driven and property crime would be socially driven (Raine, 1993).

The heritability of *DSM*-diagnosed psychopathy and antisocial personality disorder has not yet been adequately studied. Some studies have confounded property crime or alcoholism with criteria for psychopathy (Raine, 1993). Grove, Eckert, Heston, Bouchard, Segal, and Lykken (1990) used *DSM-III* criteria to create a dimensional score for the number of antisocial personality characteristics and found a modest heritability estimate of .28 in their sample of MZ twins reared apart. Lyons et al. (1993) found moderate heritability of antisocial personality symptoms in adults but less heritability (and stronger environment influence) in adolescents. Carey's (1994) review of twin and adoption studies of aggressive personality characteristics, as assessed by aggression scales such as the one in the Minnesota Multiphasic Personality Questionnaire, indicate a pooled correlation of .40 for MZ twins and .18 for DZ twins, indicating a heritability estimate of .44.

Gene-Environment Interaction Effects

Intriguing findings from a study of 862 Swedish male adoptees suggest an interaction between heredity and environment (Cloninger, Sigvardsson, Bohman, & van Knoring, 1982). Of adoptees with both biological and adoptive parents who were criminal, 40% were arrested for a nonalcohol-related petty crime. For adoptees with a criminal biological parent but noncriminal adoptive parents, the rate was 12%, 7% for adoptees with a criminal adoptive parent but noncriminal biological parent, and 3% for adoptees with neither criminal biological parents nor criminal adoptive parents. A similar interaction effect, with lower base rates, has been found for female adoptees (Cloninger & Gottesman, 1987).

Conclusions

Individual genetic differences likely play a role in physiological characteristics such as impulsivity and tendency to addiction, and through interaction with environmental characteristics these physiological features may lead to individual differences in behavioral tendencies such as negative emotionality and property crime; however, the link between genes and physical aggression in adulthood has not been made. A second conclusion is adapted from the point by Carey (1994, p. 44) that the genetic literature on antisocial behavior to date cannot be generalized to the problem of urban violence in the United States, because rapid secular changes in rates of violence and major differences in both environmental and genetic characteristics between this U.S. population and every behavior-genetic sample ever studied renders this generalization invalid. A final conclusion is also adapted from Carey: Because behavior-genetic studies are exclusively concerned with within-group variation in behavior, none of this literature has any implication for understanding differences between groups, especially between race groups. "At the very least, there is no positive evidence to suggest that heritability plays an important role in group differences in violence within the United States" (Carey, 1994, p. 50).

Dispositional Factors

Since the introduction of the concept of difficult temperament by Thomas et al. in 1968, individual differences in several dimensions of infant temperament, such as fussiness, difficultness, unadaptability, resistance to control, and latency to calming (Bates, Freeland, & Lounsbury, 1979; Goldsmith et al., 1987) have been considered "early emerging personality traits" (Buss & Plomin, 1984). Bates found that mothers' ratings of infant temperament as early as age 6 months significantly predict mothers' ratings of child conduct problems at age 3 years (Bates, Maslin, & Frankel, 1985) and, to a lesser degree, mothers' CBCL Externalizing Scores at ages 7 to 8 years (Bates, Bayles, Bennett, Ridge, & Brown, 1991). Bates et al. (1991) concluded that the earliest signs of dispositional behavior problems are evident by age 6 months, but plasticity is great at this young age. Long-term outcomes may result from an interaction between early difficult temperament and parenting quality. Coon, Carey, Corley, and Fulker (1992) found that among "difficult-temperament" young children, only those with conjoint maladaptive parenting were at risk for later conduct-disordered behavior.

Campbell and Ewing (1990) found that "hard to manage" preschoolers were at risk for externalizing problems at age 9. Longitudinal analyses of the 1,037 subjects of the Dunedin (New Zealand) Multidisciplinary Health and Development Study revealed significant, but low, correlations between experimenter ratings of Lack of Control at ages 3 to 5 years and parent and teacher ratings of antisocial behavior at ages 9 to 11 (mean $r = .25$ for boys and .15 for girls) and ratings of conduct disorder at ages 13 to 15 (mean $r = .16$ for boys and .12 for girls; Caspi, Henry, McGee, Moffitt, & Silva, 1995). By age 18, a group that had been temperamentally "undercontrolled" at age 3 did not differ significantly from a group that had been rated as "well adjusted" at age 3 on self-reports of Aggression, although the groups did differ significantly in self-reported Constraint and Negative Emotionality (Caspi & Silva, 1995). It appears that the temperament construct of lack of control may be stable over time (just as aggressive behavior is stable) but does not necessarily predict aggressive behavior.

In general, ratings of infant temperament have weak long-term predictive value. Not until the toddler years are they stronger predictors of conduct problems making it difficult to attribute a biologically based dispositional role to temperament. A further limitation of much of the temperament literature is that empirical ratings are produced solely by mothers, whose own role in the early developmental process may be quite significant. Nonetheless, emerging developmental theories of antisocial behavior emphasize the early onset of conduct problems in the form of difficult-to-manage temperament in the preschool years (Hinshaw, 1994). Difficult children both shape and respond to their environmental circumstances, so that moderation and mediation effects by the environment qualify estimates of temperament stability.

Psychobiological Influences

Some of the most significant discoveries in the study of antisocial behavior over the past 20 years have taken place in the area of human biological processes. Current research on the biological determinants of aggression and antisocial behavior is focused primarily on androgens, neurotransmitters, and autonomic nervous system functioning. Very little research has related these three approaches, although the conceptual models invoked in each domain have significant commonalities. Research on the effects of toxins and neurological damage will be described in this context.

Sex Hormones

Differences in circulating testosterone levels frequently are cited in explanations of age and sex differences in human aggressive behavior. The parallel between sexual development at puberty and the increased frequency of aggression and antisocial activity in adolescence provides a compelling basis for this argument, as does the greater propensity for aggressive behavior and delinquency among males compared with females. These parallels, involving the apparent role of hormonal factors, have led to the search for explanations of more general individual

differences in aggression in circulating levels of testosterone and other androgens, although individual differences in aggression occur long before puberty. Hormones are considered to have two possible major influences on aggression. In the perinatal period, the presence of sex hormones may sensitize the central nervous system to be differentially responsive to these hormones at later times in life. This hypothesis assumes a critical period in human neural development in which testosterone plays an *organizing* role that has long-term consequences for aggressive behavior. This is true for a wide range of nonhuman species (Brain, 1994). Second, sex hormones also may play an *activating* role in aggressive behavior, as often happens during pubertal development for many species, although Brain (1994) cautions that these hormone-behavior linkages are complex and that "it would not be surprising if all hormones alter some aspect of aggression in a particular species or a specific situation" (p. 193).

There is substantial evidence for a relation between adult aggressiveness and individual levels of testosterone. Archer's (1991) meta-analysis of studies comparing prisoners of high or low aggressiveness represents a test of the activational influence of hormones and has yielded effect sizes in the moderate to strong range. The large sample study ($n = 4,462$) of U.S. military veterans by Dabbs and Morris (1990) is an activation study. These authors compared adult males whose testosterone levels placed them in the upper 10% of the distribution with the remainder of the sample. The high testosterone group self-reported more trouble with parents, teachers, and classmates, more assaultive behavior toward others, greater use of hard drugs and alcohol, and a greater number of sexual partners than the normal testosterone group. They also had records of more frequent AWOL attempts. The relation between testosterone and problem behavior, however, was much weaker for higher socioeconomic status males than for the lower SES males.

Similar investigations with adolescent samples have yielded mixed results, although there is some support for a positive correlation between levels of testosterone and aggression. Olweus et al. (1988) found a significant correlation ($r = .44$) among 58 normal adolescent Swedish males between plasma testosterone and self-reported aggression, primarily in response to provocation. Susman et al. (1987) also found a significant relation between hormonal levels and aggressive or delinquent behavior as reported by mothers of a sample of adolescent males; however, no relation was found for females. On the other hand, Halpern, Udry,

Campbell, and Suchindraw (1994) failed to replicate the Olweus et al. findings in a study of 82 U.S. adolescent males; nor did they find evidence of a relation between pubertal increases in testosterone and increases in aggressive behavior. In contrast to the Susman et al. results, Inoff-Germain et al. (1988) did not find a significant relation between hormonal levels and directly observed angry or defiant behavior of boys (ages 9–14) toward other family members. They did find a significant relation for girls, however. This inconsistent pattern of results is characteristic of the literature on the concurrent relation between testosterone and aggression in juvenile populations.

Effects of Aggression on Hormonal Levels

The evidence supporting a correlation between aggression and testosterone does not resolve the question of the direction of effect involved, although the dominant assumption is that hormones influence behavior. Archer (1988) has reviewed animal studies relating to this question and concluded that dominance or success in conflict often results in increased levels of testosterone. There is some research among humans that would support a similar conclusion. Salvador, Simon, Suay, and Llorens (1987) studied male judo competitors and found that testosterone levels were positively related to success in competition. Other evidence for the effects of prior competitive experience on testosterone comes from a series of laboratory studies of winners and losers in staged (and rigged) competitions. Gladue, Boechler, and McCaul (1989) found that winners in a reaction-time competition had elevated testosterone levels after the competition, but losers maintained their original levels. Similar results were obtained even when the contest simply involved coin-tossing (McCaul, Gladue, & Joppa, 1992). Mazur and Lamb (1980), by contrast, did not find testosterone differences between winners and losers in an experimental lottery; nor did they find differences between winners and losers of a closely contested tennis match. They only found differences when the results of these matches were decisive.

These findings suggest that experiences of competitive success, not necessarily involving physical combat or aggression, can lead to increased levels of testosterone. This conclusion must be balanced against evidence, albeit mixed and lacking some critical methodological controls, that the experimental or clinical manipulation of testosterone levels also can lead to subsequent changes in levels of aggressive behavior (Archer, 1994). Thus, the pattern of influence appears to be reciprocal, at least in a limited

temporal framework. How this reciprocity influences the long-term developmental picture is still a matter of conjecture, although a study by Schaal, Tremblay, Soussignan, and Susman (1995) provides indications. Their study of testosterone levels among 13-year-old boys whose aggressive behavior and peer status had been assessed continually for the previous 7 years reveals that testosterone is more closely linked to social dominance than to aggression. Those boys rated by newly acquainted peers as both tough and social leaders had the highest testosterone levels, even though they were not rated by everyday peers and teachers as being high on physical aggression. Boys rated as tough, but not leaders, had testosterone levels no greater than the nontough boys, even though the tough nonleaders were rated highest in physical aggression by peers and teachers. In fact, boys who had been highly aggressive from ages 6 through 12 had the lowest testosterone levels at age 13, compared with boys who were consistently low on fighting in elementary school. The authors explain earlier findings linking testosterone to responses to provocation (Olweus et al., 1988) as a consequence of dominant, tough boys being more apt to respond to provocation by lower status peers.

In reviewing the literature on sex hormones and aggression, Archer (1994) provides a compelling interactionist theory of the role of hormones in the development of individual differences in human aggressiveness. First, Archer argues that the organizing effect of androgens on the central nervous system takes place after birth in humans. If this is true, he argues that questions can be raised about the developmental relevance of earlier studies of the effects of synthetic progestins administered during gestation. Furthermore, because there is some evidence of a relation between testosterone levels and aggression among both boys and girls during childhood (Dabbs, 1992), Archer challenges the possibility of an organizing effect of androgens on human aggressiveness. Instead, he would agree with Maccoby (1988) that early gender differences in social behavior may be due to perinatal androgen influences on activity levels and consequent gender group play preferences. This process leads to different gender-based subcultures in which physical aggressiveness may play a more functional role for boys because of their involvement in more physical games and in larger play groups. These differences in gender subculture are influenced further by societal factors and interact with individual differences in temperament to determine children's disposition to use aggression, particularly when provoked. A potential biological influence on this process is the heritability of testosterone baseline levels. At puberty, established patterns of aggressive behavior will interact with rising levels of testosterone to influence behavior. This behavior and its consequences will affect future levels of testosterone, as a result of the influence that dominance and successful aggression can have on individual testosterone levels. Archer argues, it thus becomes difficult to separate cause and effect in the relation between testosterone and aggression.

Aggression and Neurotransmitters

The role of neurotransmitters in modulating systems related to human aggression and impulsive responding was considered initially in clinical studies that demonstrated low cerebrospinal fluid (CSF) concentrations of serotonin metabolites (5-HIAA) in those depressed patients most likely to attempt suicide through violent methods (Asberg et al., 1976). Linnoila and Virkkunen (1992) suggest that this finding is "one of the most consistently replicated findings in biological psychiatry" (p. 46). Marazziti et al. (1993) compared suicide attempters, aggressive patients, and healthy controls and found reduced peripheral serotonergic markers (imipramine binding) among the first two groups compared with the controls. The suicide attempters also had lower serotonergic activity than the aggressive patients. Linnoila and Virkkunen contend that their research indicates that low CSF 5-HIAA levels are related to impulsivity rather than to aggressiveness, per se.

There has been less neurotransmitter research with children and adolescents than with adults; nonetheless a few important studies support the link between decreased serotonergic functioning and antisocial behavior among children. Stoff, Pollock, Vitiello, Behar, and Bridger (1987) found lower values of imipramine binding to platelets among conduct disordered and ADHD children than normal control children. Likewise Pliszka, Rogeness, Renner, Sherman, and Broussard (1988) reported higher levels of whole blood serotonin (found to be inversely related to CSF 5-HIAA) among adolescents with conduct disorder than children with only depressive or anxiety disorder. Kruesi et al. (1990) found that children with disruptive behavior disorders (conduct disorder, oppositional disorder, or attention deficit disorder) had lower concentrations of CSF 5-HIAA than a sample of children with obsessive-compulsive disorder. Furthermore, when they followed these children for 2 years (Kruesi et al., 1992), they obtained a negative correlation (−.53) between 5-HIAA concentrations and measures of the severity of physical aggression as assessed by interviews with parents and children, controlling for age.

Findings relating neurotransmitter levels to individual differences in aggressiveness frequently have been interpreted in the framework of Gray's theory of brain function in relation to learning and emotional behavior (Gray, 1982, 1987). Gray described a behavioral facilitation system (BFS) that mobilizes active interactions with the environment—behaviors such as approach, escape, and active avoidance. Aggressive, sexual, and socially interactive behaviors also would fall in this category. According to Depue and Spoont (1986), the chief components of the BFS, locomotion and incentive reward, are integrated in the mesolimbic dopaminergic pathway, and dopamine (DA) is considered to be the neurotransmitter involved in BFS modulation.

Gray also postulated a second system—the behavioral inhibition system (BIS)—that stops or reduces behavioral responding when mismatches occur between environmental conditions and expectations of the outcome of behavior. The septohippocampal system, with its connections to prefrontal cortex, is thought to be the neurobiological focus of the BIS, with regulation governed by the noradrenergic and serotonergic systems. The serotonergic system is inhibitory in nature, relating to impulse control (Rogeness, Javors, & Pliszka, 1992), and its function in information processing, according to Spoont (1992), is that of signal stabilization. The serotonergic, or 5-HT (5-hydroxytryptamine) system, acts to ensure "that signals that do interrupt current information flow must be of a sufficient intensity or, from a psychological perspective, must be of sufficient relevance to the organism" (Spoont, 1992, p. 341). In personality terms, low 5-HT can result in both "a dissociation between behavioral inhibition and affective states, . . . [and can lead to an] increase in greater stress reactivity" (p. 342). Low levels of norepinephrine (NE), the primary neurotransmitter of the noradrenergic system are thought to decrease concentration and selective attention (Rogeness et al., 1992), although the serotonergic system is considered to have a stronger role in inhibiting irritable and aggressive behavior (Coccaro et al., 1989) with central NE release serving to increase awareness of external stimuli, and the 5-HT system functioning to inhibit the tendency to respond aggressively (Coccaro, Kavoussi, & Lesser, 1992). In a series of important studies, Rogeness and his colleagues have linked noradrenergic functioning to undersocialized conduct disorder in children and adolescents (Rogeness, Hernandez, Macedo, & Mitchell,

1982; Rogeness, Maas, Javors, Macedo, Harris, & Hoppe, 1988).

Quay (1993) has extended Gray's theory to explain major dimensions of child psychiatric disorder, including undersocialized aggressive conduct disorder (UACD). Emphasizing the predatory or instrumental aggressive behavior of UACD and the impulsive response involved, Quay posits that UACD is the result of an imbalance between the BFS and BIS that favors the BFS. This imbalance could arise either from an especially weak BIS or an unusually strong BFS. At present, the predominant evidence is in support of the weak BIS side of Quay's hypothesis. Consistent with this conclusion is research pertaining to the serotonergic and noradrenergic systems previously discussed, but there also is an extensive literature on autonomic nervous system functioning that has been hypothesized to index activity in the BIS, and this literature could also be interpreted as supporting the weak BIS hypothesis. Fowles (1980, 1988) has proposed that electrodermal responding provides an index of BIS activity and that consistent findings of underresponding among adults with antisocial personality disorder is evidence of a weak BIS among these individuals. Research on skin conductance and aggression among children and adolescents is reviewed in the next section.

Evidence in support of the strong BFS aspect of Quay's theory would come from correlations between antisocial behavior and dopaminergic hyperactivity; however, there is very little evidence to this effect. High plasma levels of homovanillic acid (HVA), the primary metabolite of dopamine, have not been associated with conduct problems (Rogeness, Javors, Maas, Macedo, & Fischer, 1987); nor have CSF concentrations of HVA been found to relate to measures of aggression or impulsivity among children (Kruesi et al., 1990). Most of the evidence supporting the contention that antisocial activity results from a dominant BFS comes from nonbiological studies of reward-oriented behavior. Newman and his colleagues developed a measure of perseverative responding to reward that is considered to reflect a hyperresponsive BFS (Newman, Patterson, & Kosson, 1987). Adult neurotic extroverts have been found to be overly responsive toward cues on this task (Newman & Wallace, 1992), and Newman and Wallace have speculated that this mechanism may characterize the behavior of socialized delinquent youth. On the other hand, Quay (1993) reviewed a series of studies that support the hypothesis of reward dominance (strong BFS) among UACD youth and concluded that perseverated responding to

reward in the face of punishment develops early on among such children.

Unlike the research on hormones and aggression, there has been less research on the direction of effects between neurotransmitter levels and human aggression. The 2-year longitudinal study by Kruesi et al. (1992) provides support for biological factors determining aggressive responses in humans. However, Rogeness et al. (1992b) conclude that the "development and balance among [the three neurotransmitter systems] may be influenced by environmental factors as well as being genetically determined," (p. 772) including such environmental influences as psychosocial factors. Rogeness et al. note that primate studies of mother-deprived and mother-reared infants (Kraemer, Ebert, Lake, & McKinney, 1984) show lower levels of NE among the mother-deprived primates, thus providing evidence of the influence of early socialization experiences on neurotransmitters. Quay speculated about the environmental and learning conditions that would lead to a poor functioning BIS or a hyperactive BFS, suggesting that these experiences could influence neurotransmitters involved in these two systems. These speculations are consistent with the hypothesis that the effects of social conditioning must have some enduring neurobiological structural effects; however, research in this area has not progressed to documenting this process.

Autonomic Nervous System Activity

Fowles's hypothesis that electrodermal responding reflects the strength of the BIS is based, in part, on research that described consistently low skin conductance (SC) among psychopathic individuals (Hare, 1978). An early study of psychopathic, neurotic, and normal delinquents showed lower initial reactivity among the psychopathic group (Borkovec, 1970), but SC findings among child conduct problem populations show considerable variability, depending on the measures employed and the groups being compared (e.g., Davies & Maliphant, 1971; Delameter & Lahey, 1983; Garralda, Connell, & Taylor, 1991). Raine (1993) reviewed studies relating ANS activity and violence and found different patterns of results for different measures of skin conductance. In studies of SC arousal, Raine found 4 of 10 studies showing effects for violence, but these were primarily for nonspecific fluctuations in SC, rather than levels of SC. Studies of SC orienting to neutral tones revealed a reduced frequency of SC response to the stimuli particularly by psychopaths or criminals with schizoid features. Raine found that resistance to skin conductance conditioning occurred primarily among antisocial individuals coming from positive social environments and found little evidence that antisocial individuals, in general, were unresponsive to aversive stimuli. SC half-recovery time was consistently found to be longer among criminals and psychopaths, suggesting either slow fear dissipation or a mechanism for shutting out aversive stimuli.

Data on resting heart rate as a measure of ANS reactivity provides a more consistent picture of low reactivity among antisocial children and adolescents (Raine, 1993), although these effects are not obtained with institutionalized offenders (Hare, 1978). Raine, Venables, and Williams (1990) found that resting heart rate, skin conductance, and other measures including EEG successfully classified 75 of 101 male subjects at age 15 according to their criminality at age 24. In his review of 13 studies involving noninstitutionalized subjects, Raine (1993) found that low resting heart related to violent behavior in all 13 studies, with an average effect size of 0.85. Wadsworth (1976) found that low resting heart rate at age 11 predicted violent criminal acts by age 21 in a sample of over 5,000 youth. Maliphant, Hume, and Furnham (1990) also found low resting heart rate to predict teacher ratings of disruptive behavior among 12- to 13-year-old girls. Zahn and Kruesi (1993), however, found higher heart rates among disruptive boys who had been referred to the study by doctors or clinics. Although the authors conceded this unexpected finding may have been due to a biased sample having anxious parents, this finding is consistent with the hypothesis by Fowles (1980) that heart rate reflects activity in the BFS, yielding the prediction that unsocialized antisocial youth might show higher heart rates than controlled youth.

Magnusson and his colleagues have examined a third measure of ANS activity, catecholamine excretions (adrenaline and noradrenaline), as a predictor of subsequent criminal activity in a large, community-based Swedish sample of 13-year-olds. Adrenaline levels at age 13 proved to be negatively related, concurrently, to aggression and motor restlessness ratings by teachers (Magnusson, 1987). More importantly, low levels of adrenaline excretion were predictive of persistent criminal activity prior to age 18 and both persistent and sporadic criminal offending after age 18 and prior to age 30 (Magnusson, Klinteberg, & Stattin, 1993).

Although the findings from studies using psychophysiological measures are largely consistent with those assessing neurotransmitter levels, it is surprising that the two literatures are nonintersecting. Findings from both types of research can and have been assimilated in support of Gray's two-factor explanation of antisocial behavior; yet, there has been no integration of research involving hormones, neurotransmitters, or other measures of autonomic nervous system functioning. A slightly different theoretical perspective on the ANS-related findings from Venables (1988) is that the autonomic nervous systems of violent individuals are dominated by parasympathetic process rather than sympathetic process, and hence such youth exhibit characteristics of fearlessness in situations that normally engender anxiety and caution. This interpretation focuses on the fearlessness of antisocial youth, rather than more general failures of inhibition and regulation.

Neuropsychological Deficits

Studies of violent adults using electroencephalography, computerized tomography, and positron emission tomography (Volkow & Tancredi, 1987) have shown abnormalities in temporal or frontal areas of antisocial individuals. These data, coupled with other neuropsychological data on violent adults, and the fact that magnetic resonance imaging suggests that skin conductance activity may be correlated with prefrontal areas, has led Raine and Scerbo (1991) to speculate that deficits in the frontal cortex may be related to violent behavior. Support from studies of brain injury among adults is mixed but broadly consistent with this hypothesis.

A growing number of concurrent studies indicate deficits in neuropsychological functioning among juvenile delinquent populations (Brickman, McManus, Grapentine, & Alessi, 1984; Frost, Moffitt, & McGee, 1989; Karniski, Levine, Clarke, Palfrey, & Meltzer, 1982; Vitiello, Stoff, Atkins, & Mahoney, 1990; Wolff, Waber, Bauermeister, Cohen, & Ferber, 1982; Yeudall, Fromm-Auch, & Davies, 1982), although the pattern of results does not point consistently to particular deficits. Moffitt and Lynam (in press) followed a sample of New Zealand males who had been administered a neuropsychological test battery at age 13 and used these scores to predict self-reported delinquency at age 15 and 18 and court data at age 18. Neurological deficits at age 13 have correlations with delinquency at age 18 with SES controlled statistically. Verbal and auditory-verbal memory factors had the strongest relation to delinquency. Furthermore, regression analyses (ages 13–15, ages 15–18, and ages 13–18) all revealed a significant prediction of later delinquency by a neurological status by prior delinquency interaction term when prior delinquency was entered first in the regression analyses. By itself, neurological status at 13 failed to account for subsequent delinquency when prior delinquency was accounted for. Boys who were high on delinquency and low on neurological status at age 13 committed significantly more of the subsequent juvenile offenses (46%) than all of the other boys, who constituted 88% of the sample. Moffitt and Lynam interpreted these results as evidence that neuropsychological deficits are not a risk factor for those youth whose delinquency does not begin until adolescence.

An important consequence of neuropsychological deficits is lowered intellectual functioning. The relation between IQ and delinquency has been well documented (e.g., Wilson & Herrnstein, 1985); however, Moffitt and Lynam (1994) argue that this deficit largely occurs in the verbal domain. In their longitudinal study of New Zealand youth, they found that language-based measures were more strongly related to self-reported delinquency than non-language measures, a finding mirrored by a number of reviews. In discussing the potential impact of neuropsychological deficits on conduct disorder, Pennington and Bennetto (1993) conclude that executive function deficits, which limit the way actions can be planned, evaluated, and controlled, must be considered independently of verbal skill deficits, because these functions could compensate for each other; however, if both types of deficits are present, the risk for conduct problems may be multiplied.

A major challenge for researchers advocating the importance of neuropsychological deficits is to examine whether within-individual changes in antisocial behavior over time are linked to changes in neuropsychological functioning.

Attention Deficits/Impulsivity

The neuropsychological deficits implicated in attention deficit/hyperactivity disorder (ADHD), especially response inhibition failures, overactivity, and attention deficits, have been found repeatedly to covary with aggressive behavior in schoolchildren (see Hinshaw, 1987, for a review). Substantial overlap has been demonstrated through dimensional correlations between latent factors of attention deficit and conduct disorder (Biederman et al., 1991). Quay (1979) once argued that the dimensions of hyperactivity and aggression are essentially identical, but considerable evidence since then supports the partial independence of these domains (Loney, 1987), with distinct family histories (Lahey et al., 1988), genetic loadings (Faraone, Biederman, Keenan, & Tsuang, 1991), concurrent social adjustment (Milich & Landau, 1984), and long-term outcomes (Hinshaw, 1994).

The developmental nature of the relation between ADHD problems and aggressive behavior is not clear. Attention deficit/impulsivity in early childhood is a marker of risk for adolescent aggressive behavior (Satterfield, Hoppe, & Schell, 1982). Several reviewers, however, have concluded that attention deficit/impulsivity does not increment this risk much beyond early comorbid aggressive behavior (Barkley, Fischer, Edelbrock, & Smallish, 1990; Lilienfeld & Waldman, 1990). Contrasting evidence, in favor of the hypothesis that ADHD symptoms play an incremental role in later aggressive behavior beyond early aggression, has been amassed in Sweden by Magnusson (1987), in inner-city London by Farrington et al. (1990), in New Zealand by Moffitt (1990), and in the United States by Mannuzza et al. (1991). Another kind of evidence comes from intervention studies that show stimulant medication directed at ADHD symptoms also can reduce aggressive behaviors (Hinshaw, 1991; Hinshaw, Heller, & McHale, 1992). On the other hand, long-term aggressive outcomes are not appreciably altered by medication treatment of ADHD (Hinshaw & Simmel, 1994; Weiss & Hechtman, 1986).

It appears that attention deficits increment long-term risk for antisocial behavior, but do not lead to antisocial outcomes directly or inevitably. In the New Zealand study, early attention deficits predicted adolescent delinquency only in interaction with early family difficulties, such as low SES, overcrowding, and maternal psychopathology, or early intellectual skill deficits (Moffitt, 1990). It may be that attention deficits, especially impulsivity, will lead to aggressive outcomes only if the early environment fails to shape the child's behavior appropriately or if the child lacks other compensatory intellectual skills.

Like difficult temperament, another possible path from attention deficits to aggression could be through the effects of attention deficits on the environment. If parents respond to an impulsive child with harsh or even abusive discipline, then this factor may foster aggressive development (Hinshaw & Simmel, 1994). If attention deficits lead to academic failure, this additional problem may increase risk for adolescent antisocial behavior, even when current aggressive behavior is controlled (Maughan, Gray, & Rutter, 1985). Findings on this point are conflicting, however, with McGee and Share (1988) contending that reading failure precedes and causes ADHD, and Hinshaw (1992) finding a correlation between inattention and reading readiness deficiencies early in life, before schooling, suggesting a neurodevelopmental basis for ADHD with academic failure as a consequence. Further support for Hinshaw's position comes from a study of first-, fourth-, and seventh-grade boys for whom reading performance, attention problems, and delinquency data were obtained (Maguin, Loeber, & LeMahieu, 1993). The negative relation between reading performance and delinquency was equally strong for all age groups in the White sample, and at fourth and seventh grade for the African American sample. However, when the effects of attention problems were controlled, the relation between reading and delinquency was insignificant. Those children who come to display *both* attention deficits and aggressive behavior are at particular risk for long-term antisocial outcomes, in a way that is not simply a sum of the two types of problems (Hinshaw et al., 1993; Loeber, 1990; Magnusson, 1987).

Neurodevelopmentally based attention deficits and impulsivity very likely play a role in the early onset of aggressive behavior problems of certain children during the elementary school years. However, all of the proposed paths for the role of these deficits are probabilistic and contingent; multiple trajectories to antisocial behavior undoubtedly will be discovered. Although neither necessary nor sufficient for aggressive development, attention deficits likely are one of the factors in aggressive development.

Toxins in the Early Environment

With the increased use of hard drugs by pregnant women, social concerns about the impact of prenatal exposure to derivatives of cocaine and heroin have risen among public health officials and educators, yet there is still surprisingly little research on this topic. A study of 72 children born to women addicted to opiates and methadone at the time of pregnancy indicated that serious behavior problems, such as hyperactivity and aggression, were present among 56% of the sample by age 10 (Olofsson, Buckley, Andersen, & Friis-Hansen, 1983). A shorter term study involving a control group demographically matched to the group whose mothers were in a methadone treatment program during pregnancy (de Cubas & Field, 1993) reflected similar negative effects of prenatal methadone exposure. The exposed group had more deviant scores for hyperactivity, aggression, and delinquency on the Child Behavior Checklist (Achenbach & Edelbrock, 1983) at ages 6 to 13, despite comparable numbers of perinatal complications in the two groups. The effects of prenatal exposure to cannabis (O'Connell & Fried, 1991) yielded similar results in a study in which the controls were matched for maternal smoking and alcohol consumption during pregnancy. However, when income, mother's personality, and home environment were covaried, the effect of cannabis use on conduct problems between ages 6 and 9 became nonsignificant.

Maternal smoking during pregnancy apparently increases a child's risk for conduct problems as well as early cognitive difficulties (Bagley, 1992; Makin, Fried, & Watkinson, 1991). However, Bagley, whose sample included 11,465 subjects followed to age 16, speculated that the mediating process involved unmeasured personality variables in which extroverted characteristics of the mothers associated with both smoking and deviant behavior influenced the behavior of the children.

Lead ingestion, related to environmental exposure and diet, also appears to be consistently related to hyperactivity, impulsivity, and conduct problems (Tesman & Hills, 1994). Needleman et al. (1979) first presented this possibility in a study relating children's blood lead levels to antisocial behavior on the Rutter scale and the Conners scale. Silva, Hughes, Williams, and Faed (1988) also found a significant effect for blood lead levels and hyperactivity in a sample of 579 New Zealand 11-year-olds. A study of 501 Scotch children (Thomson et al., 1989) also demonstrated the connection between lead exposure and antisocial behavior and hyperactivity. The exact neurological mechanisms by which lead ingestion influences antisocial behavior are not clear at this point; however, the impact on various aspects of cognitive functioning, particularly verbal and language performance, has been established (Tesman & Hills, 1994).

Conclusions

At this point, it is not possible to write a comprehensive integrated summary of the relation of biological functioning to human aggression. An early conclusion drawn from this review is that aggression as a trait is not directly linked to any biological process; rather, aggression occurs indirectly through the effects of biological processes on related behaviors. Testosterone levels seem to be related to activity levels and responses to provocation; conversely, experiences of competitive success and dominance seem to increase testosterone levels in humans. Serotonergic activity seems to be related to impulsivity, rather than aggression, as illustrated in the strongest behavioral connections having been made with violent suicidal attempts. Thus, it is most likely that various forms of antisocial behavior will be linked to biological vulnerabilities that compromise adaptive functioning in many different ways. In some children, but probably not all children, these compromised aspects of functioning may increase the likelihood of aggressive behavior. Parenthetically, almost all of the research in this area has focused on aggressive behavior; virtually no studies have focused on biological factors in the development of more covert forms of antisocial activity.

A second conclusion is that arguments for a strict biological determination of antisocial behavior are consistently rejected by most researchers. Directions of effect seem to flow both ways—from physiology to behavior and from environmental experiences to biological events. For some individuals, the correlated constraints of biology and environment (i.e., families with shared biological risk factors often live in high-risk environments—Cairns, McGuire, & Gariepy, 1993; Scarr & Ricciuti, 1991) make it very difficult for them to avoid the persistent patterns of antisocial behavior that seem to be impelled by certain biological vulnerabilities. The intricate interplay between biological capacities and environmental events will likely be seen as a lifelong sequence of interactions and reciprocal influences when a better understanding of this developmental process is reached.

Ecological Factors and Social Stressors

Children born into disadvantaged environments are at relatively great risk for becoming violent later in life. The importance of poverty and environmental stressors in providing an ecological context for the development of individual differences in aggressive behavior can be inferred from the earlier discussion of the effects of these variables on populationwide rates. Moreover, even when broader indices of community poverty are controlled, children who are born into families of poverty are at risk for later peer-nominated aggression (Patterson et al., 1990) and serious violent crime (Blumstein et al., 1985). The work of Elder (1979; Elder, Nguyen, & Caspi, 1985) on children raised during the Great Depression convincingly implicates family poverty as a risk factor for later conduct problems. Bolger, Patterson, Thompson, and Kupersmidt (1995) have found that even intermittent and temporary poverty has enduring effects on children's later externalizing problems, although the effects of persistent poverty are most severe.

Cumulative and Interactive Effects

Family poverty is correlated with myriad ecological risk factors, including large family size (Rutter & Giller, 1983), lack of parental education (Wilson & Herrnstein, 1985), family loss, illness, and stress (Shaw & Emory, 1988), inadequate housing (Rutter & Giller, 1983), criminal victimization (McLoyd, 1990), and high residential mobility (Eckenrode, Rowe, Laird, & Braithwaite, 1995). These risk factors are apparently not merely redundant in their impact on the developing child; rather, their effects are cumulative (Rutter & Garmezy, 1983). Children who experience multiple family stressors are at greater risk for conduct problems than are children experiencing any single stressor (Shaw & Emory, 1988).

On the other hand, analyses by Bolger et al. (1995) indicate that the effects of economic hardship are more dramatic among children in the racial majority than among those who are already stressed by the circumstances of racial minority status. Being black brings numerous social hardships in American society (Ogbu, 1990) and, with these hardships, relative risk for aggressive behavior. The effects of economic hardship, above and beyond the hardships already imposed by racial stratification, are muted for African American children (Bolger et al.). Another way to characterize these data is to conclude that poor children, including both African American and white children, are at high risk for later aggression, whereas being raised in relative economic affluence buffers white children from aggressive outcomes but does not buffer African American children as strongly.

Ecological risk factors appear to interact with other child characteristics in predicting aggressive outcomes. Kupersmidt, Griesler, DeRosier, Patterson, and Davis (1995) found that living in a middle socioeconomic status neighborhood serves as a protective factor for children who are at risk by virtue of household composition and family income factors. A broad base of evidence indicates that boys are more vulnerable to the effects of poverty than are girls (Elder, 1979; Bolger et al., 1995), in the same way that boys are more vulnerable to the effects of divorce and single parenthood (Hetherington, Camara, & Featherman, 1983). The reasons for this interaction are not clear, although they are consistent with a general diathesis stress model of developmental psychopathology (Garber, 1984).

Causal Processes

Even though the outcomes associated with poverty are pervasive, establishing the causal role of poverty is difficult because of the lack of experimental evidence and the possibility that another factor could account for both poverty and child outcomes. For example, low parental intelligence could lead to family poverty and to child aggressive outcomes. Zill, Moore, Nord, and Stief (1991) have found that many long-term welfare recipients score poorly on tests of intelligence, and Moffitt and Silva (1988) have found that child intelligence, which is a strong function of parental intelligence, is correlated with child aggression.

Most current theories of the effects of poverty point toward the mediating role of parenting quality to explain how being born into economic hardship leads a child to become aggressive (Conger et al., 1992). Parents living in poverty are under great psychological distress and are exposed to negative experiences (e.g., family illness, victimization, residential moves) over which they have no control. Under such circumstances, parents become less available to their children (McLoyd, 1990). Mothers living in poverty are relatively less knowledgeable about their children's school performance, have less contact with schoolteachers (Baker & Stevenson, 1986), and are less likely to monitor their children's activities (McCord, 1979). When parents under stress and poverty discipline their children, they are relatively likely to use harsh strategies and physical punishment (Dodge et al., 1994; McLoyd, 1990). These differences in parental involvement and discipline strategies lead, in turn, to child aggressive behavior.

Processes in Early Family Socialization

The search for causal factors in the development of persistently antisocial individuals inevitably leads back to an examination of early family socialization practices. There is ample evidence of differences in discipline practices and more general parent-child interactions between families of aggressive children and nonproblem children. Much of the early research on this point was concurrent in nature, however, and there has long been a recognition of the difficulty in separating cause and effect in these relations (Bell & Harper, 1977). Anderson, Lytton, and Romney (1986) demonstrated that parents of normal children will resort to more punitive discipline practices when confronted with managing conduct-disordered boys than when managing their own sons. Despite these problems of interpretation, the research on early socialization practices provides important information on the early experiences of aggressive individuals. The number of longitudinal studies in this area has also increased, making it possible to begin to sort out the effects of parenting and the effects of child characteristics.

Attachment Relationships

The strange situation procedure (Ainsworth, Blehar, Waters, & Wall, 1978) provides an important assessment of the early mother-child relationship by evaluating the child's response to separation and reunion during the toddler years. This reaction is thought to reflect a basic interpersonal orientation that frames the child's perspective on future relationships. Security of attachment has been linked to greater parental warmth and responsiveness to the child's signals (Belsky, Rovine, & Taylor, 1984; Egeland & Sroufe, 1981), although the child's contribution to this relation has also been described (Crockenberg, 1981; Kagan, 1981).

The results of longitudinal studies on infant attachment and conduct problems in childhood are mixed. Three separate studies failed to yield significant relations between insecure attachment and conduct problems, whereas three other investigations did support this connection. Bates and his colleagues followed children in a predominantly middle-class, two-parent sample from infancy into elementary school and consistently failed to establish insecure attachment as a predictor of externalizing problems (Bates et al., 1991). The same held for a similar sample studied by Fagot (Fagot & Kavanaugh, 1990; Fagot & Leve, in press) and a longitudinal investigation by Lewis, Feiring, McGuffog, and Jaskir (1984). On the other hand, Sroufe and Egeland have repeatedly found insecure attachments to predict to childhood behavior problems in a sample from low-income and predominantly single-parent households (Erickson, Sroufe & Egeland, 1985; Renken, Egeland, Marvinney, Mangelsdorf, & Sroufe, 1989; Sroufe, 1983). Lyons-Ruth found that disorganized attachment, a newer subset of insecure attachment, predicted hostile behavior to peers at age 5 (Lyons-Ruth, Alpern, & Repacholi, 1993) and teacher-rated externalizing problems at age 7 (Lyons-Ruth, Easterbrooks, & Davidson, 1995). Finally, although Shaw et al. (1995) did not find attachment to predict elevated externalizing scores on the CBCL at age 5, insecure attachment, particularly disorganized attachment, predicted the narrow-band aggression scores at age 5. This latter sample was predominantly lower income, having been recruited from a federally funded nutritional support program for mothers, infants, and children. Studies in which insecure attachment was not predictive of aggression involved a high proportion of two-parent families, whereas those in which insecure attachment predicted aggression were based on low-income, single-parent families, suggesting that sufficient family income and access to two parents may buffer a child against the deleterious effects of insecure attachment.

Greenberg, Spelz, and Deklyen (1993) have argued that the socioeconomic differences between samples in studies that support or do not support the attachment-conduct problem relation suggest that insecure attachment works in combination with other risk factors to place children at risk for conduct problems. Thus, for example, Lyons-Ruth et al. (1993) found substantial overlapping variance accounted for by lower mental development on the one hand, and disorganized attachment and maternal depression on the other hand. Alternatively, Greenberg et al. (1993) have concluded that secure attachment might be considered as a protective factor for infants of low-income, highly stressed mothers. In fact, there is support for this interaction hypothesis in a study of birth complications in a Danish male sample ($n = 4,269$). Raine, Brennan, and Mednick (in press) found that males with a history of birth complications and early rejection by the mother (unwanted pregnancy, attempt to abort fetus, and public institutional care of the infant) predicted violent crime by ages 17 to 19, whereas neither factor by itself was predictive of violence nor was the interaction between birth complications and poor social circumstances (unmarried mother, low SES, poor home conditions, etc.). That is, of offenders who had both risk factors, 47% became violent, compared with 20% of those who had one factor. Thus, the strength of the mother-child bond, in this case represented by the mother's reaction to the infant, was a risk factor for violence only in the context of another early risk factor. It is also important to note that this relation held only for violent crimes and not offending in general.

Parental Warmth versus Negativity

Closely related to the attachment construct, but distinct from it in terms of empirical consequences, as well as the locus of causality, is the concept of maternal warmth as an early parental risk factor. This factor appears as a significant predictor of early school-age conduct problems in exactly those samples for which insecure attachment failed as a predictor—those involving more middle-class, two-parent families. Bates and Bayles (1988) found maternal affection to be negatively related to externalizing problems in both boys and girls at ages 5 and 6. Fagot and Leve (in press) found mother negativity and poor marital adjustment predictive of externalizing problems at age 5; Booth, Rose-Krasnor, McKinnon, and Rubin (1994) found maternal warmth at age 4 negatively related to externalizing problems at age 8, with maternal negativity being positively related to behavior problems. In each case, the strength of these relations was fairly modest, but the pattern mirrors the results of earlier findings (Richman et al., 1982), tying a lack of parental warmth in preschool to behavior problems

in the school years. One explanation for these findings can be found in the social learning theory assumption that for a parent to be influential in getting a child to adopt parental standards for behavior, that parent must have a viable source of reward for the child (Martin, 1975). The establishment of this kind of positive relationship begins in the earliest years of life, and presumably sets the tone for the internalization of parental standards. For this reason, longitudinal studies such as those just cited, which point to the connection between parental warmth during ages 2 to 4 and later conduct problems, have the greatest significance for explaining the development of self-control.

Family Coercion and Inconsistent Discipline

In their classic longitudinal study of delinquency, Glueck and Glueck (1950) reported that parents of boys who became delinquent were less consistent in their discipline practices than parents of matched control boys who did not become delinquent. In an experimental follow-up of this hypothesis, Parke and Deur (1972) demonstrated that children are less inhibited from behaving aggressively when an adult is inconsistent in administering punishment. The same point has been made about inconsistency between adults when one of them enforces a standard, but the other does not (Sawin & Parke, 1979).

Patterson has sharpened the conceptualization of parental responses to aggression and aversive behavior with his theory of coercive interactions between parents and children. According to this theory, children who begin to display antisocial behaviors such as aggression and disruptiveness in the early school years have been trained, inadvertently, in the effectiveness of these behaviors in the context of their homes prior to school entry. Patterson (1995) describes coercion training as a four-step process that begins with the aversive intrusion of a family member into the child's activities. For example, a mother may scold her child for not going to bed. In the second step, the child counterattacks, in this case by whining, yelling, and complaining that he is being picked as the only one who has to go to bed. The third step is the crucial one, for it involves the negative reinforcement that increases the likelihood of future aversive responding by the child: The adult stops her scolding and her demands for compliance. The fourth step involves reinforcement of the mother's giving into the child: When the mother ceases her demands, the child stops the counterattack. According to Patterson's theory, it is the conditional probabilities in this sequence that distinguish the early parenting patterns of antisocial children from those of normal children. Observational data from clinical samples (Patterson, Reid, & Dishion, 1992) suggest that a child's aversive responses to the mother's intrusions in Step 2 occur two to three times more often in distressed families than in normal families. The success of these child counterattacks is reflected in observations documenting that mothers of aggressive boys are more apt to negatively reinforce their sons' aversive responses than are mothers of nonaggressive boys (Snyder & Patterson, 1995). Conversely, mothers of nonaggressive boys more often reinforce their sons' prosocial responses (talking, positive nonverbal communication) than do the mothers of aggressive boys. The net result is that children in normal families can be successful with their parents in two ways (aversive and nonaversive behavior), whereas the aggressive boys only succeed with aversive behavior. An interesting sidelight to this study was the finding of similar aggressive versus nonaggressive group differences in the contingent probabilities of sons' reinforcement of their mothers' positive and negative responding. That is, aggressive boys reinforced the aversive behavior of their mothers more often than did nonaggressive boys. The latter findings suggest that the coercion training process is a family dynamic, not simply a difference in parenting activity. The idea of coercion as a family dynamic is supported by observations of families of children referred to clinics for conduct problems. Siblings of the referred children displayed similar levels of problem behavior and were equally as involved in coercive interactions with their parents as the referred children (Dadds, Sanders, Morrison, & Rebgetz, 1992).

The Snyder and Patterson (1995) study is particularly important for the developmental model of early starting antisocial youth because the earlier empirical support for coercion theory had come largely from observational data on children 9 to 11 years old. This made it difficult to determine whether this coercive process reflected a family process that was simply concurrent with aggressive sequences in the school setting and with peers or truly reflected an earlier history of formative interactions between aggressive children and their parents. The boys in the Snyder and Patterson study were between 4 and 5 years of age, providing confirmation of the potential developmental significance of this mechanism.

Punishment and Punitiveness

The role of physical punishment in promoting or reducing children's aggressive and antisocial behavior has long been a matter of dispute among professionals and laypersons.

Hoffman (1960) warned against the excessive use of unqualified power assertion methods (direct commands, threats, deprivations, and physical force) because they evoke oppositional tendencies and feelings of hostility toward the parent and do not promote internalized control. Furthermore, they could lead the child to take a power-assertive orientation toward other people. Parental reports of their own use of these techniques when their child failed to comply initially were highly correlated with children's hostile behavior and power assertiveness toward peers in a nursery school setting. Since the Hoffman paper, there have been numerous studies of the relation between punitive discipline and aggression. One early longitudinal investigation yielded data that brought the role of physical punishment into question. In their concurrent study of third-grade children, Eron, Walder, and Lefkowitz (1971) found that punishment was positively related to aggression only among those children who were poorly or moderately identified with their parents. Punishment was negatively correlated with aggression among those children who had a close identification with their parents. The complexity of these findings highlighted the importance of considering other factors in the parent-child equation in addition to punishment. When this sample was followed up 10 years later, there was no longer any relation between parental punitiveness in third grade and reputation for aggressiveness in late adolescence (Lefkowitz, Eron, Walder, & Huesmann, 1977), but there was a predictive relation between parental punitiveness and antisocial behavior at age 30 (Eron, Huesmann, & Zell, 1991).

One possible explanation for these contradictory findings is that normative increases in adolescent antisocial activity (Elliott, 1994; Moffitt, 1993a) mask the role of early influences on adolescent aggression. A number of subsequent longitudinal investigations have supported the developmental connections between punishment and antisocial activity. Data from the Cambridge Longitudinal Study (Farrington & Hawkins, 1991) point to harsh discipline practices at ages 8 and 9 as being among the important predictors of the early onset of delinquency in this sample of 411 London males. McCord (1991a) found that fathers' uses of physical punishment predicted their sons' adult records of criminality, even when paternal criminality was controlled. McCord reviewed the Cambridge-Somerville Youth Study records of 130 families having two natural parents, looking at parental criminal records as well as sons' criminal records when they were middle-aged. She found that sons' criminality reflected the combined effects of fathers' criminality and fathers' use of physical punishment. Because of the high proportion of criminal fathers who use physical punishment (73%), however, there were only 6 cases of criminal fathers who did not use physical punishment.

It is also quite possible that the effects of physical punishment are moderated by other aspects of parenting, such as the quality of the parent-child relationship and the degree of parent-child warmth (Campbell, 1990). It might be that the negative effects of physical punishment hold only when punishment is administered in the absence of warmth and caring guidance. Deater-Deckard and Dodge (1997) reported that harsh physical discipline was correlated with later child externalizing problems, but only among the subset of children who scored below the median in parent-child warmth; among the children scoring above the median in parent-child warmth, physical discipline was not significantly correlated with externalizing outcomes. Thus, a warm parent-child relationship might buffer a child from deleterious effects of physical punishment. The "authoritative" parenting style described by Baumrind (1967), known to be associated with positive child behavior outcomes, includes a combination of firm limit setting along with educative guidance and clear expectations. The absence of caring guidance would turn this positive parenting into "authoritarian" parenting, known to be associated with negative child behaviors (Baumrind, 1967).

None of the preceding research helps to resolve the continuing dilemma of disentangling the effects of parenting from the behavior of the child. Grusec and Kuczynski (1980) found that parents adjusted their discipline practices according to the nature of the child's offense. In addition to replicating this finding, however, Trickett and Kuczynski (1986) found that abusive mothers tended to use power-assertion responses regardless of the behavior problem. A partial resolution of this dilemma comes from longitudinal analyses of conduct disorder among a random sample of almost 1,000 children from two upstate New York counties. The children ranged in age from 1 to 10 when parenting and child behaviors were assessed initially, and then were reassessed twice, 8 and 10 years later (Cohen & Brook, 1995). Power-assertive methods were more frequently used on the younger children, but children who showed more behavior problems were the ones receiving the most frequent punishment. As in many other studies, early behavior problems were a powerful predictor of subsequent conduct disorder. To determine whether the strong predictive role of early parental punishment on later conduct

disorder was not simply due to the effects of early problem behavior on parental discipline, Cohen and Brook used cross-lagged analyses to obtain alternative estimates of the directionality of effects. The cross-lags from first assessment (ages 1–10) to the second assessment (ages 9–18) showed comparable influences from behavior to punishment and punishment to behavior. The cross-lags from the second assessment (ages 9–18) to the third assessment (ages 12–20) showed only an effect of punishment on subsequent conduct disorder and not the converse effect. These results were due almost exclusively to the younger half of the sample, however. Thus, Cohen and Brook conclude that punishment and behavior problems have reciprocal influences on each other in the lag from preschool to preadolescence, but only punishment seems to influence subsequent behavior problems in the transition to adolescence. Taking into account that punishment decreased with age and had nonreciprocal effects on behavior problems only at the adolescent transition period, it is possible to conclude that the strongest negative consequences of power-assertive discipline are most clear-cut when young adolescents typically push for more autonomy and most parents decrease their use of physical punishment. This is not to detract from the point also made by these data to the effect that punishment can contribute to increased problem behavior at all ages.

Abusive Parenting

In some cases, the distinction between the use of physical punishment and abusive parenting may be one of degree, as is illustrated by Trickett and Kuczynski's (1986) conclusion that abusive mothers rely almost exclusively on physical punishment in disciplining their children. An important methodological issue for research in this area may be the need to distinguish between controlled spanking and more abusive forms of physical punishment, although theorists such as Hoffman and McCord seem to argue that all forms of physical punishment promote the development of antisocial behavior.

Widom (1989) has provided a comprehensive review of research on child abuse that challenges the methodological adequacy of much of this research. Although she concludes that evidence is sparse for the prevailing idea that all abused children will grow up to abuse their own children, she acknowledges that abused children are at higher risk of doing so than nonabused children. Nevertheless, she concludes that the majority of abusive parents were not abused themselves. Widom makes these same general points about the relation between child abuse and later delinquency.

Since the publication of this review, more longitudinal studies have been reported that support the connection between child abuse and adult antisocial behavior. Luntz and Widom (1994), demonstrated long-term effects of child abuse on antisocial behavior in a 20-year follow-up of children who had been reported as abused or neglected prior to age 11. Compared with control subjects matched for age, race, sex, and family SES, the once-abused sample had twice the number of adults diagnosed as having an adult antisocial personality disorder.

As research on the effects of child abuse has expanded, it has become important to distinguish among several forms of maltreatment (Cicchetti, 1989). It appears that physical abuse has clear effects on subsequent child aggressive behavior, whereas sexual abuse and neglect have different negative consequences. Fagot, Hagan, Youngblade, and Potter (1989) found important early childhood effects in the observed social behavior of preschool children (ages 3–5) who had been sexually abused or were victims of physical abuse and neglect. The physically abused children were more aggressive, less communicative, and more passive than either sexually abused or control subjects; whereas the sexually abused were simply more quiet and unresponsive to peers. The physically abused children were more apt to respond to negative interactions with negative behavior than other children, a finding that has been found repeatedly. Sternberg et al. studied an older child sample (ages 8–12) consisting of those who had been physically abused by parents within the previous 6 months, had witnessed spousal violence but not been abused themselves, or had witnessed violence and been abused (Sternberg et al., 1993). Data on abuse and violence for this Israeli sample came from social workers and the outcome data involved self-reports or mothers' ratings of internalizing or externalizing problems. All three vulnerable groups showed more self-reported depression than the demographically matched control group, but only the two groups that had been physically abused reported more externalizing problems. Mothers, on the other hand, reported more externalizing problems among the two groups who had witnessed domestic violence. It is not unusual for mothers and children to disagree on the problem behavior of children (Achenbach, McConaugh, & Howell, 1987), but these differences make it difficult to sort out the differential effects of being victimized as opposed to witnessing violence. It seems clear that when children are themselves the victims of physical abuse, this increases their aggressive behavior; however, it is less certain that observing violence toward others has this same effect, although other negative consequences do follow (Osofsky, 1995).

The effects of physical abuse, neglect, and sexual abuse also were contrasted in a summer camp study of children 5 to 11 years old ($N = 235$) that included a non-maltreated matched control group (Manley, Cicchetti, & Barnett, 1994). The subgroups differed on counselor ratings of social competence and behavior problems, but did not differ on peer ratings of disruptiveness or aggressiveness. The sexual abuse group was rated by counselors as more socially competent and having fewer behavior problems than the physically abused or the neglected groups, and even somewhat more competent than the non-maltreated group. The physically abused group had more behavior problems than the non-maltreated group, with the other two maltreated groups falling between these extremes.

Beyond the effects of maltreatment versus non-maltreatment described in these studies, measures of the relative severity, frequency, and chronicity of abuse have been found to predict both behavior problem levels and competence ratings, suggesting that aside from some categorical effects that distinguish sexual abuse from other kinds of abuse, factors relating to the degree of abuse are most significant in predicting its effects. The consistent pattern of findings across studies indicates a substantial influence of physical abuse on aggression and behavior problems.

A number of important studies have been conducted that speak to the mechanisms connecting the experience of child abuse to subsequent antisocial behavior. Main and George (1985) observed toddlers (ages 1–3) with peers and noted that the abused children were much less likely to respond to distressed peers with concern than were nonabused toddlers. Instead, they more often responded with fear or aggression. Howes and Eldredge (1985) reported similar observations with toddlers in a day-care setting. In addition to being more aggressive and less helpful with distressed peers, the abused children were more retaliatory and apt to accelerate conflicts, whereas the nonabused children responded with crying. Haskett and Kistner (1991) observed physically abused 3- to 6-year-old children in day-care settings and found that they initiated fewer interactions with peers, but proportionately more negative interactions, than a carefully matched comparison group. In a study that suggests a more complex connection between ambient anger and aggressive behavior, Cummings, Hennessy, Rabideau, and Cicchetti (1994) observed boys (ages 4–7) in a lab setting where a female experimenter became angry with the child's mother in the presence of the child. Boys with a history of physical abuse reacted by giving more comfort and support to their mothers, as well as more negative or aggressive responses to the adult actress, than did boys without a history of abuse or neglect. Mothers of abused boys also reported more externalizing behavior problems by their sons than did mothers of the nonabused boys, even controlling for SES. Thus, all three studies confirm the greater aggressive responding to conflict and distress by physically abused children and the greater general level of reactivity, but the Cummings et al. (1994) study suggests that the identity of the distressed individual and the circumstances evoking distress can influence behavioral responding.

The results of the Cummings et al. (1994) study of abused boys points to the significance of early emotion regulation in the development of aggressive tendencies and to a distinction Eisenberg (1986) has made between sympathy and personal distress. Both reactions are emotional responses to the emotional state or welfare of another, but in the case of sympathy the reaction is other-directed and can lead to altruistic behavior such as the abused boys' attempts to comfort their mothers. Personal distress, according to Eisenberg, is a self-directed reaction reflecting anxiety and worry and can lead to escape behavior, or as Cummings and his colleagues have demonstrated in other research, to aggressive acts. Cummings, Iannotti, and Zahn-Waxler (1985) observed dyads of 2-year olds in an experimental study in which adults were heard in angry or positive exchanges. Exposure to angry exchanges led to immediate emotional displays of distress and to subsequent aggressive behavior toward playmates. Cummings and Zahn-Waxler (1992) reviewed a number of studies confirming the relation between exposure to adult conflict and emotional arousal in children, including evidence that a history of such exposure leads to greater arousal of distress. Interestingly, in light of the heart rate data reviewed by Raine (1993), children who had the strongest behavioral arousal showed a decrease in heart rate at the onset of adult anger, whereas children showing less distress behaviorally had an increase in heart rate in response to adult anger. Although repeated exposure to adult anger cannot be said to have a direct connection to individual aggressiveness but involves other factors such as temperament, gender, and socialization history, Cummings and Zahn-Waxler (1992) conclude that such exposure may lower thresholds for emotional regulation and the latter can translate into aggressive coping responses. Fabes and Eisenberg (1992b)

reached a similar conclusion from an observation of preschool children's reactions to provocation during free play. Their measures of children's arousability actually had a somewhat stronger relation to children's peer status than their aggressive responses, although both relations were significant.

A longitudinal study of a community-based preschool sample provides insight into the cognitive and emotional mediators of the relation between physical abuse and aggressive behavior (Dodge, Bates, & Pettit, 1990; Dodge, Pettit, Bates, & Valente, 1995; Weiss, Dodge, Bates, & Pettit, 1992). Children were recruited for this study before they made the transition into kindergarten. At that time, parents were interviewed about the child's developmental history from 12 months of age to the present, and interviewers included this question: "Do you remember any times that your child was hit severely enough by any adult to be hurt or to require medical attention?" Probes to assess whether welts or bruises that lasted more than 24 hours or required medical attention were rated on a 5-point scale and abuse was coded for scores from "probably not" to "definitely and/or authorities involved." Those children who had been physically abused were more likely than nonabused children to display aggressive behaviors later in kindergarten, as assessed by direct observation and teacher and peer ratings. Early physical abuse also predicted the development of hypervigilance to hostile cues, hostile attributional biases, and aggressive problem-solving strategies. These social information-processing patterns, in turn, accounted for a significant portion (up to one half) of the relation between early physical abuse and later aggressive behavior. These results held even when controls for child temperament, SES, and marital violence were included in the structural model (Weiss et al., 1992). In the longest term analyses relating physical abuse prior to kindergarten to externalizing problem behavior in third and fourth grade (Dodge et al., 1995), these same social information-processing patterns assessed annually from kindergarten to the beginning of third grade continued to mediate the relation between early childhood physical abuse and conduct problems in middle childhood. It is compelling to juxtapose these findings with the conclusions of Cummings and Zahn-Waxler (1992) on the arousal of distress in response to adult conflict and suggest that when young children are reared in a home context of conflict and threats and are themselves the targets of physical abuse, they develop a heightened arousal to conflict and threat that eventually impairs their ability to process the intentions of others in threatening circumstances. This handicap, which is both emotional and cognitive, leads them to be more reactively aggressive and less able to control their anger responses.

What emerges from these findings is a strong association between early parental physical abuse and a heightened emotional reactivity to conflict, anger, and distress. Very young children who have been victimized come to expect hostile intentions in others and are hypervigilant to these cues. With such a strong orientation toward defending self and attacking others, limited alternative thinking may occur, leaving the young child ill equipped to relate in prosocial ways with peers and responding to the distress in others as though oneself was in danger.

Parenting in Later Childhood and Adolescence

Although early family socialization practices seem to set some children onto a pathway of aggressive and disruptive behaviors outside the home, other dimensions of parenting play a part in the progression toward more serious antisocial activities. Two aspects of parenting appear to be critical to controlling child antisocial activity in later childhood and early adolescence, namely discipline practices and parental monitoring. Larzelere and Patterson (1990) described structural equation modeling of the linkage between family socioeconomic status, as measured when the boys were in fourth grade, and delinquency, measured in seventh grade from police records and self-report. They found that parent management practices measured in sixth grade entirely mediated this relation. Parental management comprised discipline practices such as consistency, control of parental anger during discipline, and negativity in interactions reflecting aversive comments over trivial incidents, and parental monitoring of the child's activities and associations.

Parental monitoring is particularly important in relation to adolescent involvement with deviant peers. Snyder, Dishion, and Patterson (1986) reported strong path relations between parental monitoring and deviant peer associations in tenth grade. In their study of 169 adolescent boys living in small, midwestern towns, Simons, Wu, Conger, and Lorenz (1994) assessed the impact of parental discipline (monitoring, harsh discipline, consistency, and standards) on deviant peer associations and police arrests and sanctions. For both early starters and late starters in delinquency, ineffective parenting in seventh grade predicted arrests in ninth grade.

Following from Hirschi's (1969) social control theory of antisocial behavior in which a close bond between parent and adolescent is thought to function as a control on antisocial activity, Hawkins and Lishner (1987) reviewed studies supporting the hypothesis that positive parent-child bonding in adolescence is negatively related to adolescent problem behavior. This conceptualization has strong similarity to Baumrind's (1987) contention that an authoritative parent-child relationship is the best protection against serious adolescent risk taking. An observational study of parent-adolescent interactions during a discussion of ongoing discipline issues illustrates important cultural differences in the way that adolescent autonomy relates to antisocial behavior in African American and Hispanic households. Florsheim, Tolan, and Gorman-Smith (in press) found that boys rated by fifth- and seventh-grade teachers as high on antisocial behavior were less friendly and more hostile toward both parents than low antisocial boys. Conversely, mothers of the antisocial boys were more hostile to their sons than were mothers of the low antisocial boys. In a second study of the same sample, Gorman-Smith, Tolan, Zelli, and Huesmann (in press) found differences in parental monitoring and marginally significant differences in discipline practices between families of violent delinquent youth and nondelinquent youth. Ethnicity and risk for delinquency interacted for a measure of beliefs about the importance of family and duty to family. Stronger endorsement of these beliefs was found among the families of delinquent Latino youth than among the nondelinquent Latino group, whereas both groups of African American families had similar endorsement levels to that of the nondelinquent Latino families. The authors speculate that greater family focus among recently immigrated Mexican American families may lead to greater adolescent avoidance of home.

Dishion, French, and Patterson (1995) have challenged the bonding hypothesis, citing a multiagent and multimethod measurement study of parent monitoring, limit setting, and parent-child relationships (Dishion & Brown, in press) that indicates there is considerable overlap between these various measures of parenting practices. Dishion argues that most studies supporting the utility of bonding for predicting delinquency fail to control for past behavior. Nonetheless, the results obtained by Florsheim et al. suggest that parent-adolescent relationships must be understood in the context of broader ethnic and cultural values and norms.

An important validation of the causal role of parenting practices on antisocial activity comes from interventions designed to change these practices and reduce antisocial activity. For example, Patterson, Chamberlain, and Reid

(1982) compared the effects of parent training that used the coercion model as a basis for altering parent behavior and found significant reductions in observed deviant behavior compared with those youth randomly assigned to community practitioners. In a stronger test of the model, Dishion, Patterson and Kavanagh (1991) randomly assigned parents of preadolescents at risk for substance abuse to training in contingency management techniques and found significant reductions in teacher ratings of antisocial behavior compared with youth whose families were assigned to placebo control conditions. Of greatest significance for the validation of the causal role of parenting to antisocial behavior was the fact that improvements in behavior correlated significantly, controlling for baseline behavior, with improvements in observed discipline practices.

Mental Processes

The analyses of the mechanisms through which early family conflict exerts an influence on antisocial development provide a natural transition to a discussion of the role of mental processes in aggressive behavior.

Intelligence and Academic Achievement

Juvenile delinquents score about 8 points lower, on average, than nondelinquents on standardized measures of intelligence, with the major difference being in Verbal IQ and not Performance IQ (Wilson & Herrnstein, 1985). This difference holds even when other factors, such as socioeconomic class and race (Lynam, Moffitt, & Stouthamer-Loeber, 1993) and differential likelihood of delinquency detection (Moffitt & Silva, 1988), are statistically controlled. Prospective analyses (Moffitt, Gabrielli, Mednick, & Schulsinger, 1981; West & Farrington, 1973) suggest that the causal direction is most likely that impairments in intelligence lead to later delinquency. One of the mediating factors, particularly for African American youth, appears to be school failure (Lynam et al., 1993). That is, "achievement difficulties are more strongly predictive of delinquent behavior than is low intellectual ability per se" (Hinshaw, 1992, p. 135).

Early epidemiological analyses in the Isle of Wight study (Rutter et al., 1970) suggested that the key predictor variable might be IQ-discrepant reading deficits (reflecting lower reading performance than expected by IQ scores), but subsequent findings from the Dunedin study (Anderson, Williams, McGee, & Silva, 1989) and a comprehensive review (Hinshaw, 1992) indicate that in childhood IQ-achievement discrepancies relate to ADHD, but not to other antisocial behavior once ADHD is controlled. Instead, antisocial behavior correlates more closely with low IQ and overall academic failure (Hinshaw, 1992). Given that low achievement correlates with antisocial behavior more strongly in adolescence than in childhood (Hinshaw, 1992), it is likely that a history of antisocial behavior leads a child to miss out on peer and classroom experiences that promote academic learning. It is also likely, though, that a history of academic failure is a risk factor for the development of other problems, including antisocial behavior. As noted earlier, when low achievement is related to attention problems, it is the latter that has proven to be predictive of delinquency rather than the former.

In an effort to understand what aspect of low intelligence places a child at risk for antisocial behavior and how mental processes lead to behavior, Hinshaw concluded, "Intelligence is sufficiently heterogeneous as a construct that it may mask more specific aspects of cognitive functioning that hold stronger relationships with externalizing behavior" (p. 148).

Moral Development and Perspective Taking

The structuralist perspective on cognitive development evolving from Piaget's theory and research has contributed two major ideas to the quest for understanding the development of antisocial behavior. Social and cognitive egocentrism, or the failure to recognize the perspective of social others, has been related to the development of antisocial behavior. Rubin (1972) found that children's performance on a task requiring them to understand and take the perspective of another is correlated with their social adjustment, even after IQ is controlled. Chandler (1973) found that aggressive children's social perspective-taking level, scored in terms of Piagetian developmental levels, was lower than their peers. He then developed an intervention showing young adolescent delinquents videotapes of their own behavior, followed by discussion in which participants were encouraged to take each other's roles, to improve their perspective-taking levels. Those adolescents who participated in the intervention displayed fewer delinquent acts 18 months later than did a control group. Others (e.g., Iannotti, 1978) have been unable to obtain shifts in aggression through role-taking training, and Shantz (1983) has noted that the processes responsible for any positive effects remain to be specified. Perspective taking has also been viewed in terms of empathy, which has been related to both altruistic and antisocial behavior (Marcus, 1980). Eisenberg (1986) made an important distinction between empathy as a mere echoing of the distress of another person and sympathy, which is an accurate reading of the other's distress that gives rise to helpful responding without necessarily overwhelming one with the pain of the other. Sympathetic responding has been consistently found to predict altruistic or helpful behavior in children (cf. Eisenberg & Fabes, 1990), but there has been less systematic research linking the absence of sympathetic responding to antisocial behavior. There have been some attempts to make children less aggressive by training them to take the affective perspective of others (e.g., Feshbach & Feshbach, 1982), but the results have been mixed, at best. Eisenberg's (1986) conception of the development of sympathetic capacity has not been translated into training programs that might provide a valid test of these ideas. With respect to cognitive perspective-taking, Shantz (1983) has noted that accuracy in understanding the emotional response of another, by itself, may not always lead a child to more prosocial behavior.

The second major contribution of the structuralist perspective has been the articulation of moral development in relation to antisocial behavior. Kohlberg's five-stage theory of moral judgment processes (Kohlberg, 1981) has been the basic framework for much of this research. The basic hypothesis has been that developmental lags in stages of moral development will lead to antisocial behavior. Blasi (1980) reviewed studies testing the relation between moral judgment and moral action and concluded that a majority of these studies supported Kohlberg's thesis that higher moral reasoning would lead to personal honesty and altruism. The fact that moral reasoning, per se, does not always relate to apparently altruistic behavior or resistance to temptation has led to an elaboration of the theory in terms of personal identity. That is, moral reasoning is related to moral behavior in individuals for whom moral values are central to their self-understanding (Blasi & Oresick, 1986; Damon, 1984; Damon & Hart, 1988). Thus far, moral reasoning has not been evaluated as a longitudinal predictor of aggression and antisocial behavior. Instead, interviews with delinquent youth demonstrate differences in moral judgment and self-understanding between delinquent and nondelinquent youth. Melcher (1986, cited in Damon & Hart, 1988) found that conduct-disordered adolescents had a weaker conception of themselves ($r = .27$ between conduct disorder and self-understanding), particularly with respect to seeing themselves in the future and having a sense of agency. Although structural constructs are more specific than general IQ as descriptors of the process of aggressive behavior, even more

specific analyses are required. Hinshaw (1992) and Schonfeld, Shaffer, O'Connor, and Portnoy (1988) suggest that social information processing analyses are better equipped to account for aggressive behavior.

Social Information Processing

Social-information-processing models of aggressive behavior were developed to describe at a proximal level how cognitive and emotional processes lead a child to engage in aggressive behavior within a social event (e.g., Dodge, 1986; Huessman, 1988; McFall, 1982; Rubin & Krasnor, 1986). The conceptual grounding for these models is work in cognitive science on how individuals store and retrieve information (Tulving & Thomson, 1973), distribute processing in parallel and hierarchical fashion (Rumelhart & McClelland, 1986; Schneider & Shiffrin, 1977), and ultimately solve problems (Newell & Simon, 1972). According to these models, an individual comes to a social situation with a set of biological capabilities and a history of social experiences represented in memory. The individual is presented with a new set of social cues (e.g., peers gently tease a boy on the playground about his ugly shoes). The individual's behavioral response is hypothesized to occur as a function of how he or she encodes, represents, and processes those cues, which, in turn, is a function of the interaction among biological, memorial, and current-cue factors. Because processing occurs in real time, it can have both conscious and unconscious (and controlled and automatic) components (Rabiner, Lenhart, & Lochman, 1990). As Piaget (1965; Cowan, 1979) noted, processing is a fully emotional, as well as cognitive, phenomenon.

The first step in processing is encoding the cues. Because the cue array is so overwhelming, the individual employs heuristics to encode only relevant portions. Both deficits (e.g., failure to encode mitigating cues) and biases (e.g., selective attention to hostile features of others' behavior) in encoding could lead an individual to respond aggressively; different biases (e.g., selective failure to encode actual hostile cues) could lead to nonaggressive responding. As cues are encoded, they are interpreted, so the next step is mental representation of the meaning of the cues, particularly with regard to threat and others' intentions. The probability of aggressive retaliation is much greater if the individual interprets cues as threatening than as benign, even given the very same cues (Dodge, 1980). Thus, both biases (e.g., a hostile attributional bias, as dubbed by Nasby et al., 1979) and errors (e.g., misinterpreting a benign teasing stimulus as malicious) in mental representation could enhance the likelihood of aggressive responding. The next step in processing is to access one or more possible behavioral responses from memory. Through exposure, experience, and evolution, one's interpretation of a stimulus becomes associated with emotional and behavioral responses (e.g., threat-retaliate, disrespect-anger; see desired object-grab it); in some cases, the individual actively generates responses, as in problem solving. Often, single behavioral responses are not accessed; rather, a program of behaviors and expected responses to those behaviors is accessed, as in a script (Huesmann, 1988). Obviously, patterns of response access will be closely linked to the probability of aggressive responding. Accessing a response does not destine one to that response; the next step of processing is response decision. The individual might evaluate a potential response in terms of its moral acceptability (Guerra, Huesmann, & Hanish, 1995) and its instrumental, interpersonal, and intrapersonal outcomes, weight the values of those outcomes, and decide on a course of action. The response that is most positively evaluated (e.g., a boy evaluates that hitting a peer will save face, which is more important than being punished by authority, so he decides to aggress) will likely be enacted. An individual might consider multiple potential responses simultaneously or sequentially, with varying thresholds of acceptability for enactment. In this context, impulsivity is defined as the lowest possible acceptability (i.e., a child responds with the first response that comes to mind, with no further evaluation). Thus, patterns of impulsivity or positive evaluation for aggressing are likely to eventuate in aggressive behavior. Also, rehearsal of behaviors in one's mind enhances the likelihood of selection, without regard to its likely consequences (Huesmann, 1988). Finally, the selected response gets transformed into behavior, which requires motor and verbal skills. Skill deficiencies in enacting aggressive responses could inhibit those behaviors, whereas skill deficiencies in enacting competent, nonaggressive alternatives could enhance aggressive responding through default.

Because the model describes social behavior as it unfolds in real time, the steps of processing are hypothesized to recycle iteratively (e.g., one's behavioral response gets a reaction from another person, which becomes the next cue for further encoding) and most likely occur simultaneously with feedback loops in parallel processing (e.g., in the microsecond of evaluating a potential response, one encodes a change in a peer's facial expression). As a description of social events, the model has great heuristic strength (see Crick & Dodge, 1994, for a review). In addition, the model proposes that individuals develop characteristic styles of processing cues at each step, within domains of situations, and that these processing styles will correlate with individual differences in aggressive behavior. This hypothesis has generated over 100 empirical studies, with generally supportive findings (see reviews by Crick & Dodge, 1994; Rubin & Krasnor, 1986).

At the first stage of encoding, aggressive children demonstrate both relative deficits in attention to relevant social cues and hypervigilant biases. Dodge et al. (1995) found that aggressive children are less able than nonaggressive children to recall relevant social cues presented via videotape. However, aggressive children have also been found to attend selectively to aggressive social cues in a stimulus array more than nonaggressive peers do and have difficulty diverting attention from aggressive cues (Gouze, 1987). When encoded cues are used to make interpretations of others' actions, aggressive children use fewer external cues than others do (Dodge & Newman, 1981). Instead, they rely more on their own stereotypes or simply use the most recently presented cue (Dodge & Tomlin, 1987). These patterns all suggest that aggressive children are relatively ill equipped to make social judgments based on full and accurate information because of their poor encoding patterns.

Other studies have examined children's mutual representations of social information. Over three dozen studies have shown that, given ambiguous provocation circumstances, aggressive children are more likely than nonaggressive children to make a hostile interpretation of another's intentions. In a typical study, participants are asked to imagine being the object of an ambiguous provocation (e.g., a peer spills water on you) and to make an interpretation of the peer's likely intent (Graham & Hudley, 1994). A hostile attributional bias has been found in many aggressive school-based samples, including aggressive 8- to 12-year-old children (Guerra & Slaby, 1989; Lochman, 1987), rejected-aggressive white children (Dell Fitzgerald & Asher, 1987; Sancilio, Plumert, & Hartup, 1989; Waas, 1988), aggressive African American middle school boys (Graham & Hudley, 1994), aggressive Latino children (Graham, Hudley, & Williams, 1992), and rejected British 8- to 10-year-old children (Aydin & Markova, 1979). Hostile attributional biases have also been found in aggressive clinical samples, including hyperactive-aggressive children from an outpatient psychiatric clinic (Milich & Dodge, 1984), incarcerated violent offenders (Slaby & Guerra, 1988), and aggressive boys in residential treatment (Nasby et al., 1979). The findings extend beyond hypothetical situations: Steinberg and Dodge (1983) found similar evidence using a laboratory-based actual social interaction.

Hostile attributional bias effects have been found to be quite robust but not necessarily large in magnitude, partly because of the specificity of this phenomenon. These effects reflect a personalized tendency instead of a general inclination to infer that peers act with hostile intent toward other peers (Dodge & Frame, 1982; Sancilio et al., 1989). Hostile attributional biases occur more readily when the aggressive child is emotionally aroused (Dodge & Somberg, 1987). Finally, hostile attributional biases predict angry-reactive aggression but not proactive aggression (Dodge & Coie, 1987) and violent crimes but not nonviolent crimes (Dodge, Price, Bachorowski, & Newman, 1990).

Although reciprocal effects are likely, prospective analyses by Dodge et al. (1995) suggest that hostile attributional biases predict aggressive behavior several years in the future. Rabiner and Coie (1989) experimentally manipulated children's expectations for peer intent and found that these expectations predicted subsequent peer acceptance of the child (presumably, the expectations led to nonaggressive child behaviors that led to peer acceptance). Finally, experimental intervention with aggressive African American boys in which the focus was to reduce hostile attributional tendencies led to decreased aggressive behavior, relative to a control group (Hudley & Graham, 1993).

Using videotaped stimuli, several researchers have found that aggressive children not only show biases toward hostile attributions in ambiguous circumstances, but also erroneously interpret intent when the stimuli clearly depict benign intentions (Dodge et al., 1984; Dodge, Pettit, McClaskey, & Brown, 1986). Statistical controls indicate that this intention-cue detection deficiency in aggressive children cannot be accounted for by general information-processing deficits (Waldman, 1988), impulsivity (Waldman, in press), or verbal intelligence (Dodge, Price, et al., 1990).

The next step of processing is response access. Both the automatic association between social cue representation and aggressive responses and the conscious generation of aggressive solutions to social dilemmas have been implicated in the genesis of aggressive behavior. Shure and Spivack (1980) have pioneered the study of generativity of response accessing and have found that among preschool children, the number of responses that a child generates to hypothetical social problems is inversely related to that child's rate of aggressive behavior. Among children in elementary school, the quality, not quantity, of responses is linked to aggressive problems. Aggressive children generate high proportions of atypical responses (Ladd & Odens, 1979; Rubin, Bream, & Rose-Krasnor, 1991), bribery and affect manipulation responses (Rubin, Moller, & Emptage, 1987), direct physical aggression responses (Waas, 1988), and adult intervention responses (Asher & Renshaw, 1981). They access fewer competent responses, including nonaggressive assertion (Deluty, 1981), planning responses (Asarnow & Callan, 1985), and the coordination of multiple goals (Taylor & Gabriel, 1989).

There are crucial differences between accessing a response and selecting it for enactment. Across development, children learn to lengthen the time between response accessing and behavior or to withhold impulses altogether, pending a mental evaluation of their likely effects. Barkley (1997) has argued that the inability to inhibit accessed responses is the single major component of ADHD that is responsible for the aggressive behavior problems of these children. Both anecdotal case reports (Kendall & Braswell, 1985) and systematic self-reports by aggressive children (Perry, Perry, & Rasmussen, 1986) support the hypothesis that aggressive children have difficulty inhibiting aggressive responses. Slaby and Guerra (1988) found that aggressive adolescent offenders generate fewer possible outcomes for their own behaviors than others do, suggesting a failure to consider consequences by this group.

When they are experimentally forced to make evaluations and consider consequences, aggressive children, relative to nonaggressive peers, evaluate aggressive responses as less morally "bad" (Deluty, 1983), more "friendly" (Crick & Ladd, 1990), and globally more acceptable (Asarnow & Callan, 1985; Boldizar, Perry, & Perry, 1989). They expect more positive instrumental outcomes (Hart, Ladd, & Burleson, 1990), more positive intrapersonal outcomes (Deluty, 1983), fewer negative interpersonal outcomes (Quiggle, Panak, Garber, & Dodge, 1992), and fewer sanctional outcomes (Perry et al., 1986) for aggressing. Guerra, Huesmann, and Hanish (1995) suggest that aggressive children hold generally positive beliefs about aggression and believe it is socially normative. Furthermore, the display of aggression enhances one's endorsement of positive beliefs about aggression, and the endorsement of positive beliefs increases subsequent aggression. Ethnographic analyses of urban communities also support the notion that "codes of violence" support aggressive behavior as the only means of gaining status and avoiding victimization (E. Anderson, 1990).

As with other aspects of processing, these findings are moderated by subtyping of aggressive children. Crick and Dodge (1996) have found that positive evaluations of the outcomes of aggression predict proactive aggression (e.g., bullying, grabbing peers' possessions) but not reactive anger (which, as noted earlier, is predicted more by hostile attributional biases).

The final step of processing is to transform a selected response into motor and verbal behavior. Perry et al. (1986) found that aggressive children are more likely than others to believe that engaging in aggression will come easily for them. In contrast, socially rejected and aggressive children have been shown to be less competent when asked to enact and role-play nonaggressive socially appropriate behaviors in laboratory settings (Burleson, 1982; Dodge et al., 1985; Gottman, Gonso, & Rasmussen, 1975). One of the difficulties with these studies is that children's enactments may be confounded by other mental processes, such as their expectations about the likely outcomes of behavior, even in laboratory role-play settings.

Each of the single processing-aggressive behavior correlations previously described is rather modest in magnitude. These correlations are enhanced by considering the situational context, the type of aggressive behavior, and the profile of processing patterns. Dodge et al. (1986) found that the correlation between processing and aggressive behavior is stronger within situations than across situations (i.e., processing about teasing events relates more strongly to aggressive behavior in response to teasing than to aggressive behavior in peer group entry situations). Also, early-step processing variables (i.e., encoding and hostile attributions) relate more strongly to reactive anger, whereas later-stage processing variables (i.e., response evaluations) relate more strongly to proactive aggression (Crick & Dodge, 1996). Finally, when profiles are assembled or multiple regression techniques are used, the predictability of aggressive behavior from aggregated processing measures is great (Dodge et al., 1986). Findings from seven samples (three from Dodge et al., 1986; one from Dodge & Price, 1994; one from Slaby & Guerra, 1988; and two from Weiss et al., 1992) indicate that processing variables from different steps provides unique increments in predicting aggression, such that multiple correlations range from .4 to .94.

Knowledge Structures That Guide Processing

Social-cognitive theories in psychology (Bargh et al., 1995; Schneider, 1991) suggest that processing of social cues is guided by latent knowledge structures, variously called schemas, scripts, and working models, that are stored in memory (Abelson, 1981; Bowlby, 1980). These structures are hypothesized to be the evolving representational products of experience, which guide processing of new cues (Dodge et al., 1994). Huesmann (1988) has articulated the theory that early development leads children to represent in memory scripts for aggression that include acceptable antecedents, details of context and action, and likely consequences. It is methodologically difficult to assess these scripts independently from an assessment of processing itself, but Graham and Hudley (1994) have creatively employed priming techniques from cognitive social psychology (Higgins & King, 1981) to ascertain that aggressive children have highly accessible aggressive constructs represented in memory. They presented sentences to children that activate related constructs in memory (e.g., "he acted selfishly . . . and on purpose" [priming negative intent] vs. "he didn't contribute because his wallet had been lost" [priming mitigation]) and found that in a subsequent, purportedly unrelated, task, the previous experimental priming of negative intent led aggressive children to make hostile attributions and respond with aggressive behavior but had no effect on nonaggressive children. Consistent with the cognitive literature, the authors interpreted the aggressive children's responses as evidence of aggressive construct accessibility.

Other methods have been used to assess various knowledge structures of aggressive children. Stromquist and Strauman (1992) asked children to describe freely their social relationships and found that the tendency to use aggressive constructs (both in commission and omission; e.g., "he hits others" and "he stays away from fights") is correlated with aggressive behavior. Asher (Asher & Renshaw, 1981; Renshaw & Asher, 1983; Taylor & Asher, 1989) has assessed the goals for social interactions that children carry around with them and has found that aggressive children are more likely than their peers to carry performance and competitive (rather than relational) goals.

Self-concept is a knowledge structure that has been hypothesized to relate to aggression (Harter, 1982). However, despite the speculation of psychodynamic theorists (Keith, 1984) that aggressive children must have miserable self-concepts, empirical assessments have not borne out this hypothesis (Crick & Dodge, 1996; Zakriski & Coie, 1996). It appears that aggressive children blame others rather than themselves for negative outcomes (Cairns, 1991). The possibility that other-blaming may represent self-defensive mechanisms in aggressive children (Keith, 1984) indicates the inherent difficulty in measuring latent knowledge structures.

Self-blaming or not, assessments of yet another knowledge structure (social satisfaction) indicate that aggressive children carry with them feelings of loneliness (Asher, Hymel, & Renshaw, 1984). These feelings likely represent the outcomes rather than the cause of aggressive behavior, but a growing schema of the world as a lonely place could guide future aggressive acts.

Peer Contexts

By school entry, it is possible to identify a constellation of factors that mark children who are at high risk for antisocial behavior in adolescence and adulthood. As the review thus far has indicated, individual child characteristics such as impulsivity and attention deficits often combine with coercive parent-child interactions and discipline practices that are inconsistent, but often punitive and abusive. The result for the child is heightened aggressiveness and emotional reactivity. The high-risk child at school entry, on average, is not only more apt to be disruptive and coercive, but also is not well prepared for academic tasks.

When young aggressive children who fit the risk profile of impulsivity and emotional reactivity enter school, they are likely not only to fail academically but also to fail socially; and these two kinds of failure can interact to increase the tendency toward increased aggressiveness. There is now substantial evidence that aggressive children are likely to be rejected by their peers (Coie, Dodge, & Kupersmidt, 1990). Aggression and disruptiveness are the child characteristics most highly correlated with peer rejection and dislike in elementary school, as reported by peers, teachers, and unbiased observers. Although most of the studies reviewed by Coie et al. were correlational, making it difficult to determine whether aggression leads to rejection or rejection to aggression, several laboratory play group studies now demonstrate that aggression leads to rejection among new, unfamiliar peers. Unfortunately, these studies all involved males only.

Coie and Kupersmidt (1983) assembled groups of previously unacquainted fourth-grade boys of known sociometric status, one of whom was rejected, and observed them at play for six weekly sessions. By the third week, most of the rejected boys were rejected by their new groupmates. Verbal and physical aggression were most characteristic of the rejected boys, and in ratings after the last session, there was consensus among group members that the rejected

boys most often started fights. In a second study, Dodge (1983) formed groups of eight previously unacquainted second-grade boys who were not selected for social status and observed them for eight sessions. Boys who were observed to make hostile comments and hit other boys most often in initial sessions were likely to be rejected by their new peers in sociometric nominations by the fourth session of play. In a third study, Dodge, Coie, Pettit, and Price (1990) observed groups of five or six unfamiliar boys at two grade levels (first and third) for five consecutive play sessions. Negative peer status determined at the end of the sessions was associated with both angry reactive aggression and instrumental aggression. Negative peer status was not related to rough play, a finding that Smith and his colleagues (Humphreys & Smith, 1987) also have found. Bullying was negatively related to peer status in the third-grade groups, but not in the first grade groups. In the first grade, it was the well-liked or popular boys who engaged in the most bullying, suggesting that at this young age some forms of proactive aggression may serve, initially, to establish peer dominance hierarchies. Interestingly, it was the aggressive boys who most often were the targets of the dominance-oriented aggression by the popular first-grade boys. This finding is consistent with Hinde's (1974) contention that dominance hierarchies serve to minimize fighting in social groups by establishing relative power among members. In this case, aggressive boys not only may identify themselves as the group members with whom one must contend, but are the most resistant to domination and thus require more demonstration of physical superiority. Bullying was related to disliking in the third-grade groups suggesting that social dominance is achieved by more sophisticated social strategies with increasing age and that bullying becomes socially unacceptable (Strayer, 1989). Savin-Williams (1979) noted that among adolescent males, ridicule and verbal sparring are more common mechanisms for maintaining dominance than physical aggression.

Two qualifying points need to be made about the relation between childhood aggression and rejection by peers. First, not all aggressive acts are viewed with disapproval by peers. Aggression in response to direct provocation actually is positively viewed by peers. Children who are seen as standing up for themselves are generally well liked (Lancelotta & Vaughn, 1989; Lesser, 1959; Olweus, 1977). The second point is that not all aggressive children are socially rejected by peers. In fact, no more than half of the children named by classmates as being highly aggressive are rejected by them (Cillessen, Van IJzendoorn, van

Lieshout, & Hartup, 1992; Coie & Koeppl, 1990; French, 1988). Furthermore, Lancelotta and Vaughn (1989) found the correlation between aggression and peer rejection to be much stronger among girls ($r = .73$) than among boys ($r = .37$). The fact that boys' levels of aggression are generally higher than girls may make acts of aggression more deviant for girls and thus be more likely to result in rejection.

There are several reasons why not all aggressive children are rejected by their peers. First, social context plays a significant role in the factors leading to peer rejection. Wright, Giammarino, and Parad (1986) demonstrated the importance of social context in the form of peer behavioral norms in a study of cabinmates in a summer program for behaviorally disturbed boys. Using counselor reports on aggression episodes, Wright and his colleagues divided the boys' living units into high and low aggression groups. Within-group peer status measures were then correlated with individual aggression ratings from counselors. Aggression was negatively correlated with peer status in the low-aggression groups, as is the case for most unselected peer group studies, but aggression was uncorrelated with status in the high-aggression groups. Similar findings relating to within-group norms have been found in another study. Boivin, Dodge, and Coie (1995) examined the relation between aggressive behavior and peer status in 30 of the experimental play groups studied in the Dodge, Coie, et al. (1990) project. Reactive aggression was negatively related to peer status in play groups low in reactive aggression, but uncorrelated with status in groups where reactive aggression was frequent.

The second major reason that not all aggressive children are socially rejected is the considerable diversity in other aspects of social behavior that either set the context for aggressive acts or compensate for them. Bierman (1986) has found differences in the social behavior of rejected versus nonrejected aggressive boys that seem to account for the different evaluations of peers. For example, Bierman, Smoot, and Aumiller (1993) studied the social and aggressive behaviors of 95 first- through sixth-grade boys by means of teacher ratings, peer interviews, and direct observations of lunchroom and playground behavior. The boys were selected from a sample of 415 boys on the basis of peer nominations and assigned to one of four categories: aggressive-rejected, aggressive only, rejected only, or comparison (neither aggressive nor rejected). Factor scores derived from the three sources of behavioral data reflected no differences in physical aggression between the two aggressive groups, although both were more aggressive than the nonaggressive groups. The aggressive-rejected group was reported to be more argumentative and disruptive than the other three groups, as well as being less attentive and perceptive. Nonrejected aggressive boys differed from the comparison group only in physical aggressiveness, suggesting that frequency of aggression alone is not the basis for rejection.

Another aspect of the heterogeneity of childhood aggression was reflected in the analysis of bullies and victims in relation to peer status. Using peer nominations for bullies and victims, several investigators (Kupersmidt, Patterson, & Eickholt, 1989; Perry, Kusel, & Perry, 1988) have found a strong relation between victimization and rejection. Perry et al. found that 11 of 17 extreme victims were also rejected by peers. Kupersmidt et al. found that 48% of the children named as frequent victims of peer attack and abuse were children who were rejected by peers. Of those children named as both victims and bullies, 71% were socially rejected. About two thirds of all rejected children were named as either victims, bullies, or both.

These data and other findings on victimization from the Perrys' research led them to conclude that aggressive children may be divided into those who are effectual and those who are ineffectual in peer conflict situations (Perry, Perry, & Kennedy, 1992). Effectual aggressors are rarely victimized by peers and not often involved in extended conflicts because they usually get what they want. Ineffectual aggressors get into lengthy, emotionally charged conflicts from which they often emerge as losers. The latter are also described by Perry et al. as being argumentative, disruptive, needing to have things their own way, and responding to provocation with anger.

This behavior contrasts markedly with that of nonaggressive victims who are passive and vulnerable. Schwartz, Dodge, and Coie (1993) observed boys in small groups and found that submissiveness in response to peer requests increased the probability of subsequent bullying by others. The preceding findings suggest that ineffectual aggressors, who are both victims and bullies, may be the rejected aggressive children. This conclusion is supported by the observation (Dodge & Coie, 1987) that rejected aggressive boys are more highly prone to angry, reactive aggression and to making hostile attributions to peers.

Coie et al. (1991) reported observational data that support the Perrys' description of the high conflict, ineffectual, aggressive boys in their analysis of differences in qualitative features of the aggressive behavior of rejected versus nonrejected, aggressive boys. In this study, rejected aggressive boys were found to continue aggressive episodes for longer periods than nonrejected aggressive boys, and do so in several ways. In bullying episodes, most bullies did not escalate the levels of aggression during an episode, whereas rejected boys were more likely to do so when they were acting as bullies. Conversely, in reactive episodes where aggressors appear to feel justified in their aggressive behavior, most targets of such aggression submit to or ignore the attack, apparently assuming that it might be justified or that it would be better not to make a response. Rejected aggressive boys were found to be more likely to respond to reactive aggression with defensive, aggressive retaliations and less likely to ignore them or submit. These patterns are independent of the probability of winning or losing aggressive episodes. Thus, it appears that rejected aggressive boys intensify their tendencies to deal with peer conflict in aggressive ways and to consolidate their perception of peers as having hostile intentions toward them.

A secondary consequence is that peers appear to let aggressive boys get away with acts that might otherwise start an aggressive episode. Coie et al. (1991) found that not only did rejected aggressive boys initiate more aggressive episodes than other boys, but a higher proportion of these initiations were met with nonresponsive behavior by the recipients of these acts. It appeared that peers were choosing to ignore these aversive behaviors rather than becoming entangled in extended conflictual sequences. In the process, peers seem to be reinforcing the aggressive tendencies of the rejected aggressive boys, albeit unwittingly. Patterson, Littman, and Bricker (1967) observed a similar phenomenon in their study of aggressive playground behavior among preschool children. They found that withdrawal or submission to an aggressive attack increased the probability that the aggressor would make subsequent attacks on the same victim, whereas retaliation or adult intervention decreased this probability. The net result is that aggressive boys receive partial reinforcement by peers, although the long-term consequences mean continued rejection and dislike.

Peer Rejection and Aggression—Effects of Rejection

The reason for giving special attention to the peer status consequences of aggressive behavior is that peer rejection now appears to contribute to subsequent problems of adaptation, including increased antisocial behavior, for aggressive children who become rejected. Ladd (1990) traced the impact of peer rejection early in the first year of school to adjustment at the end of the school year. He found that rejection by peers in the fall of the year predicted poorer academic adjustment, while controlling for measures of academic competence taken in the fall or prior to the start of the school year. Similarly, Dodge, Bates, et al. (1990) have demonstrated that rejection leads to greater aggressiveness among boys who are aggressive initially. They found that peer rejection in kindergarten predicted increased individual aggressiveness by third grade, even when aggression in kindergarten was controlled statistically. In a second longitudinal study in which children were followed from elementary school to middle school, measures assessing children's hostile attribution biases were found to mediate the predictive relation between earlier rejected status and increased individual aggressiveness in middle school. In a third longitudinal study, Bierman and Wargo (1995) followed a sample of first- through sixth-grade boys selected to fit a two-by-two matrix defined by peer rejection and aggression. Increases in aggressive behavior across a 2-year period were predicted by a combination of factors assessed at Time 1. With Time 1 measures of aggression and disruptive-hyperactive behavior scores entered earlier in the model, peer status, as indexed by social preference scores, increased the explained variance on Time 2 aggression by 5%. Thus, being rejected by peers seems to increase the negative expectations of peers held by these aggressive boys and, in turn, leads them to become even more aggressive as they get older. Each of these studies demonstrates the important impact of peer rejection on the adaptive capacities of aggressive children.

A number of longitudinal investigations have provided evidence for the predictive significance of peer rejection and aggressiveness in elementary school for antisocial behavior and other adjustment problems in adolescence (e.g., Coie, Lochman, Terry, & Hyman, 1992; Kupersmidt & Coie, 1990; Ollendick, Weist, Borden, & Greene, 1992; Patterson & Bank, 1989). Parker and Asher (1987) concluded that the case for aggression as a predictor of delinquency was well established and that peer rejection is also predictive of multiple adjustment problems, but the significance of peer rejection for delinquency could not be separated from the correlated effects of rejection and aggression. Since that review, Patterson and Bank (1989) used structural equation modeling to show that peer rejection in fourth grade predicts antisocial activity in sixth grade with fourth-grade antisocial activity partialed out. Kupersmidt and Coie (1990) demonstrated the independent effects of aggression and rejection on delinquency for the majority white portion of their mixed race sample, and Ollendick et al. (1992) did the same for externalizing behaviors in an all-white sample. In the Kupersmidt and Coie study, only childhood aggression was predictive of delinquency for the African American adolescents, a finding the authors attribute to problems of validity of the reaction measure for racial minority members. Coie et al. (1992) found that third-grade peer rejection is a more powerful predictor of parents' ratings of externalizing problems in a sixth-grade sample of African American children than is aggression. They also documented the additive effects of rejection and aggression for predicting a composite index of maladjustment in sixth grade, using parents, teachers, and self-reports as sources. Rejected aggressive children had three times the early adolescent adjustment problems of the nonrejected, nonaggressive peer population.

Coie, Terry, Lenox, et al. (1995) followed the same predominantly urban, African American sample across two more assessment points in eighth and tenth grade and analyzed growth curve models for the four groups formed by crossing third-grade peer rejection and aggressiveness. These results were more striking than the earlier findings on sixth-grade adjustment in terms of the combined predictive significance of rejection and aggression. Although parent- and self-reports of problem behavior were only modestly correlated, growth curves calculated separately on data from the two sources produced the same general conclusion regarding consistent antisocial behavior among males. Males who had been both rejected and aggressive in third grade had profiles of increasingly antisocial activity from sixth grade through tenth grade, whereas the other groups showed lower and decreasing patterns of antisocial behavior. The results for females were less consistent. Third-grade aggression was the variable that predicted consistently higher levels of self-reported antisocial behavior across adolescence for females, whereas it was third grade peer rejection that predicted consistently greater antisocial activity as reported by parents. When data on age of first arrest were examined for this sample (Coie, Miller-Johnson, et al., 1995), survival analyses demonstrated clearly that it was the aggressive-rejected children who were significantly more likely to be arrested earlier than all other children.

These results, and others reported in this section, are consistent with the hypothesis that aggressive-rejected males constitute a significant part of the early starting antisocial group, the relatively small group that Wolfgang, Figlio, and Sellin (1972), among others, describe as accounting for approximately half of adolescent delinquency. This is not to suggest that peer rejection carries equal weight with aggression as a causal factor in development, however. The characteristics that distinguish rejected and nonrejected aggressive boys cannot be argued to have developed solely or even predominantly as a consequence of peer rejection because the immature and incompetent aspects of social functioning that characterize the rejected subgroup are, no doubt, the same factors that contributed to their initial rejection. In this sense, then, peer rejection may serve as both a marker variable for these other risk factors and as a catalyst for the escalation of antisocial behavior.

Deviant Peer Group Influences

A central feature of the development of antisocial careers among the early starter group is the increased diversity of antisocial activity that they engage in as they enter adolescence. This diversity is thought to reflect a kind of training in deviancy that a number of theorists ascribe to peer groups.

Often, the role of deviant peers comes in the form of co-offending—many adolescent offenses are initiated in the company of peers. Aultman (1980) found that 63% of recorded juvenile offenses were committed by groups of two or three adolescents. Girls were more likely to offend in the company of peers than boys.

Elliott et al. (1985) maintain that the modeling and reinforcement required to produce more diverse antisocial activity does not usually come from the family but resides in the deviant peer context. Their longitudinal data on delinquency and substance use from the National Youth Survey point to the incremental predictive role of involvement with deviant peers. In support of this conclusion, Patterson et al. (1991) found that involvement with deviant peers in sixth grade predicted subsequent delinquency when prior antisocial behavior was in the model. Both prior antisocial behavior and poor parental monitoring were predictive of deviant peer associations, as was poor academic achievement in fourth grade. The deviant peer association construct in this study was formed from parent, peer, and self-descriptions of children who "hang around" with peers who get into trouble. In the Simons et al. (1994) study described earlier, association with deviant peers was found to predict arrests in subsequent assessment waves.

Keenan, Loeber, Zhang, Stouthamer-Loeber, and Van Kammen (1995) examined the effects of deviant peer associations on the onset of disruptive behaviors in two cohorts of the Pittsburgh Youth Study. Participants were asked to describe the extent to which their friends engaged in disruptive behavior, and these estimates related both to concurrent and future reports of the participants' own disruptive behavior. The onset of delinquency was assessed at 6-month intervals for five successive waves in data collection beginning in fourth grade for one cohort, or in seventh grade for the other. Authority conflict was twice as likely to occur among disruptive boys who had truant or disobedient best friends as among those who did not, and the odds ratios for the prediction of covert activity and overt activity were 4.3 and 3.4, respectively. The predictive influence of association with deviant peers on disruptive behavior in the following year for onset (that is, among boys offending for the first time in the year following the report of deviant best friends) was less strong than the concurrent influence, perhaps because concurrent influences were so strong. The predictive odds ratios for authority conflict, covert antisocial, and overt antisocial activities were 1.5, 2.2, and 1.9, respectively. Two important features of this study were that onset was the dependent variable, thus controlling for previous disruptive behavior, and that peer influence was tested within a specific type of antisocial activity as a way of examining the extent to which peers truly were models of deviant behavior.

In a contrasting study, Tremblay, Mâsse, Vitaro, and Dobkin (1995) failed to establish peer influence on delinquency in a longitudinal study of preadolescents. Mutual best friends were identified for 758 of the 1,034 French-Canadian boys aged 10 to 12. Self-reported overt and covert delinquency assessed one year later were predicted by the participants' earlier peer-rated aggressiveness, but the peer-rated aggressiveness of the best friends did not add to the prediction of either covert or overt delinquency. The delinquency of peers in this study was estimated by aggressive reputation and peer influence was restricted to a single best friend, rather than a group of friends; however, it is possible that peer influence may be greater at older ages than those studied here. In the Keenan et al. study, older boys were more likely to initiate covert delinquency than the younger boys.

In a follow-up analysis of data from the Tremblay et al. (1995) study, Vitaro et al. (in press) divided the boys according to teacher ratings of their disruptiveness at ages 11 to 12. When the impact of having aggressive-disruptive friends was analyzed in terms of the boys' prior history of conduct problems, Vitaro et al. found that it was the moderately disruptive boys whose delinquent activity at age 13 showed the negative consequences of deviant friends' influence, in contrast to highly disruptive or socially conforming

boys. This study points to the importance of considering the characteristics of both parties to the influence process.

One of the limitations of each of the preceding studies is that measures of actual group affiliation were not used. A problem with relying on adult or peer estimates of deviant peer influence is that these indices are highly correlated ($r = .89$) with ratings of the target individual's own aggressive behavior (Bagwell, Coie, Terry, & Lochman, 1996), making it virtually impossible to partial out the influence of the target's aggression from estimates of deviant peer influence. In identifying peer associations such as the ones just described, Cairns and his associates utilized a more complex approach that was less susceptible to stereotyping on the basis of reputation. They used peer informants to identify the peer clique structure for a school-based peer cohort, and then used behavioral characteristics of clique members as an index of clique deviance. Using this approach, they demonstrated that aggressive youth not only tend to associate with other aggressive youth (Cairns et al., 1988) but that deviant peer associations appear to influence dropping out of school (Cairns, Cairns, & Neckerman, 1989).

Coie, Terry, Zakriski, et al. (1995) employed a similar method to that of Cairns for identifying peer cliques, except that all participating adolescents named those peers with whom they associated. Relative centrality in a clique was then derived for each member based on factor analytic techniques. Cliques were defined as more or less deviant by the statistical relation between the deviance scores of members and their relative centrality to a clique. Coie, Terry, Zakriski, et al. (1995) did not find that deviant peer associations among eighth grade, urban, African American youth were predictive of subsequent police arrest beyond that predicted by prior arrest record. However, in a second study involving twice as many subjects, the deviant peer construct did predict self-reported antisocial activity above and beyond that predicted by prior self-reported antisocial activity (Coie, Terry, & Lochman, 1993). The failure to find deviant peer influences in the first study may have been due to the combined effect of fewer subjects and an overly conservative index of antisocial activity such as police arrests; however, the second study did reveal the importance of timing in evaluating the impact of deviant peer associations. Deviant peer influences were not found for sixth-grade evaluations but were found for the eighth-grade associations. Deviant peer involvement in sixth grade did not add to the prediction of subsequent antisocial activity phenomenon. Because sixth grade was the first year of middle school, peer cliques at that time may have lacked the stability to have the persistent influence found later in eighth grade.

The hypothesis that deviant peer associations promote antisocial activity is as enduring as the folk wisdom that leads parents to warn their children about bad company. The preceding research findings provide empirical support for this idea. Just how these associations produce their effects beyond the individual predispositions of the members has not been well researched. Buehler, Patterson, and Furniss (1966) observed adolescents in a correctional institution and found that inmates tended to reinforce delinquent behaviors and punish behaviors conforming to mainstream social norms. In two studies attempting to follow up this question of how deviant peers increase each other's antisocial activity, Dishion examined the interactions of antisocial youth and their friends. As part of the 13- to 14-year-old assessment of the Oregon Youth Study, friends of the study participants (named by both the boys and their parents) were invited to participate in a peer interaction task (Dishion, Andrews, & Crosby, 1995). Friends of the more antisocial boys tended to come from the same neighborhood and to provide less satisfying friendships, suggesting that these were friendships of convenience. Also, the behaviors of friends were highly correlated, with antisocial dyads having more negative qualities and more noxious behavior. When highly antisocial dyads (i.e., both had prior police contact and high antisocial ratings) were compared with low antisocial dyads, the high antisocial dyads contingently reciprocated more negative behavior.

In another report of the same set of friendship interaction data, Dishion, Patterson, and Griesler (1994) found that antisocial dyads engaged in more talk that would tend to reinforce delinquent behavior than low antisocial dyads. In this latter paper, longitudinal data on antisocial activity and deviant peer associations at ages 10 and 14 suggested a synchrony between the two variables.

Even though the dynamics of movement toward and away from deviant peer associations has not been well studied, the relation between association with other deviant youth and delinquent activity is well established in the literature on gangs. Thornberry, Krohn, Lizotte, and Chard-Wierschem (1993) found that gang members accelerated their illegal activity during the time they were associated with their gang, and decelerated this activity when they left the gang and were not enmeshed in the gang environment.

Taken together, the preceding findings suggest two important facts about deviant peer associations and antisocial behavior. Friendship activities between antisocial youth serve to promote greater deviant behavior, even though, or perhaps because, the interaction quality of the relationship is abrasive. Second, when youth are in a period of antisocial activity, they tend to associate with other antisocial youth, a phenomenon that Kandel (1978) referred to as homophily (like seeking like), but when they are no longer engaged in antisocial activity, they no longer associate with deviant peers. Although the term homophily suggests a mutual attraction between antisocial adolescents, the quality of interactions among aggressive youth suggests both positive friendship features like those of nondeviant friends and aversive qualities that are lacking in the relationships of nondeviant friends. In comparing delinquent and nondelinquent 12- to 19-year-olds, Giordano, Cernkovich, and Pugh (1986) found more self-reported conflict between delinquent friends, but also more willingness to confide and equivalent amounts of interaction. Gillmore, Hawkins, Day, and Catalano (1992) interviewed preadolescent youth about their friends and nonfriends and found that those who described themselves as frequently getting into trouble were more attached to their conventional friends than to their friends who also get into trouble. These sentiments about friendship mirror the Dishion et al. (1994) conclusion that many antisocial friendships are relationships of convenience and not necessarily the preferred choices of these youth. Many of the chronically antisocial youth in the Oregon Youth Study Sample (Dishion et al., 1994) were rejected at age 10 and age 14, and their friendships were of relatively short duration. Thus, part of the dynamics of peer associations for highly antisocial youth may be that they have limited conventional friendship opportunities. In fact, Hawkins and Weis (1985) have argued that delinquency often results from a lack of social bonding to the conventional elements of society. The absence of these bonds leads to a lessened influence of conventional rules for behavior and this, in turn, contributes to greater antisocial activity.

The reciprocal influence of deviant peer associations and delinquent activity is illustrated in longitudinal findings from the Rochester Youth Developmental Study. Thornberry (1994) found that associating with deviant peers leads to increased delinquency, partly through the formation and reinforcement of beliefs that it is not wrong to commit delinquent acts. Across time, adolescents who commit delinquent acts are more likely to associate with peers who are also delinquent. Their analyses suggested that bi-directional relationships are necessary to account for longitudinal changes in delinquency, supporting the idea that a dynamic social developmental process is involved.

Delinquent Gangs

The phenomenon of delinquent gangs, particularly in the United States, is an important contemporary manifestation of deviant peer groups. As Goldstein (1994) noted, gangs have changed across the past 50 years, as have explanations for their existence, one of the most salient changes being the increased involvement with illegal drug sales. Miller's (1974) early survey of gangs in cities attributed the highest proportions of adolescent male involvement in gangs to Los Angeles and Philadelphia, and most gangs comprised non-white, ethnically homogeneous members. More recently, Spergel, Ross, Curry, and Chance (1989, as cited in Goldstein, 1994) found gangs in all 50 states, with most police and other informants indicating that gang participation and activity were on the increase. Males outnumbered females in gang membership by 20 to 1 and gang crime rates by gender mirrored this ratio. The age range of gang members appeared to have extended in both directions from the time of the earlier Miller study. Goldstein concluded that the reasons these youths join gangs are "peer friendship, pride, identity development, self-esteem enhancement, excitement, the acquisition of resources, and in response to family and community tradition. These goals are often not available to young people through legitimate means in the disorganized and low-income environments from which most gang youth derive" (p. 261).

Even though adolescents may join gangs for identity and friendship, one effect of gang involvement, like involvement with deviant peers in general, is increased antisocial activity. Spergel et al. (1989) found that individuals in a gang are three times more likely to engage in violent offenses than are those persons not affiliated with a gang. Thornberry et al. (1993) used longitudinal analyses to show that becoming involved in a gang increases an adolescent's likelihood of violently offending, and that leaving a gang leads to decreases in the likelihood of violently offending.

Adult Antisocial Activity

The developmental model for early starting antisocial individuals posits not only that early starters manifest a greater involvement in delinquency and violence during adolescence than most late starters, but that they are more likely to continue breaking the law in their adult years than are the late starters. The distinction between early and late

starters, however, cannot be sharply drawn because curves for the onset of offending do not show clear demarcation and some so-called late starters do continue offending in the adult years. Continuity of offending into adult years has been shown by Farrington (1995), who found that nearly 75% of those convicted of juvenile offenses (at ages 10–16) were reconvicted between ages 17 and 24, and half of the juvenile offenders were reconvicted between ages 25 and 32. Thus, although the peak of offending in this study was age 17, a substantial number of juvenile offenders continue in criminal careers well into adulthood.

The continuity of antisocial activity in adulthood takes on other forms besides criminal offending. This heterotypic continuity includes spouse abuse, drunk driving, moving traffic violations, and severe punishment of children (Huesmann, Eron, et al., 1984), and what Pulkkinen (1990) described as a relapsed lifestyle. Caspi, Elder, and Bem (1987) followed up 182 children from the Berkeley Guidance Study, interviewing them, their spouses, and children at age 40 about their education, work, marriage, and parenthood. Children characterized as having frequent temper tantrums (biting, kicking, striking, throwing things, swearing, and screaming) at ages 8, 9, and 10 were contrasted in their adult years with children low on temper tantrums. The criterion for inclusion in the high-tempered group was fairly inclusive compared with most criteria for aggression (38% of boys and 29% of girls qualified); nonetheless, the adult comparisons demonstrated the way early self-control problems undermined future adjustment, particularly for middle-class males. Boys with bad tempers wound up with lower educational attainment as adults. For middle-class males, this lower educational attainment translated into lower occupational status than their parents, although this was not true for lower-class males. Of the middle-class, high-tempered males, 53% had downward occupational mobility compared with their fathers, while this rate was only 28% for the even-tempered group. Of the 70% of the male sample who served in the military, high-tempered males of both social class categories had lower rank than their even-tempered counterparts. Furthermore, marriages of men who had self-control problems as boys tended to be more unstable. Divorce among these men was twice as frequent as in the even-tempered group (46% vs. 22%). Thus, early self-control problems were predictive of a broad range of basic adjustment problems among the males.

Females from the Berkeley Study who had self-control problems as girls did not show deficits in their own educational or occupational attainment, but were married to men of lower occupational status than the even-tempered females. Like the males, high-tempered females had twice the divorce rate (26%) as the even-tempered group (12%) and were rated by their spouses and children as less adequate mothers. Caspi et al. (1987) concluded that early problems of explosive, uncontrolled behavior translate into difficulties with authority and in negotiating conflict, characteristics that undermine both occupational and domestic success. These results, along with the potential influence of genetic factors, help explain the surprising similarity in aggressive behavior that Huesmann et al. (1984) found between fathers and sons ($r = .31$) when each was only 8 years of age.

Longitudinal studies also reflect substantial discontinuity. Not all early starting antisocial youth become adult offenders or follow the pathway of poor occupational or marital adjustment. In this light, it is important to identify those factors that lead to desistance of antisocial behavior in adulthood, as well as to understand the determinants of continued antisocial activity. Rutter, Quinton, and Hill (1990) reported several protective factors operating in longitudinal child cohorts that they had followed into adulthood to assess the long-term effects of family dysfunction. They found that marital support served as a factor in promoting desistance from deviance in the early adult years.

The idea that a solid marriage and regular employment provide support for desistance from crime is consistent with social control theories of crime. Sampson and Laub (1990) reexamined data on occupational history and marital relationships from the Glueck and Glueck (1968) longitudinal study as a test of the theory that strong ties to adult institutions such as work and family influence subsequent criminal behavior among those with a previous history of delinquency. Men with a history of childhood delinquency were more often charged with offenses while serving in the military than those without childhood delinquency records (64% vs. 20%). Patterns of civilian arrest, excessive substance use, high school graduation, unstable employment, and divorce all show equally unfavorable ratios or worse for those with childhood delinquency records. Job stability, occupational commitment, and attachment to spouse were assessed from multiple sources of information on the sample for ages 17 to 25. Not only did each of these factors relate inversely to crime and deviance concurrently, but each was a powerful predictor of subsequent arrest and deviance in the period from 25 to 32 years of age.

The impressive feature of this study is that Sampson and Laub then repeated these analyses controlling first for official delinquency status in the delinquent and control

samples separately, and second for frequency of crimes committed per year while free in the community. This was done to provide a strict test of the independent effects of social ties on adult crime by looking at changes in crime. Considered this way, job stability had a consistently inverse influence on crime and deviance in young adulthood (ages 17–25) and in later adulthood (ages 25–32), whereas income and marriage per se did not have effects when other factors were controlled. Following up that part of the sample who had been married at some time, Sampson and Laub found that marital cohesiveness had a significant effect on crime and deviance, independent of other factors. Thus, both job stability and marital attachment seem to reduce criminal activity, controlling for prior crime and other factors. Similar results were found for the predictive power of these factors for subsequent offending in later adulthood. Sampson and Laub concluded that "job stability is central in explaining adult desistance from crime; however, this effect is reduced among those who were never married, for whom attachment to wife assumes greater relative importance" (p. 621).

Conclusions

The longitudinal research on highly antisocial individuals paints a picture of continuity in interpersonal behavior that is as stable as any human characteristic that has been studied by behavioral scientists. Such a conclusion, coupled with evidence of genetic heritability and the role of hormones and neurotransmitters, would suggest a biological inevitability to antisocial traits. However, the data on stability can also be interpreted as evidence for discontinuity that is not explained simply by measurement error and similar factors. This discontinuity can be explained by the same factors that have been described as life-course events that amplify antisocial behavior. That is, when a good teacher helps a high-risk child become academically and socially successful, discontinuity in antisocial behavior will probably be achieved. Similarly, when a delinquent older adolescent is fortunate enough to acquire a spouse who supports positive social activity in a cohesive marital context, discontinuity is likely. The developmental story that currently can be told points to a series of interaction sequences between individuals and their environments that either strengthen and diversify antisocial tendencies or move individuals off this pathway into less deviant behavior patterns. This interaction between biological and environmental influence does not merely describe the effects of biological deficits or environmental consequences. It also demonstrates that experiences reciprocably leave their mark on biological systems and thus can intensify an existing deficit or reduce its impact.

The behavioral feature most firmly established as the link between psychobiological deficits and antisocial behavior is impulsivity. There is still some ambiguity as to the precise way that impulsivity becomes a primary cause of antisocial behavior, however. One possibility is that it takes the form of hyperactivity that translates into various types of behavioral control problems in the school setting and at home. These control problems initially may be unrelated to motivated antisocial acts, but simply put a child in the continual circumstances of being reprimanded for disruptive activity and poor academic performance. Across time, the child becomes defined, by the self and others, as deviant, and in some homes may inadvertently be rewarded for aversive behavior. A second possible scenario is that impulsivity takes the form of a high fear threshold, or low anxiety (Fowles & Missell, 1994), with the result that these children take risks and ignore the possibility of adult sanctions for rule violations. Both scenarios have some plausibility, but with important differences. The developmental sequences that might be projected for each scenario are different, as are the behavioral treatment and prevention implications.

A separate developmental path to emotional reactivity and reactive aggression is related to early abuse at home and social rejection by peers. At present, there is little biological research that can be related to reactive aggression, except for a suggestion by Fowles and Missell (1994) that deficits in cue reading, a central feature in the hostile attribution process, may be related to low electrodermal discrimination conditioning. Other core features may evolve out of an early family atmosphere of abuse that sensitizes the child to hostility and promotes a hyperreactivity to insult or injury.

An important third factor in the early developmental interface between biology and environment is the presence of neuropsychological deficits that undermine language and executive functioning. These deficits may be traced to physical abuse, nutritional deprivation, lack of stimulation, maternal drug use, birth complications, or may be heritable (Moffitt & Lynam, 1994). Moffitt and Lynam offer a number of developmental explanations for the antisocial consequences of these deficits. Among them is the possibility that less verbal children more often resort to physical solutions to conflict, that attentional deficits minimize reflection on the consequences of behavior, and that children

with language problems will have difficulty early on with school curriculum and eventually be shunted toward peer associations that promote deviant behavior. Thus, child characteristics interact with home and school environments in ways that can accentuate and accelerate child antisocial behavior or deflect a child from an antisocial course. Furthermore, environmental effects do not simply promote the display of more of the same antisocial behavior, they often deprive children of valuable learning opportunities and leave them less able to fit in with conventional peers or to cope with the demands of work or family life. Failure in these latter domains can then leave these individuals with few alternatives to a criminal lifestyle.

There is another side to this picture. Although the preceding review provides strong support for a model of early-starting antisocial youth whose conduct problems arise from biologically rooted executive function deficits that lead to impulsivity, the failure to learn from punishment situations, and verbal and language performance deficits, as well as seriously inadequate parenting, the distributions of onset and desistence of antisocial activity do not support an exclusively bimodal theory of early versus later starters. Certainly there are young children without these early biological risk factors who grow up in family and neighborhood contexts where aggression and disruptiveness are effective strategies for getting what is wanted, or in homes where abuse and neglect are so profound that emotional and behavioral disregulation are predictable consequences. It is also probable that some children grow up in relatively effective home contexts, but are pulled into delinquent acts in later childhood by influences from both school and neighborhood. It is also likely that more than a few late-starting delinquents become entrenched in a lifestyle of substance use and criminal activity that limits their adult options and is continued beyond adolescence. The early starter-late starter model is an important framework on which to hang a substantial body of research findings. To question its adequacy as an explanation of all antisocial behavior is only to suggest that the next 20 years of research will provide greater understanding of the variabilities in these development pathways.

CONCLUSION

Implications for Future Research

There are significant barriers to conducting biologically oriented research with human beings, and so much less is known about the role of biological factors in human antisocial behavior than is necessary for an adequate understanding of the phenomenon. Some assessments are so invasive or susceptible to situational variations that reliable and valid data are difficult to collect. Important political, as well as ethical, considerations limit what has been possible to do in research with children, although some political concerns can be traced to overly simplistic theoretical positions taken by scientists and critics in the field. One political fear is that the identification of biological factors in aggressive development would lead to the targeting of individuals, or ethnic groups, for isolation and negative treatment. However, there has been a marked increase among social and biologically oriented scientists in recognizing the complex and interactive nature of biological and environmental factors. As this change begins to receive greater recognition in nonscientific discourse, it may become possible to undertake some important research that clarifies the developmental contributions of biological and environmental processes. Except for a small body of research on testosterone and aggression and a few studies on neurotransmitters, very little is known of the reciprocal influences of biology and environment on human antisocial behavior. Longitudinal investigations, beginning in early childhood and involving multiple measures of neurobiological functioning along with assessments of individual impulsivity, emotion regulation, language and verbal performance, as well as detailed assessments of family dynamic and larger contextual factors, are needed. Very few studies of this sort exist, and most of these studies have their beginnings in adolescence.

Although much more is known about parent-child interactions, only recently has there been much recognition of the need to study changes in parenting as a function of the age of the child and the correlated psychosocial tasks of a developmental period. For example, knowledge of parenting at age 10 has often served as a proxy for knowledge of parenting at age 3 or age 7 in the development of theoretical models. The next generation of parent-child interaction research has the promise of providing greater detailed understanding of the developmental course of parent-child interactions and the way that deviations in parenting interact with the changing psychosocial demands on the child.

The past 15 to 20 years have witnessed marked advances in research on antisocial development that can be traced to greater sophistication in two aspects of research design. First, microanalytic studies of interaction between parents and children (e.g., Snyder & Patterson, 1995) and

adolescents and peers (Dishion, Andrews, et al., 1995) have provided more carefully articulated accounts of the interpersonal interaction variables that promote and support antisocial behavior. Second, longitudinal studies with repeated assessments of large, population-based samples from relatively high-risk communities have created rich, overlapping data sets for testing developmental theories of antisocial behavior. Both approaches have provided invaluable and groundbreaking findings. Nonetheless, what is missing is a level of design that bridges the microsocial experimental design and the macrolevel longitudinal design. The former design typically reflects events occurring within a period of 15 to 45 minutes; the latter design assesses change across time periods of a year or more. The detailed findings from sophisticated microanalytic studies are extrapolated to describe larger order social processes, in theory, but these processes are never really validated in the larger time frame designs of longitudinal research.

The 6-month intervals at which Loeber et al. (1993) repeat their assessments are quite remarkable in contrast to most other designs. What is missing even here, however, is a view of the kinds of day-to-day or week-to-week interactions that children actually have with family members, peers, and older nonfamily members. All too often, the multiple measures employed in longitudinal studies are reduced to larger order composites of some of the finer grained constructs acquired from microanalytic studies. The resulting latent variable models then test the relative strength of parent, peer, or individual characteristics on antisocial behavior summed across a period of months. These analyses test competing theories at only a very high order of abstraction and fail to articulate the more proximal processes leading up to specific antisocial events. One reason for this void is expense. Current longitudinal designs are more ambitious in terms of numbers of participants and richness of contracts to be assessed than was true of earlier studies, generally. These new studies, themselves, are enormously expensive and time consuming. They also address a prior absence of data sets that span large developmental periods with frequent time samples. A second reason for this void is the lack of theoretical and empirical clarity regarding the appropriate time unit to employ in studies of changes in aggressive and antisocial behavior. Scientists select the frequency of data collection time points based on some expectation that the interval is long enough to detect reliably a change in behavior but short enough so that multiple changes in behavior are not masked within a single time unit. A major task for researchers in the next decade will be to identify the appropriate time unit in studies of aggressive behavior. Because processes may be gradual, the units that are employed may be somewhat arbitrary (e.g., consider what time unit should be employed to study changes in atmospheric temperature across the day). Still, the units should not be selected arbitrarily or simply for ease of data collection (e.g., annual data collections conform to annual grant budgets). It is likely that different levels of abstraction will require different time units: Studies of aggressive behavior exchanges require units of seconds, whereas studies of psychiatric diagnoses may require units of months. Again, how the microlevel units relate to more macrolevel units is not understood and will require theoretical and empirical analysis.

As noted earlier, not enough empirical inquiry or theoretical analysis has considered variations in gender, ethnic, and cultural context. A few studies have raised the unsettling possibility that models of aggression might not hold across gender or ethnic groups. It is not clear whether unique models of development are necessary for each subgroup, or whether subgroup differences in process can be explained by more complex moderator variables for a single general model. Consider the finding that the effect of harsh punitive parenting on child aggression seems to be greater for white Americans than for African Americans (Deater-Deckard & Dodge, in press). It is unlikely that different developmental processes operate for these two groups at a basic level; rather, this finding may inspire future attempts to understand this difference and explain it, possibly, through some third variable (such as co-occurring features of family life that vary across cultures). The examination of these new variables will enrich a general model of aggressive development by noting moderators and complex interactions.

Likewise, future studies may lead to the simplification of some aspects of developmental theories and not merely to an endless stream of caveats and exceptions. It is hoped that exceptions, moderators, and complex interactions will lead eventually to the identification of a small number of more general principles that explain and predict aggressive development. For example, in the finding that harsh parenting may have different effects on different cultural groups, it may be that norms for discipline practices vary across cultural groups and that it is deviation from normative parenting (more so than harshness per se) that leads to child deviance.

Another future direction for research will be the testing of models of aggressive development across domains of assessment. Many of the studies reviewed here have examined single constructs as predictors of aggression. How constructs increment each other, moderate each other, and mediate each other is not well understood, especially across domains and levels of analysis. For example, it is not yet clear whether biological constructs such as impulsivity will account for the same variance or unique variance beyond mental process constructs in predicting aggression. Our guess is the mental constructs have biological correlates, and these variables merely reflect different levels of analysis and not competing sources of variance. It may be that biology does not cause the cognitions, or vice versa; instead these variables may represent different ways of measuring the same phenomenon. With the advent of cross-domain studies will come tests of comprehensive models of aggressive development that integrate measurement across biological, mental, dyadic, and cultural levels. These multivariate tests will lead to truly integrative and comprehensive theories of aggressive development.

Implications for Treatment and Prevention

The preceding review of developmental factors operating across the life course suggests that the distinction between prevention and treatment of antisocial behavior is largely ephemeral, except when dealing with distinctions such as whether individuals have or have not been involved in violations of criminal code or have or have not been apprehended for such violations. Prevention is a probabilistic undertaking, and the probabilities are such that individuals who have not exhibited persistent aggression or conduct problems as children are not likely to become delinquent adolescents, except for brief and infrequent experimentation. Nor are they likely to become adult criminals (except possibly for so-called white collar crimes, a phenomenon that has not been studied adequately). That being the case, prevention usually begins with children who frequently engage in antisocial acts. Treatment is initiated on this same premise, except that the referral process for treatment inevitably requires that the child's antisocial activity has exceeded the tolerance of adult authorities such as parents, teachers, or juvenile court judges.

The developmental literature indicates that by age 3, at least, many children who will have childhood conduct problems can be identified by their impulsivity, irritability, and noncompliance. Regardless of whether or not the origins of this behavior lie primarily in the family dynamics or are biologically based, most treatment strategies for preschool-age children focus on parent management training. For children below the age of 4, stimulant medications are not typically prescribed, and these medications are initiated as school problems become evident (Barkley, 1990). Reid (1993) concluded that teaching parents nonviolent and effective discipline strategies deals preventively with the most powerful proximal antecedents of persistent conduct problems. This, too, is what Kazdin (1985) has identified as among the most promising treatment strategies for aggressive children. As Reid notes, however (1993, p. 249), "The major problem with this strategy is getting parents to participate in, or cooperate with, such interventions."

What does not get dealt with adequately by parent management training, nor by stimulant medication, are the early language deficits that can impede the verbal mediation of self-control or the ability to learn to read. These deficits may be exacerbated in some homes by parents' inability or disinclination to read to their children or to speak to their children about emotional reactions and help them develop internalized controls over strong negative emotions (Cook, Greenberg, & Kusche, 1994). Both language deficits and verbal mediation of emotions may require special attention during the late preschool and early school years.

The transition to elementary school marks the point at which high-risk children may be identified as displaying aggression and oppositional or disruptive behavior across settings. Assessment of these behaviors at school and at home provides a method of screening most children in a community for the early-starting antisocial group, because the evidence is that generalized and diverse conduct problems by age 6 or 7 are reasonably predictive of long-term antisocial activity. However, although school entry provides an optimal opportunity for preventionists to identify high-risk children in a community who could most benefit from a prevention program, the number of factors that now contribute to increasing risk expand beyond the child and the family and require a larger framework for prevention activity (Reid, 1993). For children beyond the age of 5, the classroom now becomes a primary socialization setting, and factors such as the child's ability to make and sustain positive relationships within a large group context, the number of other high-risk children in the classroom, the teacher's ability to maintain classroom order and teach effectively, and the nature of communication between home and school become important factors in developmental pathways (Conduct Problems Prevention Research Group, 1992).

The same factors that must be addressed in a multiple-setting prevention plan also must be dealt with in treatment planning, but most of the treatment literature does not reflect this orientation. Kazdin's (1993) analysis of current treatment advances is that the most effective treatment programs incorporate both parent management training and cognitive behavioral skill training. Kazdin and his colleagues have demonstrated impressive behavioral improvement among the 3- to 13-year-old sample who have participated in their program, although a significant number remain outside the normal range in several domains of relevant functioning. Kazdin concludes that future treatment planning should expand the combination of treatment activities in a way that meets the circumstances and characteristics of specific antisocial youth, recognizing that conduct disorder "represents a pervasive developmental disorder in the sense that broad areas of functioning are deleteriously affected" (p. 301).

Kazdin's point can be interpreted in several ways. One is that multiple domains of functioning are implicated. A second is that the pervasiveness of adjustment problems for antisocial children arises from the cumulative nature of social development. A child's range of friendships may become narrowed because of early school-age tendencies to resolve conflict by physical aggression and to compensate for academic weaknesses by disrupting the classroom setting. This child grows up missing critical skills for relating in adolescent peer groups, for getting and keeping a job, for attracting a competent and supportive mate, for regulating life in a family, and for providing appropriate guidance and discipline to offspring. These social skills build one on another, as do the interpersonal orientations reflected in such basic social cognitions as are required in distinguishing hostile intent from playful banter or inadvertent mistake. A similarly cumulative process is present in the development of an effective parenting relationship with a child. The potential for effectively monitoring the out-of-home activities of a preadolescent or adolescent is dependent on having already established effective communication and a trusting, loving relationship. Furthermore, the content of effective social skill training programs for children, as well as that of parent training programs, must keep pace with the developmental issues of the growing child. Intervention at any point in time involves both a resocialization effort to deal with existing deficits and preparation for the child's current and pending needs. Very few existing programs meet these criteria because most training curricula are based on a few simple principles and are planned for an intervention time frame of no longer than a year.

Current levels of delinquency and violence in many Western societies, particularly the United States, are sufficiently high in many communities that successful intervention and prevention require a focus on the attitudes and behavioral norms of the whole adolescent peer culture. In many urban schools, an aggressive reputation is positively related to adolescent peer popularity. It is not just the deviant peer group that influences delinquency and risk taking. Children in these schools grow up in neighborhoods of poverty and high crime rates, being exposed to homicide and the frequent use of guns. All this is embedded in a media culture of highly explicit violence (Coie & Jacobs, 1993). The challenge of contemporary prevention, whether for the high-risk early-starter group or the late-starting, adolescence-limited group is to alter these adolescent norms. The primary strategy currently employed to achieve this goal is through the use of classroom and school-based programs in social problem solving, conflict management, violence prevention, and more broad-based curriculum for promoting emotional and social development in the total school population. Weissberg and Greenberg (Ch. 13, Volume 4) describe these programs elsewhere in this *Handbook*. These universal interventions should not be considered as alternatives to more targeted interventions with high-risk youth, because each approach provides a complementary strategy to reducing violence and antisocial activity in the entire community. The success of one approach should influence the success of another.

ACKNOWLEDGMENTS

We appreciate the careful reviews by John Bates, William Damon, Thomas Dishion, Nancy Eisenberg, David Farrington, L. Rowell Huesmann, Rolf Loeber, Gerald Patterson, and Adrian Raine, and the cooperation of numerous scholars in providing papers to us. Catherine Bagwell and Kari Lenox provided valuable research assistance.

REFERENCES

Abelson, R. P. (1981). The psychological status of the script concept. *American Psychologist, 36,* 715–729.

Abramovich, R., Corter, C., & Lando, B. (1979). Sibling interaction in the home. *Child Development, 4,* 997–1003.

Achenbach, T. M. (1991). *Manual for the Child Behavior Checklist and 1991 Profile.* Burlington: University of Vermont, Department of Psychiatry.

Achenbach, T. M., & Edelbrock, C. S. (1983). *Manual for the Child Behavior Checklist and Revised Child Behavior Profile.* Burlington: University of Vermont, Department of Psychiatry.

Achenbach, T. M., McConaugh, S. H., & Howell, C. T. (1987). Child/adolescent behavioral and emotional problems: Implications of cross-informant correlations for situational specificity. *Psychological Bulletin, 101,* 213–232.

Ainsworth, M. D. S., Blehar, M. C., Waters, E., & Wall, S. (1978). *Patterns of attachment.* Hillsdale, NJ: Erlbaum.

American Psychiatric Association. (1994). *Diagnostic and statistical manual of mental disorders* (4th ed.). Washington, DC: American Psychiatric Press.

Anderson, D. R., Choi, H. P., & Lorch, E. P. (1987). Attentional inertia reduces distractibility during young children's TV viewing. *Child Development, 58,* 798–806.

Anderson, E. (1990). *Streetwise: Race, class, and change in an urban community.* Chicago: University of Chicago Press.

Anderson, J., Williams, S., McGee, R., & Silva, P. (1989). Cognitive and social correlates of *DSM-III* disorders in preadolescent children. *Journal of the American Academy of Child and Adolescent Psychiatry, 28,* 842–846.

Anderson, K. E., Lytton, H., & Romney, D. M. (1986). Mother's interactions with normal and conduct-disordered boys: Who affects whom? *Developmental Psychology, 22,* 604–609.

Archer, J. (1988). *The behavioral biology of aggression.* Cambridge, England: Cambridge University Press.

Archer, J. (1991). The influence of testosterone on human aggression. *British Journal of Psychology, 82,* 1–28.

Archer, J. (1994). Testosterone and aggression: A theoretical review. *Journal of Offender Rehabilitation, 21,* 3–39.

Asarnow, J. R., & Callan, J. W. (1985). Boys with peer adjustment problems: Social cognitive processes. *Journal of Consulting and Clinical Psychology, 53,* 80–87.

Asberg, M., Traskman, L., & Thoren, P. (1976). 5-HIAA in the cerebrospinal fluid: A biochemical suicide predictor? *Archives of General Psychiatry, 33,* 1193–1197.

Asher, S. R., Hymel, S., & Renshaw, P. D. (1984). Loneliness in children. *Child Development, 55,* 1457–1464.

Asher, S. R., & Renshaw, P. D. (1981). Children without friends: Social knowledge and social skill training. In S. R. Asher & J. M. Gottman (Eds.), *The development of children's friendships* (pp. 273–296). Cambridge, England: Cambridge University Press.

Atkins, M. S., & Stoff, D. M. (1993). Instrumental and hostile aggression in childhood disruptive behavior disorders. *Journal of Abnormal Child Psychology, 21,* 165–178.

Atkins, M. S., Stoff, D. M., Osborne, M. L., & Brown, K. (1993). Distinguishing instrumental and hostile aggression: Does it make a difference? *Journal of Abnormal Child Psychology, 21,* 355–365.

Aultman, M. (1980). Group involvement in delinquent acts: A study of offense type and male-female participation. *Criminal Justice and Behavior, 7,* 185–192.

Averill, J. R. (1982). *Anger and aggression: An essay on emotion.* New York: Springer-Verlag.

Aydin, O., & Markova, I. (1979). Attribution tendencies of popular and unpopular children. *British Journal of Social and Clinical Psychology, 18,* 291–298.

Bagley, C. (1992). Maternal smoking and deviant behavior in 16-year-olds: A personality hypothesis. *Personality and Individual Differences, 13,* 377–378.

Bagwell, C., Coie, J. D., Terry, R., & Lochman, J. E. (1996, March). *Consistency and change in peer cliques across the transition to adolescence.* Paper presented at the biennial meeting of the Society for Research on Adolescence, Boston.

Baker, D. P., & Stevenson, D. L. (1986). Mothers' strategies for children's school achievement: Managing the transition to high school. *Sociology of Education, 59,* 156–166.

Bandura, A. (1973). *Aggression: A social learning analysis.* Englewood Cliffs, NJ: Prentice-Hall.

Bandura, A. (1977). *Social learning theory.* Englewood Cliffs, NJ: Prentice-Hall.

Bandura, A. (1983). Psychological mechanisms of aggression. In R. G. Geen & E. Donnerstein (Eds.), *Aggression: Theoretical and empirical reviews.* New York: Academic Press.

Bandura, A. (1991). Social cognitive theory of moral thought and action. In W. M. Kurtines & J. L. Gewirtz (Eds.), *Handbook of moral behavior and development: Vol. 1. Theory.* Hillsdale, NJ: Erlbaum.

Bandura, A., & Caprara, G. (1995). Unpublished data. Stanford University, Palo Alto, CA.

Bandura, A., Ross, D., & Ross, S. A. (1963). Imitation of film-mediated aggressive models. *Journal of Abnormal and Social Psychology, 66,* 3–11.

Bandura, A., & Walters, R. H. (1959). *Adolescent aggression.* New York: Ronald Press.

Bargh, J. A. (1989). Conditional automaticity: Varieties of automatic influence in social perception and cognition. In J. S. Uleman & J. A. Bargh (Eds.), *Unintended thought* (pp. 3–51). New York: Guilford Press.

Bargh, J. A., Chaiken, S., Raymond, P., & Hymes, C. (1995). The automatic evaluation effect: Unconditional automatic attitude activation with a pronunciation task. *Journal of Experimental Social Psychology, 31,* 221–232.

Bargh, J. A., & Thein, R. D. (1985). Individual construct accessibility, person memory, and the recall-judgment link: The case of information overload. *Journal of Personality and Social Psychology, 49,* 1129–1146.

Barkley, R. A. (1990). *Attention-deficit hyperactivity disorder: A handbook for diagnosis and treatment.* New York: Guilford Press.

Barkley, R. A. (1997). Behavioral inhibition, sustained attention, and executive function: Constructing a unified theory of ADHD. *Psychological Bulletin, 121,* 65–94.

Barkley, R. A., Fischer, M., Edelbrock, C. S., & Smallish, L. (1990). The adolescent outcome of hyperactive children diagnosed by research criteria: I. An 8-year prospective follow-up study. *Journal of the American Academy of Child and Adolescent Psychiatry, 29,* 546–557.

Bates, J. E. (1980). The concept of difficult temperament. *Merrill-Palmer Quarterly, 26,* 299–319.

Bates, J. E., & Bayles, K. (1988). Attachment and the development of behavior problems. In J. Belsky & T. Nezworski (Eds.), *Clinical implications of attachment.* Hillsdale, NJ: Erlbaum.

Bates, J. E., Bayles, K., Bennett, D. S., Ridge, B., & Brown, M. M. (1991). Origins of externalizing behavior problems at eight years of age. In D. J. Pepler & K. H. Rubin (Eds.), *The development and treatment of childhood aggression* (pp. 93–120). Hillsdale, NJ: Erlbaum.

Bates, J. E., Freeland, C. A. B., & Lounsbury, M. L. (1979). Measurement of infant temperament. *Child Development, 50,* 794–803.

Bates, J. E., Maslin, C. A., & Frankel, K. A. (1985). Attachment security, mother-child interaction, and temperament as predictors of behavior problem ratings at age three years. In I. Bretherton & E. Waters (Eds.), Growing points of attachment theory and research. *Monographs of the Society for Research in Child Development, 50*(1/2, Serial No. 209).

Baumrind, D. (1967). Child care practices anteceding three patterns of preschool behavior. *Genetic Psychology Monographs, 75,* 43–88.

Baumrind, D. (1971). Current patterns of parental authority. *Developmental Psychology, 4,* 1–103.

Baumrind, D. (1987). A developmental perspective on adolescent risk taking in contemporary America. In C. E. Irwin, Jr. (Ed.), *Adolescent social behavior and health: Vol. 37. New directions for child development* (pp. 93–125). San Francisco: Josey-Bass.

Becker, G. (1974). Crime and punishment: An economic approach. In G. Becker & W. Landes (Eds.), *Essays in the economics of crime and punishment* (pp. 1–54). New York: Macmillan.

Bell, R. Q., & Harper, L. V. (1977). *Child effects on adults.* Hillsdale, NJ: Erlbaum.

Belsky, J., Rovine, M., & Taylor, D. G. (1984). The Pennsylvania Infant and Family Development Project: 3. The origins of individual differences in infant-mother attachment: Maternal and infant contributions. *Child Development, 55,* 718–728.

Berke, R. L. (1994, January 23,). Crime joins economic issues as leading worry, poll says. *New York Times.*

Berkowitz, L. (1962). *Aggression: A social psychological analysis.* New York: McGraw-Hill.

Berkowitz, L. (1989). Frustration-aggression hypothesis: Examination and reformulation. *Psychological Bulletin, 106,* 59–73.

Berkowitz, L. (1990). On the formation and regulation of anger and aggression: A cognitive-neoassociationistic analysis. *American Psychologist, 45,* 494–503.

Berkowitz, L. (1993). Towards a general theory of anger and emotional aggression: Implications of the cognitive-neoassociationistic perspective for the analysis of anger and other emotions. In R. S. Wyer, Jr., & T. K. Srull (Eds.), *Advances in social cognition: Vol. 6. Perspectives on anger and emotion* (pp. 1–45). Hillsdale, NJ: Erlbaum.

Berkowitz, L. (1994). Is something missing? Some observations prompted by the cognitive-neoassociationistic view of anger and emotional aggression. In L. R. Huesmann (Ed.), *Aggressive behavior: Current perspectives* (pp. 35–37). New York: Plenum Press.

Biederman, J., Newcorn, J., & Sprich, S. E. (1991). Comorbidity of attention deficit hyperactivity disorder with conduct, depressive, anxiety, and other disorders. *American Journal of Psychiatry, 148,* 564–577.

Bierman, K. L. (1986). The relation between social aggression and peer rejection in middle childhood. In R. J. Prinz (Ed.), *Advances in behavioral assessment of children and families* (Vol. 2, pp. 151–178). Greenwich, CT: JAI Press.

Bierman, K. L., Smoot, D. L., & Aumiller, K. (1993). Characteristics of aggressive-rejected, aggressive (nonrejected), and rejected (nonaggressive) boys. *Child Development, 64,* 139–151.

Bierman, K. L., & Wargo, J. B. (1995). Predicting the longitudinal course associated with aggressive-rejected, aggressive (non-rejected), and rejected (non-aggressive) status. *Developmental Psychopathology, 7,* 669–682.

Björkqvist, K. (1985). *Violent films, anxiety, and aggression.* Helsinki, Finland: Finnish Society of Sciences and Letters.

Björkqvist, K., & Didrikkson, B. (1985, August). *Desensitization to film violence in aggressive and nonaggressive boys.* Paper presented at the meeting of the International Society for Research on Aggression, Parma, Italy.

Blasi, A. (1980). Bridging moral cognition and moral action: A critical review of the literature. *Psychological Bulletin, 88,* 593–637.

Blasi, A., & Oresick, R. J. (1986). Emotions and cognitions in self-consistency. In D. J. Bearison & H. Zimiles (Eds.), *Thought and emotion* (pp. 147–165). Hillsdale, NJ: Erlbaum.

Block, J. H., & Block, J. (1980). The role of ego control and ego resiliency in the organization of behavior. In W. A. Collins (Ed.), *Minnesota Symposia on child psychology: Development of cognition, affect, and social relations* (Vol. 13). Hillsdale, NJ: Erlbaum.

Blum, H. M., Boyle, M. H., & Offord, D. R. (1988). Single-parent families: Child psychiatric disorder and school performance. *Journal of the American Academy of Child and Adolescent Psychiatry, 27,* 214–219.

Blumstein, A. (in press). Youth violence, guns, and the illicit-drug industry. *Journal of Criminal Law and Criminology.*

Blumstein, A., & Cohen, J. (1987). Characterizing criminal careers. *Science, 237,* 985–991.

Blumstein, A., Farrington, D. P., & Moitra, S. D. (1985). *Delinquency careers: Innocents, desisters, and persisters* (pp. 187–219). Chicago: University of Chicago Press.

Blurton Jones, N. G. (1967). An ethological study of some aspects of social behavior of children in nursery school. In D. Morris (Ed.), *Primate ethology* (pp. 347–368). London: Weidenfeld and Nicolson.

Bohman, M., Cloninger, R., Sigvardsson, S., & von Knoring, A. L. (1982). Predisposition to petty criminality in Swedish adoptees: I. Genetic and environmental heterogeneity. *Archives of General Psychiatry, 39,* 1233–1241.

Boivin, M., Dodge, K. A., & Coie, J. D. (1995). Individual-group behavioral similarity and peer status in experimental play groups of boys: The social misfit revisited. *Journal of Personality and Social Psychology, 69,* 269–279.

Boldizar, J. P., Perry, D. G., & Perry, L. C. (1989). Outcome values and aggression. *Child Development, 60,* 571–579.

Bolger, K. E., Patterson, C. J., Thompson, W. W., & Kupersmidt, J. B. (1995). Psychosocial adjustment among children experiencing persistent and intermittent family economic hardship. *Child Development, 66,* 1107–1129.

Booth, C. L., & Rose-Krasnor, L., McKinnon, J., & Rubin, K. H. (1994). Predicting social adjustment in middle childhood: The role of preschool attachment security and maternal style. From family to peer group: Relations between relationship systems [Special issue]. *Social Development, 3,* 189–204.

Borkovec, T. M. (1970). Autonomic reactivity to sensory stimulation in psychopathic, neurotic and normal juvenile delinquents. *Journal of Consulting and Clinical Psychology, 35,* 217–222.

Bowlby, J. (1980). *Attachment and loss: Vol. 3. Loss.* New York: Basic Books.

Brain, P. F. (1994). Hormonal aspects of aggression and violence. In A. J. Reis, Jr. & J. A. Roth (Eds.), *Understanding and control of biobehavioral influences on violence* (Vol. 2, pp. 177–244). Washington, DC: National Academy Press.

Brickman, A. S., McManus, M., Grapentine, W. L., & Alessi, N. (1984). Neuropsychological assessment of seriously delinquent adolescents. *Journal of the American Academy of Child Psychiatry, 23,* 453–457.

Britten, R. J. (1986). Rates of DNA sequence evolution differ between taxonomic groups. *Science, 231,* 1393–1398.

Brown, A. L., Bransford, J. D., Ferrara, R. A., & Campione, J. C. (1983). Learning, remembering, and understanding. In P. Mussen (Series Ed.) & J. H. Flavell & E. M. Markman (Eds.), *Handbook of child psychology: Vol. 3. Cognitive development* (pp. 77–166). New York: Wiley.

Brunner, H. G., Nelen, M., Breakfield, X. O., Ropers, H. H., & Van Oost, B. A. (1993). Abnormal behavior associated with a point mutation in the structural gene for monoamine oxidase A. *Science, 262,* 578–580.

Buehler, R. E., Patterson, G. R., & Furniss, J. M. (1966). The reinforcement of behavior in institutional settings. *Behavior Research and Therapy, 4,* 157–167.

Burleson, B. R. (1982). The development of communication skills in childhood and adolescence. *Child Development, 53,* 1578–1588.

Bushman, B. J., & Geen, R. (1990). Role of cognitive-emotional mediators and individual differences in the effects of media violence on aggression. *Journal of Personality and Social Psychology, 58,* 156–163.

Buss, A. H. (1961). *The psychology of aggression.* New York: Wiley.

Buss, A. H., & Plomin, R. (1984). *Temperament: Early developing personality traits.* Hillsdale, NJ: Erlbaum.

Cadoret, R. J. (1978). Psychopathology in adopted-away offspring of biological parents with antisocial behavior. *Archives of General Psychiatry, 35,* 176–184.

Cairns, R. B. (1979). *Social development: The origins and plasticity of interchanges.* San Francisco: Freeman.

Cairns, R. B. (1991). Multiple metaphors for a singular idea. *Developmental Psychology, 27,* 23–26.

Cairns, R. B., & Cairns, B. D. (1994). *Lifelines and risks: Pathways of youth in our time.* New York: Cambridge University Press.

Cairns, R. B., Cairns, B. D., & Neckerman, H. J. (1989). Early school drop-out: Configurations and determinants. *Child Development, 60,* 1437–1452.

Cairns, R. B., Cairns, B. D., Neckerman, H. J., Ferguson, L. L., & Gariepy, J. L. (1989). Growth and aggression: Childhood to early adolescence. *Developmental Psychology, 25,* 320–330.

Cairns, R. B., Cairns, B. D., Neckerman, H. J., Gest, S. D., & Gariepy, J. L. (1988). Social networks and aggressive behavior: Peer support or peer rejection? *Developmental Psychology, 24,* 815–823.

Cairns, R. B., McGuire, A. M., & Gariepy, J. L. (1993). Developmental behavioral genetics: Fusion, correlated constraints, and timing. In A. Angold & D. Hay (Eds.), *Precursors and causes in development and psychopathology* (pp. 87–122). Chichester, England: Wiley.

Campbell, S. B. (1987). Parent-referred problem 3-year-olds: Developmental changes in symptoms. *Journal of Child Psychology and Psychiatry, 28,* 835–845.

Campbell, S. B. (1990). *Behavior problems in preschool children: Clinical and developmental issues.* New York: Guilford Press.

Campbell, S. B., & Ewing, L. D. (1990). Follow-up of hard-to-manage preschoolers: Adjustment at age 9 and predictors of continuing symptoms. *Journal of Child Psychology & Psychiatry, 31,* 871–889.

Campos, J., Campos, R., & Barrett, K. (1989). Emergent themes in the study of emotional development and emotion regulation. *Developmental Psychology, 25,* 394–402.

Cantwell, D., Baker, L., & Mattison, R. (1979). The prevalence of psychiatric disorder in children with speech and language disorders: An epidemiological study. *Journal of the American Academy of Child Psychiatry, 18,* 450–461.

Caplan, M., Vespo, J. E., Pedersen, J., & Hay, D. F. (1991). Conflict over resources in small groups of 1- and 2-year-olds. *Child Development, 62,* 1513–1524.

Carey, G. (1992). Twin imitation for antisocial behavior: Implications for genetic and family environment research. *Journal of Abnormal Psychology, 101,* 18–25.

Carey, G. (1994). Genetics and violence. In A. J. Reis, K. A. Miczek, & J. A. Roth (Eds.), *Understanding and preventing violence* (pp. 21–58). Washington, DC: National Academy Press.

Carver, C. S., Ganellan, R. J., Froming, W. J., & Chambers, W. (1983). Modeling: An analysis in terms of category accessibility. *Journal of Experimental Social Psychology, 19,* 403–421.

Caspi, A. (1987). Personality in the life course. *Journal of Personality and Social Psychology, 53,* 1203–1213.

Caspi, A., & Bem, D. J. (1990). Personality continuity and change across the life course. In L. Pervin (Ed.), *Handbook of personality theory and research* (pp. 549–575). New York: Guilford Press.

Caspi, A., Elder, G. H., & Bem, D. J. (1987). Moving against the world: Life-course patterns of explosive children. *Developmental Psychology, 23,* 308–313.

Caspi, A., Henry, B., McGee, R. O., Moffitt, T. E., & Silva, P. A. (1995). Temperamental origins of child and adolescent behavior problems: From age 3 to age 15. *Child Development, 66,* 55–68.

Caspi, A., & Silva, P. A. (1995). Temperamental qualities at age 3 predict personality traits in young adulthood: Longitudinal evidence from a birth cohort. *Child Development, 66,* 486–498.

Centers for Disease Control. (1991). Forum on youth violence in minority communities: Setting the agenda for prevention. *Public Health Reports, 106,* 225–253.

Chandler, M. J. (1973). Egocentrism and antisocial behavior: The assessment and training of social perspective-taking skills. *Developmental Psychology, 9,* 326–332.

Charlesworth, W. R., & Dzur, C. (1987). Gender comparisons of preschoolers' behavior and resource utilization in preschool children's groups. *Child Development, 58,* 191–200.

Charlesworth, W. R., & LaFreniere, P. J. (1982). Dominance, friendship, and resource utilization in preschool children's groups. *Ethology and Sociobiology, 4,* 175–186.

Christiansen, K. (1977). A preliminary study of criminality among twins. In S. A. Mednick & K. O. Christiansen (Eds.), *Biosocial bases of criminal behavior* (pp. 89–108). New York: Gardner Press.

Cicchetti, D. (1989). How research on child maltreatment has informed the study of child maltreatment: Perspectives from developmental psychopathology. In D. Cicchetti & V. Carlson (Eds.), *Child maltreatment: Theory and research on the causes and consequences of child abuse and neglect* (pp. 377–431). New York: Cambridge University Press.

Cillessen, A. H. N., Van IJzendoorn, H. W., van Lieshout, C. F. M., & Hartup, W. W. (1992). Heterogeneity among peer-rejected boys: Subtypes and stabilities. *Child Development, 63,* 893–905.

Clarke, R. V., & Cornish, D. B. (1983). *Crime control in Britain: A review of policy research.* Albany: State University of New York Press.

Cline, V. B., Croft, R. G., & Courrier, S. (1973). Desensitization of children to television violence. *Journal of Personality and Social Psychology, 27,* 360–365.

Cloninger, C. R., & Gottesman, I. I. (1987). Genetic and environmental factors in antisocial behavior disorders. In S. A. Mednick, T. E. Moffitt, & S. Stack (Eds.), *The causes of crime: New biological approaches.* Cambridge, England: Cambridge University Press.

Cloninger, C. R., Sigvardsson, S., Bohman, M., & van Knoring, A. L. (1982). Predisposition to petty criminality in Swedish adoptees: II. Cross-fostering analyses of gene-environmental interactions. *Archives of General Psychiatry, 39,* 1242–1247.

Coccaro, E. F., Kavoussi, R. J., & Lesser, J. C. (1992). Self- and other-directed human aggression: The role of the central serotonergic system. *International Clinical Psychopharmacology, 6*(Suppl. 6), 70–83.

Coccaro, E. F., Siever, L. J., Klar, H. M., Maurer, G., Cochrane, K., Cooper, T. B., Mohs, R. C., & Davis, K. L. (1989). Serotonergic studies in patients with affective and personality disorders. *Archives of General Psychiatry, 46,* 587–599.

Cohen, N. J., Davine, M., & Meloche-Kelly, M. (1989). The prevalence of unsuspected language disorders in a child psychiatric population. *Journal of the American Academy of Child and Adolescent Psychiatry, 28,* 107–111.

Cohen, P., & Brook, J. S. (1995). The reciprocal influence of punishment and child behavior disorder. In J. McCord (Ed.), *Coercion and punishment in long-term perspectives* (pp. 154–164). Cambridge, England: Cambridge University Press.

Coie, J. D., & Dodge, K. A. (1983). Continuities and changes in children's sociometric status: A five-year longitudinal study. *Merrill-Palmer Quarterly, 29,* 261–282.

Coie, J. D., Dodge, K. A., & Kupersmidt, J. (1990). Peer group behavior and social status. In S. R. Asher & J. D. Coie (Eds.), *Peer rejection in childhood* (pp. 17–59). New York: Cambridge University Press.

Coie, J. D., Dodge, K. A., Terry, R., & Wright, V. (1991). The role of aggression in peer relations: An analysis of aggression episodes in boys' play groups. *Child Development, 62,* 812–826.

Coie, J. D., & Jacobs, M. R. (1993). The role of social context in the prevention of conduct disorder. *Development and Psychopathology, 5,* 263–275.

Coie, J. D., & Koeppl, G. K. (1990). Expanding the framework of intervention with rejected children. In S. R. Asher & J. D. Coie (Eds.), *The rejected child* (pp. 309–337). New York: Cambridge University Press.

Coie, J. D., & Kupersmidt, J. B. (1983). A behavioral analysis of emerging social status in boys' groups. *Child Development, 54,* 1400–1416.

Coie, J. D., Lochman, J. E., Terry, R., & Hyman, C. (1992). Predicting early adolescent disorder from childhood aggression and peer rejection. *Journal of Consulting and Clinical Psychology, 60,* 783–792.

Coie, J. D., Miller-Johnson, S., Terry, R., Maumary-Gremaud, A., Lochman, J. E., & Hyman, C. (1995, November). *The influence of peer rejection, aggression, and deviant peer associations on juvenile offending among African-American adolescents.* Paper presented at the annual meeting of the American Society of Criminology, Boston.

Coie, J. D., Terry, R., Lenox, K., Lochman, J. E., & Hyman, C. (1995). Childhood peer rejection and aggression as predictors of stable patterns of adolescent disorder. *Development and Psychopathology, 7,* 697–713.

Coie, J. D., Terry, R., & Lochman, J. E. (1993, November). *Changing social networks and their impact on juvenile delinquency.*

Paper presented at the annual meeting of the American Society of Criminology, Phoenix, AZ.

Coie, J. D., Terry, R., Zakriski, A., & Lochman, J. E. (1995). Early adolescent social influences on delinquent behavior. In J. McCord (Ed.), *Coercion and punishment in long-term perspectives* (pp. 229–244). New York: Cambridge University Press.

Collins, W. A. (1982). Cognitive processing aspects of television viewing. In D. Pearl, L. Bouthilet, & J. Lazar (Eds.), *Television and behavior: Ten years of scientific progress and implications for the eighties: Vol. 2. Technical reviews* (pp. 9–23). Washington, DC: U.S. Government Printing Office.

Comstock, G. A., & Paik, H. (1991). The effects of television violence on aggressive behavior: A meta-analysis. In *A preliminary report to the National Research Council on the understanding and control of violent behavior.* Washington, DC: National Research Council.

Condry, J., & Condry, S. (1976). Sex differences: A study of the eye of the beholder. *Child Development, 47,* 812–819.

Conduct Problems Prevention Research Group. (1992). A developmental and clinical model for the prevention of conduct disorder: The FAST Track Program. *Development and Psychopathology, 4,* 509–527.

Conger, R. D., Conger, K. J., Elder, G. H., Lorenz, F. O., Simons, R. L., & Whitbeck, L. B. (1992). A family process model of economic hardship and adjustment of early adolescent boys. *Child Development, 63,* 526–541.

Cook, E. T., Greenberg, M. T., & Kusche, C. A. (1994). The relations between emotional understanding, intellectual functioning and disruptive behavior problems in elementary school-aged children. *Journal of Abnormal Child Psychology, 22,* 205–219.

Coon, H., Carey, G., Corley, R., & Fulker, D. W. (1992). Identifying children in the Colorado Adoption Project at risk for conduct disorder. *Journal of the American Academy of Child and Adolescent Psychiatry, 31,* 503–511.

Cowan, P. (1979). *Piaget with feelings: Cognitive, social, and emotional dimensions.* New York: Holt, Rinehart and Winston.

Crick, N. R. (1995). Relational aggression: The role of intent attributions, feelings of distress, and provocation type. *Development and Psychopathology, 7,* 313–322.

Crick, N. R., & Dodge, K. A. (1994). A review and reformulation of social information processing mechanisms in children's social adjustment. *Psychological Bulletin, 115,* 74–101.

Crick, N. R., & Dodge, K. A. (1996). Social information-processing mechanisms in reactive and proactive aggression. *Child Development, 67,* 993–1002.

Crick, N. R., & Grotpeter, J. K. (1995). Relational aggression, gender, and social-psychological adjustment. *Child Development, 66,* 710–722.

Crick, N. R., & Ladd, G. W. (1990). Children's perceptions of the outcomes of aggressive strategies: Do the ends justify being mean? *Developmental Psychology, 26,* 612–620.

Crockenberg, S. (1981). Infant irritability, mother responsiveness, and social influences on the security of infant-mother attachment. *Child Development, 52,* 857–865.

Crowther, J. K., Bond, L. A., & Rolf, J. E. (1981). The incidence, prevalence, and severity of behavior disorders among preschool-aged children in day care. *Journal of Abnormal Child Psychology, 9,* 23–42.

Cummings, E. M., Hennessy, K. D., Rabideau, G. J., & Cicchetti, D. (1994). Responses of physically abused boys to inter-adult anger involving their mothers. *Development and Psychopathology, 6,* 31–41.

Cummings, E. M., Iannotti, R. J., & Zahn-Waxler, C. (1985). Influence of conflict between adults on the emotions and aggression of young children. *Developmental Psychology, 21,* 495–507.

Cummings, E. M., & Zahn-Waxler, C. (1992). Emotions and the socialization of aggression: Adult's angry behavior and children's arousal and aggression. In A. Fraezek & H. Zumkley (Eds.), *Socialization and aggression* (pp. 61–84). Berlin: Springer-Verlag.

Dabbs, J. M., Jr. (1992). Testosterone measurements in social and clinical psychology. *Journal of Social and Clinical Psychology, 11,* 302–326.

Dabbs, J. M., & Morris, R. (1990). Testosterone, social class, and antisocial behavior in a sample of 4,462 men. *Psychological Science, 1,* 209–211.

Dadds, M. R., Sanders, M. R., Morrison, M., & Rebgetz, M. (1992). Childhood depression and conduct disorder: II. An analysis of family interaction patterns in the home. *Journal of Abnormal Psychology, 101,* 505–513.

Damon, W. (1984). Self-understanding and moral development from childhood to adolescence. In W. M. Kurtines & J. L. Gewirtz (Eds.), *Morality, moral behavior, and moral development* (pp. 109–127). New York: Wiley.

Damon, W., & Hart, D. (1988). *Self-understanding in childhood and adolescence.* New York: Cambridge University Press.

Darwin, C. R. (1872). *The expression of emotions in man and animals.* London: John Murray.

Davies, J. G. V., & Maliphant, R. (1971). Autonomic responses of male adolescents exhibiting refractory behavior in school. *Journal of Child Psychology and Psychiatry, 12,* 115–127.

Davitz, J. R. (1952). The effects of previous training on postfrustration behavior. *Journal of Abnormal and Social Psychology, 47,* 309–315.

Dawe, H. C. (1934). An analysis of two hundred quarrels of preschool children. *Child Development, 5,* 139–157.

Deater-Deckard, K., & Dodge, K. A. (1997). Externalizing behavior problems and discipline revisited: Nonlinear effects and variation by culture, context, and gender. *Psychological Inquiry, 8,* 161–175.

Deater-Deckard, K., Dodge, K. A., Bates, J. E., & Pettit, G. S. (in press). Physical discipline among African-American and European-American mothers: Links to children's externalizing behaviors. *Developmental Psychology.*

de Cubas, M. M., & Field, T. (1993). Children of methadone-dependent women: Developmental outcomes. *American Journal of Orthopsychiatry, 63,* 266–276.

Delamater, A. M., & Lahey, B. B. (1983). Physiological correlates of conduct problems and anxiety in hyperactive and learning-disabled children. *Journal of Abnormal Child Psychology, 11,* 85–100.

Dell Fitzgerald, P., & Asher, S. R. (1987, August–September). *Aggressive-rejected children's attributional biases about liked and disliked peers.* Paper presented at the 95th annual convention of the American Psychological Association, New York.

Deluty, R. H. (1981). Alternative-thinking ability of aggressive, assertive, and submissive children. *Cognitive Therapy and Research, 5,* 309–312.

Deluty, R. H. (1983). Children's evaluations of aggressive, assertive, and submissive responses. *Journal of Clinical Child Psychology, 12,* 124–129.

Depue, R. A., & Spoont, M. R. (1986). Conceptualizing a serotonin trait: A behavioral dimension of constraint. *Annals of the New York Academy of Sciences, 487,* 205–212.

DiLalla, L. F., & Gottesman, I. I. (1989). Heterogeneity of causes of delinquency and criminality: Lifespan perspectives. *Development and Psychopathology, 1,* 339–349.

Dishion, T. J., Andrews, D. W., & Crosby, L. (1995). Antisocial boys and their friends in early adolescence: Relationship characteristics, quality, and interactional process. *Child Development, 66,* 139–151.

Dishion, T. J., & Brown, G. A. (in press). Measurement issues in studying parenting effects on adolescent problem behavior. In W. J. Bukowski & Z. Ansel (Eds.), *Drug abuse prevention: Source book on strategies and research.* Westport, CT: Greenwood Press.

Dishion, T. J., French, D. C., & Patterson, G. R. (1995). The development and ecology of antisocial behavior. In D. Cicchetti & D. J. Cohen (Eds.), *Developmental psychopathology* (pp. 421–471). New York: Wiley.

Dishion, T. J., Patterson, G. R., & Griesler, P. C. (1994). Peer adaptations in the development of antisocial behavior: A confluence model. In L. R. Huesmann (Ed.), *Aggressive behavior: Current perspectives* (pp. 61–95). New York: Plenum Press.

Dishion, T. J., Patterson, G. R., & Kavanagh, K. (1991). An experimental test of the coercion model: Linking theory, measurement, and intervention. In J. McCord & R. Tremblay (Eds.), *Preventing antisocial behavior: Interventions from birth through adolescence* (pp. 253–282). New York: Guilford Press.

Dodge, K. A. (1980). Social cognition and children's aggressive behavior. *Child Development, 51,* 162–170.

Dodge, K. A. (1983). Behavioral antecedents of peer social status. *Child Development, 54,* 1386–1399.

Dodge, K. A. (1986). A social information processing model of social competence in children. In M. Perlmutter (Ed.), *The Minnesota Symposium on Child Psychology* (Vol. 18, pp. 77–125). Hillsdale, NJ: Erlbaum.

Dodge, K. A. (1991). The structure and function of reactive and proactive aggression. In D. J. Pepler & K. H. Rubin (Eds.), *The development and treatment of childhood aggression* (pp. 201–218). Hillsdale, NJ: Erlbaum.

Dodge, K. A., Bates, J. E., & Pettit, G. S. (1990). Mechanisms in the cycle of violence. *Science, 250,* 1678–1683.

Dodge, K. A., & Coie, J. D. (1987). Social information-processing factors in reactive and proactive aggression in children's peer groups. *Journal of Personality and Social Psychology, 53,* 1146–1158.

Dodge, K. A., Coie, J. D., Pettit, G. S., & Price, J. M. (1990). Peer status and aggression in boys' groups: Developmental and contextual analyses. *Child Development, 61,* 1289–1309.

Dodge, K. A., & Frame, C. L. (1982). Social cognitive biases and deficits in aggressive boys. *Child Development, 53,* 620–635.

Dodge, K. A., McClaskey, C. L., & Feldman, E. (1985). A situational approach to the assessment of social competence in children. *Journal of Consulting and Clinical Psychology, 53,* 344–353.

Dodge, K. A., Murphy, R. R., & Buchsbaum, K. (1984). The assessment of intention-cue detection skills in children: Implications for developmental psychopathology. *Child Development, 55,* 163–173.

Dodge, K. A., & Newman, J. P. (1981). Biased decision-making processes in aggressive boys. *Journal of Abnormal Psychology, 90,* 375–379.

Dodge, K. A., Pettit, G. S., & Bates, J. E. (1994). Socialization mediators of the relation between socioeconomic status and child conduct problems. *Child Development, 65,* 649–665.

Dodge, K. A., Pettit, G. S., Bates, J. E., & Valente, E. (1995). Social information processing patterns partially mediate the effect of early physical abuse on later conduct problems. *Journal of Abnormal Psychology, 104,* 632–643.

Dodge, K. A., Pettit, G. S., McClaskey, C. L., & Brown, M. M. (1986). Social competence in children. *Monographs of the Society for Research in Child Development, 51*(2, Serial No. 213).

Dodge, K. A., & Price, J. M. (1994). On the relation between social information-processing and socially competent behavior in early school-aged children. *Child Development, 65*, 1385–1397.

Dodge, K. A., Price, J. M., Bachorowski, J. A., & Newman, J. P. (1990). Hostile attributional biases in severely aggressive adolescents. *Journal of Abnormal Psychology, 99*, 385–392.

Dodge, K. A., & Somberg, D. R. (1987). Hostile attributional biases among aggressive boys are exacerbated under conditions of threats to the self. *Child Development, 58*, 213–224.

Dodge, K. A., & Tomlin, A. M. (1987). Utilization of self-schemas as a mechanism of interpretational bias in aggressive children. *Social Cognition, 5*, 280–300.

Dollard, J., Doob, L. W., Miller, N. E., Mowrer, O. H., & Sears, R. R. (1939). *Frustration and aggression*. New Haven, CT: Yale University Press.

Dryfoos, J. G. (1990). *Adolescents at risk: Prevalence and prevention*. New York: Oxford University Press.

Dunn, J. (1988). *The beginnings of social understanding*. Cambridge, MA: Harvard University Press.

Dunn, J., & Kendrick, C. (1982). *Siblings*. Cambridge: Harvard University Press.

Earls, F. (1980). The prevalence of behavior problems in 3-year-old children. *Archives of General Psychiatry, 37*, 1153–1159.

Eaves, L. J., Silberg, J. L., Hewitt, J. K., Rutter, M., Meyer, J. M., Neale, M. C., & Pickles, A. (1993). Analyzing twin resemblance in multisymptom data: Genetic applications of a latent class model for symptoms of conduct disorder in juvenile boys. *Behavior Genetics, 23*, 5–19.

Eckenrode, J., Rowe, E., Laird, M., & Braithwaite, J. (1995). Mobility as a mediator of the effects of child maltreatment on academic performance. *Child Development, 66*, 1130–1142.

Edelbrock, C., Rende, R., Plomin, R., & Thompson, L. A. (1992). *Genetic and environmental effects on competence and problem behavior in childhood and early adolescence*. Unpublished manuscript.

Edelman, M. W. (1992). *The measure of our success*. Boston: Beacon Press.

Egeland, B., & Sroufe, L. A. (1981). Developmental sequelae of maltreatment in infancy. *New Directions for Child Development, 11*, 77–92.

Eisenberg, N. (1986). *Altruistic emotion, cognition, and behavior*. Hillsdale, NJ: Erlbaum.

Eisenberg, N., & Fabes, R. A. (1990). Empathy: Conceptualization, assessment, and relation to prosocial behavior. *Motivation and Emotion, 14*, 131–149.

Eisenberg, N., Fabes, R. A., Nyman, M., Bernzweig, J., & Pinuelas, A. (1994). The relations of emotionality and regulation to children's anger-related reactions. *Child Development, 65*, 109–128.

Ekman, P. (1972). Universals and cultural differences in facial expressions of emotion. In J. K. Cole (Ed.), *Nebraska Symposium on motivation* (Vol. 19, pp. 207–283). Lincoln: Nebraska University Press.

Ekman, P., & Friesen, W. (1975). *Unmasking the face*. Englewood Cliffs, NJ: Prentice-Hall.

Elder, G. H. (1979). Historical change in life patterns and personality. In P. B. Blates & O. G. Bim (Eds.), *Life-span development and behavior* (Vol. 2, pp. 117–159). New York: Academic Press.

Elder, G. H., Nguyen, T. V., & Caspi, A. (1985). Linking family hardship to children's lives. *Child Development, 56*, 361–375.

Elliott, D. S. (1994). Serious violent offenders: Onset, developmental course, and termination—The American Society of Criminology 1993 Presidential Address. *Criminology, 32*, 1–21.

Elliott, D. S., & Ageton, S. (1980). Reconciling race and class difference in self-reported and official estimates of delinquency. *American Sociological Review, 45*, 95–110.

Elliott, D. S., Ageton, S., Huizinga, D., Knowles, B., & Canter, R. (1983). *The prevalence and incidence of delinquent behavior: 1976–1980*. Boulder, CO: Behavioral Research Institute.

Elliott, D. S., & Huizinga, D. (1983). Social class and delinquent behavior. *Criminology, 21*, 149–177.

Elliott, D. S., Huizinga, D., & Ageton, S. S. (1985). *Explaining delinquency and drug use*. Newbury Park, CA: Sage.

Elliott, D. S., Huizinga, D., & Menard, S. (1989). *Multiple problem youth: Delinquency, substance use, and mental health problems*. New York: Springer-Verlag.

Elliott, D. S., Huizinga, D., & Morse, B. J. (1987). Self-reported violent offending: A descriptive analysis of juvenile violent offenders and their offending careers. *Journal of Interpersonal Violence, 1*, 472–514.

Elliott, D. S., & Morse, B. J. (1989). Delinquency and drug use as risk factors in teenage sexual activity. *Youth and Society, 21*, 32–60.

Erickson, M. F., Sroufe, L. A., & Egeland, B. (1985). The relationship between quality of attachment and behavior problems in preschool in a high-risk sample. In I. Bretherton & E. Waters (Eds.), Growing points in attachment theory and research. *Monographs of the Society for Research in Child Development, 50*(1/2, Serial No. 209), 147–186.

Eron, L. D., & Huesmann, L. R. (1990). The stability of aggressive behavior—even into the third generation. In M. Lewis & S. M. Miller (Eds.), *Handbook of developmental psychology* (pp. 147–156). New York: Plenum Press.

Eron, L. D., Huesmann, L. R., Brice, P., Fischer, P., & Mermelstein, R. (1983). Age trends in the development of aggression, sex typing, and related television habits. *Developmental Psychology, 19*, 71–77.

Eron, L. D., Huesmann, L. R., Dubow, E., Romanoff, R., & Yarmel, P. W. (1987). Aggression and its correlates over 22 years. In D. H. Crowell & I. M. Evans (Eds.), *Childhood aggression and violence* (pp. 249–262). New York: Plenum Press.

Eron, L. D., Huesmann, L. R., Lefkowitz, M. M., & Walder, L. O. (1972). Does television violence cause aggression? *American Psychologist, 27,* 253–263.

Eron, L. D., Huesmann, L. R., & Zell, A. (1991). The role of parental variables in the learning of aggression. In D. J. Pepler & K. H. Rubin (Eds.), *The development and treatment of childhood aggression* (pp. 169–189). Hillsdale, NJ: Erlbaum.

Eron, L. D., Walder, L. O., & Lefkowitz, M. M. (1971). *Learning of aggression in children.* Boston: Little, Brown.

Fabes, R. A., & Eisenberg, N. (1992a). Young children's emotional arousal and anger/aggressive behaviors. In A. Fraezek & H. Zumkley (Eds.), *Socialization and aggression* (pp. 85–102). Berlin: Springer-Verlag.

Fabes, R. A., & Eisenberg, N. (1992b). Young children's coping with interpersonal anger. *Child Development, 63,* 116–128.

Fagot, B. I., & Hagan, R. (1985). Aggression in toddlers: Responses to the assertive acts of boys and girls. *Sex Roles, 12,* 341–351.

Fagot, B. I., Hagan, R., Youngblade, L. M., & Potter, L. (1989). A comparison of the play behaviors of sexually abused, physically abused, and nonabused preschool children. *Topics in Early Childhood Special Education, 9,* 88–100.

Fagot, B. I., & Kavanaugh, K. (1990). The prediction of antisocial behavior from avoidant attachment classifications. *Child Development, 61,* 864–873.

Fagot, B. I., & Leve, L. (in press). Prediction of oppositional behavior from early childhood to school entry. *Journal of Consulting and Clinical Psychology.*

Faraone, S., Biederman, J., Keenan, K., & Tsuang, M. T. (1991). Separation of *DSM-III* attention deficit disorder and conduct disorder: Evidence from a family genetic study of American child psychiatry patients. *Psychological Medicine, 21,* 109–121.

Farrington, D. P. (1989a). Early predictors of adolescent aggression and adult violence. *Violence and Victims, 4,* 79–100.

Farrington, D. P. (1989b). Self-reported and official offending from adolescence to adulthood. In M. W. Klein (Ed.), *Cross-national research in self-reported crime and delinquency* (pp. 399–423). Dordrecht, The Netherlands: Kluwer.

Farrington, D. P. (1992). Juvenile delinquency. In J. C. Coleman (Ed.), *The school years,* (2nd ed., pp. 123–163). London: Routledge & Kegan Paul.

Farrington, D. P. (1993). The challenge of teenage antisocial behavior. In M. Rutter (Ed.), *Psychosocial disturbances in young people.* Cambridge, England: Cambridge University Press.

Farrington, D. P. (1995). The development of offending and antisocial behavior from childhood: Key findings from the Cambridge study in delinquent development. *Journal of Child Psychology and Psychiatry, 36,* 1–36.

Farrington, D. P., Gallagher, I., Morley, R. J., St. Ledger, R. J., & West, D. J. (1986). Unemployment, school leaving, and crime. *British Journal of Criminology, 26,* 335–356.

Farrington, D. P., & Hawkins, J. D. (1991). Predicting participation, early onset and later persistence in officially recorded offending. *Criminal Behavior and Mental Health, 1,* 1–33.

Farrington, D. P., Loeber, R., & Van Kammen, W. B. (1990). Long-term criminal outcomes of hyperactivity-impulsivity-attention deficit and conduct problems in childhood. In L. N. Robins & M. Rutter (Eds.), *Straight and devious pathways from childhood to adulthood* (pp. 62–81). Cambridge, England: Cambridge University Press.

Ferguson, T. J., & Rule, B. G. (1980). Effects of inferential set, outcome severity, and basis of responsibility on children's evaluation of aggressive acts. *Developmental Psychology, 16,* 141–146.

Ferguson, T. J., & Rule, B. G. (1988). Children's evaluations of retaliatory aggression. *Child Development, 59,* 961–968.

Feshbach, N. D., & Feshbach, S. (1982). Empathy training and the regulation of aggression: Potentialities and limitations. *Academic Psychology Bulletin, 4,* 399–413.

Feshbach, S. (1970). Aggression. In P. H. Mussen (Ed.), *Carmichael's manual of child psychology* (Vol. 2, 3rd ed.). New York: Wiley.

Fingerhut, L. A., & Kleinman, J. C. (1990). International and interstate comparisons of homicide among young males. *Journal of the American Medical Association, 263,* 3292–3295.

Fischer, M., Rolf, J. E., Hasazi, J. C., & Cummings, L. (1984). Follow-up of a preschool epidemiological sample: Cross-age continuities and predictions of later adjustment with internalizing and externalizing dimensions of behavior. *Child Development, 55,* 137–150.

Flavell, J. H. (1977). *Cognitive development.* Englewood Cliffs, NJ: Prentice-Hall.

Florsheim, P., Tolan, P. H., & Gorman-Smith, D. (in press). Family processes and risk for externalizing behavior problems among African-American and Hispanic boys. *Journal of Consulting and Clinical Psychology.*

Fowles, D. C. (1980). The three arousal model: Implications of Gray's two-factor learning theory for heart rate, electrodermal activity and psychopathy. *Psychophysiology, 17,* 87–104.

Fowles, D. C. (1988). Psychophysiology and psychopathy: A motivational approach. *Psychophysiology, 25,* 373–391.

Fowles, D. C., & Missell, K. A. (1994). Electrodermal hyporeactivity, motivation, and psychopathy: Theoretical issues.

In D. C. Fowles, P. Sutker, & S. H. Goodman (Eds.), *Progress in experimental personality and psychopathology research* (pp. 263–283). New York: Springer-Verlag.

Freedman, J. (1984). Effect of television violence on aggressiveness. *Psychological Bulletin, 96,* 227–246.

French, D. C. (1988). Heterogeneity of peer-rejected boys: Aggressive and nonaggressive subtypes. *Child Development, 59,* 976–985.

Freud, S. (1958). *Civilization and its discontents* (J. Riviere, Trans.). Garden City, NY: Doubleday. (Original work published 1930)

Frick, P. J., Lahey, B. B., Loeber, R., Tannenbaum, L., Van Horn, Y., & Christ, M. A. G. (1993). Oppositional defiant disorder and conduct disorder: I. Meta-analytic review of factor analyses. *Clinical Psychology Review, 13,* 319–340.

Frijda, N. (1986). *The emotions.* New York: Cambridge University Press.

Frost, L. A., Moffitt, T. E., & McGee, R. (1989). Neuropsychological correlates of psychopathology in an unselected cohort of young adolescents. *Journal of Abnormal Psychology, 98,* 307–313.

Garber, J. (1984). Classification of childhood psychopathology. *Child Development, 55,* 30–48.

Garralda, M. E., Connell, J., & Taylor, D. C. (1991). Psychophysiological anomalies in children with emotional and conduct disorders. *Psychological Medicine, 21,* 947–957.

Gelman, R., & Baillargeon, R. (1983). A review of some Piagetian concepts. In P. Mussen (Series Ed.) & J. H. Flavell & E. M. Markman (Eds.), *Handbook of child psychology: Vol. 3. Cognitive development.* New York: Wiley.

Gerbner, G., & Gross, L. (1976). Living with television: The violence profile. *Journal of Communication, 26,* 173–199.

Ghodsian-Carpey, J., & Baker, L. A. (1987). Genetic and environmental influences on aggression in 4- to 7-year-old twins. *Aggressive Behavior, 13,* 173–186.

Gillmore, M. R., Hawkins, J. D., Day, L. E., & Catalano, R. F. (1992). Friendship and deviance: New evidence on an old controversy. *Journal of Early Adolescence, 12,* 80–95.

Giordano, P. G., Cernkovich, S. A., & Pugh, M. D. (1986). Friendships and delinquency. *American Journal of Sociology, 91,* 1170–1202.

Gladue, B. A., Boechler, M., & McCaul, K. D. (1989). Hormonal responses to competition in human males. *Aggressive Behavior, 17,* 313–326.

Glueck, S., & Glueck, E. (1950). *Unraveling juvenile delinquency.* Cambridge, MA: Harvard University Press.

Glueck, S., & Glueck, E. (1968). *Delinquents and nondelinquents in perspective.* Cambridge, MA: Harvard University Press.

Goldsmith, H. H. (1993). Temperament: Variability in developing emotion systems. In M. Lewis & J. M. Haviland (Eds.), *Handbook of emotion* (pp. 353–364). New York: Guilford Press.

Goldsmith, H. H., Buss, A. H., Plomin, R., Rothbart, T. A., Chess, S., Hinde, R. A., & McCall, R. B. (1987). Round table: What is temperament? Four approaches. *Child Development, 58,* 505–529.

Goldsmith, H. H., Jaco, K. L., & Elliott, T. K. (1986). Genetic analyses of infant and early childhood temperament characteristics. *Behavior Genetics, 16,* 620.

Goldstein, A. P. (1992, May 4). *School violence: Its community context and potential solutions.* Testimony presented to the Subcommittee on Elementary, Secondary and Vocational Education of the Committee on Education and Labor of the United States House of Representatives.

Goldstein, A. P. (1994). Delinquent gangs. In L. R. Huesmann (Ed.), *Aggressive behavior: Current perspectives. Plenum series in social/clinical psychology* (pp. 255–273). New York: Plenum Press.

Goodenough, F. L. (1931). *Anger in young children.* Minneapolis: University of Minnesota.

Gorman-Smith, D., Tolan, P. H., Zelli, A., & Huesmann, L. R. (in press). The relation of family functioning to violence among inner-city minority youth. *Journal of Family Practice.*

Gottesman, I. I., & Goldsmith, H. H. (1994). Developmental psychopathology of antisocial behavior: Inserting genes into its ontogenesis and epigenesis. In C. A. Nelson (Ed.), *Threats to optimal development: Integrating biological, psychological, and social risk factors* (pp. 69–104). Hillsdale, NJ: Erlbaum.

Gottman, J., Gonso, J., & Rasmussen, B. (1975). Social interaction, social competence, and friendship in children. *Child Development, 46,* 709–718.

Gouze, K. R. (1987). Attention and social problem solving as correlates of aggression in preschool males. *Journal of Abnormal Child Psychology, 15,* 181–197.

Graham, S., & Hudley, C. (1994). Attributions of aggressive and nonaggressive African-American male early adolescents: A study of construct accessibility. *Developmental Psychology, 30,* 365–373.

Graham, S., Hudley, C., & Williams, E. (1992). Attributional and emotional determinants of aggression among African-American and Latino young adolescents. *Developmental Psychology, 28,* 731–740.

Gray, J. A. (1982). *The neuropsychology of anxiety: An inquiry into the function of the septohippocampal system.* New York: Oxford University Press.

Gray, J. A. (1987). *The psychology of fear and stress.* Cambridge, England: Cambridge University.

Greenberg, M. T., Spelz, M. L., & Deklyen, M. (1993). The role of attachment in the early development of disruptive behavior problems. *Development and Psychopathology, 5,* 191–213.

Grove, W. M., Eckert, E. D., Heston, L., Bouchard, T. J., Segal, N., & Lykken, D. T. (1990). Heritability of substance abuse and antisocial behavior: A study of monozygotic twins reared apart. *Biological Psychiatry, 27,* 1293–1304.

Grusec, J. E., & Kuczynski, L. (1980). Direction of effect in socialization: A comparison of the parent's versus the child's behavior as determinants of disciplinary tactics. *Developmental Psychology, 16,* 1–9.

Guerra, N. G., Huesmann, L. R., & Hanish, L. (1995). The role of normative beliefs in children's social behavior. In N. Eisenberg (Ed.), *Review of personality and social psychology, development, and social psychology: The interface* (pp. 140–158). Thousand Oaks, CA: Sage.

Guerra, N. G., Huesmann, L. R., Tolan, P. H., Van Acker, R., & Eron, L. D. (1995). Stressful events and individual beliefs as correlates of economic disadvantage and aggression among urban children. *Journal of Consulting and Clinical Psychology, 63,* 518–528.

Guerra, N. G., & Slaby, R. G. (1989). Evaluative factors in social problem solving by aggressive boys. *Journal of Abnormal Child Psychology, 17,* 277–289.

Gurwitz, S. G., & Dodge, K. A. (1975). Adults' evaluations of a child as a function of the sex of adult and sex of child. *Journal of Personality and Social Psychology, 32,* 822–828.

Haapasalo, J., & Tremblay, R. E. (1994). Physically aggressive boys from ages 6 to 12: Family background, parenting behavior, and prediction of delinquency. *Journal of Consulting and Clinical Psychology, 62,* 1044–1052.

Halpern, C. T., Udry, J. R., Campbell, B., & Suchindraw, C. (1994). Relationships between aggression and pubertal increases in testosterone: A panel analysis of adolescent males. *Social Biology, 40,* 8–24.

Hammond, W. R., & Yung, B. R. (1991). Preventing violence in at-risk African-American youth. *Journal of Health Care for the Poor and Underserved, 2,* 1–16.

Hamparian, D. M., Schuster, R., Dinitz, S., & Conrad, J. (1978). *The violent few.* Lexington, MA: Heath.

Hare, R. D. (1978). Electrodermal and cardiovascular correlates of psychopathy. In R. D. Hare & D. Schalling (Eds.), *Psychopathic behavior: Approaches to research* (pp. 107–144). New York: Wiley.

Hart, C. H., Ladd, G. W., & Burleson, B. (1990). Children's expectations of the outcomes of social strategies: Relations with sociometric status and maternal disciplinary styles. *Child Development, 61,* 127–137.

Harter, S. (1982). The perceived competence scale for children. *Child Development, 53,* 89–97.

Hartup, W. W. (1974). Aggression in childhood: Developmental perspectives. *American Psychologist, 29,* 336–341.

Hartup, W. W., & deWit, J. (1974). The development of aggression: Problems and perspectives. In J. deWit & W. W. Hartup (Eds.), *Determinants and origins of aggressive behavior* (pp. 595–615). The Hague: Mouton.

Haskett, M. E., & Kistner, J. A. (1991). Social interactions and peer perceptions of young physically abused children. *Child Development, 62,* 979–990.

Hawkins, J. D., & Lishner, D. M. (1987). Schooling and delinquency. In E. H. Johnson (Ed.), *Handbook on crime and delinquency prevention* (pp. 179–221). New York: Greenwood Press.

Hawkins, J. D., & Weis, J. G. (1985). The social development model: An integrated approach to delinquency prevention. *Journal of Primary Prevention, 6,* 73–95.

Hay, D. F., Nash, A., & Pedersen, J. (1983). Interactions between 6-month-olds. *Child Development, 54,* 557–562.

Hay, D. F., & Ross, H. S. (1982). The social nature of early conflict. *Child Development, 53,* 105–113.

Heider, F. (1958). *The psychology of interpersonal relationships.* New York: Wiley.

Herr, P. M. (1986). Consequences of priming: Judgment and behavior. *Journal of Personality and Social Psychology, 51,* 1106–1115.

Hetherington, E. M., Camara, C., & Featherman, D. L. (1983). Achievement and intellectual functioning of children in one-parent households. In J. T. Spence (Ed.), *Achievement and achievement motives* (pp. 205–284). San Francisco: Freeman.

Higgins, E. T., & King, G. (1981). Accessibility of social constructs: Information-processing consequences of individual differences and construct accessibility. In N. Cantor & J. Kihlstrom (Eds.), *Personality and social interaction* (pp. 69–122). Hillsdale, NJ: Erlbaum.

Hinde, R. A. (1974). *Biological bases of social behavior.* New York: McGraw-Hill.

Hinshaw, S. P. (1987). On the distinction between attentional deficits/hyperactivity and conduct problems/aggression in child psychopathology. *Psychological Bulletin, 101,* 443–463.

Hinshaw, S. P. (1991). Stimulant medication and the treatment of aggression in children with attentional deficits. *Journal of Clinical Child Psychology, 20,* 301–312.

Hinshaw, S. P. (1992). Externalizing behavior problems and academic underachievement in childhood and adolescence: Causal relationships and underlying mechanisms. *Psychological Bulletin, 111,* 127–155.

Hinshaw, S. P. (1994). Conduct disorder in childhood: Conceptualization, diagnosis, comorbidity, and risk status for antisocial functioning in adulthood. In D. Fowles, P. Sutter, &

S. Goodman (Eds.), *Progress in experimental personality and psychopathology research, 1994. Special focus on psychopathy and antisocial personality: A developmental perspective* (pp. 3–44). New York: Springer-Verlag.

Hinshaw, S. P., & Anderson, C. A. (1996). Conduct and oppositional defiant disorder. In E. J. Mash & R. A. Barkley (Eds.), *Child psychology* (pp. 113–149). New York: Guilford Press.

Hinshaw, S. P., Heller, T., & McHale, J. P. (1992). Covert antisocial behavior in boys with attention-deficit hyperactivity disorder: External validation and effects of methylphenidate. *Journal of Consulting and Clinical Psychology, 60,* 274–281.

Hinshaw, S. P., Lahey, B. B., & Hart, E. L. (1993). Issues of taxonomy and comorbidity in the development of conduct disorder. *Developmental and Psychopathology, 5,* 31–49.

Hinshaw, S. P., & Simmel, C. (1994). Attention-deficit hyperactivity disorder. In M. Hersen, R. T. Ammerman, & L. A. Sisson (Eds.), *Handbook of aggressive and destructive behavior in psychiatric patients* (pp. 339–354). New York: Plenum Press.

Hirschi, T. (1969). Causes of delinquency. Berkeley: University of California Press.

Hobbes, T. (1969). *Leviathon.* Cambridge, England: Cambridge University Press. (Original work published 1651)

Hoffman, M. L. (1960). Power assertion by the parent and its impact on the child. *Child Development, 31,* 129–143.

Holmberg, M. S. (1977). *The development of social interchange patterns from 12 months to 42 months: Cross-sectional and short-term longitudinal analyses.* Doctoral dissertation, University of North Carolina, Chapel Hill.

Howes, C., & Eldredge, R. (1985). Responses of abused, neglected, and non-maltreated children to the behaviors of their peers. *Journal of Applied Developmental Psychology, 6,* 261–270.

Hudley, C. A., & Graham, S. (1993). An attributional intervention to reduce peer-directed aggression among African-American boys. *Child Development, 64,* 124–138.

Huesmann, L. R. (1986). Psychological processes promoting the relation between exposure to media violence and aggressive behavior by the viewer. *Journal of Social Issues, 42,* 125–139.

Huesmann, L. R. (1988). An information-processing model for the development of aggression. *Aggressive Behavior, 14,* 13–24.

Huesmann, L. R., & Bachrach, R. S. (1988). Differential effects of television violence in kibbutz and city children. In R. Patterson & P. Drummond (Eds.), *Television and its audience: International research perspectives* (pp. 154–176). London: BFI.

Huesmann, L. R., & Eron, L. D. (1986). *Television and the aggressive child: A cross-national perspective.* Hillsdale, NJ: Erlbaum.

Huesmann, L. R., Eron, L. D., Berkowitz, L., & Chafee, S. (1991). The effects of television violence on aggression: A reply to a skeptic. In P. Suedfeld & P. Tetlock (Eds.), *Psychology and social policy* (pp. 192–200). New York: Hemisphere.

Huesmann, L. R., Eron, L. D., Klein, R., Brice, P., & Fischer, P. (1983). Mitigating the imitation of aggressive behaviors by children's attitudes about media violence. *Journal of Personality and Social Psychology, 44,* 899–910.

Huesmann, L. R., Eron, L. D., Lefkowitz, M. M., & Walder, L. O. (1984). Stability of aggression over time and generations. *Developmental Psychology, 20,* 1120–1134.

Huesmann, L. R., Lagerspetz, & Eron, L. D. (1984). Intervening variables in the TV violence aggression relation: Evidence from two countries. *Developmental Psychology, 20,* 746–775.

Huesmann, L. R., & Miller, L. S. (1994). Long-term effects of repeated exposure to media violence in childhood. In L. R. Huesmann (Ed.), *Aggressive behavior: Current perspectives* (pp. 153–186). New York: Plenum Press.

Huizinga, D., & Dunford, F. W. (1985). *The delinquent behavior of arrested individuals.* Paper presented at the 1985 annual meeting of the Academy of Criminal Justice Sciences, Las Vegas, NV.

Huizinga, D., & Elliott, D. S. (1987). Juvenile offenders: Prevalence, offender incidence, and arrest rates by race. *Crime and Delinquency, 33,* 206–223.

Humphreys, A. P., & Smith, P. K. (1987). Rough and tumble, friendship, and dominance in school children: Evidence for continuity and change with age. *Child Development, 58,* 201–212.

Iannotti, R. J. (1978). Effects of role-taking experiences on role-taking, empathy, altruism, and aggression. *Developmental Psychology, 14,* 119–124.

Inoff-Germain, G., Arnold, G. S., Nottelmann, E. D., Susman, E. J., Cutler, G. B., & Chrousos, G. P. (1988). Relations between hormone levels and observational measures of aggressive behavior of young adolescents in family interactions. *Developmental Psychology, 24,* 129–139.

Izard, C. E. (1977). *Human emotions.* New York: Plenum Press.

James, W. (1890). *Principles of psychology* (Vol. 2). New York: Holt.

Jenkins, S., Bax, M., & Hart, H. (1980). Behavior problems in preschool children. *Journal of Child Psychology and Psychiatry, 21,* 5–18.

Jersild, A. T., & Markey, F. U. (1935). Conflicts between preschool children. *Child Development Monographs.*

Jessor, R., Donovan, J. E., & Costa, F. M. (1991). *Beyond adolescence: Problem behavior and young adult development.* New York: Academic Press.

Jessor, R., & Jessor, S. L. (1977). *Problem behavior and psychosocial development: A longitudinal study of youth.* New York: Academic Press.

Jimack, P. (1911). *Introduction to Rousseau's Emile.* London: Dent.

Jones, E. E., & Davis, K. E. (1965). From acts to dispositions: The attribution process in social perception. In L. Berkowitz (Ed.), *Advances in experimental social psychology* (Vol. 2, pp. 220–266). New York: Academic Press.

Josephson, W. L. (1987). Television violence and children's aggression: Testing the priming, social script, and disinhibition predictors. *Journal of Personality and Social Psychology, 53,* 882–890.

Kagan, J. (1981). *The second year: The emergence of self-awareness.* Cambridge, MA: Harvard University Press.

Kandel, D. B. (1978). Homophily, selection, and socialization in adolescent friendships. *American Journal of Sociology, 84,* 427–436.

Karniski, W. M., Levine, M. D., Clarke, S., Palfrey, J. S., & Meltzer, L. J. (1982). A study of neurodevelopmental findings in early adolescent delinquents. *Journal of Adolescent Health Care, 3,* 151–159.

Kazdin, A. E. (1985). *Treatment of antisocial behavior in children and adolescents.* Homeword, IL: Dorsey Press.

Kazdin, A. E. (1993). Treatment of conduct disorder: Progress and directions in psychotherapy research. *Development and Psychopathology, 5,* 276–310.

Keenan, K., Loeber, R., Zhang, Q., Stouthamer-Loeber, M., & Van Kammen, W. B. (1995). The influence of deviant peers on the development of boys' disruptive and delinquent behavior: A temporal analysis. *Development and Psychopathology, 7,* 715–726.

Keenan, K., Shaw, D., Giovanelli, J., Greenstein, B., & Delliquadri, E. (1995, March). *Developmental trajectories of girls' and boys' early emotional and behavioral problems: A longitudinal study of low-income families.* Paper presented at the meeting of the Society for Research in Child Development, Indianapolis.

Keith, C. R. (Ed.). (1984). *The aggressive adolescent: Clinical perspectives.* New York: Free Press.

Kellam, S. G. (1990). Developmental epidemiological framework for family research on depression and aggression. In G. R. Patterson (Ed.), *Depression and aggression in family interaction* (pp. 11–48). Hillsdale, NJ: Erlbaum.

Kelley, H. H. (1973). The processes of causal attribution. *American Psychologist, 28,* 107–128.

Kelley, H. H. (1979). *Personal relationships: Their structure and process.* Hillsdale, NJ: Erlbaum.

Kendall, P. C., & Braswell, L. (1985). *Cognitive-behavioral therapy for impulsive children.* New York: Guilford Press.

Kohlberg, L. (1981). *The philosophy of moral development.* San Francisco: Harper & Row.

Kolvin, I., Miller, F. J. W., Scott, D. M., Gatzanis, S. R. M., & Fleeting, M. (1990). *Continuities of deprivation?* Aldershot: Avebury.

Kopp, C. B. (1982). Antecedents of self-regulation: A developmental perspective. *Developmental Psychology, 18,* 199–214.

Kovacs, M., Paulauskas, S., Gatsonis, C., & Richards, C. (1988). Depressive disorder in childhood: A longitudinal study of the comorbidity with and risk for conduct disorders. *Journal of Affective Disorders, 15,* 205–217.

Kraemer, G. W., Ebert, M. H., Lake, C. R., & McKinney, W. T. (1984). Cerebrospinal fluid changes associated with pharmacological alteration of the despair response to social separation in rhesus monkeys. *Psychiatry Research, 11,* 303–315.

Kruesi, M. J. P., Hibbs, E. D., Zahn, T. P., Keysor, C. S., Hamburger, S. D., Bartko, J. J., & Rapoport, J. L. (1992). A 2-year prospective follow-up study of children and adolescents with disruptive behavior disorders. *Archives of General Psychiatry, 49,* 249–435.

Kruesi, M. J. P., Rapoport, J. L., Hamburger, S., Hibbs, E., Potter, W. Z., Lenane, M., & Brown, G. L. (1990). Cerebrospinal fluid monoamine metabolites, aggression, and impulsivity in disruptive behavior disorders of children and adolescents. *Archives of General Psychiatry, 47,* 419–426.

Kruttschnitt, C. (1994). Gender and interpersonal violence. In A. J. Reis, Jr. & J. A. Roth (Eds.), *Understanding and preventing violence: Vol. 3. Social influences* (pp. 293–376). Washington, DC: National Academy Press.

Kupersmidt, J. B., & Coie, J. D. (1990). Preadolescent peer status, aggression, and school adjustment as predictors of externalizing problems in adolescence. *Child Development, 61,* 1350–1362.

Kupersmidt, J. B., Griesler, P. C., DeRosier, M. E., Patterson, C. J., & Davis, P. W. (1995). Childhood aggression and peer relations in the context of family and neighborhood factors. *Child Development, 66,* 360–375.

Kupersmidt, J. B., Patterson, C., & Eickholt, C. (1989, April). *Socially rejected children: Bullies, victims, or both?* Paper presented at the biennial meeting of the Society for Research in Child Development, Kansas City.

Ladd, G. W. (1990). Having friends, keeping friends, making friends, and being liked by peers in the classroom: Predictors of children's early school adjustment. *Child Development, 61,* 312–331.

Ladd, G. W., & Odens, S. (1979). The relationship between peer acceptance and children's ideas about helpfulness. *Child Development, 50,* 402–408.

Lagerspetz, K. M. J., & Björkqvist, K. (1994). Indirect aggression in boys and girls. In L. R. Huesmann (Ed.), *Aggressive behavior: Current perspectives* (pp. 131–150). New York: Plenum Press.

Lahey, B., & Loeber, R. (1994). Framework for a developmental model of oppositional defiant disorder and conduct disorder. In D. Routh (Ed.), *Disruptive behavior disorders in childhood* (pp. 139–180). New York: Plenum Press.

Lahey, B., Loeber, R., Quay, H. C., Frick, P. J., & Grimm, J. (1992). Oppositional defiant and conduct disorders: Issues to be resolved for *DSM-IV. Journal of the American Academy of Child and Adolescent Psychiatry, 31,* 539–546.

Lahey, B., Piacentini, J. C., McBurnett, K., Stone, P., Hartdagen, S., & Hynd, G. (1988). Psychopathology in the parents of children with conduct disorder and hyperactivity. *Journal of the American Academy of Child and Adolescent Psychiatry, 27,* 163–170.

Lancelotta, G. X., & Vaughn, S. (1989). Relation between types of aggression and sociometric status: Peer and teacher perceptions. *Journal of Educational Psychology, 81,* 86–90.

Larzelere, R. E., & Patterson, G. R. (1990). Parental management: Mediators of the effect of socioeconomic status on early delinquency. *Criminology, 28,* 301–323.

Lefkowitz, M. M., Eron, L. D., Walder, L. O., & Huesmann, L. R. (1977). *Growing up to be violent: A longitudinal study of the development of aggression.* New York: Pergamon Press.

Lesser, G. S. (1959). The relationship between various forms of aggression and popularity among lower-class children. *Journal of Educational Psychology, 50,* 20–25.

Lewis, M., Feiring, C., McGuffog, C., & Jaskir, J. (1984). Predicting psychopathology in 6-year-olds from early social relations. *Child Development, 55,* 123–136.

Lilienfeld, S. O., & Waldman, I. D. (1990). The relation between childhood attention-deficit hyperactivity disorder and adult antisocial behavior reexamined: The problem of heterogeneity. *Clinical Psychology Review, 10,* 699–725.

Linnoila, V. M. I., & Virkkunen, M. (1992). Aggression, suicidality, and serotonin. *Journal of Clinical Psychology, 53* (Suppl. 10), 46–51.

Lipsett, L. P., & Levy, N. (1959). Electroactual threshold in the neonate. *Child Development, 30,* 547–554.

Lochman, J. E. (1987). Self and peer perceptions and attributional biases of aggressive and nonaggressive boys. *Journal of Consulting Clinical Psychology, 55,* 4404–4410.

Locke, J. (1913). *Some thoughts concerning education.* London: Cambridge University Press. (Original work published 1690)

Loeber, R. (1982). The stability of antisocial and delinquent child behavior: A review. *Child Development, 53,* 1431–1446.

Loeber, R. (1985). Patterns and development of antisocial child behavior. *Annals of Child Development, 2,* 77–116.

Loeber, R. (1988a). Behavioral precursors and accelerators of delinquency. *Criminology, 25,* 615–642.

Loeber, R. (1988b). Natural histories of conduct problems, delinquency, and associated substance use: Evidence for developmental progressions. In B. B. Lahey & A. E. Kazdin (Eds.), *Advances in clincial child psychology* (Vol. 2, pp. 73–124). New York: Plenum Press.

Loeber, R. (1990). Development and risk factors of juvenile antisocial behavior and delinquency. *Clinical Psychology Review, 10,* 1–41.

Loeber, R., & Hay, D. F. (1993). Developmental approaches to aggression and conduct problems. In M. Rutter & D. F. Hay (Eds.), *Development through life: A handbook for clinicians* (pp. 488–516). Oxford, England: Blackwell.

Loeber, R., Lahey, B. B., & Thomas, C. (1991). Diagnostic conundrum of oppositional defiant disorder and conduct disorder. *Journal of Abnormal Psychology, 100,* 379–390.

Loeber, R., & Schmaling, K. B. (1985a). The utility of differentiating between mixed and pure forms of antisocial child behavior. *Journal of Abnormal Child Psychology, 13,* 315–336.

Loeber, R., & Schmaling, K. B. (1985b). Empirical evidence for overt and covert patterns of antisocial conduct problems: A meta-analysis. *Journal of Abnormal Child Psychology, 13,* 337–352.

Loeber, R., Stouthamer-Loeber, M., Van Kammen, W. B., & Farrington, D. (1991). Initiation, escalation, and desistance in juvenile offending and their correlates. *Journal of Criminal Law and Criminology, 82,* 36–82.

Loeber, R., Tremblay, R. E., Gagnon, C., & Charlebois, P. (1989). Continuity and desistance in disruptive boys' early fighting in school. *Development and Psychopathology, 1,* 39–50.

Loeber, R., Wung, P., Keenan, K., Giroux, B., Stouthamer-Loeber, M., Van Kammen, W. B., & Maughan, B. (1993). Developmental pathways in disruptive child behavior. *Development Psychopathology, 5,* 103–133.

Loney, J. (1987). Hyperactivity and aggression in the diagnosis of attention deficit disorder. In B. B. Lahey & A. E. Kazdin (Eds.), *Advances in clinical child psychology* (Vol. 10, pp. 99–135). New York: Plenum Press.

Lorenz, K. (1966). *On aggression.* New York: Harcourt.

Luntz, B. K., & Widom, C. S. (1994). Antisocial personality disorders in abused and neglected children grown up. *American Journal of Psychiatry, 151,* 670–674.

Lynam, D., Moffitt, T., & Stouthamer-Loeber, M. (1993). Explaining the relation between IQ and delinquency: Class, race, test motivation, school failure, or self control? *Journal of Abnormal Psychology, 102,* 187–196.

Lyons, M. J., Eaves, L., Tsuang, M. Y., Eisen, S. E., Goldberg, J., & True, W. T. (1993). Differential heritability of adult and juvenile antisocial traits. *Psychiatric Genetics, 3,* 117.

Lyons-Ruth, K., Alpern, L., & Repacholi, B. (1993). Disorganized infant attachment classification and maternal psychosocial problems as predictors of hostile-aggressive behavior in the preschool classroom. *Child Development, 64,* 572–585.

Lyons-Ruth, K., Easterbrooks, M. A., & Davidson, C. (1995, April). *Disorganized attachment strategies and mental lag in infancy: Prediction of externalizing problems at seven.* Paper presented at biennial meeting of the Society for Research in Child Development, Indianapolis.

Maccoby, E. E. (1986). Social groupings in childhood: Their relationship to prosocial and antisocial behavior in boys and girls. In D. Olweus, J. Block, & M. Radke-Yarrow (Eds.), *Development of antisocial and prosocial behavior: Research, theories, and issues* (pp. 263–284). New York: Academic Press.

Maccoby, E. E. (1988). Gender as a social category. *Developmental Psychology, 24,* 755–765.

Maccoby, E. E., & Jacklin, C. N. (1980). Sex differences in aggression: A rejoinder and reprise. *Child Development, 51,* 964–980.

Magnusson, D. (1987). Adult delinquency and early conduct and physiology. In D. Magnusson & A. Öhman (Eds.), *Psychopathology: An international perspective* (pp. 221–234). New York: Academic Press.

Magnusson, D., Klinteberg, B., & Stattin, H. (1993). Autonomic activity/reactivity, behavior, and crime in a longitudinal perspective. In J. McCord (Ed.), *Facts, framework, and forecasts: Advances in criminological theory* (pp. 287–318). New Brunswick: Transaction.

Maguin, E., Loeber, R., & LeMahieu, P. G. (1993). Does the relationship between poor reading and delinquency hold for males of different ages and ethnic groups? *Journal of Emotional and Behavioral Disorders, 1,* 88–100.

Mahler, M. (1968). *On human symbiosis and the vicissitudes of individualization.* New York: International Universities Press.

Main, M., & George, C. (1985). Responses of abused and disadvantaged toddlers to distress in agemates: A study in the daycare setting. *Developmental Psychology, 21,* 407–412.

Makin, J., Fried, P. A., & Watkinson, B. (1991). A comparison of active and passive smoking during pregnancy: Long-term effects. *Neurotoxicology and Teratology, 13,* 12.

Maliphant, R., Hume, F., & Furnham, A. (1990). Autonomic nervous system activity, personality characteristics, and disruptive behavior in girls. *Journal of Child Psychology and Psychiatry, 31,* 619–628.

Manley, J. T., Cicchetti, D., & Barnett, D. (1994). The impact of subtype, frequency, chronicity, and severity of child maltreatment on social competence and behavior problems. *Development and Psychopathology, 6,* 121–143.

Mannuzza, S., Klein, R. G., Bonagura, N., Malloy, P., Giampino, T. L., & Addalli, K. A. (1991). Hyperactive boys almost grown up: V. Replication of psychiatric status. *Archives of General Psychiatry, 48,* 77–83.

Marazziti, D., Rotondo, A., Presto, S., Pancioli-Guadagnucci, M. L., Palego, L., & Conti, L. (1993). Role of serotonin in human aggressive behavior. *Aggressive Behavior, 19,* 347–353.

Marcus, R. F. (1980). Empathy and popularity of preschool children. *Child Study Journal, 10,* 133–145.

Martin, B. (1975). Parent-child relations. In F. D. Horowitz (Ed.), *Review of child development research* (Vol. 4, pp. 463–540). Chicago: University of Chicago Press.

Matheny, A. P. (1989). Children's behavioral inhibition over age and across situations: Genetic similarity for a trait during change. *Journal of Personality, 57,* 215–226.

Maudry, M., & Nekula, M. (1939). Social relations between children of the same age during the first two years of life. *Journal of Genetic Psychology, 54,* 193–215.

Maughan, B., Gray, G., & Rutter, M. (1985). Reading retardation and antisocial behavior: A follow-up in employment. *Journal of Child Psychology and Psychiatry, 26,* 741–758.

Mazur, A., & Lamb, T. A. (1980). Testosterone, status, and mood in human males. *Hormones and Behavior, 14,* 236–246.

McCall, N. (1994). *Makes me wanna holler: A young black man in America.* New York: Vintage Books.

McCaul, K. D., Gladue, B. A., & Joppa, M. (1992). Winning, losing, mood, and testosterone. *Hormones and Behavior, 26,* 486–504.

McCord, J. (1977). A comparative study of two generations of native Americans. In R. F. Meier (Ed.), *Theory in criminology: Contemporary views* (pp. 83–92). New York: Sage.

McCord, J. (1979). Some child-rearing antecedents of criminal behavior in adult men. *Journal of Personality and Social Psychology, 9,* 1477–1486.

McCord, J. (1991a). The cycle of crime and socialization practices. *Journal of Criminal Law and Criminology, 82,* 211–228.

McCord, J. (1991b). Family relationships, juvenile delinquency, and adult criminality. *Criminology, 29,* 397–417.

McCord, J. (1991c). Questioning the value of punishment. *Social Problems, 38,* 167–179.

McFall, R. M. (1982). A review and reformulation of the concept of social skills. *Behavioral Assessment, 4,* 1–33.

McGee, R., & Share, D. L. (1988). Attention-deficit-disorder hyperactivity and academic failure: Which comes first and what should be treated? *Journal of the American Academy of Child and Adolescent Psychiatry, 27,* 318–325.

McGee, R., Silva, P. A., & Williams, S. (1984). Perinatal, neurological, environmental, and developmental characteristics of seven-year old children with stable behavior problems. *Journal of Child Psychology and Psychiatry, 25,* 573–586.

McLoyd, V. (1990). The impact of economic hardship on black families and children: Psychological distress, parenting, and socioemotional development. *Child Development, 61,* 311–346.

Mead, M. (1935). *Sex and temperament in three savage tribes.* New York: Morrow.

Mednick, S. A., Gabrielli, W. H., & Hutchings, B. (1984). Genetic influences in criminal convictions: Evidence from an adoption cohort. *Science, 224,* 891–894.

Melcher, B. (1986). *Moral reasoning, self-identity, and moral action: A study of conduct disorder in adolescence.* Doctoral dissertation, University of Pittsburgh.

Meltzoff, A. N., & Moore, M. K. (1977). Imitation of facial and manual gestures by human neonates. *Science, 198,* 75–78.

Menard, S., & Elliott, D. S. (1994). Delinquent bonding, moral beliefs, and illegal behavior: A three-wave panel model. *Justice Quarterly, 11,* 173–188.

Milgram, S. (1974). *Obedience to authority: An experimental view.* New York: Harper & Row.

Milich, R., & Dodge, K. A. (1984). Social information-processing patterns in child psychiatric populations. *Journal of Abnormal Child Psychology, 12,* 171–189.

Milich, R., & Landau, S. (1984). The role of social status variables in differentiating subgroups of hyperactive children. In L. M. Bloomingdale & J. M. Swanson (Eds.), *Attention deficit disorder* (Vol. 4, pp. 1–16). Oxford, England: Pergamon Press.

Miller, W. B. (1974). American youth gangs: Past and present. In A. Blumberg (Ed.), *Current perspectives on criminal behavior* (pp. 210–239). New York: Knopf.

Mischel, W. (1974). Processes in delay of gratification. In L. Berkowitz (Ed.), *Advances in experimental social psychology* (Vol. 7, pp. 249–292). New York: Academic Press.

Moffitt, T. E. (1990). Juvenile delinquency and attention deficit disorders: Boys' developmental trajectories from age 3 to age 15. *Child Development, 61,* 893–910.

Moffitt, T. E. (1993a). Adolescence-limited and life-course-persistent antisocial behavior: A development taxonomy. *Psychological Review, 100,* 674–701.

Moffitt, T. E. (1993b). The neuropsychology of conduct disorder. *Development and Psychopathology, 5,* 135–151.

Moffitt, T. E., Gabrielli, W. F., Mednick, S. A., & Schulsinger, F. (1981). Socioeconomic status, IQ, and delinquency. *Journal of Abnormal Psychology, 90,* 152–156.

Moffitt, T. E., & Lynam, D. R. (1994). The neuropsychology of conduct disorder and delinquency: Implications for understanding antisocial behavior. In D. C. Fowles, P. Sutker, & S. H. Goodman (Eds.), *Progress in experimental personality and psychopathology research* (pp. 233–262). New York: Springer-Verlag.

Moffitt, T. E., & Lynam, D. R. (in press). Neuropsychological tests predict persistent male delinquency. *Criminology.*

Moffitt, T. E., & Silva, P. A. (1988). IQ and delinquency: A direct test of the differential detection hypothesis. *Journal of Abnormal Psychology, 97,* 330–333.

Morash, M., & Rucker, L. (1989). An exploratory study of the connection of mother's age at child-bearing to her children's delinquency in four data sets. *Crime and Delinquency, 35,* 45–93.

Moskowitz, D. S., Schwartzman, A. E., & Ledingham, J. E. (1985). Stability and change in aggression and withdrawal in middle childhood and early adolescence. *Journal of Abnormal Psychology, 94,* 30–41.

Moyer, K. E. (1976). *The psychobiology of aggression.* New York: Harper & Row.

Nasby, W., Hayden, B., & DePaulo, B. M. (1979). Attributional bias among aggressive boys to interpret unambiguous social stimuli as displays of hostility. *Journal of Abnormal Psychology, 89,* 459–468.

Needleman, H. L., Gunnoe, C., Leviton, A., Reed, R., Peresie, H., Maher, C., & Barret, P. (1979). Deficits in psychologic and classroom performance of children with elevated dentine lead levels. *New England Journal of Medicine, 322,* 83–88.

Newell, A., & Simon, H. A. (1972). *Human problem solving.* Englewood Cliffs, NJ: Prentice Hall.

Newman, J. P., Patterson, C. M., & Kosson, D. S. (1987). Response perseveration in psychopaths. *Journal of Abnormal Psychology, 96,* 145–148.

Newman, J. P., & Wallace, J. F. (1992). Three pathways to impulsive behavior: Implications for violence and aggression. In *Proceedings: Fourth symposium on violence and aggression.* Saskatchewan: University of Saskatchewan and Regional Psychiatric Centre.

O'Connell, C. M., & Fried, P. A. (1991). Prenatal exposure to cannabis: A preliminary report of postnatal consequences in school-age children. *Neurotoxicology and Teratology, 13,* 631–639.

Offord, D. R., Boyle, M. H., & Racine, Y. A. (1989). Ontario Child Health Study: Correlates of conduct disorder. *Journal of the American Academy of Child and Adolescent Psychiatry, 28,* 856–860.

Offord, D. R., Boyle, M. H., & Racine, Y. A. (1991). The epidemiology of antisocial behavior in childhood and adolescence. In D. J. Pepler & K. H. Rubin (Eds.), *The development and treatment of childhood aggression* (pp. 31–54). Hillsdale, NJ: Erlbaum.

Ogbu, J. U. (1990). Overcoming racial barriers to equal access. In I. Goodlad & P. Keating (Eds.), *Access to knowledge: An agenda for our nation's schools* (pp. 59–89). New York: College Entrance Examination Board.

Ogbu, J. U. (1993). Differences in cultural frame of reference. *International Journal of Behavioral Development, 16,* 483–506.

Ollendick, T. H., Weist, M. D., Borden, M. C., & Greene, R. W. (1992). Sociometric status and academic, behavioral, and psychological adjustment: A five-year longitudinal study. *Journal of Consulting and Clinical Psychology, 60,* 80–87.

Olofsson, M., Buckley, W., Andersen, G. E., & Friis-Hansen, B. (1983). Investigation of 89 children born by drug-dependent mothers. *Acta Psychiatrica Scandinavica, 72,* 407–410.

Olweus, D. (1977). Aggression and peer acceptance in adolescent boys: Two short-term longitudinal studies of ratings. *Child Development, 48,* 1301–1313.

Olweus, D. (1979). Stability and aggressive reaction patterns in males: A review. *Psychological Bulletin, 86,* 852–875.

Olweus, D. (1981). Continuity in aggressive and inhibited, withdrawn behavior patterns. *Psychiatry and Social Sciences, 1,* 141–159.

Olweus, D., Mattison, A., Schalling, D., & Low, H. (1988). Circulating testosterone levels and aggression in adolescent males: A causal analysis. *Psychosomatic Medicine, 50,* 261–272.

Omark, R. R., Omark, M., & Edelman, M. (1975). Formation of dominance hierarchies in young children. In T. R. Williams (Ed.), *Psychological anthropology* (pp. 289–315). The Hague: Mouton.

Osofsky, J. D. (1995). The effects of exposure to violence on young children. *American Psychologist, 50,* 782–788.

Parke, R. D., & Deur, J. L. (1972). Schedule of punishment and inhibition of aggression in children. *Developmental Psychology, 7,* 266–269.

Parke, R. D., & Slaby, R. G. (1983). The development of aggression. In P. Mussen (Series Ed.) & E. M. Hetherington (Ed.), *Handbook of child psychology: Vol. 4. Socialization, personality, and social development* (pp. 547–641). New York: Wiley.

Parker, J. G., & Asher, S. R. (1987). Peer relations and later personal adjustment: Are low-accepted children at risk? *Psychological Bulletin, 102,* 357–389.

Patterson, C. J., Kupersmidt, J. B., & Vaden, N. A. (1990). Income level, gender, ethnicity, and household compositions as predictors of children's school-based competence. *Child Development, 61,* 485–494.

Patterson, G. R. (1993). Orderly change in a stable world: The antisocial trait as a Chimera. *Journal of Consulting and Clinical Psychology, 61,* 911–919.

Patterson, G. R. (1995). Coercion—A basis for early age of onset for arrest. In J. McCord (Ed.), *Coercion and punishment in long-term perspective* (pp. 81–105). New York: Cambridge University Press.

Patterson, G. R., & Bank, C. L. (1989). Some amplifying mechanisms for pathologic processes in families. In M. Gunnar &

E. Thelen (Eds.), *Systems and development: Symposia on child psychology* (pp. 167–210). Hillsdale, NJ: Erlbaum.

Patterson, G. R., Capaldi, D. M., & Bank, L. (1991). An early starter model for predicting delinquency. In D. J. Pepler & K. H. Rubin (Eds.), *The development and treatment of childhood aggression* (pp. 139–168). Hillsdale, NJ: Erlbaum.

Patterson, G. R., Chamberlain, P., & Reid, J. R. (1982). A comparative evaluation of parent training procedures. *Behavior Therapy, 3,* 638–650.

Patterson, G. R., Crosby, L., & Vuchinich, S. (1992). Predicting risk for early police arrest. *Journal of Quantitative Criminology, 8,* 335–355.

Patterson, G. R., Littman R. A., & Bricker, W. (1967). Assertive behavior in children: A step toward a theory of aggression. *Monographs of the Society for Research in Child Development, 32*(5, Serial No. 113).

Patterson, G. R., Reid, J. B., & Dishion, T. J. (1992). *A social learning approach: Vol. 4. Antisocial boys.* Eugene, OR: Castalia Press.

Patterson, G. R., & Yoerger, K. (1993). Developmental models for delinquent behavior. In S. Hodgins (Ed.), *Mental disorder and crime* (pp. 140–172). Newbury Park, CA: Sage.

Pennington, B. F., & Bennetto, L. (1993). Main effects of transactions in the neuropsychology of conduct disorder. Commentary on "The neuropsychology of conduct disorder." *Development and Psychopathology, 5,* 153–164.

Pepler, D. J., & Craig, W. M. (1995). A peer behind the fence: Naturalistic observations of aggressive children with remote audio-visual recording. *Developmental Psychology, 31,* 548–553.

Perry, D. G., & Bussey, K. (1977). Self-reinforcement in high- and low-aggressive boys following acts of aggression. *Child Development, 48,* 653–657.

Perry, D. G., Kusel, S. J., & Perry, L. C. (1988). Victims of peer aggression. *Developmental Psychology, 24,* 807–814.

Perry, D. G., Perry, L. C., & Kennedy, E. (1992). Conflict and the development of antisocial behavior. In C. U. Shantz & W. W. Hartup (Eds.), *Conflict in child and adolescent development* (pp. 301–329). New York: Cambridge University Press.

Perry, D. G., Perry, L. C., & Rasmussen, P. (1986). Cognitive social learning mediators of aggression. *Child Development, 57,* 700–711.

Piaget, J. (1965). *The moral judgment of the child.* London: Routledge & Kegan Paul.

Pliszka, S. R., Rogeness, G. A., Renner, P., Sherman, J., & Broussard, T. (1988). Plasma neurochemistry in juvenile offenders. *Journal of the American Academy of Child and Adolescent Psychiatry, 27,* 588–594.

Plomin, R. (1983). Childhood temperament. In B. B. Lahey & A. E. Kazdin (Eds.), *Advances in clinical child psychology* (Vol. 6, pp. 45–92). New York: Plenum Press.

Price, J. M., & Dodge, K. A. (1989). Reactive and proactive aggression in childhood: Relations to peer status and social context dimensions. *Journal of Abnormal Child Psychology, 17*, 455–471.

Puig-Antich, J. (1982). Major depression and conduct disorder in prepuberty. *Journal of the American Academy of Child Psychiatry, 30*, 431–438.

Pulkkinen, L. (1981). Long-term studies on the characteristics of aggressive and non-aggressive juveniles. In P. F. Brain & D. Benton (Eds.), *Multidisciplinary approaches to aggression research* (pp. 225–243). Amsterdam: Elsevier/North-Holland Biomedical Press.

Pulkkinen, L. (1982). Self-control and continuity from childhood to late adolescence. In P. B. Baltes & O. G. Brim (Eds.), *Life-span development and behavior* (pp. 63–85). New York: Academic Press.

Pulkkinen, L. (1986). The role of impulse control in the development of antisocial and prosocial behavior. In D. Olweus, J. Block, & M. Radke-Yarrow (Eds.), *Development of antisocial and prosocial behavior: Research, theories, and issues* (pp. 149–175). New York: Academic Press.

Pulkkinen, L. (1988). Delinquent development: Theoretical and empirical considerations. In M. Rutter (Ed.), *Studies of psychosocial risk* (pp. 184–199). Cambridge, England: Cambridge University Press.

Pulkkinen, L. (1990). Adult life-styles and their precursors in the social behavior of children and adolescents. *European Journal of Personality, 4*, 237–251.

Quay, H. C. (1979). Classification. In H. C. Quay & J. S. Werry (Eds.), *Psychopathological disorders of childhood* (2nd ed., pp. 1–42). New York: Wiley.

Quay, H. C. (1993). The psychobiology of undersocialized aggressive conduct disorder: A theoretical perspective. *Development and Psychopathology, 5*, 165–180.

Quiggle, N., Panak, W. F., Garber, J., & Dodge, K. A. (1992). Social information processing in aggressive and depressed children. *Child Development, 63*, 1305–1320.

Rabiner, D. L., & Coie, J. D. (1989). The effect of expectancy inductions on rejected children's acceptance by unfamiliar peers. *Developmental Psychology, 25*, 450–457.

Rabiner, D. L., Lenhart, L., & Lochman, J. E. (1990). Automatic versus reflective social problem solving in relation to children's sociometric status. *Developmental Psychology, 26*, 1010–1016.

Radke-Yarrow, M., & Kochanska, G. (1990). Anger in young children. In N. L. Stein, B. Leventhal, & T. Trabasso (Eds.), *Psychological and biological approaches to emotion* (pp. 297–310). Hillsdale, NJ: Erlbaum.

Raine, A. (1993). *The psychopathology of crime: Criminal behavior as a clinical disorder.* San Diego: Academic Press.

Raine, A., Brennan, P., & Mednick, S. A. (in press). Birth complications combined with early maternal rejection at age one year predispose to violent crime at age 18 years. *Archives of General Psychiatry.*

Raine, A., & Scerbo, A. (1991). Biological theories of violence. In. J. S. Milner (Ed.), *Neuropsychology of aggression* (pp. 1–25). Boston: Kluwer Academic Press.

Raine, A., Venables, P. H., & Williams, M. (1990). Relationships between CNS and ANS measures of arousal at age 15 and criminality at age 24. *Archives of General Psychiatry, 47*, 1003–1007.

Reid, J. B. (1993). Prevention of conduct disorder before and after school entry: Relating interventions to developmental findings. *Development and Psychopathology, 5*, 243–262.

Reis, D. J. (1974). Central neurotransmitters in aggression. In S. H. Frazier (Ed.), *Aggression* (Vol. 52, pp. 119–148). Baltimore: Williams & Wilkins.

Renken, B., Egeland, B., Marvinney, D., Mangelsdorf, S., & Sroufe, L. A. (1989). Early childhood antecedents of aggression and passive-withdrawal in early elementary school. *Journal of Personality, 57*, 257–281.

Renshaw, P. D., & Asher, S. R. (1983). Children's goals and strategies for social interaction. *Merrill-Palmer Quarterly, 29*, 353–374.

Richman, N., Stevenson, J., & Graham, P. J. (1982). *Preschool to school: A behavioural study.* London: Academic Press.

Riese, M. L. (1990). Neonatal temperament in monozygotic and dizygotic twin pairs. *Child Development, 61*, 1230–1237.

Robins, L. N. (1966). *Deviant children grown up.* Baltimore: Williams & Wilkins.

Robins, L. N. (1978). Sturdy childhood predictors of adult antisocial behavior: Replications from longitudinal studies. *Psychological Medicine, 8*, 611–622.

Roff, J. D., & Wirt, R. D. (1984). Childhood aggression and social adjustment as antecedents of delinquency. *Journals of Abnormal Child Psychology, 12*, 111–126.

Rogeness, G. A., Hernandez, J. M., Macedo, C. A., & Mitchell, E. L. (1982). Biochemical differences in children with conduct disorder socialized and undersocialized. *American Journal of Psychiatry, 139*, 307–311.

Rogeness, G. A., Javors, M. A., Maas, J. W., Macedo, C. A., & Fischer, C. (1987). Plasma dopamine-beta-hydroxylase, HVA, MHPG, and conduct disorder in emotionally disturbed boys. *Biological Psychiatry, 22*, 1158–1162.

Rogeness, G. A., Javors, M. A., & Pliszka, S. R. (1992). Neurochemistry and child and adolescent psychiatry. *Journal of the American Academy of Child and Adolescent Psychiatry, 31,* 765–781.

Rogeness, G. A., Maas, J. W., Javors, M. A., Macedo, C. A., Harris, W. R., & Hoppe, S. K. (1988). Diagnoses, catecholamine metabolism, and plasma dopamine-beta-hydroxylase. *Journal of the American Academy of Child and Adolescent Psychiatry, 27,* 121–125.

Rosenthal, R. (1986). Media violence, antisocial behavior, and the social consequences of small effects. *Journal of Social Issues, 42,* 141–154.

Rowe, D. C. (1985). Sibling interaction and self-reported delinquent behavior: A study of 265 twin pairs. *Criminology, 23,* 223–240.

Rowe, D. C., Vazsonyi, A. T., & Flannery, D. J. (1994). No more than skin deep: Ethnic and racial similarity in developmental process. *Psychological Review, 101,* 396–413.

Rubin, J. Z., Provenzano, F. J., & Luria, Z. (1974). The eye of the beholder: Parents' view on sex of newborns. *American Journal of Orthopsychiatry, 43,* 720–731.

Rubin, K. H. (1972). Relationship between egocentric communication and popularity among peers. *Developmental Psychology, 7,* 364.

Rubin, K. H., Bream, L. A., & Rose-Krasnor, L. (1991). Social problem solving and aggression in childhood. In D. J. Pepler & K. H. Rubin (Eds.), *The development and treatment of childhood aggression* (pp. 219–248). Hillsdale, NJ: Erlbaum.

Rubin, K. H., & Krasnor, L. R. (1986). Social cognitive and social behavioral perspectives on problem solving. In M. Perlmutter (Ed.), *The Minnesota Symposium on Child Psychology* (Vol. 18, pp. 1–68). Hillsdale, NJ: Erlbaum.

Rubin, K. H., Moller, L., & Emptage, A. (1987). The preschool behavior questionnaire: A useful index of behavior problems in elementary school-age children. *Canadian Journal of Behavioral Science, 19,* 86–100.

Rule, B. G., & Ferguson, T. J. (1986). The effects of media violence on attitudes, emotions, and cognitions. *Journal of Social Issues, 42,* 29–50.

Rumelhart, D. E., & McClelland, J. L. (1986). *Parallel distributed processing: Exploration in the microstructure of cognition: Vol. 1. Foundations.* Cambridge, MA: MIT Press.

Rutter, M. (1989). Pathways from childhood to adult life. *Journal of Child Psychology and Psychiatry, 30,* 25–31.

Rutter, M., Boltin, P., Harrington, R., Le Couteur, A., Macdonald, H., & Simonoff, E. (1990). Genetic factors in child psychiatric disorders: I. A review of research strategies. *Journal of Child Psychology and Psychiatry, 31,* 5–37.

Rutter, M., & Garmezy, N. (1983). Developmental psychopathology. In P. H. Mussen (Series Ed.) & E. M. Hetherington (Ed.), *Handbook of child psychology: Vol. 4. Socialization, personality and social development* (pp. 775–911). New York: Wiley.

Rutter, M., & Giller, H. (1983). *Juvenile delinquency: Trends and perspectives.* Harmondsworth, England: Penguin Books.

Rutter, M., Quinton, D., & Hill, J. (1990). Adult outcomes of institution-reared children: Males and females compared. In L. Robins & M. Rutter (Eds.), *Straight and devious pathways from childhood to adulthood* (pp. 135–157). Cambridge, England: Cambridge University Press.

Rutter, M., Tizard, J., & Whitmore, K. (Eds.). (1970). *Education, health, and behaviour.* London: Longmans.

Sadowski, L. S., Cairns, R. B., & Earp, J. A. (1989). Firearm ownership among non-urban adolescents. *American Journal of Diseases of Children, 143,* 1410–1413.

Salvador, A., Simon, V., Suay, F., & Llorens, L. (1987). Testosterone and cortisol responses to competitive fighting in human males: A pilot study. *Aggressive Behavior, 13,* 9–13.

Sampson, R. J., & Laub, J. H. (1990). Crime and deviance over the life course: The saliences of adult social bonds. *American Sociological Review, 55,* 609–627.

Sampson, R. J., & Laub, J. H. (1992). Crime and deviance in the life course. *Annual Review of Sociology, 18,* 63–84.

Sampson, R. J., & Laub, J. H. (1993). *Crime in the making: Pathways and turning points through life.* Cambridge, MA: Harvard University Press.

Sampson, R. J., & Laub, J. H. (1994). Urban poverty and the family context of delinquency: A new look at structure and process in a classic study. *Child Development, 65,* 523–540.

Sancilio, F. M., Plumert, J. M., & Hartup, W. W. (1989). Friendship and aggressiveness as determinants of conflict outcomes in middle childhood. *Developmental Psychology, 25,* 812–819.

Satterfield, J. H., Hoppe, C. M., & Schell, A. M. (1982). A prospective study of delinquency in 110 adolescent boys with attention deficit disorder and 88 normal adolescent boys. *American Journal of Psychiatry, 139,* 795–798.

Savin-Williams, R. C. (1979). Dominance hierarchies in groups of early adolescents. *Child Development, 50,* 142–151.

Sawin, D. B., & Parke, R. D. (1979). The effects of interagent inconsistent discipline on children's aggressive behavior. *Journal of Experimental Child Psychology, 28,* 525–538.

Scarr, S., & Ricciuti, A. (1991). What effects do parents have on their children? In L. Okagaki & J. Sternberg (Eds.), *Directors of development: Influences on the development of children's thinking* (pp. 3–23). Hillsdale, NJ: Erlbaum.

Schaal, B., Tremblay, R. E., Soussignan, R., & Susman, E. J. (1995). *Male testosterone linked to high social dominance but low physical aggression in early adolescence.* Unpublished manuscript, University of Montreal.

Schneider, D. J. (1991). Social cognition. *Annual Review of Psychology, 42,* 527–561.

Schneider, W., & Shiffrin, R. (1977). Controlled and automatic human information processing: Detection, search, and attention. *Psychological Review, 84,* 1–66.

Schonfeld, I. S., Shaffer, D., O'Connor, P., & Portnoy, S. (1988). Conduct disorder and cognitive functioning: Testing three causal hypotheses. *Child Development, 59,* 993–1007.

Schwartz, D., Dodge, K. A., & Coie, J. D. (1993). The emergence of chronic peer victimization in boys' play groups. *Child Development, 64,* 1755–1772.

Selman, R. (1980). *The growth of interpersonal understanding.* New York: Academic Press.

Shank, R. C., & Abelson, R. (1977). *Scripts, plans, goals, and understanding.* Hillsdale, NJ: Erlbaum.

Shantz, C. U. (1983). Social cognition. In J. H. Flavell & E. M. Markman (Eds.), *Handbook of child psychology* (4th ed.) (Vol. 3, pp. 495–555) New York: Wiley.

Shantz, C. U., & Shantz, D. W. (1985). Conflict between children: Social-cognitive and sociometric correlates. *New Directions for Child Development, 20,* 3–21.

Shantz, D. W., & Voydanoff, D. A. (1973). Situational effects on retaliatory aggression at three age levels. *Child Development, 44,* 149–153.

Shaw, C., & McKay, H. (1942). *Juvenile delinquency and urban areas.* Chicago: University of Chicago Press.

Shaw, D. S., & Emory, R. E. (1988). Chronic family adversity and school-age children's adjustment. *Journal of the American Academy of Child and Adolescent Psychiatry, 27,* 200–226.

Shaw, D. S., Keenan, K., Owens, E. B., Winslow, E. B., Hood, N., & Garcia, M. (1995, April). *Developmental precursors of externalizing behavior among two samples of low-income families: Ages 1 to 5.* Paper presented at the biennial meeting of the Society for Research in Child Development, Indianapolis.

Sherman, L. (1992). *Policing domestic violence.* New York: Free Press.

Sherman, L. (1993). Defiance, deterrence, and irrelevance: A theory of the criminal sanction. *Journal of Research in Crime and Delinquency, 30,* 445–473.

Sherman, M. (1927). The differentiation of emotional responses in infants: II. The ability of observers to judge the emotional characteristics of the crying of infants and of the voice of the adult. *Journal of Comparative Psychology, 7,* 265–284.

Shure, M. B., & Spivack, G. (1980). Interpersonal problem-solving as a mediator of behavioral adjustment in preschool and kindergarten children. *Journal of Applied Developmental Psychology, 1,* 29–44.

Sigvardsson, S., Cloninger, R., Bohman, M., & von Knoring, A. L. (1982). Predisposition to petty criminality in Swedish adoptees: III. Sex differences and validation of the male typology. *Archives of General Psychiatry, 39,* 1248–1253.

Silva, P. A., Hughes, P., Williams, S., & Faed, J. M. (1988). Blood lead, intelligence, reading attainment, and behavior in 11-year-old children in Dunedin, New Zealand. *Journal of Child Psychology and Psychiatry, 29,* 43–52.

Simons, R. L., Wu, C. I., Conger, R. D., & Lorenz, F. O. (1994). Two routes to delinquency: Differences between early and late starters in the impact of parenting and deviant peers. *Criminology, 32,* 247–276.

Singer, J. L., & Singer, D. G. (1981). *Television, imagination, and aggression: A study of preschoolers' play.* Hillsdale, NJ: Erlbaum.

Skogan, W. G. (1989). Social change and the future of violent crime. In T. R. Gurr (Ed.), *Violence in America: Vol. 1. The history of crime.* Newbury Park, CA: Sage.

Slaby, R. G., & Guerra, N. G. (1988). Cognitive mediators of aggression in adolescent offenders: 1. Assessment. *Developmental Psychology, 24,* 580–588.

Smith, P. K., & Green, M. (1974). Aggressive behavior in English nurseries and playgrounds: Sex differences and response of adults. *Child Development, 45,* 211–214.

Snyder, H., Finnegan, T., Nimick, E., Sickmund, D., Sullivan, D., & Tierney, N. (1987). *Juvenile Court Statistics, 1984.* Pittsburgh: National Center for Juvenile Justice.

Snyder, J., Dishion, T. J., & Patterson, G. R. (1986). Determinants and consequences of associating with deviant peers during preadolescence and adolescence. *Journal of Early Adolescence, 6,* 29–43.

Snyder, J. J., & Patterson, G. R. (1995). Individual differences in social aggression: A test of a reinforcement model of socialization in the natural environment. *Behavior Therapy, 26,* 371–391.

Spencer, M. B., Dobbs, B., & Phillips, D. (1988). African-American adolescents: Adaptational processes and socioeconomic diversity in behavioral outcomes. *Journal of Adolescence, 11,* 117–137.

Spergel, I. A., Ross, R. E., Curry, G. D., & Chance, R. (1989). *Youth gangs: Problem and response.* Washington, DC: Office of Juvenile Justice and Delinquency Prevention.

Spoont, M. R. (1992). Modulating role of serotonin in neural information-processing: Implications for human psychopathology. *Psychological Bulletin, 112,* 330–350.

Sroufe, L. A. (1983). Infant caregiver attachment and patterns of adaptation in preschool: The roots of maladaptation and competence. In M. Perlmutter (Ed.), *Minnesota Symposium on Child Psychology* (Vol. 16, pp. 41–81). Hillsdale, NJ: Erlbaum.

Sroufe, L. A. (1985). Attachment classification from the perspective of infant-caregiver relationships and infant temperament. *Child Development, 56,* 1–14.

Sroufe, L. A., & Rutter, M. (1984). The domain of developmental psychopathology. *Child Development, 54,* 17–29.

Stattin, H., & Magnusson, D. (1989). The role of early aggressive behavior in the frequency, seriousness, and types of later crime. *Journal of Consulting and Clinical Psychology, 57,* 710–718.

Steinberg, M. D., & Dodge, K. A. (1983). Attributional bias in aggressive boys and girls. *Journal of Social and Clinical Psychology, 1,* 312–321.

Stenberg, C., & Campos, J. (1990). The development of anger expressions in infancy. In N. Stein, T. Trabasso, & B. Leventhal (Eds.), *Concepts in emotion.* Hillsdale, NJ: Erlbaum.

Stenberg, C., Campos, J., & Emde, R. (1983). The facial expression of anger in 7-month-old infants. *Child Development, 54,* 178–184.

Sternberg, K. J., Lamb, M. E., Greenbaum, C., Cicchetti, D., Dawus, S., Cortes, R. M., Krispin, O., & Lorey, F. (1993). Effects of domestic violence on children's behavior problems and depression. *Developmental Psychology, 29,* 44–52.

Stoff, D. M., Pollock, L., Vitiello, B., Behar, D., & Bridger, W. H. (1987). Reduction of (3H)—imipramine binding sites on platelets of conduct-disordered children. *Neuropsychopharmacology, 1,* 55–62.

Stouthamer-Loeber, M., & Loeber, R. (1989). The use of prediction data in understanding delinquency. In L. A. Bond & B. E. Compas (Eds.), *Primary prevention and promotion in the schools* (pp. 179–202). Newbury Park, CA: Sage.

Strauman, T. J., & Higgins, E. T. (1987). Automatic activation of self-discrepancies and emotional syndromes: When cognitive structures influence affect. *Journal of Personality and Social Psychology, 53,* 1004–1014.

Straus, M. A., & Gelles, R. J. (1990). How violent are American families? In M. A. Straus & R. J. Gelles (Eds.), *Physical violence in American families* (pp. 95–112). New Brunswick, NJ: Transaction.

Strayer, F. F. (1989). Co-adaptation within the early peer group: A psychobiological study of social competence. In B. H. Schneider, G. Attili, J. Nadd, & R. P. Weissberg (Eds.), *Social competence in developmental perspective* (pp. 145–174). Norwell, MA: Kluwer Academic Press.

Strayer, F. F., & Trudel, M. (1984). Developmental changes in the nature and function of social dominance among young children. *Ethology and Sociobiology, 5,* 279–295.

Stromquist, V. J., & Strauman, T. J. (1992). Children's social constructs: II. Nature, assessment, and association with adaptive and maladaptive behavior. *Social Cognition, 9,* 330–358.

Susman, E. J., Inoff-Germain, G., Nottelmann, E. D., Loriaux, L., Cutler, G. B., & Chrousos, G. P. (1987). Hormones, emotional dispositions, and aggressive attributes in young adolescents. *Child Development, 58,* 1114–1134.

Taylor, A. R., & Asher, S. R. (1989). *Children's goals in game playing situations.* Unpublished manuscript.

Taylor, A. R., & Gabriel, S. W. (1989, April). *Cooperative versus competitive game-playing strategies of peer accepted and peer rejected children in a goal conflict situation.* Paper presented at the biennial meeting of the Society for Research in Child Development, Kansas City, MO.

Tedeschi, J. T., & Felson, R. B. (1994). *Violence, aggression, and coercive actions.* Washington, DC: American Psychological Association.

Tesman, J. R., & Hills, A. (1994). Developmental effects of lead exposure in children. *Social Policy Report, 8*(3), 1–19.

Thomas, A., Chess, S., & Birch, H. (1968). *Temperament and behavior disorders in children.* New York: New York University Press.

Thomson, G. O. B., Raab, G. M., Hepburn, W. S., Hunter, R., Fulton, M., & Laxen, D. P. H. (1989). Blood lead levels and children's behavior: Results from the Edinburgh lead study. *Journal of Child Psychology and Psychiatry, 30,* 515–528.

Thornberry, T. P. (1987). Toward an interactional theory of delinquency. *Criminology, 25,* 863–891.

Thornberry, T. P., Krohn, M. D., Lizotte, A. J., & Chard-Wierschem, D. (1993). The role of juvenile gangs in facilitating delinquent behavior. *Journal of Research in Crime and Delinquency, 30,* 55–87.

Thornberry, T. P., Lizotte, A. J., Krohn, M. D., Farnworth, M., & Jang, S. J. (1991). Testing interactional theory: An examination of reciprocal causal relationships among family, school, and delinquency. *Journal of Criminal Law and Criminology, 82,* 3–35.

Thornberry, T. P., Lizotte, A. J., Krohn, M. D., Farnworth, M., & Jang, S. J. (1994). Delinquent peers beliefs and delinquent behavior: A longitudinal test of interaction theory. *Criminology, 32,* 47–83.

Thornberry, T. P., Wolfgang, M., & Figlio, R. (1987). *From boy to man.* Chicago: University of Chicago Press.

Tomkins, S. (1963). *Affect, imagery, consciousness: Vol. 2. The negative affects.* New York: Plenum Press.

Tremblay, R. E., Mâsse, L. C., Vitaro, F., & Dobkin, P. L. (1995). The impact of friend's deviant behavior on early onset of delinquency: Longitudinal data from 6- to 13-years-of-age. *Development and Psychopathology, 7,* 649–667.

Trickett, P. K., & Kuczynski, L. (1986). Children's misbehaviors and parental discipline in abusive and non-abusive families. *Developmental Psychology, 22,* 115–123.

Trivers, R. L. (1974). Parental-offspring conflict. *American Zoologist, 46,* 35–57.

Tulving, E., & Thomson, D. M. (1973). Encoding specificity and retrieval processes in episodic memory. *Psychological Review, 80,* 352–373.

Uniform Crime Reports (UCR). (1992). *Crime in the United States: 1991*. Washington, DC: U.S. Government Printing Office.

Van Den Oord, E. J. C. G., Boomsma, D. I., & Verhulst, F. C. (1992). *Genetic and environmental influences on problem behaviors in international adoptees: Evidence for sibling cooperation*. Unpublished manuscript.

Van Den Oord, E. J. C. G., Verhulst, F. C., & Boomsma, D. I. (1992). *A genetic study of maternal and paternal ratings of problem behaviors in three-year-old twins*. Unpublished manuscript.

Venables, P. H. (1988). Psychophysiology and crime: Theory and data. In T. E. Moffitt & S. A. Mednick (Eds.), *Biological contributions to crime causation* (pp. 3–13). Dordrecht, The Netherlands: Martinus Nijhoff.

Viemero, V. (1992). Antecedents of the development of adolescent antisocial and criminal behavior. In A. Fraczek & H. Zumkley (Eds.), *Socialization and aggression* (pp. 171–185). Berlin: Springer-Verlag.

Vitaro, F., Tremblay, R. E., Kerr, M., Pagani, L., & Bukowski, W. M. (in press). Disruptiveness, friends' characteristics, and delinquency in early adolescence: A test of two competing models of development. *Child Development*.

Vitiello, B., Stoff, D., Atkins, M., & Mahoney, A. (1990). Neurological signs and impulsivity in children. *Developmental and Behavioral Pediatrics, 11*, 112–115.

Volkow, N. D., & Tancredi, L. (1987). Neural substrates of violent behavior: A preliminary study with position emission topography. *British Journal of Psychiatry, 151*, 668–673.

Waas, G. A. (1988). Social attributional biases of peer-rejected and aggressive children. *Child Development, 59*, 969–992.

Wadsworth, M. E. J. (1976). Delinquency, pulse rate and early emotional deprivation. *British Journal of Criminology, 16*, 245–256.

Waldman, I. D. (1988). *Relationships between noon-social information processing, social perception, and social status in 7- to 12-year-old boys*. Unpublished doctoral dissertation, University of Waterloo, Waterloo, Ontario, Canada.

Waldman, I. D. (in press). Aggressive boys' hostile perceptual and response biases: The role of attention in impulsivity. *Child Development*.

Walters, R. H. (1964). On the high-magnitude theory of aggression. *Child Development, 35*, 303–304.

Walters, R. H., & Parke, R. D. (1964). Social motivation, dependency, and susceptibility to social influence. In L. Berkowitz (Ed.), *Advances in experimental social psychology* (Vol. 1, pp. 231–276). New York: Academic Press.

Wann, D. L., & Branscombe, N. R. (1990). Person perception when aggressive or nonaggressive sport are primed. *Aggressive Behavior, 16*, 27–32.

Watson, J. B., & Morgan, C. (1917). Emotional reactions and psychological experimentation. *American Journal of Psychology, 28*, 163–174.

Weiner, N. A. (1989). Violent criminal careers and "violent career criminals": An overview of the research literature. In N. A. Weiner & M. E. Wolfgang (Eds.), *Violent crime, violent criminals* (pp. 35–138). Newbury Park, CA: Sage.

Weiss, B., Dodge, K. A., Bates, S. E., & Pettit, G. S. (1992). Some consequences of early harsh discipline: Child aggression and a maladaptive social information processing style. *Child Development, 63*, 1321–1335.

Weiss, G., & Hechtman, L. T. (1986). *Hyperactive children grown up*. New York: Guilford Press.

Wenar, C. (1972). Executive competence and spontaneous social behavior in 1-year-olds. *Child Development, 43*, 256–260.

Werner, H. (1961). *Comparative psychology of mental development*. New York: Science Editions. (Original work published 1948)

Werthamer-Larsson, L., Kellam, S., & Wheeler, L. (1991). Effect of first-grade classroom environment on shy behavior, aggressive behavior, and concentration problems. *American Journal of Community Psychology, 19*, 585–602.

West, D. J. (1982). *Delinquency: It's roots, careers, and prospects*. London: Heinemann.

West, D. J., & Farrington, D. P. (1973). *Who becomes delinquent?* London: Heinemann.

White, J. L., Moffitt, T. E., Earls, F., Robins, L., & Silva, P. A. (1990). How early can we tell? Predictors of childhood conduct disorder and adolescent delinquency. *Criminology, 28*, 507–533.

Whiting, B. B., & Edwards, C. P. (1973). A cross-cultural analysis of the behavior of children aged 3–11. *Journal of Social Psychology, 91*, 171–188.

Whiting, B. B., & Whiting, J. W. M. (1975). *Children of six cultures: A psychocultural analysis*. Cambridge, MA: Harvard University Press.

Widom, C. S. (1989). Does violence beget violence? A critical examination of the literature. *Psychological Bulletin, 106*, 3–28.

Wilson, J. Q., & Herrnstein, R. (1985). *Crime and human nature*. New York: Simon & Schuster.

Wilson, W. J. (1987). *The truly disadvantaged*. Chicago: University of Chicago Press.

Wolff, P. H., Waber, D., Bauermeister, M., Cohen, C., & Ferber, R. (1982). The neuropsychological status of adolescent delinquent boys. *Journal of Child Psychology and Psychiatry, 23*, 267–279.

Wolfgang, M. E., Figlio, R. M., & Sellin, T. (1972). *Delinquency in a birth cohort*. Chicago: University of Chicago Press.

Wood, W., Wong, F. Y., & Chachere, G. (1991). Effects of media violence on viewers' aggression in unconstrained social interaction. *Psychological Bulletin, 109,* 371–383.

Wright, J. C., Giammarino, M., & Parad, H. W. (1986). Social status in small groups: Individual-group similarity and the social "misfit." *Journal of Personality and Social Psychology, 50,* 523–536.

Wyer, R. S., Jr., & Srull, T. K. (1989). *Memory and cognition in its social context.* Hillsdale, NJ: Erlbaum.

Yeudall, L. T., Fromm-Auch, D., & Davies, P. (1982). Neuropsychological impairment of persistent delinquency. *Journal of Nervous and Mental Disease, 170,* 257–265.

Zahn, T. P., & Kruesi, M. J. P. (1993). Autonomic activity in boys with disruptive behavior disorders. *Psychophysiology, 30,* 605–614.

Zahn-Waxler, C., Radke-Yarrow, M., & King, R. A. (1979). Child-rearing and children's prosocial initiations toward victims of distress. *Child Development, 50,* 319–330.

Zakriski, A. L., & Coie, J. D. (1996). A comparison of aggressive-rejected and nonaggressive-rejected boys' interpretations of self-directed and other-directed rejection. *Child Development, 67,* 1048–1070.

Zill, N., Moore, K. A., Nord, C. W., & Stief, T. (1991). *Welfare mothers as potential employees: A statistical profile based on national survey data.* Washington, DC: Child Trends.

Zoccolillo, M. (1992). Co-occurrence of conduct disorder and its adult outcomes with depressive anxiety disorders: A review. *Journal of American Academy of Child and Adolescent Psychiatry, 31,* 547–556.

CHAPTER 13

The Development of Morality

ELLIOT TURIEL

Sigmund Freud, B. F. Skinner, and Jean Piaget were concerned with morality. Each a major figure in psychology, setting forth highly influential general theories, provided an account of morality and its development. They recognized that its acquisition and role in society were central to explaining the psychology of moral functioning. Freud, Skinner, and Piaget's differing perspectives on morality, in concert with their general theoretical accounts, included features that remain, albeit in transformed ways, important to the main contemporary perspectives.

Among the three, Freud wrote most extensively about morality, incorporating it into his case histories, specific analyses of psychological conditions, explanations of

particular psychological processes (e.g., the unconscious, narcissism, identification), and his general formulations of individual development in society. Central to his view was the concept of conscience, tied to the idea of a duality, and concomitant tension, between individual and society. The root of this tension is the incompatibility of psychological and biological needs of individuals, on the one hand, and strivings for long-term survival of individuals and the species, on the other. The collectivity largely has the function of ensuring survival and protecting people from each other's aggressive tendencies. Through the influences of the collectivity, particularly as reproduced within a family, the individual's biologically based needs for instinctual gratification become transformed and displaced in the developmental process to make room for internalized standards (via parents as representatives of society) and internalized emotional mechanisms for regulating behaviors. This transformation, which is facilitated by positive emotions of love and attachment, largely stems from emotional conflicts producing psychological transformations through the acquisition of a mental agency, a superego, incorporating moral ideals and guilt as the means for the regulation of conduct.

In the Freudian view, the acquisition of morality results in a duality within the individual, including the forces of the superego and needs for instinctual gratification. The moral side of the duality entails duties to uphold societal norms. Although fulfilling duties entails deep conflicts (most often of an unconscious nature), the duties are felt as inexorable and impersonal. An appropriately internalized morality is invariable and applied inflexibly. In this regard, Freud proposed that women do not adequately internalize a superego. He said, in what has become an infamous statement about gender differences in morality:

> I cannot escape the notion (though I hesitate to give it expression) that for women the level of what is ethically normal is different from what it is in men. Their superego is never so inexorable, so impersonal, so independent of its emotional origins as we require it to be in men. (1925/1959, p. 196)

The questions of gender differences and contextual variations are important ones, and will be discussed later in this chapter in the context of contemporary analyses and debates.

It was in the latter part of his career, and in a largely nontechnical book for a popular audience, that B. F. Skinner (1971, Chapter 6) presented his position on morality. In keeping with his behavioristic formulations, Skinner proposed that morality reflects behaviors that have been reinforced (positively or negatively) with value judgments associated with cultural norms: "It is an ethical or moral judgment in the sense that ethos and mores refer to the customary practices of a group" (1971, p. 107). Actions are not intrinsically good or bad, but are acquired and performed as a consequence of contingencies of reinforcement. Certain contingencies, consistent with the mores of the group, are social in that they pertain to relationships with others and are governed by verbal reinforcers, such as good, bad, right, and wrong. Moreover, social control over behavior is particularly powerful when it is exercised by institutional forces (e.g., religious, governmental, economic,

educational). This is because the reinforcers of "good" and "bad" also take the form, for example, of legal, illegal, pious, or sinful acts, with their associated rewards and punishments (e.g., fines, imprisonment, grades, diplomas). Learned behaviors stemming from the customary practices of a group are invariant insofar as reinforcement contingencies are maintained. For Skinner, however, they do not constitute duties or obligations, nor do they reflect one's character:

> A person behaves well with respect to his fellow men . . . not because his fellow men have endowed him with a sense of responsibility or obligation or with loyalty or respect for others but because they have arranged effective social contingencies. The behaviors classified as good or bad and right or wrong are not due to goodness or badness, or good or bad character or a knowledge of right and wrong; they are due to contingencies involving a great variety of reinforcers. (Skinner, 1971, p. 108)

Knowledge and judgments about social relationships were considered central to morality by Jean Piaget, who wrote about the topic in an extensive way in the early part of his career (Piaget, 1932; see also Piaget, 1960/1995). In keeping with his general views of development as stemming from reciprocal interactions of individual and environment and entailing constructions of understandings of experiences, Piaget analyzed morality from the perspective of how experiences result in the formation of judgments about social relationships, rules, laws, authority, and social institutions.

Several notions were central to Piaget's formulation. One was that social transmission does not solely result in the reproduction of that which is transmitted, but entails reconstructions. A second is that moral development is influenced by a variety of experiences, including emotional reactions (e.g., sympathy and empathy), relationships with adults, and relationships with contemporaries (and even with those younger than oneself). A third concept is that moral judgments are fundamentally about relationships, with development progressing toward feelings of mutual respect among persons (with a developmentally prior set of feelings entailing a sense of unilateral respect from child to adult or authority), toward concerns with attaining and maintaining social relationships of cooperation (with rules and laws serving ends of cooperation rather than seen as fixed and categorical), toward the formation of concepts of justice, and toward an ability to consider the perspectives of others as possibly different from one's own (thus accounting for subjectivity and intentionality rather than viewing all perspectives as reflecting objective "reality"). As based on mutual respect, cooperation, and concepts of rules, laws, and duties as serving ends of fairness and justice, the developmentally advanced form of morality, in Piaget's view, is both inexorable and flexible. Moral concepts and goals have an obligatory quality to individuals, but are applied flexibly in accord with requirements of situations and appraisal of intentions, and varying perspectives. It is the less developmentally advanced heteronomous morality of the young child that entails conceptions of fixed rules, duties, and necessary obedience to authority. In this regard, too, Piaget proposed gender differences of a less straightforward kind than those proposed by Freud. In some respects, Piaget viewed the morality of school-age girls as less advanced than boys (specifically, "the legal sense is far less developed in little girls than in boys," 1932, p. 69); whereas in other respects he viewed girls as more advanced than boys (specifically, girls more readily subordinate rules to cooperation and mutual agreement, and are "more tolerant and more easily reconciled to innovations," 1932, p. 75).

Another aspect of Piaget's formulation especially relevant to contemporary analyses of culture and morality is the concept of autonomy. In a general sense, Piaget proposed that as morality develops, it shifts from a heteronomous to an autonomous orientation. Autonomy in this context does not mean that individuals' conceptions of morality are based on the independence of individuals. Indeed, the ideas of mutual respect and cooperation, key to Piaget's formulation, imply interdependence rather than independence. By autonomy, Piaget (1960/1995, p. 315) meant "that the subject participates in the elaboration of norms instead of receiving them ready-made as happens in the case of the norms of unilateral respect that lie behind heteronomous morality." Therefore, Piaget used autonomy in reference to a process in which norms furthering interdependence are elaborated with the participation of the child.

Many issues and questions addressed by Freud, Skinner, and Piaget persist in contemporary analyses of moral development. Their theoretical approaches influenced subsequent researchers working from about 1950 to the 1970s, who in turn have influenced contemporary researchers. The following section presents a brief historical overview connecting the ideas of Skinner and Freud to subsequent research of behavioristically oriented thinkers, who also attempted to account for psychoanalytic concepts. The overview includes a consideration of connections between the ideas of Piaget and subsequent cognitively oriented thinkers.

HISTORICAL OVERVIEW

Freud's and Piaget's formulations of morality were produced in the context of a fair amount of interest in the topic among social scientists writing in the early part of the 20th century (Baldwin, 1896; McDougall, 1908). Another influential direction was established by the French sociologist Emile Durkheim (1912/1965, 1925/1961), whose ideas contrasted with those of Piaget (see Piaget, 1932, Chapter 4, for his critique of Durkheim's position). Durkheim conceptualized morality as largely based on sentiments of attachment to the group and respect for its symbols, rules, and authority. According to Durkheim, children's immersion in the group and participation in social life produce a natural attachment to the group and a willing adherence (regarded as a form of autonomy by Durkheim) to its moral norms.

In a sociological-anthropological formulation like that of Durkheim, contextual variations in morality are located at the level of societal or cultural differences. Within societies or cultures, however, moral codes generalize across situations because the culture embodies a "moral system," dictating fixed duties from participants. More or less consistent with that perspective is the idea that morality consists of a set of learned traits of character or personality that are manifested, if acquired with the appropriate strength, in behaviors across situational contexts. The character trait approach was central to a set of ambitious studies conducted by Hartshorne and May (1928–1930), the results of which greatly influenced later formulations. Among the traits most commonly associated with the domain of morality are honesty, courage, loyalty, responsibility, and self-control. Hartshorne and May's research, which focused on honesty, service, and self-control, produced the unexpected findings of a great deal of situational variability in children's behavior. For example, they found that children did not consistently act honestly or dishonestly; an individual child did not always cheat or always avoid cheating on their assessments.

Many of the issues put forth in the first part of the 20th century by Freud, Piaget, and others had a major influence on later research on moral development. It took some time, however, for those influences to have their impact.

Whereas there was little research from about the early 1930s until the late 1950s, a great deal of research on moral development has been conducted since the late 1950s to the time of this writing. During the late 1950s and early 1960s, there was steadily increasing interest in research on the child-rearing antecedents of conscience, guilt, and internalized moral values and behaviors (e.g., Hoffman, 1963; Sears, Maccoby, & Levin, 1957). Although the influence of psychoanalytic theory waned over the years, many of Freud's ideas were incorporated into the work on child rearing, alongside the increasingly influential behavioristic theories of that time. Emphasis was placed on identification as a mechanism for the acquisition of moral values, and on guilt and anxiety as the basic motives for the child's inhibition of needs or impulses and adherence to moral values. At about the same time, several researchers turned their attention to direct applications of behavioristic learning principles to explanations of the acquisition of moral behaviors and the role of anxiety and guilt in moral actions (e.g., Aronfreed, 1961; Bandura & Walters, 1963).

The dominant conceptions of morality were, therefore, either based on psychoanalytic explanations of conscience and guilt, as transformed by a learning theory paradigm, or straightforward behavioristic explanations of moral learning. In either formulation, moral development was assumed to be a function of societal control over the individual's interests, needs, or impulses—that is most effective when it becomes part of the individual's functioning and is maintained independently of external sanctions. Since then, a major shift has occurred in psychologists' approach to morality, which was brought about in no small measure by the work of Lawrence Kohlberg. Kohlberg critiqued the dominant behavioristic and psychoanalytic conceptions of morality (Kohlberg, 1963, 1964), argued for the need to ground empirical study of moral development on sound philosophical definitions of the domain (Kohlberg, 1970, 1971), presented his own formulations of the process of moral development (Kohlberg, 1963, 1969), entailing modifications and elaborations of Piaget's (1932) earlier formulations and, in the process, stimulated new interest in Piaget's perspective on social development.

Kohlberg provided a comprehensive review of research pertaining to what was then the common wisdom that parental practices of discipline determined the strength and accuracy of the acquisition of conscience, guilt, and moral behaviors. Kohlberg's review documented that there were no clear-cut patterns of findings supporting the psychoanalytic or behavioristic propositions. No consistent relations were obtained between those parental conditions of child rearing postulated to lead to learning and the various measures of conscience or internalized values used at the time (see Kohlberg, 1963, for details). Kohlberg also argued persuasively that the measures of moral development generally used in that body of research were inadequate because they entailed projective tests of guilt or anxiety, reactions to story stimuli of little moral importance, ambiguous self-reports by parents of their past child-rearing techniques, and contrived experimental situations of little meaning to children.

The message Kohlberg wanted to convey regarding his critique of the methodology in that body of research was not only methodological, however. The inadequacies in methods were, in Kohlberg's view, tied to theories that were not grounded in any substantive epistemology of the domain. Whereas morality was treated, through the ages, as a substantive epistemological category by philosophers—from Plato and Aristotle, to Hume, Mill, and Kant, and among contemporary philosophers—psychologists attempted to explain its acquisition without consideration of the definition or meaning of that which is acquired. Kohlberg (1970) articulated the problem as follows:

> It is usually supposed that psychology contributes to moral education by telling us appropriate *methods* of moral teaching and learning. A Skinnerian will speak of proper schedules of reinforcement in moral learning, a Freudian will speak of the importance of the balance of parental love and firmness which will promote superego identification, and so on. When Skinnerians or Freudians speak on the topic of moral education, then, they start by answering Yes to Meno's question "Is virtue something that can be taught?" and go on to tell us how. . . .
>
> My response to these questions was more modest. When confronted with a group of parents who asked me "How can we help make our children virtuous?" I had to answer, as Socrates, "You must think I am very fortunate to know how virtue is acquired. The fact is that far from knowing whether it can be taught, I have no idea what virtue really is." . . . If I could not define virtue or the ends of moral education, could I really offer advice as to the means by which virtue could be taught? . . .
>
> It appears, then, that we must either be totally silent about moral education or else speak to the nature of virtue. (pp. 57–58)

With a good deal of rhetorical flourish, and perhaps an element of false modesty, Kohlberg thus made the point that we cannot consider mechanisms of moral acquisition without concern with the nature (definition, meanings, substance) of morality. This idea, however, was based not only on epistemological considerations, but also on psychological considerations. Kohlberg presumed that behavioral scientists and philosophers were not the only ones who engage in systematic thinking about psychological, social, or moral matters. Laypersons do too! He rejected the implied duality between the psychologist and the layperson evident in most psychological explanations.

Kohlberg (1968) coined the phrase "the child as a moral philosopher." However, the metaphor was not meant to convey the idea that children engage in reflective intellectual deliberations or formulate conceptual systems of the type seen in the writings of professional moral philosophers. Rather, it was meant to convey the idea, consistent with Piagetian theory, that children form ways of thinking through their social experiences, which include substantive understandings of moral concepts like justice, rights, equality, and welfare. An implicit but important assumption in this formulation is that morality is not solely, or even mainly, imposed on children nor solely based on avoiding negative emotions like anxiety and guilt. As part of their orientation to social relationships, and especially through taking the perspectives of others, children generate judgments, built on emotions like sympathy, empathy, respect, love, and attachment, to which they have a commitment and which are not in conflict with their "natural" or biological dispositions (recall Piaget's definition of moral autonomy).

Kohlberg first studied moral development by focusing on how children and adolescents make judgments about conflicts, in hypothetical situations, around issues of life, interpersonal obligations, trust, law, authority, and retribution. As is well known, Kohlberg proposed a sequence of six stages, depicting a progression from judgments primarily based on obedience, punishment avoidance, and instrumental need and exchange (Stages 1 and 2, grouped into a "preconventional" level); to judgments based on role obligations, stereotypical conceptions of good persons, and respect for the rules and authority legitimated in the social system (Stages 3 and 4, grouped into a "conventional" level); to judgments based on contractual agreements, established procedural arrangements for adjudicating conflicts, mutual respect, and differentiated concepts of justice and rights (Stages 5 and 6, grouped into a "postconventional" level). This sequence of six stages was also a reformulation of Piaget's progression from heteronomy to autonomy (Kohlberg, 1963). Kohlberg maintained that respect for rules and

authority, which Piaget had attributed to young children at the heteronomous level, does not come about at least until adolescence (Kohlberg's conventional level), and that young children's moral judgments are characterized, instead, by a failure to distinguish moral value from power, sanctions, and instrumental needs. In turn, Kohlberg proposed that mutual respect and concepts of justice and rights as part of an autonomous system of thought (i.e., as reflecting the individual's elaboration of norms through social participation), whose emergence Piaget had placed in late childhood or early adolescence, do not come about until at the earliest late adolescence and usually not until adulthood (Kohlberg's postconventional level).

Kohlberg also proposed that the stages represent universal forms of moral judgment among individuals participating in social interactions and perspective taking. He viewed the stages as constituting a universal sequence, through which individuals progress in an invariant step-by-step process. He also assumed that rates of progress through the stages may vary. Kohlberg proposed that the stages defined structural features of moral thought, which represented commonalities among cultures in the context of possible differences in the content of morality. He undertook a series of studies of the development of moral judgments in several cultures, some Western and some non-Western (Kohlberg, 1969). In conducting studies in different cultures, Kohlberg gave greater emphasis than existed before to empirical data to test propositions regarding cultural differences or commonalities in moral judgments. Kohlberg's research, as well as many studies conducted by others, suggest that there may be similarities across cultures in development through the first three or four stages, and much ambiguity of thought corresponding to the higher stages (see Snarey, 1985). As discussed in subsequent sections, the question of cultural differences and commonalities has provoked much controversy. Nevertheless, Kohlberg's work in this regard has been influential in framing discussions of morality and culture around empirical findings.

Kohlberg's influence on subsequent research and theories is, in important respects, separate from the influence of his particular formulation of stages of moral development, or even from the theoretical viewpoint he espoused. Many advance alternative theoretical paradigms, including paradigms based on the idea of the internalization of conscience and values or the idea of culture-based morality. Even among those who advance developmental positions influenced by Piaget's theory, many propose formulations divergent from that of Kohlberg. Yet, Kohlberg has influenced discourse about the psychology of moral development in several ways. One is that there is greater recognition of the need to ground psychological explanations in philosophical considerations about morality. For example, developmental perspectives emphasizing the construction of moral judgments are often grounded in philosophical perspectives (e.g., Dworkin, 1977; Gewirth, 1978; Habermas, 1990a; Rawls, 1971), which assume that morality involves principles of obligation, oughts, and the right. Analyses emphasizing cultural variations in moral codes are often grounded in philosophical perspectives (e.g., Blum, 1990; MacIntyre, 1981) that view morality as conditional on context and not based on objective criteria.

Another of the influences is that in many current formulations morality is not framed in terms of impositions on children due to conflicts between their needs or interests and the requirements of society or the group. Instead, many investigators now think that children are, in an active and positive sense, integrated into their social relationships with adults and peers, and that morality is not solely or even primarily an external or unwanted imposition on them. Kohlberg had stressed children's constructions of moral judgments from social interactions and maintained that, therefore, moral acquisition and behavior are not regulated mainly by emotions of fear, anxiety, shame, or guilt. Although these emotional sanctions are not to be excluded, they would have a lesser role than would be the case in the context of morality that is imposed on children's "natural" inclinations. Following Piaget's formulations, Kohlberg proposed that emotions of sympathy for others, as well as spontaneous interests in helping others, or altruism, were centrally involved in children's moral development especially as part of the process of taking the perspective of others (Kohlberg, 1969, 1971, 1976). Moreover, Kohlberg regarded the sense of respect for others as a key component of morality at the most advanced levels of development.

All the changes in perspectives on moral development cannot be attributed solely to Kohlberg's influence. The issues noted are ones he addressed directly and for which he provided persuasive arguments. Nor do contemporary analyses of moral development exclude elements of the positions taken by behavioristic and psychoanalytic theorists. There are researchers concerned with the internalization of values, the ideas of conscience and self-control, and with emotions like anxiety, shame, and guilt. Nevertheless, the scope of inquiry has been broadened to include and emphasize positive emotions, the intricacies of moral, social, and

personal judgments as part of individuals' relations with the social world, and social interactions contributing to development, including with parents, peers, schooling, and culture. Debates now center on the roles of emotions and judgments, on the individual and the collectivity, on the contributions of constructions of moral understandings and culturally based meanings, and on how to distinguish between universally applicable and locally based moralities. These types of debates are also evident in analyses of morality outside psychology, but which in many instances, use psychological concepts in positions bearing on public policy, education, and politics. Several of those analyses entail critiques of society and prescriptions for changes in public policy (Bellah, Madsen, Sullivan, Swidler, & Tipton, 1985; Etzioni, 1993; Wilson, 1993), education (Bennett, 1992, 1993; K. Ryan, 1989; Wynne, 1989), and family practices (Whitehead, 1993).

ISSUES, EMPHASES, AND THEORIES

A striking and perhaps ironic feature of discussions of moral development is that there are strongly held conflicting positions, and that debates over these positions are often very heated and not so gentle. Moreover, it is frequently asserted that positions held by others exclude a particular feature of central importance—usually the feature emphasized by those characterizing the other's approach. Portraying others as excluding a feature deemed of central importance extends well beyond debates over moral development. Probably the most common example is seen in the continual debates over the roles of biology and environment. Those debates seem to be everlasting and there is a recycling of the issues even though periodically there appears something of a consensus that such debates are futile because both biology and environment contribute to psychological functioning and development. One reason for this state of affairs is that the question is usually mischaracterized as whether biology or environment is taken into account, rather than *how* each feature is explained. An equally important reason for the continual reemergence of the debates is that these matters are not settled, and yet researchers pursuing different and even opposite explanations tend to declare matters settled.

For example, consider assertions about supposedly new disciplines, one labeled cultural psychology (Shweder, 1990a; Shweder & Sullivan, 1993), and the other evolutionary psychology (Cosmides & Tooby, 1989; Tooby, 1987; Wright, 1994). Proponents of cultural psychology maintain that thoughts, meanings, emotions, and behaviors vary by culture. Because their focus is on culturally constructed meanings, they propose that there are no general psychological processes to be discovered. Through cultural psychology, it is declared that "the mind . . . is content driven, domain specific, and constructively stimulus bound" (Shweder, 1990a, p. 87), with an emphasis on that which is local, contingent, and context-dependent. There is a rejection of the idea of general psychological mechanisms, forms of development, or mental processes. It has been asserted that cultural psychology is a newly emerging and increasingly popular discipline entailing "the study of the way cultural traditions and social practices regulate, express, and transform the human psyche, resulting less in psychic unity for humankind than in ethnic divergences in mind, self, and emotion" (Shweder, 1990a, p. 73). (For an alternative and broader perspective on cultural psychology, see Bruner, 1996.)

By contrast, proponents of evolutionary psychology maintain that mind and behavior have a firm evolutionary and genetic basis, which makes for a "unity within the species" connecting the peoples of the world. According to the tenets of evolutionary psychology, social relationships, and especially relationships between the sexes including and going well beyond reproductive functions, are highly influenced by evolutionary processes. Evolutionary processes extend to the realm of morality: "Altruism, compassion, empathy, love, conscience, the sense of justice—all these things, the things that hold society together, the things that allow our species to think so highly of itself, can now confidently be said to have a firm genetic basis" (Wright, 1994, p. 12). Confidence in a firm genetic basis brings with it confidence in uniformities among people of different cultures: "Evolutionary psychologists are pursuing what is known in the trade as 'the psychic unity of humankind'" (Wright, 1994, p. 26).

Along with the striking confidence expressed by cultural and evolutionary psychologists in discoveries against and for the psychic unity of humankind, they make other parallel claims. Visible representatives of each discipline claim that the discipline has discovered knowledge contrary to the established perspective in psychology, which will be resisted by those with vested interests in the old paradigm. Cultural psychologists argue that psychology, and other social sciences, had been dominated by those seeking psychic unity and proposing general psychological mechanisms. Evolutionary psychologists argue that psychology, and other social sciences, had been dominated by those believing that "biology doesn't much matter—that the uniquely malleable human mind, together with the

unique force of culture, has severed our behavior from its evolutionary roots" (Wright, 1994, p. 5).

If the content were omitted, it would appear that cultural and evolutionary psychologists are in agreement about the past and future of psychology. Each assert that there is a previously dominant paradigm, about which its proponents are defensive and resistant to change, but which is being displaced by a new paradigm. Unfortunately, they hold contradictory views as to which paradigm was previously dominant and which paradigm is taking over. Not only are levels of the state of knowledge and documentation and verification for discoveries exaggerated so that matters are prematurely claimed to be settled, but opposing positions are characterized as accounting for mainly one type of feature. Among theorists of moral development, there seems to be a greater recognition of the viability of competing points of view. However, it is not uncommon to find characterizations of others' explanations of moral development as excluding a feature judged to be of central importance. It is implied that the omission, in itself, invalidates the theoretical point of view. The most frequent examples of this revolve around whether theorists account for emotions or judgments, for social influences or the individual's logical operations, for parental influences or peer influences, and for culture or individual constructions. Here, too, there is a tendency to mischaracterize positions as failing to account for this or that, instead of recognizing that differences in theoretical perspectives have more to do with how different features (e.g., emotions and judgments) are explained and emphasized. Even when a theorist excludes a particular component regarded important by others, it is usually mistaken to say that there is a failure to account for the component. Often, the relevance of a component is explicitly excluded. An example is Skinner's (1971) arguments for the exclusion of moral judgments, along with cognition in general, as epiphenomena.

It is important, therefore, to consider how a theoretical perspective frames the relevant issues. Within current theoretical perspectives and research programs it is particularly important to consider how issues like emotion, culture, gender, judgment, social influence, and individual construction are explained. Indeed, emphases placed on these issues serve to distinguish points of view on moral development. Whereas most explanations of moral development attempt to account for each of these issues, there are differences in the importance and roles given to them.

This chapter is organized around theoretical approaches to moral development, in line with the central issues emphasized in those approaches. I begin with theorists who emphasize the role of emotions in morality. Among them are social critics, educators, and sociologists who link emotions to the formation of character traits and/or habitual moral practices. Although these ideas have not been put forth by psychologists, their positions have connections to psychological concepts and can be evaluated by psychological evidence. After discussing their positions, I consider, in greater detail, the concepts and research of developmental psychologists who emphasize emotions, the influences of parental practices toward their children, and conscience. This is followed by discussion of approaches that, though including emotions and judgments, emphasize the role of gender and gender-related experiences in moral development. Then I consider approaches in which culture is regarded as central, and in which fairly sharp distinctions are drawn among moral orientations in different cultures. Next I discuss approaches emphasizing moral judgments and reciprocal interactions in development. Finally, a perspective is presented based on reciprocal interactions, the domains of personal, social, and moral judgments, and their interplay with cultures. I approach each of the positions, and associated research, from the perspectives of their conceptualizations of the moral realm, theoretical constructs on development, and on the ways children are influenced by biological and environmental features.

EMPHASIZING EMOTIONS

Emotions have been considered the basis for morality by some philosophers (Hume, 1751/1966; Smith, 1759/1976), and have been central in psychologists' formulations—including in Freud's conception of superego development. Whereas in the past, psychologists have linked emotions to habits and character traits, in recent years they have rarely done so. The concept of habit has received little attention among psychologists since the analyses of the early behaviorists (Miller & Dollard, 1941), who attempted to explain behavioral consistencies through mechanisms of learning, or habit formation, and generalization. Similarly, psychologists have now moved away from explaining morality in terms of internal traits or dispositions of character or personality. This is most likely a consequence of the types of behavioral inconsistencies obtained in the Hartshorne and May (1928–1930) research, as well as in later research also showing a lack of consistency in social behaviors across situations (Mischel, 1973). The idea of character traits implies that internalized dispositions would result in habitual behaviors applied across situations.

Explanations of morality as entailing virtues and character are not uncommon among philosophers who trace their roots to Aristotle. Aristotelian and neo-Aristotelian accounts (e.g., MacIntyre, 1981) have included conceptions of morality as the good life, reflected in habitual practices and in living up to the virtues through action. Although Aristotle linked virtues to tradition, he also believed that traditions should not necessarily remain fixed or immune from criticism. According to Nussbaum (1989, p. 36), Aristotle's position was, "If we reason well we can make progress in lawmaking, just as we do in other arts and sciences." Outside of philosophy and psychology, however, there are those who hold that morality is best explained through the concept of character, as linked more to emotions than to reasoning. These conceptions of character have not carried over the philosophical substance of the Aristotelian and neo-Aristotelian propositions. They have greater affinities to the types of character traits, defined through consistencies in behaviors, identified by Hartshorne and May.

It has also been proposed, primarily among some sociologists, that American children's acquisition of moral habits requires a renewed valuing of cultural traditions and commitment to a sense of community, along with a deemphasis of individualism. Positions emphasizing community are not unlike Durkheim's (1925/1961) proposition that morality involves a collective sense of solidarity, experienced by individuals as feelings of attachments to and respect for the moral authority embedded in society.

Character, Habits, and Moral Degeneration

The propositions that morality is best explained through character traits, habits, or commitments to community are held by several educators, sociologists, and social commentators. A common theme in these positions is that American society is in moral crisis, decay, or serious decline. Myriad causes have been offered as bringing about the decline. These include the culture of the 1960s (Bloom, 1987), changes in the family (Bloom, 1987; Etzioni, 1993; Whitehead, 1993; Wilson, 1993), a failure to attend to, or questioning of, traditions (Bennett, 1993; Etzioni, 1993; K. Ryan, 1989; Wynne, 1986); the failure to provide moral education (Bennett & Delattre, 1978; Sommers, 1984); the failure of universities to provide adequate education (Bloom, 1987; Sommers, 1984); the onset of radical individualism (Bellah et al., 1985; Etzioni; 1993; Sampson, 1977); the influences of feminism (Bloom, 1987); and the teachings of elites (intellectuals, scholars) who, in contradiction with the "common sense" or natural propensities of "ordinary people," create theories hostile to the virtues and character (Bennett, 1992; Bloom, 1987; Wilson, 1993).

Character and Moral Sensibilities

Some of those who lament the moral decline of American society propose that the remedy lies in promoting character in children through firm controls by adults in the family and schools. They find fault in programs of moral education (especially those based on Kohlberg's theories) whose pedagogical aims are to stimulate the development of moral judgments, deliberation, reflection, or the consideration of alternative moral decisions and solutions (for critiques, see especially Bennett & Delattre, 1978; Sommers, 1984). Judgment is deemed largely tangential to morality and, therefore, detrimental to its acquisition because it diverts children from learning to behave in habitual ways consistent with traditions and virtues.

It is argued that, instead, there should be an emphasis on the inculcation of traits in children, with a focus on influencing how they act and not on their "states of mind" (Wynne, 1986). The traits, which are based on traditions of the culture, are to be taught or transmitted not only through rewards and punishments, but especially, through the example provided by the constant and consistent actions of adults practicing the values and in the telling and retelling of stories or narratives about people habitually behaving in accord with those values. The fundamental traits of character are ones for which the "majority of Americans share a respect . . . : honesty, compassion, courage, and perseverance" (Bennett, 1993, p. 12). Additional traits are mentioned by proponents of character development (e.g., responsibility, self-discipline, loyalty, faith), but little is provided in the way of rationales for the validity of those traits—except the proclamations that they are traditional and embraced by the majority of Americans. Almost no evidence is provided either for the extent to which Americans value the traits or for their consistency in practicing these. Also, virtually no evidence is given for the claim that the traits or behaviors are acquired through inculcation, practice, or examples through narratives or in the actions of others.

The premise that traits of character are ingrained in cultural traditions and held in respect by the majority of Americans may appear contradictory with the proposition put forth by the same writers that American society has lost its moral compass and is experiencing moral decay (the latter premise suggests that Americans do not possess the necessary traits). This potential contradiction is explained by some as due to a discrepancy between the beliefs and values of the majority of Americans, who constitute the mainstream, and an apparently highly influential minority of "elites" who "have waged an all-out assault on common sense and the common values of the American people" (Bennett, 1992, p. 13). In ways unspecified, the presumed elites' rejection of the idea of character, their antipathy to the culture, and their embrace of an ideology contrary to the beliefs of most Americans are said to have placed the country in moral crisis. Much of the fault is attributed to the changes in educational practices.

These propositions are at root paradoxical, however, because if people acquire character and habits through the example of others and if the majority of mainstream Americans maintain the morally proper traits and beliefs, then it would be expected that there are many examples from whom children would learn. Presumably, children are exposed to exemplary virtues in most families and elsewhere. Moreover, for Bennett (1992) at least, the majority of school teachers, in contrast with leaders in educational organizations and teacher unions, do hold mainstream American values. Presumably, the teachers' actions, to which students are continually exposed, would most influence children in schools.

A similar paradox is potentially in the propositions of James Q. Wilson (1993), another social scientist who shares some of the emphasis on character while attempting to account for evidence from psychology, anthropology, economics, and biology in formulating a theory of morality and its acquisition based on emotions and innate sociability. Wilson sees a loss of confidence in the use of the language of morality due to a prevailing moral skepticism perpetuated by "intellectuals" who question the scientific bases for morality, and who further an ideology of individual autonomy and choice (among those whose writings have had a deleterious influence are Enlightenment philosophers, Freud, Karl Marx, and contemporary philosophers espousing a morality of individual choice and rights). Wilson believes that intellectuals have contributed to an increase in crime, drug abuse, and political corruption by undermining commitments to personal responsibility (in this regard Wilson has no evidence to offer). At the same time, Wilson's explanation of morality is founded on the proposition that a natural moral sense has emerged in the process of evolution, which results in moral practices among most people. He attempts, in a not entirely satisfactory way, to escape the paradox with the claim that the natural moral sense, itself, immunizes most people from the "philosophical doubts, therapeutic postures, ideological zealotry, with which the modern age has been so thoroughly infected" (Wilson, 1993, p. 11). Yet, morality has been undermined because the immunity is not foolproof. In part, this is because self-interest, which is also natural, can conflict with people's natural moral inclinations. Moreover, those at-risk for criminal activity are most likely to be influenced by "intellectual currents." People are at risk, according to Wilson, often because of biological factors, such as a propensity for inadequate self-control entailing an inherited inability to sustain attention or inhibit impulses (salient examples are attention deficit disorder, dispositions to addictions to smoking, drugs, and food, and inherited dispositions for criminal activities).

Drawing a dichotomy between "intellectuals" and those he refers to as "ordinary people," Wilson asserts that most people's moral behaviors are determined largely by emotions and habits (Wilson, 1993, pp. 7–8): "Much of the time our inclination toward fair play or our sympathy for the plight of others are immediate and instinctive, a reflex of our emotions more than an act of our intellect. . . . The feelings on which people act are often superior to the arguments that they employ." In Wilson's formulation, although reasoning, reflection, and deliberation may emerge later in life than the reflexive and habitual, they are less adaptive, from the moral point of view, than the earlier emerging moral sensibilities. Such a reversal of often-held conceptions of development (where reasoning and reflection are built on earlier reflexive processes) is based on the idea that morality stems from natural emotions, whose emergence is best facilitated by early experiences in appropriate types of families (i.e., defined by Wilson as intact heterosexual families, where parents provide love, nurturance, and act authoritatively). Evolution, Wilson argues, has selected for attachment or affiliative behavior. In addition to natural selection for reproductive success, with a disposition toward self-interest, there is a biologically based disposition for bonding and attachment that takes the form of sociability. Innate sociability is the overriding component in producing four central "sentiments" that make up the moral life: *sympathy* (allowing for people to be affected by the feelings and experiences of others), *fairness* (based on equity, reciprocity, and impartiality), *self-control* (a necessary sensibility because conflicts arise between self-interest and the moral sense), and *duty* or conscience (which dictates actions in the absence of sanctions).

In keeping with a deemphasis of individuals' reasoning and reflection, Wilson believes that morality is, in most instances, local and parochial. In simple agricultural communities, and in Western cultures prior to the Enlightenment,

the moral sense applies to those who are similar and familiar to oneself (kin and the local community). The idea that moral considerations should be universalized is a Western concept stemming from the Enlightenment and the advent of individualism.

The idea that morality is constituted by moral sentiments guiding behavior in instinctive and reflexive ways is akin to the idea that morality comprises habitual behaviors reflecting traits or dispositions. Wilson goes beyond solely describing traits by attempting to explain the sources of moral sensibility in biologically based dispositions toward sociability and attachments. This type of link between emotions and habitual behaviors also has affinities with those who regard emotions as linked to habits based on commitments to community.

Habits and the Communitarian Spirit

As noted, the theme of a moral decline in American society is echoed by those who believe individuals need to form tighter and better attachments to communities that transcend individual goals and pursuits. Not surprisingly, the emphasis on community is evident in works of sociologists—two of the most visible being Etzioni's (1993) *The Spirit of Community* and Bellah et al.'s (1985) *Habits of the Heart.* With regard to the moral status of American society, Etzioni (1993, p. 12) has asserted that because of a waning of traditional values, without an affirmation of new values, "we live in a state of everlasting moral confusion and social anarchy." Bellah et al. (1985) assert that American "individualism may have grown cancerous" (p. vii), and that "we seem to be hovering on the very brink of disaster . . . from the internal incoherence of society" (p. 284). They ask: "How can we reverse the slide toward the abyss?" (p. 284).

The call for a greater sense of community is to reverse a supposed breakdown in society connected to a supposed overemphasis on personal goals and individual rights. The personal has been offset from the group or society in psychological theories, as well—especially in psychoanalytic and behavioristic explanations. In those psychological explanations, individuals' biologically derived needs, drives, or instincts are said to require societal control and displacement by concerns with others and the well-being of the community. The sociological explanations, however, only touch on biological or psychological motives for the prominence of personal goals or rights. Instead, it is presumed that an overemphasis on rights and radical individualism are themselves mainly part of a cultural ethos;

culture has produced habits and practices detrimental to societal well-being and a balanced moral life.

Moreover, the cultural ethos of rights and individualism is seen as, in large measure, a contemporary phenomenon at odds with traditions of social commitment and responsibility. To a good extent, a return to past practices is required. Much of the reason there is a need for recommitment to moral values, restoration of law and order, and rebuilding of the foundation of society, according to Etzioni and his colleagues, is that Americans have become overly concerned with rights (there has been an "explosion" of rights, and "incessant issuance of new rights") and a concomitant "elevation of the unbridled pursuit of self-interest and greed to the level of social virtue" (Etzioni, 1993, p. 24). However, the call is not for an elimination of all personal rights, but for a renewed balance of rights and responsibilities. To accomplish such a balance, Etzioni recommends a moratorium on virtually all new rights for a decade, a reaffirmation of responsibilities, and a restoration of communities. Essential to the renewal are changes in family structure—ranging from maintaining two-parent families (such as by legislating a lengthy waiting period for remarriage after divorce) to reinstating the ritual of the family meal.

Bellah et al.'s (1985) analyses of late 20th century American culture adopt the idea of "national character"— the American character is firmly, and legitimately from the moral point of view, individualistic. In their view, however, individualism can take different forms in relation to connections to others and community, as well as to a moral order. In the past, American individualism was characterized by personal autonomy, self-reliance, and individual initiative. Central to that form of individualism was a belief in the dignity of the individual, a valuing of equality, and questioning of fixed social ranks and subjugation of persons.

In its traditional form, however, individualism was balanced with commitment to the moral order and attachments to family, church, and community. American society is "hovering on the brink of disaster" and sliding "toward the abyss" because individualism has been reshaped and is no longer balanced (Bellah et al., 1985, p. 284). There is now a radical individualism, characterized by isolation, separation, independence from the past (from a "community of memory"), with personal choice and individual fulfillment placed over attachment to family, social institutions (e.g., the church), and one's community. Bellah et al. conclude that Americans are rarely able to see themselves as interrelated with other Americans who may be different, and that the "quintessential American task is of finding oneself." Moral goals have been transformed into ones of economic effectiveness, self-fulfillment, and personal satisfaction. The proposed solution—the way to avoid the abyss—is to achieve a balance by attenuating individualism and by restoring traditions, a sense of community, and concerns with the common good. Accomplishing this task, so that we do not have "very little future to think about at all" (Bellah et al., 1985, p. 286), requires changing the cultural ethos, national identity, and the habits and emotions of individuals.

Moral Appraisal and Moral Recommendations

The perspectives on character education and the restoration of a sense of community entail social activism and constitute applied social science since much of the focus is on moral crises and societal change. However, the activist and applied components rest on assertions about the moral state of society in the present and past (i.e., moral crisis, decay now, and a better moral state of affairs then), about the nature of individuals' morality in the past and present (i.e., firm character traits, and commitment to virtues and community then but not now); and about the causes of moral problems in the present (selfishness, individualism, failures of commitment and community, and changes in family life). Those assertions are subject to social scientific analysis, and imply assumptions about the process of successful moral development. It is assumed that in the past morality was acquired through training in character or commitment to family and community, and that society was then more successful morally. On that basis, it is assumed that adequate moral development should proceed (and be facilitated) as it did in the past. These assumptions about the psychology of moral development, however, are not grounded on detailed psychological and developmental analyses or empirical evidence. Instead, the line of reasoning rests on certain key untested assumptions.

One is the repeatedly stated assumption of the moral downslide. The causes attributed to the moral decline of the society are quite varied, and many of those causes reflect disagreements, about the events, with others who would regard them as having promoted moral goals. As examples, many would regard as furthering moral ends events in the 1960s (especially the anti-Vietnam War and civil rights movements), feminism, and the assertion of rights for groups faced with discrimination. Furthermore, the only evidence provided for the sweeping claims of moral decline is some data, open to varying interpretations, on increases, since the 1950s, of rates of suicide, homicide, and out-of-wedlock births (Wynne, 1986).

The vast societal changes over the past two centuries, however, make it very difficult to document whether there has been decay, improvement, or simply patterns of positive and negative changes associated with different realms of social life. To cite some salient examples of morally relevant (and often viewed as positive) societal shifts, there have been changes in race relations and treatment of minority groups, in the roles, burdens, and privileges of women, in the treatment of children, in the conditions of work for children, in the workforce and labor relations more generally, in care of the elderly, in levels of political representation of many groups (including women), in numbers of people receiving higher levels of education, and in the power and authority relationships among those of higher and lower social classes.

No analyses have been provided of the ways all these changes might constitute some betterment of the lives of people, nor of how past practices may have produced harm. Even with regard to violence and homicide—for which there are statistics documenting its prevalence in contemporary society—there are good indications that they are traditional in American society and were prevalent in the past (Butterfield, 1995). Moreover, insofar as there is documentation regarding levels of honesty, it reveals that even in the early part of the 20th century children exhibited a fair amount of dishonesty in school activities and in experimental tasks (Hartshorne & May, 1928–1930). It is also the case that in past times strikingly similar concerns with moral decay existed in Western countries. During the 1920s, much concern was expressed in the United States regarding the moral state of youth, cultural disintegration, and social chaos (see Fass, 1977). Similarly, in fin-de-siècle France (the late 1800s), there were widespread concerns with moral degeneration, national decline, the declining morality of youth (e.g., an explosion of juvenile crime rates), and calls for renewal of the society (see Norris, 1996).

These examples demonstrate the complexity of social and moral change through history and suggest that perhaps we are seeing stereotypic impressions and speculations of the morality of the present, along with nostalgic views of the past. Without solid evidence of negative changes in the morality of the society, it cannot be concluded that the ways morality was transmitted in the past are the most efficacious (similar considerations apply to

claims that recent activities, such as of the 1960s or feminism, have caused moral decay). It may be that the proposed explanations of the process of moral development would hold for the past (and present) even in the absence of any considerations of moral decline. However, the assertions about how morality was transmitted or acquired in the past are themselves undocumented.

At best, the propositions regarding moral development as the acquisition of character traits or as commitment to community must be seen as standing alongside several other competing explanations. However, the basic concepts used still require research so as to know more about the parameters of the habitual, the criteria for an adequate commitment to community, as well as how these are acquired. Similarly, the propositions regarding the family as a central influence on moral development through parental example and training represents only one perspective on the family. Others have attempted to account for the effects of the structure (e.g., extent of a hierarchical structure) of the family, its particular practices in terms of their fairness and justice, and the content of communications and proclaimed ideology. Furthermore, many researchers have given a fair amount of emphasis to the influences of other social experiences (e.g., with peers, in school, in relation to culture), to the ways children account for a heterogeneity of social experiences, and to their ways of constructing judgments about those different dimensions of social experience.

Positive Emotions, Evolution, and Parental Practices

Emotions have been considered central in some explanations of moral learning. The earlier psychoanalytic and behavioristic conceptions gave most emphasis to guilt and/or anxiety as internalized sanctions. However, a major shift in thinking about emotions in the late 1970s and through the 1980s entailed a focus on attachment, bonding, love, sympathy, and empathy. The emphasis on these emotions included a continued concern with the influences of the family (in keeping with Freudian and behavioristic accounts), as well as a renewed interest in the evolutionary sources of emotions.

Of particular relevance to the shift are findings that very young children display positive emotions, and affiliate and bond with others (Dunn, 1987, 1988; Dunn, Brown, & Maguire, 1995; Hoffman, 1984, 1991a, 1991b; Kagan, 1984; Kochanska, 1991, 1993, 1994). Another set of relevant findings show that young children are sensitive to the interests and well-being of others, producing actions of a prosocial or altruistic nature. That body of research is not reviewed in this chapter as it is the topic of the chapter by Eisenberg and Fabes in this Volume, but the general pattern of findings is that young children engage in acts of sharing, and helping or altruism. Studies conducted in the home show that even children under 2 years of age share possessions (e.g., toys) with others, help mothers with household tasks, cooperate in games, and respond to the emotional distress of others (Radke-Yarrow, Zahn-Waxler, & Chapman, 1983). Toddlers and young children, in addition, show comfort and engage in caregiving of others. It also appears that reactions of empathy emerge by the age of 3 years (Lennon & Eisenberg, 1987). Moreover, distinctions drawn among reactions of empathy have a bearing on the relations of emotions to prosocial or altruistic behaviors (Eisenberg & Fabes, 1990, 1991).

Empathy, defined as an emotional response stemming from another's emotional state, can result in sympathy or "personal distress." Sympathy goes beyond solely experiencing an emotional reaction to another similar to the other's feelings in that it entails an other-oriented response and concern for that person's well-being. Empathy can also result, by contrast, in personal distress, which entails a self-focused aversive reaction (e.g., anxiety, discomfort) to the distress of another; the motivation is to alleviate one's own aversive state (see Eisenberg & Fabes, 1990, 1991, and this volume for further discussion). There is also evidence that children's feelings of empathy are related to their prosocial actions (Eisenberg & Miller, 1987; Eisenberg & Strayer, 1987). In particular, measures of facial and psychological indexes of affect have shown that sympathy, and not personal distress, is related to prosocial actions motivated by concerns for the welfare of others (Eisenberg & Fabes, 1991).

The research findings on sympathy and prosocial actions are inconsistent with the idea that children, before they have internalized parental values, or societal standards, or have been taught to behave in socially sanctioned ways, will act solely in selfish and self-directed ways when they are not coerced or fearful of detection. It does not necessarily follow, however, that sympathy and spontaneous prosocial behaviors at a very young age either reflect innate dispositions or that morality is primarily based on emotions (to be discussed). Moreover, questions still exist regarding the validity of age-related findings in empathic responses, the need to draw further distinctions between closely aligned emotions, and the development of more

adequate methods of measurement (Eisenberg & Fabes, 1991). The findings on sympathy and prosocial actions are not inconsistent with emotive positions on morality, either. In several formulations, it has been proposed that morality is directed more by emotions than reasoning (Dunn, 1987, 1988; Hoffman, 1984, 1991a; Kagan, 1984; Kochanska, 1993, 1994).

Anxiety, Empathy, and the Form of Emotions as Distinct from the Content of Morality

Some of the themes of those who propose that moral learning entails the acquisition of traits and habits are also evident in psychological formulations giving the prominent role to emotions. In particular, it has been proposed that the morality of ordinary persons is directed more by emotions than reasoning. Kagan (1984) has argued that rationalist philosophers, who have developed moral theories based on reasoning and deduction, fail to understand that average citizens, across history and cultures, decide right and wrong mainly through their feelings. Although emotions are constant, they can result in variations in the content of morality by historical context and culture (hence making for a type of form-content distinction). For example, it is argued that the morality of post-enlightenment Western cultures is based on the idea of freedom, as a "primary good," which implies the freedom to enter into contracts with others, hold personal property, allow freedom of speech, and to value actions in one's self-interest. It is said that individual freedom is not part of the morality of other historical periods (e.g., among fourth-century Athenians who enslaved barbarians or sixth-century French monks who declared total loyalty to God) or of other cultures in the contemporary period. In this view, freedom is not any more facilitative of social harmony than obligations to care for others or cooperation in groups found in small farming villages, such as in Latin America and Africa. It is Western cultures that tend to conceptualize morality in an abstract way, with standards deemed applicable across situations and persons.

In Kagan's formulation, there is a juxtaposition of variability of the content of morality with universal formal properties stemming from five evolutionary-based emotions, most of which entail unpleasant feelings: anxiety (over fear of punishment, social disapproval, and failure), empathy, responsibility and guilt, "fatigue" or boredom, and confusion and uncertainty. Avoidance of unpleasant feelings and achievement of pleasant feelings are the major motivations for the acquisition of moral content, and they provide the main rationale for postulating historical and cultural variations in content. Some examples, given by Kagan (1984), illustrate the role attributed to society's ways of engendering unpleasant and pleasant feelings. He proposes that content classified as "moral principles," which are treated as important and inviolable, is determined by the intensity of affective reactions in the community. If affective reactions to a standard are strong, such as with regard to inflicting physical harm, it will hold the status of a moral standard. Other standards are "conventional" in that they are judged as relatively unimportant and changeable (e.g., rules of dress). Their conventional status is due to weak affective reactions in the community.

With regard to moral content, therefore, this position flirts with moral relativism. If the community's affective reactions determine an act's status as moral or conventional, then any act may be conventionalized in a particular social system. Even violence toward persons can become conventionalized. For example, continued exposure to aggression on television can numb children's emotional reactions to violence, so that "the principled standard on violence will become more conventional" (Kagan, 1984, p. 122). Moreover, insofar as evidence is presented for these propositions, it is not with regard to the relations of emotions and morality, nor for their evolutionary basis. Evidence is provided only showing that very young children are aware of "standards." This evidence, however, primarily entails children's concerns with regularities in nonsocial and nonmoral realms (e.g., reactions to broken objects, torn clothing, and missing buttons, or anxiety about pictures of people with distorted faces and bodies).

A Primacy for Empathy

One type of emotion, empathy, has been considered central in moral development by some who do not rely as heavily as Kagan on associations of unpleasant and pleasant affect with moral content. Hoffman (1983, 1984, 1991a, 1991b) has put forth a formulation that combines emotion as coming about through evolution with an internalization presumption that "the society's moral norms and values [are made] part of the individual's personal motive system" (Hoffman, 1991b, p. 106). In addition to emotion and internalization, this approach includes motives, cognition, moral principles of care and justice, and perspective taking. Despite the attempt to incorporate all these features, however, it can be said that primacy is given to emotion because the linchpin is empathy.

In fact, Hoffman distinguishes his approach from those giving primacy to moral judgments or principles in that he defines moral actions in motivational terms. A moral act is "a disposition to do something on behalf of another person, or to behave in accord with a moral norm or standard bearing on human welfare or justice" (Hoffman, 1991a, p. 276). The distinction between defining a moral act in terms of moral judgment or motives is not unambiguous (Blasi, 1983). It could be said that the moral judgments one makes—say that one should come to the aid of another in distress because it is wrong to allow suffering—motivates one to act. It appears that the key to the distinction is in the term "disposition" in the definition of a moral act. In this case, disposition refers to an emotional reaction that propels action. The main source of moral motives is feelings of empathy, with empathy defined as an affective response that does not necessarily match another's affective state but which is "more appropriate to another's situation than one's own" (Hoffman, 1984, p. 285). By putting the matter in affective-motivational terms, Hoffman poses the question, "Why act morally?" and answers in terms of feelings that need to be acted on.

Although empathy is regarded as a biological predisposition and a product of natural selection, it is characterized as developing through four stagelike manifestations that are partly determined by changing cognitive capabilities. The first of these stages is characterized simply by the "global" distress felt by infants (during the first year) entailing a confusion of one's own feelings with those of another. An example of this early type of empathy is of an 11-month-old girl who, on seeing a child fall and cry, looked as if she was about to cry herself, put her thumb in her mouth, and buried her head in her mother's lap. At the second stage of "egocentric" empathy (age of one year), the onset of object permanence allows for an awareness that other people are physically distinct from the self, and concern ("sympathetic distress") with another person who is in distress. However, the child does not distinguish between the other's and one's own internal states. The example here is that of a 18-month-old boy who got his own mother to comfort a crying child even though the crying child's mother was present.

Hoffman further asserts that role taking emerges at about 2 or 3 years of age (this, however, is a controversial issue), allowing for a differentiation of one's own feelings from those of others. At the third stage, therefore, children are responsive to cues about the other person's feelings, and empathize with a range of emotions other than distress (e.g., disappointment, feelings of betrayal). Whereas the third stage is labeled "empathy for another's feelings," the fourth stage, emerging in late childhood is labeled "empathy for another's life conditions." The relevant social cognitions for the fourth stage are children's awareness of self and others as "continuing people with separate histories and identities." These conceptions allow for an awareness that others feel pleasure and pain in their general life experiences. At this stage, empathy is felt in particular situations, as well as for more general life circumstances of others or of groups of people (e.g., the poor or the oppressed).

Whether this sequence of stages is an accurate representation of how children develop is at this point undetermined since the stages were not, for the most part, based on empirical evidence. There is some evidence that infants respond to the crying of other infants to a greater extent than to sounds resembling the crying of human infants (Sagi & Hoffman, 1976). However, it is not entirely clear that this type of response is a form of very early empathy. The other stages have not been tested empirically and, instead, rely on illustrations with the types of anecdotal examples previously mentioned (see Eisenberg & Fabes, this Volume, for discussion of further distinctions within the general construct of empathy).

As a proposed sequence of stages, it may appear that Hoffman's formulation is in accord with other approaches, like those of Piaget and Kohlberg, positing stage sequences. Although there are some similarities, the positions are, as Hoffman (1991b) notes, at the core fundamentally different. The main similarities are that, like Piaget and Kohlberg, Hoffman proposes a sequence in which emotional-social features are dependent on underlying cognitive capacities of children at different ages, and that taking others' perspectives is, in some sense, central to moral actions (Gibbs, 1991). Nevertheless, there are differences of much significance. Whereas Piaget and Kohlberg proposed stages to describe the substance of the moral thinking of individuals, Hoffman's stages describe changes in the forms that empathy takes. In Hoffman's formulation, empathy drives not only moral actions, but moral judgments and principles, as well.

According to Hoffman, empathy motivates actions in many types of situations in addition to the obvious ones in which one observes the pain and distress of another. Empathy also motivates actions in situations in which harm or distress are not observed directly. In turn, empathy is supposedly associated with a variety of moral reactions, including sympathy, aggression or anger at another who injures people, guilt (blaming oneself on feeling empathy for the distress of others), and feelings of injustice (empathy due to perceived unfairness of a situation). Indeed, in Hoffman's perspective, moral principles of care and injustice are validated by emotions.

Hoffman invoked a distinction between "cool" and "hot" cognitions with regard to moral principles. Moral principles, in that view, can be so-called cold cognitions insofar as they are detached from emotions. It is the association of empathy with principles that render them "hot"—that is, morally meaningful and linked to action. At least as common, if not more common, a perspective, especially among philosophers (but also see Baldwin, 1896; Kohlberg, 1971; Piaget, 1932), is that insofar as moral principles are understood by people in ways that are part of their belief systems and mental functioning, it is not necessary that they receive their force from other elements (like empathy) so as to render them meaningful. Instead, there is a synthesis between judgments and emotions, making it difficult to disentangle the two.

Evolution and Internalization

The formulations of morality emphasizing emotions illustrate that, in many instances, asking whether theories are based on nature or nurture, or biology or environment, is not useful. Each of the positions shows a firm orientation to evolutionary-based biological processes, and to the influences of the family, historical contexts, and culture. Much of the research on the internalization side has focused on the family, examining the types of parental child-rearing practices producing more and stronger incorporations of moral standards by children. (In some later writings, Hoffman [1983, 1991b] speculates that children's information processing is part of their response to discipline practices of parents.) A large body of research (for reviews, see Hoffman, 1970, and Maccoby & Martin, 1983) has examined, mainly through self-reports, parental child-rearing practices, along with various measures of moral functioning. Three types of parental practices were identified. One is referred to as power assertion, mainly involving physical punishment, deprivation of goods or privileges, and threats of force. The second, love withdrawal, involves disapproval and other expressions of the removal of affection or emotional supports. The third type, referred to as induction, entails the communication of reasons or explanations for the prescribed behavior, including appeals for concerns with the welfare of others.

Parental reports of their use of these discipline techniques have been correlated with measures of children's guilt (children's tendencies to confession to misdeeds; projective measures of story completions), an external or internal orientation to moral stories (i.e., if they judge by fear of external sanctions or by an evaluation of the act's wrongness), and whether or not children resist the temptation to engage in a prohibited act (often measured in experimental situations). A consistent finding from these studies is that parental practices of induction are the most successful method of discipline (Hoffman, 1970; Hoffman & Saltzstein, 1967; Maccoby & Martin, 1983). Measures reflecting moral development (i.e., guilt, confession, internal orientation, resistance to temptation) are correlated to a greater extent with induction than love withdrawal or power assertion. For example, a moral orientation based on fear of sanctions is correlated with parental practices of physical punishment, whereas expressions of guilt and an internal orientation are correlated with parental practices that emphasize explaining reasons for avoiding or engaging in moral actions.

There are tensions within the theories, however, because propositions regarding internalization are placed alongside propositions of universal biological processes producing particular behaviors inherent in social relationships. In Kagan's position, features of morality pertaining to empathy and concerns with the welfare of others are combined with the proposition that the intensity of emotions linked by the group to content renders acts as moral or not (i.e., as conventional). Sexual behavior can be a moral issue in one historical time, by virtue of associated emotional reactions, and a nonmoral issue in another historical period when the emotions are lessened or removed. Similarly, violence on others can be taken out of the moral realm in a particular setting (again, by virtue of intensity of associated emotion within a group). It is not evident that this historical or cultural component is compatible with the idea that morality entails welfare and avoidance of harm, or with assumptions about biologically based emotional reactions underlying morality. How is it that issues indifferent to matters of welfare can be rendered moral by emotional intensity, and that acts violating people's welfare can become nonmoral because of the historical or cultural context?

In Hoffman's proposition that empathic reactions emanate from biological dispositions that motivate actions in situations with particular features (especially distress felt by a victim), the individual is said to spontaneously react to situations in ways that are governed by internal (and to a fair extent, built-in) emotional structures. In proposing that individuals internalize society's values and norms as a consequence of how they are reared by their parents, it is being said that morality entails a process of making the external internal to the individual. These two propositions can be in tension with each other in certain respects. Insofar as society's values are not in accord with children's natural, spontaneous dispositions to act empathically and for the welfare of others, conflict should occur. Insofar as the two are in concordance (which is probably an implicit assumption in this framework), then it is likely that the process is not one of internalization but of external forces reinforcing and facilitating the emergence and refining of natural propensities.

Conscience and Internalization

Nevertheless, with the inclusion of natural features of social relationships, these perspectives go beyond earlier socialization perspectives by which it was assumed that morality could be adequately defined through consensual norms (Maccoby, 1968). However, some contemporary researchers have addressed hypotheses regarding moral internalization—defining morality through consensual norms—with the assumption that morality entails the acquisition of a conscience serving to internally regulate conduct consistent with societal values, norms, or rules (Kochanska, 1991, 1993, 1994). The concept of conscience, central to Freud's theory, was also central to behavioristic conceptions in which internalization was theorized to be acquired through the anxiety associated with punishments for transgressions (Aronfreed, 1968, 1976; Parke & Walters, 1967). Whether it be from a psychoanalytic or behavioristic perspective, the concept of conscience has been used to refer to a mechanism internalized by children for exerting control on needs that would otherwise be acted on: "Conscience is the term that has been used traditionally to refer to the cognitive and affective processes which constitute an internalized moral governor over an individual's conduct" (Aronfreed, 1968, p. 2) Predating Kagan's proposition that emotional intensity is a criterion distinguishing the moral from conventional status of acts, Aronfreed did not regard conscience to apply to all internalized standards of conduct: "The behavior of parents and of other agents of the social transmission of values will establish different intensities of value for the child in different areas of conduct. The usual connotations of conscience might therefore be conveyed more accurately if we were to narrow its definition even further by a criterion of affective intensity. We might restrict the province of conscience to those areas of conduct where social experience has attached substantial affective value to the child's cognitive representation and evaluation of its own behavior" (Aronfreed, 1968, pp. 5–6). Examples cited by Aronfreed of conduct distinct from conscience, because they do not have as much affective intensity associated with them, include those applicable to taste, physical skill, and etiquette.

In a contemporary formulation that has affinities with earlier positions on conscience and that includes elements of other socioemotional perspectives, Kochanska (1993, 1994) has examined conscience as regulation due to internalization marking successful socialization as "the gradual developmental shift from external to internal regulation that results in the child's ability to conform to societal standards of conduct and to restrain antisocial or destructive impulses, even in the absence of surveillance" (1993, pp. 325–326). Moreover, the formation of conscience is functional from the societal perspective: "Without reliance on internalized consciences, societies would have to instill ever-present surveillance in all aspects of social life" (Kochanska, 1994, p. 20). This position includes a shift in balance away from natural moral propensities of concerns with the welfare of others back to more of an emphasis on the need to control antisocial and destructive tendencies. Ultimately, it is society that has to control the behavior of individuals, either by instilling control internally in children or through continual and all-encompassing ("in all aspects of social life") external control.

In keeping with the traditional conception of conscience, it was proposed that it is encompassed by "affective discomfort" or the various negative emotional reactions to acts of transgression, and "behavioral control." Reactions of sympathy and empathy are also considered to contribute to the process of development, but through the anxiety and distress they can arouse in the child. Nevertheless, the focus is on anxiety, fear arousal, and discomfort in the process of internalizing moral prohibitions. A significant aspect of this process is that parental socialization contributes greatly through arousal of children's anxiety (using punishment or power assertion, threats to connections to parents or love-withdrawal, threats to the child's self-concept, etc.). Moreover, the particular manifestations of the emergence of conscience entail an interaction between parental socialization, other experiences, and the temperament of the child.

With regard to temperament and individual differences, Kochanska's position has affinities with that of Wilson

(indeed, she notes that psychopathy in adults has underpinnings of temperament and physiology). Anxiety, fearfulness, and arousal (e.g., as found for shy children) underlie the affective component of conscience, and impulsivity and inhibition are related to behavioral control. Specifically, impulsive children are more likely to transgress and find it more difficult to internalize conscience than nonimpulsive children. In turn, parents' methods of socialization may work differently for children with different temperaments. The practice of induction (which involves explanations and reasoning) may be less effective with impulsive than nonimpulsive children. Some support for these hypotheses comes from research (Kochanska, 1991) with 8- to 10-year-old children whose vulnerability to anxiety had been assessed when they were 1½ to 3½ years old. Assessments were also made of parental practices (self-reports and laboratory observations). It was found that parental practices deemphasizing power, displaying warmth, and providing explanations were related to conscience (i.e., measures of external or internal moral orientation) primarily for children who are vulnerable to anxiety and who are nonimpulsive.

However, a longitudinal study (Dunn et al., 1995) showed, in contrast, that shy children (inhibited, nonimpulsive, anxious) scored lower on the same measures of moral orientation than children who were not shy. Furthermore, although some positive correlations were obtained between non-power-assertive parental practices and moral orientation, other factors associated with moral orientation included the quality of the child's relationships with older siblings (children who had had friendlier, more positive relationships with siblings showed higher moral orientation scores) and the child's earlier level of understanding of emotions (children who had shown better emotional understandings at earlier ages scored higher on moral orientation at first grade). Dunn et al. also found differences among the stories used in the assessments. At kindergarten and first grade, the children gave more empathic responses to a physical harm story than to a story dealing with cheating in a game. Correspondingly, guilt responses (i.e., reparative endings in the story completions) were given by more children to the physical harm story than to the cheating story.

Beyond Family and Beyond Incorporation of Societal Standards

The Dunn et al. (1995) findings suggest that influences on moral development extend beyond the practices of parents in disciplining children, and that a child's reactions to transgressions are not uniform. Additional research indicates that young children's development may proceed in several directions with regard to relationships with parents and in their orientations to morality. It has been found that along with an increased awareness of standards, at the age of 2 or 3 years, young children also display increased teasing of their mothers, more physical aggression and destruction of objects, and greater interest in what is socially prohibited (Dunn, 1987). It appears that along with greater sympathy and empathy for others, with increasing age children also begin to understand how to manipulate situations and upset others. This increasing complexity of young children's social relationships is also evident in their abilities, by 18 to 36 months, to engage in arguments and counter-arguments in disputes with mothers (Dunn & Munn, 1987). By 36 months, children also provide justifications for their positions in disputes with mothers and siblings (see also Kuczynski, Kochanska, Radke-Yarrow, & Girnius-Brown, 1987). Disputes occurred over issues such as rights and needs of persons, conventions (manners, etiquette), and destruction or aggression. Children's emotional reactions also varied by the different kinds of disputes; distress and anger were associated with disputes affecting children's rights and interests. These differentiations and extensions of the influences of social relationships are consistent with a reconceptualization of moral internalization presented by Grusec and Goodnow (1994).

Grusec and Goodnow maintained that the common view of internalization as the process by which children take over the values of society has significant limitations and is not consistent with existing data. A more complete understanding of the process requires that additional factors be taken into account, including the nature of the act (the misdeed or transgression), characteristics of the parent, the child's perspective on the position of the parents, and the child's perceptions of the misdeed. Furthermore, they argue that it is necessary to consider the child's ability to "move beyond the parent's specific position to one of his or her own, a consideration that points to successful socialization as more than an unquestioning adoption of another's position" (Grusec & Goodnow, 1994, p. 4).

There is evidence, some of which is reviewed by Grusec and Goodnow, that the effectiveness of particular parental practices are not uniform and that parents do not consistently use one type of discipline. Mothers use different reasons for different kinds of transgressions. Smetana (1989b) found that mothers of toddlers used explanations of needs

and rights for acts entailing harm to others, whereas they used explanations pertaining to social order and conformity for violations of social conventions. It also appears that mothers vary their methods in accord with the types of standard violated. Working with families of children from 6 to 10 years of age, Chilamkurti and Milner (1993) found that mothers report using reasons or explanations mainly for moral transgressions and forceful verbal commands for conventional transgressions. Furthermore, parents use a combination of power assertion and reasoning in reaction to acts like lying and stealing, whereas reasoning is used in reaction to a child's failure to show concern for others (Grusec & Goodnow, 1994).

Other findings in accord with these propositions stem from studies of children's evaluations of parental discipline, as well as of correspondences between the judgments of children and adults. A study by Catron and Masters (1993) showed that 10- to 12-year-old children and mothers endorsed corporal punishment (spanking) for prudential (i.e., acts harmful to the self, such as opening a bottle of poison) and moral transgressions to a greater extent than for transgressions of social conventions. These findings indicate both that mothers make discriminations in the ways discipline should be used with their children, and that by at least 10 years of age children make similar judgments about that type of discipline. Research by Saltzstein, Weiner, and Munk (1995) on judgments about moral intentionality and consequences has shown that children evaluate the fairness of mothers' (in hypothetical situations) approval or disapproval of actions in accord with their own judgments regarding those actions. For example, children regard a mother who disapproves of a well-intentioned act resulting in a negative outcome as more unfair than a mother who approves it. Moreover, children whose own judgments were based on the actor's intentions made greater distinctions in evaluations of mothers' approval or disapproval than children whose judgments were based on the consequences of the act.

It has also been found that children's own judgments about intentions and consequences are not concordant with the judgments they attribute to adults (Saltzstein et al., 1987). For acts with positive intentions and negative outcomes, children (incorrectly) believe adults' judgments of wrongness would be harsher than their own; whereas the children judge by intentions, they believe that adults' judgments are mainly based on disobedience or rule violations.

These findings support Grusec and Goodnow's contention that it is necessary to account for the child's perspective and, thereby, view the process of discipline as interactive. In particular, they maintain that because children's judgments differ for different types of misdeeds (e.g., moral as opposed to conventional transgressions; Turiel, 1983a), they will evaluate and judge the appropriateness of the reasons given by parents, or others, when disciplining the child (as shown in research by Killen, 1991 and Nucci, 1984). It has been found that children are more responsive to adults' directives when the adults use reasons that correspond to the ways children classify moral actions. For example, when teachers simply point to rule violations in discussing acts like stealing or hitting, children are less responsive than when teachers underscore the welfare of others or fairness (Killen, 1991; Nucci, 1984). It has also been found that children are more likely to share with others when given reasons based on empathy and concern for others than when given reasons based on adherence to norms (Eisenberg-Berg & Geisheker, 1979).

Several other features of communications from parents to children may bear on the effectiveness of discipline. These include verifiability of its truth value, the level of generality of reprimands, whether they are tangential or directly relevant to the misdeed, and whether statements are direct or indirect. Distinctions need to be made in discipline activities to understand how they are interpreted and how they might lead to changes in children's behaviors. Along those lines, it is proposed that characteristics of the parents and children would also make a difference in the ways discipline is interpreted and felt (also see Chilamkurti & Milner's, 1993, distinction between mothers at high and low risk for physical abuse).

Grusec and Goodnow present an extensive model regarding the effectiveness of discipline and internalization (also see Bugental and Goodnow's chapter in this Volume). Unlike the traditional views of conscience or internalization, their model includes the possibility that internalization is not necessarily the sole desired goal of parents nor the only positive outcome from the societal or individual perspectives. Parents may strive for flexibility and initiative on the part of the child, rather than simply adoption of parental standards. They may also be motivated by the goal that children acquire negotiation and thinking skills. As put by Grusec and Goodnow (1994):

> Researchers need to consider other outcomes than internalization in their investigations, including the encouragement of new values and ways of behaving that may differ to an extent from parental values and ways of behaving, the maintenance of a child's self-esteem, and the parent's ability to tolerate noncompliance when it serves a positive goal. (p. 17)

GENDER, EMOTIONS, AND MORAL JUDGMENTS

The major issues considered thus far—emotion, socialization, and interaction—also have received scrutiny in theory and research on gender differences in moral development. The question of gender differences has been posed regarding many aspects of development (Maccoby & Jaklin, 1974), but it has been of particular controversy in the moral realm because in the early part of the century it was asserted, by Freud most notably, that the morality of females is less developed than that of males, and then in the latter part of the century that the morality of females is qualitatively different from that of males (Gilligan, 1977, 1982; Gilligan & Wiggins, 1987). Gilligan and her colleagues have maintained that two moral injunctions define two sequences of moral development—the injunction not to treat others unfairly (justice) and the injunction to not turn away from someone in need (care). Gilligan (1982) argued that a morality of care, mainly linked to females, had been overlooked in favor of analyses of justice because it was mainly males who had formulated explanations of moral development. These assertions, however, have generated a great deal of controversy among students of moral development, as well as in other social scientific disciplines (Abu-Lughod, 1991; Okin, 1989; Stack, 1990), within feminist scholarship (Faludi, 1991), and in journalistic accounts (Pollitt, 1992).

In a way, Gilligan accepts Freud's (1925/1959) contention that women "show less sense of justice than men." She does not accept Freud's more general contention that women show less of a moral sense than men since women show more of a sense of the alternative form, that of care. A morality of justice fails to account for the morality characterizing women's orientations because it focuses on rules, rights, and autonomy. According to Gilligan (1982), justice links development to the logic of equality and reciprocity, which contrasts with "the logic underlying an ethic of care [which] is a psychological logic of relationships" (p. 73). The morality of care is one of fulfillment of responsibility and avoidance of exploitation and hurt. The morality of care is linked to concepts of self as attached to social networks, whereas the morality of justice is linked to concepts of self as autonomous and detached from social networks. The female self-definition is closely linked to social interactions and attachments, whereas the male self-definition is based on the separateness inherent in abstract reflections about others (Gilligan, 1986).

It would appear then that the formulation of a morality of care has important affinities with those who emphasize emotions. Care entails avoidance of harm and concerns for the welfare of others (sympathy and empathy) and is applied mainly to those in close relationships. Although empathy and sympathy are relevant, this formulation differs in several respects from other perspectives emphasizing emotions. First, the central emotions for morality are defined differently from empathy, sympathy, shame, and guilt, and are associated with a different set of experiences and mechanisms for the development of morality. Second, more emphasis is given to judgments in the moralities of care and justice. And third, there is a sequence of development for the morality of care progressing toward increasing inclusiveness of moral judgments.

It is not particular emotions, like sympathy or empathy, that constitute the origins of the moralities of care and justice. Instead, very young children's relationships constitute the groundwork for the types of morality formed by individuals. Two dimensions of relationships are proposed as mechanisms for development at early ages, establishing long-term moral orientations. One is the experience of attachment, which produces an awareness that one can affect others and be affected by them, and which results in discoveries of the ways people care for and hurt one another. Relying on neo-psychoanalytic accounts of identity formation (Chodorow, 1978), it was proposed that since young children are for the most part cared for by women, there is a basic difference in the social experiences of boys and girls which results, by an early age (3 or 4 years), in differences in their personality and identity. For girls, identity formation occurs in the context of a relationship with another female, the mother, which maintains continuity and in which mothers and daughters see themselves as alike. Most importantly, in forming her identity as a female, the young girl maintains an attachment with her mother and, thereby, development progresses toward creating and sustaining relationships. Thus, the emotions associated with attachment and care are "cofeelings" that depend on: "the ability to *participate* in another's feelings, signifying an attitude of engagement rather than an attitude of judgment or observation. To feel with another any emotion means in essence to be *with* that person, rather than to stand apart

and look *at* the other, feeling sympathy *for* her or him" (Gilligan & Wiggins, 1987, p. 289).

For young boys, identity formation occurs in the context of a sense of difference (in both mother and son), and in the process of forming a masculine identity there is separation from the mother and individuation. The consequence is an orientation to differentiations from others and independence on the part of boys. A second related dimension is the inequality that stems from the child's awareness of being smaller, less powerful, and less competent than older children and adults (Gilligan & Wiggins, 1987). For girls, the experience of inequality is not as overwhelming as for boys because girls identify with the object of their attachment (mother). Because boys identify with their fathers without a strong attachment with him, they relate more to the father's authority and power. Inequality and authority are therefore salient for boys, resulting in strivings for equality (part of fairness) and regulation as moral ends.

Although emotions are not excluded, Gilligan regards the care and justice orientations as systems of moral judgments. In fact, she considers the conception of justice and fairness as one of the two major types of morality and, at least implicitly, accepts the validity of the stages of moral judgment formulated by Kohlberg (1969). However, those stages capture only one moral orientation, particularly the moral development of males. According to Gilligan (1977, 1982), the morality of care, too, proceeds through a sequence of transformations culminating in a level of thinking based on universal principles encompassing self and others, with an understanding that self and other are interdependent, that violence is destructive, and that care benefits others and self. That level of moral judgment is preceded by two less advanced levels, and associated transitions, reflecting a conflict between self and other that constitutes the central moral problem for women. At the first level, there is a focus on caring for the self as a means of survival. This leads to a second level, in which concepts of responsibility focus on care for dependent persons.

The sequence of women's conceptions of the morality of care was derived from interview studies. The main study entailed interviews of 29 pregnant women (ages 15–33 years) about their decision to have or not to have an abortion (they were referred by counseling services and abortion clinics). Follow-up interviews were conducted with 21 of the women a year after they had made their choices. A necessary feature of this study, according to Gilligan (1982), is that the interviews were about situations faced in the women's own lives. This is because women's moral judgments are tied more closely to contexts than men's. Interviews about hypothetical situations, in her view, are likely to provide misleading information since women attempt to reframe hypothetical situations into real, contextualized ones. Moreover, it was presumed that interviews about hypothetical situations are more likely to elicit justice concerns than would interviews about real-life situations.

According to Gilligan (1982, 1986), studying women's judgments also serves to correct biases in influential theories of moral development put forth by males who largely overlooked females or who, when they addressed the issue, superficially relegated females' morality of care to a "lesser" form. Freud, for example, included women in his observations and case studies, but misinterpreted their care orientation simply as a concern with approval. Gilligan also contends that others such as Piaget and Kohlberg, constructed their theories through research with samples of males and then studied females from the inappropriate perspective of male-based theories.

In considering Piaget's ideas, Gilligan imposes certainty where some ambiguity exists. It is true that Piaget maintained that girls are less interested than boys with "legal elaboration" and that "the legal sense is far less developed in little girls than in boys" (Piaget, 1932, pp. 69, 75 and quoted in Gilligan, 1977 and Gilligan & Wiggins, 1987). As noted earlier, however, in Piaget's view, the developmentally advanced level of autonomous morality was organized by concerns with mutuality, reciprocity, and cooperation. A strict legal sense for fixed rules that left little room for innovation and tolerance was seen by Piaget as part of the less advanced form of heteronomous morality. Thus, it is not at all clear that Piaget regarded girls to be less advanced than boys since he thought that girls were orientated to tolerance, innovation with rules, and cooperation. It should also be mentioned that aside from his studies of children's practices with game rules, it cannot be said that Piaget's research was conducted with males and not females. Piaget supported his interpretations with many interview excerpts (he did not report statistical analyses) that include both boys and girls.

In contrast, Kohlberg's (1963) original formulation of stages of the development of moral judgments was based on interviews with males only. The first studies assessing Kohlberg's stages that included females showed college-age and adult women scoring at Stage 3 (entailing judgments of morality focused on interpersonal considerations) more than men, and men scoring at higher stages (mainly

Stage 4, which entails judgments of morality focused on maintenance of rules, authority, and social order) more than women (Kohlberg & Kramer, 1969). Briefly speculating on these results, Kohlberg and Kramer (1969) suggested that Stage 3 moral thinking may be functional for the roles of housewives and mothers. The generalizability of this finding was accepted by Gilligan, but she was critical of the idea that Stage 3 was functional for the roles of housewives or mothers, and proposed that instead women's reasoning proceeds through the sequence of the morality of care.

However, the conclusion that women score lower on Kohlberg's stages (as drawn by Kohlberg and Kramer and reaffirmed by Gilligan) has not been supported empirically. Walker (1984, 1991) has presented extensive reviews (including a meta-analysis) of 80 studies which included assessments of males and females on Kohlberg's stages. Those analyses reveal little in the way of sex differences on this dimension. In most studies (86% of the samples), no differences were obtained. In some samples (9%), males scored higher than females, but in other samples (6%), it was the reverse. Walker also found that when researchers controlled for educational and occupational levels, no sex differences were observed. Several studies also compared males and females on another relevant dimension in Kohlberg's assessment, which entails coding for what is referred to as moral orientations (Colby & Kohlberg, 1987; Kohlberg, 1976). Since the orientations include fairness (a focus on justice and equality) and "perfectionism" (harmony with self and others), it might be expected that they would divide by gender. A number of studies, with children and adults, using hypothetical and real-life situations yielded varying results with no clear patterns of gender differences (Pratt, Golding, & Hunter, 1984; Pratt, Golding, Hunter, & Sampson, 1988; Walker, 1986, 1989; Walker, Pitts, Hennig, & Matsuba, 1995).

Furthermore, it is not generally accepted that Kohlberg's concept of morality at the most advanced stages actually fails to account for judgments about interdependence and concerns with welfare (Gilligan construed Kohlberg's formulation as focusing on rights, rules, and separation). It has been argued that embedded in Kohlberg's formulations of justice and fairness are considerations of respect for others and ways of maintaining social relationships that are non-exploitive, nonharmful, and that promote the welfare of persons (see Boyd, 1983; Broughton, 1983; Habermas, 1990a; Kohlberg, Levine, & Hewer, 1983; Nunner-Winkler, 1984; Walker, 1991).

Care and Justice as Moral Orientations

Regardless of Gilligan's claims about the methods and findings of other theorists, some of the propositions can stand on their own right, and be evaluated accordingly (Haste & Baddeley, 1991). Those propositions have received a good deal of attention and have had an impact on research on moral development, with some providing positive evaluations (Baumrind, 1986; Haste, 1993; Haste & Baddeley, 1991; Hoffman, 1991a; Miller & Bersoff, 1995; Shweder & Haidt, 1993). Those propositions, however, have also been subjected to a good deal of scrutiny because of perceived inadequacies in sampling, procedures, research designs, and data analyses (see Colby & Damon, 1983; Greeno & Maccoby, 1986; Luria, 1986; Mednick, 1989). The construct of a morality of care, itself, was not based on extensive research. Instead, it was based, first, on a combination of (a) the argument that a conception of morality as justice did not adequately characterize the moral judgments of females since they were usually assessed in stages lower than males (a conclusion that, as already discussed, does not hold), and (b) subjectively analyzed excerpts from a limited number of boys and girls responding to moral dilemmas in Kohlberg's interview (see Gilligan, 1982, Chapter 2).

The construct of a morality of care was also based on the studies of women discussing abortion, as well as of interview studies of college students. Those studies, however, were limited in that the samples were small, restricted to pregnant women discussing one particular contested issue (abortion), and to students in elite universities. Perhaps most importantly, the analyses of interview responses were neither based on systematic coding schemes nor analyzed statistically in any extensive ways (see Colby & Damon, 1983; Greeno & Maccoby, 1986; and Luria, 1986 for details on these shortcomings). Furthermore, the propositions regarding the origins of moral concepts in early relationships entailing inequalities, detachments, and attachments have not been subjected to empirical study.

In later research, however, a more circumscribed approach was taken, with a focus on defining the proposed orientations of care and justice, and on coding (Lyons, 1983) the extent to which males and females use one or the other, or combine the two. Studies assessing the distribution of care and justice orientations included male and female adolescents and adults responding to questions about moral conflicts in their lives (for a summary, see Gilligan & Attanucci, 1988). Varying results were obtained. Lyons

(1983), for example, found that the majority of females (75%) judged by a care orientation whereas the majority of males (79%) judged by a rights orientation. Other studies, with more refined analyses, indicated that only a minority of people exclusively use either the care or justice orientation, and that most use both in one fashion or another (Gilligan & Attanucci, 1988). Those studies also suggested that the justice orientation was used more frequently than care, but with a tendency for females to use care more than males and males to use justice more than females. Haste and Baddeley (1991) reported findings indicating that whereas both sexes have access to each orientation, females appear to more easily shift orientations than males.

These types of studies (see Gilligan, Ward, Taylor, & Bardige, 1988 for reports of additional research) have provided some evidence for the contention that there is a tendency for the care and justice orientations to be associated with gender. However, the patterns are not clear-cut because studies also show shifts by context (Johnston, 1988). Perhaps because of the combinations of care and justice found in the reasoning of males and females, Gilligan and her colleagues appear, in later writings, to be inconsistent or ambiguous about sex differences, asserting that care and justice are concerns that can be part of the thinking of males or females, with "a tendency for these problems to be differently organized in male and female development" (Gilligan & Wiggins, 1987, p. 281). This contrasts with the idea that the differences are based on deep features of early interactions, resulting in deep differences in moral judgments (Gilligan, 1982).

Moral Judgments, Orientations, and Social Contexts

The ambiguities in the interpretations of gender differences may very well stem from contextual variations in individuals' judgments. Issues of context are considered in propositions regarding justice and care, but in a limited way. In the first place, a broad contextual distinction was drawn through the proposition that the life circumstances of girls and women usually differ from those of boys and men. Especially for females, judgments in the context of a hypothetical situation may differ from judgments in the context of real-life situations (Gilligan, 1982). The inclination to be distant from hypothetical situations may be related to another proposed feature of the psychology of those with a care orientation—that they are more attuned to contextual features than those with a justice orientation.

Those with a justice orientation are more likely to abstract from a situation (i.e., decontextualize it) in ways that generate judgments of likeness with other situations.

However, since those formulations essentially propose group differences in the ways people approach morality, a more fundamental issue regarding social contexts is unaddressed: People may apply their moral judgments in sufficiently flexible ways to take features of situations into account in coming to decisions. In that case, moral judgments would not be of one type for females or males. Females and males may hold both concepts of justice and concepts regarding the network of social relationships. Individuals may be oriented both to autonomy or independence and to interdependence and social harmony. How individuals apply these different judgments might depend on the situation. Because of the different roles and status in social networks and hierarchies of women and men, it may also be that they would apply justice and care considerations differently. In some situations, men may even apply considerations regarding social networks and interdependence more than women (e.g., situations in which men wish to maintain the existing network of unequal relationships and role obligations), whereas in some situations women may apply justice considerations more than men (e.g., situations in which women are more sensitive to the injustices of the existing inequalities, networks of role obligations, and interdependence; see Wainryb & Turiel, 1994). In Gilligan's formulation, different moral and personal orientations are treated as general characteristics of individuals, often reflecting individual differences between females and males rather than as coexisting judgments whose application intersects with contextual features.

These multifaceted concerns are not unrelated to the types of childhood experiences proposed to be sources of the different orientations. It was proposed that attachments and detachments are the central social experiences for girls, while inequalities and power are central for boys (Gilligan & Wiggins, 1987). This is surely a one-sided characterization. In certain respects, issues of equalities and inequalities, as well as power relationships are at least as salient for girls as for boys. Perhaps starting within the family (Okin, 1989), and then in school (Ornstein, 1994) and the wider society, girls confront unequal treatment in more poignant ways than boys. Women, too, experience inequalities and unjust treatment in ways that permeate their family and work experiences (Hochschild, 1989; Okin, 1989). Conversely, issues of attachment and detachment may be salient in the experiences of boys in ways that go beyond learning separation and individuation. For boys, the prominence of groups, cliques, team sports, and gangs are evidence of the pull for cooperation, attachments, and solidarity pervasive in their experiences. This is not to say that researchers should simply reverse the ways the proposed moral orientations have been linked to gender, but that concerns with justice, fairness, individuation, care, solidarity, and interdependence are all important coexisting aspects of children's social experiences and developing judgments. As will be discussed, issues regarding contexts and heterogeneity of moral, social, and personal orientations go beyond questions of gender differences, and are especially relevant to analyses of culture and moral development.

A number of studies on how care and justice orientations are used in different hypothetical and real-life situations show that situational contexts affect whether a justice or care orientation is used. A study by Rothbart, Hanley, and Albert (1986) included two hypothetical dilemmas (one from Kohlberg's interview and the other dealing with physical intimacy), as well as situations bearing on real-life conflicts generated by the respondents. It was found that more reasoning about rights was used in Kohlberg's hypothetical dilemma (one in which a husband is faced with deciding whether to steal a drug to save his dying wife) than in the real-life situations, but that the real-life situations produced more reasoning about rights than the hypothetical situation pertaining to physical intimacy.

Therefore, the substance of the situations (e.g., physical intimacy or saving a life), and not only whether they are hypothetical or real-life, has a bearing on people's judgments. Other studies (Walker, 1991; Walker, deVries, & Trevethan, 1987) have shown that only a minority of individuals make consistent judgments across the hypothetical and real-life situations, and that about 50% of them showed consistency among the real-life situations. Whereas no sex differences were obtained in children's or adolescents' use of the care orientations on the real-life situations, adult women showed more use of care than men (60% vs. 37%). In addition, the real-life conflicts were divided as to whether they involved a specific person or group with whom the subject had or did not have a relationship (labeled personal and impersonal, respectively). Both female and male adults used the care orientation more on the personal than the impersonal conflicts. Whereas this shows that type of conflict can predict moral orientation better than gender (Walker, 1991), overall the adult women showed more care responses than men. This means that women generated more personal conflicts than men.

Therefore, type of orientation is related to the content of the situation (reflecting contextual variations), but women are more likely than men to use the care orientation if, in fact, they are more likely to perceive moral conflicts as personal rather than impersonal. These findings are generally consistent with findings from studies by Pratt and his colleagues (Pratt, Diessner, Hunsberger, Pancer, & Savoy, 1991; Pratt, Golding, Hunter, & Sampson, 1988).

Other studies assessing judgments about hypothetical situations pertaining to interpersonal relationships and fairness directly examined contextual variations (Smetana, Killen, & Turiel, 1991). In this research, measures were developed specifically so as to explore the proposition that individuals make judgments both about justice and maintaining obligations in interpersonal relationships. In one study, boys and girls alike gave priority to avoiding unfair acts (e.g., failing to share over helping to further a close friend's personal interests). In addition, in the context of closer relationships (e.g., sibling or close friend vs. acquaintance) there was a greater tendency on the part of girls and boys to give priority to obligations in interpersonal relationships over fairness. In turn, contexts in which the unfairness was more pronounced resulted in a lesser tendency to give priority to interpersonal relationships. In a second study (also reported in Smetana, Killen, et al., 1991) more positive and compelling interpersonal obligations than those used in the first study were given greater weight by children. They were presented with conflicts in which an interpersonal act that would benefit a close friend or sibling would also entail unfairness or a violation of rights toward an acquaintance or stranger (e.g., helping a sister from being teased through an act that is unfair to another child). In this study, as well, judgments differed by the same situational contexts as in the first study (i.e., closeness and degree of injustice).

The findings of these studies, therefore, indicate that concerns with fairness and with the maintenance of interpersonal relationships do not represent individual differences in moral orientations. Furthermore, numerous studies on the development of moral judgments, considered in subsequent sections, have included females and males in the initial investigations (theory building). Little in the way of sex difference has been obtained in all that research. Some studies are worth noting at this juncture because of their focus on judgments about positive actions toward others. Using stories that pose conflicts between close friendship considerations, personal interests, and the interests of nonclose friendships, Keller and Edelstein (1990, 1993)

longitudinally studied the interpersonal concepts of children and adolescents (7–15 years). They have outlined a sequence of development demonstrating progressive changes toward understandings of the perspectives of self and others and the coordination of those perspectives. In late childhood and early adolescence, girls and boys begin to form understandings of stable reciprocal relationships among friends (see also Selman, 1980). Along with understandings of friendship relationships, there are age-related shifts, but no gender differences, in moral commitments based on obligations, intimacy, and mutuality in relationships. In addition to the finding that there were no differences in the moral judgments of females and males, Keller and Edelstein (1990, p. 280) concluded that in contrast to the proposition "that persons can be classified in terms of the basically different moral orientations of justice and care, the developmental progression of arguments about the friendship dilemma rather emphasizes the interconnection of both."

A similar proposition was put forth by Kahn (1992) on the basis of his findings on children's judgments about positive moral actions (i.e., whether to give money for food to hungry persons). The children in Kahn's study applied discretionary judgments to the positive actions, evaluating them as morally praiseworthy but not obligatory or necessitating legal regulation. Females were no more likely to judge that people should give to, or care for, hungry persons. Moreover, the reasons for these evaluations were mainly consideration of the welfare of others and issues of justice. Whereas younger children emphasized welfare, older girls and boys embedded welfare into concepts of justice.

Also relevant are some intriguing observations in studies of adults demonstrating a lifelong commitment to helping others and contributing to social causes (Colby & Damon, 1992). These "caring" persons often voiced a strong commitment to justice and preventing harm that went far beyond those close to them and resulted in sacrificing their own families, including their children (see Chapters 2, 3, and 8). The major commitment on the part of these individuals was to humanity, not to kin or the ingroup, on the belief that justice and the welfare of people posed objectives to be met without exception, in impartial ways. These commitments were met even if they conflicted with the views of others in the community. Hart also has provided research on the self-understandings of inner-city adolescents identified as showing exceptional commitment and caring (Hart & Fegley, 1995; Hart, Yates, Fegley, & Wilson, 1995).

Politics, Economics, Social Structure, and Women's Perspectives

The proposition that care and justice tend to be organized differently in males and females as a consequence of differences in childhood relationships, carries a host of issues and problems, including scientific verification, stereotyping of moral orientations, and the role of politics, economics, and social structure in possible inequalities and power relationships between men and women. Issues pertaining to scientific verification are raised by the assertion that male psychologists have imposed male-oriented formulations of moral development that overlook a major strand of development associated with females. This assertion implies that evaluating the validity of scientific knowledge is extremely hazardous because explanatory concepts and methods of theory-building or verification are colored by the particular perspective of the investigator.

The idea that general features of an investigator's perspective leads to bias is not restricted to the biases that may stem from the gender of the investigator. It is also often asserted that a particular perspective reflects the cultural biases of persons promulgating it (see Turiel, 1989a for a discussion of the issue). This, however, is a criticism that turns on itself as a vicious cycle. It could be said, for example, that Gilligan's perspective is a consequence of various biases. It could be said that her ideas are colored by her status as a female of a rather advantaged position writing from the perspective of her memberships in a male dominated field and in a highly elitist, well-endowed, and powerful male-dominated educational institution. The myriad ways that such contexts can determine one point of view or another should be evident if too much credence is given to the ways an individual's characteristics and place color scientific or scholarly analyses. The alternative is to evaluate the arguments and the evidence on their own merits.

A related point made by Gilligan, closer to issues of evidence, is that some researchers (e.g., Kohlberg, 1969) used data from males only to build theory. An analogous criticism applies to the data used by Gilligan to build her theory because the initial data used to formulate the care orientation and its sequence of development were drawn from samples of largely white middle-class and upper-middle-class women, most of whom were undergraduates at Harvard and Radcliffe (Pollitt, 1992; Stack, 1990). Gilligan's (1977) focus has been on women's status in society, which is that they are usually in subordinate and vulnerable positions relative to men (see also Okin, 1989, 1996; Turiel,

1996; Wainryb & Turiel, 1994). However, working class and racial minority groups are also in vulnerable positions relative to middle- and upper-class groups. The hierarchical relationships between white middle-class women or men vis-à-vis working class or minority racial groups poses interesting questions that have not been much investigated. One such question bears on the racial and economic injustices experienced by children in those groups, and its effects on their sensitivity to the issues.

This question was addressed in a study by Stack (1990) of the moral thinking of African American adolescents and adults who were return migrants from the north to rural, southern homeplaces in the United States. She interviewed the participants in the study about dilemmas relevant to their lives. One dilemma, constructed with the aid of adolescents, pertained to children living with their grandparents in the South who are asked by their mother to live with her in a northern city. A second dilemma relevant to adults entailed a conflict faced by a single male as to whether to stay in a northern city or, as he is urged to by his sisters, move back South to take care of his ailing parents. In contrast with findings of the Gilligan and Attanucci (1988) study there were no differences between responses of the adolescent girls and boys or between adult females and males, all of whom gave more justice than care responses.

Stack proposed that African American boys and girls are aware, from an early age, of social and economic injustice. Men and women experience a good deal of injustice in the workplace and other settings, and are committed to combating it. Simultaneously, males and females are embedded in extended families, concerning themselves with their own aspirations and the needs of their kin. Stack proposed, then, that concepts of care and responsibility are formed alongside concepts of justice in both young boys and girls. Stack's findings and theoretical analyses suggest that broader life experiences than identifications, attachments, and separations are central to the development of moral concepts.

Another potential methodological problem in Gilligan's (1982) research is that much of the data used to formulate the levels of care reasoning were derived from interviews about abortion, an issue with some unique features that may not generalize to other moral issues. Other research has shown that people are divided as to whether abortion should be classified as a moral issue, and that those divisions are associated with assumptions people make about the fetus as a person or as constituting a life (Smetana, 1982; Turiel, Hildebrandt, & Wainryb, 1991). Whereas those who assume that the fetus is a life with attributes of personhood judge abortion as morally wrong, those who do not hold to that assumption judge abortion as mainly a decision of personal choice. Moreover, many individuals' assumptions about the status of the fetus as a life include ambiguities and uncertainties resulting in conflicting and contradictory judgments about abortion not evident in the same individuals' judgments about welfare, harm, and life in other contexts (Turiel et al., 1991).

Finally, in contrast with the way the issue has sometimes been couched, women have been involved in the construction of theoretical approaches at variance with propositions regarding sex differences. Many women, including those writing from a feminist perspective, have taken issue with the proposition that women's morality is mainly one of care and interdependence (e.g., Abu-Lughod, 1991; Colby & Damon, 1983; Mednick, 1989; Okin, 1989; Pollitt, 1992; Stack, 1990). These critiques have highlighted the stereotypical nature of gender-linked distinctions, the significance of justice and fairness in women's judgments and life circumstances, how men's concepts of nurturance and interdependence serve to maintain those circumstances, and how economics and social structural arrangements bear on the moral judgments of females and males (for an alternative view, see Haste, 1994). Writing from her perspective as a journalist and feminist, Pollitt (1992) has critiqued characterizations of women as nurturing, caring individuals whose concerns are with relationships but not justice, rationality, or logic. Not that Pollitt would exclude nurturing and caring from the purview of women by any means. Rather, it is that women neither have a monopoly on caring, nor are they solely caring nurturers of others. Women are caring, cooperative, competitive, assertive of independence, and committed to rights and justice.

The characterization of women as caring and nurturing, according to Pollitt, stereotypes them in traditional and restrictive ways. It is restrictive because it limits real concern with justice, rights, and independence—just as it is restrictive to attribute characteristics of males solely to justice, rights, and autonomy. This stereotyping serves several ends for females and males. The positive end, according to Pollitt, is that it provides women with an equal moral status to men and challenges the division of men as rational and women as irrational. Women are said to develop a type of rationality by which their morality is different and equal to that of men. Despite the greater concern with equality in moral orientations, Pollitt argues that the formulation constitutes a stereotype serving also to reinforce a status quo in which women retain positions subordinate to men. Men encourage the idea that women are concerned with care because men are, in addition to children, the main beneficiaries of women's nurturance. Vis-à-vis themselves, men value an orientation on the part of women to interdependence, relationships, caring, and inequality.

Pollitt also argues that propositions regarding the sources of women's judgments in early identifications (Chodorow, 1978) overlook the important contributions of their roles in the economic and social structure. Along with its positive aspects, caring is a consequence of economic dependence and subordination in the family. The role of caretaker and nurturer is, in part, imposed by a power structure in which men are in positions of influence and economic independence (at least middle-class men). Pollitt's argument, it should be stressed, is not that caring and interdependence are negative and independence is positive. Rather, it is that women, too, can appropriately function independently, claiming rights. In particular, the workplace in capitalist society entails autonomy, concerns with personal advancement, and rights, along with caring and justice. Insofar as women appear less autonomous in the workplace, it is a consequence of discrimination serving ends of men in positions of power and influence.

The justice of distribution of resources, privileges, and burdens within the family, especially as it affects women, has been analyzed in depth by Okin (1989, 1996). She argues that moral philosophers and social scientists have either ignored the justice of gender relationships or accepted the legitimacy of unequal distributions and unjust treatment by relegating women to traditional roles. In that context, she also maintains that justice and rights are spheres relevant to women's thinking, that there is no evidence that women are more inclined to contextuality than universalism, and that the idea that women are oriented to care and not universally applicable concepts of rights and justice reinforces traditional stereotypes. In Okin's (1989) view, the distinction between care and justice has been overdrawn:

> The best theorizing about justice, I argue, has integral to it the notions of care and empathy, of thinking of the interests and well-being of others who may be very different from ourselves. It is, therefore, misleading to draw a dichotomy as though they were two contrasting ethics. The best theorizing about justice is not some abstract "view from nowhere," but results from the carefully attentive consideration of *everyone's* point of view [emphasis in original]. (p. 15)

An implication of Okin's contention is that justice needs to be inclusive. Those emphasizing emotions argue, as noted, that an inclusive or universal conception of morality is a Western one, largely promulgated by intellectuals. In other cultures, and perhaps for ordinary people in Western cultures, morality is applied in a local and parochial fashion. A similar position has been taken by those who emphasize culture in the development of morality.

EMPHASIZING CULTURE

Implicit in the propositions that care and justice are linked to gender because of differences in early childhood experiences is the idea that the orientations of females and males reflect cultural differences. This is an implicit idea made explicit by others. For example, Haste and Baddeley (1991, p. 228) maintain that the propositions put forth by Gilligan and her colleagues entail "treatment of gender as a cultural experience." Haste and Baddeley also maintain that gender differences constitute "quasi-culture" differences because, in this case, the presumed culturally different orientations are available in the wider cultural context. Nevertheless, because males and females in a given society share so many experiences, sometimes intimately, these ideas confront the common view of culture as constituting integrated patterns of social interaction.

The idea of cultures forming integrated cohesive patterns diverging from each other goes back at least to the formulations of cultural anthropologists of the early part of the 20th century (Benedict, 1934, 1946; Mead, 1928). One of the most influential proponents of the idea that cultures form integrated patterns was Ruth Benedict (1934), who proclaimed that "the diversity of cultures can be endlessly documented" (p. 45). Cultural anthropologists of the time also wrote about morality, often taking positions of cultural relativism, in reaction to predominant late 19th-century anthropological assumptions that cultures could be classified in a hierarchy of lower to higher. Usually, Western cultures were placed at the apex of the hierarchy. Cultural anthropologists argued that these hierarchies were simply based on the moral standards and values of one's society as the best or highest, relegating the values of other societies lower in the scale. The classifications of cultures in a hierarchy of progress or development, it was argued, was due to a bias in favor of Western cultural values, as well as to intolerance and lack of respect for the equally valid values of other cultures. Along with

relativism, therefore, it was asserted that cultures should be treated as different and equal, and each accepted as functioning on its own moral standards with moral ends endemic to its system. Some critics of cultural relativism (e.g., Hatch, 1983) have pointed out that the position actually includes nonrelativistic moral prescriptions. In particular, relativists espouse the values of tolerance (that the validity of other cultures' values and perspectives should be accepted), freedom (that a culture should not be obstructed from following its moral standards), and equality (that a culture's moral standards should be regarded as of equal validity as those of any other).

Benedict (1934) sharply characterized the proposed variations among cultures through an example that many would consider to epitomize moral concerns, transcending time and place, and pertaining to justice, rights, empathy, sympathy, and care:

> We might suppose that in the matter of taking life all peoples would agree in condemnation. On the contrary, in a matter of homicide, it may be held that one is blameless if diplomatic relations have been severed between neighboring countries, or that one kills by custom his first two children, or that a husband has right of life and death over his wife, or that it is the duty of the child to kill his parents before they are old. It may be that those are killed who steal a fowl, or who cut their upper teeth first, or who are born on a Wednesday. (p. 46)

In this way, Benedict encompassed several cultural practices commonly used to illustrate variations in moral codes: parricide, infanticide, and family relationships of deep inequalities. Observations of variations in social practices, thus, were used to argue for the incomparability of the moralities of different cultures, and in that sense empirical observations were used for propositions about the nature of morality (i.e., to define it as local and entailing an acquisition of the standards of the culture). The core of these propositions is that variations in social practices stem from differences in the ways cultures are integrated (Benedict, 1934, p. 46): "A culture, like an individual, is a more or less consistent pattern of thought and action."

In contemporary views of human development, the role of culture has once again been emphasized, especially through the "new" discipline of cultural psychology (Bruner, 1990; Shweder, 1990a; Shweder & Sullivan, 1993), and has become increasingly part of research on moral development. As already seen, those emphasizing emotions include cultural influences as a part of moral acquisition, along with the idea that morality is highly influenced by biologically based propensities. Others assert that culture must be given center stage (Markus & Kitayama, 1991; Miller & Bersoff, 1995; Sampson, 1977; Shweder, 1990a; Shweder, Mahapatra, & Miller, 1987; Triandis, 1990). Many of the features of contemporary views of culture and moral development were presaged by an early critique of Kohlberg's theory and research, which included links with the prior formulations of cultural anthropologists (Simpson, 1973).

Simpson asserted that the direction of the stages of moral judgment proposed by Kohlberg reflected his own cultural biases, and that other cultures contain other forms of morality associated with their customs and conceptions of reality. In particular, Western philosophies differ from Eastern philosophies (which "differ far more between themselves than within"), and any effort to provide a "unified, synthetic theory of human moral development would be a difficult task . . . without major assimilation of one general system by another and the destruction of its integrity" (Simpson, 1973, p. 84). In this case, the bias in Kohlberg's theory is said to reflect not that he is a male but that he is a member of a culture with a general system and moral philosophy.

A critique of this sort, based on the idea that an investigator's position is due to a cultural bias, also turns on itself as a vicious cycle (as already noted with regard to bias supposedly due to the gender of the investigator). It could be said that Simpson's propositions (for other examples, see Sampson, 1977 and Shweder, 1982) reflect biases due to her status as an intellectual elite from a Western culture. A consequence of that cultural perspective would be the imposition of Western notions of the relativity of moral orientations, of group variations in moral practices, and of the value of tolerance for the practices of other groups. Indeed, there is some evidence, discussed in the subsequent section, that could be construed to show that people from Western cultures accept the legitimacy of cultural variations in social practices to a greater extent then people from non-Western cultures.

Accusations regarding the bias of the investigator can lead to an impasse. As noted earlier, an alternative is to evaluate the evidence on its own merits. Simpson did claim that Kohlberg made general assertions about the universalizability of moral principles without sufficient empirical evidence on varying cultural practices and varying cultural meanings. However, as she critiqued Kohlberg's formulations for a failure to provide sufficient evidence, Simpson made a set of assertions regarding the cultural sources of morality as if they were self-evident,

also without any substantive support with empirical evidence. This included the propositions that moral concepts, such as justice, have no cross-cultural generality and that socialization or the learning of cultural meanings through social participation is how individual morality is formed. In this regard, the position taken on the learning of the morality of Western culture was ambiguously stated. On the one hand, it was claimed that a general system of Western moral philosophic thought, which differs from Eastern philosophy, is at the basis of the developmental findings of Western researchers. On the other hand, it was said that the judgments of those at the proposed highest stages (Stage 6 in Kohlberg's system) reflect the learning of narrow and unrepresentative ideas of a small group within Western culture. People whose judgments correspond to the highest stage "are not functioning independently of their socialization; they have been very thoroughly socialized into the company of intellectual elites who value and practice analytic, abstract and logical reasoning" (Simpson, 1973, p. 95).

The idea that a minority of intellectuals hold moral views different from most others in a culture poses two problems for the proposition that integrated cultural patterns are the source of morality. One is that it is unclear how integrated or consistent are the cultural patterns since one group, at least, holds moral concepts different in kind from others. The second problem is that it is unclear what constitutes the pattern of morality in Western cultures. One of the key features often said to distinguish Western from Eastern cultures is that the former place an emphasis on abstractions, justice, and the autonomy of individuals (Kagan, 1984; Markus & Kitayama, 1991; Shweder & Bourne, 1982; Triandis, 1990). However, it is usually just those features of moral judgment that are attributed to the *unrepresentative* groups of intellectual educated elites. Shweder (1982), one of the leading proponents of culture as the main source of morality, asserted in his critique that Kohlberg's highest stages (Stages 5 and 6), which include the ideas of "society as a social contract" and the "individual as possessing natural and inalienable rights prior to or outside society" (Shweder, 1982, p. 424) are culture specific. However, Shweder also stated that these ideas are the domain of a small segment of Western culture (p. 425): "If they are advocated at all, and they rarely are, it is among Western educated middle-class adults." Again, the majority of "ordinary" people (i.e., nonintellectuals in Western culture and those in non-Western cultures) hold views that do not revolve around individual autonomy and separateness from society (Shweder, 1982, p. 425): "Moral exegesis seems to stabilize around the not unreasonable ideas that social roles carry with them an obligation to behave in a certain way, that society is not of our own making, and that self and society are somehow intimately linked (Stages 3 and 4)."

At the same time, Shweder's (1986) position is that a variety of systems of rationality exist that are framed by culture. Western cultures have an individualistic orientation (in contrast with the collectivistic orientations of non-Western cultures) focusing on rights and autonomy. Therefore, while asserting that individualism is the central ethos of Western cultures, it is argued that concepts of freedom, contract, and rights (by Shweder, as well as Kagan, Wilson, Simpson, Bennett, and others) are ways of thinking espoused mainly by intellectual elites and not others in the West. Furthermore, whereas these writers often emphasize the role of the elites in Western culture and draw differences in the thinking of elites and laypersons, they seldom do so with non-Western cultures. Insofar as there is mention of elites or leaders in non-Western cultures, it is on the premise that there is consistency in their thinking with that of ordinary people (Shweder, 1986).

Social Communication and Cultural Coherence

Like Benedict, contemporary researchers point to many areas of *moral* diversity that are said to be well documented by anthropologists and historians (Shweder, 1994):

> On the basis of the historical and ethnographic record we know that different people in different times and places have found it quite natural to be spontaneously appalled, outraged, indignant, proud, disgusted, guilty and ashamed by all sorts of things: masturbation, homosexuality, sexual abstinence, polygamy, abortion, circumcision, corporal punishment, capital punishment, Islam, Christianity, Judaism, capitalism, democracy, flag burning, miniskirts, long hair, no hair, alcohol consumption, meat eating, medical inoculations, atheism, idol worship, divorce, widow remarriage, arranged marriage, romantic love marriage, parents and children sleeping in the same bed, parents and children not sleeping in the same bed, women being allowed to work, women not being allowed to work. (p. 26)

The sweep of this statement is breathtaking. Being appalled, outraged, indignant, proud, disgusted, guilty and ashamed are all seen as moral reactions. Most positive and negative reactions are regarded to have a moral component (Shweder, Jensen, & Goldstein, 1995). Moreover, as evident in the long list given of "all sorts of things," many different behaviors can be and have been part of the moral domain. Little is exempt, given that sexuality, hairstyle, clothing style, love, marriage, sleeping patterns, and work are all included. Despite appearances, it would not be correct to say that these researchers endorse moral relativism (although questions can be raised about this) nor that they regard the reactions to social practices (e.g., women being allowed to work, women not being allowed to work) as arbitrary or fortuitous. This is because it is proposed that particular social practices are part of sets of "moral qualities" entailing rights, autonomy, duty, interdependence, and sanctity. In turn, moral qualities are connected to more general patterns that make up cultural communities. Cultures do not simply provide a series of isolated standards, values or codes. Some worlds of moral meaning emphasize rights and justice, others emphasize duties and obligations, each part of general orientations to individualistic (read Western cultures) and collectivistic (read non-Western cultures) conceptions of self, others, and society.

The proposed contrast between individualistic and collectivistic cultural orientations is related to moral conceptions, practices, and appraisals. However, these orientations encompass much more; they are the bases for cultural constructions of how persons are defined, how they interact with each other, how society is defined, and how the goals of persons and the group are established and met (e.g., Geertz, 1984; Markus & Kitayama, 1991; Sampson, 1977; Shweder & Bourne, 1982; Triandis, 1989, 1990). As put by Markus and Kitayama (1991, p. 225): "In many Western cultures there is a faith in the coherent separateness of distinct persons. . . . Achieving the cultural goal of independence requires construing oneself as an individual whose behavior is organized and made meaningful primarily by reference to one's own internal repertoire of thought, feelings, and action." In the contrasting construal of interdependence (Markus & Kitayama, 1991, p. 227) "many non-Western cultures insist . . . on the fundamental connectedness of human beings to each other. A normative imperative of these cultures is to maintain this interdependence among individuals."

In these formulations, the United States is often identified as the quintessential individualistic society (also by Bellah et al., 1985), but individualism is also prevalent in other countries, such as Australia, Canada, England, and New Zealand (Triandis, 1990). Prototypical collectivistic cultures are found in Japan, India, China, and the Middle East, as well as in Africa, Latin America, and southern

Europe (Markus & Kitayama, 1991). The person conceived as an autonomous agent is central in the individualistic frame, whereas the group as an interconnected and interdependent network of relationships is central in the collectivistic frame. In the former, personal goals are primary; in the latter, shared goals are primary. A core feature of individualistic cultures is that the highest value is accorded to the person as *detached* from others and as independent of the social order. People are, therefore, oriented to self-sufficiency, self-reliance, independence, and resistance to social pressure for conformity or obedience to authority. Collectivistic cultures, by contrast, are oriented to tradition, duty, obedience to authority, interdependence, and social harmony. Hierarchy, status, and role distinctions predominate.

A significant component of cultural meanings is the kind of moral orientation communicated to children and reproduced by them as they grow into adulthood. Shweder et al. (1987) proposed a distinction between "rights-based" and "duty-based" moralities in their comparisons between the United States and India. The cultural concept of autonomous individuals organizes the morality of Western culture by separating the social order from the natural order, which entails a definition of the moral as "free contracts, promises, or consent among autonomous individuals" (Shweder et al., 1987, p. 3). Moral authority resides in individuals who voluntarily enter into contracts and promises, with the idea of rights as fundamental (hence a "rights-based" morality). In a contrasting duty-based morality, the social order is the organizing feature of moral rationality. Customary social practices are viewed as part of the natural moral order, so that social practices are seen neither as within individual discretion nor as a function of social consensus (thus the concept of conventionality as agreement in a group is largely absent). The social order dictates specified duties based on roles and status within the social structure, "while the individual per se and his various interior states, preferences, appetites, intentions, or motives are of little interest or concern" (Shweder et al., 1987, pp. 20–21). Moreover, Shweder et al. assert that in a duty-based culture, individuals are not free to deviate from rules and that there is no conception of a natural right, such as free speech, that might lead to advocating deviation from the socially defined right.

Social Practices and Cultural Coherence

Propositions regarding cultural divergence in "moral rationality" have been examined in a study conducted with samples of secular middle- and upper-middle-class children and adults from the United States (Hyde Park in Chicago), and samples of "untouchables" and Brahmans living in the old temple town of Bhubaneswar, Orissa, in India (for research in Brazil, see Haidt, Koller, & Dias, 1993; and in Israel, see Nissan, 1987). Shweder et al. (1987) obtained evaluations and judgments about descriptions of acts that could be regarded as transgressions or "breaches" in one culture or the other. In large measure, the research aimed at ascertaining whether a distinction could be drawn across the two cultures between morality, as based on concepts of justice, rights, and welfare, and conventionality, as based on context-specific uniformities serving goals of social coordination—a distinction that had been addressed by others and is considered further in subsequent sections of this chapter (e.g., Nucci, 1981; Smetana, 1981, 1983; Tisak, 1986; Turiel, 1979, 1983a).

Shweder et al. (1987) hypothesized that a distinction between morality and convention is particular to cultures which structure social relationships through the concept of autonomous individuals free to choose by consensus. Accordingly, they included subjects of consensual choice in Western cultures such as issues about food, dress, terms of address, ritual practices, and sex-role definitions. Whereas some items were straightforward (e.g., a son addressing his father by his first name) others included religious and metaphysical considerations for Indians because of their connections to ideas about an afterlife (e.g., a widow wearing jewelry and bright-colored clothing six months after the death of her husband, a widow eating fish two or three times a week). Also many of the items entailed acts on the part of women that might contradict the power and desires of men (e.g., a woman wanting to eat with her husband and elder brother, a son claiming an inheritance over his sister). Shweder et al. (1987) included items reflecting concepts they consider candidates for moral universals (e.g., a father breaking a promise to his son, cutting in line, refusing to treat an injured person). These dealt with justice, harm, reciprocity, theft, arbitrary assault, and discrimination. Still other issues dealt with family practices that might vary by culture, including those bearing on personal liberty, privacy, and equality (considered central themes for Americans), and sanctity, chastity, and respect for status (considered central themes for Indians).

The assessments were adapted, in modified form, from previous research on morality and convention (Turiel, 1983a), and included rankings of the seriousness of the acts, evaluations as to whether the act is considered wrong, and judgments about the act's alterability (e.g., is it all right to change the practice if most people in a society want to?) and relativity or generalizability (e.g., would it be best if everyone in the world followed the rule, would a different society be a better place if people acted in ways consistent with practices in one's own society?). Shweder et al. (1987) found that Americans and Indians rank the seriousness of breaches in very different ways, such that there are high correlations among Americans and among Indians, with little correlation between Americans and Indians. There was agreement in judgments about some moral issues between Indians and Americans, and a good deal of disagreement on issues pertaining to conventions, liberty, equality, sanctity, chastity, and status. The findings of variations in judgments, aside from the few issues dealing with harm, promises, assault, etc., led Shweder et al. (1987, p. 51) to conclude that "many things viewed as wrong on one side of the Atlantic are not viewed as wrong on the other side."

On the side of India, according to the findings, more things are regarded as wrong than on the side of the United States. In particular, Indians regarded many breaches pertaining to food, dress, terms of address, and sex roles as wrong, as unalterable, and in some cases as universal. That is, some of the breaches were considered unalterable and wrong everywhere and some were considered unalterable but specific to the Indian context. Shweder et al. (1987) maintain that both types of judgment (unalterable and universal; unalterable and context specific) reflect a moral orientation to the practices, and that conventional thinking "is almost a nonexistent form of thought in our Indian data" (1987, p. 52). Although convention was existent in the American data, it was much less prevalent than found in many other studies conducted in the United States.

It was also found that with increasing age Americans judged the issues in more relativistic ways (i.e., judging that the practices are acceptable for other people or in other countries) and were more likely to take situational features into account. By contrast, with increasing age Indians judged the prohibitions as applicable universally and across varying contexts (for similar contrasts in comparisons of Americans and Brazilians, as well as members of lower and higher social classes, see Haidt et al., 1993). On the basis of these findings, Damon (1988, p. 109) has suggested "that moral maturity in some parts of the world implies an ever-expanding tendency to universalize one's moral beliefs, whereas in other parts of the world moral maturity means applying one's beliefs flexibly to an array of changing situations." Since it is Indians, in contrast to Americans, who universalize moral judgments, Damon's

suggestion is in direct opposition to presumptions that moral universality is a post-Enlightenment Western idea (e.g., as asserted Wilson, Kagan, and others).

In addition to differences in judgments between the two cultural groups, on issues related to food, dress, terms of address, and sex roles, Shweder et al. (1987) found that a number of issues were judged as wrong by both Indians and Americans (these are the candidates for moral universals). Agreement occurred on issues pertaining to harm (e.g., hospital workers ignoring an accident victim, destroying another child's picture, kicking a harmless animal), injustice (e.g., cutting in line, discriminating against invalids), breaking promises, and incest. However, not all issues bearing on discrimination or harm were judged as wrong by Indians and Americans. Three issues, in particular, were judged as right by Indians and wrong by Americans. One of these depicted a father who canes his son for a misdeed. Two others pertained to gender relationships. One depicted a husband who beats his wife "black and blue" after she disobeys him by going to a movie alone without his permission. The other one depicted a son who claims most of his deceased father's property, not allowing his sister to obtain much inheritance. As put by Shweder et al. (1987):

> Oriya Brahmans do not view beating an errant wife as an instance of arbitrary assault, and they do not believe it is unfair to choose the son over the daughter in matters of life and inheritance. . . . [They] believe, that beating a wife who goes to the movies without permission is roughly equivalent to corporal punishment for a private in the army who leaves the military base without permission. For Oriyas there are rationally appealing analogical mappings between the family unit and military units (differentiated roles and status obligations in the service of the whole, hierarchical control, drafting and induction, etc.). One thing the family is not, for Oriyas, is a voluntary association among equal individuals. (p. 71)

The overarching principle applied in the analyses of responses to these items is cultural meaning in a moral system. Not considered is that different and varying agendas may be at work in addition to "moral duties." For example, Indians may judge caning a son as right because of their psychological assumptions regarding the effectiveness of physical punishment on learning (see Wainryb, 1991). Also, exerting power and asserting personal choices may account for the acceptability, among Indians, of husbands beating their wives and sons claiming an inheritance over their sisters. In fact, the analogy between the family and military units ignores some possibly important differences. Is it permissible for a private in the army to be "beaten black and blue?" What about an officer who leaves the base without permission? Is he not accountable for his actions, as opposed to a husband in the family situation? In that sense, there may be more accountability and reciprocity between people in different ranks in the military than husband and wife in the family. When a husband beats his wife, is it "in the service of the whole" or in the service of the husband's personal interests?

Nevertheless, the examples and analogy point to some hierarchical social relationships, entailing dominance and subordination. Additional items used by Shweder et al. (1987) illustrate hierarchy in the family. Indians judged that it is wrong for a woman to eat with her husband's elder brother, that it is wrong for a husband to massage the legs of his wife, and that it is wrong for a husband to cook dinner for his wife. Intimacy should not exist among certain family members, such as between a woman and her husband's elder brother. A husband must not give his wife a massage or cook for her because "The wife is the servant of the husband. The servant should do her work" (Shweder, Much, Mahapatra, & Park, 1997, p. 137).

Another area where hierarchical relationships exist in a traditional culture like India is among people of different castes. Shweder et al. (1987) also propose that the morality of Indians includes the idea of "purity," communicating to children that they should avoid sources of impurity and uncleanliness. A source of pollution is contact with people of a lower caste:

> Oriya children learn that "touching" can be dangerous. They learn that "purity," "cleanliness," and status go together. Just as the pure must be protected from the impure, the higher status and the lower status must be kept at a distance. These ideas are effectively conveyed in several ways . . . the culture is providing the child with a practical moral commentary in which one of the many messages is ultimately that menstrual blood, feces, and lower status go together. (pp. 74–75)

Again, these practices are attributed to cultural meanings around duties, without consideration of the possibility that they reflect the creation of distance in social relationships within a culture that is supposed to be collectivistic and to stress interdependence.

Emotional Forms, Cultural Content, and Rapid Processing

The emphasis on the dictates of roles, status, and hierarchy appears to leave little room for the types of moral concerns

with justice, harm and even rights (e.g., that it is wrong to discriminate against invalids) apparent in some of their findings. Recognizing that such judgments are made in that non-Western, "sociocentric" culture (as in their own findings and as in interpretations by Turiel, Killen, & Helwig, 1987), Shweder and his colleagues (1990b; Shweder et al., 1997) appear to have attenuated the proposition regarding the separation of a rights-based morality (individualism) and a duty-based morality (collectivism), and elaborated on it. One elaboration is the proposition that three major types of "ethics" are found the world over: the ethics of autonomy, community, and divinity. Although the inclusion of three ethics broadens the scope of the analyses beyond the dichotomy of rights and duties, it is still presumed that the social order determines the interplay of different types of "goods" within a worldview. Thus, in India, community and divinity are dominant, whereas in the United States autonomy prevails (Shweder et al., 1997). In Indian society, therefore, the ethics of autonomy, based on concepts of justice, harm, and rights, is subordinated to and in the service of the ethics of community, which refers to status, hierarchy, and social order, and the ethics of divinity based on concepts of sin, sanctity, duty, and natural order. In the United States, by contrast, there is a "specialization" in the ethics of autonomy, with community, and divinity in even smaller part, providing a background. Reminiscent of Etzioni's (1993) position, Shweder et al. (1997) are of the opinion that the "expertise" in the ethics of autonomy in the United States has led to a wide extension of the concept of rights (e.g., to children, animals), to the desire to be protected from "every imaginable harm" (e.g., from secondary cigarette smoke, psychologically offensive work environments), and to an enlargement of the idea of harm (to include "all-embracing notions as 'harassment,' 'abuse,' 'exploitation,'" p. 142). Shweder et al. (1997) view these extensions as distortions, just as other distortions may occur through the extensions of concepts of community and divinity in Indian culture.

In India, the ethics of autonomy is linked to the idea of a soul, which obligates respect (souls include human and nonhuman animals). More dominant, however, is the ethic of community, in which a person's identity is associated with status and relationships to others to a much greater extent than individuality. Relationships are part of hierarchical orderings, in which people in subordinate and dominant positions are obligated to protect and look after each other's interests (e.g., wives should be obedient to husbands and husbands should be responsive to the needs and desires of wives). Shweder et al. (1997) regard this as analogous to feudal ethics, where the feudal lord does for others as much as they do for him (an asymmetrical reciprocity because one person is in a position of dominance and control).

Along with the three types of morality, another set of modifications and extensions of the theory is that cultural content is communicated to individuals who are prepared by evolution with deep emotions to receive and rapidly process the content, making decisions intuitively (Shweder, 1994; Shweder & Haidt, 1993). In several respects, this position has affinities with Wilson's (1993) proposals. In the first place, Shweder (1994) accepts the validity of Wilson's four moral sensibilities (sympathy, fairness, duty, and self-control), which he regards as consistent with the formulation of the three types of ethics; autonomy includes sympathy and fairness, community includes duty, and divinity includes self-control. Moreover, emotions are regarded as "the gatekeeper of the moral world," revealing features of social reality. It is proposed that moral emotions are linked to moral intuitions, which together operate rapidly and without a necessity for reflection, deliberation, or argumentation. The combination of emotions (like anger, sympathy, shame, guilt, and disgust) and intuitions yields "self-evident" moral truths.

According to Shweder (1994), however, emotions and intuitions are too deep in the psyche and the possible self-evident truths are too many to be translated into particular social practices. Culture provides constraints on social practices by imposing content and, thereby, brings to the surface the deeper forms of emotions and intuitions. In this way, the natural or innate and the cultural are combined. For example, fairness is a formal principle with self-evident truth value. For the principle to be "activated" and applied, it must be given concrete substance and knowledge by culture. Even though there may be "universal self-evident truths," it "makes sense to speak of the 'Hindu moral sense' or the 'Islamic moral sense' or the 'Western liberal moral sense'" (Shweder, 1994, p. 31).

Justice and Interpersonal Responsibilities

The Hindu moral sense, in Shweder's view, includes treating the family unit like a military unit and acceptance of the legitimacy of a husband beating his wife "black and blue" when she is disobedient. Another aspect of hierarchy, in this moral orientation, is the necessity of members of the higher caste to avoid contact with members of lower castes

(to avoid pollution). Although social hierarchy is portrayed as entailing asymmetrical reciprocity, it also makes for a good deal of distance and separation between the genders and among social classes. Shweder et al.'s (1987) depiction of the family unit as akin to a military unit implies formality and dependence of women (like privates) on men (like commissioned officers). The distance between members of different castes due to the need to avoid pollution makes for very little interdependence and care or concern for the welfare of those of lower castes. These conclusions are not entirely consonant with the more general portrayal of non-Western cultures as oriented to interdependence and social harmony, nor with the findings of another series of studies comparing Americans and Indians on their judgments about helping others, interpersonal obligations, and justice (e.g., Bersoff & Miller, 1993; Miller & Bersoff, 1992, 1995; Miller, Bersoff, & Hardwood, 1990; Miller & Luthar, 1989).

In contrast to Gilligan (1982; also Haste & Baddeley, 1991), Miller and her colleagues proposed that variations in judgments about interpersonal obligations and justice reflect cultural, and not gender, differences. Miller and Bersoff (1995) maintain that Gilligan takes a narrow approach to culture by failing to consider differences in cultural meanings that affect individuals' concepts of self and morality. They believe Gilligan's ideas lead to implausible predictions—that concepts of self and morality would be more similar among individuals of the same gender from different cultures (e.g., a secular American woman vs. a traditional Hindu Indian woman) than individuals of different genders from similar cultures (e.g., a traditional Hindu Indian man vs. a traditional Hindu Indian woman). Miller and Bersoff (1995) further argue that in Gilligan's propositions regarding the influences of early childhood experience there is a failure to consider how they are related to cultural meanings.

In line with the dichotomy between individualism or independence and collectivism or interdependence, Miller and Bersoff (1995) proposed that American women too are influenced by the individualistic views of self in their culture and that Indian men are influenced by the relational or interdependent views of the self in their culture (see also Miller, 1994a). As a consequence, Americans have a "minimalist" view of interpersonal moral obligations that contrasts with the maximalist views of Indians. The thinking of Indians is contextual since self is conceptualized as part of the social order such that duty is not in contradiction with individual desires.

In one of the studies (Miller & Luthar, 1989) comparing Indians and Americans, adults were presented with a set of scenarios depicting transgressions of role-related interpersonal obligations (e.g., a son refusing to care for his elderly parents, a man leaving his wife and children for another woman), and justice (e.g., a college student cheating on a final exam because family responsibilities do not allow time for study, a man leaving the city without paying back a personal loan). It was found that differences in evaluations between Americans and Indians were mainly on the interpersonal transgressions. Both groups evaluated the justice issues as wrong, but Indians were more likely than Americans to evaluate the interpersonal transgressions as wrong. Correspondingly, the justice transgressions were classified by each group mainly in moral terms. There was a greater tendency for Indians to classify the interpersonal transgressions as moral rather than as matters of personal choice and the reverse for Americans. Furthermore, there was some tendency (though not by a majority) for Indians to absolve actors of accountability for the justice transgressions, but not the interpersonal ones. Neither type of transgression was absolved by Americans.

Furthermore, a study by Miller et al. (1990) showed that a large majority of Indians judged as wrong actors who, for selfish reasons, failed to help persons in extreme, moderate, or minor need. This was true for relationships between parent and child, best friends, and strangers. The same judgment was made by the large majority of Americans regarding situations of extreme need and situations of moderate need involving parents and children. With regard to the situations of minor need with parents, and moderate need in relationships of friends and strangers, Americans (especially among the oldest groups) were less likely to see helping as an obligation.

Another extension of these types of analyses entailed assessments of judgments about real-life examples of behaviors among family members in their different roles, which subjects considered exemplary (e.g., an example of something a mother they know well had done which "was a very good thing for a mother to have done"). Indians and Americans alike provided examples based on meeting the significant needs of others as part of interpersonal responsibilities, without a high cost to the actor (e.g., a grown daughter accompanying her mother to the hospital for treatment). Behaviors entailing "selflessness," by which interpersonal responsibilities were fulfilled at personal hardship or risk (e.g., a son going into the family business, giving up his own career ambitions) were mainly provided by Indians. Americans more than Indians gave examples that entailed providing psychological support and affection. Miller and Bersoff (1995) proposed that selflessness is consistent with a duty-oriented culture and that providing psychological support is consistent with a cultural orientation to voluntary, personal decisions in interpersonal relationships. More generally, for Americans, because of their orientation to individualism, interpersonal relationships are not strictly moral obligations. They are either seen as matters of personal choice or as involving a combination of the moral and personal. For Indians, interpersonal relationships are seen as moral obligations that can be given priority over matters of justice or rights.

However, the proposed commitment of Indians to interpersonal obligations is discrepant with the findings of Shweder et al. (1987) showing detachment between castes and among family members. Other aspects of the research conducted by Miller and her colleagues are discrepant with findings obtained by Shweder et al. (1987). In the first place, Miller and her colleagues (Bersoff & Miller, 1993; Miller & Bersoff, 1992) found that Indians do think in terms of social conventions. Both Indians and Americans judged a violation of a dress code (not related to religious obligations) in social conventional and not moral terms, and these judgments differed from judgments about theft (which was judged in moral terms). Other research, by Madden (1992), conducted in the temple town of Bhubaneswar also showed that there was conventional thinking about nonreligious issues, which was distinct from moral thinking.

Additionally, Miller contends that Indians take contextual features into account to a greater extent than Americans. According to Miller, Hindu Indian culture frames a contextual orientation through its emphasis on a self vulnerable to the effects of the environment, and of dharma, which "is considered to be contextually-dependent, with duty relative to one's culture, historical time, life stage, innate dispositions, situational state, and so on" (Miller, 1994a, p. 16). Evidence for this proposition comes from studies of person descriptions and social explanations indicating that Americans tend to explain behaviors with trait attributions, whereas Indians tend to do so with references to context (Miller, 1984, 1986). Evidence also comes from studies indicating that Indians are less likely than Americans to hold individuals accountable for violations of moral codes, attributing the causes of behavior to contextual features (Bersoff & Miller, 1993; Miller & Luthar, 1989). These propositions about the contextual dependence of duty appear to be in opposition to the Shweder et al. (1987) findings that with age Americans become more relativistic and flexible in their moral judgments and that Indians become more universalistic, applying moral injunctions across contexts. Miller's propositions regarding moral accountability also appear to be different from the view of Shweder et al. (1997, p. 152) that karma institutionalizes human tendencies to attribute consequences to personal responsibility. "It is a great irony of Western understanding that karma is often misinterpreted as a description of how Indians excuse themselves from responsibility by describing themselves as passive objects of the force of their past actions." According to Shweder et al., some Indians do use an interpretation of karma to account for failures of responsibility, but other Indians are critical of such thinking.

EMPHASIZING JUDGMENT AND RECIPROCAL SOCIAL INTERACTIONS

In several approaches considered thus far, it is, for the most part, proposed that children acquire morality from the family and/or the culture, and that this occurs very early in life. It is presumed that the necessary components of morality emerge very early in life—infants and very young children show positive social behaviors, react with positive emotions to others, and form attachments with them. This presumption, in turn, is linked to the propositions that much of it is naturally derived (through evolution), that much of it is acquired from parents since most of the child's early social experiences are within the family, and that much of it is reflexive and habitual.

The findings that young children show positive moral emotions and actions toward others indicate that the foundations of morality are established in early childhood, and do not solely entail the control and inhibition of children's tendencies toward gratifying needs or drives or acting on impulses. However, that the foundations of positive morality are established in early childhood does not necessarily establish that significant aspects of development do not occur beyond early childhood, that judgments, deliberations, and reflections are unimportant, or that many experiences, in addition to parental practices, do not contribute. As noted earlier, the theories and research of Piaget and Kohlberg have had much to do with the shift away from conceptualizing morality as entailing self-control over impulses through their demonstrations that children think about the social world, attempt to understand social relationships, form

judgments of right and wrong, and thereby engage in reciprocal interactions with others. However, Piaget and Kohlberg thought that young children's moral judgments are based on extrinsic features, such as basing right and wrong on obedience and sanctions. As will be discussed, it appears that Piaget and Kohlberg failed to uncover not only the positive nature of young children's moral feelings but also that young children form relatively complex judgments that are not based on extrinsic features.

Moral reasoning is a multifaceted process that can entail ambiguities and uncertainties, certainties and unreflective apprehension, as well as deliberation and reflection. Whether moral evaluations and judgments are processed very quickly or slowly, with certainty or given pause, with an apparent lack of self-awareness or with reflection and deliberation, depends on the individual's development, the situation or problem confronted, and the points of view of other people. First, how well a concept is understood has a bearing on the rapidity of a moral evaluation. A well-understood concept that is perceived as readily applicable to a particular situation may well be used in "rapid-fire" fashion and give a false appearance to the outside observer that it is "intuitive" or a habitual practice. The same concept for that individual at an earlier time may have been applied with more uncertainty and less of a sense of being evidently true. That does not mean, however, that a concept, once formed and accepted, will be produced rapidly and without self-awareness in all situations. Ambiguities in a situation, as well as an awareness that others take a different point of view, can produce deliberation, awareness of ambiguities, and argumentation.

These points can be illustrated through research findings on young children's psychological understandings (research on "theory of mind"; see chapter by Flavell and Miller in Volume 2). Many studies have demonstrated that 5-year-old children have an understanding of others' mental states, including beliefs, desires, and intentions. One frequently used method of determining if children have concepts of others' mental states has been to assess their understandings of false belief. Five-year-olds readily understand that another person may hold a "false" belief about, for example, the contents of a crayon box that actually contains candy. For adults, this is rapidly understood and readily applied—and it appears to be so also for 5-year-olds. Yet, processes of development and thought are involved in these understandings since 3-year-olds generally do not answer correctly on tasks assessing false beliefs (or other assessments of understandings of mental states).

The rapidity of the cognitive processing of 5- or 6-year-old children can mask the uncertainties and ambiguities in younger children's judgments, as well as the processes of judgment in the older children. Furthermore, the development of psychological understandings does not stop there. Even adults can face difficulties and ambiguities in understanding the psychological states and behaviors of persons (Ross & Nisbett, 1991).

Research on the moral decisions of people identified by Colby and Damon (1992) as moral exemplars indicated that judgments can include convictions, certainty, *and* openness to new ways of thinking. As put by Colby and Damon (1992):

> We believe that the quality that distinguishes great moral certainty from dogmatism is persistent truth-seeking—an eagerness to learn more about the world combined with a willingness to examine one's ideas when they are challenged. This "open receptivity" to new ideas . . . is an orientation that characterizes the moral exemplars in this study. . . . It is the primary catalyst for the frequent creative transformations in their modes of moral action. (p. 76)

The search for "truth" and openness to change in thinking does not reflect automatic, reflexive, or intuitively evident truths immediately apparent to one. However, the certainty in the thinking of these individuals also leads them to make decisions that much of the time do not require belabored weighing of alternatives.

Studies of moral development, including several of the ones already considered, suggest alternatives to the propositions that emotions are primary in morality, or that moral acquisition is mainly due to effects of parental practices on children, or that morality largely reflects the acquisition of societal standards. Dunn et al. (1995) found differences in the two types of situations they assessed (physical harm and cheating), and also documented that relationships with siblings influence development. By 2 or 3 years of age, moreover, children display a fair amount of teasing of mothers, physical aggression, destruction of objects, and an increasing ability to engage in arguments and disputes with mothers (Dunn, 1987; Dunn & Munn, 1987). This increasing variety in young children's social relationships is consistent with the findings reviewed by Grusec and Goodnow (1994) showing that parental practices are related to type of misdeed (e.g., moral or conventional), that children judge the appropriateness of reasons given by parents when communicating with them, and that parents may encourage ways of behaving that differ from those they engage in themselves.

An interactional perspective on parent-child relationships casts a different light on the types of child-rearing practices studied in research on moral development (Turiel, 1983a, 1983b). In addition to how particular practices shape children's behaviors (the focus of much of the research), it is necessary to consider how these very practices constitute forms of social communication. Among the types of child-rearing practices, the most effective (the so-called induction method) entails explanation of reasons for the required behaviors (Hoffman, 1970; Maccoby & Martin, 1983). That explicit communications of this sort are more effective than practices like physical punishment and love-withdrawal suggests that parents and children engage in reciprocal interactions. Another body of findings on parental practices has shown that "authoritative" forms of parenting are more effective than either "authoritarian" or "permissive" forms (Baumrind, 1973, 1989; Maccoby & Martin, 1983). One of the features distinguishing authoritative parenting from the others is an emphasis on discussion, communication, and explanation. It is also likely that the types of parental practices that do not emphasize communications entail implicit communications. As implicit communications, the messages are less clear and more open to children's own interpretations. Perhaps this accounts for the findings that the use of physical punishment is connected with greater aggressiveness on the part of children (Hoffman, 1970; Maccoby & Martin, 1983). Physical punishment may convey the implicit message that inflicting physical harm and using a form of aggression is acceptable.

It is also likely that family influences on children's moral development go beyond the effects of parental discipline practices. The structure of family interactions is another important influence, especially as it relates to fairness in arrangements among males and females (Hochschild, 1989; Okin, 1989, 1996). Within most families, there exist gender-related inequalities in the distribution of power, the ways goods and privileges are allocated, and work opportunities are encouraged or discouraged. Such structural arrangements and practices may well have an effect on children's development, but this is an area largely neglected in research on family influences.

An interactional perspective, therefore, needs to account for many aspects of family life and social life in addition to family experiences. One of these that has received some attention from researchers is interactions among peers. In fact, some have followed Piaget's (1932) lead in proposing that peer interactions are important to children's moral development (Damon, 1981, 1988; Youniss, 1980). Piaget maintained that relationships of young children with adults were ones of constraint, whereas relationships with peers are more likely to be ones of cooperation. According to Piaget, since peers are perceived more or less as equals, children are more likely to take their perspectives and see themselves as responsible partners in social interchanges.

Without necessarily presuming that interactions with peers are more conducive than interactions with adults to the development of moral judgments, several researchers have examined the influences of children's relationships with each other. Damon (1981, 1984, 1988) and Youniss (1980) propose that the effects of peer interactions are a consequence of "the coordinating of one's perspective and actions with those of another, rather than through the transmission of information and ideas" (Damon, 1981, p. 165). Furthermore, Damon maintains that important aspects of morality are first learned through play with friends, including norms which may be discrepant with societal standards espoused by adults. Even norms consistent with those of adults are "discovered" by children through their interactions with friends.

Damon (1988) identified as primary to childhood relationships reciprocity of a symmetrical kind which is more likely to occur among children than between adults and children because children perceive each other as equals in status and power. Moreover, the mutuality and intimacy that develop among children entail close collaboration and communication, and are more likely to foster decisions based on consensual agreements. Children, thereby, come to understand that social rules can be based on cooperation among equals in creating and applying them, and not solely on the authority of others (Damon, 1988). Both Damon (1981) and Youniss (1980) have stressed that children, through interactions involving "give and take," collaborations, the sharing of ideas, openness to new insights, and compromise, "co-construct" knowledge and ways of thinking. Co-construction involves children together discovering solutions to problems and encouraging creative thinking.

Within the context of research on the development of concepts of distributive justice, experimental work has shown that children change more as a consequence of discussions with peers than with adults (Damon, 1981). Other studies on the influences of peer discussion among college students were conducted in the context of Kohlberg's stages of moral judgments. In these studies, students were paired for discussions about moral dilemmas so as to create disparities in their previously assessed levels of moral judgment. It was found that discussions between those whose levels were only slightly different served to stimulate change (Berkowitz, Gibbs, & Broughton, 1980), and that the most effective types of discussions entailed efforts at transforming each other's meanings into comprehensible forms (Berkowitz & Gibbs, 1983).

Another source of development related to peer interactions occurs through social conflicts (Berkowitz & Gibbs, 1985; Killen & Nucci, 1995). Conflicts, which are not uncommon among children, can stimulate them to take different points of view in order to restore balance to social situations, to produce ideas as to how to coordinate the needs of others and self, and to consider the rights of others—especially claims to ownership or possession of objects (see Killen & Nucci, 1995 for more extensive discussion). Research by Killen and her colleagues (Killen, 1989; Killen & Naigles, 1995; Killen & Nucci, 1995; Killen & Sueyoshi, 1995; Rende & Killen, 1992) has also demonstrated that in the absence of adult intervention young children are quite capable of addressing social conflicts and producing resolutions that take the needs and interests of others into account. In another study (Eisenberg, Lundy, Shell, & Roth, 1985), it was found that preschool children justified meeting the requests of peers with references to the needs of others and to one's relationships with others (requests of adults, by contrast, were justified with references to authority and punishment).

The Construction of Moral Judgments through Social Interactions

Conflicts, disputes, argumentation, and discussion are all part of social interactions. For many who emphasize the role of judgments in morality, such social interactions are involved in the individual's constructions of moral judgments that are not solely local or derived primarily from parental teachings or an integrated, consistent cultural pattern. In these positions, generalizable, nonlocal moral judgments are not innately based, but a consequence of social interactions and constructions. From a philosophical perspective, too, propositions regarding universalizable moral reasoning are consistent with the idea that morality stems from social experiences and social constructions (Dworkin, 1977, 1993; Gewirth, 1978, 1982; Habermas, 1990a, 1990b, 1993; Rawls, 1971, 1993).

One of the most extensive philosophical formulations of the social sources of moral reasoning can be seen in the "neo-Kantian" propositions of Habermas, based on his theory of communicative action and discourse ethics, that morality entails concepts of justice, rights, and welfare (of others and the general welfare). Habermas bridges important distinctions: one between justification and application of moral norms, the other between individual autonomy and social solidarity. Whereas moral principles are justified or grounded in criteria of universalizability and impartiality, in their application to concrete instances situational features are taken into account. Consequently, the way moral principles are understood is a necessary component, as is an understanding of the features of the context. As put by Habermas (1993):

> The principle of universalization that regulates discourses of justification does not exhaust the normative sense of the impartiality of a just judgment. A further principle must be adduced to guarantee the correctness of singular judgments. An impartial judge must assess which of the competing norms of action—whose validity has been established in advance—is most appropriate to a given concrete case once all the relevant features of the given constellation of circumstances have been accorded due weight in the situational description. Thus, principles of appropriateness and the exhaustion of all relevant contextual features come into play here. (p. 129)

In bridging autonomy and social solidarity, Habermas maintained that both are essential features for those who participate in "the network of reciprocal expectations and perspectives built into the pragmatics of the speech situation and communicative action" (Habermas, 1993, p. 114). Discourse, communication, and argumentation are the means by which individuals, with moral concepts, function in a moral world. This places individuals in a collectivity, attempting to maintain social solidarity by submitting their moral principles for verification by others in moral dialogue, reflective discussion, and argumentation. In the process, individuals take positions based on moral principles, but through consensus attempt to achieve resolutions that account for the general welfare and maintenance of solidarity.

Habermas also incorporated developmental research into his philosophical formulations, relying on his revised form of the progression of moral judgments formulated by Kohlberg (the general outline of the stage progression was provided earlier). Like Kohlberg (1976), Habermas regarded stages of perspective taking (Selman, 1976, 1980)

as part of the process of the formation of moral judgments. However, Habermas's theory of discourse ethics is dependent not on a particular formulation like Kohlberg's but on a psychology that allows for moral concepts of a generalizable kind.

Kohlberg's formulations are not further reviewed here, as they have been discussed extensively in previous editions of this *Handbook* (see Hoffman, 1970, and, especially, Rest, 1983). Several researchers, however, have pursued hypotheses based on the stages proposed by Kohlberg. This includes research conducted by Kohlberg and his colleagues tracing developmental changes longitudinally (Colby, Kohlberg, Gibbs, & Lieberman, 1983) and reformulating the specific descriptions of the stages (Colby & Kohlberg, 1987; Kohlberg, 1984; Kohlberg, Levine, & Hewer, 1983). Other researchers have used Kohlberg's formulations to examine relationships between perspective taking and moral development (e.g., Keller & Edelstein, 1991; Selman, 1976; Walker, 1980), hypotheses regarding the invariance of the stages (Walker, 1982; Walker, de Vries, & Bichard, 1984), and processes by which changes occur (Berkowitz & Gibbs, 1983; Walker & Taylor, 1991).

Some studies have examined family variables and moral judgment, including correspondence between parents' and children's levels (e.g., Hart, 1988a; Walker & Taylor, 1991). Other studies (Hart, 1988b; Hart & Chmiel, 1992) have related personality measures, personality ratings, and defense mechanisms to stages of moral judgment. There have also been theoretical formulations aimed at combining aspects of Kohlberg's stage sequence with other variables, such as affect, coping and stress, to explain unusual moral commitments on the part of individuals (Haste, 1990). Still other research has attempted to extend the analyses to the adult lifespan, including among the elderly (Pratt, Golding, & Hunter, 1983, 1984; Pratt, Golding, Hunter, & Norris, 1988; Pratt, Golding, Hunter, & Sampson, 1988).

Studies have also been conducted on the possible influences of attending college on the development of moral judgments (e.g., Rest & Narvaez, 1991). These studies deviate from Kohlberg's procedures in that assessments were made using a paper and pencil questionnaire requesting individuals to rate and rank a series of solutions to moral dilemmas corresponding to the six stages—as opposed to Kohlberg's semistructured clinical interview aimed at ascertaining individuals' ways of thinking (see Rest, 1979 for details on the standardized assessment; see Damon, 1977, Piaget, 1929, and Turiel, 1983a for discussions of the aims and value of the clinical interview method). The research conducted by Rest is also linked to what he refers to as a "Four Component Model" of moral development, including judgment, "sensitivity," motivation, and ego strength (it is detailed in the previous edition of this *Handbook*; Rest, 1983).

Moral Judgments in Early Childhood and Beyond

Kohlberg's stage formulation, in which young children's moral judgments are based on obedience and sanctions, was derived from responses to complex situations in which competing and conflicting issues are depicted. As an example, the often-cited situation of a man who must decide whether to steal an overpriced drug that might save his wife's life includes considerations of the value of life, property rights, violating the law, interpersonal obligations, and personal responsibilities to each of these. In that sense, Kohlberg was attempting to study contextualized judgments. He constructed hypothetical situations in which the use of readily conceived values (e.g., it is wrong to steal) would be challenged by situational circumstances (e.g., if you do not steal, you sacrifice a life). These situations, however, presented multifaceted problems requiring children to weigh and coordinate competing moral considerations, as well as nonmoral considerations (Turiel, 1978a, 1978b, 1983a). The complexity of the judgments required by those situations led to the appearance that young children's moral judgments are contingent on sanctions, are not based on understandings of morality as generalizable, and that it is not until after progressing to the fourth stage (usually not until at least adolescence) that morality is distinguished from nonmoral issues (Turiel & Davidson, 1986). Research into several aspects of moral judgments indicates that starting at a young age children make moral judgments that are not based on extrinsic features like obedience and sanctions. These include judgments about distributive justice, social justice in institutional settings, and prosocial actions.

The Development of Concepts of Distributive Justice and Fairness of Social Practices

In accord with long-standing presumptions among philosophers (e.g., Aristotle, 1947; Mill, 1863/1963; Rawls, 1971), Damon (1988, p. 31) has placed issues of distributive justice at the forefront of moral concerns: "And there is no graver human concern than one of distributive justice.

Many of humanity's great battles, military as well as political, have been waged by people contending for their fair share of some treasured commodity." According to Damon, questions pertaining to allocation of resources, merit, and balance of rights, which pertain to distributive justice, have eluded resolution over the centuries. Yet, young children begin to consider these issues. Extensive research on children's concepts of sharing and distribution revealed a developmental progression of moral judgments (Damon, 1977, 1980, 1988, 1995), with indications that very young children are somewhat attuned to sharing. In their second year, children take turns in playing with objects and show an awareness that food or candy can be divided. Information regarding how children 4 or 5 years of age and older conceptualize sharing comes from research on children's (ages 4–8 years) judgments about hypothetical and real-life situations entailing the distribution of goods (Damon, 1977, 1980). For example, in one situation, children in a class that made paintings to sell at a school fair must decide how to distribute the proceeds. Children were asked to respond to examples of ways of distributing the money (e.g., on the basis of merit, need, equality, and sex of the children), and to give their ideas on how the money should be distributed. The children were presented with examples of ways of distribution so as to elicit reactions to three categories considered basic in the literature on moral philosophy: equality, merit, and benevolence.

It was found that children's thinking about distributive justice progresses through four levels encompassing equality, merit, and benevolence (though not at the first level). At the first level, concepts of distribution initially are tied to the child's own desires and perspectives. After these initial judgments of preschoolers by self-interest, they begin to bring in external criteria (such as size or ability). Although these external features ultimately are used to justify one's desires and goals, this way of thinking leads to other-oriented concepts based on equality, merit, and benevolence. Elementary school-aged children, at the next level, base their judgments on equality; everyone should be given the same amount and receive the same treatment, regardless of merit or need. Next comes a shift to considerations of merit and reciprocity; distribution is based on the need to acknowledge good deeds, hard work, or personal attributes like intelligence. The next shift includes judgments that take benevolence into account, with greater awareness of competing claims and an understanding of the need for compromises to resolve claims in a fair manner. Therefore, by the ages of 10 or 11 years, children take into account merit (hard work, talent), advantages and disadvantages, and other factors (e.g., investment, inheritance).

This developmental sequence was supported by longitudinal findings (see Damon, 1977, 1980). Furthermore, similar patterns of judgment were obtained in studies of behavioral situations in experimental contexts (Gerson & Damon, 1978). Judgments on the "real-life" situations (elicited individually and in group discussions) were highly correlated with judgments on the hypothetical situations, and the same age trends were evidenced. It was also found, however, that personal concerns were coordinated with judgments about distribution to a greater extent in the real-life than the hypothetical situations. For example, children who showed an understanding of merit as a basis for fairness were most likely to apply that understanding when they were themselves in a meritorious position. In ways consistent with these findings, Blasi (1983, 1993) proposed that an integration of concepts of self and identity contributes to how individuals act on their moral judgments.

An age-related sequence corresponding, in a general sense, to the levels of concepts of distributive justice has been observed by Thorkildsen (1989a, 1989b, 1991) in children's understandings of social arrangements and practices in institutional settings. The focus of the research was on judgments about the fairness of classroom practices pertaining to "educational goods" (ways of fostering learning, contests, and testing situations). In one study (Thorkildsen, 1989a), children and adolescents judged the fairness of several different teaching practices as to how faster workers would proceed, relative to slower workers, in a class assignment (e.g., after finishing, faster workers tutor slower ones; faster workers move on to other learning experiences). It was found that younger children focus on equality and older ones on equity. Within the focus on equality, there are also shifts with age in the goods considered relevant. The youngest children judged as fair attainment of an equality of rewards, whereas somewhat older children consider as fair those practices that result in equality in schoolwork completed. This is followed by an emphasis on learning as the relevant good, where practices that foster an equality in learning are judged as fair. Finally, equity in learning is judged as the basis for fairness; it is judged fair that those capable of learning more than others do so.

Thorkildsen, in other research (1989b), has linked judgments of fair practices to individuals' situational definitions. What is considered a fair classroom practice in the context of a learning activity differed from what is considered fair in a testing situation (e.g., helping slower workers to learn was judged more fair than helping them on a test). These findings indicate that children coordinate their understandings of the goals of events (e.g., to learn or to demonstrate what one knows), participants' perspectives on those events, and what would constitute a breach of just expectations. Thorkildsen (1989b, 1991) interprets these results, following the philosophical position of Walzer (1983), as showing that concepts of justice vary in accord with "spheres" of activities (e.g., justice is one thing in economics, another in the family). Thorkildsen's data, however, are not conclusive in this regard. She has shown that the concrete manifestations of fairness may be seen to differ by situation, but this has not shown that the concepts of fairness, themselves, vary (for a critique of the "spheres" of justice philosophical position of Walzer, see Okin, 1989).

Prosocial Moral Judgments

Children's judgments about sharing or distribution pertain to actions beneficial to others and possibly entail sacrifice of the interests of the self. Of course, these are not the only types of positive social actions experienced by children. The term "prosocial" moral reasoning has been used by researchers (e.g., Eisenberg-Berg, 1979) with reference to judgments about positive social actions (e.g., helping, giving) serving to benefit others in contexts in which one's actions are not based on rules, laws, or the dictates of authorities. Children have been presented with hypothetical situations posing conflicts between the needs and desires of different actors and questioned about whether it would be right to help, give, or share with others at the expense of one's own goals (Eisenberg-Berg, 1979). One situation depicted people faced with deciding whether to help feed those of another town who had lost their food in a flood; doing so would present a hardship to them. Other situations included donating blood, helping another who is being mugged or bullied, and helping physically disabled children.

A sequence of five age-related levels in judgments about prosocial actions were identified—a sequence proposed to reflect developmental advances in "capabilities for complex perspective taking and for understanding abstract concepts" (Eisenberg, Miller, Shell, McNalley, & Shea, 1991, p. 849). It was also proposed that the levels do not constitute hierarchical, integrated structures, and that the sequence is not invariant nor necessarily universal. This implies that an individual's reasoning can be spread over the different types and that the sequence may vary by situations and life circumstances. At the first level, judgments are based on a "hedonistic," self-focused orientation (personal gain linked to reciprocity with others, or basis in identification and relationship with another, or liking for the other), whereas at the next level there is an orientation to the needs of others. This is followed by judgments based on stereotypes of good or bad persons, along with concerns with the approval or disapproval of others. The fourth level is characterized by a self-reflective and empathetic orientation, including sympathetic concern and caring for others, and taking the perspective of others. At the fifth level, there is an internalization of affect linked to self-respect, of laws, norms, duties, and responsibilities, as well as abstract types of reasoning about society, rights, justice, and equality.

A series of longitudinal assessments were conducted following children from preschool to ages 19 to 20 years (Eisenberg, Carlo, Murphy, & Van Court, 1995; Eisenberg, Lennon, & Roth, 1983; Eisenberg et al., 1991; Eisenberg et al., 1987; Eisenberg-Berg & Roth, 1980). The longitudinal findings yielded a varied and heterogeneous pattern of changes in these ways of making prosocial judgments. In broad terms, there was advance on the levels with increasing age and decreased use of the lowest levels. However, along with increased use of the higher levels with age, there were renewed uses of aspects of lower levels. Hedonistic reasoning decreased in mid-adolescence, but in late adolescence, along with increases in self-reflection and empathy, there was some increase in hedonistic reasoning (i.e., in situations where costs of helping were high). The patterns obtained in the longitudinal studies indicate, again, an interaction of different ways of thinking with situational contexts (for further discussion of this extensive body of research, see the chapter by Eisenberg and Fabes in Ch. 1, this Volume).

DOMAIN SPECIFICITY: EMPHASIZING DISTINCTIONS IN JUDGMENTS

Concepts of welfare and justice emerge as central in the development of morality across the diversity of theoretical approaches. Several theorists pursued hypotheses regarding other issues, but their research findings have pointed to welfare and justice as ubiquitous components of moral judgments. Gilligan's (1982) initial emphasis on the division of gender more or less along a care or justice orientation has been largely transformed into the proposition that the two orientations coexist in most individuals, including a substantive concern with justice on the part of females. The proposition that cultures divide more or less on the basis of an orientation to the individual as an autonomous agent with rights or an orientation to the duties of the social order has also been transformed. The proposition was attenuated somewhat by Shweder (1990b) through his proposal that morality includes patterns of autonomy (justice and welfare), community, and divinity. More strikingly, the research by Miller and her colleagues consistently demonstrated that Indians maintain concepts of justice and welfare (in this regard, little difference was obtained between cultures).

Concepts of justice and welfare have been considered central to morality by philosophers, dating back to the formulations of Aristotle. Aristotle, like many philosophers after him (e.g., Dworkin, 1977; Gewirth, 1978; Habermas, 1990a; Rawls, 1971), considered justice as "other-regarding," impartial, and as characterized by universality (see Helwig, Turiel, & Nucci, 1996, for further discussion). As already indicated, Piaget's research was consistent with moral epistemologies of this type. However, Piaget proposed that understandings of welfare, justice, and rights did not emerge until after a period in which right and wrong are judged by the word of authorities and the necessity of adhering to their rules. Such "unilateral respect," according to Piaget, reflected young children's undifferentiated concepts of authority based on adults' size, power, and knowledge. By contrast, several studies conducted in the United States (Braine, Pomerantz, Lorber, & Krantz, 1991; Damon, 1977; Laupa, 1991, 1994; Laupa & Turiel, 1986, 1993; Tisak, 1986) and Korea (Kim, in press; Kim & Turiel, 1996) have yielded a different portrayal of young children's understandings of authority relations.

These studies have shown that young children, in evaluating commands by either adults or peers in positions of authority, account for the type of act commanded and the boundaries of the authority's jurisdiction in a social context. Damon (1977) found that young children do not accept the legitimacy of a parent's directive to engage in acts judged to violate moral injunctions, such as directives to steal or cause another harm. Other studies (Kim, in press; Kim & Turiel, 1996; Laupa, 1991, 1994; Laupa & Turiel, 1986, 1993) examined how children account for the type of act commanded and the attributes of persons giving commands (i.e., adult or peer, social position in a school, and attributes like possessing knowledge about rules or an event). With acts entailing theft or physical harm to persons, young children (4–6 years) give priority to the act itself rather than the status of the person as in a position of authority. For example, whether or not they hold positions of authority, commands from peers or adults that children stop fighting were judged legitimate. Moreover, commands from peers (with or without positions of authority in a school) that children stop fighting were judged more legitimate than a conflicting command from an adult authority (e.g., a teacher) that children be allowed to continue fighting. By contrast, children do give priority to adult authority over children or other adults who are not in positions of authority for acts like turn-taking and interpretations of game rules.

Most relevant for the present purposes is that children's judgments are based not on the respect or reverence held for adult authority but on an act's harmful consequences to persons (for a more general discussion of concepts of authority, see Laupa, Turiel, & Cowan, 1995). Children's judgments about such harmful consequences emerge early in life along with emotions like sympathy and empathy (Baldwin, 1896; Piaget, 1932); at young ages children go well beyond social impulses and the habitual or reflexive, attempting to understand emotions, other persons, the self, and interrelationships (Arsenio, 1988; Nucci, 1981; Nunner-Winkler & Sodian, 1988; Smetana, 1983; Turiel, 1983a). A great deal of research has demonstrated that young children make moral judgments about harm, welfare, justice, and rights which are different in type from their judgments about other social domains.

Domains of Social Judgment

Distinguishing morality from other domains presupposes that individuals think about social relationships, emotions, social practices, and social order. It presupposes that thinking about morality has features distinctive from other aspects of thinking about the social world (hence the idea of domain specificity). It also presupposes that individuals' judgments about the social world include domains of importance, which need to be distinguished from morality. Individuals form judgments within the "personal" domain that pertain to actions considered outside the jurisdiction of moral concern or social regulation and legitimately within the jurisdiction of personal choice (Nucci, 1996). Individuals also form judgments about social systems, social organization, and the conventions that further the coordination of social interactions within social systems. As summarized in Turiel et al. (1987):

Conventions are part of constitutive systems and are shared behaviors (uniformities, rules) whose meanings are defined by the constituted system in which they are embedded. Adherence to conventional acts is contingent on the force obtained from socially constructed and institutionally embedded meanings. Conventions are thus context-dependent and their content may vary by socially constructed meanings. (pp. 169–170)

Morality, too, applies to social systems, but the contrast with convention is that it is not constitutive or defined by existing social arrangements. In this perspective on morality, prescriptions are characterized as unconditionally obligatory, generalizable, and impersonal insofar as they stem from concepts of welfare, justice, and rights (Turiel et al., 1987). This type of definition of morality is, in part, derived from criteria given in philosophical analyses, where concepts of welfare, justice, and rights are not seen as solely determined by consensus, agreement, or received wisdom. In his *Nichomachean Ethics,* Aristotle drew a distinction of this type, although he couched it as two forms of justice:

There are two forms of justice, the natural and the conventional. It is natural when it has the same validity everywhere and is unaffected by any view we may take of the justice of it. It is conventional when there is no original reason why it should take one form rather than another and the rule it imposes is reached by agreement after which it holds good. Some philosophers are of the opinion that justice is conventional in all its branches, arguing that a law of nature admits no variation and operates in exactly the same way everywhere—thus fire burns here and in Persia—while rules of justice keep changing before our eyes. It is not obvious what rules of justice are natural and what are legal and conventional, in cases where variation is possible. Yet it remains true that there is such a thing as natural, as well as conventional, justice. (as cited in Winch, 1972)

Although Aristotle considered other aspects of morality, including happiness and the good life, which differed from the approaches of philosophers like Dworkin (1977), Gewirth (1978), Habermas (1990a, 1990b), and Rawls (1971), there is overlap among all of them in the propositions that justice is universal (it has the same validity everywhere), it is not legitimated by agreement (as opposed to convention), and it is impartial (not based on personal preference or individual inclinations).

These features of morality are not solely the products of philosophical conceptions, but apply also to laypersons' ways of thinking. As noted earlier, children and adolescents in India make judgments about welfare and justice that differ from their judgments about social convention (Bersoff & Miller, 1993; Madden, 1992; Miller & Bersoff, 1992). Similar findings have been obtained in several other non-Western cultures, including Korea (Song, Smetana, & Kim, 1987), Indonesia (Carey & Ford, 1983), Nigeria (Hollos, Leis, & Turiel, 1986), Zambia (Zimba, 1987) and Brazil (Nucci, Camino, & Milnitsky-Sapiro, 1996). A much larger number of studies have evidenced that domain distinctions are made by children and adolescents in Western cultures. In all, well over 60 studies have examined and supported the validity of the domain distinctions (for comprehensive reviews, see Helwig, Tisak, & Turiel, 1990; Smetana, 1995a; Tisak, 1995).

One direction of early research on domains was to examine how children make judgments about moral, conventional, and personal issues (e.g., Davidson, Turiel, & Black, 1983; Nucci, 1981; Smetana, 1981, 1985; Tisak, 1986; Tisak & Tisak, 1990; Tisak & Turiel, 1984, 1988; Turiel, 1978b, 1983a; Weston & Turiel, 1980). Children were typically presented with a series of social acts or transgressions classified in accord with the distinctions among the domains. Thus, moral actions pertained to physical harm (e.g., hitting others, pushing them down), psychological harm (e.g., teasing, name-calling, hurting feelings), and fairness or justice (e.g., failing to share, stealing, destroying others' property). These acts were depicted as intentional and as resulting in negative consequences to others (a few studies also included prosocial actions—Kahn, 1992; Smetana, Bridgeman, & Turiel, 1983). By contrast, conventional issues pertained to uniformities or regulations serving functions of social coordination (e.g., pertaining to modes of dress, forms of address, table manners, forms of greeting). Actions that do not entail inflicting harm or violating fairness or rights and that are not regulated formally or informally are consistent with the definition of the personal domain (these issues, within Western culture include choices of friends, the content of one's correspondence, and recreational activities).

Two dimensions, in particular, have been examined. One pertains to the criteria by which thinking within domains is identified (referred to as *criterion judgments*); the second pertains to the ways individuals reason about courses of action (referred to as *justifications*). Assessments of criterion judgments have included questions as to whether the actions would be right or wrong in the absence of a rule or law, if the act would be all right if permitted by a person in authority (e.g., a teacher in a school context), whether an act would be all right if there were general agreement as to its acceptability, and whether the act would be all right if it were accepted in another group or culture. These studies have consistently shown that children and adolescents judge that moral issues are obligatory, that they are not contingent on authority dictates, rules or consensus (e.g., that the acts would be wrong even if no rule or law exists about it), or on accepted practices within a group or culture (e.g., the act is wrong even if it were acceptable practice in another culture). Judgments about moral issues, based on these criteria, are structured by concepts of welfare, justice, and rights. Justifications for these judgments entail preventing harm, promoting welfare, fairness, and rights.

However, all social actions and regulations are not judged in these ways. Conventional issues are conceptualized as linked to existing social arrangements, and contingent on rules, authority, and existing social or cultural practices. Justifications for judgments about conventional issues are based on understandings of social organization, including the role of authority, custom, and social coordination. Convention, therefore, is not simply those residual regulations, to which there is little emotional intensity attached (as had been proposed by Aronfreed and Kagan). They are uniformities and regulations of importance for social coordination. Indeed, even when conventional transgressions are deemed very important, children still judge them by conventional criteria and justifications (Tisak & Turiel, 1988). Furthermore, insofar as nonmoral actions are not part of the conventionally regulated system, they are judged to be part of the realm of personal jurisdiction, which defines the bounds of individual authority and establishes distinctions between the self and group (see especially, Nucci, 1996).

The research on domains shows that individuals' social judgments are multifaceted, including understandings of right and wrong based on concerns with welfare, justice, and rights that are not simply based on acceptance of societal values, along with understandings of the conventional system of social regulation and coordination judged as relative and context-specific. Starting in early childhood, differentiations are made among moral, conventional, and personal concepts whose origins appear to be based in early social experiences (for more detailed discussions of methods, types of studies, and numbers of studies documenting domain distinctions in criterion judgments and justifications, see Helwig et al., 1990; Smetana, 1995a; and Tisak, 1995).

Several studies were conducted with young children. In one type of study, criterion judgments were assessed among children ranging from about 2 years to about 5 years

(Crane & Tisak, 1995a; Nucci & Turiel, 1978; Siegal & Storey, 1985; Smetana, 1981, 1985; Smetana & Braeges, 1990; Smetana, Schlagman, & Adams, 1993; Tisak, 1993). These studies show that a distinction between moral and conventional transgressions becomes more consistent and focused by about the ages of 4 or 5 years. Whereas 2-year-olds do not distinguish the domains, during their 3rd year children judge moral transgressions to be generally wrong to a greater extent than conventional transgressions. By the end of the 3rd year, children also judge moral transgressions independently of rules or authority (Smetana, 1995a; Smetana & Braeges, 1990). Although 6- or 7-year-old children generally make the distinction on several dimensions, it has been found that they apply it readily to familiar but not unfamiliar issues (Davidson et al., 1983). By the ages of 9 or 10 years, children apply the distinction to both familiar and unfamiliar issues.

Social Judgments, Social Experiences, and Social Actions

Just as children's judgments are multifaceted, their social experiences are highly varied. Some of those variations have already been considered—experiences with parents, with siblings, with peers. Children also experience the substance of people's (adults' or children's) reactions to the events around them, including emotional responses to social interactions. An important part of all this is communications among persons, and as already considered, how explicit communications (induction or explanations) may be more effective than implicit communications between parent and child. Among young children's experiences are interactions that differ in the context of dealing with moral, conventional, or personal issues. A series of observational studies in schools, playgrounds, and homes (ages ranging from 2 and 3 years to late childhood) has shown that communications between adults and children, as well as other types of social interactions, are not uniform (Nucci & Nucci, 1982a, 1982b; Nucci & Turiel, 1978; Nucci, Turiel, & Encarnacion-Gawrych, 1983; Nucci & Weber, 1995; Smetana, 1984, 1989b; Tisak, Nucci, Baskind, & Lampkind, 1991).

To summarize a large body of findings, children's experiences around moral transgressions (e.g., when one child hits another, a failure to share, taking another's objects) usually entail communications about the effects of acts on others, the welfare or expectations of others, and attention to the perspectives and needs of others. At an early age, children respond to moral transgressions and focus on the consequences of actions, the pain and injuries experienced, and emotions felt. The observational studies generally show that young children do not respond to conventional transgressions to the extent they respond to moral transgressions. However, adults' responses to conventional transgressions focus not on consequences to persons or perspectives and needs, but on issues of disorder, rule maintenance, authority, and more generally on social organization.

The observational studies show that children's social experiences are multifaceted. Much more than exposure to directives about rules, standards, or norms is involved in children's social experiences. At the least, social interactions and social communications differ in accord with domains. Furthermore, distinctions in social experiences are linked to a relationship between social judgments and social actions. In an extensive study (Turiel, in preparation) of action and judgment, observations were made of children's social interactions in several settings within schools. Interactions among children, as well as children and adults, were recorded for 1st, 3rd, 5th, and 7th graders in their classrooms, periods of recess, during lunch, and during transitions from one activity to another. The detailed recording of observations included events or incidents entailing moral or conventional issues (as well as events that involved combinations of the two domains). Over 100 such events were observed, with at least 30 in each grade. Typically, the events had several participants, such as a perpetrator, a victim, observers, and peer or adult authorities.

The majority of observed events falling into the moral domain involved violations or transgressions (e.g., around physical harm, issues of fairness, and psychological harm), but some also involved efforts at preventing moral transgressions. Similarly, the majority of conventional events involved transgressions (e.g., pertaining to classroom rules, authority dictates, procedures for school activities), but some involved efforts at preventing conventional violations. As might be expected, there was a tendency for conventional transgressions to occur in classrooms. Moral transgressions occurred about equally in classrooms and non-classroom settings. However, the frequency of moral transgressions in classrooms increased with grade, with a marked increase among the 7th graders.

As in prior observational studies, social interactions and communications were, in important respects, different for the moral and conventional events. In reaction to moral events, participants responded with statements about the injurious effects on others, the unfairness of actions, and at times with physical or verbal retaliation. By contrast, reactions to the conventional events focused on rules, sanctions, and commands to refrain from the acts. In this particular research, unlike most of the prior studies, participants' judgments about the events were assessed shortly after the events had occurred. For the most part, participants negatively evaluated the moral and conventional transgressions, and accepted as valid rules prohibiting the actions. Nevertheless, judgments about the actual moral events differed from judgments about the actual conventional events. These differences in judgments were consistent with previous findings in studies conducted in non-behavioral contexts. Acts in the moral domain, in contrast with acts in the conventional domain, were judged independently of rules, institutional context, or authority dictates. As examples, generally it was judged that moral acts should be regulated, and that moral acts would be wrong even if a rule did not exist in the school or in a school in another city. It was judged that conventional acts were acceptable if rules did not exist. It was also found that transgressions in the moral domain, in contrast with conventional transgressions, would be wrong even if the teacher dictates that they are acceptable. In turn, justifications for judgments about moral events were mainly based on welfare and justice, whereas for conventional events, justifications were mainly based on considerations of social organization, rules, authority, and tradition. Moreover, similar judgments and justifications were made by these participants when responding to situations put to them in hypothetical terms.

Social Judgments and Family Interactions

Differences among the domains of social judgment also have a bearing on social interactions within families. In addition to moral and conventional issues, the domain of personal jurisdiction is a salient aspect of social interactions across different age periods. As shown in a study (Nucci & Weber, 1995) of social interactions in the home between children (3 to 4 years of age) and mothers, there are aspects of behavior revolving around personal issues in which children are given a fair amount of freedom and discretion. Mothers allow their children choices in activities, show a willingness to negotiate, and accept challenges from them. Most mothers, while allowing choice on certain activities interact differently with their children over moral and social conventional issues, often placing restrictions on them. Therefore, the discretion mothers allow in

the personal domain does not simply reflect a general permissive orientation.

The observational study by Nucci and Weber (1995), along with the research by Dunn and her colleagues (e.g., Dunn & Munn, 1987), shows that relationships between parents and children, early on, include conflict and harmony, as well as domain differences in the extent to which parents are directive. This pattern of heterogeneity of social relationships is not, by any means, restricted to early childhood, as shown by Smetana's extensive program of research with adolescents and parents. Judgments about the legitimacy of parental authority were elicited from adolescents and their parents regarding hypothetical situations and conflicts that actually occur in their families. These studies consistently showed that morality is judged to be legitimately regulated and enforced by parents (Smetana, 1988, 1995b). There is acceptance of parental authority over moral issues by adolescents of varying ages and by their parents in nondivorced and divorced families (Smetana, 1988, 1993; Smetana & Asquith, 1994; Smetana, Yau, Restrepo, & Braeges, 1991), and with regard to both hypothetical and actual conflicts (Smetana, 1989a; Smetana, Braeges, & Yau, 1991). Smetana (1995b) reports that moral issues are not a frequent source of conflict between parents and adolescents.

Parental regulation over conventions is also accepted by adolescents, so that there is a good deal of agreement on those issues as well (Smetana, 1988; Smetana & Asquith, 1994; Tisak, 1986). Nevertheless, there is greater acceptance on the part of adolescents of parental authority over moral than conventional issues. It is issues in the personal domain, as well as those entailing a combination of personal and conventional considerations, that produce disagreements and conflicts (Smetana, 1988, 1993; Smetana & Asquith, 1994). As with younger children, adolescents identify issues they consider part of personal jurisdiction (some of the issues examined in these studies include spending decisions, appearances, and friendship preferences). Parents tend to believe that they should have authority to control these activities, while adolescents believe that the activities are not legitimately regulated. Moreover, from early to late adolescence, there is an increase in judgments that parents do not have authority over personal issues (Smetana, 1988; Smetana & Asquith, 1994). An even sharper sort of disagreement occurs over issues combining conventional and personal considerations (e.g., disputes over order in an adolescent's room, since it can be seen as both personal and shared space in the home; see Smetana, 1995b). Typically, clashes between adolescents and parents actually entail different interpretations of the issues. Parents focus on components pertaining to conventional regulations, whereas adolescents focus on personal components.

The research by Smetana and her colleagues provides evidence that synchrony does not always exist in the ways parents and their children interpret and evaluate social events. Although parents and children alike identify the different domains of judgment, they differ regarding the legitimacy of parental authority over some of the issues. They also differ in their interpretations of events with mixtures of personal and conventional considerations. Adolescents agree with parents in the ways they judge moral events and attribute legitimacy to parental authority. However, children and adolescents do not accept the legitimacy of parental authority with regard to parental directives to engage in acts considered morally wrong (Laupa et al., 1995).

Emotional Attributions and Social Judgments

Observational studies also show that conflicts among siblings usually occur over morally relevant issues, such as possessions, rights, physical harm, and unkindness (Dunn & Munn, 1987; Smetana, 1990). These interactions include feedback from siblings, which reveal negative reactions and feelings, as well as communications, especially from parents, about reasons as to why acts are wrong (Smetana, 1995b). The observational studies suggest that the emotions surrounding moral transgressions may differ from those around conventional transgressions, and that social events entail emotional reactions (Arsenio & Lover, 1995). Studies by Arsenio and his colleagues (Arsenio, 1988; Arsenio & Fleiss, 1996; Arsenio & Ford, 1985) have demonstrated that children associate different types of emotional outcomes with different types of social events.

In one study (Arsenio, 1988), children from 5 to 12 years of age, who were presented with descriptions of several different types of acts, gave their assessments of the emotions which would be experienced by different participants (actors, recipients, and observers). For events entailing positive moral actions, such as helping and sharing, children generally attributed positive emotions, like happiness, to the actors. For conventional transgressions, children attributed neutral or somewhat negative emotions (sadness, anger) to the participants. In the case of moral transgressions entailing one person victimizing another (e.g., a child stealing a toy from another), children attributed very

negative emotions to the recipients and observers, and attributed somewhat positive emotions to the perpetrators of the acts. The research also showed children could use information about emotional responses to infer the types of experiences that would lead to the emotional reactions. Children who were presented with descriptions of the emotional reactions of actors and alternative events that may have elicited the emotions, associated different emotions to the different actions; older children were able to do this more accurately than younger ones.

Children's reasons for characters in the events experiencing the emotions attributed to them, too, varied by domain of event and role of participants (Arsenio & Fleiss, 1996). The negative emotions expected of victims of moral transgressions were thought to occur because of the harm, loss, or injury resulting from the acts. For victimizers, however, it was thought that the material gains obtained by them would result in some feelings of happiness. With regard to conventional transgressions, it was thought that negative emotions would be felt by those in authority who tend not to want rules violated (also see Arsenio, Berlin, & O'Desky, 1989).

Thus, children differentiate among the emotions attributed to people in different roles in an event. In particular, they attribute different emotions to victims and those who do the victimizing. The youngest children assumed that those engaging in a transgression would feel positive emotions, and that the victims would feel negative emotions. The finding that positive emotions are attributed to victimizers is consistent with Nunner-Winkler and Sodian's (1988) finding that the younger children focused on the material outcomes for victimizers. Arsenio's research (e.g., Arsenio & Kramer, 1992) extends those findings by showing that attributions to victims and victimizers are very different, and that young children do not minimize the negative emotions that might be experienced by victims. Also, older children tended to attribute mixed emotions to victimizers, expecting that in addition to positive emotions for a desired outcome, there may be negative feelings due to the effects of their acts on others. Because even among the younger children, the moral transgressions were evaluated as wrong, it would appear that their attributions of positive emotional outcomes to victimizers do not determine their moral judgments about the acts. Instead, with regard to moral evaluations, the victims' reactions seem to be what is taken into account. It also appears that older children give priority to the victim in their moral judgments and understand that a victim's reactions can feed back on an actor (the victimizer) and produce a mixture of positive and negative reactions (for more extensive discussion, including of similar findings of a study conducted in Korea, see Arsenio & Lover, 1995).

Children's understandings of people's emotional reactions to moral and social transgressions bring to bear different realms. When young children state that one who engages in a moral transgression feels happy and that the victim feels sad, it is likely that they are making psychological attributions. When older children state that a victimizer may experience a mixture of positive and negative emotions, they may also be making psychological attributions, with an awareness that people can simultaneously experience more than one emotion. However, the research has not looked into whether children think a person engaging in a moral transgression *should* feel negatively about it. How children respond to such a question would depend on whether they assume emotional reactions are in some sense involuntary or modifiable. It is, therefore, necessary to consider children's understandings of psychological makeup, as coordinated with their moral evaluations.

Ambiguities, Uncertainties, and Deliberations

Despite the complexities in understandings of the psychological features of emotions, children do assume that victims of moral transgressions react negatively and they evaluate those transgressions as wrong using the previously mentioned criteria and justifications. The moral reasoning reflected in criterion judgments and justifications includes relatively complex components. Nevertheless, because young children (3- and 4-year-olds) make moral judgments about many situations, such as harming another person for reasons of self-interest or stealing another's property (situations referred to as "prototypical"; see Turiel et al., 1987), in an unambiguous way and with certainty, it may appear to some that their moral responses are easily derived and reflexive, and, in turn, that the judgments are intuitive or naturally given. However, those presumptions would ignore, first of all, that 3- and 4-year-olds have experienced a fair amount of social interaction as infants and toddlers, and that they have already undergone some development. Moreover, moral judgments give the appearance that they are readily derived and reflexive if we consider only their application once they have been constructed, and then only for judgments about relatively straightforward situations in the case of most children.

For some children, the application of their moral judgments to particular kinds of situations can be problematic. Astor (1994) investigated the reasoning of children with histories of violent actions, pursuing the propositions that they had formed moral judgments regarding harm and welfare but, nevertheless, would judge actions in response to various kinds of provocations differently from children who do not engage in violence. Children with or without histories of violent activities evaluated unprovoked acts of violence (e.g., a boy who is mad because he fell down hits his brother) as wrong, and justified their evaluations with moral reasons. Differences between the two groups emerged with regard to acts of violence after provocation (e.g., a boy hits his brother after being teased and called names by him). The nonviolent group of children evaluated those acts as wrong on the grounds that physically harming another is worse than the provoking acts. By contrast, the group identified as violent accepted the legitimacy of hitting in those situations on the grounds that it is fair retribution for an unjust action. For those children, therefore, the application of their moral judgments in situations perceived as entailing provocations differed from those who do not often engage in acts of violence (see Butterfield, 1995, for a historical and contemporary analysis of the role of provocation in individuals who have engaged in extremely violent acts).

Another difference from judgments about straightforward situations is seen in judgments about ones including components from more than one domain (Turiel, 1989b; Turiel & Davidson, 1986). In such situations, the application of moral and social judgments is not entirely straightforward, entailing ambiguities, uncertainties, contradictions, and a good deal of disagreement. Many situations, studied naturalistically (Kelman & Hamilton, 1989) and experimentally (Haney, Banks, & Zimbardo, 1973; Milgram, 1974), pose conflicts between issues of harm and issues of authority, status, and social organization. Milgram's experiments on obedience to authority, which posed individuals with choices between avoiding harm and adhering to conventional authority-relations, have shown that moral and social decisions can entail uncertainties, emotional and cognitive conflicts, and belabored decision making (Turiel & Smetana, 1984).

Judgments about situations with salient features from more than one domain have been examined in several studies. A study by Killen (1990) presented children with both prototypical situations (e.g., one child hitting another) and "mixed-domain" situations (e.g., choosing between preventing harm or continuing a task to maintain a group activity). Whereas judgments about prototypical events were similar among children, there were differences as to whether children gave priority to the moral or non-moral features in the mixed-domain situations. Moreover, decisions in the mixed situations involved consideration of the different components, with expressions of conflict (see also Smetana, 1983, 1985; Tisak & Tisak, 1990; Turiel, 1983a). It has also been found that older children are better able to coordinate varying components than younger children (Crane & Tisak, 1995b).

As amply documented by many polls and surveys, sharp differences exist in positions about controversial social issues, such as abortion, homosexuality, and pornography (Smetana, 1982; Turiel et al., 1991). Research into the judgments of adolescents and adults also shows that individuals display inconsistencies and ambiguities. People differ in their judgments about these issues (and not about issues like killing or rape), in large measure, as a consequence of differences in assumptions about reality or aspects of nature. With regard to abortion, for example, differences were associated with assumptions about the origins of life, with those who assumed the fetus to be a life evaluating abortion as wrong. Those assumptions, however, contained ambiguities in thinking, such that evaluations about abortion were inconsistent across situations and patterns of judgment differed from those usually found with regard to prototypical moral issues (e.g., abortion is wrong but should not be legally restricted because it is up to personal decision).

Information, Assumptions about Reality, and Moral Decisions

Assumptions of an informational kind about persons, psychological states, biology, and nature represent an additional component to be added to the mix in analyses of social decision making. Wainryb (1991, 1993) has shown that individuals may hold similar concepts about welfare, fairness, and rights, but come to different decisions in situations where they apply different informational assumptions. An example is that assumptions about the effectiveness of parental punishment bears on evaluations of physical harm in the context of a parent disciplining a child, whereas in other contexts parents inflicting harm on children is commonly judged unacceptable.

Possible variations in informational assumptions, especially those entailing assumptions about the natural and an

afterlife, bear on cultural variations in moral decisions. It has been noted, not infrequently, that differences in such assumptions give the appearance of radical differences in moral concepts, when moral judgments or principles, themselves, may actually not vary (Asch, 1952; Duncker, 1939; Hatch, 1983; Wertheimer, 1935). Asch (1952) pointed out that beliefs about an afterlife bear on cultural practices (such as the social practices listed by Benedict as evidence of variability in cultural patterns). An example is the cultural practice of putting one's elderly parents to death because "there prevails the belief that people continue into the next world the same existence as in the present and that they maintain the same condition of health and vigor at the time of death" (Asch, 1952, p. 377). According to Asch, a concern with the welfare of one's parents underlies the practice. A similar view was proposed by Hatch (1983, p. 67): "Judgments of value are always made against a background of existential beliefs and assumptions, consequently what appears to be a radical difference in values between societies may actually reflect different judgments of reality."

Most analyses of culture and morality, however, have not seriously considered the role of judgments of reality. It is through consideration of such judgments that the findings of Shweder et al. (1987) were reinterpreted by Turiel et al. (1987). In their comparative research of judgments about morality and convention in India and the United States, Shweder et al. presented individuals with some issues pertaining to matters like dress and eating (practices such as a son avoiding eating chicken or getting a haircut the day after his father's death, widows not eating fish). These issues were supposedly conventional by U.S. standards, given their content. As detailed elsewhere (Turiel et al., 1987), this is an overly literal interpretation of how to classify issues within domains (moral or otherwise) that fails to account for the intentions and goals of actors, the surrounding context of the actions, and informational assumptions. This literal interpretation would be akin to classifying any act that causes physical damage or pain to another person as a moral transgression. By that standard, a surgeon's thrust of the knife would be classified a moral transgression.

For several "conventional" issues studied by Shweder et al. (1987), a different picture of their domain status emerges by considering the assumptions of reality surrounding the events. Those assumptions concern beliefs about an afterlife and actions on earth that can adversely affect unobservable entities such as souls and deceased ancestors. Using ethnographic material (presented by

Shweder et al., 1987, and Shweder & Miller, 1985), further analyses of the issues were made by Turiel et al. (1987) to account for assumptions about reality. Consider some examples. The practice that a son not eat chicken the day after his father's death is connected to the belief that doing so would result in a failure of the father's soul to receive salvation (Shweder & Miller, 1985, p. 48). It is believed that if a widow were to eat fish regularly, it would cause her great suffering and offend her husband's spirit. If a menstruating woman were to enter the kitchen it would result in great misfortune for the family because the deceased ancestors would leave the household for several generations.

Since in these examples events on earth affect unobserved unearthly occurrences and beings, they illustrate how assumptions about an afterlife contextualize some issues to include potential harm. The cultural differences may thus reflect existential beliefs and not moral principles. The Turiel et al. (1987) reanalysis showed that many Shweder et al. (1987) issues of this kind pertaining to dress, food, and the like resulted in different judgments between Indians and Americans. By contrast, issues that directly depicted consequences of harm or unfairness to people on earth were judged in the same ways by individuals in both cultures (see Table 4.5, pp. 208–211 of Turiel et al., 1987, for a detailed account of classifications of the issues). These reanalyses are consistent with the findings of conventional judgments by Indians.

In the Shweder et al. (1987) American sample, the "conventional" issues were more often judged by moral criteria than has been typically found in other studies. Undoubtedly, this is because for Americans the presumably conventional issues presented were devoid of the surrounding context of assumptions about reality and, therefore, unconnected to their experiences. Moreover, many of the issues pertained to practices that restrict the activities of one group and not another (usually restrictions on females and not males). That is, in the original study, Americans were simply presented with a description of an act like "a widow eats fish two or three times a week" and asked to evaluate it. Other research with Americans (Vail & Turiel, 1995) has demonstrated that if children are given a little context regarding such practices and if they are not couched in terms that can be perceived as discriminatory practices, then the issues are judged differently. When American children were presented with the issues as cultural practices that apply to everyone (not just one group) they generally judged them by conventional criteria rather than moral criteria.

The Personal and the Social

With a few exceptions (Miller, Bersoff, & Harwood, 1990; Nucci, Camino, & Milnitsky-Sapiro, 1996; Yau & Smetana, 1996), the research comparing moral and conventional judgments with judgments in the personal domain has been conducted in Western cultures. Those few studies show that non-Westerners distinguish areas of personal jurisdiction from moral and conventional regulations. Nevertheless, from the viewpoint of the proposition that cultures divide according to orientations to collectivism and individualism, it would be expected that concepts of personal agency and jurisdiction are mainly part of Western individualism, and not of non-Western collectivism. However, the findings from the few studies on personal jurisdiction in non-Western cultures are consistent with fundamental propositions in the social theories and philosophical views of James (1890), Dewey (A. Ryan, 1995), and Habermas (1990a, 1993). Each of these writers argued that personal agency and individual freedom cannot be offset from collectivism or social solidarity. They held that the self and the social, individual growth and social engagement, personhood and social solidarity are not opposing orientations, restricted to particular societies. Habermas (1993, p. 114) put forth the thesis that anyone who has formed an identity in a network of reciprocal expectations and perspectives will have acquired moral orientations entailing "the reciprocal dependence of socialization and individuation, the interrelation between personal autonomy and social solidarity."

The development of personal boundaries and their connections to moral development have been elaborated by Nucci and his colleagues (Nucci, 1996; Nucci & Lee, 1993; Nucci & Weber, 1995), by Helwig (1995a, 1995b), and by Wainryb and the present author (Turiel, 1994, 1996; Turiel & Wainryb, 1994; Wainryb & Turiel, 1994, 1995). Beyond the identification of issues that individuals judge part of personal jurisdiction, Nucci maintains that children attempt to establish boundaries between self and group, and that establishing such boundaries facilitates mutual respect and cooperation. Moreover, the process of coming to understand personal boundaries is social and includes interpersonal negotiations. As documented in research by Nucci and Weber (1995), young children's (ages 3–5 years) interactions with their mothers frequently include discussions and negotiations over the extent to which certain activities can be based on the child's choices, preferences, and discretion. Often, mothers convey the idea that activities and choices are up to the child. In other situations, children's resistance of directives from mothers results in negotiations and compromises. The resistances, negotiations, and compromises occur primarily around personal issues and not moral ones. At a young age, therefore, children are challenging parental authority to a greater extent in the personal than the moral realm. Interviews with Americans (Nucci & Smetana, 1996) and Brazilians (Nucci et al., 1996) further demonstrated that mothers believe children should be allowed discretion over certain activities to encourage a sense of autonomy and personal agency (for a discussion of the psychological functions of the establishment of personal boundaries, see Nucci, 1996).

Along with conceptions of philosophers (e.g., Dworkin, 1977; Gewirth, 1982), Nucci sees necessary links between the development of a personal sphere and concepts of rights. Concepts of the agency of self and others constitute the locus of the application of freedoms and rights. Indeed, if concepts of personal agency did not develop because persons were defined mainly through connections with the group and embeddedness in the collectivity (as in, e.g., Markus & Kitayama, 1991; Shweder & Bourne, 1982), then it would follow that moral concepts of rights and freedoms would not apply.

Although many philosophers have regarded rights as universally significant, little research was conducted on the development of concepts of rights prior to that of Helwig (1991, 1995a, 1995b). Helwig's research examined the judgments of American adolescents and adults about freedoms of speech and religion, in general, and about a series of situations entailing conflicts between the freedoms and other moral considerations. In response to general questions (e.g., should people be allowed to express their views or engage in their religious practices, would it be right or wrong for the government to institute laws restricting the freedoms), most individuals, from early adolescence to young adulthood, endorsed the freedoms and judged them as moral rights independent of existing laws that are generalizable to other cultural contexts. They based these judgments on psychological needs (e.g., self-expression, identity, autonomy), social utility, and democratic principles. Along with the general judgments, individuals accepted restrictions on the freedoms when in conflict with other moral considerations (i.e., physical harm, psychological harm, or equality of opportunity). At younger ages, however, there was more likelihood of acceptance of restrictions than at older ages.

Helwig's findings, too, demonstrate that individuals' judgments vary by context. Whereas speech and religion are judged as generalizable rights, restrictions on them are accepted when in conflict with other moral considerations. Helwig's findings, based on in-depth interviews, are consistent with findings of large-scale surveys of the attitudes of American adults toward civil liberties (McClosky & Brill, 1983; Stouffer, 1955). The surveys tapped the attitudes of large samples (in some cases over 3,000 adults) toward several freedoms, including speech, press, assembly, and religion, as well as rights to privacy, dissent, and divergent lifestyles. As in Helwig's research, when the questions of freedoms and rights were put generally or in the abstract (e.g., a belief in freedom of speech for everyone) they were endorsed by large majorities of respondents. However, the surveys also tapped attitudes toward the freedoms in conflict with other moral considerations, such as when they may result in harm to others or may be detrimental to the general welfare. Also assessed were conflicts of freedoms with traditions, community standards, and the maintenance of social order. The results were striking for the ways majorities fail to uphold freedoms and rights in most of those situations. Most Americans do not endorse the very freedoms and rights highlighted in public discourse, evident in public documents (e.g., the U.S. Constitution and the Bill of Rights), and central to depictions of American culture as individualistic and perhaps overly oriented to rights (as maintained by Bellah et al., 1985; Etzioni, 1993). This does not mean, however, that Americans do not value freedoms and rights. Also striking in the findings of the survey studies is the contrast between Americans' endorsement of freedoms and civil liberties in nonconflict situations and their failure to endorse freedoms and rights in conflict situations.

The coexistence of concerns with the freedoms and rights of individuals *and* the welfare of the community supports the contentions of Dewey and Habermas that personal agency and social solidarity go together. Additional research, on the concepts of freedoms and rights of Druze Arabs living in northern Israel (Turiel & Wainryb, 1995), supports Habermas's view that the coexistence of personal agency and collectivism is not applicable "for Americans alone," and that it extends beyond those who are "heirs to the political thought of a Thomas Paine and a Thomas Jefferson" (1993, p. 114).

The Druze community is tightly knit, living in large measure separately from the rest of the nation. They constitute a traditional hierarchical society, with strong sanctions for violations of societal norms—especially as applied to women, since it is a patriarchal society (Turiel & Wainryb, 1994). Three types of freedoms were studied with adolescents and adults: speech, religion, and reproduction (i.e., freedom to bear the number of children desired). Freedom of speech is frequently considered a fundamental right, especially in philosophical and political analyses. The issues of religion and reproduction were chosen because of the centrality accorded these matters in the culture. The Druze clearly judge, when put in general terms, that individuals should have noncontingent rights to each freedom. The majority endorsed the freedoms and judged it would be wrong to legally restrict the freedoms. The majority also thought that freedom of speech and religion should apply across cultures and that it would be permissible to exercise one's rights even if the acts were illegal. Only with regard to freedom of reproduction did the majority judge that the right was not generalizable across cultures and that it would be wrong to exercise the right if it were illegal.

Individuals were also presented with conflicts depicting freedoms producing physical or psychological harm, or having negative effects on community interests. Conflict situations also depicted ways that within the family the exercise of the freedoms by a son, daughter, or wife was in contradiction with the desires and directives of father or husband. The findings from the conflict situations showed that the Druze also think that freedoms should be, in certain situations, subordinated to other concerns, such as when they could cause harm to others. Similarly, in some situations (but not all) it is thought that considerations of community interest should take precedence over the right to exercise the freedoms.

For the most part, however, freedoms and rights of sons, daughters, and wives were not subordinated to the authority of the father or husband. Particularly for religion and reproduction, most upheld the rights and negatively evaluated the father's or husband's efforts to restrict the freedoms. The Druze were more willing to allow restrictions on the freedoms of females (wives and daughters) than males (sons) and, thereby, granted greater authority to men over their wives and daughters.

CULTURE AND CONTEXT REVISITED

The research with the Druze, along with the other research in non-Western cultures, indicates that concepts of rights, welfare, and justice are found across cultures. In the context of these similarities among cultures, however, there are also differences. In addition to differences in assumptions about reality, there are differences in the degree of hierarchically based distinctions in relationships between males and females and those of different social castes and classes. For example, Indians are more likely than Americans to accept a husband beating his disobedient wife because, according to Shweder et al. (1987), for Indians the family is analogous to a military unit. Shweder et al. also suggested that cultural practices in India pertain to the "moral" injunction that those of higher castes within the hierarchy avoid contact (and pollution) with those of lower castes. Many analyses of culture have focused on these types of differences, interpreting them in accord with the proposition that cultures form integrated patterns. The prime example relevant to morality is the presumably consistent patterns of thought and action represented either by an individualistic or collectivistic orientation. The hierarchical distinctions in gender or castes are said to be connected with the role designations of persons, through which persons are submerged within the group.

It is not at all clear, however, that the presumption of coherent, integrated cultural patterns and associated consistencies in individuals' judgments and actions coheres with other formulations central to the propositions of those emphasizing culture. In particular, the idea of coherence and consistency conflicts with the call for pluralism, and with the core ideas of cultural psychology that the mind is context-dependent, domain-specific, and local. With regard to pluralism, those emphasizing culture often have voiced that there be acceptance of a variety of moral perspectives. Shweder and Haidt (1993, p. 362) asserted that Gilligan "won the argument for pluralism" by augmenting the traditional views on justice with the care orientation. They also argue that Gilligan's proposition does not go far enough in the quest for pluralism because it does not account for further variations among cultures.

These kinds of arguments are contradictory because descriptions of cultural orientations actually frame most of the elements in Gilligan's formulation of justice as part of Western (or individualistic) morality and most of the elements of the care orientation as part of non-Western (or collectivistic) morality (see Miller & Bersoff, 1995). By describing cultures with integrated patterns of thought, a rather limited form of pluralism or heterogeneity is seen to be in differences between cultures while a unitary or homogeneous orientation (with a lack of pluralism) is imposed within cultures and for individuals. The evidence actually points in the other direction—that there is coexistence, not only within cultures but also for the individual, of care, interdependence, justice, and individuation. As detailed earlier, the research assessing those dimensions through Gilligan's formulations has shown that care (or collectivistic) and justice (or individualistic) judgments vary by context for females and males. The evidence suggests that the types of contextual distinctions drawn by Gilligan between females' and males' life circumstances are too broad and require further distinctions within each context.

Those emphasizing culture also have maintained that general, "abstract," universal moral principles are inadequate because they fail to account for variations among cultures. However, by locating contextual variations at the cultural level little consideration is given to variations that may be associated with contextual differences within cultures. For a given culture, therefore, constructs like individualism and collectivism end up functioning as general, abstract orientations that apply across contexts and fail to account for domain specificity. Distinctions in judgments by domain mean that individuals have heterogeneous orientations in social thought.

The proposed general cultural orientations of individualism and collectivism, therefore, do not sufficiently account for diversity in judgments of individuals, for domain specificity in people's thinking (the coexistence of moral, social, and personal judgments), and for contextual variations in the ways judgments are applied. These shortcomings in the proposed division of cultures by general orientations are evidenced by the findings from the research on concepts of freedoms and rights. Americans do endorse rights and freedoms, which have been associated with individualism, but they also subordinate freedoms to preventing harm, upholding traditions, asserting community standards, and maintaining social order. People in so-called individualistic cultures have multiple social orientations, including concerns with social duties, the collective community, and interdependence, as well as independence, rights, freedoms, and equality. People in so-called traditional, collectivistic cultures also have multiple social orientations. The research shows that the Druze endorse traditions, status, and role distinctions, but they also endorse individual freedoms and rights even when in contradiction with status and hierarchy.

The coexistence of domains stems from a process of development that is not restricted to circumscribed experiences characterized by the family or parental child-rearing practices, more narrowly, or by culture, more broadly. As shown by much of the research considered thus far, social experiences influencing development are varied (with parents, siblings, peers, social institutions). Through reciprocal interactions, children are engaged in communications, negotiations, compromises, disputes, and conflicts. The research has also shown that the diversity of children's social interactions includes concerns with the desires, goals, and

interests of persons (self and others), as well as with the welfare of others and the group.

It is proposed, therefore, that in children's social interactions there is a dynamic interplay of personal goals and social goals, as well as an interplay among different social goals. Reciprocity of social interactions means that individuals both participate in cultural practices and can stand apart from culture and take a critical approach to social practices. Typically, there are elements both of harmony and tension or conflict. Moreover, through the development of different domains of judgment, individuals deal with social situations from more than one perspective, taking into account varying features of situations and contexts.

Culture as Context or Context as Context

Along with much of the research already considered, a number of social psychological experiments have demonstrated that there are contextual variations in morally relevant behaviors within Western cultures. These are experiments well known for their demonstration of group influences (Latanée & Darley, 1970), conformity (Asch, 1956), obedience (Milgram, 1974), and adherence to roles in social hierarchy (Haney, Banks, & Zimbardo, 1973)—behaviors contrary to the idea of individualism. These experiments show, however, that individuals respond in multifaceted ways, often with conflict, and that different domains of judgment are used in interpreting the parameters of situations (Turiel, 1994; Turiel & Wainryb, 1994). In each of these types of experiment, behaviors varied by context. In some experimental conditions, people generally obeyed an authority's directives to act in ways that caused physical pain to others (by administering electric shocks), but in other experimental conditions people generally defied the authority's directives to engage in similar acts (Milgram, 1974). Other experiments showed that individuals are influenced by group decisions as to whether to help someone in distress, helping in some situations but not in others (Latanée & Darley, 1970). Similarly, individuals "conform" to the judgments of a group in some situations, but contradict the group in other situations (Asch, 1956).

These variations in behavior indicate that Americans act in ways consistent and inconsistent with the purported features of individualism. For instance, Markus and Kitayama (1991) presumed that there is an American orientation to independence, such that "noncomformity is regarded as every individual's birthright" (p. 230). Yet, the findings are that just as Americans sometimes endorse freedoms and rights and at other times do not, they sometimes conform and other times contradict the group, and they sometimes obey authority and other times defy authority (for details of the contextual variations in the experiments, see Turiel & Smetana, 1984; Turiel & Wainryb, 1994). Perhaps more to the point, however, is that these behaviors are not readily classified in terms of independence and interdependence because of the interweaving of both types of judgment. Consider the research on whether bystanders intervene to help others in distress. An individual is more likely to intervene to help others when he or she is alone than when in the presence of others who do not intervene (Latanée & Darley, 1970). Thus, people seem to act in independent ways and take personal initiative when alone, but do so in the service of interdependence since the act furthers the welfare of others. Conversely, when in the presence of others, people are influenced socially in failing to intervene. This social influence, however, simultaneously works against interdependence in the sense that it is at the expense of the welfare of others. A similar analysis applies to experiments on obedience to an authority's commands to inflict pain on another person (Milgram, 1974). Insofar as participants in the experiments adhered to their assigned roles and accepted the authority's status and commands, they acted in ways consistent with a collectivistic orientation. In doing so, however, they acted against an interdependent concern with the welfare of the victim. Insofar as people defied the experimenter and in that sense acted independently, they were acting in the service of the nonindividualistic goal of promoting the welfare of the victim.

The overarching observation is that individuals do not simply obey or disobey, or act as conformists or nonconformists. Rather, they make judgments about the actions of others, social organizational features, and right and wrong (see Ross & Nisbett, 1991 for an analysis of social construals and psychological attributions in these situations). In the experiments on obedience to authority, for example, many experienced intense conflict due to a construal of legitimate competing claims between social structural features (i.e., the appraisal that one must maintain the integrity of the social situation) and moral considerations (i.e., the appraisal that the other person should not be subjected to physical pain).

Asch (1952, 1956) has provided an incisive analysis of the process of social construal. In the experiments on conformity, some participants were asked to judge the length of lines in group settings, where the other participants were confederates of the experimenters who at predetermined times gave incorrect judgments. In Asch's view, those who gave incorrect perceptual judgments consistent with those of the group were not simply "going along" with others so as to fit into the group, but instead were attempting to make sense of a perplexing situation. One component of reality about which people were making judgments was the straightforward physical event regarding the relative lengths of lines. A second component was the actions of other people. Especially once the rest of the group began to give opposing judgments about the length of lines, participants had to make judgments about others' reactions to the physical event. Because the judgments about the lengths of lines were unambiguous and they could see no apparent reason for the others' judgments, they were led to question their own perceptions, perceive a conflict, and give credence to the group judgment.

Research by Ross, Bierbrauer, and Hoffman (1976) supported Asch's interpretation, through the finding that when participants could attribute the actions of the others in the group to motivation by extrinsic goals (e.g., attaining a material payoff) there was much less conformity than when no motives were specified. If individuals were acting so as to fit into the group, they should have conformed to an equal extent regardless of the perceived motivations of others. More generally, Asch proposed that individuals made a judgment about the total context experienced, such that a context in which no one gives the discrepant, incorrect perceptual responses constitutes a different situation from one in which everyone else gives those responses. In Asch's terminology, variations in situational features make for differences in the actual "objects of judgment" (see Ross & Nisbett, 1991; Turiel & Wainryb, 1994, for further discussion).

The social psychological experiments demonstrate that Americans often behave in ways that appear nonindividualistic, that there are contextual variations so that seemingly individualistic behaviors are also evident among Americans, and that the constructs of individualism and collectivism fail to capture the interweaving of independence and interdependence in many social situations. It has been recognized and emphasized that behaviors vary by situations (especially Mischel, 1973) and that research shows conformity, obedience to authority, and group influences among Americans (Kelman & Hamilton, 1989; Milgram, 1974; Ross & Nisbett, 1991). Yet, the import of these findings has not often been carried over to characterizations of culture. It seems that those who characterize Western cultures as individualistic attend mainly to one side of the picture; this includes those who portray American society as in moral decay (Bellah et al., 1985; Etzioni, 1993).

It is informative that in the fairly recent history of social scientific thought, the opposite side of the picture, reflecting the idea that the individual is submerged into the group, has been portrayed as the dominant cultural orientation in the United States. For example, Fromm (1941) maintained that modern capitalistic societies, including the United States, foster conformity and a loss of personal identity. In Fromm's view, the self is subordinated to others in personal relationships, and to the social and economic system. He lamented that the individual is but a "cog in the vast economic machine." Fromm's appraisal of the lack of personal agency was starkly put (1941, pp. 131–132): "The individual is confronted by uncontrollable dimensions in comparison with which he is a small particle. All he can do is to fall in step like a marching soldier or a worker on the endless belt. He can act; but the sense of independence, significance, has gone." Others writing in the 1950s were popularly received for their similar characterizations of the culture (Mills, 1956; Reisman, Glazer, & Denney, 1950; Whyte, 1956). These social commentators also regarded the society to be oriented to conformity and to group dependence, with individual initiative being overwhelmed by economic forces. They proclaimed that bureaucratic and hierarchical social institutions stifle freedoms, personal control, and individual creativity.

Therefore, the culture of the United States (and other Western societies) has been characterized in nearly opposite ways by different social scientists. In a sense, these characterizations capture the opposing attitudes and behaviors evident in research on concepts of freedoms and in the social psychological experiments. However, each of these characterizations provides a one-sided typing that fails to account for the heterogeneity of social judgments and behaviors. In line with Asch's analyses, the process of making social judgments, psychological attributions, and construals about social events implies that neither individuals nor cultures are appropriately characterized by a category reflecting consistent, integrated patterns. From this broader conception of individuals in Western culture, it is not plausible to portray their morality as framed only through the ideas of individuals with rights and the freedom to voluntarily enter into contracts.

Tradition, Social Hierarchy, and Heterogeneity

Many of the findings considered thus far that document heterogeneous moral and social judgments come from research in the United States. However, findings were reviewed from non-Western cultures showing that concepts of freedom and rights vary by context. Moreover, some of the research conducted in India has yielded inconsistencies that may very well reflect variations within the culture. For example, the morality of interpersonal relationships of Indians was characterized in ways suggesting distance and formality even in the family (Shweder et al., 1987), and as oriented to closeness and interdependence (Miller & Bersoff, 1992). Other inconsistencies pertain to whether Indians do or do not hold individuals accountable for moral violations, and whether Indians' judgments are attuned to context or are universalistic and noncontextual.

Those inconsistencies may reflect the existence of variations in cultural practices within non-Western cultures, indicating that the morality of those cultures is not adequately characterized as revolving around connections in the collectivity, and duties in the natural and social order. An important component of that characterization of morality is the proposition of a non-Western conception of persons as "unbounded" and interdependent, in contrast to a Western conception of persons as bounded and independent (Markus & Kitayama, 1991; Shweder & Bourne, 1982). However, anthropological and developmental research has yielded direct evidence of contextual variations in the judgments of people in non-Western cultures, including variations in concepts of persons. Spiro's (1993) extensive review of anthropological research shows that concepts of self, as well as other social concepts, vary across individuals within the same society, and across societies (1993, p. 117): "There is much more differentiation, individuation, and autonomy in the putative non-Western self, and much more dependence and interdependence in the putative Western self, than these binary opposite types allow."

Spiro maintained that cultural ideologies and public symbols do not necessarily translate into individuals' conceptions or experiences of self and others. One example comes from his research of Buddhism in Burma. A central doctrine of Theravada Buddhism is that there is no soul, ego, or transcendental self, but Spiro found that these ideas are not maintained by the Burmese he studied. Instead, "They strongly believe in the very ego or soul that this doctrine denies. . . . because they themselves experience a subjective sense of self, the culturally normative concept does not correspond to their personal experience" (Spiro, 1993, p. 119). Ethnographic evidence also shows that self-interested goals and concerns with personal entitlements are part of the thinking of the Balinese, Indians, Pakistanis, Nepalese, and Japanese. In their work, northern Japanese villagers are motivated not so much by group goals as by individual goals of power, self-esteem, and pride (see Spiro, 1993, pp. 134–136). Moreover, village women act in accord with the interests of others, their roles in the family, and "self-serving personal desires." Others have also documented that self-interest, personal goals, and autonomy are significant in the lives of Indians from various backgrounds (Mines, 1988), and among the Toraja of Indonesia (Hollan, 1992).

In accord with these findings, several anthropologists (e.g., Abu-Lughod, 1991, 1993; Appadurai, 1988; Clifford, 1988; Strauss, 1992) have criticized conceptions of cultures as homogenous, coherent, and timeless, or as embodying integrated, stable sets of meanings and practices readily reproduced in individuals through socialization. As put by Strauss (1992, p. 1): "Rarely, if ever, does the public realm of culture present a single, clearly-defined, well-integrated reality." They argue for the need to include, in analyses of culture, conflicts, disputes, arguments, contradictions, ambiguity, and changes in cultural understandings. As put by Abu-Lughod (1993, p. 27): "Others live as we perceive ourselves living—not as automatons programmed according to 'cultural' rules or acting out of social roles, but as people going though life wondering what they should do, making mistakes, being opinionated, vacillating. . . . " Like Spiro, others have proposed that individuals' judgments and understandings are often discrepant from public messages or ideologies, and that cultural practices are often contested and subject to negotiations.

Strauss (1992) stressed the need to explore the varying meanings individuals give to the dominant values and practices of the society, so as to ascertain if the actor's point of view ("from the bottom") looks different from the perspective of dominant institutions and ideologies ("from the top"). Exploring the individual's understandings of dominant cultural values and practices was one of the aims of another study conducted with the Druze (Wainryb & Turiel, 1994). A second aim was to explore the hypothesis that there is more than one side to cultural practices, such that the varying perspectives individuals may take render cultural practices more nebulous and multifaceted. That is, a particular type of cultural practice is likely to contain varying messages. Cultural practices around social hierarchies are a case in point. One side of social hierarchy, which has been the focus of cultural analyses, is specified duties and roles, and the submergence of self into a network of interdependence (Markus & Kitayama, 1991; Shweder et al., 1997). The other side, however, may be that there is a

strong sense of independence and personal entitlements embedded in hierarchical arrangements. Examples of where such entitlements hold are for those in higher castes and social classes relative to those in lower castes and classes (Turiel, 1994), and in relationships between males and females. Whereas practices revolving around social hierarchical arrangements convey duties and role prescriptions, they also convey that those in dominant positions have personal autonomy and entitlements—especially due to them by those in subordinate positions. The analogy drawn by Shweder et al. (1987) between the family unit and a military unit (as described earlier) fails to consider that within the family men may conceptualize themselves as having personal entitlements. Punishing a disobedient wife may be, at least in part, motivated by the husband's aim of protecting what he considers realms of personal entitlements. The research with the Druze examined both sides of social hierarchy, focusing on judgments about gender relationships in the family—relationships in which males are in dominant positions and females in subordinate positions.

The research examined personal, social and moral judgments, focusing on decision making in the family regarding various activities of relevance within the community (e.g., choices of occupational and educational activities, household tasks, friendships, leisure activities). Family decisions were examined because the society is hierarchically organized, with a strong patriarchal tradition. Many restrictions are placed on the activities of females, including their education, work, dress, social affiliations, and leisure time. Men are in control of finances and can easily divorce their wives, while wives cannot easily divorce their husbands. Individuals were presented with conflicts between persons in dominant (i.e., husbands and fathers) and subordinate (i.e., wives, daughters, sons) positions in the family structure. In one set of situations, a person in a dominant position objects to the choices of a person in a subordinate position (e.g., a husband objects to his wife's decision to take a job), and in another set the person in the subordinate position objects to the choices of the person who is in a dominant position (e.g., a wife objects to her husband's decision to change jobs). Assessments were made of judgments as to who should make the decision, the reasons for those judgments, and how the relationships are conceptualized.

The results showed that Druze males and females think men should have decision-making power and discretion. Most judged that wives or daughters should not engage in activities to which a father or husband objects. This was not reciprocal. Most judged that a man is free to choose his activities even if his wife, daughter, or son objects. It was also thought that sons should be able to make their own decisions over objections from their fathers. The inequality in decision making is based on different reasons for the decisions and on different ways of conceptualizing the relationships. Again, there is an interweaving of people's judgments in situations that constitute, for them, different contexts associated with the direction of the dialogue and negotiation. In the context of objections from a man to the activities of his wife or daughter, relationships were viewed in interdependent and hierarchical terms, and it was thought that role responsibilities and competencies should dictate what people do. In the context of objections from a wife or daughter to the activities of her husband or father (as well as a father who objects to a son's activities), the relationships were conceptualized as ones of independence for a person choosing the activities (i.e., men), and it was thought that personal choices and entitlements dictate what people should do. Persons are conceived as autonomous and independent, and they are conceived as part of a social network in which their independence and personal jurisdiction are subordinated to others and the requirements of their role. In these respects, males and females made similar judgments. Both attributed interdependence to females and to males in some contexts and both attributed independence to males. However, Druze females were aware of the pragmatics of social relationships in the family and sometimes attributed decision-making authority to males because males have the power to inflict serious negative consequences to those in subordinate positions (e.g., abandonment and divorce). Moreover, females evaluated many of these practices giving men power over the activities of females as unfair.

The findings of these studies demonstrate the multiple aspects of social hierarchy; in the traditional culture there is a complex picture of judgments about role obligations, prescribed activities, personal independence and entitlements, pragmatic concerns, and fairness (see also Wainryb, 1995). For the activities used in these studies the Druze judged it more acceptable to impose restrictions on a wife or daughter than was the case when judging the legitimacy of restricting freedoms of speech, religion, or reproduction (as in the Turiel & Wainryb, 1995 study discussed earlier). The multiplicity of individuals' perspectives brings with it both acceptance and opposition to cultural practices. Whereas persons in dominant and subordinate positions share orientations to duties, status, prescribed roles, and

personal autonomy, those in subordinate positions are aware of the pragmatics of power relationships and view themselves as having legitimate claims to independence and unmet rights. There is a tendency to restrict analyses of cultures to the public and institutionalized features of cultural practices and to the perspectives of those in a dominant position (caste, class, as well as gender). However, the perspectives of those in subordinate positions are significant reflections of culture and provide windows into conflicts, struggles, below-the-surface activities, and the interplay of opposing orientations such as independence and interdependence, or conflict and harmony. Along with participation in cultural practices, there can be distancing from them. Along with acceptance of one's role in the culture there can be critique of it.

Conflicts, struggles, and below-the-surface activities have been documented when social practices are examined from the perspective of those in subordinate positions. One example is Abu-Lughod's (1993) studies of Bedouin women in Egypt. Living with families for long periods, Abu-Lughod compiled women's stories and conversations around several themes pertaining to their roles in a culture that emphasizes patriarchy and patrilineality, has arranged marriages, and stresses submission of women to men's wishes and commands. She determined that there are differences and disagreements among group members, conflicts between people, efforts to alter existing practices, and struggles between wives and husbands, and parents and children. Women develop strategies, often hidden from men, to assert their interests. These strategies allow women to avoid unwanted arranged marriages, assert their will against restrictions imposed by men, attain some education, and engage in prohibited leisure activities. A woman who finds some of her husband's demands unacceptable typically attempts to control and even dominate him through connections to her parents and, at a later age, to her grown sons. Another example is found in the sociologist Fatima Mernissi's (1994) reflections on her upbringing in a harem in Morocco of the 1940s. In *Dreams of Trespass* she recounts the host of shared, but hidden strategies among women to subvert cultural practices restricting their activities. Women's discontents were with many of the cultural practices bearing on male and female relationships, including keeping women behind the walls of the harem, polygamy, and wearing of the veil.

Examining the perspective of people in subordinate positions, as well as the way people in dominant positions construe their relationships with persons in subordinate positions, yields an alternative view of social hierarchies from those who have emphasized community as a "moral good." In the communitarianism of Etzioni (1993) and the ethics of community of Shweder et al. (1997), the idea of community serves to reify the existing social hierarchy as morally positive. However, social hierarchy does not solely entail an asymmetrical reciprocity whereby those in dominant positions oversee the welfare of those in subordinate positions. Recall that Shweder et al. (1997, p. 145) assert that in India the ethics of community involves feudal ethics, in which "powerful persons take care their 'subjects'." By contrast, hierarchy often involves oppression and exploitation (Baumrind, 1997), and the use of status differences to further the self-interest, entitlements, and autonomy of those in positions of power and dominance (Wainryb & Turiel, 1994). Hierarchy often produces struggle, conflict, and hidden activities, by persons in positions of lesser power, aimed at subverting aspects of cultural practices (Abu-Lughod, 1991; Turiel, 1996, in press).

When we look beyond public characterizations of social practices and when our analyses are not restricted to the perspectives of those in dominant positions, there is evidence for a conception of cultures as embodying variations in behaviors, diversity in orientations, and conflicting points of view resulting in disagreements, disputes, and struggles among people. In traditional hierarchically organized cultures, issues of freedoms, independence, rights, and justice are part of the ways people think about social relationships, along with duties, social roles, and interdependence. These varying and potentially conflicting perspectives are related to the domains of moral, social, and personal judgments formed by individuals.

Conflicts over inequalities among persons of differing status are not restricted to traditional, hierarchically organized cultures. Gender relationships in Western cultures usually are not strictly hierarchical nor are the activities of females restricted in the same ways as in some traditional cultures. Despite the emphasis on equality in the culture, there is considerable evidence documenting inequalities and struggles between men and women in several spheres of life (see especially Hochschild, 1989; Okin, 1989, 1996; Turiel, 1996). Unequal treatment of women is reflected in their underrepresentation in the political system, in positions of power and influence in business and the professions, and in fewer opportunities for paid work. In addition, in many fields women are paid substantially less than men for similar work, even when their qualifications are the same (Okin, 1989). Inequalities are also part of gender

relationships in the family, with the interests of men given priority over those of women (Blood & Wolfe, 1960; Blumstein & Schwartz, 1983). Studies of dual-career families document a pervasive pattern in which women are expected to do more of the undesired household tasks, and men have entitlements such as greater time for leisure activities (see Hochschild, 1989, for a review). These conditions provide another example of the interweaving of duties, roles, and assertion of rights and personal entitlements. Often conflicts occur over men's orientation to maintaining role distinctions and role responsibilities in the family and women's concerns that there be greater equality and fairness (Hochschild, 1989; Okin, 1989).

The possibility that conflicts and below-the-surface activities within cultures include the vantage points of those in subordinate positions as different from those in dominant positions casts a different light on the intersection of gender and cultures. In describing the research in India on interpersonal obligations, it was noted earlier that Miller and Bersoff (1995) thought that Gilligan's (1982) gender-based distinction between care and justice leads to an implausible prediction: that concepts of self and morality would be more similar among people of the same gender from different cultures than between males and females in the same culture. It is implausible to Miller and Bersoff that there would be more similarity between, for example, a secular American woman and a traditional Hindu Indian woman than between the Indian woman and a traditional Hindu man. Although there are commonalities and shared experiences within a culture, the issues are more complicated because women from different cultures (e.g., Indian and American women) may also share certain perspectives based on their roles in a hierarchy, the status held, their burdens, and the unfairness experienced. Similarly, men from different cultures may share perspectives based on their roles in the hierarchy, their privileges and burdens, and a sense of personal entitlements based on the extent to which they are in dominant positions relative to women.

Cultures and societies, therefore, have a multitude of components that need to be taken into account. Social hierarchy may bring with it interdependence, but it also implies independence for some, at least. Cultural norms may entail certain social practices, but relationships experienced and their associated elements of equality and inequality, or dominance and subordination make for differences between those of different roles and status. Those aspects of relationships may also make for similarities and potential connections between people in like positions from different cultures.

However, perspectives based on social hierarchy are further complicated by aspects other than gender. Males and females share dominant or subordinate positions with regard to their status as members of social classes within the hierarchy. It is likely that the perspectives of men or women of lower classes in non-Western and Western cultures have some similarities (as would the perspectives of those of higher classes). Correspondingly, differences exist between people of different social classes within a culture (an interesting comparison, again, is between an upper-middle-class woman and a working-class man with regard to roles in the hierarchy). These considerations have received very little attention in research on social and moral development (for an exception see the analyses of Nucci et al., 1996, of people from different social classes in Brazil). It would be of particular interest to consider how in some non-Western societies (e.g., in India) the economic dependence of women on men, and differential economic status in the caste hierarchy bear on concepts of interpersonal obligations.

One example of research documenting conflict within Western culture pertaining to social class comes from Willis's (1977) ethnographic analyses of British working-class youth in school settings. Willis documented the conflicts of working-class youth with dominant cultural values and ideology, insofar as they are represented by teachers, administrators, and even middle-class students. The working-class adolescents opposed and defied authority, criticized the demeanor of teachers, rejected many of their values, and often failed to adhere to their rules. Moreover, working-class adolescents were critical of other students perceived to be part of mainstream culture. Here, too, there is a mixture of individuation and connection. The working-class youth continually displayed behaviors that were independent and rebellious relative to school authorities, other students, and cultural symbols. Their independence, however, also was linked to cohesiveness among working-class adolescents or what Willis referred to as the counter-culture group.

All these examples demonstrate that along with the cohesiveness usually ascribed to cultures, it is necessary to account for conflicts, struggles, ambiguities, and multiple perspectives. Multiple perspectives stem from both the varieties of social experiences and the differentiated domains of social thinking developed by individuals. Distinctions need to be made between culture as publicly conveyed ideology or as social practices and the ways individuals interpret and make judgments about social experiences. Social and cultural practices can be nebulous, with many sides and connotations. They embody multiple messages and are carried out in multiple ways. It has been documented that experiences influencing social development go well beyond any one type (family, peers, culture) and must be viewed form the perspective of reciprocal interactions. The idea of development stemming from reciprocal interactions suggests, then, that there are discrepancies between cultural ideologies, public documents, official pronouncements, or other manifestations of cultural orientations. Much of the research reviewed here points to the existence of such discrepancies, as does a larger body of evidence (see Spiro, 1993; Turiel, 1996, in press; Turiel et al., 1987, for further details). More generally, the multiplicity of orientations within cultures, including conflicts and ambiguities, means that morality cannot be simply characterized through particular ideologies like that of individuals with rights and freedom to enter into contracts or that of persons as interconnected in a social order of involuntary duties and roles.

CONCLUSION

Heterogeneity and variability in social judgments and actions do not stem solely from the presence of different groups or cultures within a society. The types of variations documented pertain to given cultures and individual members of those cultures. However, those variations are not haphazard, nor do the features of situations determine how people will act. Rather, heterogeneity and variation suggest that the thinking of individuals is flexible and takes into account different and varied aspects of the social world. The variety of social experiences is relevant to an understanding of moral development because children attend to much more than any one type or context of social experience. It is not only the family, or peers, or the culture that bears on children's development. Moreover, these and other aspects of a vast social world affect development through reciprocal interactions that include a coordination of emotions, thoughts, and actions. An important part of reciprocal interactions is that children engage in, and experience, disputes, conflicts, negotiations, ambiguities, and uncertainties—along with agreements, harmony, and certainties. Conflicts, uncertainties, and negotiations, however, are not solely dimensions that are resolved at particular childhood phases to be left behind with further social development or fuller participation in culture. Conflicts and uncertainties persist in social life.

As an interactional process, development entails attempts at understanding the judgments and positions of others, as well as participating in the collectivity. In an interactional process, however, individuals are likely to form judgments that at times are discrepant from those of others (e.g., parents or those represented in the collectivity). As a consequence, individuals may at times be in tension with culture and take a critical approach to it—even while simultaneously being a participant in the culture.

As children interact with a varied social world, their development entails the formation of different but systematic types or domains of social reasoning. Whereas morality is an important domain, it needs to be understood alongside and in intersection with other aspects of understandings of the social world. Because the social world is varied and because there are different domains of social judgment, generalizable and impartial moral prescriptions are not always applied in the same way. Social situations often require a balancing and coordination of different social and personal considerations related to features of the context. Consequently, although moral prescriptions dictate obligations based on right or wrong and how one ought to act, they do not dictate rigid rules or maxims. There is more than one way to reach a particular set of goals. Habermas (1993) articulated this feature of morality in his comments on how a traditional Kantian view failed to account for context:

> But the way in which Kant makes the break with conventional thought leaves him vulnerable to the charge of context insensitivity. Because he explicates the moral point of view in terms of the "moral law" and construes the question "What should I do?" exclusively in terms of the justification of maxims, he seems to restrict the exercise of practical reason to assessing alternative courses of action in light of the moral. Moral justification seems to amount to nothing more than the deductive application of an abstract basic principle to particular cases, with the result that the specific context of the given situation loses its *peculiar* relevance. (p. 120)

In the view of Habermas, rational principles can take different forms in their application in contexts, and are subject to change and elaboration through social discourse. However, critiques of "abstract" moral principles all too often postulate analogously abstract, decontextualized,

and general cultural orientations equally vulnerable to the criticism that situations and contexts lose their peculiar relevance. A critique of moral rationality like that of MacIntyre (1981) originally included the concern that rational principles do not address local and contextual circumstances, but resulted (see MacIntyre, 1988) in the propositions that morality best rests on religious tradition and authority and that agreements regarding moral principles should be inculcated through education designed by religious authorities. By relying on a system of religious tradition and authority for moral prescriptions, there is little room for contextual variations.

Especially in the United States, the current political and intellectual climate seems to be one that deemphasizes thought, reasoning, rationality, and reflective analyses and not infrequently places them under attack. Accordingly, emotions, with assumptions about their underlying evolutionary biological bases, are frequently regarded as central determinants of morality along with the authority of the group, or religion, or culture. As important as are emotions—especially sympathy, empathy, and respect—for moral functioning, emotions occur in and among persons who can think about them with regard to other people and in relation to complicated social agendas, goals, and arrangements. The relationships among emotions, moral judgments, reflections, and deliberations require a great deal of attention in research and in theoretical formulations. Investigators are less likely to address these relationships if reflective analyses are attacked as, at best, irrelevant to the layperson and, at worst, corrupting of individuals and society (Wilson, 1993). Still, scholars critiquing the proposition of rational, deliberative, and reflective moral functioning, themselves engage in those very activities, attempting to persuade others though rational discourse. These human activities are not solely the province of scholars, however. Laypersons, too, deliberate and reason systematically about emotions and morality and engage in discussion and argumentation.

ACKNOWLEDGMENTS

I wish to thank the people who provided many thoughtful and very helpful suggestions on earlier drafts of this manuscript: William Damon, Nancy Eisenberg, Charles Helwig, Melanie Killen, Marta Laupa, Larry Nucci, Judith Smetana, and Cecilia Wainryb. I am also grateful for comments and bibliographic assistance from Daphne Anshel, Theo Dawson, and James Mensing.

REFERENCES

Abu-Lughod, L. (1991). Writing against culture. In R. E. Fox (Ed.), *Recapturing anthropology: Working in the present* (pp. 137–162). Santa Fe, NM: School of American Research Press.

Abu-Lughod, L. (1993). *Writing women's worlds: Bedouin stories.* Berkeley: University of California Press.

Appadurai, A. (1988). Putting hierarchy in its place. *Cultural Anthropology, 3,* 36–49.

Aristotle. (1947). Nichomachean ethics. In R. McKeon (Ed.), *Introduction to Aristotle.* New York: Random House.

Aronfreed, J. (1961). The nature, variety, and social patterning of moral responses to transgressions. *Journal of Abnormal and Social Psychology, 63,* 223–240.

Aronfreed, J. (1968). *Conduct and conscience: The socialization of internalized control over behavior.* New York: Academic Press.

Aronfreed, J. (1976). Moral development from the standpoint of a general psychological theory. In T. Lickona (Ed.), *Moral development and behavior: Theory, research, and social issues* (pp. 54–69). New York: Holt, Rinehart and Winston.

Arsenio, W. (1988). Children's conceptions of the situational affective consequences of sociomoral events. *Child Development, 59,* 1611–1622.

Arsenio, W., Berlin, N., & O'Desky, I. (1989, April). *Children's and adults' understanding of sociomoral events.* Paper presented at the biennial meeting of the Society for Research in Child Development, Kansas City.

Arsenio, W., & Fleiss, K. (1996). Typical and behaviourally disruptive children's understanding of the emotional consequences of socio-moral events. *British Journal of Developmental Psychology, 14,* 173–186.

Arsenio, W., & Ford, M. (1985). The role of affective information in social-cognitive development: Children's differentiation of moral and conventional events. *Merril-Palmer Quarterly, 31,* 1–18.

Arsenio, W., & Kramer, R. (1992). Victimizers and their victims: Children's conceptions of the mixed emotional consequences of moral transgressions. *Child Development, 63,* 915–927.

Arsenio, W., & Lover, A. (1995). Children's conceptions of sociomoral affect: Happy victimizers, mixed emotions, and other expectancies. In M. Killen & D. Hart (Eds.), *Morality in everyday life: Developmental perspectives* (pp. 87–128). Cambridge, England: Cambridge University Press.

Asch, S. E. (1952). *Social psychology.* Englewood Cliffs, NJ: Prentice-Hall.

Asch, S. E. (1956). Studies of independence and conformity: A minority of one against a unanimous majority. *Psychological Monographs, 70*(No. 9).

Astor, R. A. (1994). Children's moral reasoning about family and peer violence: The role of provocation and retribution. *Child Development, 65,* 1054–1067.

Baldwin, J. M. (1896). *Social and ethical interpretations in mental development.* New York: Macmillan.

Bandura, A., & Walters, R. (1963). *Social learning and personality development.* New York: Holt, Rinehart and Winston.

Baumrind, D. (1973). The development of instrumental competence through socialization. In A. D. Pick (Ed.), *Minnesota Symposia on Child Psychology* (Vol. 7, pp. 3–46). Minneapolis: University of Minnesota Press.

Baumrind, D. (1986). Sex differences in moral judgment: Critique of Walker's conclusion that there are none. *Child Development, 57,* 511–521.

Baumrind, D. (1989). Rearing competent children. In W. Damon (Ed.), *Child development today and tomorrow* (pp. 349–378). San Francisco: Jossey-Bass.

Baumrind, D. (1997, April). *A correct moral standpoint is not impartial or universalizable.* Paper presented at the biennial meeting of the Society for Research in Child Development, Washington, DC.

Bellah, R. N., Madsen, R., Sullivan, W. M., Swidler, A., & Tipton, S. M. (1985). *Habits of the heart: Individualism and commitment in American life.* New York: Harper & Row.

Benedict, R. (1934). *Patterns of culture.* Boston: Houghton Mifflin.

Benedict, R. (1946). *The chrysanthemum and the sword: Patterns of Japanese culture.* Boston: Houghton Mifflin.

Bennett, W. J. (1992). *The de-valuing of America: The fight for our culture and our children.* New York: Simon & Schuster.

Bennett, W. J. (1993). *The book of virtues.* New York: Simon & Schuster.

Bennett, W. J., & Delattre, E. J. (1978). Moral education in the schools. *The Public Interest, 50,* 81–99.

Berkowitz, M. W., & Gibbs, J. C. (1983). Measuring the developmental features of moral discussion. *Merrill-Palmer Quarterly, 29,* 399–410.

Berkowitz, M. W., & Gibbs, J. C. (1985). The process of moral conflict resolution and moral development. In M. Berkowitz (Ed.), *Peer conflict and psychological growth: New directions for child development* (pp. 71–84). San Francisco: Jossey-Bass.

Berkowitz, M. W., Gibbs, J. C., & Broughton, J. M. (1980). The relation of moral judgment stage disparity to developmental effects of peer dialogues. *Merrill-Palmer Quarterly, 26,* 341–357.

Bersoff, D. M., & Miller, J. G. (1993). Culture, context, and the development of moral accountability judgments. *Developmental Psychology, 29,* 664–676.

Blasi, A. (1983). Moral cognition and moral action: A theoretical perspective. *Developmental Review, 3,* 178–210.

Blasi, A. (1993). The development of identity: Some implications for moral functioning. In G. G. Noam & T. E. Wren (Eds.), *The moral self: Building a better paradigm* (pp. 99–121). Cambridge, MA: MIT Press.

Blood, R. O., & Wolfe, D. M. (1960). *Husbands and wives: The dynamics of married living.* Glencoe, IL: Free Press.

Bloom, A. (1987). *The closing of the American mind: How higher education has failed democracy and impoverished the soul of today's students.* New York: Simon & Schuster.

Blum, L. (1990). Universality and particularity. In D. Schroder (Ed.), *The legacy of Lawrence Kohlberg* (pp. 59–70). San Francisco: Jossey-Bass.

Blumstein, P., & Schwartz, P. (1983). *American couples.* New York: Morrow.

Boyd, D. (1983). Careful justice or just caring: A response to Gilligan. *Proceedings of the Philosophy of Education Society, 38,* 63–69.

Braine, L. G., Pomerantz, E., Lorber, D., & Krantz, D. H. (1991). Conflicts with authority: Children's feelings, actions, and justifications. *Developmental Psychology, 27,* 829–840.

Broughton, J. (1983). Women's rationality and men's virtues. A critique of gender dualism in Gilligan's theory of moral development. *Social Research, 50,* 597–642.

Bruner, J. (1990). *Acts of meaning.* Cambridge, MA: Harvard University Press.

Bruner, J. (1996). *The culture of education.* Cambridge, MA: Harvard University Press.

Butterfield, F. (1995). *All God's children: The Boskett family and the American tradition of violence.* New York: Knopf.

Carey, N., & Ford, M. (1983, August). *Domains of social and self-regulation: An Indonesian study.* Paper presented at the meeting of the American Psychological Association, Los Angeles.

Catron, T. F., & Masters, J. C. (1993). Mothers' and children's conceptualizations of corporal punishment. *Child Development, 64,* 1815–1828.

Chilamkurti, C., & Milner, J. S. (1993). Perceptions and evaluations of child transgressions and disciplinary techniques in high- and low-risk mothers and their children. *Child Development, 64,* 1801–1814.

Chodorow, N. (1978). *The reproduction of mothering.* Berkeley: University of California Press.

Clifford, J. (1988). *The predicament of culture: Twentieth-century ethnography, literature, and art.* Cambridge, MA: Harvard University Press.

Colby, A., & Damon, W. (1983). Listening to a different voice: A review of Gilligan's "In a Different Voice." *Merrill-Palmer Quarterly, 29,* 473–481.

Colby, A., & Damon, W. (1992). *Some do care: Contemporary lives of moral commitment.* New York: Free Press.

Colby, A., & Kohlberg, L. (1987). *The measurement of moral judgment: Vol. 1. Theoretical foundations and research validation. Vol. 2. Standard issue scoring manual.* New York: Cambridge University Press.

Colby, A., Kohlberg, L., Gibbs, J., & Lieberman, M. (1983). A longitudinal study of moral judgment. *Monographs of the Society for Research in Child Development, 48*(Serial No. 200).

Cosmides, L., & Tooby, J. (1989). Evolutionary psychology and the generation of culture: II. Case study: A computational theory of social exchange. *Ethology and Sociobiology, 10,* 51–97.

Crane, D. A., & Tisak, M. (1995a). Does day-care experience affect young children's judgments of home and school rules? *Early Education and Child Development, 6,* 25–37.

Crane, D. A., & Tisak, M. (1995b). Mixed-domain events: The influence of moral and conventional components on the development of social reasoning. *Early Education and Development, 6,* 169–180.

Damon, W. (1975). Early conceptions of positive justice as related to the development of logical operations. *Child Development, 46,* 301–312.

Damon, W. (1977). *The social world of the child.* San Francisco: Jossey-Bass.

Damon, W. (1980). Patterns of change in children's social reasoning: A two-year longitudinal study. *Child Development, 51,* 1010–1017.

Damon, W. (1981). Exploring children's social cognition on two fronts. In J. M. Flavell & L. Ross (Eds.), *Social cognitive development: Frontiers and possible futures* (pp. 154–175). Cambridge, England: Cambridge University Press.

Damon, W. (1984). Peer education: The untapped potential. *Journal of Applied Developmental Psychology, 5,* 331–343.

Damon, W. (1988). *The moral child: Nurturing children's natural moral growth.* New York: Free Press.

Davidson, P., Turiel, E., & Black, A. (1983). The effect of stimulus familiarity on the use of criteria and justifications in children's social reasoning. *British Journal of Developmental Psychology, 1,* 49–65.

Duncker, K. (1939). Ethical relativity? (An inquiry into the psychology of ethics). *Mind, 48,* 39–53.

Dunn, J. (1987). The beginnings of moral understanding: Development in the second year. In J. Kagan & S. Lamb (Eds.), *The emergence of morality in young children* (pp. 91–112). Chicago: University of Chicago Press.

Dunn, J. (1988). *The beginnings of social understanding.* Cambridge, MA: Harvard University Press.

Dunn, J., Brown, J. R., & Maguire, M. (1995). The development of children's moral sensibility: Individual differences and emotion understanding. *Developmental Psychology, 31,* 649–659.

Dunn, J., & Munn, P. (1987). Development of justification in disputes with mother and sibling. *Developmental Psychology, 23,* 791–798.

Durkheim, E. (1961). *Moral education.* Glencoe, IL: Free Press. (Original work published 1925)

Durkheim, E. (1965). *The elementary forms of the religious life.* New York: Free Press. (Original work published 1912)

Dworkin, R. M. (1977). *Taking rights seriously.* Cambridge, MA: Harvard University Press.

Dworkin, R. M. (1993). *Life's dominion: An argument about abortion, euthanasia, and individual freedom.* New York: Knopf.

Eisenberg, N., Carlo, G., Murphy, B., & Van Court, N. (1995). Prosocial development in late adolescence: A longitudinal study. *Child Development, 66,* 1179–1197.

Eisenberg, N., & Fabes, R. A. (1990). Empathy: Conceptualization, measurement, and relation to prosocial behavior. *Motivation and Emotion, 14,* 131–149.

Eisenberg, N., & Fabes, R. A. (1991). Prosocial behavior: A multimethod developmental perspective. In M. S. Clark (Ed.), *Review of personality and social psychology* (Vol. 2, pp. 34–61). Newbury Park, CA: Sage.

Eisenberg, N., Lennon, R., & Roth, K. (1983). Prosocial development: A longitudinal study. *Developmental Psychology, 19,* 846–855.

Eisenberg, N., Lundy, T., Shell, R., & Roth, K. (1985). Children's justifications for their adult and peer-directed compliant (prosocial and nonprosocial) behaviors. *Developmental Psychology, 21,* 325–331.

Eisenberg, N., & Miller, P. A. (1987). The relation of empathy to prosocial and related behaviors. *Psychological Bulletin, 101,* 91–119.

Eisenberg, N., Miller, P. A., Shell, R., McNalley, S., & Shea, C. (1991). Prosocial development in adolescence: A longitudinal study. *Developmental Psychology, 27,* 849–857.

Eisenberg, N., Shell, R., Pasternack, J., Lennon, R., Beller, R., & Mathy, R. M. (1987). Prosocial development in middle childhood: A longitudinal study. *Developmental Psychology, 23,* 712–718.

Eisenberg, N., & Strayer, J. (Eds.). (1987). *Empathy and its development.* New York: Cambridge University Press.

Eisenberg-Berg, N. (1979). Development of children's prosocial moral judgment. *Developmental Psychology, 15,* 128–137.

Eisenberg-Berg, N., & Geisheker, E. (1979). Content of preachings and power of the model/preacher: The effect on children's generosity. *Developmental Psychology, 15,* 168–175.

Eisenberg-Berg, N., & Roth, K. (1980). Development of young children's prosocial moral judgment: A longitudinal follow-up. *Developmental Psychology, 16,* 375–376.

Etzioni, A. (1993). *The spirit of community: The reinvention of American society.* New York: Touchstone.

Faludi, S. (1991). *Backlash: The undeclared war against American women.* New York: Doubleday.

Fass, P. (1977). *The damned and the beautiful: American youth in the 1920s.* New York: Oxford University Press.

Freud, S. (1959). Some psychological consequences of the anatomical distinction between the sexes. In S. Freud (Ed.), *Collected papers* (pp. 186–197). New York: Basic Books.

Fromm, E. (1941). *Escape from freedom.* New York: Holt, Rinehart and Winston.

Geertz, C. (1984). "From the native's point of view": On the nature of anthropological understanding. In R. A. Shweder & R. A. Levine (Eds.), *Culture theory: Essays on mind, self, and emotion* (pp. 123–136). Cambridge, England: Cambridge University Press.

Gerson, R., & Damon, W. (1978). Moral understanding and children's conduct. In W. Damon (Ed.), *Moral development: New directions in child development* (pp. 41–60). San Francisco: Jossey-Bass.

Gewirth, A. (1978). *Reason and morality.* Chicago: University of Chicago Press.

Gewirth, A. (1982). *Human rights: Essays on justification and applications.* Chicago: University of Chicago Press.

Gibbs, J. C. (1991). Toward an integration of Kohlberg's and Hoffman's moral development theories. *Human Development, 34,* 88–104.

Gilligan, C. (1977). In a different voice: Women's conceptions of self and of morality. *Harvard Educational Review, 47,* 481–517.

Gilligan, C. (1982). *In a different voice: Psychological theory and women's development.* Cambridge, MA: Harvard University Press.

Gilligan, C. (1986). On in a different voice: An interdisciplinary forum: Reply. *Signs, 11,* 324–333.

Gilligan, C., & Attanucci, J. (1988). Two moral orientations: Gender differences and similarities. *Merrill-Palmer Quarterly, 34,* 223–237.

Gilligan, C., Ward, J. V., Taylor, J. M., & Bardige, B. (Eds.). (1988). *Mapping the moral domain: A contribution of women's thinking to psychological theory and education.* Cambridge, MA: Harvard University Press.

Gilligan, C., & Wiggins, G. (1987). The origins of morality in early childhood relationships. In J. Kagan & S. Lamb (Eds.), *The emergence of morality in young children* (pp. 277–305). Chicago: University of Chicago Press.

Greeno, C. G., & Maccoby, E. E. (1986). How different is the "different voice?" *Signs, 11,* 313–314.

Grusec, J. E., & Goodnow, J. J. (1994). Impact of parental discipline methods on the child's internalization of values: A reconceptualization of current points of view. *Developmental Psychology, 30,* 4–19.

Habermas, J. (1990a). *Moral consciousness and communicative action.* Cambridge, MA: MIT Press.

Habermas, J. (1990b). Justice and solidarity: On the discussion concerning stage 6. In T. E. Wren (Ed.), *The moral domain: Essays in the ongoing discussion between philosophy and the social sciences* (pp. 224–254). Cambridge, MA: MIT Press.

Habermas, J. (1993). *Justification and application.* Cambridge, MA: MIT Press.

Haidt, J., Koller, S. H., & Dias, M. G. (1993). Affect, culture, and morality, or is it wrong to eat your dog? *Journal of Personality and Social Psychology, 65,* 613–628.

Haney, C., Banks, C., & Zimbardo, P. (1973). Interpersonal dynamics in a simulated prison. *International Journal of Criminology and Penology, 1,* 69–97.

Hart, D. (1988a). Self-concept in the social context of the adolescent. In D. Lapsely & F. C. Power (Eds.), *Self, ego, and identity: Integrative approaches* (pp. 71–90). New York: Springer-Verlag.

Hart, D. (1988b). A longitudinal study of adolescents' socialization and identification as predictors of adult moral judgment development. *Merrill-Palmer Quarterly, 34,* 245–260.

Hart, D., & Chmiel, S. (1992). Influence of defense mechanisms on moral judgment development: A longitudinal study. *Developmental Psychology, 28,* 722–730.

Hart, D., & Fegley, S. (1995). Prosocial behavior and caring in adolescence: Relations to self-understanding and social judgment. *Child Development, 66,* 1346–1359.

Hart, D., Yates, M., Fegley, S., & Wilson, G. (1995). Moral commitment in adolescence. In M. Killen & D. Hart (Eds.), *Morality in everyday life: Developmental perspectives* (pp. 317–341). Cambridge, England: Cambridge University Press.

Hartshorne, H., & May, M. A. (1928–1930). *Studies in the nature of character. Volume 1: Studies in deceit. Volume 2: Studies in self-control. Volume 3: Studies in the organization of character.* New York: Macmillan.

Haste, H. (1990). Moral responsibility and moral commitment: The integration of affect and cognition. In T. E. Wren (Ed.), *The moral domain: Essays in the ongoing discussion between philosophy and the social sciences* (pp. 315–359). Cambridge, MA: MIT Press.

Haste, H. (1993). Morality, self, and sociohistorical context: The role of lay social theory. In G. G. Noam & T. E. Wren (Eds.), *The moral self: Building a better paradigm* (pp. 175–208). Cambridge, MA: MIT Press.

Haste, H. (1994). "You've come a long way, babe": A catalyst of feminist conflicts. *Feminism and Psychology, 4,* 399–403.

Haste, H., & Baddeley, J. (1991). Moral theory and culture: The case of gender. In W. M. Kurtines & J. L. Gewirtz (Eds.), *Handbook of moral behavior and development: Vol. 1. Theory* (pp. 222–249). Hillsdale, NJ: Erlbaum.

Hatch, E. (1983). *Culture and morality: The relativity of values in anthropology.* New York: Columbia University Press.

Helwig, C. C. (1991). *Adolescents' and young adults' conceptions of civil liberties: Freedom of speech and religion.* Unpublished doctoral dissertation, University of California, Berkeley.

Helwig, C. C. (1995a). Adolescents' and young adults' conceptions of civil liberties: Freedom of speech and religion. *Child Development, 66,* 152–166.

Helwig, C. C. (1995b). Social context in social cognition. In M. Killen & D. Hart (Eds.), *Morality in everyday life: Developmental perspectives* (pp. 166–200). Cambridge, England: Cambridge University Press.

Helwig, C. C., Tisak, M., & Turiel, E. (1990). Children's social reasoning in context. *Child Development, 61,* 2068–2078.

Helwig, C. C., Turiel, E., & Nucci, L. P. (1996). The virtues and vices of moral development theorists. *Developmental Review, 16,* 69–107.

Hochschild, A. (1989). *The second shift.* New York: Avon Books.

Hoffman, M. L. (1963). Childrearing practices and moral development: Generalizations from empirical research. *Child Development, 34,* 295–318.

Hoffman, M. L. (1970). Moral development. In P. H. Mussen (Ed.), *Carmichael's manual of child psychology* (Vol. 2, pp. 261–359). New York: Wiley.

Hoffman, M. L. (1983). Affective and cognitive processes in moral internalization: An information processing approach. In E. T. Higgins, D. Ruble, & W. W. Hartup (Eds.), *Social cognition and social development* (pp. 236–274). Cambridge, England: Cambridge University Press.

Hoffman, M. L. (1984). Empathy, its limitations, and its role in a comprehensive moral theory. In W. M. Kurtines & J. L. Gewirtz (Eds.), *Morality, moral behavior, and moral development: Basic issues in theory and research* (pp. 283–302). New York: Wiley.

Hoffman, M. L. (1991a). Empathy, social cognition, and moral action. In W. M. Kurtines & J. L. Gewirtz (Eds.), *Handbook of moral behavior and development: Vol. 1. Theory* (pp. 275–301). Hillsdale NJ: Erlbaum.

Hoffman, M. L. (1991b). Commentary on: Toward an integration of Kohlberg's and Hoffman's moral development theories. *Human Development, 34,* 105–110.

Hoffman, M. L., & Saltzstein, H. D. (1967). Parent discipline and the child's moral development. *Journal of Personality and Social Psychology, 5,* 45–57.

Hollan, D. (1992). Cross-cultural differences in the self. *Journal of Anthropological Research, 48,* 283–300.

Hollos, M., Leis, P. E., & Turiel, E. (1986). Social reasoning in Ijo children and adolescents in Nigerian communities. *Journal of Cross-Cultural Psychology, 17,* 352–374.

Hume, D. (1966). *An enquiry concerning the principles of morals.* Oxford, England: Clarendon Press. (Original work published 1751)

James, W. (1890). *The principles of psychology.* New York: Holt.

Johnston, D. K. (1988). Adolescents' solutions to dilemmas in fables: Two moral orientations—two problem solving strategies. In C. Gilligan, J. V. Ward, J. M. Taylor, & B. Bardige (Eds.), *Mapping the moral domain: A contribution of women's thinking to psychological theory and education* (pp. 49–71). Cambridge, MA: Harvard University Press.

Kagan, J. (1984). *The nature of the child.* New York: Basic Books.

Kahn, P. H. (1992). Children's obligatory and discretionary moral judgments. *Child Development, 63,* 416–430.

Keller, M., & Edelstein, W. (1990). The emergence of morality in interpersonal relationships. In T. E. Wren (Ed.), *The moral domain: Essays in the ongoing discussion between philosophy and the social sciences* (pp. 255–282). Cambridge, MA: MIT Press.

Keller, M., & Edelstein, W. (1991). The development of sociomoral meaning making: Domains, categories, and perspective-taking. In W. M. Kurtines & J. L. Gewirtz (Eds.), *Handbook of moral behavior and development: Vol. 1. Theory* (pp. 89–114). Hillsdale, NJ: Erlbaum.

Keller, M., & Edelstein, W. (1993). The development of the moral self from childhood to adolescence. In G. G. Noam & T. E. Wren (Eds.), *The moral self: Building a better paradigm* (pp. 310–336). Cambridge, MA: MIT Press.

Kelman, H. C., & Hamilton, V. L. (1989). *Crimes of obedience: Toward a social psychology of authority and responsibility.* New Haven, CT: Yale University Press.

Killen, M. (1989). Context, conflict, and coordination in social development. In L. T. Winegar (Ed.), *Social interaction and the development of children's understanding* (pp. 119–146). Norwood, NJ: ABLEX.

Killen, M. (1990). Children's evaluations of morality in the context of peer, teacher-child and familial relations. *Journal of Genetic Psychology, 151,* 395–410.

Killen, M. (1991). Social and moral development in early childhood. In W. M. Kurtines & J. L. Gewirtz (Eds.), *Handbook of moral behavior and development: Vol. 2. Research* (pp. 115–138). Hillsdale, NJ: Erlbaum.

Killen, M., & Naigles, L. (1995). Preschool children pay attention to their addresses: The effects of gender composition on peer disputes. *Discourse Processes, 19,* 329–346.

Killen, M., & Nucci, L. P. (1995). Morality, autonomy, and social conflict. In M. Killen & D. Hart (Eds.), *Morality in everyday life: Developmental perspectives* (pp. 52–86). Cambridge, England: Cambridge University Press.

Killen, M., & Sueyoshi, L. (1995). Conflict resolution in Japanese social interactions. *Early Education and Development, 6,* 313–330.

Kim, J. M. (in press). Korean children's concepts of adult and peer authority and moral reasoning. *Developmental Psychology.*

Kim, J. M., & Turiel, E. (1996). Korean and American children's concepts of adult and peer authority. *Social Development, 5,* 310–329.

Kochanska, G. (1991). Socialization and temperament in the development of guilt and conscience. *Child Development, 62,* 1379–1392.

Kochanska, G. (1993). Toward a synthesis of parental socialization and child temperament in early development of conscience. *Child Development, 64,* 325–347.

Kochanska, G. (1994). Beyond cognition: Expanding the search for the early roots of internalization and conscience. *Developmental Psychology, 30,* 20–22.

Kohlberg, L. (1963). Moral development and identification. In H. W. Stevenson (Ed.), *Child psychology: 62nd yearbook of the National Society for the Study of Education* (pp. 277–332). Chicago: University of Chicago Press.

Kohlberg, L. (1964). Development of moral character and moral ideology. In M. L. Hoffman & L. W. Hoffman (Eds.), *Review of child development research* (Vol. 1, pp. 283–432). New York: Sage.

Kohlberg, L. (1968). The child as a moral philosopher. *Psychology Today, 2,* 25–30.

Kohlberg, L. (1969). Stage and sequence: The cognitive-developmental approach to socialization. In D. Goslin (Ed.), *Handbook of socialization theory and research* (pp. 347–480). Chicago: Rand McNally.

Kohlberg, L. (1970). Education for justice: A modern statement of the Platonic view. In N. F. Sizer & T. R. Sizer (Eds.), *Moral education: Five lectures* (pp. 56–83). Cambridge, MA: Harvard University Press.

Kohlberg, L. (1971). From is to ought: How to commit the naturalistic fallacy and get away with it in the study of moral development. In T. Mischel (Ed.), *Psychology and genetic epistemology* (pp. 151–235). New York: Academic Press.

Kohlberg, L. (1976). Moral stages and moralization. The cognitive developmental approach. In T. Lickona (Ed.), *Moral development and behavior: Theory, research, and social issues* (pp. 31–53). New York: Holt, Rinehart and Winston.

Kohlberg, L. (1984). *Essays on moral development: The psychology of moral development.* San Francisco: Harper & Row.

Kohlberg, L., & Kramer, R. (1969). Continuities and discontinuities in childhood and adult moral development. *Human Development, 12,* 93–120.

Kohlberg, L., Levine, C., & Hewer, A. (1983). Moral stages: A current formulation and a response to critics. *Contributions to Human Development, 10,* 104–166.

Kuczynski, L., Kochanska, G., Radke-Yarrow, M., & Girnius-Brown, O. (1987). A developmental interpretation of young children's noncompliance. *Developmental Psychology, 23,* 799–806.

Latanée, B., & Darley, J. M. (1970). *The unresponsive bystander: Why doesn't he help?* New York: Appleton-Crofts.

Laupa, M. (1991). Children's reasoning about three authority attributes: Adult status, knowledge, and social position. *Developmental Psychology, 27,* 321–329.

Laupa, M. (1994). "Who's in charge?" Preschool children's concepts of authority. *Early Childhood Research Quarterly, 9,* 1–17.

Laupa, M., & Turiel, E. (1986). Children's conceptions of adult and peer authority. *Child Development, 57,* 405–412.

Laupa, M., & Turiel, E. (1993). Children's concepts of authority and social contexts. *Journal of Educational Psychology, 85,* 191–197.

Laupa, M., Turiel, E., & Cowan, P. A. (1995). Obedience to authority in children and adults. In M. Killen & D. Hart (Eds.), *Morality in everyday life: Developmental perspectives* (pp. 131–165). Cambridge, England: Cambridge University Press.

Lennon, R., & Eisenberg, N. (1987). Gender and age differences in empathy and sympathy. In N. Eisenberg & J. Strayer (Eds.), *Empathy and its development* (pp. 195–217). New York: Cambridge University Press.

Luria, Z. (1986). A methodological critique. *Signs, 11,* 318.

Lyons, N. P. (1983). Two perspectives: On self, relationships, and morality. *Harvard Educational Review, 53,* 125–145.

Maccoby, E. E. (1968). The development of moral values and behavior in childhood. In J. A. Clausen (Ed.), *Socialization and society* (pp. 227–269). Boston: Little, Brown.

Maccoby, E. E., & Jacklin, C. N. (1974). *The psychology of sex differences.* Stanford, CA: Stanford University Press.

Maccoby, E. E., & Martin, J. A. (1983). Socialization in the context of the family: Parent-child interaction. In P. Mussen (Series Ed.) & E. M. Hetherington (Ed.), *Socialization, personality, and social development: Vol. 4. Handbook of child psychology* (4th ed., pp. 1–102). Wiley: New York.

MacIntyre, A. (1981). *After virtue: A study in moral theory.* Notre Dame, IN: University of Notre Dame Press.

MacIntyre, A. (1988). *Whose justice? Which rationality?* Notre Dame, IN: University of Notre Dame Press.

Madden, T. (1992). *Cultural factors and assumptions in social reasoning in India.* Unpublished doctoral dissertation, University of California, Berkeley.

Markus, H. R., & Kitayama, S. (1991). Culture and the self: Implications for cognition, emotion, and motivation. *Psychological Review, 98,* 224–253.

McClosky, M., & Brill, A. (1983). *Dimensions of tolerance: What Americans believe about civil liberties.* New York: Sage.

McDougall, W. (1908). *An introduction to social psychology.* London: Methuen.

Mead, M. (1928). *Coming of age in Samoa.* New York: Dell.

Mednick, M. T. (1989). On the politics of psychological constructs: Stop the bandwagon, I want to get off. *American Psychologist, 44,* 1118–1123.

Mernissi, F. (1994). *Dreams of trespass: Tales of a harem childhood.* Reading, MA: Addison-Wesley.

Milgram, S. (1974). *Obedience to authority.* New York: Harper & Row.

Mill, J. S. (1963). *On liberty.* London: Oxford University Press. (Original work published 1863)

Miller, J. G. (1984). Culture and the development of everyday social explanation. *Journal of Personality and Social Psychology, 46,* 961–978.

Miller, J. G. (1986). Early cross-cultural commonalities in social explanation. *Developmental Psychology, 22,* 514–520.

Miller, J. G. (1994a). Cultural diversity in the morality of caring: Individually oriented versus duty-based interpersonal moral codes. *Cross-Cultural Research, 28,* 3–39.

Miller, J. G. (1994b). Cultural psychology: Bridging disciplinary boundaries in understanding the cultural grounding of self. In P. K. Bock (Ed.), *Handbook of psychological anthropology* (pp. 139–170). Westport, CT: Praeger/Greenwood.

Miller, J. G., & Bersoff, D. M. (1992). Culture and moral judgment: How are conflicts between justice and interpersonal responsibilities resolved? *Journal of Personality and Social Psychology, 62,* 541–554.

Miller, J. G., & Bersoff, D. M. (1995). Development in the context of everyday family relationships: Culture, interpersonal morality, and adaption. In M. Killen & D. Hart (Eds.), *Morality in everyday life: Developmental perspectives* (pp. 259–282). Cambridge, England: Cambridge University Press.

Miller, J. G., Bersoff, D. M., & Harwood, R. L. (1990). Perceptions of social responsibilities in India and in the United States: Moral imperatives or personal decisions? *Journal of Personality and Social Psychology, 58,* 33–47.

Miller, J. G., & Luthar, S. (1989). Issues of interpersonal responsibility and accountability: A comparison of Indians' and Americans' moral judgments. *Social Cognition, 7,* 237–261.

Miller, N. E., & Dollard, J. (1941). *Social learning and imitation.* New Haven, CT: Yale University Press.

Mills, C. W. (1956). *White collar: The American middle-class.* New York: Oxford University Press.

Mines, M. (1988). Conceptualizing the person: Hierarchial society and individual autonomy in India. *American Antropologist, 90,* 568–579.

Mischel, W. (1973). Toward a cognitive social learning reconceptualization of personality. *Psychological Review, 80,* 252–283.

Nissan, M. (1987). Moral norms and social conventions: A cross-cultural comparison. *Developmental Psychology, 23,* 719–725.

Norris, K. (1996). *Lying in the age of innocence: The deceitful child in Fin-de-Siecle France.* Paper presented at the Society for French Historical Studies Annual Meeting, Boston, MA.

Nucci, L. P. (1981). The development of personal concepts: A domain distinct from moral or social concepts. *Child Development, 52,* 114–121.

Nucci, L. P. (1984). Evaluating teachers as social agents: Students' ratings of domain appropriate and domain inappropriate teacher responses to transgressions. *American Educational Research Journal, 21,* 367–378.

Nucci, L. P. (1996). Morality and the personal sphere of action. In E. Reed, E. Turiel, & T. Brown (Eds.), *Values and knowledge* (pp. 41–60). Hillsdale, NJ: Erlbaum.

Nucci, L. P., Camino, C., & Milnitsky-Sapiro, C. (1996). Social class effects on Northeastern Brazilian children's conceptions of areas of personal choice and social regulation. *Child Development, 67,* 1223–1242.

Nucci, L. P., & Lee, J. (1993). Morality and personal autonomy. In G. G. Noam & T. Wren (Eds.), *The moral self: Building a better paradigm* (pp. 123–148). Cambridge, MA: MIT Press.

Nucci, L. P., & Nucci, M. S. (1982a). Children's reponses to moral and social conventional transgressions in free-play settings. *Child Development, 53,* 1337–1342.

Nucci, L. P., & Nucci, M. S. (1982b). Children's social interactions in the context of moral and conventional transgressions. *Child Development, 53,* 403–412.

Nucci, L. P., & Smetana, J. G. (1996). Mother's concepts of young children's areas of personal freedom. *Child Development, 67,* 1870–1886.

Nucci, L. P., & Turiel, E. (1978). Social interactions and the development of social concepts in preschool children. *Child Development, 49,* 400–407.

Nucci, L. P., & Turiel, E. (1993). God's word, religious rules and their relation to Christian and Jewish children's concepts of morality. *Child Development, 64,* 1485–1491.

Nucci, L. P., Turiel, E., & Encarnacion-Gawrych, G. (1983). Children's social interactions and social concepts: Analyses of morality and convention in the Virgin Islands. *Journal of Cross-Cultural Psychology, 14,* 469–487.

Nucci, L. P., & Weber, E. (1995). Social interactions in the home and the development of young children's conceptions of the personal. *Child Development, 66,* 1438–1452.

Nunner-Winkler, G. (1984). Two moralities? A critical discussion of an ethic of care and responsibility versus an ethic of rights and justice. In W. M. Kurtines & J. L. Gewirtz (Eds.), *Morality, moral behavior, and moral development: Basic issues in theory and research* (pp. 348–364). New York: Wiley.

Nunner-Winkler, G., & Sodian, B. (1988). Children's understanding of moral emotions. *Child Development, 59,* 1323–1328.

Nussbaum, M. (1989, December 7). Recoiling from reason [Review of the book *Whose justice? Which rationality?*]. *The New York Review of Books,* 36–41.

Okin, S. M. (1989). *Justice, gender, and the family.* New York: Basic Books.

Okin, S. M. (1996). The gendered family and the development of a sense of justice. In E. S. Reed, E. Turiel, & T. Brown (Eds.), *Values and knowledge* (pp. 61–74). Hillsdale, NJ: Erlbaum.

Ornstein, P. (1994). *Schoolgirls: Young women, self esteem, and the confidence gap.* New York: Doubleday.

Parke, R. D., & Walters, R. M. (1967). Some factors influencing the efficacy of punishment training for inducing response inhibition. *Monographs of the Society for Research in Child Development, 32*(1).

Piaget, J. (1929). *The child's conception of the world.* London: Routledge & Kegan Paul.

Piaget, J. (1932). *The moral judgment of the child.* London: Routledge & Kegan Paul.

Piaget, J. (1995). *Sociological studies.* London: Routledge & Kegan Paul. (Original work published 1960)

Pollitt, K. L. (1992). Are women really superior to men? *The Nation,* 799–807.

Pratt, M. W., Diessner, R., Hunsberger, B., Pancer, S. M., & Savoy, K. (1991). Four pathways in the analysis of adult development and aging: Comparing analyses of reasoning about personal-life dilemmas. *Psychology and Aging, 6,* 666–675.

Pratt, M. W., Golding, G., & Hunter, W. (1983). Aging as ripening: Character and consistency of moral judgment in young, mature, and older adults. *Human Development, 26,* 277–288.

Pratt, M. W., Golding, G., & Hunter, W. (1984). Does morality have a gender? Sex, sex role, and moral judgment relationships across the adult lifespan. *Merrill-Palmer Quarterly, 30,* 321–340.

Pratt, M. W., Golding, G., Hunter, W., & Norris, J. (1988). From inquiry to judgment: Age and sex differences in patterns of adult moral thinking and information-seeking. *International Journal of Aging and Human Development, 27,* 109–124.

Pratt, M. W., Golding, G., Hunter, W., & Sampson, R. (1988). Sex differences in adult moral orientations. *Journal of Personality, 56,* 373–391.

Radke-Yarrow, M., Zahn-Waxler, C., & Chapman, M. (1983). Children's prosocial dispositions and behavior. In P. Mussen (Series Ed.) & E. M. Hetherington (Ed.), *Socialization, personality, and social development: Vol. 4. Handbook of child psychology* (4th ed., pp. 469–545). New York: Wiley.

Rawls, J. (1971). *A theory of justice.* Cambridge, MA: Harvard University Press.

Rawls, J. (1993). *Political liberalism.* New York: Columbia University Press.

Reisman, D. (with N. Glazer & R. Denney). (1950). *The lonely crowd: A study of the changing American character.* New York: Doubleday.

Rende, R., & Killen, M. (1992). Social interactional antecedents of object conflict. *Early Childhood Research Quarterly, 1,* 551–563.

Rest, J. (1979). *Development in judging moral issues.* Minneapolis: University of Minnesota Press.

Rest, J. (1983). Morality. In P. Mussen (Ed.) & J. H. Flavell & E. Markman (Eds.), *Cognitive development: Vol. 3. Handbook of child psychology* (4th ed., pp. 920–990). New York: Wiley.

Rest, J., & Narvaez, D. (1991). The college experience and moral development. In W. M. Kurtines & J. L. Gewirtz (Eds.), *Handbook of moral behavior and development: Vol. 2. Research* (pp. 229–245). Hillsdale, NJ: Erlbaum.

Ross, L., Bierbrauer, G., & Hoffman, S. (1976). The role of attributional processes in conformity and dissent: Revisiting the Asch situation. *American Psychologist, 31,* 148–157.

Ross, L., & Nisbett, R. M. (1991). *The person and the situation: Perspectives on social psychology.* Philadelphia: Temple University Press.

Rothbart, M. K., Hanley, D., & Albert, M. (1986). Gender differences in moral reasoning. *Sex Roles, 15,* 645–653.

Ryan, A. (1995). *John Dewey and the high tide of American liberalism.* New York: Norton.

Ryan, K. (1989). In defense of character education. In L. P. Nucci (Ed.), *Moral development and character education: A dialogue* (pp. 3–18). Berkeley, CA: McCutchan.

Sagi, A., & Hoffman, M. L. (1976). Empathic distress in the newborn. *Developmental Psychology, 32,* 720–729.

Saltzstein, H. D., Weiner, S., & Munk, J. (1995). *Children's judgments of the fairness of mothers who approve/disapprove good and bad intended acts.* Unpublished manuscript, City University of New York.

Saltzstein, M. D., Weiner, A. S., Munk, J. S., Supraner, A., Blank, R., & Schwarz, R. P. (1987). Comparison between children's own moral judgments and those they attribute to adults. *Merrill-Palmer Quarterly, 33,* 33–51.

Sampson, E. E. (1977). Psychology and the American ideal. *Journal of Personality and Social Psychology, 35,* 767–782.

Sears, R. R., Maccoby, E. E., & Levin, M. (1957). *Patterns of child reasoning.* Evanston, IL: Row-Peterson.

Selman, R. L. (1976). Social-cognitive understanding: A guide to educational and clinical practices. In T. Lickona (Ed.), *Moral development and behavior: Theory, research, and social issues* (pp. 299–316). New York: Holt, Rinehart and Winston.

Selman, R. L. (1980). *The growth of interpersonal understanding: Developmental and clinical analyses.* New York: Academic Press.

Shweder, R. A. (1982). Liberalism as destiny. *Contemporary Psychology, 27,* 421–424.

Shweder, R. A. (1986). Divergent rationalities. In D. W. Fiske & R. A. Shweder (Eds.), *Metatheory in social science: Pluralism and subjectivities* (pp. 163–196). Chicago: University of Chicago Press.

Shweder, R. A. (1990a). Cultural psychology—What is it? In J. W. Stigler, R. A. Shweder, & G. Herdt (Eds.), *Cultural psychology: Essays on camparative human development* (pp. 1–43). Cambridge, England: Cambridge University Press.

Shweder, R. A. (1990b). In defense of moral realism: Reply to Gabennesch. *Child Development, 61,* 2060–2067.

Shweder, R. A. (1994). Are moral intuitions self-evident truths? *Criminal Justice Ethics, 13,* 24–31.

Shweder, R. A., & Bourne, E. J. (1982). Does the concept of person vary cross-culturally? In A. J. Marsella & G. M. White (Eds.), *Cultural conceptions of mental health and therapy* (pp. 97–137). Boston: Reidel.

Shweder, R. A., & Haidt, J. (1993). The future of moral psychology: Truth, intuition, and the pluralist way. *Psychological Science, 4,* 360–356.

Shweder, R. A., Jensen, L. A., & Goldstein, W. M. (1995). Who sleeps by whom revisited: A method for extracting the moral goods implicit in practice. In J. J. Goodnow, P. J. Miller, & F. Kessel (Eds.), *Cultural practices as contexts for development: New directions for child development* (pp. 21–39). San Francisco: Jossey-Bass.

Shweder, R. A., Mahapatra, M., & Miller, J. G. (1987). Culture and moral development. In J. Kagan & S. Lamb (Eds.), *The emergence of morality in young children* (pp. 1–83). Chicago: University of Chicago Press.

Shweder, R. A., & Miller, J. G. (1985). The social construction of the person: How is it possible? In K. J. Gergen & K. Davis (Eds.), *The social construction of the person* (pp. 41–69). New York: Springler-Verlag.

Shweder, R. A., Much, N. C., Mahapatra, M., & Park, L. (1997). The "Big Three" of morality (Autonomy, Community, and Divinity) and the "Big Three" explanations of suffering. In A. Brandt & P. Rozin (Eds.), *Morality and health* (pp. 119–169). Stanford, CA: Stanford University Press.

Shweder, R. A., & Sullivan, M. A. (1993). Cultural psychology: Who needs it? *Annual Review of Psychology, 44,* 497–523.

Siegal, M., & Storey, R. M. (1985). Day care and children's conceptions of moral and social rules. *Child Development, 56,* 1001–1008.

Simpson, E. L. (1973). Moral development research: A case study of scientific cultural bias. *Human Development, 17,* 81–106.

Skinner, B. F. (1971). *Beyond freedom and dignity.* New York: Knopf.

Smetana, J. G. (1981). Preschool conceptions of moral and social rules. *Child Development, 52,* 1333–1336.

Smetana, J. G. (1982). *Concepts of self and morality: Women's reasoning about abortion.* New York: Praeger.

Smetana, J. G. (1983). Social-cognitive development: Domain distinctions and coordinations. *Developmental Review, 3,* 131–147.

Smetana, J. G. (1984). Toddlers' social interactions regarding moral and conventional transgressions. *Child Development, 55,* 1767–1776.

Smetana, J. G. (1985). Preschool children's conceptions of transgressions: Effects of varying moral and conventional domain-related attributes. *Developmental Psychology, 21,* 18–29.

Smetana, J. G. (1988). Adolescents' and parents' conceptions of parental authority. *Child Development, 59,* 321–335.

Smetana, J. G. (1989a). Adolescents' and parents' reasoning about actual family conflict. *Child Development, 60,* 1052–1067.

Smetana, J. G. (1989b). Toddlers' social interactions in the context of moral and conventional transgressions in the home. *Developmental Psychology, 25,* 499–508.

Smetana, J. G. (1990). *Toddlers' social interactions in the context of harm.* Unpublished manuscript, University of Rochester, Rochester, NY.

Smetana, J. G. (1993). Conceptions of parental authority in divorced and married mothers and their adolescents. *Journal of Research in Adolescence, 3,* 19–40.

Smetana, J. G. (1995a). Morality in context: Abstractions, ambiguities, and applications. In R. Vasta (Ed.), *Annals of child development* (Vol. 10, pp. 83–130). London: Jessica Kingsley.

Smetana, J. G. (1995b). Context, conflict, and constraint in adolescent–parent authority relationships. In M. Killen & D. Hart (Eds.), *Morality in everyday life: Developmental*

perspectives (pp. 225–255). Cambridge, England: Cambridge University Press.

Smetana, J. G., & Asquith, P. (1994). Adolescents' and parents' conceptions of parental authority and adolescent autonomy. *Child Development, 65,* 1147–1162.

Smetana, J. G., & Braeges, J. L. (1990). The development of toddler's moral and conventional judgments. *Merrill-Palmer Quarterly, 36,* 329–346.

Smetana, J. G., Braeges, J. L., & Yau, J. (1991). Doing what you say and saying what you do: Reasoning about adolescent-parent conflict in interviews and interactions. *Journal of Adolescent Research, 6,* 276–295.

Smetana, J. G., Bridgeman, D. L., & Turiel, E. (1983). Differentiation of domains and prosocial behaviors. In D. L. Bridgeman (Ed.), *The nature of prosocial development: Interdisciplinary theories and strategies* (pp. 163–183). New York: Academic Press.

Smetana, J. G., Killen, M., & Turiel, E. (1991). Children's reasoning about interpersonal and moral conflicts. *Child Development, 62,* 629–644.

Smetana, J. G., Schlagman, N., & Adams, P. W. (1993). Preschool children's judgments about hypothetical and actual transgressions. *Child Development, 64,* 202–214.

Smetana, J. G., Yau, J., Restrepo, A., & Braeges, J. (1991). Adolescent-parent conflict in married and divorced families. *Developmental Psychology, 27,* 1000–1010.

Smith, A. (1976). *The theory of moral sentiments.* Oxford: Clarendon Press. (Original work published 1759)

Snarey, J. (1985). Cross-cultural universality of social-moral development: A critical review of Kohlbergian research. *Psychological Bulletin, 97,* 202–232.

Sommers, C. H. (1984). Ethics without virtue: Moral education in America. *American Scholar, 53,* 381–389.

Song, M. J., Smetana, J. G., & Kim, S. Y. (1987). Korean children's conceptions of moral and conventional transgressions. *Developmental Psychology, 23,* 577–582.

Spiro, M. (1993). Is the Western conception of the self "peculiar" within the context of the world cultures? *Ethos, 21,* 107–153.

Stack, C. (1990). Different voices, different visions: Race, gender, and moral reasoning. In R. Ginsberg & A. Tsing (Eds.), *The negotiation of gender in American society* (pp. 19–27). Boston: Beacon Press.

Stouffer, S. (1955). *Communism, conformity and civil liberties.* New York: Doubleday.

Strauss, C. (1992). Models and motives. In R. G. D'Andrade & C. Strauss (Eds.), *Human motives and cultural models* (pp. 1–20). Cambridge, England: Cambridge University Press.

Thorkildsen, T. A. (1989a). Justice in the classroom: The student's view. *Child Development, 60,* 323–334.

Thorkildsen, T. A. (1989b). Pluralism in children's reasoning about social justice. *Child Development, 60,* 965–972.

Thorkildsen, T. A. (1991). Defining social goods and distributing them fairly: The development of conceptions of fair testing practices. *Child Development, 62,* 852–862.

Tisak, M. S. (1986). Children's conceptions of parental authority. *Child Development, 57,* 166–176.

Tisak, M. S. (1993). Preschool children's judgments of moral and personal events involving physical harm and property damage. *Merrill-Palmer Quarterly, 39,* 375–390.

Tisak, M. S. (1995). Domains of social reasoning and beyond. In R. Vista (Ed.), *Annals of child development* (Vol. 11, pp. 95–130). London: Jessica Kingsley.

Tisak, M. S., Nucci, L., Baskind, D., & Lamping, M. (1991). *Preschool children's social interactions: An observational study.* Paper presented at the annual meeting of the American Psychological Association, San Francisco.

Tisak, M. S., & Tisak, J. (1990). Children's conceptions of parental authority, friendship, and sibling relations. *Merrill-Palmer Quarterly, 36,* 347–367.

Tisak, M. S., & Turiel, E. (1984). Children's conceptions of moral and prudential rules. *Child Development, 55,* 1030–1039.

Tisak, M. S., & Turiel, E. (1988). Variation in seriousness of transgressions and children's moral and conventional concepts. *Developmental Psychology, 24,* 352–357.

Tooby, J. (1987). The emergence of evolutionary psychology. In D. Pines (Ed.), *Emerging synthesis in science.* Santa Fe, NM: Santa Fe Institute.

Triandis, H. C. (1989). The self and social behavior in differing cultural contexts. *Psychological Review, 96,* 506–520.

Triandis, H. C. (1990). Cross-cultural studies of individualism and collectivism. In J. J. Berman (Ed.), *Nebraska Symposium on motivation: 1989, Vol. 37. Cross-cultural perspectives* (pp. 41–133). Lincoln: University of Nebraska Press.

Turiel, E. (1978a). The development of concepts of social structure: Social convention. In J. Glick & K. A. Clarke-Stewart (Eds.), *The development of social understanding* (pp. 25–107). New York: Gardner Press.

Turiel, E. (1978b). Social regulation and domains of social concepts. In W. Damon (Ed.), *Social cognition: New directions for child development* (pp. 45–74). San Francisco: Jossey-Bass.

Turiel, E. (1979). Distinct conceptual and developmental domains: Social convention and morality. In H. E. Howe & G. B. Keasey (Eds.), *Nebraska Symposium on Motivation: 1977, Vol. 25. Social cognitive development* (pp. 77–116). Lincoln: University of Nebraska Press.

Turiel, E. (1983a). *The development of social knowledge: Morality and convention.* Cambridge, England: Cambridge University Press.

Turiel, E. (1983b). Interaction and development in social cognition. In E. T. Higgins, D. N. Ruble, & W. W. Hartup (Eds.), *Social cognition and social development: A sociocultural perspective* (pp. 333–355). Cambridge, England: Cambridge University Press.

Turiel, E. (1989a). The social construction of social construction. In W. Damon (Ed.), *Child development today and tomorrow* (pp. 86–106). San Francisco: Jossey-Bass.

Turiel, E. (1989b). Domain-specific social judgments and domain ambiguities. *Merril-Palmer Quarterly, 35,* 89–114.

Turiel, E. (1994). Morality, authoritarianism, and personal agency. In R. J. Sternberg & P. Ruzgis (Eds.), *Personality and intelligence* (pp. 271–299). Cambridge, England: Cambridge University Press.

Turiel, E. (1996). Equality and hierarchy: Conflict in values. In E. S. Reed, E. Turiel, & T. Brown (Eds.), *Values and knowledge* (pp. 71–102). Hillsdale, NJ: Erlbaum.

Turiel, E. (in press). Notes from the underground: Culture, conflict, and subversion. In J. Langer & M. Killen (Eds.), *Piaget, evolution, and development.* Mahwah, NJ: Erlbaum.

Turiel, E. (in preparation). *Judgments and action in practical social situations,* University of California, Berkeley.

Turiel, E., & Davidson, P. (1986). Heterogeneity, inconsistency, and asynchrony in the development of cognitive structures. In I. Levin (Ed.), *Stage and structure: Reopening the debate* (pp. 106–143). Norwood, NJ: ABLEX.

Turiel, E., Hildebrandt, C., & Wainryb, C. (1991). Judging social issues: Difficulties, inconsistencies and consistencies. *Monographs of the Society for Research in Child Development, 56*(Serial No. 224).

Turiel, E., Killen, M., & Helwig, C. C. (1987). Morality: Its structure, functions and vagaries. In J. Kagan & S. Lamb (Eds.), *The emergence of moral concepts in young children* (pp. 155–244). Chicago: University of Chicago Press.

Turiel, E., & Smetana, J. G. (1984). Social knowledge and social action. The coordination of domains. In W. M. Kurtines & J. L. Gewirtz (Eds.), *Morality, moral behavior, and moral development: Basic issues in theory and research* (pp. 261–282). New York: Wiley.

Turiel, E., & Wainryb, C. (1994). Social reasoning and the varieties of social experience in cultural contexts. In H. W. Reese (Ed.), *Advances in child development and behavior* (Vol. 25, pp. 289–326). New York: Academic Press.

Turiel, E., & Wainryb, C. (1995). *Concepts of freedoms and rights in a traditional hierarchically organized society.* Unpublished manuscript, University of California, Berkeley.

Vail, S., & Turiel, E. (1995). *Children's judgments about others' social practices.* Unpublished manuscript, University of California, Berkeley.

Wainryb, C. (1991). Understanding differences in moral judgments: The role of informational assumptions. *Child Development, 62,* 840–851.

Wainryb, C. (1993). The application of moral judgments to other cultures: Relativism and universality. *Child Development, 64,* 924–933.

Wainryb, C. (1995). Reasoning about social conflicts in different cultures: Druze and Jewish children in Israel. *Child Development, 66,* 390–401.

Wainryb, C., & Turiel, E. (1994). Dominance, subordination, and concepts of personal entitlements in cultural contexts. *Child Development, 65,* 1701–1722.

Wainryb, C., & Turiel, E. (1995). Diversity in social development: Between or within cultures? In M. Killen & D. Hart (Eds.), *Morality in everyday life: Developmental perspectives* (pp. 283–313). Cambridge, England: Cambridge University Press.

Walker, L. J. (1980). Cognitive and perspective-taking prerequisites for moral development. *Child Development, 51,* 131–139.

Walker, L. J. (1982). The sequentiality of Kohlberg's stages of moral development. *Child Development, 53,* 1330–1336.

Walker, L. J. (1984). Sex differences in the development of moral reasoning: A critical review. *Child Development, 55,* 677–691.

Walker, L. J. (1986). Experiential and cognitive sources of moral development in adulthood. *Human Development, 29,* 113–124.

Walker, L. J. (1989). A longitudinal study of moral reasoning. *Child Development, 60,* 157–166.

Walker, L. J. (1991). Sex differences in moral reasoning. In W. M. Kurtines & J. L. Gewirtz (Eds.), *Handbook of moral behavior and development: Vol. 2. Research* (pp. 333–364). Hillsdale, NJ: Erlbaum.

Walker, L. J., de Vries, B., & Bichard, S. L. (1984). The hierarchical nature of stages of moral development. *Developmental Psychology, 20,* 960–966.

Walker, L. J., de Vries, B., & Trevethan, S. D. (1987). Moral stages and moral orientations in real-life and hypothetical dilemmas. *Child Development, 58,* 842–858.

Walker, L. J., Pitts, R., Hennig, K., & Matsuba, M. K. (1995). Reasoning about morality and real-life moral problems. In M. Killen & D. Hart (Eds.), *Morality in everyday life: Developmental perspectives* (pp. 371–407). New York: Cambridge University Press.

Walker, L. J., & Taylor, J. H. (1991). Stage transitions in moral reasoning: A longitudinal study of developmental processes. *Developmental Psychology, 27,* 330–337.

Walzer, M. (1983). *Spheres of justice: A defense of pluralism and equality.* New York: Basic Books.

Wertheimer, M. (1935). Some problems in the theory of ethics. *Social Research, 2,* 353–367.

Weston, D. R., & Turiel, E. (1980). Act-rule relations: Children's concepts of social rules. *Developmental Psychology, 16,* 417–424.

Whitehead, B. D. (1993, April). Dan Quayle was right. *The Atlantic Monthly,* 47–84.

Whyte, W. H. (1956). *The organization man.* New York: Simon & Schuster.

Willis, P. (1977). *Learning to labor: How working class kids get working class jobs.* New York: Columbia University Press.

Wilson, J. Q. (1993). *The moral sense.* New York: Free Press.

Winch, P. (1972). *Ethics and action.* London: Routledge & Kegan Paul.

Wright, R. (1994). *The moral animal: The new science of evolutionary psychology.* New York: Pantheon Books.

Wynne, E. A. (1986). The great tradition in education: Transmitting moral values. *Educational Leadership, 43,* 4–9.

Wynne, E. A. (1989). Transmitting traditional values in contemporary schools. In L. P. Nucci (Ed.), *Moral development and character education: A dialogue* (pp. 19–36). Berkeley, CA: McCutchan.

Yau, J., & Smetana, J. G. (1996). Adolescent-parent conflict among Chinese adolescents in Hong Kong. *Child Development, 67,* 1262–1275.

Youniss, J. (1980). *Parents and peers in social development: A Sullivan-Piaget perspective.* Chicago: University of Chicago Press.

Zimba, R. F. (1987). *A study of forms of social knowledge in Zambia.* Unpublished doctoral dissertation, Purdue University, West Lafayette, IN.

CHAPTER 14

Gender Development

DIANE N. RUBLE and CAROL LYNN MARTIN

Being born a girl or a boy has implications that carry considerably beyond the chromosomal, hormonal, and genital differences. Virtually all of human functioning has a gendered cast—appearance, mannerisms, communication, temperament, activities at home and outside, aspirations, and values. In this chapter, we consider the developmental processes involved in sustaining this gender system. How does a girl come to think of herself as a girl? When and why do children prefer same-sex playmates and activities? Do the sexes really differ in cognitive abilities, and if so, can these abilities be modified? Do children's beliefs about the sexes influence their own behavior? How do children develop their sexual orientations? The issues considered within the realm of gender span many controversial and intriguing topics.

Not surprisingly, then, the study of gender is enormously popular. Figures 14.1 and 14.2 show the results of a PsychLit search of articles on human sex differences and gender roles/sex roles, respectively, published since 1974. Although the trends vary somewhat year to year, both figures indicate the astonishing number of articles, as well as the surge in interest in the mid-1980s, which has leveled off somewhat in recent years for sex/gender role articles. Similar patterns appeared for studies with children only, with a high of about 400 articles on sex differences and 100 on sex/gender roles in 1985.

Because of the broad scope of topics, the enormous numbers of studies that have been conducted, and space restrictions, we have limited our coverage primarily to articles published since Huston's (1983) *Handbook* chapter "Sex-Typing," except in the case of historical and theoretical information. In addition, we have largely focused on children and adolescents (see Deaux & LaFrance, in press, for a discussion of gender in adults). To maintain continuity, we chose to build on the framework that Huston (1983) carefully developed. The multidimensional framework not only provides a good way to organize the myriad topics in the area, but also has heuristic value for directing new research efforts.

Our review is organized in terms of three major sections following this introduction. First, we present a historical review. In this section, we briefly review the broad perspectives that have shaped the direction of thinking about gender-related issues and the most central research issues in the areas of sex differences, gender stereotyping,

Preparation of this chapter was facilitated by a Research Scientist Award (MH01202) and a research award (37215), both from the National Institute of Mental Health to D. Ruble.

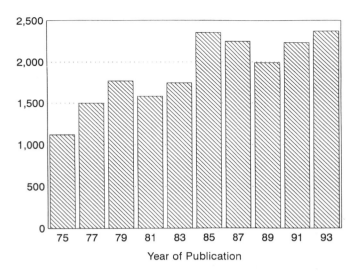

Figure 14.1 The number of articles on sex differences published each two years in journals reviewed by PsychLit from 1975 to 1994.

masculinity/femininity, gender schemas, and gender categories. Second, we present a detailed review of gender development, using a modified version of Huston's (1983) matrix of gender-related constructs and content. Third, we examine issues concerning gender development using three major theoretical orientations: biological, socialization, and cognitive approaches. In this section, we cover in more detail the major psychological theories that have directly guided research efforts and present aspects of the theories that have generated the most controversy. Finally, following these

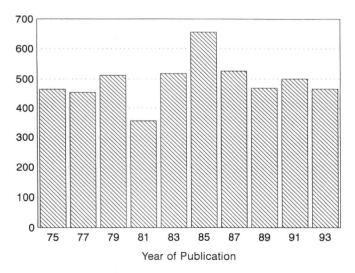

Figure 14.2 The number of articles on gender- and sex-roles published each two years in journals reviewed by PsychLit from 1975 to 1994.

three large sections, we suggest some conclusions and future research directions.

Throughout the review, we highlight certain theory-relevant themes that have guided current research efforts. The broadest theme that recurs in the literature is the nature-nurture debate, which has been central in the literature concerning the influence of hormones on behavior, the development of gender identity, and the development of sexual orientation. The question of how early children learn gender roles has also been a focal theme because it highlights the differences between social learning and cognitive approaches to gender development. A related question is what forms of gender differentiation are seen first: Do children first play with same-sex peers or with gender-typed toys? Similarly, a theme in recent research has been the degree to which cognitions (e.g., gender constancy, gender stereotypes) supply the underpinning to behavior, memory, and attentional focus. A final recurring theme in the chapter concerns the rigidity or flexibility of gender roles. Are there periods during development when children adhere particularly strongly to gender norms, and are these related to specific developmental milestones, such as changes in cognitions, social environment, or biology?

A source of continuing debate has been the use of terms, especially sex and gender. For many scholars, the sex versus gender debate involves assumptions of causality, with *gender* being used for socially based characteristics and *sex* being used for biologically based characteristics. We did not want to adopt a system based on presupposing the origin of a characteristic because causality is more complex than such a system implies. Instead, we have loosely adopted Deaux's (1993) use of these terms, in which "sex" is used to refer to any study or finding in which people are selected on the basis of the demographic categories of female and male, and "gender" refers to judgments or inferences about the sexes, such as stereotypes, roles, and masculinity and femininity. Even this system proved difficult to apply unequivocally, however, and we have used the term gender except when comparisons explicitly involve girls and boys or men and women as a category such as, "sex differences" and "sex segregation."

HISTORICAL REVIEW OF THEORIES AND RESEARCH ISSUES

In the first part of this section, a brief history of the major psychological theories and of trends and themes from other disciplines are presented to provide a broad overview of the field. The major theories that have been guiding research are covered in depth later in the chapter. In the second part of the section, a brief historical picture of the issues and methods involved in the major areas of gender research is presented to provide background for understanding present-day controversies.

Influential Theoretical Perspectives

Psychological perspectives on gender have ranged from early Freudian theory to current day views of gender schemas. This section briefly introduces each of the major psychological theories and its contributions to the study of gender. We also present brief reviews of the sociological and anthropological themes that have most strongly influenced developmental research.

Psychoanalytic Approaches

The earliest psychological theory about sex differences was Freud's psychoanalytic theory (1905/1962). Freud proposed that individuals experience an invariant sequence of stages in their psychosexual development with sex differences developing from experiences in the phallic stage (approximately 3–6 years). During this time, fears concerning castration presumably lead children to identify with their same-sex parent and incorporate that parent's personality and attitudes into their developing self-concept. Gender researchers later revised this idea, arguing that gender identity developed earlier (Stoller, 1985). Other psychoanalytic perspectives also have been proposed. Karen Horney (1922) argued that the social situations that restrict women's behavior are as important to consider as the anatomic differences between the sexes. Chodorow (1978) suggested that the differential availability of mothers and fathers may lead to different patterns of identification and dependency for daughters than for sons. Although it was the intellectual driving force for early developmental researchers on identification and imitation, the psychoanalytic perspective on gender development has not received much empirical support (see Frieze, Parsons, Johnson, Ruble, & Zellman, 1978).

Social Learning Theories

In 1966, Mischel outlined a learning-based approach that emphasized the role of social agents. In this view, gender roles are shaped by contingencies: Children are rewarded and encouraged for gender-appropriate play and punished or discouraged for gender-inappropriate play. More important

is observational learning in which children imitate the behavior of powerful and nurturant others, especially their parents. Children's behavior varies across situations because they learn when it is appropriate to enact certain behaviors. In the late 1970s, the theory was revised and relabeled "cognitive social learning theory," in order to explicitly incorporate cognitive factors, such as remembered expectancies about contingencies, as mediating the relation between situations and behaviors (Bandura, 1977, 1986; Bussey, 1983; Mischel, 1979). Social learning theories have played a major role in directing research, especially on the processes involved in observational learning.

Cognitive Developmental Theory

The basic tenets of cognitive developmental theory are that the child's understanding of gender emerges as part of general cognitive development (Kohlberg, 1966; Kohlberg & Ullian, 1974). Of central concern, and quite revolutionary at the time, was the proposal that children's *understanding* of gender, rather than their gender-typed *behavior* (as emphasized by learning theorists), was the crucial feature of gender typing. As children acquire the understanding of the irreversibility of being male or female (gender constancy) between 2 to 7 years of age, they become motivated to seek out information about what is appropriate for their own sex by observing the behaviors of others. Cognitive developmental theory has been highly influential (Maccoby, 1990b), especially in emphasizing the notion that children actively construct their own gender typing.

Gender Schema Theories

One result of the "cognitive revolution" in psychology was the development of schema-based theories of gender typing in the early 1980s (Bem, 1981; Markus, Crane, Bernstein, & Siladi, 1982; Martin & Halverson, 1981). These theorists proposed that gender schemas, which are networks of gender-related information, color individual's perceptions and influence their behavior. The tendency of infants to categorize events and people combined with the functional significance of gender in our society leads to the formation of gender schemas. Schema theory applied to children emphasizes the functions and liabilities of schematic processing and the development of schemas (Martin, 1991). Schema theories applied to adults emphasize individual differences in gender schemas (Bem, 1981; Markus et al., 1982). Schema theories have provided new insights into the cognitive processes involved in the development and maintenance of gender-related beliefs.

Social Categorization Approaches

In contrast to the conceptualization of gender as individual schemas or self-perceptions of personal characteristics associated with masculinity and femininity, other theories view gender in terms of identification with a social category or membership in a group of males or females in relation to the other group. One of the best known illustrations of this approach is social identity theory, originally developed in the late 1970s by Tajfel (1978) and Turner (Tajfel & Turner, 1979). The theory has been popular for explaining the relation between identification with a social group and intergroup relations, including prejudice, especially in adults. A major contribution of this perspective is the idea that people can behave and think at the group as well as at the personal level. Although relatively few researchers have explicitly applied social categorization approaches to gender development (e.g., Powlishta, 1995b), the ideas have had an important influence on other cognitive approaches (Lutz & Ruble, 1995; Maccoby, 1988; Martin & Halverson, 1981).

Situation-Based Social Psychological Context Perspectives

Some psychologists have shifted the focus of explanations of sex differences from individuals to roles and social contexts. Rather than assuming that behavior is a function of stable traits residing within individuals, these researchers have described how gender-typed behavior is influenced by immediate social situations (see Deaux & LaFrance, in press, for a review). Eagly and her colleagues (e.g., Eagly, 1987; Eagly & Wood, 1991) have shown how a consideration of the different social roles of males and females is crucial to interpreting research findings of sex differences in behavior. They argue that any given sex difference is sustained or inhibited by the social roles (e.g., homemaking; military) occupied mainly by one sex or the other. Different roles are associated with different behaviors and statuses, both of which contribute directly to observations of sex differences. The social role analysis implies that sex differences may not be seen if males and females were equivalently distributed across roles.

In another social psychological theory of gender, Deaux and Major (1987) also focus on the impact of contemporaneous situational factors on gender-related responding. They argue that the display of gender occurs primarily in the context of social interaction. According to their model, gender is negotiated between perceivers and targets; the extent to which an individual exhibits gender-related behavior depends on the expectations of the perceiver, the self-conceptions and goals of the target, and situational factors that affect the salience of gender. This model thus provides an important tool for making predictions about which situations should elicit greater or lesser sex differences.

Despite some fundamental distinctions in the emphases of different social psychological accounts of gender, they share a common view about the importance of gender-related expectations held by others and by the self in particular situations. These approaches are also important for understanding developmental changes in children. For example, sex differences emerging at a particular age may reflect changes in social contexts or age-related changes in the expectations of socializing agents.

Evolutionary and Ethological Approaches

Evolutionary approaches stress principles of natural selection and adaptation as major determinants of social behavior. According to sociobiological principles, sex differences in social behavior emerge because they promote the survival of the individual's genes, thereby enhancing the likelihood of one's characteristics being passed on to subsequent generations (Kendrick & Trost, 1993). A controversial claim is that males and females have different reproductive strategies, with males having less investment in offspring because they can never be sure that a child is their own, and females having heavy investment in each child. Based on these differences, males spend more time on short-term mating strategies that focus on finding many fertile mates, whereas females spend more time on long-term mating strategies that focus on finding and keeping mates and resources to help protect and nurture the child. To favor these strategies, other sex differences are believed to have emerged (Buss, 1995). Evidence supporting some claims of the theory has been found (Hoyenga & Hoyenga, 1993). These approaches also have been widely criticized based on disagreements about how natural and sexual selection work, the complexity of genetic transmission of information (e.g., Fausto-Sterling, 1992), neglect of animal data that fail to support the theory (Bleier, 1984), and reliance on outdated views of cultural evolution.

In contrast to sociobiological approaches that emphasize the survival of particular genes, ethological approaches focus on the adaptive value of behavior for the individual. For instance, ethologists focus on the adaptive value of nurturing behavior and compare species in their tendencies to engage in specific nurturing behaviors. Ethological approaches have been used to understand specific gender-related behaviors in children. For example, comparisons have been made of play fighting and play mothering in humans and primates with the goal of understanding how hormonal variations and early social environments influence these behaviors (Meaney, Stewart, & Beatty, 1985).

Anthropological and Sociological Perspectives

Anthropologists and sociologists gain insight into gender issues by examining, both historically and in contemporary societies, the kinds of roles each sex adopts. Several ideas have had wide-ranging impact on developmental researchers. The first idea concerns cultural universals, that is, similarities in gender roles across cultures. If across disparate cultures, men and women tend to adopt the same roles, then the roles might be considered cultural universals determined by biological factors; whereas inconsistencies may be assumed to be determined by social factors (Mackie, 1987).

Much of the early research on gender roles was interpreted as supporting two cultural universals: males having higher status than females and assignments of tasks on the basis of sex. To explain these cultural universals, sociologists developed the public/private spheres hypothesis in which, because of reproductive roles, females were responsible for the private/domestic sphere, including child care and agriculture, whereas males were responsible for the public sphere, including hunting and politics (Rosaldo, 1974). From these roles, personality differences arose: Females develop nurturance to help them in the domestic roles and males develop task mastery and competitiveness to help them in their public roles. Similarly, the prevailing anthropological view has been the man-the-hunter theory of evolution, in which it is presumed that men banded together to hunt large animals while women cared for infants at a home base, and each sex developed skills to complement these tasks. Furthermore, cultural evolution from the early hominids to homo sapiens was seen to be a result of males developing the skills required to hunt successfully.

Over the past 20 years, although some similarities are found across modern cultures, cultural universals have been questioned because of ethnographic data that confirm the enormous complexity and variability in gender roles (Gailey, 1987; Mukhopadhyay & Higgins, 1988; Rosaldo, 1980). Also, many anthropologists now believe that there is stronger primate, ethnographic, and material evidence that hominid ancestors were food gatherers, and mainly vegetarians, eating as they roamed, rather than primarily being hunters (Bleier, 1984; Gailey, 1987). Furthermore, acknowledgment has been made of the importance of women's roles in cultural evolution. As a result, traditional evolutionary arguments may not be appropriate as explanations of sex-based divisions of labor (Gailey, 1987). Finally, the notion of cultural universals may be simplistic because various groups differ biologically (e.g., hormone levels) and because consistencies in behavior may be due to similar life events and experiences.

Another related and influential idea concerns gender-based family roles. In the 1950s, the functionalist approach was proposed, which directed early research efforts and colored the lay public's view of families. The functionalist perspective assumes that families carry out the socialization of children best when roles are apportioned in families, with men taking the economic provider/instrumental role and women taking the expressive role in which they provide for the emotional needs of the family (Parsons & Bales, 1955). This approach supports a fundamental distinction apparent in gender stereotypes—that males are instrumental and female are expressive. Thus, gender roles are considered to be advantageous for healthy family functioning.

Finally, psychologists have been influenced by arguments about the importance of culture, especially as providing a shared system for attributing meaning to events (Shweder, 1984). In gender research, an outcome has been the development in the 1980s of the idea of the social construction of gender. According to this perspective, individuals "construct gender" using cues such as hairstyles, body shape, and height to assign people to a gender group and then base their social interactions with the person accordingly. Gender is thus seen to be fluid because it is constantly constructed through the interactions (Deaux & Major, 1987; Eagly, 1987), and implies that gender is relational rather than an essential quality of individuals (Ferree & Hess, 1987). At the most extreme, this view brings into consideration the role of culture in constructing the division of individuals into two sexes (Kessler & McKenna, 1978).

Research Issues in the Study of Gender Typing

The study of gender typing in children and adolescents has been influenced by numerous issues and controversies about how relevant constructs should be conceptualized and measured. A brief historical picture of research and measurement issues is provided in this section for the major topics of gender development.

Research Issues Concerning Sex Differences

Sex differences became a serious topic of scientific study within psychology as early as the field emerged in the United States (Ashmore, 1990). From the 1930s to 1950s, social psychologists avoided studying the sexes or focused their attention on personality assessment, whereas developmentalists investigated sex differences in many areas (see the 1954 *Handbook* chapter by Terman & Tyler). In the 1960s, the publication of Maccoby's (1966) *The Development of Sex Differences* was a watershed event in that the book detailed specific hypotheses and issues that needed investigation. For the next 10 years, sex and gender became widely used variables in all of psychology (Carter, 1987; Jacklin, 1989).

Another monumental book, *The Psychology of Sex Differences* by Maccoby and Jacklin (1974), had a long-lasting impact on the area. In this classic narrative review of over 2000 studies examining sex differences, Maccoby and Jacklin proposed a "new look" at the field, which reversed the trends of the time by minimizing sex differences. They concluded that the sexes differ in only a few areas, and that the differences are small and usually related to other variables. Critiques of the new look followed, which provided reasonable and thoughtful alternative interpretations of the same data, concluding that sex differences may have been underestimated, partly due to each study being given equal weight (e.g., Block, 1983). However, these critiques tended to be overlooked (Ashmore, 1990). Over the next 20 years, two trends can likely be traced back to the "new look." The first is that researchers present and interpret findings on sex differences more carefully. The second is that more researchers became interested in studying gender development of girls and boys, both in terms of similarities and differences.

The 1980s were marked by continued interest in studying sex differences, often with sex differences being maximized instead of minimized, and by a new approach—the "separate cultures" perspective (Ashmore, 1990). This perspective is based on Gilligan's influential work on moral development (1982) and her views of women's sense of self as a connected being (Gilligan, Lyons, & Hanmer, 1990). This perspective is also apparent in *Women's Ways of Knowing* (Belenky, Clinchy, Goldberger, & Tarule, 1986), *Women's Growth in Connection* (Jordan, Kaplan, Miller, Stiver, & Surrey, 1991), Tannen's (1990) research on conversational style differences between the sexes, and Maccoby's (1990a) ideas about how children learn gender-typed behaviors through largely sex-segregated interactions. According to this approach, the issues and concerns are different for males and females, so that comparing them on the same standard is inappropriate. For example, females are believed to develop different stances toward morality based on interpersonal connectedness, and different ways of knowing based on intuition and personal knowledge. This perspective thus emphasizes that being different is not equivalent to being inadequate, but the research also has been used to suggest that females have a superior culture (see Ashmore, 1990). The idea that men and women differ in their orientations to others recently has been developed into a model of sex differences in self-construals. Men are presumed to construct an independent-from-others self construal and women are presumed to construct an interdependent-on-others self construal. Cross and Madsen (in press) use this model to explain many types of sex differences, although direct evidence of sex differences in self construals is sparse thus far (Martin & Ruble, in press).

Measuring Sex Differences. Should scientists study sex differences? Because the study of sex differences has been used in the past to justify inequality in the treatment of women, many researchers are cautious about measuring and reporting sex differences. The merits and problems of studying sex differences continue to be debated, with some scholars strongly arguing for the importance of studying areas that may lead to socially uncomfortable discoveries (e.g., Scarr, 1988), and others suggesting that psychologists should not study sex differences at all (Baumeister, 1988).

One problem with research on sex differences is that the sexes can differ in many ways but researchers tend to compare their means rather than examining other types of differences, such as the variability of their distributions of scores (Feingold, 1995). Another problem concerns measurement biases. The most popular methods to measure sex differences are self-reports, which may be biased by gender-related beliefs and socially desirable responding, and behavioral observation, which may be biased by gender-stereotypic expectations of the observers. Indeed, biases can occur at every level—from the design of a study to the way the data are interpreted and reported (e.g., Lips, 1993).

The values of the researchers who investigate sex differences may also contribute to biases. Some researchers maximize differences between the sexes, called an *alpha bias,* and others minimize differences, called a *beta bias* (Hare-Mustin & Marecek, 1988). Alpha bias would be applied, for example, to the functional perspective on family roles (Parsons & Bales, 1955) and to Gilligan's ideas about moral development; whereas beta bias characterizes androgyny approaches.

Since the 1980s, methodological advances, especially the use of meta-analyses, have dramatically changed research on sex differences. In contrast to narrative reviews, meta-analytic reviews are quantitative strategies for simplifying and summarizing large bodies of research. In a meta-analysis, each study on a particular topic is summarized using a *d* statistic that expresses the sex difference in standard units (the mean sex difference divided by the pooled within-sex standard deviation). The effect sizes are compiled over studies to determine a central tendency which is located along a continuum ranging from no differences to large differences (Eagly, 1995).

During the 1970s and 1980s, virtually every book on sex differences or gender roles reminded readers that: (a) because little variance (5% or less) is accounted for by sex, sex differences are small; (b) a high degree of overlap exists in the distributions of the sexes; (c) within-sex variability is high; and (d) differences vary by context. Although these cautions remain important, the issue of the "small" magnitude of sex differences has been challenged recently. At what point is the label of small versus moderate versus large applied to a sex difference? Cohen (1977) proposed broad guidelines for interpreting effect sizes from meta-analyses: a *d* of .2 is small (85% overlap in distributions), .5 is moderate (67% overlap) and probably noticeable, and .8 is large (53% overlap) and very noticeable. Even with these guidelines, however, there has been considerable debate about whether the size of sex differences is meaningful. On the one hand, Eagly (1987; 1995) has argued that although most sex differences are in the small-to-moderate range, they are typically as large as psychological treatment effects (e.g., effects of psychotherapy) and are thus meaningful. She also notes that sex differences in some cognitive, physical, and social domains are large, in contrast to the dominant tendencies of feminist researchers to downplay the differences. On the other hand, Hyde and Plant (1995) have argued that although there are some large sex differences, effects are more likely to be close to zero than are treatment effects (Hyde & Plant, 1995).

The magnitude debate presents psychologists with several challenges. The first is to develop a better context for comparing sex differences with other research areas. The second is to communicate findings more effectively, such as using the binomial effect size to illustrate the practical importance of a finding (Rosenthal & Rubin, 1982). For example, the sex difference in smiling accounts for 9% of the variance and yet the binomial effect size display indicates that above-average amounts of smiling occur for 35% of men and 65% of women (Eagly, 1995). Finally, we need to better understand how others interpret what we report (Martin & Parker, 1995).

Origins of Sex Differences. Probably the single most controversial issue in the field is the origins of sex differences. Are sex differences due to biological factors, such as exposure to prenatal hormones, or are they due to environmental factors, such as experiences within the family? Each side of the nature-nurture issue has far-reaching political and social implications (see section on Biological Approaches); thus careful consideration of origins is of paramount importance for gender researchers.

The research on sex differences in mathematical abilities illustrates well the issues surrounding the nature-nurture debate. In 1980, an article published in *Science* reported that twice as many adolescent boys as girls scored over 500 on the mathematics section of the SATs. On the basis of these findings, the authors suggested that although ". . . male superiority is probably an expression of a combination of both endogenous and exogenous variables . . . environmental influences are more significant for achievement in mathematics than for mathematic aptitude" (Benbow & Stanley, 1980, p. 1264). This conclusion has been interpreted as an unusually strong statement about biological bases of sex differences and elicited controversy within the scientific community (see Letters to *Science,* April 10, 1981) and in the popular press (e.g., *Newsweek,* Dec. 15, 1980). Research on the roles of social factors (e.g., Kimball, 1989) has not received the same attention in the press.

The math controversy also illustrates the potential danger of presupposing biological causation. During the time that the results from the Benbow and Stanley studies were publicized, a large-scale study of mathematics and achievement was being conducted by Eccles and colleagues. Mothers who heard the media reports were more likely to believe that mathematics would be difficult for their daughters than mothers who had not heard these reports (Eccles & Jacobs, 1986). Given the importance of parental attitudes on children's mathematics attitudes, such beliefs can set up a self-fulfilling prophecy for girls within their families.

Are Sex Differences Disappearing? In a number of domains, especially cognitive abilities, the results of meta-analyses have suggested that over the past 20 years, sex differences are disappearing, leading some researchers to conclude that sex differences must be socially rather than biologically determined (e.g., Hyde & Linn, 1986). Caution must be exercised in drawing such conclusions, however. In one meta-analytic review, the disappearing sex difference in aggression was found to be due to testing methods and sample size differences rather than to real changes over time (Knight, Fabes, & Higgins, 1996).

Research Issues Concerning Gender Stereotypes

Beliefs concerning sex differences date back to ancient times. These beliefs, called gender stereotypes, include characteristics of males and females ranging from attitudes and interests to traits and physical appearances (see Ruble & Ruble, 1982). Images of females and males vary across cultures and throughout history; nonetheless it is common for the sexes to be perceived as being fundamentally different, and these differences are often linked to societal roles.

Stereotype research has been popular since the early 1930s. Early studies of gender stereotypes concentrated on identifying different beliefs about personality characteristics, and found two basic clusters of sex-differentiated traits—nurturance/expressiveness associated with females, and dominance/instrumentality associated with males (e.g., Broverman, Vogel, Broverman, Clarkson, & Rosenkrantz, 1972). More recent studies attempted to identify the broad spectrum of characteristics associated with each sex, including occupations, interests/activities, physical appearance, and sexual orientation (e.g., Deaux & Lewis, 1984; Martin, Wood, & Little, 1990). Important cross-cultural research also has been conducted on the content of gender stereotypes (Williams & Best, 1982).

Several other important advances have occurred in stereotype research. One advance was the idea that an attribute need not be generalized to the group as a whole; to function as a stereotype, it need only maximize the differentiation across categories. In other words, stereotypes are not all-or-nothing concepts but instead are probabilistic beliefs (McCauley, Stitt, & Segal, 1980; Stangor & Lange, 1994). As a way of assessing the extent to which a characteristic distinguishes one group from another and how often the characteristic is associated with a group, McCauley and Stitt (1978) recommended using a diagnostic ratio method. To illustrate, even if we believe that only 60% of Germans are industrious but we believe that only 30% of other people are industrious, then industriousness is very distinctive or diagnostic of being German. When this approach was applied to the study of adults' gender stereotypes, characteristics such as aggressiveness were found to be more diagnostic of differences between males and females than other traits (Martin, 1987).

Developmental researchers also confront issues about children's abilities to understand and produce responses about their stereotypic beliefs. In the early measures, children's response demands were simplified by forcing them to attribute characteristics either to males or to females but not to both (e.g., Williams, Bennett, & Best, 1975). A significant advance occurred with the development of the Sex Role Learning Inventory (SERLI), in which children divide gender-typed objects/activities according to who does an activity more, girls, boys, or both girls and boys (Edelbrock & Sugawara, 1978). Including the "both" category has allowed for assessments of flexibility in stereotypic responding (Signorella et al., 1993). Even newer approaches have moved beyond a forced-choice format to allow for assessment of the probabilistic nature of stereotypes. For example, Trautner (1992) asked children if a characteristic was associated with more of one sex than the other (e.g., more males than females) as well as with only one sex (e.g., only males). Developmental researchers also use several forms of questions, some of which may not assess stereotype knowledge. Certain question formats (e.g., "who usually does this?") seem to be assessing knowledge, whereas others (e.g., "who should or who can do this?") seem to assess something more like gender-related attitudes (Signorella et al., 1993). Data interpretation is often complicated because of these methodological differences.

Most researchers implicitly conceive stereotype knowledge as paired associations between gender categories and attributes. This simple view colored measures of stereotypes: In many studies, children were asked only about pairings between the sexes and interests. In the past 10 years, stereotype knowledge has been more broadly conceived as a hierarchical cognitive structure, with gender labels at the top of the hierarchy, and associated attributes at the lower levels. Attributes are associated with one another through their shared relation with "masculinity" or "femininity" (Martin, 1993) (see Figure 14.3). To fully learn a stereotype, then, individuals must learn the "vertical" associations between labels and attributes (as emphasized in early measures), and the "horizontal" associations linking attributes together. Using this method of conceptualizing stereotypes has led to the assessments of the previously neglected horizontal associations (Martin et al., 1990).

Gender Labels

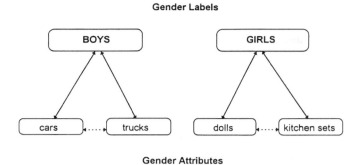

Gender Attributes

Figure 14.3 Hierarchical conceptualization of gender stereotypes.

Finally, a major issue in the study of stereotypes is evaluating their roles in interpreting information and influencing behavior. The broad picture that has emerged from social and developmental research is that gender stereotypes have a more direct effect on interpreting information than on behavior, because individuals may consciously monitor their explicit use of stereotype information (Devine, 1989). Furthermore, gender stereotypes may be self-fulfilling in that they may be confirmed through elicitation of stereotypic behavior in others.

Research Issues Concerning Personal Gender Orientations (Masculinity and Femininity)

What does it mean to consider oneself to be masculine or feminine? How should masculinity and femininity be assessed and are they related? In our culture, there is an assumption that masculinity and femininity are stable over time. Not all cultures adopt this view. The Hua of Papua New Guinea have a fluid view in which individuals change in their levels of masculinity and femininity throughout life (Gailey, 1987).

The traditional view in Western culture has been that girls should be socialized to be feminine and boys to be masculine. Instruments were developed to measure how closely individuals represented particular sets of attributes believed to characterize males and females in a given society. In early research, scales were designed to be unidimensional and bipolar, with masculinity and femininity representing ends of a single dimension (Windle, 1987). Constantinople's (1973) critique of the unidimensional conception of gender set in motion significant conceptual and assessment changes. She argued that masculinity and femininity are each multidimensional and heterogeneous constructs, best measured separately to allow for a better understanding of the relation between

the two. Masculinity was generally conceived as instrumental/agentic behaviors, independence, assertiveness, and dominance, whereas femininity was conceived as expressive behaviors, sensitivity to others, and communality. Bem (1974) developed the Bem Sex Role Inventory (BSRI), which measured masculinity and femininity separately, allowing a new and powerful construct to emerge—psychological androgyny. Androgyny, having both feminine and masculine characteristics, began to represent the ideal state of being.

During the 1970s, many researchers became interested in investigating masculinity, femininity, and androgyny generally using either the BSRI (Bem, 1974) or the Personal Attributes Questionnaire (PAQ; Spence, Helmreich, & Stapp, 1974). Participants rate their endorsement of personality traits that tap into the two broad constellations of masculinity (M-scale) and femininity (F-scale) and are classified using a fourfold table in which androgyny is defined as scoring above the M-scale and F-scale medians. Using these instruments, masculinity and femininity have proven to be heterogeneous dimensions, just as Constantinople expected. Interestingly, the items "masculine" and "feminine" usually are not found to relate to the two subscales, and instead form a separate single bipolar dimension (Marsh, Antill, & Cunningham, 1987). Most researchers believe that the subscales in these measures should be more narrowly defined as representing expressive/communal and instrumental/agentic domains (Spence, 1993). The separability of these two dimensions has been less clear (Ashmore, 1990).

Part of the appeal of androgyny was the belief that androgynous individuals would have a wide repertoire of behaviors at their command, allowing them to adapt to any situation, ultimately leading to stronger self-esteem (Kelly & Worell, 1977). A fundamental problem arose in trying to measure behavioral flexibility using trait measures because they imply consistency, not adaptability, across situations (Sedney, 1989). Flexibility also has been assessed by asking individuals about their capabilities to match behavior to specific situations. These capability measures correlate with self-esteem measures more strongly than trait measures, suggesting that they may better capture the original meaning of androgyny (Paulhus & Martin, 1988). Another problem with assessing the androgyny and self-esteem relations occurs on instruments that include only positive traits (Whitley, 1985). Presumably, individuals with more positive traits, regardless of whether they are masculine or feminine characteristics, should be "better off" in general than people with fewer positive traits. Interestingly, self-ratings of masculinity are more closely associated with general well-being and self-esteem than are self-ratings of femininity (Cate & Sugawara, 1986; Orlofsky & O'Heron, 1987).

Developmental researchers have also used several methods to assess masculinity and femininity in children. In the 1950s and 1960s, a popular measure was the It Scale for Children (Brown, 1956), but this scale may have instead assessed children's gender stereotype knowledge (Thompson & McCandless, 1970). Since the 1970s, children's preferences for toys, activities, and occupations (e.g., the Sex Role Learning Index, Edelbrock & Sugawara, 1978); behavioral observation of toy play, playmate preferences, and interaction styles; and parent ratings of children's activities (Golombok & Rust, 1993) have been widely employed to tap into masculinity and femininity in children (Beere, 1990). Many of the measures are less than ideal because they do not allow femininity and masculinity to vary independently (Katz & Boswell, 1986), and often have questionable reliability and validity (Beere, 1990). After 1980, personality questionnaires were developed for children (Boldizar, 1991; Hall & Halberstadt, 1980) that were similar to the PAQ and BSRI, except that behaviors were used to represent personality traits, thereby making it possible for younger children to answer the questions. These measures have been used to assess masculinity, femininity, and androgyny, but mainly with children older than 10 years.

Concern has been voiced that the labeling of characteristics as masculine or feminine reifies these distinctions, making them a constructed reality (Morawski, 1987). To minimize this concern, many researchers (e.g., Spence, 1993) recommend more specific labels for characteristics (e.g., expressiveness). Another solution is to develop new strategies for assessing gender orientation. Lippa and Connelly (1990) developed a promising "gender diagnosticity" measure in which self-ratings (e.g., aggressiveness; occupational preferences) are used to calculate how similar an individual is to other males or females in a given sample. This method has the advantage of construing individuals within their culture as malelike or femalelike to varying degrees, which may capture but not reify sex differences.

Research Issues Concerning Gender Schemas

The advent of gender schema theories in the early 1980s (Bem, 1981; Markus et al., 1982; Martin & Halverson, 1981) brought about a new set of issues including the nature and structure of knowledge and beliefs about gender

and the extent to which cognitions about gender (for self and for others) influence individuals' behavior and judgments. Furthermore, the notion of gender schemas reinforced the idea of a strong unity in aspects of gender typing because individuals develop gender schemas and self-concepts that are more or less interconnected.

Researchers do not agree on a method of assessing gender schemas. In the adult literature, Bem (1981) proposed that the BSRI assesses an aspect of gender typing that relates to an individual's gender schemas. For this reason, individual differences have often been measured through the use of personal/social attribute questionnaires. Developmental researchers have used many different strategies— preferences, attitudes, and stereotype knowledge—to assess gender schemas, and no one particular method predominated (see Signorella et al., 1993). The Gender Stereotype Attitude Scale for Children (GASC) has been used successfully to measure individual differences in children's attributions about which sex "can" perform various activities (Signorella & Liben, 1985). In 1989, Levy and Carter developed a unique reaction time measure to assess individual differences in the salience of children's gender schemas. Because schema theorists tend to assume a unity underlying many aspects of gender typing, it is not surprising that researchers have tapped into gender schemas in numerous ways. Nonetheless, it is important that the method being adopted is specified so that comparisons can be made across studies.

Research Issues Concerning Gender Categories

The research issues concerning gender categories are quite varied. In addition to issues about how individuals resolve their own gender identity through understanding their own gender category placement and the meaning attributed to that placement, this area of research also includes the controversial topic of gender constancy, which involves understanding the permanence and stability of gender category assignments. Research on gender categories also involves how and why individuals are assigned to these categories and the consequences of mismatched cues about gender category placement.

The Western view that people easily fit into one of two gender categories—male or female—and that this categorical distinction is a biologically based, stable attribute of individuals has been brought into question by cross-cultural analyses and social constructivist perspectives suggesting that not all cultures share this view (Herdt, 1994), and that individuals would be better served by not forcing variation in, say, gender orientation or genital anomolies to fit into an arbitrary male/female dichotomy (Bem, 1995; Fausto-Sterling, 1993). Although it is rare, some cultures allow for three or four unique gender groups. The most common label for a third gender group is *berdache,* a person who is anatomically normal but assumes the behavior, dress, and occupation of the other sex. Early anthropologists reported rare cases of male berdache in Asia, the South Pacific, and in many North American Indian tribes, and some research suggests that they may still exist (W. Williams, 1986). Female berdache reportedly adopted masculine roles of hunting, trapping, and sometimes fighting (Blackwood, 1984). Some cultures maintained alternative gender groups for both sexes: The Mohave Indians acknowledged both *alyha,* males who showed preferences for female roles, and *hwame,* females who showed preferences for male roles.

Do these individuals represent true gender alternatives or are they simply crossing the gender boundaries? Most anthropologists agree that these conceptions represent true

gender alternatives with distinct status since they often are assigned rituals and roles different from those typical of either men or women, and they do not simply adopt all the roles of the other sex. They are considered to have the spiritual essence of both sexes, but not the physical characteristics of both sexes (W. Williams, 1986).

THE DEVELOPMENT OF GENDER-RELATED CONSTRUCTS AND CONTENT

In this section, we update and expand Huston's (1983) review of the developmental course of the various components of gender. A modified version of her multidimensional matrix is presented in Table 14.1. The four Constructs (Columns) remain essentially the same: Concepts or Beliefs, Identity or Self-Perception, Preferences, and Behavioral Enactment. The six Contents—Biological/Categorical Sex, Activities and Interests, Personal-Social Attributes, Social

TABLE 14.1   A Matrix of Gender-Typing: Constructs by Content (All Entries Are Examples)

Content Area	Construct			
	A. Concepts or Beliefs	B. Identity or Self-Perception	C. Preferences	D. Behavioral Enactment, Adoption
1. *Biological/Categorical Sex*	A1. Gender labeling and constancy.	B1. Inner sense of maleness or femaleness, or self-perception of masculinity or femininity.	C1. Wish to be male or female.	D1. Displaying bodily attributes of one's gender (e.g., clothing, body type, hair), transvestism, transsexualism.
2. *Activities and interests:* Toys, play activities, occupations, household roles, tasks	A2. Knowledge of gender stereotypes or concepts about toys, activities, etc.	B2. Self-perception of interests.	C2. Preference for toys, games, activities.	D2. Engaging in play, activities, occupations, or achievement tasks that are gender typed.
3. *Personal-social attributes:* Personality traits, social behaviors, and abilities	A3. Concepts about gender stereotypes of personality or role-appropriate social behavior.	B3. Perception of own traits and abilities (e.g., on self-rating questionnaires).	C3. Preference or wish to have certain attributes.	D3. Displaying gender-typed traits (e.g., aggression, dependence) and abilities (e.g., math).
4. *Gender-based social relationships:* Sex of peers, friends, lovers, preferred parent, models	A4. Concepts about norms for gender-based relations.	B4. Self-perception of own patterns of friendships, relationships, or sexual orientation.	C4. Preference for friends, parents, and models, or judgments of popularity based on sex or gender.	D4. Engaging in social activity with others on the basis of sex or gender (e.g., same-sex peer play).
5. *Styles and symbols:* Gestures, speech patterns (e.g., tempo), play styles, fantasy	A5. Awareness of gender-related symbols or styles.	B5. Self-perception of nonverbal, stylistic characteristics.	C5. Preference for stylistic or symbolic objects or personal characteristics.	D5. Manifesting gender-typed verbal and nonverbal behavior or fantasy.
6. *Gender-related values*	A6. Knowledge of greater value attached to one sex or gender role than the other.	B6. Biased self-perceptions associated with group identification.	C6. In-group/out-group biases; prejudice; attitudes toward egalitarian roles.	D6. In-group/out-group discrimination.

Relationships, Styles and Symbols, and Values—are similar to Huston's except for the addition of the last area. Huston had included values as part of preferences, but we felt that this dimension of gender was of sufficient importance, though understudied, that it warranted attention in its own right. Definitions and examples are provided in the cells of the table. Our review of the literature is divided according to the cells of the matrix, and information is presented in the order of the column headings: A review of the literature on concepts and beliefs is presented first, then on identity, preferences/attitudes, and behavioral enactment. The sections are designated with letters and numbers corresponding to the cells in the matrix.

In writing about each area using this matrix, some difficulties arose, in particular, the problems of distinguishing between some of the topics in each cell (e.g., preferences and behavior). Also, presenting developmental trends broken down into so many cells may obscure common trends, but we have tried to identify those trends when they occur. The advantages of using the matrix system were also apparent, especially in helping to pinpoint the areas needing additional research, and in providing the clearest distinctions between different areas of gender typing.

Concepts and Beliefs about Gender (A)

The literature on concepts and beliefs about gender spans a wide array of well-researched topics, including gender constancy, gender stereotypes, and distinguishing between the sexes based on physical differences. Many of these issues are controversial and the topics are seen to have wide-ranging theoretical importance. For example, the age of attainment of gender constancy is important for understanding whether general conservation abilities underlie gender "conservation" abilities in Kohlberg's cognitive developmental theory. The age at which children begin to recognize the sexes and form concepts about their attributes are important issues for understanding the mechanisms driving children's behavior. Do children behave in gender-typed ways because they are being guided by knowledge or norms about the appropriate behavior of the sexes or does gender-typed behavior occur independently of cognitions?

Biological/Categorical Sex (A1)

Making Gender Distinctions. How early can children discriminate the sexes? Most infants are able to visually discriminate the sexes by 9 months of age according to studies using habituation paradigms with pictures of males and females. In one study, 6-month-old infants showed discrimination of the sexes (Walsh, Katz, & Downey, 1991), but other research suggests such distinctions emerge later. By one year of age, about 75% of children can discriminate the faces of males and females, largely based on hair length not on facial or body configuration (Leinbach & Fagot, 1993). Around 7 months, infants respond differently to female and male voices (Miller, Younger, & Morse, 1982). Infants' abilities to discriminate the sexes in other ways—by their height, softness, or smell—has not been studied to any great extent. By one year of age, infants demonstrate intermodal gender knowledge; they are able to integrate their knowledge of female and male faces with masculine and feminine voices (Poulin-Dubois, Serbin, Kenyon, & Derbyshire, 1994), and for some infants, this integration may occur earlier (Walker-Andrews, Bahrick, Raglioni, & Diaz, 1991). These studies suggest that infants have some rudimentary use of gender categories.

When can children label the sexes? Early research suggested that by approximately 30 months, children reliably demonstrate the ability to understand the categorical labels associated with sex (e.g., boy; she) (Huston, 1983), a conclusion supported by more recent findings (Etaugh, Grinnell, & Etaugh, 1989; Weinraub et al., 1984). Leinbach and Fagot (1986) developed a test of gender labeling using common labels (mommy and daddy; boy and girl), and found that children applied labels to adult targets earlier than to child targets. Longitudinal studies confirm the cross-sectional studies, finding that children pass gender labeling tasks at about 28 months (Fagot & Leinbach, 1989).

What cues are used to label the sexes? Early studies indicate that when genital cues are available, they figure prominently in adults' decisions about the sex of others, but much less so in children's decisions (e.g., Kessler & McKenna, 1978), at least until 8 to 9 years of age (McConaghy, 1979). A more recent study, however, suggests that some preschoolers can recognize genital differences when realistic pictures are used rather than schematic drawings (Bem, 1989). In an extensive examination of gender cues, Intons-Peterson (1988a) found that children rely heavily on hair cues; they believe that figures with blonde, curly, long hair are females. Dynamic cues (e.g., running and sitting) were used by adolescents but not by younger children.

Gender Stability and Constancy. One of the most controversial and compelling ideas in the literature is "gender constancy," the idea proposed by Kohlberg (1966) that children's developing sense of the permanence of categorical sex ("I am a girl and will always be a girl") is a critical organizer and motivator for learning gender concepts and behaviors. Slaby and Frey (1975) demonstrated that children move through a series of stages: first learning to identify their own and others' sex (gender identity or labeling), next learning that gender remains stable over time (gender stability), and finally learning that gender is a fixed and immutable characteristic that is not altered by superficial transformations in appearance or activities (gender consistency). These stages have been confirmed in other research (Stangor & Ruble, 1987), including cross-cultural studies (De Lisi & Gallagher, 1991; Munroe, Shimmin, & Munroe, 1984). Because the term "gender constancy" has been applied quite loosely in the literature—referring to the general construct, attainment of all stages, or attainment of various levels of understanding—we avoid using that term and instead use sex category constancy (SCC) to refer to the understanding of all levels of the construct and refer to specific stages when they are relevant. The controversies about SCC focus on the age that children acquire each stage of understanding, especially the last stage, and the consequences of acquiring this understanding of gender. In this section, we focus only on the age issue. In later sections, we review the evidence concerning the consequences of acquiring SCC.

From a cognitive developmental perspective, children would not be expected to show a complete understanding of SCC until they mastered conservation, usually during the concrete operational period (5–7 years of age) (Maccoby, 1990b). Although operational thought relates to constancy (Aboud & Ruble, 1987), the salience of sex categories in most cultures makes it reasonable to suppose that sex "conservation" may be one of the earliest forms of operational thought. Studies designed to pinpoint the development of SCC show a wide age range with some finding complete SCC in children as young as 3 to 4 years (e.g., Bem, 1989; Slaby & Frey, 1975), whereas others do not find it in most 7-year-olds (e.g., De Lisi & Gallagher, 1991; Emmerich, Goldman, Kirsh, & Sharabany, 1977).

A number of methodological and theoretical issues may underlie the age controversy. First, variations in sample culture, ethnicity, or SES may partially account for the observed age discrepancies (De Lisi & Gallagher, 1991; Emmerich, 1982). Second, children show higher levels of SCC using verbal questions about hypothetical transformations than when shown actual transformations (Shields & Duveen, 1986). Third, the requirements for determining that a child has acquired SCC also vary by study. Most researchers assess children's level of understanding from their responses to the structured questions, but others argue that justifications must also be examined (Emmerich et al., 1977; Emmerich & Shepard, 1982) because some children select the correct option but give an incorrect or no justification. A fourth important factor is the degree of realism of the measure and context. Using real-life events (Intons-Peterson, 1988a), familiar children (Leonard & Archer, 1989; A. Miller, 1984), or proper names rather than pronouns for targets (Beal & Lockhart, 1989), typically even 3- to 4-year-old children show high levels of SCC. Similarly, using pictures of undressed real boys and girls (rather than drawings), 3- to 5-year-olds who understood SCC (40%) typically also recognized the genital basis of gender (Bem, 1989).

Much of the age controversy may be due to the consistency questions. Children may misinterpret the meaning of gender consistency questions, which leads to underestimates of the age of understanding. Many children who first give nonconstant responses to the consistency questions later give the correct answer when asked if the child was *really* a girl or a boy, suggesting that they originally responded to what sex they thought the child was *pretending* to be (Martin & Halverson, 1983a). When pretend responding has been minimized, children typically show a younger age of attainment on consistency questions (Leonard & Archer, 1989; Martin & Little, 1990; Slaby & Frey, 1975) but this pattern is not always found (Frey & Ruble, 1992). Furthermore, the wording of the questions can make a large difference in age of attainment of SCC (Johnson & Ames, 1994; A. Miller, 1984). Not all studies suggest that SCC is being underestimated, however. Several studies show a dip in scores on consistency questions appearing sometime after age 3 to 4 years followed by a recovery between 5 to 9 years (Coker, 1984; De Lisi & Gallagher, 1991; Emmerich, 1982; Munroe et al., 1984; Wehren & De Lisi, 1983; Yee & Brown, 1994), suggesting perhaps that high levels of SCC in very young children may overestimate their level of understanding.

These problems with consistency items raise important questions about interpreting scores on SCC measures. Are high levels of SCC in 3-year-olds pseudo-constancy (Emmerich et al., 1977), or are 3- and 4-year-olds capable of true constancy (e.g., Bem, 1989; Intons-Peterson, 1988a)? Perhaps some kind of compromise position reflects the true state of affairs. High levels of responding by young children may represent a rigid application of the categorical distinction rather than a true understanding of the permanence of sex categories (Aboud & Ruble, 1987), and variations in the procedures (e.g., using realistic stimuli) may simply highlight this external categorical marker, allowing the child to see something that is the same despite the appearance change (Emmerich et al., 1977). Young children also may focus more on sex categories than on role conflicts, and thus their response is simple: "Jack is a boy; of course he would still be a boy." As children grow older, conflicting gender-role information may become more salient and may interfere with the application of the categorical distinction, contributing to errors on consistency questions. Consistent with this idea, some studies indicate that the dip in consistency scores occurs at approximately the same time that there is an increase in children's use of social norms (e.g., "If Jack wore lipstick, Jack would be a girl; boys can't wear lipstick") to explain their answers (Emmerich, 1982; Szkrybalo & Ruble, 1997; Wehren & De Lisi, 1983). Finally, the "recovery" of SCC may represent an integration of understanding categorical distinctions with understanding gender role norms. At all ages, however, SCC may be underestimated if studies use unrealistic stimuli or inappropriate wording of questions.

The age at which children attain complete SCC has yet to be completely resolved. Nonetheless, this issue remains important because of its implications for testing predictions that SCC is associated with certain kinds of outcomes, such as learning gender stereotypes or developing gender-typed preferences. Care must be taken because the errors of older children may not reflect a lack of understanding of SCC and because high-level responding among 3- to 4-year-olds may not reflect a complete understanding of SCC. In future studies of SCC, it will be important to sample a wide age range, to emphasize "real" mode responding, to consider justifications for responses, and to provide details about the wording.

Beliefs about the Origins of Gender Group Differences.   A relatively new area of research has focused on children's beliefs about the origins of sex differences. Do children believe that the sexes differ because of biological factors, or do they believe differences are more likely due to societal factors, such as how children are raised? This issue is important, in part, because it may provide insight about when and why children show changes in flexibility in their gender-related perceptions and behaviors at different ages (Carter & Patterson, 1982; Ullian, 1976).

Several studies indicate that adults believe sex differences are based more on socialization than biological factors (Antill, 1987; Martin & Parker, 1995). Such beliefs have important implications. Antill (1987) found that parents' beliefs about the origins of sex differences related to

the characteristics they encouraged in their children. Furthermore, Martin and Parker (1995) found that the more adults believed that sex differences were caused by biological factors, the more they believed the sexes differ from one another and the less likely they thought these differences could be eliminated. When children have been asked about the origins of differences, younger children were more likely to attribute differences to biological factors than were older children (Smith & Russell, 1984). A similar pattern has been found when asking children about hypothetical situations, such as the outcome of a child being raised on an island by members of only one sex (M. Taylor, 1996). Preschoolers attributed characteristics to the target children based on their sex rather than on the rearing environment.

Activities and Interests (A2)

Many studies have examined children's stereotypes about clothing, activities, and toys and games that differentiate the sexes. From these studies, Huston (1983) concluded that stereotypes are learned at a very young age: Children show some awareness of gender stereotypes about objects and activities by age 3, and even show better than chance responding on a few measures by age 2½. Recent research has supported these conclusions. Stereotype knowledge of child and adult activities and occupations increases rapidly between 3 to 5, reaching a high level by kindergarten (Martin & Little, 1990; Perry, White, & Perry, 1984; Picariello, Greenberg, & Pillemer, 1990; Serbin, Powlishta, & Gulko, 1993). In a meta-analysis of studies of developmental change in stereotypes (Signorella et al., 1993), age differences were most pronounced when studies included preschoolers and when the stereotyping measures included multiple domains, suggesting that after preschool, gender stereotypes are well developed, showing further change only when a broad range of topics is examined.

Most stereotype measures assess knowledge at a relatively simple level, identifying which gender category is associated with particular objects, and thus it is not surprising that such studies often find extremely high levels of stereotyping in very young children. Because of changes in the way stereotype knowledge is conceptualized (see History), methods of examining more complex associations within stereotypes have been developed (Gelman, Collman, & Maccoby, 1986; Martin et al., 1990). When complex associations are assessed, studies show that stereotypes continue to develop throughout childhood (Martin et al., 1990). "Horizontal" associations (e.g., attribute to attribute) develop later than vertical label-attribute associations. For example, children 8 to 10 years old can use attribute information about a target to make horizontal associations about other stereotypic attributes, but 6-year-olds are limited in these horizontal associations (Martin et al., 1990).

What kinds of stereotypes are children learning first? Although this question has not been systematically addressed, there are some interesting clues. Very young children (around 26 months) appear to be more aware of gender differences associated with adult possessions (e.g., shirt and tie), roles (Weinraub et al., 1984), physical appearance (Etaugh & Duits, 1990), and with abstract characteristics associated with gender (e.g., softness) (Leinbach, Hort, & Fagot, in press), and 5 to 6 months later show evidence of awareness of stereotypes about children's toys (Weinraub et al., 1984). During the elementary school years, the range of and extent to which occupations, sports, and school tasks or subjects are differentially associated with males and females continues to increase (e.g., Kaminski & Sheridan, 1984; Wilder, Mackie, & Cooper, 1985).

How do people use stereotypes to make inferences about others? Two issues are important. The first issue is how children make inferences given information about someone's sex. Children easily make assumptions about others based on their sex (e.g., Cowan & Hoffman, 1986) and will even attribute new qualities to them based on sex (Gelman et al., 1986). The second issue is how inferences are made when categorical information (e.g., being female) conflicts with attribute information (e.g., a masculine interest). Do we assume that this person would also like other masculine activities because of her prior interests (a horizontal association), or will she like feminine activities because of her sex (a vertical association), or are the two sources of information integrated in some way? When horizontal associations emerge at around 8 years, children's judgments may begin to involve attribute information, whereas younger children's judgments should be dominated by categorical information. Consistent with this prediction, two studies (Biernat, 1991b; Martin, 1989) found that third graders' judgments were influenced by attribute information as well as by categorical sex. In contrast, Berndt and Heller (1986) found clear use of attribute information only for sixth graders and college students, but not for third graders. Although the studies were similar, the kinds of inferences children made (i.e., toys vs. activities/chores) differed, and may account for different developmental patterns.

Taken together, these data suggest that by the time children enter elementary school, they have extensive knowledge about which activities are linked to being male or female. Soon afterward, they can even make inferences about other masculine or feminine attributes when given information that implies a masculine or feminine orientation, especially when that information does not conflict with categorical sex. Unlike adults (Locksley, Borgida, Brekke, & Hepburn, 1980), children tend to rely much more on categorical sex than on attribute information in making such judgments, at least until approximately 8 years of age. Stereotypes are likely to be held quite rigidly until that age, as younger children do not seem to recognize that there can be individual variation in masculinity and femininity within the male and female categories.

Do stereotypes become more flexible with age? Describing clear trends about developmental changes is difficult because the term *flexibility* can mean many different things including: the willingness to apply an attribute to both sexes, rather than just to one or the other, or the recognition of the relativity of stereotypes (e.g., that norms could be different in another culture). The term has been applied either to changes in knowledge (e.g., about variability or relativity) or to personal acceptance of stereotypes, with the latter being closer in meaning to attitudes or values that the sexes "should" be different. Ideally, these latter trends would be reviewed in the "Values" subsections of this section. However, because distinguishing between knowledge and attitudes on the basis of currently available measures is so difficult, all are reviewed in this subsection. And, because of the difficulty pinpointing the exact meaning of flexibility, we use the term somewhat loosely to apply to any nonrigid application of stereotypic items, whether because of knowledge or because of personal attitudes.

Based largely on a comparison of studies that allow children to classify items as equally appropriate for both sexes (i.e., "both" responding), Huston (1983) concluded that after about 7 years of age, children's knowledge of stereotypes continues to increase but that their acceptance of stereotypes as inflexible or being morally right begins to decline. Studies employing varied measures and analyses support these conclusions. First, interview studies suggest that with age, children increasingly recognize the cultural relativity of gender norms, though this understanding appears to reach a ceiling at some point during middle elementary school (Carter & Patterson, 1982; Damon, 1977; Stoddart & Turiel, 1985; Ullian, 1976). Second, a meta-analysis of stereotype attitudes and knowledge studies showed that "both" responding for questions worded "who can" or "who should" engage in an activity increase with age among elementary school children (Signorella et al., 1993). Presumably, such questions assess either children's increasing recognition that there is some flexibility in the associations of items with the sexes or an increasing willingness to accept cross-gender behavior, and studies using conceptually similar measures that do not rely on "both" responses show similar trends (e.g., Leahy & Shirk, 1984; Pellett & Ignico, 1993). Interestingly, curvilinear age trends in the meta-analysis suggest that this flexibility of association or attitudes is lowest at about the time children begin school. Third, as children grow older, "both" responding declines in response to questions assessing knowledge about which items are stereotypically associated with each sex (e.g., "who usually"). Thus, with age, children learn more about what each sex is expected to do and that such norms are relative and somewhat flexible. Presumably, the flexibility trends also reflect decreasing personal acceptance of rigid stereotypic divisions.

Such trends often vary for girls and boys. In the meta-analysis, girls scored higher than boys on stereotype knowledge, but no clear sex differences were found in flexibility for preschool children (Signorella et al., 1993). However, many studies find that by middle childhood girls have more flexible stereotypes (e.g., Canter & Ageton, 1984), and are more likely to increase in flexibility than are boys (e.g., Hageman & Gladding, 1983). Finally, some research suggests that children view the male role as more rigidly proscribed than the female role (e.g., Henshaw, Kelly, & Gratton, 1992; Smetana, 1986). In short, girls are both more knowledgeable and, after the preschool years, more flexible in their personal acceptance of gender stereotypes, and boys hold stereotypic views more rigidly and are held to them more by others.

Predictions concerning changes in flexibility during adolescence have been mixed. Gender-related beliefs and behaviors may become intensified (e.g., Hill & Lynch, 1983) or be transcended (e.g., Rebecca, Hefner, & Oleshansky, 1976). A newly emerging identity as a sexual being and the need to be accepted by the other sex may lead to heightened concerns about gender-role expectations and increased polarization of attitudes (Katz, 1979). In contrast, continuing cognitive maturation should facilitate a more flexible and relativistic view of gender norms (Eccles, 1987). Most measures of flexibility show an increase through early adolescence (Biernat, 1991b; Emmerich & Shepard, 1982). Studies of changes between early and later adolescence show somewhat more mixed results depending on the stereotype, the measure, and the sex

of the participants (Biernat, 1991b; Emmerich & Shepard, 1982; Guttentag & Longfellow, 1977; Plumb & Cowan, 1984).

Personal-Social Attributes (A3)

Many studies of the development of stereotypes about personal-social attributes have used a measure based on the Sex Stereotype Questionnaire, in which children are told stories about masculine and feminine traits and are asked to select whether the stories fit better with a male or female figure (Best et al., 1977). Best et al.'s (1977) original studies of U.S. participants found that the knowledge of kindergartners was at levels little better than chance, with a large increase in knowledge between kindergarten and third grade. Moreover, knowledge continued to increase steadily throughout elementary school, such that the knowledge level of the high school sample approached that of college students on whom the measure was standardized (see Best & Williams, 1993, for a review).

Based on this and similar findings, Huston (1983) concluded that gender stereotype knowledge of personal-social attributes emerges at approximately 5 years of age, but increases steadily throughout childhood and perhaps into adolescence. Research in the 1980s and 1990s has generally supported this conclusion (e.g., Powlishta, Serbin, Doyle, & White, 1994; Serbin et al., 1993; Signorella et al., 1993; Trautner, 1992), as well as the idea that children develop stereotypes about physical characteristics before psychological ones (Carter & McCloskey, 1984).

Children younger than 5 years of age generally show little evidence of using trait stereotypes about the sexes (e.g., Coker, 1984; Kuhn, Nash, & Brucken, 1978; Leahy & Shirk, 1984). Instead, preschool children often attribute positive characteristics to their own sex and negative characteristics to the other (Albert & Porter, 1983; Kuhn et al., 1978), with some evidence that this bias peaks at age 5 (Urberg, 1982).

Are any particular trait stereotypes learned earlier than 5 years of age? Such data may provide clues about how young children structure their initial learning about gender categories. Multiple studies have reported that 2- to 4-year-old children distinguish between males and females on particular traits (e.g., cruel), emotions (e.g., fearful), or trait-related behaviors (e.g., hits people; can't fix things) (Albert & Porter, 1983; Cowan & Hoffman, 1986; Haugh, Hoffman, & Cowan, 1980; Kuhn et al., 1978; Reis & Wright, 1982; Urberg, 1982). These findings suggest that preschoolers may be most aware of differentials along a power dimension, as they apply high power adjectives to boys (e.g., strong, fast, hit) and adjectives related to fear and helplessness to girls (e.g., can't fix bike, needs help, cries a lot, fearful). Children also use a general evaluative dimension in which males are labeled negatively (aggressive, cruel) and females are labeled positively (affectionate, nice). As Serbin et al. (1993) suggested, young children may apply a general stereotype that girls are sugar and spice . . . and boys are snakes and snails. Interestingly, then, early stereotypes appear to highlight distinctions involving what Osgood, Suci, and Tannenbaum (1957) identified as two of the three most important dimensions of meaning (i.e., power and valence).

Thus, even very young children may differentiate the sexes on some dimensions. It is not yet clear why a few studies find consistent stereotyping across preschool boys and girls on certain traits, whereas others find own-sex bias or favoritism. Perhaps methods that force children to compare male and female targets in assigning traits (see Stern & Karraker, 1989, for a review) are more sensitive to knowledge and make it more difficult to respond simply on the basis of own-sex bias. Also, young children may appear less knowledgeable because they find it difficult to respond to a conflict, such as when a trait is positive but stereotypic for the other sex (Muller & Goldberg, 1980).

Huston (1983) was unable to draw clear conclusions regarding the cognitive-developmental prediction that flexibility in beliefs about gender-typed traits should increase after approximately 7 years of age because the literature was sparse and yielded mixed results. However, an extensive database has now emerged. Although the Signorella et al. (1993) meta-analysis did not separate traits from other stereotypes, the trends found for traits appeared similar to those for activities and interests with a peak in rigidity as children enter school and a subsequent increase with age in flexibility. It is not yet clear whether trait flexibility shows a gradual increase after kindergarten, as suggested by some studies (e.g., Serbin et al., 1993), or shows a more dramatic shift at 7 to 8 years, as suggested by others (Trautner, 1992). With few exceptions (Trautner, 1992), there is a dearth of longitudinal research examining developmental changes in stereotyping.

Relatively few studies extend beyond elementary school, but for the most part, the pattern seems similar to that described for activities, with flexibility increasing through early adolescence (e.g., Nelson & Keith, 1990). Research directly comparing younger and older adolescents suggests that trait flexibility may stabilize or decline during high school (e.g., Biernat, 1991b; Ullian, 1976; Urberg, 1979). Moreover, one study showed this curvilinear pattern using a combination of cross-sectional and longitudinal analyses (Alfieri, Ruble, & Higgins, 1996), with flexibility increasing through the first year of junior high school and then declining. Thus, consistent with the conclusions concerning concrete stereotypes, trait flexibility may fluctuate throughout the adolescent years in response to two opposing influences—increasing cognitive flexibility and increasing pressures to conform to gender stereotypes in preparation for sexual roles and adult status (Eccles, 1987; Katz & Ksansnak, 1994).

Social Relationships (A4)

Few studies have examined children's stereotypes about the sexes in social relationships, such as beliefs about boys' and girls' play styles, about friends, or about sex differences in dating behaviors. In one study, young children's beliefs about the qualities of play with girls and boys were assessed, as well as their predictions about others' play partner preferences. Children showed little stereotyping of play characteristics in girls' groups or boys' groups (e.g., that girls play inside more than boys). However, children showed strong stereotypes about others' play partner preferences (i.e., they believe boys prefer to play with other boys more than with girls), and this pattern increased with age (from 4 to 6 years). Interestingly, these beliefs influenced their tendencies to report same-sex play partner preferences: the more gender-typed their beliefs, the more they preferred same-sex partners for themselves (Martin, 1994).

Styles and Symbols (A5)

Very few studies have examined children's beliefs about styles (e.g., mannerisms) or symbols (colors, textures) associated with gender. Some evidence, however, suggests that symbolic associations may be learned at a very early age. For example, preschoolers seem to have clear stereotypes about colors (Picariello et al., 1990) and can associate obvious physical cues such as colors and clothing with gender-typed interests in others (Kaiser, Rudy, & Byfield, 1985; Picariello et al., 1990). In studies of "metaphorical" associations with gender, children tend to attribute to boys things that are angular, rough, and dangerous (e.g., a bear), while attributing to girls things that are soft, light, and graceful (e.g., a butterfly) (Leinbach et al., in press). Furthermore, when gender-typing of objects was in conflict with "metaphorical" cues (e.g., a tea set painted brown and covered in spikes), children selected toys on the basis of the metaphorical cues rather than the known gender-typing of the object, suggesting that these cues play an important role in gender development (Leinbach et al., in press).

Values (A6)

In many cultures, more positive evaluations are applied to men and "masculine" activities than to women and "feminine" activities (e.g., Berscheid, 1993). When do children become aware of the cultural values placed on the sexes? Kohlberg (1966) hypothesized that at a very young age, children are attentive to sex differences in power, and research on stereotype knowledge described earlier is consistent with this hypothesis. The few studies that have directly examined the development of knowledge about cultural values suggest that children older than 10 years perceive that females are devalued. For example, when asked to describe what would happen if they woke up one day to find they had changed sex, 11-, 14-, and 18-year-olds in Sweden and the United States offered different evaluations of the male and female role, acknowledging gender-based discrimination, greater restrictions for females, and the lower value of the female role (Intons-Peterson, 1988b).

Identity or Self-Perception (B)

Two topics have been of particular interest in the literature on identity and self-perception. The first topic is how typical and atypical children learn about their placement in a gender group and then the consequences and meaning associated with that placement. This issue has been theoretically important, especially in untangling the extent to which gender identity is influenced by biological versus environmental factors. The second topic has been how children view themselves as being masculine and feminine, and whether there are behavioral consequences associated with their self-concepts.

Biological/Categorical Sex (B1)

Gender identity is one's sense of self as a male or female (Zucker, 1989). At the most basic level, this understanding is anatomic, but it also includes the presentation of the self as a male or female sexual being. Research on gender identity has followed two paths: Developmental research has traced its typical course, and clinical research has examined children with gender identity problems (Fagot & Leinbach, 1985).

Developmental Course in Typical Children.   Because understanding how a child comes to place himself or herself into a gender category is considered a motivation for gender-typed behavior, especially by cognitive theorists (e.g., Constantinople, 1979), the focus of normative developmental research has been on the age of attaining gender identity. Most studies suggest that children can accurately label their sex and place a picture of themselves with other same-sex children by around 24 to 36 months of age, although considerable variability among children has been found in these abilities (Fagot, 1985b; Thompson, 1975; Weinraub et al., 1984).

Developmental Course in Atypical Children.   The focus of clinical research has been on the roles of biological and environmental factors in the development of gender identity. Two populations have been studied. The first is children who were born with ambiguous genitalia or who have been reared as the other sex because of surgical accidents (e.g., Money & Ehrhardt, 1972). Early on, Money and Ehrhardt concluded that even in extreme cases, children tend to adopt roles consistent with the ways they are raised, regardless of their biological sex, as long as their gender assignment is done early in life (before 18 to 30 months) and is unambiguous. Others have raised serious questions about the stability of gender identity in some of the cases, however (Diamond, 1982). Recent research suggests that gender identity may be more malleable than previously considered. In one famous case of an XY individual with a damaged penis, the decision was made at 8 months to rear the child as a girl. At age 14, the child rejected this sex of rearing and successfully lives as a male (Diamond & Sigmundson, 1997). Moreover, other questions about the roles of nature and nurture have been in the forefront because of recent research suggesting that changes in gender identity may occur as late as adolescence for children with certain genetic diseases (see Biological Approach section).

The second line of clinical research has involved individuals with gender identity problems whose biological sex is not in doubt (e.g., Green, 1974, 1987). Since 1980, the *Diagnostic and Statistical Manual of Mental Disorders* (American Psychiatric Association) has included Gender Identity Disorder (GID). Diagnosis of this disorder in children (GID) requires evidence of both identity problems (e.g., discomfort with assigned sex, wishing to be the other sex) and cross-gender behavior (Zucker, 1992). Such children typically show a wide range of cross-gender behaviors, including wearing clothes and playing with toys that are typical of the other sex (Zucker, 1992). Children with GID are not androgynous; they are extreme and inflexible in adopting cross-gender but not same gender roles (Green, 1987; Rekers, 1985).

Because there is a continuum of gender identity (Meyer-Bahlburg, 1985), it is difficult to determine the prevalence of GID. Estimates of the prevalence of GID or subclinical variants range from about 2% to 5% of the general population (Bradley & Zucker, 1990). Boys are referred for treatment more than girls with ratios varying from 6:1 to 30:1 (Rekers, 1985; Zucker, 1992). This pronounced difference may be due to a variety of cultural factors including beliefs that girls may grow out of cross-gender behavior (Green, 1974) or beliefs that cross-gender boys are more likely to grow up to be homosexual and not well-adjusted (Antill, 1987; Martin, 1990).

The onset of gender-atypical behavior in GID children usually occurs during the preschool years, but may be earlier (Bradley & Zucker, 1990; Rekers, 1985). The first signs for children include wearing other-sex clothing, being preoccupied with other-sex toys, and showing gender confusion or mislabeling of sex (Bradley & Zucker, 1990). During early and middle childhood, GID boys prefer playing with girls, avoid rough-and-tumble play, and begin to show effeminate vocalization and mannerisms, as well as lack of social skills and immaturity, all of which lead to social ostracism (Green, 1987; Rekers, 1985). GID girls may play with boys, show high activity levels, and join sport teams. Extreme cases of cross-gender identity in childhood, especially in boys, are related to greatly increased likelihood of bisexual and homosexual behavior, and a slight increase in transsexualism (Green, 1987).

Why do some children fail to develop a gender identity consistent with their biological sex? Several broad factors have been implicated in the etiology of GID (see Zucker & Bradley, 1995, for a review), including hormones, temperament, and encouragement of cross-sex behaviors. Research on GID brings into question many assumptions of the past 20 years. If stereotypes are less prevalent, why are children referred to clinics if they behave in a way that is considered normal for the other sex? If our goals for boys and girls are the same, why is it considered a problem for a boy to play with dolls? On the other hand, clinicians may be justified in labeling and diagnosing children as GID because of the research indicating that these children show a broad range of behavioral and emotional disturbances.

Activities and Interests (B2)

To what extent are children's identities influenced by their gender-related activities and interests? There has been little research on this question. Instead, researchers have examined what kinds of activities children prefer (see C2) or how children perceive themselves in terms of traits (see next section). One exception is research on the relation of self-concepts to self-perceptions of academic interests and abilities (e.g., Marsh, Byrne, & Shavelson, 1988), generally with samples of older children who are assumed capable of reporting on their perceptions. Stereotypic patterns are found: Boys' academic self-concept is correlated more strongly with their math than with their verbal self-perceptions, but the reverse is true for girls (Skaalvik & Rankin, 1990). Even first-grade children show some evidence of the influence of stereotypic beliefs: math is relevant only for boys' self-concepts and not for girls' (Entwisle, Alexander, Pallas, & Cadigan, 1987). Such relations are important in part because children may avoid courses or future occupations that are believed to be unimportant or irrelevant for their academic self-concept. Eccles (1989) found a decrease over time in girls' ratings of how much they liked math and thought math competence was important for their self-concept, and such values were related to their enrollment in advanced math and physics in high school. Moreover, she found that girls' images of themselves as helpful or nurturing appeared to create antipathy toward math and science careers. Girls who rated themselves as relatively feminine on the Personal Attributes Questionnaire (PAQ) rated math as less interesting and important than androgynous girls.

Personal-Social Attributes (B3)

How early do children view themselves in terms of gender-typed personality traits and do these patterns change over time? Only tentative conclusions can be drawn because of methodological differences between studies. In studies with 3- to 4-year-olds, boys and girls tend to endorse socially desirable characteristics (Cowan & Hoffman, 1986), and their perceptions of themselves are beginning to differentiate along gender-typed lines but not yet enough to show a significant difference (Intons-Peterson, 1988a). For 5-year-olds, the findings are mixed (Biernat, 1991a; Inoff, Halverson, & Pizzigati, 1983). By 8 to 9 years, most studies show that boys and girls rate themselves in terms of gender-typed patterns of traits (Biernat, 1991a; Boldizar, 1991; Intons-Peterson, 1988a); however, some studies show different patterns (Inoff et al., 1983; Silvern & Katz, 1986). Overall, cross-sectional studies suggest that self-perceptions of instrumental and expressive traits become more gender-typed with age up through early adolescence, even though considerable overlap remains between the sexes (Boldizar, 1991; Intons-Peterson, 1988a).

The stability of children's endorsements of gender-typed personality traits is of interest because some theorists expect that certain life events will influence their adoption. For example, the gender intensification hypothesis is based on the idea that the onset of puberty will lead others to expect adult-like behavior from adolescents, including the adoption of more gender-typed traits (Hill & Lynch, 1983). Because of this hypothesis, most of the longitudinal studies of change in trait endorsement have focused on the preadolescent to adolescent time span. Only limited support for gender intensification has been found, mainly for increased sex differences in masculinity (Galambos, Almeida, & Petersen, 1990). Other studies show a general pattern of stability over time (e.g., Antill, Russell, Goodnow, & Cotton, 1993), or that both masculinity and femininity increase with age (Butcher, 1989, girls only).

Social Relationships (B4)

Although many scholars argue that it is best to study gender as it is constructed within a social context, little attention has been paid to how children perceive themselves in terms of their social relationships. To what degree do children incorporate stereotypic beliefs into their self-concepts about their relationships? There are some hints in the literature that children recognize that certain relationships are more acceptable than others (i.e., same-sex friendships more acceptable than other-sex friendships) (Bussey & Bandura, 1992; Martin, 1994). Along the same line, it would also be interesting to investigate the beliefs of girls who label themselves as tomboys (e.g., Plumb & Cowan, 1984) because they may have some notion that their behavior or relationships are different from those of other girls.

Styles and Symbols (B5)

One way to actively construct one's own gender is through nonverbal and stylistic behaviors, and yet little attention has been paid to these aspects of gender construction. Are children who often select their own clothing aware of the effects of their choices? Studies of children's awareness of their appearance, mannerisms, and general style may help us understand more about the different ways in which individuals can choose to adopt, reject, or reform gender roles.

Values (B6)

As children begin to recognize that males and females are differentially valued, their own self-perceptions may be affected when their identity as a group member is salient. According to social identity theory (Tajfel, 1978), the social categories into which individuals are divided have evaluative implications and thus consequences for self-esteem. For example, girls who attribute their failure on a computer project to the idea that girls are incompetent in this domain may experience sadness and shame (Lutz & Ruble, 1995). These ideas have received little direct empirical attention with children. Although considerable evidence suggests that girls evaluate themselves more negatively than boys in many situations (see section D; Eccles, Wigfield, & Schiefele, Ch. 15, this Volume; Ruble, Greulich, Pomerantz, & Gochberg, 1993), the specific link to gender values is not clear. Future research should examine self-perceptions in situations in which categorical group identification is more or less salient.

Preferences (C)

How strongly and when do children prefer to be their own biological sex and to play with same-gender toys and same-sex playmates? Such preferences have been assessed in various ways and are often viewed as indicators of gender typing or of stereotypic beliefs. In this section, we examine preferences expressed verbally, often in terms of options presented to the child. In the next section, we consider behavioral measures of the same constructs. In many cases, self-reports and behavioral measures yield similar trends. Like Huston, however, we have chosen to examine them separately because processes governing conscious choices versus behaviors may be quite different. Children may play with familiar toys but when asked to make a conscious selection, they may select on some other basis. Similarly, self-reports may involve demand characteristics more than behavioral measures. Not only may the distinction between verbal and behavioral preferences be quite subtle or artificial at times, but a similar blurring of the distinction between identities (i.e., what one actually is or does) and verbal preferences (what one would like to do or be like) may also create problems.

Biological/Categorical Sex (C1)

How satisfied are children with their sex? In Goldman and Goldman's (1982) study of 5- to 15-year-olds from Australia, England, North America, and Sweden, very few children reported wishing that they could have been the other sex. However, more girls wished to be boys than vice versa, especially around age 13. Similarly, in two studies in Australia, 8- to 12-year-old boys were more satisfied with their sex (Antill, Cotton, Russell, & Goodnow, 1996), and sex differences in dissatisfaction increased up to adolescence (Burns & Homel, 1986). Finally, one study examined whether sex preferences have changed over time. High school girls in the 1980s were less likely than those in the 1950s to say they preferred to be the other sex (Lewin & Tragos, 1987). Children with gender identity disorder (GID) more often report wishing to be the other sex (Zucker et al., 1993). Parents of 4- to 11-year-old clinic-referred children report 1% to 16% of boys and 6% to 8% of girls wish to be the other sex, compared with 0% to 2% of boys and 2% to 5% of girls from a nonclinic sample (Meyer-Bahlburg, 1985).

Activities and Interests (C2)

Developmental Trends for Preschoolers. Trends for toy and activity preferences are similar to those for stereotypes (Huston, 1983): A dramatic increase in gender-typed preferences during the preschool years, with well-established preferences by 5 years, and more gender-typed preferences for boys than for girls (Carter & Levy, 1988; Coker, 1984; Martin & Little, 1990). Some qualifications in these conclusions should be noted, however. First, preferences vary tremendously depending on the activity. Assessment procedures in use today often involve forced-choice questions in which children are asked explicitly about their own preferences for child and adult activities (e.g., preference section of SERLI; Edelbrock & Sugawara, 1978). With activities from the SERLI, some of which are chores, children's preferences are not strongly gender-typed, even though their stereotype knowledge is (Serbin et al., 1993; Turner, Gervai, & Hinde, 1993). For other play activities (e.g., trucks, dolls), gender-consistent preferences are very strong, over 80% at age 4 and reaching 100% by age 7 (Emmerich & Shepard, 1982). The second qualification concerns the strength of the sex difference. Because SERLI items for boys are mostly play things, whereas for girls they are household chores, it is not surprising that girls consistently show less clear same-gender preferences (Edelbrock & Sugawara, 1978; Serbin et al., 1993; Turner et al., 1993). When other items are used, boys do not always show greater gender typing (Coker, 1984; Serbin et al., 1993). Nevertheless, even using other measures, most studies still suggest that girls are less invested in same-gender activities than are boys (Carter & Levy, 1988; Katz & Boswell, 1986; Perry et al., 1984; Turner et al., 1993). Because in many studies children select between gender-typed and neutral items, the observed difference may reflect girls' greater attraction to neutral toys rather than preferences for gender-consistent toys.

How early do children state gender-typed preferences? The data are mixed. In one study, boys showed gender-typed preferences at age 2, but girls did not until age 4 (Blakemore, LaRue, & Olejnik, 1979). In contrast, Perry et al. (1984) found that both boys and girls preferred gender-typed items over neutral ones at age 3 years, but not before. One problem assessing stereotypic preferences in young children is the use of cultural stereotypes as the criterion, rather than the child's own judgments. The few studies that have examined this issue suggest that the distinction makes relatively little difference, though preferences based on personal rather than cultural stereotypes sometimes show higher gender-typing for young children, especially girls (Edelbrock & Sugawara, 1978; Turner et al., 1993).

Developmental Trends in Middle Childhood. Because some aspects of stereotyping become less rigid but also more elaborated as children move into middle school, activity/interest preferences might also be expected to change at this time. Early studies showed that boys' and girls' preferences follow different developmental paths after age 5, with boys showing increasingly stereotyped preferences and girls remaining stable or declining (Huston, 1983). More recent research has shown mixed support for this conclusion. In some cases, the same sex difference is found (Katz & Boswell, 1986; Katz & Walsh, 1991), but other studies show that preference scores for both sexes were stable between kindergarten–first grade and fifth–sixth grade (although boys' scores were somewhat higher overall) (O'Keefe & Hyde, 1983; Serbin et al., 1993; Trautner, 1992). The mixed results may be due to individual differences in the developmental trajectory for preferences. In a longitudinal analysis, Trautner (1992) found that children exhibited two different patterns: either object and activity preferences continued to become more stereotyped through age 7 years and then stabilized at a high level through age 10, or they were already highly stereotyped by age 5 and remained so.

Patterns also may vary depending on the kind of preference assessed. For example, in a study of 5- to 14-year-old children, Etaugh and Liss (1992) found that (a) for occupational preferences, gender-type preferences became more flexible with age for girls but not boys; (b) for toys, both sexes showed an increased preference for neutral toys with age, and girls' gender-typed preferences declined sooner;

and (c) for school subject preferences, no clear gender-typed pattern was found. Also, patterns may vary depending on whether children's preferences for same-gender activity are assessed versus their rejection of other-gender activities. Bussey and Perry (1982) found that third- and fourth-grade boys reject gender-inconsistent behavior more than girls, but there was no sex difference in gender-consistent preferences. One clear conclusion is possible: When preferences become less rigidly gender-typed during the middle grades, it is usually for girls only.

Developmental Changes into Adolescence. Do gender preferences for activities and interests become more rigid or more flexible as children move through their adolescent years? Similar to the literature on stereotyping, several studies report that preferences become more flexible between middle childhood and early adolescence (Etaugh & Liss, 1992; Katz & Ksansnak, 1994; Plumb & Cowan, 1984), although for some studies this increase occurs only or primarily for girls (e.g., Plumb & Cowan, 1984). Studies examining change into late adolescence generally show that girls' preferences remain more flexible than boys' (Archer, 1984). Consistent with the gender intensification hypothesis, however, one study found that girls' relative preferences for stereotypically feminine over masculine school subjects increased in secondary school (Archer, 1992). Tomboys and non-tomboy girls may differ in preferences. Non-tomboys showed an increased preference for gender-consistent activities between early and later adolescence, similar to boys, but tomboys did not (Plumb & Cowan, 1984), suggesting perhaps that the main distinction between girls' and boys' preferences may occur only for a subgroup of girls. One study, using a measure of liking of gender-inconsistent activities (rather than a comparative evaluation of gender-consistent and inconsistent activities) reported that both males and females showed more flexible preferences into late adolescence (Katz & Ksansnak, 1994).

The dominant finding is that girls are less rigid in their stereotypic preferences than boys. With few exceptions, this difference has appeared at all age levels. Although some evidence suggests an increase in flexibility in early adolescence, particularly for girls, trends into later adolescence are unclear.

Personal-Social Attributes (C3)

Do children prefer certain kinds of personality traits for themselves? In our consideration of the findings regarding cell B3 in the matrix (Table 14.1), we discussed a closely related issue: how children perceive their current or actual selves in terms of such traits—that is, their identity. Few researchers have examined trait preferences, even though preferred or valued characteristics may influence children's future behavior. In one relevant study, Intons-Peterson (1988b) asked Swedish respondents from 11 to 18 years to rate characteristics associated with their ideal self. Overall, several instrumental qualities (e.g., never gives up) and several expressive qualities (e.g., kind) were rated highly by both sexes. Sex differences were found on 19 out of 59 characteristics, but these were not the top-rated characteristics (except "gentle" which was rated more highly by females). With age, the importance of expressive characteristics tended to increase with age whereas instrumental traits decreased with age.

Social Relationships (C4)

Children's reported preferences for same-sex peers have been widely documented (Maccoby & Jacklin, 1987). When preschool, kindergarten, and middle school children are asked to rate either known or unknown peers, they consistently like same-sex peers and prefer them as friends more than other-sex peers, and this tendency usually increases with age until adolescence when other-sex interests become apparent (Goldman & Goldman, 1982; Martin, 1989; Powlishta et al., 1994; Serbin et al., 1993). School-age children report more positive feelings and more trust in their own sex than in the other sex (Rotenberg, 1986). Both sexes report being more hurt, disgusted, and more likely to avoid the other sex than their own sex (Powlishta et al., 1994). An exception to these same-sex preferences is children with GID who often report other-sex preferences, even though they may be rejected by both sexes (Bradley & Zucker, 1990).

Strong same-sex peer preferences are even shown for unknown children with nontraditional interests, especially by younger children (e.g., Berndt & Heller, 1986; Martin, Eisenbud, & Rose, 1995; Martin & Little, 1990; Zucker, Wilson-Smith, Kurita, & Stern, 1995). For example, a boy described as liking girls and as playing with kitchen sets was liked by boys as much as a boy who was described as liking to play with boys and with footballs (Martin, 1989). Similarly, in a naturalistic context, Moller, Hymel, and Rubin (1992) found little evidence that peers' engagement in gender-typed activities affected sociometric ratings, although there was some tendency for boys to prefer male peers who engaged more in masculine-typed behaviors and activities and for girls to prefer male peers who engaged more in feminine-typed play. However, even younger children may consider nontraditional interests of peers more under specific conditions, such as with extreme or multiple examples of cross-sex behavior (Zucker et al., 1995). Finally, children's personal preferences for others may differ from perceptions of others' evaluations. In an Israeli sample of 10- to 12-year-olds, children predicted that the least popular child would be a boy who played games with girls, but their personal preferences were more egalitarian (Lobel, Bempechat, Gewirtz, Shoken-Topaz, & Bashe, 1993).

The reasons for same-sex preferences have not yet been ascertained, but it appears that children are more drawn to their own sex than they are avoidant of the other sex (Bukowski, Gauze, Hoza, & Newcombe, 1993). A study of 5- to 15-year-olds from Australia, North America, Britain, and Sweden found that reasons for selecting same-sex peers as friends differed by sex with girls tending to report that similarity of feelings was important, whereas boys tended to report similarity in activities and interests (Goldman & Goldman, 1982).

Styles and Symbols (C5)

Anecdotally, parents report that young children express quite strong preferences to dress in a way that indicates clearly their sex, regardless of the parents' preferences for their appearance. This may mean that girls prefer frilly dresses and bows and boys prefer baseball caps and sneakers, but to our knowledge, studies of verbal preferences have not addressed this aspect of gender typing.

Values (C6)

How do children evaluate gender categories and related activities and interests? Do they view males and masculine activities as somehow "better" or more valued, as some research with adults has suggested (see Deaux & LaFrance, in press)? Do they view cross-gender behavior or traits as morally wrong? One problem with examining personal values about gender is that they are rarely measured directly by, for example, asking children whether they think it is better to be a man or woman or to do masculine or feminine jobs. Instead, such values must be inferred from related measures. In this section, evidence is examined on three types of gender-related values: in-group biases, prejudice against females, and attitudes about egalitarian gender roles.

In-Group/Out-Group Biases. According to cognitive theories, children's growing awareness of their membership in one sex category is likely to create a number of identity validation processes, one of which is to view one's own sex, the "in-group," more favorably than the other (Kohlberg, 1966; Martin & Halverson, 1981; Tajfel, 1978). In a direct examination of this prediction, 3- to 11-year-olds in South Wales were asked how they "feel" about girls and boys (Yee & Brown, 1994). By age 5, both girls and boys were markedly more positive about their own sex than about the other sex, and even 3-year-old girls (but not boys) showed a significant in-group favoritism. Children's greater liking of same-sex others may also be interpreted in terms of an in-group bias. Although in-group peer preferences do not weaken (and even strengthen) during childhood, other measures of in-group bias, such as positive evaluations of same-sex versus other-sex story characters, have shown a decline with age (Nesdale & McLaughlin, 1987).

Children also tend to show in-group evaluative biases in assigning more positive than negative traits to their own sex in the early school years (e.g., Albert & Porter, 1983; Urberg, 1982; Yee & Brown, 1994) and in the middle grades (e.g., Kaminski & Sheridan, 1984; Powlishta, 1995a). This positivity bias declines with age, at least after 4 to 5 years (Powlishta et al., 1994; Urberg, 1982) and is often stronger for girls (Yee & Brown, 1994). Overall, then, there is considerable evidence of in-group evaluative biases, especially among preschool children (but see Cowan & Hoffman, 1986, and Haugh et al., 1980, for exceptions).

Prejudice against Women. One reason for the high level of interest in gender development involves a search for the origins of women's disadvantaged status in most cultures. Is there any evidence that, aside from in-group biases, children value males more than females, and if so, how early does this begin? Interestingly, despite general cultural biases attributing greater prestige and power to males (and some evidence that children are aware of such status differences by middle childhood—see A6), most of the available evidence suggests that children are more likely to derogate males than females. Yee and Brown (1994) found that although both boys and girls felt more positively about their own sex, boys were described in more negative terms overall. Whether such a pro-feminine bias would hold true in certain non-western countries, where, for example, women lower themselves to the floor and cover their heads when men enter the area (Whiting & Edwards, 1988), is an interesting question for future cross-cultural research.

Why do children not show this expected devaluation of females relative to males? Young children may be particularly attentive to attributes implying moral goodness, such as helpfulness and conformity with adult norms (Paley, 1988; Ruble & Dweck, 1995). As children begin to stereotypically associate such attributes more with females than with males ("girls are sugar and spice and everything nice"), they may initially value females more, and this positive evaluation of females continues to some extent into adulthood (Eagly, Mladinic, & Otto, 1991). For adults, however, cultural standards emphasize masculine attributes of prestige, power, and competence. As these adult standards are acquired, evaluations of females would be expected to decline relative to evaluations of males (De Lisi & Johns, 1984).

Some evidence indirectly supports this account. Zalk and Katz (1978) found that both boys and girls evaluated girls more positively on conduct/morality items (e.g., tells lies) but on a set including competence-related items (e.g., wins at tic-tac-toe), there was no difference. Studies involving children older than 7 years, however, often show evidence of more positive evaluations of males and masculine activities and attributes (e.g., Archer & Macrae, 1991; Thorne, 1993). Lockheed, Harris, and Nemceff (1983) found that although there were no observed differences in the behavior of fourth- and fifth-grade boys and girls in mixed sex teams, boys were perceived as more competent and leaderlike than girls. An interesting finding along these lines is reported by Lobel et al. (1993). Both boys and girls aged 10 to 12 years preferred to play with a target who had been previously shown on videotape as playing with boys.

Egalitarian Attitudes. Do children think it is desirable for individuals to be free to engage in whatever behaviors they prefer, or do they feel it is wrong to engage in activities not stereotypically associated with one's gender? One approach to this question is to assess attitudes toward equal roles, using a measure such as the Attitudes toward Women Scale (e.g., "Girls should have the same freedoms as boys") (Galambos, Petersen, Richards, & Gitelson, 1985). Older children and adolescents' responses to this measure indicate that boys value gender equality less than girls (Antill et al., 1996; Galambos et al., 1990) and boys become increasingly negative between 6th and 8th grades, whereas girls become increasingly positive (Galambos et al., 1990).

Other studies have examined developmental trends in children's assessment of whether it is right or wrong (good or bad) to engage in cross-gender behavior. In contrast to findings that flexibility of gender stereotyping increases with age, some studies of evaluative reactions to cross-gender behavior find that negative reactions are relatively stable (Levy, Taylor, & Gelman, 1995) or increase across age (Carter & McCloskey, 1984). Stoddart and Turiel (1985), however, found a U-shaped pattern in which cross-gender behavior was evaluated more negatively by kindergartners and early adolescents than by children in the middle grades. Perhaps the young children in this study were less accepting because the behaviors were relatively extreme appearance violations (e.g., a boy wearing nail polish) rather than activity violations (e.g., a girl playing with a truck). This interpretation is supported by another study finding that preschool children considered cross-gender appearances to be more serious violations than cross-gender activities (Smetana, 1986).

Finally, gender-based values are often implicit in measures of stereotypes and preferences. Signorella and her colleagues (Signorella & Liben, 1985; Signorella et al., 1993) have argued that measures of stereotyping that allow the option of responding "both males and females" are similar to attitudes. Especially close to the notion of values are studies that ask what males, females, or both "should" be like or do. The Signorella et al. (1993) meta-analysis suggests that values about gender become more flexible with age (see A2).

Behavioral Enactment (D)

Gender-typed behavioral displays can be assessed by examining the ways individuals dress, the kinds of activities they engage in, their abilities, the kinds of sexual partners they choose, and the ways they treat women and men as groups. An examination of developmental trends across different kinds of behaviors can help elucidate key theoretical issues concerning the motivating forces behind gender-typed behavior. For example, are behaviors guided by children's beliefs about what girls and boys should do, or are they occurring independently of belief systems?

Biological/Categorical Sex (D1)

Despite wide varieties of socialization pressures, cultural differences, and even biological influences, most children develop a clear sense of self as male or female and master the roles generally associated with their assigned sex. Although it is rare, some individuals are uncomfortable with their sex and want to become the other sex (Green, 1974), and these transsexuals may elect to have the extensive surgical and hormonal treatments required for sex reassignment.

Activities and Interests (D2)

Children's engagement in gender stereotypical activities has been examined in a wide range of settings, including free play in home, school, and laboratory observations, as well as chores children do at home, television preferences, and courses they select at school. A major question has been whether sex differences in behaviors occur before or after the awareness of gender stereotypes and the development of gender identity. Huston (1983) concluded that children show differential engagement in gender-typed toy play as early as 1½ to 2 years, which appears to be earlier than most indicators of children's cognitive awareness of gender stereotypes or identity. More recent research suggests that boys and girls show differential play around 2 years of age (e.g., Fagot, Leinbach, & Hagan, 1986; O'Brien & Huston, 1985; Weinraub et al., 1984). In addition, individual differences in same-gender play appear to be quite stable among 2- to 3-year-olds, although avoidance of other-gender play was found to be stable only for boys (Powlishta, Serbin, & Moller, 1993). Whether gender-typed toy play emerges prior to 2 years of age is less clear. There are some reports of infants showing gender-typed toy play with parents before one year of age (Roopnarine, 1986). Other studies of unconstrained free play by children younger than 2 years have reported mixed results (Caldera, Huston, & O'Brien, 1989; Fagot & Leinbach, 1989).

Do boys show stronger or earlier evidence of gender-typed toy play? Many studies of preschoolers show no sex differences (e.g., Bussey & Bandura, 1992) or mixed results (O'Brien & Huston, 1985). The evidence appears to be clearer for children's willingness to play with other-gender toys. Preschool boys appear to avoid highly stereotyped cross-gender behavior more than girls (e.g., Bussey & Bandura, 1992; Fagot et al., 1986).

Most studies examining gender-typed play in children aged 3 to 6 years report clear differences not only in *what* children play with but also *where* they play (Downs & Langlois, 1988; Smetana & Letourneau, 1984). During free play at preschool, girls are more likely to be found in arts and crafts areas and boys in blocks areas (Pellegrini & Perlmutter, 1989), and girls prefer situations structured by adults more than do boys (Carpenter, Huston, & Holt,

1986; Powlishta et al., 1993). In an observational study of homes and neighborhoods, however, few sex differences were found in how or where preschoolers play (Bloch, 1987).

Sex differences in interests and activities persist into middle childhood and adolescence. Boys and girls show different preferences for shows on television: boys prefer cartoons more than girls, and spend more time watching action adventure programs (see Huston & Wright, Ch. 15, this Volume). Australian children from 8 to 14 years of age revealed clear gender typing across a variety of domains: sports, household jobs, toys owned, and interests or hobbies (Antill et al., 1993). Girls spend more time in indoor household tasks and chores (Blair, 1992) and this increases with age (e.g., Sanik & Stafford, 1985), whereas boys spend more time in outdoor chores and leisure activities. Boys' leisure activities involve less structure and more active sports; girls' activities involve more shopping and socializing (Huston, Carpenter, Atwater, & Johnson, 1986; Maudlin & Meeks, 1990; Timmer, Eccles, & O'Brien, 1985). Often, however, the commonalities in use of time by boys and girls are more remarkable than the differences (Timmer et al., 1985).

A few studies have found developmental changes in gender-typed behavior in adolescence that confirm the gender intensification hypothesis, especially for girls. With age, girls spend more time in interpersonal activities, personal care, and household chores and less time in sports (Richards & Larson, 1989; Timmer et al., 1985), whereas for boys, participation in sports either remains stable (Richards & Larson, 1989) or increases (Timmer et al., 1985). In addition, consistent with the idea that achievement pressures should increase for boys and decrease for girls during adolescence, one study found that the relation between self-image and achievement increased for boys and decreased for girls between sixth and seventh grades (Roberts, Sarigiani, Petersen, & Newman, 1990).

Finally, a few studies have looked specifically at "gender-atypical" behavior early in development, in part because of the widespread belief that such behaviors are related to homosexuality in adolescence and adulthood (Bailey & Zucker, 1995; Green, 1987; Zucker, 1985). In general, selecting other-sex playmates and playing with dolls are uncommon in boys throughout early childhood and cross-gender behavior decreases as children enter middle childhood (e.g., Zucker, 1985). Some engagement in other-gender activities or forms of play is quite common, however. One large study of 6- to 10-year-olds found that over 23% of the boys and 39% of the girls engaged in some forms of gender-atypical behavior at least once in a while (Sandberg, Meyer-Bahlburg, Ehrhardt, & Yager, 1993).

Personal-Social Attributes (D3)

Huston (1983) did not attempt to review the literature on sex differences in traits and abilities, because the literature was so large. Instead, she referred to Maccoby and Jacklin's (1974) comprehensive review. Maccoby and Jacklin (1974) concluded that research findings supported the existence of sex differences in only four areas: (a) Boys are more physically aggressive at all ages and across cultures; (b) beginning around puberty, boys' mathematical skills increase faster than girls; (c) males tend to perform better on tasks involving spatial skills than do girls; and (d) from middle elementary school through high school, girls tend to perform better than boys on tasks involving verbal skills. In other domains in which sex differences might be expected, Maccoby and Jacklin felt either that the question was still open (e.g., activity level, compliance, nurturance) or that the evidence did *not* support sex differences (e.g., sociability, analytic skills).

Because of the increasing use of meta-analysis in the study of sex differences, many of the problems concerning compiling results have been alleviated, and it is now easier to summarize the findings briefly (see Historical Review section). In this section, the focus is primarily on meta-analytic reviews of sex differences in personal-social attributes, especially on whether sex differences show developmental trends and whether there are domains in which sex differences are stronger than in others. Our review relies heavily on a summary of meta-analytic studies of sex differences by Hyde and Frost (1993), covering studies through 1990, but meta-analyses not covered by that review are also included.

Cognitive Skills. Historically, women have been viewed as less intellectually gifted and less likely to achieve eminence as a result of innate inferiority in prerequisite abilities (Hyde & Linn, 1986). Do the sexes actually differ on components of intelligence—mathematical skills, spatial skills, and verbal skills (see Halpern, 1992)?

The sexes differ in mathematic abilities although the patterns vary depending on many factors (Halpern, 1992). Meta-analytic studies indicate that differences are larger and favor males with highly selected samples (Hyde, Fennema, & Lamon, 1990) and on certain standardized tests

(e.g., SAT) (Hyde & Frost, 1993). Sex differences vary for different mathematical components. No sex difference is found in mathematical concepts. Males outperform females on problem-solving tasks (effect sizes .2 to .4), usually beginning in junior high or high school, with differences increasing between 9th and 12th grades (Hyde et al., 1990). For computational skills, elementary school girls outperform boys (−.2), but no difference is found past age 15 (Hyde et al., 1990). Girls receive higher grades in mathematics classes than boys (Kimball, 1989). Interestingly, female performance in mathematics has been improving over time relative to males, such that studies in the 1980s and 1990s tend to show smaller or no differences relative to earlier studies (Feingold, 1988; Hyde et al., 1990; Rosenthal & Rubin, 1982). Furthermore, some evidence suggests that sex differences in performance may be accounted for by prior knowledge and strategy use (Byrnes & Takahira, 1993).

A common explanation for why women do not abound in the scientific and mathematical professions is their supposed inferiority on tasks involving spatial skills. Although males tend to outperform females on these tasks, the patterns vary depending on the kind of spatial task that is assessed. The largest sex difference occurs with adolescents and adults on tasks involving mental rotation (rapid manipulation of three-dimensional figures, overall $d = .6$) or involving recognition of the vertical or horizontal (overall $d = .4$), but are much smaller or not evident on spatial visualization tasks (e.g., hidden figures tests, overall $d = .2$) (Voyer, Voyer, & Bryden, 1995). Only a few differences are significant at younger ages (Voyer et al., 1995), although 9- to 13-year-olds show moderate sex differences (.4–.6) on simplified tests of mental rotation and spatial visualization (Kerns & Berenbaum, 1991). Effect sizes increase with age for all measures. In addition, the magnitude of the difference has been decreasing over time (Feingold, 1988; Voyer et al., 1995), except on mental rotation tasks, in which sex differences have remained stable (Masters & Sanders, 1993).

Although differences are small, females show superior performance on verbal tasks (−.1 to −.3) (Hyde & Linn, 1986; Rosenthal & Rubin, 1982). Several researchers have suggested that sex differences in verbal skills are becoming smaller and perhaps even disappearing (Feingold, 1988; Hyde & Linn, 1986), but others suggest that differences have remained stable (Hedges & Nowell, 1995). The differences favoring females are clearest in spelling and language (Feingold, 1988; Hyde & Linn, 1986), and are stable across age (Hyde & Linn, 1986).

In a large-scale examination of a wide range of abilities in several national probability samples of adolescents, Hedges and Nowell (1995) found that females tended to score higher than males on reading comprehension, perceptual speed, and associative memory, and were much better at writing; whereas males performed somewhat better than females on tests of science, mathematics, social studies, and much better on vocational aptitude scales (e.g., mechanical reasoning and electronics). Sex differences in mathematics and science scores narrowed between 1960 to 1992 somewhat, whereas differences in reading or writing did not. Furthermore, males were generally more variable than females on ability tests.

Physical Performance. Beliefs that males are more active and better at physical activities are supported by meta-analytic results. Eaton and Enns (1986) reported an average effect size of .5 for activity level, based primarily on studies with children. The effect sizes were not uniform across age and context, however; males were relatively more active at older ages and in familiar, nonthreatening settings. Thomas and French (1985) found better performance by males for 17 of 20 motor tasks examined, with the largest differences occurring for throw velocity and distance. Females' performance was better on fine eye-motor and flexibility tasks. Sex differences in physical tasks increased with age, possibly due to differential environmental support (Smoll & Schutz, 1990). Certainly, the differential participation of boys and girls in sports particularly after puberty is well documented and probably influences the results of studies of physical performance (Eisenberg, Martin, & Fabes, 1996), though biological factors are also likely to be important (e.g., Hall & Kimura, 1995).

Subjective Well-Being and Self-Evaluation. A variety of indicators show that females experience lower levels of well-being than males. Females are more likely than males to be clinically depressed or to exhibit higher levels of depressive symptoms, beginning in adolescence (Angold & Rutter, 1992; Nolen-Hoeksema, 1987; Weissman & Olfson, 1995). Meta-analyses on studies conducted since 1984 reported small but significant effect sizes (.2) favoring males on self-esteem (Feingold, 1994; Hyde & Frost, 1993) and "general self-concept" (Hattie, 1992). A number of large-scale studies have confirmed a marked decline in self-esteem in young girls after age 9 compared with no change in boys (American Association of University Women, 1992). In addition, many researchers have found that girls have more appearance and weight concerns than boys, a difference that increases during adolescence (Mendelson, White, & Mendelson, 1996; Richards, Casper, & Larson, 1990) and that may influence the emergence of sex differences in self-esteem (Friedman & Brownell, 1995).

A recent summary of self-evaluation studies with children reported that when studies find sex differences in related areas (e.g., self-confidence, expectations for success, maladaptive attributions for achievement-related outcomes), they almost always favor boys (Ruble et al., 1993). These sex differences in self-confidence (or success expectations) and in maladaptive reactions to failure are supported by meta-analyses and reviews including adults (Lirgg, 1991; Roberts, 1991), although the findings for attributions are less clear (Sohn, 1982; Whitley, McHugh, & Frieze, 1986). A more detailed evaluation of this literature would seem productive, given the centrality of self-cognitions and attributions in theories of the etiology and maintenance of depression (e.g., Hammen, 1992).

Personality Traits and Social Behavior. The question of whether males and females actually display the different attributes that are stereotypically associated with them, such as aggression and dependency, has been the subject of a number of meta-analyses. Studies of aggression have yielded some of the most consistent findings for any personality or ability area, at least for children. Most studies have found that boys engage in more aggressive behaviors than girls ($d = .5$) (Block, 1983; Maccoby & Jacklin, 1974). An exception is relational aggression—behaviors intended to damage another child's friendship (e.g., exclusion from play group)—which girls engage in more than boys (Crick & Grotpeter, 1995) and which girls view as a fairly common response to anger for girls but not boys (Crick, Bigbee, & Howes, 1996). Meta-analytic reviews also indicate that males are more assertive, though effect sizes are somewhat smaller (Feingold, 1994). These differences emerge quite early in life and are found cross-culturally suggesting that biological factors may be involved (Maccoby & Jacklin, 1974; Rohner, 1976).

Sex differences in aggression are stronger in children than in adults (Maccoby & Jacklin, 1974); the magnitude of difference is quite small for adults, even smaller than for other social behaviors such as helping and nonverbal behaviors (Eagly & Crowley, 1986), and appears to be moderated by contextual factors, such as provocation (Bettencourt & Miller, 1996). It is important to consider, however, that sex differences in aggression are more apparent in the real world than in the laboratory. Men commit more violent crimes of all sorts than women, and the more serious the crime, the more a sex difference is apparent (Ellis, 1990).

Despite stereotypes that females are more helpful and oriented to the needs of others, there are not strong and consistent sex differences in prosocial behavior in children. Sex differences tend to be small, and the likelihood of finding sex differences varies by characteristics of the study (Eisenberg & Fabes, Ch. 11, this Volume; Eisenberg et al., 1996). Perhaps most interesting are the results of a recent meta-analysis of helping behavior. Girls help others more than boys (Eisenberg & Fabes, Ch. 11, this Volume) but the reverse is true for adults, partly because studies with adults often involve heroic and instrumental helping, which is more consistent with the male role (Eagly & Crowley, 1986). According to Gilligan (1982), females rely on a morality of caring rather than of justice. The scientific evidence does not provide consistent support for these views (e.g., Walker, 1984). For children, few sex differences are found in moral reasoning (e.g., Garrod & Beal, 1993), however, by early adolescence, girls use specific types of other-oriented reasoning more than do boys (Eisenberg, Carlo, Murphy, & Van Court, 1995).

Although stereotypes suggest that females are more passive and dependent, and more easily influenced than males, empirical verification of sex differences in these areas is relatively weak. Maccoby and Jacklin (1974) found that differences were particularly small for observational and experimental studies of children interacting with parents and peers, but girls are rated by others as dependent, possibly because of stereotypic expectations. Meta-analyses have found small but significant (<.3) effect sizes indicating an overall tendency for women to be more easily influenced than men (e.g., Becker, 1986), but these differences may be contextual (Eagly, 1987). In addition, females are more likely to be helped than males ($d = .5$) (Eagly & Crowley, 1986). This difference does not necessarily indicate that women are more dependent, only that they are so perceived. A few studies suggest, however, that females may be more likely to seek help of certain kinds and more willing to accept help (see Eisenberg et al., 1996, for a review).

Are females more socially oriented and sensitive as gender stereotypes suggest? The results of meta-analyses in some areas suggest that they are. In an extensive review of the literature, little evidence was found that girls and boys differ in their abilities to understand what others are thinking or feeling, but women appear to be better than men at decoding others' emotions and to have a greater tendency to take the perspective of another when the opportunity arises (Eisenberg et al., 1996). In addition, females at all ages are more accurate at decoding emotions from visual and auditory stimuli (Hall, 1984), with moderate effect sizes. Females also appear to be more socially expressive and responsive. Moderate-to-large effect sizes have been found for social gazing, expression of emotion, and general facial expressiveness (Hall, 1984; Hall & Halberstadt, 1986).

Emotionality.   Females are believed to be more emotional, which generally means more anxious, fearful, more easily upset, and more empathic and emotionally expressive, whereas males are believed to express more anger and to be more likely to hide or deny emotional reactions (Fabes & Martin, 1991). In the only meta-analytic review of sex differences in emotions, Feingold (1994) found a small effect size for sex differences in anxiety (< .3) in the expected direction in adults and adolescents.

On the basis of their review, Eisenberg et al. (1996) provide the following developmental account of emotional reactivity. During infancy and toddler years, few consistent sex differences in the expression of emotion are found, although there is some evidence that males exhibit more irritability and anger, and girls more fearfulness. During the early elementary school years, boys start to hide negative emotions, such as sadness, and girls express less anger and emotions such as disappointment that might hurt others' feelings. By adolescence, girls report more sadness, shame, and guilt, and say they experience emotions more intensely, whereas boys are more likely to deny experiencing these emotions.

With respect to empathy, Eisenberg et al. (1996) concluded that females are only slightly more likely than males to show sympathy, and that differences are dependent on methodology and context. Self-report measures show large differences favoring females, but physiological or unobtrusive observations do not (Eisenberg & Lennon, 1983; also see Eisenberg & Fabes, Ch. 11, this Volume). This pattern suggests that individuals' views of themselves may be biased by the gender stereotypes they hold.

Summary.   Consistent with Maccoby and Jacklin's (1974) review, moderately strong sex differences are found for some components of spatial skills, primarily in adolescents and adults, and for aggression, primarily in children. In addition, males outperform females on some mathematical skills, but moderate sex differences appear primarily for standardized tests, such as the SAT, and/or in selected populations. Sex differences in verbal ability that had been evident in earlier publications are now weak or inconsistent. Furthermore, strong and consistent sex differences appear in other domains, most notably activity level (especially in older children), physical performance (especially for adolescents and adults), and facial expressiveness at all age levels. Overall, then, sex difference patterns vary considerably by content area and developmental level. In general, personal/ social behavior show negligible to moderate differences but no large differences, whereas interests and abilities show differences across the full range of effect sizes (see Ashmore, 1990, for a composite review of effect sizes).

Social Relationships (D4)

Development of Sex Segregation. One of the most pervasive and consistent sex differences involves children's tendencies to play with same-sex partners (Maccoby, 1988). The role of peers in children's socialization rivals that of the family (Harris, 1995), in part because children spend so much of their time in same-sex groups. Because distinct differences between girls' and boys' peer groups are found throughout childhood with girls' groups being more cooperative and boys' groups being more competitive and rough (see Leaper, 1994; Maccoby, 1988, 1990a, for reviews), girls and boys learn different ways of interacting with others. Play in boys' groups is marked by rough-and-tumble play, attempts at attaining dominance, and constrictive interaction styles, whereas play in girls' groups is marked by cooperative interactions and enabling interaction styles. From these different experiences, it has been argued boys and girls form two separate cultures (Maccoby, 1990a).

Only a few studies have examined the early origins of sex segregation. One large study showed the following: At 17 months, children showed no tendency to affiliate with same-sex peers over other-sex peers; by 27 months, girls showed same-sex preferences; and by 36 months, both sexes showed similar same-sex preferences (La Freniere, Strayer, & Gauthier, 1984). Boys lag behind girls in their positive contacts with same-sex peers (Serbin, Moller, Gulko, Powlishta, & Colburne, 1994). The emergence of same-sex biases over the second and third years has been confirmed in several other studies (Fagot, 1995; Moller & Serbin, 1996; Serbin et al., 1994).

Sex segregation increases as children grow older. Maccoby and Jacklin (1987) found that 4-year-old children interacted with same-sex peers 3 times more often than with other-sex peers, but 6-year-olds interacted with same-sex peers 11 times more often than with other-sex peers. Interestingly, a tendency for boys more than girls to interact in groups has also been found to emerge between 4- to 6-years-of-age (Benenson, Apostoleris, & Parnass, 1997). In early adolescence, children congregate in small cliques of same-sex peers but by middle adolescence, these cliques are often replaced by heterosexual dating couples (Carter, 1987). Generally, children's friendships follow similar patterns. Sex is more important than race or age in the selection of friends.

The phenomenon of sex segregation appears to be virtually universal in Western and non-Western societies, as well as occurring in many higher species of nonhuman primates (Archer, 1992; Carter, 1987), although the extent varies depending on the number of children available and on their ages (Harkness & Super, 1985; Whiting & Edwards, 1988). The degree of sex segregation varies across settings (Archer, 1992), as well. It is less likely to occur when children are in their neighborhoods than in their schools (Ellis, Rogoff, & Cromer, 1981), when there are few playmate choices (Whiting & Edwards, 1988), when teachers provide structure for mixed-sex situations (e.g., Lockheed, 1986), when children are highly engaged in a task or actively cooperating (Thorne, 1986), and when children are in novel situations and with unfamiliar peers (Luria & Herzog, 1991).

When do children feel comfortable crossing gender boundaries? Based on observations of children in elementary school, Thorne (1986, 1993) has described the ways children engage in "borderwork," interacting across gender boundaries by chasing each other, invading each others' territory, and by involvement in games such as "chase and kiss." For preadolescents, certain conditions, such as having the protection of a same-sex peer, having an excuse, or being forced, allow for permissible gender boundary violations (Sroufe, Bennett, Englund, Urban, & Shulman, 1993). Children who violate boundaries in inappropriate settings are rated as being socially incompetent by adults and are considered unpopular with peers.

Development of Sexual Orientation. The developmental course of sexual orientation has been difficult to chart. Young children, especially boys, with gender identity problems are more likely to have homosexual or bisexual orientations than other children (Green, 1987; Zucker & Bradley, 1995). A meta-analytic review suggests that homosexuals are much more likely than heterosexuals to report retrospectively cross-gender interests in childhood (effect size for men = 1.3; women = 1.0) (Bailey & Zucker, 1995). In one group of young homosexual and bisexual males, homoerotic attraction was acknowledged before the age of 10 and most had their first homosexual experience at approximately 14 years of age (Savin-Williams, 1995). The typical age for public acknowledgement of homosexuality is around 21 (Bell & Weinberg, 1978).

The origins of sexual orientation have been hotly debated. At the core of the debate is the issue of whether sexual orientation is innate. Genetic, hormone, and brain studies suggest a biological component (Hamer, Hu, Magnuson, Hu, & Pattatucci, 1993; LeVay, 1991). Biological contributors to sexual orientation also may work indirectly through an influence on temperament (D. Bem, 1996). Others have suggested, however, that social factors relate to homosexuality or bisexuality (Green, 1987).

Styles and Symbols (D5)

Communication Styles. Research on adults has demonstrated that women and men differ in their styles of speaking and nonverbal communication. In our culture, men use more space and stare more than women, whereas women tend to establish eye contact and smile more than men (see Hall, 1984; Pearson, 1985, for reviews). Many researchers have assumed connections between sex differences and social roles. Lakoff (1975) argued that men's speech contains markers of their more powerful roles (e.g., use of interruptions), whereas women's speech contains markers of their subordinate status (e.g., use of tag questions). Other research, however, suggests that the context of communication may have more of an influence on communicative styles than does the sex of the speaker (McCloskey, 1987).

In the literature on children's communicative styles, the same issues are apparent. Do boys and girls have different styles, and if so, are these differences due to status or power differentials between the sexes? Girls tend to use collaborative and cooperative speech acts, whereas boys tend to use controlling and domineering exchanges (Leaper, 1991; Maltz & Borker, 1982). Although researchers often find more similarities than differences (Cook, Fritz, McCornack, & Visperas, 1985), there appears to be a general stylistic difference in which girls use strategies that demonstrate their attentiveness, responsiveness, and support and boys use strategies that demand attention and attempt to establish dominance (Maltz & Borker, 1982). Such differences appear to increase between preschool and elementary school and are more common in same-sex dyads than in mixed-sex dyads (Leaper, 1991). They also appear to be stronger among White than among African American children (Filardo, 1996). Moreover, such differences may depend on context. When communicating with younger same-sex peers, girls adopted a more tutorial or supervisory tone than did boys (McCloskey, 1996).

Girls and boys also vary in their use of gestures, although few studies have examined these sex differences. Girls more than boys showed limp wrists, arm flutters, and flexed elbows when walking, and boys show the gesture of hands-on-hips-with-fingers-forward more than girls (Rekers, 1985). Interestingly, Rekers (1985) reported that effeminate behavioral mannerisms are displayed by gender-disturbed boys at a much higher rate than similar behaviors in typical girls, and that these behaviors are stable and enduring despite peer ostracism for them. Similarly, judges have distinguished gender-atypical boys from other boys and girls on the basis of gross motor movements (e.g., walking, running) (Green, Neuberg, & Finch, 1983).

Fantasy Play. One of the most striking characteristics about very young children is their involvement in fantasy play. Girls and boys engage in fantasy play equally often, but the content of their play is markedly different. Preschool girls prefer domestic and family roles during fantasy play whereas boys prefer super hero or character roles. Boys also tend to use objects as substitutes during fantasy play more often than girls (Cole & LaVoie, 1985).

Clothing and Appearance. Clothing, jewelry, cosmetics, and hairstyles provide a wealth of information about one's sex, socioeconomic background, status, lifestyle, nationality, and age. Parents use clothing to mark the sex of their children for strangers, and these cues are accurately interpreted much of the time (Shakin, Shakin, & Sternglanz, 1985).

As children grow older, their own styles for dressing and adornment should become evident. Furthermore, because some clothing is more constraining than other kinds, children's clothing choices (e.g., dresses) may preclude certain activity choices (e.g., rough-and-tumble play). Few studies have examined children's clothing choices or the consequences of the choices. Consistent with the idea that children become less rigid in their behaviors after 5 years of age, Ogletree, Denton, and Williams (1993) found that first and second graders selected less gender-stereotyped Halloween costumes to wear than preschoolers and kindergartners. Another small study of 2- to 5½-year-old-girls found that 45% of girls seldom wore pants and 55% often wore pants. Although observations in the day care revealed little relation between play activities and clothing style, the group who often wore pants were somewhat more likely to play in nontraditional activities than the group who tended to wear dresses (Kaiser et al., 1985). Interestingly, preschool girls and boys associate particular clothing styles (pants vs. skirts) with different activities and seem to recognize the functional advantages of girls wearing pants when engaged in active play (Kaiser & Phinney, 1983).

The role of clothing in children's activity choices needs further investigation. Girls who choose to dress in more feminine styles may be reluctant to engage in active or dirty activities because of their clothing, and/or they may be more rigidly adhering to gender norms. Moreover, a cycle may develop in which girls' clothing choices somewhat modify their behavior, which decreases their competence for certain activities over time, leading to even less interest in those activities. Any factor that modifies children's interests may end up having a large impact on later abilities.

Values (D6)

Values are expressed in behavior through overt indexes of preferential or discriminatory treatment. A common paradigm for examining discriminatory behavior is a reward allocation task in which individuals are asked to distribute resources to different groups or individuals based on performance and personal attributes. Although some research has shown in-group favoritism based on ethnicity, only one study to our knowledge has examined such behaviors as a function of sex (Yee & Brown, 1994). In this study, girls tended to give rewards on the basis of in-group favoritism, whereas boys tended to reward on the basis of equity. Although these trends did not vary significantly across age (3–11 years), it is noteworthy that at age 3, both boys and girls gave nicer prizes to girls regardless of actual performance, and the clearest indication of in-group favoritism for both sexes occurred at age 5.

Values are also expressed in the way children respond to cross-gender behavior. Children, especially boys, who deviate from same-sex play norms suffer more from peer ridicule (Zucker, 1990). Thorne (1993) found that boys who

violated norms for masculinity were teased, shunned, or referred to as "girls."

Summary of Developmental Trends

The extensive database on gender development depicts the following portrait. By one year of age, many infants respond to gender cues. Most children learn to label themselves and others as male and female by 2½ years of age, show some limited understanding of gender stereotypes, play more often with same- than with other-gender toys, especially dolls and cars, and show the first signs of more positive contacts toward same- than toward other-sex peers. In addition, early indication of GID may be seen at this age. During the third year, children master gender stability, show better than chance responding to measures of gender stereotyping of children's toys and activities, colors, and certain traitlike characteristics, and state gender-typed play preferences. During the remaining preschool years (4–5), most indices of gender knowledge and behavior increase dramatically. A large proportion of children show complete sex category constancy (SCC) understanding, are able to link traits to gender (especially power-related and evaluative traits), show in-group positivity biases, and expect same-sex peers to play together. In addition, sex differences in a few personal-social characteristics, such as aggression and helping, are seen at this time. This appears to be an age of heightened gender rigidity in several measures of gender-related beliefs and behaviors.

A number of important changes in gender development occur during the elementary school years. Children develop more complex stereotypic associations and add more information to their stereotypes. During middle school, children appear to become aware of male-favored status differences and at the same age girls are more likely than boys to prefer to be the other sex. Sex differences in certain spatial skills and emotional perception and expression are seen in middle childhood and increase with age. Children in elementary school also show increasingly flexible stereotypic beliefs through, at least, early adolescence, and girls (especially tomboys) only often become more flexible in their activity preferences and behaviors. Three areas do not show increasing flexibility, however: (a) children's segregation into same-sex groupings increases and reaches ceiling during early elementary school; (b) they increasingly attribute to themselves gender-typed personality characteristics during these years; and (c) they continue to evaluate negatively peers who engage in cross-gender behavior.

Finally, further changes are often found during adolescence, but the findings are mixed. Some evidence supports the notion of gender intensification after early adolescence. A few studies suggest that stereotyping becomes somewhat less flexible. Trends for preferences are less clear and appear to diverge for males and females. However, in middle adolescence, both sexes seem to show high levels of gender-typed activities and interests in many contexts (at home, school), and sexual identity becomes established. In addition, sex differences in problem-solving, physical skills, and depression emerge or increase during adolescence. Taken together, then, the various trends show a number of parallel developments among cognitions, preferences, and behavior. An important and controversial theoretical issue concerns the extent to which gender cognitions, such as category knowledge and stereotypes, produce preferences and behavior. The nature and implications of these associations are discussed in the section Cognitive Approaches.

By applying the modified version of Huston's (1983) organizational framework (Table 14.1) to the review of developmental trends, gaps in the literature can easily be identified. Although relatively clear conclusions can now be drawn about the development of gender-related stereotypes, verbal preferences, and behaviors, especially regarding concrete activities and interests, much less is known about corresponding trends in children's gender-related self-perceptions and identity. In addition, relatively little is known about the development of children's gender-related values and attitudes, styles and symbols, and relationships, with the exception of sex-segregated behavior.

The development of the multidimensional matrix by Huston (1983) marked an important turning point in the study of gender (Windle, 1987). By disentangling the various content domains, researchers were given a clearer picture of the many aspects of gender that exist. Furthermore, developmental researchers were sensitized to the implicit assumption underlying much of the thinking in the area—that gender typing in one domain will predict gender typing in another. Rather than assuming unity in measures, developmentalists have been faced with the issue of how to assess each aspect of gender, and have begun using multimethod assessments to discover whether relations exist among the various aspects (e.g., Antill, Cotton, Russell, & Goodnow, 1996; Bigler, 1997).

What is the state of the field regarding the unity of gender-typing constructs? The trend being reported in the literature by many researchers is that gender typing is multidimensional (Antill et al., 1993; Ashmore, 1990; Downs & Langlois, 1988; Hort, Leinbach, & Fagot, 1991; Serbin et al., 1993; Spence & Hall, 1996; Trautner, 1992; Weinraub et al., 1984). This statement is used to describe failures to find relations among all types of gender-related variables, but is most often used to refer to the lack of connection between gender-typed preferences or behavior and gender stereotype knowledge. Generally, however, the findings vary depending on the kind of knowledge that is assessed: Gender stereotype knowledge does not precede other aspects of gender typing in age and often is correlated only modestly with other aspects of gender typing, suggesting that gender stereotype knowledge may not be a strong norm for guiding personal behavior. In contrast, however, basic knowledge about one's own sex and the sex of others develops at about the same time as gender-typed behavior and may influence that behavior (see Cognitive Approaches section).

It may be informative to examine issues of unity among subsets of variables. For example, greater coherence among gender differentiation constructs may occur if a distinction is made between self- versus other-related variables (Bigler, 1997). With respect to *self* variables, coherence may be found among categorical gender, the development of gender identity, preferences for same-sex playmates, interests in gender-typed activities, and later preferences for other-sex sexual partners. Consistent with suggestions made by Huston (1985), findings regarding sex differences in personality seem to be weaker and to adhere less well to an overall pattern than these other aspects of the self, with the exception that most people seem to describe themselves as being "masculine" if they are male, and "feminine" if they are female, regardless of their other expressive and instrumental qualities (Spence, 1985).

In addition, individuals' beliefs and concepts about *others* may have a high level of coherence and interconnectedness. A child who has been asked to guess the sex of an unknown child playing with a doll is likely to infer that the child is a girl. The gender concepts of masculinity and femininity appear to be coherent and used in a bipolar, unidimensional manner when we refer to others. As children grow older, these concepts become more strongly differentiated from one another, and more negatively correlated. The content associated with each of these is multidimensional but all are interwoven under the broad rubrics of masculinity and femininity. The outcome of using these concepts is that social observers create and provide a stereotypic environment for others.

The matrix has been particularly useful in allowing research to ask and begin to answer questions about the relations among all the different constructs and content domains. We agree with Huston that gender researchers should take the multidimensionality of gender typing seriously, but we also recommend caution about assuming that no unity exists at all. The likelihood of finding expected correlations may be influenced by a number of factors other than a true relation among constructs (see Aubry, Ruble, & Silverman, in press, for a review). For example, a correlation between peer and activity preferences found in some studies (e.g., Zucker et al., 1995) may not occur when the variance in these measures is low (e.g., Alexander & Hines, 1994).

THEORETICAL ANALYSIS OF GENDER DEVELOPMENT

Three broad approaches are considered in this analysis of gender development: Biological, Socialization, and Cognitive. The theoretical processes described here represent the dominant perspectives currently being applied to gender development. In each section, mechanisms derived from these theoretical perspectives are used to describe gender development, and evidence is presented relevant to the most pressing issues within each theoretical orientation.

Biological Approaches

Biological approaches to the study of gender development encompass a broad and diverse set of issues ranging from the effects of genes and hormones on sex differentiation and behavior to the influence of evolutionary history on the present-day behaviors of males and females. Because recent research has emphasized the influence of hormones on behavior, in this section, we concentrate on hormonal effects involved in gender development.

The nature/nurture issue is a central controversy in gender development, relevant for understanding sex differences as well as differences within each sex. Dramatic social and political implications follow depending on which set of influences is believed to be dominant. When biological factors are emphasized, the assumption is that sex differences are stable, universal, and immutable. When social factors are emphasized, the assumption is that differences are more variable and more easily changed. Biological factors need not imply determinism, however; behaviors with a strong biological influence may be relatively easy to modify

(Hoyenga & Hoyenga, 1993). Similarly, environmental factors need not necessarily imply free will and easy malleability; when social forces work in concert, they can be very difficult to counteract.

Anastasi (1958) introduced the "continuum of indirectness" as a method for considering the impact of each biological variable. For example, if high levels of androgen during prenatal development lead an individual to learn to respond to threats with physical aggression, the effect of androgens on aggression is fairly direct. Alternatively, androgen's effect may operate indirectly by increasing one's susceptibility to later hormone effects, such that an increase in physical size and strength at puberty increases the likelihood of using aggression because it is effective. Biological variables often affect gender indirectly by influencing one's appearance and physical capabilities, thereby allowing a host of environmental variables to come into play (Unger, 1993). Generally, biological and environmental factors work together in complex ways and are difficult to consider separately.

Prenatal Sex Differentiation

In humans, the genetic information within the 23rd pair of chromosomes begins the process of sexual differentiation. Most females have an XX pattern; most males have an XY pattern. A tiny portion of the Y chromosome contains the testes-determining factor (TDF) that pushes development from the female default pattern to the male pattern. If TDF is missing, an XY individual may be phenotypically female. At about 6 to 7 weeks after conception, if TDF is present, the primitive gonads develop into testes; otherwise, at 10 to 12 weeks, the gonads develop into ovaries. From this point on, sex differentiation is largely influenced by the steroid hormones secreted by the gonads, particularly by androgens (e.g., testosterone). Both males and females have steroid receptors in their cells to respond to androgens, although usually only males will be exposed to enough androgens to be masculinized. However, if high levels of androgens are present, male external genitalia will develop even in genetic females. Conversely, removal of testosterone at the right point in development will produce female genitalia even in genetic males. Fetal ovaries appear to play little role in sex differentiation of the body (Hoyenga & Hoyenga, 1993).

Hormones also play a role in sexual differentiation of the developing brain, especially during prenatal and neonatal development, although the processes are more complex and less well understood than are hormone effects on reproductive organs. In the first, "organizational" phase (during prenatal development), according to animal research, gonadal hormones permanently alter the biochemical sensitivity and neural structures in specific areas of the brain (e.g., hypothalamus) (Arnold & Gorski, 1984). At puberty, sex differences in the ratio of gonadal hormones (e.g., males have a higher ratio of testosterone to estrogen) will cause the second phase of sex differentiation, called "activation," in which circulating hormones may trigger the structures that were organizationally affected by hormones earlier in life. The distinction between organizational and activational effects has been blurred by animal research indicating some permanent effects of hormones administered in adulthood (Arnold & Breedlove, 1985).

According to the classic view of hormone action developed from animal studies in which hormones are manipulated, organizational effects have been viewed as being driven by androgens: administration of high levels of androgens organize the prenatal brain for male-typical behaviors and abilities, whereas low levels of androgens organize the brain for female-typical behaviors and abilities (e.g., Finegan, Niccols, & Sitarenios, 1992). The classic view has been expanded by research suggesting additional complexity in understanding hormone effects (Arnold & Gorski, 1984; Meyer-Bahlburg et al., 1995). For example, hormones change form easily. As demonstrated in rodent studies, some gonadal testosterone is metabolized ("aromatized") to a form (estradiol) which interacts with *estrogen* receptors in the brain (McEwen, 1983), suggesting that both estrogen and androgen can cause masculinization. Apparently, however, most females are not masculinized by estrogen because their estrogen sources are bound by proteins (Breedlove, 1994). The possibility of androgenic effects of estrogens in humans is now of interest (Dorner, 1988) and is being examined by studying females with brain exposure to estrogenic components (e.g., diethylstilbestrol—DES) during prenatal development, as will be described. Moreover, the actions of hormones vary in effect depending on when they are introduced in development (Breedlove, 1994). For example, early prenatal administration of androgens to genetic female rhesus macaques increases masculine sexual behavior but later administration influences masculine rough-and-tumble play behavior (Goy, Bercovitch, & McBrair, 1988). Finally, although most people think of hormones as causal agents, they too are susceptible to a wide array of environmental influences, ranging from stress to social interactions (Breedlove, 1994).

Prenatal Hormonal Conditions in Humans

Researchers have investigated the effects of hormones on human behavior by studying children who are naturally exposed to high or low levels of hormones during their development. Certain genetic disorders tend to raise or lower prenatal hormone levels, and women are sometimes treated with hormones to offset pregnancy problems, thereby providing natural experiments in which children develop under unusual hormonal conditions. We describe several such types of populations in this section (see Collaer & Hines, 1995, for a review).

High Levels of Androgens: Congenital Adrenal Hyperplasia.   Individuals with congenital adrenal hyperplasia (CAH) have a recessive genetic disorder causing the adrenal gland to produce high levels of androgens during prenatal development. Genetic females with this disorder may have fully or partly masculinized external genitalia, but they have female gonads. Some of the girls will be labeled as boys at birth and raised as boys (Money & Ehrhardt, 1972). If the condition is not treated, these girls will continue to be exposed to higher than normal levels of androgens and will become further masculinized at puberty. For children raised as girls, treatment involves cortisone therapy to control androgen production and surgical adjustments to external genitalia. These girls develop a female gender identity in spite of their prenatal androgen exposure but it may not be as firmly established as in other girls (Collaer & Hines, 1995). Genetic males with CAH are also treated with cortisone to prevent early puberty but they usually do not require surgery, are raised as boys, and develop male gender identity.

In early research, CAH girls were characterized as tomboys (Huston, 1983). These findings were taken as evidence of the role of androgens in human behavior, although they have been criticized on many levels. Parents' uncertainty about the sex of their child, the possibility of side effects following treatment, small sample sizes, and awareness of their unique status were often neglected as alternative explanations (Hines, 1993; Huston, 1983). Another concern was the use of relative controls (siblings or cousins) which may increase the likelihood of common hidden causal factors (Helleday, Bartfai, Ritzen, & Forsman, 1994). Finally, the history and severity of the disease (Slijper, 1984) as well as the timing of androgen release during prenatal development may influence findings. Some of these criticisms have been addressed in the recent research, but many remain valid (Helleday et al., 1994).

Later studies confirmed that parents report CAH girls to be more tomboyish (e.g., Dittman et al., 1990). Is their actual behavior more like boys than girls? Three studies on the same sample of CAH children examined aspects of their actual behavior. Berenbaum and Hines (1992) found that 3- to 8-year-old CAH girls played with boys' toys about twice as much as the relative control girls, but CAH boys did not differ from control boys. Several years later, the same patterns were found (Berenbaum & Snyder, 1995). In a subsample of the same children, CAH girls did not show more rough-and-tumble play but they preferred boys as playmates more than did control girls (44% to 11%), whereas CAH boys did not differ from control boys in many ways (Hines & Kaufman, 1994).

In adolescence, but not before, CAH girls scored significantly higher on visual/spatial tasks (e.g., mental rotation, hidden patterns) compared with relative control girls, but the groups did not differ in overall psychological adjustment, intelligence, verbal fluency, or perceptual speed. Boys with CAH did not differ from controls on any of the measures (Resnick, Berenbaum, Gottesman, & Bouchard, 1986). Similar findings on visual/spatial tasks have been reported for adult women with CAH (e.g., Helleday et al., 1994).

Gender identity issues for CAH girls may become more prevalent during adolescence, especially when virilization (e.g., excessive facial and body hair) may occur if children fail to conform with hormone therapy. CAH girls did not have more masculine gender identity than other girls with chronic illnesses but they reported more delays in friendship formation, mixed-sex socializing, dating, and sexual relations than control girls, possibly due to long-time concerns about their appearance (Hurtig & Rosenthal, 1987). Finally, CAH women have an increased likelihood of bisexual or homosexual orientation (e.g., Collaer & Hines, 1995; Hines, 1993; Meyer-Bahlburg et al., 1995; Money, 1987).

High Levels of Androgens and Synthetic Progestins. Because some hormones (androgenic progestins) mimic the actions of androgen, children whose mothers took these hormones during pregnancy also experience higher than normal levels of androgens. These children have higher levels of reported aggression (Reinisch, 1981) and are more independent and self-sufficient compared with relative controls (Reinisch & Sanders, 1984). Research is mixed

about gender-typed behavior. In some studies, these girls show "tomboy" preferences and behavior similar to the CAH girls (Money & Ehrhardt, 1972), but in others, they do not (Ehrhardt, 1984). When older, these individuals had no difficulties developing friendships or romantic interests (Money & Mathews, 1982).

High Levels of Estrogens. Animal studies suggest powerful influences of estrogen on behavior which may be masculinizing or demasculinizing depending on the specific compounds, dosages, and timing (Collaer & Hines, 1995). Most studies with humans have involved diethylstilbestrol (DES), a synthetic estrogen that produces masculine-typical brain structure and sexual behavior in female rodents (Hines, 1993); this drug was widely prescribed between 1943 and 1971 to minimize pregnancy complications. DES daughters develop under unusual hormonal circumstances, but their external genitalia are unaffected. DES-exposed girls and women showed a male-like pattern of increased language lateralization compared with their unaffected sisters but no differences on visual/spatial or verbal tasks (Hines & Shipley, 1984). For many gender-typed behaviors (e.g., activities, traits, vocational preferences), DES women do not differ from control women (Lish, Meyer-Bahlburg, Ehrhardt, Travis, & Veridiano, 1992; cf. Ehrhardt et al., 1989). Whereas DES girls show increased language lateralization, DES boys appear to be less malelike in spatial abilities and hemisphere lateralization than unexposed brothers (Reinisch & Sanders, 1992).

In a recent study, DES-exposed women were shown to have a slight tendency toward bisexual and homosexual imagery as part of their sexual behavior, compared with control women (Meyer-Bahlburg et al., 1995). Few women were lifelong or current homosexuals, but those that were had DES exposure. Generally, the effects of prenatal DES, if any, are small compared with those found with prenatal androgen.

Low Levels of Gonadal Hormones. Androgen insensitivity (testicular feminization) is a rare genetic disorder in which XY males produce appropriate levels of androgens but their tissues are insensitive to these hormones. Because these children are born with genitalia that are not masculinized, they often are raised as girls. These children report preferences for feminine roles, enjoyed playing with dolls, and were contented with the female gender role

(Money & Ehrhardt, 1972). Though they are reported to have somewhat better verbal skills than spatial skills, it is not clear whether this pattern is due to prenatal hormones, postnatal hormones, and/or being raised as girls (Collaer & Hines, 1995; Halpern, 1992).

5-Alpha-Reductase Deficiency. The controversy about the roles of biological and social factors in the formation of gender identity has been rekindled in the past 15 years by research in the Dominican Republic on 5-alpha-reductase deficiency, a recessive genetic condition in which XY individuals are exposed to normal male levels of testosterone, and they are born with normal internal male structures but with ambiguous or femalelike external genitalia (Imperato-McGinley, Peterson, Gautier, & Sturla, 1979). Because of their genitalia, they are often raised as girls. At puberty, these children are masculinized when their normal testes pour testosterone into their systems, causing masculine external genitalia and secondary sexual characteristics to develop. Many of these children appear to make the switch to a male gender identity with ease and show attraction to females. Because of the ease of transition to the other-gender identity, Imperato-McGinley and colleagues concluded that when sex assignment is contrary to biological sex, and if pubertal hormones related to biological sex are present, biological sex will prevail over the sex of rearing. Importantly, contrary to the critical period hypothesis (Money & Ehrhardt, 1972), they argued that gender identity is not fixed in childhood but instead continues to develop and becomes stabilized at puberty.

These findings are unclear for several reasons. First, there is a question concerning the clarity of gender identity in several cases (Rubin, Reinisch, & Haskett, 1981). Second, the role of cultural factors cannot be ruled out. In the Dominican Republic, changing into the high-valued male role from the low-value female role may be relatively easy, but in other cultures, the conversions happen with great difficulty (Herdt & Davidson, 1988) or no conversion occurs (Rubin et al., 1981). Third, parents may have raised their children differently because of their ambiguous genitalia (Fausto-Sterling, 1992).

Normal Hormonal Variations in Prenatal Hormones. Because the ability to generalize the results from atypical children is limited, another approach has been to examine normal variations in prenatal hormone levels and their relation to later behavior and cognition. There is no method to directly determine prenatal hormone levels. When umbilical cord blood has been analyzed, which indicates hormone levels in the fetal blood supply, the findings are the opposite from the expected patterns based on CAH girls: Girls (but not boys) with higher levels of androgen were found to have lower spatial ability than other girls (Jacklin, Wilcox, & Maccoby, 1988). When fetal hormone levels are monitored through amniotic fluid in mid-pregnancy, similar findings were obtained: Girls with higher levels of androgens showed lower spatial abilities as well as lower scores on number tasks than other girls, but boys did not differ depending on their hormone levels. Language comprehension (but not expression) was found to relate to girls' fetal levels of testosterone in a more complex pattern (Finegan et al., 1992).

Hormone Influences in Adolescence

Because of the large rises in levels of gonadal hormones and associated physical changes that accompany the transition to adolescence (see Buchanan, Eccles, & Becker, 1992, and Paikoff & Brooks-Gunn, 1990, for reviews), it is interesting to ask whether sex differences emerging at this time may be related to these biological changes. Most researchers have focused on possible relations with emotions (negative affect, anxiety) and certain behaviors/cognitions (aggression, self-esteem), partly because of well-documented sex differences in forms of distress and psychopathology. Males tend to show signs of distress in the form of aggression, conduct disorders, and antisocial disorders; females show distress in the form of depression and anxiety disorder (Rutter & Garmezy, 1983). Moreover, the sex difference in depression is usually not found until adolescence, which has led to a search for an association with sex-linked pubertal hormone changes (e.g., Angold & Rutter, 1992).

One line of relevant evidence comes from menstrual cycle research in which changes in affect are examined in relation to changes in estrogen levels (Buchanan et al., 1992; Brooks-Gunn, Petersen, & Compas, 1995). Studies in this area remain inconclusive, however (see Klebanov & Ruble, 1994, for a review), in part because self-report data are difficult to interpret independent of social expectations about menstrual symptoms (McFarlane, Martin, & Williams, 1988; Ruble & Brooks-Gunn, 1979). Nevertheless, it is possible that adjustment to the rapid rise of gonadal hormones and hormonal cyclicity may contribute to the emergence of females' negative affect or "moodiness" during adolescence (Buchanan et al., 1992).

Another line of evidence concerns whether hormone increases associated with puberty lead to increases in negative affect. There is little support for this relation in girls (Brooks-Gunn & Ruble, 1983). In boys, a few studies support a relationship (Rutter, 1986; Susman, Nottelmann, & Blue, 1983), but in a carefully controlled study, no relation was found between pubertal status and depression in either girls or boys (Angold & Rutter, 1992; see also Crockett & Petersen, 1987).

The timing of the onset of puberty also may be important. Early maturation for girls and late maturation for boys seem to contribute to negative affect (e.g., Nottelmann et al., 1987; Petersen, Sarigiani, & Kennedy, 1991; Ruble & Brooks-Gunn, 1982), and to problem behavior in girls (Silbereisen, Petersen, Albrecht, & Kracke, 1989; Simmons & Blyth, 1987). It is not clear the extent to which these findings are due to biological factors (e.g., timing of various pubertal changes), but many interpret them in social psychological terms (e.g, asynchrony of development with peers) (Buchanan et al., 1992; Magnusson, Stattin, & Allen, 1985).

Direct examination of hormone-affect links show complex and often inconsistent findings (see Brooks-Gunn et al., 1995, and Buchanan et al., 1992, for reviews). Hormone-mood relations may be stronger for adolescent boys than girls (Susman et al., 1987). For girls, rising hormone levels rather than actual estrogen level may relate to depressive symptoms (Paikoff, Brooks-Gunn, & Warren, 1991).

Hormone effects are more clear in studies linking boys' androgen levels to aggressiveness (Buchanan et al., 1992) and to delinquent behavior, nastiness, rebelliousness, and behavior problems (Nottelmann et al., 1987; Susman et al., 1987). Fewer associations have been found for girls. Inoff-Germain et al. (1988) found that both estrogen and adrenal hormones were associated with girls' higher levels of anger and aggression but these relations were reduced or eliminated when prior behavior and pubertal status were controlled (Paikoff et al., 1991). The meaning of these hormone-behavior links in adolescents is unclear. Hormones may exert a direct influence by increasing aggression in boys. Hormone-behavior relations may also be reciprocal. For example, Steinberg (1988) has suggested that family conflict leads to changes in hormone levels in addition to the reverse effect. Finally, hormone-behavior relations may be co-occurring processes because of a common pathway mapped out during prenatal development (Coe, Hayashi, & Levine, 1988).

The interaction of biological changes and the social/psychological changes accompanying adolescence has become increasingly obvious. The transition to junior high school, for example, has been found to affect children's self-perceptions and mood, especially for girls (see Ruble & Seidman, 1996, for a review). In a longitudinal study, Simmons and Blyth (1987) found that the transition to junior high school, and then again, the transition to high school negatively affected self-esteem of girls but not boys, especially when it occurred in conjunction with the onset of puberty. Similarly, depressive symptoms increase when pubertal change occurs simultaneously with a school transition (Petersen et al., 1991). In addition, gender identification or socialization processes prior to adolescence may differentially affect girls' and boys' reactions to adolescent social and biological transitions (Brooks-Gunn et al., 1995; Nolen-Hoeksema, 1987; Ruble et al., 1993). Such findings have led to the development of models of how biological factors may exert effects indirectly or may interact with social factors in affecting gender-related changes during adolescence (e.g., Paikoff & Brooks-Gunn, 1990; Petersen et al., 1991).

Brain Structure and Function

The action of hormones on behavior and abilities may be mediated through the hormone-directed changes in brain structure or functioning. In this section, we review the evidence concerning structural and functional similarities and differences in male and female brains.

Brain Laterality. Different areas of the brain are specialized for different tasks. In most people, the left hemisphere of the brain is specialized for language tasks and the right hemisphere for perceptual and spatial processing. Researchers have been interested in assessing whether females and males differ in how their hemispheres function because such differences may account for sex differences in cognitive abilities and in behavior. Indirect support for the idea that females may show more symmetry (less laterality) than males in brain functioning comes from research showing better recovery or maintenance of functioning in the face of brain damage for women than for men (Halpern, 1992).

Many studies of laterality use dichotic listening and divided visual field tasks, both of which involve presenting information to each sensory field and assessing individuals' responsiveness to the information. In an extensively cited review, McGlone (1980) concluded that the evidence supported sex differences in laterality. Other reviews, however, suggest that sex differences in laterality are more clear-cut in the auditory domain (Hines, 1990) than in the visual domain (Halpern, 1992), and are less obvious in children (Hahn, 1987). Although there is no consensus, many researchers have concluded that the there is "at least reasonable evidence that women are somewhat less lateralized than men" (Bryden, 1988, p. 11). Differences are not always found, but when they are, they support the hypothesis of small differences between the sexes (Halpern, 1992).

Newer techniques to identify brain functioning involve imaging techniques, such as magnetic resonance imaging which detects cerebral blood flow during various activities. In a study of language processing (Shaywitz, Shaywitz, Pugh, & Constable, 1995), participants were asked to decide if nonsense words rhymed. For this task, the activated brain regions differed for women and men. Women used both the left and right inferior frontal gyrus for the task, whereas men used only the left. Unlike most studies of sex differences, there was little overlap between the sexes in patterns of brain activation. Using other techniques to assess brain activity, sex differences have been found with spatial tasks (Reite, Cullum, Stocker, Teale, & Kozora, 1993), and with younger children. In the comprehension of words, even 16-month-old infants showed sex differences in patterns of brain activation (Molfese, 1990).

How does laterality relate to performance and observed sex differences? An early and influential theory was developed by J. Levy (1976) who proposed that language functioning will be optimal when it is bilateral because more "cortical space" is provided for language abilities. Because language has priority over spatial abilities, spatial abilities will be best when they are not bilateral, because language processing will crowd out spatial abilities. As a result, women and left-handed men (who are less lateralized) should show similar patterns of performance: good verbal skills and poorer spatial skills compared with right-handed men. Research suggests that reasoning abilities mediate laterality effects (e.g., O'Boyle & Benbow, 1990), and that sex differences in laterality may be less important than sex differences in functioning within hemispheres (Kimura, 1987).

The development of laterality may be determined by prenatal hormones, especially testosterone, which is believed to slow the development of the left hemisphere so that the right hemisphere becomes dominant (Geschwind & Behan, 1982). Although some support for these expectations has been found (Halpern, 1992), contrary to the theory, testosterone levels at birth relate to lower spatial skills

at age 6 in girls (Jacklin et al., 1988). This theory has been criticized for a number of reasons including that it is unclear that testosterone would slow development of only one hemisphere (Bleier, 1988).

Brain Size. Research comparing the brain sizes and structures of men and women has a checkered history (S. Shields, 1975). Nonetheless, in the past 10 years, researchers have actively pursued brain structure differences between men and women, as well as whether differences within sex relate to behavior or abilities. Overall, the brain size of men tends to be 10% to 15% larger than for women, but there is no difference in brain weight relative to body weight (Janowsky, 1989). Other than absolute brain size, there are no other gross structural differences related to sex. Only recently has there been a suggestion of differences at a microscopic level. Females were found to have a larger density of neurons than males in two layers of the temporal lobe thought to be involved in receiving input from the auditory system (Witelson, Glezer, & Kigar, 1995). Most attention, however, has focused on assessing specific structures of the brain, especially the anterior hypothalamic/preoptic area (AH/POA) and the corpus callosum (CC).

Corpus Callosum. The corpus callosum (CC) is a bundle of fibers that provide communication between the left and right cerebral hemispheres; it plays an important role in higher thought processes, especially language (Hines, Chiu, McAdams, Bentler, & Lipcamon, 1992). Differences in CC sizes between men and women are generally assumed to be biologically based, but environmental changes, such as handling and environmental complexity, significantly change the size and distribution of fibers in rat CC, as well as the likelihood of finding sex differences (Juraska & Kopcik, 1988).

Early research using autopsied brains found that certain portions of the CC, especially the splenium, were more bulbous and larger for women (e.g., de Lacoste-Utamsing & Holloway, 1982). Such differences are potentially important because a larger CC may allow greater communication between the hemispheres and thus less lateralization in female than male brains, though the size and shape of CC have not been well linked to functions. The conclusions from studies on CC remain controversial, however. Some research with larger samples report small sex differences (Hines & Collaer, 1993), whereas other studies find no difference or only a shape difference (Breedlove, 1994).

Do CC size differences relate to verbal or spatial abilities? Hines and colleagues (Hines et al., 1992) studied within-sex variations in four sections of the CC. Women with larger spleniums demonstrated higher levels of verbal fluency and less language lateralization than women with smaller spleniums. These results suggest that the splenium may be involved in the interhemispheric transfer of language-related but not visual/spatial information (Hines, 1993).

Anterior Hypothalamic Region. The AH/POA is a focus of interest because it contains a high density of hormone receptors and because animal studies suggest that various subregions within the preoptic area show sex differences (Arnold & Gorski, 1984). In studies with humans, two of four interstitial nuclei of the anterior hypothalamus (INAH) have been found to be larger in men than in women (Breedlove, 1994; Hines, 1993), and the sex difference in one nucleus (INAH 3) has been replicated (LeVay, 1991).

A controversial issue concerns the relation between brain structure and sexual orientation. Because heterosexual women and homosexual men share sexual attraction to men, the interest is whether the morphology of the brains of homosexual men resembles that of women or heterosexual men. In a widely publicized study, LeVay (1991) found that a small sample of homosexual men showed the female pattern in that their INAH-3 areas were larger than a comparison group of heterosexual men. News reports suggested that a biological basis of homosexuality had been discovered. From a scientific view, however, there are a number of concerns with the research suggesting that replication of this finding is needed. Furthermore, it is unclear whether the INAH-3 or any other structural difference is the cause or result of the development of sex differences.

Integration and Conclusions

The increased interest in the study of hormones and hormone-behavior links has resulted in a much broader knowledge base concerning hormone effects and gender development. Congruent with earlier research, prenatal hormones (especially androgens) have been identified as playing a major role in gender differentiation of the body. Investigations into the roles of hormones on brain structures and functioning have been more limited, but these studies also suggest that although the similarities are much more striking than any differences, a few differences are apparent. In particular, sex differences have been found in some areas of the brain, both in terms of gross structural differences, and possibly in terms of microscopic differences. For some tasks, females process information with both hemispheres more than do males and these sex differences in brain functioning may be related to prenatal hormone differences between the sexes. At this point, the link between structural differences in the brain, at either gross or microscopic levels, and functioning has not been clearly described. The research relating sex differences in brain structure/functioning to cognitive abilities and behaviors remains controversial. Part of the controversy is due to the assumption of unidirectional brain to behavior effects, which ignores the significant growth of the brain after birth and the plasticity of the brain (Hood, Draper, Crockett, & Petersen, 1987), especially in enriched environments (Greenough, Black, & Wallace, 1987). Furthermore, the hypotheses and evidence thus far do not mirror the complexities in the findings of sex differences in performance, such as age or specific task differences.

Based on animal research, hormone-behavior relations may be expected for many behaviors. Research on humans, largely based on naturally occurring situations in which hormone levels are unusual, has suggested that for girls more than boys, peer preferences, toy/activity preferences, and visual/spatial skills, in particular, may be influenced by androgens. The strongest evidence is the studies of CAH girls, who show some masculine gender-typed behaviors. For boys, the evidence of hormone effects is mixed. The difficulty with these natural experiments is that there are valid alternative explanations for the behavioral differences, and that normal variations in hormone levels do not confirm the CAH patterns. Estrogens appear to play a much smaller role in influencing behavior, although prenatal estrogen levels may influence the development of sexual orientation. The timing of prenatal hormones may be critical in determining which aspects of gender-typing are most susceptible to hormone influences. Taken together, the results suggest that the actions of hormones are complex and that different theories may be needed to explain diverse behaviors (Collaer & Hines, 1995).

Circulating hormones during adolescence provide an even more challenging arena for investigating hormone influences because of the many possible indirect effects. The emerging picture suggests that hormone levels per se have little influence on girls' behavior, although rising hormone levels and/or changing hormone levels at puberty have been found to relate to girls' negative affect. For boys, circulating hormones, especially androgens, relate to boys' aggressiveness, rebelliousness, and behavior problems. The complexity of hormone-behavior links is further highlighted by several studies in which associations have been found between social/psychological changes and biological changes (e.g., puberty). It may be that children's social and psychological states provide windows of opportunity for hormones to work more or less directly on their behavior.

Biological approaches have tended to focus on particular aspects of the gender-typing matrix, mainly on behavioral enactment, identity (gender and sexual orientation), and somewhat on preferences. Little research effort has been focused on the biological factors that may influence concepts and beliefs about the sexes. Furthermore, at this point in their theoretical development, biological approaches have more to offer in terms of explaining sex differences and differences between individuals of the same sex than in explaining situational variability or developmental changes in gender typing. Part of this limitation may be due to the implicit assumptions about biological effects—that they are permanent and immune to environmental impact. Researchers could enhance theoretical development in this realm by giving more serious attention to biological factors that vary with situations, and across time and individuals. Finally, we must be cautious not to presume that the direction of hormone effects works from hormones to behavior and not in reverse. Hormones, brain structures, and brain functioning may each be greatly influenced by the different environments that girls and boys are raised in, by their different toy and activity choices, and by more complex biology-environment interactions.

Socialization Approaches

Socialization approaches to the study of gender development have had wide appeal. Many potential sources of gender socialization can be identified including parents, teachers, peers, and the media. The main concern for theorists who adopt socialization approaches is how to conceptualize socialization influences. Which features from the environment are noticed and incorporated into gender development, *and* by what processes? In this section, we tackle such questions as we summarize the past 15 years of socialization research.

Socialization Processes

To what extent do social agents (parents, teachers, media, peers) take an active role in shaping the interests, attributes, and behaviors of boys and girls? In the 1970 *Handbook,* Mischel presented a social learning perspective that used differential reinforcement, together with observational learning, to explain the development of gender typing. Social learning theorists assume that children learn and adopt gender-traditional patterns of behavior because they are directly reinforced for gender-typed behaviors and because they attend to the consequences associated with others' actions. Gender-traditional behaviors are not likely to be consistently displayed, however, because children adjust their behavior to fit particular settings. Certain developmental trends are expected to follow from this approach. Because social learning theorists expect that children will learn about consequences over time, they assume that young children will be more likely than older children to display gender-nontraditional behavior, and that behavior becomes increasingly traditional as they learn more and more about consequences of their actions. Children's understanding of their own gender also grows out of their developing recognition of the consequences associated with actions, such that they infer their sex based on the category of behaviors (e.g., masculine or feminine) that are rewarded and punished (Mischel, 1979).

Differential Treatment. Socialization agents may influence gender development by treating boys and girls differently. This process may involve direct reinforcement for conformity to gender norms, as when adults compliment a girl when she wears a dress but not when she wears pants. Having once experienced these consequences, future behavior is shaped by the child's recognition that similar behavior will reap similar consequences (Bandura, 1977). Over time, for most children, their behavior is gradually shaped to be gender-typed, because most socializing agents tend to apply contingencies following gender-traditional patterns.

Differential treatment also occurs through reciprocal role enactment processes (e.g., Siegal, 1987), in which, due to adult experiences with the other sex, fathers encourage femininity in daughters and mothers encourage masculinity in sons (Maccoby & Jacklin, 1974). Parents may also feel a greater commonality and responsibility for the socialization of same-sex children (Huston, 1983), and thereby exert closer control over them (Power & Shanks, 1989; Rothbart & Maccoby, 1966). Because most children spend more time with female than male caregivers, such responses may represent a significant type of differential treatment. Finally, differential treatment may also be more subtle and covert, as when socializing agents structure the environment in a way that limits choices, such as providing only dolls for girls and trucks for boys, a process called channeling or shaping (Block, 1983; Bugental & Goodnow, Ch. 7, this Volume).

The initial empirical evaluations of the role of differential treatment suggested minimal impact of these processes. Most notably, Maccoby and Jacklin (1974) concluded that child-rearing practices were quite similar for boys and girls, with consistent differences emerging only in a few areas: (a) Infant boys received more physical stimulation and encouragement; (b) boys were punished more; and (c) boys were praised more. In addition, parents encouraged gender-typed behavior and discouraged cross-gender behavior, especially for boys. In short, there was limited support for a differential treatment account of gender development, at least as carried out within the family.

The database was spotty, however, focusing mainly on maternal socialization of preschoolers (Maccoby & Jacklin, 1974). In addition, Block (1983) challenged the conclusions, arguing that Maccoby and Jacklin gave short shrift to differential socialization of activities and interests and instead focused on differential socialization of personal-social attributes (e.g, aggression, dependency). A large number of direct tests of differential socialization appeared in the literature shortly after and perhaps in response to this controversy. Within this context of uncertainty, Huston's (1983) review was extremely influential. She identified a number of reasonably clear forms of differential treatment, such as encouragement of motor activity for boys and nurturance play for girls, as well as a number of areas of continued uncertainty or negative findings, within and outside the family.

Observational Learning. Learning theories (e.g., Bandura, 1977; Bussey & Bandura, 1992) in particular, as well as cognitive theories (e.g., Bem, 1981; Kohlberg, 1966; Martin & Halverson, 1981), all provide insight into how children learn about gender from observing others. One reason children may engage in more same- than other-gender behavior is that they are differentially exposed to same-sex models, and some evidence suggests that this is the case. In naturalistic observations in public settings, boys were observed more often with men and girls were observed more often with women (Hoffman & Teyber, 1985). In addition, this differential exposure appears to increase during adolescence (Crouter, Manke, & McHale, 1995). Furthermore, because of children's tendencies to segregate by sex, they are exposed more often to same-sex peers than to other-sex peers (Maccoby, 1988).

Differential exposure is not necessary for children to learn about gender, however. Children are more likely to model the behaviors of individuals who are powerful, nurturant, and prestigious than other individuals (Bandura, 1977). To what extent is children's gender-typed behavior explained by selective modeling of same-sex models? As Huston (1983) argued, generalized imitation of same-sex models as an explanation for gender-typed behavior is simplistic and has not been supported in extensive reviews of the research (Maccoby & Jacklin, 1974). Instead, it is more informative to inquire about the conditions under which children imitate the behavior of same-sex versus other-sex models. A number of studies now delineate the conditions likely to increase the imitation of same-sex models. Although children may not necessarily imitate a single same-sex model, they are likely to engage in same-sex modeling with multiple models, all or most of whom are engaged in the same activity, especially a neutral activity (Bussey & Bandura, 1984; Bussey & Perry, 1982) or a gender-typed behavior (Perry & Bussey, 1979). Girls are more likely to imitate cross-sex models than boys, although boys will imitate a female model when she is shown to be very powerful (Bussey & Bandura, 1984).

Are there developmental changes in same-sex imitation? Most of the research on modeling has been conducted with 7- to 8-year-old children. Surprisingly, little research has focused on assessing the age at which children first begin to imitate multiple models. Presumably, same-sex modeling would require that children recognize their own and others' sex (Bussey, 1983). Also, children seem to decide who is "worth" modeling, strongly suggesting a cognitive component to observational learning that may be influenced by developmental changes. Furthermore, there may be individual differences in children's tendencies to process information on the basis of gender, inducing some children to be more attuned to the sex of an actor than other children (Bem, 1981; Martin & Halverson, 1981).

What are the consequences of same-sex imitation? When children attend to same-sex models, they are assumed to focus on and extract information about how behaviors are enacted (Bussey & Bandura, 1984; Perry & Bussey, 1979), the sequencing of events (Boston & Levy, 1991), and the consequences associated with the enactment of the behavior (Bussey & Bandura, 1992). Although often neglected, it is likely that children also attend to the other sex as well. By attending to models of both sexes, children construct notions of appropriate appearance, occupations, and behavior for each sex, and from these stereotypes, they develop complex concepts about the nature of masculinity and femininity. This inductive path to stereotype acquisition has been illustrated in several studies. When children have been shown multiple same-sex models, they appear to abstract information about consensus, allowing them to guess about the gender typing of novel activities (Perry & Bussey, 1979; Ruble, Balaban, & Cooper, 1981). For example, a novel object demonstrated by a boy might be tentatively marked as belonging with the other "boy" attributes but one demonstrated by four boys would be more powerfully associated with the boy stereotype.

Gender Socialization within the Family

The family provides many socialization experiences, including differences in the ways sons and daughters are raised and modeling of gender-related roles in the home. The following subsections outline the effects of family socialization experiences on children's gender development in each of the major content areas.

Encouragement of Gender-Typed Activities and Interests. One way that caregivers influence gender development is by providing boys and girls with distinct social contexts, in terms of toys, room furnishings, and encouragement of same-sex interactions (e.g., O'Brien & Huston, 1985; Rheingold & Cook, 1975). For example, Pomerleau, Bolduc, Malcuit, and Cossette (1990) found that the bedrooms of infants and toddlers (5 to 25 months) were very different for boys and girls: Girls had more dolls, pink and multicolored clothes, and yellow bedding; whereas boys had more sports equipment, vehicles, and blue bedding and clothing. Gender-typed environments may be subtle ways of channeling children's preferences and their behavioral tendencies for activities and interests. These findings are of particular interest because the children are younger than the age at which gender-differentiated play is typically found.

In a meta-analysis of many possible ways that boys and girls could be differentially treated by parents, Lytton and Romney (1991) reported that differential encouragement of gender-typed activities versus areas such as personality traits showed the clearest effect. The overall effect size was moderate ($d = .43$), was somewhat stronger for fathers than for mothers, and tended to decrease with age of child. This phenomenon has been well illustrated in recent studies. Adults tend to purchase gender-typed toys, especially for boys (e.g., Fisher-Thompson, 1993), but this may be because these toys are requested by children. Indeed, adult

toy purchases are often neutral when they are not requested by the child (e.g., Fisher-Thompson, 1993). Moreover, parents tend to offer gender-stereotypic toys to children during free play (e.g., Bradley & Gobbart, 1989, fathers only), or to be more responsive or supportive when children are engaged in same- than in other-gender behaviors (e.g., Fagot & Hagan, 1991; Leaper, Leve, Strasser, & Schwartz, 1995; Roopnarine, 1986), although this pattern is not consistent (Caldera et al., 1989). Such differential responsiveness is more often found for boys, for infants and toddlers versus 5-year-olds, and for fathers relative to mothers (Bradley & Gobbart, 1989; Fagot & Hagan, 1991; Roopnarine, 1986), consistent with the Lytton and Romney meta-analysis. Finally, even when parents preferred gender-typed toys for daughters and sons, they tended to avoid offering feminine toys to girls as well as to boys in a free-play setting (Idle, Wood, & Desmarais, 1993). Taken together, these studies suggest that contemporary efforts to foster sex-differentiated play may often be subtle or limited, and that parents may now be making conscious efforts to encourage egalitarian behaviors, at least for older children and girls.

What effect does encouragement of gender-typed play have on the children? Fagot and Leinbach (1989) found that fathers who reported more traditional gender socialization practices had children who learned gender labels at a relatively early age. Fagot, Leinbach, and O'Boyle (1992) also found that mothers who handed their children (especially sons) more gender-typical toys in free play, and who responded more positively to same-gender play, had toddlers who learned gender labels early. Finally, Eisenberg, Wolchik, Hernandez, and Pasternak (1985) reported that parental (especially mothers') reinforcement of gender-typed play was associated with higher levels of sex category constancy at 2 to 2½ years of age. Thus, there is reasonably clear evidence that parents of very young children might be promoting precocious learning of gender distinctions when they encourage gender-typed play.

Encouragement of particular activities may also influence children's learning of cognitive and social skills (Miller, 1987). For example, parental encouragement of construction play may foster the differential development of visual-spatial and mechanical skills and exploration of the environment (Liss, 1983) and may contribute to sex differences in these areas. In addition, play with gender-typed toys may contribute to the emergence and maintenance of sex differences by influencing parent-child interaction patterns, independent of the sex of the child (Caldera et al.,

1989). "Masculine" toys tend to involve less physical proximity and control and little language, whereas feminine toys, such as dolls, elicit more verbal interactions (O'Brien & Nagle, 1987).

Little is known about the role of parental encouragement of gender-typed play on subsequent play preferences and behaviors. Katz and Boswell (1986) found significant but weak correlations between parents' reports of their encouragement of gender-typed toy choice and children's reports of toy preferences. Eisenberg et al. (1985) found that the amount of time children played with masculine, feminine, or neutral toys was associated with the number of toys in each category that parents brought to a play session but not with differential reinforcement of gender-typed play. They suggested that an important tool for gender socialization is channeling children toward certain activities, and that given this kind of control, parents may not differentially encourage certain kinds of play during actual interactions.

To what extent can parents change children's gender-stereotypic beliefs and behaviors? In a home-based program in which mothers were trained in the use of nonstereotypic play materials, no changes were observed in 4- to 6-year-olds' knowledge of gender roles or identity (Roddy, Klein, Stericker, & Kurdek, 1981). For the most part, inducing children to engage in nonstereotypic activities also appears to be quite difficult, at least outside the context in which the teaching occurred and especially for young children (Sedney, 1987). Fathers play a particularly influential role in eliciting nonstereotypic behavior. In two studies, Katz and Walsh (1991) found that male experimenters were more effective than females in inducing 7- and 10-year-old children, especially boys, to engage in counterstereotypic behaviors. The authors suggest that male adults may be viewed by children as the "custodians of gender-role norms" (p. 349); thus, it is especially powerful when they encourage the violation of norms.

Encouragement of Gender-Typed Personal-Social Attributes. Huston (1983) concluded that parental socialization practices influence the development of gender-typed personality characteristics in children. In particular, the findings suggested that feminine, communal behaviors were associated with parents showing high levels of warmth and moderate to high control, whereas masculine, agentic behaviors were associated with parents showing high demands, control, and encouragement of independence when paired with moderate warmth. Furthermore, several studies suggested that boys receive more encouragement for gross motor activities and more freedom from adult supervision, whereas girls receive more encouragement to show dependency, affectionate behavior, and tender emotions, and are more likely to receive immediate help in achievement contexts. A meta-analysis found little consistent evidence of these differential socialization practices by parents, however. Lytton and Romney (1991) failed to find enough consistency across studies to result in a significant effect size for any of the following areas: amount of interaction, encouragement of achievement, warmth and responsiveness, encouragement of dependency, restrictiveness/low encouragement of independence, disciplinary strictness, or clarity of communication/use of reasoning.

This lack of differential socialization practices in the Lytton and Romney review is surprising in light of conclusions from the Huston (1983) review, as well as common assumptions that parents are more likely to encourage achievement and independence in boys, and dependency in girls. Some limitations in the analysis suggest, however, that it may be premature to conclude that the only way parents treat boys and girls differently is by encouraging gender-typed activities. Most importantly, as Lytton and Romney (1991) themselves noted, conclusions depend on how studies are combined to compute effect sizes. Lytton and Romney reported that for most domains, there were studies showing effects in both directions and yet reasons for this heterogeneity were left unexplored. Socialization outcomes are operationalized in many different ways, and combining behaviors that show effects in opposite directions can obscure true relations. For example, the overall effect size for encouraging dependency was not significant, primarily because a few studies showed strong differences favoring boys and these seemed to involve more questionable measures of dependency.

In addition, because effect sizes are likely to vary as a function of other variables (e.g., sex of parent, quality of journal publishing study), broad groupings may mask significant effects. Lytton and Romney's (1991) analyses of moderator variables lend some support to this suggestion by finding stronger differential socialization effects for fathers, for younger children, with higher quality articles, and when using observational/experimental measures. Interestingly, in a meta-analysis of differential socialization which was more narrowly focused on published studies that included fathers, 20 of the 39 studies showed that fathers' treatment of boys and girls differed significantly, an overall effect that was significantly greater than the few effects found for mothers (Siegal, 1987).

Broad grouping may also obscure effects when socialization practices occurring in different domains have similar effects. For example, sex differences in self-evaluative processes may be linked to seemingly quite distinct socialization practices, such as differential control versus autonomy-granting in the home (Higgins, 1991; Ruble et al., 1993), differential types of feedback provided in problem-solving situations (Alessandri & Lewis, 1993), and encouragement of greater empathy and feelings of responsibility in girls than in boys (e.g., Zahn-Waxler, Cole, & Barrett, 1991). Because such socialization processes cut across the different domains, it would be difficult to identify them in a meta-analysis.

Identifying areas of differential socialization practices may also be difficult because they occur at a subtle level. For example, through the microanalysis of everyday social interactions among the Kaluli people of Papua New Guinea, Schieffelin (1990) has shown how mothers use language and games to teach children adult gender roles and characteristics, even though direct reference to gender only occurs in cases of a breach in gender norms. Furthermore, context is important to consider because it influences, for example, the communication of control to sons and daughters (Biringen, Robinson, & Emde, 1994; Robinson, Little, & Biringen, 1993). Pomerantz and Ruble (in press) found that although overall communication of control in the home did not differ for girls and boys, control communications were more often accompanied by autonomy-granting messages for boys than for girls.

Although differential socialization practices may be subtle, complex, and context dependent, parents show different treatment of sons and daughters in some important ways that are broader than the assignments of chores or encouragement of activities or traits. A meta-analysis of parents' language behavior with their children found that mothers tended to talk more and use more supportive and directive speech with daughters than with sons (Leaper, Anderson, & Sanders, in press). In addition, mothers vary the nature and frequency of their discussion of emotions with toddler sons and daughters (Dunn, Bretherton, & Munn, 1987; Fivush, 1989). Parents also respond differentially to hypothetical stories about children's emotional reactions, with anger more accepted in boys and fear more accepted in girls (Birnbaum & Croll, 1984).

Parents also hold strong beliefs about boys and girls having different attributes and skills (McGuire, 1988). These beliefs and expectations appear to influence adults' perceptions and behaviors toward their children, and even the children's own perceptions and behaviors (e.g., Klebanov

& Brooks-Gunn, 1992). In an impressive program of research, Eccles and her colleagues (e.g., Eccles, Jacobs, Harold, Yoon, Arbreton, & Freedman-Doan, 1993) found that parents who hold stronger stereotypes regarding the capabilities of boys and girls in English, math, and sports had differential expectations regarding their own children's abilities in these subjects, which were, in turn, related to the children's performance and self-perceptions of competence, even when actual ability levels were controlled. Such relations appeared to be mediated, in part, by parents' tendencies to provide different experiences for sons and daughters, such as enrolling sons more often in sports programs.

Role Models in the Home. Is there any evidence that parents act as role models thereby influencing their children's attitudes and behaviors? Huston (1983) focused on the evidence with respect to maternal employment, which is one concrete way that parents provide less traditional role models. Much research has shown that maternal employment is associated with less stereotyped concepts in both boys and girls from age 3 through adolescence, and is associated with less gender-typed preferences and behaviors for girls only (Huston & Alvarez, 1990; Lerner, 1994). Among preschoolers, a relation has been found between maternal employment and less knowledge of gender labeling and stereotyping and/or greater flexibility of gender beliefs (Levy, 1989 [girls only]; Weinraub et al., 1984). Among elementary school students and young adolescents, maternal employment relates to less traditional gender beliefs and attitudes, at least for girls (e.g., Nelson & Keith, 1990). The relation between employment status and nontraditional attitudes often involves some other variable, such as status of mothers' work (Serbin, Powlishta, et al., 1993), closeness of the relationship with mother, or maternal satisfaction with employment (Galambos, Petersen, & Lennerz, 1988). It is not surprising, then, that some studies fail to find a relation between maternal employment and gender concepts and beliefs (e.g., Weisner & Wilson-Mitchell, 1990; Wright, Peterson, & Barnes, 1990).

Does maternal employment relate to children's career aspirations? Interestingly, most studies report no relation among elementary school students (e.g., Colangelo, Rosenthal, & Dettmann, 1984; Serbin, Powlishta, et al., 1993), although associations have been found with younger children (Barak, Feldman, & Noy, 1991; Selkow, 1984) and with adolescent girls (Amstey & Whitbourne, 1988; Corder & Stephan, 1984). Perhaps the inconsistent findings are due, in part, to other variables that moderate the relation between maternal employment and gender traditionality, especially job satisfaction (Leslie, 1986) and mothers' reasons for working (Katz & Boswell, 1986).

It is generally assumed that this relation with maternal employment is due to access to nontraditional role models, but other variables associated with maternal employment, such as differential treatment, nontraditional attitudes within the home, or exposure to different kinds of information outside the home are probably also involved (Hoffman, 1989). Furthermore, maternal employment may reflect socioeconomic status, which is itself related to nontraditional gender concepts. When demographic variables were controlled, few effects of maternal employment on gender concepts and preferences were found in a sample of 5- to 12-year-old children (Serbin, Powlishta, et al., 1993). Such failures to find effects of maternal employment in recent research may be partly because maternal employment is now so prevalent that children's gender concepts are affected by the presence of women in the workplace, regardless of whether or not their own mother works outside the home.

A few studies have examined the effects of other nontraditional family roles on the gender development of children. The evidence shows that an egalitarian division of labor in the home (or father involvement) relates to many aspects of gender development, such as satisfaction with one's own sex among 9- to 11-year-old Australian children (Burns & Homel, 1986), and children's gender concepts and preferences. Mothers who engaged in less traditional household/childcare responsibilities had children who were themselves less traditional in occupational and/or peer preferences (Serbin, Powlishta, et al., 1993; Turner & Gervai, 1995). Similarly, fathers who modeled nontraditional behaviors had children with less advanced knowledge of gender distinctions (Serbin, Powlishta, et al., 1993; Turner & Gervai, 1995; Weinraub et al., 1984), and sons with lower preference for gender traditional adult activities (Turner & Gervai, 1995).

Parental division of labor also relates to children's attitudes and behaviors. In a longitudinal study, Williams, Radin, and Allegro (1992) found that nontraditional paternal involvement in child care in childhood was associated with adolescents' approval of nontraditional roles (employment and child rearing) in their own lives, though not with approval of nontraditional roles in general. Blair (1992) found that fathers highly involved in sharing housework had sons who spent more time in household labor than fathers with more traditional patterns. Such effects are not consistently found, however (Baruch & Barnett, 1986;

Katz & Boswell, 1986; Weisner, Garnier, & Loucky, 1994). Parental involvement in sports appears to relate positively to the sports involvement of adolescent girls but not boys (e.g., Colley, Eglinton, & Elliott, 1992).

Parental Attitudes and Values.   To what extent are children's gender concepts related to general measures of gender orientation in the home, such as parents' perceptions of their own attributes, attitudes about equality, or nonegalitarian lifestyles? Several studies suggest that caregivers who view themselves in more traditional terms or who hold traditional attitudes foster the learning of gender distinctions in their children, such as stereotype knowledge (Repetti, 1984; Weinraub et al., 1984 [fathers only]) and young children's learning of gender labels (Fagot & Leinbach, 1989 [fathers only]; Fagot et al., 1992 [mothers only]). Several studies found that parents who held nontraditional values had children who had less traditional gender concepts or less knowledge of gender stereotypes (Baruch & Barnett, 1986 [mothers only]; Turner & Gervai, 1995; Weisner & Wilson-Mitchell, 1990), but others have not found this pattern (e.g., Barak et al., 1991; Katz & Boswell, 1986), and reasons for inconsistencies across studies are not yet clear.

Parental attitudes also appear to affect gender-typed preferences and behavioral enactment. Peretti and Sydney (1984) found that parents who showed greater endorsement of play with gender-consistent toys had children with stronger gender-typed toy preferences. An association has been found between parents' traditional beliefs and attitudes and the distribution of gender-typed chores to sons and daughters (Blair, 1992; Lackey, 1989). Finally, several studies report that parents' gender-typed beliefs and attitudes are often directly correlated with their children's ratings on similar measures (e.g., Pellett & Ignico, 1993). Katz and Boswell (1986) found that mothers' desires for the kinds of jobs they would like their sons to hold was associated with sons' actual preferences.

Single Parenting.   The study of single parents is of interest because role modeling and differential reinforcement in these families are likely to vary in many ways from that in two-parent families. Single parents may take on more nontraditional roles than in two-parent families. Furthermore, single parents may have less control over their children than two parents. Because mothers most often have custody, children receive more exposure to female role models in the home. For these reasons, absence of a father should be associated with less traditional gender typing in children (Katz, 1987). Early studies (Huston, 1983), as well as a more recent meta-analysis on the effect of paternal absence and gender development (Stevenson & Black, 1988) support this prediction, but only for boys. Boys from father-present homes were more stereotypically gender-typed than boys from father-absent homes but the effects were small and may not be of major practical significance. Nevertheless, there were some interesting differences across age, SES, race, and type of measure. Preschool father-absent boys made less stereotypical choices of toys and activities than father-present boys, a finding that was supported in a study by Serbin, Powlishta, et al. (1993) showing that knowledge of gender-typed activities and occupations was higher among younger boys but not girls in father-present homes. Interestingly, in contrast to measures of gender identification and preference in the Stevenson and Black meta-analysis, findings for measures of adoption (e.g., ratings of attitudes) suggested that older father-absent boys were *more* stereotypical in their overt behavior, particularly aggression. According to the authors, these data may indicate that older boys act out more as a response to their home environment. For girls, the most striking finding was the lack of effects, although there was a small indication that by adolescence father-absent girls were less feminine than father-present girls.

The finding that boys but not girls are affected by paternal absence would support theoretical accounts emphasizing identification and modeling processes, both in terms of the availability of a same-sex role model for boys and in terms of the likelihood that the home environment is less gender-typed when mothers must assume the duties of both roles and may be less able to provide control and discipline. In addition, the findings are consistent with the idea that fathers may take a special responsibility for masculinizing their sons (Huston, 1983). The lack of effects for girls, however, would appear to be inconsistent with accounts emphasizing the importance of reciprocal role processes in socialization (e.g., Radin, 1986; Williams, Radin, & Allegro, 1992), except for the weak finding that older girls in father-absent homes are less feminine. Perhaps reciprocal role processes become more important in adolescence, and may account for the finding of earlier studies (see Huston, 1983) that father absence contributes to difficulty in heterosexual relationships in adolescent girls.

Sibling Effects. Early studies of sibling effects focused primarily on the question of whether children learn gender-related attributes and interests from their siblings. According to Huston (1983), these studies produced conflicting predictions and findings in that some focused on same-sex modeling, whereas others focused on the needs to individuate and be different from one's siblings. Recent research has focused more on the effects of siblings on gender concepts and knowledge. Although there are few studies, the results are reasonably consistent: Children with few or no siblings in the home are more likely to show gender-egalitarian beliefs (Hertsgaard & Light, 1984 [girls only]; Levy, 1989). Among families with siblings, it seems to matter whether or not they are the same-sex. Not surprisingly, same-sex siblings engage in more gender-typed activities (Stoneman, Brody, & MacKinnon, 1986). Same-sex siblings appear to provide information in the form of modeling or reinforcement about gender-appropriate behavior. Findings are inconsistent about the effects of other-sex siblings on gender stereotyping, however (Crouter, Manke, & McHale, 1995; Lawrie & Brown, 1992; Stoneman et al., 1986). Siblings may provide wider ranging experiences that facilitate flexibility or they may inhibit flexibility by providing information about behaviors to avoid, by actively reinforcing gender-typical behavior, and by heightening the salience of gender in the family.

Gender Socialization at School

Schools provide a number of gender-related messages to children. The social structure of school is biased, with males in positions of power and women as teachers of younger children. Teachers may structure classroom activities by sex and provide differential reinforcements and punishments to boys and girls. Classrooms also provide many opportunities to learn about the consequences of behavior through observing peers.

Differential Treatment. Some evidence suggests that, like parents, teachers may encourage gender-appropriate play and discourage gender-inappropriate play. Fagot (1984) found that girls who were high in activity level and/or engaged in many male-typical behaviors received more negative responses from teachers, especially when they were also low on female typical behaviors; moreover, their behavior was relatively unstable over a one-year period, suggesting that girls change in response to teacher feedback.

Do teachers support gender-typed personal-social behavior? Many early studies found that boys receive more disapproval and scolding than girls, presumably because of generalized expectations that boys misbehave more (Huston, 1983). Studies also suggest that teachers focus more on misconduct in interactions with boys than girls (Eccles

& Blumenfeld, 1985). Yet, other studies have found that teachers respond positively to quiet, task-oriented, and responsible behavior in both sexes (e.g., Fagot, 1984). A study by Fagot, Hagan, Leinbach, and Kronsberg (1985) suggests that teachers may shape children's behavior over time. No sex differences in behavior were found in infant play groups, even though teachers were differentially attending to assertive behaviors in boys and attempts at communication in girls. By the next year, however, boys were more assertive and girls talked to teachers more, even though teachers no longer responded differentially to boys and girls. The authors suggested that teachers' responses toward infants may be guided by gender stereotypes because their behavior is ambiguous, and the resultant differential responding then serves to perpetuate the stereotype.

Teachers support gender-typed responding in other ways (Tittle, 1986). They interrupt preschool girls more frequently than boys during conversations (Hendrick & Stange, 1991) and interact more frequently with boys than with girls (Ebbeck, 1984). Sadker and Sadker (1986) reported that teachers of older children were more attentive to boys and allowed them more time to speak in class than girls. In addition, when children called out in class, boys were more likely to have their answers accepted whereas girls were told to raise their hands. These effects, however, vary across grade level and race of students and teachers (e.g., Irvine, 1986; Wilkinson & Marrett, 1986). Meece (1987) reviewed evidence suggesting that black teachers are less stereotyped in their beliefs and behaviors.

Teachers' hold stereotypic beliefs about girls' and boys' skills. Teachers believe that elementary school boys possess greater scientific and math skills than girls (Meece, Parsons, Kaczala, Goff, & Futterman, 1982; Shepardson & Pizzini, 1992), and that compliance is a significant component of perceived intelligence for preschool girls but not boys (Gold, Crombie, & Noble, 1987). In addition, girls who violate expectations because they are gifted (Kramer, 1991) or because they are not obedient and socially mature (Grant, 1985) are perceived more negatively by teachers.

Finally, school structures and practices may foster perceptions that boys and girls are different. Boys and girls are kept in segregated groups for even the most minor activities, such as standing in line (Meece, 1987; Thorne, 1993). Different contexts in which boys and girls tend to play at school may also influence their behavior. In preschoolers, highly structured activities tend to elicit higher rates of feminine-typed social behaviors, such as asking for help, whereas less structured activities tend to elicit higher rates of masculine-typed behaviors, such as leadership attempts toward peers (Carpenter et al., 1986). To the extent that girls are more likely than boys to play in highly structured activities, as suggested in an earlier section, a greater propensity toward feminine-typed behavior may be enhanced in school, even without direct teacher encouragement.

As with studies in the home, studies of classroom interventions suggest that it is difficult to change children's gender-related behavior (Sedney, 1989). Although young children will engage in activities normally dominated by the other sex if they receive specific encouragement (e.g., Smith, 1985), those effects may not carry over once the direct encouragement stops or in other contexts where it is not present (Carpenter et al., 1986; Lockheed, 1986). Gender-typed behaviors are difficult to change in part because they are reinforced by widely shared cultural beliefs and practices (Shamai & Coambs, 1992).

Role Models in School. Schools provide children with many examples of the importance of gender in the educational system. Men hold a disproportionate number of positions in higher administration, whereas women are more often teachers, particularly, in the early grades. Only in older grades are children likely to have many male teachers, and these are often in "masculine" classes such as mathematics and science.

Two main issues are relevant to the impact of observational learning in classrooms on gender development. First, does exposure to male teachers change gender concepts? The dearth of male teachers in elementary school and its implications for the gender typing and achievement of both boys and girls has generated considerable debate (e.g., Mancus, 1992). However, little research has directly examined the impact of teachers' sex on children. A few studies suggest that male teachers may foster more nontraditional gender beliefs and preferences (Koblinsky & Sugawara, 1984) and nontraditional views of teachers (Mancus, 1992).

Second, will exposure to role models as part of the curriculum change children's gender typing? The approach of using nontraditional role models is more effective if children receive longer interventions and more interactive programs. For example, 10 weeks of exposure to a nonsexist curriculum led to only a nonsignificant decrease in traditional vocational role preferences (Weeks & Porter, 1983) but extensive exposure changed young children's stereotypes and verbally stated preferences (Koblinsky &

Sugawara, 1984) for as long as one year after exposure (Gash & Morgan, 1993).

Peers' Differential Treatment.   Peers also reinforce gender-appropriate behavior. By the age of 3, children respond differentially to gender-typed behavior in others (Huston, 1983; Roopnarine, 1984). Fagot and Hagan (1985) reported that peers responded to boys' assertive behavior more than to girls'. Fagot (1984) found that peers were more negative toward boys who engaged in relatively high levels of female-typical behaviors, especially when they were low on male-typical behaviors. Thus, peer reinforcement processes may begin quite young, and evidence suggests that they may increase with age (Carter & McCloskey, 1984).

The sex segregation of children's groups no doubt also contributes to gender socialization (Carter, 1987; Maccoby & Jacklin, 1987) possibly in two somewhat conflicting forms (Huston, 1983). On the one hand, children practice gender-typed play with toys (Lloyd & Smith, 1985) and learn gender-typed interaction styles that translate into girls developing styles that facilitate interaction and boys developing styles that limit interaction (Leaper, 1994; Maccoby, 1988). On the other hand, sex segregation in some settings, such as all-female schools and math classes, appears to promote more flexible gender responding, such as greater achievement and nontraditional attitudes, independent of demographic and self-selection factors (Lawrie & Brown, 1992; Lee & Bryk, 1986). Single-sex classes for females are likely to be effective for a number of reasons (Meece, 1987): greater exposure to successful role models, a narrower range of elective courses which encourages nontraditional course selections, and the absence of reciprocal role pressures and differential teacher responsiveness of mixed-sex groupings.

Children and adolescents may also try to live up to images of what type of behavior is "cool" or leads to popularity and high status among the peer group. Preadolescent boys achieve high status on the basis of athletic ability, toughness, and social skills, whereas girls' status relates to physical appearance, social skills, and parents' socioeconomic status (Adler, Kless, & Adler, 1992). Gender-appropriate athletic participation in high school relates to social status for both sexes (Holland & Andre, 1994). Peer interactions involving athletics appear to be a particularly potent influence on gender-related values in high school. Eder and Parker (1987) reported that the high status granted to male athletes and female cheerleaders led the informal peer culture to incorporate values involving competition for males and appearance and emotion management for females.

Peer Models.   Children may also learn standards for gender-appropriate behavior by observing their peers. Children's own gender-typed preferences are closely associated with the perceived preferences of peers (e.g., Katz & Boswell, 1986). Perry and Bussey (1979) theorized and research has supported the idea that children determine the gender typing of activities by observing the proportion of boys and girls that engage in particular activities. Such learning involves both acceptance of same-sex modeled behavior and avoidance of other-sex modeled behavior, especially for boys (Bussey & Perry, 1982). Peer involvement with toys also influences children's toy choices. In an observational study, Shell and Eisenberg (1990) found that preschoolers approached toys based on the number and proportion of same-sex peers currently engaged in the activity, and boys ceased involvement when the engagement of girls increased. Interestingly, however, prior differential peer involvement did not relate to play, suggesting that these children were not storing information about the gender-appropriateness of toys to determine their initial approach. Once children have acquired gender concepts, however, it is not so clear that peer modeling of gender-inconsistent behavior can easily promote change. Simply observing peer models engage in gender-inconsistent behavior did not promote change in 7- and 10-year-old children's behavior unless the peer model's behavior was reinforced (Katz & Walsh, 1991).

Observational Learning from the Media

Because children spend much of their free time in front of television, the role of the media has been considered a crucial issue in the study of gender development. Despite the widespread social changes that occurred in the 1970s to 1980s, Huston (1983) concluded that few changes had occurred in the presentation of the sexes in the mass media during that time. The past 10 years can be summarized similarly: The sexes continued to be portrayed in stereotypic ways, although there have been some improvements (see Huston & Wright, Ch. 15, Volume 4, for review). The improvements noted in several areas may have been offset by the introduction of a new, powerful, and very stereotyped media—music videos.

There are two broad concerns about media portrayals of the sexes. The first is the degree to which each sex is represented in the media because underrepresentation may suggest a devaluing of one group (Huston et al., 1992). Early studies showed a very sizable bias toward presenting more males than females in virtually every domain, with the exception of daytime soap operas. Women have continued to occupy about ¼ to ⅓ of televised roles over the past 20 years (Signorielli, 1993).

The second concern is the stereotypic portrayals for each sex in terms of occupations, personality characteristics, social relationships, appearance, and dress styles, as well as whether the roles are valued or desirable. Roles continue to be stereotypic and unbalanced, though some changes have been made, especially in portraying women involved in careers (Allan & Coltrane, 1996; Calvert & Huston, 1987). In terms of appearance, women tend to be young, thin, provocatively dressed, and beautiful, whereas many males are middle-aged (Calvert & Huston, 1987). Generally, the personality characteristics demonstrated by female and male characters on television also continue to be stereotypic (Signorielli, 1993).

Children's programs present a more gender-stereotyped picture of the world than do adult programs. In cartoons, male characters tend to be the problem-solvers whereas the female characters follow the male's lead and are sweet and more childlike, although both sexes appear to demonstrate equal levels of intelligence (Durkin, 1985; Huston et al., 1992). Even children's educational programs are dominated by male characters, including such appealing shows as Sesame Street. Many of the shows that children actually watch are older, stereotypic shows that are being rebroadcast. Programming is also geared toward one sex through subtle formal features. For example, shows designed for boys tend to have rapid action, frequent cuts, loud music, and sound effects, whereas shows for girls use fades and dissolves, female narration, and soft background music (Huston, Greer, Wright, Welch, & Ross, 1984).

Programs for adolescents also present extremely stereotypic depictions of the sexes. In the early 1980s, MTV and similar kinds of music-oriented broadcasting were introduced to tap into a relatively neglected teen market. Now, 6 out of 10 television households receive MTV (Signorielli, McLeod, & Healy, 1994). The music videos (and the accompanying advertisements) are highly stereotypic in their portrayal of the sexes, and tend to be designed to attract young male viewers. Men are shown twice as often as women in music videos (Sommers-Flanagan, Sommers-Flanagan, & Davis, 1993). The women in music videos are 10 times more likely to be dressed in revealing clothing

than are men, and they are more likely to receive sexual advances (Seidman, 1992; Sommers-Flanagan et al., 1993).

Children's literature also contains stereotypic messages about gender roles. In the 1970s, most studies found a clear bias toward more male representation in books (Segel, 1986). Books written in the 1980s provided a shift to a more equal representation of the sexes, with both sexes beginning to become involved in a wider variety of roles. Girls, however, still tended to be involved in weaker, less interesting story lines (Purcell & Stewart, 1990), and were still depicted as being dependent and needing help more often than boys (Turner-Bowker, 1996; White, 1986).

The Influence of Gender-Stereotypic Portrayals of the Sexes.   What role do television and books play in children's gender socialization? Researchers have been faced with the tremendous difficulty of exploring the causal influence of something that is so pervasive in our culture. By examining the outcomes of correlational and longitudinal studies as well as natural experiments, researchers hope to determine whether converging patterns suggest that media influences gender-related behavior and attitudes.

Some correlational studies report that children who are heavy and consistent television viewers generally hold more stereotypic beliefs about the sexes than light viewers (Durkin, 1985; Huston et al., 1992). The major problem with such studies is determining the direction of influence. Television may be causing individuals to develop stronger beliefs; however, it may also be that heavier viewers find television more appealing because it presents images that are consistent with their beliefs.

Several longitudinal studies have examined the relation between television viewing at one point in time and gender-related attitudes and behavior later in time. Morgan (1987) found that adolescents' earlier television viewing related to attitudes about the gender typing of chores but not to their behavior (chores) 6 months later. Although longitudinal studies show some influence of television viewing on attitudes, more research needs to consider the influence on a wider range of children's behaviors than has been examined thus far (Durkin, 1985).

The most convincing evidence about the impact of television on children's lives resulted from a naturally occurring experiment in Canada. Researchers examined the changes that occurred as television was introduced into several towns that had been unable to receive television. Before television was introduced into one town (Notel), the children held less traditional gender attitudes than the children in a comparable town with access to multiple television channels. Furthermore, two years after television was introduced, children in Notel showed sharp increases in traditional attitudes. For girls, attitudes about peer relationships changed most dramatically. For boys, attitudes about occupations changed most dramatically (Kimball, 1986).

The Media as a Vehicle for Attitude Change. Given the widespread stereotyping portrayed on television, interest in the influence of counterstereotypic portrayals becomes particularly informative about the power of television. Can television undo the stereotypic messages? Most of the classic research on these issues took place during the 1970s (e.g., Flerx, Fidler, & Rogers, 1976), and these studies illustrated that children's stereotypes about activities, personal and social attributes, and parenting roles became less gender typed after exposure to nontraditional media portrayals (see Huston, 1983).

The largest and most ambitious project on the effect of counterstereotypic messages was a multisite, semester-long project involving classroom showings and discussions of the series *Freestyle,* which was designed to change children's gender stereotypes regarding activities, occupations, and personality characteristics, using appealing characters. Generally, the programs were effective: Children's stereotypes became less traditional than nonviewers' concerning activities, domestic roles, and occupations, but less change was found in personality characteristics (e.g., independence). Children's own preferences and interests in mechanical activities and athletics also changed somewhat (Johnston & Ettema, 1982). Moreover, many of these changes were evident even after 9 months, but all changes were more likely to occur in classrooms where follow-up discussions were held after viewing (Johnston, 1982).

Short-term efforts have also been tried with mixed effects. In some cases, changes occurred in some domains (e.g., domestic but not occupational roles), and in other studies, no change or *more* traditional attitudes were expressed by adolescents after viewing counterstereotypic programming (Durkin, 1985). Matteson (1991) suggested that it is necessary to use models of the same sex to be effective, whereas other-sex portrayals may lead to backlash effects.

Although earlier studies demonstrated the power of the media, additional research needs to explore how enduring these changes are and whether children simply disregard counterstereotypic examples they view as exceptions to the stereotypic rule or if their stereotypes change more dramatically than this. Furthermore, children's gender-related attitudes and beliefs do not always become less traditional when they view counterstereotypic programming; thus, the conditions that encourage egalitarian beliefs need to be more carefully identified.

Summary. Television is a window onto the world: it allows viewers to experience life in other countries and under different social systems. Television is also a window onto a world that does not exist, one that remains more stereotypic in roles and behaviors than the world children see around them everyday. Other forms of media reinforce this stereotypic view, even though some positive changes are occurring.

The ways in which media messages affect children's lives have yet to be fully determined. The background "wash" of gender-stereotyping messages certainly provides an overabundance of inaccurate information about the sexes. But knowing what programs children watch is not enough. Instead, we need to understand how children actively construct their own understanding of the messages they view and how these messages influence their gender development. Access to nontraditional portrayals may act to counter some of their stereotypic beliefs, but the conditions leading to change need to be explored in more depth.

Integration and Conclusions

Socialization processes influence both the course of gender development and individual differences in children's gender beliefs and adherence to gender norms. Gender socialization processes at home, at school, in interaction with peers, and through the media all appear to contribute to gender differentiation in most of the areas identified in Table 14.1—concepts, preferences, behaviors, and values. Differential treatment is particularly influential in young children, affecting their early learning of gender distinctions. The more active, constructive processes involved in observational learning appear effective in influencing the development of concepts, preferences, and behaviors for older children as well, but little is known about developmental processes. Although adults and peers treat boys and girls differently in many ways, especially concerning activities and interests, the role of these processes in children's gender-related preferences and behaviors remains to be demonstrated. Subtle forms of differential treatment, such as channeling and structuring the home environment, may be indirect but influential socialization forces. In many cases, it is likely that multiple processes working together best explain the observed relations between, for example, gender-related beliefs or behaviors and parental attitudes or the presence of same-sex siblings.

Although socialization effects are found for many aspects of gender development, some studies fail to find expected associations, or find them only under a narrow range of conditions. Moreover, there are some aspects of gender differentiation that socialization research does not (at least yet) explain or that it has not tried to explain, such as sex segregation. In addition, studies using social learning principles to change stereotypic beliefs and behaviors have met with only mixed success. These findings highlight the complexity of gender socialization processes and the need for more fine-grained analysis to better understand when and how social agents influence gender development. Furthermore, effects may often be moderated by children's beliefs or level of understanding (Ruble & Goodnow, in press). If so, different socialization processes may be influential at different ages, suggesting that interventions will be more effective if developmental level is taken into account.

Two key theoretical questions remain. First, why are girls and boys treated differently? One answer is that boys and girls elicit differential responding because they behave differently. Burnham and Harris (1992) report that adults perceived infant boys as stronger and less sensitive than girls, even when the labeled sex of the infant was manipulated independently of real sex. Similarly, teachers and peers may simply be responding to different behaviors of boys and girls (Meece, 1987), and studies rarely control for such differences. Other research suggests, however, that boys and girls are treated differently regardless of their behavior, implying that gender-related expectations and beliefs also play an important role (e.g., Pomerantz & Ruble, in press). Some of the clearest demonstrations that socialization agents initiate differential treatment come from experimental studies in which the same infants are labeled as boys or girls. In these "eye of the beholder" studies, boys and girls are perceived and responded to differently (Huston, 1983). Infants that are presented as girls are rated lower on potency-related traits, such as weakness (Leone & Robertson, 1989), are perceived as exhibiting more feminine-typed behaviors (Delk, Madden, Livingston, & Ryan, 1986), and are given more stereotypically feminine toys and verbal interaction (Culp, Cook, & Housley, 1983). Stern and Karraker (1989), in their review, concluded that the effects of labeling an infant male or female are not as strong and consistent as often portrayed, however, particularly for stereotypic perceptions. Such effects are often bi-directional, in that attributes of the child elicit the parental beliefs. In short, differential treatment is likely due to some combination of actual differences between boys and girls and gender-based beliefs of socializing agents.

What kinds of beliefs do socializing agents hold? Do they respond on the basis of what they believe the sexes *are* like (expectations) or what they *should be* like (prescriptions)? As described earlier, considerable research has demonstrated the importance of parents' stereotypic expectations in fostering children's gender-differentiated behaviors (e.g., Jussim & Eccles, 1992; McGuire, 1988). Maccoby and Jacklin (1974) reported that parents think boys and girls have different typical behaviors but that the socialization goals for the two sexes appear to be similar. Cultural analyses, however, indicate that societies have quite different goals for boys and girls in domains such as power and status (Bugental & Goodnow, Ch. 7, this Volume; Low, 1989) and emotional expression (Schieffelin, 1990), which may implicitly guide parents' socialization strategies without becoming manifest as conscious goals. Similarly, research suggests that, when given closer examination, adults hold different goals for the socialization of boys and girls. Martin (1995) found that although adults generally agreed on certain characteristics being desirable for both sexes, many traits were rated as more desirable for boys than for girls (e.g., mechanical, competitive) and others as more desirable for girls (e.g., gentle, sympathetic). Distinguishing between stereotypic expectations and child-rearing goals and assessing their impact on differential treatment would lead to better understanding of gender socialization.

A second theoretical issue concerns the underlying processes linking the actions of socializing agents to child outcomes. It is relatively rare to identify a specific process underlying differential socialization, such as via the development of personal gender standards (Bussey & Bandura, 1992) or different attributions for performance (Eccles, Jacobs, Harold, Yoon, Albreton, & Freedman-Doan, 1993). Most studies test a relatively simplistic hypothesis—that boys and girls are treated differently or exposed to models of differential behavior. Although many of the findings are intuitively compelling, the exact nature of the mediating process and its causal direction are often unclear. For example, one of the most interesting and consistent findings is that encouragement of gender-differentiated play and traditional role modeling in the home are associated with advanced gender knowledge in young children (e.g., Fagot et al., 1992; Weinraub et al., 1984). Which of the many inter-related aspects of the home environment are most important—is it the father's differential responding, his lack of involvement in activities at home, and/or his traditional attitudes? Are multiple socialization processes involved or does a single process underlie these various relations?

Cognitive Approaches

Cognitive approaches to the study of gender development have received considerable attention and there is a rapidly growing body of work in this area. Theories based on cognitive approaches assume that underlying cognitions about gender influence gender development. Although cognitive approaches share many similarities, the theories based on this approach identify different sorts of cognitions as being important and provide somewhat different mechanisms to link cognitions to beliefs and behavior. In this section, we examine how the cognitive theories briefly described in the Historical Review section have explained gender development. The first two subsections describe the extensive evidence now available on the roles of sex category constancy and gender schemas, respectively. The third subsection concerns the role of children's identification with males or females as a group.

Cognitive Developmental Theory and the Role of Sex Category Constancy

One of the most controversial aspects of Kohlberg's cognitive developmental theory concerns the role of gender constancy in the development of gender-related knowledge and preferences. Although Kohlberg's ideas about how children socialize themselves into gender roles were pioneering, the mechanisms that drive their socialization efforts were not pinpointed and clearly articulated (Huston, 1983; Martin & Little, 1990). Kohlberg believed that children's understanding of the unchangeability of gender was an essential ingredient for motivating children to acquire gender roles. He stated, "A child's gender identity can provide a stable organizer of the child's psychosexual attitudes only when he is categorically certain of its unchangeability" (1966, p. 95). Not surprisingly, many researchers concluded that gender consistency—children's understanding of the permanence of gender over situational changes—was the critical component for motivating children to learn and adhere to gender roles. However, in seeming contrast to his emphasis on gender consistency, Kohlberg also believed that

children showed gender-typed preferences prior to the time they attained complete constancy.

The relation between sex category constancy (SCC) and gender stereotypic thought and behavior has been conceptualized in two ways. The first hypothesis is that children show the strongest adherence to gender-related behaviors prior to their attainment of gender consistency because they are afraid that cross-sex behaviors may transform them to the other sex (Marcus & Overton, 1978). Once consistency is attained, they will have the freedom to not follow gender norms (see Huston, 1983). Thus, the attainment of consistency should be associated with decreased rigidity (Urberg, 1982). The second hypothesis is that children show a linear increase in adherence to gender norms as they learn about SCC (Levy & Carter, 1989), and that norms do not become more flexible until a few years after the attainment of gender consistency (Frey & Ruble, 1992).

Huston (1983) concluded that SCC appeared to be independent of other components of gender development, with only a few studies suggesting a relation between SCC and responsiveness to same-sex models. Recent reviews suggest that any such relation is more complex than initially hypothesized (Martin & Little, 1990; Stangor & Ruble, 1987). Part of the problem is that comparisons across studies have been difficult to make because of variations in the ways SCC is operationalized. Many studies have used high/low splits of participants on their understanding of the gender concepts, with most labeling children as belonging to the highest level of understanding even if they only understand identity (labeling of the sexes) and stability of gender over time (e.g., Bussey & Bandura, 1992; Ruble et al., 1981; Slaby & Frey, 1975). Only a few require complete SCC understanding (e.g., Frey & Ruble, 1992). Other issues include whether correlational or stagelike patterns are assessed. Some studies have looked for correlations with level of SCC (e.g., Carter & Levy, 1988; Lobel & Menashri, 1993; Newman, Cooper, & Ruble, 1995; Perloff, 1982). Other studies have examined relations with the attainment of lower levels of SCC (e.g., Eaton, Von Bargen, & Keats, 1981; Martin & Little, 1990; Yee & Brown, 1994), thereby providing evidence about the possibility that children's gender-related thoughts and behaviors are more closely associated with aspects of gender labeling or stability than with consistency. In this review, we distinguish between findings relating to specific levels of understanding whenever possible.

SCC and Selective Attention, Modeling, and Preferences. According to Kohlberg, children with high levels of SCC would be expected to attend to and imitate the behaviors of same-sex models more than other children. Thus far, in contrast to this hypothesis, research has not demonstrated that gender *consistency* relates to selective attention to same-sex models; gender *stability,* however, does appear to relate. Children, especially boys, who have acquired gender stability show greater attention to same-sex models (Slaby & Frey, 1975). In a naturalistic study of television viewing, boys at higher levels of SCC showed differential attention to male characters and watched programs with a higher percentage of male characters and adult male roles (e.g., sports) than did boys at lower levels of SCC (Luecke-Aleksa, Anderson, Collins, & Schmitt, 1995). Unlike the positive relations observed when same- versus other-sex stimuli are presented simultaneously or when naturalistic stimuli are used, however, when methods involving attention to sequentially presented stimuli are used, same-sex attentional biases are not found (Bryan & Luria, 1978).

Several studies have shown that gender consistency may play a role in imitating same-sex others under certain conditions (Perloff, 1982; Ruble et al., 1981). Same-sex imitation may be especially likely when the relevant behavior requires forgoing an attractive activity associated with the other sex—that is, when same-gender activities are selected under conditions of conflict—at least for boys (Frey & Ruble, 1992). When no conflict is involved (e.g, the modeled behaviors are neutral), level of understanding does not exert an influence on children's same-sex modeling (Bussey & Bandura, 1984; Perloff, 1982, on identical task modeling).

According to Kohlberg, we would expect to find higher levels of SCC, especially gender consistency, to relate to children's preferences for gender-typed toys and same-sex playmates. Generally, this hypothesis has not been supported (Bussey & Bandura, 1984, 1992; Carter & Levy, 1988; Lobel & Menashri, 1993; Marcus & Overton, 1978; Taylor & Carter, 1987). Instead, SCC may be related to preferences in more complex ways. First, gender-typed preferences are linked to lower levels of SCC (i.e., gender identity and stability). For example, children who have achieved gender identity engage in more gender-typed toy play or less gender-inconsistent behavior than other children (cf., Bussey & Bandura, 1984; Fagot, 1985b (boys only); Weinraub et al., 1984). Also, children who understand the stability of sex select toys on the basis of gender appropriateness, rather than an alternative attractive dimension (Eaton et al., 1981), like gender-typed toys and same-sex peers more (Martin & Little, 1990), and, for girls

only, play with same-sex peers more (Smetana & Letourneau, 1984).

Second, an influence of SCC is found under conflict conditions (e.g., Frey & Ruble, 1992). In these situations, where there is conflict between selecting an activity on the basis of gender versus some other dimension of attractiveness, children who acquired stability (Eaton et al., 1981) and those with complete SCC (Stangor & Ruble, 1989) selected on the basis of gender. In conflict between a same-gender toy and same-sex peer, preference for the same-sex peer was associated with consistency understanding, especially among older boys (Emmerich & Shepard, 1984). Support for the conflict hypothesis was also found in a study of interest in computers. Although computers were attractive to both boys and girls, girls who attained SCC and who had considerable gender stereotypic knowledge showed less interest in computers than did all other children, suggesting that they abandoned an attractive activity to comply with gender norms (Newman et al., 1995). Finding support for the conflict hypothesis may depend on the age of the sample, however, with older samples (6 years and older) supporting the relationship (Emmerich & Shepard, 1984; Frey & Ruble, 1992; Newman et al., 1995; Stangor & Ruble, 1989), but not younger ones (Lobel & Menashri, 1993). Perhaps discrepancies are due to curvilinear relations between age and SCC, as described in an earlier section. Finally, a study comparing children with gender identity disorder (GID) and a control sample may also be interpreted in terms of the conflict hypothesis. Same-gender free play was higher for GID children who had achieved gender consistency relative to those who had not, but there was no effect for a control sample. Because gender-related play is likely to involve more conflict for GID children, these findings provide a different kind of support for the conflict hypothesis (Zucker et al., 1996).

Taken together, these studies show an interesting pattern. In studies using simple measures of toy preference, the earliest levels of gender understanding relate to preferences because simply knowing that one is a boy or a girl may provide the cognitive underpinning for making gender-typed selections. Only in studies involving conflict situations is the additional motivational impetus associated with higher levels of SCC needed for making the selection.

SCC and Stereotypic Knowledge and Memory.   Several studies have also found a relation between children's level of gender stereotype knowledge and either level of SCC (Kuhn et al., 1978; Taylor & Carter, 1987) or with attainment of gender stability (Bussey & Bandura, 1992, among 4-year-olds only; Coker, 1984; Martin & Little, 1990; O'Keefe & Hyde, 1983), and these associations occurred even with age controlled (Martin & Little, 1990; Taylor & Carter, 1987). In addition, SCC has been associated with greater flexibility in the application of stereotypes or gender role norms (Urberg, 1982). Relations between levels of SCC and knowledge or flexibility are not always found, however (Carter & Levy, 1988; Levy & Carter, 1989), perhaps because knowledge levels rapidly reach ceiling. It is thus noteworthy that the effects occur primarily for very young children (e.g., Kuhn et al., 1978), with the attainment of lower levels of understanding (e.g., Martin & Little, 1990), or with more complex kinds of knowledge, such as stereotypes regarding the other sex (Taylor & Carter, 1987).

Studies of memory show that children distort information that violates gender stereotypes; actions by a male nurse were remembered by 5-year-olds as either having been done by a female or as representing duties by a doctor (Cordua, McGraw, & Drabman, 1979). In some studies, a relation is found between distortions and SCC. Stangor and Ruble (1989) found that children's level of gender understanding correlated with the number of times the actors' sex was distorted for two stereotype-inconsistent toy commercials, with age controlled, suggesting that a high level of motivation to conform to gender-stereotypic norms associated with SCC led the children to misperceive actions that violated these norms. Other studies have not found this pattern. When shown a large number of pictures depicting males and females engaged in many activities, SCC did not relate to children remembering the stereotype-consistent pictures or distorting the inconsistent ones (Carter & Levy, 1988; Stangor & Ruble, 1989). The reasons for the different results may relate to the tasks inducing different biases in either retrieving and/or encoding (Liben & Signorella, 1993; Stangor & McMillan, 1992; Stangor & Ruble, 1989).

Finally, a few studies have found relations between SCC stages and responsiveness to gender as a social category. Coker (1984) found that boys who had attained gender stability were more likely to sort pictures on the basis of sex than age. Level of SCC is also associated with more positive feelings about one's own sex. Munroe et al. (1984) found that higher levels of SCC (stability or consistency) were associated with a greater likelihood of preferring a same-gender role choice (e.g., being a son or daughter). Yee and Brown (1994) found that gender stability was associated with liking one's own sex more and rewarding

same-sex groups more. Finally, De Lisi and Johns (1984) found that, relative to children low in SCC, children high in SCC were less negative about males and less positive about females, a pattern the authors interpret as closer to adults' more positive evaluations of males.

Evaluating Sex Category Constancy. There is little empirical support for the idea that gender consistency is the crucial component of gender development. Instead, significant relations often involve the lower levels of SCC—identity and stability. It would be valuable in future research to pay more attention to the psychological processes that underlie relations between different components of SCC and gender-related outcomes. For example, does understanding gender identity elicit the kind of group identification described by social identity and schema theorists (see later sections) or reflect the motivational attachment to one's group suggested by Kohlberg?

Is there any value at all to the concept of gender consistency? The converging evidence suggests that a different approach may be needed to understand the role of gender consistency. One promising proposal is that gender consistency increases children's responsiveness to gender information, rather than acting to initiate their responsiveness (Stangor & Ruble, 1987). Consistency may serve as a period of consolidation for conclusions about gender-appropriate activities. Children with complete SCC understanding are more motivated to adhere to gender-appropriate standards (Ruble, 1994), leading them to be more likely to engage in unpleasant behaviors or situations, as long as they are gender-appropriate, because it is more important to adhere to the gender roles than to do something that is pleasant (Frey & Ruble, 1992).

There are many problems with the construct of SCC and its presumed relation to gender-related beliefs, preferences, and behaviors. Complete understanding of SCC does not serve the initial organizing function that Kohlberg proposed but may serve important functions other than an organizing role. On the other hand, lower levels of SCC—especially identity and sometimes stability—show some of the associations Kohlberg predicted to occur with constancy. Whether such relations are best understood in terms of the motivational processes Kohlberg described or are instead better described in terms of alternative formulations remains for future research to decide. Finally, despite the controversies about SCC, cognitive developmental theories have been influential in illustrating the child's active role in gender development.

Gender Schema Theories

Gender schemas are interrelated networks of mental associations representing information about the sexes that influence information processing. Their influence ranges from directing attention to biasing memory and behavioral choices. Gender schemas have been broadly and narrowly conceptualized. Schemas are broadly conceived as "lenses" that color perception and thinking (Bem, 1993), abstract theories about gender groups (Martin, 1993; Martin et al., 1995), stereotypes about the sexes, or a network of dimensions underlying gender-related beliefs (e.g., "metaphorical associations," Leinbach et al., in press). Schemas also are more narrowly conceived as concepts about the self (Bem, 1981; Intons-Peterson, 1988a), or scripts about gender-appropriate activities (Levy & Boston, 1994; Martin & Halverson, 1981). Furthermore, gender schemas have been operationalized many ways, causing some confusion when comparing results across studies (Carter & Levy, 1988; Martin, 1993; Signorella et al., 1993; Ruble & Stangor, 1986). The crucial aspect of gender schemas, however, is that they are dynamic knowledge representations that change in response to situations and with age (Carter & Levy, 1988; Ruble & Stangor, 1986), and their content varies according to culture and social experiences.

The idea of a schema as a mental representation was borrowed from research in cognitive psychology, but the translation of schemas into the social arena required the development of additional concepts to explain how the structures influence behavior and thinking. Schema theorists in developmental psychology use the concept of schematic or cognitive consistency to describe children's tendencies to attend, act, and remember in ways that conform to their gender schemas (Martin & Halverson, 1981). Similarly, evaluation was assumed to easily follow from categorizing the sexes (although it is not a necessary feature) and from recognizing one's membership in a gender group. Thus, at least two levels of schematic consistency can be identified. The first level is consistency with gender groups. This form of consistency would be apparent in in-group and out-group biases, such as those first investigated by social identity theorists. This would also include conforming to and learning about the behaviors believed to be appropriate for one's own gender group. Research on children's learning about own-sex scripts provides some support for this notion (discussed later). The second level is consistency with broader gender schemas, namely, beliefs about the sexes. At this level, children would be expected to show biased memory for and positive evaluation of stereotype-consistent information over stereotype-inconsistent information. As described subsequently, children show biased memory for stereotype-consistent information in many circumstances. Research also illustrates that children show broad evaluative biases, such as rating individuals in schema-consistent occupations as more competent than those in schema-inconsistent occupations (Cann & Newbern, 1984). Details about the mechanisms associating the knowledge structure with evaluation biases and with motivation, as well as developmental changes in these mechanisms, have not been explored in depth (Serbin et al., 1993; Signorella, 1987; Stangor & Ruble, 1989).

Development of Gender Schemas. Gender schemas develop through an interaction of the perceiver's characteristics with the characteristics of the environment. Infants are predisposed to simplify and organize by categorizing people and objects into meaningful groups. The dimensions most likely to be used are those given the most significance by the culture, such as gender (Bem, 1981, 1993).

Children are exposed to social environments in which sex and gender are salient, both perceptually and conceptually. Clothing, voices, and roles are only some of the gender-related cues that can be used to determine sex. Sex is also salient in vocalizations to children (e.g., "You're a good girl"). Once children can distinguish the sexes, they have many opportunities to add information to their gender schemas. Even before children can easily recognize physical appearance cues, they may be familiar with the concepts of females and males simply from frequently hearing references to gender labels. Adults also socially transmit stereotypes about the sexes, both directly through admonitions to their children (e.g., "boys don't cry") or through stating their own beliefs (e.g., "girls like to play with dolls").

Developmental changes in cognitive and motivational processes also influence how the social environment is perceived and interpreted. For schema theories, an important developmental change involves children recognizing their membership in a gender category. Once they attain this understanding, they are more motivated to learn details and scripts for own-sex-expected activities, and some evidence suggests that they begin to make inferences based on abstract theories about members of the same-sex groups being similar to themselves and members of the other-sex groups being different (Martin et al., 1995). Schema theorists expect that being attuned to gender groupings also may increase tendencies to notice group differences (Bem,

1981; Martin, 1993). Furthermore, as associations become stronger and schemas more elaborate, their tendency to influence and bias information organization, memory, and behavior may increase.

Other cognitive processes offset these developmental trends somewhat. As children cognitively develop, they can use additional classification systems that cross gender categories, thereby decreasing the influence of gender schemas (Bigler & Liben, 1992). For example, occupational stereotyping decreased when children were taught decision rules about occupations based on interests and skills rather than on gender (Bigler & Liben, 1990; 1992). As children grow older, individual differences in values, gender salience, and schema elaboration will modify the use of gender schemas. Furthermore, the actual application of gender schemas may become more consciously controlled (Devine, 1989; Lutz & Ruble, 1995; Martin, 1993).

Individual Differences and Situational Factors. Schema theorists expect some children to have more salient, more fully developed, and more elaborated gender schemas than others (Signorella, Bigler, & Liben, 1993). To the extent that gender tends to be a salient processing dimension for an individual, behavior and thinking should show stronger gender effects (Bem, 1981). Research has supported this hypothesis: When salience is assessed using reaction times for gender-related decisions, children who have salient gender schemas pay more attention to gender as an organizing strategy (Levy, 1994), better remember consistent information (Carter & Levy, 1988; Levy, 1989), and attribute more stereotypic characteristics to others than children who have less salient schemas (Levy & Carter, 1989).

Gender salience also varies by situation (Bem, 1981). Some situations make gender salient for a brief period, thereby increasing the likelihood of schematic processing. For example, after being told to line up outside their classroom by sex, children may be more likely to process information using gender categories. Classrooms in which gender frequently was made salient for 4 weeks had children with more traditional attitudes than children in classrooms in which gender was not as salient. Interestingly, students who showed lower levels of cognitive development (i.e., the inability to use multiple classifications) were more influenced by increased gender salience than were other children (Bigler, 1995). Other situations may increase salience for longer periods (e.g., being in a coed school).

Although the topic has not received much attention, children may differ in their readiness to change their schemas once they are formed. Individual differences in schema modification may relate more to gender-typed behavior and memory than does the general knowledge represented in the schema (Ruble & Stangor, 1986). In addition, children may be trained in intervention programs to learn alternative strategies for determining occupation roles, which may enable them to better remember counterstereotypic information (Bigler & Liben, 1990, 1992). These findings suggest that gender schemas may be modified with appropriate intervention strategies, although more research is needed to assess the long-term impact of these interventions as well as individual differences in the ability to modify gender schemas.

Gender Schemas and Inferences.   An important role of gender schemas is in interpreting environmental input. Information that is ambiguous, missing, or not attended to in familiar situations will be filled in from the gender schema (Martin & Halverson, 1981). Children's use of gender-based inferences has been demonstrated in many settings. Preschoolers generalize their beliefs about the sexes to infants (Haugh et al., 1980), and children and adolescents make gender-based inferences about unfamiliar children (Berndt & Heller, 1986; Biernat, 1991b; Haugh et al., 1980; Lobel et al., 1993; Martin, 1989), and will make inferences about novel attributes based on their knowledge of gender groups (Gelman, Collman, & Maccoby, 1986). Children assume that unfamiliar others are more likely to be competent in same-gender than other-gender occupational roles (Cann & Palmer, 1986). Children also base their liking of unknown others on their gender schemas: They believe they will like same-sex more than other-sex children (Berndt & Heller, 1986; Martin, 1989).

Gender Schemas, Learning, and Memory.   Gender schemas are hypothesized to influence what individuals pay attention to, how they encode the information they see, and how they organize and remember the information (Bem, 1981; Markus et al., 1982; Martin & Halverson, 1981). Children's memory for gender-related information has been investigated in many studies. Schema theorists hypothesize that any information that is consistent with gender schemas should have priority in processing thereby making it easily remembered (Martin & Halverson, 1983b; Signorella & Liben, 1984). Some evidence suggests that children pay more attention to and then later remember information that is congruent with their gender schemas, such as gender-consistent stereotypes (Ruble & Stangor, 1986). Children show a same-sex bias in remembering information: They tend to remember more about same-sex peers and activities than other-sex peers and activities (Ruble & Stangor, 1986; Signorella, Bigler, & Liben, in press; Stangor & McMillan, 1992; Stangor & Ruble, 1987). In addition, children better learn details about how to use novel toys labeled as being for their own sex than for those labeled for the other sex (Bradbard, Martin, Endsley, & Halverson, 1986). Selectivity in memory has also been illustrated for gender-related scripted sequences. Boys but not girls were more accurate in sequencing pictures of own-gender than other-gender activities (Boston & Levy, 1991; Levy & Fivush, 1993). When presented with information that does not match their schemas, perceivers may not encode it at all, or they may encode it inaccurately (Liben & Signorella, 1993; Martin & Halverson, 1983b; Signorella & Liben, 1984; Stangor & Ruble, 1989). Information that is schema-relevant, whether consistent or not, also should have processing advantages (Ruble & Stangor, 1986).

Research suggests that schema effects on memory are more complex than initially hypothesized: Several contextual factors influence the kinds of information that are remembered (List et al., 1983; Nesdale & McLaughlin, 1987). Under certain conditions, such as when pressed to be accurate, when memory is assessed immediately, or when given stories with only a few characters (e.g., Kropp & Halverson, 1983), individuals are more likely to remember schema-inconsistent information.

In most developmental studies, children are given relatively vague, general instructions to remember the information they are given, and thus it is not surprising that they remember schema-consistent (e.g., Signorella, 1987) and schema-relevant information (e.g., Ruble & Stangor, 1986). Children's better memory for schema-consistent information grows stronger with age (Stangor & Ruble, 1989). Schema-inconsistent information is particularly difficult to remember when it is labeled (e.g., a woman doctor), possibly because labels make stereotypes more salient (Cann & Newbern, 1984). The effects of labeling may also interact with individual differences in gender-schematic processing: Labeling deters performance for children with salient gender schemas more than for other children (Levy, 1989).

Memory patterns may change as schemas develop. Early in development, children may be more likely to focus on information related to the schema, whereas once the schema is more fully developed, they may be able to use other processing dimensions (e.g, age or interests) as well. A promising developmental approach might be to consider phases within gender schema development similar to the approach applied to sex category constancy (SCC) (Ruble, 1994). In the early phase of *construction,* gender is highly salient and processing focuses on gender-relevant information rather than irrelevant information. In the next phase of *consolidation,* children will tend to remember consistent information rather than inconsistent. In the final phase of *integration,* individual differences in processing and gender salience should become apparent. Some support for this kind of phase model was recently reported for gender-related memory distortions (Welch-Ross & Schmidt, 1996).

Memory Distortions Associated with Schematic Processing. The active role of information processing in children's gender development is especially apparent when we consider how information can be distorted due to gender schemas. When faced with a scene that does not match their expectations, individuals often distort the information to make it consistent with gender schemas (Liben & Signorella, 1980; Martin & Halverson, 1983b). After a 1-week delay, children were three times more likely to distort the sex of the actors in the inconsistent pictures (e.g., a *girl* sawing wood was remembered as a *boy* sawing wood) than in the consistent pictures (Martin & Halverson, 1983b). A number of studies have found gender-based memory distortions in children (Cann & Newbern, 1984; Carter & Levy, 1988; Cordua et al., 1979; Signorella & Liben, 1984), although others have not (Liben & Signorella, 1980; List et al., 1984). Distortions appear to be greatest at 5–6 years of age (Welch-Ross & Schmidt, 1996). For example, when 5-, 7-, and 9-year-olds were shown commercials of a boy playing with a doll and a girl playing with a truck, 58% of the children distorted the sex of the actor in one commercial and 22% changed both actors, but older children were less likely to make these distortions than younger children (Stangor & Ruble, 1989). The consequences of information distortions are far-ranging: Faced with inconsistent information, children are unlikely to disconfirm their beliefs and may instead reaffirm them. As a consequence, it may be difficult to change schemas and they can be easily maintained with little new supportive input.

Gender-schematic processing may also lead children to have lower levels of competence in cross-gender behaviors because of reduced interest in activities associated with the other sex. If competence is limited, children may not perform cross-gender activities because they are lacking knowledge, rather than lacking interest in performing the activity (although that may also be true). Young children who were taught how to perform novel activities, some labeled as being for boys and some for girls, tended to better remember how to perform activities associated with their own sex several days later, even after being offered rewards to remember (Bradbard et al., 1986). Competence limitations may be more severe than performance ones: Children need to be taught to be competent in a behavior rather than simply being encouraged or rewarded for performing the behavior.

Gender Schemas and Behavior.   The most controversial aspect of gender schema theories is the notion that gender schemas influence behavior. Gender schemas are hypothesized to influence behavior in several ways. First, schemas provide a prescriptive standard for behavior (Bem, 1981). Second, children are motivated to match their behavior to their own gender group as a means of self-definition and to attain cognitive consistency. Third, schemas provide information about detailed plans of action (i.e., the temporal ordering, details of performing a behavior) that allow for behaviors to be enacted competently (Boston & Levy, 1991; Martin, 1991; Martin & Halverson, 1981, 1987).

In addition to the numerous studies of children's actual play behavior that show gender-typed patterns of toy choices, studies using novel objects confirm the power of gender labels to influence children's toy choices. When novel toylike objects or games are labeled as being "for girls" versus "for boys," children's play with these toys is biased such that children will play more with same-gender toys, even though these toys are not in reality gender-typed at all (Bradbard et al., 1986). Even when novel toys are extremely attractive, children show a "hot-potato" effect, meaning that they lose interest in toys once they have been given a label indicating that they are for the other sex (Martin et al., 1995).

Despite many studies showing gender effects on behavior, the exact link between cognition and behavior has yet to be established (as discussed later). Furthermore, gender schemas do not always guide behavior; otherwise no variation in behavior would be evident. A promising avenue for future investigations is to investigate more about the particular conditions and individual difference factors that influence when gender behaviors are influenced by gender schemas.

Summary.   Gender schema approaches have been heuristic in guiding researchers to examine gender issues from new angles. In particular, rather than focusing on the abundance of gendered information in the environment and assuming that this information is absorbed directly, researchers using schema theories, like those who use cognitive developmental approaches, have reversed the focus by assuming that thinking and perceiving influence the types of information cognitively available. Thus, the emphasis moves from a catalog of the environment to a catalog of the strategies individuals use. to interpret and reconstruct the environment. Environmental factors also are acknowledged in that cultural messages transmitted through all sorts of socialization agents provide the content for the schemas. Schematic approaches have been especially influential in guiding research on all varieties of gender concepts, and on the attention, memory, and inferences processes involved in applying gender concepts. Moreover, gender schema theories have provided reasonable hypotheses for how and why stereotypes are maintained so easily, even in the face of disconfirming evidence. The main limitation in the empirical analyses, to date, concerns the operationalization of schemas. There is confusion between having schemas (knowing the content of the gender schema) and having readily accessible schemas that are used frequently for information processing (Martin, 1991). Because measures vary greatly across studies (e.g., gender salience; level of knowledge), it is sometimes difficult to draw clear conclusions about what gender schemas are and how they function. Moreover, this diversity of measures contributes to some conceptual confusion in that it is sometimes difficult to identify unique predictions and mechanisms associated with gender schemas as distinct from other cognitive theories.

The Role of Identification with a Social Category

Social categorization approaches emphasize that part of gender identification that occurs at a group level (see Deaux & LaFrance, in press). According to social identity theory, for example, social categorization is the cognitive mechanism that segments, classifies, and orders the environment, and the resulting social groupings provide a system of orientation for self-reference (Tajfel & Turner, 1979). Social identity is conceived as the aspects of self-concept that derive from the social categories to which individuals believe they belong. This sense of group membership has important evaluative implications, such that ingroup members are perceived more positively and receive preferential treatment (Tajfel, 1982). Moreover, perceptions of the social status and prestige of one's own category in relation to the other affects self-evaluation. When low group prestige results in a negative social identity, individuals may engage in one of three processes to elevate feelings of self-esteem: (a) *social mobility* in which they leave or dissociate from their group, (b) *social creativity* in which they try to make the social comparison more positive by changing the in-group versus out-group comparison (e.g., by finding a new dimension), or (c) *social competition* in which they attempt to engage in direct competition with the out-group (Tajfel & Turner, 1979).

Social identity theory has provided a conceptual backdrop for studies on stereotyping, prejudice, status, and discrimination. Social identity theorists provided direct explanations of how stereotyping and prejudice can occur from a combination of cognitive "mechanics" and valued social dimensions (Tajfel, 1978). Simply categorizing people or objects into groups results in the exaggeration of group differences (Tajfel, 1982). By extension, then, the social groupings in everyday life likely lead to stereotyping of members of these groups. Moreover, even when placed into social groups on the basis of minimal criteria, participants consistently discriminate in favor of other members in their own groups, suggesting that trivial information takes on importance when it constitutes the only known information about a group (Moghaddam & Stringer, 1986; Tajfel, 1982).

Because gender is likely to be one of the earliest learned and most salient social categories available, children's identification of themselves as a member of the group of males or females seems likely to have a pronounced impact on their self-concepts, preferences, and behaviors (Duveen & Lloyd, 1986). A few studies have shown how children's gender groups act similarly to other social groups in providing a basis for biases. For example, Powlishta (1995b) showed clear evidence of own-sex favoritism among 8- to 10-year-olds. The children rated the characteristics of same-sex unfamiliar boys and girls more positively and liked them better than other-sex targets. Moreover, the extent to which children showed evidence of own-sex favoritism was associated with perceiving targets in stereotypic terms and with emphasizing similarities between same-sex others and the self, suggesting further the potential impact of biased perceptions associated with gender-based categorization. In another study, when gender groups were made salient (by informing children that they would be rating both girls and boys), 10- to 12-year-old children

were more likely to accentuate between-group differences and within-group similarities than when groups were not salient (Doise, Deschamps, & Meyer, 1978).

Since individuals experience membership in more than one group, it is interesting to consider how multiple group memberships interact in social identity. Deschamps and Doise (1978) described situations in which group memberships are embedded hierarchically (I am human, I am a female), compared with crossed-group memberships involving two categories that overlap somewhat (I am female, I am young). Membership in crossed groups is effective in minimizing but not eliminating group-based biases (Deschamps & Doise, 1978). Furthermore, crossed-category effects may explain the effectiveness of teaching children multiple classification strategies for reducing racial and gender prejudice (Bigler & Liben, 1992).

Social identity theory has also been useful for understanding the behavior of high- and low-status members. Specifically, because the high-status group would be expected to prefer to maintain their advantage, findings that boys emphasize stereotypic differences more than do girls, as reported earlier, is consistent with the idea of a status differential favoring males (Lewin & Tragos, 1987). Such a status differential may also affect girls' and boys' evaluations of gender stereotypes. Alfieri and Ruble (1997) found that adolescent girls were able to protect self-esteem potentially threatened by being a member of the lower status group by engaging more than boys in "social creativity" responding, in this case operationalized as evaluating positive female traits more highly than other traits. Similarly, the greater rigidity observed in boys' gender behavior may be traced to status inequalities between men and women (Archer, 1992). Several findings support this suggestion. Feinman (1984) found that cross-gender behavior received greater disapproval when it was performed by a boy than a girl. Furthermore, cross-cultural comparisons show that in the societies with the greatest status inequalities, males showed greater avoidance of females or feminine behavior (Whiting & Edwards, 1988).

Integration and Conclusions

The various cognitive perspectives share a common assumption that there are cognitive underpinnings to preferences and behavior in that cognitions provide standards for behavior and structure for organizing and interpreting information. Yet, these various theories are generally thought to emphasize different cognitive elements and mechanisms. The cognitive-developmental approach emphasizes the importance of a stable understanding of one's sex; the schema approach emphasizes the importance of a network of gender-related mental representations; and the social category approach emphasizes the importance of identification with males or females as a social group. Such distinctions are often fuzzy, however, and considerable overlap exists. For example, all three theoretical approaches refer to the importance of basic categorization as a girl or boy.

A fundamental issue for cognitive approaches is delineating the mechanisms underlying cognitive effects, but these are rarely assessed or manipulated directly. The three approaches suggest different mechanisms for understanding the relation between evaluation and cognitions. Cognitive-developmental approaches refer to motivational processes (valuing the self and mastery motivation) that are elicited once children understand that their sex is unchanging; schema approaches refer to cognitive consistency processes implying that evaluation follows from categorization; and social category approaches refer to self-evaluative processes—the role of identification with same-sex group members in maintaining a positive self-concept. A better understanding of the mechanisms underlying cognitive effects would help clarify each theoretical position.

Cognitive approaches have all been the target of arguments that the role of cognition has been overstated, and that the various aspects of gender typing are only loosely interconnected. Have cognitive theorists gone too far in asserting the role of cognitions on children's behavior? The controversy about the role of cognition has been addressed in several papers (Downs & Langlois, 1988; Hort, Leinbach, & Fagot, 1991; Huston, 1985; Martin, 1993). Two lines of evidence are used to argue against the cognitive underpinning notion. The first is the age of onset of gender stereotype knowledge in relation to early gender differentiation. As described in detail earlier, children show gender-differentiated play behavior and segregation into same-sex groups soon after their second birthdays, but knowledge of gender stereotypes does not seem to emerge clearly until about six months later (Weinraub et al., 1984).

Before concluding that gender cognitions do not underlie early gender-typed behavior, researchers must consider that the age argument refers to only one type of gender knowledge—gender stereotype knowledge—while ignoring types of gender knowledge, such as category labeling, that children do have at this early age. Moreover, in the past 10 years, more effective methods of assessing gender

knowledge have been developed for use with toddlers and infants that are likely to renew interest in the age issue. By 9 to 12 months, infants can distinguish the faces of males and females if the gender cues are strong (Leinbach & Fagot, 1993), which could allow them to form rudimentary links between appearance and behaviors. Simply having basic discrimination abilities may not be sufficient for developing gender knowledge bases, and the ability to correlate features with gender categories may only occur later in development. However, studies also suggest that by one year of age, infants have the ability to make some complex connections, in that they can link, for example, male faces with deep-pitched masculine voices (Poulin-Dubois et al., 1994). Furthermore, toddlers show evidence of using gender schemas. Bauer (1993) used an elicited imitation task to investigate whether toddlers would imitate schema-consistent action sequences more than schema-inconsistent sequences. Even at 25 months of age, boys were more likely to imitate a masculine sequence (e.g., shaving a teddy bear) than a feminine one (e.g., diapering a teddy bear), suggesting they have differential memory for gender-typed sequences, though girls did not show a preference for imitating own-gender activities.

The recent infant and toddler studies suggest that children may have rudimentary gender concepts well before they show gender-typed behavior and preferences. However, simply demonstrating earlier onset for cognitions does not confirm that these cognitions motivate the behavior. Creative longitudinal analyses are needed to determine whether or not cognitions develop separately from behavioral patterns. Because gender categories are understood by most children by age 3 and many other measures of gender differentiation reach ceiling within the next few years, correlational strategies may be inadequate to uncover connections that exist. Nonetheless, a careful analysis of the temporal ordering of various aspects of gender differentiation has the potential of providing useful theoretical and practical information about gender development. The challenge for the future is examining which, if any, of these earlier cognitions influence early gender-related preferences and behaviors, and whether they do so by means of motivational, consistency, evaluative, or some other process.

The second line of evidence that could undermine the idea of cognitive underpinning comes from studies that fail to map individual differences in knowledge to differences in gender-typed preferences or behavior, usually conducted with children in preschool or middle school (Huston, 1985; Ruble & Stangor, 1986, for reviews). Across a number of studies, the relation between stereotype knowledge and behavior or preferences tends to be weak (e.g., Hort et al., 1991; Weinraub et al., 1984), or to occur for boys but not girls (e.g., Coker, 1984; Hort et al., 1991). In a large-scale study of 5- to 12-year-olds, Serbin et al. (1993) found two distinct aspects of gender-typing—the cognitive aspect (stereotype knowledge and flexibility) and the affective aspect (peer and activity preferences)—developed in different patterns, were not strongly related to one another, and were influenced by different factors in the child's environment. In a longitudinal study of children from 4 to 10 years old, Trautner (1992) found little relation among various components of gender typing, even within preferences (e.g., toy preferences and occupational preferences).

Just as in the age of onset argument, the focus has been on only one type of knowledge—gender stereotype knowledge. And, it may be premature to conclude that gender stereotype knowledge does not relate at all to behavior for several reasons. First, finding individual differences may be precluded because most measures show very high levels of stereotype knowledge after early childhood. Second, because recent research suggests that stereotype knowledge in older children has not yet been tapped adequately, studies using more sophisticated knowledge measures may show relations that were not shown with more basic methods (Martin, 1991).

Although one type of gender knowledge, gender stereotypes, does not relate well to individual differences in behavior, another type does. Gender labeling, children's understanding of the categories of males and females, often correlates with other aspects of children's behavior and preferences. Many cognitive theorists believe that once children can reliably identify females and males (between 2 and 3 years of age), labels should enhance learning by facilitating memory organization (Fagot & Leinbach, 1989), and by providing opportunities to directly observe and learn about the behaviors of males and females (Martin, 1993). All three cognitive theories suggest that the child's knowledge of their own membership in a gender group provides motivation for gender-typed behavior and preferences.

Evidence reviewed earlier supports the importance of gender labeling. Children who can label the sexes show stronger same-sex peer preferences (Fagot, 1985b), adopt gender-typed behaviors (Fagot & Leinbach, 1989; Fagot, Leinbach, & O'Boyle, 1992), and know more about gender stereotypes (Martin & Little, 1990) than those who do not. Longitudinal studies confirm these patterns: Children who

are aware of gender labels at an early age are more aware of gender stereotypes by age 4 than those children who learn labels later (Fagot & Leinbach, 1989). Higher levels of gender understanding relates to in-group positivity biases, modeling, and preferences under conditions of conflict. The challenge for future research will be to examine the mechanisms underlying such links and the possibility that some mechanisms, such as cognitive consistency, are important at some ages or for some relations; whereas other mechanisms, such as identification at a group level, are important at other ages or for other relations.

Many of the studies reviewed in this section conclude that cognitions concerning gender stereotype knowledge (as well as the earlier sections on gender consistency) are only weakly related to certain aspects of gender development thereby reaffirming the multidimensionality of gender typing. Yet, some types of gender knowledge, especially gender labeling, appear to be strongly tied to many aspects of gender development. The relation between gender cognitions and behavior is complicated by the many types of cognitions, measurement problems, ceiling effects in knowledge, and by the possibility that relations may change with age and across situations (Aubry, Ruble, & Silverman, 1997). The final story on cognition and gender differentiation is far from complete.

An Integration of Perspectives

The three broad approaches to the understanding of gender typing—biological, socialization, and cognitive—each focus on specific topics of interest and on concerns that arise from issues within each approach. For biological researchers, most of the attention has been directed toward understanding the role of hormones on brain structure and on behavior, with much less attention being paid to how the environment influences brain structure or hormone levels, or how congenital events influence the development of gender-typed behaviors. For psychologically oriented researchers, two issues have been at the forefront because they delineate the most fundamental differences between the cognitive and social learning approaches. The first issue concerns very early gender typing. Which comes first, learning about the consequences of behavior and then deriving from patterns of rewards which gender category one belongs to, or does understanding the gender category precede other forms of gender typing? The second issue is less well defined but underlies the philosophical foundation of the theories. The issue is which factors ultimately determine self-concept: Is it one's reinforcement history or a desire to adhere to a gendered cognitive structure? Because of this intense focus on a few issues, many other interesting aspects of each theory have been relatively neglected, and much of the developmental action has been ignored except within the preschool years.

To understand gender typing, we need to listen to the messages coming from researchers within each of the major approaches, and devise ways to think about how the three approaches can be integrated in theoretically meaningful ways. Despite Huston's (1983) plea for biologically oriented and psychologically oriented researchers to combine their efforts, little movement has been made in that direction. Neither social learning, cognitive developmental, or schema approaches have approached the consideration of biological influences on gender-role development in systematic ways. Nonetheless, research findings are accumulating about the wide range of influences on particular gendered behaviors, suggesting several promising avenues for future research using multiple approaches, such as the development of sexual orientation and gender identity.

One topic that is particularly promising for integrating and synthesizing multiple approaches to gender development is sex segregation. Sex segregation is a powerful developmental phenomenon that increases with age and potentially serves as a mechanism for socializing children into the ways of their own gender group. Several hypotheses have been proposed to account for sex segregation (Maccoby, 1988, 1990a). One hypothesis concerns rough-and-tumble play (Maccoby, 1990a), which likely has a biological component. Boys engage in and seem to enjoy bouts of rough-and-tumble play more than do girls (DiPietro, 1981), and these active and boisterous styles may allow for the development of competition and dominance in boys' groups. Similar patterns of sex differences in rough-and-tumble play have been found in many, but not all, species of mammals (Meaney et al., 1985). Sex differences in regulating arousal may partly explain these patterns (Fabes, 1994), and temperament differences may also influence the likelihood of playing with same-sex others (Fabes, Shepard, Guthrie, & Martin, in press). Because of these differences, boys may find rough-and-tumble play more entertaining, whereas it may be too stimulating for many girls. Similarly, in other mammals, it has been hypothesized that females withdraw from rough play because they react differently than males do to tactile stimulation associated with this form of play, suggesting another biological avenue to influence sex segregation (Meaney et al., 1985).

Social factors are also important. Sex segregation may relate to behavioral compatibility, meaning that children prefer to play with others who share the same interests and/or share the same play styles. However, children often play in same-sex groups regardless of the focal activity, suggesting that sex segregation involves more than simply shared interests (Maccoby, 1987). The initiation of sex segregation may be related to compatibility in play styles (Moller & Serbin, 1996). Girls and boys show higher levels of social interaction in same-sex versus mixed-sex groups, suggesting that play with same-sex others might be more stimulating, more engaging, and more interesting than within mixed-sex groups (Serbin et al., 1993).

Another promising social hypothesis concerns the styles of influence that girls and boys use in play groups. Between the ages of 3 to 5 years, children increase their tendencies to influence their peers, but boys and girls begin to adopt different strategies of influence; girls use polite suggestions and boys use direct commands. However, girls' methods also become less effective with boys (Serbin, Sprafkin, Elman, & Doyle, 1984), thereby possibly making interactions with them less pleasant (Maccoby, 1990a).

Finally, children's understanding and expectations about their own sex may also influence sex segregation (Maccoby, 1990a; Martin, 1994). Knowledge about male and female categories co-occurs with or precedes the emergence of sex-segregated play groups and may affect the motivation to affiliate with same-sex children. In addition, simply expecting same-sex children to share interests may increase the likelihood of sex segregation. With age, increasing knowledge about differences in play styles and the effectiveness of different strategies in boys' and girls' groups may be used to make decisions about whether to play with unfamiliar play partners. Moreover, as children notice sex segregation and begin to believe that others are likely to approve of it, their tendencies to play with others of the same sex may increase (Martin, 1994).

Sex segregation provides an illustration of the ways that biological factors, socialization agents, and cognitive influences can be used to describe more fully the development and changes in an aspect of gender differentiation. In addition to considering these hypotheses separately, it would also be useful to speculate about the ways cognitive, social, and biological factors may interact to explain sex segregation, for example, considering that physiological responsiveness may confirm a child's initial cognitive expectations about play with children of the other sex. Using multidisciplinary teams, multiple perspectives, and broader conceptualizations of underlying mechanisms and processes should provide the potential for making significant strides in understanding the complexities of gender differentiation.

CONCLUSION

One of the difficulties in compiling research on gender is that it cuts across areas and is relevant to virtually every topic, ranging from neurological sex differences to children's understanding of the constancy of categorical sex over situations. Controversies frequently arise that do not occur with regularity in many other areas, such as the questioning of the research enterprise itself, confusion about terms for major constructs, and the political implications of the findings. Despite, or perhaps because of the controversies, the study of gender attracts scientists from many disciplines, each bringing to the enterprise different interests and strategies. The pluralism of views provides many insights into the diverse issues covered in gender studies.

Several broad themes have been apparent in the literature reviewed for this chapter. First, interest in all sorts of biological factors has marked the literature of the past 10 years. In accord with this interest are suggestions that biological factors may play a more prominent role in behavior, thinking, and gender identity than has been previously considered. Second, social and cognitive theories have moved more closely together but continue to disagree about some issues, and these theoretical debates continue to drive a surprising amount of gender-typing research. Third, developmental researchers took Huston's (1983) admonitions in the preceding edition of the *Handbook* chapter to heart: They have been more likely to include multiple components of gender typing in studies, are less prone to broadly inferring gender typing from one measure, and recognize the distinctions among content domains and constructs. Fourth, more researchers have focused on understanding the wide range of processes underlying gender typing, ranging from studies of attention and memory, to self-evaluation in relation to one's groups. Fifth, new methods have played an important role in the research that has been undertaken in the past 15 years. Meta-analysis has allowed for systematic compilations of research findings in meaningful ways across studies, thereby sparking and contributing to the interest in the study of sex differences. More sophisticated testing procedures have been adopted to allow researchers to begin to understand what infants and young children know about gender.

In 1983, Huston concluded that the field moves too quickly to attempt to predict the future with any hope of accuracy. Today, we view the field in much the same way—it is not a safe area for prognostication. Nonetheless, many new and intriguing ideas are emerging within the field that may spark interest and lead researchers to think about gender in novel and interesting ways. There is renewed interest in process and change in gender development. Instead of focusing on static concepts, many researchers have begun to consider developmental changes in the mechanisms that produce variability and allow for adaptive changes. Social learning theorists have concentrated their efforts on the cognitive mechanisms underlying observational learning (Bandura, 1986). Cognitive theorists have considered how shifts from early gender concepts to more consolidated ones influence the information individuals process and remember (Ruble, 1994), and some of the situations that modify gender-related responding (Martin, 1991). With adults, researchers have begun to examine the changing nature of one's gendered "personal identities" in relation to interactional partners (Ashmore, 1990). Gender researchers may want to consider exploring in even more depth the issue of variability because it is considered crucial in understanding many aspects of development.

The idea that gender is constructed in a social context has many interesting possibilities. Most often, it has been taken to mean that we must investigate how we see others in gendered ways, using cues associated with gender. The concept can be taken even further, however, to suggest that we need to examine how individuals construct their own multifaceted gender cues, and how they believe these cues work in their social interactions. Do individuals strive for a certain balance in their gender cues, so as to present a particular type of image to others? A woman who is assertive and dominant may choose to dress in a feminine way to "offset" perceptions of masculinity. Appearance, clothing, adornment, and mannerisms all become more important to study since visible cues are often used to "read" and "construct" gender.

Some areas, such as the study of prejudice and discrimination, have been more popular in the adult literature than in the child literature. The study of the affective side of gender deserves more attention by developmental researchers. Steps in this direction have been taken in considering the role of attitudes on behavior and thought (e.g., Bigler & Liben, 1992), and in exploring children's values about gender and their implications for prejudice (e.g., Lutz & Ruble, 1995). The application of social identity theories may be helpful for directing this line of research.

Questions about mental health and self-esteem require more research efforts, as well. In the 1970s, interest was focused on the relation between mental health and androgyny. A more detailed examination of these topics is needed that takes seriously the idea of the multidimensionality of gender. Which particular domains of gender influence positive self-regard? Why are preadolescent girls more likely to show declines in self-esteem than boys? Which factors related to gender may be risk versus buffering factors?

Gender in relationships is an idea that invokes a new and interesting view of both individual masculinity and femininity, as well as increased focus on the study of all sorts of relationships. Peers' contributions to socialization have been more at the forefront of research because we now suspect that sex segregation may well provide the impetus for many of the sex differences we find in adults (Maccoby, 1990a). The role of parents in socialization continues to be of interest, but perhaps with some different emphases on subtle forms of socialization, such as channeling of interests by parental modification of the environment. Research has suggested that children with rigid cross-gender roles often grow up to be maladjusted. Does this mean that parents should not encourage cross-gender interests for fear of inducing psychological problems in their children? Also, we know surprisingly little about the effects of children having androgynous interests.

In conclusion, the study of gender is a monumental undertaking, shared by individuals from many fields. Constantinople (1979) used the metaphor about four blind men studying an elephant to describe how gender researchers have focused on individual parts of the elephant, with each one assuming that the animal was best described by the part they were studying. No one recognized the whole animal. Gender researchers must continue to be careful about building global concepts based on partial information. However, we might argue that now we have some sense of the size of the animal, its capacities, and its general framework. The picture is far from complete but the process of identification has certainly continued to be intriguing.

ACKNOWLEDGMENTS

This chapter is dedicated to our mothers, Marjorie W. Nelesen and, in loving memory, Carolyn I. Martin, and to Eleanor E. Maccoby, esteemed mentor, teacher, role model, and friend. The final version has benefited enormously from her detailed and thoughtful suggestions for which we are extremely grateful. We are also grateful to Stephanie Aubry, Stephanie Evans, Faith Greulich, Catharine Lennon, Melanie Smith, and Connie Yeung for assistance in gathering materials and organizing references, and especially to Joel Szkrybalo for help with checking citations and with editing. We are also grateful to Alice Eagly, Jananne Khouri, Campbell Leaper, Stacey Lutz, Hans Trautner, and Ken Zucker for a number of helpful suggestions.

REFERENCES

Aboud, F. E., & Ruble, D. N. (1987). Identity constancy in children: Developmental processes and implications. In T. Honess & K. Yardley (Eds.), *Self and identity: Perspectives across the lifespan* (pp. 95–107). London: Routledge & Kegan Paul.

Adler, P. A., Kless, S. J., & Adler, P. (1992). Socialization to gender roles: Popularity among elementary school boys and girls. *Sociology of Education, 65,* 169–187.

Albert, A. A., & Porter, J. R. (1983). Age patterns in the development of children's gender-role stereotypes. *Sex Roles, 9*(1), 59–67.

Alessandri, S. M., & Lewis, M. (1993). Parental evaluation and its relation to shame and pride in young children. *Sex Roles, 29*(5/6), 335–343.

Alexander, G. M., & Hines, M. (1994). Gender labels and play styles: Their relative contribution to children's selection of playmates. *Child Development, 65,* 869–879.

Alfieri, T. J., & Ruble, D. N. (1997). *Young adolescents gender stereotypes: Protecting threats to self-esteem with a social identity.* Manuscript submitted for publication.

Alfieri, T. J., Ruble, D. N., & Higgins, E. T. (1996). Gender stereotypes during adolescence: Developmental changes and the transition to Junior High School. *Developmental Psychology, 32,* 1129–1137.

Allan, K., & Coltrane, S. (1996). Gender displaying television commercials: A comparative study of television commercials in the 1950s and 1980s. *Sex Roles, 35,* 185–203.

American Association of University Women. (1992). *How schools shortchange girls.* Washington, DC: AAUW Educational Foundation.

Amstey, F. H., & Whitbourne, S. K. (1988). Work and motherhood: Transition to parenthood and women's employment. *Journal of Genetic Psychology, 149,* 111–118.

Anastasi, A. (1958). Heredity, environment, and the question, "How?" *Psychological Review, 65,* 197–208.

Angold, A., & Rutter, M. (1992). Effects of age and pubertal status on depression in a large clinical sample. *Development and Psychopathology, 4,* 5–28.

Antill, J. K. (1987). Parents' beliefs and values about sex roles, sex differences, and sexuality: Their sources and implications. In P. Shaver & C. Hendrick (Eds.), *Review of personality and social psychology: Sex and gender* (Vol. 7, pp. 294–328). Newbury Park, CA: Sage.

Antill, J. K., Cotton, S., Russell, G., & Goodnow, J. J. (1996). Measures of children's sex-typing in middle childhood: II. *Australian Journal of Psychology, 48,* 35–44.

Antill, J. K., Russell, G., Goodnow, J. J., & Cotton, S. (1993). Measures of children's sex-typing in middle childhood. *Australian Journal of Psychology, 45*(1), 25–33.

Archer, J. (1984). Children's attitudes toward sex-role division in adult occupational roles. *Sex Roles, 10*(1/2), 1–10.

Archer, J. (1992). Childhood gender roles: Social context and organization. In H. McGurk (Ed.), *Childhood social development: Contemporary perspectives* (pp. 31–61). Hove, England: Erlbaum.

Archer, J., & Macrae, M. (1991). Gender-perceptions of school subjects among 10–11-year-olds. *British Journal of Educational Psychology, 61,* 99–103.

Arnold, A. P., & Breedlove, S. M. (1985). Organizational and activational effects of sex steroids on brain and behavior: A reanalysis. *Hormones and Behavior, 19,* 469–498.

Arnold, A. P., & Gorski, R. A. (1984). Gonadal steroid induction of structural sex differences in the central nervous system. *Annual Review of Neuroscience, 7,* 413–442.

Ashmore, R. D. (1990). Sex, gender and the individual. In L. A. Pervin (Ed.), *Handbook of personality: Theory and research* (pp. 486–526). New York: Guilford Press.

Aubry, S., Ruble, D. N., & Silverman, L. (1997). The role of gender knowledge in children's gender-typed preferences. In C. Tamis-LeMonda & L. Balter (Eds.), *Child psychology: A handbook of contemporary issues.* New York: Garland.

Bailey, J. M., & Zucker, K. J. (1995). Childhood sex-typed behavior and sexual orientation: A conceptual analysis and quantitative review. *Developmental Psychology, 31*(1), 43–55.

Bandura, A. (1977). *Social learning theory.* Englewood Cliffs, NJ: Prentice-Hall.

Bandura, A. (1986). *Social foundations of thought and action: A social cognitive theory.* Englewood Cliffs, NJ: Prentice-Hall.

Barak, A., Feldman, S., & Noy, A. (1991). Traditionality of children's interests as related to their parents' gender stereotypes and traditionality of occupations. *Sex Roles, 24,* 511–524.

Baruch, G. K., & Barnett, R. C. (1986). Fathers' participation in family work and children's sex role attitudes. *Child Development, 57,* 1210–1223.

Bauer, P. J. (1993). Memory for gender-consistent and gender-inconsistent event sequences by twenty-five-month-old children. *Child Development, 64,* 285–297.

Baumeister, R. F. (1988). Should we stop studying sex differences altogether? *American Psychologist, 43,* 1092–1095.

Beal, C. R., & Lockhart, M. E. (1989). The effect of proper name and appearance changes on children's reasoning about gender constancy. *International Journal of Behavioral Development, 12,* 195–205.

Becker, B. J. (1986). Influence again: An examination of reviews and studies of gender differences in social influence. In J. S. Hyde & M. C. Linn (Eds.), *The psychology of gender: Advances through meta-analysis* (pp. 178–209). Baltimore: Johns Hopkins University Press.

Beere, C. A. (1990). *Gender roles: A handbook of tests and measures.* San Francisco: Jossey-Bass.

Belenky, M. F., Clinchy, B. M., Goldberger, N. R., & Tarule, J. M. (1986). *Women's ways of knowing: The development of self, voice, and mind.* New York: Basic Books.

Bell, A. P., & Weinberg, M. S. (1978). *Homosexualities: A study of diversity among men and women.* New York: Simon & Schuster.

Bem, D. J. (1996). Exotic becomes erotic: A developmental theory of sexual orientation. *Psychological Review, 103,* 320–335.

Bem, S. L. (1974). The measurement of psychological androgyny. *Journal of Consulting and Clinical Psychology, 42,* 155–162.

Bem, S. L. (1981). Gender schema theory: A cognitive account of sex typing. *Psychological Review, 88,* 354–364.

Bem, S. L. (1989). Genital knowledge and gender constancy in preschool children. *Child Development, 60,* 649–662.

Bem, S. L. (1993). *The lenses of gender: Transforming the debate on sexual inequality.* New Haven, CT: Yale University Press.

Bem, S. L. (1995). Dismantling gender polarization and compulsory heterosexuality: Should we turn the volume down or up? *Journal of Sex Research, 32,* 329–334.

Benbow, C. P., & Stanley, J. C. (1980). Sex differences in mathematics ability: Fact or artifact? *Science, 210,* 1262–1264.

Benenson, J. F., Apostoleris, N. H., & Parnass, J. (1997). Age and sex differences in dyadic and group interaction. *Developmental Psychology, 33,* 538–543.

Berenbaum, S. A., & Hines, M. (1992). Early androgens are related to childhood sex-typed toy preferences. *Psychological Science, 3,* 203–206.

Berenbaum, S. A., & Snyder, E. (1995). Early hormonal influences on childhood sex-typed activity and playmate preferences: Implications for the development of sexual orientation. *Developmental Psychology, 31,* 31–42.

Berndt, T. J., & Heller, K. A. (1986). Gender stereotypes and social inferences: A developmental study. *Journal of Personality and Social Psychology, 50,* 889–898.

Berscheid, E. (1993). Forward. In A. E. Beall & R. J. Sternberg (Eds.), *The psychology of gender* (pp. i-xvii). New York: Guilford Press.

Best, D. L., & Williams, J. E. (1993). A cross-cultural viewpoint. In A. E. Beall & R. J. Sternberg (Eds.), *The psychology of gender* (pp. 215–248). New York: Guilford Press.

Best, D. L., Williams, J. E., Cloud, J. M., Davis, S. W., Robertson, L. S., Edwards, J. R., Giles, H., & Fowles, J. (1977). The development of sex-trait stereotypes. *Child Development, 48,* 1375–1384.

Bettencourt, B. A., & Miller, N. (1996). Gender differences in aggression as a function of provocation: A meta-analysis. *Psychological Bulletin, 119,* 422–447.

Biernat, M. (1991a). A multicomponent, developmental analysis of sex typing. *Sex Roles, 24,* 567–586.

Biernat, M. (1991b). Gender stereotypes and the relationship between masculinity and femininity: A developmental analysis. *Journal of Personality and Social Psychology, 61,* 351–365.

Bigler, R. S. (1995). The role of classification skill in moderating environmental influences on children's gender stereotyping: A study of the functional use of gender in the classroom. *Child Development, 66*(4), 1072–1087.

Bigler, R. S. (1997). Conceptual and methodological issues in the measurement of children's sex typing. *Psychology of Women Quarterly, 21,* 53–69.

Bigler, R. S., & Liben, L. S. (1990). The role of attitudes and interventions in gender-schematic processing. *Child Development, 61,* 1440–1452.

Bigler, R. S., & Liben, L. S. (1992). Cognitive mechanisms in children's gender stereotyping: Theoretical and educational implications of a cognitive-based intervention. *Child Development, 63,* 1351–1363.

Biringen, Z., Robinson, J. L., & Emde, R. N. (1994). Maternal sensitivity in the second year: Gender based relations in the dyadic balance of control. *American Journal of Orthopsychiatry, 64*(1), 78–90.

Birnbaum, D. W., & Croll, W. L. (1984). The etiology of children's stereotypes about sex differences in emotionality. *Sex Roles, 10*(9/10), 677–691.

Blackwood, E. (1984). Sexuality and gender in certain native American tribes: The case of cross-gender females. *Signs, 10,* 27–42.

Blair, S. L. (1992). The sex-typing of children's household labor: Parental influences on daughters' and sons' housework. *Youth and Society, 24*(2), 178–203.

Blakemore, J. E., LaRue, A. A., & Olejnik, A. B. (1979). Sex appropriate toy preference and the ability to conceptualize toys as sex-role related. *Developmental Psychology, 15,* 339–340.

Bleier, R. (1984). *Science and gender.* New York: Pergamon Press.

Bleier, R. (1988). The plasticity of the human brain and human potential. *Behavioral and Brain Science, 11,* 184–185.

Bloch, M. N. (1987). The development of sex differences in young children's activities at home: The effect of social context. *Sex Roles, 16,* 279–301.

Block, J. H. (1983). Differential premises arising from differential socialization of sexes: Some conjectures. *Child Development, 54,* 1335–1354.

Boldizar, J. P. (1991). Assessing sex typing and androgyny in children: The children's sex role inventory. *Developmental Psychology, 27,* 505–515.

Boston, M. B., & Levy, G. D. (1991). Changes and differences in preschoolers' understanding of gender scripts. *Cognitive Development, 6,* 412–417.

Bradbard, M. R., Martin, C. L., Endsley, R. C., & Halverson, C. F. (1986). Influence of sex stereotypes on children's exploration and memory: A competence versus performance distinction. *Developmental Psychology, 22,* 481–486.

Bradley, B. S., & Gobbart, S. K. (1989). Determinants of gender-typed play in toddlers. *Journal of Genetic Psychology, 150*(4), 453–455.

Bradley, S. J., & Zucker, K. J. (1990). Gender identity disorder and psychosexual problems in children and adolescents. *Canadian Journal of Psychiatry, 35,* 477–486.

Breedlove, S. M. (1994). Sexual differentiation of the human nervous system. *Annual Review of Psychology, 45,* 389–418.

Brooks-Gunn, J., Petersen, A. C., & Compas, B. E. (1995). Physiological processes and the development of childhood and adolescence depression. In I. M. Goodyer (Ed.), *The depressed child and adolescent: Developmental and clinical perspectives* (pp. 91–109). New York: Cambridge University Press.

Brooks-Gunn, J., & Ruble, D. N. (1983). The experience of menarche from a developmental perspective. In J. Brooks-Gunn & A. C. Petersen (Eds.), *Girls at puberty: Biological and psychosocial perspectives* (pp. 155–178). New York: Plenum Press.

Broverman, I. K., Vogel, S. R., Broverman, D. M., Clarkson, F. E., & Rosenkrantz, P. S. (1972). Sex-role stereotypes: A current appraisal. *Journal of Social Issues, 28,* 59–78.

Brown, D. G. (1956). *The IT scale for children.* Missoula, MT: Psychological Testing Specialists.

Bryan, J. W., & Luria, Z. (1978). Sex-role learning: A test of the selective attention hypothesis. *Child Development, 49,* 13–23.

Bryden, M. P. (1988). Does laterality make any difference? Thoughts on the relation between cerebral asymmetry and reading. In D. L. Molfese & S. J. Segalowitz (Eds.), *Brain lateralization in children: Developmental implications* (pp. 509–525). New York: Guilford Press.

Buchanan, C. M., Eccles, J. S., & Becker, J. B. (1992). Are adolescents the victims of raging hormones: Evidence for activational effects of hormones on moods and behaviors at adolescence. *Psychological Bulletin, 111*(1), 62–107.

Bukowski, W. M., Gauze, C., Hoza, B., & Newcombe, A. F. (1993). Differences and consistency between same-sex and other-sex peer relationships during early adolescence. *Developmental Psychology, 29*, 255–263.

Burnham, D. K., & Harris, M. B. (1992). Effects of real gender and labeled gender on adults' perceptions of infants. *Journal of Genetic Psychology, 153*(2), 165–183.

Burns, A., & Homel, R. (1986). Sex role satisfaction among Australian children: Same sex, age, and cultural group comparisons. *Psychology of Women Quarterly, 10*, 285–296.

Buss, D. M. (1995). Psychological sex differences: Origins through sexual selection. *American Psychologist, 3*, 164–168.

Bussey, K. (1983). A social-cognitive appraisal of sex-role development. *Australian Journal of Psychology, 35*, 135–143.

Bussey, K., & Bandura, A. (1984). Influence of gender constancy and social power on sex-linked modeling. *Journal of Personality and Social Psychology, 47*, 1292–1302.

Bussey, K., & Bandura, A. (1992). Self-regulatory mechanisms governing gender development. *Child Development, 63*, 1236–1250.

Bussey, K., & Perry, D. G. (1982). Same-sex imitation: The avoidance of cross-sex models or the acceptance of same-sex models? *Sex Roles, 8*, 773–785.

Butcher, J. E. (1989). Adolescent girls' sex role development: Relationship with sports participation, self-esteem, and age at menarche. *Sex Roles, 20*, 575–593.

Byrnes, J. P., & Takahira, S. (1993). Explaining gender differences on SAT-math items. *Developmental Psychology, 29*, 805–810.

Caldera, Y. M., Huston, A. C., & O'Brien, M. (1989). Social interactions and play patterns of parents and toddlers with feminine, masculine, and neutral toys. *Child Development, 60*, 70–76.

Calvert, S. L., & Huston, A. C. (1987). Television and children's gender schemata. In L. S. Liben & M. L. Signorella (Eds.), *Children's gender schemata* (pp. 75–88). San Francisco: Jossey-Bass.

Cann, A., & Newbern, S. R. (1984). Sex stereotype effects in children's picture recognition. *Child Development, 55*, 1085–1090.

Cann, A., & Palmer, S. (1986). Children's assumptions about the generalizability of sex-typed abilities. *Sex Roles, 15*, 551–558.

Canter, R. J., & Ageton, S. S. (1984). The epidemiology of adolescent sex-role attitudes. *Sex Roles, 11*, 657–767.

Carpenter, C. J., Huston, A. C., & Holt, W. (1986). Modification of preschool sex-typed behaviors by participation in adult-structured activities. *Sex Roles, 14*, 603–615.

Carter, D. B. (1987). The roles of peers in sex role socialization. In D. B. Carter (Ed.), *Current conceptions of sex roles and sex typing: Theory and research* (pp. 101–121). New York: Praeger.

Carter, D. B., & Levy, G. D. (1988). Cognitive aspects of children's early sex-role development: The influence of gender schemas on preschoolers memories and preferences for sex-typed toys and activities. *Child Development, 59*, 782–793.

Carter, D. B., & McCloskey, L. A. (1984). Peers and the maintenance of sex-typed behavior: The development of children's conceptions of cross-gender behavior in their peers. *Social Cognition, 2*, 294–314.

Carter, D. B., & Patterson, C. J. (1982). Sex-roles as social conventions: The development of children's conceptions of sex-role stereotypes. *Developmental Psychology, 18*, 812–824.

Cate, R., & Sugawara, A. I. (1986). Sex role orientation and dimensions of self-esteem among middle adolescents. *Sex Roles, 15*, 145–158.

Chodorow, N. (1978). *The reproduction of mothering: Psychoanalysis and the sociology of gender*. Berkeley: University of California Press.

Coe, C. L., Hayashi, K. T., & Levine, S. (1988). Hormones and behavior at puberty: Activation or concatenation. In M. R. Gunnar & W. A. Collins (Eds.), *Minnesota Symposium on Child Psychology: Vol. 21. Development during the transition to adolescence* (pp. 17–41). Hillsdale, NJ: Erlbaum.

Cohen, J. (1977). *Statistical power analysis for the behavior sciences* (2nd ed.). New York: Academic Press.

Coker, D. R. (1984). The relationships among gender concepts and cognitive maturity in preschool children. *Sex Roles, 10*, 19–31.

Colangelo, N., Rosenthal, D. M., & Dettmann, D. F. (1984). Maternal employment and job satisfaction and their relationship to children's perceptions and behaviors. *Sex Roles, 10*, 691–700.

Cole, D., & La Voie, J. C. (1985). Fantasy play and related cognitive development in 2- to 6-year-olds. *Developmental Psychology, 21*, 233–240.

Collaer, M. L., & Hines, M. (1995). Human behavioral sex differences: A role for gonadal hormones during early development? *Psychological Bulletin, 118*(1), 55–107.

Colley, A., Eglinton, E., & Elliott, E. (1992). Sport participation in middle childhood: Associations with styles of play and parental participation. *International Journal of Sport Psychology, 23*, 193–206.

Constantinople, A. (1973). Masculinity-femininity: An exception to a famous dictum? *Psychological Bulletin, 80*, 389–407.

Constantinople, A. (1979). Sex-role acquisition: In search of the elephant. *Sex Roles, 5*, 121–132.

Cook, A. S., Fritz, J. J., McCornack, B. L., & Visperas, C. (1985). Early gender differences in the functional usage of language. *Sex Roles, 12,* 909–915.

Corder, J., & Stephan, C. W. (1984). Females' combination of work and family roles: Adolescents' aspirations. *Journal of Marriage and the Family, 50,* 391–400.

Cordua, G. D., McGraw, K. O., & Drabman, R. S. (1979). Doctor or nurse: Children's perception of sex typed occupations. *Child Development, 50,* 590–593.

Cowan, G., & Hoffman, C. D. (1986). Gender stereotyping in young children: Evidence to support a concept-learning approach. *Sex Roles, 14,* 211–224.

Crick, N. R., Bigbee, M. A., & Howes, C. (1996). Gender differences in children's normative beliefs about aggression: How do I hurt thee? Let me count the ways. *Child Development, 67,* 1003–1014.

Crick, N. R., & Grotpeter, J. K. (1995). Relational aggression, gender, and social-psychological adjustment. *Child Development, 66,* 710–722.

Crockett, L. J., & Petersen, A. C. (1987). Pubertal status and psychosocial development: Findings from the early adolescence study. In R. M. Lerner & T. T. Foch (Eds.), *Biological-psychosocial interactions in early adolescence* (pp. 173–188). Hillsdale, NJ: Erlbaum.

Cross, S. E., & Madsen, L. (in press). Models of the self: Self-construals and gender. *Psychological Bulletin, 122.*

Crouter, A. C., Manke, B. A., & McHale, S. M. (1995). The family context of gender intensification in early adolescence. *Child Development, 66,* 317–329.

Culp, R. E., Cook, A. S., & Housley, P. C. (1983). A comparison of observed and reported adult-infant interactions: Effects of perceived sex. *Sex Roles, 9*(4), 475–479.

Damon, W. (1977). *The social world of the child.* San Francisco: Jossey-Bass.

Deaux, K. (1993). Commentary: Sorry, wrong number: A reply to Gentile's call. Sex or gender? [Special section]. *Psychological Science, 4*(2), 125–126.

Deaux, K., & LaFrance, M. (in press). Gender. In D. Gilbert, S. Fiske, & G. Lindzey (Eds.), *The handbook of social psychology* (4th ed.). New York: McGraw-Hill.

Deaux, K., & Lewis, L. L. (1984). Structure of gender stereotypes: Interrelationships among components and gender label. *Journal of Personality and Social Psychology, 46,* 991–1004.

Deaux, K., & Major, B. (1987). Putting gender into context: An interactive model of gender-related behavior. *Psychological Review, 94,* 369–389.

de Lacoste-Utamsing, C., & Holloway, R. L. (1982). Sexual dimorphism in the human corpus callosum. *Science, 216,* 1341–1342.

De Lisi, R., & Gallagher, A. M. (1991). Understanding of gender stability and constancy in Argentinean children. *Merrill-Palmer Quarterly, 37,* 483–502.

De Lisi, R., & Johns, M. L. (1984). The effects of books and gender constancy development on kindergarten children's sex-role attitudes. *Journal of Applied Developmental Psychology, 5,* 173–184.

Delk, J. L., Madden, R. B., Livingston, M., & Ryan, T. T. (1986). Adult perceptions of the infant as a function of gender labeling and observer gender. *Sex Roles, 15*(9/10), 527–534.

Deschamps, J. C., & Doise, W. (1978). Crossed category memberships in intergroup relations. In H. Tajfel (Ed.), *Differentiation between social groups* (pp. 141–158). London: Academic Press.

Devine, P. G. (1989). Stereotypes and prejudice: Their automatic and controlled components. *Journal of Personality and Social Psychology, 56,* 5–18.

Diamond, M. (1982). Sexual identity, monozygotic twins rated in discordant sex role and a BBC follow-up. *Archives of Sexual Behavior, 11,* 181–186.

Diamond, M., & Sigmundson, K. (1997). Sex reassignment at birth: Long-term review and clinical implications. *Archives of Pediatric Adolescent Medicine, 151,* 298–304.

DiPietro, J. A. (1981). Rough and tumble play: A function of gender. *Developmental Psychology, 17,* 50–58.

Dittmann, R. W., Kappes, M. H., Kappes, M. E., Borger, D., Stegner, H., Willig, R. H., & Wallis, H. (1990). Congenital adrenal hyperplasia: I. Gender-related behavior and attitudes in female patients and sisters. *Psychoneuroendocrinology, 15*(5/6), 401–420.

Doise, W., Deschamps, J. C., & Meyer, G. (1978). The accentuation of intra-category similarities. In H. Tajfel (Ed.), *Differentiation between social groups.* London: Academic Press.

Dorner, G. (1988). Neuroendocrine response to estrogen and brain differentiation in heterosexuals, homosexuals and transsexuals. *Archives of Sexual Behavior, 17,* 57–75.

Downs, A. C., & Langlois, J. H. (1988). Sex typing: Construct and measurement issues. *Sex Roles, 18,* 87–100.

Dunn, J., Bretherton, I., & Munn, P. (1987). Conversations about feeling states between mothers and their young children. *Developmental Psychology, 23*(1), 132–139.

Durkin, K. (1985). *Television, sex roles and children.* Milton Keynes, England: Open University Press.

Duveen, G., & Lloyd, B. (1986). The significance of social identities. *British Journal of Social Psychology, 25,* 219–230.

Eagly, A. H. (1987). *Sex differences in social behavior: A social-role interpretation.* Hillsdale, NJ: Erlbaum.

Eagly, A. H. (1995). The science and politics of comparing women and men. *American Psychologist, 50,* 145–158.

Eagly, A. H., & Crowley, M. (1986). Gender and helping behavior: A meta-analytic review of the social psychological literature. *Psychological Bulletin, 100,* 283–308.

Eagly, A. H., Mladinic, A., & Otto, S. (1991). Are women evaluated more favorably than men? An analysis of attitudes, beliefs, and emotions. *Psychology of Women Quarterly, 15,* 203–216.

Eagly, A. H., & Wood, W. E. (1991). Explaining sex differences in social behavior: A meta-analytic perspective [Special issue]. *Personality and Social Psychology Bulletin, 17,* 306–315.

Eaton, W. O., & Enns, L. R. (1986). Sex differences in human motor activity level. *Psychological Bulletin, 100,* 19–28.

Eaton, W. O., Von Bargen, D., & Keats, J. G. (1981). Gender understanding and dimensions of preschooler toy choice: Sex stereotype versus activity level. *Canadian Journal of Behavioral Science, 13,* 203–209.

Ebbeck, M. (1984). Equity for boys and girls: Some important issues. *Early Child Development and Care, 18,* 119–131.

Eccles, J. S. (1987). Adolescence: Gateway to gender-role transcendence. In D. B. Carter (Ed.), *Current conceptions of sex roles and sex typing: Theory and research* (pp. 225–241). New York: Praeger.

Eccles, J. S. (1989). Bringing young women to math and science. In M. Crawford & M. Gentry (Eds.), *Gender and thought* (pp. 36–58). New York: Springer-Verlag.

Eccles, J. S., & Blumenfeld, P. (1985). Classroom experiences and student gender: Are there differences and do they matter? In L. C. Wilkinson & C. Marrett (Eds.), *Gender influences in classroom interaction* (pp. 79–114). Hillsdale, NJ: Erlbaum.

Eccles, J. S., & Jacobs, J. E. (1986). Social forces shape math attitudes and performance. *Signs, 11,* 367–389.

Eccles, J. S., Jacobs, J., Harold, R., Yoon, K. S., Arbreton, A., & Freedman-Doan, C. (1993). Parents' and gender-role socialization during the middle childhood and adolescent years. In S. Oskamp & M. Costanzo (Eds.), *Gender issues in contemporary society* (pp. 59–83). Newbury Park, CA: Sage.

Edelbrock, C., & Sugawara, A. I. (1978). Acquisition of sex-typed preferences in preschool children. *Developmental Psychology, 14,* 614–623.

Eder, D., & Parker, S. (1987). The cultural production and reproduction of gender: The effect of extracurricular activities on peer-group culture. *Sociology of Education, 60*(3), 200–213.

Ehrhardt, A. (1984). Gender differences: A biosocial perspective. In T. B. Sonderegger (Ed.), *Psychology and gender* (pp. 37–57). Lincoln: University of Nebraska Press.

Ehrhardt, A. A., Meyer-Bahlburg, H. F. L., Rosen, L. R., Feldman, J. F., Veridiano, N. P., Elkin, E. J., & McEwen, B. S. (1989). The development of gender-related behavior in females following prenatal exposure to diethylstilbestrol (DES). *Hormones and Behavior, 23,* 526–541.

Eisenberg, N., Carlo, G., Murphy, B., & Van Court, P. (1995). Prosocial development in late adolescence: A longitudinal study. *Child Development, 66,* 1179–1197.

Eisenberg, N., & Lennon, R. (1983). Sex differences in empathy and related capacities. *Psychological Bulletin, 94,* 100–131.

Eisenberg, N., Martin, C. L., & Fabes, R. A. (1996). Gender development and gender effects. In D. C. Berliner & R. C. Calfee (Eds.), *The handbook of educational psychology* (pp. 358–396). New York: Simon & Schuster.

Eisenberg, N., Wolchik, S. A., Hernandez, R., & Pasternak, J. (1985). Parental socialization of young children's play: A short-term longitudinal study. *Child Development, 56,* 1506–1513.

Ellis, L. (1990). Universal behavioral and demographic correlates of animal behavior: Toward common ground in the assessment of criminological theories. In L. Ellis & H. Hoffman (Eds.), *Criminal, biological, social, and moral contexts* (pp. 36–49). New York: Praeger.

Ellis, S., Rogoff, B., & Cromer, C. C. (1981). Age segregation in children's social interactions. *Developmental Psychology, 17,* 399–407.

Emmerich, W. (1982). Nonmonotonic developmental trends in social cognition: The case of gender identity. In S. Strauss (Ed.), *U-shaped behavioral growth* (pp. 249–269). New York: Academic Press.

Emmerich, W., Goldman, K. S., Kirsh, B., & Sharabany, R. (1977). Evidence for a transitional phase in the development of gender constancy. *Child Development, 48,* 930–936.

Emmerich, W., & Shepard, K. (1982). Development of sex-differentiated preferences during late childhood and adolescence. *Developmental Psychology, 18,* 406–417.

Emmerich, W., & Shepard, K. (1984). Cognitive factors in the development of sex-typed preferences. *Sex Roles, 11,* 997–1007.

Entwisle, D. R., Alexander, K. L., Pallas, A. M., & Cadigan, D. (1987). The emergence of academic self-image of first graders: Its response to social structure. *Child Development, 58,* 1190–1206.

Etaugh, C., & Duits, T. (1990). Development of gender discrimination: Role of stereotypic and counterstereotypic gender cues. *Sex Roles, 23*(5/6), 215–222.

Etaugh, C., Grinnell, K., & Etaugh, A. (1989). Development of gender labeling: Effect of age of pictured children. *Sex Roles, 21,* 769–773.

Etaugh, C., & Liss, M. B. (1992). Home, school, and playroom: Training grounds for adult gender roles. *Sex Roles, 26,* 129–147.

Fabes, R. A. (1994). Physiological, emotional, and behavioral correlates of gender segregation. In C. Leaper (Ed.), *Childhood gender segregation: Causes and consequences. New directions for child development* (Vol. 65, pp. 19–34). San Francisco: Jossey-Bass.

Fabes, R. A., & Martin, C. L. (1991). Gender and age stereotypes of emotionality. *Personality and Social Psychology Bulletin, 17,* 532–540.

Fabes, R. A., Shepard, S. A., Guthrie, I. K., & Martin, C. L. (in press). The roles of temperamental arousal and gender-segregated play in young children's social adjustment. *Developmental Psychology.*

Fagot, B. I. (1984). The child's expectations of differences in adult male and female interactions. *Sex Roles, 11*(7/8), 593–600.

Fagot, B. I. (1985a). Beyond the reinforcement principle: Another step toward understanding sex-role development. *Developmental Psychology, 21,* 1097–1104.

Fagot, B. I. (1985b). Changes in thinking about early sex role development. *Developmental Review, 5,* 83–98.

Fagot, B. I. (1995). Parenting boys and girls. In M. H. Bornstein (Ed.), *Handbook of parenting: Vol. 1. Children and parenting* (pp. 163–183). Mahwah, NJ: Erlbaum.

Fagot, B. I., & Hagan, R. (1985). Aggression in toddlers' responses to the assertive acts of boys and girls. *Sex Roles, 12*(3/4), 341–351.

Fagot, B. I., & Hagan, R. (1991). Observations of parent reactions to sex-stereotyped behaviors: Age and sex effects. *Child Development, 62,* 617–628.

Fagot, B. I., Hagan, R., Leinbach, M. D., & Kronsberg, S. (1985). Different reactions to assertive and communicative acts of toddler boys and girls. *Child Development, 56,* 1499–1505.

Fagot, B. I., & Leinbach, M. D. (1985). Gender identity: Some thoughts on an old concept. *Journal of the American Academy of Child Psychiatry, 24,* 684–688.

Fagot, B. I., & Leinbach, M. D. (1989). The young child's gender schema: Environmental input, internal organization. *Child Development, 60,* 663–672.

Fagot, B. I., & Leinbach, M. D. (1993). Gender-role development in young children: From discrimination to labeling. *Developmental Review, 13,* 205–224.

Fagot, B. I., Leinbach, M. D., & Hagan, R. (1986). Gender labeling and the adoption of sex-typed behaviors. *Developmental Psychology, 22,* 440–443.

Fagot, B. I., Leinbach, M. D., & O'Boyle, C. (1992). Gender labeling, gender stereotyping, and parenting behaviors. *Developmental Psychology, 28*(2), 225–230.

Fausto-Sterling, A. (1992). *Myths of gender: Biological theories about women and men* (2nd ed.). New York: Basic Books.

Fausto-Sterling, A. (1993). The five sexes: Why male and female are not enough. *The Sciences, 33,* 19–24.

Feingold, A. (1988). Cognitive gender differences are disappearing. *American Psychologist, 43,* 95–103.

Feingold, A. (1994). Gender differences in personality: A meta-analysis. *Psychological Bulletin, 116,* 429–456.

Feingold, A. (1995). The additive effects of differences in central tendency and variability are important in comparisons between groups. *American Psychologist, 50,* 5–13.

Feinman, S. (1984). A status theory of the evaluation of sex-role and age-role behavior. *Sex Roles, 10*(5/6), 445–456.

Ferree, M. M., & Hess, B. B. (1987). Introduction. In B. B. Hess & M. M. Ferree (Eds.), *Analyzing gender: A handbook of social science research.* Newbury Park, CA: Sage.

Filardo, E. M. (1996). Gender patterns in African American and White adolescents' social interactions in same-race, mixed-gender groups. *Journal of Personality and Social Psychology, 71,* 71–82.

Finegan, J. K., Niccols, G. A., & Sitarenios, G. (1992). Relations between prenatal testosterone levels and cognitive abilities at 4 years. *Developmental Psychology, 28*(6), 1075–1089.

Fisher-Thompson, D. (1993). Adult toy purchase for children: Factors affecting sex-typed toy selection. *Journal of Applied Developmental Psychology, 14,* 385–406.

Fivush, R. (1989). Exploring sex differences in the emotional content of mother-child conversations about the past. *Sex Roles, 20*(11/12), 675–691.

Flerx, V. C., Fidler, D. S., & Rogers, R. W. (1976). Sex role stereotypes: Developmental aspects and early intervention. *Child Development, 47,* 998–1007.

Freud, S. (1962). *Three essays on the theory of sexuality.* New York: Avon. (Original work published 1905)

Frey, K. S., & Ruble, D. N. (1992). Gender constancy and the "cost" of sex-typed behavior: A test of the conflict hypothesis. *Developmental Psychology, 28,* 714–721.

Friedman, M. A., & Brownell, K. D. (1995). Psychological correlates of obesity: Moving to the next research generation. *Psychological Bulletin, 117,* 3–20.

Frieze, I., Parsons, J. E., Johnson, P., Ruble, D. N., & Zellman, G. (1978). *Women and sex roles: A social psychological perspective.* New York: Norton.

Gailey, C. W. (1987). Evolutionary perspectives on gender hierarchy. In B. B. Hess & M. M. Ferree (Eds.), *Analyzing gender* (pp. 32–67). Newbury Park, CA: Sage.

Galambos, N. L., Almeida, D. M., & Petersen, A. C. (1990). Masculinity, femininity, and sex role attitudes in early adolescence: Exploring gender intensification. *Child Development, 61*(6), 1905–1914.

Galambos, N. L., Petersen, A. C., & Lennerz, K. (1988). Maternal employment and sex typing in early adolescents: Contemporaneous and longitudinal relations. In A. E. Gottfried & A. W. Gottfried (Eds.), *Maternal employment and children's development* (pp. 155–189). New York: Plenum Press.

Galambos, N. L., Petersen, A. C., Richards, M., & Gitelson, I. B. (1985). The attitudes toward women scale for adolescents (AWSA): A study of reliability and validity. *Sex Roles, 13*(5/6), 343–356.

Garrod, A., & Beal, C. (1993). Voices of care and justice in children's responses to fable dilemmas. In A. Garrod (Ed.), *Approaches to moral development: New research and emerging themes* (pp. 59–71). New York: Teachers College Press.

Gash, H., & Morgan, M. (1993). School-based modifications of children's gender-related beliefs. *Journal of Applied Developmental Psychology, 14,* 277–287.

Gelman, S. A., Collman, P., & Maccoby, E. E. (1986). Inferring properties from categories versus inferring categories from properties. *Child Development, 57,* 396–404.

Geschwind, N., & Behan, P. (1982). Left-handedness: Association with immune disease, migraine, and developmental learning disorder. *Proceedings of the National Academy of Sciences, 79,* 5097–5100.

Gilligan, C. (1982). *In a different voice: Psychological theory and women's development.* Cambridge, MA: Harvard University Press.

Gilligan, C., Lyons, N., & Hanmer, T. J. (1990). *Making connections: The relational worlds of adolescent girls at Emma Willard School.* New York: Harvard University Press.

Gold, D., Crombie, G., & Noble, S. (1987). Relations between teachers' judgments of girls and boys compliance and intellectual competence. *Sex Roles, 16*(7/8), 351–358.

Goldman, R., & Goldman, J. (1982). *Children's sexual thinking.* London: Routledge & Kegan Paul.

Golombok, S., & Rust, J. (1993). The pre-school activities inventory: A standardized assessment of gender role in children. *Psychological Assessment, 5,* 131–136.

Goy, R. W., Bercovitch, F. B., & McBrair, M. C. (1988). Behavioral masculinization is independent of genital masculinization in prenatally androgenized female rhesus macaques. *Hormones and Behavior, 22,* 552–571.

Grant, L. (1985). Race-gender status, classroom interaction and children. In L. C. Wilkinson & C. Marrett (Eds.), *Gender influences in classroom interaction* (pp. 55–75). Orlando, FL: Academic Press.

Green, R. (1974). *Sexual identity conflict in children and adults.* New York: Basic Books.

Green, R. (1987). *The "sissy boy syndrome" and the development of homosexuality.* New Haven, CT: Yale University Press.

Green, R., Neuberg, D. S., & Finch, S. J. (1983). Sex-typed motor behaviors of "feminine" boys, conventionally masculine boys, and conventionally feminine girls. *Sex Roles, 9,* 571–579.

Greenough, W. T., Black, J. E., & Wallace, C. S. (1987). Experience and brain development. *Child Development, 58,* 539–559.

Guttentag, M., & Longfellow, C. (1977). Children's social attributions: Development and change. *Nebraska Symposium on Motivation, 25,* 305–341.

Hageman, M. B., & Gladding, S. T. (1983). The art of career exploration: Occupational sex-role stereotyping among elementary school children. *Elementary School Guidance and Counseling, 17*(4), 280–287.

Hahn, W. K. (1987). Cerebral lateralization of function: From infancy through childhood. *Psychology Bulletin, 101,* 376–392.

Hall, J. A. (1984). *Nonverbal sex differences: Communication accuracy and expressive style.* Hillsdale, NJ: Erlbaum.

Hall, J. A., & Halberstadt, A. G. (1980). Masculinity and femininity in children: Development of the children's personal attribute questionnaire. *Developmental Psychology, 16,* 270–280.

Hall, J. A., & Halberstadt, A. G. (1986). Smiling and gazing. In J. S. Hyde & M. C. Linn (Eds.), *The psychology of gender: Advances through meta-analysis* (pp. 136–158). Baltimore: Johns Hopkins University Press.

Hall, J. A., & Kimura, D. (1995). Sexual orientation and performance on sexually dimorphic motor tasks. *Archives of Sexual Behavior, 24*(4), 395–407.

Halpern, D. F. (1992). *Sex differences in cognitive abilities* (2nd ed.). Hillsdale, NJ: Erlbaum.

Hamer, D. H., Hu, S., Magnuson, V. L., Hu, N., & Pattatucci, A. M. L. (1993). A linkage between DNA markers on the X chromosome and male sexual orientation. *Science, 261,* 321–327.

Hammen, C. (1992). Cognitive, life stress, and interpersonal approaches to a developmental psychopathology model of depression. *Developmental Psychopathology, 4,* 189–206.

Hare-Mustin, R. T., & Marecek, J. (1988). The meaning of difference: Gender theory, postmodernism, and psychology. *American Psychologist, 43,* 455–464.

Harkness, S., & Super, C. M. (1985). The cultural context of gender segregation in children's peer groups. *Child Development, 56,* 219–224.

Harris, J. R. (1995). Where is the child's environment? A group socialization theory of development. *Psychological Review, 102,* 458–489.

Hattie, J. (1992). Correlates of self-concept. In J. Hattie (Ed.), *Self-concept* (pp. 176–181). Hillsdale, NJ: Erlbaum.

Haugh, S. S., Hoffman, C. D., & Cowan, G. (1980). The eye of the very young beholder: Sex typing of infants by young children. *Child Development, 51,* 598–600.

Hedges, L. V., & Nowell, A. (1995). Sex differences in mental test scores, variability, and numbers of high scoring individuals. *Science, 269,* 41–45.

Helleday, J., Bartfai, A., Ritzen, E. M., & Forsman, M. (1994). General intelligence and cognitive profile in women with congenital adrenal hyperplasia (CAH). *Psychoneuroendocrinology, 19,* 343–356.

Hendrick, J., & Stange, T. (1991). Do actions speak louder than words? An effect of the functional use of language on dominant sex role behavior in boys and girls. *Early Childhood Research Quarterly, 6,* 565–576.

Henshaw, A., Kelly, J., & Gratton, C. (1992). Skipping's for girls: Children's perceptions of gender roles and gender preferences. *Educational Research, 34*(3), 229–235.

Herdt, G. H. (1994). Introduction: Third sexes and third genders: In G. Herdt (Ed.), *Third sex, third gender: Beyond sexual dimorphism in culture and history* (pp. 21–81). New York: Zone Books.

Herdt, G. H., & Davidson, J. (1988). The sambia "turnim-man": Sociocultural and clinical aspects of gender formation in male pseudohermaphrodites with 5-alpha-reductase deficiency in Papua, New Guinea. *Archives of Sexual Behavior, 17,* 33–56.

Hertsgaard, D., & Light, H. (1984). Junior high girls' attitudes toward the rights and roles of women. *Adolescence, 76,* 847–853.

Higgins, E. T. (1991). Development of self-regulatory and self-evaluative processes: Costs, benefits, and tradeoffs. In M. R. Gunnar & L. A. Sroufe (Eds.), *Self processes and development: The Minnesota Symposium on Child Psychology* (Vol. 23, pp. 125–166). Hillsdale, NJ: Erlbaum.

Hill, J. P., & Lynch, M. E. (1983). The intensification of gender-related role expectations during early adolescence. In J. Brooks-Gunn & A. C. Petersen (Eds.), *Girls at puberty: Biological and psychosocial perspectives* (pp. 201–228). New York: Plenum Press.

Hines, M. (1990). Gonadal hormones and human cognitive development. In J. Balthazart (Ed.), *Hormones, brain and behaviour in vertebrates: 1. Sexual differentiation neuroanatomical aspects, neurotransmitters and neuropeptides* (pp. 51–63). New York: Krager.

Hines, M. (1993). Hormonal and neural correlates of sex-typed behavioral development in human beings. In M. Haug, R. E. Whalen, C. Aron, & K. L. Olsen (Eds.), *The development of sex differences and similarities in behavior.* Boston: Kluwer.

Hines, M., Chiu, L., McAdams, L. A., Bentler, P. M., & Lipcamon, J. (1992). Cognition and the corpus callosum: Verbal fluency, visuospatial ability, and language lateralization related to midsagittal surface areas of callosal subregions. *Behavioral Neuroscience, 106,* 3–14.

Hines, M., & Collaer, M. L. (1993). Gonadal hormones and sexual differentiation of human behavior: Developments from research on endocrine syndromes and studies of brain structure. *Annual Review of Sex Research, 4,* 1–48.

Hines, M., & Kaufman, F. R. (1994). Androgen and the development of human sex-typical behavior: Rough-and-tumble play and sex of preferred playmates in children with congenital adrenal hyperplasia (CAH). *Child Development, 65,* 1042–1053.

Hines, M., & Shipley, C. (1984). Prenatal exposure to diethylstilbestrol (DES) and the development of sexually dimorphic cognitive abilities and cerebral lateralization. *Developmental Psychology, 20,* 81–94.

Hoffman, C. D., & Teyber, E. C. (1985). Naturalistic observations of sex differences in adult involvement with girls and boys of different ages. *Merrill-Palmer Quarterly, 31*(1), 93–97.

Hoffman, L. O. (1989). Effects of maternal employment in the two-parent family. Children and their development: Knowledge base, research agenda, and social policy application [Special issue]. *American Psychologist, 44*(2), 283–292.

Holland, A., & Andre, T. (1994). Athletic participation and the social status of adolescent males and females. *Youth and Society, 25*(3), 388–407.

Hood, K. E., Draper, P., Crockett, L. J., & Petersen, A. C. (1987). The ontogeny and phylogeny of sex differences in development: A biopsychosocial synthesis. In D. B. Carter (Ed.), *Current conceptions of sex roles and sex typing: Theory and research* (pp. 49–77). New York: Praeger.

Horney, K. (1922). The dread of women. *International Journal of Psychoanalysis, 13,* 348–360.

Hort, B. E., Leinbach, M. D., & Fagot, B. I. (1991). Is there coherence among components of gender acquisition? *Sex Roles, 24,* 195–208.

Hoyenga, K. B., & Hoyenga, K. T. (1993). *Gender related differences: Origins and outcomes.* Needham Heights, MA: Allyn & Bacon.

Hurtig, A. L., & Rosenthal, I. M. (1987). Psychological findings in early treated cases of female pseudohermaphroditism caused by virilizing congenital adrenal hyperplasia. *Archives of Sexual Behavior, 16,* 209–223.

Huston, A. C. (1983). Sex-typing. In E. M. Hetherington (Ed.), *Handbook of child psychology: Socialization, personality, and social development* (Vol. 4, pp. 388–467). New York: Wiley.

Huston, A. C. (1985). The development of sex typing: Themes from recent research. *Development Review, 5,* 1–17.

Huston, A. C., & Alvarez, M. M. (1990). The socialization context of gender role development in early adolescence. In R. Montemayor, G. R. Adams, & T. P. Gullotta (Eds.), *From childhood to adolescence: A transitional period?* (pp. 156–179). Newbury Park, CA: Sage.

Huston, A. C., Carpenter, C. J., Atwater, J. B., & Johnson, L. M. (1986). Gender, adult structuring of activities, and social behavior in middle childhood. *Child Development, 57,* 1200–1209.

Huston, A. C., Dunnerstein, E., Fairchild, H., Feshbach, N. D., Katz, P. A., Murray, J. P., Rubinstein, E. A., Wilcox, B. L., & Zuckerman, D. (1992). *Big world, small screen: The role of television in American society.* Lincoln: University of Nebraska Press.

Huston, A. C., Greer, D., Wright, J. C., Welch, R., & Ross, R. (1984). Children's comprehension of televised formal features with masculine and feminine connotations. *Developmental Psychology, 2,* 707–716.

Hyde, J. S., Fennema, E., & Lamon, S. J. (1990). Gender differences in mathematics performance: A meta-analysis. *Psychological Bulletin, 107,* 139–155.

Hyde, J. S., & Frost, L. A. (1993). Meta-analysis in the psychology of women. In F. L. Denmark & M. A. Paludi (Eds.), *Psychology of women: A handbook of issues and theories* (pp. 67–103). Westport, CT: Greenwood Press.

Hyde, J. S., & Linn, M. C. (Eds.). (1986). *The psychology of gender: Advances through meta-analysis* (pp. 1–13). Baltimore: Johns Hopkins University Press.

Hyde, J. S., & Plant, E. A. (1995). Magnitude of psychological gender differences. *American Psychologist, 50,* 159–161.

Idle, T., Wood, E., & Desmarais, S. (1993). Gender role socialization in toy play situations: Mothers and fathers with their sons and daughters. *Sex Roles, 28*(11/12), 679–690.

Imperato-McGinley, J., Peterson, R. E., Gautier, T., & Sturla, E. (1979). Androgens and the evolution of male gender identity among male pseudohermaphrodites with 5-alpha-reductase deficiency. *New England Journal of Medicine, 300,* 1233–1237.

Inoff, G. E., Halverson, C. F., & Pizzigati, K. A. L. (1983). The influence of sex-role stereotypes on children's self-and-peer-attributions. *Sex Roles, 9*(12), 1205–1222.

Inoff-Germain, G., Arnold, G. S., Nottelmann, E. D., Susman, E. J., Cutler, J., Gordon, B., & Chrousos, G. P. (1988). Relations between hormone levels and observational measures of aggressive behavior in young adolescents in family interactions. *Developmental Psychology, 24*(1), 129–139.

Intons-Peterson, M. J. (1988a). *Children's concepts of gender.* Norwood, NJ: ABLEX.

Intons-Peterson, M. J. (1988b). *Gender concepts of Swedish and American youth.* Hillsdale, NJ: Erlbaum.

Irvine, J. J. (1986). Teacher-student interactions: Effects of student race, sex, and grade level. *Journal of Educational Psychology, 78*(1), 14–21.

Jacklin, C. N. (1989). Female and male: Issues of gender. *American Psychologist, 44,* 127–133.

Jacklin, C. N., Wilcox, K. T., & Maccoby, E. E. (1988). Neonatal sex-steroid hormones and cognitive abilities at six years. *Developmental Psychology, 21,* 567–574.

Janowsky, S. S. (1989). Sexual dimorphism in the human brain: Dispelling the myths. *Developmental Medicine and Child Neurology, 31,* 257–263.

Johnson, A., & Ames, E. (1994). The influence of gender labelling on preschoolers' gender constancy judgments. *British Journal of Developmental Psychology, 12,* 241–249.

Johnston, J. (1982). Using television to change stereotypes. *Prevention in Human Services, 2,* 67–81.

Johnston, J., & Ettema, J. S. (1982). Positive images: Breaking stereotypes with children's television. Beverly Hills/London: Sage.

Jordan, J., Kaplan, A. G., Miller, J. B., Stiver, I. P., & Surrey, J. L. (1991). *Women's growth in connection: Writings from the Strone Center.* New York: Guilford Press.

Juraska, J. M., & Kopcik, J. R. (1988). Sex and environmental influences on the size and ultrastructure of the rat corpus callosum. *Brain Research, 450,* 1–8.

Jussim, L., & Eccles, J. S. (1992). Teacher expectations: Construction and reflection of student achievement. *Journal of Personality and Social Psychology, 63*(6), 947–961.

Kaiser, S., & Phinney, J. S. (1983). Sex typing of play activities by girls' clothing style: Pants versus skirts. *Child Study Journal, 13,* 115–132.

Kaiser, S., Rudy, M., & Byfield, P. (1985). The role of clothing in sex-role socialization: Person perceptions versus overt behavior. *Child Study Journal, 15,* 83–97.

Kaminski, D., & Sheridan, M. E. (1984). Children's perceptions of sex stereotyping: A five-year study. *International Journal of Women's Studies, 7*(1), 24–36.

Katz, P. A. (1979). The development of female identity. *Sex Roles, 5,* 155–178.

Katz, P. A. (1987). Variations in family constellation: Effects on gender schema. In L. S. Liben & M. L. Signorella (Eds.), *Children's gender schema: New directions for child development* (Vol. 38, pp. 39–56). San Francisco: Jossey-Bass.

Katz, P. A., & Boswell, S. (1986). Flexibility and traditionality in children's gender roles. *Genetic, Social, and General Psychology Monographs, 112*(1), 103–147.

Katz, P. A., & Ksansnak, K. R. (1994). Developmental aspects of gender role flexibility and traditionality in middle childhood and adolescence. *Developmental Psychology, 30*(2), 272–282.

Katz, P. A., & Walsh, V. (1991). Modification of children's gender-stereotyped behavior. *Child Development, 62,* 338–351.

Kelly, J. A., & Worell, J. (1977). New formulations of sex roles and androgyny: A critical review. *Journal of Consulting and Clinical Psychology, 45,* 1101–1115.

Kendrick, D. T., & Trost, M. R. (1993). The evolutionary perspective. In A. E. Beall & R. J. Sternberg (Eds.), *The psychology of gender* (pp. 148–172). New York: Guilford Press.

Kerns, K. A., & Berenbaum, S. A. (1991). Sex differences in spatial ability in children. *Behavior Genetics, 21*(4), 383–396.

Kessler, S. J., & McKenna, W. (1978). *Gender: An ethnomethodological approach.* New York: Wiley.

Kimball, M. M. (1986). Television and sex-role attitudes. In T. M. Williams (Ed.), *The impact of television: A natural experiment in three communities* (pp. 265–301). Orlando, FL: Academic Press.

Kimball, M: M. (1989). A new perspective on women's math achievement. *Psychological Bulletin, 105,* 198–214.

Kimura, D. (1987). Are men's and women's brains really different? *Canadian Psychology, 28,* 133–147.

Klebanov, P. K., & Brooks-Gunn, J. (1992). Impact of maternal attitudes, girls' adjustment, and cognitive skills upon academic performance in middle and high school. *Journal of Research on Adolescence, 2,* 81–102.

Klebanov, P. K., & Ruble, D. N. (1994). Toward an understanding of women's experience of menstrual cycle symptoms. In V. J. Adesso, D. M. Reddy, & R. Fleming (Eds.), *Psychological perspectives on women's health* (pp. 183–221). Washington, DC: Taylor & Francis.

Knight, G. P., Fabes, R. A., & Higgins, D. A. (1996). Concerns about drawing causal inferences from meta-analyses: An example in the study of gender differences in aggression. *Psychological Bulletin, 119,* 410–421.

Koblinsky, S. A., & Sugawara, A. I. (1984). Nonsexist curricula, sex of teacher, and children's sex-role learning. *Sex Roles, 10,* 357–367.

Kohlberg, L. A. (1966). A cognitive-developmental analysis of children's sex role concepts and attitudes. In E. E. Maccoby (Ed.), *The development of sex differences* (pp. 82–173). Stanford, CA: Stanford University Press.

Kohlberg, L. A., & Ullian, D. Z. (1974). Stages in the development of psychosexual concepts and attitudes. In R. C. Friedman, R. M. Richart, & R. L. Varde Wiete (Eds.), *Sex differences in behavior.* New York: Wiley.

Kramer, L. R. (1991). The social construction of ability perceptions: An ethnographic study of gifted adolescent girls. *Journal of Early Adolescence, 11*(3), 340–362.

Kropp, J. J., & Halverson, C. F. (1983). Preschool children's preferences and recall for stereotyped versus nonstereotyped stories. *Sex Roles, 9,* 261–272.

Kuhn, D., Nash, S. C., & Brucken, L. (1978). Sex role concepts of two- and three-year-old children. *Child Development, 49,* 445–451.

Lackey, P. N. (1989). Adults' attitudes about assignments of household chores to male and female children. *Sex Roles, 20,* 271–281.

La Freniere, P., Strayer, F. F., & Gauthier, R. (1984). The emergence of same-sex affiliative preferences among preschool peers: A developmental/ethological perspective. *Child Development, 55*(5), 1958–1965.

Lakoff, R. (1975). *Language and women's place.* New York: Harper & Row.

Lawrie, L., & Brown, R. (1992). Sex stereotypes, school subject preferences and career aspirations as a function of single/mixed sex schooling and presence/absence of an opposite sex sibling. *British Journal of Educational Psychology, 63,* 132–138.

Leahy, R. L., & Shirk, S. R. (1984). The development of classificatory skills and sex-trait stereotypes in young children. *Sex Roles, 10,* 281–292.

Leaper, C. (1991). Influence and involvement in children's discourse: Age, gender, and partner effects. *Child Development, 62,* 797–811.

Leaper, C. (1994). Exploring the correlates and consequences of gender segregation: Social relationships in childhood, adolescence, and adulthood. In B. Damon (Series Ed.) & C. Leaper (Vol. Ed.), *New directions for child development. The development of gender relationships.* San Francisco: Jossey-Bass.

Leaper, C., Anderson, K. J., & Sanders, P. (in press). Moderators of gender effects on parents' talk to their children: A meta-analysis. *Developmental Psychology.*

Leaper, C., Leve, L., Strasser, T., & Schwartz, R. (1995). Mother-child communication sequences: Play activity, child gender, and marital status effects. *Merrill-Palmer Quarterly, 41,* 307–327.

Lee, V. E., & Bryk, A. S. (1986). Effects of single-sex secondary schools on student achievement and attitudes. *Journal of Educational Psychology, 78*(5), 381–395.

Leinbach, M. D., & Fagot, B. I. (1986). Acquisition of gender labeling: A test for toddlers. *Sex Roles, 15,* 655–666.

Leinbach, M. D., & Fagot, B. I. (1993). Categorical habituation to male and female faces: Gender schematic processing in infancy. *Infant Behavior and Development, 16,* 317–332.

Leinbach, M. D., Hort, B. E., & Fagot, B. I. (in press). Bears are for boys: Metaphorical associations in young children's gender stereotypes. *Cognitive Development.*

Leonard, S. P., & Archer, J. (1989). A naturalistic investigation of gender constancy in three- to four-year-old children. *British Journal of Developmental Psychology, 7,* 341–346.

Leone, C., & Robertson, K. (1989). Some effects of sex-linked clothing and gender schema on the stereotyping of infants. *Journal of Social Psychology, 129*(5), 609–619.

Lerner, J. V. (1994). Maternal employment and children's socioemotional development. In J. V. Lerner (Ed.), *Working women and their families* (pp. 54–86). Thousand Oaks, CA: Sage.

Leslie, L. A. (1986). The impact of adolescent females' assessments of parenthood and employment on plans for the future. *Journal of Youth and Adolescence, 15,* 29–49.

LeVay, S. (1991). A difference in hypothalamic structure between heterosexual and homosexual men. *Science, 253,* 1034–1037.

Levy, G. D. (1989). Relations among aspects of children's social environments, gender schematization, gender role knowledge, and flexibility. *Sex Roles, 21,* 803–823.

Levy, G. D. (1994). High and low gender schematic children's release from proactive interference. *Sex Roles, 30,* 93–108.

Levy, G. D., & Boston, M. B. (1994). Preschoolers' recall of own-sex and other-sex gender scripts. *Journal of Genetic Psychology, 155,* 369–371.

Levy, G. D., & Carter, D. B. (1989). Gender schema, gender constancy, and gender-role knowledge: The roles of cognitive factors in preschoolers' gender-role stereotype attributions. *Developmental Psychology, 25,* 444–449.

Levy, G. D., & Fivush, R. (1993). Scripts and gender: A new approach for examining sex-role development. *Developmental Review, 13,* 126–146.

Levy, G. D., Taylor, M. G., & Gelman, S. A. (1995). Traditional and evaluative aspects of flexibility in gender roles, social conventions, moral rules, and physical laws. *Child Development, 66,* 515–531.

Levy, J. (1976). Cerebral lateralization and spatial ability. *Behavior Genetics, 6,* 171–188.

Lewin, M., & Tragos, L. M. (1987). Has the feminist movement influenced adolescent sex role attitudes? A reassessment after a quarter century. *Sex Roles, 16*(3/4), 125–135.

Liben, L. S., & Signorella, M. L. (1980). Gender-related schemata and constructive memory in children. *Child Development, 57,* 11–18.

Liben, L. S., & Signorella, M. L. (1993). Gender-schematic processing in children: The role of initial interpretations of stimuli. *Developmental Psychology, 29,* 141–149.

Lippa, R., & Connelly, S. (1990). Gender diagnosticity: A new bayesian approach to gender-related individual differences. *Journal of Personality and Social Psychology, 59,* 1051–1065.

Lips, H. M. (1993). *Sex and gender: An introduction* (2nd ed.). Mountain View, CA: Mayfield.

Lirgg, C. D. (1991). Gender differences in self-confidence in physical activity: A meta-analysis of recent studies. *Journal of Sport and Exercise Psychology, 13*(3), 294–310.

Lish, J. D., Meyer-Bahlburg, H. F. L., Ehrhardt, A. A., Travis, B. G., & Veridiano, N. P. (1992). Prenatal exposure to diethylstilbestrol (DES): Childhood play behavior and adult gender-role behavior in women. *Archives of Sexual Behavior, 21,* 423–441.

Liss, M. B. (1983). Learning gender-related skills through play. In M. B. Liss (Ed.), *Social and cognitive skills: Sex roles and children's play* (pp. 147–167). New York: Academic Press.

List, J. A., Collins, W. A., & Westby, S. D. (1983). Comprehension and inferences from traditional and nontraditional sex-role portrayals on television. *Child Development, 54,* 1579–1587.

Lloyd, B., & Smith, C. (1985). The social representation of gender and young children's play: A replication. *British Journal of Developmental Psychology, 6,* 83–88.

Lobel, T. E., Bempechat, J., Gewirtz, J., Shoken-Topaz, T., & Bashe, E. (1993). The role of gender-related information and self endorsement of traits in preadolescents' inferences and judgments. *Child Development, 64,* 1285–1294.

Lobel, T. E., & Menashri, J. (1993). The relations of conceptions of gender-role transgressions and gender constancy to gender-typed toy preferences. *Developmental Psychology, 29,* 150–155.

Lockheed, M. E. (1986). Reshaping the social order: The case of gender segregation. *Sex Roles, 14,* 617–628.

Lockheed, M. E., Harris, A. M., & Nemceff, W. P. (1983). Sex and social influence: Does sex function as a status characteristic in mixed-sex groups of children? *Journal of Educational Psychology, 75*(6), 877–888.

Locksley, A., Borgida, E., Brekke, N., & Hepburn, C. (1980). Sex stereotypes and social judgment. *Journal of Personality and Social Psychology, 39*(5), 821–831.

Low, B. S. (1989). Cross-cultural patterns in the training of children: An evolutionary perspective. *Journal of Comparative Psychology, 103,* 311–319.

Luecke-Aleksa, D., Anderson, D. R., Collins, P. A., & Schmitt, K. L. (1995). Gender constancy and television viewing. *Developmental Psychology, 31,* 773–780.

Luria, Z., & Herzog, E. W. (1991). Sorting gender out in a children's museum. *Gender and Society, 5,* 224–232.

Lutz, S. E., & Ruble, D. N. (1995). Children and gender prejudice: Context, motivation, and the development of gender concepts. *Annals of Child Development, 10,* 131–166.

Lytton, H., & Romney, D. M. (1991). Parents' differential socialization of boys and girls: A meta-analysis. *Psychological Bulletin, 109,* 267–296.

Maccoby, E. E. (1966). *The development of sex differences.* Stanford, CA: Stanford University Press.

Maccoby, E. E. (1987). The varied meanings of "masculine" and "feminine." In J. M. Reinisch, L. A. Rosenblum, & S. A. Sanders (Eds.), *Masculinity/femininity, basic perspectives* (pp. 227–239). New York: Oxford University Press.

Maccoby, E. E. (1988). Gender as a social category. *Developmental Psychology, 24,* 755–765.

Maccoby, E. E. (1990a). Gender and relationships: A developmental account. *American Psychologist, 45,* 513–520.

Maccoby, E. E. (1990b). The role of gender identity and gender constancy in sex-differentiated development. In D. Schroder (Ed.), *The legacy of Lawrence Kohlberg: New directions for child development* (pp. 5–20). San Francisco: Jossey-Bass.

Maccoby, E. E., & Jacklin, C. N. (1974). *The psychology of sex differences.* Stanford, CA: Stanford University Press.

Maccoby, E. E., & Jacklin, C. N. (1987). Gender segregation in childhood. In H. Reese (Ed.), *Advances in child development and behavior* (Vol. 20, pp. 239–287). New York: Academic Press.

Mackie, D. M. (1987). Systematic and nonsystematic processing of majority and minority persuasive communications. *Journal of Personality and Social Psychology, 53,* 41–52.

Magnusson, D., Stattin, H., & Allen, V. L. (1985). Biological maturation and social development: A longitudinal study of some adjustment processes from mid-adolescence to adulthood. *Journal of Youth and Adolescence, 14*(4), 267–283.

Maltz, D. N., & Borker, R. A. (1982). A cultural approach to male-female miscommunication. In J. A. Gumperz (Ed.), *Language and social identity* (pp. 195–216). New York: Cambridge University Press.

Mancus, D. S. (1992). Influence of male teachers on elementary school children's stereotyping of teacher competence. *Sex Roles, 26*(3/4), 109–128.

Marcus, D. E., & Overton, W. F. (1978). The development of cognitive gender constancy and sex role preferences. *Child Development, 49,* 434–444.

Markus, H., Crane, M., Bernstein, S., & Siladi, M. (1982). Self-schemas and gender. *Journal of Personality and Social Psychology, 42,* 38–50.

Marsh, H. W., Antill, J. K., & Cunningham, J. D. (1987). Masculinity, femininity and androgyny: Relations to self-esteem and social desirability. *Journal of Personality, 55,* 661–685.

Marsh, H. W., Byrne, B. M., & Shavelson, R. J. (1988). A multifaceted academic self concept: Its hierarchical structure and its relation to academic achievement. *Journal of Educational Psychology, 80,* 366–380.

Martin, C. L. (1987). A ratio measure of sex stereotyping. *Journal of Personality and Social Psychology, 52,* 489–499.

Martin, C. L. (1989). Children's use of gender-related information in making social judgments. *Developmental Psychology, 25,* 80–88.

Martin, C. L. (1990). Attitudes and expectations about children with nontraditional and traditional gender roles. *Sex Roles, 22,* 151–165.

Martin, C. L. (1991). The role of cognition in understanding gender effects. In H. Reese (Ed.), *Advances in child development and behavior* (Vol. 23, pp. 113–149). San Diego, CA: Academic Press.

Martin, C. L. (1993). New directions for investigating children's gender knowledge. *Developmental Review, 13,* 184–204.

Martin, C. L. (1994). Cognitive influences on the development and maintenance of gender segregation. In B. Damon (Series Ed.) & C. Leaper (Vol. Ed.), *New directions for child development. The development of gender relationships* (pp. 35–51). San Francisco: Jossey-Bass.

Martin, C. L. (1995). Stereotypes about children with traditional and nontraditional gender roles. *Sex Roles, 33,* 727–751.

Martin, C. L., Eisenbud, L., & Rose, H. (1995). Children's gender-based reasoning about toys. *Child Development, 66,* 1453–1471.

Martin, C. L., & Halverson, C. F. (1981). A schematic processing model of sex typing and stereotyping in children. *Child Development, 52,* 1119–1134.

Martin, C. L., & Halverson, C. F. (1983a). Gender constancy: A methodological and theoretical analysis. *Sex Roles, 9,* 775–790.

Martin, C. L., & Halverson, C. F. (1983b). The effects of sex-typing schemas on young children's memory. *Child Development, 54,* 563–574.

Martin, C. L., & Halverson, C. F. (1987). The roles of cognition in sex role acquisition. In D. B. Carter (Ed.), *Current conceptions of sex roles and sex typing: Theory and research* (pp. 123–137). New York: Praeger.

Martin, C. L., & Little, J. K. (1990). The relation of gender understanding to children's sex-typed preferences and gender stereotypes. *Child Development, 61,* 1427–1439.

Martin, C. L., & Parker, S. (1995). Folk theories about sex and race differences. *Personality and Social Psychology Bulletin, 21,* 45–57.

Martin, C. L., & Ruble, D. N. (in press). Self-construals and sex differences: A developmental perspective. *Psychological Development.*

Martin, C. L., Wood, C. H., & Little, J. K. (1990). The development of gender stereotype components. *Child Development, 61,* 1891–1904.

Masters, M. S., & Sanders, B. (1993). Is the gender difference in mental rotation disappearing? *Behavior Genetics, 23,* 337–341.

Matteson, D. R. (1991). Attempting to change sex role attitudes in adolescents: Explorations of reverse effects. *Adolescence, 26*(104), 885–898.

Maudlin, T., & Meeks, C. B. (1990). Sex differences in children's time use. *Sex Roles, 22*(9/10), 537–554.

McCauley, C., & Stitt, C. L. (1978). An individual and quantitative measure of stereotypes. *Journal of Personality and Social Psychology, 36,* 929–940.

McCauley, C., Stitt, C. L., & Segal, M. (1980). Stereotyping: From prejudice to prediction. *Psychological Bulletin, 87,* 195–215.

McCloskey, L. A. (1987). Gender and conversation: Mixing and matching styles. In D. B. Carter (Ed.), *Current conceptions of sex roles and sex typing* (pp. 139–153). New York: Praeger.

McCloskey, L. A. (1996). Gender and the expression of status in children's mixed-age conversations. *Journal of Applied Developmental Psychology, 17,* 117–133.

McConaghy, M. J. (1979). Gender permanence and the genital basis of gender: Stages in the development of constancy of gender identity. *Child Development, 50,* 1223–1226.

McEwen, B. S. (1983). Gonadal steroid influences on brain development and sexual differentiation. In R. O. Greep (Ed.), *Reproductive physiology* (Vol. 4, pp. 99–145). Baltimore: University Park Press.

McFarlane, J., Martin, C. L., & Williams, T. M. (1988). Mood fluctuations: Women versus men and menstrual versus other cycles. *Psychology of Women Quarterly, 12,* 201–223.

McGlone, J. (1980). Sex differences in human brain asymmetry: A critical survey. *Behavioral and Brain Sciences, 3,* 215–263.

McGuire, J. (1988). Gender stereotypes of parents with two-year-olds and beliefs about gender differences in behavior. *Sex Roles, 19,* 233–240.

Meaney, M. J., Stewart, J., & Beatty, W. W. (1985). Sex differences in social play: The socialization of sex roles. In J. S. Rosenblatt, C. Beer, C. M. Bushnell, & P. Slater (Eds.), *Advances in the study of behavior* (Vol. 15, pp. 1–58). Orlando, FL: Academic Press.

Meece, J. L. (1987). The influence of school experiences on the development of gender schemata. *New Directions for Child Development, 38,* 57–73.

Meece, J. L., Parsons, J. E., Kaczala, C. M., Goff, S. B., & Futterman, R. (1982). Sex differences in math achievement: Toward a model of academic choice. *Psychological Bulletin, 91*(2), 324–348.

Mendelson, B. K., White, D. R., & Mendelson, M. J. (1996). Self-esteem and body esteem: Effects of gender, age, and weight. *Journal of Applied Developmental Psychology, 17,* 321–346.

Meyer-Bahlburg, H. F. L. (1985). Gender identity disorder of childhood: Introduction. *Journal of the American Academy of Child Psychiatry, 24,* 681–683.

Meyer-Bahlburg, H. F. L., Ehrhardt, A. A., Rosen, L. R., Gruen, R. S., Veridiano, N. P., Vann, F. H., & Neuwalder, H. F. (1995). Prenatal estrogens and the development of homosexual orientation. *Developmental Psychology, 31,* 12–21.

Miller, A. (1984). A transitional phase in gender constancy and it's relationship to cognitive level and sex identification. *Child Study Journal, 13,* 259–275.

Miller, C. L. (1987). Qualitative differences among gender-stereotyped toys: Implications for cognitive and social development in girls and boys. *Sex Roles, 16,* 473–487.

Miller, C. L., Younger, B. A., & Morse, P. A. (1982). The categorization of male and female voices in infancy. *Infant Behavior and Development, 5,* 143–159.

Mischel, W. (1966). A social-learning view of sex differences in behavior. In E. E. Maccoby (Ed.), *The development of sex differences* (pp. 57–81). Stanford, CA: Stanford University Press.

Mischel, W. (1970). Sex typing and socialization. In P. H. Mussen (Ed.), *Carmichael's handbook of child psychology* (Vol. 2, pp. 3–72). New York: Wiley.

Mischel, W. (1979). On the interface of cognition and personality: Beyond the person-situation debate. *American Psychologist, 34,* 740–754.

Moghaddam, F. M., & Stringer, P. (1986). Trivial and important criteria for social categorization in the minimal group paradigm. *Journal of Social Psychology, 126,* 345–354.

Molfese, D. (1990). Auditory evoked responses recorded from 16-month-old human infants to words they did and did not know. *Brain and Language, 38,* 345–363.

Moller, L. C., Hymel, S., & Rubin, K. H. (1992). Sex typing in play and popularity in middle childhood. *Sex Roles, 26,* 331–353.

Moller, L. C., & Serbin, L. A. (1996). Antecedents of toddler gender segregation: Cognitive consonance, gender-typed toy preferences and behavioral compatibility. *Sex Roles, 35,* 445–460.

Money, J. (1987). Sin, sickness, or status? Homosexual gender identity and psychoneuroendocrinology. *American Psychologist, 42,* 384–399.

Money, J., & Ehrhardt, A. A. (1972). *Man and woman. Boy and girl.* Baltimore: Johns Hopkins University Press.

Money, J., & Mathews, D. (1982). Prenatal exposure to virilizing progestins: An adult follow-up study of twelve women. *Archives of Sexual Behavior, 11,* 73–83.

Morawski, J. G. (1987). The troubled quest for masculinity, femininity, and androgyny. In P. Shaver & C. Hendrick (Eds.), *Review of personality and social psychology: Sex and gender.* Newbury Park, CA: Sage.

Morgan, M. (1987). Television, sex-role attitudes, and sex-role behavior. *Journal of Early Adolescence, 7,* 269–282.

Mukhopadhyay, C. C., & Higgins, P. J. (1988). Anthropological studies of women's status revisited: 1977–1987. *Annual Review of Anthropology, 17,* 461–495.

Muller, R., & Goldberg, S. (1980). Why William doesn't want a doll: Preschoolers' expectations of adult behavior toward girls and boys. *Merrill-Palmer Quarterly, 26,* 259–269.

Munroe, R. H., Shimmin, H. S., & Munroe, R. L. (1984). Gender understanding and sex role preference in four cultures. *Developmental Psychology, 20,* 673–682.

Nelson, C., & Keith, J. (1990). Comparison of female and male early adolescent sex role attitude and behavior development. *Adolescence, 25,* 183–204.

Nesdale, A. R., & McLaughlin, K. (1987). Effects of sex stereotypes on young children's memories, predictions, and liking. *British Journal of Developmental Psychology, 5,* 231–241.

Newman, L. S., Cooper, J., & Ruble, D. N. (1995). Gender and computers: II. The interactive effects of gender knowledge and constancy on gender-stereotyped attitudes. *Sex Roles, 33,* 325–351.

Nolen-Hoeksema, S. (1987). Sex differences in unipolar depression: Evidence and theory. *Psychological Bulletin, 101*(2), 259–282.

Nottelmann, E. D., Susman, R. N., Inoff-Germain, B. A., Cutler, J. G. B., Loriaux, D. L., & Chrousos, G. P. (1987). Developmental processes in early adolescence: Relationships between adolescent adjustment problems and chronological age, pubertal stage, and puberty-related serum hormone levels. *Journal of Pediatrics, 110,* 473–480.

O'Boyle, M. W., & Benbow, C. P. (1990). Enhanced right hemisphere involvement during cognitive processing may relate to intellectual precocity. *Neuropsychologia, 28,* 211–216.

O'Brien, M., & Huston, A. C. (1985). Development of sex-typed play behavior in toddlers. *Developmental Psychology, 21,* 866–871.

O'Brien, M., & Nagle, K. J. (1987). Parents' speech to toddlers: The effect of play context. *Journal of Child Language, 14,* 269–279.

Ogletree, S. M., Denton, L., & Williams, S. W. (1993). Age and gender differences in children's Halloween costumes. *Journal of Psychology, 127*(6), 633–637.

O'Keefe, E. S., & Hyde, J. S. (1983). The development of occupational sex-role stereotypes: The effects of gender stability and age. *Sex Roles, 9,* 481–492.

Orlofsky, J. L., & O'Heron, C. A. (1987). Stereotypic and non-stereotypic sex role trait and behavior orientations: Implications for personal adjustment. *Journal of Personality and Social Psychology, 52,* 1034–1042.

Osgood, C. E., Suci, G. J., & Tannenbaum, P. H. (1957). *The measurement of meaning.* Urbana: University of Illinois Press.

Paikoff, R. L., & Brooks-Gunn, J. (1990). Physiological processes: What role do they play during the transition to adolescence? In G. R. Adams & T. P. Gullotta (Eds.), *From childhood to adolescence: A transitional period?* (pp. 63–82). Newbury Park, CA: Sage.

Paikoff, R. L., Brooks-Gunn, J., & Warren, M. P. (1991). Effects of girls' hormonal status on depressive and aggressive symptoms over the course of one year. *Journal of Youth and Adolescence, 20*(2), 191–215.

Paley, V. G. (1988). *Bad guys don't have birthdays: Fantasy play at four.* Chicago: University of Chicago Press.

Parsons, T., & Bales, R. (1955). *Family, socialization, and interaction processes.* New York: Academic Press.

Paulhus, D. L., & Martin, C. L. (1988). Functional flexibility: A new conception of interpersonal flexibility. *Journal of Personality and Social Psychology, 55,* 88–101.

Pearson, J. C. (1985). *Gender and communication.* Dubuque, IA: Wm. C. Brown.

Pellegrini, A. D., & Perlmutter, J. C. (1989). Classroom contextual effects on children's play. *Developmental Psychology, 25*(2), 289–296.

Pellett, T. L., & Ignico, A. A. (1993). Relationship between children's and parents' stereotyping of physical activities. *Perceptual and Motor Skills, 77*(3, Pt. 2), 1283–1289.

Peretti, P. O., & Sydney, T. M. (1984). Parental toy choice stereotyping and its effects on child toy preference and sex-role typing. *Social Behavior and Personality, 12,* 213–216.

Perloff, R. M. (1982). Gender constancy and same-sex imitation: A developmental study. *Journal of Psychology, 111,* 81–86.

Perry, D. G., & Bussey, K. (1979). The social learning theory of sex differences: Imitation is alive and well. *Journal of Personality and Social Psychology, 37,* 1699–1712.

Perry, D. G., White, A. J., & Perry, L. C. (1984). Does early sex typing result from children's attempts to match their behavior to sex role stereotypes? *Child Development, 55,* 2114–2121.

Petersen, A. C., Sarigiani, P. A., & Kennedy, R. E. (1991). Adolescent depression: Why more girls? *Journal of Youth and Adolescence, 20*(2), 247–271.

Picariello, M. L., Greenberg, D. N., & Pillemer, D. (1990). Children's sex-related stereotyping of colors. *Child Development, 61,* 1453–1460.

Plumb, P., & Cowan, G. (1984). A developmental study of destereotyping and androgynous activity preferences of tomboys, nontomboys, and males. *Sex Roles, 10,* 703–712.

Pomerantz, E. M., & Ruble, D. N. (in press). A multidimensional perspective of control: Implications for the development of sex differences in self-evaluation and depression. In J. Heckhausen & C. Dweck (Eds.), *Motivation and self-regulation across the life span.*

Pomerleau, A., Bolduc, D., Malcuit, G., & Cossette, L. (1990). Pink or blue: Environmental gender stereotypes in the first two years of life. *Sex Roles, 22,* 359–367.

Poulin-Dubois, D., Serbin, L. A., Kenyon, B., & Derbyshire, A. (1994). Infants' intermodal knowledge about gender. *Developmental Psychology, 30,* 436–442.

Power, T. G., & Shanks, J. A. (1989). Parents as socializers: Maternal and paternal views. *Journal of Youth and Adolescence, 18*(2), 203–220.

Powlishta, K. K. (1995a). Gender bias in children's perception of personality traits. *Sex Roles, 32*(1/2), 17–28.

Powlishta, K. K. (1995b). Intergroup processes in childhood: Social categorization and sex role development. *Developmental Psychology, 31*(5), 781–788.

Powlishta, K. K., Serbin, L. A., Doyle, A., & White, D. C. (1994). Gender, ethnic, and body type biases: The generality of prejudice in children. *Developmental Psychology, 30*(4), 526–536.

Powlishta, K. K., Serbin, L. A., & Moller, L. C. (1993). The stability of individual differences in gender typing: Implications for understanding gender segregation. *Sex Roles, 29*(11/12), 723–737.

Purcell, P., & Stewart, L. (1990). Dick and Jane in 1989. *Sex Roles, 22,* 177–185.

Radin, N. (1986). The influence of fathers on their sons and daughters. *Social Work in Education, 18,* 77–91.

Rebecca, M., Hefner, R., & Oleshansky, B. (1976). A model of sex-role transcendence. *Journal of Social Issues, 32*(3), 197–206.

Reinisch, J. M. (1981). Prenatal exposure to synthetic progestins increases potential for aggression in humans. *Science, 211,* 1171–1173.

Reinisch, J. M., & Sanders, S. A. (1984). Prenatal gonadal steroidal influences on gender-related behavior. In G. J. De Vries, J. P. C. De Bruin, H. G. M. Uylings, & M. A. Corner (Eds.), *Progress in brain research: Vol. 61. Sex differences in the brain* (pp. 407–415). Amsterdam, The Netherlands: Elsevier.

Reinisch, J. M., & Sanders, S. A. (1992). Effects of prenatal exposure to diethylstilbestrol (DES) on hemispheric laterality and spatial ability in human males. *Hormones and Behavior, 26,* 62–75.

Reis, H. T., & Wright, S. (1982). Knowledge of sex-role stereotyping in children aged 3 to 5. *Sex Roles, 8,* 1049–1056.

Reite, M., Cullum, C. M., Stocker, J., Teale, P., & Kozora, E. (1993). Neuropsychological test performance and MEG-based brain lateralization: Sex differences. *Brain Research Bulletin, 32,* 325–328.

Rekers, G. A. (1985). Gender identity problems. In P. A. Bornstein & A. E. Kazdin (Eds.), *Handbook of clinical behavior therapy with children* (pp. 658–699). Homewood, IL: Dorsey Press.

Repetti, R. L. (1984). Determinants of children's sex stereotyping: Parental sex-role traits and television viewing. *Personality and Social Psychology Bulletin, 10,* 457–468.

Resnick, S. M., Berenbaum, S. A., Gottesman, I. I., & Bouchard, T. J. (1986). Early hormonal influences on cognitive functioning in congenital adrenal hyperplasia. *Developmental Psychology, 22,* 191–198.

Rheingold, H. L., & Cook, K. V. (1975). The contents of boys' and girls' rooms as an index of parents' behavior. *Child Development, 46,* 445–463.

Richards, M. H., Casper, R. C., & Larson, R. (1990). Weight and eating concerns among pre- and young adolescent boys and girls. *Journal of Adolescent Health Care, 11,* 203–209.

Richards, M. H., & Larson, R. (1989). The life space and socialization of the self: Sex differences in the young adolescences [Special issue]. *Journal of Youth and Adolescence, 18*(6), 617–626.

Roberts, L. R., Sarigiani, P. A., Petersen, A. C., & Newman, J. L. (1990). Gender differences in the relationship between achievement and self-image during early adolescence. *Journal of Early Adolescence, 10*(2), 159–175.

Roberts, T. (1991). Gender and the influence of evaluations on self assessments in achievement settings. *Psychological Bulletin, 109,* 297–308.

Robinson, J., Little, C., & Biringen, Z. (1993). Emotional communication in mother-toddler relationships: Evidence for early gender differentiation. *Merrill-Palmer Quarterly, 39*(4), 496–517.

Roddy, J. M., Klein, H. A., Stericker, A. B., & Kurdek, L. A. (1981). Modification of stereotypic sex-typing in young children. *Journal of Genetic Psychology, 139,* 109–118.

Rohner, R. P. (1976). Sex differences in aggression: Phylogenetic and enculturation perspectives. *Ethos, 4,* 57–72.

Roopnarine, J. L. (1984). Sex-typed socialization in mixed-age preschool classrooms. *Child Development, 55,* 1078–1084.

Roopnarine, J. L. (1986). Mothers' and fathers' behaviors toward the toy play of their infant sons and daughters. *Sex Roles, 14,* 59–68.

Rosaldo, M. Z. (1974). Women, culture, and society: A theoretical overview. In M. Z. Rosaldo & L. Lamphere (Eds.), *Women, culture and society.* Stanford, CA: Stanford University Press.

Rosaldo, M. Z. (1980). The use and abuse of anthropology: Reflections on feminism and cross-cultural understanding. *Signs, 5,* 389–417.

Rosenthal, R., & Rubin, D. B. (1982). A simple, general purpose display of magnitude of experimental effect. *Journal of Educational Psychology, 74,* 166–169.

Rotenberg, K. J. (1986). Same-sex patterns and sex differences in the trust-value basis of children's friendship. *Sex Roles, 15,* 613–626.

Rothbart, M. D., & Maccoby, E. E. (1966). Parents' differential reactions to sons and daughters. *Journal of Personality and Social Psychology, 4,* 237–243.

Rubin, R. T., Reinisch, J. M., & Haskett, R. F. (1981). Postnatal gonadal steroid effects on human behavior. *Science, 211,* 1318–1324.

Ruble, D. N. (1994). A phase model of transitions: Cognitive and motivational consequences. In M. Zanna (Ed.), *Advances in experimental social psychology* (Vol. 26, pp. 163–214). New York: Academic Press.

Ruble, D. N., Balaban, T., & Cooper, J. (1981). Gender constancy and the effects of sex-typed televised toy commercials. *Child Development, 52,* 667–673.

Ruble, D. N., & Brooks-Gunn, J. (1979). Menstrual symptoms: A social cognition analysis. *Journal of Behavioral Medicine, 2,* 171–194.

Ruble, D. N., & Brooks-Gunn, J. (1982). The experience of menarche. *Child Development, 53,* 1557–1566.

Ruble, D. N., & Dweck, C. (1995). Self-conceptions, person conceptions, and their development. In N. Eisenberg (Ed.), *Review of personality and social psychology: Social development* (Vol. 15). Thousand Oaks, CA: Sage.

Ruble, D. N., & Goodnow, J. (in press). Social development from a lifespan perspective. In D. Gilbert, S. Fiske, & G. Lindzey (Eds.), *Handbook of social psychology.* New York: McGraw-Hill.

Ruble, D. N., Greulich, F., Pomerantz, E. M., & Gochberg, G. (1993). The role of gender-related processes in the development of sex differences in self-evaluation and depression. *Journal of Affective Disorders, 29,* 97–128.

Ruble, D. N., & Ruble, T. L. (1982). Sex-role stereotypes. In A. G. Miller (Ed.), *In the eye of the beholder: Contemporary issues in stereotyping.* New York: Holt, Rinehart and Winston.

Ruble, D. N., & Seidman, E. (1996). Social transitions: Windows into social psychological processes. In E. T. Higgins, & A. Kruglanski (Eds.), *Handbook of social processes.* New York: Guilford Press.

Ruble, D. N., & Stangor, C. (1986). Stalking the elusive schema: Insights from developmental and social-psychological analyses of gender schemas. *Social Cognition, 4,* 227–261.

Rutter, M. (1986). The developmental psychopathology of depression: Issues and perspectives. In M. Rutter, C. E. Izard, & P. B. Read (Eds.), *Depression in young people: Developmental and clinical perspectives* (pp. 3–30). New York: Guilford Press.

Rutter, M., & Garmezy, N. (1983). Developmental psychopathology. In P. H. Mussen (Series Ed.) & E. M. Hetherington (Vol. Ed.), *Handbook of child psychology: Vol. 4. Socialization, personality, and social development* (pp. 775–911). New York: Wiley.

Sadker, M., & Sadker, D. (1986, March). Sexism in the classroom: From grade school to graduate school. *Phi-Delta-Cappan,* 512–515.

Sandberg, D. E., Meyer-Bahlburg, H. F. L., Ehrhardt, A. A., & Yager, T. J. (1993). The prevalence of gender-atypical behavior in elementary school children. *Journal of the American Academy of Child Psychiatry, 32,* 306–314.

Sanik, M. M., & Stafford, K. (1985). Adolescents' contribution to household production: Male and female differences. *Adolescence, 20,* 207–215.

Savin-Williams, R. C. (1995). An exploratory study of pubertal maturation timing and self-esteem among gay and bisexual male youths. *Developmental Psychology, 31,* 56–64.

Scarr, S. (1988). Race and gender as psychological variables. *American Psychologist, 43,* 56–59.

Schieffelin, B. B. (1990). *The give and take of everyday life: Language socialization of Kaluli children.* New York: Cambridge University Press.

Sedney, M. A. (1987). Development of androgyny: Parental influences. *Psychology of Women Quarterly, 11,* 311–326.

Sedney, M. A. (1989). Conceptual and methodological sources of controversies about androgyny. In R. K. Unger (Ed.), *Representations: Social constructions of gender* (pp. 126–144). Amityville, NY: Baywood.

Segel, E. (1986). "As the twig is bent . . . ": Gender and childhood reading. In E. A. Flynn & P. P. Schweickart (Eds.), *Gender and reading* (pp. 165–186). Baltimore: Johns Hopkins University Press.

Seidman, S. A. (1992). An investigation of sex-role stereotyping in music videos. *Journal of Broadcasting and Electronic Media, 36,* 209–216.

Selkow, P. V. (1984). Effects of maternal employment on kindergarten and first grade children's vocational aspirations. *Sex Roles, 11,* 677–690.

Serbin, L. A., Moller, L. C., Gulko, J., Powlishta, K. K., & Colburne, K. A. (1994). The emergence of gender segregation in toddler playgroups. In C. Leaper (Ed.), *Childhood gender segregation: Causes and consequences. New directions for child development* (Vol. 65, pp. 7–17). San Francisco: Jossey-Bass.

Serbin, L. A., Powlishta, K. K., & Gulko, J. (1993). The development of sex-typing in middle childhood. *Monographs of the Society for Research in Child Development, 58*(Serial No. 232).

Serbin, L. A., Sprafkin, C., Elman, M., & Doyle, A. B. (1984). The early development of sex differentiated patterns and social influence. *Canadian Journal of Social Science, 14,* 350–363.

Shakin, M., Shakin, D., & Sternglanz, S. H. (1985). Infant clothing: Sex labeling for strangers. *Sex Roles, 12,* 955–963.

Shamai, S., & Coambs, R. B. (1992). The relative autonomy of schools and educational intervention for substance abuse prevention, sex education, and gender stereotyping. *Adolescence, 27*(108), 757–770.

Shaywitz, B. A., Shaywitz, S. E., Pugh, K. R., & Constable, R. T. (1995). Sex differences in the functional organization of the brain for language. *Nature, 373,* 607–609.

Shell, R., & Eisenberg, N. (1990). The role of peers' gender in children's naturally occurring interest in toys. *International Journal of Behavioral Development, 13,* 373–388.

Shepardson, D. P., & Pizzini, E. L. (1992). Gender bias in female elementary teachers' perceptions of the scientific ability of students. *Science Education, 76*(2), 147–153.

Shields, M., & Duveen, G. (1986). The young child's image of the person and the social world: Some aspects of the child's representation of persons. In J. Cook-Gumperz, W. A. Corsaro, & J. Streeck (Eds.), *Children's worlds and children's language.* Berlin: Mouton de Gruyter.

Shields, S. A. (1975). Functionalism, Darwinism, and the psychology of women. *American Psychologist, 30,* 739–754.

Shweder, R. A. (1984). Anthropology's romantic rebellion against the enlightenment, or there's more to thinking than reason and evidence. In R. A. Shweder & R. A. LeVine (Eds.), *Culture theory: Essays on mind, self, and emotions.* Cambridge, England: Cambridge University Press.

Siegal, M. (1987). Are sons and daughters treated more differently by fathers than by mothers? *Developmental Review, 7,* 183–209.

Signorella, M. L. (1987). Gender schemata: Individual differences and context effects. In L. S. Liben & M. L. Signorella (Eds.), *Children's gender schemata: New directions for child development* (Vol. 38, pp. 23–37). San Francisco: Jossey-Bass.

Signorella, M. L., Bigler, R. S., & Liben, L. S. (1993). Developmental differences in children's gender schemata about others: A meta-analytic review. *Developmental Review, 13,* 147–183.

Signorella, M. L., Bigler, R. S., & Liben, L. S. (in press). A meta-analysis of children's memories for own-sex and other-sex information. *Journal of Applied Developmental Psychology.*

Signorella, M. L., & Liben, L. S. (1984). Recall and reconstruction of gender-related pictures: Effects of attitude, task difficulty, and age. *Child Development, 55,* 393–405.

Signorella, M. L., & Liben, L. S. (1985). Assessing children's gender-stereotyped attitudes. *Psychological Documents, 15,* 7.

Signorielli, N. (1993). Television, the portrayal of women, and children's attitudes. In G. L. Berry & J. K. Samen (Eds.), *Children and television: Images in a changing sociocultural world.* Newbury Park, CA: Sage.

Signorielli, N., McLeod, D., & Healy, E. (1994). Gender stereotypes in MTV commercials: The beat goes on. *Journal of Broadcasting and Electronic Media, 38,* 91–101.

Silbereisen, R. K., Petersen, A. C., Albrecht, H. T., & Kracke, B. (1989). Maturational timing and the development of problem behavior: Longitudinal studies in adolescence. *Journal of Early Adolescence, 9*(3), 247–268.

Silvern, L. E., & Katz, P. A. (1986). Gender roles and adjustment in elementary-school children: A multi-dimensional approach. *Sex Roles, 14,* 181–202.

Simmons, R. G., & Blyth, D. A. (1987). *Moving into adolescence: The impact of pubertal change and school context.* Hawthorn, NY: Aldine de Gruyter.

Skaalvik, E. M., & Rankin, R. J. (1990). Math, verbal, and general academic self-concept: The internal/external frame of reference model and gender differences in self-concept structure. *Journal of Educational Psychology, 82,* 546–554.

Slaby, R. G., & Frey, K. S. (1975). Development of gender constancy and selective attention to same-sex models. *Child Development, 52,* 849–856.

Slijper, F. M. E. (1984). Androgens and gender role behavior in girls with congenital adrenal hyperplasia (CAH). In G. J. De Vries, H. B. M. Uylings, & M. A. Corner (Eds.), *Progress in brain research* (Vol. 61, pp. 417–422). Amsterdam, The Netherlands: Elsevier.

Smetana, J. G. (1986). Preschool children's conceptions of sex-role transgressions. *Child Development, 57,* 862–871.

Smetana, J. G., & Letourneau, K. J. (1984). Development of gender constancy and children's sex-typed free play behavior. *Developmental Psychology, 20,* 691–695.

Smith, D. M. (1985). Perceived peer and parental influences on youth's social world. *Youth and Society, 17,* 131–156.

Smith, J., & Russell, G. (1984). Why do males and females differ? Children's beliefs about sex differences. *Sex Roles, 11,* 1111–1120.

Smoll, F. L., & Schutz, R. W. (1990). Quantifying gender differences in physical performance: A developmental perspective. *Developmental Psychology, 26*(3), 360–369.

Sohn, D. (1982). Sex differences in achievement self-attributions: An effect size analysis. *Sex Roles, 8,* 345–357.

Sommers-Flanagan, R., Sommers-Flanagan, J., & Davis, B. (1993). What's happening on music television? A gender role content analysis. *Sex Roles, 28,* 745–753.

Spence, J. T. (1985). Gender identity and its implications for the concepts of masculinity and femininity. In T. B. Sonderegger

(Ed.), *Psychology and gender: Nebraska Symposium on Motivation*. Lincoln: University of Nebraska Press.

Spence, J. T. (1993). Gender-related traits and gender ideology: Evidence for a multifactorial theory. *Journal of Personality and Social Psychology, 64,* 624–635.

Spence, J. T., & Hall, S. K. (1996). Children's gender-related self-perceptions, activity preferences, and occupational stereotypes: A test of three models of gender constructs. *Sex Roles, 35,* 659–692.

Spence, J. T., Helmreich, R., & Stapp, J. (1974). The Personal Attributes Questionnaire: A measure of sex role stereotypes and masculinity-femininity. *Journal of Supplemental Abstract Service Catalog of Selected Documents in Psychology, 4,* 43.

Sroufe, L. A., Bennett, C., Englund, M., Urban, J., & Shulman, S. (1993). The significance of gender boundaries in preadolescence: Contemporary correlates and antecedents of boundary violation and maintenance. *Child Development, 64,* 455–466.

Stangor, C., & Lange, J. E. (1994). Mental representation of social groups: Advances in understanding stereotypes and stereotyping. *Advances in Experimental Social Psychology, 26,* 357–416.

Stangor, C., & McMillan, D. (1992). Memory for expectancy-congruent and expectancy-incongruent information: A review of the social and social developmental literatures. *Psychological Bulletin, 111,* 42–61.

Stangor, C., & Ruble, D. N. (1987). Development of gender role knowledge and gender constancy. In L. S. Liben & M. L. Signorella (Eds.), *Children's gender schemata* (pp. 5–22). San Francisco: Jossey-Bass.

Stangor, C., & Ruble, D. N. (1989). Differential influences of gender schemata and gender constancy on children's information processing and behavior. *Social Cognition, 7,* 353–372.

Steinberg, L. (1988). Reciprocal relation between parent-child distance and pubertal maturation. *Developmental Psychology, 24*(1), 122–128.

Stern, M., & Karraker, K. H. (1989). Sex stereotyping of infants: A review of gender labeling studies. *Sex Roles, 20,* 501–522.

Stevenson, M. R., & Black, K. N. (1988). Paternal absence and sex-role development: A meta-analysis. *Child Development, 59,* 793–814.

Stoddart, T., & Turiel, E. (1985). Children's concepts of cross-gender activities. *Child Development, 56,* 1241–1252.

Stoller, R. J. (1985). *Presentations of gender.* New Haven, CT: Yale University Press.

Stoneman, Z., Brody, G. H., & MacKinnon, C. E. (1986). Same-sex and cross-sex siblings: Activity choices, roles, behavior, and gender stereotypes. *Sex Roles, 15*(9/10), 495–511.

Susman, E. J., Inoff-Germain, G., Nottelmann, E. D., Loriaux, D. L., Cutler, J., Gordon B., & Chrousos, G. P. (1987). Hormones, emotional dispositions, and aggressive attributes in young adolescents. *Child Development, 58,* 1114–1134.

Susman, E. J., Nottelmann, E. D., & Blue, J. H. (1983, April). *Social competence, psychological states, and behavior problems in normal adolescents.* Paper presented at the biennial meeting of the Society for Research in Child Development, Detroit, MI.

Szkrybalo, J., & Ruble, D. N. (1997). *"God made me a girl": Gender constancy judgments and explanations revisited.* Manuscript submitted for publication.

Tajfel, H. (1978). Social categorization, social identity and social comparison. In H. Tajfel (Ed.), *Differentiation between social groups: Studies in the social psychology of intergroup relations* (pp. 61–76). London: Academic Press.

Tajfel, H. (Ed.). (1982). *Social identity and intergroup relations.* Cambridge, England: Cambridge University Press.

Tajfel, H., & Turner, J. (1979). An integrative theory of intergroup conflict. In W. Austin & S. Wochel (Eds.), *The social psychology of intergroup relations* (pp. 33–47). Monterey, CA: Brooks/Cole.

Tannen, D. (1990). *You just don't understand: Women and men in conversation.* New York: Morrow.

Taylor, M. (1996). The development of children's beliefs about the social and biological aspects of gender differences. *Child Development, 67,* 1555–1571.

Taylor, R. D., & Carter, D. B. (1987). The association between children's gender understanding, sex-role knowledge, and sex-role preferences. *Child Study Journal, 17,* 185–195.

Terman, L. M., & Tyler, L. E. (1954). Psychological sex differences. In L. Carmichael (Ed.), *Manual of child psychology* (2nd ed., pp. 1064–1140). New York: Wiley.

Thomas, J. R., & French, K. E. (1985). Gender differences across age in motor performance: A meta-analysis. *Psychological Bulletin, 98,* 260–282.

Thompson, N. L., & McCandless, B. R. (1970). IT score variations by instructional style. *Child Development, 41,* 425–436.

Thompson, S. K. (1975). Gender labels and early sex-role development. *Child Development, 46,* 339–347.

Thorne, B. (1986). Girls and boys together, but mostly apart. In W. W. Hartup & K. Rubin (Eds.), *Relationship and development* (pp. 167–184). Hillsdale, NJ: Erlbaum.

Thorne, B. (1993). *Gender play: Girls and boys in school.* New Brunswick, NJ: Rutgers University Press.

Timmer, S. G., Eccles, J., & O'Brien, K. (1985). How children use time. In J. T. Juster & F. P. Stafford (Eds.), *Time, goods, and well-being* (pp. 353–382). Ann Arbor, MI: Institute for Social Research.

Tittle, C. K. (1986). Gender research and education [Special issue]. *American Psychologist, 41*(10), 1161–1168.

Trautner, H. M. (1992). The development of sex-typing in children: A longitudinal analysis. *German Journal of Psychology, 16*, 183–199.

Turner, P. J., & Gervai, J. (1995). A multidimensional study of gender typing in preschool children and their parents: Personality, attitudes, preferences, behavior, and cultural differences. *Developmental Psychology, 31*, 759–772.

Turner, P. J., Gervai, J., & Hinde, R. A. (1993). Gender-typing in young children: Preferences, behavior and cultural differences. *British Journal of Developmental Psychology, 11*, 323–342.

Turner-Bowker, D. M. (1996). Gender stereotyped descriptors in children's picture books: Does "Curious Jane" exist in the literature? *Sex Roles, 35*, 461–488.

Ullian, D. A. (1976). The development of conceptions of masculinity and femininity. In B. Lloyd & J. Archer (Eds.), *Exploring sex differences* (pp. 25–48). London: Academic Press.

Unger, R. H. (1993). Alternative conceptions of sex (and sex differences). In M. Haug, R. E. Whalen, C. Aron, & K. L. Olsen (Eds.), *The development of sex differences and similarities in behaviors* (pp. 457–476). Boston: Kluwer.

Urberg, K. A. (1979). Sex role conceptualization in adolescents and adults. *Developmental Psychology, 15*, 90–92.

Urberg, K. A. (1982). The development of the concepts of masculinity and femininity in young children. *Sex Roles, 8*, 659–668.

Voyer, D., Voyer, S., & Bryden, M. P. (1995). Magnitude of sex differences in spatial abilities: A meta-analysis and consideration of critical variables. *Psychological Bulletin, 117*, 250–270.

Walker, L. J. (1984). Sex differences in the development of moral reasoning: A critical review. *Child Development, 55*, 677–691.

Walker-Andrews, A. S., Bahrick, L. E., Raglioni, S. S., & Diaz, I. (1991). Infants' bimodal perception of gender. *Ecological Psychology, 3*, 55–75.

Walsh, P. V., Katz, P. A., & Downey, E. P. (1991, April). *A longitudinal perspective on race and gender socialization in infants and toddlers.* Paper presented at the meetings of the Society for Research in Child Development, Kansas City.

Weeks, M. O., & Porter, E. P. (1983). A second look at the impact of nontraditional vocational role models and curriculum on the vocational role preferences of kindergarten children. *Journal of Vocational Behavior, 23*, 64–71.

Wehren, A., & De Lisi, R. (1983). The development of gender understanding: Judgments and explanations. *Child Development, 54*, 1568–1578.

Weinraub, M., Clemens, L. P., Sockloff, A., Ethridge, R., Gracely, E., & Myers, B. (1984). The development of sex role stereotypes in the third year: Relationships to gender labeling, gender identity, sex-typed toy preferences, and family characteristics. *Child Development, 55*, 1493–1503.

Weisner, T. S., Garnier, H., & Loucky, J. (1994). Domestic tasks, gender egalitarian values and children's gender typing in current and nonconventional families. *Sex Roles, 30*(1/2), 23–54.

Weisner, T. S., & Wilson-Mitchell, J. E. (1990). Nonconventional family life-styles and sex typing in six-year-olds. *Child Development, 61*, 1915–1933.

Weissman, M. M., & Olfson, M. (1995). Depression in women: Implications for health care research. *Science, 269*, 799–801.

Welch-Ross, M. K., & Schmidt, E. R. (1996). Gender-schema development and children's constructive story memory: Evidence for a developmental model. *Child Development, 67*, 820–835.

White, H. (1986). Damsels in distress: Dependency themes in fiction for children and adolescents. *Adolescence, 21*, 251–256.

Whiting, B. B., & Edwards, C. P. (1988). *Children of different worlds.* Cambridge, MA: Harvard University Press.

Whitley, B. E. (1985). Sex role orientation and psychological well-being: Two meta-analyses. *Sex Roles, 12*, 207–225.

Whitley, B. E., McHugh, M. C., & Frieze, I. H. (1986). Assessing the theoretical models for sex differences in causal attributions of success and failure. In J. S. Hyde & M. C. Linn (Eds.), *The psychology of gender: Advances through meta-analysis* (pp. 102–135). Baltimore: Johns Hopkins University Press.

Wilder, G., Mackie, D., & Cooper, J. (1985). Gender and computers: Two surveys of computer-related attitudes [Special issue]. *Sex Roles, 13*(3/4), 215–228.

Wilkinson, L. C., & Marrett, C. B. (Eds.). (1986). *Gender influences in classroom interaction.* New York: Academic Press.

Williams, E., Radin, N., & Allegro, T. (1992). Sex role attitudes of adolescents reared primarily by their fathers: An 11-year follow-up. *Merrill-Palmer Quarterly, 38*(4), 457–476.

Williams, J. E., Bennett, S. M., & Best, D. L. (1975). Awareness and expression of sex stereotypes in young children. *Developmental Psychology, 11*, 635–642.

Williams, J. E., & Best, D. L. (1982). *Measuring sex stereotypes: A thirty-nation study.* Beverly Hills, CA: Sage.

Williams, W. L. (1986). *The spirit and the flesh: Sexual diversity in American Indian culture.* Boston: Beacon Press.

Windle, M. S. (1987). Measurement issues in sex roles and sex-typing. In D. B. Carter (Ed.), *Current conceptions of sex roles and sex typing: Theory and research* (pp. 33–45). New York: Praeger.

Witelson, S. F., Glezer, I. I., & Kigar, D. L. (1995). Women have greater density of neurons in posterior temporal cortex. *Journal of Neuroscience, 15*(5), 3418–3428.

Wright, D. W., Peterson, L. R., & Barnes, H. L. (1990). The relation of parental employment and contextual variables with sexual permissiveness and gender role attitudes of rural early adolescents. *Journal of Early Adolescence, 10*(3), 382–398.

Yee, M., & Brown, R. (1994). The development of gender differentiation in young children. *British Journal of Social Psychology, 33,* 183–196.

Zahn-Waxler, C., Cole, P. M., & Barrett, K. C. (1991). Guilty and empathy: Sex differences and implications for the development of depression. In J. Garber & K. A. Dodge (Eds.), *The development of emotion regulation and dysregulation* (pp. 243–272). Cambridge, England: Cambridge University Press.

Zalk, S. R., & Katz, P. A. (1978). Gender attitudes in children. *Sex Roles, 4*(3), 349–357.

Zucker, K. J. (1985). Cross-gender-identified children. In B. W. Steiner (Ed.), *Gender dysphoria: Development, research, management* (pp. 75–174). New York: Plenum Press.

Zucker, K. J. (1989). Gender identity disorders. In C. G. Last & M. Hersen (Eds.), *Handbook of child psychiatric diagnosis* (pp. 388–406). New York: Wiley.

Zucker, K. J. (1990). Psychosocial and erotic development in cross-gender identified children. *Canadian Journal of Psychiatry, 35,* 487–495.

Zucker, K. J. (1992). Gender identity disorder. In S. R. Hooper, G. W. Hynd, & R. E. Mattison (Eds.), *Child psychopathology: Diagnosis criteria and clinical assessment* (pp. 305–342). Hillsdale, NJ: Erlbaum.

Zucker, K. J., & Bradley, S. J. (1995). *Gender identity disorder and psychosexual problems in children and adolescents.* New York: Guilford Press.

Zucker, K. J., Bradley, S. J., Kukis, M., Pecor, K., Birkenfeld-Adams, A., Doering, R. W., Mitchel, J. N., & Wild, J. (1996). *Gender constancy judgments in children with gender identity disorder: Evidence for a developmental lag.* Manuscript submitted for publication.

Zucker, K. J., Bradley, S. J., Lowry-Sullivan, C. B., Kuksis, M., Birkenfeld-Adams, A., & Mitchell, J. N. (1993). A gender identity interview for children. *Journal of Personality Assessment, 61,* 443–456.

Zucker, K. J., Wilson-Smith, D. N. W., Kurita, J. A., & Stern, A. (1995). Children's appraisals of sex-typed behavior in their peers. *Sex Roles, 33*(11/12), 703–725.

CHAPTER 15

Motivation to Succeed

JACQUELYNNE S. ECCLES, ALLAN WIGFIELD, and ULRICH SCHIEFELE

The Latin root of *motivation* means "to move" and fundamentally, motivational psychologists study what moves people to act and why people think and do what they do (Weiner, 1992). In keeping with this broad view of motivation, we focus on individuals' choices about which tasks to do, the persistence with which they pursue these tasks, the intensity of their engagement in these tasks, and their thoughts about their performance and their goals (see also

Eccles-Parsons et al., 1983; Wigfield & Eccles, 1992). The work reviewed here addresses the following types of questions: Why do people have different goals? Why do some people invest time and energy in developing their academic skills, while others, with similar levels of intellectual ability, focus on other skills such as sports, or no particular skills at all? Why do some continue to persist even when they are struggling, while others quit at the first sign of difficulty? In addition, since most of the relevant developmental work has focused on achievement motivation—the motive related to performance on tasks involving standards of excellence—we focus on this particular aspect of motivation. We begin with a brief historical review of the early

The writing of this chapter was supported in part by grants from the National Institute for Child Health and Human Development and the Spencer Foundation.

developmentally focused theories and empirical work and then discuss more extensively the current theoretical perspectives and empirical work on developmental changes in, socialization of, and contextual influences on motivation.

A BRIEF HISTORY OF THE FIELD

The early motivational theorists, reflecting the "grand theory" tradition in psychology, attempted to explain motivation in many different settings and for many kinds of behaviors (Weiner 1990). Over time, theories of motivation have become more specific, focused, and cognitive. In this section, we review the most influential of the early grand theories of motivation (psychoanalytic theory, field theory, behavioral/drive theory), as well as more specific theories (social learning theory, interest theories, competence/effectance motivation theory, and expectancy-value theory (see Heckhausen, 1991; Pintrich & Schunk, 1996; Weiner, 1992, for more details). We then relate this work to the early developmental research.

Early Grand Theories of Motivation

Psychoanalytic Theory

Freud (1934), in one of the first grand theories of motivation, proposed that *instincts* (conceptualized as bodily needs that get represented cognitively as wishes or desires) are the major force behind energized behavior and that the primary source of these instincts is the id or the unconscious part of the mind. According to Freud, an instinct, or need, arises from the id, creating tension. To release this tension, individuals engage in behaviors that will reinstate a balanced, homeostatic condition. If the object needed to fulfill the instinctual drive is absent, then the ego must plan an alternative strategy. If this new strategy is successful, then homeostasis is achieved. The ego also gets involved if the id seeks to satisfy the need in socially unacceptable ways; under these circumstances the ego (the conscious mind) must either suppress the need or find another more appropriate outlet, often leading to a conflict between the ego and id. If the ego's solutions do not satisfactorily fulfill the id's needs, then problems (such as neuroses) can develop.

In general, Freud's ideas about motivation are not central to current developmental theorists' views on the nature of motivation, in part because they are so difficult to test,

and in part because both the notion that people are closed energy systems and that instincts are the primary source of motivation have been questioned. Freud's most lasting contribution to the field of motivation is likely to be his emphasis on unconscious motivation. Until quite recently, most contemporary models focused on the more conscious aspects of motivation.

Lewin's Field Theory

Lewin's (1938) field theory was based on such Gestaltist notions as the importance of considering the whole rather than just the parts of things, and the tendency of people to organize and interpret their experiences. Lewin postulated that behavior is determined by both the person and the environment, $[B = f(P,E)]$, and introduced the idea of *life space* to describe the person's psychological reality. This life space contains the person and his or her perception of the environment, organized into different regions. He posited that motivation results because the regions associated with particular needs or goals (e.g., school achievement) are in tension until these goals are achieved. Lewin also hypothesized that properties of the goal object such as valence, or relative attractiveness, influence the level of tension: The higher the valence the more likely the individual is to pursue the object (particularly if needs and goal also are strong). Lewin, Dembo, Festinger, and Sears (1944) defined *level of aspiration* as the kind of performance the individual plans to undertake. They argued that level of aspiration is influenced by the valence of the activity undertaken, as well as the individual's sense of *potency* about their ability to accomplish the activity. Although Lewin's notion of the life space no longer receives much attention, his view that behavior is a function of both the person and the environment, and his notions of valence and potency are central to most current expectancy-based motivation theories, such as expectancy-value theory and self-efficacy theory.

Behavioral Theory

In classic behavioral theory (e.g., Hull, 1943), motivation was conceived in terms of *drives*. Hull included both primary drives coming from deprivation of basic biological needs (such as hunger, thirst, sex, need for air, and need for rest) and learned secondary drives (such as fear, different incentives to perform an action, and anxiety). These drives motivated behavior designed to satisfy the need. Exactly which behavior was determined by habit strength. According to Thorndike's (1931) law of effect, the habit strength of any given behavior depends on the history of that behavior leading to positive results (i.e., satisfying the need). Hull hypothesized that behavior is a joint function of drives and habits [Behavior = Drive times Habit $(B = D \times H)$]. The drive provides the energy for the behavior, and the behavior that the organism engages in is the one most readily available in the organism's repertoire of habits. The inclusion of learned secondary drives is most relevant to current theories.

Other behavioral theorists, building on Thorndike's (1931) law of effect, explored how consequences affect organisms' tendencies to engage in different behaviors. For example, B.F. Skinner (1974) studied how different kinds and rates of reinforcements affect behaviors. Reinforcement principles derived from this work have been applied extensively in educational settings (see Kazdin, 1982) leading to prolific use of positive reinforcements (e.g., praise, stars, and token economies) to foster students' motivation to engage in school tasks and of negative strategies such as time-out to extinguish undesirable behaviors.

Like Freud, Hull emphasized the satisfaction of needs as the main motivators of behavior. Unlike Freud, however, Hull, Skinner, and other behaviorally oriented theorists (e.g., Bijou & Baer, 1961; Gewirtz, 1969) did not include cognitive mechanisms in their theories. Instead, behavior was assumed to be controlled by its consequences with positive consequences leading to increases, and negative consequences leading to decreases, in the behavior. In contrast, modern motivational theorists stress internal cognitive representations and processes. According to these theorists, consequences of one's behavior influence one's motivation primarily through individuals' *interpretations* of these consequences.

Early Specific Motivational Theories

Rotter's Social Learning Theory

In his theory of motivation, Rotter (1966) extended the learning theorists' approach to include mental representation (called expectations) of the likely reinforcement outcomes. He also added the construct of value and hypothesized that motivated behavior choice is a function of reward expectancies and the value of that reinforcement to the individual. He believed that specific reward expectations form as a result of experiences with similar tasks. Rotter also posited that individuals develop generalized expectancies based on previous performance across varied tasks and that these generalized expectancies have a particularly strong

influence in novel situations. Both his pairing of expectation and value and his stress on mental representations of experience and events have been incorporated into most contemporary expectancy/value and social construction theories of motivation (e.g., Atkinson, 1964, 1966; Eccles-Parsons et al., 1983; Raynor, 1982).

Rotter also introduced the construct of locus of control, which he conceptualized as a stable individual difference in the tendency to see events as under personal control (internal locus of control) or environmental control (external locus of control; see Findley & Cooper, 1983). This construct has been incorporated into many current theories, including Weiner's (1985) attribution theory, Bandura's personal efficacy theory, and Connell and E. Skinner's developmentally-oriented motivational theories (e.g., Connell, 1985; E. Skinner, 1985, 1995). It is also central to Dweck and Elliott's (1983) discussion of the nature of children's ability beliefs in that the belief that ability is incremental means that one's ability is under one's own control, whereas the belief that ability is an entity implies that one's ability is determined by uncontrollable factors such as one's genetic makeup.

Interest Theories

Before academic psychology became an independent scientific discipline, educational theorists and philosophers were concerned with motivational issues in learning and education. Many of these theories, however, referred to interest rather than motivation. For example, Herbart (1841/1965) argued that education should foster unspecialized, multifaceted interests because it would facilitate learning. Herbart hypothesized that interest facilitates meaningful learning, correct and complete understanding of facts or domains of knowledge, long-term storage of knowledge, and the desire for further learning. These ideas, in turn, influenced Dewey's (1913) emphasis on interest and enjoyment as central motivational forces in education. Dewey stressed that people will identify with, and be totally absorbed by, the material to be learned only if they are sufficiently interested in it. In contrast, learning activities that are controlled by external forces will result in only superficial understanding. These ideas have been incorporated into many contemporary theories (e.g., Graham & Golan, 1991; Lepper, 1988; Ryan, Connell, & Deci, 1985).

For many years, these early conceptions of interest (see also Rubinstein, 1958) were supplanted by behaviorist theories and drive concepts of motivation (cf. Berlyne, 1949, 1967) except in the area of vocational psychology.

Vocational psychology researchers, like Kerschensteiner (1922), continued to stress the centrality of interests in determining occupational choice. Systematic educationally relevant research on interest was not resumed until the 1980s (e.g., Renninger, Hidi, & Krapp, 1992).

White's Notion of Competence Motivation

In 1959, Robert White argued that neither drive nor instinct-based motivational theories could explain animals' persistent attempts to master their environments, particularly if homeostasis was assumed to be the preferred state. He pointed out abundant evidence that exploratory behaviors occur even when basic bodily needs are fully sated. White argued for a new motivational construct *(effectance motivation)* to explain behaviors such as exploration, mastery, and manipulation. The goals of effectance motivation are acquiring competence and influencing one's environment. White also postulated that the behaviors stimulated by effectance motivation are critical for successful adaptation to one's environments, and for the development of self-determination and autonomy. Finally, he introduced cognitive constructs such as goals and planning into the motivational literature. White's ideas had a tremendous impact on subsequent theorizing about motivation by developmental psychologists, particularly Harter, Deci, Ryan, Connell, E. Skinner, and Wellborn.

Atkinson's Expectancy-Value Theory of Achievement Motivation

Atkinson (1964, 1966) developed the first formal model of motivation designed to explain achievement-related behaviors such as striving for success, choice among achievement tasks, and persistence. Atkinson was influenced by several ideas including Murray's (1938) suggestion that the need for achievement is a basic human need, Lewin's (1938) ideas regarding activity valence and importance, Tolman's (1932) construct of expectancies for success, and Edwards' (1954) work on maximizing expected utility. Atkinson (1964) hypothesized that achievement behaviors are determined by achievement motives, expectancies for success, and incentive values. He posited that two achievement motives (M_{as}—the relatively stable disposition to strive for success; and M_{af}—the disposition to avoid failure) are aroused when cues indicate that performance will be evaluated against a rigorous standard of excellence. He measured the motive for success using Murray's Thematic Apperception Test (TAT), in which people tell stories about a series of somewhat ambiguous pictures of individuals engaging (or not engaging) in different activities. The

stories are scored for their achievement imagery, which Atkinson assumed reflected unconscious achievement motivation (see also McClelland, 1985). The motive to avoid failure is usually measured with test anxiety scales.

Atkinson defined expectancies for success in terms of the expected probabilities for success (P_s) and failure (P_f) on specific tasks and assumed that $P_s + P_f = 1$. He defined incentive value as the relative attractiveness of succeeding on a given achievement task—with I_s being the incentive for success and I_f being the incentive to avoid failure. He then expressed the relations among these constructs algebraically to define the resultant motive to achieve (M_{ach}):

$$M_{ach} = (M_{as} \times P_s \times I_s) - (M_{af} \times P_f \times I_f)$$

Though he included incentive value as a separate term, he also assumed that it was equal to $1 - P_s$ and then, through algebraic manipulation of the terms, he eliminated I_s as a central construct. Thus, P_s became the primary cognitive component of the model, leading to a large body of the work assessing individuals' achievement strivings under different probabilities for success (see Atkinson, 1966).

This equation yields the hypotheses that individuals with relatively stronger motives to approach success than avoid failure will have positive resultant M_{ach}, will be most likely to approach achievement tasks, and will be most highly motivated on tasks of intermediate difficulty (e.g., $P_s = .50$). In contrast, individuals with relatively stronger motives to avoid failure than to approach success will seek to avoid achievement tasks, especially those of intermediate risk (when M_{af} will be at its maximum) and should prefer either very easy or very difficult tasks (when M_{af} is at its minimum). These two sets of propositions have received extensive empirical support with different-aged subjects, mostly using laboratory gamelike tasks (see Atkinson, 1966, for review). However, they are not always supported, particularly in more real-world achievement situations with important tasks. Further, equating incentive value as the inverse of the probability of success greatly limited research on, and theorizing about, task value (see Parsons & Goff, 1980; Wigfield & Eccles, 1992).

Atkinson's expectancy-value model was the first comprehensive, mathematical expectancy-value model of achievement motivation; it dominated the field for many years. This expectancy-value tradition has influenced the efforts of Weiner (see 1992), Feather (e.g., 1982a, 1982b, 1988), Raynor (1982), Eccles and her colleagues (e.g., Eccles-Parsons et al., 1983; Pekrun, 1993; Wigfield, 1994; Wigfield & Eccles, 1992), and Pintrich and his colleagues

(Pintrich & De Groot, 1990; Pintrich & Schrauben, 1992) to expand Atkinson's theory into more comprehensive and educationally relevant models.

Early Developmental Research

Expectancies and Values

The most important early work on children's motivation was done by Virginia Crandall and her colleagues Vaughn Crandall and Esther Battle (e.g., Battle, 1965, 1966; Crandall, 1969). Following Atkinson (1964) and Rotter (1966), these researchers investigated how children's expectancies for success and task attainment value (i.e., importance to the individual) affected achievement. Both Crandall and Battle demonstrated that children's and adolescents' expectancies relate to their choice of, persistence at, and performance on, achievement tasks. Persistence was related to high attainment value. Performance, however, was more strongly related to expectancies for success than to attainment value. In addition, in contrast to Atkinson's assumption that expectancies and values are inversely related, expectancies for success and attainment value were positively related.

The Crandalls also pioneered developmental work on locus of control. Crandall, Katkovsky, and Crandall (1965) developed the first children's measure of personal responsibility (or control) for positive and negative achievement outcomes—the Intellectual Achievement Responsibility Scale. This measure was adapted by Dweck and her colleagues to measure academic learned helplessness.

Early Research on Interest

Among the earliest writings on the development of interest are those of Nagy (1912), Carter (1940), and Piaget (1948). Nagy proposed five stages of interest development: sensory (years 1–2), subjective (years 3–7), objective (years 7–10), persisting (years 11–15), and logical interest (years 15 and beyond). During the stage of *sensory interest,* young children focus their attention on lively, stimulating perceptions (especially visual and acoustical perceptions). As interest in sensory events diminishes, the objects themselves become a source of interest. In this stage of *subjective interest,* objects gain interest value because they are instrumental to some preferred activity (e.g., trees become interesting because they can be climbed). These subjective interests are unstable and can change rapidly. In the stage of *objective interest,* children focus on understanding how things work and on analyzing and categorizing their perceptions. As these interests become increasingly associated

with self-concepts, children move into the stage of *persisting interests.* More than at earlier stages, interests begin to vary systematically across individuals. Finally, in the stage of *logical interest,* interests become independent of specific activities and more strongly related to abstract categories or domains of knowledge, such as aesthetic, religious, or scientific interest. Carter extended this approach to a theory of the development of vocational interests and aspirations.

Early Research on Children's Test Anxiety

Anxiety was an important early topic because Atkinson (1964) conceptualized (and often measured) the motive to avoid failure in terms of test anxiety, and because anxiety was considered one of the important secondary drives in the learning theories of Hull and Spence. Much of this work focused on either test anxiety, or anxiety about other performance evaluations (see Dusek, 1980; Wigfield & Eccles, 1989). Sarason, Davidson, Lighthall, Waite, and Ruebush (1960) developed the Test Anxiety Scale for Children (for critique, see Nicholls, 1976). Using this measure, Hill and Sarason (1966) found that anxiety both increases across the school years and becomes more negatively related to subsequent grades and test scores. They also found that highly anxious children's achievement test scores are up to two years behind those of their low anxious peers and that girls' anxiety scores are higher than boys' scores.

Subsequent researchers made two important conceptual distinctions: First, Spielberger (1966) distinguished trait and state anxiety, with trait anxiety defined as a stable, cross-situational individual characteristic and state anxiety being more task specific and time bound. He developed the scales still used to measure each component. Second, Liebert and Morris (1967) distinguished between worry and emotionality, with worry being the cognitive aspects of anxiety (consisting of self-deprecating and task-irrelevant thoughts) and emotionality being the physiological component of anxiety. Most recent research on anxiety has focused on the worry aspect of anxiety.

CURRENT THEORETICAL PERSPECTIVES ON MOTIVATION

Current theories of motivation do not focus on constructs such as drives or instincts, although some include psychological "needs" (e.g., Connell & Wellborn, 1991; Deci & Ryan, 1985; Ryan, 1992). Few current achievement motivation theories deal explicitly with unconscious aspects of motivation (for exception, see McClelland, 1985). Instead, most of these theories focus on beliefs and cognitions, emphasizing psychological and interpretational processes instead of drives and emotional states. Cognitions like attributions for success and failure, self-efficacy beliefs, control beliefs, self-regulatory beliefs, and goals have received the most attention. Some current theories (e.g., attribution theory) incorporate affect; others highlight broad definitions of what it means to value achievement (e.g., modern expectancy value theory). Finally, current theorists are increasingly sensitive to context influences.

To organize our presentation, we group the current theories according to three broad motivational questions: Can I do this task? Do I want to do this task and why? and What do I have to do to succeed on this task (see Eccles & Wigfield, 1985)? Many contemporary theories deal primarily with a construct or constructs within one of these broad domains. However, some theories include constructs aimed at more than one of these questions, and we note this in our discussion.

Theories Concerned with the Question "Can I Do This Task?"

Several theories focus on individuals' beliefs about their competence and efficacy, their expectancies for success or failure, and their sense of control over outcomes, which are beliefs directly related to the question "Can I do this task?" In general, when children answer this question affirmatively, they perform better and select more challenging tasks.

Attribution Theory

Attribution theory grew out of Heider's (1958) work on people's understandings and explanations of different outcomes. Weiner's attribution theory has dominated the field of achievement motivation for most of the past 25 years (see Graham, 1991; Weiner, 1985). A student of Atkinson, Weiner based his approach in the expectancy-value tradition. However, he emphasized how *interpretations* of one's achievement outcomes (causal attribution), rather than motivational dispositions or actual outcomes, determine subsequent achievement strivings. Weiner et al. (1971) initially identified ability, effort, task difficulty, and luck as the most important achievement causal attributions. They classified these attributions into two dimensions: locus of control and stability. The locus of control dimension, derived from Rotter's work, has two poles: internal versus external locus of control. The stability dimension captures

whether causes change over time or not. For example, ability was classified as a stable, internal cause, and effort was classified as unstable, internal. Later, Weiner (1985) added a third dimension, controllability, to distinguish causes one can control, such as skill/efficacy, from causes one can't control, such as aptitude, mood, others' actions, and luck.

Weiner and his colleagues (e.g., Weiner, 1985; Weiner et al., 1971) proposed and demonstrated that each of these causal dimensions has unique influences on various aspects of achievement behavior. The stability dimension was hypothesized to influence individuals' expectancies for success because attributing an outcome to a stable cause such as ability should have a stronger influence on expectancies for future success than attributing an outcome to an unstable cause such as effort (see Weiner, 1985). This perspective contrasts with Rotter's (1966) contention that locus of control influences expectancies. Weiner argued that Rotter confounded the locus of control and stability dimensions in his theory, and so did not accurately identify the determinants of expectancy change. Further, like Atkinson (1966) and later Bandura (see 1986) and Eccles-Parsons et al. (1983), Weiner argued that expectations for success influence the individual's choice of subsequent achievement tasks.

Weiner (1985) proposed that the locus of control dimension was linked most strongly to affective reactions. He argued that, although individuals' first emotional responses to an outcome are based largely on their evaluation of whether the outcome is positive or negative, the next more distinct emotional reactions are based on whether the outcome is attributed to an internal or external cause: Attributing success to internal causes should enhance pride or self-esteem; attributing it to external causes should enhance gratitude; attributing failure to internal causes should produce shame; attributing it to external causes should induce anger. These are the emotional reactions that influence behavior in subsequent achievement situations (Weiner, Russell, & Lerman, 1979).

Finally, Weiner and his colleagues stressed the relation of the controllability dimension to help-giving. Individuals are more likely to help others if they failed due to factors they could not control (I didn't do my homework because my house burned down) than if they failed for controllable reasons (I didn't do my homework because I went to the movies instead).

In summary, attributions are important because they influence subsequent achievement strivings in both positive and negative ways: Individuals who attribute success to ability and effort, will have positive affect, and will expect to do well on similar tasks in the future because they think they have control over these outcomes. In contrast, individuals who attribute failure to lack of ability will feel shameful, and will lower their future expectancies because they think they have little control over subsequent outcomes.

A number of important developmental issues relate to this theory. First, the process of making attributions is relatively complex. One must understand the covariance of a cause and effect, discount other possible causes, understand the distinctiveness and consistency of an event, and determine whether a cause is necessary, sufficient, or both to make accurate attributions (Kelly, 1972). These processes impose cognitive demands that are difficult for young children. Second, children (especially young children) do not always distinguish clearly between different causal dimensions; in addition, their understanding of each dimension changes over time. Young children see ability and effort as complementary and do not fully distinguish between the two constructs; the smart person is one who tries hardest, and ability can be improved through effort (Nicholls, 1978). By age 11 or 12, children also come to understand the reciprocal, compensatory relations between effort and ability: People with less ability need to try harder to reach the same level of success as people with more ability. They also come to understand that trying harder may be a sign that one is less able. Children's understanding of task difficulty also changes with age (Nicholls & Miller, 1984). These developmental shifts mean that the neat distinctions between causal categories in Weiner's model cannot be applied to children of different ages. Further, a factor analytic study of junior high school students' recollections of their own successes and failure showed little support for the attributional dimensions of locus of control, stability, and controllability (Vispoel & Austin, 1995). Instead, internal attributions factored separately into different achievement domains, and the external attributions factored together across domains. These results deserve further exploration.

There has also been general criticism of the "person as scientist" metaphor used so extensively in attribution theory. As researchers understand better the limits of individuals' rational decision-making power (e.g., Fischoff, Goitein, & Shapira, 1982; Kahneman & Tversky, 1984), the notion of people as logical, rational information seekers has been questioned. Motivation likely means more than understanding outcomes, reacting to them emotionally, predicting the future, and executing the next behavior. Perhaps, as Nicholls (1992) suggested, attribution theory is a modern theory in a more complex postmodern age.

Self-Efficacy Theory

Bandura's (1994) social-cognitive model emphasizes human agency and perceptions of efficacy (defined as individuals' confidence in their ability to organize and execute a given course of action to solve a problem or accomplish a task) in determining individuals' achievement strivings. Bandura (1994) characterizes self-efficacy as a multidimensional construct that can vary in strength (i.e., positive or negative), generality (relating to many situations or only a few), and level of difficulty (feeling efficacious for all tasks or only easy tasks).

Like expectancy-value theory and attribution theory, Bandura's theory stresses expectancies for success. However, Bandura distinguished between two kinds of expectancy beliefs: outcome expectations (beliefs that certain behaviors, like practice, will lead to certain outcomes, like improved performance) versus efficacy expectations (beliefs about whether one can perform the behaviors necessary to produce the outcome, e.g., I can practice sufficiently hard to win the next tennis match). Individuals can believe that a certain behavior will produce a certain outcome (outcome expectation) but may not believe they can do that behavior (efficacy expectation). Bandura proposed that individuals' efficacy expectations are the major determinant of goal setting, activity choice, willingness to expend effort, and persistence (see Bandura, 1994).

Bandura proposed that individuals' perceived self-efficacy is determined by four things: previous performance (succeeding leads to a stronger sense of personal efficacy); vicarious learning (watching models succeed or fail on tasks); verbal encouragement by others, and one's physiological reactions (overarousal and anxiety/worry leading to a lower sense of personal efficacy). His stress on these four determinants reflects the link of this theory with both behaviorist and social learning traditions. In addition, Bandura acknowledged the influence of causal attributions on people's self-efficacy. However, Bandura argued that causal attributions only influence behavior through their impact on efficacy beliefs.

The self-efficacy construct has been applied to behavior in many domains including school, health, sports, therapy, and even snake phobia (see Bandura, 1994). By and large, the evidence is supportive of his theoretical predictions. For example, high personal academic expectations predict subsequent performance, course enrollment, and occupational choice (see Bandura, 1994; Pajares & Miller, 1994; Schunk, 1991; Zimmerman, Bandura, & Martinez-Pons, 1992). Additionally, perceived efficacy, particularly personal efficacy regarding academic work, is an important predictor of academic achievement among African American adolescents, particularly males (e.g., Gurin & Epps, 1974; Hale-Benson, 1989).

In summary, Bandura (1994) argued that his self-efficacy construct is superior to most other self-related constructs in the motivation field, (including locus of control, effectance motivation, control beliefs, perceived competence beliefs, and possible selves) because it is more task and situation specific and therefore should relate more strongly to behavior. However, the distinctions among these constructs is less clear than Bandura proposed. Furthermore, like attribution theory, social cognitive theory can be criticized for its overly rational and information-processing approach to motivation. Finally, it is not clear how distinct self-efficacy is from past performance. Bandura argued that self-efficacy mediates the link between past performance and subsequent performance and task choice. Whether this is true is still a controversial issue.

Self-Worth Theory

Covington (1992) defined the motive for self-worth as the desire to establish and maintain a positive self-image, or sense of self-worth. Because children spend so much time and experience so much evaluation in classrooms, Covington argued that protecting one's sense of academic competence is likely to be critical for maintaining a positive sense of self-worth. One way to protect one's sense of academic confidence is by adopting causal attribution patterns that enhance both the sense of academic competence and control. Attributing success to ability and effort and failure to not trying is one common protective pattern (Covington & Omelich, 1979; Eccles-Parsons, Meece, Adler, & Kaczala, 1982). Attributing failure to lack of ability is a particularly problematic attribution that many students seek to avoid.

However, school evaluation, competition, and social comparison can make it difficult for some children to maintain the belief that they are competent academically. Covington (1992) outlined various strategies children develop to avoid appearing to lack ability, including procrastination, making excuses, avoiding challenging tasks, and not trying. The last two strategies are particularly interesting. Covington and Omelich (1979) referred to effort as a "double-edged sword" because, although trying is important for success (and is encouraged by both teachers and parents), if children try and fail, it is difficult to escape the conclusion that they lack ability. Therefore, if failure

seems likely, some children will not try, precisely because trying and failing threatens their ability self-concepts. Avoiding challenging tasks is another good way to avoid or minimize failure experiences; this strategy is often used by high-achieving students who are failure avoidant: Rather than being motivated by challenging tasks, such students try to avoid difficult tasks altogether to maintain both their own sense of competence, and others' perceptions of their competence.

Covington (1992) suggested that reducing the frequency and salience of competitive, social comparative, and evaluative practices, and focusing instead on effort, mastery, and improvement, would allow more children to maintain their self-worth without having to resort to such failure-avoiding strategies. These suggestions have been incorporated into many researchers' recommendations for school reform (e.g., Ames, 1992; Maehr & Midgley, 1996).

Because Covington focuses on the inverse relation of ability and effort and emphasizes the importance of the interpretation of achievement outcomes for self-perception, his views are complementary with those of attribution theory and self-efficacy theory (see Graham, 1991). However, recent work in the self-concept area has raised questions about Covington's contention that academic competence beliefs are particularly strong determinants of self-worth. Harter (1990) has shown that self-concepts regarding physical appearance and social competence are stronger predictors of self-worth than academic self-concepts (see Harter, Ch. 9, this Volume). In addition, several investigations suggest that the power of any particular self-concept to influence an individual's self-worth depends on the value this individual attaches to this competence domain, and that people can reduce the value they attach to various tasks in order to maintain their sense of self-worth (e.g., Eccles, 1993; Eccles, Wigfield, & Blumenfeld, 1984; Harter, 1990: Harter, Ch. 9, this Volume; James, 1892/1963). It is likely, however, that lowering the value one attaches to school achievement in response to school failure as a way to maintain self-worth will lead to reduced effort as predicted by Covington.

Modern Expectancy-Value Theory

Modern expectancy-value theories (e.g., Eccles, 1987, 1993; Eccles-Parsons et al., 1983; Feather, 1982a, 1982b; Wigfield, 1994; Wigfield & Eccles, 1992) are based on Lewin's and Atkinson's suggestions that achievement performance, persistence, and choice are most directly linked to individuals' expectancy-related and task value beliefs. However, they differ from Atkinson's (1964) expectancy-value theory in several ways: First, the expectancy and value components are both more elaborated, and more closely linked to psychological and social/cultural determinants. Second, they are grounded in more real-world achievement tasks than those tasks used to test Atkinson's theory. Third, expectancies and values are assumed to be positively related to each other.

The Eccles et al. Expectancy-Value Model. Eccles-Parsons and her colleagues have elaborated one expectancy-value model of achievement-related choices, (e.g., Eccles, 1987; Eccles, Adler, & Meece, 1984; Eccles & Wigfield, 1995; Eccles-Parsons et al., 1983; Meece, Eccles-Parsons, Kaczala, Goff, & Futterman, 1982; Meece, Wigfield, & Eccles, 1990; Parsons & Goff, 1980). Eccles and her colleagues derive the expectancy and value constructs from the work of Lewin (1938), Tolman (1932), and Atkinson (1966). In addition, however, Eccles and her colleagues also emphasize the social psychological influences on choice and persistence. Choices are assumed to be influenced by both negative and positive task characteristics, and all choices are assumed to have costs associated with them precisely because one choice often eliminates other options. Consequently, the *relative* value and probability of success of various options are key influences on choice, particularly for achievement-related choices related to which courses to take, what careers to seek, and what avocational/recreational activities to pursue.

The most recent version of this model is depicted in Figure 15.1. Expectancies and values are assumed to directly influence performance, persistence, and task choice. Expectancies and values are assumed to be influenced by task-specific beliefs such as perceptions of competence, perceptions of the difficulty of different tasks, and individuals' goals and self-schemas. These social cognitive variables, in turn, are influenced by individuals' perceptions of other peoples' attitudes and expectations for them, and by their own interpretations of their previous achievement outcomes. Individuals' task-perceptions and interpretations of their past outcomes are assumed to be influenced by socializers' behaviors and beliefs and by the cultural milieu and unique historical events.

Eccles-Parsons et al. (1983) defined expectancies for success as children's beliefs about how well they will do on upcoming tasks, either in the immediate or long-term future. These expectancy beliefs are measured in a manner analogous to measures of Bandura's (1986) personal efficacy expectations: Thus, in contrast to Bandura's claim that expectancy-value theories focus on outcome expectations, the focus in this model is on personal or efficacy expectations.

Eccles-Parsons et al. (1983) defined beliefs about ability as children's evaluations of their competence in different areas; this definition is similar to those of researchers such as Covington, Harter (e.g., Harter, 1982, 1990), and Marsh and his colleagues (e.g., Marsh, 1990a; Marsh & Shavelson, 1985). Thus, ability beliefs are conceived as integrated beliefs about competence in a given domain, in contrast to one's expectancies for success on a specific upcoming task. However, their empirical work has shown that children and adolescents do not distinguish between these two levels of beliefs (e.g., Eccles & Wigfield, 1995). Apparently, even though these constructs can be theoretically distinguished from each other, in real-world achievement situations they are highly related and empirically indistinguishable.

Heckhausen's Expectancy-Value Model. In his general expectancy-value model, Heckhausen (1977) integrated a number of different approaches to motivation. In the resulting model, he distinguished among four different types of expectancies: situation-outcome expectancies (i.e., subjective probability of attaining an outcome in a specific situation without acting), action-outcome expectancies (i.e., subjective probability of attaining an outcome by one's actions), action-by-situation-outcome expectancies (i.e., subjective probability that situational factors facilitate or impede one's action-outcome expectancy), and outcome-consequence expectancies (i.e., subjective probability of an outcome to be associated with a specific consequence). In Heckhausen's model, outcomes are the immediate results of one's actions. These immediate results are, or are not, followed by various consequences (e.g., self-evaluation, external evaluation). They do not have any incentive value on their own. Incentive value is attributed only to the *consequences* of one's actions. Therefore, the motivation to act depends mainly on the value that is attached to the consequences of one's behavior.

Rheinberg (1988) argued that Heckhausen's model does not include the possibility of being motivated by characteristics of an action itself, independently of any external consequences. This restriction of Heckhausen's model is less evident when achievement-related behavior is the only focus of analysis. When different domains of behavior are studied, however, the importance of action-specific incentives is clear. Such incentives are similar to

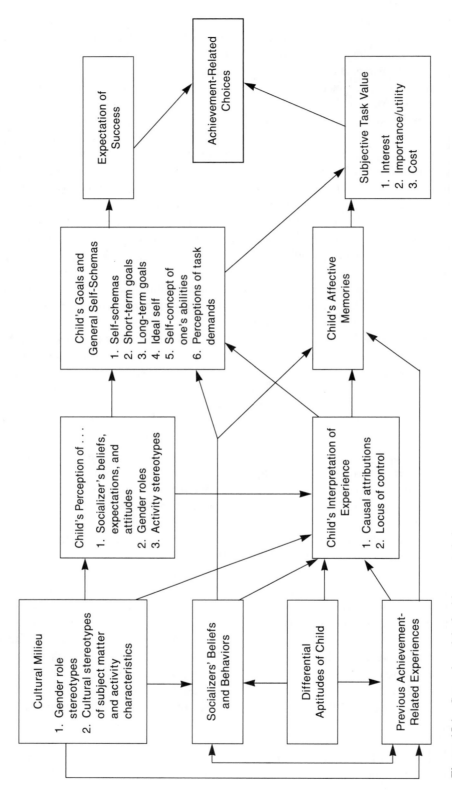

Figure 15.1 General model of achievement choices.

intrinsic motivation discussed later. Rheinberg (1995) has investigated a number of different leisure activities, such as painting, motorcycling, and playing a musical instrument that are motivated by action-specific incentives, such as feelings of competence, enjoyment of perfect or harmonic movements, being absorbed in the activity, and feelings of self-fulfillment.

Other Expectancy/Self-Concept Related Theory. Harter (Ch. 9, this Volume) provides a thorough review of the enormous literature on self-concept development. This work is relevant here in two ways: First, prominent current structural models of self-concept, such as those of Harter and her colleagues, Marsh and his colleagues (e.g., Marsh, 1989, 1990a; Marsh & Shavelson, 1985) and Eccles and Wigfield (e.g., Eccles, 1994; Eccles & Wigfield, 1995; Eccles et al., 1989), focus on domain-specific perceived competence as a crucial aspect of self-concept. Because self-concept is usually measured by asking about perceived competence, self-concepts and perceived competencies notions are quite similar. Further, like motivation theorists, self-concept researchers are interested in the relation of self-concepts (or perceived competence) to performance in different activity arenas. Indeed, like expectancy theorists, Marsh (e.g., Marsh, 1990b) has argued that competence beliefs predict subsequent performance more strongly than performance predicts subsequent self-concept beliefs. Thus, in self-concept models, as in other theories concerned with the question "Can I do this task?", competence beliefs are assumed to play a pivotal role in motivating behavior.[1]

In addition, the more process-oriented researchers studying "self" propose that self-concept guides, directs, regulates, and motivates behavior (e.g., Eccles, 1987, 1994; Eccles-Parsons, et al., 1983; Garcia & Pintrich, 1994; Markus & Wurf, 1987). For example, Markus and her colleagues discuss how "possible future selves" motivate behavior. Possible selves, the vision individuals have of themselves in the future, include both hoped-for (I will pass geometry) and feared (I will not pass geometry) components. Because possible selves are not identical to one's current self-concept, they motivate the individual by providing goals that the individual tries to attain and outcomes

that the individual tries to avoid in order to achieve one's image. Whether or not the possible self is attained depends on many things, one of which is the individual's current perceived competence.

Control Theories

Building on the work of Rotter (1966) and the Crandalls (e.g., Crandall et al., 1965), research in control theory has both confirmed the positive association between internal locus of control and academic achievement (see Findley & Cooper, 1983) and elaborated broader conceptual models of control. Connell (1985), for example, added *unknown control* as a third control belief category and argued that younger children are particularly likely to use this category. Connell developed a scale to assess external control (in terms of "powerful others"), internal control (in terms of effort and ability), and unknown control for cognitive, physical, social, and general activities.

Connell and Wellborn (1991) then integrated control beliefs into a broader theoretical framework based on the psychological needs for competence, autonomy, and relatedness (see also Deci & Ryan, 1985; Ryan, 1992). They linked control beliefs to competence needs: Children who believe they control their achievement outcomes should feel more competent. They hypothesized that the extent to which these needs are fulfilled is influenced by the following characteristics of their family, peer, and school contexts: the amount of structure, the degree of autonomy provided, and the level of involvement in the children's activities. Finally, they proposed that the ways in which these needs are fulfilled determine engagement in different activities. When the needs are fulfilled, children will be fully engaged. When one or more of the needs is not fulfilled, children will become disaffected (see Connell, Spencer, & Aber, 1994; Skinner & Belmont, 1993).

Building on Connell's work, E. Skinner and her colleagues (e.g., E. Skinner, 1985, 1995; E. Skinner, Chapman, & Baltes, 1988) proposed a model that includes three critical control-related beliefs: means-ends beliefs, control beliefs, and agency beliefs. Means-ends beliefs concern the expectation that particular causes can produce certain outcomes; these causes include Weiner's various causal attributions and Connell's (1985) unknown control. Agency beliefs are the expectations that one has access to the means to produce various outcomes. Control beliefs are the expectations individuals have that they can produce desired events.

---

[1] Harter, like Eccles and other expectancy-value theorists, also includes the importance of the task to the individual as an important motivational factor.

E. Skinner distinguished her position from attribution theory in two ways: First, she argued that attribution theorists confound means-ends and agency beliefs because they define different causes (or means) without any consideration of the agent implementing these causes. She also faulted attribution theory for being retrospective rather than prospective and argued that her means-ends beliefs correct this problem.

She distinguished her position from self-efficacy theories by noting that self-efficacy theorists discuss connections between agents and means primarily in terms of expectancies that the individual can produce some outcome; thus outcomes are contingent on one's responses. In contrast, she argued that her agency beliefs relate to potential as well as actual means. Further, an individual can have strong agency beliefs for different means without believing that any of the means are necessarily effective (see also Ryan, 1992). In contrast, Bandura (1994) argued that means-ends beliefs are the same as outcome expectations, and agency beliefs are somewhat like efficacy expectations. In addition, Bandura argued that his construct implies a more powerful agent than Skinner's does and that E. Skinner's control belief constructs have little theoretical power because they do not reference specific means to attain outcomes.

Like other cognitive motivational theories, E. Skinner's original control model emphasizes cognitive aspects of motivation and does not systematically deal with constructs like values and affect. However, by including children's needs for competence, autonomy, and relatedness in her most recent writings (e.g., Patrick, Skinner, & Connell, 1993; Skinner, 1995), she has broadened her model in important ways.

Theories Concerned with the Question "Do I Want to Do This Task and Why?"

Although theories dealing with competence, expectancy, and control beliefs provide powerful explanations of individuals' performance on different kinds of achievement tasks, these theories do not systematically address another important motivational question: Does the individual *want* to do the task? Even if people are certain they can do a task, they may not *want* to engage in it. Once the decision is made to engage in a task or activity, there are different reasons for doing so; the "why" part of this question deals with that issue. This section focuses on these theories of motivation.

Modern Expectancy-Value Theories: Expanding the Value Construct

Feather's Work on Values. Feather (e.g., 1982a, 1982b, 1988, 1992) broadened Atkinson's conceptualization of value. Drawing on Rokeach's (1979) work, he defined values as a set of stable, general beliefs about what is desirable and postulated that these beliefs emerge from both society's norms and the individual's core psychological needs and sense of self. He integrated Rokeach's approach to values into an expectancy-value approach by arguing that values are a class of motives that affect behavior by influencing the attractiveness of different goal objects and, consequently, the motivation to attain these goals. Feather confirmed these ideas for several types of behavior including joining political action groups and selecting academic majors. In addition, contrary to Atkinson's predictions, he found that values and expectancies are positively rather than inversely related, suggesting that influences other than just the perceived difficulty of the task determine value; these influences include features of the goal object itself, the valence of success and failure to the individual, and the probability of succeeding on the task. He also concluded that we know little about the origins of these task values.

Eccles, Wigfield, and Colleagues' Work on Subjective Task Values. Eccles and her colleagues have also elaborated the concept of task value. Building on earlier work on attainment values (e.g., Battle, 1965, 1966), intrinsic and extrinsic motivation (e.g., Deci, 1975), and Rokeach's (1979) view that values are shared beliefs about desired end-states, Eccles-Parsons et al. (1983) outlined four motivational components of task value: attainment value, intrinsic value, utility value, and cost. Like Battle (1965, 1966), they defined attainment value as the personal importance of doing well on the task. Drawing on self-schema and identity theories (e.g., Kohlberg, 1966; Markus & Nurius, 1986), they also linked attainment value to the relevance of engaging in a task for confirming or disconfirming salient aspects of one's self-schema; that is, since tasks provide the opportunity to demonstrate aspects of one's actual or ideal self-schema, such as masculinity, femininity, and/or competence in various domains, tasks will have higher attainment value to the extent that they allow the individual to confirm salient aspects of these self-schemas (see Eccles, 1984, 1987). This component of value relates most directly to the perspectives on values espoused by Feather (1982a, 1982b, 1988) and Rokeach (1979).

Intrinsic value is the enjoyment the individual gets from performing the activity, or the subjective interest the individual has in the subject. This component of value is similar to the construct of intrinsic motivation as defined by Harter (1981), and by Deci and his colleagues (e.g., Deci & Ryan, 1985; Ryan, Connell, & Deci, 1985), and to the constructs of interest and flow as defined by Csikszentmihalyi (1988), Renninger (1990), and Schiefele (1991).

Utility value is determined by how well a task relates to current and future goals, such as career goals. A task can have positive value to a person because it facilitates important future goals, even if he or she is not interested in the task for its own sake. Students often take classes that they do not particularly enjoy but that they need to take to pursue other interests, to please their parents, or to be with their friends. In one sense then, this component captures the more "extrinsic" reasons for engaging in a task (see Harter, 1981, for further discussion of extrinsic motivation). But it also relates directly to individuals' internalized short- and long-term goals.

Finally, Eccles and her colleagues identified "cost" as a critical component of value (Eccles, 1987; Eccles-Parsons et al., 1983). Cost is conceptualized in terms of the negative aspects of engaging in the task, such as performance anxiety and fear of both failure and success as well as the amount of effort needed to succeed and the lost opportunities that result from making one choice rather than another.

Eccles and her colleagues have confirmed different aspects of this model. For example, they have shown that ability self-concepts and expectancies for success predict performance in mathematics and English, whereas task values predict course plans and enrollment decisions in mathematics, physics, and English and involvement in sport activities even after controlling for prior performance levels (Eccles, Adler, & Meece, 1984; Eccles, Barber, Updegraff, & O'Brien, 1995; Eccles & Harold, 1991; Eccles-Parsons et al., 1983; Meece et al., 1990). They have also shown that both expectancies and values predict career choices (see Eccles, 1994). These findings suggest possible modifications to the model in Figure 15.1, where direct paths are drawn from both expectancies and values to performance, persistence, and choice. These results suggest reconsidering the direct paths from expectancies to choice once prior achievement level is controlled, and from values to performance (see Wigfield & Eccles, 1992).

Expectancy-value models continue to be prominent. The most important contributions of the contemporary models are the elaboration of the values construct and the discussion of whether expectancies and values relate differentially to performance and choice. More work is needed on how the links of expectancies and values to performance and choice change across ages (see Eccles, Wigfield, & Blumenfeld, 1984; Wigfield, 1994) and on the links between expectancies and values. Both Eccles (1984) and Bandura (1994) propose a positive association between expectancy-related beliefs and task values. Their findings support this prediction. Most of the work, however, does not provide the kind of evidence necessary to evaluate the causal direction inherent in this relation.

Like attribution theory, modern expectancy-value theory has been criticized for overly emphasizing rational cognitive processes. Fischoff, Goitein, and Shapira (1982) argued that the logical, rational decision-making processes of determining expectancies and valences are often not used because people prefer simpler, but more fallible and optimistic, decision-making strategies. They also argued that task values shift fairly rapidly, particularly for unfamiliar tasks. These criticisms are likely to be particularly apropos when these models are considered from a developmental perspective (see Wigfield, 1994). However, the impressive body of research showing the relations of expectancy and values to different kinds of performance and choice supports the continuing viability of these models. Furthermore, as conceptualized by Eccles and her colleagues, values are linked to more stable self-schema and identity constructs and choice is not necessarily the result of conscious rational decision-making processes (see Eccles, 1987; Eccles & Harold, 1992). By including affective memories, culturally based stereotypes, and identity-related constructs and processes as part of their theoretical system, Eccles and her colleagues have allowed for less rational and more nonconscious processes in motivated behavioral choices.

Intrinsic Motivation Theories

The following theories deal with the distinction between *intrinsic* motivation and *extrinsic* motivation. When individuals are intrinsically motivated they do activities for their own sake and out of interest in the activity. When extrinsically motivated, individuals do activities for instrumental or other reasons, such as receiving a reward. This distinction is assumed to be fundamental throughout the motivation literature.

Harter's Effectance Motivation Theory. Harter (see 1983) proposed a model of mastery (or effectance) motivation, describing the effects of both success and failure experiences on mastery motivation. She proposed that successful mastery attempts that (initially) are positively reinforced lead to internalization of the reward system. They also enhance perceptions of competence and perceived internal control over outcomes, give the individual pleasure, and ultimately increase mastery motivation. In contrast, when mastery attempts fail, the need for approval by others persists, with a corresponding increase in external control beliefs, lower competence beliefs, higher anxiety in mastery situations, and ultimately, lower mastery motivation. This model is important because it includes the effects of both success and failure on subsequent motivation. Moreover, many of the links in the model, such as those between competence beliefs and intrinsic motivation, and optimal challenge and competence beliefs, have received empirical support (e.g., Harter 1983). Based in part on this model, Harter (1981) developed a scale measuring different aspects of intrinsic and extrinsic motivation.

Self-Determination Theory.   Over the past 25 years, many studies have documented the debilitating effects of extrinsic incentives and pressures on the motivation to perform even inherently interesting activities (e.g., see Amabile, Hill, Hennessey & Tighe, 1994; Cameron & Pierce, 1994; Deci & Ryan, 1985; Lepper, 1988). There is still debate, however, over why human beings are intrinsically motivated for particular activities. This debate began with two different theories: (a) Humans are motivated to maintain an optimal level of stimulation (Berlyne, 1967; Hebb, 1955; Hunt & Paraskevopoulos, 1980), and (b) basic needs for competence (White, 1959) and personal causation or self-determination (deCharms, 1968) underlie intrinsically motivated behavior. Deci and Ryan (1985) have integrated these two approaches into their theory of self-determination by suggesting that the basic need for competence is the major reason people seek out optimal stimulation and challenging activities. In addition, they argued that intrinsic motivation is maintained only when actors feel competent and self-determined. Evidence that intrinsic motivation is reduced by exerting external control and by giving negative competence feedback supports this hypothesis (see Deci & Ryan, 1985).

Deci and Ryan (1985) also argued, however, that the basic needs for competence and self-determination play a role in more extrinsically motivated behavior. Consider, for example, a student who consciously and without any external pressure selects a specific major because it will help him or her earn a lot of money. This student is guided by basic needs for competence and self-determination but the choice of major is based on reasons totally extrinsic to the major itself.

Deci, Ryan, and their colleagues (e.g., Ryan, 1992) went beyond the extrinsic-intrinsic motivation dichotomy in their discussion of *internalization,* the process of transferring the regulation of behavior from outside to inside the individual. Deci and Ryan (1985) postulated that a basic need for interpersonal relatedness explains why people turn external goals into internal goals through internalization. They defined several levels of regulations: *external regulation* coming from outside the individual; *introjected regulation* based on feelings that he or she should or has to do the behavior; *identified regulation* based on the utility of that behavior (e.g., studying hard to get grades to get into college), and finally, *integrated regulation* based on what the individual thinks is valuable and important to the self. Even this latter level is not fully internalized and self-determined since it does require that the individual is also highly interested in the behavior. These levels of regulation have some similarities to the different kinds of values defined by Eccles and her colleagues. Deci and colleagues have developed scales to measure these levels.

Flow Theory.   Csikszentmihalyi (1988) discussed intrinsically motivated behavior in terms of the immediate subjective experience that occurs when people are engaged in the activity. Interviews with climbers, dancers, chess players, basketball players, and composers revealed that these activities yield a specific form of experience—labeled *flow*—characterized by (a) holistic feelings of being immersed in, and of being carried by, an activity; (b) merging of action and awareness; (c) focus of attention on a limited stimulus field; (d) lack of self-consciousness; and (e) feeling in control of one's actions and the environment. Flow is only possible when people feel that the opportunities for action in a given situation match their ability to master the challenges. The challenge of an activity may be something concrete or physical like the peak of a mountain to be scaled, or it can be something abstract and symbolic, like a set of musical notes to be performed, a story to be written, or a puzzle to be solved. Research has shown that both the challenges and skills must be relatively high before a flow experience becomes possible (Massimini & Carli, 1988).

At first sight, the theories of Deci and Ryan and Csikszentmihalyi seem very different. Deci and Ryan (1985) explain intrinsic motivation by assuming innate, basic needs, whereas Csikszentmihalyi stresses subjective experience. We suggest, however, that this difference reflects two sides of the same coin. As Schneider (in press) has argued, one has to distinguish between immediate reasons (e.g., enjoyment) and ultimate reasons of behavior (e.g., survival). Intrinsically motivated behavior can be conducive to ultimate goals even though the actor is only motivated by immediate incentives. A typical case is exploratory or play behavior. Both types of behavior help to increase an individual's competence but they are usually performed because they are exciting, pleasurable, or enjoyable. This distinction between immediate and ultimate causes of behavior makes it possible to reconcile the positions of Deci and Ryan and Csikszentmihalyi. Deci and Ryan (1985) focus on ultimate reasons of behavior, whereas Csikszentmihalyi (1988) focuses on immediate reasons. Csikszentmihalyi and Massimini (1985) suggested that the experience of flow is a reward that ensures that individuals will seek to increase their competence. According to Csikszentmihalyi, the repeated experience of flow is only possible when individuals seek out increasingly challenging tasks and expand their competencies to meet these challenges. Thus, the experience of flow should reinforce behaviors underlying development.

Individual Difference Theories of Intrinsic Motivation. Until recently, intrinsic motivation researchers such as Deci and Ryan and Csikszentmihalyi have dealt with conditions, components, and consequences of intrinsic motivation without distinguishing between intrinsic motivation as a state versus intrinsic motivation as a traitlike characteristic. However, interest in traitlike individual differences in intrinsic motivation has increased, particularly among educational psychologists (see Amabile et al., 1994; Gottfried, 1986, 1990; Harter, 1981; Nicholls, 1984, 1989; Schiefele, 1996a, 1982b; Schiefele & Schreyer, 1994). These researchers define this enduring intrinsic motivational orientations in terms of three components: (a) preference for hard or challenging tasks; (b) learning driven by curiosity or interest; and (c) striving for competence and mastery. The second component is most central to the idea of intrinsic motivation. Both preference for hard tasks and striving for competence can be linked to either extrinsic or more general need achievement motivation. Nonetheless, empirical findings suggest that the three components are

highly correlated. In addition, evidence suggests that high levels of traitlike intrinsic motivation facilitate positive emotional experience (Matsumoto & Sanders, 1988), self-esteem (Ryan, Connell, & Deci, 1985), mastery-oriented coping with failure, high academic achievement (Benware & Deci, 1984; Schiefele & Schreyer, 1994), and use of appropriate learning strategies (Pintrich & Schrauben, 1992; Schiefele & Schreyer, 1994). As a consequence, many have suggested that the development of an intrinsic motivational orientation should be fostered in the home and the classroom (e.g., Batson & Johnson, 1976; Brophy, 1987; Dewey, 1913; Lepper & Chabay, 1985).

Interest Theories

Closely related to the notion of intrinsic motivation is the work on interest (Alexander, Kulikowich, & Jetton, 1994; Hidi, 1990; Renninger et al., 1992; Renninger & Wozniak, 1985; Schiefele, 1991; Tobias, 1994). These researchers differentiate between individual and situational interest. Individual interest is a relatively stable evaluative orientation toward certain domains; situational interest is an emotional state aroused by specific features of an activity or a task. Two aspects or components of individual interest are distinguishable (Schiefele, 1991, 1996a, 1996b): feeling-related and value-related interest. Feeling-related interest refers to the feelings associated with an object or an activity itself such as involvement, stimulation, or flow. Value-related interest refers to the personal significance or importance of an object. In addition, both feeling-related and value-related interests are directly related to the object rather than to the relation of this object to other objects or events. For example, if students associate mathematics with high personal significance because mathematics can help them get prestigious jobs, then we would not speak of interest. Although feeling-related and value-related interests are highly correlated (Schiefele, 1996a), it is useful to differentiate between them because some individual interests are based primarily on feelings, whereas other interests are based more on personal significance (see Eccles, 1984; Wigfield & Eccles, 1992). Further research is necessary to validate this assumption.

Much of the research on individual interest has focused on its relation to the quality of learning (see Alexander, Kulikowich, et al., 1994; Renninger, Hidi & Krapp, 1992; Schiefele, 1996a). In general, there are significant but moderate relations between interest and text learning. More importantly, interest is related more strongly to indicators of deep-level learning (e.g., recall of main ideas, coherence of recall, responding to deeper comprehension questions, representation of meaning) than to surface-level learning (e.g., responding to simple questions, verbatim representation of text; Schiefele, 1996b; Schiefele & Krapp, in press).

Most of the research on situational interest has focused on the characteristics of academic tasks that create interest (e.g., Anderson, Shirey, Wilson, & Fielding, 1987; Hidi & Baird, 1986; Teigen, 1987). The following text features arouse situational interest: personal relevance, novelty, activity level, and comprehensibility (Hidi & Baird, 1986). Empirical evidence has provided strong support for the relation between situational interest and text comprehension and recall (see reviews by Schiefele, 1996a, 1996b; Wade, 1992).

Goal Theories

Recently researchers have become interested in children's achievement goals and their relation to achievement behavior (see Ames & Ames, 1989; Harackiewicz & Elliot, 1993; Locke & Latham, 1990; Meece, 1991, 1994). Several different approaches have emerged. Bandura (1986) and Schunk (1990, 1991), focusing on goals' proximity, specificity, and level of challenge, have shown that specific, proximal, and somewhat challenging goals promote both self-efficacy and improved performance.

Another set of researchers have defined goals in terms of the individual's immediate achievement-related focus and definition of success (e.g., Ames, 1992; Blumenfeld, 1992; Butler, 1993; Dweck & Leggett, 1988; Nicholls, 1984). Nicholls and his colleagues (e.g., Nicholls, 1979b; Nicholls, Cobb, Yackel, Wood, & Wheatley, 1990) for example, defined three major kinds of motivationally relevant goal patterns or orientations: ego-involved goals, task-involved goals, and work avoidant goals. Individuals with ego-involved goals seek to maximize favorable evaluations and minimize negative evaluations of their competence. Questions such as "Will I look smart?" and "Can I outperform others?" reflect ego-involved goals. In contrast, individuals with task-involved goals focus on mastering tasks and increasing their competence. Questions such as "How can I do this task?" and "What will I learn?" reflect task-involved goals. Individuals with work avoidant goals seek to minimize the effort expended. Dweck and her colleagues proposed a complementary analysis (e.g., Dweck & Elliott, 1983; Dweck & Leggett, 1988) distinguishing between performance goals (similar to ego-involved goals) and learning goals (similar to task-involved goals). Similarly, Ames (1992) distinguished between the

association of performance (similar to ego-involved) goals and mastery (similar to task-focused) goals with both performance and task choice. With ego-involved (or performance) goals, children try to outperform others, and are more likely to do tasks they know they can do. Task-involved (or mastery-oriented) children choose challenging tasks and are more concerned with their own progress than with outperforming others.

Goal theories focused on this distinction between performance versus mastery orientations are currently very popular among researchers interested in both the determinants of performance and task choice (e.g., Butler, 1989a, 1989b), and the restructuring of schools to enhance motivation (e.g., Ames, 1992; Maehr & Midgley, 1996; see later discussion). By and large, consistent support for the benefits of task involved or learning goals is emerging. We are concerned, however, that categorizing children's goals as ego or task involved oversimplifies the complexity of motivation even when these two goal orientations are allowed to exist simultaneously. Further, work in this tradition often does not take the effects of the particular achievement domain into account (for an important exception, see Meece, 1991, 1994).

Other researchers (e.g., Ford, 1992; Wentzel, 1991b) have adopted a different perspective on goals and motivation, arguing that individuals can have many different kinds of goals in achievement settings. For example, Ford proposed a complex motivation theory based on the assumption that humans are goal directed and self-organized (e.g., Ford, 1992). He defined goals as the desired end-states people try to attain through the cognitive, affective, and biochemical regulation of their behavior. Furthermore, Ford defined goals as only one part of motivation; in his model, motivation is defined as the product of goals, emotions, and personal agency beliefs. Finally, Ford derived a set of principles for optimizing motivation based on his theory.

Returning to goals in particular, Ford and his colleagues have developed an extensive taxonomy of goals based on their *content* rather than on the criteria used to define success of failure. Ford and Nichols (1987) distinguished most broadly between *within-person* goals, which concern desired within-person consequences, and *person-environment* goals, which concern the relation between the person and his or her environment. Similar to Rokeach's (1979) human values and Eccles' attainment value (Eccles-Parsons et al., 1983), the within-person goals include affective goals (e.g., happiness, physical well-being), cognitive goals (e.g., exploration, intellectual creativity), and subjective organization goals (e.g., unity, transcendence). These goals include self-assertive goals such as self-determination and individuality, integrative social relationship goals such as belongingness and social responsibility, and task goals such as mastery, material gain, and safety. Although Ford and Nichols (1987) developed measures to assess all 24 goals specified in Ford's model, their evidence suggests that people typically rely on a much smaller cluster of core goals in regulating their behavior.

Building on Ford's work, Wentzel (e.g., Wentzel 1991a, 1993, in press) has examined the multiple goals of adolescents in achievement settings. Because Wentzel also focuses on the content of children's goals, her definition of goals is similar to the idea of attainment value hierarchies in the Eccles et al. expectancy value model. Wentzel has demonstrated that both social and academic goals relate to adolescents' school performance and behavior; specifically school achievement is positively related to wanting to be both successful and dependable, wanting to learn new things, and wanting to get things done (see Juvonen & Wentzel, in press; Wentzel, 1991a, 1991b). Furthermore, Wentzel (1994) demonstrated very interesting relations among the various goals of middle school children: Prosocial goals (such as helping others), academic prosocial goals (such as sharing learning with classmates), peer social responsibility goals (such as following through on promises made to peers), and academic social responsibility goals (such as doing what the teacher says to do) were all related to each other (Wentzel, 1994). She also documented intriguing patterns in the relations of these children's goals to both their behavior and their relationships with their peers and teachers: Prosocial goals (particularly academic prosocial goals) related positively to peer acceptance; academic responsibility goals related negatively to peer acceptance but positively to acceptance by teachers; positive prosocial and academic goals related positively to prosocial behaviors (as rated by teachers) and negatively to irresponsible behaviors; And finally, the pursuit of positive social goals was facilitated by perceived support from teachers and peers. These findings warrant further investigation.

Summary

We have seen a gradual increase in the complexity of theoretical frameworks for addressing issues related to task value, interest, and goals. Ford and Wentzel have developed the most comprehensive perspectives on multiple goals. Wigfield and Eccles (1992) suggested several links between theories of subjective task value, interest, and goals. But additional theoretical and empirical work are badly needed to integrate these various perspectives.

Theories Concerned with the Question "What Do I Have to Do to Succeed on This Task?"

Motivation theorists have become interested in the specific ways children regulate their behavior to meet their goals (e.g., see Schunk & Zimmerman, 1994). Some have suggested links between motivational beliefs and the use of particular cognitive strategies (e.g., P. A. Alexander et al., 1994; Pintrich, Marx, & Boyle, 1993; Pintrich & Schrauben, 1992). Further, Kuhl (1987) and Corno and Kanfer (1993) argued for the distinction between motivation and volition, with motivation guiding decisions about engaging in particular activities, and volition guiding the behaviors used to attain the goal. Broadly, these theorists focus on two issues: how motivation gets translated into regulated behavior, and how motivation and cognition are linked.

Social Cognitive Theories of Self-Regulation and Motivation

Reviewing the extensive literature on the self-regulation of behavior is beyond the scope of the chapter (see Borkowski, Carr, Relliger, & Pressley, 1990; Bullock, 1991). We focus on the work of Zimmerman, Schunk, and their colleagues because they directly link motivation to self-regulation. Zimmerman (1989) described self-regulated students as being metacognitively, motivationally, and behaviorally active in their own learning processes and in achieving their own goals. Following Bandura (1986), Zimmerman posited reciprocally related personal, environmental, and behavioral determinants of self-regulated learning that allow individuals to control the extent to which they are self-regulated through personal and behavioral actions and choices. He also acknowledged, however, that context is important in that environments vary in how much latitude they afford for choice of activities or approaches.

According to Zimmerman (1989), self-regulated learners have three important characteristics. First, they use *self-regulated strategies* (active learning processes that involve agency and purpose). Second, self-regulated students believe they can perform efficaciously. Third, self-regulated students set numerous and varied *goals* for themselves. Further, self-regulated learners engage in three important processes: *self-observation* (monitoring of one's activities); *self-judgment* (evaluation of how well one's own performance compares with a standard or with the performance of others); and *self-reactions* (reactions to performance outcomes). When these reactions are favorable, particularly in response to failure, students are more likely to persist. As proposed by attribution theorists, the favorableness of one's reaction to failure is determined by how individuals interpret their difficulties and failures. Zimmerman and Bonner (in press) discussed the advantages of attributing difficulties to ineffective strategy use rather than to a more general attribution of not trying.

In his discussions of self-efficacy and self-regulation, Schunk (e.g., 1994) emphasizes the reciprocal roles of goal-setting, self-evaluation, and self-efficacy. He has discussed goals in two ways: Initially, he argued and demonstrated that when goals are proximal, specific, and challenging they are most effective in motivating children's behavior and increasing their sense of self-efficacy (Schunk, 1990, 1991). More recently, Schunk (1994) discussed how self-efficacy might be influenced by the learning and performance goal types discussed earlier, suggesting that self-efficacy should be higher under learning than under performance goals; some research supports this claim (e.g., Elliott & Dweck, 1988; Meece, Blumenfeld, & Hoyle, 1988).

The social cognitive view of self-regulation emphasizes the importance of self-efficacy beliefs, causal attributions, and goal-setting in regulating behavior directed at accomplishing a task or activity. Once children engage in a task, then they must monitor their behavior, judge its outcomes, and react to those outcomes to regulate what they do. Because these processes require relatively sophisticated cognitive processes, it is likely that very young children seldom engage in them.

Theories Linking Motivation and Cognition

Some motivation researchers are interested in how motivation and cognition interact with one another to influence self-regulated learning (e.g., Borkowski & Thorpe, 1994; Paris & Byrnes, 1989). Winne and Marx (1989) suggested that motivation should be conceived in cognitive processing terms, and that motivational thoughts and beliefs are governed by the basic principles of cognitive psychology, differing from other thoughts and beliefs only in their content. Winne and Marx further discussed the conditions under which tasks are performed, the operations needed to complete the task, the product the student produces when the task is completed, and the evaluation of the task and how motivation can influence each aspect.

Borkowski and his colleagues (e.g., Borkowski et al., 1990; Borkowski & Muthukrisna, 1995) developed a model highlighting the interaction of the following cognitive, motivational, and self-processes: knowledge of oneself (including one's goals, possible selves, and sense of self-worth), domain-specific knowledge, strategy knowledge, and personal-motivational states (including attributional beliefs, self-efficacy, and intrinsic motivation). More specifically, Borkowski and Thorpe (1994) stressed the importance of a belief in both an incremental view of ability and the utility of carefully applied effort, intrinsic motivation, low anxiety, and positive academic-focused possible selves for preventing underachievement. In their intervention work with learning-disabled or low-achieving children, Borkowski and his colleagues showed that teaching both learning strategies and an understanding that effort and a sense of personal control can produce successful performance is more effective than strategy instruction alone (Carr & Borkowski, 1989; Carr, Borowski, & Maxwell, 1991).

Pintrich and Schrauben (1992) also outlined a model of the relations between motivation and cognition with several components including student entry characteristics (e.g., prior achievement levels), the social aspects of the learning setting (e.g., the social characteristics of the tasks and the interactions between students and teachers during instruction), several motivational constructs derived from expectancy-value and goal theories (expectancies, values, and affect), and various cognitive constructs (e.g., background knowledge, learning strategies, and self-regulatory and metacognitive strategies). Pintrich and Schrauben (1992) postulated that the cognitive and motivational constructs influence each other as well as being influenced by the social context in which the learning is taking place. In turn, both the cognitive and motivational constructs are assumed to influence students' involvement with their learning, and consequently, achievement outcomes.

Pintrich and De Groot (1990) tested this model with both junior high school and college students. Perceived self-efficacy and task values related positively to the reported use of cognitive strategies and self-regulation. The relations between achievement values, strategy use, and self-regulation were stronger than those between self-efficacy, strategy use, and self-regulation. As found by Eccles, Wigfield, and their colleagues, expectancies related more strongly than achievement values to performance. However, as predicted, they also found that cognitive strategy and self-regulation most directly predicted performance. The relations of self-efficacy and task values to performance were mediated through their association with both learning and self-regulation strategies (cf., Pokay & Blumenfeld, 1990). Consistent with the expectancy-value models of Eccles-Parsons and her colleagues (e.g., 1983) and Bandura's (1994) model of self-efficacy, Pintrich and De Groot concluded that achievement values determine initial engagement decisions with self-efficacy then facilitating both engagement and performance in conjunction with cognitive and self-regulation strategies. Although these hypotheses need to be tested longitudinally and in varied activity domains, these results provide good preliminary evidence of the ways motivation and cognition work together to facilitate (or impede) performance on different academic tasks.

Many of the possible links in both the Borkowski and Muhukrishna and the Pintrich and Schrauben models remain unexamined. Pintrich et al. (1993) presented a more fully articulated discussion of links of motivation and cognition, with specific reference to conceptual change. They discussed how traditional "cold" cognitive psychological models of conceptual change do not consider the motivational and contextual factors that likely influence conceptual development. They described and provided preliminary evidence of how various classroom and motivational factors such as goals, achievement values, efficacy beliefs, and control beliefs can influence whether students change their mental concepts. They also stressed the relative paucity of research on these relations.

Theories of Motivation and Volition

The term "volition" refers to both the strength of will needed to complete a task and diligence of pursuit (Corno, 1993). Kuhl (1987) argued that many motivational theorists have ignored volitional processes by assuming that motivation leads directly to outcomes. He argued instead that motivational processes only *lead* to the decision to act. Once the individual *engages* in action, volitional processes take over and determine whether or not the intention is fulfilled (cf., Zimmerman, 1989). Distracters can waylay even the strongest intentions to complete a task or activity. Kuhl proposed several specific volitional strategies to explain persistence in the face of distractions and other opportunities:

1. *Cognitive control strategies* that help individuals stay focused on the relevant information, avoid distracting information, and optimize decision making; selective attention, encoding control, and parsimony of information processing are three cognitive strategies.
2. *Emotional control strategies* that keep inhibiting emotional states such as anxiety and depression in check.
3. *Motivational control strategies* that strengthen the current behavior's motivational base particularly when the

intention is weak relative to other possible competing intentions.
4. *Environmental control strategies* that constrain or enhance one's environment to facilitate the motivated behavior such as turning off the TV while studying.

Finally, Kuhl proposed that some individuals (those with an *action orientation*) are more likely to engage in these volitional strategies than *state-oriented* individuals.

Corno discussed volition in the context of student achievement as "a dynamic system of psychological control processes that protect concentration and direct effort in the face of personal and/or environmental distractions, and so aid learning and performance" (Corno, 1989, p. 16). She provided several examples of the volitional challenges students face (coordinating multiple demands and desires such as doing homework, watching TV, or calling a friend; dealing with the many distractions in any particular context such as a classroom; and clarifying often vaguely specified goals and assignments). She focused on Kuhl's (1985) motivation and emotion control strategies because strengthening one's motivation to complete a task and managing one's negative emotional states are often crucial to successful academic performance. Corno also argued that volition is a broader concept than self-regulation because volition includes personality characteristics, aptitudes, and other cognitive processes, while most models of self-regulation focus more narrowly on self-monitoring and self-evaluation (see also Corno & Kanfer, 1993).

The development of good volitional control and self-regulation is widely acknowledged as an important socialization outcome. Jackson (1968) stressed the need for schoolchildren to learn patience and control over their immediate impulses in order to deal effectively with the delays, obstructions, and rules that are an ever-present part of schooling. Indeed, Corno and Kanfer (1993) argued that the acquisition of volitional skills such as persistence and patience are essential elements of becoming good citizens in both school and, later, in the workplace. However, because the volition construct has only recently resurfaced in psychology, there has been relatively little research on its relation to motivation and performance.

Academic Help Seeking

Some researchers have argued that knowing when help is needed is another important aspect of self-regulation and volition. Children learn to do many tasks on their own; indeed, schools and parents often encourage children to become independent and self-reliant. However, there are times when children need help. Both Nelson-Le Gall and her colleagues (e.g., Nelson-Le Gall & Glor-Shieb, 1985; Nelson-Le Gall & Jones, 1990) and Newman and his colleagues (e.g., Newman, 1990, 1994; Newman & Goldin, 1990; Newman & Schwager, 1995) have articulated models that stress the difference between children's appropriate and inappropriate help seeking. Appropriate help seeking (labeled *instrumental* help seeking by Nelson-Le Gall and *adaptive* help seeking by Newman) involves deciding that one doesn't understand how to complete a problem after having tried to solve it on one's own, figuring out what and whom to ask, developing a good question to get the needed help, and processing the information received appropriately in order to complete the problem-solving task. Instrumental help seeking can foster motivation by keeping children engaged in an activity when they experience difficulties. Newman (1994) has found that children are most likely to seek adaptive help when they are self-regulated and have strong competence beliefs, and have mastery-oriented learning goals.

Summary

Some of the most promising current work in motivation focuses on the link between motivational constructs and the cognitive processes underlying both the acquisition of new material and skills and optimal performance of learned material and skills. Although some of this work builds on the tradition of remediation of motivational problems, the newest work integrates the fields of cognitive science, social cognition, personality, and motivation. Such work is opening new theoretical perspectives and promising more effective intervention strategies. More work is needed adapting these findings for children of different ages in different contexts.

THE DEVELOPMENT OF MOTIVATION: WITHIN-PERSON CHANGE AND GROUP DIFFERENCES

Developmental and educational psychologists have focused on two major developmental questions: (a) How do the beliefs, values, and goals develop during childhood and adolescence? (b) What explains the emergence of individual differences in motivation? Three broad sources of influence have been considered: (a) within-person changes resulting from growth and maturation in cognitive processing, emotional development, or other individual characteristics;

(b) socially mediated developmental changes resulting from systematic age-related changes in the social contexts children experience at home, in school, and among peers as they grow up; and (c) socially mediated influences that differ across individuals and contexts. These different sources often interact with one another but the nature of this interaction is rarely studied. Consequently, our discussion of the development of motivation and of individual differences in motivation is organized around these three broad categories of influence. First, we present work on within-person changes, beginning with work on children's early self-evaluations, and then describing the work on within-person changes in the constructs discussed thus far. We also include a consideration of the development of motivational problems, and of sex and ethnic differences in motivation. In the last three sections, we describe parent and family influences; then school influences, and finally peer influences.

Early Development of Self-Evaluation

Some researchers have looked at very young children's reactions to success and failure because these reactions provide one foundation for the development of the different motivational beliefs, values, and goals discussed in this chapter. Heckhausen (1984, 1987) found that children between 2½ and 3½ years of age start to show self-evaluative, nonverbal expressions following a successful or unsuccessful action. The earliest indicators of achievement motivation were facial expressions of joy after success and sadness after failure. The experience of success (around 30 months) preceded the experience of failure (around 36 months). Several months later, children showed postural expressions of pride and shame following success and failure. When competing with others, 3- and 4-year-old children initially showed joy after winning and sadness after losing. It was only when they looked at their competitor that they expressed pride and shame.

Stipek, Recchia, and McClintic (1992) identified three stages of development in their young children's self-evaluations: The children younger than 22 months were neither concerned with others' evaluation of their performance nor self-reflective in their evaluations. However, they did show positive emotional reactions to accomplishing a task and negative emotions when they did not. Thus, unlike Heckhausen, Stipek et al. found that reactions to success and failure occurred at the same time in development. Two-year-olds reacted more to others' evaluations by seeking approval when they did well and turning away when they did poorly. After age 3, the children were able to evaluate their own performance, without needing to see how adults reacted to that performance, and engaged in more autonomous self-evaluation. Children 3 and older also reacted more strongly to winning and losing than did younger children.

Taken together, these studies show that reactions to success and failure begin early in the preschool years, likely laying the groundwork for the development of motivation in the middle childhood years. The results concerning children's reactions to failure are particularly important because they suggest that children are more sensitive to failure in the preschool years than was once believed (see also Burhans & Dweck, 1995).

The Development of Competence-Related Beliefs

Much of the work on the development of children's achievement-related beliefs has looked at the development of children's ability and expectancy-related beliefs (e.g., see Dweck & Elliott, 1983; Stipek & Mac Iver, 1989). We discuss three kinds of changes in these beliefs: change in their factorial structure, in mean levels, and in children's understanding of them.

The Factorial Structure of Children's Competence-Related Beliefs

Developmental theorists such as Werner (1957) have proposed that many characteristics change with age from a global to a more differentiated state. Harter (1983) discussed how children begin with broad understandings of whether they are "smart" or "dumb," that later develop into a more fine-grained and differentiated understanding of their competencies across different activities. Researchers examining this hypothesis with factor analytic approaches have found that even very young elementary schoolchildren distinguish their competence self-perceptions across different domains of competence (e.g., Eccles, Wigfield, Harold, & Blumenfeld, 1993; Harter, 1982; Harter & Pike, 1984; Marsh & Hocevar, 1985). For example, Eccles, Wigfield, et al. (1993), Marsh, Barnes, Cairns, & Tidman (1984), and Wigfield, Eccles, Yoon, et al. (1996) demonstrated that even kindergarten and first-grade children's beliefs about their competencies are differentiated across many different domains including math, reading, music, sports, general school ability, physical appearance, and both peer and parent relations. Apparently, the differentiation process begins very young for ability beliefs—as young as we have been

able to reliably measure these beliefs. This does not mean, however, that there is no change or refinement in children's beliefs from kindergarten through high school. As one might expect, the younger children in the Eccles, Wigfield, et al. (1993) study gave more extreme responses, used fewer of the scale points, and their responses correlated less well with both their teachers' and their parents' estimates of their competencies (Wigfield, Eccles, Yoon, et al., 1996). So, although the first graders' responses yielded a well-differentiated factor structure, their responses became more finely tuned and more strongly related to external indicators of their performance as they got older, particularly during the first 3 to 4 years of elementary school.

Some of these researchers (Eccles & Wigfield, 1995; Eccles, Wigfield, et al., 1993) also have used factor analytic strategies to access whether children's competence beliefs and expectancies for success are distinct constructs. Both children's and adolescents' data suggest that ratings of their own current competence, expectancies for success, and perceived performance load on the same factor, suggesting that these components comprise a single concept for children aged 6 to 18.

Change in the Mean Level of Children's Competence-Related Beliefs

Several researchers have found that children's competence-related beliefs for different tasks decline across the elementary school years and into the middle school years (see Dweck & Elliott, 1983; Eccles & Midgley, 1989; Stipek & Mac Iver, 1989). To illustrate, in Nicholls (1979a), most first graders ranked themselves near the top of the class in reading ability, and there was no correlation between their ability ratings and their performance level. In contrast, the 12-year-olds' ratings were more dispersed and correlated highly with school grades (.70 or higher). Similar results have emerged in cross-sectional and longitudinal studies of children's competence beliefs in various academic and nonacademic domains by Eccles and her colleagues (e.g., Eccles, Wigfield, et al., 1993; Wigfield, Eccles, Yoon, et al., 1996) and Marsh (1989). These declines, particularly for math, often continue into, and through, secondary school (Eccles-Parsons et al., 1983; Eccles et al., 1989; Wigfield, Eccles, Mac Iver, Reuman, & Midgley, 1991).

Expectancies for success also decrease during the elementary school years. In most laboratory-type studies, 4- and 5-year old children expect to do quite well on specific tasks, even after repeated failure (e.g., Parsons & Ruble, 1977; Stipek, 1984). Stipek (1984) argued that young children's optimistic expectancies may reflect hoped-for outcomes rather than real expectations; in addition, Parsons and Ruble (1977) suggested that, since young children's skills improve rapidly, high expectancies for future success may be based on experience (see also Dweck & Elliott, 1983). Across the elementary school years, however, children become more sensitive to both success and failure experiences and their expectancies of success become more directly linked to their actual performance history (see Assor & Connell, 1992; Eccles, Midgley, & Adler, 1984; Parsons & Ruble, 1972, 1977; Stipek, 1984).

In contrast to these early studies using self-report measures, researchers using different methods (either asking different kinds of questions, or observing young children's reactions to their performance on different tasks) have shown that not all young children are optimistic about their abilities. In Heyman, Dweck, and Cain (1993), some preschool children reacted quite negatively to failure, reporting that their failures mean that they are not good people. Similarly in Stipek, et al. (1992), preschool children as young as 2 reacted both behaviorally and emotionally to failure experiences.

In summary, children's competence beliefs and expectancies for success become more negative as they get older, at least through the early adolescence time period. The negative changes in children's competence-related beliefs have been explained in two ways: First, because children become much better at understanding, interpreting, and integrating the evaluative feedback they receive, and engage in more social comparison with their peers, children become more accurate or realistic in their self-assessments, leading some to become relatively more negative (see Dweck & Elliott, 1983; Nicholls, 1984; Parsons & Ruble, 1977; Ruble, 1983; Shaklee & Tucker, 1979; Stipek & Mac Iver, 1989). Second, because changes in the school environment make evaluation more salient and competition between students more likely, some children's self-assessments will decline as they get older (e.g., see Blumenfeld, Pintrich, Meece, & Wessels, 1982; Eccles & Midgley, 1989; Eccles, Midgley, & Adler, 1984; Stipek & Daniels, 1988).

Changes in Children's Understanding of Competence-Related Beliefs

Several researchers have investigated children's understanding of ability, effort, task difficulty, and intelligence. For example, Nicholls and his colleagues asked children questions about ability, intelligence, effort, and task difficulty, and about how different levels of performance can occur when children exert similar effort (e.g., Nicholls, 1978; Nicholls, Patashnick, & Mettetal, 1986). They found four relatively distinct levels of reasoning: At Level 1 (ages 5–6), effort, ability, and performance are not clearly differentiated in terms of cause and effect. At Level 2 (ages 7–9), effort is seen as the primary cause of performance outcomes. At Level 3 (ages 9–12), children begin to differentiate ability and effort as causes of outcomes, but they do not always apply this distinction. Finally, at Level 4, adolescents clearly differentiate ability and effort, and understand the notion of ability as capacity. They also believe that ability can limit the effects of additional effort on performance, that ability and effort are often related to each other in a compensatory manner, and, consequently, that success requiring a great deal of effort likely reflects limited ability (cf., Kun, Parsons, & Ruble, 1974).

Dweck and her colleagues (e.g., Dweck & Elliott, 1983; Dweck & Leggett, 1988) have also studied children's understanding of intelligence and ability. They hypothesized that children hold one of two views: An *entity* view that intelligence or ability is a stable trait, or an *incremental* view that intelligence or ability is changeable and can be increased through effort. Although Dweck's entity view of intelligence seems similar to the notion of "ability as capacity," Nicholls (1990) argued that Dweck and her colleagues equate "ability" and "intelligence" in their work, thus glossing over important differences between the two constructs (see Nicholls et al., 1986, for discussion of how ability and intelligence are different constructs). However despite the differences in their approaches to defining and assessing the construct of intelligence, both Nicholls (1984) and Dweck (e.g., Dweck & Elliott, 1983; Dweck & Leggett, 1988) have stressed how children's conceptions of ability and intelligence have important motivational consequences. Believing that ability is a capacity should increase the debilitating effects of failure on performance and motivation. Children holding this view likely believe they have little chance of improving after failure because their ability cannot be increased. In contrast, believing that effort can improve one's ability (an incremental view of intelligence) should protect against a learned helpless response to failure precisely because these children should continue to try even after failing. The work by Nicholls suggests that younger children may be less likely to believe ability is stable or fixed; however, Burhans and Dweck (1995) reviewed evidence showing that some young children already have doubts about their ability to do certain tasks, even if they are trying hard.

Development of Efficacy Beliefs

There has not been extensive research on the development of efficacy beliefs per se, although the work on ability beliefs and expectancies is directly relevant. Instead, research on children's self-efficacy has focused primarily on interventions to enhance the self-efficacy and school performance of low-achieving children (e.g., see Schunk, 1990, 1991, 1994). As valuable as this work is, more work is needed on the age-related differences in both efficacy beliefs and their relation to performance. Shell, Colvin, and Bruning (1995) found that 4th graders had lower self-efficacy beliefs for reading and writing than did 7th and 10th graders, and the 7th graders' efficacy beliefs were lower than 10th graders' beliefs (see Zimmerman & Martinez-Pons, 1990, for similar findings). That these findings are inconsistent with findings on children's competence beliefs probably reflects the self-efficacy measure used by Shell et al. because their instrument measured children's estimates of their efficacy on specific reading and writing skills, which should be higher among older children.

Bandura (1994) presented a comprehensive theoretical analysis of the development of self-efficacy. First, he proposed that experiences controlling proximal stimuli provide the earliest sense of personal agency. Through these experiences, infants learn that they can influence and control their environments. If adults do not provide infants with these experiences, they are not likely to develop a strong sense of personal agency. Second, because self-efficacy requires the understanding that the *self* produced an action and an outcome, Bandura (1994) argued that a more mature sense of self-efficacy should not emerge until children have at least a rudimentary self-concept and can recognize that they are distinct individuals, which happens sometime during the second year of life (see Harter, 1983; Ch. 9, this Volume). Through the preschool period, children are exposed to extensive performance information that should be crucial to their emerging sense of self-efficacy. However, just how useful such information is likely depends on the child's ability to integrate it across time, contexts, and domains. Since these cognitive capacities emerge gradually over the preschool and early elementary school years, young children's efficacy judgments should depend more on immediate and apparent outcomes than on a systematic analysis of their performance history in similar situations (see Parsons & Ruble, 1972, 1977; Ruble, Parsons, & Ross, 1976; Shaklee & Tucker, 1979). More work is needed to understand how children become able to integrate diverse sources of information about their performances (e.g., information about their own performance, social comparison information, etc.) to develop a stable self-efficacy (cf., Ruble, 1983).

In his developmental analysis, Bandura (1994) also considered the influence of goals. He argued that proximal rather than distal goals help foster a sense of efficacy, because distal goals are too general and abstract (cf., Schunk, 1990, 1991). Bandura also hypothesized that children's interests derive from their efficacy beliefs, arguing that people become and stay interested in activities they can do and that provide them some satisfaction. This perspective is similar to the hypothesized relation of ability self-concepts to task value in the Eccles et al. expectancy-value model. Also like others (e.g., Csikszentmihalyi, 1988), Bandura hypothesized that challenging activities will be of most interest. In addition, reminiscent of Atkinson's claim that people with stronger tendencies to approach success (who likely have a stronger sense of efficacy as well) will be most motivated on tasks of intermediate difficulty, Bandura predicted that feeling *too* efficacious about an activity might decrease interest because the task will seem too easy and boring. Finally, he stressed the importance of school environments for developing and supporting a high sense of efficacy.

Development of Control Beliefs

In their review of studies of children primarily 8 to 9 years and older, Skinner and Connell (1986) concluded that there is an increase in perceptions of internal control as children get older. In contrast, based on a series of studies of children's understanding of skill versus chance events, Weisz (1984) concluded that the developmental sequence is more complex. The kindergarten children in these studies believed outcomes of chance tasks were due to effort; whereas the oldest groups (eighth graders and college students) believed that such outcomes were due to chance; fourth graders were confused about the distinction. Thus, in this work, the youngest children had such strong internal control beliefs that they believed they had control over totally chance based outcomes, suggesting that with age children came to understand better which kinds of events they can and cannot control. Similarly, Connell (1985) found a decrease in the endorsement of all three of his locus of control constructs (internal control, powerful others control, and unknown control) from Grades 3 through 9. Like Weisz's (1984) findings, the unknown belief results suggest that older children have a clearer understanding of what controls achievement outcomes. However, the older children also rated the other two sources of control as less important, making interpretation of these findings difficult.

In discussing the ontogeny of control beliefs, E. Skinner (1990, 1995) stressed the importance of perceived contingency between individuals' actions and their successes. She also stressed that success itself fosters positive control beliefs and discussed how children's understanding of causality and explanations for outcomes likely change over age with these beliefs, particularly the means-ends beliefs, becoming more differentiated as children get older. What is similar across all ages is the importance of fulfilling the need for competence.

Skinner has examined age differences in both the structure and the mean levels of means-ends beliefs (see E. Skinner, 1995). The factor structure of these beliefs is more differentiated among older children. Among the 7- and 8-year-olds, two factors emerged with the unknown items loading on one factor, and the effort, luck, ability, and powerful other items loading on a second factor. Among 9- and 10-year-olds, this second factor divided into internal (ability and effort) and external (luck and powerful others) components. Among 11- and 12-year-olds, there were four factors: unknown, external, ability, and effort. Based on these factor analytic results, Skinner suggested that different aspects of control should influence children's behavior at different ages, with unknown control being one of the first predictors, and perceived ability emerging much later. This hypothesis has yet to be tested.

She also found the largest mean-level differences on some of the means-ends beliefs. At all ages between 7 and 12, children believe effort is the most effective means. In contrast, older children are much less likely to believe that luck is an effective means than younger children. As in Connell (1985), belief in the relevance of unknown control and powerful others also decreased across age levels.

In summary, there are numerous changes in children's competence and control beliefs including structural change, mean-level change, and change in children's understanding of the constructs. These changes pose interesting theoretical and methodological problems for researchers trying to measure these constructs in different-aged children.

Development of Subjective Task Values

Eccles, Wigfield, and their colleagues examined age-related changes in both the structure and mean levels of children's valuing of different activities In Eccles, Wigfield, et al. (1993), Eccles and Wigfield (1995) and Wigfield, Eccles, Yoon, et al. (1996), children's competence-expectancy beliefs and subjective values *within* the domains of math, reading, and sports formed distinct factors at all grade levels from 1st through 12th. Thus, even during the very early elementary grades children appear to have distinct beliefs about what they are *good* at and what they *value*. The distinction between components of subjective task value appear to differentiate more gradually (Eccles, Wigfield, et al., 1993; Eccles & Wigfield, 1995; Wigfield, Eccles, Yoon, et al., 1996). Children in early elementary school differentiate task value into two components: interest and utility/importance. In contrast, children in Grades 5 through 12 differentiate task value into the three major subcomponents (attainment value/personal importance, interest, and utility value) outlined by Eccles-Parsons et al. (1983). These results suggest that the interest component differentiates out first, followed later by the distinction between utility and attainment value.

As with competence-related beliefs, studies generally show age-related declines in children's valuing of certain academic tasks (e.g., Eccles et al., 1983, 1993b; see Eccles & Midgley, 1989; Wigfield & Eccles, 1992). In a longitudinal analysis of elementary school children, beliefs about the usefulness and importance of math, reading, instrumental music, and sports activities decreased over time (Wigfield, Eccles, Yoon, et al., 1996). In contrast, the children's interest decreased only for reading and instrumental music, not for either math or sports. The decline in valuing of math continues through high school (Eccles, 1984; Eccles, Midgley, et al., 1984). Eccles et al. (1989) and Wigfield et al. (1991) also found that children's ratings of both the importance of math and English and their liking of these school subjects decreased across the transition to junior high school. In math, students' importance ratings continued to decline across seventh grade, whereas their importance ratings of English increased somewhat during seventh grade. It is important to examine the components of task value separately if we are to understand the development of achievement-related task values.

Researchers have not addressed changes in children's understandings of the components of task value identified by Eccles-Parsons et al. (1983), although there likely are age-related differences in these understandings. An 8-year-old is likely to have a different sense of what it means for a task to be "useful" than an 11-year-old does. Further, it also is likely that there are differences across age in which components of achievement values are most dominant. Wigfield and Eccles (1992) suggested that interest may be especially salient during the early elementary school grades with young children's activity choices being most directly related to their interests. If, as Nagy (1912) proposed, young children's interests shift as rapidly as their attention spans, they are likely to try many different activities for a short time each before developing a more stable opinion regarding which activities they enjoy the most. As children get older, the perceived utility and personal importance of different tasks likely become more salient, particularly as they develop more stable self-schemas and long-range goals and plans. These developmental predictions need to be tested.

A related developmental question is how children's developing competence beliefs relate to their developing subjective task values. According to both the Eccles (Eccles-Parsons et al., 1983) model and Bandura's (1994) self-efficacy theory, ability self-concepts should influence the development of task values. In support of this prediction, Mac Iver, Stipek, and Daniels (1991) found that changes in junior high school students' competence beliefs over a semester predicted change in children's interests much more strongly than vice versa. Does the same causal ordering occur in younger children? Bandura (1994) argued that interests emerge out of one's sense of self-efficacy and that children should be more interested in challenging than in easy tasks. Taking a more developmental perspective, Wigfield (1994) proposed that initially young children's competence and task value beliefs are likely to be relatively independent of each other. This independence would mean that young children may be more likely than older children to pursue activities they are interested in regardless of how good or bad they think they are at the activity. Over time, particularly in the achievement domains, children may begin to attach more value to those activities they are good at for several reasons: First, through processes associated with classical conditioning, the positive affect one experiences when one does well should become attached to the activities yielding success (see Eccles, 1984). Second, lowering the value one attaches to activities that one is having difficulty with is an effective way to maintain a positive global sense of efficacy and self-esteem (see Eccles, 1984; Eccles, Wigfield, & Blumenfeld, 1984; Harter, 1990). Thus, at some point the two kinds of beliefs should become more positively related to one another. In partial support of this view, Wigfield, Eccles, Yoon, et al. (1996) found that relations between

children's competence beliefs and subjective values in different domains become stronger over age as children move through elementary school. The causal direction of this relation needs to be tested.

Development of Interest and Intrinsic Motivation

The theories following the early approaches to interest development were based primarily on empirical studies (for an overview, see Todt, 1990). Most noteworthy is the work of Tyler (1955), Roe and Siegelman (1964), Kohlberg (1966), Travers (1978), and Gottfredson (1981). Based on Piaget's (1948) theory, (Travis 1978) analyzed the earliest phase of interest development. He assumed that only "universal" interests would be evident in very young children, for example, the infant's search for structure. Later, depending on the general cognitive development of the child, these universal interests should become more differentiated and individualized. According to Roe and Siegelman (1964), the earliest differentiation occurs between interest in the world of physical objects versus interest in world of people. Todt (1990) argued that this early differentiation eventually leads to individual differences in interests in the social versus the natural sciences.

The next phase of interest development—between 3 and 8 years of age—should be strongly influenced by gender-role acquisition. According to Kohlberg (1966), the acquisition of gender identity leads to gender-specific behaviors, attitudes, and interests. Children strive to behave consistently with their gender identity and, thus, evaluate activities or objects consistent with their gender identity more positively than other activities or objects. As a consequence, boys and girls develop gender-role stereotyped interests (see Ruble & Martin, Ch. 14, this Volume; Eccles, 1987).

Similarly, in her theory of occupational aspirations, Gottfredson (1981) assumed that the development of interests depends on the development of one's self-concept, particularly those dimensions of the self-concept linked to gender, social class, and ability. Initially, gender is the primary dimension. At the next stage (ages 9–13), the emerging self-concept is assumed to be linked more directly to social group affiliation and cognitive ability, leading to occupational interests consistent with one's social class and ability self-concepts. The final stage (occurring after age 13 or 14) is characterized by an orientation to the internal, unique self leading to more differentiated and individualized vocational interest, based on abstract concepts of self (e.g., of personality). Thus, the development of vocational interests is a process of continuous elimination of interests that do not fit the self-concepts of one's gender, social group affiliation, ability, and then personal identity (Todt, 1990). This process is assumed to depend mainly on the general cognitive development of the child or adolescent.

It is also likely that changing needs or motives across the life span can influence the development of interests. A good example is the increasing interest in biology and psychology during puberty. The need to know oneself and to cope with rapid bodily and psychological changes seems to foster interest in biological and psychological domains of knowledge (Todt, 1990) at this age.

Consistent with studies of American children (e.g., Eccles, Wigfield, et al., 1993; Harter, 1981; Wigfield et al., 1991), several European researchers have found that interest and intrinsic motivation in different subject areas decline across the school years. This is especially true for the natural sciences and mathematics (e.g., Hedelin & Sjoberg, 1989; Helmke, 1993; Lehrke, Hoffmann, & Gardner, 1985; Oldfather & McLaughlin, 1993) and particularly during the early adolescent years. Pekrun (1993) found that intrinsic motivation stabilized after eighth grade.

Baumert (1995) argued that the decline in school-related interests during adolescence reflects a more general developmental process in which the adolescents discover new fields of experience that lead to new interests and reduce the dominant influence of school (cf., Eder, 1992). In contrast, other researchers have suggested that changes in a number of instructional variables such as clarity of presentation, monitoring of what happens in the classroom, supportive behavior, cognitively stimulating experiences, self-concept of the teacher (educator vs. scientist), and achievement pressure may contribute to declining interest in school mathematics and science (e.g., Eccles & Midgley, 1989).

Development of Children's Goals

Little work has focused on how children's goals develop. Although Nicholls documented that both task goals and ego goals are evident by second grade (e.g., Nicholls et al., 1990), he also suggested that an ego goal orientation becomes more prominent for many children as they get older due to both developmental changes in their conceptions of ability and systematic changes in school context. Dweck and her colleagues (e.g., Dweck & Leggett, 1988) also predicted that performance goals should become more prominent with age as more children view intelligence as stable (entity view), because an entity view of intelligence is linked to performance goals. In contrast, Meece and Miller (1996) found that both children's learning and performance goals decreased across third to fourth grade, while their work avoidance goals increased. More work charting the development of children's goal orientations is needed.

The relations of goals to performance should also change with age as the meaning of ability and effort changes. In a series of studies looking at how competitive and noncompetitive conditions, and task and ego-focused conditions, influence preschool and elementary school-age children's interests, motivation, and self-evaluations, Butler identified several developmental changes: First, competition decreased children's subsequent interest in a task only among children who had also developed a social-comparative sense of ability (Butler, 1989a, 1990). Competition also increased older, but not younger, children's tendency to engage in social comparison (Butler, 1989a, 1989b). Second, although children of all ages engaged in social comparison, younger children seemed to be doing so more for task mastery reasons, whereas older children did so to assess their abilities (Butler, 1989b). Third, whereas, 5-, 7-, and 10-year-old children's self-evaluations were equally accurate under mastery conditions, under competitive conditions 5- and 7-year-olds inflated their performance self-evaluations more than 10-year-olds (Butler, 1990). Apparently the influence of situationally-induced performance goals on children's self-evaluations depends on the children's age and cognitive sophistication. Finally, Butler and Ruzany (1993) found that patterns of socialization influence both ability assessments and reasons for social comparison: Kibbutz-raised Israeli children adopted a normative ability concept at a younger age than city-reared Israeli children. However, only the urban children's reasons for engaging in social comparison were influenced by their concept of ability: Once they adopted a normative view, they used social comparison to compare their abilities with those of other children. In contrast, the kibbutz children used social comparison primarily for mastery reasons, regardless of their conception of ability.

Developmental studies of multiple goals are badly needed. Neither Wentzel or Ford, the major theorists in this area, have done such work. Thus, we know very little about how these kinds of multiple goals emerge during childhood and whether the relation of these different goals to performance varies across age and context.

Development of Self-Regulation and Volition

Before reviewing the work on self-regulatory and volitional processes in achievement settings, two general developmental points need to be made. First, children's ability to self-regulate increases dramatically across the toddler period (Bullock & Lutkenhaus, 1988) due to increases in ability to focus on both the outcomes of their behaviors and the behaviors themselves (see Mischel & Mischel, 1983), increases in understanding of the self as a causal agent (Bandura, 1994; Jennings, 1991; E. Skinner, 1995), and increases in both the ability and desire to evaluate the success or failure of one's achievement efforts (Heckhausen, 1984, 1987; Stipek et al., 1992). Second, parents play a critical role in the extent to which children regulate their own behavior. Both the ways parents define and organize tasks for the children and the control strategies they use have a big impact on very young children's ability to regulate their behavior (e.g., use of indirect commands, verbal controls, and reasoning facilitates the early development of self-regulation, Kopp, 1991).

Turning to self-regulated learning, Zimmerman and Bonner (in press) recently proposed a four-step developmental sequence. Children first learn effective strategies by observing successful models. Second, children imitate the strategies, following what the model did relatively closely. Third, they learn to use the strategies apart from the model; Zimmerman and Bonner called this self-controlled learning. Although children do the strategies on their own, they still are dependent on the model. Finally, children begin to both use the strategies in different situations and tailor them to their own purposes. This hypothesized sequence has yet to be tested and there is very little developmental research on the kinds of self-regulatory strategies and processes Zimmerman and his colleagues have discussed (e.g., Zimmerman & Martinez-Pons, 1986). Zimmerman and Martinez-Pons (1990) found a complex pattern of differences across age in use of these strategies by older children and adolescents. Researchers have not yet systematically tested how strategies, goals, and self-efficacy interact to influence the regulation of learning in children of different ages. Additionally, it would be useful to compare Zimmerman and Bonner's model with Deci and Ryan's discussion of the development of internalized regulation.

In contrast, there is some developmental work on volitional strategies. For example, Kuhl and Kraska (1989), in German and Mexican elementary school-age children, found increases in children's ability to use all the strategies except for emotion control. But more developmental work is needed here as well.

The Development and Remediation of Motivational Problems

Many children begin to experience motivational problems during the school years. These problems include anxiety, lack of confidence in their abilities, and the belief that they cannot control their own achievement outcomes. Two motivational problems have received extensive research attention—test anxiety and learned helplessness.

Anxiety

Test anxiety is estimated to interfere with the learning and performance, particularly in evaluative situations, of as many as 10 million children and adolescents in the United States (Hill & Wigfield, 1984; Tobias, 1985; Wigfield & Eccles, 1989; Wigfield & Meece, 1988). Much work has focused on the cognitive/worry aspect of anxiety because worry is more strongly and negatively related to performance than emotionality (e.g., Geen, 1980; Morris, Davis, & Hutchings, 1981; I. G. Sarason, 1980; Zatz & Chassin, 1983, 1985). For example, Wine (1971, 1980) suggested that worry interferes with cognitive processing and the maintenance of attention to the task at hand because highly anxious individuals divide their attention between the task and their negative ruminations about the task and the likelihood they will do poorly on it. This divided attention leads to poorer performance (see also Benjamin, McKeachie, & Lin, 1987; Tobias, 1985). Furthermore, introducing tasks, tests, or assignments as tests of ability heightens the worry of highly anxious individuals (see Wigfield & Eccles, 1989).

Researchers (e.g., Dusek, 1980; Hill & Wigfield, 1984; Wigfield & Eccles, 1989) have postulated that high trait-anxiety emerges when parents have overly high expectations and put too much pressure on their children, but few studies have tested this proposition. Anxiety continues to develop across the school years as children face more frequent evaluation, social comparison, and (for some) experiences of failure; to the extent that schools emphasize these characteristics, both state and trait-anxiety become a problem for more children (Hill & Wigfield, 1984; Phillips, Pitcher, Worcham, & Miller, 1980). Wigfield and

Eccles (1989) proposed that anxiety initially may be characterized more by emotionality, but as children develop cognitively, the worry aspect of anxiety should become increasingly salient. This proposal needs to be tested, but we do know that worry is a major component of the thought processes of highly anxious fifth and sixth graders (Freedman-Doan, 1994; Zatz & Chassin, 1983, 1985).

With a few important exceptions (e.g., Silverman, La Greca, & Wasserstein, 1995; Vasey & Daliedon, 1994), work on anxiety has diminished over the past decade for two reasons: (a) increased focus on cold cognitions such as ability and efficacy beliefs, and achievement goals; and (b) the argument that anxiety is simply the flip side of negative judgments about one's ability and efficacy. For example, Nicholls (1976) concluded that many items on the TASC refer to negative ability beliefs. When he separated the ability and anxiety items, the ability items related more strongly to indicators of achievement than the anxiety items (cf., Bandura, 1994; Meece et al., 1990). But the apparent similarity of anxiety and negative ability beliefs likely reflects a focus in current tests on the cognitive aspects of anxiety. Although this component is critical, a consideration of physiological/emotional aspects of anxiety, and possibly other motivational constructs, is also needed, particularly as we learn more and more about biological influences (e.g., temperament and level of arousal) on thought and behavior. It is also likely that the emotional component of anxiety will have a more independent influence on performance than the worry component. Nonetheless, work on the worry component is still important because this component provides a process mechanism explanation for the negative effects of low confidence on performance.

Anxiety Intervention Programs. Many programs have been developed to reduce anxiety (see Deffenbacher, 1980; Denny, 1980; Hill, 1980; Wigfield & Eccles, 1989). Earlier intervention programs, emphasizing the emotionality aspect of anxiety, focused on relaxation and desensitization techniques. Although these programs reduced anxiety, they did not always lead to improved performance, and the studies had serious methodological flaws. Anxiety intervention programs linked to the worry aspect of anxiety focus on changing the negative, self-deprecating thoughts of anxious individuals and replacing them with more positive, task-focused thoughts (e.g., see Denny, 1980; Meichenbaum & Butler, 1980). These programs have been more successful both in lowering anxiety and improving performance.

An important issue needing more attention is how to tailor programs for children of different ages, particularly during elementary school (see Wigfield & Eccles, 1989). Further, because children's anxiety depends so much on the kinds of evaluations they experience in school, changes in school testing practices could help reduce anxiety (see Hill & Wigfield, 1984).

Learned Helplessness

"Learned helplessness . . . exists when an individual perceives the termination of failure to be independent of his responses" (Dweck & Goetz, 1978, p. 157). It is related to individuals' attributions: Helpless individuals are more likely to attribute their failures to uncontrollable factors, such as lack of ability, and their successes to unstable factors (see Dweck & Goetz, 1978). Dweck and her colleagues have documented several differences between helpless and more mastery-oriented children's responses to failure (see Dweck & Elliott, 1983; Dweck & Leggett, 1988): When confronted by difficulty (or failure), mastery-oriented children persist, stay focused on the task, and sometimes even use more sophisticated strategies. In contrast, helpless children's performance deteriorates, they ruminate about their difficulties, and they often begin to attribute their failures to lack of ability. Further, helpless children adopt the "entity" view that their intelligence is fixed, whereas mastery-oriented children adopt the incremental view of intelligence.

Because young children have limited cognitive abilities, confuse different attributional categories (particularly ability and effort), and have trouble distinguishing between contingent and noncontingent events (making it difficult for them to know which outcomes they do and do not control, Weisz, 1984), it is likely that both learned helpless behaviors and the concomitant detrimental effects will show a developmental pattern. In support of this hypothesis, Rholes, Blackwell, Jordan, and Walters (1980) found that younger children did not show the same decrements in performance in response to failure as some older children do. However, recent work (see Burhans & Dweck, 1995) shows that some young (5- and 6-year-old) children respond quite negatively to failure feedback, judging themselves to be bad people (cf., Stipek et al., 1992). Burhans and Dweck proposed that young children's helplessness is based more on their judgments that their worth as persons is contingent on their performance than on having a mature entity view of intelligence. Fincham and Cain (1986) stressed the need to examine how children's understanding of contingencies, estimations of their own competence, and attributions for their outcomes work together in determining children's evaluations of their achievement outcomes. This kind of integrative work on learned helplessness has not yet been undertaken. However, the work by Burhans and Dweck suggests an important developmental modification to Dweck and Legget's model of learned helpless versus mastery-oriented motivational styles.

What else influences the emergence of individual differences in learned helplessness in children? Dweck and Goetz (1978) stressed the importance of whether children receive feedback that their failures are due to lack of ability or lack of skills and effort from parents and teachers. In support, Hokoda and Fincham (1995) found that mothers of helpless third grade children (compared with mothers of mastery-oriented children) gave fewer positive affective comments to their children, were more likely to respond to their children's lack of confidence in their ability by telling them to quit, were less responsive to their children's bids for help, and did not focus them on mastery goals. Dweck and Goetz argued further that girls may be more likely than boys to receive negative ability feedback in elementary school classrooms (see Dweck, Davidson, Nelson, & Enna, 1978), and so may be more likely to develop helplessness. Although some other researchers have not replicated Dweck et al.'s (1978) classroom findings regarding sex differences in feedback to children (e.g., Eccles-Parsons, Kaczala, & Meece, et al., 1982), it is likely that children who receive feedback that their failures are due to lack of ability will be more prone to develop helplessness.

Alleviating Learned Helplessness. Various training techniques (including operant conditioning and providing specific attributional feedback) have been used successfully to change children's failure attributions from lack of ability to lack of effort, improving their task persistence, and performance (e.g., Andrews & Debus, 1978; Dweck, 1975; Forsterling, 1985; Fowler & Peterson, 1981). Two problems with these approaches have been noted. First, what if the child is already trying very hard? Then the attribution retraining may be counterproductive. Second, telling children to "try harder" without providing specific strategies to improve performance is likely to backfire if the children increase their efforts and still do not succeed.

Therefore, some researchers advocate using strategy retraining in combination with attribution retraining to provide low achieving and/or learned helpless children with specific ways to remedy their achievement problems. Borkowski and his colleagues, have shown that a combined program of strategy instruction and attribution retraining is more effective than strategy instruction alone in increasing reading motivation and performance in underachieving students (e.g., Borkowski & Muthukrisna 1995; Borkowski, Weyhing, & Carr, 1988; Paris & Byrnes, 1989; Pressley & El-Dinary, 1993; Weinstein & Mayer, 1986).

Summary

Work on anxiety and helplessness shows that some children suffer from motivational problems that can debilitate their performance in achievement situations. Although most of the work in developmental and educational psychology has focused on these two problems, there likely are other important motivational problems as well. In particular, some children may set maladaptive achievement goals, others may have difficulties regulating their achievement behaviors, and still others come to devalue achievement. More comprehensive work is needed on these kinds of motivational problems and how they affect children's achievement. Self-efficacy training provides an example of such work.

Self-Efficacy Training. Schunk and his colleagues have done several studies designed to improve elementary school-age children's (often low-achieving children) math, reading, and writing performance through skill training, enhancement of self-efficacy, attribution retraining, and training in how to set goals (e.g., Schunk, 1982, 1983; Schunk & Rice, 1987, 1989; Schunk & Schwartz, 1993). Modeling is an important aspect of this training (see Schunk, 1991, 1994). A number of findings have emerged from this work. First, the training increases both children's performance and their sense of self-efficacy (e.g., Schunk & Rice, 1989). Second, attributing children's success to ability has a stronger impact on their self-efficacy than does either effort feedback, or ability and effort feedback (e.g., Schunk, 1982, 1983). However, the effects of this kind of attributional feedback vary across different groups of children (see Schunk, 1994). Third, training children to set proximal, specific, and somewhat challenging goals enhances both their self-efficacy and performance. Fourth, training that emphasizes process goals (analogous to task or learning goals) increases self-efficacy and skills in writing more than an emphasis on product (ego) goals (e.g., Schunk & Schwartz, 1993); however, this is not true for reading (Schunk & Rice, 1989). Finally, like the work of Borkowski and his colleagues, Schunk and his colleagues have found that combining strategy training, goal emphases, and feedback to show children how their learning of strategies related to their performance has some of the strongest effects on subsequent self-efficacy and skill development.

This work now needs to be extended to children of different ages to determine whether the strategy instruction and motivation enhancement techniques need to be modified for younger and older children. Further, work is needed on developing programs that integrate various approaches, particularly those approaches associated with self-efficacy, goal setting, and self-regulation. More broadly, however, as valuable as these individual programs are, they are likely to have little lasting benefit if home and school environments do not facilitate and support the changes. Therefore, some researchers have turned to changing school and classroom environments to facilitate motivation, rather than changing individual children, This work is discussed later.

Gender Differences in Motivation

Despite efforts to increase the participation of women in advanced educational training and high status professional fields, women are still underrepresented in many fields, particularly those associated with technology, physics, and applied mathematics and at the highest levels of almost all fields (see Eccles, 1989). Efforts to understand these persistent gender differences in achievement patterns have produced a proliferation of theories and research. Eccles and her colleagues originally proposed their expectancy-value model of achievement choices (see Figure 15.1) as an effort to organize this disparate research into a comprehensive theoretical framework (see Eccles-Parsons et al., 1983; Meece et al., 1982). For example, consider gender differences in high school course enrollment: This model predicts that people will be most likely to enroll in courses that they think they will do well in and that have high task value for them. Expectations for success depend on the confidence the individual has in his or her intellectual abilities and on the individual's estimations of the difficulty of the course. These beliefs have been shaped by the individual's experiences with the subject matter, by the individual's subjective interpretation of those experiences

(e.g., does the person think that his or her successes are a consequence of high ability or lots of hard work?), and by cultural stereotypes regarding both the difficulty of the course and the distribution of relevant talents across various subgroups. The value of a particular course is also influenced by several factors including the following: Does the person like doing the subject material? How well does the course fit with the individual's self-concepts, goals, and values? Is the course seen as instrumental in meeting one of the individual's long- or short-range goals? Have parents or counselors insisted that the individual take the course or, conversely, have other people tried to discourage the individual from taking the course? Is the person worried about failing the course? Does taking the course interfere with other goals and values activities? Existing evidence, reviewed next, supports the conclusion that gender-role socialization and internalization are likely to lead to gender differences in each of these broad motivational categories, which, in turn, likely contribute to the underrepresentation of women in many occupations and activities oriented toward high achievement (see Eccles, 1989, 1994).

Gender Differences in Competence-Related Beliefs, Causal Attributions, and Control Beliefs

Gender differences, often favoring males, in competence beliefs are frequently reported, particularly in gender-role stereotyped domains and on novel tasks. For example, gifted and high-achieving females are more likely to underestimate both their ability level and their class standing (Frome & Eccles, 1995; Strauss & Subotnik, 1991; Terman, 1926). Crandall (1969) concluded that such gender differences in general expectations for success reflect the tendency for girls to underestimate and boys to overestimate their likely future performance. However, these differences are not always found (e.g., Dauber & Benbow, 1990; Schunk & Lilly, 1982) and, when found, are generally quite small (Marsh, 1989).

Furthermore, the magnitude and direction of these gender difference depend on the gender-role stereotyping of the activity. For example, boys hold higher competence beliefs than girls for math and sports, even after all relevant skill-level differences are controlled; in contrast, girls have higher competence beliefs than boys for reading, English, and social activities; and the magnitude of these differences often increases following puberty (Eccles, 1984; Eccles et al., 1989; Eccles, Wigfield, et al., 1993; Eccles-Parsons et al., 1983; Harter, 1982; Huston, 1983; Marsh, 1989; Marsh, Craven, & Debus, 1991; Wigfield et al., 1991). Further, the extent to which children endorse the cultural stereotypes regarding which sex is likely to be most talented in each domain predicts the extent to which girls and boys distort their own ability self-concepts and expectations in the gender-stereotypic direction (Early, Belansky, & Eccles, 1992; Eccles & Harold, 1991; Nash, 1979).

Findings regarding gender differences in attributions are also mixed. Some researchers (e.g., Dweck & Goetz, 1978; Ruble & Martin, Ch. 14, this Volume; Stipek & Gralinski, 1991) have found that girls are less likely than boys to attribute success to ability and more likely to attribute failure to lack of ability. Others have found that this pattern depends on the kind of task used: It occurs more with unfamiliar tasks or stereotypically masculine achievement tasks and sometimes does not occur at all (see Eccles-Parsons, 1983; Eccles-Parsons, Meece, et al., 1982; Yee & Eccles, 1988).

Gender differences are also sometimes found for locus of control. In Crandall et al. (1965), the girls tended to have higher internal locus of responsibility scores for both positive and negative achievement events and the older girls had higher internality for negative events than did the younger girls. The boys' internal locus of responsibility scores for positive events decreased from 10th to 12th grade. These two developmental patterns resulted in the older girls accepting more blame for negative events than the older boys (cf., Dweck & Goetz, 1978; Dweck & Repucci, 1973). Similarly, Connell (1985) found that boys attributed their outcomes more than girls to either powerful others or unknown causes in both the cognitive and social domains.

This greater propensity for girls to take personal responsibility for their failures, coupled with their more frequent attribution of failure to lack of ability (a stable, uncontrollable cause) has been interpreted as evidence of greater learned helplessness in females (see Dweck & Licht, 1980). However, evidence for gender differences on behavioral indicators of learned helplessness is quite mixed. In most studies of underachievers, boys outnumber girls 2 to 1 (see McCall, Evahn, & Kratzer, 1992). Similarly, boys are more likely than girls to be referred by their teachers for motivational problems and are more likely to drop out of school before completing high school. More consistent evidence exists that females, compared with males, select easier laboratory tasks, avoid challenging and competitive situations, lower their expectations more following failure, shift more quickly to a different college

major when their grades begin to drop, and perform more poorly than they are capable of on difficult, timed tests (see Dweck & Licht, 1980; Parsons & Ruble, 1977; Ruble & Martin, Ch. 14, this Volume; Spencer & Steele, 1995).

Gender differences also emerge regularly in studies of anxiety (e.g., Douglas & Rice, 1979; Hill & Sarason, 1966; Manley & Rosemier, 1972; Meece et al., 1990). However, Hill and Sarason suggested that boys may be more defensive than girls about admitting anxiety on questionnaires. In support of this suggestion, Lord, Eccles, and McCarthy (1994) found that test anxiety was a more significant predictor of poor adjustment to junior high school for boys even though the girls reported higher mean levels of anxiety.

Closely related to the anxiety findings, Spencer and Steele (1995) documented another motivational mechanism likely to undermine females' performance on difficult timed tests: stereotype vulnerability. They hypothesized that members of social groups (e.g., females) stereotyped as being less competent in a particular subject area (e.g., math) will become anxious when asked to do difficult problems because they are afraid the stereotype might be true of them. This vulnerability is also likely to make them respond more negatively to failure feedback, leading to lowering their expectations and their confidence in their ability to succeed. They gave college students a difficult math test under two conditions: (a) after being told that males typically do better on this test, or (b) after being told that males and females typically do about the same. The women scored lower than the males only in the first condition. Furthermore, the manipulation's effect was mediated by variations across condition in reported anxiety.

In summary, when gender differences emerge on competence-related measures of motivation, they are both consistent with gender-role stereotypes and are likely mediators of gender differences in various types of achievement-related behaviors and choices. But more work is needed before we will understand the reasons behind the inconsistency in findings across studies.

Gender Differences in Achievement Values

Eccles, Wigfield, and their colleagues have found gender-role stereotypic differences in both children's and adolescents' valuing of sports, social activities, and English (e.g., Eccles et al., 1989; Eccles, Wigfield, et al., 1993; Stein & Bailey, 1973; Wigfield et al., 1991). In Eccles, Wigfield, et al. (1993), girls also valued instrumental music more than boys. Interestingly, gender differences in the value of math did not emerge until high school (Eccles, 1984).

Although it is encouraging that boys and girls value math equally during elementary and middle school, the fact that adolescent girls have less positive views of both their math ability and the value of math is problematic because these differences underlie girls' lower probability of taking optional advanced level math and physical science courses and entering math-related scientific and engineering fields (see Eccles, 1994).

Sex differences have also been found on many of the psychological processes proposed by Eccles and her colleagues to underlie sex differences in subjective task value. For example, Eccles-Parsons et al. (1983) predicted that the attainment value of particular tasks would be linked to (a) conceptions of one's personality and capabilities; (b) long-range goals and plans; (c) schemas regarding the proper roles of men and women; (d) instrumental and terminal values (Rokeach, 1979); (e) ideal images of what one should be like; and (f) social scripts regarding proper behavior in many situations. If gender-role socialization leads males and females to differ on these core self- and role-related beliefs, then related activities will have differential value for males and females. In support, in a study of the link between personal values and college major, Dunteman, Wisenbaker, and Taylor (1978) identified two sets of values that both predicted major and differentiated the sexes: the first set (labeled thing-orientation) reflected an interest in manipulating objects and understanding the physical world; the second set (labeled person-orientation) reflected an interest in understanding human social interaction and a concern with helping people. Students with high thing-orientation and low person-orientation were more likely than other students to select a math or a science major. Not surprisingly, the females were more likely than the males to major in something other than math or science because of their higher person-oriented values. Similarly, the young women in Jozefowicz, Eccles, and Barber (1993) placed more value than the young men on female-stereotyped career-related skills and interests such as doing work that directly helps people and meshes well with child-rearing responsibilities. These values, along with ability self-concepts, predicted the gender-stereotyped career plans of both males and females (see Eccles & Harold, 1992, for review of the gender-role stereotypic patterns for personal values, occupational values, and personality traits).

Finally, the role of conflict between gender roles and achievement in gifted girls' lives is well illustrated by a recent ethnographic study of a group of gifted schoolgirls by Bell (1989). She interviewed a multiethnic group of third- to sixth-grade gifted girls in an urban elementary school regarding the barriers they perceived to their achievement in school. Five gender-role related themes emerged with great regularity: (a) concern about hurting someone else's feelings by winning in achievement contests; (b) concern about seeming to be a braggart by expressing pride in one's own accomplishments; (c) overreaction to nonsuccess experiences (apparently not being the very best is very painful to these girls); (d) concern over their physical appearance and what it takes to be beautiful; and (e) concern with being overly aggressive in terms of getting the teacher's attention. In each case, the gifted girls felt caught between doing their best and either appearing feminine or doing the caring thing.

Disidentification

Earlier, we discussed the relationship between values and competence-related beliefs. Drawing on the writings of William James (1892/1963), we suggested that children, in an effort to maintain self-esteem, will lower the value they attach to particular activities or subject areas if they lack confidence in these areas (see also Harter, 1990). Spencer and Steele (1995) suggested a similar phenomenon related to stereotype vulnerability. They hypothesized that women will disidentify with those subject areas in which females are stereotyped as less competent than males. By disidentifying with these areas, the women will not only lower the value they attach to these subject areas, they will also be less likely to experience pride and positive affect when they are doing well in these subjects. Consequently, these subjects should become irrelevant to their self-esteem. These hypotheses remain to be tested.

Racial and Ethnic Group Differences in Motivation

As is the case in many areas of psychology (see Graham, 1992), less is known about the motivation of children from different racial and ethnic groups. However, work in this area is growing quickly, with much of it focusing on the academic achievement difficulties of many African American children (see Berry & Asamen, 1989; Hare, 1985; Slaughter-Defoe, Nakagawa, Takanishi, & Johnson, 1990). Work has also focused on other minority groups within the United States and on recent immigrant populations, some of whom are doing much better in school than both European American middle-class children and third- and fourth-generation members of their same national heritage (e.g., Chen & Stevenson, 1995; Kao & Tienda 1995; Slaughter-Defoe et al., 1990).

Ethnic Group Differences in Children's Competence, Control, and Attribution Beliefs

Graham (1994) reviewed the literature on differences between African American and European American students on such motivational constructs as need for achievement, locus of control, achievement attributions, and ability beliefs and expectancies. She concluded that the differences are not very large. Further, she argued that many existing studies have not adequately distinguished between race and socioeconomic status, making it difficult to interpret any differences that emerge. Cooper and Dorr (1995) did a meta-analysis of some of the same studies reviewed by Graham to compare more narrative and more quantitative reviews. Although there were some important points of agreement across the two reviews, Cooper and Dorr concluded that there is evidence suggesting race differences in need for achievement favoring European Americans, especially in low-SES and younger samples.

In their study of educational opportunity, Coleman et al. (1966) reported that perceived control was an important predictor of African American children's school achievement. Graham (1994) found some evidence that African Americans are more external than European Americans. However, she also noted that studies looking at relations of locus of control to various achievement outcomes have not shown this greater externality to be a problem; indeed, in some studies, greater externality is associated with higher achievement among African Americans. In interpreting such findings, Gurin and Epps (1974) suggested that being external for failure in a racist context is likely to be both psychologically protective and accurate.

Research on competence beliefs and expectancies has revealed more optimism among African American children than among European American children, even when the European American children are achieving higher marks (e.g., Stevenson, Chen, & Uttal, 1990). But more importantly, in Stevenson, Chen, and Uttal (1990) the European American children's ratings of their ability related significantly to their performance, whereas the African American children's did not. Graham (1994) suggested the following explanations: (a) African American and European American children may use different social comparison groups to help judge their own abilities; and (b) African American children may say they are doing well to protect their general self-esteem, and for the same reason may also devalue or

disidentify academic activities at which they do poorly. However, neither of these explanations has been adequately tested. If African American children's competence-related beliefs do not predict their school performance, then questions must be raised about how relevant the theories considered in this chapter are for understanding these children's motivation.

Ethnic Group Differences in Achievement Values and Goals

There are few ethnic comparative studies specifically focused on the kinds of achievement values measured by Eccles, Wigfield, and their colleagues, or of the kinds of goals measured by Nicholls, Dweck, Ames, and Wentzel. Researchers studying minority children's achievement values have focused instead on the broader valuing of school by minority children and their parents. In general, these researchers find that minority children and parents highly value school (particularly during the elementary school years), and have high educational aspirations for their children (e.g., Stevenson, Chen, & Uttal, 1990). However, the many difficulties associated with poverty (see Duncan, Brooks-Gunn, & Klevbanov, 1994; Huston, McLoyd, & Coll, 1994; McLoyd, 1990) make these educational aspirations difficult to attain. It is important for researchers to extend this work to more specific value-related constructs.

Ethnicity and Motivation at the Interface between Expectancies and Values

Researchers interested in ethnic and racial differences in achievement have proposed models linking social roles, competence-related beliefs, and values. For example, Steele (1992) proposed stereotype vulnerability and disidentification to help explain the underachievement of African American students: Confronted throughout their school career with mixed messages about their competence and their potential and with the widespread negative cultural stereotypes about their academic potential and motivation, African American students should find it difficult to concentrate fully on their school work due to the anxiety induced by their stereotype vulnerability (for support see Steele & Aronson, 1995). In turn, to protect their self-esteem, they should disidentify with academic achievement leading to both a lowering of the value they attach to academic achievement and a detachment of their self-esteem from both positive and the negative academic experiences. In support, several researchers have found that academic self-concept of ability is less predictive of general self-esteem for some African American children (Bledsoe, 1967; Winston, Eccles, & Senior, in press).

Fordham and Ogbu (1986) have made a similar argument linking African American students' perception of limited future job opportunities to lowered academic motivation: Since society and schools give African American youth the dual message that academic achievement is unlikely to lead to positive adult outcomes for them and that they are not valued by the system, some of these students may create an oppositional culture that rejects the value of academic achievement. Ogbu (1992) discussed how this dynamic will be stronger for involuntary minorities who continue to be discriminated against by mainstream American culture (e.g., African Americans) than for voluntary minority immigrant groups (e.g., recent immigrants from Southeast Asia). Although voluntary minorities have initial barriers to overcome due to language and cultural differences, these barriers can be overcome somewhat more easily than the racism faced by involuntary minorities, giving voluntary minorities greater access to mainstream culture and its benefits.

Contrary to this view, several investigators found no evidence of greater disidentification with school among African American students (e.g., Steinberg, Dornbusch, & Brown, 1992; Taylor, Casten, Flickinger, Roberts, & Fulmore, 1994). Nonetheless several studies show that disidentification, particularly as a result of inequitable treatment and failure experiences at school, undermines achievement and academic motivation (e.g., see Finn, 1989; Taylor et al., 1994). It is likely that some students, particularly members of involuntary minority groups, will have these experiences as they pass through the secondary school system. Longitudinal studies of the process of disidentification, and of ameliorating intervention efforts, are badly needed.

Any discussion of performance and motivational differences across different ethnic groups must take into account larger contextual issues. Spencer and Markstrom-Adams (1990) argued that many minority children, particularly those living in poverty, have to deal with several difficult issues not faced by majority adolescents such as racist prejudicial attitudes, conflict between the values of their group and those of larger society, and scarcity of high-achieving adults in their group to serve as role models. These difficulties can impede identity formation in these adolescents, leading to identity diffusion or inadequate exploration of different possible identities (Taylor et al., 1994). Similarly, Cross (1990) argued that one must consider the development of both personal identities and racial group identity. For example, some African American adolescents may have

positive personal identities but be less positive about their racial group as a whole, whereas others may have negative personal identities but positive orientations toward their group. Cross argued that many researchers have confounded these two constructs, leading to confusion in our understanding of identity development in, and its motivational implications for, African Americans.

Finally it is critical to consider the quality of the educational institutions that serve many of these youth. Thirty-seven percent of African American youth and 32% of Hispanic youth, compared with 5% of European American and 22% of Asian youth are enrolled in the 47 largest city school districts in this country; in addition, African American and Hispanic youth attend some of the poorest school districts in this country. Of the youth enrolled in city schools, 28% live in poverty and 55% are eligible for free or reduced cost lunch, suggesting that class may be as important (or more important) as race in the differences that emerge. Teachers in these schools report feeling less safe than teachers in other school districts, dropout rates are highest, and achievement levels at all grades are the lowest (Council of the Great City Schools, 1992). Finally, schools that serve these populations are less likely than schools serving more advantaged populations to offer either high-quality remedial services or advanced courses and courses that facilitate the acquisition of higher order thinking skills and active learning strategies. Even children who are extremely motivated may find it difficult to perform well under these educational circumstances.

Graham (1994) made several important recommendations for future work on African American children's motivation that could be applied more broadly to work on different racial and ethnic groups. Two particularly important recommendations are (a) the need to separate out effects of race and social class; and (b) the need to move beyond race comparative studies to studies that look at individual differences within different racial and ethnic groups, and at the antecedents and processes underlying variations in achievement outcomes among minority youth (e.g., Connell et al., 1994; Kao & Tienda, 1995; Luster & McAdoo, 1994; Schneider & Coleman, 1993; Steinberg, Dornbusch, et al., 1992; Steinberg, Lamborn, Dornbusch, & Darling, 1992). Studies of recent immigrant populations and comparative studies of different generations of immigrant populations move in these directions. For example, work by Stevenson and his colleagues, by Tienda and her colleagues, and by Fuligni all demonstrate the power of the types of motivational constructs discussed thus far in explaining both within- and between-group variation in academic achievement (e.g., Chen & Stevenson, 1995; Lummis & Stevenson, 1990).

THE SOCIALIZATION OF MOTIVATION: PARENTAL INFLUENCES

Early Studies of Parental Influences

The first major empirical attempts to understand the socialization of achievement motivation began with the work of McClelland (1961) and Winterbottom (1958) on need-achievement motivation. Winterbottom found that mothers of sons with high achievement motivation had earlier expectations of independence and achievement, made fewer but earlier restrictive demands on their sons' behaviors, made relatively more positive demands than restrictive demands on their sons' behavior throughout development, rewarded their sons more often with physical affection for compliance with these expectations, and had higher estimations of their sons' abilities even though the actual performance levels of both high and low need-achievement boys were equal. These results suggest the importance of three socialization factors: (a) early independence and achievement training; (b) high estimation of the child's abilities; and (c) reward for behaviors that correspond to parental expectations.

Many socialization studies followed. Results regarding the importance of early independence and achievement training were quite mixed. Instead, timing and sensitivity to the child's skill level, rather than age, emerged as the critical component (cf., Smith, 1969). The importance of the developmental timing theme continues today. In addition, the training for achievement-related activities rather than for independence per se emerged as critical. The need for this distinction became clear as investigators tried to understand social class differences in children's achievement strivings: Although lower-class mothers endorsed caretaking-type independence at an earlier age than middle-class mothers, they endorsed achievement-related independence at an older age and only the early training of the latter predicted children's need-achievement motivation (Rosen, 1959).

In contrast, consistent support emerged for the importance of parents' confidence in their children's abilities. For example, in Rosen and D'Andrade's study (1959), parents of high need-achievement sons had higher achieve-

ment expectations, higher career and higher academic aspirations, and set higher standards for their children than parents of low need-achievement sons (see also Crandall, Dewey, Katkovsky, & Preston, 1964; McClelland, 1961; Smith, 1969). Rosen (1959) also demonstrated that parents have higher career aspirations for, and higher ability estimations of, their sons in cultural groups with relatively high mean levels of adult need-achievement (i.e., Irish and Protestant cultures) than parents from other cultural groups. The importance of this variable is still evident.

Consistent support also emerged for the importance of rewarding specific achievement-related behaviors. However, there was some controversy regarding how specific this reinforcement needed to be. Several investigators demonstrated that reinforcement for specific achievement-related behaviors was most important (e.g., Crandall et al., 1964; Zigler & Child, 1969). Other investigators focused more on the general affective climate in the home, suggesting that a warm, affectionate, low-conflict home environment is the key (e.g., Crandall et al., 1964; Solomon, Houlihan, Busse, & Parelius, 1971). In contrast, some studies suggested that the association between positive parent-child interaction patterns and achievement behaviors in children is not a simple, linear relation (e.g., Baumrind, 1971; Crandall et al., 1964). For example, Solomon et al. (1971) found strong support for a quadratic relation between parental warmth and childhood achievement, suggesting that there may be an optimal level of parental warmth that is conducive to the development of achievement motivation: While excessive warmth may reinforce dependent behavior patterns that are incompatible with the expression of achievement orientation, overly critical and evaluative parenting leads to high test anxiety (Sarason et al., 1960).

Several investigators stressed the importance of the interplay among several parenting characteristics (Heilburn & Walters, 1968; Teevan & McGhee, 1972). For example, Baumrind (1971) highlighted the conjoint importance of warmth, control, and democracy in her classification system: Authoritarian parents have strict rules, allow little give-and-take about those rules, and use assertive discipline strategies; permissive parents allow a great deal of autonomy, discipline infrequently, and maintain a warm, positive relationship with children; and authoritative parents provide rules and structure, but discuss those rules with their children, show some flexibility in applying the rules, and are warm and accepting. The association of authoritative parenting style with a wide variety of positive developmental outcomes including those linked to achievement motivation is well documented (e.g., Baumrind, 1971; Dornbusch, Ritter, Leiderman, Roberts, & Fraleigh, 1987), at least in the United States. This perspective has been incorporated by Steinberg and his colleagues (e.g., Steinberg, Lamborn, et al., 1992).

The importance of role modeling and "observational learning" was another salient theme during the 1960s. Several specific mechanisms were suggested as important. At the most basic level, it was shown that parents influence their children's attitudes by engaging in different activities. Because children want to be like their parents, they are most likely to value their parents' activities.

Kohlberg (1966) suggested another powerful way in which role models could affect achievement motivation: Children, in an effort to understand their experiences and to synthesize a social role for themselves, make generalizations about appropriate role-related behaviors based on what they observe others like themselves doing. These role-related concepts provide a guide as the children try to master what they consider to be role-appropriate behaviors. Integrating Kohlberg's role concept idea with the other parental influences on need-achievement yields the following predictions: Developing positive achievement orientation should be associated with having a competent role model who is like you, getting the appropriate mix of support for autonomy, instrumental training and structured learning, and experiencing adequate emotional support. Positive achievement orientation in one's same-sex parent helps establish the gender-role appropriateness of achievement behaviors; a warm encouraging relationship with both parents encourages the incorporation of these behaviors into the child's repertoire. For boys, this perspective predicts that positive achievement orientation will be associated with the presence of an authoritative, competent, achieving father and a mother who provides an optimal level of support along with encouragement for independent behavior. In contrast, for girls it predicts that a positive achievement orientation is most likely to develop in the presence of an authoritative, competent, achieving mother and a father who provides an optimal level of support and encouragement for achievement behavior.

Few studies have directly tested these predictions because studies rarely include both parents so that sex of child by sex of parent effects can be assessed. When such tests have been done, this interaction is often significant and consistent with this hypothesis. For example, Crandall and his associates demonstrated that achievement behavior

in girls is correlated with less nurturing maternal behaviors coupled with supportive paternal behaviors (Crandall, Preston, & Rabson, 1960; Crandall et al., 1964). Chance (1961) also supported the importance of a competent female role model for girls. Both investigators found that excessive maternal intrusion and control is negatively related to the academic achievement of girls. To the extent that less nurturant and less intrusive maternal behaviors may reflect greater concern of the mother with her own competence, it is possible that these mothers are providing their daughters with a more competent and, consequently, less stereotypical feminine role model than mothers who exhibit more nurturant behavior patterns.

Summary

This early work on the socialization of achievement motivation established the importance of four components of parenting: developmentally appropriate timing of achievement demands/pressure, high confidence in one's children's abilities, a supportive affective family climate, and highly motivated role models. The work also suggested that these variables usually operate in combination with each other to foster high need achievement. For example, Katkovsky, Crandall, and Preston (1964) found that the greater the value parents placed on their own intellectual competence, the more likely they were to participate in children's intellectual activities. By involving themselves in these activities, it is likely that these parents modeled competent achievement-motivated behaviors. Such parents also strongly encouraged their children to engage in intellectual achievement activities and reacted strongly to their children's achievement efforts. Consequently, in these families, the children were exposed simultaneously to all of the socialization experiences linked to high need-achievement motivation.

Finally, the early work demonstrated that the relations between "antecedent" variables and the development of achievement orientation reflect interacting, bidirectional and dynamic processes. Both the data suggesting the importance of timing demands to correspond to the child's abilities and dispositions (Feld, 1967; Smith, 1969) and the data suggesting the importance of the child's perception of gender-role appropriate behaviors (Kohlberg, 1966) indicate that the child's abilities, perceptions, and cognitive processes must be considered if the acquisition of achievement orientation is to be fully understood. In addition, the impact of parenting on the ontogeny of motivational orientation likely depends on the ability of parents to gear their demands and expectations to the changing needs, abilities, and dispositions of their children as they mature.

With the advent of the social cognitive revolution, researchers shifted their attention to a more cognitive and situated view of motivation. Consistent with this change, investigators interested in the socialization of achievement motivation also shifted the nature of the dependent measures they tried to predict. The distinction between motivational variables and achievement outcome variables has blurred, particularly in socialization studies. So, for example, a plethora of studies now link family characteristics and practices to school achievement. Implicit in these studies is the assumption that family practices influence achievement through their impact on either motivation or skill acquisition. However, the specific motivational mediators are often not included in these studies. We pay special attention in this review to those studies that focus directly on this mediational link. The consistency of the findings from the past 25 years with the themes and constructs in this earlier work is striking.

Parent Influence: Work over the Past 25 Years

Contemporary work has been both more focused and more general. There are many small-scale, laboratory- and field-based studies in which researchers link specific parenting practices to specific motivational constructs. Researchers also have done several large-scale national and local survey-type studies using quite global indicators of parenting practices and beliefs, and of motivational and performance outcomes. In both types of studies, there have been attempts to link parenting practices both to their antecedents and to their socialization consequences. Figure 15.2 provides a general overview of the types of associations tested. Although this specific model was proposed and elaborated by Eccles and her colleagues (Barber & Eccles, 1992; Eccles, 1989, 1993; Eccles & Harold, 1993), similar social-cognitive mediational models of parental behavior and influence have been proposed by several other researchers (e.g., Alexander & Entwisle, 1988; Clark, 1983; Goodnow & Collins, 1990; Grolnick & Slowiaczek, 1994; Hess & Holloway, 1984; Marjoribanks, 1979; Phillips, 1987; Seginer, 1983; Stevenson, Lee, et al., 1990).

Although there is extensive work on some components of this model, few studies include the several components underlying parenting behaviors outlined in Box E. Much of the existing work focuses on the association of the exogenous characteristics (Boxes A and B) with either parents'

beliefs (Box C) or child outcomes (Box F; e.g., linking family socioeconomic status and/or ethnicity with parents' child-specific beliefs [Box D], specific parenting practices [Box E], and children's academic outcomes [Box F]; Entwisle & Alexander, 1990; Entwisle, Alexander, Pallas, & Cadigan, 1987; Marjoribanks, 1979; Schneider & Coleman, 1993; Steinberg, Dornbusch, et al., 1992; Stevenson et al., 1990b). The few researchers who have looked broadly at the mediating and moderating hypotheses implied in Figure 15.2 have focused primarily on predicting academic motivation and achievement, and more recently on sports motivation and achievement. Additionally, much of this work is quite general; for example, linking family SES and general family socialization styles to general school achievement, achievement motivation, and other general motivational constructs such as mastery orientation, learned helplessness, and school engagement. Few researchers have focused on why individuals are motivated to do different things: for example, why someone might prefer math to English, swimming to baseball, dancing to playing sports, or reading to playing sports.

Family Demographic Characteristics

Sociological researchers have documented the importance of such factors as family structure, family size, parents' financial resources, parents' education, parents' occupation, community characteristics, and dramatic changes in the family's economic resources in shaping children's academic motivation and achievement (e.g., Alexander & Entwisle, 1988; Beyer, 1995; Coleman et al., 1966; Laosa, 1984; Marjoribanks, 1980; Schaefer & Edgerton, 1985; Sewell & Hauser, 1980; Thompson, Alexander, & Entwisle, 1988). Several mechanisms could account for these associations. First, family demographics could affect children's motivation indirectly through their association with both parent beliefs and practices and the opportunity structures in the child's environment. For example, parents with more education are more likely to believe that involvement in their children's education and intellectual development is important, to be actively involved with the children's education, and to have intellectually stimulating materials in their home (e.g., DeBaryshe, Patterson, & Capaldi, 1993; Marjoribanks, 1979; Schneider & Coleman, 1993).

Second, some demographic characteristics could influence motivation indirectly through the competing demands they place on parents' time and energy. For example, the negative association of single-parent status, time spent at work, and large family size on children's school achievement

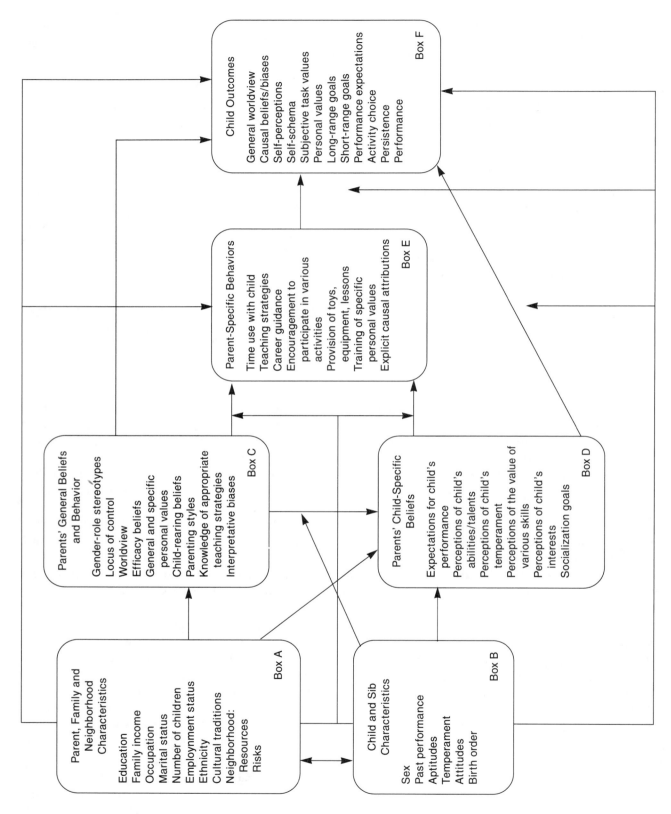

Figure 15.2 Model of parental influences on their children's motivation and achievement.

might reflect the fact that these factors reduce the time and energy parents have for engaging their children in activities that foster high motivation (e.g., Schneider & Coleman, 1993). Similarly, the psychological stress associated with some demographic factors could influence parents' ability to engage in the kinds of behaviors associated with high motivation. Ample evidence documents how much harder it is to do a good job of parenting if one lives in a high-risk neighborhood or is financially stressed (e.g., Elder, Conger, Foster, & Ardelt, 1992; Elder, Eccles, Ardelt, & Lord, 1995; Furstenberg, 1993; McLoyd, 1990). Not only do such parents have limited resources to implement whatever strategies they think might be effective, they also have to cope with more external stressors than middle-class families living in stable, resource-rich neighborhoods. Not surprisingly, their children also evidence less positive motivation toward conventional school success.

Third, demographic characteristics can also affect parents' perceptions of, and expectations for, their children. Both parent educational level and family income are related positively to parents' expectations regarding both their children's immediate school success and long-term educational prospects (e.g., Alexander & Entwisle, 1988; Marjoribanks, 1979). Similarly, divorced parents have lower expectations for their children's academic achievement (Barber & Eccles, 1992). Ogbu has highlighted this mechanism as one way poverty and anticipated discrimination can undermine academic motivation in some minority populations: If parents believe that there are limited opportunities for their children to obtain conventional forms of success, they are likely to shift their socialization efforts toward other goals and interests (Fordham & Ogbu, 1986; Ogbu, 1985).

Fourth, demographic characteristics can influence parents' beliefs and behaviors, and children's outcomes, in even less direct ways such as those associated with role modeling. Family demographic characteristics are often associated with things like parents' jobs and leisure-time activities, and with the kinds of role models children see outside the home. These behaviors and models can influence children's achievement goals, values, and self-perceptions through observational learning (D'Amico, Haurin, & Mott, 1983). Very little work has addressed this hypothesis directly. Instead, such mechanisms are typically inferred from correlational findings.

Fifth, demographic characteristics linked to culture and ethnicity can influence parents' behaviors and children's motivation through mechanism underlying values, goals, and general belief systems (e.g., Hess & Azuma, 1991; Luster, Rhoades, & Haas, 1989; Modell, 1993). For example, Ogbu (1985) has argued that parents value those characteristics that they assume will help their children succeed in their world. Other scholars describe cultural differences in valued activities, motivational orientation, and behavioral styles (e.g., Maehr & Nicholls, 1980; Modell, 1993; Stevenson, Chen, et al., 1990). Such differences can affect the socialization of motivated behavior through variations in (a) valued activities (e.g., athletic vs. musical competence), (b) valued goals (e.g., communal goals versus individualistic goals; mastery versus performance goals; and doing versus being goals), and (c) approved means of achieving one's goals (e.g., competitive versus cooperative means). There has been a recent increase in research on these types of influences.

Similarly, researchers studying cultural differences in school achievement have linked cultural differences in parents' expectations and achievement-related beliefs to cultural differences in achievement. For example, the work by Stevenson and his colleagues has demonstrated that European American parents, compared with Japanese parents, overestimate their children's academic abilities, are less aware of their children's academic difficulties, and are more satisfied with school performance that falls below their expectations (e.g., Crystal & Stevenson, 1991). Similarly, Stevenson et al. (1990a) found differences in parents' achievement beliefs across African American, Hispanic, and European American parents in the United States.

In summary, there are many ways for family demographic characteristics to directly or indirectly affect motivation. However, even though family demographic characteristics have been linked repeatedly to children's school achievement, their effects are almost always indirect, mediated by their association with parents' beliefs, practices, and psychological resources. In addition, parents' beliefs and psychological and social resources often override the effects of even the most stressful demographic characteristics on children's school achievement and motivation (e.g., Clark, 1983). Finally, there are often complex interactions among various demographic characteristics in predicting either parenting beliefs and practices or child outcomes.

General Child-Rearing Climate

Historically, researchers studying parental influence have focused on the impact of the general patterns and philosophy of child rearing on children's overall orientation toward achievement. Researchers have related a set of general behaviors and beliefs to the development of self-esteem, achievement motivation, locus of control, sense of personal efficacy, and so on. The variables investigated include the general emotional warmth and supportiveness in the home (e.g., Clark, 1983; Connell, Halpern-Felsher, Clifford, Crichlow, & Usinger, 1995; DeBaryshe et al., 1993; Estrada, Arsenio, Hess, & Holloway, 1987; Wagner & Phillips, 1992; Wentzel, 1994; Wentzel & Feldman, 1993; Wentzel, Feldman, & Weinberger, 1991) valuing of achievement (e.g., Clark, 1983; DeBaryshe, in press; Hess, Holloway, Dickson, & Price, 1984); general parental child-rearing beliefs and theories, values, and goals, as well as gender-typed goals and cultural beliefs, goals, and values (e.g., Eccles & Hoffman, 1984; Goodnow & Collins, 1990; Hess, Chih-Mei, & McDevitt, 1987; Huston, 1983; Miller & Davis, 1992); general child-rearing style as well as authority structure, discipline tactics, and general interaction patterns (e.g., Baumrind, 1971; DeBaryshe et al., 1993; Lord et al., 1994; Steinberg, Lamborn, et al., 1992; Wentzel, 1994; Yee & Flanagan, 1985); parental locus of control and personal efficacy (Bandura, 1994; Hess, 1970); and communicative style and teaching style (Hess et al., 1984; McGillicuddy-DeLisi & Sigel, 1991; Sigel, 1982). Similarly, researchers have documented the benefits of active involvement with, and monitoring of, children's and adolescents' school work (e.g., Clark, 1983; Connell et al., 1994; Eccles, 1993; Hess & Holloway, 1984; Marjoribanks, 1979; Schneider & Coleman, 1993; Steinberg, et al., 1992b; Stevenson, Chen, et al., 1990).

Consistent with the conclusions reached in the 1960s, several investigators have stressed an integrated view of how these various parenting characteristics work together to produce optimal motivational outcomes. For example, Grolnick, Ryan and their colleagues stress the interplay of three components of general parenting: involvement and interest in the child's activities, support for autonomous behaviors, and adequate structure (e.g., Connell & Wellborn, 1991; Grolnick & Ryan, 1989; Grolnick, Ryan, & Deci, 1991; Ryan & Grolnick, 1986; E. Skinner, 1990). Similarly, Csikszentmihalyi, Rathunde, and Whalen (1993) suggested that positive motivational development is optimized when there is appropriate synergy in the family's provision of support, harmony, involvement, and freedom. Finally, Eccles and her colleagues (1993) stress the importance of emotional support, role models, and the right balance between structure, control, challenge, and developmentally appropriate levels of support

for autonomy (e.g., Eccles, 1993). This balance depends on cultural systems, on the specific context in which the family is living, the age of the child, and other individual characteristics.

Although the magnitude of effects varies by race/ ethnicity, sex, social economic class, and nationality, there is consensus that these general parental practices do impact children's motivation and motivated behavior (e.g., Coleman et al., 1966; Eccles, 1993; Hess & Holloway, 1984; Marjoribanks, 1980; Roberts, 1991; Stevenson & Baker, 1987). The results are consistent with three general principles: appropriate levels of structure (similar to Vygotsky's notion of appropriate scaffolding and Hunt & Paraskevopoulos's [1980] notion of good match), consistent and supportive parenting, and observational learning. Families who know enough about their child to provide the right amount of challenge with the right amount of support are more likely to produce highly competent and motivated children. These parents are also able to adjust their behavior to meet the changing developmental needs and competencies of their children. Families that provide a positive emotional environment are more likely to produce children who want to internalize the parents' values and goals and therefore want to imitate the behaviors modeled by their parents. Consequently, if parents provide such a model, children growing up in these homes are likely to develop a positive achievement orientation and value those tasks, goals, and means of achieving one's goals valued by their parents.

General Beliefs

Researchers have shown that parents' general beliefs such as valuing of achievement and school competence, general parental child-rearing beliefs and theories, values and goals, gender-typed ideologies and goals, and culturally based beliefs, goals, and values are linked to parenting behaviors in the school achievement arena in the predicted direction (e.g., see Eccles & Hoffman, 1984, Hess & Holloway, 1984; McGillicuddy-DeLisi, 1982; Miller, in press; Sameroff & Feil, 1985). Much less is known about how these general beliefs relate to specific behaviors and motivational beliefs across various achievement-related activity domains. This issue, however, is beginning to attract attention (e.g., see Eccles, 1989; Goodnow & Collins, 1990; Sigel, McGillicuddy-DeLisi, & Goodnow, 1992). Figure 15.2 depicts a general overview of how one might think about these interrelationships.

Several important questions are suggested by this model: First, what is the relation of parents' general beliefs and practices to domain- and child-specific parental beliefs, values, and practices? For example, do parents' gender-role stereotypes affect their perceptions of their own child's abilities in various activity domains? Relevant research is reviewed later. Similarly, do parents' beliefs regarding the nature of ability affect their motivational parenting? As discussed earlier, children who think that incompetence is a temporary and modifiable state respond to failure with increased mastery efforts more than children who think that current incompetence reflects insufficient and unmodifiable aptitude (Dweck & Elliott, 1983; Dweck & Leggett, 1988). Parents also differ in their beliefs regarding the origins of individual differences in competence, the meaning of failure, and the most adaptive responses to failure. These beliefs should influence both their response to their children's failures and their efforts to help their children acquire new competencies and interests. Hokoda and Fincham (1995) provide preliminary support for this hypotheses.

Second, do cultural beliefs about things like the nature of ability affect the attributions parents' provide to their children for the child's successes and failures? Hess and his colleagues (e.g., Dunton, McDevitt, & Hess, 1988; Hess, Chih-Mei, & McDevitt, 1987; Holloway, 1988; Holloway, Kashiwagi, Hess, & Azuma, 1986) and Stevenson and his colleagues (Lee, Ichikawa, & Stevenson, 1987; Stevenson, Lee, et al., 1990) have found that Japanese and Chinese parents make different causal attributions than European American parents for their children's school performances, with Japanese and Chinese parents emphasizing effort and hard work and European American parents emphasizing natural talent. Similarly, cultural differences in beliefs regarding ability and competence should relate to the statements parents make to their children about the origins of individual differences in performance such as "you have to be born with math talent" versus "anyone can be good at math if they just work hard enough" (Dunton et al., 1988; Holloway, 1988; Stevenson, Lee, et al., 1990). An interesting cross-cultural difference in the relation between the age of the child and parents' beliefs regarding ability is also emerging. Knight (1981) found that European Australian parents become more nativist in their view of their children's cognitive abilities as their children get older. In contrast, Japanese mothers become less nativist as their children get older (Dunton et al., 1988).

Third, do parents' general developmental theories affect the specific teaching strategies they use with their children? Work related to this question has been done by Sameroff

(Sameroff & Feil, 1985) and by Sigel, McGillicuddy-DeLisi, and their colleagues (e.g., Sigel, 1982). McGillicuddy-DeLisi (1982), for example, has shown that fathers' general developmental theories affect the teaching strategy they use with their child in a specific laboratory setting. Few researchers have addressed the implications of parents' developmental theories for the socialization of motivation. But given the importance of the timing of experience for the development of achievement motivation, it is likely that parents' general developmental theories will affect the ontogeny of motivational orientation.

Fourth, how do these general beliefs and practices interact with more specific practices in shaping children's preferences and beliefs? Are the effects of the parents' general beliefs on their children's development primarily mediated by their impact on specific practices and beliefs or do these general beliefs and practices have substantial direct effects themselves? If so, are general beliefs particularly influential on some types of motivational outcomes while specific beliefs and practices are more influential on other outcomes? One might predict, for example, that general beliefs and practices are more likely to affect traitlike aspects of motivation while specific beliefs and practices are more likely to affect the specific domains in which these traitlike characteristics are manifest. This hypothesis has yet to be tested.

Child-Specific Beliefs, Values, and Perceptions: Parents as Interpreters of Competence-Relevant Information

Parents hold many child-specific beliefs about their own children's abilities, which, in turn, have been shown to affect motivationally linked outcomes, such as the well-established positive link of parents' educational expectations to academic motivation and performance (e.g., Alexander & Entwisle, 1988; Brooks-Gunn, Guo, & Furstenberg, 1993; Gottfried, 1991; Kandel & Lesser, 1969; Marjoribanks, 1979; Schneider & Coleman, 1993; Seginer, 1983; Sewell & Hauser, 1980). Along with others, Eccles (1993) suggested the following child-specific parental beliefs as particularly likely to influence children's motivation:

1. Causal attributions for their children's performance in each domain.
2. Perceptions of the difficulty of various tasks for their children.
3. Expectations for their children's success and confidence in their children's abilities.

4. Beliefs regarding the value of various tasks and activities coupled with the extent to which parents believe they should encourage their children to master various tasks.

5. Differential achievement standards across various activity domains.

6. Beliefs about the external barriers to success coupled with beliefs regarding both effective strategies to overcome these barriers and their own sense of efficacy to implement these strategies for each child.

Parents convey these beliefs to their children in many ways: They may make causal attributions for their children's performance—praising their child for that "A" in math by pointing out either the child's natural talent or great diligence. They may also communicate their impression of their children's relative abilities by telling them what they are good at, or, more subtly, by encouraging them to try, or discouraging them from trying, particular activities. Finally, they may make more general comments to their children about the importance of talent versus effort in accounting for individual differences in competence such as "you have to be born with music talent" or "anyone can be good at sports if they just work hard enough."

Such beliefs and messages, particularly those associated with parents' perceptions of their children's competencies and likely success, have been shown to influence children's self and task beliefs (e.g., Alexander & Entwisle, 1988; Eccles-Parsons, Adler & Kaczala, 1982; Miller, Manhal, & Mee, 1991; Pallas, Entwisle, Alexander, & Stluka, 1994; Phillips, 1987). For example, parents' perceptions of their adolescents' abilities are significant predictors of adolescents' estimates of their own ability and interest in math, English, and sports even after the significant positive relation of the child's actual performance to both the parents' and adolescents' perceptions of the adolescents' domain-specific abilities is controlled (Eccles, 1993; Eccles-Parsons, Adler, et al., 1982; Jacobs, 1992; Jacobs & Eccles, 1992). Furthermore, Eccles and her colleagues found support for the hypothesized causal direction of this relationship using longitudinal panel analyses (Eccles, 1993, Eccles et al., in press; Yoon, Wigfield, & Eccles 1993). In addition, in this same longitudinal study (Michigan Study of Adolescent Life Transitions—MSALT), there was a negative relation between mothers' perceptions of their adolescents' *English* ability and the adolescents' perceptions of their own *math* ability. Individuals use a variety of information to decide how good they are in various domains including their relative performances across those domains (i.e., they may decide they are very good at math because they find math easier than other school subjects; see Eccles, 1987; Eccles-Parsons et al., 1983; Marsh, 1990a). The MSALT results suggest that a similar phenomenon characterizes the impact of parents' perceptions of their children's abilities on the development of the children's self-perceptions. The adolescents in this study had lower estimates of their math ability than one would have predicted based on their teachers' and their mothers' rating of their math ability if their mothers thought that they were better in English than in math (Eccles, Jacobs, et al., 1991).

Influences on Parents' Perceptions of Their Children's Competencies.   How do parents' form their impressions of their children's abilities? Parents appear to rely quite heavily on objective feedback, such as school grades (K. Alexander & Entwisle, 1988; Arbreton & Eccles, 1994; Eccles-Parsons, Adler, et al., 1982; Miller, in press). The causal attributions parents make for their children's performances also influence parents' perceptions. For example, in Arbreton, Eccles, and Harold's (1994) longitudinal study, parents' attributions of success to talent led to increments in the parents' perceptions of their children's abilities in math, English, and sports and decrements in parents' estimates of how hard their children will have to work to be successful in math, English, and sports even after appropriate controls for prior performance and prior ability ratings were included (cf., Dunton et al., 1988; Holloway, 1986; Yee & Eccles, 1988).

Researchers have also assessed sex of child effects on parents' attributional patterns to help explain the gender-role stereotypic distortions in parents' impression of their children's academic and nonacademic abilities that exist from an early age on, even after one controls for actual performance differences (e.g. K. Alexander & Entwisle, 1988; Eccles, 1993, 1994; Eccles & Harold, 1991; Eccles et al., 1989; Eccles-Parsons, Adler, et al., 1982; Jacobs, 1992; Jacobs & Eccles, 1992). For example, Yee and Eccles (1988) found that parents of boys rated natural talent as a more important reason for their children's math successes than parents of girls. In contrast, parents of girls rated effort as a more important reason for their children's math successes than parents of boys (see also Dunton et al., 1988; Holloway et al., 1986). Similarly, in Eccles, Jacobs, et al. (1991), mothers gave gender-role stereotypic causal attributions for their adolescent children's successes and failures in mathematics, reading, and sports: Sons' successes in math and sports were more likely to be attributed to natural talent than daughters'; daughters' success in English was more likely to be attributed to natural talent than sons.' Furthermore, as predicted, the sex differences in these mothers' ratings of their adolescents' abilities were substantially reduced once the sex difference in the mothers' causal attributions was controlled, supporting the hypothesis that parents' gender-role stereotyped causal attributions mediate parents' gender-role stereotyped perceptions of their children's math competence. Lee et al. (1987), however, found no evidence of a sex-of-child effect on parents' attributions for younger children in several cultures.

Evidence is also emerging in support of the hypothesis that more general beliefs and stereotypes—often linked to gender or cultural group—influence parents' gender-role stereotypic perceptions of their children's abilities and interests. Using path analytic techniques, Jacobs and Eccles (1992) tested whether parents' gender-role stereotypes generalized to their perceptions of their own children's ability: Parents who endorsed gender-role stereotypes regarding which sex is most interested in, and has the most natural talent for, math, English, and sports also distorted their ratings of their own children's abilities in each of these domains in the gender-role stereotypic direction (cf., Jacobs, 1992).

Child-Specific Beliefs, Values, and Perceptions: Parents as Interpreters of Task Value

The messages parents provide about the value of various activities should also influence children's motivation. Parents can convey differential task values through explicit rewards and encouragement for participating in some activities rather than others. Similarly, parents can influence children's interests and aspirations, particularly about future educational and vocational options, through explicit and implicit messages they provide as they counsel children. For example, parents, teachers, and counselors are more likely to encourage boys than girls to pursue math-related interests (see Eccles & Harold, 1992; Eccles & Hoffman, 1984).

Whether this encouragement directly affects either the value children attach to math or their participation in math activities has not been established. Some work suggests rather weak relations between parents' own task value and adolescents' task value for math (Eccles-Parsons, Jacobs, et al., 1982). The relations may be stronger for younger children and when a wider range of activities are included. The relation may also be curvilinear. Work in the

area of intrinsic motivation suggests that excessive attempts to influence a child's interest in a specific activity can backfire and lead to a decrease in interest and involvement (e.g., Deci & Ryan, 1985; Lepper & Green, 1978).

A related issue regarding parents' task value socialization efforts is beginning to attract some attention. Building on the work of William James (1892/1963), several investigators have become interested in the association between achievement, task values, self-concepts, and self-esteem (e.g., Harter, 1990, 1992; Winston et al., in press). These investigators suggest that self-esteem and motivation are enhanced when one values those activities at which one is competent. Extending this idea to more than one activity domain suggests the importance of the hierarchy of individuals' subjective task values and competence perceptions. If James is correct, then children with high self-esteem and motivation should have congruent hierarchies for their competency assessments and their subjective task values. In contrast, children who feel relatively incompetent about activities relatively high on their task value hierarchy are likely to be at risk for low self-esteem. Harter (1990) has found support for this hypothesis. Individuals may protect their self-esteem over time by lowering the value they attach to those activity domains at which they are relatively less competent. For example, they may cope with being relatively incompetent in tennis by concluding that it is not very important to be competent in tennis. But what happens when an individual cannot adopt this ego-protective strategy? For example, what happens if a child's parents' activity value hierarchy is both rigid and inconsistent with the child's relative competencies and, consequently will not allow the child to protect his or her self-esteem by lowering the value he or she attaches to those activity domains at which he or she is relatively less competent? In this case, the child is likely at high risk for developing either low self-esteem or other self-protective motivational and behavioral strategies such as those proposed by Covington (1992) in his work on self-worth.

Provisions of Specific Experiences at Home

There is ample evidence that parents influence their children's motivation through the learning experiences they provide for their children. Researchers have shown that reading to one's preschool children and providing reading materials in the home predicts the children's later reading achievement and motivation (e.g., Dix, 1976; Wigfield & Asher, 1984). Such experiences likely influence both the child's skill levels and the child's interest in doing these activities; both of which, in turn, should facilitate the child's transition into elementary school and subsequent educational success. Entwisle and Alexander (1993) have documented that the skills and work habits children have when they enter kindergarten are among the strongest predictors of academic motivation and performance throughout elementary and secondary school. That these effects hold even when one controls for the children's scores on standardized intelligence tests provides support for the hypothesis that some of the effect is mediated through social and motivational processes. These results are especially interesting because they illustrate how experience in one context, the home, can influence the child's experiences and motivation in other contexts, such as school.

Similarly, by providing the specific toys, home environment, and cultural and recreational activities for their children, parents structure their children's experiences. Through the processes associated with familiarity (Zajonc, 1968), and both operant and classical conditioning, children should come to prefer the toys and activities to which they are exposed. However, the extent to which this is true should depend on the affective and motivational climate created by parents when the children are engaged with any particular experience. If children learn a skill in a positive setting, they should come to enjoy and value the activity and to develop intrinsic motivation for doing it. If, instead, they learn a skill in a highly negative charged or highly controlling setting, children likely will develop an aversion to that activity.

Exposure to different toys and activities also provides children with the opportunity to develop different competencies. For example, manipulative toys and large space play activities affect the development of such basic cognitive skills as spatial facility (Connor, Schanckman, & Serbin, 1978). Having specific success experiences and acquiring specific skills likely influence motivation to engage in related activities through their influence on personal efficacy, ability self-concepts, and reduced performance/evaluation anxiety.

For the skill acquisition process to have these positive effects, however, experiences must be appropriately matched to the children's current competence levels so that the child is challenged but not overwhelmed. Building on Hunt and Paraskevopoulos' (1980) notion of match, Miller and his colleagues (e.g., Miller, Manhal, & Mee, 1991) have looked at the connection between parents' specific beliefs about their children's abilities and the experiences they provide for their children. They argue that parents who have an

accurate view of their children's level of competence are better at providing appropriate tasks and adequate scaffolding as the children go about mastering these tasks. Such interactions, in turn, are likely to facilitate positive motivational outcomes and better skill acquisition.

Group Differences in Provision of Specific Experiences. There is abundant evidence that parents provide different experiences for sons and daughters (Eccles & Hoffman, 1984; Huston, 1983). For example, parents are less likely to nominate their daughters for gifted programs at school and to enroll their daughters in computer and competitive sports programs (see Eccles & Harold, 1992). Similarly, families with limited economic resources are more willing to invest these resources in their sons than in their daughters (see Eccles & Hoffman, 1984). It is likely that the gender differences in children's competencies, self-perceptions, interests, and aspirations result in part from these differences in the experiences parents provide for their sons and daughters (Huston, 1983). Characteristics such as social class, family income, and ethnicity also affect the toys and other experiences parents are able to provide for their children (Coleman et al., 1966; Laosa, 1984; Marjoribanks, 1980). Social class also influences what neighborhood a family lives in. In turn, the neighborhood influences the resources and role models readily available to the family and to their children as well as the peers children are likely to have available for friends. As a consequence of all these factors, families living in poor neighborhoods are likely to have an especially difficult time providing their children with rich and varied experiences both within and outside the home (Eccles & Lord, in press; Furstenberg, 1993).

Summary

The studies reviewed suggest a multivariate model of the relation between antecedent child-rearing variables and the development of achievement orientation: The development of achievement motivation likely depends on the presence of several variables interacting with each other to mediate and moderate children's motivation. Proper timing of demands creates a situation in which children can develop a sense of competence in dealing with their environment. An optimally warm and supportive environment creates a situation in which children will choose their parents as role models. The presence of high yet realistic expectations creates a demand situation in which children will perform in accord with the expectancies of their parents. Finally, the ability level of a child must be such that attainment of the expected level of performance is within that child's capacity. All these factors, as well as the availability of appropriate role models, are essential for children to develop a positive, achievement orientation. The exact way this orientation will be manifest is likely dependent on the values a child has learned, which are directly influenced by the culture in which the family lives and the social roles that the child is being socialized to assume.

THE DEVELOPMENT OF MOTIVATION: INFLUENCES OF SCHOOL AND INSTRUCTIONAL CONTEXTS, AND SCHOOL TRANSITIONS

Trying to identify those instructional characteristics that will motivate children to engage the activity and master the skills being taught has been a core issue in educational and motivational psychology. Consequently, there are hundreds of relevant studies, ranging from small-scale laboratory experiments to large-scale school interventions. Space limitations allow only an overview of the work being done in this area, with particular attention to those researchers who have articulated and tested specific motivational hypotheses (cf., Modell, 1993; Stipek, 1993).

General Instructional Practices and Teacher Beliefs

Classroom Climate and Emotional Support

Historically, researchers studying teacher influence on motivation focused on the impact of personal characteristics and teaching style on children's overall achievement, motivation, satisfaction, and self-concept (see Dunkin & Biddle, 1974). These researchers assumed that general teacher characteristics such as warmth, and practices such as indirectness would enhance student satisfaction, persistence, curiosity, and problem-solving capability through their impact on general classroom climate. Similarly, based on the assumption that warm relationships increase a teacher's influence by increasing children's desire to do what the teacher says (due either to identification or the increased power of the teacher's social reinforcement properties), many investigators studied the association between teacher warmth/supportiveness and student motivation (particularly the value attached to working hard) and performance. However, since much of this early work was

flawed methodologically, the results are difficult to interpret (see Duncan & Biddle, 1974).

More recently, researchers studying classroom climate have separated factors such as teacher personality and warmth from teacher instruction and managerial style. And, as is true for parents, the effects of "climate" are dependent on other aspects of a teacher's beliefs and practices. For instance, Moos and his colleagues have shown that student satisfaction, personal growth, and achievement are maximized only when teacher warmth/supportiveness is accompanied by efficient organization, stress on academics, and provision of focused goal-oriented lessons (Fraser & Fisher, 1982; Moos, 1979; Trickett & Moos, 1974). Furthermore, these practices are more common among teachers who believe they can influence their students' performance and future achievement potential (Brookover, Beady, Flood, Schweitzer, & Wisenbaker, 1979; Rutter, Maughan, Mortimer, & Ouston, 1979).

Researchers have extended this general approach to the climate of the entire school. These researchers provide evidence that schools vary in the climate, teachers' sense of efficacy, and general expectations regarding student potential, and that variations in general climate affect the motivation of both teachers and students in fundamental ways (e.g., Bandura, 1994; Bryk, Lee, & Holland, 1993; Rutter et al., 1979). In an evaluation of a school intervention based on these principles, Cauce, Comer, and Schwartz (1987) demonstrated their impact on adolescents' confidence in their academic abilities (see Becker & Hedges, 1992). Similarly, in their analysis of higher achievement in Catholic schools, Bryk et al. (1993) discussed how the culture (or climate) within Catholic schools is fundamentally different from the culture within most public schools in ways that positively affect the motivation of students, students' parents, and teachers. This culture (school climate) values academics, has high expectations that all children can learn, and affirms the belief that the business of school is learning. The work of Maehr, Midgley, and their colleagues provides a final example of this school organizational perspective (e.g., Anderman & Maehr, 1994; Maehr & Anderman, 1993; Maehr & Midgley, 1996). These investigators suggest that certain school-level policies and practices (such as those promoting ability tracking, comparative performance evaluations, retention, and ego instead of mastery focus) undermine the motivation of both teachers and students through their impact on the goals these individuals bring to the learning environment (cf., Mac Iver, Reuman, & Main, 1995).

Classroom Management

The findings from studies of teacher management also parallel those from studies of family environment (Brophy, 1987). In rooms where teachers have established smoothly running and efficient procedures for monitoring student progress, providing feedback, enforcing accountability for work completion, and organizing group activities, student achievement, motivation, and conduct are enhanced. Although there has been almost no research on the impact of management on student beliefs and values, it seems likely that the quality of classroom management contributes to differences in children's perceptions. Blumenfeld, Hamilton, Bossert, Wessels, and Meece (1983) found that classroom academic orientation has significant benefits for children's perceptions of the importance of adherence to classroom work norms. Under conditions where children are held accountable for work, they exert more effort, value success more, and consequently do better. As a result, the children may also see themselves as more able.

Control and Autonomy

deCharms (1968), Deci and Ryan (1985), and Lepper (Lepper & Cordova, 1992) have all argued that intrinsic motivation is good for learning. Furthermore, they have argued that classroom environments that are overly controlling and do not provide adequate autonomy undermine intrinsic motivation, mastery orientation, ability self-concepts and expectations, and self-direction, and induce a learned helplessness response to difficult tasks. Support for this hypothesis has been found in both laboratory and field-based studies (e.g., Boggiano & Katz, 1991; Boggiano, Main, & Katz, 1987; Boggiano et al., 1992; Deci, Schwartz, Sheinman, & Ryan, 1981; Flink, Boggiano, & Barrett, 1990; Grolnick & Ryan, 1987; Ryan & Grolnick, 1986). Boggiano and her colleagues (see Boggiano et al., 1992) have also found that students with an extrinsic motivational orientation are most likely to respond to controlling teaching strategies with the learned helplessness pattern of behaviors and self-perceptions.

In other work, Boggiano and her colleagues had teachers teach small groups of children a set of tasks using either a controlling strategy or a less controlling strategy, and videotaped the sessions (Flink et al., 1990). Observers of the tapes rated the more controlling teachers as the better teachers even though the children did better in terms of learning and learning transfer under the less controlling teacher. Similar results were reported by Deci, Speigel, Ryan, Koestner,

and Kauffman (1982). Although these researchers did not investigate why this pattern emerged, they did suggest that there is a bias in this country to view more controlling styles as better because these styles appear more active, directive, and better organized, and because they appear to be consistent with the types of teaching and parenting practices advocated by operant conditioning and token economy specialists (e.g., Kazdin, 1982).

A related line of work focuses on the adverse effects of rewards on motivation and interest. Lepper first demonstrated these effects by rewarding children for activities that they otherwise found interesting. Subsequent research has demonstrated that such rewards have a negative effect primarily when they provide no valid information regarding the quality of performance. Under these conditions, the rewards are seen as controlling and it is this aspect of the rewards that undermines intrinsic interest in the activity (e.g., Cameron & Pierce, 1994).

But what is the best mix of autonomy and structure? Studies of both well-managed classrooms and international differences in achievement (Stevenson, Lee, et al., 1990) have demonstrated the importance of teacher control in keeping a large group focused on learning activities. Although these two perspectives seem somewhat contradictory, they can be integrated if one focuses on the optimal levels of structure combined with developmentally appropriate provision of autonomy as discussed earlier. However, because researchers in these two areas do not usually work together, they tend to approach the issue with somewhat different questions and conceptualizations, making it difficult to compare across studies to determine exactly which aspects of control are good and which undermine intrinsic motivation.

Classroom/Instructional Organization and Structure

The work on classroom and instructional organization is linked conceptually to the work on support for autonomy, reward structures, and classroom climate. This work suggests that students are more motivated in less traditional classrooms where many activities occur simultaneously, materials are varied in level and content, and there is some choice regarding partners and work activities. Students in these classrooms develop more autonomy, have more positive self-concepts and capitalize better on their individual strengths and preferences, without sacrificing achievement (see Horwitz, 1979). Similarly, when teachers adopt a cooperative instructional and reward structure in their classrooms, motivation, liking for subject matter, and self-perceptions of competence are all enhanced. Both learning and motivation appear to be maximally facilitated in cooperative learning situations that are characterized by both group goals and individual accountability (Stevens & Slavin, 1995). Such situations appear to create positive interdependence and stimulating group inquiry which, in turn, arouse social and academic motivational goals (see Sharan, 1980) and prevent the "free rider effect" (Stevens & Slavin, 1995).

Ability Grouping Practices.   Curricular tracking and between-classroom ability grouping are other practices attracting recent attention. Despite much research, however, few strong and definitive answers have emerged regarding their impact on motivation (see Fuligni, Eccles, & Barber, 1995; Gamoran & Mare, 1989; Kulik & Kulik, 1987; Slavin, 1990). The results vary depending on the outcome assessed, the group studied, the length of the study, the control groups used for comparison, and the context in which these practices are manifest. The situation is complicated by conflicting hypotheses that emerge about the likely direction and the magnitude of the effect depending on the theoretical lens one uses to evaluate the practice. The best justification for these practices derives from a person-environment fit perspective: People will be more motivated to learn if the material can be adapted to their current competence level. There is some evidence consistent with this perspective for students placed in high-ability classrooms, high within-class ability groups, and college tracks (Dreeban & Barr, 1988; Fuligni et al., 1995; Gamoran & Mare, 1989; Pallas et al., 1994). The results for students placed in low-ability and noncollege tracks do not confirm this hypothesis. By and large, when long-term effects are found for this group of students, they are negative, primarily because these students are often provided with inferior educational experience and support (Dreeban & Barr, 1988; Pallas et al., 1994). These latter results are consistent with a social stratification theoretical perspective. But it is important to note that these negative effects appear to result from the stereotypically biased implementation of ability grouping programs. A different result might emerge if the teachers implemented the program more in keeping with the goals inherent in the person-environment fit perspective by providing high-quality instruction and motivational practices tailored to the current competence level of all of the students.

Social comparison theory leads to a different prediction regarding the effect of ability grouping and tracking on one aspect of motivation: ability self-concepts. Ability grouping should narrow the range of possible social comparisons, and so lead to declines in the ability self-perceptions of higher ability individuals and increases in the ability self-perceptions of lower ability individuals. The few existing studies support this position. Reuman, Mac Iver, Eccles, and Wigfield (1987) found that being placed in a low-ability math class in the seventh grade led to an increase in self-concept of math ability and a decrease in test anxiety; and conversely being placed in a high-ability math class led to a decrease in self-concept of math ability (see also Reuman, 1989). Similarly, Marsh, Chessor, Craven, and Roche (1995) found that being placed in a gifted and talented program led to a decline over time in the students' academic self-concepts. Pallas et al. (1994), however, found no evidence of within-class ability grouping in reading effects on ability self-concepts and performance expectations during the early elementary school years once the effect of ability group placement on actual achievement level was controlled.

The impact of these changes on other aspects of motivation likely depends on individual and contextual factors. Atkinson (1964) provided evidence that achievement motivation is maximized when the probability of success is .5. If the net result of the big-fish/little-pond effect is to bring both low and high achievers closer to the .5 probability level, then ability grouping should have a positive impact on the motivation of high need-achievement individuals in both ability groups and a negative impact on the motivation of the low need-achievement individuals in both ability groups. Theorists focused on the importance of challenging material in a supported environment also suggest an increase in motivation for everyone provided that the quality of instruction leads to equally challenging material for all ability levels. Conversely, if the social comparison context also increases the salience of an entity view rather than an incremental view of ability, then the decline in ability self-concepts of the high-ability individuals might lead them to engage in more failure-avoidant and ego-protective strategies.

Specific Instructional Tasks.   Teachers can affect children's motivation by the type of material they present, the amount of work assigned, frequency of coverage, and instructional style (see Stipek, 1996). If the teacher gives too much work, students are less likely to enjoy the task; if topics are infrequently covered, children will conclude that they are not important; and if the teacher makes the subject matter interesting and provides variety, children's interest and motivation increase (see Ames, 1992). Teacher knowledge about, and involvement with, subject matter also can affect preferences. Students like math and science more when taught by teachers who are trained in the area and hold memberships in professional societies, presumably because these teachers use more relevant, authentic, and interesting material for teaching their specialty (see Eccles, 1989). Similarly, individuals' interest in the material is enhanced when the material is taught in a way that is meaningful to them and their life goals (Blumenfeld, 1992; Krapp, Hidi, & Renninger, 1992; Pintrich et al., 1993).

More Integrated Approaches to General Practices and Beliefs

The work reviewed thus far is based on studies focused on only one or two contextual characteristics at a time. The following work reflects a shift to a more global, integrated view of the impact of learning contexts on motivation.

General Teaching Practices Linked to Self-Evaluation and Motivation. Among the first such efforts, Rosenholtz and Simpson (1984) suggested a cluster of teaching practices (e.g., individualized vs. whole group instruction; ability grouping practices; publicness of feedback) that should affect motivation because they make ability differences in the classroom especially salient to the students (cf., Mac Iver, 1987). They assumed that these practices affect the motivation of all students by increasing the salience of extrinsic motivators and ego-focused learning goals, leading to greater incidence of social comparison behaviors, and increased perception of ability as an entity state rather than an incremental condition. All these changes should reduce the quality of the children's motivation and learning. The magnitude of the negative consequences of these shifts, however, should be greater for low-performing children because, as they become more aware of their relative low standing, they are likely to adopt ego-protective strategies that undermine learning and mastery (Covington, 1992). The little available research provides preliminary support for these hypotheses (e.g., Mac Iver, 1987; Rosenholtz & Rosenholtz, 1981).

Evaluation practices also influence self-evaluation. Although students primarily use feedback and grades to evaluate their ability, the form of these reporting practices can affect how they use this information. How teachers report on, and recognize, performance will affect the degree to which ability-related information is accessible, comparable, and salient (Rosenholtz & Rosenholtz, 1981). Public methods for charting progress, such as wall posters

detailing amount or level of work completed provide readily accessible information. In addition, teachers who frequently contrast students' performances, grant privileges to "smart" children, or award prizes for "best" performance may increase the importance of ability as a factor in classroom life and heighten the negative affect associated with failure (see Ames, 1992). When there are few clear winners and many losers, relative performance will be more salient to children (Nicholls, 1979b). In contrast, in more cooperative or mastery-oriented classrooms, everyone who performs adequately can experience success. As a result, youngsters in mastery-oriented rooms are more likely to focus on self-improvement than social comparison, to perceive themselves as able, and to have high expectation for success (Nicholls, 1984; Slavin, 1990). Finally, when variations in evaluations are either attributed to entity-based differences in competence, or are used as a controlling strategy rather than primarily for information on progress, intrinsic motivation is reduced (Kage & Namiki, 1990). These results suggest that mastery evaluation practices are better at fostering and maintaining motivation than social normative, competitive, or controlling evaluation practices (see also Mac Iver & Reuman, 1993; Maehr & Midgley, 1996).

Teachers' Ability Beliefs, Instructional Strategies, and Classroom Goal Structure. Closely related to the work of Rosenholtz and Rosenholtz (1981) is the work growing out of goal theory (e.g., Ames, 1992; Dweck & Elliott, 1983; Meece, 1994; Nicholls, 1984). Researchers now have examined a wide range of learning context characteristics that influence children's motivational orientation and learning through their impact on the children's achievement goals. What is especially important about this work is the great care the researchers are taking in articulating a model of how teacher beliefs translate into specific practices, which, in turn, influence specific aspects of children's motivation. It has been suggested that teachers' beliefs regarding both the nature of ability (incremental vs. entity) and their own efficacy to teach all students affect the teaching practices used, which, in turn, create a climate that focuses children's attention on either mastery or performance goals (Ames, 1992; Anderman & Maehr, 1994; Midgley, Anderman, & Hicks, 1995; Nicholls, 1984). In her review of this research, Ames (1992) outlined how variations in the tasks used for instruction, the authority relations between students and teachers, and the nature of evaluation and recognition can affect students' motivation.

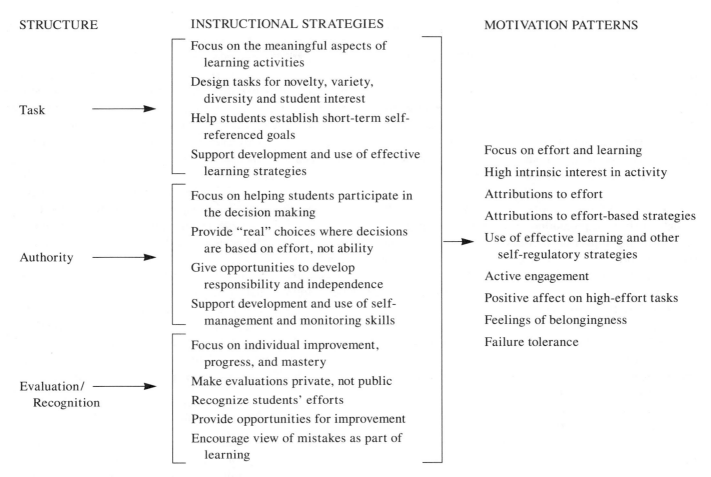

STRUCTURE

INSTRUCTIONAL STRATEGIES

MOTIVATION PATTERNS

Task

Focus on the meaningful aspects of
learning activities

Design tasks for novelty, variety,
diversity and student interest

Help students establish short-term self-
referenced goals

Support development and use of effective
learning strategies

Authority

Focus on helping students participate in
the decision making

Provide "real" choices where decisions
are based on effort, not ability

Give opportunities to develop
responsibility and independence

Support development and use of self-
management and monitoring skills

Evaluation/
Recognition

Focus on individual improvement,
progress, and mastery

Make evaluations private, not public

Recognize students' efforts

Provide opportunities for improvement

Encourage view of mistakes as part of
learning

Focus on effort and learning

High intrinsic interest in activity

Attributions to effort

Attributions to effort-based strategies

Use of effective learning and other
self-regulatory strategies

Active engagement

Positive affect on high-effort tasks

Feelings of belongingness

Failure tolerance

Figure 15.3   Ames' summary of the link between instructional strategies and student motivation. Adapted from Ames (1992).

Figure 15.3 summarizes her conclusions. The motivational constructs include many of the components of motivation described in this chapter. In addition, the range of instructional strategies is quite broad, overlapping with several dimensions discussed earlier.

Preliminary findings from several studies support the hypothesized links in Figure 15.3 (see reviews by Ames, 1992; Anderman & Maehr, 1994; Blumenfeld, 1992; Blumenfeld et al., 1991; Boggiano et al., 1992; Dweck & Elliott, 1983; Stipek, 1993, 1996). Especially relevant are studies showing the positive effects of mastery learning programs (Kulik, Kulik, & Bangert-Drowns, 1990). However, although the individual associations hypothesized in Figure 15.3 have been documented, much more work is needed to understand how various instructional strategies interact with each other in a single context, such as the classroom, to affect motivation and learning (Ames, 1992;

Blumenfeld, 1992). Most teachers in American schools use a mix of mastery-oriented and performance-oriented strategies. They may use mastery-oriented tasks and allow the students appropriate levels of autonomy but still rely primarily on social comparative evaluation strategies, and children often engage in social comparison and competition even in mastery-oriented classrooms (Crockenberg & Bryant, 1978). We know little about the best combination of these features to support a mastery-oriented motivational orientation. Nor do we know when, and if, the collection of motivational dimensions actually cluster together within the individual. More work is needed to determine how these motivational components interrelate with each other and with other motivational constructs to influence behavior. Of particular importance is the need to study the interaction of multiple goals as well as the contextual characteristics influencing the relative salience of various achievement, social, and moral goals in particular settings.

The direction of causality in Figure 15.3 primarily goes from teacher to student, implying that the student is rather passive. But students' own beliefs about effective instructional and motivational strategies need to be considered. Results of two studies are illustrative. Nolen and Nicholls (1994) found that students and teachers often had different views of effective motivational practices; for example, students thought extrinsic rewards were more effective, and praise less effective, than teachers did. Further, Thorkildsen, Nolen, and Fournier (1994) found that some children thought practices promoting meaningful learning were most fair, others favored practices emphasizing the importance of effort, and still others focused on practices involving extrinsic reward. If students' ideas on appropriate motivational strategies do not mesh with teachers' ideas and practices, their motivation is not likely to be enhanced.

Girls and Math (Girl-Friendly Classrooms). The work on understanding group differences in achievement and achievement choices is another example of an attempt to identify a broad set of classroom characteristics related to motivation. The work on girls and math is one example of this approach. Sex differences in children's preferences for learning contexts likely interact with subject area to affect their interest in those subjects (Casserly, 1980; Eccles, 1989; Hoffmann & Haeussler, 1995; Kahle, 1984). Females appear to respond more positively to math and science instruction if it is taught in a cooperative or individualized manner rather than a competitive manner, if it is taught from an applied/person-centered perspective rather than from a theoretical/abstract perspective, if it is taught using a hands-on approach rather than a book-learning approach, and if the teacher avoids sexism in its many subtle forms. These effects likely reflect the fit between the teaching style, the instructional focus, and females' values, goals, motivational orientation, and learning styles. The few relevant studies have found support for this idea (e.g., Eccles, 1994; Eccles & Harold, 1992; Hoffmann & Haeussler, 1995). If such classroom practices are more prevalent in one subject area (e.g., physical science) than another (e.g., biological or social science), then one would expect gender differences in motivation to study these subject areas. Researchers studying classroom practices have found that math and physics are especially likely to be taught in a manner least preferred by females. Consequently, it is not surprising that many girls are less interested in these subject areas

than in other subject areas that are taught in a manner more consistent with their preferences. It should also be noted that math and physical science do not have to be taught in these ways; more girl-friendly instructional approaches can be used. And when they are, both girls and boys are more likely to continue taking courses in these fields and to consider working in these fields when they become adults.

The girl-friendly classroom argument is a good example of person-environment fit. Many investigators have suggested that a person will be maximally motivated to learn in situations that fit well with their interests, current skill level, and psychological needs because the material is then challenging, interesting, and meaningful (e.g., Csikszentmihalyi et al., 1993; Eccles & Midgley, 1989; Eccles, Wigfield, et al., 1984; Krapp et al., 1992). Variations on this theme include aptitude by treatment interactions and theories stressing cultural match or mismatch as explanations for group differences in school achievement and activity choices (e.g., Fordham & Ogbu, 1986). Finally, stage-environment fit theory (Eccles & Midgley, 1989) is a direct extension of person-environment fit theory into a developmental frame. We discuss this perspective more extensively later.

Student-Specific Beliefs, Expectations, Causal Attributions, and Interactions

The mechanisms discussed thus far are assumed to operate at the group or classroom level. Instructors can also influence children's ability beliefs, task value, performance expectations, and personal efficacy through individuated feedback and interactions. The most obvious example of this effect is the teacher expectancy literature. Beginning with the work by Rosenthal (1969), many researchers examined teacher-expectancy effects. This work suggests that teacher-expectancy effects depend on whether teachers structure activities for and interact differently with high- and low-expectancy students and on whether the students perceive this difference (Brophy, 1987; Eccles & Wigfield, 1985; Eccles-Parsons, Kaczala, et al., 1982; Weinstein, 1989; Weinstein, Marshall, Sharp, & Botkin, 1987). Recent work also suggests that these effects are not as prevalent as once believed. For the effect to be of great concern, the researcher needs to demonstrate that it has a biasing effect that leads to changes in motivation and performance over time beyond what is expected based on the pre-existing characteristics of the student (Jussim & Eccles, 1992; Jussim, Eccles, & Madon, 1996). Evidence for such biasing effects is minimal. Teacher expectations for individual students and subsequent student motivation and performance tend to reflect the accurate association between teacher expectations and student characteristics such as prior achievement levels and behavioral patterns (see Jussim et al., 1996). In addition, not all teachers respond to their expectations with behaviors that undermine the motivation and performance of the low-expectancy students. Some teachers respond to low expectations with increased instructional and motivational efforts for particular students and succeed in increasing both their motivation and their learning (Goldenberg, 1992). Nonetheless, small teacher expectancy effects over time can have a large cumulative effect on both motivation and achievement (Jussim et al., 1996), particularly if these effects begin in kindergarten and the first grade (Entwisle & Alexander, 1993). Finally, some groups may be more subject to the biasing effects of teacher expectations. Jussim et al. (1996) found that girls, low SES students, and minority students are more susceptible to these effects than are White middle-class boys.

Several researchers have argued that teachers' more general feelings of efficacy operate much like their expectancy effects in that they influence the motivation of the children to learn through their impact on the children's own sense of efficacy (Ashton, 1985; Bandura, 1994; Brookover et al., 1979). Although some teachers lack a general sense of efficacy and believe they cannot motivate or teach any of their students, more often feelings of low teacher efficacy are focused on a subset of the students within a particular classroom—the low-achieving students. In this case, the teacher is less likely to try to motivate these students than the more competent students in the class, leading to teacher expectancy effects. Few researchers, however, have tested the interaction of general teacher efficacy beliefs with student performance level in assessing teacher expectancy effects. Support for this prediction was obtained by Midgley, Feldlaufer, and Eccles (1989a).

Weiner (1985) and Graham (1984) studied a slightly different aspect of within-classroom variations in teacher-student interaction: the impact of teachers' emotional reactions on students' self-evaluations and motivation. They have shown that such emotional reactions influence children's own causal attributions and expectations for future success. Pity and excessive help, for example, lead to lack of ability attributions, lowered expectations for success (Graham & Barker, 1990), and efforts to maintain one's self-worth (Covington, 1992). Similarly, Eccles-Parsons, Kaczala, et al. (1982) demonstrated that, when praise is used in a way that conveys low teacher expectations (e.g., patronizing praise for low-level successes), it undermines

junior high school students' confidence in their abilities as well as their expectations for success. In contrast, when overt criticism conveys high teacher expectations (e.g., when teachers use public criticism only with the high-performing students because they want to protect the low-performing students' egos), high rates of criticism are associated with higher than predicted confidence in one's ability.

Summary

These studies suggest that motivation is optimized when students are provided with challenging tasks in a mastery-oriented environment that provides good emotional and cognitive support, meaningful material to learn and master, and sufficient support for their own autonomy and initiative (cf., Lipsitz, 1984). Similar characteristics emerged as the important familial influences on the ontogeny of motivation, suggesting that one could use the same theoretical framework for studying contextual effects in both arenas. But because schools are a more widely shared social environment than families, one can ask an even more interesting question about the school as a social context. Earlier, we reviewed the fairly consistent age-related changes in various indicators of children's motivational orientation, interests, and activity involvement, particularly with regard to school-related achievement tasks. These changes are often interpreted as reflecting developmental changes that are going on within the individual (see Stipek & Mac Iver, 1989). However, such changes may also reflect systematic changes in the social contexts of schools.

School Transitions and Motivational Development

Despite sound theoretical reasons to expect that school transitions can influence children's motivation (see Eccles, Midgley, et al., 1984), until recently there has been little research on these effects. We consider various school transitions, but because most of the empirical work has focused on the junior high and middle school transition, we emphasize this transition.

Transition into Elementary School

Entrance into elementary school and then moving from kindergarten to first grade introduce several systematic changes in children's social worlds. First, classes are age stratified, making within-age ability social comparison much easier. Second, formal evaluations of competence by "experts" begins. Third, formal ability grouping begins usually with reading group assignment. Fourth, peers have the opportunity to play a much more constant and salient role in children's lives. Each of these changes should impact children's motivational development. Such changes could contribute to the increase in children's response to failure feedback as they move from preschool and kindergarten into the first grade (Parsons & Ruble, 1972, 1977; Stipek & Hoffman, 1980). Parents' expectations for, and perceptions of, their children's academic competence are also influenced by report card marks and standardized test scores given out during the early elementary school years, particularly for mathematics (Alexander & Entwisle, 1988; Arbreton & Eccles, 1994). But more systematic studies of the effects of transition into elementary school, and transitions from kindergarten to first grade, on motivation are needed.

Significant long-term consequences are associated with children's experiences in the first grade, particularly with ability grouping and within-class differential teacher treatment. Teachers use varied information to assign first graders to reading groups including temperamental characteristics such as interest and persistence, race, gender, and social class (e.g., Alexander, Dauber, & Entwisle, 1993; Brophy & Good, 1974). Alexander et al. (1993) demonstrated that differences in first-grade reading group placement and teacher-student interactions have a significant effect (net of beginning differences in competence) on motivation and achievement several years later. Furthermore, these effects are mediated by both differential instruction and the exaggerating impact of ability group placement on parents' and teachers' views of the children's abilities, talents, and motivation (Pallas et al., 1994).

The Middle School Transition

There are substantial declines in academic motivation and achievement across the upper elementary and early secondary school years (see Anderman & Maehr, 1994; Eccles & Midgley, 1989; Eccles, Midgley, et al., 1993; Wigfield, Eccles, & Pintrich, 1996): School grades decline for many students as they move into junior high school (Simmons & Blyth, 1987). Similar declines occur for interest in school (Epstein & McPartland, 1976), intrinsic motivation (Harter, 1981), self-concepts/self-perceptions (Eccles et al., 1989; Wigfield et al., 1991), and confidence in one's intellectual abilities, especially following failure (Parsons & Ruble, 1977). There are also increases in test anxiety

(Wigfield & Eccles, 1989), learned helpless responses to failure (Rholes et al., 1980), focus on ego goals rather than task mastery (Midgley et al., 1995), and both truancy and school dropout (Rosenbaum, 1976). Although these changes are not extreme for most adolescents, they are common enough to make us ask why (see Eccles & Midgley, 1989). Since academic failure and dropout are especially problematic among some ethnic groups and among youth from low-SES communities and families (e.g., Schneider & Coleman, 1993), it is probable that these groups are particularly likely to show these declines in academic motivation and self-perception as they move into and through the secondary school years.

A variety of explanations exist for these "negative" changes in academic motivation: Some point to the intrapsychic upheaval associated with early adolescent development. Others point the co-occurrence of multiple life changes: Simmons and Blyth (1987) attributed these declines, particularly among females, to the coincidence of the junior high school transition with pubertal development. Still others point to the nature of the junior high school environment itself. Extending person-environment fit theory (see Hunt, 1979) into a developmental perspective (stage-environment fit theory), Eccles and Midgley (1989) proposed that these negative motivational changes occur because traditional junior high schools do not provide developmentally appropriate educational environments for early adolescents. They suggested that different types of educational environments may be needed for different age groups to meet individual developmental needs and foster continued developmental growth. Exposure to the developmentally appropriate environment would facilitate both motivation and continued growth; in contrast, exposure to developmentally inappropriate environments, especially developmentally regressive environments, should create a particularly poor person-environment fit, leading to declines in motivation as well as detachment from the goals of the institution.

This analysis suggests several questions. First, what are the developmental needs of the early adolescent? Second, what kinds of educational environment are developmentally appropriate for meeting these needs and stimulating further development? Third, what are the most common school environmental changes before and after the transition to middle or junior high school? Fourth, and most importantly, are these changes compatible with the physiological, cognitive, and psychological changes early adolescents are experiencing? Or is there a developmental mismatch between maturing early adolescents and the classroom environments they experience before and after the transition to middle or junior high school that results in a deterioration in academic motivation and performance for some children?

Eccles and Midgley (1989) argued that there are developmentally inappropriate changes at the junior high or middle school in a cluster of classroom organizational, instructional, and climate variables, including task structure, task complexity, grouping practices, evaluation techniques, motivational strategies, locus of responsibility for learning, and quality of teacher-student and student-student relationships. They hypothesized that these changes contribute to the negative change in early adolescents' motivation and achievement-related beliefs. Evaluating these hypotheses is difficult because, until recently, there have been so few studies of differences in the classroom or school environment across grades or school levels. Most relevant descriptions have focused on school level characteristics such as school size, degree of departmentalization, and extent of bureaucratization. For example, Simmons and Blyth (1987) pointed out that most junior high schools are substantially larger (by several orders of magnitude) than elementary schools and instruction is more likely to be organized departmentally. As a result, junior high school teachers typically teach several different groups of students, making it very difficult to form a close relationship with any school-affiliated adult at precisely the point in development when there is a great need for guidance and support from nonfamilial adults. Such changes in student-teacher relationships are also likely to undermine the sense of community and trust between students and teachers, leading to a lowered sense of efficacy among the teachers, an increased reliance on authoritarian control practices by the teachers, and an increased sense of alienation among the students. Finally, such changes are likely to decrease the probability that any particular student's difficulties will be noticed early enough to get the student necessary help, thus increasing the likelihood that students on the edge will be allowed to slip onto negative motivational and performance trajectories leading to increased school failure and dropout.

These structural changes are also likely to affect classroom dynamics, teacher beliefs and practices, and student alienation and motivation in the ways proposed by Eccles and Midgley (1989). Some support for these predictions is

emerging, along with evidence of other motivationally relevant systematic changes (e.g., Ward et al., 1982).

Authority Relationships.   Despite the increasing maturity of students, junior high school classrooms, compared with elementary school classrooms, are characterized by a greater emphasis on teacher control and discipline, and fewer opportunities for student decision making, choice, and self-management (e.g., Midgley & Feldlaufer, 1987; Moos, 1979). Junior high school teachers spend more time maintaining order and less time actually teaching than elementary school teachers (Brophy & Everston, 1976). Similarly, sixth-grade elementary school math teachers report less concern with controlling and disciplining their students than these same students' seventh-grade junior high school math teachers reported one year later (Midgley, Feldlaufer, & Eccles, 1988).

Similar differences emerge on indicators of student opportunity to participate in decision making regarding their own learning. For example, Midgley and Feldlaufer (1987) reported that both seventh graders and their teachers in the first year of junior high school indicated less opportunity for students to participate in classroom decision making than did these same students and their sixth-grade elementary school teachers one year earlier. In addition, Midgley and Feldlaufer (1987) found a greater discrepancy between the adolescents' desire for participation in decision making and their perception of the opportunities for such participation when the adolescents were in their first year in junior high school than when these same adolescents were in their last year in elementary school, leading to a decline in the fit between the adolescents' desire for autonomy and their perception of the extent to which their school affords them opportunities to exchange in autonomous behavior over this school transition. And, as predicted by Eccles and Midgley (1989), this mismatch predicted the decline in adolescents' intrinsic motivation and interest in school (Mac Iver & Reuman, 1988).

Affective Relationships.   Junior high school classrooms are also characterized by less positive teacher/student relationships than elementary school classrooms (Midgley et al., 1988; Trebilco, Atkinson, & Atkinson, 1977). Given the association of classroom climate and student motivation reviewed earlier, it is not surprising that this transition into a less supportive classroom impacts negatively on early adolescents' interest in the subject matter being taught in that classroom, particularly among low-achieving students (Midgley, Feldlaufer, & Eccles, 1989b).

Teacher Efficacy.   Junior high school teachers also feel less effective as teachers, especially for low-ability students (Midgley et al., 1988). Given the association of teacher efficacy and students' beliefs, attitudes, motivation, and achievement (Ashton, 1985; Brookover et al., 1979), it is again not surprising that these differences in teachers' sense of efficacy before and after the transition to junior high school predicted the decline in early adolescents,' particularly low-achieving adolescents,' beliefs about their academic competency and potential (Midgley, Feldlaufer, & Eccles, 1989a).

Organization of Instruction.   The shift to junior high school is also associated with an increase in practices such as whole class task organization, and between-classroom ability grouping (see Eccles & Midgley, 1989; Rounds & Osaki, 1982); these changes are likely to increase social comparison, concerns about evaluation, and competitiveness (see Rosenholtz & Simpson, 1984). They also increase the likelihood that teachers will use normative grading criteria and more public forms of evaluation, both of which are likely to impact negatively on many early adolescents' self-perceptions and motivation. Finally, these changes also make aptitude differences more salient to both teachers and students, likely leading to increased teacher expectancy effects and decreased feelings of efficacy among teachers and increased entity rather than incremental views of ability. These predictions need to be tested.

Cognitive Level of Academic Content.   Surprisingly, there is also evidence that classwork during the first year of junior high school requires lower level cognitive skills than classwork at the elementary level. One rationale often given for the large, departmentalized junior high school system is its efficiency in providing early adolescents with higher level academic work. Two assumptions are implicit in this argument: (a) More formal, departmentalized teaching is conducive to the learning of higher-order cognitive processes; and (b) children in junior high school are getting higher-order learning tasks in their departmentalized courses. Both of these assumptions are being questioned. In one observational study of 11 junior high school science classes, only a very small proportion

of tasks required higher-level creative or expressive skills; the most frequent activity involved copying answers from the board or textbook onto worksheets (Mitman, Mergendoller, Packer, & Marchman, 1984; see also Walberg, House, & Steele, 1973). No one has researched the impact of this decline in the cognitive demands placed on students' motivation, but it is likely to be negative based on the importance of challenging, engaging material for positive motivation.

Grading Practices.   There is no stronger predictor of students' self-confidence and efficacy than the grades they receive. If grades change, there should be a concomitant shift in the adolescents' self-perceptions and academic motivation. Junior high school teachers use stricter and more social comparison-based standards than elementary school teachers to assess student competency and to evaluate student performance, leading to a drop in grades for many early adolescents as they make the junior high school transition (Eccles & Midgley, 1989; Finger & Silverman, 1996; Simmons & Blyth, 1987). Importantly, this decline in grades is not matched by a decline in the adolescents' scores on standardized achievement tests, suggesting that the decline reflects a change in grading practices rather than a change in the rate of the students' learning. Simmons and Blyth (1987) documented the negative impact of this grade drop on subsequent school performance and dropout, even controlling for a youth's performance prior to the school transition.

Motivational Goals.   Several of the previously noted changes are linked together in goal theory: Classroom practices related to grading practices, support for autonomy, and instructional organization affect the relative salience of mastery versus performance goals that students adopt as they engage in the learning tasks at school. The changes associated with the middle school transition should precipitate greater focus on performance goals. In support of this, in Midgley et al. (1995), both teachers and students reported that performance-focused goals were more prevalent and task-focused goals less prevalent in middle school classrooms than in elementary school classrooms. In addition, the elementary school teachers reported using task-focused instructional strategies more frequently than did the middle school teachers. Finally, at both grade levels, the extent to which teachers were task-focused predicted the students' and the teachers' sense of personal efficacy. Not surprisingly, personal efficacy was lower among the middle school participants than among the elementary school participants.

Summary

Changes such as those just reviewed are likely to have a negative effect on many children's motivational orientation toward school at any grade level. But Eccles and Midgley (1989) argued that these types of school environmental changes are particularly harmful at early adolescence. Evidence from several sources suggests that early adolescent development is characterized by increases in desire for autonomy, peer orientation, self-focus and self-consciousness, salience of identity issues, concern over heterosexual relationships, and capacity for abstract cognitive activity (see Brown, 1990; Eccles & Midgley, 1989; Harter, 1990; Keating, 1990; Simmons & Blyth, 1987). Simmons and Blyth argued that adolescents need safe, intellectually challenging environments to adapt to these shifts. In light of these needs, the environmental changes associated with transition to junior high school seem especially harmful in that they emphasize competition, social comparison, and ability self-assessment at a time of heightened self-focus; they decrease decision making and choice at a time when the desire for control is growing; they emphasize lower level cognitive strategies at a time when the ability to use higher level strategies is increasing; and they disrupt social networks at a time when adolescents are especially concerned with peer relationships and may be in special need of close adult relationships outside the home. Consequently, these environmental changes, coupled with the normal course of individual development, are likely to result in a poor "fit" between early adolescents and their classroom environment, increasing the risk of negative motivational outcomes, especially for low-achieving adolescents. An important future task is to assess how common and general these mismatches between school environments and early adolescent development are across different kinds of educational settings, different regions of the country, and different groups of early adolescents.

The High School Transition

Although there is less work on the transition to high school, the existing work is suggestive of similar problems (Jencks & Brown, 1975; Wehlage, 1989). High schools are typically even larger and more bureaucratic than junior high schools and middle schools. Bryk, Lee, and Smith (1989) provide numerous examples of how the sense of community among teachers and students is undermined by the size and bureaucratic structure of most high schools. There is little opportunity for students and teachers to get to know each other and, likely as a consequence, there is distrust between them and little attachment to a common set of goals and values. There is also little opportunity for students to form mentor relationships with a nonfamilial adult and little effort is made to make instruction relevant to the students. Such environments are likely to further undermine the motivation and involvement of many students, especially those not doing particularly well academically, those not enrolled in the favored classes, and those who are alienated from the values of the adults in the high school. These hypotheses need to be tested.

Most large public high schools also organize instruction around curricular tracks that sort students into different groups. As a result, there is even greater diversity in the educational experiences of high school students than of middle school students; and this diversity is often associated more with the students' social class and ethnic group than with differences in the students' talents and interests (Lee & Bryk, 1989). As a result, curricular tracking has served to reinforce social stratification rather than foster optimal education for all students, particularly in large schools (Dornbusch, 1994; Lee & Bryk, 1989). Lee and Bryk documented that average school achievement levels do not benefit from this curricular tracking. Quite the contrary—evidence comparing Catholic high schools with public high schools suggests that average school achievement levels are increased when all students are required to take the same challenging curriculum. This conclusion is true even after one has controlled for student selectivity factors. A more thorough examination of how the organization and structure of our high schools influence cognitive, motivational, and achievement outcomes is needed.

PEERS AND MOTIVATION

How might peers affect motivation and achievement? Researchers focus on the role of social comparison in self-evaluation, the link between social competence and school motivation/achievement, peers as colearners, the reinforcing and socializing mechanism within peer groups, and the coordination of multiple goals.

Social Comparison and Self-Evaluation

Much of the recent work has focused on children's use of peer comparison to gauge the acceptability of their beliefs and behaviors, and to evaluate their ability levels (see Reuman, 1989; Ruble, 1983; Suls & Sanders, 1982). This work shows both individual differences and age differences in people's motives for social comparison, the extent to which they engage in social comparison, and who is used for comparison. Older children use social comparison more often and more efficiently to evaluate their ability levels (e.g., Ruble, 1983; Suls & Sanders, 1982; Veroff, 1969). Ruble (1994) has also suggested that social comparison may increase during transitional phases in one's life such as the school transitions discussed earlier, making children especially vulnerable to the motivational consequences of such comparisons during these transitions. Researchers interested in adolescent development (see Brown, 1990; Fuligni & Eccles, 1993; Youniss, 1980) also suggest that early adolescents may be especially vulnerable to peer-based social comparison processes as they try to cope with this transitional phase. Cultural background (either in terms of gender or ethnic group) also likely influences the extent and the type of social comparison, but this possibility needs more attention. Finally, as noted earlier, social comparison processes are very sensitive to social context, particularly those linked to classroom experiences.

Social Competence and Motivation

There has been a long history of work focused on the relation between social competence and academic success. Much of this work has documented that children who are accepted by their peers and who have good social skills do better in school and have more positive academic achievement motivation; in contrast, socially rejected and highly aggressive children are at risk for numerous negative motivationally relevant outcomes (e.g., Asher & Coie, 1990; Green, Forehand, Beck, & Vosk, 1980; Hinshaw, 1992; Ladd & Price, 1987; Parker & Asher, 1987; Wentzel, 1991b, 1993; Wentzel, Weinberger, Ford, & Feldman, 1990). Further, social competence and social support can help ease school transitions (Ladd, 1990). The exact mechanisms underlying these associations are just beginning to be studied. Some suggest that the association represents the influence of some underlying form of inherited intelligence or temperament/motivational orientation that facilitates the acquisition of both social and academic competence

(e.g., Keogh, 1986; Martin, Drew, Gaddis, & Moseley, 1988). In support, similar socialized characteristics are significantly related to competence in both domains; these characteristics include a high sense of social responsibility (Wentzel, 1991b), a moral commitment to conventional forms of success (Hart, Yates, Fegley, & Wilson, in press), and good self-regulatory skills (Ford, 1982). A second hypothesized mechanism is based on the link between social support and mental health (Berndt, 1989; Fine & Zane, 1989): Children should be able to focus more of their attention on learning if they feel socially supported and well liked by both their peers and the adults in their learning context and if they feel that they belong (Goodenow, 1993; Ladd, 1990; Wehlage et al., 1989). They may also place more value on learning in such a context.

Peers as Colearners

The extensive work on the advantages of cooperative learning provides another link between peers and motivation. In this work, the role of peers as colearners is stressed. First, doing learning activities in a social context is usually more fun and, thus, more intrinsically interesting (Slavin, 1990; Stevens & Slavin, 1995). Peers can also help each other understand and learn the material through group discussion, sharing of resources, and modeling of academic skills, and by interpreting and clarifying the tasks for each other (Schunk, 1987; Sieber, 1979). Each of these characteristics should influence achievement through its impact on children's expectations for success, their valuing of the activity, and their focus on learning rather than performance goals.

Cooperative learning has been used to facilitate positive peer social interactions in classrooms (see Slavin, 1990). Cooperative learning arrangements may also affect motivation by reducing socially isolation and, thus, mitigating the effects of peer rejection and lack of belonging on students' academic motivation.

Peer Group Influences

Much of the classic work on peer influences on school achievement focused on the negative effects of peer groups on adolescents' commitment to doing well in school (e.g., Goodlad, 1984). More recently, investigators have also investigated the specific mechanisms by which peer groups can have either a positive or negative affect on motivation across various activity settings. These researchers have found that children cluster together in peer groups sharing similar motivational orientations and activity preferences and that such clustering reinforces and strengthens existing motivational orientation and activity preferences over time (e.g., Ball, 1981; Berndt & Keefe, in press; Berndt, Laychak, & Park, 1990; Epstein, 1983; Kindermann, McCollam, & Gibson, in press; Youniss, 1980). Whether such effects are positive or negative depends on the peer group's motivational orientation. High-achieving children who seek out other high achievers as friends develop even more positive academic motivation over time. In contrast, low achievers who join a low-achieving peer group should become even less motivated to do school work and more motivated to engage in other activities more consistent with their peer group's values (see Brown, 1990; Kindermann, 1993; Kindermann et al., in press).

The role of peer group influences is likely to vary across ages, with peers having an especially important role vis-à-vis motivation and achievement during adolescence. Adolescents are more aware of, and concerned about, peer group acceptance and spend much more unsupervised time with peer groups than do younger children. Consequently, adolescents should be especially vulnerable to peer group influences on their goals, interests, and values. In addition, however, the potential negative impact of peers may be especially problematic for some adolescents' academic achievement motivation: Early adolescents rate social activities as very important and more enjoyable than most other activities, particularly academic activities (Eccles et al., 1989; Wigfield et al., 1991). Furthermore, early adolescents' physical appearance and social acceptance are more important predictors of their general self-esteem than their perceptions of their cognitive competence (Harter, 1990). Consequently, to the extent that one's peer group devalues academic achievement relative to other goals and activities, adolescents should shift their focus away from academic pursuits to maintain peer acceptance. Finally, given other changes associated with adolescent development, it is quite likely that a substantial number of adolescents will be recruited into such a peer group.

The work by Stattin and Magnusson (e.g., 1990) provides a good example of this process. The early maturing young women in their study were particularly likely to be recruited early into heterosocial peer groups and activities. Because these females looked sexually mature, they were more likely to become involved with older male peers who interacted with them in a gender-role stereotypic manner. As these young women got caught up in this peer

social system, they shifted their attention away from academic activities and into heterosocial activities and roles, and, as a result, lowered their educational aspirations and the value they attached to academic pursuits. Consequently, they obtained less education than predicted based on their prepubertal academic performance and motivation. Instead, they often married and became parents earlier than their other female classmates.

The work on the institutional consequences of ability grouping provides a similar example. Several researchers (e.g., Dreeban & Barr, 1988; Eder & Felmlee, 1984) have suggested that ability grouping influences motivation and achievement, in part, by its influence on one's peer group. The evidence of this effect is mixed for the elementary school years. But it is more likely to be true in the adolescent years when between-class ability grouping and curricular tracking become more common. These institutional practices result in much greater segregation of peer groups based the courses they are taking (Fuligni et al., 1995; Rosenbaum, 1980; Vanfossen, Jones, & Spade, 1987). Consequently, there should be greater evidence of social stratification effects of ability grouping on students' motivation during the high school years.

Peers' Role in the Coordination of Multiple Goals

The work by Magnusson and Stattin also illustrates the importance of coordinating multiple goals. Coordinating multiple goals is part of motivational management and choice. Peers can play a central role in this process by making various goals and motivational states more or less salient and more or less desirable. Adolescence is an ideal time in which to observe these dynamics. Such processes have been suggested as one reason for ethnic group differences in school achievement based on the assumption that some groups receive less peer support for academic achievement than affluent European American youth (e.g., Fordham & Ogbu, 1986; Willis, 1977). Steinberg, Dornbusch, and Brown (1992) concluded that both the lower performance of African Americans and Hispanics and the higher performance of Whites and Asians are due more to ethnic differences in peer support for academic achievement than ethnic differences in either the value parents attach to education or the youths' beliefs regarding the likely occupational payoff for academic success. Even though the adolescents in each of these groups reported strong support for school achievement from their parents, the Hispanic and African American students reported less support for school achievement among their peers than either the European American or Asian American students, resulting in less congruence between parents and peers in the valuing of school achievement. Some African Americans in this study indicated that they have difficulty finding a peer group that will encourage them to comply with their parents' valuing of educational success and that they need to be very careful in selecting which of their African American peers to have as close friends. The European American and Asian American students were much less likely to report this kind of peer dilemma.

CROSS-CONTEXT INFLUENCES

Just as there has been an increase in attention to managing multiple goals in studies of the psychology of individual motivation, so too there has been an increase in attention to the interaction between multiple contexts on motivation. Several examples of this type of work were noted in discussing how experiences at home and with one's peers can explain variations in motivation at school. Until recently, this work has tended to be fairly simplistic, focusing on unidirectional causal models of the influence of experiences in one context (usually the family) on motivation in another context (usually the school). But in the past several years, there has been a dramatic increase in studies based on more complex models. For example, consider the growing body of work on school-family connections (see Coleman, 1987; Eccles & Harold, 1993, in press; Epstein, 1992). Epstein and her colleagues (e.g., see Epstein, 1992) pioneered this field by focusing attention on the inadequate job schools do to help parents, particularly non-White and poor parents, play an effective role in their children's education. They documented both the minimal attention many schools pay to supporting family involvement and the power of such attention for fostering and maintaining student motivation when it is available (cf., Kagen, 1989; Lightfoot, 1978; Zigler & Turner, 1982).

The role that teachers play in shaping parents' impression of their children's competencies is another example of these cross-context dynamics. We have already discussed how report cards influence parents' view of their children's competencies and motivation, but Epstein's work shows that even this effect varies depending on the larger communication context between the school and the family. When teachers attempt, systematically and frequently, to inform parents of academic progress, parents develop a better

understanding of the nature and difficulty of tasks that need to be accomplished as well as their children's academic performance and motivation. In addition, the extent to which teachers try to involve parents in the learning process by sending home assignments to be completed jointly or by having parents check homework affects what parents know about school tasks and about their children's strengths and weaknesses. These practices should influence children's motivation if the parents use the information to help their children master new material or overcome difficulties, and if parents acknowledge and reward children's progress. Finally, the extent to which the schools provide the parents with adequate information about the consequences of various curricular decisions that adolescents and their parents must make during the secondary school years will have a major impact on the educational and occupational options available to the adolescents. There is ample evidence that secondary schools do a very bad job at this type of communication (Dornbusch, 1994; Eccles & Harold, in press). As a consequence, females and minority group adolescents often end up in courses that severely limit their subsequent options.

CONCLUSION

In this chapter, we have reviewed a wide range of topics related to motivation, particularly academic achievement motivation. The view of motivation has changed dramatically over the last half of the 20th century, going from a biologically based drive perspective to a behavioral-mechanistic perspective, and then to a cognitive-mediational/constructivist perspective. The conception of the individual as a purposeful, goal-directed actor who must coordinate multiple goals and desires across multiple contexts within both short- and long-range time frames currently is prominent. As we approach the 21st century, the role of affect and less conscious processes is reemerging as a central theme. Complementing this more complex view of the psychology of motivation, researchers interested in the contextual influences on motivation are also adopting more complex and multicontextual frameworks. These frameworks are guiding both basic research agendas and policy-focused reform efforts. We find these new perspectives quite exciting and look forward to the next 10 years of research on motivation.

Many basic issues still need to be resolved, and have been discussed throughout this chapter. In closing, we highlight the issues we think deserve immediate attention.

Foremost, there continues to be a proliferation of constructs particularly with regard to the social cognitive aspects of motivation. Many of these constructs deal with competence and control. It is now time to integrate this array. We have outlined what we see as the major constructs as well as the overlap among the many instantiations of these constructs. We encourage other scholars to continue this effort at theoretical integration (see Ford, 1992, for one such effort).

Along with integrating this array of constructs, it also is crucial to expand our social cognitive models of motivation to include other constructs. The highest priority in this area is attention to the influence of emotions on motivation. Attribution theorists have moved to incorporate emotion into their models by linking emotional reactions to cognitive causal appraisals. Other conceptualizations of the link between emotion and motivation are needed. Some cognitive theorists (e.g., Pintrich et al., 1993) are going beyond "cold" models of conceptual change to include both affective and motivational processes; motivation theorists need to go beyond cold, rational models of motivation as well.

Equally important is the need for continuing work on the connection between motivational and cognitive processes. For example, how does interest actually affect strategy use, learning, and performance? Although there has been substantial headway on such questions, more work is needed if we are to make both theoretical and applied progress.

Turning to some methodological issues, we have seen a dramatic increase in the number of available measures of motivation (particularly self-report measures) over the past 20 years. Although this has increased the tools available, it has also contributed to the emergence of a vast literature that is difficult to integrate because there are so many different measures for quite similar constructs. The field would be better served if researchers spent less time generating slight variations on similar constructs and more time on fundamental theory development. Further, if new measures are to be developed, more attention should be paid to assessing motivation using different methods than the typical self-reports. The experience sampling methodology used by Csikszentmihalyi and his colleagues in which participants report on their ongoing states is an interesting example.

A critically important theoretical and methodological issue that is still being debated is the domain specificity of motivational processes. Some theorists argue that motivational constructs such as ability self-concepts and personal efficacy are quite domain specific and should be studied at that level. Bandura (1994), for example, has criticized global measures of personality traits and motivational constructs like locus of control because they are too general to predict specific behaviors very well. He made similar critical comments about Harter's (1990) perceived competence scales. Other researchers focus on more global and/or trait-like aspects of motivation. For example, researchers interested in anxiety tend to think of this characteristic as more cross-situational (e.g., Freedman-Doan, 1994; Wigfield & Eccles, 1989). It is likely that some aspects of motivation operate at a general level, whereas other aspects operate at a quite specific level. Work is needed to determine which is which.

Regarding socialization and contextual issues, researchers need to assess in more detail the influences of the transition into elementary school, and the transition from middle to high school, on children's motivation. Such studies should focus on the characteristics of particular school environments that might influence children's adjustments at these transitions points. This research will require complex longitudinal designs. Finally, as Western society becomes more diverse and connections among different parts of the world become stronger, we need to continue to assess motivation in different ethnic groups, and evaluate whether current theory adequately addresses motivation across these groups.

ACKNOWLEDGMENTS

We would like to thank Nancy Eisenberg and an anonymous reviewer for their helpful comments on earlier drafts of this chapter.

REFERENCES

Alexander, K. L., Dauber, S. L., & Entwisle, D. R. (1993). First-grade classroom behavior: Its short- and long-term consequences for school performance. *Child Development, 64,* 801–803.

Alexander, K. L., & Entwisle, D. R. (1988). Achievement in the first two years of school: Patterns and processes. *Monographs of the Society for Research in Child Development, 53*(2, Serial No. 218).

Alexander, K. L., Entwisle, D. R., & Dauber, S. L. (1994). *On the success of failure: A reassessment of the effects of retention in the primary grades.* Cambridge, MA: Cambridge University Press.

Alexander, P. A., Kulikowich, J. M., & Jetton, T. L. (1994). The role of subject-matter knowledge and interest in the processing of linear and nonlinear texts. *Review of Educational Research, 64,* 201–252.

Amabile, T. M., Hill, K. G., Hennessey, B. A., & Tighe, E. M. (1994). The Work Preference Inventory: Assessing intrinsic and extrinsic motivational orientations. *Journal of Personality and Social Psychology, 66,* 950–967.

Ames, C. (1992). Classrooms: Goals, structures, and student motivation. *Journal of Educational Psychology, 84,* 261–271.

Ames, C., & Ames, R. (Eds.). (1989). *Research on motivation in education: Vol. 3. Goals and cognitions.* San Diego: Academic Press.

Ames, C., & Archer, J. (1988). Achievement goals in the classroom: Students' learning strategies and motivation processes. *Journal of Educational Psychology, 80,* 260–267.

Anderman, E. M., & Maehr, M. L. (1994). Motivation and schooling in the middle grades. *Review of Educational Research, 64,* 287–309.

Anderson, R. C., Shirey, L. L., Wilson, P. T., & Fielding, L. G. (1987). Interestingness of children's reading material. In R. E. Snow & M. J. Farr (Eds.), *Aptitude, learning, and instruction: Vol. 3. Conative and affective process analyses* (pp. 287–299). Hillsdale, NJ: Erlbaum.

Andrews, G. R., & Debus, R. L. (1978). Persistence and the causal perception of failure: Modifying cognitive attributions. *Journal of Educational Psychology, 70,* 154–166.

Arbreton, A. J. A., & Eccles, J. S. (1994). *Mother's perceptions of their children during the transition from kindergarten to formal schooling: The effect of teacher evaluations on parents' expectations for their early elementary school children.* Paper presented at the meeting of the American Educational Research Association Conference, New Orleans, LA.

Arbreton, A. J. A., Eccles, J. S., & Harold, R. D. (1994). *Parents' perceptions of their children's competence: The role of parents' attributions.* Paper presented at the meeting of the Society for Research on Adolescence, San Diego.

Asher, S. R., & Coie, J. D. (Eds.). (1990). *Peer rejection in childhood.* New York: Cambridge University Press.

Ashton, P. (1985). Motivation and the teacher's sense of efficacy. In C. Ames & R. Ames (Eds.), *Research on motivation in education: Vol. 2. The classroom milieu* (pp. 141–171). Orlando, FL: Academic Press.

Assor, A., & Connell, J. P. (1992). The validity of students' self-reports as measures of performance affecting self-appraisals. In D. H. Schunk & J. L. Meece (Eds.), *Student self-perceptions in the classroom* (pp. 25–47). Hillsdale, NJ: Erlbaum.

Atkinson, J. W. (1964). *An introduction to motivation.* Princeton, NJ: Van Nostrand.

Atkinson, J. W. (1966). Motivational determinants of risk taking behavior. In J. W. Atkinson & N. T. Feather (Eds.), *A theory of achievement motivation* (pp. 11–31). New York: Wiley.

Ball, S. J. (1981). *Beachside comprehensive: A case-study of secondary schooling.* Cambridge, England: Cambridge University Press.

Bandura, A. (1986). *Social foundations of thought and action: A social cognitive theory.* Englewood Cliffs, NJ: Prentice-Hall.

Bandura, A. (1994). *Self-efficacy: The exercise of control.* New York: Freeman.

Barber, B., & Eccles, J. S. (1992). A developmental view of the impact of divorce and single parenting on children and adolescents. *Psychological Bulletin, 111,* 108–126.

Batson, C. D., & Johnson, A. (1976). Arousing intrinsic motivation as a goal for introductory classes: A case study. *Teaching of Psychology, 3,* 155–159.

Battle, E. (1965). Motivational determinants of academic task persistence. *Journal of Personality and Social Psychology, 2,* 209–218.

Battle, E. (1966). Motivational determinants of academic competence. *Journal of Personality and Social Psychology, 4,* 534–642.

Baumert, J. (1995, April). *Gender, science interest, teaching strategies and socially shared beliefs about gender roles in 7th graders—a multi-level analysis.* Paper presented at the annual meeting of the American Educational Research Association, San Francisco.

Baumrind, D. (1971). Current patterns of parental authority. *Developmental Psychology Monograph, 4*(1, Pt. 2).

Becker, B. J., & Hedges, L. V. (1992). *A review of the literature on the effectiveness of Comer's school development program.* A report to the Rockefeller Foundation.

Bell, L. A. (1989). Something's wrong here and it's not me: Challenging the dilemmas that block girls success. *Journal for the Education of the Gifted, 12,* 118–130.

Benjamin, M., McKeachie, W. J., & Lin, Y.-G. (1987). Two types of test anxious students: Support for an information processing model. *Journal of Educational Psychology, 59,* 128–132.

Benware, C. A., & Deci, E. L. (1984). Quality of learning with an active versus passive motivational set. *American Educational Research Journal, 21,* 755–765.

Berlyne, D. E. (1949). Interest as a psychological concept. *British Journal of Psychology, 39,* 184–195.

Berlyne, D. E. (1967). Arousal and reinforcement. In D. Levine (Ed.), *Nebraska Symposium on Motivation* (pp. 1–110). Lincoln: University of Nebraska Press.

Berndt, T. J. (1989). Friendships in childhood and adolescence. In W. Damon (Ed.), *Child development today and tomorrow* (pp. 332–348). San Francisco: Jossey-Bass.

Berndt, T. J., & Keefe, K. (in press). Friends' influence on adolescents' adjustment to school. *Child Development*.

Berndt, T. J., Laychak, A. E., & Park, K. (1990). Friends' influence on adolescents' academic achievement motivation: An experimental study. *Journal of Educational Psychology, 82*(4), 664–670.

Berry, G. L., & Asamen. J. K. (Eds.). (1989). *Black students: Psychosocial issues and academic achievement*. Newbury Park, CA: Sage.

Beyer, S. (1995). Maternal employment and children's academic achievement: Parenting styles as mediating variable. *Developmental Review, 15*, 212–253.

Bijou, S. W., & Baer, D. M. (1961). *Child development: Vol. 1. A systematic and empirical theory*. New York: Appleton-Century-Crofts.

Bledsoe, J. (1967). Self-concept of children and their intelligence, achievement, interests, and anxiety. *Childhood Education, 43*, 436–438.

Blumenfeld, P. C. (1992). Classroom learning and motivation: Clarifying and expanding goal theory. *Journal of Educational Psychology, 84*, 272–281.

Blumenfeld, P., Hamilton, V. L., Bossert, S., Wessels, K., & Meece, C. (1983). Teacher talk and student thought: Socialization into the student role. In J. Levine & U. Wang (Eds.), *Teacher and student perceptions: Implications for learning*. Hillsdale, NJ: Erlbaum.

Blumenfeld, P., Pintrich, P. R., Meece, J., & Wessels, K. (1982). The formation and role of self-perceptions of ability in elementary school classrooms. *Elementary School Journal, 82*, 401–420.

Blumenfeld, P., Soloway, E., Marx, R. W., Krajcik, J. S., Guzdail, M., & Palincsar, A. (1991). Motivating project-based learning: Sustaining the doing, supporting the learning. *Educational Psychologist, 26*, 369–398.

Boggiano, A. K., & Katz, P. (1991). Maladaptive achievement patterns in students: The role of teacher's controlling strategies. *Journal of Social Issues, 47*, 35–51.

Boggiano, A. K., Main, D. S., & Katz, P. A. (1987). Children's preference for challenge. The role of perceived competence and control. *Journal of Personality and Social Psychology, 54*, 134–141.

Boggiano, A. K., Shields, A., Barrett, M., Kellam, T., Thompson, E., Simons, J., & Katz, P. (1992). Helplessness deficits in students: The role of motivational orientation. *Motivation and Emotion, 16*, 271–296.

Borkowski, J. G., Carr, M., Relliger, E., & Pressley, M. (1990). Self-regulated cognition: Interdependence of metacognition, attributions, and self-esteem. In B. Jones & L. Idol (Eds.), *Dimensions of thinking and cognitive instruction* (Vol. 1). Hillsdale, NJ: Erlbaum.

Borkowski, J. G., & Muthukrisna, N. (1995). Learning environments and skill generalization: How contexts facilitate regulatory processes and efficacy beliefs. In F. Weinert & W. Schneider (Eds.), *Recent perspectives on memory development*. Hillsdale, NJ: Erlbaum.

Borkowski, J. G., & Thorpe, P. K. (1994). Self-regulation and motivation: A life-span perspective on underachievement. In D. H. Schunk & B. J. Zimmerman (Eds.), *Self-regulation of learning and performance*. Hillsdale, NJ: Erlbaum.

Borkowski, J. G., Weyhing, R. S., & Carr, M. (1988). Effects of attributional retraining on strategy-based reading comprehension in learning-disabled student. *Journal of Educational Psychology, 80*, 46–53.

Brookover, W., Beady, C., Flood, P., Schweitzer, J., & Wisenbaker, J. (1979). *School social systems and student achievement: Schools can make a difference*. New York: Praeger.

Brooks-Gunn, J, Guo, G., & Furstenberg, F. F., Jr. (1993). Who drops out of and who continues beyond high school? A 20-year follow up of black urban youth. *Journal of Research on Adolescence, 3*, 271–294.

Brophy, J. E. (1987). Socializing student motivation to learn. In M. L. Maehr & D. Kleiber (Eds.), *Advances in motivation and achievement* (Vol. 5). Greenwich, CT: JAI Press.

Brophy, J. E., & Evertson, C. M. (1976). *Learning for teaching: A developmental perspective*. Boston: Allyn & Bacon.

Brophy, J. E., & Good, J. L. (1974). *Teacher-student relationships*. New York: Holt, Rinehart and Winston.

Brown, B. B. (1990). Peer groups and peer culture. In S. S. Feldman & G. R. Elliott (Eds.), *At the threshold: The developing adolescent* (pp. 171–196). Cambridge, MA: Harvard University Press.

Bryk, A. S., Lee, V. E., & Holland, P. B. (1993). *Catholic schools and the common good*. Cambridge, MA: Harvard University Press.

Bryk, A. S., Lee, V. E., & Smith, J. B. (1989, May). *High school organization and its effects on teachers and students: An interpretative summary of the research*. Paper presented at the invitational conference on Choice and Control in American Education: Robert M. La Follette Institute of Public Affairs, University of Wisconsin-Madison.

Bullock, M. (Ed.). (1991). *The development of intentional action. Cognitive, motivational, and interactive processes: Vol. 22. Contributions to human development*. Basel: Karger Press.

Bullock, M., & Lutkenhaus, P. (1988). The development of volitional behaviors in the toddler years. *Child Development, 59*, 664–674.

Burhans, K. K., & Dweck, C. S. (1995). Helplessness in early childhood: The role of contingent worth. *Child Development, 66*, 1719–1738.

Butler, R. (1989a). Interest in the task and interest in peers' work: A developmental study. *Child Development, 60,* 562–570.

Butler, R. (1989b). Mastery versus ability appraisal: A developmental study of children's observations of peers' work. *Child Development, 60,* 1350–1361.

Butler, R. (1990). The effects of mastery and competitive conditions on self-assessment at different ages. *Child Development, 61,* 201–210.

Butler, R. (1993). Effects of task- and ego-achievement goals on information seeking during task engagement. *Journal of Personality and Social Psychology, 65,* 18–31.

Butler, R., & Ruzany, N. (1993). Age and socialization effects on the development of social comparison motives and normative ability assessments in kibbutz and urban children. *Child Development, 64,* 532–543.

Cameron, J., & Pierce, W. D. (1994). Reinforcement, reward, and intrinsic motivation: A meta-analysis. *Review of Educational Research, 64,* 363–423.

Carnegie Council on Adolescent Development. (1989). *Turning points: Preparing American youth for the 21st century.* Washington, DC.

Carr, M., & Borkowski, J. G. (1989). Culture and the development of the metacognitive system. *Zeitschrift fur Pedagogische Psychologie, 3,* 219–228.

Carr, M., Borkowski, J. G., & Maxwell, S. E. (1991). Motivational components of underachievement. *Developmental Psychology, 27,* 108–118.

Carter, H. D. (1940). The development of vocational attitudes. *Journal of Consulting Psychology, 4,* 181–191.

Casserly, P. (1980). An assessment of factors affecting female participation in advanced placement programs in mathematics, chemistry, and physics. In L. Fox, I. Brody, & D. Tobin (Eds.), *Women and the mathematical mystique* (pp. 138–163). Baltimore: Johns Hopkins University Press.

Cauce, A. M., Comer, J. P., & Schwartz, D. (1987). Long term effects of a systems oriented school prevention program. *American Journal of Orthopsychiatric Association, 57,* 127–131.

Chance, J. E. (1961). Independence training and first graders' achievement. *Journal of Consulting Psychology, 25,* 149–154.

Chen, C., & Stevenson, H. W. (1995). Motivation and mathematics achievement: A comparative study of Asian-American, Caucasian-American, and East Asian high school students. *Child Development, 66,* 1215–1234.

Clark, R. (1983). *Family life and school achievement: Why poor black children succeed or fail.* Chicago: University of Chicago Press.

Coleman, J. S. (1987). Families and schools. *Educational Researcher, 16,* 32–38.

Coleman, J. S., Campbell, E. Q., Hobson, C. J., McPartland, J., Mood, A., Weinfeld, F. D., & York, R. L. (1966). *Equality of educational opportunity.* Washington, DC: U.S. Government Printing Office.

Connell, J. P. (1985). A new multidimensional measure of children's perception of control. *Child Development, 56,* 1018–1041.

Connell, J. P., Halpern-Felsher, B. L., Clifford, E., Crichlow, W., & Usinger, P. (1995). Hanging in there: Behavioral, psychological, and contextual factors affecting whether African-American adolescents stay in high school. *Journal of Adolescent Research, 10,* 41–63.

Connell, J. P., Spencer, M. B., & Aber, J. L. (1994). Educational risk and resilience in African American Youth: Context, self, and action outcomes in school. *Child Development, 65,* 493–506.

Connell, J. P., & Wellborn, J. G. (1991). Competence, autonomy, and relatedness: A motivational analysis of self-system processes. In R. Gunnar & L. A. Sroufe (Eds.), *Minnesota Symposia on Child Psychology* (Vol. 23, pp. 43–77). Hillsdale, NJ: Erlbaum.

Connor, J. M., Schanckman, M., & Serbin, L. A. (1978). Sex-related differences in response to practice on a visual-spatial test and generalization to a related test. *Child Development, 49,* 24–29.

Cooper, H., & Dorr, N. (1995). Race comparisons on need for achievement: A meta-analytic alternative to Graham's narrative review. *Review of Educational Research, 65,* 483–508.

Corno, L. (1989). Self-regulated learning: A volitional analysis. In B. J. Zimmerman & D. H. Schunk (Eds.), *Self-regulated learning and academic achievement: Theory, research, and practice* (pp. 111–141). New York: Springer-Verlag.

Corno, L. (1993). The best-laid plans: Modern conceptions of volition and educational research. *Educational Researcher, 22,* 14–22.

Corno, L., & Kanfer, R. (1993). The role of volition in learning and performance. In L. Darling-Hammond (Ed.), *Review of research in education* (Vol. 29). Washington, DC: American Educational Research Association.

Council of the Great City Schools. (1992). *National urban education goals: Baseline indicators, 1990–1991.* Washington, DC: Council of the Great City Schools.

Covington, M. V. (1992). *Making the grade: A self-worth perspective on motivation and school reform.* New York: Cambridge University Press.

Covington, M. V., & Omelich, C. L. (1979). Effort: The double-edged sword in school achievement. *Journal of Educational Psychology, 71,* 169–182.

Crandall, V. C. (1969). Sex differences in expectancy of intellectual and academic reinforcement. In C. P. Smith (Ed.),

Achievement related motives in children (pp. 11–45). New York: Russell-Sage Foundation.

Crandall, V. C., Katkovsky, W., & Crandall, V. J. (1965). Children's beliefs in their own control of reinforcements in intellectual-academic achievement situations. *Child Development, 36*, 91–109.

Crandall, V. J., Dewey, R., Katkovsky, W., & Preston, A. (1964). Parents' attitudes and behaviors and grade school children's academic achievements. *Journal of Genetic Psychology, 104*, 53–66.

Crandall, V. J., Preston, A., & Rabson, A. (1960). Maternal reaction and the development of independence and achievement behavior in young children. *Child Development, 31*, 243–251.

Crockenberg, S., & Bryant, B. (1978). Socialization: The "implicit curriculum" of learning environments. *Journal of Research Development in Education, 12*, 69–78.

Cross, W. E., Jr. (1990). Race and ethnicity: Effects on social networks. In M. Cochran, M. Larner, D. Riley, I. Gunnarsson, & C. Henderson (Eds.), *Extending families: The social networks of parents and their children*. New York: Cambridge University Press.

Crystal, D. S., & Stevenson, H. W. (1991). Mothers' perceptions of children's problems with mathematics: A cross-national comparison. *Journal of Educational Psychology, 83*, 372–376.

Csikszentmihalyi, M. (1988). The flow experience and its significance for human psychology. In M. Csikszentmihalyi & I. S. Csikszentmihalyi (Eds.), *Optimal experience* (pp. 15–35). Cambridge, MA: Cambridge University Press.

Csikszentmihalyi, M., & Massimini, F. (1985). On the psychological selection of bio-cultural information. *New Ideas in Psychology, 3*, 15–138.

Csikszentmihalyi, M., Rathunde, K., & Whalen, S. (1993). *Talented teenagers: The roots of success and failure*. New York: Cambridge University Press.

D'Amico, R. J., Haurin, R. J., & Mott, F. L. (1983). The effects of mother's employment on adolescent and early outcomes of young men and women. In C. D. Hayes & S. B. Kamerman (Eds.), *Children of working parents: Experiences and outcomes* (pp. 130–219). Washington, DC: National Academy Press.

Dauber, S. L., & Benbow, C. P. (1990). Aspects of personality and peer relations of extremely talented adolescents. *Gifted Child Quarterly, 34*, 10–15.

DeBaryshe, B. D. (in press). Maternal belief systems: Linchpin in the home reading process. *Journal of Applied Developmental Psychology, 15*.

DeBaryshe, B. D., Patterson, G. R., & Capaldi, D. M. (1993). A performance model for academic achievement in early adolescence. *Developmental Psychology, 29*, 795–804.

deCharms, R. (1968). *Personal causation: The internal affective determinants of behavior*. New York: Academic Press.

Deci, E. L. (1975). *Intrinsic motivation*. New York: Plenum Press.

Deci, E. L., & Ryan, R. M. (1985). *Intrinsic motivation and self-determination in human behavior*. New York: Plenum Press.

Deci, E. L., Schwartz, A. J., Sheinman, L., & Ryan, R. M. (1981). An instrument to assess adults' orientations toward control versus autonomy with children: Reflections on intrinsic motivation and perceived competence. *Journal of Educational Psychology, 73*, 645–650.

Deci, E. L., Speigel, N. H., Ryan, R. M., Koestner, R., & Kauffman, M. (1982). Effects of performance standards on teaching styles: Behavior of controlling teachers. *Journal of Educational Psychology, 74*, 852–859.

Deffenbacher, J. L. (1980). Worry and emotionality in test anxiety. In I. G. Sarason (Ed.), *Test anxiety: Theory, research, and applications*. Hillsdale, NJ: Erlbaum.

Denny, D. R. (1980). Self-control approaches to the treatment of test anxiety. In I. G. Sarason (Ed.), *Test anxiety: Theory, research, and applications*. Hillsdale, NJ: Erlbaum.

Dewey, J. (1913). *Interest and effort in education*. Boston: Riverside Press.

Dix, M. (1976). *Are reading habits of parents related to reading performance of their children?* Paper presented at the annual meeting of the National Council of the Teachers of English.

Dornbusch, S. M. (1994). *Off the track*. Presidential address at the biennial meeting of the Society for Research on Adolescence, San Diego, CA.

Dornbusch, S. M., Ritter, P. L., Leiderman, P. H., Roberts, D. F., & Fraleigh, M. J. (1987). The relation of parenting style to adolescent school performance. *Child Development, 58*, 1244–1257.

Douglas, J. D., & Rice, K. M. (1979). Sex differences in children's anxiety and defensiveness measures. *Developmental Psychology, 15*, 223–224.

Dreeben, R., & Barr, R., (1988). Classroom composition and the design of instruction. *Sociology of Education, 61*, 129–142.

Duncan, G. J., Brooks-Gunn, J., & Klevbanov, P. K. (1994). Economic deprivation and early childhood development. *Child Development, 65*, 296–318.

Dunkin, M., & Biddle, B. (1974). *The study of teaching*. Holt, Rinehart and Winston.

Dunteman, G. H., Wisenbaker, J., & Taylor, M. F. (1978). *Race and sex differences in college science program participation*. Report to the National Science Foundation. North Carolina: Research Triangle Park.

Dunton, K. J., McDevitt, T. M., & Hess, R. D. (1988). Origins of mothers' attributions about their daughters' and sons' performance in mathematics in sixth grade. *Merrill-Palmer Quarterly, 34,* 47–70.

Dusek, J. B. (1980). The development of test anxiety in children. In I. G. Sarason (Ed.), *Test anxiety: Theory, research, and applications.* Hillsdale, NJ: Erlbaum.

Dweck, C. S. (1975). The role of expectations and attributions in the alleviation of learned helplessness. *Journal of Personality and Social Psychology, 31,* 674–685.

Dweck, C. S., Davidson, W., Nelson, S., & Enna, B. (1978). Sex differences in learned helplessness: II. The contingencies of evaluative feedback in the classroom: III. An experimental analysis. *Developmental Psychology, 14,* 268–276.

Dweck, C. S., & Elliott, E. S. (1983). Achievement motivation. In P. H. Mussen (Ed.), *Handbook of child psychology* (3rd ed.) (Vol. 4, pp. 643–691). New York: Wiley.

Dweck, C. S., & Goetz, T. E. (1978). Attributions and learned helplessness. In J. H. Harvey, W. Ickes, & R. F. Kidd (Eds.), *New directions in attribution research* (Vol. 2). Hillsdale, NJ: Erlbaum.

Dweck, C. S., & Leggett, E. (1988). A social-cognitive approach to motivation and personality. *Psychological Review, 95,* 256–273.

Dweck, C. S., & Licht, B. G. (1980). Learned helplessness and intellectual achievement. In J. Garber & M. E. P. Seligman (Eds.), *Human helplessness: Theory and applications.* New York: Academic Press.

Dweck, C. S., & Repucci, N. D. (1973). Learned helplessness and reinforcement responsibility in children. *Journal of Personality and Social Psychology, 25,* 109–116.

Early, D. M., Belansky, E., & Eccles, J. S. (1992, March). *The impact of gender stereotypes on perceived ability and attributions for success.* Poster presented at the biennial meeting of the Society for Research on Adolescence, Washington, DC,

Eccles, J. S. (1984). Sex differences in achievement patterns. In T. Sonderegger (Ed.), *Nebraska Symposium on Motivation* (Vol. 32, pp. 97–132). Lincoln: University of Nebraska Press.

Eccles, J. S. (1987). Gender roles and women's achievement-related decisions. *Psychology of Women Quarterly, 11,* 135–172.

Eccles, J. S. (1989). Bringing young women to math and science. In M. Crawford & M. Gentry (Eds.), *Gender and thought: Psychological perspectives* (pp. 36–57). New York: Springer-Verlag.

Eccles, J. S. (1993). School and family effects on the ontogeny of children's interests, self-perceptions, and activity choice. In J. Jacobs (Ed.) *Nebraska Symposium on Motivation, 1992: Developmental perspectives on motivation* (pp. 145–208). Lincoln: University of Nebraska Press.

Eccles, J. S. (1994). Understanding women's educational and occupational choices: Applying the Eccles et al. model of achievement-related choices. *Psychology of Women Quarterly, 18,* 585–609.

Eccles, J. S., Adler, T. F., & Meece, J. L. (1984). Sex differences in achievement: A test of alternate theories. *Journal of Personality and Social Psychology, 46,* 26–43.

Eccles, J. S., Barber, B., Updegraff, K., & O'Brien, K. (1995). *An expectancy-value model of achievement choices: The role of ability self-concepts, perceived task utility and interest in predicting activity choice and course enrollment.* Paper presented at the meeting of the American Educational Research Association, San Francisco.

Eccles, J. S., Buchanan, C. M., Flanagan, C., Fuligni, A., Midgley, C. M., & Yee, D. (1991). Control and autonomy: Individuation revisited in early adolescence. *Journal of Social Issues, 47,* 53–68.

Eccles, J. S., & Harold, R. D. (1991). Gender differences in sport involvement: Applying the Eccles' expectancy-value model. *Journal of Applied Sport Psychology, 3,* 7–35.

Eccles, J. S., & Harold, R. D. (1992). Gender differences in educational and occupational patterns among the gifted. In N. Colangelo, S. G. Assouline, & D. L. Amronson (Eds.), *Talent development: Proceedings from the 1991 Henry B. and Jocelyn Wallace National Research Symposium on Talent Development* (pp. 3–29). Unionville, NY: Trillium Press.

Eccles, J. S., & Harold, R. D. (1993). Parent-school involvement during the early adolescent years. *Teachers' College Record, 94,* 568–587.

Eccles, J. S., & Harold, R. (in press). Family involvement in children's and adolescents' schooling. In A. Booth & J. Dunn (Eds.), *Family-school links: How do they affect educational outcomes.* Hillsdale, NJ: Erlbaum.

Eccles, J. S., & Hoffman, L. W. (1984). Socialization and the maintenance of a sex-segregated labor market. In H. W. Stevenson & A. E. Siegel (Eds.), *Research in child development and social policy* (Vol. 1, pp. 367–420). Chicago: University of Chicago Press.

Eccles, J. S., Jacobs, J., Harold, R. D., Yoon, K. S., Aberbach, A., & Freedman-Doan, C. (1991, August). *Expectancy effects are alive and well: Gender-role socialization.* Invited address at the annual meeting of the American Psychological Association, San Francisco.

Eccles, J. S., & Lord, S. (in press). A family management perspective on raising adolescents in different types of neighborhoods. In M. K. Rosenheim & M. F. Testa (Eds.), *Children harmed and harmful: Risks and risk-taking among ten to fifteen year olds.*

Eccles, J. S., & Midgley, C. (1989). Stage/environment fit: Developmentally appropriate classrooms for early adolescents. In R. Ames & C. Ames (Eds.), *Research on motivation in education* (Vol. 3, pp. 139–181). New York: Academic Press.

Eccles, J. S., Midgley, C., & Adler, T. F. (1984). Grade-related changes in the school environment: Effects on achievement motivation. In J. H. Nicholls (Ed.), *The development of achievement motivation* (pp. 285–331). Greenwich, CT: JAI Press.

Eccles, J. S., Midgley, C., Wigfield, A., Reuman, D., Mac Iver, D., & Feldlaufer, H. (1993). Negative effects of traditional middle-schools on students' motivation. *Elementary School Journal, 93,* 553–574.

Eccles, J. S., & Wigfield, A. (1985). Teacher expectations and student motivation. In J. B. Dusek (Ed.), *Teacher expectations* (pp. 185–217). Hillsdale, NJ: Erlbaum.

Eccles, J. S., & Wigfield, A. (1995). In the mind of the achiever: The structure of adolescents' academic achievement related-beliefs and self-perceptions. *Personality and Social Psychology Bulletin, 21,* 215–225.

Eccles, J. S., Wigfield, A., & Blumenfeld, P. B. (1984). *Ontogeny of self- and task beliefs and activity choice.* Funded grant application to the National Institute for Child Health and Human Development (Grant # RO1-HD17553).

Eccles, J. S., Wigfield, A., Flanagan, C., Miller, C., Reuman, D., & Yee, D. (1989). Self-concepts, domain values, and self-esteem: Relations and changes at early adolescence. *Journal of Personality, 57,* 283–310.

Eccles, J. S., Wigfield, A., Harold, R., & Blumenfeld, P. B. (1993). Age and gender differences in children's self- and task perceptions during elementary school. *Child Development, 64,* 830–847.

Eccles, J. S., Yoon, K. S., Wigfield, A., & Eccles, J. S. (in press). *Causal relations between mothers' and children's beliefs about math ability: A structural equation model.* Manuscript submitted for publication.

Eccles-Parsons, J. (1983). Attributional processes as mediators of sex differences in achievement. *Journal of Educational Equity and Leadership, 3,* 19–27.

Eccles-Parsons, J., Adler, T. F., Futterman, R., Goff, S. B., Kaczala, C. M., Meece, J. L., & Midgley, C. (1983). Expectancies, values, and academic behaviors. In J. T. Spence (Ed.), *Achievement and achievement motivation* (pp. 75–146). San Francisco: Freeman.

Eccles-Parsons, J., Adler, T. F., & Kaczala, C. M. (1982). Socialization of achievement attitudes and beliefs: Parental influences. *Child Development, 53,* 310–321.

Eccles-Parsons, J., Kaczala, C. M., & Meece, J. L. (1982). Socialization of achievement attitudes and beliefs: Classroom influences. *Child Development, 53,* 322–339.

Eccles-Parsons, J., Meece, J. L., Adler, T. F., & Kaczala, C. M. (1982). Sex differences in attributions and learned helplessness. *Sex Roles, 8,* 421–432.

Eder, D., & Felmlee, D. (1984). The development of attention norms in ability groups. In P. L. Peterson, L. C. Wilkinson, & M. Hallinan (Eds.) *The social context of instruction: Group organization and group processes* (pp. 189–208). Orlando, FL: Academic Press.

Eder, F. (1992). Schulklima und Entwicklung allgemeiner Interessen. In A. Krapp & M. Prenzel (Eds.), *Interesse, Lernen, Leistung* (pp. 165–194). Munster: Aschendorff.

Edwards, W. (1954). The theory of decision making. *Psychological Bulletin, 51,* 380–417.

Elder, G. H., Jr., Conger, R. D., Foster, E. M., & Ardelt, M. (1992). Families under economic pressure. *Journal of Family Issues, 13,* 5–37.

Elder, G. H., Jr., Eccles, J. S., Ardelt, M., & Lord, S. (1995). Inner-city parents under economic pressure: Perspectives on the strategies of parenting. *Journal of Marriage and the Family, 6,* 81–86.

Elliott, E. S., & Dweck, C. S. (1988). Goals: An approach to motivation and achievement. *Journal of Personality and Social Psychology, 54,* 5–12.

Entwisle, D. R., & Alexander, K. L. (1990). Beginning school math competence: Minority and majority comparisons. *Child Development, 61,* 454–471.

Entwisle, D. R., & Alexander, K. L. (1993). Entry into school: The beginning school transition and educational stratification in the United States. *Annual Review of Sociology, 19,* 401–423.

Entwisle, D. R., Alexander, K. L., Pallas, A. M., & Cadigan, D. (1987). The emergent academic self-image of first graders: Its response to social structure. *Child Development, 58,* 1190–1206.

Epstein, J. L. (1983). The influence of friends on achievement and affective outcomes. In J. L. Epstein & N. L. Karweit (Eds.), *Friends in school* (pp. 177–200). New York: McGraw-Hill.

Epstein, J. L. (1992). School and family partnerships. In M. Alkin (Ed.), *Encyclopedia of educational research* (pp. 1139–1151). New York: Macmillan.

Epstein, J. L., & McPartland, J. M. (1976). The concept and measurement of the quality of school life. *American Educational Research Journal, 13,* 15–30.

Estrada, P., Arsenio, W. F., Hess, R. D., & Holloway, S. D. (1987). Affective quality of the mother-child relationship: Longitudinal consequences for children's school-relevant cognitive functioning. *Developmental Psychology, 23,* 210–215.

Feather, N. T. (1982a). Expectancy-value approaches: Present status and future directions. In N. T. Feather (Ed.), *Expectations and actions: Expectancy-value models in psychology* (pp. 395–420). Hillsdale, NJ: Erlbaum.

Feather, N. T. (1982b). *Expectations and actions: Expectancy-value models in psychology*. Hillsdale, NJ: Erlbaum.

Feather, N. T. (1988). Values, valences, and course enrollment: Testing the role of personal values within an expectancy-value framework. *Journal of Educational Psychology, 80*, 381–391.

Feather, N. T. (1992). Values, valences, expectations, and actions. *Journal of Social Issues, 48*, 109–124.

Feld, S. C. (1967). Longitudinal study of the origins of achievement strivings. *Journal of Personality and Social Psychology, 7*, 408–414.

Fincham, F. D., & Cain, K. M. (1986). Learned helplessness in humans: A developmental analysis. *Developmental Review, 6*, 301–333.

Findley, M. J., & Cooper, H. M. (1983). Locus of control and academic achievement: A literature review. *Journal of Personality and Social Psychology, 44*, 419–427.

Fine, M., & Zane, N. (1989). Bein' wrapped too tight: When low-income women drop out of high school. In L. Weis, E. Farrar, & H. Petrie (Eds.), *Dropouts from schools*. Albany: SUNY Press.

Finger, J. A., & Silverman, M. (1996). Changes in academics performance in the junior high school. *Personnel and Guidance Journal, 45*, 157–164.

Finn, J. D. (1989). Withdrawing from school. *Review of Educational Research, 59*, 117–142.

Fischoff, B., Goitein, B., & Shapira, Z. (1982). The experienced utility of expected utility approaches. In N. T. Feather (Ed.), *Expectations and actions: Expectancy-value models in psychology* (pp. 315–339). Hillsdale, NJ: Erlbaum.

Flink, C., Boggiano, A. K., & Barrett, M. (1990). Controlling teaching strategies: Undermining children's self-determination and performance. *Journal of Personality and Social Psychology, 59*, 916–924.

Ford, M. E. (1982). Social cognition and social competence in adolescence. *Developmental Psychology, 18*, 323–340.

Ford, M. E. (1992). *Human motivation: Goals, emotions, and personal agency beliefs*. Newbury Park, CA: Sage.

Ford, M. E., & Nichols, C. W. (1987). A taxonomy of human goals and some possible application. In M. E. Ford & D. H. Ford (Eds.), *Humans as self-constructing living systems: Putting the framework to work* (pp. 289–311). Hillsdale, NJ: Erlbaum.

Fordham, S., & Ogbu, J. U. (1986). Black students' school success: Coping with "the burden of 'acting white.'" *The Urban Review, 18*, 176–206.

Forsterling, F. (1985). Attributional retraining: A review. *Psychological Bulletin, 98*, 495–512.

Fowler, J. W., & Peterson, P. L. (1981). Increasing reading persistence and altering attributional style of learned helpless children. *Journal of Educational Psychology, 73*, 251–260.

Fraser, B. J., & Fisher, D. L. (1982). Predicting students' outcomes from their perceptions of classroom psychosocial environment. *American Educational Research Journal, 19*, 498–518.

Freedman-Doan, C. R. (1994). *Factors influencing the development of general, academic, and social anxiety in normal preadolescent children*. Unpublished doctoral dissertation, Wayne State University, Detroit, MI.

Freud, S. (1934). *A general introduction to psychoanalysis*. New York: Washington Square.

Frome, P., & Eccles J. (1995, April). *Underestimation of academic ability in the middle school years*. Based on poster presented at the SRCD, Indianapolis, IN.

Fuligni, A. J., & Eccles, J. S. (1993). Perceived parent-child relationships and early adolescents' orientation toward peers. *Developmental Psychology, 29*, 622–632.

Fuligni, A. J., Eccles, J. S., & Barber, B. L. (1995). The long-term effects of seventh-grade ability grouping in mathematics. *Journal of Early Adolescence, 15*(1), 58–89.

Furstenberg, F. (1993). How families manage risk and opportunity in dangerous neighborhoods. In W. J. Wilson (Ed.), *Sociology and the public agenda*. Newbury Park, CA: Sage.

Gamoran, A., & Mare, R. D. (1989). Secondary school tracking and educational inequality: Compensation, reinforcement, or neutrality? *American Journal of Sociology, 94*, 1146–1183.

Garcia, T., & Pintrich, P. R. (1994). Regulating motivation and cognition in the classroom: The role of self-schemas and self-regulatory strategies. In D. H. Schunk & B. J. Zimmerman (Eds.), *Self-regulation of learning and performance: Issues and educational applications* (pp. 127–154). Hillsdale, NJ: Erlbaum.

Geen, R. G. (1980). Test anxiety and cue utilization. In I. G. Sarason (Ed.), *Test anxiety: Theory, research, and applications*. Hillsdale, NJ: Erlbaum.

Gewirtz, J. (1969). Mechanisms of social learning: Some roles of stimulation and behavior in early human development. In D. A. Goslin (Ed.), *Handbook of socialization theory and research*. Chicago: Rand McNally.

Goldenberg, C. (1992). The limits of expectations: A case for case knowledge about teacher expectancy effects. *American Educational Research Journal, 29*, 517–544.

Goodenow, C. (1993). Classroom belonging among early adolescent students: Relationships to motivation and achievement. *Journal of Early Adolescence, 13*(1), 21–43.

Goodlad, J. I. (1984). *A place called school*. New York: McGraw-Hill.

Goodnow, J. J., & Collins, W. A. (1990). *Development according to parents: The nature, sources, and consequences of parents' ideas*. London: Erlbaum.

Gottfredson, L. S. (1981). Circumscription and compromise: A developmental theory of occupational aspirations. *Journal of Counseling Psychology Monograph, 28*, 545–579.

Gottfried, A. E. (1986). *Children's Academic Intrinsic Motivation Inventory*. Odessa, FL: Psychological Assessment Resources.

Gottfried, A. E. (1990). Academic intrinsic motivation in young elementary school children. *Journal of Educational Psychology, 82*, 525–538.

Gottfried, A. E. (1991). Maternal employment in the family setting: Developmental and environmental issues. In J. V. Lerner & N. L. Galambos (Eds.), *Employed mothers and their children* (pp. 63–84). New York: Garland.

Graham, S. (1984). Communicating sympathy and anger to Black and White children: The cognitive (attributional) consequences of affective cues. *Journal of Personality and Social Psychology, 47*, 14–28.

Graham, S. (1991). A review of attribution theory in achievement contexts. *Educational Psychology Review, 3*, 5–39.

Graham, S. (1992). Most of the subjects were European American and middle class: Trends in published research on African Americans in selected APA journals 1970–1989. *American Psychologist, 47*, 629–639.

Graham, S. (1994). Motivation in African Americans. *Review of Educational Research, 64*, 55–117.

Graham, S., & Barker, G. (1990). The downside of help: An attributional-developmental analysis of helping behavior as a low ability cue. *Journal of Educational Psychology, 82*, 7–14.

Graham, S., & Golan, S. (1991). Motivational influences on cognition: Task involvement, ego involvement, and depth of information processing. *Journal of Educational Psychology, 83*, 187–194.

Graham, S., & Weiner, B. (1996). Principles and theories of motivation. In D. C. Berliner & R. Calfee (Eds.), *Handbook of educational psychology*. New York: Macmillan.

Green, K. D., Forehand, R., Beck, S. J., & Vosk, B. (1980). An assessment of the relationships among measures of children's social competence and children's academic achievement. *Child Development, 51*, 1149–1156.

Grolnick, W. S., & Ryan, R. M. (1987). Autonomy in children's learning: An experimental and individual difference investigation. *Journal of Personality and Social Psychology, 52*, 890–898.

Grolnick, W. S., & Ryan, R. M. (1989). Parent styles associated with children's self-regulation and competence in schools. *Journal of Educational Psychology, 8*, 143–154.

Grolnick, W. S., Ryan, R. M., & Deci, E. L. (1991). Inner resources for school achievement: Motivational mediators of children's perceptions of their parents. *Journal of Educational Psychology, 83*, 508–517.

Grolnick, W. S., & Slowiaczek, M. L. (1994). Parents' involvement in children's schooling: A multidimensional conceptualization and motivational model. *Child Development, 65*, 237–252.

Gurin, P., & Epps, E. (1974). *Black consciousness, identity, and achievement*. New York: Wiley.

Hale-Benson, J. (1989). The school learning environment and academic success. In G. L. Berry & J. K. Asamen (Eds.), *African American students: Psychosocial issues and academic achievement* (pp. 83–97). Newbury Park, CA: Sage.

Harackiewicz, J. M., & Elliot, A. J. (1993). Achievement goals and intrinsic motivation. *Journal of Personality and Social Psychology, 65*, 904–915.

Hare, B. R. (1985). Stability and change in self-perceptions and achievement among African American adolescents: A longitudinal study. *Journal of African American Psychology, 11*, 29–42.

Hart, D., Yates, M., Fegley, S., & Wilson, G. (in press). Moral commitment in inner-city adolescents. In M. Killen & D. Hart (Eds.), *Morality in everyday life: Developmental perspectives*. New York: Cambridge University Press.

Harter, S. (1981). A new self-report scale of intrinsic versus extrinsic orientation in the classroom: Motivational and informational components. *Developmental Psychology, 17*, 300–312.

Harter, S. (1982). The Perceived Competence Scale for Children. *Child Development, 53*, 87–97.

Harter, S. (1983). Developmental perspectives on the self-system. In P. H. Mussen (Ed.), *Handbook of child psychology* (Vol. 4, pp. 275–385). New York: Wiley.

Harter, S. (1990). Causes, correlates and the functional role of global self-worth: A life-span perspective. In J. Kolligian & R. Sternberg (Eds.), *Perceptions of competence and incompetence across the life-span* (pp. 67–98). New Haven, CT: Yale University Press.

Harter, S. (1992). Visions of self: Beyond the me in the mirror. In J. Jacobs (Ed.), *Nebraska Symposium on Motivation* (Vol. 40). Lincoln: University of Nebraska Press.

Harter, S., & Pike, R. (1984). The pictorial scale of perceived competence and social acceptance for young children. *Child Development, 55*, 1969–1982.

Hebb, D. O. (1955). Drives and the C.N.S. (Conceptual Nervous System). *Psychological Review, 62*, 243–254.

Heckhausen, H. (1977). Achievement motivation and its constructs: A cognitive model. *Motivation and Emotion, 1*, 283–329.

Heckhausen, H. (1984). Emergent achievement behavior: Some early developments. In J. Nicholls (Ed.), *Advances in achievement motivation* (pp. 1–32). Greenwich, CT: JAI Press.

Heckhausen, H. (1987). Emotional components of action: Their ontogeny as reflected in achievement behavior. In D. Gîrlitz & J. F. Wohlwill (Eds.), *Curiosity, imagination, and play.* Hillsdale, NJ: Erlbaum.

Heckhausen, H. (1991). *Motivation and action.* Berlin: Springer-Verlag.

Hedelin, L., & Sjoberg, L. (1989). The development of interests in the Swedish comprehensive school. *European Journal of Psychology of Education, 4,* 17–35.

Heider, F. (1958). *The psychology of interpersonal relations.* New York: Academic Press.

Heilburn, A. B., & Walters, D. B. (1968). Under achievement as related to perceived maternal child rearing and academic conditions of reinforcement. *Child Development, 39,* 913–921.

Helmke, A. (1993). Die Entwicklung der Lernfreude vom Kindergarten bis zur 5. Klassenstufe (The development of learning from kindergarten to fifth grade). *Zeitschrift fŏr PŇdagogische Psychologie (Journal of Educational Psychology), 7,* 77–86.

Herbart, J. F. (1965). Umria paedagogischer Vorlesungen. In J. F. Herbart (Ed.), *Paedagogische Schriften* (Vol. 3, pp. 157–300). Duesseldorf: Kuepper. (Original work published 1841)

Hess, R. D. (1970). Social class and ethnic influences on socialization. In P. H. Mussen (Ed.), *Carmichael's manual of child psychology.* New York: Wiley.

Hess, R. D., & Azuma, H. (1991). Cultural support for schooling: Contrasts between Japan and the United States. *Educational Researcher, 20,* 2–8.

Hess, R. D., Chih-Mei, & McDevitt, T. M. (1987). Cultural variations in family beliefs about children's performance in mathematics: Comparisons among People's Republic of China, Chinese-American, and Caucasian-American families. *Journal of Educational Psychology, 70,* 179–188.

Hess, R. D., & Holloway, S. D. (1984). Family and school as educational institutions. In R. D. Parke (Ed.), *Review of child development and research: Vol. 17. The family* (pp. 179–222). Chicago: University of Chicago Press..

Hess, R. D., Holloway, S. D., Dickson, W. P., & Price, G. G. (1984). Maternal variables as predictors of children's school readiness and later achievement in vocabulary and mathematics in sixth grade. *Child Development, 55,* 1902–1912.

Heyman, G. D., Dweck, C. S., & Cain, K. M. (1993). Young children's vulnerability to self-blame and helplessness: Relationships to beliefs about goodness. *Child Development, 63,* 401–415.

Hidi, S. (1990). Interest and its contribution as a mental resource for learning. *Review of Educational Research, 60,* 549–571.

Hidi, S., & Baird, W. (1986). Interestingness—A neglected variable in discourse processing. *Cognitive Science, 10,* 179–194.

Hill, K. T. (1980). Motivation, evaluation, and educational testing policy. In L. J. Fyans (Ed.), *Achievement motivation: Recent trends in theory and research.* New York: Plenum Press.

Hill, K. T., & Sarason, S. B. (1966). The relation of test anxiety and defensiveness to test and school performance over the elementary school years: A further longitudinal study. *Monographs for the Society for Research in Child Development, 31*(2, Serial No. 104).

Hill, K. T., & Wigfield, A. (1984). Test anxiety: A major educational problem and what to do about it. *Elementary School Journal, 85,* 105–126.

Hinshaw, S. P. (1992). Externalizing behavior problems and academic underachievement in childhood and adolescence: Causal relationships and underlying mechanisms. *Psychological Bulletin, 111,* 127–155.

Hoffmann, L., & Haeussler. (1995, April). *Modification of interests by instruction.* Paper presented at the annual American Educational Research Association meeting in San Francisco, CA.

Hokoda, A., & Fincham, F. D. (1995). Origins of children's helpless and mastery achievement patterns in the family. *Journal of Educational Psychology, 87,* 375–385.

Holloway, S. D. (1986). The relationship of mothers' beliefs to children's mathematics achievement: Some effects of sex differences. *Merrill-Palmer Quarterly, 32,* 231–250.

Holloway, S. D. (1988). Concepts of ability and effort in Japan and the United States. *Review of Educational Research, 58,* 327–345.

Holloway, S. D., Kashiwagi, K., Hess, R. D., & Azuma, H. (1986). Causal attributions by Japanese and American mothers and children about performance in mathematics. *International Journal of Psychology, 21,* 269–286.

Horwitz, R. A. (1979). Psychological effects of the open classroom. *Review of Educational Research, 49,* 71–85.

Hull, C. L. (1943). *Principles of behavior.* New York: Appleton-Century-Crofts.

Hunt, D. E. (1979). Person-environment interaction: A challenge found wanting before it was tried. *Review of Educational Research, 45,* 209–230.

Hunt, J. M., & Paraskevopoulos, J. (1980). Children's psychological development as a function of the inaccuracy of their mothers' knowledge of their abilities. *Journal of Genetic Psychology, 136,* 285–298.

Huston, A. (1983). Sex-typing. In P. H. Mussen (Ed.), *Handbook of child psychology* (Vol. 4, pp. 387–467). New York: Wiley.

Huston, A. C., McLoyd, V., & Coll, C. G. (1994). Children and poverty: Issues in contemporary research. *Child Development, 65,* 275–282.

Jackson, P. W. (1968). *Life in classrooms.* New York: Holt, Rinehart and Winston.

Jacobs, J. E. (1992). The influence of gender stereotypes on parent and child math attitudes. *Journal of Educational Psychology, 83,* 518–527.

Jacobs, J. E., & Eccles, J. S. (1992). The influence of parent stereotypes on parent and child ability beliefs in three domains. *Journal of Personality and Social Psychology, 63,* 932–944.

James, W. (1963). *Psychology.* New York: Fawcett. (Original work published 1892)

Jencks, C. L., & Brown, M. (1975). The effects of high schools on their students. *Harvard Educational Review, 45,* 273–324.

Jennings, K. D. (1991). Early development of mastery motivation and its relation to the self-concept. In M. Bullock (Ed.), *The development of intentional action: Cognitive, motivational, and interactive processes: Vol. 22. Contributions to human development.* Basel: Karger Press.

Jozefowicz, D. M., Eccles, J. S., & Barber, B. L. (1993, March). *Adolescent work-related values and beliefs: Gender differences and relation to occupational aspirations.* Paper presented at the biennial meeting of the Society for Research in Child Development, New Orleans, LA.

Jussim, L., & Eccles, J. S. (1992). Teacher expectations: II. Construction and reflection of student achievement. *Journal of Personality and Social Psychology, 63,* 947–961.

Jussim, L., Eccles, J., & Madon, S. (1996). Social perception, social stereotypes, and teacher expectations: Accuracy and the quest for the powerful self-fulfilling prophecy. In L. Berkowitz (Ed.), *Advances in experimental social psychology* (pp. 281–388). New York: Academic Press.

Kage, M., & Namiki. H. (1990). The effects of evaluation structure on children's intrinsic motivation and learning. *Japanese Journal of Educational Psychology, 38,* 36–45.

Kagen, S. L. (1989). Early care and education: Beyond the schoolhouse doors. *Phi Delta Kappan, 71,* 107–112.

Kahle, J. (1984). *Girl-friendly science.* Paper presented at the meeting of the American Association for the Advancement of the Sciences, New York.

Kahneman, D., & Tversky, A. (1984). Choices, values, and frames. *American Psychologist, 39,* 341–350.

Kandel, D. B., & Lesser, G. S. (1969). Parental and peer influence, on educational plans of adolescents. *American Sociological Review, 34,* 213–223.

Kao, G., & Tienda, M. (1995). Optimism and achievement: The educational performance of immigrant youth. *Social Science Quarterly, 76,* 1–19.

Katkovsky, W., Crandall, V. C., & Preston, A. (1964). Parent attitudes toward their personal achievements and toward the achievement behavior of their children. *Journal of Genetic Psychology, 104,* 67–82.

Kazdin, A. E. (1982). The token economy: A decade later. *Journal of Applied Behavior Analysis, 15,* 431–445.

Keating, D. P. (1990). Adolescent thinking. In S. S. Feldman & G. R. Elliott (Eds.), *At the threshold: The developing adolescent* (pp. 54–89). Cambridge, MA: Harvard University Press.

Kelly, H. H. (1972). Causal schemata and the attribution process. In E. E. Jones, D. E. Kanouse, R. E. Nisbett, S. Valin, & B. Weiner (Eds.), *Attributions: Perceiving the causes of behavior.* Morristown, NJ: General Learning Press.

Keogh, B. (1986). Temperament and schooling: Meaning of "goodness of fit." In J. Lerner & R. Lerner (Eds.), *Temperament and social interaction during infancy and childhood* (pp. 89–108). San Francisco: Jossey-Bass.

Kerschensteiner, G. (1922). *Theorie der Bildung (Theories of education).* Leipzig: Teubner.

Kindermann, T. A. (1993). Natural peer groups as contexts for individual development: The case of children's motivation in school. *Developmental Psychology, 29*(6), 970–977.

Kindermann, T. A., McCollam, T. L., & Gibson, E., Jr. (in press). Peer networks and students' classroom engagement during childhood and adolescence. In K. Wentzel & J. Juvonen (Eds.), *Social motivation: Understanding children's school adjustment.* Cambridge, England: Cambridge University Press.

Knight, R. (1981). Parents' beliefs about cognitive development: The role of experience. In A. R. Nesdale, C. Pratt, R. Grieve, J. Field, D. Illingworth, & J. Hogben (Eds.), *Advances in child development: Theory and research* (pp. 226–229). Perth: University of Western Australia Press.

Kohlberg, L. (1966). A cognitive-development analysis of children's sex-role concepts and attitudes. In E. E. Maccoby (Ed.), *The development of sex differences* (pp. 82–172). Stanford, CA: Stanford University Press.

Kopp, C. B. (1991). Young children's progression to self-regulation. In M. Bullock (Ed.), *The development of intentional action: Cognitive, motivational, and interactive processes: Vol. 22. Contributions to human development.* Basel: Karger Press.

Krapp, A., Hidi, S., & Renninger, K. A. (1992). Interest, learning and development. In K. A. Renninger, S. Hidi, & A. Krapp (Eds.), *The role of interest in learning and development* (pp. 3–25). Hillsdale, NJ: Erlbaum.

Kuhl, J. (1985). Volitional mediators of cognition-behavior consistency: Self-regulatory processes and action versus state orientation. In J. Kuhl & J. Beckman (Eds.), *Action control: From cognition to behavior.* Berlin: Springer-Verlag.

Kuhl, J. (1987). Action control: The maintenance of motivational states. In F. Halisch & J. Kuhl (Eds.), *Motivation, intention, and volition* (pp. 279–307). Berlin: Springer-Verlag.

Kuhl, J., & Kraska, K. (1989). Self-regulation and metamotivation: Computational mechanisms, development, and assessment. In R. Kanfer, P. L. Ackerman, & R. Cudeck (Eds.), *Abilities, motivation, and methodology.* Hillsdale, NJ: Erlbaum.

Kulik, C. L., Kulik, J., & Bangert-Drowns, R. (1990). Effectiveness of mastery learning programs: A meta-analysis. *Review of Educational Research, 60,* 265–299.

Kulik, J. A., & Kulik, C. L. (1987). Effects of ability grouping on student achievement. *Equity and Excellence, 23,* 22–30.

Kun, A., Parsons, J. E., & Ruble, D. (1974). The development of integration processes using ability and effort information to predict outcome. *Developmental Psychology, 10,* 721–732.

Ladd, G. W. (1990). Having friends, keeping friends, making friends, and being liked by peers in the classroom: Predictors of children's early school adjustment? *Child Development, 61,* 1081–1100.

Ladd, G. W., & Price, J. M. (1987). Predicting children's social and school adjustment following the transition from preschool to kindergarten. *Child Development, 58,* 1168–1189.

Laosa, L. M. (1984). Social policies toward children of diverse ethnic, racial, and language groups in the United States. In H. W. Stevenson & A. E. Siegel (Eds.), *Child developmental research and social policy* (pp. 1–109). Chicago: University of Chicago Press.

Lee, S., Ichikawa, V., & Stevenson, H. S. (1987). Beliefs and achievement in mathematics and reading: A cross-national study of Chinese, Japanese, and American children and their mothers. In M. Maehr (Ed.), *Advances in motivation* (Vol. 7, pp. 149–179). Greenwich, CT: JAI Press.

Lee, V. E., & Bryk, A. S. (1989). A multilevel model of the social distribution of high school achievement. *Sociology of Education, 62,* 172–192.

Lehrke, M., Hoffmann, L., & Gardner, P. L. (Eds.). (1985). *Interests in science and technology education.* Kiel: Institut fur die Padagogik der Naturwissenschaften.

Lepper, M. R. (1988). Motivational considerations in the study of instruction. *Cognition and Instruction, 5,* 289–309.

Lepper, M. R., & Chabay, R. W. (1985). Intrinsic motivation and instruction: Conflicting views on the role of motivational processes in computer-based education. *Educational Psychologist, 20,* 217–230.

Lepper, M. R., & Cordova, D. (1992). A desire to be taught: Instructional consequences of intrinsic motivation. *Motivation and Emotion, 3,* 187–208.

Lepper, M. R., & Green, D. (1978). *The hidden cost of rewards: New perspectives on the psychology of human motivation.* Hillsdale, NJ: Erlbaum.

Lewin, K. (1938). *The conceptual representation and the measurement of psychological forces.* Durham, NC: Duke University Press.

Lewin, K., Dembo, T., Festinger, L., & Sears, R. S. (1944). Level of aspiration. In J. M. Hunt (Ed.), *Personality and the behavior disorders* (Vol. 1). New York: Ronald Press.

Liebert, R., & Morris, L. W. (1967). Cognitive and emotional components of test-anxiety: A distinction and some initial data. *Psychological Reports, 20,* 975–978.

Lightfoot, S. L. (1978). *Worlds apart: Relationships between families and schools.* New York: Basic Books.

Lipsitz, J. (1984). *Successful schools for young adolescents.* New Brunswick, NJ: Transaction Books.

Locke, E. A., & Latham, G. P. (1990). *A theory of goal setting and task performance.* Englewood Cliffs, NJ: Prentice-Hall.

Lord, S., Eccles, J. S., & McCarthy, K. (1994). Risk and protective factors in the transition to junior high school. *Journal of Early Adolescence, 14,* 162–199.

Lummis, M., & Stevenson, H. W. (1990). Gender differences in beliefs and achievement: A cross-cultural study. *Developmental Psychology, 26,* 254–263.

Luster, T., & McAdoo, H. P. (1994). Factors related to the achievement and adjustment of young African American children. *Child Development, 65,* 1080–1094.

Luster, T., Rhoades, K., & Haas, B. (1989). The relation between parental values and parenting behavior: A test of the Kohn hypothesis. *Journal of Marriage and the Family, 51,* 139–147.

Mac Iver, D. J. (1987). Classroom factors and student characteristics predicting students' use of achievement standards during ability self-assessment. *Child Development, 58,* 1258–1271.

Mac Iver, D. J., & Reuman, D. A. (1988, April). *Decision-making in the classroom and early adolescents' valuing of mathematics.* Paper presented at the annual meeting of the American Educational Research Association, New Orleans.

Mac Iver, D. J., & Reuman, D. A. (1993). Giving their best: Grading and recognition practices that motivate students to work hard. *American Education 17,* 24–31.

Mac Iver, D. J., Reuman, D. A., & Main, S. R. (1995). Social structuring of school: Studying what is, illuminating what could be. In M. R. Rosenzweig & L. W. Porter (Eds.), *Annual review of psychology* (Vol. 46).

Mac Iver, D. J., Stipek, D. J., & Daniels, D. H. (1991). Explaining within-semester changes in student effort in junior high school and senior high school courses. *Journal of Educational Psychology, 83,* 201–211.

Maehr, M. L., & Anderman, E. M. (1993). Reinventing schools for early adolescents: Emphasizing task goals. *The Elementary School Journal, 93,* 593–610.

Maehr, M. L., & Midgley, C. (1996). *Transforming school cultures.* Boulder, CO: Westview Press.

Maehr, M. L., & Nicholls, J. G., (1980). Culture and achievement motivation: A second look. In N. Warren (Ed.), *Studies in cross cultural psychology* (Vol. 3, pp. 221–267). New York: Academic Press.

Manley, J. J., & Rosemier, R. A. (1972). Developmental trends in general and test anxiety among junior high and senior high school students. *Journal of Genetic Psychology, 12,* 119–126.

Marjoribanks, K. (1979). *Families and their learning environments.* London: Routledge & Kegan Paul.

Marjoribanks, K. (1980). *Ethnic families and children's achievement.* Sydney: Allen & Unwin.

Markus, H., & Nurius, P. (1986). Possible selves. *American Psychologist, 41,* 954–969.

Markus, H., & Wurf, E. (1987). The dynamic self-concept: A social psychological perspective. *Annual Review of Psychology, 38,* 299–337.

Marsh, H. W. (1989). Age and sex effects in multiple dimensions of self-concept: Preadolescence to early adulthood. *Journal of Educational Psychology, 81,* 417–430.

Marsh, H. W. (1990a). A multidimensional, hierarchical self-concept: Theoretical and empirical justification. *Educational Psychology Review, 2,* 77–171.

Marsh, H. W. (1990b). The causal ordering of academic self-concept and academic achievement: A multiwave, longitudinal analysis. *Journal of Educational Psychology, 82.*

Marsh, H. W., Barnes, J., Cairns, L., & Tidman, M. (1984). Self-Description Questionnaire: Age and sex effects in the structure and level of self-concept for preadolescent children. *Journal of Educational Psychology, 76,* 940–956.

Marsh, H. W., Chessor, D., Craven, R., & Roche, L. (1995). The effects of gifts and talented programs on academic self-concept: The big fish strikes again. *American Educational Research Journal, 32,* 285–319.

Marsh, H. W., Craven, R. G., & Debus, R. (1991). Self-concepts of young children 5 to 8 years of age: Measurement and multidimensional structure. *Journal of Educational Psychology, 83,* 377–392.

Marsh, H. W., & Hocevar, D. (1985). The application of confirmatory factor analyses to the study of self-concept: First and higher-order factor structures and their invariance across age groups. *Psychological Bulletin, 97,* 562–582.

Marsh, H. W., & Shavelson, R. (1985). Self-concept: Its multifaceted, hierarchical structure and its relation to academic achievement. *Educational Psychologist, 20,* 107–125.

Martin, R., Drew, K., Gaddis, L., & Moseley, M. (1988). Prediction of elementary school achievement from preschool temperament: Three studies. *School Psychology Review, 17,* 125–137.

Massimini, F., & Carli, M. (1988). The systematic assessment of flow in daily experience. In M. Csikszentmihalyi & I. S. Csikszentmihalyi (Eds.), *Optimal experience: Psychological studies of flow in consciousness* (pp. 266–287). Cambridge, MA: Cambridge University Press.

Matsumoto, D., & Sanders, M. (1988). Emotional experiences during engagement in intrinsically and extrinsically motivated tasks. *Motivation and Emotion, 12,* 353–369.

McCall, R. B., Evahn, C., & Kratzer, L. (1992). *High school underachievers: What do they achieve as adults?* Newbury Park, CA: Sage.

McClelland, D. C. (1961). *The achieving society.* Princeton, NJ: Van Nostrand.

McClelland, D. C. (1985). How motives, skills, and values determine what people do. *American Psychologist, 40,* 812–825.

McGillicuddy-DeLisi, A. V. (1982). Parental beliefs about development. *Human Development, 25,* 192–200.

McGillicuddy-DeLisi, A. V., & Sigel, I. E. (1991). Family environments and children's representational thinking. In P. Mosenthal (Ed.), *Advances in reading/language research* (Vol. 5, pp. 63–90). JAI Press.

McLoyd, V. C. (1990). The impact of economic hardship on African American families and children: Psychological distress, parenting, and socioemotional development. *Child Development, 61,* 311–346.

Meece, J. L. (1991). The classroom context and students' motivational goals. In M. Maehr & P. Pintrich (Eds.), *Advances in motivation and achievement* (Vol. 7, pp. 261–286). Greenwich, CT: JAI Press,

Meece, J. L. (1994). The role of motivation in self-regulated learning. In D. H. Schunk & B. J. Zimmerman (Eds.), *Self-regulation of learning and performance* (pp. 25–44). Hillsdale, NJ: Erlbaum.

Meece, J. L., Blumenfeld, P. B., & Hoyle, R. H. (1988). Students' goal orientations and cognitive engagement in classroom activities. *Journal of Educational Psychology, 80,* 514–523.

Meece, J. L., Eccles-Parsons, J., Kaczala, C. M., Goff, S. E., & Futterman, R. (1982). Sex differences in math achievement: Toward a model of academic choice. *Psychological Bulletin, 91,* 324–348.

Meece, J. L., & Miller, S. D. (1996, April). *Developmental changes in children's self-reports of achievement goals, competence, and strategy use during the late elementary years.* Paper presented at the annual meeting of the American Educational Research Association, New York.

Meece, J. L., Wigfield, A., & Eccles, J. S. (1990). Predictors of math anxiety and its consequences for young adolescents' course enrollment intentions and performances in mathematics. *Journal of Educational Psychology, 82,* 60–70.

Meichenbaum, D., & Butler, L. (1980). Toward a conceptual model of the treatment of test anxiety: Implications for research and treatment. In I. G. Sarason (Ed.), *Test anxiety: Theory, research, and applications.* Hillsdale, NJ: Erlbaum.

Midgley, C., Anderman, E., & Hicks, L. (1995). Differences between elementary and middle school teachers and students: A goal theory approach. *Journal of Early Adolescence, 15,* 90–113.

Midgley, C., & Feldlaufer, H. (1987). Students' and teachers' decision-making fit before and after the transition to junior high school. *Journal of Early Adolescence, 7,* 225–241.

Midgley, C., Feldlaufer, H., & Eccles, J. S. (1988). The transition to junior high school: Beliefs of pre- and post-transition teachers. *Journal of Youth and Adolescence, 17,* 543–562.

Midgley, C., Feldlaufer, H., & Eccles, J. S. (1989a). Changes in teacher efficacy and student self- and task-related beliefs during the transition to junior high school. *Journal of Educational Psychology, 81,* 247–258.

Midgley, C., Feldlaufer, H., & Eccles, J. S. (1989b). Student/teacher relations and attitudes toward mathematics before and after the transition to junior high school. *Child Development, 60,* 981–992.

Miller, S. A. (1988). Parents' beliefs about children's cognitive development. *Child Development, 59,* 259–285.

Miller, S. A. (in press). Parents' attributions for their children's behavior. *Child Development.*

Miller, S. A., & Davis, T. L. (1992). Beliefs about children: A comparative study of mothers, teachers, peers, and self. *Child Development, 63,* 1251–1265.

Miller, S. A., Manhal, M., & Mee, L. L. (1991). Parental beliefs, parental accuracy, and children's cognitive performance: A search for causal relations. *Developmental Psychology, 27,* 267–276.

Mischel, W., & Mischel, C. (1983). Development of children's knowledge of self-control strategies. *Child Development, 54,* 603–619.

Mitman, A. L., Mergendoller, J. R., Packer, M. J., & Marchman, V. A. (1984). *Scientific literacy in seventh-grade life science: A study of instructional process, task completion, student perceptions and learning outcomes: Final report.* San Francisco: Far West Laboratory.

Modell, J. (1993). *Desire to learn: A comparative view of schooling in children's lives.* Princeton, NJ: Educational Testing Service.

Moos, R. H. (1979). *Evaluating educational environments.* San Francisco: Jossey-Bass.

Morris, L. W., Davis, M. A., & Hutchings, C. J. (1981). Cognitive and emotional components of anxiety: Literature review and a revised worry-emotionality scale. *Journal of Educational Psychology, 73,* 541–555.

Murray, H. A. (1938). *Explorations in personality.* New York: Oxford University Press.

Nagy, L. (1912). *Psychologie des kindlichen Interesses* (Psychology of interests). Leipzig: Nemnich.

Nash, S. C. (1979). Sex role as a mediator of intellectual functioning. In M. A. Wittig & A. C. Peterson (Eds.), *Sex-related differences in cognitive functioning: Developmental issues.* New York: Academic Press.

Nelson-Le Gall, S., & Glor-Sheib, S. (1985). Help seeking in elementary classrooms: An observational study. *Contemporary Educational Psychology, 10,* 58–71.

Nelson-Le Gall, S., & Jones, E. (1990). Cognitive-motivational influences on task-related help-seeking behavior of Black children. *Child Development, 61,* 581–589.

Newman, R. S. (1990). Children's help-seeking in the classroom: The role of motivational factors and attitudes. *Journal of Educational Psychology, 82,* 71–80.

Newman, R. S. (1994). Adaptive help-seeking: A strategy of self-regulated learning. In D. H. Schunk & B. J. Zimmerman (Eds.), *Self-regulation of learning and performance: Issues and educational applications* (pp. 283–301). Hillsdale, NJ: Erlbaum.

Newman, R. S., & Goldin, L. (1990). Children's reluctance to seek help with schoolwork. *Journal of Educational Psychology, 82,* 92–100.

Newman, R. S., & Schwager, M. T. (1995). Students' help-seeking during problem solving: Effects of grader, goal, and prior achievement. *American Educational Research Journal, 32,* 352–376.

Nicholls, J. G. (1976). When a test measures more than its name: The case of the Test Anxiety Scale for Children. *Journal of Consulting and Clinical Psychology, 20,* 321–326.

Nicholls, J. G. (1978). The development of the concepts of effort and ability, perceptions of academic attainment, and the understanding that difficult tasks require more ability. *Child Development, 49,* 800–814.

Nicholls, J. G. (1979a). Development of perception of own attainment and causal attributions for success and failure in reading. *Journal of Educational Psychology, 71,* 94–99.

Nicholls, J. G. (1979b). Quality and equality in intellectual development: The role of motivation in education. *American Psychologist, 34,* 1071–1084.

Nicholls, J. G. (1984). Achievement motivation: Conceptions of ability, subjective experience, task choice, and performance. *Psychological Review, 91,* 328–346.

Nicholls, J. G. (1989). *The competitive ethos and democratic education.* Cambridge MA: Harvard University Press.

Nicholls, J. G. (1990). What is ability and why are we mindful of it? A developmental perspective. In R. J. Sternberg &

J. Kolligian (Eds.), *Competence considered.* New Haven, CT: Yale University Press.

Nicholls, J. G. (1992). Students as educational theorists. In D. H. Schunk & J. L. Meece (Ed.), *Student self-perceptions in the classroom* (pp. 267–286). Hillsdale, NJ: Erlbaum.

Nicholls, J. G., Cobb, P., Yackel, E., Wood, T., & Wheatley, G. (1990). Students' theories of mathematics and their mathematical knowledge: Multiple dimensions of assessment. In G. Kulm (Ed.), *Assessing higher order thinking in mathematics* (pp. 137–154). Washington, DC: American Association for the Advancement of Science.

Nicholls, J. G., & Miller, A. T. (1984). The differentiation of the concepts of difficulty and ability. *Child Development, 54,* 951–959.

Nicholls, J. G., Patashnick, M., & Mettetal, G. (1986). Conceptions of ability and intelligence. *Child Development, 57,* 636–645.

Nolen, S. B., & Nicholls, J. G. (1994). A place to begin (again) in research on student motivation: Teachers' beliefs. *Teaching and Teacher Education, 10,* 57–69.

Ogbu, J. G. (1985). Cultural ecology of competence among inner-city blacks. In H. McAdoo & J. Mc Adoo (Eds.), *Black children social, educational, and parental environments.* Newbury Park, CA: Sage.

Ogbu, J. G. (1992). Understanding cultural diversity and learning. *Educational Researcher, 21,* 5–14.

Oldfather, P., & McLaughlin, J. (1993). Gaining and losing voice: A longitudinal study of students' continuing impulse to learn across elementary and middle school contexts. *Research in Middle Level Education, 17,* 1–25.

Pajares, F., & Miller, M. D. (1994). Role of self-efficacy and self-concept beliefs in mathematical problem solving: A path analysis. *Journal of Educational Psychology, 86,* 193–203.

Pallas, A. M., Entwisle, D. R., Alexander, K. L., & Stluka, M. F. (1994). Ability-group effects: Instructional, social, or institutional? *Sociology of Education, 67,* 27–46.

Paris, S. G., & Byrnes, J. P. (1989). The constructivist approach to self-regulation and learning in the classroom. In B. J. Zimmerman & D. H. Schunk (Eds.), *Self-regulated learning and academic achievement: Theory, research, and practice.* New York: Springer-Verlag.

Parker, J. G., & Asher, S. R. (1987). Peer relations and later personal adjustment: Are low-accepted children at risk? *Psychological Bulletin, 102,* 357–389.

Parsons, J. E., & Goff, S. B. (1980). Achievement motivation and values: An alternative perspective. In L. J. Fyans (Ed.), *Achievement motivation* (pp. 349–373). New York: Plenum Press.

Parsons, J. E., & Ruble, D. N. (1972). Attributional processes related to the development of achievement-related affect and expectancy. *APA Proceedings, 80th Annual Convention,* 105–106.

Parsons, J. E., & Ruble, D. N. (1977). The development of achievement-related expectancies. *Child Development, 48,* 1075–1079.

Patrick, B. C., Skinner, E. A., & Connell, J. P. (1993). What motivates children's behavior and emotion? Joint effects of perceived control and autonomy in the academic domain. *Journal of Personality and Social Psychology, 65,* 781–791.

Pekrun, R. (1993). Facets of adolescents' academic motivation: A longitudinal expectancy-value approach. In M. Maehr & P. Pintrich (Eds.), *Advances in motivation and achievement* (Vol. 8, pp. 139–189). Greenwich, CT: JAI Press.

Phillips, B., Pitcher, G. D., Worsham, M. E., & Miller, S. L. (1980). Test anxiety and the school environment. In I. G. Sarason (Ed.), *Test anxiety: Theory, research, and applications.* Hillsdale, NJ: Erlbaum.

Phillips, D. A. (1987). Socialization of perceived academic competence among highly competent children. *Child Development, 58,* 1308–1320.

Piaget, J. (1948). *Psychologie der Intelligenz (Psychology of intelligence).* Zuerich: Rascher.

Pintrich, P. R., & De Groot, E. V. (1990). Motivational and self-regulated learning components of classroom academic performance. *Journal of Educational Psychology, 82,* 33–40.

Pintrich, P. R., Marx, R. W., & Boyle, R. A. (1993). Beyond cold conceptual change: The role of motivational beliefs and classroom contextual factors in the process of conceptual change. *Review of Educational Research, 63,* 167–199.

Pintrich, P. R., & Schrauben, B. (1992). Students' motivational beliefs and their cognitive engagement in classroom academic tasks. In D. H. Schunk & J. L. Meece (Eds.), *Student perceptions in the classroom* (pp. 149–183). Hillsdale, NJ: Erlbaum.

Pintrich, P. R., & Schunk, D. H. (1996). *Motivation in education: Theory, research, and applications.* Englewood Cliffs, NJ: Merrill/Prentice-Hall.

Pokay, P., & Blumenfeld, P. C. (1990). Predicting achievement early and late in the semester: The role of motivation and learning strategies. *Journal of Educational Psychology, 82,* 41–50.

Pressley, M., & El-Dinary, P. B. (Eds.). (1993). Strategies instruction [Special issue]. *Elementary School Journal, 94*(2).

Raynor, J. O. (1982). Future orientation, self-evaluation, and achievement motivation: Use of an expectancy X value theory of personality functioning and change. In N. T. Feather

(Ed.), *Expectations and actions: Expectancy-value models in psychology* (pp. 97–124). Hillsdale, NJ: Erlbaum.

Renninger, K. A. (1990). Children's play interests, representation, and activity. In R. Fivush & J. Hudson (Eds.), *Knowing and remembering in young children* (pp. 127–165). Cambridge, MA: Cambridge University Press.

Renninger, K. A., Hidi, S., & Krapp, A. (Eds.). (1992). *The role of interest in learning and development.* Hillsdale, NJ: Erlbaum.

Renninger, K. A., & Wozniak, R. H. (1985). Effect of interest on attentional shift, recognition, and recall in young children. *Developmental Psychology, 21,* 624–632.

Reuman, D. A. (1989). How social comparison mediates the relation between ability-grouping practices and students' achievement expectancies in mathematics. *Journal of Educational Psychology, 81,* 178–189.

Reuman, D. A., Mac Iver, D., Eccles, J., & Wigfield, A. (1987, April). *Changes in students' mathematics motivation and behavior at the transition to junior high school.* Paper presented at the annual meeting of the American Educational Research Association, Washington, DC.

Rheinberg, F. (1988). Motivation and learning activities: How research could proceed. *International Journal of Educational Research, 12,* 299–306.

Rheinberg, F. (1995). Flow-Erleben, Freude an riskantem Sport und andere "unvernunftige" Motivationen (Flow experience, pleasure at risky sports and other "foolish" motivations). In J. Kuhl & H. Heckhausen (Hrsg.), *Motivation, Volition und Handlung (Motivation, volition, and action)* (Enzyklopadie der Psychologie, C, Serie Motivation und Emotion, Bd. 4) (S. 101–118). Gottingen: Hogrefe.

Rholes, W. S., Blackwell, J., Jordan, C., & Walters, C. (1980). A developmental study of learned helplessness. *Developmental Psychology, 16,* 616–624.

Roberts, T. A. (1991). Gender and the influence of evaluations on self-assessments in achievement settings. *Psychological Bulletin, 109,* 297–308.

Roe, A., & Siegelman, M. (1964). *The origin of interests.* Washington, DC: American Personnel and Guidance Association.

Rokeach, M. (1979). From individual to institutional values with special reference to the values of science. In M. Rokeach (Ed.), *Understanding human values* (pp. 47–70). New York: Free Press.

Rosen, B. C. (1959). Race, ethnicity, and the achievement syndrome. *American Society Review, 24,* 47–60.

Rosen, B. C., & D'Andrade, R. (1959). The psychosocial origins of achievement motivation. *Sociometry, 22,* 185–218.

Rosenbaum, J. E. (1976). *Making inequality: The hidden curriculum of high school tracking.* New York: Wiley.

Rosenbaum, J. E. (1980). Social implications of educational grouping. *Review of Research in Education, 7,* 361–401.

Rosenholtz, S. R., & Rosenholtz, S. J. (1981). Classroom organization and the perception of ability. *Sociology of Education, 54,* 132–140.

Rosenholtz, S. J., & Simpson, C. (1984). The formation of ability conceptions: Developmental trend or social construction? *Review of Educational Research, 54,* 31–63.

Rosenthal, R. (1969). Interpersonal expectations: Effects of the experimenter's hypothesis. In R. Rosenthal & R. L. Rosnow (Eds.), *Artifact in behavioral research* (pp. 182–279). New York: Academic Press.

Rotter, J. B. (1966). Generalized expectancies for internal versus external control of reinforcement. *Psychological Monographs, 80,* 1–28.

Rounds, T. S., & Osaki, S. Y. (1982). *The social organization of classrooms: An analysis of sixth- and seventh-grade activity structures* (Report EPSSP-82-5). San Francisco: Far West Laboratory.

Rubinstein, S. L. (1958). *Grundlagen der allgemeinen Psychologie (Foundations of psychology).* Berlin: Volk & Wissen. (Original erschienen 1935)

Ruble, D. (1983). The development of social comparison processes and their role in achievement-related self-socialization. In E. T. Higgins, D. N. Ruble, & W. W. Hartup (Eds.), *Social cognition and social development: A sociocultural perspective* (pp. 134–157). New York: Cambridge University Press.

Ruble, D. (1994). A phase model of transitions: Cognitive and motivational consequences. *Advances in experimental social psychology* (Vol. 26, pp. 163–214). New York: Academic Press.

Ruble, D. N., Parsons, J. E., & Ross, J. (1976). Self-evaluative responses of children in an achievement setting. *Child Development, 47,* 990–997.

Rutter, M., Maughan, B., Mortimor, P., & Ouston, J. (1979). *Fifteen thousand hours: Secondary schools and their effects on children.* Cambridge: Harvard University Press.

Ryan, R. M. (1992). Agency and organization: Intrinsic motivation, autonomy, and the self in psychological development. In J. Jacobs (Ed.), *Nebraska Symposium on Motivation* (Vol. 40, pp. 1–56). Lincoln: University of Nebraska Press.

Ryan, R. M., Connell, J. P., & Deci, E. L. (1985). A motivational analysis of self-determination and self-regulation in education. In C. Ames & R. Ames (Eds.), *Research on motivation in education: Vol. 2. The classroom milieu* (pp. 13–51). London: Academic Press.

Ryan, R. M., & Grolnick, W. S. (1986). Origins and pawns in the classroom: Self-report and projective assessments of individual differences in children's perceptions. *Journal of Personality and Social Psychology, 50,* 550–558.

Sameroff, A. J., & Feil, L. A. (1985). Parental concepts of development. In I. E. Sigel (Ed.), *Parental belief systems* (pp. 83–105). Hillsdale, NJ: Erlbaum.

Sarason, I. G. (1980). Introduction to the study of test anxiety. In I. G. Sarason (Ed.), *Test anxiety: Theory, research, and application* (pp. 3–14). Hillsdale, NJ: Erlbaum.

Sarason, S. B., Davidson, K. S., Lighthall, F. F., Waite, R. R., & Ruebush, B. K. (1960). *Anxiety in elementary school children.* New York: Wiley.

Schaefer, E. S., & Edgerton, M. (1985). Parent and child correlates of parental modernity. In I. E. Sigel (Ed.), *Parental belief systems* (pp. 287–318). Hillsdale: Erlbaum.

Schiefele, U. (1991). Interest, learning, and motivation. *Educational Psychologist, 26,* 299–323.

Schiefele, U. (1996a). *Motivation und Lernen mit Texten (Motivation and learning text).* Gottingen: Hogrefe.

Schiefele, U. (1996b). Topic interest, text representation, and quality of experience. *Contemporary Educational Psychology, 21,* 3–18.

Schiefele, U., & Krapp, A. (in press). Topic interest and free recall of expository text. *Learning and Individual Differences.*

Schiefele, U., & Schreyer, I. (1994). Intrinsische Lernmotivation und Lernen. Ein Uberblick zu Ergebnissen der Forschung (Topic interest and learning. A summary of research results). *Zeitschrift fur Padagogische Psychologie, 8,* 1–13.

Schneider, B., & Coleman, J. S. (1993). *Parents, their children, and schools.* Boulder, CO: Westview Press.

Schneider, K. (in press). Intrinsisch (autotelisch) motiviertes Verhalten dargestellt an den Beispielen des Neugierverhaltens sowie verwandter Verhaltenssysteme (Intrinsically motivated action as an example of creativity and related behavioral systems). In H. Heckhausen & J. Kuhl (Eds.), *Motivation, Volition, Handlung* (Motivation, Volition, and Action). Gottingen: Hogrefe.

Schunk, D. H. (1982). Effects of effort attributional feedback on children's perceived self-efficacy and achievement. *Journal of Educational Psychology, 74,* 548–556.

Schunk, D. H. (1983). Ability versus effort attributional feedback: Differential effects on self-efficacy and achievement. *Journal of Educational Psychology, 75,* 848–856.

Schunk, D. H. (1987). Peer models and children's behavioral change. *Review of Educational Research, 57,* 149–174.

Schunk, D. H. (1990). Goal setting and self-efficacy during self-regulated learning. *Educational Psychologist, 25,* 71–86.

Schunk, D. H. (1991). Self-efficacy and academic motivation. *Educational Psychologist, 26,* 207–231.

Schunk, D. H. (1994). Self-regulation of self-efficacy and attributions in academic settings. In D. H. Schunk & B. J. Zimmerman (Eds.), *Self-regulation of learning and performance.* Hillsdale, NJ: Erlbaum.

Schunk, D. H., & Lilly, M. V. (1982). *Attributional and expectancy change in gifted adolescents.* Paper presented at the annual meeting of the American Educational Research Association, New York.

Schunk, D. H., & Rice, J. M. (1987). Enhancing comprehension skills and self-efficacy with strategy value information. *Journal of Reading Behavior, 19,* 285–302.

Schunk, D. H., & Rice, J. M. (1989). Learning goals and children's reading comprehension. *Journal of Reading Behavior, 21,* 279–293.

Schunk, D. H., & Schwartz, C. W. (1993). Goals and progress feedback: Effects on self-efficacy and writing achievement. *Contemporary Educational Psychology, 18,* 337–354.

Schunk, D. H., & Zimmerman, B. J. (Eds.). (1994). *Self-regulation of learning and performance.* Hillsdale, NJ: Erlbaum.

Seginer, R. (1983). Parents' educational expectations and children's academic achievements: A literature review. *Merrill-Palmer Quarterly, 29,* 1–23.

Sewell, W., & Hauser, R. (1980). The Wisconsin longitudinal study of social and psychological factors in aspirations and achievements. In A. Kerckoff (Ed.), *Research in the sociology of education and socialization* (Vol. 1, pp. 59–100). Greenwich, CT: JAI Press.

Shaklee, H., & Tucker, D. (1979). Cognitive bases of development in inferences of ability. *Child Development, 50,* 904–907.

Sharan, S. (1980). Cooperative learning in small groups: Recent methods and effects on achievement, attitudes, and ethnic relations. *Review of Educational Research, 50,* 241–271.

Shell, D. F., Colvin, C., & Bruning, R. H. (1955). Self-efficacy, attribution, and outcome expectancy mechanisms in reading and writing achievement: Grade-level and achievement-level differences. *Journal of Educational Psychology, 87,* 386–398.

Sieber, R. T. (1979). Classmates as workmates: In formal peer activity in the elementary school. *Anthropology and Education Quarterly, 10,* 207–235.

Sigel, I. E. (1982). The relationship between parental distancing strategies and the child's cognitive behavior. In L. M. Laosa & I. E. Sigel (Eds.), *Families as learning environments for children* (pp. 47–86). New York: Plenum Press.

Sigel, I. E., McGillicuddy-DeLisi, A. V., & Goodnow, J. J. (Eds.). (1992). *Parental belief systems* (2nd ed.). Hillsdale, NJ: Erlbaum.

Silverman, W. K., La Greca, A. M., & Wasserstein, S. (1995). What do children worry about? Worries and their relations to anxiety. *Child Development, 66,* 671–686.

Simmons, R. G., & Blyth, D. A. (1987). *Moving into adolescence: The impact of pubertal change and school context.* Hawthorn, NY: Aldine de Gruyter.

Skinner, B. F. (1974). *About behaviorism.* New York: Knopf.

Skinner, E. A. (1985). Action, control judgments, and the structure of control experience. *Psychological Review, 92,* 39–58.

Skinner, E. A. (1990). Age differences in the dimensions of perceived control during middle childhood: Implications for developmental conceptualizations and research. *Child Development, 61,* 1882–1890.

Skinner, E. A. (1995). *Perceived control, motivation, and coping.* Thousand Oaks, CA: Sage.

Skinner, E. A., & Belmont, M. J. (1993). Motivation in the classroom: Reciprocal effects of teacher behavior and student engagement across the school year. *Journal of Educational Psychology, 85,* 571–581.

Skinner, E. A., Chapman, M., & Baltes, P. B. (1988). Control, means-ends, and agency beliefs: A new conceptualization and its measurement during childhood. *Journal of Personality and Social Psychology, 54,* 117–133.

Skinner, E. A., & Connell, J. P. (1986). Control understanding: Suggestions for a developmental framework. In M. M. Baltes & P. B. Baltes (Eds.), *The psychology of control and aging.* Hillsdale, NJ: Erlbaum.

Slaughter-Defoe, D. T., Nakagawa, K., Takanishi, R., & Johnson, D. J. (1990). Toward cultural/ecological perspectives on schooling and achievement in African- and Asian-American children. *Child Development, 61,* 363–383.

Slavin, R. E. (1990). Achievement effects of ability grouping in secondary schools: A best-evidence synthesis. *Review of Educational Research, 60,* 471–499.

Smith, C. P. (1969). *Achievement-related motives in children.* New York: Russell-Sage Foundation.

Solomon, D., Houlihan, K. A., Busse, T. V., & Parelius, R. J. (1971). Parent behavior and child academic achievement, achievement striving, and related personality characteristics. *Genetic Psychology Monograph, 83,* 173–273.

Spencer, M. B., & Markstrom-Adams, C. (1990). Identity processes among racial and ethnic minority children in America. *Child Development, 61,* 290–310.

Spencer, S., & Steele, C. M. (1995). *Under suspicion of inability: Stereotype vulnerability and women's math performance.* Manuscript submitted for publication.

Spielberger, C. D. (1966). Theory and research on anxiety. In C. D. Spielberger (Ed.), *Anxiety and behavior* (pp. 3–20). New York: Academic Press.

Stattin, H., & Magnusson, D. (1990). *Pubertal maturation in female development.* Hillsdale, NJ: Erlbaum.

Steele, C. M. (1992, April). Race and the schooling of black Americans. *The Atlantic Monthly.*

Steele, C. M., & Aronson, J. (1995). Stereotype threat and the intellectual test performance of African-Americans. *Journal of Personality and Social Psychology, 69,* 797–811.

Stein, A. H., & Bailey, M. M. (1973). The socialization of achievement orientation in females. *Psychological Bulletin, 80,* 345–366.

Steinberg, L., Dornbusch, S., & Brown, B. (1992). Ethnic differences in adolescents' achievements: An ecological perspective. *American Psychologist, 47,* 723–729.

Steinberg, L., Lamborn, S. D., Dornbusch, S. M., & Darling, N. (1992). Impact of parenting practices on adolescent achievement: Authoritative parenting, school involvement, and encouragement to succeed. *Child Development, 63,* 1266–1281.

Stevens, R. J., & Slavin, R. E. (1995). The cooperative elementary school: Effects on students' achievement, attitudes, and social relations. *American Educational Research Journal, 32,* 321–351.

Stevenson, D. L., & Baker, D. P. (1987). The family-school relation and the child's school performance. *Child Development, 58,* 1348–1357.

Stevenson, H. W., Chen, C., & Uttal, D. H. (1990). Beliefs and achievement: A study of black, white, and Hispanic children. *Child Development, 61,* 508–523.

Stevenson, H., Lee, S.-Y., Chen, C., Lummis, M., Stigler, J., Fan, L., & Ge, F. (1990). Mathematics achievement of children in China and the United States. *Child Development, 61,* 1053–1066.

Stipek, D. J. (1984). The development of achievement motivation. In R. Ames & C. Ames (Eds.), *Research on motivation in education* (Vol. 1, pp. 145–174). New York: Academic Press.

Stipek, D. J. (1993). *Motivation to learn.* Boston: Allyn & Bacon.

Stipek, D. J. (1996). Motivation and instruction. In R. C. Calfee & D. C. Berliner (Eds.), *Handbook of educational psychology.* New York: Macmillan.

Stipek, D. J., & Daniels, D. H. (1988). Declining perceptions of competence: A consequence of changes in the child or in the educational environment? *Journal of Educational Psychology, 80,* 352–356.

Stipek, D. J., & Gralinski, H. J. (1991). Gender differences in children's achievement-related beliefs and emotional responses to success and failure in mathematics. *Journal of Educational Psychology, 83,* 361–371.

Stipek, D. J., & Hoffman, J. M. (1980). Children's achievement-related expectancies as a function of academic performance histories and sex. *Journal of Educational Psychology, 72,* 861–865.

Stipek, D. J., & Mac Iver, D. (1989). Developmental change in children's assessment of intellectual competence. *Child Development, 60,* 521–538.

Stipek, D. J., Recchia, S., & McClintic, S. M. (1992). Self-evaluation in young children. *Monographs of the Society for Research in Child Development, 57*(2, Serial No. 226)

Strauss, S., & Subotnik, R. F. (1991). *Gender differences in classroom participation and achievement: An experiment involving advanced placement calculus classes, Part I.* Unpublished manuscript, Hunter College of the CUNY, New York.

Suls, J., & Sanders, G. S. (1982). Self-evaluation through social comparison: A developmental analysis. In L. Wheeler (Ed.), *Review of personality and social psychology* (Vol. 3, pp. 171–197). Beverly Hills, CA: Sage.

Taylor, R. D., Casten, R., Flickinger, S., Roberts, D., & Fulmore, C. D. (1994). Explaining the school performance of African-American adolescents. *Journal of Research on Adolescence, 4,* 21–44.

Teevan, R. C., & McGhee, P. E. (1972). Childhood development of fear of failure motivation. *Journal of Personality and Social Psychology, 21,* 345–348.

Teigen, K. H. (1987). Intrinsic interest and the novelty-familiarity interaction. *Scandinavian Journal of Psychology, 28,* 199–210.

Terman, L. M. (1926). *Genetic studies of genius* (Vol. 1). Stanford, CA: Stanford University Press.

Thompson, M. S., Alexander, K. L., & Entwisle, D. R. (1988). Household composition, parental expectations, and school achievement. *Social Forces, 67,* 424–451.

Thorkildsen, T. A., Nolen, S. B., & Fournier, J. (1994). What is fair? Children's critiques of practices that influence motivation. *Journal of Educational Psychology, 86,* 475–486.

Thorndike, E. L. (1931). *Human learning.* New York: Century.

Tobias, S. (1985). Test anxiety: Interference, deficient skills, and cognitive capacity. *Educational Psychologist, 20,* 135–142.

Tobias, S. (1994). Interest, prior knowledge, and learning. *Review of Educational Research, 64,* 37–54.

Todt, E. (1990). Entwicklung des Interesses (Development of Interests). In H. Hetzer (Ed.), *Angewandte Entwicklungspsychologie des Kindes- und Jugendalters (Applied Developmental Psychology of Children and Youth).* Wiesbaden: Quelle & Meyer.

Tolman, E. C. (1932). *Purposive behavior in animals and men.* New York: Appleton-Century-Crofts.

Travers, R. M. W. (1978). *Children's interests.* Unpublished manuscript, Michigan University, College of Education, Kalamazoo, MI.

Trebilco, G. R., Atkinson, E. P., & Atkinson, J. M. (1977, November). *The transition of students from primary to secondary school.* Paper presented at the annual conference of the Australian Association for Research in Education, Canberra.

Trickett, E. J., & Moos, R. H. (1974). Personal correlates of contrasting environments: Student satisfaction in high school classrooms. *American Journal of Community Psychology, 2,* 1–12.

Tyler, L. E. (1955). The development of "vocational interests": I. The organization of likes and dislikes in ten-year-old children. *Journal of Genetic Psychology, 86,* 33–41.

Vanfossen, B. E., Jones, J. D., & Spade, J. Z. (1987). Curriculum tracking and status maintenance. *Sociology of Education, 60,* 104–122.

Vasey, M. W., & Daliedon, E. L. (1994). Worry in children. In G. Davey & F. Tallis (Eds.), *Worrying: Perspectives on theory, assessment, and treatment* (pp. 185–207). Chichester, England: Wiley.

Veroff, J. (1969). Social comparison and the development of achievement motivation. In C. P. Smith (Ed.), *Achievement-related motives in children* (pp. 46–101). New York: Russell-Sage Foundation.

Vispoel, W. P., & Austin, J. R. (1995). Success and failure in junior high school: A critical incident approach to understanding students' attributional beliefs. *American Educational Research Journal, 32,* 377–412.

Wade, S. E. (1992). How interest affects learning from text. In K. A. Renninger, S. Hidi, & A. Krapp (Eds.), *The role of interest in learning and development* (pp. 255–277). Hillsdale, NJ: Erlbaum.

Wagner, B. M., & Phillips, D. A. (1992). Beyond beliefs: Parent and child behaviors and children's perceived academic competence. *Child Development, 63,* 1380–1391.

Walberg, H. J., House, E. R., & Steele, J. M. (1973). Grade level, cognition, and affect: A cross-section of classroom perceptions. *Journal of Educational Psychology, 64,* 142–146.

Ward, B. A., Mergendoller, J. R., Tikunoff, W. J., Rounds, T. S., Dadey, G. J., & Mitman, A. L. (1982). *Junior high school transition study: Executive summary.* San Francisco: Far West Laboratory.

Wehlage, G. (1989). Dropping out: Can schools be expected to prevent it? In L. Weis, E. Farrar, & H. Petrie (Eds.), *Dropouts from school.* Albany, NY: SUNY Press.

Wehlage, G., Rutter, R., Smith, G., Lesko, N., & Fernandez, R. (1989). *Reducing the risk: Schools as communities of support.* Philadelphia: Falmer Press.

Weiner, B. (1985). An attributional theory of achievement motivation and emotion. *Psychological Review, 92,* 548–573.

Weiner, B. (1990). History of motivation research in education. *Journal of Educational Psychology, 82,* 616–622.

Weiner, B. (1992). *Human motivation: Metaphors, theories, and research.* Newbury Park, CA: Sage.

Weiner, B., Frieze, I., Kukla, A., Reed, L., Rest, S., & Rosenbaum, R. M. (1971). *Perceiving the causes of success and failure.* Morristown, NJ: General Learning Press.

Weiner, B., Russell, D., & Lerman, D. (1979). The cognition-emotion process in achievement-related contexts. *Journal of Personality and Social Psychology, 37,* 1211–1220.

Weinstein, C. E., & Mayer, R. E. (1986). The teaching of learning strategies. In M. C. Wittrock (Ed.), *Handbook of research on teaching* (3rd ed.). New York: Macmillan.

Weinstein, R. S. (1989). Perception of classroom processes and student motivation: Children's views of self-fulfilling prophecies. In R. E. Ames & C. Ames (Eds.), *Research on motivation in education* (Vol. 3). New York: Academic Press.

Weinstein, R. S., Marshall, H. H., Sharp, L., & Botkin, M. (1987). Pygmalion and the student: Age and classroom differences in children's awareness of teacher expectations. *Child Development, 58,* 1079–1093.

Weisz, J. P. (1984). Contingency judgments and achievement behavior: Deciding what is controllable and when to try. In J. G. Nicholls (Ed.), *The development of achievement motivation* (pp. 107–136). Greenwich, CT: JAI Press.

Wentzel, K. R. (1991a). Relations between social competence and academic achievement in early adolescence. *Child Development, 62,* 1066–1078.

Wentzel, K. R. (1991b). Social competence at school: Relation between social responsibility and academic achievement. *Review of Educational Research, 61,* 1–24.

Wentzel, K. R. (1993). Does being good make the grade? Social behavior and academic competence in middle school. *Journal of Educational Psychology, 85,* 357–364.

Wentzel, K. R. (1994). Relations of social goal pursuit to social acceptance, and perceived social support. *Journal of Educational Psychology, 86,* 173–182.

Wentzel, K. R. (in press). Social goals and social relationships as motivators of school adjustment. In J. Juvonen & K. R. Wentzel (Eds.), *Social motivation: Understanding school adjustment.* New York: Cambridge University Press.

Wentzel, K. R., & Feldman, S. S. (1993). Parental predictors of boys' self-restraint and motivation to achieve at school: A longitudinal study. *Journal of Early Adolescence, 13,* 183–203.

Wentzel, K. R., Feldman, S. S., & Weinberger, D. A. (1991). Parental child rearing and academic achievement in boys: The mediational role of social-emotional adjustment. *Journal of Early Adolescence, 11,* 321–339.

Wentzel, K. R., Weinberger, D. A., Ford, M. E., & Feldman, S. S. (1990). Parental childrearing and academic achievement in boys: The mediational role of social-emotional adjustment. *Journal of Early Adolescence, 11,* 321–339.

Werner, H. (1957). The concept of development from a comparative and organismic point of view. In D. D. Harris (Ed.), *The concept of development.* Minneapolis: University of Minnesota Press.

White, R. H. (1959). Motivation reconsidered: The concept of competence. *Psychological Review, 66,* 297–333.

Wigfield, A. (1994). Expectancy-value theory of achievement motivation: A developmental perspective. *Educational Psychology Review, 6,* 49–78.

Wigfield, A., & Asher, S. R. (1984). Social and motivational influences on reading. In P. D. Pearson, R. Barr, M. L. Kamil, & P. Mosenthal (Eds.), *Handbook of reading research* (pp. 423–452). New York: Longman.

Wigfield, A., & Eccles, J. S. (1989). Test anxiety in elementary and secondary school students. *Educational Psychologist, 24,* 159–183.

Wigfield, A., & Eccles, J. (1992). The development of achievement task values: A theoretical analysis. *Developmental Review, 12,* 265–310.

Wigfield, A., & Meece, J. (1988). Math anxiety in elementary and secondary school students. *Journal of Educational Psychology, 80,* 210–216.

Wigfield, A., Eccles, J., Mac Iver, D., Reuman, D., & Midgley, C. (1991). Transitions at early adolescence: Changes in children's domain-specific self-perceptions and general self-esteem across the transition to junior high school. *Developmental Psychology, 27,* 552–565.

Wigfield, A., Eccles, J. S., & Pintrich, P. R. (1996). Development between the ages of eleven and twenty-five. In D. C. Berliner & R. C. Calfee (Eds.), *The handbook of educational psychology.* New York: Macmillan.

Wigfield, A., Eccles, J. S., Yoon, K. S., Harold, R. D., Arbreton, A., Freedman-Doan, K., & Blumenfeld, P. C. (1996). *Changes in children's competence beliefs and subjective task values across the elementary school years: A three-year study.* Manuscript submitted for publication.

Willis, P. L. (1977). *Learning to labor: How working class kids get working class jobs.* Driffield, England: Nafferton.

Wine, J. D. (1971). Test anxiety and direction of attention. *Psychological Bulletin, 76,* 92–104.

Wine, J. D. (1980). Cognitive-attentional theory of test anxiety. In I. G. Sarason (Ed.), *Test anxiety: Theory, research, and applications* (pp. 349–385). Hillsdale, NJ: Erlbaum.

Winne, P. H., & Marx, R. W. (1989). A cognitive-processing analysis of motivation with classroom tasks. In C. Ames & R. Ames (Eds.), *Research on motivation in education* (Vol. 3). San Diego: Academic Press.

Winston, C., Eccles, J. S., & Senior, A. M. (in press). The utility of an expectancy/value model of achievement for understanding academic performance and self-esteem in African-American and European-American adolescents. *Zeitschrift Fur Padagogische Psychologie (German Journal of Educational Psychology).*

Winterbottom, M. R. (1958). The relation of need for achievement to learning experiences in independence and mastery. In

J. W. Atkinson (Ed.), *Motives in fantasy, action and society* (pp. 453–478). Princeton, NJ: Van Nostrand.

Yee, D. K., & Eccles, J. S. (1988). Parent perceptions and attributions for children's math achievement. *Sex Roles, 19,* 317–333.

Yee, D. K., & Flanagan, C. (1985). Family environments and self-consciousness in early adolescence. *Journal of Early Adolescence, 5,* 59–68.

Yoon, K. S., Wigfield, A., & Eccles, J. S. (1993, April). *Causal relations between mothers' and children's beliefs about math ability: A structural equation model.* Paper presented at the annual meeting of the American Educational Research Association, Atlanta.

Youniss, J. (1980). *Parents and peers in social development.* Chicago: University of Chicago.

Zajonc, R. B. (1968). Attitudinal effects of mere exposure. *Journal of Personality and Social Psychology, 9,* 1–27.

Zatz, S., & Chassin, L. (1983). Cognitions of test anxious children. *Journal of Consulting and Clinical Psychology, 51,* 526–534.

Zatz, S., & Chassin, L. (1985). Cognitions of test anxious children under naturalistic test-taking conditions. *Journal of Consulting and Clinical Psychology, 53,* 393–401.

Zigler, E. F., & Child, I. L. (1969). Socialization. In G. Lindzey & E. Aronson (Eds.), *The handbook of social psychology* (Vol. 3, pp. 450–589). Reading, MA: Addison-Wesley.

Zigler, E. F., & Turner, P. (1982). Parent and day care workers: A failed partnership. In E. F. Zigler & E. W. Gordon (Eds.), *Day care: Scientific and sound policy issues* (pp. 174–182). New York: Free Press.

Zimmerman, B. J. (1989). A social cognitive view of self-regulated learning. *Journal of Educational Psychology, 81,* 329–339.

Zimmerman, B. J. (1994). Dimensions of academic self-regulation: A conceptual framework for education. In D. H. Schunk & B. J. Zimmerman (Eds.), *Self-regulation of learning and performance.* Hillsdale, NJ: Erlbaum.

Zimmerman, B. J., Bandura, A., & Martinez-Pons, M. (1992). Self-motivation for academic attainment: The role of self-efficacy beliefs and personal goal setting. *American Educational Research Journal, 29,* 663–676.

Zimmerman, B. J., & Bonner, S. (in press). A social cognitive view of strategic learning. In C. E. Weinstein & B. L. McCombs (Eds.), *Strategic learning: Skill, will, and self-regulation.* Hillsdale, NJ: Erlbaum.

Zimmerman, B. J., & Martinez-Pons, M. (1986). Development of a structured interview for assessing student use of self-regulated learning strategies. *American Educational Research Journal, 23,* 614–628.

Zimmerman, B. J., & Martinez-Pons, M. (1990). Student differences in self-regulated learning: Relating grade, sex, and giftedness to self-efficacy and strategy use. *Journal of Educational Psychology, 82,* 51–59.

CHAPTER 16

Adolescent Development in Family Contexts

HAROLD D. GROTEVANT

This chapter is unlike most others in this volume because it focuses on a developmental period rather than a developing system of the individual. A full understanding of adolescence requires consideration of the rapidly changing individual in ongoing interaction within dynamically changing, multilayered contexts. These contexts include belief systems and scripts associated with personal characteristics of individuals; relationships with parents, siblings, other family members, and friends; activity settings such as schools, religious institutions, and leisure activities; and macrosystems such as history, culture, and political and economic environments.

Adolescence is a social construction. It is a period of transition between childhood and adulthood, but it is long enough and distinctive enough to demand analysis in its own right. Adolescence "begins in biology and ends in culture" (Conger & Petersen, 1984, p. 92). The universal phenomenon of physical maturation initiates the process, but the experience of adolescence is strongly shaped by the culture in which the young person is living. Across history and cultures, there have always been socially instituted ways to move members of one's society into adulthood. However, this transition has varied markedly in several dimensions, including duration and stress.

The period we now call adolescence has been characterized differently across historical time. The English word comes from the Latin *adolesco,* which means "to grow up." But growing up has meant different things in different eras. Aristotle characterized adolescents as "passionate, irascible, and apt to be carried away by their impulses, ... [yet having] high aspirations . . . . If the young commit a fault, it is always on the side of excess and exaggeration, for they carry everything too far" (Kiell, 1964, pp. 18–19).

In Western societies during the 1700s and 1800s, children became involved in productive labor (frequently on farms) between the ages of 7 and 13, and girls of this age took major responsibility for the care of younger siblings. With the industrial revolution came the assignment of children and young people to factory jobs; but middle- and upper-class families saw the value of education for enhancing life opportunities of their children and could afford to provide it. As more schools were established, laws preventing child labor and demanding universal school attendance were passed, thus segregating young people in the teenage years from children and adults.

In the early 1900s, adolescence emerged as a distinctive and important life stage and population entity (Kett, 1977), as demographic and economic trends influenced psychological and social research and writing. G. Stanley Hall, the first American PhD in psychology and the person who sponsored Freud's only visit to the United States, published his volume *Adolescence* in 1904. This work highlighted the assumption that adolescence was a period of *"Sturm und Drang"* (storm and stress), and fit well with psychoanalytic assumptions about adolescence as a turbulent time and about the link between the turbulence and sexuality: "The teens are emotionally unstable and pathic. It is a natural impulse to experience hot and perfervid psychic states, and it is characterized by emotionalism" (Hall, 1904, Vol. 2, pp. 74–75).

Anthropologists helped broaden the lens on this period of life, presenting observations that adolescence was experienced differently in non-Western cultures. Margaret Mead's landmark *Coming of Age in Samoa* (1928) directly challenged Hall's storm and stress assumption, arguing that adolescence is strongly shaped by the culture in which it is played out. She suggested that Samoan and Western cultures differed dramatically in continuity between generations. Growing up in Samoa was characterized by gradual assumption of adult responsibilities and a limited set of futures the young person might participate in, whereas growing up in Western industrialized societies involved confronting opportunities and choices, many of which were beyond the experience of the young person's parents. Margaret Mead's findings have been challenged by some contemporary social scientists (e.g., Freeman, 1983) and defended by others (e.g., Côté, 1994). Analysis of the debate is beyond the scope of this chapter; however, the general conclusion that culture significantly shapes the adolescent experience remains widely accepted.

The contemporary experience of Samoan young people further illustrates the cultural embeddedness of adolescence, as seen in the following response of a Samoan-born young woman who had moved to New Zealand and was being interviewed about her experience as an adolescent:

> As a Samoan born, I had never heard of it [adolescence] until I came to New Zealand. I don't think it was part of my life because it is a western concept, and from a non-western society all those developmental stages didn't relate to me. All I know is that my aiga [family] and my community and my culture are important. They determine the way I behave, think, and feel. . . . Sometimes I think that we [in Samoa] are children for most of our lives, and it can take a very long time for us to become adults. It does not matter how old you are, [for] if you are not considered worthy as responsible enough by your elders then you will not be treated as an adult. You really have to earn your place in the Samoan culture. So adolescence as a developmental stage is foreign to our culture. (Subject no. 3 in Tupuola, 1993, pp. 308, 311; cited in Kroger, 1996, p. 5)

The emergence of a significant body of social science research, firm establishment of such popular notions as the "generation gap" and "youth culture" among lay audiences, and the significant size and purchasing power of persons in the second decade of life have all contributed to more differentiated views of contemporary Western adolescence. First, the period itself is viewed as having considerable texture. Since adolescence itself is socially constructed, how this period is developmentally punctuated is also socially constructed. Scholars in the field who study contemporary Western adolescence typically work from the premise that adolescence begins with the transition from childhood (usually marked by physical changes heralding the onset of puberty), includes early, middle, and late phases, and concludes with a transition into young adulthood. However, this way of subdividing adolescence has been challenged by cross-cultural perspectives on adolescence and by research focusing on the experience of American adolescents from communities of color and backgrounds of poverty (e.g., Burton, Allison, & Obeidallah, 1995). In this latter line of work, it has been shown that the lines of division within adolescence as well as the period's beginning and ending points are not always clear.

Second, whereas the entire period is not stormy and stressful, it is a time during which stress may be experienced, in part because of the many choices confronting young people and their changing relationships with their parents and friends. Third, adolescence is generally viewed in negative terms:

> Adolescents are described as major players in the multiple "epidemics" that beset the country: pregnancy, sexually transmitted diseases, drug abuse and suicide are a few of the more obvious examples. Adolescence per se is seen as the inevitable "risk" factor for these widespread problems as if the origin of these problems were innate to adolescents, rather than products of complex interactions of individual biology, personality, cultural preference, political expediency and social dysfunction. [Thus, we view] . . . adolescence as a developmental period defined by its problems, . . . "medicalized" into a condition that is inherently pathological. (Hill & Fortenberry, 1992, p. 73)

Finally, adolescence is now viewed in relation to the contexts in which it occurs and is studied in terms of ongoing transactional processes in which the changing young person interacts with evolving contexts. Interest in the knowledge yielded from research on adolescence is particularly keen in the United States as the year 2000 approaches, because the population of American adolescents between the ages of 12 and 17 is increasing after approximately 20 years of declining. As the adolescent population increases, there is a window of opportunity for research-based information to be used on behalf of preventing problematic adolescent outcomes before they occur (Resnick, 1996).

Because of the inherent link between adolescence and social/cultural contexts, this chapter focuses on research that attempts to elucidate such linkages. Even though an increasing number of studies examine differences by race,[1] ethnicity, culture, class, or gender, the focus of such studies is often on the differences per se rather than on the processes that mediate them. Our knowledge of adolescence will advance further when we understand the embeddedness of adolescent development within history, culture, gender, race, and class; therefore, primary attention in this chapter is devoted to the process issues concerning these linkages, especially as they are played out within families. Studies using contextual variables or processes as moderators or mediators of adolescent outcomes are highlighted. This chapter is not intended to be a comprehensive review of the available literature, which would require one or more volumes of its own. Interested readers might wish to consult other reviews on the following topics: broad overviews of adolescence (Adelson, 1980; Feldman & Elliott, 1990; Petersen, 1988, 1993; Takanishi, 1993); contexts (Cooper, 1994; Crockett & Crouter, 1995; Irwin & Vaughan, 1988; Moen, Elder, & Luescher, 1995; Parke & Kellam, 1994; Silbereisen & Todt, 1994; Steinberg & Darling, 1994); families (Collins & Russell, 1991; Gecas &

Seff, 1990; Grotevant & Cooper, 1986, in press; Hill, 1987; Noller, 1994; Youniss & Smollar, 1985).

CONCEPTUALIZATION

Framework for Considering Adolescent Development

Making sense of the large and varied literature on adolescent development is facilitated by an organizational framework. A number of taxonomies or structures have been proposed, including Havighurst's (1972) developmental tasks; Masten et al.'s (1995) components of adolescent competence; Hill's (1973, 1980; Hill & Monks, 1977) model of adolescent development; and Goodnow's (1994, 1995) models of context. The heuristic framework presented here draws on and integrates all of these, in a way that facilitates discussion of the contextual embeddedness of adolescent development (see Table 16.1).

The first component includes developmental continuities from childhood (Hill called this "residuals of prepubescent development"). These include self-perceptions, competencies, values, and internal working models brought forward from earlier experiences.

The second component encompasses the primary changes of adolescence: biological development into sexual maturity, changes in social definition from child to adult, and cognitive change. The biological and social role changes are universal; in all cultures, adolescence includes the physiological and social role transitions from being a child to being an adult. The potential for cognitive change appears to be universal, but cultural practices, conditions, and opportunities influence how much cognitive change actually occurs. The third component includes the contexts of development. How contexts interact with the developmental continuities from childhood and the primary changes of adolescence to result in adulthood is viewed differently in different theoretical models, as described in later sections. Contexts may be grouped into three clusters. First, *personal characteristics,* including one's gender, race, ethnicity, sexual orientation, or other type of assigned or chosen group affinity can involve alignments with belief systems, scripts, or daily patterns of living (Goodnow, 1994, 1995). Second, *interpersonal relationships and activity settings* include family, peers, parent-peer interconnections, school, work, religion, neighborhood, leisure activities, and the like. Third, *macrosystems* (e.g., Bronfenbrenner, 1979, 1988) include history and cohort; culture; societal norms; the experience of racism, discrimination, or prejudice; the media; and the

[1] Because of the importance of understanding ethnicity and race as features relevant to family contexts, definitions of each are offered as follows: "Ethnicity refers to a concept of a group's 'peoplehood' based on a combination of race, religion, and cultural history, whether or not members realize their commonalities with one another. It describes a commonality transmitted by the family over generations and reinforced by the surrounding community. . . . It involves a many-layered sense of group identification—of shared values and understandings that fulfill a deep psychological need for identity and historical continuity" (McGoldrick, 1993, p. 337). On the other hand, race is "a cultural construction of identity based on a set of descriptors used by a society. Race is, therefore, not conceived here as an empirical, social, or physical reality, but instead is viewed as having a cultural reality (Gossett, 1965, cited in Dilworth-Anderson, Burton, & Boulin Johnson, 1993, p. 628).

Table 16.1   Framework for Understanding Adolescent Development

---

1. **Developmental Continuities from Childhood**

   Self-perceptions
   Competencies
   Values
   Internal working models of relationships and self-in-relationships

2. **Primary Changes**

   Biological development to sexual maturity
   Change in social status from child to adult
   Cognitive change (potential, but dependent on environment)

3. **Contexts of Development**

   Personal Characteristics That May Involve Alignments with Belief Systems, Scripts, or Daily Patterns of Living
       Gender
       Race
       Ethnicity
       Sexual orientation

   Interpersonal Relationships and Activity Settings
       Family   Parent-child, sibling, intergenerational, intentional; links to adult development of parents and to 3-generational family system issues;
                       fictive kin; extended family, etc.
       Peers   Friendships, groups, dating
                     same-sex, opposite sex
                     intimate: heterosexual, gay/lesbian/bisexual
       Parent-peer interconnections ("cross-pressures" vs. "links" models)
       School
       Work
       Neighborhood and community
       Religion
       Leisure activities

   Macrosystems
       History and cohort
       Culture
       Societal norms
       Experience of racism, discrimination, or prejudice
       Media
       Economy
       Political environment

4. **Adolescent Outcomes**

   Transformations in relationships
       Parent-child
       Friendships
       Intimate relationships
       Relationships to community
   Development of identity
       Domains involving choice (e.g., career, political values, religious or spiritual beliefs, ideas about relationships)
       Domains that are "assigned" (e.g., gender, race, ethnicity, adoptive status, sexual orientation)
   Emotional health
       Dimension: psychological well-being, self-worth ↔ internalizing disorders, depression, suicidal ideation
   Competent conduct in school, work, and daily life
       Dimension: interpersonal competence, contributing member of society, culturally appropriate success in school, work (and/or
           preparation for work), and daily life ↔ externalizing disorders, "delinquency," acting out

---

The arrows signify that these are "dimensions" proceeding from well-being and self-worth (on one end) to internalizing disorders and depression (on the other end).

Note: Compiled by H. Grotevant. Synthesized from various frameworks, including those of Urie Bronfenbrenner, Jacqueline Goodnow, Robert Havighurst, John Hill, and Ann Masten.

economic and political systems in which one lives. Macro-systems shape the texture of everyday life, since they operate "with particular reference to the developmentally-instigative belief systems, resources, hazards, life styles, opportunity structures, life course options and patterns of social interchange that are embedded in such overarching systems" (Bronfenbrenner, 1989, p. 13). Experiences of racism, discrimination, and prejudice should be explicitly included in the model because they "have not been routinely specified in analyses of macrosystem influences, even though these may well be the critical factors that underlie the more commonly studied socio-psychological aspects of developmental processes in children of color" (García Coll et al., 1996, p. 8).

Finally, in the fourth component we consider four domains of adolescent outcomes: (a) transformations in relationships (parent-child, friendships, intimate relationships); (b) development of identity, including domains over which the adolescent exerts choice and domains that are assigned (e.g., gender, race, ethnicity, adoptive status, sexual orientation); (c) emotional health; and (d) competent conduct in the worlds of school, work, and daily life.

The four components of this framework do not relate to each other in a linear or simple fashion. Although it is tempting to think of biological changes as causal instigators of social changes, evidence is accruing to indicate that social interaction patterns can affect biological development. Conflict within the family appears related to accelerated pubertal development for girls (Graber, Brooks-Gunn, & Warren, 1995; Moffit, Caspi, Belsky, & Silva, 1992; Steinberg, 1988). In addition, some of the developmental "outcome" domains (e.g., relationships undergoing transformation) serve as contexts for other outcomes. In a transactional manner, today's outcomes contribute to the context for tomorrow's development. Personal characteristics that are part of context to the degree that they involve alignments with belief systems, scripts, or daily patterns of living may also become incorporated into one's sense of identity. The domains of developmental outcomes are also related to one another, and are all embedded within the cultural and historical contexts included in the third component. Nevertheless, although the boundaries separating these four components are not always firm, the framework does at least facilitate identification and discussion of the key features of adolescence.

In this chapter, primary attention is devoted to family contexts of adolescent developmental outcomes. However, this more comprehensive framework is offered because understanding links between contexts and outcomes frequently requires understanding of the other components of the framework. The sections that follow include brief discussions of continuities from childhood, primary changes of adolescence, and contexts of development. More detailed discussion of developmental outcomes follows in the section "Research Review."

Developmental Continuities from Childhood

Despite the significant changes that occur during adolescence, many continuities also are brought forth from childhood; a major challenge involves understanding developmental continuity in the midst of change. The increasing complexity and differentiation of behavior at adolescence makes it unlikely that we will detect much simple stability of behavior (unchanging rank order over time) or even continuity that involves stability within the same response mode. However, the developmental psychopathology model (e.g., Cicchetti, 1990; Sroufe, 1990) has highlighted the coherence of development, predictable relations in behavior across age, perhaps even across domains of behavior. Coherence is found in patterns of adaptation rather in stability of specific behaviors (e.g., Sroufe, 1979). This approach seeks to understand developmental transformations and branching developmental pathways. Although it is intuitively appealing, this approach raises important questions for understanding adolescence, especially concerning the malleability of development as time goes on. "If subsequent development is constrained by earlier adaptation, at what point does change become quite difficult to accomplish? Or, put another way, when do pathways for various problems become rather strongly channeled?" (Sroufe & Jacobvitz, 1989).

Features of childhood development that set the stage for adolescence include self-perceptions (e.g., Harter, Ch. 9, this Volume); skills; values; and internal working models of relationships (e.g., Sroufe & Fleeson, 1986), among others. We should not expect simple continuities from earlier times; however, earlier experiences provide the child with resources, skills, and coping strategies that can be useful in confronting the significant primary changes of adolescence, which are discussed in the next section.

Primary Changes

Three sets of developmental changes are considered "primary" because they are universal aspects of adolescence: changes in physical development and sexual maturation, change in social status from child to adult, and potential for changes in reasoning ability (Hill & Monks, 1977).

The onset of adolescence is typically identified by the first signs of transformation from the body of a child to that of an adult. The changes begin earlier for girls than for boys, on average, and can start before the age of 10. For most adolescents, pubertal change is complete by midadolescence; for some, however, this period extends into the late teenage years (Tanner, 1962). These physical changes are significant in many ways, including how they become incorporated into adolescents' emerging sense of self and relationships.

The research literature linking physical and psychological development during adolescence is organized around several issues. One group of studies focuses on the consequences of individual differences in the timing of puberty (whether its onset is earlier than, later than, or in step with same-sex peers). In general, early development for boys and "on time" development for girls have been associated with easier adjustment to puberty. Very late development for boys and very early development for girls appear more difficult (Brooks-Gunn, Petersen, & Eichorn, 1985), seemingly because these adolescents are so out of step with the pubertal timetables of their agemates. In another set of studies, pubertal status (e.g., prepuberal, apex puberal, postpuberal) is highlighted in relation to psychological or interactional variables. For example, Steinberg and colleagues (e.g., Steinberg, 1988) have found that the apex of pubertal development, especially for boys, is associated with more contentiousness in family interaction and an underlying change in the family's power hierarchy. Researchers are also exploring the meaning of puberty to adolescents. Brooks-Gunn and colleagues (e.g., Brooks-Gunn, 1987) have found that girls construct their definition of puberty and menarche based on various sources of information, and that their direct experience of physical change is then interpreted through that framework. Thus, girls unprepared for menarche or who have primarily negative information about it may experience menarche as more difficult than it is experienced by their peers. Presumably, this framework could be extended to boys' experiences as well (see Brooks-Gunn & Reiter, 1990, for review). Our rapidly increasing understanding of hormones and their interplay with psychological processes will add new increments of knowledge about these important changes. Excellent overviews of the literature on physical development during adolescence may be found in the following: Brooks-Gunn and Reiter (1990), Petersen and Taylor (1980).

Second, the period of adolescence itself is a transition from childhood to adulthood. Whether the transition is crossed quickly (e.g., through a physically and mentally demanding initiation rite) or gradually, following many slowly granted adult privileges, the end of adolescence is generally regarded as the point at which individuals are considered adults in their society.

Finally, cognitive changes, although less conspicuous, are equally important and extend gradually across the second decade of life (see Keating, 1980, 1990, for reviews). Accompanying the adolescent's developing cognitive skills are changes in how the social world (including the self) is conceptualized. Thus, toward the end of adolescence, the young person is challenged to consider the question "Who am I?" in terms of meshing one's individual abilities and interests with cultural opportunities and norms. This is one way in which adolescence "ends in culture." Although the potential for scientific (i.e., hypothetico-deductive) reasoning appears to be universal, the environments provided by different cultural settings are not equally facilitative of such development (Niemark, 1982). Thus, unlike physical and sexual maturation, which is universally attained by adult members of the species, the cognitive development that can potentially occur during adolescence is not sufficiently supported by all human environments to make it universal.

Contexts of Development

Clarifying the embeddedness of adolescent development within family contexts is a major goal of this chapter. Current interest in context has been shaped by the maturation of social science theories, moving from a focus on understanding universal laws of human behavior to understanding the nuances and differences shaped by contexts. This interest is also no doubt stimulated by the fact that modern transportation and communication have linked far-flung places in the world closely together. People all over the world are not only much more aware of one another, but they also participate jointly in a global economy and realize that they share a global ecosystem.

Parke (1994) has summarized four ways of thinking about contexts:

1. Focus on *physical characteristics,* such as Barker's (1968) approach to examining the physical settings in which behavior occurs.

2. Bronfenbrenner's (e.g., 1979, 1994, 1995) characterization of *levels of social systems*—microsystem, mesosystem, exosystem, chronosystem.

3. Contexts of *interpersonal relationships* (e.g., Hinde, 1992; Kelley et al., 1983), especially to the degree that

developmental outcomes in adolescence are viewed as products of different qualities of relationships.

4. *Family-based regulatory mechanisms or codes* such as family narratives, paradigms, myths, and rituals (Fiese et al., 1997; Sameroff, 1994).

Goodnow (1995) has also analyzed models of contexts, differentiating among four models being used to guide research:

1. *Geographical models* view contexts as physical or social spaces that individuals traverse. In this model, successful development is "the effective negotiation of movement from one space to another" (p. 7).
2. In *ideological models,* individuals are knowers or believers, and contexts are meaning systems or belief systems. Individuals must develop interpretive frameworks but also must be viewed in terms of how much they accept, reject, or resist the value system in which they live.
3. *Dramaturgical models* view contexts as stages or texts and individuals as performers. Individuals learn how to present themselves and manage others.
4. Finally, the emphasis in *practice models* is on contexts as everyday activities in which individuals are participants. Contexts consist of routine ways of doing everyday things.

A third taxonomy of contexts pertinent to adolescent development emerged from a conference which concluded that "serious misrepresentation of adolescence can occur if the multiple contexts are not clarified" (Irwin & Vaughan, 1988, p. 15S). Participants identified the following contextual factors as needing special attention in the research literature: demographic characteristics (gender, race); socioeconomic characteristics (especially adolescents living in poverty); family structure (reconstituted families, single-parent families, adoptive families, two-working-parent families); peer group structures; work settings (hours worked, type of work, financial need); environmental characteristics (community, school, cohort issues); age of cohort (chronological and physiological); and circumstances that put young people at risk (e.g., illegal aliens, recent immigrants, those at risk for serious psychiatric and physical illness).

Particularly important are Goodnow's (1995) recommendations that all contextual models need to go beyond treating individuals and contexts as separate variables, and that they must not view individuals as changing and contexts as static,

but rather both as being coconstituted. Furthermore, contextual influences are mediated by interpersonal processes; thus, articulation of such processes should be an important component of the research agenda (Steinberg, 1995). Parke has argued for coordination among these contextual models:

> Combining social systems (Bronfenbrenner), relationship (Hinde), and regulatory (Sameroff) approaches will permit the description of the levels of organization that characterize complex settings and at the same time, not lose sight of the kinds of relationships that exist within each of these levels of organization and how these relationships are regulated. Bronfenbrenner's scheme is useful for alerting us to the multiple levels that are involved, although the Hinde and Sameroff approaches help us begin to describe the kinds of dimensions that can characterize common relationships and regulatory mechanisms across settings. Being able to conceptualize workplace, school, and family, for example, using a similar set of dimensions will be a major step in understanding how these settings will relate to one another. (Parke, 1994, p. 217)

Much research attention is being devoted to identifying these diverse contexts, mapping their dimensions, and examining how they might be linked (e.g., Cooper, 1994; Cooper & Cooper, 1992; MacDonald & Parke, 1984; Parke & Ladd, 1992). Despite these advances, one additional step is necessary. We must understand the *meanings* that adolescents make of their experiences and their circumstances. Growing up in poverty or wealth, in a single-parent or two-parent family, or in a community that does or does not provide work opportunities for adolescents may mean different things to different individuals; consequently, young people may act differently in response to their circumstances and have different developmental outcomes as a result. Despite encouragement to attend to adolescents' own experiences (e.g., Brooks-Gunn & Paikoff, 1992; Zaslow & Takanishi, 1993), the design of most studies incorporates investigators' assumptions about what certain contextual features must mean. Studies that focus on *adolescents' meanings* receive special attention in this chapter.

Key Theories

Understanding adolescence demands multidisciplinary inquiry because this developmental period is shaped by macro and micro forces that include historical and cultural contexts, group and interpersonal interactions and relationships, and individual cognitive and biological changes. A central challenge facing the field is that scholars trained in disciplinary specialties have their own sets of research approaches, theories, concepts, and methodologies. Differences across fields are not readily understood by colleagues outside the disciplines, complicating the degree to which knowledge in this field has become cross-fertilized.

Traditional Developmental Paradigms

Developmental psychologists have traditionally grounded investigations in psychoanalytic, behavioral, organismic, or contextual paradigms (see Overton & Reese, 1973; Reese & Overton, 1970, for reviews). Although such clear and narrow grounding might work well for some developmental issues, understanding adolescence in family contexts demands greater ability to look across disciplines and levels of analysis. In this section, selected concepts of each paradigm are reviewed, especially those most relevant to the study of adolescence.

Psychoanalytic Theories. Psychoanalytic theories emphasize how children's experiences in early primary relationships establish the basis for subsequent social and personality development. According to classical psychoanalytic theories (e.g., Freud, 1938), much of adult personality is determined before adolescence, although some neoanalytic theories grant importance to later developmental events. Erikson's (1950, 1968) fifth life-cycle stage of identity versus role confusion and Blos's (1979) view that adolescence is a second individuation stage in the life span both highlight the importance of adolescence. Family relationships play important roles in psychoanalytic approaches. The contribution of early attachment relationships to the development of internal working models of relationships that are carried forward into adult relationships has stimulated a great deal of theory and research (e.g., Bowlby, 1988) and has been a main theme of work in the developmental psychopathology approach, which is reviewed in a subsequent section.

Behavioral Theories. Behavioral approaches to understanding children and adolescence have not been particularly developmental, but focus instead on the continuous pattern of contingent responses exchanged between adolescents and others in their environments, especially their parents. Behavioral approaches have been widely used in the treatment of problem behavior in adolescents (e.g., Robin & Foster, 1989); and careful analysis of family interactions has been helpful in identifying recurring patterns of behavior that become entrenched and increasingly problematic for all family members involved.

Behavioral approaches pay careful attention to contextual considerations at the micro level, but more macro contextual considerations are viewed with less interest except insofar as they are played out in micro contexts.

Organismic Theories. The body of theory and research stemming from the work of Piaget and his followers (e.g., Inhelder & Piaget, 1958; Piaget, 1983) has been central in the field of adolescent psychology. Piaget's theory of cognitive development and its stage of formal operational reasoning that potentially begins in adolescence caused developmentalists to regard youth in a new way. In addition to stimulating a great deal of research on cognitive development and adolescent reasoning (see Keating, 1980, 1990, for reviews), the organismic view inspired a generation of scholars to frame a whole host of adolescent outcomes in more developmentally sensitive ways. Large bodies of theoretical and empirical work on moral development (e.g., Kohlberg, 1976), ego development (Loevinger, 1976), social cognitive development (e.g., Selman, 1980), and sex role development (e.g., Block, 1973) noted important new developmental abilities emerging in adolescence.

Contextual Theories. Contextual theories (e.g., Lerner, 1991; Lerner & Kauffman, 1985) gained considerable attention among developmentalists who were dissatisfied with the broad stroke approaches implied by the three paradigms that have been discussed. In each of them, contextual variations and influences are subordinated to broader universal themes focusing on intraindividual development or sometimes interpersonal relationships. Further elaboration of themes from contextual approaches is found in the discussion that follows of five contemporary conceptual frameworks, all of which acknowledge the importance of contextual variation and influence.

Contemporary Conceptual Frameworks

Rather than use an overarching conceptual framework, most researchers interested in adolescence have worked within one of several rather specific theoretical approaches, and this section briefly outlines their key features and ways in which they have been used. These theoretical approaches are "mid-range" in scope, neither comprehensive nor overly narrow. They all attend to the important role of context in adolescent development, yet they do it in different ways. They also do not map neatly onto the four traditional developmental paradigms previously mentioned, as some of them bridge across more than one perspective.

Developmental Psychopathology. The past decade has witnessed the emergence of developmental psychopathology as a subdiscipline within developmental psychology. This new field has been defined as "the study of the origins and course of individual patterns of behavioral maladaptation, whatever the age of onset, whatever the causes, whatever the transformations in behavioral manifestation, and however complex the course of the developmental pattern may be" (Sroufe & Rutter, 1984, p. 18). Its goal is to "define families of developmental pathways, some of which are associated with psychopathology with high probability, others with low probability" (Sroufe, 1990, p. 135). Within this perspective, psychopathology is viewed as a "lack of integration among behavioral systems" (Cicchetti & Schneider-Rosen, 1984, p. 14). It has been differentiated from the larger discipline of developmental psychology, which focuses on general trends in normative human development rather than individual patterns of adaptation and maladaptation.

A distinctive feature of the developmental psychopathology perspective is that normal and abnormal are considered together, and investigators in this field have a common goal that research conducted with normal or clinical populations can inform research on the other. To date, the reciprocal influence has not been symmetrical, as more research addresses how normal development can inform understanding of atypical development rather than the reverse (Cicchetti, 1990).

In terms of understanding adolescence, a strength of this approach has been its focus on both continuities and discontinuities in development and on understanding the underlying coherence of development, although observable features of behavior might change or effects of early experience might become manifest at theoretically predictable later times (Sroufe, 1990). Many of the studies conducted within this framework have been longitudinal and have begun with infancy. However, the children in several of these projects are now becoming adolescents, and the contribution of this framework to the study of adolescence will become even more salient (e.g., Mother-Child Project—Egeland, Carlson, & Sroufe, 1993; Project Competence—Masten et al., 1995; Rochester Longitudinal Study—Baldwin et al., 1993).

Within this broader framework, active programs of research concerning risk and resilience have flourished. Resilience has been defined as "the process of, capacity for, or outcome of successful adaptation despite challenging or threatening circumstances" (Masten, Best, & Garmezy,

1990, p. 425). These studies acknowledge ongoing transactional processes among genetic, biological, psychological, and sociological factors considered within an organizational framework (Egeland et al., 1993).

In general, the developmental psychopathology perspective takes careful account of developmental continuities and discontinuities and looks broadly at both adaptive and maladaptive outcomes. In terms of contexts, interpersonal relationships and activity settings have received greater attention than macrosystems or the belief systems or scripts associated with specified personal characteristics.

Life Course Perspective. Environmental and contextual factors have been highlighted in the sociological work conducted under the rubric of the life-course perspective (e.g., Elder, 1995). Although a substantial amount of research has been conducted, theoretical summaries of this perspective are limited (Bronfenbrenner, 1994). In defining this perspective, Bronfenbrenner (1994) summarized three principles:

1. "The individual's own developmental life course is seen as embedded in and powerfully shaped by conditions and events occurring during the historical period through which the person lives." (p. 23)
2. "A major factor influencing the course and outcome of human development is the timing of biological and social transitions as they relate to the culturally-defined age and role expectations and opportunities through the life course." (p. 24)
3. "The lives of all family members are interdependent. Hence, how each family member reacts to a particular historical event or role transition effects the developmental course of the other family members, both within and across generations." (p. 25)

The life-course perspective is similar in many ways to the life-span perspective familiar to most developmentalists (e.g., Baltes, 1968; Baltes, Reese, & Nesselroade, 1977). However, whereas life-span views focus on individual change and continuity over time, the life-course perspective centers around generational effects, age-graded norms, role transitions, and historical context (Bush & Simmons, 1990). The life course is seen as "a crude road map with quite a few alternative routes . . . a successively bigger equation" (Atchley, 1975, pp. 261–262). The perspective's emphasis on social norms, generational differences, and historical contexts makes the life-course perspective highly pertinent for the understanding of adolescence, given our preceding discussion about this period's embeddedness in history, culture, and relationships. Among the five theoretical frameworks reviewed here, it has the clearest focus on the macrosystems that are part of context.

Elder, Caspi, and Burton (1988) articulated a life-course perspective on adolescent transitions, first highlighting the intergenerational linkages affecting human development and then connecting this understanding with knowledge of the ways in which historical context shapes these interdependent relationships. They argue persuasively that an adequate understanding of adolescence requires such information and that some classic studies in the field (e.g., Elmtown's Youth—Hollingshead, 1949) were flawed because of their inattention to significant historical events that shaped attitudes about interaction and relationships.

Ecological Systems Model. Bronfenbrenner (1977, 1979, 1992, 1994, 1995; Bronfenbrenner & Crouter, 1983) has developed and elaborated a model of human development focusing on the settings in which development occurs and the interaction of individuals and groups within and across those settings. According to this model, "development takes place through processes of progressively more complex reciprocal interaction between an active evolving biopsychological human organism and the persons, objects, and symbols in its immediate external environment" (1994, p. 3). The model takes into account issues of person, process, context, and time, and views the environment as nested systems that range from the microsystem (immediate contexts and relationships) to the mesosystem (interrelationship between microsystems linked by a common person or relationship), exosystem (system that influences a person who is not actually in that system), and the macrosystem (cultural norms, values, and systems of meaning).

Bronfenbrenner (1988) has consistently argued that developmental understanding of contextual influences must move beyond "social address" models that examine outcomes as a function of status variables such as social class, racial or ethnic group, gender, or family structure. Much more will be gained by examining the processes behind these summary variables.

Overall, Bronfenbrenner's model has provided the field a rich network of concepts and processes with which to work. This perspective and its advocates consistently challenge those conducting research or planning interventions to understand development as it proceeds within embedded contexts. Steinberg, Darling, and Fletcher (1995) noted that

the contribution of this perspective is not primarily in what it says about processes that occur within the family, but rather "the effects of . . . parenting . . . must be examined within the broader context in which the family lives and in which youngsters develop. The impact of parenting practices on youngsters' behavior and development is moderated to a large extent by the social milieu young people encounter in their peer crowd, among their close friends, within their social network, and in their neighborhood" (1995, p. 460). A significant contribution of this perspective is its focus on "multisetting links" (1995, p. 460). On the other hand, Goodnow (1994) has argued that its focus on the "geographical" metaphor of context is limited in that the belief systems, scripts, and patterns of everyday living that are also part of context are given less attention than they merit.

Goodness-of-Fit Models. A number of developmental and nondevelopmental models have focused on the importance of the fit between the individual and his or her environment in terms of optimizing developmental outcomes (e.g., Caplan & Harrison, 1993). Such perspectives have examined the match between temperament and parenting style (e.g., Thomas & Chess, 1977); person-environment fit in educational strategy (e.g., Hunt, 1975); and congruence between vocational interests and occupational environments (Holland, 1973).

Eccles and colleagues (1993) have articulated this general model in terms of the fit between developmental level during adolescence and environment. They hypothesize that "some of the negative psychological changes associated with adolescent development result from a mismatch between the needs of developing adolescents and the opportunities afforded them by their social environments" (p. 90). Their research program has focused on stage-environmental fit of educational environments for early adolescents (Eccles & Midgley, 1989), especially around the developmental appropriateness of the American junior high school model (e.g., Fuligni, Eccles, & Barber, 1995). Lerner (1991) has gone further to argue that the issue is not the fit of a changing organism with a static environment, but rather that "because changes in the organism always occur in dynamic connection with changes in the context (and vice versa), then *changes in organism-context relations* [emphasis added] are the basic change process in development" (p. 27).

Relationships Perspectives. The past 15 years have brought an explosion of interest in close relationships relevant to adolescent development. Theoretical underpinnings for this interest have come from two directions. The first is by way of social psychology, spurred quite directly by the publication of the landmark *Close Relationships* volume (Kelley et al., 1983), which laid out a conceptual framework for considering relationships. Although the framework focuses on dyadic relationships and particularly on the interpersonal interactions through which they are built, the perspective includes developmental and clinical perspectives as well. It was not formulated with one developmental period such as adolescence in mind; however, its concepts are quite useful in thinking about the important parent-child, sibling, and peer relationships in which adolescents are involved.

In this framework, relationships are defined by the interdependence, or causal interconnections among chains of events associated with two persons. Relationships are discussed in terms of the patterns, frequency, strength, diversity, and symmetry of interconnections between the parties concerned. A "close" relationship is "one of strong, frequent, and diverse interdependence that lasts over a considerable period of time" (Kelley et al., 1983, p. 38).

Whereas some research conducted under the relationships rubric focuses on behavioral interaction, other work examines cognitive mediators such as parental beliefs (e.g., C. Miller, Eccles, Goldsmith, & Flanagan, 1987) and parental expectations (e.g., Collins, 1990, 1991). The second direction is by way of the object relations perspective, stimulated by research on attachment in mother-infant relationships and the internal working models of relationships constructed in the context of such early interaction. Observations of traditional psychoanalytic writers that adolescence was a "second individuation phase" (Blos, 1979) led to further parallels being drawn between the attachment-exploration link observed in toddlerhood (e.g., Hazen & Durrett, 1982; Matas, Arend, & Sroufe, 1978) and its likely manifestation during adolescence (e.g., Grotevant & Cooper, 1985, 1986, in press). The interest in attachment shared by social psychologists and object relations theorists provides an opportunity to develop theoretical linkages between object relations and close relationship perspectives, which had formerly been viewed as incompatible. The fact that attachment plays such a central role in the developmental psychopathology literature has also contributed to increasing conjunction among these theoretical perspectives. In general, relationships perspectives focus more on interpersonal relationships and activity settings than on macrosystems.

RESEARCH REVIEW

Introduction and Scope of the Review

This research review is divided into four major sections. Key findings are presented for each topic, and inconsistencies or gaps in the literature are pointed out. The first focuses on how family relationships themselves undergo transformation during adolescence but how they simultaneously serve as contexts for adolescent development. The second section concerns identity, one of the key developmental outcomes of adolescence. The focus is on its developmental course, how its development is contextualized, how it is experienced by adolescents, and why it is important. The third and fourth sections address emotional health and competent conduct in school, work, and daily life, respectively.

This review is not exhaustive; the large and rapidly growing literature on adolescence makes such an aspiration impossible to achieve. By organizing the literature in this way, however, I hope to convey a sense of what is known, what the gaps in the literature are, and where future research attention could profitably be placed.

Family Relationships as Outcomes and Contexts

Two distinct literatures are relevant to understanding adolescent development in families. In the first, the focus is on family relationships and how they change during adolescence. In these studies, relationship qualities are often viewed as dependent variables that are predicted by other things such as pubertal status of the adolescent, discrepancies in expectations of parents and adolescents, or parental identity. In the second group of studies, family relationships are viewed as contexts in which individual adolescent development occurs. Thus, relationship qualities are independent variables, which then predict various developmental outcomes for adolescents such as identity development, ego development, moral development, or a host of other personality, social, or social cognitive constructs.

The literature has developed along these two relatively independent lines because of the ways in which investigators' research questions have been framed. However, both things occur simultaneously: Families serve as contexts for adolescent development, and characteristics of the developing adolescent and other family members affect the family's evolving relationships. Research to bring these two strands of work together is needed. In the absence of such work, I have reviewed these two literatures separately in the sections that follow.

Transformations in Relationships

Because the primary changes of adolescence entail sexual maturity, adult social status, and changes in reasoning ability, it should not be surprising that such developments have major implications for the individual's social relationships. This section includes explicit consideration of the way in which relational transformations take place, how they are influenced by the primary changes of adolescence, and how they are embedded within cultural contexts. The term *transformation,* now used widely in the literature, stands in contrast to the psychoanalytic view that adolescence brought with it the severing of parent-child ties and their replacement by peer relationships. Evidence from the extensive literature reviewed here indicates that *transformation* is a more accurate term than *severing* to describe relationship change at this point in the life cycle.

In Western societies, major developmental changes occur within individual adolescents and their parents over a time period that may exceed a decade; simultaneously, societal demands and expectations of both parties change. Despite inevitable transformations, developmental continuities from childhood are also evident. The stage is thus set for shifts in the relationships between adolescents and their parents. Shifts of this magnitude may entail conflict.

A widespread assumption in the study of adolescence in Western societies is that young people become more autonomous with respect to their families of origin. Autonomy and its developmental course have been greatly debated, however. Both psychoanalytic theory (e.g., Blos, 1979) and sociological studies of family development (e.g., Aldous, 1978; Rollins & Thomas, 1979) emphasized autonomy as separation, stressing the importance of adolescents' shifting from the family to peers as the primary reference group. Others (e.g., Douvan & Adelson, 1966; Offer, Ostrov, & Howard, 1981) found evidence favoring more continuity in parent-child relationships across adolescence. The current synthesis acknowledges the significant changes that take place in adolescents, parents, and their relationships while also acknowledging the many threads of continuity in their connections (Grotevant & Cooper, 1986).

Although adolescent theory and research both point to the important role of autonomy in development, the construct has been used in varying ways. In an attempt to systematize research in this area, Steinberg and colleagues (Hill & Steinberg, 1976; Steinberg & Silverberg, 1986) have offered both theoretical and measurement clarifications. Viewing autonomy as a multidimensional construct, Steinberg and Silverberg (1986) developed a 20-item questionnaire that assessed four components of emotional autonomy (EA): perceives parents as people, parental deidealization, nondependency on parents, and individuation. With this measure, the authors demonstrated age-related increases in EA for both boys and girls from fifth to ninth grades and linked the decreasing reliance on parents with an increasing reliance on peers.

A contrasting view of autonomy was offered by Ryan and Lynch (1989), who used the Steinberg and Silverberg (1986) measure in three studies concerning parent-adolescent relationships with seventh graders, ninth through twelfth graders, and college undergraduates. In this work, higher degrees of EA were related to less felt security in young adolescents, greater perceived parental rejection, and less experienced family cohesion and parental acceptance, leading Ryan and Lynch (1989) to conclude that the EA measure is less an index of autonomy than of emotional detachment from parents. Despite differences in interpretation of the EA measure, both sets of authors agree on the importance of understanding the way in which attachments function to optimize the individuation process during adolescence and young adulthood.

With a much larger sample of 14- to 18-year-olds, Lamborn and Steinberg (1993) found that emotional autonomy was differentially related to psychological adjustment as a function of the quality of the mother-adolescent relationship. Low to moderate scores on EA were associated with better adjustment among "secure" adolescents, whereas higher levels of EA were associated with better adjustment among "anxious" and "avoidant" adolescents.

The studies reviewed thus far are concerned primarily with emotional autonomy, which involves shifting away from dependency on parents. The literature also recognizes behavioral autonomy, the ability to behave competently when one is on his or her own; and cognitive autonomy, which involves the ability to make decisions without simply conforming to others' views (Collins, Laursen, Mortensen, Leubker, & Ferreria, 1997).

Research by Youniss and Smollar (1985) yielded distinctive portraits of dyadic parent-adolescent relationships as they varied in gender composition and as they changed over time. In general, adolescent females reported feeling distant, uncomfortable, and withdrawn from their fathers; they saw their fathers as authority figures and felt they should generally obey them. Whereas a majority of them felt their fathers met their material needs, most did not feel their fathers met their emotional needs. With mothers, daughters generally felt that both their material and emotional needs were met. Mother-daughter relationships were characterized by a combination of authority and equality, intimacy and conflict. Adolescent males' relationships with their fathers revolved around instrumental interactions, conversation, and recreational or work activities. Fathers were seen as providing knowledge or advice about practical matters; mothers were seen as confidants with whom sons could explore both personal and practical domains. With their fathers, sons felt judgmental, serious, and careful about what they said; with their mothers, sons felt that they were helpful, loved, honest, and trusting. Although these depictions are generalizations and may not hold for any particular adolescent or family situation, they do emphasize the importance of attending to issues of gender in understanding the dynamics of families with adolescents.

The families in Youniss and Smollar's (1985) studies were predominantly White. However, Knight, Virdin, and Roosa (1994) examined relationships between early adolescents and their parents in White and Hispanic families in the southwestern United States and found ethnic differences in some socialization practices. On average, Anglo mothers had lower scores on scales measuring rejection, control, inconsistent discipline, hostile control, and cohesion than did Hispanic mothers. This pattern was correlated moderately with acculturation in the sense that more highly acculturated Hispanic mothers scored more similarly to Anglo mothers. The study went on to examine links between family socialization predictors and adolescent depression, hostility, and self-esteem. Interestingly, however, these differences in family patterns were not related to differences in mental health outcomes in the early adolescents.

Results of this study underscore an important methodological point: absence of mean differences between groups on a dependent variable does not necessarily mean there are no "effects" of group membership. There may instead be differential patterns of prediction for the dependent variable that involve the group membership in simple or complex ways. Likewise, presence of mean differences between groups on a dependent variable does not necessarily mean that the differences were caused by the differential levels of the dependent variable.

In societies less individualistic than European-American, parent-adolescent relationships revolve around issues of obligation, responsibility, and respect for elders (e.g., Cooper, Baker, Polichar, & Welsh, 1994; Saraswathi & Pai, 1993). Adolescence becomes particularly complex both for young people and for their parents when their subcultural group holds collectivistic norms but is embedded within a dominant culture that emphasizes growing autonomy. For example, over 50,000 refugees from Southeast Asia settled in Minnesota between the mid-1970s and mid-1990s; this is the fastest growing ethnic group and economically the poorest one in the state (Detzner, 1995).

Increases in delinquency, juvenile arrests, and gang activity appear related in part to the fact that Southeast Asian immigrant parents of today's adolescents "have difficulty asserting their rights and responsibilities as parents in a social context they do not fully understand" (Detzner, 1995, p. 2). In traditional Hmong culture, boys are regarded as adults by age 12, at which time they can become husbands and fathers. Girls marry around that time, and until then, their parents are very restrictive and protective. Thus, the traditional culture does not prepare Hmong immigrant adults to set limits for their adolescent sons or to allow options for their adolescent daughters (Xiong, 1996). This illustration vividly points out that understanding of parent-child relationship change must consider the family's cultural context and its relation to the dominant culture.

What Happens to Adolescents?   In the realm of parent-adolescent relationships, Steinberg (1981, 1988; Steinberg & Hill, 1978) has shown that pubertal maturation increases emotional distance between adolescents and their parents, especially through increased conflict and decreased closeness. As sons became more physically mature, they interrupted their mothers more and deferred to them less frequently in a family interaction task; mothers also interrupted their sons more, so their interaction could be fairly contentious. Following the apex of puberty, mothers deferred more to their sons, suggesting that the sons had replaced their mothers in the family's influence hierarchy. In contrast, sons interrupted their fathers less and deferred to them more. This interactional pattern exemplifies how adolescents and parents renegotiate their relationships as a function of the primary changes of adolescence—in this case, physical development. Similarly, in an observational study of families with seventh-grade girls, Holmbeck and Hill (1988) found evidence for a withdrawal of positive affect and a temporary period of conflict following menarche, especially between daughters and their mothers. They argued that these changes in conflict and positivity might be adaptive within healthy families because they signal the changed developmental status of the child and facilitate her intrapsychic individuation.

Distancing in relationships does not tell the full story, however. Papini, Roggman, and Anderson (1991) examined the possibility that processes involving both distancing and buffering might be occurring. In a study of seventh graders using self-report measures of pubertal status, family relationships, depression, and anxiety, the authors tested hypotheses regarding (a) emotional distancing that might occur as a function of pubertal status, and (b) the buffering function that close attachment to parents would play in moderating feelings of depression and anxiety during puberty. Support was found for both notions. Consistent with the growing literature, attachment to both parents declined as a function of increasing pubertal maturation with the exception of mother-son relationships, which tended to become closer (see also Youniss & Smollar, 1985). In addition, greater attachments to both parents predicted lower levels of depression and social anxiety for both male and female adolescents.

Both distancing and rapprochement were suggested by research of Holmbeck and O'Donnell (1991), who found that mothers report greater degrees of conflict when their daughters desire more autonomy than the mothers are willing to grant. Their research led them to hypothesize a cycle characterized by discrepancy → perturbation → realignment → adaptation, which may repeat itself a number of times during adolescence over both mundane and major issues. This cycle may be due to changing expectations that parents and adolescents have about one another. Collins (1990, 1997) has developed a model of parent-adolescent relationships, which proposes that the interactions between parents and children are mediated by processes associated with each person's expectations about the behavior of his or her partner. He hypothesizes that discrepancies between actual and expected behavior arise from maturational and social changes (especially during early adolescence), precipitate interpersonal conflict, and ultimately force the realignment of perceptions, and ultimately relationships, within the family (Collins, 1991).

In fact, Collins and colleagues (e.g., Collins et al., 1997) found relatively little concordance between the expectations held by parents and their adolescents about the appropriate timing for certain transitions. These mismatches are most common during early adolescence, which is also the time of greatest parent-adolescent conflict. The work goes further to suggest that parents' and

adolescents' views converge over time as successive rounds of violations of expectations and relationship realignments occur (Collins et al., 1997).

Adolescents' changing expectations may be related in part to their cognitive growth and may subsequently contribute to transformations in parent-child relationships. In reviewing this literature, Laursen (1988) concluded that the link is best characterized as a two-phase process: (a) cognitive development in adolescence underlies changes in understanding the parent-child relationship, and (b) these changes bring about transformations in interactional patterns of parents and their adolescents. Examples of the first phase include the work of Youniss and Smollar (1985), who described age-related changes in adolescents' conceptualizations of relationships with their parents. Children and early adolescents perceive their parents as *figures*; later, adolescents view them as three-dimensional *persons* (true more so for views of mothers than fathers.)

The work of Judith Smetana has provided one of the most comprehensive views of the links between social cognitive development and relationship change within the family. She studied over 100 children ranging from 5th through 12th grades and their parents using interviews and direct observations (Smetana, 1989). Even though parents and their adolescents agreed about which issues caused conflict, they disagreed on their interpretations or meanings of the conflicts. "The results suggest that the mundane issues at the heart of adolescent-parent conflict may provide a context for debates over the extent of adolescents' developing autonomy, which is seen in opposition to maintaining the family system" (Smetana, 1989, p. 1064). Her work also suggests that social-cognitive change is linked to relational or behavioral changes. The extent to which certain issues are seen as being under personal jurisdiction rather than within the purview of adult authority increases with age during adolescence (Smetana, 1988; Smetana & Asquith, 1994). Such conflicts ultimately entail renegotiation of the boundaries between parental authority over the adolescent and the adolescent's authority over him- or herself (Smetana, 1995):

There may be little disagreement between parents and children during middle childhood on the conventionality of a variety of family issues, but adolescents view themselves as becoming increasingly emancipated from these parental perspectives. . . . Conflict thus entails adolescents' and parents' inability to coordinate conflicting social-cognitive perspectives and provides a context for parents and children to articulate and discuss divergent perspectives. This, in turn, leads to changes in those perspectives. That is, conflict forces parents to reevaluate the limits of their authority and the boundaries of adolescents' personal jurisdiction. Thus, parents' appeals to social convention, adolescents' rejection of their parents' perspective, and their reinterpretation of conventions as legitimately under their personal jurisdiction form a continual dialectic in which the boundaries of parental authority are subtly transformed. Parents shift from viewing a variety of conflicts as conventional and legitimately subject to their authority to granting the adolescent increasing personal jurisdiction over these issues. (pp. 32–33)

Smetana goes on to make the provocative point that this tension between parent and adolescent "mirrors the fundamental tension between the individual and society" (Smetana, 1995, p. 32). A more inclusive way to make this statement is that the link between individual and society should be mirrored in the changing parent-adolescent relationship, and thus that the changing parent-adolescent relationship will look very different in cultures that hold different views about the link between individuals and society. Specific predictions about diversity in adolescent experiences in families could be generated from this line of reasoning.

This body of research suggests that the realignment in parent-child relationships from childhood into adolescence typically involves an increase in conflict during early adolescence followed by a decline. Adolescents are increasingly able to understand their parents' conventional perspectives, which may in turn be facilitated by underlying cognitive changes (Smetana, 1991); reciprocally, parents sense their adolescent's increasing physical maturity, cognitive skill, and readiness to handle various decisions and may relinquish control that they would have retained when the child was younger.

Less research has been conducted on the transition to adulthood or "leaving home transition" that marks the end of adolescence (but see Sherrod, 1993). Despite the psychoanalytic perspective that satisfactory adjustment in the adult world requires separation from parents, research has consistently demonstrated that relationships characterized by high degrees of separateness and low connectedness to parents are associated with poorer rather than better outcomes for late adolescents and young adults (e.g., Frank, Avery, & Laman, 1988; Grotevant & Cooper, 1985; Hoffman, 1984). Research also must address issues of separation and autonomy both in a gender-specific way and by differentiating among domains of separation. In a study in which college students were asked to indicate

how important different issues were in helping them decide whether they had "left home or separated from parents yet," eight factors emerged: self-governance, emotional detachment, financial independence, separate residence, disengagement, school affiliation, starting a family, and graduation (Moore, 1987).

Most research on the leaving-home transition has been conducted with college students or college-bound high school students. A study conducted in the Netherlands highlights the importance of differentiating reasons for leaving home as well. DeJong Gierveld, Liefbroer, and Beekink (1990) used a demographic perspective to examine why young people in their country actually left home and identified three primary patterns: (a) for reasons of education or work, (b) for reasons of starting a partner relationship, and (c) for reasons of freedom or independence. This study is important in that it calls our attention to the possibility that underlying family-of-origin dynamics might differ across these three reasons, and it emphasizes the importance of considering that cultures may have different normative patterns concerning leaving home.

What Happens to Parents?   A reading of the traditional socialization literature might lead one to believe that the children in the family are the only ones who are developing and that parents' development is somehow complete. Thanks to life-span perspectives, a new appreciation for the work of Erik Erikson, and a surge of empirical research on adult development, we now know that adults change considerably as well. Transactional models of development and family systems thinking have helped us move away from the notion that adolescents are changing and their parents are reacting, toward the perspective that the developmental trajectories of *both* parents and adolescents are interdependent. In fact, adolescence is a period during which three generations in the family (the adolescent, middle-aged parents, and elderly grandparents) may be undergoing simultaneous developmental transitions that involve reconsideration of life goals (Grotevant, 1989). As adolescents work to define a sense of identity, their middle-aged parents may reconsider life choices with regard to relationships and work (Levinson, 1986), and the grandparental generation may be dealing with the transition to retirement, health concerns, and relationship changes due to death of a spouse (Carter & McGoldrick, 1980).

For a number of years, clinical accounts have noted parallels between adolescents' ascendence into their prime of life while parents are passing beyond their peak. This disjunction has been discussed with respect to both men and women. For men, "an adolescent with seemingly open choices in work and love objects forces the middle-aged father to complete his grieving over lost alternatives and reaffirm his own life choices. If the father cannot do this, he may envy and disparage his son, or alternatively, overidentify with him in trying to relive through him what he feels he has missed" (Levi, Stierlin, & Savard, 1972, p. 49). For women, this conflict has been examined in terms of the simultaneous emergence of the young woman's reproductive capacity and the decline of her mother's. Paikoff, Brooks-Gunn, and Carlton-Ford (1991) found that the combination of menopause in the mother and menarche in her daughter was related to problems in maternal eating behavior. Graber and Brooks-Gunn (in press) concluded that reproductive transitions among women (puberty, sexuality, pregnancy, and menopause) are in some sense shared by both mothers and daughters "inasmuch as the progression of one member of the dyad through the transition influences and is influenced by the response of the other member" (p. 47). Thus, future research needs to focus more explicitly on such interconnections.

This portrait is based on the assumption of a nuclear family structure in which development of personal potential is highly valued. The picture looks dramatically different in cultures involving elaborate extended family structures or in which adult development is structured around norms of obligation or responsibility to community.

Rapidly growing bodies of theory and research are now beginning to illuminate the rich complexity of adult development (e.g., Gould, 1978; Josselson, 1988; Levinson, 1986, 1996; Smelser & Erikson, 1980; Whitbourne, 1986). In her longitudinal work, Silverberg (1989; Silverberg & Steinberg, 1987, 1990) assessed four aspects of parental sense of self: experience of midlife identity concerns, general life satisfaction, self-esteem, and experience of psychological symptoms. Of particular interest is the cross-sectional finding that adolescent physical maturation is related to parental well-being, but that this link is moderated by parental work orientation. In their sample of 10- to 15-year-olds and their parents, they found that "higher levels of youngsters' dating behavior and involvement in mixed-sex peer group activities are associated with more intense midlife concerns, lower life satisfaction, or more frequent psychological symptoms on the part of their parents, but these effects are found only among parents who are not strongly invested in a paid-work role" (Silverberg & Steinberg, 1990, p. 664).

In subsequent longitudinal analyses (Silverberg, 1989), it was found that sons' emotional autonomy assessed when the sons were 10- to 15-years-old predicted fathers' reports of more intense midlife identity concerns one year later; however, the reverse was not true. In turn, the mother-daughter pattern was more bidirectional: Mothers' life reappraisal predicted increased mother-daughter conflict one year later, but mother-daughter conflict at the initial time of observation also predicted mothers' experience of more frequent psychological symptoms one year later. These provocative findings emphasize the importance of examining the interlocking nature of adolescent and adult development as well as the possible nuances of such links that may be due to orientation toward paid employment, biological versus stepparenting, socioeconomic status, ethnicity, and individual differences among both parents and adolescents.

Moving beyond Dyadic Relationships to the Family Level. The preceding discussion points out the necessity of examining specific dyads within the family (mother-son, mother-daughter, father-son, father-daughter) to understand what is happening during adolescence. But how is one to characterize larger subunits within the family or the family system as a whole? Several approaches have been used to move beyond the level of the dyad.

Many studies of parenting attitudes and behavior have been limited in that data were collected only from one parent (usually the mother, assuming that her perception was most "accurate") or from both parents but only analyzed separately for each parent. Adolescents in two-parent families, however, do not lead totally separate lives with their mothers and fathers. How can the broader parenting context be assessed? Johnson, Shulman, and Collins (1991) evaluated conjoint parenting patterns by seeking adolescents' perceptions of the child-rearing attitudes of both their mother and father (separately) and then subjecting these data to cluster analysis. Four distinctive clusters emerged. In the *authoritative systemic parenting pattern,* adolescents perceived a similar mode of parenting for mother and father in which both encouraged autonomy within an accepting atmosphere. The *permissive systemic parenting pattern* included cases in which both parents were seen as slightly less accepting and warm than in the first pattern but exercising relatively lax control. In the *incongruent systemic parenting pattern— mother authoritarian/rejecting,* different views were held of mothers and fathers: Mothers were more rejecting and fathers were more accepting and encouraging. Finally, in the *incongruent systemic parenting pattern—father authoritarian/rejecting,* different views again predominated; but in this case, fathers were seen as rejecting and controlling and mothers were more accepting and supportive. The incongruent patterns occurred in 21% of the families sampled, thus indicating the importance of paying attention to these variations. The investigators found that perceptions of incongruent parenting were most frequent among adolescents lowest in self-esteem. They also found that the frequency of authoritative/congruent parenting decreased linearly from 5th to 8th to 11th grades, whereas the frequency of incongruent parenting/father authoritarian increased as a linear function of grade. Although the study was cross-sectional and no authoritarian systemic parenting pattern emerged in the data to permit a test of whether the differences were due to inconsistent parenting or authoritarian parenting, these findings suggest interesting hypotheses about family dynamics that can be confirmed with longitudinal research.

Similarly, in a national (U.S.) sample of 720 families with adolescents, cluster analyses were performed on dimensions of positivity, negativity, and control to determine "parenting style" for each parent (Taylor, 1994). Parental combinations were derived as both "good" (authoritative and good enough styles), both "bad" (conflicted or disengaged), and one parent of each. The best outcomes for adolescents (in terms of low frequencies of internalizing and externalizing problems) were in families in which both parents were "good," and the worst outcomes were in families in which both parents were "bad;" results also highlighted the protective function of having one good parent. This study supports the approach taken by Johnson et al. (1991) in looking at particular combinations of parenting style in two-parent families.

Another approach to moving beyond the dyad was taken by Gjerde (1986), who studied interaction of 13-year-old adolescents in a dyadic situation with one parent and in a triadic situation with both parents. He found that the addition of the father improved the quality of the mother-son interaction, whereas the addition of the mother reduced the quality of the father-son interaction; the presence of the second parent had greater impact on dyadic relations in families of boys than in families of girls. This study provides further justification for looking beyond the dyad and provides a suggestion of how it can be done.

Vuchinich, Emery, and Cassidy (1988) examined the role that "third parties" play in dyadic relations by explicitly coding ways in which such persons become involved in family conflict (as tape recorded during dinner time); for example, through "siding with," "siding against," mediating, or distracting. For purposes of this discussion, the value of this study is in its explicit attention to the dynamics of triadic interaction. Replicating this study with a sample of families with adolescents would be very desirable, as most of the children in the study were younger.

One of the more innovative approaches to the study of adolescence is the experience sampling method (ESM) (Csikszentmihalyi & Larson, 1987; Larson & Csikszentmihalyi, 1983; Larson & Richards, 1994), which elicits self-reports of behavior, thoughts, and feelings at specified points in time during the day. Adolescents carry electronic pagers ("beepers") and a booklet of self-report forms for a number of days. When the pager beeps at random intervals, the adolescent completes a form in the booklet indicating where they were, what they were doing and with whom, and how they were feeling. Using this technique, Larson and Richards (1991) found that over the interval from age 9 to 15, time spent with family declined dramatically for both males and females. For males, family time was replaced by time spent alone; for females, it was replaced by time spent alone and with friends. When with the family, adolescents' affect became less positive between fifth and seventh grade but became more positive toward ninth grade.

In asking parents and adolescents to complete these logs, Larson and Richards (1994) had to confront the divergent emotional realities existing simultaneously within families. Intensive analysis of individuals' patterns and efforts to understand the coordination of these different realities family-by-family led them to conclude that "once we go inside family life, we find that it is an illusion to talk about 'the family,' as though it were a single entity. The family is the meeting ground of multiple realities" (p. 189). Their study led them to conclude that "the immediate source of family dysfunction, we believe, lies in the emotional interior of families. Contemporary family life often breaks down because individuals do not understand and cannot negotiate the differing patterns of time and emotion that structure each of their lives" (p. 2).

In Larson and Richards' sample of two-parent families with adolescents, husbands typically experienced work as stressful and viewed home as a respite from their stressful jobs. However, the frustrations and negative emotions encountered at work were often brought home and spilled over onto other family members. Their wives, many of whom were employed outside the home, felt that it was their responsibility to serve as the "glue" to keep the family together. Despite their high investment in family life, however, they did not necessarily find it gratifying or restorative; their emotional gratification often came through activities outside the home. Adolescents typically arrived home from school with their own feelings of exhaustion and brought with them the emotions they had experienced during the school day. Parental availability and responsiveness had an effect on whether negative emotions were dissipated or accentuated. This brief, albeit oversimplified, sketch vividly demonstrates the importance of understanding the divergent realities experienced by family members in order to understand how the family system and the individuals and relationships within it function.

Many of the cited studies were conducted with middle-class European American families, which, as noted earlier, is a limitation of our knowledge base at this point. In these families, socialization goals focus on the development of individualistic qualities such as autonomy, independence, and initiative in adolescents. In many cultural traditions, however, familistic norms of collective support, loyalty, and obligation are more important. In these cultures, adolescents are expected to show support, respect, and reticence in the family, especially toward their fathers. Academic and behavioral outcomes bring pride or shame to the entire family; they do not simply reflect on the individual adolescent. Such collectivistic values have been considered adaptive for ethnic minority families, especially those who live in conditions of racism, immigration, or poverty.

Cooper, Baker, Polichar, and Welsh (1994) studied differences in values and relationships among California college students differing in ethnicity. On a survey, these students described themselves with more than 30 ethnic terms. In a group of students representing five cultural groups (those of Mexican, Vietnamese, Filipino, Chinese, and European descent), adolescents rated the degree to which they viewed a list of familistic values as held by themselves, their mothers, fathers, and maternal and paternal grandparents. Adolescents from all five cultural groups strongly endorsed the statement, "Family members should make sacrifices to guarantee a good education for their children." However, adolescents of Mexican, Chinese, Vietnamese, and Filipino descent endorsed values of mutual support among siblings as well as turning to parents and other relatives in making important decisions.

Intergenerational differences suggested both continuity and change, with some indication of distinctive patterns across the cultural groups. In response to the statement, "Older siblings should help directly support other family members economically," Vietnamese and Chinese descent adolescents reported sharing their parents' *strong* endorsements, European American adolescents reported sharing their parents' *weak* endorsements, and Filipino and Mexican descent adolescents endorsed this value *less* than their parents. However, adolescents in all five groups saw their parents as holding stronger expectations for them to consider the family as a frame of reference in making decisions than they did.

Adolescents also characterized their communication of individuality and connectedness with parents, siblings, and friends, including how comfortable they felt discussing school, careers, cultural and ethnic heritage, and sexuality, dating, and marriage with each person. Within each cultural group, students reported more formal communication with fathers in contrast to more open communication and more negotiation with their mothers, siblings, and friends. They reported that their fathers "make most of the decisions in our relationship," particularly among Chinese, Filipino, and Vietnamese descent students.

The findings of Cooper and colleagues regarding values and communication in adolescents' relationships with families and peers challenge traditional definitions of adolescent maturity in terms of autonomy from parents. College students of Chinese, Filipino, Mexican, and Vietnamese descent saw themselves and their parents as holding norms of reliance on family members for both support and guidance in decision making. Communication appeared more formal with fathers than with mothers in all cultural groups. Hierarchical patterns were especially evident within Asian American families, and more egalitarian patterns were evident with change over time and generations. When norms of respect rendered adolescents' relationships with parents more formal, sibling and peer relationships played especially important roles in adolescents' lives.

Results of this work challenge the research community to think more broadly about parent-adolescent relationships: "Describing parents and adolescents as renegotiating asymmetrical patterns of authority towards peer-like mutuality appears more appropriate for European-American families than more recent immigrants from Asia and Mexico, for whom more formal relationships between adolescents with mothers and especially fathers appear more common" (Cooper et al., 1991, p. 1). This work of Cooper and colleagues is especially important because of its theoretically driven focus on processes in parent-adolescent relationships and its potential for linking them with phenomena related to ethnicity and culture such as acculturation, familistic values, and economic mobility.

Progress in moving beyond dyadic relationships is also occurring in the study of families post divorce, both single-parent and remarried families. Welsh, Powers, and Jacobson (1991) found that patterns of parent-adolescent interaction differed in single-parent and two-parent families. A key difference concerned higher levels of mother-adolescent connectedness, especially with sons. These results are consistent with those of Carlson, Cooper, and Frank (1987) who also found that single-parent mothers demonstrated greater connectedness and lower individuality in their interaction with both sons and daughters than did mothers in two-parent families. Similarly, Smetana, Yau, Restrepo, and Braeges (in press) recently reported a trend toward less conflictual parent-adolescent relationships in stabilized single-parent families than in two-parent families. On the other hand, Vuchinich, Hetherington, Vuchinich, and Clingempeel (1991) documented the greater difficulties that early adolescent females have interacting with a stepfather than do early adolescent males. These studies are beginning to add texture to our understanding of parent-adolescent relationships in diverse family ecologies. Many potentially important variables remain to be studied systematically: When did the divorce (and/or remarriage) occur? What is the relationship between the custodial and noncustodial parents and between the custodial parent and stepparent? What kind of contact does the adolescent have with the noncustodial parent? How many siblings are in the family, how are they related, and in what sibling position is the target adolescent? What is the constellation of stress and support experienced by the particular single-parent or remarried family?

Links between Family and Peer Relationships. Although a full discussion of adolescents' relationships with same- and opposite-sex peers is beyond the scope of this chapter, the following brief summaries focus on friendships and intimate relationships, especially as they are linked with adolescents' changing family relationships.

Friendships. Although the experience of friendship typically occurs first during childhood, the nature of friendship changes dramatically during adolescence. Excellent discussions of this transformation can be found in several sources (Collins & Repinski, 1994; Douvan & Adelson, 1966; Savin-Williams & Berndt, 1990; Youniss, 1980; Youniss & Smollar, 1985).

Although friendships are interesting in their own right, one of the most intriguing developments of adolescence is how friendships change in conjunction with parent-adolescent relationships. During childhood, parents are viewed as authority figures; friendships provide venues in which children learn how to take the other's perspective and how to negotiate on a relatively level playing field (Selman, 1980; Youniss, 1980). The enduring contribution of friendships and peer relationships to subsequent development has been noted by many, including Piaget (1932), who highlighted peer contributions to children's moral development.

Parents influence their children's peer relations and friendships through their child-rearing practices and interaction styles, by instructing their children about how to interact with others, and by managing their children's social lives and providing opportunities for interaction (Parke, Burks, Carson, Neville, & Boyum, 1994). At adolescence, however, time spent with friends increases dramatically and parental influence becomes less visible. In friendships, adolescents experience themselves as individuals, accepted by others in a voluntary relationship outside their family (Youniss & Smollar, 1985). For such relationships to endure, partners must take each others' views and wishes seriously. It appears that this experience, undergirded by adolescents' cognitive abilities to differentiate among relationships and view relationships with parents as one of many possible such relationships, leads to adolescents' behavior attempting to convert a more unilateral parent to-child relationship into a more symmetrical parent-adolescent one (Youniss, 1980; Youniss & Smollar, 1985). Bids toward such transformation are among the disequilibrating events of early adolescence, typically evoking conflict in the short run but ultimately leading to a somewhat more egalitarian parent-adolescent relationship (Youniss & Smollar, 1985).

Friendships are often embedded within larger peer contexts which themselves undergo change across adolescence as well. Important points for understanding developmental transformation in friendships have been made by Brown and colleagues, who studied adolescent crowds within American schools. Three features of crowds relevant to relationships were noted: first, crowds and the stereotypes associated with them ("brains," "jocks," etc.) help adolescents understand alternative social identities available to them; second, crowd affiliations channel interaction such that relationships among some individuals are more likely than among others; third, crowds themselves vary in how relationships are structured in features such as closeness and endurance over time (Brown, Mory, & Kinney, 1994). Such an analysis should be useful in understanding the potential developmental impact of affiliation with various types of groups, from the honor society to the gang.

Intimate Relationships and Sexuality. One of the primary changes of adolescence involves sexual maturity, which necessarily leads to new kinds of intimate relationships. Topics studied with regard to adolescence include the emergence of behaviors eventuating in first sexual intercourse (e.g., Brooks-Gunn & Furstenberg, 1989; Brooks-Gunn & Paikoff, 1993; Katchadourian, 1990); use of contraception, including responsibility for prevention of exposure to sexually transmitted diseases (e.g., B. Miller & Moore, 1990); teenage pregnancy and childbearing (e.g., Brooks-Gunn & Chase-Lansdale, 1994; Furstenberg, Brooks-Gunn, & Chase-Lansdale, 1989; Hofferth, 1987); and consequences to adolescents of having experienced sexual abuse during childhood.

The large literatures previously mentioned generally carry the presumption that these emerging sexual relationships are heterosexual; yet awareness of gay, lesbian, and bisexual identities and relationships is growing in the popular culture and the research literature as well (D'Augelli & Patterson, 1995; Herdt, 1989; Oswald, 1994; Savin-Williams, 1990, 1994). Developmental challenges facing gay or lesbian youth are multifaceted and illustrate the need to understand adolescent development in context. Their erotic fantasies and experiences typically do not mesh with the messages they see portrayed in the media; they may feel isolated from peers and unable to discuss their feelings with family members; their sense of identity involves coming to terms not only with this sexual identity but also with how it relates to other identity domains; their emerging sexual orientation may clash with their racial, ethnic, or religious affiliations in such a way that they must hide their true feelings; and their behavior may put them at high risk for exposure to AIDS or drug use. Although there has been a significant increase in research activity relating to the development of homosexual behavior and identity, much remains work remains to be undertaken.

Family Relationships as Contexts for Development

In the set of studies considered in this section, qualities of family relationships are typically viewed as predictors of various adolescent outcomes. There are two groups of studies

within this set. In the first, family variables are viewed as "main effects;" in the second, family factors are predictors, but moderating variables of many kinds are included in order to understand how the effect of certain family factors can vary in different contexts. The trend toward examining moderating and mediating effects may be seen in the more current research literature.

Main Effects Models. Regardless of the underlying conceptualization, virtually all work on adolescent development within the family has implicitly assumed that family processes influence adolescent outcomes in direct, or at least indirect, ways. Studies typically employ correlational designs but consider family or parent characteristics as independent variables and adolescent characteristics as dependent variables. This situation persists, despite R. Bell and Harper's (1977) effort to turn the socialization literature upside down and view family variables as "outcomes" of child characteristics. The reality is that parents and children affect one another in ongoing reciprocal fashion (Minuchin, 1985). The literature currently does a better job of acknowledging such patterns than it did in decades past, although the methods used in the empirical studies lag behind.

Because of the predominance of studies using family variables as independent and adolescent characteristics as dependent or outcome variables, it is important to look at such outcomes in terms of what has been studied, how, and why. Although many studies have examined the four adolescent outcome categories previously discussed, some of them use superordinate concepts such as "adjustment" or "competence," which require unpacking to clarify their meaning.

Early studies of parents and adolescents were consistent with the general literature on childhood socialization within the family. A large number of studies focused on parental attitudes and their hypothesized "effects" on adolescent outcomes. In the 1950s and 1960s, the outcome variables of greatest interest included aspects of personality and achievement, on the positive side, or delinquency, on the negative (e.g., Becker, 1964; Maccoby & Martin, 1983 for reviews). Interest in notions such as self-esteem and identity became prominent later, as the work of Erik Erikson became more widely known.

This approach was consistent with the "social mold" view of socialization (e.g., Hartup, 1978), according to which parents' relatively stable attitudes, values, warmth, and control largely shaped children's abilities and behavior. This view was consistent with both psychoanalytic and behaviorist paradigms, which in many other ways reflect quite different views of human development. Even though most studies done in this genre were correlational and cross-sectional, investigators liberally interpreted their results in causal ways, further strengthening the general unidirectional perspective on socialization.

Another hallmark of this era of research was that samples were homogeneous, typically convenience samples of White, middle-class Americans; of course, most researchers at that time were also White, middle-class Americans. The "melting pot" model of the mixing of races and backgrounds in the United States popular at that time further supported a context-free examination of links between predictors and outcomes; additionally, both behaviorism and psychoanalysis strove to identify universal laws of human behavior rather than ones contingent on moderating variables such as race, ethnicity, gender, sexual orientation, or class.

A significant body of research on adolescent development in families was conducted and published between the mid-1970s and mid-1980s. A number of influences contributed to this new approach, one of which was the growing ascendancy of organismic and transactional models of human development, which took into account the developing person's own role as participant in and shaper of the contexts in which subsequent development occurred. In response to several effective challenges that research move beyond simple linear cause-effect models of development (e.g., Baumrind, 1980; R. Bell, 1968, R. Bell & Harper, 1977; Lewis & Rosenblum, 1974), more bidirectional and systemic models were articulated. This keen interest in bidirectionality and reciprocity in human interaction (largely begun in the area of mother-infant interaction), made possible because of advances in videotaping technology, spawned a great deal of observational work in the field of adolescence as well.

The new look in adolescent research was also fostered by the integrative and persuasive writing of John Hill, whose reviews (e.g., 1973, 1980, 1987; Hill & Holmbeck, 1986; Hill & Monks, 1977; Hill & Palmquist, 1978; Hill & Steinberg, 1976) helped organize existing knowledge and challenge the next generation of researchers. These events happened at a time in the United States (late 1960s to early 1970s) when there was great public interest in and puzzlement about adolescents. It was the time of the widespread perception of the "youth culture" and "generation gap," when commentary by social critics such as Goodman (1956) and Friedenberg (1959, 1963) highlighted the perceived chasm between youth and adults.

Stimulated by these compelling interests and questions as well as the availability of research funds from public and private sources, a generation of investigators reshaped the empirical study of adolescence. As Hill noted, "For the first time, there is the promise of and the potential for the development of cumulative knowledge" (1987, p. 13). Compared with research on adolescence in families conducted before the mid-1970s, this new work was more programmatic, was widespread enough to engage multiple investigators at different locations and teams of investigators at individual sites, involved replication of findings across sites, and employed both self-report and observational measures that were psychometrically sound and theoretically grounded (Hill, 1987). These studies were grounded in clear theoretical frameworks less parochial than those of the past, incorporating advances in a number of fields: developmental psychology, family therapy, sociology, communication, psychiatry, and discourse analysis, to name a few.

The most important legacy of this body of work is that it refutes the premise that adolescence is primarily a time of separation from parents and society and rather points to the linkage between adolescents' developing both autonomy and connection with respect to significant adults. Findings of these studies are reviewed in the sections that follow linking the family variables to specific adolescent outcomes. Despite these significant advances, the work in this area did not fully represent diversity in family structures or ethnic groups and, with the notable exception of Hauser's, was still largely cross-sectional rather than longitudinal.

Studies not using observational methods also continued to be published, but the more significant studies were characterized by one or more of the following: large sample size, greater diversity in participants, more differentiated view of family processes, or longitudinal designs.

Complex Models Involving Moderating and Mediating Variables. Since the mid-1980s, an increasing number of studies linking family processes and adolescent outcomes have tested more complex models that involve moderating and mediating effects. In general, these studies incorporate the positive methodological features of the preceding era, but go further. Many involve observation of family interaction. Those that do not are typically survey studies that engage large samples that are more diverse and/or more representative. Oftentimes, funding limitations and logistical considerations force investigators to choose between studying a smaller sample with more intensive observational strategies or a larger sample with self-report instruments, often administered by mail or at school. Since these are not direct trade-offs, looking for replication of conclusions across both methodological modes is important.

These more complex models often examine possible contributions of moderating and/or mediating variables. A moderator variable can be either categorical (e.g., gender, ethnic group) or quantitative (e.g., level of a continuous variable) in nature; it "affects the direction and/or strength of the relation between an independent or predictor variable and a dependent or criterion variable" (Baron & Kenny, 1986, p. 1174). It may be thought of as "an interaction between a focal independent variable and a factor that specifies the appropriate condition for its operation" (p. 1174). Moderator effects may be thought of as "contextually conditioned impacts of forces and factors that were once considered to exert across-the-board influences" (Belsky, 1995, p. 550). A mediating variable "accounts for the relation between the predictor and the criterion" (Baron & Kenny, 1986, p. 1176). In general, "whereas moderator variables specify when certain effects will hold, mediators speak to how or why such effects occur" (p. 1176). Studies of this type permit contextual variables to be included directly as part of the research design and analysis. The studies reviewed here are examples of how contextual features can be taken into account in quantitative studies.

Several variables moderate the relation between various family patterns or specified risk factors, on the one hand, and adolescent outcomes, on the other. Interest in identifying and clarifying such moderating effects acknowledges the importance of understanding diversity of many kinds in the human experience. The zeitgeist of the 1990s puts less stock in the search for universal principles of behavior and more in understanding how different conditions and different experiences might produce variation in outcomes. A full review of this literature is beyond the scope of this chapter; however, a few illustrations are provided in sections that follow on specific adolescent outcomes.

The moderating variables most commonly included in the research literature on adolescent development are gender, ethnicity, family structure, and relationship quality. Long before the literature was organized in terms of moderating and mediating effects, investigators noted how results of studies often differed in predictable or unpredictable ways by gender of adolescent, gender of parent, or

interaction between the two. Occasionally, an effect would be present for one gender but not the other; at other times, one pattern of results might emerge for one gender and a different pattern would be evident for the other.

More studies are being conducted on the role of ethnicity in adolescence and family relationships, although there is not clear consensus about how best to do this. Studies aiming to document group differences risk promoting stereotyped ideas about the groups. Quantitative studies including racial or ethnic group affiliation as moderating variables may detect differences but do not contribute to understanding how ethnicity is experienced at the process level. García Coll et al. (1996) have argued strongly that the possible experiences of racism, discrimination, and prejudice must be considered in studies of children and youth of color, since these experiences may strongly influence developmental outcomes.

A new generation of researchers (Burton et al., 1995) attuned to the lives of adolescents from communities of color and from backgrounds of poverty are challenging developmental scholars to realize that much of the traditional literature on adolescent development assumes contexts with at least moderate levels of economic, social, and political resources. Burton et al. (1995) noted five specific ways in which adolescent development must be reconsidered under such circumstances. First, the ethnographic literature they reviewed noted major inconsistencies between parents and social institutions (especially schools) with regard to the social roles of teenagers. Second, adolescents in "age-condensed families" (ones in which there is a relatively narrow age separation between generations) often experience developmental challenges that are inconsistent with their generational positions, and the generational proximity may weaken parents' willingness to exert authority over their developing children (Burton et al., 1995). Related to this is the third issue, which involves the unclear boundaries between the social worlds of teenagers and their parents. Fourth, Burton (1991) and other scholars have noted the perception among inner-city African Americans that they have a shorter life expectancy and an accelerated life course. Finally, Burton et al. (1995) noted that many researchers use traditional outcome indicators (such as high school graduation or attainment of paid employment) to assess developmental outcomes among inner-city youth, when in fact other markers of developmental success (e.g., ability to care for a frail elder) go unmeasured.

A recent study of parenting styles in Chinese immigrant families highlights the importance of understanding meanings of concepts and behaviors from the cultural insider's perspective. To clarify the meaning of studies concluding that Chinese families were authoritarian with their children, Chao (1994) explored the meaning of authoritarian parenting in a sample of immigrant mothers from Taiwan. She hypothesized and found that Chinese parents may score high on concepts such as "authoritarian" because they emphasize a set standard of conduct; however, the intentions and behaviors of Chinese parents relate to the concepts of *chiao shun* ("training") and *guan* ("to govern"), which have very different connotations than the American usage of "authoritarian" with regard to the parent-child relationship. This study exemplifies the need to consider both parenting and outcome variables within their relevant cultural contexts.

The family structure variable most frequently used as a moderator is parents' marital status; levels may include intact, single-parent, remarried, or other configurations. B. L. Barber and Lyons (1994) found that parental permissiveness was positively related to adolescent self-esteem in remarried families but not in intact families. In a sample of African American families, R. Taylor, Casten, and Flickinger (1993) found that kinship support from outside the household was positively related to authoritative parenting and adolescent adjustment in one-parent, but not in two-parent homes. In addition, relationship qualities have been included as moderating variables. One line of research has demonstrated that emotional autonomy predicts adolescent adjustment differentially, depending on the quality of parent-adolescent affect; when the affect was positive, adjustment was predicted by lower autonomy, but when it was negative, adjustment was predicted by higher autonomy (Fuhrman & Holmbeck, 1995).

The inclusion of moderating variables in quantitative research designs is a significant advance over simpler main effects models. However, this approach also has its limitations. Even though differences as a result of the categories studied can be detected, the variables are still treated as categories, and more subtle nuances in the actual experience of gender, ethnicity, etc. are ignored.

In another set of studies, specific variables were found to mediate the connection between the independent variables under investigation and adolescent outcomes. This work frequently builds on prior studies that demonstrated relations between background variables and adolescent outcomes at a fairly global level; however, subsequent theoretical work suggested more detailed mediating variables or processes that could refine our understanding of the linkages. Work of this sort has been especially stimulated by interest in the possible mediating effects of perceptions and internal working models. This research is reviewed in more detail in the sections that follow on the development of emotional health and competent conduct in adolescents.

Identity

Although identity formation is widely recognized as an important developmental task of adolescence, the research literature on this topic is rather narrow. In much of this literature, correlational data have been used to speculate about antecedents or consequences of identity; furthermore, many of the studies connect identity variables with other self-reported personality or attitudinal variables from the same participants. There is little literature on *behavioral* correlates or consequences of identity. Thus, the literature is limited by common self-report method bias and by the predominance of one-shot, correlational designs. In addition, much of the literature is organized around the identity status construct and its four categories of identity achievement, moratorium, foreclosure, and diffusion; however, this construct has been more useful in elucidating individual differences than in tracing developmental patterns (for extensive reviews, see Bourne, 1978; Marcia, 1980; Marcia, Waterman, Matteson, Archer, & Orlofsky, 1993; Waterman, 1982).

Definition

The concept of identity has been used in many ways in the social sciences, including characterizations of cultures, groups, or individuals (see Bosma, Graafsma, Grotevant, & deLevita, 1994 for discussion). In developmental psychology, there are two primary uses: first, to refer to the distinctive combination of personality characteristics and social style by which one defines him- or herself and by which one is recognized by others. It represents the meshing of personality with historical and situational context. Second, identity refers to one's subjective sense of coherence of personality and continuity over time. Thus, the construct of identity stands at the interface of individual personality, social relationships, subjective awareness, and external context; it is a psychosocial construct (Erikson, 1968).

In most discussions, occupational choice is stressed as a key component of identity. In fact, Erikson (1950) pointed to work and ideology as the two central components of identity. Even when opportunity structures are restrictive (such as during periods of high unemployment or for groups that experience racial discrimination), identity is still important because it embodies a person's central values, definition of relationships with others, conceptualization of connection with his or her community, and view of the relation between self and the spiritual or transcendent.

Beginning in the late 1960s, research on identity was stimulated by Marcia's (1966) concept of identity status, which was developed to characterize four different resolutions of identity during the college years: identity achievement, moratorium, foreclosure, and diffusion. The concepts were grounded in Erikson's theory and differed with regard to whether the young person had experienced a crisis or not, and had made a commitment to a future or not. In subsequent work (e.g., Grotevant, Thorbecke, & Meyer, 1982; Matteson, 1977), the focus was shifted from the necessity of crisis to the process of exploration of alternatives. This work examined identity in the domains of occupation, religion, and political ideology, in keeping with Erikson's (1950) emphasis on the importance of work and ideology for human identity. Subsequent approaches to the empirical investigation of identity expanded the number of domains being investigated, especially by adding domains to tap interpersonal relationships (Grotevant et al., 1982); ethnicity (Phinney, 1989, 1990, 1993; Phinney & Rosenthal, 1992); and potential conflict between domains, such as between work and family (e.g., Archer, 1985). Josselson (1994, p. 166) expressed the importance of the relational perspective well: "Although identity is, in part, distinct, differentiated selfhood, it is also an integration of relational contexts which profoundly shape, bound and limit, but also create opportunities for the emergent identity."

Most of the domains of identity examined in the research literature were domains over which individuals have at least some degree of control: occupational choice, ideologies, values, relationships. However, there are other domains over which individuals have much less choice, such as gender, race, ethnicity, sexual orientation, and adoptive status. The importance of each of these domains for understanding of the self is documented in extensive, yet largely separate, literatures.

Several researchers also called for examining the domains separately because research had shown that a person could have differing degrees of exploration and commitment in different domains. The result was that the person's identity then became fragmented, and the compelling issues of organization, integration, continuity and consistency described by Erikson seemed lost.

The concept of identity is historically and culturally bound, similarly to the concept of adolescence. Historians, who more often consider collective identity (e.g., ethnic, religious, national identity) than personal identity, are now asking how certain groups are viewed by other groups and how such views affect individual personal identity (e.g., Mitzman, 1994). Questions also arise about the relative contribution of impersonal historical forces and individual choice to personal identity development, or how culturally accepted and defined notions such as "identity crisis" affect individual developmental trajectories (e.g., Neubauer, 1994). Interest in the concept of identity is related to the larger social, political, and economic structures present in contemporary Western society (Grotevant & Bosma, 1994). The concept itself also assumes the usefulness of the notion of a self; collectivistic cultures would put much more emphasis on the importance of community and connection. Whereas European and North American metaphors for the self typically include a theory, an onion, a dictator, a system of knowledge structures, and a computer, metaphors for the self in other cultures are quite different (Markus, 1995). In Asia, the self is regarded as a root that takes on the color of the soil in which it grows, or as a willow that is flexible and can bend (Markus, 1995).

American psychologists and educators from European American middle-class backgrounds have long considered autonomy and emancipation from parents as signs of adolescent maturity. They have also seen adolescent identity formation and career development as a process of exploration among a relatively unrestricted set of opportunities. More recently, scholars have been critical of this failure to address issues of gender, ethnicity, and restrictions in opportunities, including those in schooling and work (Cooper, Jackson, Azmitia, Lopez, & Dunbar, in press; Grotevant & Cooper, 1988, in press).

Developmental Course

Development of identity is a lifelong process characterized by cycles of exploration and consolidation. Although this task has its roots in childhood, it takes on new dimensions in adolescence because of the confluence of physical, cognitive, and social changes. Including notions of exploration and commitment in the construct of identity necessitates an interactional perspective because together they outline a process of dynamic attunement between individual and context. Thus, the possibility for reformulation of identity exists across the life span whenever individual or contextual changes occur (Graafsma, Bosma, Grotevant, & deLevita, 1994). Although most research in this field is focused on predicting developmental progress, work has begun to articulate patterns of regression (e.g., disequilibrium, rigidification, and disorganization), their precursors, and their developmental functions (Kroger, in press).

Several models have been formulated to specify the social-cognitive processes involved in identity formation. Grotevant (1987) proposed that identity exploration in any given domain had to consider the adolescent's individual characteristics, the identity processes within each domain of consideration (e.g., career choice), the contexts of development, and interdependencies among development in different identity domains. The identity process must first consider the adolescent's orientation and readiness to engage in exploration, then examine exactly what he or she does. (How is information sought? What is learned?) This exploration will produce both affective and cognitive outcomes: How did it feel to seek and obtain this information? what was learned? The new information is consolidated into one's evolving sense of identity. Once this new sense of oneself is evaluated, it can lead to an enhanced or decreased orientation to engage in further exploration. During late adolescence, exploration of possibilities for one's sense of identity is typical, at least in social niches that provide requisite opportunities; moreover, understanding of identity must consider how characteristics of individuals that are givens (e.g., gender, race, adoptive status, sexual orientation) contextualize those aspects over which adolescents and young adults have choice (Grotevant, 1992, 1993).

Berzonsky (1991, 1993; Berzonsky & Neimeyer, 1994) views identity development as a self-regulatory process across the life span in which the identity structure uses assimilatory and coping processes to deal with experiences and problems encountered in the world; at the same time, encounters that cannot be handled with existing strategies may lead to accommodation or change in the identity structure. Identity is viewed as a self-constructed theory of self, a cognitive framework through which meaning is constructed. Berzonsky has further distinguished among three broad types of self-theorists who use different strategies in dealing with identity formation: information-oriented, normative-oriented, and diffuse/avoidant ad hoc self-theorists.

Contexts of Identity Development

Many investigators have studied connections between contextual variation and identity-related outcomes. Although most of these studies examine family contexts, Kroger (1993b) reported that the historical and economic changes occurring between 1984 and 1990 in New Zealand, which constricted opportunities, were accompanied by higher numbers of female college students rated as identity foreclosed (high commitment with low exploration) and lower numbers of those rated as identity achievers (high commitment following high exploration) in 1990 than in 1984. This difference was observed for females only. Using evidence from intensive case studies, Kroger (1993a) also showed how foreclosed individuals sometimes limit their own life contexts, identity achievers stabilize their life contexts following exploration, and moratoriums expand their life contexts. This pair of studies demonstrates not only that opportunity structures place limits on identity development but also that individuals using different identity patterns can construct "personal contexts within their larger socio-historical milieu that differ quite markedly" (Kroger, 1993a, p. 159). Thus, the effects of changing economic and historical conditions can be mediated by individuals' constructed meanings of what is possible and appropriate for them to do.

Grotevant and Cooper's Family Process Project was designed to examine theoretically derived predictions linking family discourse with adolescent role-taking ability and identity exploration (Cooper, Grotevant, & Condon, 1983; Grotevant & Cooper, 1985, 1986, in press). In general, adolescents rated higher in identity exploration came from families in which they had opportunities to express and develop their own points of view in a supportive environment. Support was found for the significance of both individuality and connection of adolescents with their parents, in contrast to notions portraying adolescent autonomy as separation. Some differences were found as a function of both adolescent and parent gender. For example, adolescent males (high school seniors) rated higher in identity exploration showed assertiveness and separateness that was supported by their fathers' acknowledgment and willingness to let them step forward in the family decision-making task. Neither males' interactions with their mothers nor the marital interaction they observed between their parents were predictive of their identity exploration. Adolescent females rated higher in identity exploration experienced more challenges and less support from their mothers and fathers; more contention was also observed in their parents' marital interaction. Perhaps for sons, simple encouragement was all that was needed to support the assertiveness that they had associated with their masculine gender role expectations since childhood. Perhaps for daughters, some challenging or even abrasiveness on their parents' parts served to counteract the traditional feminine gender role pressures toward connection and away from assertiveness or conflict (Cooper & Grotevant, 1987). More generally, however, the study showed that adolescents scoring highest in identity exploration came from families in which they participated with at least one parent in interactions in which both individuality and connectedness exceeded the mean for the sample (Grotevant & Cooper, 1983).

Family therapy theories also influenced the work of others, including D. Bell and Bell (1983), who developed a theoretical model articulating how differentiated self-awareness in parents ultimately affects differentiated self-awareness and ego development of their adolescents by way of fostering accuracy in interpersonal perception within the family. Fullinwider-Bush and Jacobvitz (1993) tested theoretically based predictions concerning links between parent-adolescent relationships and identity development in college-age females. They assessed parent-daughter boundary dissolution, which involves parental reliance on the daughter for adultlike support and aid, even more than reliance on the spouse. They hypothesized and found that young adults who scored high on this measure had lower scores on measures of identity development and exploration, especially in the domain of interpersonal relationships. Furthermore, young women who came from families that were close but individuated scored higher on the identity development measures.

Work of Cooper and colleagues (e.g., Cooper, 1994, in press; Cooper, Jackson, Azmitia, & Lopez, in press) supports a view that the link between opportunity structures and identity development is mediated by close relationships. One feature of the economic opportunity structure is the "academic pipeline" through school to work, which has often been idealized as a smooth developmental pathway. Such a model may be particularly inappropriate for adolescents who encounter racial, economic, or political barriers to schooling and occupational choice. Educators are increasingly concerned that with each advancing cohort of students, the percentage of ethnic minority adolescents

shrinks. Ironically, parents often have high educational and professional aspirations for their children, but those with little formal education may lack specific knowledge about schools and the resources available through them. Families with histories of immigration or minority status may lose confidence that schooling is accessible or even beneficial to their children. For these reasons, youth and their families often benefit from others who can offer a bridge from the family to educational, occupational, and personal goals and resources (Cooper, Jackson, Azmitia, & Lopez, in press).

Cooper, Jackson, Azmitia, Lopez, and Dunbar (in press) built on Phelan, Davidson, and Cao's (1991) concept of multiple worlds to explore the experiences of Latino and African American junior high school, high school, and college students in northern California who participate in university programs designed to link students' worlds of families, peers, school, college, and work. Seeking to learn about the experiences of these youth, they adapted anthropological research methods to develop a new assessment instrument that did not make assumptions about family relationships, social contexts, or their interrelationships.

To learn about adolescents' social worlds, the research team conducted focus group interviews with each age group. When the students discussed and drew the worlds in their lives, including families, countries of origin, friends' homes, churches, mosques, academic outreach programs, shopping malls, video arcades, clubs, and sports, over half described more than one family world. They discussed and drew how some worlds fit together and others were in conflict or far apart, and how the academic outreach programs served as bridges across worlds. A number saw their schools and neighborhoods as worlds where people expected them to fail, become pregnant and leave school, or engage in delinquent activities. The outreach programs provided students with high academic expectations and moral goals to do "something good for your people," such as working in their communities and helping their siblings attend college.

In discussions related both to moving across worlds and from high school to college, two relationship patterns stood out. First, students experienced *gatekeeping* when teachers and counselors discouraged them from taking classes required for university admission or attempted to enroll them in noncollege tracks. Students also described *brokering* across these barriers when family members, program staff, teachers, and friends provided refuge from such experiences or spoke up for them at school. Staff in programs helped when parents were unable to persuade school officials, and conveyed their role as bridges between families and school as they told parents, "You can trust us with your kids."

In the context of these experiences, students developed a sense of their future by drawing on positive and negative role models and reflecting on their own role in helping themselves and causing themselves difficulties. They cited family and academically involved friends, the dropouts and arrests of peers and friends, and their own negative experiences as strengthening their determination to study hard to "prove the gatekeeper wrong." In addition, they anticipated working on behalf of their families and communities. As one Mexican American male high school student recounted:

> The most important experience for me did not even happen to me. It happened to my mother. She wanted to go to college and become a professional. She did not accomplish her dream because back then, women were born to be housewives, not professionals. Her parents did not pay for her education because of this. (Cooper, in press)

In a related strand of research, Hauser, Powers, and colleagues used a clearly defined theoretical framework to examine the relation between family interaction and ego development longitudinally during adolescence. Variables theoretically derived from psychodynamic theories (e.g., constraining or enabling in Stierlin's terms) and cognitive-developmental theory (e.g., cognitively stimulating or inhibiting moral development) were coded from detailed analyses of family discussions. This project has contributed much to our understanding about the nature of family interactions that predict ego development in both clinical and nonclinical adolescents (Hauser et al., 1987; Hauser, Powers, & Noam, 1991; Hauser et al., 1984; Powers, Hauser, Schwartz, Noam, & Jacobson, 1983). Four qualities of family interaction that facilitate ego development in adolescence stood out in Hauser's work: (a) enduring engagement with the adolescent ("hanging in"), even during the most difficult times; (b) parents' self-disclosure and sharing in appropriate ways; (c) tolerance of novelty, ambiguity, and uncertainty; and (d) tolerance of unwanted and unexpected emotions (Hauser et al., 1991).

How Experienced

According to Erikson, an optimal sense of identity "is experienced merely as a sense of psychosocial well-being. Its most obvious concomitants are a feeling of being at home in one's body, a sense of 'knowing where one is going,' and an inner assuredness of anticipated recognition from those who count" (1968, p. 165). In the process of development, such harmony is not likely to be experienced as a static form of congruence, but rather as an ongoing process of attunement between individual and environment (Graafsma et al., 1994).

To the degree that one accepts Erikson's argument that an important aspect of identity is continuity across past, present, and future, it makes sense that coming to terms with aspects of one's identity that are assigned rather than chosen would play an important role in the overall identity development process. How are these aspects integrated into one's overall identity; in what way is a coherent whole formed? How is this coherence experienced by the individual? A narrative approach is useful in order to understand how the different domains of identity are related to one another, and particularly how domains of identity that are assigned are related to those that are more freely chosen.

The narrative approach is receiving increasing attention within psychology, although its theoretical and methodological roots cross into other disciplines, especially linguistics, discourse analysis, and comparative literature. Narrative psychology is currently focusing on such phenomena as identity formation (e.g., Grotevant, 1992; McAdams, 1988), in which coherence of the life story is viewed as the benchmark for evaluating how well meaning and a sense of integrity are maintained over time (e.g., Polkinghorne, 1991). McAdams was one of the first to make the link between the narrative approach and identity: "The problem of identity is the problem of arriving at a life story that makes sense—provides unity and purpose—within a sociohistorical matrix that embodies a much larger story" (1988, p. 19).

The narrative approach is also being used by developmentalists who view reconstructed stories as keys to understanding current functioning. A central figure in this area is Mary Main, whose Adult Attachment Interview (Main & Goldwyn, 1985) is used to assess adults' internal working models (e.g., Bowlby, 1988) of their family of origin relationships with their parents. Another example of the use of the narrative approach is found in the work of Gottman and colleagues, who found that variables coded from an "Oral History Interview" conducted with married couples strongly predicted which couples would be divorced or still married 3 years later (Buehlman, Gottman, & Katz, 1992).

An important criterion for evaluating the quality of a narrative is *coherence,* which describes how well the story hangs together. Coherence addresses the issue of integration and provides a window for investigating how the different domains of identity are connected to one another. It focuses on the clarity of the representation of self-in-context that the adolescent has constructed.

The conceptual framework and methodological tools being used to understand narrative coherence stem from my involvement with the Family Story Collaborative Project (Fiese, Sameroff, Grotevant, Wamboldt, Dickstein, & Fravel, 1997). The overall goals of this collaboration have been to understand issues of continuity and discontinuity across generations, especially viewing continuity as a *constructed transactional process* rather than a *blueprint passed from one generation to the next.* This constructive process involves how families come to interpret other family members' behavior, how individuals interpret their own experiences in the family, and how adults in committed relationships bring forth processes from their families of origin. In research currently underway, we have hypothesized that coherence of identity mediates the link between family processes and mental health outcomes in adopted adolescents.

Importance

Identity development during adolescence is important because it serves as a foundation for adult psychosocial development and interpersonal relationships, and because difficulties in identity development have been associated with problematic behavior. Understanding the linkages between identity and behavior requires a developmental perspective. As mentioned earlier, identity development is an ongoing process with antecedents in childhood, dramatic change during adolescence, and the potential for ongoing change and adaptation through adulthood. Therefore, the question about identity-behavior linkages itself must be asked in a way that acknowledges the ongoing, dynamics of identity development rather than implies some fixed ending point to identity after which behavioral "outcomes" can be assessed. A process perspective on identity formation (Grotevant, 1987) acknowledges the potential for development throughout adolescence and adulthood, with periods of exploratory behavior yielding cognitive and affective consequences; resulting self-evaluation may then foster or inhibit further exploration. There is so little literature on behavioral correlates or consequences of identity that it can be reviewed briefly.

Two studies have examined relations between identity status and behavioral interaction with peers in college student samples. In the first (Slugoski, Marcia, & Koopman, 1984), young adult males in the "higher" status categories (achievement and moratorium) exhibited higher frequencies of "showing solidarity" and "releasing tension" and lower frequencies of "showing antagonism" than did participants in the "lower" identity status categories (foreclosure and diffusion). Identity achieved adolescents also showed higher frequencies of "asks for opinion" than participants in the other three groups, and foreclosed adolescents showed higher frequencies of "shows antagonism" than did other participants. In another cross-sectional study, undergraduate females were administered the Objective Measure of Ego Identity Status (OM-EIS) and then paired with a confederate in a task in which they could earn money for every piece of candy they could convince the confederate to eat (Read, Adams, & Dobson, 1984). Thirteen categories of social interaction were coded. Identity achieved participants used fewer frequencies of deception than did others, and foreclosed women used more manipulative behavior than did others. In both studies, it was concluded that the more mature identity statuses were associated with use of more mature interaction styles.

Jones (1992) examined links between identity status (assessed by the OM-EIS) and substance use in American 7th- to 12th-grade high school students. In all instances, identity diffused adolescents reported more frequent use of drugs than did adolescents in the other three identity statuses. Experience with marijuana for moratorium adolescents fell between that of foreclosed and diffused participants. Using the same sample, Christopherson, Jones, and Sales (1988) examined self-reported motivations for substance use. Achieved and moratorium adolescents more frequently cited curiosity as their reason for using drugs than did foreclosed and diffused agemates. Diffused adolescents cited motivations involving boredom and peers. In a related short-term longitudinal study with third and fourth graders, Jones and Hartmann (1988) found that students who increased use of illicit substances over a 5-month period had strikingly different patterns of scores on the Erikson Psychosocial Inventory Scale than did those whose use did not increase. Students who did not increase use had gains on all five Erikson stages (trust, autonomy, initiative, industry, and identity); those whose drug use increased had smaller gains on trust, autonomy, and initiative, and losses on industry and identity. "Hence, the fact that diffused adolescents report greater frequencies of substance use (Jones & Hartmann, 1988) is partially attributable to the fact that early involvement with substances may hamper successful resolution of the developmental tasks . . . necessary for healthy identity formation" (Jones, 1992, p. 229).

Identity moratorium status has sometimes been associated with problematic behavior. Hernandez and DiClemente (1992) found a relation between higher scores on identity moratorium and experience of sexual intercourse unprotected against the possibility of HIV infection in college students. Rotheram-Borus (1989) found that high-school age adolescents classified as moratorium reported higher numbers of behavior problems on Achenbach's Youth Self-Report, including higher scores on both internalizing and externalizing.

However, there are some contradictions about the relation between moratorium status and behavior in the literature. In contrast to the more problematic behavior previously described, adolescents rated as moratorium sometimes score higher in moral reasoning, are more internally directed, and are more reflective (although more anxious) than their peers (Marcia, 1980). In some studies, identity achievement and moratorium have been combined as "more advanced" statuses, and foreclosure and diffusion have been combined as "less advanced" (e.g., Marcia, 1980). The factor defining the difference involves exploration of alternatives. Because the moratorium status is characterized by exploration, it is likely that the behavior exhibited by such adolescents involves some risk-taking and experimentation. The research literature characterizing moratorium in both positive and problematic terms likely reflects the positive and problematic nature of adolescent experimentation.

Moratorium is also the least stable of the four identity statuses (Marcia et al., 1993). During late adolescence, the young person might pass through several identity statuses (Marcia, 1976; Waterman, 1982). Therefore, the relation between the variable under study and identity status might depend on when the "snapshot" was taken (Grotevant, 1983).

Finally, Grotevant and Cooper (1985) examined the concurrent link between identity exploration in high school seniors and communication observed in their families. Adolescents rated higher in exploration of alternatives for their future demonstrated higher frequencies of self-assertion and disagreements when interacting with their parents than did adolescents rated lower in exploration. In general, interaction within the family provided them with opportunities to express and develop their own points of view in a supportive and sometimes challenging environment.

These few studies demonstrate concrete linkages between adolescent identity and observed or self-reported behavior. Identity is not just an abstract construct; it is related to behavior in the daily lives of adolescents. The lack of longitudinal work limits our ability to know precisely how identity and behavior coevolve developmentally; future work of this type is needed.

Adjustment Outcomes

Selection of many of the outcome variables examined in adolescent research has been driven by the societal issues of the day rather than by theory. For example, the presence in the adolescent population of drug abuse, early pregnancy, sexual behavior potentially leading to AIDS, and other behaviors considered problematic and economically costly to society has stimulated funding from private and public sources aimed at understanding and reducing these problems. In earlier times, many of these behaviors were lumped under the rubric of "juvenile delinquency," an umbrella classification that also attracted funding and captured research attention. The focus on problematic outcomes was also reinforced by perceptions of adolescence as a troubled time, popular agonizing about the "generation gap," and theories that focused on adolescence as a time of conflict and separation. Given the greater availability of social science funding for studying problem areas than or studying healthy development, this trend is likely to continue.

Several conceptual and research issues are currently receiving significant attention in the clinical literature (Compas & Hammen, 1994; Petersen et al., 1993; Rutter & Garmezy, 1983):

- How accurate is it to conceptualize these issues in terms of a spectrum from health to pathology, or are there qualitative differences between the two?
- Are disorders defined in terms of dimensions, syndromes, or diagnostic categories?
- How is the developmental course of the disorder described in terms of onset and duration?
- What are the short-term and long-term prognoses for the condition?
- How responsive is the condition to psychotherapy, drug, or alternative treatment?

- Within the broad category of internalizing or externalizing disorders, how heterogeneous is the collection of specific disorders in terms of etiology, developmental course, prognosis, or treatment success?

Methodological issues and trends also provide context for understanding the research activity in this area. Self-report measures were widely criticized when behavioral models dominated American psychology (Robins, 1963). Questionnaires and interviews were considered untrustworthy because of the lack of correspondence between self-reports and observed behavior; problems with selective memory and reconstruction of the past distorted data gathered through interviews; and individuals' thoughts and feelings were generally considered less important than observable behavior. Ironically, self-report methods are now enjoying renewed popularity for some of the reasons for which they were earlier criticized. Current interest in social cognition has convinced some researchers of the value of understanding individuals' thoughts and feelings, regardless of how these are registered behaviorally. The ways in which individuals frame events and reconstruct their own pasts ("meaning making") are now considered important tools for understanding, even if these reconstructions are not completely faithful to history (e.g., Rosenwald & Ochberg, 1992). There is keen interest in the degree to which individuals' perceptions and cognitions mediate links between external influences and adjustment outcomes.

Despite the strong interest in problematic outcomes, it is probably fair to say that current research on adolescence is somewhat more balanced in terms of outcome foci than that conducted 20 years ago. Many studies address adolescent "adjustment," loosely conceptualized as a profile of strengths and problem areas.

Some research instruments that evaluate both competence and problems (e.g., the Achenbach Child Behavior Checklist, Achenbach, 1991a; Teacher Report Form, Achenbach, 1991b; and Youth Self Report, Achenbach, 1991c) are in widespread use in basic research, program evaluation research, and clinical assessment. This approach toward adjustment reflects the influence of frameworks such as developmental psychopathology, which strives to look at both adaptive and maladaptive outcomes. In fact, a large body of research stemming from this framework looks at the joint effects of risk and protective factors on positive and problematic outcomes. Thus, both the independent and dependent variables are now viewed in multivariate terms.

However, there are some potential problems inherent in lumping adolescent outcomes under the topic of "adjustment." First, this construct is not clearly defined. Some modest conclusions that can be drawn about the adjustment as a variable. Published intercorrelation tables suggested that, in general, indicators presumably measuring the positive end of adjustment were moderately correlated with one another, those presumably measuring the negative end were moderately correlated with one another, and the cross-correlations tended to be moderate and negative. None of the correlations was very large. Correlations between internalizing or externalizing problems and perceived competence and school performance were higher when teachers reported than when mothers did (Fuhrman & Holmbeck, 1995). Evidence is also reasonably consistent that internalizing and externalizing problems are positively correlated, whether viewed by parents, adolescents, or teachers (Capaldi, 1991; Fuhrman & Holmbeck, 1995).

The trend toward including evaluations of both positive and negative outcomes is a strength of the current literature. However, links between various independent variables and "adjustment" have been quite varied across studies, as have the definitions of variables included under this umbrella concept. Our understanding of adolescence will only be clear when more specific connections can be seen and comparability across samples and measures can be established. Thus, the next two sections describe outcomes related to emotional health and competent conduct.

Emotional Health

This section focuses on one broad dimension of adolescent adjustment that I refer to as "emotional health." It ranges from psychological well-being and feelings of self-worth, at one end, to internalizing disorders such as depression, suicidal ideation, and eating disorders, at the other.

What of the positive end of the "emotional health" dimension? Is emotional health the same as the absence of problems? The answer depends on whether one equates health with "optimal," "typical," or "without pathology" (see Walsh, 1993, for similar discussion of the meaning of "normal"). The literature is not organized in a way that facilitates good understanding of this end of the spectrum. Many studies are problem-focused, in part because funding related to the problems drives many research agendas and because the urgency of dealing with problems often takes precedence over a long-term strategy of enhancing strengths and preventing the problems from occurring. We also seem to have more and better measures of problems than of health. When measures of problems are used, health is often defined in terms of low scores on problem scales.

Self-esteem has been a widely studied indicator of emotional health in adolescents (see Harter, this volume, for an extensive review). Considerable research attention has been devoted to understanding contexts that facilitate or inhibit self-esteem, particularly for populations considered at risk.

Research focusing on self-esteem in early adolescent girls provided an opportunity to examine how differences in school structure might moderate the impact of pubertal timing on change in self-esteem in early adolescent females (Simmons, Blyth, Van Cleave, & Bush, 1979). The investigators compared self-esteem change over the transition from 6th to 7th grade in two groups: one group was in an elementary school that included kindergarten through eighth grades and in which the students did not move to a new building; the other group moved from the K-6 elementary school to the Grades 7–9 junior high school. The greatest decline in self-esteem was found for girls who had made three simultaneous transitions: they moved to junior high, they had reached menarche before many of their peers, and they had begun dating. Self-esteem change looked very different for girls who made the transition to seventh grade within the elementary school. The investigators identified positive and negative opportunities present in each setting that could account for the effects observed. For example, the early maturing girls in junior high who had begun dating were likely dating older boys, since most of their male agemates lagged behind them in physical maturity. Therefore, the ecology in which this transition was experienced involved many changes that could present challenges to self-esteem and self-confidence in these girls.

The problematic end of the emotional health dimension is often described in terms of internalizing disorders (Achenbach, 1985; Achenbach & Edelbrock, 1978; Rutter & Garmezy, 1983). Depression, eating disorders, and suicidal ideation have received significant research attention with respect to adolescents.

In the literature on depression, it has been necessary to distinguish between depressed mood, depressive syndromes, and depressive disorders (Petersen et al., 1993). Depressed mood refers to feelings of sadness or unhappiness, whereas depressive syndromes involve identification of statistically co-occurring symptoms that have been reliably reported and relate consistently to other problems such as somatic complaints, self-destructive tendencies,

and aggressive behavior (Petersen et al., 1993). Depressive disorders involve categorical diagnosis using a system such as the *DSM-IV*. Research findings using these three different definitions are not entirely consistent. Depression sometimes co-occurs with other disorders, including other internalizing problems such as anxiety or eating disorders as well as externalizing problems such as conduct disorders (Rhode, Lewinsohn, & Seeley, 1991).

In reviewing 30 studies of nonclinical adolescents, Petersen et al. (1993) concluded that 20% to 35% of boys and 25% to 40% of adolescent girls self-reported depressed mood. Girls consistently report more depressed affect than boys. Rates of clinical depression averaged 42% to 48% and 3% to 7% in clinical and nonclinical samples, respectively (Petersen et al., 1993). Epidemiological evidence with regard to racial or other group differences (except gender) is inconsistent; however, there is a suggestion that Native American and gay or lesbian youth may have higher rates of depression (Petersen et al., 1993).

Several possible developmental pathways culminating in depression during adolescence have been identified (Petersen et al., 1993). These may include environmental events that trigger "biological dysregulation;" the problematic confluence of an individual's vulnerabilities, life events, and coping resources; and a "shut-down" response to overwhelming stress. "Once on a depressed trajectory in development, an individual becomes more likely to stay on this course because of the tendency to both alienate and withdraw from the very social supports that can minimize negative effects. These effects are likely to be especially devastating to a developing adolescent" (Petersen et al., 1993, p. 161). Hammen (1992) has proposed a model of depression consistent with the developmental psychopathology framework that grants important roles to biological processes; cognitions; stressful life events; the individual's appraisal of life circumstances, internal working models of relationships, and interpersonal skills; and the responses of significant others to the individual's depression. Comprehensive models like this permit investigation of the ways in which biological, environmental, and cognitive factors interact to produce depression in contrast to prior approaches that focus on only one set of potential factors.

A number of investigators have examined familial predictors of adolescent depression. In one study, links between marital relationships and adolescent depression were hypothesized; however, the effects of marital conflict and cohesion were entirely mediated by the quality of parent-adolescent relationships (Cole & McPherson, 1993). In addition, conflict and cohesion experienced in the father-adolescent relationship were more strongly related to adolescent depression than were the same qualities in the mother-adolescent relationship. On the basis of these findings, the investigators emphasized the necessity of examining dyadic relationships separately within the family rather than masking possible differences with "family scores."

Similarly, Fauber, Forehand, Thomas, and Wierson (1990) found that the link between spousal conflict and adolescent internalizing problems was fully mediated by higher use of parental psychological control and by higher levels of rejection/withdrawal in the parent-adolescent relationship. Feldman, Fisher, and Seitel (1995), on the other hand, did not find marital effects fully mediated by parent-adolescent relationships. They found that mothers' marital satisfaction (when participants were adolescents) predicted young adult adaptation 6 years later, and these effects were only partially mediated by family closeness. Findings were also differentiated by parental dyad, supporting the call for separate dyadic analyses to be conducted.

B. L. Barber (1994) found that parental divorce predicted higher levels of depression among males and females in 12th grade. However, the effect was mediated by the presence of fathers' advice about educational, occupational, and family plans and by adolescents' satisfaction with the emotional support received from their fathers. The effect of family structure was no longer statistically significant when the advice and support variables were entered in the regression.

Although relationship representations are related to adjustment, this appeared true for relationships with parents but not for relationships with friends (Ryan, Stiller, & Lynch, 1994). Likewise, Cumsille and Epstein (1994) noted that family cohesion and social support were inversely related to adolescent depression in a clinical sample, but that social support from friends did not serve as a buffer against depression as it does in nonclinical families. The strongest predictor of depression was adolescents' dissatisfaction with cohesion and adaptability in their families, which underscores the importance of understanding adolescents' perceptions and meanings.

Higher levels of ego development were found to moderate the relation between early maturation and depression in girls: Early maturing girls with lower levels of ego development experienced more depressive symptoms than did early maturing agemates who had higher levels of ego development (Rierdan & Koff, 1993).

Our knowledge of the development of depression and other internalizing disorders is clouded for a number of reasons. "The fact that comorbidity appears to be the rule, rather than the exception, calls into question our very conceptualization of depression, as well as our understanding of its causes and consequences" (Compas & Hammen, 1994, p. 254). Even though depression covaries with some internalizing and externalizing problems, studies often do not involve full assessments of participants or look at the prediction of the "package" of problems an individual might be facing. More longitudinal research is also needed to examine sequences of depressive episodes and how depression covaries with other problems over time. Finally, we need to understand which risk factors are unique to depression and which overlap with other problems. Better understanding of these issues is necessary to make progress from either a prevention or an intervention perspective (Compas & Hammen, 1994).

Depression is one of several predictors of adolescent suicide, which is the third leading cause of death among 15- to 19-year-old American youth (Garland & Zigler, 1993). Public concern about suicide has risen because of the 200% increase in suicide rates among youth between 1960 and 1988.

> Risk factors associated with completed adolescent suicide include psychiatric illness, specifically conduct disorder and antisocial personality disorder, affective illnesses, substance abuse, eating disorders, and anxiety disorders; family history of suicide or other exposure to suicidal behavior; previous suicide attempt; and availability of a lethal suicide method. Suggested explanations for the increase in the adolescent suicide rate include increased substance abuse, increased use of firearms, increased psychosocial stress among adolescents, and a social imitation effect that may function by modeling the behavior or by lowering taboos against it. (Garland & Zigler, 1993, p. 174)

The research of Chandler and colleagues (Ball & Chandler, 1989; Chandler, 1994a, 1994b; Chandler & Ball, 1989) suggests linkages between suicide risk and narrative continuity. They developed a Continuity Assessment Procedure that requires adolescents to talk about themselves as they are currently and were 5 years ago, then to justify the conclusion that they are the same person despite all the changes their descriptions highlight. Comparing a psychiatrically hospitalized and a nonclinical sample, they found that adolescents at high risk for committing suicide were "at a complete loss as to how to justify the conclusion of their own or others' persistent identity across time" (p. 272). Such evidence reinforces the importance of understanding the role of identity in everyday life, which was discussed earlier. As Chandler (1994b) observed, "Even temporarily losing the narrative thread of one's personal persistence—a stitch easily dropped in the course of first knitting up one's identity—leaves adolescents especially vulnerable to a range of self-destructive impulses against which others remain better insulated" (p. 2).

Chandler is exploring how useful this approach might be in understanding the high rates of suicide among Canadian native youth, noting that the rate is far higher among adolescents trying to survive in the mainstream culture and lower for those in groups working to reconstitute their native culture (personal communication, December 18, 1995). Other literature supports the promise of this approach. The highest suicide rate in the United States is found among Native Americans (Berlin, 1987); however, "Less traditional tribes have higher rates of suicide than do more traditional tribes, which may offer a greater sense of belongingness and support to adolescents (Wyche, Obolensky, & Glood, 1990)" (Garland & Zigler, 1993, p. 171). Kvernmo and Heyerdahl (1994) conducted research with adolescents from the Sami (Laplander) indigenous group in Norway. Those who identified themselves as ethnic Samis had higher scores on "cultural pride," a measure of satisfaction with cultural background, than did those who identified themselves as bicultural or as belonging to the dominant Norwegian group. Although Kvernmo and Heyerdahl did not assess other more traditional psychological outcomes, it seems plausible to argue that cultural identity has protective value and can contribute to one's sense of narrative continuity.

Competent Conduct in School, Work, and Daily Life

We have explored the changing nature of social relationships, identity, and emotional health during adolescence. Interwoven among all these developmental outcomes is the question of what adolescents *do*. They spend many hours in school, many of them are employed full- or part-time, and they also get on with daily life in the contexts they inhabit. Adolescence involves the development of skills and competencies in all these domains in preparation for adulthood.

Competent conduct encompasses a broad set of adolescent outcomes, with the emphasis on social behavior. At one end, this spectrum includes contributing to society in a culturally appropriate way and demonstrating social competence and interpersonal skill. At the other end of the spectrum are the externalizing disorders, which include conduct disorders, delinquency, drug use, and sexual acting out. Complicating this picture is the difficulty sometimes inherent in distinguishing between competent and problematic behavior, because some risk-taking behavior is normal during adolescence "and may even be an essential component of a healthful adolescent experience and contribute to optimal competence" (Baumrind, 1987, p. 98). Ultimately, longitudinal studies are required to sort out which behaviors might have long-lasting negative consequences. In this section, we first focus on the competence end of the continuum, but to the degree that research designs often address problem behavior as well, they are also included along the way.

The longitudinal research of Diana Baumrind (e.g., 1975, 1991a, 1991b) has consistently focused on the development of instrumental competence (defined to include agency and social responsibility) in children and adolescents. A central purpose of this work has been to explore differences in parenting styles and their effects on developmental outcomes. With extensive data gathered by direct observation, questionnaires, and interviews, Baumrind (1971, 1991a, 1991b) used cluster and factor analytic techniques to identify three now well-known styles of parenting: authoritarian, authoritative, and permissive.

Although these qualities appear compatible with a unidirectional approach to socialization, they contain an important difference. In both authoritarian and permissive parenting, control in relationships moves primarily in one direction. In authoritarian parenting, it flows from parents to the child; in permissive parenting, it flows from the child to the parents. Both styles differ from authoritative parenting, which involves give-and-take between parents and children. Although parents are assumed to be the primary socializing agents, authoritative parents listen to their children, recognize their children's individual and developmental characteristics, and see parenting as a two-way process. Within this style of parenting, then, are the important elements of parental assertiveness and parental responsiveness, which have served as key ideas for subsequent researchers.

As Baumrind's longitudinal program of research has moved ahead in time, the categories of parenting have expanded to include authoritative, democratic, directive, good-enough, nondirective, and unengaged (Baumrind, 1991b). The general pattern of her findings remains consistent with her earlier work. Adolescents from authoritative and democratic families were found to be competent, resilient, optimistic, and not alienated. In contrast, the heaviest users of illicit drugs were found among adolescents from nondirective and unengaged families. Compared with their peers, adolescents from unengaged families were more antisocial, lacked self-regulation and social responsibility, demonstrated more internalizing and externalizing behavior problems, and rejected their parents as role models (Baumrind, 1991b).

Current research is also focusing on the embeddedness of family relationships within larger community contexts. Elder and Conger's (1996) research on rural families has shown that academic and peer success of adolescents are predicted by the strength of ties linking their family and community. Strong ties involved active engagement in social interactions with community members, knowing how things "worked" in the community, and opportunities for young people to witness their parents' active participation and then participate themselves in community affairs. Elder also noted the social redundancy in the lives of these adolescents, as there were multiple adults whom the young people could view as role models or turn to for information and advice.

As with the study of emotional health, studies examining competent conduct have evolved from main effects approaches to ones including moderating variables, among them gender, ethnicity, and parenting style or characteristics of the parent-adolescent relationship.

Although the issue of parental control in relationships with adolescents has been of interest in both psychological and sociological studies for many years (e.g., Maccoby & Martin, 1983; Rollins & Thomas, 1979, for reviews), several studies have tried to examine this construct in a more differentiated way. The possibility that psychological control and behavioral control are related differentially to adolescent outcomes has been a focus for Barber's survey research (e.g., B. K. Barber, 1992; B. K. Barber, Chadwick, & Oerter, 1992). Psychological control is defined in terms of patterns of family interaction that deal with the degree of psychological distance between parents and child; behavioral control deals with parental monitoring of adolescent behavior. In samples of 5th, 8th, and 10th graders, he found that problematic psychological control was associated with both internalizing and externalizing problems, and difficulty with behavioral control was associated with externalizing problems (B. K. Barber, 1996; B. K. Barber, Olsen, & Shagle, 1994). In a large study of 7th graders ($N = 851$), Kurdek and Fine (1994) also noted links between behavioral control (parental monitoring) and

problematic adjustment (which included low school grades, drug sampling, and externalizing behavior): "Whereas low levels of control tended to be associated with many self-regulation problems, both moderate and high levels of control tended to be associated with few self-regulation problems" (p. 1143).

Steinberg and colleagues (e.g., Steinberg, Lamborn, Darling, Mounts, & Dornbusch, 1994) found that parenting style (in their case, level of authoritative parenting perceived by the adolescent) moderates relations between features of adolescents' environments and developmental outcomes. They found that among adolescents in low and moderate authoritative homes, higher peer drug use was related to higher drug use in the participants; for adolescents in highly authoritative homes, this link did not hold (Mounts & Steinberg, 1995). One interpretation of these results is that authoritative rearing buffers adolescents against potentially negative models outside the home. Another study examined links between parental involvement in their adolescents' schooling and adolescent academic performance. They found that the correlation between parental school involvement and academic performance varied as a function of the level of parental authoritativeness, such that the link was stronger in more highly authoritative homes (Steinberg, Lamborn, Dornbusch, & Darling, 1992). They have proposed a model (see Figure 16.1) depicting the moderating role of parenting style in predicting adolescent outcomes:

> We hypothesize that parenting style moderates the influence of parenting practices on the child's development in at least two ways: by transforming the nature of the parent-child interaction, and thus moderating the specific practices' influence on child outcomes (Arrow 4), and by influencing the child's personality, especially the child's openness to parental influence (Arrow 5). This openness to socialization on the part of the child in turn moderates the association between parenting practices and child outcome (Arrow 6). (Darling & Steinberg, 1993, p. 493)

A number of studies have identified other protective factors that moderate the effect of risks on developmental outcomes. Jessor, Van den Bos, Vanderryn, Costa, and Turbin (1995) found that variables such as adolescents' intolerance of deviance and positive orientation toward school served as buffers between risk factors and adolescent problem behaviors such as drinking, drug use, early sexual behavior, and delinquency. This relationship held across four

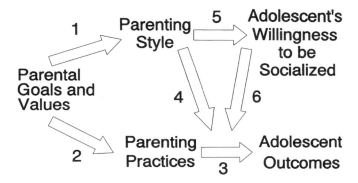

Figure 16.1 Contextual model of parenting style. Parenting goals for socialization influence both parenting style (Arrow 1) and parenting practices (Arrow 2). Parenting practices have a direct effect on specific child developmental outcomes (Arrow 3). In contrast, parenting style influences child development primarily through its moderating influence on the relationship between parenting practices and developmental outcomes (Arrow 4) and through its influence on the child's openness to parental socialization (Arrow 5). The child's openness to socialization also moderates the influence of parenting practice on the child's development (Arrow 6). From N. Darling and L. Steinberg (1993). "Parenting style as context: An integrative model." *Psychological Bulletin, 113,* pp. 487–496. Copyright © 1993 by the American Psychological Association. Reprinted with permission.

longitudinal waves of data collection (7th through 12th grade) and across gender and race of adolescent.

In a large representative sample of middle adolescents and their families, Barnes and Farrell (1992) found that lower levels of parental support and monitoring were important predictors of drinking, drug use, deviant acts, and school misconduct, even after other adolescents' age, race, gender, and family SES were taken into account. Adolescents with a family history of alcohol abuse and with high peer orientation also had increased risk of drinking, over the other predictors studied. Some gender interactions also emerged: Mothers' support had a stronger effect for girls than for boys; low parental monitoring and high peer orientation provided an added risk for deviance for boys but not girls. Similarly, in a short-term longitudinal study of risk and protective factors related to subsequent problem behavior during middle adolescence, stressful life events coupled with low family support were predictive of problem behaviors for girls but not for boys (Windle, 1992).

Physical settings have also been found to moderate effects on problem behavior. The sex composition of secondary schools was found to moderate the impact of menarcheal timing on female delinquency, such that early

maturing girls in mixed-sex settings were at greater risk for delinquency than were their peers in all-girl schools (Caspi, Lynam, Moffitt, & Silva, 1993).

Many behaviors widely considered problematic have been studied as dependent variables in the literature on adolescence. There are large, but not well-coordinated, literatures on all these problem behaviors or disorders, and understanding of these developmental outcomes is incomplete because of such fragmentation:

> Most of what we know about the predictors, correlates, and consequences of antisocial and CD [conduct disorder] behavior has been generated by studies focusing on relatively narrow domains of variables. Psychobiology studies tend not to measure attachment, neuropsychology studies tend not to assess parent disciplinary practices, attachment studies tend not to include assessments of neurological functioning, studies of social cognition tend not to assess psychobiology, and so on . . . . Progress toward a process-level understanding of antisocial behavior will require research designs and strategies that allow for the *simultaneous* consideration of multiple domains of variables within and outside the child. (Cicchetti & Richters, 1993, p. 342)

The literature on externalizing disorders is also problematic because diagnostic labels are reified as if they represent categorically distinct disorders without supportive evidence for this practice, co-occurring problems are discussed in terms of comorbidity without clear evidence that the disorders are conceptually distinct, aggressive and delinquent behaviors are often lumped together despite evidence that they are distinctive, and diagnostic criteria fail to take developmental differences into account (Achenbach, 1993).

Although few studies of adolescents have systematically included ethnic or racial membership as a moderating variable, one longitudinal project reporting data from children in kindergarten through third grade is important to consider and will provide baseline data as the children move into adolescence. Deater-Deckard, Dodge, Bates, and Pettit (1996) examined links between a number of risk factors ("harsh" parental discipline, as rated by an interviewer; being male; three or more stressful life events; living in a single-mother household; low socioeconomic status (SES); high parental conflict; peer rejection; and physical abuse) and externalizing behaviors. They found that the link between harsh parental discipline and externalizing child behavior was modified by ethnic group status, such that a linear positive correlation was found between harshness of physical discipline and later child aggressive behavior problems in White families but there was no relation between these variables in African American families. Further, the effects were not masked by SES or family structure differences, which were controlled in the study's design. The investigators speculate that the difference might have come about because of the different meanings of harsh discipline in the two groups. Further research underway by this team suggests that both parents and children interpret physical discipline differently in the two groups, and that the linkage between harsh discipline and behavior problems in White families is due to the negative meanings imputed to such discipline by both mothers and children. The researchers also noted that this interaction effect held only for discipline that was not considered physically abusive. Abuse was similarly related to externalizing for both White and African American children. These findings highlight the importance of understanding the embeddedness of both socialization practices and child behavior in cultural contexts of meaning.

Building on Maccoby and Martin's (1983) scheme that crossed dimensions of parental demandingness and parental responsiveness and Baumrind's (1971, 1991a, 1991b) classification of parenting styles, Steinberg and colleagues examined links between parental socialization (authoritarian, authoritative, neglectful, indulgent) and adolescent outcomes. Using data from approximately 4,100 adolescents, 14 to 18 years old, in an ethnically diverse sample, the investigators found that those who rated their parents high on dimensions subsequently coded as authoritative scored higher on measures of psychosocial competence and lower on measures of psychological and behavioral dysfunction (Lamborn, Mounts, Steinberg, & Dornbusch, 1991). The results did not vary by adolescents' age, gender, ethnicity, or family structure. In a longitudinal follow-up one year later, differences in adjustment associated with parenting were maintained or increased. "Whereas the benefits of authoritative parenting are largely in the maintenance of previous levels of high adjustment, the deleterious consequences of neglectful parenting continue to accumulate" (Steinberg et al., 1994, p. 754). These findings are consistent with those of Flannery, Vazsonyi, and Rowe (1996), who examined predictors of substance use among Caucasian and Hispanic early adolescents in the southwestern United States. For both groups, the best fitting model was one in which school adjustment mediated the link between parenting and adolescent adjustment, on the one hand, and drug use, on the other. Both illicit drug use and experimentation with

drugs were predicted by poor school adjustment, which had been predicted by a combination of low parental involvement and monitoring and adolescent depression, withdrawal, and aggression.

At follow-up, ethnicity did serve as a moderator of the connection between family process and adjustment in Steinberg's project. Steinberg et al. (1994) found that authoritative parenting was advantageous and neglectful parenting was disadvantageous for European American and Hispanic American youth. Authoritarian parenting was relatively more advantageous for Asian American adolescents and relatively more disadvantageous for European American adolescents. Parenting style was not related to academic competence in African American youth. Harmful effects of authoritarian rearing were not as severe among non-White youth. Despite these moderating effects, their overall conclusion was that authoritative rearing did not have harmful effects in any group, and neither neglectful nor disengaged parenting was desirable in any group.

The emergence of global characterizations of family climate or parenting style as important has led to substantial research activity designed to investigate mediating variables and to clarify microlevel family processes that mediate between more distal factors (or more global characterizations) and adolescent outcomes. Several studies have examined the possible role that adolescent personality might play in mediating adjustment outcomes. Feldman and Weinberger (1994) found that adolescent restraint (which was defined as a kind of personality variable involving internalization of standards) mediated the relationship between parenting measured in 6th grade and delinquent behavior assessed in 10th grade. Once restraint was entered in the prediction, the effect of parenting in 6th grade became nonsignificant. Another dispositional characteristic, "perceived opportunities," emerged as an important mediator and was a better predictor of young adult competence than were the family variables in the analysis (McCarthy, Bentler, & Newcomb, 1994). This latent variable, reporting adolescents' happiness with the future, happiness with schooling, and happiness with chances to be what you want, appears to tap something like "dispositional optimism" (e.g., Scheier & Carver, 1985), which involves a generalized expectancy for favorable outcomes.

Identity has also been implicated as an important mediating variable in several studies. Examining the relation between economic hardship and psychological well-being in a sample of eighth graders, DeHaan and MacDermid (in press) found that it was mediated by identity; economic hardship was negatively related to identity development, which was in turn positively related to psychological well-being. The direct link between economic hardship and well-being was nonsignificant. In research currently underway, Grotevant and McRoy are testing a mediational model concerning the relation between adoptive family relationships and adolescent adjustment, proposing that this connection is mediated by adolescent identity, which imputes meaning to one's family status.

Expectations and values have also been shown to mediate between problematic family relationships and deviant behavior in adolescence. In a sample of 100 high-risk middle adolescents, Allen, Leadbeater, and Aber (1990) inquired about how social strategies might work for them in a problem situation. Low self-efficacy expectations were especially associated with delinquent behavior and hard drug use for males; lack of identification with adult values was associated with unprotected sexual activity for females. Thus, adolescents' internal working models of self-in-relationships may mediate problematic outcomes.

A growing body of research is showing how the more proximal and immediate qualities of relationships or observed interactions mediate between qualities of macrosystems (e.g., economic resources) and adolescent adjustment. In Sampson and Laub's (1994) reanalysis of data from the classic study of delinquency conducted in Boston (Glueck & Glueck, 1950), they found that strong social controls within the family buffered against the negative effects of poverty on adolescent delinquency. Likewise, Felner et al. (1995), using an "ecological-mediational perspective," concluded that proximal environmental experiences (such as family climate, parent-child relationships, school climate, social support, and stressful events) mediate the effects of economic disadvantage on adjustment outcomes.

Detailed interpersonal process models are also adding to our understanding of adolescence. Patterson and colleagues at the Oregon Social Learning Center have contributed significantly to our understanding of developmental pathways toward antisocial behavior in children and adolescents (Capaldi, 1991, 1992; Capaldi & Patterson, 1994; Dishion, French, & Patterson, in press; Forgatch & Stoolmiller, 1994; Patterson, 1982; Patterson, DeBaryshe, & Ramsey, 1989; Patterson, Reid, & Dishion, 1992). Their program of work provides one example of how the complexity involved in externalizing disorders has been approached. One pattern they have identified (depicted in Figure 16.2) involves ineffective parenting practices and the contextual factors that may contribute to their use, which lead to conduct problems

in the child. This antisocial behavior then leads to academic failure and rejection by peers. By late childhood and early adolescence, this pattern leads to increased risk for depressed mood, involvement with peers who support continuation of the deviant behavior, initiation of new problem behavior, and heightened difficulty in interaction within the family. Such lifestyles then make it likely that the adolescent will have difficulties in school, in contact with the police, in holding a job, and with substance abuse. "Selection of an antisocial spouse could permanently cement the developing adult into a life of maladaptation through criminal behavior, incarceration, and ever more coercive family relationships" (Dishion et al., in press, p. 34).

Process models are now addressing diversity issues as well. For example, in working with a large African American sample of early adolescents (Grades 5–9), Connell, Spencer, and Aber (1994) found that disaffected behavior in low-income African American youth can lessen parents' involvement with them, which in turn creates or reinforces negative self-appraisal in the young people, leading to additional disaffected behavior and ultimately poorer school performance. Although this conclusion was based on cross-sectional data reported only by adolescents, it sets up a compelling and plausible model that can be tested with longitudinal and observational techniques.

Another study of African American young people (Brody et al., 1994) yielded evidence supporting a family process model of self-regulation. Reduced financial resources in the family led to parental depression and disruptions in caregiving, which were in turn related to reduced self-regulation in adolescents. Studies such as this provide valuable additions to the literature and go far beyond simple deficit models of poverty (poverty itself or the culture of poverty leads to dysfunction) to demonstrate the intervening processes that might be at work. Once the processes are understood, the possibilities for successful prevention and intervention programs are much greater.

What of the positive end of this "competent conduct" dimension?

From the existing literature, we could certainly suggest the kinds of environments where antisocial behavior would be extremely unlikely in children, adolescents, or adults; for example, a stable, loving family environment where parents teach their children cultural competence and effectively handle children's coercion and problem behaviors. Even under optimal family conditions, however, the absence of antisocial behavior could be guaranteed only if the family lived in a community with social and economic resources that explicitly

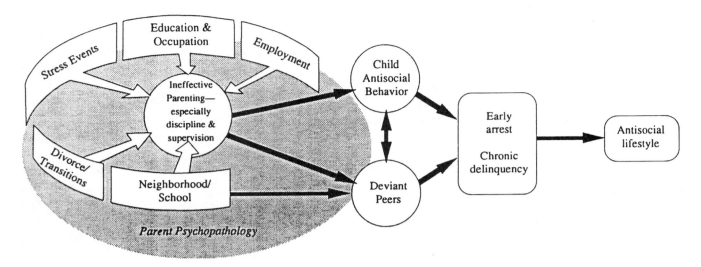

Figure 16.2 A mediational model for the association of family context and antisocial behavior. From D. M. Capaldi and G. R. Patterson. "Interrelated influences of contextual factors on antisocial behavior in childhood and adolescence for males" (1994) p. 168. In D. C. Fowles, P. Sutker, & S. H. Goodman (Eds.), *Progress in experimental psychopathy and antisocial personality: A developmental perspective,* pp. 165–198. New York: Springer. Copyright © 1994 by Springer Publishing Company, Inc., New York 10012. Used with permission.

supported the development of children and that espoused strong behavioral norms for prosocial as opposed to antisocial behavior. Unfortunately, current social structures do not often fit this warm picture. (Dishion et al., in press, p. 37)

EVALUATION AND SUMMARY

The Limitations of Conceptual Frameworks and Research Literature

Although the research literature on adolescent development in context has expanded rapidly in the past decade, its growth has been uneven and some ongoing research issues work against the cumulative impact that such research activity could have. In this section, I introduce seven criteria for evaluating conceptual frameworks used to study adolescent development and the research growing out of those frameworks. Following each criterion is a brief statement about how well it has been handled in the literature to date.

1. *The conceptual framework and resulting literature should be biopsychosocial: They should acknowledge biological influences, explicate psychological processes, and take into account both proximal social environments and the overlaying effects of cultural, historical, economic, and political forces.*

Although the conceptual writing about adolescence acknowledges the biopsychosocial nature of the period, research studies tend to be more circumscribed and do not often build systematically across the biological, psychological, and social spheres. The cumulative impact of the literature is also reduced to the extent that studies define "adjustment" or "competence" as overarching outcome variables without carefully specifying what components are included. Our knowledge of differential effects on specific outcomes is limited, as is our understanding of the intercorrelation among the set of variables considered under these larger umbrella concepts.

2. *The literature should acknowledge that adolescence is not necessarily one unitary stage, but that how adolescence is developmentally punctuated is socially constructed. For contemporary Western adolescents from backgrounds with adequate economic and political resources, subphases typically acknowledged within this developmental period are early adolescence (puberty–approximately age 13), middle adolescence (approximately ages 14–16), and late adolescence (approximately age 17 to adulthood). Explicit attention should be paid to the major transitions from childhood into adolescence and from adolescence into adulthood.*

Even though most researchers pay lip service to the need to differentiate between early, middle, and late adolescence, definitions of these periods vary across studies, even within culturally comparable groups. There is little literature suggesting how or whether this period should be divided for adolescents from non-Western or resource-poor contexts. Thus, reviewing the literature requires careful examination of sample descriptions rather than a glance at a title or an abstract. To further complicate matters, some investigators describe participants based on school grade level rather than chronological age. This is particularly troublesome because students in specific grades can vary in age and because differences between the American educational system and those outside the United States (as well as differences in alternative systems within the United States) make comparisons across studies difficult when the sample is described in terms of American school grades.

3. *The literature should deal with developmental continuities as well as discontinuities, both across the major developmental transitions and within adolescence proper.*

Although most research on adolescence is not longitudinal, there is a growing longitudinal literature. In addition, a number of highly visible studies that begin longitudinally with parents and their infants now have children who are adolescents. These studies will add considerably to our understanding of developmental continuities.

4. *The literature must acknowledge the transactional nature of development (e.g., the adolescent affects and is affected by his or her evolving context, which includes both physical settings and interpersonal relationships).*

Once again, conceptual writing acknowledges the transactional nature of development. However, many studies are cross-sectional and often draw unwarranted causal inferences from the data presented.

5. *The literature must explicitly acknowledge the contextualization of adolescence within race, class, gender, and historical time.*

Studies reviewed here that examined the possibility that contextual factors moderate links between process and outcome have already contributed to expanded understanding. However, these contextual variables are often treated as status variables or "social addresses," in Bronfenbrenner's

(1977) terms. For example, gender of adolescent and gender of parent are typically included in studies of adolescent development in family relationships. However, such practice assumes that there is more variation between genders than within each gender and that identifying someone by gender is more important than characterizing gender-related processes or enactments. The extensive literature about gender differences, gender roles, and gender effects notwithstanding, this study design may mask important differences within gender groups.

In much of the existing research on parent-adolescent relationships, samples have consisted of two-parent, Caucasian families. We know comparatively less about divorced families, families living in poverty, step or blended families, gay/lesbian families, and families of color. This situation is changing; a significant number of studies in progress and in the planning stages will incorporate more diverse families (see Spencer & Dornbusch, 1990, for a brief discussion of current research on parent-adolescent relationships in families of color).

Ethnicity and race are likewise problematic when used as moderating variables in quantitative studies. An obvious strength of doing so is that possible differences are examined. However, the current social debate about the meanings of race and ethnicity and the appropriateness of categories commonly used in the census and other databases makes it problematic to oversimplify such categories. The categorization of racial or ethnic groups is related not only to identity but also to enforcement of laws and funding for social programs (Wright, 1994). However, the broader social significance of race and ethnicity is that "they are linked to major differentials in socially organized access to opportunity, are institutionalized in stereotypical social definitions, and are inescapably implicated in adolescent self definitions" (Jessor, 1993, p. 119; see also Grotevant & Cooper, 1988, in press). Thus, researchers need to consider whether variables assessing the existence of prejudice, discrimination, or racism should be included in their research designs (García Coll et al., 1996).

The need for more sophisticated understanding of these issues is particularly acute if we wish to comprehend the experiences of adolescents who are different from the researchers who study them in terms of race, ethnicity, social class, or sexual orientation. Until very recently, the bulk of the literature on adolescence was produced by middle-class, White, heterosexual, American researchers studying adolescents who generally shared these attributes. As we approach the year 2000, both researchers and the young people they study are from more diverse backgrounds. The stage is set for us to have a much richer and deeper understanding of the processes involved in the second decade of life.

6. *The literature must be process-oriented; in this way, it will contribute knowledge to the "how" and "why" of development as well as the "what."*

Observational process-oriented work is demanding and expensive; the bulk of studies addressing issues of family structure, for example, divide samples into groups but ignore the considerable variation within groups of single-parent, remarried, and first-married families. However, it is neater to divide a research sample in this way than it is to specify the relevant processes that might differentiate among all families in ways that matter to our understanding of adolescent development. Nevertheless, there is a growing body of excellent work, which will contribute to a dynamic understanding of adolescent development. The work of Patterson and colleagues at the Oregon Social Learning Center, reviewed earlier, sets the standard.

7. *The conceptual frameworks should be flexible enough to include concepts and findings from various disciplines.*

The study of adolescence has always been inherently cross-disciplinary. However, concepts are defined within the cultures of the disciplines from which they come. Promising advances have been made toward this goal, especially with the creation of the Society for Research on Adolescence and the launch of several research journals cutting across disciplines specializing in adolescence.

Directions for the Future

I began this chapter by noting that adolescence is a social construction. Stating this implies that both the experience and the significance of this period in the life span vary as a function of the meanings imputed to them by cultural insiders. Thus, paying attention to issues of meaning is imperative if we wish to understand adolescence.

Yet the research literature has not yet dealt with meaning in a fully satisfying way. The early studies linking parents' attitudes and values with child outcomes were interested in meanings, but the attitudes tapped were often global and appeared to reveal more about what was socially desirable than about how attitudes were played out in families' lives.

The interaction literature improved on this by looking at what actually happened in families. In the more successful programs of research, behavioral categories were formulated in terms of the meanings attributed to them by investigators. However, no one asked the participants what their family dynamics meant to them. Larson and Richards (1994) brought into focus the divergent realities and meanings that members of the same family ascribe to the same situation. This work suggests that we researchers ignore the issue of meaning at our own peril.

In many of the studies of identity and adjustment reviewed in this chapter, designs called for the fitting of adolescents' responses on various measures into investigators' categories of meaning. We have not made sure that our realities fit with those of the adolescents themselves. To be sure, our theoretically derived constructs may neither be meaningful to individual adolescents nor even accessible to their conscious or cognitive processes. However, we probably have not listened carefully enough to what adolescents are saying in their own words to make sure our research lines up with their realities. This is particularly true with regard to adolescents and families from communities of color. Although some investigators are more actively including participants of color in research samples, such studies often employ the measures and constructs that are familiar; these may not fully tap the experience of families and adolescents from minority populations (Scott-Jones, 1996).

There are many good sources of information to draw on. There are scores of outstanding coming-of-age accounts represented in novels, plays, and films. Many, but not all of these, are told through the eyes of adults looking backward in time. Adolescents currently have many outlets for expressing their experiences, and scholars of adolescence would do well to become familiar with these "data." There is also a small but growing scientific literature that attempts to deal more directly with the realities of the persons we seek to understand. It rejects the positivistic notion that there is an objective reality "out there" for scientists to discover and instead calls for research that will allow scholars into the lived experiences of adolescents themselves.

CONCLUSION

The study of adolescent development has advanced tremendously in the past two decades. There is strong consensus that adolescence is best viewed as a social construction, triggered by primary changes involving physical maturation, social role redefinition, and the potential for cognitive change. However, the effects of these universally experienced changes can only be understood with respect to the multifaceted contexts in which adolescents exist. These include personal characteristics that involve individuals' alignments with belief systems, scripts, or daily patterns of living; interpersonal relationships and activity settings, such as relationships with family members and friends; and macrosystems, such as the culture, historical period, and political and economic systems in which young people live. Several conceptual frameworks, especially the developmental psychopathology and the close relationships models, are useful tools for mapping across continuities from childhood, the primary changes of adolescence, and contexts, to important developmental outcomes.

Even though today's research literature is much more extensive than it was two decades ago, it is also more tentative. First, the material reviewed for this chapter and the framework presented in Table 16.1 make it clear that an interdisciplinary orientation is essential to understand adolescence. Although we are perhaps closer to achieving this goal than ever before, much more remains to be accomplished. As long as journals and professional conferences cleave along disciplinary lines, success will continue to be elusive. And until this goal is accomplished, the literature will contain gaps and inconsistencies. Second, the study of adolescence has provided many examples of how conditional human development is on contexts operating at many levels. The grand paradigms positing universally applicable laws of behavior have given way to frameworks that focus on the points of interdependence between development and context. Thus, the literature appropriately reflects less an attitude of certainty than one of conditionality.

I conclude this chapter pondering the legacy that today's adult generation can leave for the adolescent generation that comes after it. One of the greatest gifts is a sense of hopefulness about the future and an instrumental orientation aimed at making the world a better place for all. Living conditions in many places around the world work mightily against this objective. Theories and the research literature supporting them consistently illustrate the toxic effects of poverty, hatred, and violence in homes, communities, and nations. Today's adolescents are tomorrow's adults; their expectations about possible futures and their internalized models of human relationships set the stage for how they will operate as adults and how they prepare the next generation. Although much research is yet to be done, we already know a great deal about the characteristics of contexts that contribute to optimal human development. It is our challenge to expand and apply this knowledge on behalf of the future.

Today's adolescents (and adolescents of most generations) also have significant assets and strengths, many of which are underrecognized and underutilized. Because they are not viewed as fully mature members of society, it is easy to discount their skills and their potential contributions. In addition to society's losing a rich source of untapped energy, "Underestimating teens' competence can mean misdiagnosing the sources of their risk behaviors, denying them deserved freedoms, and failing to provide needed assistance" (Quadrel, Fischoff, & Davis, 1993, p. 102).

The following statement, written over 50 years ago, is deceptively simple yet contains great wisdom concerning adolescent development in context. (References to "he" and "the adolescent" have been changed to the plural in order to make the statement gender inclusive).

> If the environment is such that adolescents can gradually be inducted into experiences for which they are prepared and with which they are able to cope, if they are allowed to assume responsibility and play mature roles when they are ready to do so, and if there is a real effort on the part of adults to accept their interests and, where possible, to meet their needs, adolescents will find their transitions into maturity relatively smooth and uncomplicated. (Horrocks, 1954, p. 700; cited in Weiner, 1970)

ACKNOWLEDGMENTS

Sincere thanks are extended to Lynn Heitritter and Nicole Ross, who assisted with gathering research materials; to W. Andrew Collins, Catherine R. Cooper, William Damon, Nancy Eisenberg, Ann O'Grady-Schneider, and James Youniss, who provided valuable feedback on earlier drafts; and to the many colleagues who sent me reprints and preprints. I also thank the graduate students in my seminar on adolescent development in families, Winter 1996, for stimulating and challenging discussions: William Allen, Susan Carlson, Patricia Herrington, Edward Kouneski, Ronit Leichtentritt, Ramona Oswald, Susan Pierce, Manfred van Dulmen, and Blong Xiong. I especially acknowledge the collaboration and colleagueship of Catherine R. Cooper and Ruth G. McRoy over two decades; my views of adolescent development, interdisciplinary work, and context have been greatly enriched through our relationships.

REFERENCES

Achenbach, T. M. (1985). Assessment of anxiety in children. In A. H. Tuma & J. Maser (Eds.), *Anxiety and the anxiety disorders* (pp. 707–734). Hillsdale, NJ: Erlbaum.

Achenbach, T. M. (1991a). *Manual for the child behavior checklist.* Burlington: University of Vermont Department of Psychiatry.

Achenbach, T. M. (1991b). *Manual for the teacher's report form and 1991 profile.* Burlington: University of Vermont Department of Psychiatry.

Achenbach, T. M. (1991c). *Manual for the youth self-report and 1991 profile.* Burlington: University of Vermont Department of Psychiatry.

Achenbach, T. M. (1993). Taxonomy and comorbidity of conduct problems: Evidence from empirically based approaches. *Development and Psychopathology, 5,* 51–64.

Achenbach, T. M., & Edelbrock, C. (1978). The classification of child psychopathology: A review and analysis of empirical efforts. *Psychological Bulletin, 85,* 1275–1301.

Adelson, J. (Ed.). (1980). *Handbook of adolescent psychology.* New York: Wiley.

Aldous, J. (1978). *Family careers: Developmental change in families.* New York: Wiley.

Allen, J. P., Leadbeater, B. J., & Aber, J. L. (1990). The relationship of adolescents' expectations and values to delinquency, hard drug use, and unprotected sexual intercourse. *Development and Psychopathology, 2,* 85–98.

Archer, S. L. (1985). Identity and the choice of social roles. In A. S. Waterman (Ed.), *Identity in adolescence: Processes and contents* (pp. 79–99). San Francisco: Jossey-Bass.

Atchley, R. (1975). The life course, age grading and age-linked demands for decision making. In N. Datan & L. Ginsberg (Eds.), *Life-span developmental psychology: Normative life crises* (pp. 261–278). New York: Academic Press.

Baldwin, A. L., Baldwin, C. P., Kasser, T., Zax, M., Sameroff, A., & Seifer, R. (1993). Contextual risk and resiliency during late adolescence. *Development and Psychopathology, 5,* 741–761.

Ball, L., & Chandler, M. (1989). Identity formation in suicidal and nonsuicidal youth: The role of self-continuity. *Development and Psychopathology, 1,* 257–275.

Baltes, P. B. (1968). Longitudinal and cross-sectional sequences in the study of age and generation effects. *Human Development, 11,* 145–171.

Baltes, P. B., Reese, H. W., & Nesselroade, J. R. (1977). *Life-span developmental psychology: Introduction to research methods.* Monterey, CA: Brooks/Cole.

Barber, B. K. (1992). Family, personality, and adolescent problem behaviors. *Journal of Marriage and the Family, 54,* 69–79.

Barber, B. K. (1996). Parental psychological control: Revisiting a neglected construct. *Child Development, 67,* 3296–3319.

Barber, B. K., Chadwick, B. A., & Oerter, R. (1992). Parental behaviors and adolescent self-esteem in the United States and Germany. *Journal of Marriage and the Family, 54,* 128–141.

Barber, B. K., Olsen, J. E., & Shagle, S. C. (1994). Associations between parental psychological and behavioral control and youth internalized and externalized behaviors. *Child Development, 65,* 1120–1136.

Barber, B. L. (1994). Support and advice from married and divorced fathers: Linkages to adolescent adjustment. *Family Relations, 43,* 433–438.

Barber, B. L., & Lyons, J. M. (1994). Family processes and adolescent adjustment in intact and remarried families. *Journal of Youth and Adolescence, 23,* 421–436.

Barker, R. G. (1968). *Ecological psychology.* Stanford, CA: Stanford University Press.

Barnes, G. M., & Farrell, M. P. (1992). Parental support and control as predictors of adolescent drinking, delinquency, and related problem behaviors. *Journal of Marriage and the Family, 54,* 763–776.

Baron, R. M., & Kenny, D. A. (1986). The moderator-mediator variable distinction in social psychological research: Conceptual, strategic, and statistical considerations. *Journal of Personality and Social Psychology, 51,* 1173–1182.

Baumrind, D. (1971). Current patterns of parental authority. *Developmental Psychology Monograph, 4*(1, Pt. 2), 1–103.

Baumrind, D. (1975). The contributions of the family to the development of competence in children. *Schizophrenia Bulletin, 14,* 12–37.

Baumrind, D. (1980). New directions in socialization research. *American Psychologist, 35,* 639–652.

Baumrind, D. (1987). A developmental perspective on adolescent risk taking in contemporary America. In C. E. Irwin, Jr. (Ed.), *Adolescent social behavior and health: New directions for child development* (Vol. 37). San Francisco: Jossey-Bass.

Baumrind, D. (1991a). Effective parenting during the early adolescent transition. In P. E. Cowan & E. M. Hetherington (Eds.), *Family transitions: Advances in family research* (Vol. 2, pp. 111–163). Hillsdale, NJ: Erlbaum.

Baumrind, D. (1991b). The influence of parenting style on adolescent competence and substance use. *Journal of Early Adolescence, 11,* 56–95.

Becker, W. C. (1964). Consequences of different kinds of parental discipline. In M. L. Hoffman & L. W. Hoffman (Eds.), *Review of child development research* (Vol. 1). New York: Russell-Sage Foundation.

Bell, D. C., & Bell, L. G. (1983). Parental validation and support in the development of adolescent daughters. In H. D. Grotevant & C. R. Cooper (Eds.), *Adolescent development in the family: New directions for child development* (pp. 27–42). San Francisco: Jossey-Bass.

Bell, R. Q. (1968). A reinterpretation of the direction of effects in studies of socialization. *Psychological Review, 75,* 81–95.

Bell, R. Q., & Harper, L. V. (1977). *Child effects on adults.* Hillsdale, NJ: Erlbaum.

Belsky, J. (1995). Expanding the ecology of human development: An evolutionary perspective. In P. Moen, G. H. Elder, & K. Luescher (Eds.), *Examining lives in context: Perspectives on the ecology of human development* (pp. 545–562). Washington, DC: American Psychological Association.

Berlin, I. N. (1987). Suicide among American Indian adolescents: An overview. *Suicide and Life-Threatening Behavior, 17,* 218–232.

Berzonsky, M. D. (1991, April). *A process view of identity formation and maintenance.* Paper presented at the meeting of the Society for Research in Child Development, Seattle, WA.

Berzonsky, M. D. (1993). A constructivist view of identity development: People as postpositivist self-theorists. In J. Kroger (Ed.), *Discussions on ego identity* (pp. 169–203). Hillsdale, NJ: Erlbaum.

Berzonsky, M. D., & Neimeyer, G. J. (1994). Ego identity status and identity processing orientation: The moderating role of commitment. *Journal of Research in Personality.*

Block, J. H. (1973). Conceptions of sex role: Some cross-cultural and longitudinal perspectives. *American Psychologist,* 512–526.

Blos, P. (1979). *The adolescent passage: Developmental issues.* New York: International University Press.

Bosma, H. A., Graafsma, T. L. G., Grotevant, H. D., & deLevita, D. J. (1994). *Identity and development: An interdisciplinary approach.* Thousand Oaks, CA: Sage.

Bourne, E. (1978). The state of research on ego identity: A review and appraisal. Part 1. *Journal of Youth and Adolescence, 7,* 223–252.

Bowlby, J. (1988). *A secure base: Parent-child attachment and healthy human development.* New York: Basic Books.

Brody, G. H., Stoneman, Z., Flor, D., McCrary, C., Hastings, L., & Conyers, O. (1994). Financial resources, parent psychological functioning, parent co-caregiving, and early adolescent competence in rural two-parent African-American families. *Child Development, 65,* 590–605.

Bronfenbrenner, U. (1977). Toward an experimental ecology of human development. *American Psychologist, 32,* 515–531.

Bronfenbrenner, U. (1979). *The ecology of human development.* Cambridge, MA: Harvard University Press.

Bronfenbrenner, U. (1988). Interacting systems in human development. Research paradigms: Present and future. In N. Bolger, A. Caspi, G. Downey, & M. Moorehouse (Eds.), *Persons in context: Developmental processes* (pp. 25–49). New York: Cambridge University Press.

Bronfenbrenner, U. (1989, April). *The developing ecology of human development: Paradigm lost or paradigm regained.* Paper presented at the meeting of the Society for Research in Child Development, Kansas City.

Bronfenbrenner, U. (1992). Ecological systems theory. In R. Vasta (Ed.), *Six theories of child development: Revised formulations and current issues.* London: Kingsley.

Bronfenbrenner, U. (1994). *Environments in developmental perspective: Theoretical and operational models.* Unpublished manuscript, Cornell University, Ithaca, NY.

Bronfenbrenner, U. (1995). Developmental ecology through space and time: A future perspective. In P. Moen, G. H. Elder, & K. Luescher (Eds.), *Examining lives in context: Perspectives on the ecology of human development* (pp. 619–647). Washington, DC: American Psychological Association.

Bronfenbrenner, U., & Crouter, A. C. (1983). The evolution of environmental models in developmental research. In P. H. Mussen (Series Ed.) & W. Kessen (Vol. Ed.), *Handbook of child psychology: Vol. 1, History, theory, and methods* (4th ed., pp. 357–414). New York: Wiley.

Brooks-Gunn, J. (1987). Pubertal processes and girls' psychological adaptation. In R. Lerner & T. T. Foch (Eds.), *Biological-psychosocial interactions in early adolescence: A life-span perspective* (pp. 123–153). Hillsdale, NJ: Erlbaum.

Brooks-Gunn, J., & Chase-Lansdale, P. L. (1994). Adolescent parenthood. In M. Bornstein (Ed.), *Handbook of parenting.* Hillsdale, NJ: Erlbaum.

Brooks-Gunn, J., & Furstenberg, F. F., Jr. (1989). Adolescent sexual behavior. *American Psychologist, 44,* 249–257.

Brooks-Gunn, J., & Paikoff, R. L. (1992). Changes in self-feelings during the transition towards adolescence. In H. McGurk (Eds.), *Childhood social development: Contemporary issues* (pp. 63–97). Hillsdale, NJ: Erlbaum.

Brooks-Gunn, J., & Paikoff, R. L. (1993). "Sex is a gamble, kissing is a game": Adolescent sexuality and health promotion. In S. P. Millstein, A. C. Petersen, & E. O. Nightingale (Eds.), *Promoting the health of adolescents: New directions for the twenty-first century* (pp. 180–208). New York: Oxford University Press.

Brooks-Gunn, J., Petersen, A. C., & Eichorn, D. (1985). The study of maturational timing effects in adolescence [Special issue]. *Journal of Youth and Adolescence, 14 (3/4).*

Brooks-Gunn, J., & Reiter, E. O. (1990). The role of pubertal processes. In S. S. Feldman & G. R. Elliott (Eds.), *At the threshold: The developing adolescent* (pp. 16–53). Cambridge, MA: Harvard University Press.

Brown, B. B., Mory, M. S., & Kinney, D. (1994). Casting adolescent crowds in a relational perspective: Caricature, channel, and context. In R. Montemayor, G. R. Adams, & T. P. Gullotta (Eds.), *Advances in adolescent development: Vol. 6. Personal relationships during adolescence* (pp. 123–167). Thousand Oaks, CA: Sage.

Buehlman, K. T., Gottman, J. M., & Katz, L. F. (1992). How a couple views their past predicts their future: Predicting divorce from an oral history interview. *Journal of Family Psychology, 5,* 295–318.

Burton, L. M. (1991). Caring for children. *The American Enterprise, 2*(3), 34–37.

Burton, L. M., Allison, K. W., & Obeidallah, D. (1995). Social context and adolescence: Perspectives on development among inner-city African-American teens. In L. J. Crockett & A. C. Crouter (Eds.), *Pathways through adolescence: Individual development in relation to social contexts* (pp. 119–138). Mahwah, NJ: Erlbaum.

Bush, D. M., & Simmons, R. G. (1990). Socialization processes over the life course. In M. Rosenberg & R. H. Turner (Eds.), *Social psychology: Sociological perspectives* (pp. 133–164). New Brunswick, NJ: Transaction.

Capaldi, D. M. (1991). Co-occurrence of conduct problems and depressive symptoms in early adolescent boys: I. Familial factors and general adjustment at grade 6. *Development and Psychopathology, 3,* 277–300.

Capaldi, D. M. (1992). Co-occurrence of conduct problems and depressive symptoms in early adolescent boys: II. A 2-year follow-up at grade 8. *Development and Psychopathology, 4,* 125–144.

Capaldi, D. M., & Patterson, G. R. (1994). Interrelated influences of contextual factors on antisocial behavior in childhood and adolescence for males. In D. C. Fowles, P. Sutker, & S. H. Goodman (Eds.), *Progress in experimental personality and psychopathology research 1994: Special focus on psychopathy and antisocial personality: A developmental perspective* (pp. 165–198). New York: Springer.

Caplan, R. D., & Harrison, R. V. (1993). Person-environment fit theory: Some history, recent developments, and future directions. *Journal of Social Issues, 49,* 253–275.

Carlson, C. I., Cooper, C. R., & Frank, C. (1987, June). *A comparison of the family processes in single parent and intact early adolescent family systems using sequential analysis.* Paper presented at the Family Research Consortium second annual summer institute, Santa Fe, NM.

Carter, E. A., & McGoldrick, M. (1980). *The family life cycle: A framework for family therapy.* New York: Gardner Press.

Caspi, A., Lynam, D., Moffitt, T. E., & Silva, P. A. (1993). Unraveling girls' delinquency: Biological, dispositional, and contextual contributions to adolescent misbehavior. *Developmental Psychology, 29,* 19–30.

Chandler, M. J. (1994a). Adolescent suicide and the loss of personal continuity. In D. Cicchetti & S. L. Toth (Eds.), *Rochester Symposium on Developmental Psychopathology: Disorders and dysfunctions of the self* (pp. 371–390). Rochester, NY: University of Rochester Press.

Chandler, M. J. (1994b). Self-continuity in suicidal and nonsuicidal adolescents. In G. Noam & S. Borst (Eds.), *Children, youth, and suicide: Developmental perspectives* (pp. 55–70). San Francisco: Jossey-Bass.

Chandler, M. J., & Ball, L. (1989). Continuity and commitment: A developmental analysis of identity formation process in suicidal and non-suicidal youth. In H. Bosma & S. Jackson (Eds.), *Coping and self-concept in adolescence.* Heidelberg: Springer-Verlag.

Chao, R. K. (1994). Beyond parental control and authoritarian parenting style: Understanding Chinese parenting through the cultural notion of training. *Child Development, 65,* 1111–1119.

Christopherson, B. B., Jones, R. M., & Sales, A. P. (1988). Diversity in reported motivations for substance use as a function of ego-identity development. *Journal of Adolescent Research, 3,* 141–152.

Cicchetti, D. (1990). Perspectives on the interface between normal and atypical development. *Development and Psychopathology, 2,* 329–333.

Cicchetti, D., & Richters, J. E. (1993). Developmental considerations in the investigation of conduct disorder. *Development and Psychopathology, 5,* 331–344.

Cicchetti, D., & Schneider-Rosen, K. (1984). Toward a transactional model of childhood depression. In D. Cicchetti & K. Schneider-Rosen (Eds.), *Childhood depression: New directions for child development* (Vol. 26, pp. 5–27). San Francisco: Jossey-Bass.

Cole, D. A., & McPherson, A. E. (1993). Relation of family subsystems to adolescent depression: Implementing a new family assessment strategy. *Journal of Family Psychology, 7,* 119–133.

Collins, W. A. (1990). Parent-child relationships in the transition to adolescence: Continuity and change in interaction, affect, and cognition. In R. Montemayor, G. R. Adams, & T. P. Gullotta (Eds.), *From childhood to adolescence* (pp. 103–110). Newbury Park, CA: Sage.

Collins, W. A. (1991). Shared views and parent-adolescent relationships. In R. L. Paikoff (Ed.), *Shared views in the family during adolescence: New directions for child development* (Vol. 51, pp. 103–110). San Francisco: Jossey-Bass.

Collins, W. A. (1997). Relationships and development during adolescence: Interpersonal adaptation to individual change. *Personal Relationships, 4,* 1–14.

Collins, W. A., Laursen, B., Mortensen, N., Luebker, C., & Ferreira, M. (1997). Conflict processes and transitions in parent and peer relationships: Implications for autonomy and regulation. *Journal of Adolescent Research, 12,* 178–198.

Collins, W. A., & Repinski, D. J. (1994). Relationships during adolescence: Continuity and change in interpersonal perspective. In R. Montemayor, G. R. Adams, & T. P. Gullotta (Eds.), *Advances in adolescent development: Vol. 6. Personal relationships during adolescence* (pp. 7–36). Thousand Oaks, CA: Sage.

Collins, W. A., & Russell, G. (1991). Mother-child and father-child relationships in middle childhood and adolescence: A developmental analysis. *Developmental Review, 11,* 99–136.

Compas, B. E., & Hammen, C. L. (1994). Child and adolescent depression: Covariation and comorbidity in development. In R. J. Haggerty, L. R. Sherrod, N. Garmezy, & M. Rutter (Eds.), *Stress, risk, and resilience in children and adolescents: Processes, mechanisms, and interventions* (pp. 225–267). Cambridge, England: Cambridge University Press.

Conger, J., & Petersen, A. (1984). *Adolescence and youth: Psychological development in a changing world.* New York: Harper & Row.

Connell, J. P., Spencer, M. B., & Aber, J. L. (1994). Educational risk and resilience in African-American youth: Context, self, action, and outcomes in school. *Child Development, 65,* 493–506.

Cooper, C. R. (1994). Cultural perspectives on continuity and change in adolescents' relationships. In R. Montemayor, G. R. Adams, & T. P. Gulotta (Eds.), *Advances in adolescent development: Vol. 6. Personal relationships during adolescence* (pp. 78–100). Newbury Park, CA: Sage.

Cooper, C. R. (in press-a). Cultural perspectives on individuality and connectedness in adolescent development. In C. Nelson & A. Masten (Eds.), *Minnesota Symposium on Child Psychology: Culture and development.* Hillsdale, NJ: Erlbaum.

Cooper, C. R. (in press-b). *The weaving of maturity: Cultural perspectives on adolescent development.* New York: Oxford University Press.

Cooper, C. R., Baker, H., Polichar, D., & Welsh, M. (1991, July). *Ethnic perspectives on individuality and connectedness in adolescents' relationships with families and peers.* Paper presented at the meetings of the International Society for the Study of Behavioral Development, Minneapolis, MN.

Cooper, C. R., Baker, H., Polichar, D., & Welsh, M. (1994). Values and communication of Chinese, European, Filipino, Mexican, and Vietnamese American adolescents with their families and friends. In S. Shulman & W. A. Collins (Eds.), *The role of fathers in adolescent development: New directions in child development* (pp. 73–89). San Francisco: Jossey-Bass.

Cooper, C. R., & Cooper, R. G. (1992). Links between adolescents' relationships with their parents and peers: Models,

evidence, and mechanisms. In R. D. Parke & G. W. Ladd (Eds.), *Family-peer relationships: Modes of linkages* (pp. 135–158). Hillsdale, NJ: Erlbaum.

Cooper, C. R., & Grotevant, H. D. (1987). Gender issues in the interface of family experience and adolescent peer relational identity. *Journal of Youth and Adolescence, 16,* 247–264.

Cooper, C. R., Grotevant, H. D., & Condon, S. L. (1983). Individuality and connectedness in the family as a context for adolescent identity formation and role-taking skill. In H. D. Grotevant & C. R. Cooper (Eds.), *Adolescent development in the family: New directions in child development* (Vol. 22, pp. 43–59). San Francisco: Jossey-Bass.

Cooper, C. R., Jackson, J. F., Azmitia, M., & Lopez, E. M. (in press). Multiple selves, multiple worlds: Ethnically sensitive research on identity, relationships, and opportunity structures in adolescence. In V. McLoyd & L. Steinberg (Eds.), *Conceptual and methodological issues in the study of minority adolescents and their families.* Hillsdale, NJ: Erlbaum.

Cooper, C. R., Jackson, J. F., Azmitia, M., Lopez, E. M., & Dunbar, N. (in press). Bridging students' multiple worlds: African American and Latino youth in academic outreach programs. In R. F. Macias & R. G. G. Ramos (Eds.), *Changing schools for changing students: An anthology of research on language minorities.* Santa Barbara: University of California Linguistic Minority Research Institute.

Côté, J. E. (1994). *Adolescent storm and stress: An evaluation of the Mead-Freeman controversy,* Hillsdale, NJ: Erlbaum.

Crockett, L. J., & Crouter, A. C. (Eds.). (1995). *Pathways through adolescence: Individual development in relation to social contexts.* Mahwah, NJ: Erlbaum.

Csikszentmihalyi, M., & Larson, R. (1987). The experience sampling method. *Journal of Nervous and Mental Disease, 175,* 526–536.

Cumsille, P. E., & Epstein, N. (1994). Family cohesion, family adaptability, social support, and adolescent depressive symptoms in outpatient clinic families. *Journal of Family Psychology, 8,* 202–214.

Darling, N., & Steinberg, L. (1993). Parenting style as context: An integrative model. *Psychological Bulletin, 113,* 487–496.

D'Augelli, A. R., & Patterson, C. J. (Eds.). (1995). *Lesbian, gay, and bisexual identities over the lifespan: Psychological perspectives.* New York: Oxford University Press.

Deater-Deckard, K. D., Dodge, K. A., Bates, J. E., & Pettit, G. S. (1996). Risk factors for the development of externalizing behavior problems: Are there ethnic group differences in process? *Developmental Psychology, 32,* 1065–1072.

DeHaan, L. G., & MacDermid, S. (in press). Individual and family factors relating to psychological well-being for junior high students living in urban poverty. *Adolescence.*

deJong Gierveld, J., Liefbroer, A. C., & Beekink, E. (1990). *The effect of parental resources on patterns of leaving home among young adults in the Netherlands.* Paper presented at the meeting of the International Society for the Study of Personal Relationships, Oxford, England.

Detzner, D. F. (1995). *Bicultural parent education curriculum for Southeast Asian families.* Unpublished grant application, University of Minnesota, Minneapolis.

Dilworth-Anderson, P., Burton, L. M., & Boulin Johnson, L. (1993). Reframing theories for understanding race, ethnicity, and families. In P. G. Boss, W. J. Doherty, R. LaRossa, W. R. Schumm, & S. K. Steinmetz (Eds.), *Sourcebook of family theories and methods: A contextual approach* (pp. 627–645). New York: Plenum Press.

Dishion, T. J., French, D. C., & Patterson, G. R. (in press). The development and ecology of antisocial behavior. In D. Cicchetti & D. Cohen (Eds.), *Manual of developmental psychopathology.* New York: Cambridge University Press.

Douvan, E., & Adelson, J. (1966). *The adolescent experience.* New York: Wiley.

Eccles, J. S., & Midgley, C. (1989). Stage/environment fit: Developmentally appropriate classrooms for early adolescents. In R. E. Ames & C. Ames (Eds.), *Research on motivation in education* (Vol. 3, pp. 139–186). San Diego, CA: Academic Press.

Eccles, J. S., Midgley, C., Wigfield, A., Buchanan, C. M., Reuman, D., Flanagan, C., & MacIver, D. (1993). Development during adolescence: The impact of stage-environment fit on young adolescents' experiences in schools and in families. *American Psychologist, 48,* 90–101.

Egeland, B., Carlson, E., & Sroufe, L. A. (1993). Resilience as process. *Development and Psychopathology, 5,* 517–528.

Elder, G. H., Jr. (1995). The life course paradigm: Social change and individual development. In P. Moen, G. H. Elder, & K. Luescher (Eds.), *Examining lives in context: Perspectives on the ecology of human development* (pp. 101–140). Washington, DC: American Psychological Association.

Elder, G. H., Jr., Caspi, A., & Burton, L. M. (1988). Adolescent transition in developmental perspective: Sociological and historical insights. In M. R. Gunnar & W. A. Collins (Eds.), *Development during the transition to adolescence: The Minnesota Symposia on Child Psychology* (Vol. 21, pp. 151–179). Hillsdale, NJ: Erlbaum.

Elder, G. H., Jr., & Conger, R. D. (1996, March). New worlds, new lives: The legacy of ties to the land. In J. Eccles (Organizer), *Successful adolescent development: Reports from a MacArthur Network.* Symposium presented at the meeting of the Society for Research on Adolescence, Boston.

Erikson, E. H. (1950). *Childhood and society.* New York: Norton.

Erikson, E. H. (1968). *Identity: Youth and crisis.* New York: Norton.

Fauber, R., Forehand, R., Thomas, A. M., & Wierson, M. (1990). A mediational model of the impact of marital conflict on adolescent adjustment in intact and divorced families: The role of disrupted parenting. *Child Development, 61,* 1112–1123.

Feldman, S. S., & Elliott, G. R. (1990). *At the threshhold: The developing adolescent.* Cambridge, MA: Harvard University Press.

Feldman, S. S., Fisher, L., & Seitel, L. (1995). *The effect of parents' marital satisfaction on young adults' adaptation: A longitudinal study.* Manuscript submitted for publication.

Feldman, S. S., & Weinberger, D. A. (1994). Self-restraint as a mediator of family influences on boys' delinquent behavior: A longitudinal study. *Child Development, 65,* 195–211.

Felner, R. D., Brand, S., DuBois, D. L., Adan, A. M., Mulhall, P. F., & Evans, E. G. (1995). Socioeconomic disadvantage, proximal environmental experiences, and socioemotional and academic adjustment in early adolescence: Investigation of a mediated effects model. *Child Development, 66,* 774–792.

Fiese, B. H., Sameroff, A. J., Grotevant, H. D., Wamboldt, F. S., Dickstein, S., & Fravel, D. L. (1997). *The stories that families tell: Narrative coherence, narrative style, and relationship beliefs.* Manuscript submitted for publication.

Flannery, D. J., Vazsonyi, A. T., & Rowe, D. C. (1996). Caucasian and Hispanic early adolescent substance use: Parenting, personality, and school adjustment. *Journal of Early Adolescence, 16,* 71–89.

Forgatch, M. S., & Stoolmiller, M. (1994). Emotions as contexts for adolescent delinquency. *Journal of Research on Adolescence, 4,* 601–614.

Frank, S. J., Avery, C. B., & Laman, M. S. (1988). Young adults' perceptions of their relationships with their parents: Individual differences in connectedness, competence, and emotional autonomy. *Developmental Psychology, 24,* 729–737.

Freeman, D. (1983). *Margaret Mead and Samoa: The making and unmaking of an anthropological myth.* Cambridge, MA: Harvard University Press.

Freud, S. (1938). *An outline of psychoanalysis.* London: Hogarth.

Friedenberg, E. Z. (1959). *The vanishing adolescent.* New York: Dell.

Friedenberg, E. Z. (1963). *Coming of age in America: Growth and acquiescence.* New York: Vintage Books.

Fuhrman, T., & Holmbeck, G. N. (1995). A contextual-moderator analysis of emotional autonomy and adjustment in adolescence. *Child Development, 66,* 793–811.

Fuligni, A. J., Eccles, J. S., & Barber, B. L. (1995). The long-term effects of seventh-grade ability grouping in mathematics. *Journal of Early Adolescence, 15,* 58–70.

Fullinwider-Bush, N., & Jacobvitz, D. B. (1993). The transition to young adulthood: Generational boundary dissolution and female identity development. *Family Process, 32,* 87–103.

Furstenberg, F. F., Jr., Brooks-Gunn, J., & Chase-Lansdale, L. (1989). Teenaged pregnancy and childbearing. *American Psychologist, 44,* 313–320.

García Coll, C., Lamberty, G., Jenkins, R., McAdoo, H. P., Crnic, K., Wasik, B. H., & García, H. V. (1996). An integrative model for the study of developmental competencies in minority children. *Child Development, 67,* 1891–1914.

Garland, A. F., & Zigler, E. (1993). Adolescent suicide prevention: Current research and social policy implications. *American Psychologist, 48,* 169–182.

Gecas, V., & Seff, M. A. (1990). Families and adolescents: A review of the 1980s. *Journal of Marriage and the Family, 52,* 941–958.

Gjerde, P. F. (1986). The interpersonal structure of family interaction settings: Parent-adolescent relations in dyads and triads. *Developmental Psychology, 22,* 297–304.

Glueck, S., & Glueck, E. (1950). *Unraveling juvenile delinquency.* New York: Commonwealth Fund.

Goodman, P. (1956). *Growing up absurd: Problems of youth in the organized society.* New York: Vintage Books.

Goodnow, J. (1994, July). *Concepts of "context."* Paper presented at the meeting of the International Society for the Study of Behavioural Development, Amsterdam, The Netherlands.

Goodnow, J. (1995). Differentiating among social contexts: By spatial features, forms of participation, and social contracts. In P. Moen, G. H. Elder, & K. Luescher (Eds.), *Examining lives in context: Perspectives on the ecology of human development* (pp. 269–301). Washington, DC: American Psychological Association.

Gould, R. L. (1978). *Transformations: Growth and change in adult life.* New York: Simon & Schuster.

Graafsma, T. L. G., Bosma, H. A., Grotevant, H. D., & deLevita, D. J. (1994). Identity and development: An interdisciplinary view. In H. A. Bosma, T. L. G. Graafsma, H. D. Grotevant, & D. J. deLevita (Eds.), *Identity and development: An interdisciplinary approach* (pp. 159–174). Thousand Oaks, CA: Sage.

Graber, J. A., & Brooks-Gunn, J. (in press). Reproductive transitions: The experience of mothers and daughters. In C. D. Ryff & M. M. Seltzer (Eds.), *The parental experience in midlife.* Chicago: University of Chicago Press.

Graber, J. A., Brooks-Gunn, J., & Warren, M. P. (1995). The antecedents of menarcheal age: Heredity, family environment and stressful life events. *Child Development, 66,* 346–359.

Grotevant, H. D. (1983). The contribution of the family to the facilitation of identity formation in early adolescence. *Journal of Early Adolescence, 3,* 225–237.

Grotevant, H. D. (1987). Toward a process model of identity formation. *Journal of Adolescent Research, 2,* 203–222.

Grotevant, H. D. (1989). The role of theory in guiding assessment. *Journal of Family Psychology, 3,* 104–117.

Grotevant, H. D. (1992). Assigned and chosen identity components: A process perspective on their integration. In G. R. Adams, R. Montemoyer, & T. Gulotta (Eds.), *Advances in adolescent development: Adolescent identity formation* (Vol. 4, pp. 73–90). Newbury Park, CA: Sage.

Grotevant, H. D. (1993). The integrative nature of identity: Bringing the soloists to sing in the choir. In J. Kroger (Ed.), *Discussions on ego identity* (pp. 121–146). Hillsdale, NJ: Erlbaum.

Grotevant, H. D., & Bosma, H. A. (1994). History and literature. In H. A. Bosma, T. L. G. Graafsma, H. D. Grotevant, & D. J. deLevita (Eds.), *Identity and development: An interdisciplinary approach* (pp. 119–122). Thousand Oaks, CA: Sage.

Grotevant, H. D., & Cooper, C. R. (1983, April). *The role of family communication patterns in adolescent identity and role taking.* Paper presented at the meeting of the Society for Research in Child Development, Detroit.

Grotevant, H. D., & Cooper, C. R. (1985). Patterns of interaction in family relationships and the development of identity exploration. *Child Development, 56,* 415–428.

Grotevant, H. D., & Cooper, C. R., (1986). Individuation in family relationships: A perspective on individual differences in the development of identity and role-taking skill in adolescence. *Human Development, 29,* 82–100.

Grotevant, H. D., & Cooper, C. R. (1988). The role of family experience in career exploration during adolescence. In P. B. Baltes, D. L. Featherman, & R. M. Lerner (Eds.), *Life-span development and behavior* (Vol. 8, pp. 231–258). Hillsdale, NJ: Erlbaum.

Grotevant, H. D., & Cooper, C. R. (in press). Individuality and connectedness in adolescent development: Review and prospects for research on identity, relationships, and context. In E. Skoe & A. von der Lippe (Eds.), *Personality development in adolescence: A cross national and life span perspective.* London: Routledge & Kegan Paul.

Grotevant, H. D., Thorbecke, W. L., & Meyer, M. L. (1982). An extension of Marcia's identity status interview into the interpersonal domain. *Journal of Youth and Adolescence, 11,* 33–47.

Hall, G. S. (1904). *Adolescence: Its psychology and its relations to physiology, anthropology, sociology, sex, crime, religion, and education* (Vols. 1, 2). New York: Appleton.

Hammen, C. (1992). Cognitive, life stress, and interpersonal approaches to a developmental psychopathology model of depression. *Development and Psychopathology, 4,* 189–206.

Hartup, W. W. (1978). Perspectives on child and family interaction: Past, present, and future. In R. M. Lerner & G. B. Spanier (Eds.), *Child influences on marital and family interaction: A life-span perspective*. Orlando, FL: Academic Press.

Hauser, S. T., Book, B. K., Houlihan, J., Powers, S., Weiss-Perry, B., Follansbee, D., Jacobson, A. M., & Noam, G. G. (1987). Sex differences within the family: Studies of adolescent and parent family interactions. *Journal of Youth and Adolescence, 16,* 199–220.

Hauser, S. T., Powers, S. I., & Noam, G. G. (1991). *Adolescents and their families: Paths of ego development.* New York: Free Press.

Hauser, S. T., Powers, S. I., Noam, G. G., Jacobson, A. M., Weiss, B., & Folansbee, D. J. (1984). Familial contexts of adolescent ego development. *Child Development, 55,* 195–213.

Havighurst, R. J. (1972). *Developmental tasks and education* (3rd ed.). New York: McKay.

Hazen, N. L., & Durrett, M. E. (1982). Relationship of security of attachment to exploration and cognitive mapping abilities in 2-year-olds. *Developmental Psychology, 18,* 751–759.

Herdt, G. (Ed.). (1989). *Gay and lesbian youth.* New York: Haworth Press.

Hernandez, J. T., & DiClemente, R. J. (1992). Self control and ego identity development as predictors of unprotected sex in late adolescent males. *Journal of Adolescence, 15,* 437–447.

Hill, J. P. (1973). *Some perspectives on adolescence in American society.* Paper prepared for the Office of Child Development, U.S. Department of Health, Education, and Welfare.

Hill, J. P. (1980). *Understanding early adolescence: A framework.* Chapel Hill, NC: Center for Early Adolescence.

Hill, J. P. (1987). Research on adolescents and their families: Past and prospect. In C. E. Irwin (Ed.), *Adolescent social behavior and health: New directions for child development* (Vol. 37, pp. 13–31). San Francisco: Jossey-Bass.

Hill, J. P., & Holmbeck, G. N. (1986). Attachment and autonomy during adolescence. In G. W. Whitehurst (Ed.), *Annals of child development* (Vol. 3). Greenwich, CT: JAI Press.

Hill, J. P., & Monks, F. J. (1977). Some perspectives on adolescence in modern societies. In J. P. Hill & F. J. Monks (Eds.), *Adolescence and youth in prospect* (pp. 28–78). Guildford, England: IPC Science and Technology Press.

Hill, J. P., & Palmquist, W. J. (1978). Social cognition and social relations in early adolescence. *International Journal of Behavioral Development, 1,* 1–36.

Hill, J. P., & Steinberg, L. D. (1976). The development of autonomy during adolescence. In *Jornadas sobre problematica juventil.* Madrid, Spain: Fundacion Faustino Orbegozo Eizaquirre.

Hill, R. F., & Fortenberry, J. D. (1992). Adolescence as a culture-bound syndrome. *Social Science Medicine, 35,* 73–80.

Hinde, R. A. (1992). Developmental psychology in the context of other behavioral sciences. *Developmental Psychology, 28,* 1018–1029.

Hofferth, S. (1987). The effects of programs and policies on adolescent pregnancy and childbearing. In S. L. Hofferth & C. D. Hayes (Eds.), *Risking the future: Adolescent sexuality, pregnancy, and childbearing* (Vol. 2, pp. 207–263). Washington, DC: National Academy of Sciences Press.

Hoffman, J. A. (1984). Psychological separation of late adolescents from their parents. *Journal of Counseling Psychology, 31,* 170–178.

Holland, J. L. (1973). *Making vocational choices: A theory of careers.* Englewood Cliffs, NJ: Prentice-Hall.

Hollingshead, A. (1949). *Elmtown's youth.* New York: Wiley.

Holmbeck, G. N., & Hill, J. P. (1988, March). *The role of familial conflict in adaptation to Menarche: Sequential analysis of family interaction.* Paper presented at the meeting of the Society for Research on Adolescence.

Holmbeck, G. N., & O'Donnell, K. (1991). Discrepancies between perceptions of decision making and behavioral autonomy. In R. Paikoff (Ed.), *Shared views in the family during adolescence: New directions for child development* (pp. 51–69). San Francisco: Jossey-Bass.

Horrocks, J. E. (1954). The adolescent. In L. Carmichael (Ed.), *Manual of child psychology* (2nd ed.). New York: Wiley.

Hunt, D. E. (1975). Person-environment interaction: A challenge found wanting before it was tried. *Review of Educational Research, 45,* 209–230.

Inhelder, B., & Piaget, J. (1958). *The growth of logical thinking from childhood to adolescence.* New York: Basic Books.

Irwin, C. E., Jr., & Vaughan, E. (1988). Psychosocial context of adolescent development. *Journal of Adolescent Health Care, 9,* 11S–19S.

Jessor, R. (1993). Successful adolescent development among youth in high-risk settings. *American Psychologist, 48,* 117–126.

Jessor, R., Van den Bos, J., Vanderryn, J., Costa, F. M., & Turbin, M. S. (1995). Protective factors in adolescent problem behavior: Moderator effects and developmental change. *Developmental Psychology, 31,* 923–933.

Johnson, B. M., Shulman, S., & Collins, W. A. (1991). Systemic patterns of parenting as reported by adolescents: Developmental differences and implications for psychosocial outcomes. *Journal of Adolescent Research, 6*(2), 235–252.

Jones, R. M. (1992). Ego identity and adolescent problem behavior. In G. R. Adams, T. P. Gulotta, & R. Montemayor (Eds.), *Adolescent identity formation: Advances in adolescent development* (Vol. 4, pp. 216–233). Newbury Park, CA: Sage.

Jones, R. M., & Hartmann, B. R. (1988). Ego identity: Developmental differences and experimental substance use among adolescents. *Journal of Adolescence, 11,* 347–360.

Josselson, R. (1988). *Finding herself: Pathways to identity development in women.* San Francisco: Jossey-Bass.

Josselson, R. (1994). Identity and relatedness in the life cycle. In H. A. Bosma, T. L. G. Graafsma, H. D. Grotevant, & D. J. deLevita (Eds.), *Identity and development: An interdisciplinary approach* (pp. 81–102). Thousand Oaks, CA: Sage.

Katchadourian, H. (1990). Sexuality. In S. S. Feldman & G. R. Elliott (Eds.), *At the threshold: The developing adolescent* (pp. 330–351). Cambridge, MA: Harvard University Press.

Keating, D. P. (1980). Thinking processes in adolescence. In J. Adelson (Ed.), *Handbook of adolescent psychology* (pp. 211–246). New York: Wiley.

Keating, D. P. (1990). Adolescent thinking. In S. S. Feldman & G. R. Elliott (Eds.), *At the threshold: The developing adolescent* (pp. 54–89). Cambridge, MA: Harvard University Press.

Kelley, H. H., Berscheid, E., Christensen, A., Harvey, J. H., Huston, T. L., Levinger, G., McClintock, E., Peplau, L. A., & Peterson, D. R. (1983). *Close relationships.* San Francisco: Freeman.

Kett, J. F. (1977). *Rites of passage.* New York: Basic Books.

Kiell, N. (1964). *The universal experience of adolescence.* New York: International Universities Press.

Knight, G. P., Virdin, L. M., & Roosa, M. (1994). Socialization and family correlates of mental health outcomes among Hispanic and Anglo American children: Consideration of cross-ethnic scalar equivalence. *Child Development, 65,* 212–224.

Kohlberg, L. (1976). Moral stages and moralization. In T. Lickona (Ed.), *Moral development and behavior.* New York: Holt, Rinehart and Winston.

Kroger, J. (1993a). Identity and context: How the identity statuses choose their match. In R. Josselson & A. Lieblich (Eds.), *The narrative study of lives* (Vol. 1, pp. 130–162). Newbury Park, CA: Sage.

Kroger, J. (1993b). *The role of historical context in the identity formation process of late adolescence.* Paper presented at the meeting of the Society for Research in Child Development, New Orleans.

Kroger, J. (1996). *Identity in adolescence: The balance between self and other* (2nd ed.). London: Routledge & Kegan Paul.

Kroger, J. (in press). Identity, regression, and development. *Journal of Adolescence.*

Kurdek, L. A., & Fine, M. A. (1994). Family acceptance and family control as predictors of adjustment in young adolescents: Linear, curvilinear, or interactive effects? *Child Development, 65,* 1137–1146.

Kvernmo, S., & Heyerdahl, S. (1994, May). *Ethnic identity among indigenous Sami adolescents.* Paper presented at a conference on Adolescence: Developmental Paths, University of Tromso, Norway.

Lamborn, S. D., Mounts, N. S., Steinberg, L., & Dornbush, S. M. (1991). Patterns of competence and adjustment among adolescents from authoritative, authoritarian, indulgent, and neglectful families. *Child Development, 62,* 1049–1065.

Lamborn, S. D., & Steinberg, L. D. (1993). Emotional autonomy redux: Revisiting Ryan and Lynch. *Child Development, 64,* 483–499.

Larson, R., & Csikszentmihalyi, M. (1983). The experience sampling method. In H. T. Reis (Ed.), *Naturalistic approaches to studying social interaction: New directions for methodology of social and behavioral science* (Vol. 15, pp. 41–56). San Francisco: Jossey-Bass.

Larson, R., & Richards, M. H. (1991). Daily companionship in late childhood and early adolescence: Changing developmental contexts. *Child Development, 62,* 284–300.

Larson, R., & Richards, M. H. (1994). *Divergent realities: The emotional lives of mothers, fathers, and adolescents.* New York: Basic Books.

Laursen, B. (1988, March). *Cognitive changes during adolescence and effects upon parent-child relationships.* Paper presented at the meeting of the Society for Research on Adolescence, Alexandria, VA.

Lerner, R. M. (1991). Changing organism-context relations as the basic process of development: A developmental-contextual perspective. *Developmental Psychology, 27,* 27–32.

Lerner, R. M., & Kauffman, M. B. (1985). The concept of development in contextualism. *Developmental Review, 5,* 309–333.

Levi, L. D., Stierlin, H., & Savard, R. J. (1972). Fathers and sons: The interlocking crises of integrity and identity. *Psychiatry, 35,* 48–56.

Levinson, D. J. (1986). *The seasons of a man's life.* New York: Ballantine Books.

Levinson, D. J. (1996). *The seasons of a woman's life.* New York: Basic Books.

Lewis, M., & Rosenblum, L. A. (1974). *The effect of the infant on its caregiver.* New York: Wiley.

Loevinger, J. (1976). *Ego development.* San Francisco: Jossey-Bass.

Maccoby, E. E., & Martin, J. A. (1983). Socialization in the context of the family: Parent-child interaction. In P. Mussen (Ed.), *Handbook of child psychology* (4th ed., Vol. 4). New York: Wiley.

MacDonald, K., & Parke, R. D. (1984). Bridging the gap: Parent-child play interaction and peer interactive competence. *Child Development, 55,* 1265–1277.

Main, M., & Goldwyn, R. (1985). *An adult attachment classification and rating system*. Unpublished manuscript, University of California at Berkeley.

Marcia, J. E. (1966). Development and validation of ego identity status. *Journal of Personality and Social Psychology, 3,* 551–558.

Marcia, J. E. (1976). Identity six years after: A follow-up study. *Journal of Youth and Adolescence, 5,* 145–160.

Marcia, J. E. (1980). Identity in adolescence. In J. Adelson (Ed.), *Handbook of adolescent psychology* (pp. 159–187). New York: Wiley.

Marcia, J. E., Waterman, A. S., Matteson, D. R., Archer, S. L., & Orlofsky, J. L. (1993). *Ego identity: A handbook for psychosocial research.* New York: Springer-Verlag.

Markus, H. R. (1995). The sociocultural self. *Newsletter of the International Society for the Study of Behavioural Development, 1*(27), 10–11.

Masten, A. S., Best, K. M., & Garmezy, N. (1990). Resilience and development: Contributions from the study of children who overcome adversity. *Development and Psychopathology, 2,* 425–444.

Masten, A. S., Coatsworth, J. D., Neeman, J., Gest, S. D., Tellegen, A., & Garmezy, N. (1995). The structure and coherence of competence from childhood through adolescence. *Child Development, 66,* 1635–1659.

Matas, L., Arend, R. A., & Sroufe, L. A. (1978). Continuity of adaptation in the second year: The relationship between quality of attachment and later competence. *Child Development, 49,* 547–556.

Matteson, D. R. (1977). Exploration and commitment: Sex differences and methodological problems in the use of identity status categories. *Journal of Youth and Adolescence, 6,* 349–370.

McAdams, D. P. (1988). *Power, intimacy, and the life story: Personological inquiries into identity.* New York: Guilford Press.

McCarthy, W. J., Bentler, P. M., & Newcomb, M. D. (1994). The contribution of personal and family characteristics in adolescence to the subsequent development of young adult competence. In R. D. Parke & S. G. Kellam (Eds.), *Exploring family relationships with other social contexts* (pp. 169–197). Hillsdale, NJ: Erlbaum.

McGoldrick, M. (1993). Ethnicity, cultural diversity, and normality. In F. Walsh (Ed.), *Normal family processes* (2ed., pp. 331–360). New York: Guilford Press.

Mead, M. (1928). *Coming of age in Samoa.* New York: Morrow.

Miller, B. C., & Moore, K. A. (1990). Adolescent sexual behavior, pregnancy, and parenting: Research through the 1980s. *Journal of Marriage and the Family, 52,* 1025–1044.

Miller, C. L., Eccles, J. S., Goldsmith, R., & Flanagan, C. A. (1987, April). *Parent expectations for adolescent transitions: What they are and how they affect their children.* Paper presented at the meeting of the Society for Research in Child Development, Baltimore, MD.

Minuchin, P. (1985). Families and individual development: Provocations from the field of family therapy. *Child Development, 56,* 289–302.

Mitzman, A. (1994). Historical identity and identity of the historian. In H. A. Bosma, T. L. G. Graafsma, H. D. Grotevant, & D. J. deLevita (Eds.), *Identity and development: An interdisciplinary approach* (pp. 135–158). Thousand Oaks, CA: Sage.

Moen, P., Elder, G. H., & Luescher, K. (Eds.). (1995). *Examining lives in context: Perspectives on the ecology of human development.* Washington, DC: American Psychological Association.

Moffitt, T. E., Caspi, A., Belsky, J., & Silva, P. A. (1992). Childhood experience and the onset of menarche: A test of a sociobiological model. *Child Development, 63,* 47–58.

Moore, D. (1987). Parent-adolescent separation: The construction of adulthood by late adolescents. *Developmental Psychology, 23,* 298–307.

Mounts, N., & Steinberg, L. D. (1995). *Developmental Psychology, 31,* 915–922.

Neimark, E. D. (1982). Adolescent thought: Transition in formal operations. In B. B. Wolman (Ed.), *Handbook of developmental psychology.* Englewood Cliffs, NJ: Prentice-Hall.

Neubauer, J. (1994). Problems of identity in modernist fiction. In H. A. Bosma, T. L. G. Graafsma, H. D. Grotevant, & D. J. deLevita (Eds.), *Identity and development: An interdisciplinary approach* (pp. 123–134). Thousand Oaks, CA: Sage.

Noller, P. (1994). Relationships with parents in adolescence: Process and outcome. In R. Montemayor, G. R. Adams, & T. P. Gullotta (Eds.), *Personal relationships during adolescence: Advances in adolescent development* (Vol. 6, pp. 37–77). Thousand Oaks, CA: Sage.

Offer, D., Ostrov, E., & Howard, K. I. (1981). *The adolescent: A psychological self-portrait.* New York: Basic Books.

Oswald, R. F. (1994). *Young bisexual and lesbian women coming-out: A qualitative investigation of social networks.* Unpublished master's thesis, Department of Family Social Science, University of Minnesota, St. Paul.

Overton, W. F., & Reese, H. W. (1973). Models of development: Methodological implications. In J. R. Nesselroade & H. W. Reese (Eds.), *Life-span developmental psychology: Methodological issues* (pp. 65–86). New York: Academic Press.

Paikoff, R. L., Brooks-Gunn, J., & Carlton-Ford, S. (1991). Effect of reproductive status changes on family functioning and well-being of mothers and daughters. *Journal of Early Adolescence, 11,* 201–220.

Papini, D. R., Roggman, L. A., & Anderson, J. (1991). Early-adolescent perceptions of attachment to mother and father: A test of the emotional-distancing and buffering hypotheses. *Journal of Early Adolescence, 11,* 258–275.

Parke, R. D. (1994). Epilogue: Unresolved issues and future trends in family relationships with other contexts. In R. D. Parke & S. G. Kellam (Eds.), *Exploring family relationships with other social contexts* (pp. 215–229). Hillsdale, NJ: Erlbaum.

Parke, R. D., Burks, V. M., Carson, J. L., Neville, B., & Boyum, L. A. (1994). In R. D. Parke & S. G. Kellam (Eds.), *Exploring family relationships with other social contexts* (pp. 115–146). Hillsdale, NJ: Erlbaum.

Parke, R. D., & Kellam, S. G. (Eds.). (1994). *Exploring family relationships with other social contexts.* Hillsdale, NJ: Erlbaum.

Parke, R. D., & Ladd, G. W. (Eds.). (1992). *Family-peer relationships: Modes of linkage.* Hillsdale, NJ: Erlbaum.

Patterson, G. R. (1982). *Coercive family process.* Eugene, OR: Castalia Press.

Patterson, G. R., DeBaryshe, B. D., & Ramsey, E. (1989). A developmental perspective on antisocial behavior. *American Psychologist, 44,* 329–335.

Patterson, G. R., Reid, J. B., & Dishion, T. J. (1992). *A social interactional approach: Vol. 4. Antisocial boys.* Eugene, OR: Castalia Press.

Petersen, A. C (1988). Adolescent development. *Annual Review of Psychology, 39,* 583–607.

Petersen, A. C. (1993). Presidential address: Creating adolescents: The role of context and process in developmental trajectories. *Journal of Research on Adolescence, 3,* 1–18.

Petersen, A. C., Compas, B. E., Brooks-Gunn, J., Stemmler, M., Ey, S., & Grant, K. E. (1993). Depression in adolescence. *American Psychologist, 48,* 155–168.

Petersen, A. C., & Taylor, B. (1980). The biological approach to adolescence. In J. Adelson (Ed.), *Handbook of adolescent psychology* (pp. 117–155). New York: Wiley.

Phelan, P., Davidson, A. L., & Cao, H. T. (1991). Students' multiple worlds: Navigating the borders of family, peer, and school cultures. In A. L. Davidson & P. Phelan (Eds.), *Cultural diversity: Implications for education.* New York: Teachers College Press.

Phinney, J. (1989). Stages of ethnic identity development in minority group adolescents. *Journal of Early Adolescence, 9,* 34–49.

Phinney, J. (1990). Ethic identity of adolescents and adults: A review of research. *Psychological Bulletin, 180,* 499–514.

Phinney, J. (1993). Multiple group identities: Differentiation, conflict, and integration. In J. Kroger (Ed.), *Discussions on ego identity.* Hillsdale, NJ: Erlbaum.

Phinney, J., & Rosenthal, D. A. (1992). Ethnic identity in adolescence: Process, context, and outcome. In G. R. Adams, T. P. Gullotta, & R. Montemayor (Eds.), *Advances in adolescent development: Adolescent identity formation* (pp. 145–172). Newbury Park, CA: Sage.

Piaget, J. (1932). *The moral judgment of the child.* New York: Harcourt, Brace, & World.

Piaget, J. (1983). Piaget's theory. In P. H. Mussen (Ed.), *Handbook of child psychology: Vol. 1. History, theory, and methods* (pp. 103–128). New York: Wiley.

Polkinghorne, D E. (1991). Narrative and self-concept. *Journal of Narrative and Life History, 1*(23), 135–153.

Powers, S. I., Hauser, S. T., Schwartz, J. M., Noam, G. G., & Jacobson, A. M. (1983). Adolescent ego development and family interaction: A structural-developmental perspective. In H. D. Grotevant & C. R. Cooper (Eds.), *Adolescent development in the family: New directions for child development.* San Francisco: Jossey-Bass.

Quadrel, M. F., Fischoff, B., & Davis, W. (1993). Adolescent (in)vulnerability. *American Psychologist, 48,* 102–116.

Read, D., Adams, G. R., & Dobson, W. R. (1984). Ego identity status, personality and social influence style. *Journal of Personality and Social Psychology, 46,* 169–177.

Reese, H. W., & Overton, W. F. (1970). Models of development and theories of development. In L. R. Goulet & P. B. Baltes (Eds.), *Life-span developmental psychology: Research and theory* (pp. 115–145). New York: Academic Press.

Resnick, M. (1996, March). The impact of caring and connectedness on adolescent health and risky behaviors. In J. Brooks-Gunn (Chair), *Youth and caring.* Symposium presented at the meeting of the Society for Research on Adolescence, Boston.

Rhode, P., Lewinsohn, P. M., & Seeley, J. R. (1991). Comorbidity of unipolar depression: II. Comorbidity with other mental disorders in adolescents and adults. *Journal of Abnormal Psychology, 100.* 214–222.

Rierdan, J., & Koff, E. (1993). Developmental variables in relation to depressive symptoms in adolescent girls. *Development and Psychopathology, 5,* 485–496.

Robin, A. L., & Foster, S. L. (1989). *Negotiating parent-adolescent conflict: A behavioral-family systems approach.* New York: Guilford Press.

Robins, L. N. (1963). The accuracy of parental recall of aspects of child development and child-rearing practices. *Journal of Abnormal and Social Psychology, 33,* 261–270.

Rollins, B. C., & Thomas, D. I. (1979). Parental support, power, and control techniques in the socialization of children. In W. Burr, R. Hill, I. Nye, & I. Reiss (Eds.), *Contemporary theories about the family* (Vol. 1). New York: Free Press.

Rosenwald, G. C., & Ochberg, R. L. (Eds.). (1992). *Storied lives: The cultural politics of self-understanding.* New Haven, CT: Yale University Press.

Rotheram-Borus, M. J. (1989). Ethnic differences in adolescents' identity status and associated behavior problems. *Journal of Adolescence, 12,* 361–374.

Rutter, M., & Garmezy, N. (1983). Developmental psychopathology. In P. H. Mussen (Series Ed.) & E. M. Hetherington (Vol. Ed.), *Handbook of child psychology: Vol. 4. Socialization, personality, and social development* (pp. 775–912). New York: Wiley.

Ryan, R. M., & Lynch, J. (1989). Emotional autonomy versus detachment: Revising the vicissitudes of adolescence and young adulthood. *Child Development, 60,* 340–356.

Ryan, R. M., Stiller, J. D., & Lynch, J. H. (1994). Representations of relationships to teachers, parents, and friends as predictors of academic motivation and self-esteem. *Journal of Early Adolescence, 14,* 226–236.

Sameroff, A. J. (1994). Developmental systems and family functioning. In R. D. Parke & S. G. Kellam (Eds.), *Exploring family relationships with other social contexts* (pp. 199–214). Hillsdale, NJ: Erlbaum.

Sampson, J. J., & Laub, J. H. (1994). Urban poverty and the family context of delinquency: A new look at structure and process in a classic study. *Child Development, 65,* 523–540.

Saraswathi, T. S., & Pai, S. (1993). Socialization in the Indian context. In H. S. R. Kao & D. Sinha (Eds.), *Asian perspectives of psychology.*

Savin-Williams, R. C. (1990). *Gay and lesbian youth: Expressions of identity.* Washington, DC: Hemisphere.

Savin-Williams, R. C. (1994). Dating those you can't love loving those you can't date. In R. Montemayor, G. R. Adams, & T. P. Gullotta (Eds.), *Advances in adolescent development: Vol. 6. Personal relationships during adolescence* (pp. 196–215). Thousand Oaks, CA: Sage.

Savin-Williams, R. C., & Berndt, T. J. (1990). Friendship and peer relations. In S. S. Feldman & G. R. Elliott (Eds.), *At the threshold: The developing adolescent* (pp. 277–307). Cambridge, MA: Harvard University Press.

Scheier, M. F., & Carver, C. S. (1985). Optimism, coping, and health: Assessment and implications of generalized outcome expectancies. *Health Psychology, 4,* 241–247.

Scott-Jones, D. (1996, March). Discussant comments. In J. Smetana (Chair), *Adolescent-parent relationships in diverse contexts.* Symposium presented at the biennial meeting of the Society for Research on Adolescence, Boston.

Selman, R. (1980). *The growth of interpersonal understanding.* New York: Academic Press.

Sherrod, L. R. (Ed.). (1993). Late adolescence and the transition to adulthood [Special issue]. *Journal of Research on Adolescence, 3*(3).

Silbereisen, R. K., & Todt, E. (Eds.). (1994). *Adolescence in context.* New York: Springer-Verlag.

Silverberg, S. B. (1989, July). *A longitudinal look at parent-adolescent relations and parents' evaluations of life and self.* Paper presented at the meeting of the International Society for the Study of Behavioral Development, Jyvaskyla, Finland.

Silverberg, S. B., & Steinberg, L. (1987). Adolescent autonomy, parent-adolescent conflict, and parental well-being. *Journal of Youth and Adolescence, 16*(3), 293–312.

Silverberg, S. B., & Steinberg, L. (1990). Psychological well-being of parents with early adolescent children. *Developmental Psychology, 26*(4), 658–666.

Simmons, R. G., Blyth, D. A., Van Cleave, E. F., & Bush, D. M. (1979). Entry into early adolescence. *American Sociological Review, 44,* 948–967.

Slugoski, B. R., Marcia, J. E., & Koopman, R. F. (1984). Cognitive and social interactional charactersitics of ego identity statuses in college males. *Journal of Personality and Social Psychology, 47,* 646–661.

Smelser, N. J., & Erikson, E. H. (1980). *Themes of work and love in adulthood.* Cambridge, MA: Harvard University Press.

Smetana, J. G. (1988). Adolescents' and parents' conceptions of parental authority. *Child Development, 59,* 321–335.

Smetana, J. G. (1989). Adolescents' and parents' reasoning about actual family conflict. *Child Development, 60*(5), 1052–1067.

Smetana, J. G. (1991, April). *Do parent-child relationships change during adolescence?* Paper presented at a symposium entitled, "Research on relationships in middle childhood and adolescence: Continuity, change, and functional significance" at the meeting of the Society for Research in Child Development, Seattle, WA.

Smetana, J. G. (1995). Context, conflict, and constraint in adolescent-parent authority relationships. In M. Killen & D. Hart (Eds.), *Morality in everyday life: Developmental perspectives.* Cambridge, England: Cambridge University Press.

Smetana, J. G., & Asquith, P. (1994). Adolescents' and parents' conceptions of parental authority and personal autonomy. *Child Development, 65,* 1147–1162.

Smetana, J. G., Yau, J., Restrepo, A., & Braeges, J. L. (in press). Adolescent-parent conflict in married and divorced families. *Developmental Psychology.*

Spencer, M., & Dornbusch, S. (1990). Ethnicity and adolescence. In S. Feldman & G. Elliot (Eds.), *At the threshold: The developing adolescent.* Cambridge, MA: Harvard University Press.

Sroufe, L. A. (1979). The coherence of individual development. *American Psychologist, 34,* 834–841.

Sroufe, L. A. (1990). Considering normal and abnormal together: The essence of developmental psychopathology. *Development and Psychopathology, 2,* 335–347.

Sroufe, L. A., & Fleeson, J. (1986). Attachment and the construction of relationships. In W. W. Hartup & Z. Rubin (Eds.), *Relationships and development.* Hillsdale, NJ: Erlbaum.

Sroufe, L. A., & Jacobvitz, D. (1989). Diverging pathways, developmental transformations, multiple etiologies and the problem of continuity in development. *Human Development, 32,* 196–203.

Sroufe, L. A., & Rutter, M. (1984). The domain of developmental psychopathology. *Child Development, 55,* 17–29.

Steinberg, L. D. (1981). Transformation in family relations at puberty. *Developmental Psychology, 17,* 833–840.

Steinberg, L. D. (1988). Reciprocal relation between parent-child distance and pubertal maturation. *Developmental Psychology, 24,* 122–128.

Steinberg, L. D. (1995) Commentary: On developmental pathways and social contexts in adolescence. In L. J. Crockett & A. C. Crouter (Eds.), *Pathways through adolescence: Individual development in relation to social contexts* (pp. 245–254). Mahwah, NJ: Erlbaum.

Steinberg, L. D., & Darling, N. E. (1994). The broader context of social influence in adolescence. In R. K. Silbereisen & E. Todt (Eds.), *Adolescence in context* (pp. 25–45). New York: Springer-Verlag.

Steinberg, L. D., Darling, N. E., & Fletcher, A. C. (1995). Authoritative parenting and adolescent adjustment: An ecological journey. In P. Moen, G. H. Elder, & K. Luescher (Eds.), *Examining lives in context: Perspectives on the ecology of human development* (pp. 423–466). Washington, DC: American Psychological Association.

Steinberg, L. D., & Hill, J. P. (1978). Patterns of family interaction as a function of age, the onset of puberty, and formal thinking. *Developmental Psychology, 14,* 683–684.

Steinberg, L. D., Lamborn, S. D., Darling, N., Mounts, N. S., & Dornbusch, S. M. (1994). Over-time changes in adjustment and competence among adolescents from authoritative, authoritarian, indulgent, and neglectful families. *Child Development, 65,* 754–770.

Steinberg, L. D., Lamborn, S., Dornbusch, S., & Darling, N. (1992). Impact of parenting practices on adolescent achievement: Authoritative parenting, school involvement, and encouragement to succeed. *Child Development, 63,* 1266–1281.

Steinberg, L. D., & Silverberg, S. B. (1986). The vicissitudes of autonomy. *Child Development, 57,* 841–851.

Takanishi, R. (1993). The opportunities of adolescence—research, interventions, and policy: Introduction to the special issue. *American Psychologist, 48,* 85–87.

Tanner, J. M. (1962). *Growth at adolescence.* New York: Lippincott.

Taylor, L. C. (1994, February). *Winning combinations: The effects of different parenting style combinations on adolescent adjustment.* Paper presented at the meeting of the Society for Research on Adolescence, San Diego.

Taylor, R. D., Casten, R., & Flickinger, S. M. (1993). Influence of kinship social support on the parenting experiences and psychosocial adjustment of African-American adolescents. *Developmental Psychology, 1993,* 382–388.

Thomas, A., & Chess, S. (1977). *Temperament and development.* New York: Brunner/Mazel.

Tupuola, A. M. (1993). *Critical analysis of adolescent development—A Samoan women's perspective.* Unpublished master's thesis, Victoria University of Wellington, New Zealand.

Vuchinich, S., Emery, R., & Cassidy, J. (1988). Family members as third parties in dyadic family conflicts: Strategies, alliances, and outcomes. *Child Development, 59,* 1293–1302.

Vuchinich, S., Hetherington, E. M., Vuchinich, R. A., & Clingempeel, W. G. (1991). Parent-child interaction and gender differences in early adolescents' adaptation to stepfamilies. *Developmental Psychology, 27,* 618–626.

Walsh, F. (Ed.). (1993). *Moral family processes* (2nd ed.) New York: Guilford Press.

Waterman, A. S. (1982). Identity development from adolescence to adulthood: An extension of theory and a review of research. *Developmental Psychology, 18,* 341–358.

Weiner, I. B. (1970). *Psychological disturbance in adolescence.* New York: Wiley.

Welsh, D., Powers, S., & Jacobson, A. (1991, April). *Gender differences in parent-adolescent interaction: A longitudinal study.* Paper presented at the meeting of the Society for Research in Child Development, Seattle, WA.

Whitbourne, S. K. (1986). *The me I know: A study of adult identity.* New York: Springer-Verlag.

Windle, M. (1992). A longitudinal study of stress buffering for adolescent problem behavior. *Developmental Psychology, 28,* 522–530.

Wright, L. (1994, July 25). One drop of blood. *New Yorker,* 46–55.

Wyche, K., Obolensky, N., & Glood, E. (1990). American Indian, Black American, and Hispanic American Youth. In M. J. Rotheram-Borus, J. Bradley, & N. Obolensky (Eds.), *Planning to live: Evaluating and treating suicidal teens in community settings* (pp. 355–389). Tulsa: University of Oklahoma Press.

Xiong, B. (1996). *Hmong parent-adolescent conflicts.* Unpublished manuscript, University of Minnesota, Department of Family Social Science.

Youniss, J. (1980). *Parents and peers in social development: A Sullivan-Piaget perspective.* Chicago: University of Chicago Press.

Youniss, J., & Smollar, J. (1985). *Adolescent relations with mothers, fathers, and friends.* Chicago: University of Chicago Press.

Zaslow, M. J., & Takanishi, R. (1993). Priorities for research on adolescent development. *American Psychologist, 48,* 185–192.

Author Index

Subject Index